College

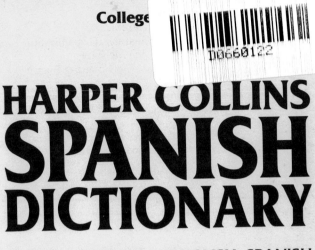

HARPER COLLINS
SPANISH
DICTIONARY

SPANISH·ENGLISH   ENGLISH·SPANISH

COLLINS
London and Glasgow
HARPER & ROW
New York

contributors/colaboradores
Jeremy Butterfield, Mike Gonzalez, Gerry Breslin,
Alicia Harland, Val McNulty,
M.ª Ángeles Recio Corral, M.ª José Sánchez Blanco

American language consultants/inglés norteamericano
Professor Halvor Clegg, Professor Willis Fails

editorial staff/redacción
John Forry, Jane Horwood, Irene Lakhani

First Edition 1990

ISBN 0-06-055251-4 (casebound)
ISBN 0-06-091951-5 (paperback)

ÍNDICE DE MATERIAS

CONTENTS

Marcas Registradas

Las marcas que creemos que constituyen marcas registradas las denominamos como tales. Sin embargo, no debe considerarse que la presencia o la ausencia de esta designación tenga que ver con la situación legal de ninguna marca.

Note on trademarks

Words which we have reason to believe constitute trademarks have been designated as such. However, neither the presence nor the absence of such designation should be regarded as affecting the legal status of any trademark.

INTRODUCCIÓN

Para comprender el inglés

Este diccionario, nuevo y completamente puesto al día, pone a disposición del usuario de la lengua una cobertura amplia y a la vez práctica de los usos lingüísticos más corrientes del inglés de hoy, e incluye la terminología necesaria en el dominio empresarial y de la microinformática, así como una numerosa selección de las abreviaturas, siglas y topónimos que suelen aparecer en la prensa. A fin de facilitar la labor del lector, se mencionan también las formas irregulares de los verbos ingleses, con indicaciones que hacen referencia a las formas básicas, donde se encuentra la traducción.

Para expresarse en inglés

A fin de ayudar al lector a expresarse correcta e idiomáticamente en inglés, el diccionario contiene frecuentes indicaciones – a manera de glosas de orientación – que pueden servirle para encontrar la traducción más apropiada en un contexto dado. Todas las palabras de uso más corriente en la lengua reciben tratamiento detallado, en el que se mencionan muchas ilustraciones de sus usos característicos.

Para acompañarle en su trabajo

Nos hemos esmerado en hacer de este nuevo diccionario de Collins una compilación fiable y fácil de utilizar que responda a sus necesidades laborales y de estudio. Nuestra esperanza es que le sirva mucho tiempo como fiel compañero de trabajo en todo lo que le haga falta mientras maneja el inglés como lengua extranjera.

INTRODUCTION

Understanding Spanish

This new and thoroughly up-to-date dictionary provides the user with wide-ranging, practical coverage of current usage, including terminology relevant to business and office automation, and a comprehensive selection of abbreviations, acronyms and geographical names commonly found in the press. You will also find, for ease of consultation, irregular forms of Spanish verbs and nouns with a cross-reference to the basic form where a translation is given.

Self-expression in Spanish

To help you express yourself correctly and idiomatically in Spanish, numerous indications – think of them as signposts – guide you to the most appropriate translation for your context. All the most commonly used words are given detailed treatment, with many examples of typical usage.

A working companion

Much care has been taken to make this new Collins dictionary thoroughly reliable, easy to use and relevant to your work and study. We hope it will become a long-serving companion for all your foreign language needs.

ABREVIATURAS

ABBREVIATIONS

adjetivo, locución adjetiva	**a**	adjective, adjectival phrase
abreviatura	**ab(b)r**	abbreviation
adverbio, locución adverbial	**ad**	adverb, adverbial phrase
administración, lengua administrativa	**ADMIN**	administration
agricultura	**AGR**	agriculture
América Latina	**AM**	Latin America
anatomía	**ANAT**	anatomy
arquitectura	**ARQ, ARCH**	architecture
astrología, astronomía	**ASTRO**	astrology, astronomy
el automóvil	**AUT(O)**	automobiles
aviación, viajes aéreos	**AVIAT**	flying, air travel
biología	**BIO(L)**	biology
botánica, flores	**BOT**	botany
inglés británico	**Brit**	British English
química	**CHEM**	chemistry
lengua familiar (! vulgar)	**col (!)**	colloquial usage (! particularly offensive)
comercio, finanzas, banca	**COM(M)**	commerce, finance, banking
informática	**COMPUT**	computing
conjunción	**conj**	conjunction
construcción	**CONSTR**	building
compuesto	**cpd**	compound element
cocina	**CULIN**	cookery
economía	**ECON**	economics
electricidad, electrónica	**ELEC**	electricity, electronics
enseñanza, sistema escolar	**ESCOL**	education, schools
España	**Esp**	Spain
especialmente	**esp**	especially
exclamación, interjección	**excl**	exclamation, interjection
femenino	**f**	feminine
lengua familiar (! vulgar)	**fam (!)**	colloquial usage (! particularly offensive)
ferrocarril	**FERRO**	railroad
uso figurado	**fig**	figurative use
fotografía	**FOTO**	photography
(verbo inglés) del cual la partícula es inseparable	**fus**	(phrasal verb) where the particle is inseparable
generalmente	**gen**	generally
geografía, geología	**GEO**	geography, geology
geometría	**GEOM**	geometry
informática	**INFORM**	computing
invariable	**inv**	invariable
irregular	**irg**	irregular
lo jurídico	**JUR**	law
América Latina	**LAm**	Latin America
gramática, lingüística	**LING**	grammar, linguistics
literatura	**LIT**	literature
masculino	**m**	masculine
matemáticas	**MAT(H)**	mathematics
medicina	**MED**	medical term, medicine
masculino/femenino	**m/f**	masculine/feminine
lo militar, ejército	**MIL**	military matters
música	**MUS**	music

sustantivo, nombre	**n**	noun
navegación, náutica	**NAUT**	sailing, navigation
sustantivo numérico	**num**	numeral noun
complemento	**obj**	(grammatical) object
	o.s.	oneself
peyorativo	**pey, pej**	derogatory, pejorative
fotografía	**PHOT**	photography
fisiología	**PHYSIOL**	physiology
plural	**pl**	plural
política	**POL**	politics
participio de pasado	**pp**	past participle
prefijo	**pref**	prefix
preposición	**prep**	preposition
pronombre	**pron**	pronoun
psicología, psiquiatría	**PSICO, PSYCH**	psychology, psychiatry
tiempo pasado	**pt**	past tense
sustantivo no empleado en el plural	**q**	collective (uncountable) noun, not used in plural
ferrocarril	**RAIL**	railroad
religión, lo eclesiástico	**REL**	religion, church service
	sb	somebody
enseñanza, sistema escolar	**SCOL**	education, schools
singular	**sg**	singular
España	**Sp**	Spain
	sth	something
subjuntivo	**subjun**	subjunctive
sujeto	**su(b)j**	(grammatical) subject
sufijo	**suff**	suffix
tauromaquia	**TAUR**	bullfighting
también	**tb**	also
técnica, tecnología	**TEC(H)**	technical term, technology
telecomunicaciones	**TELEC, TEL**	telecommunications
televisión	**TV**	television
imprenta, tipografía	**TIP, TYP**	typography, printing
sistema universitario	**UNIV**	universities
inglés norteamericano	**US**	American English
verbo	**vb**	verb
verbo intransitivo	**vi**	intransitive verb
verbo pronominal	**vr**	reflexive verb
verbo transitivo	**vt**	transitive verb
zoología, animales	**ZOOL**	zoology
marca registrada	®	registered trademark
indica un equivalente cultural	≈	introduces a cultural equivalent

SPANISH PRONUNCIATION

CONSONANTS

b	[b, ƀ]	boda bomba labor	see notes on v below
c	[k]	caja	c before a, o or u is pronounced as in cat
ce, ci	[se, sē]	cero cielo	c before e or i is pronounced as in sin
ch	[ch]	chiste	ch is pronounced as ch in chair
d	[d, ƌ]	danés ciudad	at the beginning of a phrase or after l or n, d is pronounced as in English. In any other position it is pronounced like th in the
g	[g, ǥ]	gafas paga	g before a, o or u is pronounced as in gap, if at the beginning of a phrase or after n. In other positions the sound is softened
ge, gi	[he, hē]	gente girar	g before e or i is pronounced similar to ch in Scottish loch or German och
h		haber	h is always silent in Spanish
j	[h]	jugar	j is pronounced similar to ch in Scottish loch or German och
ll	[y]	talle	ll is pronounced like the lli in million
ñ	[ny]	niño	ñ is pronounced like the ni in onion
q	[k]	que	q is pronounced as k in king
r, rr	[r, rr]	quitar garra	r is always pronounced in Spanish; rr is trilled
s	[s]	quizás isla	s is usually pronounced as in pass, but before b, d, g, l, m or n it is pronounced as in rose
v	[b, ƀ]	vía enviar dividir	v is pronounced something like b. At the beginning of a phrase or after m or n it is pronounced as b in boy. In any other position it is pronounced with the lips in position to pronounce b of boy, but not meeting
w	[b, ƀ, w]	wáter whisky	pronounced either like Spanish b, or like English w
z	[s]	tenaz	z is pronounced as in sin

f, k, l, m, n, p, t and x are pronounced as in English.

VOWELS

a	[à]	pata	not as long as *a* in p*a*lm. When followed by a consonant in the same syllable (i.e. in a closed syllable), as in am*a*nte, the *a* is short, as in *a*dd
e	[e]	me	like *e* in *e*nd. In a closed syllable, as in g*e*nte, the *e* is short as in p*e*t
i	[ē]	pino	as in m*ea*n or mach*i*ne
o	[o]	lo	as in s*o*. In a closed syllable, as in contr*o*l, the *o* is short as in p*o*t
u	[o͞o]	lunes	as in p*oo*l. It is silent after *q*, and in *gue*, *gui*, unless marked *güe*, *güi* e.g. antig*ü*edad, when it is pronounced like *w* in *w*in

SEMIVOWELS

| i, y | [y] | bien
hielo
yunta | pronounced like *y* in *y*et |
| u | [w] | huevo
fuente
antigüedad | unstressed *u* between consonant and vowel is pronounced like *w* in *w*in. See also notes on *u* above |

DIPHTHONGS

ai, ay	[àē]	baile	as *i* in r*i*de
au	[ào͞o]	auto	as *ou* in sh*ou*t
ei, ey	[eē]	buey	as *ay* in b*ay*
eu	[eo͞o]	deuda	both elements pronounced independently [e] and [o͞o]
oi, oy	[oē]	hoy	as *oy* in t*oy*

STRESS

The rules of stress in Spanish are as follows:

(a) when a word ends in a vowel or in *n* or *s*, the second last syllable is stressed: pat*a*ta, pat*a*tas, c*o*me, c*o*men

(b) when a word ends in a consonant other than *n* or *s*, the stress falls on the last syllable: par*e*d, habl*a*r

(c) when the rules set out in a and b are not applied, an acute accent appears over the stressed vowel: com*ú*n, geograf*í*a, ingl*é*s

In the phonetic transcription, the symbol ['] follows the syllable on which the stress falls.

The symbol [·] shows where two consonants should be pronounced separately.

PRONUNCIACIÓN INGLESA

VOCALES Y DIPTONGOS

	Ejemplo inglés	*Ejemplo español/explicación*
[a]	add, map	Se mantienen los labios en la posición de *e* en pena y luego se pronuncia el sonido *a*
[ā]	ace, rate	*e* cerrada seguida por una *i* débil
[är]	care, air	Una *e* abierta, parecida a la de perro. La *r* se pronuncia.
[â]	palm, father, odd	Entre *a* de padre y *o* de noche
[e]	end, pet	Como en perro
[ē]	even, tree	Como en fino
[ə]	above, darken	Sonido indistinto parecido a una *e* u *o* casi mudas
[i]	it, give	Más breve que en si
[ī]	ice, write	Como en fraile
[ō]	open, so	Como en solo
[ô]	law, dog, order	Como en torre
[oi]	oil, boy	Como en voy
[ou]	out, now	Como en pausa
[o͞o]	pool, food	Sonido largo, como en cura
[o͝o]	took, full	Sonido breve, parecido a la *u* de burro
[u]	up, done	*a* muy breve
[ûr]	urn, term	Entre *e* y *o*. La *r* se pronuncia.
[yo͞o]	use, few	Como en ciudad

CONSONANTES

	Ejemplo inglés	*Ejemplo español/explicación*
[b]	*b*at, ru*b*	Como en *b*omba, tum*b*a
[ch]	*ch*eck, ca*tch*	Como en *ch*ocolate
[d]	*d*og, ro*d*	Como en con*d*e, an*d*ar
[g]	*g*o, lo*g*	Como en *g*rande, *g*ol
[h]	*h*ope, *h*ate	Como la jota hispanoamericana
[j]	*j*oy, le*dg*e	Como en la *ll* andaluza y en *G*eneralitat (catalán)
[k]	*c*ool, ta*k*e	Como en *c*aña, Es*c*ocia
[ng]	ri*ng*, so*ng*	Como en ví*n*culo
[r]	*r*un, poo*r*	Se pronuncia con la punta de la lengua hacia atrás y sin hacerla vibrar
[s]	*s*ee, pa*ss*	Como en ca*s*a, *s*esión
[sh]	*s*ure, ru*sh*	Como en *ch*ambre (francés), ro*x*o (portugués)
[th]	*th*in, bo*th*	Como en re*c*eta, *z*apato
[t̪h]	*th*is, ba*th*e	Como en la *d* de habla*d*o, verda*d*
[v]	*v*ain, e*v*e	Con los labios en la posición de la *f* de *f*ondo, pero es sonoro
[w]	*w*in, a*w*ay	Como en la *u* de h*u*evo, p*u*ede
[y]	*y*et, *y*earn	Como en *y*a
[z]	*z*est, mu*s*e	Como en des*d*e, mi*s*mo
[zh]	vi*s*ion, plea*s*ure	Como en *j*ournal (francés)

p, f, m, n, l, t iguales que en español
El signo ['] indica la sílaba acentuada. El símbolo [·] indica que las dos consonantes a ambos lados del símbolo deben pronunciarse separadamente.

SPANISH VERB FORMS

1 Gerund. *2* Imperative. *3* Present. *4* Preterite. *5* Future. *6* Present subjunctive. *7* Imperfect subjunctive. *8* Past participle. *9* Imperfect.
Etc indicates that the irregular root is used for all persons of the tense, e.g. **oír**: *6* oiga, oigas, oigamos, oigáis, oigan.

acertar *2* acierta *3* acierto, aciertas, acierta, aciertan *6* acierte, aciertes, acierte, acierten

acordar *2* acuerda *3* acuerdo, acuerdas, acuerda, acuerdan *6* acuerde, acuerdes, acuerde, acuerden

advertir *1* advirtiendo *2* advierte *3* advierto, adviertes, advierte, advierten *4* advirtió, advirtieron *6* advierta, adviertas, advierta, advirtamos, advirtáis, adviertan *7* advirtiera *etc*

agradecer *3* agradezco *6* agradezca *etc*

aparecer *3* aparezco *6* aparezca *etc*

aprobar *2* aprueba *3* apruebo, apruebas, aprueba, aprueban *6* apruebe, apruebes, apruebe, aprueben

atravesar *2* atraviesa *3* atravieso, atraviesas, atraviesa, atraviesan *6* atraviese, atravieses, atraviese, atraviesen

caber *3* quepo *4* cupe, cupiste, cupo, cupimos, cupisteis, cupieron *5* cabré *etc* *6* quepa *etc* *7* cupiera *etc*

caer *1* cayendo *3* caigo *4* cayó, cayeron *6* caiga *etc* *7* cayera *etc*

calentar *2* calienta *3* caliento, calientas, calienta, calientan *6* caliente, calientes, caliente, calienten

cerrar *2* cierra *3* cierro, cierras, cierra, cierran *6* cierre, cierres, cierre, cierren

COMER *1* comiendo *2* come, comed *3* como, comes, come, comemos, coméis, comen *4* comí, comiste, comió, comimos, comisteis, comieron *5* comeré, comerás, comerá, comeremos, comeréis, comerán *6* coma, comas, coma, comamos, comáis, coman *7* comiera, comieras, comiera, comiéramos, comierais, comieran *8* comido *9* comía, comías, comía, comíamos, comíais, comían

conocer *3* conozco *6* conozca *etc*

contar *2* cuenta *3* cuento, cuentas, cuenta, cuentan *6* cuente, cuentes, cuente, cuenten

costar *2* cuesta *3* cuesto, cuestas, cuesta, cuestan *6* cueste, cuestes, cueste, cuesten

dar *3* doy *4* di, diste, dio, dimos, disteis, dieron *7* diera *etc*

decir *2* di *3* digo *4* dije, dijiste, dijo, dijimos, dijisteis, dijeron *5* diré *etc* *6* diga *etc* *7* dijera *etc* *8* dicho

despertar *2* despierta *3* despierto, despiertas, despierta, despiertan *6* despierte, despiertes, despierte, despierten

divertir *1* divirtiendo *2* divierte *3* divierto, diviertes, divierte, divierten *4* divirtió, divirtieron *6* divierta, diviertas, divierta, divirtamos, divirtáis, diviertan *7* divirtiera *etc*

dormir *1* durmiendo *2* duerme *3* duermo, duermes, duerme, duermen *4* durmió, durmieron *6* duerma, duermas, duerma, durmamos, durmáis, duerman *7* durmiera *etc*

empezar *2* empieza *3* empiezo, empiezas, empieza, empiezan *4* empecé *6* empiece, empieces, empiece, empecemos, empecéis, empiecen

entender *2* entiende *3* entiendo, entiendes, entiende, entienden *6* entienda, entiendas, entienda, entiendan

ESTAR *2* está *3* estoy, estás, está, están *4* estuve, estuviste, estuvo, estuvimos, estuvisteis, estuvieron *6* esté, estés, esté, estén *7* estuviera *etc*

HABER *3* he, has, ha, hemos, han *4* hube, hubiste, hubo, hubimos, hubisteis, hubieron *5* habré *etc* *6* haya *etc* *7* hubiera *etc*

HABLAR *1* hablando *2* habla, hablad *3* hablo, hablas, habla, hablamos, habláis, hablan *4* hablé, hablaste, habló, hablamos, hablasteis, hablaron *5* hablaré, hablarás, hablará, hablaremos, hablaréis, hablarán *6* hable, hables, hable, hablemos, habléis, hablen *7* hablara, hablaras, hablara, habláramos, hablarais, hablaran *8* hablado *9* hablaba, hablabas, hablaba, hablábamos, hablabais, hablaban

hacer *2* haz *3* hago *4* hice, hiciste, hizo, hicimos, hicisteis, hicieron *5* haré *etc* *6* haga *etc* *7* hiciera *etc* *8* hecho

instruir *1* instruyendo *2* instruye *3* instruyo, instruyes, instruye, instruyen *4* instruyó, instruyeron *6* instruya *etc 7* instruyera *etc*

ir *1* yendo *2* ve *3* voy, vas, va, vamos, vais, van *4* fui, fuiste, fue, fuimos, fuisteis, fueron *6* vaya, vayas, vaya, vayamos, vayáis, vayan *7* fuera *etc 8* iba, ibas, iba, íbamos, ibais, iban

jugar *2* juega *3* juego, juegas, juega, juegan *4* jugué *6* juegue *etc*

leer *1* leyendo *4* leyó, leyeron *7* leyera *etc*

morir *1* muriendo *2* muere *3* muero, mueres, muere, mueren *4* murió, murieron *6* muera, mueras, muera, muramos, muráis, mueran *7* muriera *etc 8* muerto

mostrar *2* muestra *3* muestro, muestras, muestra, muestran *6* muestre, muestres, muestre, muestren

mover *2* mueve *3* muevo, mueves, mueve, mueven *6* mueva, muevas, mueva, muevan

negar *2* niega *3* niego, niegas, niega, niegan *4* negué *6* niegue, niegues, niegue, neguemos, neguéis, nieguen

ofrecer *3* ofrezco *6* ofrezca *etc*

oír *1* oyendo *2* oye *3* oigo, oyes, oye, oyen *4* oyó, oyeron *6* oiga *etc 7* oyera *etc*

oler *2* huele *3* huelo, hueles, huele, huelen *6* huela, huelas, huela, huelan

parecer *3* parezco *6* parezca *etc*

pedir *1* pidiendo *2* pide *3* pido, pides, pide, piden *4* pidió, pidieron *6* pida *etc 7* pidiera *etc*

pensar *2* piensa *3* pienso, piensas, piensa, piensan *6* piense, pienses, piense, piensen

perder *2* pierde *3* pierdo, pierdes, pierde, pierden *6* pierda, pierdas, pierda, pierdan

poder *1* pudiendo *2* puede *3* puedo, puedes, puede, pueden *4* pude, pudiste, pudo, pudimos, pudisteis, pudieron *5* podré *etc 6* pueda, puedas, pueda, puedan *7* pudiera *etc*

poner *2* pon *3* pongo *4* puse, pusiste, puso, pusimos, pusisteis, pusieron *5* pondré *etc 6* ponga *etc 7* pusiera *etc 8* puesto

preferir *1* prefiriendo *2* prefiere *3* prefiero, prefieres, prefiere, prefieren *4* prefirió, prefirieron *6* prefiera, prefieras, prefiera, prefiramos, prefiráis, prefieran *7* prefiriera *etc*

querer *2* quiere *3* quiero, quieres, quiere, quieren *4* quise, quisiste, quiso, quisimos, quisisteis, quisieron *5* querré *etc 6* quiera, quieras, quiera, quieran *7* quisiera *etc*

reír *2* ríe *3* río, ríes, ríe, ríen *4* rio, rieron *6* ría, rías, ría, riamos, riáis, rían *7* riera *etc*

repetir *1* repitiendo *2* repite *3* repito, repites, repite, repiten *4* repitió, repitieron *6* repita *etc 7* repitiera *etc*

rogar *2* ruega *3* ruego, ruegas, ruega, ruegan *4* rogué *6* ruegue, ruegues, ruegue, roguemos, roguéis, rueguen

saber *3* sé *4* supe, supiste, supo, supimos, supisteis, supieron *5* sabré *etc 6* sepa *etc 7* supiera *etc*

salir *2* sal *3* salgo *5* saldré *etc 6* salga *etc*

seguir *1* siguiendo *2* sigue *3* sigo, sigues, sigue, siguen *4* siguió, siguieron *6* siga *etc 7* siguiera *etc*

sentar *2* sienta *3* siento, sientas, sienta, sientan *6* siente, sientes, siente, sienten

sentir *1* sintiendo *2* siente *3* siento, sientes, siente, sienten *4* sintió, sintieron *6* sienta, sientas, sienta, sintamos, sintáis, sientan *7* sintiera *etc*

SER *2* sé *3* soy, eres, es, somos, sois, son *4* fui, fuiste, fue, fuimos, fuisteis, fueron *6* sea *etc 7* fuera *etc 9* era, eras, era, éramos, erais, eran

servir *1* sirviendo *2* sirve *3* sirvo, sirves, sirve, sirven *4* sirvió, sirvieron *6* sirva *etc 7* sirviera *etc*

soñar *2* sueña *3* sueño, sueñas, sueña, sueñan *6* sueñe, sueñes, sueñe, sueñen

tener *2* ten *3* tengo, tienes, tiene, tienen *4* tuve, tuviste, tuvo, tuvimos, tuvisteis, tuvieron *5* tendré *etc 6* tenga *etc 7* tuviera *etc*

traer *1* trayendo *3* traigo *4* traje, trajiste, trajo, trajimos, trajisteis, trajeron *6* traiga *etc 7* trajera *etc*

valer *2* val *3* valgo *5* valdré *etc 6* valga *etc*

venir *2* ven *3* vengo, vienes, viene, vienen *4* vine, viniste, vino, vinimos, vinisteis, vinieron *5* vendré *etc 6* venga *etc 7* viniera *etc*

ver *3* veo *6* vea *etc 8* visto *9* veía *etc*

vestir *1* vistiendo *2* viste *3* visto, vistes, viste, visten *4* vistió, vistieron *6* vista *etc 7* vistiera *etc*

VIVIR *1* viviendo *2* vive, vivid *3* vivo, vives, vive, vivimos, vivís, viven *4* viví, viviste, vivió, vivimos, vivisteis, vivieron *5* viviré, vivirás, vivirá, viviremos, viviréis, vivirán *6* viva, vivas, viva, vivamos, viváis, vivan *7* viviera, vivieras, viviera, viviéramos, vivierais, vivieran *8* vivido *9* vivía, vivías, vivía, vivíamos, vivíais, vivían

volver *2* vuelve *3* vuelvo, vuelves, vuelve, vuelven *6* vuelva, vuelvas, vuelva, vuelvan *8* vuelto

VERBOS IRREGULARES EN INGLÉS

present	pt	pp	present	pt	pp
arise (arising)	arose	arisen	eat	ate	eaten
awake (awaking)	awoke	awaked	fall	fell	fallen
be (am, is, are, being)	was, were	been	feed	fed	fed
			feel	felt	felt
bear	bore	born(e)	fight	fought	fought
beat	beat	beaten	find	found	found
become (becoming)	became	become	flee	fled	fled
			fling	flung	flung
befall	befell	befallen	fly (flies)	flew	flown
begin (beginning)	began	begun	forbid (forbidding)	forbade	forbidden
behold	beheld	beheld	forecast	forecast	forecast
bend	bent	bent	forego	forewent	foregone
beseech	besought	besought	foresee	foresaw	foreseen
beset (besetting)	beset	beset	foretell	foretold	foretold
bet (betting)	bet (also betted)	bet (also betted)	forget (forgetting)	forgot	forgotten
			forgive (forgiving)	forgave	forgiven
bid (bidding)	bid (also bade)	bid (also bidden)	forsake (forsaking)	forsook	forsaken
bind	bound	bound	freeze (freezing)	froze	frozen
bite (biting)	bit	bitten	get (getting)	got	got, (US) gotten
bleed	bled	bled			
blow	blew	blown	give (giving)	gave	given
break	broke	broken	go (goes)	went	gone
breed	bred	bred	grind	ground	ground
bring	brought	brought	grow	grew	grown
build	built	built	hang	hung (also hanged)	hung (also hanged)
burn	burned (also burnt)	burned (also burnt)	have (has; having)	had	had
burst	burst	burst	hear	heard	heard
buy	bought	bought	hide (hiding)	hid	hidden
can	could	(been able)	hit (hitting)	hit	hit
cast	cast	cast	hold	held	held
catch	caught	caught	hurt	hurt	hurt
choose (choosing)	chose	chosen	keep	kept	kept
cling	clung	clung	kneel	knelt (also kneeled)	knelt (also kneeled)
come (coming)	came	come	know	knew	known
cost	cost	cost	lay	laid	laid
creep	crept	crept	lead	led	led
cut (cutting)	cut	cut	lean	leaned (also leant)	leaned (also leant)
deal	dealt	dealt	leap	leaped (also leapt)	leaped (also leapt)
dig (digging)	dug	dug	learn	learned (also learnt)	learned (also learnt)
do (3rd person: he/she/it/does)	did	done	leave (leaving)	left	left
draw	drew	drawn	lend	lent	lent
dream	dreamed (also dreamt)	dreamed also dreamt)	let (letting)	let	let
drink	drank	drunk	lie (lying)	lay	lain
drive (driving)	drove	driven	light	lighted (also lit)	lighted (also lit)
dwell	dwelt	dwelt	lose (losing)	lost	lost

present	pt	pp	present	pt	pp
make (making)	made	made	**spell**	spelled (*also* spelt)	spelled (*also* spelt)
may	might	—	**spend**	spent	spent
mean	meant	meant	**spill**	spilled (*also* spilt)	spilled (*also* spilt)
meet	met	met			
mistake (mistaking)	mistook	mistaken	**spin (spinning)**	spun	spun
mow	mowed	mowed (*also* mown)	**spit (spitting)**	spat	spat
			split (splitting)	split	split
must	(had to)	(had to)	**spoil**	spoiled (*also* spoilt)	spoiled (*also* spoilt)
pay	paid	paid			
put (putting)	put	put	**spread**	spread	spread
quit (quitting)	quit (*also* quitted)	quit (*also* quitted)	**spring**	sprang	sprung
read	read	read	**stand**	stood	stood
rend	rent	rent	**steal**	stole	stolen
rid (ridding)	rid	rid	**stick**	stuck	stuck
ride (riding)	rode	ridden	**sting**	stung	stung
ring	rang	rung	**stink**	stank	stunk
rise (rising)	rose	risen	**stride (striding)**	strode	stridden
run (running)	ran	run			
saw	sawed	sawn	**strike (striking)**	struck	struck (*also* stricken)
say	said	said			
see	saw	seen	**strive (striving)**	strove	striven
seek	sought	sought			
sell	sold	sold	**swear**	swore	sworn
send	sent	sent	**sweep**	swept	swept
set (setting)	set	set	**swell**	swelled	swelled (*also* swollen)
shake (shaking)	shook	shaken			
shall	should	—	**swim (swimming)**	swam	swum
shear	sheared	sheared (*also* shorn)	**swing**	swung	swung
			take (taking)	took	taken
shed (shedding)	shed	shed	**teach**	taught	taught
			tear	tore	torn
shine (shining)	shone	shone	**tell**	told	told
			think	thought	thought
shoot	shot	shot	**throw**	threw	thrown
show	showed	shown	**thrust**	thrust	thrust
shrink	shrank	shrunk	**tread**	trod	trodden
shut (shutting)	shut	shut	**wake (waking)**	woke (*also* waked)	waked (*also* woken)
sing	sang	sung	**waylay**	waylaid	waylaid
sink	sank	sunk	**wear**	wore	worn
sit (sitting)	sat	sat	**weave (weaving)**	wove (*also* weaved)	woven (*also* weaved)
slay	slew	slain			
sleep	slept	slept	**wed (wedding)**	wedded	wedded (*also* wed)
slide (sliding)	slid	slid			
sling	slung	slung	**weep**	wept	wept
slit (slitting)	slit	slit	**win (winning)**	won	won
smell	smelled (*Brit* smelt)	smelled (*Brit* smelt)	**wind**	wound	wound
			withdraw	withdrew	withdrawn
sow	sowed	sown (*also* sowed)	**withhold**	withheld	withheld
			withstand	withstood	withstood
speak	spoke	spoken	**wring**	wrung	wrung
speed	sped (*also* speeded)	sped (*also* speeded)	**write (writing)**	wrote	written

NÚMEROS   NUMBERS

uno (un, una)★	1	one
dos	2	two
tres	3	three
cuatro	4	four
cinco	5	five
seis	6	six
siete	7	seven
ocho	8	eight
nueve	9	nine
diez	10	ten
once	11	eleven
doce	12	twelve
trece	13	thirteen
catorce	14	fourteen
quince	15	fifteen
dieciséis	16	sixteen
diecisiete	17	seventeen
dieciocho	18	eighteen
diecinueve	19	nineteen
veinte	20	twenty
veintiuno(-un, -una)★	21	twenty-one
veintidós	22	twenty-two
treinta	30	thirty
treinta y uno(un, una)★	31	thirty-one
treinta y dos	32	thirty-two
cuarenta	40	forty
cincuenta	50	fifty
sesenta	60	sixty
setenta	70	seventy
ochenta	80	eighty
noventa	90	ninety
cien(ciento)★★	100	a hundred, one hundred
ciento uno(un, una)★	101	a hundred and one
ciento dos	102	a hundred and two
ciento cincuenta y seis	156	a hundred and fifty-six
doscientos(as)	200	two hundred
trescientos(as)	300	three hundred
quinientos(as)	500	five hundred
mil	1,000	a thousand
mil tres	1,003	a thousand and three
dos mil	2,000	two thousand
un millón	1,000,000	a million

★ 'uno' (+ 'veintiuno' etc) agrees in gender (but not number) with its noun: treinta y una personas; the masculine form is shortened to 'un' unless it stands alone: veintiún caballos, veintiuno.

★★ 'ciento' is used in compound numbers, except when it multiplies: ciento diez, but cien mil. 'Cien' is used before nouns: cien hombres, cien casas.

NÚMEROS

NUMBERS

primero(primer, primera), 1º, 1er/1ª, 1era	first, 1st
segundo(a), 2º/2ª	second, 2nd
tercero(tercer, tercera), 3º, 3er/3ª, 3era	third, 3rd
cuarto(a), 4º/4ª	fourth, 4th
quinto(a)	fifth, 5th
sexto(a)	sixth, 6th
séptimo(a)	seventh
octavo(a)	eighth
noveno(a); nono(a)	ninth
décimo(a)	tenth
undécimo(a)	eleventh
duodécimo(a)	twelfth
decimotercio(a)	thirteenth
decimocuarto(a)	fourteenth
decimoquinto(a)	fifteenth
decimosexto(a)	sixteenth
decimoséptimo(a)	seventeenth
decimoctavo(a)	eighteenth
decimonono(a)	nineteenth
vigésimo(a)	twentieth
vigésimo primero(a)	twenty-first
vigésimo segundo(a)	twenty-second
trigésimo(a)	thirtieth
trigésimo primero(a)	thirty-first
trigésimo segundo(a)	thirty-second
cuadragésimo(a)	fortieth
quincuagésimo(a)	fiftieth
sexagésimo(a)	sixtieth
septuagésimo(a)	seventieth
octogésimo(a)	eightieth
nonagésimo(a)	ninetieth
centésimo(a)	hundredth
centésimo primero(a)	hundred-and-first
milésimo(a)	thousandth

ESPAÑOL - INGLÉS
SPANISH - ENGLISH

A

A, a [á] *nf* (*letra*) A, a; **A de Antonio** A for Able.

a [á] *prep* (*a + el = al*) (*lugar*) at; (*dirección*) to; (*destino*) to, towards; (*tiempo*) at; (*complemento de objeto*): **quiero ~ mis padres** I love my parents; (*manera*): **hacerlo ~ la fuerza** to do it by force; (*con verbo*): **empezó ~ llover** it started raining; **~ la derecha/izquierda** on the right/left; **al lado de** beside, at the side of; **subir ~ un avión/tren** to board a plane/train; **está ~ 7 km de aquí** it is 7 km (away) from here; **hablar ~ larga distancia** to speak long distance; **~ las cuatro** at four o'clock; **~ eso de las cuatro** at about four o'clock; **¿~ qué hora?** (at) what time?; **~ los 30 años** at 30 years of age; **al día siguiente** the next day; **al poco tiempo** a short time after; **al verlo yo** when I saw it; **ir ~ caballo/pie** to go on horseback/foot; **poco ~ poco** little by little; **de dos ~ tres** from two to three; **ocho horas al día** eight hours a *o* per day; **al año/~ la semana** a year/week later; **~ 50 ptas el kilo** 50 pesetas a kilo; **enseñar ~ leer** to teach to read; **voy ~ llevarlo** I am going to carry it; **cercano ~** near (to); **por miedo ~** out of fear of; **¡~ comer!** let's eat!; **¡~ que llueve!** I bet it's going to rain!; **¿~ qué viene eso?** what's the meaning of this?; **~ ver** let's see.

A. *abr* (*ESCOL.* = *aprobado*) pass.

AA *nfpl abr* = Aerolíneas Argentinas.

ab. *abr* (= *abril*) Apr.

abad, esa [ábáb', tħe'sá] *nm/f* abbot/abbess.

abadía [ábábē'á] *nf* abbey.

abajo [ábá'ho] *ad* (*situación*) (down) below, underneath; (*en edificio*) downstairs; (*dirección*) down, downwards; **~ de** *prep* below, under; **el piso de ~** the downstairs apartment; **la parte de ~** the lower part; **¡~ el gobierno!** down with the government!; **cuesta/río ~** downhill/downstream; **de arriba ~** from top to bottom; **el ~ firmante** the undersigned; **más ~** lower *o* further down.

abalance [ábálán'se] *etc vb V* **abalanzarse**.

abalanzarse [ábálánsár'se] *vr*: **~ sobre** *o* **contra** to throw o.s. at.

abalorios [ábálo'ryos] *nmpl* (*chucherías*) trinkets.

abanderado [ábánderá'tħo] *nm* standard bearer.

abandonado, a [ábándoná'tħo, á] *a* derelict; (*desatendido*) abandoned; (*desierto*) deserted; (*descuidado*) neglected.

abandonar [ábándonár'] *vt* to leave; (*persona*) to abandon, desert; (*cosa*) to abandon, leave behind; (*descuidar*) to neglect; (*renunciar a*) to give up; (*INFORM*) to quit; **~se** *vr*: **~se a** to abandon o.s. to; **~se al alcohol** to take to drink.

abandono [ábándo'no] *nm* (*acto*) desertion, abandonment; (*estado*) abandon, neglect; (*renuncia*) withdrawal, retirement; **ganar por ~** to win by default.

abanicar [ábánēkár'] *vt* to fan.

abanico [ábánē'ko] *nm* fan; (*NAUT*) derrick; **en ~** fan-shaped.

abanique [ábánē'ke] *etc vb V* **abanicar**.

abaratar [ábárátár'] *vt* to lower the price of ♦ *vi*, **~se** *vr* to go *o* come down in price.

abarcar [ábárkár'] *vt* to include, embrace; (*contener*) to comprise; (*AM*) to monopolize; **quien mucho abarca poco aprieta** don't bite off more than you can chew.

abarque [ábár'ke] *etc vb V* **abarcar**.

abarrotado, a [ábárrotá'tħo, á] *a* packed; **~ de** packed *o* bursting with.

abarrote [ábárro'te] *nm* packing; **~s** *nmpl* (*AM*) groceries, provisions.

abarrotero, a [ábárrote'ro, á] *nm/f* (*AM*) grocer.

abastecedor, a [ábástesetħor', á] *a* supplying ♦ *nm/f* supplier.

abastecer [ábásteser'] *vt* to supply (*de* with).

abastecimiento [ábástesēmyen'to] *nm* supply.

abastezca [ábástes'ká] *etc vb V* **abastecer**.

abasto [ábá'sto] *nm* supply; (*abundancia*) abundance; **no dar ~ a algo** not to be able to cope with sth.

abatible [ábátē'ħle] *a*: **asiento ~** tip-up seat.

abatido, a [ábátē'tħo, á] *a* dejected, downcast; **estar muy ~** to be very depressed.

abatimiento [ábátēmyen'to] *nm* (*depresión*) dejection, depression.

abatir [ábátēr'] *vt* (*muro*) to demolish; (*pájaro*) to shoot *o* bring down; (*fig*) to depress; **~se** *vr* to get depressed; **~se sobre**

to swoop o pounce on.

abdicación [àbdĕkásyon'] *nf* abdication.

abdicar [àbdĕkár'] *vi* to abdicate; **~ en uno** to abdicate in favor of sb.

abdique [àbdē'ke] *etc vb* **V abdicar.**

abdomen [àbdho'men] *nm* abdomen.

abecedario [àbeseth á'ryo] *nm* alphabet.

abedul [àbethōōl'] *nm* birch.

abeja [àbe'hà] *nf* bee; (*fig: hormiguita*) hard worker.

abejorro [àbecho'rro] *nm* bumblebee.

aberración [àberrásyon'] *nf* aberration.

aberrante [àberrán'te] *a* (*disparatado*) ridiculous.

abertura [àbertōō'rá] *nf* = **apertura.**

abeto [àbe'to] *nm* fir.

abierto, a [àbyer'to, à] *pp de* **abrir ♦** *a* open; (*AM*) generous; (*fig: carácter*) frank.

abigarrado, a [àbēgàrrá'tho, à] *a* multicolored; (*fig*) motley.

abismal [àbēsmál'] *a* (*fig*) vast, enormous.

abismar [àbēsmár'] *vt* to humble, cast down; **~se** *vr* to sink; (*AM*) to be amazed; **~se en** (*fig*) to be plunged into.

abismo [àbēs'mo] *nm* abyss; **de sus ideas a las mías hay un ~** our views are worlds apart.

abjurar [àbhōōrár'] *vt* to abjure, forswear **♦** *vi:* **~ de** to abjure, forswear.

ablandar [àblándár'] *vt* to soften up; (*conmover*) to touch; (*CULIN*) to tenderize **♦** *vi,* **~se** *vr* to get softer.

abnegación [àbnegásyon'] *nf* self-denial.

abnegado, a [àbnegá'tho, à] *a* selfsacrificing.

abobado, a [àbobá'tho, à] *a* silly.

abobamiento [àbobámyen'to] *nm* (*asombro*) bewilderment.

abocado, a [àbokà'tho, à] *a:* **verse ~ al desastre** to be heading for disaster.

abochornar [àbochornár'] *vt* to embarrass; **~se** *vr* to get flustered; (*BOT*) to wilt; **~se de** to get embarrassed about.

abofetear [àbofeteár'] *vt* to slap (in the face).

abogacía [àbogàsē'á] *nf* legal profession; (*ejercicio*) practice of the law.

abogado, a [àbogá'tho, à] *nm/f* lawyer; (*notario*) ≈ notary; (*asesor*) counsel; (*en tribunal*) attorney (*US*), barrister (*Brit*); **~ defensor** defense attorney; **~ del diablo** devil's advocate.

abogar [àbogár'] *vi:* **~ por** to plead for; (*fig*) to advocate.

abogue [àbo'ge] *etc vb* **V abogar.**

abolengo [àbolen'go] *nm* ancestry, lineage.

abolición [àbolēsyon'] *nf* abolition.

abolir [àbolēr'] *vt* to abolish; (*cancelar*) to cancel.

abolladura [àboyàthōō'rá] *nf* dent.

abollar [àboyár'] *vt* to dent.

abominable [àbomēná'ble] *a* abominable.

abominación [àbomēnásyon'] *nf* abomination.

abonado, a [àboná'tho, à] *a* (*deuda*) paid (-up) **♦** *nm/f* subscriber.

abonar [àbonár'] *vt* to pay; (*deuda*) to settle; (*terreno*) to fertilize; (*idea*) to endorse; **~se** *vr* to subscribe; **~ dinero en una cuenta** to pay money into an account, credit money to an account.

abono [àbo'no] *nm* payment; fertilizer; subscription.

abordable [àbordhá'ble] *a* (*persona*) approachable.

abordar [àbordhár'] *vt* (*barco*) to board; (*asunto*) to broach; (*individuo*) to approach.

aborigen [àborē'hen] *nm/f* aborigine.

aborrecer [àborreser'] *vt* to hate, loathe.

aborrezca [àborres'ká] *etc vb* **V aborrecer.**

abortar [àbortár'] *vi* (*malparir*) to have a miscarriage; (*deliberadamente*) to have an abortion.

aborto [àbor'to] *nm* miscarriage; abortion.

abotagado, a [àbotàgá'tho, à] *a* swollen.

abotonar [àbotonár'] *vt* to button (up), do up.

abovedado, a [àbovethá'tho, à] *a* vaulted, domed.

abr. *abr* (= *abril*) Apr.

abrace [àbrá'se] *etc vb* **V abrazar.**

abrasar [àbrásár'] *vt* to burn (up); (*AGR*) to dry up, parch.

abrazadera [àbrásàthe'rá] *nf* bracket.

abrazar [àbrásár'] *vt* to embrace, hug; **~se** *vr* to embrace, hug each other.

abrazo [àbrá'so] *nm* embrace, hug; **un ~** (*en carta*) with best wishes.

abrebotellas [àbrebote'yás] *nm inv* bottle opener.

abrecartas [àbrekár'tás] *nm inv* letter opener.

abrelatas [àbrelá'tás] *nm inv* can (*US*) o tin (*Brit*) opener.

abrevadero [àbrevàthe'ro] *nm* watering place.

abreviar [àbrevyár'] *vt* to abbreviate; (*texto*) to abridge; (*plazo*) to reduce **♦** *vi:* **bueno, para ~** well, to cut a long story short.

abreviatura [àbrevyátōō'rá] *nf* abbreviation.

abridor [àbrēthor'] *nm* (*de botellas*) bottle opener; (*de latas*) can (*US*) o tin (*Brit*) opener.

abrigar [àbrēgár'] *vt* (*proteger*) to shelter; (*suj: ropa*) to keep warm; (*fig*) to cherish; **~se** *vr* to take shelter, protect o.s (*de* from); (*con ropa*) to cover (o.s.) up; **¡abrígate bien!** wrap up well!

abrigo [àbrē'go] *nm* (*prenda*) coat, overcoat; (*lugar protegido*) shelter; **al ~ de** in the shelter of.

abrigue [àbrē'ge] etc vb V **abrigar**.

abril [àbrēl'] nm April.

abrillantar [àbrēyàntàr'] vt (pulir) to polish; (fig) to enhance.

abrir [àbrēr'] vt to open (up); (camino etc) to open up; (apetito) to whet; (lista) to head ♦ vi to open; ~**se** vr to open (up); (extenderse) to open out; (cielo) to clear; ~ **un negocio** to start up a business; **en un** ~ **y cerrar de ojos** in the twinkling of an eye; ~**se paso** to find o force a way through.

abrochar [àbrotchàr'] vt (con botones) to button (up); (AM) to staple; (zapato, con broche) to do up; ~**se** vr: ~**se los zapatos** to tie one's shoelaces.

abrogación [àbrogàsyon'] nf repeal.

abrogar [àbrogàr'] vt to repeal.

abrumador, a [àbrōōmàthor', à] a (mayoría) overwhelming.

abrumar [àbrōōmàr'] vt to overwhelm; (sobrecargar) to weigh down.

abrupto, a [àbrōōp'to, à] a abrupt; (empinado) steep.

absceso [àbsse'so] nm abscess.

absentismo [àbssentēs'mo] nm (de obreros) absenteeism.

absolución [àbssolōōsyon'] nf (REL) absolution; (JUR) acquittal.

absoluto, a [àbssolōō'to, à] a absolute; (total) utter, complete; **en** ~ ad not at all.

absolver [àbssolver'] vt to absolve; (JUR) to pardon; (: acusado) to acquit.

absorbente [àbssorben'te] a absorbent; (interesante) absorbing, interesting; (exigente) demanding.

absorber [àbssorber'] vt to absorb; (embeber) to soak up; ~**se** vr to become absorbed.

absorción [àbssorsyon'] nf absorption; (COM) takeover.

absorto, a [àbssor'to, à] pp de **absorber** ♦ a absorbed, engrossed.

abstemio, a [àbsste'myo, à] a teetotal.

abstención [àbsstensyon'] nf abstention.

abstendré [àbsstendre'] etc vb V **abstenerse**.

abstenerse [àbsstener'se] vr: ~ **(de)** to abstain o refrain (from).

abstenga [àbssten'gà] etc vb V **abstenerse**.

abstinencia [àbsstēnen'syà] nf abstinence; (ayuno) fasting.

abstracción [àbsstràksyon'] nf abstraction.

abstracto, a [àbsstràk'to, à] a abstract; **en** ~ in the abstract.

abstraer [àbsstràer'] vt to abstract; ~**se** vr to be o become absorbed.

abstraído, a [àbsstràē'tho, à] a absentminded.

abstraiga [àbsstrà'ēgà] etc, **abstraje** [àbsstrà'he] etc, **abstrayendo** [àbsstràyen'do]

etc vb V **abstraer**.

abstuve [àbsstōō'be] etc vb V **abstenerse**.

absuelto [àbsswel'to] pp de **absolver**.

absurdo, a [àbssōōr'tho, à] a absurd; **lo** ~ **es que ...** the ridiculous thing is that ... ♦ nm absurdity.

abuchear [àbōōtcheàr'] vt to boo.

abucheo [àbōōtche'o] nm booing; **ganarse un** ~ (TEATRO) to be booed.

abuela [àbwe'là] nf grandmother; **¡cuéntaselo a tu** ~! (fam!) do you think I was born yesterday? (fam); **no tener/necesitar** ~ (fam) to be full of o.s./blow one's own horn (US) o trumpet (Brit).

abuelita [àbwelē'tà] nf grandma.

abuelo [àbwe'lo] nm grandfather; (antepasado) ancestor; ~**s** nmpl grandparents.

abulense [àbōōlen'se] a of Ávila ♦ nm/f native o inhabitant of Ávila.

abulia [àbōō'lyà] nf lethargy.

abultado, a [àbōōltà'tho, à] a bulky.

abultar [àbōōltàr'] vt to enlarge; (aumentar) to increase; (fig) to exaggerate ♦ vi to be bulky.

abundancia [àbōōndàn'syà] nf: **una** ~ **de** plenty of; **en** ~ in abundance.

abundante [àbōōndàn'te] a abundant, plentiful.

abundar [àbōōndàr'] vi to abound, be plentiful; ~ **en una opinión** to share an opinion.

aburguesarse [àbōōrgesàr'se] vr to become middle-class.

aburrido, a [àbōōrrē'tho, à] a (hastiado) bored; (que aburre) boring.

aburrimiento [àbōōrrēmyen'to] nm boredom, tedium.

aburrir [àbōōrrēr'] vt to bore; ~**se** vr to be bored, get bored; ~**se como una almeja** u **ostra** to be bored stiff.

abusar [àbōōsàr'] vi to go too far; ~ **de** to abuse.

abusivo, a [àbōōsē'bo, à] a (precio) exorbitant.

abuso [àbōō'so] nm abuse; ~ **de confianza** betrayal of trust.

abyecto, a [àbyek'to, à] a wretched, abject.

A.C. abr (= Año de Cristo) A.D.

a/c abr (= al cuidado de) c/o; (= a cuenta) on account.

acá [àkà'] ad (lugar) here; **pasearse de** ~ **para allá** to walk up and down; **¡vente para** ~! come over here!; **¿de cuándo** ~? since when?

acabado, a [àkàbà'tho, à] a finished, complete; (perfecto) perfect; (agotado) worn out; (fig) masterly ♦ nm finish.

acabar [àkàbàr'] vt (llevar a su fin) to finish, complete; (consumir) to use up; (rematar) to finish off ♦ vi to finish, end; (morir) to die; ~**se** vr to finish, stop; (terminarse) to be over; (agotarse) to run out; ~ **con** to put an end to; ~ **mal** (*historia*) to turn out badly; **esto acabará conmigo** this will be the end of me; ~ **de llegar** to have just arrived; **acababa de hacerlo** I had just done it; ~ **haciendo** *o* **por hacer algo** to end up (by) doing sth; **¡se acabó!** (*¡basta!*) that's enough!; (*se terminó*) it's all over!; **se me acabó el tabaco** I ran out of cigarettes.

acabóse [ákábo'sc] *nm*: **esto es el** ~ this is the limit.

academia [ákáðc'myá] *nf* academy.

académico, a [ákáðc'mčko, á] *a* academic.

acaecer [ákácscr'] *vi* to happen, occur.

acaezca [ákács'ká] *etc vb* V **acaecer.**

acalorado, a [ákálorá'tho, á] *a* (*discusión*) heated.

acalorarse [ákálorár'sc] *vr* (*fig*) to get heated.

acallar [ákáyár'] *vt* (*silenciar*) to silence; (*calmar*) to pacify.

acampar [ákámpár'] *vi* to camp.

acanalado, a [ákánálá'tho, á] *a* (*hierro*) corrugated.

acanalar [ákánálár'] *vt* to groove; (*ondular*) to corrugate.

acantilado [ákántčlá'tho] *nm* cliff.

acaparador, a [ákápáráthor', á] *nm/f* monopolizer.

acaparar [ákápárár'] *vt* to monopolize; (*acumular*) to hoard.

acaramelado, a [ákárámclá'tho, á] *a* (*CULIN*) toffee-coated; (*fig*) sugary.

acariciar [ákárčsyár'] *vt* to caress; (*esperanza*) to cherish.

acarrear [ákárrcár'] *vt* to transport; (*fig*) to cause, result in; **le acarreó muchos disgustos** it brought him lots of problems.

acaso [áká'so] *ad* perhaps, maybe ♦ *nm* chance; **(por) si** ~ (just) in case.

acatamiento [ákátámycn'to] *nm* respect; (*de la ley*) observance.

acatar [ákátár'] *vt* to respect; (*ley*) to obey, observe.

acatarrarse [ákátárrár'sc] *vr* to catch a cold.

acaudalado, a [ákáoothálá'tho, á] *a* well-off.

acaudillar [ákáoothčyár'] *vt* to lead, command.

acceder [ákscðer'] *vi* to accede, agree; ~ **a** (*INFORM*) to access.

accesar [ákscsár'] *vt* to access.

accesible [ákscsc'blc] *a* accessible; ~ **a** open to.

accésit, *pl* **accésits** [áksc'sčt, aksc'sčts] *nm* consolation prize.

acceso [áksc'so] *nm* access, entry; (*camino*) access road; (*MED*) attack, fit; (*de cólera*) fit; (*POL*) accession; (*INFORM*) access; ~ **aleatorio/directo/secuencial** *o* **en serie** (*IN-*

FORM) random/direct/sequential *o* serial access; **de** ~ **múltiple** multi-access.

accesorio, a [ákscso'ryo, á] *a* accessory ♦ *nm* accessory; ~**s** *nmpl* (*AUTO*) accessories, extras; (*TEATRO*) props.

accidentado, a [ákscðhcntá'tho, á] *a* uneven; (*montañoso*) hilly; (*azaroso*) eventful ♦ *nm/f* accident victim.

accidental [ákscðhcntál'] *a* accidental; (*empleo*) temporary.

accidentarse [ákscðhcntár'sc] *vr* to have an accident.

accidente [ákscðhcn'tc] *nm* accident; **por** ~ by chance; ~**s** *nmpl* unevenness *sg*, roughness *sg*.

acción [áksyon'] *nf* action; (*acto*) action, act; (*TEATRO*) plot; (*COM*) share; (*JUR*) action, lawsuit; **capital en acciones** share capital; ~ **liberada/ordinaria/preferente** fully-paid/ordinary/preference share.

accionamiento [áksyonámycn'to] *nm* (*de máquina*) operation.

accionar [áksyonár'] *vt* to work, operate; (*INFORM*) to drive.

accionista [áksyonč'stá] *nm/f* shareholder.

acebo [ásc'ho] *nm* holly; (*árbol*) holly tree.

acechanza [ásctchán'sá] *nf* = **acecho.**

acechar [ásctchár'] *vt* to spy on; (*aguardar*) to lie in wait for.

acecho [ásc'tcho] *nm*: **estar al** ~ **(de)** to lie in wait (for).

acedera [ásctðc'rá] *nf* sorrel.

aceitar [ásctár'] *vt* to oil, lubricate.

aceite [ásc'čtc] *nm* oil; (*de oliva*) olive oil; ~ **de hígado de bacalao** cod-liver oil.

aceitera [ásctčc'rá] *nf* oilcan.

aceitoso, a [ásccto'so, á] *a* oily.

aceituna [ásccto͞o'ná] *nf* olive.

aceitunado, a [ásccto͞oná'tho, á] *a* olive *cpd*; **de tez aceitunada** olive-skinned.

acelerador [ásclcrátho'r] *nm* gas pedal (*US*), accelerator (*Brit*).

acelerar [ásclcrár'] *vt* to accelerate; ~**se** *vr* to hurry.

acelga [ásc'l'gá] *nf* chard, beet.

acendrado, a [áscndrá'tho, á] *a*: **de** ~ **carácter español** typically Spanish.

acendrar [ásccndrár'] *vt* to purify.

acento [áscn'to] *nm* accent; (*acentuación*) stress; ~ **cerrado** strong *o* thick accent.

acentuar [áscntwár'] *vt* to accent; to stress; (*fig*) to accentuate; (*INFORM*) to highlight.

acepción [áscpsyon'] *nf* meaning.

aceptación [áscptásyon'] *nf* acceptance; (*aprobación*) approval.

aceptar [áscptár'] *vt* to accept; to approve.

acequia [ásc'kyá] *nf* irrigation ditch.

acera [ásc'rá] *nf* sidewalk (*US*), pavement (*Brit*).

acerado, a [áscrá'tho, á] *a* steel; (*afilado*) sharp; (*fig*: *duro*) steely; (: *mordaz*) biting.

acerbo, a |àscr'ħo, à| *a* bitter; (*fig*) harsh.

acerca |àscr'kà| *ad* about, concerning.

acercar |àscrkàr'| *vt* to bring *o* move nearer; **~se** *vr* to approach, come near.

acerico |àscrē'ko| *nm* pincushion.

acero |àsc'ro| *nm* steel; **~ inoxidable** stainless steel.

acerque |àscr'kc| *etc vb* V **acercar.**

acérrimo, a |àsc'rrēmo, à| *a* (*partidario*) staunch; (*enemigo*) bitter.

acertado, a |àscrtà'ħo, à| *a* correct; (*apropiado*) apt; (*sensato*) sensible.

acertar |àscrtàr'| *vt* (*blanco*) to hit; (*solución*) to get right; (*adivinar*) to guess ♦ *vi* to get it right, be right; **~ a** to manage to; **~ con** to happen *o* hit on.

acertijo |àscrtē'ho| *nm* riddle, puzzle.

acervo |àscr'ħo| *nm* heap; **~ común** undivided estate.

aciago, a |àsyà'go, à| *a* ill-fated, fateful.

acicalar |àsckàlàr'| *vt* to polish; (*adornar*) to adorn; **~se** *vr* to get dressed up.

acicate |àsckà'tc| *nm* spur; (*fig*) incentive.

acidez |àscħcs'| *nf* acidity.

ácido, a |à'scħo, à| *a* sour, acid ♦ *nm* acid; (*fam: droga*) LSD.

acierto |àsycr'to| *etc vb* V **acertar** ♦ *nm* success; (*buen paso*) wise move; (*solución*) solution; (*habilidad*) skill, ability; (*al adivinar*) good guess; **fue un ~ suyo** it was a sensible choice on his part.

aclamación |àklàmàsyon'| *nf* acclamation; (*aplausos*) applause.

aclamar |àklàmàr'| *vt* to acclaim; to applaud.

aclaración |àklàràsyon'| *nf* clarification, explanation.

aclarar |àklàràr'| *vt* to clarify, explain; (*ropa*) to rinse ♦ *vi* to clear up; **~se** *vr* (*suj: persona: explicarse*) to understand; (*fig: asunto*) to become clear; **~se la garganta** to clear one's throat.

aclaratorio, a |àklàràto'ryo, à| *a* explanatory.

aclimatación |àklēmàtàsyon'| *nf* acclimatation (*US*), acclimatization (*Brit*).

aclimatar |àklēmàtàr'| *vt* to acclimate (*US*), acclimatize (*Brit*); **~se** *vr* to become *o* get acclimated; **~se a algo** to get used to sth.

acné |àknc'| *nm* acne.

acobardar |àkoħàrħàr'| *vt* to daunt, intimidate; **~se** *vr* (*atemorizarse*) to be intimidated; (*echarse atrás*): **~se (ante)** to shrink back (from).

acodarse |àkoħàr'sc| *vr*: **~ en** to lean on.

acogedor, a |àkoħcħħor', à| *a* welcoming; (*hospitalario*) hospitable.

acoger |àkohcr'| *vt* to welcome; (*abrigar*) to shelter; **~se** *vr* to take refuge; **~se a** (*pretexto*) to take refuge in; (*ley*) to resort to.

acogida |àkohē'ħà| *nf* reception; refuge.

acogollar |àkogoyàr'| *vt* (*AGR*) to cover up ♦ *vi* to sprout.

acoja |àko'hà| *etc vb* V **acoger.**

acojonante |àkohonàn'tc| *a* (*Esp fam*) tremendous.

acolchar |àkoltchàr'| *vt* to pad; (*fig*) to cushion.

acólito |àko'lēto| *nm* (*REL*) acolyte; (*fig*) minion.

acometer |àkomctcr'| *vt* to attack; (*emprender*) to undertake.

acometida |àkomctē'ħà| *nf* attack, assault.

acomodado, a |àkomoħà'ħo, à| *a* (*persona*) well-to-do.

acomodador, a |àkomoħàħħor', à| *nm/f* usher(ette).

acomodar |àkomoħàr'| *vt* to adjust; (*alojar*) to accommodate; **~se** *vr* to conform; (*instalarse*) to install o.s.; (*adaptarse*) to adapt o.s.; **¡acomódese a su gusto!** make yourself comfortable!

acomodaticio, a |àkomoħàtē'syo, à| *a* (*pey*) accommodating, obliging; (*manejable*) pliable.

acompañamiento |àkompànyàmycn'to| *nm* (*MUS*) accompaniment.

acompañante, a |àkompànyàn'tc, à| *nm/f* companion.

acompañar |àkompànyàr'| *vt* to accompany, go with; (*documentos*) to enclose; **¿quieres que te acompañe?** do you want me to come with you?; **~ a uno a la puerta** to see sb to the door *o* out; **le acompaño en el sentimiento** please accept my condolences.

acompasar |àkompàsàr'| *vt* (*MUS*) to mark the rhythm of.

acomplejado, a |àkomplchà'ħo, à| *a* neurotic.

acomplejar |àkomplchàr'| *vt* to give a complex to; **~se** *vr*: **~se (con)** to get a complex (about).

acondicionado, a |àkondēsyonà'ħo, à| *a* (*TEC*) in good condition.

acondicionador |àkondēsyonàħħor'| *nm* conditioner.

acondicionar |àkondēsyonàr'| *vt* to get ready, prepare; (*pelo*) to condition.

acongojar |àkongohàr'| *vt* to distress, grieve.

aconsejable |àkonschà'ħlc| *a* advisable.

aconsejar |àkonschàr'| *vt* to advise, counsel; **~se** *vr*: **~se con** *o* **de** to consult.

acontecer |àkontcscr'| *vi* to happen, occur.

acontecimiento |àkontcscmycn'to| *nm* event.

acontezca |àkontcs'kà| *etc vb* V **acontecer.**

acopiar |àkopyàr'| *vt* (*recoger*) to gather; (*COM*) to buy up.

acopio [åko'pyo] *nm* store, stock.

acoplador [åkoplåɖor'] *nm*: ~ **acústico** (*INFORM*) acoustic coupler.

acoplamiento [åkoplåmyen'to] *nm* coupling, joint.

acoplar [åkoplår'] *vt* to fit; (*ELEC*) to connect; (*vagones*) to couple.

acoquinar [åkokēnår'] *vt* to scare; ~**se** *vr* to get scared.

acorazado, a [åkoråså'ɖo, å] *a* armor-plated (*US*), armour-plated (*Brit*), armored (*US*), armoured (*Brit*) ♦ *nm* battleship.

acordar [åkorɖår'] *vt* (*resolver*) to agree, resolve; (*recordar*) to remind; ~**se** *vr* to agree; ~**se (de algo)** to remember (sth).

acorde [åkor'ɖe] *a* (*MUS*) harmonious; ~ **con** (*medidas etc*) in keeping with ♦ *nm* chord.

acordeón [åkorɖeon'] *nm* accordion.

acordonado, a [åkorɖonå'ɖo, å] *a* (*calle*) cordoned-off.

acorralar [åkorrålår'] *vt* to round up, corral; (*fig*) to intimidate.

acortar [åkortår'] *vt* to shorten; (*duración*) to cut short; (*cantidad*) to reduce; ~**se** *vr* to become shorter.

acosar [åkosår'] *vt* to pursue relentlessly; (*fig*) to hound, pester; ~ **a uno a preguntas** to pester sb with questions.

acostar [åkostår'] *vt* (*en cama*) to put to bed; (*en suelo*) to lay down; (*barco*) to bring alongside; ~**se** *vr* to go to bed; to lie down.

acostumbrar [åkostōōmbrår'] *vt*: ~ **a uno a algo** to get sb used to sth ♦ *vi*: **(a hacer algo)** to be in the habit (of doing sth); ~**se** *vr*: ~**se a** to get used to.

acotación [åkotåsyon'] *nf* (*apunte*) marginal note; (*GEO*) elevation mark; (*de límite*) boundary mark; (*TEATRO*) stage direction.

acotar [åkotår'] *vt* (*terreno*) to mark out; (*fig*) to limit; (*caza*) to protect.

ácrata [å'krátá] *a, nm/f* anarchist.

acre [å'kre] *a* (*sabor*) sharp, bitter; (*olor*) acrid; (*fig*) biting ♦ *nm* acre.

acrecentar [åkresentår'] *vt* to increase, augment.

acreciente [åkresyen'te] *etc vb* V **acrecentar.**

acreditado, a [åkreɖētå'ɖo, å] *a* (*POL*) accredited; (*COM*): **una casa acreditada** a reputable firm.

acreditar [åkreɖētår'] *vt* (*garantizar*) to vouch for, guarantee; (*autorizar*) to authorize; (*dar prueba de*) to prove; (*COM: abonar*) to credit; (*embajador*) to accredit; ~**se** *vr* to become famous; (*demostrar valía*) to prove one's worth; ~**se de** to get a reputation for.

acreedor, a [åkreeɖor', å] *a*: ~ **a** worthy of ♦ *nm/f* creditor; ~ **común/diferido/con ga-**

rantía (*COM*) unsecured/deferred/secured creditor.

acribillar [åkrēbēyår'] *vt*: ~ **a balazos** to riddle with bullets.

acrimonia [åkrēmo'nyá], **acritud** [åkrētōōth'] *nf* acrimony.

acrobacia [åkroßå'syå] *nf* acrobatics; ~ **aérea** aerobatics.

acróbata [åkro'ßátá] *nm/f* acrobat.

acta [åk'tá] *nf* certificate; (*de comisión*) minutes *pl*, record; ~ **de nacimiento/de matrimonio** birth/marriage certificate; ~ **notarial** affidavit; **levantar** ~ (*JUR*) to make a formal statement *o* deposition.

actitud [åktētōōth'] *nf* attitude; (*postura*) posture; **adoptar una** ~ **firme** to take a firm stand.

activar [åktēßår'] *vt* to activate; (*acelerar*) to speed up.

actividad [åktēßēthåth'] *nf* activity; **estar en plena** ~ to be in full swing.

activo, a [åktē'ßo, å] *a* active; (*vivo*) lively ♦ *nm* (*COM*) assets *pl*; ~ **y pasivo** assets and liabilities; ~ **circulante/fijo/inmaterial/invisible** (*COM*) current/fixed/intangible/invisible assets; ~ **realizable** liquid assets; ~**s congelados** *o* **bloqueados** frozen assets; **estar en** ~ (*MIL*) to be on active service.

acto [åk'to] *nm* act, action; (*ceremonia*) ceremony; (*TEATRO*) act; **en el** ~ immediately; **hacer** ~ **de presencia** (*asistir*) to attend (formally).

actor [åktor'] *nm* actor; (*JUR*) plaintiff.

actora [åkto'rá] *a*: **parte** ~ prosecution; (*demandante*) plaintiff.

actriz [åktrēs'] *nf* actress.

actuación [åktwåsyon'] *nf* action; (*comportamiento*) conduct, behavior; (*JUR*) proceedings *pl*; (*desempeño*) performance.

actual [åktwål'] *a* present(-day), current; **el 6 del** ~ the 6th of this month.

actualice [åktwålē'se] *etc vb* V **actualizar.**

actualidad [åktwålēthåth'] *nf* present; ~**es** *nfpl* news *sg*; **en la** ~ nowadays, at present; **ser de gran** ~ to be current.

actualización [åktwålēsåsyon'] *nf* updating, modernization.

actualizar [åktwålēsår'] *vt* to update, modernize.

actualmente [åktwålmen'te] *ad* at present; (*hoy día*) nowadays.

actuar [åktwår'] *vi* (*obrar*) to work, operate; (*actor*) to act, perform ♦ *vt* to work, operate; ~ **de** to act as.

actuario, a [åktwå'ryo, å] *nm/f* clerk; (*COM*) actuary.

acuarela [åkwåre'lá] *nf* watercolor (*US*), watercolour (*Brit*).

acuario [åkwå'ryo] *nm* aquarium; **A**~ (*ASTRO*) Aquarius.

acuartelar [àkwàrtelár'] *vt* (*MIL*: *alojar*) to quarter.

acuático, a [àkwá'tēko, à] *a* aquatic.

acuciar [àkoosyár'] *vt* to urge on.

acuclillarse [àkooklēyár'se] *vr* to crouch down.

acuchillar [àkootchēyár'] *vt* (*TEC*) to plane (down), smooth.

ACUDE [àkoo'the] *nf abr* = Asociación de Consumidores y Usuarios de España.

acudir [àkoothēr'] *vi* to attend, turn up; ~ **a** to turn to; ~ **en ayuda de** to go to the aid of; ~ **a una cita** to keep an appointment; ~ **a una llamada** to answer a call; **no tener a quién** ~ to have nobody to turn to.

acuerdo [àkwer'tho] *etc vb V* **acordar** ♦ *nm* agreement; (*POL*) resolution; ~ **de pago respectivo** (*COM*) no-fault (*US*) *o* knock-for-knock (*Brit*) agreement; **A~ general sobre aranceles aduaneros y comercio** (*COM*) General Agreement on Tariffs and Trade; **tomar un** ~ to pass a resolution; **¡de** ~! agreed!; **de** ~ **con** (*persona*) in agreement with; (*acción, documento*) in accordance with; **de común** ~ by common consent; **estar de** ~ (*persona*) to agree; **llegar a un** ~ to come to an understanding.

acueste [àkwe'ste] *etc vb V* **acostar**.

acullá [àkooyá'] *ad* over there.

acumular [àkoomoolár'] *vt* to accumulate, collect.

acunar [àkoonár'] *vt* to rock (to sleep).

acuñar [àkoonyár'] *vt* (*moneda*) to mint; (*frase*) to coin.

acuoso, a [àkwo'so, à] *a* watery.

acupuntura [àkoopoontoo'rà] *nf* acupuncture.

acurrucarse [àkoorrookár'se] *vr* to crouch; (*ovillarse*) to curl up.

acurruque [àkoorroo'ke] *etc vb V* **acurrucarse**.

acusación [àkoosàsyon'] *nf* accusation.

acusado, a [àkoosá'tho, à] *a* (*JUR*) accused; (*marcado*) marked; (*acento*) strong.

acusar [àkoosár'] *vt* to accuse; (*revelar*) to reveal; (*denunciar*) to denounce; (*emoción*) to show; ~ **recibo** to acknowledge receipt; **su rostro acusó extrañeza** his face registered surprise; ~**se** *vr* to confess (*de* to).

acuse [àkoo'se] *nm*: ~ **de recibo** acknowledgement of receipt.

acusete [àkoose'te] *nm/f*, **acusón, ona** [àkooson', oná] *nm/f* telltale, sneak.

acústico, a [àkoo'stēko, à] *a* acoustic ♦ *nf* (*de una sala etc*) acoustics *pl*; (*ciencia*) acoustics *sg*.

achacar [àtchákár'] *vt* to attribute.

achacoso, a [àtcháko'so, à] *a* sickly.

achantar [àtchántár'] *vt* (*fam*) to scare, frighten; ~**se** *vr* to back down.

achaque [àtchá'ke] *etc vb V* **achacar** ♦ *nm* ailment.

achatar [àtchátár'] *vt* to flatten.

achicar [àtchēkár'] *vt* to reduce; (*humillar*) to humiliate; (*NAUT*) to bale out; ~**se** (*ropa*) to shrink; (*fig*) to humble o.s.

achicoria [àtchēko'ryá] *nf* chicory.

achicharrar [àtchētchárrár'] *vt* to scorch, burn.

achinado, a [àtchēná'tho, à] *a* (*ojos*) slanting.

achique [àtchē'ke] *etc vb V* **achicar**.

achuchar [àtchootchár'] *vt* to crush.

achuchón [àtchootchon'] *nm* shove; **tener un** ~ (*MED*) to be poorly.

ADA [à'thá] *nf abr* (*Esp*: = Ayuda del Automovilista*) ≈ AAA (*US*), AA, RAC (*Brit*).

adagio [àthá'hyo] *nm* adage; (*MUS*) adagio.

adalid [àthálēth'] *nm* leader, champion.

adaptación [àtháptàsyon'] *nf* adaptation.

adaptador [àtháptàthor'] *nm* (*ELEC*) adapter.

adaptar [àtháptár'] *vt* to adapt; (*acomodar*) to fit; (*convertir*): ~ **(para)** to convert (to).

adecentar [àthesentár'] *vt* to tidy up.

adecuado, a [àthekwá'tho, à] *a* (*apto*) suitable; (*oportuno*) appropriate; **el hombre** ~ **para el puesto** the right man for the job.

adecuar [àthekwár'] *vt* (*adaptar*) to adapt; (*hacer apto*) to make suitable.

adefesio [àthefe'syo] *nm* (*fam*): **estaba hecha un** ~ she looked a sight.

a. de J.C. *abr* (= antes de Jesucristo*) B.C.

adelantado, a [àthelántá'tho, à] *a* advanced; (*reloj*) fast; **pagar por** ~ to pay in advance.

adelantamiento [àthelántámyen'to] *nm* advance, advancement; (*AUTO*) passing (*US*), overtaking (*Brit*).

adelantar [àthelántár'] *vt* to move forward; (*avanzar*) to advance; (*acelerar*) to speed up; (*AUTO*) to pass (*US*), overtake (*Brit*) ♦ *vi* (*ir delante*) to go ahead; (*progresar*) to improve; (*tb*: ~**se** *vr*: *tomar la delantera*) to go forward, advance; ~**se a uno** to get ahead of sb; ~**se a los deseos de uno** to anticipate sb's wishes.

adelante [àthelán'te] *ad* forward(s), onward(s), ahead ♦ *excl* come in!; **de hoy en** ~ from now on; **más** ~ later on; (*más allá*) further on.

adelanto [àthelán'to] *nm* advance; (*mejora*) improvement; (*progreso*) progress; (*dinero*) advance; **los** ~**s de la ciencia** the advances of science.

adelgace [àthelgá'se] *etc vb V* **adelgazar**.

adelgazar [àthelgásár'] *vt* to thin (down); (*afilar*) to taper ♦ *vi* to get thin; (*con régimen*) to slim down, lose weight.

ademán [àthemán'] *nm* gesture; **ademanes** *nmpl* manners; **en** ~ **de** as if to.

además [àthemás'] *ad* besides; (*por otra*

parte) moreover; (*también*) also; ~ **de** besides, in addition to.

adentrarse [aðentrár'se] *vr*: ~ **en** to go into, get inside; (*penetrar*) to penetrate (into).

adentro [aðen'tro] *ad* inside, in; **mar** ~ out to sea; **tierra** ~ inland ♦ *nmpl*: **dijo para sus** ~**s** he said to himself.

adepto, a [aðep'to, á] *nm/f* supporter.

aderece [aðere'se] *etc vb* V **aderezar.**

aderezar [aðeresár'] *vt* (*ensalada*) to dress; (*comida*) to season.

aderezo [aðere'so] *nm* dressing; seasoning.

adeudar [aðeoōðár'] *vt* to owe; ~**se** *vr* to get into debt; ~ **una suma en una cuenta** to debit an account with a sum.

a.D.g. *abr* (= *a Dios gracias*) D.G. (thanks be to God).

adherirse [aðerēr'se] *vr*: ~ **a** to adhere to; (*fig*) to follow.

adhesión [aðesyon'] *nf* adhesion; (*fig*) adherence.

adhesivo, a [aðesē'ño, á] *a* adhesive ♦ *nm* sticker.

adhiera [aðye'rá] *etc*, **adhiriendo** [aðēryen'do] *etc vb* V **adherirse.**

adición [aðēsyon'] *nf* addition.

adicional [aðēsyonál'] *a* additional; (*INFORM*) add-on.

adicionar [aðēsyonár'] *vt* to add.

adicto, a [aðēk'to, á] *a*: ~ **a** (*droga etc*) addicted to; (*dedicado*) devoted to ♦ *nm/f* supporter, follower; (*toxicómano etc*) addict.

adiestrar [aðyestrár'] *vt* to train, teach; (*conducir*) to guide, lead; ~**se** *vr* to practice (*US*), practise (*Brit*); (*enseñarse*) to train o.s.

adinerado, a [aðēnerá'ðo, á] *a* wealthy.

adiós [aðyos'] *excl* (*para despedirse*) goodbye!; (*al pasar*) hello!

aditivo [aðētē'ño] *nm* additive.

adivinanza [aðēßēnán'sá] *nf* riddle.

adivinar [aðēßēnár'] *vt* (*profetizar*) to prophesy; (*conjeturar*) to guess.

adivino, a [aðēßē'no, á] *nm/f* fortune-teller.

adj *abr* (= *adjunto*) encl.

adjetivo [aðhetē'ño] *nm* adjective.

adjudicación [aðhōōðēkásyon'] *nf* award; (*COM*) adjudication.

adjudicar [aðhōōðēkár'] *vt* to award; ~**se** *vr*: ~**se algo** to appropriate sth.

adjudique [aðhōōðē'ke] *etc vb* V **adjudicar.**

adjuntar [aðhōōntár'] *vt* to attach, enclose.

adjunto, a [aðhōōn'to, á] *a* attached, enclosed ♦ *nm/f* assistant.

adminículo [aðmēnē'kōōlo] *nm* gadget.

administración [aðmēnēstrásyon'] *nf* administration; (*dirección*) management; ~ **pública** civil service; **A**~ **de Correos** General Post Office.

administrador, a [aðmēnēstráðhor', á] *nm/f* administrator; manager(ess).

administrar [aðmēnēstrár'] *vt* to administer.

administrativo, a [aðmēnēstrátē'ño, á] *a* administrative.

admirable [aðmērá'ßle] *a* admirable.

admiración [aðmērásyon'] *nf* admiration; (*asombro*) wonder; (*LING*) exclamation mark.

admirar [aðmērár'] *vt* to admire; (*extrañar*) to surprise; ~**se** *vr* to be surprised; **se admiró de saberlo** he was amazed to hear it; **no es de** ~ **que** ... it's not surprising that ...

admisible [aðmēsē'ßle] *a* admissible.

admisión [aðmēsyon'] *nf* admission; (*reconocimiento*) acceptance.

admitir [aðmētēr'] *vt* to admit; (*aceptar*) to accept; (*dudas*) to leave room for; **esto no admite demora** this must be dealt with immediately.

admón. *abr* (= *administración*) admin.

admonición [aðmonēsyon'] *nf* warning.

adobar [aðoßár'] *vt* (*preparar*) to prepare; (*cocinar*) to season.

adobe [aðo'ße] *nm* adobe, sun-dried brick.

adocenado, a [aðosená'ðo, á] *a* (*fam*) mediocre.

adoctrinar [aðoktrēnár'] *vt* to indoctrinate.

adolecer [aðoleser'] *vi*: ~ **de** to suffer from.

adolescente [aðolesen'te] *nm/f* adolescent, teenager ♦ *a* adolescent, teenage.

adolezca [aðoles'ká] *etc vb* V **adolecer.**

adonde [aðon'ðe] *conj* (to) where.

adónde [aðon'de] *ad* = **dónde.**

adondequiera [aðonðekye'rá] *adv* wherever.

adopción [aðopsyon'] *nf* adoption.

adoptar [aðoptár'] *vt* to adopt.

adoptivo, a [aðoptē'ño, á] *a* (*padres*) adoptive; (*hijo*) adopted.

adoquín [aðokēn'] *nm* paving stone.

adorar [aðorár'] *vt* to adore.

adormecer [aðormeser'] *vt* to put to sleep; ~**se** *vr* to become sleepy; (*dormirse*) to fall asleep.

adormezca [aðormes'ká] *etc vb* V **adormecer.**

adormilarse [aðormēlár'se] *vr* to doze.

adornar [aðornár'] *vt* to adorn.

adorno [aðor'no] *nm* adornment; (*decoración*) decoration.

adosado, a [aðosá'ðo, á] *a*: **una casa adosada** a semi-detached house.

adquiera [aðkye'rá] *etc vb* V **adquirir.**

adquirir [aðkērēr'] *vt* to acquire, obtain.

adquisición [aðkēsēsyon'] *nf* acquisition; (*compra*) purchase.

adrede [àḏre'ḏe] *ad* on purpose.

Adriático [àḏryà'tēko] *nm*: **el (Mar)** ~ the Adriatic (Sea).

adscribir [àḏskrēḇēr'] *vt* to appoint; **estuvo adscrito al servicio de ...** he was attached to ...

adscrito [àḏskrē'to] *pp de* **adscribir.**

aduana [àḏwà'nà] *nf* customs *pl*; *(impuesto)* (customs) duty.

aduanero, a [àḏwàne'ro, à] *a* customs *cpd* ♦ *nm/f* customs officer.

aducir [àḏōōsēr'] *vt* to adduce; *(dar como prueba)* to offer as proof.

adueñarse [àḏwenyàr'se] *vr*: ~ **de** to take possession of.

adulación [àḏōōlàsyon'] *nf* flattery.

adular [àḏōōlàr'] *vt* to flatter.

adulterar [àḏōōlteràr'] *vt* to adulterate ♦ *vi* to commit adultery.

adulterio [àḏōōlte'ryo] *nm* adultery.

adúltero, a [àḏōōl'tero, à] *a* adulterous ♦ *nm/f* adulterer/adulteress.

adulto, a [àḏōōl'to, à] *a, nm/f* adult.

adusto, a [àḏōō'sto, à] *a* stern; *(austero)* austere.

aduzca [àḏōōs'kà] *etc vb V* **aducir.**

advenedizo, a [àḏḇeneḏē'so, à] *nm/f* upstart.

advenimiento [àḏḇenēmyen'to] *nm* arrival; *(al trono)* accession.

adverbio [àḏḇer'ḇyo] *nm* adverb.

adversario, a [àḏḇersà'ryo, à] *nm/f* adversary.

adversidad [àḏḇersēḏàḏ'] *nf* adversity; *(contratiempo)* setback.

adverso, a [àḏḇer'so, à] *a* adverse; *(suerte)* bad.

advertencia [àḏḇerten'syà] *nf* warning; *(prefacio)* preface, foreword.

advertir [àḏḇertēr'] *vt (observar)* to notice; *(avisar)*: ~ **a uno de** to warn sb about o of.

Adviento [àḏḇyen'to] *nm* Advent.

advierta [àḏḇyer'tà] *etc,* **advirtiendo** [àḏḇērtyen'do] *etc vb V* **advertir.**

adyacente [àḏyàsen'te] *a* adjacent.

AECE [àe'se] *nf abr = Asociación Española de Cooperación Europea.*

aéreo, a [àe'reo, à] *a* aerial; *(tráfico)* air *cpd.*

aerobic [àero'ḇēk] *nm* aerobics *sg.*

aerodeslizador [àeroḏeslēsàḏor'], **aerodeslizante** [àeroḏeslēsàn'te] *nm* hovercraft.

aeródromo [àero'ḏromo] *nm* airdrome *(US)*, aerodrome *(Brit)*.

aerograma [àerogrà'mà] *nm* airmail letter.

aeromozo, a [àeromo'so, à] *nm/f (AM)* air steward(ess).

aeronáutica [àeronà'ōōtēkà] *nf* aeronautics *sg.*

aeronave [àeronà'ḇe] *nm* spaceship.

aeroplano [àeroplà'no] *nm* airplane *(US)*, aeroplane *(Brit)*.

aeropuerto [àeropwer'to] *nm* airport.

aerosol [àerosol'] *nm* aerosol, spray.

AES *nm abr = Acuerdo Económico y Social.*

a/f *abr (= a favor)* in favor.

afabilidad [àfàḇēlēḏàḏ'] *nf* affability, pleasantness.

afable [àfà'ḇle] *a* affable, pleasant.

afamado, a [àfàmà'ḏo, à] *a* famous.

afán [àfàn'] *nm* hard work; *(deseo)* desire; **con** ~ keenly.

afanar [àfànàr'] *vt* to harass; *(fam)* to swipe; ~**se** *vr*: ~**se por** to strive to.

afanoso, a [àfàno'so, à] *a (trabajo)* hard; *(trabajador)* industrious.

AFE [à'fe] *nf abr (= Asociación de Futbolistas Españoles)* ≈ F.A.

afear [àfeàr'] *vt* to disfigure.

afección [àfeksyon'] *nf* affection; *(MED)* disease.

afectación [àfektàsyon'] *nf* affectation.

afectado, a [àfektà'ḏo, à] *a* affected.

afectar [àfektàr'] *vt* to affect, have an effect on; *(AM: dañar)* to hurt; **por lo que afecta a esto** as far as this is concerned.

afectísimo, a [àfektē'sēmo, à] *a* affectionate; ~ **suyo** yours truly.

afectivo, a [àfektē'ḇo, à] *a* affective.

afecto, a [àfek'to, à] *a*: ~ **a** fond of; *(JUR)* subject to ♦ *nm* affection; **tenerle** ~ **a uno** to be fond of sb.

afectuoso, a [àfektwo'so, à] *a* affectionate.

afeitar [àfeẏtàr'] *vt* to shave; ~**se** *vr* to shave.

afeminado, a [àfemēnà'ḏo, à] *a* effeminate.

aferrado, a [àferrà'ḏo, à] *a* stubborn.

aferrar [àferràr'] *vt* to moor; *(fig)* to grasp ♦ *vi* to moor; ~**se** *vr (agarrarse)* to cling on; ~**se a un principio** to stick to a principle; ~**se a una esperanza** to cling to a hope.

affmo., a. *abr (= afectísimo, a)* Yours.

Afganistán [àfɡànēstàn'] *nm* Afghanistan.

afgano, a [àfɡà'no, à] *a, nm/f* Afghan.

afiance [àfyàn'se] *etc vb V* **afianzar.**

afianzamiento [àfyànsàmyen'to] *nm* strengthening; security.

afianzar [àfyànsàr'] *vt* to strengthen, secure; ~**se** *vr* to steady o.s.; *(establecerse)* to become established.

afición [àfēsyon'] *nf*: ~ **a** fondness o liking for; **la** ~ the fans *pl*; **pinto por** ~ I paint as a hobby.

aficionado, a [àfēsyonà'ḏo, à] *a* keen, enthusiastic; *(no profesional)* amateur ♦ *nm/f* enthusiast, fan; amateur.

aficionar [àfēsyonàr'] *vt*: ~ **a uno a algo** to make sb like sth; ~**se** *vr*: ~**se a algo** to grow fond of sth.

afiche [àfē'tche] *nm (AM)* poster.

afierre [àfyc'rrc] *etc vb V* **aferrar**.
afilado, a [àfēlá'tho, à] *a* sharp.
afilador [àfēláthor'] *nm (persona)* knife grinder.
afilalápices [àfēlálá'pēses] *nm inv* pencil sharpener.
afilar [àfēlár'] *vt* to sharpen; **~se** *vr (cara)* to grow thin.
afiliación [àfēlyásyon'] *nf (de sindicatos)* membership.
afiliado, a [àfēlyá'tho, à] *a* subsidiary ♦ *nm/f* affiliate.
afiliarse [àfēlyár'sc] *vr* to affiliate.
afín [àfēn'] *a (parecido)* similar; *(conexo)* related.
afinar [àfēnár'] *vt (TEC)* to refine; *(MUS)* to tune ♦ *vi* to play/sing in tune.
afincarse [àfēnkár'sc] *vr* to settle.
afinidad [àfēnēthàth'] *nf* affinity; *(parentesco)* relationship; **por ~** by marriage.
afirmación [àfērmásyon'] *nf* affirmation.
afirmar [àfērmár'] *vt* to affirm, state; *(sostener)* to strengthen; **~se** *vr (recuperar el equilibrio)* to steady o.s.; **~se en lo dicho** to stand by what one has said.
afirmativo, a [àfērmátē'ho, à] *a* affirmative.
aflicción [àflēksyon'] *nf* affliction; *(dolor)* grief.
afligir [àflēhēr'] *vt* to afflict; *(apenar)* to distress; **~se** *vr*: **~se (por** *o* **con** *o* **de)** to grieve (about *o* at); **no te aflijas tanto** you must not let it affect you like this.
aflija [àflē'hà] *etc vb V* **afligir**.
aflojar [àflohár'] *vt* to slacken; *(desatar)* to loosen, undo; *(relajar)* to relax ♦ *vi (amainar)* to drop; *(bajar)* to go down; **~se** *vr* to relax.
aflorar [àflorár'] *vi (GEO, fig)* to come to the surface, emerge.
afluencia [àflōōen'syà] *nf* flow.
afluente [àflōōen'te] *a* flowing ♦ *nm (GEO)* tributary.
afluir [àflōōēr'] *vi* to flow.
afluya [àflōō'yà] *etc*, **afluyendo** [àflōōyen'do] *etc vb V* **afluir**.
afmo., a. *abr* (= *afectísimo, a suyo, a)* Yours.
afónico, a [àfo'nēko, à] *a*: **estar ~** to have a sore throat; to have lost one's voice.
aforar [àforár'] *vt (TEC)* to gauge; *(fig)* to value.
aforo [àfo'ro] *nm (TEC)* gauging; *(de teatro etc)* capacity; **el teatro tiene un ~ de 2,000** the theater can seat 2,000.
afortunado, a [àfortōōná'tho, à] *a* fortunate, lucky.
afrancesado, a [àfránsesá'tho, à] *a* francophile.
afrenta [àfren'tá] *nf* affront, insult; *(deshonra)* dishonor *(US)*, dishonour *(Brit)*, shame.

afrentoso, a [àfrento'so, à] *a* insulting; shameful.
África [à'frēkà] *nf* Africa; **~ del Sur** South Africa.
africano, a [àfrēkà'no, à] *a, nm/f* African.
afrontar [àfrontár'] *vt* to confront; *(poner cara a cara)* to bring face to face.
afuera [àfwe'rà] *ad* out, outside; **por ~** on the outside; **~s** *nfpl* outskirts.
ag., ag.º *abr* (= *agosto)* Aug.
agachar [àgàtchár'] *vt* to bend, bow; **~se** *vr* to stoop, bend.
agalla [àgà'yà] *nf (ZOOL)* gill; **~s** *nfpl (MED)* tonsillitis *sg*; *(ANAT)* tonsils; **tener ~s** *(fam)* to have guts.
agarradera [àgàrráthe'rà] *nf (AM)*, **agarradero** [àgàrráthe'ro] *nm* handle; **~s** *npl* pull *sg*, influence *sg*.
agarrado, a [àgàrrá'tho, à] *a* mean, stingy.
agarrar [àgàrrár'] *vt* to grasp, grab; *(AM)* to take, catch ♦ *vi (planta)* to take root; **~se** *vr* to hold on (tightly); *(meterse uno con otro)* to grapple (with each other); **agarrársela con uno** *(AM)* to pick on sb.
agarrotar [àgàrrotár'] *vt (lío)* to tie tightly; *(persona)* to squeeze tightly; *(reo)* to garrotte; **~se** *vr (motor)* to seize up; *(MED)* to stiffen.
agasajar [àgàsàhár'] *vt* to treat well, fête.
agazapar [àgàsàpár'] *vt (coger)* to grab hold of; **~se** *vr (agacharse)* to crouch down.
agencia [àhen'syà] *nf* agency; **~ de créditos/publicidad/viajes** credit/advertising/travel agency; **~ inmobiliaria** real estate office *(US)*, estate agent's (office) *(Brit)*; **~ de matrimonios** ≈ dating service *(US)*, marriage bureau *(Brit)*.
agenciar [àhensyár'] *vt* to bring about; **~se** *vr* to look after o.s.; **~se algo** to get hold of sth.
agenda [àhen'dà] *nf* diary; **~ telefónica** telephone directory.
agente [àhen'te] *nm* agent; *(de policía)* policeman; **~ femenino** policewoman; **~ acreditado** *(COM)* accredited agent; **~ de bolsa** stockbroker; **~ inmobiliario** realtor *(US)*, estate agent *(Brit)*; **~ de negocios** *(COM)* business agent; **~ de seguros** insurance broker; **~ de viajes** travel agent.
ágil [à'hēl] *a* agile, nimble.
agilidad [àhēlēthàth'] *nf* agility, nimbleness.
agitación [àhētásyon'] *nf (de mano etc)* shaking, waving; *(de líquido etc)* stirring; agitation.
agitar [àhētár'] *vt* to wave, shake; *(líquido)* to stir; *(fig)* to stir up, excite; **~se** *vr* to get excited; *(inquietarse)* to get worried *o* upset.
aglomeración [àglomerásyon'] *nf*: **~ de tráfico/gente** traffic jam/mass of people.
aglomerar [àglomerár'] *vt*, **~se** *vr* to crowd

together.

agnóstico, a [ağno'stēko, á] a, nm/f agnostic.

agobiante [ağobyán'te] a (calor) oppressive.

agobiar [ağobyár'] vt to weigh down; (oprimir) to oppress; (cargar) to burden; **sentirse agobiado por** to be overwhelmed by.

agobio [ağo'byo] nm (peso) burden; (fig) oppressiveness.

agolpamiento [ağolpámyen'to] nm crowd.

agolparse [ağolpár'se] vr to crowd together.

agonía [ağonē'á] nf death throes pl; (fig) agony, anguish.

agonice [ağonē'se] etc vb V **agonizar**.

agonizante [ağonēsán'te] a dying.

agonizar [ağonēsár'] vi (tb: **estar agonizando**) to be dying.

agorero, a [ağore'ro, á] a ominous ♦ nm/f soothsayer; **ave agorera** bird of ill omen.

agostar [ağostár'] vt (quemar) to parch; (fig) to wither.

agosto [ağo'sto] nm August; (fig) harvest; **hacer su ~** to make one's fortune.

agotado, a [ağotá'ḍo, á] a (persona) exhausted; (acabado) finished; (COM) sold out; (: libros) out of print; (pila) dead.

agotador, a [ağotáḍor', á] a exhausting.

agotamiento [ağotámyen'to] nm exhaustion.

agotar [ağotár'] vt to exhaust; (consumir) to drain; (recursos) to use up, deplete; **~se** vr to be exhausted; (acabarse) to run out; (libro) to go out of print.

agraciado, a [ağrásyá'ḍo, á] a (atractivo) attractive; (en sorteo etc) lucky.

agraciar [ağrásyár'] vt (JUR) to pardon; (con premio) to reward; (hacer más atractivo) to make more attractive.

agradable [ağraḍá'ble] a pleasant, nice.

agradar [ağraḍár'] vt, vi to please; **~se** vr to like each other.

agradecer [ağraḍeser'] vt to thank; (favor etc) to be grateful for; **le agradecería me enviara ...** I would be grateful if you would send me ...; **~se** vr: **¡se agradece!** much obliged!

agradecido, a [ağraḍesē'ḍo, á] a grateful; **¡muy ~!** thanks a lot!

agradecimiento [ağraḍesēmyen'to] nm thanks pl; gratitude.

agradezca [ağraḍes'ká] etc vb V **agradecer**.

agrado [ağrá'ḍo] nm: **ser de tu** etc **~** to be to your etc liking.

agrandar [ağrándár'] vt to enlarge; (fig) to exaggerate; **~se** vr to get bigger.

agrario, a [ağrá'ryo, á] a agrarian, land cpd; (política) agricultural, farming.

agravante [ağrabán'te] a aggravating ♦ nf

complication; **con la ~ de que ...** with the further difficulty that ...

agravar [ağrabár'] vt (pesar sobre) to make heavier; (irritar) to aggravate; **~se** vr to worsen, get worse.

agraviar [ağrabyár'] vt to offend; (ser injusto con) to wrong; **~se** vr to take offense.

agravio [ağrá'byo] nm offense (US), offence (Brit); wrong; (JUR) grievance.

agraz [ağrás'] nm (uva) sour grape; **en ~** (fig) immature.

agredir [ağreḍēr'] vt to attack.

agregado [ağreğá'ḍo] nm aggregate; (persona) attaché; (profesor) assistant professor.

agregar [ağreğár'] vt to gather; (añadir) to add; (persona) to appoint.

agregue [ağre'ğe] etc vb V **agregar**.

agresión [ağresyon'] nf aggression; (ataque) attack.

agresivo, a [ağresē'ḅo, á] a aggressive.

agreste [ağre'ste] a (rural) rural; (fig) rough.

agriar [ağryár'] vt (fig) to (turn) sour; **~se** vr to turn sour.

agrícola [ağrē'kolá] a farming cpd, agricultural.

agricultor, a [ağrēkooltor', á] nm/f farmer.

agricultura [ağrēkooltoo'rá] nf agriculture, farming.

agridulce [ağreḍool'se] a bittersweet; (CULIN) sweet and sour.

agrietarse [ağryetár'se] vr to crack; (la piel) to chap.

agrimensor, a [ağrēmensor', á] nm/f surveyor.

agrio, a [ağ'ryo, á] a bitter.

agro [ağ'ro] nm farming, agriculture.

agronomía [ağronomē'á] nf agronomy, agriculture.

agrónomo, a [ağro'nomo, á] nm/f agronomist, agricultural expert.

agropecuario, a [ağropekwá'ryo, á] a farming cpd, agricultural.

agrupación [ağroopásyon'] nf group; (acto) grouping.

agrupar [ağroopár'] vt to group; (INFORM) to block; **~se** vr (POL) to form a group; (juntarse) to gather.

agua [á'gwá] nf water; (NAUT) wake; (ARQ) slope of a roof; **~s** nfpl (de joya) water sg, sparkle sg; (MED) water sg, urine sg; (NAUT) waters; **~s abajo/arriba** downstream/upstream; **~ bendita/destilada/potable** holy/distilled/drinking water; **~ caliente** hot water; **~ corriente** running water; **~ de colonia** eau de cologne; **~ mineral (con/sin gas)** carbonated/noncarbonated mineral water; **~s jurisdiccionales** territorial waters; **~s /mayores**

excrement *sg*; ~ **pasada no mueve molino** it's no use crying over spilt milk; **estar con el ~ al cuello** to be up to one's neck; **venir como ~ de mayo** to be a godsend.

aguacate [àg̃wàká'tc] *nm* avocado.

aguacero [àg̃wáse'ro] *nm* (heavy) shower, downpour.

aguachirle [àg̃wátčẽr'le] *nm* (*bebida*) dishwater.

aguado, a [àg̃wá'ᵭo, à] *a* watery, watered down ♦ *nf* (*AGR*) watering place; (*NAUT*) water supply; (*ARTE*) watercolor (*US*), watercolour (*Brit*).

aguafiestas [àg̃wáfye'stás] *nm/f inv* spoilsport.

aguafuerte [àg̃wáfwer'tc] *nf* etching.

aguamar [àg̃wàmár'] *nm* jellyfish.

aguanieve [àg̃wánye'ke] *nf* sleet.

aguantable [àg̃wántá'ᵬle] *a* bearable, tolerable.

aguantar [àg̃wántár'] *vt* to bear, put up with; (*sostener*) to hold up ♦ *vi* to last; ~**se** *vr* to restrain o.s.; **no sé cómo aguanta** I don't know how he can take it.

aguante [àg̃wán'tc] *nm* (*paciencia*) patience; (*resistencia*) endurance; (*DEPORTE*) stamina.

aguar [àg̃wàr'] *vt* to water down; (*fig*): ~ **la fiesta a uno** to spoil sb's fun.

aguardar [àg̃wárᵭàr'] *vt* to wait for.

aguardentoso, a [àg̃wárᵭento'so, à] *a* (*pey*: *voz*) husky, gruff.

aguardiente [àg̃wárᵭyen'tc] *nm* brandy, liquor.

aguarrás [àg̃wárràs'] *nm* turpentine.

aguce [àg̃oō'se] *etc vb V* **aguzar**.

agudeza [àg̃oōᵭe'sà] *nf* sharpness; (*ingenio*) wit.

agudice [àg̃oōᵭẽ'se] *etc vb V* **agudizar**.

agudizar [àg̃oōᵭẽsár'] *vt* to sharpen; (*crisis*) to make worse; ~**se** *vr* to worsen, deteriorate.

agudo, a [àg̃oō'ᵭo, à] *a* sharp; (*voz*) high-pitched, piercing; (*dolor*, *enfermedad*) acute.

agüe [à'g̃we] *etc vb V* **aguar**.

agüero [àg̃we'ro] *nm*: **buen/mal** ~ good/bad omen; **ser de buen** ~ to augur well; **pájaro de mal** ~ bird of ill omen.

aguerrido, a [àg̃errē'ᵭo, à] hardened; (*fig*) experienced.

aguijar [àg̃ẽhár'] *vt* to goad; (*incitar*) to urge on ♦ *vi* to hurry along.

aguijón [àg̃ẽhon'] *nm* (*ZOOL*) stinger (*US*), sting (*Brit*); (*fig*) spur.

aguijonear [àg̃ẽhoneàr'] *vt* = **aguijar**.

águila [à'g̃ẽlà] *nf* eagle; (*fig*) genius.

aguileño, a [àg̃ẽle'nyo, à] *a* (*nariz*) aquiline; (*rostro*) sharp-featured.

aguinaldo [àg̃ẽnál'do] *nm* Christmas box.

aguja [àg̃oō'hà] *nf* needle; (*de reloj*) hand;

(*ARQ*) spire; (*TEC*) firing-pin; (*ZOOL*) ribs; (*FERRO*) points.

agujerear [àg̃oōhereár'] *vt* to make holes in; (*penetrar*) to pierce.

agujero [àg̃oōhe'ro] *nm* hole.

agujetas [àg̃oōhe'tás] *nfpl* stitch *sg*; (*rigidez*) stiffness *sg*.

aguzar [àg̃oōsár'] *vt* to sharpen; (*fig*) to incite; ~ **el oído** to prick up one's ears.

aherrumbrarse [àerroōmbrár'se] *vr* to get rusty.

ahí [àē'] *ad* there; (*allá*) over there; **de ~ que** so that, with the result that; ~ **llega** here he comes; **por ~** (*dirección*) that way; **¡hasta ~ hemos llegado!** so it has come to this!; **¡~ va!** (*objeto*) here it comes!; (*individuo*) there he goes!; ~ **donde le ve** as sure as he's standing there.

ahijado, a [àēhá'ᵭo, à] *nm/f* godson/daughter.

ahijar [àēhàr'] *vt*: ~ **algo a uno** (*fig*) to attribute sth to sb.

ahínco [àēn'ko] *nm* earnestness; **con** ~ eagerly.

ahíto, a [àē'to, à] *a*: **estoy** ~ I'm full up.

ahogado, a [àog̃á'ᵭo, à] *a* (*en agua*) drowned; (*emoción*) pent-up; (*grito*) muffled.

ahogar [àog̃ár'] *vt* (*en agua*) to drown; (*asfixiar*) to suffocate, smother; (*fuego*) to put out; ~**se** *vr* (*en agua*) to drown; (*por asfixia*) to suffocate.

ahogo [ào'g̃o] *nm* (*MED*) breathlessness; (*fig*) distress; (*problema económico*) financial difficulty.

ahogue [ào'g̃e] *etc vb V* **ahogar**.

ahondar [àondàr'] *vt* to deepen, make deeper; (*fig*) to go deeply into ♦ *vi*: ~ **en** to go deeply into.

ahora [ào'rà] *ad* now; (*hace poco*) a moment ago, just now; (*dentro de poco*) in a moment; ~ **voy** I'm coming; ~ **mismo** right now; ~ **bien** now then; **por** ~ for the present.

ahorcado, a [àorká'ᵭo, à] *nm/f* hanged person.

ahorcar [àorkàr'] *vt* to hang; ~**se** *vr* to hang o.s.

ahorita [àorē'tá] *ad* (*fam*) right now.

ahorque [àor'ke] *etc vb V* **ahorcar**.

ahorrar [àorrár'] *vt* (*dinero*) to save; (*esfuerzos*) to save, avoid; ~**se** *vr*: ~**se molestias** to save o.s. trouble.

ahorrativo, a [àorrátē'ᵬo, à] *a* thrifty.

ahorro [ào'rro] *nm* (*acto*) saving; (*frugalidad*) thrift; ~**s** *nmpl* savings.

ahuecar [àwekár'] *vt* to hollow (out); (*voz*) to deepen ♦ *vi*: **¡ahueca!** (*fam*) beat it! (*fam*); ~**se** *vr* to give o.s. airs.

ahueque [àwe'ke] *etc vb V* **ahuecar**.

ahumar [àoōmár'] *vt* to smoke, cure; (*lle-*

nar de humo) to fill with smoke ♦ *vi* to smoke; **~se** *vr* to fill with smoke.

ahuyentar [áōōyentár'] *vt* to drive off, frighten off; (*fig*) to dispel.

AI *nf abr* (= *Amnistía Internacional*) Amnesty International.

AINS *nf abr* (*Esp*) = *Administración Institucional Nacional de Sanidad*.

airado, a [áērá'ħo, á] *a* angry.

airar [áērár'] *vt* to anger; **~se** *vr* to get angry.

aire [á'ēre] *nm* air; (*viento*) wind; (*corriente*) draft (*US*), draught (*Brit*); (*MUS*) tune; **~s** *nmpl*: **darse ~s** to give o.s. airs; **al ~ libre** in the open air; **~ acondicionado** air conditioning; **tener ~ de** to look like; **estar de buen/mal ~** to be in a good/bad mood; **estar en el ~** (*RADIO*) to be on the air; (*fig*) to be up in the air.

airear [áēreár'] *vt* to ventilate; (*fig: asunto*) to air; **~se** *vr* to take the air.

airoso, a [áēro'so, á] *a* windy; drafty (*US*), draughty (*Brit*); (*fig*) graceful.

aislado, a [áēslá'ħo, á] *a* (*remoto*) isolated; (*incomunicado*) cut off; (*ELEC*) insulated.

aislante [áēslán'te] *nm* (*ELEC*) insulator.

aislar [áēslár'] *vt* to isolate; (*ELEC*) to insulate; **~se** *vr* to cut o.s. off.

ajar [áħár'] *vt* to spoil; (*fig*) to abuse; **~se** *vr* to get crumpled; (*fig: piel*) to get wrinkled.

ajardinado, a [áħárħēná'ħo, á] *a* landscaped.

ajedrez [áħeħres'] *nm* chess.

ajenjo [áħen'ho] *nm* (*bebida*) absinth(e).

ajeno, a [áħe'no, á] *a* (*que pertenece a otro*) somebody else's; **~ a** foreign to; **~ de** free from, devoid of; **por razones ajenas a nuestra voluntad** for reasons beyond our control.

ajetreado, a [áħetreá'ħo, á] *a* busy.

ajetrearse [áħetreár'se] *vr* (*atarearse*) to bustle about; (*fatigarse*) to tire o.s. out.

ajetreo [áħetre'o] *nm* bustle.

ají [áħē'] *nm* chili, red pepper; (*salsa*) chili sauce.

ajilimoje [áħēlēmo'he] *nm* sauce of garlic and pepper; **~s** *nmpl* (*fam*) odds and ends.

ajo [á'ho] *nm* garlic; **~ porro** *o* **puerro** leek; **(tieso) como un ~** (*fam*) snobbish; **estar en el ~** to be mixed up in it.

ajorca [áħor'ká] *nf* bracelet.

ajuar [áħwár'] *nm* household furnishings *pl*; (*de novia*) trousseau; (*de niño*) layette.

ajustado, a [áħōōstá'ħo, á] *a* (*tornillo*) tight; (*cálculo*) right; (*ropa*) tight(-fitting); (*DEPORTE: resultado*) close.

ajustar [áħōōstár'] *vt* (*adaptar*) to adjust; (*encajar*) to fit; (*TEC*) to engage; (*TIP*) to make up; (*apretar*) to tighten; (*concertar*) to agree (on); (*reconciliar*) to reconcile;

(*cuenta*) to settle ♦ *vi* to fit.

ajuste [áħōō'ste] *nm* adjustment; (*COSTURA*) fitting; (*acuerdo*) compromise; (*de cuenta*) settlement; (*INFORM*) patch.

al [ál] = **a + el**; *V* **a**.

ala [á'lá] *nf* wing; (*de sombrero*) brim; (*futbolista*) wing; **andar con el ~ caída** to be downcast; **cortar las ~s a uno** to clip sb's wings; **dar ~ a uno** to encourage sb.

alabanza [álábán'sá] *nf* praise.

alabar [álábár'] *vt* to praise.

alacena [áláse'ná] *nf* closet (*US*), cupboard (*Brit*).

alacrán [álákrán'] *nm* scorpion.

ALADI [álá'ħē] *nf abr* = *Asociación Latinoamericana de Integración*.

alado, a [álá'ħo, á] *a* winged.

alambicado, a [álámbēká'ħo, á] *a* distilled; (*fig*) affected.

alambicar [álámbēkár'] *vt* to distil.

alambique [álámbē'ke] *etc vb V* **alambicar** ♦ *nm* still.

alambrada [álámbrá'ħá] *nf*, **alambrado** [álámbrá'ħo] *nm* wire fence; (*red*) wire netting.

alambre [álám'bre] *nm* wire; **~ de púas** barbed wire.

alambrista [álámbrē'stá] *nm/f* tightrope walker.

alameda [áláme'ħá] *nf* (*plantío*) poplar grove; (*lugar de paseo*) avenue, boulevard.

álamo [á'lámo] *nm* poplar; **~ temblón** aspen.

alano [álá'no] *nm* mastiff.

alarde [álár'ħe] *nm* show, display; **hacer ~ de** to boast of.

alardear [álárħeár'] *vi* to boast.

alargar [álárgár'] *vt* to lengthen, extend; (*paso*) to hasten; (*brazo*) to stretch out; (*cuerda*) to pay out; (*conversación*) to prolong; **~se** *vr* to get longer.

alargue [álár'ge] *etc vb V* **alargar**.

alarido [álárē'ħo] *nm* shriek.

alarma [álár'má] *nf* alarm; **voz de ~** warning note; **dar la ~** to raise the alarm.

alarmante [álármán'te] *a* alarming.

alavés, esa [áláħes', e'sá] *a* of Álava ♦ *nm/f* native *o* inhabitant of Álava.

alazán [álásán'] *nm* sorrel.

alba [ál'bá] *nf* dawn.

albacea [álbáse'á] *nm/f* executor/executrix.

albaceteño, a [álbásete'nyo, á] *a* of Albacete ♦ *nm/f* native *o* inhabitant of Albacete.

albahaca [álbá'ká] *nf* (*BOT*) basil.

Albania [álbá'nyá] *nf* Albania.

albañal [álbányál'] *nm* drain, sewer.

albañil [álbányēl'] *nm* bricklayer; (*cantero*) mason.

albarán [álbárán'] *nm* (*COM*) invoice.

albarda [álbár'ħá] *nf* packsaddle.

albaricoque [álbárēko'ke] *nm* apricot.

albedrío [àlβeð̪rē'o] *nm*: **libre** ~ free will.
alberca [àlβer'ká] *nf* reservoir; (*AM*) swimming pool.
albergar [àlβergár'] *vt* to shelter; (*esperanza*) to cherish; ~**se** *vr* (*refugiarse*) to shelter; (*alojarse*) to lodge.
albergue [àlβer'ge] *etc vb* V **albergar** ♦ *nm* shelter, refuge; ~ **de juventud** youth hostel.
albis [àl'βēs] *adv*: **quedarse en** ~ not to have a clue.
albóndiga [àlβon'dēɣá] *nf* meatball.
albor [àlβor'] *nm* whiteness; (*amanecer*) dawn.
alborada [àlβorá'ð̪á] *nf* dawn; (*diana*) reveille.
alborear [àlβoreár'] *vi* to dawn.
albornoz [àlβornos'] *nm* (*para el baño*) bathrobe.
alborotadizo, a [àlβorotáð̪ē'so, á] *a* excitable.
alborotar [àlβorotár'] *vi* to make a racket ♦ *vt* to agitate, stir up; ~**se** *vr* to get excited; (*mar*) to get rough.
alboroto [àlβoro'to] *nm* row, uproar.
alboroce [àlβoro'se] *etc vb* V **alborozar.**
alborozar [àlβorosár'] *vt* to gladden; ~**se** *vr* to rejoice, be overjoyed.
alborozo [àlβoro'so] *nm* joy.
albricias [àlβrē'syás] *nfpl*: **¡~!** good news!
álbum, *pl* **álbums** o **álbumes** [àl'βōōm] *nm* album.
albumen [àlβōō'men] *nm* egg white, albumen.
alcachofa [àlkátcho'fá] *nf* (*globe*) artichoke; (*TIP*) (*typewriter*) element; (*de ducha*) shower head.
alcahueta [àlkáwe'tá] *nf* procuress.
alcahuete [àlkáwe'te] *nm* pimp.
alcalde, esa [àlkál'de, àlkálde'sà] *nm/f* mayor(ess).
alcaldía [àlkáldē'á] *nf* mayoralty; (*lugar*) mayor's office.
álcali [àl'kálē] *nm* (*QUÍMICA*) alkali.
alcance [àlkán'se] *etc vb* V **alcanzar** ♦ *nm* (*MIL*, *RADIO*) range; (*fig*) scope; (*COM*) adverse balance, deficit; **estar al/fuera del** ~ **de uno** to be within/beyond one's reach; (*fig*) to be within one's powers/over one's head; **de gran** ~ (*MIL*) long-range; (*fig*) far-reaching.
alcancía [àlkánsē'á] *nf* money box.
alcanfor [àlkánfor'] *nm* camphor.
alcantarilla [àlkántárē'yá] *nf* (*de aguas cloacales*) sewer; (*en la calle*) gutter.
alcanzar [àlkánsár'] *vt* (*algo: con la mano, el pie*) to reach; (*alguien: en el camino etc*) to catch up (with); (*autobús*) to catch; (*suj: bala*) to hit, strike ♦ *vi* (*ser suficiente*) to be enough; ~ **a hacer** to manage to do.

alcaparra [àlkápá'rrá] *nf* (*BOT*) caper.
alcatraz [àlkátrás'] *nm* pelican.
alcázar [àlká'sár] *nm* fortress; (*NAUT*) quarter-deck.
alce [àl'se] *etc vb* V **alzar.**
alcista [àlsē'stá] *a* (*COM*, *ECON*): **mercado** ~ bull market; **la tendencia** ~ the upward trend ♦ *nm* speculator.
alcoba [àlko'βá] *nf* bedroom.
alcohol [àlkol'] *nm* alcohol; **no bebe** ~ he doesn't drink (alcohol).
alcoholice [àlkolē'se] *etc vb* V **alcoholizarse.**
alcohólico, a [àlko'lēko, á] *a, nm/f* alcoholic.
alcoholímetro [àlkolē'metro] *nm* Breathalyzer ®.
alcoholismo [àlkolēs'mo] *nm* alcoholism.
alcoholizarse [àlkolēsár'se] *vr* to become an alcoholic.
alcornoque [àlkorno'ke] *nm* cork tree; (*fam*) idiot.
alcotana [àlkotá'ná] *nf* pickaxe; (*DEPORTE*) ice-axe.
alcurnia [àlkōōr'nyá] *nf* lineage.
alcuzas [àlkōō'sás] *nfpl* (*AM*) cruet *sg*.
aldaba [àldá'βá] *nf* (*door*) knocker.
aldea [àlde'á] *nf* village.
aldeano, a [àldeá'no, á] *a* village *cpd* ♦ *nm/f* villager.
ale [à'le] *excl* come on!, let's go!
aleación [àleásyon'] *nf* alloy.
aleatorio, a [àleáto'ryo, á] *a* random, contingent; **acceso** ~ (*INFORM*) random access.
aleccionador, a [àleksyonáð̪or', á] *a* instructive.
aleccionar [àleksyonár'] *vt* to instruct; (*adiestrar*) to train.
aledaño, a [àleð̪á'nyo, á] *a*: ~ **a** bordering on ♦ *nmpl*: ~**s** outskirts.
alegación [àlegásyon'] *nf* allegation.
alegar [àlegár'] *vt* (*dificultad etc*) to plead; (*JUR*) to allege ♦ *vi* (*AM*) to argue; ~ **que** ... to give as an excuse that ...
alegato [àlegá'to] *nm* (*JUR*) allegation; (*escrito*) indictment; (*declaración*) statement; (*AM*) argument.
alegoría [àlegorē'á] *nf* allegory.
alegrar [àlegrár'] *vt* (*causar alegría*) to cheer (up); (*fuego*) to poke; (*fiesta*) to liven up; ~**se** *vr* (*fam*) to get merry o tight; ~**se de** to be glad about.
alegre [àle'gre] *a* happy, cheerful; (*fam*) merry, tipsy; (*licencioso*) risqué, blue.
alegría [àlegrē'á] *nf* happiness; merriment; ~ **vital** joie de vivre.
alegrón [àlegron'] *nm* (*fig*) sudden joy.
alegue [àle'ge] *etc vb* V **alegar.**
alejamiento [àlehámyen'to] *nm* removal; (*distancia*) remoteness.

alejar |àlchàr'| *vt* to move away, remove; (*fig*) to estrange; ~**se** *vr* to move away.
alelado, a |àlclá'tho, à| *a* (*bobo*) foolish.
alelar |àlclár'| *vt* to bewilder.
aleluya |àlcloō'yà| *nm* (*canto*) hallelujah.
alemán, ana |àlcmàn', à'nà| *a, nm/f* German ♦ *nm* (*lengua*) German.
Alemania |àlcmá'nyà| *nf* Germany; ~ **Occidental/Oriental** West/East Germany.
alentador, a |àlcntátho', à| *a* encouraging.
alentar |àlcntár'| *vt* to encourage.
alergia |àlcr'hyà| *nf* allergy.
alero |àlc'ro| *nm* (*de tejado*) eaves *pl*; (*de foca, DEPORTE*) flipper; (*AUTO*) mudguard, fender (*US*).
alerta |àlcr'tà| *a inv, nm* alert.
aleta |àlc'tà| *nf* (*de pez*) fin; (*de ave*) wing; (*de coche*) mudguard.
aletargar |àlctárgár'| *vt* to make drowsy; (*entumecer*) to make numb; ~**se** *vr* to grow drowsy; to become numb.
aletargue |àlctàr'gc| *etc vb V* **aletargar**.
aletear |àlctcár'| *vi* to flutter; (*ave*) to flap its wings; (*individuo*) to wave one's arms.
alevín |àlchēn'| *nm*, **alevino** |àlchē'no| *nm* fry, young fish.
alevosía |àlchosē'à| *nf* treachery.
alfabetización |àlfàhctēsàsyon'| *nf*: **campaña de** ~ literacy campaign.
alfabeto |àlfàhc'to| *nm* alphabet.
alfajor |àlfàhor'| *nm* (*Esp: polvorón*) cookie eaten at Christmas time.
alfalfa |àlfàl'fà| *nf* alfalfa, lucerne.
alfaque |àlfá'kc| *nm* (*NAUT*) bar, sandbank.
alfar |àlfár'| *nm* (*taller*) potter's workshop; (*arcilla*) clay.
alfarería |àlfàrcrē'à| *nf* pottery; (*tienda*) pottery shop.
alfarero |àlfàrc'ro| *nm* potter.
alféizar |àlfc'ēsár| *nm* window-sill.
alférez |àlfc'rcs| *nm* (*MIL*) second lieutenant; (*NAUT*) ensign.
alfil |àlfēl'| *nm* (*AJEDREZ*) bishop.
alfiler |àlfēlcr'| *nm* pin; (*broche*) clip; (*pinza*) clothespin (*US*), clothes peg (*Brit*); **prendido con** ~**es** shaky.
alfiletero |àlfēlctc'ro| *nm* needle case.
alfombra |àlfom'brà| *nf* carpet; (*más pequeña*) rug.
alfombrar |àlfombrár'| *vt* to carpet.
alfombrilla |àlfombrē'yà| *nf* rug, mat.
alforja |àlfor'hà| *nf* saddlebag.
alforza |àlfor'sà| *nf* pleat.
algarabía |àlgàráhē'à| *nf* (*fam*) gibberish; (*griterío*) hullabaloo.
algarada |àlgàrá'thà| *nf* outcry; **hacer** *o* **levantar una** ~ to kick up a tremendous fuss.
Algarbe |àlgár'hc| *nm*: **el** ~ the Algarve.
algarrobo |àlgàrro'ho| *nm* carob tree.
algas |àl'gàs| *nfpl* seaweed *sg*.
algazara |àlgàsà'rà| *nf* din, uproar.

álgebra |àl'hehrà| *nf* algebra.
álgido, a |àl'hētho, à| *a* icy; (*momento etc*) crucial, decisive.
algo |àl'go| *pron* something; (*en frases interrogativas*) anything ♦ *ad* somewhat, rather; **por** ~ **será** there must be some reason for it; **es** ~ **difícil** it's a bit awkward.
algodón |àlgothon'| *nm* cotton; (*planta*) cotton plant; ~ **de azúcar** cotton candy (*US*), candy floss (*Brit*); ~ **hidrófilo** absorbent cotton (*US*), cotton wool (*Brit*).
algodonero, a |àlgothonc'ro, à| *a* cotton *cpd* ♦ *nm/f* cotton grower ♦ *nm* cotton plant.
algoritmo |àlgorēt'mo| *nm* algorithm.
alguacil |àlgwàsēl'| *nm* constable (*US*), bailiff (*Brit*); (*TAUR*) mounted official.
alguien |àl'gyen| *pron* someone, somebody; (*en frases interrogativas*) anybody.
alguno, a |àlgoō'no, à| *a* (*delante de nm*: **algún**) some; (*después de n*): **no tiene talento alguno** he has no talent, he hasn't any talent ♦ *pron* (*alguien*) someone, somebody; **algún que otro libro** some book or other; **algún día iré** I'll go one *o* some day; **sin interés alguno** without the slightest interest; **alguno que otro** an occasional one; **algunos piensan** some (people) think; **alguno de ellos** one of them.
alhaja |àlá'hà| *nf* jewel; (*tesoro*) precious object, treasure.
alhelí |àlclē'| *nm* wallflower, stock.
aliado, a |àlyá'tho, à| *a* allied.
aliancista |àlyànsē'stà| (*Esp POL*) *a* of Alianza Popular ♦ *nm/f* member/supporter of Alianza Popular.
alianza |àlyàn'sà| *nf* (*POL etc*) alliance; (*anillo*) wedding ring.
aliar |àlyár'| *vt* to ally; ~**se** *vr* to form an alliance.
alias |à'lyàs| *ad* alias.
alicaído, a |àlckáē'tho, à| *a* (*MED*) weak; (*fig*) depressed.
alicantino, a |àlckàntē'no, à| *a* of Alicante ♦ *nm/f* native *o* inhabitant of Alicante.
alicate(s) |àlckà'tc(s)| *nm(pl)* pliers *pl*; ~ **de uñas** nail clippers.
aliciente |àlēsyen'tc| *nm* incentive; (*atracción*) attraction.
alienación |àlycnásyon'| *nf* alienation.
aliento |àlyen'to| *etc vb V* **alentar** ♦ *nm* breath; (*respiración*) breathing; **sin** ~ breathless; **de un** ~ in one breath; (*fig*) in one shot.
aligerar |àlēhcrár'| *vt* to lighten; (*reducir*) to shorten; (*aliviar*) to alleviate; (*mitigar*) to ease.
alijo |àlē'ho| *nm* (*NAUT*) unloading; (*contrabando*) smuggled goods.
alimaña |àlēmá'nyà| *nf* pest.

alimentación [álēmentásyon'] *nf* (*comida*) food; (*acción*) feeding; (*tienda*) grocery; ~ **continua** (*en fotocopiadora etc*) continuous feed.

alimentador [álēmentàthor'] *nm*: ~ **de papel** sheet-feeder.

alimentar [álēmentár'] *vt* to feed; (*nutrir*) to nourish; ~**se** *vr*: ~**se (de)** to feed (on).

alimenticio, a [álēmentē'syo, à] *a* food *cpd*; (*nutritivo*) nourishing, nutritious.

alimento [álēmen'to] *nm* food; (*nutrición*) nourishment; ~**s** *nmpl* (*JUR*) alimony *sg*.

alimón [álēmon']: **al** ~ *ad* jointly, together.

alineación [álēneásyon'] *nf* alignment; (*DEPORTE*) line-up.

alineado, a [álēneá'tho, à] *a* (*TIP*): (**no**) ~ (un)justified; ~ **a la izquierda/derecha** left/right justified.

alinear [álēneár'] *vt* to align; (*TIP*) to justify; ~**se** *vr* to line up; ~**se en** to fall in with.

aliñar [álēnyár'] *vt* (*CULIN*) to dress.

aliño [álē'nyo] *nm* (*CULIN*) dressing.

alisar [álēsár'] *vt* to smooth.

aliso [álē'so] *nm* alder.

alistamiento [álēstàmyen'to] *nm* recruitment.

alistar [álēstár'] *vt* to recruit; ~**se** *vr* to enlist; (*inscribirse*) to enroll (*US*), enrol (*Brit*).

aliviar [álēbyár'] *vt* (*carga*) to lighten; (*persona*) to relieve; (*dolor*) to relieve, alleviate.

alivio [álē'byo] *nm* alleviation, relief; ~ **de luto** half-mourning.

aljibe [álhē'he] *nm* cistern.

alma [ál'mà] *nf* soul; (*persona*) person; (*TEC*) core; **se le cayó el** ~ **a los pies** he became very disheartened; **entregar el** ~ to pass away; **estar con el** ~ **en la boca** to be scared to death; **lo siento en el** ~ I am truly sorry; **tener el** ~ **en un hilo** to have one's heart in one's throat (*US*) *o* mouth (*Brit*); **estar como** ~ **en pena** to suffer; **ir como** ~ **que lleva el diablo** to go at breakneck speed.

almacén [álmásen'] *nm* (*depósito*) warehouse, store; (*MIL*) magazine; (*AM*) shop; (**grandes**) **almacenes** *nmpl* department store *sg*; ~ **depositario** (*COM*) depository.

almacenaje [álmásená'he] *nm* storage; ~ **secundario** (*INFORM*) backup storage.

almacenamiento [álmásenámyen'to] *nm* (*INFORM*) storage; ~ **temporal en disco** disk spooling.

almacenar [álmásenár'] *vt* to store, put in storage; (*INFORM*) to store; (*proveerse*) to stock up with.

almacenero [álmásene'ro] *nm* warehouseman; (*AM*) shopkeeper.

almanaque [álmáná'ke] *nm* almanac.

almeja [álme'hà] *nf* clam.

almenas [álme'nás] *nfpl* battlements.

almendra [álmen'drá] *nf* almond.

almendro [álmen'dro] *nm* almond tree.

almeriense [álmeryen'se] *a* of Almería ♦ *nm/f* native *o* inhabitant of Almería.

almiar [álmyár'] *nm* haystack.

almíbar [álmē'hár] *nm* syrup.

almidón [álmēthon'] *nm* starch.

almidonado, a [álmēthoná'tho, à] *a* starched.

almidonar [álmēthonár'] *vt* to starch.

almirantazgo [álmēràntás'go] *nm* admiralty.

almirante [álmēràn'te] *nm* admiral.

almirez [álmēres'] *nm* mortar.

almizcle [álmēs'kle] *nm* musk.

almizclero [álmēskle'ro] *nm* musk deer.

almohada [álmoá'thà] *nf* pillow; (*funda*) pillowcase.

almohadilla [álmoáthē'yá] *nf* cushion; (*TEC*) pad; (*AM*) pincushion.

almohadillado, a [álmoáthēyá'tho, à] *a* (*acolchado*) padded.

almohadón [álmoáthon'] *nm* large pillow.

almorcé [álmorse'], **almorcemos** [álmorse'mos] *etc vb V* **almorzar**.

almorranas [álmorrá'nás] *nfpl* piles, hemorrhoids (*US*), haemorrhoids (*Brit*).

almorzar [álmorsár'] *vt*: ~ **una tortilla** to have an omelette for lunch ♦ *vi* to (have) lunch.

almuerce [álmwer'se] *etc vb V* **almorzar**.

almuerzo [álmwer'so] *etc vb V* **almorzar** ♦ *nm* lunch.

alocado, a [áloká'tho, à] *a* crazy.

alojamiento [álohámyen'to] *nf* lodging(s) (*pl*); (*viviendas*) housing.

alojar [álohár'] *vt* to lodge; ~**se** *vr*: ~**se en** to stay at; (*bala*) to lodge in.

alondra [álon'drá] *nf* lark, skylark.

alpargata [álpárgà'tà] *nf* rope-soled canvas shoe.

Alpes [ál'pes] *nmpl*: **los** ~ the Alps.

alpinismo [álpēnēs'mo] *nm* mountaineering, climbing.

alpinista [álpēnē'stà] *nm/f* mountaineer, climber.

alpiste [álpē'ste] *nm* (*semillas*) birdseed; (*AM fam: dinero*) dough; (*fam: alcohol*) booze.

alquería [álkerē'á] *nf* farmhouse.

alquilar [álkēlár'] *vt* (*suj: propietario: inmuebles, coche*) to rent; (: *TV*) to rent (out); (*suj: alquilador: inmuebles, TV*) to rent; (: *coche*) to rent, hire (*Brit*); **"se alquila casa"** "house to rent (*US*) *o* to let (*Brit*)".

alquiler [álkēler'] *nm* renting, letting; hiring; (*arriendo*) rent; hire charge; **de** ~ for hire; ~ **de automóviles** car hire.

alquimia [álkē'myà] *nf* alchemy.

alquitrán [ȧlkētrȧn'] *nm* tar.

alrededor [ȧlreⁿðeð̣or'] *ad* around, about; **~es** *nmpl* surroundings; **~ de** *prep* around, about; **mirar a su ~** to look around one.

Alsacia [ȧlsȧ'syȧ] *nf* Alsace.

alta [ȧl'tȧ] *nf* (certificate of) discharge; **dar a uno de ~** to discharge sb; **darse de ~** (MIL) to join, enrol; (DEPORTE) to declare o.s. fit.

altanería [ȧltȧnerē'ȧ] *nf* haughtiness, arrogance.

altanero, a [ȧltȧne'ro, ȧ] *a* haughty, arrogant.

altar [ȧltȧr'] *nm* altar.

altavoz [ȧltȧβos'] *nm* loudspeaker; (*amplificador*) amplifier.

alteración [ȧlterȧsyon'] *nf* alteration; (*alboroto*) disturbance; **~ del orden público** breach of the peace.

alterar [ȧlterȧr'] *vt* to alter; to disturb; **~se** *vr* (*persona*) to get upset.

altercado [ȧlterkȧ'ð̣o] *nm* argument.

alternar [ȧlternȧr'] *vt* to alternate ♦ *vi*, **~se** *vr* to alternate; (*turnar*) to take turns; **~ con** to mix with.

alternativo, a [ȧlternȧtē'βo, ȧ] *a* alternative; (*alterno*) alternating ♦ *nf* alternative; (*elección*) choice; **alternativas** *nfpl* ups and downs; **tomar la alternativa** (TAUR) to become a fully-qualified bullfighter.

alterno, a [ȧlter'no, ȧ] *a* (BOT, MAT) alternate; (ELEC) alternating.

alteza [ȧlte'sȧ] *nf* (*tratamiento*) highness.

altibajos [ȧltēβȧ'hos] *nmpl* ups and downs.

altillo [ȧltē'yo] *nm* (GEO) small hill; (AM) attic.

altiplanicie [ȧltēplȧnē'sye] *nf*, **altiplano** [ȧltēplȧ'no] *nm* high plateau.

altisonante [ȧltēsonȧn'te] *a* high-flown, high-sounding.

altitud [ȧltētōōð̣'] *nf* altitude, height; **a una ~ de** at a height of.

altivez [ȧltēβes'] *nf* haughtiness, arrogance.

altivo, a [ȧltē'βo, ȧ] *a* haughty, arrogant.

alto, a [ȧl'to, ȧ] *a* high; (*persona*) tall; (*sonido*) high, sharp; (*noble*) high, lofty; (GEO, *clase*) upper ♦ *nm* halt; (MUS) alto; (GEO) hill; (AM) pile ♦ *ad* (*estar*) high; (*hablar*) loud, loudly ♦ *excl* halt!; **la pared tiene 2 metros de ~** the wall is 2 meters high; **en alta mar** on the high seas; **en voz alta** in a loud voice; **las altas horas de la noche** the wee (US) *o* small (Brit) hours; **en lo ~ de** at the top of; **pasar por ~** to overlook; **~s y bajos** ups and downs; **poner la radio más ~** to turn the radio up; **¡más ~, por favor!** louder, please!

altoparlante [ȧltopȧrlȧn'te] *nm* (AM) loudspeaker.

altramuz [ȧltrȧmōōs'] *nm* lupin.

altura [ȧltōō'rȧ] *nf* height; (NAUT) depth;

(GEO) latitude; **la pared tiene 1.80 de ~** the wall is 1 meter 80cm high; **a esta ~ del año** at this time of the year; **estar a la ~ de las circunstancias** to rise to the occasion; **ha sido un partido de gran ~** it has been a terrific match.

alubia [ȧlōō'βyȧ] *nf* French bean, kidney bean.

alucinación [ȧlōōsēnȧsyon'] *nf* hallucination.

alucinante [ȧlōōsēnȧn'te] *a* (*fam*: *estupendo*) great, super.

alucinar [ȧlōōsēnȧr'] *vi* to hallucinate ♦ *vt* to deceive; (*fascinar*) to fascinate.

alud [ȧlōōð̣'] *nm* avalanche; (*fig*) flood.

aludir [ȧlōōð̣ēr'] *vi*: **~ a** to allude to; **darse por aludido** to take the hint; **no te des por aludido** don't take it personally.

alumbrado [ȧlōōmbrȧ'ð̣o] *nm* lighting.

alumbramiento [ȧlōōmbrȧmyen'to] *nm* lighting; (MED) childbirth, delivery.

alumbrar [ȧlōōmbrȧr'] *vt* to light (up) ♦ *vi* (*iluminar*) to give light; (MED) to give birth.

aluminio [ȧlōōmē'nyo] *nm* aluminum (US), aluminium (Brit).

alumnado [ȧlōōmnȧ'ð̣o] *nm* (UNIV) student body; (ESCOL) pupils.

alumno, a [ȧlōōm'no, ȧ] *nm/f* pupil, student.

alunice [ȧlōōnē'se] *etc vb* V **alunizar**.

alunizar [ȧlōōnēsȧr'] *vi* to land on the moon.

alusión [ȧlōōsyon'] *nf* allusion.

alusivo, a [ȧlōōsē'βo, ȧ] *a* allusive.

aluvión [ȧlōōβyon'] *nm* (GEO) alluvium; (*fig*) flood; **~ de improperios** torrent of abuse.

alvéolo [ȧlβe'olo] *nm* (ANAT) alveolus; (*fig*) network.

alza [ȧl'sȧ] *nf* rise; (MIL) sight; **~s fijas/graduables** fixed/adjustable sights; **al** *o* **en ~** (*precio*) rising; **jugar al ~** to speculate on a rising *o* bull market; **cotizarse** *o* **estar en ~** to be rising.

alzado, a [ȧlsȧ'ð̣o, ȧ] *a* (*gen*) raised; (COM: *precio*) fixed; (: *quiebra*) fraudulent; **por un tanto ~** for a lump sum ♦ *nf* (*de caballos*) height; (JUR) appeal.

alzamiento [ȧlsȧmyen'to] *nm* (*aumento*) rise, increase; (*acción*) lifting, raising; (*mejor postura*) higher bid; (*rebelión*) rising; (COM) fraudulent bankruptcy.

alzar [ȧlsȧr'] *vt* to lift (up); (*precio*, *muro*) to raise; (*cuello de abrigo*) to turn up; (AGR) to gather in; (TIP) to gather; **~se** *vr* to get up, rise; (*rebelarse*) to revolt; (COM) to go fraudulently bankrupt; (JUR) to appeal; **~se con el premio** to carry off the prize.

allá [ȧyȧ'] *ad* (*lugar*) there; (*por ahí*) over there; (*tiempo*) then; **~ abajo** down there; **más ~** further on; **más ~ de** beyond; **¡~**

tú! that's your problem!

allanamiento [àyànámyen'to] *nm*: ~ **de morada** housebreaking.

allanar [àyànár'] *vt* to flatten, level (out); (*igualar*) to smooth (out); (*fig*) to subdue; (*JUR*) to burgle, break into; ~**se** *vr* to fall down; ~**se a** to submit to, accept.

allegado, a [àyeg̃á'tho, à] *a* near, close ♦ *nm/f* relation.

allende [àyen'de] *ad* on the other side ♦ *prep*: ~ **los mares** beyond the seas.

allí [àyē'] *ad* there; ~ **mismo** right there; **por** ~ over there; (*por ese camino*) that way.

a.m. *abr* (*AM*: = *ante meridiem*) a.m.

ama [à'má] *nf* lady of the house; (*dueña*) owner; (*institutriz*) governess; (*madre adoptiva*) foster mother; ~ **de casa** housewife; ~ **de cría** o **de leche** wet-nurse; ~ **de llaves** housekeeper.

amabilidad [àmáḥēlēthàth'] *nf* kindness; (*simpatía*) niceness.

amabilísimo, a [àmáḥēlē'sēmo, à] *a super-lativo de* **amable**.

amable [àmá'ḥle] *a* kind; nice.

amaestrado, a [àmáestrá'tho, à] *a* (*animal*) trained; (*: en circo etc*) performing.

amaestrar [àmáestrár'] *vt* to train.

amagar [àmàg̃ár'] *vt, vi* to threaten.

amago [àmà'g̃o] *nm* threat; (*gesto*) threatening gesture; (*MED*) symptom.

amague [àmá'g̃e] *etc vb V* **amagar**.

amainar [àmáēnár'] *vt* (*NAUT*) to lower, take in; (*fig*) to calm ♦ *vi*, ~**se** *vr* to drop, die down; **el viento amaina** the wind is dropping.

amalgama [àmálg̃á'má] *nf* amalgam.

amalgamar [àmálg̃ámár'] *vt* to amalgamate; (*combinar*) to combine, mix.

amamantar [àmámántár'] *vt* to suckle, nurse.

amancebarse [àmánseḥár'se] *vr* (*pareja*) to live together.

amanecer [àmáneser'] *vi* to dawn; (*fig*) to appear, begin to show ♦ *nm* dawn; **el niño amaneció afiebrado** the child woke up with a fever.

amanerado, a [àmánerá'tho, à] *a* affected.

amanezca [àmánes'kà] *etc vb V* **amanecer**.

amansar [àmánsár'] *vt* to tame; (*persona*) to subdue; ~**se** *vr* (*persona*) to calm down.

amante [àmán'te] *a*: ~ **de** fond of ♦ *nm/f* lover.

amanuense [àmànwen'se] *nm* (*escribiente*) scribe; (*copista*) copyist; (*POL*) secretary.

amañar [àmányár'] *vt* (*gen*) to do skilfully; (*pey: resultado*) to alter.

amaño [àmá'nyo] *nm* (*habilidad*) skill; ~**s** *nmpl* (*TEC*) tools; (*fig*) tricks.

amapola [àmàpo'là] *nf* poppy.

amar [àmár'] *vt* to love.

amarar [àmárár'] *vi* (*AVIAT*) to land (on the sea).

amargado, a [àmárg̃á'tho, à] *a* bitter; embittered.

amargar [àmárg̃ár'] *vt* to make bitter; (*fig*) to embitter; ~**se** *vr* to become embittered.

amargo, a [àmár'g̃o, à] *a* bitter.

amargor [àmárg̃or'] *nm* (*sabor*) bitterness; (*fig*) grief.

amargue [àmár'g̃e] *etc vb V* **amargar**.

amargura [àmárg̃ōō'rà] *nf*= **amargor**.

amarillento, a [àmárēyen'to, à] *a* yellowish; (*tez*) sallow.

amarillismo [àmárēyēs'mo] *nm* (*de prensa*) sensationalist journalism.

amarillo, a [àmárē'yo, à] *a*, *nm* yellow.

amarra [àmá'rrà] *nf* (*NAUT*) mooring line; ~**s** *nfpl* (*fig*) protection *sg*; **tener buenas** ~**s** to have good connections; **soltar** ~**s** to set off.

amarrar [àmárrár'] *vt* to moor; (*sujetar*) to tie up.

amartillar [àmártēyàr'] *vt* (*fusil*) to cock.

amasar [àmásár'] *vt* to knead; (*mezclar*) to mix, prepare; (*confeccionar*) to concoct.

amasijo [àmásē'ho] *nm* kneading; mixing; (*fig*) hodgepodge.

amateur [à'mátōōr] *nm/f* amateur.

amatista [àmátē'stà] *nf* amethyst.

amazacotado, a [àmásàkotá'tho, à] *a* (*terreno, arroz etc*) lumpy.

amazona [àmáso'ná] *nf* horsewoman.

Amazonas [àmáso'nàs] *nm*: **el (Río)** ~ the Amazon.

ambages [àmbá'hes] *nmpl*: **sin** ~ in plain language.

ámbar [àm'bár] *nm* amber.

Amberes [àmbe'res] *nm* Antwerp.

ambición [àmbēsyon'] *nf* ambition.

ambicionar [àmbēsyonár'] *vt* to aspire to.

ambicioso, a [àmbēsyo'so, à] *a* ambitious.

ambidextro, a [àmbētheks'tro, à] *a* ambidextrous.

ambientación [àmbyentásyon'] *nf* (*CINE, LIT etc*) setting; (*RADIO etc*) sound effects.

ambientar [àmbyentár'] *vt* (*gen*) to give an atmosphere to; (*LIT etc*) to set.

ambiente [àmbyen'te] *nm* (*tb fig*) atmosphere; (*medio*) environment.

ambigüedad [àmbēg̃wethàth'] *nf* ambiguity.

ambigüo, a [àmbē'g̃wo, à] *a* ambiguous.

ámbito [àm'bēto] *nm* (*campo*) field; (*fig*) scope.

ambos, as [àm'bos, às] *apl, pron pl* both.

ambulancia [àmbōōlàn'syà] *nf* ambulance.

ambulante [àmbōōlàn'te] *a* travelling, itin-erant; (*biblioteca*) mobile.

ambulatorio [àmbōōláto'rēo] *nm* state health-service clinic.

ameba [àme'ḥà] *nf* amoeba.

amedrentar [àmethrentár'] *vt* to scare.

amén |àmen'| *excl* amen; ~ **de** *prep* besides, in addition to; **en un decir** ~ in the twinkling of an eye; **decir** ~ **a todo** to have no mind of one's own.

amenace |àmená'se| *etc vb* V **amenazar.**

amenaza |àmená'sà| *nf* threat.

amenazar |àmenàsàr'| *vt* to threaten ♦ *vi*: ~ **con hacer** to threaten to do.

amenguar |àmeŋgwàr'| *vt* to diminish; (*fig*) to dishonor (*US*), dishonour (*Brit*).

amengüe |àmen'gwe| *etc vb* V **amenguar.**

amenidad |àmeneθàθ'| *nf* pleasantness.

ameno, a |àme'no, à| *a* pleasant.

América |àme'rēkà| *nf* America; Latin America; ~ **del Norte/del Sur** North/South America; ~ **Central/Latina** Central/Latin America.

americano, a |àmerēkà'no, à| *a, nm/f* American ♦ *nf* coat, jacket.

americe |àmerē'se| *etc vb* V **amerizar.**

amerizaje |àmerēsà'he| *nm* (*AVIAT*) landing (on the sea).

amerizar |àmerēsàr'| *vi* (*AVIAT*) to land (on the sea).

ametralladora |àmetràyàθo'rà| *nf* machine gun.

amianto |àmyàn'to| *nm* asbestos.

amigable |àmēgà'ble| *a* friendly.

amígdala |àmēg'θàlà| *nf* tonsil.

amigdalitis |àmēgθàlē'tēs| *nf* tonsillitis.

amigo, a |àmē'go, à| *a* friendly ♦ *nm/f* friend; (*amante*) lover; ~ **de lo ajeno** thief; ~ **corresponsal** penfriend; **hacerse** ~**s** to become friends; **ser** ~ **de** to like, be fond of; **ser muy** ~**s** to be close friends.

amigote |àmēgo'te| *nm* pal.

amilanar |àmēlànàr'| *vt* to scare; ~**se** *vr* to get scared.

aminorar |àmēnoràr'| *vt* to diminish; (*reducir*) to reduce; ~ **la marcha** to slow down.

amistad |àmēstàθ'| *nf* friendship; ~**es** *nfpl* friends.

amistoso, a |àmēsto'so, à| *a* friendly.

amnesia |àmne'syà| *nf* amnesia.

amnistía |àmnēstē'à| *nf* amnesty.

amnistiar |àmnēstyàr'| *vt* to amnesty, grant an amnesty to.

amo |à'mo| *nm* owner; (*jefe*) boss.

amodorrarse |àmoθorràr'se| *vr* to get sleepy.

amolar |àmolàr'| *vt* to annoy.

amoldar |àmoldàr'| *vt* to mold (*US*), mould (*Brit*); (*adaptar*) to adapt.

amonestación |àmonestàsyon'| *nf* warning; **amonestaciones** *nfpl* wedding announcement.

amonestar |àmonestàr'| *vt* to warn; to announce the wedding of.

amontonar |àmontonàr'| *vt* to collect, pile up; ~**se** *vr* (*gente*) to crowd together; (*acumularse*) to pile up; (*datos*) to accumulate; (*desastres*) to come one on top of another.

amor |àmor'| *nm* love; (*amante*) lover; **hacer el** ~ to make love; ~ **propio** self-respect; **por (el)** ~ **de Dios** for God's sake; **estar al** ~ **de la lumbre** to be close to the fire.

amoratado, a |àmoràtà'θo, à| *a* purple, blue with cold; (*con cardenales*) bruised.

amordace |àmorθà'se| *etc vb* V **amordazar.**

amordazar |àmorθàsàr'| *vt* to muzzle; (*fig*) to gag.

amorfo, a |àmor'fo, à| *a* amorphous, shapeless.

amorío |àmorē'o| *nm* (*fam*) love affair.

amoroso, a |àmoro'so, à| *a* affectionate, loving.

amortajar |àmortàhàr'| *vt* (*fig*) to shroud.

amortice |àmortē'se| *etc vb* V **amortizar.**

amortiguador |àmortēgwàθor'| *nm* shock absorber; (*parachoques*) bumper; (*silenciador*) silencer; ~**es** *nmpl* (*AUTO*) suspension *sg*.

amortiguar |àmortēgwàr'| *vt* to deaden; (*ruido*) to muffle; (*color*) to soften.

amortigüe |àmortē'gwe| *etc vb* V **amortiguar.**

amortización |àmortēsàsyon'| *nf* redemption; repayment; (*COM*) capital allowance.

amortizar |àmortēsàr'| *vt* (*ECON: bono*) to redeem; (: *capital*) to write off; (: *préstamo*) to pay off.

amoscarse |àmoskàr'se| *vr* to get cross.

amosque |àmos'ke| *etc vb* V **amoscarse.**

amotinar |àmotēnàr'| *vt* to stir up, incite (to riot); ~**se** *vr* to mutiny.

amparar |àmpàràr'| *vt* to protect; ~**se** *vr* to seek protection; (*de la lluvia etc*) to shelter.

amparo |àmpà'ro| *nm* help, protection; **al** ~ **de** under the protection of.

amperímetro *nm* ammeter.

amperio |àmpe'ryo| *nm* ampère, amp.

ampliable |àmplyà'ble| *a* (*INFORM*) expandable.

ampliación |àmplyàsyon'| *nf* enlargement; (*extensión*) extension.

ampliar |àmplyàr'| *vt* to enlarge; to extend.

amplificación |àmplēfēkàsyon'| *nf* enlargement.

amplificador |àmplēfēkàθor'| *nm* amplifier.

amplificar |àmplēfēkàr'| *vt* to amplify.

amplifique |àmplēfē'ke| *etc vb* V **amplificar.**

amplio, a |àm'plyo, à| *a* spacious; (*falda etc*) full; (*extenso*) extensive; (*ancho*) wide.

amplitud |àmplētooθ'| *nf* spaciousness; extent; (*fig*) amplitude; ~ **de miras** broad-

mindedness; **de gran** ~ far-reaching.
ampolla [ámpo'yá] *nf* blister; (*MED*)
ampoule.
ampuloso, a [ámpōōlo'so, á] *a* bombastic,
pompous.
amputar [ámpōōtár'] *vt* to cut off, amputate.
amueblar [ámweḥlár'] *vt* to furnish.
amurallar [ámōōráyár'] *vt* to wall up *o* in.
amusgar [ámōōsg̱ár'] *vt* (*orejas*) to lay
back; (*ojos*) to screw up.
amusgue [ámōōs'g̱e] *etc vb* V **amusgar**.
anacarado, a [ánákárá'ḥo, á] *a* mother-of-
pearl *cpd*.
anacardo [ánákár'ḥo] *nm* cashew (nut).
anacronismo [ánákronēs'mo] *nm* anachronism.
ánade [á'náḥe] *nm* duck.
anadear [ánáḥeár'] *vi* to waddle.
anales [áná'les] *nmpl* annals.
analfabetismo [ánálfáḥetēs'mo] *nm* illiter-
acy.
analfabeto, a [ánálfáḥe'to, á] *a, nm/f* illiterate.
analgésico [ánálhe'sēko] *nm* painkiller,
analgesic.
analice [ánáli'se] *etc vb* V **analizar**.
análisis [áná'lēsēs] *nm inv* analysis; ~ **de
costos-beneficios** cost-benefit analysis; ~
de mercados market research; ~ **de sangre** blood test.
analista [ánálē'stá] *nm/f* (*gen*) analyst;
(*POL, HISTORIA*) chronicler; ~ **de sistemas**
(*INFORM*) systems analyst.
analizar [ánálēsár'] *vt* to analyze.
analogía [ánálohē'á] *nf* analogy; **por** ~ **con**
by analogy with.
análogo, a [áná'logo, á] *a* analogous, similar.
ananá(s) [ánáná'(s)] *nm* pineapple.
anaquel [ánákel'] *nm* shelf.
anaranjado, a [ánáránḥá'ḥo, á] *a* orange
(-colored).
anarquía [ánárkē'á] *nf* anarchy.
anarquismo [ánárkēs'mo] *nm* anarchism.
anarquista [ánárkē'stá] *nm/f* anarchist.
anatematizar [ánátemátēsár'] *vt* (*REL*) to
anathematize; (*fig*) to curse.
anatemice [ánátemē'se] *etc vb* V **anatemi-
zar**.
anatomía [ánátomē'á] *nf* anatomy.
anca [án'ká] *nf* rump, haunch; ~**s** *nfpl*
(*fam*) behind *sg*; **llevar a uno en** ~**s** to
carry sb behind one.
anciano, a [ánsyá'no, á] *a* old, aged ♦ *nm/f*
old man/woman ♦ *nm* elder.
ancla [án'klá] *nf* anchor; **levar** ~**s** to weigh
anchor.
ancladero [ánkláḥe'ro] *nm* anchorage.
anclar [ánklár'] *vi* to (drop) anchor.
ancho, a [ántch'o, á] *a* wide; (*falda*) full;

(*fig*) liberal ♦ *nm* width; (*FERRO*) gauge; **le
viene muy** ~ **el cargo** (*fig*) the job is too
much for him; **ponerse** ~ to get conceited;
quedarse tan ~ to go on as if nothing had
happened; **estar a sus anchas** to be at
one's ease.
anchoa [ántcho'á] *nf* anchovy.
anchura [ántchōō'rá] *nf* width; (*extensión*)
wideness.
anchuroso, a [ántchōōro'so, á] *a* wide.
andadas [ándá'ḥás] *nfpl* (*aventuras*)
adventures; **volver a las** ~ to backslide.
andaderas [ándáḥe'rás] *nfpl* baby-walker
sg.
andadura [ándáḥōō'rá] *nf* gait; (*de caballo*) pace.
Andalucía [ándálōōsē'á] *nf* Andalusia.
andaluz, a [ándálōōs', á] *a, nm/f* Andalusian.
andamiaje [ándámjá'he] *nm*, **andamio**
[ándá'myo] *nm* scaffold(ing).
andanada [ándáná'ḥá] *nf* (*fig*) reprimand;
soltarle a uno una ~ to give sb a piece of
one's mind.
andante [ándán'te] *a*: **caballero** ~ knight-
errant.
andar [ándár'] *vt* to go, cover, travel ♦ *vi* to
go, walk, travel; (*funcionar*) to go, work;
(*estar*) to be ♦ *nm* walk, gait, pace; ~**se** *vr*
(*irse*) to go away *o* off; ~ **a pie/a caballo/
en bicicleta** to go on foot/on horseback/by
bicycle; **¡anda!** (*sorpresa*) go on!; **anda en**
o **por los 40** he's about 40; **¿en qué andas?**
what are you up to?; **andamos mal de
dinero/tiempo** we're badly off for money/
we're short of time; ~**se por las ramas** to
beat about the bush; **no** ~**se con rodeos** to
call a spade a spade (*fam*); **todo se anda-
rá** all in good time; **anda por aquí** it's
around here somewhere; ~ **haciendo algo**
to be doing sth.
andariego, a [ándárye'g̱o, á] *a* fond of
travelling.
andas [án'dás] *nfpl* stretcher *sg*.
andén [ánden'] *nm* (*FERRO*) platform;
(*NAUT*) quayside; (*AM: de la calle*) sidewalk (*US*), pavement (*Brit*).
Andes [án'des] *nmpl*: **los** ~ the Andes.
andino, a [ándē'no, á] *a* Andean, of the
Andes.
andorga [ándor'g̱á] *nf* belly.
Andorra [ándo'rrá] *nf* Andorra.
andrajo [ándrá'ho] *nm* rag.
andrajoso, a [ándráho'so, á] *a* ragged.
andurriales [ándōōrryá'les] *nmpl* out-of-the-
way place *sg*, the sticks; **en esos** ~ in that
godforsaken spot.
anduve [ándōō'ḥe], **anduviera** [ándōōḥye'rá]
etc vb V **andar**.
anécdota [ának'ḥotá] *nf* anecdote, story.
anegar [áneg̱ár'] *vt* to flood; (*ahogar*) to

drown; ~**se** *vr* to drown; (*hundirse*) to sink.

anegue [áne'ge] *etc vb* V **anegar**.

anejo, a [áne'ho, á] *a* attached ♦ *nm* (ARQ) annexe.

anemia [áne'myá] *nf* anemia (US), anaemia (Brit).

anestésico [áneste'seko] *nm* anesthetic (US), anaesthetic (Brit).

anexar [áneksár] *vt* to annex; (*documento*) to attach; (INFORM) to append.

anexión [áneksyon'] *nf*, **anexionamiento** [áneksyonámyen'to] *nm* annexation.

anexo, a [ánek'so, á] *a* attached ♦ *nm* annexe.

anfibio, a [ánfē'hyo, á] *a* amphibious ♦ *nm* amphibian.

anfiteatro [ánfēteá'tro] *nm* amphitheater; (TEATRO) dress circle.

anfitrión, ona [ánfētryon', oná] *nm/f* host(ess).

ángel [án'hel] *nm* angel; ~ **de la guarda** guardian angel; **tener** ~ to have charm.

Ángeles [án'heles] *nmpl*: **los** ~ Los Angeles.

angelical [ánhelēkál'], **angélico, a** [ánhe'lēko, á] *a* angelic(al).

angina [ánhē'ná] *nf* (MED): ~ **de pecho** angina; **tener** ~s to have a sore throat *o* throat infection.

anglicano, a [ánglēká'no, á] *a*, *nm/f* Anglican.

Angola [ángo'lá] *nf* Angola.

angoleño, a [ángole'nyo, á] *a*, *nm/f* Angolan.

angosto, a [ángo'sto, á] *a* narrow.

anguila [ángē'lá] *nf* eel; ~**s** *nfpl* slipway *sg*.

angula [ángōō'lá] *nf* elver, baby eel.

ángulo [án'gōōlo] *nm* angle; (*esquina*) corner; (*curva*) bend.

angustia [ángōōs'tyá] *nf* anguish.

angustiar [ángōōstyár'] *vt* to distress, grieve; ~**se** *vr* to be distressed (*por* at, on account of).

anhelante [ánelán'te] *a* eager; (*deseoso*) longing.

anhelar [ánelár'] *vt* to be eager for; to long for, desire ♦ *vi* to pant, gasp.

anhelo [áne'lo] *nm* eagerness; desire.

anidar [ánēḋár'] *vt* (*acoger*) to take in, shelter ♦ *vi* to nest; (*fig*) to make one's home.

anilina [ánēlē'ná] *nf* aniline.

anillo [áne'yo] *nm* ring; ~ **de boda** wedding ring; ~ **de compromiso** engagement ring; **venir como** ~ **al dedo** to suit to a tee.

ánima [á'nēmá] *nf* soul; **las** ~**s** the Angelus (bell) *sg*.

animación [ánēmásyon'] *nf* liveliness; (*vitalidad*) life; (*actividad*) bustle.

animado, a [ánēmá'ḋo, á] *a* (*vivo*) lively;

(*vivaz*) animated; (*concurrido*) bustling; (*alegre*) in high spirits; **dibujos** ~**s** cartoon *sg*.

animador, a [ánēmáḋhor', á] *nm/f* (TV) host(ess) ♦ *nf* (DEPORTE) cheerleader.

animadversión [ánēmáḋhersyon'] *nf* ill-will, antagonism.

animal [ánēmál'] *a* animal; (*fig*) stupid ♦ *nm* animal; (*fig*) fool; (*bestia*) brute.

animalada [ánēmálá'ḋá] *nf* (*gen*) silly thing (to do *o* say); (*ultraje*) disgrace.

animar [ánēmár'] *vt* (BIO) to animate, give life to; (*fig*) to liven up, brighten up, cheer up; (*estimular*) to stimulate; ~**se** *vr* to cheer up, feel encouraged; (*decidirse*) to make up one's mind.

ánimo [á'nēmo] *nm* soul, mind; (*valentía*) courage ♦ *excl* cheer up!; **cobrar** ~ to take heart; **dar** ~**(s) a** to encourage.

animoso, a [ánēmo'so, á] *a* brave; (*vivo*) lively.

aniñado, a [ánēnyá'ḋo, á] *a* (*facción*) child-like; (*carácter*) childish.

aniquilar [ánēkēlár'] *vt* to annihilate, destroy.

anís [ánēs'] *nm* (*grano*) aniseed; (*licor*) anisette.

aniversario [ánēḃersá'ryo] *nm* anniversary.

Ankara [ánká'rá] *nf* Ankara.

ano [á'no] *nm* anus.

anoche [ánotch'e] *ad* last night; **antes de** ~ the night before last.

anochecer [ánotcheser'] *vi* to get dark ♦ *nm* nightfall, dark; **al** ~ at nightfall.

anochezca [ánotches'ká] *etc vb* V **anochecer**.

anomalía [ánomálē'á] *nf* anomaly.

anodino, a [ánoḋhē'no, á] *a* dull, anodyne.

anonimato [ánonēmá'to] *nm* anonimity.

anónimo, a [áno'nēmo, á] *a* anonymous; (COM) limited ♦ *nm* (*carta*) anonymous letter; (: *maliciosa*) poison-pen letter.

anormal [ánormál'] *a* abnormal.

anotación [ánotásyon'] *nf* note; annotation.

anotar [ánotár'] *vt* to note down; (*comentar*) to annotate.

anquilosado, a [ánkēlosá'ḋo, á] *a* (*fig*) stale, out of date.

anquilosamiento [ánkēlosámyen'to] *nm* (*fig*) paralysis, stagnation.

ansia [án'syá] *nf* anxiety; (*añoranza*) yearning.

ansiar [ánsyár'] *vt* to long for.

ansiedad [ánsyeḋháḋ'] *nf* anxiety.

ansioso, a [ánsyo'so, á] *a* anxious; (*anhelante*) eager; ~ **de** *o* **por algo** greedy for sth.

antagónico, a [ántágo'nēko, á] *a* antagonistic; (*opuesto*) contrasting.

antagonista [ántágonē'stá] *nm/f* antagonist.

antaño [ántá'nyo] *ad* long ago.

Antártico [ántár'tēko] *nm*: **el** ~ the Antarctic.

Antártida [ántár'tēthá] *nf* Antarctica.

ante [án'te] *prep* before, in the presence of; (*encarado con*) faced with ♦ *nm* suede; ~ **todo** above all.

anteanoche [ánteánotch'e] *ad* the night before last.

anteayer [ánteáyer'] *ad* the day before yesterday.

antebrazo [ánteþrá'so] *nm* forearm.

antecámara [ántekã'márá] *nf* (*ARQ*) anteroom; (*antesala*) waiting room; (*POL*) lobby.

antecedente [ántesethen'te] *a* previous ♦ *nm*: ~**s** *nmpl* (*profesionales*) background *sg*; ~**s penales** criminal record; **no tener** ~**s** to have a clean record; **estar en** ~**s** to be well-informed; **poner a uno en** ~**s** to put sb in the picture.

anteceder [ántesether'] *vt* to precede, go before.

antecesor, a [ántesesor', á] *nm/f* predecessor.

antedicho, a [ántethētch'o, á] *a* aforementioned.

antelación [ántelásyon'] *nf*: **con** ~ in advance.

antemano [ántemá'no]: **de** ~ *ad* beforehand, in advance.

antena [ánte'ná] *nf* antenna; (*de televisión etc*) aerial.

anteojeras [ánteohe'rás] *nfpl* blinders (*US*), blinkers (*Brit*).

anteojo [ánteo'ho] *nm* eyeglass; ~**s** *nmpl* (*esp AM*) glasses, spectacles.

antepasados [ántepásá'thos] *nmpl* ancestors.

antepecho [ántepetch'o] *nm* guardrail, parapet; (*repisa*) ledge, sill.

antepondré [ántepondre'] *etc vb* V **anteponer**.

anteponer [ánteponer'] *vt* to place in front; (*fig*) to prefer.

anteponga [ántepon'gá] *etc vb* V **anteponer**.

anteproyecto [ánteproyek'to] *nm* preliminary sketch; (*fig*) blueprint; (*POL*): ~ **de ley** draft bill.

antepuesto, a [ántepwe'sto, á] *pp de* **anteponer**.

antepuse [ántepōō'se] *etc vb* V **anteponer**.

anterior [ánteryor'] *a* preceding, previous.

anterioridad [ánteryoretháth'] *nf*: **con** ~ **a** prior to, before.

anteriormente [ánteryormen'te] *ad* previously, before.

antes [án'tes] *ad* sooner; (*primero*) first; (*con prioridad*) before; (*hace tiempo*) previously, once; (*más bien*) rather ♦ *prep*: ~ **de** before ♦ *conj*: ~ **(de) que** before; ~

bien (but) rather; **dos días** ~ two days before *o* previously; **mucho/poco** ~ long/ shortly before; ~ **muerto que esclavo** better dead than enslaved; **tomo el avión** ~ **que el barco** I take the plane rather than the boat; **cuanto** ~, **lo** ~ **posible** as soon as possible; **cuanto** ~ **mejor** the sooner the better.

antesala [ántesá'lá] *nf* anteroom.

antiadherente [ántiáðheren'te] *a* non-stick.

antiaéreo, a [ántiáe'reo, á] *a* anti-aircraft.

antialcohólico, a [ántiálko'lēko, á] *a*: **centro** ~ (*MED*) detoxification unit.

antibalas [ántiþá'lás] *a inv*: **chaleco** ~ bullet-proof jacket.

antibiótico [ántiþyo'tēko] *nm* antibiotic.

anticiclón [ántisēklon'] *nm* (*METEOROLOGÍA*) anti-cyclone.

anticipación [ántisēpásyon'] *nf* anticipation; **con 10 minutos de** ~ 10 minutes early.

anticipado, a [ántisēpá'tho, á] *a* (in) advance; **por** ~ in advance.

anticipar [ántisēpár'] *vt* to anticipate; (*adelantar*) to bring forward; (*COM*) to advance; ~**se** *vr*: ~**se a su época** to be ahead of one's time.

anticipo [ántisē'po] *nm* (*COM*) advance; *V tb* **anticipación**.

anticonceptivo, a [ántēkonseptē'þo, á] *a*, *nm* contraceptive; **métodos** ~**s** contraceptive devices.

anticongelante [ántēkonhelán'te] *nm* antifreeze.

anticonstitucional [ántēkonstētōōsyonál'] *a* unconstitutional.

anticuado, a [ántēkwá'tho, á] *a* out-of-date, old-fashioned; (*desusado*) obsolete.

anticuario [ántēkwá'ryo] *nm* antique dealer.

anticuerpo [ántēkwer'po] *nm* (*MED*) antibody.

antidemocrático, a [ántēthemokrá'tēko, á] *a* undemocratic.

antideportivo, a [ántētheportē'þo, á] *a* unsporting.

antideslumbrante [ántēthesloōmbrán'te] *a* (*INFORM*) anti-dazzle.

antídoto [ántē'thoto] *nm* antidote.

antidroga [ántēthro'gá] *a inv* anti-drug; **brigada** ~ drug squad.

antiestético, a [ántēeste'tēko, á] *a* unsightly.

antifaz [ántēfás'] *nm* mask; (*velo*) veil.

antigás [ántēgás'] *a inv*: **careta** ~ gasmask.

antigualla [ántēgwá'yá] *nf* antique; (*reliquia*) relic; ~**s** *nfpl* old things.

antiguamente [ántēgwámen'te] *ad* formerly; (*hace mucho tiempo*) long ago.

antigüedad [ántēgwetháth'] *nf* antiquity; (*artículo*) antique; (*rango*) seniority.

antiguo, a [ántē'gwo, á] *a* old, ancient; (*que*

fue) former; **a la antigua** in the old-fashioned way.

antihigiénico, a [ántēhye'nēko, á] *a* unhygienic.

antihistamínico, a [ántēstámē'nēko, á] *a*, *nm* antihistamine.

antiinflacionista [ántēnflásyonē'stá] *a* anti-inflationary, counter-inflationary.

antílope [ántē'lope] *nm* antelope.

antillano, a [ántēyá'no, á] *a*, *nm/f* West Indian.

Antillas [ántē'yás] *nfpl*: **las ~** the West Indies, the Antilles; **el mar de las ~** the Caribbean Sea.

antimonopolios [ántēmonopo'lyos] *a inv*: **ley ~** anti-trust law.

antinatural [ántēnátōōrál'] *a* unnatural.

antiparras [ántēpá'rrás] *nfpl* (*fam*) specs.

antipatía [ántēpátē'á] *nf* antipathy, dislike.

antipático, a [ántēpá'tēko, á] *a* disagreeable, unpleasant.

Antípodas [ántē'potàás] *nfpl*: **las ~** the antipodes.

antiquísimo, a [ántēkē'sēmo, á] *a* ancient.

antirreglamentario, a [ántērreglámentá'ryo, á] *a* (*gen*) unlawful; (*POL etc*) unconstitutional.

antirrobo [ántērro'ho] *a inv*: (**dispositivo**) **~** (*para casas etc*) burglar alarm; (*para coches*) car alarm.

antisemita [ántēsemē'tá] *a* anti-Semitic ♦ *nm/f* anti-Semite.

antiséptico, a [ántēsep'tēko, á] *a*, *nm* antiseptic.

antítesis [ántē'tesēs] *nf inv* antithesis.

antiterrorista [ántēterrorē'stá] *a* antiterrorist; **la lucha ~** the fight against terrorism.

antojadizo, a [ántohàthē'so, á] *a* capricious.

antojarse [ántohár'se] *vr* (*desear*): **se me antoja comprarlo** I have a mind to buy it; (*pensar*): **se me antoja que** I have a feeling that.

antojo [ánto'ho] *nm* caprice, whim; (*rosa*) birthmark; (*lunar*) mole; **hacer a su ~** to do as one pleases.

antología [ántolohē'á] *nf* anthology.

antonomasia [ántonomá'syá] *nf*: **por ~** par excellence.

antorcha [ántortch'á] *nf* torch.

antro [án'tro] *nm* cavern; **~ de corrupción** (*fig*) den of iniquity.

antropófago, a [ántropo'fàgo, á] *a*, *nm/f* cannibal.

antropología [ántropolohē'á] *nf* anthropology.

anual [ánwál'] *a* annual.

anualidad [ánwálēthàth'] *nf* annuity, annual payment; **~ vitalicia** life annuity.

anuario [ánwá'ryo] *nm* yearbook.

anudar [ánōōthár'] *vt* to knot, tie; (*unir*) to join; **~se** *vr* to get tied up; **se me anudó**

la voz I got a lump in my throat.

anulación [ánōōlásyon'] *nf* annulment; cancellation; repeal.

anular [ánōōlár'] *vt* to annul, cancel; (*suscripción*) to cancel; (*ley*) to repeal ♦ *nm* ring finger.

anunciación [ánōōnsyásyon'] *nf* announcement; **A~** (*REL*) Annunciation.

anunciante [ánōōnsyán'te] *nm/f* (*COM*) advertiser.

anunciar [ánōōnsyár'] *vt* to announce; (*proclamar*) to proclaim; (*COM*) to advertise.

anuncio [ánōōn'syo] *nm* announcement; (*señal*) sign; (*COM*) advertisement; (*cartel*) poster; (*TEATRO*) bill; **~s por palabras** classified ads.

anverso [ámber'so] *nm* obverse.

anzuelo [ánswe'lo] *nm* hook; (*para pescar*) fish hook; **tragar el ~** to swallow the bait.

añadidura [ányáthēthōō'rá] *nf* addition, extra; **por ~** besides, in addition.

añadir [ányáthēr'] *vt* to add.

añejo, a [ánye'ho, á] *a* old; (*vino*) vintage; (*jamón*) well-cured.

añicos [ányē'kos] *nmpl*: **hacer ~** to smash, shatter; **hacerse ~** to smash, shatter.

añil [ányēl'] *nm* (*BOT*, *color*) indigo.

año [á'nyo] *nm* year; **¡Feliz A~ Nuevo!** Happy New Year!; **tener 15 ~s** to be 15 (years old); **los ~s 80** the eighties; **~ bisiesto/escolar** leap/school year; **~ fiscal** fiscal *o* tax year; **estar de buen ~** to be in good shape; **en el ~ de la nana** in the year one (*US*) *o* dot (*Brit*); **el ~ que viene** next year.

añoranza [ányorán'sá] *nf* nostalgia; (*anhelo*) longing.

añoso, a [ányo'so, á] *a* ancient, old.

aojar [áohár'] *vt* to put the evil eye on.

aovado, a [áohá'tho, á] *a* oval.

aovar [áohár'] *vi* to lay eggs.

apabullar [ápabōōyár'] *vt* (*lit*, *fig*) to crush.

apacentar [ápásentár'] *vt* to pasture, graze.

apacible [ápásē'hle] *a* gentle, mild.

apaciente [ápásyen'te] *etc vb* V **apacentar**.

apaciguar [ápásēgwár'] *vt* to pacify, calm (down).

apacigüe [ápásē'gwe] *etc vb* V **apaciguar**.

apadrinar [ápáthrēnár'] *vt* to sponsor, support; (*REL*) to act as godfather to.

apagado, a [ápàgá'tho, á] *a* (*volcán*) extinct; (*color*) dull; (*voz*) quiet; (*sonido*) muted, muffled; (*persona: apático*) listless; **estar ~** (*fuego*, *luz*) to be out; (*radio*, *TV etc*) to be off.

apagar [ápàgár'] *vt* to put out; (*color*) to tone down; (*sonido*) to silence, muffle; (*sed*) to quench; (*INFORM*) to toggle off; **~se** *vr* (*luz*, *fuego*) to go out; (*sonido*) to die away; (*pasión*) to wither; **~ el sistema** (*INFORM*) to close *o* shut down.

apagón |ápáɡon'| *nm* blackout.

apague |ápá'ɡe| *etc vb* V **apagar**.

apalabrar |ápáláɓrár'| *vt* to agree to; *(obrero)* to engage.

Apalaches |ápálátch'es| *nmpl*: **(Montes)** ~ Appalachians.

apalear |ápáleár'| *vt* to beat, thrash; *(AGR)* to winnow.

apañar |ápányár'| *vt* to pick up; *(asir)* to take hold of, grasp; *(reparar)* to mend, patch up; **~se** *vr* to manage, get along; **apañárselas por su cuenta** to look after number one *(fam)*.

apaño |ápá'nyo| *nm* *(COSTURA)* patch; *(maña)* skill; **esto no tiene** ~ there's no answer to this one.

aparador |ápáráɖor'| *nm* sideboard; *(escaparate)* shop window.

aparato |ápárá'to| *nm* apparatus; *(máquina)* machine; *(doméstico)* appliance; *(boato)* ostentation; *(INFORM)* device; ~ **de facsímil** facsimile (machine), fax; ~ **respiratorio** respiratory system; **~s de mando** *(AVIAT etc)* controls.

aparatoso, a |ápárá'to'so, á| *a* showy, ostentatious.

aparcamiento |ápárkámyen'to| *nm* parking lot *(US)*, car park *(Brit)*.

aparcar |ápárkár'| *vt, vi* to park.

aparear |ápáreár'| *vt* *(objetos)* to pair, match; *(animales)* to mate; **~se** *vr* to form a pair; to mate.

aparecer |ápáreser'| *vi*, **~se** *vr* to appear; **apareció borracho** he turned up drunk.

aparejado, a |ápárehá'tʰo, á| *a* fit, suitable; **ir** ~ **con** to go hand in hand with; **llevar** *o* **traer** ~ to involve.

aparejar |ápárehár'| *vt* to prepare; *(caballo)* to saddle, harness; *(NAUT)* to fit out, rig out.

aparejo |ápáre'ho| *nm* preparation; *(de caballo)* harness; *(NAUT)* rigging; *(de poleas)* block and tackle.

aparentar |ápárentár'| *vt* *(edad)* to look; *(fingir)*: ~ **tristeza** to pretend to be sad.

aparente |ápáren'te| *a* apparent; *(adecuado)* suitable.

aparezca |ápáres'ká| *etc vb* V **aparecer**.

aparición |ápáresyon'| *nf* appearance; *(de libro)* publication; *(fantasma)* specter.

apariencia |ápáryen'syá| *nf* (outward) appearance; **en** ~ outwardly, seemingly.

aparque |ápár'ke| *etc vb* V **aparcar**.

apartado, a |ápártá'tʰo, á| *a* separate; *(lejano)* remote ♦ *nm* *(tipográfico)* paragraph; ~ **(de correos)** post office box.

apartamento |ápártámen'to| *nm* apartment, flat *(Brit)*.

apartamiento |ápártámyen'to| *nm* separation; *(aislamiento)* remoteness; *(AM)* apartment, flat *(Brit)*.

apartar |ápártár'| *vt* to separate; *(quitar)* to remove; *(MINERALOGÍA)* to extract; **~se** *vr* *(separarse)* to separate, part; *(irse)* to move away; *(mantenerse aparte)* to keep away.

aparte |ápár'te| *ad* *(separadamente)* separately; *(además)* besides ♦ *prep*: ~ **de** apart from ♦ *nm* *(TEATRO)* aside; *(tipográfico)* new paragraph; "**punto y** ~" "new paragraph".

apasionado, a |ápásyoná'tʰo, á| *a* passionate; *(pey)* biassed, prejudiced ♦ *nm/f* admirer.

apasionar |ápásyonár'| *vt* to arouse passion in; **~se** *vr* to get excited; **le apasiona el fútbol** she's crazy about football.

apatía |ápátē'á| *nf* apathy.

apático, a |ápá'tēko, á| *a* apathetic.

apátrida |ápá'trētʰá| *a* stateless.

Apdo. *nm abr* (= *Apartado (de Correos)*) P.O. Box.

apeadero |ápeáɖe'ro| *nm* stop, stopping place.

apearse |ápeár'se| *vr* *(jinete)* to dismount; *(bajarse)* to get down *o* out; *(de coche)* to get out, alight; **no** ~ **del burro** to refuse to back down.

apechugar |ápetchooɡár'| *vi*: ~ **con algo** to face up to sth.

apechugue |ápetchoo'ɡe| *etc vb* V **apechugar**.

apedrear |ápeɖreár'| *vt* to stone.

apegarse |ápeɡár'se| *vr*: ~ **a** to become attached to.

apego |ápe'ɡo| *nm* attachment, devotion.

apegue |ápe'ɡe| *etc vb* V **apegarse**.

apelación |ápelásyon'| *nf* appeal.

apelar |ápelár'| *vi* to appeal; ~ **a** *(fig)* to resort to.

apelativo |ápelátē'ʋo| *nm* *(LING)* common noun; *(AM)* surname.

apelmazado, a |ápelmásá'tʰo, á| *a* compact, solid.

apelotonar |ápelotonár'| *vt* to roll into a ball; **~se** *vr* *(gente)* to crowd together.

apellidar |ápeyeϧár'| *vt* to call, name; **~se** *vr*: **se apellida Pérez** her (sur)name's Pérez.

apellido |ápeyē'tʰo| *nm* surname.

apenar |ápenár'| *vt* to grieve, trouble; **~se** *vr* to grieve.

apenas |ápe'nás| *ad* scarcely, hardly ♦ *conj* as soon as, no sooner.

apéndice |ápen'dēse| *nm* appendix.

apendicitis |ápendēsē'tēs| *nf* appendicitis.

Apeninos |ápenē'nos| *nmpl* Apennines.

apercibimiento |áperseɓēmyen'to| *nm* *(aviso)* warning.

apercibir |áperseɓēr'| *vt* to prepare; *(avisar)* to warn; *(JUR)* to summon; *(AM)* to notice, see; **~se** *vr* to get ready; **~se de** to notice.

aperitivo [àperētē'ħo] *nm* (*bebida*) aperitif; (*comida*) appetizer.

apero [àpe'ro] *nm* (*AGR*) implement; ~**s** *nmpl* farm equipment *sg*.

aperrear [àperreàr'] *vt* to set the dogs on; (*fig*) to plague.

apertura [àpertōō'rà] *nf* (*gen*) opening; (*POL*) openness, liberalization; (*TEATRO etc*) beginning; ~ **de un juicio hipotecario** (*COM*) foreclosure.

aperturismo [àpertōōrēs'mo] *nm* (*POL*) (policy of) liberalization.

apesadumbrar [àpesàħōōmbràr'] *vt* to grieve, sadden; ~**se** *vr* to distress o.s.

apestar [àpestàr'] *vt* to infect ♦ *vi*: ~(**a**) to stink (of).

apestoso, a [àpesto'so, à] *a* (*hediondo*) stinking; (*asqueroso*) sickening.

apetecer [àpetecer'] *vt*: **¿te apetece una tortilla?** does an omelet appeal to you?

apetecible [àpetesē'ħle] *a* desirable; (*comida*) tempting.

apetezca [àpetes'kà] *etc vb V* **apetecer.**

apetito [àpetē'to] *nm* appetite.

apetitoso, a [àpetēto'so, à] *a* (*gustoso*) appetizing; (*fig*) tempting.

apiadarse [àpyàħàr'se] *vr*: ~ **de** to take pity on.

ápice [à'pēse] *nm* apex; (*fig*) whit, iota; **ni un** ~ not a whit; **no ceder un** ~ not to budge an inch.

apicultor, a [àpēkōōltor', à] *nm/f* beekeeper, apiarist.

apicultura [àpēkōōltōō'rà] *nf* beekeeping.

apiladora [àpēlàħo'rà] *nf* (*para máquina impresora*) stacker.

apilar [àpēlàr'] *vt* to pile o heap up; ~**se** *vr* to pile up.

apiñado, a [àpēnyà'ħo, à] *a* (*apretado*) packed.

apiñar [àpēnyàr'] *vt* to crowd; ~**se** *vr* to crowd o press together.

apio [à'pyo] *nm* celery.

apisonadora [àpēsonàħo'rà] *nf* (*máquina*) steamroller.

aplacar [àplàkàr'] *vt* to placate; ~**se** *vr* to calm down.

aplace [àplà'se] *etc vb V* **aplazar.**

aplanamiento [àplànàmyen'to] *nm* smoothing, levelling.

aplanar [àplànàr'] *vt* to smooth, level; (*allanar*) to roll flat, flatten; ~**se** *vr* (*edificio*) to collapse; (*persona*) to get discouraged.

aplaque [àplà'ke] *etc vb V* **aplacar.**

aplastar [àplàstàr'] *vt* to squash (flat); (*fig*) to crush.

aplatanarse [àplàtànàr'se] *vr* to get lethargic.

aplaudir [àplàōōħēr'] *vt* to applaud.

aplauso [àplà'ōōso] *nm* applause; (*fig*)

approval, acclaim.

aplazamiento [àplàsàmyen'to] *nm* postponement.

aplazar [àplàsàr'] *vt* to postpone, defer.

aplicación [àplēkàsyon'] *nf* application; (*esfuerzo*) effort; **aplicaciones de gestión** business applications.

aplicado, a [àplēkà'ħo, à] *a* diligent, hardworking.

aplicar [àplēkàr'] *vt* (*gen*) to apply; (*poner en vigor*) to put into effect; (*esfuerzos*) to devote; ~**se** *vr* to apply o.s.

aplique [àplē'ke] *etc vb V* **aplicar** ♦ *nm* wall light o lamp.

aplomo [àplo'mo] *nm* aplomb, self-assurance.

apocado, a [àpokà'ħo, à] *a* timid.

apocamiento [àpokàmyen'to] *nm* timidity; (*depresión*) depression.

apocarse [àpokàr'se] *vr* to feel small o humiliated.

apocopar [àpokopàr'] *vt* (*LING*) to shorten.

apodar [àpoħàr'] *vt* to nickname.

apoderado [àpoħerà'ħo] *nm* agent, representative.

apoderar [àpoħeràr'] *vt* to authorize, empower; (*JUR*) to grant (a) power of attorney to; ~**se** *vr*: ~**se de** to take possession of.

apodo [àpo'ħo] *nm* nickname.

apogeo [àpohe'o] *nm* peak, summit.

apolillado, a [àpolēyà'ħo, à] *a* moth-eaten.

apolillarse [àpolēyàr'se] *vr* to get motheaten.

apología [àpolohē'à] *nf* eulogy; (*defensa*) defense (*US*), defence (*Brit*).

apoltronarse [àpoltronàr'se] *vr* to get lazy.

apoplejía [àpoplehē'à] *nf* apoplexy, stroke.

apoque [àpo'ke] *etc vb V* **apocar.**

apoquinar [àpokēnàr'] *vt* (*fam*) to cough up.

aporrear [àporreàr'] *vt* to beat (up).

aportación [àportàsyon'] *nf* contribution.

aportar [àportàr'] *vt* to contribute ♦ *vi* to reach port; ~**se** *vr* (*AM*) to arrive, come.

aposentar [àposentàr'] *vt* to lodge, put up.

aposento [àposen'to] *nm* lodging; (*habitación*) room.

apósito [àpo'sēto] *nm* (*MED*) dressing.

apostar [àpostàr'] *vt* to bet, stake; (*tropas etc*) to station, post ♦ *vi* to bet.

aposta(s) [àpo'stà(s)] *ad* on purpose.

apostatar [àpostàtàr'] *vi* (*REL*) to apostatize; (*fig*) to change sides.

apostilla [àpostē'yà] *nf* note, comment.

apóstol [àpo'stol] *nm* apostle.

apóstrofo [àpos'trofo] *nm* apostrophe.

apostura [àpostōō'rà] *nf* neatness, elegance.

apoteósico, a [àpoteo'sēko, à] *a* tremendous.

apoyar [àpoyàr'] *vt* to lean, rest; (*fig*) to

support, back; ~**se** vr: ~**se en** to lean on.
apoyo [ápo'yo] nm support, backing.
apreciable [ápresyá'ble] a considerable; (fig) esteemed.
apreciación [ápresyásyon'] nf appreciation; (COM) appraisal (US), valuation (Brit).
apreciar [ápresyár'] vt to evaluate, assess; (COM) to appreciate, appraise (US), value (Brit) ♦ vi (ECON) to appreciate.
aprecio [ápre'syo] nm appraisal (US), valuation (Brit), estimate; (fig) appreciation.
aprehender [ápreender'] vt to apprehend, detain; (ver) to see, observe.
aprehensión [ápreensyon'] nf detention, capture.
apremiante [ápremyán'te] a urgent, pressing.
apremiar [ápremyár'] vt to compel, force ♦ vi to be urgent, press.
apremio [ápre'myo] nm urgency; ~ **de pago** demand note.
aprender [áprender'] vt, vi to learn; ~ **a conducir** to learn to drive; ~**se** vr: ~**se algo** to learn sth (off) by heart.
aprendiz, a [áprendēs', á] nm/f apprentice; (principiante) learner, trainee; ~ **de comercio** business trainee.
aprendizaje [áprendēsá'he] nm apprenticeship.
aprensión [áprensyon'] nm apprehension, fear.
aprensivo, a [áprensē'bo, á] a apprehensive.
apresar [ápresár'] vt to seize; (capturar) to capture.
aprestar [áprestár'] vt to prepare, get ready; (TEC) to prime, size; ~**se** vr to get ready.
apresto [ápre'sto] nm (gen) preparation; (sustancia) size.
apresurado, a [ápresōōrá'ðo, á] a hurried, hasty.
apresuramiento [ápresōōrámyen'to] nm hurry, haste.
apresurar [ápresōōrár'] vt to hurry, accelerate; ~**se** vr to hurry, make haste; **me apresuré a sugerir que ...** I hastily suggested that ...
apretado, a [ápretá'ðo, á] a tight; (escritura) cramped.
apretar [ápretár'] vt to squeeze, press; (mano) to clasp; (dientes) to grit; (TEC) to tighten; (presionar) to press together, pack ♦ vi to be too tight; ~**se** vr to crowd together; ~ **la mano a uno** to shake sb's hand; ~ **el paso** to quicken one's step.
apretón [ápreton'] nm squeeze; ~ **de manos** handshake.
aprieto [áprye'to] etc vb V **apretar** ♦ nm squeeze; (dificultad) difficulty, jam; **estar en un** ~ to be in a jam; **ayudar a uno a**

salir de un ~ to help sb out of trouble.
aprisa [áprē'sá] ad quickly, hurriedly.
aprisionar [áprēsyonár'] vt to imprison.
aprobación [áprobásyon'] nf approval.
aprobado [áprobá'ðo] nm (nota) passing grade (US), pass mark (Brit).
aprobar [áprobár'] vt to approve (of); (examen, materia) to pass ♦ vi to pass.
apropiación [ápropyásyon'] nf appropriation.
apropiado, a [ápropyá'ðo, á] a appropriate.
apropiarse [ápropyár'se] vr: ~ **de** to appropriate.
aprovechado, a [áprobetchá'ðo, á] a industrious, hardworking; (económico) thrifty; (pey) unscrupulous.
aprovechamiento [áprobetchámyen'to] nm use, exploitation.
aprovechar [áprobetchár'] vt to use; (explotar) to exploit; (experiencia) to profit from; (oferta, oportunidad) to take advantage of ♦ vi to progress, improve; ~**se** vr: ~**se de** to make use of; (pey) to take advantage of; **¡que aproveche!** enjoy your meal!
aprovisionar [áprobēsyonár'] vt to supply.
aproximación [áproksēmásyon'] nf approximation; (de lotería) consolation prize.
aproximadamente [áproksēmáðámen'te] ad approximately.
aproximado, a [áproksēmá'ðo, á] a approximate.
aproximar [áproksēmár'] vt to bring nearer; ~**se** vr to come near, approach.
apruebe [áprwe'be] etc vb V **aprobar**.
aptitud [áptētōōð'] nf aptitude; (capacidad) ability; ~ **para los negocios** business sense.
apto, a [áp'to, á] a (apropiado) fit, suitable (para for, to); (hábil) capable; ~**/no** ~ **para menores** (CINE) suitable/unsuitable for children.
apuesto, a [ápwe'sto, á] etc vb V **apostar** ♦ a neat, elegant ♦ nf bet, wager.
apuntador [ápōōntáðor'] nm prompter.
apuntalar [ápōōntálár'] vt to prop up.
apuntar [ápōōntár'] vt (con arma) to aim at; (con dedo) to point at o to; (anotar) to write (down); (datos) to record; (TEATRO) to prompt; ~**se** vr (DEPORTE: tanto, victoria) to score; (ESCOL) to enroll (US), enrol (Brit); ~ **una cantidad en la cuenta de uno** to charge a sum to sb's account; ~**se en un curso** to enroll in a course; **¡yo me apunto!** count me in!
apunte [ápōōn'te] nm note; (TEATRO: voz) prompt; (: texto) prompt book.
apuñalar [ápōōnyálár'] vt to stab.
apurado, a [ápōōrá'ðo, á] a needy; (difícil) difficult; (peligroso) dangerous; (AM)

hurried, rushed; **estar en una situación apurada** to be in a tight spot; **estar ~ to be** in a hurry.

apurar [àpoōrár'] *vt* (*agotar*) to drain; (*recursos*) to use up; (*molestar*) to annoy; **~se** *vr* (*preocuparse*) to worry; (*darse prisa*) to hurry.

apuro [àpoō'ro] *nm* (*aprieto*) fix, jam; (*escasez*) want, hardship; (*vergüenza*) embarrassment; (*AM*) haste, urgency.

aquejado, a [àkehá'tho, à] *a*: ~ **de** (*MED*) afflicted by.

aquejar [àkehár'] *vt* (*afligir*) to distress; **le aqueja una grave enfermedad** he suffers from a serious disease.

aquel, aquella, aquellos, as [àkel', àke'yà, àke'yos, às] *a* that; (*pl*) those.

aquél, aquélla, aquéllos, as [àkel', àke'yà, àke'yos, às] *pron* that (one); (*pl*) those (ones).

aquello [àke'yo] *pron* that, that business.

aquí [àkē'] *ad* (*lugar*) here; (*tiempo*) now; ~ **arriba** up here; ~ **mismo** right here; ~ **yace** here lies; **de ~ a ocho días** a week from now.

aquietar [àkyetár'] *vt* to calm (down).

Aquisgrán [àkēsgrán'] *nm* Aachen, Aix-la-Chapelle.

A.R. *abr* (= *Alteza Real*) R.H.

ara [à'rà] *nf* (*altar*) altar; **en ~s de** for the sake of.

árabe [à'ràbe] *a* Arab, Arabian, Arabic ♦ *nm/f* Arab ♦ *nm* (*LING*) Arabic.

Arabia [àrá'byà] *nf* Arabia; ~ **Saudí** *o* **Saudita** Saudi Arabia.

arábigo, a [àrá'bēgo, à] *a* Arab, Arabian, Arabic.

arácnido [àrák'nētho] *nm* arachnid.

arado [àrá'tho] *nm* plow (*US*), plough (*Brit*).

aragonés, esa [àràgones', e'sà] *a, nm/f* Aragonese ♦ *nm* (*LING*) Aragonese

arancel [àránsel'] *nm* tariff, duty; ~ **de aduanas** (customs) duty.

arandela [àrànde'là] *nf* (*TEC*) washer; (*chorrera*) frill.

araña [àrá'nyà] *nf* (*ZOOL*) spider; (*lámpara*) chandelier.

arañar [àrànyár'] *vt* to scratch.

arañazo [àrànyà'so] *nm* scratch.

arar [àrár'] *vt* to plow (*US*), plough (*Brit*), till.

araucano, a [àráoōkà'no, à] *a, nm/f* Araucanian.

arbitraje [àrbētrá'he] *nm* arbitration.

arbitrar [àrbētrár'] *vt* to arbitrate in; (*recursos*) to bring together; (*DEPORTE*) to referee ♦ *vi* to arbitrate.

arbitrariedad [àrbētráryethàth'] *nf* arbitrariness; (*acto*) arbitrary act.

arbitrario, a [àrbētrá'ryo] *a* arbitrary.

arbitrio [àrbē'tryo] *nm* free will; (*JUR*)

adjudication, decision; **dejar al ~ de uno** to leave to sb's discretion.

árbitro [àr'bētro] *nm* arbitrator; (*DEPORTE*) referee; (*TENIS*) umpire.

árbol [àr'bol] *nm* (*BOT*) tree; (*NAUT*) mast; (*TEC*) axle, shaft.

arbolado, a [àrbolá'tho, à] *a* wooded; (*camino*) tree-lined ♦ *nm* woodland.

arboladura [àrbolàthoō'rà] *nf* rigging.

arbolar [àrbolár'] *vt* to hoist, raise.

arboleda [àrbole'thà] *nf* grove, plantation.

arbusto [àrboō'sto] *nm* bush, shrub.

arca [àr'kà] *nf* chest, box; **A~ de la Alianza** Ark of the Covenant; **A~ de Noé** Noah's Ark.

arcada [àrkà'thà] *nf* arcade; (*de puente*) arch, span; ~**s** *nfpl* retching *sg*.

arcaico, a [àrkà'ēko, à] *a* archaic.

arce [àr'se] *nm* maple tree.

arcén [àrsen'] *nm* (*de autopista*) hard shoulder; (*de carretera*) shoulder.

arcilla [àrsē'yà] *nf* clay.

arco [àr'ko] *nm* arch; (*MAT*) arc; (*MIL, MUS*) bow; ~ **iris** rainbow.

arcón [àrkon'] *nm* large chest.

archiconocido, a [àrtchēkonosē'tho, à] *a* extremely well-known.

archipiélago [àrtchēpye'làgo] *nm* archipelago.

archisabido, a [àrtchēsàbē'tho, à] *a* extremely well-known.

archivador [àrtchēbàthor'] *nm* filing cabinet; ~ **colgante** suspension file.

archivar [àrtchēbár'] *vt* to file (away); (*INFORM*) to archive.

archivo [àrtchē'bo] *nm* archive(s) (*pl*); (*INFORM*) file, archive; **A~ Nacional** Public Record Office; ~**s policíacos** police files; **nombre de ~** (*INFORM*) filename; ~ **maestro** (*INFORM*) master file; ~ **de transacciones** (*INFORM*) transactions file.

arder [àrther'] *vt* to burn; ~ **sin llama** to smolder (*US*), smoulder (*Brit*); **estar que arde** (*persona*) to fume.

ardid [àrthēth'] *nm* ruse.

ardiente [àrthyen'te] *a* ardent.

ardilla [àrthē'yà] *nf* squirrel.

ardor [àrthor'] *nm* (*calor*) heat, warmth; (*fig*) ardor (*US*), ardour (*Brit*); ~ **de estómago** heartburn.

arduo, a [àr'thwo, à] *a* arduous.

área [à'reà] *nf* area; (*DEPORTE*) penalty area; ~ **de excedentes** (*INFORM*) overflow area.

ARENA [àre'nà] *nf abr* (*El Salvador*: *POL*) = *Alianza Republicana Nacionalista*.

arena [àre'nà] *nf* sand; (*de una lucha*) arena.

arenal [àrenál'] *nm* (*arena movediza*) quicksand.

arenga [àren'gà] *nf* (*fam*) sermon.

arengar [àrengár'] *vt* to harangue.
arengue [àren'ge] *etc vb V* **arengar**.
arenillas [àrenē'yás] *nfpl* (*MED*) stones.
arenisca [àrenēs'ko, à] *nf* sandstone; (*cascajo*) grit.
arenoso, a [àreno'so, à] *a* sandy.
arenque [àren'ke] *nm* herring.
arete [àre'te] *nm* earring.
argamasa [àrgàmá'sá] *nf* mortar, plaster.
Argel [àrhel'] *n* Algiers.
Argelia [àrhe'lyà] *nf* Algeria.
argelino, a [àrhelē'no, à] *a, nm/f* Algerian.
Argentina [àrhentē'ná] *nf*: **(la)** ~ the Argentine, Argentina.
argentino, a [àrhentē'no, à] *a* Argentinian; (*de plata*) silvery ♦ *nm/f* Argentinian.
argolla [àrgo'yá] *nf* (large) ring.
argot [àrgo'] *nm, pl* **argots** [àrgo', àrgos'] slang.
argucia [àrgoo'syá] *nf* subtlety, sophistry.
argüir [àrgwēr'] *vt* to deduce; (*discutir*) to argue; (*indicar*) to indicate, imply; (*censurar*) to reproach ♦ *vi* to argue.
argumentación [àrgoomentásyon'] *nf* (line of) argument.
argumentar [àrgoomentár'] *vt, vi* to argue.
argumento [àrgoomen'to] *nm* argument; (*razonamiento*) reasoning; (*de novela etc*) plot; (*CINE, TV*) storyline.
arguyendo [àrgooyen'do] *etc vb V* **argüir**.
aria [à'ryá] *nf* aria.
aridez [àrēthes'] *nf* aridity, dryness.
árido, a [à'rētho, à] *a* arid, dry; **~s** *nmpl* dry goods.
Aries [à'ryes] *nm* Aries.
ariete [àrye'te] *nm* battering ram.
ario, a [à'ryo, à] *a* Aryan.
arisco, a [àrēs'ko, à] *a* surly; (*insociable*) unsociable.
aristocracia [àrēstokrá'syá] *nf* aristocracy.
aristócrata [àrēsto'krátá] *nm/f* aristocrat.
aristocrático, a [àrēstokrá'tēko, à] *a* aristocratic.
aritmética [àrētme'tēká] *nf* arithmetic.
aritmético, a [àrētme'tēko, à] *a* arithmetic(al) ♦ *nm/f* arithmetician.
arma [àr'má] *nf* arm; **~s** *nfpl* arms; ~ **blanca** blade, knife; (*espada*) sword; ~ **de fuego** firearm; **~s cortas** small arms; **rendir las ~s** to lay down one's arms; **ser de ~s tomar** to be somebody to be reckoned with.
armada [àrmá'thá] *nf* armada; (*flota*) fleet; *V tb* **armado**.
armadillo [àrmáthē'yo] *nm* armadillo.
armado, a [àrmá'tho, à] *a* armed; (*TEC*) reinforced.
armador [àrmáthor'] *nm* (*NAUT*) shipowner.
armadura [àrmáthoo'rá] *nf* (*MIL*) armor (*US*), armour (*Brit*); (*TEC*) framework; (*ZOOL*) skeleton; (*FÍSICA*) armature.

armamentista [àrmámentē'stá] **armamentístico, a** [àrmámentē'stēko, à] *a* arms *cpd*.
armamento [àrmámen'to] *nm* armament; (*NAUT*) fitting-out.
armar [àrmár'] *vt* (*soldado*) to arm; (*máquina*) to assemble; (*navío*) to fit out; **~la, ~ un lío** to start a row; **~se** *vr*: **~se de valor** to summon up one's courage.
armario [àrmá'ryo] *nm* wardrobe.
armatoste [àrmáto'ste] *nm* (*mueble*) monstrosity; (*máquina*) contraption.
armazón [àrmáson'] *nf o m* body, chassis; (*de mueble etc*) frame; (*ARQ*) skeleton.
armería [àrmerē'á] *nf* (*museo*) military museum; (*tienda*) gunsmith's.
armiño [àrmē'nyo] *nm* stoat; (*piel*) ermine.
armisticio [àrmēstē'syo] *nm* armistice.
armonía [àrmonē'á] *nf* harmony.
armónica [àrmo'nēká] *nf* harmonica; *V tb* **armónico**.
armonice [àrmonē'se] *etc vb V* **armonizar**.
armónico, a [àrmo'nēko, à] *a* harmonic.
armonioso, a [àrmonyo'so, à] *a* harmonious.
armonizar [àrmonēsár'] *vt* to harmonize; (*diferencias*) to reconcile ♦ *vi* to harmonize; ~ **con** (*fig*) to be in keeping with; (*colores*) to blend in with.
arnés [àrnes'] *nm* armor (*US*), armour (*Brit*); **arneses** *nmpl* harness *sg*.
aro [à'ro] *nm* ring; (*tejo*) quoit; (*AM*: *pendiente*) earring; **entrar por el** ~ to give in.
aroma [àro'má] *nm* aroma.
aromático, a [àromá'tēko, à] *a* aromatic.
arpa [àr'pá] *nf* harp.
arpegio [àrpe'hyo] *nm* (*MUS*) arpeggio.
arpía [àrpē'á] *nf* (*fig*) shrew.
arpillera [àrpē'ye'rá] *nf* sacking, sackcloth.
arpón [àrpon'] *nm* harpoon.
arquear [àrkeár'] *vt* to arch, bend; **~se** *vr* to arch, bend.
arqueo [àrke'o] *nm* (*gen*) arching; (*NAUT*) tonnage.
arqueología [àrkeolohē'á] *nf* archeology.
arqueológico, a [àrkeolo'hēko, à] *a* archeological.
arqueólogo, a [àrkeo'logo, à] *nm/f* archeologist.
arquero [àrke'ro] *nm* archer, bowman.
arquetipo [àrketē'po] *nm* archetype.
arquitecto, a [àrkētek'to, à] *nm/f* architect; ~ **paisajista** *o* **de jardines** landscape gardener.
arquitectónico, a [àrkētekto'nēko, à] *a* architectural.
arquitectura [àrkētektoo'rá] *nf* architecture.
arrabal [àrráhál'] *nm* suburb; (*AM*) slum; **~es** *nmpl* outskirts.

arrabalero, a [àrráḅálc'ro, à] *a* (*fig*) common, coarse.

arracimarse [àrràsēmár'se] *vr* to cluster together.

arraigado, a [àrráēgá'tḥo, à] *a* deep-rooted; (*fig*) established.

arraigar [àrráēgár'] *vt* to establish ♦ *vi*, ~**se** *vr* to take root; (*persona*) to settle.

arraigo [àrrá'ēgo] *nm* (*raíces*) roots *pl*; (*bienes*) property; (*influencia*) hold; **hombre de** ~ man of property.

arraigue [àrrá'ēge] *etc vb* V **arraigar**.

arrancada [àrránká'tḥà] *nf* (*arranque*) sudden start; (*AM: fuga*) sudden dash.

arrancar [àrránkár'] *vt* (*sacar*) to extract, pull out; (*arrebatar*) to snatch (away); (*pedazo*) to tear off; (*página*) to rip out; (*suspiro*) to heave; (*AUTO*) to start; (*INFORM*) to boot; (*fig*) to extract; ~ **información a uno** to extract information from sb ♦ *vi* (*AUTO, máquina*) to start; (*ponerse en marcha*) to get going; ~ **de** to stem from.

arranque [àrrán'ke] *etc vb* V **arrancar** ♦ *nm* sudden start; (*AUTO*) start; (*fig*) fit, outburst.

arras [à'rràs] *nfpl* pledge *sg*, security *sg*.

arrasar [àrràsár'] *vt* (*aplanar*) to level, flatten; (*destruir*) to demolish.

arrastrado, a [àrràstrá'tḥo, à] *a* poor, wretched; (*AM*) servile.

arrastrador [àrràstrátḥor'] *nm* (*en máquina impresora*) tractor.

arrastrar [àrràstrár'] *vt* to drag (along); (*fig*) to drag down, degrade; (*suj: agua, viento*) to carry away ♦ *vi* to drag; ~**se** *vr* to crawl; (*fig*) to grovel; **llevar algo arrastrado** to drag sth along.

arrastre [àrràs'tre] *nm* drag, dragging; (*DEPORTE*) crawl; **estar para el** ~ (*fig*) to have had it; ~ **de papel por fricción/por tracción** (*en máquina impresora*) friction/tractor feed.

array [àrrà'ē] *nm* (*INFORM*) array; ~ **empaquetado** (*INFORM*) packed array.

arrayán [àrráyán'] *nm* myrtle.

arre [à'rre] *excl* gee up!

arrear [àrreár'] *vt* to drive on, urge on ♦ *vi* to hurry along.

arrebañaduras [àrreḅányátḥōō'ràs] *nfpl* leftovers *pl*.

arrebañar [àrreḅányár'] *vt* (*juntar*) to scrape together.

arrebatado, a [àrreḅátá'tḥo, à] *a* rash, impetuous; (*repentino*) sudden, hasty.

arrebatar [àrreḅátár'] *vt* to snatch (away), seize; (*fig*) to captivate; ~**se** *vr* to get carried away, get excited.

arrebato [àrreḅá'to] *nm* fit of rage, fury; (*éxtasis*) rapture; **en un** ~ **de cólera** in an outburst of anger.

arrebol [àrreḅol'] *nm* (*colorete*) rouge; ~**es** *nmpl* red clouds.

arrebolar [àrreḅolár'] *vt* to redden; ~**se** *vr* (*enrojecer*) to blush.

arrebujar [àrreḅōōhàr'] *vt* (*objetos*) to jumble together; ~**se** *vr* to wrap o.s. up.

arreciar [àrresyár'] *vi* to get worse; (*viento*) to get stronger.

arrecife [àrresē'fe] *nm* reef.

arrechucho [àrretchōōtch'o] *nm* (*MED*) turn.

arredrar [àrretḥrár'] *vt* (*hacer retirarse*) to drive back; ~**se** *vr* (*apartarse*) to draw back; ~**se ante algo** to shrink away from sth.

arreglado, a [àrreglá'tḥo, à] *a* (*ordenado*) neat, orderly; (*moderado*) moderate, reasonable.

arreglar [àrreglár'] *vt* (*poner orden*) to tidy up; (*algo roto*) to fix, repair; (*problema*) to solve; ~**se** *vr* to reach an understanding; **arreglárselas** (*fam*) to get by, manage.

arreglo [àrre'glo] *nm* settlement; (*orden*) order; (*acuerdo*) agreement; (*MUS*) arrangement, setting; (*INFORM*) array; **con** ~ **a** in accordance with; **llegar a un** ~ to reach a compromise.

arrellanarse [àrreyánár'se] *vr* to sprawl; ~ **en el asiento** to lie back in one's chair.

arremangar [àrremángár'] *vt* to roll up, turn up; ~**se** *vr* to roll up one's sleeves.

arremangue [àrremán'ge] *etc vb* V **arremangar**.

arremeter [àrremeter'] *vt* to attack, assault; ~ **contra uno** to attack sb.

arremetida [àrremetē'tḥà] *nf* assault.

arremolinarse [àrremolēnár'se] *vr* to crowd around, mill around; (*corriente*) to swirl, eddy.

arrendador, a [àrrendátḥor', à] *nm/f* landlord/lady.

arrendamiento [àrrendámyen'to] *nm* letting; (*el alquilar*) renting; (*contrato*) lease; (*alquiler*) rent.

arrendar [àrrendár'] *vt* to let; to hire; to lease; to rent.

arrendatario, a [àrrendátà'ryo, à] *nm/f* tenant.

arreo [àrre'o] *nm* adornment; ~**s** *nmpl* harness *sg*, trappings.

arrepentimiento [àrrepentēmyen'to] *nm* regret, repentance.

arrepentirse [àrrepentēr'se] *vr* to repent; ~ **de (haber hecho) algo** to regret (doing) sth.

arrepienta [àrrepyen'tà] *etc*, **arrepintiendo** [àrrepēntyen'do] *etc vb* V **arrepentirse**.

arrestar [àrrestár'] *vt* to arrest; (*encarcelar*) to imprison.

arresto [àrre'sto] *nm* arrest; (*MIL*) detention; (*audacia*) boldness, daring; ~ **domiciliario** house arrest.

arriar |àrryàr'| *vt* (*velas*) to haul down; (*bandera*) to lower, strike; (*un cable*) to pay out.

arriate |àrryá'tc| *nm* (*BOT*) bed; (*camino*) road.

arriba |àrrē'ḃá| *ad* (*posición*) above, overhead, on top; (*en casa*) upstairs; (*dirección*) up, upwards; ~ **de** above, higher (up) than; ~ **del todo** at the very top; **el piso de** ~ the apartment upstairs; **de** ~ **abajo** from top to bottom; (*persona*) from head to foot; **calle** ~ up the street; **lo** ~ **mencionado** the aforementioned; ~ **de 20 pesetas** more than 20 pesetas; **de 10 dólares para** ~ from 10 dollars upwards; ¡~ **España!** long live Spain!; ¡~ **las manos!** hands up!

arribar |àrrēḃàr'| *vi* to put into port; (*llegar*) to arrive.

arribista |àrrēḃē'stà| *nm/f* parvenu(e), upstart.

arriendo |àrrycn'do| *etc vb* V **arrendar** ♦ *nm* = **arrendamiento**.

arriero |àrryc'ro| *nm* muleteer.

arriesgado, a |àrryesgá'tḥo, à| *a* (*peligroso*) risky; (*audaz*) bold, daring.

arriesgar |àrryesgàr'| *vt* to risk; (*poner en peligro*) to endanger; ~**se** *vr* to take a risk.

arriesgue |àrryes'gc| *etc vb* V **arriesgar**.

arrimar |àrrēmàr'| *vt* (*acercar*) to bring close; (*poner de lado*) to set aside; ~**se** *vr* to come close *o* closer; ~**se a** to lean on; (*fig*) to keep company with; (*buscar ayuda*) to seek the protection of; **arrímate a mí** cuddle up to me.

arrinconado, a |àrrēnkonà'tḥo, à| *a* forgotten, neglected.

arrinconar |àrrēnkonàr'| *vt* to put in a corner; (*fig*) to put to one side; (*abandonar*) to push aside.

arriscado, a |àrrēskà'tḥo, à| *a* (*GEO*) craggy; (*fig*) bold, resolute.

arroba |àrro'ḃá| *nf* (*peso*) 25 pounds; **tiene talento por** ~**s** he has loads of talent.

arrobado, a |àrroḃà'tḥo, à| *a* entranced, enchanted.

arrobamiento |àrroḃàmycn'to| *nm* ecstasy.

arrobar |àrroḃàr'| *vt* to enchant; ~**se** *vr* to be enraptured; (*místico*) to go into a trance.

arrodillarse |àrrotḥēyàr'sc| *vr* to kneel (down).

arrogancia |àrrogàn'syá| *nf* arrogance.

arrogante |àrrogàn'tc| *a* arrogant.

arrojar |àrrohàr'| *vt* to throw, hurl; (*humo*) to emit, give out; (*COM*) to yield, produce; ~**se** *vr* to throw *o* hurl o.s.

arrojo |àrro'ho| *nm* daring.

arrollador, a |àrroyàtḥor', à| *a* crushing, overwhelming.

arrollar |àrroyàr'| *vt* (*enrollar*) to roll up;

(*suj*: *inundación*) to wash away; (*AUTO*) to run over; (*DEPORTE*) to crush.

arropar |àrropàr'| *vt* to cover (up), wrap up; ~**se** *vr* to wrap o.s. up.

arrostrar |àrrostràr'| *vt* to face (up to); ~**se** *vr*: ~**se con uno** to face up to sb.

arroyo |àrro'yo| *nm* stream; (*de la calle*) gutter; **poner a uno en el** ~ to turn sb onto the streets.

arroz |àrros'| *nm* rice; ~ **con leche** rice pudding.

arruga |àrrōō'gà| *nf* fold; (*de cara*) wrinkle; (*de vestido*) crease.

arrugar |àrrōōgàr'| *vt* to fold; to wrinkle; to crease; ~**se** *vr* to get wrinkled; to get creased.

arrugue |àrrōō'gc| *etc vb* V **arrugar**.

arruinar |àrrwēnàr'| *vt* to ruin, wreck; ~**se** *vr* to be ruined.

arrullar |àrrōōyàr'| *vi* to coo ♦ *vt* to lull to sleep.

arrumaco |àrrōōmà'ko| *nm* (*caricia*) caress; (*halago*) piece of flattery.

arrumbar |àrrōōmbàr'| *vt* (*objeto*) to discard; (*individuo*) to silence.

arsenal |àrsenàl'| *nm* naval dockyard; (*MIL*) arsenal.

arsénico |àrsc'nēko| *nm* arsenic.

arte |àr'tc| *nm* (*gen m en sg y siempre f en pl*) art; (*maña*) skill, guile; **por** ~ **de magia** (as if) by magic; **no tener** ~ **ni parte en algo** to have nothing whatsoever to do with sth; ~**s** *nfpl* arts; **Bellas A**~**s** Fine Art *sg*; ~**s y oficios** arts and crafts.

artefacto |àrtefák'to| *nm* appliance; (*ARQUEOLOGÍA*) artifact (*US*), artefact (*Brit*).

arteria |àrtc'ryà| *nf* artery.

artesa |àrtc'sà| *nf* trough.

artesanía |àrtesánē'á| *nf* craftsmanship; (*artículos*) handicrafts *pl*.

artesano, a |àrtesá'no, à| *nm/f* artisan, craftsman/woman.

ártico, a |àr'tēko, à| *a* Arctic ♦ *nm*: **el Á**~ the Arctic.

articulación |àrtēkōōlásyon'| *nf* articulation; (*MED, TEC*) joint.

articulado, a |àrtēkōōlá'tḥo, à| *a* articulated; jointed.

articular |àrtēkōōlàr'| *vt* to articulate; to join together.

articulista |àrtēkōōlē'stà| *nm/f* columnist, contributor (to a newspaper).

artículo |àrtē'kōōlo| *nm* article; (*cosa*) thing, article; (*TV*) feature, report; ~ **de fondo** leader, editorial; ~**s** *nmpl* goods; ~**s de marca** (*COM*) proprietary goods.

artífice |àrtē'fēsc| *nm* artist, craftsman; (*fig*) architect.

artificial |àrtēfēsyàl'| *a* artificial.

artificio |àrtēfē'syo| *nm* art, skill; (*artesa-*

nía) craftsmanship; (*astucia*) cunning.

artilugio [àrtēlōō'hyo] *nm* gadget.

artillería [àrtēyerē'á] *nf* artillery.

artillero [àrtēye'ro] *nm* artilleryman, gunner.

artimaña [àrtēmá'nyà] *nf* trap, snare; (*astucia*) cunning.

artista [àrtē'stà] *nm/f* (*pintor*) artist, painter; (*TEATRO*) artist, artiste.

artístico, a [àrtē'stēko, à] *a* artistic.

artritis [àrtrē'tēs] *nf* arthritis.

arveja [àrβe'hà] *nf* (*AM*) pea.

Arz. *abr* (= *Arzobispo*) Abp.

arzobispo [àrsoβēs'po] *nm* archbishop.

as [às] *nm* ace; ~ **del fútbol** star football player.

asa [à'sà] *nf* handle; (*fig*) lever.

asado [àsà'ðo] *nm* roast (meat).

asador [àsàðor'] *nm* (*varilla*) spit; (*aparato*) spit roaster.

asadura(s) [àsàðōō'rà(s)] *nf(pl)* entrails *pl*, offal *sg*; (*CULIN*) chitterlings *pl*.

asaetar [àsàetàr'] *vt* (*fig*) to bother.

asalariado, a [àsàlàryà'ðo, à] *a* paid, wage-earning, salaried ♦ *nm/f* wage earner.

asaltador, a [àsàltàðor', à], **asaltante** [àsàltà'nte] *nm/f* assailant.

asaltar [àsàltàr'] *vt* to attack, assault; (*fig*) to assail.

asalto [àsàl'to] *nm* attack, assault; (*DEPORTE*) round.

asamblea [àsàmble'à] *nf* assembly; (*reunión*) meeting.

asar [àsàr'] *vt* to roast; ~ **al horno/a la parrilla** to bake/grill; ~**se** *vr* (*fig*): **me aso de calor** I'm roasting; **aquí se asa uno vivo** it's boiling hot here.

asbesto [àsβe'sto] *nm* asbestos.

ascendencia [àsðenden'syà] *nf* ancestry; (*AM*) ascendancy; **de** ~ **francesa** of French origin.

ascender [àsðender'] *vi* (*subir*) to ascend, rise; (*ser promovido*) to gain promotion ♦ *vt* to promote; ~ **a** to amount to.

ascendiente [àsðendyen'te] *nm* influence ♦ *nm/f* ancestor.

ascensión [àsðensyon'] *nf* ascent; **la A**~ the Ascension.

ascenso [àsðen'so] *nm* ascent; (*promoción*) promotion.

ascensor [àsðensor'] *nm* elevator (*US*), lift (*Brit*).

ascético, a [àsðe'tēko, à] *a* ascetic.

ascienda [àsyen'dà] *etc vb V* **ascender.**

asco [às'ko] *nm*: **el ajo me da** ~ I hate *o* loathe garlic; **hacer** ~**s de algo** to turn up one's nose at sth; **estar hecho un** ~ to be filthy; **poner a uno de** ~ to call sb all sorts of names *o* every name under the sun; **¡qué** ~! how revolting *o* disgusting!

ascua [às'kwà] *nf* ember; **arrimar el** ~ **a su**

sardina to look after number one; **estar en** ~**s** to be on tenterhooks.

aseado, a [àseà'ðo, à] *a* clean; (*arreglado*) tidy; (*pulcro*) smart.

asear [àseàr'] *vt* (*lavar*) to wash; (*ordenar*) to tidy (up).

asechanza [àsetchán'sà] *nf* trap, snare.

asechar [àsetchár'] *vt* to set a trap for.

asediar [àseðyàr'] *vt* (*MIL*) to besiege, lay siege to; (*fig*) to chase, pester.

asedio [àse'ðyo] *nm* siege; (*COM*) run.

asegurado, a [àseγōōrá'ðo, à] *a* insured.

asegurador, a [àseγōōràðor', à] *nm/f* insurer.

asegurar [àseγōōràr'] *vt* (*consolidar*) to secure, fasten; (*dar garantía de*) to guarantee; (*preservar*) to safeguard; (*afirmar, dar por cierto*) to assure, affirm; (*tranquilizar*) to reassure; (*tomar un seguro*) to insure; ~**se** *vr* to assure o.s., make sure.

asemejarse [àsemehàr'se] *vr* to be alike; ~ **a** to be like, resemble.

asentado, a [àsentà'ðo, à] *a* established, settled.

asentar [àsentàr'] *vt* (*sentar*) to seat, sit down; (*poner*) to place, establish; (*alisar*) to level, smooth down *o* out; (*anotar*) to note down ♦ *vi* to be suitable, suit.

asentimiento [àsentēmyen'to] *nm* assent, agreement.

asentir [àsentēr'] *vi* to assent, agree.

aseo [àse'o] *nm* cleanliness; ~**s** *nmpl* restroom *sg* (*US*), toilet *sg* (*Brit*), cloakroom *sg*.

aséptico, a [àsep'tēko, à] *a* germ-free, free from infection.

asequible [àsekē'βle] *a* (*precio*) reasonable; (*meta*) attainable; (*persona*) approachable.

aserradero [àserràðe'ro] *nm* sawmill.

aserrar [àserràr'] *vt* to saw.

aserrín [àserrēn'] *nm* sawdust.

asesinar [àsesēnàr'] *vt* to murder; (*POL*) to assassinate.

asesinato [àsesēnà'to] *nm* murder; assassination.

asesino, a [àsesē'no, à] *nm/f* murderer, killer; (*POL*) assassin.

asesor, a [àsesor', à] *nm/f* adviser, consultant; (*COM*) assessor, consultant; ~ **administrativo** management consultant.

asesorar [àsesoràr'] *vt* (*JUR*) to advise, give legal advice to; (*COM*) to act as consultant to; ~**se** *vr*: ~**se con** *o* **de** to take advice from, consult.

asesoría [àsesorē'à] *nf* (*cargo*) consultancy; (*oficina*) consultant's office.

asestar [àsestàr'] *vt* (*golpe*) to deal; (*arma*) to aim; (*tiro*) to fire.

aseverar [àseβeràr'] *vt* to assert.

asfaltado, a [àsfàltà'ðo, à] *a* asphalted ♦ *nm* (*pavimiento*) asphalt.

asfalto [àsfál'to] *nm* asphalt.

asfixia [àsfēk'syà] *nf* asphyxia, suffocation.

asfixiar [àsfēksyár'] *vt* to asphyxiate, suffocate.

asga [ás'gà] *etc vb* V **asir**.

así [àsē'] *ad* (*de esta manera*) in this way, like this, thus; (*aunque*) although; (*tan pronto como*) as soon as; ~ **que** so; ~ **como** as well as; ~ **y todo** even so; ¿**no es** ~? isn't it?, didn't you? *etc*; ~ **de grande** this big; ¡~ **sea**! so be it!; ~ **es la vida** such is life, that's life.

Asia [à'syà] *nf* Asia.

asiático, a [àsyà'tēko, à] *a*, *nm/f* Asian, Asiatic.

asidero [àsēðe'ro] *nm* handle.

asiduidad [àsēðwēðàð'] *nf* assiduousness.

asiduo, a [àsē'ðwo, à] *a* assiduous; (*frecuente*) frequent ♦ *nm/f* regular (customer).

asiento [àsyen'to] *etc vb* V **asentar, asentir** ♦ *nm* (*mueble*) seat, chair; (*de coche, en tribunal etc*) seat; (*localidad*) seat, place; (*fundamento*) site; ~ **delantero/trasero** front/back seat.

asierre [àsye'rre] *etc vb* V **aserrar**.

asignación [àsēgnásyon'] *nf* (*atribución*) assignment; (*reparto*) allocation; (*COM*) allowance; ~ (**semanal**) pocket money; ~ **de presupuesto** budget appropriation.

asignar [àsēgnár'] *vt* to assign, allocate.

asignatura [àsēgnátoo'rà] *nf* subject; (*curso*) course.

asilado, a [àsēlà'ðo, à] *nm/f* refugee.

asilo [àsē'lo] *nm* (*refugio*) asylum, refuge; (*establecimiento*) home, institution; ~ **político** political asylum.

asimilación [àsēmēlásyon'] *nf* assimilation.

asimilar [àsēmēlár'] *vt* to assimilate.

asimismo [àsēmēs'mo] *ad* in the same way, likewise.

asintiendo [àsēntyen'do] *etc vb* V **asentir**.

asir [àsēr'] *vt* to seize, grasp; ~**se** *vr* to take hold; ~**se a** *o* **de** to seize.

asistencia [àsēsten'syà] *nf* presence; (*TEATRO*) audience; (*MED*) attendance; (*ayuda*) assistance; ~ **social** social *o* welfare work.

asistente, a [àsēsten'te, à] *nm/f* assistant ♦ *nm* (*MIL*) orderly ♦ *nf* daily help; **los** ~**s** those present; ~ **social** social worker.

asistido, a [àsēstē'ðo, à] *a* (*AUTO: dirección*) power-assisted; ~ **por ordenador** computer-assisted.

asistir [àsēstēr'] *vt* to assist, help ♦ *vi*: ~ **a** to attend, be present at.

asma [às'mà] *nf* asthma.

asno [às'no] *nm* donkey; (*fig*) ass.

asociación [àsosyàsyon'] *nf* association; (*COM*) partnership.

asociado, a [àsosyà'ðo, à] *a* associate ♦ *nm/f* associate; (*COM*) partner.

asociar [àsosyàr'] *vt* to associate; ~**se** *vr* to become partners.

asolar [àsolár'] *vt* to destroy.

asolear [àsoleàr'] *vt* to put in the sun; ~**se** *vr* to sunbathe.

asomar [àsomár'] *vt* to show, stick out ♦ *vi* to appear; ~**se** *vr* to appear, show up; ~ **la cabeza por la ventana** to put one's head out of the window.

asombrar [àsombrár'] *vt* to amaze, astonish; ~**se** *vr*: ~**se (de)** (*sorprenderse*) to be amazed (at); (*asustarse*) to be frightened (at).

asombro [àsom'bro] *nm* amazement, astonishment.

asombroso, a [àsombro'so, à] *a* amazing, astonishing.

asomo [àso'mo] *nm* hint, sign; **ni por** ~ by no means.

asonancia [àsonán'syà] *nf* (*LIT*) assonance; (*fig*) connection; **no tener** ~ **con** to bear no relation to.

aspa [às'pà] *nf* (*cruz*) cross; (*de molino*) sail; **en** ~ X-shaped.

aspaviento [àspàvyen'to] *nm* exaggerated display of feeling; (*fam*) fuss.

aspecto [àspek'to] *nm* (*apariencia*) look, appearance; (*fig*) aspect; **bajo ese** ~ from that point of view.

aspereza [àspere'sà] *nf* roughness; (*agrura*) sourness; (*de carácter*) surliness.

áspero, a [às'pero, à] *a* rough; sour; harsh.

aspersión [àspersyon'] *nf* sprinkling; (*AGR*) spraying.

aspiración [àspērásyon'] *nf* breath, inhalation; (*MUS*) short pause; **aspiraciones** *nfpl* aspirations.

aspiradora [àspēràðo'rà] *nf* vacuum cleaner.

aspirante [àspēràn'te] *nm/f* (*candidato*) candidate; (*DEPORTE*) contender.

aspirar [àspērár'] *vt* to breathe in ♦ *vi*: ~ **a** to aspire to.

aspirina [àspērē'nà] *nf* aspirin.

asquear [àskeàr'] *vt* to sicken ♦ *vi* to be sickening; ~**se** *vr* to feel disgusted.

asquerosidad [àskerosēðàð'] *nf* (*suciedad*) filth; (*dicho*) obscenity; (*truco*) dirty trick.

asqueroso, a [àskero'so, à] *a* disgusting, sickening.

asta [à'stà] *nf* lance; (*arpón*) spear; (*mango*) shaft, handle; (*ZOOL*) horn; **a media** ~ at half mast.

astado, a [àstà'ðo, à] *a* horned ♦ *nm* bull.

asterisco [àsterēs'ko] *nm* asterisk.

astilla [àstē'yà] *nf* splinter; (*pedacito*) chip; ~**s** *nfpl* firewood *sg*.

astillarse [àstēyár'se] *vr* to splinter; (*fig*) to shatter.

astillero [àstēye'ro] *nm* shipyard.

astringente [àstrēnhen'te] *a, nm* astringent.

astro [ás'tro] *nm* star.

astrología [àstroloĥē'á] *nf* astrology.

astrólogo, a [àstro'logo, à] *nm/f* astrologer.

astronauta [àstroná'ōotà] *nm/f* astronaut.

astronave [àstroná'ĥe] *nm* spaceship.

astronomía [àstronomē'á] *nf* astronomy.

astrónomo, a [ás'tro'nomo, à] *nm/f* astronomer.

astroso, a [àstro'so, à] *a* (*desaliñado*) untidy; (*vil*) contemptible.

astucia [àstōō'syà] *nf* astuteness; (*destreza*) clever trick.

asturiano, a [àstōōryá'no, à] *a, nm/f* Asturian.

Asturias [àstōō'ryàs] *nfpl* Asturias; **Príncipe de** ~ crown prince.

astuto, a [àstōō'to, à] *a* astute; (*taimado*) cunning.

asueto [àswe'to] *nm* holiday; (*tiempo libre*) time off; **día de** ~ day off; **tarde de** ~ (*trabajo*) afternoon off; (*ESCOL*) half-holiday.

asumir [àsōōmēr'] *vt* to assume.

asunción [àsōōnsyon'] *nf* assumption.

asunto [àsōōn'to] *nm* (*tema*) matter, subject; (*negocio*) business; **¡eso es** ~ **mío!** that's my business!; ~**s exteriores** foreign affairs; ~**s a tratar** agenda *sg*.

asustadizo, a [àsōōstàĥē'so, à] *a* easily frightened.

asustar [àsōōstár'] *vt* to frighten; ~**se** *vr* to be/become frightened.

atacante [àtàkán'te] *nm/f* attacker.

atacar [àtàkár'] *vt* to attack.

atadura [àtàĥōō'rà] *nf* bond, tie.

atajar [àtàĥár'] *vt* (*gen*) to stop; (*ruta de fuga*) to cut off; (*discurso*) to interrupt ♦ *vi* to take a short cut.

atajo [àtá'ho] *nm* short cut; (*DEPORTE*) tackle.

atalaya [àtàlá'yà] *nf* watchtower.

atañer [àtányer'] *vi*: ~ **a** to concern; **en lo que atañe a eso** with regard to that.

ataque [àtá'ke] *etc vb V* **atacar** ♦ *nm* attack; ~ **cardíaco** heart attack.

atar [àtár'] *vt* to tie, tie up; ~ **la lengua a uno** (*fig*) to silence sb.

atardecer [àtàrĥeser'] *vi* to get dark ♦ *nm* evening; (*crepúsculo*) dusk.

atardezca [àtàrĥes'ká] *etc vb V* **atardecer**.

atareado, a [àtàreà'ĥo, à] *a* busy.

atascar [àtàskár'] *vt* to clog up; (*obstruir*) to jam; (*fig*) to hinder; ~**se** *vr* to stall; (*cañería*) to get blocked up; (*fig*) to get bogged down; (*en discurso*) to dry up.

atasco [àtás'ko] *nm* obstruction; (*AUTO*) traffic jam.

atasque [àtás'ke] *etc vb V* **atascar**.

ataúd [àtáōōĥ'] *nm* coffin.

ataviar [àtàĥyár'] *vt* to deck, array; ~**se** *vr* to dress up.

atavío [àtáĥe'o] *nm* attire, dress; ~**s** *nmpl* finery *sg*.

ateísmo [àteēs'mo] *nm* atheism.

atemorice [àtemorē'se] *etc vb V* **atemorizar**.

atemorizar [àtemorēsár'] *vt* to frighten, scare; ~**se** *vr* to get frightened *o* scared.

Atenas [àte'nàs] *nf* Athens.

atención [àtensyon'] *nf* attention; (*bondad*) kindness ♦ *excl* (be) careful!, look out!; **en** ~ **a esto** in view of this.

atender [àtender'] *vt* to attend to, look after; (*TEC*) to service; (*enfermo*) to care for; (*ruego*) to comply with ♦ *vi* to pay attention; ~ **a** to attend to; (*detalles*) to take care of.

atendré [àtendre'] *etc vb V* **atenerse**.

atenerse [àtener'se] *vr*: ~ **a** to abide by, adhere to.

atenga [àten'gà] *etc vb V* **atenerse**.

ateniense [àtenyen'se] *a, nm/f* Athenian.

atentado [àtentá'ĥo] *nm* crime, illegal act; (*asalto*) assault; (*terrorista*) attack; ~ **contra la vida de uno** attempt on sb's life; ~ **golpista** (*POL*) attempted coup.

atentamente [àtentámen'te] *ad*: **le saluda** ~ Yours truly (*US*) *o* faithfully (*Brit*).

atentar [àtentár'] *vi*: ~ **a** *o* **contra** to commit an outrage against.

atento, a [àten'to, à] *a* attentive, observant; (*cortés*) polite, thoughtful; **su atenta (carta)** (*COM*) your letter.

atenuante [àtenwán'te] *a*: **circunstancias** ~**s** extenuating *o* mitigating circumstances ♦ *nfpl*: ~**s** extenuating *o* mitigating circumstances.

atenuar [àtenwár'] *vt* to attenuate; (*disminuir*) to lessen, minimize.

ateo, a [àte'o, à] *a* atheistic ♦ *nm/f* atheist.

aterciopelado, a [àtersyopelá'ĥo, à] *a* velvety.

aterido, a [àterē'ĥo, à] *a*: ~ **de frío** frozen stiff.

aterrador, a [àterràĥor', à] *a* frightening.

aterrar [àterrár'] *vt* to frighten; (*aterrorizar*) to terrify; ~**se** *vr* to be frightened; to be terrified.

aterrice [àterrē'se] *etc vb V* **aterrizar**.

aterrizar [àterrēsár'] *vi* to land.

aterrorice [àterrorē'se] *etc vb V* **aterrorizar**.

aterrorizar [àterrorēsár'] *vt* to terrify.

atesorar [àtesorár'] *vt* to hoard, store up.

atestado, a [àtestá'ĥo, à] *a* packed ♦ *nm* (*JUR*) affidavit.

atestar [àtestár'] *vt* to pack, stuff; (*JUR*) to attest, testify to.

atestiguar [àtestēgwár'] *vt* to testify to, bear witness to.

atestigüe [àtestē'gwe] *etc vb V* **atestiguar**.

atiborrar [àtēĥorrár'] *vt* to fill, stuff; ~**se** *vr* to stuff o.s.

atice [àtē'se] *etc vb V* **atizar**.

ático [á'tēko] *nm* attic; ~ **de lujo** penthouse apartment.

atienda [àtyen'dá] *etc vb V* **atender**.

atildar [àtēldár'] *vt* to criticize; (*TIP*) to put a tilde over; ~**se** *vr* to spruce o.s. up.

atinado, a [àtēnà'tho, á] *a* correct; (*sensato*) sensible.

atinar [àtēnár'] *vi* (*acertar*) to be right; ~ **con** *o* **en** (*solución*) to hit upon; ~ **a hacer** to manage to do.

atiplado, a [àtēplá'tho, á] *a* (*voz*) high-pitched.

atisbar [àtēshàr'] *vt* to spy on; (*echar ojeada*) to peep at.

atizar [àtēsár'] *vt* to poke; (*horno etc*) to stoke; (*fig*) to stir up, rouse.

atlántico, a [àtlán'tēko, á] *a* Atlantic ♦ *nm*: **el (Océano) A**~ the Atlantic (Ocean).

atlas [àt'làs] *nm* atlas.

atleta [àtle'tá] *nm/f* athlete.

atlético, a [àtle'tēko, á] *a* athletic.

atletismo [àtletēs'mo] *nm* athletics *sg*.

atmósfera [àtmos'ferá] *nf* atmosphere.

atolondramiento [àtolondràmyen'to] *nm* bewilderment; (*insensatez*) silliness.

atolladero [àtoyàthe'ro] *nm*: **estar en un** ~ to be in a jam.

atollar [àtoyár'] *vi*, ~**se** *vr* to get stuck; (*fig*) to get into a jam.

atómico, a [àto'mēko, á] *a* atomic.

atomizador [àtomēsàthor'] *nm* atomizer.

átomo [á'tomo] *nm* atom.

atónito, a [àto'nēto, á] *a* astonished, amazed.

atontado, a [àtontá'tho, á] *a* stunned; (*bobo*) silly, daft.

atontar [àtontár'] *vt* to stun; ~**se** *vr* to become confused.

atorar [àtorár'] *vt* to obstruct; ~**se** *vr* (*atragantarse*) to choke.

atormentar [àtormentár'] *vt* to torture; (*molestar*) to torment; (*acosar*) to plague, harass.

atornillar [àtornēyàr'] *vt* to screw on *o* down.

atosigar [àtosēgàr'] *vt* to harass.

atosigue [àtosē'ge] *etc vb V* **atosigar**.

atrabiliario, a [àtràhēlyà'ryo, á] *a* bad-tempered.

atracadero [àtràkàthe'ro] *nm* pier.

atracador, a [àtràkàthor', á] *nm/f* robber.

atracar [àtràkár'] *vt* (*NAUT*) to moor; (*robar*) to hold up, rob ♦ *vi* to moor; ~**se** *vr* (*hartarse*) to stuff o.s.

atracción [àtràksyon'] *nf* attraction.

atraco [àtrà'ko] *nm* holdup, robbery.

atractivo, a [àtràktē'tho, á] *a* attractive ♦ *nm* attraction; (*belleza*) attractiveness.

atraer [àtràer'] *vt* to attract; **dejarse** ~ **por** to be tempted by.

atragantarse [àtràgàntàr'se] *vr*: ~ **(con algo)** to choke (on sth); **se me ha atragantado el chico ese/el inglés** I can't take that kid/English.

atraiga [àtrà'ēgà] *etc*, **atraje** [àtrà'he] *etc vb V* **atraer**.

atrancar [àtrànkár'] *vt* (*con tranca, barra*) to bar, bolt.

atranque [àtrán'ke] *etc vb V* **atrancar**.

atrapar [àtràpár'] *vt* to trap; (*resfriado etc*) to catch.

atraque [àtrà'ke] *etc vb V* **atracar**.

atrás [àtrás'] *ad* (*movimiento*) back(wards); (*lugar*) behind; (*tiempo*) previously; **ir hacia** ~ to go back(wards); to go to the rear; **estar** ~ to be behind *o* at the back.

atrasado, a [àtràsà'tho, á] *a* slow; (*pago*) overdue, late; (*país*) backward.

atrasar [àtràsár'] *vi* to be slow; ~**se** *vr* to remain behind; (*llegar tarde*) to arrive late.

atraso [àtrà'so] *nm* slowness; lateness, delay; (*de país*) backwardness; ~**s** *nmpl* arrears.

atravesar [àtràhesár'] *vt* (*cruzar*) to cross (over); (*traspasar*) to pierce; (*período*) to go through; (*poner al través*) to lay *o* put across; ~**se** *vr* to come in between; (*intervenir*) to interfere.

atraviese [àtràhye'se] *etc vb V* **atravesar**.

atrayendo [àtràyen'do] *vb V* **atraer**.

atrayente [àtràyen'te] *a* attractive.

atreverse [àtreher'se] *vr* to dare; (*insolentarse*) to be insolent.

atrevido, a [àtrehē'tho, á] *a* daring; insolent.

atrevimiento [àtrehēmyen'to] *nm* daring; insolence.

atribución [àtrēhōōsyon'] *nf* (*LIT*) attribution; **atribuciones** *nfpl* (*POL*) functions; (*ADMIN*) responsibilities.

atribuir [àtrēhōōēr'] *vt* to attribute; (*funciones*) to confer.

atribular [àtrēhōōlár'] *vt* to afflict, distress.

atributo [àtrēhōō'to] *nm* attribute.

atribuya [àtrēhōō'yá] *etc*, **atribuyendo** [àtrēhōōyen'do] *etc vb V* **atribuir**.

atril [àtrēl'] *nm* lectern; (*MUS*) music stand.

atrio [à'tryo] *nm* (*REL*) porch.

atrocidad [àtrosēthàth'] *nf* atrocity, outrage.

atronador, a [àtronàthor', á] *a* deafening.

atropellar [àtropeyàr'] *vt* (*derribar*) to knock over *o* down; (*empujar*) to push (aside); (*AUTO*) to run over *o* down; (*agraviar*) to insult; ~**se** *vr* to act hastily.

atropello [àtrope'yo] *nm* (*AUTO*) accident; (*empujón*) push; (*agravio*) wrong; (*atrocidad*) outrage.

atroz [àtros'] *a* atrocious, awful.

atto., a. *abr* (= *atento, a*) Yours truly (*US*)

o faithfully (*Brit*).

attrezzo |àtrɛ'so| *nm* props *pl*.

atuendo |àtwen'do| *nm* attire.

atufar |àtōōfár'| *vt* (*suj*: *olor*) to overcome; (*molestar*) to irritate; **~se** *vr* (*fig*) to get cross.

atún |àtōōn'| *nm* tuna, tunny.

aturdir |àtōōrthēr'| *vt* to stun; (*suj*: *ruido*) to deafen; (*fig*) to dumbfound, bewilder.

atur(r)ullar |àtōōr(r)ōōyàr'| *vt* to bewilder.

atusar |àtōōsár'| *vt* (*cortar*) to trim; (*alisar*) to smooth (down).

atuve |àtōō'hɛ| *etc vb* V **atenerse**.

audacia |àōōthá'syà| *nf* boldness, audacity.

audaz |àōōthás'| *a* bold, audacious.

audible |àōōthē'hlɛ| *a* audible.

audición |àōōthēsyon'| *nf* hearing; (*TEATRO*) audition; ~ **radiofónica** radio concert.

audiencia |àōōthyen'syà| *nf* audience; (*JUR*) high court; (*POL*): ~ **pública** public inquiry.

audífono |àōōthē'fono| *nm* hearing aid.

auditor |àōōthētor'| *nm* (*JUR*) judge-advocate; (*COM*) auditor.

auditorio |àōōthēto'ryo| *nm* audience; (*sala*) auditorium.

auge |à'ōōhɛ| *nm* boom; (*clímax*) climax; (*ECON*) expansion; **estar en** ~ to thrive.

augurar |àōōgōōrár'| *vt* to predict; (*presagiar*) to portend.

augurio |àōōgōō'ryo| *nm* omen.

aula |à'ōōlà| *nf* classroom.

aullar |àōōyàr'| *vi* to howl, yell.

aullido |àōōyē'tho| *nm* howl, yell.

aumentar |àōōmentàr'| *vt* to increase; (*precios*) to raise; (*producción*) to step up; (*con microscopio, anteojos*) to magnify ♦ *vi*, **~se** *vr* to increase, be on the increase.

aumento |àōōmen'to| *nm* increase; rise.

aun |àōōn'| *ad* even.

aún |àōōn'| *ad* still, yet.

aunque |àōōn'kɛ| *conj* though, although, even though.

aúpa |àōō'pá| *excl* up!, come on! (*fam*): **una función de** ~ a slap-up do; **una paliza de** ~ a good beating.

aupar |àōōpár'| *vt* (*levantar*) to help up; (*fig*) to praise.

aura |à'ōōrà| *nf* (*atmósfera*) aura.

aureola |àōōrco'là| *nf* halo.

auricular |àōōrēkōōlár'| *nm* earpiece, receiver; **~es** *nmpl* headphones.

aurora |àōōro'rà| *nf* dawn; ~ **boreal(is)** northern lights *pl*.

auscultar |àōōskōōltàr'| *vt* (*MED*: *pecho*) to listen to, sound.

ausencia |àōōscn'syà| *nf* absence.

ausentarse |àōōscntàr'sɛ| *vr* to go away; (*por poco tiempo*) to go out.

ausente |àōōscn'tɛ| *a* absent ♦ *nm/f* (*ESCOL*) absentee; (*JUR*) missing person.

auspicios |àōōspē'syos| *nmpl* auspices; (*protección*) protection *sg*.

austeridad |àōōsterēthàth'| *nf* austerity.

austero, a |àōōstc'ro, à| *a* austere.

austral |àōōstrál'| *a* southern ♦ *nm* monetary unit of Argentina.

Australia |àōōstrá'lyà| *nf* Australia.

australiano, a |àōōstrályà'no, à| *a, nm/f* Australian.

Austria |à'ōōstryà| *nf* Austria.

austriaco, a |àōōstryà'ko, à| **austríaco, a** |àōōstrē'àko, à| *a, nm/f* Austrian.

autenticar |àōōtentèkár'| *vt* to authenticate.

auténtico, a |àōōten'tēko, à| *a* authentic.

autentique |àōōtentē'kɛ| *etc vb* V **autenticar**.

auto |à'ōōto| *nm* (*coche*) car; (*JUR*) edict, decree; (: *orden*) writ; **~s** *nmpl* (*JUR*) proceedings; (: *acta*) court record *sg*; ~ **de comparecencia** summons, subpoena; ~ **de ejecución** writ of execution.

autoadhesivo, a |àōōtoàthesē'ho, à| *a* self-adhesive; (*sobre*) self-sealing.

autoalimentación |àōōtoàlēmentàsyon'| *nf* (*INFORM*): ~ **de hojas** automatic paper feed.

autobiografía |àōōtohyogràfē'à| *nf* autobiography.

autobús |àōōtohōōs'| *nm* bus.

autocar |àōōtokàr'| *nm* coach; ~ **de línea** inter-city coach.

autocomprobación |àōōtokomprohàsyon'| *nf* (*INFORM*) self-test.

autóctono, a |àōōtok'tono, à| *a* native, indigenous.

autodefensa |àōōtothefen'sá| *nf* self-defense (*US*), self-defence (*Brit*).

autodeterminación |àōōtothetermēnásyon'| *nf* self-determination.

autodidacto, a |àōōtothēthàk'to, à| *a* self-taught.

autoescuela |àōōtocskwe'là| *nf* driving school.

autofinanciado, a |àōōtofénànsyà'tho, à| *a* self-financing.

autógrafo |àōōto'gráfo| *nm* autograph.

automación |àōōtomàsyon'| *nf* = **automatización**.

autómata |àōōto'mátà| *nm* automaton.

automatice |àōōtomàtē'sɛ| *etc vb* V **automatizar**.

automático, a |àōōtomà'tēko, à| *a* automatic ♦ *nm* snap fastener.

automatización |àōōtomàtēsàsyon'| *nf*: ~ **de fábricas** factory automation; ~ **de oficinas** office automation.

automatizar |àōōtomàtēsár'| *vt* to automate.

automotor, triz |àōōtomotor', trē'z| *a* self-propelled ♦ *nm* diesel train.

automóvil |àōōtomo'hēl| *nm* (motor) automobile (*US*), car (*Brit*).

automovilismo [àōōtomoḥēlēs'mo] *nm*
(*DEPORTE*) (sports) car racing.

automovilista [àōōtomoḥēlē'stá] *nm/f*
motorist, driver.

automovilístico, a [àōōtomoḥēlē'stēko, á]
a (*industria*) car *cpd*.

autonomía [àōōtonomē'á] *nf* autonomy;
Estatuto de A~ (*Esp*) Devolution Statute.

autonómico, a [àōōtono'mēko, á] *a* (*Esp
POL*) relating to autonomy, autonomous;
gobierno ~ autonomous government.

autónomo, a [àōōto'nomo, á] *a* autonomous; (*INFORM*) stand-alone, offline.

autopista [àōōtopē'stá] *nf* freeway (*US*),
motorway (*Brit*).

autopsia [àōōtop'syá] *nf* autopsy.

autor, a [àōōtor', á] *nm/f* author; **los ~es
del atentado** those responsible for the
attack.

autorice [àōōtorē'se] *etc vb V* **autorizar.**

autoridad [àōōtorēthàth'] *nf* authority; **~
local** local authority.

autoritario, a [àōōtorētá'ryo, á] *a* authoritarian.

autorización [àōōtorēsásyon'] *nf* authorization.

autorizado, a [àōōtorēsá'tho, á] *a*
authorized; (*aprobado*) approved.

autorizar [àōōtorēsár'] *vt* to authorize; to
approve.

autorretrato [àōōtorretrá'to] *nm* self-
portrait.

autoservicio [àōōtoserḥē'syo] *nm* self-
service shop *o* store; (*restaurante*) self-
service restaurant.

autostop [àōōtostop'] *nm* hitch-hiking; **hacer ~** to hitch-hike.

autostopista [àōōtostopē'stá] *nm/f* hitchhiker.

autosuficiencia [àōōtosōōfēsyen'syá] *nf*
self-sufficiency.

autovía [àōōtoḥē'á] *nf* ≈ state highway
(*US*), A road (*Brit*).

auxiliar [àōōksēlyár'] *vt* to help ♦ *nm/f*
assistant.

auxilio [àōōksē'lyo] *nm* assistance, help; **primeros ~s** first aid *sg*.

Av *abr* (= *Avenida*) Av(e).

a/v *abr* (*COM*: = *a vista*) on receipt.

aval [àḥál'] *nm* guarantee; (*persona*) guarantor.

avalancha [àḥálántch'á] *nf* avalanche.

avalar [àḥálár'] *vt* (*COM etc*) to underwrite;
(*fig*) to endorse.

avalista [àḥálē'stá] *nm* (*COM*) endorser.

avance [àḥán'se] *etc vb V* **avanzar** ♦ *nm*
advance; (*pago*) advance payment; (*CINE*)
preview.

avanzado, a [àḥánsá'tho, á] *a* advanced; **de
edad avanzada, ~ de edad** elderly.

avanzar [àḥánsár'] *vt, vi* to advance.

avaricia [àḥárē'syá] *nf* avarice, greed.

avaricioso, a [àḥárēsyo'so, á] *a* avaricious,
greedy.

avaro, a [àḥá'ro, á] *a* miserly, mean ♦ *nm/f*
miser.

avasallar [àḥásáyár'] *vt* to subdue, subjugate.

avatar [àḥátár'] *nm* change; **~es** *nmpl* ups
and downs.

Avda *abr* (= *Avenida*) Av(e).

ave [à'ḥe] *nf* bird; **~ de rapiña** bird of prey.

avecinarse [àḥesēnár'se] *vr* (*tormenta, fig*)
to approach, be on the way.

avejentar [àḥehentár'] *vt, vi*, **~se** *vr* to age.

avellana [àḥeyá'ná] *nf* hazelnut.

avellano [àḥeyá'no] *nm* hazel tree.

avemaría [àḥemárē'á] *nm* Hail Mary, Ave
Maria.

avena [àḥe'ná] *nf* oats *pl*.

avendré [àḥendre'] *etc*, **avenga** [àḥen'gá] *etc
vb V* **avenir.**

avenida [àḥenē'thá] *nf* (*calle*) avenue.

avenir [àḥenēr'] *vt* to reconcile; **~se** *vr* to
come to an agreement, reach a compro-
mise.

aventajado, a [àḥentáhá'tho, á] *a* outstanding.

aventajar [àḥentáhár'] *vt* (*sobrepasar*) to
surpass, outstrip.

aventar [àḥentár'] *vt* to fan, blow; (*grano*)
to winnow.

aventón [àḥenton'] *nm* (*AM*) push; **pedir ~**
to hitch a ride (*US*) *o* lift (*Brit*).

aventura [àḥentōō'rá] *nf* adventure; **~
sentimental** love affair.

aventurado, a [àḥentōōrá'tho, á] *a* risky.

aventurar [àḥentōōrár'] *vt* to risk; **~se** *vr*
to dare; **~se a hacer algo** to venture to do
sth.

aventurero, a [àḥentōōre'ro, á] *a* adventurous.

avergoncé [àḥergonse'], **avergoncemos**
[àḥergonse'mos] *etc vb V* **avergonzar.**

avergonzar [àḥergonsár'] *vt* to shame;
(*desconcertar*) to embarrass; **~se** *vr* to be
ashamed; to be embarrassed.

avergüence [àḥergwen'se] *etc vb V*
avergonzar.

avería [àḥerē'á] *nf* (*TEC*) breakdown, fault.

averiado, a [àḥeryá'tho, á] *a* broken-down.

averiguación [àḥerēgwásyon'] *nf* investigation; (*determinación*) ascertainment.

averiguar [àḥerēgwár'] *vt* to investigate;
(*descubrir*) to find out, ascertain.

averigüe [àḥerē'gwe] *etc vb V* **averiguar.**

aversión [àḥersyon'] *nf* aversion, dislike;
cobrar ~ a to take a strong dislike to.

avestruz [àḥestrōōs'] *nm* ostrich.

aviación [àḥyásyon'] *nf* aviation; (*fuerzas
aéreas*) air force.

aviado, a [àhyá'tho, á] *a*: **estar ~** to be in a mess.

aviador, a [àhyàthor', á] *nm/f* aviator, airman/woman.

aviar [àhyár'] *vt* to prepare, get ready.

avicultura [àhēkōoltōō'rà] *nf* poultry farming.

avidez [àhēthes'] *nf* avidity, eagerness.

ávido, a [à'hētho, á] *a* avid, eager.

aviente [àhyen'te] *etc vb V* **aventar.**

avieso, a [àhye'so, á] *a* (*torcido*) distorted; (*perverso*) wicked.

avinagrado, a [àhēnàgrá'tho, á] *a* sour, acid.

avinagrarse [àhēnàgrár'se] *vr* to turn sour.

avine [àhē'ne] *etc vb V* **avenir.**

Aviñón [àhēnyon'] *nm* Avignon.

avío [àhē'o] *nm* preparation; **~s** *nmpl* gear *sg*, kit *sg*.

avión [àhyon'] *nm* airplane (*US*), aeroplane (*Brit*); (*ave*) martin; **~ de reacción** jet (plane); **por ~** (*CORREOS*) by air mail.

avioneta [àhyone'tà] *nf* light aircraft.

avisar [àhēsár'] *vt* (*advertir*) to warn, notify; (*informar*) to tell; (*aconsejar*) to advise, counsel.

aviso [àhē'so] *nm* warning; (*noticia*) notice; (*COM*) demand note; (*INFORM*) prompt; **~ escrito** notice in writing; **sin previo ~** without warning; **estar sobre ~** to be on the look-out.

avispa [àhēs'pá] *nf* wasp.

avispado, a [àhēspá'tho, á] *a* sharp, clever.

avispero [àhēspe'ro] *nm* wasp's nest.

avispón [àhēspon'] *nm* hornet.

avistar [àhēstár'] *vt* to sight, spot.

avitaminosis [àhētámēno'sēs] *nf inv* vitamin deficiency.

avituallar [àhētwáyár'] *vt* to supply with food.

avivar [àhēhár'] *vt* to strengthen, intensify; **~se** *vr* to revive, acquire new life.

avizor [àhēsor'] *a*: **estar ojo ~** to be on the alert.

avizorar [àhēsorár'] *vt* to spy on.

axila [àksē'là] *nf* armpit.

axioma [àksyo'má] *nm* axiom.

ay [áē] *excl* (*dolor*) ow!, ouch!; (*aflicción*) oh!, oh dear!; **¡~ de mí!** poor me!

aya [à'yà] *nf* governess; (*niñera*) nanny.

ayer [àyer'] *ad*, *nm* yesterday; **antes de ~** the day before yesterday; **~ por la tarde** yesterday afternoon/evening.

ayo [à'yo] *nm* tutor.

ayote [àyo'te] *nm* (*AM*) pumpkin.

Ayto. *abr* = **Ayuntamiento.**

ayuda [àyōō'thá] *nf* help, assistance; (*MED*) enema; (*AM*) laxative ♦ *nm* page.

ayudante, a [àyōōthán'te, á] *nm/f* assistant, helper; (*ESCOL*) assistant; (*MIL*) adjutant.

ayudar [àyōōthár'] *vt* to help, assist.

ayunar [àyōōnár'] *vi* to fast.

ayunas [àyōō'nás] *nfpl*: **estar en ~** (*no haber comido*) to be fasting; (*ignorar*) to be in the dark.

ayuno [àyōō'no] *nm* fasting.

ayuntamiento [àyōōntàmyen'to] *nm* (*consejo*) town/city council; (*edificio*) town/city hall; (*cópula*) sexual intercourse.

azabache [àsàhátch'e] *nm* jet.

azada [àsá'thá] *nf* hoe.

azafata [àsáfá'tá] *nf* flight attendant.

azafrán [àsáfrán'] *nm* saffron.

azahar [àsáár'] *nm* orange/lemon blossom.

azar [àsár'] *nm* (*casualidad*) chance, fate; (*desgracia*) misfortune, accident; **por ~** by chance; **al ~** at random.

azaroso, a [àsáro'so, á] *a* (*arriesgado*) risky; (*vida*) eventful.

azogue [àso'ge] *nm* mercury.

azor [àsor'] *nm* goshawk.

azoramiento [àsorámyen'to] *nm* alarm; (*confusión*) confusion.

azorar [àsorár'] *vt* to alarm; **~se** *vr* to get alarmed.

Azores [àso'res] *nfpl*: **las (Islas) ~** the Azores.

azotar [àsotár'] *vt* to whip, beat; (*pegar*) to spank.

azotaina [àsotá'ēná] *nf* beating.

azote [àso'te] *nm* (*látigo*) whip; (*latigazo*) lash, stroke; (*en las nalgas*) spank; (*calamidad*) calamity.

azotea [àsote'á] *nf* (flat) roof.

azteca [àste'ká] *a*, *nm/f* Aztec.

azúcar [àsōō'kár] *nm* sugar.

azucarado, a [àsōōkárá'tho, á] *a* sugary, sweet.

azucarero, a [àsōōkáre'ro, á] *a* sugar *cpd* ♦ *nm* sugar bowl.

azuce [àsōō'se] *etc vb V* **azuzar.**

azucena [àsōōse'ná] *nf* white lily.

azufre [àsōō'fre] *nm* sulfur (*US*), sulphur (*Brit*).

azul [àsōōl'] *a*, *nm* blue; **~ celeste/marino** sky/navy blue.

azulejo [àsōōle'ho] *nm* tile.

azulgrana [àsōōlgrá'ná] *a inv* of Barcelona Football Club ♦ *nm*: **los A~** the Barcelona F.C. players *o* team.

azuzar [àsōōsár'] *vt* to incite, egg on.

B

B, b [be] *nf* (*letra*) B, b; **B de Barcelona** B

for Baker.

B.A. *abr* = **Buenos Aires.**

baba [bá'há] *nf* spittle, saliva; **se le caía la ~** (*fig*) he was thrilled to pieces (*US*) o bits (*Brit*).

babear [bábeár'] *vi* (*echar saliva*) to slobber; (*niño*) to dribble; (*fig*) to drool, slaver.

babel [bábel'] *nm o f* bedlam.

babero [bábero] *nm* bib.

Babia [bá'hyá] *nf*: **estar en ~** to be day-dreaming.

bable [bá'ble] *nm* Asturian (dialect).

babor [bábor'] *nm* port (side); **a ~** to port.

babosa, a [bábo'so, á] *a* slobbering; (*ZOOL*) slimy; (*AM*) silly.

babucha [bábōōtch'á] *nf* slipper.

baca [bá'ká] *nf* (*AUTO*) luggage o roof rack.

bacalao [bákálá'o] *nm* cod(fish).

bacanal [bákánál'] *nf* orgy.

bacilo [básē'lo] *nm* bacillus, germ.

bacinica [básēnē'ká] *nf*, **bacinilla** [básnē'yá] *nf* chamber pot.

bacteria [báktc'ryá] *nf* bacterium, germ.

báculo [bá'kōōlo] *nm* stick, staff; (*fig*) support.

bache [bátch'e] *nm* pothole, rut; (*fig*) bad patch.

bachillerato [bátchēyerá'to] *nm* (*ESCOL*) ≈ High School diploma.

badajo [báthá'ho] *nm* clapper (*of a bell*).

bagaje [bágá'he] *nm* baggage; (*fig*) background.

bagatela [bágáte'lá] *nf* trinket, trifle.

Bahama [báá'má]: **las (Islas) ~, las ~s** *nfpl* the Bahamas.

bahía [báē'á] *nf* bay.

bailar [báēlár'] *vt, vi* to dance.

bailarín, ina [báēlárēn', ēná] *nm/f* dancer; (*de ballet*) ballet dancer.

baile [báēle] *nm* dance; (*formal*) ball.

baja [bá'há] *nf* drop, fall; (*ECON*) slump; (*MIL*) casualty; (*paro*) redundancy; **dar de ~** (*soldado*) to discharge; (*empleado*) to dismiss, fire; **darse de ~** (*retirarse*) to drop out; (*MED*) to be ill; (*dimitir*) to resign; **estar de ~** (*enfermo*) to be off sick; (*BOLSA*) to be dropping o falling; **jugar a la ~** (*ECON*) to speculate on a fall in prices; *V tb* **bajo.**

bajada [báhá'thá] *nf* descent; (*camino*) slope; (*de aguas*) ebb.

bajamar [báhámár'] *nf* low tide.

bajar [báhár'] *vi* to go o come down; (*temperatura, precios*) to drop, fall ♦ *vt* (*cabeza*) to bow; (*escalera*) to go o come down; (*radio etc*) to turn down; (*precio, voz*) to lower; (*llevar abajo*) to take down; **~se** *vr* (*de vehículo*) to get out; (*de autobús*) to get off; **~ de** (*coche*) to get out of; (*autobús*) to get off; **~le los humos a uno** (*fig*) to

cut sb down to size.

bajeza [báhe'sá] *nf* baseness; (*una ~*) vile deed.

bajío [báhē'o] *nm* shoal, sandbank; (*AM*) lowlands *pl.*

bajista [báhē'stá] *nm/f* (*MUS*) bassist ♦ *a* (*BOLSA*) bear *cpd.*

bajo, a [bá'ho, á] *a* (*terreno*) low(-lying); (*mueble, número, precio*) low; (*piso*) ground; (*de estatura*) small, short; (*color*) pale; (*sonido*) faint, soft, low; (*voz, tono*) deep; (*metal*) base ♦ *ad* (*hablar*) softly, quietly; (*volar*) low ♦ *prep* under, below, underneath ♦ *nm* (*MUS*) bass; **hablar en voz baja** to whisper; **~ la lluvia** in the rain.

bajón [báhon'] *nm* fall, drop.

bajura [báhōō'rá] *nf*: **pesca de ~** coastal fishing.

bala [bá'lá] *nf* bullet.

balacera [báláse'rá] *nf* (*AM*) shoot-out.

balada [bálá'thá] *nf* ballad.

baladí [báláthē'] *a* trivial.

baladrón, ona [báláthron', o'ná] *a* boastful.

baladronada [báláthroná'thá] *nf* (*dicho*) boast, brag; (*hecho*) piece of bravado.

balance [bálán'se] *nm* (*COM*) balance; (*: libro*) balance sheet; (*: cuenta general*) inventory (*US*), stocktaking (*Brit*); **~ de comprobación** trial balance; **~ consolidado** consolidated balance sheet; **hacer ~** to make an inventory (*US*) o take stock (*Brit*).

balancear [bálánseár'] *vt* to balance ♦ *vi*, **~se** *vr* to swing (to and fro); (*vacilar*) to hesitate.

balanceo [bálánse'o] *nm* swinging.

balanza [bálán'sá] *nf* scales *pl*, balance; **~ comercial** balance of trade; **~ de pagos/de poder(es)** balance of payments/of power; (*ASTRO*): **B~** Libra.

balar [bálár'] *vi* to bleat.

balaustrada [báláōōstrá'thá] *nf* balustrade; (*pasamanos*) banister.

balazo [bálá'so] *nm* (*tiro*) shot; (*herida*) bullet wound.

balboa [bálbo'á] *nf* Panamanian currency unit.

balbucear [bálbōōseár'] *vi, vt* to stammer, stutter.

balbuceo [bálbōōse'o] *nm* stammering, stuttering.

balbucir [bálbōōsēr'] *vi, vt* to stammer, stutter.

balbuzca [bálbōōs'ká] *etc vb V* **balbucir.**

Balcanes [bálká'nes] *nmpl*: **los (Montes) ~** the Balkans, the Balkan Mountains; **la Península de los ~** the Balkan Peninsula.

balcón [bálkon'] *nm* balcony.

balda [bál'dá] *nf* (*estante*) shelf.

baldar [báldár'] *vt* to cripple; (*agotar*) to

exhaust.

balde [bál'de] *nm* bucket, pail; **de ~** *ad* (for) free, for nothing; **en ~** *ad* in vain.

baldío, a [báldē'o, á] *a* uncultivated; *(terreno)* waste; *(inútil)* vain ♦ *nm* wasteland.

baldosa [báldo'sá] *nf (azulejo)* floor tile; *(grande)* flagstone.

balear [báleár'] *a* Balearic, of the Balearic Islands ♦ *nm/f* native *o* inhabitant of the Balearic Islands.

Baleares [báleà'res] *nfpl*: **las (Islas) ~** the Balearics, the Balearic Islands.

balido [bálē'tho] *nm* bleat, bleating.

balín [bálēn'] *nm* pellet; **balines** *nmpl* buckshot *sg*.

balística [bálē'stēká] *nf* ballistics *pl*.

baliza [bálē'sá] *nf (AVIAT)* beacon; *(NAUT)* buoy.

balneario, a [bálneá'ryo, á] *a*: **estación balnearia** (bathing) resort ♦ *nm* spa, health resort.

balompié [bálompye'] *nm* football.

balón [bálon'] *nm* ball.

baloncesto [bálonse'sto] *nm* basketball.

balonmano [bálonmá'no] *nm* handball.

balonvolea [bálombole'á] *nm* volleyball.

balsa [bál'sá] *nf* raft; *(BOT)* balsa wood.

bálsamo [bál'sámo] *nm* balsam, balm.

balsón [bálson'] *nm (AM)* swamp, bog.

báltico, a [bál'tēko, á] *a* Baltic; **el (Mar) B~** the Baltic (Sea).

baluarte [bálwár'te] *nm* bastion, bulwark.

ballena [báye'ná] *nf* whale.

ballenero, a [báyene'ro, á] *a*: **industria ballenera** whaling industry ♦ *nm (pescador)* whaler; *(barco)* whaling ship.

ballesta [báye'stá] *nf* crossbow; *(AUTO)* spring.

ballet, *pl* **ballets** [bále', báles'] *nm* ballet.

bambolear [bámboleár'] *vi,* **~se** *vr* to swing, sway; *(silla)* to wobble.

bamboleo [bámbole'o] *nm* swinging, swaying; wobbling.

bambú [bámboō'] *nm* bamboo.

banal [bánál'] *a* banal, trivial.

banana [báná'ná] *nf (AM)* banana.

bananal [bánánál'] *nm (AM)* banana plantation.

banano [báná'no] *nm (AM)* banana tree.

banasta [báná'stá] *nf* large basket, hamper.

banca [bán'ká] *nf (asiento)* bench; *(COM)* banking.

bancario, a [bánká'ryo, á] *a* banking *cpd*, bank *cpd*; **giro ~** bank draft.

bancarrota [bánkárro'tá] *nf* bankruptcy; **declararse en** *o* **hacer ~** to go bankrupt.

banco [bán'ko] *nm* bench; *(ESCOL)* desk; *(COM)* bank; *(GEO)* stratum; **~ comercial** *o* **mercantil** commercial bank; **~ por acciones** joint-stock bank; **~ de crédito/de ahorros** credit/savings bank; **~ de arena** sand-

bank; **~ de datos** *(INFORM)* data bank; **~ de hielo** iceberg.

banda [bán'dá] *nf* band; *(cinta)* ribbon; *(pandilla)* gang; *(MUS)* brass band; *(NAUT)* side, edge; **la B~ Oriental** Uruguay; **~ sonora** soundtrack; **~ transportadora** conveyor belt.

bandada [bándá'thá] *nf (de pájaros)* flock; *(de peces)* shoal.

bandeja [bánde'há] *nf* tray; **~ de entrada/salida** in-tray/out-tray.

bandera [bánde'rá] *nf (de tela)* flag; *(estandarte)* banner; *(INFORM)* marker, flag; **izar la ~** to hoist the flag.

banderilla [bánderē'yá] *nf* banderilla; *(tapa)* savory appetizer *(served on a cocktail stick)*.

banderín [bánderēn'] *nm* pennant, small flag.

banderola [bándero'lá] *nf (MIL)* pennant.

bandido [bándē'tho] *nm* bandit.

bando [bán'do] *nm (edicto)* edict, proclamation; *(facción)* faction; **pasar al otro ~** to change sides; **los ~s** *(REL)* wedding announcement.

bandolera [bándole'rá] *nf*: **bolsa de ~** shoulder bag.

bandolero [bándole'ro] *nm* bandit.

bandoneón [bándoneon'] *nm (AM)* large accordion.

BANESTO [báne'sto] *nm abr* = *Banco Español de Crédito*.

banquero [bánke'ro] *nm* banker.

banqueta [bánke'tá] *nf* stool; *(AM: en la calle)* sidewalk *(US)*, pavement *(Brit)*.

banquete [bánke'te] *nm* banquet; *(para convidados)* formal dinner; **~ de boda** wedding breakfast.

banquillo [bánkē'yo] *nm (JUR)* dock, prisoner's bench; *(banco)* bench; *(para los pies)* footstool.

bañador [bányáthor'] *nm* bathing suit *(US)*, swimming costume *(Brit)*.

bañar [bányár'] *vt (niño)* to bath, bathe; *(objeto)* to dip; *(de barniz)* to coat; **~se** *vr (en el mar)* to bathe, swim; *(en la bañera)* to have a bath.

bañero, a [bánye'ro, á] *nm* lifeguard ♦ *nf* bath(tub).

bañista [bányē'stá] *nm/f* bather.

baño [bá'nyo] *nm (en bañera)* bath; *(en río, mar)* dip, swim; *(cuarto)* bathroom; *(bañera)* bath(tub); *(capa)* coating; **ir a tomar los ~s** to bathe at a spa *(US)* o take the waters *(Brit)*.

baptista [báptē'stá] *nm/f* Baptist.

baqueta [báke'tá] *nf (MUS)* drumstick.

bar [bár] *nm* bar.

barahúnda [báráoōn'dá] *nf* uproar, hubbub.

baraja [bárá'há] *nf* pack (of cards).

barajar [báráhár'] *vt (naipes)* to shuffle;

(fig) to mix up.

baranda [báràn'dá], **barandilla** [bárántʰē'yá] *nf (pasamanos)* handrail.

baratija [bárátē'há] *nf* trinket; *(fig)* trifle; ~s *nfpl (COM)* cheap goods.

baratillo [bárátē'yo] *nm (tienda)* junkshop; *(subasta)* bargain sale; *(conjunto de cosas)* second-hand goods *pl.*

barato, a [bárá'to, á] *a* cheap ♦ *ad* cheap, cheaply.

baratura [bárátoo'rá] *nf* cheapness.

baraúnda [báráoon'dá] *nf* = **barahúnda.**

barba [bár'bá] *nf (mentón)* chin; *(pelo)* beard; **tener** ~ to be unshaven; **hacer algo en las ~s de uno** to do sth under sb's very nose; **reírse en las ~s de uno** to laugh in sb's face.

barbacoa [bárbàko'á] *nf (parrilla)* barbecue; *(carne)* barbecued meat.

barbaridad [bárbárēhàtʰ'] *nf* barbarity; *(acto)* barbarism; *(atrocidad)* outrage; **una** ~ **de** *(fam)* loads of; **¡qué ~!** *(fam)* how awful!; **cuesta una** ~ *(fam)* it costs a fortune.

barbarie [bárbá'rye] *nf,* **barbarismo** [bárbárē'smo] *nm* barbarism; *(crueldad)* barbarity.

bárbaro, a [bár'báro, á] *a* barbarous, cruel; *(grosero)* rough, uncouth ♦ *nm/f* barbarian ♦ *ad*: **lo pasamos** ~ *(fam)* we had a great time; **¡qué ~!** *(fam)* how marvelous!; **un éxito** ~ *(fam)* a terrific success; **es un tipo** ~ *(fam)* he's a great bloke.

barbecho [bárbetch'o] *nm* fallow land.

barbero [bárbe'ro] *nm* barber, hairdresser.

barbilampiño [bárbēlámpē'nyo] *a* smooth-faced; *(fig)* inexperienced.

barbilla [bárbē'yá] *nf* chin, tip of the chin.

barbo [bár'bo] *nm*: ~ **de mar** red mullet.

barbotar [bárbotár'], **barbotear** [bárboteár'] *vt, vi* to mutter, mumble.

barbudo, a [bárboo'tho, á] *a* bearded.

barbullar [bárbooyár'] *vi* to jabber away.

barca [bár'ká] *nf (small)* boat; ~ **pesquera** fishing boat; ~ **de pasaje** ferry.

barcaza [bárká'sá] *nf* barge; ~ **de desembarco** landing craft.

Barcelona [bárselo'ná] *nf* Barcelona.

barcelonés, esa [bárselones', e'sá] *a* of *o* from Barcelona ♦ *nm/f* native *o* inhabitant of Barcelona.

barco [bár'ko] *nm* boat; *(buque)* ship; *(COM etc)* vessel; ~ **de carga** cargo boat; ~ **de guerra** warship; ~ **de vela** sailing ship; **ir en** ~ to go by boat.

baremo [báre'mo] *nm* scale; *(tabla de cuentas)* ready reckoner.

barítono [bárē'tono] *nm* baritone.

barman [bár'mán] *nm* bartender.

Barna. *abr* = **Barcelona.**

barnice [bárnē'se] *etc vb V* **barnizar.**

barniz [bárnēs'] *nm* varnish; *(en la loza)* glaze; *(fig)* veneer.

barnizar [bárnēsár'] *vt* to varnish; *(loza)* to glaze.

barómetro [báro'metro] *nm* barometer.

barquero [bárke'ro] *nm* boatman.

barquilla [bárkē'yá] *nf (NAUT)* log.

barquillo [bárkē'yo] *nm* cone.

barra [bá'rrá] *nf* bar, rod; *(JUR)* rail; *(: banquillo)* dock; *(de un bar, café)* bar; *(de pan)* French loaf; *(palanca)* lever; ~ **de carmín** *o* **de labios** lipstick; ~ **de espaciado** *(INFORM)* space bar; ~ **inversa** backslash; **no pararse en ~s** to stick *o* stop at nothing.

barrabasada [bárráhásá'thá] *nf* (piece of) mischief.

barraca [bárrá'ká] *nf* hut, cabin; *(en Valencia)* thatched farmhouse; *(en feria)* booth.

barracón [bárrákon'] *nm (caseta)* big hut.

barragana [bárrágá'ná] *nf* concubine.

barranca [bárrán'ká] *nf* ravine, gully.

barranco [bárrán'ko] *nm* ravine; *(fig)* difficulty.

barrena [bárre'ná] *nf* drill.

barrenar [bárrenár'] *vt* to drill (through), bore.

barrendero, a [bárrende'ro, á] *nm/f* streetsweeper.

barreno [bárre'no] *nm* large drill.

barreño [bárre'nyo] *nm* wash basin.

barrer [bárrer'] *vt* to sweep; *(quitar)* to sweep away; *(MIL, NAUT)* to sweep, rake *(with gunfire)* ♦ *vi* to sweep up.

barrera [bárre'rá] *nf* barrier; *(MIL)* barricade; *(FERRO)* crossing gate; **poner ~s a** to hinder; ~ **arancelaria** *(COM)* tariff barrier; ~ **comercial** *(COM)* trade barrier.

barriada [bárryá'thá] *nf* quarter, district.

barricada [bárrēká'thá] *nf* barricade.

barrida [bárrē'thá] *nf,* **barrido** [bárrē'tho] *nm* sweep, sweeping.

barriga [bárrē'gá] *nf* belly; *(panza)* paunch; *(vientre)* guts *pl;* **echar** ~ to get middle-age spread.

barrigón, ona [bárrēgon', o'ná], **barrigudo, a** [bárrēgoo'tho, á] *a* potbellied.

barril [bárrēl'] *nm* barrel, cask; **cerveza de** ~ draught beer.

barrio [bá'rryo] *nm (vecindad)* neighborhood *(US),* neighbourhood *(Brit); (en las afueras)* suburb; ~s **bajos** poor quarter *sg;* ~ **chino** red-light district.

barriobajero, a [bárryobáhe'ro, á] *a (vulgar)* common.

barro [bá'rro] *nm (lodo)* mud; *(objetos)* earthenware; *(MED)* pimple.

barroco, a [bárro'ko, á] *a* Baroque; *(fig)* elaborate ♦ *nm* Baroque.

barrote [bárro'te] *nm (de ventana etc)* bar.

barruntar [bárrōōntár'] *vt* (*conjeturar*) to guess; (*presentir*) to suspect.

barrunto [bárrōōn'to] *nm* guess; suspicion.

bartola [bárto'lá]: **a la ~** *ad*: **tirarse a la ~** to take it easy, be lazy.

bártulos [bár'tōōlos] *nmpl* things, belongings.

barullo [bárōō'yo] *nm* row, uproar.

basa [bá'sá] *nf* (*ARQ*) base.

basamento [básámen'to] *nm* base, plinth.

basar [básár'] *vt* to base; **~se** *vr*: **~se en** to be based on.

basca [bás'ká] *nf* nausea.

báscula [bás'kōōlá] *nf* (platform) scales *pl*; **~ biestable** (*INFORM*) flip-flop, toggle.

bascular [báskōōlár'] *vt* (*INFORM*) to toggle.

base [bá'se] *nf* base; **a ~ de** on the basis of, based on; (*mediante*) by means of; **a ~ de bien** in abundance; **~ de conocimiento** knowledge base; **~ de datos** database.

básico, a [bá'sēko, á] *a* basic.

Basilea [básēle'á] *nf* Basle.

basílica [básē'lēká] *nf* basilica.

basilisco [básēlēs'co] *nm* (*AM*) iguana; **estar hecho un ~** to be hopping mad.

bastante [bástán'te] *a* (*suficiente*) enough, sufficient; (*no poco(s)*) quite a lot of ♦ *ad* (*suficientemente*) enough, sufficiently; (*muy*) quite, rather; **es ~ alto (como) para alcanzarlo** he's tall enough to reach it.

bastar [bástár'] *vi* to be enough *o* sufficient; **~se** *vr* to be self-sufficient; **~ para** to be enough to; **¡basta!** (that's) enough!

bastardilla [bástárthē'yá] *nf* italics *pl*.

bastardo, a [bástár'tho, á] *a, nm/f* bastard.

bastidor [bástēthor'] *nm* frame; (*de coche*) chassis; (*ARTE*) stretcher; (*TEATRO*) wing; **entre ~es** behind the scenes.

basto, a [bá'sto, á] *a* coarse, rough ♦ *nmpl*: **~s** (*NAIPES*) clubs.

bastón [bástón'] *nm* stick, staff; (*para pasear*) walking stick; **~ de mando** baton.

bastonazo [bástóná'so] *nm* blow with a stick.

basura [básōō'rá] *nf* rubbish, garbage (*US*), refuse (*Brit*).

basurero [básōōre'ro] *nm* (*hombre*) garbage man (*US*), dustman (*Brit*); (*lugar*) garbage (*US*) *o* rubbish (*Brit*) dump; (*cubo*) trash can (*US*), (rubbish) bin (*Brit*).

bata [bá'tá] *nf* (*gen*) housecoat; (*cubretodo*) smock, overall (*Brit*); (*MED, TEC etc*) lab(oratory) coat.

batacazo [bátáká'so] *nm* bump.

batalla [bátá'yá] *nf* battle; **de ~** for everyday use.

batallar [bátáyár'] *vi* to fight.

batallón [bátáyon'] *nm* battalion.

batata [bátá'tá] *nf* (*AM: CULIN*) sweet potato.

bate [bá'te] *nm* (*DEPORTE*) bat.

bateador [báteáthor'] *nm* batter, batsman.

batería [báterē'á] *nf* battery; (*MUS*) drums *pl*; (*TEATRO*) footlights *pl*; **~ de cocina** kitchen utensils *pl*.

batiburrillo [bátēbōōrrē'yo] *nm* hotchpotch.

batido, a [bátē'tho, á] *a* (*camino*) beaten, well-trodden ♦ *nm* (*CULIN*) batter; **~ (de leche)** milk shake ♦ *nf* (*AM*) (police) raid.

batidora [bátētho'rá] *nf* beater, mixer; **~ eléctrica** food mixer, blender.

batir [bátēr'] *vt* to beat, strike; (*vencer*) to beat, defeat; (*revolver*) to beat, mix; (*pelo*) to back-comb; **~se** *vr* to fight; **~ palmas** to clap, applaud.

batuta [bátōō'tá] *nf* baton; **llevar la ~** (*fig*) to be the boss.

baudio [bá'ōōthyo] *nm* (*INFORM*) baud.

baúl [báōōl'] *nm* trunk; (*AUTO*) trunk (*US*), boot (*Brit*).

bautice [báōōtē'se] *etc vb V* **bautizar**.

bautismo [báōōtēs'mo] *nm* baptism, christening.

bautista [báōōtē'stá] *a, nm/f* Baptist.

bautizar [báōōtēsár'] *vt* to baptize, christen; (*fam: diluir*) to water down; (*dar apodo*) to dub.

bautizo [báōōtē'so] *nm* baptism, christening.

bávaro, a [bá'háro, á] *a, nm/f* Bavarian.

Baviera [báhye'rá] *nf* Bavaria.

baya [bá'yá] *nf* berry; *V tb* **bayo**.

bayeta [báye'tá] *nf* (*trapo*) floorcloth; (*AM*: *pañal*) diaper (*US*), nappy (*Brit*).

bayo, a [bá'yo, á] *a* bay.

bayoneta [báyone'tá] *nf* bayonet.

baza [bá'sá] *nf* trick; **meter ~** to butt in.

bazar [básár'] *nm* bazaar.

bazofia [báso'fyá] *nf* hogwash (*US*), pigswill (*Brit*); (*libro etc*) trash.

beato, a [beá'to, á] *a* blessed; (*piadoso*) pious.

bebé, *pl* **bebés** [behe', behes'] *nm* baby.

bebedero, a [behethe'ro, á] *nm* (*para animales*) drinking trough.

bebedizo, a [behethē'so, á] *a* drinkable ♦ *nm* potion.

bebedor, a [behethor', á] *a* hard-drinking.

beber [beher'] *vt, vi* to drink; **~ a sorbos/tragos** to sip/gulp; **se lo bebió todo** he drank it all up.

bebido, a [behē'tho, á] *a* drunk ♦ *nf* drink.

beca [be'ká] *nf* grant, scholarship.

becado, a [beká'tho, á] *nm/f*, **becario, a** [beká'ryo, á] *nm/f* scholarship holder.

becerro [bese'rro] *nm* yearling calf.

becuadro [bekwá'thro] *nm* (*MUS*) natural sign.

bedel [bethel'] *nm* porter, janitor.

befarse [befár'se] *vr*: **~ de algo** to scoff at sth.

béisbol [be'ēsbol] *nm* baseball.

beldad [beldáth'] *nf* beauty.

Belén [belen'] *nm* Bethlehem; **b~** (*de Navidad*) nativity scene, crib.

belga [bel'gá] *a*, *nm/f* Belgian.

Bélgica [bel'hēká] *nf* Belgium.

Belgrado [belgrá'tho] *nm* Belgrade.

Belice [belē'se] *nm* Belize.

bélico, a [be'lēko, á] *a* (*actitud*) warlike.

belicoso, a [belēko'so, á] *a* (*guerrero*) warlike; (*agresivo*) aggressive, bellicose.

beligerante [belēherán'te] *a* belligerent.

bellaco, a [beyá'ko, á] *a* sly, cunning ♦ *nm* villain, rogue.

belladona [beyátho'ná] *nf* deadly nightshade.

bellaquería [beyákerē'á] *nf* (*acción*) dirty trick; (*calidad*) wickedness.

belleza [beye'sá] *nf* beauty.

bello, a [be'yo, á] *a* beautiful, lovely; **Bellas Artes** Fine Art *sg*.

bellota [beyo'tá] *nf* acorn.

bemol [bemol'] *nm* (*MUS*) flat; **esto tiene ~es** (*fam*) this is a tough one.

bencina [bensē'ná] *nf* (*AM*) gas (*US*), petrol (*Brit*).

bendecir [bendesēr'] *vt* to bless; **~ la mesa** to say grace.

bendición [bendēsyon'] *nf* blessing.

bendiga [bendē'gá] *etc*, **bendije** [bendē'he] *etc*, **bendiré** [bendēre'] *etc vb* V **bendecir**.

bendito, a [bendē'to, á] *pp de* **bendecir** ♦ *a* (*santo*) blessed; (*agua*) holy; (*afortunado*) lucky; (*feliz*) happy; (*sencillo*) simple ♦ *nm/f* simple soul; **¡~ sea Dios!** thank goodness!; **es un ~** he's sweet; **dormir como un ~** to sleep like a log.

benedictino, a [benethēktē'no, á] *a*, *nm* Benedictine.

benefactor, a [benefáktor', á] *nm/f* benefactor/benefactress.

beneficencia [benefēsen'syá] *nf* charity.

beneficiar [benefēsyár'] *vt* to benefit, be of benefit to; **~se** *vr* to benefit, profit.

beneficiario, a [benefēsyá'ryo, á] *nm/f* beneficiary; (*de cheque*) payee.

beneficio [benefē'syo] *nm* (*bien*) benefit, advantage; (*COM*) profit, gain; **a ~ de** for the benefit of; **en ~ propio** to one's own advantage; **~ bruto/neto** gross/net profit; **~ por acción** earnings *pl* per share.

beneficioso, a [benefēsyo'so, á] *a* beneficial.

benéfico, a [bene'fēko, á] *a* charitable; **sociedad benéfica** charity (organization).

benemérito, a [beneme'rēto, á] *a* meritorious ♦ *nf*: **la Benemérita** (*Esp*) the Civil Guard.

beneplácito [beneplá'sēto] *nm* approval, consent.

benevolencia [benebolen'syá] *nf* benevolence, kindness.

benévolo, a [bene'kolo, á] *a* benevolent, kind.

Bengala [bengá'lá] *nf* Bengal; **el Golfo de ~** the Bay of Bengal.

bengala [bengá'lá] *nf* (*MIL*) flare; (*fuego*) Bengal light; (*materia*) rattan.

bengalí [bengálē'] *a*, *nm/f* Bengali.

benignidad [benēgnētháth'] *nf* (*afabilidad*) kindness; (*suavidad*) mildness.

benigno, a [benēg'no, á] *a* kind; (*suave*) mild; (*MED: tumor*) benign, non-malignant.

benjamín [benhámēn'] *nm* youngest child.

beodo, a [beo'tho, á] *a* drunk ♦ *nm/f* drunkard.

berberecho [berberetch'o] *nm* cockle.

berenjena [berenhe'ná] *nf* eggplant, aubergine.

berenjenal [berenhenál'] *nm* (*AGR*) eggplant *o* aubergine bed; (*fig*) mess; **en buen ~ nos hemos metido** we've got ourselves into a fine mess.

bergantín [bergántēn'] *nm* brig(antine).

Berlín [berlēn'] *nm* Berlin.

berlinés, esa [berlēnes', esá] *a* of *o* from Berlin ♦ *nm/f* Berliner.

bermejo, a [berme'ho, á] *a* red.

bermellón [bermeyon'] *nm* vermilion.

berrear [berreár'] *vi* to bellow, low.

berrido [berrē'tho] *nm* bellow(ing).

berrinche [berrēntch'e] *nm* (*fam*) temper, tantrum.

berro [be'rro] *nm* watercress.

berza [ber'sá] *nf* cabbage; **~ lombarda** red cabbage.

besamel [besámel'], **besamela** [besáme'lá] *nf* (*CULIN*) white sauce, bechamel sauce.

besar [besár'] *vt* to kiss; (*fig: tocar*) to graze; **~se** *vr* to kiss (one another).

beso [be'so] *nm* kiss.

bestia [bes'tyá] *nf* beast, animal; (*fig*) idiot; **~ de carga** beast of burden; **¡~!** you idiot!; **¡no seas ~!** (*bruto*) don't be such a brute!; (*idiota*) don't be such an idiot!

bestial [bestyál'] *a* bestial; (*fam*) terrific.

bestialidad [bestyálētháth'] *nf* bestiality; (*fam*) stupidity.

besugo [besōō'go] *nm* sea bream; (*fam*) idiot.

besuguera [besōōge'rá] *nf* (*CULIN*) fish pan.

besuquear [besōōkeár'] *vt* to cover with kisses; **~se** *vr* to kiss and cuddle.

bético, a [be'tēko, á] *a* Andalusian.

betún [betōōn'] *nm* shoe polish; (*QUÍMICA*) bitumen, asphalt.

Bib. *abr* = **Biblioteca**.

biberón [bēberon'] *nm* bottle.

Biblia [bē'lyá] *nf* Bible.

bíblico, a [bē'hlēko, á] *a* biblical.

bibliografía [bēhlyográfē'á] *nf* bibliography.

biblioteca [bēhlyote'ká] *nf* library; (*estantes*) bookcase, bookshelves *pl*; **~ de**

consulta reference library.
bibliotecario, a [bĕklyoteká'ryo, á] *nm/f* librarian.
B.I.C. [bĕk] *nf abr* (= *Brigada de Investigación Criminal*) ≈ FBI (*US*), CID (*Brit*).
bicarbonato [bĕkárḥoná'to] *nm* bicarbonate.
bici [bē'sē] *nf* (*fam*) bike.
bicicleta [bĕsēkle'tá] *nf* bicycle, cycle.
bicoca [bĕko'ká] *nf* (*Esp fam*) cushy job; (*AM: bofetada*) slap.
bicho [bētch'o] *nm* (*animal*) small animal; (*sabandija*) bug, insect; (*TAUR*) bull; ~ **raro** (*fam*) strange bird.
bidé [bēḍe'] *nm* bidet.
bidireccional [bēdēreksyonál'] *a* bidirectional.
bidón [bēḍon'] *nm* (*grande*) drum; (*pequeño*) can.
bien [byen] *nm* good; (*interés*) advantage, benefit; **hombre de** ~ honest man; **el** ~ **público** the common o public good; **~es de capital** (*COM*) capital goods; **~es inmuebles/muebles** real estate *sg*/personal property *sg*; **~es de consumo** consumer goods; **~es de producción** industrial goods; **~es raíces** real estate *sg* ♦ *a*: **de casa** ~ well brought up ♦ *ad* well; (*correctamente*) properly, right; (*oler*) nice; (*muy*) very; **más** ~ rather; **hablas** ~ **(el español)** you speak good Spanish; **estar** ~ **de salud/dinero** to be well/well off; **estar a** ~ **con uno** to be on good terms with sb ♦ *excl*: **¡(muy)** ~! well done! ♦ *conj*: **no** ~ **llovió, bajó la temperatura** no sooner had it rained than the temperature dropped; ~ **que** although.
bienal [byenál'] *a* biennial.
bienaventurado, a [byenáḥentōōrá'ḍho, á] *a* (*feliz*) happy; (*afortunado*) fortunate; (*REL*) blessed.
bienestar [byenestár'] *nm* well-being; **estado de** ~ welfare state.
bienhechor, a [byenetchor', á] *a* beneficent ♦ *nm/f* benefactor/benefactress.
bienio [bye'nyo] *nm* two-year period.
bienvenido, a [byembenē'ḍho, á] *a* welcome ♦ *excl* welcome! ♦ *nf* welcome; **dar la bienvenida a uno** to welcome sb.
bifásico, a [bēfá'sēko, á] *a* (*ELEC*) two-phase.
bife [bē'fe] *nm* (*AM*) steak.
bifurcación [bēfōōrkásyon'] *nf* fork; (*FERRO, INFORM*) branch.
bigamia [bēgá'myá] *nf* bigamy.
bígamo, a [bē'gámo, á] *a* bigamous ♦ *nm/f* bigamist.
bígaro [bē'gáro] *nm* winkle.
bigote [bēgo'te] *nm* (*tb*: **~s**) mustache (*US*), moustache (*Brit*).
bigotudo, a [bēgotōō'ḍho, á] *a* with a big mustache.

bigudí [bēgōōḍhē'] *nm* (hair-)curler.
bikini [bēkē'nē] *nm* bikini; (*CULIN*) toasted cheese and ham sandwich.
bilbaíno, a [bēlḥáē'no, á] *a* of o from Bilbao ♦ *nm/f* native o inhabitant of Bilbao.
bilingüe [bēlēn'gwe] *a* bilingual.
bilis [bē'lēs] *nf inv* bile.
billar [bēyár'] *nm* billiards *sg*; (*lugar*) billiard hall; (*galería de atracciones*) amusement arcade; ~ **americano** pool.
billete [bēye'te] *nm* ticket; (*de banco*) bill (*US*), banknote (*Brit*); (*carta*) note; ~ **sencillo, ~ de ida solamente/~ de ida y vuelta** one-way (*US*) o single (*Brit*) ticket/round-trip (*US*) o return (*Brit*) ticket; **sacar (un)** ~ to get a ticket; **un** ~ **de 5 dólares** a five-dollar bill.
billetera [bēyete'rá] *nf*, **billetero** [bēyete'ro] *nm* wallet.
billón [bēyon'] *nm* billion.
bimensual [bēmenswál'] *a* twice monthly.
bimestral [bēmestrál'] *a* bimonthly.
bimestre [bēmes'tre] *nm* two-month period.
bimotor [bēmotor'] *a* twin-engined ♦ *nm* twin-engined plane.
binario, a [bēná'ryo, á] *a* (*INFORM*) binary.
binóculo [bēno'kōōlo] *nm* pince-nez.
biografía [byografē'á] *nf* biography.
biógrafo, a [bēo'gráfo, á] *nm/f* biographer.
biología [bēolohē'á] *nf* biology.
biológico, a [bēolo'hēko, á] *a* biological; **guerra biológica** biological warfare.
biólogo, a [bēo'logo, á] *nm/f* biologist.
biombo [byom'bo] *nm* (folding) screen.
biopsia [bēop'syá] *nf* biopsy.
bioquímico, a [bēokē'mēko, á] *a* biochemical ♦ *nm/f* biochemist ♦ *nf* biochemistry.
bióxido [bēok'sēḍho] *nm* dioxide.
bipartidismo [bēpártēḍhēs'mo] *nm* (*POL*) two-party system.
birlar [bērlár'] *vt* (*fam*) to pinch.
birlibirloque [bērlēḥērlo'ke] *nm*: **por arte de** ~ (as if) by magic.
Birmania [bērmá'nyá] *nf* Burma.
birmano, a [bērmá'no, á] *a nm/f* Burmese.
birrete [bērre'te] *nm* (*JUR*) judge's cap.
bis [bēs] *excl* encore! ♦ *ad* (*dos veces*) twice; **viven en el 27** ~ they live at 27a.
bisabuelo, a [bēsáḥwe'lo, á] *nm/f* great-grandfather/mother; **~s** *nmpl* great-grandparents.
bisagra [bēsá'grá] *nf* hinge.
bisbisar [bēsḥēsár'], **bisbisear** [bēsḥēseár'] *vt* to mutter, mumble.
bisbiseo [bēsḥēse'o] *nm* muttering.
biselar [bēselár'] *vt* to bevel.
bisexual [bēsekswál'] *a* bisexual.
bisiesto [bēsye'sto] *a*: **año** ~ leap year.
bisnieto, a [bēsnye'to, á] *nm/f* great-grandson/daughter; **~s** *nmpl* great-

grandchildren.

bisonte [bēson'te] *nm* bison.

bisoñé [bēsonye'] *nm* toupée.

bisoño, a [bēso'nyo, á] *a* green, inexperienced.

bistec [bēstek'], **bisté** [bēste'] *nm* steak.

bisturí [bēstōōrē'] *nm* scalpel.

bisutería [bēsōōterē'á] *nf* imitation o costume jewellery.

bit [bēt] *nm* (*INFORM*) bit; ~ **de parada** stop bit; ~ **de paridad** parity bit.

bitio [bē'tyo] *nm* (*INFORM*) bit.

bizantino, a [bēsántē'no, á] *a* Byzantine; (*fig*) pointless.

bizarría [bēsárrē'á] *nf* (*valor*) bravery; (*generosidad*) generosity.

bizarro, a [bēsá'rro, á] *a* brave; generous.

bizcar [bēskár'] *vi* to squint.

bizco, a [bēs'ko, á] *a* cross-eyed.

bizcocho [bēskotch'o] *nm* (*CULIN*) sponge cake.

bizque [bēs'ke] *etc vb V* **bizcar**.

bizquear [bēskeár'] *vi* to squint.

blanco/a [blán'ko, á] *a* white ♦ *nm/f* white man/woman, white ♦ *nm* (*color*) white; (*en texto*) blank; (*MIL, fig*) target ♦ *nf* (*MUS*) half note (*US*), minim (*Brit*); **en** ~ blank; **cheque en** ~ blank check; **votar en** ~ to not mark one's ballot paper; **quedarse en** ~ to be disappointed; **noche en** ~ sleepless night; **estar sin** ~ to be broke; **ser el** ~ **de las burlas** to be the butt of jokes.

blancura [blánkōō'rá] *nf* whiteness.

blandengue [blánden'ge] *a* (*fam*) soft, weak.

blandir [blándēr'] *vt* to brandish.

blando, a [blán'do, á] *a* soft; (*tierno*) tender, gentle; (*carácter*) mild; (*fam*) cowardly ♦ *nm/f* (*POL etc*) soft-liner.

blandura [blándōō'rá] *nf* softness; tenderness; mildness.

blanquear [blánkeár'] *vt* to whiten; (*fachada*) to whitewash; (*paño*) to bleach ♦ *vi* to turn white.

blanquecino, a [blánkesē'no, á] *a* whitish.

blasfemar [blásfemár'] *vi* to blaspheme; (*fig*) to curse.

blasfemia [blásfe'myá] *nf* blasphemy.

blasfemo, a [blásfe'mo, á] *a* blasphemous ♦ *nm/f* blasphemer.

blasón [bláson'] *nm* coat of arms; (*fig*) honor (*US*), honour (*Brit*).

blasonar [blásonár'] *vt* to emblazon ♦ *vi* to boast, brag.

bledo [ble'ᵭo] *nm*: **(no) me importa un** ~ I couldn't care less.

blindado, a [blēndá'ᵭo, á] *a* (*MIL*) armorplated (*US*), armour-plated (*Brit*); (*antibalas*) bulletproof; **coche** o (*AM*) **carro** ~ armored car; **puertas blindadas** security doors.

blindaje [blēndá'he] *nm* armor (*US*), armour (*Brit*), armor-plating.

bloc, *pl* **blocs** [blok, blos] *nm* writing pad; (*ESCOL*) notebook; ~ **de dibujos** sketch pad.

bloque [blo'ke] *nm* (*tb INFORM*) block; (*POL*) bloc; ~ **de cilindros** cylinder block.

bloquear [blokeár'] *vt* (*NAUT etc*) to block-ade; (*aislar*) to cut off; (*COM, ECON*) to freeze; **fondos bloqueados** frozen assets.

bloqueo [bloke'o] *nm* blockade; (*COM*) freezing, blocking.

blusa [blōō'sá] *nf* blouse.

B.º *abr* (*FINANZAS*: = *banco*) bank; (*COM*: = *beneficiario*) beneficiary.

boato [boá'to] *nm* show, ostentation.

bobada [boᵬá'ᵭá] *nf* foolish action (o statement); **decir** ~**s** to talk nonsense.

bobalicón, ona [boᵬálēkon', oná] *a* utterly stupid.

bobería [boᵬerē'á] *nf* = **bobada**.

bobina [boᵬē'ná] *nf* (*TEC*) bobbin; (*FOTO*) spool; (*ELEC*) coil, winding.

bobo, a [bo'ᵬo, á] *a* (*tonto*) daft, silly; (*cándido*) naïve ♦ *nm/f* fool, idiot ♦ *nm* (*TEATRO*) clown, funny man.

boca [bo'ká] *nf* mouth; (*de crustáceo*) pincer; (*de cañón*) muzzle; (*entrada*) mouth, entrance; (*INFORM*) slot; ~**s** *nfpl* (*de río*) mouth *sg*; ~ **abajo/arriba** face down/up; **a** ~ **jarro** point-blank; **se me hace la** ~ **agua** my mouth is watering; **todo salió a pedir de** ~ it all turned out perfectly; **en** ~ **de** (*AM*) according to; **la cosa anda de** ~ **en** ~ the story is going the rounds; **¡cállate la** ~! (*fam*) shut up!; **quedarse con la** ~ **abierta** to be dumbfounded; **no abrir la** ~ to keep quiet; ~ **del estómago** pit of the stomach; ~ **de metro** subway (*US*) o tube (*Brit*) entrance.

bocacalle [bokáká'ye] *nf* (entrance to a) street; **la primera** ~ the first turning o street.

bocadillo [bokáᵭē'yo] *nm* sandwich.

bocado [bokáᵭo] *nm* mouthful, bite; (*de caballo*) bridle; ~ **de Adán** Adam's apple.

bocajarro [bokáhá'rro]: **a** ~ *ad* (*MIL*) at point-blank range; **decir algo a** ~ to say sth bluntly.

bocanada [bokáná'ᵭá] *nf* (*de vino*) mouthful, swallow; (*de aire*) gust, puff.

bocazas [boká'sás] *nm/f inv* (*fam*) big-mouth.

boceto [bose'to] *nm* sketch, outline.

bocina [bosē'ná] *nf* (*MUS*) trumpet; (*AUTO*) horn; (*para hablar*) megaphone; **tocar la** ~ (*AUTO*) to sound one's horn.

bocinazo [bosēná'so] *nm* (*AUTO*) toot.

bocio [bo'syo] *nm* (*MED*) goiter (*US*), goitre (*Brit*).

bocha [botch'á] *nf* bowl; ~**s** *nfpl* bowls *sg*.

bochinche [botchēntch'e] *nm* (*fam*) uproar.

bochorno [botchor'no] *nm* (*vergüenza*) embarrassment; (*calor*): **hace ~** it's very muggy.

bochornoso, a [botchorno'so, á] *a* muggy; embarrassing.

boda [bo'thá] *nf* (*tb:* **~s**) wedding, marriage; (*fiesta*) wedding reception; **~s de plata/de oro** silver/golden wedding *sg*.

bodega [bothe'gá] *nf* (*de vino*) (wine) cellar; (*bar*) bar; (*restaurante*) restaurant; (*depósito*) storeroom; (*de barco*) hold.

bodegón [bothegon'] *nm* (*ARTE*) still life.

bodrio [bothrē'o] *nm*: **el libro es un ~** the book is awful *o* rubbish.

B.O.E. [bo'e] *nm abr* (= *Boletín Oficial del Estado*) ≈ The Congressional Record (*US*), Hansard (*Brit*).

bofe [bo'fe] *nm* (*tb:* **~s**: *de res*) lungs *pl*; **echar los ~s** to slave (away).

bofetada [bofetá'thá] *nf* slap (in the face); **dar de ~s a uno** to punch sb.

bofetón [bofeton'] *nm* = **bofetada**.

boga [bo'gá] *nf*: **en ~** in vogue.

bogar [bogár'] *vi* (*remar*) to row; (*navegar*) to sail.

bogavante [bogáhán'te] *nm* (*NAUT*) stroke, first rower; (*ZOOL*) lobster.

Bogotá [bogotá'] *n* Bogota.

bogotano, a [bogotá'no, á] *a* of *o* from Bogota ♦ *nm/f* native *o* inhabitant of Bogota.

bogue [bo'ge] *etc vb V* **bogar**.

bohemio, a [boe'myo, á] *a, nm/f* Bohemian.

boicot, pl boicots [bočko'(t)] *nm* boycott.

boicotear [bočkoteár'] *vt* to boycott.

boicoteo [bočkote'o] *nm* boycott.

boina [bo'ēná] *nf* beret.

bola [bo'lá] *nf* ball; (*canica*) marble; (*NAIPES*) (grand) slam; (*betún*) shoe polish; (*mentira*) tale, story; **~s** *nfpl* (*AM*) bolas; **~ de billar** billiard ball; **~ de nieve** snowball.

bolado [bolá'tho] *nm* (*AM*) deal.

bolchevique [boltchehē'ke] *a, nm/f* Bolshevik.

boleadoras [boleátho'rás] *nfpl* (*AM*) bolas *sg*.

bolera [bole'rá] *nf* skittle *o* bowling alley.

boleta [bole'tá] *nf* (*AM: billete*) ticket; (: *permiso*) pass, permit.

boletería [boleterē'á] *nf* (*AM*) ticket office.

boletín [boletēn'] *nm* bulletin; (*periódico*) journal, review; **~ escolar** (*Esp*) school report; **~ de noticias** news bulletin; **~ de pedido** application form; **~ de precios** price list; **~ de prensa** press release.

boleto [bole'to] *nm* ticket; **~ de apuestas** betting slip.

boli [bo'lē] *nm* ballpoint.

boliche [bolētch'e] *nm* (*bola*) jack; (*juego*) bowls *sg*; (*lugar*) bowling alley; (*AM: tienda*) small grocery store.

bólido [bo'lētho] *nm* meteorite; (*AUTO*) racing car.

bolígrafo [bolē'gráfo] *nm* ball-point pen.

bolillo [bolē'yo] *nm* (*COSTURA*) bobbin (for lacemaking).

bolívar [bolē'hár] *nm monetary unit of Venezuela*.

Bolivia [bolē'hyá] *nf* Bolivia.

boliviano, a [bolē'hyá'no, á] *a, nm/f* Bolivian.

bolo [bo'lo] *nm* ninepin (*US*), skittle (*Brit*); (*píldora*) (large) pill; (*juego de*) **~s** ninepines *sg* (*US*), skittles *sg* (*Brit*).

Bolonia [bolo'nyá] *nf* Bologna.

bolsa [bol'sá] *nf* (*cartera*) purse; (*saco*) bag; (*AM*) pocket; (*ANAT*) cavity, sac; (*COM*) stock exchange; (*MINERÍA*) pocket; **~ de agua caliente** hot water bottle; **~ de aire** air pocket; **~ de papel** paper bag; **~ de plástico** plastic bag; **~ de trabajo** employment bureau; **jugar a la ~** to play the market.

bolsillo [bolsē'yo] *nm* pocket; (*cartera*) purse; **de ~** pocket *cpd*; **meterse a uno en el ~** to get sb eating out of one's hand.

bolsista [bolsē'stá] *nm/f* stockbroker.

bolso [bol'so] *nm* (*bolsa*) bag; (*de mujer*) handbag.

bollo [bo'yo] *nm* (*pan*) roll; (*dulce*) scone; (*bulto*) bump, lump; (*abolladura*) dent; **~s** *nmpl* (*AM*) troubles.

bomba [bom'bá] *nf* (*MIL*) bomb; (*TEC*) pump; (*AM: globo*) balloon; (: *borrachera*) drunkenness ♦ *a* (*fam*): **noticia ~** bombshell ♦ *ad* (*fam*): **pasarlo ~** to have a great time; **~ atómica/de humo/de retardo** atomic/smoke/time bomb; **~ de gasolina** gasoline (*US*) *o* petrol (*Brit*) pump; **~ de incendios** fire engine.

bombacho, a [bombátch'o, á] *a* (*AM*) baggy.

bombardear [bombártheár'] *vt* to bombard; (*MIL*) to bomb.

bombardeo [bombárthe'o] *nm* bombardment; bombing.

bombardero [bombárthe'ro] *nm* bomber.

bombear [bombeár'] *vt* (*agua*) to pump (out *o* up); (*MIL*) to bomb; (*FÚTBOL*) to lob; **~se** *vr* to warp.

bombero [bombe'ro] *nm* fireman; **(cuerpo de) ~s** fire brigade.

bombilla [bombē'yá] *nf* (*Esp*) (light) bulb.

bombín [bombēn'] *nm* derby (*US*), bowler hat (*Brit*).

bombo [bom'bo] *nm* (*MUS*) bass drum; (*TEC*) drum; (*fam*) exaggerated praise; **hacer algo a ~ y platillo** to make a song and dance about sth; **tengo la cabeza hecha un ~** I've got a splitting headache.

bombón [bombon'] *nm* chocolate; (*belleza*) beauty.

bombona [bombo'ná] *nf*: ~ **de butano** gas cylinder.

bombonería [bombonerē'á] *nf* candy store (*US*), sweetshop (*Brit*).

bonaerense [bonáeren'se] *a* of *o* from Buenos Aires ♦ *nm/f* native *o* inhabitant of Buenos Aires.

bonancible [bonánsē'ḅle] *a* (*tiempo*) fair, calm.

bonanza [bonán'sá] *nf* (*NAUT*) fair weather; (*fig*) bonanza; (*MINERÍA*) rich pocket *o* vein.

bondad [bondáḍ'] *nf* goodness, kindness; **tenga la ~ de** (please) be good enough to.

bondadoso, a [bondáḍho'so, á] *a* good, kind.

boniato [bonyá'to] *nm* sweet potato, yam.

bonificación [bonēfēkásyon'] *nf* (*COM*) allowance, discount; (*pago*) bonus; (*DEPORTE*) extra points *pl*.

bonito, a [bonē'to, á] *a* (*lindo*) pretty; (*agradable*) nice ♦ *ad* (*AM fam*) well ♦ *nm* (*atún*) tuna (fish).

bono [bo'no] *nm* voucher; (*FIN*) bond; ~ **de billetes de metro** booklet of metro tickets; ~ **del Tesoro** treasury bill.

bonobús [bonoḅōōs'] *nm* (*Esp*) bus pass.

boquear [bokeár'] *vi* to gasp.

boquerón [bokeron'] *nm* (*pez*) (kind of) anchovy; (*agujero*) large hole.

boquete [boke'te] *nm* gap, hole.

boquiabierto, a [bokēáḅyer'to, á] *a* open-mouthed (in astonishment); **quedar ~** to be left aghast.

boquilla [bokē'yá] *nf* (*para riego*) nozzle; (*para cigarro*) cigarette holder; (*MUS*) mouthpiece.

borbollar [borḅoyár'], **borbollear** [borḅo-yeár'] *vi* to bubble.

borbollón [borḅoyon'] *nm* bubbling; **hablar a borbollones** to jabber; **salir a borbollones** (*agua*) to gush out.

borbotar [borḅotár'] *vi* = **borbollar**.

borbotón [borḅoton'] *nm*: **salir a borbotones** to gush out.

borda [bor'ḍá] *nf* (*NAUT*) gunwale; **echar** *o* **tirar algo por la ~** to throw sth overboard.

bordado [borḍá'ḍo] *nm* embroidery.

bordar [borḍár'] *vt* to embroider.

borde [bor'ḍe] *nm* edge, border; (*de camino etc*) side; (*en la costura*) hem; **al ~ de** (*fig*) on the verge *o* brink of; **ser ~** (*Esp fam*) to be a pain in the neck.

bordear [borḍeár'] *vt* to border.

bordillo [borḍē'yo] *nm* curb (*US*), kerb (*Brit*).

bordo [bor'ḍo] *nm* (*NAUT*) side; **a ~ on** board.

Borgoña [borgo'nyá] *nf* Burgundy.

borgoña [borgo'nyá] *nm* burgundy.

borinqueño, a [borēnke'nyo, á] *a*, *nm/f*

Puerto Rican.

borla [bor'lá] *nf* (*gen*) tassel; (*de gorro*) pompon.

borra [bo'rrá] *nf* (*pelusa*) fluff; (*sedimento*) sediment.

borrachera [borrátche'rá] *nf* (*ebriedad*) drunkenness; (*orgía*) spree, binge.

borracho, a [borrá'tcho, á] *a* drunk ♦ *nm/f* (*que bebe mucho*) drunkard, drunk; (*temporalmente*) drunk, drunk man/woman ♦ *nm* (*CULIN*) cake soaked in liqueur or spirit.

borrador [borráḍhor'] *nm* (*escritura*) first draft, rough sketch; (*cuaderno*) scribbling pad; (*goma*) eraser, rubber (*Brit*); (*COM*) daybook; (*para pizarra*) eraser (*US*), duster (*Brit*); **hacer un nuevo ~ de** (*COM*) to redraft.

borrajear [borráheár'] *vt*, *vi* to scribble.

borrar [borrár'] *vt* to erase, rub out; (*tachar*) to delete; (*cinta*) to wipe out; (*INFORM: archivo*) to delete, erase; (*POL etc: eliminar*) to wipe out.

borrasca [borrás'ká] *nf* (*METEOROLOGÍA*) storm.

borrascoso, a [borrásko'so, á] *a* stormy.

borrego, a [borre'g̣o, á] *nm/f* lamb; (*oveja*) sheep; (*fig*) simpleton.

borricada [borrēká'ḍhá] *nf* foolish action/ statement.

borrico, a [borrē'ko, á] *nm* donkey; (*fig*) stupid man ♦ *nf* she-donkey; (*fig*) stupid woman.

borrón [borron'] *nm* (*mancha*) stain; ~ **y cuenta nueva** let bygones be bygones.

borroso, a [borro'so, á] *a* vague, unclear; (*escritura*) illegible; (*escrito*) smudgy; (*FOTO*) blurred.

Bósforo [bos'foro] *nm*: **el (Estrecho del) ~** the Bosp(h)orus.

bosque [bos'ke] *nm* wood; (*grande*) forest.

bosquejar [boskehár'] *vt* to sketch.

bosquejo [boske'ho] *nm* sketch.

bosta [bo'stá] *nf* dung, manure.

bostece [boste'se] *etc vb V* **bostezar**.

bostezar [bostesár'] *vi* to yawn.

bostezo [boste'so] *nm* yawn.

bota [bo'tá] *nf* (*calzado*) boot; (*saco*) leather wine bottle; **ponerse las ~s** (*fam*) to strike it rich.

botadura [botáḍhōō'rá] *nf* launching.

botánico, a [botá'nēko, á] *a* botanical ♦ *nm/f* botanist ♦ *nf* botany.

botar [botár'] *vt* to throw, hurl; (*NAUT*) to launch; (*fam*) to throw out ♦ *vi* to bounce.

botarate [botárá'te] *nm* (*imbécil*) idiot.

bote [bo'te] *nm* (*salto*) bounce; (*golpe*) thrust; (*vasija*) tin, can; (*embarcación*) boat; **de ~ en ~** packed, jammed full; ~ **salvavidas** lifeboat; **dar un ~** to jump; **dar ~s** (*AUTO etc*) to bump; ~ **de la basura**

(*AM*) trashcan (*US*), dustbin (*Brit*).
botella [bote'ya] *nf* bottle; ~ **de vino** (*contenido*) bottle of wine; (*recipiente*) wine bottle.
botellero [boteye'ro] *nm* wine rack.
botica [botē'ká] *nf* pharmacy, chemist's (shop) (*Brit*).
boticario, a [botēká'ryo, á] *nm/f* pharmacist, chemist (*Brit*).
botijo [botē'ho] *nm* (earthenware) jug; (*tren*) excursion train.
botín [botēn'] *nm* (*calzado*) half boot; (*polaina*) spat; (*MIL*) booty; (*de ladrón*) loot.
botiquín [botēkēn'] *nm* (*armario*) medicine chest; (*portátil*) first-aid kit.
botón [boton'] *nm* button; (*BOT*) bud; (*de florete*) tip; ~ **de arranque** (*AUTO etc*) starter; ~ **de oro** buttercup; **pulsar el** ~ to press the button.
botones [boto'nes] *nm inv* bellhop (*US*), bellboy (*Brit*).
botulismo [botōōlēs'mo] *nm* botulism, food poisoning.
bóveda [bo'hethá] *nf* (*ARQ*) vault.
bovino, a [bohē'no, á] *a* bovine; (*AGR*): **ganado** ~ cattle.
boxeador [bokseáhor'] *nm* boxer.
boxear [bokseár'] *vi* to box.
boxeo [bokse'o] *nm* boxing.
boya [bo'yá] *nf* (*NAUT*) buoy; (*flotador*) float.
boyante [boyán'te] *a* (*NAUT*) buoyant; (*feliz*) buoyant; (*próspero*) prosperous.
bozal [bosál'] *nm* (*de caballo*) halter; (*de perro*) muzzle.
bozo [bo'so] *nm* (*pelusa*) fuzz; (*boca*) mouth.
bracear [braseár'] *vi* (*agitar los brazos*) to wave one's arms.
bracero [brase'ro] *nm* laborer (*US*), labourer (*Brit*); (*en el campo*) farmhand.
bracete [brase'te]: **de** ~ *ad* arm in arm.
braga [brá'gá] *nf* (*cuerda*) sling, rope; (*de bebé*) diaper (*US*), nappy (*Brit*); ~**s** *nfpl* (*de mujer*) panties.
braguero [bráge'ro] *nm* (*MED*) truss.
bragueta [bráge'tá] *nf* fly, zipper (*US*).
braguetazo [brágetá'so] *nm* (*AM*) marriage of convenience.
braille [brēēl] *nm* braille.
bramante [brámán'te] *nm* twine, string.
bramar [brámár'] *vi* to bellow, roar.
bramido [brámē'tho] *nm* bellow, roar.
branquias [brán'kyás] *nfpl* gills.
brasa [brá'sá] *nf* live *o* hot coal; **carne a la** ~ grilled meat.
brasero [brase'ro] *nm* brazier; (*AM: chimenea*) fireplace.
Brasil [brásēl'] *nm*: (**el**) ~ Brazil.
brasileño, a [brásēle'nyo, á] *a, nm/f* Brazilian.

brava [brá'há]: **a la** ~ *ad* by force.
bravata [bráhá'tá] *nf* boast.
braveza [bráhe'sá] *nf* (*valor*) bravery; (*ferocidad*) ferocity.
bravío, a [bráhē'o, á] *a* wild; (*feroz*) fierce.
bravo, a [brá'ho, á] *a* (*valiente*) brave; (*bueno*) fine, splendid; (*feroz*) ferocious; (*salvaje*) wild; (*mar etc*) rough, stormy; (*CULIN*) hot, spicy ♦ *excl* bravo!
bravucón, ona [bráhōōkon', o'ná] *a* swaggering ♦ *nm/f* braggart.
bravura [bráhōō'rá] *nf* bravery; ferocity; (*pey*) boast.
braza [brá'sá] *nf* fathom; **nadar a la** ~ to swim (the) breast-stroke.
brazada [brásá'thá] *nf* stroke.
brazado [brásá'tho] *nm* armful.
brazalete [brásále'te] *nm* (*pulsera*) bracelet; (*banda*) armband.
brazo [brá'so] *nm* arm; (*ZOOL*) foreleg; (*BOT*) limb, branch; ~**s** *nmpl* (*braceros*) hands, workers; ~ **derecho** (*fig*) right-hand man; **a** ~ **partido** hand-to-hand; **cogidos** *etc* **del** ~ arm in arm; **no dar su** ~ **a torcer** not to give way easily; **huelga de** ~**s caídos** sit-down strike.
brea [bre'á] *nf* pitch, tar.
brebaje [brehá'he] *nm* potion.
brécol [bre'kol] *nm* broccoli.
brecha [bretch'á] *nf* breach; (*hoyo vacío*) gap, opening.
brega [bre'gá] *nf* (*lucha*) struggle; (*trabajo*) hard work.
bregar [bregár'] *vi* (*luchar*) to struggle; (*trabajar mucho*) to slog away.
bregue [bre'ge] *etc vb V* **bregar.**
breña [bre'nyá] *nf* rough ground.
Bretaña [bretá'nyá] *nf* Brittany.
brete [bre'te] *nm* (*cepo*) shackles *pl*; (*fig*) predicament; **estar en un** ~ to be in a jam.
bretón, ona [breton', o'ná] *a, nm/f* Breton.
breva [bre'há] *nf* (*BOT*) early fig; (*puro*) flat cigar; **¡no caerá esa** ~! no such luck!
breve [bre'he] *a* short, brief; **en** ~ (*pronto*) shortly; (*en pocas palabras*) in short ♦ *nf* (*MUS*) breve.
brevedad [brehetháth'] *nf* brevity, shortness.
breviario [brehyá'ryo] *nm* (*REL*) breviary.
brezal [bresál'] *nm* moor(land), heath.
brezo [bre'so] *nm* heather.
bribón, ona [brēhon', o'ná] *a* idle, lazy ♦ *nm/f* (*vagabundo*) vagabond; (*pícaro*) rascal, rogue.
bricolaje [brēkolá'he] *nm* do-it-yourself.
brida [brē'thá] *nf* bridle, rein; (*TEC*) clamp; **a toda** ~ at top speed.
bridge [brētch] *nm* (*NAIPES*) bridge.
brigada [brēgá'thá] *nf* (*unidad*) brigade; (*trabajadores*) squad, gang ♦ *nm* warrant

officer.

brigadier [brĕgáthyer'] *nm* brigadier(-general).

brigantino, a [brĕgánte'no, á] *a* of *o* from Corunna ♦ *nm/f* native *o* inhabitant of Corunna.

brillante [brēyàn'te] *a* brilliant; (*color*) bright; (*joya*) sparkling ♦ *nm* diamond.

brillantez [brēyántes'] *nf* (*color etc*) brightness; (*fig*) brilliance.

brillar [brēyàr'] *vi* (*tb fig*) to shine; (*joyas*) to sparkle; ~ **por su ausencia** to be conspicuous by one's absence.

brillo [brē'yo] *nm* shine; (*brillantez*) brilliance; (*fig*) splendor (*US*), splendour (*Brit*); **sacar ~ a** to polish.

brincar [brēnkár'] *vi* to skip about, hop about, jump about; **está que brinca** he's hopping mad.

brinco [brēn'ko] *nm* jump, leap; **a** ~**s** by fits and starts; **de un** ~ at one leap.

brindar [brēndár'] *vi*: ~ **a** *o* **por** to drink (a toast) to ♦ *vt* to offer, present; **le brinda la ocasión de** it offers *o* affords him the opportunity to; ~**se** *vr*: ~**se a hacer algo** to offer to do sth.

brindis [brēn'dēs] *nm inv* toast; (*TAUR*) (ceremony of) dedication.

brinque [brēn'ke] *etc vb V* **brincar.**

brío [brē'o] *nm* spirit, verve.

brioso, a [brēo'so, á] *a* spirited.

brisa [brē'sá] *nf* breeze.

británico, a [brĕtá'nĕko, á] *a* British ♦ *nm/f* Briton, British person; **los** ~**s** the British.

brizna [brēs'ná] *nf* (*hebra*) strand, thread; (*de hierba*) blade; (*trozo*) piece; (*AM*) drizzle.

broca [bro'ká] *nf* (*COSTURA*) bobbin; (*TEC*) drill bit; (*clavo*) tack.

brocado [broká'tho] *nm* brocade.

brocal [brokál'] *nm* rim.

brocha [brotch'á] *nf* (large) paintbrush; ~ **de afeitar** shaving brush; **pintor de** ~ **gorda** painter and decorator; (*fig*) poor painter.

brochazo [brotchá'so] *nm* brush-stroke; **a grandes** ~**s** (*fig*) in general terms.

broche [brotch'e] *nm* brooch.

broma [bro'má] *nf* joke; (*inocentada*) practical joke; **en** ~ in fun, as a joke; **gastar una** ~ **a uno** to play a joke on sb; **tomar algo a** ~ to take sth as a joke.

bromear [bromeár'] *vi* to joke.

bromista [bromē'stá] *a* fond of joking ♦ *nm/f* joker, wag.

bromuro [bromōō'ro] *nm* bromide.

bronca [bron'ká] *nf* row; (*regañada*) scolding; **armar una** ~ to kick up a fuss; **echar una** ~ **a uno** to tell sb off.

bronce [bron'se] *nm* bronze; (*latón*) brass.

bronceado, a [bronseá'tho, á] *a* bronze

cpd; (*por el sol*) tanned ♦ *nm* (sun)tan; (*TEC*) bronzing.

bronceador [bronseáthor'] *nm* suntan lotion.

broncearse [bronseár'se] *vr* to get a suntan.

bronco, a [bron'ko, á] *a* (*manera*) rude, surly; (*voz*) harsh.

bronquios [bron'kyos] *nmpl* bronchial tubes.

bronquitis [bronkē'tēs] *nf inv* bronchitis.

brotar [brotár'] *vt* (*tierra*) to produce ♦ *vi* (*BOT*) to sprout; (*aguas*) to gush (forth); (*lágrimas*) to well up; (*MED*) to break out.

brote [bro'te] *nm* (*BOT*) shoot; (*MED, fig*) outbreak.

broza [bro'sá] *nf* (*BOT*) dead leaves *pl*; (*fig*) rubbish.

bruces [broō'ses]: **de** ~ *ad*: **caer** *o* **dar de** ~ to fall headlong, fall flat.

bruja [broō'há] *nf* witch.

Brujas [broō'hás] *nf* Bruges.

brujería [broōherē'á] *nf* witchcraft.

brujo [broō'ho] *nm* wizard, magician.

brújula [broō'hōōlá] *nf* compass.

bruma [broō'má] *nf* mist.

brumoso, a [broōmo'so, á] *a* misty.

bruñendo [broōnyen'do] *etc vb V* **bruñir.**

bruñido [broōnyē'tho] *nm* polish.

bruñir [broōnyēr'] *vt* to polish.

brusco, a [broōs'ko, á] *a* (*súbito*) sudden; (*áspero*) brusque.

Bruselas [broōse'lás] *nf* Brussels.

brusquedad [broōsketháth'] *nf* suddenness; brusqueness.

brutal [broōtál'] *a* brutal.

brutalidad [broōtáletháth'] *nf* brutality.

bruto, a [broō'to, á] *a* (*idiota*) stupid; (*bestial*) brutish; (*peso*) gross ♦ *nm* brute; **a la bruta, a lo** ~ roughly; **en** ~ raw, unworked.

Bs.As. *abr* = **Buenos Aires.**

buba [boō'há] *nf* tumor (*US*), tumour (*Brit*).

bucal [boōkál'] *a* oral; **por vía** ~ orally.

bucanero [boōkáne'ro] *nm* buccaneer.

bucear [boōseár'] *vi* to dive ♦ *vt* to explore.

buceo [boōse'o] *nm* diving; (*fig*) investigation.

bucle [boō'kle] *nm* curl; (*INFORM*) loop.

buche [boō'tche] *nm* (*de ave*) crop; (*ZOOL*) maw; (*fam*) belly.

budín [boōthēn'] *nm* pudding.

budismo [boōthēs'mo] *nm* Buddhism.

buen [bwen] *a V* **bueno.**

buenamente [bwenámen'te] *ad* (*fácilmente*) easily; (*voluntariamente*) willingly.

buenaventura [bwenáhentoō'rá] *nf* (*suerte*) good luck; (*adivinación*) fortune; **decir** *o* **echar la** ~ **a uno** to tell sb's fortune.

bueno, a [bwe'no, á], **buen** [bwen] *a* (*amable*) kind; (*MED*) well ♦ *excl* right!, all right!; **¡buenas!** afternoon! (fam); **¡buen día!**, **¡buenos días!** good morning!; good afternoon!; hello!; **¡buenas tardes!** good afternoon!; good evening!; **¡buenas noches!** good evening!; good night!; **los buenos** (CINE) the goodies; **¡buen sinvergüenza resultó!** a fine rascal he turned out to be; **el bueno de Manolo** good old Manolo; **fue muy bueno conmigo** he was very good to me; **de buenas a primeras** all of a sudden; **por las buenas o por las malas** by hook or by crook; **bueno, ¿y qué?** well, so what?

Buenos Aires [bwenosá'ēres] nm Buenos Aires.

buey [bwē] nm ox.

búfalo [bōō'fálo] nm buffalo.

bufanda [bōōfán'dá] nf scarf.

bufar [bōōfár'] vi to snort.

bufete [bōōfe'te] nm (despacho de abogado) lawyer's office; **establecer su ~** to set up in legal practice.

buffer [bōō'fer] nm (INFORM) buffer.

bufón [bōōfon'] nm clown.

bufonada [bōōfonáʼthá] nf (dicho) jest; (hecho) piece of buffoonery; (TEATRO) farce.

buhardilla [bōōárthe'yá] nf attic.

búho [bōō'o] nm owl; (fig) hermit, recluse.

buhonero [bōōone'ro] nm pedler (US), pedlar (Brit).

buitre [bwē'tre] nm vulture.

bujía [bōōhē'á] nf (vela) candle; (ELEC) candle (power); (AUTO) spark plug.

bula [bōō'lá] nf (papal) bull.

bulbo [bōōl'ho] nm (BOT) bulb.

bulevar [bōōlehár'] nm boulevard.

Bulgaria [bōōlgá'ryá] nf Bulgaria.

búlgaro, a [bōōl'gáro, á] a, nm/f Bulgarian.

bulo [bōō'lo] nm false rumour.

bulto [bōōl'to] nm (paquete) package; (fardo) bundle; (tamaño) size, bulkiness; (MED) swelling, lump; (silueta) vague shape; (estatua) bust, statue; **hacer ~** to take up space; **escurrir el ~** to make o.s. scarce; (fig) to dodge the issue.

bulla [bōō'yá] nf (ruido) uproar; (de gente) crowd; **armar o meter ~** to kick up a row.

bullendo [bōōyen'do] etc vb V **bullir**.

bullicio [bōōyē'syo] nm (ruido) uproar; (movimiento) bustle.

bullicioso, a [bōōyēsyo'so, á] a (ruidoso) noisy, (calle etc) busy; (situación) turbulent.

bullir [bōōyēr'] vi (hervir) to boil; (burbujear) to bubble; (mover) to move, stir; (insectos) to swarm; **~ de** (fig) to teem o seethe with.

buñuelo [bōōnywe'lo] nm ≈ doughnut, donut (US).

BUP [bōōp] nm abr (Esp ESCOL:= Bachille-rato Unificado y Polivalente) secondary education and leaving diploma for 14-17 age group.

buque [bōō'ke] nm ship, vessel; **~ de guerra** warship; **~ mercante** merchant ship; **~ de vela** sailing ship.

burbuja [bōōrhōō'há] nf bubble; **hacer ~s** to bubble; (gaseosa) to fizz.

burbujear [bōōrhōōheár'] vi to bubble.

burdel [bōōrthel'] nm brothel.

Burdeos [bōōrthe'os] nm Bordeaux.

burdo, a [bōōr'tho, á] a coarse, rough.

burgalés, esa [bōōrgáles', e'sá] a of o from Burgos ♦ nm/f native o inhabitant of Burgos.

burgués, esa [bōōrges', e'sá] a middle-class, bourgeois; **pequeño ~** lower middle-class; (POL, pey) petty bourgeois.

burguesía [bōōrgesē'á] nf middle class, bourgeoisie.

burla [bōōr'lá] nf (mofa) gibe; (broma) joke; (engaño) trick; **hacer ~ de** to make fun of.

burladero [bōōrláthe'ro] nm (bullfighter's) refuge.

burlador, a [bōōrláthor', á] a mocking ♦ nm/f mocker; (bromista) joker ♦ nm (libertino) seducer.

burlar [bōōrlár'] vt (engañar) to deceive; (seducir) to seduce ♦ vi, **~se** vr to joke; **~se de** to make fun of.

burlesco, a [bōōrles'ko, á] a burlesque.

burlón, ona [bōōrlon', o'ná] a mocking.

buró [bōōro'] nm bureau.

burocracia [bōōrokrá'syá] nf bureaucracy.

burócrata [bōōro'krátá] nm/f bureaucrat.

buromática [bōōromá'tēká] nf office automation.

burrada [bōōrrá'thá] nf stupid act; **decir ~s** to talk nonsense.

burro, a [bōō'rro, á] nm/f (ZOOL) donkey; (fig) ass, idiot ♦ a stupid; **caerse del ~** to realize one's mistake; **no ver tres en un ~** to be as blind as a bat.

bursátil [bōōrsá'tēl] a stock-exchange cpd.

bus [bōōs] nm bus.

busca [bōōs'ká] nf search, hunt; **en ~ de** in search of.

buscador, a [bōōskáthor', á] nm/f searcher.

buscapiés [bōōskápyes'] nm inv firecracker (US), jumping jack (Brit).

buscapleitos [bōōskáple'ētos] nm/f inv troublemaker.

buscar [bōōskár'] vt to look for; (beneficio) to seek; (enemigo) to seek out; (traer) to bring, fetch; (provocar) to provoke; (INFORM) to search ♦ vi to look, search, seek; **ven a ~me a la oficina** come and pick me up at the office; **~le 3 o 4 pies al gato** to split hairs; "**~ y reemplazar**" (INFORM) "search and replace"; **se busca secretaria**

secretary wanted; **se la buscó** he asked for it.

buscavidas [booskåbē'tḥás] *nm/f inv* snooper; (*persona ambiciosa*) go-getter.

buscón, ona [booskon', o'ná] *a* thieving ♦ *nm* petty thief ♦ *nf* whore.

busilis [boosē'lēs] *nm inv* (*fam*) snag.

busque [boos'ke] *etc vb* V **buscar.**

búsqueda [boos'ketḥá] *nf* = **busca.**

busto [boo'sto] *nm* (*ANAT, ARTE*) bust.

butaca [bootá'ká] *nf* armchair; (*de cine, teatro*) seat.

butano [bootá'no] *nm* butane (gas); **bombona de ~** gas cylinder.

butifarra [bootēfá'rrá] *nf* Catalan sausage.

buzo [boo'so] *nm* diver.

buzón [booson'] *nm* (*gen*) mailbox (*US*), letter box (*Brit*); (*en la calle*) pillar box (*Brit*); (*TELEC*) mailbox; **echar al ~** to post.

byte [bäēt] *nm* (*INFORM*) byte.

C

C, c [se] *nf* (*letra*) C, c; **C de Carmen** C for Charlie.

C. *abr* (= *centígrado*) C.; (= *compañía*) Co.

c. *abr* (= *capítulo*) ch.

C/ *abr* (= *calle*) St, Rd.

c/ *abr* (*COM:* = *cuenta*) a/c.

ca [ká] *excl* not a bit of it!

c.a. *abr* (= *corriente alterna*) A.C.

cabal [kábál'] *a* (*exacto*) exact; (*correcto*) right, proper; (*acabado*) finished, complete; **~es** *nmpl*: **estar en sus ~es** to be in one's right mind.

cábala [ká'bálá] *nf* (*REL*) cab(b)ala; (*fig*) cabal, intrigue; **~s** *nfpl* guess *sg*, supposition *sg*.

cabalgadura [kábálgátḥoo'rá] *nf* mount, horse.

cabalgar [kábálgár'] *vt, vi* to ride.

cabalgata [kábálgá'tá] *nf* procession.

cabalgue [kábál'ge] *etc vb* V **cabalgar.**

cabalístico, a [kábálē'stēko, á] *a* (*fig*) mysterious.

caballa [kábá'yá] *nf* mackerel.

caballeresco, a [kábáyeres'ko, á] *a* noble, chivalrous.

caballería [kábáyerē'á] *nf* mount; (*MIL*) cavalry.

caballeriza [kábáyerē'sá] *nf* stable.

caballerizo [kábáyerē'so] *nm* groom, stableman.

caballero [kábáye'ro] *nm* gentleman; (*de la orden de caballería*) knight; (*trato directo*) sir; "**C~s**" "Gentlemen".

caballerosidad [kábáyerosētḥátḥ'] *nf* chivalry.

caballete [kábáye'te] *nm* (*AGR*) ridge; (*ARTE*) easel.

caballito [kábáyē'to] *nm* (*caballo pequeño*) small horse, pony; (*juguete*) rocking horse; **~s** *nmpl* merry-go-round *sg*; **~ de mar** seahorse; **~ del diablo** dragonfly.

caballo [kábá'yo] *nm* horse; (*AJEDREZ*) knight; (*NAIPES*) queen; **~ de vapor** *o* **de fuerza** horsepower; **es su ~ de batalla** it's his hobby-horse; **~ blanco** (*COM*) backer.

cabaña [kábá'nyá] *nf* (*casita*) hut, cabin.

cabaré, cabaret, *pl* **cabarets** [kábáre', kábáres'] *nm* cabaret.

cabecear [kábeseár'] *vi* to nod.

cabecera [kábese'rá] *nf* (*gen*) head; (*de distrito*) chief town; (*de cama*) headboard; (*IMPRENTA*) headline.

cabecilla [kábesē'yá] *nm* ringleader.

cabellera [kábeye'rá] *nf* (head of) hair; (*de cometa*) tail.

cabello [kábe'yo] *nm* (*tb:* **~s**) hair *sg*.

caber [káber'] *vi* (*entrar*) to fit, go; **caben 3 más** there's room for 3 more; **cabe preguntar si...** one might ask whether...; **cabe que venga más tarde** he may come later.

cabestrillo [kábestrē'yo] *nm* sling.

cabestro [kábes'tro] *nm* halter.

cabeza [kábe'sá] *nf* head; (*POL*) chief, leader; **caer de ~** to fall head first; **sentar la ~** to settle down; **~ de lectura/escritura** read/write head; **~ impresora** *o* **de impresión** printhead.

cabezada [kábesá'tḥá] *nf* (*golpe*) butt; **dar una ~** to nod off.

cabezal [kábesál'] *nm*: **~ impresor** print head.

cabezón, ona [kábeson', o'ná] *a* with a big head; (*vino*) heady; (*obstinado*) obstinate, stubborn.

cabezota [kábeso'tá] *a inv* obstinate, stubborn.

cabezudo, a [kábesoo'tḥo, á] *a* with a big head; (*obstinado*) obstinate, stubborn.

cabida [kábē'tḥá] *nf* space; **dar ~ a** to make room for; **tener ~ para** to have room for.

cabildo [kábēl'do] *nm* (*de iglesia*) chapter; (*POL*) town council.

cabina [kábē'ná] *nf* (*de camión*) cabin; **~ telefónica** (*tele*)phone booth.

cabizbajo, a [kábēsbá'ho, á] *a* crestfallen, dejected.

cable [ká'ble] *nm* cable; (*de aparato*) lead; **~ aéreo** (*ELEC*) overhead cable; **conectar con ~** (*INFORM*) to hardwire.

cabo [ká'bo] *nm* (*de objeto*) end, extremity; (*MIL*) corporal; (*NAUT*) rope, cable; (*GEO*) cape; (*TEC*) thread; **al ~ de 3 días** after 3 days; **de ~ a rabo** *o* ~ from beginning to end; (*libro: leer*) from cover to cover; **llevar a** ~ to carry out; **atar ~s** to tie up the loose ends; **C~ de Buena Esperanza** Cape of Good Hope; **C~ de Hornos** Cape Horn; **las Islas de C~ Verde** the Cape Verde Islands.

cabra [ká'brá] *nf* goat; **estar como una ~** (*fam*) to be nuts.

cabré [kábre'] *etc vb V* **caber.**

cabrear [kábreár'] *vt* to annoy; **~se** *vr* to fly off the handle.

cabrío, a [kábrē'o, á] *a* goatish; **macho ~** (he-)goat, billy goat.

cabriola [kábryo'lá] *nf* caper.

cabritilla [kábrētē'yá] *nf* kid, kidskin.

cabrito [kábrē'to] *nm* kid.

cabrón [kábron'] *nm* (*fig: fam!*) bastard (!).

caca [ká'ká] *nf* (*palabra de niños*) pooh ♦ *excl:* **no toques, ¡~!** don't touch, it's dirty!

cacahuete [kákáwe'te] *nm* (*Esp*) peanut.

cacao [káká'o] *nm* cocoa; (*BOT*) cacao.

cacarear [kákáreár'] *vi* (*persona*) to boast; (*gallina*) to cackle.

cacatúa [kákátōō'á] *nf* cockatoo.

cacereño, a [kásere'nyo, á] *a* of *o* from Cáceres ♦ *nm/f* native *o* inhabitant of Cáceres.

cacería [káserē'á] *nf* hunt.

cacerola [kásero'lá] *nf* pan, saucepan.

cacique [kásē'ke] *nm* chief, local ruler; (*POL*) local party boss; (*fig*) despot.

caciquismo [kásēkēs'mo] *nm* *system of dominance by the local boss.*

caco [ká'ko] *nm* pickpocket.

cacofonía [kákofonē'á] *nf* cacophony.

cacto [kák'to] *nm*, **cactus** [kák'tōōs] *nm inv* cactus.

cacha [kátch'á] *nf* (*mango*) handle; (*nalga*) buttock.

cacharro [kátchá'rro] *nm* (*vasija*) (earthenware) pot; (*cerámica*) piece of pottery; (*AM fam*) useless object; **~s** *nmpl* pots and pans.

cachear [kátcheár'] *vt* to search, frisk.

cachemir [kátchemēr'] *nm* cashmere.

cacheo [kátche'o] *nm* searching, frisking.

cachete [kátche'te] *nm* (*ANAT*) cheek; (*bofetada*) slap (in the face).

cachimba [kátchēm'bá] *nf* pipe.

cachiporra [kátchēpo'rrá] *nf* (billy) club (*US*), truncheon (*Brit*).

cachivache [kátchēbátch'e] *nm* piece of junk; **~s** *nmpl* trash *sg*, junk *sg*.

cacho, a [kátch'o, á] *nm* (small) bit; (*AM: cuerno*) horn.

cachondearse [kátchondeár'se] *vr:* ~ **de uno** to tease sb.

cachondeo [kátchonde'o] *nm* (*fam*) farce, joke; (*guasa*) laugh.

cachondo, a [kátchon'do, á] *a* (*ZOOL*) in heat; (*persona*) horny; (*gracioso*) funny.

cachorro, a [kátcho'rro, á] *nm/f* (*perro*) pup, puppy; (*león*) cub.

cada [ká'thá] *a inv* each; (*antes de número*) every; ~ **día** each day, every day; ~ **dos días** every other day; ~ **uno/a** each one, every one; ~ **vez más** more and more; **uno de** ~ **diez** one out of every ten; **¿~ cuánto?** how often?

cadalso [káthál'so] *nm* scaffold.

cadáver [káthá'ber] *nm* (dead) body, corpse.

cadavérico, a [káthábe'rēko, á] *a* cadaverous; (*pálido*) deathly pale.

cadena [káthe'ná] *nf* chain; (*TV*) channel; **reacción en** ~ chain reaction; **trabajo en** ~ assembly line work; ~ **perpetua** (*JUR*) life imprisonment; ~ **de caracteres** (*INFORM*) character string.

cadencia [káthen'syá] *nf* cadence, rhythm.

cadera [káthe'rá] *nf* hip.

cadete [káthe'te] *nm* cadet.

Cádiz [ká'thēs] *nm* Cadiz.

caducar [káthōōkár'] *vi* to expire.

caducidad [káthōōsētháth'] *nf:* **fecha de** ~ expiration (*US*) *o* expiry (*Brit*) date; (*de comida*) sell-by date.

caduco, a [káthōō'ko, á] *a* (*idea etc*) outdated, outmoded; **de hoja caduca** deciduous.

caduque [káthōō'ke] *etc vb V* **caducar.**

C.A.E. *abr* (= *cóbrese al entregar*) COD.

caer [káer'] *vi*, **~se** *vr* to fall (down); (*noche, fecha*) to fall; (*pago*) to fall due; (*AM*) to drop in; **dejar ~** to drop; **estar por** ~ to be due to happen; **me cae bien/mal** I get on well with him/I can't stand him; ~ **en la cuenta** to catch on; **su cumpleaños cae en viernes** her birthday falls on a Friday.

café, pl cafés [káfe', káfes'] *nm* (*bebida, planta*) coffee; (*lugar*) café ♦ *a* (*color*) brown; ~ **con leche** coffee with cream (*US*), white coffee (*Brit*); ~ **solo**, ~ **negro** (*AM*) (small) black coffee.

cafeína [káfeē'ná] *nf* caffein(e).

cafetal [káfetál'] *nm* coffee plantation.

cafetera [káfete'rá] *nf V* **cafetero.**

cafetería [káfeterē'á] *nf* cafe.

cafetero, a [káfete'ro, á] *a* coffee *cpd* ♦ *nf* coffee pot; **ser muy** ~ to be a coffee addict.

cafre [ká'fre] *nm/f:* **como ~s** (*fig*) like savages.

cagar [kágár'] (*fam!*) *vt* to shit (!); (*fig*) to bungle, mess up ♦ *vi* to take (*US*) *o* have (*Brit*) a shit (!); **~se** *vr:* **¡me cago en diez** (*etc*)! shit! (!).

cague [ká'ge] *etc vb V* **cagar.**

caído, a [káē'tho, á] *a* fallen; (*INFORM*)

down ♦ *nf* fall; (*declive*) slope; (*disminución*) fall, drop; ~ **del cielo** out of the blue; **a la caída del sol** at sunset; **sufrir una caída** to have a fall.

caiga [ká'ęgá] *etc vb V* **caer.**

caimán [káẽmán'] *nm* alligator.

Cairo [ká'ẽro] *nm*: **el** ~ Cairo.

caja [ká'há] *nf* box; (*ataúd*) casket (*US*), coffin; (*para reloj*) case; (*de ascensor*) shaft; (*COM*) cashbox; (*ECON*) fund; (*donde se hacen los pagos*) checkout; (*en supermercado*) checkout, till; (*TIP*) case; ~ **de ahorros** savings bank; ~ **de cambios** gearbox; ~ **fuerte,** ~ **de caudales** safe, strongbox; **ingresar en** ~ to be paid in.

cajero, a [káhe'ro, á] *nm/f* cashier; (*en banco*) (bank) teller ♦ *nm*: ~ **automático** cash dispenser, A.T.M.

cajetilla [káhetẽ'yá] *nf* (*de cigarrillos*) pack (*US*), packet (*Brit*).

cajista [káhẽ'stá] *nm/f* typesetter.

cajón [káhon'] *nm* big box; (*de mueble*) drawer.

cal [kál] *nf* lime; **cerrar algo a** ~ **y canto** to shut sth firmly.

cala [ká'lá] *nf* (*GEO*) cove, inlet; (*de barco*) hold.

calabacín [kálähásẽn'] *nm,* **calabacita** [kálähásẽ'tá] *nf* (*AM*) (*BOT*) zucchini (*US*), courgette (*Brit*).

calabaza [kálähá'sá] *nf* (*BOT*) pumpkin; **dar** ~**s a** (*candidato*) to fail.

calabozo [káläho'so] *nm* (*cárcel*) prison; (*celda*) cell.

calado, a [kálá'tho, á] *a* (*prenda*) lace *cpd* ♦ *nm* (*TEC*) fretwork; (*NAUT*) draft (*US*), draught (*Brit*) ♦ *nf* (*de cigarrillo*) puff; **estar** ~ **(hasta los huesos)** to be soaked (to the skin).

calamar [kálámár'] *nm* squid.

calambre [kálám'bre] *nm* (*tb*: ~**s**) cramp.

calamidad [kálámẽtháth'] *nf* calamity, disaster; (*persona*): **es una** ~ he's a dead loss.

calamina [kálámẽ'ná] *nf* calamine.

cálamo [ká'lámo] *nm* (*BOT*) stem; (*MUS*) reed.

calaña [kálá'nyá] *nf* model, pattern; (*fig*) nature, stamp.

calar [kálár'] *vt* to soak, drench; (*penetrar*) to pierce, penetrate; (*comprender*) to see through; (*vela, red*) to lower; ~**se** *vr* (*AUTO*) to stall; ~**se las gafas** to put one's glasses on.

calavera [kálähe'rá] *nf* skull.

calcañal [kálkányál'], **calcañar** [kálkányár'], **calcaño** [kálká'nyo] *nm* heel.

calcar [kálkár'] *vt* (*reproducir*) to trace; (*imitar*) to copy.

calce [kál'se] *etc vb V* **calzar.**

calceta [kálse'tá] *nf* (knee-length) stocking; **hacer** ~ to knit.

calcetín [kálsetẽn'] *nm* sock.

calcinar [kálsẽnár'] *vt* to burn, blacken.

calcio [kál'syo] *nm* calcium.

calco [kál'ko] *nm* tracing.

calcomanía [kálkománẽ'á] *nf* transfer.

calculadora [kálkōōlátho'rá] *nf* calculator.

calcular [kálkōōlár'] *vt* (*MAT*) to calculate, compute; ~ **que** ... to reckon that ....

cálculo [kál'kōōlo] *nm* calculation; (*MED*) (gall)stone; (*MAT*) calculus; ~ **de costo** pricing (*US*), costing (*Brit*); ~ **diferencial** differential calculus; **obrar con mucho** ~ to act cautiously.

caldear [káldeár'] *vt* to warm (up), heat (up); (*metales*) to weld.

caldera [kálde'rá] *nf* boiler.

calderero [kálde're'ro] *nm* boilermaker.

calderilla [káldere'yá] *nf* (*moneda*) small change.

caldero [kálde'ro] *nm* small boiler.

caldo [kál'do] *nm* stock; (*consomé*) consommé; ~ **de cultivo** (*BIO*) culture medium; **poner a** ~ **a uno** to give sb a dressing-down; **los** ~**s jerezanos** sherries.

calé [kále'] *a* gipsy *cpd*.

calefacción [kálefáksyon'] *nf* heating; ~ **central** central heating.

calendario [kálendá'ryo] *nm* calendar.

calentador [kálentátÿor'] *nm* heater.

calentar [kálentár'] *vt* to heat (up); (*fam: excitar*) to turn on; (*AM: enfurecer*) to anger; ~**se** *vr* to heat up, warm up; (*fig: discusión etc*) to get heated.

calentura [kálentōō'rá] *nf* (*MED*) fever, (high) temperature; (*de boca*) mouth sore.

calero [kále'ro, á] *a* lime *cpd*.

calibrar [kálẽbrár'] *vt* to gauge, measure.

calibre [kálẽ'bre] *nm* (*de cañón*) calibre, bore; (*diámetro*) diameter; (*fig*) calibre.

calidad [kálẽtháth'] *nf* quality; **de** ~ quality *cpd*; ~ **de borrador** (*INFORM*) draft quality; ~ **de carta** *o* **de correspondencia** (*INFORM*) letter quality; ~ **texto** (*INFORM*) text quality; **en** ~ **de** in the capacity of.

cálido, a [ká'lẽtho, á] *a* hot; (*fig*) warm.

caliente [kályen'te] *etc vb V* **calentar** ♦ *a* hot; (*fig*) fiery; (*disputa*) heated; (*fam: cachondo*) horny.

calificación [kálẽfẽkásyon'] *nf* qualification; (*de alumno*) grade, mark; ~ **de sobresaliente** first-class mark.

calificar [kálẽfẽkár'] *vt* to qualify; (*alumno*) to grade, mark; ~ **de** to describe as.

calificativo, a [kálẽfẽkátẽ'ÿo] *a* qualifying ♦ *nm* qualifier, epithet.

califique [kálẽfẽ'ke] *etc vb V* **calificar.**

californiano, a [kálẽfornyá'no, á] *a, nm/f* Californian.

calina [kálẽ'ná] *nf* haze.

cáliz [ká'lẽs] *nm* (*BOT*) calyx; (*REL*) chalice.

calma [kál'má] *nf* calm; (*pachorra*) slow-

ness; (COM, ECON) calm, lull; ~ **chicha**
dead calm; ¡~!, ¡con ~! take it easy!
calmante [kálmán'te] a soothing ♦ nm sedative, tranquillizer.
calmar [kálmár'] vt to calm, calm down;
(dolor) to relieve ♦ vi, ~**se** vr (tempestad)
to abate; (mente etc) to become calm.
calmoso, a [kálmo'so, á] a calm, quiet.
caló [kálo'] nm (de gitanos) gipsy language,
Romany; (argot) slang.
calor [kálor'] nm heat; (~ agradable)
warmth; **entrar en** ~ to get warm; **tener**
~ to be o feel hot.
caloría [kálore'á] nf calorie.
calorífero, a [kálore'fero, á] a heat-
producing, heat-giving ♦ nm heating
system.
calque [kál'ke] etc vb V **calcar.**
calumnia [káloōm'nyá] nf slander; (por
escrito) libel.
calumniar [káloōmnyár'] vt to slander; to libel.
calumnioso, a [káloōmnyo'so, á] a slanderous; libellous.
caluroso, a [káloōro'so, á] a hot; (sin exceso) warm; (fig) enthusiastic.
calva [kál'há] nf bald patch; (en bosque)
clearing.
calvario [kálhá'ryo] nm stations pl of the
cross; (fig) cross, heavy burden.
calvicie [kálhē'sye] nf baldness.
calvo, a [kál'ho, á] a bald; (terreno) bare,
barren; (tejido) threadbare ♦ nm bald
man.
calza [kál'sá] nf wedge, chock.
calzado, a [kálsá'tho, á] a shod ♦ nm foot-
wear ♦ nf roadway, highway.
calzador [kálsáthor'] nm shoehorn.
calzar [kálsár'] vt (zapatos etc) to wear; (un
mueble) to put a wedge under; (TEC: rueda
etc) to scotch; ~**se** vr: ~**se los zapatos** to
put on one's shoes; **¿qué (número) calza?**
what size do you take?
calzón [kálson'] nm (tb: **calzones**) shorts
pl; (AM: de hombre) pants; (: de mujer)
panties.
calzonazos [kálsoná'sos] nm inv henpecked
husband.
calzoncillos [kálsonsē'yos] nmpl underpants.
callado, a [káyá'tho, á] a quiet, silent.
callar [káyár'] vt (asunto delicado) to keep
quiet about, say nothing about; (omitir) to
pass over in silence; (persona, oposición) to
silence ♦ vi, ~**se** vr to keep quiet, be silent; (dejar de hablar) to stop talking;
¡**calla!**, be quiet!; ¡**cállate!**, ¡**cállese!** shut
up!; ¡**cállate la boca!** shut your mouth!
calle [ká'ye] nf street; (DEPORTE) lane; ~
arriba/abajo up/down the street; ~ **de**
sentido único one-way street; **poner a uno**

(de patitas) en la ~ to kick sb out.
calleja [káye'há] nf alley, narrow street.
callejear [káyeheár'] vi to wander (about)
the streets.
callejero, a [káyehe'ro, á] a street cpd ♦ nm
street map.
callejón [káyehon'] nm alley, passage;
(GEO) narrow pass; ~ **sin salida** cul-de-
sac; (fig) blind alley.
callejuela [káyehwe'lá] nf side-street, alley.
callista [káyē'stá] nm/f chiropodist.
callo [ká'yo] nm callus; (en el pie) corn; ~**s**
nmpl (CULIN) tripe sg.
calloso, a [káyo'so, á] a callous (US),
calloused (Brit).
cama [ká'má] nf bed; (GEO) stratum; ~
individual/de matrimonio single/double
bed; **guardar** ~ to be ill in bed.
camada [kámá'thá] nf litter; (de personas)
gang, band.
camafeo [kámáfe'o] nm cameo.
cámara [ká'márá] nf (POL etc) chamber;
(habitación) room; (sala) hall; (CINE)
movie camera; (fotográfica) camera; ~ **de**
aire inner tube; ~ **alta/baja** upper/lower
house; ~ **de comercio** chamber of
commerce; ~ **de gas** gas chamber; **a** ~
lenta in slow motion.
camarada [kámárá'thá] nm comrade,
companion.
camaradería [kámáráther̄e'á] nf comradeship.
camarero, a [kámáre'ro, á] nm waiter ♦ nf
(en restaurante) waitress; (en casa, hotel)
maid.
camarilla [kámárē'yá] nf (clan) clique;
(POL) lobby.
camarín [kámárēn'] nm (TEATRO) dressing
room.
camarón [kámáron'] nm shrimp.
camarote [kámáro'te] nm (NAUT) cabin.
cambiable [kámbyá'hle] a (variable)
changeable, variable; (intercambiable)
interchangeable.
cambiante [kámbyán'te] a variable.
cambiar [kámbyár'] vt to change; (trocar)
to exchange ♦ vi to change; ~**se** vr (mudarse) to move; (de ropa) to change; ~**(se)**
de ... to change one's ...; ~ **de idea/de**
ropa to change one's mind/clothes.
cambiazo [kámbyá'so] nm: **dar el** ~ **a uno**
to swindle sb.
cambio [kám'byo] nm change; (trueque)
exchange; (COM) rate of exchange; (oficina) foreign exchange office (US), bureau de
change (Brit); (dinero menudo) small
change; **en** ~ on the other hand; (en lugar
de eso) instead; ~ **de divisas** (COM)
foreign exchange; ~ **de línea** (INFORM)
line feed; ~ **de página** (INFORM) form
feed; ~ **a término** (COM) future (US) o

forward (*Brit*) exchange; ~ **de velocidades** gearshift; ~ **de vía** switch (*US*), points *pl* (*Brit*).

cambista [kámbē'stá] *nm* (*COM*) exchange broker.

Camboya [kámbo'yá] *nf* Cambodia, Kampuchea.

camboyano, a [kámboyá'no, á] *a, nm/f* Cambodian, Kampuchean.

camelar [kámelár'] *vt* (*con mujer*) to flirt with; (*persuadir*) to cajole.

camelo [káme'lo] *nm*: **me huele a ~** it smells fishy.

camello [káme'yo] *nm* camel; (*fam: traficante*) pusher.

camerino [kámerē'no] *nm* (*TEATRO*) dressing room.

camilla [kámē'yá] *nf* (*MED*) stretcher.

caminante [kámēnán'te] *nm/f* traveller.

caminar [kámēnár'] *vi* (*marchar*) to walk, go; (*viajar*) to travel, journey ♦ *vt* (*recorrer*) to cover, travel.

caminata [kámēná'tá] *nf* long walk.

camino [kámē'no] *nm* way, road; (*sendero*) track; **a medio ~** halfway (there); **en el ~** on the way, en route; ~ **de** on the way to; ~ **particular** private road; ~ **vecinal** country road; **C~s, Canales y Puertos** (*UNIV*) Civil Engineering; **ir por buen ~** (*fig*) to be on the right track.

camión [kámyon'] *nm* truck (*US*), lorry (*Brit*); ~ **de bomberos** fire engine.

camionero [kámyone'ro] *nm* truck (*US*) *o* lorry (*Brit*) driver, trucker (*esp US*).

camioneta [kámyone'tá] *nf* van, light truck; (*AM: carro*) station wagon.

camisa [kámē'sá] *nf* shirt; (*BOT*) skin; ~ **de dormir** nightdress; ~ **de fuerza** straitjacket.

camisería [kámēserē'á] *nf* outfitter's (shop).

camiseta [kámēsc'tá] *nf* tee-shirt; (*ropa interior*) vest; (*de deportista*) top.

camisón [kámēson'] *nm* nightie, nightgown.

camomila [kámomē'lá] *nf* camomile.

camorra [kámo'rrá] *nf*: **armar ~** to kick up a row; **buscar ~** to look for trouble.

campamento [kámpámen'to] *nm* camp.

campana [kámpá'ná] *nf* bell.

campanada [kámpáná'ðá] *nf* peal.

campanario [kámpáná'ryo] *nm* belfry.

campanilla [kámpánē'yá] *nf* (*campana*) small bell.

campante [kámpán'te] *a*: **siguió tan ~** he went on as if nothing had happened.

campaña [kámpá'nyá] *nf* (*MIL, POL*) campaign; **hacer ~** (**en pro de/contra**) to campaign (for/against); ~ **de venta** sales campaign.

campechano, a [kámpetchá'no, á] *a* open.

campeón, ona [kámpeon', o'ná] *nm/f* champion.

campeonato [kámpeoná'to] *nm* championship.

campesino, a [kámpesē'no, á] *a* country *cpd*, rural; (*gente*) peasant *cpd* ♦ *nm/f* countryman/woman; (*agricultor*) farmer.

campestre [kámpes'tre] *a* country *cpd*, rural.

camping [kám'pēn] *nm* camping; (*lugar*) campsite; **ir de** *o* **hacer ~** to go camping.

campiña [kámpē'nyá] *nf* countryside.

campista [kámpē'stá] *nm/f* camper.

campo [kám'po] *nm* (*fuera de la ciudad*) country, countryside; (*AGR, ELEC, INFORM*) field; (*de fútbol*) field (*US*), pitch (*Brit*); (*de golf*) course; (*MIL*) camp; ~ **de batalla** battlefield; ~ **de minas** minefield; ~ **petrolífero** oilfield; ~ **visual** field of vision; ~ **de concentración/de internación/de trabajo** concentration/internment/labor camp.

camposanto [kámposán'to] *nm* cemetery.

CAMPSA [kámp'sá] *nf abr* (*Esp COM*) = *Compañía Arrendataria del Monopolio de Petróleos, S.A.*

campus [kám'pōōs] *nm inv* (*UNIV*) campus.

camuflaje [kámōōflá'he] *nm* camouflage.

can [kán] *nm* dog, mutt (*fam*).

cana [ká'ná] *nf V* **cano**.

Canadá [kánáthá'] *nm* Canada.

canadiense [kánáthyen'se] *a, nm/f* Canadian ♦ *nf* fur-lined jacket.

canal [kánál'] *nm* canal; (*GEO*) channel, strait; (*de televisión*) channel; (*de tejado*) gutter; **C~ de la Mancha** English Channel; **C~ de Panamá** Panama Canal.

canalice [kánálē'se] *etc vb V* **canalizar**.

canalizar [kánálēsár'] *vt* to channel.

canalón [kánálon'] *nm* (*conducto vertical*) drainpipe; (*del tejado*) gutter; **canalones** *nmpl* (*CULIN*) cannelloni.

canalla [káná'yá] *nf* rabble, mob ♦ *nm* swine.

canallada [kánáyá'ðá] *nf* (*hecho*) dirty trick.

canapé, pl canapés [kánápe', kánápes'] *nm* sofa, settee; (*CULIN*) canapé.

Canarias [káná'ryás] *nfpl*: **las (Islas) ~** the Canaries, the Canary Isles.

canario, a [kaná'ryo, á] *a* of *o* from the Canary Isles ♦ *nm/f* native *o* inhabitant of the Canary Isles ♦ *nm* (*ZOOL*) canary.

canasta [káná'stá] *nf* (round) basket.

canastilla [kánástē'yá] *nf* small basket; (*de niño*) layette.

canasto [káná'sto] *nm* large basket.

cancela [kánse'lá] *nf* (wrought-iron) gate.

cancelación [kánselásyon'] *nf* cancellation.

cancelar [kánselár'] *vt* to cancel; (*una deuda*) to write off.

cáncer [kán'ser] *nm* (*MED*) cancer; **C~** (*ASTRO*) Cancer.

canciller [kánsēyer'] *nm* chancellor.

canción [kánsyon'] *nf* song; ~ **de cuna** lullaby.

cancionero [kánsyone'ro] *nm* song book.

cancha [kántch'á] *nf* (*de baloncesto, tenis etc*) court; (*AM: de fútbol*) field (*US*), pitch (*Brit*).

candado [kándá'tho] *nm* padlock.

candela [kánde'lá] *nf* candle.

candelabro [kándelá'bro] *nm* candelabra.

candelero [kándele'ro] *nm* (*para vela*) candlestick; (*de aceite*) oil lamp.

candente [kánden'te] *a* red-hot; (*tema*) burning.

candidato, a [kándéthá'to, á] *nm/f* candidate; (*para puesto*) applicant.

candidatura [kándéthátoō'rá] *nf* candidature.

candidez [kándéthes'] *nf* (*sencillez*) simplicity; (*simpleza*) naiveté.

cándido, a [kán'détho, á] *a* simple; naive.

candil [kándēl'] *nm* oil lamp.

candilejas [kándēle'hás] *nfpl* (*TEATRO*) footlights.

candor [kándor'] *nm* (*sinceridad*) frankness; (*inocencia*) innocence.

canela [káne'lá] *nf* cinnamon.

canelo [káne'lo] *nm*: **hacer el** ~ to act the fool.

cangrejo [kángre'ho] *nm* crab.

canguro [kángoō'ro] *nm* (*ZOOL*) kangaroo; (*de niños*) baby-sitter; **hacer de** ~ to baby-sit.

caníbal [káné'bál] *a, nm/f* cannibal.

canica [káné'ká] *nf* marble.

canícula [káné'koōlá] *nf* midsummer heat.

caniche [kánētch'e] *nm* poodle.

canijo, a [káné'ho, á] *a* frail, sickly.

canilla [káné'yá] *nf* (*TEC*) bobbin.

canino, a [káné'no, á] *a* canine ♦ *nm* canine (tooth).

canje [kánhe'] *nm* exchange; (*trueque*) swap.

canjear [kánheár'] *vt* to exchange; (*trocar*) to swap.

cano, a [ká'no, á] *a* gray- o grey-haired, white-haired ♦ *nf* (*tb*: **canas**) white o gray hair; **tener canas** to be going gray.

canoa [káno'á] *nf* canoe.

canon [ká'non] *nm* canon; (*pensión*) rent; (*COM*) tax.

canonice [kánoné'se] *etc vb* V **canonizar.**

canońico, a [káno'nēko, á] *a*: **derecho** ~ canon law.

canónigo [káno'nēgo] *nm* canon.

canonizar [kánonēsár'] *vt* to canonize.

canoro, a [káno'ro, á] *a* melodious.

cansado, a [kánsá'tho, á] *a* tired, weary; (*tedioso*) tedious, boring; **estoy** ~ **de hacerlo** I'm sick of doing it.

cansancio [kánsán'syo] *nm* tiredness, fatigue.

cansar [kánsár'] *vt* (*fatigar*) to tire, tire out; (*aburrir*) to bore; (*fastidiar*) to bother; ~**se** *vr* to tire, get tired; (*aburrirse*) to get bored.

cantabro, a [kántá'bro, á] *a, nm/f* Cantabrian.

cantábrico, a [kántá'brēko, á] *a* Cantabrian; **Mar C~** Bay of Biscay; **(Montes) C~s, Cordillera Cantábrica** Cantabrian Mountains.

cantante [kántán'te] *a* singing ♦ *nm/f* singer.

cantaor, a [kántáor', á] *nm/f* Flamenco singer.

cantar [kántár'] *vt* to sing ♦ *vi* to sing; (*insecto*) to chirp; (*rechinar*) to squeak; (*fam: criminal*) to squeal ♦ *nm* (*acción*) singing; (*canción*) song; (*poema*) poem; ~ **a uno las cuarenta** to give sb a piece of one's mind; ~ **a dos voces** to sing a duet.

cántara [kán'tárá] *nf* large pitcher.

cántaro [kán'táro] *nm* pitcher, jug.

cante [kán'te] *nm*: ~ **jondo** flamenco singing.

cantera [kánte'rá] *nf* quarry.

cántico [kán'tēko] *nm* (*REL*) canticle; (*fig*) song.

cantidad [kántētháth'] *nf* quantity, amount; (*ECON*) sum ♦ *ad* (*fam*) a lot; ~ **alzada** lump sum; ~ **de** lots of.

cantilena [kántēle'ná] *nf* = **cantinela.**

cantimplora [kántēmplo'rá] *nf* (*frasco*) water bottle, canteen.

cantina [kántē'ná] *nf* cafeteria (*US*), canteen (*Brit*); (*de estación*) buffet.

cantinela [kántēne'lá] *nf* ballad, song.

canto [kán'to] *nm* singing; (*canción*) song; (*borde*) edge, rim; (*de un cuchillo*) back; ~ **rodado** boulder.

cantón [kánton'] *nm* canton.

cantor, a [kántor', á] *nm/f* singer.

canturrear [kántoōrreár'] *vi* to sing softly.

canuto [kánoō'to] *nm* (*tubo*) small tube; (*fam: droga*) joint.

caña [ká'nyá] *nf* (*BOT: tallo*) stem, stalk; (*carrizo*) reed; (*vaso*) tumbler; (*de cerveza*) glass of beer; (*ANAT*) shinbone; ~ **de azúcar** sugar cane; ~ **de pescar** fishing rod.

cañada [kányá'thá] *nf* (*entre dos montañas*) gully, ravine; (*camino*) cattle track.

cáñamo [ká'nyámo] *nm* (*BOT*) hemp.

cañaveral [kányáverál'] *nm* (*BOT*) reedbed; (*AGR*) sugar-cane field.

caño [ká'nyo] *nm* (*tubo*) tube, pipe; (*de aguas servidas*) sewer; (*MUS*) pipe; (*NAUT*) navigation channel; (*de fuente*) jet.

cañón [kányon'] *nm* (*MIL*) cannon; (*de fusil*) barrel; (*GEO*) canyon, gorge.

cañonazo [kányoná'so] *nm* (*MIL*) gunshot.

cañonera [kányone'rá] *nf* (*tb*: **lancha** ~)

gunboat.
caoba [káo'ḥá] *nf* mahogany.
caos [ká'os] *nm* chaos.
caótico, a [káo'tēko, á] *a* chaotic.
cap. *abr* (= *capítulo*) ch.
capa [ká'pá] *nf* cloak, cape; (*CULIN*) coating; (*GEO*) layer, stratum; (*de pintura*) coat; **de ~ y espada** cloak-and-dagger; **so ~ de** under the pretext of; **~s sociales** social groups.
capacidad [kápásēḥáḥ'] *nf* (*medida*) capacity; (*aptitud*) capacity, ability; **una sala con ~ para 900** a hall seating 900; **~ adquisitiva** purchasing power.
capacitación [kápásētásyon'] *nf* training.
capacitar [kápásētár'] *vt*: **~ a uno para algo** to qualify sb for sth; (*TEC*) to train sb for sth.
capacho [kápátch'o] *nm* wicker basket.
capar [kápár'] *vt* to castrate, geld.
caparazón [kápáráson'] *nm* (*ZOOL*) shell.
capataz [kápátás'] *nm* foreman.
capaz [kápás'] *a* able, capable; (*amplio*) capacious, roomy.
capcioso, a [kápsyo'so, á] *a* wily, deceitful; **pregunta capciosa** trick question.
capellán [kápeyán'] *nm* chaplain; (*sacerdote*) priest.
caperuza [káperōō'sá] *nf* hood; (*de bolígrafo*) cap.
capicúa [kápēkōō'á] *nf* reversible number, *e.g. 1441.*
capilar [kápēlár'] *a* hair *cpd.*
capilla [kápē'yá] *nf* chapel.
capital [kápētál'] *a* capital ♦ *nm* (*COM*) capital ♦ *nf* (*ciudad*) capital (city); **~ activo/ en acciones** working/share *o* equity capital; **~ arriesgado** venture capital; **~ autorizado** *o* **social** authorized capital; **~ emitido** issued capital; **~ improductivo** idle money; **~ invertido** *o* **utilizado** invested capital; **~ pagado** paid-up capital **~ de riesgo** risk capital; **~ social** equity *o* share capital; **inversión de ~es** capital investment.
capitalice [kápētálē'se] *etc vb V* **capitalizar.**
capitalismo [kápētálēs'mo] *nm* capitalism.
capitalista [kápētálē'stá] *a, nm/f* capitalist.
capitalizar [kápētálēsár'] *vt* to capitalize.
capitán [kápētán'] *nm* captain; (*fig*) leader.
capitana [kápētá'ná] *nf* flagship.
capitanear [kápētáneár'] *vt* to captain.
capitanía [kápētánē'á] *nf* captaincy.
capitel [kápētel'] *nm* (*ARQ*) capital.
capitolio [kápēto'lyo] *nm* capitol.
capitulación [kápētōōlásyon'] *nf* (*rendición*) capitulation, surrender; (*acuerdo*) agreement, pact; **capitulaciones matrimoniales** marriage contract *sg.*
capitular [kápētōōlár'] *vi* to come to terms, make an agreement; (*MIL*) to surrender.

capítulo [kápē'tōōlo] *nm* chapter.
capó [kápo'] *nm* (*AUTO*) hood (*US*), bonnet (*Brit*).
capón [kápon'] *nm* capon.
caporal [káporál'] *nm* chief, leader.
capota [kápo'tá] *nf* (*de mujer*) bonnet; (*AUTO*) top (*US*), hood (*Brit*).
capote [kápo'te] *nm* (*abrigo: de militar*) greatcoat; (*de torero*) cloak.
Capricornio [káprēkor'nyo] *nm* Capricorn.
capricho [káprētch'o] *nm* whim, caprice.
caprichoso, a [káprētcho'so, á] *a* capricious.
cápsula [káp'sōōlá] *nf* capsule; **~ espacial** space capsule.
captar [káptár'] *vt* (*comprender*) to understand; (*RADIO*) to pick up; (*atención, apoyo*) to attract.
captura [káptōō'rá] *nf* capture; (*JUR*) arrest.
capturar [káptōōrár'] *vt* to capture; (*JUR*) to arrest; (*datos*) to input.
capucha [kápōōtch'á] *nf* hood, cowl.
capullo [kápōō'yo] *nm* (*ZOOL*) cocoon; (*BOT*) bud; (*fam*) idiot.
caqui [ká'kē] *nm* khaki.
cara [ká'rá] *nf* (*ANAT, de moneda*) face; (*aspecto*) appearance; (*de disco*) side; (*fig*) boldness; (*descara*) nerve ♦ *prep*: **~ a** facing; **de ~ a** opposite, facing; **dar la ~** to face the consequences; **echar algo en ~ a uno** to reproach sb for sth; **¿~ o cruz?** heads or tails?; **¡ qué ~ más dura!** what a nerve!; **de una ~** (*disquete*) single-sided.
carabina [kárábē'ná] *nf* carbine, rifle; (*persona*) chaperone.
carabinero [kárábēne'ro] *nm* (*de aduana*) customs officer; (*AM*) gendarme.
Caracas [kárá'kás] *nm* Caracas.
caracol [kárákol'] *nm* (*ZOOL*) snail; (*concha*) (sea)shell; **escalera de ~** spiral staircase.
caracolear [kárákoleár'] *vi* (*caballo*) to prance about.
carácter, *pl* **caracteres** [kárák'ter, kárákte'res] *nm* character; **~ de cambio de página** (*INFORM*) form feed character; **caracteres de imprenta** (*TIP*) type(face) *sg*; **~ libre** (*INFORM*) wildcard character; **tener buen/mal ~** to be good-natured/bad tempered.
caracterice [kárákterē'se] *etc vb V* **caracterizar.**
característico, a [kárákterē'stēko, á] *a* characteristic ♦ *nf* characteristic.
caracterizar [kárákterēsár'] *vt* (*distinguir*) to characterize, typify; (*honrar*) to confer (a) distinction on.
caradura [kárádȟōō'rá] *nm/f* sassy (*US*) *o* cheeky person; **es un ~** he's got a nerve.

carajo [kárá'ho] *nm* (*fam!*): ¡∼! shit!(*!*); ¡qué ∼ ! what the hell!; **me importa un ∼** I don't give a damn.

caramba [kárám'bá] *excl* well!, good gracious!

carámbano [kárám'báno] *nm* icicle.

carambola [kárámbo'lá] *nf*: **por** ∼ by a fluke.

caramelo [káráme'lo] *nm* (*dulce*) candy (*US*), sweet (*Brit*); (*azúcar fundido*) caramel.

carapacho [kárápátch'o] *nm* shell, carapace.

caraqueño, a [kuráke'nyo, á] *a* of *o* from Caracas ♦ *nm/f* native *o* inhabitant of Caracas.

carátula [kárá'toōlá] *nf* (*máscara*) mask; (*TEATRO*): **la** ∼ the stage.

caravana [kárá̱há'ná] *nf* caravan; (*fig*) group; (*de autos*) line of traffic (*US*), tailback (*Brit*).

carbón [kárḅon'] *nm* coal; ∼ **de leña** charcoal; **papel** ∼ carbon paper.

carbonatado, a [kárḅonotá'ṭ̣ho, á] *a* carbonated.

carbonato [kárḅoná'to] *nm* carbonate; ∼ **sódico** sodium carbonate.

carboncillo [kárḅonsē'yo] *nm* (*ARTE*) charcoal.

carbonice [kárḅonsē'se] *etc vb* V **carbonizar**.

carbonilla [kárḅonē'yá] *nf* coal dust.

carbonizar [kárḅonēsár'] *vt* to carbonize; (*quemar*) to char; **quedar carbonizado** (*ELEC*) to be electrocuted.

carbono [kárḅo'no] *nm* carbon.

carburador [kárḅoōráṭho̱r'] *nm* carburetor (*US*), carburettor (*Brit*).

carburante [kárḅoōrán'te] *nm* fuel.

carca [kár'ká] *a*, *nm/f inv* reactionary.

carcajada [kárkáhá'ṭ̣há] *nf* (loud) laugh, guffaw.

cárcel [kár'sel] *nf* prison, jail; (*TEC*) clamp.

carcelero, a [kársele'ro, á] *a* prison *cpd* ♦ *nm/f* guard (*US*), warder (*Brit*).

carcomer [kárkomer'] *vt* to bore into, eat into; (*fig*) to undermine; ∼**se** *vr* to become worm-eaten; (*fig*) to decay.

carcomido, a [kárkomē'ṭho, á] *a* worm-eaten; (*fig*) rotten.

cardar [kárḍár'] *vt* (*TEC*) to card, comb.

cardenal [kárḍenál'] *nm* (*REL*) cardinal; (*MED*) bruise.

cárdeno, a [kár'ṭ̣heno, á] *a* purple; (*lívido*) livid.

cardíaco, a [kárḍē'áko, á] *a* cardiac, heart *cpd*.

cardinal [kárḍenál'] *a* cardinal.

cardiólogo, a [kárḍyo'logo, á] *nm/f* cardiologist.

cardo [kár'ṭ̣ho] *nm* thistle.

carear [káreár'] *vt* to bring face to face;

(*comparar*) to compare; ∼**se** *vr* to come face to face, meet.

carecer [káreser'] *vi*: ∼ **de** to lack, be in need of.

carencia [káren'syá] *nf* lack; (*escasez*) shortage; (*MED*) deficiency.

carente [káren'te] *a*: ∼ **de** lacking in, devoid of.

carestía [kárestē'á] *nf* (*escasez*) scarcity, shortage; (*COM*) high cost; **época de** ∼ period of shortage.

careta [káre'tá] *nf* mask.

carey [káre'ē] *nm* tortoiseshell.

carezca [káres'ká] *etc vb* V **carecer**.

carga [kár'ḡá] *nf* (*peso*, *ELEC*) load; (*de barco*) cargo, freight; (*FINANZAS*) tax, duty; (*MIL*) charge; (*INFORM*) loading; (*obligación*, *responsabilidad*) duty, obligation; ∼ **aérea** (*COM*) air cargo; ∼ **útil** (*COM*) payload; **la** ∼ **fiscal** the tax burden.

cargadero [kárḡáṭ̣he'ro] *nm* loading bay.

cargado, a [kárḡá'ṭ̣ho, á] *a* loaded; (*ELEC*) live; (*café*, *té*) strong; (*cielo*) overcast.

cargador, a [kárḡáṭ̣hor', á] *nm/f* loader; (*NAUT*) stevedore ♦ *nm* (*INFORM*): ∼ **de discos** disk pack.

cargamento [kárḡámen'to] *nm* (*acción*) loading; (*mercancías*) load, cargo.

cargante [kárḡán'te] *a* (*persona*) trying.

cargar [kárḡár'] *vt* (*barco*, *arma*) to load; (*ELEC*) to charge; (*impuesto*) to impose; (*COM*: *algo en cuenta*) to charge, debit; (*MIL*: *enemigo*) to charge ♦ *vi* (*AUTO*) to load (up); (*inclinarse*) to lean; (*INFORM*) to load, feed in; ∼ **con** to pick up, carry away; ∼**se** *vr* (*fam*: *estropear*) to break; (: *matar*) to bump off; (*ELEC*) to become charged.

cargo [kár'ḡo] *nm* (*COM etc*) charge, debit; (*puesto*) post, office; (*responsabilidad*) duty, obligation; (*fig*) weight, burden; (*JUR*) charge; **altos** ∼**s** high-ranking officials; **una cantidad en** ∼ **a uno** a sum chargeable to sb; **hacerse** ∼ **de** to take charge *o* responsibility for.

cargue [kár'ḡe] *etc vb* V **cargar**.

carguero [kárḡe'ro] *nm* freighter, cargo boat; (*avión*) freight plane.

Caribe [kárē'ḅe] *nm*: **el** ∼ the Caribbean.

caribeño, a [kárēḅe'nyo, á] *a* Caribbean.

caricatura [kárēḅátoō'rá] *nf* caricature.

caricia [kárē'syá] *nf* caress; (*a animal*) pat, stroke.

caridad [kárēṭ̣háṭ̣h'] *nf* charity.

caries [ká'ryes] *nf inv* (*MED*) tooth decay.

carilla [kárē'yá] *nf* (*TIP*) page.

cariño [kárē'nyo] *nm* affection, love; (*caricia*) caress; (*en carta*) love ... .

cariñoso, a [kárēnyo'so, á] *a* affectionate.

carioca [káryo'ká] *a* (*AM*) of *o* from Rio de Janeiro ♦ *nm/f* native *o* inhabitant of Rio de

Janeiro.

carisma [kárēs'má] *nm* charisma.

caritativo, a [kárētátē'ṇo, á] *a* charitable.

cariz [kárēs'] *nm*: **tener** *o* **tomar buen/mal** ~ to look good/bad.

carmesí [kármesē'] *a, nm* crimson.

carmín [kármēn'] *nm* (*color*) carmine; ~ **(de labios)** lipstick.

carnal [kárnál'] *a* carnal; **primo** ~ first cousin.

carnaval [kárnàḅál'] *nm* carnival.

carne [kár'ne] *nf* flesh; (*CULIN*) meat; ~ **de cañón** cannon fodder; ~ **de cerdo/de cordero/de ternera/de vaca** pork/lamb/veal/beef; ~ **picada** ground meat (*US*), mince (*Brit*); ~ **de gallina** (*fig*) gooseflesh.

carné [kár'ne] *nm* = **carnet**.

carnero [kárne'ro] *nm* sheep, ram; (*carne*) mutton.

carnet, *pl* **carnets** [kár'ne', kárnes'] *nm*: ~ **de conducir** driver's license; ~ **de identidad** identity card.

carnicería [kárnēserē'á] *nf* butcher's (shop); (*fig: matanza*) carnage, slaughter.

carnicero, a [kárnēse'ro, á] *a* carnivorous ♦ *nm/f* (*tb fig*) butcher ♦ *nm* carnivore.

carnívoro, a [kárnē'ḅoro, á] *a* carnivorous ♦ *nm* carnivore.

carnoso, a [kárno'so, á] *a* beefy, fat.

caro, a [ká'ro, á] *a* dear; (*COM*) expensive ♦ *ad* dearly; **vender** ~ to sell at a high price.

carpa [kár'pá] *nf* (*pez*) carp; (*de circo*) big top; (*AM: de camping*) tent.

carpeta [kárpe'tá] *nf* folder, file.

carpetazo [kárpetá'so] *nm*: **dar** ~ **a** to shelve.

carpintería [kárpēnterē'á] *nf* carpentry.

carpintero [kárpēnte'ro] *nm* carpenter; **pájaro** ~ woodpecker.

carraca [kárrá'ká] *nf* (*DEPORTE*) rattle.

carraspear [kárráspeár'] *vi* (*aclararse*) to clear one's throat.

carraspera [kárráspe'rá] *nf* hoarseness.

carrera [kárre'rá] *nf* (*acción*) run(ning); (*espacio recorrido*) run; (*certamen*) race; (*trayecto*) course; (*profesión*) career; (*ESCOL, UNIV*) course; (*de taxi*) ride; (*en medias*) ladder; **a la** ~ at (full) speed; **caballo de** ~(s) racehorse; ~ **de armamentos** arms race.

carrerilla [kárrerē'yá] *nf*: **decir algo de** ~ to reel sth off; **tomar** ~ to get up speed.

carreta [kárre'tá] *nf* wagon, cart.

carrete [kárre'te] *nm* reel, spool; (*TEC*) coil.

carretera [kárrete'rá] *nf* (main) road, highway; ~ **nacional** ≈ state highway (*US*), A road (*Brit*); ~ **de circunvalación** beltway (*US*), ring road (*Brit*).

carretilla [kárretē'yá] *nf* trolley; (*AGR*) (wheel)barrow.

carril [kárrēl'] *nm* furrow; (*de autopista*) lane; (*FERRO*) rail.

carrillo [kárrē'yo] *nm* (*ANAT*) cheek; (*TEC*) pulley.

carrizo [kárrē'so] *nm* reed.

carro [ká'rro] *nm* cart, wagon; (*MIL*) tank; (*AM: coche*) car; (*TIP*) carriage; ~ **blindado** armored car.

carrocería [kárroserē'á] *nf* body, bodywork *q* (*Brit*).

carroña [kárro'nyà] *nf* carrion *q*.

carroza [kárro'sá] *nf* (*vehículo*) coach ♦ *nm/ f* (*fam*) old fogey.

carrusel [kárrōōsel'] *nm* merry-go-round.

carta [kár'tá] *nf* letter; (*CULIN*) menu; (*naipe*) card; (*mapa*) map; (*JUR*) document; ~ **aérea** aerogramme; ~ **de crédito** credit card; ~ **de crédito documentaria** (*COM*) documentary letter of credit; ~ **de crédito irrevocable** (*COM*) irrevocable letter of credit; ~ **certificada/urgente** registered/special delivery letter; ~ **marítima** chart; ~ **de pedido** (*COM*) order; ~ **verde** (*AUTO*) *international insurance certificate*; ~ **de vinos** wine list; **echar una** ~ **al correo** to mail a letter; **echar las** ~**s a uno** to tell sb's fortune.

cartabón [kártàḅon'] *nm* triangle (*US*), set square (*Brit*).

cartel [kártel'] *nm* (*anuncio*) poster, placard; (*ESCOL*) wall chart; (*COM*) cartel.

cartelera [kártele'rá] *nf* billboard; (*en periódico etc*) listings *pl*, entertainments guide; "**en** ~" "showing".

cartera [kárte'rá] *nf* (*de bolsillo*) wallet; (*de colegial, cobrador*) satchel; (*de señora*) handbag; (*para documentos*) briefcase; **ministro sin** ~ (*POL*) minister without portfolio; **ocupa la** ~ **de Agricultura** he is Minister of Agriculture; ~ **de pedidos** (*COM*) order book; **efectos en** ~ (*ECON*) holdings.

carterista [kárterē'stá] *nm/f* pickpocket.

cartero [kárte'ro] *nm* mailman (*US*), postman (*Brit*).

cartílago [kártē'láḡo] *nm* cartilage.

cartilla [kártē'yá] *nf* (*ESCOL*) primer, first reading book; ~ **de ahorros** bank book.

cartón [kárton'] *nm* cardboard.

cartucho [kártōōtch'o] *nm* (*MIL*) cartridge; (*bolsita*) paper cone; ~ **de datos** (*INFORM*) data cartridge.

cartulina [kártōōlē'ná] *nf* fine cardboard, card.

CASA [ká'sá] *nf abr* (*Esp AVIAT*) = *Construcciones Aeronáuticas S.A.*

casa [ká'sá] *nf* house; (*hogar*) home; (*edificio*) building; (*COM*) firm, company; ~ **consistorial** town hall; ~ **de huéspedes** boarding house; ~ **de socorro** first aid station (*US*) *o* post (*Brit*); ~ **de citas** (*fam*) brothel; **ir a** ~ to go home; **salir de** ~ to

go out; (*para siempre*) to leave home;
echar la ~ por la ventana (*gastar*) to
spare no expense.
casadero, a [kásáɖɪe'ro, á] *a* marriageable.
casado, a [kásá'ɵo, á] *a* married ♦ *nm/f*
married man/woman.
casamiento [kásámyen'to] *nm* marriage,
wedding.
casar [kásár'] *vt* to marry; (*JUR*) to quash,
annul; **~se** *vr* to marry, get married; **~se**
por lo civil to have a civil wedding, get
married in a registry office (*Brit*) .
cascabel [káskábel'] *nm* (small) bell;
(*ZOOL*) rattlesnake.
cascada [káská'ɵa] *nf* waterfall.
cascajo [káská'ho] *nm* gravel, stone chippings *pl.*
cascanueces [káskánwe'ses] *nm inv*: **un ~**
a pair of nutcrackers.
cascar [káskár'] *vt* to split; (*nuez*) to crack
♦ *vi* to chatter; **~se** *vr* to crack, split,
break (open).
cáscara [kás'kárá] *nf* (*de huevo, fruta seca*)
shell; (*de fruta*) skin; (*de limón*) peel.
cascarón [káskáron'] *nm* (broken) eggshell.
cascarrabias [káskárrá'ⁿyás] *nm/f inv* (*fam*)
hothead.
casco [kás'ko] *nm* (*de bombero, soldado*)
helmet; (*cráneo*) skull; (*NAUT: de barco*)
hull; (*ZOOL: de caballo*) hoof; (*botella*)
empty bottle; (*de ciudad*): **el ~ antiguo**
the old part; **el ~ urbano** the town center.
caserío [kásere'o] *nm* hamlet, group of
houses; (*casa*) country house.
casero, a [káse'ro, á] *a*: **ser muy ~** (*perso-*
na) to be homeloving; **"comida casera"**
"home cooking" ♦ *nm/f* (*propietario*)
landlord/lady; (*COM*) property manager
(*US*), house agent (*Brit*).
caserón [káseron'] *nm* large (ramshackle)
house.
caseta [káse'tá] *nf* hut; (*para bañista*) cubicle; (*de feria*) stall.
casete [káse'te] *nm o f* cassette.
casi [ká'se] *ad* almost; **~ nunca** hardly ever,
almost never; **~ nada** next to nothing; **~**
te caes you almost o nearly fell.
casilla [káse'ʎyá] *nf* (*casita*) hut, cabin; (*TEA-*
TRO) box office; (*para cartas*) box; (*AJE-*
DREZ) square; **sacar a uno de sus ~s** to
make sb lose his temper.
casillero [káseʎe'ro] *nm* (mail) boxes.
casino [káse'no] *nm* club; (*de juego*) casino.
caso [ká'so] *nm* case; (*suceso*) event; **en ~**
de ... in case of ...; **~ es que** the fact is
that; **en el mejor de los ~s** at best; **en**
ese ~ in that case; **en todo ~** in any case;
en último ~ as a last resort; **hacer ~ a** to
pay attention to; **hacer o omiso de** to fail
to mention, pass over; **hacer o venir al ~**
to be relevant.

caspa [kás'pá] *nf* dandruff.
Caspio [kás'pyo] *a*: **Mar ~** Caspian Sea.
casque [kás'ke] *etc vb* V **cascar.**
cassette [káset'] *nf o m* cassette.
casta [ká'stá] *nf* caste; (*raza*) breed; (*li-*
naje) lineage.
castaña [kástá'nyá] *nf* V **castaño.**
castañetear [kástányeteár'] *vi* (*dientes*) to
chatter.
castaño, a [kástá'nyo, á] *a* chestnut
(-colored), brown ♦ *nm* chestnut tree ♦ *nf*
chestnut; (*fam: golpe*) punch; **~ de Indias**
horse chestnut tree.
castañuelas [kástánywe'lás] *nfpl* castanets.
castellano, a [kásteyá'no, á] *a* Castilian;
(*fam*) Spanish ♦ *nm/f* Castilian; (*fam*)
Spaniard ♦ *nm* (*LING*) Castilian, Spanish.
castellonense [kásteyonen'se] *a* of o from
Castellón de la Plana ♦ *nm/f* native o inhabitant of Castellón de la Plana.
castidad [kásteɖáɖ'] *nf* chastity, purity.
castigar [kástegár'] *vt* to punish; (*DEPORTE*)
to penalize; (*afligir*) to afflict.
castigo [káste'go] *nm* punishment; (*DE-*
PORTE) penalty.
castigue [káste'ge] *etc vb* V **castigar.**
Castilla [káste'yá] *nf* Castile.
castillo [káste'yo] *nm* castle.
castizo, a [káste'so, á] *a* (*LING*) pure; (*de*
buena casta) purebred, pedigree; (*auténti-*
co) genuine.
casto, a [ká'sto, á] *a* chaste, pure.
castor [kástor'] *nm* beaver.
castrar [kástrár'] *vt* to castrate; (*gato*) to
neuter; (*BOT*) to prune.
castrense [kástren'se] *a* army *cpd*, military.
casual [káswál'] *a* chance, accidental.
casualidad [káswáleɖáɖ'] *nf* chance, accident; (*combinación de circunstancias*)
coincidence; **¡qué ~!** what a coincidence!
casualmente [káswálmen'te] *ad* by chance.
cataclismo [kátáklɪs'mo] *nm* cataclysm.
catador [kátáɖor'] *nm* taster.
catadura [kátáɖoo'rá] *nf* (*aspecto*) looks *pl.*
catalán, ana [kátálán', á'ná] *a, nm/f* Catalan
♦ *nm* (*LING*) Catalan.
catalizador [kátálesáɖor'] *nm* catalyst.
catalogar [kátálogár'] *vt* to catalog (*US*),
catalogue; **~ (de)** (*fig*) to classify (as).
catálogo [kátá'logo] *nm* catalog (*US*), catalogue.
catalogue [kátálo'ge] *etc vb* V **catalogar.**
Cataluña [kátáloo'nyá] *nf* Catalonia.
catar [kátár'] *vt* to taste, sample.
catarata [kátárá'tá] *nf* (*GEO*) (water)fall;
(*MED*) cataract.
catarro [kátá'rro] *nm* catarrh; (*constipado*)
cold.
catástrofe [kátás'trofe] *nf* catastrophe.
catecismo [káteses'mo] *nm* catechism.
cátedra [ká'teɖrá] *nf* (*UNIV*) chair, pro-

fessorship; (*ESCOL*) senior teacher's post; **sentar ~ sobre un argumento** to take one's stand on an argument.

catedral [kåteťɥrál'] *nf* cathedral.

catedrático, a [kåteťɥrá'tēko, á] *nm/f* professor; (*ESCOL*) senior teacher.

categoría [kåteᵍorē'á] *nf* category; (*rango*) rank, standing; (*calidad*) quality; **de ~** (*hotel*) top-class; **de baja ~** (*oficial*) low-ranking; **de segunda ~** second-rate; **no tiene ~** he has no standing.

categórico, a [kåteᵍo'rēko, á] *a* categorical.

caterva [kåter'hå] *nf* throng, crowd.

cateto, a [kåte'to, á] *nm/f* yokel.

cátodo [kå'toťɥo] *nm* cathode.

catolicismo [kátolēsēs'mo] *nm* Catholicism.

católico, a [kåto'lēko, á] *a, nm/f* Catholic.

catorce [kátor'se] *num* fourteen.

Cáucaso [kå'ōōkáso] *nm* Caucasus.

cauce [kå'ōōse] *nm* (*de río*) riverbed; (*fig*) channel.

caución [kåōōsyon'] *nf* bail.

caucionar [kåōōsyonár'] *vt* (*JUR*) to bail (out), go bail for.

caucho [kå'ōōtcho] *nm* rubber; (*AM*: *llanta*) tire (*US*), tyre (*Brit*).

caudal [kåōōťɥál'] *nm* (*de río*) volume, flow; (*fortuna*) wealth; (*abundancia*) abundance.

caudaloso, a [kåōōťɥálo'so, á] *a* (*río*) large; (*persona*) wealthy, rich.

caudillo [kåōōťɥē'yo] *nm* leader, chief.

caudillaje [kåōōťɥeᵞá'he] *nm* leadership.

causa [kå'ōōsá] *nf* cause; (*razón*) reason; (*JUR*) lawsuit, case; **a o por ~ de** because of, on account of.

causar [kåōōsár'] *vt* to cause.

cáustico, a [kå'ōōstēko, á] *a* caustic.

cautela [kåōōte'lá] *nf* caution, cautiousness.

cauteloso, a [kåōōtelo'so, á] *a* cautious, wary.

cautivar [kåōōtēhár'] *vt* to capture; (*fig*) to captivate.

cautiverio [kåōōtēhe'ryo] *nm*, **cautividad** [kåōōtēheťɥáťɥ'] *nf* captivity.

cautivo, a [kåōōtē'ho, á] *a, nm/f* captive.

cauto, a [kå'ōōto, á] *a* cautious, careful.

cava [kå'hå] *nf* (*bodega*) (wine) cellar ♦ *nm* (*vino*) champagne-type wine.

cavar [kåhár'] *vt* to dig; (*AGR*) to till.

caverna [kåher'ná] *nf* cave, cavern.

cavernoso, a [kåherno'so, á] *a* cavernous; (*voz*) resounding.

cavidad [kåheťɥáťɥ'] *nf* cavity.

cavilación [kåhēlásyon'] *nf* deep thought.

cavilar [kåhēlár'] *vt* to ponder.

cayado [kåyá'ťɥo] *nm* (*de pastor*) crook; (*de obispo*) crozier.

cayendo [kåyen'do] *etc vb V* **caer.**

caza [kå'sá] *nf* (*acción: gen*) hunting; (: *con fusil*) shooting; (*una ~*) hunt, chase; (*animales*) game; **coto de ~** hunting estate ♦

nm (*AVIAT*) fighter.

cazador, a [kåsáťɥor', á] *nm/f* hunter/huntress ♦ *nf* jacket.

cazaejecutivos [kåsáehekōōtē'hos] *nm inv* (*COM*) headhunter.

cazar [kåsár'] *vt* to hunt; (*perseguir*) to chase; (*prender*) to catch; **~las al vuelo** to be pretty sharp.

cazasubmarinos [kåsásōōhmárē'nos] *nm inv* (*NAUT*) destroyer; (*AVIAT*) anti-submarine craft.

cazo [kå'so] *nm* saucepan.

cazuela [kåswe'lá] *nf* (*vasija*) pan; (*guisado*) casserole.

cazurro, a [kåsōō'rro, á] *a* surly.

CC *nm abr* (*POL*: = *Comité Central*) Central Committee.

c/c. *abr* (*COM*: = *cuenta corriente*) checking (*US*) o current (*Brit*) account.

CCI *nf abr* (*COM*: = *Cámara de Comercio Internacional*) ICC.

CC.OO. *nfpl abr* = **Comisiones Obreras.**

c/d *abr* (= *en casa de*) c/o; (= *con descuento*) with discount.

CDN *nm abr* = *Centro Dramático Nacional.*

CE *nm abr* (= *Consejo de Europa*) Council of Europe ♦ *nf abr* (= *Comunidad Europea*) EC.

cebada [sehá'ťhá] *nf* barley.

cebar [sehár'] *vt* (*animal*) to fatten (up); (*anzuelo*) to bait; (*MIL, TEC*) to prime; **~se** *vr*: **~se en** to vent one's fury on, take it out on.

cebo [se'ho] *nm* (*para animales*) feed, food; (*para peces, fig*) bait; (*de arma*) charge.

cebolla [seho'yá] *nf* onion.

cebollín [sehoyēn'] *nm* green onion (*US*), spring onion (*Brit*).

cebón, ona [sehon', oná] *a* fat, fattened.

cebra [se'hrá] *nf* zebra; **paso de ~** zebra crossing.

CECA [se'ká] *nf abr* (= *Comunidad Europea del Carbón y del Acero*) ECSC.

ceca [se'ká] *nf*: **andar o ir de la ~ a la Meca** to chase about all over the place.

cecear [seseár'] *vi* to lisp.

ceceo [sese'o] *nm* lisp.

cecina [sesē'ná] *nf* cured o smoked meat.

cedazo [seťɥá'so] *nm* sieve.

ceder [seťɥer'] *vt* (*entregar*) to hand over; (*renunciar a*) to give up, part with ♦ *vi* (*renunciar*) to give in, yield; (*disminuir*) to diminish, decline; (*romperse*) to give way; (*viento*) to die down; (*fiebre etc*) to abate; **"ceda el paso"** (*AUTO*) "yield" (*US*), "give way" (*Brit*).

cedro [se'ťɥro] *nm* cedar.

cédula [se'ťɥōōlá] *nf* certificate, document; **~ en blanco** blank check.

CEE *nf abr* (= *Comunidad Económica Europea*) EEC.

cegar [seɣár'] *vt* to blind; *(tubería etc)* to block up, stop up ♦ *vi* to go blind; **~se** *vr* to be blinded *(de* by).

cegué [seɣe'] *etc vb V* **cegar.**

ceguemos [seɣe'mos] *etc vb V* **cegar.**

ceguera [seɣe'rà] *nf* blindness.

Ceilán [seēlán'] *nm* Ceylon, Sri Lanka.

ceja [se'há] *nf* eyebrow; **~s pobladas** bushy eyebrows; **arquear las ~s** to raise one's eyebrows; **fruncir las ~s** to frown.

cejar [sehár'] *vi (fig)* to back down; **no ~** to keep it up, stick to it.

cejijunto, a [sehēhōōn'to, á] *a* with bushy eyebrows; *(fig)* scowling.

celada [selá'ᵭá] *nf* ambush, trap.

celador, a [selátᵭor', á] *nm/f (de edificio)* watchman; *(de museo etc)* attendant; *(de cárcel)* guard *(US)*, warder *(Brit)*.

celda [sel'dá] *nf* cell.

celebérrimo, a [selebe'rrēmo, á] *a superlativo de* **célebre.**

celebración [selebrásyon'] *nf* celebration.

celebrar [selebrár'] *vt* to celebrate; *(alabar)* to praise ♦ *vi* to be glad; **~se** *vr* to occur, take place.

célebre [se'lebre] *a* celebrated, renowned.

celebridad [selebrēᵭáᵭ'] *nf* fame; *(persona)* celebrity.

celeridad [selerēᵭáᵭ'] *nf:* **con ~** promptly.

celeste [sele'ste] *a* sky-blue; *(cuerpo etc)* heavenly ♦ *nm* sky blue.

celestial [selestyál'] *a* celestial, heavenly.

celibato [selēbá'to] *nm* celibacy.

célibe [se'lēbe] *a, nm/f* celibate.

celo [se'lo] *nm* zeal; *(REL)* fervor; *(pey)* envy; **~s** *nmpl* jealousy *sg*; **dar ~s a uno** to make sb jealous; **tener ~s de uno** to be jealous of sb; **en ~** *(animales)* in heat.

celofán [selofán'] *nm* cellophane.

celosía [selosē'á] *nf* lattice (window).

celoso, a [selo'so, á] *a (envidioso)* jealous; *(trabajador)* zealous; *(desconfiado)* suspicious.

celta [sel'tá] *a* Celtic ♦ *nm/f* Celt.

célula [se'lōōlá] *nf* cell.

celular [selōōlár'] *a:* **tejido ~** cell tissue.

celuloide [selōōlo'ēᵭe] *nm* celluloid.

celulosa [selōōlo'sá] *nf* cellulose.

cementerio [semente'ryo] *nm* cemetery, graveyard; **~ de coches** junkyard *(US)*, used-car dump *(Brit)*.

cemento [semen'to] *nm* cement; *(hormigón)* concrete; *(AM: cola)* glue.

CEN *nm abr (Esp) = Consejo de Economía Nacional.*

cena [se'ná] *nf* evening meal, dinner.

cenagal [senáɡál'] *nm* bog, quagmire.

cenar [senár'] *vt* to have for dinner, dine on ♦ *vi* to have dinner, dine.

cencerro [sense'rro] *nm* cowbell; **estar como un ~** *(fam)* to be crazy.

cenicero [senēse'ro] *nm* ashtray.

cenit [senēt'] *nm* zenith.

ceniciento, a [senēsyen'to, á] *a* ash-colored, ashen.

ceniza [senē'sá] *nf* ash, ashes *pl.*

censar [sensár'] *vt* to take a census of.

censo [sen'so] *nm* census; **~ electoral** list of registered voters *(US)*, electoral roll *(Brit)*.

censor [sensor'] *nm* censor; **~ de cuentas** *(COM)* auditor; **~ jurado de cuentas** certified public accountant *(US)*, chartered accountant *(Brit)*.

censura [sensōō'rá] *nf (POL)* censorship; *(moral)* censure, criticism.

censurable [sensōōrá'ble] *a* reprehensible.

censurar [sensōōrár'] *vt (idea)* to censure; *(cortar: película)* to censor.

centella [sente'yá] *nf* spark.

centellear [senteyeár'] *vi (metal)* to gleam; *(estrella)* to twinkle; *(fig)* to sparkle.

centelleo [senteye'o] *nm* gleam(ing); twinkling; sparkling.

centenar [sentenár'] *nm* hundred.

centenario, a [sentená'ryo, á] *a* one hundred years old ♦ *nm* centennial *(US)*, centenary *(Brit)*.

centeno [sente'no] *nm* rye.

centésimo, a [sente'sēmo, á] *a, nm* hundredth.

centígrado [sentē'ɡráᵭo] *a* centigrade.

centigramo [sentēɡrá'mo] *nm* centigram *(US)*, centigramme *(Brit)*.

centilitro [sentēlē'tro] *nm* centiliter *(US)*, centilitre *(Brit)*.

centímetro [sentē'metro] *nm* centimeter *(US)*, centimetre *(Brit)*.

céntimo, a [sen'tēmo, á] *a* hundredth ♦ *nm* cent.

centinela [sentēne'lá] *nm* sentry, guard.

centollo, a [sento'yo, á] *nm/f* large *(o* spider*)* crab.

central [sentrál'] *a* central ♦ *nf* head office; *(TEC)* plant; *(TELEC)* exchange; **~ nuclear** nuclear power station.

centralice [sentrálē'se] *etc vb V* **centralizar.**

centralita [sentrálē'tá] *nf (TELEC)* switchboard.

centralización [sentrálēsásyon'] *nf* centralization.

centralizar [sentrálēsár'] *vt* to centralize.

centrar [sentrár'] *vt* to center *(US)*, centre *(Brit)*.

céntrico, a [sen'trēko, á] *a* central.

centrifugar [sentrēfōōɡár'] *vt (ropa)* to spin-dry.

centrifugue [sentrēfōō'ɡe] *etc vb V* **centrifugar.**

centrista [sentrē'stá] *a* center *(US)*, centre *(Brit) cpd.*

centro [sen'tro] *nm* center *(US)*, centre *(Brit)*; **~ de beneficios** *(COM)* profit center; ~ **comercial** shopping center; ~ **de computatión** computer center; ~ **(de determinación) de costos** (COM) cost center; ~ **delantero** (DEPORTE) center forward; ~ **docente** teaching institution; ~ **juvenil** youth club; ~ **social** community center; **ser del** ~ (POL) to be a moderate.

centroafricano, a [sentroáfrēká'no, á] a: **la República Centroafricana** the Central African Republic.

centroamericano, a [sentroámerēká'no, á] a, nm/f Central American.

centrocampista [sentrokámpē'stá] nm/f (DEPORTE) halfback.

cent(s). abr (= céntimo(s)) c.

ceñir [senyēr'] vt (rodear) to encircle, surround; (ajustar) to fit (tightly); (apretar) to tighten; ~**se** vr: ~**se algo** to put sth on; ~**se al asunto** to stick to the matter in hand.

ceño [se'nyo] nm frown, scowl; **fruncir el** ~ to frown, knit one's brow.

CEOE nf abr = Confederación Española de Organizaciones Empresariales.

cepa [se'pá] nf (de vid, fig) stock; (BIO) strain.

CEPAL [sepál'] nf abr (= Comisión Económica de las Naciones Unidas para la América Latina) Economic Commission for Latin America.

cepillar [sepēyár'] vt to brush; (madera) to plane (down).

cepillo [sepē'yo] nm brush; (para madera) plane; (REL) poorbox, alms box.

cepo [se'po] nm (caza) trap.

CEPSA [sep'sá] nf abr (COM) = Compañía Española de Petróleos, S.A.

cera [se'rá] nf wax; ~ **de abejas** beeswax.

cerámica [será'mēká] nf pottery; (arte) ceramics sg.

ceramista [serámē'stá] nm/f potter.

cerbatana [serḥátá'ná] nf blowgun.

cerca [ser'ká] nf fence ♦ ad near, nearby, close; **por aquí** ~ nearby ♦ prep: ~ **de** (cantidad) nearly, about; (distancia) near, close to ♦ nmpl: ~**s** foreground sg.

cercado [serká'ḥo] nm enclosure.

cercanía [serkánē'á] nf nearness, closeness; ~**s** nfpl outskirts, suburbs; **tren de** ~**s** commuter o local train.

cercano, a [serká'no, á] a close, near; (pueblo etc) nearby; **C~ Oriente** Near East.

cercar [serkár'] vt to fence in; (rodear) to surround.

cerciorar [sersyorár'] vt (asegurar) to assure; ~**se** vr (descubrir) to find out (de about); (asegurarse) to make sure (de of).

cerco [ser'ko] nm (AGR) enclosure; (AM) fence; (MIL) siege.

Cerdeña [serḥe'nyá] nf Sardinia.

cerdo [ser'ḥo] nm pig; **carne de** ~ pork.

cereal [sereál'] nm cereal; ~**es** nmpl cereals, grain sg.

cerebro [sere'ḥro] nm brain; (fig) brains pl; **ser un** ~ (fig) to be brilliant.

ceremonia [seremo'nyá] nf ceremony; **reunión de** ~ formal meeting; **hablar sin** ~ to speak plainly.

ceremonial [seremonyál'] a, nm ceremonial.

ceremonioso, a [seremonyo'so, á] a ceremonious; (cumplido) formal.

cereza [sere'sá] nf cherry.

cerezo [sere'so] nm cherry tree.

cerilla [serē'yá] nf (fósforo) match.

cerner [serner'] vt to sift, sieve; ~**se** vr to hover.

cernidor [sernēḥor'] nm sieve.

cero [se'ro] nm nothing, zero; (DEPORTE) zip (US), nil (Brit); **8 grados bajo** ~ 8 degrees below zero; **a partir de** ~ from scratch.

cerque [ser'ke] etc vb V cercar.

cerrado, a [serrá'ḥo, á] a closed, shut; (con llave) locked; (tiempo) cloudy, overcast; (curva) sharp; (acento) thick, broad; **a puerta cerrada** (JUR) in camera.

cerradura [serráḥōō'rá] nf (acción) closing; (mecanismo) lock.

cerrajería [serráherē'á] nf locksmith's craft; (tienda) locksmith's (shop).

cerrajero, a [serráhe'ro, á] nm/f locksmith.

cerrar [serrár'] vt to close, shut; (paso, carretera) to close; (grifo) to turn off; (trato, cuenta, negocio) to close; ~ **con llave** to lock; ~ **el sistema** (INFORM) to close o shut down the system; ~ **un trato** to strike a bargain ♦ vi to close, shut; (la noche) to fall; ~**se** vr to close, shut; (herida) to heal.

cerro [se'rro] nm hill; **andar por las** ~**s de Úbeda** to wander from the point, digress.

cerrojo [serro'ho] nm (herramienta) bolt; (de puerta) latch.

certamen [sertá'men] nm competition, contest.

certero, a [serte'ro, á] a (gen) accurate.

certeza [serte'sá], **certidumbre** [sertēḥōōm'bre] nf certainty.

certificación [sertēfēkásyon'] nf certification; (JUR) affidavit.

certificado, a [sertēfēká'ḥo, á] a certified; (CORREOS) registered ♦ nm certificate.

certificar [sertēfēkár'] vt (asegurar, atestar) to certify.

certifique [sertēfē'ke] etc vb V certificar.

cervatillo [serḥátē'yo] nm fawn.

cervecería [serḥeserē'á] nf (fábrica) brewery; (taberna) beer hall (US), public house (Brit).

cerveza [serḥe'sá] nf beer.

cervical [serḥēkál'] a cervical.

cerviz [serƀes'] *nf* nape of the neck.

cesación [sesásyon'] *nf* cessation, suspension.

cesante [sesán'te] *a* laid off.

cesantía [sesántē'à] *nf* (*AM*) unemployment.

cesar [sesár'] *vi* to cease, stop ♦ *vt* (*en el trabajo*) to lay off; (*funcionario*) to remove from office.

cese [se'se] *nm* (*de trabajo*) dismissal; (*de pago*) suspension.

cesión [sesyon'] *nf*: ~ **de bienes** surrender of property.

césped [ses'peƀ] *nm* grass, lawn.

cesta [se'stá] *nf* basket.

cesto [se'sto] *nm* (large) basket, hamper.

cetrería [setrerē'à] *nf* falconry.

cetrino, a [setrē'no, à] *a* (*tez*) sallow.

cetro [se'tro] *nm* scepter.

Ceuta [seōō'tá] *nf* Ceuta.

ceutí [seōōtē'] *a* of *o* from Ceuta ♦ *nm/f* native *o* inhabitant of Ceuta.

C.F. *nm abr* (= *Club de Fútbol*) F.C.

cfr. abr (= *confróntese, compárese*) cf.

cg. *abr* (= *centígramo*) cg.

CGS *nf abr* (*Guatemala, El Salvador*) = *Confederación General de Sindicatos*.

CGT *nf abr* (*Colombia, México, Nicaragua*) = *Confederación General de Trabajadores*; (*Argentina*) = *Confederación General del Trabajo*.

ch... *V bajo la letra* CH, *después de* C.

C.I. *nm abr* (= *coeficiente intelectual o de inteligencia*) I.Q.

Cía *abr* (= *compañía*) Co.

cianuro [syánōō'ro] *nm* cyanide.

ciática [syà'tēkà] *nf* sciatica.

cicatrice [sēkátrē'se] *etc vb V* **cicatrizar**.

cicatriz [sēkátrēs'] *nf* scar.

cicatrizar [sēkátrēsár'] *vt* to heal; **~se** *vr* to heal (up), form a scar.

cíclico, a [sē'klēko, à] *a* cyclical.

ciclismo [sēklēs'mo] *nm* cycling.

ciclista [sēklē'stá] *nm/f* cyclist.

ciclo [sē'klo] *nm* cycle.

ciclón [sēklon'] *nm* cyclone.

cicuta [sēkōō'tá] *nf* hemlock.

C.I.D. *nm abr* = *Centro Internacional para el Desarrollo* (*Ginebra*).

ciego, a [sye'ġo, à] *etc vb V* **cegar** ♦ *a* blind ♦ *nm/f* blind man/woman; **a ciegas** blindly.

ciegue [sye'ġe] *etc vb V* **cegar**.

cielo [sye'lo] *nm* sky; (*REL*) heaven; (*ARQ: tb*: ~ **raso**) ceiling; ¡**~s!** good heavens!; **ver el** ~ **abierto** to see one's chance.

ciempiés [syempyes'] *nm inv* centipede.

cien [syen] *num V* **ciento**.

ciénaga [sye'náġà] *nf* marsh, swamp.

ciencia [syen'syà] *nf* science; **~s** *nfpl* science *sg*; **saber algo a** ~ **cierta** to know sth for certain.

ciencia-ficción [syen'syáfēksyon'] *nf* science

fiction.

cieno [sye'no] *nm* mud, mire.

científico, a [syentē'fēko, à] *a* scientific ♦ *nm/f* scientist.

ciento [syen'to], **cien** *num* hundred; **pagar al 10 por ciento** to pay at 10 percent.

cierne [syer'ne] *etc vb V* **cerner** ♦ *nm*: **en** ~ in blossom; **en ~(s)** (*fig*) in its infancy.

cierre [sye'rre] *etc vb V* **cerrar** ♦ *nm* closing, shutting; (*con llave*) locking; (*RADIO, TV*) sign-off; ~ **de cremallera** zip (fastener); **precios de** ~ (*BOLSA*) closing prices; ~ **del sistema** (*INFORM*) system shutdown.

cierto, a [syer'to, à] *a* sure, certain; (*un tal*) a certain; (*correcto*) right, correct; ~ **hombre** a certain man; **ciertas personas** certain *o* some people; **sí, es** ~ yes, that's correct; **por** ~ by the way; **lo** ~ **es que ...** the fact is that ...; **estar en lo** ~ to be right.

ciervo [syer'ƀo] *nm* (*ZOOL*) deer; (: *macho*) stag.

cierzo [syer'so] *nm* north wind.

CIES *nm abr* = *Consejo Interamericano Económico y Social*.

cifra [sē'frá] *nf* number, figure; (*cantidad*) number, quantity; (*secreta*) code; ~ **global** lump sum; ~ **de negocios** (*COM*) turnover; **en ~s redondas** in round figures; ~ **de referencia** (*COM*) bench mark; ~ **de ventas** (*COM*) sales figures.

cifrado, a [sēfrà'ƀo, à] *a* in code.

cifrar [sēfrár'] *vt* to code, write in code; (*resumir*) to abridge; (*calcular*) to calculate.

cigala [sēġá'lá] *nf* Norway lobster.

cigarra [sēġá'rrá] *nf* cicada.

cigarrera [sēġárre'rá] *nf* cigar case.

cigarrillo [sēġárrē'yo] *nm* cigarette.

cigarro [sēġá'rro] *nm* cigarette; (*puro*) cigar.

cigüeña [sēġwe'nyá] *nf* stork.

CIJ *nf abr* (= *Corte Internacional de Justicia*) International Court of Justice.

cilíndrico, a [sēlēn'drēko, à] *a* cylindrical.

cilindro [sēlēn'dro] *nm* cylinder.

cima [sē'má] *nf* (*de montaña*) top, peak; (*de árbol*) top; (*fig*) height.

címbalo [sēm'bálo] *nm* cymbal.

cimbrar [sēmbrár'], **cimbrear** [sēmbreár'] *vt* to brandish; **~se** *vr* to sway.

cimentar [sēmentár'] *vt* to lay the foundations of; (*fig: reforzar*) to strengthen; (: *fundar*) to found.

cimiento [sēmyen'to] *etc vb V* **cimentar** ♦ *nm* foundation.

cinc [sēnk] *nm* zinc.

cincel [sēnsel'] *nm* chisel.

cincelar [sēnselár'] *vt* to chisel.

cinco [sēn'ko] *num* five; (*fecha*) fifth; **las** ~ five o'clock; **no estar en sus** ~ (*fam*) to be off one's rocker.

cincuenta [sēnkwen'tá] *num* fifty.
cincuentón, ona [sēnkwenton', o'ná] *a, nm/f* fifty-year old.
cincha [sēntch'á] *nf* girth, saddle strap.
cincho [sēntch'o] *nm* sash, belt.
cine [sē'ne] *nm* movies *pl*; **el ~ mudo** silent films *pl*; **hacer ~** to make films.
cineasta [sēneá'stá] *nm/f* (*director de cine*) film-maker *o* director.
cine-club [sē'neklōōb'] *nm* film club.
cinéfilo, a [sēne'fēlo, á] *nm/f* film buff.
cinematográfico, a [sēnemátográ'fēko, á] *a* film *cpd*.
cínico, a [sē'nēko, á] *a* cynical; (*descarado*) shameless ♦ *nm/f* cynic.
cinismo [sēnēs'mo] *nm* cynicism.
cinta [sēn'tá] *nf* band, strip; (*de tela*) ribbon; (*película*) reel; (*de máquina de escribir*) ribbon; (*métrica*) tape measure; (*magnetofónica*) tape; **~ adhesiva** adhesive tape; **~ aislante** insulating tape; **~ de carbón** carbon ribbon; **~ magnética** (*INFORM*) magnetic tape; **~ métrica** tape measure; **~ de múltiples impactos** (*en impresora*) multistrike ribbon; **~ de tela** (*para máquina de escribir*) fabric ribbon; **~ transportadora** conveyor belt.
cinto [sēn'to] *nm* belt, girdle.
cintura [sēntōō'rá] *nf* waist; (*medida*) waistline.
cinturón [sēntōōron'] *nm* belt; (*fig*) belt, zone; **~ salvavidas** lifebelt; **~ de seguridad** safety belt.
ciña [sē'nyá] *etc*, **ciñendo** [sēnyen'ḍo] *etc vb V* ceñir.
CIP [sēp] *nm abr = Club Internacional de Prensa* (*Madrid*).
ciprés [sēpres'] *nm* cypress (tree).
circo [sēr'ko] *nm* circus.
circuito [sērkwē'to] *nm* circuit; (*DEPORTE*) lap; **TV por ~ cerrado** closed-circuit TV; **~ experimental** (*INFORM*) breadboard; **~ impreso** printed circuit; **~ lógico** (*INFORM*) logical circuit.
circulación [sērkōōlásyon'] *nf* circulation; (*AUTO*) traffic; "**cerrado a la ~ rodada**" "closed to vehicles".
circular [sērkōōlár'] *a, nf* circular ♦ *vt* to circulate ♦ *vi* to circulate; (*dinero*) to be in circulation; (*AUTO*) to drive; (*autobús*) to run.
círculo [sēr'kōōlo] *nm* circle; (*centro*) clubhouse; (*POL*) political group.
circuncidar [sērkōōnsēdár'] *vt* to circumcise.
circunciso, a [sērkōōnsē'so, á] *pp de* **circuncidar**.
circundante [sērkōōndán'te] *a* surrounding.
circundar [sērkōōndár'] *vt* to surround.
circunferencia [sērkōōnferen'syá] *nf* circumference.

circunloquio [sērkōōnlo'kyo] *nm* circumlocution.
circunscribir [sērkōōnskrēḇēr'] *vt* to circumscribe; **~se** *vr* to be limited.
circunscripción [sērkōōnskrēpsyon'] *nf* division; (*POL*) constituency.
circunscrito [sērkōōnskrē'to] *pp de* **circunscribir**.
circunspección [sērkōōnspeksyon'] *nf* circumspection, caution.
circunspecto, a [sērkōōnspek'to, á] *a* circumspect, cautious.
circunstancia [sērkōōnstán'syá] *nf* circumstance; **~s agravantes/extenuantes** aggravating/extenuating circumstances; **estar a la altura de las ~s** to rise to the occasion.
circunstante [sērkōōnstán'te] *nm/f* onlooker, bystander.
circunvalación [sērkōōmbálásyon'] *nf*: **carretera de ~** beltway (*US*), ring road (*Brit*).
cirio [sē'ryo] *nm* (wax) candle.
ciruela [sērwe'lá] *nf* plum; **~ pasa** prune.
ciruelo [sērwe'lo] *nm* plum tree.
cirugía [sērōōhē'á] *nf* surgery; **~ estética** *o* **plástica** plastic surgery.
cirujano [sērōōhá'no] *nm* surgeon.
cisco [sēs'ko] *nm*: **armar un ~** to kick up a row; **estar hecho ~** to be a wreck.
cisma [sēs'má] *nm* schism; (*POL etc*) split.
cisne [sēs'ne] *nm* swan; **canto de ~** swan song.
cisterna [sēster'ná] *nf* cistern, tank.
cistitis [sēstē'tēs] *nf* cystitis.
cita [sē'tá] *nf* appointment, meeting; (*de novios*) date; (*referencia*) quotation; **acudir/faltar a una ~** to turn up for/miss an appointment.
citación [sētásyon'] *nf* (*JUR*) summons *sg*.
citar [sētár'] *vt* to make an appointment with, arrange to meet; (*JUR*) to summons; (*un autor, texto*) to quote; **~se** *vr*: **~se con uno** to arrange to meet sb; **se citaron en el cine** they arranged to meet at the cinema.
cítara [sē'tárá] *nf* zither.
cítrico, a [sē'trēko, á] *a* citric ♦ *nm*: **~s** citrus fruits.
CiU *nm abr* (*POL*) = *Convergència i Unió*.
ciudad [syōōḍháḍ'] *nf* town; (*capital de país etc*) city; **~ universitaria** university campus; **C~ del Cabo** Cape Town; **la C~ Condal** Barcelona.
ciudadanía [syōōḍháḍhanē'á] *nf* citizenship.
ciudadano, a [syōōḍháḍhá'no, á] *a* civic ♦ *nm/f* citizen.
ciudadrealeño, a [syōōḍháḍhreále'nyo, á] *a* of *o* from Ciudad Real ♦ *nm/f* native *o* inhabitant of Ciudad Real.
cívico, a [sē'ḇēko, á] *a* civic; (*fig*) publicspirited.

civil [sĕhĕl'] *a* civil ♦ *nm* (*guardia*) policeman.
civilice [sĕhĕlē'se] *etc vb* V **civilizar**.
civilización [sĕhĕlēsásyon'] *nf* civilization.
civilizar [sĕhĕlēsár'] *vt* to civilize.
civismo [sĕhēs'mo] *nm* public spirit.
cizaña [sĕsá'nyá] *nf* (*fig*) discord; **sembrar** ~ to sow discord.
cl. *abr* (= *centilitro*) cl.
clamar [klámár'] *vt* to clamor (*US*) *o* clamour (*Brit*) for, cry out for ♦ *vi* to cry out, clamor (*US*), clamour (*Brit*).
clamor [klámor'] *nm* (*grito*) cry, shout; (*fig*) clamor (*US*), clamour (*Brit*), protest.
clamoroso, a [klàmoro'so, á] *a* (*éxito etc*) resounding.
clandestinidad [klándestēnēthátĥ'] *nf* secrecy.
clandestino, a [klándestē'no, á] *a* clandestine; (*POL*) underground.
clara [klá'rá] *nf* (*de huevo*) eggwhite.
claraboya [kláráĥo'yá] *nf* skylight.
clarear [klárcár'] *vi* (*el día*) to dawn; (*el cielo*) to clear up, brighten up; ~**se** *vr* to be transparent.
clarete [klárc'tc] *nm* rosé (wine).
claridad [klárēthátĥ'] *nf* (*del día*) brightness; (*de estilo*) clarity.
clarificar [klárēfēkár'] *vt* to clarify.
clarifique [klárēfē'kc] *etc vb* V **clarificar**.
clarín [klárēn'] *nm* bugle.
clarinete [klárēnc'tc] *nm* clarinet.
clarividencia [klárēĥēthen'syá] *nf* clairvoyance; (*fig*) far-sightedness.
claro, a [klá'ro, á] *a* clear; (*luminoso*) bright; (*color*) light; (*evidente*) clear, evident; (*poco espeso*) thin ♦ *nm* (*en bosque*) clearing ♦ *ad* clearly ♦ *excl* of course!; **hablar** ~ (*fig*) to speak plainly; **a las claras** openly; **no sacamos nada en** ~ we couldn't get anything definite.
clase [klá'sc] *nf* class; (*tipo*) kind, sort; (*ESCOL etc*) class; (: *aula*) classroom; ~ **alta/media/obrera** upper/middle/working class; **dar** ~**s** to teach.
clásico, a [klá'sēko, á] *a* classical; (*fig*) classic.
clasificable [klásēfēká'ĥlc] *a* classifiable.
clasificación [klásēfēkásyon'] *nf* classification; (*DEPORTE*) league; (*COM*) ratings *pl*.
clasificador [klásēfēkáĥor'] *nm* filing cabinet.
clasificar [klásēfēkár'] *vt* to classify; (*INFORM*) to sort; ~**se** *vr* (*DEPORTE*: *torneo*) to qualify.
clasifique [klásēfē'kc] *etc vb* V **clasificar**.
clasista [klásē'stá] *a* (*fam*: *actitud*) snobbish.
claudia [klá'ōōthyá] *nf* greengage.
claudicar [kláōōthēkár'] *vi* (*fig*) to back down.

claudique [kláōōthē'kc] *etc vb* V **claudicar**.
claustro [klá'ōōstro] *nm* cloister; (*UNIV*) staff; (*junta*) senate.
cláusula [klá'ōōsōōlá] *nf* clause; ~ **de exclusión** (*COM*) exclusion clause.
clausura [kláōōsōō'rá] *nf* closing, closure.
clausurar [kláōōsōōrár'] *vt* (*congreso etc*) to close, bring to a close; (*POL etc*) to adjourn; (*cerrar*) to close (down).
clavado, a *a* nailed ♦ *excl* exactly!, precisely!
clavar [kláĥár'] *vt* (*tablas etc*) to nail (together); (*con alfiler*) to pin; (*clavo*) to hammer in; (*cuchillo*) to stick, thrust; (*mirada*) to fix; (*fam*: *estafar*) to cheat.
clave [klá'ĥe] *nf* key; (*MUS*) clef; ~ **de búsqueda** (*INFORM*) search key; ~ **de clasificación** (*INFORM*) sort key.
clavel [kláĥel'] *nm* carnation.
claveteado [kláĥeteá'tĥo] *nm* studding.
clavicémbalo [kláĥesem'bálo] *nm* harpsichord.
clavicordio [kláĥēkor'tĥyo] *nm* clavicord.
clavícula [kláĥē'kōōlá] *nf* collar bone.
clavija [kláĥē'há] *nf* peg, pin; (*MUS*) peg; (*ELEC*) plug.
clavo [klá'ĥo] *nm* (*de metal*) nail; (*BOT*) clove; **dar en el** ~ (*fig*) to hit the nail on the head.
claxon [klák'son], *pl* **claxons** *nm* horn; **tocar el** ~ to sound one's horn.
clemencia [klemen'syá] *nf* mercy, clemency.
clemente [klemen'te] *a* merciful, clement.
cleptómano, a [klepto'máno, á] *nm/f* kleptomaniac.
clerical [klerēkál'] *a* clerical.
clérigo [klc'rēɡo] *nm* priest, clergyman.
clero [klc'ro] *nm* clergy.
cliché [klētche'] *nm* cliché; (*TIP*) stencil; (*FOTO*) negative.
cliente, a [klyen'tc, á] *nm/f* client, customer.
clientela [klyente'lá] *nf* clientele, customers *pl*; (*COM*) goodwill; (*MED*) patients *pl*.
clima [klē'má] *nm* climate.
climatizado, a [klēmátēsá'tĥo, á] *a* air-conditioned.
clínico, a [klē'nēko, á] *a* clinical ♦ *nf* clinic; (*particular*) private hospital.
clip *nm*, *pl* **clips** [klēp, klēs] paper clip.
cloaca [kloá'ká] *nf* sewer, drain.
clorhídrico, a [klorē'drēko, á] *a* hydrochloric.
cloro [klo'ro] *nm* chlorine.
cloroformo [klorofor'mo] *nm* chloroform.
cloruro [klorōō'ro] *nm* chloride; ~ **sódico** sodium chloride.
club *pl* **clubs** *o* **clubes** [klōōb, klōōs, klu'ĥes] *nm* club; ~ **de jóvenes** youth club.
cm *abr* (= *centímetro*) cm.
CN *nf abr* (= *Carretera Nacional*) ≈ A road.

C.N.T. *nf abr* (*Esp*) = *Confederación Nacional de Trabajo;* (*AM*) = *Confederación Nacional de Trabajadores.*

coacción [koáksyon'] *nf* coercion, compulsion.

coaccionar [koáksyonár'] *vt* to coerce, compel.

coagular [koágōōlár'] *vt*, ~**se** *vr* (*sangre*) to clot; (*leche*) to curdle.

coágulo [koá'gōōlo] *nm* clot.

coalición [koálēsyon'] *nf* coalition.

coartada [koártá'tḥá] *nf* alibi.

coartar [koártár'] *vt* to limit, restrict.

coba [ko'ḥá] *nf*: **dar** ~ **a uno** to soft-soap sb.

cobarde [koḥár'tḥe] *a* cowardly ♦ *nm/f* coward.

cobardía [koḥártḥē'á] *nf* cowardice.

cobaya [koḥá'yá] *nf*, **cobayo** [koḥá'yo] *nm* guinea pig.

cobertizo [koḥertē'so] *nm* shelter.

cobertor [koḥertor'] *nm* bedspread.

cobertura [koḥertōō'rá] *nf* cover; (*COM*) collateral (*US*) coverage (*Brit*); ~ **de dividendo** (*COM*) dividend cover.

cobija [koḥē'há] *nf* (*AM*) blanket.

cobijar [koḥēhár'] *vt* (*cubrir*) to cover; (*abrigar*) to shelter; ~**se** *vr* to take shelter.

cobijo [koḥē'ho] *nm* shelter.

cobra [ko'ḥrá] *nf* cobra.

cobrador, a [koḥrátḥor', á] *nm/f* (*de autobús*) conductor/conductress; (*de impuestos, gas*) collector.

cobrar [koḥrár'] *vt* (*cheque*) to cash; (*sueldo*) to collect, draw; (*objeto*) to recover; (*precio*) to charge; (*deuda*) to collect ♦ *vi* to draw one's pay; ~**se** *vr* to recover, get on well; **cóbrese al entregar** cash on delivery (COD); **a** ~ (*COM*) receivable; **cantidades por** ~ sums due.

cobre [ko'ḥre] *nm* copper; ~**s** *nmpl* brass instruments.

cobrizo, a [koḥrē'so, á] *a* coppery.

cobro [ko'ḥro] *nm* (*de cheque*) cashing; (*pago*) payment; **presentar al** ~ to cash; *V tb* **llamada.**

coca [ko'ká] *nf* coca.

Coca-Cola ® [ko'káko'lá] *nf* Coca-Cola ®.

cocaína [kokáē'ná] *nf* cocaine.

cocainómano, a [kokáēno'máno, á] *nm/f* cocaine addict.

cocción [koksyon'] *nf* (*CULIN*) cooking; (*el hervir*) boiling.

cocear [koseár'] *vi* to kick.

cocer [koser'] *vt*, *vi* to cook; (*en agua*) to boil; (*en horno*) to bake.

cocido, a [kosē'tḥo, á] *a* boiled ♦ *nm* stew.

cocina [kosē'ná] *nf* kitchen; (*aparato*) cooker; (*acto*) cookery; ~ **casera** home cooking; ~ **eléctrica** electric stove; ~ **francesa** French cuisine; ~ **de gas** gas stove.

cocinar [kosēnár'] *vt*, *vi* to cook.

cocinero, a [kosēne'ro, á] *nm/f* cook.

coco [ko'ko] *nm* coconut; (*fantasma*) bogeyman; (*fam: cabeza*) nut; **comer el** ~ **a uno** (*fam*) to brainwash sb.

cocodrilo [kokotḥrē'lo] *nm* crocodile.

cocotero [kokote'ro] *nm* coconut palm.

cóctel [kok'tel] *nm* (*bebida*) cocktail; (*reunión*) cocktail party.

coctelera [koktele'rá] *nf* cocktail shaker.

coche [kotch'e] *nm* (*AUTO*) automobile (*US*), car; (*de tren, de caballos*) coach, carriage; (*para niños*) baby carriage (*US*); pram (*Brit*); ~ **de bomberos** fire engine; ~ **celular** paddy wagon; ~ **(comedor)** (*FERRO*) (dining) car; ~ **fúnebre** hearse.

coche-cama [kotch'ekâ'má], *pl* **coches-cama** *nm* (*FERRO*) sleeping car, sleeper (*Brit*).

cochera [kotche'rá] *nf* garage; (*de autobuses, trenes*) depot.

coche-restaurante, *pl* **coches-restaurante** [kotch'erestáōōrán'te] *nm* (*FERRO*) diningcar, diner.

cochinada [kotchēná'tḥá] *nf* dirty trick.

cochinillo [kotchēnē'yo] *nm* piglet, suckling pig.

cochino, a [kotche'no, á] *a* filthy, dirty ♦ *nm/f* pig.

cod. *abr* (= *código*) code.

codazo [kotḥá'so] *nm*: **dar un** ~ **a uno** to nudge sb.

codear [kotḥeár'] *vi* to elbow, jostle; ~**se** *vr*: ~**se con** to rub shoulders with.

códice [ko'tḥēse] *nm* manuscript, codex.

codicia [kotḥē'syá] *nf* greed; (*fig*) lust.

codiciar [kotḥēsyár'] *vt* to covet.

codicioso, a [kotḥēsyo'so, á] *a* covetous.

codificador [kotḥēfēkátḥor'] *nm* (*INFORM*) encoder; ~ **digital** digitizer.

código [ko'tḥēgo] *nm* code; ~ **de barras** (*COM*) bar code; ~ **binario** binary code; ~ **de caracteres** (*INFORM*) character code; ~ **de (la) circulación** highway code; ~ **civil** common law; ~ **de control** (*INFORM*) control code; ~ **máquina** (*INFORM*) machine code; ~ **militar** military law; ~ **de operación** (*INFORM*) operational *o* machine code; ~ **penal** penal code; ~ **de práctica** code of practice.

codillo [kotḥē'yo] *nm* (*ZOOL*) knee; (*TEC*) elbow (joint).

codo [ko'tḥo] *nm* (*ANAT, de tubo*) elbow; (*ZOOL*) knee; **hablar por los** ~**s** to talk a blue streak (*US*) *o* 19 to the dozen (*Brit*).

codorniz [kotḥornēs'] *nf* quail.

coeficiente [koefēsyen'te] *nm* (*MAT*) coefficient; (*ECON etc*) rate; ~ **intelectual** *o* **de inteligencia** intelligence quotient.

coerción [koersyon'] *nf* coercion.

coercitivo, a [koersētē'ho, á] *a* coercive.

coetáneo, a [koetá'neo, á] nm/f: ~s contemporaries.

coexistencia [koeksēsten'syá] nf coexistence.

coexistir [koeksēstēr'] vi to coexist.

cofia [ko'fyá] nf (de enfermera) (white) cap.

cofradía [kofráthē'á] nf brotherhood, fraternity.

cogedor [kohethor'] nm dustpan.

coger [koher'] vt (Esp) to take (hold of); (objeto caído) to pick up; (frutas) to pick, harvest; (resfriado, ladrón, pelota) to catch; (AM fam!) to lay (!); ~ a uno desprevenido to take sb unawares ♦ vi: ~ por el buen camino to take the right road; ~se vr (el dedo) to catch; ~se a algo to get hold of sth.

cogida [kohē'thá] nf gathering, harvesting; (de peces) catch; (TAUR) goring.

cogollo [kogo'yo] nm (de lechuga) heart; (fig) core, nucleus.

cogote [kogo'te] nm back o nape of the neck.

cohabitar [koáhētár'] vi to live together, cohabit.

cohecho [koetch'o] nm (acción) bribery; (soborno) bribe.

coherencia [koeren'syá] nf coherence.

coherente [koeren'te] a coherent.

cohesión [koesyon'] nm cohesion.

cohete [koe'te] nm rocket.

cohibido, a [koēhē'tho, á] a (PSICO) inhibited; (tímido) shy; **sentirse ~** to feel embarrassed.

cohibir [koēhēr'] vt to restrain, restrict; ~se vr to feel inhibited.

COI nm abr (= Comité Olímpico Internacional) IOC.

coima [ko'ēmá] nf (fam) bribe.

coincidencia [koēnsēthen'syá] nf coincidence.

coincidir [koēnsēthēr'] vi (en idea) to coincide, agree; (en lugar) to coincide.

coito [ko'ēto] nm intercourse, coitus.

cojear [koheár'] vi (persona) to limp, hobble; (mueble) to wobble, rock.

cojera [kohe'rá] nf lameness; (andar cojo) limp.

cojín [kohēn'] nm cushion.

cojinete [kohēne'te] nm small cushion, pad; (TEC) (ball) bearing.

cojo, a [ko'ho, á] etc vb V **coger** ♦ a (que no puede andar) lame, crippled; (mueble) wobbly ♦ nm/f lame person, cripple.

cojón [kohon'] nm (fam!) ball (!), testicle; **¡cojones!** shit! (!).

cojonudo, a [kohonoō'tho, á] a (Esp fam) great, fantastic.

col [kol] nf cabbage; **~es de Bruselas** Brussels sprouts.

col., col.ª abr (= columna) col.

cola [ko'lá] nf tail; (de gente) line (US), queue (Brit); (lugar) end, last place; (para pegar) glue, gum; (de vestido) train; **hacer ~** to line (US), queue (up) (Brit).

colaboración [koláhorásyon'] nf (gen) collaboration; (en periódico) contribution.

colaborador, a [koláhoráthor', á] nm/f collaborator; contributor.

colaborar [koláhorár'] vi to collaborate.

colación [kolásyon'] nf: **sacar a ~** to bring up.

colado, a [kolá'tho, á] a (metal) cast ♦ nf: **hacer la colada** to do the washing.

colador [koláthor'] nm (de té) strainer; (para verduras etc) colander.

colapso [koláp'so] nm collapse; **~ nervioso** nervous breakdown.

colar [kolár'] vt (líquido) to strain off; (metal) to cast ♦ vi to ooze, seep (through); **~se** vr to cut in line (US) o jump the queue (Brit); (en mitin) to sneak in; (equivocarse) to slip up; **~se en** to get into without paying; (en una fiesta) to gatecrash.

colateral [koláterál'] nm collateral.

colcha [koltch'á] nf bedspread.

colchón [koltchon'] nm mattress; **~ inflable** inflatable mattress.

colchoneta [coltchone'tá] nf (en gimnasio) mat.

colear [koleár'] vi (perro) to wag its tail.

colección [koleksyon'] nf collection.

coleccionar [koleksyonár'] vt to collect.

coleccionista [koleksyonē'stá] nm/f collector.

colecta [kolek'tá] nf collection.

colectivo, a [kolektē'ho, á] a collective, joint ♦ nm (AM) (small) bus.

colector [kolektor'] nm collector; (sumidero) sewer.

colega [kole'gá] nm/f colleague.

colegial, a [kolehyál', á] a (ESCOL etc) school cpd, college cpd ♦ nm/f schoolboy/girl.

colegio [kole'hyo] nm college; (escuela) school; (de abogados etc) association; **~ de internos** boarding school; **ir al ~** to go to school.

colegir [kolehēr'] vt (juntar) to collect, gather; (deducir) to infer, conclude.

cólera [ko'lerá] nf (ira) anger; **montar en ~** to get angry ♦ nm (MED) cholera.

colérico, a [kole'rēko, á] a angry, furious.

colesterol [kolesterol'] nm cholesterol.

coleta [kole'tá] nf pigtail.

coletazo [koletá'so] nm: **dar un ~** (animal) to flap its tail; **los últimos ~s** death throes.

colgado, a [kolgá'tho, á] pp de **colgar** ♦ a hanging; (ahorcado) hanged; **dejar ~ a uno** to let sb down.

colgajo [kolgá'ho] nm tatter.

colgante [kolgán'te] a hanging; V **puente** ♦

nm (joya) pendant.

colgar [kolgår'] *vt* to hang (up); *(tender: ropa)* to hang out ♦ *vi* to hang; *(teléfono)* to hang up.

colgué [kolge'], **colguemos** [kolge'mos] *etc vb V* **colgar.**

colibrí [kolēbrē'] *nm* hummingbird.

coliflor [kolēflor'] *nf* cauliflower.

coligiendo [kolēhyen'do] *etc vb V* **colegir.**

colija [kolē'há] *etc vb V* **colegir.**

colilla [kolē'yá] *nf* cigarette end.

colina [kolē'ná] *nf* hill.

colindante [kolēndán'te] *a* adjacent, neighboring.

colindar [kolēndár'] *vi* to adjoin, be adjacent.

colisión [kolēsyon'] *nf* collision; ~ **de frente** head-on crash.

colitis [kolē'tēs] *nf inv:* **tener** ~ to have diarrhea *(US)*, diarrhoea *(Brit)*.

colmado, a [kolmá'tho, á] *a* full ♦ *nm* grocer's shop.

colmar [kolmár'] *vt* to fill to the brim; *(fig)* to fulfil, realize.

colmena [kolme'ná] *nf* beehive.

colmillo [kolmē'yo] *nm (diente)* eye tooth; *(de elefante)* tusk; *(de perro)* fang.

colmo [kol'mo] *nm* height, summit; **para** ~ **de desgracias** to cap it all; **¡eso es ya el** ~**!** that's the last straw!

colocación [kolokásyon'] *nf (acto)* placing; *(empleo)* job, position; *(situación)* place, position; *(COM)* placement.

colocar [kolokár'] *vt* to place, put, position; *(poner en empleo)* to find a job for; ~ **dinero** to invest money; ~**se** *vr* to place o.s.; *(conseguir trabajo)* to find a job.

colofón [kolofon'] *nm:* **como** ~ **de las conversaciones** as a sequel to o following the talks.

Colombia [kolom'byá] *nf* Colombia.

colombiano, a [kolombyá'no, á]˙ *a, nm/f* Colombian.

colon [ko'lon] *nm* colon.

Colonia [kolo'nyá] *nf* Cologne.

colonia [kolo'nyá] *nf* colony; *(de casas)* housing development *(US)* o estate *(Brit)*; *(agua de* ~*)* cologne; ~ **escolar** summer camp (for schoolchildren).

colonice [kolonē'se] *etc vb V* **colonizar.**

colonización [kolonēsásyon'] *nf* colonization.

colonizador, a [kolonēsáthor', á] *a* colonizing ♦ *nm/f* colonist, settler.

colonizar [kolonēsár'] *vt* to colonize.

colono [kolo'no] *nm (POL)* colonist, settler; *(AGR)* tenant farmer.

coloque [kolo'ke] *etc vb V* **colocar.**

coloquio [kolo'kyo] *nm* conversation; *(congreso)* conference; *(INFORM)* handshake.

color [kolor'] *nm* color *(US)*, colour *(Brit)*;

a todo ~ in full color; **verlo todo** ~ **de rosa** to see everything through rose-colored spectacles; **le salieron los** ~**es** she blushed.

colorado, a [kolorá'tho, á] *a (rojo)* red; *(AM: chiste)* dirty; **ponerse** ~ to blush.

colorante [koloran'te] *nm* coloring *(US)*, colouring *(Brit)*.

colorar [kolorár'] *vt* to color *(US)*, colour *(Brit)*; *(teñir)* to dye.

colorear [koloreár'] *vt* to color *(US)*, colour *(Brit)*.

colorete [kolore'te] *nm* blusher.

colorido [kolorē'tho] *nm* color(ing) *(US)*, colour(ing) *(Brit)*.

columbrar [koloōmbrár'] *vt* to glimpse, spy.

columna [koloōm'ná] *nf* column; *(pilar)* pillar; *(apoyo)* support; ~ **blindada** *(MIL)* armored column; ~ **vertebral** spine, spinal column.

columpiar [koloōmpyár'] *vt*, ~**se** *vr* to swing.

columpio [koloōm'pyo] *nm* swing.

collar [koyár'] *nm* necklace; *(de perro)* collar.

coma [ko'má] *nf* comma ♦ *nm (MED)* coma.

comadre [komá'thre] *nf (madrina)* godmother; *(vecina)* neighbor *(US)*, neighbour *(Brit)*; *(chismosa)* gossip.

comadrear [komáthreár'] *vi* to gossip.

comadreja [komáthre'há] *nf* weasel.

comadrona [komáthro'ná] *nf* midwife.

comandancia [komándán'syá] *nf* command.

comandante [komándán'te] *nm* commandant; *(grado)* major.

comandar [komándár'] *vt* to command.

comando [komán'do] *nm (MIL: mando)* command; (: *grupo)* commando unit; *(INFORM)* command; ~ **de búsqueda** search command.

comarca [komár'ká] *nf* region.

comarcal [komárkál'] *a* local.

comba [kom'bá] *nf (curva)* curve; *(en viga)* warp; *(cuerda)* skipping rope; **saltar a la** ~ to skip.

combar [kombár'] *vt* to bend, curve.

combate [kombá'te] *nm* fight; *(fig)* battle; **fuera de** ~ out of action.

combatiente [kombátyen'te] *nm* combatant.

combatir [kombátēr'] *vt* to fight, combat.

combatividad [kombátēhētháth'] *nf (actitud)* fighting spirit; *(agresividad)* aggressiveness.

combativo, a [kombátē'ho, á] *a* full of fight.

combinación [kombēnásyon'] *nf* combination; *(QUÍMICA)* compound; *(bebida)* cocktail; *(plan)* scheme, setup; *(prenda)* slip.

combinado, a [kombēná'tho, á] *a:* **plato** ~ *main course served with vegetables.*

combinar [kombēnár'] *vt* to combine; (*colores*) to match.

combustible [kombōōstē'ble] *nm* fuel.

combustión [kombōōstyon'] *nf* combustion.

comedia [kome'thyá] *nf* comedy; (*TEATRO*) play, drama; (*fig*) farce.

comediante [komethyán'te] *nm/f* (comic) actor/actress.

comedido, a [komethē'tho, á] *a* moderate.

comedirse [komethēr'se] *vr* to behave moderately; (*ser cortés*) to be courteous.

comedor, a [komethor', á] *nm/f* (*persona*) glutton ♦ *nm* (*habitación*) dining room; (*restaurante*) restaurant; (*cantina*) cafeteria (*US*), canteen (*Brit*).

comencé [komense'], **comencemos** [komense'mos] *etc vb V* **comenzar.**

comensal [komensál'] *nm/f* fellow guest/diner.

comentar [komentár'] *vt* to comment on; (*fam*) to discuss; **comentó que...** he made the comment that....

comentario [komentá'ryo] *nm* comment, remark; (*LIT*) commentary; ~**s** *nmpl* gossip *sg*; **dar lugar a** ~**s** to cause gossip.

comentarista [komentárē'stá] *nm/f* commentator.

comenzar [komensár'] *vt, vi* to begin, start, commence; ~ **a hacer algo** to begin *o* start doing *o* to do sth.

comer [komer'] *vt* to eat; (*DAMAS, AJEDREZ*) to take, capture; (*párrafo etc*) to skip ♦ *vi* to eat; (*almorzar*) to have lunch; ~**se** *vr* to eat up; ~ **el coco a** (*fam*) to brainwash; **¡a** ~**!** food's ready!

comerciable [komersyá'ble] *a* marketable, saleable.

comercial [komersyál'] *a* commercial; (*relativo al negocio*) business *cpd*.

comerciante [komersyán'te] *nm/f* trader, merchant; (*tendero*) shopkeeper; ~ **exclusivo** (*COM*) sole trader.

comerciar [komersyár'] *vi* to trade, do business.

comercio [komer'syo] *nm* commerce, trade; (*negocio*) business; (*grandes empresas*) big business; (*fig*) dealings *pl*; ~ **autorizado** (*COM*) licensed trade; ~ **exterior** foreign trade.

comestible [komestē'ble] *a* eatable, edible ♦ *nmpl*: ~**s** food *sg*, foodstuffs; (*COM*) groceries.

cometa [kome'tá] *nm* comet ♦ *nf* kite.

cometer [kometer'] *vt* to commit.

cometido [kometē'tho] *nm* (*misión*) task, assignment; (*deber*) commitment.

comezón [komeson'] *nf* itch, itching.

comicios [komē'syos] *nmpl* elections; (*voto*) voting *sg*.

cómico, a [ko'mēko, á] *a* comic(al) ♦ *nm/f* comedian; (*de teatro*) (comic) actor/actress.

comida [komē'thá] *etc vb V* **comedirse** ♦ *nf* (*alimento*) food; (*almuerzo, cena*) meal; (*de mediodía*) lunch.

comidilla [komēthē'yá] *nf*: **ser la** ~ **de la ciudad** to be the talk of the town.

comience [komyen'se] *etc vb V* **comenzar.**

comienzo [komyen'so] *etc vb V* **comenzar** ♦ *nm* beginning, start; **dar** ~ **a un acto** to begin a ceremony; ~ **del archivo** (*INFORM*) top-of-file.

comilón, ona [komēlon', o'ná] *a* greedy ♦ *nf* (*fam*) blow-out.

comillas [komē'yás] *nfpl* quotation marks.

comino [komē'no] *nm* cumin (seed); **no me importa un** ~ I don't give a damn.

comisaría [komēsárē'á] *nf* precinct (*US*), police station; (*MIL*) commissariat.

comisario [komēsá'ryo] *nm* (*MIL etc*) commissary; (*POL*) commissar.

comisión [komēsyon'] *nf* (*COM: pago*) commission, rake-off (*fam*); (: *junta*) board; (*encargo*) assignment; ~ **mixta/permanente** joint/standing committee; **Comisiones Obreras** (*Esp*) Workers' Unions.

comisura [komēsōō'rá] *nf*: ~ **de los labios** corner of the mouth.

comité, *pl* **comités** *nm* [komēte', komētes'] committee; work council.

comitiva [komētē'há] *nf* suite, retinue.

como [ko'mo] *ad* as; (*tal* ~) like; (*aproximadamente*) about, approximately ♦ *conj* (*ya que, puesto que*) as, since; (*en seguida que*) as soon as; (*si: +subjun*) if; **¡**~ **no!** of course!; ~ **no lo haga hoy** unless he does it today; ~ **si** as if; **es tan alto** ~ **ancho** it is as high as it is wide.

cómo [ko'mo] *ad* how?, why? ♦ *excl* what?, I beg your pardon? ♦ *nm*: **el** ~ **y el porqué** the whys and wherefores; **¿**~ **está Ud?** how are you?; **¿**~ **no?** why not?; **¿**~ **son?** what are they like?

cómoda [ko'mothá] *nf* chest of drawers.

comodidad [komothētháth'] *nf* comfort; **venga a su** ~ come at your convenience.

comodín [komothēn'] *nm* joker; (*INFORM*) wild card; **símbolo** ~ wildcard character.

cómodo, a [ko'motho, á] *a* comfortable; (*práctico, de fácil uso*) convenient.

comoquiera [komokye'rá] *conj*: ~ **que** (+ *subjun*) in whatever way; ~ **que sea eso** however that may be.

comp. *abr* (= *compárese*) cp.

compacto, a [kompák'to, á] *a* compact.

compadecer [kompáthēser'] *vt* to pity, be sorry for; ~**se** *vr*: ~**se de** to pity, be sorry for.

compadezca [kompáthēs'ká] *etc vb V* **compadecer.**

compadre [kompá'thre] *nm* (*padrino*)

godfather; (*amigo*) friend, pal.

compaginar [kompáhēnár'] *vt*: ~ **A con B** to bring A into line with B; **~se** *vr*: **~se con** to tally with, square with.

compañerismo [kompányerēs'mo] *nm* friendship (*US*), comradeship (*Brit*).

compañero, a [kompánye'ro, á] *nm/f* companion; (*novio*) boyfriend/girlfriend; ~ **de clase** classmate.

compañía [kompányē'á] *nf* company; ~ **afiliada** associated company; ~ **concesionadora** franchiser; ~ **(no) cotizable** (un)listed company; ~ **inversionista** investment trust; **hacer ~ a uno** to keep sb company.

comparación [kompárásyon'] *nf* comparison; **en ~ con** in comparison with.

comparar [kompárár'] *vt* to compare.

comparativo, a [kompárátē'ho, á] *a* comparative.

comparecencia [kompáresen'syá] *nf* (*JUR*) appearance (in court); **orden de ~** summons *sg*.

comparecer [kompáreser'] *vi* to appear (in court).

comparezca [kompáres'ká] *etc vb V* **comparecer.**

comparsa [kompár'sá] *nm/f* extra.

compartimiento [kompártēmyen'to] *nm* (*FERRO*) compartment.

compartir [kompártēr'] *vt* to divide (up), share (out).

compás [kompás'] *nm* (*MUS*) beat, rhythm; (*MAT, NAUT etc*) compass; **al ~** in time.

compasión [kompásyon'] *nf* compassion, pity.

compasivo, a [kompásē'ho, á] *a* compassionate.

compatibilidad [kompátēhēlēthátħ'] *nf* (*tb INFORM*) compatibility.

compatible [kompátē'hle] *a* compatible.

compatriota [kompátryo'tá] *nm/f* compatriot, fellow countryman/woman.

compendiar [kompendyár'] *vt* to summarize; (*libro*) to abridge.

compendio [kompen'dyo] *nm* summary; abridgement.

compenetración [kompenetrásyon'] *nf* (*fig*) mutual understanding.

compenetrarse [kompenetrár'se] *vr* (*fig*): ~ **(muy) bien** to get on (very) well together.

compensación [kompensásyon'] *nf* compensation; (*JUR*) damages *pl*; (*COM*) clearing.

compensar [kompensár'] *vt* to compensate; (*pérdida*) to make up for.

competencia [kompeten'syá] *nf* (*incumbencia*) domain, field; (*COM*) receipt; (*JUR, habilidad*) competence; (*rivalidad*) competition.

competente [kompeten'te] *a* (*JUR, persona*) competent; (*conveniente*) suitable.

competer [kompeter'] *vi*: ~ **a** to be the responsibility of, fall to.

competición [kompetēsyon'] *nf* competition.

competidor, a [kompetēthor', á] *nm/f* competitor.

competir [kompetēr'] *vi* to compete.

compilación [kompēlásyon'] *nf* compilation; **tiempo de ~** (*INFORM*) compile time.

compilador [kompēláthor'] *nm* compiler.

compilar [kompēlár'] *vt* to compile.

compita [kompē'tá] *etc vb V* **competir.**

complacencia [komplásen'syá] *nf* (*placer*) pleasure; (*satisfacción*) satisfaction; (*buena voluntad*) willingness.

complacer [kompláser'] *vt* to please; **~se** *vr* to be pleased.

complaciente [komplásyen'te] *a* kind, obliging, helpful.

complazca [komplás'ká] *etc vb V* **complacer.**

complejo, a [komple'ho, á] *a, nm* complex.

complementario, a [komplementá'ryo, á] *a* complementary.

completar [kompletár'] *vt* to complete.

completo, a [komple'to, á] *a* complete; (*perfecto*) perfect; (*lleno*) full ♦ *nm* full complement.

complicado, a [komplēká'tħo, á] *a* complicated; **estar ~ en** to be involved in.

complicar [komplēkár'] *vt* to complicate.

cómplice [kom'plēse] *nm/f* accomplice.

complique [komplē'ke] *etc vb V* **complicar.**

complot [komplo'(t)], *pl* **complots** [komplo'(t), komplos'] *nm* plot; (*conspiración*) conspiracy.

compondré [kompondre'] *etc vb V* **componer.**

componenda [komponen'dá] *nf* compromise; (*pey*) shady deal.

componer [komponer'] *vt* to make up, put together; (*MUS, LIT, IMPRENTA*) to compose; (*algo roto*) to mend, repair; (*adornar*) to adorn; (*arreglar*) to arrange; (*reconciliar*) to reconcile; **~se** *vr*: **~se de** to consist of; **componérselas para hacer algo** to manage to do sth.

componga [kompon'gá] *etc vb V* **componer.**

comportamiento [komportámyen'to] *nm* behavior (*US*), behaviour (*Brit*), conduct.

comportarse [komportár'se] *vr* to behave.

composición [komposēsyon'] *nf* composition.

compositor, a [komposētor', á] *nm/f* composer.

compostelano, a [kompostelá'no, á] *a* of *o* from Santiago de Compostela ♦ *nm/f* native *o* inhabitant of Santiago de Compostela.

compostura [kompostōō'rá] *nf* (*repara-*

ción) mending, repair; (*composición*) composition; (*acuerdo*) agreement; (*actitud*) composure.

compota [kompo'tá] *nf* compote, preserve.

compra [kom'prá] *nf* purchase; ~**s** *nfpl* purchases, shopping *sg*; **hacer la** ~**/ir de** ~**s** to do the/go shopping; ~ **a granel** (*COM*) bulk buying; ~ **proteccionista** (*COM*) support buying.

comprador, a [komprà'ðor', á] *nm/f* buyer, purchaser.

comprar [komprár'] *vt* to buy, purchase; ~ **deudas** (*COM*) to factor.

compraventa [komprà̱en'tá] *nf* (*JUR*) contract of sale.

comprender [komprender'] *vt* to understand; (*incluir*) to comprise, include.

comprensible [komprensē'ƀle] *a* understandable.

comprensión [komprensyon'] *nf* understanding; (*totalidad*) comprehensiveness.

comprensivo, a [komprensē'ƀo, á] *a* comprehensive; (*actitud*) understanding.

compresa [kompre'sá] *nf* compress; ~ **higiénica** sanitary napkin (*US*) o towel (*Brit*).

compresión [kompresyon'] *nf* compression.

comprimido, a [komprēmē'ðo] *a* compressed ♦ *nm* (*MED*) pill, tablet; **en caracteres** ~**s** (*TIP*) condensed.

comprimir [komprēmēr'] *vt* to compress; (*fig*) to control; (*INFORM*) to pack.

comprobación [komproƀasyon'] *nf:* ~ **general de cuentas** (*COM*) general audit.

comprobante [komproƀan'te] *nm* proof; (*COM*) voucher; ~ **(de pago)** receipt.

comprobar [komproƀár'] *vt* to check; (*probar*) to prove; (*TEC*) to check, test.

comprometedor, a [komprometeðor', á] *a* compromising.

comprometido, a [komprometē'ðo, á] *a* (*situación*) awkward; (*escritor etc*) committed.

comprometer [komprometer'] *vt* to compromise; (*exponer*) to endanger; ~**se** *vr* to compromise o.s.; (*involucrarse*) to get involved.

compromiso [kompromē'so] *nm* (*obligación*) obligation; (*cita*) engagement, date; (*cometido*) commitment; (*convenio*) agreement; (*dificultad*) awkward situation; **libre de** ~ (*COM*) without obligation.

comprueba [komprwe'ƀá] *etc vb* V **comprobar.**

compuerta [kompwer'tá] *nf* (*en canal*) sluice, floodgate; (*INFORM*) gate.

compuesto, a [kompwe'sto, á] *pp de* **componer** ♦ *a:* ~ **de** composed of, made up of ♦ *nm* compound; (*MED*) preparation.

compulsar [kompōōlsár'] *vt* (*cotejar*) to collate, compare; (*JUR*) to make an attested copy of.

compulsivo, a [kompōōlsē'ƀo, á] *a* compulsive.

compuse [compōō'se] *etc vb* V **componer.**

computador [kompōōtáðor'] *nm,* **computadora** [kompōōtàðo'rá] *nf* computer; ~ **central** mainframe computer; **computador especializado** dedicated computer; ~ **personal** personal computer.

computar [kompōōtár'] *vt* to calculate, compute.

cómputo [kom'pōōto] *nm* calculation, computation.

comulgar [komōōlgár'] *vi* to receive communion.

comulgue [komōōl'ge] *etc vb* V **comulgar.**

común [komōōn'] *a* (*gen*) common; (*corriente*) ordinary; **por lo** ~ generally ♦ *nm:* **el** ~ the community.

comuna [komōō'ná] *nf* commune; (*AM*) district.

comunicación [komōōnēkásyon'] *nf* communication; (*informe*) report.

comunicado [komōōnēká'ðo] *nm* announcement; ~ **de prensa** press release.

comunicar [komōōnēkár'] *vt* to communicate; (*ARQ*) to connect ♦ *vi* to communicate; to send a report; ~**se** *vr* to communicate; **está comunicando** (*TELEC*) the line's busy.

comunicativo, a [komōōnēkátē'ƀo, á] *a* communicative.

comunidad [komōōnēðàð'] *nf* community; ~ **de vecinos** residents' association; **C~ Económica Europea (CEE)** European Economic Community (EEC).

comunión [komōōnyon'] *nf* communion.

comunique [komōōnē'ke] *etc vb* V **comunicar.**

comunismo [komōōnēs'mo] *nm* communism.

comunista [komōōnē'stá] *a, nm/f* communist.

con [kon] *prep* with; (*a pesar de*) in spite of; (*hacia: tb:* **para** ~) towards; ~ **arreglo a** in accordance with; ~ **que** so, and so; ~ **tal que** so long as; ~ **apretar el botón** by pressing the button; ~ **todo, él la quiere mucho** in spite of it all, he loves her dearly.

conato [koná'to] *nm* attempt; ~ **de robo** attempted robbery.

cóncavo, a [kon'káƀo, á] *a* concave.

concebir [konseƀēr'] *vt* to conceive; (*imaginar*) to imagine ♦ *vi* to conceive.

conceder [konseðer'] *vt* to concede.

concejal, a [konsehál', á] *nm/f* town councilman (*US*) o councillor (*Brit*).

concejo [konse'ho] *nm* council.

concentración [konsentrásyon'] *nf* concentration.

concentrar [konsentrár'] *vt*, **~se** *vr* to concentrate.

concepción [konsepsyon'] *nf* conception.

concepto [konsep'to] *nm* concept; **por ~ de** as, by way of; **tener buen ~ de uno** to think highly of sb; **bajo ningún ~** under no circumstances.

conceptuar [konseptwár'] *vt* to judge.

concernir [konsernēr'] *vi*: **en lo que concierne a** concerning.

concertar [konsertár'] *vt* (*MUS*) to harmonize; (*acordar: precio*) to agree; (: *tratado*) to conclude; (*trato*) to arrange, fix up; (*combinar: esfuerzos*) to coordinate; (*reconciliar: personas*) to reconcile ♦ *vi* to harmonize, be in tune.

concesión [konsesyon'] *nf* concession; (*COM: fabricación*) license (*US*), licence (*Brit*).

concesionario, a [konsesyoná'ryo, á] *nm/f* (*COM*) (licensed) dealer, agent, concessionaire; (: *de venta*) franchisee; (: *de transportes etc*) contractor.

conciencia [konsyen'syá] *nf* (*moral*) conscience; (*conocimiento*) awareness; **libertad de ~** freedom of worship; **tener/tomar ~ de** to be/become aware of; **tener la ~ limpia** *o* **tranquila** to have a clear conscience; **tener plena ~ de** to be fully aware of.

concienciar [konsyensyár'] *vt* to make aware; **~se** *vr* to become aware.

concienzudo, a [konsyensōō'tho, á] *a* conscientious.

concierne [konsyer'ne] *etc vb V* **concernir**.

concierto [konsyer'to] *etc vb V* **concertar** ♦ *nm* concert; (*obra*) concerto.

conciliación [konsēlyásyon'] *nf* conciliation.

conciliar [konsēlyár'] *vt* to reconcile ♦ *a* (*REL*) of a council; **~ el sueño** to get to sleep.

concilio [konsē'lyo] *nm* council.

concisión [konsēsyon'] *nf* conciseness.

conciso, a [konsē'so, á] *a* concise.

conciudadano, a [konsyōōtháthá'no, á] *nm/f* fellow citizen.

concluir [konklōōēr'] *vt* (*acabar*) to conclude; (*inferir*) to infer, deduce ♦ *vi*, **~se** *vr* to conclude; **todo ha concluido** it's all over.

conclusión [konklōōsyon'] *nf* conclusion; **llegar a la ~ de que ...** to come to the conclusion that ....

concluya [konklōō'yá] *etc vb V* **concluir**.

concluyente [konklōōyen'te] *a* (*ra__ __ __ información*) conclusive.

concordancia [konkorthán'syá] *nf* agreement.

concordar [konkorthár'] *vt* to reconcile ♦ *vi* to agree, tally.

concordia [konkor'thyá] *nf* harmony.

concretamente [konkretámen'te] *ad* specifically, to be exact.

concretar [konkretár'] *vt* to make concrete, make more specific; (*problema*) to pinpoint; **~se** *vr* to become more definite.

concreto, a [konkre'to, á] *a*, *nm* (*AM*) concrete; **en ~** (*en resumen*) to sum up; (*específicamente*) specifically; **no hay nada en ~** there's nothing definite.

concubina [konkōōbē'ná] *nf* concubine.

concuerde [konkwer'the] *etc vb V* **concordar**.

concupiscencia [konkōōpēsen'syá] *nf* (*avancia*) greed; (*lujuria*) lustfulness.

concurrencia [konkōōrren'syá] *nf* turnout.

concurrido, a [konkōōrrē'tho, á] *a* (*calle*) busy; (*local, reunión*) crowded.

concurrir [konkōōrrēr'] *vi* (*juntarse: ríos*) to meet, come together; (: *personas*) to gather, meet.

concursante [konkōōrsán'te] *nm* competitor.

concursar [konkōōrsár'] *vi* to compete.

concurso [konkōōr'so] *nm* (*de público*) crowd; (*ESCOL, DEPORTE, competencia*) competition; (*COM*) invitation to tender; (*examen*) open competition; (*TV etc*). quiz; (*ayuda*) help, cooperation.

concha [kontch'á] *nf* shell.

condado [kondá'tho] *nm* county.

condal [kondál'] *a*: **la ciudad ~** Barcelona.

conde [kon'de] *nm* count.

condecoración [kondekorásyon'] *nf* (*MIL*) medal, decoration.

condecorar [kondekorár'] *vt* to decorate.

condena [konde'ná] *nf* sentence; **cumplir una ~** to serve a sentence.

condenación [kondenásyon'] *nf* condemnation; (*REL*) damnation.

condenado, a [kondená'tho, á] *a* (*JUR*) condemned; (*fam: maldito*) damned ♦ *nm/f* (*JUR*) convicted person.

condenar [kondenár'] *vt* to condemn; (*JUR*) to convict; **~se** *vr* (*JUR*) to confess (one's guilt); (*REL*) to be damned.

condensar [kondensár'] *vt* to condense.

condesa [konde'sá] *nf* countess.

condescendencia [kondesenden'syá] *nf* condescension; **aceptar algo por ~** to accept sth so as not to hurt feelings.

condescender [kondesender'] *vi* to acquiesce, comply.

condescienda [kondesyen'dá] *etc vb V* **condescender**.

condición [kondēsyon'] *nf* (*gen*) condition; (*rango, social clase*) __ __ __ tp. (*cualidades*) qualities; (*estado*) condition; **a ~ de que ...** on condition that ...; **las condiciones del contrato** the terms of the contract; **condiciones de trabajo** working conditions; **condiciones de venta** conditions of sale.

condicionamiento [kondēsyonámyen'to] *nm* conditioning.

condicional [kondēsyonál'] *a* conditional.

condicionar [kondēsyonár'] *vt* (*acondicionar*) to condition; ~ **algo a algo** to make sth conditional *o* dependent on sth.

condimento [kondēmen'to] *nm* seasoning.

condiscípulo, a [kondēsē'pōolo, á] *nm/f* fellow student.

condolerse [kondoler'se] *vr* to sympathize.

condominio [kondomē'nyo] *nm* (*COM*) joint ownership.

condón [kondon'] *nm* condom.

condonar [kondonár'] *vt* (*JUR: reo*) to reprieve; (*COM: deuda*) to cancel.

conducente [kondōōsen'te] *a*: ~ **a** conducive to, leading to.

conducir [kondōōsēr'] *vt* to take, convey; (*ELEC etc*) to carry; (*AUTO*) to drive; (*negocio*) to manage ♦ *vi* to drive; (*fig*) to lead; ~**se** *vr* to behave.

conducta [kondōōk'tá] *nf* conduct, behavior (*US*), behaviour (*Brit*).

conducto [kondōōk'to] *nm* pipe, tube; (*fig*) channel; (*ELEC*) lead; **por** ~ **de** through.

conductor, a [kondōōktor', á] *a* leading, guiding ♦ *nm* (*FÍSICA*) conductor; (*de vehículo*) driver.

conduela [kondwe'lá] *etc vb* V **condolerse**.

conduje [kondōō'he] *etc vb* V **conducir**.

conduzca [kondōōs'ká] *etc vb* V **conducir**.

conectado, a [konektá'ðo, á] *a* (*ELEC*) connected, plugged in; (*INFORM*) on-line.

conectar [konektár'] *vt* to connect (up), plug in; (*INFORM*) to toggle on; ~**se** *vr* (*INFORM*) to log in (on).

conejillo [konehē'yo] *nm*: ~ **de Indias** guinea pig.

conejo [kone'ho] *nm* rabbit.

conexión [koneksyon'] *nf* connection; (*INFORM*) logging in (on).

confabularse [konfábōōlár'se] *vr*: ~ (**para hacer algo**) to plot, conspire (to do sth).

confección [konfeksyon'] *nf* (*preparación*) preparation, making-up; (*industria*) clothing industry; (*producto*) article; **de** ~ (*ropa*) off-the-rack (*US*) *o* peg (*Brit*).

confeccionar [konfe(k)syonár'] *vt* to make (up).

confederación [konfetherásyon'] *nf* confederation.

conferencia [konferen'syá] *nf* conference; (*lección*) lecture; (*TELEC*) call; ~ **de cobro revertido** (*TELEC*) collect (*US*) *o* reversed-charge (*Brit*) call; ~ **cumbre** summit (conference).

conferenciante [konferensyán'te] *nm/f* lecturer.

conferir [konferēr'] *vt* to award.

confesar [konfesár'] *vt* (*admitir*) to confess, admit; (*error*) to acknowledge; (*crimen*) to own up to.

confesión [konfesyon'] *nf* confession.

confesionario [konfesyoná'ryo] *nm* confessional.

confeso, a [konfe'so, á] *a* (*JUR etc*) self-confessed.

confeti [konfe'tē] *nm* confetti.

confiado, a [konfyá'ðo, á] *a* (*crédulo*) trusting; (*seguro*) confident; (*presumido*) conceited, vain.

confianza [konfyán'sá] *nf* trust; (*aliento, confidencia*) confidence; (*familiaridad*) intimacy, familiarity; (*pey*) vanity, conceit; **margen de** ~ credibility gap; **tener** ~ **con uno** to be on close terms with sb.

confiar [konfyár'] *vt* to entrust ♦ *vi* (*fiarse*) to trust; (*contar con*) to rely; ~**se** *vr* to put one's trust.

confidencia [konfēthen'syá] *nf* confidence.

confidencial [konfēthensyál'] *a* confidential.

confidente [konfēthen'te] *nm/f* confidant/e; (*policial*) informer.

confiera [konfye'rá] *etc vb* V **conferir**.

confiese [konfye'se] *etc vb* V **confesar**.

configuración [konfēgōōrásyon'] *nf* (*tb INFORM*) configuration; **la** ~ **del terreno** the lie of the land; ~ **de bits** (*INFORM*) bit pattern.

configurar [konfēgōōrár'] *vt* to shape, form.

confín [konfēn'] *nm* limit; **confines** *nmpl* confines, limits.

confinar [konfēnár'] *vi* to confine; (*desterrar*) to banish.

confiriendo [konfēryen'do] *etc vb* V **conferir**.

confirmar [konfērmár'] *vt* to confirm; (*JUR etc*) to corroborate; **la excepción confirma la regla** the exception proves the rule.

confiscar [konfēskár'] *vt* to confiscate.

confisque [konfēs'ke] *etc vb* V **confiscar**.

confitado, a [konfētá'ðo, á] *a*: **fruta confitada** candied (*US*) *o* crystallised (*Brit*) fruit.

confite [konfē'te] *nm* candy (*US*), sweet (*Brit*).

confitería [konfēterē'á] *nf* confectionery; (*tienda*) candy store (*US*), confectioner's (shop) (*Brit*).

confitura [konfētōō'rá] *nf* jam.

conflagración [konflágrásyon'] *nf* conflagration.

conflictivo, a [konflēktē'ðo, á] *a* (*asunto, propuesta*) controversial; (*país, situación*) troubled.

conflicto [konflēk'to] *nm* conflict; (*fig*) clash; (: *dificultad*): **estar en un** ~ to be in a jam; ~ **laboral** labor dispute.

confluir [konflōōēr'] *vi* (*ríos etc*) to meet; (*gente*) to gather.

confluya [konflōō'yá] *etc vb* V **confluir**.

conformar [konformár'] *vt* to shape, fashion ♦ *vi* to agree; **~se** *vr* to conform; (*resignarse*) to resign o.s.

conforme [konfor'me] *a* alike, similar; (*de acuerdo*) agreed, in agreement; (*satisfecho*) satisfied ♦ *ad* as ♦ *excl* agreed! ♦ *nm* agreement ♦ *prep*: **~ a** in accordance with.

conformidad [konformētháth'] *nf* (*semejanza*) similarity; (*acuerdo*) agreement; (*resignación*) resignation; **de/en ~ con** in accordance with; **dar su ~** to consent.

conformismo [konformēs'mo] *nm* conformism.

conformista [konformē'stá] *nm/f* conformist.

confortable [konfortá'ßle] *a* comfortable.

confortar [konfortár'] *vt* to comfort.

confraternidad [konfráternētháth'] *nf* brotherhood; **espíritu de ~** feeling of unity.

confrontación [konfrontásyon'] *nf* confrontation.

confrontar [konfrontár'] *vt* to confront; (*dos personas*) to bring face to face; (*cotejar*) to compare ♦ *vi* to border.

confundir [konfoondēr'] *vt* (*borrar*) to blur; (*equivocar*) to mistake, confuse; (*mezclar*) to mix; (*turbar*) to confuse; **~se** *vr* (*hacerse borroso*) to become blurred; (*turbarse*) to get confused; (*equivocarse*) to make a mistake; (*mezclarse*) to mix.

confusión [konfoosyon'] *nf* confusion.

confusionismo [konfoosyonēs'mo] *nm* confusion, uncertainty.

confuso, a [konfoo'so, á] *a* (*gen*) confused; (*recuerdo*) hazy; (*estilo*) obscure.

congelación [konhelásyon'] *nf* freezing; **~ de créditos** credit freeze.

congelado, a [konhelá'tho, á] *a* frozen ♦ *nmpl*: **~s** frozen food(s) (*sg*).

congelador [konhelátḥor'], **congeladora** [konhelátḥo'rá] *nf* (*aparato*) freezer, deep freeze.

congelar [konhelár'] *vt* to freeze; **~se** *vr* (*sangre, grasa*) to congeal.

congeniar [konhenyár'] *vi* to get along (well).

congénito, a [konhe'nēto, á] *a* congenital.

congestión [konhestyon'] *nf* congestion.

congestionado, a [konhestyoná'tho, á] *a* congested.

congestionar [konhestyonár'] *vt* to congest; **~se** *vr* to become congested; **se le congestionó la cara** his face became flushed.

conglomeración [konglomerásyon'] *nf* conglomeration.

conglomerado [konglomerá'tho] *nm* conglomerate.

Congo [kon'go] *nm*: **el ~** the Congo.

congoja [kongo'há] *nf* distress, grief.

congraciarse [kongrásyár'se] *vr* to ingratiate o.s.

congratular [kongrátoolár'] *vt* to congratulate.

congregación [kongreġásyon'] *nf* congregation.

congregar [kongreġár'] *vt*, **~se** *vr* to gather together.

congregue [kongre'ġe] *etc vb* V **congregar**.

congresista [kongresē'stá] *nm/f* delegate, congressman/woman.

congreso [kongre'so] *nm* congress; **C~ de los Diputados** (*Esp POL*) ≈ House of Representatives (*US*), House of Commons (*Brit*).

congrio [kong'ryo] *nm* conger (eel).

congruente [kongrwen'te], **congruo, a** [kong'rwo, á] *a* congruent, congruous.

conjetura [konhetoo'rá] *nf* guess; (*COM*) guesstimate.

conjeturar [konhetoorár'] *vt* to guess.

conjugar [konhooġár'] *vt* to combine, fit together; (*LING*) to conjugate.

conjugue [konhoo'ġe] *etc vb* V **conjugar**.

conjunción [konhoonsyon'] *nf* conjunction.

conjunto, a [konhoon'to, á] *a* joint, united ♦ *nm* whole; (*MUS*) band; (*vestido*) ensemble; (*INFORM*) set; **en ~** as a whole; **~ integrado de programas** (*INFORM*) integrated software package.

conjura [konhoo'rá] *nf* plot, conspiracy.

conjurar [konhoorár'] *vt* (*REL*) to exorcise; (*peligro*) to ward off ♦ *vi* to plot.

conjuro [konhoo'ro] *nm* spell.

conllevar [konyeßár'] *vt* to bear; (*implicar*) to imply, involve.

conmemoración [konmemorásyon'] *nf* commemoration.

conmemorar [konmemorár'] *vt* to commemorate.

conmigo [konmē'ġo] *pron* with me.

conminar [konmēnár'] *vt* to threaten.

conmiseración [konmēserásyon'] *nf* pity, commiseration.

conmoción [konmosyon'] *nf* shock; (*POL*) disturbance; (*fig*) upheaval; **~ cerebral** (*MED*) concussion.

conmovedor, a [konmoßethor', á] *a* touching, moving; (*emocionante*) exciting.

conmover [konmoßer'] *vt* to shake, disturb; (*fig*) to move; **~se** *vr* (*fig*) to be moved.

conmueva [konmwe'ßá] *etc vb* V **conmover**.

conmutación [konmootásyon'] *nf* (*INFORM*) switching; **~ de mensajes** message switching; **~ por paquetes** packet switching.

conmutador [konmootátḥor'] *nm* switch; (*AM TELEC*) switchboard.

conmutar [konmootár'] *vt* (*JUR*) to commute.

connivencia [konnēßen'syá] *nf*: **estar en ~**

con to be in collusion with.

cono [ko'no] *nm* cone.

conocedor, a [konose'ðor', á] *a* expert, knowledgeable ♦ *nm/f* expert, connoisseur.

conocer [konoser'] *vt* to know; (*por primera vez*) to meet, get to know; (*entender*) to know about; (*reconocer*) to recognize; **~se** *vr* (*una persona*) to know o.s.; (*dos personas*) to (get to) know each other; **darse a ~** (*presentarse*) to make o.s. known; **se conoce que ...** (*parece*) apparently ....

conocido, a [konose'ðo, á] *a* (well-)known ♦ *nm/f* acquaintance.

conocimiento [konosēmyen'to] *nm* knowledge; (*MED*) consciousness; (*NAUT*: *tb*: **~ de embarque**) bill of lading; **~s** *nmpl* (*personas*) acquaintances; (*saber*) knowledge *sg*; **hablar con ~ de causa** to speak from experience; **~ (de embarque) aéreo** (*COM*) air waybill.

conotación [konotásyon'] *nf* connotation.

conozca [konos'ká] *etc vb V* **conocer**.

conque [kon'ke] *conj* and so, so then.

conquense [konken'se] *a* of *o* from Cuenca ♦ *nm/f* native *o* inhabitant of Cuenca.

conquista [konke'stá] *nf* conquest.

conquistador, a [konkēstáðor', á] *a* conquering ♦ *nm* conqueror.

conquistar [konkēstár'] *vt* (*MIL*) to conquer; (*puesto, simpatía*) to win; (*enamorar*) to win the heart of.

consabido, a [konsaβē'ðo, á] *a* (*frase etc*) old; (*pey*): **las consabidas excusas** the same old excuses.

consagrado, a [konsáǧrá'ðo, á] *a* (*REL*) consecrated; (*actor*) established.

consagrar [konsáǧrár'] *vt* (*REL*) to consecrate; (*fig*) to devote.

consciente [konsyen'te] *a* conscious; **ser** *o* **estar ~ de** to be aware of.

consecución [konsekōōsyon'] *nf* acquisition; (*de fin*) attainment.

consecuencia [konsekwen'syá] *nf* consequence, outcome; (*firmeza*) consistency; **de ~** of importance.

consecuente [konsekwen'te] *a* consistent.

consecutivo, a [konsekōōtē'βo, á] *a* consecutive.

conseguir [konseǧēr'] *vt* to get, obtain; (*sus fines*) to attain.

consejero, a [konsehe'ro, á] *nm/f* adviser, consultant; (*POL*) councilor (*US*), councillor (*Brit*); (*COM*) director; (*en comisión*) member.

consejo [konse'ho] *nm* advice; (*POL*) council; (*COM*) board; **un ~** a piece of advice; **~ de administración** board of directors; **~ de guerra** court-martial; **C~ de Europa** Council of Europe.

consenso [konsen'so] *nm* consensus.

consentido, a [konsentē'ðo, á] *a* (*mimado*) spoiled.

consentimiento [konsentēmyen'to] *nm* consent.

consentir [konsentēr'] *vt* (*permitir, tolerar*) to consent to; (*mimar*) to pamper, spoil ♦ *vi* to agree, consent; **~ que uno haga algo** to allow sb to do sth.

conserje [konser'he] *nm* caretaker; (*portero*) porter.

conservación [konserβásyon'] *nf* conservation; (*de alimentos, vida*) preservation.

conservador, a [konserβáðor', á] *a* (*POL*) conservative ♦ *nm/f* conservative.

conservadurismo [konserβáðōōrēs'mo] *nm* (*POL etc*) conservatism.

conservante [konserβán'te] *nm* preservative.

conservar [konserβár'] *vt* (*gen*) to preserve; (*recursos*) to conserve, keep; (*alimentos, vida*) to preserve; **~se** *vr* to survive.

conservas [konser'βás] *nfpl*: **~ (alimenticias)** canned (*US*) *o* tinned (*Brit*) goods.

conservatorio [konserβáto'ryo] *nm* (*MUS*) conservatory; (*AM*) greenhouse.

considerable [konsēðerá'βle] *a* considerable.

consideración [konsēðerásyon'] *nf* consideration; (*estimación*) respect; **de ~** important; **tomar en ~** to take into account.

considerado, a [konsēðerá'ðo, á] *a* (*atento*) considerate; (*respetado*) respected.

considerar [konsēðerár'] *vt* (*gen*) to consider; (*meditar*) to think about; (*tener en cuenta*) to take into account.

consienta [konsyen'tá] *etc vb V* **consentir**.

consigna [konsēǧ'ná] *nf* (*orden*) order, instruction; (*para equipajes*) luggage checkroom (*US*), left-luggage office (*Brit*).

consignación [konsēǧnásyon'] *nf* consignment; **~ de créditos** allocation of credits.

consignador [konsēǧnáðor'] *nm* (*COM*) consignor.

consignar [konsēǧnár'] *vt* (*COM*) to send; (*créditos*) to allocate.

consignatario, a [konsēǧnátá'ryo, á] *nm/f* (*COM*) consignee.

consigo [konsē'ǧo] *etc vb V* **conseguir** ♦ *pron* (*m*) with him; (*f*) with her; (*usted*) with you; (*reflexivo*) with o.s.

consiguiendo [konsēǧyen'do] *etc vb V* **conseguir**.

consiguiente [konsēǧyen'te] *a* consequent; **por ~** and so, therefore, consequently.

consintiendo [konsēntyen'do] *etc vb V* **consentir**.

consistente [konsēsten'te] *a* consistent; (*sólido*) solid, firm; (*válido*) sound; **~ en** consisting of.

consistir [konsēstēr'] *vi*: **~ en** (*componerse*

de) to consist of; (*ser resultado de*) to be due to.

consola [konso'lá] *nf* console, control panel; (*mueble*) console table; ~ **de mando** (*INFORM*) control console; ~ **de visualización** visual display console.

consolación [konsolásyon'] *nf* consolation.

consolar [konsolár'] *vt* to console.

consolidar [konsolēthár'] *vt* to consolidate.

consomé, *pl* **consomés** *nm* [konsome', konsomes'] consommé, clear soup.

consonancia [konsonán'syá] *nf* harmony; **en ~ con** in accordance with.

consonante [konsonán'te] *a* consonant, harmonious ♦ *nf* consonant.

consorcio [konsor'syo] *nm* (*COM*) consortium, syndicate.

consorte [konsor'te] *nm/f* consort.

conspicuo, a [konspē'kwo, á] *a* conspicuous.

conspiración [konspērásyon'] *nf* conspiracy.

conspirador, a [konspēráthor', á] *nm/f* conspirator.

conspirar [konspērár'] *vi* to conspire.

constancia [konstán'syá] *nf* (*gen*) constancy; (*certeza*) certainly; **dejar ~ de algo** to put sth on record.

constante [konstán'te] *a*, *nf* constant.

constar [konstár'] *vi* (*evidenciarse*) to be clear *o* evident; ~ **(en)** to appear (in); ~ **de** to consist of; **hacer ~** to put on record; **me consta que ...** I have evidence that ...; **que conste que lo hice por ti** believe me, I did it for your own good.

constatar [konstátár'] *vt* (*controlar*) to check; (*observar*) to note.

constelación [konstelásyon'] *nf* constellation.

consternación [konsternásyon'] *nf* consternation.

constipado, a [konstēpá'tho, á] *a*: **estar ~** to have a cold ♦ *nm* cold.

constitución [konstētōōsyon'] *nf* constitution.

constitucional [konstētōōsyonál'] *a* constitutional.

constituir [konstētōōēr'] *vt* (*formar, componer*) to constitute, make up; (*fundar, erigir, ordenar*) to constitute, establish; (*ser*) to be; ~**se** *vr* (*POL etc*: *cuerpo*) to be composed; (: *fundarse*) to be established.

constitutivo, a [konstētōōtē'tho, á] *a* constitutive, constituent.

constituya [konstētōō'yá] *etc vb* V **constituir**.

constituyente [konstētōōyen'te] *a* constituent.

constreñir [konstrenyēr'] *vt* (*obligar*) to compel, oblige; (*restringir*) to restrict.

constriño [konstrē'nyo] *etc*, **constriñendo**

[konstrēnyen'do] *etc vb* V **constreñir**.

construcción [konstrōōksyon'] *nf* construction, building.

constructor, a [konstrōōktor', á] *nm/f* builder.

construir [konstrōōēr'] *vt* to build, construct.

construyendo [konstrōōyen'do] *etc vb* V **construir**.

consuelo [konswe'lo] *etc vb* V **consolar** ♦ *nm* consolation, solace.

consuetudinario, a [konswetōōthēná'ryo, á] *a* customary; **derecho ~** common law.

cónsul [kon'sōōl] *nm* consul.

consulado [konsōōlá'tho] *nm* (*sede*) consulate; (*cargo*) consulship.

consulta [konsōōl'tá] *nf* consultation; (*MED*: *consultorio*) consulting room; (*INFORM*) enquiry; **horas de ~** office (*US*) *o* surgery (*Brit*) hours; **obra de ~** reference book.

consultar [konsōōltár'] *vt* to consult; ~ **un archivo** (*INFORM*) to search a file.

consultor, a [konsōōltor', á] *nm*: ~ **en dirección de empresas** management consultant.

consultorio [konsōōlto'ryo] *nm* (*MED*) doctor's office (*US*), surgery (*Brit*).

consumado, a [konsōōmá'tho, á] *a* perfect; (*bribón*) out-and-out.

consumar [konsōōmár'] *vt* to complete, carry out; (*crimen*) to commit; (*sentencia*) to carry out.

consumición [konsōōmēsyon'] *nf* consumption; (*bebida*) drink; (*comida*) food; ~ **mínima** cover charge.

consumido, a [konsōōmē'tho, á] *a* (*flaco*) skinny.

consumidor, a [konsōōmēthor', á] *nm/f* consumer.

consumir [konsōōmēr'] *vt* to consume; ~**se** *vr* to be consumed; (*persona*) to waste away.

consumismo [konsōōmēs'mo] *nm* (*COM*) consumerism.

consumo [konsōō'mo] *nm* consumption; **bienes de ~** consumer goods.

contabilice [kontáhēlē'se] *etc vb* V **contabilizar**.

contabilidad [kontáhēlētháth'] *nf* accounting, book-keeping; (*profesión*) accountancy; (*COM*): ~ **analítica** variable pricing (*US*) *o* costing (*Brit*); ~ **de costos** cost accounting; ~ **de doble partida** double-entry book-keeping; ~ **de gestión** management accounting; ~ **por partida simple** single-entry book-keeping.

contabilizar [kontáhēlē'sár'] *vt* to enter in the accounts.

contable [kontá'hle] *nm/f* bookkeeper; (*licenciado*) accountant; ~ **de costos** (*COM*) cost accountant.

contacto [konták'to] *nm* contact; **lentes de** ~ contact lenses; **estar en** ~ **con** to be in touch with.

contado, a [kontá'ðo, á] *a:* ~**s** (*escasos*) numbered, scarce, few ♦ *nm:* **al** ~ for cash; **pagar al** ~ to pay (in) cash; **precio al** ~ cash price.

contador [kontaðor'] *nm* (*aparato*) meter; (*AM: contable*) accountant.

contaduría [kontaðoorē'á] *nf* accountant's office.

contagiar [kontahyàr'] *vt* (*enfermedad*) to pass on, transmit; (*persona*) to infect; ~**se** *vr* to become infected.

contagio [kontá'hyo] *nm* infection.

contagioso, a [kontáhyo'so, á] *a* infectious; (*fig*) catching.

contaminación [kontámēnásyon'] *nf* (*gen*) contamination; (*del ambiente etc*) pollution.

contaminar [kontámēnár'] *vt* (*gen*) to contaminate; (*aire, agua*) to pollute; (*fig*) to taint.

contante [kontán'te] *a:* **dinero** ~ **(y sonante)** hard cash.

contar [kontár'] *vt* (*páginas, dinero*) to count; (*anécdota etc*) to tell ♦ *vi* to count; ~**se** *vr* to be counted, figure; ~ **con** to rely on, count on; **sin** ~ not to mention; **le cuento entre mis amigos** I count him among my friends.

contemplación [kontemplásyon'] *nf* contemplation; **no andarse con contemplaciones** not to stand on ceremony.

contemplar [kontemplár'] *vt* to contemplate; (*mirar*) to look at.

contemporáneo, a [kontemporá'neo, á] *a, nm/f* contemporary.

contemporizar [kontemporēsár'] *vi:* ~ **con** to keep in with.

contención [kontensyon'] *nf* (*JUR*) suit; **muro de** ~ retaining wall.

contencioso, a [kontensyo'so, á] *a* (*JUR etc*) contentious ♦ *nm* (*POL*) conflict, dispute.

contender [kontender'] *vi* to contend; (*en un concurso*) to compete.

contendiente [kontendyen'te] *nm/f* contestant.

contendrá [kontendrá'] *etc vb* V **contener**.

contenedor [konteneðor'] *nm* container.

contenedorización [konteneðorēsásyon'] *nf* (*COM*) containerization.

contener [kontener'] *vt* to contain, hold; (*risa etc*) to hold back, contain; ~**se** *vr* to control o restrain o.s.

contenga [konten'gá] *etc vb* V **contener**.

contenido, a [kontenē'ðo, á] *a* (*moderado*) restrained; (*risa etc*) suppressed ♦ *nm* contents *pl*, content.

contentar [kontentár'] *vt* (*satisfacer*) to sat-

isfy; (*complacer*) to please; (*COM*) to endorse; ~**se** *vr* to be satisfied.

contento, a [konten'to, á] *a* contented, content; (*alegre*) pleased; (*feliz*) happy.

contestación [kontestásyon'] *nf* answer, reply; ~ **a la demanda** (*JUR*) defense plea.

contestador [kontestaðor'] *nm:* ~ **automático** answering machine.

contestar [kontestár'] *vt* to answer (back), reply; (*JUR*) to corroborate, confirm.

contexto [kontek'sto] *nm* context.

contienda [kontyen'dá] *nf* contest, struggle.

contiene [kontye'ne] *etc vb* V **contener**.

contigo [kontē'go] *pron* with you.

contiguo, a [kontē'gwo, á] *a* (*de al lado*) next; (*vecino*) adjacent, adjoining.

continente [kontēnen'te] *a, nm* continent.

contingencia [kontēnhen'syá] *nf* contingency; (*riesgo*) risk; (*posibilidad*) eventuality.

contingente [kontēnhen'te] *a* contingent ♦ *nm* contingent; (*COM*) quota.

continuación [kontēnwásyon'] *nf* continuation; **a** ~ then, next.

continuar [kontēnwár'] *vt* to continue, go on with; (*reanudar*) to resume ♦ *vi* to continue, go on; ~ **hablando** to continue talking o to talk.

continuidad [kontēnwēðáð'] *nf* continuity.

continuo, a [kontē'nwo, á] *a* (*sin interrupción*) continuous; (*acción perseverante*) continual.

contonearse [kontoneár'se] *vr* (*hombre*) to swagger; (*mujer*) to swing her hips.

contorno [kontor'no] *nm* outline; (*GEO*) contour; ~**s** *nmpl* neighborhood *sg*, surrounding area *sg*.

contorsión [kontorsyon'] *nf* contortion.

contra [kon'trá] *prep* against; (*COM: giro*) on ♦ *ad* against ♦ *a, nm/f* (*POL fam*) counter-revolutionary ♦ *nm con* ♦ *nf:* **la C**~ **(nicaragüense)** the Contras *pl*.

contraalmirante [kontráálmērán'te] *nm* rear admiral.

contraataque [kontráátá'ke] *nm* counterattack.

contrabajo [kontráðá'ho] *nm* double bass.

contrabandista [kontráðándē'stá] *nm/f* smuggler.

contrabando [kontráðán'do] *nm* (*acción*) smuggling; (*mercancías*) contraband; ~ **de armas** gun-running.

contracción [kontráksyon'] *nf* contraction.

contracorriente [kontrákorryen'te] *nf* cross-current.

contrachapado [kontrátchápá'ðo] *nm* plywood.

contradecir [kontráðesēr'] *vt* to contradict.

contradicción [kontráðēksyon'] *nf* contradiction; **espíritu de** ~ contrariness.

contradiciendo [kontráðēsyen'do] *etc vb*

V **contradecir**.

contradictorio, a [kontrà't̪ĕkto'ryo, à] *a* contradictory.

contradicho [kontrà't̪ĕtch'o] *pp de* **contradecir**.

contradiga [kontràt̪ĕ'g̱à] *etc*, **contradije** [kontràt̪ĕ'he], **contradirá** [kontràt̪ĕrá'] *etc vb V* **contradecir**.

contraer [kontràer'] *vt* to contract; (*hábito*) to acquire; (*limitar*) to restrict; ~**se** *vr* to contract; (*limitarse*) to limit o.s.

contragolpe [kontràg̱ol'pe] *nm* backlash.

contrahaga [kontràá'g̱à] *etc*, **contraharé** [kontràáre'] *etc vb V* **contrahacer**.

contrahecho, a [kontràĕtch'o, à] *pp de* **contrahacer** ♦ *a* fake; (*ANAT*) hunch-backed.

contrahice [kontràĕ'se] *etc vb V* **contrahacer**.

contraiga [kontrà'ĕg̱à] *etc vb V* **contraer**.

contraindicaciones [kontràĕndĕkàsyo'nes] *nfpl* (*MED*) contraindications.

contraje [kontrà'he] *etc vb V* **contraer**.

contraluz [kontràlōōs'] *nf* (*FOTO etc*) back lighting; **a** ~ against the light.

contramaestre [kontràmàes'tre] *nm* foreman.

contraorden [kontràor't̪ĕen] *nf* counter-order, countermand.

contrapartida [kontràpàrtĕ'ĭt̪à] *nf* (*COM*) balancing entry; **como** ~ **(de)** in return (for), as *o* in compensation (for).

contrapelo [kontràpe'lo]: **a** ~ *ad* the wrong way.

contrapesar [kontràpesàr'] *vt* to counterbalance; (*fig*) to offset.

contrapeso [kontràpe'so] *nm* counterweight; (*fig*) counterbalance; (*COM*) make-weight.

contrapondré [kontràpondre'] *etc vb V* **contraponer**.

contraponer [kontràponer'] *vt* (*cotejar*) to compare; (*oponer*) to oppose.

contraponga [kontràpon'g̱à] *etc vb V* **contraponer**.

contraproducente [kontràprot̪ōōsen'te] *a* counterproductive.

contrapuesto [kontràpwe'sto] *pp de* **contraponer**.

contrapunto [kontràpōōn'to] *nm* counterpoint.

contrapuse [kontràpōō'se] *etc vb V* **contraponer**.

contrariar [kontràryàr'] *vt* (*oponerse*) to oppose; (*poner obstáculo*) to impede; (*enfadar*) to annoy.

contrariedad [kontràryet̪àĭt̪'] *nf* (*oposición*) opposition; (*obstáculo*) obstacle, set-back; (*disgusto*) vexation, annoyance.

contrario, a [kontrà'ryo, à] *a* contrary; (*persona*) opposed; (*sentido, lado*) opposite

♦ *nm/f* enemy, adversary; (*DEPORTE*) opponent; **al** ~, **por el** ~ on the contrary; **de lo** ~ otherwise.

Contrarreforma [kontràrrefor'mà] *nf* Counter-Reformation.

contrarrestar [kontràrrestàr'] *vt* to counteract.

contrarrevolución [kontràrrĕolōōsyon'] *nf* counter-revolution.

contrasentido [kontràsentĕ'ĭt̪o] *nm* contradiction; **es un** ~ **que él ...** it doesn't make sense for him to ... .

contraseña [kontràse'nyà] *nf* countersign; (*frase*) password.

contrastar [kontràstàr'] *vt* to resist ♦ *vi* to contrast.

contraste [kontrà'ste] *nm* contrast.

contrata [kontrà'tà] *nf* (*JUR*) written contract; (*empleo*) hiring.

contratar [kontràtàr'] *vt* (*firmar un acuerdo para*) to contract for; (*empleados, obreros*) to hire; (*DEPORTE*) to sign up; ~**se** *vr* to sign on.

contratiempo [kontràtyem'po] *nm* (*revés*) setback; (*accidente*) mishap; **a** ~ (*MUS*) off-beat.

contratista [kontràtĕ'stà] *nm/f* contractor.

contrato [kontrà'to] *nm* contract; ~ **de compraventa** contract of sale; ~ **a precio fijo** fixed-price contract; ~ **a término** future (*US*) *o* forward (*Brit*) contract; ~ **de trabajo** contract of employment *o* service.

contravalor [kontràĭàlor'] *nm* exchange value.

contravención [kontràĭensyon'] *nf* contravention, violation.

contravendré [kontràĭendre'] *etc*, **contravenga** [kontràĭen'g̱à] *etc vb V* **contravenir**.

contravenir [kontràĭenĕr'] *vi*: ~ **a** to contravene, violate.

contraventana [kontràĭentà'nà] *nf* shutter.

contraviene [kontràĭye'ne] *etc*, **contraviniendo** [kontràĭenyen'do] *etc vb V* **contravenir**.

contrayendo [kontràyen'do] *vb V* **contraer**.

contribución [kontrĕĭōōsyon'] *nf* (*municipal etc*) tax; (*ayuda*) contribution; **exento de contribuciones** tax-free.

contribuir [kontrĕĭōōĕr'] *vt, vi* to contribute; (*COM*) to pay (in taxes).

contribuyendo [kontrĕĭōōyen'do] *etc vb V* **contribuir**.

contribuyente [kontrĕĭōōyen'te] *nm/f* (*COM*) taxpayer; (*que ayuda*) contributor.

contrincante [kontrĕnkàn'te] *nm* opponent, rival.

control [kontrol'] *nm* control; (*inspección*) inspection, check; (*COM*): ~ **de calidad** quality control; ~ **de cambios** exchange control; ~ **de costos** cost control; ~ **de créditos** credit control; ~ **de existencias**

stock control; **~ de precios** price control.
controlador, a [kontrolátʰor', á] *nm/f* controller; **~ aéreo** air-traffic controller.
controlar *vt* to control; to inspect, check; (*COM*) to audit.
controversia [kontroʜer'syá] *nf* controversy.
contubernio [kontooʜer'nyo] *nm* ring, conspiracy.
contumaz [kontoomás'] *a* obstinate, stubbornly disobedient.
contundente [kontoonden'te] *a* (*prueba*) conclusive; (*fig: argumento*) convincing; **instrumento ~** blunt instrument.
contusión [kontoosyon'] *nf* bruise.
contuve [kontoo'ʜe] *etc vb* V **contener**.
convalecencia [kombálesen'syá] *nf* convalescence.
convalecer [kombáleser'] *vi* to convalesce, get better.
convaleciente [kombálesyen'te] *a, nm/f* convalescent.
convalezca [kombáles'ká] *etc vb* V **convalecer**.
convalidar [kombáletʰár'] *vt* (*título*) to recognize.
convencer [kombenser'] *vt* to convince; (*persuadir*) to persuade.
convencimiento [kombensēmyen'to] *nm* (*acción*) convincing; (*persuasión*) persuasion; (*certidumbre*) conviction; **tener el ~ de que ...** to be convinced that ... .
convención [kombensyon'] *nf* convention.
convendré [kombendre'] *etc,* **convenga** [komben'gà] *etc vb* V **convenir**.
conveniencia [kombenyen'syá] *nf* suitability; (*conformidad*) agreement; (*utilidad, provecho*) usefulness; **~s** *nfpl* conventions; (*COM*) property *sg*; **ser de la ~ de uno** to suit sb.
conveniente [kombenyen'te] *a* suitable; (*útil*) useful; (*correcto*) fit, proper; (*aconsejable*) advisable.
convenio [kombe'nyo] *nm* agreement, treaty; **~ de nivel crítico** threshold agreement.
convenir [kombenēr'] *vi* (*estar de acuerdo*) to agree; (*ser conveniente*) to suit, be suitable; **"sueldo a ~"** "salary to be agreed"; **conviene recordar que...** it should be remembered that... .
convento [komben'to] *nm* monastery; (*de monjas*) convent.
convenza [komben'sá] *etc vb* V **convencer**.
convergencia [komberhen'syá] *nf* convergence.
converger [komberher'], **convergir** [komber'hēr] *vi* to converge; **sus esfuerzos convergen a un fin común** their efforts are directed towards the same objective.
converja [komber'há] *etc vb* V **converger**, **convergir**.

conversación [kombersásyon'] *nf* conversation.
conversar [kombersár'] *vi* to talk, converse.
conversión [kombersyon'] *nf* conversion.
converso, a [komber'so, á] *nm/f* convert.
convertir [kombertēr'] *vt* to convert; (*transformar*) to transform, turn; (*COM*) to (ex)change; **~se** *vr* (*REL*) to convert.
convicción [kombēksyon'] *nf* conviction.
convicto, a [kombēk'to, á] *a* convicted; (*condenado*) condemned.
convidado, a [kombētʰá'tʰo, á] *nm/f* guest.
convidar [kombētʰár'] *vt* to invite.
conviene [kombye'ne] *etc vb* V **convenir**.
convierta [kombyer'tá] *etc vb* V **convertir**.
convincente [kombēnsen'te] *a* convincing.
conviniendo [kombēnyen'do] *etc vb* V **convenir**.
convirtiendo [kombērtyen'do] *etc vb* V **convertir**.
convite [kombē'te] *nm* invitation; (*banquete*) banquet.
convivencia [kombēʜen'syá] *nf* coexistence, living together.
convivir [kombēʜēr'] *vi* to live together; (*POL*) to coexist.
convocar [kombokár'] *vt* to summon, call (together).
convocatoria [kombokáto'ryá] *nf* summons *sg*; (*anuncio*) notice of meeting; (*ESCOL*) examination session.
convoque [kombo'ke] *etc vb* V **convocar**.
convoy [komboy'] *nm* (*FERRO*) train.
convulsión [komboolsyon'] *nf* convulsion; (*POL etc*) upheaval.
conyugal [konyoogál'] *a* conjugal; **vida ~** married life.
cónyuge [kon'yooʜe] *nm/f* spouse, partner.
coña [ko'nyá] *nf*: **tomar algo a ~** (*fam!*) to take sth as a joke.
coñac *pl* **coñacs** [ko'nyá(k), ko'nyás] *nm* cognac, brandy.
coñazo [konyá'so] *nm* (*fam*) pain; **dar el ~** to be a real pain.
coño [ko'nyo] (*fam!*) *nm* cunt(!) ♦ *excl* (*enfado*) shit(!); (*sorpresa*) damn it to hell(!) (*US*), bloody hell(!) (*Brit*); **¡qué ~!** what a pain in the ass (*US*) o arse(!) (*Brit*).
cooperación [kooperásyon'] *nf* cooperation.
cooperar [kooperár'] *vi* to cooperate.
cooperativo, a [kooperátē'ʜo, á] *a* cooperative ♦ *nf* cooperative.
coordenada [koortʰená'dá] *nf* (*MAT*) coordinate; (*fig*): **~s** *nfpl* guidelines, framework *sg*.
coordinación [koortʰēnásyon'] *nf* coordination.
coordinador, a [koortʰēnátʰor', á] *nm/f* coordinator ♦ *nf* coordinating committee.
coordinar [koortʰēnár'] *vt* to coordinate.
copa [ko'pá] *nf* (*tb DEPORTE*) cup; (*vaso*)

glass; (de árbol) top; (de sombrero) crown; **~s** nfpl (NAIPES) ≈ hearts; **(tomar una)** ~ (to have a) drink; **ir de ~s** to go out for a drink.

coparticipación [kopártēsēpásyon'] nf (COM) co-ownership.

Copenhague [kopcná'gc] Copenhagen.

copete [kopc'te] nm tuft (of hair); **de alto ~** aristocratic, upper-crust (fam).

copia [ko'pyá] nf copy; (ARTE) replica; (COM etc) duplicate; (INFORM): **~ impresa** hard copy; **~ de respaldo** o **de seguridad** backup copy; **hacer ~ de seguridad** to back up; **~ de trabajo** working copy; **~ vaciada** dump.

copiadora [kopyáẗho'rá] nf photocopier; **~ al alcohol** spirit duplicator.

copiar [kopyár'] vt to copy; **~ al pie de la letra** to copy word for word.

copioso, a [kopyo'so, á] a copious, plentiful.

copita [kopē'tá] nf (small) glass; (GOLF) tee.

copla [ko'plá] nf verse; (canción) (popular) song.

copo [ko'po] nm: **~s de maíz** cornflakes; **~ de nieve** snowflake.

coprocesador [koprosesáẗhor'] nm (IN-FORM) co-processor.

coproducción [koproẗhōōksyon'] nf (CINE etc) joint production.

copropietarios [kopropyctá'ryos] nmpl (COM) joint owners.

cópula [ko'pōōlá] nf copulation.

copular [kopōōlár'] vi to copulate.

coqueta [koke'tá] a flirtatious, coquettish ♦ nf (mujer) flirt.

coquetear [koketeár'] vi to flirt.

coraje [korá'he] nm courage; (ánimo) spirit; (ira) anger.

coral [korál'] a choral ♦ nf choir ♦ nm (ZOOL) coral.

Corán [korán'] nm: **el ~** the Koran.

coraza [korá'sá] nf (armadura) armor (US), armour (Brit); (blindaje) armor-plating.

corazón [koráson'] nm heart; (BOT) core; **corazones** nmpl (NAIPES) hearts; **de buen ~** kind-hearted; **de todo ~** wholeheartedly; **estar mal del ~** to have heart trouble.

corazonada [korásoná'ẗhá] nf impulse; (presentimiento) presentiment, hunch.

corbata [korḃá'tá] nf necktie (US), tie (Brit).

corbeta [korḃe'tá] nf corvette.

Córcega [kor'segá] nf Corsica.

corcel [korsel'] nm steed.

corcovado, a [korkoḃá'ẗho, á] a hunchbacked ♦ nm/f hunchback.

corchete [kortche'te] nm catch, clasp; **~s** nmpl (TIP) square brackets.

corcho [kor'tcho] nm cork; (PESCA) float.

cordel [korḋel'] nm cord, line.

cordero [korḋe'ro] nm lamb; (piel) lambskin.

cordial [korḋyál'] a cordial ♦ nm cordial, tonic.

cordialidad [korḋyálēẗháẗh'] nf warmth, cordiality.

cordillera [korḋēŷe'rá] nf range (of mountains).

Córdoba [kor'ḋoḃá] nf Cordova.

cordobés, esa [korḋoḃes', e'sá] a, nm/f Cordovan.

cordón [korḋon'] nm (cuerda) cord, string; (de zapatos) lace; (ELEC) cord (US), flex (Brit); (MIL etc) cordon.

cordura [korḋōō'rá] nf (MED) sanity; (fig) good sense.

Corea [kore'á] nf Korea; **~ del Norte/Sur** North/South Korea.

coreano, a [koreá'no, á] a, nm/f Korean.

corear [koreár'] vt to chorus.

coreografía [koreográfē'á] nf choreography.

corista [korē'stá] nf (TEATRO etc) chorus girl.

cornada [korná'ẗhá] nf (TAUR etc) butt, goring.

corneta [korne'tá] nf bugle.

cornisa [kornē'sá] nf cornice.

Cornualles [kornwá'yes] nm Cornwall.

cornudo, a [kornōō'ẗho, á] a (ZOOL) horned; (marido) cuckolded.

coro [ko'ro] nm chorus; (conjunto de cantores) choir.

corolario [korolá'ryo] nm corollary.

corona [koro'ná] nf crown; (de flores) garland.

coronación [koronásyon'] nf coronation.

coronar [koronár'] vt to crown.

coronel [koronel'] nm colonel.

coronilla [koronē'yá] nf (ANAT) crown (of the head); **estar hasta la ~ (de)** to be utterly fed up (with).

corporación [korporásyon'] nf corporation.

corporal [korporál'] a corporal, bodily.

corpulento, a [korpōōlen'to á] a (persona) well-built.

corral [korrál'] nm (patio) farmyard; (AGR: de aves) poultry yard; (redil) pen.

correa [korre'á] nf strap; (cinturón) belt; (de perro) lead, leash; **~ transportadora** conveyor belt.

correaje [korreá'he] nm (AGR) harness.

corrección [korreksyon'] nf correction; (reprensión) rebuke; (cortesía) good manners; (INFORM): **~ por líneas** line editing; **~ en pantalla** screen editing; **~ (de pruebas)** (TIP) proofreading.

correccional [korreksyonál'] nm reformatory.

correcto, a [korrek'to, á] a correct; (persona) well-mannered.

corredera [korreðe'rá] *nf*: **puerta de ~** sliding door.

corredizo, a [korreðı̄'so, á] *a* (*puerta etc*) sliding; (*nudo*) running.

corredor, a [korreðor', á] *a* running; (*rápido*) fast ♦ *nm/f* (DEPORTE) runner ♦ *nm* (*pasillo*) corridor; (*balcón corrido*) gallery; (COM) agent, broker; (*pasillo*) corridor, passage; **~ de bienes raíces** real-estate broker; **~ de bolsa** stockbroker; **~ de seguros** insurance broker.

corregir [korreħēr'] *vt* (*error*) to correct; (*amonestar, reprender*) to rebuke, reprimand; **~se** *vr* to reform.

correo [korre'o] *nm* mail (US), post (Brit); (*persona*) courier; **C~s** *nmpl* Post Office *sg*; **~ aéreo** airmail; **~ certificado** registered mail; **~ electrónico** electronic mail; **~ urgente** special delivery; **a vuelta de ~** by return mail.

correr [korrer'] *vt* to run; (*viajar*) to cover, travel; (*riesgo*) to run; (*aventura*) to have; (*cortinas*) to draw; (*cerrojo*) to shoot ♦ *vi* to run; (*líquido*) to run, flow; (*rumor*) to go round; **~se** *vr* to slide, move; (*colores*) to run; (*fam: tener orgasmo*) to come; **echar a ~** to break into a run; **~ con los gastos** to pay the expenses; **eso corre de mi cuenta** I'll take care of that.

correspondencia [korresponden'syá] *nf* correspondence; (FERRO) connection; (*reciprocidad*) return; **~ directa** (COM) direct mail.

corresponder [korresponder'] *vi* to correspond; (*convenir*) to be suitable; (*pertenecer*) to belong; (*tocar*) to concern; (*favor*) to repay; **~se** *vr* (*por escrito*) to correspond; (*amarse*) to love one another; **"a quien corresponda"** "to whom it may concern".

correspondiente [korrespondyen'te] *a* corresponding; (*respectivo*) respective.

corresponsal [korresponsál'] *nm/f* (newspaper) correspondent; (COM) agent.

corretaje [korretá'he] *nm* (COM) brokerage.

corretear [korreteár'] *vi* to loiter.

corrido, a [korrē'ðo, á] *a* (*avergonzado*) abashed; (*fluido*) fluent ♦ *nf* run, dash; (*de toros*) bullfight; **de ~** fluently; **3 noches corridas** 3 nights running; **un kilo ~** a good kilo.

corriente [korryen'te] *a* (*agua*) running; (*fig*) flowing; (*dinero, cuenta etc*) current; (*común*) ordinary, normal ♦ *nf* current; (*fig: tendencia*) course ♦ *nm* current month; **~ f de aire** draft (US), draught (Brit); **~ eléctrica** electric current; **las ~s modernas del arte** modern trends in art; **estar al ~ de** to be informed about.

corrigiendo [korrēhyen'do] *etc vb* V **corregir**.

corrija [korrē'há] *etc vb* V **corregir**.

corrillo [korrē'yo] *nm* ring, circle (of people); (*fig*) clique.

corro [ko'rro] *nm* ring, circle (of people); **la gente hizo ~** the people formed a ring.

corroborar [korroßorár'] *vt* to corroborate.

corroer [korroer'] *vt* (*tb fig*) to corrode, eat away; (GEO) to erode.

corroyendo [korroyen'do] *etc vb* V **corroer**.

corromper [korromper'] *vt* (*madera*) to rot; (*fig*) to corrupt.

corrompido, a [korrompē'ðo, á] *a* corrupt.

corrosivo, a [korrosē'ßo, á] *a* corrosive.

corrupción [korrōōpsyon'] *nf* rot, decay; (*fig*) corruption.

corsario [korsá'ryo] *nm* privateer, corsair.

corsé [korse'] *nm* corset.

corso, a [kor'so, á] *a, nm/f* Corsican.

cortacésped [kortáses'peð] *nm* lawn mower.

cortado, a [kortá'ðo, á] *a* (*con cuchillo*) cut; (*leche*) sour; (*confuso*) confused; (*desconcertado*) embarrassed; (*tímido*) shy ♦ *nm* coffee with cream (US), white coffee (with a little milk) (Brit).

cortadora [kortáðo'rá] *nf* cutter, slicer.

cortadura [kortáðōō'rá] *nf* cut.

cortante [kortán'te] *a* (*viento*) biting; (*frío*) bitter.

cortapisa [kortápē'sá] *nf* (*restricción*) restriction; (*traba*) snag.

cortar [kortár'] *vt* to cut; (*suministro*) to cut off; (*un pasaje*) to cut out; (*comunicación*) to cut off ♦ *vi* to cut; **~se** *vr* (*turbarse*) to become embarrassed; (*leche*) to turn, curdle; **~ por lo sano** to settle things once and for all; **~se el pelo** to have one's hair cut.

cortauñas [kortáōō'nyás] *nm inv* nail clippers *pl*.

corte [kor'te] *nm* cut, cutting; (*filo*) edge; (*de tela*) piece, length; (COSTURA) tailoring ♦ *nf* (*real*) royal court; **~ y confección** dressmaking; **~ de corriente** *o* **luz** power cut; **me da ~ pedírselo** I'm embarrassed to ask him for it; **¡qué ~ le di!** I left him with no comeback!; **C~ Internacional de Justicia** International Court of Justice; **las C~s** the Spanish Parliament *sg*; **hacer la ~ a** to woo, court.

cortedad [korteðáð'] *nf* shortness; (*fig*) bashfulness, timidity.

cortejar [kortehár'] *vt* to court.

cortejo [korte'ho] *nm* entourage; **~ fúnebre** funeral procession, cortège.

cortés [kortes'] *a* courteous, polite.

cortesano, a [kortesá'no, á] *a* courtly.

cortesía [kortesē'á] *nf* courtesy.

corteza [korte'sá] *nf* (*de árbol*) bark; (*de pan*) crust; (*de fruta*) peel, skin; (*de queso*) rind.

cortijo [kortē'ho] *nm* farmhouse.
cortina [kortē'nà] *nf* curtain; ~ **de humo** smoke screen.
corto, a [kor'to, à] *a* (*breve*) short; (*tímido*) bashful; ~ **de luces** not very bright; ~ **de oído** hard of hearing; ~ **de vista** short-sighted; **estar** ~ **de fondos** to be short of funds.
cortocircuito [kortosērkwē'to] *nm* short-circuit.
cortometraje [kortometrà'he] *nm* (*CINE*) short.
Coruña [koroō'nyà] *nf*: **La** ~ Corunna.
coruñés, esa [koroōnyes', e'sà] *a* of *o* from Corunna ♦ *nm/f* native *o* inhabitant of Corunna.
corvo, a [kor'ko, à] *a* curved; (*nariz*) hooked ♦ *nf* back of knee.
cosa [ko'sà] *nf* thing; (*asunto*) affair; ~ **de** about; **eso es** ~ **mía** that's my business; **es poca** ~ it's not important; **¡qué** ~ **más rara!** how strange; **en** ~ **de 10 minutos** in about 10 minutes.
cosaco, a [kosá'ko, à] *a, nm/f* Cossack.
coscorrón [koskorron'] *nm* bump on the head.
cosecha [kose'tchà] *nf* (*AGR*) harvest; (*acto*) harvesting; (*de vino*) vintage; (*producción*) yield.
cosechadora [kosetchàḍo'rà] *nf* combine (*US*), combine harvester (*Brit*).
cosechar [kosetchár'] *vt* to harvest, gather (in).
coser [koser'] *vt* to sew; (*MED*) to stitch (up).
cosido [kosē'ḍo] *nm* sewing.
cosmético, a [kosme'tēko, à] *a, nm* cosmetic.
cosmopolita [kosmopolē'tà] *a* cosmopolitan.
coso [ko'so] *nm* bullring.
cosquillas [koskē'yàs] *nfpl*: **hacer** ~ to tickle; **tener** ~ to be ticklish.
cosquilleo [koskēye'o] *nm* tickling (sensation).
cosquilloso, a [koskēyo'so, à] *a* ticklish.
costa [ko'stà] *nf* (*GEO*) coast; **C**~ **Brava** Costa Brava; **C**~ **Cantábrica** Cantabrian Coast; **C**~ **de Marfil** Ivory Coast; **C**~ **del Sol** Costa del Sol; **a** ~ (*COM*) at cost; **a** ~ **de** at the expense of; **a toda** ~ at any price.
costado [kostá'ḍo] *nm* side; **de** ~ (*dormir*) on one's side; **español por los 4** ~**s** Spanish through and through.
costal [kostál'] *nm* sack.
costalada [kostàlà'ḍà] *nf* bad fall.
costar [kostár'] *vt* (*valer*) to cost; **me cuesta hablarle** I find it hard to talk to him; **¿cuánto cuesta?** how much does it cost?
Costa Rica [kostàrē'kà] *nf* Costa Rica.

costarricense [kostárrēsen'se], **costarriqueño, a** [kostárrēke'nyo, à] *a, nm/f* Costa Rican.
coste [ko'ste] *nm* (*COM*): ~ **promedio** average cost; ~**s fijos** fixed costs; *V tb* **costo**.
costear [kosteár'] *vt* to pay for; (*COM etc*) to finance; (*NAUT*) to sail along the coast of; ~**se** *vr* (*negocio*) to pay for itself, cover its costs.
costeño, a [koste'nyo, à] *a* coastal.
costilla [kostē'yà] *nf* rib; (*CULIN*) cutlet.
costo [ko'sto] *nm* cost, price; ~ **directo** direct cost; ~ **de expedición** shipping charges; ~ **de sustitución** replacement cost; ~ **unitario** unit cost; ~ **de la vida** cost of living.
costoso, a [kosto'so, à] *a* costly, expensive.
costra [kos'trà] *nf* (*corteza*) crust; (*MED*) scab.
costumbre [kostoōm'bre] *nf* custom, habit; **como de** ~ as usual.
costura [kostoō'rà] *nf* sewing, needlework; (*confección*) dressmaking; (*zurcido*) seam.
costurera [kostoōre'rà] *nf* dressmaker.
costurero [kostoōre'ro] *nm* sewing box *o* case.
cotejar [kotehár'] *vt* to compare.
cotejo [kote'ho] *nm* comparison.
cotice [kotē'se] *etc vb V* **cotizar**.
cotidiano, a [kotēthyá'no, à] *a* daily, day to day.
cotilla [kotē'yà] *nf* busybody, gossip.
cotillear [kotēyeár'] *vi* to gossip.
cotización [kotēsásyon'] *nf* (*COM*) quotation, price; (*de club*) dues *pl*.
cotizado, a [kotēsá'tho, à] *a* (*fig*) highly-prized.
cotizar [kotēsár'] *vt* (*COM*) to quote, price; ~**se** *vr* (*fig*) to be highly prized; ~**se a** to sell at; (*BOLSA*) to stand at, be quoted at.
coto [ko'to] *nm* (*terreno cercado*) enclosure; (*de caza*) reserve; (*COM*) price-fixing agreement; **poner** ~ **a** to put a stop to.
cotorra [koto'rrà] *nf* (*ZOOL*: *loro*) parrot; (*fam*: *persona*) windbag.
COU [kooō] *nm abr* (*Esp* = *Curso de Orientación Universitario*) *one year course leading to high school diploma and university entrance examinations.*
coyote [koyo'te] *nm* coyote, prairie wolf.
coyuntura [koyoōntoō'rà] *nf* (*ANAT*) joint; (*fig*) juncture, occasion; **esperar una** ~ **favorable** to await a favorable moment.
coz [kos] *nf* kick.
CP *nm abr* (= *computador personal*) PC.
C.P. *abr* (*Esp*) = **Caja Postal**.
C.P.A. *nf abr* (= *Caja Postal de Ahorros*) Post Office Savings Bank.
CP/M *nm abr* (= *Programa de control para microprocesadores*) CP/M.
CPN *nm abr* (*Esp*) = *Cuerpo de la Policía*

Nacional.

cps *abr* (= *caracteres por segundo*) c.p.s.

crac [krák] *nm* (*ECON*) crash.

cráneo [krá'neo] *nm* skull, cranium.

crápula [krá'pŏŏlá] *nf* drunkenness.

cráter [krá'ter] *nm* crater.

creación [kreásyon'] *nf* creation.

creador, a [kreáθor', á] *a* creative ♦ *nm/f* creator.

crear [kreár'] *vt* to create, make; (*originar*) to originate; (*INFORM: archivo*) to create; **~se** *vr* (*comité etc*) to be set up.

crecer [kreser'] *vi* to grow; (*precio*) to rise; **~se** *vr* (*engreírse*) to get cocky.

creces [kre'ses]: **con ~** *ad* amply, fully.

crecido, a [kresē'θo, á] *a* (*persona, planta*) full-grown; (*cantidad*) large ♦ *nf* (*de río*) flood.

creciente [kresyen'te] *a* growing; (*cantidad*) increasing; (*luna*) crescent ♦ *nm* crescent.

crecimiento [kresēmyen'to] *nm* growth; (*aumento*) increase; (*COM*) rise.

credenciales [kreθensyá'les] *nfpl* credentials.

crédito [kre'θēto] *nm* credit; **a ~** on credit; **dar ~ a** to believe (in); **~ al consumidor** consumer credit; **~ rotativo** *o* **renovable** revolving credit.

credo [kre'θo] *nm* creed.

crédulo, a [kre'θŏŏlo, á] *a* credulous.

creencia [kreen'syá] *nf* belief.

creer [kreer'] *vt, vi* to think, believe; (*considerar*) to think, consider; **~se** *vr* to believe o.s. (to be); **~ en** to believe in; **¡ya lo creo!** I should think so!

creíble [kreē'ᵬle] *a* credible, believable.

creído, a [kreē'θo, á] *a* (*engreído*) conceited.

crema [kre'má] *a inv* cream (colored) ♦ *nf* cream; (*natillas*) custard; **la ~ de la sociedad** the cream of society.

cremallera [kremáye'rá] *nf* zipper (*US*), zip (fastener) (*Brit*).

cremoso, a [kremo'so, á] *a* creamy.

crepitar [krepētár'] *vi* (*fuego*) to crackle.

crepúsculo [krepŏŏs'kŏōlo] *nm* twilight, dusk.

crespo, a [kres'po, á] *a* (*pelo*) curly.

crespón [krespon'] *nm* crêpe.

cresta [kres'stá] *nf* (*GEO, ZOOL*) crest.

Creta [kre'tá] *nf* Crete.

creyendo [kreyen'do] *etc vb V* **creer**.

creyente [kreyen'te] *nm/f* believer.

crezca [kres'ká] *etc vb V* **crecer**.

cría [krē'á] *etc vb V* **criar** ♦ *nf V* **crío, a.**

criada [kreá'θá] *nf V* **criado, a.**

criadero [kreáθe'ro] *nm* nursery; (*ZOOL*) breeding place.

criadillas *nfpl* [kryáθē'yás] *nfpl* (*CULIN*) bull's (*o* sheep's) testicles.

criado, a [kreá'θo, á] *nm* servant ♦ *nf*

servant, maid.

criador [kreáθor'] *nm* breeder.

crianza [kreán'sá] *nf* rearing, breeding; (*fig*) breeding; (*MED*) lactation.

criar [kreár'] *vt* (*amamantar*) to suckle, feed; (*educar*) to bring up; (*producir*) to grow, produce; (*animales*) to breed; **~se** *vr* to grow (up); **Dios los cría y ellos se juntan** birds of a feather flock together.

criatura [kreátŏŏ'rá] *nf* creature; (*niño*) baby, (small) child.

criba [krē'ᵬá] *nf* sieve.

cribar [krēᵬár'] *vt* to sieve.

crimen [krē'men] *nm* crime; **~ pasional** crime of passion.

criminal [krēmēnál'] *a, nm/f* criminal.

crin [krēn] *nf* (*tb:* **~es**) mane.

crío, a [krē'o, á] *nm/f* (*fam: chico*) kid ♦ *nf* (*de animales*) rearing, breeding; (*animal*) young.

criollo, a [krēo'yo, á] *a* (*gen*) Creole; (*AM*) native (to America), national ♦ *nm/f* (*gen*) Creole; (*AM*) native American.

crisis [krē'sēs] *nf inv* crisis; **~ nerviosa** nervous breakdown.

crisol [krēsol'] *nm* (*TEC*) crucible; (*fig*) melting pot.

crispar [krēspár'] *vt* (*músculo*) to cause to contract; (*nervios*) to set on edge.

cristal [krēstál'] *nm* crystal; (*de ventana*) glass, pane; (*lente*) lens; **de ~** glass *cpd*; **~ ahumado/tallado** smoked/cut glass.

cristalería [krēstálere'á] *nf* (*tienda*) glassware shop; (*objetos*) glassware.

cristalice [krēstálē'se] *etc vb V* **cristalizar**.

cristalino, a [krēstálē'no, á] *a* crystalline; (*fig*) clear ♦ *nm* lens of the eye.

cristalizar [krēstálēsár'] *vt, vi* to crystallize.

cristiandad [krēstyándáθ'] *nf*, **cristianismo** [krēstyánēs'mo] *nm* Christianity.

cristiano, a [krēstyá'no, á] *a, nm/f* Christian; **hablar en ~** to speak proper Spanish; (*fig*) to speak clearly.

Cristo [krē'sto] *nm* (*dios*) Christ; (*crucifijo*) crucifix.

Cristóbal [krēsto'ᵬál] *nm*: **~ Colón** Christopher Columbus.

criterio [krēte'ryo] *nm* criterion; (*juicio*) judgement; (*enfoque*) attitude, approach; (*punto de vista*) view, opinion; **~ de clasificación** (*INFORM*) sort criterion.

criticar [krētēkár'] *vt* to criticize.

crítico, a [krē'tēko, á] *a* critical ♦ *nm* critic ♦ *nf* criticism; (*TEATRO etc*) review, notice; **la crítica** the critics *pl*.

critique [krētē'ke] *etc vb V* **criticar**.

croar [kroár'] *vi* to croak.

croata [kroá'tá] *a, nm/f* Croat(ian).

cromado [kromá'θo] *nm* chromium plating, chrome.

cromo [kro'mo] *nm* chrome; (*TIP*) colored

(*US*) *o* coloured print (*Brit*).

crónico, a [kro'nĕko, á] *a* chronic ♦ *nf* chronicle, account; (*de periódico*) feature, article.

cronometraje [kronometrá'he] *nm* timing.

cronómetro [krono'metro] *nm* (*DEPORTE*) stopwatch; (*TEC etc*) chronometer.

croqueta [kroke'tá] *nf* croquette, rissole.

croquis [kro'kĕs] *nm inv* sketch.

cruce [kr̄oo'se] *etc vb V* **cruzar** ♦ *nm* crossing; (*de carreteras*) crossroads; (*AUTO etc*) junction, intersection; (*BIO: proceso*) crossbreeding; **luces de** ~ low-beam (*US*) *o* dipped (*Brit*) headlights.

crucero [kr̄oose'ro] *nm* (*NAUT: barco*) cruise ship; (: *viaje*) cruise.

crucificar [kr̄oosĕfĕkár'] *vt* to crucify; (*fig*) to torment.

crucifijo [kr̄oosĕfĕ'ho] *nm* crucifix.

crucifique [kr̄oosĕfĕ'ke] *etc vb V* **crucificar**.

crucigrama [kr̄oosĕg̃rá'má] *nm* crossword (puzzle).

crudeza [kr̄ooᵭe'sá] *nf* (*rigor*) harshness; (*aspereza*) crudeness.

crudo, a [kr̄oo'ᵭo, á] *a* raw; (*no maduro*) unripe; (*petróleo*) crude; (*rudo, cruel*) cruel; (*agua*) hard; (*clima etc*) harsh ♦ *nm* crude (oil).

cruel [kr̄wel] *a* cruel.

crueldad [kr̄weldáᵭ'] *nf* cruelty.

cruento, a [kr̄wen'to, á] *a* bloody.

crujido [kr̄oohĕ'ᵭo] *nm* (*de madera etc*) creak.

crujiente [kr̄oohyen'te] *a* (*galleta etc*) crunchy.

crujir [kr̄oohĕr'] *vi* (*madera etc*) to creak; (*dedos*) to crack; (*dientes*) to grind; (*nieve, arena*) to crunch.

cruz [kr̄oos] *nf* cross; (*de moneda*) tails *sg*; (*fig*) burden; ~ **gamada** swastika; **C~ Roja** Red Cross.

cruzado, a [kr̄oosá'ᵭo, á] *a* crossed ♦ *nm* crusader ♦ *nf* crusade.

cruzar [kr̄oosár'] *vt* to cross; (*palabras*) to exchange; ~**se** *vr* (*líneas etc*) to cross, intersect; (*personas*) to pass each other; ~**se de brazos** to fold one's arms; (*fig*) not to lift a finger to help; ~**se con uno en la calle** to pass sb in the street.

c.s.f. *abr* (= *costo, seguro y flete*) c.a.f. (*US*), c.i.f. (*Brit*).

CSIC [sesĕk'] *nm abr* (*Esp ESCOL*) = *Consejo Superior de Investigaciones Científicas*.

cta, c.ᵗᵃ *abr* (= *cuenta*) a/c.

cta. cto. *abr* (= *carta de crédito*) L.C.

cte. *abr* (= *corriente, de los corrientes*) inst.

CTNE *nf abr* (*TELEC*) = *Compañía Telefónica Nacional de España*.

c/u *abr* (= *cada uno*) ea.

cuaderno [kwáᵭer'no] *nm* notebook; (*de escuela*) workbook (*US*), exercise book

(*Brit*); (*NAUT*) logbook.

cuadra [kwá'ᵭrá] *nf* (*caballeriza*) stable; (*AM*) (city) block.

cuadrado, a [kwáᵭrá'ᵭo, á] *a* square ♦ *nm* (*MAT*) square.

cuadragésimo, a [kwáᵭráhe'sĕmo, á] *num* fortieth.

cuadrángulo [kwáᵭrán'ḡoolo, á] *nm* quadrangle.

cuadrante [kwáᵭrán'te] *nm* quadrant.

cuadrar [kwáᵭrár'] *vt* to square; (*TIP*) to justify ♦ *vi*: ~ **con** (*cuenta*) to square with, tally with; ~**se** *vr* (*soldado*) to stand to attention; ~ **por la derecha/izquierda** to right-/left-justify.

cuadrícula [kwáᵭrĕ'k̄oolá] *nf* (*TIP etc*) grid, ruled squares.

cuadriculado, a [kwáᵭrĕk̄oolá'ᵭo, á] *a*: **papel** ~ squared *o* graph paper.

cuadrilátero [kwáᵭrĕlá'tero] *nm* (*DEPORTE*) boxing ring; (*GEOM*) quadrilateral.

cuadrilla [kwáᵭrĕ'yá] *nf* (*amigos*) party, group; (*pandilla*) gang; (*obreros*) team.

cuadro [kwá'ᵭro] *nm* square; (*PINTURA*) painting; (*TEATRO*) scene; (*diagrama: tb*: ~ **sinóptico**) chart, table, diagram; (*DEPORTE, MED*) team; (*POL*) executive; ~ **de mandos** control panel; **a** ~**s** checkered (*US*), check *cpd* (*Brit*).

cuadruplicarse [kwáᵭr̄ooplĕkár'se] *vr* to quadruple.

cuádruplo, a [kwá'ᵭr̄ooplo, á], **cuádruple** [kwá'ᵭr̄oople] *a* quadruple.

cuajado, a [kwáhá'ᵭo, á] *a*: ~ **de** (*fig*) full of ♦ *nf* (*de leche*) curd.

cuajar [kwáhár'] *vt* to thicken; (*leche*) to curdle; (*sangre*) to congeal; (*adornar*) to adorn; (*CULIN*) to set ♦ *vi* (*nieve*) to lie; (*fig*) to become set, become established; (*idea*) to be received, be acceptable; ~**se** *vr* to curdle; to congeal; (*llenarse*) to fill up.

cuajo [kwá'ho] *nm*: **arrancar algo de** ~ to tear sth out by its roots.

cual [kwál] *ad* like, as ♦ *pron*: **el** ~ *etc* which; (*persona: sujeto*) who; (: *objeto*) whom; **lo** ~ (*relativo*) which; **allá cada** ~ every man to his own taste; **son a** ~ **más gandul** each is as idle as the other; **cada** ~ each one ♦ *a* such as; **tal** ~ just as it is.

cuál [kwál] *pron interrogativo* which (one), what.

cualesquier(a) [kwáleskyer'(á)] *pl de* **cualquier(a)**.

cualidad [kwálĕᵭáᵭ'] *nf* quality.

cualificado, a [kwálĕfĕká'ᵭo, á] *a* (*obrero*) skilled, qualified.

cualquiera [kwálkyc'rá], **cualquier** [kwálkyer'], *pl* **cualesquier(a)** *a* any ♦ *pron* anybody, anyone; (*quienquiera*) whoever; **en cualquier momento** any time; **en cualquier**

parte anywhere; **cualquiera que sea** whichever it is; (*persona*) whoever it is.

cuán [kwán] *adv* how.

cuando [kwán'do] *ad* when; (*aún si*) if, even if ♦ *conj* (*puesto que*) since ♦ *prep:* **yo, ~ niño** ... when I was a child ..., as a child I ...; **~ no sea así** even if it is not so; **~ más** at (the) most; **~ menos** at least; **~ no** if not, otherwise; **de ~ en ~** from time to time; **ven ~ quieras** come when(ever) you like.

cuándo [kwán'do] *ad* when; ¿**desde ~?**, ¿**de ~ acá?** since when?

cuantía [kwàntē'à] *nf* (*alcance*) extent; (*importancia*) importance.

cuantioso, a [kwántyo'so, á] *a* substantial.

cuanto, a [kwán'to, á] *a, pron:* **llévate todo ~ quieras** take as much as you like; **en ~** (*en seguida que*) as soon as; (*ya que*) since, inasmuch as; **en ~ a** as for; **~ más difícil sea** the more difficult it is; **~ más hace (tanto) menos avanza** the more he does, the less he progresses; **~s más invitados vengan tantas más comidas habrá que preparar** the more guests come, the more meals will have to be cooked; **~ antes** as soon as possible; **unos ~s libros** a few books.

cuánto, a [kwán'to, á] *a* (*exclamación*) what a lot of; (*interrogativo:* *sg*) how much?; (: *pl*) how many? ♦ *pron, ad* how; (*interrogativo:* *sg*) how much?; (: *pl*) how many? ♦ *excl:* ¡~ **me alegro!** I'm so glad!; ¡**cuánta gente!** what a lot of people!; ¿~ **tiempo?** how long?; ¿~ **cuesta?** how much does it cost?; ¿**a ~s estamos?** what's the date?; ¿~ **hay de aquí a Bilbao?** how far is it from here to Bilbao?; **Señor no sé ~s** Mr. So-and-So.

cuarenta [kwáren'tá] *num* forty.

cuarentena [kwárente'ná] *nf* (*MED etc*) quarantine; (*conjunto*) forty(-odd).

cuarentón, ona [kwárenton', o'ná] *a* forty-year-old, fortyish ♦ *nm/f* person of about forty.

cuaresma [kwáres'má] *nf* Lent.

cuarta [kwár'tá] *nf* V **cuarto**.

cuartear [kwártcár] *vt* to quarter; (*dividir*) to divide up; **~se** *vr* to crack, split.

cuartel [kwártcl'] *nm* (*de ciudad*) quarter, district; (*MIL*) barracks *pl*; **~ general** headquarters *pl*.

cuartelazo [kwártelá'so] *nm* coup, military uprising.

cuarteto [kwárte'to] *nm* quartet.

cuartilla [kwártē'yà] *nf* (*hoja*) sheet (of paper); **~s** *nfpl* (*TIP*) copy *sg*.

cuarto, a [kwár'to, á] *a* fourth ♦ *nm* (*MAT*) quarter, fourth; (*habitación*) room ♦ *nf* (*MAT*) quarter, fourth; (*palmo*) span; **~ de baño** bathroom; **~ de estar** living room; **~**

de hora quarter (of an) hour; **~ de kilo** quarter kilo; **no tener un ~** to be broke (*fam*).

cuarzo [kwár'so] *nm* quartz.

cuatrero [kwátre'ro] *nm* (*AM*) rustler, stock thief.

cuatro [kwà'tro] *num* four; **las ~** four o'clock; **el ~ de octubre** (on) the fourth of October; *V tb* **seis**.

cuatrocientos, as [kwàtrosyen'tos, ás] *num* four hundred; *V tb* **seiscientos**.

Cuba [kōō'bá] *nf* Cuba.

cuba [kōō'bá] *nf* cask, barrel; **estar como una ~** (*fam*) to be soused (*US*) *o* sloshed (*Brit*).

cubalibre [kōōbálē'bre] *nm* (white) rum and coke ®.

cubano, a [kōōbá'no, á] *a, nm/f* Cuban.

cubata [kōōbá'tá] *nm* = **cubalibre**.

cubertería [kōōberterē'á] *nf* knives and forks.

cúbico, a [kōō'bēko, á] *a* cubic.

cubierto, a [kōōbyer'to, á] *pp de* **cubrir** ♦ *a* covered; (*cielo*) overcast ♦ *nm* cover; (*en la mesa*) place setting ♦ *nf* cover, covering; (*neumático*) tire (*US*), tyre (*Brit*); (*NAUT*) deck; **~s** *nmpl* utensils (*US*), cutlery *sg* (*Brit*); **a ~ de** covered with *o* in; **precio del ~** cover charge.

cubil [kōōbēl'] *nm* den.

cubilete [kōōbēle'te] *nm* (*en juegos*) cup.

cubito [kōōbē'to] *nm:* **~ de hielo** ice cube.

cubo [kōō'bo] *nm* cube; (*balde*) bucket, tub; (*TEC*) drum; **~ de la basura** garbage can (*US*), dustbin (*Brit*).

cubrecama [kōōbrcká'má] *nm* (*AM*) bedspread.

cubrir [kōōbrēr'] *vt* to cover; (*vacante*) to fill; (*BIO*) to mate with; (*gastos*) to meet; **~se** *vr* (*cielo*) to become overcast; (*COM:* *gastos*) to be met *o* paid; (: *deuda*) to be covered; **~ las formas** to keep up appearances; **lo cubrieron las aguas** the waters closed over it; **el agua casi me cubría** I was almost out of my depth.

cucaracha [kōōkárátch'á] *nf* cockroach.

cuclillas [kōōklē'yàs] *nfpl:* **en ~** squatting.

cuco, a [kōō'ko, á] *a* pretty; (*astuto*) sharp ♦ *nm* cuckoo.

cucurucho [kōōkōōrōōtch'o] *nm* paper cone, cornet.

cuchara [kōōtchá'rá] *nf* spoon; (*TEC*) scoop.

cucharada [kōōtchárá'thá] *nf* spoonful; **~ colmada** heaped spoonful.

cucharadita [kōōtcháráthē'tá] *nf* teaspoonful.

cucharita [kōōtchárē'tá] *nf* teaspoon.

cucharón [kōōtcháron'] *nm* ladle.

cuchichear [kōōtchētchcár'] *vi* to whisper.

cuchicheo [kōōtchētche'o] *nm* whispering.

cuchilla [kōōtchē'yà] *nf* (large) knife; (*de*

arma blanca) blade; ~ **de afeitar** razor blade; **pasar a** ~ to put to the sword.
cuchillo [koōtchē'yo] *nm* knife.
cuchitril [koōtchētrēl'] *nm* hovel; (*habitación etc*) pigsty.
cuece [kwe'se] *etc vb* V **cocer**.
cuele [kwe'le] *etc vb* V **colar**.
cuelgue [kwel'ge] *etc vb* V **colgar**.
cuello [kwe'yo] *nm* (ANAT) neck; (*de vestido, camisa*) collar.
cuenca [kwen'ká] *nf* (ANAT) eye socket; (GEO: *valle*) bowl, deep valley; (: *fluvial*) basin.
cuenco [kwen'ko] *nm* (earthenware) bowl.
cuenta [kwen'tá] *etc vb* V **contar** ♦ *nf* (*cálculo*) count, counting; (*en café, restaurante*) check (US), bill (Brit); (COM) account; (*de collar*) bead; (*fig*) account; **a fin de** ~**s** in the end; **en resumidas** ~**s** in short; **caer en la** ~ to catch on; **dar** ~ **a uno de sus actos** to account for sb's one's actions; **darse** ~ **de** to realize; **tener en** ~ to bear in mind; **echar** ~**s** to take stock; ~ **de atrás** countdown; ~ **corriente/de ahorros/a plazo (fijo)** checking (US)/o current (Brit)/savings/deposit account; ~ **de asignación** appropriation account; ~ **de caja** cash account; ~ **de capital** capital account; ~ **por cobrar** account receivable; ~ **de crédito** credit *o* loan account; ~ **de gastos e ingresos** income and expenditure account; ~ **por pagar** account payable; **abonar una cantidad en** ~ **a uno** to credit a sum to sb's account; **ajustar** *o* **liquidar una** ~ to settle an account; **pasar la** ~ to send the bill.
cuentagotas [kwentágo'tás] *nm inv* (MED) dropper; **a** *o* **con** ~ (*fam, fig*) drop by drop, bit by bit.
cuentakilómetros [kwentákēlo'metros] *nm inv* (*de distancias*) ≈ odometer (US), milometer (Brit); (*velocímetro*) speedometer.
cuentista [kwentē'stá] *nm/f* gossip; (LIT) short-story writer.
cuento [kwen'to] *etc vb* V **contar** ♦ *nm* story; (LIT) short story; ~ **de hadas** fairy tale; **es el** ~ **de nunca acabar** it's an endless business; **eso no viene a** ~ that's irrelevant.
cuerda [kwer'tá] *nf* rope; (*hilo*) string; (*de reloj*) spring; (MUS: *de violín etc*) string; (MAT) chord; (ANAT) cord; ~ **floja** tightrope; ~**s vocales** vocal cords; **dar** ~ **a un reloj** to wind up a clock.
cuerdo, a [kwer'to, á] *a* sane; (*prudente*) wise, sensible.
cuerno [kwer'no] *nm* (ZOOL: *gen*) horn; (: *de ciervo*) antler; **poner los** ~**s a** (*fam*) to cuckold; **saber a** ~ **quemado** to leave a nasty taste.

cuero [kwe'ro] *nm* (ZOOL) skin, hide; (TEC) leather; **en** ~**s** stark naked; ~ **cabelludo** scalp.
cuerpo [kwer'po] *nm* body; (*cadáver*) corpse; (*fig*) main part; ~ **de bomberos** fire department (US) *o* brigade (Brit); **diplomático** diplomatic corps; **luchar** ~ **a** ~ to fight hand-to-hand; **tomar** ~ (*plan etc*) to take shape.
cuervo [kwer'ho] *nm* (ZOOL) raven, crow.
cuesta [kwe'stá] *etc vb* V **costar** ♦ *nf* slope; (*en camino etc*) hill; ~ **arriba/abajo** uphill/downhill; **a** ~**s** on one's back.
cuestión [kwestyon'] *nf* matter, question, issue; (*riña*) quarrel, dispute; **eso es otra** ~ that's another matter.
cuestionar [kwestyonár'] *vt* to question.
cueva [kwe'há] *nf* cave.
cueza [kwe'sá] *etc vb* V **cocer**.
cuidado [kwēthá'tho] *nm* care, carefulness; (*preocupación*) care, worry ♦ *excl* careful!, look out!; **eso me tiene sin** ~ I'm not worried about that.
cuidadoso, a [kwēthátho'so, á] *a* careful; (*preocupado*) anxious.
cuidar [kwēthár'] *vt* (MED) to care for; (*ocuparse de*) to take care of, look after; (*detalles*) to pay attention to ♦ *vi*: ~ **de** to take care of, look after; ~**se** *vr* to look after o.s.; ~**se de hacer algo** to take care to do something.
cuita [kwē'tá] *nf* (*preocupación*) worry, trouble; (*pena*) grief.
culata [koōlá'tá] *nf* (*de fusil*) butt.
culatazo [koōlátá'so] *nm* kick, recoil.
culebra [koōle'hrá] *nf* snake; ~ **de cascabel** rattlesnake.
culebrear [koōlehreár'] *vi* to wriggle along; (*río*) to meander.
culinario, a [koōlēná'ryo, á] *a* culinary, cooking *cpd*.
culminación [koōlmēnásyon'] *nf* culmination.
culminante [koōlmēnán'te] *a*: **momento** ~ climax, highlight, highspot.
culminar [koōlmēnár'] *vi* to culminate.
culo [koō'lo] *nm* (*fam: asentaderas*) bottom, backside, bum (Brit); (: *ano*) ass(hole) (US!), arse(hole) (Brit!); (*de vaso*) bottom.
culpa [koōl'pá] *nf* fault; (JUR) guilt; ~**s** *nfpl* sins; **por** ~ **de** through, because of; **tener la** ~ **(de)** to be to blame (for).
culpabilidad [koōlpáhēlētháth'] *nf* guilt.
culpable [koōlpá'hle] *a* guilty ♦ *nm/f* culprit; **confesarse** ~ to plead guilty; **declarar** ~ **a uno** to find sb guilty.
culpar [koōlpár'] *vt* to blame; (*acusar*) to accuse.
cultivadora [koōltēhátho'rá] *nf* cultivator.
cultivar [koōltēhár'] *vt* to cultivate; (*co-*

secha) to raise; (*talento*) to develop.

cultivo [kōōltē'ḅo] *nm* (*acto*) cultivation; (*plantas*) crop; (*BIO*) culture.

culto, a [kōōl'to, á] *a* (*cultivado*) cultivated; (*que tiene cultura*) cultured, educated ♦ *nm* (*homenaje*) worship; (*religión*) cult; (*POL etc*) cult.

cultura [kōōltōō'rá] *nf* culture.

culturismo [kōōltōōrēs'mo] *nm* body building.

cumbre [kōōm'bre] *nf* summit, top; (*fig*) top, height; **conferencia (en la)** ~ summit (conference).

cumpleaños [kōōompleá'nyos] *nm inv* birthday.

cumplido, a [kōōmplē'ḅo, á] *a* complete, perfect; (*abundante*) plentiful; (*cortés*) courteous ♦ *nm* compliment; **visita de** ~ courtesy call.

cumplidor, a [kōōmplēḅor', á] *a* reliable.

cumplimentar [kōōmplēmentár'] *vt* to congratulate; (*órdenes*) to carry out.

cumplimiento [kōōmplēmyen'to] *nm* (*de un deber*) fulfilment, execution, performance; (*acabamiento*) completion; (*COM*) expiration (*US*), expiry (*Brit*).

cumplir [kōōmplēr'] *vt* (*orden*) to carry out, obey; (*promesa*) to carry out, fulfil; (*condena*) to serve; (*años*) to reach, attain ♦ *vi* (*pago*) to fall due; (*plazo*) to expire; ~**se** *vr* (*plazo*) to expire; (*plan etc*) to be fulfilled; (*vaticinio*) to come true; **hoy cumple dieciocho años** he is eighteen today; ~ **con** (*deberes*) to carry out, fulfil.

cúmulo [kōō'mōōlo] *nm* (*montón*) heap; (*nube*) cumulus.

cuna [kōō'ná] *nf* cradle, cot; **canción de** ~ lullaby.

cundir [kōōndēr'] *vi* (*noticia, rumor, pánico*) to spread; (*rendir*) to go a long way.

cuneta [kōōnc'tá] *nf* ditch.

cuña [kōō'nyá] *nf* (*TEC*) wedge; (*COM*) advertising spot; (*MED*) bedpan; **tener** ~**s** to have influence.

cuñado, a [kōōnyá'ḅo, á] *nm/f* brother/sister-in-law.

cuño [kōō'nyo] *nm* (*TEC*) die-stamp; (*fig*) stamp.

cuota [kwo'tá] *nf* (*parte proporcional*) share; (*cotización*) fee, dues *pl*; ~ **inicial** (*COM*) down payment.

cupo [kōō'po] *etc vb* V **caber** ♦ *nm* quota, share; (*COM*): ~ **de importación** import quota; ~ **de ventas** sales quota.

cupón [kōōpon'] *nm* coupon.

cúpula [kōō'pōōlá] *nf* (*ARQ*) dome.

cura [kōō'rá] *nf* (*curación*) cure; (*método curativo*) treatment ♦ *nm* priest; ~ **de emergencia** emergency treatment.

curación [kōōrásyon'] *nf* cure; (*acción*) curing.

curado, a [kōōrá'ḅo, á] *a* (*CULIN*) cured; (*pieles*) tanned.

curar [kōōrár'] *vt* (*MED: herida*) to treat, dress; (: *enfermo*) to cure; (*CULIN*) to cure, salt; (*cuero*) to tan ♦ *vi*, ~**se** *vr* to get well, recover.

curda [kōōr'ḅá] (*fam*) *nm* drunk ♦ *nf*: **agarrar una/estar** ~ to get/be soused (*US*) *o* sloshed (*Brit*).

curiosear [kōōryoseár'] *vt* to glance at, look over ♦ *vi* to look round, wander round; (*explorar*) to poke about.

curiosidad [kōōryosēḅáḅ'] *nf* curiosity.

curioso, a [kōōryo'so, á] *a* curious; (*aseado*) neat ♦ *nm/f* bystander, onlooker; **¡qué** ~**!** how odd!

curita [kōōrē'tá] *nf* (*AM*) bandaid (*US*), sticking plaster (*Brit*).

currante [kōōrrán'te] *nm/f* (*fam*) worker.

currar [kōōrrár'] *vi* (*fam*), **currelar** [kōōrrelár'] *vi* (*fam*) to work.

currículo [kōōrrē'kōōlo] *nm*, **currículum** [kōōrrē'kōōlōōm] *nm* curriculum vitae.

curro [kōō'rro] *nm* (*fam*) work, job.

cursar [kōōrsár'] *vt* (*ESCOL*) to study.

cursi [kōōr'sē] *a* (*fam*) pretentious; (: *amanerado*) affected.

cursilería [kōōrsēlerē'á] *nf* (*vulgaridad*) bad taste; (*amaneramiento*) affectation.

cursillo [kōōrsē'yo] *nm* short course.

cursiva [kōōrsē'ḅá] *nf* italics *pl*.

curso [kōōr'so] *nm* (*dirección*) course; (*fig*) progress; (*ESCOL*) school year; (*UNIV*) academic year; **en** ~ (*año*) current; (*proceso*) going on, under way; **moneda de** ~ **legal** legal tender.

cursor [kōōrsor'] *nm* (*INFORM*) cursor; (*TEC*) slide.

curtido, a [kōōrtē'ḅo, á] *a* (*cara etc*) weather-beaten; (*fig: persona*) experienced.

curtir [kōōrtēr'] *vt* (*piel*) to tan; (*fig*) to harden.

curvo, a [kōōr'ḅo, á] *a* (*gen*) curved; (*torcido*) bent ♦ *nf* (*gen*) curve, bend; **curva de rentabilidad** (*COM*) break-even chart.

cúspide [kōōs'pēḅe] *nf* (*GEO*) summit, peak; (*fig*) top, pinnacle.

custodia [kōōsto'ḅyá] *nf* (*cuidado*) safekeeping; (*JUR*) custody.

custodiar [kōōstoḅyár'] *vt* (*conservar*) to keep, take care of; (*vigilar*) to guard.

custodio [kōōsto'ḅyo] *nm* guardian, keeper.

cutícula [kōōtē'kōōlá] *nf* cuticle.

cutis [kōō'tēs] *nm inv* skin, complexion.

cutre [kōō'tre] *a* (*fam: lugar*) nasty; (: *persona*) inferior.

cuyo, a [kōō'yo, á] *pron* (*de quien*) whose; (*de que*) whose, of which; **la señora en cuya casa me hospedé** the lady in whose house I stayed; **el asunto cuyos detalles**

conoces the affair the details of which you know; **por ~ motivo** for which reason.
C.V. *abr* (= *caballos de vapor*) H.P.
C y F *abr* (= *costo y flete*) C & F.

CH

Ch, ch [tche] *nf* (*letra*) Ch, ch.
chabacano, a [tchàbàká'no, à] *a* vulgar, coarse.
chabola [tchàbo'là] *nf* shack; **~s** *nfpl* shanty town *sg*.
chabolismo [tchàbolēs'mo] *nm*: **el problema del ~** the problem of substandard housing, the shanty town problem.
chacal [tchàkál'] *nm* jackal.
chacarero [tchàkáre'ro] *nm* (*AM*) small farmer.
chacra [tchà'krà] *nf* (*AM*) small farm.
chacha [tchàtch'à] *nf* (*fam*) maid.
cháchara [tchàtch'árà] *nf* chatter; **estar de ~** to chatter away.
chafar [tchàfár'] *vt* (*aplastar*) to crush, flatten; (*arruinar*) to ruin.
chaflán [tchàflàn'] *nm* (*TEC*) bevel.
chal [tchál] *nm* shawl.
chalado, a [tchàlá'tho, à] *a* (*fam*) crazy.
chalé, *pl* **chalés** [tchále', tcháles'] *nm* villa, ≈ detached house.
chaleco [tchàle'ko] *nm* vest (*US*), waistcoat (*Brit*); **~ antibala** bulletproof vest; **~ salvavidas** life jacket.
chalet, *pl* **chalets** [tchá'le, tchá'les] *nm* = **chalé.**
chalupa [tchàlōō'pá] *nf* launch, boat.
chamaco, a [tchàmá'ko, à] *nm/f* boy/girl.
chamarra [tchàmà'rrà] *nf* sheepskin jacket; (*AM*: *poncho*) blanket.
champán [tchàmpàn'] *nm,* **champaña** [tchàmpá'nyà] *nm* champagne.
champiñón [tchàmpēnyon'] *nm* mushroom.
champú [tchàmpōō'] (*pl* **champúes,** **champús**) *nm* shampoo.
chamuscar [tchàmōōskár'] *vt* to scorch, sear, singe.
chamusque [tchàmōōs'ke] *etc vb* V **chamuscar.**
chamusquina [tchàmōōskē'ná] *nf* singeing.
chancla [tchàn'klà] *nf* (*AM*: *zapato viejo*) old shoe.
chancleta [tchànkle'tà] *nf* sandal, slipper.
chancho, a [tchántch'o, à] *nm/f* (*AM*) pig.
chanchullo [tchántchōō'yo] *nm* (*fam*) swindle, wangle.

chandal [tchàndàl'] *nm* tracksuit.
chantaje [tchàntá'he] *nm* blackmail; **hacer ~ a uno** to blackmail sb.
chanza [tchàn'sà] *nf* joke.
chao [tchào] *excl* (*fam*) see ya (*US*), bye.
chapa [tchà'pá] *nf* (*de metal*) plate, sheet; (*de madera*) board, panel; (*de botella*) bottle top; (*insignia*) (lapel) badge; (*AM*: *AUTO*) license (*US*) o number (*Brit*) plate; **de 3 ~s** (*madera*) 3-ply.
chapado, a [tchàpá'tho, à] *a* (*metal*) plated; (*muebles etc*) finished.
chaparrón [tchàpàrron'] *nm* downpour, cloudburst.
chapotear [tchàpoteár'] *vt* to sponge down ♦ *vi* (*fam*) to splash about.
chapucero, a [tchàpōōse'ro, à] *a* rough, crude ♦ *nm/f* bungler.
chapurr(e)ar [tchàpōōrr(e)àr'] *vt* (*idioma*) to speak badly.
chapuza [tchàpōō'sá] *nf* botched job; (*AM*: *estafa*) trick, swindle.
chapuzón [tchàpōōson'] *nm*: **darse un ~** to go for a dip.
chaqueta [tchàke'tá] *nf* jacket; **cambiar la ~** (*fig*) to change sides.
charca [tchàr'ká] *nf* pond, pool.
charco [tchàr'ko] *nm* pool, puddle.
charcutería [tchàrkōōterē'á] *nf* (*tienda*) shop selling chiefly pork meat products; (*productos*) cooked pork meats *pl*.
charla [tchàr'lá] *nf* talk, chat; (*conferencia*) lecture.
charlar [tchàrlàr'] *vi* to talk, chat.
charlatán, ana [tchàrlàtàn', à'ná] *nm/f* chatterbox; (*estafador*) trickster.
charol [tchàrol'] *nm* varnish; (*cuero*) patent leather.
charro, a [tchà'rro, à] *a* Salamancan; (*AM*) Mexican; (*ropa*) loud, gaudy; (*AM*: *costumbres*) traditional ♦ *nm/f* Salamancan; Mexican.
chárter [tchàr'ter] *a inv*: **vuelo ~** charter flight.
chascarrillo [tchàskàrrē'yo] *nm* (*fam*) funny story.
chasco [tchàs'ko] *nm* (*broma*) trick, joke; (*desengaño*) disappointment.
chasis [tchà'sēs] *nm inv* (*AUTO*) chassis; (*FOTO*) plateholder.
chasquear [tchàskeàr'] *vt* (*látigo*) to crack; (*lengua*) to click.
chasquido [tchàskē'tho] *nm* (*de lengua*) click; (*de látigo*) crack.
chatarra [tchàtá'rrà] *nf* scrap (metal).
chato, a [tchà'to, à] *a* flat; (*nariz*) snub ♦ *nm* wine tumbler; **beber unos ~s** to have a few drinks.
chauvinismo [tchobēnēs'mo] *nm* chauvinism.
chauvinista [tchobēnē'stá] *a, nm/f* chauvin-

ist.

chaval, a [tchábál', á] *nm/f* kid *(fam)*, boy/
girl.

chavo [tchá'ʤo] *nm (AM: fam)* boy, kid.

checo, a *a, nm/f* Czech ♦ *nm (LING)* Czech.

checo(e)slovaco, a [tcheko(e)slobá'ko, á]
a, nm/f Czech, Czechoslovak.

Checo(e)slovaquia [tcheko(e)slobá'kyá] *nf*
Czechoslovakia.

chepa [tche'pá] *nf* hump.

cheque [tche'ke] *nm* check *(US)*, cheque
(Brit); ~ **abierto** check payable to bearer
(US), open cheque *(Brit)*; ~ **en blanco**
blank check; ~ **cruzado** check marked for
deposit only *(US)*, crossed cheque *(Brit)*; ~
al portador check payable to bearer; ~ **ca-**
ducado stale check; ~ **de viajero** traveler's check.

chequeo [tcheke'o] *nm (MED)* check-up;
(AUTO) service.

chequera [tcheke'rá] *nf (AM)* checkbook
(US), chequebook *(Brit)*.

chévere [tche'bere] *a (AM)* great, fabulous
(fam).

chico, a [tchē'ko, á] *a* small, little ♦ *nm/f*
child; *(muchacho)* boy; *(muchacha)* girl.

chicano, a [tchēká'no, á] *a* chicano,
Mexican-American.

chicle [tchē'kle] *nm* chewing gum.

chicha [tchētch'á] *nf (AM)* maize liquor.

chícharo [tchētch'áro] *nm (AM)* pea.

chicharra [tchētchá'rrá] *nf* harvest bug, cicada.

chicharrón [tchētchárron'] *nm* (pork) crackling.

chichón [tchētchon'] *nm* bump, lump.

chiflado, a [tchēflá'ʤo, á] *a (fam)* crazy,
round the bend ♦ *nm/f* nutcase.

chiflar [tchēflár'] *vt* to hiss, boo.

Chile [tchē'le] *nm* Chile.

chile [tchē'le] *nm* chilli, pepper.

chileno, a [tchēle'no, á] *a, nm/f* Chilean.

chillar [tchēyár'] *vi (persona)* to yell,
scream; *(animal salvaje)* to howl; *(cerdo)*
to squeal; *(puerta)* to creak.

chillido [tchēyē'ʤo] *nm (de persona)* yell,
scream; *(de animal)* howl; *(de frenos)*
screech(ing).

chillón, ona [tchēyon', o'ná] *a (niño)* noisy;
(color) loud, gaudy.

chimenea [tchēmene'á] *nf* chimney; *(ho-*
gar) fireplace.

chimpancé, pl chimpancés [tchēmpánse',
tchēmpánses'] *nm* chimpanzee.

China [tchē'ná] *nf*: **(la)** ~ China.

china [tchē'ná] *nf* pebble.

chinchar [tchēntchár'] *(fam) vt* to pester,
annoy; ~**se** *vr* to get cross; **¡chínchate!**
tough!

chinche [tchēntch'e] *nf* bug; *(TEC)*
thumbtack *(US)*, drawing pin *(Brit)* ♦ *nm/f*

nuisance, pest.

chincheta [tchēntche'tá] *nf* thumbtack *(US)*,
drawing pin *(Brit)*.

chingar [tchēngár'] *vt (AM: fam!)* to fuck
(up)*(!)* ♦ *vi (AM: bromear)* to joke; (: *fra-*
casar) to fail, fall through.

chingue [tchēn'ge] *etc vb V* **chingar**.

chino, a [tchē'no, á] *a, nm/f* Chinese ♦ *nm*
(LING) Chinese.

chip [tchēp] *nm (INFORM)* chip.

chipirón [tchēpēron'] *nm* squid.

Chipre [tchē'pre] *nf* Cyprus.

chipriota [tchēpryo'tá], **chipriote** [tchēpryo'-
te] *a* Cypriot, Cyprian ♦ *nm/f* Cypriot.

chiquillada [tchēkēyá'dá] *nf* childish prank.

chiquillo, a [tchēkē'yo, á] *nm/f* kid *(fam)*,
youngster, child.

chiquito, a [tchēkē'to, á] *a* very small, tiny
♦ *nm/f* kid *(fam)*.

chirigota [tchērēgo'tá] *nf* joke.

chirimbolo [tchērēmbo'lo] *nm* thingamajig
(fam).

chirimoya [tchērēmo'yá] *nf* cherimoya
(US), custard apple *(Brit)*.

chiringuito [tchērēngē'to] *nm* refreshment
stall *o* stand.

chiripa [tchērē'pá] *nf* fluke; **por** ~ by
chance.

chirona [tchēro'ná], *(AM)* **chirola** [tchēro'lá]
nf (fam) clink, jail.

chirriar [tchērryár'] *vi (goznes)* to creak,
squeak; *(pájaros)* to chirp, sing.

chirrido [tchērrē'ʤo] *nm* creak(ing),
squeak(ing); *(de pájaro)* chirp(ing).

chis [tchēs] *excl* sh!

chisme [tchēs'me] *nm (habladurías)* piece of
gossip; *(fam: objeto)* thingamajig.

chismoso, a [tchēsmo'so, á] *a* gossiping ♦
nm/f gossip.

chispa [tchēs'pá] *nf* spark; *(fig)* sparkle;
(ingenio) wit; *(fam)* drunkenness.

chispeante [tchēspeán'te] *a (tb fig)* sparkling.

chispear [tchēspeár'] *vi* to spark; *(lloviznar)*
to drizzle.

chisporrotear [tchēsporroteár'] *vi (fuego)*
to throw out sparks; *(leña)* to crackle;
(aceite) to hiss, splutter.

chistar [tchēstár'] *vi*: **no** ~ not to say a
word.

chiste [tchē'ste] *nm* joke, funny story; ~
verde dirty joke.

chistoso, a [tchēsto'so, á] *a (gracioso)*
funny, amusing; *(bromista)* witty.

chistu [tchē'stōō] *nm* = **txistu**.

chivarse [tchēbár'se] *vr (fam)* to squeal.

chivatazo [tchēbátá'so] *nm (fam)* tip-off;
dar ~ to inform.

chivo, a [tchē'bo, á] *nm/f* (billy/nanny-)goat;
~ **expiatorio** scapegoat.

chocante [tchokán'te] *a* startling; *(extraño)*

odd; (*ofensivo*) shocking.

chocar [tchokàr'] *vi* (*coches etc*) to collide, crash; (*MIL*, *fig*) to clash ♦ *vt* to shock; (*sorprender*) to startle; ~ **con** to collide with; (*fig*) to run into, run up against; **¡chócala!** (*fam*) put it there!

chocolate [tchokolá'te] *a* chocolate ♦ *nm* chocolate; (*fam*) dope, marijuana.

chocolatería [tchokoláterē'á] *nf* chocolate factory (*o* shop).

chochear [tchotcheàr'] *vi* to dodder, be senile.

chocho, a [tchotch'o, à] *a* doddering, senile; (*fig*) soft, doting.

chófer [tcho'fer], **chofer** [tchofer'] *nm* driver.

chollo [tcho'yo] *nm* (*fam*) bargain.

chopo [tcho'po] *nm* black poplar.

choque [tcho'ke] *etc vb V* **chocar** ♦ *nm* (*impacto*) impact; (*golpe*) jolt; (*AUTO*) crash; (*fig*) conflict.

chorizo [tchorē'so] *nm hard pork sausage*, (*type of*) salami; (*ladrón*) crook.

chorra [tcho'rrá] *nf* luck.

chorradas [tchorrá'thàs] *nfpl* (*objetos*) rubbish *sg*, junk *sg*; **decir** ~ to talk rubbish *o* nonsense.

chorrear [tchorreàr'] *vt* to pour ♦ *vi* to gush (out), spout (out); (*gotear*) to drip, trickle.

chorreras [tchorre'ràs] *nfpl* (*COSTURA*) frill *sg*.

chorro [tcho'rro] *nm* jet; (*caudalito*) dribble, trickle; (*fig*) stream; **salir a ~s** to gush forth; **con propulsión a** ~ jet-propelled.

chotearse [tchoteàr'se] *vr* to joke.

choteo [tchote'o] *nm* kidding.

choto [tcho'to] *nm* (*cabrito*) kid.

chovinismo [tchoķēnēs'mo] *nm* = **chauvinismo**.

chovinista [tchoķēnē'stá] *a*, *nm/f* = **chauvinista**.

choza [tcho'sá] *nf* hut, shack.

chubasco [tchōōbàs'ko] *nm* squall.

chubasquero [tchōōbàske'ro] *nm* foulweather gear (*US*), oilskins *pl* (*Brit*).

chuchería [tchōōtcherē'á] *nf* trinket.

chucho [tchōōtch'o] *nm* (*ZOOL*) mongrel.

chufa [tchōō'fá] *nf* chufa, earth almond, tiger nut; **horchata de ~s** *drink made from chufas*.

chuleta [tchōōle'tá] *nf* chop, cutlet; (*ESCOL etc*: *fam*) crib.

chulo, a [tchōō'lo, à] *a* (*encantador*) charming; (*aire*) proud; (*pey*) fresh; (*fam*: *estupendo*) great, fantastic ♦ *nm* (*pícaro*) rascal; (*madrileño*) working-class Madrilenian; (*rufián*: *tb*: ~ **de putas**) pimp.

chumbera [tchōōmbe'rá] *nf* prickly pear.

chungo, a [tchōōn'go, à] (*fam*) *a* lousy ♦ *nf*: **estar de chunga** to be in a merry mood.

chupado, a [tchōōpà'tho, à] *a* (*delgado*)

skinny, gaunt; **está** ~ (*fam*) it's simple, it's dead easy.

chupar [tchōōpàr'] *vt* to suck; (*absorber*) to absorb; ~**se** *vr* to grow thin; **para ~se los dedos** mouthwatering.

chupatintas [tchōōpàtēn'tàs] *nm inv* penpusher.

chupete [tchōōpe'te] *nm* pacifier (*US*), dummy (*Brit*).

churrasco [tchōōrràs'ko] *nm* (*AM*) barbecue, barbecued meat.

churrería [tchōōrrerē'á] *nf* fritter stall *o* shop.

churrete [tchōōrre'te] *nm* grease spot.

churrigueresco, a [tchōōrrēgeres'ko, à] *a* (*ARQ*) baroque; (*fig*) excessively ornate.

churro, a [tchōō'rro, à] *a* coarse ♦ *nm* (*CULIN*) (type of) fritter; (*chapuza*) botch, mess.

churruscar [tchōōrrōōskàr'] *vt* to fry crisp.

churrusque [tchōōrrōōs'ke] *etc vb V* **churruscar**.

churumbel [tchōōrōōmbel'] *nm* (*fam*) kid.

chus [tchōōs] *excl*: **no decir ni** ~ **ni mus** not to say a word.

chusco, a [tchōōs'ko, à] *a* funny.

chusma [tchōōs'má] *nf* rabble, mob.

chutar [tchōōtàr'] *vi* (*DEPORTE*) to shoot (at goal); **esto va que chuta** it's going fine.

chuzo [tchōō'so] *nm*: **llueve a ~s, llueven ~s de punta** it's raining cats and dogs.

D

D, d [de] *nf* (*letra*) D, d; **D de Dolores** D for Dog.

D. *abr* = **Don**.

Da., D.ª *abr* = **Doña**.

dactilar [dàktēlàr'] *a*: **huellas ~es** fingerprints.

dactilógrafo, a [dàktēlo'gràfo, à] *nm/f* typist.

dádiva [dá'theķà] *nf* (*donación*) donation; (*regalo*) gift.

dadivoso, a [dàtheķo'so, à] *a* generous.

dado, a [dá'tho, à] *pp de* **dar** ♦ *nm* die; ~**s** *nmpl* dice ♦ *a*: **en un momento** ~ at a certain point; **ser** ~ **a** (**hacer algo**) to be very fond of (doing sth); ~ **que** *conj* given that.

daga [dá'gà] *nf* dagger.

daltónico, a [dàlto'nēko, à] *a* color-blind (*US*), colour-blind (*Brit*).

daltonismo [dàltonēs'mo] *nm* color (*US*) *o*

colour (*Brit*) blindness.

dama [dá'má] *nf* (*gen*) lady; (*AJEDREZ*) queen; ~**s** *nfpl* checkers (*US*), draughts (*Brit*); **primera** ~ (*TEATRO*) leading lady; (*POL*) first lady (*US*), president's wife; ~ **de honor** (*de reina*) lady-in-waiting; (*de novia*) bridesmaid.

damasco [dámás'ko] *nm* (*tela*) damask.

damnificado, a [dámnēfēká'ṭo, á] *nm/f*: **los** ~**s** the victims.

damnificar [dámnēfēkár'] *vt* to harm; (*persona*) to injure.

damnifique [dámnēfē'ke] *etc vb* V **damnificar**.

dance [dán'se] *etc vb* V **danzar**.

danés, esa [dánes', e'sá] *a* Danish ♦ *nm/f* Dane ♦ *nm* (*LING*) Danish.

Danubio [dánōō'byo] *nm* Danube.

danza [dán'sá] *nf* (*gen*) dancing; (*una* ~) dance.

danzar [dánsár'] *vt, vi* to dance.

danzarín, ina [dánsárēn', ē'ná] *nm/f* dancer.

dañar [dányár'] *vt* (*objeto*) to damage; (*persona*) to hurt; (*estropear*) to spoil; ~**se** *vr* (*objeto*) to get damaged.

dañino, a [dányē'no, á] *a* harmful.

daño [dá'nyo] *nm* (*a un objeto*) damage; (*a una persona*) harm, injury; ~**s y perjuicios** (*JUR*) damages; **hacer** ~ **a** to damage; (*persona*) to hurt, injure; **hacerse** ~ to hurt o.s.

dar [dár] *vt* to give; (*entregar: objeto*) to hand; (*grito*) to let out; (*noticias*) to tell; (*olor*) to give off; (*lección*) to teach; (*TEATRO*) to perform, put on; (*película*) to show; (*COM*) to yield; (*naipes*) to deal; (*la hora*): ~ **las 3** to strike 3 ♦ *vi*: ~ **a** to look out on(to), overlook; ~ **como** *o* **por** to consider, regard as; ~ **con** (*persona etc*) to meet, run into; (*idea*) to hit on; ~ **contra** to knock against, bang into; ~ **en** to strike, hit; ~ **de sí** to give, stretch; ~ **para** to be enough for; ~ **que hablar** to set people talking; ~**se** *vr* (*suceso*) to happen; (*presentarse*) to occur; (*AGR*) to grow; ~**se a** to be given to; ~**se por** to consider o.s.; **dárselas de** to pose as; **se me dan muy bien/mal los idiomas** I am very good/bad at languages; ~ **de comer/beber a uno** to give sb sth to eat/drink; **¡dale!** go on!; ~**le a uno por hacer algo** to take it into one's head to do sth; **lo mismo da** it makes no difference; **da lo mismo** *o* **qué más da** it's all the same; **me da igual** I don't care; ~ **en el blanco** to hit the mark; **me da asco/ miedo** it sickens/frightens me; **me da pena** it makes me sad; ~**se prisa** to hurry (up).

dardo [dár'ṭo] *nm* dart.

dársena [dár'sená] *nf* (*NAUT*) dock.

datar [dátár'] *vi*: ~ **de** to date from.

dátil [dá'tēl] *nm* date.

dativo [dátē'ḅo] *nm* (*LING*) dative.

dato [dá'to] *nm* fact, piece of information; (*MAT*) datum; ~**s** *nmpl* (*INFORM*) data; ~**s de entrada/salida** input/output data; ~**s personales** personal particulars.

dcha. *abr* (= *derecha*) r.h.

d. de J. C. *abr* (= *después de Jesucristo*) A.D.

de [de] *prep* (*posesión*) of; (*origen, distancia*) from; **la ciudad** ~ **Madrid** the city of Madrid; **el coche de mi amigo/mis amigos** my friend's car/my friends' car; **el más caro del negocio/mundo** the most expensive in the shop/world; **un libro** ~ **Unamuno** a book by Unamuno; **un chico** ~ **15 años** a 15-year-old boy; **un viaje** ~ **2 días** a two-day journey; **un libro grato** ~ **leer** a nice book to read; **libro** ~ **cocina** cookbook; **el hombre** ~ **largos cabellos** the man with long hair; **guantes** ~ **cuero** leather gloves; **vuelo 507** ~ **Londres** flight 507 from London; **es** ~ **Sevilla** she's from Seville; **estar loco** ~ **alegría** to be overjoyed; ~ **un salto** with one bound; ~ **niño** as a child; **fue a Londres** ~ **profesor** he went to London as a teacher; **una** ~ **dos** one or the other; **3** ~ **cada 4** three out of every four; ~ **día/noche** by day/night; ~ **mañana** in the morning; **vestido** ~ **negro** dressed in black; **más/menos** ~ **3** more/ less than 3; ~ **cara a** facing; ~ **ser posible** if possible.

dé [de] *vb* V **dar**.

deambular [deámbōōlár'] *vi* to stroll, wander.

debajo [deḅá'ho] *ad* underneath; ~ **de** below, under; **por** ~ **de** beneath.

debate [deḅá'te] *nm* debate.

debatir [deḅátēr'] *vt* to debate; ~**se** *vr* to struggle.

debe [de'ḅe] *nm* (*en cuenta*) debit side; ~ **y haber** debit and credit.

deber [deḅer'] *nm* duty ♦ *vt* to owe ♦ *vi*: **debe (de)** it must, it should; **debo hacerlo** I must do it; **debe de ir** he should go; ~**se** *vr*: ~**se a** to be owing *o* due to; **¿qué** *o* **cuánto le debo?** how much is it?; ~**es** *nmpl* (*ESCOL*) homework *sg*.

debidamente [deḅēṭhámen'te] *ad* properly; (*rellenar: documento, solicitud*) duly.

debido, a [deḅē'ṭho, á] *a* proper, due; ~ **a** due to, because of; **en debida forma** duly.

débil [de'ḅēl] *a* weak; (*persona: físicamente*) feeble; (*salud*) poor; (*voz, ruido*) faint; (*luz*) dim.

debilidad [deḅēlēṭháṭh'] *nf* weakness; feebleness; dimness; **tener** ~ **por uno** to have a soft spot for sb.

debilitar [deḅēlētár'] *vt* to weaken; ~**se** *vr* to grow weak.

débito [de'ḅēto] *nm* debit; (*deuda*) debt.

debutante [deḇoōtán'te] *nm/f* beginner.
debutar [deḇoōtár'] *vi* to make one's debut.
década [de'káḏá] *nf* decade.
decadencia [dekáḏen'syá] *nf* (*estado*) decadence; (*proceso*) decline, decay.
decadente [dekáḏen'te] *a* decadent.
decaer [dekáer'] *vi* (*declinar*) to decline; (*debilitarse*) to weaken; (*salud*) to fail; (*negocio*) to fall off.
decaído, a [dekáē'ḏo, á] *a*: **estar ~** (*persona*) to be down.
decaiga [deká'ēgá] *etc vb V* **decaer**.
decaimiento [dekáēmyen'to] *nm* (*declinación*) decline; (*desaliento*) discouragement; (*MED*: *depresión*) depression.
decanato [dekáná'to] *nm* (*cargo*) deanship; (*despacho*) dean's office.
decano, a [deká'no, á] *nm/f* (*UNIV etc*) dean; (*de grupo*) senior member.
decantar [dekántár'] *vt* (*vino*) to decant.
decapitar [dekápētár'] *vt* to behead.
decayendo [dekáyen'do] *etc vb V* **decaer**.
decena [dese'ná] *nf*: **una ~** ten (or so).
decencia [desen'syá] *nf* (*modestia*) modesty; (*honestidad*) respectability.
decenio [dese'nyo] *nm* decade.
decente [desen'te] *a* (*correcto*) proper; (*honesto*) respectable.
decepción [desepsyon'] *nf* disappointment.
decepcionante [desepsyonán'te] *a* disappointing.
decepcionar [desepsyonár'] *vt* to disappoint.
decibel [deseḇel'], **decibelio** [deseḇe'lyo] *nm* decibel.
decidido, a [deseḏē'ḏo, á] *a* decided; (*resuelto*) resolute.
decidir [deseḏēr'] *vt* (*persuadir*) to convince, persuade; (*resolver*) to decide ♦ *vi* to decide; **~se** *vr*: **~se a** to make up one's mind to; **~se por** to decide *o* settle on, choose.
décimo, a [de'sēmo, á] *num* tenth ♦ *nf* (*esp en lotería*) tenth part.
decimoctavo, a [desēmoktá'ḇo, á] *num* eighteenth; *V tb* **sexto**.
decimoséptimo, a [desēmosep'tēmo, á] *num* seventeenth; *V tb* **sexto**.
decimosexto, a [desēmosek'sto, á] *num* sixteenth; *V tb* **sexto**.
decimotercero, a [desēmoterse'ro, á], **decimotercio, a** [desēmoter'syo, á] *num* thirteenth; *V tb* **sexto**.
decir [desēr'] *vt* (*expresar*) to say; (*contar*) to tell; (*hablar*) to speak; (*indicar*) to show; (*revelar*) to reveal; (*fam: nombrar*) to call ♦ *nm* saying; **~se** *vr*: **se dice** it is said, they say; (*se cuenta*) the story goes; **¿cómo se dice en inglés "cursi"?** what's the English for "cursi"?; **~ para/entre sí** to say to o.s.; **~ por ~** to talk for talking's

sake; **dar que ~** (**a la gente**) to make people talk; **querer ~** to mean; **es ~** that is to say, namely; **ni que ~ tiene que...** it goes without saying that...; **como quien dice** so to speak; **¡quién lo diría!** would you believe it!; **el qué dirán** gossip; **¡diga!, ¡dígame!** (*en tienda etc*) can I help you?; (*TELEC*) hello?; **le dije que fuera más tarde** I told her to go later; **es un ~** it's just a phrase.
decisión [desēsyon'] *nf* decision; (*firmeza*) decisiveness; (*voluntad*) determination.
decisivo, a [desēsē'ḇo, á] *a* decisive.
declamar [deklámár'] *vt*, *vi* to declaim; (*versos etc*) to recite.
declaración [deklárásyon'] *nf* (*manifestación*) statement; (*explicación*) explanation; (*JUR: testimonio*) evidence; **~ de derechos** (*POL*) bill of rights; **~ de impuestos** (*COM*) tax return; **~ de ingresos** *o* **de renta** *o* **fiscal** (*AM*) income tax return; **~ jurada** affidavit; **falsa ~** (*JUR*) misrepresentation.
declarar [deklárár'] *vt* to declare ♦ *vi* to declare; (*JUR*) to testify; **~se** *vr* (*opinión*) to make one's opinion known; (*a una chica*) to propose; (*guerra, incendio*) to break out; **~ culpable/inocente a uno** to find sb guilty/not guilty; **~se culpable/inocente** to plead guilty/not guilty.
declinación [deklēnásyon'] *nf* (*decaimiento*) decline; (*LING*) declension.
declinar [deklēnár'] *vt* (*gen, LING*) to decline; (*JUR*) to reject ♦ *vi* (*el día*) to draw to a close.
declive [deklē'ḇe] *nm* (*cuesta*) slope; (*inclinación*) incline; (*fig*) decline; (*COM*: **~ económico**) slump.
decodificador [dekoḏēfēkáḏor'] *nm* (*INFORM*) decoder.
decolorarse [dekolorár'se] *vr* to become discolored (*US*) *o* discoloured (*Brit*).
decomisar [dekomēsár'] *vt* to seize, confiscate.
decoración [dekorásyon'] *nf* decoration; (*TEATRO*) scenery, set; **~ de escaparates** window dressing.
decorado [dekorá'ḏo] *nm* (*CINE, TEATRO*) scenery, set.
decorador, a [dekoráḏor', á] *nm/f* (*de interiores*) (interior) decorator; (*TEATRO*) stage *o* set designer.
decorar [dekorár'] *vt* to decorate.
decorativo, a [dekorátē'ḇo, á] *a* ornamental, decorative.
decoro [deko'ro] *nm* (*respeto*) respect; (*dignidad*) decency; (*recato*) propriety.
decoroso, a [dekoro'so, á] *a* (*decente*) decent; (*modesto*) modest; (*digno*) proper.
decrecer [dekreser'] *vi* to decrease, diminish; (*nivel de agua*) to go down; (*días*) to

draw in.

decrépito, a [dekre'pĕto, á] *a* decrepit.

decretar [dekretár'] *vt* to decree.

decreto [dekre'to] *nm* decree; (*POL*) act.

decreto-ley [dekretoleē'], *pl* **decretos-leyes** *nm* decree.

decrezca [dekres'ká] *etc vb* V **decrecer.**

decúbito [dekōō'hĕto] *nm* (*MED*): ~ **prono/supino** prone/supine position.

dedal [deħál'] *nm* thimble.

dedalera [deħále'rá] *nf* foxglove.

dédalo [de'ħálo] *nm* (*laberinto*) labyrinth; (*fig*) tangle, mess.

dedicación [deħēkásyon'] *nf* dedication; **con ~ exclusiva** *o* **plena** full-time.

dedicar [deħēkár'] *vt* (*libro*) to dedicate; (*tiempo, dinero*) to devote; ~**se** *vr*: ~**se a** to devote o.s. to (*hacer algo* doing sth); (*carrera, estudio*) to go in for, take up; **¿a qué se dedica usted?** what do you do (for a living)?

dedicatoria [deħēkáto'ryá] *nf* (*de libro*) dedication.

dedillo [deħē'yo] *nm*: **saber algo al ~** to have sth at one's fingertips.

dedique [deħē'ke] *etc vb* V **dedicar.**

dedo [de'ħo] *nm* finger; (*de vino etc*) drop; ~ **(del pie)** toe; ~ **pulgar** thumb; ~ **índice** index finger; ~ **mayor** *o* **cordial** middle finger; ~ **anular** ring finger; ~ **meñique** little finger; **contar con los** ~**s** to count on one's fingers; **comerse los** ~**s** to get very impatient; **entrar a** ~ to get a job by pulling strings; **hacer** ~ (*fam*) to hitch (a ride (*US*) *o* lift (*Brit*)); **poner el ~ en la llaga** to put one's finger on it; **no tiene dos** ~**s de frente** he's pretty dense.

deducción [deħōōksyon'] *nf* deduction.

deducir [deħōōsēr'] *vt* (*concluir*) to deduce, infer; (*COM*) to deduct.

deduje [deħōō'he] *etc*, **dedujera** [deħōōhe'rá] *etc*, **deduzca** [deħōō'ská] *etc vb* V **deducir.**

defección [defeksyon'] *nf* defection, desertion.

defecto [defek'to] *nm* defect, flaw; (*de cara*) imperfection; ~ **de pronunciación** speech defect; **por** ~ (*INFORM*) default; ~ **latente** (*COM*) latent defect.

defectuoso, a [defektwo'so, á] *a* defective, faulty.

defender [defender'] *vt* to defend; (*ideas*) to uphold; (*causa*) to champion; (*amigos*) to stand up for; ~**se** *vr* to defend o.s.; ~**se bien** to give a good account of o.s.; **me defiendo en inglés** (*fig*) I can get by in English.

defendible [defendē'hle] *a* defensible.

defensa [defen'sá] *nf* defense (*US*), defence (*Brit*); (*NAUT*) fender, bumper pad (*US*) ♦ *nm* (*DEPORTE*) defense (*US*), back; **en** ~

propia in self-defense.

defensivo, a [defensē'ho, á] *a* defensive ♦ *nf*: **a la defensiva** on the defensive.

defensor, a [defensor', á] *a* defending ♦ *nm/f* (*abogado* ~) defense (*US*) *o* defending (*Brit*) counsel; (*protector*) protector; ~ **del pueblo** (*Esp*) ≈ ombudsman.

deferir [deferēr'] *vt* (*JUR*) to refer, delegate ♦ *vi*: ~ **a** to defer to.

deficiencia [defēsyen'syá] *nf* deficiency.

deficiente [defēsyen'te] *a* (*defectuoso*) defective; ~ **en** lacking *o* deficient in ♦ *nm/f*: **ser un ~ mental** to be mentally handicapped.

déficit, ~**s** [de'fēsēt] *nm* (*COM*) deficit; (*fig*) lack, shortage; ~ **presupuestario** budget deficit.

defienda [defyen'dá] *etc vb* V **defender.**

defiera [defye'rá] *etc vb* V **deferir.**

definición [defēnēsyon'] *nf* definition; (*INFORM: de pantalla*) resolution.

definido, a [defēnē'ħo, á] *a* (*tb LING*) definite; **bien ~** well *o* clearly defined; ~ **por el usuario** (*INFORM*) user-defined.

definir [defēnēr'] *vt* (*determinar*) to determine, establish; (*decidir, INFORM*) to define; (*aclarar*) to clarify.

definitivo, a [defēnētē'ho, á] *a* (*edición, texto*) definitive; (*fecha*) definite; **en definitiva** definitively; (*en conclusión*) finally; (*en resumen*) in short.

defiriendo [defēryen'do] *etc vb* V **deferir.**

deflacionario, a [deflásyoná'ryo, á], **deflacionista** [deflásyonē'stá] *a* deflationary.

deflector [deflēktor'] *nm* (*TEC*) baffle.

deformación [deformásyon'] *nf* (*alteración*) deformation; (*RADIO etc*) distortion.

deformar [deformár'] *vt* (*gen*) to deform; ~**se** *vr* to become deformed.

deforme [defor'me] *a* (*informe*) deformed; (*feo*) ugly; (*mal hecho*) misshapen.

deformidad [deformēħáħ'] *nf* (*forma anormal*) deformity; (*fig: defecto*) (moral) shortcoming.

defraudar [defráōōħár'] *vt* (*decepcionar*) to disappoint; (*estafar*) to cheat; to defraud; ~ **impuestos** to evade tax.

defunción [defōōnsyon'] *nf* decease, demise.

degeneración [dehenerásyon'] *nf* (*de las células*) degeneration; (*moral*) degeneracy.

degenerar [dehenerár'] *vi* to degenerate; (*empeorar*) to get worse.

deglutir [deglōōtēr'] *vt*, *vi* to swallow.

degolladero [degoyáħe'ro] *nm* (*ANAT*) throat; (*cadalso*) scaffold; (*matadero*) slaughterhouse.

degollar [degoyár'] *vt* to slaughter.

degradar [degráħár'] *vt* to debase, degrade; (*INFORM: datos*) to corrupt; ~**se** *vr* to demean o.s.

degüelle [deǥwe'ye] *etc vb V* **degollar**.

degustación [deǥōōstásyon'] *nf* sampling, tasting.

deificar [deēfēkár'] *vt* (*persona*) to deify.

deifique [deēfē'ke] *etc vb V* **deificar**.

dejadez [dehátħes'] *nf* (*negligencia*) neglect; (*descuido*) untidiness, carelessness.

dejado, a [dehá'ħo, â] *a* (*desaliñado*) slovenly; (*negligente*) careless; (*indolente*) lazy.

dejar [dehár'] *vt* (*gen*) to leave; (*permitir*) to allow, let; (*abandonar*) to abandon, forsake; (*actividad, empleo*) to give up; (*beneficios*) to produce, yield ♦ *vi*: ~ **de** (*parar*) to stop; ~**se** *vr* (*abandonarse*) to let o.s. go; **no puedo** ~ **de fumar** I can't give up smoking; **no dejes de visitarles** don't fail to visit them; **no dejes de comprar un billete** make sure you buy a ticket; ~ **a un lado** to leave *o* set aside; ~ **caer** to drop; ~ **entrar/salir** to let in/out; ~ **pasar** to let through; **¡déjalo!** (*no te preocupes*) don't worry about it; **te dejo en tu casa** I'll drop you off at your place; **deja mucho que desear** it leaves a lot to be desired; ~**se persuadir** to allow o.s. to *o* let o.s. be persuaded; **¡déjate de tonterías!** stop messing around!

deje [de'he] *nm* (trace of) accent.

dejo [de'ho] *nm* (*LING*) accent.

del [del] = **de + el**, *ver* **de**.

del. *abr* (*ADMIN*: = *Delegación*) district office.

delantal [delántál'] *nm* apron.

delante [delán'te] *ad* in front; (*enfrente*) opposite; (*adelante*) ahead ♦ *prep*: ~ **de** in front of, before; **la parte de** ~ the front part; **estando otros** ~ with others present.

delantero, a [delánte'ro, â] *a* front; (*patas de animal*) fore ♦ *nm* (*DEPORTE*) forward ♦ *nf* (*de vestido, casa etc*) front part; (*TEATRO*) front row; (*DEPORTE*) forward line; **llevar la delantera (a uno)** to be ahead (of sb).

delatar [delátár'] *vt* to inform on *o* against, betray; **los delató a la policía** he reported them to the police.

delator, a [delátor', â] *nm/f* informer.

delegación [deleǥásyon'] *nf* (*acción, delegados*) delegation; (*COM: oficina*) district office, branch; ~ **de poderes** (*POL*) devolution; ~ **de policía** police station.

delegado, a [deleǥá'ħo, â] *nm/f* delegate; (*COM*) agent.

delegar [deleǥár'] *vt* to delegate.

delegue [dele'ǥe] *etc vb V* **delegar**.

deleitar [deleētár'] *vt* to delight; ~**se** *vr*: ~**se con** *o* **en** to delight in, take pleasure in.

deleite [dele'ēte] *nm* delight, pleasure.

deletrear [deletreár'] *vt* (*tb fig*) to spell (out).

deletreo [deletre'o] *nm* spelling; (*fig*) interpretation, decipherment.

deleznable [delesná'ħle] *a* (*frágil*) fragile; (*fig: malo*) poor; (*excusa*) feeble.

delfín [delfēn'] *nm* dolphin.

delgadez [delǥáħes'] *nf* thinness, slimness.

delgado, a [delǥá'ħo, â] *a* thin; (*persona*) slim, thin; (*tierra*) poor; (*tela etc*) light, delicate ♦ *ad*: **hilar (muy)** ~ (*fig*) to split hairs.

deliberación [delēħerásyon'] *nf* deliberation.

deliberar [delēħerár'] *vt* to debate, discuss ♦ *vi* to deliberate.

delicadeza [delēkáħe'sá] *nf* delicacy; (*refinamiento, sutileza*) refinement.

delicado, a [delēká'ħo, â] *a* delicate; (*sensible*) sensitive; (*rasgos*) dainty; (*gusto*) refined; (*situación: difícil*) tricky; (*: violento*) embarrassing; (*punto, tema*) sore; (*persona: difícil de contentar*) hard to please; (*: sensible*) touchy, hypersensitive; (*: atento*) considerate.

delicia [delē'syá] *nf* delight.

delicioso, a [delēsyo'so, â] *a* (*gracioso*) delightful; (*exquisito*) delicious.

delictivo, a [delēktē'ħo, â] *a* criminal *cpd*.

delimitar [delēmētár'] *vt* to delimit.

delincuencia [delēnkwen'syá] *nf*: ~ **juvenil** juvenile delinquency; **cifras de la** ~ crime rate.

delincuente [delēnkwen'te] *nm/f* delinquent; (*criminal*) criminal; ~ **sin antecedentes** first offender; ~ **habitual** hardened criminal.

delineante [delēneán'te] *nm/f* draftsman (*US*), draughtsman (*Brit*).

delinear [delēneár'] *vt* to delineate; (*dibujo*) to draw; (*contornos, fig*) to outline; ~ **un proyecto** to outline a project.

delinquir [delēnkēr'] *vi* to commit an offense.

delirante [delērán'te] *a* delirious.

delirar [delērár'] *vi* to be delirious, rave; (*fig: desatinar*) to talk nonsense.

delirio [delē'ryo] *nm* (*MED*) delirium; (*palabras insensatas*) ravings *pl*; ~ **de grandeza** megalomania; ~ **de persecución** persecution mania; **con** ~ (*fam*) madly; **¡fue el** ~! (*fam*) it was great!

delito [delē'to] *nm* (*gen*) crime; (*infracción*) offense (*US*), offence (*Brit*).

demacrado, a [demákrá'ħo, â] *a* emaciated.

demagogo [demáǥo'ǥo] *nm* demagogue.

demanda [demán'dá] *nf* (*pedido, COM*) demand; (*petición*) request; (*pregunta*) inquiry; (*reivindicación*) claim; (*JUR*) action, lawsuit; (*TEATRO*) call; (*ELEC*) load; ~ **de**

pago demand for payment; **escribir en ~ de ayuda** to write asking for help; **entablar ~** (*JUR*) to sue; **presentar ~ de divorcio** to sue for divorce; **~ final** final demand; **~ indirecta** derived demand; **~ de mercado** market demand.

demandado, a [demàndá'ᵭo, á] *nm/f* defendant; (*en divorcio*) respondent.

demandante [demàndán'te] *nm/f* claimant; (*JUR*) plaintiff.

demandar [demàndár'] *vt* (*gen*) to demand; (*JUR*) to sue, file a lawsuit against, start proceedings against; **~ a uno por calumnia/daños y perjuicios** to sue sb for libel/damages.

demarcación [demárkásyon'] *nf* (*de terreno*) demarcation.

demás [demás'] *a*: **los ~ niños** the other children, the remaining children ♦ *pron*: **los/las ~** the others, the rest (of them); **lo ~** the rest (of it); **por ~** moreover; (*en vano*) in vain; **y ~** etcetera.

demasía [demásê'á] *nf* (*exceso*) excess, surplus; **comer en ~** to eat to excess.

demasiado, a [demásyá'ᵭo, á] *a*: **~ vino** too much wine; **~s libros** too many books ♦ *ad* (*antes de a, ad*) too; **¡es ~!** it's too much!; **es ~ pesado para levantar** it is too heavy to lift; **~ lo sé** I know it only too well; **hace ~ calor** it's too hot.

demencia [demen'syá] *nf* (*locura*) madness.

demencial [demensyál'] *a* crazy.

demente [demen'te] *a* mad, insane ♦ *nm/f* lunatic.

demérito [deme'rêto] *nm* (*falta*) fault; (*AM: depreciación*) depreciation.

democracia [demokrá'syá] *nf* democracy.

demócrata [demo'krátá] *nm/f* democrat.

democratacristiano, a [demokrátákrêstyá'no, á] *a, nm/f* Christian Democrat.

democrático, a [demokrá'têko, á] *a* democratic.

democristiano, a [demokrêstyá'no, á] *a, nm/f* Christian Democrat.

demográfico, a [demográ'fêko, á] *a* demographic, population *cpd*; **la explosión demográfica** the population explosion.

demoledor, a [demoleᵭor', á] *a* (*fig: argumento*) overwhelming; (: *ataque*) shattering.

demoler [demoler'] *vt* to demolish; (*edificio*) to tear down.

demolición [demolêsyon'] *nf* demolition.

demonio [demo'nyo] *nm* devil, demon; **¡~s!** hell!; **¿cómo ~s?** how the hell?; **¿qué ~s será?** what the devil can it be?; **¿dónde ~ lo habré dejado?** where the hell can I have left it?; **tener el ~ en el cuerpo** (*no parar*) to be always on the go.

demora [demo'rá] *nf* delay.

demorar [demorár'] *vt* (*retardar*) to delay,

hold back; (*dilatar*) to hold up ♦ *vi* to linger, stay on; **~se** *vr* to linger, stay on; (*retrasarse*) to take a long time.

demos [de'mos] *vb* V **dar**.

demostración [demostrásyon'] *nf* (*gen*, *MAT*) demonstration; (*de cariño, fuerza*) show; (*de teorema*) proof; (*de amistad*) gesture; (*de cólera, gimnasia*) display; **~ comercial** commercial exhibition.

demostrar [demostrár'] *vt* (*probar*) to prove; (*mostrar*) to show; (*manifestar*) to demonstrate.

demostrativo, a [demostrátê'ᵭo, á] *a* demonstrative.

demudado, a [demooᵭá'ᵭo, á] *a* (*rostro*) pale; (*fig*) upset; **tener el rostro ~** to look pale.

demudar [demooᵭár'] *vt* to change, alter; **~se** *vr* (*expresión*) to alter; (*perder color*) to change color (*US*) o colour (*Brit*).

demuela [demwe'lá] *etc vb* V **demoler**.

demuestre [demwes'tre] *etc vb* V **demostrar**.

den [den] *vb* V **dar**.

denegación [denegásyon'] *nf* refusal, denial.

denegar [denegár'] *vt* (*rechazar*) to refuse; (*negar*) to deny; (*JUR*) to reject.

denegué [denege'], **deneguemos** [denege'mos] *etc*, **deniego** [denye'go] *etc*, **deniegue** [denye'ge] *etc vb* V **denegar**.

denigrante [denêgrán'te] *a* (*injurioso*) insulting; (*deshonroso*) degrading.

denigrar [denêgrár'] *vt* (*desacreditar*) to denigrate; (*injuriar*) to insult.

denodado, a [denoᵭá'ᵭo, á] *a* bold, brave.

denominación [denomênásyon'] *nf* (*acto*) naming; (*clase*) denomination; **~ de origen** (*vino*) guarantee of vintage, ≈ appellation contrôlée.

denostar [denostár'] *vt* to insult.

denotar [denotár'] *vt* (*indicar*) to indicate, denote.

densidad [densêᵭáᵭ'] *nf* (*FÍSICA*) density; (*fig*) thickness; **~ de caracteres** (*INFORM*) pitch.

denso, a [den'so, á] *a* (*apretado*) solid; (*espeso, pastoso*) thick; (*fig*) heavy.

dentado, a [dentá'ᵭo, á] *a* (*rueda*) cogged; (*filo*) jagged; (*sello*) perforated; (*BOT*) dentate.

dentadura [dentáᵭoo'rá] *nf* (set of) teeth *pl*; **~ postiza** dentures *pl*.

dentellada [denteyá'ᵭá] *nf* (*mordisco*) bite, nip; (*señal*) tooth mark; **partir algo a ~s** to sever sth with one's teeth.

dentera [dente'rá] *nf* (*sensación desagradable*) the shivers *pl*.

dentición [dentêsyon'] *nf* (*acto*) teething; (*ANAT*) dentition; **estar con la ~** to be teething.

dentífrico, a [dentē'frēko, á] *a* dental, tooth *cpd* ♦ *nm* toothpaste; **pasta dentífrica** toothpaste.

dentista [dentē'stá] *nm/f* dentist.

dentro [den'tro] *ad* inside ♦ *prep*: ~ **de** in, inside, within; **allí** ~ in there; **mirar por** ~ to look inside; ~ **de lo posible** as far as possible; ~ **de todo** all in all; ~ **de tres meses** within three months.

denuedo [denwe'ðo] *nm* boldness, daring.

denuesto [denwe'sto] *nm* insult.

denuncia [denōōn'syá] *nf* (*delación*) denunciation; (*acusación*) accusation; (*de accidente*) report; **hacer** *o* **poner una** ~ to report an incident to the police.

denunciable [denōōnsyá'ɓle] *a* indictable, punishable.

denunciador, a [denōōnsyáðor', á], **denunciante** [denōōnsyán'te] *nm/f* accuser; (*delator*) informer.

denunciar [denōōnsyár'] *vt* to report; (*delatar*) to inform on *o* against.

Dep. *abr* (= *Departamento*) Dept.; (= *Depósito*) dep.

deparar [depárár'] *vt* (*brindar*) to provide *o* furnish with; (*suj: futuro, destino*) to have in store for; **los placeres que el viaje nos deparó** the pleasures which the trip afforded us.

departamento [depártámen'to] *nm* (*sección administrativa*) department, section; (*AM: piso*) apartment (*US*), flat (*Brit*); (*distrito*) department, province; ~ **de envíos** (*COM*) shipping department; ~ **de máquinas** (*NAUT*) engine room.

departir [depártēr'] *vi* to talk, converse.

dependencia [dependen'syá] *nf* dependence; (*POL*) dependency; (*COM*) office, section; (*sucursal*) branch office; (*ARQ: cuarto*) room; ~**s** *nfpl* outbuildings.

depender [depender'] *vi*: ~ **de** to depend on; (*contar con*) to rely on; (*de autoridad*) to be under, be answerable to; **depende** it (all) depends; **no depende de mí** it's not up to me.

dependienta [dependyen'tá] *nf* saleswoman, sales assistant.

dependiente [dependyen'te] *a* dependent ♦ *nm* salesman, sales assistant.

depilación [depēlásyon'] *nf* hair removal.

depilar [depēlár'] *vt* (*con cera: piernas*) to remove hair from; (*cejas*) to pluck.

depilatorio, a [depēláto'ryo, á] *a* depilatory ♦ *nm* hair remover.

deplorable [deplorá'ɓle] *a* deplorable.

deplorar [deplorár'] *vt* to deplore.

depondré [depondre'] *etc vb V* **deponer**.

deponer [deponer'] *vt* (*armas*) to lay down; (*rey*) to depose; (*gobernante*) to oust; (*ministro*) to remove from office ♦ *vi* (*JUR*) to give evidence; (*declarar*) to make a statement.

deponga [depon'gá] *etc vb V* **deponer**.

deportación [deportásyon'] *nf* deportation.

deportar [deportár'] *vt* to deport.

deporte [depor'te] *nm* sport.

deportista [deportē'stá] *a* sports *cpd* ♦ *nm/f* sportsman/woman.

deportivo, a [deportē'ho, á] *a* (*club, periódico*) sports *cpd* ♦ *nm* sports car.

deposición [deposēsyon'] *nf* (*de funcionario etc*) removal from office; (*JUR: testimonio*) evidence.

depositante [deposētán'te], **depositador, a** [deposētáðor', á] *nm/f* depositor.

depositar [deposētár'] *vt* (*dinero*) to deposit; (*mercaderías*) to put away, store; ~**se** *vr* to settle; ~ **la confianza en uno** to place one's trust in sb.

depositario, a [deposētá'ryo, á] *nm/f* trustee; ~ **judicial** official receiver.

depósito [depo'sēto] *nm* (*gen*) deposit; (*de mercaderías*) warehouse, store; (*de animales, coches*) pound; (*de agua, gasolina etc*) tank; (*en retrete*) tank; ~ **afianzado** bonded warehouse; ~ **bancario** bank deposit; ~ **de cadáveres** mortuary; ~ **de maderas** lumber (*US*) *o* timber (*Brit*) yard; ~ **de suministro** feeder bin.

depravar [depráhár'] *vt* to deprave, corrupt; ~**se** *vr* to become depraved.

depreciación [depresyásyon'] *nf* depreciation.

depreciar [depresyár'] *vt* to depreciate, reduce the value of; ~**se** *vr* to depreciate, lose value.

depredador, a [depreðáðor', á] (*ZOOL*) *a* predatory ♦ *nm* predator.

depredar [depreðár'] *vt* to pillage.

depresión [depresyon'] *nf* (*gen*, *MED*) depression; (*hueco*) hollow; (*en horizonte, camino*) dip; (*merma*) drop; (*ECON*) slump, recession; ~ **nerviosa** nervous breakdown.

deprimente [deprēmen'te] *a* depressing.

deprimido, a [deprēmē'ðo, á] *a* depressed.

deprimir [deprēmēr'] *vt* to depress; ~**se** *vr* (*persona*) to become depressed.

deprisa [deprē'sá] *ad V* **prisa**.

depuesto [depwe'sto] *pp de* **deponer**.

depuración [depōōrásyon'] *nf* purification; (*POL*) purge; (*INFORM*) debugging.

depurador, a [depōōráðor'] *nm* purifier.

depurar [depōōrár'] *vt* to purify; (*purgar*) to purge; (*INFORM*) to debug.

depuse [depōō'se] *etc vb V* **deponer**.

der., der.º *abr* (= *derecho*) r.

derecha [deretch'á] *nf V* **derecho**.

derechazo [deretchá'so] *nm* (*BOXEO*) right; (*TENIS*) forehand drive; (*TAUR*) *a pass with the cape.*

derechista [deretchē'stá] (*POL*) *a* right-wing ♦ *nm/f* right-winger.

derecho, a [deretch'o, á] *a* right, right-hand ♦ *nm* (*privilegio*) right; (*título*) claim, title; (*lado*) right(-hand) side; (*leyes*) law ♦ *nf* right(-hand) side ♦ *ad* straight, directly; ~**s** *nmpl* dues; (*profesionales*) fees; (*impuestos*) taxes; (*de autor*) royalties; **la(s) derecha(s)** (*pl*) (*POL*) the Right; ~**s civiles** civil rights; ~**s de muelle** (*COM*) docking fees (*US*), dock dues (*Brit*); ~**s de patente** patent rights; ~**s portuarios** (*COM*) harbor fees (*US*), harbour dues (*Brit*); ~ **de propiedad literaria** copyright; ~ **de retención** (*COM*) lien; ~ **de timbre** (*COM*) stamp duty; ~ **de votar** right to vote; ~ **a voto** voting right; **Facultad de D**~ Law School (*US*), Faculty of Law (*Brit*); **a derechas** rightly, correctly; **de derechas** (*POL*) right-wing; "**reservados todos los** ~**s**" "all rights reserved"; **¡no hay** ~**!** it's not fair!; **tener** ~ **a** to have a right to; **a la derecha** on the right; (*dirección*) to the right.

deriva [derē'bá] *nf*: **ir** *o* **estar a la** ~ to drift, be adrift.

derivación [derēbásyon'] *nf* derivation.

derivado, a [derēbá'tho, á] *a* derived ♦ *nm* (*LING*) derivative; (*INDUSTRIA*, *QUÍMICA*) by-product.

derivar [derēbár'] *vt* to derive; (*desviar*) to direct ♦ *vi*, ~**se** *vr* to derive, be derived; ~**(se) de** (*consecuencia*) to spring from.

dermatólogo, a [dermáto'logo, á] *nm/f* dermatologist.

dérmico, a [der'mēko, á] *a* skin *cpd*.

derogación [derogásyon'] *nf* repeal.

derogar [derogár'] *vt* (*ley*) to repeal; (*contrato*) to revoke.

derogue [dero'ge] *etc vb V* **derogar**.

derramamiento [derrámámyen'to] *nm* (*dispersión*) spilling; (*fig*) squandering; ~ **de sangre** bloodshed.

derramar [derrámár'] *vt* to spill; (*verter*) to pour out; (*esparcir*) to scatter; ~**se** *vr* to pour out; ~ **lágrimas** to weep.

derrame [derrá'me] *nm* (*de líquido*) spilling; (*de sangre*) shedding; (*de tubo etc*) overflow; (*perdida*) leakage; (*MED*) discharge; (*declive*) slope; ~ **cerebral** brain hemorrhage (*US*) *o* haemorrhage (*Brit*); ~ **sinovial** water on the knee.

derredor [derretħor'] *ad*: **al** *o* **en** ~ **de** around, about.

derrengado, a [derrengá'tho, á] *a* (*torcido*) bent; (*cojo*) crippled; **estar** ~ (*fig*) to ache all over; **dejar** ~ **a uno** (*fig*) to wear sb out.

derretido, a [derretē'tho, á] *a* melted; (*metal*) molten; **estar** ~ **por uno** (*fig*) to be crazy about sb.

derretir [derretēr'] *vt* (*gen*) to melt; (*nieve*) to thaw; (*fig*) to squander; ~**se** *vr* to melt.

derribar [derrēbár'] *vt* to knock down; (*construcción*) to demolish; (*persona, gobierno, político*) to bring down.

derribo [derrē'bo] *nm* (*de edificio*) demolition; (*LUCHA*) take-down (*US*), throw (*Brit*); (*AVIAT*) shooting down; (*POL*) overthrow; ~**s** *nmpl* rubble *sg*, debris *sg*.

derrita [derrē'tá] *etc vb V* **derretir**.

derrocar [derrokár'] *vt* (*gobierno*) to bring down, overthrow; (*ministro*) to oust.

derrochador, a [derrotcháthor', á] *a*, *nm/f* spendthrift.

derrochar [derrotchár'] *vt* (*dinero, recursos*) to squander; (*energía, salud*) to be bursting with *o* full of.

derroche [derrotch'e] *nm* (*despilfarro*) waste, squandering; (*exceso*) extravagance; **con un** ~ **de buen gusto** with a fine display of good taste.

derroque [derro'ke] *etc vb V* **derrocar**.

derrota [derro'tá] *nf* (*NAUT*) course; (*MIL*) defeat, rout; **sufrir una grave** ~ (*fig*) to suffer a grave setback.

derrotar [derrotár'] *vt* (*gen*) to defeat.

derrotero [derrote'ro] *nm* (*rumbo*) course; **tomar otro** ~ (*fig*) to adopt a different course.

derrotista [derrotē'stá] *a*, *nm/f* defeatist.

derruir [derrōōēr'] *vt* to demolish, tear down.

derrumbamiento [derrōōmbámyen'to] *nm* (*caída*) plunge; (*demolición*) demolition; (*desplome*) collapse; ~ **de tierra** landslide.

derrumbar [derrōōmbár'] *vt* to throw down; (*despeñar*) to fling *o* hurl down; (*volcar*) to upset; ~**se** *vr* (*hundirse*) to collapse; (: *techo*) to fall in, cave in; (*fig: esperanzas*) to collapse.

derrumbe [derrōōm'be] *nm* = **derrumbamiento**.

derruyendo [derrōōyen'do] *etc vb V* **derruir**.

des [des] *vb V* **dar**.

desabastecido, a [desábástesē'tho, á] *a*: **estar** ~ **de algo** to be short of *o* out of sth.

desabotonar [desábotonár'] *vt* to unbutton, undo ♦ *vi* (*flores*) to blossom; ~**se** *vr* to come undone.

desabrido, a [desábrē'tho, á] *a* (*comida*) insipid, tasteless; (*persona: soso*) dull; (: *antipático*) rude, surly; (*respuesta*) sharp; (*tiempo*) unpleasant.

desabrigado, a [desábrēgá'tho, á] *a* (*sin abrigo*) not sufficiently protected; (*fig*) exposed.

desabrigar [desábrēgár'] *vt* (*quitar ropa a*) to remove the clothing of; (*descubrir*) to uncover; (*fig*) to deprive of protection; ~**se** *vr*: **me desabrigué en la cama** the bedclothes came off.

desabrigue [desábrē'ge] *etc vb V* **desabri-**

gar.
desabrochar [desábrotchár'] vt (botones, broches) to undo, unfasten; ~se vr (ropa etc) to come undone.
desacatar [desákátár'] vt (ley) to disobey.
desacato [desáká'to] nm (falta de respeto) disrespect; (JUR) contempt.
desacertado, a [desásertá'tho, á] a (equivocado) mistaken; (inoportuno) unwise.
desacierto [desásyer'to] nm (error) mistake, error; (dicho) unfortunate remark.
desaconsejable [desákonsehá'ble] a inadvisable.
desaconsejado, a [desákonsehá'tho, á] a ill-advised.
desaconsejar [desákonsehár'] vt: ~ algo a uno to advise sb against sth.
desacoplar [desákoplár'] vt (ELEC) to disconnect; (TEC) to take apart.
desacorde [desákor'the] a (MUS) discordant; (fig: opiniones) conflicting; estar ~ con algo to disagree with sth.
desacreditar [desákrethétár'] vt (desprestigiar) to discredit, bring into disrepute; (denigrar) to run down.
desactivar [desáktéhár'] vt to deactivate; (bomba) to defuse.
desacuerdo [desákwer'tho] nm (conflicto) disagreement, discord; (error) error, blunder; en ~ con not in agreement with.
desafiador, a [desáfyáthor', á], **desafiante** [desáfyán'te] a (insolente) defiant; (retador) challenging ♦ nm/f challenger.
desafiar [desáfyár'] vt (retar) to challenge; (enfrentarse a) to defy.
desafilado, a [desáfilá'tho, á] a blunt.
desafinado, a [desáfēná'tho, á] a: estar ~ to be out of tune.
desafinarse [desáfēnár'se] vr to go out of tune.
desafío [desáfē'o] nm (reto) challenge; (combate) duel; (resistencia) defiance.
desaforadamente [desáforáthámen'te] ad: gritar ~ to shout one's head off.
desaforado, a [desáforá'tho, á] a (grito) ear-splitting; (comportamiento) outrageous.
desafortunadamente [desáfortōōnáthámen'te] ad unfortunately.
desafortunado, a [desáfortōōná'tho, á] a (desgraciado) unfortunate, unlucky.
desagradable [deságráthá'ble] a (fastidioso, enojoso) unpleasant; (irritante) disagreeable; ser ~ con uno to be rude to sb.
desagradar [deságráthár'] vi (disgustar) to displease; (molestar) to bother.
desagradecido, a [deságráthesē'tho, á] a ungrateful.
desagrado [deságrá'tho] nm (disgusto) displeasure; (contrariedad) dissatisfaction; con ~ unwillingly.
desagraviar [deságráhyár'] vt to make amends to.
desagravio [deságrá'hyo] nm (satisfacción) amends; (compensación) compensation.
desagregarse [deságregár'se] vr to disintegrate.
desagregue [deságre'ge] etc vb V **desagregarse**.
desaguadero [deságwáthe'ro] nm drain.
desagüe [desá'gwe] nm (de un líquido) drainage; (cañería: tb: **tubo de** ~) drainpipe; (salida) outlet, drain.
desaguisado, a [deságēsá'tho, á] a illegal ♦ nm outrage.
desahogado, a [desáogá'tho, á] a (holgado) comfortable; (espacioso) roomy.
desahogar [desáogár'] vt (aliviar) to ease, relieve; (ira) to vent; ~se vr (distenderse) to relax; (desfogarse) to let off steam (fam); (confesarse) to confess, get sth off one's chest (fam).
desahogo [desáo'go] nm (alivio) relief; (comodidad) comfort, ease; vivir con ~ to be comfortably off.
desahogue [desáo'ge] etc vb V **desahogar**.
desahuciado, a [desáōōsyá'tho, á] a hopeless.
desahuciar [desáōōsyár'] vt (enfermo) to give up hope for; (inquilino) to evict.
desahucio [desáōō'syo] nm eviction.
desairado, a [desáērá'tho, á] a (menospreciado) disregarded; (desgarbado) shabby; (sin éxito) unsuccessful; quedar ~ to come off badly.
desairar [desáērár'] vt (menospreciar) to slight, snub; (cosa) to disregard; (COM) to default on.
desaire [desá'ēre] nm (menosprecio) slight; (falta de garbo) unattractiveness; dar o hacer un ~ a uno to offend sb; ¿me va usted a hacer ese ~? I won't take no for an answer!
desajustar [desáhōōstár'] vt (desarreglar) to disarrange; (desconcertar) to throw off balance; (fig: planes) to upset; ~se vr to get out of order; (aflojarse) to loosen.
desajuste [desáhōō'ste] nm (de máquina) disorder; (avería) breakdown; (situación) imbalance; (desacuerdo) disagreement.
desalentador, a [desálentáthor', á] a discouraging.
desalentar [desálentár'] vt (desanimar) to discourage; ~se vr to get discouraged.
desaliento [desályen'to] etc vb V **desalentar** ♦ nm discouragement; (abatimiento) depression.
desalineación [desálēneásyon'] nf misalignment.
desaliñado, a [desálēnyá'tho, á] a (descuidado) slovenly; (raído) shabby; (desordenado) untidy; (negligente) careless.
desaliño [desálē'nyo] nm (descuido) slov-

enliness; (*negligencia*) carelessness.

desalmado, a [desàlmá'ðo, á] *a* (*cruel*) cruel, heartless.

desalojar [desálohàr'] *vt* (*gen*) to remove, expel; (*expulsar, echar*) to eject; (*abandonar*) to move out of ♦ *vi* to move out; **la policía desalojó el local** the police cleared people out of the place.

desalquilar [desálkēlár'] *vt* to vacate, move out; ~**se** *vr* to become vacant.

desamarrar [desámárrár'] *vt* to untie; (*NAUT*) to cast off.

desamor [desámor'] *nm* (*frialdad*) indifference; (*odio*) dislike.

desamparado, a [desàmpárá'ðo, á] *a* (*persona*) helpless; (*lugar: expuesto*) exposed; (: *desierto*) deserted.

desamparar [desàmpárár'] *vt* (*abandonar*) to desert, abandon; (*JUR*) to leave defenseless (*US*) o defenceless (*Brit*); (*barco*) to abandon.

desamparo [desàmpá'ro] *nm* (*acto*) desertion; (*estado*) helplessness.

desamueblado, a [desàmweblá'ðo, á] *a* unfurnished.

desandar [desándár'] *vt*: ~ **lo andado** o **el camino** to retrace one's steps.

desanduve [desándōō'he] *etc*, **desanduviera** [desàndōōhye'rá] *etc vb* V **desandar**.

desangelado, a [desànhelá'ðo, á] *a* (*habitación, edificio*) lifeless.

desangrar [desángrár'] *vt* to bleed; (*fig: persona*) to bleed dry; (*lago*) to drain; ~**se** *vr* to lose a lot of blood; (*morir*) to bleed to death.

desanimado, a [desánēmá'ðo, á] *a* (*persona*) downhearted; (*espectáculo, fiesta*) dull.

desanimar [desánēmár'] *vt* (*desalentar*) to discourage; (*deprimir*) to depress; ~**se** *vr* to lose heart.

desánimo [desá'nēmo] *nm* despondency; (*abatimiento*) dejection; (*falta de animación*) dullness.

desanudar [desánōōðár'] *vt* to untie; (*fig*) to clear up.

desapacible [desápásē'hle] *a* unpleasant.

desaparecer [desápáreser'] *vi* to disappear; (*el sol, la luz*) to vanish; (~ *de vista*) to drop out of sight; (*efectos, señales*) to wear off.

desaparecido, a [desápáresē'ðo, á] *a* missing; (*especie*) extinct ♦ *nm*: ~**s** (*en accidente etc*) people missing.

desaparezca [desápáres'ká] *etc vb* V **desaparecer**.

desaparición [desápáresyon'] *nf* disappearance; (*de especie etc*) extinction.

desapasionado, a [desápásyoná'ðo, á] *a* dispassionate, impartial.

desapego [desápe'go] *nm* (*frialdad*) coolness; (*distancia*) detachment.

desapercibido, a [desápersēhē'ðo, á] *a* unnoticed; (*desprevenido*) unprepared; **pasar** ~ to go unnoticed.

desaplicado, a [desáplēká'do, á] *a* lazy.

desaprender [desáprender'] *vt* to forget; (*lo aprendido*) to unlearn.

desaprensivo, a [desáprensē'ho, á] *a* unscrupulous.

desaprobar [desáproðár'] *vt* (*reprobar*) to disapprove of; (*condenar*) to condemn; (*no consentir*) to reject.

desaprovechado, a [desáproðetchá'ðo, á] *a* (*oportunidad, tiempo*) wasted; (*estudiante*) lazy.

desaprovechar [desáproðetchár'] *vt* to waste; (*talento*) not to use to the full ♦ *vi* (*perder terreno*) to lose ground.

desapruebe [desáprwe'he] *etc vb* V **desaprobar**.

desarmar [desármár'] *vt* (*MIL, fig*) to disarm; (*TEC*) to take apart, dismantle.

desarme [desàr'me] *nm* disarmament.

desarraigado, a [desàrráēgá'ðo, á] *a* (*persona*) without roots, rootless.

desarraigar [desàrráēgár'] *vt* to uproot; (*fig: costumbre*) to root out; (: *persona*) to banish.

desarraigo [desàrrá'ēgo] *nm* uprooting.

desarraigue [desàrrá'ēge] *etc vb* V **desarraigar**.

desarreglado, a [desàrreglá'ðo, á] *a* (*desordenado*) disorderly, untidy; (*hábitos*) irregular.

desarreglar [desàrreglár'] *vt* to mess up; (*desordenar*) to disarrange; (*trastocar*) to upset, disturb.

desarreglo [desàrre'glo] *nm* (*de casa, persona*) untidiness; (*desorden*) disorder; (*TEC*) trouble; (*MED*) upset; **viven en el mayor** ~ they live in complete chaos.

desarrollado, a [desàrroyà'ðo, á] *a* developed.

desarrollar [desàrroyár'] *vt* (*gen*) to develop; (*extender*) to unfold; (*teoría*) to explain; ~**se** *vr* to develop; (*extenderse*) to open (out); (*film*) to develop; (*fig*) to grow; (*tener lugar*) to take place; **aquí desarrollan un trabajo muy importante** they carry on o out very important work here; **la acción se desarrolla en Roma** (*CINE etc*) the scene is set in Rome.

desarrollo [desàrro'yo] *nm* development; (*de acontecimientos*) unfolding; (*de industria, mercado*) expansion, growth; **país en vías de** ~ developing country; **la industria está en pleno** ~ industry is expanding steadily.

desarrugar [desàrrōōgár'] *vt* (*alisar*) to smooth (out); (*ropa*) to remove the wrinkles (*US*) o creases (*Brit*) from.

desarrugue [desàrrōō'ge] *etc vb* V **desarru-**

gar.

desarticulado, a [desártēkōōlá'tho, á] a disjointed.

desarticular [desártēkōōlár'] vt (huesos) to dislocate, put out of joint; (objeto) to take apart; (grupo terrorista etc) to break up.

desaseado, a [desáseá'tho, á] a (sucio) dirty; (desaliñado) untidy.

desaseo [desáse'o] nm (suciedad) dirtiness; (desarreglo) untidiness.

desasga [desás'gá] etc vb V desasir.

desasir [desásēr'] vt to loosen; ~se vr to extricate o.s.; ~se de to let go, give up.

desasosegar [desásosegár'] vt (inquietar) to disturb, make uneasy; ~se vr to become uneasy.

desasosegué [desásosege'], **desasoseguemos** [desásosege'mos] etc vb V desasosegar.

desasosiego [desásosye'go] etc vb V desasosegar ♦ nm (intranquilidad) uneasiness, restlessness; (ansiedad) anxiety; (POL etc) unrest.

desasosiegue [desásosye'ge] etc vb V desasosegar.

desastrado, a [desástrá'tho, á] a (desaliñado) shabby; (sucio) dirty.

desastre [desás'tre] nm disaster; ¡un ~! how awful!; la función fue un ~ the show was a shambles.

desastroso, a [desástro'so, á] a disastrous.

desatado, a [desátá'tho, á] a (desligado) untied; (violento) violent, wild.

desatar [desátár'] vt (nudo) to untie; (paquete) to undo; (perro, odio) to unleash; (misterio) to solve; (separar) to detach; ~se vr (zapatos) to come untied; (tormenta) to break; (perder control de sí) to lose self-control; ~se en injurias to pour out a stream of insults.

desatascar [desátáskár'] vt (cañería) to unblock, clear; (carro) to pull out of the mud; ~ a uno (fig) to get sb out of a jam.

desatasque [desátás'ke] etc vb V desatascar.

desatención [desátensyon'] nf (descuido) inattention; (distracción) absent-mindedness.

desatender [desátender'] vt (no prestar atención a) to disregard; (abandonar) to neglect.

desatento, a [desáten'to, á] a (distraído) inattentive; (descortés) discourteous.

desatienda [desátyen'dá] etc vb V desatender.

desatinado, a [desátēná'tho, á] a foolish, silly.

desatino [desátē'no] nm (idiotez) foolishness, folly; (error) blunder; ~s nmpl nonsense sg; ¡qué ~! how silly!, what rubbish!

desatornillar [desátornēyár'] vt to unscrew.

desatrancar [desátránkár'] vt (puerta) to unbolt; (cañería) to unblock.

desatranque [desátrán'ke] etc vb V desatrancar.

desautorice [desáōōtorē'se] etc vb V desautorizar.

desautorizado, a [desáōōtorēsá'tho, á] a unauthorized.

desautorizar [desáōōtorēsár'] vt (oficial) to deprive of authority; (informe) to deny.

desavendré [desáhendre'] etc vb V desavenir.

desavenencia [desáhenen'syá] nf (desacuerdo) disagreement; (discrepancia) quarrel.

desavenga [desáhen'gá] etc vb V desavenir.

desavenido, a [desáhenē'tho, á] a (opuesto) contrary; (reñidos) in disagreement; ellos están ~s they are at odds.

desavenir [desáhenēr'] vt (enemistar) to make trouble between; ~se vr to have a falling out (US), fall out (Brit).

desaventajado, a [desáhentáhá'tho, á] a (inferior) inferior; (poco ventajoso) disadvantageous.

desaviene [desáhye'ne] etc, **desaviniendo** [desáhēnyen'do] etc vb V desavenir.

desayunar [desáyōōnár'] vi, ~se vr to have breakfast ♦ vt to have for breakfast; ~ con café to have coffee for breakfast; ~ con algo (fig) to get the first news of sth.

desayuno [desáyōō'no] nm breakfast.

desazón [desáson'] nf (angustia) anxiety; (MED) discomfort; (fig) annoyance.

desazonar [desásonár'] vt (fig) to annoy, upset; ~se vr (enojarse) to be annoyed; (preocuparse) to worry, be anxious.

desbancar [desbánkár'] vt (quitar el puesto a) to oust; (suplantar) to supplant (in sb's affections).

desbandada [desbándá'thá] nf rush; ~ general mass exodus; a la ~ in disorder.

desbandarse [desbándár'se] vr (MIL) to disband; (fig) to flee in disorder.

desbanque [desbán'ke] etc vb V desbancar.

desbarajuste [desbáráhōō'ste] nm confusion, disorder; ¡qué ~! what a mess!

desbaratar [desbárátár'] vt (gen) to mess up; (plan) to spoil; (deshacer, destruir) to ruin ♦ vi to talk nonsense; ~se vr (máquina) to break down; (persona: irritarse) to fly off the handle (fam).

desbarrar [desbárrár'] vi to talk nonsense.

desbloquear [desblokeár'] vt (negociaciones, tráfico) to get going again; (COM: cuenta) to unfreeze.

desbocado, a [desboká'tho, á] a (caballo) runaway; (herramienta) worn.

desbocar [desbokár'] vt (vasija) to break

the rim of; **~se** *vr* (*caballo*) to bolt; (*persona*: *soltar injurias*) to let out a stream of insults.

desboque [desβo'ke] *etc vb* V **desbocar**.

desbordamiento [desβorðamyen'to] *nm* (*de río*) overflowing; (*INFORM*) overflow; (*de cólera*) outburst; (*de entusiasmo*) upsurge.

desbordar [desβorðár'] *vt* (*sobrepasar*) to go beyond; (*exceder*) to exceed ♦ *vi*, **~se** *vr* (*líquido, río*) to overflow; (*entusiasmo*) to erupt; (*persona*: *exaltarse*) to get carried away.

desbravar [desβraβár'] *vt* (*caballo*) to break in; (*animal*) to tame.

descabalgar [deskaβalɣár'] *vi* to dismount.

descabalgue [deskaβál'ge] *etc vb* V **descabalgar**.

descabellado, a [deskaβeyá'ðo, á] *a* (*disparatado*) wild, crazy; (*insensato*) preposterous.

descabellar [deskaβeyár'] *vt* to ruffle; (*TAUR*: *toro*) to give the coup de grace to.

descabezado, a [deskaβesá'ðo, á] *a* (*sin cabeza*) headless; (*insensato*) wild.

descafeinado, a [deskáfeēná'ðo, á] *a* decaffeinated ♦ *nm* decaffeinated coffee.

descalabrar [deskáláβrár'] *vt* to smash; (*persona*) to hit; (: *en la cabeza*) to hit on the head; (*NAUT*) to cripple; (*dañar*) to harm, damage; **~se** *vr* to hurt one's head.

descalabro [deskálá'βro] *nm* blow; (*desgracia*) misfortune.

descalce [deskál'se] *etc vb* V **descalzar**.

descalificar [deskálēfēkár'] *vt* to disqualify; (*desacreditar*) to discredit.

descalifique [deskálēfē'ke] *etc vb* V **descalificar**.

descalzar [deskálsár'] *vt* (*zapato*) to take off.

descalzo, a [deskál'so, á] *a* barefoot(ed); (*fig*) destitute; **estar (con los pies) ~(s)** to be barefooted.

descambiar [deskámbyár'] *vt* to exchange.

descaminado, a [deskámēná'ðo, á] *a* (*equivocado*) on the wrong road; (*fig*) misguided; **en eso no anda usted muy ~** you're not far wrong there.

descamisado, a [deskámēsá'ðo, á] *a* barechested.

descampado [deskámpá'ðo] *nm* open space, piece of empty ground; **comer al ~** to eat in the open air.

descansado, a [deskánsá'ðo, á] *a* (*gen*) rested; (*que tranquiliza*) restful.

descansar [deskánsár'] *vt* (*gen*) to rest; (*apoyar*): **~ (sobre)** to lean (on) ♦ *vi* to rest, have a rest; (*echarse*) to lie down; (*cadáver, restos*) to lie; **¡que usted descanse!** sleep well!; **~ en** (*argumento*) to be based on.

descansillo [deskánsē'yo] *nm* (*de escalera*) landing.

descanso [deskán'so] *nm* (*reposo*) rest; (*alivio*) relief; (*pausa*) break; (*DEPORTE*) interval, half time; **día de ~** day off; **~ de enfermedad/maternidad** sick/maternity leave; **tomarse unos días de ~** to take a few days' leave *o* rest.

descapitalizado, a [deskápētálēsá'ðo, á] *a* undercapitalized.

descapotable [deskápotá'βle] *nm* (*tb*: **coche ~**) convertible.

descarado, a [deskárá'ðo, á] *a* (*sin vergüenza*) shameless; (*insolente*) sassy (*US*), cheeky (*Brit*).

descarga [deskár'ɣá] *nf* (*ARQ, ELEC, MIL*) discharge; (*NAUT*) unloading.

descargador [deskárɣáðor'] *nm* (*de barcos*) stevedore.

descargar [deskárɣár'] *vt* to unload; (*golpe*) to let fly; (*arma*) to fire; (*ELEC*) to discharge; (*pila*) to run down; (*conciencia*) to relieve; (*COM*) to pay off; (*persona: de una obligación*) to release; (: *de una deuda*) to free; (*JUR*) to clear ♦ *vi* (*río*): **~ (en)** to flow (into); **~se** *vr* to unburden o.s.; **~se de algo** to get rid of sth.

descargo [deskár'ɣo] *nm* (*de obligación*) release; (*COM: recibo*) receipt; (: *de deuda*) discharge; (*JUR*) evidence; **~ de una acusación** acquittal on a charge.

descargue [deskár'ge] *etc vb* V **descargar**.

descarnado, a [deskárná'ðo, á] *a* scrawny; (*fig*) bare; (*estilo*) straightforward.

descaro [deskár'o] *nm* nerve.

descarriar [deskárryár'] *vt* (*descaminar*) to misdirect; (*fig*) to lead astray; **~se** *vr* (*perderse*) to lose one's way; (*separarse*) to stray; (*pervertirse*) to err, go astray.

descarrilamiento [deskárrēlámyen'to] *nm* (*de tren*) derailment.

descarrilar [deskárrēlár'] *vi* to be derailed.

descartable [deskártá'βle] *a* (*INFORM*) temporary.

descartar [deskártár'] *vt* (*rechazar*) to reject; (*eliminar*) to rule out; **~se** *vr* (*NAIPES*) to discard; **~se de** to shirk.

descascarar [deskáskárár'] *vt* (*naranja, limón*) to peel; (*nueces, huevo duro*) to shell; **~se** *vr* to peel (off).

descascarillado, a [deskáskárēyá'ðo, á] *a* (*paredes*) peeling.

descendencia [desenden'syá] *nf* (*origen*) origin, descent; (*hijos*) offspring; **morir sin dejar ~** to die without issue.

descendente [desenden'te] *a* (*cantidad*) diminishing; (*INFORM*) top-down.

descender [desender'] *vt* (*bajar: escalera*) to go down; ♦ *vi* to descend; (*temperatura, nivel*) to fall, drop; (*líquido*) to run; (*cortina etc*) to fall (*US*), hang (*Brit*); (*fuerzas,* *persona*) to fail, get weak; ~ **de** to be descended from.

descendiente [desendyen'te] *nm/f* descendant.

descenso [desen'so] *nm* descent; (*de temperatura*) drop; (*de producción*) downturn; (*de calidad*) decline; (*MINERÍA*) collapse; (*bajada*) slope; (*fig: decadencia*) decline; (*de empleado etc*) demotion.

descentrado, a [desentrá'ĝo, á] *a* (*pieza de una máquina*) off-center (*US*), off-centre (*Brit*); (*rueda*) out of balance; (*persona*) bewildered; (*desequilibrado*) unbalanced; (*problema*) out of focus; **todavía está algo** ~ he is still somewhat out of touch.

descentralice [desentrálē'se] *etc vb V* **descentralizar**.

descentralizar [desentrálēsár'] *vt* to decentralize.

descerrajar [deserráhár'] *vt* (*puerta*) to break open.

descienda [desyen'dá] *etc vb V* **descender**.

descifrable [desēfrá'ble] *a* (*gen*) decipherable; (*letra*) legible.

descifrar [desēfrár'] *vt* (*escritura*) to decipher; (*mensaje*) to decode; (*problema*) to solve; (*misterio*) to solve.

descocado, a [deskoká'ĝo, á] *a* (*descarado*) sassy (*US*), cheeky (*Brit*); (*desvergonzado*) brazen.

descoco [desko'ko] *nm* (*descaro*) sassy (*US*), cheek (*Brit*); (*atrevimiento*) brazenness.

descolgar [deskolĝár'] *vt* (*bajar*) to take down; (*desde una posición alta*) to lower; (*de una pared etc*) to unhook; (*teléfono*) to pick up; **~se** *vr* to let o.s. down; **~se por** (*bajar escurriéndose*) to slip down; (*pared*) to climb down; **dejó el teléfono descolgado** he left the phone off the hook.

descolgué [deskolĝe'], **descolguemos** [deskolĝe'mos] *etc vb V* **descolgar**.

descolocado, a [deskoloká'ĝo, á] *a*: **estar** ~ (*cosa*) to be out of place; (*criada*) to be unemployed.

descolorido, a [deskolorē'ĝo, á] *a* (*color, tela*) faded; (*pálido*) pale; (*fig: estilo*) colorless (*US*), colourless (*Brit*).

descollar [deskoyár'] *vi* (*sobresalir*) to stand out; (*montaña etc*) to rise; **la obra que más descuella de las suyas** his most outstanding work.

descompaginar [deskompáhēnár'] *vt* (*desordenar*) to disarrange, mess up.

descompasado, a [deskompásá'ĝo, á] *a* (*sin proporción*) out of all proportion; (*excesivo*) excessive; (*hora*) unearthly.

descompondré [deskompondre'] *etc vb V* **descomponer**.

descompensar [deskompensár'] *vt* to unbalance.

descomponer [deskomponer'] *vt* (*gen, LING, MAT*) to break down; (*desordenar*) to disarrange, disturb; (*materia orgánica*) to rot, decompose; (*TEC*) to put out of order; (*facciones*) to distort; (*estómago etc*) to upset; (*planes*) to mess up; (*persona: molestar*) to upset; (: *irritar*) to annoy; **~se** *vr* (*corromperse*) to rot, decompose; (*estómago*) to get upset; (*el tiempo*) to change (for the worse); (*TEC*) to break down.

descomponga [deskompon'ĝá] *etc vb V* **descomponer**.

descomposición [deskomposēsyon'] *nf* (*gen*) breakdown; (*de fruta etc*) decomposition; (*putrefacción*) rotting; (*de cara*) distortion; ~ **de vientre** (*MED*) stomach upset, diarrhea (*US*), diarrhoea (*Brit*).

descompostura [deskompostoo'rá] *nf* (*TEC*) breakdown; (*desorganización*) disorganization; (*desorden*) untidiness.

descompuesto, a [deskompwe'sto, á] *pp de* **descomponer** ♦ *a* (*corrompido*) decomposed; (*roto*) broken.

descompuse [deskompoo'se] *etc vb V* **descomponer**.

descomunal [deskomoonál'] *a* (*enorme*) huge; (*fam: excelente*) fantastic.

desconcertado, a [deskonsertá'ĝo, á] *a* disconcerted, bewildered.

desconcertar [deskonsertár'] *vt* (*confundir*) to baffle; (*incomodar*) to upset; (*orden*) to disturb; **~se** *vr* (*turbarse*) to be upset; (*confundirse*) to be bewildered.

desconcierto [deskonsyer'to] *etc vb V* **desconcertar** ♦ *nm* (*gen*) disorder; (*desorientación*) uncertainty; (*inquietud*) uneasiness; (*confusión*) bewilderment.

desconchado, a [deskontchá'ĝo, á] *a* (*pintura*) peeling.

desconchar [deskontchár'] *vt* (*pared*) to strip off; (*loza*) to chip off.

desconectado, a [deskonektá'ĝo, á] *a* (*ELEC*) disconnected, switched off; (*INFORM*) offline; **estar** ~ **de** (*fig*) to have no contact with.

desconectar [deskonektár'] *vt* to disconnect; (*desenchufar*) to unplug; (*radio, televisión*) to switch off; (*INFORM*) to toggle off.

desconfiado, a [deskonfyá'ĝo, á] *a* suspicious.

desconfianza [deskonfyán'sá] *nf* distrust.

desconfiar [deskonfyár'] *vi* to be distrustful; ~ **de** (*sospechar*) to mistrust, suspect; (*no tener confianza en*) to have no faith o confidence in; **desconfío de ello** I doubt it; **desconfíe de las imitaciones** (*COM*) beware of imitations.

desconforme [deskonfor'me] *a* = **disconforme**.

descongelar [deskonhelár'] *vt* (*nevera*) to

defrost; (*comida*) to thaw; (*AUTO*) to de-ice; (*COM, POL*) to unfreeze.

descongestionar [desconhestyonár'] *vt* (*cabeza, tráfico*) to clear; (*calle, ciudad*) to relieve congestion in; (*fig: despejar*) to clear.

desconocer [deskonoser'] *vt* (*ignorar*) not to know, be ignorant of; (*no aceptar*) to deny; (*repudiar*) to disown.

desconocido, a [deskonosē'ŧ̵ho, á] *a* unknown; (*que no se conoce*) unfamiliar; (*no reconocido*) unrecognized ♦ *nm/f* stranger; (*recién llegado*) newcomer; **está ~** he is hardly recognizable.

desconocimiento [deskonosēmyen'to] *nm* (*falta de conocimientos*) ignorance; (*repudio*) disregard.

desconozca [deskonos'ká] *etc vb* V **desconocer.**

desconsiderado, a [deskonsēŧ̵herá'ŧ̵ho, á] *a* inconsiderate; (*insensible*) thoughtless.

desconsolado, a [deskonsolá'ŧ̵ho, á] *a* (*afligido*) disconsolate; (*cara*) sad; (*desanimado*) dejected.

desconsolar [deskonsolár'] *vt* to distress; **~se** *vr* to despair.

desconsuelo [deskonswe'lo] *etc vb* V **desconsolar** ♦ *nm* (*tristeza*) distress; (*desesperación*) despair.

descontado, a [deskontá'ŧ̵ho, á] *a:* **por ~** of course; **dar por ~ (que)** to take it for granted (that).

descontar [deskontár'] *vt* (*deducir*) to take away, deduct; (*rebajar*) to discount.

descontento, a [deskonten'to, á] *a* dissatisfied ♦ *nm* dissatisfaction, discontent.

descontrolado, a [deskontrolá'ŧ̵ho, á] *a* (*AM*) uncontrolled.

desconvendré [deskombendre'] *etc,* **desconvenga** [deskomben'gá] *etc vb* V **desconvenir.**

desconvenir [deskombenēr'] *vi* (*personas*) to disagree; (*no corresponder*) not to fit; (*no convenir*) to be inconvenient.

desconviene [deskombye'ne] *etc,* **desconviniendo** [deskombēnyen'do] *etc vb* V **desconvenir.**

descorazonar [deskorásonár'] *vt* to discourage, dishearten; **~se** *vr* to get discouraged, lose heart.

descorchador [deskortchaŧ̵hor'] *nm* corkscrew.

descorchar [deskortchár'] *vt* to uncork, open.

descorrer [deskorrer'] *vt* (*cortina, cerrojo*) to draw back; (*velo*) to remove.

descortés [deskortes'] *a* (*mal educado*) discourteous; (*grosero*) rude.

descortesía [deskortesē'á] *nf* discourtesy; (*grosería*) rudeness.

descoser [deskoser'] *vt* to unstitch; **~se** *vr*

to come apart (at the seams); (*fam: descubrir un secreto*) to blurt out a secret; **~se de risa** to split one's sides laughing.

descosido, a [deskosē'ŧ̵ho, á] *a* (*costura*) unstitched; (*desordenado*) disjointed ♦ *nm:* **como un ~** (*obrar*) wildly; (*beber, comer*) to excess; (*estudiar*) like mad.

descoyuntar [deskoyōōntár'] *vt* (*ANAT*) to dislocate; (*hechos*) to twist; **~se** *vr:* **~se un hueso** (*ANAT*) to put a bone out of joint; **~se de risa** (*fam*) to split one's sides laughing.

descrédito [deskre'ŧ̵heto] *nm* discredit; **caer en ~** to fall into disrepute; **ir en ~ de** to be to the discredit of.

descreído, a [deskreē'ŧ̵ho, á] *a* (*incrédulo*) incredulous; (*falto de fe*) unbelieving.

descremado, a [deskremá'ŧ̵ho, á] *a* skimmed.

descremar [deskremár'] *vt* (*leche*) to skim.

describir [deskrēhēr'] *vt* to describe.

descripción [deskrēpsyon'] *nf* description.

descrito [deskrē'to] *pp de* **describir.**

descuajar [deskwáhár'] *vt* (*disolver*) to melt; (*planta*) to pull out by the roots; (*extirpar*) to eradicate, wipe out; (*desanimar*) to dishearten.

descuajaringarse [deskwáhárēngár'se] *vr* to fall apart.

descuajaringue [deskwáhárēn'ge] *etc vb* V **descuajaringarse.**

descuartice [deskwártē'se] *etc vb* V **descuartizar.**

descuartizar [deskwártēsár'] *vt* (*animal*) to carve up, cut up; (*fig: hacer pedazos*) to tear apart.

descubierto, a [deskōōhyer'to, á] *pp de* **descubrir** ♦ *a* uncovered, bare; (*persona*) bare-headed; (*cielo*) clear; (*coche*) open; (*campo*) treeless ♦ *nm* (*lugar*) open space; (*COM: en el presupuesto*) shortage; (*: bancario*) overdraft; **al ~** in the open; **poner al ~** to lay bare; **quedar al ~** to be exposed; **estar en ~** to be overdrawn.

descubridor, a [deskōōhrēŧ̵hor', á] *nm/f* discoverer.

descubrimiento [deskōōhrēmyen'to] *nm* (*hallazgo*) discovery; (*de criminal, fraude*) detection; (*revelación*) revelation; (*de secreto etc*) disclosure; (*de estatua etc*) unveiling.

descubrir [deskōōhrēr'] *vt* to discover, find; (*petróleo*) to strike; (*inaugurar*) to unveil; (*vislumbrar*) to detect; (*sacar a luz: crimen*) to bring to light; (*revelar*) to reveal, show; (*poner al descubierto*) to expose to view; (*naipes*) to lay down; (*quitar la tapa de*) to uncover; (*cacerola*) to take the lid off; (*enterarse de: causa, solución*) to find out; (*divisar*) to see, make out; (*delatar*) to give away, betray; **~se** *vr* to reveal o.s.;

(*quitarse sombrero*) to take off one's hat; (*confesar*) to confess; (*fig: salir a luz*) to come out *o* to light.

descuelga [deskwel'ǥá] *etc*, **descuelgue** [deskwel'ǥe] *etc vb* V **descolgar**.

descuelle [deskwe'ye] *etc vb* V **descollar**.

descuento [deskwen'to] *etc vb* V **descontar** ♦ *nm* discount; ~ **del 3%** 3% off; **con** ~ at a discount; ~ **por pago al contado** (*COM*) cash discount; ~ **por volumen de compras** (*COM*) volume discount.

descuidado, a [deskwethá'tho, á] *a* (*sin cuidado*) careless; (*desordenado*) untidy; (*olvidadizo*) forgetful; (*dejado*) neglected; (*desprevenido*) unprepared.

descuidar [deskwethár'] *vt* (*dejar*) to neglect; (*olvidar*) to overlook ♦ *vi*, ~**se** *vr* (*distraerse*) to be careless; (*estar desaliñado*) to let o.s. go; (*desprevenirse*) to drop one's guard; **¡descuida!** don't worry!

descuidero, a [deskwethe'ro, á] *nm/f* sneak thief.

descuido [deskwe'tho] *nm* (*dejadez*) carelessness; (*olvido*) negligence; (*un* ~) oversight; **al** ~ casually; (*sin cuidado*) carelessly; **al menor** ~ if my *etc* attention wanders for a minute; **con** ~ thoughtlessly; **por** ~ by an oversight.

desde [des'the] *prep* from; ~ **entonces** since then; **¿**~ **cuándo es esto así?** how long has it been like this?; ~ **lejos** from afar; ~ **ahora en adelante** from now on(wards); ~ **hace 3 días** for 3 days; ~ **luego** of course ♦ *conj*: ~ **que** since; ~ **que puedo recordar** for as long as I can remember.

desdecir [desthesēr'] *vi*: ~ **de** (*no merecer*) to be unworthy of; (*no corresponder*) to clash with; ~**se** *vr*: ~**se de** to go back on.

desdén [desthen'] *nm* scorn.

desdentado, a [desthentá'tho, á] *a* toothless.

desdeñable [desthenyá'ble] *a* contemptible; **nada** ~ far from negligible, considerable.

desdeñar [desthenyár'] *vt* (*despreciar*) to scorn.

desdeñoso, a [desthenyo'so, á] *a* scornful.

desdibujar [desthēbōōhár'] *vt* to blur (the outlines of); ~**se** *vr* to get blurred, fade (away); **el recuerdo se ha desdibujado** the memory has become blurred.

desdiciendo [desthēsyen'do] *etc vb* V **desdecir**.

desdichado, a [desthētchá'tho, á] *a* (*sin suerte*) unlucky; (*infeliz*) unhappy; (*día*) ill-fated ♦ *nm/f* (*pobre desgraciado*) poor devil.

desdicho, a [desthētch'o, á] *pp de* **desdecir** ♦ *nf* (*desgracia*) misfortune; (*infelicidad*) unhappiness.

desdiga [desthē'ǥá] *etc*, **desdije** [desdē'he]

etc vb V **desdecir**.

desdoblado, a [desthohlá'tho, á] *a* (*personalidad*) split.

desdoblar [desthohlár'] *vt* (*extender*) to spread out; (*desplegar*) to unfold.

deseable [deseá'ble] *a* desirable.

desear [deseár'] *vt* to want, desire, wish for; **¿qué desea la señora?** (*tienda etc*) what can I do for you, madam?; **estoy deseando que esto termine** I'm longing for this to finish.

desecar [desekár'] *vt*, **desecarse** *vr* to dry up.

desechable [desetchá'ble] *a* (*envase etc*) disposable.

desechar [desetchár'] *vt* (*basura*) to throw out *o* away; (*ideas*) to reject, discard; (*miedo*) to cast aside; (*plan*) to drop.

desecho [desetch'o] *nm* (*desprecio*) contempt; (*lo peor*) dregs *pl*; ~**s** *nmpl* rubbish *sg*, waste *sg*; **de** ~ (*hierro*) scrap; (*producto*) waste; (*ropa*) cast-off.

desembalar [desembálár'] *vt* to unpack.

desembarace [desembárá'se] *etc vb* V **desembarazar**.

desembarazado, a [desembárásá'tho, á] *a* (*libre*) clear, free; (*desenvuelto*) free and easy.

desembarazar [desembárásár'] *vt* (*desocupar*) to clear; (*desenredar*) to free; ~**se** *vr*: ~**se de** to free o.s. of, get rid of.

desembarazo [desembárá'so] *nm* (*acto*) clearing; (*AM: parto*) birth; (*desenfado*) ease.

desembarcadero [desembárkáthe'ro] *nm* wharf.

desembarcar [desembárkár'] *vt* (*personas*) to land; (*mercancías etc*) to unload ♦ *vi*, ~**se** *vr* (*de barco, avión*) to disembark; (*esp AM: de tren, autobús*) to alight.

desembarco [desembár'ko] *nm* landing.

desembargar [desembárǥár'] *vt* (*gen*) to free; (*JUR*) to remove the embargo on.

desembargue [desembár'ǥe] *etc vb* V **desembargar**.

desembarque [desembár'ke] *etc vb* V **desembarcar** ♦ *nm* disembarkation; (*de pasajeros*) landing; (*de mercancías*) unloading.

desembocadura [desembokáthōō'rá] *nf* (*de río*) mouth; (*de calle*) opening.

desembocar [desembokár'] *vi*: ~ **en** to flow into; (*fig*) to result in.

desemboce [desembo'se] *etc vb* V **desembozar**.

desembolsar [desembolsár'] *vt* (*pagar*) to pay out; (*gastar*) to lay out.

desembolso [desembol'so] *nm* payment.

desemboque [desembo'ke] *etc vb* V **desembocar**.

desembozar [desembosár'] *vt* to unmask.

desembragar [desembráǥár'] *vt* (*TEC*) to

disengage; (*embrague*) to release ♦ *vi* (*AUTO*) to release the clutch.

desembrague [desembrá'ge] *etc vb* V **desembragar**.

desembrollar [desembroyár'] *vt* (*madeja*) to unravel; (*asunto, malentendido*) to sort out.

desembuchar [desemboōtchár'] *vt* to disgorge; (*fig*) to come out with ♦ *vi* (*confesar*) to spill the beans (*fam*); **¡desembucha!** out with it!

desemejante [desemehán'te] *a* dissimilar; ~ **de** different from, unlike.

desemejanza [desemehán'sá] *nf* dissimilarity.

desempacar [desempakár'] *vt* to unpack.

desempañar [desempányár'] *vt* (*cristal*) to clean; (*AUTO*) to defog (*US*), demist (*Brit*).

desempaque [desempá'ke] *etc vb* V **desempacar**.

desempaquetar [desempáketár'] *vt* to unpack, unwrap.

desempatar [desempátár'] *vi* to break a tie; **volvieron a jugar para** ~ they held a play-off.

desempate [desempá'te] *nm* (*FÚTBOL*) play-off; (*TENIS*) tie-break(er).

desempeñar [desempenyár'] *vt* (*cargo*) to hold; (*papel*) to play; (*deber, función*) to perform, carry out; (*lo empeñado*) to redeem; ~**se** *vr* to get out of debt; ~ **un papel** (*fig*) to play (a role).

desempeño [desempe'nyo] *nm* occupation; (*de lo empeñado*) redeeming; **de mucho** ~ very capable.

desempleado, a [desempleá'tho, á] *a* unemployed, out of work ♦ *nm/f* unemployed person.

desempleo [desemple'o] *nm* unemployment.

desempolvar [desempolvár'] *vt* (*muebles etc*) to dust; (*lo olvidado*) to revive.

desencadenar [desenkáthenár'] *vt* to unchain; (*ira*) to unleash; (*provocar*) to cause, set off; ~**se** *vr* to break loose; (*tormenta*) to burst; (*guerra*) to break out; **se desencadenó una lucha violenta** a violent struggle ensued.

desencajar [desenkáhár'] *vt* (*hueso*) to put out of joint; (*mandíbula*) to dislocate; (*mecanismo, pieza*) to disconnect, disengage.

desencantar [desenkántár'] *vt* to disillusion, disenchant.

desencanto [desenkán'to] *nm* disillusionment, disenchantment.

desencoger [desenkoher'] *vt* (*extender*) to spread out; (*desdoblar*) to smooth out; ~**se** *vr* to lose one's timidity.

desencoja [desenko'há] *etc vb* V **desencoger**.

desenchufar [desentchoōfár'] *vt* to unplug, disconnect.

desenfadado, a [desenfáthá'tho, á] *a* (*desenvuelto*) uninhibited; (*descarado*) forward; (*en el vestir*) casual.

desenfado [desenfá'tho] *nm* (*libertad*) freedom; (*comportamiento*) free and easy manner; (*descaro*) forwardness; (*desenvoltura*) self-confidence.

desenfocado, a [desenfoká'tho, á] *a* (*FOTO*) out of focus.

desenfrenado, a [desenfrená'tho, á] *a* (*descontrolado*) uncontrolled; (*inmoderado*) unbridled.

desenfrenarse [desenfrenár'se] *vr* (*persona: desmandarse*) to lose all self-control; (*multitud*) to run riot; (*tempestad*) to burst; (*viento*) to rage.

desenfreno [desenfre'no] *nm* (*vicio*) wildness; (*falta de control*) lack of self-control; (*de pasiones*) unleashing.

desenganchar [desengántchár'] *vt* (*gen*) to unhook; (*FERRO*) to uncouple; (*TEC*) to disengage.

desengañar [desengányár'] *vt* to disillusion; (*abrir los ojos a*) to open the eyes of; ~**se** *vr* to become disillusioned; **¡desengáñate!** don't you believe it!

desengaño [desengá'nyo] *nm* disillusionment; (*decepción*) disappointment; **sufrir un** ~ **amoroso** to be disappointed in love.

desengrasar [desengrásár'] *vt* to degrease.

desenlace [desenlá'se] *etc vb* V **desenlazar** ♦ *nm* outcome; (*LIT*) ending.

desenlazar [desenlásár'] *vt* (*desatar*) to untie; (*problema*) to solve; (*aclarar: asunto*) to unravel; ~**se** *vr* (*desatarse*) to come undone; (*LIT*) to end.

desenmarañar [desenmárányár'] *vt* (*fig*) to unravel.

desenmascarar [desenmáskárár'] *vt* to unmask, expose.

desenredar [desenrethár'] *vt* to resolve.

desenrollar [desenroyár'] *vt* to unroll, unwind.

desenroscar [desenroskár'] *vt* (*tornillo etc*) to unscrew.

desenrosque [desenros'ke] *etc vb* V **desenroscar**.

desentenderse [desentender'se] *vr*: ~ **de** to pretend not to know about; (*apartarse*) to have nothing to do with.

desentendido, a [desentendē'tho, á] *a*: **hacerse el** ~ to pretend not to notice; **se hizo el** ~ he didn't take the hint.

desenterrar [desenterrár'] *vt* to exhume; (*tesoro, fig*) to unearth, dig up.

desentierre [desentye'rre] *etc vb* V **desenterrar**.

desentonar [desentonár'] *vi* (*MUS*) to sing (*o* play) out of tune; (*no encajar*) to be out of place; (*color*) to clash.

desentorpecer [desentorpeser'] *vt* (*miembro*) to stretch; (*fam: persona*) to smarten up.

desentorpezca [desentorpes'ká] *etc vb* V **desentorpecer**.

desentrañar [desentrányár'] *vt* (*misterio*) to unravel.

desentrenado, a [desentrená'tho, á] *a* out of training.

desentumecer [desentoōmeser'] *vt* (*pierna etc*) to stretch; (*DEPORTE*) to loosen up.

desentumezca [desentoōmes'ká] *etc vb* V **desentumecer**.

desenvainar [desembáēnár'] *vt* (*espada*) to draw, unsheathe.

desenvoltura [desemboltoō'rá] *nf* (*libertad, gracia*) ease; (*descaro*) free and easy manner; (*al hablar*) fluency.

desenvolver [desembolher'] *vt* (*paquete*) to unwrap; (*fig*) to develop; ~**se** *vr* (*desarrollarse*) to unfold, develop; (*suceder*) to go off; (*prosperar*) to prosper; (*arreglárselas*) to cope.

desenvolvimiento [desembolhēmyen'to] *nm* (*desarrollo*) development; (*de idea*) exposition.

desenvuelto, a [desembwel'to, á] *pp de* **desenvolver** ♦ *a* (*suelto*) easy; (*desenfadado*) confident; (*al hablar*) fluent; (*pey*) forward.

desenvuelva [desembw'elhá] *etc vb* V **desenvolver**.

deseo [dese'o] *nm* desire, wish; ~ **de saber** thirst for knowledge; **buen** ~ good intentions *pl*; **arder en** ~**s de algo** to yearn for sth.

deseoso, a [deseo'so, á] *a*: **estar** ~ **de hacer** to be anxious to do.

deseque [dese'ke] *etc vb* V **desecar**.

desequilibrado, a [desekēlēhrá'tho, á] *a* unbalanced ♦ *nm/f* unbalanced person; ~ **mental** mentally disturbed person.

desequilibrar [desekēlēhrár'] *vt* (*mente*) to unbalance; (*objeto*) to throw out of balance; (*persona*) to throw off balance.

desequilibrio [desekēlē'hrēo] *nm* (*de mente*) unbalance; (*entre cantidades*) imbalance; (*MED*) unbalanced mental condition.

desertar [desertár'] *vt* (*JUR: derecho de apelación*) to forfeit ♦ *vi* to desert; ~ **de sus deberes** to neglect one's duties.

desértico, a [deser'tēko, á] *a* desert *cpd*; (*vacío*) deserted.

desesperación [desesperásyon'] *nf* desperation, despair; (*irritación*) fury; **es una** ~ it's maddening; **es una** ~ **tener que ...** it's infuriating to have to ... .

desesperado, a [desesperá'tho, á] *a* (*persona: sin esperanza*) desperate; (*caso, situación*) hopeless; (*esfuerzo*) furious ♦ *nm*:

como un ~ like mad ♦ *nf*: **hacer algo a la desesperada** to do sth as a last resort *o* in desperation.

desesperance [desesperán'se] *etc vb* V **desesperanzar**.

desesperante [desesperán'te] *a* (*exasperante*) infuriating; (*persona*) hopeless.

desesperanzar [desesperánsár'] *vt* to drive to despair; ~**se** *vr* to lose hope, despair.

desesperar [desesperár'] *vt* to drive to despair; (*exasperar*) to drive to distraction ♦ *vi*: ~ **de** to despair of; ~**se** *vr* to despair, lose hope.

desestabilice [desestáhēlē'se] *etc vb* V **desestabilizar**.

desestabilizar [desestáhēlēsár'] *vt* to destabilize.

desestimar [desestēmár'] *vt* (*menospreciar*) to have a low opinion of; (*rechazar*) to reject.

desfachatez [desfátchátes'] *nf* (*insolencia*) impudence; (*descaro*) rudeness.

desfalco [desfál'ko] *nm* embezzlement.

desfallecer [desfáyeser'] *vi* (*perder las fuerzas*) to become weak; (*desvanecerse*) to faint.

desfallecido, a [desfáyesē'tho, á] *a* (*débil*) weak.

desfallezca [desfáyes'ká] *etc vb* V **desfallecer**.

desfasado, a [desfásá'tho, á] *a* (*anticuado*) old-fashioned; (*TEC*) out of phase.

desfasar [desfásár'] *vt* to phase out.

desfase [desfá'se] *nm* (*diferencia*) gap.

desfavorable [desfáhorá'hle] *a* unfavorable (*US*), unfavourable (*Brit*).

desfavorecer [desfáhoreser'] *vt* (*sentar mal*) not to suit.

desfavorezca [desfáhores'ká] *etc vb* V **desfavorecer**.

desfiguración [desfēgoōrásyon'] *nf*, **desfiguramiento** [desfēgoōrámyen'to] *nm* (*de persona*) disfigurement; (*de monumento*) defacement; (*FOTO*) blurring.

desfigurar [desfēgoōrár'] *vt* (*cara*) to disfigure; (*cuerpo*) to deform; (*cuadro, monumento*) to deface; (*FOTO*) to blur; (*sentido*) to twist; (*suceso*) to misrepresent.

desfiladero [desfēláthe'ro] *nm* gorge, defile.

desfilar [desfēlár'] *vi* to parade; **desfilaron ante el general** they marched past the general.

desfile [desfē'le] *nm* procession; (*MIL*) parade; ~ **de modelos** fashion show.

desflorar [desflorár'] *vt* (*mujer*) to deflower; (*arruinar*) to tarnish; (*asunto*) to touch on.

desfogar [desfogár'] *vt* (*fig*) to vent ♦ *vi* (*NAUT: tormenta*) to burst; ~**se** *vr* (*fig*) to let off steam.

desfogue [desfo'ge] *etc vb* V **desfogar**.

desgajar [desgáhár'] *vt* (*arrancar*) to tear

off; (*romper*) to break off; (*naranja*) to split into segments; ~**se** *vr* to come off.

desgana [desɡá'ná] *nf* (*falta de apetito*) loss of appetite; (*renuencia*) unwillingness; **hacer algo a** ~ to do sth unwillingly.

desganado, a [desɡáná'ðo, á] *a*: **estar** ~ (*sin apetito*) to have no appetite; (*sin entusiasmo*) to have lost interest.

desgañitarse [desɡányētár'se] *vr* to shout o.s. hoarse.

desgarbado, a [desɡárbá'ðo, á] *a* (*sin gracia*) clumsy, ungainly.

desgarrador, a [desɡárráθor', á] *a* heart-rending.

desgarrar [desɡárrár'] *vt* to tear (up); (*fig*) to shatter.

desgarro [desɡá'rro] *nm* (*en tela*) tear; (*aflicción*) grief; (*descaro*) impudence.

desgastar [desɡástár'] *vt* (*deteriorar*) to wear away o down; (*estropear*) to spoil; ~**se** *vr* to get worn out.

desgaste [desɡá'ste] *nm* wear (and tear); (*de roca*) erosion; (*de cuerda*) fraying; (*de metal*) corrosion; ~ **económico** drain on one's resources.

desglosar [desɡlosár'] *vt* to detach.

desgobernar [desɡobernár'] *vt* (*POL*) to misgovern; (*asunto*) to handle badly; (*ANAT*) to dislocate.

desgobierno [desɡobyer'no] *etc vb* V **desgobernar** ♦ *nm* (*POL*) misgovernment, misrule.

desgracia [desɡrá'syá] *nf* misfortune; (*accidente*) accident; (*vergüenza*) disgrace; (*contratiempo*) setback; **por** ~ unfortunately; **en el accidente no hay que lamentar** ~**s personales** there were no casualties in the accident; **caer en** ~ to fall from grace; **tener la** ~ **de** to be unlucky enough to.

desgraciadamente [desɡrásyáθámen'te] *ad* unfortunately.

desgraciado, a [desɡrásyá'ðo, á] *a* (*sin suerte*) unlucky, unfortunate; (*miserable*) wretched; (*infeliz*) miserable ♦ *nm/f* (*malo*) swine; (*infeliz*) poor creature.

desgraciar [desɡrásyár'] *vt* (*estropear*) to spoil; (*ofender*) to displease.

desgranar [desɡránár'] *vt* (*trigo*) to thresh; (*guisantes*) to shell; ~ **un racimo** to pick the grapes from a bunch; ~ **mentiras** to come out with a string of lies.

desgravación [desɡrábásyon'] *nf* (*COM*): ~ **de impuestos** tax relief; ~ **personal** personal allowance.

desgravar [desɡrábár'] *vt* (*producto*) to reduce the tax o duty on.

desgreñado, a [desɡrenyá'ðo, á] *a* dishevelled.

deshabitado, a [desáβētá'ðo, á] *a* uninhabited.

deshabitar [desáβētár'] *vt* (*casa*) to leave empty; (*despoblar*) to depopulate.

deshacer [desáser'] *vt* (*lo hecho*) to undo, unmake; (*proyectos*: *arruinar*) to spoil; (*casa*) to break up; (*TEC*) to take apart; (*enemigo*) to defeat; (*diluir*) to melt; (*contrato*) to break; (*intriga*) to solve; (*cama*) to strip; (*maleta*) to unpack; (*paquete*) to unwrap; (*nudo*) to untie; (*costura*) to unpick; ~**se** *vr* (*desatarse*) to come undone; (*estropearse*) to be spoiled; (*descomponerse*) to fall to pieces; (*disolverse*) to melt; (*despedazarse*) to come apart o undone; ~**se de** to get rid of; (*COM*) to dump, unload; ~**se en** (*cumplidos*, *elogios*) to be lavish with; ~**se en lágrimas** to burst into tears; ~**se por algo** to be crazy about sth.

deshaga [desá'ɡá] *etc*, **desharé** [desáre'] *etc vb* V **deshacer**.

des(h)arrapado, a [desárrápá'ðo, á] *a* ragged; (**de aspecto**) ~ shabby.

deshecho, a [desetch'o, á] *pp de* **deshacer** ♦ *a* (*lazo*, *nudo*) undone; (*roto*) smashed; (*despedazado*) in pieces; (*cama*) unmade; (*MED*: *persona*) weak, emaciated; (: *salud*) broken; **estoy** ~ I'm shattered.

deshelar [deselár'] *vt* (*cañería*) to thaw; (*heladera*) to defrost.

desheredar [deseredár'] *vt* to disinherit.

deshice [desī'se] *etc vb* V **deshacer**.

deshidratación [desēðrátásyon'] *nf* dehydration.

deshidratar [desēðrátár'] *vt* to dehydrate.

deshielo [desye'lo] *etc vb* V **deshelar** ♦ *nm* thaw.

deshilachar [desēlátchár'] *vt*, **deshilacharse** *vr* to fray.

deshilar [desēlár'] *vt* (*tela*) to unravel.

deshilvanado, a [desēlβáná'ðo, á] *a* (*fig*) disjointed, incoherent.

deshinchar [desēntchár'] *vt* (*neumático*) to let down; (*herida etc*) to reduce (the swelling of); ~**se** *vr* (*neumático*) to go flat; (*hinchazón*) to go down.

deshojar [desohár'] *vt* (*árbol*) to strip the leaves off; (*flor*) to pull the petals off; ~**se** *vr* to lose its leaves *etc*.

deshollinar [desoyēnár'] *vt* (*chimenea*) to sweep.

deshonesto, a [desone'sto, á] *a* (*no honrado*) dishonest; (*indecente*) indecent.

deshonor [desonor'] *nm* dishonor (*US*), dishonour (*Brit*), disgrace; (*un* ~) insult, affront.

deshonra [deson'rá] *nf* (*deshonor*) dishonor (*US*), dishonour (*Brit*); (*vergüenza*) shame.

deshonrar [desonrár'] *vt* to dishonor (*US*), dishonour (*Brit*).

deshonroso, a [desonro'so, á] *a* dishonorable (*US*), dishonourable (*Brit*), disgraceful.

deshora [deso'rá]: **a** ~ *ad* at the wrong time; (*llegar*) unexpectedly; (*acostarse*) at some unearthly hour.

deshuesar [deswesár'] *vt* (*carne*) to bone; (*fruta*) to stone.

desidia [desē'δyá] *nf* (*pereza*) idleness.

desierto, a [desyer'to, á] *a* (*casa, calle, negocio*) deserted; (*paisaje*) bleak ♦ *nm* desert.

designación [desēgnásyon'] *nf* (*para un cargo*) appointment; (*nombre*) designation.

designar [desēgnár'] *vt* (*nombrar*) to designate; (*indicar*) to fix.

designio [desēg'nyo] *nm* plan; **con el** ~ **de** with the intention of.

desigual [desēgwál'] *a* (*lucha*) unequal; (*diferente*) different; (*terreno*) uneven; (*tratamiento*) unfair; (*cambiadizo*: *tiempo*) changeable; (: *carácter*) unpredictable.

desigualdad [desēgwáldáth'] *nf* (*ECON, POL*) inequality; (*de carácter, tiempo*) unpredictability; (*de escritura*) unevenness; (*de terreno*) roughness.

desilusión [desēlōōsyon'] *nf* disillusionment; (*decepción*) disappointment.

desilusionar [desēlōōsyonár'] *vt* to disillusion; (*decepcionar*) to disappoint; ~**se** *vr* to become disillusioned.

desinencia [desēnen'syá] *nf* (*LING*) ending.

desinfectar [desēnfektár'] *vt* to disinfect.

desinfestar [desēnfestár'] *vt* to decontaminate.

desinflación [desēnflásyon'] *nf* (*COM*) disinflation.

desinflar [desēnflár'] *vt* to deflate; ~**se** *vr* (*neumático*) to go down o flat.

desintegración [desēntegrásyon'] *nf* disintegration; ~ **nuclear** nuclear fission.

desintegrar [desēntegrár'] *vt* (*gen*) to disintegrate; (*átomo*) to split; (*grupo*) to break up; ~**se** *vr* to disintegrate; to split; to break up.

desinterés [desēnteres'] *nm* (*objetividad*) disinterestedness; (*altruismo*) unselfishness.

desinteresado, a [desēnteresá'δo, á] *a* (*imparcial*) disinterested; (*altruista*) unselfish.

desintoxicar [desēntoksēkár'] *vt* to detoxify; ~**se** *vr*: ~**se de** (*rutina, trabajo*) to get away from.

desintoxique [desēntoksē'ke] *etc vb V* **desintoxicar.**

desistir [desēstēr'] *vi* (*renunciar*) to stop, desist; ~ **de** (*empresa*) to give up; (*derecho*) to waive.

deslavazado, a [deslávásá'δo, á] *a* (*lacio*) limp; (*desteñido*) faded; (*insípido*) colorless (*US*), colourless (*Brit*); (*incoherente*) disjointed.

desleal [desleál'] *a* (*infiel*) disloyal; (*COM*: *competencia*) unfair.

deslealtad [desleáltáth'] *nf* disloyalty.

desleído, a [desleē'δo, á] *a* weak.

desleír [desleēr'] *vt* (*líquido*) to dilute; (*sólido*) to dissolve.

deslenguado, a [deslengwá'δo, á] *a* (*grosero*) foul-mouthed.

deslía [deslē'á] *etc vb V* **desleír.**

desliar [deslyár'] *vt* (*desatar*) to untie; (*paquete*) to open; ~**se** *vr* to come undone.

deslice [deslē'se] *etc vb V* **deslizar.**

desliendo [deslēen'do] *etc vb V* **desleír.**

desligar [deslēgár'] *vt* (*desatar*) to untie, undo; (*separar*) to separate; ~**se** *vr* (*de un compromiso*) to extricate o.s.

desligue [deslē'ge] *etc vb V* **desligar.**

deslindar [deslēndár'] *vt* (*señalar las lindes de*) to mark out, fix the boundaries of; (*fig*) to define.

desliz [deslēs'] *nm* (*fig*) lapse; ~ **de lengua** slip of the tongue; **cometer un** ~ to slip up.

deslizar [deslēsár'] *vt* to slip, slide; ~**se** *vr* (*escurrirse*: *persona*) to slip, slide; (: *coche*) to skid; (*aguas mansas*) to flow gently; (*error*) to creep in; (*tiempo*) to pass; (*persona*: *irse*) to slip away; ~**se en un cuarto** to slip into a room.

deslomar [deslomár'] *vt* (*romper el lomo de*) to break the back of; (*fig*) to wear out; ~**se** *vr* (*fig fam*) to work one's guts out.

deslucido, a [deslōōsē'δo, á] *a* dull; (*torpe*) awkward, graceless; (*deslustrado*) tarnished; (*fracasado*) unsuccessful; **quedar** ~ to make a poor impression.

deslucir [deslōōsēr'] *vt* (*deslustrar*) to tarnish; (*estropear*) to spoil, ruin; (*persona*) to discredit; **la lluvia deslució el acto** the rain ruined the ceremony.

deslumbrar [deslōōmbrár'] *vt* (*con la luz*) to dazzle; (*cegar*) to blind; (*impresionar*) to dazzle; (*dejar perplejo a*) to puzzle, confuse.

deslustrar [deslōōstrár'] *vt* (*vidrio*) to frost; (*quitar lustre a*) to dull; (*reputación*) to sully.

desluzca [deslōōs'ká] *etc vb V* **deslucir.**

desmadrarse [desmáthrár'se] *vr* (*fam*) to run wild.

desmán [desmán'] *nm* (*exceso*) outrage; (*abuso de poder*) abuse.

desmandarse [desmándár'se] *vr* (*portarse mal*) to behave badly; (*excederse*) to get out of hand; (*caballo*) to bolt.

desmantelar [desmántelár'] *vt* (*deshacer*) to dismantle; (*casa*) to strip; (*organización*) to disband; (*MIL*) to raze; (*andamio*) to take down; (*NAUT*) to unrig.

desmaña [desmá'nyá] *nf* clumsiness.

desmaquillador [desmákēyáthor'] *nm* make-up remover.

desmayado, a [dɛsmàyà'ᵭo. á] *a* (*sin sentido*) unconscious; (*carácter*) dull; (*débil*) faint, weak; (*color*) pale.

desmayar [desmáyár'] *vi* to lose heart; ~**se** *vr* (*MED*) to faint.

desmayo [desmá'yo] *nm* (*MED: acto*) faint; (*estado*) unconsciousness; (*depresión*) dejection; (*de voz*) faltering; **sufrir un** ~ to have a fainting fit.

desmedido, a [desmeᵭe'ᵭo. á] *a* excessive; (*ambición*) boundless.

desmedrado, a [desmeᵭrá'ᵭo, á] *a* (*estropeado*) impaired; (*MED*) run down.

desmejorado, a [desmehorá'ᵭo, á] *a*: **está muy desmejorada** (*MED*) she's not looking too well.

desmejorar [desmehorár'] *vt* (*dañar*) to impair, spoil; (*MED*) to weaken.

desmembración [desmembrásyon'] *nf* dismemberment; (*fig*) break-up.

desmembrar [desmembrár'] *vt* (*MED*) to dismember; (*fig*) to separate.

desmemoriado, a [desmemoryá'ᵭo, á] *a* forgetful, absent-minded.

desmentir [desmentēr'] *vt* (*contradecir*) to contradict; (*refutar*) to deny; (*rumor*) to squelch (*US*), scotch (*Brit*) ♦ *vi*: ~ **de** to refute; ~**se** *vr* to contradict o.s.

desmenuce [desmenōō'se] *etc vb V* **desmenuzar.**

desmenuzar [desmenōōsár'] *vt* (*deshacer*) to crumble; (*carne*) to chop; (*examinar*) to examine closely.

desmerecer [desmereser'] *vt* to be unworthy of ♦ *vi* (*deteriorarse*) to deteriorate.

desmerezca [desmeres'ká] *etc vb V* **desmerecer.**

desmesurado, a [desmesōōrá'ᵭo, á] *a* (*desmedido*) disproportionate; (*enorme*) enormous; (*ambición*) boundless; (*descarado*) insolent.

desmiembre [desmyem'bre] *etc vb V* **desmembrar.**

desmienta [desmyen'tá] *etc vb V* **desmentir.**

desmigajar [desmēɡàhàr'], **desmigar** [desmēɡàr'] *vt* to crumble.

desmigue [desmē'ɡe] *etc vb V* **desmigar.**

desmilitarice [desmēlētàrē'se] *etc vb V* **desmilitarizar.**

desmilitarizar [desmēlētárēsár'] *vt* to demilitarize.

desmintiendo [desmēntyen'do] *etc vb V* **desmentir.**

desmochar [desmotchár'] *vt* (*árbol*) to lop; (*texto*) to cut, hack about.

desmontable [desmontá'ᵬle] *a* (*que se quita*) detachable; (*en compartimientos*) sectional; (*que se puede plegar etc*) collapsible.

desmontar [desmontár'] *vt* (*deshacer*) to dismantle; (*motor*) to strip down; (*máquina*) to take apart; (*escopeta*) to uncock; (*tienda de campaña*) to take down; (*tierra*) to level; (*quitar los árboles a*) to clear; (*jinete*) to throw ♦ *vi* to dismount.

desmonte [desmon'te] *nm* (*de tierra*) levelling; (*de árboles*) clearing; (*terreno*) levelled ground; (*FERRO*) cutting.

desmoralice [desmorálē'se] *etc vb V* **desmoralizar.**

desmoralizador, a [desmorálēsáᵭhor', á] *a* demoralizing.

desmoralizar [desmorálēsár'] *vt* to demoralize.

desmoronado, a [desmoroná'ᵭo, á] *a* (*casa, edificio*) dilapidated.

desmoronamiento [desmoronàmyen'to] *nm* (*tb fig*) crumbling.

desmoronar [desmoronár'] *vt* to wear away, erode; ~**se** *vr* (*edificio, dique*) to fall into disrepair; (*economía*) to decline.

desmovilice [desmoᵬēlē'se] *etc vb V* **desmovilizar.**

desmovilizar [desmoᵬēlēsár'] *vt* to demobilize.

desnacionalización [desnàsyonálēsásyon'] *nf* denationalization.

desnacionalizado, a [desnàsyonálēsá'ᵭo, á] *a* (*industria*) denationalized; (*persona*) stateless.

desnatado, a [desnàtá'ᵭo, á] *a* skimmed.

desnatar [desnàtár'] *vt* (*leche*) to skim; **leche sin** ~ whole milk.

desnaturalice [desnàtōōrálē'se] *etc vb V* **desnaturalizar.**

desnaturalizado, a [desnàtōōrálēsá'ᵭo, á] *a* (*persona*) unnatural; **alcohol** ~ methylated spirits.

desnaturalizar [desnàtōōrálēsár'] *vt* (*QUÍMICA*) to denature; (*corromper*) to pervert; (*sentido de algo*) to distort; ~**se** *vr* (*perder la nacionalidad*) to give up one's nationality.

desnivel [desnēᵬel'] *nm* (*de terreno*) unevenness; (*POL*) inequality; (*diferencia*) difference.

desnivelar [desnēᵬelár'] *vt* (*terreno*) to make uneven; (*fig: desequilibrar*) to unbalance; (*balanza*) to tip.

desnuclearizado, a [desnōōkleàrēsá'ᵭo, á] *a*: **región desnuclearizada** nuclear-free zone.

desnudar [desnōōᵭhár'] *vt* (*desvestir*) to undress; (*despojar*) to strip; ~**se** *vr* (*desvestirse*) to get undressed.

desnudez [desnōōᵭhes'] *nf* (*de persona*) nudity; (*fig*) bareness.

desnudo, a [desnōō'ᵭo, á] *a* (*cuerpo*) naked; (*árbol, brazo*) bare; (*paisaje*) flat; (*estilo*) unadorned; (*verdad*) plain ♦ *nm/f* nude; ~ **de** devoid o bereft of; **la retrató al**

~ he painted her in the nude; **poner al** ~ to lay bare.

desnutrición [desnōōtrēsyon'] *nf* malnutrition.

desnutrido, a [desnōōtrē'tho, á] *a* undernourished.

desobedecer [desoḇeḏeser'] *vt*, *vi* to disobey.

desobedezca [desoḇeḏes'ká] *etc vb* V **desobedecer**.

desobediencia [desoḇeḏyen'syá] *nf* disobedience.

desocupado, a [desocōōpá'tho, á] *a* at leisure; (*desempleado*) unemployed; (*deshabitado*) empty, vacant.

desocupar [desocōōpár'] *vt* to vacate; ~**se** *vr* (*quedar libre*) to be free; **se ha desocupado aquella mesa** that table's free now.

desodorante [desoḏoránʹte] *nm* deodorant.

desoiga [deso'ēğá] *etc vb* V **desoír**.

desoír [desoēr'] *vt* to ignore, disregard.

desolación [desolásyon'] *nf* (*de lugar*) desolation; (*fig*) grief.

desolar [desolár'] *vt* to ruin, lay waste.

desolladero [desoyáḏe'ro] *nm* slaughterhouse.

desollar [desoyár'] *vt* (*quitar la piel a*) to skin; (*criticar*): ~ **vivo a** to criticize unmercifully.

desorbitado, a [desorḇetá'tho, á] *a* (*excesivo*) excessive; (*precio*) exorbitant; **con los ojos** ~**s** pop-eyed.

desorbitar [desorḇetár'] *vt* (*exagerar*) to exaggerate; (*interpretar mal*) to misinterpret; ~**se** *vr* (*persona*) to lose one's sense of proportion; (*asunto*) to get out of hand.

desorden [desor'then] *nm* confusion; (*de casa, cuarto*) mess; (*político*) disorder; **desórdenes** *nmpl* (*alborotos*) disturbances; (*excesos*) excesses; **en** ~ (*gente*) in confusion.

desordenado, a [desorthená'tho, á] *a* (*habitación, persona*) untidy; (*objetos: revueltos*) in a mess, jumbled; (*conducta*) disorderly.

desordenar [desorthenár'] *vt* (*gen*) to disarrange; (*pelo*) to mess up; (*cuarto*) to make a mess in; (*causar confusión a*) to throw into confusion.

desorganice [desorğáne'se] *etc vb* V **desorganizar**.

desorganizar [desorğánēsár'] *vt* to disorganize.

desorientar [desoryentár'] *vt* (*extraviar*) to mislead; (*confundir, desconcertar*) to confuse; ~**se** *vr* (*perderse*) to lose one's way.

desovar [desoḇár'] *vi* (*peces*) to spawn; (*insectos*) to lay eggs.

desoyendo [desoyen'do] *etc vb* V **desoír**.

despabilado, a [despáḇelá'tho, á] *a* (*despierto*) wide-awake; (*fig*) alert, sharp.

despabilar [despáḇelár'] *vt* (*despertar*) to wake up; (*fig: persona*) to liven up; (*trabajo*) to get through quickly ♦ *vi*, ~**se** *vr* to wake up; (*fig*) to get a move on.

despacio [despá'syo] *ad* (*lentamente*) slowly; (*en voz baja*) softly; ¡~! take it easy!

despacito [despásē'to] *ad* (*fam*) slowly; (*suavemente*) softly.

despachar [despátchár'] *vt* (*negocio*) to do, complete; (*resolver: problema*) to settle; (*correspondencia*) to deal with; (*fam: comida*) to polish off; (: *bebida*) to gulp down (*US*), knock back (*Brit*); (*enviar*) to send, dispatch; (*vender*) to sell, deal in; (*COM: cliente*) to attend to; (*billete*) to issue; (*mandar ir*) to send away ♦ *vi* (*decidirse*) to get things settled; (*apresurarse*) to hurry up; ~**se** *vr* to finish off; (*apresurarse*) to hurry up; ~**se de algo** to get rid of sth; ~**se a su gusto con uno** to give sb a piece of one's mind; **¿quién despacha?** is anybody serving?

despacho [despátch'o] *nm* (*oficina*) office; (: *en una casa*) study; (*de paquetes*) dispatch; (*COM: venta*) sale (of goods); (*comunicación*) message; ~ **de billetes** *o* **boletos** (*AM*) booking office; ~ **de localidades** box office; **géneros sin** ~ unsaleable goods; **tener buen** ~ to find a ready sale.

despachurrar [despátchōōrrár'] *vt* (*aplastar*) to crush; (*persona*) to flatten.

despampanante [despámpánán'te] *a* (*fam: chica*) stunning.

desparejado, a [despáreḥá'tho, á], **desparejo, a** [despáre'ho, á] *a* odd.

desparpajo [despárpá'ho] *nm* (*desenvoltura*) self-confidence; (*pey*) nerve.

desparramar [despárrámár'] *vt* (*esparcir*) to scatter; (*líquido*) to spill.

despatarrar [despátárrár'] *vt* (*asombrar*) to amaze; ~**se** *vr* (*abrir las piernas*) to open one's legs wide; (*caerse*) to tumble; (*fig*) to be flabbergasted.

despavorido, a [despáḇorē'tho, á] *a* terrified.

despectivo, a [despektē'ḇo, á] *a* (*despreciativo*) derogatory; (*LING*) pejorative.

despechar [despetchár'] *vt* (*provocar ira a*) to enrage; (*fam: destetar*) to wean.

despecho [despetch'o] *nm* spite; **a** ~ **de** in spite of; **por** ~ out of (sheer) spite.

despedace [despethá'se] *etc vb* V **despedazar**.

despedazar [despethásár'] *vt* to tear to pieces.

despedida [despethē'thá] *nf* (*adiós*) goodbye, farewell; (*antes de viaje*) send-off; (*en carta*) closing formula; (*de obrero*) dismissal; (*INFORM*) log off (*US*), logout (*Brit*); **cena/función de** ~ farewell dinner/

performance; **regalo de** ~ parting gift; ~ **de soltero/soltera** stag/shower party.

despedir [despeðˈeɾ'] vt (visita) to see off, show out; (empleado) to dismiss; (inquilino) to evict; (objeto) to hurl; (olor etc) to give out o off; **~se** vr (dejar un empleo) to give up one's job; (INFORM) to log out o off; **~se de** to say goodbye to; **se despidieron** they said goodbye to each other.

despegado, a [despeɣáˈðo, á] a (separado) detached; (persona: poco afectuoso) cold, indifferent ♦ nm/f: **es un** ~ he has cut himself off from his family.

despegar [despeɣáɾ'] vt to unstick; (sobre) to open ♦ vi (avión) to take off; (cohete) to blast off; **~se** vr to come loose, come unstuck; **sin** ~ **los labios** without uttering a word.

despego [despeˈɣo] nm detachment.

despegue [despeˈɣe] etc vb V **despegar** ♦ nm takeoff; (de cohete) blastoff.

despeinado, a [despeˈeˈnáˈðo, á] a dishevelled, unkempt.

despeinar [despeˈeˈnáɾ'] vt (pelo) to ruffle; **¡me has despeinado todo!** you've completely ruined my hairdo!

despejado, a [despeˈháˈðo, á] a (lugar) clear, free; (cielo) clear; (persona) wideawake, bright.

despejar [despeˈháɾ'] vt (gen) to clear; (misterio) to clarify, clear up; (MAT: incógnita) to find ♦ vi (el tiempo) to clear; **~se** vr (tiempo, cielo) to clear (up); (misterio) to become clearer; (cabeza) to clear; **¡despejen!** (moverse) move along!; (salirse) everybody out!

despeje [despeˈhe] nm (DEPORTE) clearance.

despelotarse [despelotáɾ'se] vr (fam) to strip off; (fig) to let one's hair down.

despeluce [despelóˈse] etc vb V **despeluzar**.

despeluzar [despelóˈsáɾ'] vt (pelo) to tousle; ~ **a uno** (fig) to horrify sb.

despellejar [despeˈyeˈháɾ'] vt (animal) to skin; (criticar) to criticize unmercifully; (fam: arruinar) to fleece.

despensa [despenˈsá] nf (armario) pantry; (NAUT) storeroom; (provisión de comestibles) stock of food.

despeñadero [despenyáˈðeˈro] nm (GEO) cliff, precipice.

despeñar [despenyáɾ'] vt (arrojar) to fling down; **~se** vr to fling o.s. down; (caer) to fall headlong.

desperdiciar [despeɾðiˈsyáɾ'] vt (comida, tiempo) to waste; (oportunidad) to throw away.

desperdicio [despeɾðiˈsyo] nm (despilfarro) squandering; (residuo) waste; **~s** nmpl (basura) rubbish sg, refuse sg, garbage sg (US); (residuos) waste sg; **~s de cocina** kitchen scraps; **el libro no tiene** ~ the book is excellent from beginning to end.

desperdigar [despeɾðiˈɣáɾ'] vt (esparcir) to scatter; (energía) to dissipate; **~se** vr to scatter.

desperdigue [despeɾðiˈɣe] etc vb V **desperdigar**.

desperece [despeɾeˈse] etc vb V **desperezarse**.

desperezarse [despeɾeˈsáɾ'se] vr to stretch.

desperfecto [despeɾfekˈto] nm (deterioro) slight damage; (defecto) flaw, imperfection.

despertador [despeɾtáˈðoɾ'] nm alarm clock; ~ **de viaje** travelling clock.

despertar [despeɾtáɾ'] vt (persona) to wake up; (recuerdos) to revive; (esperanzas) to raise; (sentimiento) to arouse ♦ vi, **~se** vr to awaken, wake up; **~se a la realidad** to wake up to reality ♦ nm awakening.

despiadado, a [despyáˈðáˈðo, á] a (ataque) merciless; (persona) heartless.

despido [despeˈðo] etc vb V **despedir** ♦ nm dismissal; ~ **improcedente** o **injustificado** wrongful dismissal; ~ **injusto** unfair dismissal; ~ **voluntario** voluntary dismissal (US) o redundancy (Brit).

despierto, a [despyeɾˈto, á] etc vb V **despertar** ♦ a awake; (fig) sharp, alert.

despilfarrado, a [despilfáɾráˈðo, á] a (malgastador) wasteful; (con dinero) spendthrift ♦ nm/f spendthrift.

despilfarrar [despilfáɾráɾ'] vt (gen) to waste; (dinero) to squander.

despilfarro [despilfáˈrro] nm (derroche) squandering; (lujo desmedido) extravagance.

despintar [despintáɾ'] vt (quitar pintura a) to take the paint off; (hechos) to distort ♦ vi: **A no despinta a B** A is in no way inferior to B; **~se** vr (desteñir) to fade.

despiojar [despyoháɾ'] vt to delouse.

despistado, a [despistáˈðo, a] a (distraído) vague, absent-minded; (poco práctico) impractical; (confuso) confused; (desorientado) off the track ♦ nm/f (tipo: distraído) scatterbrain, absent-minded person.

despistar [despistáɾ'] vt to throw off the track o scent; (fig) to mislead, confuse; **~se** vr to take the wrong road; (fig) to become confused.

despiste [despeˈste] nm (AUTO etc) swerve; (error) slip; (distracción) absent-mindedness; **tiene un terrible** ~ he's terribly absent-minded.

desplace [despláˈse] etc vb V **desplazar**.

desplante [desplánˈte] nm: **hacer un** ~ **a uno** to be rude to sb.

desplazado, a [despláˈsáˈðo, á] a (pieza) wrongly placed ♦ nm/f (inadaptado) misfit;

sentirse un poco ~ to feel rather out of place.

desplazamiento [desplásámyen'to] *nm* displacement; (*viaje*) journey; (*de opinión, votos*) shift, swing; (*INFORM*) scrolling; **~ hacia arriba/abajo** (*INFORM*) scroll up/down.

desplazar [desplásár'] *vt* (*gen*) to move; (*FÍSICA, NAUT, TEC*) to displace; (*tropas*) to transfer; (*suplantar*) to take the place of; (*INFORM*) to scroll; **~se** *vr* (*persona, vehículo*) to travel, go; (*objeto*) to move, shift; (*votos, opinión*) to shift, swing.

desplegar [desplegár'] *vt* (*tela, papel*) to unfold, open out; (*bandera*) to unfurl; (*alas*) to spread; (*MIL*) to deploy; (*manifestar*) to display.

desplegué [desplege'], **despleguemos** [desplege'mos] *etc vb V* **desplegar**.

despliegue [desplye'ge] *etc vb V* **desplegar** ♦ *nm* unfolding, opening; deployment, display.

desplomarse [desplomár'se] *vr* (*edificio, gobierno, persona*) to collapse; (*derrumbarse*) to topple over; (*precios*) to slump; **se ha desplomado el techo** the ceiling has fallen in.

desplumar [desploomár'] *vt* (*ave*) to pluck; (*fam: estafar*) to fleece.

despoblado, a [despobla'tho, á] *a* (*sin habitantes*) uninhabited; (*con pocos habitantes*) depopulated; (*con insuficientes habitantes*) underpopulated ♦ *nm* deserted spot.

despojar [despohár'] *vt* (*alguien: de sus bienes*) to divest of, deprive of; (*casa*) to strip, leave bare; (*de su cargo*) to strip of; **~se** *vr* (*desnudarse*) to undress; **~se de** (*ropa, hojas*) to shed; (*poderes*) to relinquish.

despojo [despo'ho] *nm* (*acto*) plundering; (*objetos*) plunder, loot; **~s** *nmpl* (*de ave, res*) offal *sg*.

desposado, a [desposá'tho, á] *a, nm/f* newly-wed.

desposar [desposár'] *vt* (*suj: sacerdote: pareja*) to marry; **~se** *vr* (*casarse*) to marry, get married.

desposeer [desposeer'] *vt* (*despojar*) to dispossess; **~ a uno de su autoridad** to strip sb of his authority.

desposeído, a [deposeé'tho, á] *nm/f:* **los ~s** the have-nots.

desposeyendo [desposeyen'do] *etc vb V* **desposeer**.

desposorios [desposo'ryos] *nmpl* (*esponsales*) betrothal *sg*; (*boda*) marriage ceremony *sg*.

déspota [des'potá] *nm/f* despot.

despotricar [despotrēkár'] *vi:* **~ contra** to moan *o* complain about.

despotrique [despotrē'ke] *etc vb V* **despo-**

tricar.

despreciable [despresyá'ble] *a* (*moralmente*) despicable; (*objeto*) worthless; (*cantidad*) negligible.

despreciar [despresyár'] *vt* (*desdeñar*) to despise, scorn; (*afrentar*) to slight.

despreciativo, a [despresyátē'bo, á] *a* (*observación, tono*) scornful, contemptuous; (*comentario*) derogatory.

desprecio [despre'syo] *nm* scorn, contempt; slight.

desprender [desprender'] *vt* (*soltar*) to loosen; (*separar*) to separate; (*desatar*) to unfasten; (*olor*) to give off; **~se** *vr* (*botón: caerse*) to fall off; (*: abrirse*) to unfasten; (*olor, perfume*) to be given off; **~se de** to follow from; **~se de algo** (*ceder*) to give sth up; (*desembarazarse*) to get rid of sth; **se desprende que** it transpires that.

desprendido, a [desprendē'do, á] *a* (*pieza*) loose; (*sin abrochar*) unfastened; (*desinteresado*) disinterested; (*generoso*) generous.

desprendimiento [desprendēmyen'to] *nm* (*gen*) loosening; (*generosidad*) disinterestedness; (*indiferencia*) detachment; (*de gas*) leak; (*de tierra, rocas*) landslide.

despreocupado, a [despreokōopá'tho, á] *a* (*sin preocupación*) unworried, unconcerned; (*tranquilo*) nonchalant; (*en el vestir*) casual; (*negligente*) careless.

despreocuparse [despreokōopár'se] *vr* to be carefree; (*dejar de inquietarse*) to stop worrying; (*ser indiferente*) to be unconcerned; **~ de** to have no interest in.

desprestigiar [desprestēhyár'] *vt* (*criticar*) to run down, disparage; (*desacreditar*) to discredit.

desprestigio [desprestē'hyo] *nm* (*denigración*) disparagement; (*impopularidad*) unpopularity.

desprevenido, a [desprebenē'tho, á] *a* (*no preparado*) unprepared, unready; **coger** (*Esp*) *o* **agarrar** (*AM*) **a uno ~** to catch sb unawares.

desproporción [desproporsyon'] *nf* disproportion, lack of proportion.

desproporcionado, a [desproporsyoná'tho, á] *a* disproportionate, out of proportion.

despropósito [despropo'sēto] *nm* (*salida de tono*) irrelevant remark; (*disparate*) piece of nonsense.

desprovisto, a [desprobē'sto, á] *a:* **~ de** devoid of; **estar ~ de** to lack.

después [despwes'] *ad* afterwards, later; (*desde entonces*) since (then); (*próximo paso*) next; **poco ~** soon after; **un año ~** a year later; **~ se debatió el tema** next the matter was discussed ♦ *prep:* **~ de** (*tiempo*) after, since; (*orden*) next (to); **~ de comer** after lunch; **~ de corregido el texto** after the text had been corrected; **~**

de esa fecha (*pasado*) since that date; (*futuro*) from *o* after that date; **~ de todo** after all; **~ de verlo** after seeing it, after I *etc* saw it; **mi nombre está ~ del tuyo** my name comes next to yours ♦ *conj*: **~ (de) que** after; **~ (de) que lo escribí** after *o* since I wrote it, after writing it.

despuntar [despōontár'] *vt* (*lápiz*) to blunt ♦ *vi* (*BOT*: *plantas*) to sprout; (: *flores*) to bud; (*alba*) to break; (*día*) to dawn; (*persona*: *descollar*) to stand out.

desquiciar [deskēsyár'] *vt* (*puerta*) to take off its hinges; (*descomponer*) to upset; (*persona*: *turbar*) to disturb; (: *volver loco a*) to unhinge.

desquitarse [deskētár'se] *vr* to obtain satisfaction; (*COM*) to recover a debt; (*fig*: *vengarse de*) to get one's own back; **~ de una pérdida** to make up for a loss.

desquite [deskē'te] *nm* (*satisfacción*) satisfaction; (*venganza*) revenge.

Dest. *abr* = **destinatario**.

destacado, a [destáká'tho, á] *a* outstanding.

destacamento [destákámen'to] *nm* (*MIL*) detachment.

destacar [destákár'] *vt* (*ARTE*: *hacer resaltar*) to make stand out; (*subrayar*) to emphasize, point up; (*MIL*) to detach, detail; (*INFORM*) to highlight ♦ *vi*, **~se** *vr* (*resaltarse*) to stand out; (*persona*) to be outstanding *o* exceptional; **quiero ~ que...** I wish to emphasize that...; **~(se) contra** *o* **en** *o* **sobre** to stand out *o* be outlined against.

destajo [destá'ho] *nm*: **a ~** (*por pieza*) by the job; (*con afán*) eagerly; **trabajar a ~** to do piecework; (*fig*) to work one's fingers to the bone.

destapar [destápár'] *vt* (*botella*) to open; (*cacerola*) to take the lid off; (*descubrir*) to uncover; **~se** *vr* (*descubrirse*) to get uncovered; (*revelarse*) to reveal one's true character.

destape [destá'pe] *nm* nudity; (*fig*) permissiveness; **el ~ español** the process of liberalization in Spain after Franco's death.

destaque [destá'ke] *etc vb* V **destacar**.

destartalado, a [destártálá'tho, á] *a* (*desordenado*) untidy; (*casa etc*: *grande*) rambling; (: *ruinoso*) tumbledown.

destellar [desteyár'] *vi* (*diamante*) to sparkle; (*metal*) to glint; (*estrella*) to twinkle.

destello [deste'yo] *nm* (*de diamante*) sparkle; (*de metal*) glint; (*de estrella*) twinkle; (*de faro*) signal light; **no tiene un ~ de verdad** there's not a grain of truth in it.

destemplado, a [destemplá'tho, á] *a* (*MUS*) out of tune; (*voz*) harsh; (*MED*) out of

sorts; (*METEOROLOGÍA*) unpleasant, nasty.

destemplar [destemplár'] *vt* (*MUS*) to put out of tune; (*alterar*) to upset; **~se** *vr* (*MUS*) to lose its pitch; (*descomponerse*) to get out of order; (*persona*: *irritarse*) to get upset; (*MED*) to get out of sorts.

desteñir [destenyēr'] *vt* to fade ♦ *vi*, **~se** *vr* to fade; **esta tela no destiñe** this fabric will not run.

desternillarse [desternēyár'se] *vr*: **~ de risa** to split one's sides laughing.

desterrado, a [desterrá'tho, á] *nm/f* (*exiliado*) exile.

desterrar [desterrár'] *vt* (*exilar*) to exile; (*fig*) to banish, dismiss.

destetar [destetár'] *vt* to wean.

destiempo [destyem'po]: **a ~** *ad* at the wrong time.

destierro [destye'rro] *etc vb* V **desterrar** ♦ *nm* exile; **vivir en el ~** to live in exile.

destilar [destēlár'] *vt* to distil; (*pus*, *sangre*) to ooze; (*fig*: *rebosar*) to exude; (: *revelar*) to reveal ♦ *vi* (*gotear*) to drip.

destilería [destēlerē'á] *nf* distillery; **~ de petróleo** oil refinery.

destinar [destēnár'] *vt* (*funcionario*) to appoint, assign; (*fondos*) to set aside; **es un libro destinado a los niños** it is a book (intended *o* meant) for children; **una carta que viene destinada a usted** a letter for you, a letter addressed to you.

destinatario, a [destēnátá'ryo, á] *nm/f* addressee; (*COM*) payee.

destino [destē'no] *nm* (*suerte*) destiny; (*de viajero*) destination; (*función*) use; (*puesto*) post, placement; **~ público** public appointment; **salir con ~ a** to leave for; **con ~ a Londres** (*avión*, *barco*) (bound) for London; (*carta*) to London.

destiña [destē'nyá] *etc*, **destiñendo** [destēnyen'do] *etc vb* V **desteñir**.

destitución [destētōōsyon'] *nf* dismissal, removal.

destituir [destētōōēr'] *vt* (*despedir*) to dismiss; (: *ministro*, *funcionario*) to remove from office.

destituyendo [destētōōyen'do] *etc vb* V **destituir**.

destornillador [destornēyáthor'] *nm* screwdriver.

destornillar [destornēyár'] *vt*, **~se** *vr* (*tornillo*) to unscrew.

destrabar [destrábár'] *vt* to untie, unfetter.

destreza [destre'sá] *nf* (*habilidad*) skill; (*maña*) dexterity.

destripar [destrēpár'] *vt* (*animal*) to gut; (*reventar*) to mangle.

destronar [destronár'] *vt* (*rey*) to dethrone; (*fig*) to overthrow.

destroncar [destronkár'] *vt* (*árbol*) to chop off, lop; (*proyectos*) to ruin; (*discurso*) to interrupt.

destronque [destron'ke] *etc vb* V **destroncar.**

destroce [destro'se] *etc vb* V **destrozar.**

destrozar [destrosár'] *vt* (*romper*) to smash, break (up); (*estropear*) to ruin; (*nervios*) to shatter; ~ **a uno en una discusión** to crush sb in an argument.

destrozo [destro'so] *nm* (*acción*) destruction; (*desastre*) smashing; ~**s** *nmpl* (*pedazos*) pieces; (*daños*) havoc *sg.*

destrucción [destrooksyon'] *nf* destruction.

destructor, a [destrooktor', á] *a* destructive ♦ *nm* (*NAUT*) destroyer.

destruir [destrooér'] *vt* to destroy; (*casa*) to demolish; (*equilibrio*) to upset; (*proyecto*) to spoil; (*esperanzas*) to dash; (*argumento*) to demolish.

destruyendo [destrooyen'do] *etc vb* V **destruir.**

desuelle [deswe'ye] *etc vb* V **desollar.**

desueve [deswe'ke] *etc vb* V **desovar.**

desunión [desoonyon'] *nf* (*separación*) separation; (*discordia*) disunity.

desunir [desoonér'] *vt* to separate; (*TEC*) to disconnect; (*fig*) to cause a quarrel *o* rift between.

desuso [desoo'so] *nm* disuse; **caer en** ~ to fall into disuse, become obsolete; **una expresión caída en** ~ an obsolete expression.

desvaído, a [desbáé'tho, á] *a* (*color*) pale; (*contorno*) blurred.

desvalido, a [desbálé'tho, á] *a* (*desprotegido*) destitute; (*sin fuerzas*) helpless; **niños** ~**s** waifs and strays.

desvalijar [desbáléhár'] *vt* (*persona*) to rob; (*casa, tienda*) to burgle; (*coche*) to break into.

desvalorice [desbálorē'se] *etc vb* V **desvalorizar.**

desvalorizar [desbálorēsár'] *vt* to devalue.

desván [desbán'] *nm* attic.

desvanecer [desbáneser'] *vt* (*disipar*) to dispel; (*recuerdo, temor*) to banish; (*borrar*) to blur; ~**se** *vr* (*humo etc*) to vanish, disappear; (*duda*) to be dispelled; (*color*) to fade; (*recuerdo, sonido*) to fade away; (*MED*) to pass out.

desvanecido, a [desbánesē'tho, á] *a* (*MED*) faint; **caer** ~ to fall in a faint.

desvanecimiento [desbánesēmyen'to] *nm* (*desaparición*) disappearance; (*de dudas*) dispelling; (*de colores*) fading; (*evaporación*) evaporation; (*MED*) fainting spell (*US*) *o* fit (*Brit*).

desvanezca [desbánes'ká] *etc vb* V **desvanecer.**

desvariar [desbáryár'] *vi* (*enfermo*) to be delirious; (*delirar*) to talk nonsense.

desvarío [desbárē'o] *nm* delirium; (*desatino*) absurdity; ~**s** *nmpl* ravings.

desvelar [desbelár'] *vt* to keep awake; ~**se** *vr* (*no poder dormir*) to stay awake; (*vigilar*) to be vigilant *o* watchful; ~**se por algo** (*inquietarse*) to be anxious about sth; (*poner gran cuidado*) to take great care over sth.

desvelo [desbe'lo] *nm* lack of sleep; (*insomnio*) sleeplessness; (*fig*) vigilance; ~**s** *nmpl* (*preocupación*) anxiety *sg*, effort *sg.*

desvencijado, a [desbensēhá'tho, á] *a* (*silla*) rickety; (*máquina*) broken-down.

desvencijar [desbensēhár'] *vt* (*romper*) to break; (*soltar*) to loosen; (*persona: agotar*) to exhaust; ~**se** *vr* to come apart.

desventaja [desbentá'há] *nf* disadvantage; (*inconveniente*) drawback.

desventajoso, a [desbentáho'so, á] *a* disadvantageous, unfavorable (*US*), unfavourable (*Brit*).

desventura [desbentoo'rá] *nf* misfortune.

desventurado, a [desbentoorá'tho, á] *a* (*desgraciado*) unfortunate; (*de poca suerte*) ill-fated.

desvergonzado, a [desbergonsá'tho, á] *a* (*sin vergüenza*) shameless; (*descarado*) insolent ♦ *nm/f* shameless person.

desvergüenza [desbergwen'sá] *nf* (*descaro*) shamelessness; (*insolencia*) impudence; (*mala conducta*) effrontery; **esto es una** ~ this is disgraceful; **¡qué** ~**!** what a nerve!

desvestir [desbestér'] *vt*, **desvestirse** *vr* to undress.

desviación [desbyásyon'] *nf* deviation; (*AUTO: rodeo*) diversion, detour; (: *carretera de circunvalación*) beltway (*US*), ring road (*Brit*); ~ **de la circulación** traffic diversion; **es una** ~ **de sus principios** it is a departure from his usual principles.

desviar [desbyár'] *vt* to turn aside; (*balón, flecha, golpe*) to deflect; (*pregunta*) to parry; (*ojos*) to avert, turn away; (*río*) to alter the course of; (*navío*) to divert, reroute; (*conversación*) to sidetrack; ~**se** *vr* (*apartarse del camino*) to turn aside; (: *barco*) to go off course; (*AUTO: dar un rodeo*) to make a detour; ~**se de un tema** to get away from the point.

desvincular [desbēnkoolár'] *vt* to free, release; ~**se** *vr* (*aislarse*) to be cut off; (*alejarse*) to cut o.s. off.

desvío [desbē'o] *etc vb* V **desviar** ♦ *nm* (*desviación*) detour, diversion; (*fig*) indifference.

desvirtuar [desbērtwár'] *vt* (*estropear*) to spoil; (*argumento, razonamiento*) to detract from; (*efecto*) to counteract; (*sentido*) to distort; ~**se** *vr* to spoil.

desvistiendo [desbēstyen'do] *etc vb* V **desvestir.**

desvivirse [desbēhér'se] *vr*: ~ **por** to long for, crave for; ~ **por los amigos** to do anything for one's friends.

detalladamente [detàyàɵámen'te] *ad* (*con detalles*) in detail; (*extensamente*) at great length.

detallar [detàyàr'] *vt* to detail; (*asunto por asunto*) to itemize.

detalle [detà'ye] *nm* detail; (*fig*) gesture, token; **al ~** in detail; (*COM*) retail *cpd*; **comercio al ~** retail trade; **vender al ~** to sell retail; **no pierde ~** he doesn't miss a trick; **me observaba sin perder ~** he watched my every move; **tiene muchos ~s** she is very considerate.

detallista [detàyē'stà] *nm/f* retailer ♦ *a* (*meticuloso*) meticulous; **comercio ~** retail trade.

detectar [detektàr'] *vt* to detect.

detector [detektor'] *nm* (*NAUT, TEC etc*) detector; **~ de mentiras/de minas** lie/mine detector.

detención [detensyon'] *nf* (*acción*) stopping; (*estancamiento*) stoppage; (*retraso*) holdup, delay; (*JUR: arresto*) arrest; (*cuidado*) care; **~ de juego** (*DEPORTE*) stoppage of play; **~ ilegal** unlawful detention.

detendré [detendre'] *etc vb V* **detener**.

detener [detener'] *vt* (*gen*) to stop; (*JUR: arrestar*) to arrest; (: *encarcelar*) to detain; (*objeto*) to keep; (*retrasar*) to hold up, delay; (*aliento*) to hold; **~se** *vr* to stop; **~se en** (*demorarse*) to delay over, linger over.

detenga [deten'gà] *etc vb V* **detener**.

detenidamente [detenēɵámen'te] *ad* (*minuciosamente*) carefully; (*extensamente*) at great length.

detenido, a [detenē'ɵo, à] *a* (*arrestado*) under arrest; (*minucioso*) detailed; (*examen*) thorough; (*tímido*) timid ♦ *nm/f* person under arrest, prisoner.

detenimiento [detenēmyen'to] *nm* care; **con ~** thoroughly.

detentar [detentàr'] *vt* to hold; (*sin derecho: título*) to hold unlawfully; (: *puesto*) to occupy unlawfully.

detergente [deterhen'te] *a, nm* detergent.

deteriorado, a [deteryorà'ɵo, à] *a* (*estropeado*) damaged; (*desgastado*) worn.

deteriorar [deteryoràr'] *vt* to spoil, damage; **~se** *vr* to deteriorate.

deterioro [deteryo'ro] *nm* deterioration.

determinación [determēnàsyon'] *nf* (*empeño*) determination; (*decisión*) decision; (*de fecha, precio*) settling, fixing.

determinado, a [determēnà'ɵo, à] *a* (*preciso*) fixed, set; (*LING: artículo*) definite; (*persona: resuelto*) determined; **un día ~** on a certain day; **no hay ningún tema ~** there is no particular theme.

determinar [determēnàr'] *vt* (*plazo*) to fix;

(*precio*) to settle; (*daños, impuestos*) to assess; (*pleito*) to decide; (*causar*) to cause; **~se** *vr* to decide; **el reglamento determina que...** the rule states that...; **aquello determinó la caída del gobierno** that brought about the fall of the government; **esto le determinó** this made him decide.

detestable [detestà'ɥle] *a* (*persona*) hateful; (*acto*) detestable.

detestar [detestàr'] *vt* to detest.

detonar [detonàr'] *vi* to detonate.

detracción [detràksyon'] *nf* (*denigración*) disparagement.

detractor, a [detràktor', à] *a* disparaging ♦ *nm/f* detractor.

detrás [detràs'] *ad* behind; (*atrás*) at the back ♦ *prep*: **~ de** behind; **por ~ de uno** (*fig*) behind sb's back; **salir de ~** to come out from behind; **por ~** behind.

detrimento [detrēmen'to] *nm*: **en ~ de** to the detriment of.

detuve [detōō'ɥe] *etc vb V* **detener**.

deuda [deōō'ɵà] *nf* (*condición*) indebtedness, debt; (*cantidad*) debt; **~ a largo plazo** long-term debt; **~ exterior/pública** foreign/national debt; **~ incobrable** *o* **morosa** bad debt; **~s activas/pasivas** assets/liabilities; **contraer ~s** to get into debt.

deudor, a [deōōɵhor', à] *nm/f* debtor; **~ hipotecario** mortgager; **~ moroso** defaulter.

devaluación [deɥàlwàsyon'] *nf* devaluation.

devaluar [deɥàlōōàr'] *vt* to devalue.

devanador [deɥànàɵhor'] *nm* (*carrete*) spool, bobbin.

devanar [deɥànàr'] *vt* (*hilo*) to wind; **~se** *vr*: **~se los sesos** to rack one's brains.

devaneo [deɥàne'o] *nm* (*MED*) delirium; (*desatino*) nonsense; (*fruslería*) idle pursuit; (*amorío*) flirtation.

devastar [deɥàstàr'] *vt* (*destruir*) to devastate.

devendré [deɥendre'] *etc*, **devenga** [deɥen'gà] *etc vb V* **devenir**.

devengar [deɥengàr'] *vt* (*salario: ganar*) to earn; (: *tener que cobrar*) to be due; (*intereses*) to bring in, accrue, earn.

devengue [deɥen'ge] *etc vb V* **devengar**.

devenir [deɥenēr'] *vi*: **~ en** to become, turn into ♦ *nm* (*movimiento progresivo*) process of development; (*transformación*) transformation.

deviene [deɥye'ne] *etc*, **deviniendo** [deɥēnyen'do] *etc vb V* **devenir**.

devoción [deɥosyon'] *nf* devotion; (*afición*) strong attachment.

devolución [deɥolōōsyon'] *nf* (*reenvío*) return, sending back; (*reembolso*) repayment; (*JUR*) devolution.

devolver [deɥolɥer'] *vt* (*lo extraviado, prestado*) to give back; (*a su sitio*) to put back; (*carta al correo*) to send back;

(*COM*) to repay, refund; (*visita, la palabra*) to return; (*salud, vista*) to restore; (*fam: vomitar*) to throw up ♦ *vi* (*fam*) to be sick; ~ **mal por bien** to return ill for good; ~ **la pelota a uno** to give sb tit for tat.

devorar [deḅorár'] *vt* to devour; (*comer ávidamente*) to gobble up; (*fig: fortuna*) to run through; **todo lo devoró el fuego** the fire consumed everything; **le devoran los celos** he is consumed with jealousy.

devoto, a [deḅo'to, á] *a* (*REL: persona*) devout; (: *obra*) devotional; (*amigo*): ~ **(de uno)** devoted (to sb) ♦ *nm/f* admirer; **los** ~**s** (*REL*) the faithful; **su muy** ~ your devoted servant.

devuelto [deḅwel'to], **devuelva** [deḅwel'ḅá] *etc vb V* **devolver.**

D.F. *abr* (*México*) = *Distrito Federal.*

dg. *abr* (= *decigramo*) dg.

D.G. *abr* = *Dirección General*; (= *Director General*) D.G.

DGS *nf abr* = *Dirección General de Seguridad*; = *Dirección General de Sanidad.*

DGT *nf abr* = *Dirección General de Tráfico*; = *Dirección General de Turismo.*

di [dē] *vb V* **dar; decir.**

día [dē'á] *nm* day; ~ **de asueto** day off; ~ **festivo** holiday; ~ **hábil/inhábil** working/ non-working day; ~ **de inocentes** (*28 December*) ≈ All Fools' Day; ~ **lectivo** teaching day; ~ **libre** day off; **D**~ **de Reyes** Epiphany (*6 January*); **¿qué** ~ **es?** what's the date?; **estar/poner al** ~ to be/keep up to date; **el** ~ **de hoy/de mañana** today/ tomorrow; **el** ~ **menos pensado** when you least expect it; **al** ~ **siguiente** on the following day; **todos los** ~**s** every day; **un** ~ **sí y otro no** every other day; **vivir al** ~ to live from hand to mouth; **de** ~ by day, in daylight; **del** ~ (*estilos*) fashionable; (*menú*) today's; **de un** ~ **para otro** any day now; **en pleno** ~ in full daylight; **en su** ~ in due time; **¡hasta otro** ~! so long!

diablo [dyá'ḅlo] *nm* (*tb fig*) devil; **pobre** ~ poor devil; **hace un frío de todos los** ~**s** it's hellishly cold.

diablura [dyáḅlōō'rá] *nf* prank; (*travesura*) mischief.

diabólico, a [dyáḅo'lēko, á] *a* diabolical.

diáfano, a [dyá'fáno, á] *a* (*tela*) diaphanous; (*agua*) crystal-clear.

diafragma [dyáfrág'má] *nm* diaphragm.

diagnosis [dyágno'sēs] *nf inv*, **diagnóstico** [dēágno'stēko] *nm* diagnosis.

diagrama [dyágrá'má] *nm* diagram; ~ **de barras** (*COM*) bar chart; ~ **de dispersión** (*COM*) scatter diagram; ~ **de flujo** (*INFORM*) flowchart.

dialecto [dyálek'to] *nm* dialect.

dialogar [dyáloğár'] *vt* to write in dialogue

form ♦ *vi* (*conversar*) to have a conversation; ~ **con** (*POL*) to hold talks with.

diálogo [dyá'loğo] *nm* dialogue.

dialogue [dyálo'ğe] *etc vb V* **dialogar.**

diamante [dyámán'te] *nm* diamond.

diametralmente [dyámetrálmen'te] *ad* diametrically; ~ **opuesto a** diametrically opposed to.

diámetro [dēá'metro] *nm* diameter; ~ **de giro** (*AUTO*) turning circle; **faros de gran** ~ wide-angle headlights.

diana [dyá'ná] *nf* (*MIL*) reveille; (*de blanco*) center (*US*), centre (*Brit*), bull's-eye.

diantre [dyán'tre] *nm*: **¡**~**!** (*fam*) oh hell!

diapasón [dyá'páson'] *nm* (*instrumento*) tuning fork; (*de violín etc*) fingerboard; (*de voz*) tone.

diapositiva [dyáposētē'ḅá] *nf* (*FOTO*) slide, transparency.

diario, a [dyá'ryo, á] *a* daily ♦ *nm* newspaper; (*libro diario*) diary; (: *COM*) daybook; (*COM: gastos*) daily expenses; ~ **de navegación** (*NAUT*) logbook; ~ **hablado** (*RADIO*) news (bulletin); ~ **de sesiones** parliamentary report; **a** ~ daily; **de** *o* **para** ~ everyday.

diarrea [dyárre'á] *nf* diarrhea (*US*), diarrhoea (*Brit*).

diatriba [dyátrē'ḅá] *nf* diatribe, tirade.

dibujante [dēḅōōhán'te] *nm/f* (*de bosquejos*) artist; (*de dibujos animados*) cartoonist; (*de moda*) designer; ~ **de publicidad** commercial artist.

dibujar [dēḅōōhár'] *vt* to draw, sketch; ~**se** *vr* (*emoción*) to show; ~**se contra** to be outlined against.

dibujo [dēḅōō'ho] *nm* drawing; (*TEC*) design; (*en papel, tela*) pattern; (*en periódico*) cartoon; (*fig*) description; ~**s animados** cartoons; ~ **del natural** drawing from life.

dic., dic.ᵉ *abr* (= *diciembre*) Dec.

diccionario [dēksyoná'ryo] *nm* dictionary.

diciembre [dēsyem'bre] *nm* December.

diciendo [dēsyen'do] *etc vb V* **decir.**

dictado [dēktá'ḍo] *nm* dictation; **escribir al** ~ to take dictation; **los** ~**s de la conciencia** (*fig*) the dictates of conscience.

dictador [dēktáḍor'] *nm* dictator.

dictadura [dēktáḍōō'rá] *nf* dictatorship.

dictáfono ® [dēktá'fono] *nm* Dictaphone ®.

dictamen [dēktá'men] *nm* (*opinión*) opinion; (*informe*) report; ~ **contable** auditor's report; ~ **facultativo** (*MED*) medical report.

dictar [dēktár'] *vt* (*carta*) to dictate; (*JUR: sentencia*) to pass; (*decreto*) to issue; (*AM: clase*) to give; (: *conferencia*) to deliver.

dicharachero, a [dētchárátche'ro, á] *a* talkative ♦ *nm/f* (*ingenioso*) wit;

(*parlanchín*) chatterbox.

dicho, a [dētch'o, á] *pp de* **decir** ♦ *a*
(*susodicho*) aforementioned ♦ *nm* saying;
(*proverbio*) proverb; (*ocurrencia*) bright
remark ♦ *nf* (*buena suerte*) good luck; **mejor** ~ rather; ~ **y hecho** no sooner said
than done.

dichoso, a [dētcho'so, á] *a* (*feliz*) happy;
(*afortunado*) lucky; ¡**aquel** ~ **coche!** (*fam*)
that blessed car!

diecinueve [dyesēnwe'ḫe] *num* nineteen;
(*fecha*) nineteenth; *V tb* **seis.**

dieciochesco, a [dyesēotches'ko, á] *a*
eighteenth-century.

dieciocho [dyesēotch'o] *num* eighteen;
(*fecha*) eighteenth; *V tb* **seis.**

dieciséis [dyesēse'ēs] *num* sixteen; (*fecha*)
sixteenth; *V tb* **seis.**

diecisiete [dyesēsye'te] *num* seventeen;
(*fecha*) seventeenth; *V tb* **seis.**

diente [dyen'te] *nm* (*ANAT, TEC*) tooth;
(*ZOOL*) fang; (: *de elefante*) tusk; (*de ajo*)
clove; ~ **de león** dandelion; ~**s postizos**
false teeth; **enseñar los** ~**s** (*fig*) to show
one's teeth; **hablar entre** ~**s** to mutter,
mumble; **hincar el** ~ **en** (*comida*) to bite
into.

diera [dye'rá] *etc vb V* **dar.**

diéresis [dēe'resēs] *nf* dieresis.

dieron [dye'ron] *vb V* **dar.**

diesel [dē'sel] *a*: **motor** ~ diesel engine.

diestro, a [dyes'tro, á] *a* (*derecho*) right;
(*hábil*) skillful; (: *con las manos*) handy ♦
nm (*TAUR*) matador ♦ *nf* right hand; **a** ~ **y
siniestro** (*sin método*) wildly.

dieta [dye'tá] *nf* diet; ~**s** *nfpl* expenses;
estar a ~ to be on a diet.

dietético, a [dyete'tēko, á] *a* dietetic ♦ *nm/f*
dietician.

diez [dyes] *num* ten; (*fecha*) tenth; **hacer
las** ~ **de últimas** (*NAIPES*) to sweep the
board; *V tb* **seis.**

difamación [dēfámásyon'] *nf* slander; libel.

difamar [dēfàmár'] *vt* (*JUR: hablando*) to
slander; (: *por escrito*) to libel.

difamatorio, a [dēfámáto'ryo, á] *a* slanderous; libellous.

diferencia [dēferen'syá] *nf* difference; **a** ~
de unlike; **hacer** ~ **entre** to make a distinction between; ~ **salarial** (*COM*) wage differential.

diferencial [dēferensyál'] *nm* (*AUTO*) differential.

diferenciar [dēferensyár'] *vt* to differentiate
between ♦ *vi* to differ; ~**se** *vr* to differ, be
different; (*distinguirse*) to distinguish o.s.

diferente [dēferen'te] *a* different.

diferido [dēfere'ḏho] *nm*: **en** ~ (*TV etc*) recorded.

diferir [dēferēr'] *vt* to defer.

difícil [dēfē'sēl] *a* difficult; (*tiempos, vida*)

hard; (*situación*) delicate; **es un hombre**
~ he's a difficult man to get along with.

difícilmente [dēfē'sēlmente] *ad* (*con
dificultad*) with difficulty; (*apenas*) hardly.

dificultad [dēfēkōōltáṯh'] *nf* difficulty;
(*problema*) trouble; (*objeción*) objection.

dificultar [dēfēkōōltár'] *vt* (*complicar*) to
complicate, make difficult; (*estorbar*) to
obstruct; **las restricciones dificultan el
comercio** the restrictions hinder trade.

dificultoso, a [dēfēkōōlto'so, á] *a* (*difícil*)
difficult, hard; (*fam: cara*) odd, ugly;
(*persona: exigente*) fussy.

difiera [dēfye'rá] *etc*, **difiriendo** [dēfēryen'do]
etc vb V **diferir.**

difuminar [dēfōōmēnár'] *vt* to blur.

difundir [dēfōōndēr'] *vt* (*calor, luz*) to
diffuse; (*RADIO*) to broadcast; ~**se** *vr* to
spread (out); ~ **una noticia** to spread a
piece of news.

difunto, a [dēfōōn'to, á] *a* dead, deceased ♦
nm/f: **el** ~ the deceased.

difusión [dēfōōsyon'] *nf* (*de calor, luz*) diffu-
sion; (*de noticia, teoría*) dissemination; (*de
programa*) broadcasting; (*programa*)
broadcast.

difuso, a [dēfōō'so, á] *a* (*luz*) diffused;
(*conocimientos*) widespread; (*estilo, explicación*) wordy.

diga [dē'gá] *etc vb V* **decir.**

digerir [dēherēr'] *vt* to digest; (*fig*) to
absorb; (*reflexionar sobre*) to think over.

digiera [dēhye'rá] *etc*, **digiriendo**
[dēhēryen'do] *etc vb V* **digerir.**

digital [dēhētál'] *a* (*INFORM*) digital; (*dactilar*) finger *cpd* ♦ *nf* (*BOT*) foxglove; (*droga*) digitalis.

digitalizador [dēhētálēsáṯhor'] *nm* (*IN-
FORM*) digitizer.

dignarse [dēgnár'se] *vr* to deign to.

dignidad [dēgnēṯháṯh'] *nf* dignity; (*honra*)
honor (*US*), honour (*Brit*); (*rango*) rank;
(*persona*) dignitary; **herir la** ~ **de uno** to
hurt sb's pride.

dignificar [dēgnēfēkàr'] *vt* to dignify.

dignifique [dēgnēfē'ke] *etc vb V* **dignificar.**

digno, a [dēg'no, á] *a* worthy; (*persona:
honesto*) honorable (*US*), honourable
(*Brit*); ~ **de elogio** praiseworthy; ~ **de
mención** worth mentioning; **es** ~ **de verse**
it is worth seeing; **poco** ~ unworthy.

digresión [dēgresyon'] *nf* digression.

dije [dē'he] *etc*, **dijera** [dēhe'rá] *etc vb V* **decir.**

dilación [dēlásyon'] *nf* delay; **sin** ~ without
delay, immediately.

dilapidar [dēlápēṯhár'] *vt* to squander,
waste.

dilatación [dēlátásyon'] *nf* (*expansión*) dilation.

dilatado, a [dēlátá'ḏho, á] *a* dilated;

(*período*) long drawn-out; (*extenso*) extensive.

dilatar [dēlátár'] *vt* (*gen*) to dilate; (*prolongar*) to prolong; (*aplazar*) to delay; ~**se** *vr* (*pupila etc*) to dilate; (*agua*) to expand.

dilema [dēle'má] *nm* dilemma.

diligencia [dēlēhen'syá] *nf* diligence; (*rapidez*) speed; (*ocupación*) errand, job; (*carruaje*) stagecoach; ~**s** *nfpl* (*JUR*) formalities; ~**s judiciales** judicial proceedings; ~**s previas** inquest *sg*.

diligente [dēlēhen'te] *a* diligent; **poco** ~ lazy.

dilucidar [dēlōōsēthár'] *vt* (*aclarar*) to elucidate, clarify; (*misterio*) to clear up.

diluir [dēlōōēr'] *vt* to dilute; (*aguar*, *fig*) to water down.

diluviar [dēlōōvyár'] *vi* to pour with rain.

diluvio [dēlōō'vyo] *nm* deluge, flood; **un** ~ **de cartas** (*fig*) a flood of letters.

diluyendo [dēlōōyen'do] *etc vb V* **diluir.**

dimanar [dēmánár'] *vi*: ~ **de** to arise *o* spring from.

dimensión [dēmensyon'] *nf* dimension; **dimensiones** *nfpl* size *sg*; **tomar las dimensiones de** to take the measurements of.

dimes [dē'mes] *nmpl*: **andar en** ~ **y diretes con uno** to bicker *o* squabble with sb.

diminuto, a [dēmēnōō'to, á] *a* tiny, diminutive.

dimisión [dēmēsyon'] *nf* resignation.

dimitir [dēmētēr'] *vt* (*cargo*) to give up; (*despedir*) to sack ♦ *vi* to resign.

dimos [dē'mos] *vb V* **dar.**

Dinamarca [dēnámár'ká] *nf* Denmark.

dinamarqués, esa [dēnámárkes', e'sá] *a* Danish ♦ *nm/f* Dane ♦ *nm* (*LING*) Danish.

dinámico, a [dēná'mēko, á] *a'* dynamic ♦ *nf* dynamics *sg*.

dinamita [dēnámē'tá] *nf* dynamite.

dinamitar [dēnámētár'] *vt* to dynamite.

dínamo [dē'námo] *nf* dynamo.

dinastía [dēnástē'á] *nf* dynasty.

dinerada [dēnérá'thá] *nf*, **dineral** [dēnérál'] *nm* fortune.

dinero [dēne'ro] *nm* money; (~ *en circulación*) currency; ~ **caro** (*COM*) expensive (*US*) *o* dear (*Brit*) money; ~ **contante (y sonante)** hard cash; ~ **de curso legal** legal tender; ~ **efectivo** cash, ready cash; **es hombre de** ~ he is a man of means; **andar mal de** ~ to be short of money; **ganar** ~ **a espuertas** to make money hand over fist.

dintel [dēntel'] *nm* lintel; (*umbral*) threshold.

diñar [dēnyár'] *vt* (*fam*) to give; ~**la** to kick the bucket.

dio [dyo] *vb V* **dar.**

Dios [dyos] *nm* God; ~ **mediante** God willing; **a** ~ **gracias** thank heaven; **a la buena de** ~ any old how; **una de** ~ **es Cristo** an

almighty row; ~ **los cría y ellos se juntan** birds of a feather flock together; **como** ~ **manda** as is proper; **¡**~ **mío!** (oh,) my God!; **¡por** ~**!** for God's sake!; **¡válgame** ~**!** bless my soul!

dios [dyos] *nm* god.

diosa [dyo'sá] *nf* goddess.

Dip. *abr* (= *Diputación*) ≈ CC.

diploma [dēplo'má] *nm* diploma.

diplomacia [dēplomá'syá] *nf* diplomacy; (*fig*) tact.

diplomado, a [dēplomá'tho, á] *a* qualified ♦ *nm/f* holder of a diploma; (*UNIV*) graduate.

diplomático, a [dēplomá'tēko, á] *a* (*cuerpo*) diplomatic; (*que tiene tacto*) tactful ♦ *nm/f* diplomat.

diptongo [dēpton'go] *nm* diphthong.

diputación [dēpōōtásyon'] *nf* delegation; ~ **permanente** (*POL*) standing committee; ~ **provincial** ≈ county commission (*US*) *o* council (*Brit*).

diputado, a [dēpōōtá'tho, á] *nm/f* delegate; (*POL*) ≈ representative (*US*), ≈ member of parliament (*Brit*).

dique [dē'ke] *nm* dike (*US*), dyke (*Brit*); (*rompeolas*) breakwater; ~ **de contención** dam.

Dir. *abr* = **dirección**; (= *director*) dir.

diré [dēre'] *etc vb V* **decir.**

dirección [dēreksyon'] *nf* direction; (*fig*: *tendencia*) trend; (*señas*, *tb INFORM*) address; (*AUTO*) steering; (*gerencia*) management; (*de periódico*) editorship; (*en escuela*) principalship (*US*), headship (*Brit*); (*POL*) leadership; (*junta*) board of directors; (*despacho*) director's/manager's/headmaster's/editor's office; ~ **absoluta** (*INFORM*) absolute address; ~ **administrativa** office management; ~ **asistida** power-assisted steering; **D**~ **General de Seguridad/Turismo** State Security/Tourist Office; ~ **relativa** (*INFORM*) relative address; ~ **única o prohibida** one-way; **tomar la** ~ **de una empresa** to take over the running of a company.

direccionamiento [dēreksyonámyen'to] *nm* (*INFORM*) addressing.

directivo, a [dērectē'ho, á] *a* (*junta*) managing; (*función*) administrative ♦ *nm* (*COM*) manager.

directo, a [dērek'to, á] *a* direct; (*línea*) straight; (*inmediato*) immediate; (*tren*) through; (*TV*) live; **en** ~ (*INFORM*) on line; **transmitir en** ~ to broadcast live.

director, a [dērektor', á] *a* leading ♦ *nm/f* director; (*ESCOL*) principal (*US*), head (teacher) (*Brit*); (*gerente*) manager(ess); (*de compañía*) president; (*jefe*) head; (*PRENSA*) editor; (*de prisión*) warden (*US*), governor (*Brit*); (*MUS*) conductor; ~ **adjunto** assistant manager; ~ **de cine** film director; ~ **comercial** marketing manager; ~ **ejecutivo** executive director; ~ **de empresa** company president (*US*) *o* director (*Brit*); ~ **general** general manager; ~ **gerente** managing director; ~ **de sucursal** branch manager.

directorial [dērektoryàl'] *a* (*COM*) managing, executive; **clase** ~ management.

directorio [dērekto'ryo] *nm* (*INFORM*) directory.

directrices [dērektrē'ses] *nfpl* guidelines.

dirigencia [dērēhen'syá] *nf* (*POL*) leadership.

dirigente [dērēhen'te] *a* leading ♦ *nm/f* (*POL*) leader; **los** ~**s del partido** the party leaders.

dirigible [dērēhē'ble] *a* (*AVIAT*, *NAUT*) steerable ♦ *nm* blimp (*US*), airship (*Brit*).

dirigir [dērēhēr'] *vt* to direct; (*acusación*) to level; (*carta*) to address; (*obra de teatro*, *film*) to produce, direct; (*MUS*) to conduct; (*comercio*) to manage; (*expedición*) to lead; (*sublevación*) to head; (*periódico*) to edit; (*guiar*) to guide; ~**se** *vr*: ~**se a** to go towards, make one's way towards; (*hablar con*) to speak to; ~**se a uno solicitando algo** to apply to sb for sth; "**diríjase a ...**" "apply to ...".

dirigismo [dērēhēs'mo] *nm* management, control; ~ **estatal** state control.

dirija [dērē'há] *etc vb V* **dirigir**.

dirimir [dērēmēr'] *vt* (*contrato*, *matrimonio*) to dissolve.

discado [dēská'tho] *nm*: ~ **automático** autodial.

discernir [dēsernēr'] *vt* to discern ♦ *vi* to distinguish.

discierna [dēsyer'ná] *etc vb V* **discernir**.

disciplina [dēsēplē'ná] *nf* discipline.

disciplinar [dēsēplēnár'] *vt* to discipline; (*enseñar*) to school; (*MIL*) to drill; (*azotar*) to whip.

discípulo, a [dēsē'pōōlo, á] *nm/f* disciple; (*seguidor*) follower; (*ESCOL*) pupil.

disco [dēs'ko] *nm* disk (*US*), disc (*Brit*); (*DEPORTE*) discus; (*TELEC*) dial; (*AUTO*: *semáforo*) light; (*MUS*) record; (*INFORM*) disk; ~ **de arranque** boot disk; ~ **compacto** compact disc; ~ **de densidad sencilla/doble** single/double density disk; ~ **de larga duración** long-playing record (L.P.); ~ **flexible** *o* **floppy** floppy disk; ~ **de freno** brake disc; ~ **maestro** master disk; ~ **de reserva** backup disk; ~ **rígido** hard disk; ~ **de una cara/dos caras** single-/double-sided disk; ~ **virtual** ramdisk.

discóbolo [dēsko'bolo] *nm* discus thrower.

discográfico, a [dēskográ'fēko, á] *a* record *cpd*; **casa discográfica** record company; **sello** ~ label.

díscolo, a [dēs'kolo, á] *a* (*rebelde*) unruly.

disconforme [dēskonfor'me] *a* differing; **estar** ~ **(con)** to be in disagreement (with).

discordar [dēskorthár'] *vi* (*MUS*) to be out of tune; (*estar en desacuerdo*) to disagree; (*colores, opiniones*) to clash.

discorde [dēskor'the] *a* (*sonido*) discordant; (*opiniones*) clashing.

discordia [dēskor'thyá] *nf* discord.

discoteca [dēskote'ká] *nf* disco(theque).

discreción [dēskresyon'] *nf* discretion; (*reserva*) prudence; **¡a** ~! (*MIL*) at ease!; **añadir azúcar a** ~ (*CULIN*) add sugar to taste; **comer a** ~ to eat as much as one wishes.

discrecional [dēskresyonál'] *a* (*facultativo*) discretionary; **parada** ~ flag stop (*US*), request stop (*Brit*).

discrepancia [dēskrepán'syá] *nf* (*diferencia*) discrepancy; (*desacuerdo*) disagreement.

discrepante [dēskrepán'te] *a* divergent; **hubo varias voces** ~**s** there were some dissenting voices.

discreto, a [dēskre'to, á] *a* (*diplomático*) discreet; (*sensato*) sensible; (*reservado*) quiet; (*sobrio*) sober; (*mediano*) fair, fairly good; **le daremos un plazo** ~ we'll allow him a reasonable time.

discriminación [dēskrēmēnásyon'] *nf* discrimination.

discuerde [dēskwer'the] *etc vb V* **discordar**.

disculpa [dēskōōl'pá] *nf* excuse; (*pedir perdón*) apology; **pedir** ~**s a/por** to apologize to/for.

disculpar [dēskōōlpár'] *vt* to excuse, pardon; ~**se** *vr* to excuse o.s.; to apologize.

discurrir [dēskōōrrēr'] *vt* to contrive, think up ♦ *vi* (*pensar, reflexionar*) to think, meditate; (*recorrer*) to roam, wander; (*río*) to flow; (*el tiempo*) to pass, flow by.

discurso [dēskōōr'so] *nm* speech; ~ **de clausura** closing speech; **pronunciar un** ~ to make a speech; **en el** ~ **del tiempo** with the passage of time.

discusión [dēskōōsyon'] *nf* (*diálogo*) discussion; (*riña*) argument; **tener una** ~ to have an argument.

discutible [dēskōōtē'ble] *a* debatable; **de mérito** ~ of dubious worth.

discutido, a [dēskōōtē'tho, á] *a* controversial.

discutir [dēskōōtēr'] *vt* (*debatir*) to discuss; (*pelear*) to argue about; (*contradecir*) to argue against ♦ *vi* to discuss; (*disputar*) to argue; ~ **de política** to argue about politics; **¡no discutas!** don't argue!

disecar [dēsekár'] *vt* (*para conservar*: *animal*) to stuff; (: *planta*) to dry.

diseminar [dēsemēnár'] *vt* to disseminate, spread.

disentir [dĕsentĕr'] *vi* to dissent, disagree.

diseño [dĕse'nyo] *nm* (*TEC*) design; (*ARTE*) drawing; (*COSTURA*) pattern; **de ~ italiano** Italian-designed; **~ asistido por ordenador** computer-assisted design, CAD.

diseque [dĕse'ke] *etc vb* V **disecar**.

disertar [dĕsertár'] *vi* to speak.

disfrace [dĕsfrá'se] *etc vb* V **disfrazar**.

disfraz [dĕsfrás'] *nm* (*máscara*) disguise; (*traje*) fancy dress; (*excusa*) pretext; **bajo el ~ de** under the cloak of.

disfrazado, a [dĕsfrásá'tho, á] *a* disguised; **ir ~ de** to masquerade as.

disfrazar [dĕsfrásár'] *vt* to disguise; **~se** *vr* to dress (o.s.) up; **~se de** to disguise o.s. as.

disfrutar [dĕsfrootár'] *vt* to enjoy ♦ *vi* to enjoy o.s.; **¡que disfrutes!** have a good time; **~ de** to enjoy, possess; **~ de buena salud** to enjoy good health.

disfrute [dĕsfroo'te] *nm* (*goce*) enjoyment; (*aprovechamiento*) use.

disgregar [dĕsgregár'] *vt* (*desintegrar*) to disintegrate; (*manifestantes*) to disperse; **~se** *vr* to disintegrate, break up.

disgregue [dĕsgre'ge] *etc vb* V **disgregar**.

disgustar [dĕsgoostár'] *vt* (*no gustar*) to displease; (*contrariar, enojar*) to annoy; to upset; **~se** *vr* to be annoyed; (*dos personas*) to fall out; **estaba muy disgustado con el asunto** he was very upset about the affair.

disgusto [dĕsgoo'sto] *nm* (*repugnancia*) disgust; (*contrariedad*) annoyance; (*desagrado*) displeasure; (*tristeza*) grief; (*riña*) quarrel; (*avería*) misfortune; **hacer algo a ~** to do sth unwillingly; **matar a uno a ~s** to drive sb to distraction.

disidente [dĕsĕthen'te] *nm* dissident.

disienta [dĕsyen'tá] *etc vb* V **disentir**.

disimulado, a [dĕsĕmoolá'tho, á] *a* (*solapado*) furtive, underhand; (*oculto*) covert; **hacerse el ~** to pretend not to notice.

disimular [dĕsĕmoolár'] *vt* (*ocultar*) to hide, conceal ♦ *vi* to dissemble.

disimulo [dĕsĕmoo'lo] *nm* (*fingimiento*) dissimulation; **con ~** cunningly.

disipar [dĕsĕpár'] *vt* (*duda, temor*) to dispel; (*esperanza*) to destroy; (*fortuna*) to squander; **~se** *vr* (*nubes*) to vanish; (*dudas*) to be dispelled; (*indisciplinarse*) to dissipate.

diskette [dĕsket'] *nm* (*INFORM*) diskette, floppy disk.

dislate [dĕslá'te] *nm* (*absurdo*) absurdity; **~s** *nmpl* nonsense *sg*.

dislocar [dĕslokár'] *vt* (*gen*) to dislocate; (*tobillo*) to sprain.

disloque [dĕslo'ke] *etc vb* V **dislocar** ♦ *nm*: **es el ~** (*fam*) it's the last straw.

disminución [dĕsmĕnoosyon'] *nf* diminu-

tion.

disminuir [dĕsmĕnooĕr'] *vt* to decrease, diminish; (*estrechar*) to lessen; (*temperatura*) to lower; (*gastos, raciones*) to cut down; (*dolor*) to relieve; (*autoridad, prestigio*) to weaken; (*entusiasmo*) to dampen ♦ *vi* (*días*) to grow shorter; (*precios, temperatura*) to drop, fall; (*velocidad*) to reduce; (*población, beneficios, número*) to decrease; (*memoria, vista*) to fail.

disminuyendo [dĕsmĕnooyen'do] *etc vb* V **disminuir**.

disociar [dĕsosyár'] *vt* to disassociate; **~se** *vr* to disassociate o.s.

disoluble [dĕsoloo'ble] *a* soluble.

disolución [dĕsoloosyon'] *nf* (*acto*) dissolution; (*QUÍMICA*) solution; (*COM*) liquidation; (*moral*) dissoluteness.

disoluto, a [dĕsoloo'to, á] *a* dissolute.

disolver [dĕsolber'] *vt* (*gen*) to dissolve; (*manifestación*) to break up; **~se** *vr* to dissolve; (*COM*) to go into liquidation.

disonar [dĕsonár'] *vi* (*MUS*) to be out of tune; **~ con** (*fig*) to be out of keeping with.

dispar [dĕspár'] *a* (*distinto*) different; (*irregular*) uneven.

disparado, a [dĕspárá'tho, á] *a*: **entrar ~** to shoot in; **salir ~** to shoot out; **ir ~** to go like mad.

disparador [dĕspáráthor'] *nm* (*de arma*) trigger; (*FOTO, TEC*) release; **~ atómico** aerosol; **~ de bombas** bomb release.

disparar [dĕspárár'] *vt, vi* to shoot, fire; **~se** *vr* (*arma de fuego*) to go off; (*persona: marcharse*) to rush off; (*caballo*) to bolt; (*enojarse*) to lose control.

disparatado, a [dĕspárátá'tho, á] *a* crazy.

disparatar [dĕspárátár'] *vi* (*decir disparates*) to talk nonsense; (*hacer disparates*) to blunder.

disparate [dĕspárá'te] *nm* (*tontería*) foolish remark; (*error*) blunder; **decir ~s** to talk nonsense; **¡qué ~!** how absurd!; **costar un ~** to cost a hell of a lot.

disparo [dĕspá'ro] *nm* shot; (*acto*) firing; **~s** *nmpl* shooting *sg*, (exchange of) shots (*sg*); **~ inicial** (*de cohete*) blastoff.

dispendio [dĕspen'dyo] *nm* waste.

dispensar [dĕspensár'] *vt* to dispense; (*ayuda*) to give; (*honores*) to grant; (*disculpar*) to excuse; **¡usted dispense!** I beg your pardon!; **~ a uno de hacer algo** to excuse sb from doing sth.

dispensario [dĕspensá'ryo] *nm* (*clínica*) community clinic; (*de hospital*) outpatients' department.

dispersar [dĕspersár'] *vt* to disperse; (*manifestación*) to break up; **~se** *vr* to scatter.

disperso, a [dĕsper'so, á] *a* scattered.

displicencia [dĕsplĕsen'syá] *nf* (*mal humor*) peevishness; (*desgana*) lack of enthusiasm.

displicente [dĕssēplēsen'te] a (*malhumora-do*) peevish; (*poco entusiasta*) unenthusiastic.

dispondré [dĕspondre'] *etc vb V* **disponer**.

disponer [dĕsponer'] *vt* (*arreglar*) to arrange; (*ordenar*) to put in order; (*preparar*) to prepare, get ready ♦ *vi*: ~ **de** to have, own; ~**se** *vr*: ~**se para** to prepare to, prepare for; **la ley dispone que...** the law provides that...; **no puede** ~ **de esos bienes** she cannot dispose of those properties.

disponga [dĕspon'gá] *etc vb V* **disponer**.

disponibilidad [dĕsponēnēlēthàth'] *nf* availability; ~**es** *nfpl* (*COM*) resources, financial assets.

disponible [dĕsponē'ble] a available; (*tiempo*) spare; (*dinero*) on hand.

disposición [dĕsposēsyon'] *nf* arrangement, disposition; (*de casa*, *INFORM*) layout; (*ley*) order; (*cláusula*) provision; (*aptitud*) aptitude; ~ **de ánimo** attitude of mind; **última** ~ last will and testament; **a la** ~ **de** at the disposal of; **a su** ~ at your service.

dispositivo [dĕsposētē'ho] *nm* device, mechanism; ~ **de alimentación** hopper; ~ **de almacenaje** storage device; ~ **periférico** peripheral (device); ~ **de seguridad** safety catch; (*fig*) security measure.

dispuesto, a [dĕspwe'sto, à] *pp de* **disponer** ♦ *a* (*arreglado*) arranged; (*preparado*) disposed; (*persona: dinámico*) bright; **estar** ~**/poco** ~ **a hacer algo** to be inclined/reluctant to do sth.

dispuse [dĕspoo'se] *etc vb V* **disponer**.

disputa [dĕspoo'tá] *nf* (*discusión*) dispute, argument; (*controversia*) controversy.

disputar [dĕspootár'] *vt* (*discutir*) to dispute, question; (*contender*) to contend for ♦ *vi* to argue.

disquete [dĕske'te] *nm* (*INFORM*) diskette, floppy disk.

Dist. *abr* (= *distancia*, *Distrito*) dist.

distancia [dĕstán'syà] *nf* distance; (*de tiempo*) interval; ~ **de parada** braking distance; ~ **del suelo** (*AUTO etc*) height off the ground; **a gran** o **a larga** ~ long-distance; **mantenerse a** ~ to keep one's distance; (*fig*) to remain aloof; **guardar las** ~**s** to keep one's distance.

distanciado, a [dĕstánsyá'tho, à] *a* (*remoto*) remote; (*fig: alejado*) far apart; **estamos** ~**s en ideas** our ideas are poles apart.

distanciamiento [dĕstánsyámyen'to] *nm* (*acto*) spacing out; (*estado*) remoteness; (*fig*) distance.

distanciar [dĕstánsyár'] *vt* to space out; ~**se** *vr* to become estranged.

distante [dĕstán'te] *a* distant.

distar [dĕstár'] *vi*: **dista 5 kms de aquí** it is 5 kms from here; **¿dista mucho?** is it far?; **dista mucho de la verdad** it's very far from the truth.

diste [dē'ste], **disteis** [dē'stēčs] *vb V* **dar**.

distensión [dēstensyon'] *nf* distension; (*POL*) détente; ~ **muscular** (*MED*) muscular strain.

distinción [dēstēnsyon'] *nf* distinction; (*elegancia*) elegance; (*honor*) honor (*US*), honour (*Brit*); **a** ~ **de** unlike; **sin** ~ indiscriminately; **sin** ~ **de edades** irrespective of age.

distinga [dēstēn'gá] *etc vb V* **distinguir**.

distinguido, a [dēstēngē'tho, à] *a* distinguished; (*famoso*) prominent, well-known; (*elegante*) elegant.

distinguir [dēstēngēr'] *vt* to distinguish; (*divisar*) to make out; (*escoger*) to single out; (*caracterizar*) to mark out; ~**se** *vr* to be distinguished; (*destacarse*) to distinguish o.s.; **a lo lejos no se distingue** it's not visible from a distance.

distintivo, a [dēstēntē'ho, à] *a* distinctive; (*signo*) distinguishing ♦ *nm* (*de policía etc*) badge; (*fig*) characteristic.

distinto, a [dēstēn'to, à] *a* different; (*claro*) clear; ~**s** several, various.

distorsión [dēstorsyon'] *nf* (*ANAT*) twisting; (*RADIO etc*) distortion.

distracción [dēstráksyon'] *nf* distraction; (*pasatiempo*) hobby, pastime; (*olvido*) absent-mindedness, distraction.

distraer [dēstràer'] *vt* (*atención*) to distract; (*divertir*) to amuse; (*fondos*) to embezzle ♦ *vi* to be relaxing; ~**se** *vr* (*entretenerse*) to amuse o.s.; (*perder la concentración*) to allow one's attention to wander; ~ **a uno de su pensamiento** to divert sb from his train of thought; **el pescar distrae** fishing is a relaxation.

distraído, a [dēstràē'tho, à] *a* (*gen*) absent-minded; (*desatento*) inattentive; (*entretenido*) amusing ♦ *nm*: **hacerse el** ~ to pretend not to notice; **con aire** ~ idly; **me miró distraída** she gave me a casual glance.

distraiga [dēstrà'ēgá] *etc*, **distraje** [dēstrà'he] *etc*, **distrajera** [dēstráhe'rà] *etc*, **distrayendo** [dēstráyen'do] *vb V* **distraer**.

distribución [dēstrēhoosyon'] *nf* distribution; (*entrega*) delivery; (*en estadística*) distribution, incidence; (*ARQ*) layout; ~ **de premios** prize giving; **la** ~ **de los impuestos** the incidence of taxes.

distribuidor, a [dēstrēhooēthor', à] *nm/f* (*persona: gen*) distributor; (: *CORREOS*) sorter; (: *COM*) dealer; **su** ~ **habitual** your regular dealer.

distribuir [dēstrēhooēr'] *vt* to distribute; (*prospectos*) to hand out; (*cartas*) to deliver; (*trabajo*) to allocate; (*premios*) to award; (*dividendos*) to pay; (*peso*) to distribute; (ARQ) to plan.

distribuyendo [dēstrēhōōyen'do] etc vb V **distribuir**.

distrito [dēstrē'to] nm (sector, territorio) region; (barrio) district; ~ **electoral** constituency; ~ **postal** postal district.

disturbio [dēstōōr'hyo] nm disturbance; (desorden) riot; **los ~s** the troubles.

disuadir [dēswáthēr'] vt to dissuade.

disuasión [dēswásyon'] nf dissuasion; (MIL) deterrent; ~ **nuclear** nuclear deterrent.

disuasivo, a [dēswásē'ho, á] a dissuasive; **arma disuasiva** deterrent.

disuelto [dēswel'to] pp de **disolver**.

disuelva [dēswel'há] etc vb V **disolver**.

disuene [dēswe'ne] etc vb V **disonar**.

disyuntiva [dēsyōōntē'há] nf (dilema) dilemma.

DIU [dē'ōō] nm abr (= dispositivo intrauterino) I.U.D.

diurno, a [dyōōr'no, á] a day cpd, diurnal.

diva [dē'há] nf prima donna.

divagar [dēhágár'] vi (desviarse) to digress.

divague [dēhá'ge] etc vb V **divagar**.

diván [dēhán'] nm divan.

divergencia [dēherhen'syá] nf divergence.

divergir [dēherhēr'] vi (líneas) to diverge; (opiniones) to differ; (personas) to disagree.

diverja [dēher'há] etc vb V **divergir**.

diversidad [dēhersētháth'] nf diversity, variety.

diversificación [dēhersēfēkásyon'] nf (COM) diversification.

diversificar [dēhersēfēkár'] vt to diversify.

diversifique [dēhersēfē'ke] etc vb V **diversificar**.

diversión [dēhersyon'] nf (gen) entertainment; (actividad) hobby, pastime.

diverso, a [dēher'so, á] a diverse; (diferente) different ♦ nm: ~**s** (COM) sundries; ~**s libros** several books.

divertido, a [dēhertē'tho, á] a (chiste) amusing, funny; (fiesta etc) enjoyable; (película, libro) entertaining; **está ~** (irónico) this is going to be fun.

divertir [dēhertēr'] vt (entretener, recrear) to amuse, entertain; ~**se** vr (pasarlo bien) to have a good time; (distraerse) to amuse o.s.

dividendo [dēhēthen'do] nm (COM): ~**s** nmpl dividends; ~**s por acción** earnings per share; ~ **definitivo** final dividend.

dividir [dēhēthēr'] vt (gen) to divide; (separar) to separate; (distribuir) to distribute, share out.

divierta [dēhyer'tá] etc vb V **divertir**.

divinidad [dēhēnētháth'] nf (esencia divina) divinity; **la D~** God.

divino, a [dēhē'no, á] a divine; (fig) lovely.

divirtiendo [dēhērtyen'do] etc vb V **divertir**.

divisa [dēhē'sá] nf (emblema, moneda) emblem, badge; ~**s** nfpl currency sg; (COM) foreign exchange sg; **control de ~s** exchange control; ~ **de reserva** reserve currency.

divisar [dēhēsár'] vt to make out, distinguish.

división [dēhēsyon'] nf division; (de partido) split; (de país) partition.

divisorio, a [dēhēso'ryo, á] a (línea) dividing; **línea divisoria de las aguas** watershed.

divorciado, a [dēhorsyá'tho, á] a divorced; (opinion) split ♦ nm/f divorcé(e).

divorciar [dēhorsyár'] vt to divorce; ~**se** vr to get divorced.

divorcio [dēhor'syo] nm divorce; (fig) split.

divulgación [dēhōōlgásyon'] nf (difusión) spreading; (popularización) popularization.

divulgar [dēhōōlgár'] vt (desparramar) to spread; (popularizar) to popularize; (hacer circular) to divulge, circulate; ~**se** vr (secreto) to leak out; (rumor) to spread.

divulgue [dēhōōl'ge] etc vb V **divulgar**.

DM abr = **decimal**.

dm. abr (= decímetro) dm.

Dña. abr = **Doña**.

DNI nm abr Esp: = **Documento Nacional de Identidad**.

dobladillo [dohláthē'yo] nm (de vestido) hem; (de pantalón: vuelta) turn-up (Brit), cuff (US).

doblaje [dohlá'he] nm (CINE) dubbing.

doblar [dohlár'] vt to double; (papel) to fold; (caño) to bend; (la esquina) to turn, go round; (film) to dub ♦ vi to turn; (campana) to toll; ~**se** vr (plegarse) to fold (up), crease; (encorvarse) to bend.

doble [do'hle] a (gen) double; (de dos aspectos) dual; (cuerda) thick; (fig) two-faced ♦ nm double ♦ nm/f (TEATRO) double, stand-in; ~**s** nmpl (DEPORTE) doubles sg; ~ **o nada** double or nothing; ~ **página** double-page spread; **con ~ sentido** with a double meaning; **el ~** twice the quantity o as much; **su sueldo es el ~ del mío** his salary is twice (as much as) mine; (INFORM): ~ **cara** double-sided; ~ **densidad** double density; ~ **espacio** double spacing.

doblegar [dohlegár'] vt to fold, crease; ~**se** vr to yield.

doblegue [dohle'ge] etc vb V **doblegar**.

doblez [dohles'] nm (pliegue) fold, hem ♦ nf (falsedad) duplicity.

doc. abr (= docena) doz.; (= documento) doc.

doce [do'se] num twelve; (fecha) twelfth; **las ~** twelve o'clock; V tb **seis**.

docena [dose'ná] nf dozen; **por ~s** by the dozen.

docente [dosen'te] a: **centro/personal ~**

teaching institution/staff.

dócil [do'sēl] *a* (*pasivo*) docile; (*manso*) gentle; (*obediente*) obedient.

docto, a [dok'to, á] *a* learned, erudite ♦ *nm/f* scholar.

doctor, a [doktor', á] *nm/f* doctor; ~ **en filosofía** Doctor of Philosophy.

doctorado [doktorá'ᵭo] *nm* doctorate.

doctorarse [doktorár'se] *vr* to get a doctorate.

doctrina [doktrē'ná] *nf* doctrine, teaching.

documentación [dokōōmentásyon'] *nf* documentation; (*de identidad etc*) papers *pl*.

documental [dokōōmentál'] *a*, *nm* documentary.

documentar [dokōōmentár'] *vt* to document; ~**se** *vr* to gather information.

documento [dokōōmen'to] *nm* (*certificado*) document; (*JUR*) exhibit; ~**s** *nmpl* papers; ~ **justificativo** voucher; ~ **nacional de identidad** national identity card.

dogo [do'g̣o] *nm* bulldog.

dólar [do'lár] *nm* dollar.

dolencia [dolen'syá] *nf* (*achaque*) ailment; (*dolor*) ache.

doler [doler'] *vt*, *vi* to hurt; (*fig*) to grieve; ~**se** *vr* (*de su situación*) to grieve, feel sorry; (*de las desgracias ajenas*) to sympathize; (*quejarse*) to complain; **me duele el brazo** my arm hurts; **no me duele el dinero** I don't mind about the money; **¡ahí le duele!** you've put your finger on it!

doliente [dolyen'te] *a* (*enfermo*) sick; (*dolorido*) aching; (*triste*) sorrowful; **la familia** ~ the bereaved family.

dolor [dolor'] *nm* pain; (*fig*) grief, sorrow; ~ **de cabeza** headache; ~ **de estómago** stomach ache; ~ **de oídos** earache; ~ **sordo** dull ache.

dolorido, a [dolorē'ᵭo, á] *a* (*MED*) sore; **la parte dolorida** the part which hurts.

doloroso, a [doloro'so, á] *a* (*MED*) painful; (*fig*) distressing.

domar [domár'] *vt* to tame.

domesticado, a [domestēká'ᵭo, á] *a* (*amansado*) tame.

domesticar [domestēkár'] *vt* to tame.

doméstico, a [dome'stēko, á] *a* domestic ♦ *nm/f* servant; **economía doméstica** home economy; **gastos** ~**s** household expenses.

domestique [domestē'ke] *etc vb* V **domesticar**.

domiciliación [domēsēlyásyon'] *nf*: ~ **de pagos** (*COM*) standing order, direct debit.

domiciliar [domēsēlyár'] *vt* to domicile; ~**se** *vr* to take up (one's) residence.

domiciliario, a [domēsēlyá'ryo, á] *a*: **arresto** ~ house arrest.

domicilio [domēsē'lyo] *nm* home; ~ **particular** private residence; ~ **social** (*COM*) head office, registered office; **servicio a** ~

delivery service; **sin** ~ **fijo** of no fixed abode.

dominante [domēnán'te] *a* dominant; (*person*) domineering.

dominar [domēnár'] *vt* (*gen*) to dominate; (*países*) to rule over; (*adversario*) to overpower; (*caballo, nervios, emoción*) to control; (*incendio, epidemia*) to bring under control; (*idiomas*) to be fluent in ♦ *vi* to dominate, prevail; ~**se** *vr* to control o.s.

domingo [domēn'g̣o] *nm* Sunday; **D**~ **de Ramos** Palm Sunday; **D**~ **de Resurrección** Easter Sunday; *V tb* **sábado**.

dominguero, a [domēnge'ro, á] *a* Sunday *cpd*.

dominical [domēnēkál'] *a* Sunday *cpd*; **periódico** ~ Sunday newspaper.

dominio [domē'nyo] *nm* (*tierras*) domain; (*POL*) dominion; (*autoridad*) power, authority; (*supremacía*) supremacy; (*de las pasiones*) grip, hold; (*de idioma*) command; **ser del** ~ **público** to be widely known.

dominó [domēno'] *nm* (*pieza*) domino; (*juego*) dominoes.

dom.º *abr* (= *domingo*) Sun.

don [don] *nm* (*talento*) gift; **D**~ **Juan Gómez** Mr Juan Gomez *o* Juan Gomez Esq.; **tener** ~ **de gentes** to known how to handle people; ~ **de lenguas** gift for languages; ~ **de mando** (qualities of) leadership; ~ **de palabra** gift of gab (*US*) *o* the gab (*Brit*).

donaire [donái'ēre] *nm* charm.

donante [donán'te] *nm/f* donor; ~ **de sangre** blood donor.

donar [donár'] *vt* to donate.

donativo [donátē'ᵭo] *nm* donation.

doncella [donse'yá] *nf* (*criada*) maid.

donde [don'de] *ad* where ♦ *prep*: **el coche está allí** ~ **el farol** the car is over there by the lamppost *o* where the lamppost is; **por** ~ through which; **a** ~ to where, to which; **en** ~ where, in which; **es a** ~ **vamos nosotros** that's where we're going.

dónde [don'de] *ad interrogativo* where?; **¿a** ~ **vas?** where are you going (to)?; **¿de** ~ **vienes?** where have you come from?; **¿en** ~**?** where?; **¿por** ~**?** where?, whereabouts?; **¿por** ~ **se va al estadio?** how do you get to the stadium?

dondequiera [dondekye'rá] *ad* anywhere ♦ *conj*: ~ **que** wherever; **por** ~ everywhere, all over the place.

donostiarra [donostyá'rrá] *a* of *o* from San Sebastián ♦ *nm/f* native *o* inhabitant of San Sebastián.

doña [do'nyá] *nf* título de mujer que no se traduce.

dopar [dopár'] *vt* to dope, drug.

doquier [dokyer'] *ad*: **por** ~ all over, everywhere.

dorado, a [dorá'ðo, á] *a* (*color*) golden; (*TEC*) gilt.

dorar [dorár'] *vt* (*TEC*) to gild; (*CULIN*) to brown, cook lightly; ~ **la píldora** to sweeten the pill.

dormilón, ona [dormēlon', o'ná] *a* fond of sleeping ♦ *nm/f* sleepyhead.

dormir [dormēr'] *vt*: ~ **la siesta por la tarde** to have an afternoon nap ♦ *vi* to sleep; ~**se** *vr* (*persona, brazo, pierna*) to fall asleep; ~**la** (*fam*) to sleep it off; ~ **la mona** (*fam*) to sleep off a hangover; ~ **como un lirón** *o* **tronco** to sleep like a log; ~ **a pierna suelta** to sleep soundly.

dormitar [dormētár'] *vi* to doze.

dormitorio [dormēto'ryo] *nm* bedroom; ~ **común** dormitory.

dorsal [dorsál'] *a* dorsal ♦ *nm* (*DEPORTE*) number.

dorso [dor'so] *nm* back; **escribir algo al** ~ to write sth on the back; **"véase al** ~**"** "see other side", "please turn over".

DOS *nm abr* (= *sistema operativo de disco*) DOS.

dos [dos] *num* two; (*fecha*) second; **los** ~ the two of them, both of them; **cada** ~ **por tres** every 5 minutes; **de** ~ **en** ~ in twos; **estamos a** ~ (*TENIS*) the score is deuce; *V tb* **seis**.

doscientos, as [dosyen'tos, ás] *num* two hundred; *V tb* **seiscientos**.

dosel [dosel'] *nm* canopy.

dosificar [dosēfēkár'] *vt* (*CULIN, MED, QUÍMICA*) to measure out; (*no derrochar*) to be sparing with.

dosifique [dosēfē'ke] *etc vb V* **dosificar**.

dosis [do'sēs] *nf inv* dose, dosage.

dossier [dosyer'] *nm* dossier, file.

dotación [dotásyon'] *nf* (*acto, dinero*) endowment; (*plantilla*) staff; (*NAUT*) crew; **la** ~ **es insuficiente** we are under-staffed.

dotado, a [dotá'ðo, á] *a* gifted; ~ **de** (*persona*) endowed with; (*máquina*) equipped with.

dotar [dotár'] *vt* to endow; (*TEC*) to fit; (*barco*) to man; (*oficina*) to staff.

dote [do'te] *nf* (*de novia*) dowry; ~**s** *nfpl* (*talentos*) gifts.

doy [doy] *vb V* **dar**.

Dpto. *abr* (= *Departamento*) dept.

Dr(a). *abr* (= *Doctor, Doctora*) Dr.

draga [drá'ɡá] *nf* dredge.

dragado [dráɡá'ðo] *nm* dredging.

dragar [dráɡár'] *vt* to dredge; (*minas*) to sweep.

drague [drá'ɡe] *etc vb V* **dragar**.

drama [drá'má] *nm* drama; (*obra*) play.

dramático, a [drámá'tēko, á] *a* dramatic ♦ *nm/f* dramatist; (*actor*) actor; **obra dramática** play.

dramaturgo, a [drámátōōr'ɡo, á] *nm/f* dramatist, playwright.

dramón [drámon'] *nm* (*TEATRO*) melodrama; **¡qué** ~**!** what a scene!

drenaje [drená'he] *nm* drainage.

drenar [drenár'] *vt* to drain.

droga [dro'ɡá] *nf* drug; (*DEPORTE*) dope; **el problema de la** ~ the drug problem.

drogadicto, a [droɡáðhēk'to, á] *nm/f* drug addict.

drogar [droɡár'] *vt* to drug; (*DEPORTE*) to dope; ~**se** *vr* to take drugs.

drogue [dro'ɡe] *etc vb V* **drogar**.

droguería [droɡerē'á] *nf* pharmacy.

Dto., D.to *abr* = **descuento**.

Dtor(a). *abr* (= *Director, Directora*) Dir.

ducado [dōōká'ðo] *nm* duchy, dukedom.

ducentésimo, a [dōōsente'sēmo, á] *a* two hundredth; *V tb* **sexto, a**.

dúctil [dōōk'tēl] *a* (*metal*) ductile; (*persona*) easily influenced.

ducha [dōōtch'á] *nf* (*baño*) shower; (*MED*) douche.

ducharse [dōōtchár'se] *vr* to take a shower.

ducho, a [dōōtch'o, á] *a*: ~ **en** (*experimentado*) experienced in; (*hábil*) skilled at.

duda [dōō'ðá] *nf* doubt; **sin** ~ no doubt, doubtless; **¡sin** ~**!** of course!; **no cabe** ~ there is no doubt about it; **no le quepa** ~ make no mistake about it; **no quiero poner en** ~ **su conducta** I don't want to call his behavior into question; **sacar a uno de la** ~ to settle sb's doubts; **tengo una** ~ I have a question.

dudar [dōōðár'] *vt* to doubt ♦ *vi* to doubt, have doubts; ~ **acerca de algo** to be uncertain about sth; **dudó en comprarlo** he hesitated to buy it; **dudan que sea verdad** they doubt whether *o* if it's true.

dudoso, a [dōōðo'so, á] *a* (*incierto*) hesitant; (*sospechoso*) doubtful; (*conducta*) dubious.

duelo [dwe'lo] *etc vb V* **doler** ♦ *nm* (*combate*) duel; (*luto*) mourning; **batirse en** ~ to fight a duel.

duende [dwen'de] *nm* imp, goblin; **tiene** ~ there's something magic about him.

dueño, a [dwe'nyo, á] *nm/f* (*propietario*) owner; (*de pensión, taberna*) landlord/lady; (*de casa, perro*) master/mistress; (*empresario*) employer; **ser** ~ **de sí mismo** to have self-control; (*libre*) to be one's own boss; **eres** ~ **de hacer como te parezca** you're free to do as you think fit; **hacerse** ~ **de una situación** to take command of a situation.

duerma [dwer'má] *etc vb V* **dormir**.

duermevela [dwermeke'lá] *nf* (*fam*) nap, snooze.

Duero [dwe'ro] *nm* Douro.

dulce [dōōl'se] *a* sweet; (*carácter, clima*) gentle, mild ♦ *ad* gently, softly ♦ *nm* sweet.

dulcificar [dōōlsēfēkàr'] *vt* (*fig*) to soften.
dulcifique [dōōlsēfē'ke] *etc vb* V **dulcificar**.
dulzura [dōōlsōō'rà] *nf* sweetness; (*ternura*) gentleness.
Dunquerque [dōōnkcr'kc] *nm* Dunkirk.
dúo [dōō'o] *nm* duet, duo.
duodécimo, a [dōōōt̄hc'sēmo, à] *a* twelfth; *V tb* **sexto, a**.
dup., **dup.do** *abr* (= *duplicado*) duplicated.
dúplex [dōō'plcks] *nm inv* (*piso*) flat on two floors; (*TELEC*) link-up; (*INFORM*): ~ **integral** full duplex.
duplicar [dōōplēkàr'] *vt* (*hacer el doble de*) to duplicate; (*cantidad*) to double; ~**se** *vr* to double.
duplique [dōōplē'kc] *etc vb* V **duplicar**.
duque [dōō'kc] *nm* duke.
duquesa [dōōkc'sà] *nf* duchess.
duración [dōōràsyon'] *nf* duration, length; (*de máquina*) life; ~ **media de la vida** average life expectancy; **de larga** ~ (*enfermedad*) lengthy; (*pila*) long-life; (*disco*) long-playing; **de poca** ~ short.
duradero, a [dōōràt̄hc'ro, à] *a* (*tela*) hardwearing; (*fe, paz*) lasting.
durante [dōōràn'tc] *ad* during; ~ **toda la noche** all night long; **habló** ~ **una hora** he spoke for an hour.
durar [dōōràr'] *vi* (*permanecer*) to last; (*recuerdo*) to remain; (*ropa*) to wear (well).
durazno [dōōràs'no] *nm* (*AM*: *fruta*) peach; (: *árbol*) peach tree.
durex [dōō'rcks] *nm* (*AM*: *tira adhesiva*) Scotch tape ® (*US*), Sellotape ® (*Brit*).
dureza [dōōrc'sà] *nf* (*cualidad*) hardness; (*de carácter*) toughness.
durmiendo [dōōrmycn'do] *etc vb* V **dormir**.
durmiente [dōōrmycn'tc] *a* sleeping ♦ *nm/f* sleeper.
duro, a [dōō'ro, à] *a* hard; (*carácter*) tough; (*pan*) stale; (*cuello, puerta*) stiff; (*clima, luz*) harsh ♦ *ad* hard ♦ *nm* (*moneda*) five peseta coin; **el sector** ~ **del partido** the hardliners *pl* in the party; **ser** ~ **con uno** to be tough with *o* hard on sb; ~ **de mollera** (*torpe*) dense; ~ **de oído** hard of hearing; **trabajar** ~ to work hard; **estar sin un** ~ to be broke.

E

E, e [c] *nf* (*letra*) E, e; **E de Enrique** E for Easy.
E *abr* (= *este*) E.

e [c] *conj* (*delante de* **i-** *e* **hi-**, *pero no* **hie-**) and; *V tb* **y**.
e/ *abr* (*COM*: = *envío*) shpt.
ebanista [cbànē'stà] *nm/f* cabinetmaker.
ébano [c'bàno] *nm* ebony.
ebrio, a [cb'ryo, à] *a* drunk.
Ebro [c'bro] *nm* Ebro.
ebullición [cbōōyēsyon'] *nf* boiling; **punto de** ~ boiling point.
eccema [cksc'mà] *nm* (*MED*) eczema.
eclesiástico, a [cklcsyà'stēko, à] *a* ecclesiastical; (*autoridades etc*) church *cpd* ♦ *nm* clergyman.
eclipse [cklēp'sc] *nm* eclipse.
eco [c'ko] *nm* echo; **encontrar un** ~ **en** to produce a response from; **hacerse** ~ **de una opinión** to echo an opinion; **tener** ~ to catch on.
ecología [ckolohē'à] *nf* ecology.
ecológico, a [ckolo'hēko, à] *a* ecological.
economato [ckonomà'to] *nm* cooperative store.
economía [ckonomē'à] *nf* (*sistema*) economy; (*cualidad*) thrift; ~ **dirigida** planned economy; ~ **doméstica** housekeeping; ~ **mixta** mixed economy; ~ **sumergida** black economy; **hacer** ~**s** to economize; ~**s de escala** economies of scale.
economice [ckonomē'sc] *etc vb* V **economizar**.
económico, a [ckono'mēko, à] *a* (*barato*) cheap, economical; (*persona*) thrifty; (*COM*: *año etc*) financial; (: *situación*) economic.
economista [ckonomē'stà] *nm/f* economist.
economizar [ckonomēsàr'] *vt* to economize on ♦ *vi* (*ahorrar*) to save up; (*pey*) to be miserly.
ecuador [ckwàt̄hor'] *nm* equator; **(el) E**~ Ecuador.
ecuánime [ckwà'nēmc] *a* (*carácter*) levelheaded; (*estado*) calm.
ecuatorial [ckwàtoryàl'] *a* equatorial.
ecuatoriano, a [ckwàtoryà'no, à] *a, nm/f* Ecuador(i)an.
ecuestre [ckwcs'trc] *a* equestrian.
echar [ctchàr'] *vt* to throw; (*agua, vino*) to pour (out); (*CULIN*) to put in, add; (*dientes*) to cut; (*discurso*) to give; (*empleado: despedir*) to fire; (*hojas*) to sprout; (*cartas*) to mail (*US*), post (*Brit*); (*humo*) to emit, give out; (*reprimenda*) to deal out; (*cuenta*) to make up; (*freno*) to put on ♦ *vi*: ~ **a correr/llorar** to break into a run/ burst into tears; ~ **a reír** to burst out laughing; ~**se** *vr* to lie down; ~ **abajo** (*gobierno*) to overthrow; (*edificio*) to demolish; ~ **la buenaventura a uno** to tell sb's fortune; ~ **la culpa a** to lay the blame on; ~ **de menos** to miss; ~**se atrás** to move back(wards); (*fig*) to go back on what one

has said; ~**se una novia** to get o.s. a girlfriend; ~**se una siestecita** to have a nap.
echarpe [etchár'pe] *nm* (woman's) stole.
ed. *abr* (= *edición*) ed.
edad [etháth'] *nf* age; **¿qué ~ tienes?** how
old are you?; **tiene ocho años de ~** he is
eight (years old); **de ~ corta** young; **ser
de ~ mediana/avanzada** to be middle-
aged/getting on in years; **ser mayor de ~**
to be of age; **llegar a mayor ~** to come of
age; **ser menor de ~** to be under age; **la
E~ Media** the Middle Ages.
Edén [ethen'] *nm* Eden.
edición [ethesyon'] *nf* (*acto*) publication;
(*ejemplar*) edition; **"al cerrar la ~"** (*TIP*)
"stop press".
edicto [ethék'to] *nm* edict, proclamation.
edificante [ethefekán'te] *a* edifying.
edificar [edefekár'] *vt* (*ARQ*) to build.
edificio [ethefe'syo] *nm* building; (*fig*)
edifice, structure.
edifique [ethefe'ke] *etc vb* V **edificar**.
Edimburgo [ethemboor'go] *nm* Edinburgh.
editar [ethetár'] *vt* (*publicar*) to publish;
(*preparar textos, tb INFORM*) to edit.
editor, a [ethetor', á] *nm/f* (*que publica*)
publisher; (*redactor*) editor ♦ *a:* **casa ~a**
publishing company.
editorial [ethetoryál'] *a* editorial ♦ *nm* leading article, editorial ♦ *nf* (*tb:* **casa ~**) pub-
lishers.
editorialista [ethetoryále'stá] *nm/f* editor.
edredón [ethrethon'] *nm* eiderdown, quilt.
educación [ethookásyon'] *nf* education;
(*crianza*) upbringing; (*modales*) (good)
manners *pl*; (*formación*) training; **sin ~**
ill-mannered; **¡qué falta de ~!** how rude!
educado, a [ethooká'tho, á] *a* well-
mannered; **mal ~** ill-mannered.
educar [ethookár'] *vt* to educate; (*criar*) to
bring up; (*voz*) to train.
eduque [ethoo'ke] *etc vb* V **educar**.
EE.UU. *nmpl abr* (= *Estados Unidos*) USA.
efectista [efekte'stá] *a* sensationalist.
efectivamente [efektehámen'te] *ad* (*como
respuesta*) exactly, precisely; (*verdaderamente*) really; (*de hecho*) in fact.
efectivo, a [efekte'ho, á] *a* effective; (*real*)
actual, real ♦ *nm:* **pagar en ~** to pay (in)
cash; **hacer ~ un cheque** to cash a check.
efecto [efek'to] *nm* effect, result; (*objetivo*)
purpose, end; **~s** *nmpl* (*personales*)
effects; (*bienes*) goods; (*COM*) assets;
(*ECON*) bills, securities; **~s de consumo**
consumer goods; **~s a cobrar** bills
receivable; **~s personales** personal effects;
~ secundarios (*COM*) spin-off effects; **~s
sonoros** sound effects; **hacer o surtir ~** to
have the desired effect; **hacer ~** (*impresionar*) to make an impression; **llevar algo a
~** to carry sth out; **en ~** in fact; (*res-

puesta) exactly, indeed.
efectuar [efektwár'] *vt* to carry out; (*viaje*)
to make.
efervescente [eferhesen'te] *a* (*bebida*)
fizzy, bubbly.
eficacia [efeká'syá] *nf* (*de persona*)
efficiency; (*de medicamento etc*) effectiveness.
eficaz [efekás'] *a* (*persona*) efficient;
(*acción*) effective.
eficiencia [efesyen'syá] *nf* efficiency.
eficiente [efesyen'te] *a* efficient.
efigie [efe'hye] *nf* effigy.
efímero, a [efe'mero, á] *a* ephemeral.
efusión [efoosyon'] *nf* outpouring; (*en el
trato*) warmth; **con ~** effusively.
efusivo, a [efoose'ho, á] *a* effusive; **mis
más efusivas gracias** my warmest thanks.
EGB *nf abr* (*Esp ESCOL*)=*Educación General Básica.*
Egeo [ehe'o] *nm:* **(Mar) ~** Aegean (Sea).
egipcio, a [ehep'syo, á] *a, nm/f* Egyptian.
Egipto [ehep'to] *nm* Egypt.
egocéntrico, a [egosen'treko, á] *a* self-
centered (*US*), self-centred (*Brit*).
egoísmo [egoes'mo] *nm* egoism.
egoísta [egoe'stá] *a* egoistical, selfish ♦ *nm/f*
egotist, egoist.
egolatra [egolá'trá] *a* big-headed.
egregio, a [egre'hyo, á] *a* eminent, distinguished.
eh [e] *excl* hey!, hi!
Eire [e'ēre] *nm* Eire.
ej. *abr* (= *ejemplo*) ex.
eje [e'he] *nm* (*GEO, MAT*) axis; (*POL, fig*)
axis, main line; (*de rueda*) axle; (*de máquina*) shaft, spindle.
ejecución [ehekoosyon'] *nf* execution;
(*cumplimiento*) fulfilment; (*actuación*) performance; (*JUR: embargo de deudor*)
attachment.
ejecutar [ehekootár'] *vt* to execute, carry
out; (*matar*) to execute; (*cumplir*) to fulfil;
(*MUS*) to perform; (*JUR: embargar*) to
attach, distrain; (*deseos*) to fulfill (*US*),
fulfil (*Brit*); (*INFORM*) to run.
ejecutivo, a [ehekoote'ho, á] *a, nm/f* executive; **el (poder) ~** the Executive (Power).
ejecutor [ehekootor'] *nm* (*tb: ~
testamentario*) executor.
ejecutoria [ehekooto'ryá] *nf* (*JUR*) final
judgment.
ejemplar [ehemplár'] *a* exemplary ♦ *nm*
example; (*ZOOL*) specimen; (*de libro*)
copy; (*de periódico*) number, issue; **~ de
regalo** complimentary copy; **sin ~** unprecedented.
ejemplificar [ehemplefekár'] *vt* to exemplify, illustrate.
ejemplifique [ehemplefe'ke] *etc vb* V **ejemplificar.**

ejemplo [ehem'plo] *nm* example; (*caso*) instance; **por** ~ for example; **dar** ~ to set an example.

ejercer [eherser'] *vt* to exercise; (*funciones*) to perform; (*negocio*) to manage; (*influencia*) to exert; (*un oficio*) to practice (*US*), practise (*Brit*); (*poder*) to wield ♦ *vi*: ~ **de** to practice as.

ejercicio [ehersē'syo] *nm* exercise; (*MIL*) drill; (*COM*) fiscal *o* financial year; (*período*) tenure; ~ **acrobático** (*AVIAT*) stunt; ~ **comercial** business year; ~**s espirituales** (*REL*) retreat *sg*; **hacer** ~ to take exercise.

ejercitar [ehersētár'] *vt* to exercise; (*MIL*) to drill.

ejército [eher'sēto] *nm* army; ~ **de ocupación** army of occupation; ~ **permanente** standing army; **entrar en el** ~ to join the army, join up.

ejerza [eher'sá] *etc vb* V **ejercer**.

ejote [eho'te] *nm* (*AM*) green bean.

el [el], *pl* **los** *artículo definido msg* the; **me gusta** ~ **fútbol** I like football; ~ **General Prim** General Prim ♦ *pron demostrativo*: **mi libro y** ~ **de usted** my book and yours; ~ **de Pepe es mejor** Pepe's is better ♦ *pron relativo*: ~ **que** he *etc* who, whoever, the one(s) that; ~ **que compramos no vale** the one we bought is no good.

él [el] *pron* (*persona*) he; (*cosa*) it; (*después de prep*: *persona*) him; (: *cosa*) it; **mis libros y los de** ~ my books and his.

elaboración [eláborásyon'] *nf* (*producción*) manufacture; ~ **de presupuestos** (*COM*) budgeting.

elaborar [eláborár'] *vt* (*producto*) to make, manufacture; (*preparar*) to prepare; (*madera, metal etc*) to work; (*proyecto etc*) to work on *o* out.

elasticidad [elástēsēthath'] *nf* elasticity.

elástico, a [elá'stēko, á] *a* elastic; (*flexible*) flexible ♦ *nm* elastic; (*gomita*) elastic band.

elección [eleksyon'] *nf* election; (*selección*) choice, selection; **elecciones parciales** off-year election *sg* (*US*), by-election *sg* (*Brit*); **elecciones generales** general election *sg*.

electo, a [elek'to, á] *a* elect; **el presidente** ~ the president-elect.

electorado [elektorá'tho] *nm* electorate, voters *pl*.

electrice [elektrē'se] *etc vb* V **electrizar**.

electricidad [elektrēsēthath'] *nf* electricity.

electricista [elektrēsē'stá] *nm/f* electrician.

eléctrico, a [elek'trēko, á] *a* electric.

electrizar [elektrēsár'] *vt* (*FERRO, fig*) to electrify.

electro... [elek'tro] *pref* electro....

electrocución [elektrokōōsyon'] *nf* electrocution.

electrocutar [elektrokōōtár'] *vt* to electro-

cute.

electrodo [elektro'tho] *nm* electrode.

electrodomésticos [elektrothome'stēkos] *nmpl* (electrical) household appliances; (*COM*) major appliances (*US*), white goods (*Brit*).

electroimán [electroēmán'] *nm* electromagnet.

electromagnético, a [elektromágne'tēko, á] *a* electromagnetic.

electrónico, a [elektro'nēko, á] *a* electronic ♦ *nf* electronics *sg*; **proceso** ~ **de datos** (*INFORM*) electronic data processing.

electrotecnia [elektrotek'nyá] *nf* electrical engineering.

electrotécnico, a [elektrotek'nēko, á] *nm/f* electrical engineer.

electrotermo [elektroter'mo] *nm* immersible (*US*) *o* immersion (*Brit*) heater.

elefante [elefán'te] *nm* elephant.

elegancia [elegán'syá] *nf* elegance, grace; (*estilo*) stylishness.

elegante [elegán'te] *a* elegant, graceful; (*traje etc*) smart, fashionable; (*decoración*) tasteful.

elegía [elehē'á] *nf* elegy.

elegir [eleher'] *vt* (*escoger*) to choose, select; (*optar*) to opt for; (*presidente*) to elect.

elemental [elementál'] *a* (*claro, obvio*) elementary; (*fundamental*) elemental, fundamental.

elemento [elemen'to] *nm* element; (*fig*) ingredient; (*AM*) person, individual; (*tipo raro*) odd person; (*de pila*) cell; ~**s** *nmpl* elements, rudiments; **estar en su** ~ to be in one's element; **vino a verle un** ~ someone came to see you.

elenco [elen'ko] *nm* catalog(ue), list; (*TEATRO*) cast.

elevación [elebásyon'] *nf* elevation; (*acto*) raising, lifting; (*de precios*) rise; (*GEO etc*) height, altitude.

elevar [elebár'] *vt* to raise, lift (up); (*precio*) to put up; (*producción*) to step up; (*informe etc*) to present; ~**se** *vr* (*edificio*) to rise; (*precios*) to go up; (*transportarse, enajenarse*) to get carried away; **la cantidad se eleva a** ... the total amounts to ... .

eligiendo [elēhyen'tho] *etc*, **elija** [elē'há] *etc vb* V **elegir**.

eliminar [elēmēnár'] *vt* to eliminate, remove; (*olor, persona*) to get rid of; (*DEPORTE*) to eliminate, knock out.

eliminatoria [elēmēnáto'ryá] *nf* heat, preliminary (round).

elite [elē'te] *nf* elite.

elocuencia [elokwen'syá] *nf* eloquence.

elocuente [elokwen'te] *a* eloquent; (*fig*) significant; **un dato** ~ a fact which speaks for itself.

elogiar [elohyár'] *vt* to praise, eulogize.
elogio [elo'hyo] *nm* praise; **queda por encima de todo** ~ it's beyond praise; **hacer** ~ **de** to sing the praises of.
elote [elo'te] *nm* (*AM*) corn on the cob.
El Salvador *nm* El Salvador.
eludir [eloōṭḫ̱ēr'] *vt* (*evitar*) to avoid, evade; (*escapar*) to escape, elude.
ella [e'yá] *pron* (*persona*) she; (*cosa*) it; (*después de prep*: *persona*) her; (: *cosa*) it; **de** ~ hers.
ellas [e'yás] *pron V* **ellos**.
ello [e'yo] *pron neutro* it; **es por** ~ **que** ... that's why ... .
ellos, as [e'yos, ás] *pron personal pl* they; (*después de prep*) them; **de** ~ theirs.
E.M. *abr* (*MIL*:=*Estado Mayor*) G.S.
Em.ª *abr* = **Eminencia**.
emanar [emánár'] *vi*: ~ **de** to emanate from, come from; (*derivar de*) to originate in.
emancipar [emánsēpár'] *vt* to emancipate; ~**se** *vr* to become emancipated, free o.s.
embadurnar [embáṭḫ̱oōrnár'] *vt* to smear.
embajada [embáhá'ṭḫ̱á] *nf* embassy.
embajador, a [embáháṭḫ̱or', á] *nm/f* ambassador/ambassadress.
embaladura [embáláṭḫ̱oō'rá] *nf* (*AM*), **embalaje** [embálá'he] *nm* packing.
embalar [embálár'] *vt* (*envolver*) to package, wrap (up); (*envasar*) to package ♦ *vi* to sprint.
embalsamar [embálsámár'] *vt* to embalm.
embalsar [embálsár'] *vt* (*río*) to dam (up); (*agua*) to retain.
embalse [embál'se] *nm* (*presa*) dam; (*lago*) reservoir.
embarace [embárá'se] *etc vb V* **embarazar**.
embarazada [embárásá'ṭḫ̱á] *af* pregnant ♦ *nf* pregnant woman.
embarazar [embárásár'] *vt* to obstruct, hamper; ~**se** *vr* (*aturdirse*) to become embarrassed; (*confundirse*) to get into a mess.
embarazo [embárá'so] *nm* (*de mujer*) pregnancy; (*impedimento*) obstacle, obstruction; (*timidez*) embarrassment.
embarazoso, a [embárá'so'so, á] *a* (*molesto*) awkward; (*violento*) embarrassing.
embarcación [embárkásyon'] *nf* (*barco*) boat, craft; (*acto*) embarkation; ~ **de arrastre** trawler; ~ **de cabotaje** coastal vessel.
embarcadero [embárkáṭḫ̱e'ro] *nm* pier, wharf.
embarcar [embárkár'] *vt* (*cargamento*) to ship, stow; (*persona*) to embark, put on board; (*fig*): ~ **a uno en una empresa** to involve sb in an undertaking; ~**se** *vr* to embark, go on board; (*marinero*) to sign on.

embargar [embárgár'] *vt* (*frenar*) to restrain; (*sentidos*) to overpower; (*JUR*) to seize, impound.
embargo [embár'go] *nm* (*JUR*) seizure; (*COM etc*) embargo; **sin** ~ still, however, nonetheless.
embargue [embár'ge] *etc vb V* **embargar**.
embarque [embár'ke] *etc vb V* **embarcar** ♦ *nm* shipment, loading.
embarrancar [embárránkár'] *vt, vi* (*NAUT*) to run aground; (*AUTO etc*) to run into a ditch.
embarranque [embárrán'ke] *etc vb V* **embarrancar**.
embarullar [embároōyár'] *vt* to make a mess of.
embate [embá'te] *nm* (*de mar, viento*) beating, violence.
embaucador, a [embáoōkáṭḫ̱or', á] *nm/f* (*estafador*) trickster; (*impostor*) impostor.
embaucar [embáoōkár'] *vt* to trick, fool.
embauque [embá'oōke] *etc vb V* **embaucar**.
embebecido, a [embeḫesē'ṭḫ̱o, á] *a* fascinated.
embeber [embeḫer'] *vt* (*absorber*) to absorb, soak up; (*empapar*) to saturate ♦ *vi* to shrink; ~**se** *vr*: ~**se en un libro** to be engrossed *o* absorbed in a book.
embelesado, a [embelesá'ṭḫ̱o, á] *a* spellbound.
embelesar [embelesár'] *vt* to enchant; ~**se** *vr*: ~**se (con)** to be enchanted (by).
embellecer [embeyeser'] *vt* to embellish, beautify.
embellezca [embeyes'ká] *etc vb V* **embellecer**.
embestida [embestē'ṭḫ̱á] *nf* attack, onslaught; (*carga*) charge.
embestir [embestēr'] *vt* to attack, assault; to charge, attack ♦ *vi* to attack.
embistiendo [embēstyen'do] *etc vb V* **embestir**.
emblandecer [emblándeser'] *vt* to soften; (*fig*) to mollify; ~**se** *vr* to relent.
emblandezca [emblándes'ká] *etc vb V* **emblandecer**.
emblanquecer [emblánkeser'] *vt* to whiten, bleach; ~**se** *vr* to turn white.
emblanquezca [emblánkes'ká] *etc vb V* **emblanquecer**.
emblema [emble'má] *nm* emblem.
embobado, a [emboḫá'ṭḫ̱o, á] *a* (*atontado*) stunned, bewildered.
embobar [emboḫár'] *vt* (*asombrar*) to amaze; (*fascinar*) to fascinate; ~**se** *vr*: ~**se con** *o* **de** *o* **en** to be amazed at; to be fascinated by.
embocadura [embokáṭḫ̱oō'rá] *nf* narrow entrance; (*de río*) mouth; (*MUS*) mouthpiece.

embolado [embolá'tho] *nm* (*TEATRO*) bit part, minor role; (*fam*) trick.

embolia [embo'lyá] *nf* (*MED*) embolism; ~ **cerebral** clot on the brain.

émbolo [em'bolo] *nm* (*AUTO*) piston.

embolsar [embolsár'] *vt* to pocket, put in one's pocket.

emboquillado, a [embokēyá'tho, á] *a* (*cigarrillo*) tipped, filter *cpd*.

emborrachar [emborrátchár'] *vt* to make drunk; ~**se** *vr* to get drunk.

emboscada [emboská'thá] *nf* (*celada*) ambush.

embotar [embotár'] *vt* to blunt, dull; ~**se** *vr* (*adormecerse*) to go numb.

embotellamiento [emboteyámyen'to] *nm* (*AUTO*) traffic jam.

embotellar [emboteyár'] *vt* to bottle; ~**se** *vr* (*circulación*) to get into a jam.

embozo [embo'so] *nm* muffler, mask.

embragar [embrágár'] *vt* (*AUTO, TEC*) to engage; (*partes*) to connect ♦ *vi* to let in the clutch.

embrague [embrá'ge] *etc vb* V **embragar** ♦ *nm* (*tb*: **pedal de** ~) clutch.

embravecer [embráṵeser'] *vt* to enrage, infuriate; ~**se** *vr* to become furious; (*mar*) to get rough; (*tormenta*) to rage.

embravecido, a [embráṵesē'tho, á] *a* (*mar*) rough; (*persona*) furious.

embriagador, a [embryágáthor', á] *a* intoxicating.

embriagar [embryágár'] *vt* (*emborrachar*) to make drunk; (*alegrar*) to delight; ~**se** *vr* (*emborracharse*) to get drunk.

embriague [embryá'ge] *etc vb* V **embriagar**.

embriaguez [embryáges'] *nf* (*borrachera*) drunkenness.

embrión [embryon'] *nm* embryo.

embrionario, a [embryoná'ryo, á] *a* embryonic.

embrollar [embroyár'] *vt* (*asunto*) to confuse, complicate; (*persona*) to involve, embroil; ~**se** *vr* (*confundirse*) to get into a mess.

embrollo [embro'yo] *nm* (*enredo*) confusion; (*aprieto*) fix, jam.

embromar [embromár'] *vt* (*burlarse de*) to tease, make fun of.

embrujado, a [embrōōhá'tho, á] *a* (*persona*) bewitched; **casa embrujada** haunted house.

embrutecer [embrōōteser'] *vt* (*atontar*) to stupefy; ~**se** *vr* to be stupefied.

embrutezca [embrōōtes'ká] *etc vb* V **embrutecer**.

embudo [embōō'tho] *nm* funnel.

embuste [embōō'ste] *nm* trick; (*mentira*) lie; (*hum*) fib.

embustero, a [embōōstc'ro, á] *a* lying, deceitful ♦ *nm/f* (*tramposo*) cheat; (*mentiroso*) liar; (*hum*) fibber.

embutido [embōōtē'tho] *nm* (*CULIN*) sausage; (*TEC*) inlay.

embutir [embōōtēr'] *vt* to insert; (*TEC*) to inlay; (*llenar*) to pack tight, cram.

emergencia [emerhen'syá] *nf* emergency; (*surgimiento*) emergence.

emergente [emerhen'te] *a* resultant, consequent; (*nación*) emergent.

emerger [emerher'] *vi* to emerge, appear.

emeritense [emerēten'se] *a* of *o* from Mérida ♦ *nm/f* native *o* inhabitant of Mérida.

emerja [emer'há] *etc vb* V **emerger**.

emigración [emēgrásyon'] *nf* emigration; (*de pájaros*) migration.

emigrado, a [emēgrá'tho, á] *nm/f* emigrant; (*POL etc*) émigré(e).

emigrante [emēgrán'te] *a, nm/f* emigrant.

emigrar [emēgrár'] *vi* (*personas*) to emigrate; (*pájaros*) to migrate.

eminencia [emēnen'syá] *nf* eminence; (*en titulos*): **Su E**~ His Eminence; **Vuestra E**~ Your Eminence.

eminente [emēnen'te] *a* eminent, distinguished; (*elevado*) high.

emisario [emēsá'ryo] *nm* emissary.

emisión [emēsyon'] *nf* (*acto*) emission; (*COM etc*) issue; (*RADIO, TV*: *acto*) broadcasting; (: *programa*) broadcast, program (*US*), programme (*Brit*); ~ **de acciones** (*COM*) share issue; ~ **gratuita de acciones** (*COM*) rights issue; ~ **de valores** (*COM*) flotation.

emisor, a [emēsor', á] *nm* transmitter ♦ *nf* radio *o* broadcasting station.

emitir [emētēr'] *vt* (*olor etc*) to emit, give off; (*moneda etc*) to issue; (*opinión*) to express; (*voto*) to cast; (*señal*) to send out; (*RADIO*) to broadcast; ~ **una señal sonora** to beep.

emoción [emosyon'] *nf* emotion; (*excitación*) excitement; (*sentimiento*) feeling; **¡qué** ~! how exciting!; (*irónico*) what a thrill!

emocionado, a [emosyoná'tho, á] *a* deeply moved, stirred.

emocionante [emosyonán'te] *a* (*excitante*) exciting, thrilling.

emocionar [emosyonár'] *vt* (*excitar*) to excite, thrill; (*conmover*) to move, touch; (*impresionar*) to impress; ~**se** *vr* to get excited.

emotivo, a [emotē'ho, á] *a* emotional.

empacar [empákár'] *vt* (*gen*) to pack; (*en caja*) to bale, crate.

empacharse [empátchár'se] *vr* (*MED*) to get indigestion.

empacho [empátch'o] *nm* (*MED*) indigestion; (*fig*) embarrassment.

empadronamiento [empáthronámyen'to]

nm census; (*de electores*) list of registered voters (*US*), electoral register (*Brit*).

empadronarse |empáđronár'se| *vr* (*POL: como elector*) to register.

empalagar |empálágár'| *vt* (*suj: comida*) to cloy ♦ *vi* to pall.

empalagoso, a |empálágo'so, à| *a* cloying; (*fig*) tiresome.

empalague |empálá'ge| *etc vb* V **empalagar**.

empalizada |empálēsá'đá| *nf* fence; (*MIL*) palisade.

empalmar |empálmár'| *vt* to join, connect ♦ *vi* (*dos caminos*) to meet, join.

empalme |empál'me| *nm* joint, connection; (*de vías*) junction; (*de trenes*) connection.

empanada |empáná'đá| *nf* pie.

empanar |empánár'| *vt* (*CULIN*) to cook o roll in breadcrumbs o pastry.

empantanarse |empántánár'se| *vr* to get swamped; (*fig*) to get bogged down.

empañarse |empáñár'se| *vr* (*nublarse*) to get misty, steam up.

empapar |empápár'| *vt* (*mojar*) to soak, saturate; (*absorber*) to soak up, absorb; ~**se** *vr*: ~**se de** to soak up.

empapelar |empápelár'| *vt* (*paredes*) to paper.

empaque |empá'ke| *etc vb* V **empacar**.

empaquetar |empáketár'| *vt* to pack, package up; (*COM*) to package.

emparedado |empáređá'đo| *nm* sandwich.

emparejar |empárehár'| *vt* to pair ♦ *vi* to catch up.

emparentar |empárentár'| *vi*: ~ **con** to marry into.

empariente |empáryen'te| *etc vb* V **emparentar**.

empastar |empástár'| *vt* (*embadurnar*) to paste; (*diente*) to fill.

empaste |empá'ste| *nm* (*de diente*) filling.

empatar |empátár'| *vi* to draw, tie.

empate |empá'te| *nm* draw, tie; **un** ~ **a cero** a no-score draw.

empecé |empese'|, **empecemos** |empese'mos| *etc vb* V **empezar**.

empecinado, a |empesēná'đo, à| *a* (*AM*) stubborn.

empedernido, a |empeđernē'đo, à| *a* hard, heartless; (*fijado*) hardened, inveterate; **un fumador** ~ a heavy smoker.

empedrado, a |empeđrá'đo, à| *a* paved ♦ *nm* paving.

empedrar |empeđrár'| *vt* to pave.

empeine |empe'ēne| *nm* (*de pie, zapato*) instep.

empellón |empeyon'| *nm* push, shove; **abrirse paso a empellones** to push o shove one's way past o through.

empeñado, a |empenyá'đo, à| *a* (*persona*) determined; (*objeto*) pawned.

empeñar |empenyár'| *vt* (*objeto*) to pawn, pledge; (*persona*) to compel; ~**se** *vr* (*obligarse*) to bind o.s., pledge o.s.; (*endeudarse*) to get into debt; ~**se en hacer** to be set on doing, be determined to do.

empeño |empe'nyo| *nm* (*determinación*) determination; (*cosa prendada*) pledge; **casa de** ~**s** pawnshop; **con** ~ insistently; (*con celo*) eagerly; **tener** ~ **en hacer algo** to be bent on doing sth.

empeoramiento |empeorámyen'to| *nm* worsening.

empeorar |empeorár'| *vt* to make worse, worsen ♦ *vi* to get worse, deteriorate.

empequeñecer |empekenyeser'| *vt* to dwarf; (*fig*) to belittle.

empequeñezca |empekenyes'ká| *etc vb* V **empequeñecer**.

emperador |emperáđor'| *nm* emperor.

emperatriz |emperátrēs'| *nf* empress.

emperrarse |emperrár'se| *vr* to get stubborn; ~ **en algo** to persist in sth.

empezar |empesár'| *vt, vi* to begin, start; **empezó a llover** it started to rain; **bueno, para** ~ well, to start with.

empiece |empye'se| *etc vb* V **empezar**.

empiedre |empye'đre| *etc vb* V **empedrar**.

empiezo |empye'so| *etc vb* V **empezar**.

empinado, a |empēná'đo, à| *a* steep.

empinar |empēnár'| *vt* to raise; (*botella*) to tip up; ~**se** *vr* (*persona*) to stand on tiptoe; (*animal*) to rear up; (*camino*) to climb steeply; ~ **el codo** to booze (*fam*).

empingorotado, a |empēngorotá'đo, à| *a* (*fam*) stuck-up.

empírico, a |empē'rēko, à| *a* empirical.

emplace |emplá'se| *etc vb* V **emplazar**.

emplaste |emplá'ste|, **emplasto** |emplá'sto| *nm* (*MED*) plaster.

emplazamiento |emplásámyen'to| *nm* site, location; (*JUR*) summons *sg*.

emplazar |emplásár'| *vt* (*ubicar*) to site, place, locate; (*JUR*) to summons; (*convocar*) to summon.

empleado, a |empleá'đo, à| *nm/f* (*gen*) employee; (*de banco etc*) clerk; ~ **público** civil servant.

emplear |empleár'| *vt* (*usar*) to use, employ; (*dar trabajo a*) to employ; ~**se** *vr* (*conseguir trabajo*) to be employed; (*ocuparse*) to occupy o.s.; ~ **mal el tiempo** to waste time; **¡te está bien empleado!** it serves you right!

empleo |emple'o| *nm* (*puesto*) job; (*puestos: colectivamente*) employment; (*uso*) use, employment; **"modo de** ~**"** "instructions for use".

emplumar |emploomár'| *vt* (*estafar*) to swindle.

empobrecer |empobreser'| *vt* to impoverish; ~**se** *vr* to become poor o impoverished.

empobrecimiento [empobresēmyen'to] *nm* impoverishment.

empobrezca [empobres'ká] *etc vb* V **empobrecer.**

empolvar [empolbár'] *vt* (*cara*) to powder; ~**se** *vr* to powder one's face; (*superficie*) to get dusty.

empollar [empoyár'] *vt* to incubate; (*ESCOL fam*) to swot (up) ♦ *vi* (*gallina*) to brood; (*ESCOL fam*) to bone up.

empollón, ona [empoyon', oná] *nm/f* (*ESCOL fam*) swot.

emponzoñar [emponsonyár'] *vt* (*esp fig*) to poison.

emporio [empo'ryo] *nm* emporium, trading center; (*AM: gran almacén*) department store.

empotrado, a [empotrá'tho, á] *a* (*armario etc*) built-in.

empotrar [empotrár'] *vt* to embed; (*armario etc*) to build in.

emprender [emprender'] *vt* to undertake; (*empezar*) to begin, embark on; (*acometer*) to tackle, take on; ~ **marcha a** to set out for.

empreñar [emprenyár'] *vt* to make pregnant; ~**se** *vr* to become pregnant.

empresa [empre'sá] *nf* enterprise; (*COM: sociedad*) firm, company; (: *negocio*) business; (*esp TEATRO*) management; ~ **filial** (*COM*) subsidiary company; ~ **matriz** (*COM*) parent company.

empresario, a [empresá'ryo, á] *nm/f* (*COM*) businessman/woman, entrepreneur; (*TEC*) manager; (*MUS: de ópera etc*) impresario; ~ **de pompas fúnebres** mortician (*US*), undertaker (*Brit*).

empréstito [empre'stēto] *nm* (public) loan; (*COM*) loan capital.

empujar [empoohár'] *vt* to push, shove.

empuje [empoo'he] *nm* thrust; (*presión*) pressure; (*fig*) vigor (*US*), vigour (*Brit*), drive.

empujón [empoohon'] *nm* push, shove; **abrirse paso a empujones** to shove one's way through.

empuñadura [empoonyáthoo'rá] *nf* (*de espada*) hilt; (*de herramienta etc*) handle.

empuñar [empoonyár'] *vt* (*asir*) to grasp, take (firm) hold of; ~ **las armas** (*fig*) to take up arms.

emulación [emoolásyon'] *nf* emulation.

emular [emoolár'] *vt* to emulate; (*rivalizar*) to rival.

émulo, a [e'mōolo, á] *nm/f* rival, competitor.

en [en] *prep* (*gen*) in; (*sobre*) on, upon; (*tiempo*) in, on; (*tipo*) by; **meter** ~ **el bolsillo** to put in *o* into one's pocket; **vivir** ~ **Toledo** to live in Toledo; ~ **casa** at home; **lo terminó** ~ **6 días** he finished it in 6 days; ~ (**el mes de**) **enero** in (the month of) January; ~ **aquel momento/aquella época** at that moment/that time; ~ **aquel día/aquella ocasión** on that day/that occasion; **ha aumentado** ~ **un 20 por ciento** it has increased by 20%; ~ **serio** seriously; ~ **fin** well, well then; **ir de puerta** ~ **puerta** to go from door to door; (*viajar*) ~ **tren** (to travel) by train.

enajenación [enáhenásyon'] *nf*, **enajenamiento** [enáhenámyen'to] *nm* alienation; (*fig: distracción*) absent-mindedness; (: *embelesamiento*) rapture, trance; ~ **mental** mental derangement.

enajenar [enáhenár'] *vt* to alienate; (*fig*) to carry away.

enamorado, a [enámorá'tho, á] *a* in love ♦ *nm/f* lover; **estar** ~ (**de**) to be in love (with).

enamorar [enámorár'] *vt* to win the love of; ~**se** *vr*: ~**se** (**de**) to fall in love (with).

enano, a [ená'no, á] *a* tiny, dwarf ♦ *nm/f* dwarf; (*pey*) runt.

enarbolar [enárbolár'] *vt* (*bandera etc*) to hoist; (*espada etc*) to brandish.

enardecer [enártheser'] *vt* (*pasiones*) to fire, inflame; (*persona*) to fill with enthusiasm; ~**se** *vr* to get excited; ~**se por** to get enthusiastic about.

enardezca [enárdes'ká] *etc vb* V **enardecer.**

encabece [enkábe'se] *etc vb* V **encabezar.**

encabezado [enkábesá'tho] *nm* (*COM*) header.

encabezamiento [enkábesámyen'to] *nm* (*de carta*) heading; (*COM*) billhead, letterhead; (*de periódico*) headline; (*preámbulo*) foreword, preface; ~ **normal** (*TIP etc*) running head.

encabezar [enkábesár'] *vt* (*movimiento, revolución*) to lead, head; (*lista*) to head; (*carta*) to put a heading to; (*libro*) to entitle.

encadenar [enkáthenár'] *vt* to chain (together); (*poner grilletes a*) to shackle.

encajar [enkáhár'] *vt* (*ajustar*): ~ **en** to fit (into); (*meter a la fuerza*) to push in; (*máquina etc*) to house; (*partes*) to join; (*fam: golpe*) to give, deal; (*entrometer*) to insert ♦ *vi* to fit (well); (*fig: corresponder a*) to match; ~**se** *vr*: ~**se en un sillón** to squeeze into a chair.

encaje [enká'he] *nm* (*labor*) lace.

encajonar [enkáhonár'] *vt* to box (up), put in a box.

encalar [enkálár'] *vt* (*pared*) to whitewash.

encallar [enkáyár'] *vi* (*NAUT*) to run aground.

encaminado, a [enkámēná'tho, á] *a*: **medidas encaminadas a ...** measures designed to *o* aimed at ...

encaminar [enkámēnár'] *vt* to direct, send; ~**se** *vr*: ~**se a** to set out for; ~ **por** (*expedición etc*) to route via.

encandilar [enkándēlár'] *vt* to dazzle; (*persona*) to daze, bewilder.

encanecer [enkáneser'] *vi*, **encanecerse** *vr* (*pelo*) to go grey.

encanezca [enkánes'ká] *etc vb* V **encanecer.**

encantado, a [enkántá'ᶿo, á] *a* delighted; ¡~! how do you do!, pleased to meet you.

encantador, a [enkántáᶿor', á] *a* charming, lovely ♦ *nm/f* magician, enchanter/ enchantress.

encantar [enkántár'] *vt* to charm, delight; (*cautivar*) to fascinate; (*hechizar*) to bewitch, cast a spell on.

encanto [enkán'to] *nm* (*magia*) spell, charm; (*fig*) charm, delight; (*expresión de ternura*) sweetheart; **como por** ~ as if by magic.

encapotado, a [enkápotá'ᶿo, á] *a* (*cielo*) overcast.

encapricharse [enkáprētchár'se] *vr*: **se ha encaprichado con ir ...** he's taken it into his head to go ...; **se ha encaprichado** he's digging his heels in.

encaramar [enkárámár'] *vt* (*subir*) to raise, lift up; ~**se** *vr* (*subir*) to perch; ~**se a** (*árbol etc*) to climb.

encararse [enkárár'se] *vr*: ~ **a** *o* **con** to confront, come face to face with.

encarcelar [enkárselár'] *vt* to imprison, jail.

encarecer [enkáreser'] *vt* to raise the price of ♦ *vi*, ~**se** *vr* to get more expensive.

encarecidamente [enkáresēᶿhámen'te] *ad* earnestly.

encarecimiento [enkáresēmyen'to] *nm* price increase.

encarezca [enkáres'ká] *etc vb* V **encarecer.**

encargado, a [enkárgá'ᶿo, á] *a* in charge ♦ *nm/f* agent, representative; (*responsable*) person in charge.

encargar [enkárgár'] *vt* to entrust; (*COM*) to order; (*recomendar*) to urge, recommend; ~**se** *vr*: ~**se a** to look after, take charge of; ~ **algo a uno** to put sb in charge of sth.

encargo [enkár'go] *nm* (*pedido*) assignment, job; (*responsabilidad*) responsibility; (*recomendación*) recommendation; (*COM*) order.

encargue [enkár'ge] *etc vb* V **encargar.**

encariñarse [enkárēnyár'se] *vr*: ~ **con** to grow fond of, get attached to.

encarnación [enkárnásyon'] *nf* incarnation, embodiment.

encarnado, a [enkárná'ᶿo, á] *a* (*color*) red; **ponerse** ~ to blush.

encarnar [enkárnár'] *vt* to personify; (*TEATRO*: *papel*) to play ♦ *vi* (*REL etc*) to become incarnate.

encarnizado, a [enkárnēsá'ᶿo, á] *a* (*lucha*) bloody, fierce.

encarrilar [enkárrēlár'] *vt* (*tren*) to put back on the rails; (*fig*) to correct, put on the right track.

encasillar [enkásēyár'] *vt* (*TEATRO*) to typecast; (*clasificar*: *pey*) to pigeonhole.

encauce [enká'ōōse] *etc vb* V **encauzar.**

encausar [enkáōōsár'] *vt* to prosecute, sue.

encauzar [enkáōōsár'] *vt* to channel; (*fig*) to direct.

encendedor [ensendeᶿor'] *nm* lighter.

encender [ensender'] *vt* (*con fuego*) to light; (*incendiar*) to set fire to; (*luz, radio*) to put on, switch on; (*INFORM*) to toggle on, switch on; (*avivar*: *pasiones etc*) to inflame; (*despertar*: *entusiasmo*) to arouse; (: *odio*) to awaken; ~**se** *vr* to catch fire; (*excitarse*) to get excited; (*de cólera*) to flare up; (*el rostro*) to blush.

encendidamente [ensendēᶿhámen'te] *ad* passionately.

encendido, a [ensendē'ᶿo, á] *a* alight; (*aparato*) (switched) on; (*mejillas*) glowing; (*cara*: *por el vino etc*) flushed; (*mirada*) passionate ♦ *nm* (*AUTO*) ignition; (*de faroles*) lighting.

encerado, a [enserá'ᶿo, á] *a* (*suelo*) waxed, polished ♦ *nm* (*ESCOL*) blackboard; (*hule*) oilcloth.

encerar [enserár'] *vt* (*suelo*) to wax, polish.

encerrar [enserrár'] *vt* (*confinar*) to shut in *o* up; (*con llave*) to lock in *o* up; (*comprender, incluir*) to include, contain; ~**se** *vr* to shut *o* lock o.s. up *o* in.

encerrona [enserro'ná] *nf* trap.

encía [ensē'á] *nf* (*ANAT*) gum.

enciclopedia [ensēklope'ᶿhyá] *nf* encyclopedia.

encienda [ensyen'dá] *etc vb* V **encender.**

encierro [ensye'rro] *etc vb* V **encerrar** ♦ *nm* shutting in *o* up; (*calabozo*) prison; (*AGR*) pen; (*TAUR*) penning.

encima [ensē'má] *ad* (*sobre*) above, over; (*además*) besides; ~ **de** (*en*) on, on top of; (*sobre*) above, over; (*además de*) besides, on top of; **por** ~ **de** over; **¿llevas dinero** ~**?** have you (got) any money on you?; **se me vino** ~ it took me by surprise.

encina [ensē'ná] *nf* (holm) oak.

encinta [ensēn'tá] *af* pregnant.

enclenque [enklen'ke] *a* weak, sickly.

encoger [enkoher'] *vt* (*gen*) to shrink, contract; (*fig*: *asustar*) to scare; (: *desanimar*) to discourage; ~**se** *vr* to shrink, contract; (*fig*) to cringe; ~**se de hombros** to shrug one's shoulders.

encoja [enko'há] *etc vb* V **encoger.**

encojar [enkohár'] *vt* to lame; (*tullir*) to cripple; ~**se** *vr* to go lame; to become crippled.

encolar [enkolár'] *vt* (*engomar*) to glue, paste; (*pegar*) to stick down.

encolerice [enkolerē'se] *etc vb* V **encolerizar.**

encolerizar [enkolerēsár'] *vt* to anger, provoke; ~**se** *vr* to get angry.

encomendar [enkomendár'] *vt* to entrust, commend; ~**se** *vr*: ~**se a** to put one's trust in.

encomiar [enkomyár'] *vt* to praise, pay tribute to.

encomienda [enkomyen'dà] *etc vb* V **encomendar ♦** *nf* (*encargo*) charge, commission; (*elogio*) tribute; ~ **postal** (*AM*) parcel post.

encomio [enko'myo] *nm* praise, tribute.

encono [enko'no] *nm* (*rencor*) rancor (*US*), rancour (*Brit*), spite.

encontrado, a [enkontrà'ḍo, à] *a* (*contrario*) contrary, conflicting; (*hostil*) hostile.

encontrar [enkontrár'] *vt* (*hallar*) to find; (*inesperadamente*) to meet, run into; ~**se** *vr* to meet (each other); (*situarse*) to be (situated); (*persona*) to find o.s., be; (*entrar en conflicto*) to crash, collide; ~**se con** to meet; ~**se bien (de salud)** to feel well; **no se encuentra aquí en este momento** he's not in at the moment.

encontronazo [enkontroná'so] *nm* collision, crash.

encorvar [enkorḅár'] *vt* to curve; (*inclinar*) to bend (down); ~**se** *vr* to bend down, bend over.

encrespado, a [enkrespà'ḍo, à] *a* (*pelo*) curly; (*mar*) rough.

encrespar [enkrespár'] *vt* (*cabellos*) to curl; (*fig*) to anger, irritate; ~**se** *vr* (*el mar*) to get rough; (*fig*) to get cross *o* irritated.

encrucijada [enkrōōsēhá'ḍà] *nf* crossroads *sg*; (*empalme*) junction.

encuadernación [enkwàḍhernásyon'] *nf* binding; (*taller*) bindery.

encuadernador, a [enkwàḍhernáḍhor', à] *nm/f* bookbinder.

encuadrar [enkwàḍhrár'] *vt* (*retrato*) to frame; (*ajustar*) to fit, insert; (*encerrar*) to contain.

encubierto [enkōōḅyer'to] *pp de* **encubrir.**

encubrir [enkōōḅrēr'] *vt* (*ocultar*) to hide, conceal; (*criminal*) to harbor (*US*), harbour (*Brit*), shelter; (*ayudar*) to be an accomplice in.

encuentro [enkwen'tro] *etc vb* V **encontrar ♦** *nm* (*de personas*) meeting; (*AUTO etc*) collision, crash; (*DEPORTE*) match, game; (*MIL*) encounter.

encuesta [enkwe'stà] *nf* inquiry, investigation; (*sondeo*) public opinion poll; ~ **judicial** post mortem.

encumbrado, a [enkōōmbrà'ḍo, à] *a* eminent, distinguished.

encumbrar [enkōōmbrár'] *vt* (*persona*) to exalt; ~**se** *vr* (*fig*) to become conceited.

encharcar [entchárkár'] *vt* to swamp, flood; ~**se** *vr* to become flooded.

encharque [entchár'ke] *etc vb* V **encharcar.**

enchufar [entchōōfár'] *vt* (*ELEC*) to plug in; (*TEC*) to connect, fit together; (*COM*) to merge.

enchufe [entchōō'fe] *nm* (*ELEC*: *clavija*) plug; (: *toma*) socket; (*de dos tubos*) joint, connection; (*fam*: *influencia*) contact, connection; (: *puesto*) cushy job; ~ **de clavija** jack plug; **tiene un** ~ **en el ministerio** he can pull strings at the ministry.

endeble [ende'ḅle] *a* (*argumento, excusa, persona*) weak.

endemoniado, a [endemonyà'ḍo, à] *a* possessed (of the devil); (*travieso*) devilish.

enderece [endere'se] *etc vb* V **enderezar.**

enderezar [enderesár'] *vt* (*poner derecho*) to straighten (out); (: *verticalmente*) to set upright; (*fig*) to straighten *o* sort out; (*dirigir*) to direct; ~**se** *vr* (*persona sentada*) to sit up straight.

endeudarse [endeōōḍhár'se] *vr* to get into debt.

endiablado, a [endyàḅlà'ḍo, à] *a* devilish, diabolical; (*hum*) mischievous.

endilgar [endēlġár'] *vt* (*fam*): ~ **algo a uno** to saddle sb with sth; ~ **un sermón a uno** to give sb a lecture.

endilgue [endēl'ġe] *etc vb* V **endilgar.**

endomingarse [endomēngár'se] *vr* to dress up, put on one's best clothes.

endomingue [endomēn'ge] *etc vb* V **endomingarse.**

endosante [endosán'te] *nm/f* endorser.

endosar [endosár'] *vt* (*cheque etc*) to endorse.

endulce [endōōl'se] *etc vb* V **endulzar.**

endulzar [endōōlsár'] *vt* to sweeten; (*suavizar*) to soften.

endurecer [endōōreser'] *vt* to harden; ~**se** *vr* to harden, grow hard.

endurecido, a [endōōresē'ḍo, à] *a* (*duro*) hard; (*fig*) hardy, tough; **estar ~ a algo** to be hardened *o* used to sth.

endurezca [endōōres'kà] *etc vb* V **endurecer.**

ene. *abr* (= *enero*) Jan.

enemigo, a [enemē'ġo, à] *a* enemy, hostile **♦** *nm/f* enemy **♦** *nf* enmity, hostility; **ser ~ de** (*persona*) to dislike; (*suj: tendencia*) to be inimical to.

enemistad [enemēstàd'] *nf* enmity.

enemistar [enemēstár'] *vt* to make enemies of, cause a rift between; ~**se** *vr* to become enemies; (*amigos*) to have a falling out (*US*), fall out (*Brit*).

energético, a [enerhe'tēko, à] *a*: **política**

energética energy policy.
energía [enerhē'á] *nf* (*vigor*) energy, drive; (*TEC, ELEC*) energy, power.
enérgico, a [ener'hēko, á] *a* (*gen*) energetic; (*ataque*) vigorous; (*ejercicio*) strenuous; (*medida*) bold; (*voz, modales*) forceful.
energúmeno, a [energōō'meno, á] *nm/f* madman/woman; **ponerse como un ~ con uno** to get furious with sb.
enero [ene'ro] *nm* January.
enervar [enerβár'] *vt* (*poner nervioso a*) to get on sb's nerves.
enésimo, a [ene'sēmo, á] *a* (*MAT*) nth; **por enésima vez** (*fig*) for the umpteenth time.
enfadado, a [enfáthá'tho, á] *a* angry, annoyed.
enfadar [enfáthár'] *vt* to anger, annoy; **~se** *vr* to get angry o annoyed.
enfado [enfá'tho] *nm* (*enojo*) anger, annoyance; (*disgusto*) trouble, bother.
énfasis [en'fásēs] *nm* emphasis, stress; **poner ~ en** to stress.
enfático, a [enfá'tēko, á] *a* emphatic.
enfatizado, a [enfátēsá'tho, á] *a*: **en caracteres ~s** (*INFORM*) emphasized.
enfermar [enfermár'] *vt* to make ill ♦ *vi* to fall ill, be taken ill; **su actitud me enferma** his attitude makes me sick; **~ del corazón** to develop heart trouble.
enfermedad [enfermetháth'] *nf* illness; **~ venérea** venereal disease.
enfermera [enferme'rá] *nf* V **enfermero**.
enfermería [enfermerē'á] *nf* infirmary; (*de colegio etc*) sick bay.
enfermero, a [enferme'ro, á] *nm* (male) nurse ♦ *nf* nurse; **enfermera jefa** head nurse (*US*), matron (*Brit*).
enfermizo, a [enfermē'so, á] *a* (*persona*) sickly, unhealthy; (*fig*) unhealthy.
enfermo, a [enfer'mo, á] *a* ill, sick ♦ *nm/f* invalid, sick person; (*en hospital*) patient.
enfilar [enfēlár'] *vt* (*aguja*) to thread; (*calle*) to go down.
enflaquecer [enflákeser'] *vt* (*adelgazar*) to make thin; (*debilitar*) to weaken.
enflaquezca [enflákes'ká] *etc vb* V **enflaquecer**.
enfocar [enfokár'] *vt* (*foto etc*) to focus; (*problema etc*) to consider, look at.
enfoque [enfo'ke] *etc vb* V **enfocar** ♦ *nm* focus; (*acto*) focusing; (*óptica*) approach.
enfrascado, a [enfráská'tho, á] *a*: **estar ~ en algo** (*fig*) to be wrapped up in sth.
enfrascar [enfráskár'] *vt* to bottle; **~se** *vr*: **~se en un libro** to bury o.s. in a book.
enfrasque [enfrás'ke] *etc vb* V **enfrascar**.
enfrentamiento [enfrentámyen'to] *nm* confrontation.
enfrentar [enfrentár'] *vt* (*peligro*) to face (up to), confront; (*oponer*) to bring face to

face; **~se** *vr* (*dos personas*) to face o confront each other; (*DEPORTE: dos equipos*) to meet; **~se a** o **con** to face up to, confront.
enfrente [enfren'te] *ad* opposite; **~ de** *prep* opposite, facing; **la casa de ~** the house opposite, the house across the street.
enfriamiento [enfrēámyen'to] *nm* chilling, refrigeration; (*MED*) cold, chill.
enfriar [enfrēár'] *vt* (*alimentos*) to cool, chill; (*algo caliente*) to cool down; (*habitación*) to air, freshen; (*entusiasmo*) to dampen; **~se** *vr* to cool down; (*MED*) to get chilled (*US*), catch a chill (*Brit*); (*amistad*) to cool.
enfurecer [enfōōreser'] *vt* to enrage, madden; **~se** *vr* to become furious, fly into a rage; (*mar*) to get rough.
enfurezca [enfōōres'ká] *etc vb* V **enfurecer**.
engalanar [engálánár'] *vt* (*adornar*) to adorn; (*ciudad*) to decorate; **~se** *vr* to get dressed up.
enganchar [engántchár'] *vt* to hook; (*ropa*) to hang up; (*dos vagones*) to hitch up; (*TEC*) to couple, connect; (*MIL*) to recruit; (*fam: atraer: persona*) to rope into; **~se** *vr* (*MIL*) to enlist, join up; **~se (a)** (*drogas*) to get hooked (on).
enganche [engántch'e] *nm* hook; (*TEC*) coupling, connection; (*acto*) hooking (up); (*MIL*) recruitment, enlistment; (*AM: depósito*) deposit.
engañar [engáñár'] *vt* to deceive; (*estafar*) to cheat, swindle ♦ *vi*: **las apariencias engañan** appearances are deceptive; **~se** *vr* (*equivocarse*) to be wrong; (*asimismo*) to deceive o kid o.s.; **engaña a su mujer** he's unfaithful to o cheats on his wife.
engaño [engá'nyo] *nm* deceit; (*estafa*) trick, swindle; (*error*) mistake, misunderstanding; (*ilusión*) delusion.
engañoso, a [engányo'so, á] *a* (*tramposo*) crooked; (*mentiroso*) dishonest, deceitful; (*aspecto*) deceptive; (*consejo*) misleading.
engarce [engár'se] *etc vb* V **engarzar**.
engarzar [engársár'] *vt* (*joya*) to set, mount; (*fig*) to link, connect.
engatusar [engátōōsár'] *vt* (*fam*) to coax.
engendrar [enhendrár'] *vt* to breed; (*procrear*) to beget; (*fig*) to cause, produce.
engendro [enhen'dro] *nm* (*BIO*) fetus; (*fig*) monstrosity; (*idea*) brainchild.
englobar [englohár'] *vt* (*comprender*) to include, comprise; (*incluir*) to lump together.
engomar [engomár'] *vt* to glue, stick.
engordar [engorthár'] *vt* to fatten ♦ *vi* to get fat, put on weight.
engorro [engo'rro] *nm* bother, nuisance.
engorroso, a [engorro'so, á] *a* bothersome, trying.
engranaje [engráná'he] *nm* (*AUTO*) gear;

(*juego*) gears *pl*.

engrandecer [engrándeser'] *vt* to enlarge, magnify; (*alabar*) to praise, speak highly of; (*exagerar*) to exaggerate.

engrandezca [engrándes'ká] *etc vb* V **engrandecer.**

engrasar [engrásár'] *vt* (TEC: *poner grasa*) to grease; (: *lubricar*) to lubricate, oil; (*manchar*) to make greasy.

engrase [engrá'se] *nm* greasing, lubrication.

engreído, a [engreē'tho, á] *a* vain, conceited.

engrosar [engrosár'] *vt* (*ensanchar*) to enlarge; (*aumentar*) to increase; (*hinchar*) to swell.

engrudo [engrōō'tho] *nm* paste.

engruese [engrwe'se] *etc vb* V **engrosar.**

engullir [engōōyēr'] *vt* to gobble, gulp (down).

enhebrar [enebrár'] *vt* to thread.

enhiesto, a [enye'sto, á] *a* (*derecho*) erect; (*bandera*) raised; (*edificio*) lofty.

enhorabuena [enoráhwe'ná] *excl* congratulations.

enigma [enēg'má] *nm* enigma; (*problema*) puzzle; (*misterio*) mystery.

enigmático, a [enēgmá'tēko, á] *a* enigmatic.

enjabonar [enháhonár'] *vt* to soap; (*barba*) to lather; (*fam: adular*) to soft-soap; (: *regañar*) to tick off.

enjalbegar [enhálhegár'] *vt* (*pared*) to whitewash.

enjalbegue [enhálhe'ge] *etc vb* V **enjalbegar.**

enjambre [enhám'bre] *nm* swarm.

enjaular [enháōōlár'] *vt* to (put in a) cage; (*fam*) to jail, lock up.

enjuagadientes [enhwágádyen'tes] *nm inv* mouthwash.

enjuagar [enhwágár'] *vt* (*ropa*) to rinse (out).

enjuague [enhwá'ge] *etc vb* V **enjuagar ♦** *nm* (MED) mouthwash; (*de ropa*) rinse, rinsing.

enjugar [enhōōgár'] *vt* to wipe (off); (*lágrimas*) to dry; (*déficit*) to wipe out.

enjugue [enhōō'ge] *etc vb* V **enjugar.**

enjuiciar [enhwēsyár'] *vt* (JUR: *procesar*) to prosecute, try; (*fig*) to judge.

enjuto, a [enhōō'to, á] *a* dry, dried up; (*fig*) lean, skinny.

enlace [enlá'se] *etc vb* V **enlazar ♦** *nm* link, connection; (*relación*) relationship; (*tb:* **matrimonial**) marriage; (*de trenes*) connection; **~ de datos** data link; **~ sindical** shop steward; **~ telefónico** telephone link-up.

enlazar [enlásár'] *vt* (*unir con lazos*) to bind together; (*atar*) to tie; (*conectar*) to link, connect; (AM) to lasso.

enlodar [enlothár'] *vt* to cover in mud; (*fig: manchar*) to stain; (: *rebajar*) to debase.

enloquecer [enlokeser'] *vt* to drive mad ♦ *vi,* **~se** *vr* to go mad.

enloquezca [enlokes'ká] *etc vb* V **enloquecer.**

enlutado, a [enlōōtá'tho, á] *a* (*persona*) in mourning.

enlutar [enlōōtár'] *vt* to dress in mourning; **~se** *vr* to go into mourning.

enmarañar [enmárányár'] *vt* (*enredar*) to tangle up, entangle; (*complicar*) to complicate; (*confundir*) to confuse; **~se** *vr* (*enredarse*) to become entangled; (*confundirse*) to get confused.

enmarcar [enmárkár'] *vt* (*cuadro*) to frame; (*fig*) to provide a setting for.

enmarque [enmár'ke] *etc vb* V **enmarcar.**

enmascarar [enmáskárár'] *vt* to mask; (*intenciones*) to disguise; **~se** *vr* to put on a mask.

enmendar [enmendár'] *vt* to emend, correct; (*constitución etc*) to amend; (*comportamiento*) to reform; **~se** *vr* to reform, mend one's ways.

enmienda [enmyen'dá] *etc vb* V **enmendar ♦** *nf* correction; amendment; reform.

enmohecerse [enmocser'se] *vr* (*metal*) to rust, go rusty; (*muro, plantas*) to go moldy.

enmohezca [enmoes'ká] *etc vb* V **enmohecerse.**

enmudecer [enmōōtheser'] *vt* to silence ♦ *vi,* **~se** *vr* (*perder el habla*) to fall silent; (*guardar silencio*) to remain silent; (*por miedo*) to be struck dumb.

enmudezca [enmōōthes'ká] *etc vb* V **enmudecer.**

ennegrecer [ennegreser'] *vt* (*poner negro*) to blacken; (*oscurecer*) to darken; **~se** *vr* to turn black; (*oscurecerse*) to get dark, darken.

ennegrezca [ennegres'ká] *etc vb* V **ennegrecer.**

ennoblecer [ennohleser'] *vt* to ennoble.

ennoblezca [ennohles'ká] *etc vb* V **ennoblecer.**

en.º *abr* (= *enero*) Jan.

enojadizo, a [enoháthē'so, á] *a* irritable, short-tempered.

enojar [enohár'] *vt* (*encolerizar*) to anger; (*disgustar*) to annoy, upset; **~se** *vr* to get angry; to get annoyed.

enojo [eno'ho] *nm* (*cólera*) anger; (*irritación*) annoyance; **~s** *nmpl* trials, problems.

enojoso, a [enoho'so, á] *a* annoying.

enorgullecerse [enorgōōyeser'se] *vr* to be proud; **~ de** to pride o.s. on, be proud of.

enorgullezca [enorgōōyes'ká] *etc vb* V **enorgullecerse.**

enorme [enor'me] *a* enormous, huge; (*fig*)

monstrous.

enormidad [enormētháth'] *nf* hugeness, immensity.

enraice [enráē'se] *etc vb* V **enraizar**.

enraizar [enráēsár'] *vi* to take root.

enrarecido, a [enráresē'tho, á] *a* rarefied.

enredadera [enretháthe'rá] *nf* (*BOT*) creeper, climbing plant.

enredar [enrethár'] *vt* (*cables, hilos etc*) to tangle (up), entangle; (*situación*) to complicate, confuse; (*meter cizaña*) to sow discord among *o* between; (*implicar*) to embroil, implicate; ~**se** *vr* to get entangled, get tangled (up); (*situación*) to get complicated; (*persona*) to get embroiled; (*AM: fam*) to meddle.

enredo [enre'tho] *nm* (*maraña*) tangle; (*confusión*) mix-up, confusion; (*intriga*) intrigue; (*apuro*) jam; (*amorío*) love affair.

enrejado [enrehá'tho] *nm* grating; (*de ventana*) lattice; (*en jardín*) trellis.

enrevesado, a [enrehesá'tho, á] *a* (*asunto*) complicated, involved.

enriquecer [enrēkeser'] *vt* to make rich; (*fig*) to enrich; ~**se** *vr* to get rich.

enriquezca [enrēkes'ká] *etc vb* V **enriquecer**.

enrojecer [enroheser'] *vt* to redden ♦ *vi*, ~**se** *vr* (*persona*) to blush.

enrojezca [enrohes'ká] *etc vb* V **enrojecer**.

enrolar [enrolár'] *vt* (*MIL*) to enlist; (*reclutar*) to recruit; ~**se** *vr* (*MIL*) to join up; (*afiliarse*) to enrol, sign on.

enrollar [enroyár'] *vt* to roll (up), wind (up); ~**se** *vr*: ~**se con uno** to get involved with sb.

enroque [enro'ke] *nm* (*AJEDREZ*) castling.

enroscar [enroskár'] *vt* (*torcer, doblar*) to twist; (*arrollar*) to coil (round), wind; (*tornillo, rosca*) to screw in; ~**se** *vr* to coil, wind.

enrosque [enros'ke] *etc vb* V **enroscar**.

ensalada [ensálá'thá] *nf* salad; (*lío*) mix-up.

ensaladilla [ensáláthē'yá] *nf* (*tb*: ~ **rusa**) ≈ Russian salad.

ensalce [ensál'se] *etc vb* V **ensalzar**.

ensalzar [ensálsár'] *vt* (*alabar*) to praise, extol; (*exaltar*) to exalt.

ensamblador [ensámbláthor'] *nm* (*INFORM*) assembler.

ensambladura [ensámbláthōō'rá] *nf*, **ensamblaje** [ensámblá'he] *nm* assembly; (*TEC*) joint.

ensamblar [ensámblár'] *vt* (*montar*) to assemble; (*madera etc*) to join.

ensanchar [ensántchár'] *vt* (*hacer más ancho*) to widen; (*agrandar*) to enlarge, expand; (*COSTURA*) to let out; ~**se** *vr* to get wider, expand; (*pey*) to put on airs.

ensanche [ensántch'e] *nm* (*de calle*) widening; (*de negocio*) expansion.

ensangrentado, a [ensángrentá'tho, á] *a* bloodstained, covered with blood.

ensangrentar [ensángrentár'] *vt* to stain with blood.

ensangriente [ensángryen'te] *etc vb* V **ensangrentar**.

ensañar [ensáñár'] *vt* to enrage; ~**se** *vr*: ~**se con** to treat brutally.

ensartar [ensártár'] *vt* (*gen*) to string (together); (*carne*) to spit, skewer.

ensayar [ensáyár'] *vt* to test, try (out); (*TEATRO*) to rehearse.

ensayista [ensáyē'stá] *nm/f* essayist.

ensayo [ensá'yo] *nm* test, trial; (*QUÍMICA*) experiment; (*TEATRO*) rehearsal; (*DEPORTE*) try; (*ESCOL, LITERATURA*) essay; **pedido de** ~ (*COM*) trial order; ~ **general** (*TEATRO*) dress rehearsal; (*MUS*) full rehearsal.

ensenada [ensená'thá] *nf* inlet, cove.

enseña [ense'nyá] *nf* ensign, standard.

enseñante [ensenyán'te] *nm/f* teacher.

enseñanza [ensenyán'sá] *nf* (*educación*) education; (*acción*) teaching; (*doctrina*) teaching, doctrine; ~ **primaria/secundaria/superior** primary/secondary/higher education.

enseñar [ensenyár'] *vt* (*educar*) to teach; (*instruir*) to teach, instruct; (*mostrar, señalar*) to show.

enseres [ense'res] *nmpl* belongings.

ENSIDESA [ensēthe'sá] *abr* (*Esp COM*) = *Empresa Nacional Siderúrgica, S. A.*

ensillar [ensēyár'] *vt* to saddle (up).

ensimismarse [ensēmēsmár'se] *vr* (*abstraerse*) to become lost in thought; (*estar absorto*) to be lost in thought; (*AM*) to become conceited.

ensordecer [ensortheser'] *vt* to deafen ♦ *vi* to go deaf.

ensordezca [ensorthes'ká] *etc vb* V **ensordecer**.

ensortijado, a [ensortēhá'tho, á] *a* (*pelo*) curly.

ensuciar [ensōōsyár'] *vt* (*manchar*) to dirty, soil; (*fig*) to defile; ~**se** *vr* (*mancharse*) to get dirty; (*niño*) to dirty (*o* wet) o.s.

ensueño [enswe'nyo] *nm* (*sueño*) dream, fantasy; (*ilusión*) illusion; (*soñando despierto*) daydream; **de** ~ dream-like.

entablado [entáblá'tho] *nm* (*piso*) floorboards *pl*; (*armazón*) boarding.

entablar [entáblár'] *vt* (*recubrir*) to board (up); (*AJEDREZ, DAMAS*) to set up; (*conversación*) to strike up; (*JUR*) to file ♦ *vi* to draw.

entablillar [entáblēyár'] *vt* (*MED*) to (put in a) splint.

entallar [entáyár'] *vt* (*traje*) to tailor ♦ *vi*: **el traje entalla bien** the suit fits well.

ente [en'te] *nm* (*organización*) body, organization; (*compañía*) company; (*fam: persona*) odd character; (*ser*) being; ~ **público** (*Esp*) state(-owned) body.

entender [entender'] *vt* (*comprender*) to understand; (*darse cuenta*) to realize; (*querer decir*) to mean ♦ *vi* to understand; (*creer*) to think, believe ♦ *nm*: **a mi** ~ in my opinion; ~ **de** to know all about; ~ **algo de** to know a little about; ~ **en** to deal with, have to do with; ~**se** *vr* (*comprenderse*) to be understood; (*2 personas*) to get on together; (*ponerse de acuerdo*) to agree, reach an agreement; **dar a** ~ **que ...** to lead to believe that ...; ~**se mal** not to get along; **¿entiendes?** (do you) understand?

entendido, a [entendē'ðo, á] *a* (*comprendido*) understood; (*hábil*) skilled; (*inteligente*) knowledgeable ♦ *nm/f* (*experto*) expert ♦ *excl* agreed!

entendimiento [entendēmyen'to] *nm* (*comprensión*) understanding; (*inteligencia*) mind, intellect; (*juicio*) judgement.

enterado, a [entera'ðo, á] *a* well-informed; **estar** ~ **de** to know about, be aware of; **no darse por** ~ to pretend not to understand.

enteramente [enterámen'te] *ad* entirely, completely.

enterar [enterár'] *vt* (*informar*) to inform, tell; ~**se** *vr*: ~**se de** to find out about.

entereza [entere'sá] *nf* (*totalidad*) entirety; (*fig: carácter*) strength of mind; (*honradez*) integrity.

enternecedor, a [enterneseðor', á] *a* touching.

enternecer [enterneser'] *vt* (*ablandar*) to soften; (*apiadar*) to touch, move; ~**se** *vr* to be touched, be moved.

enternezca [enternes'ká] *etc vb V* **enternecer.**

entero, a [ente'ro, á] *a* (*total*) whole, entire; (*fig: recto*) honest; (: *firme*) firm, resolute ♦ *nm* (*MAT*) integer; (*COM: punto*) point; (*AM: pago*) payment; **las acciones han subido dos** ~**s** the shares have gone up two points.

enterrador [enterráðor'] *nm* gravedigger.

enterrar [enterrár'] *vt* to bury; (*fig*) to forget.

entibiar [entēßyár'] *vt* (*enfriar*) to cool; (*calentar*) to warm; ~**se** *vr* (*fig*) to cool.

entidad [entēðáth'] *nf* (*empresa*) firm, company; (*organismo*) body; (*sociedad*) society; (*FILOSOFÍA*) entity.

entienda [entyen'dá] *etc vb V* **entender.**

entierro [entye'rro] *etc vb V* **enterrar** ♦ *nm* (*acción*) burial; (*funeral*) funeral.

entomología [entomolohe'á] *nf* entomology.

entomólogo, a [entomo'logo, á] *nm/f* entomologist.

entonación [entonásyon'] *nf* (*LING*) intonation; (*fig*) conceit.

entonar [entonár'] *vt* (*canción*) to intone; (*colores*) to tone; (*MED*) to tone up ♦ *vi* to be in tune; ~**se** *vr* (*engreírse*) to put on airs.

entonces [enton'ses] *ad* then, at that time; **desde** ~ since then; **en aquel** ~ at that time; (**pues**) ~ and so; **el** ~ **embajador de España** the then Spanish ambassador.

entornar [entornár'] *vt* (*puerta, ventana*) to half close, leave ajar; (*los ojos*) to half-close.

entorno [entor'no] *nm* setting, environment; ~ **de redes** (*INFORM*) network environment.

entorpecer [entorpeser'] *vt* (*entendimiento*) to dull; (*impedir*) to obstruct, hinder; (: *tránsito*) to slow down, delay.

entorpezca [entorpes'ká] *etc vb V* **entorpecer.**

entrado, a [entrá'ðo, á] *a*: ~ **en años** elderly; (**una vez**) ~ **el verano** in the summer(time), when summer comes ♦ *nf* (*acción*) entry, access; (*sitio*) entrance, way in; (*principio*) beginning; (*COM*) receipts *pl*, takings *pl*; (*CULIN*) entrée; (*DEPORTE*) innings *sg*; (*TEATRO*) house, audience; (*para el cine etc*) ticket; (*INFORM*) input; (*ECON*): **entradas** *nfpl* income *sg*; **entradas brutas** gross receipts; **entradas y salidas** (*COM*) income and expenditure; **entrada de aire** (*TEC*) air intake o inlet; **de entrada** right away; "**entrada gratis**" "admission free"; **entrada de datos vocal** (*INFORM*) voice input; **tiene entradas** he's losing his hair.

entrante [entrán'te] *a* next, coming; (*POL*) incoming ♦ *nm* inlet; (*CULIN*) starter; **mes/año** ~ next month/year.

entraña [entrá'nyá] *nf* (*fig: centro*) heart, core; (*raíz*) root; ~**s** *nfpl* (*ANAT*) entrails; (*fig*) heart *sg*.

entrañable [entrányá'ßle] *a* close, intimate.

entrañar [entrányár'] *vt* to entail.

entrar [entrár'] *vt* (*introducir*) to bring in; (*persona*) to show in; (*INFORM*) to input ♦ *vi* (*meterse*) to go o come in, enter; (*comenzar*): ~ **diciendo** to begin by saying; **le entraron ganas de reír** he felt a sudden urge to laugh; **no me entra** I can't get the hang of it.

entre [en'tre] *prep* (*dos*) between; (*en medio de*) among(st); (*por*): **se abrieron paso** ~ **la multitud** they forced their way through the crowd; ~ **una cosa y otra** what with one thing and another.

entreabierto [entreáßyer'to] *pp de* **entreabrir.**

entreabrir [entreáßrēr'] *vt* to half-open, open halfway.

entreacto [entreák'to] *nm* interval.

entrecano, a [entrekáʹno, á] *a* graying (*US*), greying (*Brit*); **ser ~** (*persona*) to be going gray.

entrecejo [entreseʹho] *nm*: **fruncir el ~** to frown.

entrecomillado, a [entrekoméyáʹʧo, á] *a* in quotation marks.

entrecortado, a [entrekortáʹʧo, á] *a* (*respiración*) labored (*US*), laboured (*Brit*), difficult; (*habla*) faltering.

entrecot [entrekoʹ(t)] *nm* (*CULIN*) sirloin steak.

entrecruce [entrekrōōʹse] *etc vb V* **entrecruzarse.**

entrecruzarse [entrekrōōsárʹse] *vr* (*BIO*) to interbreed.

entrechocar [entretchokárʹ] *vi* (*dientes*) to chatter.

entrechoque [entretchoʹke] *etc vb V* **entrechocar.**

entredicho [entreʧéʹtch'o] *nm* (*JUR*) injunction; **poner en ~** to cast doubt on; **estar en ~** to be in doubt.

entrega [entreʹgá] *nf* (*de mercancías*) delivery; (*de premios*) presentation; (*de novela etc*) installment (*US*), instalment (*Brit*); **"~ a domicilio"** "home delivery service".

entregar [entregárʹ] *vt* (*dar*) to hand (over), deliver; (*ejercicios*) to hand in; **~se** *vr* (*rendirse*) to surrender, give in, submit; **~se a** (*dedicarse*) to devote o.s. to; **a ~** (*COM*) to be supplied.

entregue [entreʹge] *etc vb V* **entregar.**

entrelace [entreláʹse] *etc vb V* **entrelazar.**

entrelazar [entrelásárʹ] *vt* to entwine.

entremedias [entremeʹʧyás] *ad* (*en medio*) in between, halfway.

entremeses [entremeʹses] *nmpl* hors d'œuvres.

entremeter [entremeterʹ] *vt* to insert, put in; **~se** *vr* to meddle, interfere.

entremetido, a [entremetéʹʧo, á] *a* meddling, interfering.

entremezclar [entremesklárʹ] *vt*, **~se** *vr* to intermingle.

entrenador, a [entrenáʹʧor, á] *nm/f* trainer, coach.

entrenamiento [entrenámyenʹto] *nm* training.

entrenar [entrenárʹ] *vt* (*DEPORTE*) to train; (*caballo*) to exercise; **~se** *vr* to train.

entrepierna [entrepyerʹná] *nf* (*tb:* **~s**) crotch.

entresacar [entresákárʹ] *vt* to pick out, select.

entresaque [entresáʹke] *etc vb V* **entresacar.**

entresuelo [entresweʹlo] *nm* mezzanine, entresol; (*TEATRO*) dress *o* first circle.

entretanto [entretánʹto] *ad* meanwhile, meantime.

entretejer [entreteherʹ] *vt* to interweave.

entretela [entreteʹlá] *nf* (*de ropa*) interlining; **~s** *nfpl* heart-strings.

entretendré [entretendreʹ] *etc vb V* **entretener.**

entretener [entretenerʹ] *vt* (*divertir*) to entertain, amuse; (*detener*) to hold up, delay; (*mantener*) to maintain; **~se** *vr* (*divertirse*) to amuse o.s.; (*retrasarse*) to delay, linger; **no le entretengo más** I won't keep you any longer.

entretenga [entretenʹgá] *etc vb V* **entretener.**

entretenido, a [entretenéʹʧo, á] *a* entertaining, amusing.

entretenimiento [entretenēmyenʹto] *nm* entertainment, amusement; (*mantenimiento*) upkeep, maintenance.

entretiene [entretyeʹne] *etc*, **entretuve** [entretōōʹʋe] *etc vb V* **entretener.**

entreveía [entreʋeēʹá] *etc vb V* **entrever.**

entrever [entreʋerʹ] *vt* to glimpse, catch a glimpse of.

entrevista [entreʋēʹstá] *nf* interview.

entrevistar [entreʋēstárʹ] *vt* to interview; **~se** *vr*: **~se con** to have an interview with, see; **el ministro se entrevistó con el Rey ayer** the minister had an audience with the King yesterday.

entrevisto [entreʋēʹsto] *pp de* **entrever.**

entristecer [entrēsteserʹ] *vt* to sadden, grieve; **~se** *vr* to grow sad.

entristezca [entrēstesʹká] *etc vb V* **entristecer.**

entrometerse [entrometerʹse] *vr*: **~ (en)** to interfere (in *o* with).

entrometido, a [entrometéʹʧo, á] *a* interfering, meddlesome.

entroncar [entronkárʹ] *vi* to be connected *o* related.

entronque [entronʹke] *etc vb V* **entroncar.**

entuerto [entwerʹto] *nm* wrong, injustice; **~s** *nmpl* (*MED*) afterpains.

entumecer [entōōmeserʹ] *vt* to numb, benumb; **~se** *vr* (*por el frío*) to go *o* become numb.

entumecido, a [entōōmesēʹʧo, á] *a* numb, stiff.

entumezca [entōōmesʹká] *etc vb V* **entumecer.**

enturbiar [entōōrʰyárʹ] *vt* (*el agua*) to make cloudy; (*fig*) to confuse; **~se** *vr* (*oscurecerse*) to become cloudy; (*fig*) to get confused, become obscure.

entusiasmar [entōōsyásmárʹ] *vt* to excite, fill with enthusiasm; (*gustar mucho*) to delight; **~se** *vr*: **~se con** *o* **por** to get enthusiastic *o* excited about.

entusiasmo [entōōsyàsʹmo] *nm* enthusiasm; (*excitación*) excitement.

entusiasta [entōōsyáʹstá] *a* enthusiastic ◆

nm/f enthusiast.

enumerar [enōōmerár'] *vt* to enumerate.

enunciación [enōōnsyàsyon'] *nf*, **enunciado** [enōōnsyá'tho] *nm* enunciation; (*declaración*) declaration, statement.

enunciar [enōōnsyàr'] *vt* to enunciate; to declare, state.

envainar [embáênár'] *vt* to sheathe.

envalentonar [embálentonár'] *vt* to give courage to; ~**se** *vr* (*pey*: *jactarse*) to boast, brag.

envanecer [embáneser'] *vt* to make conceited; ~**se** *vr* to grow conceited.

envanezca [embánes'kà] *etc vb* V **envanecer.**

envasar [embásàr'] *vt* (*empaquetar*) to pack, wrap; (*enfrascar*) to bottle; (*enlatar*) to can; (*embolsar*) to pocket.

envase [embá'se] *nm* packing, wrapping; bottling; canning; pocketing; (*recipiente*) container; (*paquete*) package; (*botella*) bottle; (*lata*) can, tin (*Brit*).

envejecido, a [embehesē'tho, à] *a* old, aged; (*de aspecto*) old-looking.

envejecer [embeheser'] *vt* to make old, age ♦ *vi*, ~**se** *vr* (*volverse viejo*) to grow old; (*parecer viejo*) to age.

envejezca [embehes'kà] *etc vb* V **envejecer.**

envenenar [embenenàr'] *vt* to poison; (*fig*) to embitter.

envergadura [embergàthōō'rà] *nf* (*expansión*) expanse; (*NAUT*) breadth; (*fig*) scope; **un programa de gran** ~ a wide-ranging program.

envés [embes'] *nm* (*de tela*) back, wrong side.

enviado, a [embyà'tho, à] *nm/f* (*POL*) envoy; ~ **especial** (*de periódico*, *TV*) special correspondent.

enviar [embyàr'] *vt* to send.

enviciar [embēsyàr'] *vt* to corrupt ♦ *vi* (*trabajo etc*) to be addictive; ~**se** *vr*: ~**se** (**con** *o* **en**) to get addicted (to).

envidia [embē'thyà] *nf* envy; **tener** ~ **a** to envy, be jealous of.

envidiar [embēthyàr'] *vt* (*desear*) to envy; (*tener celos de*) to be jealous of.

envidioso, a [embēthyo'so, à] *a* envious, jealous.

envío [embē'o] *nm* (*acción*) sending; (*de mercancías*) consignment; (*de dinero*) remittance; (*en barco*) shipment; **gastos de** ~ postage and handling (*US*) *o* packing (*Brit*); ~ **contra reembolso** COD shipment.

enviudar [embyōōthàr'] *vi* to be widowed.

envoltura [emboltōō'rà] *nf* (*cobertura*) cover; (*embalaje*) wrapper, wrapping.

envolver [embolher'] *vt* to wrap (up); (*cubrir*) to cover; (*enemigo*) to surround; (*implicar*) to involve, implicate.

envuelto [embwel'to], **envuelva** [embwel'hà] *etc vb* V **envolver.**

enyesar [enyesàr'] *vt* (*pared*) to plaster; (*MED*) to cast (*US*), put in plaster (*Brit*).

enzarzarse [ensàrsár'se] *vr*: ~ **en algo** to get mixed up in sth.

E.P.D. *abr* (= *en paz descanse*) R.I.P.

épico, a [e'pēko, à] *a* epic ♦ *nf* epic (poetry).

epidemia [epēthe'myà] *nf* epidemic.

epidémico, a [epēthe'mēko, à] *a* epidemic.

epifanía [epēfánē'à] *nf* Epiphany.

epilepsia [epēlep'syà] *nf* epilepsy.

epílogo [epē'logo] *nm* epilogue.

episcopado [epēskopá'tho] *nm* (*cargo*) bishopric; (*obispos*) bishops *pl* (*collectively*).

episodio [epēso'thyo] *nm* episode; (*suceso*) incident.

epístola [epē'stolà] *nf* epistle.

epitafio [epētá'fyo] *nm* epitaph.

época [e'pokà] *nf* period, time; (*temporada*) season; (*HISTORIA*) age, epoch; **hacer** ~ to be epoch-making.

equidad [ekēthàth'] *nf* equity, fairness.

equilibrar [ekēlēbrár'] *vt* to balance.

equilibrio [ekēlēb'ryo] *nm* balance, equilibrium; ~ **político** balance of power.

equilibrista [ekēlēbrē'stá] *nm/f* (*funámbulo*) tightrope walker; (*acróbata*) acrobat.

equinoccio [ekēnok'syo] *nm* equinox.

equipaje [ekēpá'he] *nm* baggage (*US*), luggage (*Brit*); (*avíos*) equipment, kit; ~ **de mano** hand luggage; **hacer el** ~ to pack.

equipar [ekēpàr'] *vt* (*proveer*) to equip.

equiparar [ekēpárár'] *vt* (*igualar*) to put on the same level; (*comparar*) to compare (*con* with); ~**se** *vr*: ~**se con** to be on a level with.

equipo [ekē'po] *nm* (*conjunto de cosas*) equipment; (*DEPORTE*, *grupo*) team; (*de obreros*) shift; (*de máquinas*) plant; (*turbinas etc*) set; ~ **de caza** hunting gear; ~ **físico** (*INFORM*) hardware; ~ **médico** medical team.

equis [e'kēs] *nf* (the letter) X.

equitación [ekētàsyon'] *nf* (*acto*) riding; (*arte*) horsemanship.

equitativo, a [ekētátē'ho, à] *a* equitable, fair.

equivaldré [ekēhàldre'] *etc vb* V **equivaler.**

equivalencia [ekēhálen'syà] *nf* equivalence.

equivalente [ekēhàlen'te] *a*, *nm* equivalent.

equivaler [ekēhàler'] *vi*: ~ **a** to be equivalent *o* equal to; (*en rango*) to rank as.

equivalga [ekēhàl'gà] *etc vb* V **equivaler.**

equivocación [ekēhokàsyon'] *nf* mistake, error; (*malentendido*) misunderstanding.

equivocado, a [ekēhokà'tho, à] *a* wrong, mistaken.

equivocarse [ekēhokár'se] *vr* to be wrong, make a mistake; ~ **de camino** to take the wrong road.

equívoco, a [ekē'hoko, á] *a* (*dudoso*) suspect; (*ambiguo*) ambiguous ♦ *nm* ambiguity; (*malentendido*) misunderstanding.

equivoque [ekēho'ke] *etc vb* V **equivocar**.

era [e'rá] *vb* V **ser** ♦ *nf* era, age; (*AGR*) threshing floor.

erais [e'ráes], **éramos** [e'rámos], **eran** [e'rán] *vb* V **ser**.

erario [e'ráryo] *nm* exchequer, treasury.

eras [e'rás], **eres** [e'res] *vb* V **ser**.

ergonomía [ergonomē'á] *nf* ergonomics *sg*, human engineering.

erguir [ergēr'] *vt* to raise, lift; (*poner derecho*) to straighten; ~**se** *vr* to straighten up.

erice [erē'se] *etc vb* V **erizarse**.

erigir [erēhēr'] *vt* to erect, build; ~**se** *vr*: ~**se en** to set o.s. up as.

erija [erē'há] *etc vb* V **erigir**.

erizado, a [erēsá'tho, á] *a* bristly.

erizarse [erēsár'se] *vr* (*pelo: de perro*) to bristle; (: *de persona*) to stand on end.

erizo [erē'so] *nm* hedgehog; ~ **de mar** sea urchin.

ermita [ermē'tá] *nf* hermitage.

ermitaño, a [ermētá'nyo, á] *nm/f* hermit.

erosionar [erosyonár'] *vt* to erode.

erótico, a [ero'tēko, á] *a* erotic.

erotismo [erotēs'mo] *nm* eroticism.

erradicar [errátĥēkár'] *vt* to eradicate.

erradique [errátĥē'ke] *etc vb* V **erradicar**.

errado, a [errá'tho, á] *a* mistaken, wrong.

errante [errán'te] *a* wandering, errant.

errar [errár'] *vi* (*vagar*) to wander, roam; (*equivocarse*) to be mistaken ♦ *vt*: ~ **el camino** to take the wrong road; ~ **el tiro** to miss.

errata [errá'tá] *nf* misprint.

erre [e'rre] *nf* (the letter) R; ~ **que** ~ stubbornly.

erróneo, a [erro'neo, á] *a* (*equivocado*) wrong, mistaken; (*falso*) false, untrue.

error [error'] *nm* error, mistake; (*INFORM*) bug; ~ **de imprenta** misprint; ~ **de lectura/escritura** (*INFORM*) read/write error; ~ **sintáctico** syntax error; ~ **judicial** miscarriage of justice.

eructar [erooktár'] *vt* to belch, burp.

erudición [erootĥēsyon'] *nf* erudition, learning.

erudito, a [erootĥē'to, á] *a* erudite, learned ♦ *nm/f* scholar; **los** ~**s en esta materia** the experts in this field.

erupción [eroopsyon'] *nf* eruption; (*MED*) rash; (*de violencia*) outbreak; (*de ira*) outburst.

es [es] *vb* V **ser**.

E/S *abr* (*INFORM*: *entrada/salida*) I/O.

esa [e'sá], **esas** [e'sás] *a demostrativo* V **ese**.

ésa [e'sá], **ésas** [e'sás] *pron* V **ése**.

esbelto, a [esbel'to, á] *a* slim, slender.

esbirro [esbē'rro] *nm* henchman.

esbozar [esbosár'] *vt* to sketch, outline.

esbozo [esbo'so] *nm* sketch, outline.

escabeche [eskábetch'e] *nm* brine; (*de aceitunas etc*) pickle; **en** ~ pickled.

escabechina [eskábetchē'ná] *nf* (*batalla*) massacre; **hacer una** ~ (*ESCOL*) to fail a lot of students.

escabroso, a [eskábro'so, á] *a* (*accidentado*) rough, uneven; (*fig*) tough, difficult; (: *atrevido*) risqué.

escabullirse [eskábooyēr'se] *vr* to slip away; (*largarse*) to clear out.

escafandra [eskáfán'drá] *nf* (*buzo*) diving suit; (~ *espacial*) spacesuit.

escala [eská'lá] *nf* (*proporción, MUS*) scale; (*de mano*) ladder; (*AVIAT*) stopover; (*de colores etc*) range; ~ **de tiempo** time scale; ~ **de sueldos** salary scale; **una investigación a** ~ **nacional** a nationwide inquiry; **reproducir según** ~ to reproduce to scale; **hacer** ~ **en** to stop off o over at.

escalada [eskálá'thá] *nf* (*de montaña*) climb; (*de pared*) scaling.

escalafón [eskálafon'] *nm* (*escala de salarios*) salary scale, wage scale.

escalar [eskálár'] *vt* to climb, scale ♦ *vi* (*MIL, POL*) to escalate.

escaldar [eskáldár'] *vt* (*quemar*) to scald; (*escarmentar*) to teach a lesson.

escalera [eskále'rá] *nf* stairs *pl*, staircase; (*escala*) ladder; (*NAIPES*) run; (*de camión*) tailgate; ~ **mecánica** escalator; ~ **de caracol** spiral staircase; ~ **de incendios** fire escape.

escalfar [eskálfár'] *vt* (*huevos*) to poach.

escalinata [eskálēná'tá] *nf* staircase.

escalofriante [eskálofryán'te] *a* chilling.

escalofrío [eskálofrē'o] *nm* (*MED*) chill; ~**s** *nmpl* (*fig*) shivers.

escalón [eskálon'] *nm* step, stair; (*de escalera*) rung; (*fig: paso*) step; (*al éxito*) ladder.

escalonar [eskálonár'] *vt* to spread out; (*tierra*) to terrace; (*horas de trabajo*) to stagger.

escalope [eskálo'pe] *nm* (*CULIN*) cutlet (*US*), escalope (*Brit*).

escama [eská'má] *nf* (*de pez, serpiente*) scale; (*de jabón*) flake; (*fig*) resentment.

escamar [eskámár'] *vt* (*pez*) to scale; (*producir recelo*) to make wary.

escamotear [eskámoteár'] *vt* (*fam: robar*) to lift, swipe; (*hacer desaparecer*) to make disappear.

escampar [eskámpár'] *vb impersonal* to stop raining.

escanciar [eskánsyár'] *vt* (*vino*) to pour (out).

escandalice [eskándálḗ'se] *etc vb* **V escandalizar**.

escandalizar [eskándálēsár'] *vt* to scandalize, shock; **~se** *vr* to be shocked; (*ofenderse*) to be offended.

escándalo [eskán'dálo] *nm* scandal; (*alboroto, tumulto*) row, uproar; **armar un ~** to make a scene; **¡es un ~!** it's outrageous!

escandaloso, a [eskándálo'so, á] *a* scandalous, shocking; (*risa*) hearty; (*niño*) noisy.

Escandinavia [eskándēná'ḃyá] *nf* Scandinavia.

escandinavo, a [eskándēná'ḃo, á] *a, nm/f* Scandinavian.

escaño [eská'nyo] *nm* bench; (*POL*) seat.

escapada [eskápá'ḋá] *nf* (*huida*) escape, flight; (*deportes*) breakaway; (*viaje*) quick trip.

escapar [eskápár'] *vi* (*gen*) to escape, run away; (*DEPORTE*) to break away; **~se** *vr* to escape, get away; (*agua, gas, noticias*) to leak (out); **se me escapa su nombre** his name escapes me.

escaparate [eskápárá'te] *nm* shop window; (*COM*) showcase.

escapatoria [eskápáto'ryá] *nf*: **no tener ~** (*fig*) to have no way out.

escape [eská'pe] *nm* (*huida*) escape; (*de agua, gas*) leak; (*de motor*) exhaust; **salir a ~** to rush out.

escapismo [eskápēs'mo] *nm* escapism.

escarabajo [eskáráḃá'ho] *nm* beetle.

escaramuza [eskárámōō'sá] *nf* skirmish; (*fig*) brush.

escarbar [eskárḃár'] *vt* (*gallina*) to scratch; (*fig*) to inquire into, investigate.

escarcha [eskártch'á] *nf* frost.

escarlata [eskárlá'tá] *a inv* scarlet.

escarlatina [eskárlátē'ná] *nf* scarlet fever.

escarmentar [eskármentár'] *vt* to punish severely ♦ *vi* to learn one's lesson; **¡para que escarmientes!** that'll teach you!

escarmiento [eskármyen'to] *etc vb* **V escarmentar** ♦ *nm* (*ejemplo*) lesson; (*castigo*) punishment.

escarnio [eskár'nyo] *nm* mockery; (*injuria*) insult.

escarola [eskáro'lá] *nf* (*BOT*) endive.

escarpado, a [eskárpá'ḋo, á] *a* (*pendiente*) sheer, steep; (*rocas*) craggy.

escasamente [eskásámen'te] *ad* (*insuficientemente*) scantily; (*apenas*) scarcely.

escasear [eskáseár'] *vi* to be scarce.

escasez [eskáses'] *nf* (*falta*) shortage, scarcity; (*pobreza*) poverty; **vivir con ~** to live on next to nothing.

escaso, a [eská'so, á] *a* (*poco*) scarce; (*raro*) rare; (*ralo*) thin, sparse; (*limitado*) limited; (*recursos*) scanty; (*público*) sparse; (*posibilidad*) slim; (*visibilidad*) poor.

escatimar [eskátēmár'] *vt* (*limitar*) to skimp (on), be sparing with; **no ~ esfuerzos (para)** to spare no effort (to).

escayola [eskáyo'lá] *nf* cast (*US*), plaster (*Brit*).

escayolar [eskáyolár'] *vt* to cast (*US*), put in plaster (*Brit*).

escena [ese'ná] *nf* scene; (*decorado*) scenery; (*escenario*) stage; **poner en ~** to put on.

escenario [esená'ryo] *nm* (*TEATRO*) stage; (*CINE*) set; (*fig*) scene; **el ~ del crimen** the scene of the crime; **el ~ político** the political scene.

escenografía [esenográfē'á] *nf* set *o* stage design.

escepticismo [eseptēsēs'mo] *nm* scepticism.

escéptico, a [esep'tēko, á] *a* sceptical ♦ *nm/f* sceptic.

escindir [esēndēr'] *vt* to split; **~se** *vr* (*facción*) to split off; **~se en** to split into.

escisión [esēsyon'] *nf* (*MED*) excision; (*fig, POL*) split; **~ nuclear** nuclear fission.

esclarecer [eskláreser'] *vt* (*iluminar*) to light up, illuminate; (*misterio, problema*) to shed light on.

esclarezca [eskláres'ká] *etc vb* **V esclarecer**.

esclavice [eskláḃē'se] *etc vb* **V esclavizar**.

esclavitud [eskláḃētōōth'] *nf* slavery.

esclavizar [eskláḃēsár'] *vt* to enslave.

esclavo, a [esklá'ḃo, á] *nm/f* slave.

esclusa [esklōō'sá] *nf* (*de canal*) lock; (*compuerta*) floodgate.

escoba [esko'ḃá] *nf* broom; **pasar la ~** to sweep up.

escobazo [eskoḃá'so] *nm* (*golpe*) blow with a broom; **echar a uno a ~s** to kick sb out.

escocer [eskoser'] *vi* to burn, sting; **~se** *vr* to chafe, get chafed.

escocés, esa [eskoses', esá] *a* Scottish; (*whisky*) Scotch ♦ *nm/f* Scotsman/woman, Scot; (*whisky*) Scotch ♦ *nm* (*LING*) Scots *sg*; **tela escocesa** tartan.

Escocia [esko'syá] *nf* Scotland.

escoger [eskoher'] *vt* to choose, pick, select.

escogido, a [eskohē'ḋo, á] *a* chosen, selected; (*calidad*) choice, select; (*persona*): **ser muy ~** to be very fussy.

escoja [esko'há] *etc vb* **V escoger**.

escolar [eskolár'] *a* school *cpd* ♦ *nm/f* schoolboy/girl, pupil.

escolaridad [eskoláréthǎth'] *nf* schooling; **libro de ~** school record.

escolarización [eskolárēsásyon'] *nf*: **~ obligatoria** compulsory education.

escolarizado, a [eskolárēsá'ḋo, á] *a, nm/f*: **los ~s** those in *o* attending school.

escolta [eskol'tá] *nf* escort.

escoltar [eskoltár'] *vt* to escort; (*proteger*)

to guard.

escollo [esko'yo] *nm* (*arrecife*) reef, rock; (*fig*) pitfall.

escombros [eskom'bros] *nmpl* (*basura*) rubbish *sg*; (*restos*) debris *sg*.

esconder [eskonder'] *vt* to hide, conceal; ~**se** *vr* to hide.

escondidas [eskondē'ᵺás] *nfpl* (*AM*) hide-and-seek *sg*; **a** ~ secretly; **hacer algo a** ~ **de uno** to do sth behind sb's back.

escondite [eskondē'te] *nm* hiding place; (*juego*) hide-and-seek.

escondrijo [eskondrē'ho] *nm* hiding-place, hideout.

escopeta [eskope'tá] *nf* shotgun; ~ **de aire comprimido** air gun.

escoria [esko'ryá] *nf* (*desecho mineral*) slag; (*fig*) scum, dregs *pl*.

Escorpio [eskor'pyo] *nm* (*ASTRO*) Scorpio.

escorpión [eskorpyon'] *nm* scorpion.

escotado, a [eskotá'ᵺo, á] *a* low-cut.

escotar [eskotár'] *vt* (*vestido: ajustar*) to cut to fit; (*cuello*) to cut low.

escote [esko'te] *nm* (*de vestido*) low neck; **pagar a** ~ to share the expenses.

escotilla [eskotē'yá] *nf* (*NAUT*) hatchway.

escotillón [eskotēyon'] *nm* trapdoor.

escozor [eskosor'] *nm* (*dolor*) sting(ing).

escribano, a [eskrēḁ'no, á], **escribiente** [eskrēᵇyen'te] *nm/f* clerk; (*secretario judicial*) court *o* lawyer's clerk.

escribir [eskrēḇēr'] *vt, vi* to write; ~ **a máquina** to type; **¿cómo se escribe?** how do you spell it?

escrito, a [eskrē'to, á] *pp de* **escribir ♦** *a* written, in writing; (*examen*) written **♦** *nm* (*documento*) document; (*manuscrito*) text, manuscript; **por** ~ in writing.

escritor, a [eskrētor', á] *nm/f* writer.

escritorio [eskrēto'ryo] *nm* desk; (*oficina*) office.

escritura [eskrētōō'rá] *nf* (*acción*) writing; (*caligrafía*) (hand)writing; (*JUR: documento*) deed; (*COM*) indenture; ~ **de propiedad** title deed; **Sagrada E**~ (Holy) Scripture; ~ **social** articles *pl* of association.

escroto [eskro'to] *nm* scrotum.

escrúpulo [eskrōō'pōōlo] *nm* scruple; (*minuciosidad*) scrupulousness.

escrupuloso, a [eskrōōpōōlo'so, á] *a* scrupulous.

escrutar [eskrōōtár'] *vt* to scrutinize, examine; (*votos*) to count.

escrutinio [eskrōōtē'nyo] *nm* (*examen atento*) scrutiny; (*POL: recuento de votos*) count(ing).

escuadra [eskwá'ᵺrá] *nf* (*TEC*) square; (*MIL etc*) squad; (*NAUT*) squadron; (*de coches etc*) fleet.

escuadrilla [eskwáᵺrē'yá] *nf* (*de aviones*)

squadron; (*AM: de obreros*) gang.

escuadrón [eskwáᵺron'] *nm* squadron.

escuálido, a [eskwá'lēᵺo, á] *a* skinny, scraggy; (*sucio*) squalid.

escucha [eskōōtch'á] *nf* (*acción*) listening **♦** *nm* (*TELEC: sistema*) monitor; (*oyente*) listener; **estar a la** ~ to listen in; **estar de** ~ to spy; ~**s teléfonicas** (*telephone*) tapping *sg*.

escuchar [eskōōtchár'] *vt* to listen to; (*consejo*) to heed **♦** *vi* to listen; ~**se** *vr*: **se escucha muy mal** (*AM TELEC*) it's a very bad connection (*US*) *o* line (*Brit*).

escudarse [eskōōᵺár'se] *vr*: ~ **en** (*fig*) to hide behind.

escudería [eskōōᵺerē'á] *nf*: **la** ~ **Ferrari** the Ferrari team.

escudero [eskōōᵺe'ro] *nm* squire.

escudilla [eskōōᵺē'yá] *nf* bowl, basin.

escudo [eskōō'ᵺo] *nm* shield; ~ **de armas** coat of arms.

escudriñar [eskōōᵺrēnyár'] *vt* (*examinar*) to investigate, scrutinize; (*mirar de lejos*) to scan.

escuece [eskwe'se] *etc vb* V **escocer**.

escuela [eskwe'lá] *nf* (*tb fig*) school; ~ **normal** teacher training college; ~ **de párvulos** kindergarten.

escueto, a [eskwe'to, á] *a* plain; (*estilo*) simple; (*explicación*) concise.

escueza [eskwe'sá] *etc vb* V **escocer**.

escuincle [eskwēn'kle] *nm* (*AM fam*) kid.

esculpir [eskōōlpēr'] *vt* to sculpt; (*grabar*) to engrave; (*tallar*) to carve.

escultor, a [eskōōltor', á] *nm/f* sculptor.

escultura [eskōōltōō'rá] *nf* sculpture.

escupidera [eskōōpēᵺe'rá] *nf* spittoon.

escupir [eskōōpēr'] *vt* to spit (out) **♦** *vi* to spit.

escurreplatos [eskōōrreplá'tos] *nm inv* plate rack.

escurridizo, a [eskōōrrēᵺē'so, á] *a* slippery.

escurrir [eskōōrrēr'] *vt* (*ropa*) to wring out; (*verduras, platos*) to drain **♦** *vi* (*los líquidos*) to drip; ~**se** *vr* (*secarse*) to drain; (*resbalarse*) to slip, slide; (*escaparse*) to slip away.

ese [e'se] *nf* (the letter) S; **hacer** ~**s** (*carretera*) to zigzag; (*borracho*) to reel about.

ese [e'se], **esa** [e'sá], **esos** [e'sos], **esas** [e'sás] *a demostrativo* (*sg*) that; (*pl*) those.

ése [e'se], **ésa** [e'sá], **ésos** [e'sos], **ésas** [e'sás] *pron* (*sg*) that (one); (*pl*) those (ones); **ése ... éste ...** the former ... the latter ...; **¡no me vengas con ésas!** don't give me any more of that nonsense!

esencia [esen'syá] *nf* essence.

esencial [esensyál'] *a* essential; (*principal*) chief; **lo** ~ the main thing.

esfera [esfe'rá] *nf* sphere; (*de reloj*) face; ~

de acción scope; **~ terrestre** globe.

esférico, a [esfe'rēko, á] *a* spherical.

esfinge [esfēn'he] *nf* sphinx.

esforcé [esforse'], **esforcemos** [esforse'mos] *etc vb V* **esforzar.**

esforzado, a [esforsá'ᵗᵺo, á] *a* (*enérgico*) energetic, vigorous.

esforzarse [esforsár'se] *vr* to exert o.s., make an effort.

esfuerce [esfwer'se] *etc vb V* **esforzar.**

esfuerzo [esfwer'so] *etc vb V* **esforzar** ♦ *nm* effort; **sin ~** effortlessly.

esfumarse [esfōōmár'se] *vr* (*apoyo, esperanzas*) to fade away; (*persona*) to vanish.

esgrima [esɡrē'má] *nf* fencing.

esgrimidor [esɡrēmēᵗᵺor'] *nm* fencer.

esgrimir [esɡrēmēr'] *vt* (*arma*) to brandish; (*argumento*) to use ♦ *vi* to fence.

esguince [esɡēn'se] *nm* (*MED*) sprain.

eslabón [eslá̱ᵺon'] *nm* link; **~ perdido** (*BIO, fig*) missing link.

eslabonar [eslá̱ᵺonár'] *vt* to link, connect.

eslavo, a [eslá'ᵦo, á] *a* Slav, Slavonic ♦ *nm/f* Slav ♦ *nm* (*LING*) Slavonic.

eslogan [eslo'ɡán] *nm, pl* **eslogans** = **slogan.**

eslora [eslo'rá] *nf* (*NAUT*) length.

esmaltar [esmáltár'] *vt* to enamel.

esmalte [esmál'te] *nm* enamel; **~ de uñas** nail polish.

esmerado, a [esmerá'ᵗᵺo, á] *a* careful, neat.

esmeralda [esmerál'dá] *nf* emerald.

esmerarse [esmerár'se] *vr* (*aplicarse*) to take great pains, exercise great care; (*afanarse*) to work hard; (*hacer lo mejor*) to do one's best.

esmero [esme'ro] *nm* (great) care.

esmirriado, a [esmērryá'ᵗᵺo, á] *a* puny.

esmoquin [esmo'kēn] *nm* tuxedo (*US*), dinner jacket (*Brit*).

esnob [esnob'] *a inv* (*persona*) snobbish; (*coche etc*) posh ♦ *nm/f* snob.

esnobismo [esnoᵦes'mo] *nm* snobbery.

eso [e'so] *pron* that, that thing *o* matter; **~ de su coche** that business about his car; **~ de ir al cine** all that about going to the movies; **a ~ de las cinco** at about five o'clock; **en ~** thereupon, at that point; **por ~ therefore; ~ es** that's it; **nada de ~** far from it; **¡~ sí que es vida!** now this is really living!; **por ~ te lo dije** that's why I told you; **y ~ que llovía** in spite of the fact it was raining.

esófago [eso'fáɡo] *nm* (*ANAT*) esophagus (*US*), oesophagus (*Brit*).

esos [e'sos] *a demostrativo V* **ese.**

ésos [e'sos] *pron V* **ése.**

esp. *abr* (= *español*) Sp., Span.

espabilar [espá̱ᵺēlár'] *vt*, **espabilarse** *vr* = **despabilar(se).**

espaciado [espásyá'ᵗᵺo] *nm* (*INFORM*) spacing.

espacial [espásyál'] *a* (*del espacio*) space *cpd*.

espaciar [espásyár'] *vt* to space (out).

espacio [espá'syo] *nm* space; (*MUS*) interval; (*RADIO, TV*) program (*US*), programme (*Brit*); **el ~** space; **ocupar mucho ~** to take up a lot of room; **a dos ~s, a doble ~** (*TIP*) double-spaced; **por ~ de** during, for.

espacioso, a [espásyo'so, á] *a* spacious, roomy.

espada [espá'ᵗᵺá] *nf* sword; **~s** *nfpl* (*NAIPES*) spades; **estar entre la ~ y la pared** to be between the devil and the deep blue sea ♦ *nm* swordsman; (*TAUR*) matador.

espadachín [espá̱ᵗᵺátchēn'] *nm* (*esgrimidor*) skilled swordsman.

espaguetis [espáɡe'tēs] *nmpl* spaghetti *sg*.

espalda [espál'dá] *nf* (*gen*) back; (*NATACIÓN*) backstroke; **~s** *nfpl* (*hombros*) shoulders; **a ~s de uno** behind sb's back; **estar de ~s** to have one's back turned; **tenderse de ~s** to lie (down) on one's back; **volver la ~ a uno** to give sb the cold-shoulder.

espaldarazo [espáldárá'so] *nm* (*tb fig*) slap on the back.

espaldilla [espáltᵺe'yá] *nf* shoulder blade.

espantadizo, a [espántáᵗᵺe'so, á] *a* timid, easily frightened.

espantajo [espántá'ho] *nm*, **espantapájaros** [espántápá'háros] *nm inv* scarecrow.

espantar [espántár'] *vt* (*asustar*) to frighten, scare; (*ahuyentar*) to frighten off; (*asombrar*) to horrify, appal; **~se** *vr* to get frightened *o* scared; to be appalled.

espanto [espán'to] *nm* (*susto*) fright; (*terror*) terror; (*asombro*) astonishment; **¡qué ~!** how awful!

espantoso, a [espánto'so, á] *a* frightening, terrifying; (*ruido*) dreadful.

España [espá'nyá] *nf* Spain; **la ~ de pandereta** touristy Spain.

español, a [espányol', á] *a* Spanish ♦ *nm/f* Spaniard ♦ *nm* (*LING*) Spa̱.ish.

españolice [espányolē'se] *etc vb V* **españolizar.**

españolizar [espányolēsár'] *vt* to make Spanish, Hispanicize; **~se** *vr* to adopt Spanish ways.

esparadrapo [espárá̱ᵗᵺrá'po] *nm* bandaid (*US*), (sticking) plaster.

esparcido, a [espársē'ᵗᵺo, á] *a* scattered.

esparcimiento [espársēmyen'to] *nm* (*dispersión*) spreading; (*derramamiento*) scattering; (*fig*) cheerfulness.

esparcir [espársēr'] *vt* to spread; (*derramar*) to scatter; **~se** *vr* to spread (out); to scatter; (*divertirse*) to enjoy o.s.

espárrago [espá'rráɣo] *nm* (*tb:* ~s) asparagus; **estar hecho un** ~ to be as thin as a rake; **¡vete a freír** ~**s!** (*fam*) go to hell!

espasmo [espás'mo] *nm* spasm.

esparto [espár'to] *nm* esparto (grass).

esparza [espár'sá] *etc vb* V **esparcir.**

espátula [espá'tōōlá] *nf* (*MED*) spatula; (*ARTE*) palette knife; (*CULIN*) fish slice.

especia [espe'syá] *nf* spice.

especial [espesyál'] *a* special.

especialidad [espesyáléthát'h'] *nf* specialty (*US*), speciality (*Brit*); (*ESCOL: ramo*) specialization.

especialista [espesyálē'stá] *nm/f* specialist; (*CINE*) stuntman/woman.

especializado, a [espesyálēsá'tho, á] *a* specialized; (*obrero*) skilled.

especie [espe'sye] *nf* (*BIO*) species; (*clase*) kind, sort; **pagar en** ~ to pay in kind.

especificar [espesēfēkár'] *vt* to specify.

específico, a [espesē'fēko, á] *a* specific.

especifique [espesēfē'ke] *etc vb* V **especificar.**

espécimen [espe'sēmen], *pl* **especímenes** *nm* specimen.

espectáculo [espektá'kōōlo] *nm* (*gen*) spectacle; (*TEATRO etc*) show; (*función*) performance; **dar un** ~ to make a scene.

espectador, a [espektáthor', á] *nm/f* spectator; (*de incidente*) onlooker; **los** ~**es** (*TEATRO*) the audience *sg.*

espectro [espek'tro] *nm* ghost; (*fig*) specter (*US*), spectre (*Brit*).

especulación [espekōōlásyon'] *nf* speculation; ~ **bursátil** speculation on the Stock Market.

especular [espekōōlár'] *vt, vi* to speculate.

especulativo, a [espekōōlátē'ho, á] *a* speculative.

espejismo [espehēs'mo] *nm* mirage.

espejo [espe'ho] *nm* mirror; (*fig*) model; ~ **retrovisor** rear-view mirror; **mirarse al** ~ to look (at o.s.) in the mirror.

espeluznante [espelōōsnán'te] *a* horrifying, hair-raising.

espera [espe'rá] *nf* (*pausa, intervalo*) wait; (*JUR: plazo*) respite; **en** ~ **de** waiting for; (*con expectativa*) expecting; **en** ~ **de su contestación** awaiting your reply.

esperance [esperán'se] *etc vb* V **esperanzar.**

esperanza [esperán'sá] *nf* (*confianza*) hope; (*expectativa*) expectation; **hay pocas** ~**s de que venga** there is little prospect of his coming.

esperanzador, a [esperánsáthor', á] *a* hopeful, encouraging.

esperanzar [esperánsár'] *vt* to give hope to.

esperar [esperár'] *vt* (*aguardar*) to wait for; (*tener expectativa de*) to expect; (*desear*) to hope for ♦ *vi* to wait; to expect; to hope; ~**se** *vr*: **como podía** ~**se** as was to be expected; **hacer** ~ **a uno** to keep sb waiting; **ir a** ~ **a uno** to go and meet sb; ~ **un bebé** to be expecting.

esperma [esper'má] *nf* sperm.

esperpento [esperpen'to] *nm* (*persona*) sight (*fam*); (*disparate*) (piece of) nonsense.

espesar [espesár'] *vt* to thicken; ~**se** *vr* to thicken, get thicker.

espeso, a [espe'so, á] *a* thick; (*bosque*) dense; (*nieve*) deep; (*sucio*) dirty.

espesor [espesor'] *nm* thickness; (*de nieve*) depth.

espesura [espesōō'rá] *nf* (*bosque*) thicket.

espetar [espetár'] *vt* (*reto, sermón*) to give.

espía [espē'á] *nm/f* spy.

espiar [espēár'] *vt* (*observar*) to spy on ♦ *vi*: ~ **para** to spy for.

espiga [espē'ɣá] *nf* (*BOT: de trigo etc*) ear; (: *de flores*) spike.

espigado, a [espēɣá'tho, á] *a* (*BOT*) ripe; (*fig*) tall, slender.

espigón [espēɣon'] *nm* (*BOT*) ear; (*NAUT*) breakwater.

espina [espē'ná] *nf* thorn; (*de pez*) bone; ~ **dorsal** (*ANAT*) spine; **me da mala** ~ I don't like the look of it.

espinaca [espēná'ká] *nf* (*tb:* ~s) spinach.

espinar [espēnár'] *nm* (*matorral*) thicket.

espinazo [espēná'so] *nm* spine, backbone.

espinilla [espēnē'yá] *nf* (*ANAT: tibia*) shin(bone); (: *en la piel*) blackhead.

espino [espē'no] *nm* hawthorn.

espinoso, a [espēno'so, á] *a* (*planta*) thorny, prickly; (*fig*) bony; (*problema*) knotty.

espionaje [espyoná'he] *nm* spying, espionage.

espiral [espērál'] *a, nf* spiral; **la** ~ **inflacionista** the inflationary spiral.

espirar [espērár'] *vt, vi* to breathe out, exhale.

espiritista [espērētē'stá] *a, nm/f* spiritualist.

espíritu [espē'rētōō] *nm* spirit; (*mente*) mind; (*inteligencia*) intelligence; (*REL*) spirit, soul; **E**~ **Santo** Holy Ghost; **con** ~ **amplio** with an open mind.

espiritual [espērētwál'] *a* spiritual.

espita [espē'tá] *nf* faucet (*US*), tap (*Brit*).

esplendidez [esplendēthes'] *nf* (*abundancia*) lavishness; (*magnificencia*) splendor (*US*), splendour (*Brit*).

espléndido, a [esplen'dētho, á] *a* (*magnífico*) magnificent, splendid; (*generoso*) generous, lavish.

esplendor [esplendor'] *nm* splendor (*US*), splendour (*Brit*).

espliego [esplye'ɣo] *nm* lavender.

espolear [espoleár'] *vt* to spur on.

espoleta [espole'tá] *nf* (*de bomba*) fuse.

espolvorear [espolɣoreár'] *vt* to dust, sprinkle.

esponja [espon'há] *nf* sponge; (*fig*) sponger.

esponjoso, a [esponho'so, á] *a* spongy.

esponsales [esponsá'les] *nmpl* betrothal *sg*.

espontaneidad [espontáneeðháð'] *nf* spontaneity.

espontáneo, a [espontá'neo, á] *a* spontaneous; (*improvisado*) impromptu; (*persona*) natural.

espora [espo'rá] *nf* spore.

esporádico, a [esporá'ðhēko, á] *a* sporadic.

esposa [espo'sá] *nf* V **esposo**.

esposar [esposár'] *vt* to handcuff.

esposo, a [espo'so, á] *nm* husband ♦ *nf* wife; **esposas** *nfpl* handcuffs.

espuela [espwe'lá] *nf* spur; (*fam*: *trago*) one for the road.

espuerta [espwer'tá] *nf* basket, pannier.

espuma [espōō'má] *nf* foam; (*de cerveza*) froth, head; (*de jabón*) lather; (*de olas*) surf.

espumarajo [espōōmárá'ho] *nm* froth, foam; **echar ~s (de rabia)** to splutter with rage.

espumoso, a [espōōmo'so, á] *a* frothy, foamy; (*vino*) sparkling.

esputo [espōō'to] *nm* (*saliva*) spit; (*MED*) sputum.

esqueje [eske'he] *nm* (*BOT*) cutting.

esquela [eske'lá] *nf*: **~ mortuoria** announcement of death.

esqueleto [eskele'to] *nm* skeleton; (*lo esencial*) bare bones (of a matter); **en ~** unfinished.

esquema [eske'má] *nm* (*diagrama*) diagram; (*dibujo*) plan; (*plan*) scheme; (*FILOSOFÍA*) schema.

esquí [eskē'], *pl* **esquís** *nm* (*objeto*) ski; (*deporte*) skiing; **~ acuático** water-skiing; **hacer ~** to go skiing.

esquiador, a [eskyáðhor', á] *nm/f* skier.

esquiar [eskyár'] *vi* to ski.

esquila [eskē'lá] *nf* (*campanilla*) small bell; (*encerro*) cowbell.

esquilar [eskēlár'] *vt* to shear.

esquimal [eskēmál'] *a*, *nm/f* Eskimo.

esquina [eskē'ná] *nf* corner; **doblar la ~** to turn the corner.

esquinar [eskēnár'] *vi* (*hacer esquina*) to form a corner ♦ *vt* (*madera*) to square (off); **~se** *vr* (*pelearse*) to quarrel.

esquinazo [eskēná'so] *nm*: **dar ~ a uno** to give sb the slip.

esquirla [eskēr'lá] *nf* splinter.

esquirol [eskērol'] *nm* scab.

esquivar [eskēɣár'] *vt* to avoid; (*evadir*) to dodge, elude.

esquivo, a [eskē'ɣo, á] *a* (*altanero*) aloof; (*desdeñoso*) scornful, disdainful.

esquizofrenia [eskēsofre'nyá] *nf* schizophrenia.

esta [e'stá] *a demostrativo* V **este**.

ésta [e'stá] *pron* V **éste**.

está [está'] *vb* V **estar**.

estabilice [estáɣēlē'se] *etc vb* V **estabilizar**.

estabilidad [estáɣēlēðháð'] *nf* stability.

estabilización [estáɣēlēsásyon'] *nf* (*COM*) stabilization.

estabilizar [estáɣēlēsár'] *vt* to stabilize; (*fijar*) to make steady; (*precios*) to peg; **~se** *vr* to become stable.

estable [está'ɓle] *a* stable.

establecer [estáɓleser'] *vt* to establish; (*fundar*) to set up; (*colonos*) to settle; (*récord*) to set (up); **~se** *vr* to establish o.s.; (*echar raíces*) to settle (down); (*COM*) to start up.

establecimiento [estáɓlesēmyen'to] *nm* establishment; (*fundación*) institution; (*de negocio*) start-up; (*de colonias*) settlement; (*local*) establishment; **~ comercial** business house.

establezca [estáɓles'ká] *etc vb* V **establecer**.

establo [está'ɓlo] *nm* (*AGR*) stall; (: *esp AM*) barn.

estaca [está'ká] *nf* stake, post; (*de tienda de campaña*) peg.

estacada [estaká'ðá] *nf* (*cerca*) fence, fencing; (*palenque*) stockade; **dejar a uno en la ~** to leave sb in the lurch.

estación [estásyon'] *nf* station; (*del año*) season; **~ de autobuses/ferrocarril** bus/railway station; **~ balnearia (de turistas)** seaside resort; **~ de servicio** service station; **~ terminal** terminus; **~ de trabajo** (*COM*) work station; **~ transmisora** transmitter; **~ de visualización** display unit.

estacionamiento [estásyonámyen'to] *nm* (*AUTO*) parking; (*MIL*) stationing.

estacionar [estásyonár'] *vt* (*AUTO*) to park; (*MIL*) to station.

estacionario, a [estásyoná'ryo, á] *a* stationary; (*COM*: *mercado*) slack.

estadio [está'ðhyo] *nm* (*fase*) stage, phase; (*DEPORTE*) stadium.

estadista [estáðhē'stá] *nm* (*POL*) statesman; (*ESTADÍSTICA*) statistician.

estadística [estáðhē'stēká] *nf* (*una ~*) figure, statistic; (*ciencia*) statistics *sg*.

estado [está'ðho] *nm* (*POL*: *condición*) state; **~ civil** marital status; **~ de cuenta(s)** bank statement, statement of accounts; **~ de excepción** (*POL*) state of emergency; **~ financiero** (*COM*) financial statement; **~ mayor** (*MIL*) staff; **~ de pérdidas y ganancias** (*COM*) profit and loss statement, operating statement; **E~s Unidos (EE.UU.)** United States (of America)

(USA); **estar en ~ (de buena esperanza)** to be pregnant.

estadounidense [estáthooōnēt̮en'se] *a* United States *cpd*, American ♦ *nm/f* United States citizen, American.

estafa [está'fá] *nf* swindle, trick; (*COM etc*) racket.

estafar [estáfár'] *vt* to swindle, defraud.

estafeta [estáfe'tá] *nf* (*oficina de correos*) post office; **~ diplomática** diplomatic bag.

estalactita [estáláktē'tá] *nf* stalactite.

estalagmita [estálágmē'tá] *nf* stalagmite.

estallar [estáyár'] *vi* to burst; (*bomba*) to explode, go off; (*volcán*) to erupt; (*vidrio*) to shatter; (*látigo*) to crack; (*epidemia, guerra, rebelión*) to break out; **~ en llanto** to burst into tears.

estallido [estáyē'tḥo] *nm* explosion; (*de látigo, trueno*) crack; (*fig*) outbreak.

estambre [estám'bre] *nm* (*tela*) worsted; (*BOT*) stamen.

Estambul [estámbōōl'] *nm* Istanbul.

estamento [estámen'to] *nm* (social) class.

estampa [estám'pá] *nf* (*impresión, imprenta*) print, engraving; (*imagen, figura: de persona*) appearance.

estampado, a [estámpá'tḥo, á] *a* printed ♦ *nm* (*impresión: acción*) printing; (: *efecto*) print; (*marca*) stamping.

estampar [estámpár'] *vt* (*imprimir*) to print; (*marcar*) to stamp; (*metal*) to engrave; (*poner sello en*) to stamp; (*fig*) to stamp, imprint.

estampida [estámpē'tḥá] *nf* stampede.

estampido [estámpē'tḥo] *nm* bang, report.

estampilla [estámpē'yá] *nf* (*sello de goma*) (rubber) stamp; (*AM*) stamp.

están [están'] *vb V* estar.

estancado, a [estánká'tḥo, á] *a* (*agua*) stagnant.

estancamiento [estánkámyen'to] *nm* stagnation.

estancar [estánkár'] *vt* (*aguas*) to hold up, hold back; (*COM*) to monopolize; (*fig*) to block, hold up; **~se** *vr* to stagnate.

estancia [están'syá] *nf* (*permanencia*) stay; (*sala*) room; (*AM*) farm, ranch.

estanciero [estánsye'ro] *nm* (*AM*) farmer, rancher.

estanco, a [están'ko, á] *a* watertight ♦ *nm* cigar store (*US*), tobacconist's (shop) (*Brit*).

estándar [están'dár] *a, nm* standard.

estandarice [estándárē'se] *etc vb V* **estandarizar.**

estandarizar [estándárēsár'] *vt* to standardize.

estandarte [estándár'te] *nm* banner, standard.

estanque [están'ke] *etc vb V* **estancar** ♦ *nm* (*lago*) pool, pond; (*AGR*) reservoir.

estanquero, a [estánke'ro, á] *nm/f* tobacconist.

estante [están'te] *nm* (*armario*) rack, stand; (*biblioteca*) bookcase; (*anaquel*) shelf; (*AM*) pier.

estantería [estánterē'á] *nf* shelving, shelves *pl*.

estaño [está'nyo] *nm* tin.

estar [estár'] *vi* (*gen*) to be; (*en casa*) to be in; (*ubicarse*) to be found; (*presente*) to be present; **~se** *vr*: **¡estate quieto!** keep still!; **se está bien aquí** it's nice here; **estamos a 2 de mayo** it is the 2nd of May; **¿cómo está usted?** how are you?; **~ enfermo *o* mal** to be ill; **~ viejo/joven** (*parecerse*) to seem old/young; **¿a cuánto estamos de Madrid?** (*seguido de una preposición*) how far are we from Madrid?; **~ de fiesta *o* vacaciones** to be on vacation; **las uvas están a 5 pesetas** grapes are at 5 pesetas; **María no está** Maria isn't in; **está fuera** (*de casa*) she's out; (*de ciudad*) she's away; **está de camarero** he's working as a waiter; **estaba de uniforme** he was (dressed) in uniform; **el problema está en que ...** the problem lies in the fact that ...; **no estoy para bromas** I'm not in the mood for jokes *o* joking; **~ por** (*moción*) to be in favor of; (*persona*) to support, back; **está por hacer** it remains to be done; **¿estamos?** are we agreed?; **¡ya está!** that's it!, there you are!; **¡ya está bien!** that's enough!

estarcir [estársēr'] *vt* to stencil.

estarza [estár'sá] *etc vb V* **estarcir.**

estas [e'stás] *a demostrativo V* **este.**

éstas [e'stás] *pron V* **éste.**

estás [estás'] *vb V* **estar.**

estatal [estátál'] *a* state *cpd*.

estático, a [está'tēko, á] *a* static.

estatua [está'twá] *nf* statue.

estatura [estátōō'rá] *nf* stature, height.

estatutario, a [estátōōtá'ryo, á] *a* statutory.

estatuto [estátōō'to] *nm* (*JUR*) statute; (*de ciudad*) bye-law; (*de comité*) rule; **~s sociales** (*COM*) articles of association.

este [es'te] *a* (*lado*) east; (*dirección*) easterly ♦ *nm* east; **en la parte del ~** in the eastern part.

este [e'ste], **esta** [e'stá], **estos** [e'stos], **estas** [e'stás] *a demostrativo* (*sg*) this; (*pl*) these.

éste [e'ste], **ésta** [e'stá], **éstos** [e'stos], **éstas** [e'stás] *pron* (*sg*) this (one); (*pl*) these (ones); **ése ... éste ...** the former ... the latter ...

esté [este'] *vb V* **estar.**

estela [este'lá] *nf* wake, wash; (*fig*) trail.

estelar [estelár'] *a* (*ASTRO*) stellar; (*TEATRO*) star *cpd*.

estén [esten'] *vb V* **estar.**

estenografía [estenográfē'á] *nf* shorthand.

estentóreo, a [estento'reo, á] *a* (*sonido*) strident; (*voz*) booming.

estepa [este'pá] *nf* (*GEO*) steppe.

estera [este'rá] *nf* (*alfombra*) mat; (*tejido*) matting.

estercolero [esterkole'ro] *nm* manure heap, dunghill.

estéreo [este'reo] *a inv, nm* stereo.

estereofónico, a [estereofo'nēko, á] *a* stereophonic.

estereotipar [estereotēpár'] *vt* to stereotype.

estereotipo [estereotē'po] *nm* stereotype.

estéril [este'rēl] *a* sterile, barren; (*fig*) vain, futile.

esterilice [esterēlē'se] *etc vb* V **esterilizar**.

esterilizar [esterēlēsár'] *vt* to sterilize.

esterilla [esterē'yá] *nf* (*alfombrilla*) small mat.

esterlina [esterlē'ná] *a*: **libra ~** pound sterling.

esternón [esternon'] *nm* breastbone.

estertor [estertor'] *nm* death rattle.

estés [estes'] *vb* V **estar**.

esteta [este'tá] *nm/f* esthete (*US*), aesthete (*Brit*).

esteticienne [estetēsyen'] *nf* beautician.

estético, a [este'tēko, á] *a* esthetic (*US*), aesthetic (*Brit*) ♦ *nf* (a)esthetics *sg*.

estetoscopio [estetosko'pyo] *nm* stethoscope.

estibador [estēbáthor'] *nm* stevedore.

estibar [estēbár'] *vt* (*NAUT*) to stow.

estiércol [estyer'kol] *nm* dung, manure.

estigma [estēg'má] *nm* stigma.

estigmatice [estēgmátē'se] *etc vb* V **estigmatizar**.

estigmatizar [estēgmátēsár'] *vt* to stigmatize.

estilar [estēlár'] *vi*, **~se** *vr* (*estar de moda*) to be in fashion; (*usarse*) to be used.

estilice [estēlē'se] *etc vb* V **estilizar**.

estilizar [estēlēsár'] *vt* to stylize; (*TEC*) to design.

estilo [estē'lo] *nm* style; (*TEC*) stylus; (*NATACIÓN*) stroke; **~ de vida** lifestyle; **al ~ de** in the style of; **algo por el ~** something along those lines.

estilográfica [estēlográ'fēká] *nf* fountain pen.

estima [estē'má] *nf* esteem, respect.

estimación [estēmásyon'] *nf* (*evaluación*) estimation; (*aprecio, afecto*) esteem, regard.

estimado, a [estēmá'tho, á] *a* esteemed; **"E~ Señor"** "Dear Sir".

estimador [estēmáthor'] *nm* (*COM*) estimator.

estimar [estēmár'] *vt* (*evaluar*) to estimate; (*valorar*) to appraise (*US*), value (*Brit*); (*apreciar*) to esteem, respect; (*pensar, considerar*) to think, reckon.

estimulante [estēmōōlàn'te] *a* stimulating ♦ *nm* stimulant.

estimular [estēmōōlár'] *vt* to stimulate; (*excitar*) to excite; (*animar*) to encourage.

estímulo [estē'mōōlo] *nm* stimulus; (*ánimo*) encouragement; (*INFORM*) prompt.

estío [estē'o] *nm* summer.

estipendio [estēpen'dyo] *nm* salary; (*COM*) stipend.

estipulación [estēpōōlásyon'] *nf* stipulation, condition.

estipular [estēpōōlár'] *vt* to stipulate.

estirado, a [estērá'tho, á] *a* (*tenso*) (stretched o drawn) tight; (*fig: persona*) stiff, pompous; (*engreído*) stuck-up.

estirar [estērár'] *vt* to stretch; (*dinero, suma etc*) to stretch out; (*cuello*) to crane; (*dinero*) to eke out; (*discurso*) to stretch out; **~ la pata** (*fam*) to kick the bucket; **~se** *vr* to stretch.

estirón [estēron'] *nm* pull, tug; (*crecimiento*) spurt, sudden growth; **dar un ~** (*niño*) to shoot up.

estirpe [estēr'pe] *nf* stock, lineage.

estival [estēbál'] *a* summer *cpd*.

esto [e'sto] *pron* this, this thing o matter; **~ de la boda** this business about the wedding; **en ~** at this o that point; **por ~** for this reason.

estocada [estoká'thá] *nf* (*acción*) stab; (*TAUR*) death blow.

Estocolmo [estokol'mo] *nm* Stockholm.

estofa [esto'fá] *nf*: **de baja ~** poor-quality.

estofado [estofá'tho] *nm* stew.

estofar [estofár'] *vt* (*bordar*) to quilt; (*CULIN*) to stew.

estoico, a [esto'ēko, á] *a* (*FILOSOFÍA*) stoic(al); (*fig*) cold, indifferent.

estomacal [estomákál'] *a* stomach *cpd*; **trastorno ~** stomach upset.

estómago [esto'mágo] *nm* stomach; **tener ~** to be thick-skinned.

estoque [esto'ke] *nm* rapier, sword.

estorbar [estorbár'] *vt* to hinder, obstruct; (*fig*) to bother, disturb ♦ *vi* to be in the way.

estorbo [estor'bo] *nm* (*molestia*) bother, nuisance; (*obstáculo*) hindrance, obstacle.

estornino [estornē'no] *nm* starling.

estornudar [estornōōthár'] *vi* to sneeze.

estornudo [estornōō'tho] *nm* sneeze.

estos [e'stos] *a demostrativo* V **este**.

éstos [e'stos] *pron* V **éste**.

estoy [esto'ē] *vb* V **estar**.

estrabismo [estrábēs'mo] *nm* squint.

estrado [estrá'tho] *nm* (*tarima*) platform; (*MUS*) bandstand; **~s** *nmpl* law courts.

estrafalario, a [estráfálá'ryo, á] *a* odd, eccentric; (*desarreglado*) slovenly, sloppy.

estrago [estrá'go] *nm* ruin, destruction; **ha-**

cer ~**s en** to wreak havoc among.

estragón [estrá̱gon'] *nm* (*CULIN*) tarragon.

estrambólico, a [estrámbo'léko, á] *a* (*AM*),
estrambótico, a [estrámbo'téko, á] *a* odd,
eccentric.

estrangulación [estrángōōlásyon'] *nf*
strangulation.

estrangulador, a [estrángōōlátḫor', á] *nm/f*
strangler ♦ *nm* (*TEC*) throttle; (*AUTO*)
choke.

estrangulamiento [estrángōōlámyen'to]
nm (*AUTO*) bottleneck.

estrangular [estrángōōlár'] *vt* (*persona*) to
strangle; (*MED*) to strangulate.

estraperlista [estráperlḗ'stá] *nm/f* black
marketeer.

estraperlo [estráper'lo] *nm* black market.

estratagema [estrátáhe'má] *nf* (*MIL*)
stratagem; (*astucia*) cunning.

estratega [estráte'ġá] *nm/f* strategist.

estrategia [estráte'hyá] *nf* strategy.

estratégico, a [estráte'héko, á] *a* strategic.

estratificar [estrátēfēkár'] *vt* to stratify.

estratifique [estrátēfē'ke] *etc vb* V **estratificar**.

estrato [estrá'to] *nm* stratum, layer.

estratosfera [estrátosfe'rá] *nf* stratosphere.

estrechar [estretchár'] *vt* (*reducir*) to
narrow; (*vestido*) to take in; (*persona*) to
hug, embrace; ~**se** *vr* (*reducirse*) to
narrow, grow narrow; (*2 personas*) to embrace; ~ **la mano** to shake hands.

estrechez [estretches'] *nf* narrowness; (*de
ropa*) tightness; (*intimidad*) intimacy;
(*COM*) want *o* shortage of money; **estreche-
ces** *nfpl* financial difficulties.

estrecho, a [estretch'o, á] *a* narrow; (*apretado*) tight; (*íntimo*) close, intimate; (*miserable*) miserly ♦ *nm* strait; ~ **de miras**
narrow-minded; **E~ de Gibraltar** Strait of
Gibraltar.

estrella [estre'yá] *nf* star; ~ **fugaz** shooting
star; ~ **de mar** starfish; **tener (buena)/
mala** ~ to be lucky/unlucky.

estrellado, a [estreyá'tḫo, á] *a* (*forma*)
star-shaped; (*cielo*) starry; (*huevos*) fried.

estrellar [estreyár'] *vt* (*hacer añicos*) to
smash (to pieces); (*huevos*) to fry; ~**se** *vr*
to smash; (*chocarse*) to crash; (*fracasar*)
to fail.

estrellato [estreyá'to] *nm* stardom.

estremecer [estremeser'] *vt* to shake; ~**se**
vr to shake, tremble; ~ **de** (*horror*) to
shudder with; (*frío*) to shiver with.

estremecimiento [estremesḗmyen'to] *nm*
(*temblor*) trembling, shaking.

estremezca [estremes'ká] *etc vb* V **estremecer**.

estrenar [estrenár'] *vt* (*vestido*) to wear for
the first time; (*casa*) to move into; (*película, obra de teatro*) to present for the first

time; ~**se** *vr* (*persona*) to make one's début; (*película*) to have its premiere; (*TEA-
TRO*) to open.

estreno [estre'no] *nm* (*primer uso*) first
use; (*CINE etc*) premiere.

estreñido, a [estrenyḗ'tḫo, á] *a* constipated.

estreñimiento [estrenyḗmyen'to] *nm* constipation.

estrépito [estre'pēto] *nm* noise, racket;
(*fig*) fuss.

estrepitoso, a [estrepēto'so, á] *a* noisy;
(*fiesta*) rowdy.

estrés [estres'] *nm* stress.

estresante [estresán'te] *a* stressful.

estría [estrḗ'á] *nf* groove; ~**s (en el cutis)**
stretchmarks.

estribación [estrēḫásyon'] *nf* (*GEO*) spur;
estribaciones *nfpl* foothills.

estribar [estrēḫár'] *vi*: ~ **en** to rest on, be
supported by; **la dificultad estriba en el
texto** the difficulty lies in the text.

estribillo [estrēḫē'yo] *nm* (*LITERATURA*) refrain; (*MUS*) chorus.

estribo [estrē'ḫo] *nm* (*de jinete*) stirrup;
(*de coche, tren*) step; (*de puente*) support;
(*GEO*) spur; **perder los** ~**s** to fly off the
handle.

estribor [estrēḫor'] *nm* (*NAUT*) starboard.

estricnina [estrēknē'ná] *nf* strychnine.

estricto, a [estrēk'to, á] *a* (*riguroso*) strict;
(*severo*) severe.

estridente [estrēḫen'te] *a* (*color*) loud;
(*voz*) raucous.

estro [es'tro] *nm* inspiration.

estrofa [estro'fá] *nf* verse.

estropajo [estropá'ho] *nm* scourer.

estropear [estropeár'] *vt* (*arruinar*) to
spoil; (*dañar*) to damage ♦ *vi* (*coche*) to
break down; ~**se** *vr* (*objeto*) to get damaged; (*la piel etc*) to be ruined.

estropicio [estropē'syo] *nm* (*rotura*) breakage; (*efectos*) harmful effects *pl*.

estructura [estrōōktōō'rá] *nf* structure.

estruendo [estrwen'do] *nm* (*ruido*) racket,
din; (*fig: alboroto*) uproar, turmoil.

estrujar [estrōōhár'] *vt* (*apretar*) to
squeeze; (*aplastar*) to crush; (*fig*) to drain,
bleed.

estuario [estwá'ryo] *nm* estuary.

estuche [estōōtch'e] *nm* box, case.

estudiante [estōōtḫyán'te] *nm/f* student.

estudiantil [estōōtḫyántēl'] *a inv* student
cpd.

estudiantina [estōōtḫyánte'ná] *nf* student
music group.

estudiar [estōōtḫyár'] *vt* to study; (*propuesta*) to think about *o* over; ~ **para
abogado** to study to become a lawyer.

estudio [estōō'tḫyo] *nm* study; (*encuesta*)
research; (*proyecto*) plan; (*piso*) studio
apartment; (*CINE, ARTE, RADIO*) studio;

~s *nmpl* studies; (*erudición*) learning *sg*;
cursar *o* **hacer** ~s to study; ~ **de casos prácticos** case study; ~ **de desplazamientos y tiempos** (*COM*) time and motion study; ~s **de motivación** motivational research *sg*; ~ **del trabajo** (*COM*) work study; ~ **de viabilidad** (*COM*) feasibility study.

estudioso, a [estoóthyo'so, á] *a* studious.

estufa [estoó'fá] *nf* heater, fire.

estulticia [estoólte'syá] *nf* foolishness.

estupefaciente [estoópefásyen'te] *a, nm* narcotic.

estupefacto, a [estoópefák'to, á] *a* speechless, thunderstruck.

estupendamente [estoópendámen'te] *ad* (*fam*): **estoy** ~ I feel great; **le salió** ~ he did it very well.

estupendo, a [estoópen'do, á] *a* wonderful, terrific; (*fam*) great; ¡~! that's great!, fantastic!

estupidez [estoópethes'] *nf* (*torpeza*) stupidity; (*acto*) stupid thing (to do); **fue una** ~ **mía** that was a silly thing for me to do *o* say.

estúpido, a [estoó'petho, á] *a* stupid, silly.

estupor [estoópor'] *nm* stupor; (*fig*) astonishment, amazement.

estupro [estoó'pro] *nm* rape.

estuve [estoó'he] *etc*, **estuviera** [estoóhye'rá] *etc vb V* **estar**.

esvástica [esbá'stëká] *nf* swastika.

ETA [e'tá] *nf abr* (*POL: =Euskadi Ta Askatasuna*) ETA, *Basque separatist movement.*

etapa [etá'pá] *nf* (*de viaje*) stage; (*DEPORTE*) leg; (*parada*) stopping place; (*fig*) stage, phase; **por** ~s gradually *o* in stages.

etarra [etá'rrá] *a* ETA *cpd* ♦ *nm/f* member of ETA.

etc. *abr* (= *etcétera*) etc.

etcétera [etse'terá] *ad* etcetera.

etéreo, a [ete'reo, á] *a* ethereal.

eternice [eternē'se] *etc vb V* **eternizar**.

eternidad [eternētháth'] *nf* eternity.

eternizarse [eternēsár'se] *vr*: ~ **en hacer algo** to take ages to do sth.

eterno, a [eter'no, á] *a* eternal, everlasting; (*despectivo*) never-ending.

ético, a [e'tēko, á] *a* ethical ♦ *nf* ethics.

etimología [etēmolohē'á] *nf* etymology.

etiqueta [etēke'tá] *nf* (*modales*) etiquette; (*rótulo*) label, tag; **de** ~ formal.

étnico, a [et'nēko, á] *a* ethnic.

eucalipto [eoókálép'to] *nm* eucalyptus.

Eucaristía [eoókárēstē'á] *nf* Eucharist.

eufemismo [eoófemēs'mo] *nm* euphemism.

euforia [eoófo'ryá] *nf* euphoria.

eufórico, a [eoófo'rēko, á] *a* euphoric.

eunuco [eoónoó'ko] *nm* eunuch.

Europa [eoóro'pá] *nf* Europe.

europeice [eoórope'ēse] *etc vb V* **europei-**

zar.

europeizar [eoóropeēsár'] *vt* to Europeanize; ~**se** *vr* to become Europeanized.

europeo, a [eoórope'o, á] *a, nm/f* European.

éuscaro, a [e'oóskáro, á] *a, nm/f* Basque.

Euskadi [eoóská'thē] *nm* the Basque Provinces *pl*.

euskera, eusquera [eoóske'rá] *nm* (*LING*) Basque.

eutanasia [eoótáná'syá] *nf* euthanasia.

evacuación [ebákwásyon'] *nf* evacuation.

evacuar [ebákwar'] *vt* to evacuate.

evadir [ebáthēr'] *vt* to evade, avoid; ~**se** *vr* to escape.

evaluación [ebálwásyon'] *nf* evaluation, assessment.

evaluar [ebálwar'] *vt* to evaluate, assess.

evangélico, a [ebánhe'lēko, á] *a* evangelical.

evangelio [ebánhe'lyo] *nm* gospel.

evaporación [ebáporásyon'] *nf* evaporation.

evaporar [ebáporár'] *vt* to evaporate; ~**se** *vr* to vanish.

evasión [ebásyon'] *nf* escape, flight; (*fig*) evasion; ~ **fiscal** *o* **tributaria** tax evasion.

evasivo, a [ebásē'ho, á] *a* evasive, noncommittal ♦ *nf* (*pretexto*) excuse; **contestar con evasivas** to avoid giving a straight answer.

evento [eben'to] *nm* event; (*eventualidad*) eventuality.

eventual [ebentwál'] *a* possible, conditional (upon circumstances); (*trabajador*) casual, temporary.

Everest [eberest'] *nm*: **el (Monte)** ~ (Mount) Everest.

evidencia [ebēthen'syá] *nf* evidence, proof; **poner en** ~ to make clear; **ponerse en** ~ (*persona*) to show o.s. up.

evidenciar [ebēthensyár'] *vt* (*hacer patente*) to make evident; (*probar*) to prove, show; ~**se** *vr* to be evident.

evidente [ebēthen'te] *a* obvious, clear, evident.

evitar [ebētár'] *vt* (*evadir*) to avoid; (*impedir*) to prevent; (*peligro*) to escape; (*molestia*) to save; (*tentación*) to shun; **si puedo** ~**lo** if I can help it.

evocador, a [ebokáthor', á] *a* (*sugestivo*) evocative.

evocar [ebokár'] *vt* to evoke, call forth.

evolución [eboloósyon'] *nf* (*desarrollo*) evolution, development; (*cambio*) change; (*MIL*) maneuver (*US*), manoeuvre (*Brit*).

evolucionar [eboloósyonár'] *vi* to evolve; (*MIL, AVIAT*) to maneuver (*US*), manoeuvre (*Brit*).

evoque [eho'ke] *etc vb V* **evocar**.

ex [eks] *a* ex-; **el** ~ **ministro** the former minister, the ex-minister.

exabrupto [eksáhroóp'to] *nm* interjection.

exacción [eksáksyon'] *nf* (*acto*) exaction; (*de impuestos*) demand.

exacerbar [eksáserbár'] *vt* to irritate, annoy.

exactamente [eksáktámen'te] *ad* exactly.

exactitud [eksáktĕtōōth'] *nf* exactness; (*precisión*) accuracy; (*puntualidad*) punctuality.

exacto, a [eksák'to, á] *a* exact; accurate; punctual; ¡~! exactly!; **eso no es del todo** ~ that's not quite right; **para ser** ~ to be precise.

exageración [eksáherásyon'] *nf* exaggeration.

exagerado, a [eksáherá'tho, á] *a* (*relato*) exaggerated; (*precio*) excessive; (*persona*) over-demonstrative; (*gesto*) theatrical.

exagerar [eksáherár'] *vt* to exaggerate; (*exceder*) to overdo.

exaltado, a [eksáltá'tho, á] *a* (*apasionado*) over-excited, worked up; (*exagerado*) extreme; (*fanático*) hot-headed; (*discurso*) impassioned ♦ *nm/f* (*fanático*) hothead; (*POL*) extremist.

exaltar [eksáltár'] *vt* to exalt, glorify; ~se *vr* (*excitarse*) to get excited o worked up.

examen [eksá'men] *nm* examination; (*de problema*) consideration; ~ **de** (*encuesta*) inquiry into; ~ **de ingreso** entrance examination; ~ **de conducir** driving test; ~ **eliminatorio** qualifying examination.

examinar [eksámĕnár'] *vt* to examine; (*poner a prueba*) to test; (*inspeccionar*) to inspect; ~se *vr* to be examined, take an examination.

exánime [eksá'nĕme] *a* lifeless; (*fig*) exhausted.

exasperar [eksásperár'] *vt* to exasperate; ~se *vr* to get exasperated, lose patience.

Exc.ª *abr* = **Excelencia.**

excarceler [ekskárselár'] *vt* to release (from prison).

excavador, a [ekskáhàthor', á] *nm/f* (*persona*) excavator ♦ *nf* (*TEC*) digger.

excavar [ekskáhár'] *vt* to excavate, dig (out).

excedencia [eksethen'syá] *nf* (*MIL*) leave; (*ESCOL*) sabbatical.

excedente [eksethen'te] *a, nm* excess, surplus.

exceder [eksether'] *vt* to exceed, surpass; ~se *vr* (*extralimitarse*) to go too far; (*sobrepasarse*) to excel o.s.

excelencia [ekselen'syá] *nf* excellence; **E~** Excellency; **por** ~ par excellence.

excelente [ekselen'te] *a* excellent.

excelso, a [eksel'so, á] *a* lofty, sublime.

excentricidad [eksentrĕsĕthàth'] *nf* eccentricity.

excéntrico, a [eksen'trĕko, á] *a, nm/f* eccentric.

excepción [eksepsyon'] *nf* exception; **la** ~ **confirma la regla** the exception proves the rule.

excepcional [eksepsyonál'] *a* exceptional.

excepto [eksep'to] *ad* excepting, except (for).

exceptuar [ekseptwár'] *vt* to except, exclude.

excesivo, a [eksesē'ho, á] *a* excessive.

exceso [ekse'so] *nm* excess; (*COM*) surplus; ~ **de equipaje/peso** excess luggage/weight; ~ **de velocidad** speeding; **en** o **por** ~ excessively.

excitación [eksētásyon'] *nf* (*sensación*) excitement; (*acción*) excitation.

excitado, a [eksētá'tho, á] *a* excited; (*emociones*) aroused.

excitante [eksētán'te] *a* exciting; (*MED*) stimulating ♦ *nm* stimulant.

excitar [eksētár'] *vt* to excite; (*incitar*) to urge; (*emoción*) to stir up; (*esperanzas*) to raise; (*pasión*) to arouse; ~se *vr* to get excited.

exclamación [eksklámásyon'] *nf* exclamation.

exclamar [eksklámár'] *vi* to exclaim; ~se *vr*: ~se (**contra**) to complain (about).

excluir [eksklōōēr'] *vt* to exclude; (*dejar fuera*) to shut out; (*solución*) to reject; (*posibilidad*) to rule out.

exclusión [eksklōōsyon'] *nf* exclusion.

exclusiva [eksklōōsē'hà] *nf V* exclusivo.

exclusive [eksklōōsē'he] *prep* exclusive of, not counting.

exclusivo, a [eksklōōsē'ho, á] *a* exclusive ♦ *nf* (*PRENSA*) exclusive, scoop; (*COM*) sole right o agency; **derecho** ~ sole o exclusive right.

excluyendo [eksklōōyen'do] *etc vb V* excluir.

Excma., Excmo. *abr* (= *Excelentísima, Excelentísimo*) *courtesy title.*

excombatiente [ekskombátyen'te] *nm* war veteran, ex-serviceman (*Brit*).

excomulgar [ekskomōōlgár'] *vt* (*REL*) to excommunicate.

excomulgue [ekskomōōl'ge] *etc vb V* excomulgar.

excomunión [ekskomōōnyon'] *nf* excommunication.

excoriar [ekskoryár'] *vt* to flay, skin.

excremento [ekskremen'to] *nm* excrement.

exculpar [ekskōōlpár'] *vt* to exonerate; (*JUR*) to acquit; ~se *vr* to exonerate o.s.

excursión [ekskōōrsyon'] *nf* excursion, outing; **ir de** ~ to go (off) on a trip.

excursionista [ekskōōrsyonē'stá] *nm/f* (*turista*) sightseer.

excusa [ekskōō'sá] *nf* excuse; (*disculpa*) apology; **presentar sus** ~s to excuse o.s.

excusado, a [ekskōōsá'tho, á] *a* unnecessary; (disculpado) excused, forgiven.

excusar [ekskōōsár'] vt to excuse; (evitar) to avoid, prevent; ~se vr (disculparse) to apologize.

execrable [eksekrá'ble] a appalling.

exención [eksensyon'] nf exemption.

exento, a [eksen'to, á] pp de **eximir** ♦ a exempt.

exequias [ekse'kyás] nfpl funeral rites.

exhalación [eksálásyon'] nf (del aire) exhalation; (vapor) fumes pl, vapor (US), vapour (Brit); (rayo) shooting star; **salir como una** ~ to shoot out.

exhalar [eksálár'] vt to exhale, breathe out; (olor etc) to give off; (suspiro) to breathe, heave.

exhaustivo, a [eksáōōstē'ho, á] a exhaustive.

exhausto, a [eksá'ōōsto, á] a exhausted, worn-out.

exhibición [eksēhēsyon'] nf exhibition; (demostración) display, show; (de película) showing; (de equipo) performance.

exhibicionista [eksēhēsyonē'stá] a, nm/f exhibitionist.

exhibir [eksēhēr'] vt to exhibit; to display, show; (cuadros) to exhibit; (artículos) to display; (pasaporte) to show; (película) to screen; (mostrar con orgullo) to show off; ~se vr (mostrarse en público) to show o.s. off; (fam: indecentemente) to expose o.s.

exhortación [eksortásyon'] nf exhortation.

exhortar [eksortár'] vt: ~ a to exhort to.

exhumar [eksōōmár'] vt to exhume.

exigencia [eksēhen'syá] nf demand, requirement.

exigente [eksēhen'te] a demanding; (profesor) strict; **ser** ~ **con uno** to be hard on sb.

exigir [eksēhēr'] vt (gen) to demand, require; (impuestos) to exact, levy; ~ **el pago** to demand payment.

exiguo, a [eksē'gwo, á] a (cantidad) meager (US), meagre (Brit); (objeto) tiny.

exija [eksē'há] etc vb V **exigir**.

exiliado, a [eksēlyá'ho, á] a exiled, in exile ♦ nm/f exile.

exiliar [eksēlyár'] vt to exile; ~se vr to go into exile.

exilio [eksē'lyo] nm exile.

eximio, a [eksē'myo, á] a (eminente) distinguished, eminent.

eximir [eksēmēr'] vt to exempt.

existencia [eksēsten'syá] nf existence; ~s nfpl stock sg; ~ **de mercancías** (COM) stock-in-trade; **tener en** ~ to have in stock; **amargar la** ~ **a uno** to make sb's life miserable.

existir [eksēstēr'] vi to exist, be.

éxito [ek'sēto] nm (resultado) result, outcome; (triunfo) success; (MUS, TEATRO)

hit; ~ **editorial** bestseller; ~ **rotundo** smash hit; **tener** ~ to be successful.

exitoso, a [eksēto'so, á] a successful.

éxodo [ek'sotho] nm exodus; **el** ~ **rural** urban flight.

ex oficio [eksofē'syo] a, ad ex officio.

exonerar [eksonerár'] vt to exonerate; ~ **de una obligación** to free from an obligation.

exorcice [eksorsē'se] etc vb V **exorcizar**.

exorcismo [eksorsēs'mo] nm exorcism.

exorcizar [eksorsēsár'] vt to exorcize.

exótico, a [ekso'tēko, á] a exotic.

expandido, a [ekspándē'tho, á] a: **en caracteres** ~**s** (INFORM) double width.

expandir [ekspándēr'] vt to expand; (COM) to expand, enlarge; ~se vr to expand, spread.

expansión [ekspánsyon'] nf expansion; (recreo) relaxation; **la** ~ **económica** economic growth; **economía en** ~ expanding economy.

expansionar [ekspánsyonár'] vt to expand; ~se vr (dilatarse) to expand; (recrearse) to relax.

expansivo, a [ekspánsē'ho, á] a expansive; (efusivo) communicative.

expatriado, a [ekspátryá'tho, á] nm/f (emigrado) expatriate; (exiliado) exile.

expatriarse [ekspátryár'se] vr to emigrate; (POL) to go into exile.

expectación [ekspektásyon'] nf (esperanza) expectation; (ilusión) excitement.

expectativa [ekspektátē'há] nf (espera) expectation; (perspectiva) prospect; ~ **de vida** life expectancy; **estar a la** ~ to wait and see (what will happen).

expedición [ekspethēsyon'] nf (excursión) expedition; **gastos de** ~ shipping charges.

expedientar [ekspethyentár'] vt to open a file on; (funcionario) to discipline, start disciplinary proceedings against.

expediente [ekspethyen'te] nm expedient; (JUR: procedimento) action, proceedings pl; (: papeles) dossier, file, record; ~ **judicial** court proceedings pl; ~ **académico** (student's) record.

expedir [ekspethēr'] vt (despachar) to send, forward; (pasaporte) to issue; (cheque) to make out.

expedito, a [ekspethē'to, á] a (libre) clear, free.

expeler [ekspeler'] vt to expel, eject.

expendedor, a [ekspendethor', á] nm/f (vendedor) dealer; (TEATRO) ticket agent ♦ nm (aparato) (vending) machine; ~ **de cigarrillos** cigarette machine.

expendeduría [ekspendethōōrē'á] nf (estanco) cigar store (US), tobacconist's (shop) (Brit).

expensas [ekspen'sás] nfpl (JUR) costs; **a** ~ **de** at the expense of.

experiencia [eksperyen'syá] *nf* experience.
experimentado, a [eksperēmentá'tho, á] *a* experienced.
experimentar [eksperēmentár'] *vt* (*en laboratorio*) to experiment with; (*probar*) to test, try out; (*notar, observar*) to experience; (*deterioro, pérdida*) to suffer; (*aumento*) to show; (*sensación*) to feel.
experimento [eksperēmen'to] *nm* experiment.
experto, a [eksper'to, á] *a* expert ♦ *nm/f* expert.
expiar [ekspēár'] *vt* to atone for.
expida [ekspē'thá] *etc vb V* **expedir**.
expirar [ekspērár'] *vi* to expire.
explanada [eksplåná'thá] *nf* (*paseo*) esplanade; (*a orillas del mar*) promenade.
explayarse [eksplåyár'se] *vr* (*en discurso*) to speak at length; ~ **con uno** to confide in sb.
explicación [eksplēkásyon'] *nf* explanation.
explicar [eksplēkár'] *vt* to explain; (*teoría*) to expound; (*UNIV*) to lecture in; ~**se** *vr* to explain (o.s.); **no me lo explico** I can't understand it.
explícito, a [eksplē'sēto, á] *a* explicit.
explique [eksplē'ke] *etc vb V* **explicar**.
exploración [eksplorásyon'] *nf* exploration; (*MIL*) reconnaissance.
explorador, a [eksploráthor', á] *nm/f* (*pionero*) explorer; (*MIL*) scout ♦ *nm* (*MED*) probe; (*radar*) scanner.
explorar [eksplorár'] *vt* to explore; (*MED*) to probe; (*radar*) to scan.
explosión [eksplosyon'] *nf* explosion.
explosivo, a [eksplosē'ḫo, á] *a* explosive.
explotación [eksplotásyon'] *nf* exploitation; (*de planta etc*) running; (*de mina*) working; (*de recurso*) development; ~ **minera** mine; **gastos de** ~ operating costs.
explotar [eksplotár'] *vt* to exploit; (*planta*) to run, operate; (*mina*) to work ♦ *vi* (*bomba etc*) to explode, go off.
expondré [ekspondre'] *etc vb V* **exponer**.
exponer [eksponer'] *vt* to expose; (*cuadro*) to display; (*vida*) to risk; (*idea*) to explain; (*teoría*) to expound; (*hechos*) to set out; ~**se** *vr*: ~**se a (hacer) algo** to run the risk of (doing) sth.
exponga [ekspon'gá] *etc vb V* **exponer**.
exportación [eksportásyon'] *nf* (*acción*) export; (*mercancías*) exports *pl*.
exportador, a [eksportáthor', á] *a* (*país*) exporting ♦ *nm/f* exporter.
exportar [eksportár'] *vt* to export.
exposición [eksposēsyon'] *nf* (*gen*) exposure; (*de arte*) show, exhibition; (*COM*) display; (*feria*) show, fair; (*explicación*) explanation; (*de teoría*) exposition; (*narración*) account, statement.
exprés [ekspres'] *a inv* (*café*) espresso ♦ *nm*

(*AM*) express (train).
expresado, a [ekspresá'tho, á] *a* abovementioned.
expresamente [ekspresámen'te] *ad* (*concretamente*) expressly; (*a propósito*) on purpose.
expresar [ekspresár'] *vt* to express; (*redactar*) to phrase, put; (*emoción*) to show; ~**se** *vr* to express o.s.; (*dato*) to be stated; **como abajo se expresa** as stated below.
expresión [ekspresyon'] *nf* expression; ~ **familiar** colloquialism.
expresivo, a [ekspresē'ḫo, á] *a* expressive; (*cariñoso*) affectionate.
expreso, a [ekspre'so, á] *a* (*explícito*) express; (*claro*) specific, clear; (*tren*) fast ♦ *nm* (*FERRO*) fast train ♦ *ad*: **mandar** ~ to send by express (delivery).
exprimidor [eksprēmēthor'] *nm* (lemon) squeezer.
exprimir [eksprēmēr'] *vt* (*fruta*) to squeeze; (*zumo*) to squeeze out.
ex profeso [eksprofe'so] *ad* (*ADMIN, JUR*) on purpose.
expropiar [ekspropyár'] *vt* to expropriate.
expuesto, a [ekspwe'sto, á] *pp de* **exponer** ♦ *a* exposed; (*cuadro etc*) on show, on display; **según lo** ~ **arriba** according to what has been stated above.
expulsar [ekspōōlsár'] *vt* (*echar*) to eject, throw out; (*alumno*) to expel; (*despedir*) to fire; (*DEPORTE*) to eject (*US*), send off (*Brit*).
expulsión [ekspōōlsyon'] *nf* expulsion; (*DEPORTE*) ejection (*US*), sending-off (*Brit*).
expuse [ekspōō'se] *etc vb V* **exponer**.
expurgar [ekspōōrgár'] *vt* to expurgate.
exquisito, a [ekskēsē'to, á] *a* exquisite; (*comida*) delicious; (*afectado*) affected.
Ext. *abr* (= *Exterior*) ext.; (= *Extensión*) ext.
éxtasis [ek'stásēs] *nm* ecstasy.
extemporáneo, a [ekstemporá'neo, á] *a* unseasonal.
extender [ekstender'] *vt* to extend; (*los brazos*) to stretch out, hold out; (*mapa, tela*) to spread (out), open (out); (*mantequilla*) to spread; (*certificado*) to issue; (*cheque, recibo*) to make out; (*documento*) to draw up; ~**se** *vr* to extend; (*terreno*) to stretch *o* spread (out); (*persona: en el suelo*) to stretch out; (*en el tiempo*) to extend, last; (*costumbre, epidemia*) to spread; (*guerra*) to escalate; ~**se sobre un tema** to enlarge on a subject.
extendido, a [ekstendē'tho, á] *a* (*abierto*) spread out, open; (*brazos*) outstretched; (*costumbre etc*) widespread.
extensible [ekstensē'ḫle] *a* extending.
extensión [ekstensyon'] *nf* (*de terreno, mar*) expanse, stretch; (*MUS*) range; (*de*

conocimientos) extent; (*de programa*) scope; (*de tiempo*) length, duration; (*TELEC*) extension; ~ **de plazo** (*COM*) extension; **en toda la ~ de la palabra** in every sense of the word; **de ~** (*INFORM*) add-on.

extenso, a [eksten'so, à] *a* extensive.

extenuar [ekstenwår'] *vt* (*debilitar*) to weaken.

exterior [eksteryor'] *a* (*de fuera*) external; (*afuera*) outside, exterior; (*apariencia*) outward; (*deuda, relaciones*) foreign ♦ *nm* exterior, outside; (*aspecto*) outward appearance; (*DEPORTE*) forward (*US*), wing(er) (*Brit*); (*países extranjeros*) abroad; **asuntos ~es** foreign affairs; **al ~** outwardly, on the outside; **en el ~** abroad; **noticias del ~** foreign *o* overseas news.

exteriorice [eksteryorē'se] *etc vb* V **exteriorizar.**

exteriorizar [eksteryorēsår'] *vt* (*emociones*) to show, reveal.

exteriormente [eksteryormen'te] *ad* outwardly.

exterminar [ekstermēnår'] *vt* to exterminate.

exterminio [ekstermē'nyo] *nm* extermination.

externo, a [ekster'no, à] *a* (*exterior*) external, outside; (*superficial*) outward ♦ *nm/f* day pupil.

extienda [ekstyen'dà] *etc vb* V **extender.**

extinción [ekstēnsyon'] *nf* extinction.

extinga [ekstēn'gà] *etc vb* V **extinguir.**

extinguido, a [ekstēngē'tho, à] (*animal, volcán*) extinct; (*fuego*) out, extinguished.

extinguir [ekstēngēr'] *vt* (*fuego*) to extinguish, put out; (*raza, población*) to wipe out; **~se** *vr* (*fuego*) to go out; (*BIO*) to die out, become extinct.

extinto, a [ekstēn'to, à] *a* extinct.

extintor [ekstēntor'] *nm* (*fire*) extinguisher.

extirpar [ekstērpår'] *vt* (*vicios*) to eradicate, stamp out; (*MED*) to remove (surgically).

extorsión [ekstorsyon'] *nf* blackmail.

extra [eks'trà] *a inv* (*tiempo*) extra; (*vino*) vintage; (*chocolate*) good-quality; (*gasolina*) high-octane ♦ *nm/f* extra ♦ *nm* (*bono*) bonus; (*periódico*) special edition.

extracción [ekstråksyon'] *nf* extraction; (*en lotería*) draw; (*de carbón*) mining.

extracto [ekstråk'to] *nm* extract.

extradición [ekstråthēsyon'] *nf* extradition.

extradicionar [ekstråthēsyonår'], **extraditar** [ekstråthētår'] *vt* to extradite.

extraer [ekstråer'] *vt* to extract, take out.

extrafino, a [ekstråfē'no, à] *a* extra-fine; **azúcar ~** caster sugar.

extraiga [ekstrà'ēgà] *etc*, **extraje** [ekstrà'he] *etc*, **extrajera** [ekstråhe'rà] *etc vb* V **extraer.**

extralimitarse [ekstrålēmētår'se] *vr* to go too far.

extranjerismo [ekstrånherēs'mo] *nm* foreign word *o* phrase *etc.*

extranjero, a [ekstrånhe'ro, à] *a* foreign ♦ *nm/f* foreigner ♦ *nm* foreign lands *pl*; **en el ~** abroad.

extrañamiento [ekstrånyàmyen'to] *nm* estrangement.

extrañar [ekstrånyàr'] *vt* (*sorprender*) to find strange *o* odd; (*echar de menos*) to miss; **~se** *vr* (*sorprenderse*) to be amazed, be surprised; (*distanciarse*) to become estranged, grow apart; **me extraña** I'm surprised.

extrañeza [ekstrånye'sà] *nf* (*rareza*) strangeness, oddness; (*asombro*) amazement, surprise.

extraño, a [ekstrà'nyo, à] *a* (*extranjero*) foreign; (*raro, sorprendente*) strange, odd.

extraoficial [ekstråofēsyál'] *a* unofficial, informal.

extraordinario, a [ekstráorthēnà'ryo, à] *a* extraordinary; (*edición, número*) special ♦ *nm* (*de periódico*) special edition; **horas extraordinarias** overtime *sg.*

extrarradio [ekstrårrà'thyo] *nm* suburbs *pl.*

extrasensorial [ekstråsensoryál'] *a*: **percepción ~** extrasensory perception.

extraterrestre [ekstráterres'tre] *a* of *o* from outer space ♦ *nm/f* creature from outer space.

extravagancia [ekstråbàgàn'syá] *nf* oddness; outlandishness; (*rareza*) peculiarity; **~s** *nfpl* (*tonterías*) nonsense *sg.*

extravagante [ekstråbàgàn'te] *a* (*excéntrico*) eccentric; (*estrafalario*) outlandish.

extraviado, a [ekstråbyà'tho, à] *a* lost, missing.

extraviar [ekstråbyàr'] *vt* to mislead, misdirect; (*perder*) to lose, misplace; **~se** *vr* to lose one's way, get lost; (*objeto*) to go missing, be mislaid.

extravío [ekstråbē'o] *nm* loss; (*fig*) misconduct.

extrayendo [ekstråyen'do] *vb* V **extraer.**

extremado, a [ekstremà'tho, à] *a* extreme, excessive.

Extremadura [ekstremåthōō'rà] *nf* Estremadura.

extremar [ekstremår'] *vt* to carry to extremes; **~se** *vr* to do one's utmost, make every effort.

extremaunción [ekstremáōōnsyon'] *nf* extreme unction, last rites *pl.*

extremidad [ekstremēthàth'] *nf* (*punta*) extremity; (*fila*) edge; **~es** *nfpl* (*ANAT*) extremities.

extremo, a [ekstre'mo, à] *a* extreme; (*más alejado*) furthest; (*último*) last ♦ *nm* end; (*situación*) extreme; **E~ Oriente** Far East; **en último ~** as a last resort; **pasar de un**

~ **a otro** (*fig*) to go from one extreme to the other; **con** ~ in the extreme; **la extrema derecha** (*POL*) the far right; ~ **derecho/izquierdo** (*DEPORTE*) outside right/ left.

extrínseco, a [ekstrēn'seko, á] *a* extrinsic.

extrovertido, a [ekstroḫertē'ḋo, á] *a* extrovert, outgoing ♦ *nm/f* extrovert.

exuberancia [eksōōḫerán'syá] *nf* exuberance.

exuberante [eksōōḫerán'te] *a* exuberant; (*fig*) luxuriant, lush.

exudar [eksōōṫhár'] *vt, vi* to exude.

exultar [eksōōltár'] *vi*: ~ **(en)** to exult (in); (*pey*) to gloat (over).

exvoto [eksḫo'to] *nm* votive offering.

eyacular [eyákōōlár'] *vt, vi* to ejaculate.

F

F,f [e'fe] *nf* (*letra*) F, f; **F de Francia** F for Fox.

f.ª *abr* (*COM*: = *factura*) Inv.

f.a.b. *abr* (= *franco a bordo*) f.o.b.

fabada [fáḫá'ṫhá] *nf* bean and sausage stew.

fábrica [fá'ḫrēká] *nf* factory; ~ **de moneda** mint; **marca de** ~ trademark; **precio de** ~ factory price.

fabricación [fáḫrēkásyon'] *nf* (*manufactura*) manufacture; (*producción*) production; **de** ~ **casera** home-made; **de** ~ **nacional** domestically produced; ~ **en serie** mass production.

fabricante [fáḫrēkán'te] *nm/f* manufacturer.

fabricar [fáḫrēkár'] *vt* (*manufacturar*) to manufacture, make; (*construir*) to build; (*cuento*) to fabricate, devise; ~ **en serie** to mass-produce.

fabrique [fáḫrē'ke] *etc vb V* **fabricar**.

fabril [fáḫrēl'] *a*: **industria** ~ manufacturing industry.

fábula [fá'ḫōōlá] *nf* (*cuento*) fable; (*chisme*) rumor (*US*), rumour (*Brit*); (*mentira*) fib.

FACA [fá'ká] *nm abr* (*Esp AVIAT*)=*Futuro Avión de Combate y Ataque*.

facción [fáksyon'] *nf* (*POL*) faction; **facciones** *nfpl* (*del rostro*) features.

faceta [fáse'tá] *nf* facet.

fácil [fá'sēl] *a* (*simple*) easy; (*sencillo*) simple, straightforward; (*probable*) likely; (*respuesta*) facile; ~ **de usar** (*INFORM*) user-friendly.

facilidad [fáselēṫháḋ'] *nf* (*capacidad*) ease; (*sencillez*) simplicity; (*de palabra*) fluency;

~**es** *nfpl* facilities; "~**es de pago**" (*COM*) "credit facilities","payment terms".

facilitar [fásēlētár'] *vt* (*hacer fácil*) to make easy; (*proporcionar*) to provide; (*documento*) to issue; **le agradecería me facilitara ...** I would be grateful if you could let me have ....

fácilmente [fá'sēlmente] *ad* easily.

facsímil [fáksē'mēl] *nm* (*documento*) facsimile; **enviar por** ~ to fax.

factible [fáktē'ḅle] *a* feasible.

factor [fáktor'] *nm* factor; (*COM*) agent; (*FERRO*) freight clerk.

factoría [fáktorē'á] *nf* (*COM: agencia*) agency; (: *fábrica*) factory.

factura [fáktōō'rá] *nf* (*cuenta*) bill; (*nota de pago*) invoice; (*hechura*) manufacture; **presentar** ~ **a** to invoice.

facturación [fáktōōrásyon'] *nf* (*COM*) invoicing; (: *ventas*) turnover; ~ **de equipajes** luggage check-in.

facturar [fáktōōrár'] *vt* (*COM*) to invoice, charge for; (*AVIAT*) to check in; (*equipaje*) to check (*US*), register (*Brit*).

facultad [fákōōltáṫh'] *nf* (*aptitud, ESCOL etc*) faculty; (*poder*) power.

facultativo, a [fákōōltátē'ḋo, á] *a* optional; (*de un oficio*) professional; **prescripción facultativa** medical prescription.

facha [fátch'á] (*fam*) *nm/f* fascist, right-wing extremist ♦ *nf* (*aspecto*) look; (*cara*) face; **¡qué** ~ **tienes!** you look a sight!

fachada [fátchá'ṫhá] *nf* (*ARQ*) façade, front; (*TIP*) title page; (*fig*) façade, outward show.

FAD *nm abr* (*Esp*)=*Fondo de Ayuda y Desarrollo*.

faena [fáe'ná] *nf* (*trabajo*) work; (*quehacer*) task, job; ~**s domésticas** housework *sg*.

faenar [fáenár'] *vi* to fish.

fagot [fáḡot'] *nm* (*MUS*) bassoon.

faisán [fáesán'] *nm* pheasant.

faja [fá'há] *nf* (*para la cintura*) sash; (*de mujer*) corset; (*de tierra*) strip.

fajo [fá'ho] *nm* (*de papeles*) bundle; (*de billetes*) role, wad.

falange [fálán'he] *nf*: **la F~** (*POL*) the Falange.

falda [fál'dá] *nf* (*prenda de vestir*) skirt; (*GEO*) foothill; ~ **escocesa** kilt.

fálico, a [fá'lēko, á] *a* phallic.

falo [fá'lo] *nm* phallus.

falsear [fálseár'] *vt* to falsify; (*firma etc*) to forge ♦ *vi* (*MUS*) to be out of tune.

falsedad [fálseṫháḋ'] *nf* falseness; (*hipocresía*) hypocrisy; (*mentira*) falsehood.

falsificación [fálsēfēkásyon'] *nf* (*acto*) falsification; (*objeto*) forgery.

falsificar [fálsēfēkár'] *vt* (*firma etc*) to forge; (*voto etc*) to rig; (*moneda*) to counterfeit.

falsifique [fálsēfē'kε] *etc vb* V **falsificar**.

falso, a [fál'so, á] *a* false; (*erróneo*) wrong, mistaken; (*firma, documento*) forged; (*documento, moneda etc*) fake; **en ~** falsely; **dar un paso en ~** to trip; (*fig*) to take a false step.

falta [fál'tá] *nf* (*defecto*) fault, flaw; (*privación*) lack, want; (*ausencia*) absence; (*carencia*) shortage; (*equivocación*) mistake; (*JUR*) default; (*DEPORTE*) foul; (*TENIS*) fault; **~ de ortografía** spelling mistake; **~ de respeto** disrespect; **echar en ~** to miss; **hacer ~ hacer algo** to be necessary to do sth; **me hace ~ una pluma** I need a pen; **sin ~** without fail; **por ~ de** through *o* for lack of.

faltar [fáltár'] *vi* (*escasear*) to be lacking, be wanting; (*ausentarse*) to be absent, be missing; **¿falta algo?** is anything missing?; **falta mucho todavía** there's plenty of time yet; **¿falta mucho?** is there long to go?; **faltan 2 horas para llegar** there are 2 hours to go till arrival; **~ (al respeto) a uno** to be disrespectful to sb; **~ a una cita** to miss an appointment; **~ a la verdad** to lie; **¡no faltaba más!** that's the last straw!

falto, a [fál'to, á] *a* (*desposeído*) deficient, lacking; (*necesitado*) poor, wretched; **estar ~ de** to be short of.

falla [fá'yá] *nf* (*defecto*) fault, flaw.

fallar [fáyár'] *vt* (*JUR*) to pronounce sentence on; (*NAIPES*) to trump ♦ *vi* (*memoria*) to fail; (*plan*) to go wrong; (*motor*) to miss; **~ a uno** to let sb down.

fallecer [fáyεsεr'] *vi* to pass away, die.

fallecido, a [fáyεsē'tho, á] *a* late ♦ *nm/f* deceased.

fallecimiento [fáyεsēmyεn'to] *nm* decease, demise.

fallezca [fáyεs'ká] *etc vb* V **fallecer**.

fallido, a [fáyē'tho, á] *a* vain; (*intento*) frustrated, unsuccessful; (*esperanza*) disappointed.

fallo [fá'yo] *nm* (*JUR*) verdict, ruling; (*decisión*) decision; (*de jurado*) findings; (*fracaso*) failure; (*DEPORTE*) miss; (*INFORM*) bug.

fama [fá'má] *nf* (*renombre*) fame; (*reputación*) reputation.

famélico, a [fámε'lēko, á] *a* starving.

familia [fámē'lyá] *nf* family; **~ política** in-laws *pl*.

familiar [fámēlyár'] *a* (*relativo a la familia*) family *cpd*; (*conocido, informal*) familiar; (*estilo*) informal; (*LING*) colloquial ♦ *nm/f* relative, relation.

familiarice [fámēlyárē'sε] *etc vb* V **familiarizarse**.

familiaridad [fámēlyárētháth'] *nf* familiarity; (*informalidad*) homeliness.

familiarizarse [fámēlyárēsár'sε] *vr*: **~ con** to familiarize o.s. with.

famoso, a [fámo'so, á] *a* (*renombrado*) famous.

fanático, a [fáná'tēko, á] *a* fanatical ♦ *nm/f* fanatic; (*CINE, DEPORTE etc*) fan.

fanatismo [fánátēs'mo] *nm* fanaticism.

fanfarrón, ona [fánfárron', oná] *a* boastful; (*pey*) showy.

fango [fán'go] *nm* mud.

fangoso, a [fángo'so, á] *a* muddy.

fantasear [fántáseár'] *vi* to fantasize; **~ con una idea** to toy with an idea.

fantasía [fántásē'á] *nf* fantasy, imagination; (*MUS*) fantasia; (*capricho*) whim; **joyas de ~** imitation jewellery *sg*.

fantasma [fántás'má] *nm* (*espectro*) ghost, apparition; (*presumido*) show-off.

fantástico, a [fántás'stēko, á] *a* (*irreal, fam*) fantastic.

FAO [fá'o] *nf abr* (= *Organización de las Naciones Unidas para la Agricultura y la Alimentación*) FAO.

fardar [fárthár'] *vi* to show off; **~ de** to boast about.

fardo [fár'tho] *nm* bundle; (*fig*) burden.

farmacéutico, a [fármásε'ōōtēko, á] *a* pharmaceutical ♦ *nm/f* pharmacist, chemist (*Brit*).

farmacia [fármá'syá] *nf* (*ciencia*) pharmacy; (*tienda*) drugstore (*US*), chemist's (shop) (*Brit*), pharmacy; **~ de turno** pharmacy on call (*US*), duty chemist (*Brit*).

fármaco [fár'máko] *nm* medicine, drug.

faro [fá'ro] *nm* (*NAUT: torre*) lighthouse; (*señal*) beacon; (*AUTO*) headlamp; **~s antiniebla** fog lamps; **~s delanteros/ traseros** headlights/rear lights.

farol [fárol'] *nm* (*luz*) lantern, lamp; (*FERRO*) headlamp; (*poste*) lamppost; **echarse un ~** (*fam*) to show off.

farola [fáro'lá] *nf* street light, lamppost.

farruco, a [fárrōō'ko, á] *a* (*fam*): **estar** *o* **ponerse ~** to get aggressive.

farsa [fár'sá] *nf* (*gen*) farce.

farsante [fársán'tε] *nm/f* fraud, fake.

FASA [fá'sá] *nf abr* (*Esp AUTO*)=*Fábrica de Automóviles, S.A.*

fascículo [fásē'kōōlo] *nm* (*gen*) part, installment (*US*), instalment (*Brit*).

fascinante [fásēnán'tε] *a* fascinating.

fascinar [fásēnár'] *vt* to fascinate; (*encantar*) to captivate.

fascismo [fásēs'mo] *nm* fascism.

fascista [fásēs'tá] *a, nm/f* fascist.

fase [fá'sε] *nf* phase.

fastidiar [fástēthyár'] *vt* (*disgustar*) to annoy, bother; (*estropear*) to spoil; **~se** *vr* (*disgustarse*) to get annoyed *o* cross; **¡no fastidies!** you're joking!; **¡que se fastidie!** (*fam*) he'll just have to put up with it!

fastidio [fåstɛ'dhyo] *nm* (*disgusto*) annoyance.

fastidioso, a [fåstɛdhyo'so, å] *a* (*molesto*) annoying.

fastuoso, a [fåstwo'so, å] *a* (*espléndido*) magnificent; (*banquete etc*) lavish.

fatal [fåtál'] *a* (*gen*) fatal; (*desgraciado*) ill-fated; (*fam: malo, pésimo*) awful ♦ *ad* terribly; **lo pasó ~** he had a terrible time (of it).

fatalidad [fåtálɛ'dhàdh'] *nf* (*destino*) fate; (*mala suerte*) misfortune.

fatídico, a [fåtɛ'dheko, å] *a* fateful.

fatiga [fåtɛ'gå] *nf* (*cansancio*) fatigue, weariness; **~s** *nfpl* hardships.

fatigar [fåtɛgár'] *vt* to tire, weary; **~se** *vr* to get tired.

fatigoso, a [fåtɛgo'so, å] *a* (*cansador*) tiring.

fatigue [fåtɛ'ge] *etc vb* V **fatigar**.

fatuo, a [få'two, å] *a* (*vano*) fatuous; (*presuntuoso*) conceited.

fauces [få'ōōses] *nfpl* (*ANAT*) gullet *sg*; (*fam*) jaws.

fauna [få'ōōnå] *nf* fauna.

favor [fåhor'] *nm* favor (*US*), favour (*Brit*); **haga el ~ de ...** would you be so good as to ..., kindly ...; **por ~** please; **a ~ in** favo(u)r; **a ~ de** to be in favo(u)r of; (*COM*) to the order of.

favorable [fåhorá'hle] *a* favorable (*US*), favourable (*Brit*); (*condiciones etc*) advantageous.

favorecer [fåhoreser'] *vt* to favor (*US*), favour (*Brit*); (*amparar*) to help; (*vestido etc*) to become, flatter; **este peinado le favorece** this hairstyle suits him.

favorezca [fåhores'kå] *etc vb* V **favorecer**.

favorito, a [fåhorɛ'to, å] *a, nm/f* favorite (*US*), favourite (*Brit*).

faz [fås] *nf* face; **la ~ de la tierra** the face of the earth.

F.C., f.c. *abr* = **ferrocarril**.

FE *nf abr* = **Falange Española**.

fe [fe] *nf* (*REL*) faith; (*confianza*) belief; (*documento*) certificate; **de buena ~** (*JUR*) bona fide; **prestar ~ a** to believe, credit; **actuar con buena/mala ~** to act in good/bad faith; **dar ~ de** to bear witness to; **~ de erratas** errata.

fealdad [feåldàdh'] *nf* ugliness.

feb., feb.º *abr* (= *febrero*) Feb.

febrero [fehre'ro] *nm* February.

febril [fehrɛl'] *a* feverish; (*movido*) hectic.

fécula [fe'kōōlå] *nf* starch.

fecundación [fekōōndásyon'] *nf* fertilization; **~ in vitro** in vitro fertilization, I.V.F.

fecundar [fekōōndár'] *vt* (*generar*) to fertilize, make fertile.

fecundidad [fekōōndɛ'dhàdh'] *nf* fertility; (*fig*) productiveness.

fecundo, a [fekōōn'do, å] *a* (*fértil*) fertile; (*fig*) prolific; (*productivo*) productive.

fecha [fetch'å] *nf* date; **~ límite** *o* **tope** closing *o* last date; **~ límite de venta** (*de alimentos*) sell-by date; **~ de caducidad** (*de alimentos*) sell-by date; (*de contrato*) expiration (*US*) *o* expiry (*Brit*) date; **en ~ próxima** soon; **hasta la ~** to date, so far; **~ de vencimiento** (*COM*) due date; **~ de vigencia** (*COM*) effective date.

fechar [fetchár'] *vt* to date.

federación [fedheråsyon'] *nf* federation.

federal [fedherál'] *a* federal.

federalismo [fedheråles'mo] *nm* federalism.

FEF [fef] *nf abr* = *Federación Española de Fútbol*.

felicidad [felesɛ'dhàdh'] *nf* (*satisfacción, contento*) happiness; **~es** *nfpl* best wishes, congratulations.

felicitaciones [felesɛtåsyo'nes] *nfpl* congratulations.

felicitar [felesɛtår'] *vt* to congratulate.

feligrés, esa [feleˈgres', esá] *nm/f* parishioner.

feliz [feles'] *a* (*contento*) happy; (*afortunado*) lucky.

felonía [felonɛ'á] *nf* felony, crime.

felpa [fel'på] *nf* (*terciopelo*) plush; (*toalla*) towelling.

felpudo [felpōō'dho] *nm* doormat.

femenino, a [femenɛ'no, å] *a* feminine; (*ZOOL etc*) female ♦ *nm* (*LING*) feminine.

feminismo [femɛnes'mo] *nm* feminism.

feminista [femɛnɛ'stá] *a, nm/f* feminist.

fenomenal [fenomenál'] *a* phenomenal; (*fam*) great, terrific.

fenómeno [feno'meno] *nm* phenomenon; (*fig*) freak, accident ♦ *ad*: **lo pasamos ~** we had a great time ♦ *excl* great!, marvelous! (*US*), marvellous! (*Brit*).

feo, a [fe'o, å] *a* (*gen*) ugly; (*desagradable*) bad, nasty ♦ *nm* insult; **hacer un ~ a uno** to offend sb; **más ~ que Picio** as ugly as sin.

féretro [fe'retro] *nm* (*ataúd*) coffin; (*sarcófago*) bier.

feria [fe'ryå] *nf* (*gen*) fair; (*AM: mercado*) market; (*descanso*) holiday, day off; (*AM: cambio*) small change; **~ comercial** trade fair; **~ de muestras** trade show.

feriado, a [feryå'dho, å] (*AM*) *a*: **día ~** (*public*) holiday ♦ *nm* (*public*) holiday.

fermentar [fermentár'] *vi* to ferment.

fermento [fermen'to] *nm* leaven, leavening.

ferocidad [ferosɛ'dhàdh'] *nf* fierceness, ferocity.

ferocísimo, a [ferosɛ'semo, å] *a superlativo de* **feroz**.

feroz [feros'] *a* (*cruel*) cruel; (*salvaje*) fierce.

férreo, a [fe'rreo, å] *a* iron *cpd*; (*TEC*)

ferrous; (*fig*) (of) iron.

ferretería [ferretereꞌá] *nf* (*tienda*) hardware store, ironmonger's (shop) (*Brit*).

ferrocarril [ferrokárrēl'] *nm* railroad, railway (*Brit*); ~ **de vía estrecha/única** narrow-gauge/single-track railway *o* line.

ferroviario, a [ferrovyáryo', á] *a* rail *cpd*, railroad *cpd* (*US*), railway *cpd* (*Brit*) ♦ *nm*: ~**s** railroad (*US*) *o* railway (*Brit*) workers.

fértil [fer'tēl] *a* (*productivo*) fertile; (*rico*) rich.

fertilice [fertēlē'se] *etc vb V* **fertilizar**.

fertilidad [fertēlēꞌáth'] *nf* (*gen*) fertility; (*productividad*) fruitfulness.

fertilizar [fertēlēsár'] *vt* to fertilize.

fervor [ferꞌor'] *nm* fervor (*US*), fervour (*Brit*).

fervoroso, a [ferꞌoro'so, á] *a* fervent.

festejar [festehár'] *vt* (*agasajar*) to wine and dine, fête; (*galantear*) to court; (*celebrar*) to celebrate.

festejo [feste'ho] *nm* (*diversión*) entertainment; (*galanteo*) courtship; (*fiesta*) celebration.

festín [festēn'] *nm* feast, banquet.

festival [festēꞌál'] *nm* festival.

festividad [festēꞌēꞌáth'] *nf* festivity.

festivo, a [festēꞌho, á] *a* (*de fiesta*) festive; (*fig*) witty; (*CINE, LIT*) humorous; **día** ~ holiday.

fetiche [fetētch'e] *nm* fetish.

fetichista [fetētchē'stá] *a* fetishistic ♦ *nm/f* fetishist.

fétido, a [fe'tētho, á] *a* (*hediondo*) foul-smelling.

feto [fe'to] *nm* fetus; (*fam*) monster.

FF.AA. *nfpl abr* (*MIL*) = **Fuerzas Armadas**.

FF.CC. *nmpl abr* = **Ferrocarriles**.

fiable [fēā'ꞌle] *a* (*persona*) trustworthy; (*máquina*) reliable.

fiado [fēā'ꞌho] *nm*: **comprar al** ~ to buy on credit; **en** ~ on bail.

fiador, a [fēāꞌhor', á] *nm/f* (*JUR*) surety, guarantor; (*COM*) backer; **salir** ~ **por uno** to post (*US*) *o* stand (*Brit*) bail for sb.

fiambre [fyám'bre] *a* (*CULIN*) (served) cold ♦ *nm* (*CULIN*) cold cut; (*fam*) corpse, stiff.

fiambrera [fyámbre'rá] *nf* ≈ dinner pail (*US*), lunch box.

fianza [fyán'sá] *nf* surety; (*JUR*): **libertad bajo** ~ release on bail.

fiar [fēār'] *vt* (*salir garante de*) to guarantee; (*JUR*) to post (*US*) *o* stand (*Brit*) bail for; (*vender a crédito*) to sell on credit; (*secreto*) to confide ♦ *vi*: ~ **(de)** to trust (in); **ser de** ~ to be trustworthy; ~**se** *vr*: ~ **de** to trust (in), rely on.

fiasco [fyás'ko] *nm* fiasco.

fibra [fē'ꞌrá] *nf* fiber (*US*), fibre (*Brit*); (*fig*) vigor (*US*), vigour (*Brit*); ~ **óptica** (*IN*-*FORM*) optical fiber.

ficción [fēksyon'] *nf* fiction.

ficticio, a [fēktē'syo, á] *a* (*imaginario*) fictitious; (*falso*) fabricated.

ficus [fē'kōōs] *nm inv* (*BOT*) rubber plant.

ficha [fētch'á] *nf* (*TELEC*) token; (*en juegos*) counter, marker; (*en casino*) chip; (*COM, ECON*) check (*US*), tally; (*INFORM*) file; (*tarjeta*) (index) card; (*ELEC*) plug; (*en hotel*) registration form; ~ **policíaca** police dossier.

fichaje [fētchá'he] *nm* signing(-up).

fichar [fētchár'] *vt* (*archivar*) to file, index; (*DEPORTE*) to sign (up) ♦ *vi* (*deportista*) to sign (up); (*obrero*) to clock in *o* on; **estar fichado** to have a record.

fichero [fētche'ro] *nm* card index; (*archivo*) filing cabinet; (*COM*) box file; (*INFORM*) file, archive; (*de policía*) criminal records; ~ **activo** (*INFORM*) active file; ~ **archivado** (*INFORM*) archived file; ~ **indexado** (*INFORM*) index file; ~ **de reserva** (*INFORM*) backup file; ~ **de tarjetas** card index; **nombre de** ~ filename.

fidedigno, a [fēthethēg'no, á] *a* reliable.

fideicomiso [fēthecēkomē'so] *nm* (*COM*) trust.

fidelidad [fēthelēꞌáth'] *nf* (*lealtad*) fidelity, loyalty; (*exactitud: de dato etc*) accuracy; **alta** ~ high fidelity, hi-fi.

fidelísimo, a [fēthelē'sēmo, á] *a superlativo de* **fiel**.

fideos [fēthe'os] *nmpl* noodles.

fiduciario, a [fēthōōsyá'ryo, á] *nm/f* fiduciary.

fiebre [fyeꞌre] *nf* (*MED*) fever; (*fig*) fever, excitement; ~ **amarilla/del heno** yellow/hay fever; ~ **palúdica** malaria; **tener** ~ to have a temperature.

fiel [fyel] *a* (*leal*) faithful, loyal; (*fiable*) reliable; (*exacto*) accurate ♦ *nm* (*aguja*) needle, pointer; **los** ~**es** the faithful.

fieltro [fyel'tro] *nm* felt.

fiera [fye'rá] *nf V* **fiero**.

fiereza [fyere'sá] *nf* (*ZOOL*) wildness; (*bravura*) fierceness.

fiero, a [fye'ro, á] *a* (*cruel*) cruel; (*feroz*) fierce; (*duro*) harsh ♦ *nm/f* (*fig*) fiend ♦ *nf* (*animal feroz*) wild animal *o* beast; (*fig*) dragon.

fiesta [fye'stá] *nf* party; (*de pueblo*) festival; (*vacaciones: tb*: ~**s**) holiday; ~ **nacional** national (*US*) *o* bank (*Brit*) holiday; **mañana es** ~ it's a holiday tomorrow; ~ **de guardar** (*REL*) day of obligation.

figura [fēgōō'rá] *nf* (*gen*) figure; (*forma, imagen*) shape, form; (*NAIPES*) face card.

figurado, a [fēgōōrá'tho, á] *a* figurative.

figurar [fēgōōrár'] *vt* (*representar*) to represent; (*fingir*) to feign ♦ *vi* to figure; ~**se** *vr* (*imaginarse*) to imagine; (*suponer*) to suppose; **ya me lo figuraba** I thought as much.

fijador [fēhád̦or'] *nm* (*FOTO etc*) fixative; (*de pelo*) cream (*US*), gel (*Brit*).

fijar [fēhár'] *vt* (*gen*) to fix; (*cartel*) to post, put up; (*estampilla*) to affix, stick (on); (*pelo*) to set; (*fig*) to settle (on), decide; **~se** *vr*: **~se en** to notice; **¡fíjate!** just imagine!; **¿te fijas?** see what I mean?

fijo, a [fē'ho, á] *a* (*gen*) fixed; (*firme*) firm; (*permanente*) permanent; (*trabajo*) steady; (*color*) fast ♦ *ad*: **mirar ~** to stare.

fila [fē'lá] *nf* row; (*MIL*) rank; (*cadena*) line; (*MIL*) rank; (*en marcha*) file; **~ india** single file; **ponerse en ~** to line up, get into line; **primera ~** front row.

filántropo, a [fēlán'tropo, á] *nm/f* philanthropist.

filarmónico, a [fēlármo'nēko, á] *a, nf* philharmonic.

filatelia [fēláte'lyá] *nf* philately, stamp collecting.

filatelista [fēlátelē'stá] *nm/f* philatelist, stamp collector.

filete [fēle'te] *nm* (*carne*) fillet steak; (*de cerdo*) tenderloin; (*pescado*) fillet; (*MEC: rosca*) thread.

filiación [fēlyásyon'] *nf* (*POL etc*) affiliation; (*señas*) particulars *pl*; (*MIL, POLICÍA*) records *pl*.

filial [fēlyál'] *a* filial ♦ *nf* subsidiary; (*sucursal*) branch.

filibustero [fēlēḇōoste'ro] *nm* pirate.

Filipinas [fēlēpē'nás] *nfpl*: **las (Islas) ~** the Philippines.

filipino, a [fēlēpē'no, á] *a, nm/f* Philippine.

film [fēlm], *pl* **films** *nm* movie.

filmación [fēlmásyon'] *nf* filming, shooting.

filmar [fēlmár'] *vt* to film, shoot.

filmoteca [fēlmote'ká] *nf* film library.

filo [fē'lo] *nm* (*gen*) edge; **sacar ~ a** to sharpen; **al ~ del medio día** at about midday; **de doble ~** double-edged.

filología [fēlolohē'á] *nf* philology.

filólogo, a [fēlo'logo, á] *nm/f* philologist.

filón [fēlon'] *nm* (*MINERÍA*) vein, lode; (*fig*) gold mine.

filosofía [fēlosofē'á] *nf* philosophy.

filosófico, a [fēloso'fēko, á] *a* philosophic(al).

filósofo, a [fēlo'sofo, á] *nm/f* philosopher.

filtración [fēltrásyon'] *nf* (*TEC*) filtration; (*INFORM*) sorting; (*fig: de fondos*) misappropriation; (*de datos*) leak.

filtrar [fēltrár'] *vt, vi* to filter, strain; (*información*) to leak; **~se** *vr* to filter; (*fig: dinero*) to dwindle.

filtro [fēl'tro] *nm* (*TEC, utensilio*) filter.

fin [fēn] *nm* end; (*objetivo*) aim, purpose; **a ~ de cuentas** in the end; **al ~ y al cabo** when all's said and done; **a ~ de** in order

to; **por ~** finally; **en ~** in short; **~ de archivo** (*INFORM*) end-of-file; **~ de semana** weekend; **sin ~** endless(ly).

final [fēnál'] *a* final ♦ *nm* end, conclusion ♦ *nf* (*DEPORTE*) championship (*US*), final (*Brit*).

finalice [fēnálē'se] *etc vb V* **finalizar**.

finalidad [fēnálēd̦ád̦'] *nf* finality; (*propósito*) purpose, aim.

finalista [fēnálē'stá] *nm/f* finalist.

finalizar [fēnálēsár'] *vt* to end, finish ♦ *vi* to end, come to an end; **~ la sesión** (*INFORM*) to log off *o* out (*Brit*).

financiación [fēnánsyásyon'] *nf* financing.

financiar [fēnánsyár'] *vt* to finance.

financiero, a [fēnánsye'ro, á] *a* financial ♦ *nm/f* financier.

finanzas [fēnán'sás] *nfpl* finances.

finca [fēn'ká] *nf* country estate.

fineza [fēne'sá] *nf* (*cualidad*) fineness; (*modales*) refinement.

fingir [fēnhēr'] *vt* (*simular*) to simulate, feign; (*pretextar*) to fake ♦ *vi* (*aparentar*) to pretend; **~se** *vr*: **~se dormido** to pretend to be asleep.

finiquitar [fēnēkētár'] *vt* (*ECON: cuenta*) to settle and close.

Finisterre [fēnēste'rre] *nm*: **el cabo de ~** Cape Finisterre.

finja [fēn'há] *etc vb V* **fingir**.

finlandés, esa [fēnlándes', esá] *a* Finnish ♦ *nm/f* Finn ♦ *nm* (*LING*) Finnish.

Finlandia [fēnlán'dyá] *nf* Finland.

fino, a [fē'no, á] *a* fine; (*delgado*) slender; (*de buenas maneras*) polite, refined; (*inteligente*) shrewd; (*punta*) sharp; (*gusto*) discriminating; (*oído*) sharp; (*jerez*) fino, dry ♦ *nm* (*jerez*) dry sherry.

finura [fēnōō'rá] *nf* (*calidad*) fineness; (*cortesía*) politeness; (*elegancia*) elegance; (*agudeza*) shrewdness.

FIP [fēp] *nf abr* (*Esp*)=*Formación Intensiva Profesional*.

firma [fēr'má] *nf* signature; (*COM*) firm, company.

firmante [fērmán'te] *a, nm/f* signatory; **los abajo ~s** the undersigned.

firmar [fērmár'] *vt* to sign; **~ un contrato** (*COM: colocarse*) to sign on; **firmado y sellado** signed and sealed.

firme [fēr'me] *a* firm; (*estable*) stable; (*sólido*) solid; (*constante*) steady; (*decidido*) resolute; (*duro*) hard; **¡~s!** (*MIL*) attention!; **oferta en ~** (*COM*) firm offer ♦ *nm* road (surface).

firmemente [fērmemen'te] *ad* firmly.

firmeza [fērme'sá] *nf* firmness; (*constancia*) steadiness; (*solidez*) solidity.

fiscal [fēskál'] *a* fiscal ♦ *nm* (*JUR*) ≈ district attorney.

fiscalice [fēskálē'se] *etc vb V* **fiscalizar**.

fiscalizar [fēskálēsár'] *vt* (*controlar*) to control; (*registrar*) to inspect (officially); (*fig*) to criticize.

fisco [fēs'ko] *nm* (*hacienda*) treasury, exchequer (*Brit*); **declarar algo al** ~ to declare sth for tax purposes.

fisgar [fēsᵹár'] *vt* to pry into.

fisgue [fēs'ᵹe] *etc vb V* **fisgar**.

físico, a [fē'seko, á] *a* physical ♦ *nm* physique; (*aspecto*) appearance, looks ♦ *nm/f* physicist ♦ *nf* physics *sg*.

fisonomía [fēsonomē'á] *nf* physiognomy, features *pl*.

fisonomista [fēsonomē'stá] *nm/f*: **ser buen** ~ to have a good memory for faces.

flac(c)idez [flá(k)sēᵹes'] *nf* softness, flabbiness.

flác(c)ido, a [flá'(k)sēᵹo, á] *a* flabby.

flaco, a [flá'ko, á] *a* (*muy delgado*) skinny, thin; (*débil*) weak, feeble.

flagrante [fláᵹránt'e] *a* flagrant.

flamante [flámán'te] *a* (*fam*) brilliant; (: *nuevo*) brand-new.

flamear [flámeár'] *vt* (*CULIN*) to flambé.

flamenco, a [flámen'ko, á] *a* (*de Flandes*) Flemish; (*baile, música*) gipsy ♦ *nm/f* Fleming; **los** ~**s** the Flemish ♦ *nm* (*LING*) Flemish; (*baile, música*) flamenco.

flan [flán] *nm* custard (*US*), creme caramel (*Brit*).

flanco [flán'ko] *nm* side; (*MIL*) flank.

Flandes [flán'des] *nm* Flanders.

flanquear [flánkeár'] *vt* to flank; (*MIL*) to outflank.

flaquear [flákeár'] *vi* (*debilitarse*) to weaken; (*persona*) to slack.

flaqueza [fláke'sá] *nf* (*delgadez*) thinness, leanness; (*fig*) weakness.

flaquísimo, a [flákē'sēmo, á] *a superlativo de* **flaco**.

flash [flás], *pl* **flashes** [flás] *nm* (*FOTO*) flash.

flato [flá'to] *nm*: **el** (*o* **un**) ~ the (*o* a) stitch.

flauta [flá'oōtá] (*MUS*) *nf* flute ♦ *nm/f* flautist, flute player.

fleco [fle'ko] *nm* fringe.

flecha [fletch'á] *nf* arrow.

flechazo [fletchá'so] *nm* (*acción*) bowshot; (*fam*): **fue un** ~ it was love at first sight.

flema [fle'má] *nm* phlegm.

flemático, a [flemá'tēko, á] *a* phlegmatic; (*tono etc*) matter-of-fact.

flemón [flemon'] *nm* (*MED*) gumboil.

flequillo [flekē'yo] *nm* (*pelo*) bangs *pl* (*US*), fringe (*Brit*).

fletar [fletár'] *vt* (*COM*) to charter; (*embarcar*) to load; (*AUTO*) to lease (purchase).

flete [fle'te] *nm* (*carga*) freight; (*alquiler*) charter; (*precio*) freightage.

flexible [fleksē'ble] *a* flexible; (*individuo*) compliant.

flipper [flē'per] *nm* pinball machine.

flirtear [flērteár'] *vi* to flirt.

FLN *nm abr* (*POL: Esp, Perú, Venezuela*) = *Frente de Liberación Nacional*.

flojera [flohe'rá] *nf* (*AM*) laziness; **me da** ~ I can't be bothered.

flojo, a [flo'ho, á] *a* (*gen*) loose; (*sin fuerzas*) limp; (*débil*) weak; (*viento*) light; (*bebida*) weak; (*trabajo*) poor; (*actitud*) lazy; (*precio*) low; (*COM: mercado*) dull.

flor [flor] *nf* flower; (*piropo*) compliment; **la** ~ **y nata de la sociedad** (*fig*) the cream of society; **en la** ~ **de la vida** in the prime of life; **a** ~ **de** on the surface of.

florecer [floreser'] *vi* (*BOT*) to flower, bloom; (*fig*) to flourish.

floreciente [floresyen'te] *a* (*BOT*) in flower, flowering; (*fig*) thriving.

Florencia [floren'syá] *nf* Florence.

florero [flore'ro] *nm* vase.

florezca [flores'ká] *etc vb V* **florecer**.

florista [florē'stá] *nm/f* florist.

flota [flo'tá] *nf* fleet.

flotación [flotásyon'] *nf* (*COM*) flotation.

flotador [flotáᵭor'] *nm* (*gen*) float; (*para nadar*) life preserver (*US*), rubber ring (*Brit*); (*de cisterna*) ballcock.

flotante [flotán'te] *a* floating; (*INFORM*): **de coma** ~ floating-point.

flotar [flotár'] *vi* to float.

flote [flo'te] *nm*: **a** ~ afloat; **ponerse a** ~ (*fig*) to get back on one's feet.

FLS *nm abr* (*POL: Nicaragua*)=*Frente de Liberación Sandinista*.

fluctuación [floōktwásyon'] *nf* fluctuation.

fluctuante [floōktwán'te] *a* fluctuating.

fluctuar [floōktwár'] *vi* (*oscilar*) to fluctuate.

fluidez [floōēᵭes'] *nf* fluidity; (*fig*) fluency.

flúido, a [floō'ēᵭo, á] *a* fluid; (*lenguaje*) fluent; (*estilo*) smooth ♦ *nm* (*líquido*) fluid.

fluir [floōēr'] *vi* to flow.

flujo [floō'ho] *nm* flow; (*POL*) swing; (*NAUT*) rising tide; ~ **y reflujo** ebb and flow; ~ **de sangre** (*MED*) hemorrhage (*US*), haemorrhage (*Brit*); ~ **positivo/negativo de efectivo** (*COM*) positive/negative cash flow.

flujograma [floōhoᵹrá'má] *nm* flowchart.

fluoruro [flworoō'ro] *nm* fluoride.

fluvial [floōᵬēál'] *a* fluvial, river *cpd*.

fluyendo [floōyen'do] *etc vb V* **fluir**.

F.M. *nf abr* (= *Frecuencia Modulada*) F.M.

FMI *nm abr* (= *Fondo Monetario Internacional*) I.M.F.

F.N. *nf abr* (*Esp POL*)=*Fuerza Nueva* ♦ *nm* = *Frente Nacional*.

FNPT *nm abr* (*Esp*)=*Fondo Nacional de Protección del Trabajo*.

f.º *abr* (= *folio*) fo., fol.

foca [fo'ká] *nf* seal.

foco [fo'ko] *nm* focus; (*centro*) focal point;

(*fuente*) source; (*de incendio*) heart; (*ELEC*) floodlight; (*TEATRO*) spotlight; (*AM*) (light) bulb.

fofo, a [fo'fo, à] *a* (*esponjoso*) soft, spongy; (*músculo*) flabby.

fogata [foɣá'tà] *nf* (*hoguera*) bonfire.

fogón [foɣon'] *nm* (*de cocina*) ring.

fogoso, a [foɣo'so, à] *a* spirited.

fol. *abr* (= *folio*) fo., fol.

folio [fo'lyo] *nm* folio; (*hoja*) leaf.

follaje [foyà'hc] *nm* foliage.

follar [foyàr'] *vt, vi* (*fam!*) to fuck(*!*).

folletinesco, a [foyctēncs'ko, à] *a* melodramatic.

folleto [foyc'to] *nm* pamphlet; (*COM*) brochure; (*prospecto*) leaflet; (*ESCOL etc*) handout.

follón [foyon'] *nm* (*fam: lío*) mess; (: *conmoción*) fuss, rumpus; **armar un ~** to kick up a fuss; **se armó un ~** there was a hell of a row.

fomentar [fomentàr'] *vt* (*MED*) to foment; (*fig: promover*) to promote, foster; (*odio etc*) to stir up.

fomento [fomen'to] *nm* (*fig: ayuda*) fostering; (*promoción*) promotion.

fonda [fon'dà] *nf* inn.

fondear [fondeàr'] *vt* (*NAUT: sondear*) to sound; (*barco*) to search.

fondo [fon'do] *nm* (*de caja etc*) bottom; (*medida*) depth; (*de coche, sala*) back; (*ARTE etc*) background; (*reserva*) fund; (*fig: carácter*) nature; **~s** *nmpl* (*COM*) funds, resources; **~ de amortización** (*COM*) sinking fund; **F~ Monetario Internacional** International Monetary Fund; **~ del mar** sea bed *o* floor; **una investigación a ~** a thorough investigation; **en el ~** deep down; **tener buen ~** to be good-natured.

fonética [fone'tēkà] *nf* phonetics *sg*.

fonógrafo [fono'ɣráfo] *nm* (*AM*) phonograph, gramophone.

fonología [fonolohē'à] *nf* phonology.

fontanería [fontànerē'à] *nf* plumbing.

fontanero [fontàne'ro] *nm* plumber.

footing [fōō'tēn] *nm* jogging; **hacer ~** to jog.

F.O.P. [fop] *nfpl abr* (*Esp*)=**Fuerzas del Orden Público.**

forajido [foràhē'tho] *nm* outlaw.

foráneo, a [forá'neo, à] *a* foreign ♦ *nm/f* outsider.

forastero, a [foràste'ro, à] *nm/f* stranger.

forcé [forse'] *vb* V **forzar.**

forcejear [forsehcàr'] *vi* (*luchar*) to struggle.

forcemos [forse'mos] *etc vb* V **forzar.**

forense [foren'se] *a* forensic ♦ *nm/f* pathologist.

forestal [forestàl'] *a* forest *cpd*.

forjar [forhàr'] *vt* to forge; (*formar*) to form.

forma [for'mà] *nf* (*figura*) form, shape; (*molde*) mold (*US*), mould (*Brit*), pattern; (*MED*) fitness; (*método*) way, means; **estar en ~** to be fit; **~ de pago** (*COM*) method of payment; **las ~s** the conventions; **de ~ que ...** so that ...; **de todas ~s** in any case.

formación [formàsyon'] *nf* (*gen*) formation; (*enseñanza*) training; **~ profesional** vocational training; **~ fuera del trabajo** off-the-job training; **~ en el trabajo** *o* **sobre la práctica** on-the-job training.

formal [formàl'] *a* (*gen*) formal; (*fig: persona*) serious; (: *de fiar*) reliable; (*conducta*) steady.

formalice [formàlē'se] *etc vb* V **formalizar.**

formalidad [formàlēthàth'] *nf* formality; seriousness; reliability; steadiness.

formalizar [formàlēsàr'] *vt* (*JUR*) to formalize; (*plan*) to draw up; (*situación*) to put in order, regularize; **~se** *vr* (*situación*) to be put in order, be regularized.

formar [formàr'] *vt* (*componer*) to form, shape; (*constituir*) to make up, constitute; (*ESCOL*) to train, educate ♦ *vi* (*MIL*) to fall in; (*DEPORTE*) to line up; **~se** *vr* (*ESCOL*) to be trained (*o* educated); (*cobrar forma*) to form, take form; (*desarrollarse*) to develop.

formatear [formàteàr'] *vt* (*INFORM*) to format.

formateo [formàte'o] *nm* (*INFORM*) formatting.

formato [formà'to] *nm* (*INFORM*): **sin ~** (*disco, texto*) unformatted; **~ de registro** record format.

formidable [formēthà'hle] *a* (*temible*) formidable; (*asombroso*) tremendous.

fórmula [for'mōōlà] *nf* formula.

formulario [formōōlá'ryo] *nm* form; **~ de solicitud/de pedido** (*COM*) application/order form; **llenar un ~** to fill in a form; **~ contínuo desplegable** (*INFORM*) fanfold paper.

fornicar [fornēkàr'] *vi* to fornicate.

fornido, a [fornē'tho, à] *a* well-built.

fornique [fornē'ke] *etc vb* V **fornicar.**

foro [fo'ro] *nm* (*gen*) forum; (*JUR*) court.

forofo, a [foro'fo, à] *nm/f* fan.

FORPPA [for'pà] *nm abr* (*Esp*)=*Fondo de Ordenación y Regulación de Productos y Precios Agrarios.*

forrado, a [forrà'tho, à] *a* (*ropa*) lined; (*fam*) well-heeled.

forrar [forràr'] *vt* (*abrigo*) to line; (*libro*) to cover; (*coche*) to upholster; **~se** *vr* (*fam*) to line one's pockets.

forro [fo'rro] *nm* (*de cuaderno*) cover; (*costura*) lining; (*de sillón*) upholstery.

fortalecer [fortàleser'] *vt* to strengthen; **~se** *vr* to fortify o.s.; (*opinión etc*) to become stronger.

fortaleza [fortále'sá] *nf* (*MIL*) fortress, stronghold; (*fuerza*) strength; (*determinación*) resolution.

fortalezca [fortáles'ká] *etc vb* V **fortalecer**.

fortificar [fortēfēkár'] *vt* to fortify; (*fig*) to strengthen.

fortifique [fortēfē'ke] *etc vb* V **fortificar**.

fortísimo, a [fortēs'imo, á] *a superlativo de* **fuerte**.

fortuito, a [fortwē'to, á] *a* accidental, chance *cpd*.

fortuna [fortōō'ná] *nf* (*suerte*) fortune, (good) luck; (*riqueza*) fortune, wealth.

forzar [forsár'] *vt* (*puerta*) to force (open); (*compeler*) to compel; (*violar*) to rape; (*ojos etc*) to strain.

forzoso, a [forso'so, á] *a* necessary; (*inevitable*) inescapable; (*obligatorio*) compulsory.

forzudo, a [forsōō'ṭho, á] *a* burly.

fosa [fo'sá] *nf* (*sepultura*) grave; (*en tierra*) pit; (*MED*) cavity; **~s nasales** nostrils.

fosfato [fosfá'to] *nm* phosphate.

fósforo [fos'foro] *nm* (*QUÍMICA*) phosphorus; (*cerilla*) match.

fósil [fo'sēl] *a* fossil, fossilized ♦ *nm* fossil.

foso [fo'so] *nm* ditch; (*TEATRO*) pit; (*AUTO*): **~ de reconocimiento** inspection pit.

foto [fo'to] *nf* photo, snap(shot); **sacar una ~** to take a photo *o* picture.

fotocopia [fotoko'pyá] *nf* photocopy.

fotocopiadora [fotokopyáṭho'rá] *nf* photocopier.

fotocopiar [fotokopyár'] *vt* to photocopy.

fotoestilo [fotoestē'lo] *nm* (*INFORM*) light pen.

fotografía [fotográfē'á] *nf* (*arte*) photography; (*una ~*) photograph.

fotografiar [fotográfyár'] *vt* to photograph.

fotógrafo, a [foto'gráfo, á] *nm/f* photographer.

fotómetro [foto'metro] *nm* (*FOTO*) light meter.

foulard [fōōlár'] *nm* head(scarf).

FP *nf abr* (*Esp*: *ESCOL*, *COM*)=*Formación Profesional* ♦ *nm abr* (*POL*)=*Frente Popular*.

FPLP *nm abr* (*POL*:=*Frente Popular para la Liberación de Palestina*) PFLP.

Fr. *abr* (= *Fray*) Fr.; (= *franco*) Fr.

frac [frák], *pl* **fracus** *o* **fraques** [frá'kes] *nm* dress coat, tails.

fracasar [frákásár'] *vi* (*gen*) to fail; (*plan etc*) to fall through.

fracaso [fráká'so] *nm* (*desgracia*, *revés*) failure; (*de negociaciones etc*) collapse, breakdown.

fracción [fráksyon'] *nf* fraction; (*POL*) faction, splinter group.

fraccionamiento [fráksyonámyen'to] *nm* (*AM*) housing development (*US*) *o* estate (*Brit*).

fractura [fráktōō'rá] *nf* fracture, break.

fragancia [frágán'syá] *nf* (*olor*) fragrance, perfume.

fragante [frágán'te] *a* fragrant, scented.

fraganti [frágán'tē]: **in ~** *ad*: **coger a uno in ~** to catch sb red-handed.

frágil [frá'hēl] *a* (*débil*) fragile; (*COM*) breakable; (*fig*) frail, delicate.

fragilidad [fráhēlēṭháṭh'] *nf* fragility; (*de persona*) frailty.

fragmento [frágmen'to] *nm* fragment; (*pedazo*) piece; (*de discurso*) excerpt; (*de canción*) snatch.

fragor [frágor'] *nm* (*ruido intenso*) din.

fragua [frá'gwá] *nf* forge.

fraguar [frágwár'] *vt* to forge; (*fig*) to concoct ♦ *vi* to harden.

fragüe [frá'gwe] *etc vb* V **fraguar**.

fraile [frá'ēle] *nm* (*REL*) friar; (: *monje*) monk.

frambuesa [frámbwe'sá] *nf* raspberry.

francés, esa [fránses', esá] *a* French ♦ *nm/f* Frenchman/woman ♦ *nm* (*LING*) French.

Francia [frán'syá] *nf* France.

franco, a [frán'ko, á] *a* (*cándido*) frank, open; (*COM*: *exento*) free ♦ *nm* (*moneda*) franc; **~ de derechos** duty-free; **~ al costado del buque** (*COM*) free alongside ship; **~ puesto sobre vagón** (*COM*) free on rail; **~ a bordo** free on board.

francotirador, a [fránkotēráṭhor', á] *nm/f* sniper.

franela [fráne'lá] *nf* flannel.

franja [frán'há] *nf* fringe; (*de uniforme*) stripe; (*de tierra etc*) strip.

franquear [fránkeár'] *vt* (*camino*) to clear; (*carta*, *paquete postal*) to frank, stamp; (*obstáculo*) to overcome; (*COM etc*) to free, exempt.

franqueo [fránke'o] *nm* postage.

franqueza [fránke'sá] *nf* (*candor*) frankness.

franquicia [fránke'syá] *nf* exemption; **~ aduanera** exemption from customs duties.

franquísimo, a [fránkē'sēmo, á] *a* superlativo de **franco**.

franquista [fránkē'stá] *a* pro-Franco ♦ *nm/f* supporter of Franco.

frasco [frás'ko] *nm* bottle, flask; **~ al vacío** (vacuum) flask.

frase [frá'se] *nf* sentence; (*locución*) phrase, expression; **~ hecha** set phrase; (*despectivo*) cliché.

fraude [frá'ōōṭhe] *nm* (*cualidad*) dishonesty; (*acto*) fraud, swindle.

fraudulento, a [fráōōṭhōōlen'to, á] *a* fraudulent.

frazada [frásá'ṭhá] *nf* (*AM*) blanket.

frecuencia [frekwen'syá] *nf* frequency; **con ~** frequently, often; **~ de red** (*INFORM*) mains frequency; **~ del reloj** (*INFORM*) clock speed; **~ telefónica** voice frequency.

frecuente [frekwen'te] *a* frequent; (*costumbre*) common; (*vicio*) rife.

fregadero [freɣàðħe'ro] *nm* (kitchen) sink.

fregador, a [freɣàðħor', à] *nm/f* (*tb*: **~ de platos**) dishwasher.

fregar [freɣár'] *vt* (*frotar*) to scrub; (*platos*) to wash (up); (*AM*) to annoy.

fregona [freɣo'ná] *nf* (*utensilio*) mop; (*pey: sirvienta*) maid.

fregué [freɣe'], **freguemos** [freɣe'mos] *etc vb V* **fregar**.

freír [freēr'] *vt* to fry.

fréjol [fre'hol] *nm* = **fríjol**.

frenar [frenár'] *vt* to brake; (*fig*) to check.

frenazo [frená'so] *nm*: **dar un ~** to brake sharply.

frenesí [frenesē'] *nm* frenzy.

frenético, a [frene'tēko, à] *a* frantic; **ponerse ~** to lose one's head.

freno [fre'no] *nm* (*TEC, AUTO*) brake; (*de cabalgadura*) bit; (*fig*) check.

frente [fren'te] *nm* (*ARQ, MIL, POL*) front; (*de objeto*) front part ♦ *nf* forehead, brow; **~ de batalla** battle front; **hacer ~ común con uno** to make common cause with sb; **~ a** in front of; (*en situación opuesta*) opposite; **chocar de ~** to crash head-on; **hacer ~ a** to face up to.

fresa [fre'sá] *nf* (*Esp: fruta*) strawberry; (*de dentista*) drill.

fresco, a [fres'ko, à] *a* (*nuevo*) fresh; (*huevo*) newly-laid; (*frío*) cool; (*descarado*) sassy (*US*), cheeky (*Brit*) ♦ *nm* (*aire*) fresh air; (*ARTE*) fresco ♦ *nm/f* (*fam*) shameless person; (*persona insolente*) impudent person; **tomar el ~** to get some fresh air; **¡qué ~!** what a mouth (*US*) o cheek (*Brit*)!

frescor [freskor'] *nm* freshness.

frescura [freskoo'rá] *nf* freshness; (*descaro*) nerve; (*calma*) calmness.

fresno [fres'no] *nm* ash (tree).

fresón [freson'] *nm* strawberry.

frialdad [fryáldàðħ'] *nf* (*gen*) coldness; (*indiferencia*) indifference.

fricción [frēksyon'] *nf* (*gen*) friction; (*acto*) rub(bing); (*MED*) massage; (*POL, fig etc*) friction, trouble.

friega [frye'ɣá] *etc*, **friegue** [frye'ɣe] *etc vb V* **fregar**.

friendo [frēen'do] *etc vb V* **freír**.

frigidez [frēhēðħes'] *nf* frigidity.

frígido, a [frē'hēðħo, à] *a* frigid.

frigorífico, a [frēɡorē'fēko, à] *a* refrigerating; **instalación frigorífica** cold-storage plant ♦ *nm* refrigerator; (*camión*) freezer truck (*US*) o lorry (*Brit*).

frijol [frēhol'], **fríjol** [frē'hol] *nm* kidney bean.

frió [frēo'] *vb V* **freír**.

frío, a [frē'o, à] *etc vb V* **freír** ♦ *a* cold; (*fig: indiferente*) unmoved, indifferent; (*poco entusiasta*) chilly ♦ *nm* cold(ness); indifference; **¡qué ~!** how cold it is!

friolero, a [fryole'ro, à] *a* sensitive to cold.

frito, a [frē'to, à] *pp de* **freír** ♦ *a* fried ♦ *nm* fry; **me trae ~ ese hombre** I'm sick and tired of that man; **~s variados** mixed grill.

frívolo, a [frē'ħolo, à] *a* frivolous.

frondoso, a [frondo'so, à] *a* leafy.

frontera [fronte'rá] *nf* frontier; (*línea divisoria*) border; (*zona*) frontier area.

fronterizo, a [frontĕrē'so, à] *a* frontier *cpd*; (*contiguo*) bordering.

frontal [frontál'] *nm*: **choque ~** head-on collision.

frontón [fronton'] *nm* (*DEPORTE: cancha*) jai alai court; (: *juego*) jai alai.

frotar [frotár'] *vt* to rub; (*fósforo*) to strike; **~se** *vr*: **~se las manos** to rub one's hands.

frs. *abr* (= *francos*) fr.

fructífero, a [frooktē'fero, à] *a* productive, fruitful.

frugal [frooɡál'] *a* frugal.

fruncir [froonsēr'] *vt* (*COSTURA*) to gather; (*ceño*) to frown; (*labios*) to purse.

frunza [froon'sá] *etc vb V* **fruncir**.

frustrar [froostrár'] *vt* to frustrate; **~se** *vr* to be frustrated; (*plan etc*) to fail.

fruta [froo'tá] *nf* fruit.

frutal [frootál'] *a* fruit-bearing, fruit *cpd* ♦ *nm*: (**árbol**) **~** fruit tree.

frutería [frooterē'á] *nf* fruit shop.

frutero, a [froote'ro, à] *a* fruit *cpd* ♦ *nm/f* fruit vendor ♦ *nm* fruit dish o bowl.

frutilla [frootē'yá] *nf* (*AM*) strawberry.

fruto [froo'to] *nm* (*BOT*) fruit; (*fig: resultado*) result, outcome; **~s secos** ≈ nuts and raisins.

FSLN *nm abr* (*POL: Nicaragua*)=*Frente Sandinista de Liberación Nacional.*

fue [fwe] *vb V* **ser, ir**.

fuego [fwe'ɡo] *nm* (*gen*) fire; (*CULIN: gas*) ring; (*MIL*) fire; (*fig: pasión*) fire, passion; **~s artificiales** o **de artificio** fireworks; **prender ~ a** to set fire to; **a ~ lento** on a low heat; **¡alto el ~!** cease fire!; **estar entre dos ~s** to be in the crossfire; **¿tienes ~?** have you (got) a light?

fuel-oil [fooelo'ēl] *nm* kerosene (*US*), paraffin (*Brit*).

fuelle [fwe'ye] *nm* bellows *pl*.

fuente [fwen'te] *nf* fountain; (*manantial, fig*) spring; (*origen*) source; (*plato*) large dish; **~ de alimentación** (*INFORM*) power supply; **de ~ desconocida/fidedigna** from an unknown/reliable source.

fuera [fwe'rá] *etc vb V* **ser, ir** ♦ *ad* out(side); (*en otra parte*) away; (*excepto, salvo*) except, save ♦ *prep*: **~ de** outside; (*fig*) besides; ~ **de alcance** out of reach; ~ **de combate** out of action; (*boxeo*) knocked out; ~ **de sí** beside o.s.; **por** ~ (on the) outside; **los de** ~ strangers, newcomers; **estar** ~ (*en el extranjero*) to be abroad.

fuera-borda [fwerá ̱ɦor'tĥá] *nm inv* outboard engine *o* motor.

fuerce [fwer'se] *etc vb* V **forzar.**

fuero [fwe'ro] *nm* (*carta municipal*) municipal charter; (*leyes locales*) local *o* regional law code; (*privilegio*) privilege; (*autoridad*) jurisdiction; (*fig*): **en mi** *etc* ~ **interno** in my *etc* heart of hearts ..., deep down ....

fuerte [fwer'te] *a* strong; (*golpe*) hard; (*ruido*) loud; (*comida*) rich; (*lluvia*) heavy; (*dolor*) intense ♦ *ad* strongly; hard; loud(ly) ♦ *nm* (*MIL*) fort, strongpoint; (*fig*): **el canto no es mi** ~ singing is not my strong point.

fuerza [fwer'sà] *etc vb* V **forzar** ♦ *nf* (*fortaleza*) strength; (*TEC, ELEC*) power; (*coacción*) force; (*violencia*) violence; (*MIL: tb:* ~**s**) forces *pl*; ~ **de arrastre** (*TEC*) pulling power; ~ **de brazos** manpower; ~ **mayor** force majeure; ~ **bruta** brute force; ~**s armadas (FF.AA.)** armed forces; ~ **de Orden Público (F.O.P.)** police (forces); ~ **vital** vitality; **a** ~ **de** by (means of); **cobrar** ~**s** to recover one's strength; **tener** ~**s para** to have the strength to; **a la** ~ forcibly, by force; **con** ~ **legal** (*COM*) legally binding; **por** ~ of necessity; ~ **de voluntad** willpower.

fuga [fōō'gá] *nf* (*huida*) flight, escape; (*de enamorados*) elopement; (*de gas etc*) leak; ~ **de cerebros** (*fig*) brain drain.

fugarse [fōōgàr'se] *vr* to flee, escape.

fugaz [fōōgàs'] *a* fleeting.

fugitivo, a [fōōhētē' ̱ɦo, à] *a* fugitive, fleeing ♦ *nm/f* fugitive.

fugue [fōō'ge] *etc vb* V **fugarse.**

fui [fwē] *etc vb* V **ser, ir.**

fulano, a [fōōlà'no, à] *nm/f* so-and-so, what's-his-name.

fulgor [fōōlgor'] *nm* brilliance.

fulminante [fōōlmēnàn'te] *a* (*pólvora*) fulminating; (*fig*: *mirada*) withering; (*MED*) fulminant; (*fam*) terrific, tremendous.

fumador, a [fōōmà ̱ɦor', à] *nm/f* smoker; **no** ~ non-smoker.

fumar [fōōmàr'] *vt, vi* to smoke; ~**se** *vr* (*disipar*) to squander; ~ **en pipa** to smoke a pipe.

funámbulo, a [fōōnàm'bōōlo, à], **funambulista** [fōōnàmbōōlē'stà] *nm/f* tightrope walker.

función [fōōnsyon'] *nf* function; (*de puesto*) duties *pl*; (*TEATRO etc*) show; **entrar en funciones** to take up one's duties; ~ **de**

tarde/de noche matinée/evening performance.

funcionamiento [fōōnsyonàmyen'to] *nm* functioning; (*TEC*) working; **en** ~ (*COM*) on line; **entrar en** ~ to come into operation.

funcionar [fōōnsyonàr'] *vi* (*gen*) to function; (*máquina*) to work; **"no funciona"** "out of order".

funcionario, a [fōōnsyoná'ryo, à] *nm/f* official; (*público*) civil servant.

funda [fōōn'dá] *nf* (*gen*) cover; (*de almohada*) pillowcase; ~ **protectora del disco** (*INFORM*) disk-jacket.

fundación [fōōndàsyon'] *nf* foundation.

fundado, a [fōōndà'tĥo, à] *a* (*justificado*) well-founded.

fundamental [fōōndàmentàl'] *a* fundamental, basic.

fundamentar [fōōndàmentàr'] *vt* (*poner base*) to lay the foundations of; (*establecer*) to found; (*fig*) to base.

fundamento [fōōndàmen'to] *nm* (*base*) foundation; (*razón*) grounds; **eso carece de** ~ that is groundless.

fundar [fōōndàr'] *vt* to found; (*crear*) to set up; (*fig*: *basar*): ~ **(en)** to base *o* found (on); ~**se** *vr*: ~**se en** to be founded on.

fundición [fōōndēsyon'] *nf* (*acción*) smelting; (*fábrica*) foundry; (*TIP*) font.

fundir [fōōndēr'] *vt* (*gen*) to fuse; (*metal*) to smelt, melt down; (*COM*) to merge; (*estatua*) to cast; ~**se** *vr* (*colores etc*) to merge, blend; (*unirse*) to fuse together; (*ELEC*: *fusible, lámpara etc*) to blow; (*nieve etc*) to melt.

fúnebre [fōō'ne ̱ɦre] *a* funeral *cpd*, funereal.

funeral [fōōnerál'] *nm* funeral.

funeraria [fōōnerà'ryà] *nf* mortician's (*US*), undertaker's (*Brit*).

funesto, a [fōōne'sto, à] *a* ill-fated; (*desastroso*) fatal.

furgón [fōōrgon'] *nm* wagon.

furgoneta [fōōrgone'tà] *nf* (*AUTO, COM*) pickup (truck).

furia [fōō'ryà] *nf* (*ira*) fury; (*violencia*) violence.

furibundo, a [fōōrē ̱ɦōōn'do, à] *a* furious.

furioso, a [fōōryo'so, à] *a* (*iracundo*) furious; (*violento*) violent.

furor [fōōror'] *nm* (*cólera*) rage; (*pasión*) frenzy, passion; **hacer** ~ to be a sensation.

furtivo, a [fōōrtē' ̱ɦo, à] *a* furtive ♦ *nm* poacher.

furúnculo [fōōrōōn'kōōlo] *nm* (*MED*) boil.

fuselaje [fōōselà'he] *nm* fuselage.

fusible [fōōsē' ̱ɦle] *nm* fuse.

fusil [fōōsēl'] *nm* rifle.

fusilamiento [fōōsēlàmyen'to] *nm* (*JUR*) execution by firing squad.

fusilar [fōōsēlàr'] *vt* to shoot.

fusión [fōōsyon'] *nf* (*gen*) melting; (*unión*) fusion; (*COM*) merger, amalgamation.

fusionar [fōōsyonár'] *vt* to fuse (together); (*COM*) to merge; **~se** *vr* (*COM*) to merge, amalgamate.

fusta [fōō'stá] *nf* (*látigo*) riding crop.

fútbol [fōōt'ḥol] *nm* football.

futbolín [fōōtḥolēn'] *nm* table football.

futbolista [fōōtḥolē'stá] *nm/f* football player.

fútil [fōō'tēl] *a* trifling.

futilidad [fōōtēlēḥáṭh'], **futileza** [fōōtēle'sá] *nf* triviality.

futuro, a [fōōtōō'ro, á] *a* future ♦ *nm* future; (*LING*) future tense; **~s** *nmpl* (*COM*) futures.

G

G, g [he] *nf* (*letra*) G, g; **G de Gerona** G for George.

g/ *abr* = **giro**.

gabán [gàḥán'] *nm* overcoat.

gabardina [gàḥàrḥē'ná] *nf* (*tela*) gabardine; (*prenda*) raincoat.

gabinete [gàḥēne'te] *nm* (*POL*) cabinet; (*estudio*) study; (*de abogados etc*) office; **~ de consulta/de lectura** consulting/reading room.

gacel [gàsel'] *nm*, **gacela** [gàse'lá] *nf* gazelle.

gaceta [gàse'tá] *nf* gazette.

gacetilla [gàsetē'yà] *nf* (*en periódico*) news in brief; (*de personalidades*) gossip column.

gacha [gàtch'á] *nf* mush; **~s** *nfpl* porridge *sg*.

gacho, a [gàtch'o, á] *a* (*encorvado*) bent down; (*orejas*) drooping.

gaditano, a [gàḥētá'no, á] *a* of o from Cadiz ♦ *nm/f* native o inhabitant of Cadiz.

GAE *nm abr* (*Esp MIL*)=**Grupo Aéreo Embarcado**.

gaélico, a [gàe'lēko, á] *a* Gaelic ♦ *nm/f* Gael ♦ *nm* (*LING*) Gaelic.

gafar [gàfár'] *vt* (*fam: traer mala suerte*) to put a jinx on.

gafas [gà'fás] *nfpl* glasses; **~ oscuras** dark glasses; **~ de sol** sunglasses.

gafe [gà'fe] *a*: **ser ~** to be jinxed ♦ *nm* (*fam*) jinx.

gaita [gà'ētá] *nf* flute; (**~ gallega**) bagpipes *pl*; (*dificultad*) bother; (*cosa engorrosa*) tough job.

gajes [gà'hes] *nmpl* (*salario*) pay *sg*; **los ~**

del oficio occupational hazards; **~ y emolumentos** perquisites.

gajo [gà'ho] *nm* (*gen*) bunch; (*de árbol*) bough; (*de naranja*) segment.

gala [gà'lá] *nf* full dress; (*fig: lo mejor*) cream, flower; **~s** *nfpl* finery *sg*; **estar de ~** to be in one's best clothes; **hacer ~ de** to display, show off; **tener algo a ~** to be proud of sth.

galaico, a [gàlá'ēko, á] *a* Galician.

galán [gàlán'] *nm* lover, gallant; (*hombre atractivo*) ladies' man; (*TEATRO*): **primer ~** leading man.

galano, a [gàlà'no, á] *a* (*elegante*) elegant; (*bien vestido*) smart.

galante [gàlán'te] *a* gallant; (*atento*) charming; (*cortés*) polite.

galantear [gàlànteár'] *vt* (*hacer la corte a*) to court, woo.

galanteo [gàlánte'o] *nm* (*coqueteo*) flirting; (*de pretendiente*) wooing.

galantería [gàlànterē'á] *nf* (*caballerosidad*) gallantry; (*cumplido*) politeness; (*piropo*) compliment.

galápago [gàlá'pàḥo] *nm* (*ZOOL*) turtle.

galardonar [gàlàrḥonár'] *vt* (*premiar*) to reward; (*una obra*) to award a prize for.

galaxia [gàlák'syà] *nf* galaxy.

galbana [gàlḥà'ná] *nf* (*pereza*) sloth, laziness.

galeote [gàleo'te] *nm* galley slave.

galera [gàle'rá] *nf* (*nave*) galley; (*carro*) wagon; (*MED*) hospital ward; (*TIP*) galley.

galería [gàlerē'á] *nf* (*gen*) gallery; (*balcón*) veranda(h); (*de casa*) corridor; (*fam: público*) audience; **~ secreta** secret passage.

Gales [gà'les] *nm*: (**el País de**) **~** Wales.

galés, esa [gàles', csá] *a* Welsh ♦ *nm/f* Welshman/woman ♦ *nm* (*LING*) Welsh.

galgo, a [gàl'go, á] *nm/f* greyhound.

Galia [gà'lyà] *nf* Gaul.

Galicia [gàlē'syà] *nf* Galicia.

galicismo [gàlēsēs'mo] *nm* gallicism.

Galilea [gàlēle'á] *nf* Galilee.

galimatías [gàlēmátē'ás] *nm inv* (*asunto*) rigmarole; (*lenguaje*) gibberish, nonsense.

galo, a [gà'lo, á] *a* Gallic; (= *francés*) French ♦ *nm/f* Gaul.

galón [gàlon'] *nm* (*COSTURA*) braid; (*MIL*) stripe; (*medida*) gallon.

galopar [gàlopár'] *vi* to gallop.

galope [gàlo'pe] *nm* gallop; **al ~** (*fig*) in great haste; **a ~ tendido** at full gallop.

galvanice [gàlḥánē'se] *etc vb* **V galvanizar**.

galvanizar [gàlḥánēsár'] *vt* to galvanize.

gallardía [gàyàrḥē'á] *nf* (*gracia*) gracefulness; (*valor*) bravery; (*elegancia*) elegance; (*nobleza*) nobleness.

gallego, a [gàye'go, á] *a* Galician; (*AM pey*) Spanish ♦ *nm/f* Galician; (*AM pey*) Spaniard ♦ *nm* (*LING*) Galician.

galleta [gáye'tá] *nf* cookie (*US*), biscuit (*Brit*); (*fam: bofetada*) whack, slap.

gallina [gáyē'ná] *nf* hen ♦ *nm* (*fam*) coward; ~ **ciega** blind man's buff; ~ **llueca** brooding (*US*) *o* broody (*Brit*) hen.

gallinero [gáyēne'ro] *nm* (*criadero*) henhouse; (*TEATRO*) gods *sg*, top gallery; (*voces*) hubbub.

gallo [gá'yo] *nm* cock, rooster; (*MUS*) false *o* wrong note; (*cambio de voz*) break in the voice; **en menos que canta un** ~ in an instant.

gama [gá'má] *nf* (*MUS*) scale; (*fig*) range; (*ZOOL*) doe.

gamba [gám'bá] *nf* prawn.

gamberrada [gámberrá'tɦá] *nf* act of hooliganism.

gamberro, a [gámbe'rro, á] *nm/f* hooligan, lout.

gamo [gá'mo] *nm* (*ZOOL*) buck.

gamuza [gámoō'sá] *nf* chamois; (*bayeta*) duster; (*AM: piel*) suede.

gana [gá'ná] *nf* (*deseo*) desire, wish; (*apetito*) appetite; (*voluntad*) will; (*añoranza*) longing; **de buena** ~ willingly; **de mala** ~ reluctantly; **me dan** ~s **de** I feel like, I want to; **tener** ~s **de** to feel like; **no me da la (real)** ~ I don't (damned well) want to; **son** ~s **de molestar** they're just trying to make trouble.

ganadería [gánátɦerē'á] *nf* (*ganado*) livestock; (*ganado vacuno*) cattle *pl*; (*cría, comercio*) cattle raising.

ganadero, a [gánátɦe'ro, á] *a* stock *cpd* ♦ *nm* stockman.

ganado [gáná'tɦo] *nm* livestock; ~ **caballar/cabrío** horses *pl*/ goats *pl*; ~ **lanar** *u* **ovejuno** sheep *pl*; ~ **porcino/vacuno** pigs *pl*/cattle *pl*.

ganador, a [gánátɦor', á] *a* winning ♦ *nm/f* winner; (*ECON*) earner.

ganancia [gánán'syá] *nf* (*lo ganado*) gain; (*aumento*) increase; (*beneficio*) profit; ~s *nfpl* (*ingresos*) earnings; (*beneficios*) profit *sg*, winnings; ~s **y pérdidas** profit and loss; ~ **bruta/líquida** gross/net profit; ~s **de capital** capital gains; **sacar** ~ **de** to draw profit from.

ganapán [gánápán'] *nm* (*obrero casual*) odd-job man; (*individuo tosco*) lout.

ganar [gánár'] *vt* (*obtener*) to get, obtain; (*sacar ventaja*) to gain; (*COM*) to earn; (*DEPORTE, premio*) to win; (*derrotar*) to beat; (*alcanzar*) to reach; (*MIL: objetivo*) to take; (*apoyo*) to gain, win ♦ *vi* (*DEPORTE*) to win; ~**se** *vr*: ~**se la vida** to earn one's living; **se lo ha ganado** he deserves it; ~ **tiempo** to gain time.

ganchillo [gántchē'yo] *nm* (*para croché*) crochet hook; (*arte*) crochet work.

gancho [gántch'o] *nm* (*gen*) hook; (*colga-*

dor) hanger; (*pey: revendedor*) tout; (*fam: atractivo*) sex appeal; (*BOXEO: golpe*) hook.

gandul, a [gándoōl', á] *a, nm/f* good-for-nothing.

ganga [gán'gá] *nf* (*cosa*) bargain; (*buena situación*) cushy job.

Ganges [gán'hes] *nm*: **el (Río)** ~ the Ganges.

ganglio [gáng'lyo] *nm* (*ANAT*) ganglion; (*MED*) swelling.

gangrena [gángre'ná] *nf* gangrene.

gansada [gánsá'tɦá] *nf* (*fam*) stupid thing (to do).

ganso, a [gán'so, á] *nm/f* (*ZOOL*) gander/ goose; (*fam*) idiot.

Gante [gán'te] *nm* Ghent.

ganzúa [gánsoō'á] *nf* skeleton key ♦ *nm/f* burglar.

gañán [gáñyán'] *nm* farmhand.

garabatear [gáráɦáteár'] *vt* to scribble, scrawl.

garabato [gáráɦá'to] *nm* (*gancho*) hook; (*garfio*) grappling iron; (*escritura*) scrawl, scribble; (*fam*) sex appeal.

garaje [gárá'he] *nm* garage.

garante [gárán'te] *a* responsible ♦ *nm/f* guarantor.

garantía [gárántē'á] *nf* guarantee; (*seguridad*) pledge; (*compromiso*) undertaking; (*JUR: caución*) warranty; **de máxima** ~ absolutely guaranteed; ~ **de trabajo** job security.

garantice [gárántē'se] *etc vb* V **garantizar**.

garantir [gárántēr'], **garantizar** [gárántēsár'] *vt* (*hacerse responsable de*) to vouch for; (*asegurar*) to guarantee.

garbanzo [gárɦán'so] *nm* chickpea.

garbeo [gárɦe'o] *nm*: **darse un** ~ to go for a walk.

garbo [gár'ɦo] *nm* grace, elegance; (*aire*) jauntiness; (*de mujer*) glamor; **andar con** ~ to walk gracefully.

garboso, a [gárɦo'so, á] *a* graceful, elegant.

garfa [gár'fá] *nf* claw.

garfio [gár'fyo] *nm* grappling iron; (*gancho*) hook; (*ALPINISMO*) climbing iron.

gargajo [gárgá'ho] *nm* phlegm, sputum.

garganta [gárgán'tá] *nf* (*interna*) throat; (*externa, de botella*) neck; (*GEO: barranco*) ravine; (*desfiladero*) narrow pass.

gargantilla [gárgántē'yá] *nf* necklace.

gárgara [gár'gárá] *nf* gargle, gargling; **hacer** ~s to gargle; **¡vete a hacer** ~s! (*fam*) go to blazes!

gárgola [gár'golá] *nf* gargoyle.

garita [gárē'tá] *nf* cabin, hut; (*MIL*) sentry box; (*puesto de vigilancia*) lookout post.

garito [gárē'to] *nm* (*lugar*) gaming house *o* den.

Garona [gàro'nà] *nm*: **el (Río)** ~ the Garonne.

garra [gà'rrá] *nf* (*de gato, TEC*) claw; (*de ave*) talon; (*fam*) hand, paw; (*fig: de canción etc*) bite; **caer en las ~s de uno** to fall into sb's clutches.

garrafa [gàrrá'fá] *nf* carafe, decanter.

garrafal [gàrráfál'] *a* enormous, terrific; (*error*) terrible.

garrapata [gàrràpà'tà] *nf* (*ZOOL*) tick.

garrido, a [gàrrē'tħo, à] *a* handsome.

garrotazo [gàrrotà'so] *nm* blow with a stick *o* club.

garrote [gàrro'te] *nm* (*palo*) stick; (*porra*) club, cudgel; (*suplicio*) garrotte.

garza [gàr'sà] *nf* heron.

garzo, a [gàr'so, à] *a* blue.

gas [gàs] *nm* gas; (*vapores*) fumes *pl*; **~es de escape** exhaust (fumes).

gasa [gá'sà] *nf* gauze; (*de pañal*) diaper (*US*) *o* nappy (*Brit*) liner.

gaseoso, a [gàseo'so, à] *a* carbonated ♦ *nf* lemonade, pop (*fam*).

gasoducto [gàsotħōōk'to] *nm* gas pipeline.

gasoil [gàso'ēl], **gasóleo** [gàso'leo] *nm* diesel (oil).

gasolina [gàsolē'nà] *nf* gas(oline) (*US*), petrol (*Brit*).

gasolinera [gàsolēne'rá] *nf* gas (*US*) *o* petrol (*Brit*) station.

gastado, a [gàstà'tħo, à] *a* (*ropa*) worn out; (*usado: frase etc*) trite.

gastar [gàstár'] *vt* (*dinero, tiempo*) to spend; (*consumir*) to use (up), consume; (*desperdiciar*) to waste; (*llevar*) to wear; **~se** *vr* to wear out; (*terminarse*) to run out; (*estropearse*) to waste; ~ **bromas** to crack jokes; **¿qué número gastas?** what size (shoe) do you take?

gasto [gàs'to] *nm* (*desembolso*) expenditure, spending; (*cantidad gastada*) outlay, expense; (*consumo, uso*) use; (*desgaste*) waste; **~s** *nmpl* (*desembolsos*) expenses; (*cargos*) charges, costs; ~ **corriente** (*COM*) revenue expenditure; ~ **fijo** (*COM*) fixed charge; **~s bancarios** bank charges; **~s corrientes** running expenses; **~s de distribución** (*COM*) distribution costs; **~s generales** overhead (*US*), overheads (*Brit*); **~s de mantenimiento** maintenance expenses; **~s operacionales** operating costs; **~s de tramitación** (*COM*) handling charge *sg*; **~s vencidos** (*COM*) accrued charges; **cubrir ~s** to cover expenses; **meterse en ~s** to incur expense.

gastronomía [gàstronomē'á] *nf* gastronomy.

gata [gà'tà] *nf* (*ZOOL*) she-cat; **andar a ~s** to go on all fours.

gatear [gàteár'] *vi* to go on all fours.

gatillo [gàtē'yo] *nm* (*de arma de fuego*) trigger; (*de dentista*) forceps.

gato [gà'to] *nm* (*ZOOL*) cat; (*TEC*) jack; ~ **de Angora** Angora cat; ~ **montés** wildcat; **dar a uno ~ por liebre** to take sb in; **aquí hay ~ encerrado** there's something fishy here.

gatuno, a [gàtōō'no, à] *a* feline.

gaucho, a [gà'ōōtcho, à] *a, nm/f* gaucho.

gaveta [gàħe'tà] *nf* drawer.

gavilán [gàħēlàn'] *nm* sparrowhawk.

gavilla [gàħē'yà] *nf* sheaf.

gaviota [gáħyo'tà] *nf* seagull.

gay [ge] *a, nm* gay, homosexual.

gazapo [gàsá'po] *nm* young rabbit.

gaznate [gàsná'te] *nm* (*pescuezo*) gullet; (*garganta*) windpipe.

gazpacho [gàspátch'o] *nm* gazpacho.

gelatina [helàtē'nà] *nf* jello (*US*), jelly (*Brit*); (*polvos etc*) gelatine.

gema [he'mà] *nf* gem.

gemelo, a [heme'lo, à] *a, nm/f* twin; **~s** *nmpl* (*de camisa*) cufflinks; **~s de campo** field glasses, binoculars; **~s de teatro** opera glasses.

gemido [hemē'tħo] *nm* (*quejido*) moan, groan; (*lamento*) wail, howl.

Géminis [he'mēnēs] *nm* (*ASTRO*) Gemini.

gemir [hemēr'] *vi* (*quejarse*) to moan, groan; (*animal*) to whine; (*viento*) to howl.

gen. *abr* (*LING*) = **género**; **genitivo**.

gendarme [hendár'me] *nm* (*AM*) policeman.

genealogía [heneàlohē'á] *nf* genealogy.

generación [henerásyon'] *nf* generation; **primera/segunda/tercera/cuarta** ~ (*INFORM*) first/second/third/fourth generation.

generado, a [henerá'tħo, à] *a* (*INFORM*): ~ **por ordenador** computer generated.

generador [henerátħor'] *nm* generator; ~ **de programas** (*INFORM*) program generator.

general [henerál'] *a* general; (*común*) common; (*pey: corriente*) rife; (*frecuente*) usual ♦ *nm* general; ~ **de brigada/de división** brigadier-/major-general; **por lo** *o* **en** ~ in general.

generalice [henerálē'se] *etc vb V* **generalizar**.

generalidad [henerálētħàtħ'] *nf* generality.

Generalitat [henerálētàt'] *nf* Catalan parliament.

generalización [henerálēsásyon'] *nf* generalization.

generalizar [henerálēsár'] *vt* to generalize; **~se** *vr* to become generalized, spread; (*difundirse*) to become widely known.

generalmente [henerálmen'te] *ad* generally.

generar [henerár'] *vt* to generate.

genérico, a [hene'rēko, à] *a* generic.

género [he'nero] *nm* (*clase*) kind, sort;

(*tipo*) type; (*BIO*) genus; (*LING*) gender; (*COM*) material; **~s** *nmpl* (*productos*) goods; **~ humano** human race; **~ chico** (*zarzuela*) Spanish operetta; **~s de punto** knitwear *sg*.

generosidad [heneroseˈthath'] *nf* generosity.

generoso, a [heneroˈso, á] *a* generous.

genial [henyál'] *a* inspired; (*idea*) brilliant; (*afable*) genial.

genialidad [henyáleˈthath'] *nf* (*singularidad*) genius; (*acto genial*) stroke of genius; **es una ~ suya** it's one of his brilliant ideas.

genio [heˈnyo] *nm* (*carácter*) nature, disposition; (*humor*) temper; (*facultad creadora*) genius; **mal ~** bad temper; **~ vivo** quick *o* hot temper; **de mal ~** bad-tempered.

genital [henétál'] *a* genital ♦ *nm*: **~es** genitals, genital organs.

genocidio [henoseˈthyo] *nm* genocide.

Génova [heˈnoná] *nf* Genoa.

genovés, esa [henoˈbes', esá] *a*, *nm/f* Genoese.

gente [henˈte] *nf* (*personas*) people *pl*; (*raza*) race; (*nación*) nation; (*parientes*) relatives *pl*; **~ bien/baja** upper-class/lower-class people *pl*; **~ menuda** (*niños*) children *pl*; **es buena ~** (*fam: esp AM*) he's a good sort.

gentil [hentél'] *a* (*elegante*) graceful; (*encantador*) charming; (*REL*) gentile.

gentileza [hentéleˈsá] *nf* grace; charm; (*cortesía*) courtesy; **por ~ de** by courtesy of.

gentilicio, a [hentéléˈsyo, á] *a* (*familiar*) family *cpd*.

gentío [hentéˈo] *nm* crowd, throng.

gentuza [hentōoˈsá] *nf* (*pey: plebe*) rabble; (: *chusma*) riffraff.

genuflexión [henōofleksyon'] *nf* genuflexion.

genuino, a [henweˈno, á] *a* genuine.

GEO [heˈo] *nmpl abr* (*Esp:= Grupos Especiales de Operaciones*) *Special Police Units used in anti-terrorist operations etc.*

geografía [heografeˈá] *nf* geography.

geográfico, a [heográˈféko, á] *a* geographic(al).

geología [heolohéˈá] *nf* geology.

geólogo, a [heoˈlogo, á] *nm/f* geologist.

geometría [heometréˈá] *nf* geometry.

geométrico, a [heomeˈtréko, á] *a* geometric(al).

geranio [heráˈnyo] *nm* (*BOT*) geranium.

gerencia [herenˈsyá] *nf* management; (*cargo*) post of manager; (*oficina*) manager's office.

gerente [herenˈte] *nm/f* (*supervisor*) manager; (*jefe*) director.

geriatría [heryátreˈá] *nf* (*MED*) geriatrics *sg*.

germano, a [hermáˈno, á] *a* German,

Germanic ♦ *nm/f* German.

germen [herˈmen] *nm* germ.

germinar [hermenár'] *vi* to germinate; (*brotar*) to sprout.

gerundense [herōoˈnden'se] *a* of *o* from Gerona ♦ *nm/f* native *o* inhabitant of Gerona.

gerundio [herōon'dyo] *nm* (*LING*) gerund.

gesticulación [hestékōōlásyon'] *nf* (*ademán*) gesticulation; (*mueca*) grimace.

gestión [hestyon'] *nf* management; (*diligencia, acción*) negotiation; **hacer las gestiones preliminares** to do the groundwork; **~ de cartera** (*COM*) portfolio management; **~ financiera** (*COM*) financial management; **~ interna** (*INFORM*) housekeeping; **~ de personal** personnel management; **~ de riesgos** (*COM*) risk management.

gestionar [hestyonár'] *vt* (*lograr*) to try to arrange; (*llevar*) to manage.

gesto [hesˈto] *nm* (*mueca*) grimace; (*ademán*) gesture; **hacer ~s** to make faces.

gestor, a [hestor', á] *a* managing ♦ *nm/f* manager; (*promotor*) promoter; (*agente*) business agent.

gestoría [hestoreˈá] *nf* agency undertaking business with government departments, insurance companies etc.

Gibraltar [hébráltár'] *nm* Gibraltar.

gibraltareño, a [hébráltáreˈnyo, á] *a* of *o* from Gibraltar ♦ *nm/f* native *o* inhabitant of Gibraltar.

gigante [hégán'te] *a*, *nm/f* giant.

gijonés, esa [héhones', esá] *a* of *o* from Gijón ♦ *nm/f* native *o* inhabitant of Gijón.

gilipollas [hélépo'yás] (*fam*) *a inv* daft ♦ *nm/f* idiot.

gima [héˈmá] *etc vb V* **gemir**.

gimnasia [hémnáˈsyá] *nf* gymnastics *pl*; **confundir la ~ con la magnesia** to get things mixed up.

gimnasio [hémnáˈsyo] *nm* gymnasium, gym.

gimnasta [hémnáˈstá] *nm/f* gymnast.

gimotear [hémoteár'] *vi* to whine, whimper; (*lloriquear*) to snivel.

Ginebra [héneˈhrá] *n* Geneva.

ginebra [héneˈhrá] *nf* gin.

ginecológico, a [hénekoloˈhéko, á] *a* gyn(a)ecological.

ginecólogo, a [hénekoˈlogo, á] *nm/f* gyn(a)ecologist.

gira [héˈrá] *nf* tour, trip.

girado, a [héráˈtho, á] *nm/f* (*COM*) drawee.

girar [hérár'] *vt* (*dar la vuelta*) to turn (around); (: *rápidamente*) to spin; (*COM: giro postal*) to draw; (*comerciar: letra de cambio*) to issue ♦ *vi* to turn (round); (*dar vueltas*) to rotate; (*rápido*) to spin; **la conversación giraba en torno a las elecciones** the conversation centered on the election; **~ en descubierto** to overdraw.

girasol [hĕrásol'] *nm* sunflower.

giratorio, a [hĕráto'ryo, á] *a* (*gen*) revolving; (*puente*) swing *cpd*; (*silla*) swivel *cpd*.

giro [hĕ'ro] *nm* (*movimiento*) turn, revolution; (*LING*) expression; (*COM*) draft; (*de sucesos*) trend, course; ~ **bancario** money order; ~ **de existencias** (*COM*) stock turnover; ~ **postal** money order; ~ **a la vista** (*COM*) sight draft.

gis [hĕs] *nm* (*AM*) chalk.

gitano, a [hĕtá'no, á] *a*, *nm/f* gypsy.

glacial [glásyál'] *a* icy, freezing.

glaciar [glásyár'] *nm* glacier.

glándula [glán'dōōlá] *nf* (*ANAT, BOT*) gland.

glicerina [glĕserē'ná] *nf* (*TEC*) glycerin(e).

global [glohál'] *a* (*en conjunto*) global; (*completo*) total; (*investigación*) full; (*suma*) lump *cpd*.

globo [glo'ho] *nm* (*esfera*) globe, sphere; (*aeróstato, juguete*) balloon.

glóbulo [glo'hōōlo] *nm* globule; (*ANAT*) corpuscle; ~ **blanco/rojo** white/red corpuscle.

gloria [glo'ryá] *nf* glory; (*fig*) delight; (*delicia*) bliss.

glorieta [glorye'tá] *nf* (*de jardín*) arbor (*US*), arbour (*Brit*); (*AUTO*) traffic circle (*US*), roundabout (*Brit*); (*plaza redonda*) circus; (*cruce*) junction.

glorificar [glorēfēkár'] *vt* (*enaltecer*) to glorify, praise.

glorifique [glorēfē'ke] *etc vb* V **glorificar**.

glorioso, a [gloryo'so, á] *a* glorious.

glosa [glo'sá] *nf* comment; (*explicación*) gloss.

glosar [glosár'] *vt* (*comentar*) to comment on.

glosario [glosá'ryo] *nm* glossary.

glotón, ona [gloton', oná] *a* gluttonous, greedy ♦ *nm/f* glutton.

glotonería [glotonerē'á] *nf* gluttony, greed.

glúteo [glōō'teo] *nm* (*fam: nalga*) buttock.

gnomo [no'mo] *nm* gnome.

gobernación [gohernásyon'] *nf* government, governing; (*POL*) Provincial Governor's office.

gobernador, a [gohernáhor', á] *a* governing ♦ *nm/f* governor.

gobernanta [gohernán'tá] *nf* (*AM: niñera*) governess.

gobernante [gohernán'te] *a* governing ♦ *nm* ruler, governor ♦ *nf* (*en hotel etc*) maid (*US*), housekeeper (*Brit*).

gobernar [gohernár'] *vt* (*dirigir*) to guide, direct; (*POL*) to rule, govern ♦ *vi* to govern; (*NAUT*) to steer; ~ **mal** to misgovern.

gobierno [gohyer'no] *etc vb* V **gobernar** ♦ *nm* (*POL*) government; (*gestión*) management; (*dirección*) guidance, direction; (*NAUT*) steering; (*puesto*) governorship.

goce [go'se] *etc vb* V **gozar** ♦ *nm* enjoyment.

godo, a [go'tho, á] *nm/f* Goth; (*AM pey*) Spaniard.

gol [gol] *nm* goal.

gola [go'lá] *nf* gullet; (*garganta*) throat.

golear [golcár'] *vt* (*marcar*) to score a goal against.

golf [golf] *nm* golf.

golfo, a [gol'fo, á] *nm/f* (*pilluelo*) street urchin; (*vago*) tramp; (*gorrón*) loafer; (*gamberro*) lout ♦ *nm* (*GEO*) gulf ♦ *nf* (*fam: prostituta*) hooker.

golondrina [golondrē'ná] *nf* swallow.

golosina [golosē'ná] *nf* tidbit (*US*), titbit (*Brit*); (*dulce*) candy (*US*), sweet (*Brit*).

goloso, a [golo'so, á] *a* sweet-toothed; (*fam: glotón*) greedy.

golpe [gol'pe] *nm* blow; (*de puño*) punch; (*de mano*) smack; (*de remo*) stroke; (*FÚTBOL*) kick; (*TENIS etc*) hit, shot; (*mala suerte*) misfortune; (*fam: atraco*) heist (*US*), job; (*fig: choque*) clash; **no dar** ~ to be bone idle; **de un** ~ with one blow; **de** ~ suddenly; (~ **de estado**) coup (d'état); ~ **de gracia** coup de grâce (*tb fig*); ~ **de fortuna/maestro** stroke of luck/genius; **cerrar una puerta de** ~ to slam a door.

golpear [golpeár'] *vt, vi* to strike, knock; (*asestar*) to beat; (*de puño*) to punch; (*golpetear*) to tap; (*mesa*) to bang.

goma [go'má] *nf* (*caucho*) rubber; (*elástico*) elastic; (*tira*) rubber o elastic (*Brit*) band; (*fam: preservativo*) condom; (*droga*) hashish; (*explosivo*) plastic explosive; ~ **(de borrar)** eraser, rubber (*Brit*); ~ **de mascar** chewing gum; ~ **de pegar** gum, glue.

goma-espuma [gomáespōō'má] *nf* foam rubber.

gomina [gomē'ná] *nf* (*AM*) hair cream.

gomita [gomē'tá] *nf* rubber o elastic (*Brit*) band.

góndola [gon'dolá] *nf* (*barco*) gondola; (*de tren*) freight car (*US*), goods wagon (*Brit*).

gordo, a [gor'tho, á] *a* (*gen*) fat; (*persona*) plump; (*agua*) hard; (*fam*) enormous ♦ *nm/f* fat man o woman; **el (premio)** ~ (*en lotería*) first prize; ¡~! (*fam*) fatty!

gordura [gorthōō'rá] *nf* fat; (*corpulencia*) fatness, stoutness.

gorgojo [gorgo'ho] *nm* (*insecto*) grub.

gorgorito [gorgorē'to] *nm* (*gorjeo*) trill, warble.

gorila [gorē'lá] *nm* gorilla; (*fam*) tough, thug; (*guardaespaldas*) bodyguard.

gorjear [gorheár'] *vi* to twitter, chirp.

gorjeo [gorhe'o] *nm* twittering, chirping.

gorra [go'rrá] *nf* (*gen*) cap; (*de niño*) bonnet; (*militar*) bearskin; ~ **de montar/ de paño/de punto/de visera** riding/cloth/

knitted/peaked cap; **andar** *o* **ir** *o* **vivir de** ~ to sponge, scrounge; **entrar de** ~ (*fam*) to gatecrash.

gorrión [gorryon'] *nm* sparrow.

gorro [go'rro] *nm* cap; (*de niño, mujer*) bonnet; **estoy hasta el** ~ I am fed up.

gorrón, ona [gorron', oná] *nm* pebble; (*TEC*) pivot ♦ *nm/f* scrounger.

gorronear [gorroneár'] *vi* (*fam*) to sponge, scrounge.

gota [go'tá] *nf* (*gen*) drop; (*de pintura*) blob; (*de sudor*) bead; (*MED*) gout; ~ **a** ~ drop by drop; **caer a** ~**s** to drip.

gotear [goteár'] *vi* to drip; (*escurrir*) to trickle; (*salirse*) to leak; (*cirio*) to gutter; (*lloviznar*) to drizzle.

gotera [gote'rá] *nf* leak.

gótico, a [go'tēko, á] *a* Gothic.

gozar [gosár'] *vi* to enjoy o.s.; ~ **de** (*disfrutar*) to enjoy; (*poseer*) to possess; ~ **de buena salud** to enjoy good health.

gozne [gos'ne] *nm* hinge.

gozo [go'so] *nm* (*alegría*) joy; (*placer*) pleasure; **¡mi** ~ **en el pozo!** just my luck!

g.p. *nm abr* (= *giro postal*) m.o.

GPI *nm abr* (*Esp POL*)=*Grupo Parlamentario Independiente*.

gr. *abr* (= *gramo(s)*) g.

grabación [gràbàsyon'] *nf* recording.

grabado, a [gràbá'ðo, á] *a* (*MUS*) recorded; (*en cinta*) taped, on tape ♦ *nm* print, engraving; ~ **al agua fuerte** etching; ~ **al aguatinta** aquatint; ~ **en cobre** copperplate; ~ **en madera** woodcut; ~ **rupestre** rock carving.

grabador, a [gràbàðhor', á] *nm/f* engraver ♦ *nf* tape-recorder; ~**a de cassettes** cassette recorder.

grabar [gràbár'] *vt* to engrave; (*discos, cintas*) to record; (*impresionar*) to impress.

gracejo [gráse'ho] *nm* (*humor*) wit, humor (*US*), humour (*Brit*); (*elegancia*) grace.

gracia [grá'syá] *nf* (*encanto*) grace, gracefulness; (*REL*) grace; (*chiste*) joke; (*humor*) humor (*US*), humour (*Brit*), wit; **¡muchas** ~**s!** thanks very much!; ~**s a** thanks to; **tener** ~ (*chiste etc*) to be funny; **¡qué** ~**!** how funny!; (*irónico*) what a nerve!; **no me hace** ~ I'm not keen on it; **con** ~**s anticipadas/repetidas** thanking you in advance/again; **dar las** ~**s a uno por algo** to thank sb for sth.

grácil [grá'sēl] *a* (*sutil*) graceful; (*delgado*) slender; (*delicado*) delicate.

gracioso, a [grásyo'so, á] *a* (*garboso*) graceful; (*chistoso*) funny; (*cómico*) comical; (*agudo*) witty; (*título*) gracious ♦ *nm/f* (*TEATRO*) comic character, fool; **su graciosa Majestad** His/Her Gracious Majesty.

grada [grá'ðá] *nf* (*de escalera*) step; (*de anfiteatro*) tier, row; ~**s** *nfpl* (*de estadio*) stands (*US*), terraces (*Brit*).

gradación [gràðàsyon'] *nf* gradation; (*serie*) graded series.

gradería [gràðerē'á] *nf* (*gradas*) (flight of) steps *pl*; (*de anfiteatro*) tiers *pl*, rows *pl*; ~ **cubierta** covered stand.

grado [grá'ðo] *nm* degree; (*etapa*) stage, step; (*nivel*) rate; (*de parentesco*) degree; (*de aceite, vino*) grade; (*grada*) step; (*ESCOL*) grade (*US*), class, year; (*UNIV*) degree; (*LING*) degree of comparison; (*MIL*) rank; **de buen** ~ willingly; **en sumo** ~, **en** ~ **superlativo** in the highest degree.

graduación [gràðwàsyon'] *nf* (*acto*) gradation; (*clasificación*) rating; (*del alcohol*) proof, strength; (*ESCOL*) graduation; (*MIL*) rank; **de alta** ~ high-ranking.

gradual [gràðwál'] *a* gradual.

graduar [gràðwàr'] *vt* (*gen*) to graduate; (*medir*) to gauge; (*TEC*) to calibrate; (*UNIV*) to confer a degree on; (*MIL*) to commission; ~**se** *vr* to graduate; ~**se la vista** to have one's eyes tested.

grafía [gráfē'á] *nf* (*escritura*) writing; (*ortografía*) spelling.

gráfico, a [grá'fēko, á] *a* graphic; (*fig: vívido*) vivid, lively ♦ *nm* diagram ♦ *nf* graph; ~ **de barras** (*COM*) bar chart; ~ **de sectores** *o* **de tarta** (*COM*) pie chart; ~**s** *nmpl* (*tb INFORM*) graphics; ~**s empresariales** (*COM*) business graphics.

grafito [gráfē'to] *nm* (*TEC*) graphite, black lead.

grafología [gráfoloħē'á] *nf* graphology.

gragea [gráħe'á] *nf* (*MED*) pill; (*caramelo*) dragée.

grajo [grá'ho] *nm* rook.

Gral. *abr* (*MIL*: = *General*) Gen.

gramático, a [grámá'tēko, á] *nm/f* (*persona*) grammarian ♦ *nf* grammar.

gramo [grá'mo] *nm* gram (*US*), gramme (*Brit*).

gran [grán] *a V* **grande**.

grana [grá'ná] *nf* (*BOT*) seedling; (*color*) scarlet; **ponerse como la** ~ to go as red as a beet.

granada [gráná'ðá] *nf* pomegranate; (*MIL*) grenade; ~ **de mano** hand grenade; ~ **de metralla** shrapnel shell.

granadino, a [gránáðē'no, á] *a* of *o* from Granada ♦ *nm/f* native *o* inhabitant of Granada ♦ *nf* grenadine.

granar [gránár'] *vi* to seed.

granate [gráná'te] *nm* garnet.

Gran Bretaña [grámbretá'nyá] *nf* Great Britain.

Gran Canaria [gránkáná'ryá] *nf* Grand Canary.

grancanario, a [gránkáná'ryo, á] *a* of *o* from Grand Canary ♦ *nm/f* native *o* inhabitant of Grand Canary.

grande [grán'dě|, **gran** *a* (*de tamaño*) big, large; (*alto*) tall; (*distinguido*) great; (*impresionante*) grand ♦ *nm* grandee; *¿cómo es de* ~? how big is it?, what size is it?; **pasarlo en** ~ to have a tremendous time.

grandeza [grándě'sá] *nf* greatness; (*tamaño*) bigness; (*esplendidez*) grandness; (*nobleza*) nobility.

grandioso, a [grándyo'so, á] *a* magnificent, grand.

grandullón, ona [gránthoo͞ōyon', oná] *a* oversized.

granel [gránel'] *nm* (*montón*) heap; **a ~** (*COM*) in bulk.

granero [gráne'ro] *nm* granary, barn.

granice [gráně'se] *etc vb* V **granizar**.

granito [gráně'to] *nm* (*AGR*) small grain; (*roca*) granite.

granizada [gráněsá'thá] *nf* hailstorm; (*fig*) hail; **una ~ de balas** a hail of bullets.

granizado [gráněsá'tho] *nm* iced drink; **~ de café** iced coffee.

granizar [gráněsár'] *vi* to hail.

granizo [gráně'so] *nm* hail.

granja [grán'há] *nf* (*gen*) farm; **~ avícola** chicken *o* poultry farm.

granjear [gránheár'] *vt* (*cobrar*) to earn; (*ganar*) to win; (*avanzar*) to gain; **~se** *vr* (*amistad etc*) to gain for o.s.

granjero, a [gránhe'ro, á] *nm/f* farmer.

grano [grá'no] *nm* grain; (*semilla*) seed; (*baya*) berry; (*MED*) pimple, spot; (*partícula*) particle; (*punto*) speck; **~s** *nmpl* cereals; **~ de café** coffee bean; **ir al ~** to get to the point.

granuja [gránoo͞'há] *nm* rogue; (*golfillo*) urchin.

grapa [grá'pá] *nf* staple; (*TEC*) clamp; (*sujetador*) clip, fastener; (*ARQ*) cramp.

GRAPO [grá'po] *nm abr* (*Esp POL*)=*Grupo de Resistencia Antifascista Primero de Octubre*.

grasa [grá'sá] *nf* V **graso**.

grasiento, a [grásyen'to, á] *a* greasy; (*de aceite*) oily; (*mugriento*) filthy.

graso, a [grá'so, á] *a* fatty; (*aceitoso*) greasy, oily ♦ *nf* (*gen*) grease; (*de cocina*) fat, lard; (*sebo*) suet; (*mugre*) filth; (*AUTO*) oil; (*lubricante*) grease; **~ de ballena** blubber; **~ de pescado** fish oil.

gratificación [grátěfěkásyon'] *nf* (*propina*) tip; (*aguinaldo*) gratuity; (*bono*) bonus; (*recompensa*) reward.

gratificar [grátěfěkár'] *vt* (*dar propina*) to tip; (*premiar*) to reward; **"se gratificará"** "a reward is offered".

gratifique [grátěfě'ke] *etc vb* V **gratificar**.

gratis [grá'těs] *ad* free, for nothing.

gratitud [grátětoo͞th'] *nf* gratitude.

grato, a [grá'to, á] *a* (*agradable*) pleasant,

agreeable; (*bienvenido*) welcome; **nos es ~ informarle que** ... we are pleased to inform you that ....

gratuito, a [grátwě'to, á] *a* (*gratis*) free; (*sin razón*) gratuitous; (*acusación*) unfounded.

grava [grá'há] *nf* (*guijos*) gravel; (*piedra molida*) crushed stone; (*en carreteras*) gravel.

gravamen [gráhá'men] *nm* (*carga*) burden; (*impuesto*) tax; **libre de ~** (*ECON*) free from encumbrances.

gravar [gráhár'] *vt* to burden; (*COM*) to tax; (*ECON*) to assess for tax; **~ con impuestos** to burden with taxes.

grave [grá'he] *a* heavy; (*fig*, *MED*) grave, serious; (*importante*) important; (*herida*) severe; (*MUS*) low, deep; (*LING*: *acento*) grave; **estar ~** to be seriously ill.

gravedad [gráhetháth'] *nf* gravity; (*fig*) seriousness; (*grandeza*) importance; (*dignidad*) dignity; (*MUS*) depth.

grávido, a [grá'hětho, á] *a* (*preñada*) pregnant.

gravilla [gráhě'yá] *nf* gravel.

gravitación [gráhětásyon'] *nf* gravitation.

gravitar [gráhětár'] *vi* to gravitate; **~ sobre** to rest on.

gravoso, a [gráho'so, á] *a* (*pesado*) burdensome; (*costoso*) costly.

graznar [grásnár'] *vi* (*cuervo*) to squawk; (*pato*) to quack; (*hablar ronco*) to croak.

graznido [grásně'tho] *nm* squawk; croak.

Grecia [gre'syá] *nf* Greece.

gregario, a [gregá'ryo, á] *a* gregarious; **instinto ~** herd instinct.

gremio [gre'myo] *nm* (*asociación*) professional association, guild.

greña [gre'nyá] *nf* (*cabellos*) shock of hair; (*maraña*) tangle; **andar a la ~** to bicker, squabble.

greñudo, a [grenyoo͞'tho, á] *a* (*persona*) dishevelled; (*hair*) tangled.

gresca [gres'ká] *nf* uproar; (*trifulca*) row.

griego, a [grye'go, á] *a* Greek, Grecian ♦ *nm/f* Greek ♦ *nm* (*LING*) Greek.

grieta [grye'tá] *nf* crack; (*hendidura*) chink; (*quiebra*) crevice; (*MED*) chap; (*POL*) rift.

grifa [grě'fá] *nf* (*fam*: *droga*) marijuana.

grifo [grě'fo] *nm* faucet (*US*), tap (*Brit*); (*AM*) gas (*US*) *o* petrol (*Brit*) station.

grilletes [grěye'tes] *nmpl* fetters, shackles.

grillo [grě'yo] *nm* (*ZOOL*) cricket; (*BOT*) shoot; **~s** *nmpl* shackles, irons.

grima [grě'má] *nf* (*horror*) loathing; (*desagrado*) reluctance; (*desazón*) uneasiness; **me da ~** it makes me sick.

gringo, a [grēn'go, á] (*AM*) *a* (*pey*: *extranjero*) foreign; (: *norteamericano*) Yankee; (*idioma*) foreign ♦ *nm/f* foreigner; Yankee.

gripe [grě'pe] *nf* flu, influenza.

gris [grēs] *a* gray (*US*), grey (*Brit*).
grisáceo, a [grēsá'seo, á] *a* grayish (*US*),
greyish (*Brit*).
gritar [grētár'] *vt, vi* to shout, yell; **¡no gri-
tes!** stop shouting!
grito [grē'to] *nm* shout, yell; (*de horror*)
scream; **a ~ pelado** at the top of one's
voice; **poner el ~ en el cielo** to scream
bloody murder; **es el último ~** (*de moda*)
it's the latest thing.
groenlandés, esa [groenlándes', csá] *a*
Greenland *cpd* ♦ *nm/f* Greenlander.
Groenlandia [groenlán'dyá] *nf* Greenland.
grosella [grose'yá] *nf* (red)currant; **~ negra**
blackcurrant.
grosería [groserē'á] *nf* (*actitud*) rudeness;
(*comentario*) vulgar comment; (*palabrota*)
swearword.
grosero, a [grose'ro, á] *a* (*poco cortés*)
rude, bad-mannered; (*ordinario*) vulgar,
crude.
grosor [grosor'] *nm* thickness.
grotesco, a [grotes'ko, á] *a* grotesque;
(*absurdo*) bizarre.
grúa [grōō'á] *nf* (*TEC*) crane; (*de petróleo*)
derrick; **~ corrediza** *o* **móvil/de
pescante/puente/de torre** mobile/jib/
overhead/tower crane.
grueso, a [grwe'so, á] *a* thick; (*persona*)
stout; (*calidad*) coarse ♦ *nm* bulk; (*espesor*) thickness; (*densidad*) density; (*de gente*) main body, mass; **el ~ de** the bulk of.
grulla [grōō'yá] *nf* (*ZOOL*) crane.
grumete [grōōme'te] *nm* (*NAUT*) cabin boy.
grumo [grōō'mo] *nm* (*coágulo*) clot, lump;
(*masa*) dollop.
gruñido [grōōnyē'tho] *nm* grunt, growl;
(*fig*) grumble.
gruñir [grōōnyēr'] *vi* (*animal*) to grunt,
growl; (*fam*) to grumble.
gruñón, ona [grōōnyon', oná] *a* grumpy ♦
nm/f grumbler.
grupa [grōō'pá] *nf* (*ZOOL*) rump.
grupo [grōō'po] *nm* group; (*TEC*) unit, set;
(*de árboles*) cluster; **~ sanguíneo** blood
group.
gruta [grōō'tá] *nf* grotto.
Gta. *abr* (*AUTO*) = **Glorieta.**
guadalajareño, a [gwáthálá"háre'nyo, á] *a*
of *o* from Guadalajara ♦ *nm/f* native *o* inhabitant of Guadalajara.
Guadalquivir [gwáthálkēvēr'] *nm:* **el (Río)
~** the Guadalquivir.
guadaña [gwátha'nyá] *nf* scythe.
guadañar [gwáthányár'] *vt* to scythe, mow.
Guadiana [gwáthyá'ná] *nm:* **el (Río) ~** the
Guadiana.
guagua [gwá'gwá] *nf* (*AM, Canarias*) bus;
(*AM: criatura*) baby.
guajolote [gwáholo'te] *nm* (*AM*) turkey.
guano [gwá'no] *nm* guano.

guantada [gwántá'thá] *nf,* **guantazo**
[gwántá'so] *nm* slap.
guante [gwán'te] *nm* glove; **se ajusta como
un ~** it fits like a glove; **echar el ~ a uno**
to catch hold of sb; (*fig: policía*) to catch
sb.
guapo, a [gwá'po, á] *a* good-looking; (*mujer*) pretty, attractive; (*hombre*) handsome; (*elegante*) smart ♦ *nm* lover,
gallant.
guarda [gwár'thá] *nm/f* (*persona*) warden,
keeper ♦ *nf* (*acto*) guarding; (*custodia*)
custody; (*TIP*) flyleaf, endpaper; **~ forestal**
game warden.
guarda(a)gujas [gwárdágōō'hás] *nm inv*
(*FERRO*) switchman.
guardabarros [gwárthábá'rros] *nm inv*
fender (*US*), mudguard (*Brit*).
guardabosques [gwárdáos'kes] *nm inv*
game warden.
guardacostas [gwárdáko'stás] *nm inv*
coastguard vessel.
guardacoches [gwárthákotch'es] *nm/f inv*
(*celador*) parking attendant.
guardador, a [gwárthátho'or', á] *a* protective;
(*tacaño*) mean, stingy ♦ *nm/f* guardian,
protector.
guardaespaldas [gwárdáespál'dás] *nm/f inv*
bodyguard.
guardameta [gwártháme'tá] *nm* goalkeeper.
guardapolvo [gwárdápol'ho] *nm* dust
cover; (*prenda de vestir*) overalls *pl*.
guardar [gwárthár'] *vt* (*gen*) to keep; (*vigilar*) to guard, watch over; (*conservar*) to
put away; (*dinero: ahorrar*) to save; (*promesa etc*) to keep; (*ley*) to observe; (*rencor*) to bear; (*INFORM: archivo*) to save;
~se *vr* (*preservarse*) to protect o.s.; **~se
de algo** (*evitar*) to avoid sth; (*abstenerse*)
to refrain from sth; **~se de hacer algo** to
be careful not to do sth; **guardársela a uno**
to have it in for sb.
guardarropa [gwárthárro'pá] *nm* (*armario*)
wardrobe; (*en establecimiento público*)
cloakroom.
guardería [gwárthererē'á] *nf* nursery.
guardia [gwár'thyá] *nf* (*MIL*) guard; (*cuidado*) care, custody; **estar de ~** to be on
guard; **montar ~** to mount guard; **la G~
Civil** the Civil Guard; **~ municipal** *o* **urba-
na** municipal police ♦ *nm/f* guard; (*policía*)
policeman/woman; **un ~ civil** a Civil
Guard(sman); **un(a) ~ nacional** a
policeman/woman; **~ urbano** traffic policeman.
guardián, ana [gwárthyán', áná] *nm/f* (*gen*)
guardian, keeper.
guarecer [gwáreser'] *vt* (*proteger*) to protect; (*abrigar*) to shelter; **~se** *vr* to take
refuge.
guarezca [gwáres'ká] *etc vb V* **guarecer.**

guarida [gwáré'θá] *nf* (*de animal*) den, lair; (*de persona*) haunt, hideout; (*refugio*) refuge.

guarnecer [gwárneser'] *vt* (*equipar*) to provide; (*adornar*) to adorn; (*TEC*) to reinforce.

guarnezca [gwárnes'ká] *etc vb* **V guarnecer.**

guarnición [gwárnēsyon'] *nf* (*de vestimenta*) trimming; (*de piedra*) mount; (*CULIN*) garnish; (*arneses*) harness; (*MIL*) garrison.

guarro, a [gwá'rro, á] *nm/f* pig; (*fig*) dirty *o* slovenly person.

guasa [gwá'sá] *nf* joke; **con** *o* **de ~** jokingly, in fun.

guasón, ona [gwáson', oná] *a* witty; (*bromista*) joking ♦ *nm/f* wit; joker.

Guatemala [gwátemá'lá] *nf* Guatemala.

guatemalteco, a [gwátemálte'ko, á] *a, nm/f* Guatemalan.

guateque [gwáte'ke] *nm* (*fiesta*) party, binge.

guayaba [gwáyá'bá] *nf* (*BOT*) guava.

Guayana [gwáyá'ná] *nf* Guyana, Guaiana.

guyanés, esa [gwáyánes', esá] *a, nm/f* Guyanese.

gubernamental [goobernámentál'], **gubernativo, a** [goobernátē'bo, á] *a* governmental.

guedeja [geθe'há] *nf* long hair.

guerra [ge'rrá] *nf* war; (*arte*) warfare; (*pelea*) struggle; **~ atómica/bacteriológica/ nuclear/de guerrillas** atomic/germ/nuclear/ guerrilla warfare; **Primera/Segunda G~ Mundial** First/Second World War; **~ de precios** (*COM*) price war; **~ civil/fría** civil/ cold war; **~ a muerte** fight to the death; **de ~** military, war *cpd*; **estar en ~** to be at war; **dar ~** to be annoying.

guerrear [gerreár'] *vi* to wage war.

guerrero, a [gerre'ro, á] *a* fighting; (*carácter*) warlike ♦ *nm/f* warrior.

guerrilla [gerrē'yá] *nf* guerrilla warfare; (*tropas*) guerrilla band *o* group.

guerrillero, a [gerrēye'ro, á] *nm/f* guerrilla (fighter); (*contra invasor*) partisan.

guía [gē'á] *etc vb* **V guiar** ♦ *nm/f* (*persona*) guide ♦ *nf* (*libro*) guidebook; (*manual*) handbook; (*INFORM*) prompt; **~ de ferrocarriles** railway timetable; **~ telefónica** telephone directory; **~ del turista/del viajero** tourist/traveller's guide.

guiar [geár'] *vt* to guide, direct; (*dirigir*) to lead; (*orientar*) to advise; (*AUTO*) to steer; **~se** *vr:* **~se por** to be guided by.

guijarro [gēhá'rro] *nm* pebble.

guillotina [gēyotē'ná] *nf* guillotine.

guinda [gēn'dá] *nf* sour (*US*) *o* morello (*Brit*) cherry; (*licor*) cherry liqueur.

guindar [gēndár'] *vt* to hoist; (*fam: robar*) to rip off.

guindilla [gēndē'yá] *nf* chilli pepper.

Guinea [gēne'á] *nf* Guinea.

guineo, a [gēne'o, á] *a* Guinea *cpd*, Guinean ♦ *nm/f* Guinean.

guiñapo [gēnyá'po] *nm* (*harapo*) rag; (*persona*) rogue.

guiñar [gēnyár'] *vi* to wink.

guiño [gē'nyo] *nm* (*parpadeo*) wink; (*muecas*) grimace; **hacer ~s a** (*enamorados*) to make eyes at.

guiñol [gēnyol'] *nm* (*TEATRO*) puppet theater.

guión [gēon'] *nm* (*LING*) hyphen, dash; (*esquema*) summary, outline; (*CINE*) script.

guionista [gyonē'stá] *nm/f* scriptwriter.

guipuzcoano, a [gēpooskoá'no, á] *a* of *o* from Guipúzcoa ♦ *nm/f* native *o* inhabitant of Guipúzcoa.

guirigay [gērēgá'ē] *nm* (*griterío*) uproar; (*confusión*) chaos.

guirnalda [gērnál'dá] *nf* garland.

guisa [gē'sá] *nf:* **a ~ de** as, like.

guisado [gēsá'tho] *nm* stew.

guisante [gēsán'te] *nm* pea.

guisar [gēsár'] *vt, vi* to cook; (*fig*) to arrange.

guiso [gē'so] *nm* cooked dish.

guita [gē'tá] *nf* twine; (*fam: dinero*) dough.

guitarra [gētá'rrá] *nf* guitar.

guitarrista [gētárrē'stá] *nm/f* guitarist.

gula [goo'lá] *nf* gluttony, greed.

gusano [goosá'no] *nm* maggot, worm; (*de mariposa, polilla*) caterpillar; (*fig*) worm; (*ser despreciable*) creep; **~ de seda** silkworm.

gustar [goostár'] *vt* to taste, sample ♦ *vi* to please, be pleasing; **~ de algo** to like *o* enjoy sth; **me gustan las uvas** I like grapes; **le gusta nadar** she likes *o* enjoys swimming; **¿gusta Ud?** would you like some?; **como Ud guste** as you wish.

gusto [goo'sto] *nm* (*sentido, sabor*) taste; (*agrado*) liking; (*placer*) pleasure; **tiene un ~ amargo** it has a bitter taste; **tener buen ~** to have good taste; **sobre ~s no hay nada escrito** there's no accounting for tastes; **de buen/mal ~** in good/bad taste; **sentirse a ~** to feel at ease; **¡mucho** *o* **tanto ~ (en conocerle)!** how do you do?, pleased to meet you; **el ~ es mío** the pleasure is mine; **tomar ~ a** to take a liking to; **con ~** willingly, gladly.

gustoso, a [goosto'so, á] *a* (*sabroso*) tasty; (*agradable*) pleasant; (*con voluntad*) willing, glad; **lo hizo ~** he did it gladly.

gutural [gootoorál'] *a* guttural.

H

H, h [átch'e] *nf* (*letra*) H, h; **H de Historia** H for How.

h. *abr* (= *hora(s)*) h., hr(s).; (= *hacia*) c. ♦ *nmpl abr* (= *habitantes*) pop.

H. *abr* (*QUÍMICA*: = *Hidrógeno*) H; (= *Hectárea(s)*) ha.; (*COM*: = *Haber*) cr.

ha [á] *vb* V **haber.**

Ha. *abr* (= *Hectárea(s)*) ha.

haba [á'ßá] *nf* bean; **son ~s contadas** it goes without saying; **en todas partes cuecen ~s** it's the same (story) the whole world over.

Habana [aßá'ná] *nf*: **la ~** Havana.

habanero, a [aßáne'ro, á] *a* of *o* from Havana ♦ *nm/f* native *o* inhabitant of Havana ♦ *nf* (*MUS*) habanera.

habano [aßá'no] *nm* Havana cigar.

habeas corpus [aße'áskor'pōōs] *nm* (*LAW*) habeas corpus.

haber [aßer'] *vt* (*LAW etc*): **todos los inventos habidos y por ~** all inventions present and future; **en el encuentro habido ayer** in the fight which occurred yesterday ♦ *vb auxiliar* (*en tiempos compuestos*) to have; **de ~lo sabido** if I had known (it); **lo hubiéramos hecho** we would have done it; **antes de ~lo visto** before seeing him; **~ de** to have to ♦ *vb impersonal*: **hay** there is/are; **hay un hombre/2 hombres en la calle** there is one man/there are two men in the street; **ha habido problemas** there have been problems; **hay sol** it is sunny; **hay que** it is necessary to, one must; **hay que hacerlo** it has to be done; **¿habrá tiempo?** will there be time?; **tomará lo que haya** he'll take whatever there is; **lo que hay es que ...** it's like this, ...; **¿cuánto hay de aquí a Cuzco?** how far is it from here to Cuzco?; **¿qué hay?** how's it going?; **no hay de qué** don't mention it; **~se** *vr*: **habérselas con uno** (*tener delante*) to be up against sb ♦ *nm* (*ingreso*) income; (*COM*: *crédito*) credit; (*balance*) credit side; (*: tb*: **~es**) assets *pl*.

habichuela [aßitchwe'lá] *nf* kidney bean.

hábil [á'ßil] *a* (*listo*) clever, smart; (*capaz*) fit, capable; (*experto*) expert; **día ~** working day.

habilidad [aßeliðáð'] *nf* (*gen*) skill, ability; (*inteligencia*) cleverness; (*destreza*) expertness, expertise; (*JUR*) competence; **~ (para)** fitness (for); **tener ~ manual** to be good with one's hands.

habilitación [aßeletásyon'] *nf* qualification; (*colocación de muebles*) furnishing; (*financiamiento*) financing; (*oficina*) payroll (*US*) *o* paymaster's (*Brit*) office.

habilitado [aßeletá'ðo] *nm* paymaster.

habilitar [aßeletár'] *vt* to qualify; (*autorizar*) to authorize; (*capacitar*) to enable; (*dar instrumentos*) to equip; (*financiar*) to finance.

hábilmente [aßilmen'te] *ad* skilfully, expertly.

habitable [aßetá'ßle] *a* inhabitable.

habitación [aßetásyon'] *nf* (*cuarto*) room; (*casa*) dwelling, abode; (*BIO*: *morada*) habitat; **~ sencilla** *o* **individual** single room; **~ doble** *o* **de matrimonio** double room.

habitante [aßetán'te] *nm/f* inhabitant.

habitar [aßetár'] *vt* (*residir en*) to inhabit; (*ocupar*) to occupy ♦ *vi* to live.

hábito [á'ßeto] *nm* habit; **tener el ~ de hacer algo** to be in the habit of doing sth.

habitual [aßetwál'] *a* habitual.

habituar [aßetwár'] *vt* to accustom; **~se** *vr*: **~se a** to get used to.

habla [á'ßlá] *nf* (*capacidad de hablar*) speech; (*idioma*) language; (*dialecto*) dialect; **perder el ~** to become speechless; **de ~ francesa** French-speaking; **estar al ~** to be in contact; (*TELEC*) to be on the line; **¡González al ~!** (*TELEC*) Gonzalez speaking!

hablador, a [aßláðhor', á] *a* talkative ♦ *nm/f* chatterbox.

habladuría [aßláðhōōrá'á] *nf* rumor (*US*), rumour (*Brit*); **~s** *nfpl* gossip *sg*.

hablante [aßlán'te] *a* speaking ♦ *nm/f* speaker.

hablar [aßlár'] *vt* to speak, talk ♦ *vi* to speak; **~se** *vr* to speak to each other; **~ con** to speak to; **¡hable!**, **¡puede ~!** (*TELEC*) go ahead (*US*), you're through! (*Brit*); **de eso ni ~** no way; **~ alto/bajo/claro** to speak loudly/quietly/plainly *o* bluntly; **~ de** to speak of *o* about; **"se habla inglés"** "English spoken here"; **no se hablan** they are not on speaking terms.

habré [aßre'] *etc vb* V **haber.**

hacedor, a [aseðhor', á] *nm/f* maker.

hacendado, a [asendá'ðho, á] *a* property-owning ♦ *nm* (*terrateniente*) large landowner.

hacendoso, a [asendo'so, á] *a* industrious, hard-working.

hacer [áser'] *vt* (*gen*) to make; (*crear*) to create; (*TEC*) to manufacture; (*preparar*) to prepare; (*ejecutar*) to do, execute; (*obligar*) to force, compel; (*dinero*) to earn; (*volver*) to make, turn ♦ *vi* (*comportarse*) to act, behave; (*disimular*) to pretend; (*convenir, ser apto*) to be suitable; ~**se** *vr* (*fabricarse*) to be made, be done; (*volverse*) to become; (*acostumbrarse a*) to get used to; ~ **bien/mal** to act rightly/ wrongly; **hace frío/calor** it's cold/hot; **hace un momento/dos años** a moment/two years ago; **hace poco** a little while ago; **te hacíamos en el Perú** we assumed you were in Peru; **hágale entrar** show him in; ~ **polvo algo** to smash sth to pieces; ~ **polvo a uno** to exhaust sb; ~ **un papel** (*TEATRO*) to play a role *o* part; **¿qué le vamos a ~?** what can we do about it?; **¿qué haces ahí?** what are you up to?; ~ **como que** *o* **como si** to act as though *o* as if; **dar que** ~ to cause trouble; ~ **de** to act as; **¿hace?** will it do?; **me hice un traje** I had a suit made; ~**se el sordo** to turn a deaf ear; ~**se el tonto** *o* **el sueco** to act dumb, play the innocent; ~**se a** (~) **algo** to get used to (doing) sth; ~**se viejo** to grow old; ~**se con algo** to get hold of sth; ~**se a un lado** to stand aside; **se hace tarde** it's getting late; **se me hace imposible trabajar** I'm finding it impossible to work; **no le hace** it doesn't matter.

hacia [á'syá] *prep* (*en dirección de, actitud*) towards; (*cerca de*) near; ~ **arriba/abajo** up(wards)/down(wards); ~ **mediodía** about noon.

hacienda [àsyen'dá] *nf* (*propiedad*) property; (*finca*) farm; (*AM*) ranch; ~ **pública** public finance; **(Ministerio de) H~** Treasury Department (*US*), Exchequer (*Brit*).

hacina [àsē'ná] *nf* pile, stack.

hacinar [àsēnár'] *vt* to pile (up); (*AGR*) to stack; (*fig*) to overcrowd.

hacha [átch'á] *nf* axe; (*antorcha*) torch.

hache [átch'e] *nf* (the letter) H; **llámele usted** ~ call it what you will.

hachís [átchēs'] *nm* hashish.

hada [à'ꝺá] *nf* fairy; ~ **madrina** fairy godmother.

hado [à'ꝺo] *nm* fate, destiny.

haga [à'gá] *etc vb V* **hacer**.

Haití [áētē'] *nm* Haiti.

haitiano, a [áētyá'no, á] *a, nm/f* Haitian.

hala [à'lá] *excl* (*vamos*) come on!; (*anda*) get on with it!

halagar [àlàgár'] *vt* (*lisonjear*) to flatter.

halago [àlà'go] *nm* (*adulación*) flattery.

halague [àlà'ge] *etc vb V* **halagar**.

halagüeño, a [àlàgwe'nyo, á] *a* flattering.

halcón [àlkon'] *nm* falcon, hawk.

hálito [à'lēto] *nm* breath.

halitosis [àlēto'sēs] *nf* halitosis, bad breath.

halo [à'lo] *nm* halo.

halterofilia [àlterofē'lyà] *nf* weightlifting.

hallar [àyàr'] *vt* (*gen*) to find; (*descubrir*) to

discover; (*toparse con*) to run into; ~**se** *vr* to be (situated); (*encontrarse*) to find o.s.; **se halla fuera** he is away; **no se halla** he feels out of place.

hallazgo [àyàs'go] *nm* discovery; (*cosa*) find.

hamaca [àmá'ká] *nf* hammock.

hambre [àm'bre] *nf* hunger; (*carencia*) famine; (*inanición*) starvation; (*fig*) longing; **tener** ~ to be hungry.

hambriento, a [àmbryen'to, á] *a* hungry, starving ♦ *nm/f* starving person; **los** ~**s** the hungry; ~ **de** hungry *o* longing for.

Hamburgo [àmboōr'go] *nm* Hamburg.

hamburguesa [àmboōrge'sà] *nf* hamburger.

hampa [àm'pá] *nf* underworld.

hampón [àmpon'] *nm* thug.

han [àn] *vb V* **haber**.

haragán, ana [áràgàn', ànà] *a, nm/f* good-for-nothing.

haraganear [áràgàneàr'] *vi* to idle, loaf about.

harapiento, a [árápyen'to, á] *a* tattered, in rags.

harapo [árá'po] *nm* rag.

hardware [hàr'dwer] *nm* (*INFORM*) hardware.

haré [àre'] *etc vb V* **hacer**.

harén [àren'] *nm* harem.

harina [àrē'ná] *nf* flour; **eso es** ~ **de otro costal** that's a horse of a different color.

harinero, a [árēne'ro, á] *nm/f* flour merchant.

harinoso, a [árēno'so, á] *a* floury.

hartar [àrtár'] *vt* to satiate, glut; (*fig*) to tire, sicken; ~**se** *vr* (*de comida*) to fill o.s., gorge o.s.; (*cansarse*) to get fed up (*de* with).

hartazgo [àrtàs'go] *nm* surfeit, glut.

harto, a [àr'to, á] *a* (*lleno*) full; (*cansado*) fed up ♦ *ad* (*bastante*) enough; (*muy*) very; **estar** ~ **de** to be fed up with; **¡estoy** ~ **de decírtelo!** I'm sick and tired of telling you (so)!

hartura [àrtoō'rá] *nf* (*exceso*) surfeit; (*abundancia*) abundance; (*satisfacción*) satisfaction.

has [às] *vb V* **haber**.

Has. *abr* (= *Hectáreas*) ha.

hasta [à'stá] *ad* even ♦ *prep* (*alcanzando a*) as far as, up/down to; (*de tiempo*: *a tal hora*) till, until; (: *antes de*) before ♦ *conj*: ~ **que** until; ~ **luego** *o* **ahora** (*fam*)/**el sábado** see you soon/on Saturday; ~ **la fecha** (up) to date; ~ **nueva orden** until further notice; ~ **en Valencia hiela a veces** even in Valencia it freezes sometimes.

hastiar [àstyár'] *vt* (*gen*) to weary; (*aburrir*) to bore; ~**se** *vr*: ~**se de** to get fed up with.

hastío [ástē'o] *nm* weariness; boredom.
hatajo [átá'ho] *nm*: **un ~ de gamberros** a bunch of hooligans.
hatillo [átē'yo] *nm* belongings *pl*, kit; (*montón*) bundle, heap.
Hawai [áwá'ē] *nm* (*tb*: **las Islas ~**) Hawaii.
hawaiano, a [áwáyá'no, á] *a, nm/f* Hawaian.
hay [áē] *vb* V **haber**.
Haya [á'yá] *nf*: **la ~** The Hague.
haya [á'yá] *etc vb* V **haber** ♦ *nf* beech tree.
hayal [áyál'] *nm* beech grove.
haz [ás] *vb* V **hacer** ♦ *nm* bundle, bunch; (*rayo: de luz*) beam ♦ *nf*: **~ de la tierra** face of the earth.
hazaña [ásá'nyá] *nf* feat, exploit; **sería una ~** it would be a great achievement.
hazmerreír [ásmerreēr'] *nm inv* laughing stock.
HB *abr* (= *Herri Batasuna*) Basque political party.
he [e] *vb* V **haber** ♦ *ad*: **~ aquí** here is, here are; **~ aquí por qué ...** that is why ....
hebilla [ebē'yá] *nf* buckle, clasp.
hebra [e'hrá] *nf* thread; (*BOT: fibra*) fiber (*US*), fibre (*Brit*), grain.
hebreo, a [ehre'o, á] *a, nm/f* Hebrew ♦ *nm* (*LING*) Hebrew.
Hébridas [e'hrēthás] *nfpl*: **las ~** the Hebrides.
hectárea [ektá'reá] *nf* hectare.
hechice [etchē'se] *etc vb* V **hechizar**.
hechicera [etchēse'rá] *nf* witch.
hechizar [etchēsár'] *vt* to cast a spell on, bewitch.
hechizo [etchē'so] *nm* witchcraft, magic; (*acto de magia*) spell, charm.
hecho, a [etch'o, á] *pp de* **hacer** ♦ *a* complete; (*maduro*) mature; (*COSTURA*) ready-to-wear ♦ *nm* deed, act; (*dato*) fact; (*cuestión*) matter; (*suceso*) event ♦ *excl* agreed!, done!; **¡bien ~!** well done!; **de ~** in fact, as a matter of fact; (*POL etc*: *a, ad*) de facto; **de ~ y de derecho** de facto and de jure; **~ a la medida** made-to-measure; **a lo ~, pecho** it's no use crying over spilt milk.
hechura [etchōō'rá] *nf* making, creation; (*producto*) product; (*forma*) form, shape; (*de persona*) build; (*TEC*) craftsmanship.
heder [ether'] *vi* to stink, smell; (*fig*) to be unbearable.
hediondez [ethyondes'] *nf* stench, stink; (*cosa*) stinking thing.
hediondo, a [ethyon'do, á] *a* stinking.
hedor [ethor'] *nm* stench.
helada [elá'thá] *nf* frost.
heladera [eláthe'rá] *nf* (*AM: refrigerador*) refrigerator.
heladería [eláthere'á] *nf* ice-cream parlor (*US*) o parlour (*Brit*).

helado, a [elá'tho, á] *a* frozen; (*glacial*) icy; (*fig*) chilly, cold ♦ *nm* ice-cream; **dejar ~ a uno** to dumbfound sb.
helador, a [eláthor', á] *a* (*viento etc*) icy, freezing.
helar [elár'] *vt* to freeze, ice (up); (*dejar atónito*) to amaze; (*desalentar*) to discourage ♦ *vi*, **~se** *vr* to freeze; (*AVIAT, FERRO etc*) to ice (up), freeze up; (*líquido*) to set.
helecho [eletch'o] *nm* bracken, fern.
helénico, a [ele'nēko, á] *a* Hellenic, Greek.
heleno, a [ele'no, á] *nm/f* Hellene, Greek.
hélice [e'lēse] *nf* spiral; (*TEC*) propeller; (*MAT*) helix.
helicóptero [elēkop'tero] *nm* helicopter.
helmántico, a [elmán'tēko, á] *a* of o from Salamanca.
helvético, a [elhe'tēko, á] *a, nm/f* Swiss.
hembra [em'brá] *nf* (*BOT, ZOOL*) female; (*mujer*) woman; (*TEC*) nut; **un elefante ~** a female elephant.
hemeroteca [emerote'ká] *nf* newspaper library.
hemofilia [emofē'lyá] *nf* hemophilia (*US*), haemophilia (*Brit*).
hemorragia [emorrá'hyá] *nf* hemorrhage (*US*), haemorrhage (*Brit*).
hemorroides [emorro'ēthes] *nfpl* hemorrhoids (*US*), haemorrhoids (*Brit*).
hemos [e'mos] *vb* V **haber**.
henar [enár'] *nm* meadow, hayfield.
henchir [entchēr'] *vt* to fill, stuff; **~se** *vr* (*llenarse de comida*) to stuff o.s. (with food); (*inflarse*) to swell (up).
Hendaya [endá'yá] *nf* Hendaye.
hender [ender'] *vt* to cleave, split.
hendidura [endēthōō'rá] *nf* crack, split; (*GEO*) fissure.
heno [e'no] *nm* hay.
herbario, a [erhá'ryo, á] *a* herbal ♦ *nm* (*colección*) herbarium; (*especialista*) herbalist; (*botánico*) botanist.
herbicida [erhēsē'thá] *nm* weedkiller.
heredad [eretháth'] *nf* landed property; (*granja*) farm.
heredar [erethár'] *vt* to inherit.
heredero, a [erethe'ro, á] *nm/f* heir(ess); **~ del trono** heir to the throne.
hereditario, a [erethētá'ryo, á] *a* hereditary.
hereje [ere'he] *nm/f* heretic.
herejía [erehē'á] *nf* heresy.
herencia [eren'syá] *nf* inheritance; (*fig*) heritage; (*BIO*) heredity.
herético, a [ere'tēko, á] *a* heretical.
herido, a [erē'tho, á] *a* injured, wounded; (*fig*) offended ♦ *nm/f* casualty ♦ *nf* wound, injury.
herir [erēr'] *vt* to wound, injure; (*fig*) to offend; (*conmover*) to touch, move.
hermana [ermá'ná] *nf* V **hermano**.

hermanar [ermánár'] vt to match; (unir) to join; (ciudades) to make sister cities (US), twin (Brit).
hermanastro, a [ermánás'tro, á] nm/f stepbrother/sister.
hermandad [ermándáth'] nf brotherhood; (de mujeres) sisterhood; (sindicato etc) association.
hermano, a [ermá'no, á] a similar ♦ nm brother ♦ nf sister; ~ **gemelo** twin brother; ~ **político** brother-in-law; ~ **primo** first cousin; **mis ~s** my brothers, my brothers and sisters; **hermana política** sister-in-law.
hermético, a [ermc'tēko, á] a hermetic; (fig) watertight.
hermoso, a [ermo'so, á] a beautiful, lovely; (estupendo) splendid; (guapo) handsome.
hermosura [ermosōō'rá] nf beauty; (de hombre) handsomeness.
héroe [e'roe] nm hero.
heroicidad [eroēsēthath'] nf heroism; (una ~) heroic deed.
heroico, a [ero'ēko, á] a heroic.
heroína [eroē'ná] nf (mujer) heroine; (droga) heroin.
heroísmo [eroēs'mo] nm heroism.
herpes [er'pes] nmpl o nfpl (MED: gen) herpes sg; (: de la piel) shingles sg.
herradura [erráthōō'rá] nf horseshoe.
herraje [errá'he] nm (trabajos) ironwork.
herramienta [errámyen'tá] nf tool.
herrería [errerē'á] nf blacksmith's workshop (US), smithy (Brit); (TEC) forge.
herrero [erre'ro] nm blacksmith.
herrumbre [errōōm'bre] nf rust.
herrumbroso, a [errōōmbro'so, á] a rusty.
hervidero [erhēthe'ro] nm (fig) swarm; (POL etc) hotbed.
hervir [erhēr'] vi to boil; (burbujear) to bubble; (fig): ~ **de** to teem with; ~ **a fuego lento** to simmer.
hervor [erhor'] nm boiling; (fig) ardor (US), ardour (Brit), fervor (US), fervour (Brit).
heterogéneo, a [eterohe'neo, á] a heterogeneous.
heterosexual [eterosekswál'] a, nm/f heterosexual.
hez [es] nf (tb: **heces** pl) dregs.
hibernar [ēbernár'] vi to hibernate.
hice [ē'se] etc vb V **hacer.**
hidalgo, a [ēthál'go, á] a noble; (honrado) honorable (US), honourable (Brit) ♦ nm/f noble(man/woman).
hidratante [ēthrátán'te] a: **crema** ~ moisturizing cream, moisturizer.
hidratar [ēthrátár'] vt to moisturize.
hidrato [ēthrá'to] nm hydrate; ~ **de carbono** carbohydrate.
hidráulico, a [ēthrá'ōōlēko, á] a hydraulic ♦ nf hydraulics sg.

hidro... [ēthro] pref hydro..., water-....
hidroavión [ēthroáhyon'] nm seaplane.
hidroeléctrico, a [ēthroelek'trēko, á] a hydroelectric.
hidrófilo, a [ēthro'fēlo, á] a absorbent; **algodón** ~ absorbent cotton (US), cotton wool (Brit).
hidrofobia [ēthrofo'hyá] nf hydrophobia, rabies.
hidrófugo, a [ēthro'fōōgo, á] a waterproof.
hidrógeno [ēthro'heno] nm hydrogen.
hieda [ye'thá] etc vb V **heder.**
hiedra [ye'thrá] nf ivy.
hiel [yel] nf gall, bile; (fig) bitterness.
hielo [ye'lo] etc vb V **helar** ♦ nm (gen) ice; (escarcha) frost; (fig) coldness, reserve; **romper el** ~ (fig) to break the ice.
hiena [ye'ná] nf (ZOOL) hyena.
hiera [ye'rá] etc vb V **herir.**
hierba [yer'há] nf (pasto) grass; (CULIN. MED: planta) herb; **mala** ~ weed; (fig) evil influence.
hierbabuena [yerháhwe'ná] nf mint.
hierro [ye'rro] nm (metal) iron; (objeto) iron object; ~ **acanalado** corrugated iron; ~ **colado** o **fundido** cast iron; **de** ~ iron cpd.
hierva [yer'há] etc vb V **hervir.**
hígado [ē'gátho] nm liver; ~s nmpl (fig) guts; **echar los ~s** to wear o.s. out.
higiene [ēhye'ne] nf hygiene.
higiénico, a [ēhye'nēko, á] a hygienic.
higo [ē'go] nm fig; ~ **seco** dried fig; ~ **chumbo** prickly pear; **de ~s a brevas** once in a blue moon.
higuera [ēge'rá] nf fig tree.
hijastro, a [ēhás'tro, á] nm/f stepson/daughter.
hijo, a [ē'ho, á] nm/f son/daughter, child; (uso vocativo) dear; ~s nmpl children, sons and daughters; **sin ~s** childless; ~/**hija político/a** son-/daughter-in-law; ~ **pródigo** prodigal son; ~ **de papá/mamá** daddy's/mama's boy; ~ **de puta** (fam!) bastard(!), son of a bitch(!); **cada ~ de vecino** any Tom, Dick or Harry.
hilacha [ēlátch'á] nf ravelled thread; ~ **de acero** steel wool.
hilado, a [ēlá'tho, á] a spun.
hilandero, a [ēlánde'ro, á] nm/f spinner.
hilar [ēlár'] vt to spin; (fig) to reason, infer; ~ **delgado** to split hairs.
hilera [ēle'rá] nf row, file.
hilo [ē'lo] nm thread; (BOT) fiber (US), fibre (Brit); (tela) linen; (metal) wire; (de agua) trickle, thin stream; (de luz) beam, ray; (de conversación) thread, theme; (de pensamientos) train; **colgar de un** ~ (fig) to hang by a thread; **traje de** ~ linen suit.
hilvanar [ēlhánár'] vt (COSTURA) to baste (US); tack (Brit); (fig) to do hurriedly.

Himalaya [ēmálá'yá] *nm*: **el ~, los Montes ~** the Himalayas.

himno [ēm'no] *nm* hymn; **~ nacional** national anthem.

hincapié [ēnkápye'] *nm*: **hacer ~ en** to emphasize, stress.

hincar [ēnkár'] *vt* to drive (in), thrust (in); (*diente*) to sink; **~se** *vr*: **~se de rodillas** to kneel down.

hincha [ēntch'á] *nm/f* (*fam*: *DEPORTE*) fan.

hinchado, a [ēntchá'ðo, á] *a* (*gen*) swollen; (*persona*) pompous.

hinchar [ēntchár'] *vt* (*gen*) to swell; (*inflar*) to blow up, inflate; (*fig*) to exaggerate; **~se** *vr* (*inflarse*) to swell up; (*fam*: *llenarse*) to stuff o.s.; (*fig*) to get conceited; **~se de reír** to have a good laugh.

hinchazón [ēntcháson'] *nf* (*MED*) swelling; (*protuberancia*) bump, lump; (*altivez*) arrogance.

hindú [ēndōō'] *a, nm/f* Hindu.

hinojo [ēno'ho] *nm* fennel.

hinque [ēn'ke] *etc vb* V **hincar.**

hipar [ēpár'] *vi* to hiccup.

hiper... [ēper] *pref* hyper....

hiperactivo, a [ēperáktē'ßo, á] *a* hyperactive.

hipermercado [ēpermerká'ðo] *nm* hypermarket, superstore (*Brit*).

hipersensible [ēpersensē'ßle] *a* hypersensitive.

hípico, a [ē'pēko, á] *a* horse *cpd*, equine; **club ~** riding club.

hipnotice [ēpnotē'se] *etc vb* V **hipnotizar.**

hipnotismo [ēpnotēs'mo] *nm* hypnotism.

hipnotizar [ēpnotēsár'] *vt* to hypnotize.

hipo [ē'po] *nm* hiccups *pl*; **quitar el ~ a uno** to cure sb's hiccups.

hipocondría [ēpokondrē'á] *nf* hypochondria.

hipocondríaco, a [ēpokondry'áko, á] *a, nm/f* hypochondriac.

hipocresía [ēpokresē'á] *nf* hypocrisy.

hipócrita [ēpo'krētá] *a* hypocritical ♦ *nm/f* hypocrite.

hipodérmico, a [ēpoðer'mēko, á] *a*: **aguja hipodérmica** hypodermic needle.

hipódromo [ēpo'ðromo] *nm* racetrack.

hipopótamo [ēpopo'támo] *nm* hippopotamus.

hipoteca [ēpote'ká] *nf* mortgage; **redimir una ~** to pay off a mortgage.

hipotecario, a [ēpoteká'ryo, á] *a* mortgage *cpd*.

hipótesis [ēpo'tesēs] *nf inv* hypothesis; **es una ~ (nada más)** that's just a theory.

hipotético, a [ēpote'tēko, á] *a* hypothetic(al).

hiriendo [ēryen'do] *etc vb* V **herir.**

hiriente [ēryen'te] *a* offensive, wounding.

hirsuto, a [ērsōō'to, á] *a* hairy.

hirviendo [ērßyen'do] *etc vb* V **hervir.**

hisopo [ēso'po] *nm* (*REL*) sprinkler; (*BOT*) hyssop; (*de algodón*) swab.

hispánico, a [ēspá'nēko, á] *a* Hispanic, Spanish.

hispanidad [ēspánēðáð'] *nf* (*cualidad*) Spanishness; (*POL*) Spanish o Hispanic world.

hispanista [ēspánē'stá] *nm/f* (*UNIV etc*) Hispan(ic)ist.

hispano, a [ēspá'no, á] *a* Hispanic, Spanish, Hispano- ♦ *nm/f* Spaniard.

Hispanoamérica [ēspánoáme'rēká] *nf* Spanish o Latin America.

hispanoamericano, a [ēspánoámerēká'no, á] *a, nm/f* Spanish o Latin American.

hispanohablante [ēspánoáhlàn'te], **hispanoparlante** [ēspánopárlàn'te] *a* Spanish-speaking.

histeria [ēste'ryá] *nf* hysteria.

histérico, a [ēste'rēko, á] *a* hysterical.

histerismo [ēsterēs'mo] *nm* (*MED*) hysteria; (*fig*) hysterics.

histograma [ēstográ'má] *nm* histogram.

historia [ēsto'ryá] *nf* history; (*cuento*) story, tale; **~s** *nfpl* (*chismes*) gossip *sg*; **dejarse de ~s** to come to the point; **pasar a la ~** to go down in history.

historiador, a [ēstoryáðhor', á] *nm/f* historian.

historial [ēstoryál'] *nm* record; (*profesional*) résumé (*US*), curriculum vitae, c.v.; (*MED*) case history.

historiar [ēstoryár'] *vt* to chronicle, write the history of.

histórico, a [ēsto'rēko, á] *a* historical; (*fig*) historic.

historieta [ēstorye'tá] *nf* tale, anecdote; (*dibujos*) comic strip.

histrionismo [ēstryonēs'mo] *nm* (*TEATRO*) acting; (*fig*) histrionics *pl*.

hito [ē'to] *nm* (*fig*) landmark; (*objetivo*) goal, target; (*fig*) milestone.

hizo [ē'so] *vb* V **hacer.**

Hna(s). *abr* (= *Hermana(s)*) Sr(s).

Hno(s). *abr* (= *Hermano(s)*) Bro(s).

hocico [osē'ko] *nm* snout; (*fig*) grimace.

hockey [ho'kē] *nm* hockey; **~ sobre hielo** ice hockey.

hogar [oɡár'] *nm* fireplace, hearth; (*casa*) home; (*vida familiar*) home life.

hogareño, a [oɡàre'nyo, á] *a* home *cpd*; (*persona*) home-loving.

hogaza [oɡá'sá] *nf* (*pan*) large loaf.

hoguera [oɡe'rá] *nf* (*gen*) bonfire; (*para herejes*) stake.

hoja [o'há] *nf* (*gen*) leaf; (*de flor*) petal; (*de hierba*) blade; (*de papel*) sheet; (*página*) page; (*formulario*) form; (*de puerta*) leaf; **~ de afeitar** razor blade; **~ de cálculo electrónico** spreadsheet; **~ de trabajo** (*IN-*

FORM) worksheet; **de ~ ancha** broad-leaved; **de ~ caduca/perenne** deciduous/evergreen.

hojalata [ohálá'tá] *nf* tin(plate).

hojaldre [ohál'dre] *nm* (*CULIN*) puff pastry.

hojarasca [ohárás'ká] *nf* (*hojas*) dead *o* fallen leaves *pl*; (*fig*) rubbish.

hojear [oheár'] *vt* to leaf through, turn the pages of.

hola [o'lá] *excl* hello!

Holanda [olán'dá] *nf* Holland.

holandés, esa [olándes', esá] *a* Dutch ♦ *nm/f* Dutchman/woman; **los holandeses** the Dutch ♦ *nm* (*LING*) Dutch.

holgado, a [olgá'tho, á] *a* loose, baggy; (*rico*) well-to-do.

holganza [olgán'sá] *nf* (*ocio*) leisure; (*diversión*) amusement.

holgar [olgár'] *vi* (*descansar*) to rest; (*sobrar*) to be superfluous; **huelga decir que** it goes without saying that.

holgazán, ana [olgásán', áná] *a* idle, lazy ♦ *nm/f* loafer.

holgazanear [olgásáneár'] *vi* to laze *o* loaf around.

holgué [olge'], **holguemos** [olge'mos] *etc vb* V **holgar.**

holgura [olgōō'rá] *nf* looseness, bagginess; (*TEC*) play, free movement; (*vida*) comfortable living, luxury.

hollar [oyár'] *vt* to tread (on), trample.

hollín [oyēn'] *nm* soot.

hombre [om'bre] *nm* man; (*raza humana*): **el ~** man(kind) ♦ *excl*: **¡sí ~!** (*claro*) of course!; (*para énfasis*) man; **~ de negocios** businessman; **~-rana** frogman; **~ de bien** *o* **pro** honest man; **~ de confianza** right-hand man; **~ de estado** statesman; **el ~ medio** the average man.

hombrera [ombre'rá] *nf* shoulder strap.

hombro [om'bro] *nm* shoulder; **arrimar el ~** to lend a hand; **encogerse de ~s** to shrug one's shoulders.

hombruno, a [ombrōō'no, á] *a* mannish.

homenaje [omená'he] *nm* (*gen*) homage; (*tributo*) tribute; **un partido ~** a benefit match.

homicida [omēsē'thá] *a* homicidal ♦ *nm/f* murderer.

homicidio [omēsē'thyo] *nm* murder, homicide; (*involuntario*) manslaughter.

homologación [omologásyon'] *nf* (*de sueldo, condiciones*) parity.

homólogo, a [omo'logo, á] *nm/f* counterpart, opposite number.

homónimo [omo'nēmo] *nm* (*tocayo*) namesake.

homosexual [omosekswál'] *a, nm/f* homosexual.

hondo, a [on'do, á] *a* deep; **lo ~** the depth(s) (*pl*), the bottom; **con ~ pesar**

with deep regret.

hondonada [ondoná'thá] *nf* hollow, depression; (*cañón*) ravine; (*GEO*) lowland.

hondura [ondōō'rá] *nf* depth, profundity.

Honduras [ondōō'rás] *nf* Honduras.

hondureño, a [ondōōre'nyo, á] *a, nm/f* Honduran.

honestidad [onestē'tháth'] *nf* purity, chastity; (*decencia*) decency.

honesto, a [one'sto, á] *a* chaste; decent, honest; (*justo*) just.

hongo [on'go] *nm* (*BOT*: *gen*) fungus; (: *comestible*) mushroom; (: *venenoso*) toadstool; (*sombrero*) derby (*US*), bowler (hat) (*Brit*); **~s del pie** athlete's foot *sg*.

honor [onor'] *nm* (*gen*) honor (*US*), honour (*Brit*); (*gloria*) glory; **~ profesional** professional etiquette; **en ~ a la verdad** to be fair.

honorable [onorá'ble] *a* honorable (*US*), honourable (*Brit*).

honorario, a [onorá'ryo, á] *a* honorary ♦ *nm*: **~s** fees.

honorífico, a [onorē'fēko, á] *a* honorable (*US*), honourable (*Brit*); **mención honorífica** honorable mention.

honra [on'rá] *nf* (*gen*) honor (*US*), honour (*Brit*); (*renombre*) good name; **~s fúnebres** funeral rites; **tener algo a mucha ~** to be proud of sth.

honradez [onráthes'] *nf* honesty; (*de persona*) integrity.

honrado, a [onrá'tho, á] *a* honest, upright.

honrar [onrár'] *vt* to honor (*US*), honour (*Brit*); **~se** *vr*: **~se con algo/de hacer algo** to be honored by sth/to do sth.

honroso, a [onro'so, á] *a* (*honrado*) honorable (*US*), honourable (*Brit*); (*respetado*) respectable.

hora [o'rá] *nf* hour; (*tiempo*) time; **¿qué ~ es?** what time is it?; **¿a qué ~?** at what time?; **media ~** half an hour; **a la ~ de comer/de recreo** at lunchtime/at playtime; **a primera ~** first thing (in the morning); **a última ~** at the last moment; **noticias de última ~** last-minute news; **a altas ~s** in the wee small hours; **a la ~ en punto** on the dot; **¡a buena ~!** about time, too!; **en mala ~** unluckily; **dar la ~** to strike the hour; **poner el reloj en ~** to set one's watch; **~s de oficina/de trabajo** office/working hours; **~s de visita** visiting times; **~s extra** *o* **extraordinarias** overtime *sg*; **~s punta** rush hours; **no ver la ~ de** to look forward to; **¡ya era ~!** and about time too!

horadar [orátár'] *vt* to drill, bore.

horario, a [orá'ryo, á] *a* hourly, hour *cpd* ♦ *nm* timetable; **~ comercial** business hours.

horca [or'ká] *nf* gallows *sg*; (*AGR*) pitchfork.

horcajadas [orkáhá'ŧŧás]: **a ~** *ad* astride.
horchata [ortchá'tá] *nf cold drink made from almonds and water*, almond milk.
horda [or'ŧŧá] *nf* horde.
horizontal [orĕsontál'] *a* horizontal.
horizonte [orĕson'te] *nm* horizon.
horma [or'má] *nf* mold (*US*), mould (*Brit*); **~ (de calzado)** last; **~ de sombrero** hat block.
hormiga [ormĕ'gá] *nf* ant; **~s** *nfpl* (*MED*) pins and needles.
hormigón [ormĕgon'] *nm* concrete; **~ armado/pretensado** reinforced/prestressed concrete.
hormigueo [ormĕge'o] *nm* (*comezón*) itch; (*fig*) uneasiness.
hormona [ormo'ná] *nf* hormone.
hornada [orná'ŧŧá] *nf* batch of loaves (*etc*).
hornillo [ornĕ'yo] *nm* (*cocina*) portable stove.
horno [or'no] *nm* (*CULIN*) oven; (*TEC*) furnace; (*para cerámica*) kiln; **~ microondas** microwave (oven); **alto ~** blast furnace; **~ crematorio** crematorium.
horóscopo [oros'kopo] *nm* horoscope.
horquilla [orkĕ'yá] *nf* hairpin; (*AGR*) pitchfork.
horrendo, a [orren'do, á] *a* horrendous, frightful.
horrible [orrĕ'ʰle] *a* horrible, dreadful.
horripilante [orrĕpĕlán'te] *a* hair-raising, horrifying.
horripilar [orrĕpĕlár'] *vt*: **~ a uno** to horrify sb; **~se** *vr* to be horrified.
horror [orror'] *nm* horror, dread; (*atrocidad*) atrocity; **¡qué ~!** (*fam*) oh, my God!; **estudia horrores** he studies a hell of a lot.
horrorice [orrorĕ'se] *etc vb V* **horrorizar.**
horrorizar [orrorĕsár'] *vt* to horrify, frighten; **~se** *vr* to be horrified.
horroroso, a [orroro'so, á] *a* horrifying, ghastly.
hortaliza [ortálĕ'sá] *nf* vegetable.
hortelano, a [ortelá'no, á] *nm/f* (market) gardener.
hortera [orte'rá] *a* (*fam*) vulgar.
hortícola [ortĕ'kolá] *a* horticultural.
horticultura [ortĕkōōltōō'rá] *nf* horticulture.
hosco, a [os'ko, á] *a* dark; (*persona*) sullen, gloomy.
hospedaje [ospeŧŧá'he] *nm* (cost of) board and lodging.
hospedar [ospeŧŧár'] *vt* to put up; **~se** *vr*: **~se (con/en)** to stay *o* lodge (with/at).
hospedería [ospeŧŧerĕ'á] *nf* (*edificio*) inn; (*habitación*) guest room.
hospicio [ospĕ'syo] *nm* (*para niños*) orphanage.
hospital [ospĕtál'] *nm* hospital.
hospitalario, a [ospĕtálá'ryo, á] *a* (*acoge-*

dor) hospitable.
hospitalice [ospĕtálĕ'se] *etc vb V* **hospitalizar.**
hospitalidad [ospĕtálĕŧŧáŧŧ'] *nf* hospitality.
hospitalizar [ospĕtálĕsár'] *vt* to send *o* take to hospital, hospitalize.
hosquedad [oskeŧŧáŧŧ'] *nf* sullenness.
hostal [ostál'] *nm* small hotel.
hostelería [ostelerĕ'á] *nf* hotel business *o* trade.
hostelero, a [ostele'ro, á] *nm/f* innkeeper, landlord/lady.
hostia [os'tyá] *nf* (*REL*) host, consecrated wafer; (*fam: golpe*) whack, punch ♦ *excl*: **¡~(s)!** (*fam!*) damn!
hostigar [ostĕgár'] *vt* to whip; (*fig*) to harass, pester.
hostigue [ostĕ'ge] *etc vb V* **hostigar.**
hostil [ostĕl'] *a* hostile.
hostilidad [ostĕlĕŧŧáŧŧ'] *nf* hostility.
hotel [otel'] *nm* hotel.
hotelero, a [otele'ro, á] *a* hotel *cpd* ♦ *nm/f* hotelier.
hoy [oĕ] *ad* (*este día*) today; (*en la actualidad*) now(adays) ♦ *nm* present time; **~ (en) día** now(adays); **el día de ~, ~ día** (*AM*) this very day; **~ por ~** right now; **de ~ en ocho días** a week from today; **de ~ en adelante** from now on.
hoya [o'yá] *nf* pit; (*sepulcro*) grave; (*GEO*) valley.
hoyo [o'yo] *nm* hole, pit; (*tumba*) grave; (*GOLF*) hole; (*MED*) pockmark.
hoyuelo [oywe'lo] *nm* dimple.
hoz [os] *nf* sickle.
hube [ōō'ʰe] *etc vb V* **haber.**
hucha [ōōtch'á] *nf* money box.
hueco, a [we'ko, á] *a* (*vacío*) hollow, empty; (*resonante*) booming; (*sonido*) resonant; (*persona*) conceited; (*estilo*) pompous ♦ *nm* hollow, cavity; (*agujero*) hole; (*de escalera*) well; (*de ascensor*) shaft; (*vacante*) vacancy; **~ de la mano** hollow of the hand.
huela [we'lá] *etc vb V* **oler.**
huelga [wel'gá] *etc vb V* **holgar** ♦ *nf* strike; **declararse en ~** to go on strike; **~ general** general strike; **~ de hambre** hunger strike; **~ oficial** official strike.
huelgue [wel'ge] *etc vb V* **holgar.**
huelguista [welgĕ'stá] *nm/f* striker.
huella [we'yá] *nf* (*acto de pisar, pisada*) tread(ing); (*marca del paso*) footprint, footstep; (*: de animal, máquina*) track; **~ digital** fingerprint; **sin dejar ~** without leaving a trace.
huérfano, a [wer'fáno, á] *a* orphan(ed); (*fig*) unprotected ♦ *nm/f* orphan.
huerta [wer'tá] *nf* truck farm (*US*), market garden (*Brit*); (*Murcia, Valencia*) irrigated region.

huerto |wcr'to| *nm* kitchen garden; *(de árboles frutales)* orchard.

hueso |wc'so| *nm* (ANAT) bone; *(de fruta)* pit (US), stone; **sin ~** *(carne)* boned; **estar en los ~s** to be nothing but skin and bones; **ser un ~** *(profesor)* to be terribly strict; **un ~ duro de roer** a hard nut to crack.

huésped, a |wcs'pcth, á| *nm/f* *(invitado)* guest; *(habitante)* resident; *(anfitrión)* host(ess).

huesudo, a |wcsoo'tho, á| *a* bony, big-boned.

huevera |wchc'rá| *nf* eggcup.

huevo |wc'ho| *nm* egg; *(fam!)* ball(!), testicle; **~ duro/escalfado/estrellado** *o* **frito/pasado por agua** hard-boiled/poached/fried/soft-boiled egg; **~s revueltos** scrambled eggs; **me costó un ~** *(fam!)* it was hard work; **tener ~s** *(fam!)* to have guts.

huida |ooc'thá| *nf* escape, flight; **~ de capitales** (COM) flight of capital.

huidizo, a |ooeethc'so, á| *a* *(tímido)* shy; *(pasajero)* fleeting.

huir |ooer'| *vt* *(escapar)* to flee, escape; *(evadir)* to avoid ♦ *vi* to flee, run away; **~se** *vr* *(escaparse)* to escape.

hule |oo'lc| *nm* *(encerado)* oilskin.

hulla |oo'yá| *nf* bituminous coal.

humanice |oománc'sc| *etc vb* V **humanizar.**

humanidad |oománcthath'| *nf* *(género humano)* man(kind); *(cualidad)* humanity; *(fam: gordura)* corpulence.

humanitario, a |oománctá'ryo, á| *a* humanitarian; *(benévolo)* humane.

humanizar |oománcsár'| *vt* to humanize; **~se** *vr* to become more human.

humano, a |oomá'no, á| *a* (gen) human; *(humanitario)* humane ♦ *nm* human; **ser ~** human being.

humareda |oomárc'thá| *nf* cloud of smoke.

humeante |oomeán'te| *a* smoking, smoky.

humedad |oomethath'| *nf* *(del clima)* humidity; *(de pared etc)* dampness; **a prueba de ~** waterproof.

humedecer |oomethcscr'| *vt* to moisten, wet; **~se** *vr* to get wet.

humedezca |oomethcs'cá| *etc vb* V **humedecer.**

húmedo, a |oo'metho, á| *a* *(mojado)* damp, wet; *(tiempo etc)* humid.

humildad |ooméldáth'| *nf* humility, humbleness.

humilde |oomél'dc| *a* humble, modest; *(clase etc)* low, modest.

humillación |ooméyásyon'| *nf* humiliation.

humillante |ooméyán'tc| *a* humiliating.

humillar |ooméyár'| *vt* to humiliate; **~se** *vr* to humble o.s., grovel.

humo |oo'mo| *nm* *(de fuego)* smoke; *(gas nocivo)* fumes *pl*; *(vapor)* steam; **~s** *nmpl*

(fig) conceit *sg*; **irse todo en ~** *(fig)* to vanish without trace; **bajar los ~s a uno** to take sb down a peg or two.

humor |oomor'| *nm* *(disposición)* mood, temper; *(lo que divierte)* humor (US), humour (Brit); **de buen/mal ~** in a good/bad mood.

humorado, a |oomorá'tho, á| *a*: **bien ~** good-humored (US), good-humoured (Brit); **mal ~** bad-tempered, cross ♦ *nf* witticism.

humorismo |oomorcs'mo| *nm* humor (US), humour (Brit).

humorista |oomorc'stá| *nm/f* comic.

humorístico, a |oomorc'stcko, á| *a* funny, humorous.

hundimiento |oondcmycn'to| *nm* (gen) sinking; *(colapso)* collapse.

hundir |oondcr'| *vt* to sink; *(edificio, plan)* to ruin, destroy; **~se** *vr* to sink, collapse; *(fig: arruinarse)* to be ruined; *(desaparecer)* to disappear; **se hundió la economía** the economy collapsed; **se hundieron los precios** prices slumped.

húngaro, a |oon'gáro, á| *a, nm/f* Hungarian ♦ *nm* (LING) Hungarian, Magyar.

Hungría |oongrc'á| *nf* Hungary.

huracán |oorákán'| *nm* hurricane.

huraño, a |oorá'nyo, á| *a* shy; *(antisocial)* unsociable.

hurgar |oorgár'| *vt* to poke, jab; *(remover)* to stir (up); **~se** *vr*: **~se (las narices)** to pick one's nose.

hurgonear |oorgoneár'| *vt* to poke.

hurgue |oor'gc| *etc vb* V **hurgar.**

hurón |ooron'| *nm* (ZOOL) ferret.

huronera |ooronc'rá| *nf* *(fig)* den.

hurra |oo'rrá| *excl* hurray!, hurrah!

hurtadillas |oortáthc'yás|: **a ~** *ad* stealthily, on the sly.

hurtar |oortár'| *vt* to steal; **~se** *vr* to hide, keep out of the way.

hurto |oor'to| *nm* theft, stealing; *(lo robado)* (piece of) stolen property, loot.

husmear |oosmeár'| *vt* *(oler)* to sniff out, scent; *(fam)* to pry into ♦ *vi* to smell bad.

huso |oo'so| *nm* (TEC) spindle; *(de torno)* drum.

huy |oo'ĉ| *excl* *(dolor)* ow!, ouch!; *(sorpresa)* well!; *(alivio)* phew!

huyendo |ooyen'do| *etc vb* V **huir.**

I

I, i |ĉ| *nf* *(letra)* I, i; **I de Inés** I for Item.

I.A. *abr* = **inteligencia artificial.**
iba [ē'ḥá] *etc vb V* **ir.**
Iberia [ēḥe'ryá] *nf* Iberia.
ibérico, a [ēḥe'rēko, á] *a* Iberian; **la Península ibérica** the Iberian Peninsula.
ibero, a [ēḥe'ro, á], **íbero, a** [ē'ḥero, á] *a, nm/f* Iberian.
iberoamericano, a [ēḥeroámerēká'no, á] *a, nm/f* Latin American.
íbice [iḥ'ise] *nm* ibex.
ibicenco, a [ēḥēsen'ko, á] *a* of *o* from Ibiza ♦ *nm/f* native *o* inhabitant of Ibiza.
Ibiza [ēḥē'sá] *nf* Ibiza.
ice [ē'se] *etc vb V* **izar.**
iceberg [ēseber'] *nm* iceberg.
ICONA [ēko'ná] *nm abr* (*Esp*)=*Instituto Nacional para la Conservacion de la Naturaleza.*
ícono [ē'kono] *nm* (*tb INFORM*) icon.
iconoclasta [ēkonoklá'stá] *a* iconoclastic ♦ *nm/f* iconoclast.
ictericia [ēkterē'syá] *nf* jaundice.
íd. *abr* = **ídem.**
ida [ē'ḋá] *nf* going, departure; **~ y vuelta** round trip, return; **~s y venidas** comings and goings.
IDE [ēḋe] *nf abr* (= *Iniciativa de Defensa Estratégica*) SDI.
idea [ēḋe'á] *nf* idea; (*impresión*) opinion; (*propósito*) intention; **~ genial** brilliant idea; **a mala ~** out of spite; **no tengo la menor ~** I haven't a clue.
ideal [ēḋeál'] *a, nm* ideal.
idealice [ēḋeálē'se] *etc vb V* **idealizar.**
idealista [ēḋeálē'stá] *a* idealistic ♦ *nm/f* idealist.
idealizar [ēḋeálēsár'] *vt* to idealize.
idear [ēḋeár'] *vt* to think up; (*aparato*) to invent; (*viaje*) to plan.
ídem [ē'ḋem] *pron* ditto.
idéntico, a [ēḋen'tēko, á] *a* identical.
identidad [ēḋentēḋáḋ'] *nf* identity; **~ corporativa** corporate identity *o* image.
identificación [ēḋentēfēkásyon'] *nf* identification.
identificar [ēḋentēfēkár'] *vt* to identify; **~se** *vr*: **~se con** to identify with.
identifique [ēḋentēfē'ke] *etc vb V* **identificar.**
ideología [ēḋeolohē'á] *nf* ideology.
ideológico, a [ēḋeolo'hēko, á] *a* ideological.
idílico, a [ēḋē'lēko, á] *a* idyllic.
idioma [ēḋyo'má] *nm* language.
idiomático, a [ēḋyomá'tēko, á] *a* idiomatic.
idiota [ēḋyo'tá] *a* idiotic ♦ *nm/f* idiot.
idiotez [ēḋyotes'] *nf* idiocy.
ídolo [ē'ḋolo] *nm* (*tb fig*) idol.
idoneidad [ēḋonēḋáḋ'] *nf* suitability; (*capacidad*) aptitude.
idóneo, a [ēḋo'neo, á] *a* suitable.

iglesia [ēgle'syá] *nf* church; **~ parroquial** parish church; **¡con la ~ hemos topado!** now we're really up against it!
ignición [ēgnēsyon'] *nf* ignition.
ignominia [ēgnomē'nyá] *nf* ignominy.
ignominioso, a [ēgnomēnyo'so, á] *a* ignominious.
ignorado, a [ēgnorá'ḋo, á] *a* unknown; (*dato*) obscure.
ignorancia [ēgnorán'syá] *nf* ignorance; **por ~** through ignorance.
ignorante [ēgnorán'te] *a* ignorant, uninformed ♦ *nm/f* ignoramus.
ignorar [ēgnorár'] *vt* not to know, be ignorant of; (*no hacer caso a*) to ignore; **ignoramos su paradero** we don't know his whereabouts.
ignoto, a [ēgno'to, á] *a* unknown.
igual [ēgwál'] *a* equal; (*similar*) like, similar; (*mismo*) (the) same; (*constante*) constant; (*temperatura*) even ♦ *nm/f* equal; **al ~ que** *prep, conj* like, just like; **~ que** the same as; **sin ~** peerless; **me da *o* es ~** I don't care, it makes no difference; **no tener ~** to be unrivalled; **son ~es** they're the same.
iguala [ēgwá'lá] *nf* equalization; (*COM*) agreement.
igualada [ēgwálá'ḋá] *nf* equalizer.
igualar [ēgwálár'] *vt* (*gen*) to equalize, make equal; (*terreno*) to make even; (*COM*) to agree upon; **~se** *vr* (*platos de balanza*) to balance out; **~se (a)** (*equivaler*) to be equal (to).
igualdad [ēgwáldáḋ'] *nf* equality; (*similaridad*) sameness; (*uniformidad*) uniformity; **en ~ de condiciones** on an equal basis.
igualmente [ēgwálmen'te] *ad* equally; (*también*) also, likewise ♦ *excl* the same to you!
ikurriña [ēkōōrrē'nyá] *nf* Basque flag.
ilegal [ēlegál'] *a* illegal.
ilegitimidad [ēlehētēmēḋáḋ'] *nf* illegitimacy.
ilegítimo, a [ēlehē'tēmo, á] *a* illegitimate.
ileso, a [ēle'so, á] *a* unhurt, unharmed.
ilícito, a [ēlē'sēto, á] *a* illicit.
ilimitado, a [ēlēmētá'ḋo, á] *a* unlimited.
Ilma., Ilmo. *abr* (= *Ilustrísima, Ilustrísimo*) courtesy title.
ilógico, a [ēlo'hēko, á] *a* illogical.
iluminación [ēlōōmēnásyon'] *nf* illumination; (*alumbrado*) lighting; (*fig*) enlightenment.
iluminar [ēlōōmēnár'] *vt* to illuminate, light (up); (*fig*) to enlighten.
ilusión [ēlōōsyon'] *nf* illusion; (*quimera*) delusion; (*esperanza*) hope; (*emoción*) excitement, thrill; **hacerse ilusiones** to build up one's hopes; **no te hagas ilusiones** don't build up your hopes *o* get too excited.

ilusionado, a [ēlōōsyoná'tho, á] a excited.

ilusionista [ēlōōsyonē'stá] nm/f illusionist (US), conjurer (Brit).

iluso, a [ēlōō'so, á] a gullible, easily deceived ♦ nm/f dreamer, visionary.

ilusorio, a [ēlōōso'ryo, á] a (de ilusión) illusory, deceptive; (esperanza) vain.

ilustración [ēlōōstrásyon'] nf illustration; (saber) learning, erudition; **la l~** the Enlightenment.

ilustrado, a [ēlōōstrá'tho, á] a illustrated; learned.

ilustrar [ēlōōstrár'] vt to illustrate; (instruir) to instruct; (explicar) to explain, make clear; **~se** vr to acquire knowledge.

ilustre [ēlōōs'tre] a famous, illustrious.

imagen [ēmá'hen] nf (gen) image; (dibujo, TV) picture; (REL) statue; **ser la viva ~ de** to be the spitting o living image of; **a su ~** in one's own image.

imaginación [ēmáhēnásyon'] nf imagination; (fig) fancy; **ni por ~** on no account; **no se me pasó por la ~ que...** it never even occurred to me that ... .

imaginar [ēmáhēnár'] vt (gen) to imagine; (idear) to think up; (suponer) to suppose; **~se** vr to imagine; **¡imagínate!** just imagine!, just fancy!; **imagínese que...** suppose that ...; **me imagino que sí** I should think so.

imaginario, a [ēmáhēná'ryo, á] a imaginary.

imaginativo, a [ēmáhēnátē'tho, á] a imaginative ♦ nf imagination.

imán [ēmán'] nm magnet.

iman(t)ar [ēmán(t)ár'] vt to magnetize.

imbécil [ēmbe'sēl] nm/f imbecile, idiot.

imbecilidad [ēmbesēlētháth'] nf imbecility, stupidity.

imberbe [ēmber'he] a beardless.

imborrable [ēmborrá'hle] a indelible; (inolvidable) unforgettable.

imbuir [ēmbōōēr'] vi to imbue.

imbuyendo [ēmbōōyen'do] etc vb V **imbuir**.

imitación [ēmētásyon'] nf imitation; (parodia) mimicry; **a ~ de** in imitation of; **desconfíe de las imitaciones** (COM) beware of copies o imitations.

imitador, a [ēmētáthor', á] a imitative ♦ nm/f imitator; (TEATRO) mimic.

imitar [ēmētár'] vt to imitate; (parodiar, remedar) to mimic, ape; (copiar) to follow.

impaciencia [ēmpásyen'syá] nf impatience.

impacientar [ēmpásyentár'] vt to make impatient; (enfadar) to irritate; **~se** vr to get impatient; (inquietarse) to fret.

impaciente [ēmpásyen'te] a impatient; (nervioso) anxious.

impacto [ēmpák'to] nm impact.

impagado, a [ēmpágá'tho, á] a unpaid, still to be paid.

impar [ēmpár'] a odd ♦ nm odd number.

imparable [ēmpárá'hle] a unstoppable.

imparcial [ēmpársyál'] a impartial, fair.

imparcialidad [ēmpársyálētháth'] nf impartiality, fairness.

impartir [ēmpártēr'] vt to impart, give.

impasible [ēmpásē'hle] a impassive.

impavidez [ēmpáhēthes'] nf fearlessness, intrepidness.

impávido, a [ēmpá'hētho, á] a fearless, intrepid.

IMPE [ēm'pe] nm abr (Esp COM)=Instituto de la Mediana y Pequeña Empresa.

impecable [ēmpeká'hle] a impeccable.

impedido, a [ēmpethē'tho, á] a: **estar ~** to be an invalid ♦ nm/f: **ser un ~ físico** to be an invalid.

impedimento [ēmpethēmen'to] nm impediment, obstacle.

impedir [ēmpethēr'] vt (obstruir) to impede, obstruct; (estorbar) to prevent; **~ el tráfico** to block the traffic.

impeler [ēmpeler'] vt to drive, propel; (fig) to impel.

impenetrabilidad [ēmpenetráhēlētháth'] nf impenetrability.

impenetrable [ēmpenetrá'hle] a impenetrable; (fig) incomprehensible.

impensable [ēmpensá'hle] a unthinkable.

impepinable [ēmpepēná'hle] a (fam) certain, inevitable.

imperante [ēmperán'te] a prevailing.

imperar [ēmperár'] vi (reinar) to rule, reign; (fig) to prevail, reign; (precio) to be current.

imperativo, a [ēmperátē'ho, á] a (persona) imperious; (urgente, LING) imperative.

imperceptible [ēmperseptē'hle] a imperceptible.

imperdible [ēmperthē'hle] nm safety pin.

imperdonable [ēmperthoná'hle] a unforgivable, inexcusable.

imperecedero, a [ēmperesethe'ro, á] a undying.

imperfección [ēmperfeksyon'] nf imperfection; (falla) flaw, fault.

imperfecto, a [ēmperfek'to, á] a faulty, imperfect ♦ nm (LING) imperfect tense.

imperial [ēmperyál'] a imperial.

imperialismo [ēmperyálēs'mo] nm imperialism.

imperialista [ēmperyálē'stá] a imperialist(ic) ♦ nm/f imperialist.

impericia [ēmperē'syá] nf (torpeza) unskilfulness; (inexperiencia) inexperience.

imperio [ēmpe'ryo] nm empire; (autoridad) rule, authority; (fig) pride, haughtiness; **vale un ~** (fig) it's worth a fortune.

imperioso, a [ēmperyo'so, á] a imperious; (urgente) urgent; (imperativo) imperative.

impermeable [ēmpermeá'hle] a (a prueba

de agua) waterproof ♦ *nm* raincoat, mac (*Brit*).

impersonal [ēmpersonál'] *a* impersonal.

impertérrito, a [ēmperte'rrēto, á] *a* undaunted.

impertinencia [ēmpertēnen'syá] *nf* impertinence.

impertinente [ēmpertēnen'te] *a* impertinent.

imperturbable [ēmpertōōrbá'ble] *a* imperturbable; (*sereno*) unruffled; (*impasible*) impassive.

ímpetu [im'petōō] *nm* (*impulso*) impetus, impulse; (*impetuosidad*) impetuosity; (*violencia*) violence.

impetuosidad [ēmpetwosētháth'] *nf* impetuousness; (*violencia*) violence.

impetuoso, a [ēmpetwo'so, á] *a* impetuous; (*río*) rushing; (*acto*) hasty.

impida [ēmpē'thá] *etc vb V* **impedir**.

impío, a [ēmpē'o, á] *a* impious, ungodly; (*cruel*) cruel, pitiless.

implacable [ēmplāká'ble] *a* implacable, relentless.

implantación [ēmplántásyon'] *nf* implantation; (*introducción*) introduction.

implicar [ēmplēkár'] *vt* to involve; (*entrañar*) to imply; **esto no implica que ...** this does not mean that ....

implícito, a [ēmplē'sēto, á] *a* (*tácito*) implicit; (*sobreentendido*) implied.

implique [ēmplē'ke] *etc vb V* **implicar**.

implorar [ēmplorár'] *vt* to beg, implore.

impoluto, a [ēmpolōō'to, á] *a* unpolluted, pure.

impondré [ēmpondre'] *etc vb V* **imponer**.

imponente [ēmponen'te] *a* (*impresionante*) impressive, imposing; (*solemne*) grand ♦ *nm/f* (*COM*) depositor.

imponer [ēmponer'] *vt* (*gen*) to impose; (*tarea*) to assign; (*exigir*) to exact; (*miedo*) to inspire; (*COM*) to deposit; **~se** *vr* to assert o.s.; (*prevalecer*) to prevail; (*costumbre*) to develop; **~se un deber** to assume a duty.

imponga [ēmpon'gá] *etc vb V* **imponer**.

imponible [ēmponē'ble] *a* (*COM*) taxable, subject to tax; (*importación*) dutiable, subject to duty; **no ~** tax-exempt, tax-free.

impopular [ēmpopōōlár'] *a* unpopular.

importación [ēmportásyon'] *nf* (*acto*) importing; (*mercancías*) imports *pl*.

importancia [ēmportán'syá] *nf* importance; (*valor*) value, significance; (*extensión*) size, magnitude; **no dar ~ a** to consider unimportant; (*fig*) to make light of; **no tiene ~** it's nothing.

importante [ēmportán'te] *a* important; valuable, significant.

importar [ēmportár'] *vt* (*del extranjero*) to import; (*costar*) to amount to; (*implicar*)

to involve ♦ *vi* to be important, matter; **me importa un bledo** I don't give a damn; **¿le importa que fume?** do you mind if I smoke?; **¿te importa prestármelo?** would you mind lending it to me?; **¿qué importa?** what difference does it make?; **no importa** it doesn't matter; **no le importa** he doesn't care, it doesn't bother him; **"no importa precio"** "cost no object".

importe [ēmpor'te] *nm* (*total*) amount; (*valor*) value.

importunar [ēmportōōnár'] *vt* to bother, pester.

importuno, a [ēmportōō'no, á] *a* (*inoportuno*, *molesto*) inopportune; (*indiscreto*) troublesome.

imposibilidad [ēmposēbēlētháth'] *nf* impossibility; **mi ~ para hacerlo** my inability to do it.

imposibilitado, a [ēmposēbēlētá'tho, á] *a*: **verse ~ para hacer algo** to be unable to do sth.

imposibilitar [ēmposēbēlētár'] *vt* to make impossible, prevent.

imposible [ēmposē'ble] *a* impossible; (*insoportable*) unbearable, intolerable; **es ~** it's out of the question; **es ~ de predecir** it's impossible to forecast o predict.

imposición [ēmposēsyon'] *nf* imposition; (*COM*) tax; (*inversión*) deposit; **efectuar una ~** to make a deposit.

impostor, a [ēmpostor', á] *nm/f* impostor.

impostura [ēmpostōō'rá] *nf* fraud, imposture.

impotencia [ēmpoten'syá] *nf* impotence.

impotente [ēmpoten'te] *a* impotent.

impracticable [ēmpráktēká'ble] *a* (*irrealizable*) impracticable; (*intransitable*) impassable.

imprecar [ēmprekár'] *vi* to curse.

imprecisión [ēmpresēsyon'] *nf* lack of precision, vagueness.

impreciso, a [ēmpresē'so, á] *a* imprecise, vague.

impredecible [ēmprethesē'ble], **impredictible** [ēmprethēktē'ble] *a* unpredictable.

impregnar [ēmpregnár'] *vt* to impregnate; (*fig*) to pervade; **~se** *vr* to become impregnated.

imprenta [ēmpren'tá] *nf* (*acto*) printing; (*aparato*) press; (*casa*) printer's; (*letra*) print.

impreque [ēmpre'ke] *etc vb V* **imprecar**.

imprescindible [ēmpresēndē'ble] *a* essential, vital.

impresión [ēmpresyon'] *nf* impression; (*IMPRENTA*) printing; (*edición*) edition; (*FOTO*) print; (*marca*) imprint; **~ digital** fingerprint.

impresionable [ēmpresyoná'ble] *a* (*sensible*) impressionable.

impresionado, a [ĕmpresyonáʹtʃo, á] *a* impressed; (*FOTO*) exposed.

impresionante [ĕmpresyonánʹte] *a* impressive; (*tremendo*) tremendous; (*maravilloso*) great, marvelous (*US*), marvellous (*Brit*).

impresionar [ĕmpresyonárʹ] *vt* (*conmover*) to move; (*afectar*) to impress, strike; (*película fotográfica*) to expose; **~se** *vr* to be impressed; (*conmoverse*) to be moved.

impresionista [ĕmpresyonēʹstá] *a* impressionist(ic); (*ARTE*) impressionist ♦ *nm/f* impressionist.

impreso, a [ĕmpreʹso, á] *pp de* **imprimir** ♦ *a* printed ♦ *nm* printed paper/book *etc*; **~s** *nmpl* printed matter *sg*; **~ de solicitud** application form.

impresora [ĕmpresoʹrá] *nf* (*INFORM*) printer; **~ de chorro de tinta** ink-jet printer; **~ (por) láser** laser printer; **~ de línea** line printer; **~ de matriz (de agujas)** dot-matrix printer; **~ de rueda** *o* **de margarita** daisy-wheel printer.

imprevisible [ĕmprebēsēʹble] *a* unforeseeable; (*individuo*) unpredictable.

imprevisión [ĕmprebēsyonʹ] *nf* shortsightedness; (*irreflexión*) thoughtlessness.

imprevisto, a [ĕmprebēʹsto, á] *a* unforeseen; (*inesperado*) unexpected ♦ *nm*: **~s** (*dinero*) incidentals, unforeseen expenses.

imprimir [ĕmprēmērʹ] *vt* to stamp; (*textos*) to print; (*INFORM*) to output, print out.

improbabilidad [ĕmprobáᵬēlēᵭáᵭʹ] *nf* improbability, unlikelihood.

improbable [ĕmprobáʹble] *a* improbable; (*inverosímil*) unlikely.

improcedente [ĕmprosēᵭenʹte] *a* inappropriate; (*JUR*) inadmissible.

improductivo, a [ĕmproᵭōōktēʹᵬo, á] *a* unproductive.

impronunciable [ĕmpronōōnsyáʹble] *a* unpronounceable.

improperio [ĕmpropeʹryo] *nm* insult; **~s** *nmpl* abuse *sg*.

impropiedad [ĕmpropyeᵭáᵭʹ] *nf* impropriety (of language).

impropio, a [ĕmproʹpyo, á] *a* improper; (*inadecuado*) inappropriate.

improvisación [ĕmproᵬēsásyonʹ] *nf* improvisation.

improvisado, a [ĕmproᵬēsáʹtʃo, á] *a* improvised, impromptu.

improvisar [ĕmproᵬēsárʹ] *vt* to improvise; (*comida*) to rustle up ♦ *vi* to improvise; (*MUS*) to extemporize; (*TEATRO etc*) to ad-lib.

improviso [ĕmproᵬēʹso]: *ad* **de ~** unexpectedly, suddenly; (*MUS etc*) impromptu.

imprudencia [ĕmproōᵭenʹsyá] *nf* imprudence; (*indiscreción*) indiscretion; (*descuido*) carelessness.

imprudente [ĕmproōᵭenʹte] *a* imprudent; indiscreet.

Impte. *abr* (= *Importe*) amt.

impúdico, a [ĕmpoōʹᵭēko, á] *a* shameless; (*lujurioso*) lecherous.

impudor [ĕmpoōᵭorʹ] *nm* shamelessness; (*lujuria*) lechery.

impuesto, a [ĕmpweʹsto, á] *pp de* **imponer** ♦ *a* imposed ♦ *nm* tax; (*derecho*) duty; **anterior al ~** pre-tax; **sujeto a ~** taxable; **~ de lujo** luxury tax; **~ de plusvalía** capital gains tax; **~ sobre la propiedad** property tax; **~ sobre la renta** income tax; **~ sobre la renta de las personas físicas (IRPF)** personal income tax; **~ sobre la riqueza** wealth tax; **~ de transferencia de capital** capital transfer tax; **~ de venta** sales tax; **~ sobre el valor añadido (IVA)** value added tax (VAT).

impugnar [ĕmpoōgnárʹ] *vt* to oppose, contest; (*refutar*) to refute, impugn.

impulsar [ĕmpoōlsárʹ] *vt* = **impeler**.

impulso [ĕmpoōlʹso] *nm* impulse; (*fuerza, empuje*) thrust, drive; (*fig: sentimiento*) urge, impulse; **a ~s del miedo** driven on by fear.

impune [ĕmpoōʹne] *a* unpunished.

impunemente [ĕmpoōnemenʹte] *ad* with impunity.

impureza [ĕmpoōreʹsá] *nf* impurity; (*fig*) lewdness.

impuro, a [ĕmpoōʹro, á] *a* impure; lewd.

impuse [ĕmpoōʹse] *etc vb* **V imponer**.

imputación [ĕmpoōtásyonʹ] *nf* imputation.

imputar [ĕmpoōtárʹ] *vt*: **~ a** to attribute to, to impute to.

inabordable [ēnáᵬorᵭáʹble] *a* unapproachable.

inacabable [ēnákáᵬáʹble] *a* (*infinito*) endless; (*interminable*) interminable.

inaccesible [ēnáksesēʹble] *a* inaccessible; (*fig: precio*) beyond one's reach, prohibitive; (*individuo*) aloof.

inacción [ēnáksyonʹ] *nf* inactivity.

inaceptable [ēnáseptáʹble] *a* unacceptable.

inactividad [ēnáktēᵭēᵭáᵭʹ] *nf* inactivity; (*COM*) dullness.

inactivo, a [ēnáktēʹᵬo, á] *a* inactive; (*COM*) dull; (*población*) non-working.

inadaptación [ēnáᵭáptásyonʹ] *nf* maladjustment.

inadaptado, a [ēnáᵭáptáʹtʃo, á] *a* maladjusted ♦ *nm/f* misfit.

inadecuado, a [ēnáᵭekwáʹtʃo, á] *a* (*insuficiente*) inadequate; (*inapto*) unsuitable.

inadmisible [ēnáᵭmēsēʹble] *a* inadmissible.

inadvertido, a [ēnáᵭᵬertēʹtʃo, á] *a* (*no visto*) unnoticed.

inagotable [ēnágotáʹble] *a* inexhaustible.

inaguantable [ēnáᵬwántáʹble] *a* unbearable.

inalcanzable [ēnálkánsá'ḅlc] *a* unattainable.
inalterable [ēnálterá'ḅlc] *a* immutable, unchangeable.
inamovible [ēnámoḅē'ḅlc] *a* fixed, immovable; (*TEC*) undetachable.
inanición [ēnánēsyon'] *nf* starvation.
inanimado, a [ēnánēmá'ḍo, á] *a* inanimate.
inánime [ēná'nēmc] *a* lifeless.
inapelable [ēnápelá'ḅlc] *a* (*JUR*) unappealable; (*fig*) irremediable.
inapetencia [ēnápeten'syá] *nf* lack of appetite.
inaplicable [ēnáplēká'ḅlc] *a* not applicable.
inapreciable [ēnápresyá'ḅlc] *a* invaluable.
inapto, a [ēnáp'to] *a* unsuited.
inarrugable [ēnárrōōgá'ḅlc] *a* permanent press.
inasequible [ēnásckē'ḅlc] *a* unattainable.
inaudito, a [ēnáōōḍe'to, á] *a* unheard-of.
inauguración [ēnáōōgōōrásyon'] *nf* inauguration; (*de exposición*) opening.
inaugurar [ēnáōōgōōrár'] *vt* to inaugurate; to open.
I.N.B. *abr* (= *Instituto Nacional de Bachillerato*) ≈ high school.
inca [ēn'ká] *nm/f* Inca.
INCAE [ēnká'c] *nm abr* = *Instituto Centroamericano de Administración de Empresas.*
incaico, a [ēnká'ēko, á] *a* Inca.
incalculable [ēnkálkōōlá'ḅlc] *a* incalculable.
incandescente [ēnkándesscn'tc] *a* incandescent.
incansable [ēnkánsá'ḅlc] *a* tireless, untiring.
incapacidad [ēnkápásēṭḥáḍ'] *nf* incapacity; (*incompetencia*) incompetence; ~ **física/mental** physical/mental disability.
incapacitar [ēnkápásētár'] *vt* (*inhabilitar*) to incapacitate, handicap; (*descalificar*) to disqualify.
incapaz [ēnkápás'] *a* incapable; ~ **de hacer algo** unable to do sth.
incautación [ēnkáōōtásyon'] *nf* seizure, confiscation.
incautarse [ēnkáōōtár'sc] *vr*: ~ **de** to seize, confiscate.
incauto, a [ēnká'ōōto, á] *a* (*imprudente*) incautious, unwary.
incendiar [ēnsendyár'] *vt* to set fire to; (*fig*) to inflame; ~**se** *vr* to catch fire.
incendiario, a [ēnsendyá'ryo, á] *a* incendiary ♦ *nm/f* arsonist.
incendio [ēnsen'dyo] *nm* fire; ~ **intencionado** arson.
incentivo [ēnscntē'ḅo] *nm* incentive.
incertidumbre [ēnscrtēṭḥōōm'brc] *nf* (*inseguridad*) uncertainty; (*duda*) doubt.
incesante [ēnscsán'tc] *a* incessant.
incesto [ēnsc'sto] *nm* incest.
incidencia [ēnsēṭḥen'syá] *nf* (*MAT*) incidence; (*fig*) effect.

incidente [ēnsēṭḥen'te] *nm* incident.
incidir [ēnsēṭḥēr'] *vi*: ~ **en** (*influir*) to influence; (*afectar*) to affect; ~ **en un error** to be mistaken.
incienso [ēnsyen'so] *nm* incense.
incierto, a [ēnsyer'to, á] *a* uncertain.
incineración [ēnsēnerásyon'] *nf* incineration; (*de cadáveres*) cremation.
incinerar [ēnsēnerár'] *vt* to burn; to cremate.
incipiente [ēnsēpyen'te] *a* incipient.
incisión [ēnsēsyon'] *nf* incision.
incisivo, a [ēnsēsē'ḅo, á] *a* sharp, cutting; (*fig*) incisive.
inciso [ēnsē'so] *nm* (*LING*) clause, sentence; (*coma*) comma; (*JUR*) subsection.
incitante [ēnsētán'tc] *a* (*estimulante*) exciting; (*provocativo*) provocative.
incitar [ēnsētár'] *vt* to incite, rouse.
incivil [ēnsēḅēl'] *a* rude, uncivil.
inclemencia [ēnklemen'syá] *nf* (*severidad*) harshness, severity; (*del tiempo*) inclemency.
inclemente [ēnklemen'te] *a* harsh, severe; inclement.
inclinación [ēnklēnásyon'] *nf* (*gen*) inclination; (*de tierras*) slope, incline; (*de cabeza*) nod, bow; (*fig*) leaning, bent.
inclinar [ēnklēnár'] *vt* to incline; (*cabeza*) to nod, bow ♦ *vi* to lean, slope; ~**se** *vr* to bow; (*encorvarse*) to stoop; ~**se a** (*parecerse*) to take after, resemble; ~**se ante** to bow down to; **me inclino a pensar que ...** I'm inclined to think that ... .
incluir [ēnklōōēr'] *vt* to include; (*incorporar*) to incorporate; (*meter*) to enclose; **todo incluido** (*COM*) inclusive.
inclusive [ēnklōōsē'ḅe] *ad* inclusive ♦ *prep* including.
incluso, a [ēnklōō'so, á] *a* included ♦ *ad* inclusively; (*hasta*) even.
incluyendo [ēnklōōyen'do] *etc vb* V **incluir**.
incobrable [ēnkoḅrá'ḅlc] *a* irrecoverable; (*deuda*) bad.
incógnita [ēnkog'nētá] *nf* (*fig*) mystery.
incógnito [ēnkog'nēto]: **de** ~ *ad* incognito.
incoherencia [ēnkocrcn'syá] *nf* incoherence; (*falta de conexión*) disconnectedness.
incoherente [ēnkocrcn'te] *a* incoherent.
incoloro, a [ēnkolo'ro, á] *a* colorless (*US*), colourless (*Brit*).
incólume [ēnko'lōōmc] *a* safe; (*indemne*) unhurt, unharmed.
incombustible [ēnkombōōstē'ḅlc] *a* (*gen*) fire-resistant; (*telas*) fireproof.
incomestible [ēnkomcstē'ḅlc] *a* inedible.
incomodar [ēnkomoṭḥár'] *vt* to inconvenience; (*molestar*) to bother, trouble; (*fastidiar*) to annoy; ~**se** *vr* to put o.s. out; (*fastidiarse*) to get annoyed; **no se incomode** don't bother.

incomodidad [ēnkomoðēðáð'] *nf* inconvenience; *(fastidio, enojo)* annoyance; *(de vivienda)* discomfort.

incómodo, a [ēnko'moðo, á] *a (inconfortable)* uncomfortable; *(molesto)* annoying; *(inconveniente)* inconvenient; **sentirse** ~ to feel ill at ease.

incomparable [ēnkompárá'ble] *a* incomparable.

incomparecimiento [ēnkompárecēmyen'to] *nm (JUR etc)* failure to appear.

incompatible [ēnkompátē'ble] *a* incompatible.

incompetencia [ēnkompeten'syá] *nf* incompetence.

incompetente [ēnkompeten'te] *a* incompetent.

incompleto, a [ēnkomple'to, á] *a* incomplete, unfinished.

incomprensible [ēnkomprensē'ble] *a* incomprehensible.

incomunicado, a [ēnkomōōnēká'ðo, á] *a (aislado)* cut off, isolated; *(confinado)* in solitary confinement.

incomunicar [ēnkomōōnēkár'] *vt (gen)* to cut off; *(preso)* to put into solitary confinement; **~se** *vr (fam)* to go into one's shell.

incomunique [ēnkomōōnē'ke] *etc vb* V **incomunicar.**

inconcebible [ēnkonsehē'ble] *a* inconceivable.

inconcluso, a [ēnkonklōō'so, á] *a (inacabado)* unfinished.

inconcuso, a [ēnkonkōō'so, á] *a* indisputable, undeniable.

incondicional [ēnkondēsyonál'] *a* unconditional; *(apoyo)* wholehearted; *(partidario)* staunch.

inconexo, a [ēnkonek'so, á] *a* unconnected; *(desunido)* disconnected; *(incoherente)* incoherent.

inconfeso, a [ēnkonfe'so, á] *a* unconfessed; **un homosexual** ~ a closet homosexual.

inconfundible [ēnkonfōōndē'ble] *a* unmistakable.

incongruente [ēnkongrwen'te] *a* incongruous.

inconmensurable [ēnkonmensōōrá'ble] *a* immeasurable, vast.

inconsciencia [ēnkonsyen'syá] *nf* unconsciousness; *(fig)* thoughtlessness.

inconsciente [ēnkonsyen'te] *a* unconscious; thoughtless; *(ignorante)* unaware; *(involuntario)* unwitting.

inconsecuencia [ēnkonsekwen'syá] *nf* inconsistency.

inconsecuente [ēnkonsekwen'te] *a* inconsistent.

inconsiderado, a [ēnkonsēðerá'ðo, á] *a* inconsiderate.

inconsistente [ēnkonsēsten'te] *a* inconsistent; *(CULIN)* lumpy; *(endeble)* weak; *(tela)* flimsy.

inconstancia [ēnkonstán'syá] *nf* inconstancy; *(de tiempo)* changeability; *(capricho)* fickleness.

inconstante [ēnkonstán'te] *a* inconstant; changeable; fickle.

incontable [ēnkontá'ble] *a* countless, innumerable.

incontestable [ēnkontestá'ble] *a* unanswerable; *(innegable)* undeniable.

incontinencia [ēnkontēnen'syá] *nf* incontinence.

incontrolado, a [ēnkontrolá'ðo, á] *a* uncontrolled.

incontrovertible [ēnkontrohertē'ble] *a* undeniable, incontrovertible.

inconveniencia [ēnkombenyen'syá] *nf* unsuitability, inappropriateness; *(descortesía)* impoliteness.

inconveniente [ēnkombenyen'te] *a* unsuitable; impolite ♦ *nm* obstacle; *(desventaja)* disadvantage; **el** ~ **es que** ... the trouble is that ...; **no hay** ~ **en** *o* **para hacer eso** there is no objection to doing that; **no tengo** ~ I don't mind.

incorporación [ēnkorporásyon'] *nf* incorporation; *(fig)* inclusion.

incorporado, a [ēnkorporá'ðo, á] *a (TEC)* built-in.

incorporar [ēnkorporár'] *vt* to incorporate; *(abarcar)* to embody; *(CULIN)* to mix; **~se** *vr* to sit up; **~se a** to join.

incorrección [ēnkorreksyon'] *nf* incorrectness, inaccuracy; *(descortesía)* bad-mannered behavior *(US) o* behaviour *(Brit)*.

incorrecto, a [ēnkorrek'to, á] *a* incorrect, wrong; *(comportamiento)* bad-mannered.

incorregible [ēnkorrehē'ble] *a* incorrigible.

incorruptible [ēnkorrōōptē'ble] *a* incorruptible.

incorrupto, a [ēnkorrōōp'to, á] *a* uncorrupted; *(fig)* pure.

incredulidad [ēnkreðōōlēðáð'] *nf* incredulity; *(escepticismo)* scepticism.

incrédulo, a [ēnkre'ðōōlo, á] *a* incredulous, unbelieving; sceptical.

increíble [ēnkreē'ble] *a* incredible.

incrementar [ēnkrementár'] *vt (aumentar)* to increase; *(alzar)* to raise; **~se** *vr* to increase.

incremento [ēnkremen'to] *nm* increment; *(aumento)* rise, increase; ~ **de precio** rise in price.

increpar [ēnkrepár'] *vt* to reprimand.

incriminar [ēnkrēmēnár'] *vt (JUR)* to incriminate.

incruento, a [ēnkrwen'to, á] *a* bloodless.

incrustar [ēnkrōōstár'] *vt* to incrust; *(piedras: en joya)* to inlay; *(fig)* to graft;

(*TEC*) to set.

incubar [ĕnkōōkár'] *vt* to incubate; (*fig*) to hatch.

incuestionable [ĕnkwestyonà'ᴮle] *a* unchallengeable.

inculcar [ĕnkōōlkár'] *vt* to inculcate.

inculpar [ĕnkōōlpár'] *vt*: ~ **de** (*acusar*) to accuse of; (*achacar, atribuir*) to charge with, blame for.

inculque [ĕnkōōl'ke] *etc vb V* **inculcar.**

inculto, a [ĕnkōōl'to, à] *a* (*persona*) uneducated, uncultured; (*fig: grosero*) uncouth ♦ *nm/f* ignoramus.

incumbencia [ĕnkōōmben'syà] *nf* obligation; **no es de mi ~** it is not my field.

incumbir [ĕnkōōmbēr'] *vi*: ~ **a** to be incumbent upon; **no me incumbe a mí** it is no concern of mine.

incumplimiento [ĕnkōōmplēmyen'to] *nm* non-fulfilment; (*COM*) repudiation; ~ **de contrato** breach of contract; **por ~** by default.

incurrir [ĕnkōōrrēr'] *vi*: ~ **en** to incur; (*crimen*) to commit; ~ **en un error** to make a mistake.

indagación [ĕndàgásyon'] *nf* investigation; (*búsqueda*) search; (*JUR*) inquest.

indagar [ĕndàgár'] *vt* to investigate; to search; (*averiguar*) to ascertain.

indague [ĕndà'ge] *etc vb V* **indagar.**

indebido, a [ĕndebē'tho, à] *a* undue; (*dicho*) improper.

indecente [ĕndesen'te] *a* indecent, improper; (*lascivo*) obscene.

indecible [ĕndesē'ᴮle] *a* unspeakable; (*indescriptible*) indescribable.

indeciso, a [ĕndesē'so, à] *a* (*por decidir*) undecided; (*vacilante*) hesitant.

indefenso, a [ĕndefen'so, à] *a* defenceless.

indefinido, a [ĕndefēnē'tho, à] *a* indefinite; (*vago*) vague, undefined.

indeleble [ĕndele'ᴮle] *a* indelible.

indemne [ĕndem'ne] *a* (*objeto*) undamaged; (*persona*) unharmed, unhurt.

indemnice [ĕndemnē'se] *etc vb V* **indemnizar.**

indemnización [ĕndemnēsásyon'] *nf* (*acto*) indemnification; (*suma*) indemnity; ~ **de cese**, ~ **de despido** severance pay; **doble** ~ double indemnity.

indemnizar [ĕndemnēsár'] *vt* to indemnify; (*compensar*) to compensate.

independencia [ĕndependen'syà] *nf* independence.

independice [ĕndependē'se] *etc vb V* **independizar.**

independiente [ĕndependyen'te] *a* (*libre*) independent; (*autónomo*) self-sufficient; (*INFORM*) stand-alone.

independizar [ĕndependēsár'] *vt* to make independent; ~**se** *vr* to become independent.

pendent.

indescifrable [ĕndesēfrà'ᴮle] *a* (*MIL: código*) indecipherable; (*fig: misterio*) impenetrable.

indeterminado, a [ĕndetermēnà'tho, à] *a* (*tb LING*) indefinite; (*desconocido*) indeterminate.

India [ēn'dyà] *nf*: **la** ~ India.

indiano, a [ēndyà'no, à] *a* (Spanish-) American ♦ *nm* Spaniard who has made good in America.

indicación [ĕndēkásyon'] *nf* indication; (*dato*) piece of information; (*señal*) sign; (*sugerencia*) suggestion, hint; **indicaciones** *nfpl* (*COM*) instructions.

indicado, a [ĕndēkà'tho, à] *a* (*apto*) right, appropriate.

indicador [ĕndēkàthor'] *nm* indicator; (*TEC*) gauge, meter; (*aguja*) hand, pointer; (*de carretera*) roadsign; ~ **de encendido** (*INFORM*) power-on indicator.

indicar [ĕndēkár'] *vt* (*mostrar*) to indicate, show; (*suj: termómetro etc*) to read, register; (*señalar*) to point to.

indicativo, a [ĕndēkàtē'tho, à] *a* indicative ♦ *nm* (*RADIO*) call letters (*US*) o sign (*Brit*); ~ **de nacionalidad** (*AUTO*) national identification plate.

índice [ēn'dēse] *nm* index; (*catalogo*) catalog(ue); (*ANAT*) index finger, forefinger; ~ **del coste de (la) vida** cost-of-living index; ~ **de crédito** credit rating; ~ **de materias** table of contents; ~ **de natalidad** birth rate; ~ **de precios al por menor (IPM)** (*COM*) retail price index (RPI).

indicio [ĕndē'syo] *nm* indication, sign; (*en pesquisa etc*) clue; (*INFORM*) marker, mark.

indiferencia [ĕndēferen'syà] *nf* indifference; (*apatía*) apathy.

indiferente [ĕndēferen'te] *a* indifferent; **me es** ~ it makes no difference to me.

indígena [ĕndē'henà] *a* indigenous, native ♦ *nm/f* native.

indigencia [ĕndēhen'syà] *nf* poverty, need.

indigenista [ĕndēhenē'stá] (*AM*) *a* pro-Indian ♦ *nm/f* (*estudiante*) student of Indian cultures; (*POL etc*) promoter of Indian cultures.

indigestar [ĕndēhestár'] *vt* to cause indigestion to; ~**se** *vr* to get indigestion.

indigestión [ĕndēhestyon'] *nf* indigestion.

indigesto, a [ĕndēhe'sto, à] *a* undigested; (*indigestible*) indigestible; (*fig*) turgid.

indignación [ĕndēgnásyon'] *nf* indignation.

indignante [ĕndēgnán'te] *a* outrageous, infuriating.

indignar [ĕndēgnár'] *vt* to anger, make indignant; ~**se** *vr*: ~**se por** to get indignant about.

indigno, a [ĕndēg'no, à] *a* (*despreciable*)

low, contemptible; (*inmerecido*) unworthy.
indio, a [ēn'dyo, à] *a, nm/f* Indian.
indique [ēndē'ke] *etc vb V* **indicar**.
indirecto, a [ēndērek'to, à] *a* indirect ♦ *nf* insinuation, innuendo; (*sugerencia*) hint.
indisciplina [ēndēsēplē'nà] *nf* (*gen*) lack of discipline; (*MIL*) insubordination.
indiscreción [ēndēskresyon'] *nf* (*imprudencia*) indiscretion; (*irreflexión*) tactlessness; (*acto*) gaffe, faux pas; ..., **si no es ~** ..., if I may say so.
indiscreto, a [ēndēskre'to, à] *a* indiscreet.
indisculpable [ēndēskōōlpá'ble] *a* inexcusable, unforgivable.
indiscutible [ēndēskōōtē'ble] *a* indisputable, unquestionable.
indispensable [ēndēspensá'ble] *a* indispensable.
indispondré [ēndēspondre'] *etc vb V* **indisponer**.
indisponer [ēndēsponer'] *vt* to spoil, upset; (*salud*) to make ill; **~se** *vr* to fall ill; **~se con uno** to fall out with sb.
indisponga [ēndēspon'gá] *etc vb V* **indisponer**.
indisposición [ēndēsposēsyon'] *nf* indisposition; (*desgana*) unwillingness.
indispuesto, a [ēndēspwe'sto, à] *pp de* **indisponer** ♦ *a* indisposed; **sentirse ~** to feel unwell.
indispuse [ēndēspōō'se] *etc vb V* **indisponer**.
indistinto, a [ēndēstēn'to, à] *a* indistinct; (*vago*) vague.
individual [ēndēvēthwál'] *a* individual; (*habitación*) single ♦ *nm* (*DEPORTE*) singles *sg*.
individuo, a [ēndēvē'thwo, à] *a* individual ♦ *nm* individual.
indocumentado, a [ēndokōōmentá'tho, à] *a* without identity papers.
Indochina [ēndotchē'nà] *nf* Indochina.
indoeuropeo, a [ēndoeōōrope'o, à] *a, nm/f* Indo-European.
índole [ēn'dole] *nf* (*naturaleza*) nature; (*clase*) sort, kind.
indolencia [ēndolen'syà] *nf* indolence, laziness.
indoloro, a [ēndolo'ro, à] *a* painless.
indómito, a [ēndo'mēto, à] *a* indomitable.
Indonesia [ēndone'syà] *nf* Indonesia.
indonesio, a [ēndone'syo, à] *a, nm/f* Indonesian.
inducción [ēndōōksyon'] *nf* (*FILOSOFÍA*, *ELEC*) induction; **por ~** by induction.
inducir [ēndōōsēr'] *vt* to induce; (*inferir*) to infer; (*persuadir*) to persuade; **~ a uno en el error** to mislead sb.
indudable [ēndōōthá'ble] *a* undoubted; (*incuestionable*) unquestionable; **es ~ que** ... there is no doubt that ... .

indulgencia [ēndōōlhen'syà] *nf* indulgence; (*JUR etc*) leniency; **proceder sin ~ contra** to proceed ruthlessly against.
indultar [ēndōōltàr'] *vt* (*perdonar*) to pardon, reprieve; (*librar de pago*) to exempt.
indulto [ēndōōl'to] *nm* pardon; exemption.
indumentaria [ēndōōmentà'ryà] *nf* (*ropa*) clothing, dress.
industria [ēndōōs'tryà] *nf* industry; (*habilidad*) skill; **~ agropecuaria** farming and fishing; **~ pesada** heavy industry; **~ petrolífera** oil industry.
industrial [ēndōōstryàl'] *a* industrial ♦ *nm* industrialist.
INE [ē'ne] *nm abr* (*Esp*)=*Instituto Nacional de Estadística*.
inédito, a [ēne'thēto, à] *a* (*libro*) unpublished; (*nuevo*) unheard-of.
inefable [ēnefá'ble] *a* ineffable, indescribable.
ineficacia [ēnefēká'syà] *nf* (*de medida*) ineffectiveness; (*de proceso*) inefficiency.
ineficaz [ēnefēkàs'] *a* (*inútil*) ineffective; (*ineficiente*) inefficient.
ineludible [ēnelōōthē'ble] *a* inescapable, unavoidable.
INEN [ē'nen] *nm abr* (*México*)=*Instituto Nacional de Energía Nuclear*.
inenarrable [ēnenàrrá'ble] *a* inexpressible.
ineptitud [ēneptētōōth'] *nf* ineptitude, incompetence.
inepto, a [ēnep'to, à] *a* inept, incompetent.
inequívoco, a [ēnekē'voko, à] *a* unequivocal; (*inconfundible*) unmistakable.
inercia [ēner'syà] *nf* inertia; (*pasividad*) passivity.
inerme [ēner'me] *a* (*sin armas*) unarmed; (*indefenso*) defenseless (*US*), defenceless (*Brit*).
inerte [ēner'te] *a* inert; (*inmóvil*) motionless.
inesperado, a [ēnesperà'tho, à] *a* unexpected, unforeseen.
inestable [ēnestá'ble] *a* unstable.
inevitable [ēnevētá'ble] *a* inevitable.
inexactitud [ēneksáktētōōth'] *nf* inaccuracy.
inexacto, a [ēneksàk'to, à] *a* inaccurate; (*falso*) untrue.
inexistente [ēneksēsten'te] *a* non-existent.
inexperiencia [ēneksperyen'syà] *nf* inexperience, lack of experience.
inexperto, a [ēneksper'to, à] *a* (*novato*) inexperienced.
inexplicable [ēneksplēká'ble] *a* inexplicable.
inexpresable [ēnekspresá'ble] *a* inexpressible.
inexpresivo, a [ēnekspresē'ho, à] *a* inexpressive; (*ojos*) dull.
inexpugnable [ēnekspōōgná'ble] *a* (*MIL*) impregnable; (*fig*) firm.

infalible [ēnfálē'ble] *a* infallible; *(indefectible)* certain, sure; *(plan)* foolproof.

infame [ēnfá'me] *a* infamous.

infamia [ēnfá'myá] *nf* infamy; *(deshonra)* disgrace.

infancia [ēnfán'syá] *nf* infancy, childhood; **jardín de la ~** nursery school.

infanta [ēnfán'tá] *nf* *(hija del rey)* infanta princess.

infante [ēnfán'te] *nm* *(hijo del rey)* infante, prince.

infantería [ēnfánterē'á] *nf* infantry.

infantil [ēnfántēl'] *a* a child's, children's; *(pueril, aniñado)* infantile; *(cándido)* childlike.

infarto [ēnfár'to] *nm* *(tb:* **~ de miocardio)** heart attack.

infatigable [ēnfátēgá'ble] *a* tireless, untiring.

infección [ēnfeksyon'] *nf* infection.

infeccioso, a [ēnfeksyo'so, á] *a* infectious.

infectar [ēnfektár'] *vt* to infect; **~se** *vr:* **~se (de)** *(tb fig)* to become infected (with).

infecundidad [ēnfekōōndētháth'] *nf* *(de tierra)* infertility, barrenness; *(de mujer)* sterility.

infecundo, a [ēnfekōōn'do, á] *a* infertile, barren; sterile.

infeliz [ēnfelēs'] *a* *(desgraciado)* unhappy, wretched; *(inocente)* gullible ♦ *nm/f (desgraciado)* wretch; *(inocentón)* simpleton.

inferior [ēnferyor'] *a* inferior; *(situación, MAT)* lower ♦ *nm/f* inferior, subordinate; **cualquier número ~ a 9** any number less than *o* under *o* below 9; **una cantidad ~ a** a lesser quantity.

inferir [ēnferēr'] *vt* *(deducir)* to infer, deduce; *(causar)* to cause.

infértil [ēnfer'tēl] *a* infertile.

infestar [ēnfestár'] *vt* to infest.

infidelidad [ēnfēthelētháth'] *nf* *(gen)* infidelity, unfaithfulness.

infiel [ēnfyel'] *a* unfaithful, disloyal; *(falso)* inaccurate ♦ *nm/f* infidel, unbeliever.

infiera [ēnfye'rá] *etc vb* V **inferir**.

infierno [ēnfyer'no] *nm* hell; **¡vete al ~!** go to hell; **está en el quinto ~** it's in the middle of nowhere.

infiltrar [ēnfēltrár'] *vt* to infiltrate; **~se** *vr* to infiltrate, filter; *(líquidos)* to percolate.

ínfimo, a [ēn'fēmo] *a* *(vil)* vile, mean; *(más bajo)* lowest; *(peor)* worst; *(miserable)* wretched.

infinidad [ēnfēnētháth'] *nf* infinity; *(abundancia)* great quantity; **~ de** vast numbers of; **~ de veces** countless times.

infinito, a [ēnfēnē'to, á] *a* infinite; *(fig)* boundless ♦ *ad* infinitely ♦ *nm* infinite; *(MAT)* infinity; **hasta lo ~** ad infinitum.

infiriendo [ēnfēryen'do] *etc vb* V **inferir**.

inflación [ēnflásyon'] *nf* *(hinchazón)* swelling; *(monetaria)* inflation; *(fig)* conceit.

inflacionario, a [ēnflásyoná'ryo, á] *a* inflationary.

inflacionismo [ēnflásyonēs'mo] *nm* (*ECON*) inflation.

inflacionista [ēnflásyonē'stá] *a* inflationary.

inflamar [ēnflámár'] *vt* to set on fire; *(MED, fig)* to inflame; **~se** *vr* to catch fire; to become inflamed.

inflar [ēnflár'] *vt* *(hinchar)* to inflate, blow up; *(fig)* to exaggerate; **~se** *vr* to swell (up); *(fig)* to get conceited.

inflexible [ēnfleksē'ble] *a* inflexible; *(fig)* unbending.

infligir [ēnflēhēr'] *vt* to inflict.

inflija [ēnflē'há] *etc vb* V **infligir**.

influencia [ēnflwen'syá] *nf* influence.

influenciar [ēnflwensyár'] *vt* to influence.

influir [ēnflōōēr'] *vt* to influence ♦ *vi* to have influence, carry weight; **~ en** *o* **sobre** to influence, affect; *(contribuir a)* to have a hand in.

influjo [ēnflōō'ho] *nm* influence; **~ de capitales** *(ECON etc)* capital influx.

influyendo [ēnflōōyen'do] *etc vb* V **influir**.

influyente [ēnflōōyen'te] *a* influential.

información [ēnformásyon'] *nf* information; *(noticias)* news *sg*; *(informe)* report; (*INFORM*: *datos*) data; (*JUR*) inquiry; **I~** *(oficina)* Information; (*TELEC*) Directory Assistance (*US*), Directory Enquiries (*Brit*); *(mostrador)* Information Desk; **una ~** a piece of information; **abrir una ~** (*JUR*) to begin proceedings; **~ deportiva** *(en periódico)* sports section.

informal [ēnformál'] *a* *(gen)* informal.

informante [ēnformán'te] *nm/f* informant.

informar [ēnformár'] *vt* *(gen)* to inform; *(revelar)* to reveal, make known ♦ *vi* (*JUR*) to plead; *(denunciar)* to inform; *(dar cuenta de)* to report on; **~se** *vr* to find out; **~se de** to inquire into.

informática [ēnformá'tēká] *nf* V **informático**.

informatice [ēnformátē'se] *etc vb* V **informatizar**.

informático, a [ēnformá'tēko, á] *a* computer *cpd* ♦ *nf* (*TEC*) information technology; computing; (*ESCOL*) computer science *o* studies; **~ de gestión** commercial computing.

informatización [ēnformátēsásyon'] *nf* computerization.

informatizar [ēnformátēsár'] *vt* to computerize.

informe [ēnfor'me] *a* shapeless ♦ *nm* report; *(dictamen)* statement; (*MIL*) briefing; (*JUR*) plea; **~s** *nmpl* information *sg*; *(datos)* data; **~ anual** annual report; **~ del juez** summation (*US*), summing-up (*Brit*).

infortunio [ēnfortōō'nyo] *nm* misfortune.

infracción [ĕnfráksyon'] *nf* infraction, infringement; (*AUTO*) violation (*US*), offence (*Brit*).

infraestructura [ĕnfráestrōōktōō'rá] *nf* infrastructure.

in fraganti [ĕnfrágán'tĕ] *ad*: **pillar a uno ~** to catch sb red-handed.

infranqueable [ĕnfránkeá'blĕ] *a* impassable; (*fig*) insurmountable.

infrarrojo, a [ĕnfrárro'ho, á] *a* infrared.

infringir [ĕnfrēnhēr'] *vt* to infringe, contravene.

infrinja [ĕnfrēn'há] *etc vb* V **infringir**.

infructuoso, a [ĕnfrōōktwo'so, á] *a* fruitless, unsuccessful.

infundado, a [ĕnfōōndá'tho, á] *a* groundless, unfounded.

infundir [ĕnfōōndēr'] *vt* to infuse, instil; **~ ánimo a uno** to encourage sb; **~ miedo a uno** to intimidate sb.

infusión [ĕnfōōsyon'] *nf* infusion; **~ de manzanilla** camomile tea.

Ing. *abr* = **Ingeniero**.

ingeniar [ĕnhenyár'] *vt* to think up, devise; **~se** *vr* to manage; **~se para** to manage to.

ingeniería [ĕnhenyerē'á] *nf* engineering; **~ de sistemas** (*INFORM*) systems engineering.

ingeniero, a [ĕnhenye'ro, á] *nm/f* engineer; **~ de sonido** sound engineer; **~ de caminos** civil engineer.

ingenio [ĕnhe'nyo] *nm* (*talento*) talent; (*agudeza*) wit; (*habilidad*) ingenuity, inventiveness; (*TEC*): **~ azucarero** sugar refinery.

ingenioso, a [ĕnhenyo'so, á] *a* ingenious, clever; (*divertido*) witty.

ingente [ĕnhen'te] *a* huge, enormous.

ingenuidad [ĕnhenwēthá'th'] *nf* ingenuousness; (*sencillez*) simplicity.

ingenuo, a [ĕnhe'nwo, á] *a* ingenuous.

ingerir [ĕnherēr'] *vt* to ingest; (*tragar*) to swallow; (*consumir*) to consume.

ingiera [ĕnhye'rá] *etc*, **ingiriendo** [ĕnhēryen'tho] *etc vb* V **ingerir**.

Inglaterra [ĕngláte'rrá] *nf* England.

ingle [ĕn'gle] *nf* groin.

inglés, esa [ĕngles', esá] *a* English ♦ *nm/f* Englishman/woman ♦ *nm* (*LING*) English; **los ingleses** the English.

ingratitud [ĕngrátĕtōōth'] *nf* ingratitude.

ingrato, a [ĕngrá'to, á] *a* ungrateful; (*tarea*) thankless.

ingravidez [ĕngráĕthes'] *nf* weightlessness.

ingrediente [ĕngrethyen'te] *nm* ingredient.

ingresar [ĕngresár'] *vt* (*dinero*) to deposit ♦ *vi* to come o go in; **~ en** (*club*) to join; (*MIL*, *ESCOL*) to enroll (*US*) o enrol (*Brit*) in; **~ en el hospital** to go into hospital.

ingreso [ĕngre'so] *nm* (*entrada*) entry; (: *en hospital etc*) admission; (*MIL*, *ESCOL*)

enrolment; **~s** *nmpl* (*dinero*) income *sg*; (: *COM*) receipts *pl*; **~ gravable** taxable income *sg*; **~s accesorios** fringe benefits; **~s brutos** gross receipts; **~s devengados** earned income *sg*; **~s exentos de impuestos** non-taxable income *sg*; **~s personales disponibles** disposable personal income *sg*.

inhábil [ĕná'bĕl] *a* unskilful, clumsy.

inhabitable [ĕnábĕtá'blĕ] *a* uninhabitable.

inhabituado, a [ĕnábĕtwá'tho, á] *a* unaccustomed.

inhalador [ĕnálátĥor'] *nm* (*MED*) inhaler.

inhalar [ĕnálár'] *vt* to inhale.

inherente [ĕncren'te] *a* inherent.

inhibición [ĕnĕbēsyon'] *nf* inhibition.

inhibir [ĕnĕbēr'] *vt* to inhibit; (*REL*) to restrain; **~se** *vr* to keep out.

inhospitalario, a [ĕnospĕtálá'ryo, á], **inhóspito, a** [ĕnos'pĕto, á] *a* inhospitable.

inhumación [ĕnōōmásyon'] *nf* burial, interment.

inhumano, a [ĕnōōmá'no, á] *a* inhuman.

INI [ē'nĕ] *nm abr* = **Instituto Nacional de Industria**.

inicial [ĕnĕsyál'] *a*, *nf* initial.

inicialice [ĕnĕsyálē'se] *etc vb* V **inicializar**.

inicializar [ĕnĕsyálĕsár'] *vt* (*INFORM*) to initialize.

iniciar [ĕnĕsyár'] *vt* (*persona*) to initiate; (*empezar*) to begin, commence; (*conversación*) to start up; **~ a uno en un secreto** to let sb into a secret; **~ la sesión** (*INFORM*) to log on *o* in (*Brit*).

iniciativa [ĕnĕsyátē'há] *nf* initiative; (*liderazgo*) leadership; **la ~ privada** private enterprise.

inicuo, a [ĕnē'kwo, á] *a* iniquitous.

inigualado, a [ĕnĕgwálá'tho, á] *a* unequalled.

ininteligible [ĕnĕntelēhē'blĕ] *a* unintelligible.

ininterrumpido, a [ĕnĕnterrōōmpē'tho, á] *a* uninterrupted; (*proceso*) continuous; (*progreso*) steady.

injerencia [ĕnheren'syá] *nf* interference.

injertar [ĕnhertár'] *vt* to graft.

injerto [ĕnher'to] *nm* graft; **~ de piel** skin graft.

injuria [ĕnhōō'ryá] *nf* (*agravio*, *ofensa*) offense (*US*), offence (*Brit*); (*insulto*) insult; **~s** *nfpl* abuse *sg*.

injuriar [ĕnhōōryár'] *vt* to insult.

injurioso, a [ĕnhōōryo'so, á] *a* offensive; insulting.

injusticia [ĕnhōōstē'syá] *nf* injustice, unfairness; **con ~** unjustly.

injusto, a [ĕnhōō'sto, á] *a* unjust, unfair.

inmaculado, a [ĕnmákōōlá'tho, á] *a* immaculate, spotless.

inmadurez [ĕnmáthōōres'] *nf* immaturity.

inmaduro, a [ĕnmáthōō'ro, á] *a* immature;

(*fruta*) unripe.

inmediaciones [ēnmeθyásyo'nes] *nfpl* environs.

inmediatez [ēnmeθyátes'] *nf* immediacy.

inmediato, a [ēnmeθyá'to, á] *a* immediate; (*contiguo*) adjoining; (*rápido*) prompt; (*próximo*) neighboring (*US*), neighbouring (*Brit*), next; **de ~** immediately.

inmejorable [ēnmehorá'ble] *a* unsurpassable; (*precio*) unbeatable.

inmemorable [ēnmemorá'ble], **inmemorial** [ēnmemoryál'] *a* immemorial.

inmenso, a [ēnmen'so, á] *a* immense, huge.

inmerecido, a [ēnmeresē'θo, á] *a* undeserved.

inmergir [ēnmerhēr'] *vt* to immerse.

inmersión [ēnmersyon'] *nf* immersion; (*buzo*) dive.

inmigración [ēnmēgrásyon'] *nf* immigration.

inmigrante [ēnmēgrán'te] *a*, *nm/f* immigrant.

inmiscuirse [ēnmēskōōēr'se] *vr* to interfere, meddle.

inmiscuyendo [ēnmēskōōyen'do] *etc vb V* **inmiscuirse.**

inmobiliario, a [ēnmobēlyá'ryo, á] *a* real-estate *cpd*, property *cpd* ♦ *nf* real estate agency (*US*), estate agency (*Brit*).

inmolar [ēnmolár'] *vt* to immolate, sacrifice.

inmoral [ēnmorál'] *a* immoral.

inmortal [ēnmortál'] *a* immortal.

inmortalice [ēnmortálē'se] *etc vb V* **inmortalizar.**

inmortalizar [ēnmortálēsár'] *vt* to immortalize.

inmotivado, a [ēnmotēbá'θo, á] *a* motiveless; (*sospecha*) groundless.

inmóvil [ēnmo'bēl] *a* immobile.

inmueble [ēnmwe'ble] *a*: **bienes ~s** real estate *sg*, real (*US*) o landed (*Brit*) property *sg* ♦ *nm* property.

inmundicia [ēnmōōndē'syá] *nf* filth.

inmundo, a [ēnmōōn'do, á] *a* filthy.

inmunidad [ēnmōōnēθáth'] *nf* immunity; (*fisco*) exemption; **~ diplomática/parlamentaria** diplomatic/parliamentary immunity.

inmutarse [ēnmōōtár'se] *vr*: **siguió sin ~** he carried on unperturbed.

innato, a [ēnná'to, á] *a* innate.

innecesario, a [ēnnesesá'ryo, á] *a* unnecessary.

innegable [ēnnegá'ble] *a* undeniable.

innoble [ēnno'ble] *a* ignoble.

innocuo, a [ēnno'kwo, á] *a* innocuous, harmless.

innovación [ēnnobásyon'] *nf* innovation.

innovador, a [ēnnobaðor', á] *a* innovatory, innovative ♦ *nm/f* innovator.

innovar [ēnnobár'] *vt* to introduce.

innumerable [ēnnōōmerá'ble], **innúmero, a** [ēnnōō'mero, á] *a* countless.

inocencia [ēnosen'syá] *nf* innocence.

inocentada [ēnosentá'thá] *nf* practical joke.

inocente [ēnosen'te] *a* (*ingenuo*) naive, innocent; (*inculpable*) innocent; (*sin malicia*) harmless ♦ *nm/f* simpleton; **día de los (Santos) I~s** ≈ April Fool's Day.

inocuidad [ēnokwētháth'] *nf* harmlessness.

inocular [ēnokōōlár'] *vt* to inoculate.

inocuo, a [ēno'kwo, á] *a* (*sustancia*) harmless.

inodoro, a [ēnoðo'ro, á] *a* odorless (*US*), odourless (*Brit*) ♦ *nm* washroom (*US*), lavatory (*Brit*).

inofensivo, a [ēnofensē'bo, á] *a* inoffensive.

inolvidable [ēnolbēthá'ble] *nf* unforgettable.

inoperante [ēnoperán'te] *a* ineffective.

inopinado, a [ēnopēná'θo, á] *a* unexpected.

inoportuno, a [ēnoportōō'no, á] *a* untimely; (*molesto*) inconvenient; (*inapropiado*) inappropriate.

inoxidable [ēnoksēthá'ble] *a* stainless; **acero ~** stainless steel.

inquebrantable [ēnkebrántá'ble] *a* unbreakable; (*fig*) unshakeable.

inquiera [ēnkye'rá] *etc vb V* **inquirir.**

inquietante [ēnkyetán'te] *a* worrying.

inquietar [ēnkyetár'] *vt* to worry, trouble; **~se** *vr* to worry, get upset.

inquieto, a [ēnkye'to, á] *a* anxious, worried; **estar ~ por** to be worried about.

inquietud [ēnkyetōōth'] *nf* anxiety, worry.

inquilino, a [ēnkēlē'no, á] *nm/f* tenant; (*COM*) lessee.

inquina [ēnkē'ná] *nf* (*aversión*) dislike; (*rencor*) ill will; **tener ~ a uno** to have a grudge against sb.

inquiriendo [ēnkēryen'do] *etc vb V* **inquirir.**

inquirir [ēnkērēr'] *vt* to enquire into, investigate.

insaciable [ēnsásyá'ble] *a* insatiable.

insalubre [ēnsálōō'bre] *a* unhealthy; (*condiciones*) unsanitary.

INSALUD [ēnsálōōth'] *nm abr* (*Esp*) = *Instituto Nacional de la Salud.*

insano, a [ēnsá'no, á] *a* (*loco*) insane; (*malsano*) unhealthy.

insatisfacción [ēnsátēsfáksyon'] *nf* dissatisfaction.

insatisfecho, a [ēnsátēsfetch'o, á] *a* (*condición*) unsatisfied; (*estado de ánimo*) dissatisfied.

inscribir [ēnskrēbēr'] *vt* to inscribe; (*en lista*) to put; (*en censo*) to register; **~se** *vr* to register; (*ESCOL etc*) to enroll (*US*), enrol (*Brit*).

inscripción [ēnskrēpsyon'] *nf* inscription; (*ESCOL etc*) enrollment (*US*), enrolment (*Brit*); (*en censo*) registration.

inscrito [ēnskrē'to] *pp de* **inscribir.**

insecticida [ēnsektēsē'thá] *nm* insecticide.

insecto [ēnsek'to] *nm* insect.

inseguridad [ēnsegōōrēthàth'] *nf* insecurity.

inseguro, a [ēnsegōō'ro, á] *a* insecure; (*inconstante*) unsteady; (*incierto*) uncertain.

inseminación [ēnsemēnásyon'] *nf*: ~ **artificial** artificial insemination (A.I.).

inseminar [ēnsemēnár'] *vt* to inseminate, fertilize.

insensato, a [ēnsensá'to, á] *a* foolish, stupid.

insensibilice [ēnsensēħēlē'se] *etc vb* V **insensibilizar**.

insensibilidad [ēnsensēħēlēthàth'] *nf* (*gen*) insensitivity; (*dureza de corazón*) callousness.

insensibilizar [ēnsensēħēlēsár'] *vt* to desensitize; (*MED*) to anesthetize (*US*), anaesthetize (*Brit*); (*eufemismo*) to knock out *o* unconscious.

insensible [ēnsensē'ħle] *a* (*gen*) insensitive; (*movimiento*) imperceptible; (*sin sentido*) numb.

insertar [ēnsertár'] *vt* to insert.

inservible [ēnserħē'ħle] *a* useless.

insidioso, a [ēnsēthyo'so, á] *a* insidious.

insigne [ēnsēg'ne] *a* distinguished; (*famoso*) notable.

insignia [ēnsēg'nyá] *nf* (*señal distintiva*) badge; (*estandarte*) flag.

insignificante [ēnsēgnēfēkàn'te] *a* insignificant.

insinuar [ēnsēnwár'] *vt* to insinuate, imply; ~**se** *vr*: ~**se con uno** to ingratiate o.s. with sb.

insípido, a [ēnsē'pētho, á] *a* insipid.

insistencia [ēnsēsten'syá] *nf* insistence.

insistir [ēnsēstēr'] *vi* to insist; ~ **en algo** to insist on sth; (*enfatizar*) to stress sth.

insobornable [ēnsoħornà'ħle] *a* incorruptible.

insolación [ēnsolásyon'] *nf* (*MED*) sunstroke.

insolencia [ēnsolen'syá] *nf* insolence.

insolente [ēnsolen'te] *a* insolent.

insólito, a [ēnso'lēto, á] *a* unusual.

insoluble [ēnsolōō'ħle] *a* insoluble.

insolvencia [ēnsolħen'syá] *nf* insolvency.

insomne [ēnsom'ne] *a* sleepless ♦ *nm/f* insomniac.

insomnio [ēnsom'nyo] *nm* insomnia.

insondable [ēnsondà'ħle] *a* bottomless.

insonorización [ēnsonorēsásyon'] *nf* soundproofing.

insonorizado, a [ēnsonorēsá'tho, á] *a* (*cuarto etc*) soundproof.

insoportable [ēnsoportà'ħle] *a* unbearable.

insoslayable [ēnsoslàyá'ħle] *a* unavoidable.

insospechado, a [ēnsospetchá'tho, á] *a* (*inesperado*) unexpected.

insostenible [ēnsostenē'ħle] *a* untenable.

inspección [ēnspeksyon'] *nf* inspection, check; I~ inspectorate.

inspeccionar [ēnspeksyonár'] *vt* (*examinar*) to inspect, examine; (*controlar*) to check; (*INFORM*) to peek.

inspector, a [ēnspektor', á] *nm/f* inspector.

inspectorado [ēnspektorá'tho] *nm* inspectorate.

inspiración [ēnspērásyon'] *nf* inspiration.

inspirador, a [ēnspēráthor', á] *a* inspiring.

inspirar [ēnspērár'] *vt* to inspire; (*MED*) to inhale; ~**se** *vr*: ~**se en** to be inspired by.

instalación [ēnstálásyon'] *nf* (*equipo*) fittings *pl*, equipment; ~ **eléctrica** wiring.

instalar [ēnstálár'] *vt* (*establecer*) to install (*US*), instal (*Brit*); (*erguir*) to set up, erect; ~**se** *vr* to establish o.s.; (*en una vivienda*) to move into.

instancia [ēnstán'syá] *nf* (*solicitud*) application; (*ruego*) request; (*JUR*) petition; **a ~ de** at the request of; **en última ~** in the last resort.

instantáneo, a [ēnstántá'neo, á] *a* instantaneous ♦ *nf* snap(shot); **café ~** instant coffee.

instante [ēnstán'te] *nm* instant, moment; **en un ~** in a flash.

instar [ēnstár'] *vt* to press, urge.

instaurar [ēnstáōōrár'] *vt* (*establecer*) to establish, set up.

instigador, a [ēnstēgáthor', á] *nm/f* instigator; ~ **de un delito** (*JUR*) accessory before the fact.

instigar [ēnstēgár'] *vt* to instigate.

instigue [ēnstē'ge] *etc vb* V **instigar**.

instintivo, a [ēnstēntē'ħo, á] *a* instinctive.

instinto [ēnstēn'to] *nm* instinct; **por ~** instinctively.

institución [ēnstētōōsyon'] *nf* institution, establishment; ~ **benéfica** charitable foundation.

instituir [ēnstētōōēr'] *vt* to establish; (*fundar*) to found.

instituto [ēnstētōō'to] *nm* (*gen*) institute; I~ **Nacional de Enseñanza** (*Esp*) ≈ high (*US*) *o* comprehensive (*Brit*) school; I~ **Nacional de Industria** (**INI**) (*Esp COM*) *government agency to encourage industrial development*.

institutriz [ēnstētōōtrēs'] *nf* governess.

instituyendo [ēnstētōōyen'do] *etc vb* V **instituir**.

instrucción [ēnstrōōksyon'] *nf* instruction; (*enseñanza*) education, teaching; (*JUR*) proceedings *pl*; (*MIL*) training; (*DEPORTE*) coaching; (*conocimientos*) knowledge; (*INFORM*) statement; **instrucciones para el uso** directions for use; **instrucciones de funcionamiento** operating instructions.

instructivo, a [ēnstrōōktē'ħo, á] *a* instructive.

instruir [ēnstrōōēr'] *vt* (*gen*) to instruct; (*enseñar*) to teach, educate; (*JUR*: *proceso*) to prepare, draw up; **~se** *vr* to learn, teach o.s.

instrumento [ēnstrōōmen'to] *nm* (*gen*, *MUS*) instrument; (*herramienta*) tool, implement; (*COM*) indenture; (*JUR*) legal document; **~ de percusión/cuerda/viento** percussion/string(ed)/wind instrument.

instruyendo [ēnstrōōyen'do] *etc vb* V **instruir**.

insubordinarse [ēnsōōhortḥēnár'se] *vr* to rebel.

insuficiencia [ēnsōōfēsyen'syá] *nf* (*carencia*) lack; (*inadecuación*) inadequacy; **~ cardíaca/renal** heart/kidney failure.

insuficiente [ēnsōōfēsyen'te] *a* (*gen*) insufficient; (*ESCOL*: *nota*) unsatisfactory.

insufrible [ēnsōōfrē'ble] *a* insufferable.

insular [ēnsōōlár'] *a* insular.

insulso, a [ēnsōōl'so] *a* insipid; (*fig*) dull.

insultar [ēnsōōltár'] *vt* to insult.

insulto [ēnsōōl'to] *nm* insult.

insumiso, a [ēnsōōmē'so, á] *a* (*rebelde*) rebellious.

insuperable [ēnsōōperá'ble] *a* (*excelente*) unsurpassable; (*problema etc*) insurmountable.

insurgente [ēnsōōrhen'te] *a*, *nm/f* insurgent.

insurrección [ēnsōōrreksyon'] *nf* insurrection, rebellion.

insustituible [ēnsōōstētwē'ble] *a* irreplaceable.

intacto, a [ēntàk'to, á] *a* (*sin tocar*) untouched; (*entero*) intact.

intachable [ēntátchá'ble] *a* irreproachable.

integrado, a [ēntegrá'tho, á] *a* (*INFORM*): **circuito ~** integrated circuit.

integral [ēntegrál'] *a* integral; (*completo*) complete; (*TEC*) built-in; **pan ~** wholewheat bread.

integrante [ēntegrán'te] *a* integral ♦ *nm/f* member.

integrar [ēntegrár'] *vt* to make up, compose; (*MAT*, *fig*) to integrate.

integridad [ēntegrēthàth'] *nf* wholeness; (*carácter*, *tb INFORM*) integrity; **en su ~** completely.

íntegro, a [ēn'tegro] *a* whole, entire; (*texto*) uncut, unabridged; (*honrado*) honest.

intelectual [ēntelektwál'] *a*, *nm/f* intellectual.

intelectualidad [ēntelektwálēthàth'] *nf* intelligentsia, intellectuals *pl*.

inteligencia [ēntelēhen'syá] *nf* intelligence; (*ingenio*) ability; **~ artificial** artificial intelligence.

inteligente [ēntelēhen'te] *a* intelligent.

inteligible [ēntelēhē'ble] *a* intelligible.

intemperancia [ēntemperàn'syá] *nf* excess, intemperance.

intemperie [ēntempe'rye] *nf*: **a la ~** outdoors, in the open air.

intempestivo, a [ēntempestē'ho, á] *a* untimely.

intención [ēntensyon'] *nf* (*gen*) intention, purpose; **con segundas intenciones** maliciously; **con ~** deliberately.

intencionado, a [ēntensyonà'tho, á] *a* deliberate; **bien/mal ~** well-meaning/ill-disposed, hostile.

intendencia [ēntenden'syá] *nf* management, administration; (*MIL*: *tb*: **cuerpo de ~**) ≈ quarter-master corps.

intensidad [ēntensēthàth'] *nf* (*gen*) intensity; (*ELEC*, *TEC*) strength; (*de recuerdo*) vividness; **llover con ~** to rain hard.

intensificar [ēntensēfēkár'] *vt*, **intensificarse** *vr* to intensify.

intensifique [ēntensēfē'ke] *etc vb* V **intensificar**.

intensivo, a [ēntensē'ho, á] *a* intensive; **curso ~** crash course.

intenso, a [ēnten'so, á] *a* intense; (*impresión*) vivid; (*sentimiento*) profound, deep.

intentar [ēntentár'] *vt* (*tratar*) to try, attempt.

intento [ēnten'to] *nm* (*intención*) intention, purpose; (*tentativa*) attempt.

intentona [ēntento'ná] *nf* (*POL*) attempted coup.

interaccionar [ēnteràksyonár'] *vi* (*INFORM*) to interact.

interactivo, a [ēnteràktē'ho, á] *a* (*INFORM*): **computación interactiva** interactive computing.

intercalación [ēnterkálásyon'] *nf* (*INFORM*) merging.

intercalar [ēnterkálár'] *vt* to insert; (*INFORM*: *archivos*, *texto*) to merge.

intercambiable [ēnterkámbyá'ble] *a* interchangeable.

intercambio [ēnterkám'byo] *nm* (*canje*) exchange; (*trueque*) swap.

interceder [ēntersethēr'] *vi* to intercede.

interceptar [ēnterseptár'] *vt* to intercept, cut off; (*AUTO*) to hold up.

interceptor [ēnterseptor'] *nm* interceptor; (*TEC*) trap.

intercesión [ēntersesyon'] *nf* intercession.

interés [ēnteres'] *nm* (*gen*, *COM*) interest; (*importancia*) concern; (*parte*) share, part; (*pey*) self-interest; **~ compuesto** compound interest; **~ simple** simple interest; **con un ~ de 9 por ciento** at an interest of 9%; **dar a ~** to lend at interest; **tener ~ en** (*COM*) to hold a share in; **intereses acumulados** accrued interest *sg*; **intereses por cobrar** interest receivable *sg*; **intereses creados** vested interests; **intereses por pagar** interest payable *sg*.

interesado, a [ēnteresá'ðo, á] *a* interested; (*prejuiciado*) prejudiced; (*pey*) mercenary, self-seeking ♦ *nm/f* person concerned; (*firmante*) the undersigned.

interesante [ēnteresán'te] *a* interesting.

interesar [ēnteresár'] *vt* to interest, be of interest to ♦ *vi* to interest, be of interest; (*importar*) to be important; ~**se** *vr*: ~**se en** *o* **por** to take an interest in; **no me interesan los toros** bullfighting does not appeal to me.

interestatal [ēnterestátál'] *a* inter-state.

interface, interfase [ēnterfá'se] *nm* (*INFORM*) interface; ~ **hombre/máquina/por menús** man/machine/menu interface.

interferir [ēnterferēr'] *vt* to interfere with; (*TELEC*) to jam ♦ *vi* to interfere.

interfiera [ēnterfye'rá] *etc*, **interfiriendo** [ēnterfēryen'do] *etc vb V* **interferir**.

interfono [ēnterfo'no] *nm* intercom.

ínterin [ēn'terēn] *ad* meanwhile ♦ *nm* interim; **en el** ~ in the meantime.

interino, a [ēnterē'no, á] *a* temporary; (*empleado etc*) provisional ♦ *nm/f* temporary worker; (*MED*) on-call doctor (*US*), locum (*Brit*); (*ESCOL*) substitute teacher (*US*), supply teacher (*Brit*); (*TEATRO*) stand-in.

interior [ēnteryor'] *a* inner, inside; (*COM*) domestic, internal ♦ *nm* interior, inside; (*fig*) soul, mind; (*DEPORTE*) inside-forward; **Ministerio del** ~ ≈ Ministry of the Interior; **dije para mí** ~ I said to myself.

interjección [ēnterheksyon'] *nf* interjection.

interlínea [ēnterlē'neá] *nf* (*INFORM*) line feed.

interlocutor, a [ēnterlokōótor', á] *nm/f* speaker; (*al teléfono*) person at the other end (of the line); **mi** ~ the person I was speaking to.

intermediario, a [ēntermeðyá'ryo, á] *a* (*mediador*) mediating ♦ *nm/f* intermediary, go-between; (*mediador*) mediator.

intermedio, a [ēnterme'ðyo, á] *a* intermediate; (*tiempo*) intervening ♦ *nm* interval; (*POL*) recess.

interminable [ēntermēná'ble] *a* endless, interminable.

intermitente [ēntermēten'te] *a* intermittent ♦ *nm* (*AUTO*) indicator.

internacional [ēnternásyonál'] *a* international.

internado [ēnterná'ðo] *nm* boarding school.

internamiento [ēnternámyen'to] *nm* internment.

internar [ēnternár'] *vt* to intern; (*en un manicomio*) to commit; ~**se** *vr* (*penetrar*) to penetrate; ~**se en** to go into *o* right inside; ~**se en un estudio** to study a subject in depth.

interno, a [ēnter'no, á] *a* internal, interior;

(*POL etc*) domestic ♦ *nm/f* (*alumno*) boarder.

interpelación [ēnterpelásyon'] *nf* appeal, plea.

interpelar [ēnterpelár'] *vt* (*rogar*) to implore; (*hablar*) to speak to; (*POL*) to ask for explanations, question formally.

interpondré [ēnterpondre'] *etc vb V* **interponer**.

interponer [ēnterponer'] *vt* to interpose, put in; ~**se** *vr* to intervene.

interponga [ēnterpon'gá] *etc vb V* **interponer**.

interposición [ēnterposēsyon'] *nf* insertion.

interpretación [ēnterpretásyon'] *nf* interpretation; (*MUS, TEATRO*) performance; **mala** ~ misinterpretation.

interpretar [ēnterpretár'] *vt* to interpret.

intérprete [ēnter'prete] *nm/f* (*LING*) interpreter, translator; (*MUS, TEATRO*) performer, artist(e).

interpuesto [ēnterpwe'sto], **interpuse** [ēnterpōō'se] *etc vb V* **interponer**.

interrogación [ēnterrogásyon'] *nf* interrogation; (*LING: tb:* **signo de** ~) question mark; (*TELEC*) polling.

interrogante [ēnterrogán'te] *a* questioning ♦ *nm* question mark; (*fig*) question mark, query.

interrogar [ēnterrogár'] *vt* to interrogate, question.

interrogatorio [ēnterrogáto'ryo] *nm* interrogation; (*MIL*) debriefing; (*JUR*) examination.

interrogue [ēnterro'ge] *etc vb V* **interrogar**.

interrumpir [ēnterrōōmpēr'] *vt* to interrupt; (*vacaciones*) to cut short; (*servicio*) to cut off; (*tráfico*) to block.

interrupción [ēnterrōōpsyon'] *nf* interruption.

interruptor [ēnterrōōptor'] *nm* (*ELEC*) switch.

intersección [ēnterseksyon'] *nf* intersection; (*AUTO*) junction.

interurbano, a [ēnteroōrbá'no, á] *a* intercity; (*TELEC*) long-distance.

intervalo [ēnterbá'lo] *nm* interval; (*descanso*) break; **a** ~**s** at intervals, every now and then.

intervención [ēnterbensyon'] *nf* supervision; (*COM*) audit(ing); (*MED*) operation; (*TELEC*) tapping; (*participación*) intervention; ~ **quirúrgica** surgical operation; **la política de no** ~ the policy of non-intervention.

intervencionista [ēnterbensyonē'stá] *a:* **no** ~ (*COM*) laissez-faire.

intervendré [ēnterbendre'] *etc*, **intervenga** [ēnterben'gá] *etc vb V* **intervenir**.

intervenir [ēnterbenēr'] *vt* (*controlar*) to control, supervise; (*COM*) to audit; (*MED*) to operate on ♦ *vi* (*participar*) to take part, participate; (*mediar*) to intervene.

interventor, a [ɛ̄nterßentor', à] *nm/f* inspector; (*COM*) auditor.

interviniendo [ɛ̄nterßenyen'do] *etc vb V* **intervenir.**

interviú [ɛ̄nterßyoō'] *nf* interview.

intestino [ɛ̄ntestē'no] *nm* intestine.

inti [ɛ̄n'tē] *nm monetary unit of Peru.*

intimar [ɛ̄ntēmár'] *vt* to intimate, announce; (*mandar*) to order ♦ *vi*, **~se** *vr* to become friendly.

intimidad [ɛ̄ntēmēthàth'] *nf* intimacy; (*familiaridad*) familiarity; (*vida privada*) private life; (*JUR*) privacy.

intimidar [ɛ̄ntēmēthàr'] *vt* to intimidate, scare.

íntimo, a [ɛ̄n'tēmo] *a* intimate; (*pensamientos*) innermost; (*vida*) personal, private; **una boda íntima** a quiet wedding.

intolerable [ɛ̄ntolerá'ßle] *a* intolerable, unbearable.

intoxicación [ɛ̄ntoksēkásyon'] *nf* poisoning; **~ alimenticia** food poisoning.

intraducible [ɛ̄ntràthōōsē'ßle] *a* untranslatable.

intranquilice [ɛ̄ntránkēlē'se] *etc vb V* **intranquilizarse.**

intranquilizarse [ɛ̄ntránkēlēsàr'se] *vr* to get worried *o* anxious.

intranquilo, a [ɛ̄ntránkē'lo, à] *a* worried.

intrascendente [ɛ̄ntránsenden'te] *a* unimportant.

intransferible [ɛ̄ntránsferē'ßle] *a* not transferable.

intransigente [ɛ̄ntránsēhen'te] *a* intransigent.

intransitable [ɛ̄ntránsētá'ßle] *a* impassable.

intratable [ɛ̄ntrátá'ßle] *a* (*problema*) intractable; (*dificultad*) awkward; (*individuo*) unsociable.

intrepidez [ɛ̄ntrepēthes'] *nf* courage, bravery.

intrépido, a [ɛ̄ntre'pētho, à] *a* intrepid, fearless.

intriga [ɛ̄ntrē'gà] *nf* intrigue; (*plan*) plot.

intrigar [ɛ̄ntrēgàr'] *vt, vi* to intrigue.

intrigue [ɛ̄ntrē'ge] *etc vb V* **intrigar.**

intrincado, a [ɛ̄ntrēnkà'tho, à] *a* intricate.

intrínseco, a [ɛ̄ntrēn'seko, à] *a* intrinsic.

introducción [ɛ̄ntrothōōksyon'] *nf* introduction; (*de libro*) foreword; (*INFORM*) input.

introducir [ɛ̄ntrothōōser'] *vt* (*gen*) to introduce; (*moneda*) to insert; (*INFORM*) to input, enter.

introduje [ɛ̄ntrothōō'he] *etc*, **introduzca** [ɛ̄ntrothōōs'kà] *etc vb V* **introducir.**

intromisión [ɛ̄ntromēsyon'] *nf* interference, meddling.

introvertido, a [ɛ̄ntroßertē'tho, à] *a*, *nm/f* introvert.

intruso, a [ɛ̄ntrōō'so, à] *a* intrusive ♦ *nm/f* intruder.

intuición [ɛ̄ntwēsyon'] *nf* intuition.

intuir [ɛ̄ntōōēr'] *vt* to know by intuition, intuit.

intuyendo [ɛ̄ntōōyen'do] *etc vb V* **intuir.**

inundación [ɛ̄nōōndásyon'] *nf* flood(ing).

inundar [ɛ̄nōōndàr'] *vt* to flood; (*fig*) to swamp, inundate.

inusitado, a [ɛ̄nōōsētá'tho, à] *a* unusual.

inútil [ɛ̄nōō'tēl] *a* useless; (*esfuerzo*) vain, fruitless.

inutilice [ɛ̄nōōtēlē'se] *etc vb V* **inutilizar.**

inutilidad [ɛ̄nōōtēlēthàth'] *nf* uselessness.

inutilizar [ɛ̄nōōtēlēsàr'] *vt* to make unusable, put out of action; (*incapacitar*) to disable; **~se** *vr* to become useless.

invadir [ɛ̄mbàthēr'] *vt* to invade.

invalidez [ɛ̄mbálēthes'] *nf* (*MED*) disablement; (*JUR*) invalidity.

inválido, a [ɛ̄mbà'lētho, à] *a* invalid; (*JUR*) null and void ♦ *nm/f* invalid.

invariable [ɛ̄mbáryà'ßle] *a* invariable.

invasión [ɛ̄mbàsyon'] *nf* invasion.

invasor, a [ɛ̄mbàsor', à] *a* invading ♦ *nm/f* invader.

invención [ɛ̄mbensyon'] *nf* invention.

inventar [ɛ̄mbentàr'] *vt* to invent.

inventario [ɛ̄mbentà'ryo] *nm* inventory; (*COM*) taking inventory (*US*), stocktaking (*Brit*).

inventiva [ɛ̄mbentē'ßà] *nf* inventiveness.

inventor, a [ɛ̄mbentor', à] *nm/f* inventor.

invernadero [ɛ̄mbernàthe'ro] *nm* greenhouse.

invernal [ɛ̄mbernál'] *a* wintry, winter *cpd.*

inverosímil [ɛ̄mberosē'mēl] *a* implausible.

inversión [ɛ̄mbersyon'] *nf* (*COM*) investment; **~ de capitales** capital investment; **inversiones extranjeras** foreign investment *sg.*

inverso, a [ɛ̄mber'so, à] *a* inverse, opposite; **en el orden ~** in reverse order; **a la inversa** inversely, the other way round.

inversor, a [ɛ̄mbersor', à] *nm/f* (*COM*) investor.

invertido, a [ɛ̄mbertē'tho, à] *a* inverted; (*al revés*) reversed; (*homosexual*) homosexual ♦ *nm/f* homosexual.

invertir [ɛ̄mbertēr'] *vt* (*COM*) to invest; (*volcar*) to turn upside down; (*tiempo etc*) to spend.

investigación [ɛ̄mbestēgàsyon'] *nf* investigation; (*indagación*) inquiry; (*UNIV*) research; **~ y desarrollo** (*COM*) research and development (R and D); **~ de los medios de publicidad** media research; **~ del mercado** market research.

investigador, a [ɛ̄mbestēgàthor', à] *nm/f* investigator; (*UNIVERSIDAD*) research fellow.

investigar [ɛ̄mbestēgàr'] *vt* to investigate;

(*estudiar*) to do research into.
investigue [ēmbestē'ǥe] *etc vb* V **investigar.**
invicto, a [ēmbēk'to, à] *a* unconquered.
invidente [ēmbēǐ̯ḥen'te] *a* sightless ♦ *nm/f* blind person; **los ~s** the sightless.
invierno [ēmbyer'no] *nm* winter.
invierta [ēmbyer'tà] *etc vb* V **invertir.**
inviolabilidad [ēmbyoláḥēlḗǐ̯ḥáǐ̯ḥ'] *nf* inviolability; **~ parlamentaria** parliamentary immunity.
invirtiendo [ēmbērtyen'do] *etc vb* V **invertir.**
invisible [ēmbēsē'ḅle] *a* invisible; **exportaciones/importaciones ~s** invisible exports/imports.
invitado, a [ēmbētá'ǐ̯ḥo, à] *nm/f* guest.
invitar [ēmbētár'] *vt* to invite; (*incitar*) to entice; **~ a uno a hacer algo** to invite sb to do sth; **~ a algo** to pay for sth; **nos invitó a cenar fuera** she took us out for dinner; **invito yo** it's on me.
invocar [ēmbokár'] *vt* to invoke, call on; (*INFORM*) to call.
involucrar [ēmbolōōkrár'] *vt*: **~ algo en un discurso** to bring something irrelevant into a discussion; **~ a uno en algo** to involve sb in sth; **~se** *vr* (*interesarse*) to get involved.
involuntario, a [ēmbolōōntà'ryo, à] *a* involuntary; (*ofensa etc*) unintentional.
invoque [ēmbo'ke] *etc vb* V **invocar.**
inyección [ēnyeksyon'] *nf* injection.
inyectar [ēnyektár'] *vt* to inject.
IPC *nm abr* (*Esp*: = *índice de precios al consumo*) CPI.
IPM *nm abr* (= *índice de precios al por menor*) RPI.
ir [ēr] *vi* to go; (*viajar*) to travel; (*ropa*) to suit; **~se** *vr* to go away, leave; (*mano etc*) to slip; **¡vete!** go away!; **¡vámonos!** let's go!; **~ caminando** to walk; **~ en coche/bicicleta/caballo/a pie** to drive/cycle/ride/walk; **~ de mal en peor** to go from bad to worse; **¡voy!** I'm coming!; **~ de viaje** to travel, go away; **voy para viejo** I'm getting on in years; **~ por/a por algo** to go for/go and get sth; **¡qué va!** (*no diga*) you don't say!; (*¡no!*) no way!; **esto va de veras** this is serious; **¿me va bien esto?** (*ropa*) does this suit me?; **eso no va por usted** I wasn't referring to you; **va mucho de A a B** there's a lot of difference between A and B; **¡vamos!** come on!; **vaya susto que me has dado** what a fright you gave me; **vaya donde vaya, encontrará ...** wherever you go, you will find ... .
ira [ē'rà] *nf* anger, rage.
iracundo, a [ērákōōn'do, à] *a* irascible.
Irak [ērák'] *nm* = **Iraq.**
Irán [ēràn'] *nm* Iran.

iraní [ērànē'] *a, nm/f* Iranian.
Iraq [ērák'] *nm* Iraq.
iraquí [ērákē'] *a, nm/f* Iraqi.
irguiendo [ērǥyen'do] *etc vb* V **erguir.**
iris [ē'rēs] *nm inv* (*arco* **~**) rainbow; (*ANAT*) iris.
Irlanda [ērlàn'dà] *nf* Ireland; **~ del Norte** Northern Ireland, Ulster.
irlandés, esa [ērlàndes', esà] *a* Irish ♦ *nm/f* Irishman/woman ♦ *nm* (*LING*) Gaelic, Irish; **los irlandeses** *npl* the Irish.
ironía [ēronē'à] *nf* irony.
irónico, a [ēro'nēko, à] *a* ironic(al).
IRPF *nm abr* (*Esp*) = *impuesto sobre la renta de las personas físicas.*
irrazonable [ērràsonà'ḅle] *a* unreasonable.
irreal [ērreàl'] *a* unreal.
irrealizable [ērreàlēsà'ḅle] *a* (*gen*) unrealizable; (*meta*) unrealistic.
irrebatible [ērrebátē'ḅle] *a* irrefutable.
irreconocible [ērrekonosē'ḅle] *a* unrecognizable.
irrecuperable [ērrekōōperá'ḅle] *a* irrecoverable, irretrievable.
irreembolsable [ērreembolsà'ḅle] *a* (*COM*) non-returnable.
irreflexión [ērreflexyon'] *nf* thoughtlessness; (*ímpetu*) rashness.
irregular [ērreǥōōlár'] *a* irregular; (*situación*) abnormal, anomalous; **margen izquierdo/derecho ~** (*texto*) ragged left/right (margin).
irremediable [ērremeǐ̯ḥyá'ḅle] *a* irremediable; (*vicio*) incurable.
irresoluto, a [ērresolōō'to, à] *a* irresolute, hesitant; (*sin resolver*) unresolved.
irrespetuoso, a [ērrespetwo'so, à] *a* disrespectful.
irresponsable [ērresponsà'ḅle] *a* irresponsible.
irreverente [ērreʜeren'te] *a* disrespectful.
irrigar [ērreǥár'] *vt* to irrigate.
irrigue [ērre'ǥe] *etc vb* V **irrigar.**
irrisible [ērrēsē'ḅle] *a* laughable; (*precio*) absurdly low.
irrisorio, a [ērrēso'ryo, à] *a* derisory, ridiculous; (*precio*) bargain *cpd*.
irritar [ērrētár'] *vt* to irritate, annoy; **~se** *vr* to get angry, lose one's temper.
irrompible [ērrompē'ḅle] *a* unbreakable.
irrumpir [ērrōōmpēr'] *vi*: **~ en** to burst *o* rush into.
irrupción [ērrōōpsyon'] *nf* irruption; (*invasión*) invasion.
IRTP *nm abr* (*Esp*) = *impuesto sobre el rendimiento del trabajo personal*) ≈ PAYE.
isla [ēs'là] *nf* (*GEO*) island; **I~s Británicas** British Isles; **I~s Filipinas/Malvinas/Canarias** Philippines/Falklands/Canaries.
Islam [ēslám'] *nm* Islam.
islámico, a [ēslà'mēko, à] *a* Islamic.

islandés, esa [ēslándes', esá] *a* Icelandic ♦ *nm/f* Icelander ♦ *nm* (*LING*) Icelandic.

Islandia [ēslán'dyá] *nf* Iceland.

isleño, a [ēsle'nyo, á] *a* island *cpd* ♦ *nm/f* islander.

islote [ēslo'te] *nm* small island.

isótopo [ēso'topo] *nm* isotope.

Israel [ēsráel'] *nm* Israel.

israelí [ēsráelē'] *a, nm/f* Israeli.

istmo [ēst'mo] *nm* isthmus; **el l~ de Panamá** the Isthmus of Panama.

Italia [ētá'lyá] *nf* Italy.

italiano, a [ētályá'no, á] *a, nm/f* Italian ♦ *nm* (*LING*) Italian.

itálica [ētá'lēká] *nf* (*INFORM*): **en ~** in italics.

itinerante [ētēnerán'te] *a* travel(l)ing; (*embajador*) roving.

itinerario [ētēnerá'ryo] *nm* itinerary, route.

IVA [ē'ḥá] *nm abr* (*Esp COM*: = *Impuesto sobre el Valor Añadido*) VAT.

IVP *nm abr* = *Instituto Venezolano de Petroquímica*.

izar [ēsár'] *vt* to hoist.

izda, izq.ª *abr* = **izquierda**.

izdo, izq, izq.º *abr* = **izquierdo**.

izquierda [ēskyer'ḥá] *nf V* **izquierdo**.

izquierdista [ēskyerthē'stá] *a* leftist, left-wing ♦ *nm/f* left-winger, leftist.

izquierdo, a [ēskyer'ḥo, á] *a* left ♦ *nf* left; (*POL*) left (wing); **a la izquierda** on the left; **es un cero a la izquierda** (*fam*) he is a nonentity; **conducción por la izquierda** left-hand drive.

J

J, j [ho'tá] *nf* (*letra*) J, j; **J de José** J for Jig.

jabalí [háḥálē'] *nm* wild boar.

jabalina [háḥálē'ná] *nf* javelin.

jabato, a [háḥá'to, á] *a* brave, bold ♦ *nm* young wild boar.

jabón [háḥon'] *nm* soap; (*fam: adulación*) flattery; **~ de afeitar** shaving soap; **~ de tocador** toilet soap; **dar ~ a uno** to soft-soap sb.

jabonar [háḥonár'] *vt* to soap.

jaca [há'ká] *nf* pony.

jacinto [hásēn'to] *nm* hyacinth.

jactancia [háktán'syá] *nf* boasting, boastfulness.

jactarse [háktár'se] *vr*: **~ (de)** to boast *o* brag (about *o* of).

jadear [háḥeár'] *vi* to pant, gasp for breath.

jadeo [háḥe'o] *nm* panting, gasping.

jaguar [hágwár'] *nm* jaguar.

jalar [hálár'] *vt* (*AM*) to pull.

jalbegue [hálḥe'ge] *nm* (*pintura*) whitewash.

jalea [hále'á] *nf* jelly.

jaleo [hále'o] *nm* racket, uproar; **armar un ~** to make a racket.

jalón [hálon'] *nm* (*AM*) tug.

jalonar [hálonár'] *vt* to stake out; (*fig*) to mark.

Jamaica [hámá'ēká] *nf* Jamaica.

jamaicano, a [hámáēká'no, á] *a, nm/f* Jamaican.

jamás [hámàs'] *ad* never, not ... ever; (*interrogativo*) ever; **¿~ se vio tal cosa?** did you ever see such a thing?

jamón [hámon'] *nm* ham; **~ dulce/serrano** boiled/cured ham.

Japón [hápon'] *nm*: **el ~** Japan.

japonés, esa [hápones', esá] *a, nm/f* Japanese ♦ *nm* (*LING*) Japanese.

jaque [há'ke] *nm*: **~ mate** checkmate.

jaqueca [háke'ká] *nf* (very bad) headache, migraine.

jarabe [hárá'ḥe] *nm* syrup; **~ para la tos** cough syrup *o* mixture.

jarana [hárá'ná] *nf* (*juerga*) spree (*fam*); **andar/ir de ~** to be/go on a spree.

jarcia [hár'syá] *nf* (*NAUT*) ropes *pl*, rigging.

jardín [hárthēn'] *nm* garden; **~ botánico** botanical garden; **~ de (la) infancia** (*Esp*) *o* **de niños** (*AM*) *o* **infantil** (*AM*) kindergarten, nursery school.

jardinería [hárthēnerē'á] *nf* gardening.

jardinero, a [hárthēne'ro, á] *nm/f* gardener.

jarra [há'rrá] *nf* jar; (*jarro*) jug; (*de leche*) churn; (*de cerveza*) mug; **de** *o* **en ~s** with arms akimbo.

jarro [há'rro] *nm* jug.

jarrón [hárron'] *nm* vase; (*ARQUEOLOGÍA*) urn.

jaspeado, a [háspeá'do, á] *a* mottled, speckled.

jaula [há'ōōlá] *nf* cage; (*embalaje*) crate.

jauría [háōōrē'á] *nf* pack of hounds.

jazmín [hásmēn'] *nm* jasmine.

J. C. *abr* = **Jesucristo**.

JD *nf abr* (*Esp COM*) = *Junta Democrática*.

jefa [he'fá] *nf ver* **jefe**.

jefatura [hefátōō'rá] *nf* (*liderato*) leadership; (*sede*) central office; **J~ de la aviación civil** ≈ Federal Aviation Administration (*US*), ≈ Civil Aviation Authority (*Brit*); **~ de policía** police headquarters *sg*.

jefazo [hefá'so] *nm* bigwig.

jefe, a [he'fe, á] *nm/f* (*gen*) chief, head; (*patrón*) boss; (*POL*) leader; (*COM*) manager(ess); **~ de camareros** head wait-

er; ~ **de cocina** chef; ~ **ejecutivo** (*COM*)
chief executive; ~ **de estación** sta-
tionmaster; ~ **de estado** head of state; ~
de oficina (*COM*) office manager; ~ **de**
producción (*COM*) production manager; ~
supremo commander-in-chief; **ser el** ~
(*fig*) to be the boss.

JEN [hen] *nf abr* (*Esp*:=*Junta de Energía*
Nuclear) ≈ NRC.

jengibre [henhē'bre] *nm* ginger.

jeque [he'ke] *nm* sheik(h).

jerarquía [herárkē'á] *nf* (*orden*) hierarchy;
(*rango*) rank.

jerárquico, a [herár'kēko, á] *a* hier-
archic(al).

jerez [heres'] *nm* sherry; **J~ de la Frontera**
Jerez.

jerezano, a [heresá'no, á] *a* of *o* from Jerez
♦ *nm/f* native *o* inhabitant of Jerez.

jerga [her'gá] *nf* (*tela*) coarse cloth;
(*lenguaje*) jargon; ~ **informática** computer
jargon.

jerigonza [herēgon'sá] *nf* (*jerga*) jargon,
slang; (*galimatías*) nonsense, gibberish.

jeringa [herēn'gá] *nf* syringe; (*AM*)
annoyance, bother; ~ **de engrase** grease
gun.

jeringar [herēngár'] *vt* (*AM*) to annoy,
bother.

jeringue [herēn'ge] *etc vb V* **jeringar.**

jeringuilla [herēng'ēyá] *nf* hypodermic (syringe).

jeroglífico [heroglē'fēko] *nm* hieroglyphic.

jersé [herse'], *pl* **jersés, jersey** [herse'ē], *pl*
jerseys *nm* jersey, pullover.

Jerusalén [herōōsálen'] *n* Jerusalem.

Jesucristo [hesōōkrē'sto] *nm* Jesus Christ.

jesuita [heswē'tá] *a, nm* Jesuit.

Jesús [hesōōs'] *nm* Jesus; ¡~! good heavens!; (*al estornudar*) bless you!

jeta [he'tá] *nf* (*ZOOL*) snout; (*fam: cara*)
mug; ¡**que** ~ **tienes!** (*fam: insolencia*)
you've got a nerve!

jícara [hē'kárá] *nf* small cup.

jiennense [hyennen'se] *a* of *o* from Jaén ♦
nm/f native *o* inhabitant of Jaén.

jilguero [hēlge'ro] *nm* goldfinch.

jinete, a [hēne'te, á] *nm/f* horseman/woman.

jipijapa [hēpēhá'pá] *nm* (*AM*) straw hat.

jira [hē'rá] *nf* (*de tela*) strip; (*excursión*)
picnic.

jirafa [hērá'fá] *nf* giraffe.

jirón [hēron'] *nm* rag, shred.

JJ.OO. *nmpl abr* = **Juegos Olímpicos.**

jocosidad [hokosētháth'] *nf* humor (*US*), humour (*Brit*); (*chiste*) joke.

jocoso, a [hoko'so, á] *a* humorous, jocular.

joder [hother'] (*fam!*) *vt* to fuck (*!*), screw
(*!*); ~**se** *vr* (*fracasar*) to fail; ¡~! damn
it!; **se jodió todo** everything was ruined.

jodido, a [hothē'tho, á] *a* (*fam!*: *difícil*)

awkward; **me han** ~ I've been screwed(*!*).

jofaina [hofáē'ná] *nf* washbasin.

jolgorio [holgo'ryo] *nm* (*juerga*) fun, revelry.

Jordania [horthá'nyá] *nf* Jordan.

jornada [horná'thá] *nf* (*viaje de un día*)
day's journey; (*camino o viaje entero*)
journey; (*día de trabajo*) working day; ~
de 8 horas 8-hour day; (**trabajar a**) ~
partida (to work a) split shift.

jornal [hornál'] *nm* (day's) wage.

jornalero [hornále'ro] *nm* (day) laborer
(*US*), labourer (*Brit*).

joroba [horo'há] *nf* hump.

jorobado, a [horohá'tho, á] *a* hunchbacked
♦ *nm/f* hunchback.

jorobar [horohár'] *vt* to annoy, pester,
bother; ~**se** *vr* to get cross; ¡**hay que** ~**se!**
to hell with it!; **esto me joroba** I'm fed up
with this!

jota [ho'tá] *nf* letter J; (*danza*) Aragonese
dance; (*fam*) jot, iota; **no saber** ~ to have
no idea.

joven [ho'hen] *a* young ♦ *nm* young man,
youth ♦ *nf* young woman, girl.

jovencito, a [hohensē'to, á] *nm/f* youngster.

jovial [hohyál'] *a* cheerful, jolly.

jovialidad [hohyálētháth'] *nf* cheerfulness,
jolliness.

joya [ho'yá] *nf* jewel, gem; (*fig: persona*)
gem; ~**s de fantasía** imitation jewellery
sg.

joyería [hoyerē'á] *nf* (*joyas*) jewelry (*US*),
jewellery (*Brit*); (*tienda*) jewel(l)er's
(shop).

joyero [hoye'ro] *nm* (*persona*) jewel(l)er;
(*caja*) jewel case.

JSP *nf abr* (*COM*)=*Junta Superior de Pre-*
cios.

juanete [hwáne'te] *nm* (*del pie*) bunion.

jubilación [hōōhēlásyon'] *nf* (*retiro*) retirement.

jubilado, a [hōōhēlá'do, á] *a* retired ♦ *nm/f*
retired person, senior citizen.

jubilar [hōōhēlár'] *vt* to pension off, retire;
(*fam*) to discard; ~**se** *vr* to retire.

jubileo [hōōhēle'o] *nm* jubilee.

júbilo [hōō'hēlo] *nm* joy, rejoicing.

jubiloso, a [hōōhēlo'so, á] *a* jubilant.

judaísmo [hōōtháēs'mo] *nm* Judaism.

judía [hōōthē'á] *nf V* **judío.**

judicatura [hōōthēkátōō'rá] *nf* (*cargo de*
juez) office of judge; (*cuerpo de jueces*) judiciary.

judicial [hōōthēsyál'] *a* judicial.

judío, a [hōōthē'o, á] *a* Jewish ♦ *nm* Jew ♦
nf Jewess, Jewish woman; (*CULIN*) bean;
judía blanca haricot bean; **judía verde**
French *o* string bean.

juego [hwe'go] *etc vb V* **jugar** ♦ *nm* (*gen*)
play; (*pasatiempo, partido*) game; (*en ca-*

sino) gambling; (*deporte*) sport; (*conjunto*) set; (*herramientas*) kit; **~ de azar** game of chance; **~ de café** coffee set; **~ de caracteres** (*INFORM*) font; **~ limpio/sucio** fair/foul *o* dirty play; **J~s Olímpicos** Olympic Games; **~ de programas** (*INFORM*) integrated software; **fuera de ~** (*DEPORTE*: *persona*) offside; (: *pelota*) out of play; **por ~** in fun, for fun.

juegue [hwe'ḡe] *etc vb* V **jugar**.

juerga [hwer'ḡá] *nf* binge; (*fiesta*) party; **ir de ~** to go out on a binge.

juerguista [hwerḡe'stá] *nm/f* reveler.

jueves [hwe'bes] *nm inv* Thursday.

juez [hwes] *nm/f* (*f tb*: **jueza**) judge; (*TENIS*) umpire; **~ de línea** linesman; **~ de paz** justice of the peace; **~ de salida** starter.

jugada [hōōḡá'thá] *nf* play; **buena ~** good move (*o* shot *o* stroke) *etc*.

jugador, a [hōōḡáthor', á] *nm/f* player; (*en casino*) gambler.

jugar [hōōḡár'] *vt* to play; (*en casino*) to gamble; (*apostar*) to bet ♦ *vi* to play; to gamble; (*COM*) to speculate; **~se** *vr* to gamble (away); **~se el todo por el todo** to stake one's all, go for broke; **¿quién juega?** whose move is it?; **¡me la han jugado!** (*fam*) I've been had!

jugarreta [hōōḡárre'tá] *nf* (*mala jugada*) bad move; (*trampa*) dirty trick; **hacer una ~ a uno** to play a dirty trick on sb.

juglar [hōōḡlár'] *nm* minstrel.

jugo [hōō'ḡo] *nm* (*BOT, de fruta*) juice; (*fig*) essence, substance; **~ de naranja** (*esp AM*) orange juice.

jugoso, a [hōōḡo'so, á] *a* juicy; (*fig*) substantial, important.

jugué [hōōḡe'], **juguemos** [hōōḡe'mos] *etc vb* V **jugar**.

juguete [hōōḡe'te] *nm* toy.

juguetear [hōōḡeteár'] *vi* to play.

juguetería [hōōḡeterē'á] *nf* toyshop.

juguetón, ona [hōōḡeton', oná] *a* playful.

juicio [hwē'syo] *nm* judgement; (*sana razón*) sanity, reason; (*opinión*) opinion; (*JUR: proceso*) trial; **estar fuera de ~** to be out of one's mind; **a mi ~** in my opinion.

juicioso, a [hwēsyo'so, á] *a* wise, sensible.

JUJEM [hōōhem'] *nf abr* (*Esp MIL*:=*Junta de Jefes del Estado Mayor*) joint Chiefs of Staff.

jul. *abr* (= *julio*) Jul.

julio [hōō'lyo] *nm* July.

jumento, a [hōōmen'to, á] *nm/f* donkey.

jun. *abr* (= *junio*) Jun.

junco [hōōn'ko] *nm* rush, reed.

jungla [hōōn'glá] *nf* jungle.

junio [hōō'nyo] *nm* June.

junta [hōōn'tá] *nf* V **junto**.

juntar [hōōntár'] *vt* to join, unite; (*maquinaria*) to assemble, put together; (*dinero*) to collect; **~se** *vr* to join, meet; (*reunirse: personas*) to meet, assemble; (*arrimarse*) to approach, draw closer; **~se con uno** to join sb.

junto, a [hōōn'to, á] *a* joined; (*unido*) united; (*anexo*) near, close; (*contiguo, próximo*) next, adjacent ♦ *nf* (*asamblea*) meeting, assembly; (*comité, consejo*) board, council, committee; (*MIL, POL*) junta; (*articulación*) joint ♦ *ad*: **todo ~** all at once ♦ *prep*: **~ a** near (to), next to; **~s** together; **junta constitutiva** (*COM*) statutory meeting; **junta directiva** (*COM*) board of directors; **junta general extraordinaria** (*COM*) special meeting (*US*), extraordinary general meeting (*Brit*).

juntura [hōōntōō'rá] *nf* (*punto de unión*) join, junction; (*articulación*) joint.

jura [hōō'rá] *nf* oath, pledge; **~ de bandera** (ceremony of taking the) pledge of allegiance.

jurado [hōōrá'tho] *nm* (*JUR: individuo*) juror; (: *grupo*) jury; (*de concurso: grupo*) panel (of judges); (: *individuo*) member of a panel.

juramentar [hōōrámentár'] *vt* to swear in, administer the oath to; **~se** *vr* to be sworn in, take the oath.

juramento [hōōrámen'to] *nm* oath; (*maldición*) oath, curse; **bajo ~** on oath; **prestar ~** to take the oath; **tomar ~ a** to swear in, administer the oath to.

jurar [hōōrár'] *vt, vi* to swear; **~ en falso** to commit perjury; **jurárselas a uno** to have it in for sb.

jurídico, a [hōōrē'thēko, á] *a* legal, juridical.

jurisdicción [hōōrēsthēksyon'] *nf* (*poder, autoridad*) jurisdiction; (*territorio*) district.

jurisprudencia [hōōrēsprōōthen'syá] *nf* jurisprudence.

jurista [hōōrē'stá] *nm/f* jurist.

justamente [hōōstámen'te] *ad* justly, fairly; (*precisamente*) just, exactly.

justicia [hōōstē'syá] *nf* justice; (*equidad*) fairness, justice; **de ~** deservedly.

justiciero, a [hōōstēsye'ro, á] *a* just, righteous.

justificable [hōōstēfēká'ḅle] *a* justifiable.

justificación [hōōstēfēkásyon'] *nf* justification; **~ automática** (*INFORM*) automatic justification.

justificado, a [hōōstēfēká'tho, á] *a* (*TIP*): **(no) ~** (un)justified.

justificante [hōōstēfēkán'te] *nm* voucher.

justificar [hōōstēfēkár'] *vt* (*tb TIP*) to justify; (*probar*) to verify.

justifique [hōōstēfē'ke] *etc vb* V **justificar**.

justo, a [hōō'sto, á] *a* (*equitativo*) just, fair, right; (*preciso*) exact, correct; (*ajustado*) tight ♦ *ad* (*precisamente*) exactly, precisely; (*apenas a tiempo*) just in time; **¡~!**

that's it!, correct!; **llegaste muy ~** you just made it; **vivir muy ~** to be hard up.
juvenil [hoohenēl'] a youthful.
juventud [hoohentooth'] nf (adolescencia) youth; (jóvenes) young people pl.
juzgado [hoosgá'tho] nm tribunal; (JUR) court.
juzgar [hoosgár'] vt to judge; **a ~ por** ... to judge by ..., judging by ...; **~ mal** to misjudge; **júzguelo usted mismo** see for yourself.
juzgue [hoos'ge] etv vb V juzgar.

K

K, k [ká] nf (letra) K, k; **K de Kilo** K for King.
K abr (= 1.000) K; (INFORM:=1.024) K.
Kampuchea [kámpootche'á] nf Kampuchea.
karate [kárá'te] nm karate.
k/c. abr (= kilociclos) kc.
Kenia [ke'nyá] nf Kenya.
keniata [kenyá'tá] a, nm/f Kenyan.
kg. abr (= kilogramo(s)) kg.
kilate [kēlá'te] nm = **quilate**.
kilo [kē'lo] nm kilo.
kilobyte [kē'loháēt] nm (INFORM) kilobyte.
kilogramo [kēlográ'mo] nm kilogram (US), kilogramme (Brit).
kilolitro [kēlolē'tro] nm kiloliter (US), kilolitre (Brit).
kilometraje [kēlometrá'he] nm distance in kilometres, ≈ mileage.
kilométrico, a [kēlome'trēko, á] a kilometric; (fam) very long; **(billete) ~** (FERRO) mileage ticket.
kilómetro [kēlo'metro] nm kilometer (US), kilometre (Brit).
kiloocteto [kēlookte'to] nm (INFORM) kilobyte.
kilovatio [kēlohá'tyo] nm kilowatt.
kiosco [kyos'ko] nm = **quiosco**.
km abr (= kilómetro(s)) km.
km/h abr (= kilómetros por hora) km/h.
knock-out [no'káoo], **K.O.** [ká'o] nm knockout; (golpe) knockout blow; **dejar o poner a uno ~** to knock sb out.
k.p.h. abr (= kilómetros por hora) km/h.
k.p.l. abr (= kilómetros por litro) ≈ m.p.g.
kv abr (= kilovatio) kw.
kv/h abr (= kilovatios-hora) kw-h.

L

L, l [e'le] nf (letra) L, l; **L de Lorenzo** L for Love.
l. abr (= litro(s)) l.; (JUR) = **ley**; (LITERATURA: = libro) bk.
L/ abr (COM) = **letra**.
la [lá] artículo definido fsg the ♦ pron her; (usted) you; (cosa) it ♦ nm (MUS) la; **está en ~ cárcel** he's in jail; **~ del sombrero rojo** the woman/girl/one in the red hat.
laberinto [láherēn'to] nm labyrinth.
labia [lá'hyá] nf fluency; (pey) glibness; **tener mucha ~** to have the gift of gab (US) o the gab (Brit).
labial [láhyál'] a labial.
labio [lá'hyo] nm lip; (de vasija etc) edge, rim; **~ inferior/superior** lower/upper lip.
labor [láhor'] nf labor (US), labour (Brit); (AGR) farm work; (tarea) job, task; (COSTURA) needlework, sewing; (punto) knitting; **~ de equipo** teamwork; **~ de ganchillo** crochet.
laborable [láhorá'hle] a (AGR) workable; **día ~** working day.
laborar [láhorár'] vi to work.
laboratorio [láhorátó'ryo] nm laboratory.
laborioso, a [láhoryo'so, á] a (persona) hard-working; (trabajo) tough.
laborista [láhorē'stá] (Brit POL) a: **Partido L~** Labour Party ♦ nm/f Labour Party member o supporter.
labrado, a [láhrá'tho, á] a worked; (madera) carved; (metal) wrought ♦ nm (AGR) cultivated field.
Labrador [láhráthor'] nm Labrador.
labrador, a [láhráthor', á] nm/f farmer.
labranza [láhrán'sá] nf (AGR) cultivation.
labrar [láhrár'] vt (gen) to work; (madera etc) to carve; (fig) to cause, bring about.
labriego, a [láhrye'go, á] nm/f peasant.
laca [lá'ká] nf lacquer; (de pelo) hairspray; **~ de uñas** nail polish.
lacayo [láká'yo] nm lackey.
lacerar [láserár'] vt to lacerate.
lacio, a [lá'syo, á] a (pelo) lank, straight.
lacón [lákon'] nm shoulder of pork.
lacónico, a [láko'nēko, á] a laconic.
lacrar [láhrár'] vt (cerrar) to seal (with sealing wax).
lacre [lá'kre] nm sealing wax.
lacrimógeno, a [lákrēmo'heno, á] a (fig) sentimental; **gas ~** tear gas.

lacrimoso, a [lákrēmo'so, á] *a* tearful.
lactar [láktár'] *vt*, *vi* to suckle, breast-feed.
lácteo, a [lák'teo, á] *a*: **productos** ~**s** dairy products.
ladear [láðeár'] *vt* to tip, tilt ♦ *vi* to tilt; ~**se** *vr* to lean; (*DEPORTE*) to swerve; (*AVIAT*) to bank, turn.
ladera [láðe'rá] *nf* slope.
ladino, a [láðē'no, á] *a* cunning.
lado [lá'ðo] *nm* (*gen*) side; (*fig*) protection; (*MIL*) flank; ~ **izquierdo** left(-hand) side; ~ **a** ~ side by side; **al** ~ **de** beside; **hacerse a un** ~ to stand aside; **poner de** ~ to put on its side; **poner a un** ~ to put aside; **me da de** ~ I don't care; **por un** ~ ..., **por otro** ~ ... on the one hand ..., on the other (hand), ...; **por todos** ~**s** on all sides, all round (*Brit*).
ladrar [láðrár'] *vi* to bark.
ladrido [láðrē'ðo] *nm* bark, barking.
ladrillo [láðrē'yo] *nm* (*gen*) brick; (*azulejo*) tile.
ladrón, ona [láðron', oná] *nm/f* thief.
lagar [lágár'] *nm* (wine/oil) press.
lagartija [lágártē'há] *nf* (small) lizard, wall lizard.
lagarto [lágár'to] *nm* (*ZOOL*) lizard.
lago [lá'go] *nm* lake.
Lagos [lá'gos] *nm* Lagos.
lágrima [lá'grēmá] *nf* tear.
lagrimear [lágrēmeár'] *vi* to weep; (*ojos*) to water.
laguna [lágoo'ná] *nf* (*lago*) lagoon; (*en escrito, conocimientos*) gap.
laico, a [lá'ēko, á] *a* lay ♦ *nm/f* layman/woman.
lameculos [lámekoo'los] *nm/f inv* (*fam*) crawler.
lamentable [lámentá'ble] *a* lamentable, regrettable; (*miserable*) pitiful.
lamentación [lámentásyon'] *nf* lamentation; **ahora no sirven lamentaciones** it's no good crying over spilt milk.
lamentar [lámentár'] *vt* (*sentir*) to regret; (*deplorar*) to lament; ~**se** *vr* to lament; **lo lamento mucho** I'm very sorry.
lamento [lámen'to] *nm* lament.
lamer [lámer'] *vt* to lick.
lámina [lá'mēná] *nf* (*plancha delgada*) sheet; (*para estampar, estampa*) plate; (*grabado*) engraving.
laminar [lámēnár'] *vt* (*en libro*) to laminate; (*TEC*) to roll.
lámpara [lám'párá] *nf* lamp; ~ **de alcohol/gas** alcohol (*US*) *o* spirit (*Brit*)/gas lamp; ~ **de pie** floor (*US*) *o* standard (*Brit*) lamp.
lamparilla [lámpárē'yá] *nf* nightlight.
lamparón [lámpáron'] *nm* (*MED*) scrofula; (*mancha*) (large) grease spot.
lampiño, a [lámpē'nyo, á] *a* (*sin pelo*) hairless.

lana [lá'ná] *nf* wool; (*tela*) woolen (*US*) *o* woollen (*Brit*) cloth; (**hecho**) **de** ~ wool *cpd*.
lance [lán'se] *etc vb V* **lanzar** ♦ *nm* (*golpe*) stroke; (*suceso*) event, incident.
lancha [lántch'á] *nf* launch; ~ **motora** motorboat; ~ **de pesca** fishing boat; ~ **salvavidas/torpedera** lifeboat/torpedo boat; ~ **neumática** rubber raft (*US*) *o* dinghy (*Brit*).
Landas [lán'dás] *nfpl*: **las** ~ Landes *sg*.
lanero, a [láne'ro, á] *a* wool *cpd*.
langosta [lángo'stá] *nf* (*insecto*) locust; (*crustáceo*) lobster (: *de río*) crayfish.
langostino [lángostē'no] *nm* prawn; (*de agua dulce*) crayfish.
languidecer [lángēðeser'] *vi* to languish.
languidez [lángēðes'] *nf* languor.
languidezca [lángēðes'ká] *etc vb V* **languidecer**.
lánguido, a [lán'gēðo, á] *a* (*gen*) languid; (*sin energía*) listless.
lanilla [lánē'yá] *nf* nap; (*tela*) thin flannel cloth.
lanolina [lánolē'ná] *nf* lanolin(e).
lanudo, a [lánoo'ðo, á] *a* wooly (*US*), woolly (*Brit*), fleecy.
lanza [lán'sá] *nf* (*arma*) lance, spear; **medir** ~**s** to cross swords.
lanzabombas [lánsábom'bás] *nm inv* (*AVIAT*) bomb release; (*MIL*) mortar.
lanzacohetes [lánsákoe'tes] *nm inv* rocket launcher.
lanzadera [lánsáðe'rá] *nf* shuttle.
lanzallamas [lánsáyá'más] *nm inv* flame-thrower.
lanzamiento [lánsámyen'to] *nm* (*gen*) throwing; (*NAUT, COM*) launch, launching; ~ **de pesos** putting the shot.
lanzar [lánsár'] *vt* (*gen*) to throw; (*con violencia*) to fling; (*DEPORTE*: *pelota*) to bowl; (: *US*) to pitch; (*NAUT, COM*) to launch; (*JUR*) to evict; (*grito*) to give, utter; ~**se** *vr* to throw o.s.; (*fig*) to take the plunge; ~**se a** (*fig*) to embark upon.
Lanzarote [lánsáro'te] *nm* Lanzarote.
lanzatorpedos [lánsátorpe'ðos] *nm inv* torpedo tube.
lapa [lá'pá] *nf* limpet.
La Paz *nf* La Paz.
lapicero [lápēse'ro] *nm* mechanical (*US*) *o* propelling (*Brit*) pencil; (*AM*: *bolígrafo*) ballpoint pen.
lápida [lá'pēðá] *nf* stone; ~ **conmemorativa** memorial stone; ~ **mortuoria** headstone.
lapidar [lápēðár'] *vt* to stone; (*TEC*) to polish, lap.
lapidario, a [lápēðá'ryo, á] *a*, *nm* lapidary.
lápiz [lá'pēs] *nm* pencil; ~ **de color** colored pencil; ~ **de labios** lipstick; ~ **óptico** *o* **luminoso** light pen.

lapón, ona [lápon', oná] *a* Lapp ♦ *nm/f* Lap-lander, Lapp ♦ *nm* (*LING*) Lapp.
Laponia [lápo'nyá] *nf* Lapland.
lapso [láp'so] *nm* lapse; (*error*) error; ~ **de tiempo** interval of time.
lapsus [láp'sōos] *nm inv* error, mistake.
LAR [lár] *nf abr* (*Esp JUR*) = *Ley de Arrendamientos Rústicos.*
largamente [lárgámen'te] *ad* for a long time; (*relatar*) at length.
largar [lárgár'] *vt* (*soltar*) to release; (*aflojar*) to loosen; (*lanzar*) to launch; (*fam*) to let fly; (*velas*) to unfurl; (*AM*) to throw; ~**se** *vr* (*fam*) to beat it; ~**se a** (*AM*) to start to.
largo, a [lár'go, á] *a* (*longitud*) long; (*tiempo*) lengthy; (*persona: alta*) tall; (: *fig*) generous ♦ *nm* length; (*MUS*) largo; **dos años** ~**s** two long years; **a** ~ **plazo** in the long term; **tiene 9 metros de** ~ it is 9 meters long; **a lo** ~ (*posición*) lengthways; **a lo** ~ **de** along; (*tiempo*) all through, throughout; **a la larga** in the long run; **me dio largas con una promesa** she put me off with a promise; **¡**~ **de aquí!** (*fam*) beat it!
largometraje [lárgometrá'he] *nm* full-length *o* feature film.
largue [lár'ge] *etc vb V* **largar.**
larguero [lárge'ro] *nm* (*ARQ*) main beam, chief support; (*de puerta*) jamb; (*DEPORTE*) crossbar; (*en cama*) bolster.
largueza [lárge'sá] *nf* generosity.
larguirucho, a [lárgēróotch'o, á] *a* lanky, gangling.
larguísimo, a [lárge'sēmo, á] *a superlativo de* **largo.**
largura [lárgōo'rá] *nf* length.
laringe [lárēn'he] *nf* larynx.
laringitis [lárēnhē'tēs] *nf* laryngitis.
larva [lár'há] *nf* larva.
las [lás] *artículo definido fpl* the ♦ *pron* them; ~ **que cantan** the ones/women/girls who sing.
lasca [lás'ká] *nf* chip of stone.
lascivia [lásē'hyá] *nf* lewdness; (*lujuria*) lust; (*fig*) playfulness.
lascivo, a [lásē'ho, á] *a* lewd.
láser [lá'ser] *nm* laser.
Las Palmas *nf* Las Palmas.
lástima [lá'stēmá] *nf* (*pena*) pity; **dar** ~ to be pitiful; **es una** ~ **que** it's a pity that; **¡qué** ~**!** what a pity!; **estar hecho una** ~ to be a sorry sight.
lastimar [lástēmár'] *vt* (*herir*) to wound; (*ofender*) to offend; ~**se** *vr* to hurt o.s.
lastimero, a [lástēme'ro, á] *a* pitiful, pathetic.
lastre [lás'tre] *nm* (*TEC, NAUT*) ballast; (*fig*) dead weight.
lata [lá'tá] *nf* (*metal*) tin; (*envase*) can; (*fam*) nuisance; **en** ~ canned; **dar (la)** ~

to be a nuisance.
latente [láten'te] *a* latent.
lateral [láterál'] *a* side, lateral ♦ *nm* (*TEATRO*) wings *pl.*
latido [látē'tho] *nm* (*del corazón*) beat; (*de herida*) throb(bing).
latifundio [látēfōon'dyo] *nm* large estate.
latifundista [látēfōondē'stá] *nm/f* owner of a large estate.
latigazo [látēgá'so] *nm* (*golpe*) lash; (*sonido*) crack; (*fig: regaño*) dressing-down.
látigo [lá'tēgo] *nm* whip.
latiguillo [látēgē'yo] *nm* (*TEATRO*) hamming.
latín [látēn'] *nm* Latin; **saber (mucho)** ~ (*fam*) to be pretty sharp.
latinajo [látēná'ho] *nm* bad Latin; **echar** ~**s** to come out with Latin words.
latino, a [látē'no, á] *a* Latin.
Latinoamérica [látēnoáme'rēká] *nf* Latin America.
latinoamericano, a [látēnoámerēká'no, á] *a, nm/f* Latin American.
latir [látēr'] *vi* (*corazón, pulso*) to beat.
latitud [látētōoth'] *nf* (*GEO*) latitude; (*fig*) breadth, extent.
lato, a [lá'to, á] *a* broad.
latón [láton'] *nm* brass.
latoso, a [láto'so, á] *a* (*molesto*) annoying; (*aburrido*) boring.
latrocinio [látrosē'nyo] *nm* robbery.
LAU *nf abr* (*Esp JUR*)=*Ley de Arrendamientos Urbanos.*
laúd [láōoth'] *nm* lute.
laudatorio, a [láōotháto'ryo, á] *a* laudatory.
laudo [lá'ōotho] *nm* (*JUR*) decision, finding.
laurear [láōoreár'] *vt* to honor (*US*), honour (*Brit*), reward.
laurel [láōorel'] *nm* (*BOT*) laurel; (*CULIN*) bay.
Lausana [láōosá'ná] *nf* Lausanne.
lava [lá'há] *nf* lava.
lavable [láhá'hle] *a* washable.
lavabo [láhá'ho] *nm* (*jofaina*) washbasin; (*retrete*)washroom (*US*), lavatory (*Brit*).
lavadero [láháthe'ro] *nm* laundry.
lavado [láhá'tho] *nm* washing; (*de ropa*) wash, laundry; (*ARTE*) wash; ~ **de cerebro** brainwashing.
lavadora [láhátho'rá] *nf* washing machine.
lavamanos [láhámá'nos] *nm inv* washbasin.
lavanda [láhán'dá] *nf* lavender.
lavandería [láhánderē'á] *nf* laundry; ~ **automática** laundromat (*US*), launderette (*Brit*).
lavaparabrisas [láhápáráhrē'sás] *nm inv* windshield (*US*) *o* windscreen (*Brit*) washer.
lavaplatos [láháplá'tos] *nm inv* dishwasher.
lavar [láhár'] *vt* to wash; (*borrar*) to wipe away; ~**se** *vr* to wash o.s.; ~**se las manos**

to wash one's hands; (*fig*) to wash one's hands of it; ~ **y marcar** (*pelo*) to shampoo and set; ~ **en seco** to dry-clean.

lavativa [láƀátē'ƀá] *nf* (*MED*) enema.

lavavajillas [láƀáƀáhē'yás] *nm inv* dishwasher.

laxante [láksán'te] *nm* laxative.

laxitud [láksētōōᵗ] *nf* laxity, slackness.

lazada [lásá'ᵗᵗá] *nf* bow.

lazarillo [lásárē'yo] *nm*: **perro de** ~ guide dog.

lazo [lá'so] *nm* knot; (*lazada*) bow; (*para animales*) lasso; (*trampa*) snare; (*vínculo*) tie; ~ **corredizo** slipknot.

LBE *nf abr* (*Esp JUR*)=*Ley Básica de Empleo*.

lb(s) *abr* = *libra(s)*.

L/C *abr* (= *Letra de Crédito*) B/E.

Lda., Ldo. *abr* = **Licenciado, a.**

le [le] *pron* (*directo*) him (*o* her); (: *usted*) you; (*indirecto*) to him (*o* her *o* it); (: *usted*) to you.

leal [leál'] *a* loyal.

lealtad [leáltáᵗ'] *nf* loyalty.

lebrel [leƀrel'] *nm* greyhound.

lección [leksyon'] *nf* lesson; ~ **práctica** object lesson; **dar lecciones** to teach, give lessons; **dar una** ~ **a uno** (*fig*) to teach sb a lesson.

lector, a [lektor', á] *nm/f* reader; (*ESCOL, UNIV*) (conversation) assistant ♦ *nm*: ~ **óptico de caracteres** (*INFORM*) optical character reader ♦ *nf*: ~**a de fichas** (*INFORM*) card reader.

lectura [lektōō'rá] *nf* reading; ~ **de marcas sensibles** (*INFORM*) mark sensing.

leche [letch'e] *nf* milk; (*fam!*) semen, spunk(*!*); **dar una** ~ **a uno** (*fam*) to belt sb; **estar de mala** ~ (*fam*) to be in a foul mood; **tener mala** ~ (*fam*) to be spiteful; ~ **condensada/en polvo** condensed/powdered milk; ~ **desnatada** skimmed milk; ~ **de magnesia** milk of magnesia; ¡~! hell!

lechera [letche'rá] *nf V* **lechero.**

lechería [letcherē'á] *nf* dairy.

lecherita [letcherē'tá] *nf* milk jug.

lechero, a [letche'ro, á] *a* milk *cpd* ♦ *nm* milkman ♦ *nf* (*vendedora*) milkmaid; (*recipiente*) milk pan; (*para servir*) milk churn; (*AM*) cow.

lecho [letch'o] *nm* (*cama, de río*) bed; (*GEO*) layer; ~ **mortuorio** deathbed.

lechón [letchon'] *nm* suckling (*US*) *o* sucking (*Brit*) pig.

lechoso, a [letcho'so, á] *a* milky.

lechuga [letchōō'ǥá] *nf* lettuce.

lechuza [letchōō'sá] *nf* (barn) owl.

leer [leer'] *vt* to read; ~ **entre líneas** to read between the lines.

legación [leǥásyon'] *nf* legation.

legado [leǥá'ᵗᵗo] *nm* (*don*) bequest; (*herencia*) legacy; (*enviado*) legate.

legajo [leǥá'ho] *nm* file, bundle (of papers).

legal [leǥál'] *a* legal, lawful; (*persona*) trustworthy.

legalice [leǥálē'se] *etc vb V* **legalizar.**

legalidad [leǥálēᵗáᵗ'] *nf* legality.

legalizar [leǥálēsár'] *vt* to legalize; (*documento*) to authenticate.

legaña [leǥá'nyá] *nf* sleep (*in eyes*).

legar [leǥár'] *vt* to bequeath, leave.

legatario, a [leǥátá'ryo, á] *nm/f* legatee.

legendario, a [lehendá'ryo, á] *a* legendary.

legible [lehē'ƀle] *a* legible; ~ **por máquina** (*INFORM*) machine-readable.

legión [lehyon'] *nf* legion.

legionario, a [lehyoná'ryo, á] *a* legionary ♦ *nm* legionnaire.

legislación [lehēslásyon'] *nf* legislation; (*leyes*) laws *pl*; ~ **antimonopolio** (*COM*) anti-trust legislation.

legislar [lehēslár'] *vt* to legislate.

legislativo, a [lehēslátē'ƀo, á] *a*: (**elecciones) legislativas** ≈ general elections.

legitimar [lehētēmár'] *vt* to legitimize.

legítimo, a [lehē'tēmo, á] *a* (*genuino*) authentic; (*legal*) legitimate, rightful.

lego, a [le'ǥo, á] *a* (*REL*) secular; (*ignorante*) ignorant ♦ *nm* layman.

legua [le'ǥwá] *nf* league; **se ve** (*o* **nota) a la** ~ you can tell (it) a mile off.

legue [le'ǥe] *etc vb V* **legar.**

leguleyo [leǥōōle'yo] *nm* (*pey*) shyster (*US*) *o* petty (*Brit*) lawyer.

legumbres [leǥōōm'bres] *nfpl* vegetables.

leído, a [leē'ᵗᵗo, á] *a* well-read.

lejanía [lehánē'á] *nf* distance.

lejano, a [lehá'no, á] *a* far-off; (*en el tiempo*) distant; (*fig*) remote; **L~ Oriente** Far East.

lejía [lehē'á] *nf* bleach.

lejísimos [lehē'sēmos] *ad* a long, long way.

lejos [le'hos] *ad* far, far away; **a lo** ~ in the distance; **de** *o* **desde** ~ from afar; **está muy** ~ it's a long way (away); ¿**está** ~? is it far?; ~ **de** *prep* far from.

lelo, a [le'lo, á] *a* silly ♦ *nm/f* idiot.

lema [le'má] *nm* motto; (*POL*) slogan.

lencería [lenserē'á] *nf* (*telas*) linen, drapery; (*ropa interior*) lingerie.

lendakari [lendáká'rē] *nm* head of the Basque Autonomous Government.

lengua [len'gwá] *nf* tongue; ~ **materna** mother tongue; ~ **de tierra** (*GEO*) spit *o* tongue of land; **dar a la** ~ to chatter; **morderse la** ~ to hold one's tongue; **sacar la** ~ **a uno** to stick one's tongue out at sb.

lenguado [lengwá'ᵗᵗo] *nm* sole.

lenguaje [lengwá'he] *nm* language; (*forma de hablar*) (mode of) speech; ~ **comercial** business language; ~ **ensamblador/de alto**

nivel (*INFORM*) assembly/high-level language; ~ **máquina** (*INFORM*) machine language; ~ **original** source language; ~ **periodístico** journalese; ~ **de programación** (*INFORM*) programming language; **en** ~ **llano** ≈ in plain English.

lenguaraz [lengwáráš'] *a* talkative; (*pey*) foul-mouthed.

lengüeta [lengwe'tá] *nf* (*ANAT*) epiglottis; (*de zapatos*) tongue; (*MUS*) reed.

lenidad [lenéthǎth'] *nf* lenience.

Leningrado [lenēngrá'ðo] *nm* Leningrad.

lente [len'te] *nm o nf* lens; (*lupa*) magnifying glass; ~s *pl* glasses; ~s **de contacto** contact lenses.

lenteja [lente'há] *nf* lentil.

lentejuela [lentehwe'lá] *nf* sequin.

lentilla [lentē'yá] *nf* contact lens.

lentitud [lentētōōth'] *nf* slowness; **con** ~ slowly.

lento, a [len'to, á] *a* slow.

leña [le'nyá] *nf* firewood; **dar** ~ **a** to thrash; **echar** ~ **al fuego** to add fuel to the flames.

leñador, a [lenyáthor', á] *nm/f* woodcutter.

leño [le'nyo] *nm* (*trozo de árbol*) log; (*madera*) timber; (*fig*) blockhead.

Leo [le'o] *nm* (*ASTRO*) Leo.

león [leon'] *nm* lion; ~ **marino** sea lion.

leonera [leone'rá] *nf* (*jaula*) lion's cage; **parece una** ~ it's shockingly dirty.

leonés, esa [leones', esá] *a, nm/f* Leonese ♦ *nm* (*LING*) Leonese.

leonino, a [leonē'no, á] *a* leonine.

leontina [leontē'ná] *nf* watch chain.

leopardo [leopár'ðo] *nm* leopard.

leotardos [leotár'ðos] *nmpl* tights.

lepra [le'prá] *nf* leprosy.

leproso, a [lepro'so, á] *nm/f* leper.

lerdo, a [ler'ðo, á] *a* (*lento*) slow; (*patoso*) clumsy.

leridano, a [leríthǎ'no, á] *a* of o from Lérida ♦ *nm/f* native o inhabitant of Lérida.

les [les] *pron* (*directo*) them; (: *ustedes*) you; (*indirecto*) to them; (: *ustedes*) to you.

lesbiana [leshyá'ná] *nf* lesbian.

lesión [lesyon'] *nf* wound, lesion; (*DEPORTE*) injury.

lesionado, a [lesyoná'ðo, á] *a* injured ♦ *nm/f* injured person.

lesionar [lesyonár'] *vt* (*dañar*) to hurt; (*herir*) to wound; ~**se** *vr* to get hurt.

letal [letál'] *a* lethal.

letanía [letánē'á] *nf* litany; (*retahíla*) long list.

letárgico, a [letár'hēko, á] *a* lethargic.

letargo [letár'go] *nm* lethargy.

Letonia [leto'nyá] *nf* Latvia.

letra [le'trá] *nf* letter; (*escritura*) handwriting; (*COM*) letter, bill, draft; (*MUS*) lyrics *pl*; ~**s** *nfpl* (*UNIV*) arts; ~ **bastar-**

dilla/negrilla italics *pl*/bold type; ~ **de cambio** bill of exchange; ~ **de imprenta** print; ~ **inicial/mayúscula/minúscula** initial/capital/small letter; **lo tomó al pie de la** ~ he took it literally; ~ **bancaria** (*COM*) bank draft; ~ **de patente** (*COM*) letters patent *pl*; **escribir 4** ~**s a uno** to drop a line to sb.

letrado, a [letrá'ðo, á] *a* learned; (*fam*) pedantic ♦ *nm/f* lawyer.

letrero [letre'ro] *nm* (*cartel*) sign; (*etiqueta*) label.

letrina [letrē'ná] *nf* latrine.

leucemia [leōōse'myá] *nf* leukemia (*US*), leukaemia (*Brit*).

leva [le'há] *nf* (*NAUT*) weighing anchor; (*MIL*) recruiting; (*TEC*) lever.

levadizo, a [leháthē'so, á] *a*: **puente** ~ drawbridge.

levadura [leháthōō'rá] *nf* yeast, leaven; ~ **de cerveza** brewer's yeast.

levantamiento [lehántámyen'to] *nm* raising, lifting; (*rebelión*) revolt, uprising; (*GEO*) survey; ~ **de pesos** weightlifting.

levantar [lehántár'] *vt* (*gen*) to raise; (*del suelo*) to pick up; (*hacia arriba*) to lift (up); (*plan*) to make, draw up; (*mesa*) to clear; (*campamento*) to strike; (*fig*) to cheer up, hearten; ~**se** *vr* to get up; (*enderezarse*) to straighten up; (*rebelarse*) to rebel; (*sesión*) to be adjourned; (*niebla*) to lift; (*viento*) to rise; ~**se** (**de la cama**) to get up, get out of bed; ~ **el ánimo** to cheer up.

levante [lehán'te] *nm* east; (*viento*) east wind; **el L**~ *region of Spain extending from Castellón to Murcia*.

levantino, a [lehántē'no, á] *a* of o from the *Levante* ♦ *nm/f*: **los** ~**s** the people of the *Levante*.

levar [lehár'] *vi* to weigh anchor.

leve [le'he] *a* light; (*fig*) trivial; (*mínimo*) slight.

levedad [lehethǎth'] *nf* lightness; (*fig*) levity.

levita [lehē'tá] *nf* frock coat.

léxico, a [lek'sēko, á] *a* lexical ♦ *nm* (*vocabulario*) vocabulary; (*LING*) lexicon.

ley [lēē] *nf* (*gen*) law; (*metal*) standard; **decreto-**~ decree law; **de buena** ~ (*fig*) genuine; **según la** ~ in accordance with the law, by law, in law.

leyenda [leyen'dá] *nf* legend; (*TIP*) inscription.

leyendo [leyen'do] *etc vb* V **leer.**

liar [lēár'] *vt* to tie (up); (*unir*) to bind; (*envolver*) to wrap (up); (*enredar*) to confuse; (*cigarrillo*) to roll; ~**se** *vr* (*fam*) to get involved; (*confundirse*) to get mixed up; ~**se a palos** to get involved in a fight.

lib. *abr* (= *libro*) bk.

libanés, esa [lĕḫánes', esá] *a, nm/f* Lebanese.

Líbano [lē'ḫáno] *nm*: **el ~** the Lebanon.

libar [lēḫár'] *vt* to suck.

libelo [lēḫe'lo] *nm* satire, lampoon; (*JUR*) petition.

libélula [lēḫe'lōōlá] *nf* dragonfly.

liberación [lēḫerásyon'] *nf* liberation; (*de la cárcel*) release.

liberado, a [lēḫerá'ᵹo, á] *a* liberated; (*COM*) paid-up.

liberal [lēḫerál'] *a, nm/f* liberal.

liberalidad [lēḫerálēᵹáᵹ'] *nf* liberality, generosity.

liberar [lēḫerár'] *vt* to liberate.

libertad [lēḫertáᵹ'] *nf* liberty, freedom; **~ de asociación/de culto/de prensa/de comercio/de palabra** freedom of association/of worship/of the press/of trade/of speech; **~ condicional** probation; **~ bajo palabra** parole; **~ bajo fianza** bail; **estar en ~** to be free; **poner a uno en ~** to set sb free.

libertador, a [lēḫertáᵹor', á] *a* liberating ♦ *nm/f* liberator.

libertar [lēḫertár'] *vt* (*preso*) to set free; (*de una obligación*) to release; (*eximir*) to exempt.

libertino, a [lēḫertē'no, á] *a* permissive ♦ *nm/f* permissive person.

Libia [lē'ḫyá] *nf* Libya.

libio, a [lē'ḫyo, á] *a, nm/f* Libyan.

libra [lē'ḫrá] *nf* pound; **L~** (*ASTRO*) Libra; **~ esterlina** pound sterling.

librador, a [lēḫráᵹor', á] *nm/f* drawer.

libramiento [lēḫrámyen'to] *nm* rescue; (*COM*) delivery.

libranza [lēḫrán'sá] *nf* (*COM*) draft; (*letra de cambio*) bill of exchange.

librar [lēḫrár'] *vt* (*de peligro*) to save; (*batalla*) to wage, fight; (*de impuestos*) to exempt; (*cheque*) to make out; (*JUR*) to exempt; **~se** *vr*: **~se de** to escape from, free o.s. from; **de buena nos hemos librado** we're well out of that.

libre [lē'ḫre] *a* (*gen*) free; (*lugar*) unoccupied; (*tiempo*) spare; (*asiento*) vacant; (*COM*): **~ a bordo** free on board; **~ de franqueo** postage-free; **~ de impuestos** free of tax; **tiro ~** free kick; **los 100 metros ~** the 100 meters free-style (race); **al aire ~** in the open air; **¿estás ~?** are you free?

librecambio [lēḫrekám'byo] *nm* free trade.

librecambista [lēḫrekámbē'stá] *a* free-trade *cpd* ♦ *nm* free-trader.

librería [lēḫrerē'á] *nf* (*tienda*) bookstore (*US*), bookshop (*Brit*); (*estante*) bookcase; **~ de ocasión** secondhand bookshop.

librero, a [lēḫre'ro, á] *nm/f* bookseller.

libreta [lēḫre'tá] *nf* notebook; (*pan*) one-pound loaf; **~ de ahorros** savings book.

libro [lē'ḫro] *nm* book; **~ de actas** minute book; **~ de bolsillo** paperback; **~ de cabecera** bedside book; **~ de caja** (*COM*) cashbook; **~ de caja auxiliar** (*COM*) petty cash book; **~ de cocina** cookbook; **~ de consulta** reference book; **~ de cuentas** account book; **~ de cuentos** storybook; **~ de cheques** check (*US*) o cheque (*Brit*) book; **~ diario** journal; **~ de entradas y salidas** (*COM*) daybook; **~ de honor** visitors' book; **~ mayor** (*COM*) general ledger; **~ de reclamaciones** complaints book; **~ de texto** textbook.

Lic. *abr* = **Licenciado, a.**

licencia [lēsen'syá] *nf* (*gen*) license (*US*), licence (*Brit*); (*permiso*) permission; **~ por enfermedad/con goce de sueldo** sick/paid leave; **~ de armas/de caza** gun/game license; **~ de exportación** (*COM*) export license; **~ poética** poetic license.

licenciado, a [lēsensyá'ᵹo, á] *a* licensed ♦ *nm/f* graduate; **L~ en Filosofía y Letras** Bachelor of Arts.

licenciar [lēsensyár'] *vt* (*empleado*) to dismiss; (*permitir*) to permit, allow; (*soldado*) to discharge; (*estudiante*) to confer a degree upon; **~se** *vr*: **~se en letras** to get an arts degree.

licenciatura [lēsensyátōō'rá] *nf* (*título*) degree; (*estudios*) course of study (*US*), degree course (*Brit*).

licencioso, a [lēsensyo'so, á] *a* licentious.

liceo [lēse'o] *nm* (high) school.

licitación [lēsētásyon'] *nf* bidding; (*oferta*) tender, offer.

licitador [lēsētáᵹor'] *nm* bidder; (*AM*) auctioneer.

licitante [lēsētán'te] *nm* bidder.

licitar [lēsētár'] *vt* to bid for; (*AM*) to sell by auction ♦ *vi* to bid.

lícito, a [lē'sēto, á] *a* (*legal*) lawful; (*justo*) fair, just; (*permisible*) permissible.

licor [lēkor'] *nm* liquor (*US*), spirits *pl* (*Brit*); (*con hierbas etc*) liqueur.

licuadora [lēkwáᵹo'rá] *nf* blender.

licuar [lēkwár'] *vt* to liquidize.

lid [lēᵹ] *nf* combat; (*fig*) controversy.

líder [lē'ᵹer] *nm/f* leader.

liderato [lēᵹerá'to] *nm* leadership.

lidia [lē'ᵹyá] *nf* bullfighting; (*una ~*) bullfight; **toros de ~** fighting bulls.

lidiar [lēᵹyár'] *vt, vi* to fight.

liebre [lye'ḫre] *nf* hare; **dar gato por ~** to con.

Lieja [lye'há] *nf* Liège.

lienzo [lyen'so] *nm* linen; (*ARTE*) canvas; (*ARQ*) wall.

lifting [lēf'tēn] *nm* facelift.

liga [lē'ᵹá] *nf* (*de medias*) garter, suspender; (*confederación*) league; (*AM*: *gomita*) rubber band.

ligadura [lēgàt̪ʰōō'rà] *nf* bond, tie; (*MED*, *MUS*) ligature.

ligamento [lēgámen'to] *nm* (*ANAT*) ligament; (*atadura*) tie; (*unión*) bond.

ligar [lēgàr'] *vt* (*atar*) to tie; (*unir*) to join; (*MED*) to bind up; (*MUS*) to slur; (*fam*) to get off with, pick up ♦ *vi* to mix, blend; (*fam*) to get off with sb; (*2 personas*) to get off with one another; ~**se** *vr* (*fig*) to commit o.s.; ~ **con** (*fam*) to get off with, pick up; ~**se a uno** to get off with o pick up sb.

ligereza [lēchere'sà] *nf* lightness; (*rapidez*) swiftness; (*agilidad*) agility; (*superficialidad*) flippancy.

ligero, a [lēche'ro, à] *a* (*de peso*) light; (*tela*) thin; (*rápido*) swift, quick; (*ágil*) agile, nimble; (*de importancia*) slight; (*de carácter*) flippant, superficial ♦ *ad* quickly, swiftly; **a la ligera** superficially; **juzgar a la ligera** to jump to conclusions.

ligón [lēgon'] *nm* (*fam*) Romeo.

ligue [lē'ge] *etc vb* **V ligar** ♦ *nm/f* boyfriend/girlfriend ♦ *nm* (*persona*) pick-up.

liguero [lēge'ro] *nm* garter (*US*) o suspender (*Brit*) belt.

lija [lē'hà] *nf* (*ZOOL*) dogfish; (**papel de**) ~ sandpaper.

Lila [lē'là] *nf* Lille.

lila [lē'là] *a inv, nf* lilac ♦ *nm* (*fam*) twit.

lima [lē'mà] *nf* file; (*BOT*) lime; ~ **de uñas** nail file; **comer como una** ~ to eat like a horse.

limar [lēmàr'] *vt* to file; (*alisar*) to smooth over; (*fig*) to polish up.

limitación [lēmētàsyon'] *nf* limitation, limit; ~ **de velocidad** speed limit.

limitado, a [lēmētà'tho, à] *a* limited; **sociedad limitada** (*COM*) corporation (*US*), limited company (*Brit*).

limitar [lēmētàr'] *vt* to limit; (*reducir*) to reduce, cut down ♦ *vi*: ~ **con** to border on; ~**se** *vr*: ~**se a** to limit o confine o.s. to.

límite [lē'mēte] *nm* (*gen*) limit; (*fin*) end; (*frontera*) border; **como** ~ at (the) most; (*fecha*) at the latest; **no tener** ~**s** to know no bounds; ~ **de crédito** (*COM*) credit limit; ~ **de página** (*INFORM*) page break; ~ **de velocidad** speed limit.

limítrofe [lēmē'trofe] *a* neighboring (*US*), neighbouring (*Brit*).

limón [lēmon'] *nm* lemon ♦ *a*: **amarillo** ~ lemon-yellow.

limonada [lēmonà'thà] *nf* lemonade.

limonero [lēmone'ro] *nm* lemon tree.

limosna [lēmos'nà] *nf* alms *pl*; **pedir** ~ to beg; **vivir de** ~ to live on charity.

limpiabotas [lēmpyàbo'tàs] *nm/f inv* shoeshine boy/girl.

limpiacristales [lēmpyàkrēstà'les] *nm inv*

(*detergente*) window cleaner.

limpiador, a [lēmpyàtʰor', à] *a* cleaning, cleansing ♦ *nm/f* cleaner.

limpiaparabrisas [lēmpyàpàràbrē'sàs] *nm inv* windshield (*US*) o windscreen (*Brit*) wiper.

limpiar [lēmpyàr'] *vt* to clean; (*con trapo*) to wipe; (*quitar*) to wipe away; (*zapatos*) to shine, polish; (*casa*) to tidy up; (*fig*) to clean up; (: *purificar*) to cleanse, purify; (*MIL*) to mop up; ~ **en seco** to dry-clean.

limpieza [lēmpye'sà] *nf* (*estado*) cleanliness; (*acto*) cleaning; (: *de las calles*) cleansing; (: *de zapatos*) polishing; (*habilidad*) skill; (*fig*: *POLICIA*) clean-up; (*pureza*) purity; (*MIL*): **operación de** ~ mopping-up operation; ~ **en seco** dry cleaning.

limpio, a [lēm'pyo, à] *a* clean; (*moralmente*) pure; (*ordenado*) tidy; (*despejado*) clear; (*COM*) clear, net; (*fam*) honest ♦ *ad*: **jugar** ~ to play fair; **pasar a** (*Esp*) o **en** (*AM*) ~ to make a clean (*US*) o fair (*Brit*) copy; **sacar algo en** ~ to get benefit from sth; ~ **de** free from.

linaje [lēnà'he] *nm* lineage, family.

linajudo, a [lēnàhōō'tho, à] *a* highborn, noble.

linaza [lēnà'sà] *nf* linseed; **aceite de** ~ linseed oil.

lince [lēn'se] *nm* lynx; **ser un** ~ (*fig*: *observador*) to be very observant; (: *astuto*) to be shrewd.

linchar [lēntchàr'] *vt* to lynch.

lindante [lēndàn'te] *a* adjoining; ~ **con** bordering on.

lindar [lēndàr'] *vi* to adjoin; ~ **con** to border on; (*ARQ*) to abut on.

linde [lēn'de] *nm o nf* boundary.

lindero, a [lēnde'ro, à] *a* adjoining ♦ *nm* boundary.

lindo, a [lēn'do, à] *a* pretty, lovely ♦ *ad*: **nos divertimos de lo** ~ we had a wonderful time; **canta muy** ~ (*AM*) he sings beautifully.

línea [lē'neà] *nf* (*gen, moral, POL etc*) line; (*talle*) figure; (*INFORM*): **en** ~ on-line; **fuera de** ~ off line; ~ **de estado** status line; ~ **de formato** format line; ~ **aérea** airline; ~ **de alto el fuego** ceasefire line; ~ **de fuego** firing line; ~ **de meta** goal line; (*de carrera*) finishing line; ~ **de montaje** assembly line; ~ **dura** (*POL*) hard line; ~ **recta** straight line; **la** ~ **de 1989** (*moda*) the 1989 look.

lineal [lēneàl'] *a* linear; (*INFORM*) on-line.

lingote [lēngo'te] *nm* ingot.

lingüista [lēngwē'stà] *nm/f* linguist.

lingüística [lēngwē'stēkà] *nf* linguistics *sg*.

linimento [lēnēmen'to] *nm* liniment.

lino [lē'no] *nm* linen; (*BOT*) flax.

linóleo [lēno'leo] *nm* linoleum.

linterna [lēnter'nà] *nf* lantern, lamp; ~ **eléctrica** *o* **a pilas** flashlight (*US*), torch (*Brit*).

lío [lē'o] *nm* bundle; (*desorden*) muddle, mess; (*fam: follón*) fuss; (: *relación amorosa*) affair; **armar un** ~ to make a fuss; **meterse en un** ~ to get into a jam; **tener un** ~ **con uno** to be having an affair with sb.

liquen [lē'ken] *nm* lichen.

liquidación [lēkēthàsyon'] *nf* liquidation; (*cuenta*) settlement; **venta de** ~ clearance sale.

liquidar [lēkēthàr'] *vt* (*QUÍMICA*) to liquefy; (*COM*) to liquidate; (*deudas*) to pay off; (*empresa*) to sell off; ~ **a uno** to bump sb off, rub sb out (*fam*).

líquido, a [lē'kētho, à] *a* liquid; (*ganancia*) net ♦ *nm* liquid; (*COM: efectivo*) ready cash *o* money; (: *ganancia*) net amount *o* profit; ~ **imponible** net taxable income.

lira [lē'rà] *nf* (*MUS*) lyre; (*moneda*) lira.

lírico, a [lē'rēko, à] *a* lyrical.

lirio [lē'ryo] *nm* (*BOT*) iris.

lirismo [lērēs'mo] *nm* lyricism; (*sentimentalismo*) sentimentality.

lirón [lēron'] *nm* (*ZOOL*) dormouse; (*fig*) sleepyhead.

Lisboa [lēsbo'à] *nf* Lisbon.

lisboeta [lēsboe'tà] *a* of *o* from Lisbon ♦ *nm/f* native *o* inhabitant of Lisbon.

lisiado, a [lēsyà'tho, à] *a* injured ♦ *nm/f* cripple.

lisiar [lēsyàr'] *vt* to maim; ~**se** *vr* to injure o.s.

liso, a [lē'so, à] *a* (*terreno*) flat; (*cabello*) straight; (*superficie*) even; (*tela*) plain; **lisa y llanamente** in plain language, plainly.

lisonja [lēson'hà] *nf* flattery.

lisonjear [lēsonheàr'] *vt* to flatter; (*fig*) to please.

lisonjero, a [lēsonhe'ro, à] *a* flattering; (*agradable*) gratifying, pleasing ♦ *nm/f* flatterer.

lista [lē'stà] *nf* list; (*de alumnos*) school list (*US*) *o* register (*Brit*); (*de libros*) catalog(ue); (*de correos*) poste restante; (*de platos*) menu; (*de precios*) price list; **pasar** ~ to call the roll; (*ESCOL*) to call roll (*US*) *o* the register (*Brit*); ~ **de correos** general delivery (*US*), poste restante (*Brit*); ~ **de direcciones** mailing list; ~ **electoral** list of voters (*US*), electoral roll (*Brit*); ~ **de espera** waiting list; **tela** a ~**s** striped material.

listado, a [lēstà'tho, à] *a* striped ♦ *nm* (*COM*, *INFORM*) listing; ~ **paginado** (*INFORM*) paged listing.

listar [lēstàr'] *vt* (*INFORM*) to list.

listo, a [lē'sto, à] *a* (*perspicaz*) smart, clever; (*preparado*) ready; ~ **para usar** ready-to-use; **¿estás** ~? are you ready?; **pasarse de** ~ to be too smart for one's britches.

listón [lēston'] *nm* (*tela*) ribbon; (*de madera, metal*) strip.

litera [lēte'rà] *nf* (*en barco, tren*) berth; (*en dormitorio*) bunk, bunk bed.

literal [lēteràl'] *a* literal.

literario, a [lēterà'ryo, à] *a* literary.

literato, a [lēterà'to, à] *nm/f* writer.

literatura [lēterátoo'rà] *nf* literature.

litigante [lētēgàn'te] *nm/f* litigant, claimant.

litigar [lētēgàr'] *vt* to fight ♦ *vi* (*JUR*) to go to court; (*fig*) to dispute, argue.

litigio [lētē'hyo] *nm* (*JUR*) lawsuit; (*fig*): **en** ~ **con** in dispute with.

litigue [lētē'ge] *etc vb* V **litigar**.

litografía [lētográfē'à] *nf* lithography; (*una* ~) lithograph.

litoral [lētoràl'] *a* coastal ♦ *nm* coast, seaboard.

litro [lē'tro] *nm* liter (*US*), litre (*Brit*).

Lituania [lētwà'nyà] *nf* Lithuania.

liturgia [lētoōr'hyà] *nf* liturgy.

liviano, a [lēvyà'no, à] *a* (*persona*) fickle; (*cosa, objeto*) trivial.

lívido, a [lē'vētho, à] *a* livid.

líving [lē'hēn], *pl* **lívings** *nm* living room.

ll... *V bajo la letra LL, después de L.*

lo [lo] *artículo definido neutro*: ~ **bueno** the good; ~ **mío** what is mine; ~ **difícil es que** ... the difficult thing about it is that ...; **no saben** ~ **aburrido que es** they don't know how boring it is; **viste a** ~ **americano** he dresses in the American style ♦ *pron* (*persona*) him; (*cosa*) it; ~ **de** that matter of; ~ **que** what, that which; **toma** ~ **que quieras** take what(ever) you want; ~ **que sea** whatever; **¡toma** ~ **que he dicho!** I stand by what I said!

loa [lo'à] *nf* praise.

loable [loà'ble] *a* praiseworthy.

LOAPA [loà'pà] *nf abr* (*Esp JUR*) = *Ley Orgánica de Armonización del Proceso Autónomo.*

loar [loàr'] *vt* to praise.

lobato [lobà'to] *nm* (*ZOOL*) wolf cub.

lobo [lo'ßo] *nm* wolf; ~ **de mar** (*fig*) salty old sailor; ~ **marino** seal.

lóbrego, a [lo'ßrego, à] *a* dark; (*fig*) gloomy.

lóbulo [lo'ßoolo] *nm* lobe.

LOC *nm abr* (= *lector óptico de caracteres*) OCR.

locación [lokàsyon'] *nf* lease.

local [lokàl'] *a* local ♦ *nm* place, site; (*oficinas*) premises *pl.*

localice [lokàlē'se] *etc vb* V **localizar**.

localidad [lokàlēthàth'] *nf* (*barrio*) locality; (*lugar*) location; (*TEATRO*) seat, ticket.

localizar [lokȧlēsár'] *vt* (*ubicar*) to locate, find; (*encontrar*) to find, track down; (*restringir*) to localize; (*situar*) to place.

loción [losyon'] *nf* lotion, wash.

loco, a [lo'ko, á] *a* mad; (*fig*) wild, mad ♦ *nm/f* lunatic, madman/woman; ~ **de atar**, (*AM*) ~ **rematado** raving mad; **a lo** ~ without rhyme or reason; **ando** ~ **con el examen** the exam is driving me crazy; **estar** ~ **de alegría** to be overjoyed o over the moon.

locomoción [lokomosyon'] *nf* locomotion.

locomotora [lokomoto'rȧ] *nf* engine, locomotive.

locuaz [lokwás'] *a* loquacious, talkative.

locución [lokōosyon'] *nf* expression.

locura [lokōō'rȧ] *nf* madness; (*acto*) crazy act.

locutor, a [lokōōtor', á] *nm/f* (*RADIO*) announcer; (*comentarista*) commentator; (*TV*) newscaster.

locutorio [lokōōto'ryo] *nm* (*TELEC*) telephone booth.

lodo [lo'do] *nm* mud.

logia [lo'hyȧ] *nf* (*MIL*, *de masones*) lodge; (*ARQ*) loggia.

lógico, a [lo'hēko, á] *a* logical; (*correcto*) natural; (*razonable*) reasonable ♦ *nm* logician ♦ *nf* logic; **es** ~ **que** ... it stands to reason that ...; **ser de una lógica aplastante** to be as clear as day.

logística [lohē'stēkȧ] *nf* logistics *pl*.

lograr [lográr'] *vt* (*obtener*) to get, obtain; (*conseguir*) to achieve, attain; ~ **hacer** to manage to do; ~ **que uno venga** to manage to get sb to come; ~ **acceso a** (*INFORM*) to access.

logro [lo'gro] *nm* achievement, success; (*COM*) profit.

logroñés, esa [logronyes', esá] *a* of o from Logroño ♦ *nm/f* native o inhabitant of Logroño.

Loira [lo'ērȧ] *nm* Loire.

loma [lo'mȧ] *nf* hillock, low ridge.

Lombardía [lombȧrthē'ȧ] *nf* Lombardy.

lombriz [lombrēs'] *nf* (earth)worm.

lomo [lo'mo] *nm* (*de animal*) back; (*CULIN*: *de cerdo*) pork loin; (: *de vaca*) rib steak; (*de libro*) spine.

lona [lo'nȧ] *nf* canvas.

loncha [lontch'ȧ] *nf* = **lonja**.

lonche [lontch'e] *nm* (*AM*) lunch.

lonchería [lontcherē'ȧ] *nf* (*AM*) diner (*US*), snack bar.

londinense [londēnen'se] *a* London *cpd*, of o from London ♦ *nm/f* Londoner.

Londres [lon'dres] *nm* London.

longaniza [longȧnē'sȧ] *nf* pork sausage.

longitud [lonhētōōth'] *nf* length; (*GEO*) longitude; **tener 3 metros de** ~ to be 3 meters long; ~ **de onda** wavelength; **salto**

de ~ long jump.

lonja [lon'hȧ] *nf* slice; (*de tocino*) rasher; (*COM*) market, exchange; ~ **de pescado** fish market.

lontananza [lontȧnȧn'sȧ] *nf* background; **en** ~ far away, in the distance.

loor [loor'] *nm* praise.

Lorena [lore'nȧ] *nf* Lorraine.

loro [lo'ro] *nm* parrot.

los [los] *artículo definido mpl* the ♦ *pron* them; (*ustedes*) you; **mis libros y** ~ **de usted** my books and yours.

losa [lo'sȧ] *nf* stone; ~ **sepulcral** gravestone.

lote [lo'te] *nm* portion, share; (*COM*) lot; (*INFORM*) batch.

lotería [loterē'ȧ] *nf* lottery; (*juego*) lotto; **le tocó la** ~ he won a big prize in the lottery; (*fig*) he got lucky; ~ **nacional** national lottery; ~ **primitiva** (*Esp*) *type of state-run lottery*.

lotero, a [lote'ro, á] *nm/f* seller of lottery tickets.

Lovaina [lohȧ'ēnȧ] *nf* Louvain.

loza [lo'sȧ] *nf* crockery; ~ **fina** china.

lozanía [losȧnē'ȧ] *nf* (*lujo*) luxuriance.

lozano, a [losȧ'no, á] *a* luxuriant; (*animado*) lively.

lubina [lōōbē'nȧ] *nf* (*ZOOL*) sea bass.

lubricante [lōōbrēkȧn'te] *a, nm* lubricant.

lubricar [lōōbrēkár'], **lubrificar** [lōōbrēfēkár'] *vt* to lubricate.

lubrifique [lōōbrēfē'ke] *etc vb V* **lubrificar**.

lubrique [lōōbrē'ke] *etc vb V* **lubricar**.

lucense [lōōsen'se] *a* of o from Lugo ♦ *nm/f* native o inhabitant of Lugo.

Lucerna [lōōser'nȧ] *nf* Lucerne.

lucero [lōōse'ro] *nm* (*ASTRO*) bright star; (*fig*) brilliance; ~ **del alba/de la tarde** morning/evening star.

luces [lōō'ses] *nfpl de* **luz**.

lucidez [lōōsēthes'] *nf* lucidity.

lucido, a [lōōsē'tho, á] *a* (*espléndido*) splendid, brilliant; (*elegante*) elegant; (*exitoso*) successful.

lúcido, a [lōō'sētho, á] *a* lucid.

luciérnaga [lōōsyer'nȧgȧ] *nf* glow-worm.

lucimiento [lōōsēmyen'to] *nm* (*brillo*) brilliance; (*éxito*) success.

lucio [lōō'syo] *nm* (*ZOOL*) pike.

lucir [lōōsēr'] *vt* to illuminate, light (up); (*ostentar*) to show off ♦ *vi* (*brillar*) to shine; ~**se** *vr* (*irónico*) to make a fool of o.s.; (*ostentarse*) to show off.

lucrativo, a [lōōkrȧtē'ho, á] *a* lucrative, profitable; **institución no lucrativa** non profit-making institution.

lucro [lōō'kro] *nm* profit, gain; ~**s y daños** (*COM*) profit and loss *sg*.

luctuoso, a [lōōktwo'so, á] *a* mournful.

lucha [lōōtch'ȧ] *nf* fight, struggle; ~ **de clases** class struggle; ~ **libre** wrestling.

luchar [lōōtchár'] *vi* to fight.

luego [lwe'ḡo] *ad* (*después*) next; (*más tarde*) later, afterwards; **desde** ~ of course; ¡**hasta** ~! see you later!, so long!; ¿**y** ~? what next?

lugar [lōōḡár'] *nm* place; (*sitio*) spot; (*pueblo*) village, town; **en** ~ **de** instead of; **en primer** ~ in the first place, firstly; **dar** ~ **a** to give rise to; **hacer** ~ to make room; **fuera de** ~ out of place; **tener** ~ to take place; ~ **común** commonplace; **yo en su** ~ if I were him; **no hay** ~ **para preocupaciones** there is no cause for concern.

lugareño, a [lōōḡáre'nyo, á] *a* village *cpd* ♦ *nm/f* villager.

lugarteniente [lōōḡártenyen'te] *nm* deputy.

lúgubre [lōō'ḡōōbre] *a* mournful.

lujo [lōō'ho] *nm* luxury; (*fig*) profusion, abundance; **de** ~ luxury *cpd*, de luxe.

lujoso, a [lōōho'so, á] *a* luxurious.

lujuria [lōōhōō'ryá] *nf* lust.

lumbre [lōōm'bre] *nf* (*luz*) light; (*fuego*) fire; **cerca de la** ~ near the fire, at the fireside; ¿**tienes** ~? (*para cigarro*) have you got a light?

lumbrera [lōōmbre'rá] *nf* luminary; (*fig*) leading light.

luminoso, a [lōōmēno'so, á] *a* luminous, shining; (*idea*) bright, brilliant.

luna [lōō'ná] *nf* moon; (*vidrio*: *escaparate*) plate glass; (: *de un espejo*) glass; (: *de gafas*) lens; (*fig*) crescent; ~ **creciente/ llena/menguante/nueva** crescent/full/waning/new moon; ~ **de miel** honeymoon; **estar en la** ~ to have one's head in the clouds.

lunar [lōōnár'] *a* lunar ♦ *nm* (*ANAT*) mole; **tela a** ~**es** spotted material.

lunes [lōō'nes] *nm inv* Monday.

luneta [lōōne'tá] *nf* lens.

lupa [lōō'pá] *nf* magnifying glass.

lusitano, a [lōōsētá'no, á], **luso, a** [lōō'so, a] *a*, *nm/f* Portuguese.

lustrar [lōōstrár'] *vt* (*mueble*) to polish; (*zapatos*) to shine.

lustre [lōōs'tre] *nm* polish; (*fig*) luster (*US*), lustre (*Brit*); **dar** ~ **a** to polish.

lustro [lōōs'tro] *nm* period of five years.

lustroso, a [lōōstro'so, á] *a* shining.

luterano, a [lōōterá'no, á] *a* Lutheran.

luto [lōō'to] *nm* mourning; (*congoja*) grief, sorrow; **llevar el** *o* **vestirse de** ~ to be in mourning.

luxación [lōōksásyon'] *nf* (*MED*) dislocation; **tener una** ~ **de tobillo** to have a dislocated ankle.

Luxemburgo [lōōksembōōr'ḡo] *nm* Luxembourg.

luz [lōōs], *pl* **luces** *nf* (*tb fig*) light; (*fam*) electricity; **dar a** ~ **un niño** to give birth to a child; **sacar a la** ~ to bring to light; **dar la** ~ to switch on the light; **encender** (*Esp*) *o* **prender** (*AM*)/**apagar la** ~ to switch the light on/off; **les cortaron la** ~ their (electricity) supply was cut off; **a la** ~ **de** in the light of; **a todas luces** by any reckoning; **hacer la** ~ **sobre** to shed light on; **tener pocas luces** to be dim *o* stupid; ~ **de la luna/del sol** *o* **solar** moonlight/sunlight; ~ **eléctrica** electric light; ~ **roja/ verde** red/green light; ~ **de cruce** (*AUTO*) low-beam (*US*) *o* dipped (*Brit*) headlight; ~ **de freno** brake light; ~ **intermitente/ trasera** flashing/rear light; **luces de tráfico** traffic lights; **el Siglo de las Luces** the Age of Enlightenment; **traje de luces** bullfighter's costume.

luzca [lōōs'ká] *etc vb V* **lucir.**

LL

Ll, ll [e'ye] *nf* (*letra*) Ll, ll.

llaga [yá'ḡá] *nf* wound.

llagar [yáḡár'] *vt* to make sore; (*herir*) to wound.

llague [yá'ḡe] *etc vb V* **llagar.**

llama [yá'má] *nf* flame; (*fig*) passion; (*ZOOL*) llama; **en** ~**s** burning, ablaze.

llamada [yámá'ḋá] *nf* call; (*a la puerta*) knock; (: *timbre*) ring; ~ **a cobro revertido** collect (*US*) *o* reverse-charge (*Brit*) call; ~ **al orden** call to order; ~ **a pie de página** reference note; ~ **a procedimiento** (*INFORM*) procedure call; ~ **interurbana** long-distance call.

llamamiento [yámámyen'to] *nm* call; **hacer un** ~ **a uno para que haga algo** to appeal to sb to do sth.

llamar [yámár'] *vt* to call; (*convocar*) to summon; (*invocar*) to invoke; (*atraer con gesto*) to beckon; (*atención*) to attract; (*TELEC*: *tb*: ~ **por teléfono**) to call, telephone; (*MIL*) to call up ♦ *vi* (*por teléfono*) to telephone; (*a la puerta*) to knock; (*por señas*) to beckon; ~**se** *vr* to be called, be named; ¿**cómo se llama usted?** what's your name?; ¿**quién llama?** (*TELEC*) who's calling?, who's that?; **no me llama la atención** (*fam*) it doesn't appeal to me.

llamarada [yámárá'ḋá] *nf* (*llamas*) blaze; (*rubor*) flush; (*fig*) flare-up.

llamativo, a [yámátē'ḃo, á] *a* showy; (*color*) loud.

llamear [yámeár'] *vi* to blaze.

llanamente [yánámen'te] *ad* (*lisamente*)

smoothly; (*sin ostentaciones*) plainly; (*sinceramente*) frankly; *V tb* **liso**.

llaneza [yàne'sá] *nf* (*gen*) simplicity; (*honestidad*) straightforwardness, frankness.

llano, a [yà'no, á] *a* (*superficie*) flat; (*persona*) straightforward; (*estilo*) clear ♦ *nm* plain, flat ground.

llanta [yàn'tá] *nf* (*wheel*) rim; (*AM*: *tb*: ~ **de goma**) tire (*US*), tyre (*Brit*); (: *cámara*) inner (tube).

llanto [yän'to] *nm* weeping; (*fig*) lamentation; (*canción*) dirge, lament.

llanura [yànōō'rá] *nf* (*lisura*) flatness, smoothness; (*GEO*) plain.

llave [yà'he] *nf* key; (*de gas, agua*) faucet (*US*), tap (*Brit*); (*MECÁNICA*) wrench; (*de la luz*) switch; (*MUS*) key; ~ **inglesa** monkey wrench; ~ **maestra** master key; ~ **de contacto** (*AUTO*) ignition key; ~ **de paso** stopcock; **echar** ~ **a** to lock up.

llavero [yàhe'ro] *nm* keyring.

llavín [yàhén'] *nm* latchkey.

llegada [ye̱ga'thá] *nf* arrival.

llegar [ye̱gár'] *vi* to bring up, bring over ♦ *vi* to arrive; (*bastar*) to be enough; ~**se** *vr*: ~**se a** to approach; ~ **a** (*alcanzar*) to reach; to manage to, succeed in; ~ **a saber** to find out; ~ **a ser famoso/el jefe** to become famous/the boss; ~ **a las manos** to come to blows; ~ **a las manos de** to come into the hands of; **no llegues tarde** don't be late; **esta cuerda no llega** this rope isn't long enough.

llegue [ye'ge] *etc vb V* **llegar**.

llenar [yenár'] *vt* to fill; (*superficie*) to cover; (*espacio, tiempo*) to fill, take up; (*formulario*) to fill in *o* out; (*deber*) to fulfil; (*fig*) to heap; ~**se** *vr* to fill (up); ~**se de** (*fam*) to stuff o.s. with.

lleno, a [ye'no, á] *a* full, filled; (*repleto*) full up ♦ *nm* (*abundancia*) abundance; (*TEATRO*) full house; **dar de** ~ **contra un muro** to hit a wall head-on.

llevadero, a [yebàthe'ro, á] *a* bearable, tolerable.

llevar [yebár'] *vt* to take; (*ropa*) to wear; (*cargar*) to carry; (*quitar*) to take away; (*en coche*) to drive; (*transportar*) to transport; (*ruta*) to follow, keep to; (*traer: dinero*) to carry; (*suj: camino etc*): ~ **a** to lead to; (*MAT*) to carry; (*aguantar*) to bear; (*negocio*) to conduct, direct; to manage; ~**se** *vr* to carry off, take away; **llevamos dos días aquí** we have been here for two days; **él me lleva 2 años** he's 2 years older than me; ~ **adelante** (*fig*) to carry forward; ~ **por delante a uno** (*en coche etc*) to run sb over; (*fig*) to ride roughshod over sb; ~ **la ventaja** to be winning *o* in the lead; ~ **los libros** (*COM*)

to keep the books; **llevo las de perder** I'm likely to lose; **no las lleva todas consigo** he's not all there; **nos llevó a cenar fuera** she took us out for a meal; ~**se a uno por delante** (*atropellar*) to run sb over; ~**se bien** to get on well (together).

llorar [yorár'] *vt* to cry, weep ♦ *vi* to cry, weep; (*ojos*) to water; ~ **a moco tendido** to sob one's heart out; ~ **de risa** to cry with laughter.

lloriquear [yorēkeár'] *vi* to snivel, whimper.

lloro [yo'ro] *nm* crying, weeping.

llorón, ona [yoron', oná] *a* tearful ♦ *nm/f* cry-baby.

lloroso, a [yoro'so, á] *a* (*gen*) weeping, tearful; (*triste*) sad, sorrowful.

llover [yober'] *vi* to rain; ~ **a cántaros** *o* **a cubos** *o* **a mares** to rain cats and dogs, pour (down); **ser una cosa llovida del cielo** to be a godsend; **llueve sobre mojado** it never rains but it pours.

llovizna [yobēs'ná] *nf* drizzle.

lloviznar [yobēsnár'] *vi* to drizzle.

llueve [ywe'he] *etc vb V* **llover**.

lluvia [yōō'hyá] *nf* rain; (*cantidad*) rainfall; (*fig*: *balas etc*) hail, shower; ~ **radioactiva** radioactive fallout; **día de** ~ rainy day; **una** ~ **de regalos** a shower of gifts.

lluvioso, a [yōōhyo'so, á] *a* rainy.

M

M, m [e'me] *nf* (*letra*) M, m; **M de Madrid** M for Mike.

M. *abr* (*FERRO*) = **Metro**.

m. *abr* (= *metro(s)*) m; (= *minuto(s)*) min., m; (= *masculino*) m., masc.

M.ª *abr* = **María**.

macabro, a [màká'hro, á] *a* macabre.

macaco [màká'ko] *nm* (*ZOOL*) rhesus monkey; (*fam*) runt, squirt.

macana [màká'ná] *nf* (*AM*: *porra*) club; (: *mentira*) lie, fib; (: *tontería*) piece of nonsense.

macanudo, a [màkánōō'tho, á] *a* (*AM fam*) great.

macarra [màká'rrá] *nm* (*fam*) thug.

macarrones [màkárro'nes] *nmpl* macaroni *sg*.

macedonia [màsetho'nyá] *nf*: ~ **de frutas** fruit salad.

macerar [màserár'] *vt* (*CULIN*) to soak, macerate; ~**se** *vr* to soak, soften.

maceta [màse'tá] *nf* (*de flores*) pot of flowers; (*para plantas*) flowerpot.

macetero [máse'te'ro] *nm* flowerpot stand *o* holder.

macilento, a [másēlen'to, á] *a* (*pálido*) pale; (*ojeroso*) haggard.

macizo, a [mása'so, á] *a* (*grande*) massive; (*fuerte, sólido*) solid ♦ *nm* mass, chunk; (*GEO*) massif.

macrobiótico, a [mákrobyo'tēko, á] *a* macrobiotic.

macro-comando [mákrokomán'do] *nm* (*INFORM*) macro (command).

macroeconomía [mákrockonomē'á] *nf* (*COM*) macroeconomics *sg*.

mácula [má'kōōlá] *nf* stain, blemish.

macuto [mákōō'to] *nm* (*MIL*) knapsack.

machacar [mátchákár'] *vt* to crush, pound; (*moler*) to grind (up); (*aplastar*) to mash ♦ *vi* (*insistir*) to go on, keep on.

machacón, ona [mátchákon', oná] *a* (*pesado*) tiresome; (*insistente*) insistent; (*monótono*) monotonous.

machamartillo [mátchámártē'yo]: **a ~** *ad*: **creer a ~** (*firmemente*) to believe firmly.

machaque [mátchá'ke] *etc vb* V **machacar.**

machete [mátche'te] *nm* (*AM*) machete, (large) knife.

machismo [mátchēs'mo] *nm* sexism; male chauvinism.

machista [mátchē'stá] *a, nm* sexist; male chauvinist.

macho [mátch'o] *a* male; (*fig*) virile ♦ *nm* male; (*fig*) he-man, tough guy (*US*); (*TEC*: *perno*) pin, peg; (*ELEC*) pin, plug; (*COSTURA*) hook.

machucar [mátchōōkár'] *vt* to pound.

machuque [mátchōō'ke] *etc vb* V **machucar.**

Madagascar [mátḥáɡáskár'] *nm* Madagascar.

madeja [mátḥe'há] *nf* (*de lana*) skein, hank.

madera [mátḥe'rá] *nf* wood; (*fig*) nature, character; (*: aptitud*) aptitude; **una ~** a piece of wood; **~ contrachapada** *o* **laminada** plywood; **tiene buena ~** he's made of solid stuff; **tiene ~ de futbolista** he's got the makings of a football player.

maderaje [mátḥerá'he], **maderamen** [mátḥerá'men] *nm* timber; (*trabajo*) woodwork, timbering.

maderero [mátḥere'ro] *nm* timber merchant.

madero [mátḥe'ro] *nm* beam; (*fig*) ship.

madrastra [mátḥrás'trá] *nf* stepmother.

madre [má'ḥre] *a* mother *cpd*; (*AM*) tremendous ♦ *nf* mother; (*de vino etc*) dregs *pl*; **~ adoptiva/política/soltera** foster mother/mother-in-law/unmarried mother; **sin ~** motherless; **¡~ mía!** oh dear!; **¡tu ~!** (*fam!*) fuck off! (*!*); **salirse de ~** (*río*) to burst its banks; (*persona*) to lose all

self-control.

madreperla [mátḥreper'lá] *nf* mother-of-pearl.

madreselva [mátḥresel'há] *nf* honeysuckle.

Madrid [mátḥrē't'] *n* Madrid.

madriguera [mátḥrēɡe'rá] *nf* burrow.

madrileño, a [mátḥrēle'nyo, á] *a* of *o* from Madrid ♦ *nm/f* native *o* inhabitant of Madrid.

Madriles [mátḥrē'les] *nmpl*: **Los ~** (*fam*) Madrid *sg*.

madrina [mátḥrē'ná] *nf* godmother; (*ARQ*) prop, shore; (*TEC*) brace; **~ de boda** bridesmaid.

madroño [mátḥro'nyo] *nm* (*BOT*) strawberry tree, arbutus.

madrugada [mátḥrōōɡá'tḥá] *nf* early morning, wee small hours; (*alba*) dawn, daybreak; **a las 4 de la ~** at 4 o'clock in the morning.

madrugador, a [mátḥrōōɡátḥor', á] *a* early-rising.

madrugar [mátḥrōōɡár'] *vi* to get up early; (*fig*) to get a head start.

madrugue [mátḥrōō'ɡe] *etc vb* V **madrugar.**

madurar [mátḥōōrár'] *vt, vi* (*fruta*) to ripen; (*fig*) to mature.

madurez [mátḥōōres'] *nf* ripeness; (*fig*) maturity.

maduro, a [mátḥōō'ro, á] *a* ripe; (*fig*) mature; **poco ~** unripe.

MAE *nm abr* (*Esp POL*)=*Ministerio de Asuntos Exteriores.*

maestra [máes'trá] *nf* V **maestro.**

maestría [máestrē'á] *nf* mastery; (*habilidad*) skill, expertise.

maestro, a [máes'tro, á] *a* masterly; (*perito*) skilled, expert; (*principal*) main; (*educado*) trained ♦ *nm/f* master/mistress; (*profesor*) teacher ♦ *nm* (*autoridad*) authority; (*MUS*) maestro; (*AM*) skilled workman; **~ albañil** master mason; **~ de obras** foreman.

mafioso [máfyo'so] *nm* (*AM*) gangster.

Magallanes [máɡáyá'nes] *nm*: **Estrecho de ~** Strait of Magellan.

magia [má'hyá] *nf* magic.

mágico, a [má'hēko, á] *a* magic(al) ♦ *nm/f* magician.

magisterio [máhēste'ryo] *nm* (*enseñanza*) teaching; (*profesión*) teaching profession; (*maestros*) teachers *pl*.

magistrado [máhēstrá'tḥo] *nm* magistrate.

magistral [máhēstrál'] *a* magisterial; (*fig*) masterly.

magistratura [máhēstrátōō'rá] *nf* magistracy; **M~ del Trabajo** (*Esp*) ≈ Industrial Tribunal.

magnánimo, a [máɡná'nēmo, á] *a* magnanimous.

magnate [máɡná'te] *nm* magnate, tycoon;

~ **de la prensa** press baron.
magnesio [máǥne'syo] *nm* (*QUÍMICA*) magnesium.
magnetice [máǥnetē'se] *etc vb V* **magnetizar**.
magnético, a [máǥne'tēko, á] *a* magnetic.
magnetizar [máǥnetēsár'] *vt* to magnetize.
magnetofón [máǥnetofon'], **magnetófono** [máǥneto'fono] *nm* tape recorder.
magnetofónico, a [máǥnetofo'nēco, á] *a*: **cinta magnetofónica** recording tape.
magnicidio [máǥnēsē'ðyo] *nm* assassination (*of an important person*).
magnífico, a [máǥnē'fēko, á] *a* splendid, magnificent.
magnitud [máǥnētōōð'] *nf* magnitude.
mago, a [má'ǥo, á] *nm/f* magician, wizard; **los Reyes M~s** the Magi, the Three Wise Men.
magrear [máǥreár'] *vt* (*fam*) to feel up.
magrez [máǥres'] *nf* leanness.
magro, a [má'ǥro, á] *a* (*persona*) thin, lean; (*carne*) lean.
maguey [máǥe'ē] *nm* (*AM BOT*) agave.
magulladura [máǥōōyáðħōō'rá] *nf* bruise.
magullar [máǥōōyár'] *vt* (*amoratar*) to bruise; (*dañar*) to damage; (*fam: golpear*) to bash, beat.
Maguncia [máǥōōn'syá] *nf* Mainz.
mahometano, a [máometá'no, á] *a* Mohammedan.
mahonesa [máone'sá] *nf* = **mayonesa**.
maicena [máēse'ná] *nf* cornflour, corn starch (*US*).
maillot [máyot'] *nm* bathing suit (*US*), swimming costume (*Brit*); (*DEPORTE*) vest.
maitre [me'tre] *nm* head waiter.
maíz [máēs'] *nm* corn (*US*), maize (*Brit*); sweet corn.
majadero, a [máháðħe'ro, á] *a* silly, stupid.
majar [máhár'] *vt* to crush, grind.
majareta [máháre'tá] *a* (*fam*) cracked, nuts.
majestad [máhestáð'] *nf* majesty; **Su M~** His/Her Majesty; **(Vuestra) M~** Your Majesty.
majestuoso, a [máhestwo'so, á] *a* majestic.
majo, a [má'ho, á] *a* nice; (*guapo*) attractive, good-looking; (*elegante*) smart.
mal [mál] *ad* badly; (*equivocadamente*) wrongly; (*con dificultad*) with difficulty ♦ *a* = **malo, a** ♦ *nm* evil; (*desgracia*) misfortune; (*daño*) harm, damage; (*MED*) illness ♦ *conj*: ~ **que le pese** whether he likes it or not; **me entendió** ~ he misunderstood me; **hablar** ~ **de uno** to speak ill of sb; **huele** ~ it smells bad; **ir de** ~ **en peor** to go from bad to worse; **oigo/veo** ~ I can't hear/see very well; **si** ~ **no recuerdo** if my memory serves me right; **¡menos** ~! just as well!; ~ **que bien** right-

ly or wrongly; **no hay** ~ **que por bien no venga** every cloud has a silver lining; ~ **de ojo** evil eye.
mala [má'lá] *nf V* **malo**.
malabarismo [máláħárēs'mo] *nm* juggling.
malabarista [máláħárē'stá] *nm/f* juggler.
malaconsejado, a [málákonsehá'ðħo, á] *a* ill-advised.
malacostumbrado, a [málákostōōmbrá'ðħo, á] *a* (*consentido*) spoiled.
malacostumbrar [málákostōōmbrár'] *vt*: ~ **a uno** to get sb into bad habits.
malagueño, a [máláǥe'nyo, á] *a* of *o* from Málaga ♦ native *o* inhabitant of Málaga.
malaria [málá'ryá] *nf* malaria.
Malasia [málá'syá] *nf* Malaysia.
malavenido, a [máláħenē'ðħo, á] *a* incompatible.
malayo, a [málá'yo, á] *a* Malay(an) ♦ *nm/f* Malay ♦ *nm* (*LING*) Malay ♦ *excl*: **¡malaya!** (*AM*) damn!
malcarado, a [málkárá'ðħo, á] *a* ugly, grim-faced.
malcriado, a [málkryá'ðħo, á] *a* (*consentido*) spoiled.
malcriar [málkryár'] *vt* to spoil, pamper.
maldad [máldáð'] *nf* evil, wickedness.
maldecir [máldesēr'] *vt* to curse ♦ *vi*: ~ **de** to speak ill of.
maldiciendo [máldēsyen'do] *etc vb V* **maldecir**.
maldición [máldēsyon'] *nf* curse; **¡~!** curse it!, damn!
maldiga [máldē'ǥá] *etc*, **maldije** [máldē'he] *etc*, **maldiré** [máldēre'] *etc vb V* **maldecir**.
maldito, a [máldē'to, á] *a* (*condenado*) damned; (*perverso*) wicked ♦ *nm*: **el** ~ the devil; **¡~ sea!** damn it!; **no le hace** ~ **(el) caso** he doesn't take a damned bit of notice.
maleable [máleá'ħle] *a* malleable.
maleante [máleán'te] *a* wicked ♦ *nm/f* criminal, crook.
malecón [málekon'] *nm* pier, jetty.
maledicencia [máleðħēsen'syá] *nf* slander, scandal.
maleducado, a [máleðħōōká'ðħo, á] *a* bad-mannered, rude.
maleficio [málefē'syo] *nm* curse, spell.
malentendido [málentendē'ðħo] *nm* misunderstanding.
malestar [málestár'] *nm* (*gen*) discomfort; (*enfermedad*) indisposition; (*fig: inquietud*) uneasiness; (*POL*) unrest; **siento un** ~ **en el estómago** my stomach is upset.
maleta [mále'tá] *nf* case, suitcase; (*AUTO*) trunk (*US*), boot (*Brit*); **hacer la** ~ to pack.
maletera [málete'rá] *nf* (*AM AUTO*) trunk (*US*), boot (*Brit*).
maletero [málete'ro] *nm* (*AUTO*) trunk

(US), boot (Brit); (persona) porter.

maletín [mál'tēn'] nm small case, bag; (portafolio) briefcase.

malevolencia [málebolen'syá] nf malice, spite.

malévolo, a [mále'bolo, á] a malicious, spiteful.

maleza [mále'sá] nf (hierbas malas) weeds pl; (arbustos) thicket.

malgache [málgátch'e] a of o from Madagascar ♦ nm/f native o inhabitant of Madagascar.

malgastar [málgástár'] vt (tiempo, dinero) to waste; (recursos) to squander; (salud) to ruin.

malhechor, a [máletchor', á] nm/f delinquent; (criminal) criminal.

malhumorado, a [málōōmorá'tho, á] a bad-tempered.

malicia [málē'syá] nf (maldad) wickedness; (astucia) slyness, guile; (mala intención) malice, spite; (carácter travieso) mischievousness.

malicioso, a [málēsyo'so, á] a wicked, evil; sly, crafty; malicious, spiteful; mischievous.

malignidad [málēgnētháth'] nf (MED) malignancy; (malicia) malice.

maligno, a [málēg'no, á] a evil; (dañino) pernicious, harmful; (malévolo) malicious; (MED) malignant ♦ nm: **el** ~ the devil.

malintencionado, a [málēntensyoná'tho, á] a (comentario) hostile; (persona) malicious.

malnutrido, a [málnōōtrē'tho, á] a undernourished.

malo, a [má'lo, á] a (**mal** before nmsg) bad; (calidad) poor; (falso) false; (espantoso) dreadful; (niño) naughty ♦ nm/f villain ♦ nm (CINE fam) bad guy ♦ nf spell of bad luck; **estar** ~ to be ill; **andar a malas con uno** to be on bad terms with sb; **estar de malas** (mal humor) to be in a bad mood; **lo** ~ **es que** ... the trouble is that ....

malograr [málográr'] vt to spoil; (plan) to upset; (ocasión) to waste; ~**se** vr (plan etc) to fail, come to grief; (persona) to die before one's time.

maloliente [málolyen'te] a stinking, smelly.

malparado, a [málpárá'tho, á] a: **salir** ~ to come off badly.

malparir [málpárēr'] vi to have a miscarriage.

malpensado, a [málpensá'tho, á] a evil-minded.

malquerencia [málkeren'syá] nf dislike.

malquistar [málkēstár'] vt: ~ **a dos personas** to cause a rift between two people; ~**se** vr to fall out.

malsano, a [málsá'no, á] a unhealthy.

malsonante [málsonán'te] a (palabra) nasty, rude.

Malta [mál'tá] nf Malta.

malteada [máltēá'thá] nf (AM) milk shake.

maltés, esa [máltes', esá] a, nm/f Maltese.

maltraer [máltráer'] vt (abusar) to insult, abuse; (maltratar) to ill-treat.

maltratar [máltrátár'] vt to ill-treat, mistreat.

maltrecho, a [máltretch'o, á] a battered, damaged.

malva [mál'bá] nf mallow; ~ **loca** hollyhock; **(de color de)** ~ mauve.

malvado, a [málbá'tho, á] a evil, villainous.

malvavisco [málbábēs'ko] nm marshmallow.

malvender [málbender'] vt to sell off cheap o at a loss.

malversación [málbersásyon'] nf embezzlement, misappropriation.

malversar [málbersár'] vt to embezzle, misappropriate.

Malvinas [málbē'nás] nfpl: **Islas** ~ Falkland Islands.

malla [má'yá] nf (de una red) mesh; (red) network; (de baño) swimsuit; (de ballet, gimnasia) leotard; ~**s** nfpl tights; ~ **de alambre** wire mesh.

Mallorca [máyor'ká] nf Majorca.

mallorquín, ina [máyorkēn', ēná] a, nm/f Majorcan ♦ nm (LING) Majorcan.

mama [má'má] nf (de animal) teat; (de mujer) breast.

mamá [mámá'] nf (fam) mom(my) (US), mum(my) (Brit).

mamar [mámár'] vt (pecho) to suck; (fig) to absorb, assimilate ♦ vi to suck; **dar de** ~ to (breast-)feed; (animal) to suckle.

mamarracho [mámárrátch'o] nm sight, mess.

mamífero, a [mámē'fero, á] a mammalian, mammal cpd ♦ nm mammal.

mamón, ona [mámon', oná] a small, baby cpd ♦ nm/f small baby; (fam) idiot.

mamotreto [mámotre'to] nm hefty volume; (fam) whopping great thing.

mampara [mámpá'rá] nf (entre habitaciones) partition; (biombo) screen.

mamporro [mámpo'rro] nm (fam): **dar un** ~ **a** to clout.

mampostería [mámposterē'á] nf masonry.

mamut [mámōōt'] nm mammoth.

maná [máná'] nm manna.

manada [máná'thá] nf (ZOOL) herd; (: de leones) pride; (: de lobos) pack; **llegaron en** ~**s** (fam) they came in droves.

Managua [máná'gwá] n Managua.

manantial [mánántyál'] nm spring; (fuente) fountain; (fig) source.

manar [mánár'] vt to run with, flow with ♦ vi to run, flow; (abundar) to abound.

manaza [máná'sá] nf big hand ♦ a, nm/f

inv: ∼**s**: **ser un** ∼**s** to be clumsy.
mancebo [mánse'ho] *nm* (*joven*) young man.
mancilla [mánsē'yá] *nf* stain, blemish.
mancillar [mánsēyár'] *vt* to stain, sully.
manco, a [mán'ko, á] *a* one-armed; one-handed; (*fig*) defective, faulty; **no ser** ∼ to be useful *o* active.
mancomunar [mánkomōōnár'] *vt* to unite, bring together; (*recursos*) to pool; (*JUR*) to make jointly responsible.
mancomunidad [mánkomōōnēṯháṯh'] *nf* union, association; (*comunidad*) community; (*JUR*) joint responsibility.
mancha [mántch'á] *nf* stain, mark; (*de tinta*) blot; (*de vegetación*) patch; (*imperfección*) stain, blemish, blot; (*boceto*) sketch, outline; **la M**∼ La Mancha.
manchado, a [mántchá'ṯho, á] *a* (*sucio*) dirty; (*animal*) spotted; (*ave*) speckled; (*tinta*) smudged.
manchar [mántchár'] *vt* to stain, mark; (*ZOOL*) to patch; (*ensuciar*) to soil, dirty; ∼**se** *vr* to get dirty; (*fig*) to dirty one's hands.
manchego, a [mántche'go, á] *a* of *o* from La Mancha ♦ *nm/f* native *o* inhabitant of La Mancha.
mandadero [mándáṯhe'ro] *nm* messenger.
mandado [mándá'ṯho] *nm* (*orden*) order; (*recado*) commission, errand.
mandamás [mándámás'] *a nm/f inv* boss; **ser un** ∼ to be very bossy.
mandamiento [mándámyen'to] *nm* (*orden*) order, command; (*REL*) commandment; ∼ **judicial** warrant.
mandar [mándár'] *vt* (*ordenar*) to order; (*dirigir*) to lead, command; (*país*) to rule over; (*enviar*) to send; (*pedir*) to order, ask for ♦ *vi* to be in charge; (*pey*) to be bossy; **¿mande?** pardon?; **¿manda usted algo más?** is there anything else?; ∼ **a uno a paseo** *o* **a la porra** to tell sb to go to hell; **se lo mandaremos por correo** we'll mail (*US*) *o* post (*Brit*) it to you; ∼ **hacer un traje** to have a suit made.
mandarín [mándárēn'] *nm* petty bureaucrat.
mandarina [mándárē'ná] *nf* (*fruta*) tangerine, mandarin (orange).
mandatario, a [mándátá'ryo, á] *nm/f* (*representante*) agent; **primer** ∼ head of state.
mandato [mándá'to] *nm* (*orden*) order; (*POL*: *período*) term of office; (: *territorio*) mandate; (*INFORM*) command; ∼ **judicial** (*search*) warrant.
mandíbula [mándē'hōōlá] *nf* jaw.
mandil [mándēl'] *nm* (*delantal*) apron.
mando [mán'do] *nm* (*MIL*) command; (*de país*) rule; (*el primer lugar*) lead; (*POL*) term of office; (*TEC*) control; ∼ **a la**

izquierda left-hand drive; **los altos** ∼**s** the high command *sg*; ∼ **por botón** push-button control; **al** ∼ **de** in charge of; **tomar el** ∼ to take the lead.
mandolina [mándolē'ná] *nf* mandolin(e).
mandón, ona [mándon', oná] *a* bossy, domineering.
manecilla [mánesē'yá] *nf* (*TEC*) pointer; (*de reloj*) hand.
manejable [mánehá'hle] *a* manageable; (*fácil de usar*) handy.
manejar [mánehár'] *vt* to manage; (*máquina*) to work, operate; (*caballo etc*) to handle; (*casa*) to run, manage; (*AM AUTO*) to drive; **"∼ con cuidado"** "handle with care" ♦ *vi* (*AM AUTO*) to drive; ∼**se** *vr* (*comportarse*) to act, behave; (*arreglárselas*) to manage.
manejo [máne'ho] *nm* management; handling; running; driving; (*facilidad de trato*) ease, confidence; (*de idioma*) command; ∼**s** *nmpl* intrigues; **tengo** ∼ **del francés** I have a good command of French.
manera [máne'rá] *nf* way, manner, fashion; (*ARTE, LITERATURA etc*: *estilo*) manner, style; ∼**s** *nfpl* (*modales*) manners; **su** ∼ **de ser** the way he is; (*aire*) his manner; **de mala** ∼ (*fam*) badly, unwillingly; **de ninguna** ∼ no way, by no means; **de otra** ∼ otherwise; **de todas** ∼**s** at any rate; **en gran** ∼ to a large extent; **sobre** ∼ exceedingly; **a mi** ∼ **de ver** in my view; **no hay** ∼ **de persuadirle** there's no way of convincing him.
manga [mán'gá] *nf* (*de camisa*) sleeve; (*de riego*) hose; **de** ∼ **corta/larga** short-/long-sleeved; **andar** ∼ **por hombro** (*desorden*) to be topsy-turvy; **tener** ∼ **ancha** to be easy-going.
mangante [mángán'te] *a* (*descarado*) brazen ♦ *nm* (*mendigo*) beggar.
mangar [mángár'] *vt* (*unir*) to plug in; (*fam*: *birlar*) to pinch, nick, swipe; (*mendigar*) to beg.
mango [mán'go] *nm* handle; (*BOT*) mango; ∼ **de escoba** broomstick.
mangonear [mángoneár'] *vt* to boss about ♦ *vi* to be bossy.
mangue [mán'ge] *etc vb V* **mangar**.
manguera [mánge'rá] *nf* (*de riego*) hose; (*tubo*) pipe; ∼ **de incendios** fire hose.
maní(s) [mánē'] *nm, pl* **maníes** *o* **manises** (*AM*: *cacahuete*) peanut; (: *planta*) groundnut plant.
manía [mánē'á] *nf* (*MED*) mania; (*fig*: *moda*) rage, craze; (*disgusto*) dislike; (*malicia*) spite; **tiene** ∼ she's a bit fussy; **tener** ∼ **a uno** to dislike sb.
maníaco, a [mánē'áko, á] *a* maniac(al) ♦ *nm/f* maniac.
maniatar [mányátár'] *vt* to tie the hands of.

maniático, a |mànyà'tēko, á| *a* maniac(al); (*loco*) crazy; (*tiquismiquis*) fussy ♦ *nm/f* maniac.

manicomio |mànēko'myo| *nm* insane asylum (*US*), mental hospital (*Brit*).

manicuro, a |mànēkōō'ro, á| *nm/f* manicurist ♦ *nf* manicure.

manido, a |mànē'ðo, á| *a* (*tema etc*) trite, stale.

manifestación |mànēfestàsyon'| *nf* (*declaración*) statement, declaration; (*demostración*) show, display; (*POL*) demonstration.

manifestante |mànēfestàn'te| *nm/f* demonstrator.

manifestar |mànēfestàr'| *vt* to show, manifest; (*declarar*) to state, declare; ~**se** *vr* to show, become apparent; (*POL: desfilar*) to demonstrate; (: *reunirse*) to hold a mass meeting.

manifiesto, a |mànēfye'sto, á| *etc vb* V **manifestar** ♦ *a* clear, manifest ♦ *nm* manifesto; (*ANAT, NAUT*) manifest; **poner algo de** ~ (*aclarar*) to make sth clear; (*revelar*) to reveal sth; **quedar** ~ to be plain *o* clear.

manija |mànē'hà| *nf* handle.

manilla |mànē'yà| *nf* (*de reloj*) hand; ~**s (de hierro)** *nfpl* handcuffs.

manillar |mànēyàr'| *nm* handlebars *pl*.

maniobra |mànyo'brà| *nf* maneuvering (*US*), manoeuvring (*Brit*); (*maneja*) handling; (*fig: movimiento*) maneuver (*US*), manoeuvre (*Brit*), move; (: *estratagema*) trick, stratagem; ~**s** *nfpl* maneuvers (*US*), manoeuvres (*Brit*).

maniobrar |mànēohràr'| *vt* to maneuver (*US*), manoeuvre (*Brit*); (*manejar*) to handle ♦ *vi* to maneuver (*US*), manoeuvre (*Brit*).

manipulación |mànēpōōlàsyon'| *nf* manipulation; (*COM*) handling.

manipular |mànēpōōlàr'| *vt* to manipulate; (*manejar*) to handle.

maniquí |mànēkē'| *nm/f* model ♦ *nm* dummy.

manirroto, a |mànērro'to, á| *a* lavish, extravagant ♦ *nm/f* spendthrift.

manita |mànē'tà| *nf* little hand; ~**s de plata** artistic hands.

manitas |mànē'tàs| *a inv* good with one's hands ♦ *nm/f inv*: **ser un** ~ to be very good with one's hands.

manito |mànē'to| *nm* (*AM: en conversación*) pal.

manivela |mànēbe'là| *nf* crank.

manjar |mànhàr'| *nm* (tasty) dish.

mano |mà'no| *nf* hand; (*ZOOL*) foot, paw; (*de pintura*) coat; (*serie*) lot, series; **a** ~ by hand; **a** ~ **derecha/izquierda** on (*o* to) the right(-hand side)/left(-hand side); **he-**

cho a ~ handmade; **a** ~**s llenas** lavishly, generously; **de primera** ~ (at) first hand; **de segunda** ~ (at) second hand; **robo a** ~ **armada** armed robbery; **Pedro es mi** ~ **derecha** Pedro is my right-hand man; ~ **de obra** manpower; ~ **de santo** sure remedy; **darse la(s)** ~**(s)** to shake hands; **echar una** ~ to lend a hand; **echar una** ~ **a** to lay hands on; **echar** ~ **de** to make use of; **estrechar la** ~ **a uno** to shake sb's hand; **traer** *o* **llevar algo entre** ~**s** to deal *o* be busy with sth; **está en tus** ~**s** it's up to you; **se le fue la** ~ his hand slipped; (*fig*) he went too far; **¡**~**s a la obra!** to work!

manojo |mà'noho| *nm* handful, bunch; ~ **de llaves** bunch of keys.

manómetro |mà'no'metro| *nm* (pressure) gauge.

manopla |mà'no'plà| *nf* (*paño*) wash cloth; ~**s** *nfpl* mittens.

manoseado, a |mànosèà'ðo, á| *a* wellworn.

manosear |mànosèàr'| *vt* (*tocar*) to handle, touch; (*desordenar*) to mess up, rumple; (*insistir en*) to overwork; (*acariciar*) to caress, fondle; (*pey: persona*) to feel up.

manotazo |mànotá'so| *nm* slap, smack.

mansalva |mànsàl'hà|: **a** ~ *ad* indiscriminately.

mansedumbre |mànseðhōōm'bre| *nf* gentleness, meekness; (*de animal*) tameness.

mansión |mànsyon'| *nf* mansion.

manso, a |màn'so, á| *a* gentle, mild; (*animal*) tame.

manta |màn'tà| *nf* blanket; (*AM*) poncho.

manteca |mànte'kà| *nf* fat; (*AM*) butter; ~ **de cacahuete/cacao** peanut/cocoa butter; ~ **de cerdo** lard.

mantecado |màntekà'ðo| *nm* (*AM*) ice cream.

mantecoso, a |màntcko'so, á| *a* fat, greasy; **queso** ~ soft cheese.

mantel |màntel'| *nm* tablecloth.

mantelería |màntelerē'à| *nf* table linen.

mantendré |màntendre'| *etc vb* V **mantener.**

mantener |màntencr'| *vt* to support, maintain; (*alimentar*) to sustain; (*conservar*) to keep; (*TEC*) to maintain, service; ~**se** *vr* (*seguir de pie*) to be still standing; (*no ceder*) to hold one's ground; (*subsistir*) to sustain o.s., keep going; ~ **algo en equilibrio** to keep sth balanced; ~**se a distancia** to keep one's distance; ~**se firme** to hold one's ground.

mantenga |màntcn'gà| *etc vb* V **mantener.**

mantenimiento |màntencmycn'to| *nm* maintenance; sustenance; (*sustento*) support.

mantequería |màntckcrē'à| *nf* (*ultramarinos*) grocer's (shop).

mantequilla [mántekē'yá] *nf* butter.

mantilla [mántē'yà] *nf* mantilla; **estar en ~s** (*persona*) to be terribly innocent; (*proyecto*) to be in its infancy.

manto [mán'to] *nm* (*capa*) cloak; (*de ceremonia*) robe, gown.

mantón [mánton'] *nm* shawl.

mantuve [mántōō'he] *etc vb* V **mantener**.

manual [mánwál'] *a* manual ♦ *nm* manual, handbook; **habilidad** ~ manual skill.

manufactura [mánōōfáktōō'rá] *nf* manufacture; (*fábrica*) factory.

manuscrito, a [mánōōskrē'to, á] *a* handwritten ♦ *nm* manuscript.

manutención [mánōōtensyon'] *nf* maintenance; (*sustento*) support.

manzana [mánsá'ná] *nf* apple; (*ARQ*) block; ~ **de la discordia** (*fig*) bone of contention.

manzanal [mánsánál'] *nm* apple orchard.

manzanilla [mánsánē'yà] *nf* (*planta*) camomile; (*infusión*) camomile tea; (*vino*) manzanilla.

manzano [mánsá'no] *nm* apple tree.

maña [má'nyá] *nf* (*gen*) skill, dexterity; (*pey*) guile; (*costumbre*) habit; (*una ~*) trick, knack; **con** ~ craftily.

mañana [mányá'ná] *ad* tomorrow ♦ *nm* future ♦ *nf* morning; **de** o **por la** ~ in the morning; **¡hasta ~!** see you tomorrow!; **pasado** ~ the day after tomorrow; ~ **por la** ~ tomorrow morning.

mañanero, a [mányáne'ro, á] *a* early-rising.

mañoso, a [mányo'so, á] *a* (*hábil*) skilful; (*astuto*) smart, clever.

mapa [má'pá] *nm* map.

maqueta [máke'tà] *nf* (scale) model.

maquiavélico, a [mákyáhe'lēko, á] *a* Machiavellian.

maquillador, a [mákēyáthor', á] *nm/f* (*TEATRO etc*) make-up artist.

maquillaje [mákēyá'he] *nm* make-up; (*acto*) making up.

maquillar [mákēyár'] *vt* to make up; **~se** *vr* to put on (some) make-up.

máquina [má'kēná] *nf* machine; (*de tren*) locomotive, engine; (*FOTO*) camera; (*AM: coche*) car; (*fig*) machinery; (: *proyecto*) plan, project; **a toda** ~ at full speed; **escrito a** ~ typewritten; ~ **de escribir** typewriter; ~ **de coser/lavar** sewing/washing machine; ~ **de facsímil** facsimile (machine), fax; ~ **de franqueo** franking machine; ~ **tragaperras** slot machine.

maquinación [mákēnásyon'] *nf* machination, plot.

maquinal [mákēnál'] *a* (*fig*) mechanical, automatic.

maquinar [mákēnár'] *vt, vi* to plot.

maquinaria [mákēná'ryá] *nf* (*máquinas*) machinery; (*mecanismo*) mechanism, works *pl*.

maquinilla [mákēnē'yà] *nf* small machine; (*torno*) winch; ~ **de afeitar** razor; ~ **eléctrica** electric razor.

maquinista [mákēnē'stà] *nm* (*FERRO*) engineer (*US*), engine driver (*Brit*); (*TEC*) operator; (*NAUT*) engineer.

mar [már] *nm* sea; ~ **de fondo** groundswell; ~ **llena** high tide; ~ **adentro** o **afuera** out at sea; **en alta** ~ on the high seas; **por** ~ by sea o boat; **hacerse a la** ~ to put to sea; **a ~es** in abundance; **un** ~ **de** lots of; **es la** ~ **de guapa** she is ever so pretty; **el M~ Negro/Báltico** the Black/Baltic Sea; **el M~ Muerto/Rojo** the Dead/Red Sea; **el M~ del Norte** the North Sea.

mar. *abr* (= *marzo*) Mar.

maraña [márá'nyá] *nf* (*maleza*) thicket; (*confusión*) tangle.

maravilla [márábē'yà] *nf* marvel, wonder; (*BOT*) marigold; **hacer ~s** to work wonders; **a (las mil) ~s** wonderfully well.

maravillar [márábēyár'] *vt* to astonish, amaze; **~se** *vr* to be astonished, be amazed.

maravilloso, a [márábēyo'so, á] *a* wonderful, marvelous (*US*), marvellous (*Brit*).

marbellí [márheyē'] *a* of o from Marbella ♦ *nm/f* native o inhabitant of Marbella.

marca [már'kà] *nf* mark; (*sello*) stamp; (*COM*) make, brand; (*de ganado*) brand; (: *acto*) branding; (*NAUT*) seamark; (: *boya*) marker; (*DEPORTE*) record; **de** ~ excellent, outstanding; ~ **de fábrica** trademark; ~ **propia** own brand; ~ **registrada** registered trademark.

marcación [márkásyon'] *nf* (*TELEC*): ~ **automática** autodial.

marcado, a [márká'tho, á] *a* marked, strong.

marcador [márkáthor'] *nm* marker; (*rotulador*) marker (pen); (*de libro*) bookmark; (*DEPORTE*) scoreboard; (: *persona*) scorer.

marcar [márkár'] *vt* to mark; (*número de teléfono*) to dial; (*gol*) to score; (*números*) to record, keep a tally of; (*el pelo*) to set; (*suj: termómetro*) to register; (*tarea*) to assign; (*COM*) to put a price on ♦ *vi* (*DEPORTE*) to score; (*TELEC*) to dial; **mi reloj marca las 2** it's 2 o'clock by my watch; ~ **el compás** (*MUS*) to keep time.

marcial [mársyál'] *a* martial, military.

marciano, a [mársyá'no, á] *a* Martian, of o from Mars.

marco [már'ko] *nm* frame; (*DEPORTE*) goal-posts *pl*; (*moneda*) mark; (*fig*) setting; (*contexto*) framework; ~ **de chimenea** mantelpiece.

marcha [mártch'à] *nf* march; (*DEPORTE*) walk; (*TEC*) running, working; (*AUTO*) gear; (*velocidad*) speed; (*fig*) progress; (*dirección*) course; **dar ~ atrás** to reverse, put into reverse; **estar en** ~ to be under way, be in motion; **hacer algo sobre la** ~ to do sth as you *etc* go along; **poner en** ~ to put into gear; **ponerse en** ~ to start, get going; **a** ~**s forzadas** (*fig*) with all speed; **¡en** ~! (*MIL*) forward march!; (*fig*) let's go!; **"**~ **moderada"** (*AUTO*) "drive slowly"; **que tiene** *o* **de mucha** ~ (*fam*) very lively.

marchante, a [mȧrtchȧn'te, ȧ] *nm/f* dealer, merchant.

marchar [mȧrtchȧr'] *vi* (*ir*) to go; (*funcionar*) to work, go; (*fig*) to go, proceed; ~**se** *vr* to go (away), leave; **todo marcha bien** everything is going well.

marchitar [mȧrtchetȧr'] *vt* to wither, dry up; ~**se** *vr* (*BOT*) to wither; (*fig*) to fade away.

marchito, a [mȧrtche'to, ȧ] *a* withered, faded; (*fig*) in decline.

marchoso, a [mȧrtcho'so, ȧ] *a* (*fam: animado*) lively; (: *moderno*) modern.

marea [mȧre'ȧ] *nf* tide; (*llovizna*) drizzle; ~ **alta/baja** high/low tide; ~ **negra** oil slick.

mareado, a [mȧreȧ'tho, ȧ] *a*: **estar** ~ (*con náuseas*) to feel nauseated; (*aturdido*) to feel dizzy.

marear [mȧreȧr'] *vt* (*fig*: *irritar*) to annoy, upset; (*MED*): ~ **a uno** to make sb feel sick; ~**se** *vr* (*tener náuseas*) to feel sick; (*desvanecerse*) to feel faint; (*aturdirse*) to feel dizzy; (*fam*: *emborracharse*) to get tipsy.

marejada [mȧrehȧ'thȧ] *nf* (*NAUT*) swell, heavy sea.

maremágnum [mȧremȧg'nōōm], **maremagno** [mȧremȧg'no] *nm* (*fig*) ocean, abundance.

maremoto [mȧremo'to] *nm* tidal wave.

mareo [mȧre'o] *nm* (*náusea*) sick feeling; (*aturdimiento*) dizziness; (*fam*: *lata*) nuisance.

marfil [mȧrfēl'] *nm* ivory.

margarina [mȧrgȧrē'nȧ] *nf* margarine.

margarita [mȧrgȧrē'tȧ] *nf* (*BOT*) daisy; **(rueda)** ~ (*en máquina impresora*) daisy wheel.

margen [mȧr'hen] *nm* (*borde*) edge, border; (*fig*) margin, space; ~ **de beneficio** *o* **de ganancia** profit margin; ~ **comercial** mark-up; ~ **de confianza** credibility gap ♦ *nf* (*de río etc*) bank; **dar** ~ **para** to give an opportunity for; **dejar a uno al** ~ to leave sb out (in the cold); **mantenerse al** ~ to keep out (of things); **al** ~ **de lo que digas** despite what you say.

marginado, a [mȧrhēnȧ'tho, ȧ] *nm/f* outcast.

marginar [mȧrhēnȧr'] *vt* to exclude.

marica [mȧrē'kȧ] *nm* (*fam*) sissy; (*homosexual*) queer.

Maricastaña [mȧrēkȧstȧ'nyȧ] *nf*: **en los días** *o* **en tiempos de** ~ way back, in the good old days.

maricón [mȧrēkon'] *nm* (*fam*) queer.

marido [mȧrē'tho] *nm* husband.

mariguana [mȧrēgwȧ'nȧ], **marijuana** [mȧrēhwȧ'nȧ] *nf* marijuana, cannabis.

marimacho [mȧrēmȧtch'o] *nf* (*fam*) mannish woman.

marimorena [mȧrēmore'nȧ] *nf* fuss, row; **armar una** ~ to kick up a fuss.

marina [mȧrē'nȧ] *nf* navy; ~ **mercante** merchant marine (*US*), merchant navy (*Brit*).

marinero, a [mȧrēne'ro, ȧ] *a* sea *cpd*; (*barco*) seaworthy ♦ *nm* sailor, seaman.

marino, a [mȧrē'no, ȧ] *a* sea *cpd*, marine ♦ *nm* sailor; ~ **de agua dulce/de cubierta/de primera** landlubber/deckhand/able seaman.

marioneta [mȧryone'tȧ] *nf* puppet.

mariposa [mȧrēpo'sȧ] *nf* butterfly.

mariposear [mȧrēposeȧr'] *vi* (*revolotear*) to flutter about; (*ser inconstante*) to be fickle; (*coquetear*) to flirt.

mariquita [mȧrēkē'tȧ] *nm* (*fam*) sissy; (*homosexual*) queer ♦ *nf* (*ZOOL*) ladybug (*US*), ladybird (*Brit*).

mariscos [mȧrēs'kos] *nmpl* shellfish *sg*, seafood *sg*.

marisma [mȧrēs'mȧ] *nf* marsh, swamp.

marisquería [mȧrēskerē'ȧ] *nf* shellfish bar, seafood restaurant.

marítimo, a [mȧrē'tēmo, ȧ] *a* sea *cpd*, maritime.

marmita [mȧrmē'tȧ] *nf* pot.

mármol [mȧr'mol] *nm* marble.

marmóreo, a [mȧrmo'reo, ȧ] *a* marble.

marmota [mȧrmo'tȧ] *nf* (*ZOOL*) marmot; (*fig*) sleepyhead.

maroma [mȧro'mȧ] *nf* rope.

marque [mȧr'ke] *etc vb* V **marcar**.

marqués, esa [mȧrkes', esȧ] *nm/f* marquis/ marchioness.

marquesina [mȧrkesē'nȧ] *nf* (*de parada*) bus-shelter.

marquetería [mȧrketerē'ȧ] *nf* marquetry, inlaid work.

marrano, a [mȧrrȧ'no, ȧ] *a* filthy, dirty ♦ *nm* (*ZOOL*) pig; (*malo*) swine; (*sucio*) dirty pig.

marrar [mȧrrȧr'] *vi* to miss; (*fig*) to miss the mark.

marras [mȧ'rrȧs]: **de** ~ *ad*: **es el problema de** ~ it's the same old problem.

marrón [mȧrron'] *a* brown.

marroquí [mȧrrokē'] *a, nm/f* Moroccan ♦ *nm* Morocco (leather).

Marruecos [mȧrrwe'kos] *nm* Morocco.

marta [mȧr'tȧ] *nf* (*animal*) (pine) marten; (*piel*) sable.

Martes [már'tes] *nm inv* Mars.

martes [már'tes] *nm inv* Tuesday; ~ **de carnaval** Shrove Tuesday.

martillar [mártēyár'], **martillear** [mártēyeár'] *vt* to hammer.

martilleo [mártēye'o] *nm* hammering.

martillo [mártē'yo] *nm* hammer; (*de presidente de asamblea, comité*) gavel; ~ **neumático** jackhammer (*US*), pneumatic drill (*Brit*).

Martinica [mártēnē'ká] *nf* Martinique.

mártir [már'tēr] *nm/f* martyr.

martirice [mártērē'se] *etc vb V* **martirizar**.

martirio [mártē'ryo] *nm* martyrdom; (*fig*) torture, torment.

martirizar [mártērēsár'] *vt* (*REL*) to martyr; (*fig*) to torture, torment.

marxismo [márksēs'mo] *nm* Marxism.

marxista [márksē'stá] *a nm/f* Marxist.

marzo [már'so] *nm* March.

mas [más] *conj* but.

más [más] *a, ad* (*comparativo*) more; (*superlativo*) most; (*otro*) another, more ♦ *conj* and, plus; **A es ~ difícil que B** A is more difficult *o* harder than B; **cada vez ~ difícil** more and more difficult, harder and harder; **es ~ de medianoche** it's after midnight; **el libro ~ leído del año** the most widely-read book of the year; **un kilómetro ~** one more kilometer; **él es el ~ inteligente** he is the most intelligent (one); **¡qué perro ~ feo!** what an ugly dog!; **~ de 6** more than 6; **~ que/~ de lo que pensaba** more than he thought; **~ bien** rather; **así no ~** (*AM*) just like that; **es ~** furthermore; **de ~** extra; **estar de ~** to be unnecessary; **¡qué ~ da!** what does it matter?; **~ o menos** more or less; **a las 8 a ~ tardar** at 8 o'clock at the latest; **~ vale tarde que nunca** better late than never; **no ~ se fue se acordó** (*AM*) no sooner had she left than she remembered.

masa [má'sá] *nf* (*mezcla*) dough; (*volumen*) volume, mass; (*FÍSICA*) mass; **en ~** en masse; **las ~s** (*POL*) the masses.

masacrar [másákrár'] *vt* to massacre.

masacre [másá'kre] *nf* massacre.

masaje [másá'he] *nm* massage; **dar ~ a** to massage.

masajista [másáhē'stá] *nm/f* masseur/masseuse.

mascar [máskár'] *vt, vi* to chew; (*fig*) to mumble, mutter.

máscara [más'kárá] *nf* (*tb INFORM*) mask ♦ *nm/f* masked person; ~ **antigás** gas mask.

mascarada [máskárá'tḥá] *nf* masquerade.

mascarilla [máskárē'yá] *nf* mask; (*vaciado*) deathmask; (*maquillaje*) face pack.

mascarón [máskáron'] *nm* large mask; ~ **de proa** figurehead.

masculino, a [máskōōlē'no, á] *a* masculine;

(*BIO*) male ♦ *nm* (*LING*) masculine.

mascullar [máskōōyár'] *vt* to mumble, mutter.

masilla [másē'yá] *nf* putty.

masivo, a [másē'ḥo, á] *a* (*en masa*) mass.

masón [máson'] *nm* (free)mason.

masonería [másonerē'á] *nf* (free)masonry.

masoquista [másokē'stá] *a* masochistic ♦ *nm/f* masochist.

masque [más'ke] *etc vb V* **mascar**.

masticar [mástēkár'] *vt* to chew; (*fig*) to ponder over.

mástil [má'stēl] *nm* (*de navío*) mast; (*de guitarra*) neck.

mastín [mástēn'] *nm* mastiff.

mastique [mástē'ke] *etc vb V* **masticar**.

masturbación [mástōōrḥásyon'] *nf* masturbation.

masturbarse [mástōōrḥár'se] *vr* to masturbate.

Mat. *abr* = **Matemáticas.**

mata [má'tá] *nf* (*arbusto*) bush, shrub; (*de hierbas*) tuft; (*campo*) field; (*manojo*) tuft, blade; **~s** *nfpl* scrub sg; ~ **de pelo** mop of hair; **a salto de ~** (*día a día*) from day to day; (*al azar*) haphazardly.

matadero [mátátḥe'ro] *nm* slaughterhouse.

matador, a [mátátḥor', á] *a* killing ♦ *nm/f* killer ♦ *nm* (*TAUR*) matador, bullfighter.

matamoscas [mátámos'kás] *nm inv* (*palo*) fly swatter.

matanza [mátán'sá] *nf* slaughter.

matar [mátár'] *vt* to kill; (*tiempo, pelota*) to kill ♦ *vi* to kill; **~se** *vr* (*suicidarse*) to kill o.s., commit suicide; (*morir*) to be *o* get killed; (*gastarse*) to wear o.s. out; ~ **el hambre** to stave off hunger; ~ **a uno a disgustos** to make sb's life miserable; **~las callando** to go about things quietly; **~se trabajando** to kill o.s. with work; **~se por hacer algo** to struggle to do sth.

matarife [mátárē'fe] *nm* slaughterman.

matasellos [mátáse'yos] *nm inv* postmark.

matasanos [mátásá'nos] *nm inv* quack.

mate [má'te] *a* (*sin brillo: color*) dull, matt ♦ *nm* (*en ajedrez*) (check)mate; (*AM: hierba*) maté; (: *vasija*) gourd.

matemático, a [mátemá'tēko, á] *a* mathematical ♦ *nm/f* mathematician ♦ **matemáticas** *nfpl* mathematics *sg*.

materia [máte'ryá] *nf* (*gen*) matter; (*TEC*) material; (*ESCOL*) subject; **en ~ de** on the subject of; (*en cuanto a*) as regards; ~ **prima** raw material; **entrar en ~** to get down to business.

material [máteryál'] *a* material; (*dolor*) physical; (*real*) real; (*literal*) literal ♦ *nm* material; (*TEC*) equipment; ~ **de construcción** building material; **~es de derribo** rubble *sg*.

materialismo [máteryálēs'mo] *nm* materialism.

materialista [máteryálē'stá] *a* material-ist(ic).

materialmente [máteryálmen'te] *ad* materially; (*fig*) absolutely.

maternal [máternál'] *a* motherly, maternal.

maternidad [máternēthátħ'] *nf* motherhood, maternity.

materno, a [máter'no, á] *a* maternal; (*lengua*) mother *cpd*.

matice [mátē'se] *etc vb V* **matizar**.

matinal [mátēnál'] *a* morning *cpd*.

matiz [mátēs'] *nm* shade; (*de sentido*) shade, nuance; (*ironía etc*) touch.

matizar [mátēsár'] *vt* (*variar*) to vary; (*ARTE*) to blend; ~ **de** to tinge with.

matón [máton'] *nm* bully.

matorral [mátorrál'] *nm* thicket.

matraca [mátrá'ká] *nf* rattle; (*fam*) nuisance.

matraz [mátrás'] *nm* (*QUÍMICA*) flask.

matriarcado [mátryárká'tħo] *nm* matriarchy.

matrícula [mátrē'kōōlá] *nf* (*registro*) registration (*US*), register (*Brit*); (*ESCOL: inscripción*) registration; (*AUTO*) registration number; (: *placa*) license plate (*US*), number plate (*Brit*).

matricular [mátrēkōōlár'] *vt* to register.

matrimonial [mátrēmonyál'] *a* matrimonial.

matrimonio [mátrēmo'nyo] *nm* (*pareja*) (married) couple; (*acto*) marriage; ~ **civil/clandestino** civil/secret marriage; **contraer** ~ (**con**) to marry.

matriz [mátrēs'] *nf* (*ANAT*) womb; (*TEC*) mold (*US*), mould (*Brit*); (*MAT*) matrix; **casa** ~ (*COM*) head office.

matrona [mátro'ná] *nf* (*persona de edad*) matron.

matutino, a [mátōōtē'no, á] *a* morning *cpd*.

maula [má'ōōlá] *a* (*persona*) good-for-nothing ♦ *nm/f* (*vago*) idler, slacker ♦ *nf* (*persona*) dead loss (*fam*).

maullar [máōōyár'] *vi* to mew, miaow.

maullido [máōōyē'tħo] *nm* mew(ing), miaow(ing).

Mauricio [máōōrē'syo] *nm* Mauritius.

Mauritania [máōōrētá'nyá] *nf* Mauritania.

mausoleo [máōōsole'o] *nm* mausoleum.

maxilar [máksēlár'] *nm* jaw(bone).

máxima [mák'sēmá] *nf V* **máximo**.

máxime [mák'sēme] *ad* especially.

máximo, a [mák'sēmo, á] *a* maximum; (*más alto*) highest; (*más grande*) greatest ♦ *nm* maximum ♦ *nf* maxim; **como** ~ at most; **al** ~ to the utmost.

mayo [má'yo] *nm* May.

mayonesa [máyone'sá] *nf* mayonnaise.

mayor [máyor'] *a* main, chief; (*adulto*) grown-up, adult; (*JUR*) of age; (*de edad avanzada*) elderly; (*MUS*) major; (*comparativo*: *de tamaño*) bigger; (: *de edad*) older; (*superlativo*: *de tamaño*) biggest; (*tb*: *fig*) greatest; (: *de edad*) oldest ♦ *nm* chief, boss; (*adulto*) adult; **al por** ~ wholesale; ~ **de edad** adult; *V tb* **mayores**.

mayores [máyo'res] *nmpl* grown-ups; **llegar a** ~**es** to get out of hand.

mayoral [máyorál'] *nm* foreman.

mayordomo [máyortħo'mo] *nm* butler.

mayoría [máyorē'á] *nf* majority, greater part; **en la** ~ **de los casos** in most cases; **en su** ~ on the whole.

mayorista [máyorē'stá] *nm/f* wholesaler.

mayoritario, a [máyorētá'ryo, á] *a* majority *cpd*; **gobierno** ~ majority government.

mayúsculo, a [máyōōs'kōōlo, á] *a* (*fig*) big, tremendous ♦ *nf* capital (letter); **mayúsculas** *nfpl* capitals; (*TIP*) upper case *sg*.

maza [má'sá] *nf* (*arma*) mace; (*DEPORTE*) bat; (*POLO*) stick.

mazacote [másáko'te] *nm* hard mass; (*CULIN*) dry doughy food; (*ARTE, LITERATURA etc*) mess, hodgepodge.

mazapán [másápán'] *nm* marzipan.

mazmorra [másmo'rrá] *nf* dungeon.

mazo [má'so] *nm* (*martillo*) mallet; (*de mortero*) pestle; (*de flores*) bunch; (*DEPORTE*) bat.

mazorca [másor'ká] *nf* (*BOT*) spike; (*de maíz*) cob, ear.

MCAC *nm abr* = **Mercado Común de la América Central**.

MCI *nm abr* = **Mercado Común Iberoamericano**.

me [me] *pron* (*directo*) me; (*indirecto*) (to) me; (*reflexivo*) (to) myself; **¡dámelo!** give it to me!; ~ **lo compró** (*de mí*) he bought it from me; (*para mí*) he bought it for me.

mear [meár'] (*fam*) *vt* to piss on (!) ♦ *vi* to pee, piss (!), take (*US*) *o* have (*Brit*) a piss (!); ~**se** *vr* to wet o.s.

Meca [me'ká] *nf*: **La** ~ Mecca.

mecánica [meká'nēká] *nf V* **mecánico**.

mecanice [mekánē'se] *etc vb V* **mecanizar**.

mecánico, a [meká'nēko, á] *a* mechanical; (*repetitivo*) repetitive ♦ *nm/f* mechanic ♦ *nf* (*estudio*) mechanics *sg*; (*mecanismo*) mechanism.

mecanismo [mekánēs'mo] *nm* mechanism; (*engranaje*) gear.

mecanizar [mekánēsár'] *vt* to mechanize.

mecanografía [mekánografē'á] *nf* typewriting.

mecanografiado, a [mekánográfyá'tħo, á] *a* typewritten ♦ *nm* typescript.

mecanógrafo, a [mekáno'gráfo, á] *nm/f* (*copy*) typist.

mecate [meká'te] *nm* (*AM*) rope.

mecedora [mesetħo'rá] *nf* rocking chair.

mecenas [mese'nás] *nm inv* patron.

mecenazgo [mesenàs'ġo] *nm* patronage.

mecer [meser'] *vt (cuna)* to rock; ~**se** *vr* to rock; *(rama)* to sway.

mecha [metch'à] *nf (de vela)* wick; *(de bomba)* fuse; **a toda** ~ at full speed; **ponerse** ~**s** to streak one's hair.

mechero [metche'ro] *nm* (cigarette) lighter.

mechón [metchon'] *nm (gen)* tuft; *(manojo)* bundle; *(de pelo)* lock.

medalla [metħà'yà] *nf* medal.

media [me'ħyà] *nf* V **medio**.

mediado, a [meħyà'ħo, a] *a* half-full; *(trabajo)* half-completed; **a** ~**s de** in the middle of, halfway through.

medianamente [meħyànàmen'te] *ad (moderadamente)* moderately, fairly; *(regularmente)* moderately well.

mediano, a [meħyà'no, à] *a (regular)* medium, average; *(mediocre)* mediocre; **(de tamaño)** ~ medium-sized.

medianoche [meħyànotch'e] *nf* midnight.

mediante [meħyàn'te] *ad* by (means of), through.

mediar [meħyàr'] *vi (tiempo)* to elapse; *(interceder)* to mediate, intervene; *(existir)* to exist; **media el hecho de que ...** there is the fact that ....

medicación [meħēkàsyon'] *nf* medication, treatment.

medicamento [meħēkàmen'to] *nm* medicine, drug.

medicina [meħēse'nà] *nf* medicine.

medición [meħēsyon'] *nf* measurement.

médico, a [me'ħēko, à] *a* medical ♦ *nm/f* doctor; ~ **de cabecera** family doctor; ~ **pediatra** pediatrician *(US)*, paediatrician *(Brit)*; ~ **residente** intern *(US)*, house physician.

medida [meħē'ħà] *nf* measure; *(medición)* measurement; *(de camisa, zapato etc)* size, fitting; *(prudencia)* moderation, prudence; **en cierta/gran** ~ up to a point/to a great extent; **un traje a la** ~ tailor-made suit; ~ **de cuello** collar size; **a** ~ **de** in proportion to; *(de acuerdo con)* in keeping with; **con** ~ with restraint; **sin** ~ immoderately; **a** ~ **que ...** (at the same time) as ...; **tomar** ~**s** to take steps.

medio, a [me'ħyo, à] *a* half (a); *(punto)* mid, middle; *(promedio)* average ♦ *ad* half ♦ *nm (centro)* middle; *(promedio)* average; *(método)* means, way; *(ambiente)* environment ♦ *nf* ~**s panti** pantyhose *(US)*, tights *(Brit)*; *(prenda de vestir)* stocking, *(AM)* sock; *(promedio)* average; **a** ~**s** barely; **pagar a** ~**s** to share the cost; **media hora** half an hour; ~ **litro** half a liter; **las tres y media** half after three; **M**~ **Oriente** Middle East; **a** ~ **camino** halfway (there); ~ **dormido** half asleep; **a** ~ **terminar** half finished; **en** ~ in the middle;

(entre) in between; **por** ~ **de** by (means of), through; **en los** ~**s financieros** in financial circles; **encontrarse en su** ~ to be in one's element; ~ **circulante** *(COM)* money supply; V *tb* **medios**.

mediocre [meħyo'kre] *a* middling, average; *(pey)* mediocre.

mediocridad [meħyokreħàħ'] *nf* middling quality; *(pey)* mediocrity.

mediodía [meħyoħē'à] *nm* midday, noon.

mediopensionista [meħyopensyonē'stà] *nm/f* day boy/girl.

medios [me'ħyos] *nmpl* means, resources.

medir [meħēr'] *vt (gen)* to measure ♦ *vi* to measure; ~**se** *vr (moderarse)* to be moderate, act with restraint; **¿cuánto mides? — mido 1.50 m** how tall are you? — I am 1.50 m tall.

meditar [meħētàr'] *vt* to ponder, think over, meditate on; *(planear)* to think out ♦ *vi* to ponder, think, meditate.

mediterráneo, a [meħēterrà'neo, à] *a* Mediterranean ♦ *nm*: **el (mar) M**~ the Mediterranean (Sea).

medrar [meħràr'] *vi* to increase, grow; *(mejorar)* to improve; *(prosperar)* to prosper, thrive; *(animal, planta etc)* to grow.

medroso, a [meħro'so, à] *a* fearful, timid.

médula [me'ħōolà] *nf (ANAT)* marrow; *(BOT)* pith; ~ **espinal** spinal cord; **hasta la** ~ *(fig)* to the core.

medusa [meħōo'sà] *nf (Esp)* jellyfish.

megabyte [me'ġàbàēt] *nm (INFORM)* megabyte.

megáfono [meġà'fono] *nm* megaphone.

megalomanía [meġàlomànē'à] *nf* megalomania.

megalómano, a [meġàlo'màno, à] *nm/f* megalomaniac.

megaocteto [meġàokte'to] *nm (INFORM)* megabyte.

mejicano, a [mehēkà'no, à] *a, nm/f* Mexican.

Méjico [me'hēko] *nm* Mexico.

mejilla [mehē'yà] *nf* cheek.

mejillón [mehēyon'] *nm* mussel.

mejor [mehor'] *a, ad (comparativo)* better; *(superlativo)* best; **lo** ~ the best thing; **lo** ~ **de la vida** the prime of life; **a lo** ~ probably; *(quizá)* maybe; ~ **dicho** rather; **tanto** ~ so much the better; **es el** ~ **de todos** he's the best of all.

mejora [meho'rà] *nf*, **mejoramiento** [mehorámyen'to] *nm* improvement.

mejorar [mehoràr'] *vt* to improve, make better ♦ *vi*, ~**se** *vr* to improve, get better; *(COM)* to do well, prosper; ~ **a** to be better than; **los negocios mejoran** business is picking up.

mejoría [mehorē'à] *nf* improvement; *(restablecimiento)* recovery.

melancólico, a [melánko'léko, á] *a* (*triste*) sad, melancholy; (*soñador*) dreamy.

melena [mele'ná] *nf* (*de persona*) long hair; (*ZOOL*) mane.

melillense [meléyen'se] *a* of *o* from Melilla ♦ *nm/f* native *o* inhabitant of Melilla.

melocotón [melokoton'] *nm* (*Esp*) peach.

melodía [melolŋē'á] *nf* melody; (*aire*) tune.

melodrama [melolŋrá'má] *nm* melodrama.

melodramático, a [melolŋrámá'tēko, á] *a* melodramatic.

melón [melon'] *nm* melon.

melopea [melope'á] *nf* (*fam*): **tener una ~** to be soused (*US*) *o* sloshed (*Brit*).

meloso, a [melo'so, á] *a* honeyed, sweet; (*empalagoso*) sickly, cloying; (*voz*) sweet; (*zalamero*) smooth.

mella [me'yá] *nf* (*rotura*) notch, nick; **hacer ~** (*fig*) to make an impression.

mellizo, a [meyē'so, á] *a*, *nm/f* twin ♦ *nm* (*AM*): **~s** cufflinks.

membrete [membre'te] *nm* letterhead.

membrillo [membrē'yo] *nm* quince; **carne de ~** quince jelly.

memo, a [me'mo, á] *a* silly, stupid ♦ *nm/f* idiot.

memorable [memorá'ḫle] *a* memorable.

memorándum [memorán'dōōm] *nm* (*libro*) notebook; (*comunicación*) memorandum.

memoria [memo'ryá] *nf* (*gen*) memory; (*artículo*) (learned) paper; **~s** *nfpl* (*de autor*) memoirs; (*comunicación*) memorandum. (*de autor*) memoirs; (*comunicación*) annual report; **aprender algo de ~** to learn sth by heart; **si tengo buena ~** if my memory serves me right; **venir a la ~** to come to mind; (*INFORM*): **~ de acceso aleatorio** random access memory, RAM; **~ auxiliar** backing storage; **~ fija** read-only memory, ROM; **~ fija programable** programmable memory; **~ del teclado** keyboard memory.

memorice [memorē'se] *etc vb V* **memorizar.**

memorizar [memorēsár'] *vt* to memorize.

menaje [mená'he] *nm* (*muebles*) furniture; (*utensilios domésticos*) household equipment; **~ de cocina** kitchenware.

mencionar [mensyonár'] *vt* to mention; (*nombrar*) to name; **sin ~ ...** let alone ....

mendicidad [mendēsē'ḫáḫ'] *nf* begging.

mendigar [mendēgár'] *vt* to beg (for).

mendigo, a [mendē'go, á] *nm/f* beggar.

mendigue [mendē'ge] *etc vb V* **mendigar.**

mendrugo [mendrōō'go] *nm* crust.

menear [meneár'] *vt* to move; (*cola*) to wag; (*cadera*) to swing; (*fig*) to handle; **~se** *vr* to shake; (*balancearse*) to sway; (*moverse*) to move; (*fig*) to get a move on.

menester [menester'] *nm* (*necesidad*) necessity; **~es** *nmpl* (*deberes*) duties; **es ~ hacer algo** it is necessary to do sth, sth must be done.

menestra [menes'trá] *nf*: **~ de verduras** vegetable stew.

mengano, a [mengá'no, á] *nm/f* Mr (*o* Mrs *o* Miss) So-and-so.

mengua [men'gwá] *nf* (*disminución*) decrease; (*falta*) lack; (*pobreza*) poverty; (*fig*) discredit; **en ~ de** to the detriment of.

menguante [mengwán'te] *a* decreasing, diminishing; (*luna*) waning; (*marea*) ebb *cpd.*

menguar [mengwár'] *vt* to lessen, diminish; (*fig*) to discredit ♦ *vi* to diminish, decrease; (*fig*) to decline.

mengüe [men'gwe] *etc vb V* **menguar.**

menopausia [menopá'ōōsyá] *nf* menopause.

menor [menor'] *a* (*más pequeño: comparativo*) smaller; (*número*) less, lesser; (: *superlativo*) smallest; (*número*) least; (*más joven: comparativo*) younger; (: *superlativo*) youngest; (*MUS*) minor ♦ *nm/f* (*joven*) young person, juvenile; **Juanito es ~ que Pepe** Juanito is younger than Pepe; **ella es la ~ de todas** she is the youngest of all; **no tengo la ~ idea** I haven't the faintest idea; **al por ~** retail; **~ de edad** under age.

Menorca [menor'ká] *nf* Minorca.

menoría [menorē'á] *n* (*AM COM*): **a ~** retail.

menorquín, ina [menorkēn', ēná] *a*, *nm/f* Minorcan.

menos [me'nos] *a* (*comparativo: sg*) less; (: *pl*) fewer; (*superlativo: sg*) least; (: *pl*) fewest ♦ *ad* (*comparativo*) less; (*superlativo*) least ♦ *conj*, *prep* except ♦ *nm* (*MAT*) minus; **~ de lo que piensas** less than you think; **es el ~ inteligente de los 4** he is the least intelligent of the 4; **eso es lo de ~** that's the least of it; **es lo ~ que puedo hacer** it's the least I can do; **lo ~ posible** as little as possible; **a ~ que** unless; **~ de 5** less than 5; **hay 7 de ~** we're 7 short; **no es rico, ni mucho ~** he's far from being rich; **ir** *o* **venir a ~** to come down in the world; **al** *o* **por lo ~** at least; **¡~ mal!** just as well!; **¡todo ~ eso!** anything but that!; **¿qué ~?** (*fam*) what else did you expect?; **las 7 ~ 20** (*hora*) 20 to 7.

menoscabar [menoskáḫár'] *vt* (*estropear*) to damage, harm; (*fig*) to discredit.

menospreciar [menospresyár'] *vt* to underrate, undervalue; (*despreciar*) to scorn, despise.

menosprecio [menospre'syo] *nm* underrating, undervaluation; scorn, contempt.

mensaje [mensá'he] *nm* message; **~ de error** (*INFORM*) error message.

mensajero, a [mensáhe'ro, á] *nm/f* messenger.

menstruación [menstrwásyon'] *nf* menstruación.

menstruar [menstrwàr'] *vi* to menstruate.

mensual [menswàl'] *a* monthly; **100 ptas ~es** 100 ptas. a month.

mensualidad [menswàlēt̪hàt̪h'] *nf* (*salario*) monthly salary; (*COM*) monthly payment *o* installment.

menta [men'tà] *nf* mint.

mentado, a [mentà'tho, à] *a* (*mencionado*) aforementioned; (*famoso*) well-known.

mental [mentàl'] *a* mental.

mentalidad [mentàlēt̪hàt̪h'] *nf* mentality, way of thinking.

mentar [mentàr'] *vt* to mention, name.

mente [men'te] *nf* mind; (*inteligencia*) intelligence; **no tengo en ~ hacer eso** it is not my intention to do that.

mentecato, a [mentekà'to, à] *a* silly, stupid ♦ *nm/f* fool, idiot.

mentir [mentēr'] *vi* to lie; **¡miento!** sorry, I'm wrong!

mentira [mentē'rà] *nf* (*una ~*) lie; (*acto*) lying; (*invención*) fiction; **~ piadosa** white lie; **una ~ como una casa** a whopping great lie (*fam*); **parece ~ que** ... it seems incredible that ..., I can't believe that ....

mentiroso, a [mentēro'so, à] *a* lying; (*falso*) deceptive ♦ *nm/f* liar.

mentís [mentēs'] *nm inv* denial; **dar el ~ a** to deny.

mentón [menton'] *nm* chin.

menú [menōō'] *nm* (*tb INFORM*) menu; (*en restaurante*) set meal; **guiado por ~** (*INFORM*) menu-driven.

menudear [menōōt̪heàr'] *vt* (*repetir*) to repeat frequently ♦ *vi* (*ser frecuente*) to be frequent; (*detallar*) to go into great detail.

menudencia [menōōt̪hen'syà] *nf* (*bagatela*) trifle; **~s** *nfpl* odds and ends.

menudillos [menōōt̪he'yos] *nmpl* giblets.

menudo, a [menōō'tho, à] *a* (*pequeño*) small, tiny; (*sin importancia*) petty, insignificant; **¡~ negocio!** (*fam*) some deal!; **a ~** often, frequently.

meñique [menyē'ke] *nm* little finger.

meollo [meo'yo] *nm* (*fig*) essence, core.

mequetrefe [meketre'fe] *nm* good-for-nothing, whippersnapper.

mercader [merkàt̪her'] *nm* merchant.

mercadería [merkàt̪herē'à] *nf* commodity; **~s** *nfpl* goods, merchandise *sg*.

mercado [merkà'tho] *nm* market; **~ en baja** falling market; **M~ Común** Common Market; **~ de demanda/de oferta** seller's/buyer's market; **~ laboral** labor market; **~ objetivo** target market; **~ de productos básicos** commodity market; **~ de valores** stock market; **~ exterior/interior** *o* **nacional/libre** overseas/domestic/free market.

mercancía [merkànsē'à] *nf* commodity; **~s** *nfpl* goods, merchandise *sg*; **~s en depósi-**

to bonded goods; **~s perecederas** perishable goods.

mercancías [merkànsē'às] *nm inv* freight train (*US*), goods train.

mercantil [merkàntēl'] *a* mercantile, commercial.

mercenario, a [mersenà'ryo, à] *a, nm* mercenary.

mercería [merserē'à] *nf* (*artículos*) notions *pl* (*US*), haberdashery (*Brit*); (*tienda*) notions store (*US*), haberdasher's shop (*Brit*), drapery (*Brit*).

mercurio [merkōō'ryo] *nm* mercury.

merecedor, a [mereset̪hor', à] *a* deserving; **~ de confianza** trustworthy.

merecer [mereser'] *vt* to deserve, merit ♦ *vi* to be deserving, be worthy; **merece la pena** it's worthwhile.

merecido, a [meresē'tho, à] *a* (well-) deserved; **llevarse su ~** to get one's deserts.

merendar [merendàr'] *vt* to have for lunch (*US*) *o* tea (*Brit*) ♦ *vi* to have lunch (*US*) *o* tea (*Brit*); (*en el campo*) to have a picnic.

merendero [merende'ro] *nm* (*café*) tearoom; (*en el campo*) picnic spot.

merengue [meren'ge] *nm* meringue.

merezca [meres'kà] *etc vb V* **merecer.**

meridiano [merēt̪hyà'no] *nm* (*ASTRO, GEO*) meridian; **la explicación es de una claridad meridiana** the explanation is as clear as day.

meridional [merēt̪hyonàl'] *a* Southern ♦ *nm/f* Southerner.

merienda [meryen'dà] *etc vb V* **merendar** ♦ *nf* (light) tea, afternoon snack; (*de campo*) picnic; **~ de negros** free-for-all.

mérito [me'rēto] *nm* merit; (*valor*) worth, value; **hacer ~s** to make a good impression; **restar ~ a** to detract from.

meritorio, a [merēto'ryo, à] *a* deserving.

merluza [merlōō'sà] *nf* hake; **coger una ~** (*fam*) to get soused (*US*) *o* sozzled (*Brit*).

merma [mer'mà] *nf* decrease; (*pérdida*) wastage.

mermar [mermàr'] *vt* to reduce, lessen ♦ *vi* to decrease, dwindle.

mermelada [mermelà'thà] *nf* jam; **~ de naranja** marmalade.

mero, a [me'ro, à] *a* mere, simple; (*AM fam*) very ♦ *nm* (*ZOOL*) grouper.

merodear [merot̪heàr'] *vi* (*MIL*) to maraud; (*de noche*) to prowl (about); (*curiosear*) to snoop around.

mes [mes] *nm* month; (*salario*) month's pay; **el ~ corriente** this *o* the current month.

mesa [me'sà] *nf* table; (*de trabajo*) desk; (*COM*) counter; (*en mitin*) platform; (*GEO*) plateau; (*ARQ*) landing; **~ de noche/de tijera/de operaciones** *u* **operatoria** bedside/folding/operating table; **~ redonda**

(*reunión*) round table; ~ **digitalizadora** (*IN-FORM*) graph pad; ~ **directiva** board; ~ **y cama** room and board; **poner/quitar la** ~ to set/clear the table.

mesarse [mesár'se] *vr*: ~ **el pelo** *o* **los cabellos** to tear one's hair out.

mesera [mese'rá] *nf* (*AM*) waitress.

mesero [mese'ro] *nm* (*AM*) waiter.

meseta [mesē'tá] *nf* (*GEO*) meseta, tableland; (*ARQ*) landing.

mesilla [mesē'yá], **mesita** [mesē'tá] *nf*: ~ **de noche** bedside table.

mesón [meson'] *nm* inn.

mestizo, a [mestē'so, á] *a* half-breed, of mixed race; (*ZOOL*) crossbred ♦ *nm/f* half-breed.

mesura [mesōō'rá] *nf* (*calma*) calm; (*moderación*) moderation, restraint; (*cortesía*) courtesy.

mesurar [mesōōrár'] *vt* (*contener*) to restrain; ~**se** *vr* to restrain o.s.

meta [me'tá] *nf* goal; (*de carrera*) finish; (*fig*) goal, aim, objective.

metafísico, a [metáfē'sēko, á] *a* metaphysical ♦ *nf* metaphysics *sg*.

metafórico, a [metáfo'rēko, á] *a* metaphorical.

metáfora [metá'forá] *nf* metaphor.

metal [metál'] *nm* (*materia*) metal; (*MUS*) brass.

metálico, a [metá'lēko, á] *a* metallic; (*de metal*) metal ♦ *nm* (*dinero contante*) cash.

metalurgia [metálōōr'hyá] *nf* metallurgy.

metalúrgico, a [metálōōr'hēko, á] *a* metallurgic(al); **industria** ~**a** steel industry.

metamorfosear [metámorfoseár'] *vt*: ~ **(en)** to metamorphose *o* transform (into).

metamorfosis [metámorfo'sēs] *nf inv* metamorphosis, transformation.

metedura [metethōō'rá] *nf*: ~ **de pata** (*fam*) blunder.

meteoro [meteo'ro] *nm* meteor.

meteorólogo, a [meteoro'logo, á] *nm/f* meteorologist; (*RADIO, TV*) weatherman.

meter [meter'] *vt* (*colocar*) to put, place; (*introducir*) to put in, insert; (*involucrar*) to involve; (*causar*) to make, cause; ~**se** *vr*: ~**se en** to go into, enter; (*fig*) to interfere in, meddle in; ~**se a** to start; ~**se a escritor** to become a writer; ~**se con uno** to provoke sb, pick a quarrel with sb; ~ **prisa a uno** to hurry sb up.

meticuloso, a [metēkōōlo'so, á] *a* meticulous, thorough.

metido, a [metē'tho, á] *a*: **estar muy** ~ **en un asunto** to be deeply involved in a matter; ~ **en años** elderly; ~ **en carne** plump.

metódico, a [meto'thēko, á] *a* methodical.

metodismo [metothēs'mo] *nm* Methodism.

método [me'totho] *nm* method.

metomentodo [metomento'tho] *nm inv* meddler, busybody.

metraje [metrá'he] *nm* (*CINE*) length; **cinta de largo/corto** ~ full-length film/short.

metralleta [metráye'tá] *nf* sub-machine-gun.

métrico, a [me'trēko, á] *a* metric; **cinta métrica** tape measure.

metro [me'tro] *nm* meter (*US*), metre (*Brit*); (*tren: tb*: **metropolitano**) subway (*US*), underground (*Brit*); (*instrumento*) ruler; ~ **cuadrado/cúbico** square/cubic meter.

mexicano, a [mehēká'no, á] *a, nm/f* (*AM*) Mexican.

México [me'hēko] *nm* (*AM*) Mexico; **Ciudad de** ~ Mexico City.

meza [me'sá] *etc vb V* **mecer.**

mezcla [mes'klá] *nf* mixture; (*fig*) blend.

mezclar [mesklár'] *vt* to mix (up); (*armonizar*) to blend; (*combinar*) to merge; ~**se** *vr* to mix, mingle; ~ **en** to get mixed up in, get involved in.

mezcolanza [meskolán'sá] *nf* hodgepodge, jumble.

mezquindad [meskēndáth'] *nf* (*cicatería*) meanness; (*miras estrechas*) pettiness; (*acto*) mean action.

mezquino, a [meskē'no, á] *a* (*cicatero*) mean ♦ *nm/f* (*avaro*) miser; (*miserable*) petty individual.

mezquita [meskē'tá] *nf* mosque.

MF *abr* (= *Modulación de Frecuencia*) FM.

mg. *abr* (= *miligramo(s)*) mg.

mi [mē] *a posesivo* my ♦ *nm* (*MUS*) E.

mí [mē] *pron* me, myself; **¿y a** ~ **qué?** so what?

miaja [myá'há] *nf* crumb; **ni una** ~ (*fig*) not the least little bit.

micro [mē'kro] *nm* (*RADIO*) mike, microphone; (*AM*) minibus.

microbio [mēkro'vyo] *nm* microbe.

microbús [mēkrohōōs'] *nm* minibus.

microcomputador [mēkrokompōōtáthor'] *nm*, **microcomputadora** [mēkrokompōōtátho'rá] *nf* micro(computer).

microchip [mēkrotchēp'] *nm* microchip.

microeconomía [mēkroekonomē'á] *nf* microeconomics *sg*.

microficha [mēkrofētch'á] *nf* microfiche.

micrófono [mēkro'fono] *nm* microphone.

microinformática [mēkroēnformá'tēká] *nf* microcomputing.

micrómetro [mēkro'metro] *nm* micrometer.

microonda [mēkroon'dá] *nf* microwave; **horno** ~**s** microwave oven.

microordenador [mēkroordenáthor'] *nm* microcomputer.

micropastilla [mēkropástē'yá], **microplaqueta** [mēkroplákē'tá] *nf* (*INFORM*) chip, wafer.

microplaquita [mēkroplákē'tá] *nf*: ~ **de si-**

licio silicon chip.

microprocesador [mēkroprosesáđhor'] *nm* microprocessor.

microprograma [mēkrogŗá'má] *nm* (*IN-FORM*) firmware.

microscopio [mēkrosko'pyo] *nm* microscope.

midiendo [mēđhyen'do] *etc vb* V **medir**.

MIE *nm abr* (*Esp*)=*Ministerio de Industria y Energía*.

miedo [mye'đho] *nm* fear; (*nerviosismo*) apprehension, nervousness; **meter** ~ **a** to scare, frighten; **tener** ~ to be afraid; **de** ~ wonderful, marvelous; **¡qué** ~! (*fam*) how awful!; **me da** ~ it scares me; **hace un frío de** ~ (*fam*) it's terribly cold.

miedoso, a [myeđho'so, á] *a* fearful, timid.

miel [myel] *nf* honey; **no hay** ~ **sin hiel** there's no rose without a thorn.

miembro [myem'bro] *nm* limb; (*socio*) member; (*de institución*) fellow; ~ **viril** penis.

mientes [myen'tes] *etc vb* V **mentar**; **mentir** ♦ *nfpl*: **no parar** ~ **en** to pay no attention to; **traer a las** ~ to recall.

mientras [myen'trás] *conj* while; (*duración*) as long as ♦ *ad* meanwhile; ~ **(que)** whereas; ~ **tanto** meanwhile; ~ **más tiene, más quiere** the more he has, the more he wants.

miérc. *abr* (= *miércoles*) Wed.

miércoles [myer'koles] *nm inv* Wednesday; ~ **de ceniza** Ash Wednesday.

mierda [myer'đhá] *nf* (*fam!*) shit (*!*), crap (*!*); (*fig*) filth, dirt; **¡vete a la** ~! go to hell!

mies [myes] *nf* (ripe) corn, wheat, grain.

miga [mē'ġá] *nf* crumb; (*fig: meollo*) essence; **hacer buenas** ~**s** (*fam*) to get on well; **esto tiene su** ~ there's more to this than meets the eye.

migración [mēġrásyon'] *nf* migration.

mil [mēl] *num* thousand; **dos** ~ **dólares** two thousand dollars.

milagro [mēlá'ġro] *nm* miracle; **hacer** ~**s** (*fig*) to work wonders.

milagroso, a [mēláġro'so, á] *a* miraculous.

Milán [mēlán'] *nm* Milan.

milenario, a [mēlená'ryo, á] *a* millennial; (*fig*) very ancient.

milenio [mēle'nyo] *nm* millennium.

milésimo, a [mēle'sēmo, á] *num* thousandth.

mili [mē'lē] *nf*: **hacer la** ~ (*fam*) to do one's military service.

milicia [mēlē'syá] *nf* (*MIL*) militia; (*servicio militar*) military service.

milímetro [mēlē'metro] *nm* millimeter (*US*), millimetre (*Brit*).

militante [mēlētán'te] *a* militant.

militar [mēlētár'] *a* military ♦ *nm/f* soldier ♦ *vi* to serve in the army; (*fig*) to militate,

fight.

milla [mē'yá] *nf* mile; ~ **marina** nautical mile.

millar [mēyár'] *num* thousand; **a** ~**es** in thousands.

millón [mēyon'] *num* million.

millonario, a [mēyoná'ryo, á] *nm/f* millionaire.

millonésimo, a [mēyone'sēmo, á] *num* millionth.

mimado, a [mēmá'đho, á] *a* spoiled.

mimar [mēmár'] *vt* to spoil, pamper.

mimbre [mēm'bre] *nm* wicker; **de** ~ wicker *cpd*, wickerwork.

mímica [mē'mēká] *nf* (*para comunicarse*) sign language; (*imitación*) mimicry.

mimetismo [mēmetēs'mo] *nm* mimicry.

mimo [mē'mo] *nm* (*caricia*) caress; (*de niño*) spoiling; (*TEATRO*) mime; (: *actor*) mime artist.

mina [mē'ná] *nf* mine; (*pozo*) shaft; (*de lápiz*) lead refill; **hullera** *o* ~ **de carbón** coalmine.

minar [mēnár'] *vt* to mine; (*fig*) to undermine.

mineral [mēnerál'] *a* mineral ♦ *nm* (*GEO*) mineral; (*mena*) ore.

minería [mēnerē'á] *nf* mining.

minero, a [mēne'ro, á] *a* mining *cpd* ♦ *nm/f* miner.

miniatura [mēnyátōō'rá] *a inv*, *nf* miniature.

minicomputador [mēnēkompōōtáđhor'] *nm* minicomputer.

minidisco [mēnēđhēs'ko] *nm* diskette.

minifalda [mēnēfál'dá] *nf* miniskirt.

minifundio [mēnēfōōn'dyo] *nm* smallholding, small farm.

mínimo, a [mē'nēmo, á] *a* minimum; (*insignificante*) minimal ♦ *nm* minimum; **precio/salario** ~ minimum price/wage; **lo** ~ **que pueden hacer** the least they can do.

minino, a [mēnē'no, á] *nm/f* (*fam*) kitty.

ministerio [mēnēste'ryo] *nm* department (*US*), ministry (*Brit*); **M**~ **de Asuntos Exteriores** State Department (*US*), Foreign Office (*Brit*); **M**~ **del Comercio e Industria** Department of Trade and Industry; **M**~ **de (la) Gobernación** *o* **del Interior** Ministry of the Interior; **M**~ **de Hacienda** Treasury Department (*US*), Treasury (*Brit*).

ministro, a [mēnēs'tro, á] *nm/f* secretary, (*esp US*) minister; **M**~ **de Hacienda** Secretary of the Treasury (*US*), Chancellor of the Exchequer (*Brit*); **M**~ **de (la) Gobernación** *o* **del Interior** ≈ Secretary of the Interior (*US*), Home Secretary (*Brit*).

minoría [mēnorē'á] *nf* minority.

mintiendo [mēntyen'do] *etc vb* V **mentir**.

minucia [mēnōō'syá] *nf* (*detalle insignificante*) trifle; (*bagatela*) mere nothing.

minuciosidad [mēnōōsyosē'thàth'] *nf* (*meti-culosidad*) thoroughness, meticulousness.

minucioso, a [mēnōōsyo'so, à] *a* thorough, meticulous; (*prolijo*) very detailed.

minúsculo, a [mēnōōs'kōōlo, à] *a* tiny, minute ♦ *nf* small letter; **minúsculas** *nfpl* (*TIP*) lower case *sg*.

minusvalía [mēnōōshàlē'à] *nf* physical handicap; (*COM*) depreciation, capital loss.

minusválido, a [mēnōōshà'lētho, à] *a* (physically) handicapped *o* disabled ♦ *nm/f* disabled person.

minuta [mēnōō'tà] *nf* (*de comida*) menu; (*de abogado etc*) fee.

minutero [mēnōōte'ro] *nm* minute hand.

minuto [mēnōō'to] *nm* minute.

Miño [mē'nyo] *nm*: **el (río)** ~ the Miño.

mío, a [mē'o, à] *a, pron*: **el** ~ mine; **un amigo** ~ a friend of mine; **lo** ~ what is mine; **los** ~**s** my people, my relations.

miope [myo'pe] *a* nearsighted.

miopía [myopē'à] *nf* nearsightedness.

MIR [mēr] *nm abr* (*POL*)=*Movimiento de Izquierda Revolucionaria*; (*Esp MED*) *Médico Interno y Residente*.

mira [mē'rà] *nf* (*de arma*) sight(s) (*pl*); (*fig*) aim, intention; **de amplias/estrechas** ~**s** broad-/narrow-minded.

mirada [mērà'thà] *nf* look, glance; (*expresión*) look, expression; ~ **de soslayo** sidelong glance; ~ **fija** stare, gaze; ~ **perdida** distant look; **echar una** ~ **a** to glance at; **levantar/bajar la** ~ to look up/down; **resistir la** ~ **de uno** to stare sb out.

mirado, a [mērà'tho, à] *a* (*sensato*) sensible; (*considerado*) considerate; **bien/mal** ~ well/not well thought of.

mirador [mērà'thor'] *nm* viewpoint, vantage point.

miramiento [mērà myen'to] *nm* (*consideración*) considerateness; **tratar sin** ~ **a uno** to ride roughshod over sb.

mirar [mērár'] *vt* to look at; (*observar*) to watch; (*considerar*) to consider, think over; (*vigilar, cuidar*) to watch, look after ♦ *vi* to look; (*ARQ*) to face; ~**se** *vr* (*dos personas*) to look at each other; ~ **algo/a uno de reojo** *o* **de través** to look askance at sth/sb; ~ **algo/a uno por encima del hombro** to look down on sth/sb; ~ **bien/mal** to think highly of/have a poor opinion of; ~ **fijamente** to stare *o* gaze at; ~ **por** (*fig*) to look after; ~ **por la ventana** to look out of the window; ~**se al espejo** to look at o.s. in the mirror; ~**se a los ojos** to look into each other's eyes.

mirilla [mērē'yà] *nf* (*agujero*) spyhole, peephole.

mirlo [mēr'lo] *nm* blackbird.

misa [mē'sà] *nf* mass; ~ **del gallo** midnight mass (*on Christmas Eve*); ~ **de difuntos** requiem mass; **como en** ~ in dead silence; **estos datos van a** ~ (*fig*) these facts are utterly trustworthy.

misántropo [mēsàn'tropo] *nm* misanthrope, misanthropist.

miscelánea [mēselà'neà] *nf* miscellany.

miserable [mēserà'hle] *a* (*avaro*) stingy; (*nimio*) miserable, paltry; (*lugar*) squalid; (*fam*) vile, despicable ♦ *nm/f* (*malvado*) rogue.

miseria [mēse'ryà] *nf* misery; (*pobreza*) poverty; (*tacañería*) stinginess; (*condiciones*) squalor; **una** ~ a pittance.

misericordia [mēserēkor'thyà] *nf* (*compasión*) compassion, pity; (*perdón*) forgiveness, mercy.

misil [mēsēl'] *nm* missile.

misión [mēsyon'] *nf* mission; (*tarea*) job, duty; (*POL*) assignment; **misiones** *nfpl* (*REL*) overseas missions.

misionero, a [mēsyone'ro, à] *nm/f* missionary.

mismamente [mēsmàmen'te] *ad* (*fam*: *sólo*) only, just.

mismísimo, a [mēsmē'sēmo, à] *a superlativo* selfsame, very (same).

mismo, a [mēs'mo, à] *a* (*semejante*) same; (*después de pronombre*) -self; (*para énfasis*) very ♦ *ad*: **aquí/ayer/hoy** ~ right here/only yesterday/this very day; **ahora** ~ right now ♦ *conj*: **lo** ~ **que** just like, just as; **por lo** ~ for the same reason; **el traje** the same suit; **en ese** ~ **momento** at that very moment; **vino el** ~ **Ministro** the Minister himself came; **yo** ~ **lo vi** I saw it myself; **lo hizo por sí** ~ he did it by himself; **lo** ~ the same (thing); **da lo** ~ it's all the same; **quedamos en las mismas** we're no further forward.

misógino [mēso'hēno] *nm* misogynist.

miss [mēs] *nf* beauty queen.

misterio [mēste'ryo] *nm* mystery; (*lo secreto*) secrecy.

misterioso, a [mēsteryo'so, à] *a* mysterious; (*inexplicable*) puzzling.

misticismo [mēstēsēs'mo] *nm* mysticism.

místico, a [mēs'tēko, à] *a* mystic(al) ♦ *nm/f* mystic ♦ *nf* mysticism.

mitad [mētàth'] *nf* (*medio*) half; (*centro*) middle; ~ **(y)** ~ half-and-half; (*fig*) half and no; **a** ~ **de precio** (at) half-price; **en** *o* **a** ~ **del camino** halfway along the road; **cortar por la** ~ to cut through the middle.

mítico, a [mē'tēko, à] *a* mythical.

mitigar [mētēgàr'] *vt* to mitigate; (*dolor*) to relieve; (*sed*) to quench; (*ira*) to appease; (*preocupación*) to allay; (*soledad*) to alleviate.

mitigue [mētē'ge] *etc vb V* **mitigar**.

mitin [mē'tēn] *nm* (*esp POL*) meeting.

mito [mḗ'to] *nm* myth.
mitología [mētolohē'á] *nf* mythology.
mitológico, a [mētolo'hēko, á] *a* mythological.
mixto, a [mēk'sto, á] *a* mixed; (*comité*) joint.
ml. *abr* (= *mililitro*) ml.
MLN *nm abr* (*POL*)=*Movimiento de Liberación Nacional*.
mm. *abr* (= *milímetro*) mm.
m/n *abr* (*ECON*) = *moneda nacional*.
M.° *abr* (*POL*: = *Ministerio*) Min.
m/o *abr* (*COM*) = *mi orden*.
mobiliario [mohēlyá'ryo] *nm* furniture.
mocedad [mosetháth'] *nf* youth.
moción [mosyon'] *nf* motion; ~ **compuesta** (*POL*) composite motion.
moco [mo'ko] *nm* mucus; **limpiarse los** ~**s** to blow one's nose; **no es** ~ **de pavo** it's no trifle.
mocoso, a [moko'so, á] *a* snivelling; (*fig*) ill-bred ♦ *nm/f* (*fam*) brat.
mochila [motchē'lá] *nf* backpack.
moda [mo'thá] *nf* fashion; (*estilo*) style; **de o a la** ~ in fashion, fashionable; **pasado de** ~ out of fashion; **vestido a la última** ~ trendily dressed.
modal [mothál'] *a* modal ♦ *nm*: ~**es** *nmpl* manners.
modalidad [mothálētháth'] *nf* (*clase*) kind, variety; (*manera*) way; (*INFORM*) mode; ~ **de texto** (*INFORM*) text mode.
modelar [mothelár'] *vt* to model.
modelo [mothe'lo] *a inv* model ♦ *nm/f* model ♦ *nm* (*patrón*) pattern; (*norma*) standard.
módem [mo'them] *nm* (*INFORM*) modem.
moderado, a [motherá'tho, á] *a* moderate.
moderar [motherár'] *vt* to moderate; (*violencia*) to restrain, control; (*velocidad*) to reduce; ~**se** *vr* to restrain o.s., control o.s.
modernice [mothernē'se] *etc vb V* **modernizar**.
modernizar [mothernēsár'] *vt* to modernize; (*INFORM*) to upgrade.
moderno, a [mother'no, á] *a* modern; (*actual*) present-day; (*equipo etc*) up-to-date.
modestia [mothes'tyá] *nf* modesty.
modesto, a [mothe'sto, á] *a* modest.
módico, a [mo'thēko, á] *a* moderate, reasonable.
modificar [mothēfēkár'] *vt* to modify.
modifique [mothēfē'ke] *etc vb V* **modificar**.
modismo [mothḗs'mo] *nm* idiom.
modisto, a [mothē'sto, á] *nm/f* dressmaker.
modo [mo'tho] *nm* (*manera, forma*) way, manner; (*INFORM, MUS*) mode; (*LING*) mood; ~**s** *nmpl* manners; "~ **de empleo**" "instructions for use"; ~ **de gobierno** form of government; **a** ~ **de** like; **de este** ~ in this way; **de ningún** ~ in no way; **de**

todos ~**s** at any rate; **de un** ~ **u otro** (in) one way or another.
modorra [motho'rrá] *nf* drowsiness.
modoso, a [motho'so, á] *a* (*educado*) quiet, well-mannered.
modulación [mothōōlásyon'] *nf* modulation; ~ **de frecuencia** (*RADIO*) frequency modulation, FM.
mofarse [mofár'se] *vr*: ~ **de** to mock, scoff at.
moflete [mofle'te] *nm* fat cheek, chubby cheek.
mogollón [mogoyon'] (*fam*) *nm*: ~ **de discos** *etc* loads of records *etc* ♦ *ad*: **un** ~ a hell of a lot.
mohín [moēn'] *nm* (*mueca*) (wry) face; (*pucheros*) pout.
mohino, a [moē'no, á] *a* (*triste*) gloomy, depressed; (*enojado*) sulky.
moho [mo'o] *nm* (*BOT*) mold (*US*), mould (*Brit*), mildew; (*en metal*) rust.
mohoso, a [moo'so, á] *a* moldy (*US*), mouldy (*Brit*); rusty.
mojado, a [mohá'tho, á] *a* wet; (*húmedo*) damp; (*empapado*) drenched.
mojar [mohár'] *vt* to wet; (*humedecer*) to damp(en), moisten; (*calar*) to soak; ~**se** *vr* to get wet; ~ **el pan en el café** to dip *o* dunk one's bread in one's coffee.
mojigato, a [mohēgá'to, á] *a* (*hipócrita*) hypocritical; (*santurrón*) sanctimonious; (*gazmoño*) prudish ♦ *nm/f* hypocrite; sanctimonious person; prude.
mojón [mohon'] *nm* (*hito*) landmark; (*en un camino*) signpost; (~ *kilométrico*) milestone.
mol. *abr* (= *molécula*) mol.
molar [molár'] *nm* molar ♦ *vt* (*fam*): **lo que más me mola es** ... what I'm really into is ...; **¿te mola un pitillo?** would you like a smoke?
molde [mol'de] *nm* mold (*US*), mould (*Brit*); (*vaciado*) cast; (*de costura*) pattern; (*fig*) model.
moldear [moldeár'] *vt* to mold (*US*), mould (*Brit*); (*en yeso etc*) to cast.
mole [mo'le] *nf* mass, bulk; (*edificio*) pile.
moler [moler'] *vt* to grind, crush; (*pulverizar*) to pound; (*trigo etc*) to mill; (*cansar*) to tire out, exhaust; ~ **a uno a palos** to give sb a beating.
molestar [molestár'] *vt* to bother; (*fastidiar*) to annoy; (*incomodar*) to inconvenience, put out; (*perturbar*) to trouble, upset ♦ *vi* to be a nuisance; ~**se** *vr* to bother; (*incomodarse*) to go to a lot of trouble; (*ofenderse*) to take offense; **¿le molesta el ruido?** do you mind the noise?; **siento** ~**le** I'm sorry to trouble you.
molestia [moles'tyá] *nf* bother, trouble; (*incomodidad*) inconvenience; (*MED*) dis-

comfort; **no es ninguna ~** it's no trouble at all.

molesto, a [mole'sto, á] *a (que fastidia)* annoying; *(incómodo)* inconvenient; *(inquieto)* uncomfortable, ill at ease; *(enfadado)* annoyed; **estar ~** *(MED)* to be in some discomfort; **estar ~ con uno** *(fig)* to be cross with sb; **me sentí ~** I felt embarrassed.

molido, a [mole'ðo, á] *a (machacado)* ground; *(pulverizado)* powdered; **estar ~** *(fig)* to be exhausted *o* dead beat.

molinero [moléne'ro] *nm* miller.

molinillo [moléne'yo] *nm* hand mill; **~ de carne/café** meat grinder *(US) o* mincer *(Brit)*/coffee grinder.

molino [mole'no] *nm (edificio)* mill; *(máquina)* grinder.

Molucas [moloō'kás] *nfpl:* **las (Islas) ~** the Moluccas, the Molucca Islands.

molusco [moloōs'ko] *nm* mollusc.

mollera [moye'rá] *nf (ANAT)* crown of the head; *(fam: seso)* brains *pl;* **duro de ~** *(estúpido)* thick.

momentáneo, a [momentá'neo, á] *a* momentary.

momento [momen'to] *nm (gen)* moment; *(TEC)* momentum; **de ~** at the moment, for the moment; **por el ~** for the time being.

momia [mo'myá] *nf* mummy.

mona [mo'ná] *nf V* **mono.**

Mónaco [mo'náko] *nm* Monaco.

monada [moná'ðá] *nf (de niño)* charming habit; *(cosa primorosa)* lovely thing; *(chica)* pretty girl; **¡qué ~!** isn't it cute?

monaguillo [monáğe'yo] *nm* altar boy.

monarca [monár'ká] *nm/f* monarch, ruler.

monarquía [monárke'á] *nf* monarchy.

monárquico, a [monár'keko, á] *nm/f* royalist, monarchist.

monasterio [monáste'ryo] *nm* monastery.

monda [mon'dá] *nf (poda)* pruning; *(: de árbol)* lopping; *(: de fruta)* peeling; *(cáscara)* skin; **¡es la ~!** *(fam: fantástico)* it's great!; *(: el colmo)* it's the limit!; *(: persona: gracioso)* he's a knockout!

mondadientes [mondáðhyen'tes] *nm inv* toothpick.

mondar [mondár'] *vt (limpiar)* to clean; *(pelar)* to peel; **~se** *vr:* **~se de risa** *(fam)* to split one's sides laughing.

moneda [mone'ðá] *nf (tipo de dinero)* currency, money; *(pieza)* coin; **una ~ de 5 pesetas** a 5 peseta coin; **~ de curso legal** tender; **~ extranjera** foreign exchange; **es ~ corriente** *(fig)* it's common knowledge.

monedero [mone'ðe'ro] *nm* purse.

monegasco, a [monegás'ko, á] *a of o* from Monaco, Monegasque ♦ *nm/f* Monegasque.

monetario, a [monetá'ryo, á] *a* monetary, financial.

monetarista [monetáre'stá] *a, nm/f* monetarist.

monitor [monetor'] *nm (INFORM)* monitor; **~ en color** color monitor; **~ fósfor verde** green screen.

monja [mon'há] *nf* nun.

monje [mon'he] *nm* monk.

mono, a [mo'no, á] *a (bonito)* lovely, pretty; *(gracioso)* nice, charming ♦ *nm/f* monkey, ape ♦ *nm* dungarees *pl; (overol)* overalls *pl;* **una chica muy mona** a very pretty girl; **dormir la ~** to sleep it off.

monolingüe [monolēn'gwe] *a* monolingual.

monólogo [mono'loğo] *nm* monologue.

monopatín [monopátēn'] *nm* skateboard.

monopolice [monopolē'se] *etc vb V* **monopolizar.**

monopolio [monopo'lyo] *nm* monopoly; **~ total** absolute monopoly.

monopolista [monopolē'stá] *a, nm/f* monopolist.

monopolizar [monopolēsár'] *vt* to monopolize.

monosílabo, a [monosē'láƀo, á] *a* monosyllabic ♦ *nm* monosyllable.

monotonía [monotonē'á] *nf (sonido)* monotone; *(fig)* monotony.

monótono, a [mono'tono, á] *a* monotonous.

mono-usuario, a [monoōōswá'ryo, á] *a (INFORM)* single-user.

monóxido [monok'sēðo] *nm* monoxide; **~ de carbono** carbon monoxide.

Mons. *abr (REL)* = **Monseñor.**

monseñor [monsenyor'] *nm* monsignor.

monserga [monser'ğá] *nf (lenguaje confuso)* gibberish; *(tonterías)* drivel.

monstruo [monst'rwo] *nm* monster ♦ *a inv* fantastic.

monstruoso, a [monstrwo'so, á] *a* monstrous.

monta [mon'tá] *nf* total, sum; **de poca ~** unimportant, of little account.

montacargas [montákár'ğás] *nm inv* freight elevator *(US)*, service lift *(Brit)*.

montador [montáðhor'] *nm (para montar)* mounting block; *(profesión)* fitter; *(CINE)* film editor.

montaje [montá'he] *nm* assembly; *(organización)* fitting up; *(TEATRO)* décor; *(CINE)* montage.

montante [montán'te] *nm (poste)* upright; *(soporte)* stanchion; *(ARQ: de puerta)* transom; *(: de ventana)* mullion; *(suma)* amount, total.

montaña [montá'nyá] *nf (monte)* mountain; *(sierra)* mountains *pl,* mountainous area; *(AM: selva)* forest; **~ rusa** roller coaster.

montañero, a [montánye'ro, á] *a* mountain *cpd* ♦ *nm/f* mountaineer, climber.

montañés, esa [montányes', csá] *a*

mountain *cpd*; (*de Santander*) of *o* from the Santander region ♦ *nm/f* highlander; native *o* inhabitant of the Santander region.

montañismo [montányēs'mo] *nm* mountaineering, climbing.

montañoso, a [montányo'so, ȧ] *a* mountainous.

montar [montár'] *vt* (*subir a*) to mount, get on; (*caballo etc*) to ride; (*TEC*) to assemble, put together; (*negocio*) to set up; (*colocar*) to lift on to; (*CINE*: *película*) to edit; (*TEATRO*: *obra*) to stage, put on; (*CU-LIN*: *batir*) to whip, beat ♦ *vi* to mount, get on; (*sobresalir*) to overlap; ~ **en cólera** to get angry; ~ **un número** *o* **numerito** to make a scene; **tanto monta** it's all the same.

montaraz [montárás'] *a* mountain *cpd*, highland *cpd*; (*pey*) uncivilized.

monte [mon'te] *nm* (*montaña*) mountain; (*bosque*) woodland; (*área sin cultivar*) wild area, wild country; ~ **de piedad** pawnshop; ~ **alto** forest; ~ **bajo** scrub(land).

montera [monte'rȧ] *nf* (*sombrero*) cloth cap; (*de torero*) bullfighter's hat.

monto [mon'to] *nm* total, amount.

montón [monton'] *nm* heap, pile; **un** ~ **de** (*fig*) heaps of, lots of; **a montones** by the score, galore.

montura [montōō'rȧ] *nf* (*cabalgadura*) mount; (*silla*) saddle; (*arreos*) harness; (*de joya*) mounting; (*de gafas*) frame.

monumento [monōōmen'to] *nm* monument; (*de conmemoración*) memorial.

monzón [monson'] *nm* monsoon.

moña [mo'nyȧ] *nf* hair ribbon.

moño [mo'nyo] *nm* (*de pelo*) bun; **estar hasta el** ~ (*fam*) to be fed up.

MOPU [mo'pōō] *nm abr* (*Esp*)=*Ministerio de Obras Públicas y Urbanismo.*

moqueta [moke'tȧ] *nf* fitted carpet.

moquillo [mokē'yo] *nm* (*enfermedad*) distemper.

mora [mo'rȧ] *nf* (*BOT*) mulberry; (: *zarzamora*) blackberry; (*COM*): **en** ~ in arrears.

morado, a [morȧ'đo, ȧ] *a* purple, violet ♦ *nm* bruise ♦ *nf* (*casa*) dwelling, abode; **pasarlas moradas** to have a tough time of it.

moral [morȧl'] *a* moral ♦ *nf* (*ética*) ethics *pl*; (*moralidad*) morals *pl*, morality; (*ánimo*) morale; **tener baja la** ~ to be in low spirits.

moraleja [morȧle'hȧ] *nf* moral.

moralice [morȧlē'se] *etc vb V* **moralizar.**

moralidad [morȧlēđȧđ'] *nf* morals *pl*, morality.

moralizar [morȧlēsȧr'] *vt* to moralize.

morar [morȧr'] *vi* to live, dwell.

moratoria [morȧto'ryȧ] *nf* moratorium.

morbosidad [morḅosēđȧđ'] *nf* morbidity.

morboso, a [morḅo'so, ȧ] *a* morbid.

morcilla [morsē'yȧ] *nf* blood sausage.

mordaz [morđȧs'] *a* (*crítica*) biting, scathing.

mordaza [morđȧ'sȧ] *nf* (*para la boca*) gag; (*TEC*) clamp.

morder [morđer'] *vt* to bite; (*mordisquear*) to nibble; (*fig*: *consumir*) to eat away, eat into ♦ *vi*, ~**se** *vr* to bite; **está que muerde** he's hopping mad; ~**se la lengua** to hold one's tongue.

mordiscar [morđēskȧr'] *vt* to nibble at; (*con fuerza*) to gnaw at; (*pinchar*) to nip.

mordisco [morđēs'ko] *nm* bite.

mordisque [morđēs'ke] *etc vb V* **mordiscar.**

mordisquear [morđēskȧr'] *vt*=**mordiscar.**

moreno, a [more'no, ȧ] *a* (*color*) (dark) brown; (*de tez*) dark; (*de pelo* ~) dark-haired; (*negro*) black ♦ *nm/f* (*de tez*) dark-skinned man/woman; (*de pelo*) dark-haired man/woman.

moretón [moreton'] *nm* (*fam*) bruise.

morfina [morfē'nȧ] *nf* morphine.

morfinómano, a [morfēno'mȧno, ȧ] *a* addicted to hard drugs ♦ *nm/f* drug addict.

moribundo, a [morēḅōōn'do, ȧ] *a* dying ♦ *nm/f* dying person.

morir [morēr'] *vi* to die; (*fuego*) to die down; (*luz*) to go out; ~**se** *vr* to die; (*fig*) to be dying; (*FERRO etc*: *vías*) to end; (*calle*) to come out; **fue muerto a tiros/en un accidente** he was shot (dead)/was killed in an accident; ~ **de frío/hambre** to die of cold/starve to death; **¡me muero de hambre!** (*fig*) I'm starving!; ~**se por algo** to be dying for sth; ~**se por uno** to be crazy about sb.

moro, a [mo'ro, ȧ] *a* Moorish ♦ *nm/f* Moor; **¡hay** ~**s en la costa!** watch out!

moroso, a [moro'so, ȧ] *a* (*lento*) slow ♦ *nm* (*COM*) bad debtor, defaulter; **deudor** ~ (*COM*) slow payer.

morral [morrȧl'] *nm* knapsack.

morro [mo'rro] *nm* (*ZOOL*) snout, nose; (*AUTO, AVIAT*) nose; (*fam*: *labio*) (thick) lip; **beber a** ~ to drink from the bottle; **caer de** ~ to nosedive; **estar de** ~**s (con uno)** to be in a bad mood (with sb); **tener** ~ to have a nerve.

morrocotudo, a [morrokotōō'đo, ȧ] *a* (*fam*) (*fantástico*) wonderful; (*riña, golpe*) tremendous; (*fuerte*) strong; (*pesado*) heavy; (*difícil*) awkward.

morsa [mor'sȧ] *nf* walrus.

mortaja [mortȧ'hȧ] *nf* shroud; (*TEC*) mortise; (*AM*) cigarette paper.

mortal [mortȧl'] *a* mortal; (*golpe*) deadly.

mortalidad [mortȧlēđȧđ'], **mortandad** [mortȧndȧđ'] *nf* mortality.

mortecino, a [mortesē'no, ȧ] *a* (*débil*)

weak; (*luz*) dim; (*color*) dull.
mortero [morte'ro] *nm* mortar.
mortífero, a [mortē'fero, á] *a* deadly, lethal.
mortificar [mortēfēkár'] *vt* to mortify; (*atormentar*) to torment.
mortifique [mortēfē'ke] *etc vb V* **mortificar**.
mortuorio, a [mortwo'ryo, á] *a* mortuary, death *cpd*.
Mosa [mo'sá] *nm*: **el (Río)** ~ the Meuse.
mosca [mos'ká] *nf* fly; **por si las** ~**s** just in case; **estar** ~ (*desconfiar*) to smell a rat; **tener la** ~ **en** *o* **detrás de la oreja** to be wary.
moscovita [moskobē'tá] *a* Muscovite, Moscow *cpd* ♦ *nm/f* Muscovite.
Moscú [moskōō'] *nm* Moscow.
mosquearse [moskeár'se] *vr* (*fam: enfadarse*) to get cross; (: *ofenderse*) to take offense (*US*) *o* offence (*Brit*).
mosquitero [moskēte'ro] *nm* mosquito net.
mosquito [moskē'to] *nm* mosquito.
mostaza [mostá'sá] *nf* mustard.
mosto [mos'to] *nm* unfermented grape juice.
mostrador [mostráthor'] *nm* (*de tienda*) counter; (*de café*) bar.
mostrar [mostrár'] *vt* to show; (*exhibir*) to display, exhibit; (*explicar*) to explain; ~**se** *vr*: ~**se amable** to be kind; to prove to be kind; **no se muestra muy inteligente** he doesn't seem (to be) very intelligent; ~ **en pantalla** (*INFORM*) to display.
mota [mo'tá] *nf* speck, tiny piece; (*en diseño*) dot.
mote [mo'te] *nm* (*apodo*) nickname.
motín [motēn'] *nm* (*del pueblo*) revolt, uprising; (*del ejército*) mutiny.
motivar [motēbár'] *vt* (*causar*) to cause, motivate; (*explicar*) to explain, justify.
motivo [motē'bo] *nm* motive, reason; (*ARTE, MUS*) motif; **con** ~ **de** (*debido a*) because of; (*en ocasión de*) on the occasion of; (*con el fin de*) in order to; **sin** ~ for no reason at all.
moto [mo'to], **motocicleta** [motosēkle'tá] *nf* motorcycle.
motor, a [motor', á] *a* (*TEC*) motor (*US*), motive (*Brit*); (*ANAT*) motor ♦ *nm* motor, engine; ~ **a chorro** *o* **de reacción/de explosión** jet engine/internal combustion engine ♦ *nf* motorboat.
motorismo [motorēs'mo] *nm* motorcycling.
motorizado, a [motorēsá'tho, á] *a* motorized.
motosierra [motosye'rrá] *nf* mechanical saw.
movedizo, a [mobethē'so, á] *a* (*inseguro*) unsteady, (*fig*) unsettled, changeable; (*persona*) fickle.
mover [mober'] *vt* to move; (*cambiar de lugar*) to shift; (*cabeza: para negar*) to

shake; (: *para asentir*) to nod; (*accionar*) to drive; (*fig*) to cause, provoke; ~**se** *vr* to move; (*mar*) to get rough; (*viento*) to rise; (*fig: apurarse*) to get a move on; (: *transformarse*) to be on the move.
movible [mobē'ble] *a* (*no fijo*) movable; (*móvil*) mobile; (*cambiadizo*) changeable.
movido, a [mobē'tho, á] *a* (*FOTO*) blurred; (*persona: activo*) active; (*mar*) rough; (*día*) hectic ♦ *nf* move; **la movida madrileña** the Madrid scene.
móvil [mo'bēl] *a* mobile; (*pieza de máquina*) moving; (*mueble*) movable ♦ *nm* motive.
movilice [mobēlē'se] *etc vb V* **movilizar**.
movilidad [mobēlēthath'] *nf* mobility.
movilizar [mobēlēsár'] *vt* to mobilize.
movimiento [mobēmyen'to] *nm* (*gen, LITERATURA, POL*) movement; (*TEC*) motion; (*actividad*) activity; (*MUS*) tempo; **el M~** the Falangist Movement; ~ **de bloques** (*INFORM*) block move; ~ **de mercancías** (*COM*) turnover, volume of business; ~ **obrero/sindical** workers'/trade union movement; ~ **sísmico** earth tremor.
Mozambique [mosámbē'ke] *nm* Mozambique.
mozambiqueño, a [mosámbēke'nyo, á] *a, nm/f* Mozambican.
mozo, a [mo'so, á] *a* (*joven*) young; (*soltero*) single, unmarried ♦ *nm/f* (*joven*) youth, young man/girl; (*camarero*) waiter; (*camarera*) waitress; ~ **de estación** porter.
MPAIAC [emepàyák'] *nm abr* (*Esp POL*) = *Movimiento para la Autodeterminación y la Independencia del Archipiélago Canario*.
mucama [mōōká'má] *nf* (*AM*) maid.
muchacho, a [mōōtchátch'o, á] *nm/f* (*niño*) boy/girl; (*criado*) servant/servant *o* maid.
muchedumbre [mōōtchethōōm'bre] *nf* crowd.
muchísimo, a [mōōtchē'sēmo, á] *a* (*superlativo de* **mucho**) lots and lots of, ever so much ♦ *ad* ever so much.
mucho, a [mōōtch'o, á] *a* (*sg*) a lot of; (*gen en frase negativa o interrogativa*) much; (*pl*) many, a lot of, lots of ♦ *ad* (*en cantidad*) a lot, a great deal, much; (*del tiempo*) long; (*muy*) very ♦ *pron*: **tengo** ~ **que hacer** I have a lot to do; ~**s dicen que** a lot of people say that; **como** ~ at (the) most; **ni con** ~ not nearly; **ni** ~ **menos** far from it; **por** ~ **que** however much; **me alegro/lo siento** ~ I'm very glad/sorry.
muda [mōō'thá] *nf* (*de ropa*) change of clothing; (*ZOOL*) moult; (*de serpiente*) slough.
mudanza [mōōthán'sá] *nf* (*cambio*) change; (*de casa*) move; **estar de** ~ to be moving.
mudar [mōōthár'] *vt* to change; (*ZOOL*) to

shed ♦ *vi* to change; **~se** *vr* (*la ropa*) to change; **~se de casa** to move.

mudo, a |mōō'tho, á| *a* dumb; (*callado, película*) silent; (*LING*: *letra*) mute; (: *consonante*) voiceless; **quedarse ~ (de)** (*fig*) to be dumb with; **quedarse ~ de asombro** to be speechless.

mueble |mwe'ble| *nm* piece of furniture; **~s** *nmpl* furniture *sg*.

mueble-bar |mweblebár'| *nm* cocktail cabinet.

mueca |mwe'ká| *nf* face, grimace; **hacer ~s a** to make faces at.

muela |mwe'lá| *etc vb V* **moler** ♦ *nf* (*diente*) tooth; (: *de atrás*) molar; (*de molino*) millstone; (*de afilar*) grindstone; **~ del juicio** wisdom tooth.

muelle |mwe'ye| *a* (*blando*) soft; (*fig*) soft, easy ♦ *nm* spring; (*NAUT*) wharf; (*malecón*) jetty.

muera |mwe'rá| *etc vb V* **morir**.

muerda |mwer'thá| *etc vb V* **morder**.

muermo |mwer'mo| *nm* (*fam*) wimp.

muerte |mwer'te| *nf* death; (*homicidio*) murder; **dar ~ a** to kill; **de mala ~** (*fam*) lousy, rotten; **es la ~** (*fam*) it's deadly boring.

muerto, a |mwer'to, á| *pp de* **morir** ♦ *a* dead; (*color*) dull ♦ *nm/f* dead man/woman; (*difunto*) deceased; (*cadáver*) corpse; **cargar con el ~** (*fam*) to take the rap; **echar el ~ a uno** to pass the buck; **hacer el ~** (*nadando*) to float; **estar ~ de cansancio** to be dead tired.

muestra |mwes'trá| *etc vb V* **mostrar** ♦ *nf* (*señal*) indication, sign; (*demostración*) demonstration; (*prueba*) proof; (*estadística*) sample; (*modelo*) model, pattern; (*testimonio*) token; **dar ~s de** to show signs of; **~ al azar** (*COM*) random sample.

muestrario |mwestrá'ryo| *nm* collection of samples; (*exposición*) showcase.

muestreo |mwestre'o| *nm* sample, sampling.

mueva |mwe'bá| *etc vb V* **mover**.

mugir |mōōhēr'| *vi* (*vaca*) to moo.

mugre |mōō'gre| *nf* dirt, filth, muck.

mugriento, a |mōōgryen'to, á| *a* dirty, filthy mucky.

muja |mōō'há| *etc vb V* **mugir**.

mujer |mōōher'| *nf* woman; (*esposa*) wife.

mujeriego |mōōherye'go| *nm* womanizer.

mula |mōō'lá| *nf* mule.

muladar |mōōláthár'| *nm* dungheap, dunghill.

mulato, a |mōōlá'to, á| *a, nm/f* mulatto.

muleta |mōōle'tá| *nf* (*para andar*) crutch; (*TAUR*) stick with red cape attached.

muletilla |mōōletē'yá| *nf* (*palabra*) pet word, tag; (*de cómico*) catch phrase.

multa |mōōl'tá| *nf* fine; **echar** *o* **poner una ~ a** to fine.

multar |mōōltár'| *vt* to fine; (*DEPORTE*) to penalize.

multiacceso |mōōltyáksc'so| *a* (*INFORM*) multi-access.

multicopista |mōōltēkopē'stá| *nm* duplicator.

multinacional |mōōltēnásyonál'| *a, nf* multinational.

múltiple |mōōl'tēple| *a* multiple; (*pl*) many, numerous; **de tarea ~** (*INFORM*) multitasking; **de usuario ~** (*INFORM*) multiuser.

multiplicar |mōōltēplēkár'| *vt* (*MAT*) to multiply; (*fig*) to increase; **~se** *vr* (*BIO*) to multiply; (*fig*) to be everywhere at once.

multiplique |mōōltēplē'ke| *etc vb V* **multiplicar**.

multitud |mōōltētōōth'| *nf* (*muchedumbre*) crowd; **~ de** lots of.

multitudinario, a |mōōltētōōthēná'ryo, á| *a* (*numeroso*) multitudinous; (*de masa*) mass *cpd*.

mullido, a |mōōyē'tho, á| *a* (*cama*) soft; (*hierba*) soft, springy.

mundanal |mōōndánál'| *a* worldly; **lejos del ~ ruido** far from the madding crowd.

mundano, a |mōōndá'no, á| *a* worldly; (*de moda*) fashionable.

mundial |mōōndyál'| *a* world-wide, universal; (*guerra, récord*) world *cpd*.

mundialmente |mōōndyálmen'te| *ad* worldwide; **~ famoso** world-famous.

mundo |mōōn'do| *nm* world; (*ámbito*) world, circle; **el otro ~** the next world; **el ~ del espectáculo** show business; **todo el ~** everybody; **tener ~** to be experienced, know one's way around; **el ~ es un pañuelo** it's a small world; **no es nada del otro ~** it's nothing special; **se le cayó el ~ (encima)** his world fell apart.

munición |mōōnēsyon'| *nf* (*MIL*: *provisiones*) stores *pl*, supplies *pl*; (: *de armas*) ammunition.

municipal |mōōnēsēpál'| *a* (*elección*) municipal; (*concejo*) town *cpd*, local; (*piscina etc*) public ♦ *nm* (*guardia*) policeman.

municipio |mōōnēsē'pyo| *nm* (*ayuntamiento*) town council, corporation; (*territorio administrativo*) town, municipality.

Munich |mōō'nētch| *nm* Munich.

muniqués, esa |mōōnēkes', esá| *a* of *o* from Munich ♦ *nm/f* native *o* inhabitant of Munich.

muñeca |mōōnye'ká| *nf* (*ANAT*) wrist; (*juguete*) doll.

muñeco |mōōnye'ko| *nm* (*figura*) figure; (*marioneta*) puppet; (*fig*) puppet, pawn; (*niño*) pretty little boy; **~ de nieve** snowman.

muñón |mōōnyon'| *nm* (*ANAT*) stump.

mural [mōōrál'] *a* mural, wall *cpd* ♦ *nm* mural.

muralla [mōōrá'yà] *nf* (city) wall(s) (*pl*).

murciano, a [mōōrsyá'no, à] *a* of *o* from Murcia ♦ *nm/f* native *o* inhabitant of Murcia.

murciélago [mōōrsye'láğo] *nm* bat.

murga [mōōr'ğá] *nf* (*banda*) band of street musicians; **dar la** ~ to be a nuisance.

murmullo [mōōrmōō'yo] *nm* murmur(ing); (*cuchicheo*) whispering; (*de arroyo*) murmur, rippling; (*de hojas, viento*) rustle, rustling; (*ruido confuso*) hum(ming).

murmuración [mōōrmōōrásyon'] *nf* gossip; (*críticas*) backbiting.

murmurador, a [mōōrmōōráthor', à] *a* gossiping; (*criticón*) backbiting ♦ *nm/f* gossip; backbiter.

murmurar [mōōrmōōrár'] *vi* to murmur, whisper; (*criticar*) to criticize; (*cotillear*) to gossip.

muro [mōō'ro] *nm* wall; ~ **de contención** retaining wall.

musaraña [mōōsárá'nyà] *nf* (ZOOL) shrew; (*insecto*) creepy-crawly; **pensar en las** ~**s** to daydream.

muscular [mōōskōōlár'] *a* muscular.

músculo [mōōs'kōōlo] *nm* muscle.

museo [mōōse'o] *nm* museum; ~ **de arte** *o* **de pintura** art gallery; ~ **de cera** waxworks.

musgo [mōōs'ğo] *nm* moss.

músico, a [mōō'sēko, à] *a* musical ♦ *nm/f* musician ♦ *nf* music; **irse con la música a otra parte** to clear out.

musitar [mōōsētár'] *vt*, *vi* to mutter, mumble.

muslo [mōōs'lo] *nm* thigh; (*de pollo*) leg, drumstick.

mustio, a [mōōs'tyo, à] *a* (*persona*) depressed, gloomy; (*planta*) faded, withered.

musulmán, ana [mōōsōōlmán', ánà] *nm/f* Moslem, Muslim.

mutación [mōōtásyon'] *nf* (BIO) mutation; (: *cambio*) (sudden) change.

mutilar [mōōtēlár'] *vt* to mutilate; (*a una persona*) to maim.

mutis [mōō'tēs] *nm inv* (TEATRO) exit; **hacer** ~ (TEATRO: *retirarse*) to exit, go off; (*fig*) to say nothing.

mutualidad [mōōtwáleħáħ'] *nf* (*reciprocidad*) mutual character; (*asociación*) benefit (US) *o* friendly (*Brit*) society.

mutuamente [mōōtwámen'te] *ad* mutually.

mutuo, a [mōō'two, à] *a* mutual.

muy [mwē] *ad* very; (*demasiado*) too; **M~ Señor mío** Dear Sir; ~ **bien** (*de acuerdo*) all right; ~ **de noche** very late at night; **eso es** ~ **de él** that's just like him; **eso es** ~ **español** that's typically Spanish.

N

N, n [e'ne] *nf* (*letra*) N, n; **N de Navarra** N for Nan.

N *abr* (= *norte*) N.

N. *abr* (= *noviembre*) Nov.

n. *abr* (LING: = *nombre*) n; (= *nacido*) b.

n/ *abr* = **nuestro, a.**

nabo [ná'ħo] *nm* turnip.

nácar [ná'kár] *nm* mother-of-pearl.

nacer [náser'] *vi* to be born; (*huevo*) to hatch; (*vegetal*) to sprout; (*río*) to rise; (*fig*) to begin, originate, have its origins; **nació para poeta** he was born to be a poet; **nadie nace enseñado** we all have to learn; **nació una sospecha en su mente** a suspicion formed in her mind.

nacido, a [náse'tho, à] *a* born; **recién** ~ newborn.

naciente [násyen'te] *a* new, emerging; (*sol*) rising.

nacimiento [násēmyen'to] *nm* birth; (*fig*) birth, origin; (*de Navidad*) Nativity; (*linaje*) descent, family; (*de río*) source; **ciego de** ~ blind from birth.

nación [násyon'] *nf* nation; (*pueblo*) people; **Naciones Unidas** United Nations.

nacional [násyonál'] *a* national; (COM, ECON) domestic.

nacionalice [násyonálē'se] *etc vb V* **nacionalizar.**

nacionalismo [násyonálēs'mo] *nm* nationalism.

nacionalista [násyonálē'stá] *a, nm/f* nationalist.

nacionalizar [násyonálēsár'] *vt* to nationalize; ~**se** *vr* (*persona*) to become naturalized.

nada [ná'ħá] *pron* nothing ♦ *ad* not at all, in no way ♦ *nf* nothingness; **no decir** ~ to say nothing, not to say anything; **de** ~ don't mention it; ~ **de eso** nothing of the kind; **antes de** ~ right away; **como si** ~ as if it didn't matter; **no ha sido** ~ it's nothing; **la** ~ the void.

nadador, a [náħáħor', à] *nm/f* swimmer.

nadar [náħár'] *vi* to swim; ~ **en la abundancia** (*fig*) to be rolling in money.

nadie [ná'ħye] *pron* nobody, no-one; ~ **habló** nobody spoke; **no había** ~ there was nobody there, there wasn't anybody there; **es un don** ~ he's a nobody *o* nonentity.

nado [ná'ħo]: **a** ~ *ad*: **pasar a** ~ to swim

across.

nafta [náf'tá] *nf* (*AM*) gas(oline) (*US*), petrol (*Brit*).

naftalina [náftálē'ná] *nf*: **bolas de ~** mothballs.

naipe [ná'ēpe] *nm* (playing) card; **~s** *nmpl* cards.

nal. *abr* (= *nacional*) nat.

nalgas [nál'gás] *nfpl* buttocks.

Namibia [námē'bya] *nf* Namibia.

nana [ná'ná] *nf* lullaby.

Nápoles [ná'poles] *nf* Naples.

napolitano, a [nápolētá'no, á] *a* of *o* from Naples, Neapolitan ♦ *nm/f* Neapolitan.

naranja [nárán'há] *a inv*, *nf* orange; **media ~** (*fam*) better half; **¡~s de la China!** nonsense!

naranjada [náránhá'thá] *nf* orangeade.

naranjo [nárán'ho] *nm* orange tree.

Narbona [nárbo'ná] *nf* Narbonne.

narciso [nársē'so] *nm* narcissus.

narcotice [nárkotē'se] *etc vb* V **narcotizar**.

narcótico, a [nárko'tēko, á] *a*, *nm* narcotic.

narcotizar [nárkotēsár'] *vt* to drug.

narcotraficante [nárkotráfēkán'te] *nm/f* narcotics *o* drug trafficker.

narcotráfico [nárkotrá'fēko] *nm* narcotics *o* drug trafficking.

nardo [nár'tho] *nm* lily.

narices [nárē'ses] *nfpl* V **nariz**.

narigón, ona, [nárēgon', o'ná], **narigudo, a** [nárēgōō'tho, á] *a* big-nosed.

nariz [nárēs'] *nf* nose; **narices** *nfpl* nostrils; **¡narices!** (*fam*) rubbish!; **delante de las narices de uno** under one's (very) nose; **estar hasta las narices** to be completely fed up; **meter las narices en algo** to poke one's nose into sth.

narración [nárrásyon'] *nf* narration.

narrador, a [nárráthor', á] *nm/f* narrator.

narrar [nárrár'] *vt* to narrate, recount.

narrativo, a [nárrátē'ho, á] *a* narrative ♦ *nf* narrative, story.

nasal [násál'] *a* nasal.

N.ª S.ʳª *abr* = *Nuestra Señora*.

nata [ná'tá] *nf* cream (*tb fig*); (*en leche cocida etc*) skin; **~ batida** whipped cream.

natación [nátásyon'] *nf* swimming.

natal [nátál'] *a* natal; (*país*) native; **ciudad ~** home town.

natalicio [nátálē'syo] *nm* birthday.

natalidad [nátálētháth'] *nf* birth rate.

natillas [nátē'yás] *nfpl* (egg) custard *sg*.

natividad [nátēhētháth'] *nf* nativity.

nativo, a [nátē'ho, á] *a*, *nm/f* native.

nato, a [ná'to, á] *a* born; **un músico ~** a born musician.

natural [nátōōrál'] *a* natural; (*fruta etc*) fresh ♦ *nm/f* nature ♦ *nm* disposition, temperament; **buen ~** good nature; **fruta al ~** fruit in its own juice.

naturaleza [nátōōrále'sá] *nf* nature; (*género*) nature, kind; **~ muerta** still life.

naturalice [nátōōrálē'se] *etc vb* V **naturalizarse**.

naturalidad [nátōōrálētháth'] *nf* naturalness.

naturalización [nátōōrálēsásyon'] *nf* naturalization.

naturalizarse [nátōōrálēsár'se] *vr* to become naturalized; (*aclimatarse*) to become acclimated (*US*) *o* acclimatized (*Brit*).

naturalmente [nátōōrálmen'te] *ad* naturally; **¡~!** of course!

naufragar [náōōfrágár'] *vi* (*barco*) to sink; (*gente*) to be shipwrecked; (*fig*) to fail.

naufragio [náōōfrá'hyo] *nm* shipwreck.

náufrago, a [ná'ōōfrágo, á] *nm/f* castaway, shipwrecked person.

naufrague [náōōfrá'ge] *etc vb* V **naufragar**.

náusea [ná'ōōseá] *nf* nausea; **me da ~s** it makes me feel sick.

nauseabundo, a [náōōseáōōn'do, á] *a* nauseating, sickening.

náutico, a [ná'ōōtēko, á] *a* nautical; **club ~** sailing *o* yacht club ♦ *nf* navigation, seamanship.

navaja [náhá'há] *nf* (*cortaplumas*) pocketknife; **~ (de afeitar)** razor.

Navarra [náhá'rrá] *nf* Navarre.

navarro, a [náhá'rro, á] *a* of *o* from Navarre, Navarrese ♦ *nm/f* Navarrese ♦ *nm* (*LING*) Navarrese.

nave [ná'he] *nf* (*barco*) ship, vessel; (*ARQ*) nave; **~ espacial** spaceship; **quemar las ~s** to burn one's boats.

navegación [náhegásyon'] *nf* navigation; (*viaje*) sea journey; **~ aérea** air traffic; **~ costera** coastal shipping; **~ fluvial** river navigation.

navegante [náhegán'te] *nm/f* navigator.

navegar [náhegár'] *vi* (*barco*) to sail; (*avión*) to fly ♦ *vt* to sail; to fly; (*dirigir el rumbo de*) to navigate.

navegue [náhe'ge] *etc vb* V **navegar**.

navidad [náhētháth'] *nf* Christmas; **~es** *nfpl* Christmas time *sg*; **día de ~** Christmas Day; **por ~es** at Christmas (time); **¡felices ~es!** Merry Christmas.

navideño, a [náhēthe'nyo, á] *a* Christmas *cpd*.

navío [náhē'o] *nm* ship.

nazi [ná'sē] *a*, *nm/f* Nazi.

n/cta *abr* (*COM*) = *nuestra cuenta*.

N. de la R. *abr* (= *nota de la redacción*) editor's note.

N. de la T./del T. *abr* (= *nota de la traductora/del traductor*) translator's note.

NE *abr* (= *nor(d)este*) NE.

neblina [neblē'ná] *nf* mist.

nebuloso, a [nehōōlo'so, á] *a* foggy; (*calinoso*) misty; (*indefinido*) nebulous, vague ♦

nf nebula.

necedad [neseθáθ'] *nf* foolishness; (*una* ~) foolish act.

necesario, a [nesesá'ryo, á] *a* necessary; **si fuera** *o* **fuese** ~ if need(s) be.

neceser [neseser'] *nm* vanity case; (*bolsa grande*) traveling case (*US*), holdall (*Brit*).

necesidad [neseseθáθ'] *nf* need; (*lo inevitable*) necessity; (*miseria*) poverty, need; **en caso de** ~ in case of need *o* emergency; **hacer sus** ~**es** to relieve o.s.

necesitado, a [nesesitá'θo, á] *a* needy, poor; ~ **de** in need of.

necesitar [nesesetár'] *vt* to need, require ♦ *vi*: ~ **de** to have need of; ~**se** *vr* to be needed; (*anuncios*) **"necesítase coche"** "car wanted".

necio, a [ne'syo, á] *a* foolish ♦ *nm/f* fool.

necrología [nekroloĥē'á] *nf* obituary.

necrópolis [nekro'polēs] *nf inv* cemetery.

nectarina [nektárē'ná] *nf* nectarine.

neerlandés, esa [neerlándes', esá] *a* Dutch ♦ *nm/f* Dutchman/woman ♦ *nm* (*LING*) Dutch; **los neerlandeses** the Dutch.

nefando, a [nefán'do, á] *a* unspeakable.

nefasto, a [nefá'sto, á] *a* ill-fated, unlucky.

negación [neɡásyon'] *nf* negation; (*LING*) negative; (*rechazo*) refusal, denial.

negado, a [neɡá'θo, á] *a*: ~ **para** inept at, unfitted for.

negar [neɡár'] *vt* (*renegar, rechazar*) to refuse; (*prohibir*) to refuse, deny; (*desmentir*) to deny; ~**se** *vr*: ~**se a hacer algo** to refuse to do sth.

negativo, a [neɡátē'βo, á] *a* negative ♦ *nm* (*FOTO*) negative; (*MAT*) minus ♦ *nf* (*gen*) negative; (*rechazo*) refusal, denial; **negativa rotunda** flat refusal.

negligencia [neɡlēhen'syá] *nf* negligence.

negligente [neɡlēhen'te] *a* negligent.

negociable [neɡosyá'βle] *a* (*COM*) negotiable.

negociado [neɡosyá'θo] *nm* department, section.

negociante [neɡosyán'te] *nm/f* businessman/woman.

negociar [neɡosyár'] *vt, vi* to negotiate; ~ **en** to deal in, trade in.

negocio [neɡo'syo] *nm* (*COM*) business; (*asunto*) affair, business; (*operación comercial*) deal, transaction; (*AM*) firm; (*lugar*) place of business; **los** ~**s** business *sg*; **hacer** ~ to do business; **el** ~ **del libro** the book trade; ~ **autorizado** licensed trade; **hombre de** ~**s** businessman; ~ **sucio** shady deal; **hacer un buen** ~ to pull off a profitable deal; **¡mal** ~**!** it looks bad!

negra [ne'ɡrá] *nf* V **negro.**

negrita [neɡrē'tá] *nf* (*TIP*) bold face; **en** ~ in bold (type).

negro, a [ne'ɡro, á] *a* black; (*suerte*) awful,

atrocious; (*humor etc*) sad; (*lúgubre*) gloomy ♦ *nm* (*color*) black ♦ *nm/f* Negro/ Negress, black ♦ *nf* (*MUS*) quarter note (*US*), crotchet (*Brit*); ~ **como la boca del lobo** pitch-black; **estoy** ~ **con esto** I'm getting desperate about it; **ponerse** ~ (*fam*) to get cross.

negrura [neɡroō'rá] *nf* blackness.

negué [neɡe'], **neguemos** [neɡe'mos] *etc vb* V **negar.**

nene, a [ne'ne, á] *nm/f* baby, small child.

nenúfar [nenoō'fár] *nm* water lily.

neologismo [neolohēs'mo] *nm* neologism.

neoyorquino, a [neoyorkē'no, á] *a* New York *cpd* ♦ *nm/f* New Yorker.

neozelandés, esa [neoselándes', esá] *a* New Zealand *cpd* ♦ *nm/f* New Zealander.

nepotismo [nepotēs'mo] *nm* nepotism.

nervio [ner'βyo] *nm* (*ANAT*) nerve; (: *tendón*) tendon; (*fig*) vigor (*US*), vigour (*Brit*); (*TEC*) rib; **crispar los** ~**s a uno,** **poner los** ~**s de punta a uno** to get on sb's nerves.

nerviosismo [nerβyosēs'mo] *nm* nervousness, nerves *pl*.

nervioso, a [nerβyo'so, á] *a* nervous; (*sensible*) nervy, highly-strung; (*impaciente*) restless; **¡no te pongas** ~**!** take it easy!

nervudo, a [nerβoō'θo, á] *a* tough; (*mano*) sinewy.

neto, a [ne'to, á] *a* clear; (*limpio*) clean; (*COM*) net.

neumático, a [neoōmá'tēko, á] *a* pneumatic ♦ *nm* (*Esp*) tire (*US*), tyre (*Brit*); ~ **de recambio** spare tire (*US*) *o* tyre (*Brit*).

neumonía [neoōmonē'á] *nf* pneumonia.

neuralgia [neoōrál'hyá] *nf* neuralgia.

neurastenia [neoōráste'nyá] *nf* neurasthenia; (*fig*) excitability.

neurasténico, a [neoōráste'nēko, á] *a* neurasthenic; excitable.

neurólogo, a [neoōro'loɡo, á] *nm/f* neurologist.

neurosis [neoōro'sēs] *nf inv* neurosis.

neurótico, a [neoōro'tēko, á] *a, nm/f* neurotic.

neutral [neoōtrál'] *a* neutral.

neutralice [neoōtrálē'se] *etc vb* V **neutralizar.**

neutralizar [neoōtrálēsár'] *vt* to neutralize; (*contrarrestar*) to counteract.

neutro, a [ne'oōtro, á] *a* (*BIO, LING*) neuter.

neutrón [neoōtron'] *nm* neutron.

nevado, a [neβá'θo, á] *a* snow-covered; (*montaña*) snow-capped; (*fig*) snowy, snow-white ♦ *nf* snowstorm; (*caída de nieve*) snowfall.

nevar [neβár'] *vi* to snow ♦ *vt* (*fig*) to whiten.

nevera [neβe'rá] *nf* (*Esp*) refrigerator.

nevería [neβerē'á] *nf* (*AM*) ice-cream parlor

(US) o parlour (Brit).

nevisca [neḃes'ká] nf flurry of snow.

nexo [nek'so] nm link, connection.

n/f abr (COM) = nuestro favor.

ni [nē] conj nor, neither; (tb: ~ **siquiera**) not even; ~ **que** not even if; ~ **blanco** ~ **negro** neither white nor black; ~ **el uno** ~ **el otro** neither one nor the other.

Nicaragua [nēkárá'gwá] nf Nicaragua.

nicaragüense [nēkárágwen'se] a, nm/f Nicaraguan.

nicotina [nēkotē'ná] nf nicotine.

nicho [nētch'o] nm niche.

nido [nē'tho] nm nest; (fig) hiding place; ~ **de ladrones** den of thieves.

niebla [nye'hlá] nf fog; (neblina) mist; **hay** ~ it is foggy.

niego [nye'go] etc, **niegue** [nye'ge] etc vb V **negar**.

nieto, a [nye'to, á] nm/f grandson/daughter; **~s** nmpl grandchildren.

nieve [nye'he] etc vb V **nevar** ♦ nf snow; (AM) ice cream; **copo de** ~ snowflake.

Nigeria [nēhe'ryá] nf Nigeria.

nigeriano, a [nēheryá'no, á] a, nm/f Nigerian.

nigromancia [nēgromán'syá] nf necromancy, black magic.

nihilista [nēēlē'stá] a nihilistic ♦ nm nihilist.

Nilo [nē'lo] nm: **el (Río)** ~ the Nile.

nimbo [nēm'bo] nm (aureola) halo; (nube) nimbus.

nimiedad [nēmyetháth'] nf small-mindedness; (trivialidad) triviality; (una ~) trifle, tiny detail.

nimio, a [nē'myo, á] a trivial, insignificant.

ninfa [nēn'fá] nf nymph.

ninfómana [nēnfo'máná] nf nymphomaniac.

ninguno, a [nēngōō'no, á] a (**ningún** delante de nmsg) no ♦ pron (nadie) nobody; (ni uno) none, not one; (ni uno ni otro) neither; **de ninguna manera** by no means, not at all; **no voy a ninguna parte** I'm not going anywhere.

niña [nē'nyá] nf V **niño**.

niñera [nēnye'rá] nf nursemaid, nanny.

niñería [nēnyerē'á] nf childish act.

niñez [nēnyes'] nf childhood; (infancia) infancy.

niño, a [nē'nyo, á] a (joven) young; (inmaduro) immature ♦ nm (chico) boy, child ♦ nf girl, child; (ANAT) pupil; **los ~s** the children; ~ **bien** rich kid; ~ **expósito** foundling; ~ **de pecho** babe-in-arms; ~ **prodigio** child prodigy; **de** ~ as a child; **ser el** ~ **mimado de uno** to be sb's pet; **ser la niña de los ojos de uno** to be the apple of sb's eye.

nipón, ona [nēpon', oná] a, nm/f Japanese; **los nipones** the Japanese.

níquel [nē'kel] nm nickel.

niquelar [nēkelár'] vt (TEC) to nickel-plate.

níspero [nēs'pero] nm medlar.

nitidez [nētēthes'] nf (claridad) clarity; (: de atmósfera) brightness; (: de imagen) sharpness.

nítido, a [nē'tētho, á] a bright; (fig) pure; (imagen) clear, sharp.

nitrato [nētrá'to] nm nitrate.

nitrógeno [nētro'heno] nm nitrogen.

nitroglicerina [nētroglēserē'ná] nf nitroglycerine.

nivel [nēḃel'] nm (GEO) level; (norma) level, standard; (altura) height; ~ **de aceite** oil level; ~ **de aire** spirit level; ~ **de vida** standard of living; **al** ~ **de** on a level with, at the same height as; (fig) on a par with; **a 900m sobre el** ~ **del mar** at 900m above sea level.

nivelado, a [nēḃelá'tho, á] a level, flat; (TEC) flush.

nivelar [nēḃelár'] vt to level out; (fig) to even up; (COM) to balance.

Niza [nē'sá] nf Nice.

n/l. abr (COM) = nuestra letra.

NNE abr (= nornordeste) NNE.

NNO abr (= nornoroeste) NNW.

NN. UU. nfpl abr (= Naciones Unidas) UN sg.

NO abr (= noroeste) NW.

no [no] ad no; (con verbo) not ♦ excl no!; ~ **tengo nada** I don't have anything, I have nothing; ~ **es el mío** it's not mine; **ahora** ~ not now; **¿~ lo sabes?** don't you know?; ~ **mucho** not much; ~ **bien termine, lo entregaré** as soon as I finish I'll hand it over; **¡a que** ~ **lo sabes!** I bet you don't know!; **¡cómo** ~**!** of course!; **pacto de** ~ **agresión** non-aggression pact; **los países** ~ **alineados** the non-aligned countries; **el** ~ **va más** the ultimate; **la** ~ **intervención** non-intervention.

N.º abr (= número) No.

n/o abr (COM) = nuestra orden.

noble [no'hle] a, nm/f noble; **los ~s** the nobility sg.

nobleza [nohle'sá] nf nobility.

noción [nosyon'] nf notion; **nociones** nfpl elements, rudiments.

nocivo, a [nosē'ho, á] a harmful.

noctambulismo [noktámbōōlēs'mo] nm sleepwalking.

noctámbulo, a [noktám'bōōlo, á] nm/f sleepwalker.

nocturno, a [noktōōr'no, á] a (de la noche) nocturnal, night cpd; (de la tarde) evening cpd ♦ nm nocturne.

noche [notch'e] nf night, night-time; (la tarde) evening; (fig) darkness; **de** ~, **por la** ~ at night; **ayer por la** ~ last night; **esta** ~ tonight; **(en) toda la** ~ all night; **hacer** ~ **en un sitio** to spend the night in a place; **se hace de** ~ it's getting dark.

Nochebuena [notchebwe'ná] *nf* Christmas Eve.

Nochevieja [notchebye'há] *nf* New Year's Eve.

nodriza [nothrē'sá] *nf* wet nurse; **buque** *o* **nave** ~ supply ship.

Noé [noe'] *nm* Noah.

nogal [nogál'] *nm* walnut tree; (*madera*) walnut.

nómada [no'máthá] *a* nomadic ♦ *nm/f* nomad.

nomás [nomás'] *ad*: (*AM*: *gen*) just; (: *tan sólo*) only.

nombramiento [nombrámyen'to] *nm* naming; (*a un empleo*) appointment; (*POL etc*) nomination; (*MIL*) commission.

nombrar [nombrár'] *vt* (*gen*) to name; (*mencionar*) to mention; (*designar*) to appoint, nominate; (*MIL*) to commission.

nombre [nom'bre] *nm* name; (*sustantivo*) noun; (*fama*) renown; ~ **y apellidos** name in full; ~ **común/propio** common/proper noun; ~ **de pila/de soltera** Christian/maiden name; ~ **de fichero** (*INFORM*) file name; **en** ~ **de** in the name of, on behalf of; **sin** ~ nameless; **su conducta no tiene** ~ his behavior is utterly despicable.

nomenclatura [nomenklátōo'rá] *nf* nomenclature.

nomeolvides [nomeolhē'thes] *nm* *inv* forget-me-not.

nómina [no'mēná] *nf* (*lista*) list; (*COM*: *tb*: ~**s**) payroll.

nominal [nomēnál'] *a* nominal; (*valor*) face *cpd*; (*LING*) noun *cpd*, substantival.

nominar [nomēnár'] *vt* to nominate.

nominativo, a [nomēnátē'ho, á] *a* (*LING*) nominative; (*COM*): **un cheque** ~ **a X** a check made out to X.

non [non] *a* odd, uneven ♦ *nm* odd number; **pares y** ~**es** odds and evens.

nonagésimo, a [nonáhe'sēmo, á] *num* ninetieth.

nono, a [no'no, á] *num* ninth.

nordeste [northe'ste] *a* north-east, north-eastern, north-easterly ♦ *nm* north-east; (*viento*) north-east wind, north-easterly.

nórdico, a [nor'thēko, á] *a* (*del norte*) northern, northerly; (*escandinavo*) Nordic, Norse ♦ *nm/f* northerner; (*escandinavo*) Norseman/woman ♦ *nm* (*LING*) Norse.

noreste [nore'ste] *a, nm* = **nordeste**.

noria [no'ryá] *nf* (*AGR*) waterwheel; (*de carnaval*) Ferris (*US*) *o* big (*Brit*) wheel.

norma [nor'má] *nf* standard, norm, rule; (*patrón*) pattern; (*método*) method.

normal [normál'] *a* (*corriente*) normal; (*habitual*) usual, natural; (*TEC*) standard; **Escuela N**~ teacher training college; (**gasolina**) ~ regular (*US*), two-star petrol

(*Brit*).

normalice [normálē'se] *etc vb* V **normalizar**.

normalidad [normálēthàth'] *nf* normality; **restablecer la** ~ to restore order.

normalización [normálēsásyon'] *nf* (*COM*) standardization.

normalizar [normálēsàr'] *vt* (*reglamentar*) to normalize; (*COM, TEC*) to standardize; ~**se** *vr* to return to normal.

Normandía [normándē'á] *nf* Normandy.

normando, a [normán'do, á] *a, nm/f* Norman.

normativo, a [normátē'ho, á] *a*: **es** ~ **en todos los coches nuevos** it is standard in all new cars.

noroeste [noroe'ste] *a* north-west, north-western, north-westerly ♦ *nm* north-west; (*viento*) north-west wind, north-westerly.

norte [nor'te] *a* north, northern, northerly ♦ *nm* north; (*fig*) guide.

Norteamérica [norteáme'rēká] *nf* North America.

norteamericano, a [norteámerēká'no, á] *a, nm/f* (North) American.

norteño, a [norte'nyo, á] *a* northern ♦ *nm/f* northerner.

Noruega [norwe'gá] *nf* Norway.

noruego, a [norwe'go, á] *a, nm/f* Norwegian ♦ *nm* (*LING*) Norwegian.

nos [nos] *pron* (*directo*) us; (*indirecto*) (to) us; (*reflexivo*) (to) ourselves; (*recíproco*) (to) each other; ~ **levantamos a las 7** we get up at 7.

nosotros, as [noso'tros, às] *pron* (*sujeto*) we; (*después de prep*) us; ~ (**mismos**) ourselves.

nostalgia [nostál'hyá] *nf* nostalgia, homesickness.

nostálgico, a [nostál'hēko, á] *a* nostalgic, homesick.

nota [no'tá] *nf* note; (*ESCOL*) grade (*US*), mark (*Brit*); (*de fin de año*) final grade (*US*), report (*Brit*); (*UNIV etc*) footnote; (*COM*) account; ~ **de aviso** advice slip (*US*), advice note (*Brit*); ~ **de crédito/débito** credit/debit note; ~ **de gastos** expenses claim; ~ **de sociedad** gossip column; **tomar** ~**s** to take notes.

notable [notá'hle] *a* noteworthy, notable; (*ESCOL etc*) outstanding ♦ *nm/f* notable.

notar [notár'] *vt* to notice, note; (*percibir*) to feel; (*ver*) to see; ~**se** *vr* to be obvious; **se nota que** ... one observes that ....

notaría [notárē'á] *nf* (*profesión*) profession of notary; (*despacho*) notary's office.

notarial [notáryál'] *a* (*estilo*) legal; **acta** ~ affidavit.

notario [notá'ryo] *nm* notary; (*abogado*) lawyer.

noticia [notē'syá] *nf* (*información*) piece of

news; (*TV etc*) news item; **las ~s** the news *sg*; **según nuestras ~s** according to our information; **tener ~s de uno** to hear from sb.

noticiar [notēsyár'] *vt* to notify.

noticiario [notēsyá'ryo] *nm* (*CINE*) newsreel; (*TV*) news bulletin.

noticiero [notēsye'ro] *nm* newspaper, gazette; (*AM: also: ~* **telediario**) news bulletin.

notificación [notēfēkásyon'] *nf* notification.

notificar [notēfēkár'] *vt* to notify, inform.

notifique [notēfē'ke] *etc vb V* **notificar**.

notoriedad [notoryetháth'] *nf* fame, renown.

notorio, a [noto'ryo, á] *a* (*público*) well-known; (*evidente*) obvious.

nov. *abr* (= *noviembre*) Nov.

novatada [nohátá'thá] *nf* (*burla*) teasing, hazing (*US*); **pagar la ~** to learn the hard way.

novato, a [nohá'to, á] *a* inexperienced ♦ *nm/f* beginner, novice.

novecientos, as [nohesyen'tos, ás] *num* nine hundred.

novedad [nohetháth'] *nf* (*calidad de nuevo*) newness, novelty; (*noticia*) piece of news; (*cambio*) change, (new) development; (*sorpresa*) surprise; **~es** *nfpl* (*noticia*) latest (news) *sg*.

novedoso, a [nohethó'so, á] *a* novel.

novel [nohel'] *a* new; (*inexperto*) inexperienced ♦ *nm/f* beginner.

novela [nohe'lá] *nf* novel; **~ policíaca** detective story.

novelero, a [nohele'ro, á] *a* highly imaginative.

novelesco, a [noheles'ko, á] *a* fictional; (*romántico*) romantic; (*fantástico*) fantastic.

novelista [nohelē'stá] *nm/f* novelist.

novelística [nohelē'stēká] *nf*: **la ~** fiction, the novel.

noveno, a [nohe'no, á] *num* ninth.

noventa [nohen'tá] *num* ninety.

novia [no'hyá] *nf V* **novio**.

noviazgo [nohyás'go] *nm* engagement.

novicio, a [nohē'syo, á] *nm/f* novice.

noviembre [nohyem'bre] *nm* November.

novilla [nohē'yá] *nf* heifer.

novillada [nohēyá'thá] *nf* (*TAUR*) bullfight with young bulls.

novillero [nohēye'ro] *nm* novice bullfighter.

novillo [nohē'yo] *nm* young bull, bullock; **hacer ~s** (*fam*) to play hooky (*US*) o truant (*Brit*).

novio, a [no'hyo, á] *nm/f* boyfriend/girlfriend; (*prometido*) fiancé/fiancée; (*recién casado*) bridegroom/bride; **los ~s** the newly-weds.

novísimo, a [nohē'sēmo, á] *a superlativo de* **nuevo, a**.

NPI *nm abr* (*INFORM*: = *número personal de identificación*) PIN.

N. S. *abr* = *Nuestro Señor*.

ntra., ntro. *abr* = **nuestra, nuestro**.

NU *nfpl abr* (= *Naciones Unidas*) UN.

nubarrón [nōohárron'] *nm* storm cloud.

nube [nōo'he] *nf* cloud; (*MED: ocular*) cloud, film; (*fig*) mass; **una ~ de críticas** a storm of criticism; **los precios están por las ~s** prices are sky-high; **estar en las ~s** to be daydreaming.

nublado, a [nōohlá'tho, á] *a* cloudy ♦ *nm* storm cloud.

nublar [nōohlár'] *vt* (*oscurecer*) to darken; (*confundir*) to cloud; **~se** *vr* to cloud over.

nuca [nōo'ká] *nf* nape of the neck.

nuclear [nōokleár'] *a* nuclear.

nuclearizado, a [nōokleárēsá'tho, á] *a*: **países ~s** countries possessing nuclear weapons.

núcleo [nōo'kleo] *nm* (*centro*) core; (*FISICA*) nucleus.

nudillo [nōothē'yo] *nm* knuckle.

nudo [nōo'tho] *nm* knot; (*unión*) bond; (*de problema*) crux; (*FERRO*) junction; (*fig*) lump; **~ corredizo** slipknot; **con un ~ en la garganta** with a lump in one's throat.

nudoso, a [nōotho'so, á] *a* knotty; (*tronco*) gnarled; (*bastón*) knobby (*US*), knobbly (*Brit*).

nueces [nwe'ses] *nfpl de* **nuez**.

nuera [nwe'rá] *nf* daughter-in-law.

nuestro, a [nwes'tro, á] *a posesivo* our ♦ *pron* ours; **~ padre** our father; **un amigo ~** a friend of ours; **es el ~** it's ours; **los ~s** our people; (*DEPORTE*) our o the local team o side.

nueva [nwe'há] *nf V* **nuevo**.

Nueva Escocia *nf* Nova Scotia.

nuevamente [nwehámen'te] *ad* (*otra vez*) again; (*de nuevo*) anew.

Nueva York [-york'] *nf* New York.

Nueva Zeland(i)a [-seländ'(y)á] *nf* New Zealand.

nueve [nwe'he] *num* nine.

nuevo, a [nwe'ho, á] *a* (*gen*) new ♦ *nf* piece of news; **¿qué hay de ~?** (*fam*) what's new?; **de ~** again.

Nuevo Méjico *nm* New Mexico.

nuez [nwes], *pl* **nueces** *nf* (*del nogal*) walnut; (*fruto*) nut; **~ de Adán** Adam's apple; **~ moscada** nutmeg.

nulidad [nōolētháth'] *nf* (*incapacidad*) incompetence; (*abolición*) nullity; (*individuo*) nonentity; **es una ~** he's a dead loss.

nulo, a [nōo'lo, á] *a* (*inepto, torpe*) useless; (*inválido*) (null and) void; (*DEPORTE*) drawn, tied.

núm. *abr* (= *número*) no.

numen [nōo'men] *nm* inspiration.

numeración [nōomerásyon'] *nf* (*cifras*)

numbers *pl*; (*arábiga, romana etc*) numerals *pl*; ~ **de línea** (*INFORM*) line numbering.

numeral [nōōmerál'] *nm* numeral.

numerar [nōōmerár'] *vt* to number; **~se** *vr* (*MIL etc*) to number off.

numerario, a [nōōmerá'ryo, á] *a* numerary; **profesor** ~ permanent *o* tenured member of teaching staff ♦ *nm* hard cash.

numérico, a [nōōme'rēko, á] *a* numerical.

número [nōō'mero] *nm* (*gen*) number; (*tamaño: de zapato*) size; (*ejemplar: de diario*) number, issue; (*TEATRO etc*) turn, act, number; **sin** ~ numberless, unnumbered; ~ **binario** (*INFORM*) binary number; ~ **de matrícula/de teléfono** registration/telephone number; ~ **personal de identificación** (*INFORM etc*) personal identification number; ~ **de serie** (*COM*) serial number; ~ **atrasado** back issue.

numeroso, a [nōōmero'so, á] *a* numerous; **familia numerosa** large family.

nunca [nōōn'ká] *ad* (*jamás*) never; (*con verbo negativo*) ever; ~ **lo pensé** I never thought it; **no viene** ~ he never comes; ~ **más** never again.

nuncio [nōōn'syo] *nm* (*REL*) nuncio.

nupcias [nōōp'syás] *nfpl* wedding *sg*, nuptials.

nutria [nōō'tryá] *nf* otter.

nutrición [nōōtrēsyon'] *nf* nutrition.

nutrido, a [nōōtrē'tho, á] *a* (*alimentado*) nourished; (*fig: grande*) large; (*abundante*) abundant; **mal** ~ undernourished; ~ **de** full of.

nutrir [nōōtrēr'] *vt* to feed, nourish; (*fig*) to feed, strengthen.

nutritivo, a [nōōtrētē'tho, á] *a* nourishing, nutritious.

nylon [nēlon'] *nm* nylon.

Ñ

Ñ, ñ [e'nye] *nf* (*letra*) Ñ, ñ.

ñato, a [nyá'to, á] *a* (*AM*) snub-nosed.

ñoñería [nyonyerē'á], **ñoñez** [nyonyes'] *nf* insipidness.

ñoño, a [nyo'nyo, á] *a* (*AM: tonto*) silly, stupid; (*soso*) insipid; (*persona: débil*) spineless.

ñoquis [nyo'kēs] *nmpl* (*CULIN*) gnocchi.

O

O, o [o] *nf* (*letra*) O, o; **O de Oviedo** O for Oboe.

O *abr* (= *oeste*) W.

o [o] *conj* or; ~ ... ~ either ... or; ~ **sea** that is.

o/ *nm* (*COM*: = *orden*) o.

OACI *nf abr* (= *Organización de la Aviación Civil Internacional*) ICAO.

oasis [oá'sēs] *nm inv* oasis.

obcecado, a [obsekà'tho, á] *a* blind; (*terco*) stubborn.

obcecarse [obsekár'se] *vr* to be obstinate; ~ **en hacer** to insist on doing.

obceque [obse'ke] *etc vb* V **obcecarse**.

obedecer [obetheser'] *vt* to obey; ~ **a** (*MED etc*) to yield to; (*fig*) ~ **a ...**, ~ **al hecho de que ...** to be due to ..., arise from ....

obedezca [obethes'ká] *etc vb* V **obedecer**.

obediencia [obethyen'syá] *nf* obedience.

obediente [obethyen'te] *a* obedient.

obertura [obertōō'rá] *nf* overture.

obesidad [obesēthàth'] *nf* obesity.

obeso, a [obe'so, á] *a* obese.

óbice [o'hēse] *nm* obstacle, impediment.

obispado [obēspá'tho] *nm* bishopric.

obispo [obēs'po] *nm* bishop.

óbito [o'hēto] *nm* demise.

objeción [obhesyon'] *nf* objection; **hacer una** ~, **poner objeciones** to raise objections, object.

objetante [obhetán'te] *nm/f* objector; (*POL*) heckler.

objetar [obhetár'] *vt, vi* to object.

objetivo, a [obhetē'ho, á] *a* objective ♦ *nm* objective; (*fig*) aim; (*FOTO*) lens.

objeto [obhe'to] *nm* (*cosa*) object; (*fin*) aim.

objetor, a [obhetor', á] *nm/f* objector; ~ **de conciencia** conscientious objector.

oblea [oble'á] *nf* (*REL, fig*) wafer; (*INFORM*) chip, wafer.

oblicuo, a [oblē'kwo, á] *a* oblique; (*mirada*) sidelong.

obligación [oblēgàsyon'] *nf* obligation; (*COM*) bond, debenture.

obligar [oblēgár'] *vt* to force; **~se** *vr*: **~se a** to commit o.s. to.

obligatorio, a [oblēgàto'ryo, á] *a* compulsory, obligatory.

obligue [oblē'ge] *etc vb* V **obligar**.

oboe [obo'e] *nm* oboe; (*músico*) oboist.

Ob.ᴾᴼ *abr* (= *Obispo*) Bp.

obra [o'bra] *nf* work; (*hechura*) piece of work; (*ARQ*) construction, building; (*libro*) book; (*MUS*) opus; (*TEATRO*) play; ~ **de arte** work of art; ~ **maestra** masterpiece; ~ **de consulta** reference book; ~**s completas** complete works; ~ **benéfica** charity; "~**s**" (*en carretera*) "men at work"; ~**s públicas** public works; **por** ~ **de** thanks to (the efforts of); ~**s son amores y no buenas razones** actions speak louder than words.

obrar [o'brar] *vt* to work; (*tener efecto*) to have an effect on ♦ *vi* to act, behave; (*tener efecto*) to have an effect; **la carta obra en su poder** the letter is in his/her possession.

obr. cit. *abr* (= *obra citada*) op. cit.

obrero, a [o'bre'ro, á] *a* working; (*movimiento*) labor *cpd* (*US*), labour *cpd* (*Brit*); **clase obrera** working class ♦ *nm/f* (*gen*) worker; (*sin oficio*) laborer (*US*), labourer (*Brit*).

obscenidad [obsenethath'] *nf* obscenity.

obsceno, a [obse'no, á] *a* obscene.

obscu... = **oscu...**

obsequiar [obsekyár'] *vt* (*ofrecer*) to present; (*agasajar*) to make a fuss of, lavish attention on.

obsequio [obse'kyo] *nm* (*regalo*) gift; (*cortesía*) courtesy, attention.

obsequioso, a [obsekyo'so, á] *a* attentive.

observación [obserbásyon'] *nf* observation; (*reflexión*) remark; (*objeción*) objection.

observador, a [obserbáthor', á] *a* observant ♦ *nm/f* observer.

observancia [obserbán'syá] *nf* observance.

observar [obserbár'] *vt* to observe; (*notar*) to notice; (*leyes*) to observe, respect; (*reglas*) to abide by.

observatorio [obserbáto'ryo] *nm* observatory; ~ **del tiempo** weather station.

obsesión [obsesyon'] *nf* obsession.

obsesionar [obsesyonár'] *vt* to obsess.

obsolescencia [obsolesen'syá] *nf*: ~ **incorporada** (*COM*) built-in obsolescence.

obstaculice [obstákoolē'se] *etc vb V* **obstaculizar.**

obstaculizar [obstákoolēsár'] *vt* (*dificultar*) to hinder, hamper.

obstáculo [obstá'koolo] *nm* (*gen*) obstacle; (*impedimento*) hindrance, drawback.

obstante [obstán'te]: **no** ~ *ad* nevertheless; (*de todos modos*) all the same ♦ *prep* in spite of.

obstetricia [obstetrē'syá] *nf* obstetrics *sg*.

obstétrico, a [obste'trēko, á] *a* obstetric ♦ *nm/f* obstetrician.

obstinado, a [obstēná'tho, á] *a* (*gen*) obstinate; (*terco*) stubborn.

obstinarse [obstēnár'se] *vr* to dig one's

heels in; ~ **en** to persist in.

obstrucción [obstrooksyon'] *nf* obstruction.

obstruir [obstrooēr'] *vt* to obstruct; (*bloquear*) to block; (*estorbar*) to hinder.

obstruyendo [obstrooyen'do] *etc vb V* **obstruir.**

obtención [obtensyon'] *nf* (*COM*) procurement.

obtendré [obtendre'] *etc vb V* **obtener.**

obtener [obtener'] *vt* (*conseguir*) to obtain; (*ganar*) to gain.

obtenga [obten'gá] *etc vb V* **obtener.**

obturación [obtoorásyon'] *nf* plugging, stopping; (*FOTO*): **velocidad de** ~ shutter speed.

obturador [obtoorathor'] *nm* (*FOTO*) shutter.

obtuso, a [obtoo'so, á] *a* (*filo*) blunt; (*MAT, fig*) obtuse.

obtuve [obtoo'be] *etc vb V* **obtener.**

obús [oboos'] *nm* (*MIL*) shell.

obviar [obbyár'] *vt* to obviate, remove.

obvio, a [ob'byo, á] *a* obvious.

ocasión [okásyon'] *nf* (*oportunidad*) opportunity, chance; (*momento*) occasion, time; (*causa*) cause; **de** ~ secondhand; **con** ~ **de** on the occasion of; **en algunas ocasiones** sometimes; **aprovechar la** ~ to seize one's opportunity.

ocasionar [okásyonár'] *vt* to cause.

ocaso [oká'so] *nm* sunset; (*fig*) decline.

occidental [oksēthentál'] *a* western ♦ *nm/f* westerner ♦ *nm* west.

occidente [oksēthen'te] *nm* west; **el O**~ the West.

occiso, a [oksē'so, á] *nm/f*: **el** ~ (*AM*) the deceased; (*de asesinato*) the victim.

océano [ose'áno] *nm* ocean; **el** ~ **Índico** the Indian Ocean.

O.C.D.E. *nf abr* (= *Organización de Cooperación y Desarrollo Económicos*) OECD.

OCI [o'sē] *nf abr* (*POL: Venezuela, Perú*) = *Oficina Central de Información*.

ocio [o'syo] *nm* (*tiempo*) leisure; (*pey*) idleness; "**guía del** ~" entertainment guide.

ociosidad [osyosēthath'] *nf* idleness.

ocioso, a [osyo'so, á] *a* (*inactivo*) idle; (*inútil*) useless.

oct. *abr* (= *octubre*) Oct.

octanaje [oktáná'he] *nm*: **de alto** ~ high octane.

octano [oktá'no] *nm* octane.

octavilla [oktábē'yá] *nm* leaflet, pamphlet.

octavo, a [oktá'bo, á] *num* eighth.

octeto [okte'to] *nm* (*INFORM*) byte.

octogenario, a [oktohená'ryo, á] *a, nm/f* octogenarian.

octubre [oktoo'bre] *nm* October.

OCU [o'koo] *nf abr* (*Esp*:=*Organización de Consumidores y Usuarios*) ≈ Consumers' Association.

ocular [okōōlár'] *a* ocular, eye *cpd*; **testigo** ~ eyewitness.

oculista [okōōlē'stá] *nm/f* oculist.

ocultar [okōōltár'] *vt* (*esconder*) to hide; (*callar*) to conceal; (*disfrazar*) to screen; ~**se** *vr* to hide (o.s.); ~**se a la vista** to keep out of sight.

oculto, a [okōōl'to, á] *a* hidden; (*fig*) secret.

ocupación [okōōpásyon'] *nf* occupation; (*tenencia*) occupancy.

ocupado, a [okōōpá'đho, á] *a* (*persona*) busy; (*plaza*) occupied, taken; (*teléfono*) busy; **¿está ocupada la silla?** is that seat taken?

ocupar [okōōpár'] *vt* (*gen*) to occupy; (*puesto*) to hold, fill; (*individuo*) to engage; (*obreros*) to employ; (*confiscar*) to seize; ~**se** *vr*: ~**se de** *o* **en** to concern o.s. with; (*cuidar*) to look after; ~**se de lo suyo** to mind one's own business.

ocurrencia [okōōrren'syá] *nf* (*ocasión*) occurrence; (*agudeza*) witticism.

ocurrir [okōōrrēr'] *vi* to happen; ~**se** *vr*: **se me ocurrió que ...** it occurred to me that ...; **¿se te ocurre algo?** can you think of *o* come up with anything? **¿qué ocurre?** what's going on?

ochenta [otchen'tá] *num* eighty.

ocho [otch'o] *num* eight; (*fecha*) eighth; ~ **días** a week.

oda [o'đhá] *nf* ode.

ODECA [otħe'ká] *nf abr*=*Organización de Estados Centroamericanos.*

odiar [ođhyár'] *vt* to hate.

odio [o'đhyo] *nm* (*gen*) hate, hatred; (*disgusto*) dislike.

odioso, a [ođhyo'so, á] *a* (*gen*) hateful; (*malo*) nasty.

odontología [otħontolohē'á] *nf* dentistry, dental surgery.

odontólogo, a [otħonto'logo, á] *nm/f* dentist, dental surgeon.

odre [o'đhre] *nm* wineskin.

O.E.A. *nf abr* (= *Organización de Estados Americanos*) O.A.S.

OECE *nf abr* (= *Organización Europea de Cooperación Económica*) OEEC.

OELA [oe'lá] *nf abr* = *Organización de Estados Latinoamericanos.*

oeste [oe'ste] *nm* west; **una película del** ~ a western.

ofender [ofender'] *vt* (*agraviar*) to offend; (*insultar*) to insult; ~**se** *vr* to take offense.

ofensa [ofen'sá] *nf* offense (*US*), offence (*Brit*); (*insulto*) slight.

ofensivo, a [ofensē'ħo, á] *a* (*insultante*) insulting; (*MIL*) offensive ♦ *nf* offensive.

ofensor, a [ofensor', á] *a* offending ♦ *nm/f* offender.

oferta [ofer'tá] *nf* offer; (*propuesta*) proposal; (*para contrato*) bid, tender; **la** ~ **y la**

demanda supply and demand; **artículos en** ~ goods for sale; **excedentaria** (*COM*) excess supply; ~ **monetaria** money supply; ~ **pública de compra** (*COM*) takeover bid; ~**s de trabajo** (*en periódicos*) job openings (*US*) *o* situations vacant (*Brit*) column.

oficial [ofēsyál'] *a* official ♦ *nm* official; (*MIL*) officer.

oficialista [ofēsyálē'stá] *a* (*AM*) (pro-) government; **el candidato** ~ the governing party's candidate.

oficiar [ofēsyár'] *vt* to inform officially ♦ *vi* (*REL*) to officiate.

oficina [ofēsē'ná] *nf* office; ~ **de colocación** employment agency; ~ **de información** information bureau; ~ **de objetos perdidos** lost-and-found department (*US*), lost property office (*Brit*); ~ **de turismo** tourist office.

oficinista [ofēsēnē'stá] *nm/f* clerk; **los** ~**s** white-collar workers.

oficio [ofē'syo] *nm* (*profesión*) profession; (*puesto*) position; (*REL*) service; (*función*) function; (*comunicado*) official letter; **ser del** ~ to be an old hand; **tener mucho** ~ to have a lot of experience; ~ **de difuntos** funeral service; **de** ~ officially.

oficioso, a [ofēsyo'so, á] *a* (*pey*) officious; (*no oficial*) unofficial, informal.

ofimática [ofēmá'tēká] *nf* office automation.

ofrecer [ofreser'] *vt* (*dar*) to offer; (*proponer*) to propose; ~**se** *vr* (*persona*) to offer o.s., volunteer; (*situación*) to present itself; **¿qué se le ofrece?, ¿se le ofrece algo?** what can I do for you?, can I get you anything?

ofrecimiento [ofresēmyen'to] *nm* offer, offering.

ofrendar [ofrendar'] *vt* to offer, contribute.

ofrezca [ofres'ká] *etc vb* V **ofrecer**.

oftalmología [oftálmolohē'á] *nf* ophthalmology.

oftalmólogo, a [oftálmo'logo, á] *nm/f* ophthalmologist.

ofuscación [ofōōskàsyon'] *nf*, **ofuscamiento** [ofōōskámyen'to] *nm* (*fig*) bewilderment.

ofuscar [ofōōskár'] *vt* (*confundir*) to bewilder; (*enceguecer*) to dazzle, blind.

ofusque [ofōōs'ke] *etc vb* V **ofuscar**.

ogro [o'gro] *nm* ogre.

OIC *nf abr*=*Organización Interamericana del Café*; (*COM*)=*Organización Internacional del Comercio.*

oída [oē'đhá] *nf*: **de** ~**s** by hearsay.

oído [oē'đho] *nm* (*ANAT, MUS*) ear; (*sentido*) hearing; ~ **interno** inner ear; **de** ~ by ear; **apenas pude dar crédito a mis** ~**s** I could scarcely believe my ears; **hacer** ~**s sordos a** to turn a deaf ear to.

OIEA *nm abr* (= *Organismo Internacional de Energía Atómica*) IAEA.

oiga |o'ēġà| *etc vb* V **oír**.

OIR |oēr'| *nf abr* (= *Organización Internacional para los Refugiados*) IRO.

oír |oēr'| *vt* (*gen*) to hear; (*atender a*) to listen to; **¡oye!** (*sorpresa*) I say!, say! (*US*); **¡oiga!** (*TELEC*) hello?; ~ **misa** to attend mass; **como quien oye llover** without paying (the slightest) attention.

O.I.T. *nf abr* (= *Organización Internacional del Trabajo*) ILO.

ojal |ohàl'| *nm* buttonhole.

ojalá |ohàlá'| *excl* if only (it were so)!, some hope! ♦ *conj* if only...!, would that...!; ~ **que venga hoy** I hope he comes today; **¡~ pudiera!** I wish I could!

ojeada |oheá'ᵺà| *nf* glance; **echar una ~ a** to take a quick look at.

ojera |ohe'rà| *nf:* **tener ~s** to have bags under one's eyes.

ojeriza |oherē'sà| *nf* ill-will; **tener ~ a** to have a grudge against, have it in for.

ojeroso, a |ohero'so, à| *a* haggard.

ojete |ohe'te| *nm* eye(let).

ojo |o'ho| *nm* eye; (*de puente*) span; (*de cerradura*) keyhole ♦ *excl* careful!; **tener ~ para** to have an eye for; **~s saltones** bulging *o* goggle eyes; **~ de buey** porthole; **~ por ~** an eye for an eye; **en un abrir y cerrar de ~s** in the twinkling of an eye; **a ~s vistas** openly; (*crecer etc*) before one's (very) eyes; **a ~ (de buen cubero)** roughly; **~s que no ven, corazón que no siente** out of sight, out of mind; **ser el ~ derecho de uno** (*fig*) to be the apple of sb's eye.

ola |o'là| *nf* wave; **~ de calor/frío** heatwave/cold spell; **la nueva ~** the latest fashion; (*CINE, MUS*) (the) new wave.

OLADE |olá'ᵺe| *nf abr* = *Organización Latinoamericana de Energía*.

olé |ole'| *excl* bravo!, olé!

oleada |oleá'ᵺà| *nf* big wave, swell; (*fig*) wave.

oleaje |oleá'he| *nm* swell.

óleo |o'leo| *nm* oil.

oleoducto |oleoᵺōōk'to| *nm* (oil) pipeline.

oler |oler'| *vt* (*gen*) to smell; (*inquirir*) to pry into; (*fig: sospechar*) to sniff out ♦ *vi* to smell; **~ a** to smell of; **huele mal** it smells bad, it stinks.

olfatear |olfáteár'| *vt* to smell; (*fig: sospechar*) to sniff out; (*inquirir*) to pry into.

olfato |olfà'to| *nm* sense of smell.

oligarquía |olēġàrkē'à| *nf* oligarchy.

olimpíada |olēmpē'àᵺà| *nf:* **las O~s** the Olympics.

olímpico, a |olēm'pēko, à| *a* Olympian; (*deportes*) Olympic.

oliva |olē'βà| *nf* (*aceituna*) olive; **aceite de ~** olive oil.

olivar |olēβàr'| *nm* olive grove *o* plantation.

olivo |olē'βo| *nm* olive tree.

olmo |ol'mo| *nm* elm (tree).

olor |olor'| *nm* smell.

oloroso, a |oloro'so, à| *a* scented.

OLP *nf abr* (= *Organización para la Liberación de Palestina*) PLO.

olvidadizo, a |olβēᵺàᵺē'so, à| *a* (*desmemoriado*) forgetful; (*distraído*) absent-minded.

olvidar |olβēᵺàr'| *vt* to forget; (*omitir*) to omit; (*abandonar*) to leave behind; **~se** *vr* (*fig*) to forget o.s.; **se me olvidó** I forgot.

olvido |olβē'ᵺo| *nm* oblivion; (*acto*) oversight; (*descuido*) slip; **caer en el ~** to fall into oblivion.

olla |o'yà| *nf* pan; (*para hervir agua*) kettle; (*comida*) stew; **~ a presión** pressure cooker.

O.M. *abr* (*POL*) = *Orden Ministerial*.

ombligo |omblē'ġo| *nm* navel.

OMI *nf abr* (= *Organización Marítima Internacional*) IMO.

ominoso, a |omēno'so, à| *a* ominous.

omisión |omēsyon'| *nf* (*abstención*) omission; (*descuido*) neglect.

omiso, a |omē'so, à| *a:* **hacer caso ~ de** to ignore, pass over.

omitir |omētēr'| *vt* to leave *o* miss out, omit.

omnipotente |omnēpoten'te| *a* omnipotent.

omnipresente |omnēpresen'te| *a* omnipresent.

omnívoro, a |omnē'βoro, à| *a* omnivorous.

omóplato |omo'plàto| *nm* shoulder blade.

OMS *nf abr* (= *Organización Mundial de la Salud*) WHO.

ONCE |on'se| *nf abr* (= *Organización Nacional de Ciegos Españoles*) charity for the blind.

once |on'se| *num* eleven ♦ *nf* (*AM*): **~s** snack *sg*.

onda |on'dà| *nf* wave; **~ corta/larga/media** short/long/medium wave; **~s acústicas/ hertzianas** acoustic/Hertzian waves; **~ sonora** sound wave.

ondear |ondeár'| *vi* to wave; (*tener ondas*) to be wavy; (*agua*) to ripple; **~se** *vr* to swing, sway.

ondulación |ondōōlásyon'| *nf* undulation.

ondulado, a |ondōōlá'ᵺo, à| *a* wavy ♦ *nm* wave.

ondulante |ondōōlán'te| *a* undulating.

ondular |ondōōlàr'| *vt* (*el pelo*) to wave ♦ *vi*, **~se** *vr* to undulate.

oneroso, a |onero'so, à| *a* onerous.

onomástico, a |onomá'stēko, à| *a:* **fiesta onomástica** saint's day ♦ *nm* saint's day.

ONU |o'nōō| *nf abr* V **Organización de las Naciones Unidas**.

onubense |onōōβen'se| *a* of *o* from Huelva ♦ *nm/f* native *o* inhabitant of Huelva.

ONUDI |onōō'ᵺē| *nf abr* (= *Organización de las Naciones Unidas para el Desarrollo*

Industrial) UNIDO (*United Nations Indus-trial Development Organization*).

onza [on'sá] *nf* ounce.

O.P. *nfpl abr* = **obras públicas**; (*COM*) = *Oficina Principal*.

opaco, a [opá'ko, á] *a* opaque; (*fig*) dull.

ópalo [o'pálo] *nm* opal.

opción [opsyon'] *nf* (*gen*) option; (*derecho*) right, option; **no hay** ~ there is no alterna-tive.

O.P.E.P. [opep'] *nf abr* (= *Organización de Países Exportadores de Petróleo*) OPEC.

ópera [o'perá] *nf* opera; ~ **bufa** *o* **cómica** comic opera.

operación [operásyon'] *nf* (*gen*) operation; (*COM*) transaction, deal; ~ **"llave en ma-nos"** (*INFORM*) turnkey operation; ~ **a pla-zo** (*COM*) future (*US*) *o* forward (*Brit*) transaction; **operaciones accesorias** (*IN-FORM*) housekeeping; **operaciones a térmi-no** (*COM*) futures.

operador, a [operáthor', á] *nm/f* operator; (*CINE: proyección*) projectionist; (: *rodaje*) cameraman.

operante [operán'te] *a* operating.

operar [operár'] *vt* (*producir*) to produce, bring about; (*MED*) to operate on ♦ *vi* (*COM*) to operate, deal; ~**se** *vr* to occur; (*MED*) to have an operation; **se han opera-do grandes cambios** great changes have been made *o* have taken place.

operario, a [operá'ryo, á] *nm/f* operative.

opereta [opere'tá] *nf* operetta.

opinar [opinár'] *vt* (*estimar*) to think ♦ *vi* (*enjuiciar*) to give one's opinion; ~ **bien de** to think well of, have a good opinion of.

opinión [opinyon'] *nf* (*creencia*) belief; (*criterio*) opinion; **la** ~ **pública** public opinion.

opio [o'pyo] *nm* opium.

opíparo, a [opē'páro, á] *a* sumptuous.

opondré [opondre'] *etc vb* V **oponer**.

oponente [oponen'te] *nm/f* opponent.

oponer [oponer'] *vt* (*resistencia*) to put up, offer; (*negativa*) to raise; ~**se** *vr* (*objetar*) to object; (*estar frente a frente*) to be opposed; (*dos personas*) to oppose each other; ~ **A a B** to set A against B; **me opongo a pensar que ... I** refuse to believe *o* think that ....

oponga [opon'gá] *etc vb* V **oponer**.

Oporto [opor'to] *nm* Oporto.

oportunidad [oportōōnē'tháth'] *nf* (*ocasión*) opportunity; (*posibilidad*) chance.

oportunismo [oportōōnēs'mo] *nm* opportunism.

oportunista [oportōōnē'stá] *nm/f* opportun-ist; (*infección*) opportunistic.

oportuno, a [oportōō'no, á] *a* (*en su tiempo*) opportune, timely; (*respuesta*) suitable; **en el momento** ~ at the right

moment.

oposición [oposēsyon'] *nf* opposition; **opo-siciones** *nfpl* public examinations; **ganar un puesto por oposiciones** to win a post by public competitive examination; **hacer oposiciones a, presentarse a unas opo-siciones a** to take a competitive examina-tion for.

opositor, a [opositor', á] *nm/f* (*adversario*) opponent; (*concurrente*) competitor.

opresión [opresyon'] *nf* oppression.

opresivo, a [opresē'ḥo, á] *a* oppressive.

opresor, a [opresor', á] *nm/f* oppressor.

oprimir [oprēmēr'] *vt* to squeeze; (*asir*) to grasp; (*pulsar*) to press; (*fig*) to oppress.

oprobio [opro'ḥyo] *nm* (*infamia*) ignominy; (*descrédito*) shame.

optar [optár'] *vi* (*elegir*) to choose; ~ **a** *o* **por** to opt for.

optativo, a [optátē'ḥo, á] *a* optional.

óptico, a [op'tēko, á] *a* optic(al) ♦ *nm/f* opti-cian ♦ *nf* optics *sg*; (*fig*) viewpoint.

optimismo [optēmēs'mo] *nm* optimism.

optimista [optēmē'stá] *nm/f* optimist.

óptimo, a [op'tēmo, á] *a* (*el mejor*) very best.

opuesto, a [opwe'sto, á] *pp de* **oponer** ♦ *a* (*contrario*) opposite; (*antagónico*) oppos-ing.

opulencia [opōōlen'syá] *nf* opulence.

opulento, a [opōōlen'to, á] *a* opulent.

opuse [opōō'se] *etc vb* V **oponer**.

ORA [o'rá] *abr* (*Esp*: = *Ordenación de la Regulación del Aparcamiento*) *parking regulations*.

ora [o'rá] *ad*: ~ **tú** ~ **yo** now you, now me.

oración [orásyon'] *nf* (*discurso*) speech; (*REL*) prayer; (*LING*) sentence.

oráculo [orá'kōōlo] *nm* oracle.

orador, a [oráthor', á] *nm/f* orator; (*confe-renciante*) speaker.

oral [orál'] *a* oral; **por vía** ~ (*MED*) orally.

orangután [orángōōtán'] *nm* orang-utan.

orar [orár'] *vi* (*REL*) to pray.

oratoria [oráto'ryá] *nf* oratory.

orbe [or'ḥe] *nm* orb, sphere; (*fig*) world; **en todo el** ~ all over the globe.

órbita [or'ḥētá] *nf* orbit; (*ANAT: ocular*) (eye-)socket.

orden [or'ḥen] *nm* (*gen*) order; (*INFORM*) command; ~ **público** public order, law and order; (*números*) **del** ~ **de** about; **de pri-mer** ~ first-rate; **en** ~ **de prioridad** in order of priority ♦ *nf* (*gen*) order; ~ **bancaria** banker's order; ~ **de compra** (*COM*) purchase order; ~ **del día** agenda; **eso ahora está a la** ~ **del día** that is now the order of the day; **a la** ~ **de usted** at your service; **dar la** ~ **de hacer algo** to give the order to do sth.

ordenación [orḥenásyon'] *nf* (*estado*)

order; (*acto*) ordering; (*REL*) ordination.
ordenado, a [orðenáˈðo, á] a (*metódico*) methodical; (*arreglado*) orderly.
ordenador [orðenáˈðor'] nm computer; ~ **central** mainframe computer; ~ **de gestión** business computer; ~ **de sobremesa** desktop computer.
ordenanza [orðenánˈsá] nf ordinance; ~**s municipales** by-laws ♦ nm (*COM etc*) messenger; (*MIL*) orderly; (*bedel*) porter.
ordenar [orðenár'] vt (*mandar*) to order; (*poner orden*) to put in order, arrange; ~**se** vr (*REL*) to be ordained.
ordeñadora [orðenyáˈðo'rá] nf milking machine.
ordeñar [orðenyár'] vt to milk.
ordinariez [orðenáryes'] nf (*cualidad*) coarseness, vulgarity; (*una* ~) coarse remark *o* joke *etc*.
ordinario, a [orðenáˈryo, á] a (*común*) ordinary, usual; (*vulgar*) vulgar, common.
ordinograma [orðenográˈmá] nm flowchart.
orear [oreár'] vt to air; ~**se** vr (*ropa*) to air.
orégano [ore'gáno] nm oregano.
oreja [ore'há] nf ear; (*MECÁNICA*) lug, flange.
orensano, a [orensáˈno, á] a of *o* from Orense ♦ nm/f native *o* inhabitant of Orense.
orfanato [orfáná'to], **orfanatorio** [orfánáto'ryo] nm orphanage.
orfandad [orfándáˈð'] nf orphanhood.
orfebre [orfe'bre] nm gold-/silversmith.
orfebrería [orfebrerē'á] nf gold/silver work.
orfelinato [orfelēná'to] nm orphanage.
orfeón [orfeon'] nm (*MUS*) choral society.
organice [orgáně'se] *etc* vb V **organizar**.
orgánico, a [orgá'něko, á] a organic.
organigrama [orgáněgrá'má] nm flow chart; (*de organización*) organization chart.
organillo [orgáně'yo] nm barrel organ.
organismo [orgáně's'mo] nm (*BIO*) organism; (*POL*) organization; **O~ Internacional de Energía Atómica** International Atomic Energy Agency.
organista [orgáně'stá] nm/f organist.
organización [orgáněsásyon'] nf organization; **O~ de las Naciones Unidas (ONU)** United Nations Organization **O~ del Tratado del Atlántico Norte (OTAN)** North Atlantic Treaty Organization (NATO).
organizador, a [orgáněsáˈðor', á] a organizing; **el comité** ~ the organizing committee ♦ nm/f organizer.
organizar [orgáněsár'] vt to organize.
órgano [or'gáno] nm organ.
orgasmo [orgás'mo] nm orgasm.
orgía [orhē'á] nf orgy.
orgullo [orgōō'yo] nm (*altanería*) pride; (*autorespeto*) self-respect.

orgulloso, a [orgōōyo'so, á] a (*gen*) proud; (*altanero*) haughty.
orientación [oryentásyon'] nf (*posición*) position; (*dirección*) direction; ~ **profesional** occupational guidance.
oriental [oryentál'] a oriental; (*región etc*) eastern ♦ nm/f oriental.
orientar [oryentár'] vt (*situar*) to orientate; (*señalar*) to point; (*dirigir*) to direct; (*guiar*) to guide; ~**se** vr to get one's bearings; (*decidirse*) to decide on a course of action.
oriente [oryen'te] nm east; **el O~** the East, the Orient; **Cercano/Medio/Lejano O~** Near/ Middle/Far East.
orificio [orēfē'syo] nm orifice.
origen [orē'hen] nm origin; (*nacimiento*) lineage, birth; **dar** ~ **a** to cause, give rise to.
original [orēhēnál'] a (*nuevo*) original; (*extraño*) odd, strange ♦ nm original; (*TIP*) manuscript; (*TEC*) master (copy).
originalidad [orēhēnáléˈðáð'] nf originality.
originar [orēhēnár'] vt to originate; ~**se** vr to originate.
originario, a [orēhēnáˈryo, á] a (*nativo*) native; (*primordial*) original; **ser** ~ **de** to originate from; **país** ~ country of origin.
orilla [orē'yá] nf (*borde*) border; (*de río*) bank; (*de bosque, tela*) edge; (*de mar*) shore; **a** ~**s de** on the banks of.
orillar [orēyár'] vt (*bordear*) to skirt, go around; (*COSTURA*) to edge; (*resolver*) to wind up; (*tocar: asunto*) to touch briefly on; (*dificultad*) to avoid.
orín [orēn'] nm rust.
orina [orē'ná] nf urine.
orinal [orēnál'] nm (chamber) pot.
orinar [orēnár'] vi to urinate; ~**se** vr to wet o.s.
orines [orē'nes] nmpl urine *sg*.
oriundo, a [oryōōn'do, á] a: ~ **de** native of.
orla [or'lá] nf edge, border; (*ESCOL*) graduation photograph.
ornamentar [ornámentár'] vt (*adornar, ataviar*) to adorn; (*revestir*) to bedeck.
ornamento [ornámen'to] nm ornament.
ornar [ornár'] vt to adorn.
ornitología [ornētolohē'á] nf ornithology, bird watching.
ornitólogo, a [ornēto'logo, á] nm/f ornithologist.
oro [o'ro] nm gold; ~ **en barras** gold ingots; **de** ~ gold, golden; **no es** ~ **todo lo que reluce** all that glitters is not gold; **hacerse de** ~ to make a fortune; V tb **oros**.
orondo, a [oron'do, á] a (*vasija*) rounded; (*individuo*) smug, self-satisfied.
oropel [oropel'] nm tinsel.
oros [o'ros] nmpl (*NAIPES*) hearts.
orquesta [orke'stá] nf orchestra; ~ **de**

cámara/sinfónica chamber/symphony orchestra; **~ de jazz** jazz band.

orquídea [orkē'ðeá] *nf* orchid.

ortiga [ortē'ġá] *nf* nettle.

ortodoxo, a [ortoðok'so, á] *a* orthodox.

ortografía [ortoġráfē'á] *nf* spelling.

ortopedia [ortope'ðyá] *nf* orthopedics *sg* (*US*), orthopaedics *sg* (*Brit*).

oruga [oroo'ġá] *nf* caterpillar.

orujo [oroo'ho] *nm type of strong grape liqueur made from grape pressings.*

orzuelo [orswe'lo] *nm* (*MED*) stye.

os [os] *pron* (*gen*) you; (*a vosotros*) (to) you; (*reflexivo*) (to) yourselves; (*mutuo*) (to) each other; **vosotros ~ laváis** you wash yourselves; **¡callar~!** (*fam*) shut up!

osa [o'sá] *nf* (she-)bear; **O~ Mayor/Menor** Ursa Major/Minor.

osadía [osàðē'á] *nf* daring; (*descaro*) impudence.

osamenta [osámen'tá] *nf* skeleton.

osar [osàr'] *vi* to dare.

oscense [osen'se] *a* of *o* from Huesca ♦ *nm/f* native *o* inhabitant of Huesca.

oscilación [osēlásyon'] *nf* (*movimiento*) oscillation; (*fluctuación*) fluctuation; (*vacilación*) hesitation; (*columpio*) swinging, movement to and fro.

oscilar [osēlàr'] *vi* to oscillate; to fluctuate; to hesitate.

ósculo [os'koolo] *nm* kiss.

oscurecer [oskooreser'] *vt* to darken ♦ *vi* to grow dark; **~se** *vr* to grow *o* get dark.

oscurezca [oskoores'ká] *etc vb V* **oscurecer**.

oscuridad [oskooreðàð'] *nf* obscurity; (*tinieblas*) darkness.

oscuro, a [osko͞o'ro, á] *a* dark; (*fig*) obscure; (*indefinido*) confused; (*cielo*) overcast, cloudy; (*futuro etc*) uncertain; **a oscuras** in the dark.

óseo, a [o'seo, á] *a* bony; (*MED etc*) bone *cpd*.

oso [o'so] *nm* bear; **~ blanco/gris/pardo** polar/grizzly/brown bear; **~ de peluche** teddy bear; **~ hormiguero** anteater; **hacer el ~** to play the fool.

Ostende [osten'de] *nm* Ostend.

ostensible [ostensē'ble] *a* obvious.

ostensiblemente [ostensēblemen'te] *ad* perceptibly, visibly.

ostentación [ostentásyon'] *nf* (*gen*) ostentation; (*acto*) display.

ostentar [ostentàr'] *vt* (*gen*) to show; (*pey*) to flaunt, show off; (*poseer*) to have, possess.

ostentoso, a [ostento'so, á] *a* ostentatious, showy.

osteópata [osteo'pátá] *nm/f* osteopath.

ostra [os'trá] *nf* oyster ♦ *excl*: **¡~s!** (*fam*) sugar!

ostracismo [ostrásēs'mo] *nm* ostracism.

OTAN [o'tàn] *nf abr V* **Organización del Tratado del Atlántico Norte**.

OTASE [otá'se] *nf abr* (= *Organización del Tratado del Sudeste Asiático*) SEATO.

otear [oteàr'] *vt* to observe; (*fig*) to look into.

otero [ote'ro] *nm* low hill, hillock.

otitis [otē'tēs] *nf* earache.

otoñal [otonyál'] *a* autumnal.

otoño [oto'nyo] *nm* fall (*US*), autumn.

otorgamiento [otorġámyen'to] *nm* conferring, granting; (*JUR*) execution.

otorgar [otorġár'] *vt* (*conceder*) to concede; (*dar*) to grant; (*poderes*) to confer; (*premio*) to award.

otorgue [otor'ġe] *etc vb V* **otorgar**.

otorrinolaringólogo, a [otorrēnolárēngo'loġo, á] *nm/f* (*MED: tb*: **otorrino**) ear, nose and throat specialist.

otro, a [o'tro, á] *a* (*sg*) another; (*pl*) other ♦ *pron* another one; **~s** others; **otra cosa** something else; **de otra manera** otherwise; **en ~ tiempo** formerly, once; **¡otra!** (*TEATRO*) encore!; **otra parte** elsewhere; **otra vez** again; **ni uno ni ~** neither one nor the other; **~ tanto** the same again; **~ dijo que ...** somebody else said that ...

otrora [otro'rá] *ad* formerly; **el ~ señor del país** the one-time ruler of the country.

OUA *nf abr* (= *Organización de la Unidad Africana*) OAU.

ovación [oβásyon'] *nf* ovation.

ovacionar [oβásyonàr'] *vt* to cheer.

oval [oβál'], **ovalado, a** [oβálá'ðo, á] *a* oval.

óvalo [o'βálo] *nm* oval.

oveja [oβe'há] *nf* sheep; **~ negra** (*fig*) black sheep (of the family).

overol [oβerol'] *nm* (*AM*) overalls *pl*.

ovetense [oβeten'se] *a* of *o* from Oviedo ♦ *nm/f* native *o* inhabitant of Oviedo.

ovillo [oβē'yo] *nm* (*de lana*) ball; (*fig*) tangle; **hacerse un ~** to curl up (into a ball).

OVNI [oβ'nē] *nm abr* (= *objeto volante no identificado*) UFO.

ovulación [oβoolásyon'] *nf* ovulation.

óvulo [o'βoolo] *nm* ovum.

oxidación [oksēðásyon'] *nf* rusting.

oxidar [oksēðár'] *vt* to rust; **~se** *vr* to go rusty; (*TEC*) to oxidize.

óxido [ok'sēðo] *nm* oxide.

oxigenado, a [oksēhená'ðo, á] *a* (*QUÍMICA*) oxygenated; (*pelo*) bleached.

oxigenar [oksēhenàr'] *vt* to oxygenate; **~se** *vr* to become oxygenated; (*fam*) to get some fresh air.

oxígeno [oksē'heno] *nm* oxygen.

oyendo [oyen'do] *etc vb V* **oír**.

oyente [oyen'te] *nm/f* listener, hearer; (*ESCOL*) auditor (*US*), unregistered *o* occasional student (*Brit*).

ozono [oso'no] *nm* ozone.

P

P, p [pe] *nf* (*letra*) P, p; **P de París** P for Peter.

P *abr* (REL: = *padre*) Fr.; = **papa.**

p. *abr* (= *página*) p.

p.a. *abr* = **por autorización.**

pabellón [påḇeyon'] *nm* bell tent; (ARQ) pavilion; (*de hospital etc*) block, section; (*bandera*) flag; ~ **de conveniencia** (COM) flag of convenience; ~ **de la oreja** outer ear.

pábilo [pá'ḇelo] *nm* wick.

pábulo [pá'ḇoolo] *nm* food; **dar** ~ **a** to feed, encourage.

PAC *nf abr* (= *Política Agrícola Común*) CAP.

pacense [påsen'se] *a* of *o* from Badajoz ♦ *nm/f* native *o* inhabitant of Badajoz.

paceño, a [påse'nyo, å] *a* of *o* from La Paz ♦ *nm/f* native *o* inhabitant of La Paz.

pacer [påser'] *vi* to graze ♦ *vt* to graze on.

paciencia [påsyen'syå] *nf* patience; **¡~!** be patient!; **¡~ y barajar!** don't give up!; **perder la** ~ to lose one's temper.

paciente [påsyen'te] *a, nm/f* patient.

pacificación [påsēfēkåsyon'] *nf* pacification.

pacificar [påsēfēkår'] *vt* to pacify; (*tranquilizar*) to calm.

pacífico, a [påsē'fēko, å] *a* peaceful; (*persona*) peace-loving; (*existencia*) pacific; **el (Océano) P~** the Pacific (Ocean).

pacifique [påsēfē'ke] *etc vb* V **pacificar.**

pacifismo [påsēfēs'mo] *nm* pacifism.

pacifista [påsēfē'stå] *nm/f* pacifist.

pacotilla [påkotē'yå] *nf* trash; **de** ~ shoddy.

pactar [påktår'] *vt* to agree to, agree on ♦ *vi* to come to an agreement.

pacto [påk'to] *nm* (*tratado*) pact; (*acuerdo*) agreement.

pachá [påtchå'] *nm*: **vivir como un** ~ to live like a king.

pachorra [påtcho'rrå] *nf* (*indolencia*) slowness; (*tranquilidad*) calmness.

pachucho, a [påtchōōtch'o, å] *a* (*fruta*) overripe; (*persona*) sickly (US), off-colour (Brit).

padecer [påḏeser'] *vt* (*sufrir*) to suffer; (*soportar*) to endure, put up with; (*ser víctima de*) to be a victim of ♦ *vi*: ~ **de** to suffer from.

padecimiento [påḏesēmyen'to] *nm* suffer-

ing.

padezca [påḏes'kå] *etc vb* V **padecer.**

padrastro [påḏrås'tro] *nm* stepfather.

padre [på'ḏre] *nm* father ♦ *a* (*fam*): **un éxito** ~ a tremendous success; **~s** *nmpl* parents; ~ **espiritual** confessor; **P~ Nuestro** Lord's Prayer; ~ **político** father-in-law; **García** ~ García senior; **¡tu** ~**!** (*fam!*) up yours! (*!*).

padrino [påḏrē'no] *nm* godfather; (*fig*) sponsor, patron; **~s** *nmpl* godparents; ~ **de boda** best man.

padrón [påḏron'] *nm* (*censo*) census, roll; (*de socios*) register.

paella [påe'yå] *nf* paella, *dish of rice with meat, shellfish etc.*

paga [på'gå] *nf* (*dinero pagado*) payment; (*sueldo*) pay, wages *pl.*

pagadero, a [någåḏe'ro, å] *a* payable; ~ **a la entrega/a plazos** payable on delivery/in instalments.

pagano, a [någå'no, å] *a, nm/f* pagan, heathen.

pagar [någår'] *vt* (*gen*) to pay; (*las compras, crimen*) to pay for; (*deuda*) to pay (off); (*fig: favor*) to repay ♦ *vi* to pay; **~se** *vr*: **~se con algo** to be content with sth; **¡me las pagarás!** I'll get you for this!

pagaré [någåre'] *nm* I.O.U.

página [på'hēnå] *nf* page.

paginación [påhēnåsyon'] *nf* (INFORM. TIP) pagination.

paginar [påhēnår'] *vt* (INFORM. TIP) to paginate.

pág(s). *abr* (= *página(s)*) p(p).

pago [på'go] *nm* (*dinero*) payment; (*fig*) return; ~ **anticipado/a cuenta/a la entrega/ en especie/inicial** advance payment/ payment on account/cash on delivery/ payment in kind/down payment; ~ **a título gracioso** ex gratia payment; **en** ~ **de** in return for.

pague [på'ge] *etc vb* V **pagar.**

país [påēs'] *nm* (*gen*) country; (*región*) land; **los P~es Bajos** the Low Countries; **el P~ Vasco** the Basque Country.

paisaje [påēså'he] *nm* countryside, landscape; (*vista*) scenery.

paisano, a [påēså'no, å] *a* of the same country ♦ *nm/f* (*compatriota*) fellow countryman/woman; **vestir de** ~ (*soldado*) to be in civilian clothes; (*guardia*) to be in plain clothes.

paja [på'hå] *nf* straw; (*fig*) trash, rubbish; (*en libro, ensayo*) padding; **riñeron por un quítame allá esas ~s** they quarrelled over a trifle.

pajarita [påhårē'tå] *nf* bow tie.

pájaro [på'håro] *nm* bird; (*fam: astuto*) clever fellow; **tener la cabeza a ~s** to be featherbrained.

pajita |páhē'tá| *nf* (drinking) straw.
pajizo, a |páhē'so, á| *a* (*de paja*) straw *cpd*; (*techo*) thatched; (*color*) straw-colored (*US*), straw-coloured (*Brit*).
pakistaní |pákēstánē'| *a, nm/f* Pakistani.
pala |pá'lá| *nf* (*de mango largo*) spade; (*de mango corto*) shovel; (*raqueta etc*) bat; (: *de tenis*) racquet; (*CULIN*) slice; ~ **matamoscas** fly swatter.
palabra |pálá'hrá| *nf* (*gen, promesa*) word; (*facultad*) (power of) speech; (*derecho de hablar*) right to speak; **faltar a su** ~ to go back on one's word; **quedarse con la** ~ **en la boca** to stop short; (*en reunión, comité etc*) **tomar la** ~ to speak, take the floor; **pedir la** ~ to ask to be allowed to speak; **tener la** ~ to have the floor; **no encuentro** ~**s para expresarme** words fail me.
palabrota |pálá̱hro'tá| *nf* swearword.
palacio |pálá'syo| *nm* palace; (*mansión*) mansion, large house; ~ **de justicia** courthouse; ~ **municipal** town/city hall.
palada |pálá'ðá| *nf* shovelful, spadeful; (*de remo*) stroke.
paladar |pálá̱ðár'| *nm* palate.
paladear |pálá̱ðeár'| *vt* to taste.
palanca |pálán'ká| *nf* lever; (*fig*) pull, influence; ~ **de cambio** (*AUTO*) gearshift (*US*), gear lever (*Brit*); ~ **de freno** (*AUTO*) brake lever; ~ **de gobierno** *o* **de control** (*INFORM*) joystick.
palangana |pálángá'ná| *nf* washbasin.
palco |pál'ko| *nm* box.
palenque |pálen'ke| *nm* (*cerca*) stockade, fence; (*área*) arena, enclosure; (*de gallos*) pit.
palentino, a |pálentē'no, á| *a* of *o* from Palencia ♦ *nm/f* native *o* inhabitant of Palencia.
paleolítico, a |pálcolē'tēko, á| *a* paleolithic.
paleontología |pálcontolohē'á| *nf* paleontology.
Palestina |pálestē'ná| *nf* Palestine.
palestino, a |pálestē'no, á| *a, nm/f* Palestinian.
paletización |pálctēsásyon'| *nf* palletization.
paleto, a |pálc'to, á| *nm/f* hick (*US*), yokel ♦ *nf* (*pala*) small shovel; (*ARTE*) palette; (*ANAT*) shoulder blade; (*AM*) Popsicle ® (*US*), ice lolly (*Brit*).
paliar |pályár'| *vt* (*mitigar*) to mitigate; (*disfrazar*) to conceal.
paliativo |pályátē'ƀo| *nm* palliative.
palidecer |pálēðeser'| *vi* to turn pale.
palidez |pálēðes'| *nf* paleness.
palidezca |pálēðes'ká| *etc vb V* **palidecer**.
pálido, a |pá'lēðo, á| *a* pale.
palillo |pálē'yo| *nm* small stick; (*para dientes*) toothpick; ~**s** (*chinos*) chopsticks; **estar hecho un** ~ to be as thin as a rake.
palique |pálē'ke| *nm:* **estar de** ~ (*fam*) to

have a chat.
paliza |pálē'sá| *nf* beating, thrashing; **dar** *o* **propinar** (*fam*) **una** ~ **a uno** to give sb a thrashing.
palma |pál'má| *nf* (*ANAT*) palm; (*árbol*) palm tree; **batir** *o* **dar** ~**s** to clap, applaud; **llevarse la** ~ to triumph, win.
palmada |pálmá'ðá| *nf* slap; ~**s** *nfpl* clapping *sg*, applause *sg*.
Palma de Mallorca *nf* Palma.
palmar |pálmár'| *vi* (*tb:* ~**la**) to die, kick the bucket.
palmear |pálmeár'| *vi* to clap.
palmero, a |pálmc'ro, á| *a* of the island of Palma ♦ *nm/f* native *o* inhabitant of the island of Palma ♦ *nm* (*AM*), *nf* palm tree.
palmo |pál'mo| *nm* (*medida*) span; (*fig*) small amount; ~ **a** ~ inch by inch.
palmotear |pálmoteár'| *vi* to clap, applaud.
palmoteo |pálmotc'o| *nm* clapping, applause.
palo |pá'lo| *nm* stick; (*poste*) post, pole; (*mango*) handle, shaft; (*golpe*) blow, hit; (*de golf*) club; (*de béisbol*) bat; (*NAUT*) mast; (*NAIPES*) suit; **vermut a** ~ **seco** straight vermouth; **de tal** ~ **tal astilla** like father like son.
paloma |pálo'má| *nf* dove, pigeon; ~ **mensajera** carrier *o* homing pigeon.
palomilla |pálomē'yá| *nf* moth; (*TEC: tuerca*) wing nut; (*soporte*) bracket.
palomitas |pálomē'tás| *nfpl* popcorn *sg*.
palpable |pálpá'ƀlc| *a* palpable; (*fig*) tangible.
palpar |pálpár'| *vt* to touch, feel.
palpitación |pálpētásyon'| *nf* palpitation.
palpitante |pálpētán'tc| *a* palpitating; (*fig*) burning.
palpitar |pálpētár'| *vi* to palpitate; (*latir*) to beat.
palta |pál'tá| *nf* (*AM*) avocado.
palúdico, a |pálōō'ƀ̱ēko, á| *a* marshy.
paludismo |pálōōðēs'mo| *nm* malaria.
palurdo, a |pálōōr'ðo, á| *a* coarse, uncouth ♦ *nm/f* hick (*US*), yokel.
pampa |pám'pá| *nf* (*AM*) pampa(s), prairie.
pamplinas |pámplē'nás| *nfpl* nonsense *sg*.
pamplonés, esa |pámploncs', csá|, **pamplonica** |pámplonē'ká| *a* of *o* from Pamplona ♦ *nm/f* native *o* inhabitant of Pamplona.
pan |pán| *nm* bread; (*una barra*) loaf; ~ **de molde** sliced loaf; ~ **integral** wholemeal bread; ~ **rallado** breadcrumbs *pl*; **eso es** ~ **comido** it's a cinch; **llamar al** ~ ~ **y al vino vino** to call a spade a spade.
pana |pá'ná| *nf* corduroy.
panadería |pánáðerē'á| *nf* baker's (shop).
panadero, a |pánáðe'ro, á| *nm/f* baker.
panal |pánál'| *nm* honeycomb.
Panamá |pánámá'| *nm* Panama.
panameño, a |pánámc'nyo, á| *a* Panama-

nian.

pancarta [pánkár'tá] *nf* placard, banner.

pancho, a [pántch'o, á] *a*: **estar tan ~ to** remain perfectly calm.

panda [pán'dá] *nm* panda ♦ *nf* gang.

pandereta [pándere'tá] *nf* tambourine.

pandilla [pándě'yá] *nf* set, group; (*de criminales*) gang; (*pey*) clique.

pando, a [pán'do, á] *a* sagging.

panel [pánel'] *nm* panel; ~ **acústico** acoustic screen.

panera [páne'rá] *nf* bread basket.

panfleto [pánfle'to] *nm* (*POL etc*) pamphlet; (*AM*) lampoon.

pánico [pá'něko] *nm* panic.

panorama [pánorá'má] *nm* panorama; (*vista*) view.

pantalón [pántálon'] *nm*, **pantalones** [pántálo'nes] *nmpl* pants *pl* (*US*), trousers *pl*; **pantalones vaqueros** jeans *pl*.

pantalla [pántá'yá] *nf* (*de cine*) screen; (*cubre-luz*) lampshade; (*INFORM*) screen, display; **servir de ~ a** to be a blind for; ~ **de cristal líquido** liquid crystal display; ~ **táctil** touch-sensitive screen; ~ **de ayuda** help screen; ~ **plana** flat screen.

pantano [pántá'no] *nm* (*ciénaga*) marsh, swamp; (*depósito: de agua*) reservoir; (*fig*) jam, fix, difficulty.

pantera [pánte'rá] *nf* panther.

pantomima [pántomě'má] *nf* pantomime.

pantorrilla [pántorrě'yá] *nf* calf (of the leg).

pantufla [pántōō'flá] *nf* slipper.

panza [pán'sá] *nf* belly, paunch.

panzón, ona [pánson', oná], **panzudo, a** [pánsōō'tho, á] *a* fat, potbellied.

pañal [pányál'] *nm* diaper (*US*), nappy (*Brit*); **estar todavía en ~es** to be still wet behind the ears.

pañería [pányerě'á] *nf* (*artículos*) drapery; (*tienda*) dry-goods store (*US*), draper's (shop) (*Brit*).

pañero, a [pánye'ro, á] *nm/f* fabric dealer (*US*), draper (*Brit*).

paño [pá'nyo] *nm* (*tela*) cloth; (*pedazo de tela*) (piece of) cloth; (*trapo*) duster, rag; ~ **de cocina** dishcloth; ~ **higiénico** sanitary napkin (*US*) *o* towel (*Brit*); ~s **menores** underclothes; ~s **calientes** (*fig*) half-measures; **no andarse con ~s calientes** to pull no punches.

pañuelo [pánywe'lo] *nm* handkerchief, hanky (*fam*); (*para la cabeza*) (head)scarf.

papa [pá'pá] *nf* (*AM*) potato ♦ *nm*: **el P~** the Pope.

papá [pápá'] *nm, pl* **papás** (*fam*) pop (*US*), dad, daddy; ~s *nmpl* parents; **hijo de ~** rich kid.

papagayo [pápágá'yo] *nm* parrot.

papanatas [pápáná'tás] *nm inv* (*fam*) sucker, simpleton.

paparrucha [pápárrōōtch'á] *nf* (*tontería*) piece of nonsense.

papaya [pápá'yá] *nf* papaya.

papel [pápel'] *nm* (*gen*) paper; (*hoja de papel*) sheet of paper; (*TEATRO*) part, role; ~**es** *nmpl* identification papers; ~ **de calco/carbón/de cartas** tracing paper/carbon paper/stationery; ~ **continuo** (*INFORM*) continuous feed paper; ~ **de envolver/de empapelar** brown paper, wrapping paper/wallpaper; ~ **de aluminio/higiénico** tinfoil/toilet paper; ~ **del** *o* **de pagos al Estado** government bonds *pl*; ~ **de lija** sandpaper; ~ **moneda** paper money; ~ **plegado (en abanico** *o* **en acordeón)** fanfold paper; ~ **secante** blotting paper; ~ **térmico** thermal paper.

papeleo [pápele'o] *nm* red tape.

papelera [pápele'rá] *nf* (*cesto*) wastepaper basket; (*escritorio*) desk.

papelería [pápelerě'á] *nf* (*tienda*) stationer's (shop) (*Brit*).

papeleta [pápele'tá] *nf* (*pedazo de papel*) slip *o* bit of paper; (*POL*) ballot paper; (*ESCOL*) report; **¡vaya ~!** this is a tough one!

paperas [pápe'rás] *nfpl* mumps *sg*.

papilla [pápě'yá] *nf* (*de bebé*) baby food; (*pey*) mush; **estar hecho ~** to be dog-tired.

paquete [páke'te] *nm* (*caja*) packet; (*bulto*) parcel; (*AM fam*) nuisance, bore; (*INFORM*) package (*of software*); (*vacaciones*) package tour; ~ **de aplicaciones** (*INFORM*) applications package; ~ **integrado** (*INFORM*) integrated package; ~ **de gestión integrado** integrated management software; ~s **postales** parcel post *sg*.

paquistaní [pákěstáně'] *a, nm/f* = **pakistaní**.

par [pár] *a* (*igual*) like, equal; (*MAT*) even ♦ *nm* equal; (*de guantes*) pair; (*de veces*) couple; (*dignidad*) peer; (*GOLF, COM*) par ♦ *nf* par; ~**es** *o* **nones** odds or evens; **abrir de** ~ **en** ~ to open wide; **a la** ~ par; **sobre/bajo la** ~ above/below par.

para [pá'rá] *prep* (*gen*) for; **no es** ~ **comer** it's not for eating; **decir** ~ **sí** to say to o.s.; **¿~ qué lo quieres?** what do you want it for?; **se casaron** ~ **separarse otra vez** they married only to separate again; ~ **entonces** by then *o* that time; **lo tendré** ~ **mañana** I'll have it for tomorrow; **ir** ~ **casa** to go home, head for home; ~ **profesor es muy estúpido** he's very stupid for a teacher; **¿quién es usted** ~ **gritar así?** who are you to shout like that?; **tengo bastante** ~ **vivir** I have enough to live on.

parabellum [páráþelōōm'] *nm* (automatic) pistol.

parabién [páráþyen'] *nm* congratulations *pl*.

parábola [párá'þolá] *nf* parable; (*MAT*) parabola.

parabrisas [pàràbrē'sàs] *nm inv* windshield (*US*), windscreen (*Brit*).

paracaídas [pàràkáē'thàs] *nm inv* parachute.

paracaidista [pàrákáēthē'stá] *nm/f* parachutist; (*MIL*) paratrooper.

parachoques [pàrátcho'kes] *nm inv* fender (*US*), bumper (*Brit*); shock absorber.

parada [pàrá'thà] *nf V* **parado**.

paradero [pàráthe'ro] *nm* stopping-place; (*situación*) whereabouts.

parado, a [pàrá'tho, à] *a* (*persona*) motionless, standing still; (*fábrica*) closed, at a standstill; (*coche*) stopped; (*de pie*) standing (up); (*sin empleo*) unemployed, idle; (*confuso*) confused ♦ *nf* (*gen*) stop; (*acto*) stopping; (*de industria*) shutdown, stoppage; (*lugar*) stopping-place; **salir bien ~** to come off well; **parada de autobús** bus stop; **parada discrecional** flag (*US*) *o* request (*Brit*) stop; **parada en seco** sudden stop; **parada de taxis** taxi stand (*US*) *o* rank (*Brit*).

paradoja [pàrátho'hà] *nf* paradox.

paradójico, a [pàráthó'hēko, à] *a* paradoxical.

parador [pàráthor'] *nm* (luxury) hotel.

parafrasear [pàráfràseàr'] *vt* to paraphrase.

paráfrasis [pàrá'fràsēs] *nf inv* paraphrase.

paraguas [pàrá'gwàs] *nm inv* umbrella.

Paraguay [pàrágwá'ē] *nm*: **el ~** Paraguay.

paraguayo, a [pàrágwá'yo, à] *a, nm/f* Paraguayan.

paraíso [pàráē'so] *nm* paradise, heaven; **~ fiscal** (*COM*) tax haven.

paraje [pàrá'he] *nm* place, spot.

paralelo, a [pàrále'lo, à] *a, nm* parallel; **en ~** (*ELEC, INFORM*) (in) parallel.

paralice [pàrálē'se] *etc vb V* **paralizar**.

parálisis [pàrá'lēsēs] *nf inv* paralysis; **~ cerebral** cerebral palsy; **~ progresiva** creeping paralysis.

paralítico, a [pàrálē'tēko, à] *a, nm/f* paralytic.

paralizar [pàrálēsár'] *vt* to paralyze (*US*) *o* paralyse (*Brit*); **~se** *vr* to become paralyzed; (*fig*) to come to a standstill.

parámetro [pàrá'metro] *nm* parameter.

paramilitar [pàràmēlētár'] *a* paramilitary.

páramo [pá'ramo] *nm* bleak plateau.

parangón [pàràngon'] *nm*: **sin ~** incomparable.

paraninfo [pàránēn'fo] *nm* (*ESCOL*) auditorium.

paranoico, a [pàráno'ēko, à] *a, nm/f* paranoid.

parapetarse [pàrápetàr'se] *vr* to shelter.

parapléjico, a [pàráple'hēko, à] *a, nm/f* paraplegic.

parar [pàrár'] *vt* to stop; (*progreso etc*) to check, halt; (*golpe*) to ward off ♦ *vi* to stop; (*hospedarse*) to stay, put up; **~se** *vr* to stop; (*AM*) to stand up; **no ~ de hacer algo** to keep on doing sth; **ha parado de llover** it has stopped raining; **van a ~ en la comisaría** they're going to end up in the police station; **no sabemos en qué va a ~ todo esto** we don't know where all this is going to end; **~se a hacer algo** to stop to do sth; **~se en** to pay attention to.

pararrayos [pàràrrá'yos] *nm inv* lightning rod (*US*) *o* conductor (*Brit*).

parásito, a [pàrá'sēto, à] *nm/f* parasite.

parasol [pàrásol'] *nm* parasol, sunshade.

parcela [pàrse'là] *nf* plot, piece of ground.

parcial [pàrsyàl'] *a* (*pago*) part-; (*eclipse*) partial; (*juez*) prejudiced, biased.

parcialidad [pàrsyálēthàth'] *nf* (*prejuicio*) prejudice, bias.

parco, a [pàr'ko, à] *a* (*frugal*) sparing; (*moderado*) moderate.

parche [pàrtch'e] *nm* patch.

pardo, a [pàr'tho, à] *a* (*color*) brown; (*cielo*) overcast; (*voz*) flat, dull.

parear [pàreàr'] *vt* (*juntar, hacer par*) to match, put together; (*calcetines*) to put into pairs; (*BIO*) to mate.

parecer [pàreser'] *nm* (*opinión*) opinion, view; (*aspecto*) looks *pl* ♦ *vi* (*tener apariencia*) to seem, look; (*asemejarse*) to look like, seem like; (*aparecer, llegar*) to appear; **~se** *vr* to look alike, resemble each other; **~se a** to look like, resemble; **al ~** apparently; **me parece que** I think (that), it seems to me that.

parecido, a [pàresē'tho, à] *a* similar ♦ *nm* similarity, likeness, resemblance; **~ a** like, similar to; **bien ~** good-looking, nice-looking.

pared [pàreth'] *nf* wall; **~ divisoria/ medianera** dividing/party wall; **subirse por las ~es** (*fam*) to go up the wall.

paredón [pàrethon'] *nm*: **llevar a uno al ~** to put sb up against a wall, shoot sb.

parejo, a [pàre'ho, à] *a* (*igual*) equal; (*liso*) smooth, even ♦ *nf* (*dos*) pair; (: *de personas*) couple; (*el otro*: *de un par*) other one (of a pair); (: *persona*) partner; (*Guardias*) Civil Guard patrol.

parentela [pàrente'là] *nf* relations *pl*.

parentesco [pàrentes'ko] *nm* relationship.

paréntesis [pàren'tesēs] *nm inv* parenthesis; (*digresión*) digression; (*en escrito*) bracket.

parezca [pàres'kà] *etc vb V* **parecer**.

parida [pàrē'thà] *nf*: **~ mental** (*fam*) dumb idea.

pariente, a [pàryen'te, à] *nm/f* relative, relation.

parihuela [pàrēwe'là] *nf* stretcher.

paripé [pàrēpe'] *nm*: **hacer el ~** to put on an act.

parir [párēr'] *vt* to give birth to ♦ *vi* (*mujer*) to give birth, have a baby; (*yegua*) to foal; (*vaca*) to calve.

París [párēs'] *nm* Paris.

parisiense [párēsyen'se], **parisiano, a** [párēsyá'no, á] *a*, *nm/f* Parisian.

parking [pár'kēn] *nm* parking lot (*US*), car park (*Brit*).

parlamentar [párlámentár'] *vi* (*negociar*) to parley.

parlamentario, a [párlámentá'ryo, á] *a* parliamentary ♦ *nm/f* member of parliament.

parlamento [párlámen'to] *nm* (*POL*) parliament; (*JUR*) speech.

parlanchín, ina [párlántchēn', ēná] *a* loosetongued, indiscreet ♦ *nm/f* chatterbox.

parlotear [párloteár'] *vi* to chatter, prattle.

parloteo [párlote'o] *nm* chatter, prattle.

parné [párne'] *nm* (*fam*: *dinero*) dough.

paro [pá'ro] *nm* (*huelga*) stoppage (of work), strike; (*desempleo*) unemployment; **subsidio de ~** unemployment benefit; **hay ~ en la industria** work in the industry is at a standstill; **~ del sistema** (*INFORM*) system shutdown.

parodia [páro'thyá] *nf* parody.

parodiar [párothyár'] *vt* to parody.

parpadear [párpátheár'] *vi* (*los ojos*) to blink; (*luz*) to flicker.

parpadeo [párpáthe'o] *nm* (*de ojos*) blinking, winking; (*de luz*) flickering.

párpado [pár'pátho] *nm* eyelid.

parque [pár'ke] *nm* (*lugar verde*) park; **~ de atracciones/de bomberos/zoológico** fairground/fire station/zoo.

parquímetro [párke'metro] *nm* parking meter.

párrafo [pá'rráfo] *nm* paragraph; **echar un ~** (*fam*) to have a chat.

parranda [párrán'dá] *nf* (*fam*) spree, binge.

parrilla [párrē'yá] *nf* (*CULIN*) grill; (*de coche*) grille; **(carne de) ~** barbecue.

parrillada [párrēyá'thá] *nf* barbecue.

párroco [pá'rroko] *nm* parish priest.

parroquia [párro'kyá] *nf* parish; (*iglesia*) parish church; (*COM*) clientele, customers *pl*.

parroquiano, a [párrokyá'no, á] *nm/f* parishioner; client, customer.

parsimonia [pársēmo'nyá] *nf* (*frugalidad*) sparingness; (*calma*) deliberateness; **con ~** calmly.

parte [pár'te] *nm* message; (*informe*) report; **~ meteorológico** weather forecast ♦ *nf* part; (*lado, cara*) side; (*de reparto*) share; (*JUR*) party; **en alguna ~ de Europa** somewhere in Europe; **en cualquier ~** anywhere; **por ahí no se va a ninguna ~** that leads nowhere; (*fig*) this is getting us nowhere; **en gran ~** to a large extent; **la**

mayor ~ de los españoles most Spaniards; **de algún tiempo a esta ~** for some time past; **de ~ de uno** on sb's behalf; **¿de ~ de quién?** (*TELEC*) who is speaking?; **por ~ de** on the part of; **yo por mi ~** I for my part; **por una ~ ... por otra ~** on the one hand, ... on the other (hand); **dar ~ a uno** to report to sb; **tomar ~** to take part.

partera [párte'rá] *nf* midwife.

parterre [párte'rre] *nm* (*de flores*) (flower) bed.

partición [pártēsyon'] *nf* division, sharingout; (*POL*) partition.

participación [pártēsēpásyon'] *nf* (*acto*) participation, taking part; (*parte*) share; (*COM*) stock; (*de lotería*) shared prize; (*aviso*) notice, notification; **~ en los beneficios** profit-sharing; **~ minoritaria** minority interest.

participante [pártēsēpán'te] *nm/f* participant.

participar [pártēsēpár'] *vt* to notify, inform ♦ *vi* to take part, participate; **~ en una empresa** (*COM*) to invest in an enterprise; **le participo que ...** I have to tell you that ....

partícipe [pártē'sēpe] *nm/f* participant; **hacer ~ a uno de algo** to inform sb of sth.

participio [pártēsē'pyo] *nm* participle; **~ de pasado/presente** past/present participle.

partícula [pártē'koolá] *nf* particle.

particular [pártēkoolár'] *a* (*especial*) particular, special; (*individual, personal*) private, personal ♦ *nm* (*punto, asunto*) particular, point; (*individuo*) individual; **tiene coche ~** he has a car of his own; **no dijo mucho sobre el ~** he didn't say much about the matter.

particularice [pártēkoolárē'se] *etc vb V* **particularizar**.

particularidad [pártēkoolárétháth'] *nf* peculiarity; **tiene la ~ de que ...** one of its special features is (that) ....

particularizar [pártēkoolárēsár'] *vt* to distinguish; (*especificar*) to specify; (*detallar*) to give details about.

partida [pártē'thá] *nf* (*salida*) departure; (*COM*) entry, item; (*juego*) game; (*grupo, bando*) band, group; **mala ~** dirty trick; **~ de nacimiento/matrimonio/defunción** birth/marriage/death certificate; **echar una ~** to have a game.

partidario, a [pártēthá'ryo, á] *a* partisan ♦ *nm/f* (*DEPORTE*) supporter; (*POL*) partisan.

partidismo [pártēthēs'mo] *nm* (*JUR*) partisanship, bias; (*POL*) party politics.

partido [pártē'tho] *nm* (*POL*) party; (*encuentro*) game, match; (*apoyo*) support; (*equipo*) team; **~ amistoso** (*DEPORTE*) friendly (game); **~ de fútbol** soccer game; **sacar ~ de** to profit from, benefit from; **to-**

mar ~ to take sides.

partir [pártēr'] vt (dividir) to split, divide; (compartir, distribuir) to share (out), distribute; (romper) to break open, split open; (rebanada) to cut (off) ♦ vi (tomar camino) to set off, set out; (comenzar) to start (off o out); ~**se** vr to crack o split o break (in two etc); **a** ~ **de** (starting) from; ~**se de risa** to split one's sides (laughing).

parto [pár'to] nm birth, delivery; (fig) product, creation; **estar de** ~ to be in labor.

parvulario [párḅōōlá'ryo] nm nursery school, kindergarten.

párvulo, a [pár'ḅōōlo, á] nm/f infant.

pasa [pá'sá] nf V **paso**.

pasada [pásá'ḋá] nf V **pasado**.

pasadizo [pásáḋē'so] nm (pasillo) passage, corridor; (callejuela) alley.

pasado, a [pásá'ḋo, á] a past; (malo: comida, fruta) bad; (muy cocido) overdone; (anticuado) out of date ♦ nm past; (LING) past (tense) ♦ nf passing, passage; (acción de pulir) rub, polish; ~ **mañana** the day after tomorrow; **el mes** ~ last month; ~**s dos días** after two days; **lo** ~, ~ let bygones be bygones; ~ **de moda** old-fashioned; ~ **por agua** (huevo) boiled; **de pasada** in passing, incidentally; **una mala pasada** a dirty trick.

pasador [pásáḋor'] nm (gen) bolt; (de pelo) pin.

pasaje [pásá'he] nm (gen) passage; (pago de viaje) fare; (los pasajeros) passengers pl; (pasillo) passageway.

pasajero, a [pásáhe'ro, á] a passing; (ave) migratory ♦ nm/f passenger; (viajero) traveler (US), traveller (Brit).

pasamanos [pásámá'nos] nm inv rail, handrail; (de escalera) banister.

pasamontañas [pásámontá'nyás] nm inv ski mask.

pasaporte [pásápor'te] nm passport.

pasar [pásár'] vt (gen) to pass; (tiempo) to spend; (durezas) to suffer, endure; (noticia) to give, pass on; (película) to show; (persona) to take, conduct; (río) to cross; (barrera) to pass through; (falta) to overlook, tolerate; (contrincante) to surpass, do better than; (coche) to pass, overtake; (contrabando) to smuggle (in/out); (enfermedad) to give, infect with ♦ vi (gen) to pass, go; (terminarse) to be over; (ocurrir) to happen; ~**se** vr (efectos) to pass, be over; (flores) to fade; (comida) to go bad; (fig) to overdo it, go too far o over the top; ~ **de** to go beyond, exceed; **¡pase!** come in!; **nos hicieron** ~ they showed us in; ~ **por** to get; ~ **por alto** to skip; ~ **por una crisis** to go through a crisis; **se hace** ~ **por médico** he passes himself off as a doctor; ~**lo bien/bomba** o **de maravilla** to have a

good/great time; ~**se al enemigo** to go over to the enemy; ~**se de la raya** to go too far; **¡no te pases!** don't try me!; **se me pasó** I forgot; **se me pasó el turno** I missed my turn; **no se le pasa nada** nothing escapes him, he misses nothing; **ya se te pasará** you'll get over it; **¿qué pasa?** what's happening?, what's going on?, what's up?; **¡cómo pasa el tiempo!** time just flies!; **pase lo que pase** come what may; **el autobús pasa por nuestra casa** the bus goes past our house.

pasarela [pásáre'lá] nf footbridge; (en barco) gangway.

pasatiempo [pásátyem'po] nm pastime, hobby; (distracción) amusement.

Pascua, pascua [pás'kwá] nf: ~ (**de Resurrección**) Easter; ~ **de Navidad** Christmas; ~**s** nfpl Christmas time; **¡felices** ~**s!** Merry Christmas; **de** ~**s a Ramos** once in a blue moon; **hacer la** ~ **a** (fam) to annoy, bug.

pase [pá'se] nm pass; (CINE) performance, showing; (COM) permit; (JUR) license (US), licence (Brit).

pasear [páseár'] vt to take for a walk; (exhibir) to parade, show off ♦ vi, ~**se** vr to walk, go for a walk; ~ **en coche** to go for a drive.

paseo [páse'o] nm (avenida) avenue; (distancia corta) short walk; ~ **marítimo** promenade; **dar un** ~ to go for a walk; **mandar a uno a** ~ to tell sb to go to blazes; **¡vete a** ~**!** get lost!

pasillo [pásē'yo] nm passage, corridor.

pasión [pásyon'] nf passion.

pasional [pásyonál'] a passionate; **crimen** ~ crime of passion.

pasivo, a [pásē'ḅo, á] a passive; (inactivo) inactive ♦ nm (COM) liabilities pl, debts pl; (de cuenta) debit side; ~ **circulante** current liabilities.

pasma [pás'má] nm (fam) cop.

pasmado, a [pásmá'ḋo, á] a (asombrado) astonished; (atontado) bewildered.

pasmar [pásmár'] vt (asombrar) to amaze, astonish; ~**se** vr to be amazed o astonished.

pasmo [pás'mo] nm amazement, astonishment; (fig) wonder, marvel.

pasmoso, a [pásmo'so, á] a amazing, astonishing.

paso, a [pá'so, á] a dried ♦ nm (gen, de baile) step; (modo de andar) walk; (huella) footprint; (rapidez) speed, pace, rate; (camino accesible) way through, passage; (cruce) crossing; (pasaje) passing, passage; (GEO) pass; (estrecho) strait; (fig) step, measure; (apuro) difficulty ♦ nf raisin; **pasa de Corinto/de Esmirna** currant/sultana; ~ **a** ~ step by step; **a ese ~** (*fig*) at that rate; **salir al ~ de** *o a* to waylay; **salir del ~** to get out of trouble; **dar un ~ en falso** to trip; (*fig*) to take a false step; **estar de ~** to be passing through; **~ atrás** step backwards; (*fig*) backward step; **~ elevado/subterráneo** overpass/underpass; **prohibido el ~** no entry; **ceda el ~** give way.

pasota |pàso'tà| *a*, *nm/f* (*fam*)≈ dropout; **ser un (tipo) ~** to be a bit of a dropout; (*ser indiferente*) not to care about anything.

pasotismo |pàsotēs'mo| *nm* underground *o* alternative culture.

pasta |pà'stà| *nf* (*gen*) paste; (*CULIN: masa*) dough; (: *de bizcochos etc*) pastry; (*fam*) money, dough; (*encuadernación*) hardback; **~s** *nfpl* (*bizcochos*) pastries, small cakes; (*fideos, espaguetis etc*) noodles, spaghetti *sg etc*; **~ de dientes** *o* **dentífrica** toothpaste; **~ de madera** wood pulp.

pastar |pàstàr'| *vt*, *vi* to graze.

pastel |pàstel'| *nm* (*dulce*) cake; (*de carne*) pie; (*ARTE*) pastel; (*fig*) plot; **~es** *nmpl* pastry *sg*, confectionery *sg*.

pastelería |pàstelerē'à| *nf* cake shop, pastry shop.

pasteurizado, a |pàsteoōrēsà'ᵭo, à| *a* pasteurized.

pastilla |pàstē'yà| *nf* (*de jabón, chocolate*) cake, bar; (*píldora*) tablet, pill.

pastizal |pàstēsàl'| *nm* pasture.

pasto |pà'sto| *nm* (*hierba*) grass; (*lugar*) pasture, field; (*fig*) food, nourishment.

pastor, a |pàstor', à| *nm/f* shepherd(ess) ♦ *nm* clergyman, pastor; (*ZOOL*) sheepdog; **~ alemán** Alsatian.

pastoso, a |pàsto'so, à| *a* (*material*) doughy, pasty; (*lengua*) furry; (*voz*) mellow.

pat. *abr* (= *patente*) pat.

pata |pà'tà| *nf* (*pierna*) leg; (*pie*) foot; (*de muebles*) leg; **~s arriba** upside down; **a cuatro ~s** on all fours; **meter la ~** to put one's foot in it; **~ de cabra** (*TEC*) crowbar; **~s de gallo** crow's feet; **tener buena/mala ~** to be lucky/unlucky.

patada |pàtà'ᵭà| *nf* stamp; (*puntapié*) kick; **a ~s** in abundance; (*trato*) roughly; **echar a uno a ~s** to kick sb out.

patalear |pàtàleàr'| *vi* to stamp one's feet.

pataleo |pàtàle'o| *nm* stamping.

patán |pàtàn'| *nm* rustic, yokel.

patata |pàtà'tà| *nf* potato; **~s fritas** *o* **a la española** chips, French fries; **~s a la inglesa** potato chips (*US*), crisps (*Brit*); **ni ~** (*fam*) nothing at all; **no entendió ni ~** he didn't understand a single word.

patear |pàteàr'| *vt* (*pisar*) to stamp on, trample (on); (*pegar con el pie*) to kick ♦

vi to stamp (with rage), stamp one's foot.

patentar |pàtentàr'| *vt* to patent.

patente |pàten'te| *a* obvious, evident; (*COM*) patent ♦ *nf* patent.

paternal |pàternàl'| *a* fatherly, paternal.

paternalista |pàternàlē'stà| *a* (*tono, actitud etc*) patronizing.

paternidad |pàternēᵭàᵭ'| *nf* fatherhood, parenthood; (*JUR*) paternity.

paterno, a |pàter'no, à| *a* paternal.

patético, a |pàte'tēko, à| *a* pathetic, moving.

patíbulo |pàtē'ᵬoolo| *nm* scaffold, gallows.

patillas |pàtē'yàs| *nfpl* sideburns.

patín |pàtēn'| *nm* skate; (*de tobogán*) runner; **~ de hielo** ice skate; **~ de ruedas** roller skate.

patinaje |pàtēnà'he| *nm* skating.

patinar |pàtēnàr'| *vi* to skate; (*resbalarse*) to skid, slip; (*fam*) to slip up, blunder.

patinazo |pàtēnà'so| *nm* (*AUTO*) skid; **dar un ~** (*fam*) to blunder.

patio |pà'tyo| *nm* (*de casa*) patio, courtyard; **~ de recreo** playground.

pato |pà'to| *nm* duck; **pagar el ~** (*fam*) to take the blame.

patológico, a |pàtolo'hēko, à| *a* pathological.

patoso, a |pàto'so, à| *a* awkward, clumsy.

patraña |pàtrà'nyà| *nf* story, fib.

patria |pà'tryà| *nf* native land, mother country; **~ chica** home town.

patrimonio |pàtrēmo'nyo| *nm* inheritance; (*fig*) heritage; (*COM*) net worth.

patriota |pàtryo'tà| *nm/f* patriot.

patriotero, a |pàtryote'ro, à| *a* chauvinistic.

patriótico, a |pàtryo'tēko, à| *a* patriotic.

patriotismo |pàtryotēs'mo| *nm* patriotism.

patrocinar |pàtrosēnàr'| *vt* to sponsor; (*apoyar*) to back, support.

patrocinio |pàtrosē'nyo| *nm* sponsorship; backing, support.

patrón, ona |pàtron', onà| *nm/f* (*jefe*) boss, chief, master/mistress; (*propietario*) landlord/lady; (*REL*) patron saint ♦ *nm* (*COSTURA*) pattern; (*TEC*) standard; **~ oro** gold standard.

patronal |pàtronàl'| *a*: **la clase ~** management; **cierre ~** lockout.

patronato |pàtronà'to| *nm* sponsorship; (*acto*) patronage; (*COM*) employers' association; (*fundación*) trust; **el ~ de turismo** the tourist board.

patrulla |pàtroō'yà| *nf* patrol.

patrullar |pàtroōyàr'| *vi* to patrol.

paulatino, a |pàoōlàtē'no, à| *a* gradual, slow.

paupérrimo, a |pàoōpe'rrēmo, à| *a* very poor, poverty-stricken.

pausa |pà'oōsà| *nf* pause; (*intervalo*) break; (*interrupción*) interruption; (*TEC: en video-*

grabadora) pause; **con** ~ slowly.

pausado, a [páǒǒsá'đo, á] *a* slow, deliberate.

pauta [pá'ǒǒtá] *nf* line, guide line.

pavimento [pábemen'to] *nm (ARQ)* flooring.

pavo [pá'bo] *nm* turkey; *(necio)* silly thing, idiot; ~ **real** peacock; **¡no seas** ~! don't be silly!

pavonearse [páboneár'se] *vr* to swagger, show off.

pavor [pábor'] *nm* dread, terror.

payasada [páyásá'đá] *nf* ridiculous thing (to do); ~**s** *nfpl* clowning *sg.*

payaso, a [páyá'so, á] *nm/f* clown.

payo, a [pá'yo, á] *a, nm/f* non-gipsy.

paz [pás] *nf* peace; *(tranquilidad)* peacefulness, tranquillity; **dejar a uno en** ~ to leave sb alone *o* in peace; **hacer las paces** to make peace; *(fig)* to make up; **¡haya** ~! stop it!

pazca [pás'ká] *etc vb* V **pacer.**

PC *nm abr (POL:* = *Partido Comunista)* CP.

P.C.E. *nm abr* = *Partido Comunista Español.*

PCL *nf abr (*= *pantalla de cristal líquido)* LCD.

PCUS [pckǒǒs'] *nm abr (*= *Partido Comunista de la Unión Soviética)* Soviet Communist Party.

P.D. *abr (*= *posdata)* P.S.

PDC *nm abr (POL)* = *Partido Demócrata Cristiano.*

pdo. *abr (*= *pasado)* ult.

peaje [peá'he] *nm* toll; **autopista de** ~ turnpike *(US)*, toll motorway *(Brit).*

peatón [peáton'] *nm* pedestrian; **paso de peatones** crosswalk *(US)*, pedestrian crossing *(Brit).*

peca [pe'ká] *nf* freckle.

pecado [peká'đo] *nm* sin.

pecador, a [pekáđor', á] *a* sinful ♦ *nm/f* sinner.

pecaminoso, a [pekámēno'so, á] *a* sinful.

pecar [pekár'] *vi (REL)* to sin; *(fig)*: ~ **de generoso** to be too generous.

peculiar [pekǒǒlyár'] *a* special, peculiar; *(característico)* typical, characteristic.

peculiaridad [pekǒǒlyárēđáđ] *nf* peculiarity; special feature, characteristic.

pecho [petch'o] *nm (ANAT)* chest; *(de mujer)* breast(s) *(pl)*, bosom; *(corazón)* heart, breast; *(valor)* courage, spirit; **dar el** ~ **a** to breast-feed; **tomar algo a** ~ to take sth to heart; **no le cabía en el** ~ he was bursting with happiness.

pechuga [petchǒǒ'gá] *nf* breast (of chicken *etc).*

pedagogo [peđágo'go] *nm* pedagogue, teacher.

pedal [peđál'] *nm* pedal; ~ **de embrague**

clutch (pedal); ~ **de freno** footbrake.

pedalear [peđáleár'] *vi* to pedal.

pedante [peđán'te] *a* pedantic ♦ *nm/f* pedant.

pedantería [peđántere'á] *nf* pedantry.

pedazo [peđá'so] *nm* piece, bit; **hacerse** ~**s** to fall to pieces; *(romperse)* to smash, shatter; **un** ~ **de pan** a scrap of bread; *(fig)* a terribly nice person.

pedernal [peđernál'] *nm* flint.

pedestre [peđes'tre] *a* pedestrian; **carrera** ~ foot race.

pediatra [peđyá'trá] *nm/f* pediatrician *(US)*, paediatrician *(Brit).*

pediatría [peđyátrē'á] *nf* pediatrics *sg (US)*, paediatrics *sg (Brit).*

pedicuro, a [peđēkǒǒ'ro, á] *nm/f* podiatrist *(US)*, chiropodist *(Brit).*

pedido [peđē'đo] *nm (COM: mandado)* order; *(petición)* request; ~**s en cartera** *(COM)* backlog.

pedir [peđēr'] *vt* to ask for, request; *(comida, COM: mandar)* to order; *(exigir: precio)* to ask; *(necesitar)* to need, demand, require ♦ *vi* to ask; ~ **prestado** to borrow; ~ **disculpas** to apologize; **me pidió que cerrara la puerta** he asked me to shut the door; **¿cuánto piden por el coche?** how much are they asking for the car?

pedo [pe'đo] *(fam) a inv:* **estar** ~ to be soused ♦ *nm* fart *(!).*

pedrea [peđre'á] *nf (granizada)* hailstorm; *(de lotería)* minor prizes.

pedrisco [peđrēs'ko] *nm (granizo)* hail; *(granizada)* hailstorm.

Pedro [pe'đro] *nm* Peter; **entrar como** ~ **por su casa** to come in as if one owned the place.

pega [pe'gá] *nf (dificultad)* snag; **de** ~ false, dud; **poner** ~**s** to raise objections.

pegadizo, a [pegáđē'so, á] *a (canción etc)* catchy.

pegajoso, a [pegáho'so, á] *a* sticky, adhesive.

pegamento [pegámen'to] *nm* gum.

pegar [pegár'] *vt (papel, sellos)* to stick (on); *(con cola)* to glue; *(cartel)* to post, stick up; *(coser)* to sew (on); *(unir: partes)* to join, fix together; *(MED)* to give, infect with; *(dar: golpe)* to give, deal ♦ *vi (adherirse)* to stick, adhere; *(ir juntos: colores)* to match, go together; *(golpear)* to hit; *(quemar: el sol)* to strike hot, burn *(fig)*; ~**se** *vr (gen)* to stick; *(dos personas)* to hit each other, fight; ~**le a algo** to be a great one for sth; ~ **un grito** to let out a yell; ~ **un salto** to jump (with fright); ~ **fuego** to catch fire; ~ **en** to touch; ~**se un tiro** to shoot o.s.; **no pega** that doesn't seem right; **ese sombrero no pega con el abrigo** that hat doesn't go with the coat.

pegatina [peɡátē'ná] *nf* (*POL etc*) sticker.

pegote [peɡo'te] *nm* (*fig*) patch, ugly mend; **tirarse ~s** (*fam*) to come on strong.

pegue [pe'ɡe] *etc vb* V **pegar.**

peinado [pečná'tʰo] *nm* (*en peluquería*) hairdo; (*estilo*) hair style.

peinar [pečnár'] *vt* to comb sb's hair; (*hacer estilo*) to style; **~se** *vr* to comb one's hair.

peine [pe'ēne] *nm* comb.

peineta [pečne'tá] *nf* ornamental comb.

p.ej. *abr* (= *por ejemplo*) e.g.

Pekín [pekēn'] *n* Peking.

pela [pe'lá] *nf* (*Esp fam*) peseta; *V tb* **pelas.**

pelado, a [pelá'tʰo, á] *a* (*cabeza*) shorn; (*fruta*) peeled; (*campo, fig*) bare; (*AM fam: sin dinero*) broke.

pelaje [pelá'he] *nm* (*ZOOL*) fur, coat; (*fig*) appearance.

pelambre [pelám'bre] *nm* long hair, mop.

pelar [pelár'] *vt* (*fruta, patatas*) to peel; (*cortar el pelo a*) to cut the hair of; (*quitar la piel: animal*) to skin; (*ave*) to pluck; (*habas etc*) to shell; **~se** *vr* (*la piel*) to peel off; **corre que se las pela** (*fam*) he runs like nobody's business.

pelas [pe'lás] *nfpl* (*Esp fam*) dough.

peldaño [peldá'nyo] *nm* step; (*de escalera portátil*) rung.

pelea [pele'á] *nf* (*lucha*) fight; (*discusión*) quarrel, row.

peleado, a [pelea'tʰo, á] *a:* **estar ~ (con uno)** to have fallen out (with sb).

pelear [pelear'] *vi* to fight; **~se** *vr* to fight; (*reñirse*) to fall out, quarrel.

pelele [pele'le] *nm* (*figura*) guy, dummy; (*fig*) puppet.

peletería [peleterē'á] *nf* furrier's, fur shop.

pelícano [pelē'káno] *nm* pelican.

pelicorto, a [pelēkor'to, á] *a* short-haired.

película [pelē'kōōlá] *nf* (*CINE*) movie; (*cobertura ligera*) film, thin covering; (*FOTO: rollo*) roll *o* reel of film; **~ de dibujos (animados)** cartoon film; **~ muda** silent film; **de ~** (*fam*) astonishing, out of this world.

peligro [pelē'ɡro] *nm* danger; (*riesgo*) risk; **"~ de muerte"** "danger"; **correr ~ de** to be in danger of; **con ~ de la vida** at the risk of one's life.

peligrosidad [pelēɡrosētʰátʰ'] *nf* danger, riskiness.

peligroso, a [pelēɡro'so, á] *a* dangerous; risky.

pelirrojo, a [pelērro'ho, á] *a* red-haired, red-headed.

pelma [pel'má] *nm/f*, **pelmazo** [pelmá'so] *nm* (*fam*) pest.

pelo [pe'lo] *nm* (*cabellos*) hair; (*de barba, bigote*) whisker; (*de animal: pellejo*) fur, coat; (*de perro etc*) hair, coat; (*de ave*) down; (*de tejido*) nap; (*TEC*) fiber (*US*),

fibre (*Brit*); **a ~** bareheaded; (*desnudo*) naked; **al ~** just right; **venir al ~** to be exactly what one needs; **por los ~s** by the skin of one's teeth; **escaparse por un ~** to have a close shave; **se me pusieron los ~s de punta** my hair stood on end; **no tener ~s en la lengua** to be outspoken, not mince words; **tomar el ~ a uno** to pull sb's leg.

pelón, ona [pelon', oná] *a* hairless, bald.

pelota [pelo'tá] *nf* ball; (*fam: cabeza*) nut (*fam*); **en ~(s)** stark naked; **~ vasca** jai alai; **devolver la ~ a uno** (*fig*) to turn the tables on sb; **hacer la ~** to brown nose.

pelotón [peloton'] *nm* (*MIL*) squad, detachment.

peluca [pelōō'ká] *nf* wig.

peluche [pelōōtch'e] *nm:* **muñeco de ~** stuffed (*US*) *o* soft (*Brit*) toy.

peludo, a [pelōō'tʰo, á] *a* hairy, shaggy.

peluquería [pelōōkerē'á] *nf* hairdresser's; (*para hombres*) barber's (shop).

peluquero, a [pelōōke'ro, á] *nm/f* hairdresser; barber.

peluquín [pelōōkēn'] *nm* toupée.

pelusa [pelōō'sá] *nf* (*BOT*) down; (*COSTURA*) fluff.

pellejo [peye'ho] *nm* (*de animal*) skin, hide; **salvar el ~** to save one's skin.

pellizcar [peyēskár'] *vt* to pinch, nip.

pellizco [peyēs'ko] *nm* (*gen*) pinch.

pellizque [peyēs'ke] *etc vb* V **pellizcar.**

PEMEX [pemeks'] *nm abr* = *Petróleos Mejicanos.*

PEN [pen] *nm abr* (*Esp*) = *Plan Energético Nacional.*

pena [pe'ná] *nf* (*congoja*) grief, sadness; (*remordimiento*) regret; (*dificultad*) trouble; (*dolor*) pain; (*JUR*) sentence; (*DEPORTE*) penalty; **merecer** *o* **valer la ~** to be worthwhile; **a duras ~s** with great difficulty; **so ~ de** on pain of; **~ capital** capital punishment; **~ de muerte** death penalty; **~ pecuniaria** fine; **¡qué ~!** what a shame *o* pity!

penal [penál'] *a* penal ♦ *nm* (*cárcel*) prison.

penalidad [penálētʰátʰ'] *nf* (*problema, dificultad*) trouble, hardship; (*JUR*) penalty, punishment.

penalty [penál'tē] *nm* (*DEPORTE*) penalty.

penar [penár'] *vt* to penalize; (*castigar*) to punish ♦ *vi* to suffer.

pender [pender'] *vi* (*colgar*) to hang; (*JUR*) to be pending.

pendiente [pendyen'te] *a* pending, unsettled ♦ *nm* earring ♦ *nf* hill, slope; **tener una asignatura ~** to have to retake a subject.

pendón [pendon'] *nm* banner, standard.

pene [pe'ne] *nm* penis.

penene [pene'ne] *nm/f* = **PNN.**

penetración [penetrásyon'] *nf* (*acto*) penetration; (*agudeza*) sharpness, insight.

penetrante [penetrán'te] a (*herida*) deep; (*persona, arma*) sharp; (*sonido*) penetrating, piercing; (*mirada*) searching; (*viento, ironía*) biting.

penetrar [penetrár'] vt to penetrate, pierce; (*entender*) to grasp ♦ vi to penetrate, go in; (*líquido*) to soak in; (*emoción*) to pierce.

penicilina [penēsēlē'ná] nf penicillin.

península [penēn'sōōlá] nf peninsula; **P~ Ibérica** Iberian Peninsula.

peninsular [penēnsōōlár'] a peninsular.

penique [penē'ke] nm penny; **~s** nmpl pence.

penitencia [penēten'syá] nf (*remordimiento*) penitence; (*castigo*) penance; **en ~** as a penance.

penitencial [penētensyál'] a penitential.

penitenciaría [penētensyárē'á] nf prison, penitentiary.

penitenciario, a [penētensyá'ryo, á] a prison cpd.

penoso, a [peno'so, á] a laborious, difficult.

pensado, a [pensá'tho, á] a: **bien/mal ~** well intentioned/cynical; **en el momento menos ~** when least expected.

pensador, a [pensáthor', á] nm/f thinker.

pensamiento [pensámyen'to] nm (*gen*) thought; (*mente*) mind; (*idea*) idea; (*BOT*) pansy; **no le pasó por el ~** it never occurred to him.

pensar [pensár'] vt to think; (*considerar*) to think over, think out; (*proponerse*) to intend, plan, propose; (*imaginarse*) to think up, invent ♦ vi to think; **~ en** to think of o about; (*anhelar*) to aim at, aspire to; **dar que ~ a uno** to give sb food for thought.

pensativo, a [pensátē'ho, á] a a thoughtful, pensive.

pensión [pensyon'] nf (*casa*) boarding house, guest house; (*dinero*) pension; (*cama y comida*) room and board; **~ de jubilación** retirement pension; **~ escalada** graduated pension; **~ completa** full board.

pensionista [pensyonē'stá] nm/f (*jubilado*) (old-age) pensioner; (*quien vive en pensión*) lodger; (*ESCOL*) boarder.

pentágono [pentá'gono] nm pentagon: **el P~** (*US*) the Pentagon.

pentagrama [pentágrá'má] nm (*MUS*) stave, staff.

penúltimo, a [penōōl'tēmo, á] a penultimate, second to last.

penumbra [penōōm'brá] nf half-light, semi-darkness.

penuria [penōō'ryá] nf shortage, want.

peña [pe'nyá] nf (*roca*) rock; (*cuesta*) cliff, crag; (*grupo*) group, circle; (*DEPORTE*) supporters' club; (*AM: club*) folk club.

peñasco [penyás'ko] nm large rock, boulder.

peñón [penyon'] nm crag; **el P~** the Rock (of Gibraltar).

peón [peon'] nm laborer (*US*), labourer (*Brit*); (*AM*) farmhand; (*TEC*) spindle, shaft; (*AJEDREZ*) pawn.

peor [peor'] a (*comparativo*) worse; (*superlativo*) worst ♦ ad worse; worst; **de mal en ~** from bad to worse; **tanto ~** so much the worse; **A es ~ que B** A is worse than B; **Z es el ~ de todos** Z is the worst of all.

pepinillo [pepēnē'yo] nm gherkin.

pepino [pepē'no] nm cucumber; **(no) me importa un ~** I don't care two hoots.

pepita [pepē'tá] nf (*BOT*) pip; (*MINERÍA*) nugget.

pepito [pepē'to] nm meat sandwich.

peque [pe'ke] etc vb V **pecar.**

pequeñez [pekenyes'] nf smallness, littleness; (*trivialidad*) trifle, triviality.

pequeño, a [peke'nyo, á] a small, little; (*cifra*) small, low; (*bajo*) short; **~ burgués** lower middle-class.

pequinés, esa [pekēnes', esá] a, nm/f Pekinese.

pera [pe'rá] a inv classy; **niño ~** spoiled upper-class brat ♦ nf pear; **eso es pedir ~s al olmo** that's asking the impossible.

peral [perál'] nm pear tree.

percance [perkán'se] nm setback, misfortune.

percatarse [perkátár'se] vr: **~ de** to notice, take note of.

percebe [perse'ke] nm (*ZOOL*) barnacle; (*fam*) idiot.

percepción [persepsyon'] nf (*vista*) perception; (*idea*) notion, idea; (*COM*) collection.

perceptible [perceptē'hle] a perceptible, noticeable; (*COM*) payable, receivable.

percibir [persēhēr'] vt to perceive, notice; (*ver*) to see; (*peligro etc*) to sense; (*COM*) to earn, receive, get.

percusión [perkōōsyon'] nf percussion.

percusor [perkōōsor'], **percutor** [perkōōtor'] nm (*TEC*) hammer; (*de arma*) firing pin.

percha [pertch'á] nf (*poste*) pole, support; (*gancho*) peg; (*de abrigos*) coat stand; (*colgador*) coat hanger; (*de ave*) perch.

perchero [pertche'ro] nm clothes rack.

perdedor, a [perthethor', á] a losing ♦ nm/f loser.

perder [perther'] vt to lose; (*tiempo, palabras*) to waste; (*oportunidad*) to lose, miss; (*tren*) to miss ♦ vi to lose; **~se** vr (*extraviarse*) to get lost; (*desaparecer*) to disappear, be lost to view; (*arruinarse*) to be ruined; **echar a ~** (*comida*) to spoil, ruin; (*oportunidad*) to waste; **tener buen ~** to be a good loser; **¡no te lo pierdas!** don't miss it!; **he perdido la costumbre** I have got out of the habit.

perdición [perthēsyon'] nf perdition; (*fig*) ruin.

pérdida |per'ðeðða] *nf* loss; (*de tiempo*) waste; (*COM*) net loss; **~s** *nfpl* (*COM*) losses; **¡no tiene ~!** you can't go wrong!; **~ contable** (*COM*) book loss.

perdido, a |per'ðeðo, ả] *a* lost; **estar ~ por** to be crazy about; **es un caso ~** he is a hopeless case.

perdiz |per'ðeθ'] *nf* partridge.

perdón |per'ðon'] *nm* (*disculpa*) pardon, forgiveness; (*clemencia*) mercy; **¡~!** sorry!, I beg your pardon!; **con ~** if I may, if you don't mind.

perdonar |per'ðonár'] *vt* to pardon, forgive; (*la vida*) to spare; (*excusar*) to exempt, excuse ♦ *vi* to pardon, forgive; **¡perdone (usted)!** sorry!, I beg your pardon!; **perdone, pero me parece que ...** excuse me, but I think ...

perdurable |perðöörå'ßle] *a* lasting; (*eterno*) everlasting.

perdurar |perðöörár'] *vi* (*resistir*) to last, endure; (*seguir existiendo*) to stand, still exist.

perecer |pereser'] *vi* to perish, die.

peregrinación |peregrẽnásyon'] *nf* (*REL*) pilgrimage.

peregrino, a |peregrẽ'no] *a* (*extraño*) strange; (*singular*) rare ♦ *nm/f* pilgrim.

perejil |perehẽl'] *nm* parsley.

perenne |peren'ne] *a* everlasting, perennial.

perentorio, a |perento'ryo, ả] *a* (*urgente*) urgent; (*terminante*) peremptory; (*fijo*) set, fixed.

pereza |pere'sá] *nf* (*flojera*) laziness; (*lentitud*) sloth, slowness.

perezca |peres'ká] *etc vb V* **perecer**.

perezoso, a |pereso'so, ả] *a* lazy; slow, sluggish.

perfección |perfeksyon'] *nf* perfection; **a la ~** to perfection.

perfeccionar |perfeksyonár'] *vt* to perfect; (*acabar*) to complete, finish.

perfecto, a |perfek'to, ả] *a* perfect ♦ *nm* (*LING*) perfect (tense).

perfidia |perfẽ'ðyá] *nf* perfidy, treachery.

pérfido, a |per'fẽðo, ả] *a* perfidious, treacherous.

perfil |perfẽl'] *nm* (*parte lateral*) profile; (*silueta*) silhouette, outline; (*TEC*) (cross) section; **~es** *nmpl* features; (*fig*) social graces; **~ del cliente** (*COM*) customer profile; **en ~** from the side, in profile.

perfilado, a |perfẽlá'ðo, ả] *a* (*bien formado*) well-shaped; (*largo: cara*) long.

perfilar |perfẽlár'] *vt* (*trazar*) to outline; (*dar carácter a*) to shape, give character to; **~se** *vr* to be silhouetted (*en* against); **el proyecto se va perfilando** the project is taking shape.

perforación |perforásyon'] *nf* perforation; (*con taladro*) drilling.

perforadora |perforáðho'rá] *nf* drill; **~ de fichas** card-punch.

perforar |perforár'] *vt* to perforate; (*agujero*) to drill, bore; (*papel*) to punch a hole in ♦ *vi* to drill, bore.

perfumado, a |perföömá'ðho, ả] *a* scented, perfumed.

perfumar |perföömár'] *vt* to scent, perfume.

perfume |perföö'me] *nm* perfume, scent.

pergamino |pergámẽ'no] *nm* parchment.

pericia |perẽ'syá] *nf* skill, expertise.

periferia |perẽfe'ryá] *nf* periphery; (*de ciudad*) outskirts *pl.*

periférico, a |perẽfe'rẽko, ả] *a* peripheral ♦ *nm* (*INFORM*) peripheral; (*AUTO*) beltway (*US*), ring road (*Brit*); **barrio ~** outlying district.

perímetro |perẽ'metro] *nm* perimeter.

periódico, a |peryo'ðẽko, ả] *a* periodic(al) ♦ *nm* (news)paper; **~ dominical** Sunday (news)paper.

periodismo |peryoðẽs'mo] *nm* journalism.

periodista |peryoðẽs'tá] *nm/f* journalist.

periodístico, a |peryoðẽs'tẽko, ả] *a* journalistic.

periodo |peryo'ðo], **período** |perẽ'oðo] *nm* period; **~ contable** (*COM*) accounting period.

peripuesto, a |perẽpwe'sto, ả] *a* dressed up; **tan ~** all dressed up.

perito, a |perẽ'to, ả] *a* (*experto*) expert; (*diestro*) skilled, skilful ♦ *nm/f* expert; skilled worker; (*técnico*) technician.

perjudicar |perhööðẽkár'] *vt* (*gen*) to damage, harm; (*fig*) to prejudice.

perjudicial |perhööðẽsyál'] *a* damaging, harmful; (*en detrimento*) detrimental.

perjudique |perhööðẽ'ke] *etc vb V* **perjudicar**.

perjuicio |perhwẽ'syo] *nm* damage, harm; **en/sin ~ de** to the detriment of/without prejudice to.

perjurar |perhöörár'] *vi* to commit perjury.

perla |per'lá] *nf* pearl; **me viene de ~s** it suits me fine.

permanecer |permáneser'] *vi* (*quedarse*) to stay, remain; (*seguir*) to continue to be.

permanencia |permánen'syá] *nf* (*duración*) permanence; (*estancia*) stay.

permanente |permánen'te] *a* (*que queda*) permanent; (*constante*) constant; (*comisión etc*) standing ♦ *nf* perm; **hacerse una ~** to have one's hair permed.

permanezca |permánes'ká] *etc vb V* **permanecer**.

permisible |permẽsẽ'ßle] *a* permissible, allowable.

permiso |permẽ'so] *nm* permission; (*licencia*) permit, license (*US*), licence (*Brit*); **con ~** excuse me; **estar de ~** (*MIL*) to be on leave; **~ de conducir** *o*

conductor driver's license (*US*), driving licence (*Brit*); **~ de exportación/importación** export/import license.

permitir |permētēr'| *vt* to permit, allow; **~se** *vr*: **~se algo** to allow o.s. sth; **no me puedo ~ ese lujo** I can't afford that; **¿me permite?** may I?; **si lo permite el tiempo** weather permitting.

permuta |permōō'tä| *nf* exchange.

permutar |permōōtár'| *vt* to switch, exchange; **~ destinos con uno** to swap *o* exchange jobs with sb.

pernicioso, a |pernēsyo'so, ä| *a* (*maligno*, *MED*) pernicious; (*persona*) wicked.

perno |per'no| *nm* bolt.

pernoctar |pernoktár'| *vi* to stay for the night.

pero |pe'ro| *conj* but; (*aún*) yet ♦ *nm* (*defecto*) flaw, defect; (*reparo*) objection; **¡no hay ~ que valga!** there are no buts about it.

perogrullada |perogrōōyá'thä| *nf* platitude, truism.

perol |perol'| *nm*, **perola** |pero'lä| *nf* pan.

peronista |perone'stä| *a*, *nm/f* Peronist.

perorar |perorár'| *vi* to make a speech.

perorata |perorá'tä| *nf* long-winded speech.

perpendicular |perpendēkōōlár'| *a* perpendicular; **el camino es ~ al río** the road is at right angles to the river.

perpetrar |perpetrár'| *vt* to perpetrate.

perpetuamente |perpetwámen'te| *ad* perpetually.

perpetuar |perpetwár'| *vt* to perpetuate.

perpetuo, a |perpe'two, ä| *a* perpetual; (*JUR etc*: *condena*) life *cpd*.

Perpiñán |perpēnyán'| *nm* Perpignan.

perplejo, a |perple'ho, ä| *a* perplexed, bewildered.

perra |pe'rrä| *nf* bitch; (*fam*: *dinero*) money; (: *manía*) mania, crazy idea; (: *rabieta*) tantrum; **estar sin una ~** to be flat broke.

perrera |perre'rä| *nf* kennel.

perro |pe'rro| *nm* dog; **~ caliente** hot dog; **"~ peligroso"** "beware of the dog"; **ser ~ viejo** to be an old hand; **tiempo de ~s** filthy weather; **~ que ladra no muerde** his bark is worse than his bite.

persa |per'sä| *a*, *nm/f* Persian ♦ *nm* (*LING*) Persian.

persecución |persekōōsyon'| *nf* pursuit, hunt, chase; (*REL*, *POL*) persecution.

perseguir |persegēr'| *vt* to pursue, hunt; (*cortejar*) to chase after; (*molestar*) to pester, annoy; (*REL*, *POL*) to persecute; (*JUR*) to prosecute.

perseverante |perseherán'te| *a* persevering, persistent.

perseverar |perseverár'| *vi* to persevere, persist; **~ en** to persevere in, persist with.

persiana |persyä'nä| *nf* (Venetian) blind.

persiga |persē'gä| *etc vb V* **perseguir**.

persignarse |persēgnár'se| *vr* to cross o.s.

persiguiendo |persēgyen'tho| *etc vb V* **perseguir**.

persistente |persēsten'te| *a* persistent.

persistir |persēstēr'| *vi* to persist.

persona |perso'nä| *nf* person; **10 ~s** 10 people; **tercera ~** third party; (*LING*) third person; **en ~** in person *o* the flesh; **por ~** a head; **es buena ~** he's a good sort.

personaje |personä'he| *nm* important person, celebrity; (*TEATRO*) character.

personal |personál'| *a* (*particular*) personal; (*para una persona*) single, for one person ♦ *nm* (*plantilla*) personnel, staff; (*NAUT*) crew; (*fam*: *gente*) people.

personalidad |personálēthäth'| *nf* personality; (*JUR*) status.

personarse |personár'se| *vr* to appear in person; **~ en** to present o.s. at, report to.

personificar |personēfēkár'| *vt* to personify.

personifique |personēfē'ke| *etc vb V* **personificar**.

perspectiva |perspektē'vä| *nf* perspective; (*vista*, *panorama*) view, panorama; (*posibilidad futura*) outlook, prospect; **tener algo en ~** to have sth in view.

perspicacia |perspēkä'syä| *nf* discernment, perspicacity.

perspicaz |perspēkäs'| *a* shrewd.

persuadir |perswäthēr'| *vt* (*gen*) to persuade; (*convencer*) to convince; **~se** *vr* to become convinced.

persuasión |perswäsyon'| *nf* (*acto*) persuasion; (*convicción*) conviction.

persuasivo, a |perwäsē'ho, ä| *a* persuasive, convincing.

pertenecer |pertenecer'| *vi*: **~ a** to belong to; (*fig*) to concern.

perteneciente |pertenesyen'te| *a*: **~ a** belonging to.

pertenencia |pertenen'syä| *nf* ownership; **~s** *nfpl* possessions, property *sg*.

pertenezca |pertenes'kä| *etc vb V* **pertenecer**.

pértiga |per'tēgä| *nf* pole; **salto de ~** pole vault.

pertinaz |pertēnás'| *a* (*persistente*) persistent; (*terco*) obstinate.

pertinente |pertēnen'te| *a* relevant, pertinent; (*apropiado*) appropriate; **~ a** concerning, relevant to.

pertrechar |pertretchár'| *vt* (*gen*) to supply; (*MIL*) to supply with ammunition and stores; **~se** *vr*: **~se de algo** to provide o.s. with sth.

pertrechos |pertretch'os| *nmpl* (*gen*) implements; (*MIL*) supplies and stores.

perturbación |pertōōrhäsyon'| *nf* (*POL*) disturbance; (*MED*) upset, disturbance; **~ del**

orden público breach of the peace.

perturbador, a [pertoͦorɦáᵗɦor', á] a (que perturba) perturbing, disturbing; (subversivo) subversive.

perturbar [pertoͦorɦár'] vt (el orden) to disturb; (MED) to upset, disturb; (mentalmente) to perturb.

Perú [peroͦo'] nm: **el ~** Peru.

peruano, a [perwá'no, á] a, nm/f Peruvian.

perversión [perɦersyon'] nf perversion.

perverso, a [perɦer'so, á] a perverse; (depravado) depraved.

pervertido, a [perɦertē'ᵗɦo, á] a perverted ♦ nm/f pervert.

pervertir [perɦertēr'] vt to pervert, corrupt.

pervierta [perɦyer'tá] etc, **pervirtiendo** [perɦertyen'do] etc vb V **pervertir**.

pesa [pe'sá] nf weight; (DEPORTE) shot.

pesadez [pesáᵗɦes'] nf (calidad de pesado) heaviness; (lentitud) slowness; (aburrimiento) tediousness; **es una ~ tener que ...** it's a bind having to ...

pesadilla [pesáᵗɦē'yá] nf nightmare, bad dream; (fig) worry, obsession.

pesado, a [pesá'ᵗɦo, á] a (gen) heavy; (lento) slow; (difícil, duro) tough, hard; (aburrido) tedious, boring; (bochornoso) sultry ♦ nm/f bore; **tener el estómago ~** to feel bloated; **¡no seas ~!** come off it!

pesadumbre [pesáᵗɦoͦom'bre] nf grief, sorrow.

pésame [pe'sáme] nm expression of condolence, message of sympathy; **dar el ~** to express one's condolences.

pesar [pesár'] vt to weigh; (fig) to weigh heavily on; (afligir) to grieve ♦ vi to weigh; (ser pesado) to weigh a lot, be heavy; (fig: opinión) to carry weight ♦ nm (sentimiento) regret; (pena) grief, sorrow; **a ~ de (que)** in spite of, despite; **no me pesa haberlo hecho** I'm not sorry I did it.

pesca [pes'ká] nf (acto) fishing; (cantidad de pescado) catch; **~ de altura/en bajura** deep sea/coastal fishing; **ir de ~** to go fishing.

pescadería [peskáᵗɦerē'á] nf fish market (US), fish shop (Brit).

pescadilla [peskáᵗɦē'yá] nf whiting.

pescado [peská'ᵗɦo] nm fish.

pescador, a [peskáᵗɦor', á] nm/f fisherman/woman.

pescar [peskár'] vt (coger) to catch; (tratar de coger) to fish for; (fam: lograr) to get hold of, land; (conseguir: trabajo) to manage to get; (sorprender) to catch unawares ♦ vi to fish, go fishing.

pescuezo [peskwe'so] nm neck.

pese [pe'se] prep: **~ a** despite, in spite of.

pesebre [pese'ɓre] nm manger.

peseta [pese'tá] nf peseta.

pesetero, a [pesete'ro, á] a a money-grubbing.

pesimista [pesēmē'stá] a pessimistic ♦ nm/f pessimist.

pésimo, a [pe'sēmo, á] a abominable, vile.

peso [pe'so] nm weight; (balanza) scales pl; (AM COM) monetary unit; (moneda) peso; (DEPORTE) shot; **~ bruto/neto** gross/net weight; **de poco ~** light(weight); **levantamiento de ~s** weightlifting; **vender a ~** to sell by weight; **argumento de ~** weighty argument; **eso cae de su ~** that goes without saying.

pesque [pes'ke] etc vb V **pescar**.

pesquero, a [peske'ro, á] a fishing cpd.

pesquisa [peskē'sá] nf inquiry, investigation.

pestaña [pestá'nyá] nf (ANAT) eyelash; (borde) rim.

pestañear [pestányeár'] vi to blink.

peste [pes'te] nf plague; (fig) nuisance; (mal olor) stink, stench; **~ negra** Black Death; **echar ~s** to swear, fume.

pesticida [pestēsē'ᵗɦá] nm pesticide.

pestilencia [pestēlen'syá] nf (mal olor) stink, stench.

pestillo [pestē'yo] nm bolt, latch; (cerrojo) catch; (picaporte) (door) handle.

petaca [petá'ká] nf (de cigarrillos) cigarette case; (de pipa) tobacco pouch; (AM: maleta) suitcase.

pétalo [pe'tálo] nm petal.

petardo [petár'ᵗɦo] nm firework, firecracker.

petición [petēsyon'] nf (pedido) request, plea; (memorial) petition; (JUR) plea; **a ~ de** at the request of; **~ de aumento de salarios** wage demand o claim.

petirrojo [petērro'ho] nm robin.

peto [pe'to] nm (corpiño) bodice; (TAUR) horse's padding.

pétreo, a [pe'treo, á] a stony, rocky.

petrificar [petrēfēkár'] vt to petrify.

petrifique [petrēfē'ke] etc vb V **petrificar**.

petrodólar [petroᵗɦo'lár] nm petrodollar.

petróleo [petro'leo] nm oil, petroleum.

petrolero, a [petrole'ro, á] a petroleum cpd ♦ nm (COM) oil man; (buque) (oil) tanker.

petulancia [petoͦolán'syá] nf (insolencia) vanity, opinionated nature.

peyorativo, a [peyorátē'ᵗɦo, á] a pejorative.

pez [pes] nm fish; **~ de colores** goldfish; **~ espada** swordfish; **estar como el ~ en el agua** to feel completely at home.

pezón [peson'] nm teat, nipple.

pezuña [pesoͦo'nyá] nf hoof.

piadoso, a [pyáᵗɦo'so, á] a (devoto) pious, devout; (misericordioso) kind, merciful.

Piamonte [pyámon'te] nm Piedmont.

pianista [pyánē'stá] nm/f pianist.

piano [pyá'no] nm piano; **~ de cola** grand piano.

piar |pyàr| *vi* to cheep.

piara |pyà'rà| *nf* (*manada*) herd, drove.

PIB *nm abr* (*Esp COM:=Producto Interno Bruto*) GDP.

pibe, a |pē'he, à| *nm/f* (*AM*) boy/girl, kid, child.

pica |pē'kà| *nf* (*MIL*) pike; (*TAUR*) goad; **poner una ~ en Flandes** to bring off something difficult.

picadero |pēkàthe'ro| *nm* riding school.

picadillo |pēkàthe'yo| *nm* mince.

picado, a |pēkà'tho, à| *a* pricked, punctured; (*mar*) choppy; (*diente*) bad; (*tabaco*) cut; (*enfadado*) cross.

picador |pēkàthor'| *nm* (*TAUR*) picador; (*minero*) faceworker.

picadura |pēkàthōō'rà| *nf* (*pinchazo*) puncture; (*de abeja*) sting; (*de mosquito*) bite; (*tabaco picado*) cut tobacco.

picante |pēkàn'te| *a* (*comida, sabor*) hot; (*comentario*) racy, spicy.

picaporte |pēkàpor'te| *nm* (*tirador*) handle; (*pestillo*) latch.

picar |pēkàr'| *vt* (*agujerear, perforar*) to prick, puncture; (*billete*) to punch, clip; (*abeja*) to sting; (*mosquito, serpiente*) to bite; (*persona*) to nibble (at); (*incitar*) to incite, goad; (*dañar, irritar*) to annoy, bother; (*quemar: lengua*) to burn, sting ♦ *vi* (*pez*) to bite, take the bait; (*el sol*) to burn, scorch; (*abeja, MED*) to sting; (*mosquito*) to bite; **~se** *vr* (*agriarse*) to turn sour; (*mar*) to get choppy; (*ofenderse*) to take offense (*US*) o offence (*Brit*); **me pican los ojos** my eyes sting; **me pica el brazo** my arm itches.

picardía |pēkàrthe'à| *nf* villainy; (*astucia*) slyness, craftiness; (*una ~*) dirty trick; (*palabra*) rude/bad word o expression.

picaresco, a |pēkàres'ko, à| *a* (*travieso*) roguish, rascally; (*LIT*) picaresque.

pícaro, a |pē'kàro, à| *a* (*malicioso*) villainous; (*travieso*) mischievous ♦ *nm* (*astuto*) sly sort; (*sinvergüenza*) rascal, scoundrel.

picazón |pēkàson'| *nf* (*comezón*) itch; (*ardor*) sting(ing feeling); (*remordimiento*) pang of conscience.

pico |pē'ko| *nm* (*de ave*) beak; (*punto agudo*) peak, sharp point; (*TEC*) pick, pickax (*US*), pickaxe (*Brit*); (*GEO*) peak, summit; (*labia*) talkativeness; **no abrir el ~** to keep quiet; **~ parásito** (*ELEC*) spike; **y ~** and a bit; **son las 3 y ~** it's just after 3; **tiene 50 libros y ~** he has 50-odd books; **me costó un ~** it cost me quite a bit.

picor |pēkor'| *nm* itch; (*ardor*) sting(ing feeling).

picota |pēko'tà| *nf* pillory; **poner a uno en la ~** (*fig*) to ridicule sb.

picotada |pēkotà'thà| *nf*, **picotazo** |pēkotà'so| *nm* (*de pájaro*) peck; (*de in-*

secto) sting, bite.

picotear |pēkoteàr'| *vt* to peck ♦ *vi* to nibble, pick.

pictórico, a |pēkto'rēko, à| *a* pictorial; **tiene dotes pictóricas** she has a talent for painting.

picudo, a |pēkōō'tho, à| *a* pointed, with a point.

pichón, ona |pētchon', onà| *nm/f* (*paloma*) young pigeon; (*apelativo*) darling, dearest.

pidiendo |pēthyen'do| *etc vb* V **pedir**.

pie |pye| (*pl* **~s**) *nm* (*gen, MAT*) foot; (*de cama, página, escalera*) foot, bottom; (*TEATRO*) cue; (*fig: motivo*) motive, basis; (*: fundamento*) foothold; **~s planos** flat feet; **ir a ~** to go on foot, walk; **estar de ~** to be standing (up); **ponerse de ~** to stand up; **al ~ de la letra** (*citar*) literally, verbatim; (*copiar*) exactly, word for word; **de ~s a cabeza** from head to foot; **en ~ de guerra** on a war footing; **sin ~s ni cabeza** pointless, absurd; **dar ~ a** to give cause for; **no dar ~ con bola** to be no good at anything; **saber de qué ~ cojea uno** to know sb's weak spots.

piedad |pyethàth'| *nf* (*lástima*) pity, compassion; (*clemencia*) mercy; (*devoción*) piety, devotion; **tener ~ de** to take pity on.

piedra |pye'thrà| *nf* stone; (*roca*) rock; (*de mechero*) flint; (*METEOROLOGÍA*) hailstone; **primera ~** foundation stone; **~ de afilar** grindstone; **~ arenisca/caliza** sand-/limestone.

piel |pyel| *nf* (*ANAT*) skin; (*ZOOL*) skin, hide; (*de oso*) fur; (*cuero*) leather; (*BOT*) skin, peel ♦ *nm/f*: **~ roja** redskin.

pienso |pyen'so| *etc vb* V **pensar** ♦ *nm* (*AGR*) feed.

pierda |pyer'thà| *etc vb* V **perder**.

pierna |pyer'nà| *nf* leg; **en ~s** bare-legged.

pieza |pye'sà| *nf* piece; (*habitación*) room; (*MUS*) piece, composition; (*TEATRO*) work, play; **~ de recambio** o **repuesto** extra (*US*), spare (part); **~ de ropa** article of clothing; **quedarse de una ~** to be dumbfounded.

pigmeo, a |pēgme'o, à| *a, nm/f* pigmy.

pija |pē'hà| *nf* V **pijo, a**.

pijama |pēhà'mà| *nm* pijama (*US*), pyjamas *pl* (*Brit*).

pijo, a |pē'ho, à| *nm/f* (*fam*) upper-class twit.

pijotada |pēhotà'thà| *nf* nuisance.

pila |pē'là| *nf* (*ELEC*) battery; (*montón*) heap, pile; (*fuente*) sink; (*REL: tb*: **~ bautismal**) font; **nombre de ~** Christian o first name; **tengo una ~ de cosas que hacer** (*fam*) I have heaps o stacks of things to do; **~ de discos** (*INFORM*) disk pack.

pilar |pēlàr'| *nm* pillar; (*de puente*) pier;

(*fig*) prop, mainstay.

píldora [pēl'dorá] *nf* pill; **la ~ (anti-conceptiva)** the pill; **tragarse la ~** to be taken in.

pileta [pēle'tá] *nf* basin, bowl; (*AM*) swimming pool.

pilón [pēlon'] *nm* pillar, post; (*ELEC*) pylon; (*bebedero*) drinking trough; (*de fuente*) basin.

piloto [pēlo'to] *nm* pilot; (*AUTO*) rear light, tail light; (*conductor*) driver ♦ *a inv*: **planta ~** pilot plant; **luz ~** side light.

piltrafa [pēltrá'fá] *nf* (*carne*) poor quality meat; (*fig*) worthless object; (: *individuo*) wretch.

pillaje [pēyá'he] *nm* pillage, plunder.

pillar [pēyár'] *vt* (*fam: coger*) to catch; (: *agarrar*) to grasp, seize; (: *entender*) to grasp, catch on to; (*suj: coche etc*) to run over; **~ un resfriado** (*fam*) to catch a cold.

pillo, a [pē'yo, á] *a* villainous; (*astuto*) sly, crafty ♦ *nm/f* rascal, rogue, scoundrel.

pimentón [pēmenton'] *nm* (*polvo*) paprika.

pimienta [pēmyen'tá] *nf* pepper.

pimiento [pēmyen'to] *nm* pepper, pimiento.

pimpante [pēmpán'te] *a* (*encantador*) charming; (*tb:* **tan ~**) smug, self-satisfied.

PIN *nm abr* (*Esp COM:*=*Producto Interior Neto*) net domestic product.

pinacoteca [pēnákote'ká] *nf* art gallery.

pinar [pēnár'] *nm* pinewood.

pincel [pēnsel'] *nm* paintbrush.

pincelada [pēnselá'ðá] *nf* brushstroke; **última ~** (*fig*) finishing touch.

pinchar [pēntchár'] *vt* (*perforar*) to prick, pierce; (*neumático*) to puncture; (*incitar*) to prod; **~se** *vr* (*con droga*) to inject o.s.; (*neumático*) to burst, puncture; **no ~ ni cortar** (*fam*) to cut no ice; **tener un neumático pinchado** to have a puncture *o* a flat tire (*US*) *o* tyre (*Brit*).

pinchazo [pēntchá'so] *nm* (*perforación*) prick; (*de llanta*) flat (*US*), puncture (*Brit*).

pinche [pēntch'e] *nm* (*de cocina*) kitchen boy, scullion.

pinchito [pēntchē'to] *nm* shish kebab.

pincho [pēntch'o] *nm* point; (*aguijón*) spike; (*CULIN*) savory (*US*) *o* savoury (*Brit*) (snack); **~ moruno** shish kebab; **~ de tortilla** small slice of omelette.

pingüe [pēn'gwe] *a* (*grasoso*) greasy; (*cosecha*) bumper *cpd*; (*negocio*) lucrative.

pingüino [pēngwē'no] *nm* penguin.

pino [pē'no] *nm* pine (tree); **vivir en el quinto ~** to live in the middle of nowhere.

pinta [pēn'tá] *nf* spot; (*gota*) spot, drop; (*aspecto*) appearance, look(s) (*pl*); (*medida*) pint; **tener buena ~** to look good, look well; **por la ~** by the look of it.

pintadas [pēntá'ðás] *nfpl* political graffiti.

pintado, a [pēntá'ðo, á] *a* spotted; (*de muchos colores*) colorful (*US*), colourful (*Brit*); **me sienta que ni ~, viene que ni ~** it suits me to a tee.

pintar [pēntár'] *vt* to paint ♦ *vi* to paint; (*fam*) to count, be important; **~se** *vr* to put on make-up; **pintárselas solo para hacer algo** to manage to do sth by o.s.; **no pinta nada** (*fam*) he has no say.

pintor, a [pēntor', á] *nm/f* painter; **~ de brocha gorda** house painter; (*fig*) bad painter.

pintoresco, a [pēntores'ko, á] *a* picturesque.

pintura [pēntoo'rá] *nf* painting; **~ a la acuarela** watercolor; **~ al óleo** oil painting; **~ rupestre** cave painting.

pinza [pēn'sá] *nf* (*ZOOL*) claw; (*para colgar ropa*) clothespin (*US*), clothes peg (*Brit*); (*TEC*) pincers *pl*; **~s** *nfpl* (*para depilar*) tweezers.

piña [pē'nyá] *nf* (*fruto del pino*) pine cone; (*fruta*) pineapple; (*fig*) group.

piñón [pēnyon'] *nm* (*BOT*) pine nut; (*TEC*) pinion.

PIO *nm abr* (*Esp:*=*Patronato de Igualdad de Oportunidades*) ≈ Office of Economic Opportunity.

pío, a [pē'o, á] *a* (*devoto*) pious, devout; (*misericordioso*) merciful ♦ *nm*: **no decir ni ~** not to breathe a word.

piojo [pyo'ho] *nm* louse.

piojoso, a [pyoho'so, á] *a* lousy; (*sucio*) dirty.

piolet [pyole'] *pl* **~s** [-s] *nm* ice ax (*US*) *o* axe (*Brit*).

pionero, a [pyone'ro, á] *a* pioneering ♦ *nm/f* pioneer.

pipa [pē'pá] *nf* pipe; (*BOT*) seed, pip.

pipí [pēpē'] *nm* (*fam*): **hacer ~** to go wee-wee.

pipiolo [pēpyo'lo] *nm* youngster; (*novato*) novice, greenhorn.

pique [pē'ke] *etc vb V* **picar** ♦ *nm* (*resentimiento*) pique, resentment; (*rivalidad*) rivalry, competition; **irse a ~** to sink; (*familia*) to be ruined; **tener un ~ con uno** to have a grudge against sb.

piqueta [pēke'tá] *nf* pick, pickax (*US*), pickaxe (*Brit*).

piquete [pēke'te] *nm* (*agujerito*) small hole; (*MIL*) squad, party; (*de obreros*) picket; **~ secundario** secondary picket.

pirado, a [pērá'ðo, á] *a* (*fam*) round the bend.

piragua [pērá'gwá] *nf* canoe.

piragüismo [pērágwēs'mo] *nm* (*DEPORTE*) canoeing.

pirámide [pērár'mēðe] *nf* pyramid.

pirarse [pērár'se] *vr*: **~(las)** (*largarse*) to beat it (*fam*); (*ESCOL*) to cut class.

pirata [pĕrá'tá] *a*: **edición/disco** ~ pirate edition/bootleg record ♦ *nm* pirate; (*INFORM*) hacker.

pirenaico, a [pĕrená'ĕko, á] *a* Pyrenean.

Pirineo(s) [pĕrĕne'o(s)] *nm(pl)* Pyrenees *pl*.

piropo [pĕro'po] *nm* compliment, (piece of) flattery; **echar ~s a** to make flirtatious remarks to.

pirulí [pĕrōōlĕ'] *nm* carameled (*US*) *o* toffee (*Brit*) apple; lollipop.

pisada [pĕsá'thá] *nf* (*paso*) footstep; (*huella*) footprint.

pisar [pĕsár'] *vt* (*caminar sobre*) to walk on, tread on; (*apretar con el pie*) to press; (*fig*) to trample on, walk all over ♦ *vi* to tread, step, walk; ~ **el acelerador** to step on the accelerator; ~ **fuerte** (*fig*) to act determinedly.

piscina [pĕsē'ná] *nf* swimming pool.

Piscis [pĕ'sĕs] *nm* (*ASTRO*) Pisces.

piso [pĕ'so] *nm* (*suelo, de edificio*) floor; (*apartamento*) apartment; **primer** ~ second (*US*) *o* first (*Brit*) floor.

pisotear [pĕsoteár'] *vt* to trample (on *o* underfoot); (*fig: humillar*) to trample on.

pisotón [pĕsoton'] *nm* (*con el pie*) stamp.

pista [pĕ'stá] *nf* track, trail; (*indicio*) clew (*US*), clue (*Brit*); (*INFORM*) track; ~ **de auditoría** (*COM*) audit trail; ~ **de aterrizaje** runway; ~ **de baile** dance floor; ~ **de tenis** tennis court; ~ **de hielo** ice rink; **estar sobre la** ~ **de uno** to be on sb's trail.

pistola [pĕsto'lá] *nf* pistol; (*TEC*) spray-gun.

pistolero, a [pĕstole'ro, á] *nm/f* gunman, gangster ♦ *nf* holster.

pistón [pĕston'] *nm* (*TEC*) piston; (*MUS*) valve.

pitar [pĕtár'] *vt* (*hacer sonar*) to blow; (*partido*) to referee; (*rechiflar*) to whistle at, boo; (*actor, obra*) to hiss ♦ *vi* to whistle; (*AUTO*) to toot one's horn; (*AM*) to smoke; **salir pitando** to beat it.

pitido [pĕtē'tho] *nm* whistle.

pitillo [pĕtē'yo] *nm* cigarette.

pito [pĕ'to] *nm* whistle; (*de coche*) horn; (*cigarrillo*) cigarette; (*fam: de marijuana*) joint; (*fam!*) prick (!); **me importa un** ~ I don't care two hoots.

pitón [pĕton'] *nm* (*ZOOL*) python.

pitonisa [pĕtonē'sá] *nf* fortune-teller.

pitorrearse [pĕtorreár'se] *vr*: ~ **de** to scoff at, make fun of.

pitorreo [pĕtorre'o] *nm* joke, laugh; **estar de** ~ to be in a joking mood.

píxel [pĕk'sel] *nm* (*INFORM*) pixel.

pizarra [pĕsá'rrá] *nf* (*piedra*) slate; (*encerado*) blackboard.

pizca [pĕs'ká] *nf* pinch; (*fig*) speck, trace; **ni** ~ **not a bit**.

placa [plá'ká] *nf* plate; (*MED*) dental plate; (*distintivo*) badge; ~ **de matrícula** license

(*US*) *o* number (*Brit*) plate; ~ **madre** (*INFORM*) mother board.

placentero, a [plásente'ro, á] *a* pleasant, agreeable.

placer [pláser'] *nm* pleasure; **a** ~ at one's pleasure.

plácido, a [plá'sĕtho, á] *a* placid.

plaga [plá'gá] *nf* pest; (*MED*) plague; (*fig*) swarm.

plagar [plágár'] *vt* to infest, plague; (*llenar*) to fill; **plagado de** riddled with; **han plagado la ciudad de carteles** they have plastered the town with posters.

plagio [plá'hyo] *nm* plagiarism.

plague [plá'ge] *etc vb V* **plagar**.

plan [plán] *nm* (*esquema, proyecto*) plan; (*idea, intento*) idea, intention; (*de curso*) program (*US*), programme (*Brit*); ~ **cotizable de jubilación** contributory pension plan; ~ **de estudios** curriculum; ~ **de incentivos** (*COM*) incentive plan; **tener** ~ (*fam*) to have a date; **tener un** ~ (*fam*) to have an affair; **en** ~ **cachondeo** for a laugh; **en** ~ **económico** (*fam*) on the cheap; **vamos en** ~ **de turismo** we're going as tourists; **si te pones en ese** ~ ... if that's your attitude ...

plana [plá'ná] *nf V* **plano**.

plancha [plántch'á] *nf* (*para planchar*) iron; (*rótulo*) plate, sheet; (*NAUT*) gangway; (*CULIN*) grill; **pescado a la** ~ grilled fish.

planchado, a [plántchá'tho, á] *a* (*ropa*) ironed; (*traje*) pressed ♦ *nm* ironing.

planchar [plántchár'] *vt* to iron ♦ *vi* to do the ironing.

planeador [pláneáthor'] *nm* glider.

planear [pláneár'] *vt* to plan ♦ *vi* to glide.

planeta [pláne'tá] *nm* planet.

planetario, a [plánetá'ryo, á] *a* planetary ♦ *nm* planetarium.

planicie [pláne'sye] *nf* plain.

planificación [plánēfēkásyon'] *nf* planning; ~ **corporativa** (*COM*) corporate planning; ~ **familiar** family planning; **diagrama de** ~ (*COM*) planner.

plano, a [plá'no, á] *a* flat, level, even; (*liso*) smooth ♦ *nm* (*MAT, TEC, AVIAT*) plane; (*FOTO*) shot; (*ARQ*) plan; (*GEO*) map; (*de ciudad*) map, street plan ♦ *nf* sheet of paper, page; (*TEC*) trowel **primer** ~ close-up; **caer de** ~ to fall flat; **rechazar algo de** ~ to turn sth down flat; **le daba el sol de** ~ (*fig*) the sun shone directly on it; **en primera plana** on the front page; **plana mayor** staff.

planta [plán'tá] *nf* (*BOT, TEC*) plant; (*ANAT*) sole of the foot, foot; (*AM: personal*) permanent staff; ~ **baja** ground floor.

plantación [plántásyon'] *nf* (*AGR*) plantation; (*acto*) planting.

plantar [plántár'] *vt* (*BOT*) to plant;

(*puesto*) to put in; (*levantar*) to erect, set up; ~**se** *vr* to stand firm; ~ **a uno en la calle** to chuck sb out; **dejar plantado a uno** (*fam*) to stand sb up; ~**se en** to reach, get to.

plantear |plánteár'| *vt* (*problema*) to pose; (*dificultad*) to raise; **se lo plantearé** I'll put it to him.

plantel |plántel'| *nm* (*fig*) group, set.

plantilla |plántē'yá| *nf* (*de zapato*) insole; (*personal*) personnel; **ser de** ~ to be on the staff.

plantío |plántē'o| *nm* (*acto*) planting; (*lugar*) plot, bed, patch.

plantón |plánton'| *nm* (*MIL*) guard, sentry; (*fam*) long wait; **dar (un)** ~ **a uno** to stand sb up.

plañir |plányēr'| *vi* to mourn.

plasmar |plásmár'| *vt* (*dar forma*) to mold (*US*), mould (*Brit*), shape; (*representar*) to represent ♦ *vi*: ~ **en** to take the form of.

plasta |plá'stá| *nf* soft mass, lump; (*desastre*) botch, mess.

plasticidad |plástēsē'ḍáḍ'| *nf* (*fig*) expressiveness.

plasticina |plástēsē'ná|, (*AM*) **plastilina** |plástēlē'ná| *nf* modeling clay (*US*), Plasticine ® (*Brit*).

plástico, a |plá'stēko, á| *a* plastic ♦ *nf* (art of) sculpture, modeling (*US*), modelling (*Brit*) ♦ *nm* plastic.

plastificar |plástēfēkár'| *vt* (*documento*) to laminate.

plastifique |plástēfē'ke| *etc vb V* **plastificar.**

plata |plá'tá| *nf* (*metal*) silver; (*cosas hechas de plata*) silverware; (*AM*) cash, dough (*fam*); **hablar en** ~ to speak bluntly *o* frankly.

plataforma |plátáfor'má| *nf* platform; ~ **de lanzamiento/perforación** launch(ing) pad/ drilling rig.

plátano |plá'táno| *nm* (*fruta*) banana; (*árbol*) plane tree; (*bananero*) banana tree.

platea |pláte'á| *nf* (*TEATRO*) pit.

plateado, a |pláteá'ḍo, á| *a* silver; (*TEC*) silver-plated.

platense |pláten'se| (*fam*) = **ríoplatense.**

plática |plá'tēká| *nf* talk, chat; (*REL*) sermon.

platicar |plátēkár'| *vi* to talk, chat.

platillo |plátē'yo| *nm* saucer; (*de limosnas*) collection plate; ~**s** *nmpl* cymbals; ~ **volador** *o* **volante** flying saucer; **pasar el** ~ to pass the hat.

platino |plátē'no| *nm* platinum; ~**s** *nmpl* (*AUTO*) (contact) points.

platique |plátē'ke| *etc vb V* **platicar.**

plato |plá'to| *nm* plate, dish; (*parte de comida*) course; (*guiso*) dish; ~ **frutero/ sopero** fruit/soup dish; **pagar los** ~**s rotos** (*fam*) to take the rap.

playa |plá'yá| *nf* beach; (*costa*) seaside; ~ **de estacionamiento** (*AM*) car park.

playera |pláyc'rá| *nf* (*AM: camiseta*) T-shirt; ~**s** *nfpl* canvas shoes; (*TENIS*) tennis shoes.

plaza |plá'sá| *nf* square; (*mercado*) market(place); (*sitio*) room, space; (*en vehículo*) seat, place; (*colocación*) post, job; ~ **de abastos** food market; ~ **mayor** main square; ~ **de toros** bullring; **hacer la** ~ to do the daily shopping; **reservar una** ~ to reserve a seat; **el hotel tiene 100** ~**s** the hotel has 100 beds.

plazca |plás'ká| *etc vb V* **placer.**

plazo |plá'so| *nm* (*lapso de tiempo*) time, period, term; (*fecha de vencimiento*) expiration (*US*) *o* expiry (*Brit*) date; (*pago parcial*) installment (*US*), instalment (*Brit*); **a corto/largo** ~ short-/long-term; **comprar a** ~**s** to buy on time (*US*) *o* hire purchase (*Brit*), pay for in installments; **nos dan un** ~ **de 8 días** they allow us a week.

plazoleta |plásolc'tá|, **plazuela** |pláswc'lá| *nf* small square.

pleamar |pleámár'| *nf* high tide.

plebe |ple'ke| *nf*: **la** ~ the common people *pl*, the masses *pl*; (*pey*) the plebes *pl* (*US*), plebs *pl* (*Brit*).

plebeyo, a |plekc'yo, á| *a* plebeian; (*pey*) coarse, common.

plebiscito |plekēsē'to| *nm* plebiscite.

pleca |ple'ká| *nf* (*INFORM*) backslash.

plegable |plexá'hlc| *a* pliable; (*silla*) folding.

plegar |plexár'| *vt* (*doblar*) to fold, bend; (*COSTURA*) to pleat; ~**se** *vr* to yield, submit.

plegaria |plexá'ryá| *nf* (*oración*) prayer.

plegué |plexc'|, **pleguemos** |plexc'mos| *etc vb V* **plegar.**

pleitear |plēteár'| *vi* (*JUR*) to plead, conduct a lawsuit; (*litigar*) to go to court.

pleito |plē'ēto| *nm* (*JUR*) lawsuit, case; (*fig*) dispute, feud; ~**s** *nmpl* litigation *sg*; **entablar** ~ to bring an action *o* a lawsuit; **poner** ~ to sue.

plenario, a |plená'ryo, á| *a* plenary, full.

plenilunio |plenēlŏō'nyo| *nm* full moon.

plenitud |plenētŏōth'| *nf* plenitude, fullness; (*abundancia*) abundance.

pleno, a |ple'no, á| *a* full; (*completo*) complete ♦ *nm* plenum; **en** ~ as a whole; (*por unanimidad*) unanimously; **en** ~ **día** in broad daylight; **en** ~ **verano** at the height of summer; **en plena cara** right in the face.

pleuresía |pleōōresē'á| *nf* pleurisy.

plexiglás |pleksēglás'| ® *nm* acrylic glass, Plexiglas (*US*) ®.

plica |plē'ká| *nf* sealed envelope *o* document; (*en un concurso*) sealed entry.

pliego [plye'go] *etc vb* V **plegar** ♦ *nm* (*hoja*) sheet (of paper); (*carta*) sealed letter/document; ~ **de condiciones** details *pl*, specifications *pl*.

pliegue [plye'ge] *etc vb* V **plegar** ♦ *nm* fold, crease; (*de vestido*) pleat.

plisado [plēsá'ðo] *nm* pleating.

plomero [plome'ro] *nm* plumber.

plomizo, a [plomē'so, á] *a* leaden, lead-colored (*US*), lead-coloured (*Brit*).

plomo [plo'mo] *nm* (*metal*) lead; (*ELEC*) fuse; **caer a** ~ to fall heavily *o* flat.

pluma [plōō'má] *nf* (*ZOOL*) feather; ~ **estilográfica**, ~ **fuente** (*AM*) fountain pen.

plumazo [plōōmá'so] *nm* (*lit, fig*) stroke of the pen.

plumero [plōōme'ro] *nm* (*quitapolvos*) feather duster; **ya te veo el** ~ I know what you're up to.

plumón [plōōmon'] *nm* (*AM: fino*) felt-tip pen; (: *ancho*) marker.

plural [plōōrál'] *a* plural ♦ *nm*: **en** ~ in the plural.

pluralidad [plōōrálēðáth'] *nf* plurality; **una** ~ **de votos** a majority of votes.

pluriempleo [plōōrēemple'o] *nm* moonlighting.

plus [plōōs] *nm* bonus.

plusmarquista [plōōsmárkē'stá] *nm/f* (*DEPORTE*) record holder.

plusvalía [plōōsbálē'á] *nf* (*mayor valor*) appreciation, added value; (*COM*) goodwill.

plutocracia [plōōtokrá'syá] *nf* plutocracy.

PM *nf abr* (*MIL:* = *Policía Militar*) MP.

p.m. *abr* (= *post meridiem*) p.m.; (= *por minuto*) per minute.

PMA *nm abr* (= *Programa Mundial de Alimentos*) World Food Program.

pmo. *abr* (= *próximo*) prox.

PN *nf abr* (*MIL:* = *Policía Naval*) Ņaval Police.

PNB *nm abr* (*Esp COM:* = *producto nacional bruto*) GNP.

P.N.D. *nm abr* (*ESCOL:* = *personal no docente*) non-teaching staff.

PNN *nm/f abr* (= *profesor no numerario*) untenured teacher; (*Esp COM:* = *producto nacional neto*) net national product.

PNUD *nm abr* (= *Programa de las Naciones Unidas para el Desarrollo*) United Nations Development Programme.

PNV *nm abr* (*Esp POL*)=*Partido Nacional Vasco*.

P.º *abr* (= *Paseo*) Av(e).

p.o. *abr* = **por orden**.

población [poßlásyon'] *nf* population; (*pueblo, ciudad*) town, city; ~ **activa** working population.

poblado, a [poßlá'ðo, á] *a* inhabited; (*barba*) thick; (*cejas*) bushy ♦ *nm* (*aldea*) village; (*pueblo*) (small) town; ~ **de** (*lle-*

no) filled with; **densamente** ~ densely populated.

poblador, a [poßláðor', á] *nm/f* settler, colonist.

poblar [poßlár'] *vt* (*colonizar*) to colonize; (*fundar*) to found; (*habitar*) to inhabit; ~**se** *vr*: ~**se de** to fill up with; (*irse cubriendo*) to become covered with.

pobre [po'ßre] *a* poor ♦ *nm/f* poor person; (*mendigo*) beggar; **los** ~**s** the poor; ¡~! poor thing!; ~ **diablo** (*fig*) poor wretch *o* devil.

pobreza [poßre'sá] *nf* poverty.

pocilga [posēl'gá] *nf* pigsty.

pócima [po'sēmá], **poción** [posyon'] *nf* potion; (*brebaje*) concoction, nasty drink.

pocito [posē'to] *nf* (*AM*) coffee cup.

poco, a [po'ko, á] *a* little; (*escaso*) slight, scanty; ~**s** few ♦ *ad* (*no mucho*) little, not much ♦ *nm*: **un** ~ a little, a bit; **tener a uno en** ~ to think little *o* not think much of sb; **por** ~ almost, nearly; ~ **a** ~ little by little, gradually; **a** ~ **de hacer** shortly after doing; **dentro de** ~ (+ *presente o futuro*) shortly; (+ *pasado*) soon after; **hace** ~ a short time ago, not long ago; ~ **más o menos** more or less.

pocho, a [potch'o, á] *a* (*flor, color*) faded, discolored; (*persona*) pale; (*fruta*) overripe; (*deprimido*) depressed.

poda [po'ðá] *nf* (*acto*) pruning; (*temporada*) pruning season.

podar [poðár'] *vt* to prune.

podenco [poðen'ko] *nm* hound.

poder [poðer'] *vi* can; (*sujeto: persona*) to be able to, can; (*permiso*) can, may; (*posibilidad, hipótesis*) may ♦ *nm* (*gen, JUR, POL*) power; (*autoridad*) authority; ¡**puede!** who knows!, maybe!; **puede que sea así** it may be, maybe; **¿se puede?** may I come in?; **¿puedes con eso?** can you manage that?; **el dinero puede mucho** money talks; **A le puede a B** (*fam*) A is more than a match for B; **a más no** ~ to the utmost; **no** ~ **menos de hacer algo** not to be able to help doing sth; **no** ~ **más** to have had enough; ~ **adquisitivo** purchasing power; ~ **ejecutivo/legislativo** executive/legislative power; **estar en el** ~, **ocupar el** ~ to be in power; **por** ~(**es**) by proxy.

poderío [poðerē'o] *nm* power; (*autoridad*) authority.

poderoso, a [poðero'so, á] *a* powerful.

podré [poðre'] *etc vb* V **poder**.

podrido, a [poðrē'ðo, á] *a* rotten, bad; (*fig*) rotten, corrupt.

podrir [poðrēr'] = **pudrir**.

poema [poe'má] *nm* poem.

poesía [poesē'á] *nf* poetry.

poeta [poe'tá] *nm* poet.

poético, a [poe'tēko, á] *a* poetic(al).

poetisa [poetĕ'sá] *nf* (woman) poet.
póker [po'ker] *nm* poker.
polaco, a [polá'ko, á] *a* Polish ♦ *nm/f* Pole ♦ *nm* (*LING*) Polish.
polar [polár'] *a* polar.
polarice [polárē'se] *etc vb V* polarizar.
polaridad [polárĕtɦátɦ'] *nf* polarity.
polarizar [polárēsár'] *vt* to polarize.
polea [pole'á] *nf* pulley.
polémica [pole'mĕká] *nf* polemics *sg*; (*una* ~) controversy.
polemice [polemē'se] *etc vb V* polemizar.
polémico, a [pole'mĕko, á] *a* polemic(al).
polemizar [polemēsár'] *vi* to indulge in a polemic, argue.
polen [po'len] *nm* pollen.
poli [po'lē] *nm* (*fam*) cop (*fam*) ♦ *nf*: **la** ~ the cops *pl* (*fam*).
policía [polēsē'á] *nm/f* policeman/woman ♦ *nf* police.
policíaco, a [polēsē'áko, á] *a* police *cpd*; **novela policíaca** detective story.
polietileno [polēetēle'no] *nm* polyethylene (*US*), polythene (*Brit*).
polifacético, a [polēfáse'tēko, á] *a* (*persona, talento*) many-sided, versatile.
poligamia [polēɡá'myá] *nf* polygamy.
polígamo, a [polē'ɡámo, á] *a* polygamous ♦ *nm* polygamist.
polígono [polē'ɡono] *nm* (*MAT*) polygon; (*solar*) building lot; (*zona*) area; (*unidad vecina*) housing estate; ~ **industrial** industrial estate.
polilla [polē'yá] *nf* moth.
Polinesia [polēne'syá] *nf* Polynesia.
polinesio, a [polēne'syo, á] *a, nm/f* Polynesian.
polio [po'lyo] *nf* polio.
Polisario [polēsá'ryo] *nm abr* (*POL*: *tb*: **Frente** ~)=*Frente Político de Liberación del Sáhara y Río de Oro*.
politécnico [polētek'nēko] *nm* polytechnic.
político, a [polē'tēko, á] *a* political; (*discreto*) tactful; (*pariente*) in-law ♦ *nm/f* politician ♦ *nf* politics *sg*; (*económica, agraria*) policy; **padre** ~ father-in-law; **política exterior/de ingresos y precios** foreign/ prices and incomes policy.
politicastro [polētēkás'tro] *nm* (*pey*) politician, politico.
póliza [po'lēsá] *nf* certificate, voucher; (*impuesto*) tax *o* fiscal stamp; ~ **de seguro(s)** insurance policy.
polizón [polēson'] *nm* (*AVIAT, NAUT*) stowaway.
polo [po'lo] *nm* (*GEO, ELEC*) pole; (*helado*) Popsicle ® (*US*), ice lolly (*Brit*); (*DEPORTE*) polo; (*suéter*) turtle-neck; **P~ Norte/Sur** North/South Pole; **esto es el ~ opuesto de lo que dijo antes** this is the exact opposite of what he said before.

Polonia [polo'nyá] *nf* Poland.
poltrona [poltro'ná] *nf* reclining chair, easy chair.
polución [poloōsyon'] *nf* pollution; ~ **ambiental** environmental pollution.
polvera [polɦe'rá] *nf* powder compact.
polvo [pol'ɦo] *nm* dust; (*QUÍMICA, CULIN, MED*) powder; (*fam!*) screw(!); **en** ~ powdered; ~ **de talco** talcum powder; **estar hecho** ~ to be worn out *o* exhausted; **hacer algo** ~ to smash sth; **hacer** ~ **a uno** to shatter sb; *V tb* **polvos.**
pólvora [pol'ɦorá] *nf* gunpowder; (*fuegos artificiales*) fireworks *pl*; **propagarse como la** ~ (*noticia*) to spread like wildfire.
polvorosa [polɦoro'sá] *a* (*fam*): **poner pies en** ~ to beat it.
polvoriento, a [polɦoryen'to, á] *a* (*superficie*) dusty; (*sustancia*) powdery.
polvos [pol'ɦos] *nmpl* powder *sg*.
pollera [poye'rá] *nf* (*criadero*) hencoop; (*AM*) skirt, overskirt.
pollería [poyerē'á] *nf* poultry shop (*US*), poulterer's (shop) (*Brit*).
pollo [po'yo] *nm* chicken; (*joven*) young man; (*señorito*) playboy; ~ **asado** roast chicken.
pomada [pomá'tɦá] *nf* pomade.
pomelo [pome'lo] *nm* grapefruit.
pómez [po'mes] *nf*: **piedra** ~ pumice stone.
pompa [pom'pá] *nf* (*burbuja*) bubble; (*bomba*) pump; (*esplendor*) pomp, splendor (*US*), splendour (*Brit*); ~**s fúnebres** funeral *sg*.
pomposo, a [pompo'so, á] *a* splendid, magnificent; (*pey*) pompous.
pómulo [po'moōlo] *nm* cheekbone.
ponche [pontch'e] *nm* punch.
poncho [pontch'o] *nm* (*AM*) poncho, cape.
ponderar [ponderár'] *vt* (*considerar*) to weigh, consider; (*elogiar*) to praise highly, speak in praise of.
pondré [pondre'] *etc vb V* poner.
ponencia [ponen'syá] *nf* (*exposición*) (learned) paper, communication; (*informe*) report.
poner [poner'] *vt* (*gen*) to put; (*colocar*) to place, set; (*ropa*) to put on; (*problema, la mesa*) to set; (*telegrama*) to send; (*TELEC*) to connect; (*RADIO, TV*) to switch on, turn on; (*tienda*) to open, set up; (*nombre*) to give; (*añadir*) to add; (*TEATRO, CINE*) to put on; (+ *adjetivo*) to make, turn; (*suponer*) to suppose ♦ *vi* (*ave*) to lay (eggs); ~**se** *vr* to put *o* place o.s.; (*ropa*) to put on; (+ *adjetivo*) to turn, get, become; (*el sol*) to set; ~ **al tanto** to keep informed; ~ **algo en duda** to cast doubt on sth; ~ **de relieve** (*INFORM*) to highlight; **póngame con el Señor X** get me Mr X, put me through to Mr X; **¡no te**

pongas así! don't be like that!; ~**se cómodo** to make o.s. comfortable; ~**se delante** (*estorbar*) to get in the way; ~**se a bien con uno** to get on good terms with sb; ~**se rojo** to blush; ~**se a** to begin to; ~**se en** (*lugar*) to get to, arrive at.

ponga [pon'gá] *etc vb V* **poner**.

poniente [ponyen'te] *nm* west.

p.º n.º *abr* (= *peso neto*) nt. wt.

pontevedrés, esa [pontebethres', esá] *a* of *o* from Pontevedra ♦ *nm/f* native *o* inhabitant of Pontevedra.

pontificado [pontēfēká'tho] *nm* papacy, pontificate.

pontífice [pontē'fēse] *nm* pope, pontiff; **el Sumo P**~ His Holiness the Pope.

pontón [ponton'] *nm* pontoon.

ponzoña [ponso'nyá] *nf* poison, venom.

ponzoñoso, a [ponsonyo'so, á] *a* poisonous, venomous.

popa [po'pá] *nf* stern; **a** ~ astern, abaft; **de** ~ **a proa** fore and aft.

popular [popōōlár'] *a* popular; (*del pueblo*) of the people.

popularice [popōōlárē'se] *etc vb V* **popularizarse**.

popularidad [popōōláréthath'] *nf* popularity.

popularizarse [popōōlárēsár'se] *vr* to become popular.

poquísimo, a [pokē'sēmo, á] *a* (*superlativo de* **poco**) very little; (*pl*) very few; (*casi nada*) hardly any.

poquito [pokē'to] *nm:* **un** ~ a little bit ♦ *ad* a little, a bit; **a** ~**s** bit by bit.

por [por] *prep* (+ *infin: para*) so as to; (*a favor de, hacia*) for; (*a causa de*) out of, because of, from; (*según*) according to; (*por agencia de*) by; (*a cambio de*) for, in exchange for; (*en lugar de*) instead of, in place of; (*durante*) for; **10** ~ **10 son 100** 10 times 10 is 100; **será** ~ **poco tiempo** it won't be for long; ~ **correo/avión** by mail/plane; ~ **centenares** by the hundred; **(el) 10** ~ **ciento** 10 percent; ~ **orden** in order; **ir a Bilbao** ~ **Santander** to go to Bilbao via Santander; **pasar** ~ **Madrid** to pass through Madrid; **camina** ~ **la izquierda** walk on the left; ~ **todo el país** throughout the country; **entra** ~ **delante/detrás** come/go in by the front/back (door); ~ **la calle** along the street; ~ **la mañana** in the morning; ~ **la noche** at night; **$2** ~ **hora** $2 an hour; ~ **allí** over there; **está** ~ **el norte** it's somewhere in the north; ~ **mucho que quisiera, no puedo** much as I would like to, I can't; **te doy éste** ~ **aquél** I'll swap you this one for that one; **¿**~ **qué?** why?; ~ **(lo) tanto** so, therefore; ~ **cierto** (*seguro*) certainly; (*a propósito*) by the way; ~ **ejemplo** for example; ~ **favor** please; ~

fuera/dentro outside/inside; ~ **mí** ... so far as I'm concerned ...; **hazlo** ~ **mí** do it for my sake; ~ **si (acaso)** just in case; ~ **sí mismo** *o* **sólo** by o.s.

porcelana [porselá'ná] *nf* porcelain; (*china*) china.

porcentaje [porsentá'he] *nm* percentage; ~ **de actividad** (*INFORM*) hit rate.

porción [porsyon'] *nf* (*parte*) portion, share; (*cantidad*) quantity, amount.

porche [portch'e] *nm* (*de una plaza*) arcade; (*de casa*) porch.

pordiosear [porthyoseár'] *vi* to beg.

pordiosero, a [porthyose'ro, á] *nm/f* beggar.

porfía [porfē'á] *nf* persistence; (*terquedad*) obstinacy.

porfiado, a [porfyá'tho, á] *a* persistent; obstinate.

porfiar [porfyár'] *vi* to persist, insist; (*disputar*) to argue stubbornly.

pormenor [pormenor'] *nm* detail, particular.

pormenorice [pormenorē'se] *etc vb V* **pormenorizar**.

pormenorizar [pormenorēsár'] *vt* to (set out in) detail ♦ *vi* to go into detail.

pornografía [pornografē'á] *nf* pornography.

poro [po'ro] *nm* pore.

poroso, a [poro'so, á] *a* porous.

poroto [poro'to] *nm* (*AM*) bean.

porque [por'ke] *conj* (*a causa de*) because; (*ya que*) since; ~ **sí** because I feel like it.

porqué [porke'] *nm* reason, cause.

porquería [porkerē'á] *nf* (*suciedad*) filth, muck, dirt; (*acción*) dirty trick; (*objeto*) small thing, trifle; (*fig*) rubbish.

porqueriza [porkerē'sá] *nf* pigsty.

porra [po'rrá] *nf* (*arma*) stick, club; (*cachiporra*) billyclub (*US*), truncheon (*Brit*); **¡**~**s!** bother!; **¡vete a la** ~**!** go to hell!

porrazo [porrá'so] *nm* (*golpe*) blow; (*caída*) bump; **de un** ~ in one fell swoop.

porrón [porron'] *nm glass wine jar with a long spout*.

port [por'(t)] *nm* (*INFORM*) port.

portada [portá'thá] *nf* (*TIP*) title page; (: *de revista*) cover.

portador, a [portáthor', á] *nm/f* carrier, bearer; (*COM*) bearer, payee.

portaequipajes [portáckēpá'hes] *nm inv* trunk (*US*), boot (*Brit*); (*baca*) luggage rack.

portafolio [portáfo'lyo] *nm:* ~ **de inversiones** (*COM*) investment portfolio.

portal [portál'] *nm* (*entrada*) vestibule, hall; (*pórtico*) porch, doorway; (*puerta de entrada*) main door; (*DEPORTE*) goal; ~**es** *nmpl* arcade *sg*.

portaligas [portálē'gás] *nm inv* garter (*US*) *o* suspender (*Brit*) belt.

portamaletas |portámàle'tås| *nm inv* roof rack.

portamonedas |portámone'd̨ås| *nm inv* purse.

portar |portár'| *vt* to carry, bear; ~**se** *vr* to behave, conduct o.s.; ~**se mal** to misbehave; **se portó muy bien conmigo** he treated me very well.

portátil |portà'tēl| *a* portable.

portaviones |portàhyo'nes| *nm inv* aircraft carrier.

portavoz |portáhos'| *nm/f* spokesman/woman.

portazo |portà'so| *nm*: **dar un** ~ to slam the door.

porte |por'te| *nm* (*COM*) transport; (*precio*) freight charges *pl*; (*CORREOS*) postage; ~ **debido** (*COM*) freight C.O.D.; ~ **pagado** (*COM*) post-paid.

portento |porten'to| *nm* marvel, wonder.

portentoso, a |portento'so, à| *a* marvellous, extraordinary.

porteño, a |porte'nyo, à| *a* of *o* from Buenos Aires ♦ *nm/f* native *o* inhabitant of Buenos Aires.

portería |porterē'á| *nf* (*oficina*) porter's office; (*gol*) goal.

portero, a |porte'ro, à| *nm/f* porter; (*conserje*) caretaker; (*DEPORTE*) goalkeeper.

pórtico |por'tēko| *nm* (*porche*) portico, porch; (*fig*) gateway; (*arcada*) arcade.

portilla |portē'yà| *nf*, **portillo** |portē'yo| *nm* gate.

portorriqueño, a |portorrēke'nyo, à| *a*, *nm/f* Puerto Rican.

portuario, a |portwà'ryo| *a* (*del puerto*) port *cpd*; (*del muelle*) dock *cpd*; **trabajador** ~ stevedore.

Portugal |portōōgàl'| *nm* Portugal.

portugués, esa |portōōges', esà| *a*, *nm/f* Portuguese ♦ *nm* (*LING*) Portuguese.

porvenir |porḩenēr'| *nm* future.

pos |pos| **en** ~ **de**: *prep* after, in pursuit of.

posada |posá'd̨à| *nf* (*refugio*) shelter, lodging; (*mesón*) guest house; **dar** ~ **a** to give shelter to, take in.

posaderas |posàḩe'ràs| *nfpl* backside *sg*, buttocks.

posar |posàr'| *vt* (*en el suelo*) to lay down, put down; (*la mano*) to place, put gently ♦ *vi* to sit, pose; ~**se** *vr* to settle; (*pájaro*) to perch; (*avión*) to land, come down.

posdata |posd̨á'tà| *nf* postscript.

pose |po'se| *nf* (*ARTE, afectación*) pose.

poseedor, a |poseed̨or', à| *nm/f* owner, possessor; (*de récord, puesto*) holder.

poseer |poseer'| *vt* to have, possess, own; (*ventaja*) to enjoy; (*récord, puesto*) to hold.

poseído, a |poseē'd̨o, à| *a* possessed; **estar muy** ~ **de** to be very vain about.

posesión |posesyon'| *nf* possession; **tomar**

~ **(de)** to take over.

posesionarse |posesyonàr'se| *vr*: ~ **de** to take possession of, take over.

posesivo, a |posesē'ḩo, à| *a* possessive.

poseyendo |poseyen'd̨o| *etc vb V* **poseer**.

posibilidad |posēḩēlēd̨àth'| *nf* possibility; (*oportunidad*) chance.

posibilitar |posēḩēlētár'| *vt* to make possible, permit; (*hacer factible*) to make feasible.

posible |posē'ḩle| *a* possible; (*factible*) feasible ♦ *nm*: ~**s** means; (*bienes*) funds, assets; **de ser** ~ if possible; **en** *o* **dentro de lo** ~ as far as possible; **lo antes** ~ as quickly as possible.

posición |posēsyon'| *nf* (*gen*) position; (*rango social*) status.

positivo, a |posētē'ḩo, à| *a* positive ♦ *nf* (*FOTO*) print.

poso |po'so| *nm* sediment.

posponer |posponer'| *vt* to put behind *o* below; (*aplazar*) to postpone.

posponga |pospon'gà| *etc*, **pospuesto** |pospwe'sto|, **pospuse** |pospōō'se| *etc vb V* **posponer**.

posta |po'stà| *nf* (*de caballos*) relay, team; **a** ~ on purpose, deliberately.

postal |postàl'| *a* postal ♦ *nf* postcard.

poste |po'ste| *nm* (*de telégrafos*) post, pole; (*columna*) pillar.

postergar |postergàr'| *vt* (*esp AM*) to put off, postpone, delay.

postergue |poster'ge| *etc vb V* **postergar**.

posteridad |posterēd̨àth'| *nf* posterity.

posterior |posteryor'| *a* back, rear; (*siguiente*) following, subsequent; (*más tarde*) later; **ser** ~ **a** to be later than.

posterioridad |posteryorēd̨àth'| *nf*: **con** ~ later, subsequently.

postgraduado, a |postgràd̨wà'd̨o, à| *a*, *nm/f* postgraduate.

pos(t)guerra |pos(t)ge'rrà| *nf* postwar period; **en la** ~ after the war.

postigo |postē'go| *nm* (*portillo*) postern; (*contraventana*) shutter.

postín |postēn'| *nm* (*fam*) elegance; **de** ~ posh; **darse** ~ to show off.

postizo, a |postē'so, à| *a* false, artificial; (*sonrisa*) false, phoney ♦ *nm* hairpiece.

postor, a |postor', à| *nm/f* bidder; **mejor** ~ highest bidder.

postrado, a |postrà'd̨o, à| *a* prostrate.

postrar |postràr'| *vt* (*derribar*) to cast down, overthrow; (*humillar*) to humble; (*MED*) to weaken, exhaust.

postre |pos'tre| *nm* sweet, dessert ♦ *nf*: **a la** ~ in the end, when all is said and done; **para** ~ (*fam*) to top it off; **llegar a los** ~**s** (*fig*) to come too late.

postrero, a |postre'ro, à| *a* (*delante de nmsg*: **postrer**: *último*) last; (: *que viene* *detrás*) rear.

postrimerías [postrĕmerē'ás] *nfpl* final stages.

postulado [postōōlá'ᵭo] *nm* postulate.

postulante [postōōlán'te] *nm/f* petitioner; (*REL*) postulant.

póstumo, a [po'stōōmo, á] *a* posthumous.

postura [postōō'rá] *nf* (*del cuerpo*) posture, position; (*fig*) attitude, position.

post-venta [posᵬen'tá] *a* (*COM*) after-sales.

potable [potá'ᵬle] *a* drinkable.

potaje [potá'he] *nm* thick vegetable soup.

pote [po'te] *nm* pot, jar.

potencia [poten'syá] *nf* power; (*capacidad*) capacity; ~ **(en caballos)** horsepower; **en** ~ potential, in the making; **las grandes** ~**s** the great powers.

potencial [potensyál'] *a, nm* potential.

potenciar [potensyár'] *vt* (*promover*) to promote; (*fortalecer*) to boost.

potente [poten'te] *a* powerful.

potestad [potestáᵭ'] *nf* authority; **patria** ~ paternal authority.

potosí [potosē'] *nm* fortune; **cuesta un** ~ it costs the earth.

potra [po'trá] *nf* (*ZOOL*) filly; **tener** ~ to be lucky.

potro [po'tro] *nm* (*ZOOL*) colt; (*DEPORTE*) vaulting horse.

pozo [po'so] *nm* well; (*de río*) deep pool; (*de mina*) shaft; ~ **negro** cesspool; **ser un** ~ **de ciencia** (*fig*) to be deeply learned.

PP *abr* (= *por poderes*) pp; (= *porte pagado*) postage paid.

p.p.m. *abr* (= *palabras por minuto*) wpm.

práctica [prák'tēká] *nf V* **práctico.**

practicable [práktēká'ᵬle] *a* practicable; (*camino*) passable, usable.

practicante [práktēkán'te] *nm/f* (*MED*: *ayudante de doctor*) medical assistant; (: *enfermero*) nurse; (*quien practica algo*) practitioner ♦ *a* practicing (*US*), practising (*Brit*).

practicar [práktēkár'] *vt* to practice (*US*), practise (*Brit*); (*deporte*) to go in for, play; (*ejecutar*) to carry out, perform.

práctico, a [prák'tēko, á] *a* (*gen*) practical; (*conveniente*) handy; (*instruído*: *persona*) skilled, expert ♦ *nf* practice; (*método*) method; (*arte, capacidad*) skill; **en la práctica** in practice.

practique [práktē'ke] *etc vb V* **practicar.**

pradera [práᵭe'rá] *nf* meadow; (*en EE.UU.*) prairie.

prado [prá'ᵭo] *nm* (*campo*) meadow, field; (*pastizal*) pasture.

Praga [prá'gá] *nf* Prague.

pragmático, a [prágmá'tēko, á] *a* pragmatic.

preámbulo [preám'bōōlo] *nm* preamble, introduction; **decir algo sin** ~**s** to say

sth without beating about the bush.

precalentar [prekálentár'] *vt* to preheat.

precaliente [prekályen'te] *etc vb V* **precalentar.**

precario, a [preká'ryo, á] *a* precarious.

precaución [prekáōōsyon'] *nf* (*medida preventiva*) preventive measure, precaution; (*prudencia*) caution, wariness.

precaver [prekáᵬer'] *vt* to guard against; (*impedir*) to forestall; ~**se** *vr*: ~**se de** *o* **contra algo** to (be on one's) guard against sth.

precavido, a [prekáᵬē'ᵭo, á] *a* cautious, wary.

precedencia [preseᵭen'syá] *nf* precedence; (*prioridad*) priority; (*superioridad*) greater importance, superiority.

precedente [preseᵭen'te] *a* preceding; (*anterior*) former ♦ *nm* precedent; **sin** ~**(s)** unprecedented; **establecer** *o* **sentar un** ~ to establish *o* set a precedent.

preceder [preseᵭer'] *vt, vi* to precede, go/come before.

precepto [presep'to] *nm* precept.

preceptor [preseptor'] *nm* (*maestro*) teacher; (: *particular*) tutor.

preciado, a [presyá'ᵭo, á] *a* (*estimado*) esteemed, valuable.

preciar [presyár'] *vt* to esteem, value; ~**se** *vr* to boast; ~**se de** to pride o.s. on.

precinto [presēn'to] *nm* (*COM*: *tb*: ~ **de garantía**) seal.

precio [pre'syo] *nm* (*de mercado*) price; (*costo*) cost; (*valor*) value, worth; (*de viaje*) fare; ~ **de coste** *o* **de cobertura** cost price; ~ **al contado** cash price; ~ **al detalle** *o* **al por menor** retail price; ~ **al detallista** wholesale price; ~ **de entrega inmediata** spot price; ~ **de oferta** offer price; ~ **de oportunidad** bargain price; ~ **de salida** minimum price; ~ **tope** top price; ~ **unitario** unit price; **no tener** ~ (*fig*) to be priceless; **"no importa** ~**"** "cost no object".

preciosidad [presyoseᵭáᵭ'] *nf* (*valor*) (high) value, (great) worth; (*encanto*) charm; (*cosa bonita*) beautiful thing; **es una** ~ it's lovely, it's really beautiful.

precioso, a [presyo'so, á] *a* precious; (*de mucho valor*) valuable; (*fam*) lovely, beautiful.

precipicio [presēpē'syo] *nm* cliff, precipice; (*fig*) abyss.

precipitación [presēpētásyon'] *nf* (*prisa*) haste; (*lluvia*) rainfall; (*QUÍMICA*) precipitation.

precipitado, a [presēpētá'ᵭo, á] *a* hasty, rash; (*salida*) hasty, sudden ♦ *nm* (*QUÍMICA*) precipitate.

precipitar [presēpētár'] *vt* (*arrojar*) to hurl, throw; (*apresurar*) to hasten; (*acelerar*) to speed up, accelerate; (*QUÍMICA*) to precipitate; **~se** *vr* to throw o.s.; (*apresurarse*) to rush; (*actuar sin pensar*) to act rashly; **~se hacia** to rush towards.

precisado, a [presēsá'tho, á] *a*: **verse ~ a hacer algo** to be obliged to do sth.

precisamente [presēsámen'te] *ad* precisely; (*justo*) precisely, exactly, just; **~ por eso** for that very reason; **~ fue él quien lo dijo** as a matter of fact he said it; **no es eso ~** it's not really that.

precisar [presēsár'] *vt* (*necesitar*) to need, require; (*fijar*) to determine exactly, fix; (*especificar*) to specify; (*señalar*) to pinpoint.

precisión [presēsyon'] *nf* (*exactitud*) precision.

preciso, a [presē'so, á] *a* (*exacto*) precise; (*necesario*) necessary, essential; (*estilo, lenguaje*) concise; **es ~ que lo hagas** you must do it.

precocidad [prekosēthath'] *nf* precociousness, precocity.

preconcebido, a [prekonsethē'tho, á] *a* preconceived.

preconice [prekonē'se] *etc vb V* **preconizar**.

preconizar [prekonēsár'] *vt* (*aconsejar*) to advise; (*prever*) to foresee.

precoz [prekos'] *a* (*persona*) precocious; (*calvicie*) premature.

precursor, a [prekoōrsor', á] *nm/f* precursor.

predecir [predesēr'] *vt* to predict, foretell, forecast.

predestinado, a [predhestēná'tho, á] *a* predestined.

predeterminar [predhetermēnár'] *vt* to predetermine.

prédica [pre'thēká] *nf* sermon.

predicador, a [predhēkáthor', á] *nm/f* preacher.

predicar [predhēkár'] *vt, vi* to preach.

predicción [predhēksyon'] *nf* prediction; (*pronóstico*) forecast; **~ del tiempo** weather forecast(ing).

predicho [predhētch'o], **prediga** [predhē'gá] *etc,* **predije** [predhē'he] *etc vb V* **predecir**.

predilecto, a [predhēlek'to, á] *a* favorite (*US*), favourite (*Brit*).

predio [pre'thyo] *nm* property, estate.

predique [predhē'ke] *etc vb V* **predicar**.

prediré [predhēre'] *etc vb V* **predecir**.

predispondré [predhēspondre'] *etc vb V* **predisponer**.

predisponer [predhēsponer'] *vt* to predispose; (*pey*) to prejudice.

predisponga [predhēspon'gá] *etc vb V* **predisponer**.

predisposición [predhēsposēsyon'] *nf* predisposition, inclination; prejudice, bias; (*MED*) tendency.

predispuesto [predhēspwe'sto], **predispuse** [predhēspoō'se] *etc vb V* **predisponer**.

predominante [predhomēnán'te] *a* predominant; (*preponderante*) prevailing; (*interés*) controlling.

predominar [predhomēnár'] *vt* to dominate ♦ *vi* to predominate; (*prevalecer*) to prevail.

predominio [predhomē'nyo] *nm* predominance; prevalence.

preescolar [preeskolár'] *a* preschool.

preestreno [preestre'no] *nm* preview, press view.

prefabricado, a [prefábrēká'tho, á] *a* prefabricated.

prefacio [prefá'syo] *nm* preface.

preferencia [preferen'syá] *nf* preference; **de ~** preferably; **localidad de ~** reserved seat.

preferible [preferē'ble] *a* preferable.

preferir [preferēr'] *vt* to prefer.

prefiera [prefye'rá] *etc vb V* **preferir**.

prefijo [prefē'ho] *nm* prefix.

prefiriendo [prefēryen'do] *etc vb V* **preferir**.

pregón [pregon'] *nm* proclamation, announcement.

pregonar [pregonár'] *vt* to proclaim, announce; (*mercancía*) to hawk.

pregonero [pregone'ro] *nm* town crier.

pregunta [pregoōn'tá] *nf* question; **~ capciosa** catch question; **hacer una ~** to ask a question.

preguntar [pregoōntár'] *vt* to ask; (*cuestionar*) to question ♦ *vi* to ask; **~se** *vr* to wonder; **~ por uno** to ask for sb; **~ por la salud de uno** to ask after sb's health.

preguntón, ona [pregoōnton', oná] *a* inquisitive.

prehistórico, a [preēsto'rēko, á] *a* prehistoric.

prejuicio [prehwē'syo] *nm* prejudgement; (*preconcepción*) preconception; (*pey*) prejudice, bias.

prejuzgar [prehoōsgár'] *vt* (*predisponer*) to prejudge.

prejuzgue [prehoōs'ge] *etc vb V* **prejuzgar**.

preliminar [prelēmēnár'] *a, nm* preliminary.

preludio [preloō'thyo] *nm* (*MUS, fig*) prelude.

prematuro, a [prematoō'ro, á] *a* premature.

premeditación [premethētásyon'] *nf* premeditation.

premeditado, a [premethētá'tho, á] *a* premeditated, deliberate; (*intencionado*) wilful.

premeditar [premethētár'] *vt* to premeditate.

premiar [premyár'] *vt* to reward; (*en un concurso*) to give a prize to.

premio [pre'myo] *nm* reward; prize; (*COM*) premium; **~ gordo** first prize.

premonición [premonẽsyon'] *nf* premonition.

premura [premoō'rá] *nf* (*prisa*) haste, urgency.

prenatal [prenátál'] *a* antenatal, prenatal.

prenda [pren'dá] *nf* (*ropa*) garment, article of clothing; (*garantía*) pledge; (*fam*) darling!; ~s *nfpl* talents, gifts; **dejar algo en ~** to pawn sth; **no soltar ~** to give nothing away; (*fig*) not to say a word.

prendar [prendár'] *vt* to captivate, enchant; ~se de algo to fall in love with sth.

prendedor [prendeðþor'] *nm* broach (*US*), brooch (*Brit*).

prender [prender'] *vt* (*captar*) to catch, capture; (*detener*) to arrest; (*coser*) to pin, attach; (*sujetar*) to fasten ♦ *vi* to catch; (*arraigar*) to take root; ~se *vr* (*encenderse*) to catch fire.

prendido, a [prendē'ðho, á] *a* (*AM: luz etc*) on.

prensa [pren'sá] *nf* press; **la P~** the press; **tener mala ~** to have o get a bad press; **la ~ nacional** the national press.

prensar [prensár'] *vt* to press.

preñado, a [prenyá'ðho, á] *a* (*mujer*) pregnant; ~ **de** pregnant with, full of.

preñez [prenyes'] *nf* pregnancy.

preocupación [preokōōpásyon'] *nf* worry, concern; (*ansiedad*) anxiety.

preocupado, a [preokōōpá'ðho, á] *a* worried, concerned; anxious.

preocupar [preokōōpár'] *vt* to worry; ~se *vr* to worry; ~se de algo (*hacerse cargo*) to take care of sth; ~se por algo to worry about sth.

preparación [prepáràsyon'] *nf* (*acto*) preparation; (*estado*) preparedness, readiness; (*entrenamiento*) training.

preparado, a [prepárá'ðho, á] *a* (*dispuesto*) prepared; (*CULIN*) ready (to serve) ♦ *nm* (*MED*) preparation; **¡~s, listos, ya!** ready, set (*US*) o steady (*Brit*), go!

preparar [prepárár'] *vt* (*disponer*) to prepare, get ready; (*TEC: tratar*) to prepare, process, treat; (*entrenar*) to teach, train; ~se *vr*: ~se a o para hacer algo to prepare o get ready to do sth.

preparativo, a [prepárátē'ȟo] *a* preparatory, preliminary ♦ *nm*: ~s preparations.

preparatoria [prepáráto'ryá] *n* (*AM*) senior high school (*US*), sixth form college (*Brit*).

prerrogativa [prerrogátē'ȟá] *nf* prerogative, privilege.

presa [pre'sá] *nf* (*cosa apresada*) catch; (*víctima*) victim; (*de animal*) prey; (*de agua*) dam; **hacer ~ en** to clutch (on to), seize; **ser ~ de** (*fig*) to be a prey to.

presagiar [presáhyár'] *vt* to threaten.

presagio [presá'hyo] *nm* omen.

presbítero [presȟē'tero] *nm* priest.

prescindir [presēndēr'] *vi*: ~ **de** (*privarse de*) to do without, go without; (*descartar*) to dispense with; **no podemos ~ de él** we can't manage without him.

prescribir [preskrēȟēr'] *vt* to prescribe.

prescripción [preskrēpsyon'] *nf* prescription; ~ **facultativa** medical prescription.

prescrito [preskrē'to] *pp de* **prescribir**.

preseleccionar [preseleksyonár'] *vt* (*DEPORTE*) to seed.

presencia [presen'syá] *nf* presence; **en ~ de** in the presence of.

presencial [presensyál'] *a*: **testigo ~** eyewitness.

presenciar [presensyár'] *vt* to be present at; (*asistir a*) to attend; (*ver*) to see, witness.

presentación [presentásyon'] *nf* presentation; (*introducción*) introduction.

presentador, a [presentáðhor', á] *nm/f* master of ceremonies (*US*), compère (*Brit*).

presentar [presentár'] *vt* to present; (*ofrecer*) to offer; (*mostrar*) to show, display; (*renuncia*) to tender; (*moción*) to propose; (*a una persona*) to introduce; ~se *vr* (*llegar inesperadamente*) to appear, turn up; (*ofrecerse: como candidato*) to run, stand; (*aparecer*) to show, appear; (*solicitar empleo*) to apply; ~ **al cobro** (*COM*) to present for payment; ~se **a la policía** to report to the police.

presente [presen'te] *a* present ♦ *nm* present; (*LING*) present (tense); (*regalo*) gift; **los ~s** those present; **hacer ~** to state, declare; **tener ~** to remember, bear in mind; **la carta ~**, **la ~** this letter.

presentimiento [presentēmyen'to] *nm* premonition, presentiment.

presentir [presentēr'] *vt* to have a premonition of.

preservación [preserȟásyon'] *nf* protection, preservation.

preservar [preserȟár'] *vt* to protect, preserve.

preservativo [preserȟátē'ȟo] *nm* condom.

presidencia [presēðhen'syá] *nf* presidency; (*de comité*) chairmanship; **ocupar la ~** to preside, be in o take the chair.

presidente [presēðhen'te] *nm/f* president; chairman/woman; (*en parlamento*) speaker; (*JUR*) presiding magistrate.

presidiario [presēðhyá'ryo] *nm* convict.

presidio [presē'ðhyo] *nm* prison, penitentiary.

presidir [presēðhēr'] *vt* (*dirigir*) to preside at, preside over; (: *comité*) to take the chair at; (*dominar*) to dominate, rule ♦ *vi* to preside; to take the chair.

presienta [presyen'tá] *etc*, **presintiendo** [presēntyen'do] *etc vb* V **presentir**.

presión [presyon'] *nf* pressure; ~ **arterial** o

sanguínea blood pressure; **a** ~ under pressure.

presionar [presyonár'] *vt* to press; (*botón*) to push, press; (*fig*) to press, put pressure on ♦ *vi*: ~ **para** *o* **por** to press for.

preso, a [pre'so, á] *a*: **estar** ~ **de terror** *o* **pánico** to be panic-stricken ♦ *nm/f* prisoner; **tomar** *o* **llevar** ~ **a uno** to arrest sb, take sb prisoner.

prestación [prestásyon'] *nf* (*aportación*) lending; (*INFORM*) capability; ~ **de juramento** oath-taking; ~ **personal** obligatory service.

prestado, a [prestá'đo, á] *a* on loan; **dar algo** ~ to lend sth; **pedir** ~ to borrow.

prestamista [prestámē'stá] *nm/f* money-lender.

préstamo [pre'stámo] *nm* loan; ~ **con garantía** loan against collateral; ~ **hipotecario** mortgage.

prestar [prestár'] *vt* to lend, loan; (*atención*) to pay; (*ayuda*) to give; (*servicio*) to do, render; (*juramento*) to take, swear; ~**se** *vr* (*ofrecerse*) to offer *o* volunteer.

prestatario, a [prestátá'ryo, á] *nm/f* borrower.

presteza [preste'sá] *nf* speed, promptness.

prestidigitador [prestēđēhētáđhor'] *nm* magician.

prestigio [prestē'hyo] *nm* prestige; (*reputación*) face; (*renombre*) good name.

prestigioso, a [prestēhyo'so, á] *a* (*honorable*) prestigious; (*famoso, renombrado*) renowned, famous.

presto, a [pre'sto, á] *a* (*rápido*) quick, prompt; (*dispuesto*) ready ♦ *ad* at once, right away.

presumido, a [presōōmē'đo, á] *a* conceited.

presumir [presōōmēr'] *vt* to presume ♦ *vi* (*tener aires*) to be conceited; **según cabe** ~ as may be presumed, presumably; ~ **de listo** to think o.s. very smart.

presunción [presōōnsyon'] *nf* presumption; (*sospecha*) suspicion; (*vanidad*) conceit.

presunto, a [presōōn'to, á] *a* (*supuesto*) supposed, presumed; (*así llamado*) so-called.

presuntuoso, a [presōōntwo'so, á] *a* conceited, presumptuous.

presupondré [presōōpondre'] *etc vb V* **presuponer**.

presuponer [presōōponer'] *vt* to presuppose.

presuponga [presōōpon'gá] *etc vb V* **presuponer**.

presupuestar [presōōpwestár'] *vi* to budget ♦ *vt*: ~ **algo** to budget for sth.

presupuestario, a [presōōpwestá'ryo, á] *a* (*FINANZAS*) budgetary, budget *cpd*.

presupuesto [presōōpwe'sto] *pp de* **presu-**

poner ♦ *nm* (*FINANZAS*) budget; (*estimación: de costo*) estimate; **asignación de** ~ (*COM*) budget appropriation.

presupuse [presōōpōō'se] *etc vb V* **presuponer**.

presuroso, a [presōōro'so, á] *a* (*rápido*) quick, speedy; (*que tiene prisa*) hasty.

pretencioso, a [pretensyo'so, á] *a* pretentious.

pretender [pretender'] *vt* (*intentar*) to try to, seek to; (*reivindicar*) to claim; (*buscar*) to seek, try for; (*cortejar*) to woo, court; ~ **que** to expect that; **¿qué pretende usted?** what are you after?

pretendiente [pretendyen'te] *nm/f* (*candidato*) candidate, applicant; (*amante*) suitor.

pretensión [pretensyon'] *nf* (*aspiración*) aspiration; (*reivindicación*) claim; (*orgullo*) pretension.

pretérito, a [prete'rēto, á] *a* (*LING*) past; (*fig*) past, former.

pretextar [pretekstár'] *vt* to plead, use as an excuse.

pretexto [pretek'sto] *nm* pretext; (*excusa*) excuse; **so** ~ **de** under pretext of.

pretil [pretēl'] *nm* (*valla*) parapet; (*baranda*) handrail.

prevalecer [prebáleser'] *vi* to prevail.

prevaleciente [prebálesyen'te] *a* prevailing, prevalent.

prevalezca [prebáles'ká] *etc vb V* **prevalecer**.

prevención [prebensyon'] *nf* (*preparación*) preparation; (*estado*) preparedness, readiness; (*medida*) prevention; (*previsión*) foresight, forethought; (*precaución*) precaution.

prevendré [prebendre'] *etc*, **prevenga** [preben'gá] *etc vb V* **prevenir**.

prevenido, a [prebenē'đo, á] *a* prepared, ready; (*cauteloso*) cautious; **estar** ~ (*preparado*) to be ready; **ser** ~ (*cuidadoso*) to be cautious; **hombre** ~ **vale por dos** forewarned is forearmed.

prevenir [prebenēr'] *vt* (*impedir*) to prevent; (*prever*) to foresee, anticipate; (*predisponer*) to prejudice, bias; (*avisar*) to warn; (*preparar*) to prepare, get ready; ~**se** *vr* to get ready, prepare; ~**se contra** to take precautions against.

preventivo, a [prebentē'đo, á] *a* preventive, precautionary.

prever [preber'] *vt* to foresee; (*anticipar*) to anticipate.

previniendo [prebēnyen'do] *etc vb V* **prevenir**.

previo, a [pre'byo, á] *a* (*anterior*) previous, prior ♦ *prep*: ~ **acuerdo de los otros** subject to the agreement of the others; ~ **pago de los derechos** on payment of the fees.

previsible [preɓēsē'ɓle] a foreseeable.

previsión [preɓēsyon'] nf (perspicacia) foresight; (predicción) forecast; (prudencia) caution; ~ **de ventas** (COM) sales forecast.

previsor, a [preɓēsor', á] a (precavido) far-sighted; (prudente) thoughtful.

previsto [preɓē'sto] pp de **prever**.

prieto, a [prye'to, á] a (oscuro) dark; (fig) stingy; (comprimido) tight, compressed.

prima [prē'má] nf V **primo**.

primacía [prēmásē'á] nf primacy.

primar [prēmár'] vi (tener primacía) to occupy first place; ~ **sobre** to have priority over.

primario, a [prēmá'ryo, á] a primary.

primavera [prēmáɓe'rá] nf (temporada) spring; (período) springtime.

primaveral [prēmáɓerál'] a spring cpd, springlike.

primero, a [prēme'ro, á] a (delante de nmsg: **primer**) first; (fig) prime; (anterior) former; (básico) fundamental ♦ ad first; (más bien) sooner, rather ♦ nf (AUTO) first gear; (FERRO) first class; **de primera** (fam) first-class, first-rate; **de buenas a primeras** suddenly; **primera dama** (TEATRO) leading lady.

primicias [prēmē'syás] nfpl first fruits (tb fig).

primitivo, a [prēmētē'ɓo, á] a primitive; (original) original; (COM: acción) ordinary.

primo, a [prē'mo, á] a (MAT) prime ♦ nm/f cousin; (fam) fool, dupe ♦ nf (COM) bonus; (seguro) premium; (a la exportación) subsidy; ~ **hermano** first cousin; **materias primas** raw materials; **hacer el** ~ to be taken for a ride.

primogénito, a [prēmohe'nēto, á] a first-born.

primordial [prēmorɗyál'] a basic, fundamental.

primoroso, a [prēmoro'so, á] a exquisite, fine.

princesa [prēnse'sá] nf princess.

principado [prēnsēpá'ɗo] nm principality.

principal [prēnsēpál'] a principal, main; (más destacado) foremost; (piso) second (US), first (Brit); (INFORM) foreground ♦ nm (jefe) chief, principal.

príncipe [prēn'sēpe] nm prince; ~ **heredero** crown prince; ~ **de gales** (tela) check.

principiante [prēnsēpyán'te] nm/f beginner; (novato) novice.

principiar [prēnsēpyár'] vt to begin.

principio [prēnsē'pyo] nm (comienzo) beginning, start; (origen) origin; (base) rudiment, basic idea; (moral) principle; **a ~s de** at the beginning of; **desde el** ~ from the first; **en un** ~ at first.

pringar [prēngár'] vt (CULIN: pan) to dip; (ensuciar) to dirty; ~**se** vr to get splashed o soiled; ~ **a uno en un asunto** (fam) to involve sb in a matter.

pringoso, a [prēngo'so, á] a greasy; (pegajoso) sticky.

pringue [prēn'ge] etc vb V **pringar** ♦ nm (grasa) grease, fat, dripping.

prioridad [prēorēɗáɗ'] nf priority; (AUTO) right of way.

prioritario, a [prēorētá'ryo, á] a (INFORM) foreground.

prisa [prē'sá] nf (apresuramiento) hurry, haste; (rapidez) speed; (urgencia) (sense of) urgency; **correr** ~ to be urgent; **darse** ~ to hurry up; **estar de** o **tener** ~ to be in a hurry.

prisión [prēsyon'] nf (cárcel) prison; (período de cárcel) imprisonment.

prisionero, a [prēsyone'ro, á] nm/f prisoner.

prismáticos [prēsmá'tēkos] nmpl binoculars.

privación [prēɓásyon'] nf deprivation; (falta) want, privation; **privaciones** nfpl hardships, privations.

privado, a [prēɓá'ɗo, á] a (particular) private; (POL: favorito) favorite (US), favourite (Brit); **en** ~ privately, in private; "~ **y confidencial**" "private and confidential".

privar [prēɓár'] vt to deprive; ~**se** vr: ~**se de** (abstenerse) to deprive o.s. of; (renunciar) to give up.

privativo, a [prēɓátē'ɓo, á] a exclusive.

privilegiado, a [prēɓēlehyá'ɗo, á] a privileged; (memoria) very good ♦ nm/f (afortunado) privileged person.

privilegiar [prēɓēlehyár'] vt to grant a privilege to; (favorecer) to favor (US), favour (Brit).

privilegio [prēɓēle'hyo] nm privilege; (concesión) concession.

pro [pro] nm o nf profit, advantage ♦ prep: **asociación** ~ **ciegos** association for the blind ♦ pref: ~ **soviético/americano** pro-Soviet/-American; **en** ~ **de** on behalf of, for; **los** ~**s y los contras** the pros and cons.

proa [pro'á] nf (NAUT) bow, prow.

probabilidad [proɓáɓēlēɗáɗ'] nf probability, likelihood; (oportunidad, posibilidad) chance, prospect.

probable [proɓá'ɓle] a probable, likely; **es** ~ **que** + subjun it is probable o likely that; **es** ~ **que no venga** he probably won't come.

probador [proɓáɗor'] nm (persona) taster (of wine etc); (en una tienda) fitting room.

probar [proɓár'] vt (demostrar) to prove; (someter a prueba) to test, try out; (ropa) to try on; (comida) to taste ♦ vi to try; ~**se** vr: ~**se un traje** to try on a suit.

probeta [proᵬe'tá] *nf* test tube.

problema [proᵬle'má] *nm* problem.

procaz [prokás'] *a* insolent, impudent.

procedencia [proseᵬen'syá] *nf* (*principio*) source, origin; (*lugar de salida*) point of departure.

procedente [proseᵬen'te] *a* (*razonable*) reasonable; (*conforme a derecho*) proper, fitting; ~ **de** coming from, originating in.

proceder [proseᵬer'] *vi* (*avanzar*) to proceed; (*actuar*) to act; (*ser correcto*) to be right (and proper), be fitting ♦ *nm* (*comportamiento*) behavior, conduct; **no procede obrar así** it is not right to act like that; ~ **de** to come from, originate in.

procedimiento [proseᵬemyen'to] *nm* procedure; (*proceso*) process; (*método*) means, method; (*trámite*) proceedings.

prócer [pro'ser] *nm* (*persona eminente*) worthy; (*líder*) great man, leader.

procesado, a [prosesá'ᵬo, á] *nm/f* accused (person).

procesador [prosesáᵬor'] *nm*: ~ **de textos** (*INFORM*) word processor.

procesamiento [prosesámyen'to] *nm* (*INFORM*) processing; ~ **de datos** data processing; ~ **por lotes** batch processing; ~ **solapado** multiprogramming; ~ **de textos** word processing.

procesar [prosesár'] *vt* to try, put on trial; (*INFORM*) to process.

procesión [prosesyon'] *nf* procession; **la va por dentro** he keeps his troubles to himself.

proceso [prose'so] *nm* process; (*JUR*) trial; (*lapso*) course (of time); (*INFORM*): ~ **(automático) de datos** (automatic) data processing; ~ **no prioritario** background process; ~ **por pasadas** batch process; ~ **en tiempo real** real-time programming.

proclama [proklá'má] *nf* (*acto*) proclamation; (*cartel*) poster.

proclamar [proklámár'] *vt* to proclaim.

proclive [proklē'ᵬe] *a*: ~ **(a)** inclined *o* prone (to).

procreación [prokreásyon'] *nf* procreation.

procrear [prokreár'] *vt, vi* to procreate.

procurador, a [prokōoráᵬor', á] *nm/f* attorney.

procurar [prokōorár'] *vt* (*intentar*) to try, endeavour; (*conseguir*) to get, obtain; (*asegurar*) to secure; (*producir*) to produce.

prodigio [proᵬē'hyo] *nm* prodigy; (*milagro*) wonder, marvel.

prodigioso, a [proᵬēhyo'so, á] *a* prodigious, marvellous.

pródigo, a [pro'ᵬēgo, á] *a* (*rico*) rich, productive; **hijo** ~ prodigal son.

producción [proᵬōoksyon'] *nf* production; (*suma de productos*) output; (*producto*) product; ~ **en serie** mass production.

producir [proᵬōoser'] *vt* to produce; (*generar*) to cause, bring about; (*impresión*) to give; (*COM: interés*) to bear; ~**se** *vr* (*gen*) to come about, happen; (*hacerse*) to be produced, be made; (*estallar*) to break out; (*accidente*) to take place.

productividad [proᵬōoktēᵬēᵬáᵬ'] *nf* productivity.

productivo, a [proᵬōoktē'ᵬo, á] *a* productive; (*provechoso*) profitable.

producto [proᵬōok'to] *nm* (*resultado*) product; (*producción*) production; ~ **alimenticio** foodstuff; ~ **(nacional) bruto** gross (national) product; ~ **interno bruto** gross domestic product.

productor, a [proᵬōoktor', á] *a* productive, producing ♦ *nm/f* producer.

produje [proᵬōo'he], **produjera** [proᵬōohe'rá], **produzca** [proᵬōos'ká] *etc vb* V **producir**.

proeza [proe'sá] *nf* exploit, feat.

profanar [profánár'] *vt* to desecrate, profane.

profano, a [profá'no, á] *a* profane ♦ *nm/f* (*inexperto*) layman/woman; **soy** ~ **en música** I don't know anything about music.

profecía [profesē'á] *nf* prophecy.

proferir [proferēr'] *vt* (*palabra, sonido*) to utter; (*injuria*) to hurl, let fly.

profesar [profesár'] *vt* (*declarar*) to profess; (*practicar*) to practise.

profesiograma [profesyográ'má] *nm* job specification.

profesión [profesyon'] *nf* profession; (*confesión*) avowal; **abogado de** ~, **de** ~ **abogado** a lawyer by profession.

profesional [profesyonál'] *a* professional.

profesor, a [profesor', á] *nm/f* teacher; (*instructor*) instructor; (~ *de universidad*) professor (*US*), lecturer (*Brit*); ~ **adjunto** associate professor (*US*), assistant lecturer (*Brit*).

profesorado [profesorá'ᵬo] *nm* (*profesión*) teaching profession; (*cuerpo*) faculty; (*cargo*) professorship.

profeta [profe'tá] *nm/f* prophet.

profetice [profetē'se] *etc vb* V **profetizar**.

profetizar [profetēsár'] *vt, vi* to prophesy.

profiera [profye'rá] *etc*, **profiriendo** [profēryen'do] *etc vb* V **proferir**.

profilaxis [profēlák'sēs] *nf inv* prevention.

prófugo, a [pro'fōogo, á] *nm/f* fugitive; (*desertor*) deserter.

profundice [profōondē'se] *etc vb* V **profundizar**.

profundidad [profōondēᵬáᵬ'] *nf* depth; **tener una** ~ **de 30 cm** to be 30 cm deep.

profundizar [profōondēsár'] *vt* (*fig*) to go deeply into, study in depth.

profundo, a [profōon'do, á] *a* deep; (*misterio, pensador*) profound; **poco** ~ shallow.

profusión [profōōsyon'] *nf* (*abundancia*) profusion; (*prodigalidad*) wealth.

progenie [prohe'nye] *nf* offspring.

progenitor [prohenētor'] *nm* ancestor; ~**es** *nmpl* (*fam*) parents.

programa [prográ'má] *nm* program (*US*), programme (*Brit*); (*INFORM*) program; ~ **de estudios** curriculum; ~ **verificador de ortografía** (*INFORM*) spelling checker.

programación [prográmásyon'] *nf* (*IN-FORM*) programming; ~ **estructurada** structured programming.

programador, a [prográmáthor', á] *nm/f* (computer) programmer; ~ **de aplicaciones** applications programmer.

programar [prográmár'] *vt* (*INFORM*) to program (*US*), programme (*Brit*).

programería [prográmerē'á] *nf* (*INFORM*): ~ **fija** firmware.

progresar [progresár'] *vi* to progress, make progress.

progresista [progresē'stá] *a, nm/f* progressive.

progresivo, a [progresē'ho, á] *a* progressive; (*gradual*) gradual; (*continuo*) continuous.

progreso [progre'so] *nm* (*tb*: ~**s**) progress; **hacer** ~**s** to progress, advance.

prohibición [proēhēsyon'] *nf* prohibition, ban; **levantar la** ~ **de** to remove the ban on.

prohibir [proēhēr'] *vt* to prohibit, ban, forbid; **se prohíbe fumar** no smoking.

prohibitivo, a [proēhētē'ho, á] *a* prohibitive.

prójimo, a [pro'hēmo, á] *nm* fellow man ♦ *nm/f* (*vecino*) neighbor (*US*), neighbour (*Brit*).

prole [pro'le] *nf* (*descendencia*) offspring.

proletariado [proletáryá'tho] *nm* proletariat.

proletario, a [proletá'ryo, á] *a, nm/f* proletarian.

proliferación [prolēferásyon'] *nf* proliferation; ~ **de armas nucleares** spread of nuclear arms.

proliferar [prolēferár'] *vi* to proliferate.

prolífico, a [prolē'fēko, á] *a* prolific.

prolijo, a [prolē'ho, á] *a* long-winded, tedious.

prólogo [pro'logo] *nm* prolog(ue); (*preámbulo*) preface, introduction.

prolongación [prolongásyon'] *nf* extension.

prolongado, a [prolongá'tho, á] *a* (*largo*) long; (*alargado*) lengthy.

prolongar [prolongár'] *vt* (*gen*) to extend; (*en el tiempo*) to prolong; (*calle, tubo*) to make longer, extend; ~**se** *vr* (*alargarse*) to extend, go on.

prolongue [prolon'ge] *etc vb V* **prolongar**.

prom. *abr* (= *promedio*) av.

promedio [prome'thyo] *nm* average; (*de distancia*) middle, mid-point.

promesa [prome'sá] *nf* promise ♦ *a*: **jugador** ~ promising player; **faltar a una** ~ to break a promise.

prometer [prometer'] *vt* to promise ♦ *vi* to show promise; ~**se** *vr* (*dos personas*) to get engaged.

prometido, a [prometē'tho, á] *a* promised; engaged ♦ *nm/f* fiancé/fiancée.

prominente [promēnen'te] *a* prominent.

promiscuidad [promēskwēthátth'] *nf* promiscuity.

promiscuo, a [promēs'kwo, á] *a* promiscuous.

promoción [promosyon'] *nf* promotion; (*año*) class, year; ~ **por correspondencia directa** (*COM*) direct mail advertising (*US*) *o* mailshot (*Brit*); ~ **de ventas** sales promotion *o* drive.

promocionar [promosyonár'] *vt* (*COM: dar publicidad*) to promote.

promotor [promotor'] *nm* promoter; (*instigador*) instigator.

promover [promoher'] *vt* to promote; (*causar*) to cause; (*juicio*) to bring; (*motín*) to instigate, stir up.

promueva [promwe'há] *etc vb V* **promover**.

promulgar [promōōlgár'] *vt* to promulgate; (*fig*) to proclaim.

promulgue [promōōl'ge] *etc vb V* **promulgar**.

pronombre [pronom'bre] *nm* pronoun.

pronosticar [pronostēkár'] *vt* to predict, foretell, forecast.

pronóstico [prono'stēko] *nm* prediction, forecast; (*profecía*) omen; (*MED: diagnóstico*) prognosis; **de** ~ **leve** slight, not serious; ~ **del tiempo** weather forecast.

pronostique [pronostē'ke] *etc vb V* **pronosticar**.

prontitud [prontētōōth'] *nf* speed, quickness.

pronto, a [pron'to, á] *a* (*rápido*) prompt, quick; (*preparado*) ready ♦ *ad* quickly, promptly; (*en seguida*) at once, right away; (*dentro de poco*) soon; (*temprano*) early ♦ *nm* urge, sudden feeling; **tener** ~**s de enojo** to be quick-tempered; **al** ~ at first; **de** ~ suddenly; **¡hasta** ~**!** see you soon!; **lo más** ~ **posible** as soon as possible; **por lo** ~ meanwhile, for the present; **tan** ~ **como** as soon as.

pronunciación [pronōōnsyásyon'] *nf* pronunciation.

pronunciado, a [pronōōnsyá'tho, á] *a* (*marcado*) pronounced; (*curva etc*) sharp; (*facciones*) marked.

pronunciamiento [pronōōnsyámyen'to] *nm* (*rebelión*) insurrection.

pronunciar [pronōōnsyár'] *vt* to pronounce;

(*discurso*) to make, deliver; (*JUR: sentencia*) to pass, pronounce; ~**se** *vr* to revolt, rise, rebel; (*declararse*) to declare o.s.; ~**se sobre** to pronounce on.

propagación [propágásyon'] *nf* propagation; (*difusión*) spread(ing).

propaganda [propágán'dá] *nf* (*política*) propaganda; (*comercial*) advertising; **hacer ~ de** (*COM*) to advertise.

propagar [propágár'] *vt* to propagate; (*difundir*) to spread, disseminate; ~**se** *vr* (*BIO*) to propagate; (*fig*) to spread.

propague [propá'ge] *etc vb* V **propagar**.

propalar [propálár'] *vt* (*divulgar*) to divulge; (*publicar*) to publish an account of.

propasarse [propásár'se] *vr* (*excederse*) to go too far; (*sexualmente*) to take liberties.

propensión [propensyon'] *nf* inclination, propensity.

propenso, a [propen'so, á] *a:* ~ **a** prone *o* inclined to; **ser ~ a hacer algo** to be inclined *o* have a tendency to do sth.

propiamente [propyámen'te] *ad* properly; (*realmente*) really, exactly; ~ **dicho** real, true.

propicio, a [propē'syo, á] *a* favourable, propitious.

propiedad [propyethath'] *nf* property; (*posesión*) possession, ownership; (*conveniencia*) suitability; (*exactitud*) accuracy; ~ **particular** private property; ~ **pública** (*COM*) public ownership; **ceder algo a uno en ~** to transfer to sb the full rights over sth.

propietario, a [propyetá'ryo, á] *nm/f* owner, proprietor.

propina [propē'ná] *nf* tip; **dar algo de ~** to give something extra.

propinar [propēnár'] *vt* (*golpe*) to strike; (*azotes*) to give.

propio, a [pro'pyo, á] *a* own, of one's own; (*característico*) characteristic, typical; (*conveniente*) proper; (*mismo*) selfsame, very; **el ~ ministro** the minister himself; **¿tienes casa propia?** have you a house of your own?; **eso es muy ~ de él** that's just like him; **tiene un olor muy ~** it has a smell of its own.

propondré [propondre'] *etc vb* V **proponer**.

proponente [proponen'te] *nm* proposer, mover.

proponer [proponer'] *vt* to propose, put forward; (*candidato*) to propose, nominate; (*problema*) to pose; ~**se** *vr* to propose, plan, intend.

proponga [propon'gá] *etc vb* V **proponer**.

proporción [proporsyon'] *nf* proportion; (*MAT*) ratio; (*razón, porcentaje*) rate; **proporciones** *nfpl* dimensions; (*fig*) size *sg*; **en ~ con** in proportion to.

proporcionado, a [proporsyoná'tho, á] *a*

proportionate; (*regular*) medium, middling; (*justo*) just right; **bien ~** well-proportioned.

proporcionar [proporsyonár'] *vt* (*dar*) to give, supply, provide; **esto le proporciona una renta anual de ...** this brings him in a yearly income of ...

proposición [proposēsyon'] *nf* proposition; (*propuesta*) proposal.

propósito [propo'sēto] *nm* (*intención*) purpose; (*intento*) aim, intention ♦ *ad:* **a ~** by the way, incidentally; **a ~ de** about, with regard to.

propuesto, a [propwe'sto, á] *pp de* **proponer** ♦ *nf* proposal.

propulsar [propōōlsár'] *vt* to drive, propel; (*fig*) to promote, encourage.

propulsión [propōōlsyon'] *nf* propulsion; ~ **a chorro** *o* **por reacción** jet propulsion.

propuse [propōō'se] *etc vb* V **proponer**.

prorrata [prorrá'tá] *nf* (*porción*) share, quota ♦ *ad* (*COM*) pro rata.

prorratear [prorráteár'] *vt* (*dividir*) to share out.

prórroga [pro'rrogá] *nf* (*gen*) extension; (*JUR*) stay; (*COM*) deferment.

prorrogable [prorrogá'hle] *a* which can be extended.

prorrogar [prorrogár'] *vt* (*período*) to extend; (*decisión*) to defer, postpone.

prorrogue [prorro'ge] *etc vb* V **prorrogar**.

prorrumpir [prorrōōmpēr'] *vi* to burst forth, break out; ~ **en gritos** to start shouting; ~ **en lágrimas** to burst into tears.

prosa [pro'sá] *nf* prose.

proscribir [proskrēbēr'] *vt* to prohibit, ban; (*desterrar*) to exile, banish; (*partido*) to proscribe.

proscripción [proskrēpsyon'] *nf* prohibition, ban; banishment; proscription.

proscrito, a [proskrē'to, á] *pp de* **proscribir** ♦ *a* (*prohibido*) banned; (*desterrado*) outlawed ♦ *nm/f* (*exilado*) exile; (*bandido*) outlaw.

prosecución [prosekōōsyon'] *nf* continuation; (*persecución*) pursuit.

proseguir [prosegēr'] *vt* to continue, carry on, proceed with; (*investigación, estudio*) to pursue ♦ *vi* to continue, go on.

prosiga [prosē'gá] *etc*, **prosiguiendo** [prosēgyen'tho] *etc vb* V **proseguir**.

prosista [prosē'stá] *nm/f* (*escritor*) prose writer.

prospección [prospeksyon'] *nf* exploration; (*del petróleo, del oro*) prospecting.

prospecto [prospek'to] *nm* prospectus; (*folleto*) leaflet, sheet of instructions.

prosperar [prosperár'] *vi* to prosper, thrive, flourish.

prosperidad [prosperēthath'] *nf* prosperity; (*éxito*) success.

próspero, a [pros'pero, á] *a* prosperous, thriving, flourishing; (*que tiene éxito*) successful.

prostíbulo [proste'booolo] *nm* brothel.

prostitución [prostetoōsyon'] *nf* prostitution.

prostituir [prostetwēr'] *vt* to prostitute; ~**se** *vr* to prostitute o.s., become a prostitute.

prostituta [prostetoō'tá] *nf* prostitute.

prostituyendo [prostetoōyen'do] *etc vb V* **prostituir**.

protagonice [protágonē'se] *etc vb V* **protagonizar**.

protagonista [protágonē'stá] *nm/f* protagonist; (*LIT: personaje*) main character, hero(ine).

protagonizar [protágonēsár'] *vt* to head, take the chief role in.

protección [proteksyon'] *nf* protection.

proteccionismo [proteksyonēs'mo] *nm* (*COM*) protectionism.

protector, a [protektor', á] *a* protective, protecting; (*tono*) patronizing ♦ *nm/f* protector; (*bienhechor*) patron; (*de la tradición*) guardian.

proteger [protcher'] *vt* to protect; ~ **contra grabación** *o* **contra escritura** (*INFORM*) to write-protect.

protegido, a [protehē'ḍo, á] *nm/f* protégé/protégée.

proteína [protec̄'ná] *nf* protein.

proteja [prote'há] *etc vb V* **proteger**.

protesta [prote'stá] *nf* protest; (*declaración*) protestation.

protestante [protestán'te] *a* Protestant.

protestar [protestár'] *vt* to protest, declare; (*fe*) to protest ♦ *vi* to protest; (*objetar*) to object; **cheque protestado por falta de fondos** insufficient funds check (*US*), cheque referred to drawer (*Brit*).

protocolo [protoko'lo] *nm* protocol; **sin ~s** (*formalismo*) informal(ly), without formalities.

prototipo [prototē'po] *nm* prototype; (*ideal*) model.

prov. *abr* (= *provincia*) prov.

provecho [prohetch'o] *nm* advantage, benefit; (*FINANZAS*) profit; **¡buen ~!** ¡bon appétit!; **en ~ de** to the benefit of; **sacar ~ de** to benefit from, profit by.

provechoso, a [prohetcho'so, á] *a* (*ventajoso*) advantageous; (*beneficioso*) beneficial, useful; (*FINANZAS*) *lucrativo*) profitable.

proveedor, a [proheeḍhor', á] *nm/f* (*abastecedor*) supplier; (*distribuidor*) dealer.

proveer [proheer'] *vt* to provide, supply; (*preparar*) to provide, get ready; (*vacante*) to fill; (*negocio*) to transact, dispatch ♦ *vi*: ~ **a** to provide for; ~**se** *vr*: ~**se de** to provide o.s. with.

provendré [prohendre'] *etc,* **provenga** [prohen'gá] *etc vb V* **provenir**.

provenir [prohenēr'] *vi*: ~ **de** to come from, stem from.

Provenza [prohen'sá] *nf* Provence.

proverbial [proherḅyál'] *a* proverbial; (*fig*) notorious.

proverbio [proher'ḅyo] *nm* proverb.

proveyendo [proheyen'do] *etc vb V* **proveer**.

providencia [prohēḍhen'syá] *nf* providence; (*previsión*) foresight; ~**s** *nfpl* measures, steps.

provincia [prohēn'syá] *nf* province; **un pueblo de ~(s)** a country town.

provinciano, a [prohēnsyá'no, á] *a* provincial; (*del campo*) country *cpd*.

proviniendo [prohēnyen'do] *etc vb V* **provenir**.

provisión [prohēsyon'] *nf* provision; (*abastecimiento*) provision, supply; (*medida*) measure, step.

provisional [prohēsyonál'] *a* provisional.

provisto, a [prohē'sto, á] *a*: ~ **de** provided *o* supplied with; (*que tiene*) having, possessing.

provocación [prohokásyon'] *nf* provocation.

provocador, a [prohokáḍhor', á] *a* provocative, provoking.

provocar [prohokár'] *vt* to provoke; (*alentar*) to tempt, invite; (*causar*) to bring about, lead to; (*promover*) to promote; (*estimular*) to rouse, stir, stimulate; (*protesta, explosión*) to cause, spark off; (*AM*): **¿te provoca un café?** would you like a coffee?

provocativo, a [prohokátē'ḥo, á] *a* provocative.

provoque [proho'ke] *etc vb V* **provocar**.

proxeneta [proksene'tá] *nm/f* go-between; (*de prostitutas*) pimp/procuress.

próximamente [proksēmámen'te] *ad* shortly, soon.

proximidad [proksēmēḍhaḍ'] *nf* closeness, proximity.

próximo, a [prok'sēmo, á] *a* near, close; (*vecino*) neighbouring; (*el que viene*) next; **en fecha próxima** at an early date; **el mes ~** next month.

proyección [proyeksyon'] *nf* projection; (*CINE*) showing; (*diapositiva*) slide, transparency; (*influencia*) influence; **el tiempo de ~ es de 35 minutos** the film runs for 35 minutes.

proyectar [proyektár'] *vt* (*objeto*) to hurl, throw; (*luz*) to cast, shed; (*CINE*) to screen, show; (*planear*) to plan.

proyectil [proyektēl'] *nm* projectile, missile; ~ **(tele)dirigido** guided missile.

proyecto [proyek'to] *nm* plan; (*idea*) project; (*estimación de costo*) detailed estimate; **tener algo en ~** to be planning sth;

~ **de ley** (*POL*) bill.

proyector [proyek'tor'] *nm* (*CINE*) projector.

prudencia [prooðen'syà] *nf* (*sabiduría*) wisdom, prudence; (*cautela*) care.

prudente [prooðen'te] *a* sensible, wise, prudent; (*cauteloso*) careful.

prueba [prwe'bà] *etc vb V* **probar** ♦ *nf* proof; (*ensayo*) test, trial; (*cantidad*) taste, sample; (*saboreo*) testing, sampling; (*de ropa*) fitting; (*DEPORTE*) event; **a** ~ **on** trial; (*COM*) on approval; **a** ~ **de** proof against; **a** ~ **de agua/fuego** waterproof/ fireproof; ~ **de capacitación** (*COM*) proficiency test; ~ **de fuego** (*fig*) acid test; ~ **de vallas** hurdles; **someter a** ~ to put to the test; **¿tiene usted** ~ **de ello?** can you prove it?, do you have proof?

prurito [proori'to] *nm* itch; (*de bebé*) diaper (*US*) *o* nappy (*Brit*) rash; (*anhelo*) urge.

PS *nm abr* (*POL*) = **Partido Socialista**.

psico... [seko] *pref* psycho...

psicoanálisis [sekoánà'leses] *nm* psychoanalysis.

psicoanalista [sekoánàle'stá] *nm/f* psychoanalyst.

psicología [sekolohe'à] *nf* psychology.

psicológico, a [seko'ekò, à] *a* psychological.

psicólogo, a [seko'logo, à] *nm/f* psychologist.

psicópata [seko'pátà] *nm/f* psychopath.

psicosis [seko'ses] *nf inv* psychosis.

psicoterapia [sekoterá'pyà] *nf* psychotherapy.

psiquiatra [sekyà'trà] *nm/f* psychiatrist.

psiquiátrico, a [sekyá'treko, à] *a* psychiatric.

psíquico, a [se'keko, à] *a* psychic(al).

PSOE [peso'e] *nm abr* = **Partido Socialista Obrero Español**.

Pta. *abr* (*GEO*: = **Punta**) Pt.

pta(s). *abr* = **peseta(s)**.

ptmo. *abr* (*COM*) = **préstamo**.

pts. *abr* = **pesetas**.

púa [poo'à] *nf* sharp point; (*para guitarra*) plectrum; **alambre de** ~**s** barbed wire.

púber, a [poo'ber, à] *a, nm/f* adolescent.

pubertad [pooertàð'] *nf* puberty.

publicación [poolekásyon'] *nf* publication.

publicar [poolekàr'] *vt* (*editar*) to publish; (*hacer público*) to publicize; (*divulgar*) to make public, divulge.

publicidad [pooleseðàð'] *nf* publicity; (*COM*) advertising; **dar** ~ **a** to publicize, give publicity to; ~ **gráfica** display advertising; ~ **en el punto de venta** point-of-sale advertising.

publicitar [poolesetàr'] *vt* to publicize.

publicitario, a [pooleseta'ryo, à] *a* publicity *cpd*; advertising *cpd*.

público, a [poo'leko, à] *a* public ♦ *nm* public; (*TEATRO etc*) audience; (*DEPORTE*) spectators *pl*, crowd; (*restaurantes etc*) clients *pl*; **el gran** ~ the general public; **hacer** ~ to publish; (*difundir*) to disclose; ~ **objetivo** (*COM*) target audience.

publique [poo̲le'ke] *etc vb V* **publicar**.

pucherazo [pootcherà'so] *nm* (*fraude*) electoral fiddle; **dar** ~ to rig an election.

puchero [pootche'ro] *nm* (*CULIN*: *olla*) cooking pot; (: *guiso*) stew; **hacer** ~**s** to pout.

pudibundo, a [pooðeboon'do, à] *a* bashful.

púdico, a [poo'ðeko, à] *a* modest; (*pudibundo*) bashful.

pudiendo [pooðyen'do] *etc vb V* **poder**.

pudiente [pooðyen'te] *a* (*opulento*) wealthy; (*poderoso*) powerful.

pudín [pooðen'] *nm* pudding.

pudor [pooðor'] *nm* modesty; (*vergüenza*) (sense of) shame.

pudoroso, a [pooðoro'so, à] *a* (*modesto*) modest; (*casto*) chaste.

pudrir [pooðrer'] *vt* to rot; (*fam*) to upset, annoy; ~**se** *vr* to rot, decay; (*fig*) to rot, languish.

pueblerino, a [pweblere'no, à] *a* (*lugareño*) small-town *cpd*; (*persona*) rustic, provincial ♦ *nm/f* (*aldeano*) country person.

pueblo [pwe'blo] *etc vb V* **poblar** ♦ *nm* people; (*nación*) nation; (*aldea*) village; (*plebe*) common people; (*población pequeña*) small town, country town.

pueda [pwe'ðà] *etc vb V* **poder**.

puente [pwen'te] *nm* (*gen*) bridge; (*NAUT*: *tb*: ~ **de mando**) bridge; (: *cubierta*) deck; ~ **aéreo** airlift; ~ **colgante** suspension bridge; ~ **levadizo** drawbridge; **hacer (el)** ~ (*fam*) to take a long weekend.

puerco, a [pwer'ko, à] *a* (*sucio*) dirty, filthy; (*obsceno*) disgusting ♦ *nm/f* pig/sow.

pueril [pwerel'] *a* childish.

puerro [pwe'rro] *nm* leek.

puerta [pwer'tà] *nf* door; (*de jardín*) gate; (*portal*) doorway; (*fig*) gateway; (*gol*) goal; (*INFORM*) port; **a** ~ **cerrada** behind closed doors; ~ **corredera/giratoria** sliding/revolving door; ~ **principal/trasera** *o* **de servicio** front/back door; ~ **(de transmisión en) paralelo/serie** (*INFORM*) parallel/serial port; **tomar la** ~ (*fam*) to leave.

puerto [pwer'to] *nm* (*tb INFORM*) port; (*de mar*) seaport; (*paso*) pass; (*fig*) haven, refuge; **llegar a** ~ (*fig*) to get over a difficulty.

Puerto Rico [pwertore'ko] *nm* Puerto Rico.

puertorriqueño, a [pwertorreke'nyo, à] *a, nm/f* Puerto Rican.

pues [pwes] *ad* (*entonces*) then; (¡*entonces!*) well, well then; (*así que*) so ♦ *conj* (*porque*) since; ~ ... **no sé** well ... I don't know.

puesto, a |pwe'sto, à| *pp de* **poner** ♦ *a* dressed ♦ *nm* (*lugar, posición*) place; (*trabajo*) post, job; (*MIL*) post; (*COM*) stall; (*quiosco*) kiosk ♦ *conj*: ~ **que** since, as ♦ *nf* (*apuesta*) bet, stake; ~ **de mercado** market stall; ~ **de policía** police station; ~ **de socorro** first aid post; **puesta en escena** staging; **puesta en marcha** starting; **puesta del sol** sunset; **puesta a cero** (*INFORM*) reset.

pugna |pōōg'nà| *nf* battle, conflict.

pugnar |pōōgnàr'| *vi* (*luchar*) to struggle, fight; (*pelear*) to fight.

puja |pōō'hà| *nf* (*esfuerzo*) attempt; (*en una subasta*) bid.

pujante |pōōhàn'te| *a* strong, vigorous.

pujar |pōōhàr'| *vt* (*precio*) to raise, push up ♦ *vi* (*en licitación*) to bid, bid up; (*fig: esforzarse*) to struggle, strain.

pulcro, a |pōōl'kro, à| *a* neat, tidy.

pulga |pōōl'gà| *nf* flea; **tener malas ~s** to be short-tempered.

pulgada |pōōlgà'thà| *nf* inch.

pulgar |pōōlgàr'| *nm* thumb.

pulgón |pōōlgon'| *nm* plant louse, greenfly.

pulir |pōōlēr'| *vt* to polish; (*alisar*) to smooth; (*fig*) to polish up, touch up.

pulmón |pōōlmon'| *nm* lung; **a pleno ~** (*respirar*) deeply; (*gritar*) at the top of one's voice; ~ **de acero** iron lung.

pulmonía |pōōlmonē'à| *nf* pneumonia.

pulpa |pōōl'pà| *nf* pulp; (*de fruta*) flesh, soft part.

pulpería |pōōlperē'à| *nf* (*AM*) small grocery store.

púlpito |pōōl'pēto| *nm* pulpit.

pulpo |pōōl'po| *nm* octopus.

pulsación |pōōlsàsyon'| *nf* beat, pulsation; (*ANAT*) throb(bing); (*en máquina de escribir*) keystroke; (*de pianista, mecanógrafo*) touch; ~ (**de una tecla**) (*INFORM*) keystroke; ~ **doble** (*INFORM*) strikeover.

pulsador |pōōlsàthor'| *nm* button, push button.

pulsar |pōōlsàr'| *vt* (*tecla*) to touch, tap; (*MUS*) to play; (*botón*) to press, push ♦ *vi* to pulsate; (*latir*) to beat, throb.

pulsera |pōōlse'rà| *nf* bracelet; **reloj de ~** wristwatch.

pulso |pōōl'so| *nm* (*MED*) pulse; **hacer algo a ~** to do sth unaided *o* by one's own efforts.

pulular |pōōlōōlàr'| *vi* (*estar plagado*): ~ (**de**) to swarm (with).

pulverice |pōōlberē'se| *etc vb V* **pulverizar**.

pulverizador |pōōlberēsàthor'| *nm* spray, spray gun.

pulverizar |pōōlberēsàr'| *vt* to pulverize; (*líquido*) to spray.

pulla |pōō'yà| *nf* cutting remark.

puna |pōō'nà| *nf* (*AM MED*) mountain sickness.

punce |pōōn'se| *etc vb V* **punzar**.

punción |pōōnsyon'| *nf* (*MED*) puncture.

pundonor |pōōndonor'| *nm* (*dignidad*) self-respect.

punición |pōōnēsyon'| *nf* punishment.

punitivo, a |pōōnētē'ho, à| *a* punitive.

punta |pōōn'tà| *nf* point, tip; (*extremidad*) end; (*promontorio*) promontory; (*COSTURA*) corner; (*TEC*) small nail; (*fig*) touch, trace; **horas ~s** peak hours, rush hours; **sacar ~ a** to sharpen; **de ~** on end; **de ~ a ~** from one end to the other; **estar de ~** to be edgy; **ir de ~ en blanco** to be all dressed up; **tener algo en la ~ de la lengua** to have sth on the tip of one's tongue; **se le pusieron los pelos de ~** her hair stood on end.

puntada |pōōntà'thà| *nf* (*COSTURA*) stitch.

puntal |pōōntàl'| *nm* prop, support.

puntapié |pōōntàpye'|, *pl* **puntapiés** *nm* kick; **echar a uno a ~s** to kick sb out.

punteado, a |pōōnteà'tho, à| *a* (*moteado*) dotted; (*diseño*) of dots ♦ *nm* (*MUS*) twang.

puntear |pōōnteàr'| *vt* to tick, mark; (*MUS*) to pluck.

puntería |pōōnterē'à| *nf* (*de arma*) aim, aiming; (*destreza*) marksmanship.

puntero, a |pōōnte'ro, à| *a* leading ♦ *nm* (*señal, INFORM*) pointer; (*dirigente*) leader.

puntiagudo, a |pōōntyàgōō'tho, à| *a* sharp, pointed.

puntilla |pōōntē'yà| *nf* (*TEC*) tack, braid; (*COSTURA*) lace edging; (**andar**) **de ~s** (to walk) on tiptoe.

puntilloso, a |pōōntēyo'so, à| *a* (*pundonoroso*) punctilious; (*susceptible*) touchy.

punto |pōōn'to| *nm* (*gen*) point; (*señal diminuta*) spot, dot; (*lugar*) spot, place; (*momento*) point, moment; (*en un examen*) grade; (*tema*) item; (*COSTURA*) stitch; (*INFORM: impresora*) pitch; (: *pantalla*) pixel; **a ~** ready; **estar a ~ de** to be on the point of *o* about to; **llegar a ~** to come just at the right moment; **al ~** at once; **en ~** on the dot; **estar en su ~** (*CULIN*) to be done to perfection; **hasta cierto ~** to some extent; **hacer ~** to knit; **poner un motor en ~** to tune an engine; ~ **de partida/de congelación/de fusión** starting/freezing/melting point; ~ **de vista** point of view, viewpoint; ~ **muerto** dead center; (*AUTO*) neutral (gear); **~s a tratar** matters to be discussed, agenda *sg*; ~ **final** period (*US*), full stop (*Brit*); **dos ~s** colon; ~ **y coma** semicolon; ~ **de interrogación** question mark; **~s suspensivos** suspension points; ~ **de equilibrio/de pedido** (*COM*) breakeven/reorder point; ~ **inicial** *o* **de**

partida (*INFORM*) home; ~ **de referencia/ de venta** (*COM*) benchmark point/point-of- sale.

puntuación [pŏŏntwásyon'] *nf* punctuation; (*puntos*: *en examen*) grade; (: *DEPORTE*) score.

puntual [pŏŏntwál'] *a* (*a tiempo*) punctual; (*cálculo*) exact, accurate; (*informe*) reliable.

puntualice [pŏŏntwálē'se] *etc vb V* **puntualizar**.

puntualidad [pŏŏntwálēthàth'] *nf* punctuality; exactness, accuracy; reliability.

puntualizar [pŏŏntwálēsàr'] *vt* to fix, specify.

puntuar [pŏŏntwár'] *vt* (*LING*, *TIP*) to punctuate; (*examen*) to grade ♦ *vi* (*DE-PORTE*) to score, count.

punzada [pŏŏnsá'thà] *nf* (*puntura*) prick; (*MED*) stitch; (*dolor*) twinge (of pain).

punzante [pŏŏnsán'te] *a* (*dolor*) shooting, sharp; (*herramienta*) sharp; (*comentario*) biting.

punzar [pŏŏnsár'] *vt* to prick, pierce ♦ *vi* to shoot, stab.

punzón [pŏŏnson'] *nm* (*TEC*) punch.

puñado [pŏŏnyá'tho] *nm* handful (*tb fig*); **a** ~**s** by handfuls.

puñal [pŏŏnyál'] *nm* dagger.

puñalada [pŏŏnyálá'thà] *nf* stab.

puñeta [pŏŏnye'tà] *nf*: ¡~!, ¡**qué** ~(**s**)! (*fam!*) hell!; **mandar a uno a hacer** ~**s** (*fam*) to tell sb to go to hell.

puñetazo [pŏŏnyetá'so] *nm* punch.

puño [pŏŏ'nyo] *nm* (*ANAT*) fist; (*cantidad*) fistful, handful; (*COSTURA*) cuff; (*de herramienta*) handle; **como un** ~ (*verdad*) obvious; (*palpable*) tangible, visible; **de** ~ **y letra del poeta** in the poet's own handwriting.

pupila [pŏŏpē'là] *nf* (*ANAT*) pupil.

pupitre [pŏŏpē'tre] *nm* desk.

puré [pŏŏre'], *pl* **purés** *nm* puree; (*sopa*) (thick) soup; ~ **de patatas** mashed potatoes; **estar hecho** ~ (*fig*) to be worn out.

pureza [pŏŏre'sà] *nf* purity.

purga [pŏŏr'gà] *nf* purge.

purgante [pŏŏrgán'te] *a*, *nm* purgative.

purgar [pŏŏrgár'] *vt* to purge; (*POL*: *depurar*) to purge, liquidate; ~**se** *vr* (*MED*) to take a purge.

purgatorio [pŏŏrgáto'ryo] *nm* purgatory.

purgue [pŏŏr'ge] *etc vb V* **purgar**.

purificar [pŏŏrēfēkàr'] *vt* to purify; (*refinar*) to refine.

purifique [pŏŏrēfē'ke] *etc vb V* **purificar**.

puritano, a [pŏŏrētá'no, à] *a* (*actitud*) puritanical; (*iglesia*, *tradición*) puritan ♦ *nm/f* puritan.

puro, a [pŏŏ'ro, à] *a* pure; (*depurado*) unadulterated; (*oro*) solid; (*cielo*) clear;

(*verdad*) simple, plain ♦ *ad*: **de** ~ **cansado** out of sheer tiredness ♦ *nm* cigar; **por pura casualidad** by sheer chance.

púrpura [pŏŏr'pŏŏrà] *nf* purple.

purpúreo, a [pŏŏrpŏŏ'reo, à] *a* purple.

pus [pŏŏs] *nm* pus.

puse [pŏŏ'se] *etc vb V* **poner**.

pústula [pŏŏs'tŏŏlà] *nf* pimple, sore.

puta [pŏŏ'tà] *nf* whore, prostitute.

putañear [pŏŏtányeàr'], **putear** [pŏŏteàr'] *vi* to go whoring.

putería [pŏŏterē'à] *nf* (*prostitución*) prostitution; (*prostíbulo*) brothel.

putrefacción [pŏŏtrefáksyon'] *nf* rotting, putrefaction.

pútrido, a [pŏŏ'trētho, à] *a* rotten.

PVP *abr* (*Esp*) = **Precio Venta al Público**.

Q

Q, q [kŏŏ] *nf* (*letra*) Q, q; **Q de Querido** Q for Queen.

q.e.g.e. *abr* (= *que en gloria esté*) R.I.P.

q.e.p.d. *abr* (= *que en paz descanse*) R.I.P.

q.e.s.m. *abr* (= *que estrecha su mano*) *courtesy formula*.

qm. *abr* = **quintal(es) métrico(s)**.

qts. *abr* = **quilates**.

que [ke] *pron* (*sujeto: individuo*) who, that; (: *cosa*) which, that; (*complemento: individuo*) whom, that; (: *cosa*) which, that ♦ *conj* that; **el momento en** ~ **llegó** the moment he arrived; **lo** ~ **digo** what I say; **dar** ~ **hablar** to give cause to talk, cause talk; ¡~ **entre!** send him in!; **le ruego** ~ **se calle** I'm asking you to keep quiet; ¡~ **sí!** yes!; **te digo** ~ **sí** I'm telling you, I assure you; **el** ~ + *subjun* the fact that ...; **ya** *o* **por** ~ for, since, because; **yo** ~ **tú** if I were you; **siguió toca** ~ **toca** he kept on playing.

qué [ke] *a* what?, which? ♦ *pron* what?; ¡~ **divertido/asco!** how funny/revolting!; ¡~ **día más espléndido!** what a glorious day!; ¿~ **edad tienes?** how old are you?; ¿**de** ~ **me hablas?** what are you saying to me?; ¿~ **tal?** how are you?, how are things?; ¿~ **hay (de nuevo)?** what's new?; ¿~ **más?** anything else?

quebrada [kebrá'thà] *nf V* **quebrado**.

quebradero [kebráthe'ro] *nm*: ~ **de cabeza** headache, worry.

quebradizo, a [kebráthē'so, à] *a* fragile; (*persona*) frail.

quebrado, a [keʰrá'ðo, á] *a (roto)* broken; *(terreno)* rough, uneven ♦ *nm/f* bankrupt ♦ *nm (MAT)* fraction ♦ *nf* ravine; ~ **rehabilitado** discharged bankrupt.

quebradura [keʰràðoo'rá] *nf (fisura)* fissure; *(MED)* rupture.

quebrantadura [keʰràntàðoo'rá] *nf*, **quebrantamiento** [keʰràntámyen'to] *nm (acto)* breaking; *(de ley)* violation; *(estado)* exhaustion.

quebrantar [keʰràntár'] *vt (infringir)* to violate, transgress; ~**se** *vr (persona)* to fail in health.

quebranto [keʰràn'to] *nm* damage, harm; *(decaimiento)* exhaustion; *(dolor)* grief, pain.

quebrar [keʰrár'] *vt* to break, smash ♦ *vi* to go bankrupt; ~**se** *vr* to break, get broken; *(MED)* to be ruptured.

queda [ke'ðá] *nf*: **(toque de)** ~ curfew.

quedar [keðár'] *vi* to stay, remain; *(encontrarse)* to be; *(restar)* to remain, be left; ~**se** *vr* to remain, stay (behind); ~ **en** *(acordar)* to agree on/to; *(acabar siendo)* to end up as; ~ **por hacer** to be still to be done; ~ **ciego/mudo** to be left blind/dumb; **no te queda bien ese vestido** that dress doesn't suit you; **quedamos a las seis** we agreed to meet at six; **eso queda muy lejos** that's a long way (away); **nos quedan 12 kms para llegar al pueblo** there are still 12 kms before we get to the village; **no queda otra** there's no alternative; ~**se (con) algo** to keep sth; ~**se con uno** *(fam)* to swindle sb; ~**se en nada** to come to nothing *o* nought; ~**se sin** to run out of.

quedo, a [ke'ðo, á] *a* still ♦ *ad* softly, gently.

quehacer [keáser'] *nm* task, job; ~**es (domésticos)** household chores.

queja [ke'há] *nf* complaint.

quejarse [kehár'se] *vr (enfermo)* to moan, groan; *(protestar)* to complain; ~ **de que** ... to complain (about the fact) that ...

quejica [kehē'ká] *a* grumpy, complaining ♦ *nm/f* grumbler, whinger.

quejido [kehē'ðo] *nm* moan.

quejoso, a [keho'so, á] *a* complaining.

quema [ke'má] *nf* fire; *(combustión)* burning.

quemado, a [kemá'ðo, á] *a* burned; *(irritado)* annoyed.

quemadura [kemáðoo'rá] *nf* burn, scald; *(de sol)* sunburn; *(de fusible)* blow-out.

quemar [kemár'] *vt* to burn; *(fig: malgastar)* to burn up, squander; *(COM: precios)* to slash, cut; *(fastidiar)* to annoy, bug ♦ *vi* to be burning hot; ~**se** *vr (consumirse)* to burn (up); *(del sol)* to get sunburned.

quemarropa [kemárro'pá]: **a** ~ *ad* pointblank.

quemazón [kemáson'] *nf* burn; *(calor)* intense heat; *(sensación)* itch.

quena [ke'ná] *nf (AM)* Indian flute.

quepo [ke'po] *etc vb V* **caber.**

querella [kere'yá] *nf (JUR)* charge; *(disputa)* dispute.

querencia [keren'syá] *nf (ZOOL)* homing instinct; *(fig)* homesickness.

querer [kerer'] *vt, vi (desear)* to want, wish; *(amar)* to love; ~ **hacer algo** to want to do sth; **como quien no quiere la cosa** offhandedly; **sin** ~ unintentionally; **¿quiere abrir la ventana?** would you mind opening the window?; **no quiso** he refused; ~ **bien a uno** to be fond of sb.

querido, a [kerē'ðo, á] *a* dear ♦ *nm/f* darling; *(amante)* lover; **nuestra querida patria** our beloved country.

querré [kerre'] *etc vb V* **querer.**

quesería [keserē'á] *nf* dairy; *(fábrica)* cheese factory.

quesero, a [kese'ro, á] *a*: **la industria quesera** the cheese industry ♦ *nm/f* cheesemaker ♦ *nf* cheese dish.

queso [ke'so] *nm* cheese; ~ **rallado** grated cheese; ~ **crema** cream cheese; **dárselas con** ~ **a uno** *(fam)* to put sth over on sb.

quetzal [ketsál'] *nm monetary unit of Guatemala.*

quicio [kē'syo] *nm* hinge; **estar fuera de** ~ to be beside o.s.; **sacar a uno de** ~ to drive sb up the wall.

quid [kēð] *nm* gist, crux; **dar en el** ~ to hit the nail on the head.

quiebra [kye'ʰrá] *nf* break, split; *(COM)* bankruptcy; *(ECON)* slump.

quiebro [kye'ʰro] *etc vb V* **quebrar** ♦ *nm (del cuerpo)* swerve.

quien [kyen] *pron relativo (suj)* who; *(complemento)* whom; *(indefinido)*: ~ **dice eso es tonto** whoever says that is a fool; **hay** ~ **piensa que** there are those who think that; **no hay** ~ **lo haga** no-one will do it; ~ **más, ~ menos tiene sus problemas** everybody has problems.

quién [kyen] *pron interrogativo* who; *(complemento)* whom; **¿~ es?** who is it?, who's there?; *(TELEC)* who's calling?

quienquiera [kyenkye'rá] *(pl* **quienesquiera)** *pron* whoever.

quiera [kye'rá] *etc vb V* **querer.**

quieto, a [kye'to, á] *a* still; *(carácter)* placid; **¡estáte** ~**!** keep still!

quietud [kyetooð'] *nf* stillness.

quijada [kēhá'ðá] *nf* jaw, jawbone.

quijote [kēho'te] *nm* dreamer; **Don Q**~ Don Quixote.

quil. *abr* = **quilates.**

quilate [kēlá'te] *nm* carat.

quilo... [kē'lo] = **kilo...**

quilla [kē'yá] *nf* keel.
quimera [kēme'rá] *nf* (*sueño*) pipe dream.
quimérico, a [kēme'rēko, á] *a* fantastic.
químico, a [kē'mēko, á] *a* chemical ♦ *nm/f* chemist ♦ *nf* chemistry.
quincallería [kēnkáyerē'á] *nf* hardware store (*US*), ironmonger's (shop) (*Brit*).
quince [kēn'se] *num* fifteen; ~ **días** two weeks.
quinceañero, a [kēnseánye'ro, á] *a* fifteen-year-old; (*adolescente*) teenage ♦ *nm/f* fifteen-year-old; (*adolescente*) teenager.
quincena [kēnse'ná] *nf* two weeks; (*pago*) two weeks' pay.
quincenal [kēnsenál'] *a* biweekly.
quincuagésimo, a [kēnkwáhe'sēmo, á] *num* fiftieth.
quiniela [kēnye'lá] *nf* football pools *pl*; ~**s** *nfpl* pools coupon *sg*.
quinientos, as [kēnyen'tos, ás] *num* five hundred.
quinina [kēnē'ná] *nf* quinine.
quinqué [kēnke'] *nm* oil lamp.
quinquenal [kēnkenál'] *a* five-year *cpd*.
quinqui [kēn'kē] *nm* delinquent.
quinta [kēn'tá] *nf* V **quinto**.
quintaesencia [kēntáesen'syá] *nf* quintessence.
quintal [kēntál'] *nm* (*Castilla: peso*) = 46kg; ~ **métrico** = 100kg.
quinto, a [kēn'to, á] *a* fifth ♦ *nm* (*MIL*) conscript, draftee ♦ *nf* country house; (*MIL*) call-up, draft.
quintuplo, a [kēntōo'plo, á] *a* quintuple, five-fold.
quiosco [kyos'ko] *nm* (*de música*) bandstand; (*de periódicos*) news stand.
quirófano [kēro'fáno] *nm* operating room (*US*) *o* theatre (*Brit*).
quiromancia [kēromán'syá] *nf* palmistry.
quirúrgico, a [kērōōr'hēko, á] *a* surgical.
quise [kē'se] *etc vb* V **querer**.
quisque [kēs'ke] *pron fam*: **cada** *o* **todo** ~ (absolutely) everyone.
quisquilloso [kēskēyo'so, á] *a* (*susceptible*) touchy; (*meticuloso*) fussy.
quiste [kē'ste] *nm* cyst.
quitaesmalte [kētáesmál'te] *nm* nail polish remover.
quitamanchas [kētámántch'ás] *nm inv* stain remover.
quitanieves [kētánye'ḥes] *nm inv* snowplow (*US*), snowplough (*Brit*).
quitar [kētár'] *vt* to remove, take away; (*ropa*) to take off; (*dolor*) to relieve; (*vida*) to take; (*valor*) to reduce; (*hurtar*) to remove, steal ♦ *vi*: ¡**quita de ahí**! get away!; ~**se** *vr* to withdraw; (*ropa*) to come off *o* out; (*ropa*) to take off; **me quita mucho tiempo** it takes up a lot of my time; **el café me quita el sueño** coffee

keeps me from sleeping; ~ **de en medio a uno** to get rid of sb; ~**se algo de encima** to get rid of sth; ~**se del tabaco** to give up smoking; **se quitó el sombrero** he took off his hat.
quitasol [kētásol'] *nm* parasol.
quite [kē'te] *nm* (*esgrima*) parry; (*evasión*) dodge; **estar al** ~ to be ready to go to sb's aid.
Quito [kē'to] *n* Quito.
quizá(s) [kēsá'(s)] *ad* perhaps, maybe.
quórum [kwo'rōōm] *nm*, *pl* **quórums** [kwo'rōōm] quorum.

R

R, r [e'rre] *nf* (*letra*) R, r; **R de Ramón** R for Roger.
R. *abr* = **Remite, Remitente.**
rábano [rá'ḥano] *nm* radish; **me importa un** ~ I don't give a damn.
rabia [rá'ḥyá] *nf* (*MED*) rabies *sg*; (*fig: ira*) fury, rage; ¡**qué** ~! isn't it infuriating!; **me da** ~ it maddens me; **tener** ~ **a uno** to have a grudge against sb.
rabiar [ráḥyár'] *vi* to have rabies; to rage, be furious; ~ **por algo** to long for sth.
rabieta [ráḥye'tá] *nf* tantrum, fit of temper.
rabino [ráḥē'no] *nm* rabbi.
rabioso, a [ráḥyo'so, á] *a* rabid; (*fig*) furious.
rabo [rá'ḥo] *nm* tail.
racanear [rákáneár'] *vi* (*fam*) to loaf.
rácano [rá'káno] *nm* (*fam*) slacker.
racial [rásyál'] *a* racial, race *cpd*.
racimo [rásē'mo] *nm* bunch.
raciocinio [rásyosē'nyo] *nm* reason; (*razonamiento*) reasoning.
ración [rásyon'] *nf* portion; **raciones** *nfpl* rations.
racional [rásyonál'] *a* (*razonable*) reasonable; (*lógico*) rational.
racionalice [rásyonálē'se] *etc vb* V **racionalizar.**
racionalizar [rásyonálēsár'] *vt* to rationalize; (*COM*) to streamline.
racionamiento [rásyonámyen'to] *nm* (*COM*) rationing.
racionar [rásyonár'] *vt* to ration (out).
racismo [rásēs'mo] *nm* racialism, racism.
racista [rásē'stá] *a, nm/f* racist.
racha [rátch'á] *nf* gust of wind; (*serie*) string, series; **buena/mala** ~ spell of good/ bad luck.

radar [ràthàr'] *nm* radar.

radiación [ràthyàsyon'] *nf* radiation; (*TELEC*) broadcasting.

radiactividad [ràthyàktēhēthàth'] *nf* radio-activity.

radiactivo, a [ràthyoàktē'ho, à] *a* radio-active.

radiado, a [ràthyà'tho, à] *a* radio *cpd*, broadcast.

radiador [ràthyàthor'] *nm* radiator.

radiante [ràthyàn'te] *a* radiant.

radiar [ràthyàr'] *vt* to radiate; (*TELEC*) to broadcast; (*MED*) to give radiotherapy to.

radical [ràthēkàl'] *a*, *nm/f* radical ♦ *nm* (*LING*) root; (*MAT*) square-root sign.

radicar [ràthēkàr'] *vi* to take root; ~ **en** to lie in; ~**se** *vr* to establish o.s., put down (one's) roots.

radio [rà'thyo] *nf* radio; (*aparato*) radio (set) ♦ *nm* (*MAT*) radius; (*QUÍMICA*) radium; ~ **de acción** extent of one's authority, sphere of influence.

radiodifusión [ràthyodēfōōsyon'] *nf* broadcasting.

radioemisora [ràthyoemēso'rà] *nf* transmitter, radio station.

radiofónico, a [ràthyofo'nēko, à] *a* radio *cpd*.

radiografía [ràthyogràfē'à] *nf* X-ray.

radiólogo, a [ràthyo'logo, à] *nm/f* radiologist.

radioterapia [ràthyoterà'pyà] *nf* radiotherapy.

radioyente [ràthyoyen'te] *nm/f* listener.

radique [ràthē'ke] *etc vb V* **radicar.**

RAE *nf abr* = *Real Academia Española.*

ráfaga [rà'fàgà] *nf* gust; (*de luz*) flash; (*de tiros*) burst.

raído, a [ràē'tho, à] *a* (*ropa*) threadbare; (*persona*) shabby.

raigambre [ràēgàm'bre] *nf* (*BOT*) roots *pl*; (*fig*) tradition.

raíz [ràēs'] (*pl* **raíces**) *nf* root; ~ **cuadrada** square root; **a ~ de** as a result of; (*después de*) immediately after.

raja [rà'hà] *nf* (*de melón etc*) slice; (*hendedura*) slit, split; (*grieta*) crack.

rajar [ràhàr'] *vt* to slash; ~**se** *vr* to split, crack; ~**se de** to back out of.

rajatabla [ràhàtà'blà]: **a ~** *ad* (*estrictamente*) strictly, to the letter.

ralea [ràle'à] *nf* (*pey*) kind, sort.

ralenti [ràlen'tē] *nm* (*TV etc*) slow motion; (*AUTO*) neutral; **al ~** in slow motion; (*AUTO*) idling.

ralo, a [rà'lo, à] *a* thin, sparse.

rallador [ràyàthor'] *nm* grater.

rallar [ràyàr'] *vt* to grate.

RAM [ràm] *nf abr* (= *random access memory*) RAM.

rama [rà'mà] *nf* bough, branch; **andarse por**

las ~s (*fig*, *fam*) to beat about the bush.

ramaje [ràmà'ye] *nm* branches *pl*, foliage.

ramal [ràmàl'] *nm* (*de cuerda*) strand; (*FERRO*) branch line; (*AUTO*) branch (road).

rambla [ràm'blà] *nf* (*avenida*) avenue.

ramera [ràme'rà] *nf* whore, hooker.

ramificación [ràmēfēkàsyon'] *nf* ramification.

ramificarse [ràmēfēkàr'se] *vr* to branch out.

ramifique [ràmēfē'ke] *etc vb V* **ramificarse.**

ramillete [ràmēye'te] *nm* bouquet; (*fig*) select group.

ramo [rà'mo] *nm* branch, twig; (*sección*) department, section; (*sector*) field, sector.

rampa [ràm'pà] *nf* ramp.

ramplón, ona [ràmplon', onà] *a* uncouth, coarse.

rana [rà'nà] *nf* frog; **salto de ~** leapfrog; **cuando las ~s críen pelos** when pigs fly.

rancio, a [ràn'syo, à] *a* (*comestibles*) stale, rancid; (*vino*) aged, mellow; (*fig*) ancient.

ranchero [ràntche'ro] *nm* (*AM*) rancher; (*pequeño propietario*) small farmer.

rancho [ràntch'o] *nm* grub (*fam*); (*AM*: *grande*) ranch; (: *pequeño*) small farm.

rango [ràn'go] *nm* rank; (*prestigio*) standing.

ranura [rànōō'rà] *nf* groove; (*de teléfono etc*) slot; ~ **de expansión** (*INFORM*) expansion slot.

rapacidad [ràpàsēthàth'] *nf* rapacity.

rapapolvo [ràpàpol'ho] *nm:* **echar un ~ a uno** to bawl sb out.

rapar [ràpàr'] *vt* to shave; (*los cabellos*) to crop.

rapaz [ràpàs'] *a* (*ZOOL*) predatory ♦ *nm/f* (*f:* **rapaza**) young boy/girl.

rape [rà'pe] *nm* quick shave; (*pez*) angler (fish); **al ~** cropped.

rapé [ràpe'] *nm* snuff.

rapidez [ràpēthes'] *nf* speed, rapidity.

rápido, a [rà'pētho, à] *a* fast, quick ♦ *ad* quickly ♦ *nm* (*FERRO*) express; ~**s** *nmpl* rapids.

rapiña [ràpē'nyà] *nm* robbery; **ave de ~** bird of prey.

raptar [ràptàr'] *vt* to kidnap.

rapto [ràp'to] *nm* kidnapping; (*impulso*) sudden impulse; (*éxtasis*) ecstasy, rapture.

raqueta [ràke'tà] *nf* racquet.

raquítico, a [ràkē'tēko, à] *a* stunted; (*fig*) poor, inadequate.

raquitismo [ràkētēs'mo] *nm* rickets *sg*.

rareza [ràre'sà] *nf* rarity; (*fig*) eccentricity.

raro, a [rà'ro, à] *a* (*poco común*) rare; (*extraño*) odd, strange; (*excepcional*) remarkable; **¡qué ~!** how (very) odd!; **¡(qué) cosa más rara!** how strange!

ras [ràs] *nm:* **a ~ de** level with; **a ~ de tierra** at ground level.

rasar |ràsàr'| vt to level.

rascacielos |ráskàsyc'los| nm inv skyscraper.

rascar |ràskàr'| vt (con las uñas etc) to scratch; (raspar) to scrape; ~se vr to scratch (o.s.).

rasgar |ràsgàr'| vt to tear, rip (up).

rasgo |ràs'go| nm (con pluma) stroke; ~s nmpl features, characteristics; **a grandes** ~s in outline, broadly.

rasguear |ràsgeàr'| vt (MUS) to strum.

rasgue |ràs'ge| etc vb V **rasgar**.

rasguñar |ràsgoōnyàr'| vt to scratch; (bosquejar) to sketch.

rasguño |ràsgoō'nyo| nm scratch.

raso, a |rà'so, à| a (liso) flat, level; (a baja altura) very low ♦ nm satin; (campo llano) flat country; **cielo** ~ clear sky; **al** ~ in the open.

raspador |ràspàthor'| nm scraper.

raspadura |ràspàthoō'rà| nf (acto) scrape, scraping; (marca) scratch; ~s nfpl scrapings.

raspar |ràspàr'| vt to scrape; (arañar) to scratch; (limar) to file ♦ vi (manos) to be rough; (vino) to be sharp, have a rough taste.

rasque |ràs'ke| etc vb V **rascar**.

rastra |ràs'trà| nf: **a** ~s by dragging; (fig) unwillingly.

rastreador |ràstreàthor'| nm tracker; ~ **de minas** minesweeper.

rastrear |ràstreàr'| vt (seguir) to track; (minas) to sweep.

rastrero, a |ràstrc'ro, à| a (BOT, ZOOL) creeping; (fig) despicable, mean.

rastrillar |ràstrēyàr'| vt to rake.

rastrillo |ràstrē'yo| nm rake.

rastro |ràs'tro| nm (AGR) rake; (pista) track, trail; (vestigio) trace; **el R**~ the Madrid fleamarket; **perder el** ~ to lose the scent; **desaparecer sin** ~ to vanish without trace.

rastrojo |ràstro'ho| nm stubble.

rasurador |ràsoōràthor'| nm, (AM) **rasuradora** |ràsoōràtho'rà| nf electric shaver o razor.

rasurarse |ràsoōràr'se| vr to shave.

rata |rà'tà| nf rat.

ratear |ràteàr'| vt (robar) to steal.

ratero, a |ràtc'ro, à| a light-fingered ♦ nm/f pickpocket; (AM: de casas) burglar.

ratificar |ràtēfēkàr'| vt to ratify.

ratifique |ràtēfē'ke| etc vb V **ratificar**.

rato |rà'to| nm while, short time; **a** ~s from time to time; **al poco** ~ shortly after, soon afterwards; ~s **libres** o **de ocio** leisure sg, spare o free time sg; **hay para** ~ there's still a long way to go; **pasar el** ~ to kill time; **pasar un buen/mal** ~ to have a good/rough time.

ratón |ràton'| nm (tb INFORM) mouse.

ratonera |ràtonc'rà| nf mousetrap.

RAU nf abr (= República Árabe Unida) UAR.

raudal |ràoōthàl'| nm torrent; **a** ~es in abundance; **entrar a** ~es to pour in.

raudo, a |rà'oōtho, à| a (rápido) swift; (precipitado) rushing.

raya |rà'yà| nf line; (marca) scratch; (en tela) stripe; (TIP) dash; (de pelo) parting; (límite) boundary; (pez) ray; **a** ~s striped; **pasarse de la** ~ to overstep the mark, go too far; **tener a** ~ to keep in check.

rayado, a |ràyà'tho, à| a (papel) ruled; (tela, diseño) striped.

rayar |ràyàr'| vt to line; to scratch; (subrayar) to underline ♦ vi: ~ **en** o **con** to border on; **al** ~ **el alba** at first light.

rayo |rà'yo| nm (del sol) ray, beam; (de luz) shaft; (en una tormenta) (flash of) lightning; ~ **solar** o **de sol** sunbeam; ~s **infrarrojos** infrared rays; ~s **X** X-rays; **como un** ~ like a shot; **la noticia cayó como un** ~ the news was a bombshell; **pasar como un** ~ to flash past.

raza |rà'sà| nf race; (de animal) breed; ~ **humana** human race; **de pura** ~ (caballo) thoroughbred; (perro etc) pedigree.

razón |ràson'| nf reason; (justicia) right, justice; (razonamiento) reasoning; (motivo) reason, motive; (proporción) rate; (MAT) ratio; **a** ~ **de 10 cada día** at the rate of 10 a day; "~: ..." "inquiries to ..."; **en** ~ **de** with regard to; **perder la** ~ to go out of one's mind; **dar** ~ **a uno** to agree that sb is right; **dar** ~ **de** to give an account of, report on; **tener/no tener** ~ to be right/wrong; ~ **directa/inversa** direct/inverse proportion; ~ **de ser** raison d'être.

razonable |ràsonà'hle| a reasonable; (justo, moderado) fair.

razonado, a |ràsonà'tho, à| a (COM: cuenta etc) itemized.

razonamiento |ràsonàmyen'to| nm (juicio) judgement; (argumento) reasoning.

razonar |ràsonàr'| vt, vi to reason, argue.

RDA nf = **República Democrática Alemana**.

Rdo. abr (REL: = Reverendo) Rev.

reabierto |reàhyer'to| pp de **reabrir**.

reabrir |reàhrēr'| vt, ~se vr to reopen.

reacción |reàksyon'| nf reaction; **avión a** ~ jet plane; ~ **en cadena** chain reaction.

reaccionar |reàksyonàr'| vi to react.

reaccionario, a |reàksyonà'ryo, à| a reactionary.

reacio, a |reà'syo, à| a stubborn; **ser** o **estar** ~ **a** to be opposed to.

reactor |reàktor'| nm reactor; (avión) jet plane; ~ **nuclear** nuclear reactor.

readaptación |reàthàptàsyon'| nf: ~ **profe-**

sional industrial retraining.

reafirmar [reáfērmár'] *vt* to reaffirm.

reagrupar [reágrōōpár'] *vt* to regroup.

reajustar [reáhōōstár'] *vt* (*INFORM*) to reset.

reajuste [reáhōō'ste] *nm* readjustment; ~ **salarial** wage increase; ~ **de plantilla** modernization.

real [reál'] *a* real; (*del rey, fig*) royal; (*espléndido*) grand ♦ *nm* (*de feria*) fairground.

realce [reál'se] *etc vb* V **realzar** ♦ *nm* (*TEC*) embossing; (*lustre, fig*) splendor (*US*), splendour (*Brit*); (*ARTE*) highlight; **poner de** ~ to emphasize.

realeza [reále'sá] *nf* royalty.

realice [reálē'se] *etc vb* V **realizar**.

realidad [reálētháth'] *nf* reality; (*verdad*) truth; **en** ~ in fact.

realista [reálē'stá] *nm/f* realist.

realización [reálēsásyon'] *nf* fulfilment, realization; (*COM*) liquidation; ~ **de plusvalías** profit-taking.

realizador, a [reálēsáthor', á] *nm/f* (*TV etc*) producer.

realizar [reálēsár'] *vt* (*objetivo*) to achieve; (*plan*) to carry out; (*viaje*) to make, undertake; (*COM*) to realize; ~**se** *vr* to come about, come true; ~**se como persona** to fulfil one's aims in life.

realmente [reálmen'te] *ad* really.

realquilar [reálkēlár'] *vt* (*subarrendar*) to sublet; (*alquilar de nuevo*) to rent again.

realzar [reálsár'] *vt* (*TEC*) to raise; (*embellecer*) to enhance; (*acentuar*) to highlight.

reanimar [reánēmár'] *vt* to revive; (*alentar*) to encourage; ~**se** *vr* to revive.

reanudar [reánōōthár'] *vt* (*renovar*) to renew; (*historia, viaje*) to resume.

reaparición [reápárēsyon'] *nf* reappearance; (*vuelta*) return.

reapertura [reápertōō'rá] *nf* reopening.

rearme [reár'me] *nm* rearmament.

rebaja [reká'há] *nf* reduction, lowering; (*COM*) discount; "**grandes** ~**s**" "big reductions", "sale".

rebajar [rekáhár'] *vt* (*bajar*) to lower; (*reducir*) to reduce; (*precio*) to cut; (*disminuir*) to lessen; (*humillar*) to humble; ~**se** *vr*: ~**se a hacer algo** to stoop to doing sth.

rebanada [rekáná'thá] *nf* slice.

rebaño [reká'nyo] *nm* herd; (*de ovejas*) flock.

rebasar [rekásár'] *vt* (*tb*: ~ **de**) to exceed; (*AUTO*) to pass.

rebatir [rekátēr'] *vt* to refute; (*rebajar*) to reduce; (*ataque*) to repel.

rebato [reká'to] *nm* alarm; (*ataque*) surprise attack; **llamar** *o* **tocar a** ~ (*fig*) to sound the alarm.

rebeca [reke'ká] *nf* cardigan.

rebelarse [rekelár'se] *vr* to rebel, revolt.

rebelde [rekel'de] *a* rebellious; (*niño*) un-

ruly ♦ *nm/f* rebel; **ser** ~ **a** to be in revolt against, rebel against.

rebeldía [rekeldē'á] *nf* rebelliousness; (*desobediencia*) disobedience; (*JUR*) default.

rebelión [rekelyon'] *nf* rebellion.

reblandecer [reklándeser'] *vt* to soften.

reblandezca [reklándes'ká] *etc vb* V **reblandecer**.

reboce [reko'se] *etc vb* V **rebozar**.

rebosante [rekosán'te] *a*: ~ **de** (*fig*) brimming *o* overflowing with.

rebosar [rekosár'] *vi* to overflow; (*abundar*) to abound, be plentiful; ~ **de salud** to be bursting *o* brimming with health.

rebotar [rekotár'] *vt* to bounce; (*rechazar*) to repel.

rebote [reko'te] *nm* rebound; **de** ~ on the rebound.

rebozado, a [rekosá'tho, á] *a* (*CULIN*) fried in batter *o* breadcrumbs *o* flour.

rebozar [rekosár'] *vt* to wrap up; (*CULIN*) to fry in batter *etc*.

rebuscado, a [rekōōská'tho, á] *a* affected.

rebuznar [rekōōsnár'] *vi* to bray.

recabar [rekákár'] *vt* (*obtener*) to manage to get; ~ **fondos** to collect money.

recadero [rekáthe'ro] *nm* messenger.

recado [reká'tho] *nm* message; **dejar/tomar un** ~ (*TELEC*) to leave/take a message.

recaer [rekáer'] *vi* to relapse; ~ **en** to fall to *o* on; (*criminal etc*) to fall back into, relapse into; (*premio*) to go to.

recaída [rekáē'thá] *nf* relapse.

recaiga [reká'ēgá] *etc vb* V **recaer**.

recalcar [rekálkár'] *vt* (*fig*) to stress, emphasize.

recalcitrante [rekálsētrán'te] *a* recalcitrant.

recalentar [rekálentár'] *vt* (*comida*) to warm up, reheat; (*demasiado*) to overheat; ~**se** *vr* to overheat, get too hot.

recaliente [rekályen'te] *etc vb* V **recalentar**.

recalque [rekál'ke] *etc vb* V **recalcar**.

recámara [reká'márá] *nf* (*vestidor*) dressing room; (*AM*) bedroom.

recambio [rekám'byo] *nm* spare; (*de pluma*) refill; **piezas de** ~ spares.

recapacitar [rekápásētár'] *vi* to reflect.

recargado, a [rekárgá'tho, á] *a* overloaded; (*exagerado*) over-elaborate.

recargar [rekárgár'] *vt* to overload; (*batería*) to recharge.

recargo [rekár'go] *nm* surcharge; (*aumento*) increase.

recargue [rekár'ge] *etc vb* V **recargar**.

recatado, a [rekátá'tho, á] *a* (*modesto*) modest, demure; (*prudente*) cautious.

recato [reká'to] *nm* (*modestia*) modesty, demureness; (*cautela*) caution.

recaudación [rekáōōthásyon'] *nf* (*acción*) collection; (*cantidad*) takings *pl*; (*en deporte*) gate; (*oficina*) tax office.

recaudador, a [rekáōōtháthor', á] *nm/f* tax collector.

recaudar [rekáōōthár'] *vt* to collect.

recaudo [reká'ōōtho] *nm* (*impuestos*) collection; (*JUR*) surety; **estar a buen ~** to be in safekeeping; **poner algo a buen ~** to put sth in a safe place.

recayendo [rekáyen'do] *etc vb V* **recaer.**

rece [re'se] *etc vb V* **rezar.**

recelar [reselár'] *vt:* **~ que** (*sospechar*) to suspect that; (*temer*) to fear that ♦ *vi:* **~(se) de** to distrust.

recelo [rese'lo] *nm* distrust, suspicion.

receloso, a [reselo'so, á] *a* distrustful, suspicious.

recepción [resepsyon'] *nf* reception; (*acto de recibir*) receipt.

recepcionista [resepsyonē'stá] *nm/f* receptionist.

receptáculo [reseptá'kōōlo] *nm* receptacle.

receptivo, a [reseptē'ho, á] *a* receptive.

receptor, a [reseptor', á] *nm/f* recipient ♦ *nm* (*TELEC*) receiver; **descolgar el ~** to pick up the receiver.

recesión [resesyon'] *nf* (*COM*) recession.

receta [rese'tá] *nf* (*CULIN*) recipe; (*MED*) prescription.

recetar [resetár'] *vt* to prescribe.

recibidor [resēthēthor'] *nm* entrance hall.

recibimiento [resēhēmyen'to] *nm* reception, welcome.

recibir [resēhēr'] *vt* to receive; (*dar la bienvenida*) to welcome; (*salir al encuentro de*) to go and meet ♦ *vi* to entertain; **~se** *vr:* **~se de** to qualify as.

recibo [resē'ho] *nm* receipt; **acusar ~ de** to acknowledge receipt of.

recién [resyen'] *ad* recently, newly; (*AM*) just, recently; **~ casado** newly-wed; **el ~ llegado** the newcomer; **el ~ nacido** the newborn child.

reciente [resyen'te] *a* recent; (*fresco*) fresh.

recientemente [resyentemen'te] *ad* recently.

recinto [resēn'to] *nm* enclosure; (*área*) area, place.

recio, a [re'syo, á] *a* strong, tough; (*voz*) loud ♦ *ad* hard; loud(ly).

recipiente [resēpyen'te] *nm* (*objeto*) container, receptacle; (*persona*) recipient.

reciprocidad [resēprosētháth'] *nf* reciprocity.

recíproco, a [resē'proco, á] *a* reciprocal.

recital [resētál'] *nm* (*MUS*) recital; (*LIT*) reading.

recitar [resētár'] *vt* to recite.

reclamación [reklámásyon'] *nf* claim, demand; (*queja*) complaint; **~ salarial** pay claim.

reclamar [reklámár'] *vt* to claim, demand ♦ *vi:* **~ contra** to complain about; **~ a uno en justicia** to take sb to court.

reclamo [reklá'mo] *nm* (*anuncio*) advertisement; (*tentación*) attraction.

reclinar [reklēnár'] *vt* to recline, lean; **~se** *vr* to lean back.

recluir [reklōōēr'] *vt* to intern, confine.

reclusión [reklōōsyon'] *nf* (*prisión*) prison; (*refugio*) seclusion; **~ perpetua** life imprisonment.

recluso, a [reklōō'so, á] *a* imprisoned; **población reclusa** prison population ♦ *nm/f* (*solitario*) recluse; (*JUR*) prisoner.

recluta [reklōō'tá] *nm/f* recruit ♦ *nf* recruitment.

reclutamiento [reklōōtámyen'to] *nm* recruitment.

recluyendo [reklōōyen'do] *etc vb V* **recluir.**

recobrar [rekohrár'] *vt* (*recuperar*) to recover; (*rescatar*) to get back; (*ciudad*) to recapture; (*tiempo*) to make up (for); **~se** *vr* to recover.

recodo [reko'tho] *nm* (*de río, camino*) bend.

recogedor, a [rekohethor', á] *nm/f* picker, harvester.

recoger [rekoher'] *vt* to collect; (*AGR*) to harvest; (*fruta*) to pick; (*levantar*) to pick up; (*juntar*) to gather; (*pasar a buscar*) to come for, get; (*dar asilo*) to give shelter to; (*faldas*) to gather up; (*mangas*) to roll up; (*pelo*) to put up; **~se** *vr* (*retirarse*) to retire; **me recogieron en la estación** they picked me up at the station.

recogido, a [rekohē'tho, á] *a* (*lugar*) quiet, secluded; (*pequeño*) small ♦ *nf* (*CORREOS*) collection; (*AGR*) harvest; **recogida de datos** (*INFORM*) data capture.

recogimiento [rekohēmyen'to] *nm* collection; (*AGR*) harvesting.

recoja [reko'há] *etc vb V* **recoger.**

recolección [rekoleksyon'] *nf* (*AGR*) harvesting; (*colecta*) collection.

recomendable [rekomendá'hle] *a* recommendable; **poco ~** inadvisable.

recomendación [rekomendásyon'] *nf* (*sugerencia*) suggestion, recommendation; (*referencia*) reference; **carta de ~ para** letter of introduction to.

recomendar [rekomendár'] *vt* to suggest, recommend; (*confiar*) to entrust.

recomencé [rekomense'], **recomencemos** [rekomense'mos] *etc vb V* **recomenzar.**

recomenzar [rekomensár'] *vt, vi* to begin again, recommence.

recomience [rekomyen'se] *etc vb V* **recomenzar.**

recomiende [rekomyen'de] *etc vb V* **recomendar.**

recomienzo [rekomyen'so] *etc vb V* **recomenzar.**

recompensa [rekompen'sá] *nf* reward, recompense; (*compensación*): **~ (de una**

pérdida) compensation (for a loss); **como o en ~ por** in return for.

recompensar [rekompensár'] vt to reward, recompense.

recompondré [rekompondre'] etc vb V **recomponer.**

recomponer [rekomponer'] vt to mend; (INFORM: texto) to reformat.

recomponga [rekompon'gá] etc, **recompuesto** [rekompwe'sto], **recompuse** [rekompōō'se] etc vb V **recomponer.**

reconciliación [rekonsēlyásyon'] nf reconciliation.

reconciliar [rekonsēlyár'] vt to reconcile; **~se** vr to become reconciled.

recóndito, a [rekon'dēto, á] a (lugar) hidden, secret.

reconfortar [rekonfortár'] vt to comfort.

reconocer [rekonoser'] vt to recognize; **~ los hechos** to face the facts.

reconocido, a [rekonosē'tho, á] a recognized; (agradecido) grateful.

reconocimiento [rekonosēmyen'to] nm recognition; (registro) search; (inspección) examination; (gratitud) gratitude; (confesión) admission; **~ óptico de caracteres** (INFORM) optical character recognition; **~ de la voz** (INFORM) speech recognition.

reconozca [rekonos'ká] etc vb V **reconocer.**

reconquista [rekonkē'stá] nf reconquest.

reconquistar [rekonkēstár'] vt (MIL) to reconquer; (fig) to recover, win back.

reconstituyente [rekonstētōōyen'te] nm tonic.

reconstruir [rekonstrōōēr'] vt to reconstruct.

reconstruyendo [rekonstrōōyen'do] etc vb V **reconstruir.**

reconversión [rekombersyon'] nf restructuring, reorganization; (tb: **~ industrial**) modernization.

recopilación [rekopēlásyon'] nf (resumen) summary; (compilación) compilation.

recopilar [rekopēlár'] vt to compile.

récord [re'korth] a inv record; **cifras ~** record figures ♦ nm, pl **records, récords** [re'korth] record; **batir el ~** to break the record.

recordar [rekorthár'] vt (acordarse de) to remember; (traer a la memoria) to recall; (acordar a otro) to remind; **recuérdale que me debe 5 dólares** remind him that he owes me 5 dollars; **que yo recuerde** as far as I can remember; **creo ~, si mal no recuerdo** if my memory serves me right.

recorrer [rekorrer'] vt (país) to cross, travel through; (distancia) to cover; (registrar) to search; (repasar) to look over.

recorrido [rekorrē'tho] nm run, journey; **tren de largo ~** main-line train.

recortado, a [rekortá'tho, á] a uneven, irregular.

recortar [rekortár'] vt (papel) to cut out; (el pelo) to trim; (dibujar) to draw in outline; **~se** vr to stand out, be silhouetted.

recorte [rekor'te] nm (acción, de prensa) cutting; (de telas, chapas) trimming.

recostado, a [rekostá'tho, á] a leaning; **estar ~** to be lying down.

recostar [rekostár'] vt to lean; **~se** vr to lie down.

recoveco [rekohe'ko] nm (de camino, río etc) bend; (en casa) cubbyhole.

recreación [rekreásyon'] nf recreation.

recrear [rekreár'] vt (entretener) to entertain; (volver a crear) to re-create.

recreativo, a [rekreátē'ho, á] a recreational.

recreo [rekre'o] nm recreation; (ESCOL) recess (US), break (Brit).

recriminar [rekrēmēnár'] vt to reproach ♦ vi to recriminate; **~se** vr to reproach each other.

recrudecer [rekrōōthēser'] vt, vi, **recrudecerse** vr to worsen.

recrudecimiento [rekrōōthēsēmyen'to] nm upsurge.

recrudezca [recrōōthes'ká] etc vb V **recrudecer.**

recta [rek'tá] nf V **recto.**

rectángulo, a [rektán'gōōlo, á] a rectangular ♦ nm rectangle.

rectificable [rektēfēká'hle] a rectifiable; **fácilmente ~** easily rectified.

rectificación [rektēfēkásyon'] nf correction.

rectificar [rektēfēkár'] vt to rectify; (volverse recto) to straighten ♦ vi to correct o.s.

rectifique [rektēfē'ke] etc vb V **rectificar.**

rectitud [rektētōōth'] nf straightness; (fig) rectitude.

recto, a [rek'to, á] a straight; (persona) honest, upright; (estricto) strict; (juez) fair; (juicio) sound ♦ nm rectum; (ATLETISMO) straight ♦ nf straight line; **en el sentido ~ de la palabra** in the proper sense of the word; **recta final o de llegada** home straight.

rector, a [rektor', á] a governing ♦ nm/f head, chief; (ESCOL) president (US), rector (Brit).

rectorado [rektorá'tho] nm (cargo) presidency (US), rectorship (Brit); (oficina) rector's office.

recuadro [rekwá'thro] nm box; (TIP) inset.

recuento [rekwen'to] nm inventory; **hacer el ~ de** to count o reckon up.

recuerdo [rekwer'tho] etc vb V **recordar** ♦ nm souvenir; **~s** nmpl memories; **¡~s a tu madre!** give my regards to your mother!; **"R~ de Mallorca"** "a present from Majorca"; **contar los ~s** to reminisce.

recueste [rekwe'ste] *etc vb* V **recostar**.

recular [rekōōlár'] *vi* to back down.

recuperable [rekōōperá'ɦle] *a* recoverable.

recuperación [rekōōperásyon'] *nf* recovery; ~ **de datos** (*INFORM*) data retrieval.

recuperar [rekōōperár'] *vt* to recover; (*tiempo*) to make up; (*INFORM*) to retrieve; ~**se** *vr* to recuperate.

recurrir [rekōōrrēr'] *vi* (*JUR*) to appeal; ~ **a** to resort to; (*persona*) to turn to.

recurso [rekōōr'so] *nm* resort; (*medio*) means *pl*, resource; (*JUR*) appeal; **como último** ~ as a last resort; ~**s económicos** economic resources; ~**s naturales** natural resources.

recusar [rekōōsár'] *vt* to reject, refuse.

rechace [retchá'se] *etc vb* V **rechazar**.

rechazar [retchásár'] *vt* to repel, drive back; (*idea*) to reject; (*oferta*) to turn down.

rechazo [retchá'so] *nm* (*de fusil*) recoil; (*rebote*) rebound; (*negación*) rebuff.

rechifla [retchē'flá] *nf* hissing, booing; (*fig*) derision.

rechinar [retchēnár'] *vi* to creak; (*dientes*) to grind; (*máquina*) to clank, clatter; (*metal seco*) to grate; (*motor*) to hum.

rechistar [retchēstár'] *vi*: **sin** ~ without complaint.

rechoncho, a [retchontch'o, á] *a* (*fam*) stocky, heavy-set.

red [reth] *nf* net, mesh; (*FERRO*, *INFORM*) network; (*ELEC*, *de agua*) main (*US*), mains (*Brit*), supply system; (*de tiendas*) chain; (*trampa*) trap; **estar conectado con la** ~ to be connected to the main; ~ **local** (*INFORM*) local area network; ~ **de transmisión** (*INFORM*) data network.

redacción [retháksyon'] *nf* (*acción*) writing; (*ESCOL*) essay, composition; (*limpieza de texto*) editing; (*personal*) editorial staff.

redactar [retháktár'] *vt* to draw up, draft; (*periódico*, *INFORM*) to edit.

redactor, a [retháktor', á] *nm/f* writer; (*en periódico*) editor.

redada [thá'thá] *nf* (*PESCA*) cast, throw; (*fig*) catch; ~ **policial** police raid, round-up.

redención [rethensyon'] *nf* redemption.

redentor, a [rethentor', á] *a* redeeming ♦ *nm/f* (*COM*) redeemer.

redescubierto [retheskōōḃyer'to] *pp de* **redescubrir**.

redescubrir [retheskōōḃrēr'] *vt* to rediscover.

redesignar [rethesēḡnár'] *vt* (*INFORM*) to rename.

redicho, a [rethētch'o, á] *a* affected.

redil [rethēl'] *nm* sheep pen.

redimir [rethēmēr'] *vt* to redeem; (*rehén*) to ransom.

redistribución [rethēstrethōōsyon'] *nf* (*COM*) redeployment.

rédito [re'thēto] *nm* interest, yield.

redoblar [rethoḃlár'] *vt* to redouble ♦ *vi* (*tambor*) to play a roll on the drums.

redoble [retho'ḃle] *nm* (*MUS*) drumroll, drumbeat; (*de trueno*) roll.

redomado, a [rethomá'tho, á] *a* (*astuto*) sly, crafty; (*perfecto*) utter.

redonda [rethon'dá] *nf* V **redondo**.

redondear [rethondeár'] *vt* to round, round off; (*cifra*) to round up.

redondel [rethondel'] *nm* (*círculo*) circle; (*TAUR*) bullring, arena; (*AUTO*) (*traffic*) circle (*US*), roundabout (*Brit*).

redondo, a [rethon'do, á] *a* (*circular*) round; (*completo*) complete ♦ *nf*: **a la redonda** around, round about; **en muchas millas a la redonda** for many miles around; **rehusar en** ~ to give a flat refusal.

reducción [rethōōksyon'] *nf* reduction; ~ **del activo** (*COM*) divestment; ~ **de precios** (*COM*) price-cutting.

reducido, a [rethōōsē'tho, á] *a* reduced; (*limitado*) limited; (*pequeño*) small; **quedar ~ a** to be reduced to.

reducir [rethōōsēr'] *vt* to reduce, limit; (*someter*) to bring under control; ~**se** *vr* to diminish; (*MAT*): ~ **(a)** to reduce (to), convert (into); ~ **las millas a kilómetros** to convert miles into kilometers; ~**se a** (*fig*) to come o boil down to.

reduje [rethōō'he] *etc vb* V **reducir**.

redundancia [rethōōndán'syá] *nf* redundancy.

reduzca [rethōōs'ká] *etc vb* V **reducir**.

reembolsable [re(e)mbolsá'ɦle] *a* (*COM*) redeemable, refundable.

reembolsar [re(e)mbolsár'] *vt* (*persona*) to reimburse; (*dinero*) to repay, pay back; (*depósito*) to refund.

reembolso [re(e)mbol'so] *nm* reimbursement; refund; **enviar algo contra** ~ to send sth cash on delivery; **contra** ~ **del flete** freight C.O.D.; ~ **fiscal** tax rebate.

reemplace [re(e)mplá'se] *etc vb* V **reemplazar**.

reemplazar [re(e)mplásár'] *vt* to replace.

reemplazo [re(e)mplá'so] *nm* replacement; **de** ~ (*MIL*) reserve.

reexportación [re(e)ksportásyon'] *nf* (*COM*) re-export.

reexportar [re(e)ksportár'] *vt* (*COM*) to re-export.

REF *nm abr* (*Esp ECON*) = *Régimen Económico Fiscal*.

Ref.ª *abr* (= *referencia*) ref.

referencia [referen'syá] *nf* reference; **con** ~ **a** with reference to; **hacer** ~ **a** to refer o allude to; ~ **comercial** (*COM*) trade reference.

referéndum [referen'dōōm], *pl* **referéndums** *nm* referendum.

referente |referen'te| *a*: ~ **a** concerning, relating to.

referir |referēr'| *vt* (*contar*) to tell, recount; (*relacionar*) to refer, relate; ~**se** *vr*: ~**se a** to refer to; ~ **al lector a un apéndice** to refer the reader to an appendix; ~ **a** (*COM*) to convert into; **por lo que se refiere a eso** as for that, as regards that.

refiera |refyc'rá| *etc vb V* **referir**.

refilón |refēlon'|: **de** ~ *ad* obliquely; **mirar a uno de** ~ to look out of the corner of one's eye at sb.

refinado, a |refēná'tho, á| *a* refined.

refinamiento |refēnámyen'to| *nm* refinement; ~ **por pasos** (*INFORM*) step by step debugging.

refinar |refēnár'| *vt* to refine.

refinería |refēncrē'á| *nf* refinery.

refiriendo |refēryen'do| *etc vb V* **referir**.

reflector |reflektor'| *nm* reflector; (*ELEC*) spotlight; (*AVIAT, MIL*) searchlight.

reflejar |reflchár'| *vt* to reflect; ~**se** *vr* to be reflected.

reflejo, a |reflc'ho, á| *a* reflected; (*movimiento*) reflex ♦ *nm* reflection; (*ANAT*) reflex; (*en el pelo*): ~**s** *nmpl* highlights; **tiene el pelo castaño con** ~**s rubios** she has chestnut hair with blond streaks.

reflexión |reflcksyon'| *nf* reflection.

reflexionar |reflcksyonár'| *vt* to reflect on ♦ *vi* to reflect; (*detenerse*) to pause (to think); **¡reflexione!** you think it over!

reflexivo, a |reflcksē'ho, á| *a* thoughtful; (*LING*) reflexive.

refluir |reflōoēr'| *vi* to flow back.

reflujo |reflōo'ho| *nm* ebb.

refluyendo |reflōoyen'do| *etc vb V* **refluir**.

reforcé |reforsc'|, **reforcemos** |reforsc'mos| *etc vb V* **reforzar**.

reforma |refor'má| *nf* reform; (*ARQ etc*) repair; ~ **agraria** agrarian reform.

reformar |reformár'| *vt* to reform; (*modificar*) to change, alter; (*texto*) to revise; (*ARQ*) to repair; ~**se** *vr* to mend one's ways.

reformatear |reformátcár'| *vt* (*INFORM*: *disco*) to reformat.

reformatorio |reformáto'ryo| *nm* reformatory; ~ **de menores** reform school (*US*), remand home (*Brit*).

reforzamiento |reforsámyen'to| *nm* reinforcement.

reforzar |reforsár'| *vt* to strengthen; (*ARQ*) to reinforce; (*fig*) to encourage.

refractario, a |refráktá'ryo, á| *a* (*TEC*) heat-resistant; **ser** ~ **a una reforma** to resist *o* be opposed to a reform.

refrán |refrán'| *nm* proverb, saying.

refregar |refrcgár'| *vt* to scrub.

refregué |refrcgc'|, **refreguemos** |refrcgc'mos| *etc vb V* **refregar**.

refrenar |refrenár'| *vt* to check, restrain.

refrendar |refrendár'| *vt* (*firma*) to endorse, countersign; (*ley*) to approve.

refrescante |refreskán'te| *a* refreshing, cooling.

refrescar |refreskár'| *vt* to refresh ♦ *vi* to cool down; ~**se** *vr* to get cooler; (*tomar aire fresco*) to go out for a breath of fresh air; (*beber*) to have a drink.

refresco |refres'ko| *nm* soft drink, cool drink; "~**s**" "refreshments".

refresque |refres'kc| *etc vb V* **refrescar**.

refriega |refryc'gá| *etc vb V* **refregar** ♦ *nf* scuffle, brawl.

refriegue |refryc'gc| *etc vb V* **refregar**.

refrigeración |refrēhcrásyon'| *nf* refrigeration; (*de casa*) air-conditioning.

refrigerado, a |refrēhcrá'tho, á| *a* cooled; (*sala*) air-conditioned.

refrigerador |refrēhcráthor'| *nm*, (*AM*) **refrigeradora** |refrēhcrátho'rá| *nf* refrigerator.

refrigerar |refrēhcrár'| *vt* to refrigerate; (*sala*) to air-condition.

refuerce |refwer'sc| *etc vb V* **reforzar**.

refuerzo |refwer'so| *etc vb V* **reforzar** ♦ *nm* reinforcement; (*TEC*) support.

refugiado, a |refōōhyá'tho, á| *nm/f* refugee.

refugiarse |refōōhyár'sc| *vr* to take refuge, shelter.

refugio |refōō'hyo| *nm* refuge; (*protección*) shelter; (*AUTO*) street *o* traffic island; ~ **alpino** *o* **de montaña** mountain hut; ~ **subterráneo** (*MIL*) underground shelter.

refulgencia |refōōlhcn'syá| *nf* brilliance.

refulgir |refōōlhēr'| *vi* to shine, be dazzling.

refulja |refōōl'há| *etc vb V* **refulgir**.

refundir |refōōndēr'| *vt* to recast; (*escrito etc*) to adapt, rewrite.

refunfuñar |refōōnfōōnyár'| *vi* to grunt, growl; (*quejarse*) to grumble.

refunfuñón, ona |refōōnfōōnyon', oná| (*fam*) *a* grumpy ♦ *nm/f* grouch.

refutación |refōōtásyon'| *nf* refutation.

refutar |refōōtár'| *vt* to refute.

regadera |regáthc'rá| *nf* watering can; **estar como una** ~ (*fam*) to be as mad as a hatter.

regadío |regáthē'o| *nm* irrigated land.

regalado, a |regálá'tho, á| *a* comfortable, luxurious; (*gratis*) free, for nothing; **lo tuvo** ~ it was handed to him on a plate.

regalar |regálár'| *vt* (*dar*) to give (as a present); (*entregar*) to give away; (*mimar*) to pamper, make a fuss of; ~**se** *vr* to treat o.s. to.

regalía |regálē'á| *nf* privilege, prerogative; (*COM*) bonus; (*de autor*) royalty.

regaliz |regálēs'| *nm* licorice.

regalo |regá'lo| *nm* (*obsequio*) gift, present; (*gusto*) pleasure; (*comodidad*) comfort.

regalón, ona |regálon', oná| *a* spoiled,

pampered.
regañadientes [reɣányáðyen'tes]: **a** ~ *ad* reluctantly.
regañar [reɣanyár'] *vt* to scold ♦ *vi* to grumble; (*dos personas*) to fall out, quarrel.
regaño [reɣa'nyo] *nm* scolding, telling-off; (*queja*) grumble.
regañón, ona [reɣanyon', oná] *a* nagging.
regar [reɣár'] *vt* to water, irrigate; (*fig*) to scatter, sprinkle.
regata [reɣa'tá] *nf* (NAUT) race.
regatear [reɣateár'] *vt* (COM) to bargain over; (*escatimar*) to be mean with ♦ *vi* to bargain, haggle; (DEPORTE) to dribble; **no** ~ **esfuerzo** to spare no effort.
regateo [reɣáte'o] *nm* bargaining; (DE-PORTE) dribbling; (*del cuerpo*) swerve, dodge.
regazo [reɣa'so] *nm* lap.
regeneración [rehenerásyon'] *nf* regeneration.
regenerar [renenerár'] *vt* to regenerate.
regentar [rehentár'] *vt* to direct, manage; (*puesto*) to hold in an acting capacity; (*negocio*) to be in charge of.
regente, a [rehen'te, á] *a* (*príncipe*) regent; (*director*) managing ♦ *nm* (COM) manager; (POL) regent.
régimen [re'hēmen], *pl* **regímenes** [rehē'menes] *nm* regime; (*reinado*) rule; (MED) diet; (*reglas*) (set of) rules; (*manera de vivir*) lifestyle; **estar a** ~ to be on a diet.
regimiento [rehēmyen'to] *nm* regiment.
regio, a [re'hyo, á] *a* royal, regal; (*fig: suntuoso*) splendid; (AM fam) great, terrific.
región [rehyon'] *nf* region; (*área*) area.
regional [rehyonál'] *a* regional.
regir [rehēr'] *vt* to govern, rule; (*dirigir*) to manage, run; (ECON, JUR, LING) to govern ♦ *vi* to apply, be in force.
registrador [rehēstráðhor'] *nm* registrar, recorder.
registrar [rehēstrár'] *vt* (*buscar*) to search; (*en cajón*) to look through; (*inspeccionar*) to inspect; (*anotar*) to register, record; (IN-FORM, MUS) to record; ~**se** *vr* to register; (*ocurrir*) to happen.
registro [rehēs'tro] *nm* (*acto*) registration; (MUS, *libro*) register; (*lista*) list, record; (INFORM) record; (*inspección*) inspection, search; ~ **civil** ≈ county clerk's office (US), registry office (Brit); ~ **electoral** list of registered voters; ~ **de la propiedad** ≈ county recorder's office (US), land registry (office) (Brit).
regla [re'ɣlá] *nf* (*ley*) rule, regulation; (*de medir*) ruler, rule; (MED: *período*) period; (~ *científica*) law, principle; **no hay** ~ **sin excepción** every rule has its exception.

reglamentación [reɣlámentásyon'] *nf* (*acto*) regulation; (*lista*) rules *pl*.
reglamentar [reɣlámentár'] *vt* to regulate.
reglamentario, a [reɣlámentá'ryo, á] *a* statutory; **en la forma reglamentaria** in the properly established way.
reglamento [reɣlámen'to] *nm* rules *pl*, regulations *pl*; ~ **del tráfico** highway code.
reglar [reɣlár'] *vt* (*acciones*) to regulate; ~**se** *vr*: ~**se por** to be guided by.
regocijarse [reɣosēhár'se] *vr*: ~ **de** *o* **por** to rejoice at, be glad about.
regocijo [reɣosē'ho] *nm* joy, happiness.
regodearse [reɣoðheár'se] *vr* to be glad, be delighted; (*pey*): ~ **con** *o* **en** to gloat over.
regodeo [reɣoðhe'o] *nm* delight; (*pey*) perverse pleasure.
regresar [reɣresár'] *vi* to come/go back, return.
regresivo, a [reɣresē'ko, á] *a* backward; (*fig*) regressive.
regreso [reɣre'so] *nm* return; **estar de** ~ to be back, be home.
regué [reɣe'], **reguemos** [reɣe'mos] *etc vb V* **regar**.
reguero [reɣe'ro] *nm* (*de sangre*) trickle; (*de humo*) trail.
regulación [reɣōōlásyon'] *nf* regulation; (TEC) adjustment; (*control*) control; ~ **del tráfico** traffic control.
regulador [reɣōōláðhor'] *nm* (TEC) regulator; (*de radio etc*) knob.
regular [reɣōōlár'] *a* regular; (*normal*) normal, usual; (*común*) ordinary; (*organizado*) regular, orderly; (*mediano*) average; (*fam*) not bad, so-so ♦ *ad*: **estar** ~ to be so-so *o* alright ♦ *vt* (*controlar*) to control, regulate; (TEC) to adjust; **por lo** ~ as a rule.
regularice [reɣōōlárē'se] *etc vb V* **regularizar**.
regularidad [reɣōōláréðháð'] *nf* regularity; **con** ~ regularly.
regularizar [reɣōōláresár'] *vt* to regularize.
regusto [reɣōō'sto] *nm* aftertaste.
rehabilitación [reáhēlētásyon'] *nf* rehabilitation; (ARQ) restoration.
rehabilitar [reáhēlētár'] *vt* to rehabilitate; (ARQ) to restore; (*reintegrar*) to reinstate.
rehacer [reáser'] *vt* (*reparar*) to mend, repair; (*volver a hacer*) to redo, repeat; ~**se** *vr* (MED) to recover.
rehaga [reá'ɣá] *etc*, **reharé** [reáre'] *etc*, **rehaz** [reás'], **rehecho** [reetch'o] *vb V* **rehacer**.
rehén [reen'] *nm* hostage.
rehice [reē'se] *etc*, **rehizo** [reē'so] *vb V* **rehacer**.
rehuir [reōōēr'] *vt* to avoid, shun.
rehusar [reōōsár'] *vt, vi* to refuse.
rehuyendo [reōōyen'do] *etc vb V* **rehuir**.
reina [re'ēná] *nf* queen.

reinado [reēnáˈt̯ho] *nm* reign.
reinante [reēnánˈte] *a* (*fig*) prevailing.
reinar [reēnárˈ] *vi* to reign; (*fig: prevalecer*) to prevail, be general.
reincidir [reēnseˈt̯herˈ] *vi* to relapse; (*criminal*) to repeat an offence.
reincorporarse [reēnkorporárˈse] *vr*: ~ **a** to rejoin.
reinicializar [reēnēsyàlēsárˈ] *vt* (*INFORM*) to reset.
reino [reˈēno] *nm* kingdom; **el R~ Unido** the United Kingdom.
reintegración [reēntegrásyon'] *nf* (*COM*) reinstatement.
reintegrar [reēntegràrˈ] *vt* (*reconstituir*) to reconstruct; (*persona*) to reinstate; (*dinero*) to refund, pay back; ~**se** *vr*: ~**se a** to return to.
reintegro [reēnteˈgro] *nm* refund, reimbursement; (*en banco*) withdrawal.
reír [reērˈ] *vi*, **reírse** *vr* to laugh; ~**se de** to laugh at.
reiterar [reēterárˈ] *vt* to reiterate; (*repetir*) to repeat.
reivindicación [reēhēndēkásyon'] *nf* (*demanda*) claim, demand; (*justificación*) vindication.
reivindicar [reēhēndēkárˈ] *vt* to claim.
reivindique [reēhēndēˈke] *etc vb V* **reivindicar.**
reja [reˈhá] *nf* (*de ventana*) grille, bars *pl*; (*en la calle*) grating.
rejamos [rehá'mos] *etc vb V* **regir.**
rejilla [rehēˈyà] *nf* grating, grille; (*muebles*) wickerwork; (*de ventilación*) vent; (*de coche etc*) luggage rack.
rejuvenecer [rehōō̆keneserˈ] *vt*, *vi* to rejuvenate.
rejuvenezca [rehōō̆kenes'kà] *etc vb V* **rejuvenecer.**
relación [rclásyon'] *nf* relation, relationship; (*MAT*) ratio; (*lista*) list; (*narración*) report; ~ **costo-efectivo** *o* **costo-rendimiento** (*COM*) cost-effectiveness; **relaciones** *nfpl* (*enchufes*) influential friends, connections; **relaciones carnales** sexual relations; **relaciones comerciales** business connections; **relaciones empresariales/humanas** industrial/human relations; **relaciones laborales/públicas** labor/public relations; **con ~ a, en ~ con** in relation to; **estar en** *o* **tener buenas relaciones con** to be on good terms with.
relacionar [rclásyonàrˈ] *vt* to relate, connect; ~**se** *vr* to be connected *o* linked.
relajación [relàhásyon'] *nf* relaxation.
relajado, a [relàháˈt̯ho, à] *a* (*disoluto*) loose; (*cómodo*) relaxed; (*MED*) ruptured.
relajante [relàhán'te] *a* relaxing; (*MED*) sedative.
relajar [relàhárˈ] *vt*, **relajarse** *vr* to relax.

relamerse [rclámer'se] *vr* to lick one's lips.
relamido, a [rclámēˈt̯ho, à] *a* (*pulcro*) overdressed; (*afectado*) affected.
relámpago [rclám'pàgo] *nm* flash of lightning ♦ *a* lightning *cpd*; **como un ~** as quick as lightning, in a flash; **visita/huelga ~** lightning visit/strike.
relampaguear [rclámpàgeár'] *vi* to flash.
relatar [relàtár'] *vt* to tell, relate.
relativo, a [relàtē'ho, à] *a* relative; **en lo ~ a** concerning.
relato [relà'to] *nm* (*narración*) story, tale.
relegar [relegár'] *vt* to relegate; ~ **algo al olvido** to banish sth from one's mind.
relegue [rele'ge] *etc vb V* **relegar.**
relevante [relehán'te] *a* eminent, outstanding.
relevar [relehár'] *vt* (*sustituir*) to relieve; ~**se** *vr* to relay; ~ **a uno de un cargo** to relieve sb of his post.
relevo [rele'ho] *nm* relief; **carrera de ~s** relay race; **~ con cinta** (*INFORM*) tape relay; **coger** *o* **tomar el ~** to take over, stand in.
relieve [relye'he] *nm* (*ARTE, TEC*) relief; (*fig*) prominence, importance; **bajo ~** bas-relief; **un personaje de ~** an important man; **dar ~ a** to highlight.
religión [relēhyon'] *nf* religion.
religioso, a [relēhyo'so, à] *a* religious ♦ *nm/f* monk/nun.
relinchar [relēntchár'] *vi* to neigh.
relincho [relēntch'o] *nm* neigh; (*acto*) neighing.
reliquia [relē'kyà] *nf* relic; ~ **de familia** heirloom.
reloj [relo'(h)] *nm* clock; ~ **de pie** grandfather clock; ~ **(de pulsera)** wristwatch; ~ **de sol** sundial; ~ **despertador** alarm (clock); **como un ~** like clockwork; **contra (el) ~** against the clock.
relojería [relohēˈá] (*tienda*) watchmaker's (shop); **aparato de ~** clockwork; **bomba de ~** time bomb.
relojero, a [relohe'ro, à] *nm/f* clockmaker; watchmaker.
reluciente [relōōsyen'te] *a* brilliant, shining.
relucir [relōōsēr'] *vi* to shine; (*fig*) to excel; **sacar algo a ~** to show sth off.
relumbrante [relōōmbrán'te] *a* dazzling.
relumbrar [relōōmbrár'] *vi* to dazzle, shine brilliantly.
reluzca [relōōs'kà] *etc vb V* **relucir.**
rellano [reyà'no] *nm* (*ARQ*) landing.
rellenar [reyenár'] *vt* (*llenar*) to fill up; (*CULIN*) to stuff; (*COSTURA*) to pad; (*formulario etc*) to fill in *o* out.
relleno, a [reye'no, à] *a* full up; (*CULIN*) stuffed ♦ *nm* stuffing; (*de tapicería*) padding.
remachar [remátchár'] *vt* to rivet; (*fig*) to

hammer home, drive home.
remache [remátch'e] *nm* rivet.
remanente [remánen'te] *nm* remainder; (*COM*) balance; (*de producto*) surplus.
remanso [remán'so] *nm* pool.
remar [remár'] *vi* to row.
rematado, a [rematá'ðo, á] *a* complete, utter; **es un loco** ~ he's a raving lunatic.
rematar [rematár'] *vt* to finish off; (*animal*) to put out of its misery; (*COM*) to sell off cheap ♦ *vi* to end, finish off; (*DEPORTE*) to shoot.
remate [remá'te] *nm* end, finish; (*punta*) tip; (*DEPORTE*) shot; (*ARQ*) top; (*COM*) auction sale; **de** *o* **para** ~ to top it all off.
remediable [remeðyá'ßle] *a*: **fácilmente** ~ easily remedied.
remediar [remeðyár'] *vt* (*gen*) to remedy; (*subsanar*) to make good, repair; (*evitar*) to avoid; **sin poder ~lo** without being able to prevent it.
remedio [remeˈðyo] *nm* remedy; (*JUR*) recourse, remedy; **poner** ~ **a** to correct, stop; **no tener más** ~ to have no alternative; **¡qué** ~! there's no other way; **como último** ~ as a last resort; **sin** ~ inevitable; (*MED*) hopeless.
remedo [remeˈðo] *nm* imitation; (*pey*) parody.
remendar [remendár'] *vt* to repair; (*con parche*) to patch; (*fig*) to correct.
remesa [remeˈsá] *nf* remittance; (*COM*) shipment.
remiendo [remyen'do] *etc vb V* **remendar** ♦ *nm* mend; (*con parche*) patch; (*cosido*) darn; (*fig*) correction.
remilgado, a [remílgá'ðo, á] *a* prim; (*afectado*) affected.
remilgo [remíl'go] *nm* primness; (*afectación*) affectation.
reminiscencia [remēnēsen'syá] *nf* reminiscence.
remirar [remirár'] *vt* (*volver a mirar*) to look at again; (*examinar*) to look hard at.
remisión [remēsyon'] *nf* (*acto*) sending, shipment; (*REL*) forgiveness, remission; **sin** ~ hopelessly.
remiso, a [remeˈso, á] *a* remiss.
remite [remēˈte] *nm* (*en sobre*) name and address of sender.
remitente [remēten'te] *nm/f* (*CORREOS*) sender.
remitir [remētēr'] *vt* to remit, send ♦ *vi* to slacken.
remo [re'mo] *nm* (*de barco*) oar; (*DEPORTE*) rowing; **cruzar un río a** ~ to row across a river.
remoce [remo'se] *etc vb V* **remozar**.
remodelación [remodelásyon'] *nf* (*POL*): ~ **del gobierno** cabinet reshuffle.
remojar [remohár'] *vt* to steep, soak; (*galle-*

ta etc) to dip, dunk; (*fam*) to celebrate with a drink.
remojo [remo'ho] *nm* steeping, soaking; (*por la lluvia*) drenching, soaking; **dejar la ropa en** ~ to leave clothes to soak.
remojón [remohon'] *nm* soaking; **darse un** ~ (*fam*) to go (in) for a dip.
remolacha [remolátch'á] *nf* beet, beetroot (*Brit*).
remolcador [remolkáðhor'] *nm* (*NAUT*) tug; (*AUTO*) tow truck (*US*), breakdown lorry (*Brit*).
remolcar [remolkár'] *vt* to tow.
remolino [remolē'no] *nm* eddy; (*de agua*) whirlpool; (*de viento*) whirlwind; (*de gente*) crowd.
remolón, ona [remolon', oná] *a* lazy ♦ *nm/f* slacker, shirker.
remolque [remol'ke] *etc vb V* **remolcar** ♦ *nm* tow, towing; (*cuerda*) towrope; **llevar a** ~ to tow.
remontar [remontár'] *vt* to mend; (*obstáculo*) to overcome; ~**se** *vr* to soar; ~**se a** (*COM*) to amount to; (*en tiempo*) to go back to, date from; ~ **el vuelo** to soar.
rémora [re'morá] *nf* hindrance.
remorder [remorðer'] *vt* to distress, disturb.
remordimiento [remorðēmyen'to] *nm* remorse.
remotamente [remotámen'te] *ad* vaguely.
remoto, a [remo'to, á] *a* remote.
remover [remoßer'] *vt* to stir; (*tierra*) to turn over; (*objetos*) to move round.
remozar [remosár'] *vt* (*ARQ*) to refurbish; (*fig*) to brighten *o* polish up.
remuerda [remwer'ðá] *etc vb V* **remorder**.
remueva [remwe'ßá] *etc vb V* **remover**.
remuneración [remōōnerásyon'] *nf* remuneration.
remunerado, a [remōōnerá'ðo, á] *a*: **trabajo bien/mal** ~ well-/badly-paid job.
remunerar [remōōnerár'] *vt* to remunerate; (*premiar*) to reward.
renacer [renáser'] *vi* to be reborn; (*fig*) to revive.
renacimiento [renásēmyen'to] *nm* rebirth; **el R**~ the Renaissance.
renacuajo [renákwá'ho] *nm* (*ZOOL*) tadpole.
renal [renál'] *a* renal, kidney *cpd*.
Renania [rená'nyá] *nf* Rhineland.
renazca [renás'ká] *etc vb V* **renacer**.
rencilla [rense'yá] *nf* quarrel; ~**s** *nfpl* bickering *sg*.
rencor [renkor'] *nm* rancor (*US*), rancour (*Brit*), bitterness; (*resentimiento*) ill feeling, resentment; **guardar** ~ **a** to hold a grudge against.
rencoroso, a [renkoro'so, á] *a* spiteful.
rendición [rendēsyon'] *nf* surrender.

rendido, a |rendē'tho, á| a (sumiso) submissive; (agotado) worn-out, exhausted; (enamorado) devoted.

rendija |rendē'há| nf (hendedura) crack; (abertura) aperture; (fig) rift, split; (JUR) loophole.

rendimiento |rendēmyen'to| nm (producción) output; (COM) yield, profit(s) (pl); (TEC, COM) efficiency; ~ **de capital** (COM) return on capital.

rendir |rendēr'| vt (vencer) to defeat; (producir) to produce; (dar beneficio) to yield; (agotar) to exhaust ♦ vi to pay; (COM) to yield, produce; ~**se** vr (someterse) to surrender; (ceder) to yield; (cansarse) to wear o.s. out; ~ **homenaje** o **culto a** to pay homage to; **el negocio no rinde** the business doesn't pay.

renegado, a |renegá'tho, á| a, nm/f renegade.

renegar |renegár'| vt (negar) to deny vigorously ♦ vi (blasfemar) to blaspheme; ~ **de** (renunciar) to renounce; (quejarse) to complain about.

renegué |renege'|, **reneguemos** |renege'mos| etc vb V **renegar**.

RENFE |ren'fe| nf abr Esp:=Red Nacional de Ferrocarriles Españoles.

renglón |renglon'| nm (línea) line; (COM) item, article; **a ~ seguido** immediately after.

reniego |renye'go| etc, **reniegue** |renye'ge| etc vb V **renegar**.

reno |re'no| nm reindeer.

renombrado, a |renombrá'tho, á| a renowned.

renombre |renom'bre| nm renown.

renovación |renohásyon'| nf (de contrato) renewal; (ARQ) renovation.

renovar |renobár'| vt to renew; (ARQ) to renovate; (sala) to redecorate.

renquear |renkeár'| vi to limp; (fam) to get along, scrape by.

renta |ren'tá| nf (ingresos) income; (beneficio) profit; (alquiler) rent; **política de ~s** income (US) o incomes (Brit) policy; ~ **gravable** o **imponible** taxable income; ~ **nacional (bruta)** (gross) national income; ~ **no salarial** unearned income; ~ **sobre el terreno** (COM) paid to owner of land; **vivir de sus ~s** to live on one's private income; ~ **vitalicia** annuity.

rentable |rentá'ble| a profitable; **no ~** unprofitable.

rentar |rentár'| vt to produce, yield.

rentista |rentē'stá| nm/f (accionista) stockholder.

renuencia |renwen'syá| nf reluctance.

renuente |renwen'te| a reluctant.

renueve |renwe'he| etc vb V **renovar**.

renuncia |renōōn'syá| nf resignation.

renunciar |renōōnsyár'| vt to renounce, give up ♦ vi to resign; ~ **a hacer algo** to give up doing sth.

reñido, a |renye'tho, á| a (batalla) bitter, hard-fought; **estar ~ con uno** to be on bad terms with sb; **está ~ con su familia** he has fallen out with his family.

reñir |renyēr'| vt (regañar) to scold ♦ vi (estar peleado) to quarrel, fall out; (combatir) to fight.

reo |re'o| nm/f culprit, offender; (JUR) accused.

reojo |reo'ho|: **de ~** ad out of the corner of one's eye.

reorganice |reorgánē'se| etc vb V **reorganizar**.

reorganizar |reorgánēsár'| vt to reorganize.

Rep abr = **República**.

reparación |repárásyon'| nf (acto) mending, repairing; (TEC) repair; (fig) amends, reparation; **"reparaciones en el acto"** "repairs while you wait".

reparar |repárár'| vt to repair; (fig) to make amends for; (suerte) to retrieve; (observar) to observe ♦ vi: ~ **en** (darse cuenta de) to notice; (poner atención en) to pay attention to; **sin ~ en los gastos** regardless of the cost.

reparo |repá'ro| nm (advertencia) observation; (duda) doubt; (dificultad) difficulty; (escrúpulo) scruple, qualm; **poner ~s (a)** to raise objections (to); (criticar) to criticize; **no tuvo ~ en hacerlo** he did not hesitate to do it.

repartición |repártēsyon'| nf distribution; (división) division.

repartidor, a |repártēthor', á| nm/f distributor; ~ **de leche** milkman.

repartir |repártēr'| vt to distribute, share out; (COM, CORREOS) to deliver; (MIL) to partition; (libros) to give out; (comida) to serve out; (naipes) to deal.

reparto |repár'to| nm distribution; (COM, CORREOS) delivery; (TEATRO, CINE) cast; (AM: urbanización) housing development (US), housing estate (Brit); **"~ a domicilio"** "home delivery service".

repasar |repásár'| vt (ESCOL) to revise; (MECÁNICA) to check, overhaul; (COSTURA) to mend.

repaso |repá'so| nm revision; (MECÁNICA) overhaul, checkup; (COSTURA) mending; ~ **general** servicing, general overhaul; **curso de ~** refresher course.

repatriar |repátryár'| vt to repatriate; ~**se** vr to return home.

repelente |repelen'te| a repellent, repulsive.

repeler |repeler'| vt to repel; (idea, oferta) to reject.

repensar |repensár'| vt to reconsider.

repente |repen'te| nm sudden movement;

(*fig*) impulse; **de ~** suddenly; **~ de ira** fit of anger.

repentice |rcpcntē'sc| *etc vb* V **repentizar**.

repentino, a |rcpcntē'no, á| *a* sudden; (*imprevisto*) unexpected.

repentizar |rcpcntēsár'| *vi* (*MUS*) to sight-read.

repercusión |rcpcrkōōsyon'| *nf* repercussion; **de amplia** *o* **ancha ~** far-reaching.

repercutir |rcpcrkōōtēr'| *vi* (*objeto*) to rebound; (*sonido*) to echo; **~ en** (*fig*) to have repercussions *o* effects on.

repertorio |rcpcrto'ryo| *nm* list; (*TEATRO*) repertoire.

repetición |rcpctēsyon'| *nf* repetition.

repetido, a |rcpctē'tho, á| *a* repeated; **repetidas veces** repeatedly.

repetir |rcpctēr'| *vt* to repeat; (*plato*) to have a second helping of; (*TEATRO*) to give as an encore, sing *etc* again ♦ *vi* to repeat; **~se** *vr* to repeat o.s.; (*suceso*) to recur.

repetitivo, a |rcpctētē'tho, á| *a* repetitive, repetitious.

repicar |rcpēkár'| *vi* (*campanas*) to ring (out).

repiense |rcpycn'sc| *etc vb* V **repensar**.

repique |rcpē'kc| *etc vb* V **repicar** ♦ *nm* pealing, ringing.

repiqueteo |rcpēkctc'o| *nm* pealing; (*de tambor*) drumming.

repisa |rcpē'sá| *nf* ledge, shelf; **~ de chimenea** mantelpiece; **~ de ventana** windowsill.

repitiendo |rcpētycn'do| *etc vb* V **repetir**.

replegarse |rcplcg̃ár'sc| *vr* to fall back, retreat.

replegué |rcplcg̃c'|, **repleguemos** |rcplcg̃c'mos| *etc vb* V **replegarse**.

repleto, a |rcplc'to, á| *a* replete, full up; **~ de** filled *o* crammed with.

réplica |rc'plēká| *nf* answer; (*ARTE*) replica; **derecho de ~** right of *o* to reply.

replicar |rcplēkár'| *vi* to answer; (*objetar*) to argue, answer back.

repliego |rcplyc'g̃o| *etc vb* V **replegarse**.

repliegue |rcplyc'g̃c| *etc vb* V **replegarse** ♦ *nm* (*MIL*) withdrawal.

replique |rcplē'kc| *etc vb* V **replicar**.

repoblación |rcpobḷásyon'| *nf* repopulation; (*de río*) restocking; **~ forestal** reforestation.

repoblar |rcpobḷár'| *vt* to repopulate; to restock.

repollo |rcpo'yo| *nm* cabbage.

repondré |rcpondrc'| *etc vb* V **reponer**.

reponer |rcponcr'| *vt* to replace, put back; (*máquina*) to re-set; (*TEATRO*) to revive; **~se** *vr* to recover; **~ que** to reply that.

reponga |rcpon'g̃á| *etc vb* V **reponer**.

reportaje |rcportá'hc| *nm* report, article; **~ gráfico** illustrated report.

reportar |rcportár'| *vt* (*traer*) to bring,

carry; (*conseguir*) to obtain; (*fig*) to check; **~se** *vr* (*contenerse*) to control o.s.; (*calmarse*) to calm down; **la cosa no le reportó sino disgustos** the affair brought him nothing but trouble.

reportero, a |rcportc'ro, á| *nm/f* reporter; **~ gráfico/a** news photographer.

reposacabezas |rcposákáhc'sás| *nm inv* headrest.

reposado, a |rcposá'tho, á| *a* (*descansado*) restful; (*tranquilo*) calm.

reposar |rcposár'| *vi* to rest, repose; (*muerto*) to lie, rest.

reposición |rcposēsyon'| *nf* replacement; (*CINE*) second showing; (*TEATRO*) revival.

reposo |rcpo'so| *nm* rest.

repostar |rcpostár'| *vt* to replenish; (*AUTO*) to fill up (with gasoline).

repostería |rcpostcrē'á| *nf* (*arte*) confectionery, pastry-making; (*tienda*) confectioner's (shop).

repostero, a |rcpostc'ro, á| *nm/f* confectioner.

reprender |rcprcndcr'| *vt* to reprimand; (*niño*) to scold.

reprensión |rcprcnsyon'| *nf* rebuke, reprimand; (*de niño*) telling-off, scolding.

represa |rcprc'sá| *nf* dam; (*lago artificial*) lake, pool.

represalia |rcprcsá'lyá| *nf* reprisal; **tomar ~s** to take reprisals, retaliate.

representación |rcprcscntásyon'| *nf* representation; (*TEATRO*) performance; **en ~ de** representing; **por ~** by proxy; **~ visual** (*INFORM*) display.

representante |rcprcscntán'tc| *nm/f* (*POL, COM*) representative; (*TEATRO*) performer.

representar |rcprcscntár'| *vt* to represent; (*significar*) to mean; (*TEATRO*) to perform; (*edad*) to look; **~se** *vr* to imagine; **tal acto representaría la guerra** such an act would mean war.

representativo, a |rcprcscntátē'tho, á| *a* representative.

represión |rcprcsyon'| *nf* repression.

reprimenda |rcprēmcn'dá| *nf* reprimand, rebuke.

reprimir |rcprēmēr'| *vt* to repress; **~se** *vr*: **~se de hacer algo** to stop o.s. from doing sth.

reprobación |rcprobásyon'| *nf* reproval; (*culpa*) blame.

reprobar |rcprobár'| *vt* to censure, reprove.

réprobo, a |rc'probo, á| *nm/f* reprobate.

reprochar |rcprotchár'| *vt* to reproach; (*censurar*) to condemn, censure.

reproche |rcprotch'c| *nm* reproach.

reproducción |rcprothōōksyon'| *nf* reproduction.

reproducir |rcprothōōsēr'| *vt* to reproduce; **~se** *vr* to breed; (*situación*) to recur.

reproductor, a [reproðꞯöktor', á] *a* reproductive.

reproduje [reproðꞯöö'he], **reprodujera** [reproðꞯööhe'rá] *etc*, **reproduzca** [reprodöös'ká] *etc vb V* **reproducir.**

repruebe [reprwe'ħe] *etc vb V* **reprobar.**

reptar [reptár'] *vi* to creep, crawl.

reptil [reptēl'] *nm* reptile.

república [repöö'ħlēká] *nf* republic; **R~ Dominicana** Dominican Republic; **R~ Democrática Alemana (RDA)** German Democratic Republic; **R~ Federal Alemana (RFA)** Federal Republic of Germany; **R~ Árabe Unida** United Arab Republic.

republicano, a [repööħlēká'no, á] *a*, *nm/f* republican.

repudiar [repööħyár'] *vt* to repudiate; *(fe)* to renounce.

repudio [repöö'ħyo] *nm* repudiation.

repueble [repwe'ħle] *etc vb V* **repoblar.**

repuesto [repwe'sto] *pp de* **reponer** ♦ *nm (pieza de recambio)* spare (part); *(abastecimiento)* supply; **rueda de ~** spare wheel; **y llevamos otro de ~** and we have another as a spare *o* in reserve.

repugnancia [repöögnán'syá] *nf* repugnance.

repugnante [repöögnán'te] *a* repugnant, repulsive.

repugnar [repöögnár'] *vt* to disgust ♦ *vi*, **~se** *vr (contradecirse)* to contradict each other; *(dar asco)* to be disgusting.

repulsa [repööl'sá] *nf* rebuff.

repulsión [repöölsyon'] *nf* repulsion, aversion.

repulsivo, a [repöölsē'ħo, á] *a* repulsive.

repuse [repöö'se] *etc vb V* **reponer.**

reputación [repöötásyon'] *nf* reputation.

reputar [repöötár'] *vt* to consider, deem.

requemado, a [rekemá'ħo, á] *a (quemado)* scorched; *(bronceado)* tanned.

requemar [rekemár'] *vt (quemar)* to scorch; *(secar)* to parch; *(CULIN)* to overdo, burn; *(la lengua)* to burn, sting.

requerimiento [rekerēmyen'to] *nm* request; *(demanda)* demand; *(JUR)* summons.

requerir [rekerēr'] *vt (pedir)* to ask, request; *(exigir)* to require; *(ordenar)* to call for; *(llamar)* to send for, summon.

requesón [rekeson'] *nm* cottage cheese.

requete... [rekete] *pref* extremely.

requiebro [rekye'ħro] *nm (piropo)* compliment, flirtatious remark.

réquiem [re'kyem] *nm* requiem.

requiera [rekye'rá] *etc*, **requiriendo** [rekēryen'do] *etc vb V* **requerir.**

requisa [rekē'sá] *nf (inspección)* survey, inspection; *(MIL)* requisition.

requisar [rekēsár'] *vt (MIL)* to requisition; *(confiscar)* to seize, confiscate.

requisito [rekēsē'to] *nm* requirement, requisite; **~ previo** prerequisite; **tener los ~s para un cargo** to have the essential qualifications for a job.

res [res] *nf* beast, animal.

resabio [resá'ħyo] *nm (maña)* vice, bad habit; *(dejo)* (unpleasant) aftertaste.

resaca [resá'ká] *nf (en el mar)* undertow, undercurrent; *(fig)* backlash; *(fam)* hangover.

resaltar [resáltár'] *vi* to project, stick out; *(fig)* to stand out.

resarcir [resársēr'] *vt* to compensate; *(pagar)* to repay; **~se** *vr* to make up for; **~ a uno de una pérdida** to compensate sb for a loss; **~ a uno de una cantidad** to repay sb a sum.

resarza [resár'sá] *etc vb V* **resarcir.**

resbaladizo, a [resħálàðē'so, á] *a* slippery.

resbalar [resħálár'] *vi*, **resbalarse** *vr* to slip, slide; *(fig)* to slip (up); **le resbalaban las lágrimas por las mejillas** tears were trickling down his cheeks.

resbalón [resħálon'] *nm (acción)* slip; *(deslizamiento)* slide; *(fig)* slip.

rescatar [reskátár'] *vt (salvar)* to save, rescue; *(objeto)* to get back, recover; *(cautivos)* to ransom.

rescate [reskà'te] *nm* rescue; *(objeto)* recovery; **pagar un ~** to pay a ransom.

rescindir [resēndēr'] *vt (contrato)* to annul, rescind.

rescisión [resēsyon'] *nf* cancellation.

rescoldo [reskol'do] *nm* embers *pl.*

resecar [resekár'] *vt* to dry off, dry thoroughly; *(MED)* to cut out, remove; **~se** *vr* to dry up.

reseco, a [rese'ko, á] *a* very dry; *(fig)* skinny.

resentido, a [resentē'ħo, á] *a* resentful; **es un ~** he's bitter.

resentimiento [resentēmyen'to] *nm* resentment, bitterness.

resentirse [resentēr'se] *vr (debilitarse: persona)* to suffer; **~ con** to resent; **~ de *(consecuencias)*** to feel the effects of.

reseña [rese'nyá] *nf (cuenta)* account; *(informe)* report; *(LIT)* review.

reseñar [resenyár'] *vt* to describe; *(LIT)* to review.

reseque [rese'ke] *etc vb V* **resecar.**

reserva [reser'ħá] *nf* reserve; *(reservación)* reservation; **a ~ de que ...** unless ...; **con toda ~** in strictest confidence; **de ~** spare; **tener algo de ~** to have sth in reserve; **~ de indios** Indian reservation; *(COM)*: **~ para amortización** depreciation allowance; **~ de caja** *o* **en efectivo** cash reserves; **~s del Estado** government stock; **~s en oro** gold reserves.

reservado, a [reserħá'ħo, á] *a* reserved;

(*retraído*) cold, distant ♦ *nm* private room; (*FERRO*) reserved compartment.

reservar [reserbár'] *vt* (*guardar*) to keep; (*FERRO, TEATRO etc*) to reserve, book; ~**se** *vr* to save o.s.; (*callar*) to keep to o.s.; ~ **con exceso** to overbook.

resfriado [resfrēá'tho] *nm* cold.

resfriarse [resfrēár'se] *vr* to cool off; (*MED*) to catch (a) cold.

resguardar [resgwárthár'] *vt* to protect, shield; ~**se** *vr*: ~**se de** to guard against.

resguardo [resgwár'tho] *nm* defense (*US*), defence (*Brit*); (*vale*) voucher; (*recibo*) receipt, slip.

residencia [resēthen'syá] *nf* residence; (*UNIV*) hall of residence; ~ **para ancianos** *o* **jubilados** rest home.

residencial [resēthensyál'] *a* residential ♦ *nf* (*urbanización*) housing development (*US*), housing estate (*Brit*).

residente [resēthen'te] *a, nm/f* resident.

residir [resēthēr'] *vi* to reside, live; ~ **en** to reside *o* lie in; (*consistir en*) to consist of.

residual [resēthwál'] *a* residual; **aguas** ~**es** sewage.

residuo [resē'thwo] *nm* residue; ~**s atmosféricos** *o* **radiactivos** fallout *sg*.

resienta [resyen'tá] *etc vb* V **resentir**.

resignación [resēgnásyon'] *nf* resignation.

resignarse [resēgnár'se] *vr*: ~ **a** *o* **con** to resign o.s. to, be resigned to.

resina [resē'ná] *nf* resin.

resintiendo [resēntyen'do] *etc vb* V **resentir**.

resistencia [resēsten'syá] *nf* (*dureza*) endurance, strength; (*oposición, ELEC*) resistance; **la R**~ (*MIL*) the Resistance.

resistente [resēsten'te] *a* strong, hardy; (*TEC*) resistant; ~ **al calor** heat-resistant.

resistir [resēstēr'] *vt* (*soportar*) to bear; (*oponerse a*) to resist, oppose; (*aguantar*) to put up with ♦ *vi* to resist; (*aguantar*) to last, endure; ~**se** *vr*: ~**se a** to refuse to, resist; **no puedo** ~ **este frío** I can't bear *o* stand this cold; **me resisto a creerlo** I refuse to believe it; **se le resiste la química** chemistry escapes her.

resol [resol'] *nm* glare of the sun.

resolución [resoloōsyon'] *nf* resolution; (*decisión*) decision; (*moción*) motion; ~ **judicial** legal ruling; **tomar una** ~ to take a decision.

resoluto, a [resoloō'to, á] *a* resolute.

resolver [resolber'] *vt* to resolve; (*solucionar*) to solve, resolve; (*decidir*) to decide, settle; ~**se** *vr* to make up one's mind.

resollar [resoyár'] *vi* to breathe noisily, wheeze.

resonancia [resonán'syá] *nf* (*del sonido*) resonance; (*repercusión*) repercussion; (*fig*) wide effect, impact.

resonante [resonán'te] *a* resonant, resounding; (*fig*) tremendous.

resonar [resonár'] *vi* to ring, echo.

resoplar [resoplár'] *vi* to snort; (*por cansancio*) to puff.

resoplido [resoplē'tho] *nm* heavy breathing.

resorte [resor'te] *nm* spring; (*fig*) lever.

respaldar [respáldár'] *vt* to back (up), support; (*INFORM*) to back up; ~**se** *vr* to lean back; ~**se con** *o* **en** (*fig*) to take one's stand on.

respaldo [respál'do] *nm* (*de sillón*) back; (*fig*) support, backing.

respectivo, a [respektē'bo, á] *a* respective; **en lo** ~ **a** with regard to.

respecto [respek'to] *nm*: **al** ~ on this matter; **con** ~ **a,** ~ **de** with regard to, in relation to.

respetable [respetá'ble] *a* respectable.

respetar [respetár'] *vt* to respect.

respeto [respe'to] *nm* respect; (*acatamiento*) deference; ~**s** *nmpl* respects; **por** ~ **a** out of consideration for; **presentar sus** ~**s a** to pay one's respects to.

respetuoso, a [respetwo'so, á] *a* respectful.

respingar [respēngár'] *vi* to shy.

respingo [respēn'go] *nm* start, jump.

respingue [respēn'ge] *etc vb* V **respingar**.

respiración [respērásyon'] *nf* breathing; (*MED*) respiration; (*ventilación*) ventilation.

respirar [respērár'] *vt, vi* to breathe; **no dejar** ~ **a uno** to hassle sb; **estuvo escuchándole sin** ~ he listened to him in complete silence.

respiratorio, a [respēráto'ryo, á] *a* respiratory.

respiro [respē'ro] *nm* breathing; (*fig: descanso*) respite, rest; (*COM*) period of grace.

resplandecer [resplándeser'] *vi* to shine.

resplandeciente [resplándesyen'te] *a* resplendent, shining.

resplandezca [resplándes'ká] *etc vb* V **resplandecer**.

resplandor [resplándor'] *nm* brilliance, brightness; (*del fuego*) blaze.

responder [responder'] *vt* to answer ♦ *vi* to answer; (*fig*) to respond; (*pey*) to answer back; (*corresponder*) to correspond; ~ **a** (*situación etc*) to respond to; ~ **a una pregunta** to answer a question; ~ **a una descripción** to fit a description; ~ **de** *o* **por** to answer for.

respondón, ona [respondon', oná] *a* mouthy (*US*), cheeky (*Brit*).

responsabilice [responsábēlē'se] *etc vb* V **responsabilizarse**.

responsabilidad [responsábēlē'thath'] *nf* responsibility; **bajo mi** ~ on my authority; ~ **ilimitada** (*COM*) unlimited liability.

responsabilizarse [responsåbēlēsár'se] *vr* to make o.s. responsible, take charge.

responsable [responsá'ble] *a* responsible; **la persona** ~ the person in charge; **hacerse** ~ **de algo** to assume responsibility for sth.

respuesta [respwe'stá] *nf* answer, reply; *(reacción)* response.

resquebrajar [reskebráhár'] *vt,* **resquebrajarse** *vr* to crack, split.

resquemor [reskemor'] *nm* resentment.

resquicio [reskē'syo] *nm* chink; *(hendedura)* crack.

resta [re'stá] *nf* (*MAT*) remainder.

restablecer [restáhleser'] *vt* to re-establish, restore; ~**se** *vr* to recover.

restablecimiento [restáhlesēmyen'to] *nm* re-establishment; *(restauración)* restoration; *(MED)* recovery.

restablezca [restáhles'ká] *etc vb* V **restablecer**.

restallar [restáyár'] *vi* to crack.

restante [restán'te] *a* remaining; **lo** ~ the remainder; **los** ~**s** the rest, those left (over).

restar [restár'] *vt* (*MAT*) to subtract; *(descontar)* to deduct; *(fig)* to take away ♦ *vi* to remain, be left.

restauración [restáōōrásyon'] *nf* restoration.

restaurador, a [restáōōráłhor', á] *nm/f* *(persona)* restorer.

restaurante [restáōōrán'te] *nm* restaurant.

restaurar [restáōōrár'] *vt* to restore.

restitución [restētōōsyon'] *nf* return, restitution.

restituir [restētōōēr'] *vt* *(devolver)* to return, give back; *(rehabilitar)* to restore.

restituyendo [restētōōyen'do] *etc vb* V **restituir**.

resto [re'sto] *nm* *(residuo)* rest, remainder; *(apuesta)* stake; ~**s** *nmpl* remains; *(CULIN)* leftovers, scraps; ~**s mortales** mortal remains.

restregar [restregár'] *vt* to scrub, rub.

restregué [restrege'], **restreguemos** [restrege'mos] *etc vb* V **restregar**.

restricción [restrēksyon'] *nf* restriction; **sin** ~ **de** without restrictions on *o* as to; **hablar sin restricciones** to talk freely.

restrictivo, a [restrēktē'ho, á] *a* restrictive.

restriego [restrye'go] *etc,* **restriegue** [restrye'ge] *etc vb* V **restregar**.

restringir [restrēnhēr'] *vt* to restrict, limit.

restrinja [restrēn'há] *etc vb* V **restringir**.

resucitar [resōōsētár'] *vt, vi* to resuscitate, revive.

resuelto, a [reswel'to, á] *pp de* **resolver** ♦ *a* resolute, determined; **estar** ~ **a algo** to be set on sth; **estar** ~ **a hacer algo** to be determined to do sth.

resuelva [reswel'há] *etc vb* V **resolver**.

resuello [reswe'yo] *etc vb* V **resollar** ♦ *nm* *(aliento)* breath.

resuene [reswe'ne] *etc vb* V **resonar**.

resulta [resōōl'tá] *nf* result; **de** ~**s de** as a result of.

resultado [resōōltá'łho] *nm* result; *(conclusión)* outcome; ~**s** *nmpl* (*INFORM*) output *sg*; **dar** ~ to produce results.

resultante [resōōltán'te] *a* resulting, resultant.

resultar [resōōltár'] *vi* (*ser*) to be; *(llegar a ser)* to turn out to be; *(salir bien)* to turn out well; *(seguir)* to ensue; ~ **a** (*COM*) to amount to; ~ **de** to stem from; ~ **en** to result in, produce; **resulta que** ... *(por consecuencia)* it follows that ...; *(parece que)* it seems that ...; **el conductor resultó muerto** the driver was killed; **no resultó** it didn't work *o* come off; **me resulta difícil hacerlo** it's difficult for me to do it.

resumen [resōō'men] *nm* summary, résumé; **en** ~ in short.

resumir [resōōmēr'] *vt* to sum up; *(condensar)* to summarize; *(cortar)* to abridge, cut down; *(condensar)* to summarize; ~**se** *vr*: **la situación se resume en pocas palabras** the situation can be summed up in a few words.

resurgir [resōōrhēr'] *vi* *(reaparecer)* to reappear.

resurrección [resōōrreksyon'] *nf* resurrection.

retablo [retá'hlo] *nm* altarpiece.

retaguardia [retágwár'thyá] *nf* rearguard.

retahíla [retáē'lá] *nf* series, string; *(de injurias)* volley, stream.

retal [retál'] *nm* remnant.

retar [retár'] *vt* (*gen*) to challenge; *(desafiar)* to defy, dare.

retardar [retárthár'] *vt* *(demorar)* to delay; *(hacer más lento)* to slow down; *(retener)* to hold back.

retardo [retár'łho] *nm* delay.

retazo [retá'so] *nm* fragment, snippet.

RETD *nf abr* (*Esp TELEC*)=*Red Especial de Transmisión de Datos.*

rete... [re'te] *pref* very, extremely.

retención [retensyon'] *nf* retention; *(de pago)* deduction; ~ **de llamadas** (*TELEC*) hold facility.

retendré [retendre'] *etc vb* V **retener**.

retener [retener'] *vt* *(guardar)* to retain, keep; *(intereses)* to withhold.

retenga [reten'gá] *etc vb* V **retener**.

reticencia [retēsen'syá] *nf* *(sugerencia)* insinuation, (malevolent) suggestion; *(engaño)* half-truth.

reticente [retēsen'te] *a* *(insinuador)* insinuating; *(engañoso)* deceptive.

retiene [retye'ne] *etc vb* V **retener**.

retina [retē'ná] *nf* retina.

retintín [retēntēn'] *nm* jangle, jingle; **decir algo con** ~ to say sth sarcastically.

retirado, a [retēra'ŏo, á] *a* (*lugar*) remote; (*vida*) quiet; (*jubilado*) retired ♦ *nf* (*MIL*) retreat; (*de dinero*) withdrawal; (*de embajador*) recall; (*refugio*) safe place; **batirse en retirada** to retreat.

retirante [retērán'te] *a*: **ser** ~ **a hacer algo** to be reluctant to do sth.

retirar [retērár'] *vt* to withdraw; (*la mano*) to draw back; (*quitar*) to remove; (*dinero*) to take out, withdraw; (*jubilar*) to retire; ~**se** *vr* to retreat, withdraw; (*jubilarse*) to retire; (*acostarse*) to retire, go to bed.

retiro [retē'ro] *nm* retreat; (*jubilación, tb DEPORTE*) retirement; (*pago*) pension; (*lugar*) quiet place.

reto [re'to] *nm* dare, challenge.

retocar [retokár'] *vt* to touch up, retouch.

retoce [reto'se] *etc vb V* **retozar**.

retoño [reto'nyo] *nm* sprout, shoot; (*fig*) offspring, child.

retoque [reto'ke] *etc vb V* **retocar** ♦ *nm* retouching.

retorcer [retorser'] *vt* to twist; (*argumento*) to turn, twist; (*manos, lavado*) to wring; ~**se** *vr* to become twisted; (*persona*) to writhe; ~**se de dolor** to writhe in *o* squirm with pain.

retorcimiento [retorsēmyen'to] *nm* twist, twisting; (*fig*) deviousness.

retórico, a [reto'rēko, á] *a* rhetorical; (*pey*) affected, windy ♦ *nf* rhetoric; (*pey*) affectedness.

retornar [retornár'] *vt* to return, give back ♦ *vi* to return, go/come back.

retorno [retor'no] *nm* return; ~ **del carro** (*INFORM, TIP*) carriage return; ~ **del carro automático** (*INFORM*) wordwrap.

retortero [retorte'ro] *nm*: **andar al** ~ to bustle about, have heaps of things to do; **andar al** ~ **por uno** to be madly in love with sb.

retortijón [retortēhon'] *nm* twist, twisting; ~ **de tripas** stomach cramp.

retorzamos [retorsá'mos] *etc vb V* **retorcer**.

retozar [retosár'] *vi* (*juguetear*) to frolic, romp; (*saltar*) to gambol.

retozón, ona [retoson', oná] *a* playful.

retracción [retráksyon'] *nf* retraction.

retractarse [retráktár'se] *vr* to retract; **me retracto** I take that back.

retraerse [retráer'se] *vr* to retreat, withdraw.

retraído, a [retráē'ŏo, á] *a* shy, retiring.

retraiga [retrá'ēgá] *etc vb V* **retraerse**.

retraimiento [retráēmyen'to] *nm* retirement; (*timidez*) shyness.

retraje [retrá'he] *etc*, **retrajera** [retráhe'rá] *etc vb V* **retraerse**.

retransmisión [retránsmēsyon'] *nf* repeat (broadcast).

retransmitir [retránsmētēr'] *vt* (*mensaje*) to relay; (*TV etc*) to repeat, retransmit; (: *en vivo*) to broadcast live.

retrasado, a [retrásá'ŏo, á] *a* late; (*MED*) mentally retarded; (*país etc*) backward, underdeveloped; **estar** ~ (*reloj*) to be slow; (*persona, industria*) to be *o* lag behind.

retrasar [retrásár'] *vt* (*demorar*) to postpone, put off; (*retardar*) to slow down ♦ *vi*, ~**se** *vr* (*atrasarse*) to be late; (*reloj*) to be slow; (*producción*) to fall (off); (*quedarse atrás*) to lag behind.

retraso [retrá'so] *nm* (*demora*) delay; (*lentitud*) slowness; (*tardanza*) lateness; (*atraso*) backwardness; ~**s** *nmpl* (*COM*) arrears; (*deudas*) deficit *sg*, debts; **llegar con** ~ to arrive late; **llegar con 25 minutos de** ~ to be 25 minutes late; **llevo un** ~ **de 6 semanas** I'm 6 weeks behind (with my work *etc*); ~ **mental** mental deficiency.

retratar [retratár'] *vt* (*ARTE*) to paint the portrait of; (*fotografiar*) to photograph; (*fig*) to depict, describe; ~**se** *vr* to have one's portrait painted; to have one's photograph taken.

retratista [retratē'stá] *nm/f* (*pintura*) (portrait) painter; (*FOTO*) photographer.

retrato [retrá'to] *nm* portrait; (*FOTO*) photograph; (*descripción*) portrayal, depiction; (*fig*) likeness; **ser el vivo** ~ **de** to be the spitting image of.

retrato-robot [retrá'toroŏo'(t)], *pl* **retratos-robot** *nm* identikit picture.

retrayendo [retráyen'do] *etc vb V* **retraerse**.

retreta [retre'tá] *nf* retreat.

retrete [retre'te] *nm* toilet.

retribución [retrēŏosyon'] *nf* (*recompensa*) reward; (*pago*) pay, payment.

retribuir [retrēŏoōēr'] *vt* (*recompensar*) to reward; (*pagar*) to pay.

retribuyendo [retrēŏoōyen'do] *etc vb V* **retribuir**.

retro... [retro] *pref* retro....

retroactivo, a [retroáktē'ŏo, á] *a* retroactive, retrospective; **dar efecto** ~ **a un pago** to backdate a payment.

retroalimentación [retroálēmentásyon'] *nf* (*INFORM*) feedback.

retroceder [retroseŏer'] *vi* (*echarse atrás*) to move back(wards); (*fig*) to back down; **no** ~ to stand firm; **la policía hizo** ~ **a la multitud** the police forced the crowd back.

retroceso [retrose'so] *nm* backward movement; (*MED*) relapse; (*COM*) recession, depression; (*fig*) backing down.

retrógrado, a [retro'gráŏo, á] *a* retrograde, retrogressive; (*POL*) reactionary.

retropropulsión [retropropoōlsyon'] *nf* jet

propulsion.

retrospectivo, a [rɛtrospɛktē'ho, à] *a* retrospective; **mirada retrospectiva** backward glance.

retrovisor [rɛtroβēsor'] *nm* rear-view mirror.

retuerce [rɛtwer'sɛ] *etc*, **retuerza** [rɛtwer'sà] *etc vb V* **retorcer.**

retumbante [rɛtōōmbàn'tɛ] *a* resounding.

retumbar [rɛtōōmbàr'] *vi* to echo, resound; (*continuamente*) to reverberate.

retuve [rɛtōō'βɛ] *etc vb V* **retener.**

reuma [rɛ'ōōmà] *nm* rheumatism.

reumático, a [rɛōōmà'tēko, à] *a* rheumatic.

reumatismo [rɛōōmátēs'mo] *nm* rheumatism.

reunificar [rɛōōnēfēkàr'] *vt* to reunify.

reunifique [rɛōōnēfē'kɛ] *etc vb V* **reunificar.**

reunión [rɛōōnyon'] *nf* (*asamblea*) meeting; (*fiesta*) party; ~ **en la cumbre** summit meeting; ~ **de ventas** (*COM*) sales meeting.

reunir [rɛōōnēr'] *vt* (*juntar*) to reunite, join (together); (*recoger*) to gather (together); (*personas*) to bring o get together; (*cualidades*) to combine; ~**se** *vr* (*personas: en asamblea*) to meet, gather; **reunió a sus amigos para discutirlo** he got his friends together to talk it over.

reválida [rɛβà'lēthà] *nf* (*ESCOL*) final examination.

revalidar [rɛβàlēthàr'] *vt* (*ratificar*) to confirm, ratify.

revalorar [rɛβàloràr'] *vt* to revalue, reassess.

revalor(iz)ación [rɛβàlor(ēs)àsyon'] *nf* revaluation; (*ECON*) reassessment.

revancha [rɛβàntch'à] *nf* revenge; (*DEPORTE*) return match; (*BOXEO*) return fight.

revelación [rɛβɛlàsyon'] *nf* revelation.

revelado [rɛβɛlà'tho] *nm* developing.

revelador, a [rɛβɛlàthor', à] *a* revealing.

revelar [rɛβɛlàr'] *vt* to reveal; (*secreto*) to disclose; (*mostrar*) to show; (*FOTO*) to develop.

revendedor, a [rɛβɛndɛthor', à] *nm/f* retailer; (*pey*) scalper (*US*), ticket tout (*Brit*).

revendré [rɛβɛndrɛ'] *etc*, **revenga** [rɛβɛn'gà] *etc vb V* **revenirse.**

revenirse [rɛβɛnēr'sɛ] *vr* to shrink; (*comida*) to go bad; (*vino*) to sour; (*CULIN*) to get tough.

reventa [rɛβɛn'tà] *nf* resale; (*especulación*) speculation; (*de entradas*) scalping (*US*), touting (*Brit*).

reventar [rɛβɛntàr'] *vt* to burst, explode; (*molestar*) to annoy, rile ♦ *vi*, ~**se** *vr* (*estallar*) to burst, explode; **me revienta tener que ponérmelo** I hate having to wear it; ~ **de** (*fig*) to be bursting with; ~ **por** to

be bursting to.

reventón [rɛβɛnton'] *nm* (*AUTO*) blow-out (*Brit*), flat (*US*).

reverberación [rɛβɛrβɛràsyon'] *nf* reverberation.

reverberar [rɛβɛrβɛràr'] *vi* (*luz*) to play, be reflected; (*superficie*) to shimmer; (*nieve*) to glare; (*sonido*) to reverberate.

reverbero [rɛβɛrβɛ'ro] *nm* play; shimmer, shine; glare; reverberation.

reverencia [rɛβɛrɛn'syà] *nf* reverence; (*inclinación*) bow.

reverenciar [rɛβɛrɛnsyàr'] *vt* to revere.

reverendo, a [rɛβɛrɛn'do, à] *a* reverend; (*fam*) big, awful; **un** ~ **imbécil** an awful idiot.

reverente [rɛβɛrɛn'tɛ] *a* reverent.

reverso [rɛβɛr'so] *nm* back, other side; (*de moneda*) reverse.

revertir [rɛβɛrtēr'] *vi* to revert; ~ **en beneficio de** to be to the advantage of; ~ **en perjuicio de** to be to the detriment of.

revés [rɛβɛs'] *nm* back, wrong side; (*fig*) reverse, setback; (*DEPORTE*) backhand; **al** ~ the wrong way around; (*de arriba abajo*) upside down; (*ropa*) inside out; **y al** ~ **and** vice versa; **volver algo al** ~ to turn sth around; (*ropa*) to turn sth inside out; **los reveses de la fortuna** life's setbacks.

revestir [rɛβɛstēr'] *vt* (*poner*) to put on; (*cubrir*) to cover, coat; (*cualidad*) to have, possess; ~**se** *vr* (*REL*) to put on one's vestments; (*ponerse*) to put on; ~ **con** o **de** to arm o.s. with; **el acto revestía gran solemnidad** the ceremony had great dignity.

reviejo, a [rɛβyɛ'ho, à] *a* very old, ancient.

reviene [rɛβyɛ'nɛ] *etc vb V* **revenirse.**

reviente [rɛβyɛn'tɛ] *etc vb V* **reventar.**

revierta [rɛβyɛr'tà] *etc vb V* **revertir.**

reviniendo [rɛβēnyɛn'do] *etc vb V* **revenirse.**

revirtiendo [rɛβērtyɛn'do] *etc vb V* **revertir.**

revisar [rɛβēsàr'] *vt* (*examinar*) to check; (*texto etc*) to revise; (*JUR*) to review.

revisión [rɛβēsyon'] *nf* revision; ~ **aduanera** customs inspection; ~ **de cuentas** audit.

revisor, a [rɛβēsor', à] *nm/f* inspector; (*FERRO*) conductor; ~ **de cuentas** auditor.

revista [rɛβē'stà] *etc vb V* **revestir** ♦ *nf* magazine, review; (*sección*) section, page; (*TEATRO*) revue; (*inspección*) inspection; ~ **literaria** literary review; ~ **de libros** book reviews (page); **pasar** ~ **a** to review, inspect.

revivir [rɛβēβēr'] *vt* (*recordar*) to revive memories of ♦ *vi* to revive.

revocación [rɛβokàsyon'] *nf* repeal.

revocar [rɛβokàr'] *vt* (*decisión*) to revoke; (*ARQ*) to plaster.

revolcar [rɛβolkàr'] *vt* to knock down, send flying; ~**se** *vr* to roll around.

revolcón [reḥolkon'] *nm* tumble.
revolotear [reḥoloteár'] *vi* to flutter.
revoloteo [reḥolote'o] *nm* fluttering.
revolqué [reḥolke'], **revolquemos** [reḥolke'mos] *etc vb* V **revolcar**.
revoltijo [reḥoltē'ho] *nm* mess, jumble.
revoltoso, a [reḥolto'so, á] *a* (*travieso*) naughty, unruly.
revolución [reḥolōōsyon'] *nf* revolution.
revolucionar [reḥolōōsyonár'] *vt* to revolutionize.
revolucionario, a [reḥolōōsyoná'ryo, á] *a*, *nm/f* revolutionary.
revolver [reḥolḥer'] *vt* (*desordenar*) to disturb, mess up; (*agitar*) to shake; (*líquido*) to stir; (*mover*) to move about; (POL) to stir up ♦ *vi*: ~ **en** to go through, rummage (about) in; ~**se** *vr* (*en cama*) to toss and turn; (METEOROLOGÍA) to break, turn stormy; ~**se contra** to turn on *o* against; **han revuelto toda la casa** they've turned the whole house upside down.
revólver [reḥol'ḥer] *nm* revolver.
revoque [reḥo'ke] *etc vb* V **revocar**.
revuelco [reḥwel'ko] *etc vb* V **revolcar**.
revuelo [reḥwe'lo] *nm* fluttering; (*fig*) commotion; **armar** *o* **levantar un gran** ~ to cause a great stir.
revuelque [reḥwel'ke] *etc vb* V **revolcar**.
revuelto, a [reḥwel'to, á] *pp de* **revolver** ♦ *a* (*mezclado*) mixed-up, in disorder; (*mar*) rough; (*tiempo*) unsettled ♦ *nf* (*motín*) revolt; (*agitación*) commotion; **todo estaba** ~ everything was in disorder *o* was topsyturvy.
revuelva [reḥwel'ḥá] *etc vb* V **revolver**.
rey [reē] *nm* king; **los R~es** the King and Queen.
reyerta [reyer'tá] *nf* quarrel, brawl.
rezagado, a [resáǵá'ᵭo, á] *a*: **quedar** ~ to be left behind; (*estar retrasado*) to be late, be behind ♦ *nm/f* straggler.
rezagar [resáǵár'] *vt* (*dejar atrás*) to leave behind; (*retrasar*) to delay, postpone; ~**se** *vr* (*atrasarse*) to fall behind.
rezague [resá'ǵe] *etc vb* V **rezagar**.
rezar [resár'] *vi* to pray; ~ **con** (*fam*) to concern, have to do with.
rezo [re'so] *nm* prayer.
rezongar [resongár'] *vi* to grumble; (*murmurar*) to mutter; (*refunfuñar*) to growl.
rezongue [reson'ge] *etc vb* V **rezongar**.
rezumar [resōōmár'] *vt* to ooze ♦ *vi* to leak; ~**se** *vr* to leak out.
RFA *nf abr* = **República Federal Alemana**.
ría [rē'á] *nf* estuary.
riada [rēá'ᵭá] *nf* flood.
ribera [rēḥe'rá] *nf* (*de río*) bank; (: *área*) riverside.
ribete [rēḥe'te] *nm* (*de vestido*) border; (*fig*) addition.
ribetear [rēḥeteár'] *vt* to edge, border.
rice [rē'se] *etc vb* V **rizar**.
ricino [rēsē'no] *nm*: **aceite de** ~ castor oil.
rico, a [rē'ko, á] *a* (*adinerado*) rich, wealthy; (*lujoso*) luxurious; (*comida*) delicious; (*niño*) lovely, cute ♦ *nm/f* rich person; **nuevo** ~ nouveau riche.
rictus [rēk'tōōs] *nm* (*mueca*) sneer, grin; ~ **de amargura** bitter smile.
ridiculez [rēᵭēkōōles'] *nf* absurdity.
ridiculice [rēᵭēkōōlē'se] *etc vb* V **ridiculizar**.
ridiculizar [rēᵭēkōōlēsár'] *vt* to ridicule.
ridículo, a [rēᵭē'kōōlo, á] *a* ridiculous; **hacer el** ~ to make a fool of o.s.; **poner a uno en** ~ to make a fool of sb; **ponerse en** ~ to make a fool *o* laughing-stock of o.s.
riego [rye'ǵo] *etc vb* V **regar** ♦ *nm* (*aspersión*) watering; (*irrigación*) irrigation.
riegue [rye'ǵe] *etc vb* V **regar**.
riel [ryel] *nm* rail.
rienda [ryen'dá] *nf* rein; (*fig*) restraint, moderating influence; **dar** ~ **suelta a** to give free rein to; **llevar las** ~**s** to be in charge.
riendo [ryen'do] *vb* V **reír**.
riesgo [ryes'ǵo] *nm* risk; **seguro a** *o* **contra todo** ~ comprehensive insurance; ~ **para la salud** health hazard; **correr el** ~ **de** to run the risk of.
Rif [rēf] *nm* Rif(f).
rifa [rē'fá] *nf* (*lotería*) raffle.
rifar [rēfár'] *vt* to raffle.
rifeño, a [rēfe'nyo, á] *a* of the Rif(f), Rif(f)ian ♦ *nm/f* Rif(f)ian, Rif(f).
rifle [rē'fle] *nm* rifle.
rigidez [rēḥēᵭes'] *nf* rigidity, stiffness; (*fig*) strictness.
rígido, a [rē'ḥēᵭo, á] *a* rigid, stiff; (*moralmente*) strict, inflexible; (*cara*) expressionless.
rigiendo [rēḥyen'do] *etc vb* V **regir**.
rigor [rēǵor'] *nm* strictness; (*dureza*) toughness; (*inclemencia*) harshness; (*meticulosidad*) accuracy; **el** ~ **del verano** the hottest part of the summer; **con todo** ~ **científico** with scientific precision; **de** ~ essential; **después de los saludos de** ~ after the inevitable greetings.
riguroso, a [rēǵōōro'so, á] *a* rigorous; (METEOROLOGÍA) harsh; (*severo*) severe.
rija [rē'ḥá] *etc vb* V **regir** ♦ *nf* quarrel.
rima [rē'má] *nf* rhyme; ~**s** *nfpl* verse *sg*; ~ **imperfecta** assonance; ~ **rimando** (*fam*) merrily.
rimar [rēmár'] *vi* to rhyme.
rimbombante [rēmbombán'te] *a* (*fig*) pompous.
rímel, rímmel [rē'mel] *nm* mascara.
rimero [rēme'ro] *nm* stack, pile.

Rin [rēn] *nm* Rhine.

rincón [rēnkon'] *nm* corner (*inside*).

rindiendo [rēndyen'do] *etc vb V* **rendir**.

rinoceronte [rēnoseron'te] *nm* rhinoceros.

riña [rē'nyá] *nf* (*disputa*) argument; (*pelea*) brawl.

riñendo [rēnyen'do] *etc vb V* **reñir**.

riñón [rēnyon'] *nm* kidney; **me costó un ~** (*fam*) it cost me an arm and a leg; **tener riñones** to have guts.

rió [rēo'] *vb V* **reír**.

río [rē'o] *etc vb V* **reír** ♦ *nm* river; (*fig*) torrent, stream; **~ abajo/arriba** downstream/upstream; **cuando el ~ suena, agua lleva** there's no smoke without fire.

Río de Janeiro [rē'oŧħeháne'ēro] *nm* Rio de Janeiro.

Río de la Plata [rē'oŧħeláplá'tá] *nm* Rio de la Plata, River Plate.

Rioja [rēo'há] *nf*: **La ~** La Rioja ♦ *nm*: **r~** rioja wine.

riojano, a [ryohá'no, á] *a, nm/f* Riojan.

rioplatense [rēopláten'se] *a* of *o* from the River Plate region ♦ *nm/f* native *o* inhabitant of the River Plate region.

riqueza [rēke'sá] *nf* wealth, riches *pl*; (*cualidad*) richness.

risa [rē'sá] *nf* laughter; (*una ~*) laugh; **¡qué ~!** what a laugh!; **caerse** *o* **morirse de ~** to split one's sides laughing, die laughing; **tomar algo a ~** to laugh sth off.

risco [rēs'ko] *nm* crag, cliff.

risible [rēsē'ble] *a* ludicrous, laughable.

risotada [rēsotá'ŧħá] *nf* guffaw, loud laugh.

ristra [rēs'trá] *nf* string.

ristre [rēs'tre] *nm*: **en ~** at the ready.

risueño, a [rēswe'nyo, á] *a* (*sonriente*) smiling; (*contento*) cheerful.

ritmo [rēt'mo] *nm* rhythm; **a ~ lento** slowly; **trabajar a ~ lento** to go slow.

rito [rē'to] *nm* rite.

ritual [rētwál'] *a, nm* ritual.

rival [rēbál'] *a, nm/f* rival.

rivalice [rēbálē'se] *etc vb V* **rivalizar**.

rivalidad [rēbálēŧħáŧħ'] *nf* rivalry, competition.

rivalizar [rēbálēsár'] *vi*: **~ con** to rival, compete with.

rizado, a [rēsá'ŧħo, á] *a* (*pelo*) curly; (*superficie*) ridged; (*terreno*) undulating; (*mar*) choppy ♦ *nm* curls *pl*.

rizar [rēsár'] *vt* to curl; **~se** *vr* (*el pelo*) to curl; (*agua*) to ripple; (*el mar*) to become choppy.

rizo [rē'so] *nm* curl; (*agua*) ripple.

Rma. *abr* (= *Reverendísima*) courtesy title.

Rmo. *abr* (= *Reverendísimo*) Rt. Rev.

RNE *nf abr* = *Radio Nacional de España*.

R. O. *abr* (= *Real Orden*) royal order.

robar [robár'] *vt* to rob; (*objeto*) to steal; (*casa etc*) to break into; (*NAIPES*) to draw;

(*atención*) to steal, capture; (*paciencia*) to exhaust.

roble [ro'ble] *nm* oak.

robledal [robleŧħál'], **robledo** [roble'ŧħo] *nm* oakwood.

robo [ro'bo] *nm* robbery, theft; (*objeto robado*) stolen article *o* goods *pl*; **¡esto es un ~!** this is highway robbery!

robot [robo'(t)], *pl* **robots** *a, nm* robot.

robótica [robo'tēká] *nf* robotics *sg*.

robustecer [roboōsteser'] *vt* to strengthen.

robustezca [roboōstes'ká] *etc vb V* **robustecer**.

robusto, a [roboō'sto, á] *a* robust, strong.

ROC *abr* (*INFORM*: = *reconocimiento óptico de caracteres*) OCR.

roca [ro'ká] *nf* rock; **la R~** the Rock (of Gibraltar).

roce [ro'se] *etc vb V* **rozar** ♦ *nm* rub, rubbing; (*caricia*) brush; (*TEC*) friction; (*en la piel*) graze; **tener ~ con** to have a brush with.

rociar [rosyár'] *vt* to sprinkle, spray.

rocín [rosēn'] *nm* nag, hack.

rocío [rosē'o] *nm* dew.

rocoso, a [roko'so, á] *a* rocky.

rodado, a [roŧħá'ŧħo, á] *a* (*con ruedas*) wheeled ♦ *nf* rut.

rodaja [roŧħá'há] *nf* (*raja*) slice.

rodaje [roŧħá'he] *nm* (*CINE*) shooting, filming; (*AUTO*): **en ~** breaking in (*US*), running in (*Brit*).

Ródano [ro'ŧħáno] *nm* Rhône.

rodar [roŧħár'] *vt* (*vehículo*) to wheel (along); (*escalera*) to roll down; (*viajar por*) to travel (through) ♦ *vi* to roll; (*coche*) to go, run; (*CINE*) to shoot, film; (*persona*) to move about (from place to place), drift; **echarlo todo a ~** (*fig*) to mess it all up.

Rodas [ro'ŧħás] *nf* Rhodes.

rodear [roŧħeár'] *vt* to surround ♦ *vi* to go around; **~se** *vr*: **~se de amigos** to surround o.s. with friends.

rodeo [roŧħe'o] *nm* (*ruta indirecta*) long way around, roundabout way; (*desvío*) detour; (*evasión*) evasion; (*AM*) rodeo; **dejarse de ~s** to talk straight; **hablar sin ~s** to come to the point, speak plainly.

rodilla [roŧħē'yá] *nf* knee; **de ~s** kneeling.

rodillo [roŧħē'yo] *nm* roller; (*CULIN*) rolling-pin; (*en máquina de escribir, impresora*) platen.

rododendro [roŧħoŧħen'dro] *nm* rhododendron.

roedor, a [roeŧħor', á] *a* gnawing ♦ *nm* rodent.

roer [roer'] *vt* (*masticar*) to gnaw; (*corroer, fig*) to corrode.

rogar [rogár'] *vt* (*pedir*) to beg, ask for ♦ *vi* (*suplicar*) to beg, plead; **~se** *vr*: **se ruega**

no fumar please do not smoke; ~ **que** + *subjun* to ask to ...; **ruegue a este señor que nos deje en paz** please ask this gentleman to leave us alone; **no se hace de** ~ he doesn't have to be asked twice.

rogué [roɣe'], **roguemos** [roɣe'mos] *etc vb V* **rogar.**

rojizo, a [rohē'so, á] *a* reddish.

rojo, a [ro'ho, á] *a* red ♦ *nm* red (color); (*POL*) red; **ponerse** ~ to turn red, blush; **al** ~ **vivo** red-hot.

rol [rol] *nm* list, roll; (*AM: papel*) role.

rollizo, a [royē'so, á] *a* (*objeto*) cylindrical; (*persona*) plump.

rollo, a [ro'yo, á] *a* (*fam*) boring, tedious ♦ *nm* roll; (*de cuerda*) coil; (*madera*) log; (*fam*) bore; (*discurso*) boring speech; **¡qué** ~! what a mess!; **la conferencia fue un** ~ the lecture was a big drag.

ROM [rom] *nf abr* (= *memoria de sólo lectura*) ROM.

Roma [ro'má] *nf* Rome; **por todas partes se va a** ~ all roads lead to Rome.

romance [román'se] *nm* (*LING*) Romance language; (*LIT*) ballad; **hablar en** ~ to speak plainly.

romano, a [romá'no, á] *a* Roman, of Rome ♦ *nm/f* Roman.

romanticismo [romántēsēs'mo] *nm* romanticism.

romántico, a [román'tēko, á] *a* romantic.

romería [romerē'á] *nf* (*REL*) pilgrimage; (*excursión*) trip, outing.

romero, a [rome'ro, á] *nm/f* pilgrim ♦ *nm* rosemary.

romo, a [ro'mo, á] *a* blunt; (*fig*) dull.

rompecabezas [rompekáße'sás] *nm inv* riddle, puzzle; (*juego*) jigsaw (puzzle).

rompehuelgas [rompewel'gás] *nm inv* strikebreaker.

rompeolas [rompeo'lás] *nm inv* breakwater.

romper [romper'] *vt* to break; (*hacer pedazos*) to smash; (*papel, tela etc*) to tear, rip; (*relaciones*) to break off ♦ *vi* (*olas*) to break; (*sol, diente*) to break through; ~ **un contrato** to break a contract; ~ **a** to start (suddenly) to; ~ **a llorar** to burst into tears; ~ **con uno** to fall out with sb; **ha roto con su novio** she has broken up with her fiancé.

rompimiento [rompēmyen'to] *nm* (*acto*) breaking; (*fig*) break; (*quiebra*) crack; ~ **de relaciones** breaking off of relations.

ron [ron] *nm* rum.

roncar [ronkár'] *vi* (*al dormir*) to snore; (*animal*) to roar.

ronco, a [ron'ko, á] *a* (*afónico*) hoarse; (*áspero*) raucous.

ronda [ron'dá] *nf* (*de bebidas etc*) round; (*patrulla*) patrol; (*de naipes*) hand, game;

ir de ~ to do one's round.

rondar [rondár'] *vt* to patrol; (*a una persona*) to hang round; (*molestar*) to harass; (*a una chica*) to court ♦ *vi* to patrol; (*fig*) to prowl round; (*MUS*) to go serenading.

rondeño, a [ronde'nyo, á] *a* of o from Ronda ♦ *nm/f* native o inhabitant of Ronda.

ronque [ron'ke] *etc vb V* **roncar.**

ronquera [ronke'rá] *nf* hoarseness.

ronquido [ronkē'ťho] *nm* snore, snoring.

ronronear [ronroneár'] *vi* to purr.

ronroneo [ronrone'o] *nm* purr.

roña [ro'nyá] *nf* (*veterinaria*) mange; (*mugre*) dirt, grime; (*óxido*) rust.

roñoso, a [ronyo'so, á] *a* (*mugriento*) filthy; (*tacaño*) stingy.

ropa [ro'pá] *nf* clothes *pl*, clothing; ~ **blanca** linen; ~ **de cama** bed linen; ~ **interior** underwear; ~ **lavada** o **para lavar** washing; ~ **planchada** ironing; ~ **sucia** dirty clothes *pl*, washing; ~ **usada** secondhand clothes.

ropaje [ropá'he] *nm* gown, robes *pl*.

ropavejero, a [ropáßehe'ro, á] *nm/f* secondhand clothes dealer.

ropero [rope'ro] *nm* linen cupboard; (*guardarropa*) wardrobe.

roque [ro'ke] *nm* (*AJEDREZ*) rook, castle; **estar** ~ to be fast asleep.

rosa [ro'sá] *a inv* pink ♦ *nf* rose; (*ANAT*) red birthmark; ~ **de los vientos** the compass; **estar como una** ~ to feel as fresh as a daisy; (**color**) **de** ~ pink.

rosado, a [rosá'ťho, á] *a* pink ♦ *nm* rosé.

rosal [rosál'] *nm* rosebush.

rosaleda [rosále'ťhá] *nf* rose bed o garden.

rosario [rosá'ryo] *nm* (*REL*) rosary; (*fig: serie*) string; **rezar el** ~ to say the rosary.

rosbif [rosßēf'] *nm* roast beef.

rosca [ros'ká] *nf* (*de tornillo*) thread; (*de humo*) coil, spiral; (*pan, postre*) ring-shaped roll/pastry; **hacer la** ~ **a uno** (*fam*) to kiss (*US*) o suck (*Brit*) up to sb; **pasarse de** ~ (*fig*) to go too far.

Rosellón [roseyon'] *nm* Roussillon.

rosetón [roseton'] *nm* rosette; (*ARQ*) rose window.

rosquilla [roskē'yá] *nf* small ring-shaped cake; (*de humo*) ring.

rostro [ros'tro] *nm* (*cara*) face; (*fig*) cheek.

rotación [rotásyon'] *nf* rotation; ~ **de cultivos** crop rotation.

rotativo, a [rotátē'ßo, á] *a* rotary ♦ *nm* newspaper.

roto, a [ro'to, á] *pp de* **romper** ♦ *a* broken; (*en pedazos*) smashed; (*tela, papel*) torn; (*vida*) shattered ♦ *nm* (*en vestido*) hole, tear.

rótula [ro'tōōlá] *nf* kneecap; (*TEC*) ball-and-socket joint.

rotulador [rotōōláťhor'] *nm* felt-tip pen.

rotular [rotōōlár'] *vt* (*carta, documento*) to head, entitle; (*objeto*) to label.

rótulo [ro'tōōlo] *nm* (*título*) heading, title; (*etiqueta*) label; (*letrero*) sign.

rotundo, a [rotōōn'do, á] *a* round; (*enfático*) emphatic.

rotura [rotōō'rá] *nf* (*rompimiento*) breaking; (*MED*) fracture.

roturar [rotōōrár'] *vt* to plough.

rozado, a [rosá'tho, á] *a* worn.

rozadura [rosáthōō'rá] *nf* abrasion, graze.

rozar [rosár'] *vt* (*frotar*) to rub; (*ensuciar*) to dirty; (*MED*) to graze; (*tocar ligeramente*) to shave, skim; (*fig*) to touch o border on; **~se** *vr* to rub (together); **~ con** (*fam*) to rub shoulders with.

Rte. *abr* = **remite, remitente.**

RTVE *nf abr* (*TV*) = *Radiotelevisión Española.*

Ruán [rōōán'] *nm* Rouen.

rubéola [rōōhe'olá] *nf* German measles, rubella.

rubí [rōōhē'] *nm* ruby; (*de reloj*) jewel.

rubio, a [rōō'hyo, á] *a* fair-haired, blond(e) ♦ *nm/f* blond/blonde; **tabaco ~** Virginia tobacco; **(cerveza) rubia** lager.

rubor [rōōhor'] *nm* (*sonrojo*) blush; (*timidez*) bashfulness.

ruborice [rōōhorē'se] *etc vb V* **ruborizarse.**

ruborizarse [rōōhorēsár'se] *vr* to blush.

ruboroso, a [rōōhoro'so, á] *a* blushing.

rúbrica [rōō'hrēká] *nf* (*título*) title, heading; (*de la firma*) flourish; **bajo la ~ de** under the heading of.

rubricar [rōōhrēkár'] *vt* (*firmar*) to sign with a flourish; (*concluir*) to sign and seal.

rubrique [rōōhrē'ke] *etc vb V* **rubricar.**

rudeza [rōōthe'sá] *nf* (*tosquedad*) coarseness; (*sencillez*) simplicity.

rudimentario, a [rōōthēmentá'ryo, á] *a* rudimentary, basic.

rudo, a [rōō'tho, á] *a* (*sin pulir*) unpolished; (*grosero*) coarse; (*violento*) violent; (*sencillo*) simple.

rueda [rwe'thá] *nf* wheel; (*círculo*) ring, circle; (*rodaja*) slice, round; (*en impresora etc*) sprocket; **~ delantera/trasera/de repuesto** front/back/spare wheel; **~ impresora** (*INFORM*) print wheel; **~ de prensa** press conference.

ruedo [rwe'tho] *etc vb V* **rodar** ♦ *nm* (*contorno*) edge, border; (*de vestido*) hem; (*círculo*) circle; (*TAUR*) arena, bullring; (*esterilla*) (round) mat.

ruego [rwe'go] *etc vb V* **rogar** ♦ *nm* request; **a ~ de** at the request of; **"~s y preguntas"** "question and answer session".

ruegue [rwe'ge] *etc vb V* **rogar.**

rufián [rōōfyán'] *nm* scoundrel.

rugby [rōōg'hē] *nm* rugby.

rugido [rōōhē'tho] *nm* roar.

rugir [rōōhēr'] *vi* to roar; (*toro*) to bellow; (*estómago*) to rumble.

rugoso, a [rōōgo'so, á] *a* (*arrugado*) wrinkled; (*áspero*) rough; (*desigual*) ridged.

ruibarbo [rwēhár'ho] *nm* rhubarb.

ruido [rwē'tho] *nm* noise; (*sonido*) sound; (*alboroto*) racket, row; (*escándalo*) commotion, rumpus; **~ de fondo** background noise; **hacer** *o* **meter ~** to cause a stir.

ruidoso, a [rwētho'so, á] *a* noisy, loud; (*fig*) sensational.

ruin [rwēn] *a* (*avaro*) stingy.

ruina [rwē'ná] *nf* ruin; (*colapso*) collapse; (*de persona*) ruin, downfall; **estar hecho una ~** to be a wreck; **la empresa le llevó a la ~** the venture ruined him (financially).

ruindad [rwēndáth'] *nf* lowness, meanness; (*acto*) low o mean act.

ruinoso, a [rwēno'so, á] *a* ruinous; (*destartalado*) dilapidated, tumbledown; (*COM*) disastrous.

ruiseñor [rwēsenyor'] *nm* nightingale.

ruja [rōō'há] *etc vb V* **rugir.**

rula [rōō'lá], **ruleta** [rōōle'tá] *nf* roulette.

rulo [rōō'lo] *nm* (*para el pelo*) curler.

rulota [rōōlo'tá] *nf* trailer (*US*), caravan (*Brit*).

Rumania [rōōmá'nyá] *nf* Rumania.

rumano, a [rōōmá'no, á] *a, nm/f* Rumanian.

rumba [rōōm'bá] *nf* rumba.

rumbo [rōōm'bo] *nm* (*ruta*) route, direction; (*ángulo de dirección*) course, bearing; (*fig*) course of events; **con ~ a** in the direction of; **ir con ~ a** to be heading for; (*NAUT*) to be bound for.

rumboso, a [rōōmbo'so, á] *a* (*generoso*) generous.

rumiante [rōōmyán'te] *nm* ruminant.

rumiar [rōōmyár'] *vt* to chew; (*fig*) to ruminate over ♦ *vi* to chew the cud.

rumor [rōōmor'] *nm* (*ruido sordo*) low sound; (*murmuración*) murmur, buzz.

rumorearse [rōōmoreár'se] *vr*: **se rumorea que** it is rumoured that.

rumoroso, a [rōōmoro'so, á] *a* full of sounds; (*arroyo*) murmuring.

runrún [rōōnrōōn'] *nm* (*voces*) murmur, sound of voices; (*fig*) rumor (*US*), rumour (*Brit*); (*de una máquina*) whirr.

rupestre [rōōpes'tre] *a* rock *cpd*; **pintura ~** cave painting.

ruptura [rōōptōō'rá] *nf* (*gen*) rupture; (*disputa*) split; (*de contrato*) breach; (*de relaciones*) breaking-off.

rural [rōōrál'] *a* rural.

Rusia [rōō'syá] *nf* Russia.

ruso, a [rōō'so, á] *a, nm/f* Russian ♦ *nm* (*LING*) Russian.

rústico, a [rōō'stēko, á] *a* rustic; (*ordinario*)

coarse, uncouth ♦ *nm/f* yokel ♦ *nf*: **libro en rústica** paperback (book).

ruta [rōō'tá] *nf* route.

rutina [rōōtē'ná] *nf* routine; **~ diaria** daily routine; **por ~** as a matter of course.

rutinario, a [rōōtēná'ryo, á] *a* routine.

S

S, s [e'se] *nf* S, s; **S de Sábado** S for Sugar.

S *abr* (= *san, santo, a*) St.; (= *sur*) S.

s. *abr* (= *siglo*) c.; (= *siguiente*) foll.

s/ *abr* (*COM*) = **su(s)**.

S.ª *abr* (= *Sierra*) Mts.

S.A. *abr* (= *Sociedad Anónima*) Ltd., Inc. (*US*); (= *Su Alteza*) His/Her Highness.

sáb. *abr* (= *sábado*) Sat.

sábado [sá'hátho] *nm* Saturday; (*de los judíos*) Sabbath; **del ~ en ocho días** a week from Saturday; **un ~ sí y otro no, cada dos ~s** every other Saturday.

sabana [sáhá'ná] *nf* savannah.

sábana [sá'háná] *nf* sheet; **se le pegan las ~s** he can't get up in the morning.

sabandija [sáhándē'há] *nf* (*bicho*) bug; (*fig*) louse.

sabañón [sáhányon'] *nm* chilblain.

sabático, a [sáhá'tēko, á] *a* (*REL, UNIV*) sabbatical.

sabelotodo [sáhéloto'tho] *nm/f inv* know-all.

saber [sáher'] *vt* to know; (*llegar a conocer*) to find out, learn; (*tener capacidad de*) to know how to ♦ *vi*: **~ a** to taste of, taste like ♦ *nm* knowledge, learning; **~se** *vr*: **se sabe que ...** it is known that ...; **no se sabe** nobody knows; **a ~** namely; **¿sabes conducir/nadar?** can you drive/swim?; **¿sabes francés?** do you *o* can you speak French?; **~ de memoria** to know by heart; **lo sé** I know; **hacer ~** to inform, let know; **que yo sepa** as far as I know; **vete *o* anda a ~** your guess is as good as mine; **¿sabe?** (*fam*) you know (what I mean)?; **le sabe mal que otro la saque a bailar** it upsets him that anybody else should ask her to dance.

sabido, a [sáhē'tho, á] *a* (*consabido*) well-known; **como es ~** as we all know.

sabiduría [sáhēthōōrē'á] *nf* (*conocimientos*) wisdom; (*instrucción*) learning; **~ popular** folklore.

sabiendas [sáhyen'dás]: **a ~** *ad* knowingly; **a ~ de que ...** knowing full well that ....

sabihondo, a [sáhyon'do, á] *a, nm/f* know-it-all (*US*), know-all (*Brit*).

sabio, a [sá'hyo,á] *a* (*docto*) learned; (*prudente*) wise, sensible.

sablazo [sáhlá'so] *nm* (*herida*) sword wound; (*fam*) sponging; **dar un ~ a uno** to tap sb for money.

sabor [sáhor'] *nm* taste; (*fig*) flavor (*US*), flavour (*Brit*); **sin ~** flavorless.

saborear [sáhoreár'] *vt* to taste; (*fig*) to relish.

sabotaje [sáhotá'he] *nm* sabotage.

saboteador, a [sáhoteáthor', á] *nm/f* saboteur.

sabotear [sáhoteár'] *vt* to sabotage.

Saboya [sáho'yá] *nf* Savoy.

sabré [sáhre'] *etc vb V* **saber**.

sabroso, a [sáhro'so, á] *a* tasty; (*fig fam*) racy.

saca [sá'ká] *nf* big sack; **~ de correo(s)** mailbag; (*COM*) withdrawal.

sacacorchos [sákákortch'os] *nm inv* corkscrew.

sacapuntas [sákápōōn'tás] *nm inv* pencil sharpener.

sacar [sákár'] *vt* to take out; (*fig: extraer*) to get (out); (*quitar*) to remove, get out; (*hacer salir*) to bring out; (*fondos: de cuenta*) to draw out, withdraw; (*obtener: legado etc*) to get; (*demostrar*) to show; (*conclusión*) to draw; (*novela etc*) to publish, bring out; (*ropa*) to take off; (*obra*) to make; (*premio*) to receive; (*entradas*) to get; (*TENIS*) to serve; (*FÚTBOL*) to put into play; **~ adelante** (*niño*) to bring up; **~ a uno a bailar** to dance with sb; **~ a uno de sí** to infuriate sb; **~ una foto** to take a photo; **~ la lengua** to stick out one's tongue; **~ buenas/malas notas** to get good/bad marks.

sacarina [sákárē'ná] *nf* saccharin(e).

sacerdote [sásertho'te] *nm* priest.

saciar [sásyár'] *vt* (*hartar*) to satiate; (*fig*) to satisfy; **~se** *vr* (*fig*) to be satisfied.

saciedad [sásyethath'] *nf* satiety; **hasta la ~** (*comer*) one's fill; (*repetir*) ad nauseam.

saco [sá'ko] *nm* bag; (*grande*) sack; (*su contenido*) bagful; (*AM: chaqueta*) jacket; **~ de dormir** sleeping bag.

sacramento [sákrámen'to] *nm* sacrament.

sacrificar [sákrēfēkár'] *vt* to sacrifice; (*animal*) to slaughter; (*perro etc*) to put to sleep; **~se** *vr* to sacrifice o.s.

sacrificio [sákrēfē'syo] *nm* sacrifice.

sacrifique [sákrēfē'ke] *etc vb V* **sacrificar**.

sacrilegio [sákrēle'hyo] *nm* sacrilege.

sacrílego, a [sákrē'lego, á] *a* sacrilegious.

sacristán [sákrēstán'] *nm* sexton.

sacristía [sákrēstē'á] *nf* sacristy.

sacro, a [sá'kro, á] *a* sacred.

sacudida [sákōōthē'thá] *nf* (*agitación*)

shake, shaking; (*sacudimiento*) jolt, bump; (*fig*) violent change; (*POL etc*) upheaval; ~ **eléctrica** electric shock.

sacudir [sǎkōōthěr'] *vt* to shake; (*golpear*) to hit; (*ala*) to flap; (*alfombra*) to beat; ~ **a uno** (*fam*) to belt sb.

sádico, a [sǎ'thěko, ǎ] *a* sadistic ♦ *nm/f* sadist.

sadismo [sǎthěs'mo] *nm* sadism.

saeta [sǎe'tǎ] *nf* (*flecha*) arrow; (*MUS*) sacred song in flamenco style.

sagacidad [sǎgǎsěthǎth'] *nf* shrewdness, cleverness.

sagaz [sǎgǎs'] *a* shrewd, clever.

sagitario [sǎhětǎ'ryo] *nm* (*ASTRO*) Sagittarius.

sagrado, a [sǎgrǎ'tho, ǎ] *a* sacred, holy.

Sáhara [sǎ'ǎrǎ] *nm*: **el** ~ the Sahara (desert).

saharaui [sǎhǎrǎ'wē] *a* Saharan ♦ *nm/f* native *o* inhabitant of the Sahara.

sajón, ona [sǎhon', ho'nǎ] *a, nm/f* Saxon.

Sajonia [sǎho'nyǎ] *nf* Saxony.

sal [sǎl] *vb ver* **salir** ♦ *nf* salt; (*gracia*) wit; (*encanto*) charm; ~**es de baño** bath salts; ~ **gorda** *o* **de cocina** kitchen *o* cooking salt.

sala [sǎ'lǎ] *nf* (*cuarto grande*) large room; (~ *de estar*) living room; (*TEATRO*) house, auditorium; (*de hospital*) ward; ~ **de apelación** court; ~ **de conferencias** lecture hall; ~ **de espera** waiting room; ~ **de embarque** departure lounge; ~ **de estar** living room; ~ **de fiestas** ballroom; ~ **de juntas** (*COM*) boardroom.

salado, a [sǎlǎ'tho, ǎ] *a* salty; (*fig*) witty, amusing; **agua salada** salt water.

salar [sǎlǎr'] *vt* to salt, add salt to.

salarial [sǎlǎryǎl'] *a* (*aumento, revisión*) wage *cpd*, salary *cpd*, pay *cpd*.

salario [sǎlǎ'ryo] *nm* wage, pay.

salchicha [sǎltchětch'ǎ] *nf* (pork) sausage.

salchichón [sǎltchětchon'] *nm* (salami-type) sausage.

saldar [sǎldǎr'] *vt* to pay; (*vender*) to sell off; (*fig*) to settle, resolve.

saldo [sǎl'do] *nm* (*pago*) settlement; (*de una cuenta*) balance; (*lo restante*) remnant(s) (*pl*), remainder; (*liquidación*) sale; (*COM*): ~ **anterior** balance brought forward; ~ **acreedor/deudor** *o* **pasivo** credit/debit balance; ~ **final** final balance.

saldré [sǎldre'] *etc vb V* **salir**.

salero [sǎle'ro] *nm* salt shaker (*US*), salt cellar (*Brit*); (*ingenio*) wit; (*encanto*) charm.

salga [sǎl'gǎ] *etc vb V* **salir**.

salida [sǎlē'thǎ] *nf* (*puerta etc*) exit, way out; (*acto*) leaving, going out; (*de tren, AVIAT*) departure; (*COM, TEC*) output, production; (*fig*) way out; (*resultado*) out-

come; (*COM: oportunidad*) opening; (*GEO, válvula*) outlet; (*de gas*) leak; (*ocurrencia*) witticism; **calle sin** ~ cul-de-sac; **a la** ~ **del teatro** after the theater; **dar la** ~ (*DEPORTE*) to give the starting signal; ~ **de incendios** fire escape; ~ **impresa** (*INFORM*) hard copy; **no hay** ~ there's no way out of it; **no tenemos otra** ~ we have no option; **tener** ~**s** to be witty.

saliente [sǎlyen'te] *a* (*ARQ*) projecting; (*sol*) rising; (*fig*) outstanding.

salina [sǎlē'nǎ] *nf* salt mine; ~**s** *nfpl* saltworks *sg*.

salir [sǎlēr'] *vi* to come/go out; (*resultar*) to turn out; (*partir*) to leave, depart; (*aparecer*) to appear; (*sobresalir*) to project, jut out; (*mancha*) to come out *o* off; (*disco*) to be released; (*número de lotería, planta*) to come up; (*pelo*) to grow; (*diente*) to come through; (*INFORM*) to quit, exit; ~**se** *vr* (*vasija*) to leak; (*animal*) to escape, get out; ~ **con** to go out with; ~ **a la superficie** to come to the surface; ~ **bien/mal** to turn out well/badly; ~ **caro/barato** to work out expensive/cheap; ~ **ganando** to come out on top; ~ **perdiendo** to lose out; **sale a su padre** he takes after his father; ~**se de la carretera** to leave the road; ~**se de la vía** to jump the rails; ~**se con la suya** to get one's own way.

saliva [sǎlē'vǎ] *nf* saliva.

salmantino, a [sǎlmǎntē'no, ǎ] *a* of *o* from Salamanca ♦ *nm/f* native *o* inhabitant of Salamanca.

salmo [sǎl'mo] *nm* psalm.

salmón [sǎlmon'] *nm* salmon.

salmonete [sǎlmone'te] *nm* red mullet.

salmuera [sǎlmwe'rǎ] *nf* pickle, brine.

salón [sǎlon'] *nm* (*de casa*) living-room, lounge; (*muebles*) lounge suite; ~ **de belleza** beauty parlour; ~ **de baile** dance hall; ~ **de sesiones** assembly hall.

salpicadero [sǎlpěkǎthe'ro] *nm* (*AUTO*) dashboard.

salpicar [sǎlpěkǎr'] *vt* (*de barro, pintura*) to splash; (*rociar*) to sprinkle, spatter; (*esparcir*) to scatter.

salpicón [sǎlpěkon'] *nm* (*acto*) splashing; (*CULIN*) meat *o* fish salad.

salpimentar [sǎlpěmentǎr'] *vt* (*CULIN*) to season.

salpique [sǎlpē'ke] *etc vb V* **salpicar**.

salsa [sǎl'sǎ] *nf* sauce; (*con carne asada*) gravy; (*fig*) spice; ~ **mayonesa** mayonnaise; **estar en su** ~ (*fam*) to be in one's element.

saltado, a [sǎltǎ'tho, ǎ] *a* (*desprendido*) missing; (*ojos*) bulging.

saltamontes [sǎltǎmon'tes] *nm inv* grasshopper.

saltar [sǎltǎr'] *vt* to jump (over), leap

(over); (*dejar de lado*) to skip, miss out ♦
vi to jump, leap; (*pelota*) to bounce; (*al
aire*) to fly up; (*quebrarse*) to break; (*al
agua*) to dive; (*fig*) to explode, blow up;
(*botón*) to come off; (*corcho*) to pop out;
~**se** *vr* (*omitir*) to skip, miss; **salta a la
vista** it's obvious; ~**se todas las reglas** to
break all the rules.

salteado, a [sàlteá'ꞏo, á] *a* (*CULIN*) sau-
té(ed).

salteador [sàlteáꞏor'] *nm* (*tb*: ~ **de caminos**) highwayman.

saltear [sàlteár'] *vt* (*robar*) to rob (in a holdup); (*asaltar*) to assault, attack; (*CULIN*)
to sauté.

saltimbanqui [sàltĕmbán'kē] *nm/f* acrobat.

salto [sàl'to] *nm* jump, leap; (*al agua*) dive;
a ~**s** by jumping; ~ **de agua** waterfall; ~
de altura high jump; ~ **de cama** negligee;
~ **mortal** somersault; (*INFORM*): ~ **de línea** line feed; ~ **de línea automático**
wordwrap; ~ **de página** formfeed.

saltón, ona [sàlton', onà] *a* (*ojos*) bulging,
popping; (*dientes*) protruding.

salubre [sàlōō'bre] *a* healthy, salubrious.

salud [sàlōōꞏ'] *nf* health; **estar bien/mal de
** ~ to be in good/poor health; **¡(a su) ~!**
cheers!, good health!; **beber a la ** ~ **de** to
drink (to) the health of.

saludable [sàlōōꞏhá'ble] *a* (*de buena salud*)
healthy; (*provechoso*) good, beneficial.

saludar [sàlōōꞏhár'] *vt* to greet; (*MIL*) to salute; **ir a ** ~ **a uno** to drop in to see sb; **sa-
lude de mi parte a X** give my regards to
X; **le saluda atentamente** (*en carta*) yours
faithfully.

saludo [sàlōō'ꞏo] *nm* greeting; ~**s** (*en
carta*) best wishes, regards; **un ** ~ **afectuoso** o **cordial** yours truly (*US*) o sincerely
(*Brit*).

salva [sàl'hà] *nf* (*MIL*) salvo; **una ** ~ **de
aplausos** thunderous applause.

salvación [sàlhàsyon'] *nf* salvation; (*rescate*) rescue.

salvado [sàlhà'ꞏo] *nm* bran.

salvador [sàlhàꞏor'] *nm* rescuer; **el S**~ the
Savior (*US*) o Saviour (*Brit*); **El S**~ El Salvador; **San S**~ San Salvador.

salvadoreño, a [sàlhàꞏore'nyo, á] *a, nm/f*
Salvadoran, Salvadorian.

salvaguardar [sàlhàgwàrꞏár'] *vt* to safeguard; (*INFORM*) to back up, make a backup copy of.

salvajada [sàlhàhà'ꞏá] *nf* savage deed,
atrocity.

salvaje [sàlhà'he] *a* wild; (*tribu*) savage.

salvajismo [sàlhàhēs'mo] *nm* savagery.

salvamento [sàlhàmen'to] *nm* (*acción*)
rescue; (*de naufragio*) salvage; ~ **y soco-
rrismo** life-saving.

salvar [sàlhàr'] *vt* (*rescatar*) to save,

rescue; (*resolver*) to overcome, resolve;
(*cubrir distancias*) to cover, travel; (*hacer
excepción*) to except, exclude; (*un barco*)
to salvage; ~**se** *vr* to save o.s., escape;
¡sálvese el que pueda! every man for
himself!

salvavidas [sàlhàhē'ꞏàs] *a inv*: **bote/
chaleco/cinturón** ~ lifeboat/lifejacket/life-
belt.

salvedad [sàlheꞏàꞏ'] *nf* reservation, qualification; **con la ** ~ **de que ...** with the proviso that ....

salvia [sàl'hyà] *nf* sage.

salvo, a [sàl'ho, á] *a* safe ♦ *prep* except
(for), save; ~ **error u omisión** (*COM*)
errors and omissions excepted; **a** ~ out of
danger; ~ **que** unless.

salvoconducto [sàlhokondōōk'to] *nm* safe-
conduct.

san [sàn] *nm* (*apócope de* **santo**) saint; ~
Juan St. John.

sanar [sànár'] *vt* (*herida*) to heal; (*persona*)
to cure ♦ *vi* (*persona*) to get well, recover;
(*herida*) to heal.

sanatorio [sànáto'ryo] *nm* sanatorium.

sanción [sánsyon'] *nf* sanction.

sancionar [sánsyonár'] *vt* to sanction.

sandalia [sándá'lyá] *nf* sandal.

sándalo [sàn'dálo] *nm* sandal (wood).

sandez [sándes'] *nf* (*cualidad*) foolishness;
(*acción*) stupid thing; **decir sandeces** to
talk nonsense.

sandía [sàndē'á] *nf* watermelon.

sandwich [sàn'dwĕtch], *pl* **sandwichs** o
sandwiches *nm* sandwich.

saneamiento [sáneámyen'to] *nm* sanitation.

sanear [sáneár'] *vt* to drain; (*indemnizar*) to
compensate; (*ECON*) to reorganize.

sangrante [sàngràn'te] *a* (*herida*) bleeding;
(*fig*) flagrant.

sangrar [sàngrár'] *vt, vi* to bleed; (*texto*) to
indent.

sangre [sàn'gre] *nf* blood; ~ **fría** sangfroid;
a ~ **fría** in cold blood.

sangría [sàngrē'á] *nf* (*MED*) bleeding; (*CU-
LIN*) sangria, *sweetened drink of red wine
with fruit*, ≈ fruit cup.

sangriento, a [sàngryen'to, á] *a* bloody.

sanguijuela [sàngēhwe'lá] *nf* (*ZOOL, fig*)
leech.

sanguinario, a [sàngēná'ryo, á] *a* bloodthirsty.

sanguíneo, a [sàngē'neo, á] *a* blood *cpd*.

sanguinolento, a [sàngēnolen'to, á] *a* (*que
echa sangre*) bleeding; (*manchado*) bloodstained; (*ojos*) bloodshot.

sanidad [sáneꞏàꞏ'] *nf* sanitation; (*calidad
de sano*) health, healthiness; ~ **pública**
public health (department).

sanitario, a [sáneтá'ryo, á] *a* sanitary; (*de

la salud) health *cpd* ♦ *nm*: ~**s** restroom *sg* (*US*), toilets (*Brit*).

San Marino [sánmárē'no] *nm*: (**La República de**) ~ San Marino.

sano, a [sá'no, á] *a* healthy; (*sin daños*) sound; (*comida*) wholesome; (*entero*) whole, intact; ~ **y salvo** safe and sound.

santanderino, a [sántánderē'no, á] *a* of *o* from Santander ♦ *nm/f* native *o* inhabitant of Santander.

Santiago [sántyá'go] *nm*: ~ (**de Chile**) Santiago.

santiamén [sántyámen'] *nm*: **en un** ~ in no time at all.

santidad [sántēᵭáᵭ'] *nf* holiness, sanctity.

santificar [sántēfēkár'] *vt* to sanctify, make holy.

santifique [sántēfē'ke] *etc vb* V **santificar**.

santiguarse [sántēgwár'se] *vr* to make the sign of the cross.

santigüe [sántē'gwe] *etc vb* V **santiguarse**.

santo, a [sán'to, á] *a* holy; (*fig*) wonderful, miraculous ♦ *nm/f* saint ♦ *nm* saint's day; **hacer su santa voluntad** to do as one damn well pleases; **¿a ~ de qué ...?** why on earth ...?; **se le fue el ~ al cielo** he forgot what he was about to say; ~ **y seña** password.

santuario [sántwá'ryo] *nm* sanctuary, shrine.

saña [sá'nyá] *nf* rage, fury.

sapo [sá'po] *nm* toad.

saque [sá'ke] *etc vb* V **sacar** ♦ *nm* (*TENIS*) service, serve; (*FÚTBOL*) throw-in; ~ **inicial** kick-off; ~ **de esquina** corner (kick); **tener buen** ~ to eat heartily.

saquear [sákeár'] *vt* (*MIL*) to sack; (*robar*) to loot, plunder; (*fig*) to ransack.

saqueo [sáke'o] *nm* sacking; looting, plundering; ransacking.

sarampión [sárámpyon'] *nm* measles *sg*.

sarape [sárá'pe] *nm* (*AM*) blanket.

sarcasmo [sárkás'mo] *nm* sarcasm.

sarcástico, a [sárká'stēko, á] *a* sarcastic.

sardina [sárᵭē'ná] *nf* sardine.

sardo, a [sár'ᵭo, á] *a, nm/f* Sardinian.

sardónico, a [sárᵭo'nēko, á] *a* sardonic; (*irónico*) ironical, sarcastic.

sargento [sárhen'to] *nm* sergeant.

SARL *abr* (= *Sociedad Anónima de Responsabilidad Limitada*) Corp. (*US*), Ltd. (*Brit*), plc (*Brit*).

sarna [sár'ná] *nf* itch; (*MED*) scabies.

sarpullido [sárpŏōyē'ᵭo] *nm* (*MED*) rash.

sarro [sá'rro] *nm* deposit; (*en dientes*) tartar.

sarta [sár'tá] *nf*, **sartal** [sártál'] *nm* (*fig*): **una** ~ **de mentiras** a pack of lies.

sartén [sárten'] *nf* frying pan; **tener la** ~ **por el mango** to rule the roost.

sastre [sás'tre] *nm* tailor.

sastrería [sástrerē'á] *nf* (*arte*) tailoring;

(*tienda*) tailor's (shop).

Satanás [sátánás'] *nm* Satan.

satélite [sáte'lēte] *nm* satellite.

satinado, a [sátēná'ᵭo, á] *a* glossy ♦ *nm* gloss, shine.

sátira [sá'tērá] *nf* satire.

satírico, a [sátē'rēko, á] *a* satiric(al).

sátiro [sá'tēro] *nm* (*MITOLOGÍA*) satyr; (*fig*) sex maniac.

satisfacción [sátēsfáksyon'] *nf* satisfaction.

satisfacer [sátēsfáser'] *vt* to satisfy; (*gastos*) to meet; (*deuda*) to pay; (*COM*: *letra de cambio*) to honor (*US*), honour (*Brit*); (*pérdida*) to make good; ~**se** *vr* to satisfy o.s., be satisfied; (*vengarse*) to take revenge.

satisfaga [sátēsfá'gá] *etc*, **satisfaré** [sátēsfáre'] *etc vb* V **satisfacer**.

satisfecho, a [sátēsfetch'o, á] *pp de* **satisfacer** ♦ *a* satisfied; (*contento*) content(ed), happy; (*tb*: ~ **de sí mismo**) self-satisfied, smug.

satisfice [sátēsfē'se] *etc vb* V **satisfacer**.

saturar [sátŏōrár'] *vt* to saturate.

sauce [sá'ŏōse] *nm* willow; ~ **llorón** weeping willow.

saúco [sáŏō'ko] *nm* (*BOT*) elder.

sauna [sá'ŏōná] *nf* sauna.

savia [sá'ᵬyá] *nf* sap.

saxofón [sáksofon'] *nm* saxophone.

saya [sá'yá] *nf* (*falda*) skirt; (*enagua*) petticoat.

sayo [sá'yo] *nm* smock.

sazón [sáson'] *nf* (*de fruta*) ripeness; **a la** ~ then, at that time.

sazonado, a [sásoná'ᵭo, á] *a* (*fruta*) ripe; (*CULIN*) seasoned.

sazonar [sásonár'] *vt* to ripen; (*CULIN*) to season.

s/c *abr* (*COM*:=*su casa*) your firm; (:=*su cuenta*) your account.

Scotch [eskotch'] *nm* (*AM*) adhesive tape.

Sdo. *abr* (*COM*:=*Saldo*) bal.

SE *abr* (= *sudeste*) SE.

se [se] *pron reflexivo* oneself; (*sg*: *m*) himself; (: *f*) herself; (: *de una cosa*) itself; (: *de usted*) yourself; (*pl*) themselves; (: *de ustedes*) yourselves; (*recíproco*) each other, one another; ~ **mira en el espejo** he looks at himself in the mirror; **¡siénte~!** sit down; ~ **ayudan** they help each other; ~ **miraron** (**el uno al otro**) they looked at one another; ~ **compró hace 3 años** it was bought 3 years ago; **en esa parte** ~ **habla francés** in that area French is spoken *o* people speak French; "~ **vende coche**" "car for sale"; ~ **lo daré** I'll give it to him/her/you; **él** ~ **ha comprado un sombrero** he has bought himself a hat.

sé [se] *vb* V **saber, ser**.

sea [se'á] *etc vb* V **ser**.

SEAT [se'át] *nf abr=Sociedad Española de Automóviles de Turismo*.

sebo [se'ƀo] *nm* fat, grease.

Sec. *abr* (= *Secretario*) Sec.

seca [se'ká] *nf* V **seco**.

secado [seká'ƀo] *nm* drying; ~ **a mano** blow-dry.

secador [sekàƀor'] *nm*: ~ **para el pelo** hair-dryer.

secadora [sekàƀo'rá] *nf* tumble dryer; ~ **centrífuga** spin-dryer.

secano [seká'no] *nm* (*AGR*: *tb*: **tierra de** ~) dry land *o* region; **cultivo de** ~ dry farming.

secante [sekán'te] *a* (*viento*) drying ♦ *nm* blotting paper.

secar [sekár'] *vt* to dry; (*superficie*) to wipe dry; (*frente*, *suelo*) to mop; (*líquido*) to mop up; (*tinta*) to blot; ~**se** *vr* to dry (off); (*río*, *planta*) to dry up.

sección [seksyon'] *nf* section; (*COM*) department; ~ **deportiva** (*en periódico*) sports page(s).

seco, a [se'ko, á] *a* dry; (*fruta*) dried; (*persona*: *magro*) thin, skinny; (*carácter*) cold; (*antipático*) disagreeable; (*respuesta*) sharp, curt ♦ *nf* dry season; **habrá pan a secas** there will be just bread; **decir algo a secas** to say sth curtly; **parar en** ~ to stop dead.

secreción [sekresyon'] *nf* secretion.

secretaría [sekretárē'á] *nf* secretariat; (*oficina*) secretary's office.

secretariado [sekretárya'ƀo] *nm* (*oficina*) secretariat; (*cargo*) secretaryship; (*curso*) secretarial course.

secretario, a [sekretá'ryo, á] *nm/f* secretary; ~ **adjunto** (*COM*) assistant secretary.

secreto, a [sekre'to, á] *a* secret; (*información*) confidential; (*persona*) secretive ♦ *nm* secret; (*calidad*) secrecy.

secta [sek'tá] *nf* sect.

sectario, a [sektá'ryo, á] *a* sectarian.

sector [sektor'] *nm* sector (*tb INFORM*); (*de opinión*) section; (*fig*: *campo*) area, field; ~ **privado/público** (*COM*, *ECON*) private/public sector.

secuela [sekwe'lá] *nf* consequence.

secuencia [sekwen'syá] *nf* sequence.

secuestrar [sekwestrár'] *vt* to kidnap; (*avión*) to hijack; (*bienes*) to seize, confiscate.

secuestro [sekwes'tro] *nm* kidnapping; hijack; seizure, confiscation.

secular [sekōōlár'] *a* secular.

secundar [sekōōndár'] *vt* to second, support.

secundario, a [sekōōndá'ryo, á] *a* secondary; (*carretera*) side *cpd*; (*INFORM*) background *cpd*.

sed [seƀ] *nf* thirst; (*fig*) thirst, craving; **te-**

ner ~ to be thirsty.

seda [se'ƀá] *nf* silk.

sedal [seƀál'] *nm* fishing line.

sedante [seƀán'te] *nm* sedative.

sede [se'ƀe] *nf* (*de gobierno*) seat; (*de compañía*) headquarters *pl*, head office; **Santa S**~ Holy See.

SEDIC [seƀēk'] *nf abr=Sociedad Española de Documentación e Información Científica*.

sedición [seƀēsyon'] *nf* sedition.

sediento, a [seƀyen'to, á] *a* thirsty.

sedimentar [seƀēmentár'] *vt* to deposit; ~**se** *vr* to settle.

sedimento [seƀēmen'to] *nm* sediment.

sedoso, a [seƀo'so, á] *a* silky, silken.

seducción [seƀōōksyon'] *nf* seduction.

seducir [seƀōōsēr'] *vt* to seduce; (*sobornar*) to bribe; (*cautivar*) to charm, fascinate; (*atraer*) to attract.

seductor, a [seƀōōktor', á] *a* seductive; charming, fascinating; attractive; (*engañoso*) deceptive, misleading ♦ *nm/f* seducer.

seduje [seƀōō'he] *etc*, **seduzca** [seƀōōs'ká] *etc vb* V **seducir**.

sefardí [sefárƀē'], **sefardita** [sefárƀē'tá] *a* Sephardi(c) ♦ *nm/f* Sephardi.

segador, a [seƀáƀor', á] *nm/f* (*persona*) harvester ♦ *nf* (*TEC*) mower, reaper.

segadora-trilladora [seƀáƀo'rátrēyáƀo'rá] *nf* combine harvester.

segar [seƀár'] *vt* (*mies*) to reap, cut; (*hierba*) to mow, cut; (*esperanzas*) to ruin.

seglar [seƀlár'] *a* secular, lay.

segoviano, a [seƀoƀyá'no, á] *a* of *o* from Segovia ♦ *nm/f* native *o* inhabitant of Segovia.

segregación [seƀreƀásyon'] *nf* segregation; ~ **racial** racial segregation.

segregar [seƀreƀár'] *vt* to segregate, separate.

segregue [seƀre'ƀe] *etc vb* V **segregar**.

seguidamente [seƀēƀámen'te] *ad* (*sin parar*) without a break; (*inmediatamente después*) immediately after.

seguido, a [seƀē'ƀo, á] *a* (*continuo*) continuous, unbroken; (*recto*) straight ♦ *ad* (*directo*) straight (on); (*después*) after; (*AM*: *a menudo*) often ♦ *nf*: **en seguida** at once, right away; **5 días** ~**s** 5 days running, 5 days in a row; **en seguida termino** I'll be done in a minute.

segué [seƀe'], **seguemos** [seƀe'mos] *etc vb* V **segar**.

seguimiento [seƀēmyen'to] *nm* chase, pursuit; (*continuación*) continuation.

seguir [seƀēr'] *vt* to follow; (*venir después*) to follow, come after; (*proseguir*) to continue; (*perseguir*) to chase, pursue; (*indicio*) to follow up; (*mujer*) to court ♦ *vi* (*gen*) to follow; (*continuar*) to continue, carry *o* go on; ~**se** *vr* to follow; **a** ~ **to be**

continued; **sigo sin comprender** I still don't understand; **sigue lloviendo** it's still raining; **sigue** (*en carta*) over; (*en libro*, *TV*) continued; "**hágase ~**" "please forward".

según |se'ḡoon'| *prep* according to ♦ *ad*: ~ (**y conforme**) it all depends ♦ *conj* as; ~ **esté el tiempo** depending on the weather; ~ **me consta** as far as I know; **está ~ lo dejaste** it is just as you left it.

segundo, a |se'ḡoon'do, à| *a* second; (*en discurso*) secondly ♦ *nm* (*gen, medida de tiempo*) second; (*piso*) second floor ♦ *nf* (*sentido*) second meaning; (**de a bordo**) (*NAUT*) first mate; **segunda (clase)** (*FERRO*) second class; **segunda (marcha)** (*AUTO*) second (gear); **de segunda mano** second hand.

seguramente |se'ḡoorámen'te| *ad* surely; (*con certeza*) for sure, with certainty; (*probablemente*) probably; **¿lo va a comprar?** **— ~** is he going to buy it? — I should think so.

seguridad |se'ḡoorēthàth'| *nf* safety; (*del estado, de casa etc*) security; (*certidumbre*) certainty; (*confianza*) confidence; (*estabilidad*) stability; ~ **social** social security; ~ **contra incendios** fire precautions; ~ **en sí mismo** (self-)confidence.

seguro, a |se'ḡoo'ro, à| *a* (*cierto*) sure, certain; (*fiel*) trustworthy; (*libre de peligro*) safe; (*bien defendido, firme*) secure; (*datos etc*) reliable; (*fecha*) firm ♦ *ad* for sure, certainly ♦ *nm* (*dispositivo*) safety device; (*de cerradura*) tumbler; (*de arma*) safety catch; (*COM*) insurance; ~ **contra accidentes/incendios** fire/accident insurance; ~ **contra terceros/a todo riesgo** third party/comprehensive insurance; ~ **dotal con beneficios** interest-bearing endowment insurance (*US*), with-profits endowment assurance (*Brit*); **S~ de Enfermedad** ≈ health insurance (*US*), ≈ National Insurance (*Brit*); ~ **marítimo** marine insurance; ~ **mixto** endowment insurance (*US*) o assurance (*Brit*); ~ **temporal** term insurance; ~ **de vida** life insurance.

seis |sēs| *num* six; ~ **mil** six thousand; **tiene ~ años** she is six (years old); **unos ~** about six; **hoy es el ~** today is the sixth.

seiscientos, as |sēssyen'tos, às| *num* six hundred.

seísmo |sēs'mo| *nm* tremor, earthquake.

selección |seleksyon'| *nf* selection; ~ **múltiple** multiple choice; ~ **nacional** (*DEPORTE*) national team.

seleccionador, a |seleksyonàthor', à| *nm/f* (*DEPORTE*) selector.

seleccionar |seleksyonàr'| *vt* to pick, choose, select.

selectividad |selektēvēthàth'| *nf* (*UNIV*) entrance examination.

selecto, a |selek'to, à| *a* select, choice; (*escogido*) selected.

selva |sel'ḃà| *nf* (*bosque*) forest, woods *pl*; (*jungla*) jungle; **la S~ Negra** the Black Forest.

selvático, a |selḃá'tēko, à| *a* woodland *cpd*; (*BOT*) wild.

sellado, a |seyà'tho, à| *a* (*documento oficial*) sealed; (*pasaporte*) stamped.

sellar |seyàr'| *vt* (*documento oficial*) to seal; (*pasaporte, visado*) to stamp; (*marcar*) to brand; (*pacto, labios*) to seal.

sello |se'yo| *nm* stamp; (*precinto*) seal; (*fig: tb*: ~ **distintivo**) hallmark; ~ **fiscal** revenue stamp; ~**s de prima** (*COM*) trading stamps.

semáforo |semà'foro| *nm* (*AUTO*) traffic lights *pl*; (*FERRO*) signal.

semana |semà'nà| *nf* week; ~ **inglesa** 5-day (work (*US*) o working (*Brit*)) week; ~ **laboral** work (*US*) o working (*Brit*) week; **S~ Santa** Holy Week; **entre ~** during the week.

semanal |semànàl'| *a* weekly.

semanario |semànà'ryo| *nm* weekly (magazine).

semántica |semàn'tēkà| *nf* semantics *sg*.

semblante |semblàn'te| *nm* face; (*fig*) look.

semblanza |semblàn'sà| *nf* biographical sketch, profile.

sembrar |sembràr'| *vt* to sow; (*objetos*) to sprinkle, scatter about; (*noticias etc*) to spread.

semejante |semehàn'te| *a* (*parecido*) similar; (*tal*) such; ~**s** alike, similar ♦ *nm* fellow man, fellow creature; **son muy ~s** they are very much alike; **nunca hizo cosa ~** he never did such a o any such thing.

semejanza |semehàn'sà| *nf* similarity, resemblance; **a ~ de** like, as.

semejar |semehàr'| *vi* to seem like, resemble; ~**se** *vr* to look alike, be similar.

semen |se'men| *nm* semen.

semental |sementàl'| *nm* (*macho*) stud.

sementera |semente'rà| *nf* (*acto*) sowing; (*temporada*) planting season; (*tierra*) planted land.

semestral |semestràl'| *a* half-yearly, biannual.

semestre |semes'tre| *nm* period of six months; (*US UNIV*) semester; (*COM*) half-yearly payment.

semicírculo |semēsēr'koolo| *nm* semicircle.

semiconductor |semēkondooktor'| *nm* semiconductor.

semiconsciente |semēkonssyen'te| *a* semi-conscious.

semifinal |semēfēnàl'| *nf* semifinal.

semilla |semē'yà| *nf* seed.

semillero |semēye'ro| *nm* (*AGR etc*)

seedbed; (*fig*) hotbed.
seminario [semĕnă'ryo] *nm* (*REL*) seminary; (*ESCOL*) seminar.
semiseco [semĕse'ko] *nm* medium-dry.
semita [semĕ'tà] *a* Semitic ♦ *nm/f* Semite.
sémola [se'molà] *nf* semolina.
sempiterno, a [sempĕter'no, à] *a* everlasting.
Sena [se'nà] *nm*: **el** ~ the (river) Seine.
senado [senà'ᵭo] *nm* senate.
senador, a [senàᵭor', à] *nm/f* senator.
sencillez [sensĕyes'] *nf* simplicity; (*de persona*) naturalness.
sencillo, a [sensĕ'yo, à] *a* simple; (*carácter*) natural, unaffected; (*billete*) single.
senda [sen'dà] *nf*, **sendero** [sende'ro] *nm* path, track.
sendos, as [sen'dos, às] *apl*: **les dio** ~ **golpes** he hit both of them.
senil [senĕl'] *a* senile.
seno [se'no] *nm* (*ANAT*) bosom, bust; (*fig*) bosom; ~**s** *nmpl* breasts; ~ **materno** womb.
sensación [sensàsyon'] *nf* sensation; (*sentido*) sense; (*sentimiento*) feeling; **causar** *o* **hacer** ~ to cause a sensation.
sensacional [sensàsyonàl'] *a* sensational.
sensato, a [sensà'to, à] *a* sensible.
sensible [sensĕ'ble] *a* sensitive; (*apreciable*) perceptible, appreciable; (*pérdida*) considerable.
sensiblero, a [sensĕble'ro, à] *a* sentimental.
sensitivo, a [sensĕtĕ'ᵭo, à], **sensorial** [sensoryàl'] *a* sense *cpd*.
sensor [sensor'] *nm*: ~ **de fin de papel** paper out sensor.
sensual [senswàl'] *a* sensual.
sentado, a [sentà'ᵭo, à] *a* (*establecido*) settled; (*carácter*) sensible ♦ *nf* sitting; (*protesta*) sit-down, sit-in; **dar por** ~ to take for granted, assume; **dejar algo** ~ to establish sth firmly; **estar** ~ to sit, be sitting (down).
sentar [sentàr'] *vt* to sit, seat; (*fig*) to establish ♦ *vi* (*vestido*) to suit; (*alimento*): ~ **bien/mal a** to agree/disagree with; ~**se** *vr* (*persona*) to sit, sit down; (*el tiempo*) to settle (down); (*los depósitos*) to settle; **¡siéntese!** (do) sit down, take a seat.
sentencia [senten'syà] *nf* (*máxima*) maxim, saying; (*JUR*) sentence; (*INFORM*) statement; ~ **de muerte** death sentence.
sentenciar [sentensyàr'] *vt* to sentence.
sentido, a [sentĕ'ᵭo, à] *a* (*pérdida*) regrettable; (*carácter*) sensitive ♦ *nm* sense; (*sentimiento*) feeling; (*significado*) sense, meaning; (*dirección*) direction; **mi más** ~ **pésame** my deepest sympathy; ~ **del humor** sense of humor; ~ **común** common sense; **en el buen** ~ **de la palabra** in the best sense of the word; **sin** ~ meaningless;

tener ~ to make sense; ~ **único** one-way (street).
sentimental [sentĕmentàl'] *a* sentimental; **vida** ~ love life.
sentimiento [sentĕmyen'to] *nm* (*emoción*) feeling, emotion; (*sentido*) sense; (*pesar*) regret, sorrow.
sentir [sentĕr'] *vt* to feel; (*percibir*) to perceive, sense; (*lamentar*) to regret, be sorry for; (*música etc*) to have a feeling for ♦ *vi* to feel; (*lamentarse*) to feel sorry ♦ *nm* opinion, judgement; ~**se** *vr* to feel; **lo siento** I'm sorry; ~**se bien/mal** to feel well/ill; ~**se como en su casa** to feel at home.
seña [se'nyà] *nf* sign; (*MIL*) password; ~**s** *nfpl* address *sg*; ~**s personales** personal description *sg*; **por más** ~**s** moreover; **dar** ~**s de** to show signs of.
señal [senyàl'] *nf* sign; (*síntoma*) symptom; (*indicio*) indication; (*FERRO*, *TELEC*) signal; (*marca*) mark; (*COM*) deposit; (*INFORM*) marker, mark; **en** ~ **de** as a token of, as a sign of; **dar** ~**es de** to show signs of; ~ **de auxilio/de peligro** distress/danger signal; ~ **de llamada** ring (*US*) *o* ringing (*Brit*) tone; ~ **para marcar** dial (*US*) *o* dialling (*Brit*) tone.
señalado, a [senyàlà'ᵭo, à] *a* (*persona*) distinguished; (*pey*) notorious.
señalar [senyàlàr'] *vt* to mark; (*indicar*) to point out, indicate; (*significar*) to denote; (*referirse a*) to allude to; (*fijar*) to fix, settle; (*pey*) to criticize.
señalice [senyàlĕ'se] *etc vb* V **señalizar**.
señalización [senyàlĕsàsyon'] *nf* signing (*US*), signposting (*Brit*); signals *pl*.
señalizar [senyàlĕsàr'] *vt* (*AUT*) to put up road signs on; (*FERRO*) to put signals on; (*AUT*: *ruta*): **está bien señalizada** it's well signed.
señas [se'nyàs] *nfpl* V **seña**.
señor, a [senyor', à] *a* (*fam*) lordly ♦ *nm* (*hombre*) man; (*caballero*) gentleman; (*dueño*) owner, master; (*trato*: *antes de nombre propio*) Mr.; (: *hablando directamente*) sir ♦ *nf* (*dama*) lady; (*trato*: *antes de nombre propio*) Mrs.; (: *hablando directamente*) madam; (*esposa*) wife; **los** ~**es González** Mr. and Mrs. González; **S**~ **Don Jacinto Benavente** (*en sobre*) Mr. J. Benavente, J. Benavente Esq. (*Brit*); **S**~ **Director ...** (*de periódico*) Dear Sir ...; ~ **juez** your honor; ~ **Presidente** Mr. Chairman *o* President; **Muy** ~ **mío** Dear Sir; **Muy** ~**es nuestros** Dear Sirs; **Nuestro S**~ (*REL*) Our Lord; **¿está la señora?** is the lady of the house in?; **la señora de Smith** Mrs. Smith; **Nuestra Señora** (*REL*) Our Lady.
señoría [senyorĕ'à] *nf* rule; **su** *o* **vuestra S**~

your *o* his/her lordship/ladyship.

señorío [senyoɾe̅'o] *nm* manor; (*fig*) rule.

señorita [senyoɾe̅'tá] *nf* (*gen*) Miss; (*mujer joven*) young lady; (*maestra*) schoolteacher.

señorito [senyoɾe̅'to] *nm* young gentleman; (*lenguaje de criados*) master; (*pey*) dandy.

señuelo [senywe'lo] *nm* decoy.

Sep. *abr* (= *septiembre*) Sept.

sepa [se'pá] *etc vb* V **saber.**

separable [sepáɾá'ƀle] *a* separable; (*TEC*) detachable.

separación [sepáɾásyon'] *nf* separation; (*división*) division; (*distancia*) gap, distance; ~ **de bienes** division of property.

separado, a [sepáɾá'ƌo, á] *a* separate; (*TEC*) detached; **vive ~ de su mujer** he is separated from his wife; **por ~** separately.

separador [sepáɾáƌoɾ'] *nm* (*INFORM*) delimiter.

separadora [sepáɾáƌo'ɾá] *nf*: ~ **de hojas** burster.

separar [sepáɾáɾ'] *vt* to separate; (*silla de la mesa*) to move away; (*TEC: pieza*) to detach; (*persona: de un cargo*) to remove, dismiss; (*dividir*) to divide; ~**se** *vr* (*parte*) to come away; (*partes*) to come apart; (*persona*) to leave, go away; (*matrimonio*) to separate.

separatismo [sepáɾátḗs'mo] *nm* (*POL*) separatism.

sepelio [sepe'lyo] *nm* burial, interment.

sepia [se'pyá] *nf* cuttlefish.

Sept. *abr* (= *septiembre*) Sept.

septentrional [septentryonál'] *a* north *cpd*, northern.

septiembre [septyem'bre] *nm* September.

séptimo, a [sep'te̅mo, á] *a, nm* seventh.

septuagésimo, a [septwáhe'se̅mo, á] *a* seventieth.

sepulcral [sepōōlkrál'] *a* sepulchral; (*fig*) gloomy, dismal.

sepulcro [sepōōl'kro] *nm* tomb, grave, sepulcher (*US*), sepulchre (*Brit*).

sepultar [sepōōltáɾ'] *vt* to bury; (*en accidente*) to trap; **quedaban sepultados en la caverna** they were trapped in the cave.

sepultura [sepōōltōō'rá] *nf* (*acto*) burial; (*tumba*) grave, tomb; **dar ~ a** to bury; **recibir ~** to be buried.

sepulturero, a [sepōōltōōre'ro, á] *nm/f* gravedigger.

seque [se'ke] *etc vb* V **secar.**

sequedad [sekeɦáɦ'] *nf* dryness; (*fig*) brusqueness, curtness.

sequía [seke̅'á] *nf* drought.

séquito [se'ke̅to] *nm* (*de rey etc*) retinue; (*POL*) followers *pl*.

ser [ser] *vi* (*gen*) to be; (*devenir*) to become ♦ *nm* being; ~ **de** (*origen*) to be from, come from; (*hecho de*) to be (made) of;

(*pertenecer a*) to belong to; **¿qué será de mí?** what will become of me?; **soy ingeniero** I'm an engineer; **soy yo** it's me; **es la una** it is one o'clock; **es de esperar que** it is to be hoped that; **era de ver** you should have seen it; **a no ~ que** unless; **de no ~ así** if it were not so, were it not so; **o sea** that is to say; **sea como sea** be that as it may; ~ **vivo** living creature.

serenarse [serenár'se] *vr* to calm down; (*mar*) to grow calm; (*tiempo*) to clear up.

sereno, a [sere'no, á] *a* (*persona*) calm, unruffled; (*el tiempo*) fine, settled; (*ambiente*) calm, peaceful ♦ *nm* night watchman.

serial [seryál'] *nm* serial.

serie [se'rye] *nf* series; (*cadena*) sequence, succession; (*TV etc*) series; (*de inyecciones*) course; **fuera de ~** out of order; (*fig*) special, out of the ordinary; **fabricación en ~** mass production; (*INFORM*): **interface/impresora en ~** serial interface/printer.

seriedad [seryeɦáɦ'] *nf* seriousness; (*formalidad*) reliability; (*de crisis*) gravity, seriousness.

serio, a [se'ryo, á] *a* serious; reliable, dependable; grave, serious; **poco ~** (*actitud*) undignified; (*carácter*) unreliable; **en ~** seriously.

sermón [sermon'] *nm* (*REL*) sermon.

sermonear [sermoneáɾ'] *vt* (*fam*) to lecture ♦ *vi* to sermonize.

serpentear [serpenteáɾ'] *vi* to wriggle; (*camino, río*) to wind, snake.

serpentina [serpente̅'ná] *nf* streamer.

serpiente [serpyen'te] *nf* snake; ~ **boa** boa constrictor; ~ **de cascabel** rattlesnake.

serranía [serráne̅'á] *nf* mountainous area.

serrano, a [serrá'no, á] *a* highland *cpd*, hill *cpd* ♦ *nm/f* highlander.

serrar [serráɾ'] *vt* to saw.

serrín [serre̅n'] *nm* sawdust.

serrucho [serrōōtch'o] *nm* handsaw.

Servia [ser'ƀyá] *nf* Serbia.

servicial [serƀe̅syál'] *a* helpful, obliging.

servicio [serƀe̅'syo] *nm* service; (*CULIN etc*) set; ~**s** *nmpl* restroom *sg* (*US*), toilet(s) (*pl*); **estar de ~** to be on duty; ~ **aduanero** *o* **de aduana** customs service; ~ **a domicilio** home delivery service; ~ **incluido** (*en hotel etc*) service charge included; ~ **militar** military service; ~ **público** (*COM*) public utility.

servidor, a [serƀe̅ƌoɾ', á] *nm/f* servant; **su seguro ~ (s.s.s.)** yours truly (*US*) *o* faithfully (*Brit*); **un ~** (*el que habla o escribe*) your humble servant.

servidumbre [serƀe̅ƌōōm'bre] *nf* (*sujeción*) servitude; (*criados*) servants *pl*, staff.

servil [serƀe̅l'] *a* servile.

servilleta [serƀe̅ye'tá] *nf* napkin.

servilletero [serbēyete'ro] *nm* napkin ring.

servir [serbēr'] *vt* to serve; (*comida*) to serve out *o* up; (*TENIS etc*) to serve ♦ *vi* to serve; (*camarero*) to serve, wait; (*tener utilidad*) to be of use, be useful; ~**se** *vr* to serve *o* help o.s.; ¿**en qué puedo** ~**le?** how can I help you?; ~ **vino a uno** to pour wine for sb; ~ **de guía** to act *o* serve as a guide; **no sirve para nada** it's useless; ~**se de algo** to make use of sth, use sth; **sírvase pasar** please come in.

sesenta [sesen'tá] *num* sixty.

sesentón, ona [sesenton', oná] *a*, *nm/f* sixty-year-old.

sesgado, a [sesgá'tho, á] *a* slanted, slanting.

sesgo [ses'go] *nm* slant; (*fig*) slant, twist.

sesión [sesyon'] *nf* (*POL*) session, sitting; (*CINE*) showing; (*TEATRO*) performance; **abrir/levantar la** ~ to open/close *o* adjourn the meeting; **la segunda** ~ the second showing.

seso [se'so] *nm* brain; (*fig*) intelligence; ~**s** *nmpl* (*CULIN*) brains; **devanarse los** ~**s** to rack one's brains.

sesudo, a [sesōō'tho, á] *a* sensible, wise.

Set. *abr* (= *setiembre*) Sept.

seta [se'tá] *nf* mushroom; ~ **venenosa** toadstool.

setecientos, as [setesyen'tos, ás] *num* seven en hundred.

setenta [seten'tá] *num* seventy.

setiembre [setyem'bre] *nm*=**septiembre**.

seto [se'to] *nm* fence; ~ **vivo** hedge.

seudo... [seōō'tho] *pref* pseudo....

seudónimo [seōō'tho'nēmo] *nm* pseudonym.

Seúl [seōōl'] *nm* Seoul.

s.e.u.o. *abr* (= *salvo error u omisión*) errors and omissions excepted.

severidad [seberēthath'] *nf* severity.

severo, a [sebe'ro, á] *a* severe; (*disciplina*) strict; (*frío*) bitter.

Sevilla [sebē'yá] *nf* Seville.

sevillano, a [sebēyá'no, á] *a* of *o* from Seville ♦ *nm/f* native *o* inhabitant of Seville.

sexagenario, a [seksáhená'ryo, á] *a* sixty-year-old ♦ *nm/f* person in his/her sixties.

sexagésimo, a [seksáhe'sēmo, á] *num* sixtieth.

sexo [sek'so] *nm* sex; **el** ~ **femenino/masculino** the female/male sex.

sexto, a [sek'sto, á] *num* sixth; **Juan S**~ John the Sixth.

sexual [sekswál'] *a* sexual; **vida** ~ sex life.

s.f. *abr* (= *sin fecha*) no date.

s/f *abr* (*COM*:=*su favor*) your favor.

sgte(s). *abr* (= *siguiente(s)*) foll.

si [sē] *conj* if; (*en pregunta indirecta*) if, whether; ~ ... ~ ... whether ... or ...; **me pregunto** ~ ... I wonder if *o* whether ...; ~ **no** if not, otherwise; ¡~ **fuera verdad!** if only it were true!

sí [sē] *ad* yes ♦ *nm* consent ♦ *pron* (*uso impersonal*) oneself; (*sg: m*) himself; (: *f*) herself; (: *de cosa*) itself; (: *de usted*) yourself; (*pl*) themselves; (: *de ustedes*) yourselves; (: *recíproco*) each other; **él no quiere pero yo** ~ he doesn't want to but I do; **ella** ~ **vendrá** she will certainly come, she is sure to come; **claro que** ~ of course; **creo que** ~ I think so; **porque** ~ because that's the way it is; (*porque lo digo yo*) because I say so; ¡~ **que lo es!** I'll say it is!; ¡**eso** ~ **que no!** never; **se ríe de** ~ **misma** she laughs at herself; **cambiaron una mirada entre** ~ they gave each other a look; **de por** ~ by itself.

siamés, esa [syàmes', esá] *a*, *nm/f* Siamese.

Sicilia [sēsē'lyá] *nf* Sicily.

siciliano, a [sēsēlyá'no, á] *a*, *nm/f* Sicilian ♦ *nm* (*LING*) Sicilian.

SIDA [sē'thá] *nm abr* (= *síndrome de inmunodeficiencia adquirida*) AIDS.

siderurgia [sētherōōr'hyá] *nf* iron and steel industry.

siderúrgico, a [sētherōōr'hēco, á] *a* iron and steel *cpd*.

sidra [sē'thrá] *nf* cider.

siega [sye'gá] *etc vb V* **segar** ♦ *nf* (*cosechar*) reaping; (*segar*) mowing; (*época*) harvest (time).

siegue [sye'ge] *etc vb V* **segar**.

siembra [syem'brá] *etc vb V* **sembrar** ♦ *nf* sowing.

siempre [syem'pre] *ad* always; (*todo el tiempo*) all the time ♦ *conj*: ~ **que** ... (+ *indic*) whenever ...; (+ *subjun*) provided that ...; **es lo de** ~ it's the same old story; **como** ~ as usual; **para** ~ forever.

sien [syen] *nf* (*ANAT*) temple.

siento [syen'to] *etc vb V* **sentar**, **sentir**.

sierra [sye'rrá] *etc vb V* **serrar** ♦ *nf* (*TEC*) saw; (*GEO*) mountain range; **S**~ **Leona** Sierra Leone.

siervo, a [syer'ho, á] *nm/f* slave.

siesta [sye'stá] *nf* siesta, nap; **dormir la** *o* **echarse una** *o* **tomar una** ~ to have an afternoon nap.

siete [sye'te] *num* seven.

sífilis [sē'fēlēs] *nf* syphilis.

sifón [sēfon'] *nm* syphon; **whisky con** ~ whiskey and soda.

siga [sē'gá] *etc vb V* **seguir**.

sigilo [sēhē'lo] *nm* secrecy; (*discreción*) discretion.

sigla [sē'glá] *nf* initial, abbreviation.

siglo [sē'glo] *nm* century; (*fig*) age; **S**~ **de las Luces** Age of Enlightenment; **S**~ **de Oro** Golden Age.

significación [sēgnēfēkásyon'] *nf* significance.

significado [sēgnēfēká'tho] *nm* significance; (*de palabra etc*) meaning.

significar [sĕgnĕfēkár'] *vt* to mean, signify; (*notificar*) to make known, express.

significativo, a [sĕgnĕfēkátē'ħo. á] *a* significant.

signifique [sĕgnĕfē'ke] *etc vb V* **significar**.

signo [sēg'no] *nm* sign; ~ **de admiración** *o* **exclamación** exclamation mark; ~ **igual** equals sign; ~ **de interrogación** question mark; ~ **de más/de menos** plus/minus sign; ~**s de puntuación** punctuation marks.

siguiendo [sēgyen'do] *etc vb V* **seguir**.

siguiente [sēgyen'te] *a* following; (*próximo*) next.

sílaba [sē'láħá] *nf* syllable.

silbar [sēlħár'] *vt, vi* to whistle; (*silbato*) to blow; (*TEATRO etc*) to hiss.

silbato [sēlħá'to] *nm* (*instrumento*) whistle.

silbido [sēlħē'ħo], **silbo** [sēl'ħo] *nm* whistle, whistling; (*abucheo*) hiss.

silenciador [sēlensyàħor'] *nm* silencer.

silenciar [sēlensyár'] *vt* (*persona*) to silence; (*escándalo*) to hush up.

silencio [sēlen'syo] *nm* silence, quiet; **en el** ~ **más absoluto** in dead silence; **guardar** ~ to keep silent.

silencioso, a [sēlensyo'so. á] *a* silent, quiet.

sílfide [sēl'fēħe] *nf* sylph.

silicio [sēlē'syo] *nm* silicon.

silueta [sēlwe'tá] *nf* silhouette; (*de edificio*) outline; (*figura*) figure.

silvestre [sēlħes'tre] *a* (*BOT*) wild; (*fig*) rustic, rural.

silla [sē'yá] *nf* (*asiento*) chair; (*tb*: ~ **de montar**) saddle; ~ **de ruedas** wheelchair.

sillería [sēyerē'á] *nf* (*asientos*) chairs *pl*, set of chairs; (*REL*) choir stalls *pl*; (*taller*) chairmaker's workshop.

sillón [sēyon'] *nm* armchair, easy chair.

sima [sē'má] *nf* abyss, chasm.

simbolice [sēmbolē'se] *etc vb V* **simbolizar**.

simbólico, a [sēmbo'lēko, á] *a* symbolic(al).

simbolizar [sēmbolēsár'] *vt* to symbolize.

símbolo [sēm'bolo] *nm* symbol; ~ **gráfico** (*INFORM*) icon.

simetría [sēmetrē'á] *nf* symmetry.

simiente [sēmyen'te] *nf* seed.

similar [sēmēlár'] *a* similar.

similitud [sēmēlētōōħ'] *nf* similarity, resemblance.

simio [sē'myo] *nm* ape.

simpatía [sēmpátē'á] *nf* liking; (*afecto*) affection; (*amabilidad*) kindness; (*de ambiente*) friendliness; (*de persona, lugar*) charm, attractiveness; (*solidaridad*) mutual support, solidarity; **tener** ~ **a** to like; **la famosa** ~ **andaluza** that well-known Andalusian charm.

simpatice [sēmpátē'se] *etc vb V* **simpatizar**.

simpático, a [sēmpá'tēko, á] *a* nice, pleasant; (*bondadoso*) kind; **no le hemos caído**

muy ~**s** she didn't like us very much.

simpatiquísimo, a [sēmpátēkē'sēmo, á] *a* (*superl de* **simpático**) ever so nice; ever so kind.

simpatizante [sēmpátēsán'te] *nm/f* sympathizer.

simpatizar [sēmpátēsár'] *vi*: ~ **con** to get along with.

simple [sēm'ple] *a* simple; (*elemental*) simple, easy; (*mero*) mere; (*puro*) pure, sheer ♦ *nm/f* simpleton; **un** ~ **soldado** an ordinary soldier.

simpleza [sēmple'sá] *nf* simpleness; (*necedad*) silly thing.

simplicidad [sēmplēsēħáħ'] *nf* simplicity.

simplificar [sēmplēfēkár'] *vt* to simplify.

simplifique [sēmplēfē'ke] *etc vb V* **simplificar**.

simplón, ona [sēmplon', oná] *a* simple, gullible ♦ *nm/f* simple soul.

simposio [sēmpo'syo] *nm* symposium.

simulacro [sēmōōlá'kro] *nm* (*apariencia*) semblance; (*fingimiento*) sham.

simular [sēmōōlár'] *vt* to simulate; (*fingir*) to feign, sham.

simultanear [sēmōōltáneár'] *vt*: ~ **dos cosas** to do two things simultaneously.

simultáneo, a [sēmōōltá'neo, á] *a* simultaneous.

sin [sēn] *prep* without; (*a no ser por*) but for ♦ *conj*: ~ **que** (+ *subjun*) without; ~ **decir nada** without a word; ~ **verlo yo** without my seeing it; **platos** ~ **lavar** unwashed *o* dirty dishes; **la ropa está** ~ **lavar** the clothes are unwashed; ~ **que lo sepa él** without his knowing; ~ **embargo** however.

sinagoga [sēnágo'gá] *nf* synagogue.

Sinaí [sēnáē'] *nm*: **El** ~ Sinai, the Sinai Peninsula; **el Monte** ~ Mount Sinai.

sinceridad [sēnserēħáħ'] *nf* sincerity.

sincero, a [sēnse'ro, á] *a* sincere; (*persona*) genuine; (*opinión*) frank; (*felicitaciones*) heartfelt.

síncope [sēn'kope] *nm* (*desmayo*) blackout; ~ **cardíaco** (*MED*) heart failure.

sincronice [sēnkronē'se] *etc vb V* **sincronizar**.

sincronizar [sēnkronēsár'] *vt* to synchronize.

sindical [sēndēkál'] *a* union *cpd*, trade-union *cpd*.

sindicalista [sēndēkálē'stá] *a* trade-union *cpd* ♦ *nm/f* trade unionist.

sindicar [sēndēkár'] *vt* (*obreros*) to organize, unionize; ~**se** *vr* (*obrero*) to join a union.

sindicato [sēndēká'to] *nm* (*de trabajadores*) trade(s) *o* labor (*US*) union; (*de negociantes*) syndicate.

sindique [sēndē'ke] *etc vb V* **sindicar**.

sinfín [sēnfēn'] *nm*: **un** ~ **de** a great many,

no end of.

sinfonía [sĭnfonē'á] *nf* symphony.

Singapur [sĭngápōōr'] *nm* Singapore.

singular [sĭngōōlár'] *a* singular; (*fig*) outstanding, exceptional; (*pey*) peculiar, odd ♦ *nm* (*LING*) singular; **en ~** in the singular.

singularice [sĭngōōlárē'sc] *etc vb V* **singularizar.**

singularidad [sĭngōōlárētháth'] *nf* singularity, peculiarity.

singularizar [sĭngōōlárēsár'] *vt* to single out; **~se** *vr* to distinguish o.s., stand out.

siniestro, a [sĭnycs'tro, á] *a* left; (*fig*) sinister ♦ *nm* (*accidente*) accident; (*desastre*) natural disaster.

sinnúmero [sĭnnōō'mero] *nm* = **sinfín.**

sino [sē'no] *nm* fate, destiny ♦ *conj* (*pero*) but; (*salvo*) except, save; **no son 8 ~ 9** there are not 8 but 9; **todos ~ él** all except him.

sinónimo, a [sĭno'nēmo, á] *a* synonymous ♦ *nm* synonym.

sinrazón [sĭnráson'] *nf* wrong, injustice.

sinsabor [sĭnsáḅor'] *nm* (*molestia*) trouble; (*dolor*) sorrow; (*preocupación*) uneasiness.

síntesis [sēn'tesēs] *nf inv* synthesis.

sintetice [sĭntetē'sc] *etc vb V* **sintetizar.**

sintético, a [sĭnte'tēko, á] *a* synthetic.

sintetizador [sĭntetēsátḥor'] *nm* synthesizer.

sintetizar [sĭntetēsár'] *vt* to synthesize.

sintiendo [sĭntyen'do] *etc vb V* **sentir.**

síntoma [sēn'tomá] *nm* symptom.

sintonía [sĭntonē'á] *nf* (*RADIO*) tuning; (*melodía*) signature tune.

sintonice [sĭntonē'sc] *etc vb V* **sintonizar.**

sintonizador [sĭntonēsátḥor'] *nm* (*RADIO*) tuner.

sintonizar [sĭntonēsár'] *vt* (*RADIO*) to tune (in) to, pick up.

sinuoso, a [sĭnwo'so, á] *a* (*camino*) winding; (*rumbo*) devious.

sinvergüenza [sĭmbcrgwen'sá] *nm/f* rogue, scoundrel.

sionismo [syonēs'mo] *nm* Zionism.

siquiera [sĕkyc'rá] *conj* even if, even though ♦ *ad* at least; **ni ~** not even.

sirena [sĕrc'ná] *nf* siren, mermaid; (*bocina*) siren.

Siria [sē'ryá] *nf* Syria.

sirio, a [sē'ryo, á] *a, nm/f* Syrian.

sirviendo [sĕrḥyen'do] *etc vb V* **servir.**

sirviente, a [sĕrḥyen'tc, á] *nm/f* servant.

sisa [sē'sá] *nf* petty theft; (*COSTURA*) dart; (*sobaquera*) armhole.

sisar [sēsár'] *vt* (*robar*) to thieve; (*COSTURA*) to take in.

sisear [sēseár'] *vt, vi* to hiss.

sismógrafo [sēsmo'gráfo] *nm* seismograph.

sistema [sēste'má] *nm* system; (*método*) method; **~ impositivo** *o* **tributario** taxa-

tion, tax system; **~ pedagógico** educational system; **~ de alerta inmediata** early-warning system; **~ binario** (*INFORM*) binary system; **~ experto** expert system; **~ de facturación** (*COM*) invoicing system; **~ de fondo fijo** (*COM*) imprest system; **~ de lógica compartida** (*INFORM*) shared logic system; **~ métrico** metric system; **~ operativo (en disco)** (*INFORM*) (disk-based) operating system.

sistemático, a [sēstemá'tēko, á] *a* systematic.

sitiar [sētyár'] *vt* to besiege, lay siege to.

sitio [sē'tyo] *nm* (*lugar*) place; (*espacio*) room, space; (*MIL*) siege; **¿hay ~?** is there any room?; **hay ~ de sobra** there's plenty of room.

situación [sētwásyon'] *nf* situation, position; (*estatus*) position, standing.

situado, a [sētwá'tḥo, á] *a* situated, placed; **estar ~** (*COM*) to be financially secure.

situar [sētwár'] *vt* to place, put; (*edificio*) to locate, situate.

S.L. *abr* (*COM*:=*Sociedad Limitada*) ≈ Corp. (*US*), Ltd. (*Brit*).

slip [eslēp'], *pl* **slips** *nm* pants *pl*, briefs *pl*.

slot [eslot'], *pl* **slots** *nm*: **~ de expansión** expansion slot.

S.M. *abr* (= *Su Majestad*) HM.

smoking [(e)smo'kēn] (*pl* **~s**) *nm* tuxedo (*US*), dinner jacket (*Brit*).

s/n *abr* (= *sin número*) no number.

snob [esnob'] = **esnob.**

SO *abr* (= *suroeste*) SW.

so [so] *excl* whoa!; **¡~ burro!** you idiot! ♦ *prep* under.

s/o *abr* (*COM*:=*su orden*) your order.

sobaco [soḅá'ko] *nm* armpit.

sobado, a [soḅá'tḥo, á] *a* (*ropa*) worn; (*arrugado*) crumpled; (*libro*) well-worn; (*CULIN*: *masa*) crumbly (*US*), short (*Brit*).

sobar [soḅár'] *vt* (*tela*) to finger; (*ropa*) to rumple, mess up; (*músculos*) to rub, massage.

soberanía [soḅeránē'á] *nf* sovereignty.

soberano, a [soḅcrá'no, á] *a* sovereign; (*fig*) supreme ♦ *nm/f* sovereign; **los ~s** the king and queen.

soberbio, a [soḅer'ḥyo, á] *a* (*orgulloso*) proud; (*altivo*) haughty, arrogant; (*fig*) magnificent, superb ♦ *nf* pride; haughtiness, arrogance; magnificence.

sobornar [soḅornár'] *vt* to bribe.

soborno [soḅor'no] *nm* (*un ~*) bribe; (*el ~*) bribery.

sobra [so'ḅrá] *nf* excess, surplus; **~s** *nfpl* left-overs, scraps; **de ~** surplus, extra; **lo sé de ~** I know too much about it; **tengo de ~** I've more than enough.

sobradamente [soḅráthámen'te] *ad* amply; (*saber*) only too well.

sobrado, a [soḅrá'ḍo, à] *a* (*más que suficiente*) more than enough; (*superfluo*) excessive ♦ *ad* too, exceedingly; **sobradas veces** repeatedly.

sobrante [soḅrán'te] *a* remaining, extra ♦ *nm* surplus, remainder.

sobrar [soḅrár'] *vt* to exceed, surpass ♦ *vi* (*tener de más*) to be more than enough; (*quedar*) to remain, be left (over).

sobrasada [soḅrásá'ḍá] *nf* ≈ sausage spread.

sobre [so'ḅre] *prep* (*gen*) on; (*encima*) on (top of); (*por encima de, arriba de*) over, above; (*más que*) more than; (*además*) in addition to, besides; (*alrededor de*) about; (*porcentaje*) in, out of; (*tema*) about, on ♦ *nm* envelope; ~ **todo** above all; **3 ~ 100** 3 in a 100, 3 out of every 100; **un libro ~ Tirso** a book about Tirso; ~ **de ventanilla** window envelope.

sobrecama [soḅreká'má] *nf* bedspread.

sobrecapitalice [soḅrekápétálḗ'se] *etc vb V* **sobrecapitalizar**.

sobrecapitalizar [soḅrekápétálḗsár'] *vi* to overcapitalize.

sobrecargar [soḅrekárgár'] *vt* (*camión*) to overload; (*COM*) to surcharge.

sobrecargue [soḅrekár'ge] *etc vb V* **sobrecargar**.

sobrecoger [soḅrekoher'] *vt* (*sobresaltar*) to startle; (*asustar*) to scare; ~**se** *vr* (*sobresaltarse*) to be startled; (*asustarse*) to get scared; (*quedar impresionado*): ~**se (de)** to be overawed (by).

sobrecoja [soḅreko'há] *etc vb V* **sobrecoger**.

sobredosis [soḅreḍo'sés] *nf inv* overdose.

sobre(e)ntender [soḅre(e)ntender'] *vt* to understand; (*adivinar*) to deduce, infer; ~**se** *vr*: **se sobre(e)ntiende que ...** it is implied that ....

sobreescribir [soḅreeskrēḅer'] *vt* (*INFORM*) to overwrite.

sobre(e)stimar [soḅre(e)stēmár'] *vt* to overestimate.

sobregiro [soḅrehē'ro] *nm* (*COM*) overdraft.

sobrehumano, a [soḅreōōmá'no, à] *a* superhuman.

sobreimprimir [soḅreēmprēmēr'] *vt* (*COM*) to merge.

sobrellevar [soḅreyeḅár'] *vt* (*fig*) to bear, endure.

sobremesa [soḅreme'sá] *nf* (*después de comer*) after-dinner conversation; (*INFORM*) desktop; **conversación de ~** table talk.

sobremodo [soḅremo'ḍo] *ad* very much, enormously.

sobrenatural [soḅrenátōōrál'] *a* supernatural.

sobrenombre [soḅrenom'bre] *nm* nickname.

sobrepasar [soḅrepásár'] *vt* to exceed, surpass.

sobrepondré [soḅrepondre'] *etc vb V* **sobreponer**.

sobreponer [soḅreponer'] *vt* (*poner encima*) to put on top; (*añadir*) to add; ~**se** *vr*: ~**se a** to overcome.

sobreponga [soḅrepon'gá] *etc vb V* **sobreponer**.

sobreprima [soḅreprē'má] *nf* (*COM*) extra premium.

sobreproducción [soḅreproḍōōksyon'] *nf* overproduction.

sobrepuesto [soḅrepwe'sto], **sobrepuse** [soḅrepōō'se] *etc vb V* **sobreponer**.

sobresaldré [soḅresáldre'] *etc*, **sobresalga** [soḅresál'gá] *etc vb V* **sobresalir**.

sobresaliente [soḅresályen'te] *a* projecting; (*fig*) outstanding, excellent; (*UNIV etc*) first class ♦ *nm* (*UNIV etc*) distinction.

sobresalir [soḅresálēr'] *vi* to project, jut out; (*fig*) to stand out, excel.

sobresaltar [soḅresáltár'] *vt* (*asustar*) to scare, frighten; (*sobrecoger*) to startle.

sobresalto [soḅresál'to] *nm* (*movimiento*) start; (*susto*) scare; (*turbación*) sudden shock.

sobreseer [soḅreseer'] *vt*: ~ **una causa** (*JUR*) to stop a case.

sobrestadía [soḅrestáthē'á] *nf* (*COM*) demurrage.

sobretensión [soḅretensyon'] *nf* (*ELEC*): ~ **transitoria** surge.

sobretodo [soḅreto'ḍo] *nm* overcoat.

sobrevendré [soḅreḅendre'] *etc*, **sobrevenga** [soḅreḅen'gá] *etc vb V* **sobrevenir**.

sobrevenir [soḅreḅenēr'] *vi* (*ocurrir*) to happen (unexpectedly); (*resultar*) to follow, ensue.

sobreviene [soḅreḅye'ne] *etc*, **sobrevine** [soḅreḅē'ne] *etc vb V* **sobrevenir**.

sobreviviente [soḅreḅēḅyen'te] *a* surviving ♦ *nm/f* survivor.

sobrevivir [soḅreḅēḅēr'] *vi* to survive; (*persona*) to outlive; (*objeto etc*) to outlast.

sobrevolar [soḅreḅolár'] *vt* to fly over.

sobrevuele [soḅreḅwe'le] *etc vb V* **sobrevolar**.

sobriedad [soḅryeḍáḍ'] *nf* sobriety, soberness; (*moderación*) moderation, restraint.

sobrino, a [soḅre'no, à] *nm/f* nephew/niece.

sobrio, a [soḅ'ryo, à] *a* (*moderado*) moderate, restrained.

socarrón, ona [sokárron', oná] *a* (*sarcástico*) sarcastic, ironic(al).

socavar [sokáḅár'] *vt* to undermine; (*excavar*) to dig underneath o below.

socavón [sokáḅon'] *nm* (*en mina*) gallery; (*hueco*) hollow; (*en la calle*) hole.

sociable [sosyá'ḅle] *a* (*persona*) sociable, friendly; (*animal*) social.

social [sosyál'] *a* social; (*COM*) company *cpd*.

socialdemócrata [sosyáldemo'krátá] *nm/f* social democrat.

socialdemocrático, a [sosyáldemokrá'tēko, á] *a* social-democratic.

socialice [sosyálē'se] *etc vb V* **socializar**.

socialista [sosyálē'stá] *a, nm/f* socialist.

socializar [sosyálēsár'] *vt* to socialize.

sociedad [sosyeᵺáᵺ'] *nf* society; (*COM*) company; ~ **de ahorro y préstamo** savings and loan society; ~ **anónima (S.A.)** incorporated company (Inc.) (*US*), limited company (Ltd.) (*Brit*); ~ **de beneficiencia** benefit association (*US*), friendly society (*Brit*); ~ **de cartera** investment trust; ~ **comanditaria** (*COM*) co-ownership; ~ **conjunta** (*COM*) joint venture; ~ **inmobiliaria** savings and loan (society) (*US*), building society (*Brit*); ~ **de responsabilidad limitada** (*COM*) corporation (*US*), private limited company (*Brit*).

socio, a [so'syo, á] *nm/f* (*miembro*) member; (*COM*) partner; ~ **activo** active partner; ~ **capitalista** *o* **comanditario** silent partner.

socioeconómico, a [sosyoekono'mēko, á] *a* socio-economic.

sociología [sosyolohē'á] *nf* sociology.

sociólogo, a [sosyo'logo, á] *nm/f* sociologist.

socorrer [sokorrer'] *vt* to help.

socorrido, a [sokorrē'ᵺo, á] *a* (*tienda*) well-stocked; (*útil*) handy; (*persona*) helpful.

socorrista [sokorrē'stá] *nm/f* first aider; (*en piscina, playa*) lifeguard.

socorro [soko'rro] *nm* (*ayuda*) help, aid; (*MIL*) relief; ¡~! help!

soda [so'ᵺá] *nf* (*sosa*) soda; (*bebida*) soda (water).

soez [soes'] *a* dirty, obscene.

sofá [sofá'] *nm* sofa, settee.

sofá-cama [sofá'kámá] *nm* studio couch, sofa bed.

Sofía [so'fyà] *nf* Sofia.

sofisticación [sofēstēkásyon'] *nf* sophistication.

sofocado, a [sofoká'ᵺo, á] *a*: **estar** ~ (*fig*) to be out of breath; (*ahogarse*) to feel stifled.

sofocar [sofokár'] *vt* to suffocate; (*apagar*) to smother, put out; ~**se** *vr* to suffocate; (*fig*) to blush, feel embarrassed.

sofoco [sofo'ko] *nm* suffocation; (*azoro*) embarrassment.

sofocón [sofokon'] *nm*: **llevarse** *o* **pasar un** ~ to have a sudden shock.

sofreír [sofreēr'] *vt* to fry lightly.

sofría [sofrē'á] *etc*, **sofriendo** [sofryen'do] *etc*, **sofrito** [sofrē'to] *vb V* **sofreír**.

soft(ware) [sof'(wer)] *nm* (*INFORM*) soft-

ware.

soga [so'ɡá] *nf* rope.

sois [soēs] *vb V* **ser**.

soja [so'hà] *nf* soy.

sojuzgar [sohōōsɡár'] *vt* to subdue, rule despotically.

sojuzgue [sohōōs'ɡe] *etc vb V* **sojuzgar**.

sol [sol] *nm* sun; (*luz*) sunshine, sunlight; ~ **naciente/poniente** rising/setting sun; **tomar el** ~ to sunbathe; **hace** ~ it is sunny.

solace [solá'se] *etc vb V* **solazar**.

solamente [solámen'te] *ad* only, just.

solapa [solá'pá] *nf* (*de chaqueta*) lapel; (*de libro*) jacket.

solapado, a [solápá'ᵺo, á] *a* sly, underhand.

solar [solár'] *a* solar, sun *cpd* ♦ *nm* (*terreno*) plot (of ground); (*local*) undeveloped site.

solaz [solás'] *nm* recreation, relaxation.

solazar [solásár'] *vt* (*divertir*) to amuse; ~**se** *vr* to enjoy o.s., relax.

soldada [soldá'ᵺá] *nf* pay.

soldado [soldá'ᵺo] *nm* soldier; ~ **raso** private.

soldador [soldáᵺor'] *nm* soldering iron; (*persona*) welder.

soldar [soldár'] *vt* to solder, weld; (*unir*) to join, unite.

soleado, a [soleá'ᵺo, á] *a* sunny.

soledad [soleᵺáᵺ'] *nf* solitude; (*estado infeliz*) loneliness.

solemne [solem'ne] *a* solemn; (*tontería*) utter; (*error*) complete.

solemnidad [solemnēᵺáᵺ'] *nf* solemnity.

soler [soler'] *vi* to be in the habit of, be accustomed to; **suele salir a las ocho** she usually goes out at 8 o'clock; **solíamos ir todos los años** we used to go every year.

solera [sole'rá] *nf* (*tradición*) tradition; **vino de** ~ vintage wine.

solicitar [solēsētár'] *vt* (*permiso*) to ask for, seek; (*puesto*) to apply for; (*votos*) to canvass for; (*atención*) to attract; (*persona*) to pursue, chase after.

solícito, a [solē'sēto, á] *a* (*diligente*) diligent; (*cuidadoso*) careful.

solicitud [solēsētōōᵺ'] *nf* (*calidad*) great care; (*petición*) request; (*a un puesto*) application.

solidaridad [solēᵺáréᵺáᵺ'] *nf* solidarity; **por** ~ **con** (*POL etc*) out of *o* in solidarity with.

solidario, a [solēᵺá'ryo, á] *a* (*participación*) joint, common; (*compromiso*) mutually binding; **hacerse** ~ **de** to declare one's solidarity with.

solidez [solēᵺes'] *nf* solidity.

sólido, a [so'lēᵺo, á] *a* solid; (*TEC*) solidly made; (*bien construido*) well-built.

soliloquio [solēlo'kyo] *nm* soliloquy.

solista [solē'stá] *nm/f* soloist.

solitario, a [soleˈtáryo, à] a (persona) lonely, solitary; (lugar) lonely, desolate ♦ nm/f (reclusa) recluse; (en la sociedad) loner ♦ nm solitaire ♦ nf tapeworm.

soliviantar [soleβyantár'] vt to stir up, rouse (to revolt); (enojar) to anger; (sacar de quicio) to exasperate.

solo, a [so'lo, à] a (único) single, sole; (sin compañía) alone; (MUS) solo; (solitario) lonely; **hay una sola dificultad** there is just one difficulty; **a solas** alone, by o.s.

sólo [so'lo] ad only, just; (exclusivamente) solely; **tan ~** only just.

solomillo [solomé'yo] nm sirloin.

soltar [soltár'] vt (dejar ir) to let go of; (desprender) to unfasten, loosen; (librar) to release, set free; (amarras) to cast off; (AUTO: freno etc) to release; (suspiro) to heave; (risa etc) to let out; **~se** vr (desanudarse) to come undone; (desprenderse) to come off; (adquirir destreza) to become expert; (en idioma) to become fluent.

soltero, a [solte'ro, à] a single, unmarried ♦ nm bachelor ♦ nf single woman, spinster.

solterón [solteron'] nm confirmed bachelor.

solterona [soltero'ná] nf spinster, maiden lady; (pey) old maid.

soltura [soltōō'rà] nf looseness, slackness; (de los miembros) agility, ease of movement; (en el hablar) fluency, ease.

soluble [solōō'βle] a (QUÍMICA) soluble; (problema) solvable; **~ en agua** soluble in water.

solución [solōōsyon'] nf solution; **~ de continuidad** break in continuity.

solucionar [solōōsyonár'] vt (problema) to solve; (asunto) to settle, resolve.

solvencia [solβen'syà] nf (COM: estado) solvency; (: acción) settlement, payment.

solventar [solβentár'] vt (pagar) to settle, pay; (resolver) to resolve.

solvente [solβen'te] a solvent, free of debt.

solloce [soyo'se] etc vb V **sollozar**.

sollozar [soyosár'] vi to sob.

sollozo [soyo'so] nm sob.

Somalia [somá'lyà] nf Somalia.

sombra [som'brà] nf shadow; (como protección) shade; **~s** nfpl darkness sg, shadows; **sin ~ de duda** without a shadow of doubt; **tener buena/mala ~** (suerte) to be lucky/unlucky; (carácter) to be likeable/disagreeable.

sombrero [sombre'ro] nm hat; **~ hongo** derby (US), bowler (hat) (Brit); **~ de copa** o **de pelo** (AM) top hat.

sombrilla [sombré'yà] nf parasol.

sombrío, a [sombré'o, à] a (oscuro) ·shady; (fig) sad; (persona) gloomy.

somero, a [some'ro, à] a superficial.

someter [someter'] vt (país) to conquer; (persona) to subject to one's will; (in-

forme) to present, submit; **~se** vr to give in, yield, submit; **~se a** to submit to; **~se a una operación** to undergo an operation.

sometimiento [sometēmyen'to] nm (estado) submission; (acción) presentation.

somier [somyer'], pl **somiers** nm spring mattress.

somnífero [somnē'fero] nm sleeping pill o tablet.

somnolencia [somnolen'syà] nf sleepiness, drowsiness.

somos [so'mos] vb V **ser**.

son [son] vb V **ser** ♦ nm sound; **en ~ de broma** as a joke.

sonado, a [sonà'δo, à] a (comentado) talked-of; (famoso) famous; (COM: pey) hyped(-up).

sonajero [sonáhe'ro] nm (baby's) rattle.

sonambulismo [sonámbōōlēs'mo] nm sleepwalking.

sonámbulo, a [sonám'bōōlo, à] nm/f sleepwalker.

sonar [sonár'] vt (campana) to ring; (trompeta, sirena) to blow ♦ vi to sound; (hacer ruido) to make a noise; (LING) to be sounded, be pronounced; (ser conocido) to sound familiar; (campana) to ring; (reloj) to strike, chime; **~se** vr: **~se (la nariz)** to blow one's nose; **es un nombre que suena** it's a name that's in the news; **me suena ese nombre** that name rings a bell.

sonda [son'dà] nf (NAUT) sounding; (TEC) bore, drill; (MED) probe.

sondear [sondeár'] vt to sound; to bore (into), drill; to probe, sound; (fig) to sound out.

sondeo [sonde'o] nm sounding; boring, drilling; (encuesta) poll, enquiry; **~ de la opinión pública** public opinion poll.

sónico, a [so'nēko, à] a sonic, sound cpd.

sonido [sonē'δo] nm sound.

sonoro, a [sono'ro, à] a sonorous; (resonante) loud, resonant; (LING) voiced; **efectos ~s** sound effects.

sonreír [sonreēr'] vi, **sonreírse** vr to smile.

sonría [sonrē'à] etc, **sonriendo** [sonryen'do] etc vb V **sonreír**.

sonriente [sonryen'te] a smiling.

sonrisa [sonrē'sà] nf smile.

sonrojar [sonrohár'] vt: **~ a uno** to make sb blush; **~se** vr: **~se (de)** to blush (at).

sonrojo [sonro'ho] nm blush.

sonsacar [sonsákár'] vt to wheedle, coax; **~ a uno** to pump sb for information.

sonsaque [sonsá'ke] etc vb V **sonsacar**.

sonsonete [sonsone'te] nm (golpecitos) tap(ping); (voz monótona) monotonous delivery, singsong (voice).

soñador, a [sonyàδor', à] nm/f dreamer.

soñar [sonyár'] vt, vi to dream; **~ con** to dream about o of; **soñé contigo anoche** I dreamed about you last night.

soñoliento, a [sonyolyen'to, à] *a* sleepy, drowsy.

sopa [so'pà] *nf* soup; ~ **de fideos** noodle soup.

sopero, a [sope'ro, à] *a* (*plato, cuchara*) soup *cpd* ♦ *nm* soup plate ♦ *nf* soup tureen.

sopesar [sopesàr'] *vt* (*fig*) to weigh.

sopetón [sopeton'] *nm*: **de** ~ suddenly, unexpectedly.

soplar [soplàr'] *vt* (*polvo*) to blow away, blow off; (*inflar*) to blow up; (*vela*) to blow out; (*ayudar a recordar*) to prompt; (*birlar*) to rip off; (*delatar*) to squeal on ♦ *vi* to blow; (*delatar*) to squeal; (*beber*) to booze, bend the elbow.

soplete [sople'te] *nm* blowtorch (*US*), blowlamp (*Brit*); ~ **soldador** welding torch.

soplo [so'plo] *nm* blow, puff; (*de viento*) puff, gust.

soplón, ona [soplon', onà] *nm/f* (*fam*: *chismoso*) telltale; (: *de policía*) informer, grass.

soponcio [sopon'syo] *nm* dizzy spell.

sopor [sopor'] *nm* drowsiness.

soporífero, a [soporē'fero, à] *a* sleep-inducing; (*fig*) soporific ♦ *nm* sleeping pill.

soportable [soportà'ble] *a* bearable.

soportar [soportàr'] *vt* to bear, carry; (*fig*) to bear, put up with.

soporte [sopor'te] *nm* support; (*fig*) pillar, support; (*INFORM*) medium; ~ **de entrada/salida** input/output medium.

soprano [soprà'no] *nf* soprano.

sor [sor] *nf*: **S~ María** Sister Mary.

sorber [sorber'] *vt* (*chupar*) to sip; (*inhalar*) to sniff, inhale; (*absorber*) to soak up, absorb.

sorbete [sorbe'te] *nm* sherbet.

sorbo [sor'bo] *nm* (*trago*) gulp, swallow; (*chupada*) sip; **beber a** ~**s** to sip.

sordera [sorde'rà] *nf* deafness.

sórdido, a [sor'dēðo, à] *a* dirty, squalid.

sordo, a [sor'ðo, à] *a* (*persona*) deaf; (*ruido*) dull; (*LING*) voiceless ♦ *nm/f* deaf person; **quedarse** ~ to go deaf.

sordomudo, a [sordomoō'ðo, à] *a* deaf and dumb ♦ *nm/f* deaf-mute.

soriano, a [soryà'no, à] *a* of *o* from Soria ♦ *nm/f* native *o* inhabitant of Soria.

sorna [sor'nà] *nf* (*malicia*) slyness; (*tono burlón*) sarcastic tone.

soroche [sorotch'e] *nm* (*AM MED*) mountain sickness.

sorprendente [sorprenden'te] *a* surprising.

sorprender [sorprender'] *vt* to surprise; (*asombrar*) to amaze; (*sobresaltar*) to startle; (*coger desprevenido*) to catch unawares; ~**se** *vr*: ~**se (de)** to be surprised *o* amazed (at).

sorpresa [sorpre'sà] *nf* surprise.

sorpresivo, a [sorpresē'bo, à] *a* (*AM*) surprising; (*imprevisto*) sudden.

sortear [sorteàr'] *vt* to draw lots for; (*rifar*) to raffle; (*dificultad*) to dodge, avoid.

sorteo [sorte'o] *nm* (*en lotería*) draw; (*rifa*) raffle.

sortija [sortē'hà] *nf* ring; (*rizo*) ringlet, curl.

sortilegio [sortēle'hyo] *nm* (*hechicería*) sorcery; (*hechizo*) spell.

sosegado, a [sosegà'ðo, à] *a* quiet, calm.

sosegar [sosegàr'] *vt* to quieten, calm; (*el ánimo*) to reassure ♦ *vi* to rest.

sosegué [sosege'], **soseguemos** [sosege'mos] *etc vb V* **sosegar**.

sosiego [sosye'go] *etc vb V* **sosegar** ♦ *nm* quiet(ness), calm(ness).

sosiegue [sosye'ge] *etc vb V* **sosegar**.

soslayo [soslà'yo]: **de** ~ *ad* obliquely, sideways; **mirar de** ~ to look out of the corner of one's eye (at).

soso, a [so'so, à] *a* (*CULIN*) tasteless; (*fig*) dull, uninteresting.

sospecha [sospetch'à] *nf* suspicion.

sospechar [sospetchàr'] *vt* to suspect ♦ *vi*: ~ **de** to be suspicious of.

sospechoso, a [sospetcho'so, à] *a* suspicious; (*testimonio, opinión*) suspect ♦ *nm/f* suspect.

sostén [sosten'] *nm* (*apoyo*) support; (*sujetador*) bra; (*alimentación*) sustenance, food.

sostendré [sostendre'] *etc vb V* **sostener**.

sostener [sostener'] *vt* to support; (*mantener*) to keep up, maintain; (*alimentar*) to sustain, keep going; ~**se** *vr* to support o.s.; (*seguir*) to continue, remain.

sostenga [sosten'gà] *etc vb V* **sostener**.

sostenido, a [sostenē'ðo, à] *a* continuous, sustained; (*prolongado*) prolonged; (*MUS*) sharp ♦ *nm* (*MUS*) sharp.

sostuve [sostoō'be] *etc vb V* **sostener**.

sotana [sotà'nà] *nf* (*REL*) cassock.

sótano [so'tàno] *nm* basement.

sotavento [sotàben'to] *nm* (*NAUT*) lee, leeward.

soterrar [soterràr'] *vt* to bury; (*esconder*) to hide away.

sotierre [sotye'rre] *etc vb V* **soterrar**.

soviético, a [sobye'tēko, à] *a*, *nm/f* Soviet; **los** ~**s** the Soviets, the Russians.

soy [soē] *vb V* **ser**.

spooling [espoō'lēn] *nm* (*INFORM*) spooling.

sport [espor'(t)] *nm* sport.

spot [espot'], *pl* **spot** *nm* (*publicitario*) ad.

Sr. *abr* (= *Señor*) Mr.

Sra. *abr* (= *Señora*) Mrs.

S.R.C. *abr* (= *se ruega contestación*) R.S.V.P.

Sres., Srs. *abr* (= *Señores*) Messrs.

Sri Lanka [srēlàn'kà] *nm* Sri Lanka.

Srta. *abr* = **Señorita**.

SS *abr* (= *Santos, Santas*) SS.

S.S. *abr* (*REL*: = *Su Santidad*) H.H.

ss. *abr* (= *siguientes*) foll.

Sta. *abr* (= *Santa*) St; (= *Señorita*) Miss.

stárter [está'ter] *nm* (*AUTO*) starter.

status [stá'tōōs, está'tōōs] *nm inv* status.

Sto. *abr* (= *Santo*) St.

su [sōō] *pron* (*de él*) his; (*de ella*) her; (*de una cosa*) its; (*de ellos, ellas*) their; (*de usted, ustedes*) your.

suave [swá'he] *a* gentle; (*superficie*) smooth; (*trabajo*) easy; (*música, voz*) soft, sweet; (*clima, sabor*) mild.

suavice [swáhe'se] *etc vb V* **suavizar**.

suavidad [swáhethath'] *nf* gentleness; (*de superficie*) smoothness; (*de música*) softness, sweetness.

suavizar [swáhesár'] *vt* to soften; (*quitar la aspereza*) to smooth (out); (*pendiente*) to ease; (*colores*) to tone down; (*carácter*) to mellow; (*dureza*) to temper.

subalimentado, a [sōōhálēmentá'tho, á] *a* undernourished.

subalterno, a [sōōhálter'no, á] *a* (*importancia*) secondary; (*personal*) minor, auxiliary ♦ *nm* subordinate.

subarrendar [sōōhárrendár'] *vt* to sublet.

subarriendo [sōōhárryen'do] *nm* (*COM*) sublease (*US*), leaseback (*Brit*).

subasta [sōōhá'stá] *nf* auction; **poner en** *o* **sacar a pública** ~ to put up for public auction; ~ **a la rebaja** Dutch auction.

subastador, a [sōōhástáthor', á] *nm/f* auctioneer.

subastar [sōōhástár'] *vt* to auction (off).

subcampeón, ona [sōōhkámpeon', oná] *nm/f* runner-up.

subconsciente [sōōhkonssyen'te] *a* subconscious.

subcontratar [sōōhkontrátár'] *vt* (*COM*) to subcontract.

subcontrato [sōōhkontrá'to] *nm* (*COM*) subcontract.

subdesarrollado, a [sōōhthesárroyá'tho, á] *a* underdeveloped.

subdesarrollo [sōōhthesárro'yo] *nm* underdevelopment.

subdirector, a [sōōhthērektor', á] *nm/f* assistant manager.

subdirectorio [sōōhthēreckto'ryo] *nm* (*INFORM*) subdirectory.

súbdito, a [sōōh'thēto, á] *nm/f* subject.

subdividir [sōōhthēthēthēr'] *vt* to subdivide.

subempleo [sōōhemple'o] *nm* underemployment.

subestimar [sōōhestēmár'] *vt* to underestimate, underrate.

subido, a [sōōhē'tho, á] *a* (*color*) bright, strong; (*precio*) high ♦ *nf* (*de montaña etc*) ascent, climb; (*de precio*) rise, increase;

(*pendiente*) slope, hill.

subíndice [sōōhēn'dese] *nm* (*INFORM, TIP*) subscript.

subir [sōōhēr'] *vt* (*objeto*) to raise, lift up; (*cuesta, calle*) to go up; (*colina, montaña*) to climb; (*precio*) to raise; (*empleado etc*) to promote ♦ *vi* to go/come up; (*a un coche*) to get in; (*a un autobús, tren*) to get on; (*precio*) to rise, go up; (*en el empleo*) to be promoted; (*río, marea*) to rise; ~**se** *vr* to get up, climb; ~**se a un coche** to get in(to) a car.

súbito, a [sōō'hēto, á] *a* (*repentino*) sudden; (*imprevisto*) unexpected.

subjetivo, a [sōōhhetē'ho, á] *a* subjective.

subjuntivo [sōōhhōōntē'ho] *nm* subjunctive (mood).

sublevación [sōōhlehásyon'] *nf* revolt, uprising.

sublevar [sōōhlehár'] *vt* to rouse to revolt; ~**se** *vr* to revolt, rise up.

sublimar [sōōhlēmár'] *vt* (*persona*) to exalt; (*deseos etc*) to sublimate.

sublime [sōōhlē'me] *a* sublime.

submarino, a [sōōhmárē'no, á] *a* underwater ♦ *nm* submarine.

subnormal [sōōhnormál'] *a* subnormal ♦ *nm/f* subnormal person.

suboficial [sōōhofēsyál'] *nm* non-commissioned officer.

subordinado, a [sōōhorthēná'tho, á] *a, nm/f* subordinate.

subproducto [sōōhprothōōk'to] *nm* by-product.

subrayado [sōōhráyá'tho] *nm* underlining.

subrayar [sōōhráyár'] *vt* to underline; (*recalcar*) to underline, emphasize.

subrepticio, a [sōōhreptē'syo, á] *a* surreptitious.

subrutina [sōōhrōōtē'ná] *nf* (*INFORM*) subroutine.

subsanar [sōōhsánár'] *vt* (*reparar*) to make good; (*perdonar*) to excuse; (*sobreponerse a*) to overcome.

subscribir [sōōhskrēhēr'] *vt* = **suscribir**.

subscrito [sōōhskrē'to] *pp de* **subscribir**.

subsecretario, a [sōōhsekrctá'ryo, á] *nm/f* undersecretary, assistant secretary.

subsidiario, a [sōōhsēthyá'ryo, á] *a* subsidiary.

subsidio [sōōhsē'thyo] *nm* (*ayuda*) aid, financial help; (*subvención*) subsidy, grant; (*de enfermedad, paro etc*) benefit, allowance.

subsistencia [sōōhsēsten'syá] *nf* subsistence.

subsistir [sōōhsēstēr'] *vi* to subsist; (*vivir*) to live; (*sobrevivir*) to survive, endure.

subsuelo [sōōhswe'lo] *nm* subsoil.

subterfugio [sōōhterfōō'hyo] *nm* subterfuge.

subterráneo, a [sooβterrá'neo, á] *a* underground, subterranean ♦ *nm* underpass, underground passage; (*AM*) subway (*US*), underground railway (*Brit*).

subtítulo [sooβtē'toolo] *nm* subtitle, subheading.

suburbano, a [sooβoorβá'no, á] *a* suburban.

suburbio [sooβoor'βyo] *nm* (*barrio*) slum quarter; (*afueras*) suburbs *pl*.

subvención [sooββensyon'] *nf* subsidy, subvention, grant; ~ **estatal** state subsidy *o* support; ~ **para la inversión** (*COM*) investment grant.

subvencionar [sooββensyonár'] *vt* to subsidize.

subversión [sooββersyon'] *nf* subversion.

subversivo, a [sooββersē'βo, á] *a* subversive.

subyacente [sooβyásen'te] *a* underlying.

subyugar [sooβyoogár'] *vt* (*país*) to subjugate, subdue; (*enemigo*) to overpower; (*voluntad*) to dominate.

subyugue [sooβyoo'βe] *etc vb V* **subyugar.**

succión [sooksyon'] *nf* suction.

succionar [sooksyonár'] *vt* (*sorber*) to suck; (*TEC*) to absorb, soak up.

sucedáneo, a [sooseβá'neo, á] *a* substitute ♦ *nm* substitute (food).

suceder [sooseβer'] *vi* to happen; ~ **a** (*seguir*) to succeed, follow; **lo que sucede es que** ... the fact is that ...; ~ **al trono** to succeed to the throne.

sucesión [soosesyon'] *nf* succession; (*serie*) sequence, series; (*hijos*) issue, offspring.

sucesivamente [soosesēβámen'te] *ad*: **y así** ~ and so on.

sucesivo, a [soosesē'βo, á] *a* successive, following; **en lo** ~ in future, from now on.

suceso [soose'so] *nm* (*hecho*) event, happening; (*incidente*) incident.

sucesor, a [soosesor', á] *nm/f* successor; (*heredero*) heir/heiress.

suciedad [sooseyeβáβ'] *nf* (*estado*) dirtiness; (*mugre*) dirt, filth.

sucinto, a [soosēn'to, á] *a* (*conciso*) succinct, concise.

sucio, a [soo'syo, á] *a* dirty; (*mugriento*) grimy; (*manchado*) grubby; (*borroso*) smudged; (*conciencia*) bad; (*conducta*) vile; (*táctica*) dirty, unfair.

Sucre [soo'kre] *n* Sucre.

suculento, a [sookoolen'to, á] *a* (*sabroso*) tasty; (*jugoso*) succulent.

sucumbir [sookoombēr'] *vi* to succumb.

sucursal [sookoorsál'] *nf* branch (office); (*filial*) subsidiary.

Sudáfrica [sooβá'frēká] *nf* South Africa.

sudafricano, a [sooβáfrēká'no, á] *a*, *nm/f* South African.

Sudamérica [sooβáme'rēká] *nf* South America.

sudamericano, a [sooβámerēká'no, á] *a*, *nm/f* South American.

sudanés, esa [sooβánes', esá] *a*, *nm/f* Sudanese.

sudar [sooβár'] *vt, vi* to sweat; (*BOT*) to ooze, give off.

sudeste [sooβe'ste] *a* south-east(ern); (*rumbo, viento*) south-easterly ♦ *nm* southeast; (*viento*) south-east wind.

sudoeste [sooβoe'ste] *a* south-west(ern); (*rumbo, viento*) south-westerly ♦ *nm* southwest; (*viento*) south-west wind.

sudor [sooβor'] *nm* sweat.

sudoroso, a [sooβoro'so, á] *a* sweaty, sweating.

Suecia [swe'syá] *nf* Sweden.

sueco, a [swe'ko, á] *a* Swedish ♦ *nm/f* Swede ♦ *nm* (*LING*) Swedish; **hacerse el** ~ to pretend not to hear *o* understand.

suegro, a [swe'gro, á] *nm/f* father-/mother-in-law; **los** ~**s** one's in-laws.

suela [swe'lá] *nf* (*de zapato, tb pescado*) sole.

sueldo [swel'do] *etc vb V* **soldar** ♦ *nm* pay, wage(s) (*pl*).

suelo [swe'lo] *etc vb V* **soler** ♦ *nm* (*tierra*) ground; (*de casa*) floor.

suelto, a [swel'to, á] *etc vb V* **soltar** ♦ *a* loose; (*libre*) free; (*separado*) detached; (*ágil*) quick, agile; (*corriente*) fluent, flowing ♦ *nm* (loose) change, small change; **está muy** ~ **en inglés** he is very good at *o* fluent in English.

suene [swe'ne] *etc vb V* **sonar.**

sueño [swe'nyo] *etc vb ver* **soñar** ♦ *nm* sleep; (*somnolencia*) sleepiness, drowsiness; (*lo soñado, fig*) dream; ~ **pesado** *o* **profundo** deep *o* heavy sleep; **tener** ~ to be sleepy.

suero [swe'ro] *nm* (*MED*) serum; (*de leche*) whey.

suerte [swer'te] *nf* (*fortuna*) luck; (*azar*) chance; (*destino*) fate, destiny; (*condición*) lot; (*género*) sort, kind; **lo echaron a** ~**s** they drew lots; **tener** ~ to be lucky; **de otra** ~ otherwise, if not; **de** ~ **que** so that, in such a way that.

suéter [swe'ter], *pl* **suéters** *nm* sweater.

suficiencia [soofēsyen'syá] *nf* (*cabida*) sufficiency; (*idoneidad*) suitability; (*aptitud*) adequacy.

suficiente [soofēsyen'te] *a* enough, sufficient.

sufijo [soofē'ho] *nm* suffix.

sufragar [soofrágár'] *vt* (*ayudar*) to help; (*gastos*) to meet; (*proyecto*) to pay for.

sufragio [soofrá'hyo] *nm* (*voto*) vote; (*derecho de voto*) suffrage.

sufrague [soofrá'ge] *etc vb V* **sufragar.**

sufrido, a [soofrē'βo, á] *a* (*de carácter fuerte*) tough; (*paciente*) long-suffering;

(*tela*) hard-wearing; (*color*) that does not show the dirt.

sufrimiento [sōōfrēmyen'to] *nm* suffering.

sufrir [sōōfrēr'] *vt* (*padecer*) to suffer; (*soportar*) to bear, stand, put up with; (*apoyar*) to hold up, support ♦ *vi* to suffer.

sugerencia [sōōheren'syá] *nf* suggestion.

sugerir [sōōherēr'] *vt* to suggest; (*sutilmente*) to hint; (*idea: incitar*) to prompt.

sugestión [sōōhestyon'] *nf* suggestion; (*sutil*) hint; (*poder*) hypnotic power.

sugestionar [sōōhestyonár'] *vt* to influence.

sugestivo, a [sōōhestē'ḅo, á] *a* stimulating; (*atractivo*) attractive; (*fascinante*) fascinating.

sugiera [sōōhye'rá] *etc*, **sugiriendo** [sōōhēryen'do] *etc vb* V **sugerir**.

suicida [sōōēsē'ḍá] *a* suicidal ♦ *nm/f* suicidal person; (*muerto*) suicide, person who has committed suicide.

suicidarse [sōōēsēḍár'se] *vr* to commit suicide, kill o.s.

suicidio [sōōēsē'ḍhyo] *nm* suicide.

Suiza [swē'sá] *nf* Switzerland.

suizo, a [swē'so, á] *a, nm/f* Swiss ♦ *nm* sugared bun.

sujeción [sōōhesyon'] *nf* subjection.

sujetador [sōōhetáḍhor'] *nm* fastener, clip; (*prenda femenina*) bra, brassiere.

sujetapapeles [sōōhetápápe'les] *nm inv* paper clip.

sujetar [sōōhetár'] *vt* (*fijar*) to fasten; (*detener*) to hold down; (*fig*) to subject, subjugate; (*pelo etc*) to keep *o* hold in place; (*papeles*) to fasten together; ~**se** *vr* to subject o.s.

sujeto, a [sōōhe'to, á] *a* fastened, secure ♦ *nm* subject; (*individuo*) individual; (*fam: tipo*) fellow, guy; ~ **a** subject to.

sulfurar [sōōlfōōrár'] *vt* (*TEC*) to sulphurate; (*sacar de quicio*) to annoy; ~**se** *vr* (*enojarse*) to get riled, see red, blow up.

sulfuro [sōōlfōō'ro] *nm* sulphide.

suma [sōō'má] *nf* (*cantidad*) total, sum; (*de dinero*) sum; (*acto*) adding (up), addition; **en** ~ in short; ~ **y sigue** (*COM*) carry forward.

sumador [sōōmáḍhor'] *nm* (*INFORM*) adder.

sumamente [sōōmámen'te] *ad* extremely, exceedingly.

sumar [sōōmár'] *vt* to add (up); (*reunir*) to collect, gather ♦ *vi* to add up.

sumario, a [sōōmá'ryo, á] *a* brief, concise ♦ *nm* summary.

sumergir [sōōmerhēr'] *vt* to submerge; (*hundir*) to sink; (*bañar*) to immerse, dip; ~**se** *vr* (*hundirse*) to sink beneath the surface.

sumerja [sōōmer'há] *etc vb* V **sumergir**.

sumidero [sōōmēḍhe'ro] *nm* drain, sewer; (*TEC*) sump.

suministrador, a [sōōmēnēstráḍhor', á] *nm/f* supplier.

suministrar [sōōmēnēstrár'] *vt* to supply, provide.

suministro [sōōmēnēs'tro] *nm* supply; (*acto*) supplying, providing.

sumir [sōōmēr'] *vt* to sink, submerge; (*fig*) to plunge; ~**se** *vr* (*objeto*) to sink; ~**se en el estudio** to become absorbed in one's studies.

sumisión [sōōmēsyon'] *nf* (*acto*) submission; (*calidad*) submissiveness, docility.

sumiso, a [sōōmē'so, á] *a* submissive, docile.

súmmum [sōō'mōōm] *nm inv* (*fig*) height.

sumo, a [sōō'mo, á] *a* great, extreme; (*mayor*) highest, supreme; **a lo** ~ at most.

suntuoso, a [sōōntwo'so, á] *a* sumptuous, magnificent; (*lujoso*) lavish.

sup. *abr* (= *superior*) sup.

supe [sōō'pe] *etc vb* V **saber**.

supeditar [sōōpeḍhētár'] *vt* to subordinate; (*sojuzgar*) to subdue; (*oprimir*) to oppress; ~**se** *vr*: ~**se a** to subject o.s. to.

super... [sōōper] *pref* super..., over....

súper [sōō'per] *a* (*fam*) super, great.

superable [sōōperà'ḅle] *a* (*dificultad*) surmountable; (*tarea*) that can be performed.

superar [sōōperár'] *vt* (*sobreponerse a*) to overcome; (*rebasar*) to surpass, do better than; (*pasar*) to go beyond; (*marca, récord*) to break; (*etapa: dejar atrás*) to get past; ~**se** *vr* to excel o.s.

superávit [sōōperá'ḥēt], *pl* **superávits** *nm* surplus.

superchería [sōōpertcherē'á] *nf* fraud, trick, swindle.

superficial [sōōperfēsyál'] *a* superficial; (*medida*) surface *cpd*.

superficie [sōōperfē'sye] *nf* surface; (*área*) area.

superfluo, a [sōōperf'lwo, á] *a* superfluous.

superíndice [sōōperēn'dēse] *nm* (*INFORM, TIP*) superscript.

superintendente [sōōperēntenden'te] *nm/f* supervisor, superintendent.

superior [sōōperyor'] *a* (*piso, clase*) upper; (*temperatura, número, nivel*) higher; (*mejor: calidad, producto*) superior, better ♦ *nm/f* superior.

superiora [sōōperyo'rá] *nf* (*REL*) mother superior.

superioridad [sōōperyorēḍháḍh'] *nf* superiority.

supermercado [sōōpermerká'ḍho] *nm* supermarket.

superpoblación [sōōperpoḥlásyon'] *nf* overpopulation; (*congestionamiento*) overcrowding.

superponer [sōōperponer'] *vt* (*INFORM*) to

overstrike.

superposición [sōōperposēsyon'] *nf* (*en impresora*) overstrike.

superpotencia [sōōperpoten'syä] *nf* superpower, great power.

superproducción [sōōperproᵭhōōksyon'] *nf* overproduction.

supersónico, a [sōōperso'nēko, ä] *a* supersonic.

superstición [sōōperstēsyon'] *nf* superstition.

supersticioso, a [sōōperstēsyo'so, ä] *a* superstitious.

supervisar [sōōperᵬēsár'] *vt* to supervise; (*COM*) to superintend.

supervisor, a [sōōperᵬēsor', ä] *nm/f* supervisor.

supervivencia [sōōperᵬēᵬen'syä] *nf* survival.

suplantar [sōōplántár'] *vt* (*persona*) to supplant; (*hacerse pasar por otro*) to take the place of.

suplementario, a [sōōplementá'ryo, ä] *a* supplementary.

suplemento [sōōplemen'to] *nm* supplement.

suplencia [sōōplen'syä] *nf* substitution, replacement; (*etapa*) period during which one deputizes *etc*.

suplente [sōōplen'te] *a* substitute; (*disponible*) reserve ♦ *nm/f* substitute.

supletorio, a [sōōpleto'ryo, ä] *a* supplementary; (*adicional*) extra ♦ *nm* supplement; **mesa supletoria** spare table.

súplica [sōō'plēkä] *nf* request; (*REL*) supplication; (*JUR: instancia*) petition; **~s** *nfpl* entreaties.

suplicar [sōōplēkár'] *vt* (*cosa*) to beg (for), plead for; (*persona*) to beg, plead with; (*JUR*) to appeal to, petition.

suplicio [sōōplē'syo] *nm* torture; (*tormento*) torment; (*emoción*) anguish; (*experiencia penosa*) ordeal.

suplique [sōōplē'ke] *etc vb V* **suplicar.**

suplir [sōōplēr'] *vt* (*compensar*) to make good, make up for; (*reemplazar*) to replace, substitute ♦ *vi*: **~ a** to take the place of, substitute for.

supo [sōō'po] *etc vb V* **saber.**

supondré [sōōpondre'] *etc vb V* **suponer.**

suponer [sōōponer'] *vt* to suppose; (*significar*) to mean; (*acarrear*) to involve ♦ *vi* to count, have authority; **era de ~ que** ... it was to be expected that ....

suponga [sōōpon'gä] *etc vb V* **suponer.**

suposición [sōōposēsyon'] *nf* supposition.

supremacía [sōōpremásē'ä] *nf* supremacy.

supremo, a [sōōpre'mo, ä] *a* supreme.

supresión [sōōpresyon'] *nf* suppression; (*de derecho*) abolition; (*de dificultad*) removal; (*de palabra etc*) deletion; (*de restricción*)

cancellation, lifting.

suprimir [sōōprēmēr'] *vt* to suppress; (*derecho, costumbre*) to abolish; (*dificultad*) to remove; (*palabra etc, INFORM*) to delete; (*restricción*) to cancel, lift.

supuestamente [sōōpwestámen'te] *ad* supposedly.

supuesto, a [sōōpwe'sto, ä] *pp de* **suponer** ♦ *a* (*hipotético*) supposed; (*falso*) false ♦ *nm* assumption, hypothesis ♦ *conj*: **~ que** since; **dar por ~ algo** to take sth for granted; **por ~** of course.

supuse [sōōpōō'se] *etc vb V* **suponer.**

sur [sōōr] *a* southern; (*rumbo*) southerly ♦ *nm* south; (*viento*) south wind.

Suráfrica [sōōrä'frēkä] *etc* = **Sudáfrica** *etc.*

Suramérica [sōōráme'rēkä] *etc* = **Sudamérica** *etc.*

surcar [sōōrkár'] *vt* to plow (*US*), plough (*Brit*); (*superficie*) to cut, score.

surco [sōōr'ko] *nm* (*en metal, disco*) groove; (*AGR*) furrow.

surcoreano, a [sōōrkoreä'no, ä] *a, nm/f* South Korean.

sureño, a [sōōre'nyo, ä] *a* southern ♦ *nm/f* southerner.

sureste [sōōre'ste] = **sudeste.**

surgir [sōōrhēr'] *vi* to arise, emerge; (*dificultad*) to come up, crop up.

surja [sōōr'há] *etc vb V* **surgir.**

suroeste [sōōroe'ste] = **sudoeste.**

surque [sōōr'ke] *etc vb V* **surcar.**

surrealismo [sōōrreälēs'mo] *nm* surrealism.

surrealista [sōōrreälē'stá] *a, nm/f* surrealist.

surtido, a [sōōrtē'ᵭho, ä] *a* mixed, assorted ♦ *nm* (*selección*) selection, assortment; (*abastecimiento*) supply, stock.

surtidor [sōōrtēᵭhor'] *nm* (*chorro*) jet, spout; (*fuente*) fountain; **~ de gasolina** gas (*US*) o petrol (*Brit*) pump.

surtir [sōōrtēr'] *vt* to supply, provide; (*efecto*) to have, produce ♦ *vi* to spout, spurt; **~se** *vr*: **~se de** to provide o.s. with.

susceptible [sōōseptē'ᵬle] *a* susceptible; (*sensible*) sensitive; **~ de** capable of.

suscitar [sōōsētár'] *vt* to cause, provoke; (*discusión*) to start; (*duda, problema*) to raise; (*interés, sospechas*) to arouse.

suscribir [sōōskrēᵬēr'] *vt* (*firmar*) to sign; (*respaldar*) to subscribe to, endorse; (*COM: acciones*) to take out an option on; **~se** *vr* to subscribe; **~ a uno a una revista** to take out a subscription to a magazine for sb.

suscripción [sōōskrēpsyon'] *nf* subscription.

suscrito, a [sōōskrē'to, ä] *pp de* **suscribir** ♦ *a*: **~ en exceso** oversubscribed.

susodicho, a [sōōsodētᵭh'o, ä] *a* abovementioned.

suspender [sōōspender'] *vt* (*objeto*) to hang (up), suspend; (*trabajo*) to stop, suspend;

(ESCOL) to fail.

suspensión [sŏōspensyon'] *nf* suspension; (*fig*) stoppage, suspension; (*JUR*) stay; ~ **de fuego** *o* **de hostilidades** ceasefire, cessation of hostilities; ~ **de pagos** suspension of payments.

suspensivo, a [sŏōspensē'ḫo, á] *a*: **puntos** ~**s** suspension points.

suspenso, a [sŏōspen'so, á] *a* hanging, suspended; (*ESCOL*) failed ♦ *nm* (*ESCOL*) fail(ure); **quedar** *o* **estar en** ~ to be pending.

suspicacia [sŏōspēká'syá] *nf* suspicion, mistrust.

suspicaz [sŏōspēkás'] *a* suspicious, distrustful.

suspirar [sŏōspērár'] *vi* to sigh.

suspiro [sŏōspē'ro] *nm* sigh.

sustancia [sŏōstán'syá] *nf* substance; ~ **gris** (*ANAT*) grey matter; **sin** ~ lacking in substance, shallow.

sustantivo, a [sŏōstántē'ḫo, á] *a* substantive; (*LING*) substantival, noun *cpd* ♦ *nm* noun, substantive.

sustentar [sŏōstentár'] *vt* (*alimentar*) to sustain, nourish; (*objeto*) to hold up, support; (*idea, teoría*) to maintain, uphold; (*fig*) to sustain, keep going.

sustento [sŏōsten'to] *nm* support; (*alimento*) sustenance, food.

sustituir [sŏōstētŏōēr'] *vt* to substitute, replace.

sustituto, a [sŏōstētŏō'to, á] *nm/f* substitute, replacement.

sustituyendo [sŏōstētŏōyen'do] *etc vb V* **sustituir.**

susto [sŏō'sto] *nm* fright, scare; **dar un** ~ **a uno** to give sb a fright; **darse** *o* **pegarse un** ~ (*fam*) to get scared (*US*) *o* a fright (*Brit*).

sustraer [sŏōstráer'] *vt* to remove, take away; (*MAT*) to subtract.

sustraiga [sŏōstrá'ēgá] *etc*, **sustraje** [sŏōstrá'he] *etc*, **sustrajera** [sŏōstrá'herá] *etc vb V* **sustraer.**

sustrato [sŏōstrá'to] *nm* substratum.

sustrayendo [sŏōstráyen'do] *etc vb V* **sustraer.**

susurrar [sŏōsŏōrrár'] *vi* to whisper.

susurro [sŏōsŏō'rro] *nm* whisper.

sutil [sŏōtēl'] *a* (*aroma*) subtle; (*tenue*) thin; (*hilo, hebra*) fine; (*olor*) delicate; (*brisa*) gentle; (*diferencia*) fine, subtle; (*inteligencia*) sharp, keen.

sutileza [sŏōtēle'sá] *nf* subtlety; (*delgadez*) thinness; (*delicadeza*) delicacy; (*agudeza*) keenness.

sutura [sŏōtŏō'rá] *nf* suture.

suturar [sŏōtŏōrár'] *vt* to suture; (*juntar con puntos*) to stitch.

suyo, a [sŏō'yo, á] *a* (*con artículo o después del verbo* ser: *de él*) his; (: *de ella*) hers; (: *de ellos, ellas*) theirs; (: *de usted, ustedes*) yours; (*después de un nombre: de él*) of his; (: *de ella*) of hers; (: *de ellos, ellas*) of theirs; (: *de usted, ustedes*) of yours; **lo** ~ (what is) his; (*su parte*) his share, what he deserves; **los** ~**s** (*familia*) one's family *o* relations; (*partidarios*) one's own people *o* supporters; ~ **afectísimo** (*en carta*) yours truly (*US*) *o* faithfully (*Brit*); **de** ~ in itself; **eso es muy** ~ that's just like him; **hacer de las suyas** to be up to one's old tricks; **ir a la suya, ir a lo** ~ to go one's own way; **salirse con la suya** to get one's way.

T

T, t [te] *nf* (*letra*) T, t; **T de Tarragona** T for Tommy.

t *abr* = **tonelada.**

T. *abr* (= *Telefón, Telégrafo*) tel.; (*COM*) = **Tarifa; Tasa.**

t. *abr* (= *tomo(s)*) vol(s).

Tabacalera [tábáкále'rá] *nf Spanish state tobacco monopoly.*

tabaco [tábá'ko] *nm* tobacco; (*fam*) cigarettes *pl.*

tabaquería [tábákerē'á] *nf* cigar store (*US*), tobacconist's (*Brit*).

tabarra [tábá'rrá] *nf* (*fam*) nuisance; **dar la** ~ to be a pain in the neck.

taberna [táḫer'ná] *nf* bar.

tabernero, a [táḫerne'ro, á] *nm/f* (*encargado*) publican; (*camarero*) barman/barmaid.

tabique [táḫē'ke] *nm* (*pared*) thin wall; (*para dividir*) partition.

tabla [tá'ḫlá] *nf* (*de madera*) plank; (*estante*) shelf; (*de anuncios*) board; (*lista, catálogo*) list; (*mostrador*) counter; (*de vestido*) pleat; (*ARTE*) panel; ~**s** *nfpl* (*TAUR, TEATRO*) boards; **hacer** ~**s** to draw; ~ **de consulta** (*INFORM*) lookup table.

tablado [táḫlá'ḫo] *nm* (*plataforma*) platform; (*suelo*) plank floor; (*TEATRO*) stage.

tablero [táḫle'ro] *nm* (*de madera*) plank, board; (*pizarra*) blackboard; (*de ajedrez, damas*) board; (*AUTO*) dashboard; ~ **de gráficos** (*INFORM*) graphics pad.

tableta [táḫle'tá] *nf* (*MED*) tablet; (*de chocolate*) bar.

tablilla [táḫlē'yá] *nf* small board; (*MED*) splint.

tablón [táblon'] *nm* (*de suelo*) plank; (*de techo*) beam; (*de anuncios*) bulletin board.

tabú [táboo'] *nm* taboo.

tabulación [táboolásyon'] *nf* (*INFORM*) tab(bing).

tabulador [táboolátor'] *nm* (*INFORM, TIP*) tab.

tabuladora [táboolátho'rá] *nf*: ~ **eléctrica** electric accounting machine.

tabular [táboolár'] *vt* to tabulate; (*INFORM*) to tab.

taburete [táboore'te] *nm* stool.

tacaño, a [táká'nyo, á] *a* (*avaro*) stingy; (*astuto*) crafty.

tácito, a [tá'seto, á] *a* tacit; (*acuerdo*) unspoken; (*LING*) understood; (*ley*) unwritten.

taciturno, a [tásetoor'no, á] *a* (*callado*) silent; (*malhumorado*) sullen.

taco [tá'ko] *nm* (*BILLAR*) cue; (*libro de billetes*) book; (*manojo de billetes*) wad; (*AM*) heel; (*tarugo*) peg; (*fam: bocado*) snack; (: *palabrota*) swear word; (: *trago de vino*) swig; (*Méjico*) filled tortilla; **armarse** *o* **hacerse un** ~ to get into a mess.

tacógrafo [táko'gráfo] *nm* (*COM*) tachograph.

tacón [tákon'] *nm* heel; **de** ~ **alto** highheeled.

taconear [tákoneár'] *vi* (*dar golpecitos*) to tap with one's heels; (*MIL etc*) to click one's heels.

taconeo [tákone'o] *nm* (heel) tapping *o* clicking.

táctico, a [ták'téko, á] *a* tactical ♦ *nf* tactics *pl.*

tacto [ták'to] *nm* touch; (*acción*) touching; (*fig*) tact.

tacha [tátch'á] *nf* (*defecto*) flaw, defect; (*TEC*) stud; **poner** ~ **a** to find fault with; **sin** ~ flawless.

tachar [tátchár'] *vt* (*borrar*) to cross out; (*corregir*) to correct; (*criticar*) to criticize; ~ **de** to accuse of.

tachón [tátchon'] *nm* erasure; (*tachadura*) crossing-out; (*TEC*) ornamental stud; (*COSTURA*) trimming.

tachuela [tátchwe'lá] *nf* (*clavo*) tack.

tafetán [táfetán'] *nm* taffeta; **tafetanes** *nmpl* (*fam*) frills; ~ **adhesivo** *o* **inglés** bandaid (*US*), sticking plaster (*Brit*).

tafilete [táfèle'te] *nm* morocco leather.

tahona [táo'ná] *nf* (*panadería*) bakery; (*molino*) flourmill.

tahur [táoor'] *nm* gambler; (*pey*) cheat.

tailandés, esa [táēlándes', esá] *a, nm/f* Thai ♦ *nm* (*LING*) Thai.

Tailandia [táēlán'dyá] *nf* Thailand.

taimado, a [táēmá'tho, á] *a* (*astuto*) sly; (*resentido*) sullen.

taita [tá'ētá] *nm* dad, daddy.

taja [tá'há] *nf* (*corte*) cut; (*repartición*) division.

tajada [táhá'thá] *nf* slice; (*fam*) rake-off; **sacar** ~ to get one's share.

tajadera [táháthe'rá] *nf* (*instrumento*) chopper; (*madera*) chopping block.

tajante [táhán'te] *a* sharp; (*negativa*) emphatic; **es una persona** ~ he's an emphatic person.

tajar [táhár'] *vt* to cut, slice.

Tajo [tá'ho] *nm* Tagus.

tajo [tá'ho] *nm* (*corte*) cut; (*filo*) cutting edge; (*GEO*) cleft.

tal [tál] *a* such; **un** ~ **García** a man called García; ~ **vez** perhaps ♦ *pron* (*persona*) someone, such a one; (*cosa*) something, such a thing; ~ **como** such as; ~ **para cual** tit for tat; (*dos iguales*) two of a kind; **hablábamos de que si** ~ **si cual** we were talking about this, that and the other ♦ *ad*: ~ **como** (*igual*) just as; ~ **cual** (*como es*) just as it is; ~ **el padre, cual el hijo** like father, like son; **¿qué** ~**?** how are things?; **¿qué** ~ **te gusta?** how do you like it? ♦ *conj*: **con** ~ **(de) que** provided that.

tala [tá'lá] *nf* (*de árboles*) tree felling.

taladradora [tálátrátho'rá] *nf* drill; ~ **neumática** jackhammer (*US*), pneumatic drill (*Brit*).

taladrar [tálátrár'] *vt* to drill; (*fig: suj: ruido*) to pierce.

taladro [tálá'thro] *nm* (*gen*) drill; (*hoyo*) drill hole; ~ **neumático** jackhammer (*US*), pneumatic drill (*Brit*).

talante [tálán'te] *nm* (*humor*) mood; (*voluntad*) will, willingness.

talar [tálár'] *vt* to fell, cut down; (*fig*) to devastate.

talco [tál'ko] *nm* (*polvos*) talcum powder; (*MINERALOGÍA*) talc.

talega [tále'gá] *nf* sack.

talego [tále'go] *nm* sack; **tener** ~ (*fam*) to have money.

talento [tálen'to] *nm* talent; (*capacidad*) ability; (*don*) gift.

TALGO, Talgo [tál'go] *nm abr* (*FERRO=tren articulado ligero Goicoechea-Oriol*) highspeed train.

talidomida [tálēthome'thá] *nm* thalidomide.

talismán [tálēsmán'] *nm* talisman.

talmente [tálmen'te] *ad* (*de esta forma*) in such a way; (*hasta tal punto*) to such an extent; (*exactamente*) exactly.

talón [tálon'] *nm* (*gen*) heel; (*de cheque*) stub; (*TEC*) rim.

talonario [táloná'ryo] *nm* (*de cheques*) check (*US*) *o* cheque (*Brit*) book; (*de billetes*) book of tickets; (*de recibos*) receipt book.

talla [tá'yá] *nf* (*estatura, fig, MED*) height,

stature; (*de ropa*) size, fitting; (*palo*) measuring rod; (*ARTE: de madera*)) carving; (*de piedra*) sculpture.

tallado, a [tàyá'tho, á] *a* carved ♦ *nm* (*de madera*) carving; (*de piedra*) sculpture.

tallar [tàyàr'] *vt* (*trabajar*) to work, carve; (*grabar*) to engrave; (*medir*) to measure; (*repartir*) to deal ♦ *vi* to deal.

tallarín [tàyàrēn'] *nm* noodle.

talle [tà'ye] *nm* (*ANAT*) waist; (*medida*) size; (*física*) build; (: *de mujer*) figure; (*fig*) appearance; **de ~ esbelto** with a slim figure.

taller [tàyer'] *nm* (*TEC*) workshop; (*fábrica*) factory; (*AUTO*) garage; (*de artista*) studio.

tallo [tà'yo] *nm* (*de planta*) stem; (*de hierba*) blade; (*brote*) shoot; (*col*) cabbage; (*CULIN*) candied peel.

tamaño, a [tàmá'nyo, á] *a* (*tan grande*) such a big; (*tan pequeño*) such a small ♦ *nm* size; **de ~ natural** full-size; **¿de qué ~ es?** what size is it?

tamarindo [tàmárēn'do] *nm* tamarind.

tambaleante [tàmbàleàn'te] *a* (*persona*) staggering; (*mueble*) wobbly; (*vehículo*) swaying.

tambalearse [tàmbàleàr'se] *vr* (*persona*) to stagger; (*mueble*) to wobble; (*vehículo*) to sway.

también [tàmbyen'] *ad* (*igualmente*) also, too, as well; (*además*) besides; **estoy cansado — yo ~** I'm tired — so am I *o* me too.

tambor [tàmbor'] *nm* drum; (*ANAT*) eardrum; **~ del freno** brake drum; **~ magnético** (*INFORM*) magnetic drum.

tamboril [tàmborēl'] *nm* small drum.

tamborilear [tàmborēleàr'] *vi* (*MUS*) to drum; (*con los dedos*) to drum with one's fingers.

tamborilero [tàmborēle'ro] *nm* drummer.

Támesis [tà'mesēs] *nm* Thames.

tamice [tàmē'se] *etc vb V* **tamizar**.

tamiz [tàmēs'] *nm* sieve.

tamizar [tàmēsàr'] *vt* to sieve.

tampoco [tàmpo'ko] *ad* nor, neither; **yo ~ lo compré** I didn't buy it either.

tampón [tàmpon'] *nm* plug; (*MED*) tampon.

tan [tàn] *ad* so; **~ es así que** so much so that; **¡qué cosa ~ rara!** how strange!; **no es una idea ~ buena** it is not such a good idea.

tanda [tàn'dà] *nf* (*gen*) series; (*de inyecciones*) course; (*juego*) set; (*turno*) shift; (*grupo*) gang.

tándem [tàn'dem] *nm* tandem; (*POL*) duo.

tangente [tànhen'te] *nf* tangent; **salirse por la ~** to go off at a tangent.

Tánger [tàn'her] *n* Tangier.

tangerino, a [tànherē'no, á] *a* of *o* from Tangier ♦ *nm/f* native *o* inhabitant of Tangier.

tangible [tànhē'ble] *a* tangible.

tanino [tànē'no] *nm* tannin.

tanque [tàn'ke] *nm* (*gen*) tank; (*AUTO, NAUT*) tanker.

tantear [tànteàr'] *vt* (*calcular*) to reckon (up); (*medir*) to take the measure of; (*probar*) to test, try out; (*tomar la medida*: *persona*) to take the measurements of; (*considerar*) to weigh ♦ *vi* (*DEPORTE*) to score.

tanteo [tànte'o] *nm* (*cálculo*) (rough) calculation; (*prueba*) test, trial; (*DEPORTE*) scoring; (*adivinanzas*) guesswork; **al ~** by trial and error.

tantísimo, a [tàntē'sēmo, á] *a* so much; **~s** so many.

tanto, a [tàn'to, á] *a* (*cantidad*) so much, as much; **~s** so many, as many; **20 y ~s** 20-odd ♦ *ad* (*cantidad*) so much, as much; (*tiempo*) so long, as long; **~ tú como yo** both you and I; **~ como eso** it's not as bad as that; **~ más ... cuanto que** it's all the more ... because; **~ mejor/peor** so much the better/the worse; **~ si viene como si va** whether he comes or whether he goes; **~ es así que** so much so that; **por ~, por lo ~** therefore; **me he vuelto ronco de** *o* **con ~ hablar** I have become hoarse with so much talking ♦ *conj*: **con ~ que** provided (that); **en ~ que** while; **hasta ~ (que)** until such time as ♦ *nm* (*suma*) certain amount; (*proporción*) so much; (*punto*) point; (*gol*) goal; **~ alzado** agreed price; **~ por ciento** percentage; **al ~** up to date; **estar al ~ de los acontecimientos** to be fully abreast of events; **un ~ perezoso** somewhat lazy; **al ~ de que** because of the fact that ♦ *pron*: **cada uno paga ~** each one pays so much; **uno de ~s** one of many; **a ~s de agosto** on such and such a day in August; **entre ~** meanwhile.

tañer [tànyer'] *vt* (*MUS*) to play; (*campana*) to ring.

T/año *abr* = **toneladas por año**.

tapa [tà'pá] *nf* (*de caja, olla*) lid; (*de botella*) top; (*de libro*) cover; (*comida*) snack.

tapacubos [tàpákōō'bos] *nm inv* hub cap.

tapadera [tàpáthe'rá] *nf* lid, cover.

tapado [tàpá'tho] *nm* (*AM: abrigo*) coat.

tapar [tàpár'] *vt* (*cubrir*) to cover; (*envolver*) to wrap *o* cover up; (*la vista*) to obstruct; (*persona, falta*) to conceal; (*AM*) to fill; **~se** *vr* to wrap o.s. up.

tapete [tàpe'te] *nm* table cover; **estar sobre el ~** (*fig*) to be under discussion.

tapia [tà'pyá] *nf* (garden) wall.

tapiar [tàpyàr'] *vt* to wall in.

tapice [tàpē'se] *etc vb V* **tapizar**.

tapicería [tápĕserĕ'á] *nf* tapestry; (*para muebles*) upholstery; (*tienda*) upholstery (*US*), upholsterer's (*Brit*).

tapicero, a [tápĕse'ro, á] *nm/f* (*de muebles*) upholsterer.

tapiz [tápĕs'] *nm* (*alfombra*) carpet; (*tela tejida*) tapestry.

tapizar [tápĕsár'] *vt* (*pared*) to wallpaper; (*suelo*) to carpet; (*muebles*) to upholster.

tapón [tápon'] *nm* (*corcho*) stopper; (*TEC*) plug; (*MED*) tampon; ~ **de rosca** *o* **de tuerca** screw-top.

taponar [táponár'] *vt* (*botella*) to cork; (*tubería*) to block.

taponazo [táponá'so] *nm* (*de tapón*) pop.

tapujo [tápōō'ho] *nm* (*embozo*) muffler; (*engaño*) deceit; **sin ~s** honestly.

taquigrafía [tákĕgráfĕ'á] *nf* shorthand.

taquígrafo, a [tákĕ'gráfo, á] *nm/f* shorthand writer.

taquilla [tákē'yá] *nf* (*de estación etc*) ticket office; (*de teatro*) box office; (*suma recogida*) take (*US*), takings *pl* (*Brit*); (*archivador*) filing cabinet.

taquillero, a [tákēye'ro, á] *a*: **función taquillera** box office success ♦ *nm/f* ticket agent.

taquímetro [tákē'metro] *nm* speedometer.

tara [tá'rá] *nf* (*defecto*) defect; (*COM*) tare.

tarado, a [tárá'tho, á] *a* (*COM*) defective, imperfect; (*idiota*) stupid; (*loco*) crazy, nuts ♦ *nm/f* idiot, cretin.

tarántula [tárán'tōōlá] *nf* tarantula.

tararear [táráreár'] *vi* to hum.

tardanza [tárthán'sá] *nf* (*demora*) delay; (*lentitud*) slowness.

tardar [tárthár'] *vi* (*tomar tiempo*) to take a long time; (*llegar tarde*) to be late; (*demorar*) to delay; **¿tarda mucho el tren?** does the train take long?; **a más ~** at the (very) latest; **~ en hacer algo** to be slow *o* take a long time to do sth; **no tardes en venir** come soon, come before long.

tarde [tár'thĕ] *ad* (*hora*) late; (*fuera de tiempo*) too late ♦ *nf* (*de día*) afternoon; (*de noche*) evening; **~ o temprano** sooner or later; **de ~ en ~** from time to time; **¡buenas ~s!** (*de día*) good afternoon!; (*de noche*) good evening!; **a** *o* **por la ~** in the afternoon; in the evening.

tardío, a [tárthē'o, á] *a* (*retrasado*) late; (*lento*) slow (to arrive).

tardo, a [tár'tho, á] *a* (*lento*) slow; (*torpe*) dull; **~ de oído** hard of hearing.

tarea [táre'á] *nf* task; **~s** *nfpl* (*ESCOL*) homework *sg*; **~ de ocasión** chore.

tarifa [tárē'fá] *nf* (*lista de precios*) price list; (*COM*) tariff; **~ básica** basic rate; **~ completa** total cost; **~ a destajo** piece rate; **~ doble** double time.

tarima [tárē'má] *nf* (*plataforma*) platform; (*taburete*) stool; (*litera*) bunk.

tarjeta [tárhe'tá] *nf* card; **~ postal/de crédito/de Navidad** postcard/credit card/ Christmas card; **~ de circuitos** (*INFORM*) circuit board; **~ comercial** (*COM*) calling card; **~ dinero** cash card; **~ gráficos** (*INFORM*) graphics card; **~ de multifunción** (*INFORM*) multiplication card.

tarraconense [tárrákonen'se] *a* of *o* from Tarragona ♦ *nm/f* native *o* inhabitant of Tarragona.

tarro [tá'rro] *nm* jar, pot.

tarta [tár'tá] *nf* (*pastel*) cake; (*torta*) tart.

tartajear [tártáheár'] *vi* to stammer.

tartamudear [tártámōōtheár'] *vi* to stutter, stammer.

tartamudo, a [tártámōō'tho, á] *a* stuttering, stammering ♦ *nm/f* stutterer, stammerer.

tartárico, a [tártá'rēko, á] *a*: **ácido ~** tartaric acid.

tártaro, a [tár'táro] *a, nm* Tartar ♦ *nm* (*QUIMICA*) tartar.

tarugo, a [tárōō'go, á] *a* stupid ♦ *nm* (*de madera*) lump.

tarumba [tárōōm'bá] *a* (*confuso*) confused.

tasa [tá'sá] *nf* (*precio*) (fixed) price, rate; (*valoración*) appraisal (*US*), valuation (*Brit*); (*medida, norma*) measure, standard; **~ básica** (*COM*) basic rate; **~ de cambio** exchange rate; **~ cero** (*COM*) zero-rated; **~ de crecimiento** growth rate; **~ de interés/de nacimiento** rate of interest/birth rate; **~ de rendimiento** (*COM*) rate of return.

tasación [tásásyon'] *nf* assessment; (*fig*) appraisal.

tasador, a [tásáthor', á] *nm/f* appraiser (*US*), valuer (*Brit*); (*COM: de impuestos*) assessor.

tasajo [tásá'ho] *nm* dried beef.

tasar [tásár'] *vt* (*arreglar el precio*) to fix a price for; (*valorar*) to assess; (*limitar*) to limit.

tasca [tás'ká] *nf* (*fam*) pub.

tata [tá'tá] *nm* (*fam*) dad(dy) ♦ *nf* (*niñera*) nanny, maid.

tatarabuelo, a [tátáráwe'lo, á] *nm/f* great-great-grandfather/mother; **los ~s** one's great-great-grandparents.

tatuaje [tátwá'he] *nm* (*dibujo*) tattoo; (*acto*) tattooing.

tatuar [tátwár'] *vt* to tattoo.

taumaturgo [táōōmátōōr'go] *nm* miracle-worker.

taurino, a [táōōrē'no, á] *a* bullfighting *cpd*.

Tauro [táōō'ro] *nm* Taurus.

tauromaquia [táōōromá'kyá] *nf* (art of) bullfighting.

tautología [táōōtolohē'á] *nf* tautology.

taxativo, a [táksátē'ho, á] *a* (*restringido*) limited; (*sentido*) specific.

taxi [ták'sē] *nm* taxi.

taxidermia [táksĕ'ḥer'myá] *nf* taxidermy.
taxímetro [táksē'metro] *nm* taximeter.
taxista [táksē'stá] *nm/f* taxi driver.
taza [tá'sá] *nf* cup; (*de retrete*) bowl; ~ **para café** coffee cup.
tazón [táson'] *nm* mug, large cup; (*escudilla*) basin.
TCI *nf abr* (= *tarjeta de circuito impreso*) PCB.
te [te] *pron* (*complemento de objeto*) you; (*complemento indirecto*) (to) you; (*reflexivo*) (to) yourself; **¿~ duele mucho el brazo?** does your arm hurt a lot?; ~ **equivocas** you're wrong; **¡cálma~!** calm yourself!
té [te], *pl* **tés** *nm* tea; (*reunión*) tea party.
tea [te'á] *nf* (*antorcha*) torch.
teatral [teátrál'] *a* theater *cpd* (*US*), theatre *cpd* (*Brit*); (*fig*) theatrical.
teatro [teá'tro] *nm* theater (*US*), theatre (*Brit*); (*LITERATURA*) plays *pl*, drama; **el** ~ (*carrera*) the theater, acting; ~ **de aficionados/de variedades** amateur/vaudeville theater; **hacer** ~ (*fig*) to make a fuss.
tebeo [teḥe'o] *nm* comic book (*US*), comic (*Brit*).
tecla [te'klá] *nf* (*INFORM, MUS, TIP*) key; (*INFORM*): ~ **de anulación/de borrar** cancel/delete key; ~ **de control/de edición** control/edit key; ~ **con flecha** arrow key; ~ **programable** user-defined key; ~ **de retorno/de tabulación** return/tab key; ~ **del cursor** cursor key; ~**s de control direccional del cursor** cursor control keys.
teclado [teklá'ḏo] *nm* keyboard (*tb INFORM*); ~ **numérico** (*INFORM*) numeric keypad.
teclear [tekleár'] *vi* to strum; (*fam*) to drum ♦ *vt* (*INFORM*) to key (in), type in, keyboard.
tecleo [tekle'o] *nm* (*MUS: sonido*) strumming; (: *forma de tocar*) fingering; (*fam*) drumming.
tecnicismo [teknēsēs'mo] *nm* (*carácter técnico*) technical nature; (*LING*) technical term.
técnico, a [tek'nēko, á] *a* technical ♦ *nm* technician; (*experto*) expert ♦ *nf* (*procedimientos*) technique; (*arte, oficio*) craft.
tecnócrata [tekno'krátá] *nm/f* technocrat.
tecnología [teknolohē'á] *nf* technology; ~ **de estado sólido** (*INFORM*) solid-state technology; ~ **de la información** information technology.
tecnológico, a [teknolo'hēko, á] *a* technological.
tecnólogo, a [tekno'logo, á] *nm/f* technologist.
techado [tetchá'ḏo] *nm* (*techo*) roof; **bajo** ~ under cover.
techo [tetch'o] *nm* (*externo*) roof; (*interno*) ceiling.
techumbre [tetchōōm'bre] *nf* roof.
tedio [te'ḏyo] *nm* (*aburrimiento*) boredom; (*apatía*) apathy; (*fastidio*) depression.
tedioso, a [teḏyo'so, á] *a* boring; (*cansado*) wearisome, tedious.
Teherán [teerán'] *nm* Teheran.
teja [te'há] *nf* (*azulejo*) tile; (*BOT*) lime (tree).
tejado [tehá'ḏo] *nm* (tiled) roof.
tejano, a [tehá'no, á] *a, nm/f* Texan ♦ *nmpl*: ~**s** (*vaqueros*) jeans.
Tejas [te'hás] *nm* Texas.
tejemaneje [tehemáne'he] *nm* (*actividad*) bustle; (*lío*) fuss, to-do; (*intriga*) intrigue.
tejer [teher'] *vt* to weave; (*tela de araña*) to spin; (*AM*) to knit; (*fig*) to fabricate ♦ *vi*: ~ **y destejer** to do and undo (*US*), chop and change (*Brit*).
tejido [tehē'ḏo] *nm* fabric; (*estofa, tela*) (knitted) material; (*ANAT*) tissue; (*textura*) texture.
tejo [te'ho] *nm* (*BOT*) yew (tree).
tel. *abr* (= *teléfono*) tel.
tela [te'lá] *nf* (*material*) material; (*de fruta, en líquido*) skin; (*del ojo*) film; **hay** ~ **para rato** there's lots to talk about; **poner en** ~ **de juicio** to (call into) question; ~ **de araña** cobweb, spider's web.
telar [telár'] *nm* (*máquina*) loom; (*de teatro*) gridiron; ~**es** *nmpl* textile mill *sg*.
telaraña [telárá'nyá] *nf* cobweb, spider's web.
tele [te'le] *nf* (*fam*) TV.
tele... [tele] *pref* tele...
telecargar [telekárgár'] *vt* (*INFORM*) to download.
telecompras [telekom'prás] *nfpl* teleshopping *sg*.
telecomunicación [telekomōōnēkásyon'] *nf* telecommunication.
telecontrol [telekontrol'] *nm* remote control.
telecopiadora [telekopyáḏo'rá] *nf*: ~ **facsímil** fax copier.
telediario [teleḏyá'ryo] *nm* television news.
teledifusión [teleḏēfōōsyon'] *nf* (television) broadcast.
teledirigido, a [teleḏērēhē'ḏo, á] *a* remote-controlled.
teléf. *abr* (= *teléfono*) tel.
teleférico [telefe'rēko] *nm* (*tren*) aerial tramway (*US*), cable-railway (*Brit*); (*de esquí*) ski-lift.
telefilm [telefēlm'], **telefilme** [telefēl'me] *nm* TV film.
telefonazo [telefoná'so] *nm* (*fam*) telephone call; **te daré un** ~ I'll give you a call.
telefonear [telefoneár'] *vi* to telephone.
telefónicamente [telefo'nēkámente] *ad* by

(tele)phone.

telefónico, a [telefo'neko, á] *a* telephone *cpd* ♦ *nf*: **Telefónica** (*Esp*) *Spanish national telephone company.*

telefonista [telefone'stá] *nm/f* telephone operator.

teléfono [tele'fono] *nm* telephone; **está hablando por** ~ he's on the phone.

telefoto [telefo'to] *nf* telephoto.

telegrafía [telegráfe'á] *nf* telegraphy.

telégrafo [tele'gráfo] *nm* telegraph; (*fam: persona*) telegraph boy.

telegrama [telegrá'má] *nm* telegram.

teleimpresor [teleempresor'] *nm* teleprinter.

telemática [telema'teká] *nf* telematics *sg.*

telémetro [tele'metro] *nm* rangefinder.

telenovela [telenoђe'lá] *nf* soap (opera).

teleobjetivo [teleobhete'ђo] *nm* telephoto lens.

telepático, a [telepá'teko, á] *a* telepathic.

teleproceso [teleprosc'so] *nm* teleprocessing.

telescópico, a [telesko'peko, á] *a* telescopic.

telescopio [telesko'pyo] *nm* telescope.

telesilla [telese'yá] *nm* chairlift.

telespectador, a [telespektáђor', á] *nm/f* viewer.

telesquí [teleske'] *nm* ski-lift.

teletex(to) [teleteks'(to)] *nm* teletext.

teletipista [teletepe'stá] *nm/f* teletypist.

teletipo [telete'po] *nm* teletype(writer).

teletratamiento [teletrátámyen'to] *nm* teleprocessing.

televidente [teleheђen'te] *nm/f* viewer.

televisar [teleheรár'] *vt* to televise.

televisión [teleheรyon'] *nf* television; ~ **en color** color (*US*) *o* colour (*Brit*) television.

televisivo, a [teleheรe'ђo, á] *a* television *cpd.*

televisor [teleheรor'] *nm* television set.

télex [te'leks] *nm* telex; **máquina** ~ telex (machine); **enviar por** ~ to telex.

telón [telon'] *nm* curtain; ~ **de boca/ seguridad** front/safety curtain; ~ **de acero** (*POL*) iron curtain; ~ **de fondo** backdrop, background.

tema [te'má] *nm* (*asunto*) subject, topic; (*MUS*) theme; ~**s de actualidad** current affairs ♦ *nf* (*obsesión*) obsession; (*manía*) ill-will; **tener** ~ **a uno** to have a grudge against sb.

temario [temá'ryo] *nm* (*ESCOL*) set of topics; (*de una conferencia*) agenda.

temático, a [temá'teko, á] *a* thematic.

tembladera [tembláђe'rá] *nf* shaking; (*AM*) quagmire.

temblar [temblár'] *vi* to shake, tremble; (*de frío*) to shiver.

tembleque [temble'ke] *a* shaking ♦ *nm*

shaking.

temblón, ona [temblon', oná] *a* shaking.

temblor [temblor'] *nm* trembling; (*AM: de tierra*) earthquake.

tembloroso, a [tembloro'so, á] *a* trembling.

temer [temer'] *vt* to fear ♦ *vi* to be afraid; **temo que Juan llegue tarde** I am afraid Juan may be late.

temerario, a [temerá'ryo, á] *a* (*imprudente*) rash; (*descuidado*) reckless; (*arbitrario*) hasty.

temeridad [temereๅ̃háђ'] *nf* (*imprudencia*) rashness; (*audacia*) boldness.

temeroso, a [temero'so, á] *a* (*miedoso*) fearful; (*que inspira temor*) frightful.

temible [teme'ђle] *a* fearsome.

temor [temor'] *nm* (*miedo*) fear; (*duda*) suspicion.

témpano [tem'páno] *nm* (*MUS*) kettledrum; ~ **de hielo** ice floe.

temperamento [temperámen'to] *nm* temperament; **tener** ~ to be temperamental.

temperar [temperár'] *vt* to temper, moderate.

temperatura [temperátoo'rá] *nf* temperature.

tempestad [tempestáๅ̃h'] *nf* storm; ~ **en un vaso de agua** (*fig*) tempest in a teapot (*US*), storm in a teacup (*Brit*).

tempestuoso, a [tempestwo'so, á] *a* stormy.

templado, a [templá'ђo, á] *a* (*moderado*) moderate; (: *en el comer*) frugal; (: *en el beber*) abstemious; (*agua*) lukewarm; (*clima*) mild; (*MUS*) in tune, well-tuned.

templanza [templán'sá] *nf* moderation; (*en el beber*) abstemiousness; (*del clima*) mildness.

templar [templár'] *vt* (*moderar*) to moderate; (*furia*) to restrain; (*calor*) to reduce; (*solución*) to dilute; (*afinar*) to tune (up); (*acero*) to temper ♦ *vi* to moderate; ~**se** *vr* to be restrained.

temple [tem'ple] *nm* (*humor*) mood; (*coraje*) courage; (*ajuste*) tempering; (*afinación*) tuning; (*pintura*) tempera.

templo [tem'plo] *nm* (*iglesia*) church; (*pagano etc*) temple; ~ **metodista** Methodist chapel.

temporada [temporá'ๅ̃há] *nf* time, period; (*estación, social, DEPORTE*) season; **en plena** ~ at the height of the season.

temporal [temporál'] *a* (*no permanente*) temporary; (*REL*) temporal ♦ *nm* storm.

tempranero, a [tempráne'ro, á] *a* (*BOT*) early; (*persona*) early-rising.

temprano, a [temprá'no, á] *a* early ♦ *ad* early; (*demasiado pronto*) too soon, too early; **lo más** ~ **posible** as soon as possible.

ten [ten] *vb V* **tener**.

tenacidad [tenàsēchàth'] *nf* (*gen*) tenacity; (*dureza*) toughness; (*terquedad*) stubbornness.

tenacillas [tenàsē'yàs] *nfpl* (*gen*) iron; (*para el pelo*) curling iron (*US*) *o* tongs (*Brit*); (*MED*) forceps.

tenaz [tenàs] *a* (*material*) tough; (*persona*) tenacious; (*pegajoso*) sticky; (*terco*) stubborn.

tenaza(s) [tenà'sà(s)] *nf*(*pl*) (*MED*) forceps; (*TEC*) pliers; (*ZOOL*) pincers.

tendal [tendál'] *nm* awning.

tendedero [tendethe'ro] *nm* (*para ropa*) drying-place; (*cuerda*) clothes line.

tendencia [tenden'syà] *nf* tendency; (*proceso*) trend; ~ **imperante** prevailing tendency; ~ **del mercado** run of the market; **tener** ~ **a** to tend *o* have a tendency to.

tendenciosidad [tendensyosēchàth'] *nf* tendentiousness.

tendencioso, a [tendensyo'so, à] *a* tendentious.

tender [tender'] *vt* (*extender*) to spread out; (*ropa*) to hang out; (*vía férrea, cable*) to lay; (*cuerda*) to stretch; (*trampa*) to set ♦ *vi* to tend; ~**se** *vr* to lie down; (*fig: dejarse llevar*) to let o.s. go; (: *dejar ir*) to let things go; ~ **la cama/la mesa** (*AM*) to make the bed/set the table.

ténder [ten'der] *nm* (*FERRO*) tender.

tenderete [tendere'te] *nm* (*puesto*) stall; (*carretilla*) barrow; (*exposición*) display of goods.

tendero, a [tende'ro, à] *nm/f* shopkeeper.

tendido, a [tendē'tho, à] *a* (*acostado*) lying down, flat; (*colgado*) hanging ♦ *nm* (*ropa*) washing; (*TAUR*) front rows *pl* of seats; (*colocación*) laying; (*ARQ: enyesado*) coat of plaster; **a galope** ~ flat out.

tendón [tendon'] *nm* tendon.

tendré [tendre'] *etc vb V* **tener**.

tenducho [tendōōtch'o] *nm* small dirty shop.

tenebroso, a [tenebro'so, à] *a* (*oscuro*) dark; (*fig*) gloomy; (*siniestro*) sinister.

tenedor [tenethor'] *nm* (*CULIN*) fork; (*poseedor*) holder; ~ **de libros** bookkeeper; ~ **de acciones** shareholder; ~ **de póliza** policyholder.

teneduría [tenethōōrē'à] *nf* keeping; ~ **de libros** bookkeeping.

tenencia [tenen'syà] *nf* (*de casa*) tenancy; (*de oficio*) tenure; (*de propiedad*) possession; ~ **asegurada** security of tenure; ~ **ilícita de armas** illegal possession of weapons.

tener [tener'] *vt* (*poseer*) to have; (*en la mano*) to hold; (*suj: recipiente*) to hold, contain; (*considerar*) to consider; ~**se** *vr* (*erguirse*) to stand; (*fig*) to control o.s.; ~ **suerte** to be lucky; ~ **permiso** to have permission; **tiene 10 años** he is 10 years old; **¿cuántos años tienes?** how old are you?; ~ **sed/hambre/frío/calor** to be thirsty/hungry/cold/hot; ~ **ganas de** to want to; ~ **celos** to be jealous; ~ **cuidado** to be careful; ~ **razón** to be right; ~ **un metro de ancho/de largo** to be one meter wide/long; ~ **a bien** to see fit to; ~ **en cuenta** to bear in mind, take into account; ~ **a menos** to consider it beneath o.s.; ~ **a uno en más (estima)** to think all the more of sb; ~ **a uno por...** to think sb...; ~ **por seguro que** to be sure that; ~ **presente** to remember, bear in mind; ~ **que** (*obligación*) to have to; **tiene que ser así** it has to be this way; **nos tiene preparada una sorpresa** he has prepared a surprise for us; **¿qué tiene?** what's the matter with him?; **¿ésas tenemos?** what's all this?; **tiene un mes de muerto** he has been dead for a month; ~**se por** (*considerarse*) to consider o.s.

tenería [tenerē'à] *nf* tannery.

tenga [ten'gà] *etc vb V* **tener**.

tenia [te'nyà] *nf* tapeworm.

teniente [tenyen'te] *nm* lieutenant; ~ **coronel** lieutenant colonel.

tenis [te'nēs] *nm* tennis; ~ **de mesa** table tennis.

tenista [tenē'stà] *nm/f* tennis player.

tenor [tenor'] *nm* (*tono*) tone; (*sentido*) meaning; (*MUS*) tenor; **a** ~ **de** on the lines of.

tenorio [teno'ryo] *nm* (*fam*) ladykiller, Don Juan.

tensar [tensár'] *vt* to tighten; (*arco*) to draw.

tensión [tensyon'] *nf* tension; (*TEC*) stress; (*MED*): ~ **arterial** blood pressure; ~ **nerviosa** nervous strain; **tener la** ~ **alta** to have high blood pressure.

tenso, a [ten'so, à] *a* tense; (*relaciones*) strained.

tentación [tentàsyon'] *nf* temptation.

tentáculo [tentà'kōōlo] *nm* tentacle.

tentador, a [tentàthor', à] *a* tempting ♦ *nm/f* tempter/temptress.

tentar [tentár'] *vt* (*tocar*) to touch, feel; (*seducir*) to tempt; (*atraer*) to attract; (*probar*) to try (out); (*MED*) to probe; ~ **hacer algo** to try to do sth.

tentativa [tentàtē'hà] *nf* attempt; ~ **de asesinato** attempted murder.

tentempié [tentempye'] *nm* (*fam*) snack.

tenue [te'nwe] *a* (*delgado*) thin, slender; (*alambre*) fine; (*insustancial*) tenuous; (*sonido*) faint; (*neblina*) light; (*lazo, vínculo*) slight.

tenuidad [tenwēthàth'] *nf* thinness; (*de*

tela) fineness; (*de relaciones*) tenuousness; (*ligereza*) lightness; (*sencillez*) simplicity.

teñir [tenyer'] *vt* to dye; (*fig*) to tinge; **~se el pelo** to dye one's hair.

teología [teolohē'á] *nf* theology.

teólogo, a [teo'logo, á] *nm/f* theologist, theologian.

teorema [teore'má] *nm* theorem.

teoría [teorē'á] *nf* theory; **en ~** in theory.

teóricamente [teo'rēkámente] *ad* theoretically.

teorice [teorē'se] *etc vb* V **teorizar.**

teórico, a [teo'rēko, á] *a* theoretic(al) ♦ *nm/f* theoretician, theorist.

teorizar [teorēsár'] *vi* to theorize.

TER [ter] *nm abr* (*FERRO*)=*tren español rápido.*

terapeuta [terápe'ōōtá] *nm/f* therapist.

terapéutico, a [terápe'ōōtēko, á] *a* therapeutic(al) ♦ *nf* therapeutics *sg.*

terapia [terá'pyá] *nf* therapy; **~ laboral** occupational therapy.

tercer [terser'] *a* V **tercero.**

tercería [terserē'á] *nf* (*mediación*) mediation; (*arbitraje*) arbitration.

tercermundista [tersermōōndē'stá] *a* Third World *cpd.*

tercero, a [terse'ro, á] *a* third (*delante de nmsg:* **tercer**) ♦ *nm* (*árbitro*) mediator; (*JUR*) third party.

terceto [terse'to] *nm* trio.

terciado, a [tersyá'tho, á] *a* slanting; **azúcar ~** brown sugar.

terciar [tersyár'] *vt* (*MAT*) to divide into three; (*inclinarse*) to slope; (*llevar*) to wear across one's chest ♦ *vi* (*participar*) to take part; (*hacer de árbitro*) to mediate; **~se** *vr* to arise.

terciario, a [tersyá'ryo, á] *a* tertiary.

tercio [ter'syo] *nm* third.

terciopelo [tersyope'lo] *nm* velvet.

terco, a [ter'ko, á] *a* obstinate, stubborn; (*material*) tough.

tergiversación [terhēhersásyon'] *nf* (*deformación*) distortion; (*evasivas*) prevarication.

tergiversar [terhēhersár'] *vt* to distort ♦ *vi* to prevaricate.

termal [termál'] *a* thermal.

termas [ter'más] *nfpl* hot springs.

térmico, a [ter'mēko, á] *a* thermic, thermal, heat *cpd.*

terminación [termēnásyon'] *nf* (*final*) end; (*conclusión*) conclusion, ending.

terminal [termēnál'] *a* terminal ♦ *nm* (*ELEC, INFORM*) terminal; **~ conversacional** interactive terminal; **~ de pantalla** visual display unit ♦ *nf* (*AVIAT, FERRO*) terminal.

terminante [termēnán'te] *a* (*final*) final, definitive; (*tajante*) categorical.

terminar [termēnár'] *vt* (*completar*) to complete, finish; (*concluir*) to end ♦ *vi* (*llegar a su fin*) to end; (*parar*) to stop; (*acabar*) to finish; **~se** *vr* to come to an end; **~ por hacer algo** to end up (by) doing sth.

término [ter'mēno] *nm* end, conclusion; (*parada*) terminus; (*límite*) boundary; (*en discusión*) point; (*LING, COM*) term; **~ medio** average; (*fig*) middle way; **en otros ~s** in other words; **en último ~** (*a fin de cuentas*) in the last analysis; (*como último recurso*) as a last resort; **en ~s de** in terms of; **según los ~s del contrato** according to the terms of the contract.

terminología [termēnolohē'á] *nf* terminology.

termodinámico, a [termothēná'mēko, á] *a* thermodynamic ♦ *nf* thermodynamics *sg.*

termoimpresora [termoēmpreso'rá] *nf* thermal printer.

termómetro [termo'metro] *nm* thermometer.

termonuclear [termonōōkleár'] *a* thermonuclear.

Termo(s) ® [ter'mo(s)] *nm* Thermos ®.

termostato [termostá'to] *nm* thermostat.

ternero, a [terne'ro, á] *nm/f* (*animal*) calf ♦ *nf* (*carne*) veal.

terneza [terne'sá] *nf* tenderness.

ternilla [ternē'yá] *nf* gristle; (*cartílago*) cartilage.

terno [ter'no] *nm* (*traje*) three-piece suit; (*conjunto*) set of three.

ternura [ternōō'rá] *nf* (*trato*) tenderness; (*palabra*) endearment; (*cariño*) fondness.

terquedad [terkethath'] *nf* obstinacy; (*dureza*) harshness.

terrado [terrá'tho] *nm* terrace.

Terranova [terráno'há] *nf* Newfoundland.

terraplén [terráplen'] *nm* (*AGR*) terrace; (*FERRO*) embankment; (*MIL*) rampart; (*cuesta*) slope.

terrateniente [terrátenyen'te] *nm* landowner.

terraza [terrá'sá] *nf* (*balcón*) balcony; (*techo*) flat roof; (*AGR*) terrace.

terremoto [terremo'to] *nm* earthquake.

terrenal [terrenál'] *a* earthly.

terreno, a [terre'no, á] *a* (*de la tierra*) earthly, worldly ♦ *nm* (*tierra*) land; (*parcela*) plot; (*suelo*) soil; (*fig*) field; **un ~** a piece of land; **sobre el ~** on the spot; **ceder/perder ~** to give/lose ground; **preparar el ~ (a)** (*fig*) to pave the way (for).

terrero, a [terre'ro, á] *a* (*de la tierra*) earthy; (*vuelo*) low; (*fig*) humble.

terrestre [terres'tre] *a* terrestrial; (*ruta*) land *cpd.*

terrible [terrē'hle] *a* (*espantoso*) terrible; (*aterrador*) dreadful; (*tremendo*) awful.

territorio [terrēto'ryo] *nm* territory; **~ bajo**

mandato mandated territory.

terrón [terron'] *nm* (*de azúcar*) lump; (*de tierra*) clod, lump; **terrones** *nmpl* land *sg.*

terror [terror'] *nm* terror.

terrorífico, a [terrorē'fēko, á] *a* terrifying.

terrorismo [terrorēs'mo] *nm* terrorism.

terrorista [terrorē'stá] *a, nm/f* terrorist.

terroso, a [terro'so, á] *a* earthy.

terruño [terrōō'nyo] *nm* (*pedazo*) clod; (*parcela*) plot; (*fig*) native soil; **apego al ~** attachment to one's native soil.

terso, a [ter'so, á] *a* (*liso*) smooth; (*pulido*) polished; (*fig: estilo*) flowing.

tersura [tersōō'rá] *nf* smoothness; (*brillo*) shine.

tertulia [tertōō'lyá] *nf* (*reunión informal*) social gathering; (*grupo*) group, circle; (*sala*) clubroom; **~ literaria** literary circle.

tesar [tesár'] *vt* to tighten up.

tesina [tesē'ná] *nf* dissertation.

tesis [te'sēs] *nf inv* thesis.

tesón [teson'] *nm* (*firmeza*) firmness; (*tenacidad*) tenacity.

tesorería [tesorerē'á] *nf* treasurership.

tesorero, a [tesore'ro, á] *nm/f* treasurer.

tesoro [teso'ro] *nm* treasure; **T~ público** (*POL*) Treasury.

testaferro [testáfe'rro] *nm* figurehead.

testamentaría [testámentárē'á] *nf* execution of a will.

testamentario, a [testámentá'ryo, á] *a* testamentary ♦ *nm/f* executor/executrix.

testamento [testámen'to] *nm* will.

testar [testár'] *vi* to make a will.

testarada [testárá'thá] *nf*, **testarazo** [testárá'so] *nm*: **darse un(a) ~** (*fam*) to bump one's head.

testarudo, a [testárōō'tho, á] *a* stubborn.

testero, a [teste'ro, á] *nm/f* (*gen*) front ♦ *nm* (*ARQ*) front wall.

testes [te'stes] *nmpl* testes.

testículo [testē'kōōlo] *nm* testicle.

testificar [testēfēkár'] *vt* to testify; (*fig*) to attest ♦ *vi* to give evidence.

testifique [testēfē'ke] *etc vb V* **testificar**.

testigo [testē'ġo] *nm/f* witness; **~ de cargo/descargo** witness for the prosecution/defense; **~ ocular** eye witness; **poner a uno por ~** to cite sb as a witness.

testimoniar [testēmonyár'] *vt* to testify to; (*fig*) to show.

testimonio [testēmo'nyo] *nm* testimony; **en ~ de** as a token *o* mark of; **falso ~** perjured evidence, false witness.

teta [te'tá] *nf* (*de biberón*) nipple (*US*), teat (*Brit*); (*ANAT*) nipple; (*fam*) breast; (*fam!*) tit (!).

tétanos [te'tános] *nm* tetanus.

tetera [tete'rá] *nf* teapot; **~ eléctrica** (electric) kettle.

tetilla [tetē'yá] *nf* (*ANAT*) nipple; (*de bibe-*

rón) nipple (*US*), teat (*Brit*).

tétrico, a [te'trēko, á] *a* gloomy, dismal.

textil [tekstēl'] *a* textile; **~es** *nmpl* textiles.

texto [tek'sto] *nm* text.

textual [tekstwál'] *a* textual; **palabras ~es** exact words.

textura [tekstōō'rá] *nf* (*de tejido*) texture; (*de mineral*) structure.

tez [tes] *nf* (*cutis*) complexion; (*color*) coloring (*US*), colouring (*Brit*).

tfno. *abr* (= *teléfono*) tel.

ti [tē] *pron* you; (*reflexivo*) yourself.

tía [tē'á] *nf* (*pariente*) aunt; (*mujer cualquiera*) girl; (*fam: pej: vieja*) old bag; (: *prostituta*) whore.

Tibet [tēbet'] *nm*: **El ~** Tibet.

tibetano, a [tēbetá'no, á] *a, nm/f* Tibetan ♦ *nm* (*LING*) Tibetan.

tibia [tē'ḥyá] *nf* tibia.

tibieza [tēḥye'sá] *nf* (*temperatura*) tepidness; (*fig*) coolness.

tibio, a [tē'ḥyo, á] *a* lukewarm, tepid.

tiburón [tēḥōōron'] *nm* shark.

tic [tēk] *nm* (*ruido*) click; (*de reloj*) tick; **~ nervioso** (*MED*) nervous tic.

tico, a [tē'ko, á] *a, nm/f* (*AM fam*) Costa Rican.

tictac [tēkták'] *nm* (*de reloj*) tick tock.

tiemble [tyem'ble] *etc vb V* **temblar**.

tiempo [tyem'po] *nm* (*gen*) time; (*época, período*) age, period; (*METEOROLOGÍA*) weather; (*LING*) tense; (*edad*) age; (*de juego*) half; **a ~** in time; **a un** *o* **al mismo ~** at the same time; **al poco ~** very soon (after); **andando el ~** in due course; **cada cierto ~** every so often; **con ~** in time; **con el ~** eventually; **de ~ en ~** from time to time; **en mis ~s** in my time; **en los buenos ~s** in the good old days; **hace buen/mal ~** the weather is fine/bad; **estar a ~** to be in time; **hace ~** some time ago; **hacer ~** to kill time; **¿qué ~ tiene?** how old is he?; **motor de 2 ~s** two-stroke engine; **~ compartido** (*INFORM*) time sharing; **~ de ejecución** (*INFORM*) run time; **~ inactivo** (*COM*) downtime; **~ libre** spare time; **~ de paro** (*COM*) idle time; **a ~ partido** (*trabajar*) part-time; **~ preferencial** (*COM*) prime time; **en ~ real** (*INFORM*) real time.

tienda [tyen'dá] *etc vb V* **tender** ♦ *nf* shop; (*más grande*) store; (*NAUT*) awning; **~ de campaña** tent.

tiene [tye'ne] *etc vb V* **tener**.

tienta [!yen'tá] *nf* (*MED*) probe; (*fig*) tact; **andar a ~s** to grope one's way along.

tiento [tyen'to] *etc vb V* **tentar** ♦ *nm* (*tacto*) touch; (*precaución*) wariness; (*pulso*) steady hand; (*ZOOL*) feeler, tentacle.

tierno, a [tyer'no, á] *a* (*blando, dulce*) tender; (*fresco*) fresh.

tierra [tye'rrá] *nf* earth; (*suelo*) soil; (*mundo*) world; (*país*) country, land; (*ELEC*) ground (*US*), earth (*Brit*); ~ **adentro** inland; ~ **natal** native land; **echar** ~ **a un asunto** to hush an affair up; **no es de estas** ~**s** he's not from these parts; **la T**~ **Santa** the Holy Land.

tieso, a [tye'so, á] *etc vb V* **tesar ♦** *a* (*rígido*) rigid; (*duro*) stiff; (*fig: testarudo*) stubborn; (*fam: orgulloso*) conceited **♦** *ad* strongly.

tiesto [tye'sto] *nm* flowerpot; (*pedazo*) piece of pottery.

tiesura [tyesoo'rá] *nf* rigidity; (*fig*) stubbornness; (*fam*) conceit.

tifo [tē'fo] *nm* typhus; ~ **de América** yellow fever; ~ **asiático** cholera.

tifoidea [tēfoēˈthe'á] *nf* typhoid.

tifón [tēfon'] *nm* (*huracán*) typhoon; (*de mar*) tidal wave.

tifus [tē'foos] *nm* typhus; ~ **icteroides** yellow fever.

tigre [tē'gre] *nm* tiger; (*AM*) jaguar.

tijera [tēhe'rá] *nf* (*AM*) (*una* ~) (pair of) scissors; (*ZOOL*) claw; (*persona*) gossip; **de** ~ folding; ~**s** *nfpl* scissors; (*para plantas*) shears; **unas** ~**s** a pair of scissors.

tijeretear [tēhereteár'] *vt* to snip **♦** *vi* (*fig*) to meddle.

tila [tē'lá] *nf* (*BOT*) lime tree; (*CULIN*) lime flower tea.

tildar [tēldár'] *vt*: ~ **de** to brand as.

tilde [tēl'de] *nf* (*defecto*) defect; (*trivialidad*) triviality; (*TIP*) tilde.

tilín [tēlēn'] *nm* tinkle.

tilo [tē'lo] *nm* lime tree.

timador, a [tēmáˈthor', á] *nm/f* swindler.

timar [tēmár'] *vt* (*robar*) to steal; (*estafar*) to swindle; (*persona*) to con; ~**se** *vr* (*fam*) to make eyes (*con uno* at sb).

timbal [tēmbál'] *nm* small drum.

timbrar [tēmbrár'] *vt* to stamp; (*sellar*) to seal; (*carta*) to postmark.

timbrazo [tēmbrá'so] *nm* ring; **dar un** ~ to ring the bell.

timbre [tēm'bre] *nm* (*sello*) stamp; (*campanilla*) bell; (*tono*) timbre; (*COM*) revenue stamp (*US*), stamp duty (*Brit*).

timidez [tēmēˈthes'] *nf* shyness.

tímido, a [tē'mētho, á] *a* shy, timid.

timo [tē'mo] *nm* swindle; **dar un** ~ **a uno** to swindle sb.

timón [tēmon'] *nm* helm, rudder; **coger el** ~ (*fig*) to take charge.

timonel [tēmonel'] *nm* helmsman.

timorato, a [tēmorá'to, á] *a* God-fearing; (*mojigato*) sanctimonious.

tímpano [tēm'páno] *nm* (*ANAT*) eardrum; (*MUS*) small drum.

tina [tē'ná] *nf* tub; (*baño*) bath(tub).

tinaja [tēná'há] *nf* large earthern jar.

tinerfeño, a [tēnerfe'nyo, á] *a* of *o* from Tenerife **♦** *nm/f* native *o* inhabitant of Tenerife.

tinglado [tēnglá'tho] *nm* (*cobertizo*) shed; (*fig: truco*) trick; (*intriga*) intrigue; **armar un** ~ to lay a plot.

tinieblas [tēnye'blás] *nfpl* darkness *sg*; (*sombras*) shadows; **estamos en** ~ **sobre sus proyectos** (*fig*) we are in the dark about his plans.

tino [tē'no] *nm* (*habilidad*) skill; (*MIL*) marksmanship; (*juicio*) insight; (*moderación*) moderation; **sin** ~ immoderately; **coger el** ~ to get the feel *o* hang of it.

tinta [tēn'tá] *nf* ink; (*TEC*) dye; (*ARTE*) color (*US*), colour (*Brit*); ~ **china** India (*US*) *o* Indian (*Brit*) ink; ~**s** *nfpl* (*fig*) shades; **medias** ~**s** (*fig*) half measures; **saber algo de buena** ~ to have sth on good authority.

tinte [tēn'te] *nm* (*acto*) dyeing; (*fig*) tinge; (*barniz*) veneer.

tinterillo [tēnterē'yo] *nm* penpusher.

tintero [tēnte'ro] *nm* inkwell; **se le quedó en el** ~ he totally forgot about it.

tintinear [tēntēneár'] *vt* to tinkle.

tinto, a [tēn'to, á] *a* (*teñido*) dyed; (*manchado*) stained **♦** *nm* red wine.

tintorera [tēntore'rá] *nf* shark.

tintorería [tēntorerē'á] *nf* dry cleaner's.

tintorero [tēntore'ro] *nm* dry cleaner('s).

tintura [tēntoo'rá] *nf* (*acto*) dyeing; (*QUÍMICA*) dye; (*farmacéutico*) tincture.

tiña [tē'nyá] *etc vb V* **teñir ♦** *nf* (*MED*) ringworm.

tío [tē'o] *nm* (*pariente*) uncle; (*fam: viejo*) old fellow; (: *individuo*) guy.

tiovivo [tēohē'ho] *nm* merry-go-round.

típico, a [tē'pēko, á] *a* typical; (*pintoresco*) picturesque.

tiple [tē'ple] *nm* soprano (voice) **♦** *nf* soprano.

tipo [tē'po] *nm* (*clase*) type, kind; (*norma*) norm; (*patrón*) pattern; (*fam: hombre*) guy; (*ANAT*) build; (: *de mujer*) figure; (*IMPRENTA*) type; ~ **bancario/de descuento** bank/discount rate; ~ **de interés** interest rate; ~ **de interés vigente** (*COM*) current rate; ~ **de cambio** exchange rate; ~ **base** (*COM*) base rate; ~ **a término** (*COM*) future (*US*) *o* forward (*Brit*) rate; **dos** ~**s sospechosos** two suspicious characters; ~ **de letra** (*INFORM. TIP*) typeface; ~ **de datos** (*INFORM*) data type.

tipografía [tēpografē'á] *nf* (*tipo*) printing; (*lugar*) printing press.

tipográfico, a [tēpográ'fēko, á] *a* printing.

tipógrafo, a [tēpo'gráfo, á] *nm/f* printer.

tíque(t) [tē'ke], *pl* ~**s** [tē'kes] *nm* ticket; (*en tienda*) receipt.

tiquismiquis [tēkēsmē'kēs] *nm* fussy person ♦ *nmpl* (*querellas*) squabbling *sg*; (*escrúpulos*) silly scruples.

tira [tē'rà] *nf* strip; (*fig*) abundance ♦ *nm*: ~ **y afloja** give and take; (*cautela*) caution; **la ~ de ...** (*fam*) lots of ....

tirabuzón [tēràb̄ōōson'] *nm* corkscrew; (*rizo*) curl.

tiradero [tērà́t̄e'ro] *nm* (*AM*) rubbish dump.

tirado, a [tērà́'t̄o, à] *a* (*barato*) dirt-cheap; (*fam: fácil*) very easy ♦ *nf* (*acto*) cast, throw; (*distancia*) distance; (*serie*) series; (*TIP*) printing, edition; **de una tirada** in one fell swoop; **está ~** (*fam*) it's a cinch.

tirador, a [tērà́t̄or', à] *nm/f* (*persona*) shooter ♦ *nm* (*mango*) handle; (*ELEC*) cord (*US*), flex (*Brit*); ~ **certero** sniper.

tiranía [tēràne͂'à] *nf* tyranny.

tirano, a [tērà́'no, à] *a* tyrannical ♦ *nm/f* tyrant.

tirante [tēràn'te] *a* (*cuerda*) tight, taut; (*relaciones*) strained ♦ *nm* (*ARQ*) brace; (*TEC*) stay; (*correa*) shoulder strap; ~**s** *nmpl* suspenders (*US*), braces (*Brit*).

tirantez [tēràntes'] *nf* tightness; (*fig*) tension.

tirar [tērà́r'] *vt* to throw; (*volcar*) to upset; (*derribar*) to knock down *o* over; (*tiro*) to fire; (*cohete*) to launch; (*bomba*) to drop; (*edificio*) to pull down; (*desechar*) to throw out *o* away; (*disipar*) to squander; (*imprimir*) to print; (*dar: golpe*) to deal ♦ *vi* (*disparar*) to shoot; (*jalar*) to pull; (*fig*) to draw; (*interesar*) to appeal; (*fam: andar*) to go; (*tender a, buscar realizar*) to tend to; (*DEPORTE*) to shoot; ~**se** *vr* to throw o.s.; (*fig*) to demean o.s.; (*fam !*) to screw (*!*); ~ **abajo** to bring down, destroy; **tira más a su padre** he takes more after his father; ~ **de algo** to pull *o* tug (on) sth; **ir tirando** to manage; ~ **a la derecha** to turn *o* go right; **a todo ~** at the most.

tirita [tērē'tà] *nf* bandaid (*US*), (sticking) plaster.

tiritar [tērētàr'] *vi* to shiver.

tiritona [tērēto'nà] *nf* shivering (fit).

tiro [tē'ro] *nm* (*lanzamiento*) throw; (*disparo*) shot; (*tiroteo*) shooting; (*DEPORTE*) shot; (*TENIS, GOLF*) drive; (*alcance*) range; (*de escalera*) flight (of stairs); (*golpe*) blow; (*engaño*) hoax; ~ **al blanco** target practice; **caballo de** ~ draught horse; **andar de** ~**s largos** to be all dressed up; **al** ~ (*AM*) at once; **se pegó un** ~ he shot himself; **le salió el** ~ **por la culata** it backfired on him.

Tirol [tērol'] *nm*: **El** ~ the Tyrol.

tirolés, esa [tēroles', esà] *a*, *nm/f* Tyrolean.

tirón [tēron'] *nm* (*sacudida*) pull, tug; **de un** ~ in one fell swoop; **dar un** ~ **a** to pull at,

tug at.

tirotear [tēroteàr'] *vt* to shoot at; ~**se** *vr* to exchange shots.

tiroteo [tērote'o] *nm* exchange of shots, shooting; (*escaramuza*) skirmish.

tirria [tē'rryà] *nf*: **tener una** ~ **a uno** to have a grudge against sb.

tísico, a [tē'sēko, à] *a*, *nm/f* consumptive.

tisis [tē'sēs] *nf* consumption, tuberculosis.

tít. *abr*=**título.**

títere [tē'tere] *nm* puppet; **no dejar** ~ **con cabeza** to turn everything upside-down.

titilar [tētēlàr'] *vi* (*luz, estrella*) to twinkle; (*parpado*) to flutter.

titiritero, a [tētērēte'ro, à] *nm/f* (*acróbata*) acrobat; (*malabarista*) juggler.

titubeante [tētōōbeàn'te] *a* (*inestable*) shaky, tottering; (*farfullante*) stammering; (*dudoso*) hesitant.

titubear [tētōōbeàr'] *vi* to stagger; (*tartamudear*) to stammer; (*vacilar*) to hesitate.

titubeo [tētōōbe'o] *nm* staggering; stammering; hesitation.

titulado, a [tētōōlà́'t̄o, à] *a* (*libro*) entitled; (*persona*) titled.

titular [tētōōlàr'] *a* titular ♦ *nm/f* (*de oficina*) occupant; (*de pasaporte*) holder ♦ *nm* headline ♦ *vt* to title; ~**se** *vr* to be entitled.

título [tē'tōōlo] *nm* (*gen*) title; (*de diario*) headline; (*certificado*) professional qualification; (*universitario*) university degree; (*COM*) bond; (*fig*) right; ~**s** *nmpl* qualifications; **a** ~ **de** by way of; (*en calidad de*) in the capacity of; **a** ~ **de curiosidad** as a matter of interest; ~ **de propiedad** title deed; ~**s convertibles de interés fijo** (*COM*) convertible loan stock *sg*.

tiza [tē'sà] *nf* chalk; **una** ~ a piece of chalk.

tizna [tēs'nà] *nf* grime.

tiznar [tēsnàr'] *vt* to blacken; (*manchar*) to smudge, stain; (*fig*) to tarnish.

tizón [tēson'], **tizo** [tē'so] *nm* brand; (*fig*) stain.

Tm. *abr*=**tonelada(s) métrica(s).**

toalla [toà'yà] *nf* towel.

tobillo [tob̄ē'yo] *nm* ankle.

tobogán [tob̄ogàn'] *nm* toboggan; (*montaña rusa*) switchback; (*resbaladilla*) chute, slide.

toca [to'kà] *nf* headdress.

tocadiscos [tokàt̄ēs'kos] *nm inv* record player.

tocado, a [tokà́'t̄o, à] *a* (*fruta etc*) rotten; ♦ *nm* headdress; **estar** ~ **de la cabeza** (*fam*) to be weak in the head.

tocador [tokàt̄or'] *nm* (*mueble*) dressing table; (*cuarto*) boudoir; (*neceser*) make-up case; (*fam*) ladies' room.

tocante [tokàn'te]: ~ **a** *prep* with regard to; **en lo** ~ **a** as for, so far as concerns.

tocar [tokàr'] *vt* to touch; (*sentir*) to feel;

(*con la mano*) to handle; (*MUS*) to play; (*campana*) to ring; (*tambor*) to beat; (*trompeta*) to blow; (*topar con*) to run into, strike; (*referirse a*) to allude to; (*ser emparentado con*) to be related to ♦ *vi* (*a la puerta*) to knock (on *o* at the door); (*ser de turno*) to fall to, be the turn of; (*ser hora*) to be due; (*atañer*) to concern; ~**se** *vr* (*cubrirse la cabeza*) to cover one's head; (*tener contacto*) to touch (each other); ~**le a uno hacer algo** to be sb's turn to do sth; ~ **en** (*NAUT*) to call at; **por lo que a mí me toca** as far as I am concerned; **esto toca en la locura** this verges on madness.

tocayo, a [tokà'yo, á] *nm/f* namesake.

tocino [tosē'no] *nm* (bacon) fat; ~ **de panceta** bacon.

todavía [toðáhē'á] *ad* (*aun*) even; (*aún*) still, yet; ~ **más** yet *o* still more; ~ **no** not yet; ~ **en 1970** as late as 1970; **está lloviendo** ~ it's still raining.

todo, a [to'ðo, á] *a* all; (*cada*) every; (*entero*) whole; (*sentido negativo*): **en** ~ **el día lo he visto** I haven't seen him all day; **todas las semanas/**~**s los martes** every week/Tuesday ♦ *ad* all, completely ♦ *nm* everything ♦ *pron*: ~**s/todas** everyone; **a toda velocidad** at full speed; **estaba** ~ **ojos** he was all eyes; **puede ser** ~ **lo honesto que quiera** he can be as honest as he likes; **en un** ~ as a whole; **corriendo y** ~, **no llegaron a tiempo** even though they ran, they still didn't arrive in time; **ante** ~ above all; **a pesar de** ~ even so, in spite of everything; **con** ~ still, even so; **del** ~ completely; **después de** ~ after all; **sobre** ~ (*especialmente*) after all; (*en primer lugar*) above all.

todopoderoso, a [toðopoðhero'so, á] *a* all powerful; (*REL*) almighty.

toga [to'gá] *nf* toga; (*ESCOL*) gown.

Tokio [to'kyo] *n* Tokyo.

toldo [tol'do] *nm* (*para el sol*) awning; (*tienda*) marquee; (*fig*) pride.

tole [to'le] *nm* (*fam*) commotion.

toledano, a [toleðhá'no, á] *a* of *o* from Toledo ♦ *nm/f* native *o* inhabitant of Toledo.

tolerable [tolerá'hle] *a* tolerable.

tolerancia [toleràn'syá] *nf* tolerance.

tolerante [toleràn'te] *a* tolerant; (*fig*) open-minded.

tolerar [tolerár'] *vt* to tolerate; (*resistir*) to endure.

Tolón [tolon'] *nm* Toulon.

tolvanera [tolháne'rá] *nf* dust cloud.

toma [to'má] *nf* (*gen*) taking; (*MED*) dose; (*ELEC*) *tb:* ~ **de corriente** socket; (*MEC*) inlet; ~ **de posesión** (*por presidente*) inauguration; ~ **de tierra** (*AVIAT*) landing.

tomadura [tomáðhoo'rá] *nf:* ~ **de pelo** hoax.

tomar [tomár'] *vt* (*gen, CINE, FOTO, TV*) to take; (*actitud*) to adopt; (*aspecto*) to take on; (*notas*) to take down; (*beber*) to drink ♦ *vi* to take; (*AM*) to drink; ~**se** *vr* to take; ~**se por** to consider o.s. to be; **¡toma!** here you are!; ~ **asiento** to sit down; ~ **a uno por loco** to think sb mad; ~ **a bien/a mal** to take well/badly; ~ **en serio** to take seriously; ~ **el pelo a uno** to pull sb's leg; ~**la con uno** to pick a quarrel with sb; ~ **por escrito** to write down; **toma y daca** give and take.

tomate [tomá'te] *nm* tomato.

tomatera [tomáte'rá] *nf* tomato plant.

tomavistas [tomáhē'stás] *nm inv* movie camera.

tomillo [tomē'yo] *nm* thyme.

tomo [to'mo] *nm* (*libro*) volume; (*fig*) importance.

ton [ton] *abr*=**tonelada** ♦ *nm*: **sin** ~ **ni son** without rhyme or reason.

tonada [toná'ðhá] *nf* tune.

tonalidad [tonálēðhàh'] *nf* tone.

tonel [tonel'] *nm* barrel.

tonelada [tonelá'ðhá] *nf* ton; ~ **métrica** metric ton.

tonelaje [tonelá'he] *nm* tonnage.

tonelero [tonele'ro] *nm* cooper.

tónico, a [to'nēko, á] *a* tonic ♦ *nm* (*MED*) tonic ♦ *nf* (*MUS*) tonic; (*fig*) keynote.

tonificador, a [tonēfēkáðhor', á], **tonificante** [tonēfēkàn'te] *a* invigorating, stimulating.

tonificar [tonēfēkár'] *vt* to tone up.

tonifique [tonēfē'ke] *etc vb V* **tonificar.**

tonillo [tonē'yo] *nm* monotonous voice.

tono [to'no] *nm* (*MUS*) tone; (*altura*) pitch; (*color*) shade; **fuera de** ~ inappropriate; ~ **de marcar** (*TELEC*) dial (*US*) *o* dialling (*Brit*) tone; **darse** ~ to put on airs.

tontear [tonteár'] *vi* (*fam*) to fool around; (*enamorados*) to flirt.

tontería [tonterē'á] *nf* (*estupidez*) foolishness; (*una*) ~ silly thing; ~**s** *nfpl* rubbish *sg*, nonsense *sg*.

tonto, a [ton'to, á] *a* stupid; (*ridículo*) silly ♦ *nm/f* fool; (*payaso*) clown; **a tontas y a locas** anyhow; **hacer(se) el** ~ to act the fool.

topacio [topá'syo] *nm* topaz.

topar [topár'] *vt* (*tropezar*) to bump into; (*encontrar*) to find, come across; (*cabra etc*) to butt ♦ *vi*: ~ **contra** *o* **en** to run into; ~ **con** to run up against; **el problema topa en eso** that's where the problem lies.

tope [to'pe] *a* maximum ♦ *nm* (*fin*) end; (*límite*) limit; (*riña*) quarrel; (*FERRO*) buffer; (*AUTO*) bumper; **al** ~ end to end; **fecha** ~ closing date; **precio** ~ top price; **sueldo** ~ maximum salary; ~ **de tabulación** tab stop.

tópico, a [to'pĕko, á] *a* topical; (*MED*) local
♦ *nm* platitude, cliché; **de uso** ~ for
external application.

topo [to'po] *nm* (*ZOOL*) mole; (*fig*) blunder-
er.

topografía [topografē'á] *nf* topography.

topógrafo, a [topo'gráfo, á] *nm/f* topog-
rapher; (*agrimensor*) surveyor.

toponimia [toponē'myá] *nf* place names *pl*;
(*estudio*) study of place names.

toque [to'ke] *etc vb* V **tocar** ♦ *nm* touch;
(*MUS*) beat; (*de campana*) ring, chime;
(*MIL*) bugle call; (*fig*) crux; **dar un** ~ **a** to
test; **dar el último** ~ **a** to put the final
touch to; ~ **de queda** curfew.

toquetear [toketeár'] *vt* to handle; (*fam!*)
to touch up.

toquilla [tokē'yá] *nf* (*chal*) shawl.

torbellino [torbeyē'no] *nm* whirlwind; (*fig*)
whirl.

torcedura [torsethōō'rá] *nf* twist; (*MED*)
sprain.

torcer [torser'] *vt* to twist; (*la esquina*) to
turn; (*MED*) to sprain; (*cuerda*) to braid
(*US*), plait (*Brit*); (*ropa, manos*) to wring;
(*persona*) to corrupt; (*sentido*) to distort ♦
vi (*cambiar de dirección*) to turn; ~**se** *vr*
to twist; (*doblar*) to bend; (*desviarse*) to
go astray; (*fracasar*) to go wrong; ~ **el
gesto** to scowl; ~**se un pie** to twist one's
foot; **el coche torció a la derecha** the car
turned right.

torcido, a [torsē'tho, á] *a* twisted; (*fig*)
crooked ♦ *nm* curl.

tordo, a [tor'tho, á] *a* dappled ♦ *nm* thrush.

torear [toreár'] *vt* (*fig: evadir*) to dodge;
(*toro*) to fight ♦ *vi* to fight bulls.

toreo [tore'o] *nm* bullfighting.

torero, a [tore'ro, á] *nm/f* bullfighter.

toril [torēl'] *nm* bullpen.

tormenta [tormen'tá] *nf* storm; (*fig: confusión*) turmoil.

tormento [tormen'to] *nm* torture; (*fig*)
anguish.

tormentoso, a [tormento'so, á] *a* stormy.

tornar [tornár'] *vt* (*devolver*) to return, give
back; (*transformar*) to transform ♦ *vi* to go
back; ~**se** *vr* (*ponerse*) to become;
(*volver*) to return.

tornasol [tornásol'] *nm* (*BOT*) sunflower;
papel de ~ litmus paper.

tornasolado, a [tornásolá'tho, á] *a*
(*brillante*) iridescent; (*reluciente*) shimmering.

torneo [torne'o] *nm* tournament.

tornero, a [torne'ro, á] *nm/f* machinist.

tornillo [tornē'yo] *nm* screw; **apretar los** ~**s
a uno** to apply pressure on sb; **le falta un**
~ (*fam*) he's got a screw loose.

torniquete [tornēke'te] *nm* (*puerta*) turnstile; (*MED*) tourniquet.

torno [tor'no] *nm* (*TEC*: *grúa*) winch; (: *de
carpintero*) lathe; (*tambor*) drum; ~ **de
banco** vise (*US*), vice (*Brit*); **en** ~ **(a)**
round, about.

toro [to'ro] *nm* bull; (*fam*) he-man; **los** ~**s**
bullfighting *sg*.

toronja [toron'há] *nf* (*AM*) grapefruit.

torpe [tor'pe] *a* (*poco hábil*) clumsy,
awkward; (*movimiento*) sluggish; (*necio*)
dim; (*lento*) slow; (*indecente*) crude; (*no
honrado*) dishonest.

torpedo [torpe'tho] *nm* torpedo.

torpemente [torpemen'te] *ad* (*sin destreza*)
clumsily; (*lentamente*) slowly.

torpeza [torpe'sá] *nf* (*falta de agilidad*)
clumsiness; (*lentitud*) slowness; (*rigidez*)
stiffness; (*error*) mistake; (*crudeza*) obscenity.

torre [to'rre] *nf* tower; (*de petróleo*)
derrick; (*de electricidad*) pylon; (*AJE-
DREZ*) rook; (*AVIAT, MIL, NAUT*) turret.

torrencial [torrensyál'] *a* torrential.

torrente [torren'te] *nm* torrent.

tórrido, a [to'rrētho, á] *a* torrid.

torrija [torrē'há] *nf* fried bread; ~**s** French
toast *sg*.

torsión [torsyon'] *nf* twisting.

torso [tor'so] *nm* torso.

torta [tor'tá] *nf* cake; (*fam*) slap; **no
entendió ni** ~ he didn't understand a word
of it.

tortazo [tortá'so] *nm* (*bofetada*) slap; (*de
coche*) crash.

tortícolis [tortē'kolēs] *nm inv* stiff neck.

tortilla [tortē'yá] *nf* omelet(te); (*AM*)
tortilla, maize pancake; ~ **francesa/
española** plain/potato omelet; **cambiar** *o*
volver la ~ **a uno** to turn the tables on sb.

tortillera [tortēye'rá] *nf* (*fam!*) lesbian.

tórtola [tor'tolá] *nf* turtledove.

tortuga [tortōō'gá] *nf* tortoise; ~ **marina**
turtle.

tortuoso, a [tortwo'so, á] *a* winding.

tortura [tortōō'rá] *nf* torture.

torturar [tortōōrár'] *vt* to torture.

torvo, a [tor'ho, á] *a* grim, fierce.

torzamos [torsá'mos] *etc vb* V **torcer**.

tos [tos] *nf inv* cough; ~ **ferina** whooping
cough.

Toscana [toská'ná] *nf*: **La** ~ Tuscany.

tosco, a [tos'ko, á] *a* coarse.

toser [toser'] *vi* to cough; **no hay quien le
tosa** he's in a class by himself.

tostado, a [tostá'tho, á] *a* toasted; (*por el
sol*) dark brown; (*piel*) tanned ♦ *nf* tan;
(*pan*) piece of toast; **tostadas** *nfpl* toast *sg*.

tostador [tostátho'r] *nm* toaster.

tostar [tostár'] *vt* to toast; (*café*) to roast;
(*al sol*) to tan; ~**se** *vr* to get brown.

total [totál'] *a* total ♦ *ad* in short; (*al fin y al
cabo*) when all is said and done ♦ *nm* total;

en ~ in all; ~ **que** to cut a long story short; ~ **de comprobación** (*INFORM*) hash total; ~ **debe/haber** (*COM*) debit/assets total.

totalidad [totálēᵗₕáᵗₕ'] *nf* whole.

totalitario, a [totálētá'ryo, á] *a* totalitarian.

tóxico, a [tok'sēko, á] *a* toxic ♦ *nm* poison.

toxicómano, a [toksēko'máno, á] *a* addicted to drugs ♦ *nm/f* drug addict.

tozudo, a [tosōō'ᵗₕo, á] *a* obstinate.

traba [trá'βá] *nf* bond, tie; (*cadena*) fetter; **poner** ~**s** a to restrain.

trabajador, a [tráβáháᵗₕor', á] *nm/f* worker ♦ *a* hard-working.

trabajar [tráβáhár'] *vt* to work; (*arar*) to till; (*empeñarse en*) to work at; (*empujar*: *persona*) to push; (*convencer*) to persuade ♦ *vi* to work; (*esforzarse*) to strive; ¡a ~! let's get to work!; ~ **por hacer algo** to strive to do sth.

trabajo [tráβá'ho] *nm* work; (*tarea*) task; (*POL*) labor (*US*), labour (*Brit*); (*fig*) effort; **tomarse el** ~ **de** to take the trouble to; ~ **por turno/a destajo** shift work/piecework; ~ **en proceso** (*COM*) work-in-progress.

trabajoso, a [tráβáho'so, á] *a* hard; (*MED*) pale.

trabalenguas [tráβálen'gwás] *nm inv* tongue twister.

trabar [tráβár'] *vt* (*juntar*) to join, unite; (*atar*) to tie down, fetter; (*agarrar*) to seize; (*amistad*) to strike up; ~**se** *vr* to become entangled; (*reñir*) to squabble; **se le traba la lengua** he gets tongue-tied.

trabazón [tráβáson'] *nf* (*TEC*) joining, assembly; (*fig*) bond, link.

trabucar [tráβōōkár'] *vt* (*confundir*) to confuse, mix up; (*palabras*) to misplace.

trabuque [tráβōō'ke] *etc vb* V **trabucar**.

tracción [tráksyon'] *nf* traction; ~ **delantera/trasera** front-wheel/rear-wheel drive.

trace [trá'se] *etc vb* V **trazar**.

tractor [tráktor'] *nm* tractor.

trad. *abr* (= *traducido*) trans.

tradición [tráᵗₕēsyon'] *nf* tradition.

tradicional [tráᵗₕēsyonál'] *a* traditional.

traducción [tráᵗₕōōksyon'] *nf* translation; ~ **asistida por ordenador** computer-assisted translation.

traducible [tráᵗₕōōsē'βle] *a* translatable.

traducir [tráᵗₕōōsēr'] *vt* to translate; ~**se** *vr*: ~**se en** (*fig*) to entail, result in.

traductor, a [tráᵗₕōōktor', á] *nm/f* translator.

traduzca [tráᵗₕōōs'ká] *etc vb* V **traducir**.

traer [trácr'] *vt* to bring; (*llevar*) to carry; (*ropa*) to wear; (*incluir*) to carry; (*fig*) to cause; ~**se** *vr*: ~ **se algo** to be up to sth; ~**se bien/mal** to dress well/badly; **traérselas** to be annoying; ~ **consigo** to involve,

entail; **es un problema que se las trae** it's a difficult problem.

traficante [tráfēkán'te] *nm/f* trader, dealer.

traficar [tráfēkár'] *vi* to trade; ~ **con** (*pey*) to deal illegally in.

tráfico [trá'fēko] *nm* (*COM*) trade; (*AUTO*) traffic.

trafique [tráfē'ke] *etc vb* V **traficar**.

tragaderas [tráɡáᵗₕe'rás] *nfpl* (*garganta*) throat *sg*, gullet *sg*; (*credulidad*) gullibility *sg*.

tragaluz [tráɡálōōs'] *nm* skylight.

tragamonedas [tráɡámone'ᵗₕás] *nm inv*, **tragaperras** [tráɡápe'rrás] *nm inv* slot machine.

tragar [tráɡár'] *vt* to swallow; (*devorar*) to devour, bolt down; ~**se** *vr* to swallow; (*tierra*) to absorb, soak up; **no le puedo** ~ (*persona*) I can't stand him.

tragedia [tráhe'ᵗₕyá] *nf* tragedy.

trágico, a [trá'hēko, á] *a* tragic.

trago [trá'ɡo] *nm* (*líquido*) drink; (*comido de golpe*) gulp; (*fam*: *de bebida*) swig; (*desgracia*) blow; ~ **amargo** (*fig*) hard time.

trague [trá'ɡe] *etc vb* V **tragar**.

traición [tráēsyon'] *nf* treachery; (*JUR*) treason; (*una* ~) act of treachery.

traicionar [tráēsyonár'] *vt* to betray.

traicionero, a [tráēsyone'ro, á] = **traidor, a**.

traída [tráē'ᵗₕá] *nf* carrying; ~ **de aguas** water supply.

traidor, a [tráēᵗₕor', á] *a* treacherous ♦ *nm/f* traitor.

traiga [trá'ēɡá] *etc vb* V **traer**.

traje [trá'he] *etc vb* V **traer** ♦ *nm* (*gen*) dress; (*de hombre*) suit; (~ *típico*) costume; (*fig*) garb; ~ **de baño** swimsuit; ~ **de luces** bullfighter's costume; ~ **hecho a la medida** tailor-made suit.

trajera [tráhe'rá] *etc vb* V **traer**.

trajín [tráhēn'] *nm* transportation; (*fam*: *movimiento*) bustle; **trajines** *nmpl* goings-on.

trajinar [tráhēnár'] *vt* (*llevar*) to carry, transport ♦ *vi* (*moverse*) to bustle; (*viajar*) to travel around.

trama [trá'má] *nf* (*fig*) link; (: *intriga*) plot; (*de tejido*) weft.

tramar [trámár'] *vt* to plot; (*TEC*) to weave; ~**se** *vr* (*fig*): **algo se está tramando** there's something going on.

tramitar [trámētár'] *vt* (*asunto*) to transact; (*negociar*) to negotiate; (*manejar*) to handle.

trámite [trá'mēte] *nm* (*paso*) step; (*JUR*) transaction; ~**s** *nmpl* (*burocracia*) paperwork *sg*, procedures; (*JUR*) proceedings.

tramo [trá'mo] *nm* (*de tierra*) plot; (*de escalera*) flight; (*de vía*) section.

tramoya [trámo'yá] *nf* (*TEATRO*) piece of

stage machinery; (*fig*) trick.

tramoyista [trámoyě'stá] *nm/f* scene shifter; (*fig*) trickster.

trampa [trám'pá] *nf* trap; (*en el suelo*) trapdoor; (*prestidigitación*) magic trick; (*engaño*) trick; (*fam*) fiddle; (*de pantalón*) fly; **caer en la ~** to fall into the trap; **hacer ~s** (*hacer juegos de manos*) to juggle, conjure; (*trampear*) to cheat.

trampear [trámpeár'] *vt, vi* to cheat.

trampilla [trámpě'yá] *nf* trap, hatchway.

trampista [trámpě'stá] *nm/f* = **tramposo.**

trampolín [trámpolěn'] *nm* trampoline; (*de piscina etc*) diving board.

tramposo, a [trámpo'so, á] *a* crooked, cheating ♦ *nm/f* crook, cheat.

tranca [trán'ká] *nf* (*palo*) stick; (*viga*) beam; (*de puerta, ventana*) bar; (*borrachera*) binge; **a ~s y barrancas** with great difficulty.

trancar [tránkár'] *vt* to bar ♦ *vi* to stride along.

trancazo [tránká'so] *nm* (*golpe*) blow.

trance [trán'se] *nm* (*momento difícil*) difficult moment; (*situación crítica*) critical situation; (*estado hipnotizado*) trance; **estar en ~ de muerte** to be at death's door.

tranco [trán'ko] *nm* stride.

tranque [trán'ke] *etc vb* V **trancar.**

tranquilice [tránkělě'se] *etc vb* V **tranquilizar.**

tranquilidad [tránkělěthátk'] *nf* '*calma*) calmness, stillness; (*paz*) peacefulness.

tranquilizador, a [tránkělěsáthor', á] *a* (*música*) soothing; (*hecho*) reassuring.

tranquilizar [tránkělěsár'] *vt* (*calmar*) to calm (down); (*asegurar*) to reassure.

tranquilo, a [tránkě'lo, á] *a* (*calmado*) calm; (*apacible*) peaceful; (*mar*) calm; (*mente*) untroubled.

Trans. *abr* (*COM*) = **transferencia.**

transacción [tránsáksyon'] *nf* transaction.

transar [tránsár'] *vi* = **transigir.**

transbordador [tránsborthátkor'] *nm* ferry.

transbordar [tránsborthár'] *vt* to transfer; **~se** *vr* to change.

transbordo [tránsbor'tko] *nm* transfer; **hacer ~** to change (trains).

transcurrir [tránskŏorrěr'] *vi* (*tiempo*) to pass; (*hecho*) to turn out.

transcurso [tránskŏor'so] *nm* passing, lapse; **en el ~ de 8 días** in the course of a week.

transeúnte [tránseŏon'te] *a* transient ♦ *nm/f* passer-by.

transferencia [tránsferen'syá] *nf* transference; (*COM*) transfer; **~ bancaria** banker's order; **~ de crédito** (*COM*) credit transfer; **~ electrónica de fondos** (*COM*) electronic funds transfer.

transferir [tránsferěr'] *vt* to transfer; (*aplazar*) to postpone.

transfiera [tránsfye'rá] *etc vb* V **transferir.**

transfigurar [tránsfěgŏorár'] *vt* to transfigure.

transfiriendo [tránsfěryen'do] *etc vb* V **transferir.**

transformador [tránsformátkor'] *nm* transformer.

transformar [tránsformár'] *vt* to transform; (*convertir*) to convert.

tránsfuga [tráns'fŏogá] *nm/f* (*MIL*) deserter; (*POL*) turncoat.

transgresión [tránsgresyon'] *nf* transgression.

transición [tránsěsyon'] *nf* transition; **período de ~** transitional period.

transido, a [tránsě'tko, á] *a* overcome; **~ de angustia** overcome with anxiety; **~ de dolor** racked with pain.

transigir [tránsěhěr'] *vi* to compromise; (*ceder*) to make concessions.

transija [tránsě'há] *etc vb* V **transigir.**

Transilvania [tránsělhá'nyá] *nf* Transylvania.

transistor [tránsěstor'] *nm* transistor.

transitable [tránsětá'ble] *a* (*camino*) passable.

transitar [tránsětár'] *vi* to go (from place to place).

tránsito [trán'sěto] *nm* transit; (*AUTO*) traffic; (*parada*) stop; **horas de máximo ~** rush hours; **"se prohíbe el ~"** ''no thoroughfare.''

transitorio, a [tránsěto'ryo, á] *a* transitory.

transmisión [tránsměsyon'] *nf* (*RADIO, TV*) transmission, broadcast(ing); (*transferencia*) transfer; **~ en circuito** hookup; **~ en directo/exterior** live/outside broadcast; **~ de datos (en paralelo/en serie)** (*INFORM*) (parallel/serial) data transfer *o* transmission; **plena/media ~ bidireccional** (*INFORM*) full/half duplex.

transmitir [tránsmětěr'] *vt* to transmit; (*RADIO, TV*) to broadcast; (*enfermedad*) to give, pass on.

transparencia [tránspáren'syá] *nf* transparency; (*claridad*) clearness, clarity; (*foto*) slide.

transparentar [tránspárentár'] *vt* to reveal ♦ *vi* to be transparent.

transparente [tránspáren'te] *a* transparent; (*aire*) clear; (*ligero*) diaphanous ♦ *nm* curtain.

transpirar [tránspěrár'] *vi* to perspire; (*fig*) to transpire.

transpondré [tránspondre'] *etc vb* V **transponer.**

transponer [tránsponer'] *vt* to transpose; (*cambiar de sitio*) to move about ♦ *vi* (*desaparecer*) to disappear; (*ir más allá*) to go beyond; ~**se** *vr* to change places; (*ocultarse*) to hide; (*sol*) to go down.

transponga [tránspon'gá] *etc vb V* **transponer.**

transportación [tránsportásyon'] *nf* transportation.

transportador [tránsportátḥor'] *nm* (*MECÁNICA*): ~ **de correa** belt conveyor.

transportar [tránsportár'] *vt* to transport; (*llevar*) to carry.

transporte [tránspor'te] *nm* transport; (*COM*) transportation, haulage; **Ministerio de T~s** ≈ Department of Transportation (*US*), ≈ Ministry of Transport (*Brit*).

transpuesto [tránspwe'sto], **transpuse** [tránspoō'se] *etc vb V* **transponer.**

transversal [tránsḥersál'] *a* transverse, cross ♦ *nf* (*tb:* **calle ~**) cross street.

transversalmente [tránsḥersálmen'te] *ad* obliquely.

tranvía [tránbē'á] *nm* streetcar (*US*), tram (*Brit*).

trapecio [trápe'syo] *nm* trapeze.

trapecista [trápesē'stá] *nm/f* trapeze artist.

trapero, a [trápe'ro, á] *nm/f* ragman.

trapicheos [trápētche'os] *nmpl* (*fam*) schemes.

trapisonda [trápēson'dá] *nf* (*jaleo*) row; (*estafa*) swindle.

trapo [trá'po] *nm* (*tela*) rag; (*de cocina*) cloth; ~**s** *nmpl* (*fam*: *de mujer*) clothes, dresses; **a todo** ~ under full sail; **soltar el** ~ (*llorar*) to burst into tears.

tráquea [trá'keá] *nf* trachea, windpipe.

traqueteo [trákete'o] *nm* (*crujido*) crack; (*golpeteo*) rattling.

tras [trás] *prep* (*detrás*) behind; (*después*) after; ~ **de** besides; **día** ~ **día** day after day; **uno** ~ **otro** one after the other.

trascendencia [trásenden'syá] *nf* (*importancia*) importance; (*filosofía*) transcendence.

trascendental [trásendentál'] *a* important; transcendental.

trascender [trásender'] *vi* (*oler*) to smell; (*noticias*) to come out, leak out; (*eventos, sentimientos*) to spread, have a wide effect; ~ **a** (*afectar*) to reach, have an effect on; (*oler a*) to smack of; **en su novela todo trasciende a romanticismo** everything in his novel smacks of romanticism.

trascienda [trásyen'dá] *etc vb V* **trascender.**

trasegar [tráseḡár'] *vt* (*mover*) to move about; (*vino*) to decant.

trasegué [tráseḡe'], **traseguemos** [tráseḡe'mos] *etc vb V* **trasegar.**

trasero, a [tráse'ro, á] *a* back, rear ♦ *nm* (*ANAT*) bottom; ~**s** *nmpl* ancestors.

trasfondo [trásfon'do] *nm* background.

trasgo [trás'ḡo] *nm* (*duende*) goblin.

trasgredir [trásḡretḥēr'] *vt* to contravene.

trashumante [trásoōmán'te] *a* migrating.

trasiego [trásye'ḡo] *etc vb V* **trasegar** ♦ *nm* (*cambiar de sitio*) move, switch; (*de vino*) decanting; (*trastorno*) upset.

trasiegue [trásye'ḡe] *etc vb V* **trasegar.**

trasladar [tráslátḥár'] *vt* to move; (*persona*) to transfer; (*postergar*) to postpone; (*copiar*) to copy; (*interpretar*) to interpret; ~**se** *vr* (*irse*) to go; (*mudarse*) to move; ~**se a otro puesto** to move to a new job.

traslado [tráslá'tḥo] *nm* move; (*mudanza*) move, removal; (*de persona*) transfer; (*copia*) copy; ~ **de bloque** (*INFORM*) block move, cut-and-paste.

traslucir [trásloosēr'] *vt* to show; ~**se** *vr* to be translucent; (*fig*) to be revealed.

trasluz [trásloōs'] *nm* reflected light; **al** ~ against *o* up to the light.

trasluzca [trásloos'ká] *etc vb V* **traslucir.**

trasmano [trásmá'no]: **a** ~ *ad* (*fuera de alcance*) out of reach; (*apartado*) out of the way.

trasnochador, a [trásnotchátḥor', á] *a* given to staying up late ♦ *nm/f* (*fig*) night bird.

trasnochar [trásnotchár'] *vi* (*acostarse tarde*) to stay up late; (*no dormir*) to have a sleepless night; (*pasar la noche*) to stay the night.

traspasar [tráspásár'] *vt* (*bala*) to pierce, go through; (*propiedad*) to sell, transfer; (*calle*) to cross over; (*límites*) to go beyond; (*ley*) to break; **"traspaso negocio"** "business for sale".

traspaso [tráspá'so] *nm* transfer; (*fig*) anguish.

traspié [tráspye'], *pl* **traspiés** *nm* (*caída*) stumble; (*tropezón*) trip; (*fig*) blunder.

trasplantar [trásplántár'] *vt* to transplant.

traste [trá'ste] *nm* (*MUS*) fret; **dar al** ~ **con algo** to ruin sth; **ir al** ~ to fall through.

trastero [tráste'ro] *nm* storage (*US*) *o* lumber (*Brit*) room.

trastienda [trástyen'dá] *nf* back room (*US*), backshop (*Brit*); **obtener algo por la** ~ to get sth by underhanded means.

trasto [trá'sto] *nm* (*mueble*) piece of furniture; (*tarro viejo*) old pot; (*pey: cosa*) piece of junk; (: *persona*) dead loss; ~**s** *nmpl* (*TEATRO*) scenery *sg*; **tirar los** ~**s a la cabeza** to have a blazing row.

trastornado, a [trástorná'tḥo, á] *a* (*loco*) mad; (*agitado*) crazy.

trastornar [trástornár'] *vt* to overturn, upset; (*fig: ideas*) to confuse; (: *nervios*) to shatter; (: *persona*) to drive crazy; ~**se** *vr* (*plan*) to fall through.

trastorno [trástor'no] *nm* (*acto*) overturning; (*confusión*) confusion; (*POL*) disturbance, upheaval; (*MED*) upset; ~ **estomacal** stomach upset; ~ **mental** mental

disorder, breakdown.
trasunto [trásōōn'to] *nm* copy.
tratable [tratá'hle] *a* friendly.
tratado [tratá'tho] *nm* (*POL*) treaty; (*COM*) agreement; (*LITERATURA*) treatise.
tratamiento [trátámyen'to] *nm* treatment; (*TEC*) processing; (*de problema*) handling; ~ **de datos** (*INFORM*) data processing; ~ **de gráficos** (*INFORM*) graphics; ~ **de márgenes** margin settings; ~ **de textos** (*INFORM*) word processing; ~ **por lotes** (*INFORM*) batch processing; ~ **de tú** familiar address.
tratante [tratán'te] *nm/f* dealer, merchandizer.
tratar [tratár'] *vt* (*ocuparse de*) to treat; (*manejar, TEC*) to handle; (*INFORM*) to process; (*MED*) to treat; (*dirigirse a: persona*) to address ♦ *vi*: ~ **de** (*hablar sobre*) to deal with, be about; (*intentar*) to try to; ~ **con** (*COM*) to trade in; (*negociar*) to negotiate with; (*tener contactos*) to have dealings with; ~**se** *vr* to treat each other; **se trata de la nueva piscina** it's about the new pool; **¿de qué se trata?** what's it about?
trato [trá'to] *nm* dealings *pl*; (*relaciones*) relationship; (*comportamiento*) manner; (*COM, JUR*) agreement, contract; (*título*) (form of) address; **de ~ agradable** pleasant; **de fácil ~** easy to get on with; ~ **equitativo** fair deal; **¡~ hecho!** it's a deal!; **malos ~s** ill-treatment *sg*.
trauma [trá'ōōmá] *nm* trauma.
traumático, a [tráōōmá'tēko, á] *a* traumatic.
través [tráhes'] *nm* (*contratiempo*) reverse; **al ~** across, crossways; **a ~ de** across; (*sobre*) over; (*por*) through; **de ~** across; (*de lado*) sideways.
travesaño [tráhesá'nyo] *nm* (*ARQ*) crossbeam; (*DEPORTE*) crossbar.
travesía [tráhesē'á] *nf* (*calle*) cross-street; (*NAUT*) crossing.
travesura [tráhesōō'rá] *nf* (*broma*) prank; (*ingenio*) wit.
travieso, a [tráhye'so, á] *a* (*niño*) naughty; (*adulto*) restless; (*ingenioso*) witty ♦ *nf* crossing; (*ARQ*) crossbeam.
trayecto [tráyek'to] *nm* (*ruta*) road, way; (*viaje*) journey; (*tramo*) stretch; (*curso*) course; **final del ~** end of the line.
trayectoria [tráyekto'ryá] *nf* trajectory; (*desarrollo*) development, path; **la ~ actual del partido** the party's present line.
trayendo [tráyen'do] *etc vb V* **traer**.
traza [trá'sá] *nf* (*ARQ*) plan, design; (*aspecto*) looks *pl*; (*señal*) sign; (*engaño*) trick; (*habilidad*) skill; (*INFORM*) trace.
trazado, a [trásá'tho, á] *a*: **bien ~** shapely, well-formed ♦ *nm* (*ARQ*) plan, design; (*fig*)

outline; (*de carretera etc*) line, route.
trazador [trásáthor'] *nm* plotter; ~ **plano** flatbed plotter.
trazar [trásár'] *vt* (*ARQ*) to plan; (*ARTE*) to sketch; (*fig*) to trace; (*itinerario: hacer*) to plot; (*plan*) to follow.
trazo [trá'so] *nm* (*línea*) line; (*bosquejo*) sketch; ~**s** *nmpl* (*de cara*) lines, features.
TRB *abr* = **toneladas de registro bruto**.
trébol [tre'hol] *nm* (*BOT*) clover; ~**es** *nmpl* (*NAIPES*) clubs.
trece [tre'se] *num* thirteen; **estar en sus ~** to stand firm.
trecho [tretch'o] *nm* (*distancia*) distance; (*de tiempo*) while; (*fam*) piece; **de ~ en ~** at intervals.
tregua [tre'gwá] *nf* (*MIL*) truce; (*fig*) lull; **sin ~** without respite.
treinta [tre'éntá] *num* thirty.
treintena [treēnte'ná] *nf* (about) thirty.
tremendo, a [tremen'do, á] *a* (*terrible*) terrible; (*imponente: cosa*) imposing; (*fam: fabuloso*) tremendous; (*divertido*) entertaining.
trémulo, a [tre'mōōlo, á] *a* quivering; (*luz*) flickering.
tren [tren] *nm* (*FERRO*) train; ~ **de aterrizaje** landing gear; ~ **directo/expreso/(de) mercancías/de pasajeros/suplementario** through/fast/freight/passenger/relief train; ~ **de vida** way of life.
trence [tren'se] *etc vb V* **trenzar**.
trenza [tren'sá] *nf* (*de pelo*) braid (*US*), plait (*Brit*).
trenzar [trensár'] *vt* (*el pelo*) to braid (*US*), plait (*Brit*) ♦ *vi* (*en baile*) to weave in and out; ~**se** *vr* (*AM*) to become involved.
trepa [tre'pá] *nf* (*subida*) climb; (*ardid*) trick.
trepador(a) [trepáthor', á] *nm/f* (*fam*): **ser un(a) ~** to be on the make ♦ *nf* (*BOT*) climber.
trepar [trepár'] *vt, vi* to climb; (*TEC*) to drill.
trepidación [trepēthásyon'] *nf* shaking, vibration.
trepidar [trepēthár'] *vi* to shake, vibrate.
tres [tres] *num* three; (*fecha*) third; **las ~** three o'clock.
trescientos, as [tresyen'tos, ás] *num* three hundred.
tresillo [tresē'yo] *nm* three-piece suite; (*MUS*) triplet.
treta [tre'tá] *nf* (*COM etc*) gimmick; (*fig*) trick.
tri... [trē] *pref* tri..., three-....
tríada [trē'áthá] *nf* triad.
triángulo [trēán'gōōlo] *nm* triangle.
tribu [trē'hōō] *nf* tribe.
tribuna [trēhōō'ná] *nf* (*plataforma*) platform; (*DEPORTE*) stand; (*fig*) public speak-

ing; ~ **de la prensa** press box; ~ **del acusado** (*JUR*) dock; ~ **del jurado** jury box.

tribunal [trĕh‿ōōnál'] *nm* (*juicio*) court; (*comisión*, *fig*) tribunal; (*ESCOL*: *examinadores*) board of examiners; **T~ Supremo** Supreme Court (*US*), High Court (*Brit*); **T~ de Justicia de las Comunidades Europeas** European Court of Justice.

tributar [trĕh‿ōōtár'] *vt* to pay; (*las gracias*) to give; (*cariño*) to show.

tributario, a [trĕh‿ōōtá'ryo, á] *a* (*GEO. POL*) tributary *cpd*; (*ECON*) tax *cpd*, taxation *cpd* ♦ *nm* (*GEO*) tributary ♦ *nm/f* (*COM*) taxpayer; **sistema** ~ tax system.

tributo [trĕh‿ōō'to] *nm* (*COM*) tax.

trice [trĕ'se] *etc vb V* **trizar**.

tricornio [trĕkor'nyo] *nm* three-cornered hat.

tricotar [trĕkotár'] *vi* to knit.

tridimensional [trĕt‿hēmensyonál'] *a* three-dimensional.

trienal [tryenál'] *a* three-year.

trigal [trĕgál'] *nm* wheat field.

trigésimo, a [trĕhe'sēmo, á] *num* thirtieth.

trigo [trĕ'go] *nm* wheat; ~**s** *nmpl* wheat field(s) (*pl*).

trigueño, a [trĕge'nyo, á] *a* (*pelo*) corn-colored; (*piel*) olive-skinned.

trilogía [trĕlohē'á] *nf* triology.

trillado, a [trĕyá'‿tho, á] *a* threshed; (*fig*) trite, hackneyed.

trilladora [trĕyá‿tho'rá] *nf* threshing machine.

trillar [trĕyár'] *vt* (*AGR*) to thresh; (*fig*) to frequent.

trillizos, as [trĕyē'sos, ás] *nmpl/nfpl* triplets.

trimestral [trĕmestrál'] *a* quarterly; (*ESCOL*) termly.

trimestre [trĕmes'tre] *nm* (*ESCOL*) term; (*COM*) quarter, financial period; (: *pago*) quarterly payment.

trinar [trĕnár'] *vi* (*MUS*) to trill; (*ave*) to sing, warble; **está que trina** he's hopping mad.

trincar [trĕnkár'] *vt* (*atar*) to tie up; (*NAUT*) to lash; (*agarrar*) to pinion.

trinchante [trĕntchán'te] *nm* (*para cortar carne*) carving knife; (*tenedor*) meat fork.

trinchar [trĕntchár'] *vt* to carve.

trinchera [trĕntche'rá] *nf* (*fosa*) trench; (*para vía*) cutting; (*impermeable*) trench-coat.

trineo [trĕne'o] *nm* sled (*US*), sledge (*Brit*).

trinidad [trĕnē‿thá‿th'] *nf* trio; (*REL*): **la T~** the Trinity.

trino [trĕ'no] *nm* trill.

trinque [trĕn'ke] *etc vb V* **trincar**.

trinquete [trĕnke'te] *nm* (*TEC*) pawl; (*NAUT*) foremast.

tripa [trĕ'pá] *nf* (*ANAT*) intestine; (*fig*, *fam*) belly; ~**s** *nfpl* (*ANAT*) insides; (*CULIN*)

tripe *sg*; **tener mucha** ~ to be fat; **me duelen las** ~**s** I have a stomach ache.

tripartito, a [trĕpártē'to, á] *a* tripartite.

triple [trĕ'ple] *a* triple; (*tres veces*) threefold.

triplicado, a [trĕplēká'‿tho, á] *a*: **por** ~ in triplicate.

Trípoli [trĕ'polē] *nm* Tripoli.

tríptico [trĕp'tēko] *nm* (*ARTE*) triptych; (*documento*) three-part document.

tripulación [trĕpōōlásyon'] *nf* crew.

tripulante [trĕpōōlán'te] *nm/f* crewman/woman.

tripular [trĕpōōlár'] *vt* (*barco*) to man; (*AUTO*) to drive.

triquiñuela [trĕkēnywe'lá] *nf* trick.

tris [trēs] *nm* crack; **en un** ~ in an instant; **estar en un** ~ **de hacer algo** to be within an inch of doing sth.

triste [trĕ'ste] *a* (*afligido*) sad; (*sombrío*) melancholy, gloomy; (*desolado*) desolate; (*lamentable*) sorry, miserable; (*viejo*) old; (*único*) single; **no queda sino un** ~ **penique** there's just one miserable penny left.

tristeza [trĕste'sá] *nf* (*aflicción*) sadness; (*melancolía*) melancholy; (*de lugar*) desolation; (*pena*) misery.

tristón, ona [trēston', oná] *a* sad, downhearted.

trituradora [trĕtōōrá‿tho'rá] *nf* shredder.

triturar [trĕtōōrár'] *vt* (*moler*) to grind; (*mascar*) to chew; (*documentos*) to shred.

triunfador, a [trēōōnfá‿thor', á] *a* triumphant; (*ganador*) winning ♦ *nm/f* winner.

triunfante [trēōōnfán'te] *a* triumphant; (*ganador*) winning.

triunfar [trēōōnfár'] *vi* (*tener éxito*) to triumph; (*ganar*) to win; (*NAIPES*) to be trumps; **triunfan corazones** hearts are trumps; ~ **en la vida** to succeed in life.

triunfo [trēōōn'fo] *nm* triumph; (*NAIPES*) trump.

trivial [trĕh‿yál'] *a* trivial.

trivialice [trĕh‿yálē'se] *etc vb V* **trivializar**.

trivializar [trĕh‿yálēsár'] *vt* to minimize, play down.

triza [trĕ'sá] *nf* bit, piece; **hacer algo** ~**s** to smash sth to bits; (*papel*) to tear sth to shreds.

trizar [trēsár'] *vt* to smash to bits.

trocar [trokár'] *vt* (*COM*) to exchange; (*dinero*, *de lugar*) to change; (*palabras*) to exchange; (*confundir*) to confuse; (*vomitar*) to vomit; ~**se** *vr* (*confundirse*) to get mixed up; (*transformarse*): ~**se (en)** to change (into).

trocha [trotch'á] *nf* (*sendero*) by-path; (*atajo*) short cut.

troche [trotch'e]: **a** ~ **y moche** *ad* helter-skelter, pell-mell.

trofeo [trofe'o] *nm* (*premio*) trophy; (*éxito*) success.

tromba [trom'bá] *nf* whirlwind; ~ **de agua** cloudburst.

trombón [trombon'] *nm* trombone.

trombosis [trombo'sēs] *nf inv* thrombosis.

trompa [trom'pá] *nf* (*MUS*) horn; (*de elefante*) trunk; (*trompo*) humming top; (*hocico*) snout; (*ANAT*) tube, duct ♦ *nm* (*MUS*) horn player; ~ **de Falopio** Fallopian tube; **cogerse una** ~ (*fam*) to get plastered.

trompada [trompá'thá] *nf*, **trompazo** [trompá'so] *nm* (*choque*) bump, bang; (*puñetazo*) punch.

trompeta [trompe'tá] *nf* trumpet; (*clarín*) bugle ♦ *nm* trumpeter.

trompo [trom'po] *nm* spinning top.

trompón [trompon'] *nm* bump.

tronado, a [troná'tho, á] *a* broken-down.

tronar [tronár'] *vt* (*AM*) to shoot ♦ *vi* to thunder; (*fig*) to rage; (*fam*) to go broke.

tronco [tron'ko] *nm* (*de árbol, ANAT*) trunk; (*de planta*) stem; **estar hecho un** ~ to be sound asleep.

tronchar [trontchár'] *vt* (*árbol*) to chop down; (*fig: vida*) to cut short; (*esperanza*) to shatter; (*persona*) to tire out; ~**se** *vr* to fall down; ~**se de risa** to split one's sides with laughter.

tronera [trone'rá] *nf* (*MIL*) loophole; (*ARQ*) small window.

trono [tro'no] *nm* throne.

tropa [tro'pá] *nf* (*MIL*) troop; (*soldados*) soldiers *pl*; (*soldados rasos*) ranks *pl*; (*gentío*) mob.

tropecé [tropese'], **tropecemos** [tropese'mos] *etc vb V* **tropezar.**

tropel [tropel'] *nm* (*muchedumbre*) crowd; (*prisa*) rush; (*montón*) throng; **acudir** *etc* **en** ~ to come *etc* in a mad rush.

tropelía [tropelē'á] *nm* outrage.

tropezar [tropesár'] *vi* to trip, stumble; (*fig*) to slip up; ~**se** *vr* (*dos personas*) to run into each other; ~ **con** (*encontrar*) to run into; (*topar con*) to bump into.

tropezón [tropeson'] *nm* trip; (*fig*) blunder; (*traspié*): **dar un** ~ to trip.

tropical [tropēkál'] *a* tropical.

trópico [tro'pēko] *nm* tropic.

tropiece [tropye'se] *etc vb V* **tropezar.**

tropiezo [tropye'so] *etc vb V* **tropezar** ♦ *nm* (*error*) slip, blunder; (*desgracia*) misfortune; (*revés*) setback; (*obstáculo*) snag; (*discusión*) quarrel.

troqué [troke'], **troquemos** [troke'mos] *etc vb V* **trocar.**

trotamundos [trotámoon'dos] *nm inv* globetrotter.

trotar [trotár'] *vi* to trot; (*viajar*) to travel about.

trote [tro'te] *nm* trot; (*fam*) travel(l)ing; **de**

mucho ~ durable.

Troya [tro'yá] *nf* Troy; **aquí fue** ~ now there's nothing but ruins.

trozo [tro'so] *nm* bit, piece; (*LITERATURA, MUS*) passage; **a** ~**s** in bits.

truco [troo'ko] *nm* (*habilidad*) knack; (*engaño*) trick; (*CINE*) trick effect *o* photography; ~**s** *nmpl* billiards *sg*; ~ **publicitario** advertising gimmick.

trucha [trootch'á] *nf* (*pez*) trout; (*TEC*) crane.

trueco [trwe'ko] *etc vb V* **trocar.**

trueno [trwe'no] *etc vb V* **tronar** ♦ *nm* (*gen*) thunder; (*estampido*) boom; (*de arma*) bang.

trueque [trwe'ke] *etc vb V* **trocar** ♦ *nm* exchange; (*COM*) barter.

trufa [troo'fá] *nf* (*BOT*) truffle; (*fig: fam*) fib.

truhán, ana [trooán', áná] *nm/f* rogue.

trulla [troo'yá] *nf* (*disturbio*) commotion; (*ruido*) noise; (*multitud*) crowd.

truncado, a [troonká'tho, á] *a* truncated.

truncar [troonkár'] *vt* (*cortar*) to truncate; (*la vida etc*) to cut short; (*el desarrollo*) to stunt.

trunque [troon'ke] *etc vb V* **truncar.**

tu [too] *a* your.

tú [too] *pron* you.

tubérculo [tooьer'koolo] *nm* (*BOT*) tuber.

tuberculosis [tooьerkoolo'sēs] *nf inv* tuberculosis.

tubería [tooьerē'á] *nf* pipes *pl*, piping; (*conducto*) pipeline.

tubo [too'ьo] *nm* tube, pipe; ~ **de desagüe** drainpipe; ~ **de ensayo** test-tube; ~ **de escape** exhaust (pipe); ~ **digestivo** alimentary canal.

tuerca [twer'ká] *nf* (*TEC*) nut.

tuerce [twer'se] *etc vb V* **torcer.**

tuerto, a [twer'to, á] *a* (*torcido*) twisted; (*ciego*) blind in one eye ♦ *nm/f* one-eyed person ♦ *nm* (*ofensa*) wrong; **a tuertas** upside-down.

tuerza [twer'sá] *etc vb V* **torcer.**

tueste [twe'ste] *etc vb V* **tostar.**

tuétano [twe'táno] *nm* (*ANAT: médula*) marrow; (*BOT*) pith; **hasta los** ~**s** through and through, utterly.

tufo [too'fo] *nm* vapor (*US*), vapour (*Brit*); (*fig: pey*) stench.

tugurio [toogoo'ryo] *nm* slum.

tul [tool] *nm* tulle.

tulipán [toolēpán'] *nm* tulip.

tullido, a [tooyē'tho, á] *a* crippled; (*cansado*) exhausted.

tumba [toom'bá] *nf* (*sepultura*) tomb; (*sacudida*) shake; (*voltereta*) somersault; **ser** (**como**) **una** ~ to keep one's mouth shut.

tumbar [toombár'] *vt* to knock down; (*doblar*) to knock over; (*fam: suj: olor*) to

overpower ♦ *vi* to fall down; ~**se** *vr*
(*echarse*) to lie down; (*extenderse*) to
stretch out.

tumbo [tōōm'bo] *nm* (*caída*) fall; (*de vehículo*) jolt; (*momento crítico*) critical moment.

tumefacción [tōōmefáksyon'] *nf* swelling.

tumido, a [tōōmē'ďo, à] *a* swollen.

tumor [tōōmor'] *nm* tumor (*US*), tumour
(*Brit*).

tumulto [tōōmōōl'to] *nm* turmoil; (*POL*:
motín) riot.

tuna [tōō'nà] *nf* V **tuno**.

tunante [tōōnàn'te] *a* rascally ♦ *nm* rogue,
villain; ¡~! you villain!

tunda [tōōn'dà] *nf* (*de tela*) shearing;
(*golpeo*) beating.

tundir [tōōndēr'] *vt* (*tela*) to shear; (*hierba*)
to mow; (*fig*) to exhaust; (*fam: golpear*) to
beat.

tunecino, a [tōōnesē'no, à] *a, nm/f* Tunisian.

túnel [tōō'nel] *nm* tunnel.

Túnez [tōō'nes] *nm* Tunis.

túnica [tōō'nēkà] *nf* tunic; (*vestido largo*)
long dress; (*ANAT, BOT*) tunic.

Tunicia [tōōnē'syà] *nf* Tunisia.

tuno, a [tōō'no, à] *nm/f* (*fam*) rogue ♦ *nf*
(*BOT*) prickly pear; (*MUS*) student music
group.

tuntún [tōōntōōn']: **al** ~ *ad* thoughtlessly.

tupido, a [tōōpē'ďo, à] *a* (*denso*) dense;
(*fig: torpe*) dim; (*tela*) close-woven.

turba [tōōr'bà] *nf* (*combustible*) turf;
(*muchedumbre*) crowd.

turbación [tōōrbàsyon'] *nf* (*molestia*) disturbance; (*preocupación*) worry.

turbado, a [tōōrbà'ďo, à] *a* (*molesto*) disturbed; (*preocupado*) worried.

turbante [tōōrbàn'te] *nm* turban.

turbar [tōōrbàr'] *vt* (*molestar*) to disturb;
(*incomodar*) to upset; ~**se** *vr* to be disturbed.

turbina [tōōrbē'nà] *nf* turbine.

turbio, a [tōōr'byo, à] *a* (*agua etc*) cloudy;
(*vista*) dim, blurred; (*tema*) unclear, confused; (*negocio*) shady ♦ *ad* indistinctly.

turbión [tōōrbyon'] *nf* downpour; (*fig*)
shower, hail.

turbohélice [tōōrḫoe'lēse] *nm* turboprop.

turbulencia [tōōrbōōlen'syà] *nf* turbulence;
(*fig*) restlessness.

turbulento, a [tōōrbōōlen'to, à] *a* turbulent; (*fig: intranquilo*) restless; (*: ruidoso*)
noisy.

turco, a [tōōr'ko, à] *a* Turkish ♦ *nm/f* Turk ♦
nm (*LING*) Turkish.

Turena [tōōre'nà] *nf* Touraine.

turgente [tōōrhen'te], **túrgido, a** [tōōr'hēďo,
à] *a* (*hinchado*) turgid, swollen.

Turín [tōōrēn'] *nm* Turin.

turismo [tōōrēs'mo] *nm* tourism; (*coche*)
sedan (*US*), saloon car (*Brit*); **hacer** ~ to
go traveling (abroad).

turista [tōōrē'stà] *nm/f* tourist; (*vacacionista*) vacationer (*US*), holidaymaker
(*Brit*).

turístico, a [tōōrē'stēko, à] *a* tourist *cpd*.

turnar [tōōrnàr'] *vi*, **turnarse** *vr* to take (it
in) turns.

turno [tōōr'no] *nm* (*oportunidad, orden de
prioridad*) opportunity; (*DEPORTE etc*)
turn; **es su** ~ it's his turn (next); ~ **de
día/de noche** (*INDUSTRIA*) day/night shift.

turolense [tōōrolen'se] *a* of *o* from Teruel ♦
nm/f native *o* inhabitant of Teruel.

turquesa [tōōrke'sà] *nf* turquoise.

Turquía [tōōrkē'à] *nf* Turkey.

turrón [tōōrron'] *nm* (*dulce*) nougat; (*fam*)
cushy job.

tutear [tōōteàr'] *vt* to address as familiar
"tú"; ~**se** *vr* to be on familiar terms.

tutela [tōōte'là] *nf* (*legal*) guardianship;
(*instrucción*) guidance; **estar bajo la** ~ **de**
(*fig*) to be under the protection of.

tutelar [tōōtelàr'] *a* tutelary ♦ *vt* to protect.

tutor [tōōtor', à] *nm/f* (*legal*) guardian;
(*ESCOL*) tutor; ~ **de curso** form master/
mistress.

tuve [tōō'ḫe] *etc vb* V **tener**.

tuyo, a [tōō'yo, à] *a* yours, of yours ♦ *pron*
yours; **los** ~**s** (*fam*) your relations, your
family.

TVE *nf abr* = *Televisión Española*.

U

U, u [ōō] *nf* (*letra*) U, u; **viraje en U** U-turn;
U de Ulises U for Uncle.

u *conj* or.

UAR [wàr] *nfpl abr* (*Esp*) = *Unidades Antiterroristas Rurales*.

ubérrimo, a [ōōḫe'rrēmo, à] *a* very rich,
fertile.

ubicación [ōōḫēkásyon'] *nf* place, position,
location.

ubicar [ōōḫēkàr'] *vt* to place, situate; (*: fig*)
to install in a post; (*esp AM: encontrar*) to
find; ~**se** *vr* to lie, be located.

ubicuo, a [ōōḫē'kwo, à] *a* ubiquitous.

ubique [ōōḫē'ke] *etc vb* V **ubicar**.

ubre [ōō'ḫre] *nf* udder.

Ucrania [ōōkrá'nyà] *nf* Ukraine.

ucraniano, a [ōōkrànyà'no, à] *a, nm/f*
Ukrainian.

Ud(s) *abr* = **usted(es)**.

UEP *nf abr* = *Unión Europea de Pagos*.

uf [ōōf] *excl* (*cansancio*) phew!; (*repugnancia*) ugh!

ufanarse [ōōfánár'se] *vr* to boast; ~ **de** to pride o.s. on.

ufano, a [ōōfá'no, á] *a* (*arrogante*) arrogant; (*presumido*) conceited.

UGT *nf abr V* **Unión General de Trabajadores**.

ujier [ōōhyer'] *nm* usher; (*portero*) doorman.

úlcera [ōōl'será] *nf* ulcer.

ulcerar [ōōlserár'] *vt* to make sore; ~**se** *vr* to ulcerate.

ULE [ōō'le] *nf abr* (*POL*) = *Unión Liberal Europea*.

ulterior [ōōlteryor'] *a* (*más allá*) farther, further; (*subsecuente, siguiente*) subsequent.

ulteriormente [ōōlteryormen'te] *ad* later, subsequently.

últimamente [ōōl'témámente] *ad* (*recientemente*) lately, recently; (*finalmente*) finally; (*como último recurso*) as a last resort.

ultimar [ōōltēmár'] *vt* to finish; (*finalizar*) to finalize; (*AM: rematar*) to finish off.

ultimátum [ōōltēmá'tōōm] *nm, pl* **ultimátums** ultimatum.

último, a [ōōl'tēmo, á] *a* last; (*más reciente*) latest, most recent; (*más bajo*) bottom; (*más alto*) top; (*fig*) final, extreme; **en las últimas** on one's last legs; **por** ~ finally.

ultra [ōōl'trá] *a* ultra ♦ *nm/f* extreme rightwinger.

ultrajar [ōōltráhár'] *vt* (*escandalizar*) to outrage; (*insultar*) to insult, abuse.

ultraje [ōōltrá'he] *nm* outrage; insult.

ultramar [ōōltrámár'] *nm*: **de** *o* **en** ~ abroad, overseas; **los países de** ~ the overseas countries.

ultramarino, a [ōōltrámárē'no, á] *a* overseas, foreign ♦ *nmpl*: ~**s** groceries; **tienda de** ~**s** grocer's (shop).

ultranza [ōōltrán'sá]: **a** ~ *ad* to the death; (*a todo trance*) at all costs; (*completo*) outright; (*POL etc*) out-and-out, extreme; **un nacionalista a** ~ a rabid nationalist.

ultrarrojo, a [ōōltrárro'ho, á] *a* = **infrarrojo, a**.

ultrasónico, a [ōōltráso'nēko, á] *a* ultrasonic.

ultratumba [ōōltrátōōm'bá] *nf*: **la vida de** ~ the next life; **una voz de** ~ a ghostly voice.

ultravioleta [ōōltráßyole'tá] *a inv* ultraviolet.

ulular [ōōlōōlár'] *vi* to howl; (*búho*) to hoot.

umbral [ōōmbrál'] *nm* (*gen*) threshold; ~ **de rentabilidad** (*COM*) break-even point.

umbroso, a [ōōmbro'so, á], **umbrío, a** [ōōm'brēo, á] *a* shady.

un, una [ōōn, ōō'ná] *artículo indefinido* a ♦ *num* one; *V* **uno**.

unánime [ōōná'nēme] *a* unanimous.

unanimidad [ōōnánēmētháth'] *nf* unanimity; **por** ~ unanimously.

unción [ōōnsyon'] *nf* anointing.

uncir [ōōnsēr'] *vt* to yoke.

undécimo, a [ōōnde'sēmo, á] *a, nm/f* eleventh.

undular [ōōndōōlár'] *vi V* **ondular**.

UNED [ōōned'] *nf abr* (*Esp UNIV*) = *Universidad Nacional de Enseñanza a Distancia*.

ungir [ōōnhēr'] *vt* to rub with ointment; (*REL*) to anoint.

ungüento [ōōngwen'to] *nm* ointment; (*fig*) salve, balm.

únicamente [ōō'nēkámente] *ad* solely; (*solamente*) only.

unicidad [ōōnēsētháth'] *nf* uniqueness.

único, a [ōō'nēko, á] *a* only; (*solo*) sole, single; (*sin par*) unique; **hijo** ~ only child.

unidad [ōōnētháth'] *nf* unity; (*TEC*) unit; ~ **móvil** (*TV*) mobile unit; (*INFORM*): ~ **central** system unit, central processing unit; ~ **de control** control unit; ~ **de disco** disk drive; ~ **de entrada/salida** input/output device; ~ **de información** data item; ~ **periférica** peripheral device; ~ **de presentación visual** *o* **de visualización** visual display unit; ~ **procesadora central** central processing unit.

unido, a [ōōnē'tho, á] *a* joined, linked; (*fig*) united.

unificar [ōōnēfēkár'] *vt* to unite, unify.

unifique [ōōnēfē'ke] *etc vb V* **unificar**.

uniformado, a [ōōnēformá'tho, á] *a* uniformed, in uniform.

uniformar [ōōnēformár'] *vt* to make uniform; (*TEC*) to standardize.

uniforme [ōōnēfor'me] *a* uniform, equal; (*superficie*) even ♦ *nm* uniform.

uniformidad [ōōnēformētháth'] *nf* uniformity; (*llaneza*) levelness, evenness.

unilateral [ōōnēláterál'] *a* unilateral.

unión [ōōnyon'] *nf* (*gen*) union; (*acto*) uniting, joining; (*calidad*) unity; (*TEC*) joint; (*fig*) closeness, togetherness; **en** ~ **con** (together) with, accompanied by; ~ **aduanera** customs union; **U~ General de Trabajadores (UGT)** (*Esp*) Socialist Union Confederation; **la U~ Soviética** the Soviet Union; **punto de** ~ (*TEC*) junction.

unir [ōōnēr'] *vt* (*juntar*) to join, unite; (*atar*) to tie, fasten; (*combinar*) to combine ♦ *vi* (*ingredientes*) to mix well; ~**se** *vr* to join together, unite; (*empresas*) to merge; **les une una fuerte simpatía** they are bound by (a) strong affection; ~**se en matrimonio** to marry.

unísono [ōōnē'sono] *nm*: **al** ~ in unison.

unitario, a [ōōnētá'ryo, á] *a* unitary; (*REL*) Unitarian ♦ *nm/f* (*REL*) Unitarian.

universal [ōōnēhersál'] *a* universal; (*mundial*) world *cpd*; **historia** ~ world history.

universidad [ōōnēhersēthátḥ'] *nf* university; ~ **laboral** polytechnic, poly.

universitario, a [ōōnēhersētá'ryo, á] *a* university *cpd* ♦ *nm/f* (*profesor*) lecturer; (*estudiante*) (university) student.

universo [ōōnēher'so] *nm* universe.

unja [ōōn'há] *etc vb* V **ungir**.

uno, a [ōō'no, á] *num* one ♦ *a* one; (*idéntico*) one and the same ♦ *pron* one; (*alguien*) someone, somebody; **es todo** ~, **es** ~ **y lo mismo** it's all one, it's all the same; ~**s (cuantos)** some, a few; ~**s 80 dólares** about 80 dollars; ~ **mismo** oneself; ~ **a** ~, ~ **por** ~ one by one; **cada** ~ each *o* every one; ~**(s) a otro(s)** each other, one another; **estar en** ~ to be at one; **una de dos** either one thing or the other; ~ **que otro** some, a few; ~**s y otros** all of them; ~ **y otro** both.

untar [ōōntár'] *vt* (*gen*) to rub; (*engrasar*) to grease, oil; (*MED*) to rub (with ointment); (*fig*) to bribe; ~**se** *vr* (*fig*) to be crooked; ~ **el pan con mantequilla** to spread butter on one's bread.

unto [ōōn'to] *nm* animal fat; (*MED*) ointment.

unza [ōōn'sá] *etc vb* V **uncir**.

uña [ōō'nyá] *nf* (*ANAT*) nail; (*del pie*) toenail; (*garra*) claw; (*casco*) hoof; (*arrancaclavos*) nail puller (*US*), claw (*Brit*); **ser** ~ **y carne** to be as thick as thieves; **enseñar** *o* **mostrar** *o* **sacar las** ~**s** to show one's claws.

UOE *nf abr* (*Esp MIL*) = Unidad de Operaciones Especiales.

UPA *nf abr* = Unión Panamericana.

UPC *nf abr* (= unidad procesadora central) CPU.

UPV *nf abr* (= unidad de presentación visual) VDU.

Urales [ōōrá'les] *nmpl* (*tb*: **Montes** ~) Urals.

uranio [ōōrá'nyo] *nm* uranium.

urbanidad [ōōrhánēthátḥ'] *nf* courtesy, politeness.

urbanismo [ōōrhánēs'mo] *nm* town planning.

urbanista [ōōrhánē'stá] *nm/f* town planner.

urbanización [ōōrhánēsasyon'] *nf* (*colonia, barrio*) housing development (*US*), housing estate (*Brit*).

urbano, a [ōōrhá'no, á] *a* (*de ciudad*) urban, town *cpd*; (*cortés*) courteous, polite.

urbe [ōōr'he] *nf* large city, metropolis.

urdimbre [ōōrthēm'bre] *nf* (*de tejido*) warp;

(*intriga*) intrigue.

urdir [ōōrthēr'] *vt* to warp; (*fig*) to plot, contrive.

urgencia [ōōrhen'syá] *nf* urgency; (*prisa*) haste, rush; **salida de** ~ emergency exit; **servicios de** ~ emergency services.

urgente [ōōrhen'te] *a* urgent; (*insistente*) insistent; **carta** ~ special delivery letter.

urgir [ōōrhēr'] *vi* to be urgent; **me urge** I'm in a hurry for it; **me urge terminarlo** I must finish it as soon as I can.

urinario, a [ōōrēná'ryo, á] *a* urinary ♦ *nm* public restroom *o* lavatory.

urja [ōōr'há] *etc vb* V **urgir**.

urna [ōōr'ná] *nf* urn; (*POL*) ballot box; **acudir a las** ~**s** (*fig*: *persona*) to (go and) vote; (: *gobierno*) to hold an election.

urólogo, a [ōōro'logo, á] *nm/f* urologist.

urraca [ōōrrá'ká] *nf* magpie.

URSS *nf abr* (= Unión de Repúblicas Socialistas Soviéticas) USSR.

Uruguay [ōōrōōgwá'ē] *nm*: **El** ~ Uruguay.

uruguayo, a [ōōrōōgwá'yo, á] *a*, *nm/f* Uruguayan.

usado, a [ōōsá'tho, á] *a* (*gen*) used; (*ropa etc*) worn; **muy** ~ worn out.

usanza [ōōsán'sá] *nf* custom, usage.

usar [ōōsár'] *vt* to use; (*ropa*) to wear; (*tener costumbre*) to be in the habit of ♦ *vi*: ~ **de** to make use of; ~**se** *vr* to be used; (*ropa*) to be worn *o* in fashion.

uso [ōō'so] *nm* use; (*MECÁNICA etc*) wear; (*costumbre*) usage, custom; (*moda*) fashion; **al** ~ in keeping with custom; **al** ~ **de** in the style of; **de** ~ **externo** (*MED*) for external application; **estar en el** ~ **de la palabra** to be speaking, have the floor; ~ **y desgaste** (*COM*) wear and tear.

usted [ōōstetḥ'] *pron* (*sg*: *abr* **Ud** *o* **Vd**: *formal*) you *sg*; ~**es** (*pl*: *abr* **Uds** *o* **Vds**: *formal*) you *pl*; (*AM*: *formal y fam*) you *pl*.

usual [ōōswál'] *a* usual.

usuario, a [ōōswá'ryo, á] *nm/f* user; ~ **final** (*COM*) end user.

usufructo [ōōsōōfrōōk'to] *nm* use; ~ **vitalicio (de)** life interest (in).

usura [ōōsōō'rá] *nf* usury.

usurero, a [ōōsōōre'ro, á] *nm/f* usurer.

usurpar [ōōsōōrpár'] *vt* to usurp.

utensilio [ōōtensē'lyo] *nm* tool; (*CULIN*) utensil.

útero [ōō'tero] *nm* uterus, womb.

útil [ōō'tēl] *a* useful; (*servible*) usable, serviceable ♦ *nm* tool; **día** ~ working day, weekday; **es muy** ~ **tenerlo aquí cerca** it's very handy having it here close by.

utilice [ōōtēlē'se] *etc vb* V **utilizar**.

utilidad [ōōtēlēthátḥ'] *nf* usefulness, utility; (*COM*) profit; ~**es líquidas** net profit *sg*.

utilitario, a [ōōtēlētá'ryo] *nm* (*INFORM*) utility.

utilizar [ōōtēlēsár'] *vt* to use, utilize; (*explo-*

tar) to harness.
utopía [oͦotopēʹá] *nf* Utopia.
utópico, a [oͦotoʹpēko, á] *a* Utopian.
uva [oͦ'bá] *nf* grape; ~ **pasa** raisin; ~ **de
Corinto** currant; **estar de mala** ~ to be in
a bad mood.
uve [oͦ'be] *nf name of the letter V*; **en
forma de** ~ V-shaped; ~ **doble** *name of
the letter W*.
UVI [oͦ'bē] *nf abr* (*Esp MED*: = *unidad de
vigilancia intensiva*) ICU.

V

V, v [be'kor'ta] *nf* (*letra*) V, v; **V de Valencia** V for Victor.
V. *abr* (= *visto*) approved, passed.
v. *abr* (= *voltio*) v.; (= *véase*) v.; (= *verso*)
v.
va [bá] *vb V* **ir.**
V.A. *abr* = *Vuestra Alteza.*
vaca [báʹká] *nf* (*animal*) cow; (*carne*) beef;
(*cuero*) cowhide; ~**s flacas/gordas** (*fig*)
bad/good times.
vacaciones [bákásyoʹnes] *nfpl* vacation *sg*
(*US*), holiday(s) (*Brit*); **estar/irse** *o* **marcharse de** ~ to be/go (away) on vacation.
vacante [bákánʹte] *a* vacant, empty ♦ *nf* vacancy.
vacar [bákárʹ] *vi* to fall vacant; ~ **a** *o* **en** to
engage in.
vaciado, a [básyàʹtho, á] *a* (*hecho en molde*)
cast in a mold (*US*) *o* mould (*Brit*); (*hueco*) hollow ♦ *nm* cast, mold(ing) (*US*),
mould(ing) (*Brit*).
vaciar [básyárʹ] *vt* to empty (out); (*ahuecar*)
to hollow out; (*moldear*) to cast; (*INFORM*)
to dump ♦ *vi* (*río*) to flow (*en* into); ~**se** *vr*
to empty; (*fig*) to blab, spill the beans.
vaciedad [básyethàth'] *nf* emptiness.
vacilación [básēlàsyon'] *nf* hesitation.
vacilante [básēlánʹte] *a* unsteady; (*habla*)
faltering; (*luz*) flickering; (*fig*) hesitant.
vacilar [básēlárʹ] *vi* to be unsteady; to
falter; to flicker; to hesitate, waver;
(*persona*) to stagger, stumble; (*memoria*)
to fail.
vacío, a [básēʹo, á] *a* empty; (*puesto*) vacant; (*desocupado*) idle; (*vano*) vain;
(*charla etc*) light, superficial ♦ *nm* emptiness; (*FÍSICA*) vacuum; (*un* ~) (empty)
space; **hacer el** ~ **a uno** to ignore sb.
vacuna [bákoͦʹná] *nf* vaccine.
vacunar [bákoͦnárʹ] *vt* to vaccinate; ~**se** *vr*

to get vaccinated.
vacuno, a [bákoͦʹno, á] *a* bovine.
vacuo, a [báʹkwo, á] *a* empty.
vadear [bátheárʹ] *vt* (*río*) to ford; (*problema*) to overcome; (*persona*) to sound out.
vado [báʹtho] *nm* ford; (*solución*) solution;
(*descanso*) respite.
vagabundear [báɡáboͦndeárʹ] *vi* (*andar sin
rumbo*) to wander, roam; (*ser vago*) to be
a bum (*US*) *o* tramp.
vagabundo, a [báɡáhoͦn'do, á] *a* wandering; (*pey*) vagrant ♦ *nm/f* (*errante*)
wanderer; (*vago*) bum (*US*), tramp.
vagamente [báɡámenʹte] *ad* vaguely.
vagancia [báɡán'syá] *nf* vagrancy.
vagar [báɡárʹ] *vi* to wander; (*pasear*) to
saunter up and down; (*no hacer nada*) to
be idle ♦ *nm* leisure.
vagido [bàhēʹtho] *nm* wail.
vagina [bàhēʹná] *nf* vagina.
vago, a [báʹɡo, á] *a* vague; (*perezoso*) lazy;
(*ambulante*) wandering ♦ *nm/f* (*vagabundo*)
bum (*US*), tramp; (*flojo*) lazybones *sg*,
idler.
vagón [báɡon'] *nm* (*de pasajeros*) passenger
car (*US*), carriage (*Brit*); (*de mercancías*)
freight car (*US*), waggon (*Brit*); ~ **cama/
restaurante** sleeping/dining car.
vague [báʹɡe] *etc vb V* **vagar.**
vaguedad [báɡethàth'] *nf* vagueness.
vahído [báēʹtho] *nm* dizzy spell.
vaho [báʹo] *nm* (*vapor*) steam; (*olor*) smell;
(*respiración*) breath; ~**s** *nmpl* (*MED*) inhalation *sg.*
vaina [báʹēná] *nf* sheath.
vainilla [bàēnēʹyá] *nf* vanilla.
vainita [bàēnē'tá] *nf* (*AM*) green *o* French
bean.
vais [báēs] *vb V* **ir.**
vaivén [báēben'] *nm* to-and-fro movement;
(*de tránsito*) coming and going; **vaivenes**
nmpl (*fig*) ups and downs.
vajilla [báhēʹyá] *nf* dishes *pl*; (*una* ~)
service; ~ **de porcelana** chinaware.
val [bál], **valdré** [báldre'] *etc vb V* **valer.**
vale [báʹle] *nm* voucher; (*recibo*) receipt;
(*pagaré*) I.O.U.; ~ **de regalo** gift
certificate (*US*) *o* voucher (*Brit*).
valedero, a [báletheʹro, á] *a* valid.
valenciano, a [bálensyáʹno, á] *a, nm/f* Valencian ♦ *nm* (*LING*) Valencian.
valentía [bálentēʹá] *nf* courage, bravery;
(*pey*) boastfulness; (*acción*) heroic deed.
valentísimo, a [bálentēʹsēmo, á] *a* (*superl
de* **valiente**) very brave, courageous.
valentón, ona [bálenton', oná] *a* blustering.
valer [bálerʹ] *vt* to be worth; (*MAT*) to
equal; (*costar*) to cost; (*amparar*) to aid,
protect ♦ *vi* (*ser útil*) to be useful; (*ser válido*) to be valid; ~**se** *vr* to defend o.s. ♦
nm worth, value; ~ **la pena** to be worth-

while; **¿vale?** O.K.?; **¡vale!** (*¡basta!*) that'll
do!; **¡eso no vale!** that doesn't count!; **no
vale nada** it's no good; (*mercancía*) it's
worthless; (*argumento*) it's no use; **no vale
para nada** he's no good at all; ~**se de** to
make use of, take advantage of; ~**se por sí
mismo** to help o manage by o.s.
valga [bál'ǥa] *etc vb* V **valer**.
valía [bálē'á] *nf* worth; **de gran** ~ (*objeto*)
very valuable.
validar [bálēthár'] *vt* to validate; (*POL*) to
ratify.
validez [bálēthes'] *nf* validity; **dar** ~ **a** to
validate.
válido, a [bá'lētho, á] *a* valid.
valiente [bályen'te] *a* brave, valiant; (*audaz*) bold; (*pey*) boastful; (*con ironía*) fine,
wonderful ♦ *nm/f* brave man/woman.
valija [bálē'há] *nf* case; (*AM*) suitcase;
(*mochila*) satchel; (*CORREOS*) mailbag; ~
diplomática diplomatic pouch (*US*) o bag
(*Brit*).
valioso, a [bályo'so, á] *a* valuable; (*rico*)
wealthy.
valor [bálor'] *nm* value, worth; (*precio*)
price; (*valentía*) courage; (*importancia*)
importance; (*cara*) nerve; **sin** ~ worthless; ~ **adquisitivo** o **de compra** purchasing power; **dar** ~ **a** to attach importance
to; **quitar** ~ **a** to minimize the importance
of; (*COM*): ~ **según balance** book value;
~ **comercial** o **de mercado** market value;
~ **contable/desglosado** asset/break-up
value; ~ **de escasez** scarcity value; ~ **intrínseco** intrinsic value; ~ **a la par** par
value; ~ **neto** net worth; ~ **de rescate/de
sustitución** surrender/replacement value; *V
tb* **valores**.
valoración [bálorásyon'] *nf* valuation.
valorar [bálorár'] *vt* to value; (*tasar*) to
price; (*fig*) to assess.
valores [bálo'res] *nmpl* (*COM*) securities; ~
en cartera o **habidos** investments.
vals [báls] *nm* waltz.
válvula [bál'hōōlá] *nf* valve.
valla [bá'yá] *nf* fence; (*DEPORTE*) hurdle;
(*fig*) barrier.
vallar [báyár'] *vt* to fence in.
valle [bá'ye] *nm* valley, vale.
vallisoletano, a [báyēsoletá'no, á] *a* of o
from Valladolid ♦ *nm/f* native o inhabitant
of Valladolid.
vamos [bá'mos] *vb* V **ir**.
vampiro, iresa [bámpē'ro, ēre'sá] *nm/f*
vampire ♦ *nf* (*CINE*) vamp, femme fatale.
van [bán] *vb* V **ir**.
vanagloriarse [bánáǥloryár'se] *vr* to boast.
vandalismo [bándálēs'mo] *nm* vandalism.
vándalo, a [bán'dálo, á] *nm/f* vandal.
vanguardia [bánǥwár'dyá] *nf* vanguard; **de**
~ (*ARTE*) avant-garde; **estar en** o **ir a la** ~

de (*fig*) to be in the forefront of.
vanidad [bánētháth'] *nf* vanity; (*inutilidad*)
futility; (*irrealidad*) unreality.
vanidoso, a [bánētho'so, á] *a* vain, conceited.
vano, a [bá'no, á] *a* (*irreal*) unreal; (*irracio-
nal*) unreasonable; (*inútil*) vain, useless;
(*persona*) vain, conceited; (*frívolo*) frivolous.
vapor [bápor'] *nm* vapor (*US*), vapour
(*Brit*); (*vaho*) steam; (*de gas*) fumes *pl*;
(*neblina*) mist; ~**es** *nmpl* (*MED*) hysterics;
al ~ (*CULIN*) steamed.
vaporice [báporē'se] *etc vb* V **vaporizar**.
vaporizador [báporēsáthor'] *nm* (*perfume
etc*) spray.
vaporizar [báporēsár'] *vt* to vaporize;
(*perfume*) to spray.
vaporoso, a [báporo'so, á] *a* vaporous; (*va-
hoso*) steamy; (*tela*) light, airy.
vaque [bá'ke] *etc vb* V **vacar**.
vaquería [bákerē'á] *nf* dairy.
vaquero, a [bá'ke'ro, á] *a* cattle *cpd* ♦ *nm*
cowboy; ~**s** *nmpl* jeans.
vaquilla [bákē'yá] *nf* heifer.
vara [bá'rá] *nf* stick, pole; (*TEC*) rod; ~ **mágica** magic wand.
varado, a [bárá'tho, á] *a* (*NAUT*) stranded;
estar ~ to be aground.
varar [bárár'] *vt* to beach ♦ *vi*, ~**se** *vr* to be
beached.
varear [báreár'] *vt* to hit, beat; (*frutas*) to
knock down (with poles).
variable [bárya'hle] *a, nf* variable (*tb IN-
FORM*).
variación [báryásyon'] *nf* variation; **sin** ~
unchanged.
variante [báryán'te] *a* variant ♦ *nf* (*alternativa*) alternative; (*AUTO*) bypass.
variar [báryár'] *vt* (*cambiar*) to change; (*poner variedad*) to vary; (*modificar*) to modify; (*cambiar de posición*) to switch around
♦ *vi* to vary; ~ **de** to differ from; ~ **de
opinión** to change one's mind; **para** ~ just
for a change.
variedad [báryetháth'] *nf* variety.
varilla [bárē'yá] *nf* stick; (*BOT*) twig; (*TEC*)
rod; (*de rueda*) spoke; ~ **mágica** magic
wand.
vario, a [bá'ryo, á] *a* (*variado*) varied;
(*multicolor*) motley; (*cambiable*) changeable; ~**s** various, several.
varón [báron'] *nm* male, man.
varonil [báronēl'] *a* manly.
Varsovia [bárso'hyá] *nf* Warsaw.
vas [bás] *vb* V **ir**.
vasco, a [bás'ko, á], **vascongado, a**
[báskongá'tho, á] *a, nm/f* Basque ♦ *nm*
(*LING*) Basque ♦ *nfpl*: **las Vascongadas** the
Basque Country *sg* o Provinces.
vascuence [báskwen'se] *nm* (*LING*) Basque.

vaselina [báselē'ná] *nf* Vaseline ®.

vasija [básē'há] *nf* (earthenware) vessel.

vaso [bá'so] *nm* glass, tumbler; (*ANAT*) vessel; (*cantidad*) glass(ful); ~ **de vino** glass of wine; ~ **para vino** wineglass.

vástago [bá'stágo] *nm* (*BOT*) shoot; (*TEC*) rod; (*fig*) offspring.

vasto, a [bá'sto, á] *a* vast, huge.

váter [bá'ter] *nm* restroom (*US*), lavatory.

Vaticano [bátēká'no] *nm*: **el** ~ the Vatican; **la Ciudad del** ~ the Vatican City.

vaticinar [bátēsēnár'] *vt* to prophesy, predict.

vaticinio [bátēsē'nyo] *nm* prophecy.

vatio [bá'tyo] *nm* (*ELEC*) watt.

vaya [bá'yá] *etc vb V* **ir**.

Vda. *abr* = **viuda**.

Vd(s) *abr* = **usted(es)**.

ve [be] *vb V* **ir, ver**.

vea [be'á] *etc vb V* **ver**.

vecindad [besēndáth'] *nf*, **vecindario** [besēndá'ryo] *nm* neighborhood (*US*), neighbourhood (*Brit*); (*habitantes*) residents *pl*.

vecinal [besēnál'] *a* (*camino, impuesto etc*) local.

vecino, a [besē'no, á] *a* neighboring (*US*), neighbouring (*Brit*) ♦ *nm/f* neighbor (*US*), neighbour (*Brit*); (*residente*) resident; **somos** ~**s** we live next door to one another.

veda [be'thá] *nf* prohibition; (*temporada*) closed (*US*) o close (*Brit*) season.

vedado [bethá'tho] *nm* preserve.

vedar [bethár'] *vt* (*prohibir*) to ban, prohibit; (*idea, plan*) to veto; (*impedir*) to stop, prevent.

vedette [bethet'] *nf* (*TEATRO, CINE*) star(let).

vega [be'gá] *nf* fertile plain o valley.

vegetación [behetásyon'] *nf* vegetation.

vegetal [behetál'] *a, nm* vegetable.

vehemencia [beemen'syá] *nf* (*insistencia*) vehemence; (*pasión*) passion; (*fervor*) fervor (*US*), fervour (*Brit*); (*violencia*) violence.

vehemente [beemen'te] *a* vehement; passionate; fervent; violent.

vehículo [beē'kōolo] *nm* vehicle; (*MED*) carrier; ~ **de servicio público** public service vehicle; ~ **espacial** spacecraft.

veinte [be'ēnte] *num* twenty; (*orden, fecha*) twentieth; **el siglo** ~ the twentieth century.

veintena [beēnte'ná] *nf*: **una** ~ (about) twenty, a score.

vejación [behásyon'] *nf* vexation; (*humillación*) humiliation.

vejamen [behá'men] *nm* satire.

vejar [behár'] *vt* (*irritar*) to annoy, vex; (*humillar*) to humiliate.

vejez [behes'] *nf* old age.

vejiga [behē'gá] *nf* (*ANAT*) bladder.

vela [be'lá] *nf* (*de cera*) candle; (*NAUT*) sail; (*insomnio*) sleeplessness; (*vigilia*) vigil; (*MIL*) sentry duty; (*fam*) snot; **a toda** ~ (*NAUT*) under full sail; **estar a dos** ~**s** (*fam*) to be broke; **pasar la noche en** ~ to have a sleepless night.

velado, a [belá'tho, á] *a* veiled; (*sonido*) muffled; (*FOTO*) blurred ♦ *nf* soirée.

velador [beláthor'] *nm* watchman; (*candelero*) candlestick.

velar [belár'] *vt* (*vigilar*) to keep watch over; (*cubrir*) to veil ♦ *vi* to stay awake; ~ **por** to watch over, look after.

velatorio [beláto'ryo] *nm* (*funeral*) wake.

veleidad [beleētháth'] *nf* (*ligereza*) fickleness; (*capricho*) whim.

velero [bele'ro] *nm* (*NAUT*) sailing ship; (*AVIAT*) glider.

veleta [bele'tá] *nm/f* fickle person ♦ *nf* weather vane.

veliz [belēs'] *nm* (*AM*) suitcase.

velo [be'lo] *nm* veil; ~ **de paladar** (*ANAT*) soft palate.

velocidad [belosētháth'] *nf* speed; (*TEC*) rate, pace, velocity; (*MECÁNICA, AUTO*) gear; **¿a qué** ~? how fast?; **de alta** ~ high-speed; **cobrar** ~ to pick up o gather speed; **meter la segunda** ~ to shift into second gear; ~ **máxima de impresión** (*INFORM*) maximum print speed.

velocímetro [belosē'metro] *nm* speedometer.

velódromo [belo'thromo] *nm* cycle track.

veloz [belos'] *a* fast, swift.

vello [be'yo] *nm* down, fuzz.

vellón [beyon'] *nm* fleece.

velloso, a [beyo'so, á] *a* fuzzy.

velludo, a [beyōō'tho, á] *a* shaggy ♦ *nm* plush, velvet.

ven [ben] *vb V* **venir**.

vena [be'ná] *nf* vein; (*fig*) vein, disposition; (*GEO*) seam, vein.

venablo [bená'blo] *nm* javelin.

venado [bená'tho] *nm* deer; (*CULIN*) venison.

venal [benál'] *a* (*ANAT*) venous; (*pey*) venal.

venalidad [benálētháth'] *nf* venality.

vencedor, a [bensethor', á] *a* victorious ♦ *nm/f* victor, winner.

vencer [benser'] *vt* (*dominar*) to defeat, beat; (*derrotar*) to vanquish; (*superar, controlar*) to overcome, master ♦ *vi* (*triunfar*) to win, triumph; (*pago*) to fall due; (*plazo*) to expire; **dejarse** ~ to yield, give in.

vencido, a [bensē'tho, á] *a* (*derrotado*) defeated, beaten; (*COM*) payable, due ♦ *ad*: **pagar** ~ to pay in arrears; **le pagan por meses** ~**s** he is paid at the end of the month; **darse por** ~ to give up.

vencimiento [bensēmyen'to] *nm* collapse; (*COM: plazo*) expiration; **a su ~** when it falls due.

venda [ben'dá] *nf* bandage.

vendaje [bendà'he] *nm* bandage, dressing.

vendar [bendár'] *vt* to bandage; **~ los ojos** to blindfold.

vendaval [bendáħál'] *nm* (*viento*) gale; (*huracán*) hurricane.

vendedor, a [bendeħor', á] *nm/f* seller; **~ ambulante** hawker, peddler (*US*), pedlar (*Brit*).

vender [bender'] *vt* to sell; (*comerciar*) to market; (*traicionar*) to sell out, betray; **~se** *vr* to be sold; **~ al contado/al por mayor/al por menor/a plazos** to sell for cash/wholesale/retail/on credit; **"se vende"** "for sale"; **"véndese coche"** "car for sale"; **~ al descubierto** to sell short.

vendimia [bendē'myá] *nf* grape harvest; **la ~ de 1973** the 1973 vintage.

vendré [bendre'] *etc vb* V **venir**.

Venecia [bene'syà] *nf* Venice.

veneciano, a [benesyà'no, á] *a, nm/f* Venetian.

veneno [bene'no] *nm* poison, venom.

venenoso, a [beneno'so, á] *a* poisonous.

venerable [benerá'ble] *a* venerable.

veneración [benerásyon'] *nf* veneration.

venerar [benerár'] *vt* (*reconocer*) to venerate; (*adorar*) to worship.

venéreo, a [bene'reo, á] *a* venereal.

venero [bene'ro] *nm* (*veta*) seam, lode; (*fuente*) spring.

venezolano, a [benesolá'no, á] *a, nm/f* Venezuelan.

Venezuela [beneswe'lá] *nf* Venezuela.

venga [ben'gá] *etc vb* V **venir**.

vengador, a [bengáħor', á] *a* avenging ♦ *nm/f* avenger.

venganza [bengán'sá] *nf* vengeance, revenge.

vengar [bengár'] *vt* to avenge; **~se** *vr* to take revenge.

vengativo, a [bengátē'ħo, á] *a* (*persona*) vindictive.

vengue [ben'ge] *etc vb* V **vengar**.

venia [be'nyá] *nf* (*perdón*) pardon; (*permiso*) consent; **con su ~** by your leave.

venial [benyál'] *a* venial.

venida [benē'ħá] *nf* (*llegada*) arrival; (*regreso*) return; (*fig*) rashness.

venidero, a [benēħe'ro, á] *a* coming, future; **en lo ~** in (the) future.

venir [benēr'] *vi* to come; (*llegar*) to arrive; (*ocurrir*) to happen; **~se** *vr*: **~se abajo** to collapse; **~ a menos** (*persona*) to lose status; (*empresa*) to go downhill; **~ bien** to be suitable, come just right; (*ropa, gusto*) to suit; **~ mal** to be unsuitable *o* inconvenient, come awkwardly; **el año que viene** next year; **¡ven acá!** come (over) here!; **¡venga!** (*fam*) come on!

venta [ben'tá] *nf* (*COM*) sale; (*posada*) inn; **~ a plazos** purchase on the installment plan (*US*), hire purchase (*Brit*); **~ al contado/al por mayor/al por menor** *o* **al detalle** cash sale/wholesale/retail; **~ a domicilio** door-to-door selling; **~ y arrendamiento al vendedor** sale and lease back; **~ de liquidación** clearance sale; **estar de** *o* **en ~** to be (up) for sale *o* on the market; **~s brutas** gross sales; **~s a término** future (*US*) *o* forward (*Brit*) sales.

ventaja [bentá'há] *nf* advantage; **llevar la ~** (*en carrera*) to be leading *o* ahead.

ventajoso, a [bentáho'so, á] *a* advantageous.

ventana [bentá'ná] *nf* window; **~ de guillotina/galería** sash/bay window; **~ de la nariz** nostril.

ventanilla [ventánē'yá] *nf* (*de taquilla, tb INFORM*) window.

ventear [benteár'] *vt* (*ropa*) to hang out to dry; (*oler*) to sniff ♦ *vi* (*investigar*) to investigate; (*soplar*) to blow; **~se** *vr* (*romperse*) to crack; (*ANAT*) to break wind.

ventilación [bentēlásyon'] *nf* ventilation; (*corriente*) draught; (*fig*) airing.

ventilador [bentēláħor'] *nm* ventilator; (*eléctrico*) fan.

ventilar [bentēlár'] *vt* to ventilate; (*a secar*) to put out to dry; (*fig*) to air, discuss.

ventisca [bentēs'ká] *nf*, **ventisquero** [bentēske'ro] *nm* blizzard; (*nieve amontonada*) snowdrift.

ventolera [bentole'rá] *nf* (*ráfaga*) gust of wind; (*idea*) whim, wild idea; **le dio la ~ de comprarlo** he had a sudden notion to buy it.

ventosear [bentoseár'] *vi* to break wind.

ventoso, a [bento'so, á] *a* windy.

ventrículo [bentrē'kōōlo] *nm* ventricle.

ventrílocuo, a [bentrē'lokwo, á] *nm/f* ventriloquist.

ventriloquia [bentrēlo'kyá] *nf* ventriloquism.

ventura [bentōō'rá] *nf* (*felicidad*) happiness; (*buena suerte*) luck; (*destino*) fortune; **a la (buena) ~** at random.

venturoso, a [bentōōro'so, á] *a* happy; (*afortunado*) lucky, fortunate.

venza [ben'sá] *etc vb* V **vencer**.

ver [ber] *vt, vi* to see; (*mirar*) to look at, watch; (*investigar*) to look into; (*entender*) to see, understand; **~se** *vr* (*encontrarse*) to meet; (*dejarse ~*) to be seen; (*hallarse: en un apuro*) to find o.s., be ♦ *nm* looks *pl*, appearance; **a ~** let's see; **a ~ si ...** I wonder if ...; **por lo que veo** apparently; **dejarse ~** to become apparent; **no tener**

nada que ~ con to have nothing to do with; **a mi modo de ~** as I see it; **merece ~se** it's worth seeing; **no lo veo** I can't see it; **¡nos vemos!** see you (later)!; **¡habráse visto!** did you ever! (*fam*); **ya se ve que ...** it is obvious that ...; **si te vi no me acuerdo** they *etc* just don't want to know.

vera [be'rá] *nf* edge, verge; (*de río*) bank; **a la ~ de** near, next to.

veracidad [beráseðáð'] *nf* truthfulness.

veraneante [beráneán'te] *nm/f* (summer) vacationer (*US*), holidaymaker (*Brit*).

veranear [bráneár'] *vi* to spend the summer.

veraneo [bráne'o] *nm*: **estar de ~** to be on summer vacation (*US*), be away on (one's summer) holiday (*Brit*); **lugar de ~** summer resort.

veraniego, a [bránye'go, á] *a* summer *cpd.*

verano [brá'no] *nm* summer.

veras [be'rás] *nfpl* truth *sg*; **de ~** really, truly; **esto va de ~** this is serious.

veraz [berás'] *a* truthful.

verbal [berβál'] *a* verbal; (*mensaje etc*) oral.

verbena [berβe'ná] *nf* street party.

verbigracia [berβégrá'syá] *ad* for example.

verbo [ber'βo] *nm* verb.

verborragia [berβorrá'hyá], **verborrea** [berβorre'á] *nf* verbosity, verbal diarrhea (*US*) o diarrhoea (*Brit*).

verboso, a [berβo'so, á] *a* verbose.

verdad [berðáð'] *nf* (*lo verídico*) truth; (*fiabilidad*) reliability ♦ *ad* really; **¿~?, ¿no es ~?** isn't it?, aren't you?, don't you? *etc*; **de ~** *a* real, proper; **a decir ~, no quiero** to tell (you) the truth, I don't want to; **la pura ~** the plain truth.

verdaderamente [berðáðerámen'te] *ad* really, indeed, truly.

verdadero, a [berðáðe'ro, á] *a* (*veraz*) true, truthful; (*fiable*) reliable; (*fig*) real.

verde [ber'ðe] *a* green; (*fruta etc*) green, unripe; (*chiste etc*) smutty, dirty ♦ *nm* green; **viejo ~** dirty old man; **poner ~ a uno** to give sb a tongue-lashing.

verdear [berðeár'], **verdecer** [berðeser'] *vi* to turn green.

verdezca [berðes'ká] *etc vb V* **verdecer**.

verdor [berðor'] *nm* (*lo verde*) greenness; (*BOT*) verdure.

verdugo [berðoo'go] *nm* executioner; (*BOT*) shoot; (*cardenal*) welt.

verdulero, a [berðoole'ro, á] *nm/f* vegetable merchant (*US*), greengrocer (*Brit*).

verdura [berðoo'rá] *nf* greenness; **~s** *nfpl* (*CULIN*) greens.

vereda [bere'ðá] *nf* path; (*AM*) sidewalk (*US*), pavement (*Brit*); **meter a uno en ~** to bring sb into line.

veredicto [bereðek'to] *nm* verdict.

vergonzoso, a [bergonso'so, á] *a* shameful; (*tímido*) timid, bashful.

vergüenza [bergwen'sá] *nf* shame, sense of shame; (*timidez*) bashfulness; (*pudor*) modesty; **tener ~** to be ashamed; **me da ~ decírselo** I feel too shy *o* it embarrasses me to tell him; **¡qué ~!** (*de situación*) what a disgrace!; (*a persona*) shame on you!

vericueto [berekwe'to] *nm* rough track.

verídico, a [bere'ðeko, á] *a* true, truthful.

verificar [berefekár'] *vt* to check; (*corroborar*) to verify (*tb INFORM*); (*testamento*) to prove; (*llevar a cabo*) to carry out; **~se** *vr* to occur, happen; (*mitin etc*) to be held; (*profecía etc*) to come *o* prove true.

verifique [berefe'ke] *etc vb V* **verificar**.

verja [ber'há] *nf* iron gate; (*cerca*) railing(s) (*pl*); (*rejado*) grating.

vermut [bermoo'], *pl* **vermuts** *nm* vermouth.

verosímil [berose'mél] *a* likely, probable; (*relato*) credible.

verosimilitud [berosémélétooð'] *nf* likeliness, probability.

verruga [berroo'gá] *nf* wart.

versado, a [bersá'ðo, á] *a*: **~ en** versed in.

Versalles [bersá'yes] *nm* Versailles.

versar [bersár'] *vi* to go round, turn; **~ sobre** to deal with, be about.

versátil [bersá'tél] *a* versatile.

versículo [berse'koolo] *nm* (*REL*) verse.

versión [bersyon'] *nf* version; (*traducción*) translation.

verso [ber'so] *nm* (*gen*) verse; **un ~** a line of poetry; **~ libre/suelto** free/blank verse.

vértebra [ber'teβrá] *nf* vertebra.

vertebral [berteβrál'] *a* vertebral; **columna ~** spine.

verter [berter'] *vt* (*vaciar*) to empty, pour (out); (*tirar*) to dump ♦ *vi* to flow.

vertical [bertekál'] *a* vertical; (*postura, piano etc*) upright ♦ *nf* vertical.

vértice [ber'tése] *nm* vertex, apex.

vertiente [bertyen'te] *nf* slope.

vertiginoso, a [bertéheno'so, á] *a* giddy, dizzy.

vértigo [ber'tégo] *nm* vertigo; (*mareo*) dizziness; (*actividad*) intense activity; **de ~** (*fam: velocidad*) giddy; (: *ruido*) tremendous; (: *talento*) fantastic.

vesícula [bese'koolá] *nf* blister; **~ biliar** gall bladder.

vespertino, a [besperté'no, á] *a* evening *cpd.*

vestíbulo [besté'hoolo] *nm* hall; (*de teatro*) foyer.

vestido [besté'ðo] *nm* (*ropa*) clothes *pl*, clothing; (*de mujer*) dress.

vestigio [besté'hyo] *nm* (*trazo*) trace; (*señal*) sign; **~s** *nmpl* remains.

vestimenta [bestēmen'tá] *nf* clothing.

vestir [bestēr'] *vt* (*poner: ropa*) to put on; (*llevar: ropa*) to wear; (*cubrir*) to clothe, cover; (*pagar: la ropa*) to clothe, pay for the clothing of; (*sastre*) to make clothes for ♦ *vi* (*ponerse: ropa*) to dress; (*verse bien*) to look good; ~**se** *vr* to get dressed, dress o.s.; **traje de** ~ (*formal*) formal suit; **estar vestido de** to be dressed *o* clad in; (*como disfraz*) to be dressed as.

vestuario [bestwá'ryo] *nm* clothes *pl*, wardrobe; (*TEATRO: para actores*) dressing room; (: *para público*) cloakroom; (*DEPORTE*) locker room.

Vesubio [besōō'ṛyo] *nm* Vesuvius.

veta [be'tá] *nf* (*vena*) vein, seam; (*raya*) streak; (*de madera*) grain.

vetar [betár'] *vt* to veto.

veterano, a [beterá'no, á] *a, nm/f* veteran.

veterinario, a [beterēná'ryo, á] *nm/f* vet(erinary surgeon) ♦ *nf* veterinary science.

veto [be'to] *nm* veto.

vetusto, a [betōō'sto, á] *a* ancient.

vez [bes] *nf* time; (*turno*) turn; **a la** ~ **que** at the same time as; **a su** ~ in its turn; **cada** ~ **más/menos** more and more/less and less; **una** ~ once; **dos veces** twice; **de una** ~ in one fell swoop; **de una** ~ **para siempre** once and for all; **en** ~ **de** instead of; **a veces** sometimes; **otra** ~ again; **una y otra** ~ repeatedly; **pocas veces** seldom; **de** ~ **en cuando** from time to time; **7 veces 9** 7 times 9; **hacer las veces de** to stand in for; **tal** ~ perhaps; ¿**lo viste alguna** ~? did you ever see it?; ¿**cuántas veces?** how often?; **érase una** ~ once upon a time (there was).

v. g., v. gr. *abr* (= *verbigracia*) viz.

vía [bē'á] *nf* (*calle*) road; (*ruta*) track, route; (*FERRO*) line; (*fig*) way; (*ANAT*) passage, tube ♦ *prep* via, by way of; **por** ~ **bucal** orally; **por** ~ **judicial** by legal means; **por** ~ **oficial** through official channels; **por** ~ **de** by way of; **en** ~**s de** in the process of; **un país en** ~**s de desarrollo** a developing country; ~ **aérea** airway; **V**~ **Láctea** Milky Way; ~ **pública** public highway *o* thoroughfare; ~ **única** one-way street; **el tren está en la** ~ **8** the train is (standing) at platform 8.

viable [byá'ṛle] *a* (*COM*) viable; (*plan etc*) feasible.

viaducto [byáḍ̣ōōk'to] *nm* viaduct.

viajante [byáhán'te] *nm* traveling salesman.

viajar [byáhár'] *vi* to travel, take a trip.

viaje [byá'he] *nm* trip; (*gira*) tour; (*NAUT*) voyage; (*COM: carga*) load; **los** ~**s** travel *sg*; **estar de** ~ to be on a journey; ~ **de ida y vuelta** round trip; ~ **de novios** honeymoon.

viajero, a [byáhe'ro, á] *a* traveling (*US*), travelling (*Brit*); (*ZOOL*) migratory ♦ *nm/f* (*quien viaja*) traveller; (*pasajero*) passenger.

vial [byál] *a* road *cpd*, traffic *cpd*.

vianda [byán'dá] *nf* (*tb:* ~**s**) food.

viáticos [byá'tēkos] *nmpl* (*COM*) traveling (*US*) *o* travelling (*Brit*) expenses.

víbora [bē'ṛorá] *nf* viper.

vibración [bēṛrásyon'] *nf* vibration.

vibrador [bēṛràḍ̣or'] *nm* vibrator.

vibrante [bēṛrán'te] *a* vibrant, vibrating.

vibrar [bēṛrár'] *vt* to vibrate ♦ *vi* to vibrate; (*pulsar*) to throb, beat, pulsate.

vicario [bēká'ryo] *nm* curate.

vicecónsul [bēsekon'sōōl] *nm* vice-consul.

vicegerente [bēseheren'te] *nm/f* assistant manager.

vicepresidente [bēsepresēḍ̣en'te] *nm/f* vice president; (*de comité etc*) vice-chairman.

viceversa [bēseḅer'sá] *ad* vice versa.

viciado, a [bēsyá'ḍ̣o, á] *a* (*corrompido*) corrupt; (*contaminado*) foul, contaminated.

viciar [bēsyàr'] *vt* (*pervertir*) to pervert; (*adulterar*) to adulterate; (*falsificar*) to falsify; (*JUR*) to nullify; (*estropear*) to spoil; (*sentido*) to twist; ~**se** *vr* to become corrupted; (*aire, agua*) to be(come) polluted.

vicio [bē'syo] *nm* (*libertinaje*) vice; (*mala costumbre*) bad habit; (*mimo*) spoiling; (*alabeo*) warp, warping; **de** *o* **por** ~ out of sheer habit.

vicioso, a [bēsyo'so, á] *a* (*muy malo*) vicious; (*corrompido*) depraved; (*mimado*) spoiled ♦ *nm/f* depraved person; (*adicto*) addict.

vicisitud [bēsēsētōōḍ̣'] *nf* vicissitude.

víctima [bēk'tēmá] *nf* victim; (*de accidente etc*) casualty.

victoria [bēkto'ryá] *nf* victory.

victorioso, a [bēktoryo'so, á] *a* victorious.

vicuña [bēkōō'nyá] *nf* vicuna.

vid [bēḍ̣] *nf* vine.

vida [bē'ḍ̣á] *nf* life; (*duración*) lifetime; (*modo de vivir*) way of life; ¡~!, ¡~ **mía!** (*saludo cariñoso*) my love!; **de por** ~ for life; **de** ~ **airada** *o* **libre** loose-living; **en la/mi** ~ never; **estar con** ~ to be still alive; **ganarse la** ~ to earn one's living; ¡**esto es** ~! this is the life!; **le va la** ~ **en esto** his life depends on it.

vídeo [bē'ḍ̣eo] *nm* video; (*aparato*) video (recorder); **cinta de** ~ videotape; **película de** ~ videofilm; **grabar en** ~ to record, (video)tape; ~ **compuesto/inverso** (*INFORM*) composite/reverse video.

videoconferencia [bēḍ̣eokonferen'syá] *nf* video-conference.

videodatos [bēḍ̣eoḍ̣á'tos] *nmpl* (*COM*) videotex (*US*), viewdata (*Brit*).

videojuego [beðeohwe'ɣo] nm video game.
videotex [beðeoteks'] nm teletext ®.
vidriero, a [beðrye'ro, á] nm/f glazier ♦ nf (ventana) stained-glass window; (AM: de tienda) shop window; (puerta) glass door.
vidrio [beð'ryo] nm glass; ~ **cilindrado/ inastillable** plate/splinter-proof glass.
vidrioso, a [beðryo'so, á] a glassy; (frágil) fragile, brittle; (resbaladizo) slippery.
viejo, a [bye'ho, á] a old ♦ nm/f old man/ woman; **mi** ~/**vieja** (fam) my old man/ woman; **hacerse** o **ponerse** ~ to grow o get old.
Viena [bye'ná] nf Vienna.
viene [bye'ne] etc vb V **venir**.
vienés, esa [byenes', esá] a, nm/f Viennese.
viento [byen'to] nm wind; (olfato) scent; **contra** ~ **y marea** at all costs; **ir** ~ **en popa** to go splendidly; (negocio) to prosper.
vientre [byen'tre] nm belly; (matriz) womb; ~**s** nmpl bowels; **hacer de** ~ to have a movement of the bowels.
vier. abr (= viernes) Fri.
viernes [byer'nes] nm inv Friday; **V**~ **Santo** Good Friday.
vierta [byer'tá] etc vb V **verter**.
Vietnam [byetnám'] nm: **el** ~ Vietnam.
vietnamita [byetnámē'tá] a, nm/f Vietnamese.
viga [bē'ɣá] nf beam, rafter; (de metal) girder.
vigencia [bēhen'syá] nf validity; (de contrato etc) term, life; **estar/entrar en** ~ to be in/come into effect o force.
vigente [bēhen'te] a valid, in force; (imperante) prevailing.
vigésimo, a [bēhe'sēmo, á] num twentieth.
vigía [bēhē'á] nm look-out ♦ nf (atalaya) watchtower; (acción) watching.
vigilancia [bēhēlán'syá] nf vigilance.
vigilante [bēhēlán'te] a vigilant ♦ nm caretaker; (en cárcel) guard (Brit), warder (Brit); (en almacén) floor-walker (US), shopwalker (Brit); ~ **de noche** o **nocturno** night watchman.
vigilar [bēhēlár'] vt to watch over; (cuidar) to look after, keep an eye on ♦ vi to be vigilant; (hacer guardia) to keep watch.
vigilia [vēhē'lyá] nf wakefulness; (REL) fast; **comer de** ~ to fast.
vigor [bēɣor'] nm vigor (US), vigour (Brit), vitality; **en** ~ in force; **entrar/poner en** ~ to take/put into effect.
vigoroso, a [bēɣoro'so, á] a vigorous.
vil [bēl] a vile, low.
vileza [bēle'sá] nf vileness; (acto) base deed.
vilipendiar [bēlēpendyár'] vt to vilify, revile.
vilo [bē'lo]: **en** ~ ad in the air, suspended;

(fig) on tenterhooks, in suspense; **estar** o **quedar en** ~ to be left in suspense.
villa [bē'yá] nf (pueblo) small town; (municipalidad) municipality; **la V**~ (Esp) Madrid; ~ **miseria** shanty town.
villorrio [bēyo'rryo] nm one-horse town, dump; (AM: barrio pobre) shanty town.
vinagre [bēná'ɣre] nm vinegar.
vinagrera [bēnáɣre'rá] nf vinegar bottle; ~**s** nfpl cruet stand sg.
vinagreta [bēnáɣre'tá] nf French dressing.
vinatería [bēnáterē'á] nf wine shop.
vinatero, a [bēnáte'ro, á] a wine cpd ♦ nm wine merchant.
vinculación [bēnkōōlásyon'] nf (lazo) link, bond; (acción) linking.
vincular [bēnkōōlár'] vt to link, bind.
vínculo [bēn'kōōlo] nm link, bond.
vindicar [bēndēkár'] vt to vindicate; (vengar) to avenge; (JUR) to claim.
vindique [bēndē'ke] etc vb V **vindicar**.
vinícola [bēnē'kolá] a (industria) wine cpd; (región) wine-growing cpd.
vinicultura [bēnēkōōltōō'rá] nf wine growing.
vino [bē'no] etc vb V **venir** ♦ nm wine; ~ **de solera/seco/tinto** vintage/dry/red wine; ~ **de Jerez** sherry; ~ **de Oporto** port (wine).
viña [bē'nyá] nf, **viñedo** [bēnye'ðo] nm vineyard.
violación [byolásyon'] nf violation; (JUR) offense (US), offence (Brit), infringement; (estupro): ~ (**sexual**) rape; ~ **de contrato** (COM) breach of contract.
violar [byolár'] vt to violate; (JUR) to infringe; (cometer estupro) to rape.
violencia [byolen'syá] nf (fuerza) violence, force; (embarazo) embarrassment; (acto injusto) unjust act.
violentar [byolentár'] vt to force; (casa) to break into; (agredir) to assault; (violar) to violate.
violento, a [byolen'to, á] a violent; (furioso) furious; (situación) embarrassing; (acto) forced, unnatural; (difícil) awkward; **me es muy** ~ it goes against the grain with me.
violeta [byole'tá] nf violet.
violín [byolēn'] nm violin.
violón [byolon'] nm double bass.
violoncelo [byolonse'lo] nm cello.
virador [bēráðor'] nm (para fotocopiadora) toner.
viraje [bērá'he] nm turn; (de vehículo) swerve; (de carretera) bend; (fig) change of direction.
virar [bērár'] vi to turn; to swerve; to change direction.
virgen [bēr'hen] a virgin; (cinta) blank ♦ nm/f virgin; **la Santísima V**~ (REL) the Blessed Virgin.

Virgo [bēr'go] *nm* Virgo.
viril [bērēl'] *a* virile.
virilidad [bērēlēthȧth'] *nf* virility.
virrey [bērre'ē] *nm* viceroy.
virtual [bērtwȧl'] *a* (*real*) virtual; (*en potencia*) potential.
virtud [bērtōōth'] *nf* virtue; **en ~ de** by virtue of.
virtuoso, a [bērtwo'so, ȧ] *a* virtuous ♦ *nm/f* virtuoso.
viruela [bērwe'lȧ] *nf* smallpox; **~s** *nfpl* pockmarks; **~s locas** chickenpox *sg*.
virulento, a [bērōōlen'to, ȧ] *a* virulent.
virus [bē'rōōs] *nm inv* virus.
viruta [bērōō'tȧ] *nf* wood *o* metal shaving.
vis [bēs] *nf*: **~ cómica** sense of humor.
visa [bē'sȧ] *nf* (*AM*), **visado** [bēsȧ'tho] *nm* visa; **~ de permanencia** residence permit.
visar [bēsȧr'] *vt* (*pasaporte*) to visa; (*documento*) to endorse.
viscoso, a [bēsko'so, ȧ] *a* viscous.
visera [bēse'rȧ] *nf* visor.
visibilidad [bēsēbēlēthȧth'] *nf* visibility.
visible [bēsē'ble] *a* visible; (*fig*) obvious; **exportaciones/importaciones ~s** (*COM*) visible exports/imports.
visillo [bēsē'yo] *nm* lace curtain.
visión [bēsyon'] *nf* (*ANAT*) vision, (eye)sight; (*fantasía*) vision, fantasy; (*panorama*) view; **ver visiones** to see *o* be seeing things.
visionario, a [bēsyonȧ'ryo, ȧ] *a* (*que prevé*) visionary; (*alucinado*) deluded ♦ *nm/f* visionary; (*chalado*) lunatic.
visita [bēsē'tȧ] *nf* call, visit; (*persona*) visitor; **horas/tarjeta de ~** visiting hours/card; **~ de cortesía/de cumplido/de despedida** courtesy/formal/farewell visit; **hacer una ~** to pay a visit; **ir de ~** to go visiting.
visitar [bēsētȧr'] *vt* to visit, call on; (*inspeccionar*) to inspect.
vislumbrar [bēslōōmbrȧr'] *vt* to glimpse, catch a glimpse of.
vislumbre [bēslōōm'bre] *nf* glimpse; (*centelleo*) gleam; (*idea vaga*) glimmer.
viso [bē'so] *nm* (*de metal*) glint, gleam; (*de tela*) sheen; (*aspecto*) appearance; **hay un ~ de verdad en esto** there is an element of truth in this.
visón [bēson'] *nm* mink.
visor [bēsor'] *nm* (*FOTO*) viewfinder.
víspera [bēs'perȧ] *nf* eve, day before; **la ~ o en ~s de** on the eve of.
vista [bē'stȧ] *nf* sight, vision; (*capacidad de ver*) (eye)sight; (*mirada*) look(s) (*pl*); (*FOTO etc*) view; (*JUR*) hearing ♦ *nm* customs officer; **a primera ~** at first glance; **~ general** overview; **fijar *o* clavar la ~ en** to stare at; **hacer la ~ gorda** to turn a blind eye; **volver la ~** to look back; **está a la ~ que** it's obvious that; **a la ~**

(*COM*) on sight; **en ~ de** in view of; **en ~ de que** in view of the fact that; **¡hasta la ~!** so long!, see you!; **con ~s a** with a view to; *V tb* **visto, a**.
vistazo [bēstȧ'so] *nm* glance; **dar *o* echar un ~ a** to glance at.
visto, a [bē'sto, ȧ] *etc vb V* **vestir** ♦ *pp de* **ver** ♦ *a* seen; (*considerado*) considered ♦ *nm*: **~ bueno** approval; **"~ bueno"** "approved"; **por lo ~** evidently; **dar el ~ bueno a algo** to give sth the go-ahead; **está ~ que** it's clear that; **está bien/mal ~** it's acceptable/unacceptable; **está muy ~** it is very common; **estaba ~** it had to be; **~ que** *conj* since, considering that.
vistoso, a [bēsto'so, ȧ] *a* colorful (*US*), colourful (*Brit*); (*alegre*) bright; (*pey*) gaudy.
visualice [bēswȧlē'se] *etc vb V* **visualizar**.
visualizador [bēswȧlēsȧthor'] *nm* (*INFORM*) display screen, VDU.
visualizar [bēswȧlēsȧr'] *vt* (*imaginarse*) to visualize; (*INFORM*) to display.
vital [bētȧl'] *a* life *cpd*, living *cpd*; (*fig*) vital; (*persona*) lively, vivacious.
vitalicio, a [bētȧlē'syo, ȧ] *a* for life.
vitamina [bētȧmē'nȧ] *nf* vitamin.
vitaminado, a [bētȧmēnȧ'tho, ȧ] *a* with added vitamins.
vitamínico, a [bētȧmē'nēko, ȧ] *a* vitamin *cpd*; **complejos ~s** vitamin compounds.
viticultor, a [bētēkōōltor', ȧ] *nm/f* vine grower.
viticultura [bētēkōōltōō'rȧ] *nf* vine growing.
vitorear [bētoreȧr'] *vt* to cheer, acclaim.
vitoriano, a [bētoryȧ'no, ȧ] *a* of *o* from Vitoria ♦ *nm/f* native *o* inhabitant of Vitoria.
vítreo, a [bē'treo, ȧ] *a* vitreous.
vitrina [bētrē'nȧ] *nf* glass case; (*en casa*) display cabinet.
vituperar [bētōōperȧr'] *vt* to condemn.
vituperio [bētōōpe'ryo] *nm* (*condena*) condemnation; (*censura*) censure; (*insulto*) insult.
viudo, a [byōō'tho, ȧ] *a* widowed ♦ *nm* widower ♦ *nf* widow.
viudez [byōōthes'] *nf* widowhood.
vivacidad [bēbȧsēthȧth'] *nf* (*vigor*) vigor (*US*), vigour (*Brit*); (*vida*) vivacity.
vivamente [bēbȧmen'te] *ad* in lively fashion; (*descripción etc*) vividly; (*protesta*) sharply; (*emoción*) acutely.
vivaracho, a [bēbȧrȧtch'o, ȧ] *a* jaunty, lively; (*ojos*) bright, twinkling.
vivaz [bēbȧs'] *a* (*que dura*) enduring; (*vigoroso*) vigorous; (*vivo*) lively.
víveres [bē'beres] *nmpl* provisions.
vivero [bēbe'ro] *nm* (*HORTICULTURA*) nursery; (*para peces*) fishpond; (: *COM*) fish farm.
viveza [bēbe'sȧ] *nf* liveliness; (*agudeza*)

sharpness.

vividor, a [běðēiðor', å] *a* (*pey*) opportunistic ♦ *nm* (*aprovechado*) hustler.

vivienda [běðyen'då] *nf* (*alojamiento*) housing; (*morada*) dwelling; **~s protegidas** public housing *sg* (*US*), council housing *sg* (*Brit*).

viviente [běðyen'te] *a* living.

vivificar [běðēfēkår'] *vt* to give life to.

vivifique [běðēfē'ke] *etc vb V* **vivificar.**

vivir [běðēr'] *vt* (*experimentar*) to live *o* go through ♦ *vi* (*gen*, *COM*): **~ (de)** to live (by, off, on) ♦ *nm* life, living; **¡viva!** hurray!; **¡viva el rey!** long live the king!

vivo, a [bē'ðo, å] *a* living, live, alive; (*fig*) vivid; (*movimiento*) quick; (*color*) bright; (*protesta etc*) strong; (*astuto*) smart, clever; **en ~** (*TV etc*) live; **llegar a lo ~** to cut to the quick.

vizcaíno, a [bēskåē'no, å] *a*, *nm/f* Biscayan.

Vizcaya [bēskå'yå] *nf* Biscay; **el Golfo de ~** the Bay of Biscay.

V.M. *abr* = **Vuestra Majestad.**

V.ºB.º *abr* = **visto bueno.**

vocablo [bokå'ðlo] *nm* (*palabra*) word; (*término*) term.

vocabulario [bokåðōōlå'ryo] *nm* vocabulary, word list.

vocación [bokåsyon'] *nf* vocation.

vocacional [bokåsyonål'] *nf* (*AM*) ≈ technical college.

vocal [bokål'] *a* vocal ♦ *nm/f* member (of a committee *etc*) ♦ *nm* non-executive director ♦ *nf* vowel.

vocalice [bokålē'se] *etc vb V* **vocalizar.**

vocalizar [bokålēsår'] *vt* to vocalize.

vocear [boseår'] *vt* (*para vender*) to cry; (*aclamar*) to acclaim; (*fig*) to proclaim ♦ *vi* to yell.

vocería [boserē'å] *nf*, **vocerío** [boserē'o] *nm* shouting; (*escándalo*) hullabaloo.

vocero [bose'ro] *nm/f* spokesman/woman.

vociferar [bosēferår'] *vt* to shout; (*jactarse*) to proclaim boastfully ♦ *vi* to yell.

vocinglero, a [bosēngle'ro, å] *a* vociferous; (*gárrulo*) garrulous; (*fig*) blatant.

vodevil [boðeðēl'] *nm* vaudeville, music hall.

vodka [boð'kå] *nm* vodka.

vol *abr* = **volumen.**

volado, a [bolå'ðo, å] *a*: **estar ~** (*fam*) to be worried; (: *AM*) to be crazy.

volador, a [bolåðor', å] *a* flying.

voladura [bolåðōō'rå] *nf* blowing up, demolition; (*MINERÍA*) blasting.

volandas [bolån'dås]: **en ~** *ad* in *o* through the air; (*fig*) swiftly.

volante [bolån'te] *a* flying ♦ *nm* (*de máquina*, *coche*) steering wheel; (*de reloj*) balance; (*nota*) note; **ir al ~** to be at the wheel, be driving.

volar [bolår'] *vt* (*demoler*) to blow up, demolish ♦ *vi* to fly; (*fig*: *correr*) to rush, hurry; (*fam*: *desaparecer*) to disappear; **voy volando** I must dash; **¡cómo vuela el tiempo!** how time flies!

volátil [bolå'tēl] *a* volatile; (*fig*) changeable.

volcán [bolkån'] *nm* volcano.

volcánico, a [bolkå'nēko, å] *a* volcanic.

volcar [bolkår'] *vt* to upset, overturn; (*tumbar*, *derribar*) to knock over; (*vaciar*) to empty out ♦ *vi* to overturn; **~se** *vr* to tip over; (*barco*) to capsize.

voleibol [boleēðol'] *nm* volleyball.

voleo [bole'o] *nm* volley; **a(l) ~** haphazardly; **de un ~** quickly.

Volga [bol'gå] *nm* Volga.

volición [bolēsyon'] *nf* volition.

volqué [bolke'], **volquemos** [bolke'mos] *etc vb V* **volcar.**

volquete [bolke'te] *nm* dump truck (*US*), dumper.

voltaje [boltå'he] *nm* voltage.

volteador, a [bolteåðor', å] *nm/f* acrobat.

voltear [bolteår'] *vt* to turn over; (*volcar*) to turn upside down; (*doblar*) to peal ♦ *vi* to roll over.

voltereta [boltere'tå] *nf* somersault; **~ sobre las manos** handspring; **~ lateral** cartwheel.

voltio [bol'tyo] *nm* volt.

voluble [bolōō'ðle] *a* fickle.

volumen [bolōō'men] *nm* volume; **~ monetario** money supply; **~ de negocios** turnover; **bajar el ~** to turn down the volume; **poner la radio a todo ~** to turn the radio up all the way.

voluminoso, a [bolōōmēno'so, å] *a* voluminous; (*enorme*) massive.

voluntad [bolōōntåð'] *nf* will, willpower; (*deseo*) desire, wish; (*afecto*) fondness; **a ~** at will; (*cantidad*) as much as one likes; **buena ~** goodwill; **mala ~** ill will, malice; **por causas ajenas a mi ~** for reasons beyond my control.

voluntario, a [bolōōntå'ryo, å] *a* voluntary ♦ *nm/f* volunteer.

voluntarioso, a [bolōōntåryo'so, å] *a* headstrong.

voluptuoso, a [bolōōptwo'so, å] *a* voluptuous.

volver [bolðer'] *vt* to turn; (*boca abajo*) to turn (over); (*voltear*) to turn around, turn upside down; (*poner al revés*) to turn inside out; (*devolver*) to return; (*transformar*) to change, transform; (*manga*) to roll up ♦ *vi* to return, go/come back; **~se** *vr* to turn around; (*llegar a ser*) to become; **~ la espalda** to turn one's back; **~ bien por mal** to return good for evil; **~ a hacer** to do again; **~ en sí** to come to *o* around, regain consciousness; **~ la vista atrás** to look

back; ~ **loco a uno** to drive sb mad; ~**se loco** to go mad.
vomitar [bomētár'] *vt, vi* to vomit.
vómito [bo'mēto] *nm* (*acto*) vomiting; (*resultado*) vomit.
vorágine [borà'hēne] *nf* whirlpool; (*fig*) maelstrom.
voraz [borás'] *a* voracious; (*fig*) fierce.
vórtice [bor'tēse] *nm* whirlpool; (*de aire*) whirlwind.
vos [bos] *pron* (*AM*) you.
voseo [bose'o] *nm* (*AM*) addressing a person as "vos", *familiar usage.*
Vosgos [bos'ḵos] *nmpl* Vosges.
vosotros, as [boso'tros, às] *pron* you *pl*; (*reflexivo*) yourselves; **entre** ~ among yourselves.
votación [botásyon'] *nf* (*acto*) voting; (*voto*) vote; ~ **a mano alzada** show of hands; **someter algo a** ~ to put sth to the vote.
votar [botár'] *vt* (*POL*: *partido etc*) to vote for; (*proyecto*: *aprobar*) to pass; (*REL*) to vow ♦ *vi* to vote.
voto [bo'to] *nm* vote; (*promesa*) vow; (*maldición*) oath, curse; ~**s** *nmpl* (good) wishes; ~ **de bloque/de grupo** block/card vote; ~ **de censura/de (des)confianza/de gracias** vote of censure/(no) confidence/ thanks; **dar su** ~ to cast one's vote.
voy [boē] *vb V* **ir.**
voz [bos] *nf* voice; (*grito*) shout; (*chisme*) rumor (*US*), rumour (*Brit*); (*LING*: *palabra*) word; (: *forma*) voice; **dar voces** to shout, yell; **llamar a uno a voces** to shout to sb; **llevar la** ~ **cantante** (*fig*) to be the boss; **tener la** ~ **tomada** to be hoarse; **tener** ~ **y voto** to have the right to speak; **a media** ~ in a low voice; **a** ~ **en cuello** *o* **en grito** at the top of one's voice; **de viva** ~ verbally; **en** ~ **alta** aloud; ~ **de mando** command.
vozarrón [bosárron'] *nm* booming voice.
vra., vro. *abr* = **vuestra, vuestro.**
Vto. *abr* (*COM*) = **vencimiento.**
vuelco [bwel'ko] *etc vb V* **volcar** ♦ *nm* spill, overturning; (*fig*) collapse; **mi corazón dio un** ~ my heart missed a beat.
vuelo [bwe'lo] *etc vb V* **volar** ♦ *nm* flight; (*encaje*) lace, frill; (*de falda etc*) loose part; (*fig*) importance; **de altos** ~**s** (*fig*: *plan*) grandiose; (: *persona*) ambitious; **alzar el** ~ to take flight; (*fig*) to dash off; **coger al** ~ to catch in flight; ~ **en picado** dive; ~ **libre** hang-gliding; ~ **regular** scheduled flight; **falda de mucho** ~ full skirt.
vuelque [bwel'ke] *etc vb V* **volcar.**
vuelta [bwel'tá] *nf* turn; (*curva*) bend, curve; (*regreso*) return; (*revolución*) revolution; (*paseo*) stroll; (*circuito*) lap; (*de

papel, tela*) other side; (*de pantalón*) cuff (*US*), turn-up (*Brit*); (*dinero*) change; ~ **a empezar** back to square one; ~ **al mundo** world trip; **V~ de Francia** Tour de France; ~ **cerrada** hairpin bend; **a la** ~ (*Esp*) on one's return; **a la** ~ **de la esquina, a la** ~ (*AM*) round the corner; **a** ~ **de correo** by return of post; **dar** ~**s** to turn, revolve; **dar** ~**s a una idea** to turn over an idea (in one's mind); **dar una** ~ to go for a walk; **dar media** ~ (*AUTO*) to do a U-turn; (*fam*) to beat it; **estar de** ~ (*fam*) to be back; **poner a uno de** ~ **y media** to heap abuse on sb; **no tiene** ~ **de hoja** there's no alternative.
vuelto [bwel'to] *pp de* **volver.**
vuelva [bwel'ḫá] *etc vb V* **volver.**
vuestro, a [bwes'tro, à] *a* your; (*después de n*) of yours ♦ *pron*: **el** ~**/la vuestra/los** ~**s/las vuestras** yours; **lo** ~ (what is) yours; **un amigo** ~ a friend of yours; **una idea vuestra** an idea of yours.
vulgar [boōlḵár'] *a* (*ordinario*) vulgar; (*común*) common.
vulgarice [boōlḵárē'se] *etc vb V* **vulgarizar.**
vulgaridad [boōlḵárēṭhàṭh'] *nf* commonness; (*acto*) vulgarity; (*expresión*) coarse expression; ~**es** *nfpl* banalities.
vulgarismo [boōlḵárēs'mo] *nm* popular form of a word.
vulgarizar [boōlḵárēsár'] *vt* to popularize.
vulgo [boōl'ḵo] *nm* common people.
vulnerable [boōlnerá'ḫle] *a* vulnerable.
vulnerar [boōlnerár'] *vt* to harm, damage; (*derechos*) to interfere with; (*JUR, COM*) to violate.
vulpino, a [boōlpē'no, à] *a* vulpine; (*fig*) foxy.

W

W, w [do'ḫleḫe'] *nf* (*letra*) W, w; **W de Washington** W for William.
wáter [bá'ter] *nm* lavatory.
wátman [wát'mán] *a inv* (*fam*) cool.
whisky [wēs'kē] *nm* whiskey (*US*), whisky (*Brit*).
Winchester [wēntch'ester] *nm* (*INFORM*): **disco** ~ Winchester disk.

X

X, x [e'kēs] *nf* (*letra*) X, x; **X de Xiquena** X for Xmas.

xenofobia [ksenofo'ḥyá] *nf* xenophobia.

xilófono [ksēlo'fono] *nm* xylophone.

Y

Y, y [ēgrye'gá] *nf* (*letra*) Y, y; **Y de Yegua** Y for Yoke.

y [ē] *conj* and.

ya [yá] *ad* (*gen*) already; (*ahora*) now; (*en seguida*) at once; (*pronto*) soon ♦ *excl* all right!; (*por supuesto*) of course! ♦ *conj* (*ahora que*) now that; ~ **no** not any more, no longer; ~ **lo sé** I know; ~ **dice que sí**, ~ **dice que no** first he says yes, then he says no; ¡~, ~! yes, yes!; (*con impaciencia*) all right!, O.K.!; ¡~ **voy!** (*enfático: no se suele traducir*) coming!; ~ **que** since.

yacer [yáser'] *vi* to lie.

yacimiento [yàsēmyen'to] *nm* bed, deposit; ~ **petrolífero** oilfield.

Yakarta [yàkár'tà] *nf* Jakarta.

yanqui [yàn'kē] *a* Yankee ♦ *nm/f* Yankee.

yate [yà'te] *nm* yacht.

yazca [yàs'kà] *etc vb* V **yacer**.

yedra [ye'ḏrà] *nf* ivy.

yegua [ye'gwà] *nf* mare.

yema [ye'mà] *nf* (*del huevo*) yoke; (*BOT*) leaf bud; (*fig*) best part; ~ **del dedo** fingertip.

Yemen [ye'men] *nm*: **el** ~ **del Norte** Yemen; **el** ~ **del Sur** Southern Yemen.

yemení [yemenē'] *a*, *nm/f* Yemeni.

yendo [yen'do] *vb* V **ir**.

yerba [yer'ḥà] *nf* = **hierba**.

yerga [yer'gà] *etc*, **yergue** [yer'ge] *etc vb* V **erguir**.

yermo, a [yer'mo, à] *a* barren; (*de gente*) uninhabited ♦ *nm* waste land.

yerno [yer'no] *nm* son-in-law.

yerre [ye'rre] *etc vb* V **errar**.

yerto, a [yer'to, à] *a* stiff.

yesca [yes'kà] *nf* tinder.

yeso [ye'so] *nm* (*GEO*) gypsum; (*ARQ*) plaster.

yo [yo'] *pron personal* I; **soy** ~ it's me, it is I; ~ **que tú/usted** if I were you.

yodo [yo'ḏo] *nm* iodine.

yoga [yo'gà] *nm* yoga.

yogur(t) [yogōōr'(t)] *nm* yogurt.

yogurtera [yogōōrte'rà] *nf* yogurt maker.

yugo [yōō'go] *nm* yoke.

Yugoslavia [yōōgoslà'ḥyá] *nf* Yugoslavia.

yugoslavo, a [yōōgoslà'ḥo, à] *a* Yugoslavian ♦ *nm/f* Yugoslav.

yugular [yōōgōōlár'] *a* jugular.

yunque [yōōn'ke] *nm* anvil.

yunta [yōōn'tá] *nf* yoke.

yuntero [yōōnte'ro] *nm* ploughman.

yute [yōō'te] *nm* jute.

yuxtapondré [yōōkstàpondre'] *etc vb* V **yuxtaponer**.

yuxtaponer [yōōkstàpóner'] *vt* to juxtapose.

yuxtaponga [yōōkstàpon'gá] *etc vb* V **yuxtaponer**.

yuxtaposición [yōōkstàposēsyon'] *nf* juxtaposition.

yuxtapuesto [yōōkstàpwe'sto], **yuxtapuse** [yōōkstàpōō'se] *etc vb* V **yuxtaponer**.

Z

Z, z [se'tà] *nf* (*letra*) Z, z; **Z de Zaragoza** Z for Zebra.

zafar [sáfár'] *vt* (*soltar*) to untie; (*superficie*) to clear; ~**se** *vr* (*escaparse*) to escape; (*ocultarse*) to hide o.s. away; (*TEC*) to slip off; ~**se de** (*persona*) to get away from.

zafio, a [sà'fyo, à] *a* coarse.

zafiro [sáfē'ro] *nm* sapphire.

zaga [sà'gà] *nf* rear; **a la** ~ behind, in the rear.

zagal [sàgál'] *nm* boy.

zagala [sàgà'là] *nf* girl.

zaguán [sàgwán'] *nm* hallway.

zahareño, a [sàáre'nyo, à] *a* (*salvaje*) wild; (*arisco*) unsociable.

zaherir [sáerēr'] *vt* (*criticar*) to criticize; (*fig: herir*) to wound.

zahiera *etc*, **zahiriendo** [sàye'rà, sàēryen'do] *etc vb* V **zaherir**.

zahorí [sáorē'] *nm* clairvoyant.

zaino, a [sà'ēno, à] *a* (*color de caballo*) chestnut; (*pérfido*) treacherous; (*animal*) vicious.

zalamería [sálámerē'á] *nf* flattery.

zalamero, a [sálámeˈro, á] *a* flattering; (*relamido*) suave.

zamarra [såmáˈrrá] *nf* (*piel*) sheepskin; (*saco*) sheepskin jacket.

Zambeze [såmbeˈse] *nm* Zambezi.

zambo, a [såmˈbo, á] *a* knock-kneed ♦ *nm/f* (*AM*) half-breed (*of Negro and Indian parentage*); (*mulato*) mulatto ♦ *nf* samba.

zambra [såmˈbrá] *nf* gypsy dance.

zambullida [såmbōōyēˈthá] *nf* dive, plunge.

zambullirse [såmbōōyēr'se] *vr* to dive; (*ocultarse*) to hide o.s.

zamorano, a [såmoráˈno, á] *a* of *o* from Zamora ♦ *nm/f* native *o* inhabitant of Zamora.

zampar [såmpár'] *vt* (*esconder*) to hide *o* put away (hurriedly); (*comer*) to gobble; (*arrojar*) to hurl ♦ *vi* to eat voraciously; **~se** *vr* (*chocar*) to bump; (*fig*) to gatecrash.

zanahoria [sånåoˈryá] *nf* carrot.

zancada [sånkáˈthá] *nf* stride.

zancadilla [sånkáthēˈyá] *nf* trip; (*fig*) stratagem; **echar la ~ a uno** to trip sb up.

zancajo [sånkáˈho] *nm* (*ANAT*) heel; (*fig*) dwarf.

zanco [sánˈko] *nm* stilt.

zancudo, a [sånkōōˈtho, á] *a* long-legged ♦ *nm* (*AM*) mosquito.

zángano [sánˈgáno] *nm* drone; (*holgazán*) idler, slacker.

zanja [sánˈhá] *nf* (*fosa*) ditch; (*tumba*) grave.

zanjar [sånhàr'] *vt* (*fosa*) to ditch, trench; (*problema*) to surmount; (*conflicto*) to resolve.

zapapico [såpápēˈko] *nm* pick, pickax.

zapata [såpáˈtá] *nf* half-boot; (*MECÁNICA*) shoe.

zapateado [såpáteáˈtho] *nm* (flamenco) tap dance.

zapatear [såpáteár'] *vt* (*tocar*) to tap with one's foot; (*patear*) to kick; (*fam*) to illtreat ♦ *vi* to tap with one's feet.

zapatería [såpáterēˈá] *nf* (*oficio*) shoemaking; (*tienda*) shoe-shop; (*fábrica*) shoe factory.

zapatero, a [såpáteˈro, á] *nm/f* shoemaker; **~ remendón** cobbler.

zapatilla [såpátēˈyá] *nf* slipper; (*TEC*) washer; (*para deporte*) training shoe.

zapato [såpáˈto] *nm* shoe.

zar [sár] *nm* tsar, czar.

zarabanda [såráhánˈdá] *nf* saraband; (*fig*) whirl.

Zaragoza [sáráɢoˈsá] *nf* Saragossa.

zaragozano, a [såráɢosáˈno, á] *a* of *o* from Saragossa ♦ *nm/f* native *o* inhabitant of Saragossa.

zaranda [såránˈdá] *nf* sieve.

zarandear [sårándeár'] *vt* to sieve; (*fam*) to shake vigorously.

zarcillo [sårsēˈyo] *nm* earring.

zarpa [sårˈpá] *nf* (*garra*) claw, paw; **echar la ~ a** to claw at; (*fam*) to grab.

zarpar [sårpár'] *vi* to weigh anchor.

zarza [sårˈsá] *nf* (*BOT*) bramble.

zarzal [sårsál'] *nm* (*matorral*) bramble patch.

zarzamora [sårsåmoˈrá] *nf* blackberry.

zarzuela [sårsweˈlá] *nf* Spanish light opera.

zigzag [sēɢsáɢ'] *a* zigzag.

zigzaguear [sēɢsåɢeár'] *vi* to zigzag.

zinc [sēnk] *nm* zinc.

zócalo [so'kálo] *nm* (*ARQ*) plinth, base; (*de pared*) skirting board.

zona [so'ná] *nf* zone; **~ fronteriza** border area; **~ del dólar** (*COM*) dollar area; **~ de fomento** *o* **de desarrollo** development area.

zoología [soolohēˈá] *nf* zoology.

zoológico, a [soolo'hēko, á] *a* zoological ♦ *nm* (*tb*: **parque ~**) zoo.

zoólogo, a [soo'loɢo, á] *nm/f* zoologist.

zoom [sōōm] *nm* zoom lens.

zopenco, a [sopen'ko, á] (*fam*) *a* dull, stupid ♦ *nm/f* idiot.

zopilote [sopēlo'te] *nm* (*AM*) buzzard.

zoquete [soke'te] *nm* (*madera*) block; (*pan*) crust; (*fam*) blockhead.

zorro, a [so'rro, á] *a* crafty ♦ *nm/f* fox/vixen ♦ *nf* (*fam*) whore, hooker (*US*).

zote [so'te] (*fam*) *a* dim, stupid ♦ *nm/f* dimwit.

zozobra [soso'hrá] *nf* (*fig*) anxiety.

zozobrar [sosohrár'] *vi* (*hundirse*) to capsize; (*fig*) to fail.

zueco [swe'ko] *nm* clog.

zulo [sōō'lo] *nm* (*de armas*) cache.

zumbar [sōōmbár'] *vt* (*burlar*) to tease; (*golpear*) to hit ♦ *vi* to buzz; (*fam*) to be very close; **~se** *vr*: **~se de** to tease; **me zumban los oídos** I have a buzzing *o* ringing in my ears.

zumbido [sōōmbē'tho] *nm* buzzing; (*fam*) punch; **~ de oídos** buzzing *o* ringing in the ears.

zumo [sōō'mo] *nm* juice; (*ganancia*) profit; **~ de naranja** (fresh) orange juice.

zurcir [sōōrsēr'] *vt* (*coser*) to darn; (*fig*) to put together; **¡que las zurzan!** to blazes with them!

zurdo, a [sōōr'tho, á] *a* (*mano*) left; (*persona*) left-handed.

zurrar [sōōrrár'] *vt* (*TEC*) to dress; (*fam*: *pegar duro*) to wallop; (: *aplastar*) to flatten; (: *criticar*) to criticize harshly.

zurriagazo [sōōrryáɢá'so] *nm* lash, stroke; (*desgracia*) stroke of bad luck.

zurriago [sōōrryá'ɢo] *nm* whip, lash.

zurrón [sōōrron'] *nm* pouch.

zurza [sōōr'sá] *etc vb V* **zurcir**.

zutano, a [sōōtá'no, á] *nm/f* so-and-so.

ENGLISH - SPANISH
INGLÉS - ESPAÑOL

A

A, a [ā] *n* (*letter*) A, a; (*SCOL: mark*) ≈ sobresaliente; (*MUS*): **A** la *m*; **A for Able** A
de Antonio; **A road** *n* (*Brit AUT*) ≈ carretera nacional.

a, an [ā, ə, an, ən] *indefinite article* un(a);
an apple una manzana; **a mirror** un espejo; **he's a doctor** es médico; **3 a day/week**
3 por día/semana; **10 km an hour** 10 km
por hora; **50¢ a kilo** 50 centavos el kilo; **3
times a month** 3 veces al mes; **I haven't
got a car** no tengo coche.

a. *abbr* = **acre.**

AA *n abbr* (*US*: = *Associate in/of Arts*) título *universitario*; (*Brit*: = *Automobile Association*) ≈ RACE *m* (*Sp*); = *Alcoholics
Anonymous*; (= *antiaircraft*) A.A.

AAA [trip'ələ] *n abbr* (= *American Automobile Association*) ≈ RACE *m* (*Sp*); [thrē'āz']
(*Brit*: = *Amateur Athletics Association*)
asociación de atletismo amateur.

AAUP *n abbr* (= *American Association of
University Professors*) asociación de profesores universitarios.

AB *abbr* = **able-bodied seaman;** (*Canada*)
= *Alberta.*

ABA *n abbr* = *American Bankers Association*; *American Bar Association.*

aback [əbak'] *ad*: **to be taken** ~ quedar
desconcertado.

abandon [əban'dən] *vt* abandonar; (*renounce*) renunciar a ♦ *n* abandono; (*wild
behavior*): **with** ~ sin reparos; **to** ~ **ship**
abandonar el barco.

abandoned [əban'dənd] *a* (*child, house etc*)
abandonado; (*unrestrained: manner*) desinhibido.

abase [əbās'] *vt*: **to** ~ **o.s.** (**so far as to do
...**) rebajarse (hasta el punto de hacer ...).

abashed [əbasht'] *a* avergonzado.

abate [əbāt'] *vi* moderarse; (*lessen*) disminuir; (*calm down*) calmarse.

abatement [əbāt'mənt] *n* (*of pollution,
noise*) disminución *f*.

abattoir [abətwâr'] *n* (*Brit*) matadero.

abbey [ab'ē] *n* abadía.

abbot [ab'ət] *n* abad *m*.

abbreviate [əbrē'vēāt] *vt* abreviar.

abbreviation [əbrēvēā'shən] *n* (*short form*)
abreviatura; (*act*) abreviación *f*.

ABC [ābēsē'] *n abbr* (= *American Broadcasting Company*) cadena de televisión.

abdicate [ab'dikāt] *vt, vi* abdicar.

abdication [abdikā'shən] *n* abdicación *f*.

abdomen [ab'dəmən] *n* abdomen *m*.

abdominal [abdâm'ənəl] *a* abdominal.

abduct [abdukt'] *vt* raptar, secuestrar.

abduction [abduk'shən] *n* rapto, secuestro.

aberration [abərā'shən] *n* aberración *f*; **in a
moment of mental** ~ en un momento de
enajenación mental.

abet [əbet'] *vt see* **aid.**

abeyance [əbā'əns] *n*: **in** ~ (*law*) en desuso; (*matter*) en suspenso.

abhor [abhôr'] *vt* aborrecer, abominar (de).

abhorrent [abhôr'ənt] *a* aborrecible, detestable.

abide [əbīd'] *vt*: **I can't** ~ **it/him** no lo/le
puedo ver; **to** ~ **by** *vt fus* atenerse a.

ability [əbil'itē] *n* habilidad *f*, capacidad *f*;
(*talent*) talento; **to the best of my** ~ lo
mejor que pueda *or* sepa.

abject [ab'jekt] *a* (*poverty*) miserable;
(*apology*) rastrero; (*coward*) vil.

ablaze [əblāz'] *a* en llamas, ardiendo.

able [ā'bəl] *a* capaz; (*skilled*) hábil; **to be** ~
to do sth poder hacer algo.

able-bodied [ā'bəlbâd'ēd] *a* sano; ~ **seaman** marinero de primera.

ably [ā'blē] *ad* hábilmente.

ABM *n abbr* = *anti-ballistic missile.*

abnormal [abnôr'məl] *a* anormal.

abnormality [abnôrmal'ətē] *n* (*condition*)
anormalidad *f*; (*instance*) anomalía.

aboard [əbôrd'] *ad* a bordo ♦ *prep* a bordo
de; ~ **the train** en el tren.

abode [əbōd'] *n* (*old*) morada; (*LAW*) domicilio; **of no fixed** ~ sin domicilio fijo.

abolish [əbâl'ish] *vt* suprimir, abolir.

abolition [abəlish'ən] *n* supresión *f*, abolición *f*.

abominable [əbâm'inəbəl] *a* abominable.

aborigine [abərij'ənē] *n* aborigen *m/f*.

abort [əbôrt'] *vt* abortar; (*COMPUT*) abandonar ♦ *vi* (*COMPUT*) abandonar.

abortion [əbôr'shən] *n* aborto (*provocado*);
to have an ~ abortar.

abortive [əbôr'tiv] *a* fracasado.

abound [əbound'] *vi*: **to** ~ (**in** *or* **with**)
abundar (de *or* en).

about [əbout'] *prep* (*subject*) acerca de, sobre; (*place*) alrededor de, por ♦ *ad* más o
menos, aproximadamente; **do something
~ it!** ¡haz algo!; ~ **a hundred/thousand**
etc unos cien/mil *etc*; **it takes** ~ **10 hours**
es cosa de 10 horas más o menos; **it's just
~ finished** está casi terminado; **at** ~ **2**

o'clock a eso de las 2; **they left it all lying ~** lo dejaron todo por todas partes; **to be ~ to** estar a punto de; **I'm not ~ to do all that for nothing** no pienso hacer todo eso gratis; **what** or **how ~ doing this?** ¿qué tal si hacemos esto?; **to walk ~** pasearse, ir y venir.

about-face [əbout'fās] n (US: MIL, fig) media vuelta.

about-turn [əbout'tûrn] n (Brit) = **about-face**.

above [əbuv'] ad encima, por encima, arriba ♦ prep encima de; **mentioned ~** susodicho; **~ all** sobre todo; **he's not ~ a bit of blackmail** es capaz hasta de hacer chantaje.

above board a legítimo.

above-mentioned [əbuv'men'chənd] a susodicho.

abrasion [əbrā'zhən] n (on skin) abrasión f.

abrasive [əbrā'siv] a abrasivo.

abreast [əbrest'] ad de frente; **to keep ~ of** mantenerse al corriente de.

abridge [əbrij'] vt abreviar.

abroad [əbrôd'] ad (to be) en el extranjero; (to go) al extranjero; **there is a rumor ~ that ...** corre el rumor de que ...

abrupt [əbrupt'] a (sudden: departure) repentino; (manner) brusco.

abruptly [əbrupt'lē] ad (leave) repentinamente; (speak) bruscamente.

abscess [ab'ses] n absceso.

abscond [abskând'] vi fugarse.

absence [ab'səns] n ausencia; **in the ~ of** (person) en ausencia de; (thing) a falta de.

absent [ab'sənt] a ausente; **~ without leave (AWOL)** ausente sin permiso.

absentee [absəntē'] n ausente m/f.

absentee ballot n (US) voto postal.

absenteeism [absəntē'izəm] n absentismo.

absent-minded [ab'səntmīn'did] a distraído.

absolute [ab'səloōt] a absoluto; **~ monopoly** monopolio total.

absolutely [absəloōt'lē] ad totalmente; **oh yes, ~!** ¡claro or por supuesto que sí!

absolution [absəloo'shən] n (REL) absolución f.

absolve [abzâlv'] vt: **to ~ sb (from)** absolver a alguien (de).

absorb [absôrb'] vt absorber; **to be ~ed in a book** estar absorto en un libro.

absorbent [absôr'bənt] a absorbente.

absorbent cotton n (US) algodón m hidrófilo.

absorbing [absôr'bing] a absorbente; (book etc) interesantísimo.

absorption [absôrp'shən] n absorción f.

abstain [abstān'] vi: **to ~ (from)** abstenerse (de).

abstemious [abstē'mēəs] a abstemio.

abstention [absten'shən] n abstención f.

abstinence [ab'stənəns] n abstinencia.

abstract [ab'strakt] a abstracto.

abstruse [abstroōs'] a oscuro.

absurd [absûrd'] a absurdo.

absurdity [absûr'dətē] n absurdo.

abundance [əbun'dəns] n abundancia.

abundant [əbun'dənt] a abundante.

abuse n [əbyoōs'] (insults) improperios mpl, injurias fpl; (misuse) abuso ♦ vt [əbyoōz'] (ill-treat) maltratar; (take advantage of) abusar de; **open to ~** sujeto al abuso.

abusive [əbyoō'siv] a ofensivo.

abysmal [əbiz'məl] a pésimo; (ignorance) supino.

abyss [əbis'] n abismo.

AC abbr (= alternating current) corriente f alterna ♦ n abbr (US) = athletic club.

a/c abbr (BANKING etc) = account, account current.

academic [akədem'ik] a académico, universitario; (pej: issue) puramente teórico ♦ n estudioso/a; profesor(a) m/f universitario/a; **~ year** (UNIV) año académico.

academy [əkad'əmē] n (learned body) academia; (school) instituto, colegio; **~ of music** conservatorio.

accede [aksēd'] vi: **to ~ to** acceder a.

accelerate [aksel'ərāt] vt acelerar ♦ vi acelerarse.

acceleration [akselərā'shən] n aceleración f.

accelerator [aksel'ərātûr] n acelerador m.

accent [ak'sent] n acento.

accentuate [aksen'choōāt] vt (syllable) acentuar; (need, difference etc) recalcar, subrayar.

accept [aksept'] vt aceptar; (approve) aprobar; (concede) admitir.

acceptable [aksep'təbəl] a aceptable; admisible.

acceptance [aksep'təns] n aceptación f; aprobación f; **to meet with general ~** tener acogida general.

access [ak'ses] n acceso ♦ vt (COMPUT: retrieve) obtener información de; (: store) dar información a; **the burglars gained ~ through a window** los ladrones lograron entrar por una ventana; **to have ~ to** tener acceso a.

accessible [akses'əbəl] a accesible.

accession [aksesh'ən] n (of monarch) subida, ascenso; (addition) adquisición f.

accessory [akses'ûrē] n accesorio; **toilet accessories** artículos mpl de tocador.

access road n carretera de acceso; (to freeway) carril m de acceso.

access time n (COMPUT) tiempo de acceso.

accident [ak'sidənt] n accidente m; (chance) casualidad f; **by ~** (unintentionally) sin querer; (by coincidence) por casualidad; **~s at work** accidentes mpl de trabajo; **to have an ~** tener or sufrir un accidente.

accidental [aksiden'təl] *a* accidental, fortuito.

accidentally [aksiden'təlē] *ad* sin querer; por casualidad.

accident insurance *n* seguro contra accidentes.

accident-prone [ak'sidəntprōn'] *a* propenso a los accidentes.

acclaim [əklām'] *vt* aclamar, aplaudir ♦ *n* aclamación *f*, aplausos *mpl*.

acclamation [akləmā'shən] *n* (*approval*) aclamación *f*; (*applause*) aplausos *mpl*; **by ~** por aclamación.

acclimate [əklī'mit] *vt* (*US*): **to become ~d** aclimatarse.

acclimatize [əklī'mətīz] *vt* (*Brit*) = **acclimate**.

accolade [akəlād'] *n* (*prize*) premio; (*praise*) alabanzas *fpl*, homenaje *m*.

accommodate [əkâm'ədāt] *vt* alojar, hospedar; (*oblige, help*) complacer; **this car ~s 4 people comfortably** en este coche caben 4 personas cómodamente.

accommodating [əkâm'ədāting] *a* servicial, complaciente.

accommodations *npl*, (*Brit*) **accommodation** *n* [əkâmədā'shən(z)] alojamiento.

accompaniment [əkum'pənimənt] *n* acompañamiento.

accompanist [əkum'pənist] *n* (*MUS*) acompañante *m/f*.

accompany [əkum'pənē] *vt* acompañar.

accomplice [əkâm'plis] *n* cómplice *m/f*.

accomplish [əkâm'plish] *vt* (*finish*) acabar; (*aim*) realizar; (*task*) llevar a cabo.

accomplished [əkâm'plisht] *a* experto, hábil.

accomplishment [əkâm'plishmənt] *n* (*ending*) conclusión *f*; (*bringing about*) realización *f*; (*skill*) talento.

accord [əkôrd'] *n* acuerdo ♦ *vt* conceder; **of his own ~** espontáneamente; **with one ~** de *or* por común acuerdo.

accordance [əkôr'dəns] *n*: **in ~ with** de acuerdo con.

according [əkôr'ding]: **~ to** *prep* según; (*in accordance with*) conforme a; **it went ~ to plan** salió según lo previsto.

accordingly [əkôr'dinglē] *ad* (*thus*) por consiguiente.

accordion [əkôr'dēən] *n* acordeón *m*.

accordionist [əkôr'dēənist] *n* acordeonista *m/f*.

accost [əkôst'] *vt* abordar, dirigirse a.

account [əkount'] *n* (*COMM*) cuenta, factura; (*report*) informe *m*; **~s** *npl* (*COMM*) cuentas *fpl*; **your ~ is still outstanding** su cuenta está todavía pendiente; **of little ~** de poca importancia; **on ~** a cuenta; **to buy sth on ~** comprar algo a cuenta; **on no ~** de ninguna manera; **on ~ of** a causa de, por motivo de; **to take into ~, take ~ of** tener en cuenta; **to keep an ~ of** llevar la cuenta de; **to call sb to ~ for sth/for having done sth** pedirle cuentas a uno por algo/por haber hecho algo.

account for *vt fus* (*explain*) explicar; **all the children were ~ed for** no faltaba ningún niño.

accountability [əkountəbil'ətē] *n* responsabilidad *f*.

accountable [əkoun'təbəl] *a* responsable.

accountancy [əkoun'tənsē] *n* contabilidad *f*.

accountant [əkoun'tənt] *n* contable *m/f*, contador(a) *m/f*.

accounting [əkoun'ting] *n* contabilidad *f*.

accounting period *n* período contable, ejercicio financiero.

account number *n* (*at bank etc*) número de cuenta.

account payable *n* cuenta por pagar.

account receivable *n* cuenta por cobrar.

accoutrements [əkōō'tûrmənts] *npl* equipo, equipaje *m*.

accredited [əkred'itid] *a* (*agent etc*) autorizado, acreditado.

accretion [əkrē'shən] *n* acumulación *f*.

accrue [əkrōō'] *vi* (*mount up*) aumentarse; (*interest*) acumularse; **to ~ to** corresponder a; **~d charges** gastos *mpl* vencidos; **~d interest** interés *m* acumulado.

acct. *abbr* = **account; accountant**.

accumulate [əkyōōm'yəlāt] *vt* acumular ♦ *vi* acumularse.

accumulation [əkyōōmyəlā'shən] *n* acumulación *f*.

accuracy [ak'yûrəsē] *n* exactitud *f*, precisión *f*.

accurate [ak'yûrit] *a* (*number*) exacto; (*answer*) acertado; (*shot*) certero.

accurately [ak'yûritlē] *ad* (*count, shoot, answer*) con precisión.

accursed [əkûr'sid] *a* maldito.

accusation [akyōōzā'shən] *n* acusación *f*.

accusative [əkyōō'zətiv] *n* acusativo.

accuse [əkyōōz'] *vt* acusar; (*blame*) echar la culpa a.

accused [əkyōōzd'] *n* acusado/a.

accustom [əkus'təm] *vt* acostumbrar; **to ~ o.s. to sth** acostumbrarse a algo.

accustomed [əkus'təmd] *a*: **~ to** acostumbrado a.

AC/DC *abbr* = *alternating current/direct current*.

ACE [ās] *n abbr* = *American Council on Education*.

ace [ās] *n* as *m*; **within an ~ of** a dos dedos de.

Ace bandage *n* ® (*US*) venda elástica.

acerbic [əsûr'bik] *a* acerbo; (*fig*) mordaz.

acetate [as'itāt] *n* acetato.

ache [āk] *n* dolor *m* ♦ *vi* doler; (*yearn*): **to ~ to do sth** suspirar por hacer algo; **I've got a stomach~** *or* (*Brit*) **stomach ~**

tengo dolor de estómago, me duele el estómago; **my head** ~s me duele la cabeza.

achieve [əchēv'] *vt* (*reach*) alcanzar; (*realize*) realizar; (*victory*, *success*) lograr, conseguir.

achievement [əchēv'mənt] *n* (*completion*) realización *f*; (*success*) éxito.

acid [as'id] *a* ácido; (*bitter*) agrio ♦ *n* ácido.

acidity [əsid'itē] *n* acidez *f*; (*MED*) acedía.

acid rain *n* lluvia ácida.

acknowledge [aknál'ij] *vt* (*letter: also*: ~ **receipt of**) acusar recibo de; (*fact*) reconocer.

acknowledgement [aknál'ijmənt] *n* acuse *m* de recibo; reconocimiento; ~**s** (*in book*) agradecimientos *mpl*.

ACLU *n abbr* (= *American Civil Liberties Union*) *unión americana por libertades civiles*.

acme [ak'mē] *n* colmo, cima.

acne [ak'nē] *n* acné *m*.

acorn [ā'kôrn] *n* bellota.

acoustic [əkōōs'tik] *a* acústico.

acoustic coupler [əkōōs'tik kup'lûr] *n* (*COMPUT*) acoplador *m* acústico.

acoustics [əkōōs'tiks] *n, npl* acústica *sg*.

acoustic screen *n* panel *m* acústico.

acquaint [əkwānt'] *vt*: **to ~ sb with sth** (*inform*) poner a uno al corriente de algo; **to be ~ed with** (*person*) conocer; (*fact*) estar al corriente de.

acquaintance [əkwān'təns] *n* conocimiento; (*person*) conocido/a; **to make sb's ~** conocer a uno.

acquiesce [akwēes'] *vi* (*agree*): **to ~ (in)** consentir (en), conformarse (con).

acquire [əkwī'ûr] *vt* adquirir.

acquired [əkwī'ûrd] *a* adquirido; **an ~ taste** un gusto adquirido.

acquisition [akwizish'ən] *n* adquisición *f*.

acquisitive [əkwiz'ətiv] *a* codicioso.

acquit [əkwit'] *vt* absolver, exculpar; **to ~ o.s. well** salir con éxito.

acquittal [əkwit'əl] *n* absolución *f*, exculpación *f*.

acre [ā'kûr] *n* acre *m*.

acreage [ā'kûrij] *n* extensión *f*.

acrid [ak'rid] *a* (*smell*) acre; (*fig*) mordaz, sarcástico.

acrimonious [akrəmō'nēəs] *a* (*remark*) mordaz; (*argument*) reñido.

acrobat [ak'rəbat] *n* acróbata *m/f*.

acrobatic [akrəbat'ik] *a* acrobático.

acrobatics [akrəbat'iks] *npl* acrobacias *fpl*.

acronym [ak'rənim] *n* siglas *fpl*.

across [əkrôs'] *prep* (*on the other side of*) al otro lado de; (*crosswise*) a través de ♦ *ad* de un lado a otro, de una parte a otra; a través, al través; **to run/swim ~** atravesar corriendo/nadando; ~ **from** enfrente de; **the lake is 12 km ~** el lago tiene 12 km de ancho; **to get sth ~ to sb** (*fig*) hacer comprender algo a uno.

acrylic [əkril'ik] *a* acrílico.

ACT *n abbr* (= *American College Test*) *examen que se hace al término de los estudios secundarios*.

act [akt] *n* acto, acción *f*; (*THEATER*) acto; (*in music-hall etc*) número; (*LAW*) decreto, ley *f* ♦ *vi* (*behave*) comportarse; (*THEATER*) actuar; (*pretend*) fingir; (*take action*) tomar medidas ♦ *vt* (*part*) hacer, representar; ~ **of God** fuerza mayor; **it's only an ~** es cuento; **to catch sb in the ~** coger a uno en flagrante *or* con las manos en la masa; **to ~ Hamlet** hacer el papel de Hamlet; **to ~ as** actuar *or* hacer de; ~**ing in my capacity as chairman, I ...** en mi calidad de presidente, yo ...; **it ~s as a deterrent** sirve para disuadir; **he's only ~ing** está fingiendo nada más.

act on *vt*: **to ~ on sth** actuar *or* obrar sobre algo.

act out *vt* (*event*) representar; (*fantasies*) realizar.

act up *vi* (*cause trouble*) dar guerra.

acting [ak'ting] *a* suplente ♦ *n*: **to do some ~** hacer algo de teatro; **he is the ~ manager** es el gerente en funciones.

action [ak'shən] *n* acción *f*, acto; (*MIL*) acción *f*; (*LAW*) proceso, demanda; **to put a plan into ~** poner un plan en acción *or* en marcha; **killed in ~** (*MIL*) muerto en acto de servicio *or* en combate; **out of ~** (*person*) fuera de combate; (*thing*) averiado, descompuesto; **to take ~** tomar medidas; **to bring an ~ against sb** entablar *or* presentar demanda contra uno.

action replay *n* (*Brit TV*) repetición *f*.

activate [ak'təvāt] *vt* activar.

active [ak'tiv] *a* activo, enérgico; (*volcano*) en actividad; **to play an ~ part in** colaborar activamente en; ~ **file** (*COMPUT*) fichero activo.

active duty (AD) *n* (*US MIL*) servicio activo.

actively [ak'tivlē] *ad* (*participate*) activamente; (*discourage, dislike*) enérgicamente.

active partner *n* (*COMM*) socio activo.

activist [ak'tivist] *n* activista *m/f*.

activity [aktiv'ətē] *n* actividad *f*.

actor [ak'tûr] *n* actor *m*.

actress [ak'tris] *n* actriz *f*.

actual [ak'chōōəl] *a* verdadero, real.

actually [ak'chōōəlē] *ad* realmente, en realidad.

actuary [ak'chōōärē] *n* (*COMM*) actuario/a (de seguros).

actuate [ak'chōōāt] *vt* mover, impulsar.

acumen [əkyōō'mən] *n* perspicacia; **business ~** talento para los negocios.

acupuncture [ak'yōōpungkchûr] *n* acupuntura.

acute [əkyōōt'] *a* agudo.

acutely [əkyōōt'lē] *ad* profundamente, extre-

madamente.
AD *ad abbr* (= *Anno Domini*) A.C. ♦ *n abbr*
(*US MIL*) = **active duty.**
ad [ad] *n abbr* = **advertisement.**
adage [ad'ij] *n* refrán *m*, adagio.
Adam [ad'əm] *n* Adán; ~'s **apple** *n* nuez *f*
de la garganta.
adamant [ad'əmənt] *a* firme, inflexible.
adapt [ədapt'] *vt* adaptar; (*reconcile*) acomodar ♦ *vi*: **to** ~ **(to)** adaptarse (a), ajustarse (a).
adaptability [ədaptəbil'ətē] *n* (*of person,
device etc*) adaptabilidad *f*.
adaptable [ədap'təbəl] *a* (*device*) adaptable; (*person*) acomodadizo, que se adapta.
adaptation [adəptā'shən] *n* adaptación *f*.
adapter, adaptor [ədap'tûr] *n* (*ELEC*)
adaptador *m*.
ADC *n abbr* (*MIL*) = **aide-de-camp**; (*US*: =
Aid to Dependent Children) ayuda para niños dependientes.
add [ad] *vt* añadir, agregar; (*figures: also*:
~ **up**) sumar ♦ *vi*: **to** ~ **to** (*increase*) aumentar, acrecentar.
add on *vt* añadir.
add up *vt* (*figures*) sumar ♦ *vi* (*fig*): **it
doesn't** ~ **up** no tiene sentido; **it doesn't** ~
up to much es poca cosa, no tiene gran *or*
mucha importancia.
addendum [əden'dəm] *n* apéndice *m*.
adder [ad'ûr] *n* víbora.
addict [ad'ikt] *n* (*to drugs etc*) adicto/a;
(*enthusiast*) aficionado/a, entusiasta *m/f*;
heroin ~ heroinómano/a.
addicted [ədik'tid] *a*: **to be** ~ **to** ser adicto
a; ser aficionado a.
addiction [ədik'shən] *n* (*dependence*) hábito
morboso; (*enthusiasm*) afición *f*.
addictive [ədik'tiv] *a* que causa adicción.
adding machine [ad'ing məshēn'] *n* calculadora.
Addis Ababa [ad'is âb'əbä] *n* Addis Abeba
m.
addition [ədish'ən] *n* (*adding up*) adición *f*;
(*thing added*) añadidura, añadido; **in** ~
además, por añadidura; **in** ~ **to** además
de.
additional [ədish'ənəl] *a* adicional.
additive [ad'ətiv] *n* aditivo.
addled [ad'əld] *a* (*Brit: rotten*) podrido; (:
fig) confuso.
address [ədres'] *n* dirección *f*, señas *fpl*;
(*speech*) discurso; (*COMPUT*) dirección *f* ♦
vt (*letter*) dirigir; (*speak to*) dirigirse a, dirigir la palabra a; **form of** ~ tratamiento;
absolute/relative ~ (*COMPUT*) dirección *f*
absoluta/relativa; **to** ~ **o.s. to sth** (*issue,
problem*) abordar.
addressee [adresē'] *n* destinatario/a.
Aden [ä'dən] *n* Adén *m*.
adenoids [ad'ənoidz] *npl* vegetaciones *fpl*
adenoideas.
adept [ədept'] *a*: ~ **at** experto *or* hábil en.

adequacy [ad'əkwəsē] *n* idoneidad *f*.
adequate [ad'əkwit] *a* (*satisfactory*) adecuado; (*enough*) suficiente; **to feel** ~ **to a
task** sentirse con fuerzas para una tarea.
adequately [ad'əkwitlē] *ad* adecuadamente.
adhere [adhēr'] *vi*: **to** ~ **to** pegarse a; (*fig*:
abide by) observar.
adherent [adhēr'ənt] *n* partidario/a.
adhesion [adhē'zhən] *n* adherencia.
adhesive [adhē'siv] *a, n* adhesivo.
adhesive tape *n* (*US*: *MED*) esparadrapo;
(*Brit*) cinta adhesiva.
ad hoc [ad häk'] *a* (*decision*) ad hoc; (*committee*) formado con fines específicos ♦ *ad*
con fines específicos.
adieu [ədyōō'] *excl* ¡vaya con Dios!
ad inf [ad inf'] *ad* hasta el infinito.
adjacent [əjā'sənt] *a*: ~ **to** contiguo a,
inmediato a.
adjective [aj'iktiv] *n* adjetivo.
adjoin [əjoin'] *vt* estar contiguo a; (*land*)
lindar con.
adjoining [əjoi'ning] *a* contiguo, vecino.
adjourn [əjûrn'] *vt* aplazar; (*US*: *end*)
terminar; (*session*) suspender, levantar ♦
vi suspenderse; **the meeting has been** ~**ed
till next week** se ha levantado la sesión
hasta la semana que viene.
adjournment [əjûrn'mənt] *n* (*period*) suspensión *f*; (*postponement*) aplazamiento.
Adjt. *abbr* = **adjutant.**
adjudicate [əjōō'dikāt] *vi* sentenciar;
(*contest*) hacer de árbitro en, juzgar;
(*claim*) decidir.
adjudication [əjōōdikā'shən] *n* adjudicación
f.
adjudicator [əjōō'dikātûr] *n* juez *m*, árbitro.
adjust [əjust'] *vt* (*change*) modificar;
(*arrange*) arreglar; (*machine*) ajustar ♦
vi: **to** ~ **(to)** adaptarse (a).
adjustable [əjust'əbəl] *a* ajustable.
adjuster [əjust'ûr] *n* see **loss.**
adjustment [əjust'mənt] *n* modificación *f*;
arreglo; (*of prices, wages*) ajuste *m*.
adjutant [aj'ətənt] *n* ayudante *m*.
ad-lib [adlib'] *vt, vi* improvisar ♦ *ad*: **ad lib**
a voluntad, a discreción.
adman [ad'man] *n* (*col*) publicista *m*.
admin [ad'min] *n abbr* (*col*) = **administration.**
administer [admin'istûr] *vt* proporcionar;
(*justice*) administrar.
administration [administrā'shən] *n* administración *f*; (*government*) gobierno; **the
A~** (*US*) la Administración.
administrative [admin'istrātiv] *a* administrativo.
administrator [admin'istrātûr] *n* adminis-
trador/a *m/f*.
admirable [ad'mûrəbəl] *a* admirable.
admiral [ad'mûrəl] *n* almirante *m*.
Admiralty [ad'mûrəltē] *n* (*Brit*) Ministerio
de Marina, Almirantazgo.

admiration [admərā'shən] *n* admiración *f.*
admire [admī'ûr] *vt* admirar.
admirer [admī'ərûr] *n* admirador(a) *m/f;* (*suitor*) pretendiente *m.*
admission [admish'ən] *n* (*exhibition, nightclub*) entrada; (*enrolment*) ingreso; (*confession*) confesión *f;* "~ free" "entrada gratis *or* libre"; **by his own ~** él mismo reconoce que.
admit [admit'] *vt* dejar entrar, dar entrada a; (*permit*) admitir; (*acknowledge*) reconocer; "**this ticket ~s two**" "entrada para 2 personas"; **children not ~ted** se prohíbe la entrada a (los) menores de edad; **I must ~ that ...** debo reconocer que ...
admit of *vt fus* admitir, permitir.
admit to *vt fus* confesarse culpable de.
admittance [admit'əns] *n* entrada; "**no ~**" "se prohíbe la entrada", "prohibida la entrada".
admittedly [admit'idlē] *ad* de acuerdo que.
admonish [admân'ish] *vt* amonestar; (*advise*) aconsejar.
ad nauseam [ad nô'zēəm] *ad* hasta el cansancio.
ado [ədo͞o'] *n:* **without (any) more ~** sin más (ni más).
adolescence [adəles'əns] *n* adolescencia.
adolescent [adəles'ənt] *a, n* adolescente *m/f.*
adopt [ədâpt'] *vt* adoptar.
adopted [ədâp'tid] *a* adoptivo.
adoption [ədâp'shən] *n* adopción *f.*
adoptive [ədâp'tiv] *a* adoptivo.
adorable [ədôr'əbəl] *a* adorable.
adoration [adərā'shən] *n* adoración *f.*
adore [ədôr'] *vt* adorar.
adoring [ədôr'ing] *a* cariñoso.
adorn [ədôrn'] *vt* adornar.
adornment [ədôrn'mənt] *n* adorno.
ADP *n abbr* = **automatic data processing**.
adrenalin [ədren'əlin] *n* adrenalina.
Adriatic [ādrēat'ik] *n:* **the ~ (Sea)** el (Mar) Adriático.
adrift [ədrift'] *ad* a la deriva; **to come ~** (*boat*) ir a la deriva, soltarse; (*wire, rope etc*) soltarse.
adroit [ədroit'] *a* diestro.
adulation [ajoo͞olā'shən] *n* adulación *f.*
adult [ədult'] *n* adulto/a ♦ *a:* **~ education** educación *f* para adultos.
adulterate [ədul'tûrāt] *vt* adulterar.
adultery [ədul'tûrē] *n* adulterio.
adulthood [ədult'hoo͞od] *n* edad *f* adulta.
advance [advans'] *n* adelanto, progreso; (*money*) anticipo, préstamo; (*MIL*) avance *m* ♦ *vt* avanzar, adelantar; (*money*) anticipar ♦ *vi* avanzar, adelantarse; **in ~** por adelantado; **to make ~s to sb** (*gen*) ponerse en contacto con uno; (*amorously*) insinuarse a uno.
advanced [advanst'] *a* avanzado; (*SCOL: studies*) adelantado; **~ in years** entrado en años.
advancement [advans'mənt] *n* progreso; (*in rank*) ascenso.
advance notice *n* previo aviso.
advance payment *n* (*part sum*) anticipo.
advantage [advan'tij] *n* (*also TENNIS*) ventaja; **to take ~ of** aprovecharse de; **it's to our ~** es ventajoso para nosotros.
advantageous [advəntā'jəs] *a* ventajoso, provechoso.
advent [ad'vent] *n* advenimiento; **A~** Adviento.
adventure [adven'chûr] *n* aventura.
adventurous [adven'chûrəs] *a* aventurero.
adverb [ad'vûrb] *n* adverbio.
adversary [ad'vûrsärē] *n* adversario, contrario.
adverse [advûrs'] *a* adverso, contrario; **~ to** adverso a.
adversity [advûr'sitē] *n* infortunio.
advert [ad'vûrt] *n abbr* (*Brit*) = **advertisement**.
advertise [ad'vûrtīz] *vi* hacer propaganda; (*in newspaper etc*) poner un anuncio; **to ~ for** (*staff*) buscar por medio de anuncios ♦ *vt* anunciar.
advertisement [advûrtīz'mənt] *n* (*COMM*) anuncio.
advertiser [ad'vûrtīzûr] *n* anunciante *m/f.*
advertising [ad'vûrtīzing] *n* publicidad *f,* propaganda; anuncios *mpl.*
advertising agency *n* agencia de publicidad.
advertising campaign *n* campaña de publicidad.
advice [advīs'] *n* consejo, consejos *mpl;* (*notification*) aviso; **a piece of ~** un consejo; **to get legal ~** consultar a un abogado; **to ask (sb) for ~** pedir consejo (a uno).
advice slip *n* nota de aviso.
advisable [advī'zəbəl] *a* aconsejable, conveniente.
advise [advīz'] *vt* aconsejar; **to ~ sb of sth** (*inform*) informar a uno de algo; **to ~ sb against sth/doing sth** desaconsejar algo a uno/aconsejar a uno que no haga algo; **you will be well/ill ~d to go** deberías/no deberías ir.
advisedly [advī'zidlē] *ad* (*deliberately*) deliberadamente.
adviser [advī'zûr] *n* consejero/a; (*business adviser*) asesor(a) *m/f.*
advisory [advī'zûrē] *a* consultivo; **in an ~ capacity** como asesor.
advocate *vt* [ad'vəkāt] (*argue for*) abogar por; (*give support to*) ser partidario de ♦ *n* [ad'vəkit] abogado/a.
advt. *abbr* = **advertisement**.
AEA *n abbr* (*Brit:* = *Atomic Energy Authority*) consejo de energía nuclear.
AEC *n abbr* (*US:* = *Atomic Energy Commission*) consejo de energía nuclear.
Aegean [ijē'ən] *n:* **the ~ (Sea)** el Mar

Egeo.

aegis [ē'jis] *n*: **under the ~ of** bajo la tutela de.

aeon [ē'ən] *n (Brit)* = **eon.**

aerial [är'ēəl] *n* antena ♦ *a* aéreo.

aerie [är'ē] *n (US)* aguilera.

aero- [är'ō] *pref* aero-.

aerobatics [ärəbat'iks] *npl* acrobacia aérea.

aerobics [ärō'biks] *nsg* aerobic *m*, aerobismo *(LAm)*.

aerodrome [är'ədrōm] *n (Brit)* aeródromo.

aerodynamic [ärōdīnam'ik] *a* aerodinámico.

aerogramme [är'əgram] *n* aerograma *m*.

aeronautics [ärənô'tiks] *nsg* aeronáutica.

aeroplane [är'əplān] *n (Brit)* avión *m*.

aerosol [är'əsôl] *n* aerosol *m*.

aerospace industry [är'əspās in'dəstrē] *n* industria aerospacial.

aesthetic *etc* [esthet'ik] *(Brit)* = **esthetic** *etc*.

a.f. *abbr* = **audiofrequency.**

afar [əfâr'] *ad* lejos; **from ~** desde lejos.

AFB *n abbr (US)* = *Air Force Base.*

AFDC *n abbr (US*: = *Aid to Families with Dependent Children) ayuda a familias con hijos menores.*

affable [af'əbəl] *a* afable.

affair [əfär'] *n* asunto; *(also*: **love ~)** relación *f* amorosa; **~s** *(business)* negocios *mpl*; **the Watergate ~** el asunto (de) Watergate.

affect [əfekt'] *vt* afectar, influir en; *(move)* conmover.

affectation [afektā'shən] *n* afectación *f*.

affected [əfek'tid] *a* afectado.

affection [əfek'shən] *n* afecto, cariño.

affectionate [əfek'shənit] *a* afectuoso, cariñoso.

affectionately [əfek'shənitlē] *ad* afectuosamente.

affidavit [afidā'vit] *n (LAW)* declaración *f* jurada.

affiliated [əfil'ēātid] *a* afiliado; **~ company** empresa *or* compañía filial *or* subsidiaria.

affinity [əfin'ətē] *n* afinidad *f*.

affirm [əfûrm'] *vt* afirmar.

affirmation [afûrmā'shən] *n* afirmación *f*.

affirmative [əfûr'mətiv] *a* afirmativo.

affix [əfiks'] *vt (signature)* estampar; *(stamp)* pegar.

afflict [əflikt'] *vt* afligir.

affliction [əflik'shən] *n* enfermedad *f*, aflicción *f*.

affluence [af'lōōəns] *n* opulencia, riqueza.

affluent [af'lōōənt] *a* adinerado, acaudalado; **the ~ society** la sociedad de consumo.

afford [əfôrd'] *vt (provide)* dar, proporcionar; **can we ~ it/to buy it?** ¿tenemos bastante dinero para comprarlo?; **can we ~ a car?** ¿tenemos dinero para comprarnos un coche?

affront [əfrunt'] *n* afrenta, ofensa.

affronted [əfrun'tid] *a* ofendido.

Afghan [af'gan] *a*, *n* afgano/a *m/f*.

Afghanistan [afgan'istan] *n* Afganistán *m*.

afield [əfēld'] *ad*: **far ~** muy lejos.

AFL-CIO *n abbr (US*: = *American Federation of Labor and Congress of Industrial Organizations) confederación sindicalista.*

afloat [əflōt'] *ad (floating)* a flote; *(at sea)* en el mar.

afoot [əfōōt'] *ad*: **there is something ~** algo se está tramando.

aforesaid [əfôr'sed] *a* antedicho, susodicho; *(COMM)* mencionado anteriormente.

afraid [əfrād'] *a*: **to be ~ of** *(person)* tener miedo a; *(thing)* tener miedo de; **to be ~ to** tener miedo de, temer; **I am ~ that** me temo que; **I'm ~ so** ¡me temo que sí!, ¡lo siento, pero es así!; **I'm ~ not** me temo que no.

afresh [əfresh'] *ad* de nuevo, otra vez.

Africa [af'rikə] *n* África.

African [af'rikən] *a*, *n* africano/a *m/f*.

Afrikaans [afrikâns'] *n* africaans *m*.

Afrikaner [afrikâ'nûr] *n* africánder *m/f*.

Afro-American [af'rōəmär'ikən] *a*, *n* afroamericano/a *m/f*.

AFT *n abbr (= American Federation of Teachers)* sindicato de profesores.

aft [aft] *ad (to be)* en popa; *(to go)* a popa.

after [af'tûr] *prep (time)* después de; *(place, order)* detrás de, tras ♦ *ad* después ♦ *conj* después (de) que; **what/who are you ~?** ¿qué/a quién busca usted?; **the police are ~ him** la policía le está buscando; **~ having done/he left** después de haber hecho/ después de que se marchó; **~ dinner** después de cenar *or* comer; **the day ~ tomorrow** pasado mañana; **~ all** después de todo, al fin y al cabo; **~ you!** ¡pase usted!; **quarter ~ two** *(US)* las 2 y cuarto.

afterbirth [af'tûrbûrth] *n* secundinas *fpl*.

aftercare [af'tûrkär] *n (MED)* asistencia postoperatoria.

after-effects [af'tûrifekts] *npl* consecuencias *fpl*, efectos *mpl*.

afterlife [af'tûrlīf] *n* vida eterna.

aftermath [af'tûrmath] *n* consecuencias *fpl*, resultados *mpl*.

afternoon [aftûrnōōn'] *n* tarde *f*; **good ~!** ¡buenas tardes!

after-sales service [af'tûrsālz sûr'vis] *n (Brit COMM: for car, washing machine etc)* servicio de asistencia pos-venta.

after-shave (lotion) [af'tûrshāv (lō'shən)] *n* aftershave *m*.

aftershock [af'tûrshâk] *n (of earthquake)* réplica.

afterthought [af'tûrthôt] *n* ocurrencia (tardía).

afterwards [af'tûrwûrdz] *ad* después, más tarde.

again [əgen'] *ad* otra vez, de nuevo; **to do sth ~** volver a hacer algo; **~ and ~** una y otra vez; **now and ~** de vez en cuando.

against [əgenst'] *prep* (*opposed*) en contra de; (*close to*) contra, junto a; **I was leaning ~ the desk** estaba apoyado contra el escritorio; (*over*) ~ en contraste con.

age [āj] *n* edad *f*; (*old ~*) vejez *f*; (*period*) época ♦ *vi* envejecer(se) ♦ *vt* envejecer; **what ~ is he?** ¿qué edad *or* cuántos años tiene?; **he is 20 years of ~** tiene 20 años; **under ~** menor de edad; **to come of ~** llegar a la mayoría de edad; **it's been ~s since I saw you** hace siglos que no te veo.

aged [ājd] *a*: **~ 10** de 10 años de edad; [ā'jid]: **the ~** *npl* los ancianos.

age group *n*: **to be in the same ~** tener la misma edad; **the 40 to 50 ~** el grupo de 40 a 50 años.

ageless [āj'lis] *a* (*eternal*) eterno; (*ever young*) siempre joven.

age limit *n* edad *f* tope.

agency [ā'jənsē] *n* agencia; **through** *or* **by the ~ of** por medio de.

agenda [əjen'də] *n* orden *m* del día; **on the ~** (*COMM*) en el orden del día.

agent [ā'jənt] *n* (*gen*) agente *m/f*; (*representative*) representante *m/f*, delegado/a.

aggravate [ag'rəvāt] *vt* agravar; (*annoy*) irritar, exasperar.

aggravating [ag'rəvāting] *a* molesto.

aggravation [agrəvā'shən] *n* agravación *f*.

aggregate [ag'rəgit] *n* (*whole*) conjunto; (*collection*) agregado.

aggression [əgresh'ən] *n* agresión *f*.

aggressive [əgres'iv] *a* agresivo; (*vigorous*) enérgico.

aggressiveness [əgres'ivnis] *n* agresividad *f*.

aggrieved [əgrēvd'] *a* ofendido, agraviado.

aghast [əgast'] *a* horrorizado.

agile [aj'əl] *a* ágil.

agitate [aj'ətāt] *vt* (*shake*) agitar; (*trouble*) inquietar; **to ~ for** hacer una campaña en pro de *or* en favor de.

agitated [aj'ətātid] *a* agitado.

agitator [aj'itātûr] *n* agitador(a) *m/f*.

AGM *n abbr* (*Brit*) = **annual general meeting.**

agnostic [agnâs'tik] *a*, *n* agnóstico/a *m/f*.

ago [əgō'] *ad*: **2 days ~** hace 2 días; **not long ~** hace poco; **how long ~?** ¿hace cuánto tiempo?; **as long ~ as 1960** ya en 1960.

agog [əgâg'] *a* (*anxious*) ansiado; (*excited*): **(all) ~ (for)** (todo) emocionado (por).

agonize [ag'ənīz] *vi*: **to ~ (over)** atormentarse (por).

agonized [ag'ənīzd] *a* angustioso.

agonizing [ag'ənīzing] *a* (*pain*) atroz; (*suspense*) angustioso.

agony [ag'ənē] *n* (*pain*) dolor *m* agudo; (*distress*) angustia; **to be in ~** retorcerse de dolor.

agony column *n* consultorio sentimental.

agree [əgrē'] *vt* (*price*) acordar, quedar en ♦ *vi* (*statements*) coincidir, concordar; **to ~ (with)** (*person*) estar de acuerdo (con), ponerse de acuerdo (con); **to ~ to do** aceptar hacer; **to ~ to sth** consentir en algo; **to ~ that** (*admit*) estar de acuerdo en que; **it was ~d that ...** se acordó que ...; **garlic doesn't ~ with me** el ajo no me sienta bien.

agreeable [əgrē'əbəl] *a* agradable; (*person*) simpático; (*willing*) de acuerdo, conforme.

agreeably [əgrē'əblē] *ad* agradablemente.

agreed [əgrēd'] *a* (*time, place*) convenido.

agreement [əgrē'mənt] *n* acuerdo; (*COMM*) contrato; **in ~** de acuerdo, conforme; **by mutual ~** de común acuerdo.

agricultural [agrəkul'chûrəl] *a* agrícola.

agriculture [ag'rəkulchûr] *n* agricultura.

aground [əground'] *ad*: **to run ~** encallar, embarrancar.

agt. *abbr* = **agent.**

ahead [əhed'] *ad* delante; **~ of** delante de; (*fig*: *schedule etc*) antes de; **~ of time** antes de la hora; **to be ~ of sb** (*fig*) llevar la ventaja *or* delantera a uno; **go right** *or* **straight ~** siga adelante; **they were (right) ~ of us** iban (justo) delante de nosotros.

ahoy [əhoi'] *excl* ¡oiga!

AI *n abbr* = *Amnesty International*; (*COMPUT*) = **artificial intelligence.**

AID *n abbr* (= *artificial insemination by donor*) inseminación artificial por donante; (*US*: = *Agency for International Development*) Agencia Internacional para el Desarrollo.

aid [ād] *n* ayuda, auxilio ♦ *vt* ayudar, auxiliar; **in ~ of** a beneficio de; **with the ~ of** con la ayuda de; **to ~ and abet** (*LAW*) ser cómplice.

aide [ād] *n* (*POL*) ayudante *m/f*.

AIDS [ādz] *n abbr* (= *acquired immune deficiency syndrome*) SIDA *m*.

AIH *abbr* (= *artificial insemination by husband*) inseminación artificial por esposo.

ailing [ā'ling] *a* (*person, economy*) enfermizo.

ailment [āl'mənt] *n* enfermedad *f*, achaque *m*.

aim [ām] *vt* (*gun, camera*) apuntar; (*missile, remark*) dirigir; (*blow*) asestar ♦ *vi* (*also*: **take ~**) apuntar ♦ *n* puntería; (*objective*) propósito, meta; **to ~ at** (*objective*) aspirar a, pretender; **to ~ to do** tener la intención de hacer.

aimless [ām'lis] *a* sin propósito, sin objeto.

aimlessly [ām'lislē] *ad* a la ventura, a la deriva.

ain't [ānt] (*col*) = **am not; aren't; isn't.**

air [âr] *n* aire *m*; (*appearance*) aspecto ♦ *vt* (*room*) ventilar; (*clothes, bed, grievances, ideas*) airear; (*views*) hacer público ♦ *cpd* aéreo; **to throw sth into the ~** (*ball etc*) lanzar algo al aire; **by ~** (*travel*) en avión;

to be on the ~ (*RADIO*, *TV*: *program*) estarse emitiendo; (: *station*) estar emitiendo.

air base *n* (*MIL*) base *f* aérea.

air bed *n* colchón *m* neumático.

airborne [är'bôrn] *a* (*in the air*) en el aire; (*MIL*) aerotransportado; **as soon as the plane was** ~ tan pronto como el avión estuvo en el aire.

air cargo *n* carga aérea.

air-conditioned [är'kəndishənd] *a* climatizado.

air conditioning [är' kəndish'əning] *n* aire *m* acondicionado.

air-cooled [är'kōōld] *a* refrigerado por aire.

aircraft [är'kraft] *n*, *pl inv* avión *m*.

aircraft carrier *n* porta(a)viones *m inv*.

air cushion *n* cojín *m* de aire; (*AVIAT*) colchón *m* de aire.

airdrome [är'drōm] *n* (*US*) aeródromo.

airfield [är'fēld] *n* campo de aviación.

Air Force *n* fuerzas aéreas *fpl*, aviación *f*.

air freight *n* flete *m* por avión.

air freshener *n* ambientador *m*.

air gun *n* escopeta de aire comprimido.

air hostess (*Brit*) *n* azafata.

airily [är'ilē] *ad* muy a la ligera.

airing [är'ing] *n*: **to give an** ~ **to** (*linen*) airear; (*room*) ventilar; (*fig: ideas etc*) airear, someter a discusión.

air letter *n* carta aérea.

airlift [är'lift] *n* puente *m* aéreo.

airline [är'līn] *n* línea aérea.

airliner [är'līnûr] *n* avión *m* de pasajeros.

airlock [är'lâk] *n* (*in pipe*) esclusa de aire.

airmail [är'māl] *n*: **by** ~ por avión.

air mattress *n* colchón *m* neumático.

airplane [är'plān] *n* (*US*) avión *m*.

airport [är'pôrt] *n* aeropuerto.

air raid *n* ataque *m* aéreo.

airsick [är'sik] *a*: **to be** ~ marearse (en avión).

airstrip [är'strip] *n* pista de aterrizaje.

air terminal *n* terminal *f*.

airtight [är'tīt] *a* hermético.

air traffic control *n* control *m* de tráfico aéreo.

air traffic controller *n* controlador(a) *m/f* aéreo/a.

air waybill [är' wā'bil] *n* conocimiento (de embarque) aéreo.

airy [är'ē] *a* (*room*) bien ventilado; (*manners*) ligero.

aisle [īl] *n* (*of church*) nave *f* lateral, pasadizo; (*of theater*, *plane*) pasillo.

ajar [əjâr'] *a* entreabierto.

AK *abbr* (*US MAIL*) = *Alaska*.

aka *abbr* (= *also known as*) alias.

akin [əkin'] *a*: ~ **to** parecido a.

AL *abbr* (*US MAIL*) = *Alabama*.

ALA *n abbr* = *American Library Association*.

Ala. *abbr* (*US*) = *Alabama*.

alabaster [al'əbastûr] *n* alabastro.

à la carte [â lâ kârt'] *ad* a la carta.

alacrity [əlak'ritē] *n*: **with** ~ con la mayor prontitud.

alarm [əlârm'] *n* alarma; (*anxiety*) inquietud *f* ♦ *vt* asustar, inquietar.

alarm clock *n* despertador *m*.

alarming [əlâr'ming] *a* alarmante.

alarmist [əlâr'mist] *n* alarmista *m/f*.

alas [əlas'] *ad* desgraciadamente ♦ *excl* ¡ay de mí!

Alas. *abbr* (*US*) = *Alaska*.

Alaska [əlas'kə] *n* Alaska.

Albania [albā'nēə] *n* Albania.

Albanian [albā'nēən] *a* albanés/esa ♦ *n* albanés/esa *m/f*; (*LING*) albanés *m*.

albeit [ôlbē'it] *conj* (*although*) aunque.

album [al'bəm] *n* álbum *m*; (*L.P.*) elepé *m*.

albumen [albyōō'mən] *n* albumen *m*.

alchemy [al'kəmē] *n* alquimia.

alcohol [al'kəhôl] *n* alcohol *m*.

alcoholic [alkəhôl'ik] *a*, *n* alcohólico/a *m/f*.

alcoholism [al'kəhôlizəm] *n* alcoholismo.

alcove [al'kōv] *n* nicho, hueco.

ald. *abbr* = *alderman*.

alderman [ôl'dúrmən] *n* concejal *m*.

ale [āl] *n* cerveza.

alert [əlûrt'] *a* alerta *inv*; (*sharp*) despierto, despabilado ♦ *n* alerta *m*, alarma ♦ *vt* poner sobre aviso; **to** ~ **sb (to sth)** poner sobre aviso *or* alertar a uno (de algo); **to** ~ **sb to the dangers of sth** poner sobre aviso *or* alertar a uno de los peligros de algo; **to be on the** ~ estar alerta *or* sobre aviso.

alertness [əlûrt'nis] *n* vigilancia.

Aleutian Islands [əlōō'shən i'ləndz] *npl* Islas *fpl* Aleutianas.

Alexandria [aligzan'drēə] *n* Alejandría.

alfresco [alfres'kō] *a*, *ad* al aire libre.

algebra [al'jəbrə] *n* álgebra.

Algeria [aljē'rēə] *n* Argelia.

Algerian [aljə'rēən] *a*, *n* argelino/a *m/f*.

Algiers [aljērz'] *n* Argel *m*.

algorithm [al'gəriţhəm] *n* algoritmo.

alias [ā'lēəs] *ad* alias, conocido por ♦ *n* alias *m*.

alibi [al'əbī] *n* coartada.

alien [āl'yən] *n* (*foreigner*) extranjero/a ♦ *a*: ~ **to** ajeno a.

alienate [āl'yənāt] *vt* enajenar, alejar.

alienation [ālyənā'shən] *n* enajenación *f*.

alight [əlīt'] *a* encendido ♦ *vi* apearse, bajar.

align [əlīn'] *vt* alinear.

alignment [əlīn'mənt] *n* alineación *f*; **the desks are out of** ~ los pupitres no están bien alineados.

alike [əlīk'] *a* semejantes, iguales ♦ *ad* igualmente, del mismo modo; **to look** ~ parecerse.

alimony [al'əmōnē] *n* (*LAW*) manutención *f*.

alive [əlīv'] *a* (*gen*) vivo; (*lively*) activo.

alkali [al'kəlī] *n* álcali *m*.

all [ôl] *a* todo; (*pl*) todos(as) ♦ *pron* todo;

(*pl*) todos(as) ♦ *ad* completamente, del todo; ~ **day** todo el día; **for ~ their efforts** a pesar de sus esfuerzos; ~ **alone** solito, completamente solo; **at ~: anything at ~** lo que sea; **not at ~** (*in answer to thanks*) de nada; **I'm not at ~ tired** no estoy nada cansado; ~ **but** casi; ~ **the time/his life** todo el tiempo/toda su vida; ~ **the more/ the better** tanto más/mejor; ~ **five** todos los cinco; ~ **of them** todos (ellos); ~ **of us went** fuimos todos; **is that ~?** ¿nada más?, ¿es (eso) todo?; (*in shop*) ¿algo más?; **not as hard as ~ that** no tan difícil; **to be/feel ~ in** estar rendido; ~ **in ~** con todo, total.

all-around [ôl'əround] *a* (*US*) completo; (*view*) amplio.

allay [əlā'] *vt* (*fears*) aquietar; (*pain*) aliviar.

all clear *n* (*after attack etc*) fin *m* de la alerta; (*fig*) luz *f* verde.

allegation [aləgā'shən] *n* alegato.

allege [əlej'] *vt* pretender; **he is ~d to have said ...** se afirma que él dijo ....

alleged [əlejd'] *a* supuesto, presunto.

allegedly [əlej'idlē] *ad* supuestamente, según se afirma.

allegiance [əlē'jəns] *n* lealtad *f*.

allegory [al'əgôrē] *n* alegoría.

all-embracing [ôl'embrās'ing] *a* universal.

allergic [əlûr'jik] *a*: ~ **to** alérgico a.

allergy [al'ûrjē] *n* alergia.

alleviate [əlē'vēāt] *vt* aliviar.

alleviation [əlēvēā'shən] *n* alivio.

alley [al'ē] *n* (*street*) callejuela; (*in garden*) paseo.

alliance [əlī'əns] *n* alianza.

allied [əlīd'] *a* aliado/a; (*related*) relacionado.

alligator [al'əgātûr] *n* caimán *m*.

all-important [ôl'impôr'tənt] *a* de suma importancia.

all-inclusive [ôl'inkloo'siv] *a* (*also ad: charge*) todo incluido.

all-in wrestling [ôl'in res'ling] *n* (*Brit*) lucha libre.

alliteration [əlitərā'shən] *n* aliteración *f*.

all-night [ôl'nīt] *a* (*café*) abierto toda la noche; (*party*) que dura toda la noche.

allocate [al'əkāt] *vt* (*share out*) repartir; (*devote*) asignar.

allocation [aləkā'shən] *n* (*of money*) ración *f*, cuota; (*distribution*) reparto.

allot [əlât'] *vt* asignar; **in the ~ted time** en el tiempo asignado.

allotment [əlât'mənt] *n* ración *f*; (*Brit: garden*) parcela.

all-out [ôl'out'] *a* (*effort etc*) supremo ♦ *ad*: **all out** con todas las fuerzas.

allow [əlou'] *vt* (*permit*) permitir, dejar; (*a claim*) admitir; (*sum to spend, time estimated*) dar, conceder; (*concede*): **to ~ that** reconocer que; **to ~ sb to do** permitir a alguien hacer; **smoking is not ~ed pro-**hibido *or* se prohíbe fumar; **he is ~ed to ...** se le permite ...; **we must ~ 3 days for the journey** debemos dejar 3 días para el viaje.

allow for *vt fus* tener en cuenta.

allowance [əlou'əns] *n* concesión *f*; (*payment*) subvención *f*, pensión *f*; (*discount*) descuento, rebaja; **to make ~s for** (*person*) disculpar a; (*thing: take into account*) tener en cuenta.

alloy [al'oi] *n* (*mix*) mezcla.

all right *ad* (*feel, work*) bien; (*as answer*) ¡conforme!, ¡está bien!

all-rounder [ôlroun'dûr] *n* (*Brit*): **to be a good ~** ser una persona que hace de todo.

allspice [ôl'spīs] *n* pimienta inglesa *or* de Jamaica.

all-time [ôl'tīm] *a* (*record*) de todos los tiempos.

allude [əlōōd'] *vi*: **to ~ to** aludir a.

alluring [əlōō'ring] *a* seductor(a), atractivo.

allusion [əlōō'zhən] *n* referencia, alusión *f*.

ally *n* [al'ī] aliado/a ♦ *vt* [əlī']: **to ~ o.s. with** aliarse con.

almanac [ôl'mənak] *n* almanaque *m*.

almighty [ôlmī'tē] *a* todopoderoso.

almond [â'mənd] *n* (*fruit*) almendra; (*tree*) almendro.

almost [ôl'mōst] *ad* casi; **he ~ fell** por poco *or* casi se cae.

alms [âmz] *npl* limosna *sg*.

aloft [əlôft'] *ad* arriba.

alone [əlōn'] *a* solo ♦ *ad* sólo, solamente; **to leave sb ~** dejar a uno en paz; **to leave sth ~** no tocar algo, dejar algo sin tocar; **let ~ ...** sin hablar de ...

along [əlông'] *prep* a lo largo de, por ♦ *ad*: **is he coming ~ with us?** ¿viene con nosotros?; **he was limping ~** iba cojeando; ~ **with** junto con; **all ~** (*all the time*) desde el principio.

alongside [əlông'sīd'] *prep* al lado de ♦ *ad* (*NAUT*) de costado; **we brought our boat ~** atracamos nuestro barco.

aloof [əlōōf'] *a* reservado ♦ *ad*: **to stand ~** mantenerse a distancia.

aloud [əloud'] *ad* en voz alta.

alphabet [al'fəbet] *n* alfabeto.

alphabetical [alfəbet'ikəl] *a* alfabético; **in ~ order** por orden alfabético.

alphanumeric [alfənōōmär'ik] *a* alfanumérico.

alpine [al'pīn] *a* alpino, alpestre.

Alps [alps] *npl*: **the ~** los Alpes.

already [ôlred'ē] *ad* ya.

alright [ôlrīt'] *ad* (*Brit*) = **all right.**

Alsatian [alsā'shən] *n* (*dog*) pastor *m* alemán.

also [ôl'sō] *ad* también, además.

Alta. *abbr* (*Canada*) = *Alberta.*

altar [ôl'tûr] *n* altar *m*.

alter [ôl'tûr] *vt* cambiar, modificar ♦ *vi* cambiarse, modificarse.

alteration [ôltərā'shən] *n* cambio, modificación *f*; alteración *f*; ~**s** *npl* (*ARCH*) reformas *fpl*; (*SEWING*) arreglos *mpl*; **time-table subject to** ~ el horario puede cambiar.

alternate *a* [ôl'tûrnit] alterno ♦ *vi* [ôl'tûrnāt]: **to** ~ **(with)** alternar (con); **on** ~ **days** un día sí y otro no.

alternately [ôl'tûrnitlē] *ad* alternativamente, por turno.

alternating [ôl'tûrnāting] *a* (*current*) alterno.

alternative [ôltûr'nətiv] *a* alternativo ♦ *n* alternativa.

alternatively [ôltûr'nətivlē] *ad*: ~ **one could** ... por otra parte se podría....

alternator [ôl'tûrnātûr] *n* (*AUT*) alternador *m*.

although [ôlthō'] *conj* aunque, si bien.

altitude [al'tətōōd] *n* altitud *f*, altura.

alto [al'tō] *n* (*female*) contralto *f*; (*male*: *US*) contralto; (: *Brit*) alto.

altogether [ôltəgeth'ûr] *ad* completamente, del todo; (*on the whole, in all*) en total, en conjunto; **how much is that** ~**?** ¿cuánto es todo or en total?

altruistic [altrōōis'tik] *a* altruista.

aluminium [alōōmin'ēəm] *etc* (*Brit*) = **aluminum** *etc*.

aluminum [əlōō'mənəm] *n* (*US*) aluminio.

aluminum foil *n* papel *m* de estaño.

alumnus [əlum'nəs] *n* (*US*) graduado.

always [ôl'wāz] *ad* siempre.

AM *abbr* = *amplitude modulation*.

am [am] *vb see* **be**.

a.m. *ad abbr* (= *ante meridiem*) de la mañana.

AMA *n abbr* = *American Medical Association*.

amalgam [əmal'gəm] *n* amalgama.

amalgamate [əmal'gəmāt] *vi* amalgamarse ♦ *vt* amalgamar.

amalgamation [əmalgəmā'shən] *n* (*COMM*) fusión *f*.

amass [əmas'] *vt* amontonar, acumular.

amateur [am'əchûr] *n* aficionado/a, amateur *m/f*; ~ **dramatics** dramas *mpl* presentados por aficionados, representación *f* de aficionados.

amateurish [aməchōō'rish] *a* (*pej*) torpe, inexperto.

amaze [əmāz'] *vt* asombrar, pasmar; **to be** ~**d (at)** asombrarse (de).

amazement [əmāz'mənt] *n* asombro, sorpresa; **to my** ~ para mi sorpresa.

amazing [əmā'zing] *a* extraordinario, asombroso; (*bargain, offer*) increíble.

amazingly [əmā'zinglē] *ad* extraordinariamente.

Amazon [am'əzän] *n* (*GEO*) Amazonas *m*; (*MYTHOLOGY*) amazona ♦ *cpd*: **the** ~ **basin/jungle** la cuenca/selva del Amazonas.

Amazonian [aməzō'nēən] *a* amazónico.

ambassador [ambas'ədûr] *n* embajador(a) *m/f*.

amber [am'bûr] *n* ámbar *m*; **at** ~ (*Brit AUT*) en el amarillo.

ambidextrous [ambidek'strəs] *a* ambidextro.

ambience [am'bēəns] *n* ambiente *m*.

ambiguity [ambəgyōō'itē] *n* ambigüedad *f*; (*of meaning*) doble sentido.

ambiguous [ambig'yōōəs] *a* ambiguo.

ambition [ambish'ən] *n* ambición *f*; **to achieve one's** ~ realizar su ambición.

ambitious [ambish'əs] *a* ambicioso; (*plan*) grandioso.

ambivalent [ambiv'ələnt] *a* ambivalente; (*pej*) equívoco.

amble [am'bəl] *vi* (*gen*: ~ **along**) deambular, andar sin prisa.

ambulance [am'byələns] *n* ambulancia.

ambulanceman/woman [am'byələnsman/wōōm'ən] *n* (*Brit*) ambulanciero/a.

ambush [am'bōōsh] *n* emboscada ♦ *vt* tender una emboscada a; (*fig*) coger (*Sp*) or agarrar (*LAm*) por sorpresa.

ameba [əmē'bə] *n* (*US*) = **amoeba**.

ameliorate [əmēl'yərāt] *vt* mejorar.

amelioration [əmēlyərā'shən] *n* mejora.

amen [ā'men'] *excl* amén.

amenable [əmē'nəbəl] *a*: ~ **to** (*advice etc*) sensible a.

amend [əmend'] *vt* (*law, text*) enmendar; **to make** ~**s** (*apologize*) enmendarlo, dar cumplida satisfacción.

amendment [əmend'mənt] *n* enmienda.

amenities [əmen'itēz] *npl* comodidades *fpl*.

amenity [əmen'itē] *n* servicio.

America [əmär'ikə] *n* América del Norte.

American [əmär'ikən] *a*, *n* norteamericano/a *m/f*, estadounidense *m/f*.

americanize [əmär'ikənīz] *vt* americanizar.

Amerindian [amərin'dēən] *a*, *n* amerindio/a *m/f*.

amethyst [am'ithist] *n* amatista.

Amex [am'eks] *n abbr* = *American Stock Exchange*.

amiable [ā'mēəbəl] *a* (*kind*) amable, simpático.

amicable [am'ikəbəl] *a* amistoso, amigable.

amid(st) [əmid(st)'] *prep* entre, en medio de.

amiss [əmis'] *ad*: **to take sth** ~ tomar algo a mal; **there's something** ~ pasa algo.

ammo [am'ō] *n abbr* (*col*) = **ammunition**.

ammonia [əmōn'yə] *n* amoníaco.

ammunition [amyənish'ən] *n* municiones *fpl*; (*fig*) argumentos *mpl*.

ammunition dump *n* depósito de municiones.

amnesia [amnē'zhə] *n* amnesia.

amnesty [am'nistē] *n* amnistía; **to grant** ~ **to** amnistiar (a).

amoeba [əmē'bə] *n* amiba.

amok [əmuk'] *ad*: **to run** ~ enloquecerse, desbocarse.

among(st) [əmung(st)'] *prep* entre, en medio de.

amoral [āmôr'əl] *a* amoral.

amorous [am'ûrəs] *a* cariñoso.

amorphous [əmôr'fəs] *a* amorfo.

amortization [amûrtəzā'shən] *n* amortización *f*.

amount [əmount'] *n* (*gen*) cantidad *f*; (*of bill etc*) suma, importe *m* ♦ *vi*: **to** ~ **to** (*total*) sumar; (*be same as*) equivaler a, significar; **this** ~**s to a refusal** esto equivale a una negativa; **the total** ~ (*of money*) la suma total.

amp(ere) [am'pēr] *n* amperio; **a 13 amp plug** un enchufe de 13 amperios.

ampersand [am'pûrsand] *n* signo &, ''y'' comercial.

amphibian [amfib'ēən] *n* anfibio.

amphibious [amfib'ēəs] *a* anfibio.

amphitheater, (*Brit*) **amphitheatre** [am'fəthēətûr] *n* anfiteatro.

ample [am'pəl] *a* (*spacious*) amplio; (*abundant*) abundante; **to have** ~ **time** tener tiempo de sobra.

amplifier [am'pləfiûr] *n* amplificador *m*.

amplify [am'pləfī] *vt* amplificar, aumentar; (*explain*) explicar.

amply [am'plē] *ad* ampliamente.

ampule, (*Brit*) **ampoule** [am'pyōol] *n* (*MED*) ampolla.

amputate [am'pyōotāt] *vt* amputar.

Amsterdam [am'stûrdam] *n* Amsterdam *m*.

amt *abbr* = **amount**.

amuck [əmuk'] *ad* = **amok**.

amuse [əmyōoz'] *vt* divertir; (*distract*) distraer, entretener; **to** ~ **o.s. with sth/by doing sth** distraerse con algo/haciendo algo; **he was** ~**d at the joke** le divirtió el chiste.

amusement [əmyōoz'mənt] *n* diversión *f*; (*pastime*) pasatiempo; (*laughter*) risa; **much to my** ~ con gran regocijo mío.

amusement arcade *n* mini-casino.

amusement park *n* parque *m* de atracciones.

amusing [əmyōo'zing] *a* divertido.

an [an, ən] *indefinite article see* **a.**

ANA *n abbr = American Newspaper Association; American Nurses Association.*

anachronism [ənak'rənizəm] *n* anacronismo.

anaemia [ənē'mēə] *n* (*Brit*) = **anemia.**

anaemic [ənē'mik] *a* (*Brit*) = **anemic.**

anaesthetic [anisthet'ik] *n* (*Brit*) = **anesthetic.**

anaesthetist [ənēs'thətist] *n* (*Brit*) anestesista *m/f*.

anagram [an'əgram] *n* anagrama *m*.

analgesic [anəljē'zik] *a*, *n* analgésico.

analogous [ənal'əgəs] *a* análogo.

analog(ue) [an'əlôg] *a* (*computer*, *watch*) analógico.

analogy [ənal'əjē] *n* analogía; **to draw an** ~ **between** señalar la analogía entre.

analyse [an'əlīz] *vt* (*Brit*) = **analyze.**

analysis, *pl* **analyses** [ənal'isis, -sēz] *n* análisis *m inv*.

analyst [an'əlist] *n* (*political* ~, *psycho*~) analista *m/f*.

analytic(al) [anəlit'ik(əl)] *a* analítico.

analyze [an'əlīz] *vt* (*US*) analizar.

anarchist [an'ûrkist] *a*, *n* anarquista *m/f*.

anarchy [an'ûrkē] *n* anarquía, desorden *m*.

anathema [ənath'əmə] *n*: **that is** ~ **to him** eso es pecado para él.

anatomical [anətâm'ikəl] *a* anatómico.

anatomy [ənat'əmē] *n* anatomía.

ANC *n abbr = African National Congress.*

ancestor [an'sestûr] *n* antepasado.

ancestral [anses'trəl] *a* ancestral.

ancestry [an'sestrē] *n* ascendencia, abolengo.

anchor [ang'kûr] *n* ancla, áncora ♦ *vi* (*also*: **to drop** ~) anclar ♦ *vt* (*fig*) sujetar, afianzar; **to weigh** ~ levar anclas.

anchorage [ang'kûrij] *n* ancladero.

anchovy [an'chōvē] *n* anchoa.

ancient [ān'shənt] *a* antiguo; ~ **monument** monumento histórico.

ancillary [an'səlärē] *a* (*worker*, *staff*) auxiliar.

and [and] *conj* y; (*before i*, *hi*) e; ~ **so on** etcétera; **try** ~ **come** procure *or* intente venir; **better** ~ **better** cada vez mejor.

Andalusia [andəlōo'zhə] *n* Andalucía.

Andes [an'dēz] *npl*: **the** ~ los Andes.

anecdote [an'ikdōt] *n* anécdota.

anemia [ənē'mēə] *n* (*US*) anemia.

anemic [ənē'mik] *a* (*US*) *a* anémico; (*fig*) soso, insípido.

anemone [ənem'ənē] *n* (*BOT*) anémone *f*; **sea** ~ anémona.

anesthesiologist [anisthēzēāl'əjist] *n* (*US*) anestesista *m/f*.

anesthetic [anisthet'ik] *n* (*US*) anestesia; **local/general** ~ anestesia local/general.

anew [ənōo'] *ad* de nuevo, otra vez.

angel [ān'jəl] *n* ángel *m*.

angelic [anjel'ik] *a* angélico.

anger [ang'gûr] *n* ira, enfado, cólera ♦ *vt* enojar, enfurecer.

angina [anjī'nə] *n* angina (del pecho).

angle [ang'gəl] *n* ángulo; **from their** ~ desde su punto de vista.

angler [ang'glûr] *n* pescador(a) *m/f* (de caña).

Anglican [ang'glikən] *a*, *n* anglicano/a.

anglicize [ang'gləsīz] *vt* dar forma inglesa a.

angling [ang'gling] *n* pesca con caña.

Anglo- [an'glō] *pref* anglo....

Angola [anggō'lə] *n* Angola.

Angolan [anggō'lən] *a*, *n* angoleño/a *m/f*.

angrily [ang'grilē] *ad* enojado, enfadado.

angry [ang'grē] *a* enfadado, enojado; **to be**

~ **with sb/at sth** estar enfadado con alguien/por algo; **to get** ~ enfadarse, enojarse.

anguish [ang'gwish] n (physical) tormentos mpl; (mental) angustia.

angular [ang'gyəlûr] a (shape) angular; (features) anguloso.

animal [an'əməl] n animal m, bestia ♦ a animal.

animate vt [an'əmāt] (enliven) animar; (encourage) estimular, alentar ♦ a [an'əmit] vivo.

animated [an'əmātid] a vivo.

animation [anəmā'shən] n animación f.

animosity [anəmás'ətē] n animosidad f, rencor m.

aniseed [an'isēd] n anís m.

Ankara [ang'kûrə] n Ankara.

ankle [ang'kəl] n tobillo m.

ankle sock n calcetín m.

annex n [an'eks] (also: Brit: **annexe**) (building) edificio anexo ♦ vt [əneks'] (territory) anexar.

annihilate [ənī'əlāt] vt aniquilar.

anniversary [anəvûr'sûrē] n aniversario.

annotate [an'ōtāt] vt anotar.

announce [ənouns'] vt (gen) anunciar; (inform) comunicar; **he ~d that he wasn't going** declaró que no iba.

announcement [ənouns'mənt] n (gen) anuncio; (declaration) declaración f; **I'd like to make an** ~ quisiera anunciar algo.

announcer [ənoun'sûr] n (RADIO, TV) locutor(a) m/f.

annoy [ənoi'] vt molestar, fastidiar, irritar; **to be** ~**ed (at sth/with sb)** estar enfadado or molesto (por algo/con uno); **don't get** ~**ed!** ¡no se enfade!

annoyance [ənoi'əns] n enojo; (thing) molestia.

annoying [ənoi'ing] a molesto, fastidioso; (person) pesado.

annual [an'yōōəl] a anual ♦ n (BOT) anual m; (book) anuario.

annual general meeting (AGM) n (Brit) junta general anual.

annually [an'yōōəlē] ad anualmente, cada año.

annual report n informe m or memoria anual.

annuity [ənōō'itē] n renta or pensión f vitalicia.

annul [ənul'] vt anular; (law) revocar.

annulment [ənul'mənt] n anulación f.

annum [an'əm] n see **per annum**.

Annunciation [ənunsēā'shən] n Anunciación f.

anode [an'ōd] n ánodo.

anoint [ənoint'] vt untar.

anomalous [ənám'ələs] a anómalo.

anomaly [ənám'əlē] n anomalía.

anon. [ənán'] abbr = **anonymous**.

anonymity [anənim'itē] n anonimato.

anonymous [ənán'əməs] a anónimo; **to remain** ~ quedar en el anonimato.

anorak [ân'ərâk] n anorak m.

anorexia [anərek'sēə] n (MED) anorexia.

another [ənuth'ûr] a: ~ **book** (one more) otro libro; (a different one) un libro distinto; ~ **beer?** ¿(quieres) otra cerveza?; **in** ~ **5 years** en cinco años más ♦ pron otro; **some actor or** ~ algún actor; see also **one**.

ANSI n abbr (= American National Standards Institute) instituto de normas.

answer [an'sûr] n contestación f, respuesta; (to problem) solución f ♦ vi contestar, responder ♦ vt (reply to) contestar a, responder a; (problem) resolver; **to ~ the phone** contestar el teléfono; **in ~ to your letter** contestando or en contestación a su carta; **to ~ the bell** or **the door** acudir a la puerta.

answer back vi replicar, ser respondón/ona.

answer for vt fus responder de or por.

answer to vt fus (description) corresponder a.

answerable [an'sûrəbəl] a: ~ **to sb for sth** responsable ante uno de algo.

answering machine [an'sûring məshēn'] n contestador m automático.

ant [ant] n hormiga.

ANTA n abbr = American National Theatre and Academy.

antagonism [antag'ənizəm] n hostilidad f.

antagonist [antag'ənist] n antagonista m/f, adversario/a.

antagonistic [antagənis'tik] a antagónico; (opposed) contrario, opuesto.

antagonize [antag'ənīz] vt provocar.

Antarctic [antârk'tik] a antártico ♦ n: **the** ~ el Antártico.

Antarctica [antârk'tikə] n Antártida.

Antarctic Circle n Círculo Polar Antártico.

Antarctic Ocean n Océano Antártico.

ante [an'tē] n: **to up the** ~ subir la puesta.

ante... pref ante...

anteater [ant'ētûr] n oso hormiguero.

antecedent [antisē'dənt] n antecedente m.

antechamber [an'tēchāmbûr] n antecámara.

antelope [an'tələp] n antílope m.

antenatal [antēnā'təl] a (Brit) = **prenatal**.

antenna, pl ~**e** [anten'ə, -nē] n antena.

anteroom [an'tērōōm] n antesala.

anthem [an'thəm] n: **national** ~ himno nacional.

anthology [anthál'əjē] n antología.

anthropologist [anthrəpál'əjist] n antropólogo/a.

anthropology [anthrəpál'əjē] n antropología.

anti... [an'tī] pref anti....

antiaircraft [antīâr'kraft] a antiaéreo.

antiballistic [antēbəlis'tik] a antibalístico.

antibiotic [antēbîât'ik] *a, n* antibiótico.
antibody [an'tēbâdē] *n* anticuerpo.
anticipate [antis'əpāt] *vt (foresee)* prever; *(expect)* esperar, contar con; *(forestall)* anticiparse a, adelantarse a; **this is worse than I ~d** esto es peor de lo que esperaba; **as ~d** según se esperaba.
anticipation [antisəpā'shən] *n* previsión *f*; esperanza; anticipación *f*.
anticlimax [antēklī'maks] *n* decepción *f*.
anticlockwise [antēklâk'wīz] *ad (Brit)* en dirección contraria a la de las agujas del reloj.
antics [an'tiks] *npl* payasadas *fpl*; *(of child)* travesuras *fpl*.
anticyclone [antēsī'klōn] *n* anticiclón *m*.
antidote [an'tidōt] *n* antídoto.
antifreeze [an'tēfrēz] *n* anticongelante *m*.
antihistamine [antēhis'təmēn] *n* antihistamínico.
Antilles [antil'ēz] *npl:* **the ~** las Antillas.
antipathy [antip'əthē] *n (between people)* antipatía; *(to person, thing)* aversión *f*.
Antipodean [antipədē'ən] *a* antípoda.
Antipodes [antip'ədēz] *npl:* **the ~** las Antípodas.
antiquarian [antəkwär'ēən] *n* anticuario/a.
antiquated [an'təkwātid] *a* anticuado.
antique [antēk'] *n* antigüedad *f* ♦ *a* antiguo.
antique dealer *n* anticuario/a.
antique shop *n* tienda de antigüedades.
antiquity [antik'witē] *n* antigüedad *f*.
anti-Semitic [an'tīsəmit'ik] *a* antisemita.
anti-Semitism [antīsem'itizəm] *n* antisemitismo.
antiseptic [antēsep'tik] *a, n* antiséptico.
antisocial [antēsō'shəl] *a* antisocial.
antitank [antētangk'] *a* antitanque.
antithesis, *pl* **antitheses** [antith'əsis, -sēz] *n* antítesis *f inv*.
antitrust [antētrust'] *a:* **~ legislation** legislación *f* antimonopolio.
antlers [ant'lûrz] *npl* cornamenta.
anus [ā'nəs] *n* ano.
anvil [an'vil] *n* yunque *m*.
anxiety [angzī'ətē] *n (worry)* inquietud *f*; *(eagerness)* ansia, anhelo.
anxious [angk'shəs] *a (worried)* inquieto; *(keen)* deseoso; **I'm very ~ about you** me tienes muy preocupado.
anxiously [angk'shəslē] *ad* con inquietud, de manera angustiada.
any [en'ē] *a (in negative and interrogative sentences = some)* algún, alguna; *(negative sense)* ningún, ninguna; *(no matter which)* cualquier(a); *(each and every)* todo; **I haven't ~ money/books** no tengo dinero/libros; **have you ~ butter/children/money?** ¿tiene mantequilla/hijos/dinero?; **at ~ moment** en cualquier momento; **~ day now** cualquier día de éstos; **in ~ case**, **at ~ rate** de todas formas, de todas maneras ♦ *pron* alguno; ninguno; *(anybody)*

cualquiera; *(in negative and interrogative sentences):* **I haven't ~** no tengo ninguno; **have you got ~?** ¿tiene algunos?; **can ~ of you sing?** ¿alguno de ustedes sabe cantar? ♦ *ad (in negative sentences)* nada; *(in interrogative and conditional constructions)* algo; **I can't hear him ~ more** no le oigo más; **do you want ~ more soup?** ¿quiere más sopa?
anybody [en'ēbâdē] *pron* cualquiera, cualquier persona; *(in interrogative sentences)* alguien; *(in negative sentences):* **I don't see ~** no veo a nadie.
anyhow [en'ēhou] *ad* de todos modos, de todas maneras; *(carelessly)* de cualquier manera; *(haphazardly)* de cualquier modo; **I shall go ~** iré de todas maneras.
anyone [en'ēwun] = **anybody**.
anyplace [en'ēplās] *ad (US)* = **anywhere**.
anything [en'ēthing] *pron (see* **anybody**) cualquier cosa; *(in interrogative sentences)* algo; *(in negative sentences)* nada; *(everything)* todo; **~ else?** ¿algo más?
anytime [en'ētīm] *ad (at any moment)* en cualquier momento, de un momento a otro; *(whenever)* no importa cuándo, cuando quiera.
anyway [en'ēwā] *ad* de todas maneras; de cualquier modo.
anywhere [en'ēhwär] *ad (see* **anybody**) dondequiera; *(interrogative)* en algún sitio; *(negative sense)* en ningún sitio; *(everywhere)* en or por todas partes; **I don't see him ~** no le veo en ningún sitio; **~ in the world** en cualquier parte del mundo.
Anzac [an'zak] *n abbr (= Australia-New Zealand Army Corps)* soldado del cuerpo Anzac.
apace [əpās'] *ad* aprisa.
apart [əpârt'] *ad* aparte, separadamente; **10 miles ~** separados por 10 millas; **to take ~** desmontar; **~ from** *prep* aparte de.
apartheid [əpärt'hīt] *n* apartheid *m*.
apartment [əpârt'mənt] *n* piso, departamento *(LAm)*, apartamento; *(room)* cuarto.
apartment block *or* **building** *or* **house** *n* bloque *m* de pisos.
apathetic [apəthet'ik] *a* apático, indiferente.
apathy [ap'əthē] *n* apatía, indiferencia.
APB *n abbr (US: = all points bulletin)* expresión usada por la policía que significa "descubrir y aprehender al sospechoso".
ape [āp] *n* mono ♦ *vt* imitar, remedar.
Apennines [ap'ənīnz] *npl:* **the ~** los Apeninos *mpl*.
aperitif [əpārētēf'] *n* aperitivo.
aperture [ap'ûrchûr] *n* rendija, resquicio; *(PHOT)* abertura.
APEX [ā'peks] *n abbr (AVIAT = advance purchase excursion)* APEX *m*.
apex [ā'peks] *n* ápice *m*; *(fig)* cumbre *f*.

aphid |ā'fid| *n* áfido.

aphorism |af'ərizəm| *n* aforismo.

aphrodisiac |afrədiz'ēak| *a, n* afrodisíaco.

API *n abbr = American Press Institute.*

apiece |əpēs'| *ad* cada uno.

aplomb |əplâm'| *n* aplomo, confianza.

APO *n abbr (US: = Army Post Office) servicio postal del ejército.*

Apocalypse |əpâk'əlips| *n* Apocalipsis *m.*

apocryphal |əpâk'rəfəl| *a* apócrifo.

apolitical |āpəlit'ikəl| *a* apolítico.

apologetic |əpâləjet'ik| *a* (*look, remark*) de disculpa.

apologetically |əpâləjet'iklē| *ad* con aire de disculpa, excusándose, disculpándose.

apologize |əpâl'əjīz| *vi:* **to ~ (for sth to sb)** disculparse (con alguien de algo).

apology |əpâl'əjē| *n* disculpa, excusa; **please accept my apologies** le ruego me disculpe.

apoplectic |apəplek'tik| *a* (*MED*) apoplético; (*col*): **~ with rage** furioso.

apoplexy |ap'əpleksē| *n* apoplejía.

apostle |əpâs'əl| *n* apóstol *m/f.*

apostrophe |əpâs'trəfē| *n* apóstrofe *m.*

Appalachian Mountains |apəlā'chēən moun'tənz| *npl:* **the ~** los Montes Apalaches.

appal(l) |əpôl'| *vt* horrorizar, espantar.

appalling |əpôl'ing| *a* espantoso; (*awful*) pésimo; **she's an ~ cook** es una cocinera malísima.

apparatus |apərat'əs| *n* aparato; (*in gymnasium*) aparatos *mpl.*

apparel |əpar'əl| *n* (*US*) indumentaria.

apparent |əpar'ənt| *a* aparente; (*obvious*) manifiesto, claro; **it is ~ that** está claro que.

apparently |əpar'əntlē| *ad* por lo visto, al parecer.

apparition |apərish'ən| *n* aparición *f;* (*ghost*) fantasma *m.*

appeal |əpēl'| *vi* (*LAW*) apelar ♦ *n* (*LAW*) apelación *f;* (*request*) llamamiento; (*plea*) súplica; (*charm*) atractivo, encanto; **to ~ for** suplicar, reclamar; **to ~ to** (*subj: person*) rogar a, suplicar a; (*subj: thing*) atraer, interesar; **to ~ to sb for mercy** rogarle misericordia a alguien; **it doesn't ~ to me** no me atrae, no me llama la atención; **right of ~** derecho de apelación.

appealing |əpē'ling| *a* (*nice*) atractivo; (*touching*) conmovedor(a), emocionante.

appear |əpēr'| *vi* aparecer, presentarse; (*LAW*) comparecer; (*publication*) salir (a luz), publicarse; (*seem*) parecer; **it would ~ that** parecería que.

appearance |əpē'rəns| *n* aparición *f;* (*look, aspect*) apariencia, aspecto; **to keep up ~s** salvar las apariencias; **to all ~s** al parecer.

appease |əpēz'| *vt* (*pacify*) apaciguar; (*satisfy*) satisfacer.

appeasement |əpēz'mənt| *n* (*POL*) entreguismo.

appellate court |əpel'it kôrt| *n* (*US*) tribunal *m* de apelación.

append |əpend'| *vt* (*COMPUT*) anexionar (al final).

appendage |əpen'dij| *n* añadidura.

appendicitis |əpendisī'tis| *n* apendicitis *f.*

appendix, *pl* **appendices** |əpen'diks, -disēz| *n* apéndice *m;* **to have one's ~ out** operarse de apendicitis.

appetite |ap'itīt| *n* apetito; (*fig*) deseo, anhelo; **that walk has given me an ~** ese paseo me ha dado apetito.

appetizer |ap'itīzûr| *n* (*drink*) aperitivo; (*food*) tapas *fpl* (*Sp*).

appetizing |ap'itīzing| *a* apetitoso.

applaud |əplôd'| *vt, vi* aplaudir.

applause |əplôz'| *n* aplausos *mpl.*

apple |ap'əl| *n* manzana.

apple tree *n* manzano.

appliance |əplī'əns| *n* aparato; **electrical ~s** electrodomésticos *mpl.*

applicable |ap'likəbəl| *a* aplicable, pertinente; **the law is ~ from January** la ley es aplicable *or* se pone en vigor desde enero; **to be ~ to** referirse a.

applicant |ap'likənt| *n* candidato/a; solicitante *m/f.*

application |aplikā'shən| *n* aplicación *f;* (*for a job, a grant etc*) solicitud *f,* petición *f.*

application form *n* solicitud *f.*

applications package *n* (*COMPUT*) paquete *m* de programas de aplicación.

applied |əplīd'| *a* (*science, art*) aplicado.

apply |əplī'| *vt:* **to ~ (to)** aplicar (a); (*fig*) emplear (para) ♦ *vi:* **to ~ to** (*ask*) dirigirse a; (*be suitable for*) ser aplicable a; (*be relevant to*) tener que ver con; **to ~ for** (*permit, grant, job*) solicitar; **to ~ the brakes** aplicar los frenos; **to ~ o.s. to** aplicarse a, dedicarse a.

appoint |əpoint'| *vt* (*to post*) nombrar; (*date, place*) fijar, señalar.

appointee |əpointē'| *n* persona nombrada.

appointment |əpoint'mənt| *n* (*engagement*) cita; (*date*) compromiso; (*act*) nombramiento; (*post*) puesto; **to make an ~ (with)** (*doctor*) pedir hora (con); (*friend*) citarse (con); **by ~** por medio de cita.

appointment book *n* agenda.

apportion |əpôr'shən| *vt* repartir.

appraisal |əprā'zəl| *n* apreciación *f.*

appraise |əprāz'| *vt* (*value*) tasar, valorar; (*situation etc*) evaluar.

appreciable |əprē'shēəbəl| *a* sensible.

appreciate |əprē'shēāt| *vt* (*like*) apreciar, tener en mucho; (*be grateful for*) agradecer; (*be aware of*) comprender ♦ *vi* (*COMM*) aumentar(se) en valor; **I ~d your help** agradecí tu ayuda.

appreciation [əprēshēā'shən] *n* aprecio; reconocimiento, agradecimiento; aumento en valor.

appreciative [əprē'shətiv] *a* apreciativo, agradecido.

apprehend [aprihend'] *vt* percibir; *(arrest)* detener.

apprehension [aprihen'shən] *n (fear)* aprensión *f*.

apprehensive [aprihen'siv] *a* aprensivo.

apprentice [əpren'tis] *n* aprendiz(a) *m/f* ♦ *vt*: **to be ~d to** estar de aprendiz con.

apprenticeship [əpren'tisship] *n* aprendizaje *m*; **to serve one's ~** hacer el aprendizaje.

approach [əprōch'] *vi* acercarse ♦ *vt* acercarse a; *(be approximate)* aproximarse a; *(ask, apply to)* dirigirse a ♦ *n* acercamiento; aproximación *f*; *(access)* acceso; *(proposal)* proposición *f*; **to ~ sb about sth** hablar con uno sobre algo.

approachable [əprō'chəbəl] *a (person)* abordable; *(place)* accesible.

approach road *n* vía de acceso.

approbation [aprəbā'shən] *n* aprobación *f*.

appropriate *a* [əprōp'rēit] apropiado, conveniente ♦ *vt* [əprōp'rēāt] *(take)* apropiarse de; *(allot)*: **to ~ sth for** destinar algo a; **~ for** *or* **to** apropiado para; **it would not be ~ for me to comment** no estaría bien *or* sería pertinente que yo diera mi opinión.

appropriation [əprōprēā'shən] *n* asignación *f*.

appropriation account *n* cuenta de asignación.

approval [əprōō'vəl] *n* aprobación *f*, visto bueno; **on ~** *(COMM)* a prueba; **to meet with sb's ~** obtener la aprobación de uno.

approve [əprōōv'] *vt* aprobar.

approve of *vt fus* aprobar.

approx. *abbr* (= *approximately*) aprox.

approximate [əprák'səmit] *a* aproximado.

approximately [əprák'səmitlē] *ad* aproximadamente, más o menos.

approximation [əpráksəmā'shən] *n* aproximación *f*.

appt. *abbr (US)* = **appointment**.

Apr. *abbr* (= *April*) abr.

apr *n abbr* (= *annual percentage rate*) tasa de interés anual.

apricot [ap'rikât] *n* albaricoque *m*, damasco *(LAm)*.

April [āp'rəl] *n* abril *m*; **~ Fool's Day** *n* (*1 April*) ≈ día *m* de los Inocentes (*28 December*).

apron [ā'prən] *n* delantal *m; (AVIAT)* pista.

apse [aps] *n* (*ARCH*) ábside *m*.

Apt. *abbr* = **apartment**.

apt [apt] *a (to the point)* acertado, oportuno; *(appropriate)* apropiado; **~ to do** *(likely)* propenso a hacer.

aptitude [ap'tətōōd] *n* aptitud *f*, capacidad *f*.

aptitude test *n* prueba de aptitud.

aptly [apt'lē] *a* aptamente, acertadamente.

aqualung [ak'wəlung] *n* escafandra autónoma.

aquarium [əkwär'ēəm] *n* acuario.

Aquarius [əkwär'ēəs] *n* Acuario.

aquatic [əkwat'ik] *a* acuático.

aqueduct [ak'widukt] *n* acueducto.

AR *abbr (US MAIL)* = *Arkansas*.

Arab [ar'əb] *a, n* árabe *m/f*.

Arabia [ərā'bēə] *n* Arabia.

Arabian [ərā'bēən] *a* árabe, arábigo.

Arabian Desert *n* Desierto Arábigo.

Arabian Sea *n* Mar *m* de Omán.

Arabic [ar'əbik] *a (language, manuscripts)* árabe, arábigo ♦ *n* árabe *m*; **~ numerals** numeración *f* arábiga.

arable [ar'əbəl] *a* cultivable.

Aragon [ar'əgán] *n* Aragón *m*.

arbiter [âr'bitûr] *n* árbitro.

arbitrary [âr'biträrē] *a* arbitrario.

arbitrate [âr'bitrāt] *vi* arbitrar.

arbitration [ârbitrā'shən] *n* arbitraje *m*; **the dispute went to ~** el conflicto laboral fue sometido al arbitraje.

arbitrator [âr'bitrātûr] *n* árbitro.

ARC *n abbr* = *American Red Cross*.

arc [ârk] *n* arco.

arcade [ârkād'] *n (ARCH)* arcada; *(round a square)* soportales *mpl*; *(shopping ~)* galería comercial.

arch [ârch] *n* arco; *(vault)* bóveda; *(of foot)* arco del pie ♦ *vt* arquear.

archaeology [ârkēál'əjē] *etc* = **archeology** *etc*.

archaic [ârkā'ik] *a* arcaico.

archangel [ârkān'jəl] *n* arcángel *m*.

archbishop [ârchbish'əp] *n* arzobispo.

arched [ârcht] *a* abovedado.

archenemy [ârch'en'əmē] *n* enemigo jurado.

archeological [ârkēəláj'ikəl] *a* arqueológico.

archeologist [ârkēál'əjist] *n* arqueólogo/a.

archeology [ârkēál'əjē] *n* arqueología.

archer [âr'chûr] *n* arquero/a.

archery [âr'chûrē] *n* tiro al arco.

archetypal [âr'kitīpəl] *a* arquetípico.

archetype [âr'kitīp] *n* arquetipo.

archipelago [ârkəpel'əgō] *n* archipiélago.

architect [âr'kitekt] *n* arquitecto/a.

architectural [âr'kitekchûrəl] *a* arquitectónico.

architecture [âr'kitekchûr] *n* arquitectura.

archive [âr'kīv] *n (also COMPUT)* archivo.

archive file *n (COMPUT)* fichero archivado.

archives [âr'kīvz] *npl* archivo *sg*.

archivist [âr'kəvist] *n* archivero/a.

archway [ârch'wā] *n* arco, arcada.

Arctic [ârk'tik] *a* ártico ♦ *n*: **the ~** el Ártico.

Arctic Circle *n* Círculo Polar Ártico.

Arctic Ocean *n* Océano Glacial Ártico.

ARD *n abbr* (*US MED*) = *acute respiratory disease*.

ardent [âr'dənt] *a* (*desire*) ardiente; (*supporter, lover*) apasionado.

ardor, (*Brit*) **ardour** [âr'dûr] *n* ardor *m*, pasión *f*.

arduous [âr'jōōəs] *a* (*gen*) arduo; (*journey*) penoso.

are [âr] *vb see* **be**.

area [âr'ēə] *n* área; (*MATH etc*) superficie *f*, extensión *f*; (*zone*) región *f*, zona; **the Chicago** ~ la zona de Chicago.

area code *n* (*TEL*) prefijo.

arena [ərē'nə] *n* arena; (*of circus*) pista; (*for bullfight*) plaza, ruedo.

aren't [ärnt] = **are not**.

Argentina [ârjəntē'nə] *n* Argentina.

Argentinian [ârjəntin'ēən] *a, n* argentino/a *m/f*.

arguable [âr'gyōōəbəl] *a*: **it is** ~ **whether** ... es dudoso que + *subjun*.

arguably [âr'gyōōəblē] *ad*: **it is** ~ ... es discutiblemente ...

argue [âr'gyōō] *vt* (*debate: case, matter*) mantener, argüir ♦ *vi* (*quarrel*) discutir; (*reason*) razonar, argumentar; **to** ~ **that** sostener que; **to** ~ **about sth (with sb)** pelearse (con uno) por algo.

argument [âr'gyəmənt] *n* (*reasons*) argumento; (*quarrel*) discusión *f*; (*debate*) debate *m*, disputa; ~ **for/against** argumento en pro/contra de.

argumentative [ârgyəmen'tətiv] *a* discutidor(a).

aria [âr'ēə] *n* (*MUS*) aria.

arid [ar'id] *a* árido.

aridity [ərid'itē] *n* aridez *f*.

Aries [âr'ēz] *n* Aries *m*.

arise [əriz'], *pt* **arose**, *pp* **arisen** [əriz'ən] *vi* (*rise up*) levantarse, alzarse; (*emerge*) surgir, presentarse; **to** ~ **from** derivar de; **should the need** ~ si fuera necesario.

aristocracy [aristâk'rəsē] *n* aristocracia.

aristocrat [əris'təkrat] *n* aristócrata *m/f*.

aristocratic [əristəkrat'ik] *a* aristocrático.

arithmetic [ərith'mətik] *n* aritmética.

arithmetical [arithmet'ikəl] *a* aritmético.

Ariz. *abbr* (*US*) = *Arizona*.

Ark [ârk] *n*: **Noah's** ~ el Arca *f* de Noé.

Ark. *abbr* (*US*) = *Arkansas*.

arm [ârm] *n* (*ANAT*) brazo ♦ *vt* armar; ~ **in** ~ cogidos del brazo; *see also* **arms**.

armaments [âr'məmənts] *npl* (*weapons*) armamentos *mpl*.

armchair [ârm'chär] *n* sillón *m*.

armed [ârmd] *a* armado; **the** ~ **forces** las fuerzas armadas.

armed robbery *n* robo a mano armada.

Armenia [ârmē'nēə] *n* Armenia.

Armenian [ârmē'nēən] *a* armenio ♦ *n* armenio/a; (*LING*) armenio.

armful [ârm'fəl] *n* brazado, brazada.

armistice [âr'mistis] *n* armisticio.

armor [âr'mûr] *n* (*US*) armadura.

armored car [âr'mûrd kâr] *n* coche *m or* carro (*LAm*) blindado.

armory [âr'mûrē] *n* arsenal *m*.

armour [âr'mûr] *etc* (*Brit*) = **armor** *etc*.

armpit [ârm'pit] *n* sobaco, axila.

armrest [ârm'rest] *n* apoyabrazos *m inv*, brazo.

arms [ârmz] *npl* (*weapons*) armas *fpl*; (*HERALDRY*) escudo *sg*.

arms control *n* control *m* de armamentos.

arms race *n* carrera de armamentos.

army [âr'mē] *n* ejército.

aroma [ərō'mə] *n* aroma *m*, fragancia.

aromatic [arəmat'ik] *a* aromático, fragante.

arose [ərōz'] *pt of* **arise**.

around [əround'] *ad* alrededor; (*in the area*) a la redonda ♦ *prep* alrededor de; **all** ~ por todos lados; **it's the other way** ~ está al revés; **the long way** ~ por el camino menos directo; **it's just** ~ **the corner** (*fig*) está a la vuelta de la esquina; **sb** ~ invitar a uno a casa; **I'll be** ~ **at 6 o'clock** llegaré a eso de las 6; **is Paul** ~? ¿está por aquí Paul?; ~ **the clock** *ad* las 24 horas; **to go** ~ **to sb's (house)** ir a casa de uno; **to go** ~ **the back** pasar por atrás; **to go** ~ **a house** visitar una casa; **enough to go** ~ bastante (para todos); **to walk** ~ **the town** andar por la ciudad.

arouse [ərouz'] *vt* despertar.

arrange [ərānj'] *vt* arreglar, ordenar; (*program*) organizar ♦ *vi*: **we have** ~**d for a taxi to pick you up** hemos hecho los arreglos para que le recoja un taxi; **to** ~ **to do sth** quedar en hacer algo; **it was** ~**d that** ... se quedó en que ...

arrangement [ərānj'mənt] *n* arreglo; (*agreement*) acuerdo; ~**s** *npl* (*plans*) planes *mpl*, medidas *fpl*; (*preparations*) preparativos *mpl*; **to come to an** ~ **(with sb)** llegar a un acuerdo (con uno); **by** ~ a convenir; **I'll make** ~**s for you to be met** haré los preparativos para que le estén esperando.

array [ərā'] *n* (*COMPUT*) arreglo, array *m*; ~ **of** (*things*) serie *f* de; (*people*) conjunto de.

arrears [ərērz'] *npl* atrasos *mpl*; **in** ~ (*COMM*) en mora; **to be in** ~ **with one's rent** estar retrasado en el pago del alquiler.

arrest [ərest'] *vt* detener; (*sb's attention*) llamar ♦ *n* detención *f*; **under** ~ detenido.

arresting [əres'ting] *a* (*fig*) llamativo.

arrival [əri'vəl] *n* llegada; **new** ~ recién llegado/a.

arrive [əriv'] *vi* llegar.

arrogance [ar'əgəns] *n* arrogancia.

arrogant [ar'əgənt] *a* arrogante.

arrow [ar'ō] *n* flecha.

arse [ârs] *n* (*Brit col!*) culo, trasero.

arsenal [âr'sənəl] *n* arsenal *m*.

arsenic [âr'sənik] *n* arsénico.

arson [âr'sən] *n* incendio premeditado.

art [ârt] *n* arte *m*; (*skill*) destreza; (*technique*) técnica; **A~s** *npl* (*SCOL*) Letras *fpl*; **work of ~** obra de arte.

artefact [âr'təfakt] *n* (*Brit*) = **artifact.**

arterial [ârtē'rēəl] *a* (*ANAT*) arterial; (*road etc*) principal.

artery [âr'tûrē] *n* (*MED*, *road etc*) arteria.

artful [ârt'fəl] *a* (*cunning: person, trick*) mañoso.

art gallery *n* pinacoteca; (*COMM*) galería de arte.

arthritis [ârthrī'tis] *n* artritis *f*.

artichoke [âr'tichōk] *n* alcachofa; **Jerusalem ~** aguaturma.

article [âr'tikəl] *n* artículo, objeto, cosa; (*in newspaper*) artículo; (*Brit LAW: training*): **~s** *npl* contrato *sg* de aprendizaje; **~s of clothing** prendas *fpl* de vestir.

articles of association *npl* (*COMM*) estatutos *mpl* sociales, escritura social.

articulate *a* [ârtik'yəlit] (*speech*) claro; (*person*) que se expresa bien ♦ *vi* [ârtik'yəlāt] articular.

articulated lorry [ârtik'yəlātid lôr'ē] *n* (*Brit*) trailer *m*.

artifact [âr'təfakt] *n* (*US*) artefacto.

artifice [âr'təfis] *n* artificio, truco.

artificial [ârtəfish'əl] *a* artificial; (*teeth etc*) postizo.

artificial insemination [ârtəfish'əl insemənā'shən] *n* inseminación *f* artificial.

artificial intelligence (A.I.) *n* inteligencia artificial (I.A.).

artificial respiration *n* respiración *f* artificial.

artillery [ârtil'ûrē] *n* artillería.

artisan [âr'tizən] *n* artesano/a.

artist [âr'tist] *n* artista *m/f*; (*MUS*) intérprete *m/f*.

artistic [ârtis'tik] *a* artístico.

artistry [âr'tistrē] *n* arte *m*, habilidad *f* (artística).

artless [ârt'lis] *a* (*innocent*) natural, sencillo; (*clumsy*) torpe.

art school *n* escuela de bellas artes.

arty [âr'tē] *a* artistoide.

ARV *n* *abbr* (= *American Revised Version*) traducción americana de la Biblia.

AS *n* *abbr* (*US UNIV:* = *Associate in/of Science*) título universitario ♦ *abbr* (*US MAIL*) = *American Samoa.*

as [az] *conj* (*cause*) como, ya que; (*time: moment*) como, cuando; (: *duration*) mientras; (*manner*) como, lo mismo que, tal como; (*in the capacity of*) como; **~ big ~** tan grande como; **twice ~ big ~** dos veces más grande que; **much ~ I like them, ...** por mucho que me gusten, ...; **~ the years went by** con el paso de los años; **~ she said** como ella dijo; **~ a present** de or como regalo; **~ if** or **though** como si; **~ for** or **to that** en cuanto a eso, en lo que a

eso se refiere; **~ or so long ~** *conj* mientras (que); **~ much/many ~** tanto(s)... como; **~ soon ~** *conj* tan pronto como; **~ such** *ad* como tal; **~ well** *ad* también, además; **~ well ~** *conj* tanto como; *see also* **such.**

ASA *n* *abbr* (= *American Standards Association*) instituto de normas.

a.s.a.p. *abbr* (= *as soon as possible*) cuanto antes, lo más pronto posible.

asbestos [asbes'təs] *n* asbesto, amianto.

ascend [əsend'] *vt* subir.

ascendancy [əsen'dənsē] *n* ascendiente *m*, dominio.

ascendant [əsen'dənt] *n*: **to be in the ~** estar en auge, ir ganando predominio.

Ascension [əsen'chən] *n*: **the ~** la Ascensión.

Ascension Island *n* Isla Ascensión.

ascent [əsent'] *n* subida; (*slope*) cuesta, pendiente *f*; (*of plane*) ascenso.

ascertain [asûrtān'] *vt* averiguar.

ascetic [əset'ik] *a* ascético.

asceticism [əset'isizəm] *n* ascetismo.

ASCII [as'kē] *n* *abbr* (= *American Standard Code for Information Interchange*) ASCII.

ascribe [əskrīb'] *vt*: **to ~ sth to** atribuir algo a.

ASCU *n* *abbr* (*US*) = *Association of State Colleges and Universities.*

ASE *n* *abbr* = *American Stock Exchange.*

ash [ash] *n* ceniza; (*tree*) fresno.

ashamed [əshāmd'] *a* avergonzado; **to be ~ of** avergonzarse de.

ashcan [ash'kən] *n* (*US*) cubo or bote *m* (*LAm*) de la basura.

ashen [ash'ən] *a* pálido.

ashore [əshôr'] *ad* en tierra.

ashtray [ash'trā] *n* cenicero.

Ash Wednesday *n* miércoles *m* de ceniza.

Asia [ā'zhə] *n* Asia.

Asian [ā'zhən], **Asiatic** [āzhēat'ik] *a*, *n* asiático/a *m/f*.

aside [əsīd'] *ad* a un lado ♦ *n* aparte *m*; **~ from** *prep* (*as well as*) aparte or además de.

ask [ask] *vt* (*question*) preguntar; (*demand*) pedir; (*invite*) invitar ♦ *vi*: **to ~ about sth** preguntar acerca de algo; **to ~ sb sth/to do sth** preguntar algo a uno/pedir a uno que haga algo; **to ~ sb about sth** preguntar algo a uno; **to ~ (sb) a question** hacer una pregunta (a uno); **to ~ sb the time** preguntar la hora a uno; **to ~ sb out to dinner** invitar a cenar a uno.

ask about *vt fus* preguntar por.

ask for *vt fus* pedir; **it's just ~ing for trouble** or **for it** es buscarse problemas.

askance [əskans'] *ad*: **to look ~ at sb** mirar con recelo a uno.

askew [əskyōō'] *ad* sesgado, ladeado.

asking price [as'king prīs] *n* (*COMM*) precio

inicial.

asleep |əslēp'| *a* dormido; **to fall ~** dormirse, quedarse dormido.

asp |asp| *n* áspid *m*.

asparagus |əspar'əgəs| *n* espárragos *mpl*.

ASPCA *n abbr* = *American Society for the Prevention of Cruelty to Animals.*

aspect |as'pɛkt| *n* aspecto, apariencia; (*direction in which a building etc faces*) orientación *f*.

aspersions |əspûr'zhənz| *npl*: **to cast ~ on** difamar a, calumniar a.

asphalt |as'fôlt| *n* asfalto.

asphyxiate |asfik'sēāt| *vt* asfixiar.

asphyxiation |asfiksēā'shən| *n* asfixia.

aspirate *vt* |as'pûrāt| aspirar ♦ *a* |as'pûrit| aspirado.

aspirations |aspərā'shənz| *npl* anhelo *sg*, deseo *sg*; (*ambition*) ambición *fsg*.

aspire |əspī'ûr| *vi*: **to ~ to** aspirar a, ambicionar.

aspirin |as'pûrin| *n* aspirina.

ass |as| *n* asno, burro; (*col*) imbécil *m/f*; (*US col!*) culo, trasero; **kiss my ~!** (*col!*) ¡vete al carajo! (*!*).

assailant |əsā'lənt| *n* asaltador(a) *m/f*, agresor(a) *m/f*.

assassin |əsas'in| *n* asesino/a.

assassinate |əsas'ənāt| *vt* asesinar.

assassination |əsasinā'shən| *n* asesinato.

assault |əsôlt'| *n* (*gen*: *attack*) asalto ♦ *vt* asaltar, atacar; (*sexually*) violar.

assemble |əsɛm'bəl| *vt* reunir, juntar; (*TECH*) montar ♦ *vi* reunirse, juntarse.

assembler |əsɛm'blûr| *n* (*COMPUT*) ensamblador *m*.

assembly |əsɛm'blē| *n* (*meeting*) reunión *f*, asamblea; (*construction*) montaje *m*.

assembly language *n* (*COMPUT*) lenguaje *m* ensamblador.

assembly line *n* cadena de montaje.

assent |əsɛnt'| *n* asentimiento, aprobación *f* ♦ *vi* consentir, asentir; **to ~ (to sth)** consentir (en algo).

assert |əsûrt'| *vt* afirmar; (*insist on*) hacer valer; **to ~ o.s.** imponerse.

assertion |əsûr'shən| *n* afirmación *f*.

assertive |əsûr'tiv| *a* enérgico, agresivo, perentorio.

assess |əsɛs'| *vt* valorar, calcular; (*tax*, *damages*) fijar; (*property etc*: *for tax*) gravar.

assessment |əsɛs'mənt| *n* valoración *f*, gravamen *m*; (*judgment*): **~ (of)** juicio (sobre).

assessor |əsɛs'ûr| *n* asesor(a) *m/f*; (*of tax*) tasador(a) *m/f*.

asset |as'ɛt| *n* posesión *f*; (*quality*) ventaja; **~s** *npl* (*funds*) activo *sg*, fondos *mpl*.

asset-stripping |as'ɛtstri'ping| *n* (*COMM*) acaparamiento de activos.

assiduous |əsij'ōōəs| *a* asiduo.

assign |əsīn'| *vt* (*date*) fijar; (*task*) asignar;

(*resources*) destinar; (*property*) traspasar.

assignment |əsīn'mənt| *n* asignación *f*; (*task*) tarea; (*SCOL*) trabajo.

assimilate |əsim'əlāt| *vt* asimilar.

assimilation |əsiməlā'shən| *n* asimilación *f*.

assist |əsist'| *vt* ayudar.

assistance |əsis'təns| *n* ayuda, auxilio.

assistant |əsis'tənt| *n* ayudante *m/f*; (*Brit*: *also*: **shop ~**) dependiente/a *m/f*.

assistant manager *n* subdirector(a) *m/f*.

assizes |əsī'ziz| *npl* (*Brit*) sesión *f* de un tribunal.

associate *a* |əsō'shēit| asociado ♦ *n* socio/a, colega *m/f*; (*in crime*) cómplice *m/f*; (*member*) miembro/a ♦ *vb* |əsō'shēāt| *vt* asociar; (*ideas*) relacionar ♦ *vi*: **to ~ with sb** tratar con alguien; **~ director** subdirector/a *m/f*; **~d company** compañía afiliada.

association |əsōsēā'shən| *n* asociación *f*; (*COMM*) sociedad *f*; **in ~ with** en asociación con.

association football *n* (*Brit*) fútbol *m*.

assorted |əsôr'tid| *a* surtido, variado; **in ~ sizes** en distintos tamaños.

assortment |əsôrt'mənt| *n* surtido.

Asst. *abbr* = *Assistant.*

assuage |əswāj'| *vt* mitigar.

assume |əsōōm'| *vt* (*suppose*) suponer; (*responsibilities etc*) asumir; (*attitude*, *name*) adoptar, tomar.

assumed name |əsōōmd' nām'| *n* nombre *m* falso.

assumption |əsump'shən| *n* (*supposition*) suposición *f*, presunción *f*; (*act*) asunción *f*; **on the ~ that** suponiendo que.

assurance |əshōōr'əns| *n* garantía, promesa; (*confidence*) confianza, aplomo; (*Brit*: *insurance*) seguro; **I can give you no ~s** no puedo hacerle ninguna promesa.

assure |əshōōr'| *vt* asegurar.

assuredly |əshōōr'idlē| *ad* seguramente, indudablemente.

AST *n abbr* (= *Atlantic Standard Time*) hora oficial de Nueva Escocia.

asterisk |as'tûrisk| *n* asterisco.

astern |əstûrn'| *ad* a popa.

asteroid |as'təroid| *n* asteroide *m*.

asthma |az'mə| *n* asma.

asthmatic |azmat'ik| *a*, *n* asmático/a *m/f*.

astigmatism |əstig'mətizəm| *n* astigmatismo.

astir |əstûr'| *ad* en acción.

ASTM *n abbr* = *American Society for Testing Materials.*

astonish |əstán'ish| *vt* asombrar, pasmar.

astonishing |əstán'ishing| *a* asombroso, pasmoso; **I find it ~ that ...** me asombra *or* pasma que ...

astonishingly |əstán'ishinglē| *ad* increíblemente, asombrosamente.

astonishment |əstán'ishmənt| *n* asombro, sorpresa; **to my ~** con gran sorpresa mía.

astound |əstound'| *vt* asombrar, pasmar.

astounding |əstound'ing| *a* asombroso.

astray |əstrā'| *ad*: **to go ~** extraviarse; **to lead ~** llevar por mal camino; **to go ~ in one's calculations** equivocarse en sus cálculos.

astride |əstrīd'| *prep* a caballo *or* horcajadas sobre.

astringent |əstrin'jənt| *a, n* astringente *m*.

astrologer |əstrål'əjūr| *n* astrólogo/a.

astrology |əstrål'əjē| *n* astrología.

astronaut |as'trənôt| *n* astronauta *m/f*.

astronomer |əstrån'əmûr| *n* astrónomo/a.

astronomical |astrənåm'ikəl| *a* astronómico.

astronomy |əstrån'əmē| *n* astronomía.

astrophysics |astrōfiz'iks| *n* astrofísica.

astute |əstōōt'| *a* astuto.

asunder |əsun'dûr| *ad*: **to tear ~** hacer pedazos.

ASV *n abbr* (= *American Standard Version*) traducción americana de la Biblia.

asylum |əsī'ləm| *n* (*refuge*) asilo; (*hospital*) manicomio; **to seek political ~** pedir asilo político.

asymmetric(al) |āsəmet'rik(əl)| *a* asimétrico.

at |at| *prep* en, a; **~ the top** en la cumbre; **~ the baker's** en la panadería; **~ 4 o'clock** a las cuatro; **~ $1 a kilo** a un dólar el kilo; **~ night** de noche; **two ~ a time** de dos en dos; **~ times** a veces; **~ full speed** a toda velocidad.

ate |āt| *pt of* **eat**.

atheism |ā'thēizəm| *n* ateísmo.

atheist |ā'thēist| *n* ateo/a.

Athenian |əthē'nēən| *a, n* ateniense *m/f*.

Athens |ath'ənz| *n* Atenas *f*.

athlete |ath'lēt| *n* atleta *m/f*.

athletic |athlet'ik| *a* atlético.

athletics |athlet'iks| *n* atletismo.

Atlantic |atlan'tik| *a* atlántico ♦ *n*: **the ~ (Ocean)** el (Océano) Atlántico.

atlas |at'ləs| *n* atlas *m*.

Atlas Mountains *npl*: **the ~** el Atlas.

A.T.M. *n abbr* (= *Automated Teller Machine*) cajero automático.

atmosphere |at'məsfēr| *n* (*air*) atmósfera; (*fig*) ambiente *m*.

atoll |at'ôl| *n* atolón *m*.

atom |at'əm| *n* átomo.

atomic |ətåm'ik| *a* atómico.

atom(ic) bomb *n* bomba atómica.

atomic power *n* energía atómica.

atomizer |at'əmīzûr| *n* atomizador *m*.

atone |ətōn'| *vi*: **to ~ for** expiar.

atonement |ətōn'mənt| *n* expiación *f*.

ATP *n abbr* (= *Association of Tennis Professionals*) sindicato de jugadores de tenis profesionales.

atrocious |ətrō'shəs| *a* (*very bad*) atroz; (*fig*) horrible, infame.

atrocity |ətrås'itē| *n* atrocidad *f*.

atrophy |at'rəfē| *n* atrofia ♦ *vi* atrofiarse.

attach |ətach'| *vt* sujetar; (*stick*) pegar; (*document, letter*) adjuntar; **to be ~ed to sb/sth** (*to like*) tener cariño a uno/algo; **the ~ed letter** la carta adjunta.

attaché |atashā'| *n* agregado/a.

attaché case *n* maletín *m*.

attachment |ətach'mənt| *n* (*tool*) accesorio; (*love*): **~ (to)** apego (a).

attack |ətak'| *vt* atacar; (*criminal*) agredir, asaltar; (*task etc*) emprender ♦ *n* ataque *m*, asalto; (*on sb's life*) atentado; **heart ~** infarto (de miocardio).

attacker |ətak'ûr| *n* agresor(a) *m/f*, asaltante *m/f*.

attain |ətān'| *vt* (*also*: **~ to**) alcanzar; (*achieve*) lograr, conseguir.

attainments |ətān'mənts| *npl* (*skill*) talento *sg*.

attempt |ətempt'| *n* tentativa, intento; (*attack*) atentado ♦ *vt* intentar, tratar de; **he made no ~ to help** ni siquiera procuró ayudar.

attempted |ətemp'tid| *a*: **~ murder/ burglary/suicide** tentativa *or* intento de asesinato/robo/suicidio.

attend |ətend'| *vt* asistir a; (*patient*) atender.

attend to *vt fus* (*needs, affairs etc*) ocuparse de; (*speech etc*) prestar atención a; (*customer*) atender a.

attendance |əten'dəns| *n* asistencia, presencia; (*people present*) concurrencia.

attendant |əten'dənt| *n* sirviente/a *m/f*, mozo/a; (*THEATER*) acomodador(a) *m/f* ♦ *a* concomitante.

attention |əten'shən| *n* atención *f* ♦ *excl* (*MIL*) ¡firme(s)!; **to the ~ of...** (*ADMIN*) atención...; **it has come to my ~ that ...** me he enterado de que ...

attentive |əten'tiv| *a* atento; (*polite*) cortés.

attenuate |əten'yōōāt| *vt* atenuar.

attest |ətest'| *vi*: **to ~ to** dar fe de.

attic |at'ik| *n* desván *m*.

attitude |at'ətōōd| *n* (*gen*) actitud *f*; (*disposition*) disposición *f*.

attorney |ətûr'nē| *n* (*US: lawyer*) abogado/ a; (*having proxy*) apoderado.

Attorney General *n* (*US*) ≈ ministro de justicia; (*Brit*) ≈ Presidente *m* del Consejo del Poder Judicial (*Sp*).

attract |ətrakt'| *vt* atraer; (*attention*) llamar.

attraction |ətrak'shən| *n* (*gen*) encanto; (*PHYSICS*) atracción *f*; (*fig: towards sth*) atractivo.

attractive |ətrak'tiv| *a* atractivo.

attribute *n* |at'rəbyōōt| atributo ♦ *vt* |ətrib'yōōt|: **to ~ sth to** atribuir algo a; (*accuse*) achacar algo a.

attrition |ətrish'ən| *n*: **war of ~** guerra de agotamiento.

atty. *abbr* (*US*) = **attorney**.

Atty. Gen. *abbr* = **Attorney General.**
ATV *n abbr* (= *all terrain vehicle*) vehículo todo terreno.
aubergine [ō'bûrzhēn] *n* berenjena.
auburn [ô'bûrn] *a* color castaño rojizo.
auction [ôk'shən] *n* (*also:* **sale by ~**) subasta ♦ *vt* subastar.
auctioneer [ôkshənēr'] *n* subastador(a) *m/f.*
auction room *n* sala de subastas.
aud. *abbr* = **audit; auditor.**
audacious [ôdā'shəs] *a* (*bold*) audaz, osado; (*impudent*) atrevido, descarado.
audacity [ôdas'itē] *n* audacia, atrevimiento; (*pej*) descaro.
audible [ôd'əbəl] *a* audible, que se puede oír.
audience [ôd'ēəns] *n* auditorio; (*gathering*) público; (*interview*) audiencia.
audiovisual [ôd'ēōvizh'ōōəl] *a* audiovisual.
audiovisual aid *n* ayuda audiovisual.
audit [ôd'it] *vt* revisar, intervenir.
audition [ôdish'ən] *n* audición *f* ♦ *vi:* **to ~ for the part of** hacer una audición para el papel de.
auditor [ô'ditûr] *n* interventor(a) *m/f*, censor(a) *m/f* de cuentas; (*US: UNIV*) estudiante *m/f* libre.
auditorium [ôditôr'ēəm] *n* auditorio.
Aug. *abbr* (= *August*) ag.
augment [ôgment'] *vt* aumentar ♦ *vi* aumentarse.
augur [ô'gûr] *vi:* **it ~s well** es de buen agüero.
August [ôg'əst] *n* agosto.
august [ôgust'] *a* augusto.
aunt [ant] *n* tía.
auntie, aunty [an'tē] *n diminutive of* **aunt.**
au pair [ô pär'] *n* (*also:* **~ girl**) au pair *f.*
aura [ô'rə] *n* aura; (*atmosphere*) ambiente *m.*
auspices [ôs'pisiz] *npl:* **under the ~ of** bajo los auspicios de.
auspicious [ôspish'əs] *a* propicio, de buen augurio.
austere [ôstēr'] *a* austero; (*manner*) adusto.
austerity [ôstär'itē] *n* austeridad *f.*
Australasia [ôstrəlā'zhə] *n* Australasia.
Australia [ôstrāl'yə] *n* Australia.
Australian [ôstrāl'yən] *a*, *n* australiano/a *m/f.*
Austria [ôs'trēə] *n* Austria.
Austrian [ôs'trēən] *a*, *n* austríaco/a *m/f.*
authentic [ôthen'tik] *a* auténtico.
authenticate [ôthen'tikāt] *vt* autenticar.
authenticity [ôthəntis'itē] *n* autenticidad *f.*
author [ô'thûr] *n* autor(a) *m/f.*
authoritarian [əthôritär'ēən] *a* autoritario.
authoritative [əthôr'itātiv] *a* autorizado; (*manner*) autoritario.
authority [əthôr'itē] *n* autoridad *f*; **the authorities** *npl* las autoridades; **to have ~ to do sth** tener autoridad para hacer algo.
authorization [ôthûrəzā'shən] *n* autoriza-

ción *f.*
authorize [ô'thərīz] *vt* autorizar.
authorized capital [ô'thərīzd kap'itəl] *n* (*COMM*) capital *m* autorizado *or* social.
autistic [ôtis'tik] *a* autístico.
autobiographical [ôtəbīəgraf'ikəl] *a* autobiográfico.
autobiography [ôtəbīâg'rəfē] *n* autobiografía.
autocratic [ôtəkrat'ik] *a* autocrático.
autograph [ô'təgraf] *n* autógrafo ♦ *vt* firmar; (*photo etc*) dedicar.
automat [ô'təmat] *n* (*US*) restaurán *m or* restaurante *m* de autoservicio.
automate [ô'təmāt] *vt* automatizar.
automated [ô'təmātid] *a* automatizado.
automatic [ôtəmat'ik] *a* automático ♦ *n* (*gun*) pistola automática; (*washing machine*) lavadora.
automatically [ôtəmat'iklē] *ad* automáticamente.
automatic data processing (ADP) *n* proceso automático de datos.
automation [ôtəmā'shən] *n* automatización *f.*
automaton, *pl* **automata** [ôtâm'ətân, -əta] *n* autómata.
automobile [ôtəməbēl'] *n* (*US*) coche *m*, carro (*LAm*), automóvil *m.*
autonomous [ôtân'əməs] *a* autónomo.
autonomy [ôtân'əmē] *n* autonomía.
autopsy [ô'tâpsē] *n* autopsia.
autumn [ô'təm] *n* otoño.
auxiliary [ôgzil'yûrē] *a* auxiliar.
AV *n abbr* (= *Authorized Version*) traducción inglesa de la Biblia ♦ *abbr* = **audiovisual.**
Av. *abbr* (= *avenue*) Av., Avda.
avail [əvāl'] *vt:* **to ~ o.s. of** aprovechar(se) de, valerse de ♦ *n:* **to no ~** en vano, sin resultado.
availability [əvāləbil'ətē] *n* disponibilidad *f.*
available [əvā'ləbəl] *a* disponible; (*obtainable*) asequible; **to make sth ~ to sb** poner algo a la disposición de uno; **is the manager ~?** ¿está libre el gerente?
avalanche [av'əlanch] *n* alud *m*, avalancha.
avant-garde [avântgârd'] *a* de vanguardia.
avarice [av'ûris] *n* avaricia.
avaricious [avərish'əs] *a* avaro.
avdp. *abbr* = *avoirdupois.*
Ave. *abbr* (= *avenue*) Av., Avda.
avenge [əvenj'] *vt* vengar.
avenue [av'ənōō] *n* avenida; (*fig*) camino.
average [av'ûrij] *n* promedio, término medio ♦ *a* (*mean*) medio, de término medio; (*ordinary*) regular, corriente ♦ *vt* calcular el promedio de, prorratear; **on ~** por regla general.
  average out *vi:* **to ~ out at** salir a un promedio de.
averse [əvûrs'] *a:* **to be ~ to sth/doing** sentir aversión *or* antipatía por algo/por ha-

cer.

aversion [əvûr'zhən] n aversión f, repugnancia.

avert [əvûrt'] vt prevenir; (blow) desviar; (one's eyes) apartar.

aviary [ā'vēārē] n pajarera.

aviation [āvēā'shən] n aviación f.

aviator [ā'vēātûr] n aviador(a) m/f.

avid [av'id] a ávido, ansioso.

avidly [av'idlē] ad ávidamente, con avidez.

avocado [avəkád'ō] n aguacate m, palta (LAm).

avoid [əvoid'] vt evitar, eludir.

avoidable [əvoid'əbəl] a evitable, eludible.

avoidance [əvoid'əns] n evasión f.

avow [əvou'] vt prometer.

avowal [əvou'əl] n promesa, voto.

avowed [əvoud'] a declarado.

AVP n abbr (US) = assistant vice-president.

avuncular [əvung'kyəlûr] a como de tío.

AWACS [ā'waks] n abbr (= airborne warning and control system) AWACS m.

await [əwāt'] vt esperar, aguardar; long ~ed largamente esperado.

awake [əwāk'] a despierto ♦ (vb: pt awoke, pp awoken or awaked) vt despertar ♦ vi despertarse; to be ~ estar despierto.

awakening [əwā'kəning] n despertar m.

award [əwôrd'] n (prize) premio; (medal) condecoración f; (LAW) fallo, sentencia; (act) concesión f ♦ vt (prize) otorgar, conceder; (LAW: damages) adjudicar.

aware [əwär'] a consciente; (awake) despierto; (informed) enterado; to become ~ of darse cuenta de, enterarse de; I am fully ~ that sé muy bien que.

awareness [əwär'nis] n conciencia, conocimiento.

awash [əwôsh'] a inundado.

away [əwā'] ad (gen) fuera; (far ~) lejos; two kilometers ~ a dos kilómetros de distancia; two hours ~ by car a dos horas en coche; the vacation was two weeks ~ faltaban dos semanas para las vacaciones; ~ from lejos de, fuera de; he's ~ for a week estará ausente una semana; he's ~ in Barcelona está en Barcelona; to take ~ llevar(se); to work/pedal ~ seguir trabajando/pedaleando; to fade ~ desvanecerse; (sound) apagarse.

away game n (SPORT) partido de fuera.

awe [ô] n pavor m, respeto, temor m reverencial.

awe-inspiring [ô'inspīuring], **awesome** [ô'səm] a imponente, pasmoso.

awestruck [ô'struk] a pasmado.

awful [ô'fəl] a terrible, pasmoso; an ~ lot of (people, cars, dogs) la mar de, muchísimos.

awfully [ô'fəlē] ad (very) terriblemente.

awhile [əhwīl'] ad (durante) un rato, algún tiempo.

awkward [ôk'wûrd] a (clumsy) desmañado,

torpe; (shape) incómodo; (difficult: question) difícil; (problem) complicado; (embarrassing) delicado.

awkwardness [ôk'wûrdnis] n (clumsiness) torpeza; (of situation) lo delicado.

awl [ôl] n lezna, subilla.

awning [ô'ning] n (of shop) toldo; (of window etc) marquesina.

awoke [əwōk'], **awoken** [əwō'kən] pt, pp of awake.

AWOL [ā'wôl] abbr (MIL) see absent without leave.

awry [ərī'] ad: to be ~ estar descolocado or atravesado; to go ~ salir mal, fracasar.

ax, (Brit) **axe** [aks] n hacha ♦ vt (employee) despedir; (project etc) cortar; (jobs) reducir; to get the ~ (col: project) ser cortado; (: person: be fired) ser despedido; to have an ~ to grind (fig) tener un interés creado or algún fin interesado.

axes [ak'sēz] npl of axis.

axiom [ak'sēəm] n axioma m.

axiomatic [aksēəmat'ik] a axiomático.

axis, pl **axes** [ak'sis, -sēz] n eje m.

axle [ak'səl] n eje m, árbol m.

ay(e) [ī] excl (yes) sí; the ayes npl los que votan a favor.

AYH n abbr = American Youth Hostels.

AZ abbr (US MAIL) = Arizona.

azalea [əzāl'yə] n azalea.

Azores [əzôrz'] npl: the ~ las (Islas) Azores.

Aztec [az'tek] a, n azteca m/f.

azure [azh'ûr] a celeste.

B

B, b [bē] n (letter) B, b f; (SCOL: mark) N; (MUS) si m; **B for Baker** B de Barcelona.

b. abbr = born.

BA n abbr (SCOL) = Bachelor of Arts.

babble [bab'əl] vi barbullar.

babe [bāb] n criatura.

baboon [baboon'] n mandril m.

baby [bā'bē] n bebé m/f.

baby buggy [bā'bē bug'ē] n cochecito.

baby carriage n (US) cochecito.

babyish [bā'bēish] a infantil.

baby-minder [bā'bēmīndûr] n (Brit) persona que cuida a los niños mientras la madre trabaja.

baby-sit [bā'bēsit] vi hacer de canguro.

baby-sitter [bā'bēsitûr] n canguro/a.

bachelor [bach'əlûr] n soltero; **B~ of Arts/ Science (BA/BSc)** licenciado/a en Filosofía y Letras/Ciencias.

back [bak] n (of person) espalda; (of animal) lomo; (of hand) dorso; (as opposed to front) parte f de atrás; (of room, car, etc) fondo; (of chair) respaldo; (of page) reverso; (SOCCER) defensa m; **to have one's ~ to the wall** (fig) estar entre la espada y la pared; **at the ~ of my mind was the thought that ...** en el fondo tenía la idea de que ... ♦ vt (candidate: also: ~ **up**) respaldar, apoyar; (horse: at races) apostar a; (car) dar marcha atrás a or con ♦ vi (car etc) dar marcha atrás ♦ a (in compounds) de atrás; ~ **seats/wheels** (AUT) asientos mpl/ruedas fpl de atrás; ~ **garden/room** jardín m/habitación f de atrás; ~ **payments** pagos mpl con efecto retroactivo; ~ **rent** renta atrasada; **to take a ~ seat** (fig) pasar a segundo plano ♦ ad (not forward) (hacia) atrás; **he's ~** (returned) está de vuelta, ha vuelto; **he ran ~** volvió corriendo; **throw the ball ~** (restitution) devuelve la pelota; **can I have it ~?** ¿me lo devuelve?; **he called ~** (again) llamó de nuevo; ~ **and forth** el uno al otro, entre sí; **as far ~ as the 13th century** ya en el siglo XIII; **when will you be ~?** ¿cuándo volverá?

back down vi echarse atrás.
back on to vt fus (Brit): **the house ~s on to the golf course** por atrás la casa da al campo de golf.
back out vi (of promise) volverse atrás.
back up vt (support: person) apoyar, respaldar; (: theory) defender; (car) dar marcha atrás a; (COMPUT) hacer una copia preventiva or de reserva de.
backache [bak'āk] n dolor m de espalda.
backbencher [bak'benchûr] n (Brit) miembro/a del parlamento sin portafolio.
backbiting [bak'bīting] n murmuración f.
backbone [bak'bōn] n columna vertebral; **the ~ of the organization** el pilar de la organización.
back burner n: **to put sth on the ~** ralentizar algo.
backcloth [bak'klôth] n telón m de fondo.
backcomb [bak'kōm] vt cardar.
backdate [bakdāt'] vt (letter) poner fecha atrasada a; **~d pay raise** alza de sueldo con efecto retroactivo.
backdrop [bak'drâp] n = **backcloth**.
backer [bak'ûr] n partidario/a; (COMM) promotor(a) m/f.
backfire [bak'fīûr] vi (AUT) petardear; (plans) fallar, salir mal.
backgammon [bak'gamən] n backgammon m.
background [bak'ground] n fondo; (of events) antecedentes mpl; (basic knowledge) bases fpl; (experience) conocimientos mpl, educación f ♦ cpd (noise, music) de fondo; (COMPUT) secundario; ~ **reading** lectura de fondo, preparación f; **fa-**

mily ~ origen m, antecedentes mpl.
backhand [bak'hand] n (TENNIS: also: ~ **stroke**) revés m.
backhanded [bak'handid] a (fig) ambiguo, equívoco.
backhander [bak'handûr] n (Brit: bribe) soborno.
backing [bak'ing] n (fig) apoyo, respaldo; (COMM) respaldo financiero; (MUS) acompañamiento.
backlash [bak'lash] n reacción f, resaca.
backlog [bak'lôg] n: ~ **of work** atrasos mpl.
back number n (of magazine etc) número atrasado.
backpack [bak'pak] n mochila.
backpacker [bak'pakûr] n mochilero/a.
back pay n pago atrasado.
backpedal [bak'pedəl] vi (fig) volverse/echarse atrás.
backside [bak'sīd] n (col) trasero, culo.
backslash [bak'slash] n pleca, barra inversa.
backslide [bak'slīd] vi reincidir, recaer.
backspace [bak'spās] vi (in typing) retroceder.
backstage [bak'stāj'] ad entre bastidores.
back-street [bak'strēt] a de barrio; ~ **abortionist** abortista m/f ilegal.
backstroke [bak'strōk] n braza de espaldas.
backtalk [bak'tôk] n réplicas fpl.
backtrack [bak'trak] vi (fig) = **backpedal**.
backup [bak'up] a (train, plane) suplementario; (COMPUT: disk, file) de reserva ♦ n (support) apoyo; (also: ~ **file**) copia preventiva or de reserva; (US: traffic) embotellamiento, acumulación f.
backup lights [bak'up līts] npl (US) luces fpl de marcha atrás.
backward [bak'wûrd] a (movement) hacia atrás; (person, country) atrasado; (shy) tímido.
backwardness [bak'wûrdnis] n atraso.
backwards [bak'wûrdz] ad (move, go) hacia atrás; (read a list) al revés; (fall) de espaldas; **to know sth ~ and forwards** or (Brit) ~ (col) saberse algo al dedillo.
backwater [bak'wôtûr] n (fig) lugar m atrasado or apartado.
backyard [bak'yârd] n traspatio.
bacon [bā'kən] n tocino, beicon m.
bacteria [baktē'rēə] npl bacteria sg.
bacteriology [baktērēál'əjē] n bacteriología.
bad [bad] a malo; (serious) grave; (meat, food) podrido, pasado; **his ~ leg** su pierna lisiada; **to go ~** pasarse; **to have a ~ time of it** pasarlo mal; **I feel ~ about it** (guilty) tengo remordimientos; ~ **debt** (COMM) cuenta incobrable; **in ~ faith** de mala fe.
bade [bad] pt of **bid**.
bad feeling n rencor m.
badge [baj] n insignia; (metal ~) chapa,

placa; (*stick-on*) pegatina.
badger [baj'ûr] *n* tejón *m*.
badly [bad'lē] *ad* (*work, dress etc*) mal; ~
wounded gravemente herido; **he needs it**
~ le hace gran falta; **to be** ~ **off (for**
money) andar mal de dinero; **things are**
going ~ las cosas van muy mal.
bad-mannered [badman'ûrd] *a* grosero,
mal educado.
badminton [bad'mintən] *n* bádminton *m*.
bad-mouth [bad'mouth'] *vt* (*US*) criticar.
bad-smelling [bad'smel'ing] *a* maloliente.
bad-tempered [bad'tem'pûrd] *a* de mal genio *or* carácter; (*temporary*) de mal humor.
baffle [baf'əl] *vt* desconcertar, confundir.
baffling [baf'ling] *a* incomprensible.
bag [bag] *n* bolsa, saco; (*handbag*) bolso;
(*satchel*) mochila; (*case*) maleta; (*of*
hunter) caza ♦ *vt* (*col: take*) coger (*Sp*),
agarrar (*LAm*), pescar; ~s **of** (*col: lots*
of) un montón de; **to pack one's** ~s hacer
las maletas.
bagful [bag'fəl] *n* saco (lleno).
baggage [bag'ij] *n* equipaje *m*.
baggage check *n* talón *m* de equipaje.
baggage claim *n* reclamación *f* de equipajes.
baggy [bag'ē] *a* (*trousers*) con rodilleras.
Baghdad [bag'dad] *n* Bagdad *m*.
bagpipes [bag'pīps] *npl* gaita *sg*.
bag-snatcher [bag'snachûr] *n* (*Brit*)
ladrón/ona *m/f* de bolsos.
Bahamas [bəhâm'əz] *npl*: **the** ~ las Islas
Bahama.
Bahrain [bárān'] *n* Bahrein *m*.
bail [bāl] *n* fianza ♦ *vt* (*prisoner: also*: **grant**
~ **to**) poner en libertad bajo fianza; (*boat:*
also: ~ **out**) achicar; **on** ~ (*prisoner*) bajo
fianza; **to be released on** ~ ser puesto en
libertad bajo fianza.
bail out *vi* (*of a plane*) lanzarse en paracaídas ♦ *vt* (*NAUT: water*) sacar; (: *boat*)
achicar; **to** ~ **sb out** obtener la libertad de
uno bajo fianza; (*US*): **to** ~ **sb out of a**
difficulty sacar a uno de un problema.
bailiff [bā'lif] *n* alguacil *m*.
bait [bāt] *n* cebo ♦ *vt* cebar.
bake [bāk] *vt* cocer (al horno) ♦ *vi* (*cook*)
cocerse; (*be hot*) hacer un calor terrible.
baked beans [bākt bēnz] *npl* judías *fpl* en
salsa de tomate.
baked potatoes [bākt pətā'tōz] *n* patatas
fpl asadas con piel.
baker [bā'kûr] *n* panadero/a.
baker's dozen [bā'kûrz du'zən] *n* docena
del fraile.
bakery [bā'kûrē] *n* (*for bread*) panadería;
(*for cakes*) pastelería.
baking [bā'king] *n* (*act*) amasar *m*; (*batch*)
hornada.
baking chocolate *n* (*US*) chocolate *m*
fondant.

baking powder *n* levadura (en polvo).
baking pan, (*Brit*) **baking tin** *n* tortera.
baking sheet *n* bandeja de horno.
balaclava [baləklâv'ə] *n* (*Brit: also*: ~
helmet) pasamontañas *m inv*.
balance [bal'əns] *n* equilibrio; (*COMM:*
sum) balance *m*; (*remainder*) resto;
(*scales*) balanza ♦ *vt* equilibrar; (*budget*)
nivelar; (*account*) saldar; (*compensate*)
contrapesar; ~ **of trade/payments** balanza
de comercio/pagos; ~ **carried forward** balance *m* pasado a cuenta nueva; ~ **brought**
forward saldo de hoja anterior; **to** ~ **the**
books hacer el balance.
balanced [bal'ənst] *a* (*personality, diet*)
equilibrado.
balance sheet *n* balance *m*.
balcony [bal'kənē] *n* (*open*) balcón *m*;
(*closed*) galería; **first/second** ~ (*US*) la
galería superior.
bald [bôld] *a* calvo; (*tire*) liso.
baldness [bôld'nis] *n* calvicie *f*.
bale [bāl] *n* (*AGR*) paca, fardo.
bale out (*Brit*) *vi* (*of a plane*) lanzarse
en paracaídas ♦ *vt* (*NAUT: water*) sacar; (:
boat) achicar; **to** ~ **sb out of a difficulty**
sacar a uno de un problema.
Balearic Islands [balēār'ək i'ləndz] *npl*:
the ~ las Islas Baleares.
baleful [bāl'fəl] *a* (*look*) triste; (*sinister*) funesto, siniestro.
balk [bôk] *vi*: **to** ~ (**at**) resistirse (a);
(*horse*) plantarse (ante).
Balkan [bôl'kən] *a* balcánico ♦ *n*: **the** ~s los
Balcanes.
ball [bôl] *n* (*sphere*) bola; (*football*) balón
m; (*for tennis, golf etc*) pelota; (*dance*)
baile *m*; **to be on the** ~ (*fig: competent*)
estar enterado; (: *alert*) ser despabilado;
to play ~ (**with sb**) jugar a la pelota (con
uno); (*fig*) cooperar; **to start the** ~ **rolling**
(*fig*) empezar; **the** ~ **is in your court** (*fig*)
le toca a usted.
ballad [bal'əd] *n* balada, romance *m*.
ballast [bal'əst] *n* lastre *m*.
ball bearing *n* cojinete *m* de bolas.
ballcock [bôl'kâk] *n* llave *f* de bola *or* de flotador.
ballerina [balərē'nə] *n* bailarina.
ballet [bala'] *n* ballet *m*.
ballet dancer *n* bailarín/ina *m/f* (de ballet).
ballistic [bəlis'tik] *a* balístico; **intercontinental** ~ **missile** misil *m* balístico
intercontinental.
ballistics [bəlis'tiks] *n* balística.
balloon [bəlōōn'] *n* globo; (*in comic strip*)
globo, bocadillo ♦ *vi* dispararse.
balloonist [bəlōō'nist] *n* ascensionista *m/f*.
ballot [bal'ət] *n* votación *f*; (*US: also*: ~ **pa-**
per) papeleta.
ballot box *n* urna (electoral).
ballot paper *n* (*Brit*) papeleta.

ballpark [bôl'pârk] *n* (*US*) estadio de béisbol; ~ **figure** cifra aproximada.

ball-point (pen) [bôl'point (pen')] *n* bolígrafo.

ballroom [bôl'rōōm] *n* salón *m* de baile.

balm [bâm] *n* (*also fig*) bálsamo.

balmy [bá'mē] *a* (*breeze*, *air*) suave, fragante; (*col*) = **barmy**.

balsa [bôl'sə] *n* (madera de) balsa.

Baltic [bôl'tik] *a* báltico ♦ *n*: **the ~ (Sea)** el (Mar) Báltico.

balustrade [bal'əstrād] *n* barandilla.

bamboo [bambōō'] *n* bambú *m*.

bamboozle [bambōō'zəl] *vt* (*col*) embaucar, engatusar.

ban [ban] *n* prohibición *f*, proscripción *f* ♦ *vt* prohibir, proscribir; (*exclude*) excluir; **he was ~ned from driving** le prohibieron conducir.

banal [bənal'] *a* banal, vulgar.

banana [bənan'ə] *n* plátano, banana (*LAm*).

band [band] *n* (*group*) banda; (*gang*) pandilla; (*strip*) faja, tira; (: *circular*) anillo; (*at a dance*) orquesta; (*MIL*) banda.

band together *vi* juntarse, asociarse.

bandage [ban'dij] *n* venda, vendaje *m* ♦ *vt* vendar.

bandaid [band'ād'] ® *n* (*US*) tirita.

bandit [ban'dit] *n* bandido; **one-armed ~** máquina tragaperras.

bandstand [band'stand] *n* quiosco.

bandwagon [band'wagən] *n*: **to jump on the ~** (*fig*) subirse al carro.

bandy [ban'dē] *vt* (*jokes*, *insults*) cambiar.

bandy-legged [ban'dēlegid] *a* estevado.

bane [bān] *n*: **it** (*or* **he** *etc*) **is the ~ of my life** me amarga la vida.

bang [bang] *n* estallido; (*of door*) portazo; (*blow*) golpe *m* ♦ *vt* hacer estallar; (*door*) cerrar de golpe ♦ *vi* estallar **to ~ into sth** chocar con algo, golpearse contra algo; *see also* **bangs**.

banger [bang'ûr] *n* (*firework*) petardo; (*Brit*: *car*: *also*: **old ~**) armatoste *m*, cacharro; (*Brit col*: *sausage*) salchicha.

Bangkok [bang'kâk] *n* Bangkok *m*.

Bangladesh [banggladesh'] *n* Bangladesh *f*.

bangle [bang'gəl] *n* ajorca.

bangs [bangz] *npl* (*US*) flequillo *sg*.

banish [ban'ish] *vt* desterrar.

banister(s) [ban'istûr(z)] *n(pl)* pasamanos *m inv*.

banjo, [ban'jō] *pl* ~es *or* ~s *n* banjo.

bank [bangk] *n* (*COMM*) banco; (*of river*, *lake*) ribera, orilla; (*of earth*) terraplén *m* ♦ *vi* (*AVIAT*) ladearse; (*COMM*): **to ~ with** tener la cuenta con.

bank on *vt fus* contar con.

bank account *n* cuenta de banco.

bank card *n* tarjeta de crédito.

bank charges *npl* comisión *fsg*.

bank draft *n* giro bancario.

banker [bangk'ûr] *n* banquero; **~'s order** orden *f* bancaria.

Bank holiday *n* (*Brit*) día *m* festivo.

banking [bangk'ing] *n* banca.

bank loan *n* empréstito.

bank manager *n* director(a) *m/f* local del banco.

banknote [bangk'nōt] *n* billete *m* de banco.

bank rate *n* tipo de interés bancario.

bankrupt [bangk'rupt] *n* quebrado/a ♦ *a* quebrado, insolvente; **to go ~** hacer bancarrota; **to be ~** estar en quiebra.

bankruptcy [bangk'ruptsē] *n* quiebra, bancarrota.

bank statement *n* extracto de cuenta.

banner [ban'ûr] *n* bandera; (*in demonstration*) pancarta.

banns [banz] *npl* amonestaciones *fpl*.

banquet [bang'kwit] *n* banquete *m*.

banter [ban'tûr] *n* guasa, chungas *fpl*.

BAOR *n abbr* (= *British Army of the Rhine*) fuerzas británicas en Alemania.

baptism [bap'tizəm] *n* bautismo; (*act*) bautizo.

baptize [baptīz'] *vt* bautizar.

bar [bâr] *n* barra; (*on door*) tranca; (*of window*, *cage*) reja; (*of soap*) pastilla; (*fig*: *hindrance*) obstáculo; (*prohibition*) proscripción *f*; (*place*) bar *m*; (*counter*) mostrador *m*; (*MUS*) barra ♦ *vt* (*road*) obstruir; (*window*, *door*) atrancar; (*person*) excluir; (*activity*) prohibir; **behind ~s** entre rejas; **the B~** (*LAW*: *profession*) la abogacía; (: *people*) el cuerpo de abogados; **~ none** sin excepción.

Barbados [bârbā'dōs] *n* Barbados *m*.

barbarian [bârbâr'ēən] *n* bárbaro/a.

barbaric [bârbar'ik] *a* bárbaro.

barbarity [bârbar'itē] *n* barbaridad *f*.

barbarous [bâr'bûrəs] *a* bárbaro.

barbecue [bâr'bəkyōō] *n* barbacoa.

barbed wire [bârbd wiûr] *n* alambre *m* de púas.

barber [bâr'bûr] *n* peluquero, barbero.

barbiturate [bârbich'ûrit] *n* barbitúrico.

Barcelona [bârsəlō'nə] *n* Barcelona *f*.

bar chart *n* gráfico de barras.

bar code *n* código de barras.

bare [bâr] *a* desnudo; (*head*) descubierto ♦ *vt* desnudar; **to ~ one's teeth** enseñar los dientes.

bareback [bâr'bak] *ad* sin silla.

barefaced [bâr'fāst] *a* descarado.

barefoot [bâr'fōōt] *a*, *ad* descalzo.

bareheaded [bâr'hedid] *a* descubierto, sin sombrero.

barely [bâr'lē] *ad* apenas.

bareness [bâr'nis] *n* desnudez *f*.

Barents Sea [bâr'ənts sē] *n*: **the ~** el Mar de Barents.

bargain [bâr'gin] *n* pacto, negocio; (*good buy*) ganga ♦ *vi* negociar; (*haggle*) regatear; **into the ~** además, por añadidura.

bargain for *vt fus* (*col*): **he got more**

than he ~**ed for** le resultó peor de lo que esperaba.

bargaining [bár'gining] *n* negociación *f*; regateo; ~ **table** mesa de negociaciones.

barge [bârj] *n* barcaza.

barge in *vi* irrumpir; (*conversation*) entrometerse.

barge into *vt fus* dar contrà.

baritone [bar'itōn] *n* barítono.

barium meal [bar'ēəm mēl'] *n* (*MED*) comida de bario.

bark [bárk] *n* (*of tree*) corteza; (*of dog*) ladrido ♦ *vi* ladrar.

barley [bár'lē] *n* cebada.

barley sugar *n* azúcar *m* cande.

barmaid [bár'mād] *n* camarera.

barman [bár'mən] *n* camarero, barman *m*.

barmy [bár'mē] *a* (*col*) chiflado, lelo.

barn [bárn] *n* granero; (*for animals*) cuadra.

barnacle [bár'nəkəl] *n* percebe *m*.

barometer [bərâm'itûr] *n* barómetro.

baron [bar'ən] *n* barón *m*; (*fig*) magnate *m*; **the press** ~**s** los magnates de la prensa.

baroness [bar'ənis] *n* baronesa.

baroque [bərōk'] *a* barroco.

barracks [bar'əks] *npl* cuartel *msg*.

barrage [bərâzh'] *n* (*MIL*) descarga, bombardeo; (*dam*) presa; (*fig: of criticism etc*) lluvia, aluvión *m*; **a** ~ **of questions** una lluvia de preguntas.

barrel [bar'əl] *n* tonel *m*, barril *m*; (*of gun*) cañón *m*.

barren [bar'ən] *a* estéril.

barrette [bəret'] *n* pasador *m*.

barricade [bar'əkād] *n* barricada ♦ *vt* cerrar con barricadas.

barrier [bar'ēûr] *n* barrera; (*crash* ~) barrera.

barrier cream *n* (*Brit*) crema protectora.

barring [bár'ing] *prep* excepto, salvo.

barrister [bar'istûr] *n* (*Brit*) abogado/a.

barrow [bar'ō] *n* (*cart*) carretilla (de mano).

barstool [bár'stōōl] *n* taburete *m* (de bar).

bartender [bár'tendûr] *n* camarero, barman *m*.

barter [bár'tûr] *vt*: **to** ~ **sth for sth** trocar algo por algo.

base [bās] *n* base *f* ♦ *vt*: **to** ~ **sth on** basar *or* fundar algo en ♦ *a* bajo, infame; **to** ~ **at** (*troops*) estacionar en; **I'm** ~**d in New York** (*work*) trabajo en Nueva York.

baseball [bās'bôl] *n* béisbol *m*.

baseboard [bās'bôrd] *n* (*US*) rodapié *m*.

base camp *n* campamento base.

Basel [báz'əl] *n* Basilea.

baseless [bās'lis] *a* infundado.

basement [bās'mənt] *n* sótano.

base pay *n* sueldo básico.

base rate *n* tipo base.

bases [bā'sēz] *npl of* **basis** ♦ [bā'siz] *npl of* **base**.

bash [bash] *n*: **I'll have a** ~ **(at it)** lo intenta-

ré ♦ *vt* (*col*) golpear.

bash up *vt* (*col: car*) estrellar; (: *person*) aporrear, vapulear.

bashful [bash'fəl] *a* tímido, vergonzoso.

bashing [bash'ing] *n* (*col*) tunda; **to go Paki-/ queer-**~ ir a dar una paliza a los paquistaníes/a los maricas.

BASIC [bā'sik] *n* BASIC *m*.

basic [bā'sik] *a* (*salary etc*) básico; (*elementary: principles*) fundamental.

basically [bā'siklē] *ad* fundamentalmente, en el fondo.

basic rate *n* (*of tax*) base *f* mínima imponible.

basil [baz'əl] *n* albahaca.

basin [bā'sin] *n* (*vessel*) cuenco, tazón *m*; (*GEO*) cuenca; (*also:* **wash**~) palangana, jofaina.

basis [bā'sis], *pl* **-ses** [-sēz] *n* base *f*; **on the** ~ **of what you've said** a base de lo que has dicho.

bask [bask] *vi*: **to** ~ **in the sun** tomarr el sol.

basket [bas'kit] *n* cesta, cesto; (*with handle*) canasta.

basketball [bas'kitbôl] *n* baloncesto.

basketball player *n* jugador(a) *m/f* de baloncesto.

basketwork [bas'kitwûrk] *n* cestería.

Basle [baz'əl] *n* Basilea.

Basque [bask] *a, n* vasco/a *m/f*.

Basque Country *n* Euskadi *m*, País *m* Vasco.

bass [bās] *n* (*MUS*) contrabajo.

bass clef [bās klef] *n* clave *f* de fa.

bassoon [basōōn'] *n* bajón *m*.

bastard [bas'tûrd] *n* bastardo/a; (*col!*) hijo de puta (*!*).

baste [bāst] *vt* (*CULIN*) pringar; (*US: stitch*) hilvanar.

bastion [bas'chən] *n* bastión *m*, baluarte *m*.

bat [bat] *n* (*ZOOL*) murciélago; (*for ball games*) palo; (*for cricket, baseball*) bate *m*; (*Brit: for table tennis*) pala; **he didn't** ~ **an eyelid** ni pestañeó, ni se inmutó.

batch [bach] *n* (*of bread*) hornada; (*of goods, work*) lote *m*; (*of applicants, letters*) montón *m*.

batch processing *n* (*COMPUT*) proceso por lotes.

bated [bā'tid] *a*: **with** ~ **breath** sin respirar.

bath [bath, *pl* baṭhz] *n* (*action*) baño; (~*tub*) baño, bañera, tina (*LAm*) ♦ *vt* bañar; **to take a** ~ bañarse, tomar un baño; *see also* **baths**.

bathchair [bath'chär] *n* silla de ruedas.

bathe [bāṭh] *vi* bañarse; (*US*) tomar un baño ♦ *vt* (*wound etc*) lavar; (*US*) bañar, dar un baño a.

bather [bāṭh'ûr] *n* bañista *m/f*.

bathing [bā'ṭhing] *n* el bañarse.

bathing cap *n* gorro de baño.

bathing suit, (*Brit*) **bathing costume** *n* traje *m* de baño.
bathing trunks *npl* bañador *msg*.
bathmat [bath'mat] *n* estera de baño.
bathrobe [bath'rōb] *n* bata.
bathroom [bath'rōōm] *n* (cuarto de) baño.
baths [ba͟thz] *npl* piscina *sg*.
bath towel *n* toalla de baño.
bathtub [bath'tub] *n* bañera.
batman [bat'man] *n* (*Brit*) ordenanza *m*.
baton [batán'] *n* (*MUS*) batuta.
battalion [bətal'yən] *n* batallón *m*.
batten [bat'ən] *n* (*CARPENTRY*) listón *m*; (*NAUT*) junquillo, sable *m*.
  batten down *vt* (*NAUT*): **to ~ down the hatches** atrancar las escotillas.
batter [bat'ûr] *vt* apalear, azotar ♦ *n* batido.
battered [bat'ûrd] *a* (*hat, pan*) estropeado.
battery [bat'ûrē] *n* batería; (*of flashlight*) pila.
battery charger *n* cargador *m* de baterías.
battery farming *n* (*Brit*) cría intensiva.
battle [bat'əl] *n* batalla; (*fig*) lucha ♦ *vi* luchar; **that's half the ~** (*col*) ya hay medio camino andado; **to fight a losing ~** (*fig*) ir perdiendo poco a poco.
battlefield [bat'əlfēld] *n* campo *m* de batalla.
battlements [bat'əlmənts] *npl* almenas *fpl*.
battleship [bat'əlship] *n* acorazado.
batty [bat'ē] *a* chalado.
bauble [bô'bəl] *n* chuchería.
baud [bôd] *n* (*COMPUT*) baudio.
baud rate *n* (*COMPUT*) velocidad *f* (de transmisión) en baudios.
bauxite [bôk'sīt] *n* bauxita.
Bavaria [bəvär'ēə] *n* Baviera.
Bavarian [bəvär'ēən] *a, a* baviero/a *m/f*.
bawdy [bô'dē] *a* indecente; (*joke*) verde.
bawl [bôl] *vi* chillar, gritar.
  bawl out *vt* (*person*) echarle un rapapolvo a uno.
bay [bā] *n* (*GEO*) bahía; (*for parking*) parking *m*, estacionamiento; (*loading ~*) patio de carga; (*BOT*) laurel *m* ♦ *vi* aullar; **to hold sb at ~** mantener a alguien a raya.
bay leaf *n* (hoja de) laurel *m*.
bayonet [bā'ənet] *n* bayoneta.
bay window *n* ventana saladiza.
bazaar [bəzár'] *n* bazar *m*.
bazooka [bəzōō'kə] *n* bazuca.
B. & B. [bē and bē] *n abbr* (= *bed and breakfast*) cama y desayuno.
B.B.A. *n abbr* (*US*) = *Bachelor of Business Administration*.
BBB *n abbr* (*US*: = *Better Business Bureau*) organismo para la defensa del consumidor.
BBC *n abbr* (= *British Broadcasting Corporation*) cadena de radio y televisión estatal británica.
BC *ad abbr* (= *before Christ*) a. de J.C. ♦

abbr = *Bachelor of Commerce*; (*Canada*) = British Columbia.
BCG *n abbr* (= *Bacillus Calmette-Guérin*) vacuna de la tuberculosis.
BD *n abbr* (= *Bachelor of Divinity*) Licenciado/a en Teología.
B/D *abbr* = *bank draft*.
BDS *n abbr* (= *Bachelor of Dental Surgery*) título universitario.
be, *pt* **was, were,** *pp* **been** [bē, wâz, wûr, bēn] *vi* (*of state*) ser; (*of place, temporary condition*) estar; **I am American** soy norteamericano; **I am tired** estoy cansado; **how are you?** ¿cómo está usted?; **who is it?** ¿quién es?; **it's only me** (*emphatic*) soy yo; **it is raining** está lloviendo; **I am warm** tengo calor; **it is cold** hace frío; **how much is it?** ¿cuánto es *or* cuesta?; **he is four (years old)** tiene cuatro años; **2 and 2 are 4** dos más dos son cuatro; **it's 8 o'clock** son las 8; **where have you been?** ¿dónde has estado?, ¿de dónde vienes? ♦ *aux vb*: **what are you doing?** ¿qué estás haciendo?; **I've been waiting for her for two hours** le he estado esperando durante dos horas; **to ~ killed** ser matado; **he is nowhere to ~ found** no se le ve en ninguna parte; **the car is to ~ sold** el coche está de venta; **he was to have come yesterday** debía de haber venido ayer; **am I to understand that ...?** ¿debo entender que ...?; **if I were you** yo que tú.
B/E *abbr* = *bill of exchange*.
beach [bēch] *n* playa ♦ *vt* varar.
beach buggy [bēch' bug'ē] *n* buggy *m*.
beachcomber [bēch'kōmûr] *n* raquero/a.
beachwear [bēch'wär] *n* ropa de playa.
beacon [bē'kən] *n* (*lighthouse*) faro; (*marker*) guía; (*radio ~*) radiofaro.
bead [bēd] *n* cuenta, abalorio; (*of dew, sweat*) gota; **~s** *npl* (*necklace*) collar *m*.
beady [bē'dē] *a* (*eyes*) pequeño y brillante.
beagle [bē'gəl] *n* sabueso pequeño.
beak [bēk] *n* pico; (*nose*) narigón.
beaker [bē'kûr] *n* jarra.
beam [bēm] *n* (*ARCH*) viga, travesaño; (*of light*) rayo, haz *m* de luz; (*RADIO*) rayo ♦ *vi* brillar; (*smile*) sonreír; **to drive on** (*US*) **high** *or* (*Brit*) **full ~** conducir con luz de carretera.
beaming [bē'ming] *a* (*sun, smile*) radiante.
bean [bēn] *n* judía; **runner/broad ~** habichuela/haba; **coffee ~** grano de café.
bean shoots *npl*, **bean sprouts** *npl* brotes *mpl* de soja.
bear [bär] *n* oso; (*STOCK EXCHANGE*) bajista *m* ♦ (*vb*: *pt* **bore,** *pp* **borne**) *vt* (*weight etc*) llevar; (*cost*) pagar; (*responsibility*) tener; (*traces, signs*) mostrar; (*produce: fruit*) dar; (*COMM: interest*) devengar; (*endure*) soportar, aguantar; (*stand up to*) resistir a; (*children*) parir ♦ *vi*: **to ~ right/left** torcer a la derecha/izquierda; **I**

can't ~ him no le puedo ver, no lo soporto; **to bring pressure to ~ on sb** ejercer presión sobre uno.

bear on vt fus tener que ver con, referirse a.

bear out vt fus (suspicions) corroborar, confirmar; (person) llevar.

bear up vi (cheer up) animarse; **he bore up well under the strain** resistió bien la presión.

bear with vt fus (sb's moods, temper) tener paciencia con.

bearable [bär'əbəl] a soportable, aguantable.

beard [bērd] n barba.

bearded [bērd'id] a barbado.

bearer [bär'ûr] n (of news, cheque) portador(a) m/f; (of passport) titular m/f.

bearing [bär'ing] n porte m, comportamiento; (connection) relación f; (ball) ~s npl cojinetes mpl a bolas; **to take a ~** marcarse; **to find one's ~s** orientarse.

bearskin [bär'skin] n (MIL) gorro militar (de piel de oso).

beast [bēst] n bestia; (col) bruto, salvaje m.

beastly [bēst'lē] a bestial; (awful) horrible.

beat [bēt] n (of heart) latido; (MUS) ritmo, compás m; (of policeman) ronda ♦ a (US col) hecho polvo ♦ (vb: pt **beat**, pp **beaten**) vt (hit) golpear; (eggs) batir; (defeat) vencer, derrotar; (better) sobrepasar; (drum) tocar; (rhythm) marcar ♦ vi (heart) latir; **off the ~en track** aislado; **to ~ about the bush** ir por rodeos; **to ~ it** largarse; **that ~s everything!** (col) ¡eso es el colmo!; **to ~ on a door** dar golpes en una puerta.

beat down vt (door) derribar a golpes; (price) conseguir rebajar, regatear; (seller) hacer rebajar ♦ vi (rain) llover a cántaros; (sun) caer de plomo.

beat off vt rechazar.

beat up vt (col: person) dar una paliza a.

beater [bē'tûr] n (for eggs, cream) batidora.

beating [bē'ting] n golpeo; (defeat) derrota; **to take a ~** salir derrotado.

beat-up [bēt'up] a (col) estropeado.

beautiful [byōō'təfəl] a hermoso, bello.

beautifully [byōō'təfəlē] ad maravillosamente.

beautify [byōō'təfī] vt embellecer.

beauty [byōō'tē] n belleza, hermosura; (concept, person) belleza; **the ~ of it is that ...** lo mejor de esto es que ....

beauty contest n concurso de belleza.

beauty queen n reina de la belleza.

beauty salon n salón m de belleza.

beauty spot n lunar m postizo; (Brit: TOURISM) lugar m pintoresco.

beaver [bē'vûr] n castor m.

becalmed [bikämd'] a encalmado.

became [bikām'] pt of **become**.

because [bikôz'] conj porque; **~ of** prep debido a, a causa de.

beck [bek] n: **to be at the ~ and call of** estar a disposición de.

beckon [bek'ən] vt (also: ~ **to**) llamar con señas.

become [bikum'] (irg: like **come**) vi (+ noun) hacerse, llegar a ser; (+ adj) ponerse, volverse ♦ vt (suit) favorecer, sentar bien a; **to ~ fat** engordarse; **to ~ angry** enfadarse; **it became known that ...** se descubrió que ....

becoming [bikum'ing] a (behavior) decoroso; (clothes) favorecedor(a).

becquerel [bekərel'] n becquerelio.

BEd n abbr (= Bachelor of Education) título universitario.

bed [bed] n cama; (of flowers) macizo; (of sea, lake) fondo; (of coal, clay) capa; **to go to ~** acostarse.

bed down vi acostarse.

bed and breakfast (B. & B.) n (place) pensión f; (terms) cama y desayuno.

bedbug [bed'bug] n chinche f.

bedclothes [bed'klōz] npl ropa de cama.

bedding [bed'ing] n ropa de cama.

bedeck [bidek'] vt engalanar, adornar.

bedevil [bidev'əl] vt (dog) acosar; (trouble) fastidiar.

bedfellow [bed'felō] n: **they are strange ~s** (fig) son extraños compañeros de cama.

bedlam [bed'ləm] n confusión f.

bedpan [bed'pan] n bacinilla (de cama).

bedraggled [bidrag'əld] a mojado, desastrado.

bedridden [bed'ridən] a postrado (en cama).

bedrock [bed'râk] n (GEO) roca firme; (fig) fondo de la cuestión.

bedroom [bed'rōōm] n dormitorio, alcoba.

Beds [bedz] abbr (Brit) = Bedfordshire.

bedside [bed'sīd] n: **at sb's ~** a la cabecera de alguien.

bedside lamp n lámpara de noche.

bedsit(ter) [bed'sit(ûr)] n (Brit) estudio, suite m (LAm).

bedspread [bed'spred] n sobrecama m, colcha.

bedtime [bed'tīm] n hora de acostarse; **it's ~** es hora de acostarse or de irse a la cama.

bee [bē] n abeja; **to have a ~ in one's bonnet (about sth)** tener una idea fija (de algo).

beech [bēch] n haya.

beef [bēf] n carne f de vaca; **roast ~** rosbif m.

beef up vt (col) reforzar.

beefburger [bēf'bûrgûr] n (Brit) hamburguesa.

beefeater [bēf'ētûr] n alabardero de la Torre de Londres.

beehive [bē'hīv] n colmena.

beeline [bē'līn] n: **to make a ~ for** ir derecho a.

been [bin] pp of **be.**

beeper [bēp'ûr] n (of doctor etc) busca m.

beer [bēr] n cerveza.

beer can n bote m or lata de cerveza.

beet [bēt] n (US) remolacha.

beetle [bēt'əl] n escarabajo.

beetroot [bēt'rōōt] n (Brit) remolacha.

befall [bifôl'] vi (vt) (irg: like **fall**) acontecer (a).

befit [bifit'] vt convenir a, corresponder a.

before [bifôr'] prep (of time) antes de; (of space) delante de ♦ conj antes (de) que ♦ ad (time) antes, anteriormente; (space) delante, adelante; **~ going** antes de marcharse; **~ she goes** antes de que se vaya; **the week ~** la semana anterior; **I've never seen it ~** no lo he visto nunca.

beforehand [bifôr'hand] ad de antemano, con anticipación.

befriend [bifrend'] vt ofrecer amistad a, ayudar.

befuddled [bifud'əld] a aturdido, atontado.

beg [beg] vi pedir limosna ♦ vt pedir, rogar; (entreat) suplicar; **I ~ your pardon** (apologising) perdóname; (not hearing) ¿perdón?

began [bigan'] pt of **begin.**

beggar [beg'ûr] n mendigo/a.

begin [bigin'] pt **began,** pp **begun** [bigin', bigan', bigun'] vt, vi empezar, comenzar; **to ~ doing** or **to do sth** empezar a hacer algo; **I can't ~ to thank you** no encuentro palabras para agradecerle; **to ~ with, I'd like to know ...** en primer lugar, quisiera saber ...; **~ning from Monday** a partir del lunes.

beginner [bigin'ûr] n principiante m/f.

beginner's slope [bigin'ûrz slōp] n (SKI) cuesta para principiantes.

beginning [bigin'ing] n principio, comienzo; **right from the ~** desde el principio.

begrudge [bigruj'] vt: **to ~ sb sth** tenerle envidia a alguien por algo.

beguile [bigīl'] vt (enchant) seducir.

beguiling [bigī'ling] a seductor(a), atractivo.

begun [bigun'] pp of **begin.**

behalf [bihaf'] n: **in ~ of,** (Brit) **on ~ of** en nombre de, por.

behave [bihāv'] vi (person) portarse, comportarse; (thing) funcionar; (well: also: **~ o.s.**) portarse bien.

behavior, (Brit) **behaviour** [bihāv'yûr] n comportamiento, conducta.

behead [bihed'] vt decapitar, descabezar.

beheld [biheld'] pt, pp of **behold.**

behind [bihīnd'] prep detrás de ♦ ad detrás, por detrás, atrás ♦ n trasero; **to be ~ (schedule)** ir retrasado; **~ the scenes** (fig) entre bastidores; **we're ~ them in technology** (fig) les quedamos atrás en tecnología; **to leave sth ~** olvidar or dejarse algo; **to be ~ with sth** estar atrasado en algo; **to be ~ with payments (on sth)** estar atrasado en el pago (de algo).

behold [bihōld'] (irg: like **hold**) vt contemplar.

beige [bāzh] a color beige.

being [bē'ing] n ser m; **to come into ~** nacer, aparecer.

Beirut [bārōōt'] n Beirut m.

belated [bilā'tid] a atrasado, tardío.

belch [belch] vi eructar ♦ vt (also: **~ out:** smoke etc) arrojar.

beleaguered [bilē'gûrd] a (city, fig) asediado; (army) asediado.

Belfast [bel'fast] n Belfast m.

belfry [bel'frē] n campanario.

Belgian [bel'jən] a, n belga m/f.

Belgium [bel'jəm] n Bélgica.

Belgrade [belgrād'] n Belgrado.

belie [bilī'] vt (give false impression of) desmentir, contradecir.

belief [bilēf'] n (opinion) opinión f; (trust, faith) fe f; (acceptance as true) creencia; **it's beyond ~** es increíble; **in the ~ that** en la creencia de que.

believable [bilēv'əbəl] a creíble.

believe [bilēv'] vt, vi creer; **to ~ (that)** creer (que); **to ~ in** (God, ghosts) creer en; (method) ser partidario de; **he is ~d to be abroad** se cree que está en el extranjero; **I don't ~ in corporal punishment** no soy partidario del castigo corporal.

believer [bilēv'ûr] n (in idea, activity) partidario/a; (REL) creyente m/f.

belittle [bilit'əl] vt minimizar, despreciar.

Belize [bəlēz'] n Belice f.

bell [bel] n campana; (small) campanilla; (on door) timbre m; (animal's) cencerro; (on toy etc) cascabel m; **that rings a ~** (fig) eso me suena.

bellboy [bel'boi] n (Brit) = **bellhop.**

bellhop [bel'hâp] n (US) botones m inv.

belligerent [bəlij'ûrənt] a (at war) beligerante; (fig) agresivo.

bellow [bel'ō] vi bramar; (person) rugir ♦ vt (orders) gritar, vociferar.

bellows [bel'ōz] npl fuelle msg.

belly [bel'ē] n barriga, panza.

bellyache [bel'ēāk] n dolor m de barriga or de tripa ♦ vi (col) quejarse.

belong [bilông'] vi: **to ~ to** pertenecer a; (club etc) ser socio de; **this book ~s here** este libro va aquí.

belongings [bilông'ingz] npl: **personal ~** pertenencias fpl.

beloved [biluv'id] a, n querido/a m/f, amado/a m/f.

below [bilō'] prep bajo, debajo de ♦ ad abajo, (por) debajo; **see ~** véase más abajo.

belt [belt] n cinturón m; (TECH) correa, cinta ♦ vt (thrash) golpear con correa; **industrial ~** zona industrial.

belt out vt (song) cantar a voz en grito

or a grito pelado.
belt up *vi* (*Brit AUT*) ponerse el cinturón de seguridad; (*fig, col*) cerrar el pico.
beltway |belt'wā| *n* (*US AUT*) carretera de circunvalación.
bemoan |bimōn'| *vt* lamentar.
bemused |bimyōōzd'| *a* aturdido, confuso.
bench |bench| *n* banco; **the B~** (*LAW*) el tribunal; (*people*) la judicatura.
bench mark *n* punto de referencia.
bend |bend| *vb* (*pt, pp* **bent** |bent|) *vt* doblar, inclinar; (*leg, arm*) torcer ♦ *vi* inclinarse; (*road*) curvarse ♦ *n* (*Brit*: *in road, river*) recodo; (*in pipe*) codo; *see also* **bends.**
bend down *vi* inclinarse, doblarse.
bend over *vi* inclinarse.
bends |bendz| *npl* (*MED*) apoplejía por cambios bruscos de presión.
beneath |binēth'| *prep* bajo, debajo de; (*unworthy of*) indigno de ♦ *ad* abajo, (por) debajo.
benefactor |ben'əfaktûr| *n* bienhechor *m*.
benefactress |ben'əfaktris| *n* bienhechora.
beneficial |benəfish'əl| *a*: ~ **to** beneficioso para.
beneficiary |benəfish'ēärē| *n* (*LAW*) beneficiario/a.
benefit |ben'əfit| *n* beneficio, provecho; (*allowance of money*) subsidio ♦ *vt* beneficiar; ~ **society** (*US*) sociedad *f* de beneficiencia ♦ *vi*: **he'll ~ from it** le sacará provecho; **unemployment ~** subsidio de paro.
Benelux |ben'əluks| *n* Benelux *m*.
benevolence |bənev'ələns| *n* benevolencia.
benevolent |bənev'ələnt| *a* benévolo.
BEng *n abbr* (= *Bachelor of Engineering*) título universitario.
benign |binīn'| *a* (*person, MED*) benigno; (*smile*) afable.
bent |bent| *pt, pp of* **bend** ♦ *n* inclinación *f* ♦ *a* (*wire, pipe*) doblado, torcido; **to be ~ on** estar empeñado en.
bequeath |bikwēth'| *vt* legar.
bequest |bikwest'| *n* legado.
bereaved |birēvd'| *a* afligido ♦ *n*: **the ~** los afligidos *mpl*.
bereavement |birēv'mənt| *n* aflicción *f*.
beret |bərā'| *n* boina.
Bering Sea |bar'ing sē| *n*: **the ~** el Mar de Bering.
Berks *abbr* (*Brit*) = Berkshire.
Berlin |bûrlin'| *n* Berlín *m*; **East/West ~** Berlín del Este/Oeste.
berm |bûrm| *n* (*US AUT*) arcén *m*.
Bermuda |bûrmōō'də| *n* las (Islas) Bermudas.
Bermuda shorts *npl* pantalones *mpl* bermudas.
Bern |bûrn| *n* Berna.
berry |bär'ē| *n* baya.
berserk |bûrsûrk'| *a*: **to go ~** perder los estribos.

berth |bûrth| *n* (*bed*) litera; (*cabin*) camarote *m*; (*for ship*) amarradero ♦ *vi* atracar, amarrar; **to give sb a wide ~** (*fig*) evitarle el encuentro a uno.
beseech *pt, pp* **besought** |bisēch', -sôt'| *vt* suplicar.
beset *pt, pp* **beset** |biset'| *vt* (*person*) acosar ♦ *a*: **a policy ~ with dangers** una política rodeada de peligros.
besetting |biset'ing| *a*: **his ~ sin** su pecado dominante.
beside |bisīd'| *prep* junto a, al lado de; (*compared with*) comparado con; **to be ~ o.s. with anger** estar fuera de sí; **that's ~ the point** eso no tiene nada que ver con el asunto.
besides |bisīdz'| *ad* además ♦ *prep* (*as well as*) además de; (*except*) excepto.
besiege |bisēj'| *vt* (*town*) sitiar; (*fig*) asediar.
besmirch |bismûrch'| *vt* (*fig*) manchar, mancillar.
besotted |bisät'id| *a*: ~ **with** encaprichado *or* encalabrinado con.
best |best| *a* (el/la) mejor ♦ *ad* (lo) mejor; **the ~ part of** (*quantity*) la mayor parte de; **at ~** en el mejor de los casos; **to make the ~ of sth** sacar el mejor partido de algo; **to do one's ~** hacer todo lo posible; **to the ~ of my knowledge** que yo sepa; **to the ~ of my ability** como mejor puedo; **the ~ thing to do is ...** lo mejor (que se puede hacer) es ...; **he's not exactly patient at the ~ of times** no se puede decir que tiene paciencia en las mejores circunstancias.
bestial |bes'tēəl| *a* bestial.
best man *n* padrino de boda.
bestow |bistō'| *vt* otorgar; (*honor, praise*) dispensar; **to ~ sth on sb** conceder *or* dar algo a uno.
best seller *n* éxito de librería, best-seller *m*.
bet |bet| *n* apuesta ♦ *vt, vi* (*pt, pp* **bet** *or* **betted**) apostar (*on* a); **it's a safe ~** (*fig*) es cosa segura.
Bethlehem |beth'lēəm| *n* Belén *m*.
betray |bitrā'| *vt* traicionar; (*inform on*) delatar.
betrayal |bitrā'əl| *n* traición *f*.
better |bet'ûr| *a* mejor ♦ *ad* mejor ♦ *vt* mejorar; (*record etc*) superar ♦ *n*: **to get the ~ of sb** quedar por encima de uno; **you had ~ do it** más vale que lo hagas; **he thought ~ of it** cambió de parecer; **to get ~** mejorar(se); (*MED*) reponerse; **that's ~!** ¡eso es!; **I had ~ go** tengo que marcharme; **a change for the ~** una mejora; ~ **off** *a* más acomodado.
betting |bet'ing| *n* juego, el apostar.
betting shop *n* (*Brit*) agencia de apuestas.

between [bitwēn'] *prep* entre ♦ *ad* (*time*) mientras tanto; (*place*) en medio; **the road ~ here and New York** la carretera de aquí a Nueva York; **we only had 5 ~ us** teníamos sólo 5 entre nosotros.

bevel [bev'əl] *n* (*also*: **~ edge**) filo biselado.

beverage [bev'ûrij] *n* bebida.

bevy [bev'ē] *n*: **a ~ of** una bandada de.

bewail [biwāl'] *vt* lamentar.

beware [biwär'] *vi*: **to ~ (of)** tener cuidado (con) ♦ *excl* ¡cuidado!

bewildered [biwil'dûrd] *a* aturdido, perplejo.

bewildering [biwil'dûring] *a* desconcertante.

bewitching [biwich'ing] *a* hechicero, encantador(a).

beyond [bēānd'] *prep* más allá de; (*exceeding*) además de, fuera de; (*above*) superior a ♦ *ad* más allá, más lejos; **~ doubt** fuera de toda duda; **~ repair** irreparable.

b/f *abbr* (= *brought forward*) saldo anterior.

BFPO *n abbr* (= *British Forces Post Office*) servicio postal del ejército.

bhp *n abbr* (= *brake horsepower*) caballo indicado al freno.

bi ... [bī] *pref* bi ....

biannual [bīan'yōōəl] *a* semestral.

bias [bī'əs] *n* (*prejudice*) prejuicio, pasión *f*; (*preference*) predisposición *f*.

bias(s)ed [bī'əst] *a* parcial; **to be ~ against** tener perjuicios contra.

bib [bib] *n* babero.

Bible [bī'bəl] *n* Biblia.

biblical [bib'likəl] *a* bíblico.

bibliography [bibēâg'rəfē] *n* bibliografía.

bicarbonate of soda [bīkâr'bənit əv sō'də] *n* bicarbonato de soda.

bicentenary [bīsen'tənärē] *n* (*Brit*) = **bicentennial**.

bicentennial [bīsenten'ēəl] *n* bicentenario.

biceps [bī'seps] *n* bíceps *m*.

bicker [bik'ûr] *vi* reñir.

bickering [bik'ûring] *n* riñas *fpl*, altercados *mpl*.

bicycle [bī'sikəl] *n* bicicleta.

bicycle path *n* camino para ciclistas.

bicycle pump *n* bomba de bicicleta.

bid [bid] *n* (*at auction*) oferta, postura; (*attempt*) tentativa, conato ♦ *vi* (*pt, pp* **bid**) hacer una oferta ♦ *vt* (*pt* **bade** [bad], *pp* **bidden** [bid'n]) mandar, ordenar; **to ~ sb good day** dar a uno los buenos días.

bidder [bid'ûr] *n*: **the highest ~** el mejor postor.

bidding [bid'ing] *n* (*at auction*) ofertas *fpl*; (*order*) orden *f*, mandato.

bide [bīd] *vt*: **to ~ one's time** esperar el momento adecuado.

bidet [bēdā'] *n* bidet *m*.

bidirectional [bīdirek'shənəl] *a* bidireccional.

biennial [bīen'ēəl] *a, n* bienal *f*.

bier [bēr] *n* féretro.

bifocals [bīfō'kəlz] *npl* gafas *fpl* or anteojos *mpl* (*LAm*) bifocales.

big [big] *a* grande; **~ business** gran negocio; **to do things in a ~ way** hacer las cosas en grande.

bigamy [big'əmē] *n* bigamía.

big dipper [big dip'ûr] *n* (*Brit*) montaña rusa.

big end *n* (*Brit AUT*) cabeza de biela.

bigheaded [big'hedid] *a* engreído.

bigot [big'ət] *n* fanático/a, intolerante *m/f*.

bigoted [big'ətid] *a* fanático, intolerante.

bigotry [big'ətrē] *n* fanatismo, intolerancia.

big toe *n* dedo gordo (del pie).

big top *n* (*circus*) circo; (*main tent*) tienda principal.

big wheel *n* (*at fair*) noria.

bigwig [big'wig] *n* (*col*) pez *m* gordo.

bike [bīk] *n* bici *f*.

bike rack *n* (*US*) soporte *m* para bicicletas.

bikeway [bīk'wā] *n* (*US*) pista de ciclismo.

bikini [bikē'nē] *n* bikini *m*.

bilateral [bīlat'ûrəl] *a* (*agreement*) bilateral.

bile [bīl] *n* bilis *f*.

bilge [bilj] *n* (*water*) agua de pantoque.

bilingual [bīling'gwəl] *a* bilingüe.

bilious [bil'yəs] *a* bilioso (*also fig*).

bill [bil] *n* (*gen*) cuenta; (*US*: *bank note*) billete *m*; (*invoice*) factura; (*POL*) proyecto de ley; (*of bird*) pico; (*notice*) cartel *m*; (*THEATER*) programa *m* ♦ *vt* extender or pasar la factura a; **may I have the ~ please?** ¿puede traerme la cuenta, por favor?; **~ of exchange** letra de cambio; **~ of lading** conocimiento de embarque; **~ of sale** escritura de venta; **"post no ~s"** "prohibido fijar carteles".

billboard [bil'bôrd] *n* cartelera.

billet [bil'it] *n* alojamiento ♦ *vt*: **to ~ sb (on sb)** alojar a uno (con uno).

billfold [bil'fōld] *n* (*US*) cartera.

billiards [bil'yûrdz] *n* billar *m*.

billion [bil'yən] *n* (*US*) mil millones *mpl*; (*Brit*) billón *m*.

billionaire [bilyənär'] *n* millonario/a.

billow [bil'ō] *n* (*of smoke*) nube *f*; (*of sail*) ondulación *f* ♦ *vi* (*smoke*) salir en nubes; (*sail*) ondear, ondular.

billowy [bil'ōē] *a* (*smoke*) que asciende en forma de nube.

billy [bil'ē] *n* (*US*) porra.

billy goat [bil'ē gōt] *n* macho cabrío.

bin [bin] *n* (*gen*) cubo or bote *m* (*LAm*) de la basura; **litter~** *n* (*Brit*) papelera.

binary [bī'nûrē] *a* (*MATH*) binario; **~ code** código binario; **~ system** sistema *m* binario.

bind, *pt, pp* **bound** [bīnd, bound] *vt* atar, liar; (*wound*) vendar; (*book*) encuadernar; (*oblige*) obligar.

bind over *vt* (*LAW*) obligar a comparecer ante el juez.

bind up vt (wound) vendar; **to be bound up in** (work, research etc) estar absorto en; **to be bound up with** (person) estar estrechamente ligado con.

binder [bĭn'dûr] n (file) carpeta.

binding [bīn'dĭng] a (contract) obligatorio.

binge [bĭnj] n borrachera, juerga; **to go on a ~ ir** de juerga.

bingo [bĭng'gō] n bingo m.

binoculars [bənâk'yəlûrz] npl prismáticos mpl.

biochemistry [bīōkem'istrē] n bioquímica.

biodegradable [bīōdĭgrā'dəbəl] a biodegradable.

biographer [bĭåg'rəfûr] n biógrafo/a.

biographical [bĭəgraf'ikəl] a biográfico.

biography [bĭåg'rəfē] n biografía.

biological [bĭəlåj'ikəl] a biológico.

biologist [bĭål'əjist] n biólogo/a.

biology [bĭål'əjē] n biología.

biophysics [bīōfĭz'iks] nsg biofísica.

biopsy [bī'åpsē] n biopsia.

biorhythm [bī'ōrith̸əm] n bioritmo.

biotechnology [bīōteknål'əjē] n biotecnología.

biped [bī'ped] n bípedo.

birch [bûrch] n abedul m; (cane) vara.

bird [bûrd] n ave f, pájaro; (Brit col: girl) chica.

birdcage [bûrd'kāj] n jaula.

bird's-eye view [bûrdz'ī vyōō'] n vista de pájaro.

bird watcher [bûrd' wâch'ûr] n ornitólogo/a.

Biro [bē'rō] n ® bolígrafo.

birth [bûrth] n nacimiento; (MED) parto; **to give ~ to** parir, dar a luz a; (fig) dar origen a.

birth certificate n partida de nacimiento.

birth control n control m de natalidad; (methods) métodos mpl anticonceptivos.

birthday [bûrth'dā] n cumpleaños m inv.

birthplace [bûrth'plās] n lugar m de nacimiento.

birth rate [bûrth rāt] n (tasa de) natalidad f.

Biscay [bis'kā] n: **the Bay of ~** el Mar Cantábrico, el golfo de Vizcaya.

biscuit [bis'kit] n (US) bizcocho; (Brit) galleta.

bisect [bīsekt'] vt (also MATH) bisecar.

bishop [bish'əp] n obispo; (CHESS) alfil m.

bit [bit] pt of **bite** ♦ n trozo, pedazo, pedacito; (COMPUT) bit m, bitio; (for horse) freno, bocado; **a ~ of** un poco de; **a ~ mad** algo loco; **to come to ~s** (break) hacerse pedazos; **to do one's ~** aportar su granito de arena; **bring all your ~s and pieces** trae todas tus cosas.

bitch [bich] n (dog) perra; (col!) zorra (!).

bite [bīt] vt, vi (pt **bit** [bit], pp **bitten** [bitn]) morder; (insect etc) picar ♦ n (wound: of dog, snake etc) mordedura; (of insect) picadura; (mouthful) bocado; **to ~ one's nails** comerse las uñas; **let's have a ~ (to eat)** comamos algo.

biting [bī'ting] a (wind) que traspasa los huesos; (criticism) mordaz.

bit part n (THEATER) papel m secundario.

bitten [bit'ən] pp of **bite**.

bitter [bit'ûr] a amargo; (wind, criticism) cortante, penetrante; (icy: weather) glacial; (battle) encarnizado ♦ n (Brit: beer) cerveza típica británica a base de lúpulos.

bitterly [bit'ûrlē] ad (disappoint, complain, weep) desconsoladamente; (oppose, criticise) implacablemente; (jealous) agriamente; **it's ~ cold** hace un frío glacial.

bitterness [bit'ûrnis] n amargura; (anger) rencor m.

bitty [bit'ē] a (US: tiny) pequeñito; (Brit col) deshilvanado.

bitumen [bitōō'mən] n betún m.

bivouac [biv'ōōak] n vivac m, vivaque m.

bizarre [bizár'] a raro, estrafalario.

bk abbr = **bank, book**.

BL n abbr (= Bachelor of Law(s), Bachelor of Letters) título universitario.

b/l abbr = **bill of lading**.

blab [blab] vi chismear, soplar ♦ vt (also: ~ out) revelar, contar.

black [blak] a (color) negro; (dark) oscuro ♦ n (color) color m negro; (person): **B~** negro/a ♦ vt (shoes) lustrar; (Brit: INDUSTRY) boicotear; **to give sb a ~ eye** ponerle a uno el ojo morado; **~ coffee** café m solo; **there it is in ~ and white** (fig) ahí está bien claro; **to be in the ~** (in credit) tener saldo positivo; **~ and blue** a amoratado.

black out vi (faint) desmayarse.

black belt n (US: area) zona negra; (SPORT) cinturón m negro.

blackberry [blak'bärē] n zarzamora.

blackbird [blak'bûrd] n mirlo.

blackboard [blak'bôrd] n pizarra.

black box n (AVIAT) registrador m de vuelo, caja negra.

blackcurrant [blakkur'ənt] n grosella negra.

black economy n (Brit) economía sumergida.

blacken [blak'ən] vt ennegrecer; (fig) denigrar.

Black Forest n: **the ~** la Selva Negra.

blackguard [blag'árd] n canalla m, pillo.

black ice n hielo invisible en la carretera.

blackjack [blak'jak] n (US) veintiuna.

blackleg [blak'leg] n (Brit) esquirol m, rompehuelgas m inv.

blacklist [blak'list] n lista negra ♦ vt poner en la lista negra.

blackmail [blak'māl] n chantaje m ♦ vt chantajear.

blackmailer [blak'mālûr] n chantajista m/f.

black market *n* mercado negro, estraperlo.

blackness [blak'nis] *n* negrura.

blackout [blak'out] *n* (*TV*, *ELEC*) apagón *m*; (*fainting*) desmayo, pérdida de conocimiento.

Black Sea *n*: **the ~** el Mar Negro.

black sheep *n* oveja negra.

blacksmith [blak'smith] *n* herrero.

black spot *n* (*Brit AUT*) lugar *m* peligroso.

bladder [blad'ûr] *n* vejiga.

blade [blād] *n* hoja; (*cutting edge*) filo; **a ~ of grass** una brizna de hierba.

blame [blām] *n* culpa ♦ *vt*: **to ~ sb for sth** echar a uno la culpa de algo; **to be to ~ (for)** tener la culpa (de); **I'm not to ~** yo no tengo la culpa; **and I don't ~ him** y lo comprendo perfectamente.

blameless [blām'lis] *a* (*person*) inocente.

blanch [blanch] *vi* (*person*) palidecer; (*CULIN*) blanquear.

bland [bland] *a* suave; (*taste*) soso.

blank [blangk] *a* en blanco; (*shot*) sin bala; (*look*) sin expresión ♦ *n* blanco, espacio en blanco; cartucho sin bala *or* de fogueo; **to draw a ~** (*fig*) no conseguir nada.

blank check *n* cheque *m* en blanco.

blanket [blang'kit] *n* manta ♦ *a* (*statement*, *agreement*) comprensivo, general.

blankly [blangk'lē] *ad*: **she looked at me ~** me miró sin comprender.

blare [blär] *vi* (*brass band*, *horns*, *radio*) resonar.

blasé [blâzā'] *a* hastiado.

blaspheme [blasfēm'] *vi* blasfemar.

blasphemous [blas'fəməs] *a* blasfemo.

blasphemy [blas'fəmē] *n* blasfemia.

blast [blast] *n* (*of wind*) ráfaga, soplo; (*of whistle*) toque *m*; (*of explosive*) carga explosiva; (*force*) choque *m* ♦ *vt* (*blow up*) volar; (*blow open*) abrir con carga explosiva ♦ *excl* (*Brit col*) ¡maldito sea!; **(at) full ~** (*also fig*) a toda marcha.

blast off *vi* (*spacecraft etc*) despegar.

blast furnace *n* alto horno.

blast-off [blast'ôf] *n* (*SPACE*) lanzamiento.

blatant [blā'tənt] *a* descarado.

blatantly [blā'təntlē] *ad*: **it's ~ obvious** está clarísimo.

blather [blaṭʰ'ûr] *vi* decir tonterías.

blaze [blāz] *n* (*fire*) fuego; (*flames*) llamarada; (*glow: of fire*, *sun etc*) resplandor *m*; (*fig*) arranque *m* ♦ *vi* (*fire*) arder en llamas; (*fig*) brillar ♦ *vt*: **to ~ a trail** (*fig*) abrir (un) camino; **in a ~ of publicity** bajo los focos de la publicidad.

blazer [blā'zûr] *n* chaqueta de uniforme de colegial o de socio de club.

bleach [blēch] *n* (*also*: **household ~**) lejía ♦ *vt* (*linen*) blanquear.

bleached [blēcht] *a* (*hair*) teñido de rubio; (*clothes*) decolorado.

bleachers [blē'chûrz] *npl* (*US SPORT*) gra-

das *fpl*.

bleak [blēk] *a* (*countryside*) desierto; (*landscape*) desolado, desierto; (*weather*) desapacible; (*smile*) triste; (*prospect*, *future*) poco prometedor(a).

bleary-eyed [blē'rēīd] *a*: **to be ~** tener ojos de cansado.

bleat [blēt] *vi* balar.

bleed, *pt*, *pp* **bled** [blēd, bled] *vt* sangrar; (*brakes*, *radiator*) desaguar ♦ *vi* sangrar.

bleeding [blē'ding] *a* sangrante.

bleeper [blē'pûr] *n* (*Brit*: *of doctor etc*) busca *m*.

blemish [blem'ish] *n* mancha, tacha.

blench [blench] *vi* (*shrink back*) acobardarse; (*grow pale*) palidecer.

blend [blend] *n* mezcla ♦ *vt* mezclar ♦ *vi* (*colors etc*) combinarse, mezclarse.

blender [blen'dûr] *n* (*CULIN*) licuadora.

bless, *pt*, *pp* **blessed** *or* **blest** [bles, blest] *vt* bendecir.

blessed [bles'id] *a* (*REL*: *holy*) santo, bendito; (: *happy*) dichoso; **every ~ day** cada santo día.

blessing [bles'ing] *n* bendición *f*; (*advantage*) beneficio, ventaja; **to count one's ~s** agradecer lo que se tiene; **it was a ~ in disguise** no hay mal que por bien no venga.

blew [blōō] *pt of* **blow**.

blight [blīt] *vt* (*hopes etc*) frustrar, arruinar.

blimey [blī'mē] *excl* (*Brit col*) ¡caray!

blind [blīnd] *a* ciego ♦ *n* (*for window*) persiana ♦ *vt* cegar; (*dazzle*) deslumbrar.

blind alley *n* callejón *m* sin salida.

blind corner *n* esquina escondida.

blinders [blīn'dûrz] *npl* (*US*) anteojeras *fpl*.

blindfold [blīnd'fōld] *n* venda ♦ *a*, *ad* con los ojos vendados ♦ *vt* vendar los ojos a.

blindly [blīnd'lē] *ad* a ciegas, ciegamente.

blindness [blīnd'nis] *n* ceguera.

blind spot *n* mácula.

blink [blingk] *vi* parpadear, pestañear; (*light*) oscilar; **to be on the ~** (*col*) estar estropeado.

blinkers [blingk'ûrz] *npl* (*Brit*) anteojeras *fpl*.

blinking [blingk'ing] *a* (*col*): **this ~...** este condenado....

bliss [blis] *n* felicidad *f*.

blissful [blis'fəl] *a* dichoso; **in ~ ignorance** feliz en la ignorancia.

blissfully [blis'fəlē] *ad* (*sigh*, *smile*) con felicidad; **~ happy** sumamente feliz.

blister [blis'tûr] *n* (*on skin*, *paint*) ampolla ♦ *vi* ampollarse.

blistering [blis'tûring] *a* (*heat*) abrasador(a).

blithely [blīṭʰ'lē] *ad* alegremente, despreocupadamente.

blithering [bliṭʰ'ûring] *a* (*col*): **this ~ idiot** este tonto perdido.

BLit(t) *n abbr* (= *Bachelor of Literature*) tí-

tulo universitario.

blitz [blits] *n* bombardeo aéreo; **to have a ~ on sth** (*fig*) tener una campaña de algo.

blizzard [bliz'ûrd] *n* ventisca.

BLM *n abbr* (*US*) = *Bureau of Land Management.*

bloated [blō'tid] *a* hinchado.

blob [blâb] *n* (*drop*) gota; (*stain, spot*) mancha.

bloc [blâk] *n* (*POL*) bloque *m*.

block [blâk] *n* bloque *m* (*also COMPUT*); (*in pipes*) obstáculo; (*of buildings*) manzana ♦ *vt* (*gen*) obstruir, cerrar; (*progress*) estorbar; (*COMPUT*) agrupar; **~ of apartments** bloque *m* de pisos; **mental ~** amnesia temporal; **~ and tackle** (*TECH*) polea con aparejo; **3 ~s from here** a 3 manzanas *or* cuadras (*LAm*) de aquí.

block up *vt* tapar, obstruir; (*pipe*) atascar.

blockade [blâkād'] *n* bloqueo ♦ *vt* bloquear.

blockage [blâk'ij] *n* estorbo, obstrucción *f*.

block booking *n* reserva en grupo.

blockbuster [blâk'bustûr] *n* (*book*) bestseller *m*; (*film*) éxito de público.

block capitals *npl* mayúsculas *fpl*.

block letters *npl* letras *fpl* de molde.

block release *n* (*Brit*) período de trabajo pagado para efectuar estudios superiores.

block vote *n* (*Brit*) voto por delegación.

bloke [blōk] *n* (*Brit col*) tipo, tío.

blond(e) [blând] *a, n* rubio/a *m/f*.

blood [blud] *n* sangre *f*; **new ~** (*fig*) gente *f* nueva.

blood donor *n* donador(a) *m/f* de sangre.

blood group *n* grupo sanguíneo.

bloodhound [blud'hound] *n* sabueso.

bloodless [blud'lis] *a* (*pale*) exangüe; (*revolt etc*) sin derramamiento de sangre, incruento.

bloodletting [blud'leting] *n* (*MED*) sangría; (*fig*) sangría, carnicería.

blood poisoning *n* envenenamiento de la sangre.

blood pressure *n* tensión *f* sanguínea; **to have high/low ~** tener la tensión alta/baja.

blood sausage *n* (*US*) morcilla.

bloodshed [blud'shed] *n* derramamiento de sangre.

bloodshot [blud'shât] *a* inyectado en sangre.

bloodstained [blud'stānd] *a* manchado de sangre.

bloodstream [blud'strēm] *n* corriente *f* sanguínea.

blood test *n* análisis *m* de sangre.

bloodthirsty [blud'thûrstē] *a* sanguinario.

blood transfusion *n* transfusión *f* de sangre.

blood vessel *n* vaso sanguíneo.

bloody [blud'ē] *a* sangriento; (*Brit col!*): **this ~...** este condenado *or* puñetero... (*!*) ♦ *ad* (*Brit col!*): **~ strong/good** terrible-

mente fuerte/bueno.

bloody-minded [blud'ēmīn'did] *a* (*Brit col*) malintencionado.

bloom [blōōm] *n* floración *f*; **in ~** en flor ♦ *vi* florecer.

blossom [blâs'əm] *n* flor *f* ♦ *vi* florecer; (*fig*) desarrollarse; **to ~ into** (*fig*) desarrollarse en.

blot [blât] *n* borrón *m* ♦ *vt* (*dry*) secar; (*stain*) manchar; **to ~ out** *vt* (*view*) tapar; (*memories*) borrar; **to be a ~ on the landscape** estropear el paisaje.

blotchy [blâch'ē] *a* (*complexion*) lleno de manchas.

blotter [blât'ûr] *n* secante *m*.

blotting paper [blât'ing pā'pûr] *n* papel *m* secante.

blouse [blous] *n* blusa.

blow [blō] *n* golpe *m* ♦ *vb* (*pt* **blew**, *pp* **blown** [blōō, blōn]) *vi* soplar; (*fuse*) fundirse ♦ *vt* (*glass*) soplar; (*fuse*) quemar; (*instrument*) tocar; **to come to ~s** llegar a golpes; **to ~ one's nose** sonarse.

blow away *vt* llevarse, arrancar.

blow down *vt* derribar.

blow off *vt* arrebatar.

blow out *vt* apagar ♦ *vi* apagarse; (*tire*) reventar.

blow over *vi* amainar.

blow up *vi* estallar ♦ *vt* volar; (*tire*) inflar; (*PHOT*) ampliar.

blow-dry [blō'drī] *n* secado con secador de mano ♦ *vt* secar con secador de mano.

blowfly [blō'flī] *n* (*US*) moscarda, mosca azul.

blowlamp [blō'lamp] *n* (*Brit*) = **blowtorch.**

blowout [blō'out] *n* (*of tire*) pinchazo; (*col*: *big meal*) banquete *m*, festín *m*.

blowtorch [blō'tôrch] *n* soplete *m*, lámpara de soldar.

blow-up [blō'up] *n* (*COMM*) ampliación *f*.

BLS *n abbr* (*US*) = *Bureau of Labor Statistics.*

BLT *n abbr* = *bacon, lettuce and tomato* (*sandwich*).

blubber [blub'ûr] *n* grasa de ballena ♦ *vi* (*pej*) lloriquear.

bludgeon [bluj'ən] *vt*: **to ~ sb into doing sth** coaccionar a uno a hacer algo.

blue [blōō] *a* azul; **~ film/joke** film/chiste verde; **once in a ~ moon** de higos a brevas; **to come out of the ~** (*fig*) ser completamente inesperado; *see also* **blues.**

blue baby *n* niño azul *or* cianótico.

bluebell [blōō'bel] *n* campanilla, campánula azul.

blueberry [blōō'bärē] *n* (*US*) arándano.

blue-blooded [blōō'blud'id] *a* de sangre azul.

bluebottle [blōō'bâtəl] *n* moscarda, mosca azul.

blue cheese *n* queso de pasta verde.

blue-chip [blōō'chip'] *n*: **~ investment**

inversión *f* asegurada.

blue-collar worker |blo͞o'kál'ûr wûr'kûr| *n* manual *m/f*.

blue jeans *npl* tejanos *mpl*, vaqueros *mpl*.

blueprint |blo͞o'print| *n* proyecto; ~ **(for)** *(fig)* anteproyecto (de).

blues |blo͞oz| *npl:* **the ~** *(MUS)* el blues; **to have the ~** estar triste.

bluff |bluf| *vi* hacer un bluff, farolear ♦ *n* bluff *m*, farol *m*; *(GEO)* precipicio, despeñadero; **to call sb's ~** coger a uno en un renuncio.

bluish |blo͞o'ish| *a* azulado.

blunder |blun'dûr| *n* patinazo, metedura de pata ♦ *vi* cometer un error, meter la pata; **to ~ into sb/sth** tropezar con uno/algo.

blunt |blunt| *a* *(knife)* desafilado; *(person)* franco, directo ♦ *vt* embotar, desafilar; **this pencil is ~** este lápiz está despuntado; **~ instrument** *(LAW)* instrumento contundente.

bluntly |blunt'lē| *ad* *(speak)* francamente, de modo terminante.

bluntness |blunt'nis| *n* *(of person)* franqueza, brusquedad *f*.

blur |blûr| *n* aspecto borroso ♦ *vt* *(vision)* enturbiar; *(memory)* empañar.

blurb |blûrb| *n* propaganda.

blurred |blûrd| *a* borroso.

blurt |blûrt|: **to ~ out** *vt* *(say)* descolgarse con, dejar escapar.

blush |blush| *vi* ruborizarse, ponerse colorado ♦ *n* rubor *m*; *(US: make up)* colorete *m*.

blusher |blush'ûr| *n* *(Brit)* colorete *m*.

bluster |blus'tûr| *n* fanfarronada, bravata ♦ *vi* fanfarronear, amenazar.

blustering |blus'tûring| *a* *(person)* fanfarrón/ona.

blustery |blus'tûrē| *a* *(weather)* tempestuoso, tormentoso.

Blvd *abbr* = boulevard.

BM *n abbr* *(UNIV:* = Bachelor of Medicine) título universitario.

BMA *n abbr* = British Medical Association.

BMus *n abbr* (= Bachelor of Music) título universitario.

BO *n abbr* *(col:* = body odor) olor *m* a sudor; *(US)* = **box office.**

boa |bō'ə| *n* boa.

boar |bôr| *n* verraco, cerdo.

board |bôrd| *n* tabla, tablero; *(on wall)* tablón *m*; *(for chess etc)* tablero; *(committee)* junta, consejo; *(in firm)* mesa *or* junta directiva; *(NAUT, AVIAT):* **on ~** a bordo ♦ *vt* *(ship)* embarcarse en; *(train)* subir a; **full ~** *(Brit)* pensión *f* completa; **half ~** *(Brit)* media pensión; **to go by the ~** *(fig)* ser abandonado *or* olvidado; **above ~** *(fig)* legítimo; **across the ~** *(fig: ad)* en todos los niveles; *(: a)* general.

board up *vt* *(door)* tapiar.

boarder |bôr'dûr| *n* huésped(a) *m/f*; *(SCOL)* interno/a.

board game *n* juego de tablero.

boarding house |bôr'ding hous| *n* casa de huéspedes.

boarding pass |bôr'ding pas| *n* *(AVIAT, NAUT)* tarjeta de embarque.

boarding school |bôr'ding sko͞ol| *n* internado.

board meeting *n* reunión *f* de la junta directiva.

board room *n* sala de juntas.

boardwalk |bôrd'wôk| *n* *(US)* paseo entablado.

boast |bōst| *vi:* **to ~ (about *or* of)** alardear (de) ♦ *vt* ostentar ♦ *n* alarde *m*, baladronada.

boastful |bōst'fəl| *a* presumido, jactancioso.

boastfulness |bōst'fəlnis| *n* fanfarronería.

boat |bōt| *n* barco, buque *m*; *(small)* barca, bote *m*; **to go by ~** ir en barco.

boater |bō'tûr| *n* *(hat)* canotié *m*.

boating |bō'ting| *n* canotaje *m*.

boatman |bōt'mən| *n* barquero.

boatswain |bō'sən| *n* contramaestre *m*.

bob |bâb| *vi* *(boat, cork on water: also:* ~ **up and down)** menearse, balancearse ♦ *n* *(Brit col)* = **shilling.**

bob up *vi* *(Brit)* (re)aparecer de repente.

bobbin |bâb'in| *n* *(of sewing machine)* carrete *m*, bobina.

bobby |bâb'ē| *n* *(Brit col)* poli *m/f*.

bobby pin |bâb'ē pin| *n* *(US)* horquilla.

bobsled |bâb'sled| *n* bob *m*.

bode |bōd| *vi:* **to ~ well/ill (for)** ser de buen/mal agüero (para).

bodice |bâd'is| *n* corpiño.

-bodied |bâd'id| *a suff* de cuerpo ....

bodily |bâd'əlē| *a* *(comfort, needs)* corporal; *(pain)* corpóreo ♦ *ad* *(in person)* en persona; *(carry)* corporalmente; *(lift)* en peso.

body |bâd'ē| *n* cuerpo; *(corpse)* cadáver *m*; *(of car)* caja, carrocería; *(fig: organization)* organización *f*; *(: public ~)* organismo; *(: quantity)* masa; *(: of speech, document)* parte *f* principal; *(also:* ~ **stocking)** body *m*; **ruling ~** directiva; **as a ~** todos juntos, en masa.

body-building |bâd'ēbil'ding| *n* culturismo.

bodyguard |bâd'ēgârd| *n* guardaespaldas *m inv*.

bodywork |bâd'ēwûrk| *n* carrocería.

boffin |bâf'in| *n* *(Brit)* científico/a.

bog |bâg| *n* pantano, ciénaga ♦ *vt:* **to get ~ged down** *(fig)* empantanarse, atascarse.

boggle |bâg'əl| *vt:* **it ~s the mind!** ¡no puedo creerlo!

Bogotá |bōgətâ'| *n* Bogotá.

bogus |bō'gəs| *a* falso, fraudulento; *(person)* fingido.

Bohemia |bōhē'mēə| *n* Bohemia.

Bohemian |bōhē'mēən| *a, n* bohemio/a *m/f*.

boil |boil| *vt* cocer; *(eggs)* pasar por agua ♦ *vi* hervir ♦ *n* *(MED)* furúnculo, divieso; **to bring to a ~** calentar hasta que hiervan; **to come to a ~** *(US)* or **the** *(Brit)* ~ comenzar a hervir; ~**ed egg** huevo pasado por agua; ~**ed potatoes** patatas *fpl or* papas *fpl* (*LAm*) hervidas.

boil down *vi* (*fig*): **to ~ down to** reducirse a.

boil over *vi* (*liquid*) rebosar; (*anger, resentment*) llegar al colmo.

boiler [boi'lûr] *n* caldera.

boiler suit *n* (*Brit*) mono.

boiling [boi'ling] *a*: **I'm ~** (**hot**) (*col*) estoy asado.

boiling point *n* punto de ebullición *f*.

boisterous [bois'tûrəs] *a* (*noisy*) bullicioso; (*excitable*) exuberante; (*crowd*) tumultuoso.

bold [bōld] *a* (*brave*) valiente, audaz; (*pej*) descarado; (*outline*) grueso; (*color*) vivo; ~ **type** (*TYP*) negrita.

boldly [bōld'lē] *ad* atrevidamente.

boldness [bōld'nis] *n* valor *m*, audacia; (*cheek*) descaro.

Bolivia [bōliv'ēə] *n* Bolivia.

Bolivian [bōliv'ēən] *a, n* boliviano/a *m/f*.

bollard [bâl'ûrd] *n* (*Brit AUT*) poste *m*.

bolster [bōl'stûr] *n* travesero, cabezal *m*.

bolster up *vt* reforzar; (*fig*) alentar.

bolt [bōlt] *n* (*lock*) cerrojo; (*with nut*) perno, tornillo ♦ *ad*: ~ **upright** rígido, erguido ♦ *vt* (*door*) echar el cerrojo a; (*food*) engullir ♦ *vi* fugarse; (*horse*) desbocarse.

bomb [bâm] *n* bomba ♦ *vt* bombardear.

bombard [bâmbârd'] *vt* bombardear; (*fig*) asediar.

bombardment [bâmbârd'mənt] *n* bombardeo.

bombastic [bâmbas'tik] *a* rimbombante; (*person*) farolero.

bomb disposal *n* desmontaje *m* de explosivos.

bomb disposal expert *n* experto/a en desactivar bombas.

bomber [bâm'ûr] *n* (*AVIAT*) bombardero; (*terrorist*) persona que pone bombas.

bombing [bâm'ing] *n* bombardeo.

bombshell [bâm'shel] *n* obús *m*, granada; (*fig*) bomba.

bomb site *n* lugar *m* donde estalló una bomba.

bona fide [bō'nə fīd'] *a* genuino, auténtico.

bonanza [bənan'zə] *n* bonanza.

bond [bând] *n* (*binding promise*) fianza; (*FINANCE*) bono; (*link*) vínculo, lazo; **in ~** (*COMM*) en depósito bajo fianza.

bondage [bân'dij] *n* esclavitud *f*.

bonded goods [bân'did gōōdz'] *npl* mercancías *fpl* en depósito de aduanas.

bonded warehouse [bân'did wär'hous] *n* depósito de aduanas.

bone [bōn] *n* hueso; (*of fish*) espina ♦ *vt* deshuesar; quitar las espinas a; ~ **of contention** manzana de la discordia.

bone china *n* porcelana fina.

bone-dry [bōn'drī'] *a* completamente seco.

bone idle *a* gandul.

boner [bō'nûr] *n* (*US col*) plancha, patochada.

bonfire [bân'fîûr] *n* hoguera, fogata.

Bonn [bân] *n* Bonn *m*.

bonnet [bân'it] *n* gorra; (*Brit: of car*) capó *m*.

bonny [bân'ē] *a* (*esp Scottish*) bonito, hermoso, lindo.

bonus [bō'nəs] *n* (*at Christmas etc*) paga extraordinaria; (*merit award*) sobrepaga, prima.

bony [bō'nē] *a* (*arm, face, MED: tissue*) huesudo; (*meat*) lleno de huesos; (*fish*) lleno de espinas; (*thin: person*) flaco, delgado.

boo [bōō] *vt* abuchear, rechiflar.

boob [bōōb] *n* (*Brit: col: mistake*) disparate *m*, sandez *f*; (*: breast*) teta.

boo-boo [bōō'bōō] *n* (*US: col: mistake*) disparate *m*, sandez *f*.

booby prize [bōō'bē prīz] *n* premio al último.

booby trap [bōō'bē trap] *n* (*MIL etc*) trampa explosiva.

book [bōōk] *n* libro; (*notebook*) libreta; (*of stamps etc*) librito; ~**s** (*COMM*) cuentas *fpl*, contabilidad *f* ♦ *vt* (*ticket, seat, room*) reservar; (*driver*) fichar; (*Brit SOCCER*) amonestar; **to keep the ~s** llevar las cuentas *or* los libros; **by the ~** según las reglas; **to throw the ~ at sb** echar un rapapolvo a uno.

book in *vi* (*Brit: at hotel*) registrarse.

book up *vt*: **all seats are** ~**ed up** todas las plazas están reservadas; **the hotel is** ~**ed up** el hotel está lleno.

bookable [bōōk'əbəl] *a*: **seats are** ~ (*Brit*) los asientos se pueden reservar (de antemano).

bookcase [bōōk'kās] *n* librería, estante *m* para libros.

booking office [bōōk'ing ôf'is] *n* (*Brit: RAIL*) despacho de billetes *or* boletos (*LAm*); (*: THEATER*) taquilla, boletería (*LAm*).

book-keeping [bōōkkē'ping] *n* contabilidad *f*.

booklet [bōōk'lit] *n* folleto.

bookmaker [bōōk'mākûr] *n* corredor *m* de apuestas.

bookseller [bōōk'selûr] *n* librero/a.

bookshop [bōōk'shâp] *n* librería.

bookstall [bōōk'stôl] *n* quiosco de libros.

book store *n* = **bookshop**.

book token *n* (*Brit*) vale *m* para libros.

book value *n* (*COMM*) valor *m* contable.

bookworm [bōōk'wûrm] *n* (*fig*) ratón/ona *m/f* de biblioteca.

boom [bōōm] *n* (*noise*) trueno, estampido; (*in prices etc*) alza rápida; (*ECON*) boom *m*, auge *m* ♦ *vi* (*cannon*) hacer gran estruendo, retumbar; (*ECON*) estar en alza.

boomerang [boo'mərang] *n* bumerang *m* (*also fig*) ♦ *vi*: **to ~ on sb** (*fig*) ser contraproducente para uno.

boom town *n* ciudad *f* beneficiaria del auge.

boon [boon] *n* favor *m*, beneficio.

boorish [boo'rish] *a* grosero.

boost [boost] *n* estímulo, empuje *m* ♦ *vt* estimular, empujar; (*increase: sales, production*) aumentar; **to give a ~ to** (*morale*) levantar; **it gave a ~ to his confidence** le dio confianza en sí mismo.

booster [boos'tûr] *n* (*MED*) reinyección *f*; (*TV*) repetidor *m*; (*ELEC*) elevador *m* de tensión; (*also*: **~ rocket**) cohete *m*.

boot [boot] *n* bota; (*ankle ~*) borceguí *m*; (*US AUT: also*: **Denver ~**) cepo; (*Brit: of car*) maleta, maletero ♦ *vt* dar un puntapié a; (*COMPUT*) arrancar; **to ~** (*in addition*) además, por añadidura; **to give sb the ~** (*col*) despedir a uno, poner a uno en la calle.

booth [booth] *n* (*at fair*) barraca; (*telephone ~, voting ~*) cabina.

bootleg [boot'leg] *a* de contrabando; **~ record** disco de contrabando.

bootlicker [boot'likûr] *n* (*col*) lameculos *m/f inv*.

booty [boo'tē] *n* botín *m*.

booze [booz] (*col*) *n* bebida, trago ♦ *vi* emborracharse.

boozer [boo'zûr] *n* (*col: person*) bebedor(a) *m/f*.

border [bôr'dûr] *n* borde *m*, margen *m*; (*of a country*) frontera ♦ *a* fronterizo; **the B~s** *región fronteriza entre Escocia e Inglaterra*.

   border on *vt fus* lindar con; (*fig*) rayar en.

borderline [bôr'dûrlīn] *n* (*fig*) frontera.

bore [bôr] *pt of* **bear** ♦ *vt* (*hole*) taladrar; (*person*) aburrir ♦ *n* (*person*) pelmazo, pesado; (*of gun*) calibre *m*.

bored [bôrd] *a* aburrido; **he's ~ to tears** *or* **to death** *or* **stiff** está aburrido como una ostra, está muerto de aburrimiento.

boredom [bôr'dəm] *n* aburrimiento.

boring [bôr'ing] *a* aburrido.

born [bôrn] *a*: **to be ~** nacer; **I was ~ in 1960** nací en 1960.

borne [bôrn] *pp of* **bear**.

Borneo [bôr'nēō] *n* Borneo.

borough [bur'ə] *n* municipio.

borrow [bâr'ō] *vt*: **to ~ sth (from sb)** tomar algo prestado (a alguien); **may I ~ your car?** ¿me prestas tu coche?

borrower [bâr'ōûr] *n* prestatario/a.

borrowing [bâr'ōing] *n* préstamos *mpl*.

borstal [bôr'stəl] *n* (*Brit*) reformatorio (de menores).

bosom [booz'əm] *n* pecho; (*fig*) seno; **~ friend** *n* amigo/a or íntimo/a del alma.

boss [bôs] *n* jefe/a *m/f*; (*employer*) patrón/ona *m/f*; (*political etc*) cacique *m* ♦ *vt* (*also*: **~ around**) mangonear; **stop ~ing everyone around!** ¡deja de dar órdenes *or* de mangonear a todos!

bossy [bôs'ē] *a* mandón/ona.

bosun [bō'sən] *n* contramaestre *m*.

botanical [bətan'ikəl] *a* botánico.

botanist [bât'ənist] *n* botanista *m/f*.

botany [bât'ənē] *n* botánica.

botch [bâch] *vt* (*also*: *Brit*: **~ up**) arruinar, estropear.

both [bōth] *a, pron* ambos/as, los/las dos; **~ of us went, we ~ went** fuimos los dos, ambos fuimos ♦ *ad*: **~ A and B** tanto A como B.

bother [bâth'ûr] *vt* (*worry*) preocupar; (*disturb*) molestar, fastidiar ♦ *vi* (*gen*: **~ o.s.**) molestarse ♦ *n*: **what a ~!** ¡qué lata! ♦ *excl* ¡maldito sea!, ¡caramba!; **I'm sorry to ~ you** perdona que te moleste; **to ~ doing** tomarse la molestia de hacer; **please don't ~** no te molestes.

Botswana [bâchwân'ə] *n* Botswana.

bottle [bât'əl] *n* botella; (*small*) frasco; (*baby's*) biberón *m* ♦ *vt* embotellar; **~ of wine/milk** botella de vino/de leche; **wine/milk ~** botella de vino/de leche.

   bottle up *vt* (*fig*) contener.

bottleneck [bât'əlnɛk] *n* embotellamiento.

bottle opener [bât'əl ōp'ənûr] *n* abrebotellas *m inv*.

bottom [bât'əm] *n* (*of box, sea*) fondo; (*buttocks*) trasero, culo; (*of page, mountain, tree*) pie *m*; (*of list*) final *m* ♦ *a* (*lowest*) más bajo; (*last*) último; **to get to the ~ of sth** (*fig*) llegar al fondo de algo; **the ~ line is ....** (*fig*) lo fundamental del asunto es ....

bottomless [bât'əmlis] *a* sin fondo, insondable.

bough [bou] *n* rama.

bought [bôt] *pt, pp of* **buy**.

bouillon cube [bool'yən kyōōb] *n* (*US*) cubito de caldo.

boulder [bōl'dûr] *n* canto rodado.

bounce [bouns] *vi* (*ball*) (re)botar; (*check*) ser rechazado ♦ *vt* hacer (re)botar ♦ *n* (*rebound*) (re)bote *m*; **he's got plenty of ~** (*fig*) tiene mucha energía.

bouncer [boun'sûr] *n* (*col*) matón *m*.

bound [bound] *pt, pp of* **bind** ♦ *n* (*leap*) salto; (*gen pl: limit*) límite *m* ♦ *vi* (*leap*) saltar ♦ *a*: **~ by friendship** vinculado por amistad; **to be ~ to do sth** (*obliged*) tener el deber de hacer algo; **he's ~ to come** es seguro que vendrá; **"out of ~s to the public"** "prohibido el paso"; **~ for** con destino a.

boundary [boun'dûrē] *n* límite *m*, lindero.

boundless [bound'lis] *a* ilimitado.

bountiful [boun'təfəl] *a* (*person*) liberal, generoso; (*God*) bondadoso; (*supply*) abundante.

bounty [boun'tē] n (generosity) generosidad f; (reward) prima.

bounty hunter n cazarrecompensas m inv.

bouquet [bōōkā'] n (of flowers) ramo, ramillete m; (of wine) aroma m.

bourbon [bûr'bən] n (US: also: ~ whiskey) whisky m americano, bourbon m.

bourgeois [bōōr'zhwä] a, n burgués/esa m/f.

bout [bout] n (of malaria etc) ataque m; (BOXING etc) combate m, encuentro.

boutique [bōōtēk'] n boutique f, tienda de ropa.

bow n [bō] (knot) lazo; (weapon, MUS) arco; [bou] (of the head) reverencia; (NAUT: also: ~s) proa ♦ vi [bou] inclinarse, hacer una reverencia; (yield): **to ~ to** or **before** ceder ante, someterse a; **to ~ to the inevitable** resignarse a lo inevitable.

bowels [bou'əlz] npl intestinos mpl, vientre m.

bowl [bōl] n tazón m, cuenco; (for washing) palangana, jofaina; (ball) bola; (US: stadium) estadio ♦ vi (CRICKET) arrojar la pelota; see also **bowls**.

bowlegged [bō'legid] a estevado.

bowler [bō'lûr] n (US) jugador m de bolos; (CRICKET) lanzador m (de la pelota); (Brit: also: ~ **hat**) hongo, bombín m.

bowling [bō'ling] n (game) bochas fpl, bolos mpl.

bowling alley n bolera.

bowling green n pista para bochas.

bowls [bōlz] n (Brit) juego de las bochas, bolos mpl.

bow tie [bō tī] n corbata de lazo, pajarita.

box [bâks] n (also: **cardboard** ~) caja, cajón m; (for jewels) estuche m; (for money) cofre m; (crate) cofre m, arca; (THEATER) palco ♦ vt encajonar ♦ vi (SPORT) boxear.

box car n (US RAIL) furgón m.

boxer [bâk'sûr] n (person) boxeador m; (dog) bóxer m.

box file n fichero.

boxing [bâk'sing] n (SPORT) boxeo.

Boxing Day n (Brit) Día de San Esteban, 26 de diciembre.

boxing gloves npl guantes mpl de boxeo.

boxing ring n ring m, cuadrilátero.

box number n (for advertisements) apartado.

box office n taquilla, boletería (LAm).

boxroom [bâks'rōōm] n (Brit) trastero.

boy [boi] n (young) niño; (older) muchacho.

boycott [boi'kât] n boicot m ♦ vt boicotear.

boyfriend [boi'frend] n novio.

boyish [boi'ish] a muchachil.

boy scout n boy scout m.

Bp abbr = **bishop**.

BPOE n abbr (US: = Benevolent and Protective Order of Elks) organización benéfica.

BR abbr = **British Rail**.

bra [brä] n sostén m, sujetador m.

brace [brās] n refuerzo, abrazadera; (tool) berbiquí m; (Brit: on teeth) corrector m ♦ vt asegurar, reforzar; **to ~ o.s. (for)** (fig) prepararse (para); see also **braces**.

bracelet [brās'lit] n pulsera, brazalete m.

braces [brā'siz] npl (US: on teeth) corrector m; (Brit) tirantes mpl.

bracing [brā'sing] a vigorizante, tónico.

bracken [brak'ən] n helecho.

bracket [brak'it] n (TECH) soporte m, puntal m; (group) clase f, categoría; (also: **brace** ~) soporte m, abrazadera; (also: Brit: **round** ~) paréntesis m inv; (gen: **square** ~) corchete m ♦ vt (fig: also: ~ **together**) agrupar; **income** ~ nivel m económico; **in** ~s entre paréntesis.

brackish [brak'ish] a (water) salobre.

brag [brag] vi jactarse.

braid [brād] n (trimming) galón m; (of hair) trenza.

Braille [brāl] n Braille m.

brain [brān] n cerebro; ~s npl sesos mpl; **she's got** ~s es muy lista.

brainchild [brān'chīld] n parto del ingenio.

brainless [brān'lis] a estúpido, insensato.

brainstorm [brān'stôrm] n (fig) ataque m de locura, frenesí m; (US: brain wave) idea luminosa or genial, inspiración f.

brainstorming [brān'stôrming] n discusión intensiva para solucionar problemas.

brainwash [brān'wâsh] vt lavar el cerebro a.

brain wave n idea luminosa or genial, inspiración f.

brainy [brā'nē] a muy listo or inteligente.

braise [brāz] vt cocer a fuego lento.

brake [brāk] n (on vehicle) freno ♦ vt, vi frenar.

brake drum n tambor m de freno.

brake fluid n líquido de frenos.

brake light n luz f de frenado.

brake pedal n pedal m de freno.

bramble [bram'bəl] n (fruit) zarza.

bran [bran] n salvado.

branch [branch] n rama; (fig) ramo; (COMM) sucursal f ♦ vi ramificarse; (fig) extenderse.

branch out vi ramificarse.

branch line n (RAIL) ramal m, línea secundaria.

branch manager n director(a) m/f de sucursal.

brand [brand] n marca; (iron) hierro de marcar ♦ vt (cattle) marcar con hierro candente.

brandish [bran'dish] vt blandir.

brand name n marca.

brand-new [brand'nōō'] a flamante, completamente nuevo.

brandy [bran'dē] n coñac m, brandy m.

brash [brash] a (rough) tosco; (cheeky) descarado.

Brasilia [brəzil'ēə] n Brasilia.
brass [bras] n latón m; **the ~** (MUS) los cobres.
brass band n banda de metal.
brassière [brəzēr'] n sostén m, sujetador m.
brass knuckles n (US) puño de hierro.
brass tacks npl: **to get down to ~** ir al grano.
brat [brat] n (pej) mocoso/a.
bravado [brəvá'dō] n fanfarronería.
brave [brāv] a valiente, valeroso ♦ n guerrero indio ♦ vt (challenge) desafiar; (resist) aguantar.
bravely [brāv'lē] ad valientemente, con valor.
bravery [brā'vûrē] n valor m, valentía.
bravo [brá'vō] excl ¡bravo!, ¡olé!
brawl [brôl] n pendencia, reyerta ♦ vi pelearse.
brawn [brôn] n fuerza muscular; (meat) carne f en gelatina.
brawny [brô'nē] a fornido, musculoso.
bray [brā] n rebuzno ♦ vi rebuznar.
brazen [brā'zən] a descarado, cínico ♦ vt: **to ~ it out** echarle cara al asunto.
brazier [brā'zhûr] n brasero.
Brazil [brəzil'] n (el) Brasil.
Brazilian [brəzil'ēən] a, n brasileño/a m/f.
breach [brēch] vt abrir brecha en ♦ n (gap) brecha; (estrangement) ruptura; (breaking): **~ of confidence** abuso de confianza; **~ of contract** infracción f de contrato; **~ of the peace** perturbación f del órden público; **in ~ of** por incumplimiento or infracción de.
bread [bred] n pan m; (col: money) pasta, plata (LAm); **~ and butter** n pan con mantequilla; (fig) pan (de cada día) ♦ a común y corriente; **to earn one's daily ~** ganarse el pan; **to know which side one's ~ is buttered (on)** saber dónde aprieta el zapato.
breadbin [bred'bin] n panera.
breadboard [bred'bôrd] n (COMPUT) circuito experimental.
breadbox [bred'bâks] n (US) panera.
breadcrumbs [bred'krumz] npl migajas fpl; (CULIN) pan msg molido.
breadline [bred'līn] n: **on the ~** en la miseria.
breadth [bredth] n anchura; (fig) amplitud f.
breadwinner [bred'winûr] n sostén m de la familia.
break [brāk] vb (pt **broke** [brōk], pp **broken** [brō'kən] vt (gen) romper; (promise) no cumplir; (fall) amortiguar; (journey) interrumpir; (law) violar, infringir; (record) batir; (news) comunicar; (horse etc) domar ♦ vi romperse, quebrarse; (storm) estallar; (weather) cambiar ♦ n (gap) abertura; (crack) grieta; (fracture) fractura; (in relations) ruptura; (rest) descanso;

(time) intervalo; (: at school) (período de) recreo; (vacation) vacaciones fpl; (chance) oportunidad f; (escape) evasión f, fuga; **to ~ with sb** (fig) romper con uno; **to ~ even** vi cubrir los gastos; **to ~ free** or **loose** vi escaparse; **lucky ~** (col) chiripa, racha de buena suerte; **to have** or **take a ~** (few minutes) descansar; **without a ~** sin descanso or descansar.
break down vt (door etc) echar abajo, derribar; (resistance) vencer, acabar con; (figures, data) analizar, descomponer; (undermine) acabar con ♦ vi estropearse; (MED) sufrir un colapso; (AUT) averiarse; (person) romper a llorar.
break in vt (car) rodar ♦ vi (burglar) forzar una entrada.
break into vt fus (house) forzar.
break off vi (speaker) pararse, detenerse; (branch) partir ♦ vt (talks) suspender; (engagement) romper.
break open vt (door etc) abrir por la fuerza, forzar.
break out vi estallar; **to ~ out in spots** salir a uno granos.
break through vi: **the sun broke through** el sol salió ♦ vt fus (defenses, barrier) abrirse paso por; (crowd) abrirse paso por.
break up vi (break) hacerse pedazos; (partnership) disolverse; (friends) romper ♦ vt (rocks, ice etc) partir; (crowd) disolver.
breakable [brā'kəbəl] a quebradizo ♦ n: **~s** cosas fpl frágiles.
breakage [brā'kij] n rotura; **to pay for ~s** pagar por los objetos rotos.
breakaway [brā'kəwā] a (group etc) disidente.
break-dancing [brāk'dansing] n break m.
breakdown [brāk'doun] n (AUT) avería; (in communications) interrupción f; (MED: also: **nervous ~**) colapso, crisis f nerviosa; (of figures) desglose m.
breakdown van n (Brit) (camión m) grúa.
breaker [brā'kûr] n rompiente m, ola grande.
breakeven [brākē'vən] cpd: **~ chart** gráfico del punto de equilibrio; **~ point** punto de break-even or de equilibrio.
breakfast [brek'fəst] n desayuno.
breakfast cereal n cereales mpl para el desayuno.
break-in [brāk'in] n robo con allanamiento de morada.
breaking and entering [brā'king and en'tûring] n (LAW) violación f de domicilio, allanamiento de morada.
breaking point [brā'king point] n punto de ruptura.
breakthrough [brāk'thrōō] n ruptura; (fig) avance m, adelanto.

break-up [brăk'up] *n* (*of partnership*, *marriage*) disolución *f*.
break-up value *n* (*COMM*) valor *m* de liquidación.
breakwater [brāk'wôtûr] *n* rompeolas *m inv*.
breast [brest] *n* (*of woman*) pecho, seno; (*chest*) pecho; (*of bird*) pechuga.
breast-feed [brest'fēd] *vt*, *vi* (*irg*: *like* **feed**) amamantar, criar a los pechos.
breaststroke [brest'strōk] *n* braza de pecho.
breath [breth] *n* aliento, respiración *f*; **out of** ~ sin aliento, sofocado; **to go out for a** ~ **of air** salir a tomar el fresco.
Breathalyzer [breth'əlīzûr] ® *n* alcoholímetro *m*; ~ **test** *n* prueba de alcoholemia.
breathe [brēth] *vt*, *vi* respirar; (*noisily*) resollar; **I won't** ~ **a word about it** no diré ni una palabra acerca de ello.
   breathe in *vt*, *vi* aspirar.
   breathe out *vt*, *vi* espirar.
breather [brē'thûr] *n* respiro.
breathing [brē'thing] *n* respiración *f*.
breathing space *n* (*fig*) respiro, pausa.
breathless [breth'lis] *a* sin aliento, jadeante; (*with excitement*) pasmado.
breathtaking [breth'tāking] *a* imponente, pasmoso.
-bred [bred] *suff*: **to be well/ill** ~ estar bien/mal criado.
breed [brēd] *vb* (*pt*, *pp* **bred** [bred]) *vt* criar; (*fig*: *hate*, *suspicion*) crear, engendrar ♦ *vi* reproducirse, procrear ♦ *n* raza, casta.
breeder [brē'dûr] *n* (*person*) criador(a) *m/f*; (*PHYSICS*: *also*: ~ **reactor**) reactor *m*.
breeding [brē'ding] *n* (*of person*) educación *f*.
breeze [brēz] *n* brisa.
breezeblock [brēz'blâk] *n* (*Brit*) ladrillo de cenizas.
breezy [brē'zē] *a* de mucho viento, ventoso; (*person*) despreocupado.
Breton [bret'ən] *a* bretón/ona ♦ *n* bretón/ona *m/f*; (*LING*) bretón *m*.
brevity [brev'itē] *n* brevedad *f*.
brew [broō] *vt* (*tea*) hacer; (*beer*) elaborar; (*plot*) tramar ♦ *vi* hacerse; elaborarse; tramarse; (*storm*) amenazar.
brewer [broō'ûr] *n* cervecero, fabricante *m* de cerveza.
brewery [broō'ûrē] *n* fábrica de cerveza.
briar [brī'ûr] *n* (*thorny bush*) zarza; (*wild rose*) escaramujo, rosa silvestre.
bribe [brīb] *n* soborno ♦ *vt* sobornar, cohechar; **to** ~ **sb to do sth** sobornar a uno para que haga algo.
bribery [brī'bûrē] *n* soborno, cohecho.
bric-a-brac [brik'əbrak] *n inv* baratijas *fpl*.
brick [brik] *n* ladrillo.
bricklayer [brik'lāûr] *n* albañil *m*.
brickwork [brik'wûrk] *n* enladrillado.
brickworks [brik'wûrks] *n* ladrillar *m*.

bridal [brīd'əl] *a* nupcial.
bride [brīd] *n* novia.
bridegroom [brīd'groōm] *n* novio.
bridesmaid [brīdz'mād] *n* dama de honor.
bridge [brij] *n* puente *m*; (*NAUT*) puente *m* de mando; (*of nose*) caballete *m*; (*CARDS*) bridge *m* ♦ *vt* (*river*) tender un puente sobre.
bridgehead [brij'hed] *n* cabeza de puente.
bridging loan [brij'ing lōn] *n* crédito provisional.
bridle [brīd'əl] *n* brida, freno ♦ *vt* poner la brida a; (*fig*) reprimir, refrenar ♦ *vi* (*in anger etc*) picarse.
bridle path *n* camino de herradura.
brief [brēf] *a* breve, corto ♦ *n* (*LAW*) escrito ♦ *vt* (*inform*) informar; (*instruct*) dar instrucciones a; **in** ~ ... en resumen ...; **to** ~ **sb (about sth)** informar a uno (sobre algo).
briefcase [brēf'kās] *n* cartera, portafolio (*LAm*).
briefing [brē'fing] *n* (*PRESS*) informe *m*.
briefly [brēf'lē] *ad* (*smile*, *glance*) brevemente; (*explain*, *say*) brevemente, en pocas palabras.
briefs [brēfs] *npl* (*for men*) calzoncillos *mpl*; (*for women*) bragas *fpl*.
Brig. *abbr* = **brigadier**.
brigade [brigād'] *n* (*MIL*) brigada.
brigadier [brigədi'ûr] *n* general *m* de brigada.
bright [brīt] *a* claro; (*room*) luminoso; (*day*) de sol; (*person*: *clever*) listo, inteligente; (: *lively*) alegre, animado; (*color*) vivo; **to look on the** ~ **side** mirar el lado bueno.
brighten [brīt'ən] (*also*: ~ **up**) *vt* (*room*) hacer más alegre ♦ *vi* (*weather*) despejarse; (*person*) animarse, alegrarse.
brilliance [bril'yəns] *n* brillo, brillantez *f*; (*fig*: *of person*) inteligencia.
brilliant [bril'yənt] *a* (*light*, *idea*, *person*, *success*) brillante; (*clever*) genial.
brilliantly [bril'yəntlē] *ad* brillantemente.
brim [brim] *n* borde *m*; (*of hat*) ala.
brimful [brim'foōl'] *a* lleno hasta el borde; (*fig*) rebosante.
brine [brīn] *n* (*CULIN*) salmuera.
bring, *pt*, *pp* **brought** [bring, brôt] *vt* (*thing*) traer; (*person*) conducir; **to** ~ **sth to an end** terminar con algo; **I can't** ~ **myself to fire him** no soy capaz de echarle.
   bring about *vt* ocasionar, producir.
   bring back *vt* volver a traer; (*return*) devolver.
   bring down *vt* bajar; (*price*) rebajar.
   bring forward *vt* adelantar; (*BOOK-KEEPING*) pasar a otra cuenta.
   bring in *vt* (*harvest*) recoger; (*person*) hacer entrar *or* pasar; (*object*) traer; (*Brit POL*: *bill*, *law*) presentar; (*LAW*: *verdict*) pronunciar; (*income*) producir, rendir.
   bring off *vt* (*task*, *plan*) lograr, conse-

guir; (*deal*) cerrar.
bring out *vt* (*object*) sacar; (*new product*) sacar; (*book*) publicar.
bring round *vt* (*unconscious person*) hacer volver en sí; (*convince*) convencer.
bring up *vt* (*person*) educar, criar; (*carry up*) subir; (*question*) sacar a colación; (*food: vomit*) devolver, vomitar.
brink [bringk] *n* borde *m*; **on the ~ of doing sth** a punto de hacer algo; **she was on the ~ of tears** estaba a punto de llorar.
brisk [brisk] *a* (*walk*) enérgico, vigoroso; (*speedy*) rápido; (*wind*) fresco; (*trade*) activo, animado; (*abrupt*) brusco; **business is ~** el negocio va bien *or* a paso activo.
brisket [bris'kit] *n* carne *f* de pecho de vaca para asar.
bristle [bris'əl] *n* cerda ♦ *vi* erizarse.
bristly [bris'lē] *a* (*beard, hair*) erizado; **to have a ~ chin** tener la barba crecida.
Brit [brit] *n abbr* (*col*: = *British person*) británico/a.
Britain [brit'in] *n* (*also*: **Great ~**) Gran Bretaña.
British [brit'ish] *a* británico; **the ~** *npl* los británicos; **the ~ Isles** *npl* las Islas Británicas.
British Rail (BR) *n* ≈ RENFE *f* (*Sp*).
Briton [brit'in] *n* británico/a.
brittle [brit'əl] *a* quebradizo, frágil.
Br(o). *abbr* (*REL*) = **brother**.
broach [brōch] *vt* (*subject*) abordar.
broad [brôd] *a* ancho, amplio; (*accent*) cerrado ♦ *n* (*US col*) tía; **in ~ daylight** en pleno día; **the ~ outlines** las líneas generales.
broad bean *n* haba.
broadcast [brôd'kast] *n* emisión *f* ♦ *vb* (*pt, pp* **broadcast**) *vt* (*RADIO*) emitir; (*TV*) transmitir ♦ *vi* emitir; transmitir.
broadcasting [brôd'kasting] *n* radiodifusión *f*, difusión *f*.
broadcasting station *n* emisora.
broaden [brôd'ən] *vt* ensanchar ♦ *vi* ensancharse.
broadly [brôd'lē] *ad* en general.
broad-minded [brôd'mīn'did] *a* tolerante, liberal.
brocade [brōkād'] *n* brocado.
broccoli [brâk'əlē] *n* (*BOT*) brécol *m*; (*CULIN*) brócoli *m*.
brochure [brōshōor'] *n* folleto.
brogue [brōg] *n* (*accent*) acento regional; (*Brit*: *shoe*) (*tipo de*) *zapato de cuero grueso*.
broil [broil] *vt* (*US*) asar a la parrilla.
broiler [broi'lûr] *n* (*fowl*) pollo (para asar).
broke [brōk] *pt of* **break** ♦ *a* (*col*) pelado, sin una perra; **to go ~** quebrar.
broken [brō'kən] *pp of* **break** ♦ *a* (*stick*) roto; (*fig: marriage*) quebrado; (: *promise, vow*) violado; **~ leg** pierna rota; **in ~ English** en un inglés imperfecto.

broken-down [brō'kəndoun'] *a* (*car*) averiado; (*machine*) estropeado; (*house*) destartalado.
brokenhearted [brō'kənhár'tid] *a* con el corazón partido.
broker [brō'kûr] *n* agente *m/f*, bolsista *m/f*.
brokerage [brō'kúrij] *n* corretaje *m*.
brolly [brâl'ē] *n* (*Brit col*) paraguas *m inv*.
bronchitis [brângkī'tis] *n* bronquitis *f*.
bronze [brânz] *n* bronce *m*.
bronzed [brânzd] *a* bronceado.
brooch [brōch] *n* prendedor *m*.
brood [brōod] *n* camada, cría; (*children*) progenie *f* ♦ *vi* (*hen*) empollar; **to ~ over** dejarse obsesionar por.
broody [brōo'dē] *a* (*fig*) triste, melancólico.
brook [brōok] *n* arroyo.
broom [brōom] *n* escoba; (*BOT*) retama.
broomstick [brōom'stik] *n* palo de escoba.
Bros. *abbr* (*COMM*: = *Brothers*) Hnos.
broth [brôth] *n* caldo.
brothel [bráth'əl] *n* burdel *m*.
brother [bruth'ûr] *n* hermano.
brotherhood [bruth'ûrhōod] *n* hermandad *f*.
brother-in-law [bruth'ûrinlō] *n* cuñado.
brotherly [bruth'ûrlē] *a* fraternal.
brought [brôt] *pt, pp of* **bring**.
brow [brou] *n* (*forehead*) frente *f*; (*of hill*) cumbre *f*.
browbeat [brou'bēt] *vt* (*irg: like* **beat**) intimidar.
brown [broun] *a* moreno; (*hair*) castaño; (*tanned*) bronceado ♦ *n* (*color*) color *m* moreno *or* pardo ♦ *vt* (*tan*) broncear; (*CULIN*) dorar; **to go ~** (*person*) broncearse; (*leaves*) dorarse.
brown bread *n* pan *m* moreno.
brownie [brou'nē] *n* niña exploradora.
brownnose(r) [broun'nōz'(ûr)] *n* (*col*) lameculos *m/f inv*.
brown paper *n* papel *m* de estraza.
brown rice *n* arroz *m* moreno.
brown sugar *n* azúcar *m* terciado.
browse [brouz] *vi* (*animal*) pacer; (*among books*) hojear libros; **to ~ through a book** hojear un libro.
bruise [brōoz] *n* (*on person*) cardenal *m*, hematoma *m* ♦ *vt* (*leg etc*) magullar; (*fig: feelings*) herir.
brunch [brunch] *n* *desayuno-almuerzo*.
brunette [brōonet'] *n* morena.
brunt [brunt] *n*: **to bear the ~ of** llevar el peso de.
brush [brush] *n* cepillo; (*large*) escoba; (*for painting, shaving etc*) brocha; (*artist's*) pincel *m*; (*BOT*) maleza ♦ *vt* cepillar; **to ~ one's teeth** lavarse los dientes; (*gen: past, ~ against*) rozar al pasar; **to have a ~ with the police** tener un roce con la policía.
brush aside *vt* rechazar, no hacer caso a.

brush up vt (knowledge) repasar, refrescar.

brushed [brusht] a (nylon, denim etc) afelpado; (TECH: steel, chrome etc) cepillado.

brushwood [brush'wo͞od] n (bushes) maleza; (sticks) leña.

brusque [brusk] a (person, manner) brusco; (tone) áspero.

Brussels [brus'əlz] n Bruselas.

Brussels sprout n col f de Bruselas.

brutal [bro͞ot'əl] a brutal.

brutality [bro͞otal'itē] n brutalidad f.

brute [bro͞ot] n bruto; (person) bestia ♦ a: **by ~ force** a fuerza bruta.

brutish [bro͞o'tish] a brutal.

BS n abbr (US: = Bachelor of Science) título universitario.

bs abbr = **bill of sale**.

BSA n abbr = Boy Scouts of America.

BSc abbr = **Bachelor of Science**.

BSI n abbr (= British Standards Institution) institución británica de normalización.

BST n abbr (= British Summer Time) hora de verano del Reino Unido.

btu n abbr (= British thermal unit) ≈ 1054.2 joules.

bubble [bub'əl] n burbuja; (in paint) ampolla ♦ vi burbujear, borbotar.

bubble bath n espuma para el baño.

bubble gum n chicle m de globo.

Bucharest [bo͞o'kərest] n Bucarest m.

buck [buk] n macho; (US col) dólar m ♦ vi corcovear; **to pass the ~ (to sb)** echar (a uno) el muerto.

buck up vi (cheer up) animarse, cobrar ánimo ♦ vt: **to ~ one's ideas up** poner más empeño.

bucket [buk'it] n cubo, balde m ♦ vi: **the rain is ~ing (down)** (Brit col) está lloviendo a cántaros.

buckle [buk'əl] n hebilla ♦ vt abrochar con hebilla ♦ vi torcerse, combarse.

buckle down vi poner empeño.

buckle up vi (US) ponerse el cinturón de seguridad.

Bucks [buks] abbr (Brit) = Buckinghamshire.

bud [bud] n brote m, yema; (of flower) capullo ♦ vi brotar, echar brotes.

Budapest [bo͞o'dəpest] n Budapest m.

Buddhism [bo͞o'dizəm] n Budismo.

Buddhist [bo͞o'dist] a, n budista m/f.

budding [bud'ing] a en ciernes, en embrión.

buddy [bud'ē] n (US) compañero, compinche m.

budge [buj] vt mover; (fig) hacer ceder ♦ vi moverse.

budgerigar [buj'ûrēgär] n periquito.

budget [buj'it] n presupuesto ♦ vi: **to ~ for sth** presupuestar algo; **I'm on a tight ~** no puedo gastar mucho; **she works out her ~ every month** planea su presupuesto todos

los meses.

budgie [buj'ē] n = **budgerigar**.

Buenos Aires [bwā'nəs i'riz] n Buenos Aires m.

buff [buf] a (color) color m de ante ♦ n (enthusiast) entusiasta m/f.

buffalo [buf'əlō] , pl ~ or **buffaloes** n (Brit) búfalo; (US: bison) bisonte m.

buffer [buf'ûr] n amortiguador m; (COMPUT) memoria intermedia, buffer m.

buffering [buf'ûring] n (COMPUT) almacenamiento en memoria intermedia.

buffet n [bo͞ofā'] (food) buffet m; (Brit: bar) bar m, cafetería ♦ vt [buf'it] (strike) abofetear; (wind etc) golpear.

buffet car [bo͞ofā' kâr] n (Brit RAIL) coche-comedor m.

buffet lunch [bo͞ofā' lunch] n buffet m (almuerzo).

buffoon [bufo͞on'] n bufón m.

bug [bug] n (insect) chinche m; (: gen) bicho, sabandija; (germ) microbio, bacilo; (spy device) micrófono oculto; (COMPUT) fallo, error m ♦ vt (annoy) fastidiar; (room) poner un micrófono oculto en; (phone) pinchar; **I've got the travel ~** (fig) me encanta viajar; **it really ~s me** me fastidia or molesta mucho.

bugbear [bug'bär] n pesadilla.

bugle [byo͞o'gəl] n corneta, clarín m.

build [bild] n (of person) talle m, tipo ♦ vt (pt, pp built [bilt]) construir, edificar.

build on vt fus (fig) basar en.

build up vt (MED) fortalecer; (stocks) acumular; (establish: business) fomentar, desarrollar; (: reputation) crear(se); (increase: production) aumentar; **don't ~ your hopes up too soon** no te hagas demasiadas ilusiones.

builder [bil'dûr] n constructor(a) m/f; (contractor) contratista m/f.

building [bil'ding] n (act of) construcción f; (habitation, offices) edificio.

building contractor n contratista m/f de obras.

building industry n construcción f.

building site n solar m (Sp), obra (LAm).

building society n (Brit) sociedad f inmobiliaria, cooperativa de construcciones.

building trade n = **building industry**.

build-up [bild'up] n (publicity): **to give sb/ sth a good ~** hacer mucha propaganda de uno/algo.

built [bilt] pt, pp of **build**.

built-in [bilt'in'] a (cupboard) empotrado; (device) interior, incorporado; **~ obsolescence** obsolescencia incorporada.

built-up [bilt'up] a (area) urbanizado.

bulb [bulb] n (BOT) bulbo; (ELEC) bombilla, foco (LAm).

bulbous [bul'bəs] a bulboso.

Bulgaria [bulgär'ēə] n Bulgaria.

Bulgarian [bulgär'ēən] a búlgaro ♦ n

búlgaro/a; (*LING*) búlgaro.

bulge [bulj] *n* bombeo, pandeo; (*in birth rate, sales*) alza, aumento ♦ *vi* bombearse, pandearse; (*pocket etc*) hacer bulto.

bulk [bulk] *n* (*mass*) bulto, volumen *m*; (*major part*) grueso; **in ~** (*COMM*) a granel; **the ~ of** la mayor parte de; **to buy in ~** comprar en grandes cantidades.

bulk buying [bulk bī'ing] *n* compra a granel.

bulkhead [bulk'hed] *n* mamparo.

bulky [bul'kē] *a* voluminoso, abultado.

bull [bo͞ol] *n* toro; (*STOCK EXCHANGE*) alcista *m/f* de bolsa; (*REL*) bula.

bulldog [bo͞ol'dôg] *n* dogo.

bulldoze [bo͞ol'dōz] *vt* mover con; **I was ~d into doing it** (*fig col*) me obligaron a hacerlo.

bulldozer [bo͞ol'dōzûr] *n* buldózer *m*, motoniveladora.

bullet [bo͞ol'it] *n* bala; **~ wound** balazo.

bulletin [bo͞ol'itən] *n* anuncio, parte *m*.

bulletin board [bo͞ol'itən bôrd] *n* tablón *m* de anuncios; (*COMPUT*) tablero de noticias.

bulletproof [bo͞ol'itpro͞of] *a* a prueba de balas; **~ vest** chaleco anti-balas.

bullfight [bo͞ol'fīt] *n* corrida de toros.

bullfighter [bo͞ol'fītûr] *n* torero.

bullfighting [bo͞ol'fīting] *n* los toros *mpl*, el toreo; (*art of ~*) tauromaquia.

bullhorn [bo͞ol'hôrn] *n* (*US*) megáfono.

bullion [bo͞ol'yən] *n* oro *or* plata en barras.

bullock [bo͞ol'ək] *n* novillo.

bullring [bo͞ol'ring] *n* plaza de toros.

bull's-eye [bo͞olz'ī] *n* centro del blanco.

bully [bo͞ol'ē] *n* valentón *m*, matón *m* ♦ *vt* intimidar, tiranizar.

bum [bum] *n* (*col: backside*) culo; (*: tramp*) vagabundo; (*col: esp US: idler*) holgazán/ana *m/f*, flojo/a.

bumble [bum'bəl] *vi* (*walk unsteadily*) andar de forma vacilante; (*fig*) farfullar, trastabillar.

bumblebee [bum'bəlbē] *n* abejorro.

bumbling [bum'bling] *n* divagación *f*.

bumf [bumf] *n* (*Brit col: forms etc*) papeleo.

bump [bump] *n* (*blow*) tope *m*, choque *m*; (*jolt*) sacudida; (*noise*) choque *m*, topetón *m*; (*on road etc*) bache *m*; (*on head*) chichón *m* ♦ *vt* (*strike*) chocar contra, topetar ♦ *vi* dar sacudidas.

 bump into *vt fus* chocar contra, tropezar con; (*person*) topar con; (*col: meet*) tropezar con, toparse con.

bumper [bum'pûr] *n* parachoques *m inv* ♦ *a*: **~ crop/harvest** cosecha abundante.

bumper cars *npl* coches *mpl* de choque.

bumph [bumf] *n* = **bumf**.

bumptious [bump'shəs] *a* engreído, presuntuoso.

bumpy [bum'pē] *a* (*road*) lleno de baches; (*journey, flight*) agitado.

bun [bun] *n* (*US: bread*) bollo; (*Brit: cake*) pastel *m*; (*of hair*) moño.

bunch [bunch] *n* (*of flowers*) ramo; (*of keys*) manojo; (*of bananas*) piña; (*of people*) grupo; (*pej*) pandilla.

bundle [bun'dəl] *n* (*gen*) bulto, fardo; (*of sticks*) haz *m*; (*of papers*) legajo ♦ *vt* (*also: ~ up*) atar, envolver; **to ~ sth/sb into** meter algo/a uno precipitadamente en.

bung [bung] *n* tapón *m*, bitoque *m* ♦ *vt* (*Brit col: throw*) arrojar; (*also: ~ up: pipe, hole*) tapar.

bungalow [bung'gəlō] *n* bungalow *m*, chalé *m*.

bungle [bung'gəl] *vt* chapucear.

bunion [bun'yən] *n* juanete *m*.

bunk [bungk] *n* litera; **~ beds** *npl* literas *fpl*.

bunker [bung'kûr] *n* (*MIL*) refugio; (*GOLF*) bunker *m*; (*Brit: coal store*) carbonera.

bunny [bun'ē] *n* (*also: ~ rabbit*) conejito.

Bunsen burner [bun'sən bûr'nûr] *n* mechero Bunsen.

bunting [bun'ting] *n* empavesada, banderas *fpl*.

buoy [bo͞o'ē] *n* boya.

 buoy up *vt* mantener a flote; (*fig*) animar.

buoyancy [boi'ənsē] *n* (*of ship*) capacidad *f* para flotar.

buoyant [boi'ənt] *a* (*carefree*) boyante, optimista; (*COMM: market, prices etc*) sostenido.

burden [bûr'dən] *n* carga ♦ *vt* cargar; **to be a ~ to sb** ser una carga para uno.

bureau, *pl* **~x** [byo͞or'ō, -z] *n* (*US: chest of drawers*) cómoda; (*Brit: writing desk*) escritorio, buró *m*; (*office*) oficina, agencia.

bureaucracy [byo͞orák'rəsē] *n* burocracia.

bureaucrat [byo͞or'əkrat] *n* burócrata *m/f*.

bureaucratic [byo͞orəkrat'ik] *a* burocrático.

burgeon [bûr'jən] *vi* (*develop rapidly*) crecer, incrementarse; (*trade etc*) florecer.

burglar [bûr'glûr] *n* ladrón/ona *m/f*.

burglar alarm *n* alarma *f* de ladrones.

burglarize [bûr'glərīz] *vt* (*US*) robar (con allanamiento).

burglary [bûr'glûrē] *n* robo con allanamiento, robo de una casa.

burgle [bûr'gəl] *vt* robar (con allanamiento).

Burgundy [bûr'gəndē] *n* Borgoña.

burial [bär'ēəl] *n* entierro.

burial ground *n* cementerio.

burlap [bûr'lap] *n* arpillera.

burlesque [bûrlesk'] *n* parodia.

burly [bûr'lē] *a* fornido, membrudo.

Burma [bûr'mə] *n* Birmania.

Burmese [bûrmēz'] *a* birmano ♦ *n* (*pl inv*) birmano/a; (*LING*) birmano.

burn [bûrn] *vb* (*pt, pp* **burned** *or* **burnt** [bûrnt]) *vt* quemar; (*house*) incendiar ♦ *vi* quemarse, arder; incendiarse; (*sting*) escocer ♦ *n* (*MED*) quemadura; **the cigarette ~t a hole in her dress** se ha quemado el

vestido con el cigarrillo; **I've ~t myself!**
¡me he quemado!
burn down *vt* incendiar.
burn out *vt* (*subj: writer etc*): **to ~ o.s.
out** agotarse.
burner [bûr'nûr] *n* (*gas*) quemador *m*.
burning [bûr'ning] *a* ardiente; (*building,
forest*) en llamas.
burp [bûrp] (*col*) *n* eructo ♦ *vi* eructar.
burrow [bûr'ō] *n* madriguera ♦ *vt* hacer una
madriguera.
bursar [bûr'sûr] *n* tesorero; (*student*)
becario/a.
bursary [bûr'sûrē] *n* (*Brit*) beca.
burst [bûrst] *vb* (*pt, pp* **burst**) *vt* (*balloon,
pipe*) reventar; (*banks etc*) romper ♦ *vi* re-
ventarse; romperse; (*tire*) pincharse;
(*bomb*) estallar ♦ *n* (*explosion*) estallido;
(*also*: **~ pipe**) reventón *m*; **the river has
~ its banks** el río se ha desbordado; **to ~
into flames** estallar en llamas; **to ~ out
laughing** soltar la carcajada; **to ~ into
tears** deshacerse en lágrimas; **to be ~ing
with** reventar de; **a ~ of energy** una explosión de energía; **a ~ of applause** una
salva de aplausos; **a ~ of speed** una escapada; **to ~ open** *vi* abrirse de golpe.
burst into *vt fus* (*room etc*) irrumpir en.
bury [bär'ē] *vt* enterrar; (*body*) enterrar, sepultar; **to ~ the hatchet** echar pelillos a la
mar.
bus [bus] *n* autobús *m*.
bush [bōōsh] *n* arbusto; (*scrub land*) monte
m; **to beat around the ~** andar(se) con
rodeos.
bushel [bōōsh'əl] *n* (*measure*: *US*) = *35,24
litros; (: Brit) = 36,36 litros.*
bushy [bōōsh'ē] *a* (*beard, eyebrows*) poblado; (*hair*) espeso; (*fur*) tupido.
busily [biz'ilē] *ad* afanosamente.
business [biz'nis] *n* (*matter, affair*) asunto;
(*trading*) comercio, negocios *mpl*; (*firm*)
empresa, casa; (*occupation*) oficio; **to be
away on ~** estar en viaje de negocios; **it's
my ~ to...** me toca *or* corresponde...; **it's
none of my ~** yo no tengo nada que ver;
he means ~ habla en serio; **he's in the insurance ~** se dedica a los seguros; **I'm
here on ~** estoy aquí por mi trabajo; **to do
~ with sb** hacer negocios con uno.
business address *n* dirección *f* comercial.
business card *n* tarjeta de visita.
business hours *n* horas *fpl* de oficina.
businesslike [biz'nislīk] *a* (*company*) serio;
(*person*) eficiente.
businessman [biz'nisman] *n* hombre *m* de
negocios.
business suit *n* traje *m* de calle.
business trip *n* viaje *m* de negocios.
businesswoman [biz'niswōōmən] *n* mujer
f de negocios.
busker [bus'kûr] *n* (*Brit*) músico/a ambu-

lante.
bus route *n* recorrido del autobús.
bus station *n* estación *f or* terminal *f* de
autobuses.
bus-stop [bus'stâp] *n* parada de autobús.
bust [bust] *n* (*ANAT*) pecho ♦ *a* (*col*: *broken*) roto, estropeado ♦ *vt* (*col*: *POLICE*:
arrest) detener; **to go ~** (*Brit*) quebrarse.
bustle [bus'əl] *n* bullicio, movimiento ♦ *vi*
menearse, apresurarse.
bustling [bus'ling] *a* (*town*) animado, bullicioso.
bust-up [bust'up] *n* (*col*) riña.
busy [biz'ē] *a* ocupado, atareado; (*shop,
street*) concurrido, animado ♦ *vt*: **to ~ o.s.
with** ocuparse en; **he's a ~ man**
(*normally*) es un hombre muy ocupado;
(*temporarily*) está muy ocupado; **the line's
~** (*esp US*) está comunicando.
busybody [biz'ēbâdē] *n* entrometido/a.
busy signal *n* (*US TEL*) señal *f* de comunicando.
but [but] *conj* pero ♦ *prep* excepto, menos;
nothing ~ nada más que; **~ for** a no ser
por, si no fuera por; **all ~ finished** casi
terminado; **no one ~ him** nadie sino él.
butane [byōō'tān] *n* (*also*: **~ gas**) (gas *m*)
butano.
butcher [bōōch'ûr] *n* carnicero/a ♦ *vt* hacer
una carnicería con; (*cattle etc for meat*)
matar; **~'s (shop)** carnicería.
butler [but'lûr] *n* mayordomo.
butt [but] *n* (*cask*) tonel *m*; (*for rain*) tina;
(*thick end*) cabo, extremo; (*of gun*) culata;
(*of cigarette*) colilla; (*fig: target*) blanco;
(*US col*) culo ♦ *vt* dar cabezadas contra, topetar.
butt in *vi* (*interrupt*) interrumpir.
butter [but'ûr] *n* mantequilla ♦ *vt* untar con
mantequilla.
butter bean *n* judía blanca.
buttercup [but'ûrkup] *n* ranúnculo.
butterfingers [but'ûrfinggûrz] *n* (*col*) torpe
m/f.
butterfly [but'ûrflī] *n* mariposa; (*SWIM-
MING: also*: **~ stroke**) (braza de) mariposa.
buttocks [but'əks] *npl* nalgas *fpl*.
button [but'ən] *n* botón *m* ♦ *vt* (*also*: **~ up**)
abotonar, abrochar ♦ *vi* abrocharse.
buttonhole [but'ənhōl] *n* ojal *m*; (*flower*)
flor *f* que se lleva en el ojal ♦ *vt* obligar a
escuchar.
buttress [but'tris] *n* contrafuerte *m*; (*fig*)
apoyo, sostén *m*.
buxom [buk'səm] *a* (*woman*) frescachona.
buy [bī] *vb* (*pt, pp* **bought** [bôt]) *vt* comprar
♦ *n* compra; **to ~ sb sth/sth from sb** com-
prarle algo a uno; **to ~ sb a drink** invitar
a uno a tomar algo; **a good/bad ~** una
buena/mala compra.
buy back *vt* volver a comprar.
buy in *vt* (*Brit*) proveerse *or* abastecerse

de.
buy into *vt fus* comprar acciones en.
buy off *vt* (*col: bribe*) sobornar.
buy out *vt* (*partner*) comprar la parte
de.
buyer [bī'ûr] *n* comprador(a) *m/f*; **~'s
market** mercado favorable al comprador.
buzz [buz] *n* zumbido; (*col: phone call*) llamada (por teléfono) ♦ *vt* (*call on intercom*)
llamar; (*with buzzer*) hacer sonar; (AVIAT:
plane, building) pasar rozando ♦ *vi*
zumbar; **my head is ~ing** me zumba la cabeza.
buzz off *vi* (*col*) largarse.
buzzard [buz'ûrd] *n* águila ratonera.
buzzer [buz'ûr] *n* timbre *m*.
buzz word *n* palabra que está de moda.
by [bī] *prep* por; (*beside*) junto a, cerca de;
(*according to*) según, de acuerdo con; (*before*): **~ 4 o'clock** para las cuatro ♦ *ad see*
pass, go *etc*; **~ bus/car** en autobús/coche;
paid ~ the hour pagado por horas; **~ the
kilo/meter** por kilo/metro; **~ night/day** de
noche/día; **~ saving hard, he ...** ahorrando
mucho, (él) ...; (*all*) **~ oneself** (completamente) solo; **~ this time tomorrow** mañana a estas horas; **~ the way** a propósito,
por cierto; **~ and large** en general; **~ and
~** luego, más tarde; **killed ~ lightning**
muerto por relámpago; **to pay ~ check** pagar con cheque; **a room 3 meters ~ 4** una
habitación de 3 metros por 4; **a painting ~
Picasso** un cuadro por Picasso; **surrounded
~ enemies** rodeado de enemigos; **it missed
me ~ inches** por un pelo, no me tocó.
bye(-bye) [bī'(bī')] *excl* adiós, hasta luego.
by-election [bī'ilekshən] *n* (*Brit*) elección *f*
parcial.
bygone [bī'gôn] *a* pasado, del pasado ♦ *n*:
let ~s be ~s lo pasado, pasado está.
by-law [bī'lô] *n* ordenanza municipal.
bypass [bī'pas] *n* carretera de circunvalación; (MED) (operación *f* de) by-pass *m* ♦
vt evitar.
by-product [bī'prâdəkt] *n* subproducto, derivado.
bystander [bī'standûr] *n* espectador(a) *m/f*.
byte [bīt] *n* (COMPUT) byte *m*, octeto.
byway [bī'wā] *n* camino poco frecuentado.
byword [bī'wûrd] *n*: **to be a ~ for** ser cono-
cidísimo por.
by-your-leave [bīyōōrlēv'] *n*: **without so
much as a ~** sin decir nada, sin dar ningún tipo de explicación.

C

C, c [sē] *n* (*letter*) C, c *f*; (MUS): **C** do *m*; **C
for Charlie** C de Carmen.
C *abbr* (= *Celsius, centigrade*) C.
c *abbr* (= *century*) S.; (= *circa*) hacia; (*US
etc*) = **cent(s)**.
CA *n abbr* = **Central America**; = **chartered
accountant**; (US MAIL) = **California**.
ca. *abbr* (= *circa*) c.
c/a *abbr* = **capital account, credit account,
current account**.
CAA *n abbr* (*Brit*: = *Civil Aviation Authority*) *organismo de control y desarrollo de la
aviación civil.*
cab [kab] *n* taxi *m*; (*of truck*) cabina.
cabaret [kabərā'] *n* cabaret *m*.
cabbage [kab'ij] *n* col *f*, berza.
cab driver *n* taxista *m/f*.
cabin [kab'in] *n* cabaña; (*on ship*) camarote
m.
cabin cruiser *n* yate *m* de motor.
cabinet [kab'ənit] *n* (POL) consejo de minis-
tros; (*furniture*) armario; (*also*: **display
~**) vitrina.
cabinet-maker [kab'ənitmākûr] *n* ebanista
m.
cabinet minister *n* ministro/a (del gabinete).
cable [kā'bəl] *n* cable *m* ♦ *vt* cablegrafiar.
cable car *n* teleférico.
cablegram [kā'bəlgram] *n* telegrama *m*.
cable television *n* televisión *f* por cable.
caboose [kəbōōs'] *n* (US RAIL) furgón.
cache [kash] *n* (*drugs*) alijo; (*arms*) zulo.
cackle [kak'əl] *vi* cacarear.
cactus, *pl* **cacti** [kak'təs, -tī] *n* cacto.
CAD *n abbr* (= *computer-aided design*) diseño asistido por ordenador.
caddie, caddy [kad'ē] *n* (GOLF) cadi *m*.
cadence [kād'əns] *n* ritmo; (MUS) cadencia.
cadet [kədet'] *n* (MIL) cadete *m*; **police ~**
cadete *m* de policía.
cadge [kaj] *vt* gorronear.
cadger [kaj'ûr] *n* gorrón/ona *m/f*.
cadre [kâd'rə] *n* cuadro.
Caesarean [sizär'ēən] *a* (*Brit*) = **Cesarean**.
CAF *abbr* (= *cost and freight*) C y F.
café [kafā'] *n* café *m*.
cafeteria [kafətir'ēə] *n* café *m*; (*communal*)
comedor *m*.
caffein(e) [ka'fēn] *n* cafeína.
cage [kāj] *n* jaula ♦ *vt* enjaular.
cagey [kā'jē] *a* (*col*) cauteloso, reservado.
cagoule [kəgōōl'] *n* (*Brit*) chubasquero.

CAI n abbr (= computer-aided instruction) enseñanza asistida por ordenador.
Cairo [kī'rō] n el Cairo.
cajole [kəjōl'] vt engatusar.
cake [kāk] n pastel m; (of soap) pastilla; **he wants to have his ~ and eat it (too)** (fig) quiere estar en misa y repicando; **it's a piece of ~** (col) es pan comido.
caked [kākt] a: **~ with** cubierto de.
Cal. abbr (US) = California.
calamine [kal'əmīn] n calamina.
calamitous [kəlam'itəs] a calamitoso.
calamity [kəlam'itē] n calamidad f.
calcium [kal'sēəm] n calcio.
calculate [kal'kyəlāt] vt (estimate: chances, effect) calcular.
   calculate on vt fus (Brit): **to ~ on sth/on doing sth** contar con algo/con hacer algo.
calculated [kal'kyəlātid] a: **a ~ risk** un riesgo calculado.
calculating [kal'kyəlāting] a (scheming) calculador(a).
calculation [kalkyəlā'shən] n cálculo, cómputo.
calculator [kal'kyəlātûr] n calculadora.
calculus [kal'kyələs] n cálculo.
calendar [kal'əndûr] n calendario; **~ month/year** n mes m/año civil.
calf, pl **calves** [kaf, kavz] n (of cow) ternero, becerro; (of other animals) cría; (also: **~skin**) piel f de becerro; (ANAT) pantorrilla.
caliber [kal'əbûr] n (US) calibre m.
calibrate [kal'əbrāt] vt (gun etc) calibrar; (scale of measuring instrument) graduar.
calibre [kal'əbûr] n (Brit) = **caliber**.
calico [kal'ikō] n calicó m.
Calif. abbr (US) = California.
California [kaləfôr'nyə] n California.
calipers [kal'əpûrz] npl (US MED) soporte m ortopédico; (MATH) calibrador m.
call [kôl] vt (gen, also TEL) llamar; (announce: flight) anunciar; (meeting, strike) convocar ♦ vi (shout) llamar; (telephone) llamar (por teléfono), telefonear (esp LAm); (visit: also: **~ in**, **~ round**) hacer una visita ♦ n (shout, TEL) llamada; (of bird) canto; (appeal) llamamiento; (summons: for flight etc) llamada; (fig: lure) llamada; **to be ~ed** (person, object) llamarse; **to ~ sb names** poner verde a uno; **let's ~ it a day** (col) ¡dejémoslo!, ¡ya está bien!; **who is ~ing?** ¿de parte de quién?; **New York ~ing** (RADIO) aquí Nueva York; **on ~** (nurse, doctor etc) de guardia; **please give me a ~ at 7** despiérteme or llámeme a las 7, por favor; **long-distance ~** conferencia (interurbana); **to make a ~** llamar por teléfono; **port of ~** puerto de escala; **to ~ on sb** pasar a ver a uno; **there's not much ~ for these items** estos artículos no tienen mucha demanda.
   call at vt fus (ship) hacer escala en, tocar en; (train) parar en.
   call back vi (return) volver; (TEL) volver a llamar.
   call for vt fus (demand) pedir, exigir; (fetch) venir por.
   call in vt (doctor, expert, police) llamar a.
   call off vt suspender; (cancel) cancelar; (deal) anular; **the strike was ~ed off** se abandonó la huelga.
   call on vt fus (visit) visitar; (turn to) acudir a.
   call out vi gritar, dar voces ♦ vt (doctor) hacer salir; (police, troops) hacer intervenir.
   call up vt (MIL) llamar al servicio militar.
callbox [kôl'bâks] n (Brit) cabina telefónica.
caller [kôl'ûr] n visita f; (TEL) usuario/a; **hold the line, ~!** ¡no cuelgue!
call girl n prostituta.
call-in [kôl'in] n (US) programa en que toma parte el público por teléfono.
calling [kôl'ing] n vocación f, profesión f.
calling card n tarjeta de visita.
callipers [kal'əpûrz] npl (Brit) = **calipers**.
callous [kal'əs] a insensible, cruel.
callousness [kal'əsnis] n crueldad f.
callow [kal'ō] a inexperto, novato.
calm [kâm] a tranquilo; (sea) liso, en calma ♦ n calma, tranquilidad f ♦ vt calmar, tranquilizar.
   calm down vi calmarse, tranquilizarse ♦ vt calmar, tranquilizar.
calmly [kâm'lē] ad tranquilamente, con calma.
calmness [kâm'nis] n calma.
Calor gas [kā'lûr gas] ® n (Brit) butano.
calorie [kal'ûrē] n caloría; **low-~ product** producto bajo en calorías.
calve [kav] vi parir.
calves [kavz] npl of **calf**.
CAM n abbr (= computer-aided manufacturing) producción f asistida por ordenador.
camber [kam'bûr] n (of road) combadura, comba.
Cambodia [kambō'dēə] n Camboya.
Cambodian [kambō'dēən] a, n camboyano/a m/f.
Cambs abbr (Brit) = Cambridgeshire.
camcorder [kam'kôrdûr] n cámara de vídeo sonora.
came [kām] pt of **come**.
camel [kam'əl] n camello.
cameo [kam'ēō] n camafeo.
camera [kam'ûrə] n máquina fotográfica; (CINEMA, TV) cámara; (movie ~) cámara, tomavistas m inv.
cameraman [kam'ûrəman] n cámara m.
Cameroon, Cameroun [kamərōōn'] n Camerón m.

camomile tea [kam'əmīl tē'] n manzanilla.
camouflage [kam'əflâzh] n camuflaje m ♦ vt camuflar.
camp [kamp] n campo, campamento ♦ vi acampar ♦ a afectado, afeminado; **to go ~ing** ir de or hacer camping.
campaign [kampān'] n (MIL, POL etc) campaña ♦ vi: **to ~ (for/against)** hacer campaña (a favor de/en contra de).
campaigner [kampān'ûr] n: **~ for** partidario/a de; **~ against** persona que hace campaña contra.
camp bed n cama de campaña.
camper [kam'pûr] n campista m/f; (vehicle) caravana.
camping [kam'ping] n camping m.
campsite [kamp'sīt] n camping m.
campus [kam'pəs] n ciudad f universitaria.
camshaft [kam'shaft] n árbol m de levas.
can [kan] auxiliary vb see next headword ♦ n (of oil, water) bidón m; (of fruit, soup etc) lata, bote m ♦ vt enlatar; (preserve) conservar en lata; **a ~ of beer** una lata or un bote de cerveza; **to carry the ~** (Brit col) pagar el pato.
can [kan] n, vt see previous headword ♦ auxiliary vb (pt **could**) poder; (know how to) saber; **~ I use your telephone?** ¿puedo usar su teléfono?; **could I have a word with you?** ¿podría hablar contigo un momento?; **they could have forgotten** puede que se hayan olvidado; **I ~'t see you** no te puedo ver; **you hear me?** (not translated) ¿me oyes?; **I ~ swim** sé nadar.
Canada [kan'ədə] n el Canadá.
Canadian [kanā'dēən] a, n canadiense m/f.
canal [kənal'] n canal m.
Canaries [kənär'ēz] npl las (Islas) Canarias.
canary [kənärē'] n canario m.
Canary Islands npl las (Islas) Canarias.
Canberra [kan'bərə] n Canberra.
cancel [kan'səl] vt cancelar; (train) suprimir; (appointment, check) anular; (cross out) tachar, borrar.
  cancel out vt (MATH) anular; (fig) contrarrestar; **they ~ each other out** se anulan mutuamente.
cancellation [kansəlā'shən] n cancelación f; supresión f.
cancer [kan'sûr] n cáncer m; **C~** (ASTRO) Cáncer m.
cancerous [kan'sûrəs] a canceroso.
cancer patient n enfermo/a m/f de cáncer.
cancer research n investigación f del cáncer.
C and F abbr (= cost and freight) C y F.
candid [kan'did] a franco, abierto.
candidacy [kan'didəsē] n candidatura.
candidate [kan'didāt] n candidato/a.
candidly [kan'didlē] ad francamente, con franqueza.
candied fruits [kan'dēd frōōts'] n frutas fpl escarchadas.

candle [kan'dəl] n vela; (in church) cirio.
candle holder n see **candlestick.**
candlelight [kan'dəllīt] n: **by ~** a la luz de una vela.
candlestick [kan'dəlstik] n (also: **candle holder**: single) candelero; (: low) palmatoria; (bigger, ornate) candelabro.
candor, (Brit) **candour** [kan'dûr] n franqueza.
candy [kan'dē] n (US) caramelo; (Brit) azúcar m cande ♦ vt (fruit) escarchar.
candy-floss [kan'dēflôs] n (Brit) algodón m (azucarado).
candy store n confitería, bombonería.
cane [kān] n (BOT) caña; (for baskets, chairs etc) mimbre m; (stick) vara, palmeta; (: for walking) bastón m ♦ vt (Brit SCOL) castigar (con palmeta).
canine [kā'nin] a canino.
canister [kan'istûr] n bote m, lata.
cannabis [kan'əbis] n marijuana.
canned [kand] a en lata, de lata; (col: music) grabado; (Brit: drunk) borracho.
cannibal [kan'əbəl] n caníbal m/f.
cannibalism [kan'əbəlizəm] n canibalismo.
cannon, pl **~** or **~s** [kan'ən] n cañón m.
cannonball [kan'ənbôl] n bala (de cañón).
cannon fodder n carne f de cañón.
cannot [kan'ât] = **can not.**
canny [kan'ē] a astuto.
canoe [kənōō'] n canoa; (SPORT) piragua.
canoeing [kənōō'ing] n (SPORT) piragüismo.
canoeist [kənōō'ist] n piragüista m/f.
canon [kan'ən] n (clergyman) canónigo; (standard) canon m.
canonize [kan'əniz] vt canonizar.
can opener [kan' ō'pənûr] n abrelatas m inv.
canopy [kan'əpē] n dosel m, toldo.
can't [kant] = **can not.**
cantankerous [kantang'kûrəs] a arisco, malhumorado.
canteen [kantēn'] n (eating place) cantina; (Brit: of cutlery) juego.
canter [kan'tûr] n medio galope ♦ vi ir a medio galope.
cantilever [kan'təlevûr] n viga voladiza.
canvas [kan'vəs] n (material) lona; (painting) lienzo; (NAUT) velas fpl; **under ~** (Brit: camping) bajo lona.
canvass [kan'vəs] vt (POL: district) hacer campaña en; (: person) solicitar votos de; (COMM: district) sondear el mercado en; (: citizens, opinions) sondear.
canvasser [kan'vəsûr] n (POL) representante m/f electoral; (COMM) corredor(a) m/f.
canyon [kan'yən] n cañón m.
CAP n abbr (= Common Agricultural Policy) PAC f.
cap [kap] n (hat) gorra; (for swimming) gorro de baño; (of pen) capuchón m; (of

bottle) tapa, cápsula; (*Brit: contraceptive*) diafragma *m* ♦ *vt* (*outdo*) superar; (*Brit SPORT*) seleccionar (para el equipo nacional); **and to ~ it all, he ...** y para colmo, él ....
capability [kāpəbil'ətē] *n* capacidad *f*.
capable [kā'pəbəl] *a* capaz.
capacious [kəpā'shəs] *a* amplio.
capacity [kəpas'itē] *n* capacidad *f*; (*position*) calidad *f*; **filled to ~** lleno a reventar; **this work is beyond my ~** este trabajo es superior a mí; **in an advisory ~** como asesor.
cape [kāp] *n* capa; (*GEO*) cabo.
Cape of Good Hope *n* Cabo de Buena Esperanza.
caper [kā'pûr] *n* (*CULIN: also: ~s*) alcaparra; (*prank*) travesura.
Cape Town *n* El Cabo.
capital [kap'itəl] *n* (*also: ~ city*) capital *f*; (*money*) capital *m*; (*also: ~ letter*) mayúscula.
capital account *n* cuenta de capital.
capital allowance *n* desgravación *f* sobre bienes del capital.
capital assets *n* activo fijo.
capital expenditure *n* inversión *f* de capital.
capital gains tax *n* impuesto sobre las ganancias de capital.
capital goods *npl* bienes *mpl* de capital.
capital-intensive [kap'itəlinten'siv] *a* de utilización intensiva de capital.
capital investment *n* inversión *f* de capital.
capitalism [kap'itəlizəm] *n* capitalismo.
capitalist [kap'itəlist] *a, n* capitalista *m/f*.
capitalize [kap'itəlīz] *vt* (*COMM: provide with capital*) aprovechar.
capitalize on *vt fus* (*fig*) sacar provecho de, aprovechar.
capital punishment *n* pena de muerte.
capitulate [kəpich'ŏōlāt] *vi* capitular, rendirse.
capitulation [kəpichŏōlā'shən] *n* capitulación *f*, rendición *f*.
capricious [kəprish'əs] *a* caprichoso.
Capricorn [kap'rikôrn] *n* Capricornio.
caps [kaps] *abbr* (= *capital letters*) may.
capsize [kap'sīz] *vt* volcar, hacer zozobrar ♦ *vi* volcarse, zozobrar.
capstan [kap'stən] *n* cabrestante *m*.
capsule [kap'səl] *n* cápsula.
Capt. *abbr* = **Captain**.
captain [kap'tin] *n* capitán *m* ♦ *vt* capitanear, ser el capitán de.
caption [kap'shən] *n* (*heading*) título; (*to picture*) leyenda.
captivate [kap'təvāt] *vt* cautivar, encantar.
captive [kap'tiv] *a, n* cautivo/a *m/f*.
captivity [kaptiv'ətē] *n* cautiverio.
captor [kap'tûr] *n* (*lawful*) apresador(a) *m/f*; (*unlawful*) secuestrador(a) *m/f*.

capture [kap'chûr] *vt* prender, apresar; (*place*) captar; (*attention*) captar, llamar ♦ *n* apresamiento; toma; (*data ~*) formulación *f* de datos.
car [kâr] *n* coche *m*, carro (*LAm*), automóvil *m*; (*US RAIL*) vagón *m*; **by ~** en coche.
Caracas [kərak'əs] *n* Caracas *m*.
carafe [kəraf'] *n* garrafa.
caramel [kar'əməl] *n* caramelo.
carat [kar'ət] *n* quilate *m*; **18-~ gold** oro de 18 quilates.
caravan [kar'əvan] *n* (*of camels*) caravana; (*Brit*) caravana (*Sp*), remolque *m* (*LAm*).
caravan site *n* (*Brit*) camping *m* para caravanas.
caraway [kar'əwā] *n*: **~ seed** carvi *m*.
carbohydrates [kârbōhī'drāts] *npl* (*foods*) hidratos *mpl* de carbono.
carbolic [kârbâl'ik] *a*: **~ acid** ácido carbónico.
carbon [kâr'bən] *n* carbono.
carbonated [kâr'bənātid] *a* (*drink*) con gas or burbujas.
carbon copy *n* copia al carbón.
carbon dioxide *n* bióxido de carbono.
carbon monoxide [kâr'bən mənák'sīd] *n* monóxido de carbono.
carbon paper *n* papel *m* carbón.
carbon ribbon *n* cinta de carbón.
carburetor, (*Brit*) **carburettor** [kâr'bərātûr] *n* carburador *m*.
carcass [kâr'kəs] *n* cadáver *m* de animal.
carcinogenic [kârsinəjen'ik] *a* cancerígeno.
card [kârd] *n* (*thin cardboard*) cartulina; (*playing ~*) carta, naipe *m*; (*visiting ~, post~ etc*) tarjeta; **membership ~** carnet *m*; **to play ~s** jugar a las cartas or los naipes.
cardamom [kâr'dəməm] *n* cardamomo.
cardboard [kârd'bôrd] *n* cartón *m*, cartulina.
cardboard box *n* caja de cartón.
card-carrying member [kârd'karēing mem'bûr] *n* miembro con carnet.
card game *n* juego de naipes.
cardiac [kâr'dēak] *a* cardíaco.
cardigan [kâr'digən] *n* rebeca.
cardinal [kâr'dənəl] *a* cardinal ♦ *n* cardenal *m*.
cardinal number [kâr'dənəl num'bûr] *n* número cardinal.
card index *n* fichero.
Cards *abbr* (*Brit*) = *Cardiganshire*.
cardsharp [kârd'shârp] *n* fullero/a.
CARE [kâr] *n abbr* (= *Cooperative for American Relief Everywhere*) sociedad benéfica.
care [kâr] *n* cuidado; (*worry*) inquietud *f*; (*charge*) cargo, custodia ♦ *vi*: **to ~ about** preocuparse por; **~ of** (*c/o*) en casa de, al cuidado de; (*: on letter*) para (entregar a); **in sb's ~** a cargo de uno; **the child has been taken into ~** (*Brit*) pusieron al niño bajo custodia del gobierno; "**handle with**

~'' "¡frágil!''; **to take** ~ **to** cuidarse de, tener cuidado de; **to take** ~ **of** vt cuidar; (details, arrangements) encargarse de; **I don't** ~ no me importa; **I could** (US) or **I couldn't** (Brit) ~ **less** eso me trae sin cuidado.

  care for vt fus cuidar; (like) querer.

careen [kərēn'] vi (ship) inclinarse, escorar ♦ vt carenar.

career [kərēr'] n carrera; (occupation) profesión f ♦ vi (also: Brit: ~ **along**) correr a toda velocidad.

career counselor n consejero/a de orientación professional.

career girl n chica de carrera.

careers officer n (Brit) consejero/a de orientación profesional.

carefree [kär'frē] a despreocupado.

careful [kär'fəl] a cuidadoso; (cautious) cauteloso; **(be)** ~! ¡tenga cuidado!; **he's very** ~ **with his money** es muy tacaño.

carefully [kär'fəlē] ad con cuidado, cuidadosamente.

careless [kär'lis] a descuidado; (heedless) poco atento.

carelessly [kär'lislē] ad sin cuidado, a la ligera.

carelessness [kär'lisnis] n descuido, falta de atención.

caress [kəres'] n caricia ♦ vt acariciar.

caretaker [kär'tākúr] n portero/a, conserje m/f.

caretaker government n gobierno provisional.

car ferry n transbordador m para coches.

cargo, pl ~**es** [kär'gō] n cargamento, carga.

cargo boat n buque m de carga.

cargo plane n avión m de carga.

car hire n (Brit) alquiler m de coche.

Caribbean [karəbē'ən] a caribe; **the** ~ **(Sea)** el (Mar) Caribe.

caricature [kar'əkəchúr] n caricatura.

caring [kär'ing] a humanitario.

carnage [kâr'nij] n matanza, carnicería.

carnal [kâr'nəl] a carnal.

carnation [kârnā'shən] n clavel m.

carnival [kâr'nəvəl] n carnaval m; (US) parque m de atracciones.

carnivore [kâr'nəvôr] n carnívoro/a.

carnivorous [kârniv'ûrəs] a carnívoro.

carol [kar'əl] n: **(Christmas)** ~ villancico.

carouse [kərouz'] vi estar de juerga.

carousel [karəsel'] n (US) tiovivo, caballitos mpl.

carp [kârp] n (fish) carpa.

  carp at or **about** vt fus quejarse de.

car park n (Brit) aparcamiento, parking m.

carpenter [kâr'pəntúr] n carpintero.

carpentry [kâr'pəntrē] n carpintería.

carpet [kâr'pit] n alfombra ♦ vt alfombrar.

carpet slippers npl zapatillas fpl.

carpet sweeper [kâr'pit swē'púr] n escoba mecánica.

car phone n teléfono portátil (por coche).

carping [kâr'ping] a (critical) criticón/ona.

car rental n (US) alquiler m de coche.

carriage [kar'ij] n coche m; (Brit RAIL) vagón m; (for goods) transporte m; (of typewriter) carro; (bearing) porte m; ~ **forward** porte debido; ~ **free** franco de porte; ~ **paid** porte pagado; ~ **inwards/ outwards** gastos mpl de transporte a cargo del comprador/vendedor.

carriage return n (on typewriter etc) tecla de regreso.

carriageway [kar'ijwā] n (Brit: part of road) carretera; **dual** ~ (Brit) carretera de doble calzada.

carrier [kar'ēûr] n trajinista m/f; (company) empresa de transportes.

carrier bag n (Brit) bolsa de papel or plástico.

carrier pigeon n paloma mensajera.

carrion [kar'ēən] n carroña.

carrot [kar'ət] n zanahoria.

carry [kar'ē] vt (subj: person) llevar; (transport) transportar; (a motion, bill) aprobar; (involve: responsibilities etc) entrañar, implicar; (COMM: stock) tener en existencia; (: interest) llevar; (MATH: figure) llevarse ♦ vi (sound) oírse; **to get carried away** (fig) entusiasmarse; **this loan carries 10% interest** este empréstito devenga un interés del 10 por ciento.

  carry forward vt (MATH, COMM) pasar a la página/columna siguiente.

  carry on vi (continue) seguir (adelante), continuar; (fam: complain) quejarse, protestar ♦ vt proseguir, continuar.

  carry out vt (orders) cumplir; (investigation) llevar a cabo, realizar.

carryall [kar'ēôl] n (US) bolsa.

carrycot [kar'ēkât] n (Brit) cuna portátil.

carry-on [kar'ēân] n (col: fuss) lío; (: annoying behavior) jaleo.

cart [kârt] n (also: US: for shopping) carro, carreta; (: for baggage) carretilla ♦ vt llevar (en carro).

carte blanche [kârt' blânsh'] n: **to give sb** ~ dar carta blanca a uno.

cartel [kârtel'] n (COMM) cartel m.

cartilage [kâr'təlij] n cartílago.

cartographer [kârtâg'rəfûr] n cartógrafo/a.

carton [kâr'tən] n (box) caja (de cartón); (of yogurt) pote m.

cartoon [kârtōōn'] n (PRESS) caricatura; (comic strip) tira cómica; (film) dibujos mpl animados.

cartoonist [kârtōō'nist] n dibujante m/f de historietas.

cartridge [kâr'trij] n cartucho.

cartwheel [kârt'hwēl] n: **to turn a** ~ dar una voltereta lateral.

carve [kârv] vt (meat) trinchar; (wood, stone) cincelar, esculpir; (on tree) grabar.

  carve up vt ' dividir, repartir; (meat)

trinchar.

carving [kár'ving] *n* (*in wood etc*) escultura, (obra de) talla.

carving knife *n* trinchante *m*.

car wash *n* lavado de coches.

Casablanca [kasəblang'kə] *n* Casablanca.

cascade [kaskād'] *n* salto de agua, cascada; (*fig*) chorro ♦ *vi* caer a chorros.

case [kās] *n* (*container*) caja; (*MED*) caso; (*for jewels etc*) estuche *m*; (*LAW*) causa, proceso; (*Brit: also:* **suit~**) maleta; **lower/upper ~** (*TYP*) caja baja/alta; **in ~ of** en caso de; **in any ~** en todo caso; **just in ~** por si acaso; **to have a good ~** tener buenos argumentos; **there's a strong ~ for reform** hay buenos fundamentos para exigir una reforma.

case-hardened [kās'hár'dənd] *a* insensible.

case history *n* (*MED*) historial *m* médico, historia clínica.

case study *n* estudio de casos prácticos.

cash [kash] *n* (*col: money*) (dinero) efectivo, dinero contante ♦ *vt* cobrar, hacer efectivo; **to pay (in) ~** pagar al contado; **~ on delivery (COD)** cóbrese al entregar; **to be short of ~** estar pelado, estar sin blanca.

cash in *vt* (*insurance policy etc*) cobrar ♦ *vi*: **to ~ in on sth** sacar partido *or* aprovecharse de algo.

cash account *n* cuenta de caja.

cashbook [kash'bōok] *n* libro de caja.

cash box *n* alcancía.

cash card *n* tarjeta *f* dinero.

cash desk *n* (*Brit*) caja.

cash discount *n* descuento por pago al contado.

cash dispenser *n* cajero automático.

cashew [kash'ōō] *n* (*also:* **~ nut**) anacardo.

cash flow *n* flujo de fondos, cash-flow *m*, corriente *f* de efectivos.

cashier [kashi'ûr] *n* cajero/a ♦ *vt* (*MIL*) destituir, expulsar.

cashmere [kazh'mēr] *n* casimir *m*, cachemira.

cash payment *n* pago al contado.

cash price *n* precio al contado.

cash register *n* caja.

cash reserves *npl* reserva en efectivo.

cash sale *n* venta al contado.

casing [kā'sing] *n* revestimiento.

casino [kəsē'nō] *n* casino.

cask [kask] *n* tonel *m*, barril *m*.

casket [kas'kit] *n* cofre *m*, estuche *m*; (*US: coffin*) ataúd *m*.

Caspian Sea [kas'pēan sē'] *n*: **the ~** el Mar Caspio.

casserole [kas'ərōl] *n* (*food, pot*) cazuela.

cassette [kəset'] *n* cassette *m*.

cassette deck *n* platina a cassette.

cassette player, cassette recorder *n* cassette *m*.

cassock [kas'ək] *n* sotana.

cast [kast] *vb* (*pt, pp* **cast**) *vt* (*throw*) echar,

arrojar, lanzar; (*skin*) mudar, perder; (*metal*) fundir; (*THEATER*): **to ~ sb as Othello** dar a uno el papel de Otelo ♦ *vi* (*FISHING*) lanzar ♦ *n* (*THEATER*) reparto; (*mold*) forma, molde *m*; (*also:* **plaster ~**) vaciado; **to ~ loose** soltar; **to ~ one's vote** votar.

cast aside *vt* (*reject*) descartar, desechar.

cast away *vt* desechar.

cast down *vt* derribar.

cast off *vi* (*NAUT*) desamarrar; (*KNITTING*) cerrar los puntos ♦ *vt* (*KNITTING*) cerrar; **to ~ sb off** abandonar a uno, desentenderse de uno.

cast on *vt* (*KNITTING*) montar.

castanets [kastənets'] *npl* castañuelas *fpl*.

castaway [kas'təwā] *n* náufrago/a.

caste [kast] *n* casta.

caster sugar [kas'tûr shōōg'ûr] *n* (*Brit*) azúcar *m* extrafino.

Castile [kastēl'] *n* Castilla.

casting vote [kas'ting vōt'] *n* (*Brit*) voto decisivo.

cast iron *n* hierro fundido *or* colado ♦ *a* (*fig: alibi, excuse*) inquebrantable; (*will*) férreo.

castle [kas'əl] *n* castillo; (*CHESS*) torre *f*.

castor [kas'tûr] *n* (*wheel*) ruedecilla.

castor oil *n* aceite *m* de ricino.

castrate [kas'trāt] *vt* castrar.

casual [kazh'ōōəl] *a* (*by chance*) fortuito; (*temporary: work etc*) eventual, temporero; (*unconcerned*) despreocupado; (*informal: clothes*) de sport.

casually [kazh'ōōəlē] *ad* por casualidad; de manera despreocupada.

casualty [kazh'ōōəltē] *n* víctima, herido; (*dead*) muerto; (*MIL*) baja; **heavy casualties** grandes pérdidas *fpl*.

cat [kat] *n* gato.

catacombs [kat'əkōmz] *npl* catacumbas *fpl*.

Catalan [kat'əlan] *a*, *n* catalán/ana *m/f*.

catalog, (*Brit*) **catalogue** [kat'əlôg] *n* catálogo ♦ *vt* catalogar.

Catalonia [kat'əlō'nēə] *n* Cataluña.

catalyst [kat'əlist] *n* catalizador *m*.

catalytic converter [katelit'ik kânvûrt'ûr] *n* (*AUT*) conversor *m* catalítico.

catapult [kat'əpult] *n* tirador *m*.

cataract [kat'ərakt] *n* (*also MED*) catarata.

catarrh [kətâr'] *n* catarro.

catastrophe [kətas'trəfē] *n* catástrofe *f*.

catastrophic [katəstrâf'ik] *a* catastrófico.

catcall [kat'kôl] *n* (*at meeting etc*) rechifla, silbido.

catch [kach] *vb* (*pt, pp* **caught** [kôt]) *vt* coger (*Sp*), agarrar (*LAm*); (*arrest*) detener; (*grasp*) asir; (*breath*) suspender; (*person: by surprise*) sorprender; (*attract: attention*) ganar; (*MED*) contagiarse de, coger; (*also:* **~ up**) alcanzar ♦ *vi* (*fire*) encenderse; (*in branches etc*) enredarse ♦

n (*fish etc*) pesca; (*act of catching*) cogida; (*trick*) trampa; (*of lock*) pestillo, cerradura; **to ~ fire** encenderse; **to ~ sight of** divisar.

catch on *vi* (*understand*) caer en la cuenta; (*grow popular*) tener éxito, cuajar.

catch out *vt* (*Brit: fig: with trick question*) hundir.

catch up *vi* (*fig*) ponerse al día.

catching [kach'ing] *a* (*MED*) contagioso.

catchment area [kach'mənt är'ēə] *n* (*Brit*) zona de captación.

catch phrase *n* lema *m*, slogan *m*.

catch-22 [kach'twentētōō'] *n*: **it's a ~ situation** es un callejón sin salida, es un círculo vicioso.

catchy [kach'ē] *a* (*tune*) pegadizo.

cat door *n* gatera.

catechism [kat'əkizəm] *n* (*REL*) catequismo.

categoric(al) [katəgôr'ik(əl)] *a* categórico, terminante.

categorically [katəgôr'ikəlē] *ad* categóricamente, terminantemente.

categorize [kat'əgərīz] *vt* clasificar.

category [kat'əgôrē] *n* categoría, clase *f*.

cater [kā'tûr] *vi*: **to ~ to** (*US*) complacer a (una persona); (*needs*) atender a; (*consumers*) proveer a; **to ~ for** (*Brit*) abastecer a.

caterer [kā'tûrûr] *n* abastecedor(a) *m/f*, proveedor(a) *m/f*.

catering [kā'tûring] *n* (*trade*) (ramo de la) alimentación *f*.

caterpillar [kat'ûrpilûr] *n* oruga, gusano.

caterpillar track *n* rodado de oruga.

cathedral [kəthē'drəl] *n* catedral *f*.

cathode-ray tube [kath'ōdrā' tōōb] *n* tubo de rayos catódicos.

catholic [kath'əlik] *a* católico; **C~** *a*, *n* (*REL*) católico/a *m/f*.

cat's-eye [kats'ī'] *n* (*Brit AUT*) catafoto.

catsup [kat'səp] *n* (*US*) catsup *m*.

cattle [kat'əl] *npl* ganado *sg*.

catty [kat'ē] *a* malicioso, rencoroso.

CATV *n abbr* (*US*) = *community antenna television*.

Caucasian [kôkā'zhən] *a*, *n* caucásico/a *m/f*.

Caucasus [kôk'əsəs] *n* Cáucaso.

caucus [kô'kəs] *n* (*POL: local committee*) comité *m* local; (*: US: to elect candidates*) comité *m* electoral; (*: group*) camarilla política.

caught [kôt] *pt, pp of* **catch**.

cauliflower [kô'ləflouûr] *n* coliflor *f*.

cause [kôz] *n* causa, motivo, razón *f* ♦ *vt* causar; (*provoke*) provocar; **to ~ sth to be done** hacer hacer algo; **to ~ sb to do sth** hacer que uno haga algo.

causeway [kôz'wā] *n* (*road*) carretera elevada; (*embankment*) terraplén *m*.

caustic [kôs'tik] *a* cáustico; (*fig*) mordaz.

cauterize [kôt'ərīz] *vt* cauterizar.

caution [kô'shən] *n* cautela, prudencia; (*warning*) advertencia, amonestación *f* ♦ *vt* amonestar.

cautious [kô'shəs] *a* cauteloso, prudente, precavido.

cautiously [kô'shəslē] *ad* con cautela.

cautiousness [kô'shəsnis] *n* cautela.

cavalcade [kav'əlkād] *n* cabalgata.

cavalier [kavəliûr'] *n* (*knight*) caballero ♦ *a* (*pej: offhand: person, attitude*) arrogante, desdeñoso.

cavalry [kav'əlrē] *n* caballería.

cave [kāv] *n* cueva, caverna ♦ *vi*: **to go caving** ir en una expedición espeleológica.

cave in *vi* (*roof etc*) derrumbarse, hundirse.

caveman [kāv'mən] *n* cavernícola *m*, troglodita *m*.

cavern [kav'ûrn] *n* caverna.

cavernous [kav'ûrnəs] *a* (*cheeks, eyes*) hundido.

caviar(e) [kav'ēâr] *n* caviar *m*.

cavity [kav'itē] *n* hueco, cavidad *f*.

cavity wall insulation *n* aislamiento térmico.

cavort [kəvôrt'] *vi* dar cabrioladas.

cayenne [kīen'] *n*: **~ pepper** pimentón *m*.

CB *n abbr* (= *Citizens' Band* (*Radio*)) banda ciudadana.

CBC *n abbr* (= *Canadian Broadcasting Corporation*) cadena de radio y televisión.

CBI *n abbr* (= *Confederation of British Industry*) ≈ C.E.O.E. (*Sp*).

CBS *n abbr* (*US*: = *Columbia Broadcasting System*) cadena de radio y televisión.

cc *abbr* (= *cubic centimeters*) c³; (*on letter etc*) = **carbon copy**.

CCA *n abbr* (*US*: = *Circuit Court of Appeals*) tribunal de apelación itinerante.

CCC *n abbr* (*US*: = *Commodity Credit Corporation*).

CCU *n abbr* (*US*: = *coronary care unit*) unidad *f* de cuidados cardiológicos.

CD *n abbr* = **compact disc**; (*MIL*) = *Civil Defense* (*US*), *Civil Defence* (*Corps*) (*Brit*) ♦ *abbr* (*Brit*: = *Corps Diplomatique*) CD.

CDC *n abbr* (*US*: = *center for disease control*).

Cdr. *abbr* = **Commander**.

CDT *n abbr* (*US*: = *Central Daylight Time*) hora de verano del centro.

CDV *n abbr* (= *compact disc video*) vídeo compact-disc.

cease [sēs] *vt* cesar.

ceasefire [sēs'fiûr'] *n* alto *m* el fuego.

ceaseless [sēs'lis] *a* incesante.

ceaselessly [sēs'lislē] *ad* sin cesar.

CED *n abbr* (*US*) = *Committee for Economic Development*.

cedar [sē'dûr] *n* cedro.

cede [sēd] *vt* ceder.

CEEB *n abbr* (*US*: = *College Entry Examination Board*) tribunal para las pruebas de

acceso a la universidad.
ceiling [sē'ling] *n* techo; *(fig: upper limit)* límite *m*, tope *m*.
celebrate [sel'əbrāt] *vt* celebrar; *(have a party)* festejar ♦ *vi* divertirse.
celebrated [sel'əbrātid] *a* célebre.
celebration [seləbrā'shən] *n* fiesta, celebración *f*.
celebrity [səleb'ritē] *n* celebridad *f*.
celeriac [səlär'ēak] *n* apio-nabo.
celery [sel'ûrē] *n* apio.
celestial [səles'chəl] *a* *(of sky)* celeste; *(divine)* celestial.
celibacy [sel'əbəsē] *n* celibato.
cell [sel] *n* celda; *(BIOL)* célula; *(ELEC)* elemento.
cellar [sel'ûr] *n* sótano; *(for wine)* bodega.
cellophane [sel'əfān] *n* celofán *m*.
cellular [sel'yəlûr] *a* celular.
celluloid [sel'yəloid] *n* celuloide *m*.
cellulose [sel'yəlōs] *n* celulosa.
Celsius [sel'sēəs] *a* centígrado.
Celt [selt, kelt] *n* celta *m/f*.
Celtic [sel'tik, kel'tik] *a* celta, céltico ♦ *n* *(LING)* céltico.
cement [siment'] *n* cemento ♦ *vt* cementar; *(fig)* cimentar, fortalecer.
cement mixer *n* hormigonera.
cemetery [sem'itärē] *n* cementerio.
cenotaph [sen'ətaf] *n* cenotafio.
censor [sen'sûr] *n* censor *m* ♦ *vt* *(cut)* censurar.
censorship [sen'sûrship] *n* censura.
censure [sen'shûr] *vt* censurar.
census [sen'səs] *n* censo.
cent [sent] *n* *(US: coin)* centavo, céntimo; *see also* **per**.
centenary [sen'tənärē] *n* *(Brit)* = **centennial**.
centennial [senten'ēəl] *n* *(US)* centenario.
center [sen'tûr] *(US)* *n* centro ♦ *vt* centrar; **to ~ on** *(concentrate)* concentrar (en).
centerfold [sen'tûrfōld] *n* página central plegable.
center forward *n* *(SPORT)* delantero centro.
center half *n* *(SPORT)* medio centro.
center halfback *n* *(US SPORT)* medio centro.
centerpiece [sen'tûrpēs] *n* punto central.
centigrade [sen'tigrād] *a* centígrado.
centiliter, *(Brit)* **centilitre** [sen'təlētûr] *n* centilitro.
centimeter, *(Brit)* **centimetre** [sen'təmētûr] *n* centímetro.
centipede [sen'təpēd] *n* ciempiés *m inv*.
central [sen'trəl] *a* central; *(of house etc)* céntrico.
Central African Republic *n* República Centroafricana.
Central America *n* Centroamérica.
Central American *a, n* centroamericano/a *m/f*.

central heating *n* calefacción *f* central.
centralize [sen'trəlīz] *vt* centralizar.
central processing unit (CPU) *n* *(COMPUT)* unidad *f* procesadora central.
central reservation *n* *(Brit AUT)* mediana.
centre [sen'tûr] *etc* *(Brit)* = **center** *etc*.
centrifuge [sen'trəfyōōj] *n* centrifugadora.
century [sen'chûrē] *n* siglo; **20th ~** siglo veinte; **in the twentieth ~** en el siglo veinte.
CEO *n abbr* *(US)* = **chief executive officer**.
ceramic [səram'ik] *a* cerámico.
ceramics [səram'iks] *n* cerámica.
cereal [sēr'ēəl] *n* cereal *m*.
cerebral [sär'əbrəl] *a* cerebral; *(person)* intelectual.
ceremonial [särəmō'nēəl] *n* ceremonial.
ceremony [sär'əmōnē] *n* ceremonia; **to stand on ~** hacer ceremonias, estar de cumplido.
cert [sûrt] *n* *(Brit col)*: **it's a dead ~** ¡eso está hecho!, ¡es cosa segura!
certain [sûr'tən] *a* seguro; *(correct)* cierto; *(person)* seguro; *(a particular)* cierto; **for ~** a ciencia cierta.
certainly [sûr'tənlē] *ad* desde luego, por supuesto.
certainty [sûr'təntē] *n* certeza, certidumbre *f*, seguridad *f*.
certificate [sûrtif'əkit] *n* certificado.
certified [sûr'təfīd] *a*: **~ mail** *(US)* correo certificado.
certified public accountant (CPA) *n* *(US)* contable *m/f* diplomado/a.
certify [sûr'təfī] *vt* certificar.
cervical [sûr'vikəl] *a*: **~ cancer** cáncer *m* cervical; **~ smear** citología.
cervix [sûr'viks] *n* cerviz *f*.
Cesarean [sizär'ēən] *a* *(US)*: **~ section** cesárea.
cessation [sesā'shən] *n* cese *m*, suspensión *f*.
cesspool [ses'pōōl] *n* pozo negro.
CET *n abbr* *(= Central European Time)* hora de Europa central.
Ceylon [silân'] *n* Ceilán *m*.
cf. *abbr* *(= compare)* cfr.
C.F. *abbr* *= cost and freight*.
c/f *abbr* *(COMM)* *= carried forward*.
cfc *n abbr* *(= chlorofluorocarbon)* clorofluorocarbono.
C.F.I. *abbr* *(= cost, freight and insurance)* c.s.f.
CG *n abbr* *(US)* = **coastguard**.
cg *abbr* *(= centigram)* cg.
ch *abbr* *(Brit: = central heating)* cal. cen.
ch. *abbr* *(= chapter)* cap.
Chad [chad] *n* Chad *m*.
chafe [chāf] *vt* *(rub)* rozar; *(irritate)* irritar; **to ~ (against)** *(fig)* irritarse *or* enojarse (con).
chaffinch [chaf'inch] *n* pinzón *m* (vulgar).

chagrin [shəgrin'] *n* (*annoyance*) disgusto; (*disappointment*) desazón *f*.

chain [chān] *n* cadena ♦ *vt* (*also*: ~ **up**) encadenar.

chain reaction *n* reacción *f* en cadena.

chain-smoke [chān'smōk] *vi* fumar un cigarrillo tras otro.

chain store *n* tienda de una cadena, ≈ gran almacén.

chair [chär] *n* silla; (*armchair*) sillón *m*; (*of university*) cátedra ♦ *vt* (*meeting*) presidir; **the** ~ (*US*: *electric* ~) la silla eléctrica; **please take a** ~ siéntese *or* tome asiento, por favor.

chairlift [chär'lift] *n* telesilla *m*.

chairman [chär'mən] *n* presidente *m*.

chairperson [chär'pûrsən] *n* presidente/a *m/f*.

chairwoman [chär'wŏŏmən] *n* presidenta.

chalet [shalā'] *n* chalet *m*.

chalice [chal'is] *n* cáliz *m*.

chalk [chôk] *n* (*GEO*) creta; (*for writing*) tiza, gis *m* (*LAm*).

chalk up *vt* apuntar; (*fig: success*) apuntarse; (: *victory*) obtener.

challenge [chal'inj] *n* desafío, reto ♦ *vt* desafiar, retar; (*statement, right*) poner en duda; **to** ~ **sb to do sth** retar a uno a que haga algo.

challenger [chal'injûr] *n* (*SPORT*) contrincante *m/f*.

challenging [chal'injing] *a* desafiante; (*tone*) de desafío.

chamber [chām'bûr] *n* cámara, sala; ~ **of commerce** cámara de comercio.

chambermaid [chām'bûrmād] *n* camarera.

chamber music *n* música de cámara.

chamberpot [chām'bûrpât] *n* orinal *m*.

chameleon [kəmē'lēən] *n* camaleón *m*.

chamois [sham'ē] *n* gamuza.

champagne [shampān'] *n* champaña *m*, champán *m*.

champion [cham'pēən] *n* campeón/ona *m/f*; (*of cause*) defensor(a) *m/f*, paladín *m/f* ♦ *vt* defender, apoyar.

championship [cham'pēənship] *n* campeonato.

chance [chans] *n* (*coincidence*) casualidad *f*; (*luck*) suerte *f*; (*fate*) azar *m*; (*opportunity*) ocasión *f*, oportunidad *f*; (*likelihood*) posibilidad *f*; (*risk*) riesgo ♦ *vt* arriesgar, probar ♦ *a* fortuito, casual; **to** ~ **it** arriesgarse, intentarlo; **to take a** ~ arriesgarse; **by** ~ por casualidad; **it's the** ~ **of a lifetime** es la oportunidad de su vida; **the** ~**s are that** ... lo más probable *or* factible es que ...; **to** ~ **to do sth** (*happen*) hacer algo por casualidad.

chance (up)on *vt fus* (*person*) encontrar por casualidad; (*thing*) tropezar(se) con.

chancel [chan'səl] *n* coro y presbiterio.

chancellor [chan'səlûr] *n* canciller *m*; **C~**

of the Exchequer (*Brit*) Ministro de Hacienda.

chancy [chan'sē] *a* (*col*) arriesgado.

chandelier [shandəli'ûr] *n* araña (de luces).

change [chānj] *vt* cambiar; (*replace*) reemplazar; (*gear*) cambiar de; (*clothes, house*) mudarse de; (*exchange*) trocar; (*transform*) transformar ♦ *vi* cambiar(se); (*trains*) hacer transbordo; (*be transformed*): **to** ~ **into** transformarse en ♦ *n* cambio; (*alteration*) modificación *f*, transformación *f*; (*coins*) suelto; (*money returned*) vuelta; **to** ~ **one's mind** cambiar de opinión *or* idea; **to** ~ **gear** (*AUT*) cambiar de marcha; **she ~d into an old skirt** se puso una falda vieja; **for a** ~ para variar; **can you give me** ~ **for $1?** ¿tiene cambio de un dólar?; **keep the** ~ quédese con la vuelta.

changeable [chān'jəbəl] *a* (*weather*) cambiable; (*person*) variable.

changeless [chānj'lis] *a* inmutable.

change machine *n* máquina de cambio.

changeover [chānj'ōvûr] *n* (*to new system*) cambio.

changing [chān'jing] *a* cambiante.

changing room *n* (*Brit*) vestuario.

channel [chan'əl] *n* (*TV*) canal *m*; (*of river*) cauce *m*; (*of sea*) estrecho; (*groove, fig: medium*) conducto, medio ♦ *vt* (*river etc*) encauzar; **to** ~ **into** (*fig: interest, energies*) encauzar a, dirigir a; **the (English) C~** el Canal (de la Mancha); **the C~ Islands** las Islas Normandas *fpl*; **~s of communication** canales *mpl* de comunicación; **green/red** ~ (*CUSTOMS*) pasillo verde/rojo.

chant [chant] *n* canto; (*of crowd*) gritos *mpl*, cantos *mpl* ♦ *vt* cantar; **the demonstrators ~ed their disapproval** los manifestantes gritaron su desaprobación.

chaos [kā'âs] *n* caos *m*.

chaotic [kāât'ik] *a* caótico, desordenado.

chap [chap] *n* (*Brit col: man*) tío, tipo; **old** ~ amigo (mío).

chapel [chap'əl] *n* capilla.

chaperone [shap'ərōn] *n* carabina.

chaplain [chap'lin] *n* capellán *m*.

chapped [chapt] *a* agrietado.

chapter [chap'tûr] *n* capítulo.

char [chär] *vt* (*burn*) carbonizar, chamuscar ♦ *n* (*Brit*) = **charlady**.

character [kar'iktûr] *n* carácter *m*, naturaleza, índole *f*; (*in novel, film*) personaje *m*; (*role*) papel *m*; (*COMPUT*) carácter *m*; **a person of good** ~ una persona de buena reputación.

character code *n* código de caracteres.

characteristic [kariktəris'tik] *a* característico ♦ *n* característica.

characterize [kar'iktərīz] *vt* caracterizar.

charade [shərād'] *n* charada.

charcoal [chär'kōl] *n* carbón *m* vegetal;

(*ART*) carboncillo.

charge [chârj] *n* carga; (*LAW*) cargo, acusación *f*; (*cost*) precio, coste *m*; (*responsibility*) cargo; (*task*) encargo ♦ *vt* (*LAW*) acusar (*with* de); (*gun, battery, MIL*: *enemy*) cargar; (*price*) pedir; (*customer*) cobrar; (*sb with task*) encargar ♦ *vi* precipitarse; (*make pay*) cobrar; ~**s** *npl*: **bank ~s** comisiones *fpl* bancarias; **extra ~** recargo, suplemento; **free of ~** gratis; **to reverse the ~s** (*Brit TEL*) revertir el cobro; **to take ~ of** hacerse cargo de, encargarse de; **to be in ~ of** estar encargado de; **how much do you ~?** ¿cuánto cobra usted?; **to ~ an expense (up) to sb's account** cargar algo a cuenta de alguien; **~ it to my account** póngalo *or* cárguelo a mi cuenta.

charge account *n* cuenta a cargo.

charge card *n* tarjeta de crédito.

chargé d'affaires [shârzhā' dâfârz'] *n* encargado de negocios.

chargehand [chârj'hand] *n* (*Brit*) capataz *m*.

charger [châr'jûr] *n* (*also*: **battery ~**) cargador *m* de baterías; (*old*: *warhorse*) caballo de batalla.

chariot [char'ēət] *n* carro.

charisma [kəriz'mə] *n* carisma *m*.

charitable [char'itəbəl] *a* caritativo.

charity [char'itē] *n* (*gen*) caridad *f*; (*organization*) sociedad *f* benéfica.

charlady [châr'lādē] *n* (*Brit*) mujer *f* de la limpieza.

charlatan [shâr'lətən] *n* farsante *m/f*.

charm [chârm] *n* encanto, atractivo; (*spell*) hechizo; (*object*) amuleto ♦ *vt* encantar; hechizar.

charm bracelet *n* pulsera amuleto.

charming [châr'ming] *a* encantador(a); (*person*) simpático.

chart [chârt] *n* (*table*) cuadro; (*graph*) gráfica; (*map*) carta de navegación; (*weather ~*) mapa *m* meteorológico ♦ *vt* (*course*) trazar; (*sales, progress*) hacer una gráfica de; **to be in the ~s** (*record, pop group*) figurar entre los discos que más se venden.

charter [châr'tûr] *vt* (*plane*) alquilar; (*ship*) fletar ♦ *n* (*document*) carta; **on ~** en alquiler, alquilado.

chartered accountant (CA) [châr'tûrd əkoun'tənt] *n* (*Brit*) contable *m/f* diplomado/a.

charter flight *n* vuelo chárter.

charwoman [châr'woomən] *n* (*Brit*) = **charlady**.

chase [chās] *vt* (*pursue*) perseguir; (*hunt*) cazar ♦ *n* persecución *f*; caza; **to ~ after** correr tras.

chase down *vt* (*US*: *information*) recoger; **to ~ sb down about sth** recordar algo a uno.

chase up *vt* (*Brit*) = **chase down**.

chasm [kaz'əm] *n* abismo.

chassis [shas'ē] *n* chasis *m*.

chaste [chāst] *a* casto.

chastened [chā'sənd] *a* escarmentado.

chastening [chā'səning] *a* aleccionador(a).

chastity [chas'titē] *n* castidad *f*.

chat [chat] *vi* (*also*: **have a ~**) charlar ♦ *n* charla.

chat up *vt* (*col*: *girl*) enrollarse con.

chat show *n* (*Brit*) programa *m* de entrevistas.

chattel [chat'əl] *n* bien *m* mueble.

chatter [chat'ûr] *vi* (*person*) charlar; (*teeth*) castañetear ♦ *n* (*of birds*) parloteo; (*of people*) charla, cháchara.

chatterbox [chat'ûrbâks] *n* parlanchín/ina *m/f*.

chatty [chat'ē] *a* (*style*) familiar; (*person*) hablador(a).

chauffeur [shō'fûr] *n* chófer *m*.

chauvinist [shō'vənist] *n* (*male ~*) machista *m*; (*nationalist*) chovinista *m/f*, patriotero/a *m/f*.

ChE *abbr* = *chemical engineer*.

cheap [chēp] *a* barato; (*joke*) de mal gusto; (*poor quality*) de mala calidad; (*reduced*: *ticket*) económico, (: *fare*) barato ♦ *ad* barato.

cheapen [chē'pən] *vt* rebajar el precio de, abaratar.

cheaply [chēp'lē] *ad* barato, a bajo precio.

cheat [chēt] *vi* (*in exam*) hacer trampa ♦ *vt* estafar, timar ♦ *n* trampa; estafa; (*person*) tramposo/a; **he's been ~ing on his wife** ha estado engañando a su esposa.

cheating [chēt'ing] *n* trampa, fraude *m*.

check [chek] *vt* (*examine*) controlar; (*facts*) comprobar; (*count*) contar; (*halt*) parar, detener; (*restrain*) refrenar, restringir ♦ *vi*: **to ~ with sb** consultar con uno; (*official etc*) informarse por ♦ *n* (*inspection*) control *m*, inspección *f*; (*curb*) freno; (*bill*) nota, cuenta; (*US*) cheque *m*; (*pattern*: *gen pl*) cuadro ♦ *a* (*also*: **~ed**: *pattern, cloth*) a cuadros; **to keep a ~ on sth/sb** controlar algo/a uno; **to pay by ~** pagar con cheque.

check in *vi* (*in hotel, airport*) registrarse ♦ *vt* (*baggage*) facturar.

check off *vt* marcar.

check out *vi* (*of hotel*) desocupar su cuarto ♦ *vt* (*investigate*: *story*) verificar; (: *person*) hacer investigaciones sobre.

check up *vi*: **to ~ up on sth** comprobar algo; **to ~ up on sb** investigar a alguien.

checkbook [chek'book] *n* talonario de cheques.

checkerboard [chek'ərbôrd] *n* (*US*) tablero de damas.

checkered [chek'ûrd] *a* (*fig*) accidentado; (*pattern*) de cuadros.

checkers [chek'ûrz] *n* (*US*) juego de damas.

check guarantee card *n* tarjeta de cheque, tarjeta bancaria.

check-in [chek'in] *n* (*also*: ~ **desk**: *at airport*) mostrador *m* de embarque.

checking account [chek'ing əkount'] *n* (*US*) cuenta corriente.

checklist [chek'list] *n* lista.

checkmate [chek'māt] *n* jaque *m* mate.

checkout [chek'out] *n* (*in supermarket*) caja.

checkpoint [chek'point] *n* (punto de) control *m*.

checkroom [chek'rōōm] *n* (*US*) consigna.

checkup [chek'up] *n* (*MED*) reconocimiento general; (*of machine*) repaso.

cheek [chēk] *n* mejilla; (*impudence*) descaro.

cheekbone [chēk'bōn] *n* pómulo.

cheeky [chē'kē] *a* (*Brit*) fresco, descarado.

cheep [chēp] *n* (*of bird*) pío ♦ *vi* piar, gorjear.

cheer [chēr] *vt* vitorear, aplaudir; (*gladden*) alegrar, animar ♦ *vi* aplaudir, dar vivas ♦ *n* vivra *m*; ~**s** *npl* aplausos *mpl*; ~**s!** ¡salud!

   cheer on *vt* (*person etc*) animar con aplausos *or* gritos.

   cheer up *vi* animarse ♦ *vt* alegrar, animar.

cheerful [chēr'fəl] *a* alegre.

cheerfulness [chēr'fəlnis] *n* alegría.

cheering [chē'ring] *n* aplausos *mpl*, vítores *mpl*.

cheerio [chēr'ēō] *excl* (*Brit*) ¡hasta luego!

cheerless [chēr'lis] *a* triste, sombrío.

cheese [chēz] *n* queso.

cheeseboard [chēz'bōrd] *n* plato de quesos.

cheesecake [chēz'kāk] *n* pastel *m* de queso.

cheesecloth [chēz'klôth] *n* estopilla.

cheetah [chē'tə] *n* leopardo cazador.

chef [shef] *n* jefe/a *m/f* de cocina.

chemical [kem'ikəl] *a* químico ♦ *n* producto químico.

chemist [kem'ist] *n* (*scientist*) químico/a; (*Brit*: *pharmacist*) farmacéutico/a; ~**'s** (**shop**) *n* (*Brit*) farmacia.

chemistry [kem'istrē] *n* química.

cheque [chek] *n* (*Brit*) cheque *m*; **to pay by** ~ pagar con cheque.

chequebook [chek'bōōk] *n* (*Brit*) = **checkbook**.

cheque card *n* (*Brit*) tarjeta de cheque.

chequered [chek'ûrd] *a* (*Brit*) = **checkered**.

cherish [chär'ish] *vt* (*love*) querer, apreciar; (*protect*) cuidar; (*hope etc*) abrigar.

cheroot [shərōōt'] *n* puro (*cortado en los dos extremos*).

cherry [chär'ē] *n* cereza.

Ches *abbr* (*Brit*) = *Cheshire*.

chess [ches] *n* ajedrez *m*.

chessboard [ches'bôrd] *n* tablero (de ajedrez).

chessman [ches'man] *n* pieza, trebejo.

chest [chest] *n* (*ANAT*) pecho; (*box*) cofre *m*, cajón *m*; **to get sth off one's** ~ (*col*) desahogarse; ~ **of drawers** *n* cómoda.

chest measurement *n* talla (*de chaqueta etc*).

chestnut [ches'nut] *n* castaña; (*also*: ~ **tree**) castaño; (*color*) castaño ♦ *a* (color) castaño *inv*.

chew [chōō] *vt* mascar, masticar.

chewing gum [chōō'ing gum] *n* chicle *m*.

chic [shēk] *a* elegante.

chicanery [shikā'nûrē] *n* embustes *mpl*, sofismas *mpl*.

chick [chik] *n* pollito, polluelo; (*col*) chica.

chicken [chik'ən] *n* gallina, pollo; (*food*) pollo; (*col*: *coward*) gallina *m/f*.

   chicken out *vi* (*col*) rajarse, amedrentarse, retirarse miedoso; **to** ~ **out of doing sth** acobardarse de hacer algo.

chickenpox [chik'ənpâks] *n* varicela.

chickpea [chik'pē] *n* garbanzo.

chicory [chik'ûrē] *n* (*for coffee*) achicoria; (*salad*) escarola.

chide [chīd] *vt*: **to** ~ **sb for sth** reprender *or* regañar a uno por algo.

chief [chēf] *n* jefe/a *m/f* ♦ *a* principal; **C~ of Staff** (*MIL*) jefe *m* del estado mayor.

chief executive officer, (*Brit*) **chief executive** *n* director *m* general.

chiefly [chēf'lē] *ad* principalmente.

chieftain [chēf'tin] *n* jefe *m*, cacique *m*.

chiffon [shifân'] *n* gasa.

chilblain [chil'blān] *n* sabañón *m*.

child, *pl* ~**ren** [chīld, chil'drən] *n* niño/a; (*offspring*) hijo/a.

childbirth [chīld'bûrth] *n* parto.

childhood [chīld'hōōd] *n* niñez *f*, infancia.

childish [chīl'dish] *a* pueril, aniñado.

childless [chīld'lis] *a* sin hijos.

childlike [chīld'līk] *a* de niño, infantil.

child minder *n* (*Brit*) niñera.

child's play [chīldz' plā] *n* (*fig*): **this is** ~ esto es coser y cantar.

Chile [chil'ē] *n* Chile *m*.

Chilean [chēl'ăən] *a*, *n* chileno/a *m/f*.

chill [chil] *n* frío; (*MED*) resfriado ♦ *a* frío ♦ *vt* enfriar; (*CULIN*) congelar.

chil(l)i [chil'ē] *n* (*Brit*) chile *m*, ají *m* (*LAm*).

chilly [chil'ē] *a* frío.

chime [chīm] *n* repique *m*, campanada ♦ *vi* repicar, sonar.

chimney [chim'nē] *n* chimenea.

chimney sweep *n* deshollinador *m*.

chimpanzee [chimpanzē'] *n* chimpancé *m*.

chin [chin] *n* mentón *m*, barbilla.

China [chī'nə] *n* China.

china *n* porcelana; (*crockery*) loza.

Chinese [chīnēz'] *a* chino ♦ *n* (*pl inv*) chino/a; (*LING*) chino.

chink [chingk] *n* (*opening*) grieta, hendedura; (*noise*) tintineo.

chintz [chints] *n* cretona.

chip [chip] *n* (*gen pl*: CULIN: *Brit*) patata *or* papa (*LAm*) frita; (: *US*: *also*: **potato ~**) patata *or* papa frita; (*of wood*) astilla; (*of glass, stone*) lasca; (*in gambling*) ficha; (*COMPUT*) chip *m* ♦ *vt* (*cup, plate*) desconchar; **when the ~s are down** (*fig*) en el momento de la verdad.

chip in *vi* (*col*: *interrupt*) interrumpir; (: *contribute*) compartir los gastos.

chipboard [chip'bôrd] *n* madera aglomerada.

chipmunk [chip'mungk] *n* ardilla listada.

chiropodist [kiráp'ədist] *n* (*Brit*) pedicuro/a.

chiropody [kiráp'ədē] *n* pedicura.

chirp [chûrp] *vi* gorjear, piar; (*cricket*) chirriar ♦ *n* (*of cricket*) chirrido.

chirpy [chûr'pē] *a* alegre, animado.

chisel [chiz'əl] *n* (*for wood*) formón *m*; (*for stone*) cincel *m*.

chit [chit] *n* nota.

chitchat [chit'chat] *n* chismes *mpl*, habladurías *fpl*.

chivalrous [shiv'əlrəs] *a* caballeroso.

chivalry [shiv'əlrē] *n* caballerosidad *f*.

chives [chīvz] *npl* cebollinos *mpl*.

chloride [klôr'īd] *n* cloruro.

chlorinate [klôr'ənāt] *vt* clorinar.

chlorine [klôr'ēn] *n* cloro.

chock-a-block [chák'əblâk'], (*Brit*) **chockfull** [chák'fōōl] *a* atestado.

chocolate [chôk'əlit] *n* chocolate *m*.

choice [chois] *n* elección *f*, selección *f*; (*preference*) preferencia ♦ *a* escogido; **I did it by** *or* **from ~** lo hice de buena gana; **a wide ~** un gran surtido, una gran variedad.

choir [kwī'ûr] *n* coro.

choirboy [kwîûr'boi] *n* corista *m*.

choke [chōk] *vi* sofocarse; (*on food*) atragantarse ♦ *vt* ahogar, sofocar; (*block*) obstruir ♦ *n* (*AUT*) estárter *m*.

choker [chō'kûr] *n* (*necklace*) gargantilla.

cholera [kál'ərə] *n* cólera *m*.

cholesterol [kəles'təról] *n* colesterol *m*.

choose, *pt* **chose**, *pp* **chosen** [chōōz, chōz, chō'zən] *vt* escoger, elegir; (*team*) seleccionar; **to ~ between** elegir *or* escoger entre; **to ~ from** elegir de entre.

choosy [chōō'zē] *a* remilgado.

chop [cháp] *vt* (*wood*) cortar, tajar; (*CULIN*: *also*: **~ up**) picar ♦ *n* golpe *m* cortante; (*CULIN*) chuleta; **~s** *npl* (*jaws*) boca *sg*, labios *mpl*; **to get the ~** (*Brit col*: *project*) ser cortado; (: *person*: *be laid off*) ser despedido.

chopper [cháp'ûr] *n* (*helicopter*) helicóptero.

choppy [cháp'ē] *a* (*sea*) picado, agitado.

chopsticks [cháp'stiks] *npl* palillos *mpl*.

choral [kôr'əl] *a* coral.

chord [kôrd] *n* (*MUS*) acorde *m*.

chore [chôr] *n* faena, tarea; (*routine task*) trabajo rutinario.

choreographer [kôrēâg'rəfûr] *n* coreógrafo/a.

chorister [kôr'istûr] *n* corista *m/f*; (*US*) director(a) *m/f* de un coro.

chortle [chôr'təl] *vi* reír entre dientes.

chorus [kôr'əs] *n* coro; (*repeated part of song*) estribillo.

chose [chōz] *pt of* **choose**.

chosen [chō'zən] *pp of* **choose**.

chow [chou] *n* (*dog*) perro chino.

chowder [chou'dûr] *n* (*esp US*) sopa de pescado.

Christ [krīst] *n* Cristo.

christen [kris'ən] *vt* bautizar.

christening [kris'əning] *n* bautizo.

Christian [kris'chən] *a, n* cristiano/a *m/f*.

Christianity [krischēan'itē] *n* cristianismo.

Christian name *n* nombre *m* de pila.

Christmas [kris'məs] *n* Navidad *f*; **Merry ~!** ¡Felices Navidades!, ¡Felices Pascuas!

Christmas card *n* crismas *m inv*, tarjeta de Navidad.

Christmas Day *n* día *m* de Navidad.

Christmas Eve *n* Nochebuena.

Christmas Island *n* Isla Christmas.

Christmas tree *n* árbol *m* de Navidad.

chrome [krōm] *n* = **chromium plating**.

chromium [krō'mēəm] *n* cromo; (*also*: **~ plating**) cromado.

chromosome [krō'məsōm] *n* cromosoma *m*.

chronic [krân'ik] *a* crónico; (*fig*: *liar, smoker*) empedernido.

chronicle [krân'ikəl] *n* crónica.

chronological [krânəlâj'ikəl] *a* cronológico.

chrysalis [kris'əlis] *n* (*BIO*) crisálida.

chrysanthemum [krisan'thəməm] *n* crisantemo.

chubby [chub'ē] *a* rechoncho.

chuck [chuk] *vt* lanzar, arrojar; **to ~** (**up** *or* **in**) *vt* (*Brit*: *job*) abandonar; (: *person*) dejar plantado.

chuckle [chuk'əl] *vi* reírse entre dientes.

chug [chug] *vi* (*also*: **~ along**: *train*) ir despacio, ir tirando.

chum [chum] *n* compinche *m/f*, compañero/a.

chump [chump] *n* (*col*) tonto/a, estúpido/a.

chunk [chungk] *n* pedazo, trozo.

chunky [chung'kē] *a* (*furniture etc*) achaparrado; (*person*) fornido; (*knitwear*) de lana espesa, grueso.

church [chûrch] *n* iglesia; **the C~ of England** la Iglesia Anglicana.

churchyard [chûrch'yârd] *n* camposanto.

churlish [chûr'lish] *a* grosero; (*miserly*) tacaño.

churn [chûrn] *n* (*for butter*) mantequera; (*for milk*) lechera.

churn out *vt* producir en serie.

chute [shōōt] *n* (*also*: **garbage ~**) vertede-

ro; (*Brit: children's slide*) tobogán *m*.
chutney [chut'nē] *n* salsa picante.
CIA *n abbr* (*US:* = *Central Intelligence Agency*) CIA *f*, Agencia Central de Inteligencia.
cicada [sikā'də] *n* cigarra.
CID *n abbr* (*Brit:* = *Criminal Investigation Department*) ≈ B.I.C. *f* (*Sp*).
cider [sī'dúr] *n* sidra.
C.I.F. *abbr* (= *cost, insurance and freight*) C.I.F.
cigar [sigâr'] *n* puro.
cigarette [sigəret'] *n* cigarrillo, pitillo.
cigarette case *n* pitillera.
cigarette end *n* colilla.
cigarette holder *n* boquilla.
C in C *abbr* = **commander in chief**.
cinch [sinch] *n* (*sure thing*) cosa segura.
cinder block [sin'dûr blâk] *n* (*US*) ladrillo de cenizas.
Cinderella [sindərel'ə] *n* Cenicienta.
cinders [sin'dûrz] *npl* cenizas *fpl*.
cine-camera [sin'ēkamûrə] *n* (*Brit*) cámara cinematográfica.
cine-film [sin'ēfilm] *n* (*Brit*) película de cine.
cinema [sin'əmə] *n* cine *m*.
cinnamon [sin'əmən] *n* canela.
cipher [sī'fúr] *n* cifra; **in** ~ en clave.
circle [sûr'kəl] *n* círculo; (*in theater*) anfiteatro ♦ *vi* (*surround*) rodear, cercar; (*move around*) dar la vuelta a.
circuit [sûr'kit] *n* circuito; (*track*) pista; (*lap*) vuelta.
circuit board *n* tarjeta de circuitos impresos.
circuit court *n* (*US LAW*) tribunal *m* superior.
circuitous [sûrkyōō'itəs] *a* indirecto.
circular [sûr'kyəlûr] *a* circular ♦ *n* circular *f*; (*as advertisement*) panfleto.
circulate [sûr'kyəlāt] *vi* circular; (*person: socially*) alternar, circular ♦ *vt* poner en circulación.
circulation [sûrkyəlā'shən] *n* circulación *f*; (*of newspaper etc*) tirada.
circumcise [sûr'kəmsīz] *vt* circuncidar.
circumference [sûrkum'fûrəns] *n* circunferencia.
circumscribe [sûrkəmskrīb'] *vt* circunscribir.
circumspect [sûr'kəmspekt] *a* circunspecto, prudente.
circumstances [sûr'kəmstansiz] *npl* circunstancias *fpl*; (*financial condition*) situación *f* económica; **in the** ~ en *or* dadas las circunstancias; **under no** ~ de ninguna manera, bajo ningún concepto.
circumstantial [sûrkəmstan'shəl] *a* detallado; ~ **evidence** prueba indiciaria.
circumvent [sûrkəmvent'] *vt* (*rule etc*) burlar.
circus [sûr'kəs] *n* circo; (*also:* **C~**: *in place*

names) Plaza.
cistern [sis'tûrn] *n* tanque *m*, depósito; (*Brit: in toilet*) cisterna.
citation [sītā'shən] *n* cita; (*LAW*) citación *f*; (*MIL*) mención *f*.
cite [sīt] *vt* citar.
citizen [sit'əzən] *n* (*POL*) ciudadano/a; (*of city*) habitante *m/f*.
citizenship [sit'əzənship] *n* ciudadanía.
citric [sit'rik] *a*: ~ **acid** ácido cítrico.
citrus fruits [sit'rəs frōōtz] *npl* agrios *mpl*.
city [sit'ē] *n* ciudad *f*; **the C~** *centro financiero de Londres*.
city center *n* centro de la ciudad.
city hall *n* (*US*) ayuntamiento.
city plan *n* (*US*) plano de la ciudad.
city planner *n* (*US*) urbanista *m/f*.
city planning *n* (*US*) urbanismo.
civic [siv'ik] *a* cívico, municipal.
civil [siv'əl] *a*; (*polite*) atento, cortés/esa; (*well-bred*) educado.
civil defense *n* protección *f* civil.
civil engineer *n* ingeniero/a de caminos.
civil engineering *n* ingeniería de caminos.
civilian [sivil'yən] *a* civil (*no militar*) ♦ *n* civil *m/f*, paisano/a.
civilization [sivələzā'shən] *n* civilización *f*.
civilized [siv'əlīzd] *a* civilizado.
civil law *n* derecho civil.
civil rights *npl* derechos *mpl* civiles.
civil servant *n* funcionario/a del Estado.
Civil Service *n* administración *f* pública.
civil war *n* guerra civil.
cl *abbr* (= *centiliter*) cl.
clad [klad] *a*: ~ **(in)** vestido (de).
claim [klām] *vt* exigir, reclamar; (*rights etc*) reivindicar; (*assert*) pretender ♦ *vi* (*for insurance*) reclamar ♦ *n* (*for expenses*) reclamación *f*; (*LAW*) demanda; (*pretension*) pretensión *f*; **to put in a** ~ **for sth** presentar una demanda por algo.
claimant [klā'mənt] *n* (*ADMIN, LAW*) demandante *m/f*.
claim form *n* solicitud *f*.
clairvoyant [klârvoi'ənt] *n* clarividente *m/f*.
clam [klam] *n* almeja.
clam up *vi* (*col*) cerrar el pico.
clamber [klam'bûr] *vi* trepar.
clammy [klam'ē] *a* (*cold*) frío y húmedo; (*sticky*) pegajoso.
clamor, (*Brit*) **clamour** [klam'ûr] *n* (*noise*) clamor *m*, clamoreo; (*protest*) reclamación *f*, protesta ♦ *vi*: **to** ~ **for sth** clamar por algo, pedir algo a voces.
clamp [klamp] *n* abrazadera, grapa ♦ *vt* afianzar (con abrazadera).
clamp down on *vt fus* (*subj: government, police*) reforzar la lucha contra.
clan [klan] *n* clan *m*.
clandestine [klandes'tin] *a* clandestino.
clang [klang] *n* estruendo ♦ *vi* sonar, hacer estruendo.

clansman [klanz'mən] *n* miembro del clan.

clap [klap] *vi* aplaudir ♦ *vt* (*hands*) batir ♦ *n* (*of hands*) palmada; **to ~ one's hands** dar palmadas, batir las palmas; **a ~ of thunder** un trueno.

clapping [klap'ing] *n* aplausos *mpl*.

claret [klar'it] *n* vino tinto (de Burdeos).

clarification [klarəfəkā'shən] *n* aclaración *f*.

clarify [klar'əfī] *vt* aclarar.

clarinet [klarənet'] *n* clarinete *m*.

clarity [klar'itē] *n* claridad *f*.

clash [klash] *n* estruendo; (*fig*) choque *m* ♦ *vi* (*meet*) encontrarse; (*battle*) chocar; (*disagree*) estar en desacuerdo; (*dates, events*) coincidir.

clasp [klasp] *n* broche *m*; (*on jewels*) cierre *m* ♦ *vt* abrochar; (*hand*) apretar; (*embrace*) abrazar.

class [klas] *n* (*gen*) clase *f*; (*group, category*) clase *f*, categoría ♦ *cpd* clasista, de clase ♦ *vt* clasificar.

class-conscious [klas'kân'shəs] *a* clasista, con conciencia de clase.

classic [klas'ik] *a* clásico ♦ *n* (*work*) obra clásica; **~s** *npl* (*UNIV*) clásicas *fpl*.

classical [klas'ikəl] *a* clásico; **~ music** música clásica.

classification [klasəfəkā'shən] *n* clasificación *f*.

classified [klas'əfīd] *a* (*information*) reservado.

classified advertisement *n* anuncio por palabras.

classify [klas'əfī] *vt* clasificar.

classmate [klas'māt] *n* compañero/a de clase.

classroom [klas'rōōm] *n* aula.

classy [klas'ē] *a* (*col*) elegante, con estilo.

clatter [klat'ûr] *n* ruido, estruendo; (*of hooves*) trápala ♦ *vi* hacer ruido *or* estruendo.

clause [klôz] *n* cláusula; (*LING*) oración *f*.

claustrophobia [klôstrəfō'bēə] *n* claustrofobia.

claw [klô] *n* (*of cat*) uña; (*of bird of prey*) garra; (*of lobster*) pinza; (*TECH*) garfio ♦ *vi*: **to ~ at** arañar; (*tear*) desgarrar.

clay [klā] *n* arcilla.

clean [klēn] *a* limpio; (*clear*) neto, bien definido ♦ *vt* limpiar ♦ *ad*: **he ~ forgot** lo olvidó por completo; **to come ~** (*col: admit guilt*) confesarlo todo; **to have a ~ driver's license** tener el carnet de conducir sin sanciones; **to ~ one's teeth** (*Brit*) lavarse los dientes.

clean off *vt* limpiar.

clean out *vt* limpiar (a fondo).

clean up *vt* limpiar, asear ♦ *vi* (*fig: make profit*): **to ~ up on** sacar provecho de.

clean-cut [klēn'kut'] *a* (*person*) de buen parecer; (*clear*) nítido.

cleaner [klē'nûr] *n* (*woman*) mujer *f* de la limpieza; (*also:* **dry ~**) tintorero/a.

cleaning [klē'ning] *n* limpieza.

cleaning lady *or* **woman** *n* señora de la limpieza, asistenta.

cleanliness [klɛn'lēnis] *n* limpieza.

cleanse [klɛnz] *vt* limpiar.

cleanser [klɛn'zûr] *n* detergente *m*; (*cosmetic*) loción *f or* crema limpiadora.

clean-shaven [klēn'shā'vən] *a* sin barba, lampiño.

cleansing department [klɛn'zing dipârt'mənt] *n* (*Brit*) departamento de limpieza.

clear [kli'ûr] *a* claro; (*road, way*) libre; (*profit*) neto; (*majority*) absoluto ♦ *vt* (*space*) despejar, limpiar; (*LAW: suspect*) absolver; (*obstacle*) salvar, saltar por encima de; (*debt*) liquidar; (*check*) pasar por un banco, aceptar; (*site, woodland*) desmontar ♦ *vi* (*fog etc*) despejarse ♦ *n*: **to be in the ~** (*out of debt*) estar libre de deudas; (*out of suspicion*) quedar fuera de toda sospecha; (*out of danger*) estar fuera de peligro ♦ *ad*: **~ of** a distancia de; **to make o.s. ~** explicarse claramente; **to make it ~ to sb that ...** hacer entender a uno que ...; **I have a ~ day tomorrow** mañana tengo el día libre; **to keep ~ of sth/sb** evitar algo/a uno; **to ~ a profit of ...** sacar una ganancia de; **to ~ the table** recoger *or* levantar la mesa.

clear off *vi* (*Brit*) = **clear out**.

clear out *vi* (*col: leave*) marcharse.

clear up *vt* limpiar; (*mystery*) aclarar, resolver.

clearance [klē'rəns] *n* (*removal*) despeje *m*; (*permission*) acreditación *f*.

clear-cut [kli'ûrkut'] *a* bien definido, nítido.

clearing [klē'ring] *n* (*in wood*) claro.

clearing bank *n* (*Brit*) banco central.

clearing house *n* (*COMM*) cámara de compensación.

clearly [kli'ûrlē] *ad* claramente.

clearway [klē'rwā] *n* (*Brit*) carretera donde no se puede aparcar.

cleaver [klē'vûr] *n* cuchilla (de carnicero).

clef [klef] *n* (*MUS*) clave *f*.

cleft [kleft] *n* (*in rock*) grieta, hendedura.

clemency [klem'ənsē] *n* clemencia.

clement [klem'ənt] *a* (*weather*) clemente, benigno.

clench [klench] *vt* apretar, cerrar.

clergy [klûr'jē] *n* clero.

clergyman [klûr'jēmən] *n* clérigo.

clerical [klär'ikəl] *a* de oficina; (*REL*) clerical; (*error*) de copia.

clerk [klûrk] *n* oficinista *m/f*; (*US*) dependiente/a *m/f*, vendedor(a) *m/f*; **C~ of the Court** escribano forense.

clever [klev'ûr] *a* (*mentally*) inteligente, listo; (*skillful*) hábil; (*device, arrangement*) ingenioso.

clew [klōō] *n* (*US*) = **clue**.

cliché [klēshā'] *n* cliché *m*, frase *f* hecha.
click [klik] *vt* (*tongue*) chasquear; (*heels*) taconear.
client [klī'ənt] *n* cliente *m/f*.
clientele [klīəntel'] *n* clientela.
cliff [klif] *n* acantilado.
cliffhanger [klif'hangûr] *n* (*TV*, *fig*) película *etc* de suspense.
climactic [klīmak'tik] *a* culminante.
climate [klī'mit] *n* clima *m*; (*fig*) ambiente *m*.
climax [klī'maks] *n* colmo, punto culminante; (*of play etc*) nudo, clímax *m*; (*sexual* ~) orgasmo.
climb [klīm] *vi* subir, trepar; (*plane*) elevarse, remontar el vuelo ♦ *vt* (*stairs*) subir; (*tree*) trepar a; (*mountain*) escalar ♦ *n* subida; **to ~ over a wall** franquear *or* salvar una tapia.
  climb down *vi* (*fig*) volverse atrás.
climbdown [klīm'doun] *n* (*Brit*) vuelta atrás.
climber [klī'mûr] *n* alpinista *m/f*, montañista *m/f*, andinista *m/f* (*LAm*).
climbing [klī'ming] *n* alpinismo, andinismo (*LAm*).
clinch [klinch] *vt* (*deal*) cerrar; (*argument*) remachar.
cling, *pt*, *pp* **clung** [kling, klung] *vi*: **to ~ (to)** agarrarse (a); (*clothes*) pegarse (a).
clinic [klin'ik] *n* clínica.
clinical [klin'ikəl] *a* clínico; (*fig*) frío, impasible.
clink [klingk] *vi* tintinar.
clip [klip] *n* (*for hair*) horquilla; (*also:* **paper** ~) sujetapapeles *m inv*, clip *m*; (*clamp*) grapa ♦ *vt* (*cut*) cortar; (*hedge*) podar; (*also:* ~ **together**) unir.
clippers [klip'ûrz] *npl* (*for gardening*) tijeras *fpl*; (*for hair*) maquinilla *sg*; (*for nails*) cortauñas *m inv*.
clipping [klip'ing] *n* (*from newspaper*) recorte *m*.
clique [klēk] *n* camarilla.
cloak [klōk] *n* capa, manto ♦ *vt* (*fig*) encubrir, disimular.
cloakroom [klōk'rōōm] *n* guardarropa *m*; (*Brit: WC*) lavabo, aseos *mpl*, baño (*LAm*).
clock [klâk] *n* reloj *m*; (*in taxi*) taxímetro; **to work against the ~** trabajar contra reloj; **around the ~** las veinticuatro horas; **to sleep round the ~** dormir un día entero; **30,000 on the ~** (*Brit AUT*) treinta mil millas en el cuentakilómetros.
  clock in, clock on *vi* fichar, picar.
  clock off, clock out *vi* fichar *or* picar la salida.
  clock up *vt* acumular.
clockwise [klâk'wīz] *ad* en el sentido de las agujas del reloj.
clockwork [klâk'wûrk] *n* aparato de relojería ♦ *a* (*toy*, *train*) de cuerda.
clod [klâd] *n* (*col*) imbécil *m/f*.

clog [klâg] *n* zueco, chanclo ♦ *vt* atascar ♦ *vi* atascarse.
cloister [klois'tûr] *n* claustro.
clone [klōn] *n* clon *m*.
close *a, ad and derivatives* [klōs] *a* cercano, próximo; (*near*): ~ **(to)** cerca (de); (*print*, *weave*) tupido, compacto; (*friend*) íntimo; (*connection*) estrecho; (*examination*) detallado, minucioso; (*weather*) bochornoso; (*atmosphere*) sofocante; (*room*) mal ventilado ♦ *ad* cerca; ~ **by**, ~ **at hand** *a, ad* muy cerca; ~ **to** *prep* cerca de; **to have a** ~ **shave** (*fig*) escaparse por un pelo; **how** ~ **is Boston to New York?** ¿qué distancia hay de Boston a Nueva York?; **at** ~ **quarters** de cerca ♦ *vb and derivatives* [klōz] *vt* (*shut*) cerrar; (*end*) concluir, terminar; (*bargain*, *deal*) cerrar ♦ *vi* (*store etc*) cerrarse; (*end*) concluirse, terminarse ♦ *n* (*end*) fin *m*, final *m*, conclusión *f*; **to bring sth to a** ~ terminar algo.
  close down *vi* cerrarse definitivamente.
  close in *vi* (*hunters*) acercarse rodeando, rodear; (*evening*, *night*, *fog*) caer, cerrarse; **to ~ in on sb** rodear *or* cercar a uno; **the days are closing in** los días son cada vez más cortos.
  close off *vt* (*area*) cerrar al tráfico *or* al público.
closed [klōzd] *a* (*store etc*) cerrado.
closed-circuit [klōzdsûr'kit] *a*: ~ **television** televisión *f* por circuito cerrado.
closed shop *n* taller *m* gremial.
close-knit [klōs'nit'] *a* (*fig*) muy unido.
closely [klōs'lē] *ad* (*study*) con detalle; (*listen*) con atención; (*watch: person*, *events*) de cerca; **we are ~ related** somos parientes cercanos; **a ~ guarded secret** un secreto rigurosamente guardado.
closet [klâz'it] *n* (*cupboard*) armario.
close-up [klōs'up] *n* primer plano.
closing [klō'zing] *a* (*stages*, *remarks*) último, final; ~ **price** (*STOCK EXCHANGE*) precio de cierre.
closure [klō'zhûr] *n* cierre *m*.
clot [klât] *n* (*gen:* **blood** ~) embolia; (*col: idiot*) imbécil *m/f* ♦ *vi* (*blood*) coagularse.
cloth [klôth] *n* (*material*) tela, paño; (*table* ~) mantel *m*; (*rag*) trapo.
clothe [klōth] *vt* vestir; (*fig*) revestir.
clothes [klōz] *npl* ropa *sg*; **to put one's ~ on** vestirse, ponerse la ropa; **to take one's ~ off** desvestirse, desnudarse.
clothes brush *n* cepillo (para la ropa).
clothes line *n* cuerda (para tender la ropa).
clothes pin, (*Brit*) **clothes peg** *n* pinza.
clothing [klō'thing] *n* = **clothes.**
clotted cream [klât'id krēm'] *n* (*Brit*) nata muy espesa.
cloud [kloud] *n* nube *f*; (*storm* ~) nubarrón *m*; (*of dust, smoke, gas*) nube *f* ♦ *vt*: (*liquid*) enturbiar; **every ~ has a silver lining**

no hay mal que por bien no venga; **to ~ the issue** empañar el problema.

cloud over vi (also fig) nublarse.

cloudburst [kloud'bûrst] n chaparrón m.

cloudland [kloud'land] n (US) Babia.

cloudy [klou'dē] a nublado, nubloso; (liquid) turbio.

clout [klout] n (fig) influencia ♦ vt dar un tortazo a.

clove [klōv] n clavo; **~ of garlic** diente m de ajo.

clover [klō'vûr] n trébol m.

clown [kloun] n payaso ♦ vi (also: **~ around**) hacer el payaso.

cloying [kloi'ing] a (taste) empalagoso.

C.L.U. n abbr (US) = Chartered Life Underwriter.

club [klub] n (society) club m; (weapon) porra, cachiporra; (also: **golf ~**) palo ♦ vt aporrear ♦ vi: **to ~ together** (join forces) unir fuerzas; **~s** npl (CARDS) tréboles mpl.

club car n (US RAIL) coche m salón.

clubhouse [klub'hous] n local social, sobre todo en clubs deportivos.

cluck [kluk] vi cloquear.

clue [klōō] n pista; (in crosswords) indicación f; **I haven't a ~** no tengo ni idea.

clued-in [klōōd'in] a (US col) al tanto, al corriente.

clued-up [klōōd'up] a (Brit col) = **clued-in**.

clump [klump] n (of trees) grupo.

clumsy [klum'zē] a (person) torpe, desmañado; (tool) difícil de manejar.

clung [klung] pt, pp of **cling**.

clunker [klunk'ûr] n (US: pej) pota, tartana.

cluster [klus'tûr] n grupo; (BOT) racimo ♦ vi agruparse, apiñarse.

clutch [kluch] n (AUT) embrague m; (pedal) pedal m de embrague; **to fall into sb's ~es** caer en las garras de alguien ♦ vt asir; agarrar.

clutter [klut'ûr] vt (also: **~ up**) atestar, llenar desordenadamente ♦ n desorden m, confusión f.

CM abbr (US MAIL) = North Mariana Islands.

cm abbr (= centimeter) cm.

CND n abbr (= Campaign for Nuclear Disarmament) plataforma pro desarme nuclear.

CO n abbr = **commanding officer** ♦ abbr (US MAIL) = Colorado.

Co. abbr = **county**; = **company**.

c/o abbr (= care of) c/a, a/c.

coach [kōch] n autocar m (Sp), autobús m; (horse-drawn) coche m; (of train) vagón m, coche m; (SPORT) entrenador(a) m/f, instructor(a) m/f ♦ vt (SPORT) entrenar; (student) preparar, enseñar.

coach trip n (Brit) excursión f en autocar.

coagulate [kōag'yəlāt] vi coagularse.

coal [kōl] n carbón m.

coalfield [kōl'fēld] n yacimiento de carbón.

coalition [kōəlish'ən] n coalición f.

coal man, coal merchant n carbonero.

coal mine n mina de carbón.

coal miner n minero (de carbón).

coal mining n minería (de carbón).

coarse [kôrs] a basto, burdo; (vulgar) grosero, ordinario.

coast [kōst] n costa, litoral m ♦ vi (AUT) ir en punto muerto.

coastal [kōs'təl] a costero, costanero.

coaster [kōs'tûr] n (drinks mat) posavasos m; (NAUT) buque m costero, barco de cabotaje.

coastguard [kōst'gârd] n guardacostas m inv.

coastline [kōst'līn] n litoral m.

coat [kōt] n (jacket) chaqueta; (overcoat) abrigo; (of animal) pelo, lana; (of paint) mano f, capa ♦ vt cubrir, revestir.

coated [kō'tid] a (tongue) saburroso.

coat hanger n percha, gancho (LAm).

coating [kō'ting] n capa, baño.

coat of arms n escudo de armas.

co-author [kōōth'ûr] n coautor(a) m/f.

coax [kōks] vt engatusar.

cob [kâb] n see **corn**.

cobbler [kâb'lûr] n zapatero (remendón).

cobble(stone)s [kâb'əl(stōn)z] npl adoquines mpl.

COBOL [kō'bōl] n COBOL m.

cobra [kōb'rə] n cobra.

cobweb [kâb'web] n telaraña.

cocaine [kōkān'] n cocaína.

cock [kâk] n (rooster) gallo; (male bird) macho ♦ vt (gun) amartillar.

cock-a-hoop [kâkəhōōp'] a: **to be ~** estar más contento que unas pascuas.

cockatoo [kâk'ətōō] n cacatúa.

cockerel [kâk'ûrəl] n gallito.

cockeyed [kâk'īd] a bizco; (fig: crooked) torcido; (: idea) disparatado.

cockle [kâk'əl] n berberecho.

cockney [kâk'nē] n habitante m/f de ciertos barrios de Londres.

cockpit [kâk'pit] n (in aircraft) cabina.

cockroach [kâk'rōch] n cucaracha.

cocktail [kâk'tāl] n combinado, cóctel m; **shrimp** (US) or **prawn** (Brit) **~** cóctel m de gambas.

cocktail cabinet n mueble-bar m.

cocktail party n cocktail m, cóctel m.

cocktail shaker [kâk'tāl shā'kûr] n coctelera.

cocoa [kō'kō] n cacao; (drink) chocolate m.

coconut [kō'kənut] n coco.

cocoon [kəkōōn'] n capullo.

cod [kâd] n bacalao.

COD abbr = **cash on delivery**; (US) = **collect on delivery**.

code [kōd] n código; (cipher) clave f; (TEL) prefijo; **~ of behavior** código de conducta; **~ of practice** código profesional.

codeine [kō'dēn] n codeína.

codicil [kâd'isəl] *n* codicilo.
codify [kâd'əfī] *vt* codificar.
cod-liver oil [kâd'livûr oil'] *n* aceite *m* de hígado de bacalao.
co-driver [kōdrī'vûr] *n* (*in race*) copiloto *m/f*; (*of truck*) segundo conductor *m*.
co-ed [kōed'] *a abbr* = **coeducational** ♦ *n abbr* (*US*: = *female student*) alumna de una universidad mixta; (*Brit*: *school*) colegio mixto.
coeducational [kōejōōkā'shənəl] *a* mixto.
coerce [kōûrs'] *vt* forzar, coaccionar.
coercion [kōûr'shən] *n* coacción *f*.
coexistence [kōigzis'təns] *n* coexistencia.
C. of C. *n abbr* = **chamber of commerce**.
C of E *abbr* = **Church of England**.
coffee [kôf'ē] *n* café *m*; ~ **with cream**, (*Brit*) **white** ~ café con leche.
coffee bar *n* (*Brit*) cafetería.
coffee bean *n* grano de café.
coffee break *n* descanso (para tomar café).
coffee cup *n* taza de café.
coffeepot [kôf'ēpât] *n* cafetera.
coffee table *n* mesita (para servir el café).
coffin [kôf'in] *n* ataúd *m*.
cog [kâg] *n* diente *m*.
cogent [kō'jənt] *a* lógico, convincente.
cognac [kōn'yak] *n* coñac *m*.
cogwheel [kâg'hwēl] *n* rueda dentada.
cohabit [kōhab'it] *vi* (*formal*): **to** ~ (**with sb**) cohabitar (con uno).
coherent [kōhē'rənt] *a* coherente.
cohesion [kōhē'zhən] *n* cohesión *f*.
cohesive [kōhē'siv] *a* (*fig*) cohesivo, unido.
coil [koil] *n* rollo; (*rope*) aduja; (*of smoke*) espiral *f*; (*AUT*, *ELEC*) bobina, carrete *m*; (*contraceptive*) espiral *f* ♦ *vt* enrollar, arrollar.
coin [koin] *n* moneda ♦ *vt* acuñar; (*word*) inventar, idear.
coinage [koi'nij] *n* moneda.
coin-box [koin'bâks] *n* (*Brit*) caja recaudadora.
coincide [kōinsīd'] *vi* coincidir; (*agree*) estar de acuerdo.
coincidence [kōin'sidəns] *n* casualidad *f*.
coin-operated [koinâp'ərātid] *a* (*machine*) de meter moneda.
Coke ® [kōk] *n* Coca Cola ® *f*.
coke [kōk] *n* (*coal*) coque *m*.
Col. *abbr* (*US*) = *Colorado*; (= *colonel*) col.
COLA *n abbr* (*US*: = *cost-of-living adjustment*) *reajuste salarial de acuerdo con el costo de la vida*.
colander [kâl'əndûr] *n* colador *m*, escurridor *m*.
cold [kōld] *a* frío ♦ *n* frío; (*MED*) resfriado; **it's** ~ hace frío; **to be** ~ tener frío; **to catch a** ~ coger un catarro, resfriarse, acatarrarse; **in** ~ **blood** a sangre fría; **the room's getting** ~ está empezando a hacer

frío en la habitación; **to give sb the** ~ **shoulder** tratar a uno con frialdad.
cold-blooded [kōld'blud'id] *a* (*ZOOL*) de sangre fría.
cold cream *n* crema.
cold cuts *npl* fiambres *mpl*.
coldly [kōld'lē] *a* fríamente.
cold sore *n* herpes *m* labial.
coleslaw [kōl'slô] *n* ensalada de col.
colic [kâl'ik] *n* cólico.
collaborate [kəlab'ərāt] *vi* colaborar.
collaboration [kəlabərā'shən] *n* colaboración *f*; (*POL*) colaboracionismo.
collaborator [kəlab'ərātûr] *n* colaborador(a) *m/f*; (*POL*) colaboracionista *m/f*.
collage [kəlâzh'] *n* collage *m*.
collagen [kâl'əjən] *n* colágeno.
collapse [kəlaps'] *vi* (*gen*) hundirse, derrumbarse; (*MED*) sufrir un colapso ♦ *n* (*gen*) hundimiento; (*MED*) colapso; (*of government*) caída; (*of plans, scheme, business*) ruina, fracaso.
collapsible [kəlaps'əbəl] *a* plegable.
collar [kâl'ûr] *n* (*of coat, shirt*) cuello; (*for dog, TECH*) collar *m* ♦ *vt* (*col*: *person, object*) abordar, acorralar.
collarbone [kâl'ûrbōn] *n* clavícula.
collate [kəlāt'] *vt* cotejar.
collateral [kəlat'ûrəl] *n* (*COMM*) garantía colateral.
collation [kəlā'shən] *n* colación *f*.
colleague [kâl'ēg] *n* colega *m/f*.
collect [kəlekt'] *vt* reunir; (*as a hobby*) coleccionar; (*Brit*: *call and pick up*) recoger; (*wages*) cobrar; (*debts*) recaudar; (*donations, subscriptions*) colectar ♦ *vi* reunirse; coleccionar ♦ *ad*: **to call** ~ (*US TEL*) llamar a cobro revertido; **to** ~ **one's thoughts** reponerse, recobrar el dominio de sí mismo; ~ **on delivery (COD)** (*US*) entrega contra reembolso.
collect call *n* (*US TEL*) llamada a cobro revertido.
collection [kəlek'shən] *n* colección *f*; (*of fares, wages*) cobro; (*of mail*) recogida.
collective [kəlek'tiv] *a* colectivo.
collective bargaining *n* negociación *f* del convenio colectivo.
collector [kəlek'tûr] *n* coleccionista *m/f*; (*of taxes etc*) recaudador(a) *m/f*; ~**'s item** or **piece** pieza de coleccionista.
college [kâl'ij] *n* colegio; (*of technology, agriculture etc*) escuela.
collide [kəlīd'] *vi* chocar.
collie [kâl'ē] *n* (*dog*) collie *m*.
colliery [kâl'yûrē] *n* (*Brit*) mina de carbón.
collision [kəlizh'ən] *n* choque *m*; **to be on a** ~ **course** (*also fig*) ir rumbo al desastre.
colloquial [kəlō'kwēəl] *a* familiar, coloquial.
collusion [kəlōō'zhən] *n* confabulación *f*, connivencia; **in** ~ **with** en connivencia con.
Colo. *abbr* (*US*) = *Colorado*.
cologne [kəlōn'] *n* (*also*: **eau de** ~) (agua

de) colonia.
Colombia [kəlum'bēə] *n* Colombia.
Colombian [kəlum'bēən] *a, n* colombiano/a *m/f*.
colon [kō'lən] *n* (*sign*) dos puntos; (*MED*) colón *m*.
colonel [kûr'nəl] *n* coronel *m*.
colonial [kəlō'nēəl] *a* colonial.
colonize [kál'ənīz] *vt* colonizar.
colonnade [kálənād'] *n* columnata.
colony [kál'ənē] *n* colonia.
color [kul'ûr] (*US*) *n* color *m* ♦ *vt* color(e)ar; (*with crayons*) color(e)ar (al pastel); (*dye*) teñir ♦ *vi* (*blush*) sonrojarse; **~s** *npl* (*of party, club*) colores *mpl*.
Colorado beetle [kálərâ'dō bē'təl] *n* escarabajo de la patata.
color bar *n* segregación *f* racial.
color-blind [kul'ûrblīnd] *a* daltoniano.
colored [kul'ûrd] *a* de color; (*photo*) en color; (*of race*) de color.
color film *n* película en color.
colorful [kul'ûrfəl] *a* lleno de color; (*person*) excéntrico.
coloring [kul'ûring] *n* (*complexion*) colorido, color; (*substance*) colorante *m*.
colorless [kul'ûrlis] *a* incoloro, sin color.
color scheme *n* combinación *f* de colores.
color television *n* televisión *f* en color.
colossal [kəlâs'əl] *a* colosal.
colour [kul'ûr] *etc* (*Brit*) = **color** *etc*.
colt [kōlt] *n* potro.
column [kál'əm] *n* columna; (*fashion ~, sports ~ etc*) sección *f*; **the editorial ~** el editorial, el artículo de fondo.
columnist [kál'əmist] *n* columnista *m/f*.
coma [kō'mə] *n* coma *m*.
comb [kōm] *n* peine *m*; (*ornamental*) peineta ♦ *vt* (*hair*) peinar; (*area*) registrar a fondo.
combat *n* [kám'bat] combate *m* ♦ *vt* [kəmbat'] combatir.
combination [kámbənā'shən] *n* (*gen*) combinación *f*.
combination lock *n* cerradura de combinación.
combine [kəmbīn'] *vt* combinar; (*qualities*) reunir ♦ *vi* combinarse ♦ *n* [kám'bīn] (*ECON*) cartel *m*; **a ~d effort** un esfuerzo conjunto.
combine (harvester) *n* cosechadora.
combo [kám'bō] *n* (*JAZZ etc*) conjunto.
combustion [kəmbus'chən] *n* combustión *f*.
come [kum], *pt* **came**, *pp* **come** *vi* venir; **to ~ undone** desatarse; **to ~ loose** aflojarse; **~ with me** ven conmigo; **we've just ~ from Seville** acabamos de llegar de Sevilla; **coming!** ¡voy!; **if it ~s to it** llegado el caso.
come about *vi* suceder, ocurrir.
come across *vt fus* (*person*) topar con; (*thing*) dar con ♦ *vi*: **to ~ across well/badly** caer bien/mal.

come around *vi* (*after faint, operation*) volver en sí.
come away *vi* marcharse; (*become detached*) desprenderse.
come back *vi* volver; (*reply*): **can I ~ back to you on that one?** ¡volvamos sobre ese punto!
come by *vt fus* (*acquire*) conseguir.
come down *vi* bajar; (*buildings*) derrumbarse; (: *be demolished*) ser derribado.
come forward *vi* presentarse.
come from *vt fus* ser de.
come in *vi* entrar; (*train*) llegar; (*fashion*) ponerse de moda.
come in for *vt fus* (*criticism etc*) merecer.
come into *vt fus* (*money*) heredar.
come off *vi* (*button*) soltarse, desprenderse; (*succeed*) salir bien.
come on *vi* (*pupil, work, project*) desarrollarse; (*lights*) encenderse; **~ on!** ¡vamos!
come out *vi* salir; (*book*) aparecer; (*be revealed*) salir a luz; (*strike*) declararse en huelga; **to ~ out for/against** declararse por/en contra de.
come over *vt fus*: **I don't know what's ~ over him!** ¡no sé lo que le pasa!
come round *vi* (*Brit*) = **come around**.
come through *vi* (*survive*) sobrevivir; (*telephone call*): **the call came through** recibimos la llamada.
come to *vi* volver en sí; (*total*) sumar; **how much does it ~ to?** ¿cuánto es en total?, ¿a cuánto asciende?
come under *vt fus* (*heading*) entrar en; (*influence*) estar bajo.
come up *vi* subir; (*sun*) salir; (*problem*) surgir.
come up against *vt fus* (*resistance, difficulties*) tropezar con.
come up to *vt fus* llegar hasta; **the film didn't ~ up to our expectations** la película no fue tan buena como esperábamos.
come up with *vt fus* (*idea*) sugerir, proponer.
come upon *vt fus* dar *or* topar con.
comeback [kum'bak] *n* (*reaction*) reacción *f*; (*response*) réplica; **to make a ~** (*THEATER*) volver a las tablas.
Comecon [kám'əkân] *n abbr* (= *Council for Mutual Economic Aid*) COMECON *m*.
comedian [kəmē'dēən] *n* cómico.
comedienne [kəmēdēen'] *n* cómica.
comedown [kum'doun] *n* revés *m*, bajón *m*.
comedy [kám'idē] *n* comedia.
comet [kâm'it] *n* cometa *m*.
comeuppance [kumup'əns] *n*: **to get one's ~** llevar su merecido.
comfort [kum'fûrt] *n* comodidad *f*, confort *m*; (*well-being*) bienestar *m*; (*solace*)

consuelo; (*relief*) alivio ♦ *vt* consolar; *see also* **comforts.**

comfortable [kum'fûrtəbəl] *a* cómodo; (*income*) adecuado; (*majority*) suficiente; **I don't feel very ~ about it** la cosa me trae algo preocupado.

comfortably [kum'fûrtəblē] *ad* (*sit*) cómodamente; (*live*) holgadamente.

comforter [kum'fûrtûr] *n* (*US: bed cover*) colcha.

comforts [kum'fûrts] *npl* comodidades *fpl*.

comfort station *n* (*US*) servicios *mpl*.

comic [kâm'ik] *a* (*also:* ~**al**) cómico, gracioso ♦ *n* (*magazine*) tebeo; (*for adults*) cómic *m*.

comic strip *n* tira cómica.

coming [kum'ing] *n* venida, llegada ♦ *a* que viene; (*next*) próximo; (*future*) venidero; ~**(s) and going(s)** *n(pl)* ir y venir *m*, ajetreo; **in the ~ weeks** en las próximas semanas.

Comintern [kâm'intûrn] *n* Comintern *f*.

comma [kâm'ə] *n* coma.

command [kəmand'] *n* orden *f*, mandato; (*MIL: authority*) mando; (*mastery*) dominio; (*COMPUT*) orden *f*, comando ♦ *vt* (*troops*) mandar; (*give orders to*) mandar, ordenar; (*be able to get*) disponer de; (*deserve*) merecer; **to have at one's ~** (*money, resources etc*) tener disponible *or* a su disposición; **to have/take ~ of** estar al/asumir el mando de.

commandeer [kâməndēr'] *vt* requisar.

commander [kəman'dûr] *n* (*MIL*) comandante *m/f*, jefe/a *m/f*; ~ **in chief** jefe *m* supremo.

commanding [kəman'ding] *a* (*appearance*) imponente; (*voice, tone*) imperativo; (*lead, position*) abrumador(a), dominante.

commanding officer *n* comandante *m*.

commandment [kəmand'mənt] *n* (*REL*) mandamiento.

command module *n* módulo de comando.

commando [kəman'dō] *n* comando.

commemorate [kəmem'ərāt] *vt* conmemorar.

commemoration [kəmemərā'shən] *n* conmemoración *f*.

commemorative [kəmem'ərātiv] *a* conmemorativo.

commence [kəmens'] *vt, vi* comenzar, empezar.

commend [kəmend'] *vt* (*praise*) elogiar, alabar; (*recommend*) recomendar; (*entrust*) encomendar.

commendable [kəmend'əbəl] *a* encomiable; **it is ~ that ...** está muy bien que ...

commendation [kâməndā'shən] *n* (*for bravery etc*) elogio, encomio; recomendación *f*.

commensurate [kəmen'sərit] *a*: ~ **with** en proporción a, que corresponde a.

comment [kâm'ent] *n* comentario ♦ *vt*: **to ~ that** comentar *or* observar que ♦ *vi*: **to ~ (on)** comentar, hacer comentarios (sobre); **"no ~"** "no tengo nada que decir".

commentary [kâm'əntārē] *n* comentario.

commentator [kâm'əntātûr] *n* comentarista *m/f*.

commerce [kâm'ûrs] *n* comercio.

commercial [kəmûr'shəl] *a* comercial ♦ *n* (*TV: also:* ~ **break**) anuncio.

commercial bank *n* banco comercial.

commercialism [kəmûr'shəlizəm] *n* materialismo.

commercialize [kəmûr'shəlīz] *vt* comercializar.

commercial television *n* televisión *f* comercial.

commercial vehicle *n* vehículo comercial.

commiserate [kəmiz'ərāt] *vi*: **to ~ with** compadecerse de, condolerse de.

commission [kəmish'ən] *n* (*committee, fee, order for work of art etc*) comisión *f*; (*act*) perpetración *f* ♦ *vt* (*MIL*) nombrar; (*work of art*) encargar; **out of ~** (*machine*) fuera de servicio; **I get 10% ~** me dan el diez por ciento de comisión; **to ~ sb to do sth** encargar a uno que haga algo; **to ~ sth from sb** (*painting etc*) encargar algo a uno.

commissionaire [kəmishənär'] *n* (*Brit*) portero.

commissioner [kəmish'ənûr] *n* comisario; (*POLICE*) comisario *m* de policía.

commit [kəmit'] *vt* (*act*) cometer; (*to sb's care*) entregar; **to ~ o.s. (to do)** comprometerse (a hacer); **to ~ suicide** suicidarse; **to ~ sb for trial** remitir a uno al tribunal.

commitment [kəmit'mənt] *n* compromiso.

committed [kəmit'id] *a* (*writer, politician etc*) comprometido.

committee [kəmit'ē] *n* comité *m*; **to be on a ~** ser miembro/a de un comité.

committee meeting *n* reunión *f* del comité.

commodious [kəmō'dēəs] *a* grande, espacioso.

commodity [kəmâd'itē] *n* mercancía.

commodity exchange *n* bolsa de productos *or* de mercancías.

commodity market *n* mercado de productos básicos.

commodore [kâm'ədôr] *n* comodoro.

common [kâm'ən] *a* (*gen*) común; (*pej*) ordinario ♦ *n* campo común; **in ~** en común; **in ~ use** de uso corriente.

commoner [kâm'ənûr] *n* plebeyo/a.

common law *n* ley *f* consuetudinaria.

common-law [kâm'ənlô'] *a*: ~ **wife** esposa consensual.

commonly [kâm'ənlē] *ad* comúnmente.

Common Market *n* Mercado Común.

commonplace [kâm'ənplās] *a* de lo más

común.

common room *n* (*Brit*) sala común.

Commons [kâm'ənz] *npl* (*Brit POL*): **the (House of)** ~ (la Cámara de) los Comunes.

commons [kâm'ənz] *n* (*US UNIV*) comedor *m*.

common sense *n* sentido común.

Commonwealth [kâm'ənwelth] *n*: **the** ~ la Mancomunidad (Británica).

commotion [kəmō'shən] *n* tumulto, confusión *f*.

communal [kəmyōō'nəl] *a* comunal.

commune *n* [kâm'yōōn] (*group*) comuna ♦ *vi* [kəmyōōn'']: **to** ~ **with** comulgar *or* conversar con.

communicate [kəmyōō'nikāt] *vt* comunicar ♦ *vi*: **to** ~ **(with)** comunicarse (con).

communication [kəmyōōnikā'shən] *n* comunicación *f*.

communication cord *n* (*Brit*) timbre *m* de alarma.

communications network *n* red *f* de comunicaciones.

communications satellite *n* satélite *m* de comunicaciones.

communicative [kəmyōō'nikātiv] *a* comunicativo.

communion [kəmyōōn'yən] *n* (*also*: **Holy C~**) comunión *f*.

communiqué [kəmyōōnikā'] *n* comunicado, parte *m*.

communism [kâm'yənizəm] *n* comunismo.

communist [kâm'yənist] *a*, *n* comunista *m/f*.

community [kəmyōō'nitē] *n* comunidad *f*; (*large group*) colectividad *f*; (*local*) vecindario.

community center *n* centro social.

community chest *n* (*US*) arca comunitaria, fondo común.

community health center *n* centro médico, dispensario público.

community spirit *n* civismo.

commutation ticket [kâmyətā'shən tik'it] *n* (*US*) billete *m* de abono.

commute [kəmyōōt'] *vi* viajar a diario de la casa al trabajo ♦ *vt* conmutar.

commuter [kəmyōōt'ûr] *n* persona (que ... *see vi*).

compact *a* [kəmpakt'] compacto; (*style*) conciso; (*packed*) apretado ♦ *n* [kâm'pakt] (*pact*) pacto; (*also*: **powder** ~) polvera.

compact disc *n* compact disc *m*.

companion [kəmpan'yən] *n* compañero/a.

companionship [kəmpan'yənship] *n* compañerismo.

companionway [kəmpan'yənwā] *n* (*NAUT*) escalera de cámara.

company [kum'pənē] *n* (*gen*) compañía; (*COMM*) sociedad *f*, compañía; **to keep sb** ~ acompañar a uno; **Smith and C~** Smith y Compañía.

company car *n* coche *m* de la compañía.

company director *n* director(a) *m/f* de empresa.

company secretary *n* (*Brit*) secretario/a de compañía.

comparable [kâm'pûrəbəl] *a* comparable.

comparative [kəmpar'ətiv] *a* (*freedom, luxury, cost*) relativo.

comparatively [kəmpar'ətivlē] *ad* (*relatively*) relativamente.

compare [kəmpär'] *vt* comparar; (*set side by side*) cotejar ♦ *vi*: **to** ~ **(with)** compararse (con); ~**d with** *or* **to** comparado con *or* a; **how do the prices** ~? ¿cómo se comparan los precios?

comparison [kəmpar'isən] *n* comparación *f*; cotejo; **in** ~ **(with)** en comparación (con).

compartment [kəmpârt'mənt] *n* (*also RAIL*) departamento.

compass [kum'pəs] *n* brújula; ~**es** *npl* compás *m*; **within the** ~ **of** al alcance de.

compassion [kəmpash'ən] *n* compasión *f*.

compassionate [kəmpash'ənit] *a* compasivo; **on** ~ **grounds** por compasión.

compatibility [kəmpatəbil'ətē] *n* compatibilidad *f*.

compatible [kəmpat'əbəl] *a* compatible.

compel [kəmpel'] *vt* obligar.

compelling [kəmpel'ing] *a* (*fig: argument*) convincente.

compendium [kəmpen'dēəm] *n* compendio.

compensate [kâm'pənsāt] *vt* compensar ♦ *vi*: **to** ~ **for** compensar.

compensation [kâmpənsā'shən] *n* (*for loss*) indemnización *f*.

compère [kâmpär'] *n* presentador(a) *m/f*.

compete [kəmpēt'] *vi* (*take part*) tomar parte, concurrir; (*vie with*) competir, hacer competencia.

competence [kâm'pitəns] *n* capacidad *f*, aptitud *f*.

competent [kâm'pitənt] *a* competente, capaz.

competition [kâmpitish'ən] *n* (*contest*) concurso; (*ECON, rivalry*) competencia; **in** ~ **with** en competencia con.

competitive [kəmpet'ətiv] *a* (*ECON, SPORT*) competitivo; (*spirit*) competidor(a), de competencia.

competitor [kəmpet'itûr] *n* (*rival*) competidor(a) *m/f*, contrincante *m/f*; (*participant*) concursante *m/f*.

compile [kəmpīl'] *vt* recopilar.

complacency [kəmplā'sənsē] *n* autosatisfacción *f*.

complacent [kəmplā'sənt] *a* autocomplaciente.

complain [kəmplān'] *vi* (*gen*) quejarse; (*COMM*) reclamar.

complaint [kəmplānt'] *n* (*gen*) queja; reclamación *f*; (*LAW*) demanda, querella; (*MED*) enfermedad *f*.

complement *n* [kâm'pləmənt] comple-

mento; (esp ship's crew) dotación f ♦ vt
[kâm'pləmənt] (enhance) complementar.
complementary [kâmpləmen'tûrē] a complementario.
complete [kəmplēt'] a (full) completo;
(finished) acabado ♦ vt (fulfil) completar;
(finish) acabar; (a form) rellenar; **it's a ~
disaster** es un desastre total.
completely [kəmplēt'lē] ad completamente.
completion [kəmplē'shən] n (gen) conclusión f, terminación f; **to be nearing ~**
estar por or para terminarse; **on ~ of contract** cuando se realice el contrato.
complex [kâm'pleks] a complejo ♦ n (gen)
complejo.
complexion [kəmplek'shən] n (of face) tez
f, cutis m; (fig) aspecto.
complexity [kəmplek'sitē] n complejidad f.
compliance [kəmplī'əns] n (submission) sumisión f; (agreement) conformidad f; **in ~
with** de acuerdo con.
compliant [kəmplī'ənt] a sumiso; conforme.
complicate [kâm'pləkāt] vt complicar.
complicated [kâm'pləkātid] a complicado.
complication [kâmpləkā'shən] n complica-
ción f.
complicity [kəmplis'ətē] n complicidad f.
compliment n [kâm'pləmənt] (formal)
cumplido; (flirtation) piropo ♦ vt
[kâm'pləmənt] felicitar; **~s** npl saludos
mpl; **to pay sb a ~** (formal) hacer cumplidos a alguien; (flirt) piropear, echar piro-
pos a alguien; **~ sb (on sth/on doing sth)**
felicitar a uno (por algo/por haber hecho
algo).
complimentary [kâmpləmen'tûrē] a lisonjero; (free) de favor.
compliments card , (Brit) **compliments
slip** n saluda m.
comply [kəmplī'] vi: **to ~ with** cumplir
con.
component [kəmpō'nənt] a componente ♦ n
(TECH) pieza.
compose [kəmpōz'] vt componer; **to be ~d
of** componerse de, constar de; **to ~ o.s.**
tranquilizarse.
composed [kəmpōzd'] a sosegado.
composer [kəmpō'zûr] n (MUS) composi-
tor(a) m/f.
composite [kəmpâz'it] a compuesto; **~ motion** (COMM) moción f compuesta.
composition [kâmpəzish'ən] n composición
f.
compositor [kəmpâz'itûr] n (TYP) cajista
m/f.
compos mentis [kâm'pəs men'tis] a: **to be
~** estar en su sano juicio.
compost [kâm'pōst] n abono.
compost heap n montón de basura vegetal para abono.
composure [kəmpō'zhûr] n serenidad f,
calma.
compound [kâm'pound] n (CHEM)

compuesto; (LING) palabra compuesta;
(enclosure) recinto ♦ a (gen) compuesto;
(fracture) complicado ♦ vt [kəmpound']
(fig: problem, difficulty) agravar.
comprehend [kâmprihend'] vt comprender.
comprehension [kâmprihen'shən] n comprensión f.
comprehensive [kâmprihen'siv] a (broad)
extenso; (general) de conjunto; **~ (school)**
n (Brit) centro estatal de enseñanza secundaria; ≈ Instituto Nacional de Bachillerato (Sp).
comprehensive insurance policy n seguro a todo riesgo.
compress vt [kəmpres'] comprimir ♦ n
[kâm'pres] (MED) compresa.
compression [kəmpresh'ən] n compresión
f.
comprise [kəmprīz'] vt (also: **be ~d of**)
comprender, constar de.
compromise [kâm'prəmīz] n (agreement)
arreglo ♦ vt comprometer ♦ vi transigir ♦
cpd (decision, solution) de término medio.
compulsion [kəmpul'shən] n obligación f;
under ~ a la fuerza, por obligación.
compulsive [kəmpul'siv] a compulsivo.
compulsory [kəmpul'sûrē] a obligatorio.
compulsory purchase n adquisición f
forzosa.
compunction [kəmpungk'shən] n escrúpulo; **to have no ~ about doing sth** no tener
escrúpulos acerca de hacer algo.
computer [kəmpyōō'tûr] n ordenador m,
computador m, computadora.
computerize [kəmpyōō'tərīz] vt (data)
computerizar; (system) informatizar.
computer language n lenguaje m de
computadora.
computer peripheral n periférico.
computer program n programa m
informático.
computer programmer n programa-
dor(a) m/f.
computer programming n programación f.
computer science n informática.
computer virus n virus m informático.
computing [kəmpyōō'ting] n (activity)
informática.
comrade [kâm'rad] n compañero/a.
comradeship [kâm'rədship] n camaradería,
compañerismo.
comsat [kâm'sat] n abbr = **communications
satellite.**
con [kân] vt estafar ♦ n estafa; **to ~ sb into
doing sth** (col) convencer a uno por engaño de que haga algo.
concave [kânkāv'] a cóncavo.
conceal [kənsēl'] vt ocultar; (thoughts etc)
disimular.
concede [kənsēd'] vt conceder ♦ vi ceder,
darse por vencido.
conceit [kənsēt'] n presunción f.

conceited [kənsē'tid] *a* presumido.
conceivable [kənsēv'əbəl] *a* concebible; **it is ~ that ...** es posible que ....
conceivably [kənsēv'əblē] *ad:* **he may ~ be right** es posible que tenga razón.
conceive [kənsēv'] *vt, vi* concebir; **to ~ of sth/of doing sth** imaginar algo/imaginarse haciendo algo.
concentrate [kân'səntrāt] *vi* concentrarse ♦ *vt* concentrar.
concentration [kânsəntrā'shən] *n* concentración *f*.
concentration camp *n* campo de concentración.
concentric [kənsen'trik] *a* concéntrico.
concept [kân'sept] *n* concepto.
conception [kənsep'shən] *n* (*idea*) concepto, idea; (*BIOL*) concepción *f*.
concern [kənsûrn'] *n* (*matter*) asunto; (*COMM*) empresa; (*anxiety*) preocupación *f* ♦ *vt* tener que ver con; **to be ~ed (about)** interesarse (por), preocuparse (por); **to be ~ed with** tratar de; **"to whom it may ~"** "a quien corresponda"; **the department ~ed** (*under discussion*) el departamento en cuestión; (*relevant*) el departamento competente; **as far as I am ~ed** en cuanto a mí, por lo que a mí se refiere.
concerning [kənsûr'ning] *prep* sobre, acerca de.
concert [kân'sûrt] *n* concierto.
concerted [kənsûr'tid] *a* (*efforts etc*) concertado.
concert hall *n* sala de conciertos.
concertina [kânsûrtē'nə] *n* concertina.
concertmaster [kân'sûrtmastûr] *n* (*US*) primer violín *m*.
concerto [kənchär'tō] *n* concierto.
concession [kənsesh'ən] *n* concesión *f*; **tax ~** privilegio fiscal.
concessionaire [kənseshənär'] *n* concesionario/a.
concessionary [kənsesh'ənärē] *a* (*ticket, fare*) concesionario.
conciliation [kənsilēā'shən] *n* conciliación *f*.
conciliatory [kənsil'ēətôrē] *a* conciliador(a).
concise [kənsīs'] *a* conciso.
conclave [kân'klāv] *n* cónclave *m*.
conclude [kənklōōd'] *vt* (*finish*) concluir; (*treaty etc*) firmar; (*agreement*) llegar a; (*decide*): **to ~ that ...** llegar a la conclusión de que ... ♦ *vi* (*events*) terminarse.
conclusion [kənklōō'zhən] *n* conclusión *f*; **to come to the ~ that** llegar a la conclusión de que.
conclusive [kənklōō'siv] *a* decisivo, concluyente.
conclusively [kənklōō'sivlē] *ad* concluyentemente.
concoct [kənkâkt'] *vt* (*gen*) confeccionar; (*plot*) tramar.
concoction [kənkâk'shən] *n* (*food, drink*) confección *f*.

concord [kân'kôrd] *n* (*harmony*) concordia; (*treaty*) acuerdo.
concourse [kân'kôrs] *n* (*hall*) vestíbulo.
concrete [kân'krēt] *n* hormigón *m* ♦ *a* concreto.
concrete mixer *n* hormigonera.
concur [kənkûr'] *vi* estar de acuerdo, asentir.
concurrently [kənkûr'əntlē] *ad* al mismo tiempo.
concussion [kənkush'ən] *n* conmoción *f* cerebral.
condemn [kəndem'] *vt* condenar.
condemnation [kândemnā'shən] *n* (*gen*) condena; (*blame*) censura.
condensation [kândensā'shən] *n* condensación *f*.
condense [kəndens'] *vi* condensarse ♦ *vt* condensar, abreviar.
condensed milk [kəndenst' milk'] *n* leche *f* condensada.
condescend [kândisend'] *vi* condescender, dignarse; **to ~ to do sth** dignarse hacer algo.
condescending [kândisen'ding] *a* condescendiente.
condition [kəndish'ən] *n* condición *f*; (*disease*) enfermedad *f* ♦ *vt* condicionar; **on ~ that** a condición (de) que; **weather ~s** condiciones atmosféricas; **in good/poor ~** en buenas/malas condiciones; **~s of sale** condiciones de venta.
conditional [kəndish'ənəl] *a* condicional.
conditioned reflex [kəndish'ənd rē'fleks] *n* reflejo condicionado.
conditioner [kəndish'ənûr] *n* (*for hair*) acondicionador *n*.
condolences [kəndō'lənsiz] *npl* pésame *msg*.
condom [kân'dəm] *n* condón *m*.
condo(minium) [kân'dō(min'ēəm)] *n* (*US*) condominio.
condone [kəndōn'] *vt* condonar.
conducive [kəndōō'siv] *a:* **~ to** conducente a.
conduct *n* [kân'dukt] conducta, comportamiento ♦ [kəndukt'] *vt* (*lead*) conducir; (*manage*) llevar, dirigir; (*MUS*) dirigir ♦ *vi* (*MUS*) llevar la batuta; **to ~ o.s.** comportarse.
conductor [kənduk'tûr] *n* (*of orchestra*) director(a) *m/f*; (*US: on train*) revisor(a) *m/f*; (*on bus*) cobrador *m*; (*ELEC*) conductor *m*.
conductress [kənduk'tris] *n* (*on bus*) cobradora.
cone [kōn] *n* cono; (*pine ~*) piña; (*for ice-cream*) barquillo.
confectioner [kənfek'shənûr] *n* (*of cakes*) pastelero/a; (*of sweets*) confitero/a; **~'s (shop)** *n* pastelería, confitería.
confectioner's sugar [kənfek'shənûrz shōōg'ûr] *n* (*US*) azúcar *m* glas(eado).

confectionery [kənfek'shənärē] *n* pasteles *mpl*; dulces *mpl*.

confederate [kənfed'ûrit] *a* confederado ♦ *n* (*pej*) cómplice *m/f*; (*US: HISTORY*) confederado/a.

confederation [kənfedərā'shən] *n* confederación *f*.

confer [kənfûr'] *vt* otorgar (*on* a) ♦ *vi* conferenciar; **to** ~ **(with sb about sth)** consultar (con uno sobre algo).

conference [kân'fûrəns] *n* (*meeting*) reunión *f*; (*convention*) congreso; **to be in** ~ estar en una reunión.

conference room *n* sala de conferencias.

confess [kənfes'] *vt* confesar ♦ *vi* confesarse.

confession [kənfesh'ən] *n* confesión *f*.

confessional [kənfesh'ənəl] *n* confesionario.

confessor [kənfes'ûr] *n* confesor *m*.

confetti [kənfet'ē] *n* confeti *m*.

confide [kənfīd'] *vi*: **to** ~ **in** confiar en.

confidence [kân'fidəns] *n* (*gen, also*: **self-**~) confianza; (*secret*) confidencia; **in** ~ (*speak, write*) en confianza; **to have (every)** ~ **that** estar seguro *or* confiado de que; **motion of no** ~ moción *f* de censura; **to tell sb in strict** ~ decir algo a uno en absoluta confianza.

confidence game, (*Brit*) **confidence trick** *n* timo.

confident [kân'fidənt] *a* seguro de sí mismo.

confidential [kânfiden'shəl] *a* confidencial; (*secretary*) de confianza.

confidentiality [kânfidenshēal'itē] *n* confidencialidad *f*.

configuration [kənfigyərā'shən] *n* (*also COMPUT*) configuración *f*.

confine [kənfīn'] *vt* (*limit*) limitar; (*shut up*) encerrar; **to** ~ **o.s. to doing sth** limitarse a hacer algo.

confined [kənfīnd'] *a* (*space*) reducido.

confinement [kənfīn'mənt] *n* (*prison*) prisión *f*; (*MED*) parto.

confines [kân'fīnz] *npl* confines *mpl*.

confirm [kənfûrm'] *vt* confirmar.

confirmation [kânfûrmā'shən] *n* confirmación *f*.

confirmed [kənfûrmd'] *a* empedernido.

confiscate [kân'fiskāt] *vt* confiscar.

confiscation [kânfiskā'shən] *n* incautación *f*.

conflagration [kânfləgrā'shən] *n* conflagración *f*.

conflict *n* [kân'flikt] conflicto ♦ *vi* [kənflikt'] (*opinions*) chocar.

conflicting [kənflik'ting] *a* (*reports, evidence, opinions*) contradictorio.

conform [kənfôrm'] *vi* conformarse; **to** ~ **to** ajustarse a.

conformist [kənfôr'mist] *n* conformista *m/f*.

confound [kənfound'] *vt* confundir; (*amaze*) pasmar.

confounded [kənfoun'did] *a* condenado.

confront [kənfrunt'] *vt* (*problems*) hacer frente a; (*enemy, danger*) enfrentarse con.

confrontation [kânfrəntā'shən] *n* enfrentamiento.

confuse [kənfyōōz'] *vt* (*perplex*) aturdir, desconcertar; (*mix up*) confundir.

confused [kənfyōōzd'] *a* confuso; (*person*) perplejo; **to get** ~ desorientarse, aturdirse.

confusing [kənfyōō'zing] *a* confuso.

confusion [kənfyōō'zhən] *n* confusión *f*.

congeal [kənjēl'] *vi* coagularse.

congenial [kənjēn'yəl] *a* agradable.

congenital [kənjen'itəl] *a* congénito.

congested [kənjes'tid] *a* (*gen*) atestado; (*telephone lines*) ocupado.

congestion [kənjes'chən] *n* congestión *f*.

conglomerate [kənglâm'ûrit] *n* (*COMM, GEO*) conglomerado.

conglomeration [kənglâmərā'shən] *n* conglomeración *f*.

Congo [kâng'gō] *n* (*state*) Congo.

congratulate [kəngrach'ōōlāt] *vt* felicitar.

congratulations [kəngrachōōlā'shənz] *npl*: ~ **(on)** felicitaciones *fpl* (por); ~! ¡enhorabuena!, ¡felicidades!

congregate [kâng'grəgāt] *vi* congregarse.

congregation [kânggrəgā'shən] *n* (*in church*) fieles *mpl*.

congress [kâng'gris] *n* congreso.

congressman [kâng'grismən] *n* (*US*) diputado.

congresswoman [kâng'griswōōmən] *n* (*US*) diputada.

conical [kân'ikəl] *a* cónico.

conifer [kō'nifûr] *n* conífera.

coniferous [kōnif'ûrəs] *a* (*forest*) conífero.

conjecture [kənjek'chûr] *n* conjetura.

conjugal [kân'jəgəl] *a* conyugal.

conjugate [kân'jəgāt] *vt* conjugar.

conjunction [kənjungk'shən] *n* conjunción *f*; **in** ~ **with** junto con.

conjunctivitis [kənjungktəvī'tis] *n* conjunctivitis *f*.

conjure [kân'jûr] *vi* hacer juegos de manos.

   conjure up *vt* (*ghost, spirit*) hacer aparecer; (*memories*) evocar.

conjurer [kân'jûrûr] *n* ilusionista *m/f*.

conjuring trick [kân'jûring trik] *n* ilusionismo, juego de manos.

conker [kâng'kûr] *n* (*Brit*) castaño de Indias.

conk out [kângk out] *vi* (*col*) descomponerse.

con man *n* timador *m*.

Conn. *abbr* (*US*) = Connecticut.

connect [kənekt'] *vt* juntar, unir; (*ELEC*) conectar; (*fig*) relacionar, asociar ♦ *vi*: **to** ~ **with** (*train*) enlazar con; **to be** ~**ed with** (*associated*) estar relacionado con; (*related*) estar emparentado con; **I am trying to** ~ **you** (*TEL*) estoy intentando comunicarle.

connection [kənek'shən] *n* juntura, unión *f*; (*ELEC*) conexión *f*; (*RAIL*) enlace *m*; (*TEL*) comunicación f; (fig) relación f; **what is the ~ between them?** ¿qué relación hay entre ellos?; **in ~ with** con respecto a, en relación a; **she has many business ~s** tiene muchos contactos profesionales; **to miss/make a ~** perder/coger el enlace.

connive [kənīv'] vi: **to ~ at** hacer la vista gorda a.

connoisseur [kânisûr'] n experto/a, entendido/a.

connotation [kânətā'shən] n connotación f.

conquer [kâng'kûr] vt (territory) conquistar; (enemy, feelings) vencer.

conqueror [kâng'kûrûr] n conquistador(a) m/f.

conquest [kân'kwest] n conquista.

cons [kânz] npl see **convenience, pro.**

conscience [kân'shəns] n conciencia; **in all ~** en conciencia.

conscientious [kânshēen'shəs] a concienzudo; (objection) de conciencia.

conscientious objector n objetor m de conciencia.

conscious [kân'shəs] a consciente; (deliberate: insult, error) premeditado, intencionado; **to become ~ of sth/that** darse cuenta de algo/de que.

consciousness [kân'shəsnis] n conciencia; (MED) conocimiento.

conscript [kân'skript] n (Brit) recluta m/f.

conscription [kənskrip'shən] n servicio militar (obligatorio).

consecrate [kân'səkrāt] vt consagrar.

consecutive [kənsek'yətiv] a consecutivo; **on 3 ~ occasions** en 3 ocasiones consecutivas.

consensus [kənsen'səs] n consenso; **the ~ of opinion** el consenso general.

consent [kənsent'] n consentimiento ♦ vi: **to ~ to** consentir en; **by common ~** de común acuerdo.

consequence [kân'səkwens] n consecuencia; **in ~** por consiguiente.

consequently [kân'səkwentlē] ad por consiguiente.

conservation [kânsûrvā'shən] n conservación f; (of nature) preservación f.

conservationist [kânsûrvā'shənist] n conservacionista m/f.

conservative [kənsûr'vətiv] a conservador(a); (cautious) cauteloso; **C~** a, n (Brit POL) conservador(a) m/f.

conservatory [kənsûr'vətôrē] n (greenhouse) invernadero.

conserve vt [kənsûrv'] conservar ♦ n [kân'sûrv] conserva.

consider [kənsid'ûr] vt considerar; (take into account) tomar en cuenta; (study) estudiar, examinar; **to ~ doing sth** pensar en (la posibilidad de) hacer algo; **all things ~ed** pensándolo bien; **~ yourself lucky** ¡date por satisfecho!

considerable [kənsid'ûrəbəl] a considera-

ble.

considerably [kənsid'ûrəblē] ad bastante, considerablemente.

considerate [kənsid'ûrit] a considerado.

consideration [kənsidərā'shən] n consideración f; (reward) retribución f; **to be under ~** estar sobre el tapete; **my first ~ is my family** mi primera consideración es mi familia.

considering [kənsid'ûring] prep: **~ (that)** teniendo en cuenta (que).

consign [kənsīn'] vt consignar.

consignee [kânsīnē'] n consignatario/a.

consignment [kənsīn'mənt] n envío.

consignment note n (COMM) talón m de expedición.

consignor [kənsī'nûr] n remitente m/f.

consist [kənsist'] vi: **to ~ of** consistir en.

consistency [kənsis'tənsē] n (of person etc) consecuencia; (thickness) consistencia.

consistent [kənsis'tənt] a (person, argument) consecuente; (results) constante.

consolation [kânsəlā'shən] n consuelo.

console vt [kənsōl'] consolar ♦ n [kân'sōl] (control panel) consola.

consolidate [kənsâl'idāt] vt consolidar.

consommé [kânsəmā'] n consomé m, caldo.

consonant [kân'sənənt] n consonante f.

consort n [kân'sôrt] consorte m/f ♦ vi [kənsôrt]: **to ~ with sb** (often pej) asociarse con uno; **prince ~** príncipe m consorte.

consortium [kənsôr'shēəm] n consorcio.

conspicuous [kənspik'yōōəs] a (visible) visible; (garish etc) llamativo; (outstanding) notable; **to make o.s. ~** llamar la atención.

conspiracy [kənspir'əsē] n conjura, complot m.

conspiratorial [kənspirətôr'ēəl] a de conspirador.

conspire [kənspī'ûr] vi conspirar.

constable [kân'stəbəl] n (Brit) policía m/f; **chief ~** ≈ jefe m/f de policía.

constabulary [kənstab'yəlärē] n ≈ policía.

constancy [kân'stənsē] n constancia; fidelidad f.

constant [kân'stənt] a (gen) constante; (loyal) leal, fiel.

constantly [kân'stəntlē] ad constantemente.

constellation [kânstəlā'shən] n constelación f.

consternation [kânstûrnā'shən] n consternación f.

constipated [kân'stəpātid] a estreñido.

constipation [kânstəpā'shən] n estreñimiento.

constituency [kənstich'ōōənsē] n (POL) distrito electoral; (people) electorado.

constituency party n partido local.

constituent [kənstich'ōōənt] n (POL) elector(a) m/f; (part) componente m.

constitute [kân'stitōōt] vt constituir.

constitution [kânstitoo'shən] *n* constitución *f*.

constitutional [kânstitoo'shənəl] *a* constitucional.

constrain [kənstrān'] *vt* obligar.

constrained [kənstrānd'] *a*: **to feel ~ to ...** sentirse en la necesidad de ....

constraint [kənstrānt'] *n* (*force*) fuerza; (*limit*) restricción *f*; (*restraint*) reserva; (*embarrassment*) cohibición *f*.

constrict [kənstrikt'] *vt* apretar, estrechar.

constriction [kənstrik'shən] *n* constricción *f*.

construct [kənstrukt'] *vt* construir.

construction [kənstruk'shən] *n* construcción *f*; (*fig: interpretation*) interpretación *f*; **under ~** en construcción.

construction industry *n* industria de la construcción.

constructive [kənstruk'tiv] *a* constructivo.

construe [kənstroo'] *vt* interpretar.

consul [kân'səl] *n* cónsul *m/f*.

consulate [kân'səlit] *n* consulado.

consult [kənsult'] *vt*, *vi* consultar; **to ~ sb (about sth)** consultar a uno (sobre algo).

consultancy [kənsul'tənsē] *n* consultorio.

consultant [kənsul'tənt] *n* (*Brit MED*) especialista *m/f*; (*other specialist*) asesor(a) *m/f*.

consultation [kânsəltā'shən] *n* consulta; **in ~ with** en consultación con.

consulting room [kənsul'ting room'] *n* (*Brit*) consultorio.

consume [kənsoom'] *vt* (*eat*) comerse; (*drink*) beberse; (*fire etc*, *COMM*) consumir.

consumer [kənsoo'mûr] *n* (*of electricity*, *gas etc*) consumidor(a) *m/f*.

consumer association *n* asociación *f* de consumidores.

consumer credit *n* crédito al consumidor.

consumer durables *npl* bienes *mpl* de consumo duraderos.

consumer goods *npl* bienes *mpl* de consumo.

consumerism [kənsoo'mərizəm] *n* consumismo.

consumer society *n* sociedad *f* de consumo.

consummate [kân'səmāt] *vt* consumar.

consumption [kənsump'shən] *n* consumo; (*MED*) tisis *f*; **not fit for human ~** no apto para el consumo humano.

cont. *abbr* (= *continued*) sigue.

contact [kân'takt] *n* contacto; (*person*) enchufe *m* ♦ *vt* ponerse en contacto con; **~ lenses** *npl* lentes *fpl* de contacto; **to be in ~ with sb/sth** estar en contacto con uno/algo; **business ~s** contactos comerciales.

contagious [kəntā'jəs] *a* contagioso.

contain [kəntān'] *vt* contener; **to ~ o.s.** contenerse.

container [kəntā'nûr] *n* recipiente *m*; (*for shipping etc*) contenedor *m*.

containerization [kəntānûrəzā'shən] *n* contenerización *f*.

containerize [kəntā'nərīz] *vt* transportar en contenedores.

contaminate [kəntam'ənāt] *vt* contaminar.

contamination [kəntamənā'shən] *n* contaminación *f*.

cont'd *abbr* (= *continued*) sigue.

contemplate [kân'təmplāt] *vt* (*gen*) contemplar; (*reflect upon*) considerar; (*intend*) pensar.

contemplation [kântəmplā'shən] *n* contemplación *f*.

contemporary [kəntem'pərärē] *a*, *n* (*of the same age*) contemporáneo/a *m/f*.

contempt [kəntempt'] *n* desprecio; **~ of court** (*LAW*) desacato (a los tribunales *or* a la justicia).

contemptible [kəntemp'təbəl] *a* despreciable, desdeñable.

contemptuous [kəntemp'chooəs] *a* desdeñoso.

contend [kəntend'] *vt* (*argue*) afirmar ♦ *vi* (*struggle*) luchar; **he has a lot to ~ with** tiene muchos problemas que enfrentar.

contender [kəntend'ûr] *n* (*SPORT*) contendiente *m/f*.

content [kəntent'] *a* (*happy*) contento; (*satisfied*) satisfecho ♦ *vt* contentar; satisfacer ♦ *n* [kân'tent] contenido; **~s** *npl* contenido *msg*; **(table of) ~s** índice *m* de materias; **to ~ o.s. with sth/with doing sth** contentarse *or* darse por contento con algo/con hacer algo.

contented [kəntent'tid] *a* contento; satisfecho.

contentedly [kənten'tidlē] *ad* con aire satisfecho.

contention [kənten'shən] *n* discusión *f*; (*belief*) argumento; **bone of ~** manzana de la discordia.

contentious [kənten'shəs] *a* discutible.

contentment [mənt'mənt] *n* contento.

contest *n* [kân'test] contienda; (*competition*) concurso ♦ *vt* [kəntest'] (*dispute*) impugnar; (*LAW*) disputar, litigar; (*POL: election*, *seat*) presentarse como candidato/a en.

contestant [kəntes'tənt] *n* concursante *m/f*; (*in fight*) contendiente *m/f*.

context [kân'tekst] *n* contexto; **in/out of ~** en/fuera de contexto.

continent [kân'tənənt] *n* continente *m*; **the C~** el continente europeo; **on the C~** en el continente europeo.

continental [kântənen'təl] *a* continental.

continental breakfast *n* desayuno estilo europeo.

continental quilt *n* (*Brit*) edredón *m*.

contingency [kəntin'jənsē] *n* contingencia.

contingent [kəntin'jənt] *n* (*group*) grupo.

continual [kəntin'yooəl] *a* continuo.

continually [kəntin'yōōəlē] *ad* constantemente.
continuation [kəntinyōōā'shən] *n* prolongación *f*; *(after interruption)* reanudación *f*.
continue [kəntin'yōō] *vi*, *vt* seguir, continuar; ~**d on page 10** sigue en la página
10.
continuity [kântənōō'itē] *n (also CINEMA)*
continuidad *f*.
continuous [kəntin'yōōəs] *a* continuo; ~
feed paper *(COMPUT)* papel *m* continuo; ~
performance *(CINEMA)* sesión *f* continua.
continuously [kəntin'yōōəslē] *ad (repeatedly)* continuamente; *(uninterruptedly)*
constantemente.
contort [kəntôrt'] *vt* retorcer.
contortion [kəntôr'shən] *n (movement)*
contorsión *f*.
contortionist [kəntôr'shənist] *n* contorsio-
nista *m/f*.
contour [kán'tōōr] *n* contorno; *(also:* ~
line) curva de nivel.
contraband [kán'trəband] *n* contrabando ♦
a de contrabando.
contraception [kântrəsep'shən] *n* contra-
cepción *f*.
contraceptive [kântrəsep'tiv] *a*, *n* anticonceptivo.
contract [kán'trakt] *n* contrato ♦ *cpd (price,
date)* contratado, de contrato; *(work)* de
contrato ♦ *vb* [kəntrakt'] *vi (COMM)*: **to ~
to do sth** comprometerse por contrato a
hacer algo; *(become smaller)* contraerse,
encogerse ♦ *vt* contraer; **to be under ~ to
do sth** estar bajo contrato para hacer algo;
~ **of employment** *or* **of service** contrato de
trabajo.
contraction [kəntrak'shən] *n* contracción *f*.
contractor [kán'traktûr] *n* contratista *m/f*.
contractual [kántrak'chōōəl] *a* contractual.
contradict [kântrədikt'] *vt (declare to be
wrong)* desmentir; *(be contrary to)* contradecir.
contradiction [kântrədik'shən] *n* contradicción *f*; **to be in ~ with** no estar de
acuerdo con.
contradictory [kântrədik'tûrē] *a (statements)* contradictorio; **to be ~ to** ser contradictorio a.
contralto [kəntral'tō] *n* contralto *f*.
contraption [kəntrap'shən] *n (pej)* artilugio
m.
contrary [kán'trärē] *a (opposite, different)*
contrario; *(perverse)* terco ♦ *n*: **on the ~**
al contrario; **unless you hear to the ~** a
no ser que le digan lo contrario; ~ **to what
we thought** en contra de lo que pensába-
mos.
contrast *n* [kán'trast] contraste *m* ♦ *vt*
[kəntrast'] comparar; **in ~ to** *or* **with** a diferencia de.
contrasting [kəntras'ting] *a (opinion)*
opuesto; *(color)* que hace contraste.

contravene [kântrəvēn'] *vt* infringir.
contravention [kântrəven'shən] *n*: ~ **(of)**
contravención *f* (de).
contribute [kəntrib'yōōt] *vi* contribuir ♦ *vt*:
to ~ to *(gen)* contribuir a; *(newspaper)*
escribir para; *(discussion)* intervenir en.
contribution [kântrəbyōō'shən] *n (money)*
contribución *f*; *(to debate)* intervención *f*;
(to journal) colaboración *f*.
contributor [kəntrib'yətûr] *n (to newspaper)* colaborador(a) *m/f*.
contributory [kəntrib'yətôrē] *a (cause)* contribuyente; **it was a ~ factor in** ... fue un
factor contribuyente en ....
contributory pension plan *n* plan *m*
cotizable de jubilación.
contrivance [kəntrī'vəns] *n (machine, device)* aparato, dispositivo.
contrive [kəntrīv'] *vt (invent)* idear ♦ *vi*: **to
~ to do** lograr hacer.
control [kəntrōl'] *vt* controlar; *(traffic etc)*
dirigir; *(machinery)* manejar; *(temper)*
dominar; *(disease, fire)* dominar, controlar
♦ *n (command)* control *m*; *(of car)*
conducción *f*; *(check)* freno; ~**s** *npl* mando
sg; **to ~ o.s.** controlarse, dominarse;
everything is under ~ todo está bajo control; **to be in ~ of** tener el mando de; **the
car went out of ~** el coche se descontroló.
control group *n (MED, PSYCH etc)* grupo
de control.
control key *n (COMPUT)* tecla de control.
controlled economy [kəntrōld' ikán'əmē]
n economía dirigida.
controller [kəntrō'lûr] *n* controlador(a) *m/f*.
controlling interest [kəntrō'ling in'trist] *n*
interés *m* mayoritario.
control panel *n (on aircraft, ship, TV etc)*
tablero de instrumentos.
control point *n (puesto de)* control *m*.
control room *n (NAUT, MIL)* sala de
mandos; *(RADIO, TV)* sala de control.
control tower *n (AVIAT)* torre *f* de control.
control unit *n (COMPUT)* unidad *f* de control.
controversial [kântrəvûr'shəl] *a* polémico.
controversy [kán'trəvûrsē] *n* polémica.
conurbation [kánûrbā'shən] *n* urbanización
f.
convalesce [kânvəles'] *vi* convalecer.
convalescence [kânvəles'əns] *n* convalecencia.
convalescent [kânvəles'ənt] *a*, *n* convaleciente *m/f*.
convector [kənvek'tûr] *n* calentador *m* de
convección.
convene [kənvēn'] *vt (meeting)* convocar ♦
vi reunirse.
convenience [kənvēn'yəns] *n (comfort)*
comodidad *f*; *(advantage)* ventaja; **at your
earliest ~** *(COMM)* cuando *or* tan pronto
como le sea conveniente; **all modern ~s,**

(*Brit*) **all mod cons** todo confort.
convenience foods *npl* platos *mpl* preparados.
convenient [kənvēn'yənt] *a* (*useful*) útil; (*place, time*) conveniente; **if it is ~ for you** si le conviene.
conveniently [kənvēn'yəntlē] *ad* (*happen*) oportunamente; (*situated*) convenientemente.
convent [kân'vent] *n* convento.
convent school *n* colegio de monjas.
convention [kənven'shən] *n* convención *f*; (*meeting*) asamblea.
conventional [kənven'shənəl] *a* convencional.
converge [kənvûrj'] *vi* converger.
conversant [kənvûr'sənt] *a*: **to be ~ with** estar al tanto de.
conversation [kânvûrsā'shən] *n* conversación *f*.
conversational [kânvûrsā'shənəl] *a* (*familiar*) familiar; (*talkative*) locuaz; **~ mode** (*COMPUT*) modo de conversación.
converse *n* [kân'vûrs] inversa ♦ *vi* [kənvûrs'] conversar; **to ~ (with sb about sth)** conversar *or* platicar (con uno de algo).
conversely [kənvûrs'lē] *ad* a la inversa.
conversion [kənvûr'zhən] *n* conversión *f*; (*house ~*) reforma, remodelación *f*.
conversion table *n* tabla de conversión.
convert *vt* [kənvûrt'] (*REL, COMM*) convertir; (*alter*) transformar ♦ *n* [kân'vûrt] converso/a.
convertible [kənvûr'təbəl] *a* convertible ♦ *n* descapotable *m*; **~ loan stock** títulos *mpl* convertibles de interés fijo.
convex [kânveks'] *a* convexo.
convey [kənvā'] *vt* llevar; (*thanks*) comunicar; (*idea*) expresar.
conveyance [kənvā'əns] *n* (*of goods*) transporte *m*; (*vehicle*) vehículo, medio de transporte.
conveyancing [kənvā'ənsing] *n* (*LAW*) preparación *f* de escrituras de traspaso.
conveyor belt [kənvā'ûr belt] *n* cinta transportadora.
convict *vt* [kənvikt'] (*gen*) condenar; (*find guilty*) declarar culpable a ♦ *n* [kân'vikt] presidiario/a.
conviction [kənvik'shən] *n* condena; (*belief*) creencia, convicción *f*.
convince [kənvins'] *vt* convencer; **to ~ sb (of sth/that)** convencer a uno (de algo/de que).
convinced [kənvinst'] *a*: **~ of/that** convencido de/de que.
convincing [kənvin'sing] *a* convincente.
convincingly [kənvin'singlē] *ad* convincentemente.
convivial [kənviv'ēəl] *a* (*person*) sociable; (*atmosphere*) alegre.
convoluted [kân'vəlōōtid] *a* (*argument etc*) enrevesado; (*shape*) enrollado, enroscado.

convoy [kân'voi] *n* convoy *m*.
convulse [kənvuls'] *vt* convulsionar; **to be ~d with laughter** dislocarse de risa.
convulsion [kənvul'shən] *n* convulsión *f*.
coo [kōō] *vi* arrullar.
cook [kook] *vt* cocinar; (*stew etc*) guisar; (*meal*) preparar, cocinar ♦ *vi* cocer; (*person*) cocinar ♦ *n* cocinero/a.
cook up *vt* (*col: excuse, story*) inventar.
cookbook [kook'book] *n* libro de cocina.
cooker [kook'ûr] *n* (*US*) olla para cocinar; (*Brit*) cocina.
cookery [kook'ûrē] *n* (*dishes*) cocina; (*art*) arte *m* culinario.
cookery book *n* (*Brit*) = cookbook.
cookie [kook'ē] *n* (*US*) galleta.
cooking [kook'ing] *n* cocina ♦ *cpd* (*apples*) para cocinar; (*utensils, salt, foil*) de cocina.
cooking chocolate *n* (*Brit*) chocolate *m* fondant.
cookout [kook'out] *n* (*US*) comida al aire libre.
cool [kool] *a* fresco; (*not hot*) tibio; (*not afraid*) tranquilo; (*unfriendly*) frío ♦ *vt* enfriar ♦ *vi* enfriarse; **it is ~** (*weather*) hace fresco; **to keep sth ~** *or* **in a ~ place** conservar algo fresco *or* en un sitio fresco.
cool down *vi* enfriarse; (*fig: person, situation*) calmarse.
cooler [koo'lûr], (*Brit*) **cool box** *n* nevera portátil.
cooling-off period [kooling-ôf' pir'ēəd] *n* (*INDUSTRY*) plazo para que se entablen negociaciones.
cooling tower [koo'ling tou'ûr] *n* torre *f* de refrigeración.
coolly [koo'lē] *ad* (*calmly*) con tranquilidad; (*audaciously*) descaradamente; (*unenthusiastically*) fríamente, con frialdad.
coolness [kool'nis] *n* frescura; tranquilidad *f*; (*hostility*) frialdad *f*; (*indifference*) falta de entusiasmo.
coop [koop] *n* gallinero ♦ *vt*: **to ~ up** (*fig*) encerrar.
co-op [kō'âp] *n* *abbr* (= *Cooperative (Society)*) cooperativa.
cooperate [kōāp'ərāt] *vi* cooperar, colaborar; **will he ~?** ¿querrá cooperar?
cooperation [kōāpərā'shən] *n* cooperación *f*, colaboración *f*.
cooperative [kōāp'rətiv] *a* cooperativo ♦ *n* cooperativa.
co-opt [kōāpt'] *vt*: **to ~ sb into sth** cooptar a uno a algo.
coordinate *vt* [kōôr'dənāt] coordinar ♦ *n* [kōôr'dənit] (*MATH*) coordenada; **~s** *npl* (*clothes*) coordinados *mpl*.
coordination [kōôrdənā'shən] *n* coordinación *f*.
coot [koot] *n* focha *f* (común).
co-ownership [kō'nûrship] *n* co-propiedad *f*.

cop [kåp] *n* (*col*) poli *m*, tira *m* (*LAm*).
cope [kōp] *vi*: **to ~ with** poder con; (*problem*) hacer frente a.
Copenhagen [kōpenhā'gən] *n* Copenhague *m*.
copier [kåp'ēûr] *n* (*photo~*) fotocopiadora, multicopista.
copilot [kōpī'lət] *n* copiloto/a.
copious [kō'pēəs] *a* copioso, abundante.
copper [kåp'ûr] *n* (*metal*) cobre *m*; (*Brit*: *col*: *policeman*) poli *m*, tira *m* (*LAm*); **~s** *npl* (*Brit*) perras *fpl*.
copse [kåps] *n* bosquecillo.
copulate [kåp'yəlāt] *vi* copularse.
copulation [kåpyəlā'shən] *n* cópula.
copy [kåp'ē] *n* copia; (*of book etc*) ejemplar *m*; (*material*: *for printing*) copia ♦ *vt* copiar (*also* COMPUT); (*imitate*) copiar, imitar; **to make good ~** (*fig*) ser una noticia de interés; **clean ~** copia en limpio.
 copy out *vt* copiar.
copycat [kåp'ēkat] *n* (*pej*) copión/ona *m/f*.
copyright [kåp'ērīt] *n* derechos *mpl* de autor.
copy typist *n* mecanógrafo/a.
coral [kôr'əl] *n* coral *m*.
coral reef *n* arrecife *m* (de coral).
Coral Sea *n*: **the ~** el Mar del Coral.
cord [kôrd] *n* cuerda; (*ELEC*) cable *m*; (*fabric*) pana; **~s** *npl* (*pants*) pantalones *mpl* de pana.
cordial [kôr'jəl] *a* afectuoso ♦ *n* cordial *m*.
cordless [kôrd'lis] *a* sin cordón.
cordon [kôr'dən] *n* cordón *m*.
 cordon off *vt* acordonar.
Cordova [kôr'dəvə] *n* Córdoba.
corduroy [kôr'dəroi] *n* pana.
CORE [kôr] *n abbr* (US) = *Congress of Racial Equality*.
core [kôr] *n* (*of earth, nuclear reactor*) centro, núcleo; (*of fruit*) corazón *m*; (*of problem etc*) corazón *m*, meollo ♦ *vt* quitar el corazón de.
Corfu [kôr'fōō] *n* Corfú *m*.
coriander [kôrēan'dûr] *n* culantro, cilantro.
cork [kôrk] *n* corcho; (*tree*) alcornoque *m*.
corked [kôrkt] *a* (*wine*) con sabor a corcho.
corkscrew [kôrk'skrōō] *n* sacacorchos *m inv*.
cormorant [kôr'mûrənt] *n* cormorán *m* grande.
Corn *abbr* (*Brit*) = *Cornwall*.
corn [kôrn] *n* (US: *maize*) maíz *m*; (*Brit*: *wheat*) trigo; (*on foot*) callo; **~ on the cob** (*CULIN*) maíz en la mazorca.
cornea [kôr'nēə] *n* córnea.
corned beef [kôrnd bēf] *n* carne *f* acecinada.
corner [kôr'nûr] *n* ángulo; (*outside*) esquina; (*inside*) rincón *m*; (*in road*) curva; (*SOCCER*) córner *m*, saque *m* de esquina ♦ *vt* (*trap*) arrinconar; (*COMM*) acaparar ♦ *vi* (*in car*) tomar las curvas; **to cut ~s**

atajar.
corner flag *n* (*SOCCER*) banderola de esquina.
corner kick *n* (*SOCCER*) córner *m*, saque *m* de esquina.
cornerstone [kôr'nûrstōn] *n* piedra angular.
cornet [kôrnet'] *n* (*MUS*) corneta; (*Brit*: *of ice-cream*) barquillo.
cornflakes [kôrn'flāks] *npl* copos *mpl* de maíz, cornflakes *mpl*.
cornflour [kôrn'flouûr] *n* (*Brit*) harina de maíz.
cornice [kôr'nis] *n* cornisa.
Cornish [kôr'nish] *a* de Cornualles.
cornmeal [kôrn'mēl] *n* (US) harina de maíz.
corn oil *n* aceite *m* de maíz.
cornstarch [kôrn'stårch] *n* (US) maicena.
cornucopia [kôrnəkō'pēə] *n* cornucopia.
corny [kôr'nē] *a* (*col*) gastado.
corollary [kôr'əlārē] *n* corolario.
coronary [kôr'ənārē] *n*: **~ (thrombosis)** infarto.
coronation [kôrənā'shən] *n* coronación *f*.
coroner [kôr'ənûr] *n* juez *m* (de instrucción).
coronet [kôr'ənit] *n* corona.
Corp. *abbr* = *corporation*.
corporal [kôr'pûrəl] *n* cabo ♦ *a*: **~ punishment** castigo corporal.
corporate [kôr'pərit] *a* corporativo.
corporate identity, corporate image *n* (*of organization*) identidad *f* corporativa.
corporation [kôrpərā'shən] *n* (*of town*) ayuntamiento; (*COMM*) corporación *f*.
corps [kôr], *pl* **corps** [kôrz] *n* cuerpo; **press ~** gabinete *m* de prensa.
corpse [kôrps] *n* cadáver *m*.
corpulent [kôr'pyələnt] *a* corpulento/a.
Corpus Christi [kôr'pəs kris'tē] *n* Corpus *m*.
corpuscle [kôr'pəsəl] *n* corpúsculo.
corral [kəral'] *n* corral *m*.
correct [kərekt'] *a* (*accurate*) justo, exacto; (*proper*) correcto ♦ *vt* corregir; (*exam*) calificar; **you are ~** tiene razón.
correction [kərek'shən] *n* rectificación *f*; (*erasure*) tachadura.
correlate [kôr'əlāt] *vi*: **to ~ with** tener correlación con.
correlation [kôrəlā'shən] *n* correlación *f*.
correspond [kôrəspånd'] *vi* (*write*) escribirse; (*be equal to*) corresponder.
correspondence [kôrəspån'dəns] *n* correspondencia.
correspondence column *n* (sección *f* de) cartas *fpl* al director.
correspondence course *n* curso por correspondencia.
correspondent [kôrəspån'dənt] *n* corresponsal *m/f*.
corresponding [kôrəspån'ding] *a* co-

rrespondiente.
corridor [kôr'idûr] *n* pasillo.
corroborate [kərâb'ərāt] *vt* corroborar.
corroboration [kərâbərā'shən] *n* corroboración *f*, confirmación *f*.
corrode [kərōd'] *vt* corroer ♦ *vi* corroerse.
corrosion [kərō'zhən] *n* corrosión *f*.
corrosive [kərō'siv] *a* corrosivo.
corrugated [kôr'əgātid] *a* ondulado.
corrugated cardboard *n* cartón *m* ondulado.
corrugated iron *n* chapa ondulada.
corrupt [kərupt'] *a* corrompido; (*person*) corrupto ♦ *vt* corromper; (*bribe*) sobornar; (*data*) degradar; ~ **practices** (*dishonesty, bribery*) corrupción *f*.
corruption [kərup'shən] *n* corrupción *f*; (*of data*) alteración *f*.
corset [kôr'sit] *n* faja.
Corsica [kôr'sikə] *n* Córcega.
Corsican [kôr'sikən] *a, n* corso/a *m/f*.
cortège [kôrtezh'] *n* cortejo, desfile *m*.
cortisone [kôr'tisōn] *n* cortisona.
c.o.s. *abbr* (= *cash on shipment*) pago al embarcar.
cosh [kâsh] *n* (*Brit*) cachiporra.
cosignatory [kōsig'nətôrē] *n* cosignatario/a.
cosine [kō'sīn] *n* coseno.
cosiness [kō'zēnis] *n* (*Brit*) = **coziness**.
cos lettuce [kâs let'is] *n* (*Brit*) lechuga cos.
cosmetic [kâzmet'ik] *n* cosmético ♦ *a* (*also fig*) cosmético; (*surgery*) estético.
cosmic [kâz'mik] *a* cósmico.
cosmonaut [kâz'mənôt] *n* cosmonauta *m/f*.
cosmopolitan [kâzməpâl'itən] *a* cosmopolita.
cosmos [kâz'məs] *n* cosmos *m*.
cosset [kâs'it] *vt* mimar.
cost [kôst] *n* (*gen*) coste *m*, costo; (*price*) precio; ~**s** *npl* (*LAW*) costas *fpl* ♦ *vb* (*pt, pp* **cost**) *vi* costar, valer ♦ *vt* preparar el presupuesto de; **how much does it ~?** ¿cuánto cuesta?, ¿cuánto vale?; **what will it ~ to have it repaired?** ¿cuánto costará repararlo?; **the ~ of living** el coste *or* costo de la vida; **at all ~s** cueste lo que cueste.
cost accountant *n* contable *m* de costos.
co-star [kō'stâr] *n* co-estrella *m/f*.
Costa Rica [kâs'tə rē'kə] *n* Costa Rica.
Costa Rican [kâs'tə rē'kən] *a, n* costarriqueño/a *m/f*.
cost center *n* centro (de determinación) de costos.
cost control *n* control *m* de costos.
cost-effective [kôstifek'tiv] *a* (*COMM*) beneficioso, rentable.
cost-effectiveness [kôstifek'tivnis] *n* relación *f* costo-eficacia *or* costo-rendimiento.
costing [kôs'ting] *n* (*Brit*) cálculo de costos.
costly [kôst'lē] *a* (*expensive*) costoso.
cost-of-living [kôstəvliv'ing] *a*: ~ **allowance** *n* plus *m* de carestía de vida; ~

index *n* índice *m* del costo *or* coste de vida.
cost price *n* (*Brit*) precio de coste.
costume [kâs'tōōm] *n* traje *m*; (*Brit: also:* **swimming** ~) traje de baño.
costume jewelry *n* bisutería.
costume party *n* (*US*) baile *m* de disfraces.
cosy [kō'zē] *a* (*Brit*) = **cozy**.
cot [kât] *n* (*US: folding bed*) cama plegable; (*Brit: child's*) cuna.
cottage [kât'ij] *n* casita de campo.
cottage cheese *n* requesón *m*.
cottage industry *n* industria casera.
cottage pie *n* pastel de carne cubierta de puré de patatas.
cotton [kât'ən] *n* algodón *m*; (*thread*) hilo; (*US MED*) algodón *m* hidrófilo.
cotton on *vi* (*Brit col*): **to ~ on (to sth)** caer en la cuenta (de algo).
cotton candy *n* (*US*) algodón *m* (azucarado).
cotton wool *n* (*Brit*) algodón *m* (hidrófilo).
couch [kouch] *n* sofá *m*; (*doctor's*) camilla.
couchette [kōōshet'] *n* (*Brit*) litera.
cough [kôf] *vi* toser ♦ *n* tos *f*.
cough up *vt* escupir.
cough drop *n* pastilla para la tos.
cough syrup *n* jarabe *m* para la tos.
could [kōōd] *pt of* **can**.
couldn't [kōōd'ənt] = **could not**.
council [koun'səl] *n* consejo; **city** *or* **town** ~ consejo municipal; **C~ of Europe** Consejo de Europa.
council estate *n* (*Brit*) urbanización de viviendas municipales de alquiler.
council house *n* (*Brit*) vivienda municipal de alquiler.
councilor, (*Brit*) **councillor** [koun'sələr] *n* concejal *m/f*.
counsel [koun'səl] *n* (*advice*) consejo; (*lawyer*) abogado/a ♦ *vt* aconsejar; ~ **for the defense/the prosecution** abogado/a defensor(a)/fiscal; **to ~ sth/sb to do sth** aconsejar algo/a uno que haga algo.
counseling, (*Brit*) **counselling** [koun'səling] *n* (*advice*) consejos *mpl*; **marriage/vocational** ~ orientación *f* matrimonial/profesional.
counselor, (*Brit*) **counsellor** [koun'sələr] *n* consejero/a; (*US LAW*) abogado/a.
count [kount] *vt* (*gen*) contar; (*include*) incluir ♦ *vi* contar ♦ *n* cuenta; (*of votes*) escrutinio; (*nobleman*) conde *m*; (*sum*) total *m*, suma; **to ~ the cost of** calcular el costo de; **not ~ing the children** niños aparte; **10 ~ing him** diez incluyéndolo a él, diez con él; ~ **yourself lucky** date por satisfecho; **that doesn't ~!** ¡eso no vale!; **to ~ (up) to 10** contar hasta diez; **it ~s for very little** cuenta poco; **to keep ~ of sth** llevar la cuenta de algo.
count on *vt fus* contar con; **to ~ on**

doing sth contar con hacer algo.
count up *vt* contar.
countdown [kount'doun] *n* cuenta atrás.
countenance [koun'tənəns] *n* semblante *m*, rostro ♦ *vt* (*tolerate*) aprobar, tolerar.
counter [koun'tûr] *n* (*in shop*) mostrador *m*; (*position: in post office, bank*) ventanilla; (*in games*) ficha; (*TECH*) contador *m* ♦ *vt* contrarrestar; (*blow*) parar; (*attack*) contestar a ♦ *ad*: ~ **to** contrario a; **to buy under the** ~ (*fig*) comprar de estraperlo *or* bajo mano; **to** ~ **sth with sth/by doing sth** contestar algo con algo/haciendo algo.
counteract [kountûrakt'] *vt* contrarrestar.
counterattack *n* [koun'tûrətak] contraataque *m* ♦ *vi* [kountûrətak'] contraatacar.
counterbalance [koun'tûrbaləns] *n* contrapeso.
counterclockwise [kountûrklâk'wīz] *ad* en sentido contrario al de las agujas del reloj.
counterespionage [kountûres'pēənâzh] *n* contraespionaje *m*.
counterfeit [koun'tûrfit] *n* falsificación *f*, simulación *f* ♦ *vt* falsificar ♦ *a* falso, falsificado.
counterfoil [koun'tûrfoil] *n* talón *m*.
counterintelligence [kountûrintel'ijəns] *n* contraespionaje *m*.
countermand [kountûrmand'] *vt* revocar, cancelar.
counter-measure [koun'tûrmezhûr] *n* contramedida.
counteroffensive [kountûrəfen'siv] *n* contraofensiva.
counterpane [koun'tûrpān] *n* colcha.
counterpart [koun'tûrpârt] *n* (*of person*) homólogo/a.
counter-productive [kountûrprəduk'tiv] *a* contraproducente.
counterproposal [koun'tûrprəpōzəl] *n* contrapropuesta.
countersign [koun'tûrsīn] *vt* ratificar, refrendar.
countess [koun'tis] *n* condesa.
countless [kount'lis] *a* innumerable.
countrified [kun'trəfīd] *a* rústico.
country [kun'trē] *n* país *m*; (*native land*) patria; (*as opposed to town*) campo; (*region*) región *f*, tierra; **in the** ~ en el campo; **mountainous** ~ región *f* montañosa.
country and western (music) *n* música country.
country dancing *n* (*Brit*) baile *m* regional.
country house *n* casa de campo.
countryman [kun'trēmən] *n* (*national*) compatriota *m*; (*rural*) campesino, paisano.
countryside [kun'trēsīd] *n* campo.
country-wide [kun'trēwīd] *a* nacional.
county [koun'tē] *n* condado.
county road *n* (*US AUT*) ≈ carretera secundaria.
county seat *n* (*US*) cabeza de partido.
coup, ~s [kōō, -z] *n* golpe *m*; (*triumph*) éxito; (*also:* ~ **d'état**) golpe de estado.
coupé [kōōpā'] *n* cupé *m*.
couple [kup'əl] *n* (*of things*) par *m*; (*of people*) pareja; (*married* ~) matrimonio ♦ *vt* (*ideas, names*) unir, juntar; (*machinery*) acoplar; **a** ~ **of** un par de.
couplet [kup'lit] *n* pareado.
coupling [kup'ling] *n* (*RAIL*) enganche *m*.
coupon [kōō'pân] *n* cupón *m*; (*Brit: pools* ~) boleto de quiniela.
courage [kûr'ij] *n* valor *m*, valentía.
courageous [kərā'jəs] *a* valiente.
courgette [kōōrzhet'] *n* (*Brit*) calabacín *m*.
courier [kûr'ēûr] *n* mensajero/a; (*diplomatic*) correo; (*for tourists*) guía *m/f* (de turismo).
course [kôrs] *n* (*direction*) dirección *f*; (*of river, SCOL*) curso; (*of ship*) rumbo; (*fig*) proceder *m*; (*GOLF*) campo; (*part of meal*) plato; **of** ~ *ad* desde luego, naturalmente; **of** ~! ¡claro!; **(no) of** ~ **not!** ¡claro que no!, ¡por supuesto que no!; **in due** ~ en el momento oportuno; **in the** ~ **of the next few days** durante los próximos días; **we have no other** ~ **but to ...** no tenemos más remedio que ...; **there are 2** ~**s open to us** se nos ofrecen dos posibilidades; **the best** ~ **would be to ...** lo mejor sería ...; ~ **of treatment** (*MED*) tratamiento.
court [kôrt] *n* (*royal*) corte *m*; (*LAW*) tribunal *m*, juzgado; (*TENNIS*) pista, cancha ♦ *vt* (*woman*) cortejar a; (*fig: favor, popularity*) solicitar, buscar; (: *death, disaster, danger etc*) buscar; **to take to** ~ demandar; **to go to** ~ recurrir a la justicia; ~ **of appeal** tribunal *m* de apelación; ~ **of law** tribunal *m* (de justicia).
courteous [kûr'tēəs] *a* cortés.
courtesan [kôr'tizən] *n* cortesana.
courtesy [kûr'tisē] *n* cortesía; **by** ~ **of** (por) cortesía de.
courtesy bus *n* autocar *or* autobús de cortesía (al aeropuerto etc).
courtesy light *n* (*AUT*) luz *f* interior.
courthouse [kôrt'hous] *n* (*US*) palacio de justicia.
courtier [kôr'tēûr] *n* cortesano.
court-martial, *pl* **courts-martial** [kôrt'mâr'shəl] *n* consejo de guerra ♦ *vt* someter a consejo de guerra.
courtroom [kôrt'rōōm] *n* sala de justicia.
court shoe *n* zapato de mujer de estilo clásico.
courtyard [kôrt'yârd] *n* patio.
cousin [kuz'in] *n* primo/a; **first** ~ primo/a carnal.
cove [kōv] *n* cala, ensenada.
covenant [kuv'ənənt] *n* convenio.
Coventry [kuv'intrē] *n*: **to send sb to** ~ (*fig*) hacer el vacío a uno.

cover [kuv'ûr] vt cubrir; (with lid) tapar; (chairs etc) revestir; (distance) cubrir, recorrer; (include) abarcar; (protect) abrigar; (journalist) investigar; (issues) tratar ♦ n cubierta; (lid) tapa; (for chair etc) funda; (for bed) cobertor m; (envelope) sobre m; (for book) forro; (of magazine) portada; (shelter) abrigo; (insurance) cobertura; **to take ~** (shelter) protegerse, resguardarse; **under ~** (indoors) bajo techo; **under ~ of darkness** al amparo de la oscuridad; **under separate ~** (COMM) por separado; **$10 will ~ everything** con diez dólares cubriremos todos los gastos.
  cover up vt (child, object) cubrir completamente, tapar; (fig: hide: truth, facts) ocultar; **to ~ up for sb** (fig) encubrir a uno.

coverage [kuv'ûrij] n alcance m; (in media) reportaje m; (INSURANCE) cobertura.
coveralls [kuv'ûrôlz] npl (US) mono sg.
cover charge n precio del cubierto.
covering [kuv'ûring] n cubierta, envoltura.
cover letter, (Brit) **covering letter** n carta de explicación.
cover note n (INSURANCE) póliza provisional.
cover price n precio de cubierta.
covert [kō'vûrt] a (secret) secreto, encubierto; (dissembled) furtivo.
cover-up [kuv'ûrup] n encubrimiento.
covet [kuv'it] vt codiciar.
covetous [kuv'ətəs] a codicioso.
cow [kou] n vaca ♦ vt intimidar.
coward [kou'ûrd] n cobarde m/f.
cowardice [kou'ûrdis] n cobardía.
cowardly [kou'ûrdlē] a cobarde.
cowboy [kou'boi] n vaquero.
cower [kou'ûr] vi encogerse (de miedo).
co-worker [kō'wûr'kûr] n colaborador(a) m/f.
cowshed [kou'shed] n establo.
cowslip [kou'slip] n (BOT) primavera, prímula.
coxswain [kák'sin] n (abbr: **cox**) timonel m.
coy [koi] a tímido.
coyote [kīōt'ē] n coyote m.
coziness [kō'zēnis] n comodidad f; (atmosphere) lo holgado.
cozy [kō'zē] a cómodo; (room, atmosphere) acogedor(a).
CP n abbr (= Communist Party) PC m.
cp. abbr (= compare) cfr.
c/p abbr (Brit) = **carriage paid.**
CPA n abbr (US) = **certified public accountant.**
CPI n abbr (= Consumer Price Index) IPC m.
Cpl. abbr (MIL) = **corporal.**
CP/M n abbr (= Central Program for Microprocessors) CP/M m.
c.p.s. abbr (= characters per second) c.p.s.

CPU n abbr = **central processing unit.**
cr. abbr = **credit, creditor.**
crab [krab] n cangrejo.
crab apple n manzana silvestre.
crack [krak] n grieta; (noise) crujido; (: of whip) chasquido; (joke) chiste m; (drug) cocaína dura; (col: attempt): **to have a ~ at sth** intentar algo ♦ vt agrietar, romper; (nut) cascar; (safe) forzar; (whip etc) chasquear; (knuckles) crujir; (joke) contar; (case: solve) resolver; (code) descifrar ♦ a (athlete) de primera clase; **to ~ jokes** (col) contar chistes or cuentos.
  crack down on vt fus reprimir fuertemente, adoptar medidas severas contra.
  crack up vi sufrir una crisis nerviosa.
crackdown [krak'doun] n: **~ (on)** (on crime) campaña (contra); (on spending) reducción f (en).
cracker [krak'ûr] n (cookie) cráquer m; (Christmas ~) sorpresa (navideña).
crackle [krak'əl] vi crepitar.
crackling [krak'ling] n (on radio, telephone) interferencia; (of fire) crepitación f; (of leaves etc) crujido; (of pork) chicharrón m.
cradle [krā'dəl] n cuna ♦ vt (child) mecer, acunar; (object) abrazar.
craft [kraft] n (skill) arte m; (trade) oficio; (cunning) astucia; (boat) barco.
craftsman [krafts'mən] n artesano.
craftsmanship [krafts'mənship] n artesanía.
crafty [kraf'tē] a astuto.
crag [krag] n peñasco.
craggy [krag'ē] a escarpado.
cram [kram] vt (fill): **to ~ sth with** llenar algo (a reventar) de; (put): **to ~ sth into** meter algo a la fuerza en ♦ vi (for exams) empollar.
crammed [kramd] a atestado.
cramp [kramp] n (MED) calambre m; (TECH) grapa ♦ vt (limit) poner trabas a.
cramped [krampt] a apretado, estrecho.
crampon [kram'pän] n crampón m.
cranberry [kran'bärē] n arándano agrio.
crane [krān] n (TECH) grúa; (bird) grulla ♦ vt, vi: **to ~ forward, to ~ one's neck** estirar el cuello, inclinarse estirando el cuello.
cranium [krā'nēəm] n cráneo.
crank [krangk] n manivela; (person) excentrico/a; (US: grumbler) gruñón/ona m/f.
crankshaft [krangk'shaft] n cigüeñal m.
cranky [krang'kē] a (eccentric) maniático; (bad-tempered) irritable.
cranny [kran'ē] n see **nook.**
crap [krap] n (col!) mierda (!).
craps [kraps] n (US) dados mpl.
crash [krash] n (noise) estrépito; (of cars etc) choque m; (of plane) accidente m de aviación; (of business) quiebra; (STOCK EXCHANGE) crac m ♦ vt (plane) estrellar ♦

vi (*plane*) estrellarse; (*two cars*) chocar; (*fall noisily*) caer con estrépito; **he ~ed the car into a wall** estrelló el coche contra una pared *or* tapia.

crash barrier *n* (*AUT*) barrera de protección.

crash course *n* curso acelerado.

crash helmet *n* casco (protector).

crash landing *n* aterrizaje *m* forzado.

crass [kras] *a* grosero, maleducado.

crate [krāt] *n* cajón *m* de embalaje; (*col*) armatoste *m*.

crater [krā'tûr] *n* cráter *m*.

cravat [krəvat'] *n* pañuelo.

crave [krāv] *vt, vi*: **to ~ (for)** ansiar, anhelar.

craving [krā'ving] *n* (*for food, cigarettes, etc*) antojo.

crawfish [krô'fish] *n, pl inv* (*US: freshwater*) cangrejo de río; (: *saltwater*) cigala.

crawl [krôl] *vi* (*drag o.s.*) arrastrarse; (*child*) andar a gatas, gatear; (*vehicle*) avanzar (lentamente); (*col*): **to ~ to sb** dar coba a uno, hacerle la pelota a uno ♦ *n* (*SWIMMING*) crol *m*.

crayfish [krā'fish] *n, pl inv* (*freshwater*) cangrejo de río; (*saltwater*) cigala.

crayon [krā'ân] *n* lápiz *m* de color.

craze [krāz] *n* manía; (*fashion*) moda.

crazed [krāzd] *a* (*look, person*) loco, demente; (*pottery, glaze*) agrietado, cuarteado.

crazy [krā'zē] *a* (*person*) loco; (*idea*) disparatado; **to go ~** volverse loco; **to be ~ about sb/sth** (*col*) estar loco por uno/algo.

crazy paving *n* (*Brit*) pavimento de baldosas irregulares.

CRC *n abbr* (*US*) = *Civil Rights Commission.*

creak [krēk] *vi* crujir; (*hinge etc*) chirriar, rechinar.

cream [krēm] *n* (*of milk*) nata, crema; (*lotion*) crema; (*fig*) flor *f* y nata ♦ *a* (*color*) color *m* crema; **whipped ~** nata batida.

cream cake *n* pastel *m* de nata.

cream cheese *n* queso crema.

creamery [krē'mûrē] *n* (*store*) quesería; (*factory*) central *f* lechera.

creamy [krē'mē] *a* cremoso.

crease [krēs] *n* (*fold*) pliegue *m*; (*in pants*) raya; (*wrinkle*) arruga ♦ *vt* (*fold*) doblar, plegar; (*wrinkle*) arrugar ♦ *vi* (*wrinkle up*) arrugarse.

crease-resistant [krēsrizis'tənt] *a* inarrugable.

create [krēāt'] *vt* (*also COMPUT*) crear; (*impression*) dar; (*fuss, noise*) hacer.

creation [krēā'shən] *n* creación *f*.

creative [krēā'tiv] *a* creador(a).

creativity [krēātiv'ətē] *n* creatividad *f*.

creator [krēā'tûr] *n* creador(a) *m/f*.

creature [krē'chûr] *n* (*animal*) animal *m*, bicho; (*living thing*) criatura.

crèche, creche [kresh] *n* (*Brit*) guardería (infantil).

credence [krēd'əns] *n*: **to lend** *or* **give ~ to** creer en, dar crédito a.

credentials [kriden'shəlz] *npl* credenciales *fpl*; (*letters of reference*) referencias *fpl*.

credibility [kredəbil'ətē] *n* credibilidad *f*.

credible [kred'əbəl] *a* creíble; (*witness, source*) de integridad.

credit [kred'it] *n* (*gen*) crédito; (*merit*) honor *m*, mérito; (*UNIV: esp US*) unidad *f* de crédito ♦ *vt* (*COMM*) abonar; (*believe*) creer, prestar fe a ♦ *a* crediticio; **to be in ~** (*Brit: person, bank account*) tener saldo a favor; **on ~** a crédito; (*col*) al fiado; **he's a ~ to his family** hace honor a su familia; **to ~ sb with** (*fig*) reconocer a uno el mérito de; *see also* **credits.**

creditable [kred'itəbəl] *a* estimable, digno de elogio.

credit account *n* cuenta de crédito.

credit agency *n* agencia de informes comerciales.

credit balance *n* saldo acreedor.

credit card *n* tarjeta de crédito.

credit control *n* control *m* de créditos.

credit facilities *npl* facilidades *fpl* de crédito.

credit limit *n* límite *m* de crédito.

credit note *n* nota de crédito.

creditor [kred'itûr] *n* acreedor(a) *m/f*.

credit rating *n* límite *m* de crédito.

credits [kred'its] *npl* (*CINEMA*) títulos *mpl*, rótulos *mpl* de crédito.

credit transfer *n* transferencia de crédito.

creditworthy [kred'itwûrthē] *a* solvente.

credulity [krədōō'litē] *n* credulidad *f*.

creed [krēd] *n* credo.

creek [krēk] *n* (*US*) riachuelo; (*Brit*) cala, ensenada.

creel [krēl] *n* nasa.

creep, *pt, pp* **crept** [krēp, krept] *vi* (*animal*) deslizarse; (*plant*) trepar; **to ~ up on sb** acercarse sigilosamente a uno; (*fig: old age etc*) acercarse a uno ♦ *n* (*col*): **he's a ~** ¡qué desagradable es!; **it gives me the ~s** me da escalofríos.

creeper [krē'pûr] *n* enredadera.

creepers [krē'pûrz] *npl* (*US: for baby*) pelele *msg*.

creepy [krē'pē] *a* (*frightening*) horripilante.

creepy-crawly [krē'pēkrôl'ē] *n* (*col*) bicho.

cremate [krē'māt] *vt* incinerar.

cremation [krimā'shən] *n* incineración *f*.

crematorium, *pl* **crematoria** [krēmətôr'ēəm, -tôr'ēə] *n* crematorio.

creosote [krē'əsōt] *n* creosota.

crêpe [krāp] *n* (*fabric*) crespón *m*; (*also: ~ rubber*) crep(é) *m*.

crêpe bandage *n* (*Brit*) venda elástica.

crêpe paper *n* papel *m* crep(é).

crêpe sole *n* (*on shoes*) suela de crep(é).

crept [krept] *pt, pp of* **creep.**

crescent [kres'ənt] *n* media luna; *(street)* calle *f (en forma de semicírculo)*.

cress [kres] *n* berro.

crest [krest] *n (of bird)* cresta; *(of hill)* cima, cumbre *f; (of helmet)* cimera; *(of coat of arms)* blasón *m*.

crestfallen [krest'fôlən] *a* alicaído.

Crete [krēt] *n* Creta.

cretin [krē'tən] *n* cretino/a.

crevasse [krəvas'] *n* grieta.

crevice [krev'is] *n* grieta, hendedura.

crew [kroō] *n (of ship etc)* tripulación *f; (CINEMA etc)* equipo; *(gang)* pandilla, banda; *(MIL)* dotación *f*.

crew cut *n* corte *m* al rape.

crew neck *n* cuello plano.

crib [krib] *n (US)* cuna; *(Brit)* pesebre *m* ♦ *vt (col)* plagiar; **portable ~** *(US)* cuna portátil.

crick [krik] *n*: **~ in the neck** tortícolis *m inv.*

cricket [krik'it] *n (insect)* grillo; *(game)* críquet *m*.

cricketer [krik'itûr] *n* jugador *m* de críquet.

crime [krīm] *n* crimen *m; (less serious)* delito.

crime wave *n* ola de crímenes *or* delitos.

criminal [krim'ənəl] *n* criminal *m/f*, delincuente *m/f* ♦ *a* criminal; *(law)* penal.

Criminal Investigation Department (CID) *n (Brit)* ≈ Brigada de Investigación Criminal (B.I.C. *f) (Sp)*.

crimp [krimp] *vt (hair)* rizar.

crimson [krim'zən] *a* carmesí.

cringe [krinj] *vi* agacharse, encogerse.

crinkle [kring'kəl] *vt* arrugar.

crinkly [kring'klē] *a (hair)* rizado, crespo.

cripple [krip'əl] *n* lisiado/a, cojo/a ♦ *vt* lisiar, mutilar; *(ship, plane)* inutilizar; *(production, exports)* paralizar; **~d with arthritis** paralizado por la artritis.

crippling [krip'ling] *a (injury etc)* debilitador(a); *(prices, taxes)* devastador(a).

crisis [krī'sis] *pl* **crises** [krī'sis, -sēz] *n* crisis *f*.

crisp [krisp] *a* fresco; *(cooked)* tostado; *(manner)* seco.

crisps [krisps] *npl (Brit)* patatas *fpl* fritas.

crisscross [kris'krôs] *a* entrelazado, entrecruzado ♦ *vt* entrecruzar(se).

criterion, *pl* **criteria** [krītēr'ēən, -tēr'ēə] *n* criterio.

critic [krit'ik] *n* crítico/a.

critical [krit'ikəl] *a (gen)* crítico; *(illness)* grave; **to be ~ of sb/sth** criticar a uno/algo; **to be on the ~ list** *(MED)* estar grave.

critically [krit'iklē] *ad (speak etc)* en tono crítico; *(ill)* gravemente.

criticism [krit'isizəm] *n* crítica.

criticize [krit'əsīz] *vt* criticar.

critique [kritēk'] *n* crítica.

croak [krōk] *vi (frog)* croar; *(raven)* graznar ♦ *n* graznido.

crochet [krōshā'] *n* ganchillo.

crock [krâk] *n* cántaro, tarro; *(col: person: also:* **old ~)** carcamal *m/f*, vejete/a *m/f; (: car etc)* cacharro.

crockery [krâk'ûrē] *n (plates, cups etc)* loza, vajilla.

crocodile [krâk'ədīl] *n* cocodrilo.

crocus [krō'kəs] *n* azafrán *m*.

croft [krôft] *n (Brit)* granja pequeña.

croissant [krooŏsânt'] *n* croissant *m*, medialuna.

crone [krōn] *n* arpía, bruja.

crony [krō'nē] *n* compinche *m/f*.

crook [krook] *n (fam)* ladrón/ona *m/f; (of shepherd)* cayado; *(of arm)* pliegue *m*.

crooked [krook'id] *a* torcido; *(path)* tortuoso; *(fam)* sucio.

crop [krâp] *n (produce)* cultivo; *(amount produced)* cosecha; *(riding ~)* látigo de montar; *(of bird)* buche *m* ♦ *vt* cortar, recortar; *(cut: hair)* cortar al rape; *(subj: animals: grass)* pacer.

crop up *vi* surgir, presentarse.

crop spraying [krâp' sprā'ing] *n* fumigación *f* de los cultivos.

croquet [krōkā'] *n* croquet *m*.

croquette [krōket'] *n* croqueta.

cross [krôs] *n* cruz *f* ♦ *vt (street etc)* cruzar, atravesar; *(thwart: person)* contrariar, ir contra ♦ *vi*: **the boat ~es from Santander to Plymouth** el barco hace la travesía de Santander a Plymouth ♦ *a* de mal humor, enojado; **it's a ~ between geography and sociology** es una mezcla de geografía y sociología; **to ~ o.s.** santiguarse; **they've got their lines ~ed** *(fig)* hay un malentendido entre ellos; **to be/get ~ with sb (about sth)** estar enfadado/enfadarse con uno (por algo).

cross out *vt* tachar.

cross over *vi* cruzar.

crossbar [krôs'bâr] *n* travesaño.

cross-Channel ferry [krôs'chanəl fär'ē] *n* transbordador *m* que cruza el Canal de la Mancha.

cross-check [krôs'chek] *n* verificación *f* ♦ *vt* verificar.

cross-country (race) [krôs'kun'trē (rās)] *n* carrera a campo traviesa, cross *m*.

cross-examination [krôs'igzamənā'shən] *n* repregunta, interrogatorio.

cross-examine [krôs'igzam'in] *vt* interrogar.

cross-eyed [krôs'īd] *a* bizco.

crossfire [krôs'fiûr] *n* fuego cruzado.

crossing [krôs'ing] *n (road)* cruce *m; (rail)* paso a nivel; *(sea passage)* travesía; *(also:* **pedestrian ~)** paso para peatones.

crossing guard *n (US)* persona encargada de ayudar a los niños a cruzar la calle.

cross purposes *npl*: **to be at ~ with sb** tener un malentendido con uno.

cross-reference [krôs'ref'ûrəns] *n* referencia, remisión *f.*

crossroads [krôs'rōdz] *nsg* cruce *m*, encrucijada.

cross section *n* corte *m* transversal; (*of population*) muestra (representativa).

crosswalk [krôs'wôk] *n* (*US*) paso de peatones.

crosswind [krôs'wind] *n* viento de costado.

crossword [krôs'wûrd] *n* crucigrama *m.*

crotch [krâch] *n* (*of garment*) entrepierna.

crotchet [krâch'it] *n* (*Brit MUS*) negra.

crotchety [krâch'ətē] *a* (*person*) arisco.

crouch [krouch] *vi* agacharse, acurrucarse.

croup [krōōp] *n* (*MED*) crup *m.*

croupier [krōō'pēā] *n* crupier *m/f.*

crouton [krōō'tân] *n* cubito de pan frito.

crow [krō] *n* (*bird*) cuervo; (*of cock*) canto, cacareo ♦ *vi* (*cock*) cantar; (*fig*) jactarse.

crowbar [krō'bâr] *n* palanca.

crowd [kroud] *n* muchedumbre *f;* (*SPORT*) público; (*common herd*) vulgo ♦ *vt* (*gather*) amontonar; (*fill*) llenar ♦ *vi* (*gather*) reunirse; (*pile up*) amontonarse; **~s of people** gran cantidad de gente.

crowded [krou'did] *a* (*full*) atestado; (*well-attended*) concurrido.

crowd scene *n* (*CINEMA, THEATER*) escena con muchos comparsas.

crown [kroun] *n* corona; (*of head*) coronilla; (*of hat*) copa; (*of hill*) cumbre *f* ♦ *vt* (*also tooth*) coronar; **and to ~ it all** ... (*fig*) y para colmo *or* remate ....

crown court *n* (*Brit LAW*) tribunal *m* superior.

crowning [krou'ning] *a* (*achievement, glory*) máximo.

crown jewels *npl* joyas *fpl* reales.

crown prince *n* príncipe *m* heredero.

crow's feet *npl* patas *fpl* de gallo.

crucial [krōō'shəl] *a* decisivo; **his approval is ~ to the success of the project** su aprobación es crucial para el éxito del proyecto.

crucifix [krōō'səfiks] *n* crucifijo.

crucifixion [krōōsəfik'shən] *n* crucifixión *f.*

crucify [krōō'səfī] *vt* crucificar; (*fig*) martirizar.

crude [krōōd] *a* (*materials*) bruto; (*fig: basic*) tosco; (: *vulgar*) ordinario.

crude (oil) *n* petróleo crudo.

cruel [krōō'əl] *a* cruel.

cruelty [krōō'əltē] *n* crueldad *f.*

cruet [krōō'it] *n* vinagreras *fpl.*

cruise [krōōz] *n* crucero ♦ *vi* (*ship*) hacer un crucero; (*car*) ir a velocidad de crucero.

cruise missile *n* misil *m* de crucero.

cruiser [krōō'zúr] *n* crucero.

cruising speed [krōō'zing spēd] *n* velocidad *f* de crucero.

crumb [krum] *n* miga, migaja.

crumble [krum'bəl] *vt* desmenuzar ♦ *vi* (*gen*) desmenuzarse; (*building*) desmoronarse.

crumbly [krum'blē] *a* desmenuzable.

crummy [krum'ē] *a* (*col: poor quality*) pésimo, cutre (*Sp*); (: *unwell*) fatal.

crumpet [krum'pit] *n* ≈ bollo para tostar.

crumple [krum'pəl] *vt* (*paper*) estrujar; (*material*) arrugar.

crunch [krunch] *vt* (*with teeth*) ronzar; (*underfoot*) hacer crujir ♦ *n* (*fig*) crisis *f inv.*

crunchy [krun'chē] *a* crujiente.

crusade [krōōsād'] *n* cruzada ♦ *vi*: **to ~ for/against** (*fig*) hacer una campaña en pro de/en contra de.

crusader [krōōsā'dúr] *n* (*fig*) paladín *m/f*, campeón/ona *m/f.*

crush [krush] *n* (*crowd*) aglomeración *f* ♦ *vt* (*gen*) aplastar; (*paper*) estrujar; (*cloth*) arrugar; (*grind, break up*: *garlic, ice*) picar; (*fruit*) exprimir; (*grapes*) exprimir, prensar; **to have a ~ on sb** estar enamorado de uno.

crushing [krush'ing] *a* aplastante; (*burden*) agobiador(a).

crust [krust] *n* corteza.

crustacean [krustā'shən] *n* crustáceo.

crusty [krus'tē] *a* (*loaf*) de corteza dura.

crutch [kruch] *n* (*MED*) muleta; (*support*) apoyo.

crux [kruks] *n* lo esencial.

cry [krī] *vi* llorar; (*shout: also*: **~ out**) gritar ♦ *n* grito; (*of animal*) aullido; (*weep*): **she had a good ~** lloró a lágrima viva; **what are you ~ing about?** ¿por qué lloras?; **to ~ for help** pedir socorro a voces; **it's a far ~ from** ... (*fig*) dista mucho de ....
cry off *vi* (*Brit*) retirarse.

crypt [kript] *n* cripta.

cryptic [krip'tik] *a* enigmático, secreto.

crystal [kris'təl] *n* cristal *m.*

crystal-clear [kris'təlkli'úr] *a* claro como el agua; (*fig*) cristalino.

crystallize [kris'təlīz] *vt* (*fig*) cristalizar ♦ *vi* cristalizarse; **~d fruits** (*Brit*) frutas *fpl* escarchadas.

CSA *n abbr* = *Confederate States of America.*

CS gas [sē'es gas'] *n* (*Brit*) gas *m* lacrimógeno.

CST *n abbr* (*US*: = *Central Standard Time*) hora de invierno de Chicago.

CT *abbr* (*US MAIL*) = *Connecticut.*

Ct. *abbr* (*US*) = *Connecticut.*

ct *abbr* = **carat.**

cu. *abbr* = **cubic.**

cub [kub] *n* cachorro; (*also*: **~ scout**) niño explorador.

Cuba [kyōō'bə] *n* Cuba.

Cuban [kyōō'bən] *a, n* cubano/a *m/f.*

cubbyhole [kub'ēhōl] *n* chiribitil *m.*

cube [kyōōb] *n* cubo; (*of sugar*) terrón *m* ♦ *vt* (*MATH*) cubicar.

cube root *n* raíz *f* cúbica.

cubic [kyōō'bik] *a* cúbico; **~ capacity** (*AUT*) capacidad *f* cúbica.

cubicle [kyōō'bikəl] *n* (*at pool*) caseta; (*for bed*) cubículo.
cubism [kyōō'bizəm] *n* cubismo.
cuckoo [kōō'kōō] *n* cuco.
cuckoo clock *n* cucú *m*.
cucumber [kyōō'kumbûr] *n* pepino.
cuddle [kud'əl] *vt* abrazar ♦ *vi* abrazarse.
cuddly [kud'lē] *a* mimoso.
cudgel [kuj'əl] *vt*: **to ~ one's brains** devanarse los sesos.
cue [kyōō] *n* (*snooker* ~) taco; (*THEATER etc*) entrada.
cuff [kuf] *n* (*US*: *of pants*) vuelta; (*blow*) bofetada; (*Brit*: *of shirt, coat etc*) puño ♦ *vt* bofetear; **off the ~** *ad* improvisado.
cuff links *npl* gemelos *mpl*.
cu. in. *abbr* = **cubic inches.**
cuisine [kwizēn'] *n* cocina.
cul-de-sac [kul'dəsak'] *n* callejón *m* sin salida.
culinary [kyōō'lənärē] *a* culinario.
cull [kul] *vt* (*select*) entresacar; (*kill selectively*: *animals*) matar selectivamente ♦ *n* matanza selectiva; **seal ~** (*Brit*) matanza selectiva de focas.
culminate [kul'mənāt] *vi*: **to ~ in** terminar en.
culmination [kulmənā'shən] *n* culminación *f*, colmo.
culottes [kyōōláts'] *npl* falda *f* pantalón.
culpable [kul'pəbəl] *a* culpable.
culprit [kul'prit] *n* culpable *m/f*, delincuente *m/f*.
cult [kult] *n* culto; **a ~ figure** un ídolo.
cultivate [kul'təvāt] *vt* (*also fig*) cultivar.
cultivated [kul'təvātid] *a* culto.
cultivation [kultəvā'shən] *n* cultivo; (*fig*) cultura.
cultural [kul'chûrəl] *a* cultural.
culture [kul'chûr] *n* (*also fig*) cultura.
cultured [kul'chûrd] *a* culto.
cumbersome [kum'bûrsəm] *a* de mucho bulto, voluminoso.
cumin [kyōōm'in] *n* (*spice*) comino.
cummerbund [kum'ûrbund] *n* faja, fajín *m*.
cumulative [kyōōm'yələtiv] *a* cumulativo.
cunning [kun'ing] *n* astucia ♦ *a* astuto; (*clever*: *device, idea*) ingenioso.
cup [kup] *n* taza; (*prize, event*) copa; **a ~ of tea** una taza de té.
cupboard [kub'ûrd] *n* (*Brit*) armario; (: in *kitchen*) alacena.
cupful [kup'fəl] *n* taza.
Cupid [kyōō'pid] *n* Cupido.
cupola [kyōō'pələ] *n* cúpula.
cup-tie [kup'tī] *n* (*Brit*) partido de copa.
cur [kûr] *n* perro de mala raza; (*person*) canalla *m*.
curable [kyōō'rəbəl] *a* curable.
curate [kyōō'rit] *n* cura *m*.
curator [kyōōrā'tûr] *n* conservador(a) *m/f*.
curb [kûrb] *vt* refrenar, limitar ♦ *n* freno;

(*US*) bordillo.
curd cheese [kûrd chēz] *n* requesón *m*.
curdle [kûr'dəl] *vi* cuajarse.
curds [kûrdz] *npl* requesón *msg*.
cure [kyōōr] *vt* curar ♦ *n* cura, curación *f*; **to be ~d of sth** curarse de algo; **to take a ~** (*Brit*) tomar una medicina, hacer una cura.
cure-all [kyōōr'ôl] *n* (*also fig*) panacea.
curfew [kûr'fyōō] *n* toque *m* de queda.
curio [kyōō'rēō] *n* curiosidad *f*.
curiosity [kyōōrēás'ətē] *n* curiosidad *f*.
curious [kyōō'rēəs] *a* curioso; **I'm ~ about him** me intriga.
curiously [kyōō'rēəslē] *ad* curiosamente; **~ enough,** ... aunque parezca extraño ....
curl [kûrl] *n* rizo; (*of smoke etc*) espiral *f*, voluta ♦ *vt* (*hair*) rizar; (*paper*) arrollar; (*lip*) fruncir ♦ *vi* rizarse; arrollarse.
  curl up *vi* arrollarse; (*person*) hacerse un ovillo; (*fam*) morirse de risa.
curler [kûr'lûr] *n* bigudí *m*.
curlew [kûr'lōō] *n* zarapito.
curling iron [kûr'ling i'ûrn] *n* (*US*) tenacillas *fpl*.
curling tongs [kûr'ling tángz] *npl* (*Brit*) = **curling iron.**
curly [kûr'lē] *a* rizado.
currant [kûr'ənt] *n* pasa; (*black, red*) grosella.
currency [kûr'ənsē] *n* moneda; **to gain ~** (*fig*) difundirse.
current [kûr'ənt] *n* corriente *f* ♦ *a* corriente, actual; (*tendency, price, event*) corriente; **direct/alternating ~** corriente directa/alterna; **the ~ issue of a magazine** el número corriente de una revista; **in ~ use** de uso corriente.
current account *n* (*Brit*) cuenta corriente.
current affairs *npl* actualidades *fpl*.
current assets *npl* (*COMM*) activo disponible.
current liabilities *npl* (*COMM*) pasivo circulante.
currently [kûr'əntlē] *ad* actualmente.
curriculum, *pl* **~s** *or* **curricula** [kərik'yələm, -lə] *n* plan *m* de estudios.
curriculum vitae (CV) [kərik'yələm vē'tī] *n* currículum *m*.
curry [kûr'ē] *n* curry *m* ♦ *vt*: **to ~ favor with** buscar favores con.
curry powder *n* curry *m* en polvo.
curse [kûrs] *vi* echar pestes ♦ *vt* maldecir ♦ *n* maldición *f*; (*swearword*) palabrota.
cursor [kûr'sûr] *n* (*COMPUT*) cursor *m*.
cursory [kûr'sûrē] *a* rápido, superficial.
curt [kûrt] *a* corto, seco.
curtail [kûrtāl'] *vt* (*cut short*) acortar; (*restrict*) restringir.
curtain [kûr'tən] *n* cortina; (*THEATER*) telón *m*; **to draw the ~s** (*together*) cerrar las cortinas; (*apart*) abrir las cortinas.

curtain call n (THEATER) llamada a escena.

curtain ring n anilla.

curts(e)y [kúrt'sē] n reverencia ♦ vi hacer una reverencia.

curvature [kûr'vəchûr] n curvatura.

curve [kûrv] n curva ♦ vt encorvar, torcer ♦ vi encorvarse, torcerse; (road) hacer curva.

curved [kûrvd] a curvo, encorvado.

cushion [koosh'ən] n cojín m; (SNOOKER) banda ♦ vt (seat) acolchar; (shock) amortiguar.

cushy [koosh'ē] a (Brit col): **a ~ job** un chollo.

custard [kus'tûrd] n (for pouring) natillas fpl.

custodian [kustō'dēən] n custodio m/f; (of museum etc) conservador(a) m/f.

custody [kus'tədē] n custodia; **to take sb into ~** detener a uno; **in the ~ of** al cuidado or cargo de.

custom [kus'təm] n costumbre f; (COMM) clientela; see also **customs**.

customary [kus'təmärē] a acostumbrado; **it is ~ to do ...** es la costumbre hacer ....

custom-built [kus'təmbilt'] a = **custom-made**.

customer [kus'təmûr] n cliente m/f; **he's a tough ~** (col) es un tipo difícil.

customer profile n perfil m del cliente.

customer service n servicio de asistencia pos-venta.

customized [kus'təmīzd] a (car etc) hecho a encargo.

custom-made [kus'təmmād'] a hecho a la medida.

customs [kus'təmz] npl aduana sg; **to go through (the) ~** pasar la aduana.

Customs and Excise n (Brit) Aduanas fpl y Arbitrios.

customs duty n derechos mpl de aduana.

customs officer n aduanero/a.

cut [kut] vb (pt, pp **cut**) vt cortar; (price) rebajar; (record) grabar; (reduce) reducir; (col: avoid: class, lecture) fumarse, faltar a ♦ vi cortar; (intersect) cruzarse ♦ n corte m; (in skin) cortadura; (with sword) tajo; (of knife) cuchillada; (in salary etc) rebaja; (slice of meat) tajada; **to ~ one's finger** cortarse un dedo; **to get one's hair ~** cortarse el pelo; **it ~s both ways** (fig) tiene doble filo; **to ~ a tooth** echar un diente; **power ~** (Brit) apagón m.

cut back vt (plants) podar; (production, expenditure) reducir.

cut down vt (tree) cortar, derribar; (consumption, expenses) reducir; **to ~ sb down to size** (fig) bajarle los humos a uno.

cut in vi: **to ~ in (on)** (interrupt: conversation) interrumpir, intervenir (en); (AUT) cerrar el paso (a).

cut off vt cortar; (fig) aislar; (troops) cercar; **we've been ~ off** (TEL) nos han cortado la comunicación.

cut out vt (shape) recortar; (delete) suprimir.

cut up vt cortar (en pedazos); (chop: food) trinchar, cortar.

cut-and-dried [kutəndrīd'] a (also: **cut-and-dry**) arreglado de antemano, seguro.

cutback [kut'bak] n reducción f.

cute [kyoot] a lindo; (shrewd) listo.

cuticle [kyoo'tikəl] n cutícula.

cutlery [kut'lûrē] n cubiertos mpl.

cutlet [kut'lit] n chuleta.

cutoff [kut'ôf] n (also: ~ **point**) límite m.

cutout [kut'out] n (cardboard ~) recortable m.

cut-price [kut'prīs] a (Brit) = **cut-rate**.

cut-rate [kut'rāt] a (US) a precio reducido.

cutthroat [kut'thrōt] n asesino/a ♦ a feroz; **~ competition** competencia encarnizada or despiadada.

cutting [kut'ing] a (gen) cortante; (remark) mordaz ♦ n (Brit: from newspaper) recorte m; (: RAIL) desmonte m; (CINEMA) desglose m.

CV n abbr = **curriculum vitae**.

C & W n abbr = **country and western (music)**.

cwo abbr (COMM) = **cash with order**.

cwt. abbr = **hundredweight(s)**.

cyanide [sī'ənīd] n cianuro.

cybernetics [sībûrnet'iks] nsg cibernética.

cyclamen [sik'ləmən] n ciclamen m.

cycle [sī'kəl] n ciclo; (bicycle) bicicleta ♦ vi ir en bicicleta.

cycle race n carrera ciclista.

cycling [sīk'ling] n ciclismo.

cyclist [sīk'list] n ciclista m/f.

cyclone [sīk'lōn] n ciclón m.

cygnet [sig'nit] n pollo de cisne.

cylinder [sil'indûr] n cilindro.

cylinder block n bloque m de cilindros.

cylinder capacity n cilindrada.

cylinder head n culata de cilindro.

cylinder-head gasket [sil'indûrhed gas'-kit] n junta de culata.

cymbals [sim'bəlz] npl platillos mpl.

cynic [sin'ik] n cínico/a.

cynical [sin'ikəl] a cínico.

cynicism [sin'əsizəm] n cinismo.

CYO n abbr (US) = Catholic Youth Organization.

cypress [sī'pris] n ciprés m.

Cypriot [sip'rēət] a, n chipriota m/f.

Cyprus [sīp'rəs] n Chipre f.

cyst [sist] n quiste m.

cystitis [sistī'tis] n cistitis f.

CZ n abbr (US: = Canal Zone) zona del Canal de Panamá.

czar [zär] n zar m.

czarina [zârē'nə] n zarina.

Czech [chek] a checo ♦ n checo/a; (LING)

checo.

Czechoslovak [chekəslō'vak] *a, n* = **Czechoslovakian**.

Czechoslovakia [chekəsləvák'ēə] *n* Checoslovaquia.

Czechoslovakian [chekəsləvák'ēən] *a, n* checo/a *m/f*.

D

D, d [dē] *n* (*letter*) D, d; (*MUS*): **D** re *m*; **D for Dog** D de Dolores.

D *abbr* (*US POL*) = **democrat(ic)**.

d. *abbr* = *died*.

DA *n abbr* (*US*) = **district attorney**.

dab [dab] *vt:* **to ~ ointment onto a wound** aplicar pomada sobre una herida; **to ~ with paint** cubrir ligeramente de pintura ♦ *n* (*light stroke*) toque *m*; (*small amount*) pizca.

dabble [dab'əl] *vi:* **to ~ in** hacer por afición.

Dacca [dâk'ə] *n* Dacca.

dachshund [dâks'ōōnd] *n* perro tejonero.

Dacron ® [dā'krân] *n* (*US*) terylene *m*.

dad [dad], **daddy** [dad'ē] *n* papá *m*.

daddy-long-legs [dadēlông'legz] *n* típula.

daffodil [daf'ədil] *n* narciso.

daft [daft] *a* chiflado.

dagger [dag'ûr] *n* puñal *m*, daga; **to look ~s at sb** apuñalar a uno con la mirada.

dahlia [dal'yə] *n* dalia.

daily [dā'lē] *a* diario, cotidiano ♦ *n* (*paper*) diario; (*domestic help*) asistenta ♦ *ad* todos los días, cada día; **twice ~** dos veces al día.

dainty [dān'tē] *a* delicado; (*tasteful*) elegante.

dairy [där'ē] *n* (*shop*) lechería; (*on farm*) vaquería ♦ *a* (*cow etc*) lechero.

dairy cow *n* vaca lechera.

dairy farm *n* vaquería.

dairy produce *n* productos *mpl* lácteos.

dais [dā'is] *n* estrado.

daisy [dā'zē] *n* margarita.

daisy wheel *n* (*on printer*) (rueda) margarita.

daisy-wheel printer [dā'zēhwēl print'ûr] *n* impresora de margarita.

Dakar [dâkâr'] *n* Dakar *m*.

dale [dāl] *n* valle *m*.

dally [dal'ē] *vi* entretenerse.

dalmatian [dalmā'shən] *n* (*dog*) (perro) dálmata *m*.

dam [dam] *n* presa; (*reservoir*) embalse ♦ *vt* represar.

damage [dam'ij] *n* daño; (*fig*) perjuicio; (*to machine*) avería ♦ *vt* dañar; perjudicar; averiar; **~ to property** daños materiales.

damages [dam'ijiz] *npl* (*LAW*) daños y perjuicios; **to pay $5000 in ~** pagar $5000 por daños y perjuicios.

damaging [dam'ijing] *a:* **~ (to)** perjudicial (a).

Damascus [dəmas'kəs] *n* Damasco.

dame [dām] *n* (*title*) dama; (*THEATER*) vieja.

damn [dam] *vt* condenar; (*curse*) maldecir ♦ *n* (*col*): **I don't give a ~** me importa un pito ♦ *a* (*col: also:* **~ed**) maldito; **~ (it)!** ¡maldito sea!

damnable [dam'nəbəl] *a* (*col: behavior*) detestable; (: *weather*) horrible.

damnation [damnā'shən] *n* (*REL*) condenación *f* ♦ *excl* (*col*) ¡maldición!, ¡maldito sea!

damning [dam'ing] *a* (*evidence*) irrecusable.

damp [damp] *a* húmedo, mojado ♦ *n* humedad *f* ♦ *vt* (*also:* **~en**) (*cloth, rag*) mojar; (*enthusiasm*) enfriar.

dampcourse [damp'kôrs] *n* aislante *m* hidrófugo.

damper [dam'pûr] *n* (*MUS*) sordina; (*of fire*) regulador *m* de tiro; **to put a ~ on things** estropearlo todo.

dampness [damp'nis] *n* humedad *f*.

damson [dam'zən] *n* ciruela damascena.

dance [dans] *n* baile *m* ♦ *vi* bailar; **to ~ around** saltar.

dance hall *n* salón *m* de baile.

dancer [dan'sûr] *n* bailador(a) *m/f*; (*professional*) bailarín/ina *m/f*.

dancing [dan'sing] *n* baile *m*.

D and C *n abbr* (*MED*: = *dilation and curettage*) raspado.

dandelion [dan'dəlīən] *n* diente *m* de león.

dandruff [dan'drəf] *n* caspa.

dandy [dan'dē] *n* dandi *m* ♦ *a* (*US col*) estupendo.

Dane [dān] *n* danés/esa *m/f*.

danger [dān'jûr] *n* peligro; (*risk*) riesgo; **~!** (*on sign*) ¡peligro de muerte!; **to be in ~ of** correr riesgo de; **out of ~** fuera de peligro.

danger list *n* (*Brit MED*): **to be on the ~** estar grave.

dangerous [dān'jûrəs] *a* peligroso.

dangerously [dān'jûrəslē] *ad* peligrosamente; **~ ill** muy enfermo.

danger zone *n* área *or* zona de peligro.

dangle [dang'gəl] *vt* colgar ♦ *vi* pender, estar colgado.

Danish [dā'nish] *a* danés/esa ♦ *n* (*LING*) danés *m*.

Danish pastry *n* pasta de almendra.

dank [dangk] *a* húmedo y malsano.

Danube [dan'yōōb] *n* Danubio.

dapper [dap'ûr] *a* pulcro, apuesto.

Dardanelles [dârdənelz'] *npl* Dardanelos *mpl*.

dare [där] *vt*: **to ~ sb to do** desafiar a uno a hacer ♦ *vi*: **to ~ (to) do sth** atreverse a hacer algo; **I ~ say** (*I suppose*) puede ser, a lo mejor; **I ~ say he'll turn up** puede ser que *or* quizás venga; **I don't ~ tell him** no me atrevo a decírselo.

daredevil [där'devəl] *n* temerario/a, atrevido/a.

Dar es Salaam [dâr es səlâm'] *n* Dar es Salaam *m*.

daring [där'ing] *a* (*person*) osado; (*plan, escape*) atrevido ♦ *n* atrevimiento, osadía.

dark [dârk] *a* oscuro; (*hair, complexion*) moreno; (*fig: cheerless*) triste, sombrío ♦ *n* (*gen*) oscuridad *f*; (*night*) tinieblas *fpl*; ~ **chocolate** chocolate *m* amargo; **it is/is getting ~** es de noche/se está poniendo oscuro; **in the ~ about** (*fig*) en ignorancia de; **after ~** después del anochecer.

darken [dâr'kən] *vt* oscurecer; (*color*) hacer más oscuro ♦ *vi* oscurecerse; (*cloud over*) anublarse.

dark glasses *npl* gafas *fpl* negras.

darkly [dârk'lē] *ad* (*gloomily*) tristemente; (*sinisterly*) siniestramente.

darkness [dârk'nis] *n* (*in room*) oscuridad *f*; (*night*) tinieblas *fpl*.

darkroom [dârk'rōōm] *n* cuarto oscuro.

darling [dâr'ling] *a, n* querido/a *m/f*.

darn [dârn] *vt* zurcir.

dart [dârt] *n* dardo; (*in sewing*) sisa ♦ *vi* precipitarse; **to ~ away/along** *vi* salir/ marchar disparado; **to ~ through the traffic** regatear por el tráfico.

dartboard [dârt'bôrd] *n* diana.

darts [dârts] *n* dardos *mpl*.

dash [dash] *n* (*small quantity*: *of liquid*) gota, chorrito; (: *of solid*) pizca; (*sign*) guión *m*; (: *long*) raya ♦ *vt* (*break*) romper, estrellar; (*hopes*) defraudar ♦ *vi* precipitarse, ir de prisa; **a ~ of soda** un poco *or* chorrito de sifón *or* soda.

dash away, dash off *vi* marcharse apresuradamente.

dashboard [dash'bôrd] *n* (*AUT*) tablero de instrumentos.

dashing [dash'ing] *a* gallardo.

dastardly [das'tûrdlē] *ad* ruin, vil.

data [dā'tə] *npl* datos *mpl*.

database [dā'təbās] *n* base *f* de datos.

data capture *n* recogida de datos.

data link *n* enlace *m* de datos.

data processing *n* proceso de datos.

data transmission *n* transmisión *f* de datos.

date [dāt] *n* (*day*) fecha; (*with friend*) cita; (*fruit*) dátil *m* ♦ *vt* fechar; (*col: girl etc*) salir con; **what's the ~ today?** ¿qué fecha es hoy?; **~ of birth** fecha de nacimiento; **closing ~** fecha tope; **to ~** *ad* hasta la fecha; **out of ~** pasado de moda; **up to ~**

moderno; puesto al día; **to bring up to ~** (*correspondence*, *information*) poner al día; (*method*) actualizar; **to bring sb up to ~** poner a uno al corriente; **letter ~d July 5th** *or* (*Brit*) **5th July** carta fechada el 5 de julio.

dated [dā'tid] *a* anticuado.

date stamp *n* matasellos *m inv*; (*on fresh foods*) sello de fecha.

dative [dā'tiv] *n* dativo.

daub [dôb] *vt* embadurnar.

daughter [dôt'ûr] *n* hija.

daughter-in-law [dô'tûrinlô] *n* nuera, hija política.

daunting [dôn'ting] *a* desalentador(a).

davenport [dav'ənpôrt] *n* (*US: sofa*) sofá *m*.

dawdle [dôd'əl] *vi* (*waste time*) perder el tiempo; (*go slowly*) andar muy despacio; **to ~ over one's work** trabajar muy despacio.

dawn [dôn] *n* alba, amanecer *m* ♦ *vi* amanecer; (*fig*): **it ~ed on him that...** cayó en la cuenta de que...; **at ~** al amanecer; **from ~ to dusk** de sol a sol.

day [dā] *n* día *m*; (*working ~*) jornada; **the ~ before** el día anterior; **the ~ after tomorrow** pasado mañana; **the ~ before yesterday** anteayer, antes de ayer; **the ~ after, the following ~** el día siguiente; **by ~** de día; **~ by ~** día por día; **(on) the ~ that ...** el día que ...; **to work an 8-hour ~** trabajar 8 horas diarias *or* al día; **he works 8 hours a ~** trabaja 8 horas al día; **paid by the ~** pagado por día; **these ~s, in the present ~** hoy en día.

daybook [dā'bŏŏk] *n* diario *or* libro de entradas y salidas.

daybreak [dā'brāk] *n* amanecer *m*.

day-care center [dā'kär sen'tûr] *n* guardería.

daydream [dā'drēm] *n* ensueño ♦ *vi* soñar despierto.

daylight [dā'līt] *n* luz *f* (del día).

Daylight Saving Time *n* (*US*) hora de verano.

day-release course [dārilēs' kôrs] *n* (*Brit*) curso de un día a la semana.

day return (ticket) *n* (*Brit*) billete *m* de ida y vuelta (en un día).

day shift *n* turno de día.

daytime [dā'tīm] *n* día *m*.

day-to-day [dātōōdā'] *a* cotidiano, diario; (*expenses*) diario; **on a ~ basis** día por día.

day trip *n* (*Brit*) excursión *f* (de un día).

daze [dāz] *vt* (*stun*) aturdir ♦ *n*: **in a ~** aturdido.

dazed [dāzd] *a* aturdido.

dazzle [daz'əl] *vt* deslumbrar.

dazzling [daz'ling] *a* (*light, smile*) deslumbrante; (*color*) fuerte.

DBS *n abbr* (= *direct broadcasting by sat-*

ellite) transmisión por satélite.

DC *abbr* (*ELEC*) = **direct current**; (*US MAIL*) = *District of Columbia*.

DD *n abbr* (= *Doctor of Divinity*) título universitario.

D/D *abbr* = *demand draft*; (*Brit*) = *direct debit*.

D-day [dē'dā] *n* (*fig*) día *m* clave.

DDS *n abbr* (*US*: = *Doctor of Dental Science*; *Doctor of Dental Surgery*) títulos universitarios.

DDT *n abbr* (= *dichlorodiphenyltrichloroethane*) DDT *m*.

DE *abbr* (*US MAIL*) = *Delaware*.

DEA *n abbr* (*US*: = *Drug Enforcement Administration*) brigada especial dedicada a la lucha contra el tráfico de estupefacientes.

deacon [dē'kən] *n* diácono.

dead [ded] *a* muerto; (*limb*) dormido; (*battery*) agotado ♦ *ad* totalmente; (*exactly*) justo; **he was ~ on arrival** ingresó cadáver; **to shoot sb ~** matar a uno a tiros; **~ tired** muerto (de cansancio); **to stop ~** parar en seco; **the line has gone ~** (*TEL*) se ha cortado la línea; **the ~** *npl* los muertos.

deaden [ded'ən] *vt* (*blow, sound*) amortiguar; (*pain*) calmar, aliviar.

dead end *n* callejón *m* sin salida.

dead-end [dedend'] *a*: **a ~ job** un trabajo sin porvenir.

dead heat *n* (*SPORT*) empate *m*.

deadline [ded'līn] *n* fecha *or* hora tope; **to work to a ~** trabajar con una fecha tope.

deadlock [ded'läk] *n* punto muerto.

dead loss *n* (*col*): **to be a ~** (*person*) ser un inútil; (*thing*) ser una birria.

deadly [ded'lē] *a* mortal, fatal; **~ dull** aburridísimo.

deadly nightshade [ded'lē nīt'shād] *n* belladona.

deadpan [ded'pan] *a* sin expresión.

Dead Sea *n*: **the ~** el Mar Muerto.

dead season *n* (*Brit TOURISM*) temporada baja.

deaf [def] *a* sordo; **to turn a ~ ear to sth** hacerse el sordo ante algo.

deaf-and-dumb [def'əndum'] *a* (*person*) sordomudo; (*alphabet*) para sordomudos.

deafen [def'ən] *vt* ensordecer.

deafening [def'əning] *a* ensordecedor(a).

deaf-mute [def'myōōt'] *n* sordomudo/a.

deafness [def'nis] *n* sordera.

deal [dēl] *n* (*agreement*) pacto, convenio; (*business*) negocio, transacción *f*; (*CARDS*) reparto ♦ *vt* (*pt, pp* **dealt**) (*gen*) dar; **a great ~ (of)** bastante, mucho; **it's a ~!** (*col*) ¡trato hecho!, ¡de acuerdo!; **to make a ~ with sb** hacer un trato con uno; **he got a bad/fair ~ from them** le trataron mal/bien.

deal in *vt fus* tratar en, comerciar en.

deal with *vt fus* (*people*) tratar con; (*problem*) ocuparse de; (*subject*) tratar de.

dealer [dē'lûr] *n* comerciante *m/f*; (*CARDS*) mano *f*.

dealership [dē'lûrship] *n* concesionario.

dealings [dē'lingz] *npl* (*COMM*) transacciones *fpl*; (*relations*) relaciones *fpl*.

dealt [delt] *pt, pp of* **deal**.

dean [dēn] *n* (*REL*) deán *m*; (*SCOL*) decano/a.

dear [dēr] *a* querido; (*costly*) caro ♦ *n*: **my ~** mi querido/a; **~ me!** ¡Dios mío!; **D~ Sir/Madam** (*in letter*) Muy señor mío, Estimado señor/Estimada señora; **D~ Mr/Mrs X** Estimado/a señor(a) X.

dearly [dēr'lē] *ad* (*love*) mucho; (*pay*) caro.

dearth [dûrth] *n* (*of food, resources, money*) escasez *f*.

death [deth] *n* muerte *f*.

deathbed [deth'bed] *n* lecho de muerte.

death certificate *n* partida de defunción.

deathly [deth'lē] *a* mortal; (*silence*) profundo.

death penalty *n* pena de muerte.

death rate *n* tasa de mortalidad.

death sentence *n* condena a muerte.

death trap *n* lugar *m* (*o* vehículo *etc*) peligroso.

debacle [dəbâk'əl] *n* desastre *m*, catástrofe *f*.

debar [dibâr'] *vt*: **to ~ sb from doing** prohibir a uno hacer.

debase [dibās'] *vt* degradar.

debatable [dibā'təbəl] *a* discutible; **it is ~ whether ...** es discutible si ... .

debate [dibāt'] *n* debate *m* ♦ *vt* discutir.

debauched [dibôcht'] *a* vicioso.

debauchery [debô'chûrē] *n* libertinaje *m*.

debenture [diben'chûr] *n* (*COMM*) bono, obligación *f*.

debenture capital *n* capital *m* hipotecario.

debilitate [dibil'ətāt] *vt* debilitar.

debilitating [dibil'ətāting] *a* (*illness etc*) debilitante.

debit [deb'it] *n* debe *m* ♦ *vt*: **to ~ a sum to sb** *or* **to sb's account** cargar una suma en cuenta a uno.

debit balance *n* saldo deudor *or* pasivo.

debit note *n* nota de débito *or* cargo.

debonair [debənär'] *a* jovial, cortés/esa.

debrief [dēbrēf'] *vt* hacer dar parte.

debriefing [dēbrēf'ing] *n* relación *f* (de un informe).

debris [dəbrē'] *n* escombros *mpl*.

debt [det] *n* deuda; **to be in ~** tener deudas; **~s of $5000** deudas de cinco mil dólares; **bad ~** deuda incobrable.

debt collector *n* cobrador(a) *m/f* de deudas.

debtor [det'ûr] *n* deudor(a) *m/f*.

debug [dēbug'] *vt* (*COMPUT*) depurar.

debunk [dibungk'] *vt* (*col: theory*) desprestigiar, desacreditar; (: *claim*) desacreditar; (: *person, institution*) desenmascarar.

début [dābyōō'] *n* presentación *f*.

debutante [debyōōtånt'] *n* debutante *f*.

Dec. *abbr* (= *December*) dic.

decade [dek'ād] *n* decenio.

decadence [dek'ədəns] *n* decadencia.

decadent [dek'ədənt] *a* decadente.

decaffeinated [dēkaf'ənātid] *a* descafeinado.

decamp [dikamp'] *vi* (*col*) escaparse, largarse, rajarse (*LAm*).

decant [dikant'] *vt* decantar.

decanter [dikan'tûr] *n* garrafa.

decay [dikā'] *n* (*fig*) decadencia; (*of building*) desmoronamiento; (*of tooth*) caries *f inv* ♦ *vi* (*rot*) pudrirse; (*fig*) decaer.

decease [disēs'] *n* fallecimiento ♦ *vi* fallecer.

deceased [disēst'] *a* difunto.

deceit [disēt'] *n* engaño.

deceitful [disēt'fəl] *a* engañoso.

deceive [disēv'] *vt* engañar.

decelerate [dēsel'ərāt] *vt* moderar la marcha de ♦ *vi* decelerar.

December [disem'bûr] *n* diciembre *m*.

decency [dē'sənsē] *n* decencia.

decent [dē'sənt] *a* (*proper*) decente; (*person*) amable, bueno.

decently [dē'səntlē] *ad* (*respectably*) decentemente; (*kindly*) amablemente.

decentralization [dēsentrəlizā'shən] *n* descentralización *f*.

decentralize [dēsen'trəlīz] *vt* descentralizar.

deception [disep'shən] *n* engaño.

deceptive [disep'tiv] *a* engañoso.

decibel [des'əbəl] *n* decibel(io) *m*.

decide [disīd'] *vt* (*person*) decidir; (*question, argument*) resolver ♦ *vi*: **to ~ to do/that** decidir hacer/que; **to ~ on sth** decidir por algo; **to ~ against doing sth** decidir en contra de hacer algo.

decided [disī'did] *a* (*resolute*) decidido; (*clear, definite*) indudable.

decidedly [disī'didlē] *ad* decididamente.

deciding [disī'ding] *a* decisivo.

deciduous [disij'ōōəs] *a* de hoja caduca.

decimal [des'əmal] *a* decimal ♦ *n* decimal *f*; **to 3 ~ places** con 3 cifras decimales.

decimalize [des'əməlīz] *vt* convertir al sistema decimal.

decimal point *n* coma decimal.

decimal system *n* sistema *m* métrico.

decimate [des'əmāt] *vt* diezmar.

decipher [disī'fûr] *vt* descifrar.

decision [disizh'ən] *n* decisión *f*; **to make a ~** tomar una decisión.

decisive [disī'siv] *a* (*influence*) decisivo; (*manner, person*) decidido; (*reply*) tajante.

deck [dek] *n* (*NAUT*) cubierta; (*of bus*) piso; (*of cards*) baraja; **cassette ~** platina; **to go up on ~** subir a (la) cubierta; **below ~** en la bodega.

deck chair *n* tumbona.

deckhand [dek'hand] *n* marinero de cubierta.

declaration [deklərā'shən] *n* declaración *f*.

declare [diklär'] *vt* (*gen*) declarar.

declassify [dēklas'əfī] *vt* permitir la publicación de.

decline [diklīn'] *n* decaimiento, decadencia; (*lessening*) disminución *f* ♦ *vt* rehusar ♦ *vi* decaer; disminuir; **~ in living standards** disminución *f* del nivel de vida; **to ~ to do sth** negarse a hacer algo.

declutch [dēkluch'] *vi* desembragar.

decode [dēkōd'] *vt* descifrar.

decoder [dēkō'dûr] *n* (*COMPUT*) decodificador *m*.

decompose [dēkəmpōz'] *vi* descomponerse.

decomposition [dēkâmpəzish'ən] *n* descomposición *f*.

decompression [dēkəmpresh'ən] *n* descompresión *f*.

decompression chamber *n* cámara de descompresión.

decongestant [dēkənjes'tənt] *n* descongestionante.

decontaminate [dēkəntam'ənāt] *vt* descontaminar.

decontrol [dēkəntrōl'] *vt* (*Brit: trade*) quitar controles a; (: *prices*) descongelar.

décor [dākôr'] *n* decoración *f*; (*THEATER*) decorado.

decorate [dek'ərāt] *vt* (*paint*) pintar; (*paper*) empapelar; (*adorn*): **to ~ (with)** adornar (de), decorar (de).

decoration [dekərā'shən] *n* adorno; (*act*) decoración *f*; (*medal*) condecoración *f*.

decorative [dek'ûrətiv] *a* decorativo.

decorator [dek'ərātûr] *n* (*workman*) pintor *m* decorador.

decorum [dikôr'əm] *n* decoro.

decoy [dē'koi] *n* señuelo; **police ~** trampa *or* señuelo policial.

decrease *n* [dē'krēs] disminución *f* ♦ (*vb*: [dikrēs']) *vt* disminuir, reducir ♦ *vi* reducirse; **to be on the ~** ir disminuyendo.

decreasing [dikrēs'ing] *a* decreciente.

decree [dikrē'] *n* decreto ♦ *vt*: **to ~ (that)** decretar (que); **~ absolute/nisi** sentencia absoluta/provisional de divorcio.

decrepit [dikrep'it] *a* (*person*) decrépito; (*building*) ruinoso.

decry [dikrī'] *vt* criticar, censurar.

dedicate [ded'ikāt] *vt* dedicar.

dedicated [ded'ikātid] *a* dedicado; (*COMPUT*) especializado; **~ word processor** procesador *m* de textos especializado *or* dedicado.

dedication [dedikā'shən] *n* (*devotion*) dedicación *f*; (*in book*) dedicatoria.

deduce [didōōs'] *vt* deducir.

deduct [didukt'] *vt* restar; (*from wage etc*) descontar.

deduction [diduk'shən] n (amount deducted) descuento; (conclusion) deducción f, conclusión f.

deed [dēd] n hecho, acto; (feat) hazaña; (LAW) escritura; ~ **of covenant** escritura de contrato.

deem [dēm] vt (formal) juzgar, considerar; **to ~ it wise to do** considerar prudente hacer.

deep [dēp] a profundo; (voice) bajo; (breath) profundo, a pleno pulmón ♦ ad: **the spectators stood 20** ~ los espectadores se formaron de 20 en fondo; **to be 4 meters** ~ tener 4 metros de profundo.

deepen [dē'pən] vt ahondar, profundizar ♦ vi (darkness) intensificarse.

deep-freeze [dēp'frēz'] n congeladora.

deep-fry [dēp'frī'] vt freír en aceite abundante.

deeply [dēp'lē] ad (breathe) a pleno pulmón; (interested, moved, grateful) profundamente, hondamente; **to regret sth** ~ sentir algo profundamente.

deep-rooted [dēp'rōō'tid] a (prejudice, habit) profundamente arraigado; (affection) profundo.

deep-sea [dēp'sē'] a: ~ **diver** buzo; ~ **diving** buceo de altura.

deep-seated [dēp'sē'tid] a (beliefs) (profundamente) arraigado.

deep-set [dēp'set] a (eyes) hundido.

deer [dēr] n, pl inv ciervo.

deerstalker [dēr'stôkûr] n (hat) gorro de cazador.

deface [difās'] vt desfigurar, mutilar.

defamation [defəmā'shən] n difamación f.

defamatory [difam'ətôrē] a difamatorio.

default [difôlt'] vi faltar al pago; (SPORT) dejar de presentarse ♦ n (COMPUT) defecto; **by** ~ (LAW) en rebeldía; (SPORT) por incomparecencia; **to** ~ **on a debt** dejar de pagar una deuda.

defaulter [difôlt'ûr] n (in debt) moroso/a.

default option n (COMPUT) opción f por defecto.

defeat [difēt'] n derrota ♦ vt derrotar, vencer; (fig: efforts) frustrar.

defeatism [difē'tizəm] n derrotismo.

defeatist [difē'tist] a, n derrotista m/f.

defect n [dē'fekt] defecto ♦ vi [difekt']: **to ~ to the enemy** pasarse al enemigo; **physical** ~ defecto físico; **mental** ~ deficiencia mental.

defective [difek'tiv] a (gen) defectuoso; (person) anormal.

defector [difek'tûr] n defector(a) m/f.

defence [difens'] etc (Brit) = **defense** etc.

defend [difend'] vt defender; (decision, action) defender; (opinion) mantener.

defendant [difen'dənt] n acusado/a; (in civil case) demandado/a.

defender [difen'dûr] n defensor(a) m/f.

defending **champion** [difen'ding

cham'pēən] n (SPORT) campeón/ona m/f titular.

defense [difens'] n defensa; **the Department of D~** el Ministerio de Defensa.

defense counsel n (LAW) abogado defensor.

defenseless [difens'lis] a indefenso.

defense spending n gasto militar.

defensive [difen'siv] a defensivo ♦ n defensiva; **on the** ~ a la defensiva.

defer [difûr'] vt (postpone) aplazar; **to** ~ **to** diferir a; (submit): **to** ~ **to sb/sb's opinion** conformarse con uno/someterse al juicio de uno.

deference [def'ûrəns] n deferencia, respeto; **out of** or **in** ~ **to** por respeto a.

deferential [defərɛn'chəl] a respetuoso.

deferred [difûrd'] a: ~ **creditor** acreedor m diferido.

defiance [difī'əns] n desafío; **in** ~ **of** en contra de.

defiant [difī'ənt] a (insolent) insolente; (challenging) retador(a).

defiantly [difī'əntlē] ad con aire de desafío.

deficiency [difish'ənsē] n (lack) falta; (COMM) déficit m; (defect) defecto.

deficient [difish'ənt] a (lacking) insuficiente; (incomplete) incompleto; (defective) defectuoso; (mentally) anormal; ~ **in** deficiente en.

deficit [def'isit] n déficit m.

defile [difīl'] vt manchar; (violate) violar.

define [difīn'] vt (also COMPUT) definir.

definite [def'ənit] a (fixed) determinado; (clear, obvious) claro; **he was** ~ **about it** no dejó lugar a dudas (sobre ello).

definitely [def'ənitlē] ad: **he's** ~ **mad** no cabe duda de que está loco.

definition [defənish'ən] n definición f.

definitive [difin'ətiv] a definitivo.

deflate [diflāt'] vt (gen) desinflar; (pompous person) quitar or rebajar los humos a; (ECON) deflacionar.

deflation [diflā'shən] n (ECON) deflación f.

deflationary [diflā'shənârē] a (ECON) deflacionario.

deflect [diflekt'] vt desviar.

defog [dēfôg'] vt desempañar.

defogger [dēfôg'ûr] n (US AUT) dispositivo antivaho.

deforestation [dēfôristā'shən] n deforestación f.

deform [difôrm'] vt deformar.

deformed [difôrmd'] a deformado.

deformity [difôr'mitē] n deformación f.

defraud [difrôd'] vt estafar; **to** ~ **sb of sth** estafar algo a uno.

defray [difrā'] vt: **to** ~ **sb's expenses** reembolsar a uno los gastos.

defrost [difrôst'] vt (frozen food, fridge) descongelar.

defroster [difrôs'tûr] n (US) eliminador m de vaho.

deft [deft] *a* diestro, hábil.
defunct [dìfungkt'] *a* difunto; (*organization etc*) ya desaparecido.
defuse [dēfyōōz'] *vt* desarmar; (*situation*) calmar, apaciguar.
defy [dìfì'] *vt* (*resist*) oponerse a; (*challenge*) desafiar; (*order*) contravenir.
degenerate *vi* [dìjen'ûrāt] degenerar ♦ *a* [dìjen'ûrit] degenerado.
degradation [dɛgrədā'shən] *n* degradación *f*.
degrade [dìgrād'] *vt* degradar.
degrading [dìgrā'ding] *a* degradante.
degree [dìgrē'] *n* grado; (*SCOL*) título; **10 ~s below freezing** 10 grados bajo cero; **to have a ~ in math** tener una licenciatura en matemáticas; **by ~s** (*gradually*) poco a poco, por etapas; **to some ~, to a certain ~** hasta cierto punto; **a considerable ~ of risk** un gran riesgo.
dehydrated [dēhì'drātid] *a* deshidratado; (*milk*) en polvo.
dehydration [dēhìdrā'shən] *n* deshidratación *f*.
de-ice [dēìs'] *vt* (*windshield*) deshelar.
de-icer [dēì'sûr] *n* deshelador *m*.
deign [dān] *vi*: **to ~ to do** dignarse hacer.
deity [dē'itē] *n* deidad *f*, divinidad *f*.
dejected [dìjek'tid] *a* abatido, desanimado.
dejection [dìjek'shən] *n* abatimiento.
Del. *abbr* (*US*) = *Delaware*.
del. *abbr* = *delete*.
delay [dìlā'] *vt* demorar, aplazar; (*person*) entretener; (*train*) retrasar; (*payment*) aplazar ♦ *vi* tardar ♦ *n* demora, retraso; **without ~** en seguida, sin tardar.
delayed-action [dìlād'ak'shən] *a* (*bomb etc*) de acción retardada.
delectable [dìlek'təbəl] *a* (*person*) encantador(a); (*food*) delicioso.
delegate *n* [del'əgit] delegado/a ♦ *vt* [del'əgāt] delegar; **to ~ sth to sb/sb to do sth** delegar algo en uno/en uno para hacer algo.
delegation [deləgā'shən] *n* (*of work etc*) delegación *f*.
delete [dìlēt'] *vt* suprimir, tachar; (*COMPUT*) suprimir, borrar.
Delhi [del'ē] *n* Delhi *m*.
deliberate *a* [dìlib'ûrit] (*intentional*) intencionado; (*slow*) pausado, lento ♦ *vi* [dìlib'ûrāt] deliberar.
deliberately [dìlib'ûritlē] *ad* (*on purpose*) a propósito; (*slowly*) pausadamente.
deliberation [dìlibərā'shən] *n* (*consideration*) reflexión *f*; (*discussion*) deliberación *f*, discusión *f*.
delicacy [del'əkəsē] *n* delicadeza; (*choice food*) golosina.
delicate [del'əkit] *a* (*gen*) delicado; (*fragile*) frágil.
delicately [del'əkitlē] *ad* con delicadeza, delicadamente; (*act, express*) con discreción.

delicatessen [deləkətes'ən] *n* tienda especializada en comida exótica.
delicious [dìlish'əs] *a* delicioso, rico.
delight [dìlìt'] *n* (*feeling*) placer *m*, deleite *m*; (*object*) encanto, delicia ♦ *vt* encantar, deleitar; **to take ~ in** deleitarse en.
delighted [dìlì'tid] *a*: **~ (at *or* with/to do)** encantado (con/de hacer); **to be ~ that** estar encantado de que; **I'd be ~** con mucho *or* todo gusto.
delightful [dìlìt'fəl] *a* encantador(a), delicioso.
delimit [dìlim'it] *vt* delimitar.
delineate [dìlin'ēāt] *vt* delinear.
delinquency [dìling'kwənsē] *n* delincuencia.
delinquent [dìling'kwint] *a*, *n* delincuente *m/f*.
delirious [dìlēr'ēəs] *a* (*MED*, *fig*) delirante; **to be ~** delirar, desvariar.
delirium [dìlēr'ēəm] *n* delirio.
deliver [dìliv'ûr] *vt* (*distribute*) repartir; (*hand over*) entregar; (*message*) comunicar; (*speech*) pronunciar; (*blow*) lanzar, dar; (*MED*) asistir al parto de.
deliverance [dìliv'ûrəns] *n* liberación *f*.
delivery [dìliv'ûrē] *n* reparto; entrega; (*of speaker*) modo de expresarse; (*MED*) parto, alumbramiento; **to take ~ of** recibir.
delivery note *n* nota de entrega.
delivery truck *n* furgoneta de reparto.
delta [del'tə] *n* delta *m*.
delude [dìlōōd'] *vt* engañar.
deluge [del'yōōj] *n* diluvio ♦ *vt* (*fig*): **to ~ (with)** inundar (de).
delusion [dìlōō'zhən] *n* ilusión *f*, engaño.
de luxe [dəluks'] *a* de lujo.
delve [delv] *vi*: **to ~ into** hurgar en.
Dem. *abbr* (*US POL*) = **democrat(ic)**.
demand [dimand'] *vt* (*gen*) exigir; (*rights*) reclamar; (*need*) requerir ♦ *n* (*gen*) exigencia; (*claim*) reclamación *f*; (*ECON*) demanda; **to ~ sth (from *or* of sb)** exigir algo (a uno); **to be in ~** ser muy solicitado; **on ~** a solicitud.
demanding [dimand'ing] *a* (*boss*) exigente; (*work*) absorbente.
demarcation [dēmärkā'shən] *n* demarcación *f*.
demarcation dispute *n* conflicto por definición *or* demarcación del trabajo.
demean [dimēn'] *vt*: **to ~ o.s.** rebajarse.
demeanor, (*Brit*) **demeanour** [dimē'nûr] *n* porte *m*, conducta, comportamiento.
demented [dimen'tid] *a* demente.
demi- [dem'i] *pref* semi..., medio....
demilitarize [dēmil'itərìz] *vt* desmilitarizar.
demise [dimìz'] *n* (*death*) fallecimiento.
demist [dēmist'] *vt* (*AUT*) eliminar el vaho de.
demister [dimìs'tûr] *n* (*Brit AUT*) eliminador *m* de vaho.
demo [dem'ō] *n abbr* (*col*: = *demonstra-*

tion) manifestación f.

demobilization [dēmōbəlizā'shən] *n* desmovilización f.

democracy [dimák'rəsē] *n* democracia.

democrat [dem'əkrat] *n* demócrata *m/f*; (*Brit, US POL*): **D~** Demócrata *m/f*.

democratic [demǝkrat'ik] *a* democrático.

demography [dimâg'rəfē] *n* demografía.

demolish [dimâl'ish] *vt* derribar, demoler.

demolition [deməlish'ən] *n* derribo, demolición f.

demon [dē'mən] *n* (*evil spirit*) demonio ♦ *cpd* temible.

demonstrate [dem'ənstrāt] *vt* demostrar ♦ *vi* manifestarse; **to ~ (for/against)** manifestarse (a favor de/en contra de).

demonstration [demənstrā'shən] *n* (*POL*) manifestación f; (*proof*) prueba, demostración f; **to hold a ~** (*POL*) hacer una manifestación.

demonstrative [dimán'strətiv] *a* (*person*) expresivo; (*LING*) demostrativo.

demonstrator [dem'ənstrātûr] *n* (*POL*) manifestante *m/f*.

demoralize [dimôr'əliz] *vt* desmoralizar.

demote [dimōt'] *vt* degradar.

demotion [dimō'shən] *n* degradación f; (*COMM*) descenso.

demur [dimûr'] *vi*: **to ~ (at)** hacer objeciones (a), vacilar (ante) ♦ *n*: **without ~** sin objeción.

demure [dimyōōr'] *a* recatado.

demurrage [dimûr'ij] *n* sobrestadía.

den [den] *n* (*of animal*) guarida; (*study*) estudio.

denationalization [dēnashnəlizā'shən] *n* desnacionalización f.

denationalize [dēnash'nəliz] *vt* desnacionalizar.

denatured alcohol [dēnā'chûrd al'kəhôl] *n* (*US*) alcohol *m* desnaturalizado.

denial [dinī'əl] *n* (*refusal*) negativa; (*of report etc*) denegación f.

denier [den'yûr] *n* denier *m*.

denim [den'əm] *n* tela vaquera; *see also* **denims**.

denim jacket *n* chaqueta vaquera, saco vaquero (*LAm*).

denims [den'əmz] *npl* vaqueros *mpl*.

denizen [den'izən] *n* (*inhabitant*) habitante *m/f*; (*foreigner*) residente *m/f* extranjero/a.

Denmark [den'mârk] *n* Dinamarca.

denomination [dinâmənā'shən] *n* valor *m*; (*REL*) confesión f.

denominator [dinâm'ənātûr] *n* denominador *m*.

denote [dinōt'] *vt* indicar, significar.

denounce [dinouns'] *vt* denunciar.

dense [dens] *a* (*thick*) espeso; (: *foliage etc*) tupido; (*stupid*) torpe.

densely [dens'lē] *ad*: **~ populated** con una alta densidad de población.

density [den'sitē] *n* densidad f; **single/**

double-~ disk *n* disco de densidad sencilla/de doble densidad.

dent [dent] *n* abolladura ♦ *vt* (*also*: **make a ~ in**) abollar.

dental [den'təl] *a* dental.

dental surgeon *n* odontólogo/a.

dentifrice [den'təfris] *n* dentífrico.

dentist [den'tist] *n* dentista *m/f*; **~'s office** (*US*) o **surgery** (*Brit*) consultorio dental.

dentistry [den'tistrē] *n* odontología.

dentures [den'chûrz] *npl* dentadura *sg* (postiza).

denude [dinōōd'] *vt*: **to ~ of** despojar de.

denunciation [dinunsēā'shən] *n* denuncia, denunciación f.

deny [dinī'] *vt* negar; (*charge*) rechazar; (*report*) desmentir; **to ~ o.s.** privarse (de); **he denies having said it** niega haberlo dicho.

deodorant [dēō'dûrənt] *n* desodorante *m*.

depart [dipárt'] *vi* irse, marcharse; (*train*) salir; **to ~ from** (*fig*: *differ from*) apartarse de.

departed [dipâr'tid] *a* (*bygone*: *days, glory*) pasado; (*dead*) difunto.

department [dipárt'mənt] *n* (*COMM*) sección f; (*SCOL*) departamento; (*POL*) ministerio; **that's not my ~** (*fig*) no tiene que ver conmigo; **D~ of State** (*US*) Ministerio de Asuntos Exteriores.

departmental [dēpârtmen'təl] *a* (*dispute*) departamental; (*meeting*) departamental, de departamento; **~ manager** jefe/a *m/f* de sección *or* de departamento *or* de servicio.

department store *n* gran almacén *m*.

departure [dipâr'chûr] *n* partida, ida; (*of train*) salida; **a new ~** un nuevo rumbo.

departure lounge *n* (*at airport*) sala de embarque.

depend [dipend'] *vi*: **to ~ (up)on** (*be dependent upon*) depender de; (*rely on*) contar con; **it ~s** depende, según; **~ing on the result** según el resultado.

dependable [dipen'dəbəl] *a* (*person*) formal, serio.

dependant [dipen'dənt] *n* dependiente *m/f*.

dependence [dipen'dəns] *n* dependencia.

dependent [dipen'dənt] *a*: **to be ~ (on)** depender (de) ♦ *n* = **dependant**.

depict [dipikt'] *vt* (*in picture*) pintar; (*describe*) representar.

depilatory [dipil'ətôrē] *n* (*also*: **~ cream**) depilatorio.

deplane [dēplān'] *vi* (*US*) desembarcar.

depleted [diplēt'id] *a* reducido.

deplorable [diplôr'əbəl] *a* deplorable.

deplore [diplôr'] *vt* deplorar.

deploy [diploi'] *vt* desplegar.

depopulate [dipâp'yəlāt] *vt* despoblar.

depopulation [dipâpyəlā'shən] *n* despoblación f.

deport [dipôrt'] *vt* deportar.

deportation [dēpôrtā'shən] *n* deportación f.

deportation order *n* orden *f* de expulsión.
deportment [dipôrt'mənt] *n* comportamiento.
depose [dipōz'] *vt* deponer.
deposit [dipáz'it] *n* depósito; (*CHEM*) sedimento; (*of ore, oil*) yacimiento; **"for ~ only"** "únicamente en cuenta del beneficiario" *vt* (*gen*) depositar; **to put down a ~ of $50** dejar un depósito de 50 dólares.
deposit account *n* (*Brit*) cuenta de ahorros.
depositor [dipáz'itûr] *n* depositante *m/f*, cuentacorrentista *m/f*.
depository [dipáz'itôrē] *n* almacén *m* depositario.
depot [dē'pō] *n* (*storehouse*) depósito; (*for vehicles*) parque *m*.
deprave [diprāv'] *vt* depravar.
depraved [diprāvd'] *a* depravado, vicioso.
depravity [diprav'itē] *n* depravación *f*, vicio.
deprecate [dep'rəkāt] *vt* desaprobar, lamentar.
deprecating [dep'rəkāting] *a* (*disapproving*) de desaprobación; (*apologetic*): **a ~ smile** una sonrisa de disculpa.
depreciate [diprē'shēāt] *vi* depreciarse, perder valor.
depreciation [diprēshēā'shən] *n* depreciación *f*.
depress [dipres'] *vt* deprimir; (*press down*) apretar.
depressant [dipres'ənt] *n* (*MED*) calmante *m*, sedante *m*.
depressed [diprest'] *a* deprimido; (*COMM*: *market, economy*) deprimido; (*area*) deprimido (económicamente); **to get ~ deprimirse.**
depressing [dipres'ing] *a* deprimente.
depression [dipresh'ən] *n* depresión *f*; **the economy is in a state of ~** la economía está deprimida.
deprivation [deprəvā'shən] *n* privación *f*; (*loss*) pérdida.
deprive [diprīv'] *vt*: **to ~ sb of** privar a uno de.
deprived [diprīvd'] *a* necesitado.
dept. *abbr* (= *department*) dto.
depth [depth] *n* profundidad *f*; **at a ~ of 3 meters** a 3 metros de profundidad; **to be out of one's ~** (*swimmer*) perder pie; (*fig*) estar perdido; **to study sth in ~** estudiar algo a fondo; **in the ~s of** en lo más hondo de.
depth charge *n* carga de profundidad.
deputation [depyətā'shən] *n* delegación *f*.
deputize [dep'yətīz] *vi*: **to ~ for sb** suplir a uno.
deputy [dep'yətē] *a*: **~ head** subdirector(a) *m/f* *n* sustituto/a, suplente *m/f*; (*POL*) diputado/a; (*agent*) representante *m/f*.
deputy leader *n* (*POL*) vicepresidente/a *m/f*.
derail [dirāl'] *vt*: **to be ~ed** descarrilarse.

derailment [dirāl'mənt] *n* descarrilamiento.
deranged [dirānjd'] *a* trastornado.
derby [dûr'bē] *n* (*US*) hongo.
Derbys *abbr* (*Brit*) = *Derbyshire*.
deregulate [dēreg'yəlāt] *vt* desreglamentar.
deregulation [dēregyəlā'shən] *n* desreglamentación *f*.
derelict [där'əlikt] *a* abandonado.
deride [dirīd'] *vt* ridiculizar, mofarse de.
derision [dirizh'ən] *n* irrisión *f*, mofas *fpl*.
derisive [dirī'siv] *a* burlón/ona.
derisory [dirī'sûrē] *a* (*sum*) irrisorio; (*laughter, person*) burlón/ona, irónico.
derivation [därəvā'shən] *n* derivación *f*.
derivative [diriv'ətiv] *n* derivado *a* (*work*) poco original.
derive [diriv'] *vt* derivar *vi*: **to ~ from** derivarse de.
derived [dirīvd'] *a* derivado.
dermatitis [dûrmətī'tis] *n* dermatitis *f*.
dermatology [dûrmətál'əjē] *n* dermatología.
derogatory [dirâg'ətôrē] *a* despectivo.
derrick [där'ik] *n* torre *f* de perforación.
derv [dûrv] *n* (*Brit*) gasoil *m*.
DES *n abbr* (*Brit*: = *Department of Education and Science*) ministerio *de educación y ciencia*.
descend [disend'] *vt, vi* descender, bajar; **to ~ from** descender de; **in ~ing order of importance** por orden descendiente de importancia.
descend on *vt fus* (*subj: enemy, angry person*) caer sobre; (: *misfortune*) sobrevenir; (*fig: gloom, silence*) invadir; **visitors ~ed (up)on us** las visitas nos invadieron.
descendant [disen'dənt] *n* descendiente *m/f*.
descent [disent'] *n* descenso; (*GEO*) pendiente *f*, declive *m*; (*origin*) descendencia.
describe [diskrīb'] *vt* describir.
description [diskrip'shən] *n* descripción *f*; (*sort*) clase *f*, género; **of every ~** de toda clase.
descriptive [diskrip'tiv] *a* descriptivo.
desecrate [des'əkrāt] *vt* profanar.
desegregation [dēsegrəgā'shən] *n* desegregación *f*.
desert *n* [dez'ûrt] desierto *vb* [dizûrt'] *vt* abandonar, desamparar *vi* (*MIL*) desertar; *see also* **deserts**.
deserter [dizûr'tûr] *n* desertor(a) *m/f*.
desertion [dizûr'shən] *n* deserción *f*.
desert island [dez'ûrt ī'lənd] *n* isla desierta.
deserts [dizûrts'] *npl*: **to get one's just ~** llevarse su merecido.
deserve [dizûrv'] *vt* merecer, ser digno de.
deservedly [dizûr'vidlē] *ad* con razón.
deserving [dizûr'ving] *a* (*person*) digno; (*action, cause*) meritorio.
desiccated [des'əkātid] *a* desecado.

design [dizīn'] *n* (*sketch*) bosquejo; (*of dress, car*) diseño; (*pattern*) dibujo ♦ *vt* (*gen*) diseñar; **industrial** ~ diseño industrial; **to have ~s on sb** tener la(s) mira(s) puesta(s) en uno; **to be ~ed for sb/sth** estar hecho para uno/algo.

designate *vt* [dez'ignāt] (*appoint*) nombrar; (*destine*) designar ♦ *a* [dez'ignit] designado.

designation [dezignā'shən] *n* (*appointment*) nombramiento; (*name*) denominación *f*.

designer [dizī'nûr] *n* diseñador(a) *m/f*; (*fashion* ~) modisto/a.

desirability [diziûrəbil'ətē] *n* ventaja, atractivo.

desirable [dizī'ûrəbəl] *a* (*proper*) deseable; (*attractive*) atractivo; **it is** ~ **that** es conveniente que.

desire [dizī'ûr] *n* deseo ♦ *vt* desear; **to** ~ **sth/to do sth/that** desear algo/hacer algo/que.

desirous [dizī'ûrəs] *a*: **to be** ~ **of** desear.

desist [dizist'] *vi*: **to** ~ (**from**) desistir (de).

desk [desk] *n* (*in office*) escritorio; (*for pupil*) pupitre *m*; (*in hotel, at airport*) recepción *f*; (*Brit: in store, restaurant*) caja.

desktop publishing [desk'tàp pub'lishing] *n* autoedición *f*.

desolate [des'əlit] *a* (*place*) desierto; (*person*) afligido.

desolation [desəlā'shən] *n* (*of place*) desolación *f*; (*of person*) aflicción *f*.

despair [dispār'] *n* desesperación *f* ♦ *vi*: **to** ~ **of** desesperarse de; **in** ~ desesperado.

despatch [dispach'] *n, vt* = **dispatch.**

desperate [des'pûrit] *a* desesperado; (*fugitive*) peligroso; (*measures*) extremo; **we are getting** ~ nos estamos desesperando.

desperately [des'pûritlē] *ad* desesperadamente; (*very*) terriblemente, gravemente; ~ **ill** gravemente enfermo.

desperation [despərā'shən] *n* desesperación *f*; **in** ~ desesperado.

despicable [des'pikəbəl] *a* vil, despreciable.

despise [dispīz'] *vt* despreciar.

despite [dispīt'] *prep* a pesar de, pese a.

despondent [dispàn'dənt] *a* deprimido, abatido.

despot [des'pət] *n* déspota *m/f*.

dessert [dizûrt'] *n* postre *m*.

dessertspoon [dizûrt'spōōn] *n* cuchara (de postre).

destabilize [dēstà'bəliz] *vt* desestabilizar.

destination [destənā'shən] *n* destino.

destine [des'tin] *vt* destinar.

destined [des'tind] *a*: ~ **for Boston** con destino a Boston.

destiny [des'tənē] *n* destino.

destitute [des'titōōt] *a* desamparado, indigente.

destitution [destitōō'shən] *n* indigencia, miseria.

destroy [distroi'] *vt* destruir; (*finish*) acabar con.

destroyer [distroi'ûr] *n* (*NAUT*) destructor *m*.

destruction [distruk'shən] *n* destrucción *f*; (*fig*) ruina.

destructive [distruk'tiv] *a* destructivo, destructor(a).

desultory [des'əltôrē] *a* (*reading*) poco metódico; (*conversation*) inconexo; (*contact*) intermitente.

detach [ditach'] *vt* separar; (*unstick*) despegar.

detachable [ditach'əbəl] *a* separable; (*TECH*) desmontable.

detached [ditacht'] *a* (*attitude*) objetivo, imparcial.

detached house *n* chalé *m*, chalet *m*.

detachment [ditach'mənt] *n* separación *f*; (*MIL*) destacamento; (*fig*) objetividad *f*, imparcialidad *f*.

detail [ditāl'] *n* detalle *m*; (*MIL*) destacamento ♦ *vt* detallar; (*MIL*) destacar; **in** ~ detalladamente; **to go into** ~(**s**) entrar en detalles.

detailed [ditāld'] *a* detallado.

detain [ditān'] *vt* retener; (*in captivity*) detener.

detainee [dētānē'] *n* detenido/a.

detect [ditekt'] *vt* (*gen*) descubrir; (*MED, POLICE*) identificar; (*MIL, RADAR, TECH*) detectar.

detection [ditek'shən] *n* descubrimiento; identificación *f*; **crime** ~ investigación *f*; **to escape** ~ (*criminal*) escaparse sin ser descubierto; (*mistake*) pasar inadvertido.

detective [ditek'tiv] *n* detective *m*.

detective story *n* novela policíaca.

detector [ditek'tûr] *n* detector *m*.

détente [dātánt'] *n* distensión *f*, detente *f*.

detention [diten'chən] *n* detención *f*, arresto.

deter [ditûr'] *vt* (*dissuade*) disuadir; (*prevent*) impedir; **to** ~ **sb from doing sth** disuadir a uno de que haga algo.

detergent [ditûr'jənt] *n* detergente *m*.

deteriorate [ditē'rēərāt] *vi* deteriorarse.

deterioration [ditērēərā'shən] *n* deterioro.

determination [ditûrmənā'shən] *n* resolución *f*.

determine [ditûr'min] *vt* determinar; **to** ~ **to do sth** decidir hacer algo.

determined [ditûr'mind] *a*: **to be** ~ **to do sth** estar decidido *or* resuelto a hacer algo; **a** ~ **effort** un esfuerzo concentrado.

deterrence [ditûr'əns] *n* disuasión *f*.

deterrent [ditûr'ənt] *n* fuerza de disuasión; **to act as a** ~ servir para prevenir.

detest [ditest'] *vt* aborrecer.

detestable [dites'təbəl] *a* aborrecible.

dethrone [dēthrōn'] *vt* destronar.

detonate [det'ənāt] *vi* estallar ♦ *vt* hacer detonar.

detonator [det'ənātûr] *n* detonador *m*, fulminante *m*.

detour |dē'tŏŏr| *n* (*gen*, *US* AUT: *diversion*) desvío ♦ *vt* (*US*: *traffic*) desviar; **to make a ~** dar un rodeo.

detract |ditrakt'| *vt*: **to ~ from** quitar mérito a, desvirtuar.

detractor |ditrak'tûr| *n* detractor(a) *m/f*.

detriment |det'rəmənt| *n*: **to the ~ of** en perjuicio de; **without ~ to** sin detrimento *or* perjuicio a.

detrimental |detrəmen'təl| *a* perjudicial.

deuce |dŏŏs| *n* (TENNIS) cuarenta iguales.

devaluation |dēvalyŏŏā'shən| *n* devaluación *f*.

devalue |dēval'yŏŏ| *vt* devaluar.

devastate |dev'əstāt| *vt* devastar; **he was ~d by the news** las noticias le dejaron desolado.

devastating |dev'əstāting| *a* devastador(a); (*fig*) arrollador(a).

devastation |devəstā'shən| *n* devastación *f*, ruina.

develop |divel'əp| *vt* desarrollar; (*PHOT*) revelar; (*disease*) coger; (*habit*) adquirir ♦ *vi* desarrollarse; (*advance*) progresar; **this land is to be ~ed** se va a construir en este terreno; **to ~ a taste for sth** tomar gusto a algo; **to ~ into** transformarse *or* convertirse en.

developer |divel'əpûr| *n* (*property* ~) especulador(a) *m/f* en construcción.

developing country *n* país *m* en (vías de) desarrollo.

development |divel'əpmənt| *n* desarrollo; (*advance*) progreso; (*of affair, case*) desenvolvimiento; (*of land*) urbanización *f*.

development area *n* zona de fomento *or* desarrollo.

deviant |dē'vēənt| *a* anómalo, pervertido.

deviate |dē'vēāt| *vi*: **to ~ (from)** desviarse (de).

deviation |dēvēā'shən| *n* desviación *f*.

device |divīs'| *n* (*scheme*) estratagema, recurso; (*apparatus*) aparato, mecanismo; (*explosive* ~) artefacto explosivo.

devil |dev'əl| *n* diablo, demonio.

devilish |dev'əlish| *a* diabólico.

devil-may-care |dev'əlmākär'| *a* despreocupado.

devious |dē'vēəs| *a* intricado, enrevesado; (*person*) taimado.

devise |divīz'| *vt* idear, inventar.

devoid |divoid'| *a*: **~ of** desprovisto de.

devolution |devəlŏŏ'shən| *n* (POL) descentralización *f*.

devolve |divâlv'| *vi*: **to ~ (up)on** recaer sobre.

devote |divōt'| *vt*: **to ~ sth to** dedicar algo a.

devoted |divōt'id| *a* (*loyal*) leal, fiel; **the book is ~ to politics** el libro trata de la política.

devotee |devōtē'| *n* devoto/a.

devotion |divō'shən| *n* dedicación *f*; (REL)

devoción *f*.

devour |divou'ûr| *vt* devorar.

devout |divout'| *a* devoto.

dew |dŏŏ| *n* rocío.

dexterity |dekstär'itē| *n* destreza.

dext(e)rous |dek'strəs| *a* (*skilful*) diestro, hábil; (*movement*) ágil.

dg *abbr* (= *decigram*) dg.

diabetes |dīəbē'tis| *n* diabetes *f*.

diabetic |dīəbet'ik| *n* diabético/a ♦ *a* diabético; (*chocolate*, *jam*) para diabéticos.

diabolical |dīəbâl'ikəl| *a* diabólico; (*col*: *dreadful*) horrendo, horroroso.

diagnose |dīəgnōs'| *vt* diagnosticar.

diagnosis, *pl* **diagnoses** |dīəgnō'sis, -sēz| *n* diagnóstico.

diagonal |dīag'ənəl| *a* diagonal ♦ *n* diagonal *f*.

diagram |dī'əgram| *n* diagrama *m*, esquema *m*.

dial |dīl| *n* esfera, cuadrante *m*, cara (*LAm*); (*of phone*) disco ♦ *vt* (*number*) marcar; **to ~ a wrong number** equivocarse de número; **can I ~ New York direct?** ¿puedo marcar Nueva York directamente?

dial. *abbr* = **dialect.**

dial code *n* (*US*) prefijo.

dialect |dī'əlekt| *n* dialecto.

dialling code |dī'ling kōd| *n* (*Brit*) prefijo.

dialling tone |dī'ling tōn| *n* (*Brit*) señal *f* *or* tono de marcar.

dialog, (*Brit*) **dialogue** |dī'əlòg| *n* diálogo.

dial tone *n* (*US*) señal *f* *or* tono de marcar.

dialysis |dīal'isis| *n* diálisis *f*.

diameter |dīam'itûr| *n* diámetro.

diametrically |dīəmet'riklē| *ad*: **~ opposed (to)** diametralmente opuesto (a).

diamond |dī'mənd| *n* diamante *m*; **~s** *npl* (CARDS) diamantes *mpl*.

diamond ring *n* anillo *or* sortija de diamantes.

diaper |dī'pûr| *n* (*US*) pañal *m*.

diaper pin *n* (*US*) imperdible *m*, seguro (*LAm*).

diaphragm |dī'əfram| *n* diafragma *m*.

diarrhea, (*Brit*) **diarrhoea** |dīərē'ə| *n* diarrea.

diary |dī'ûrē| *n* (*daily account*) diario; (*book*) agenda; **to keep a ~** escribir un diario.

diatribe |dī'ətrīb| *n*: **~ (against)** diatriba (contra).

dice |dīs| *n*, *pl inv* dados *mpl* ♦ *vt* (CULIN) cortar en cuadritos.

dicey |dī'sē| *a* (*Brit*: *col*): **it's a bit ~** (*risky*) es un poco arriesgado; (*doubtful*) es un poco dudoso.

dichotomy |dīkât'əmē| *n* dicotomía.

Dictaphone ® |dik'təfōn| *n* dictáfono ®.

dictate *vt* |diktāt'| dictar ♦ *n* |dik'tāt| dictado.

dictate to *vt fus* (*person*) dar órdenes a;

I won't be ~d to no estoy a las órdenes de nadie.
dictation [diktā'shən] *n* (*to secretary etc*) dictado; **at ~ speed** para tomar al dictado.
dictator [dik'tātúr] *n* dictador *m*.
dictatorship [dik'tātúrship] *n* dictadura.
diction [dik'shən] *n* dicción *f*.
dictionary [dik'shənärē] *n* diccionario.
did [did] *pt of* do.
didactic [dīdak'tik] *a* didáctico.
diddle [did'əl] *vt* estafar, timar.
didn't [did'ənt] = **did not**.
die [dī] *vi* morir; **to ~ (of** *or* **from)** morirse (de); **to be dying** morirse, estarse muriendo; **to be dying for sth/to do sth** morirse por algo/de ganas de hacer algo.
  die away *vi* (*sound, light*) perderse.
  die down *vi* (*gen*) apagarse; (*wind*) amainar.
  die out *vi* desaparecer, extinguirse.
diehard [dī'hárd] *n* intransigente *m/f*.
dieresis [dīär'əsis] *n* diéresis *f*.
diesel [dē'zəl] *n* diesel *m*.
diesel engine *n* motor *m* diesel.
diesel fuel, diesel oil *n* gas-oil *m*.
diet [dī'ət] *n* dieta; (*restricted food*) régimen *m* ♦ *vi* (*also*: **be on a ~**) estar a dieta, hacer régimen; **to live on a ~ of** alimentarse de.
dietician [dīətish'ən] *n* dietético/a *m/f*.
differ [dif'úr] *vi* (*be different*) ser distinto, diferenciarse; (*disagree*) discrepar.
difference [dif'ûrəns] *n* diferencia; (*quarrel*) desacuerdo; **it makes no ~ to** me me da igual *or* lo mismo; **to settle one's ~s** arreglarse.
different [dif'ûrənt] *a* diferente, distinto.
differential [difərən'chəl] *n* diferencial *f*.
differentiate [difərən'chēāt] *vt* distinguir ♦ *vi* diferenciarse; **to ~ between** distinguir entre.
differently [dif'ûrəntlē] *ad* de otro modo, en forma distinta.
difficult [dif'əkult] *a* difícil; **~ to understand** difícil de entender.
difficulty [dif'əkultē] *n* dificultad *f*; **to have difficulties with** (*police, landlord etc*) tener problemas con; **to be in ~** tener dificultad.
diffidence [dif'idəns] *n* timidez *f*, falta de confianza en sí mismo.
diffident [dif'idənt] *a* tímido.
diffuse *a* [difyōōs'] difuso ♦ *vt* [difyōōz'] difundir.
dig [dig] *vt* (*pt, pp* **dug** [dug]) (*hole*) cavar; (*ground*) remover; (*coal*) extraer; (*nails etc*) hincar ♦ *n* (*prod*) empujón *m*; (*archeological*) excavación *f*; (*remark*) indirecta; **to ~ into** (*savings*) consumir; **to ~ into one's pockets for sth** hurgar en el bolsillo por algo; **to ~ one's nails into** clavar las uñas en; *see also* **digs**.
  dig in *vi* (*also*: **~ o.s. in:** *MIL*) atrincherarse; (*col: eat*) hincar los dientes ♦ *vt* (*compost*) añadir al suelo; (*knife, claw*)

clavar; **to ~ in one's heels** (*fig*) mantenerse en sus trece.
  dig out *vt* (*hole*) excavar; (*survivors, car from snow*) sacar.
  dig up *vt* desenterrar; (*plant*) desarraigar.
digest *vt* [dijest'] (*food*) digerir; (*facts*) asimilar ♦ *n* [dī'jest] resumen *m*.
digestible [dijes'təbəl] *a* digerible.
digestion [dijes'chən] *n* digestión *f*.
digestive [dijes'tiv] *a* (*juices, system*) digestivo.
digit [dij'it] *n* (*number*) dígito; (*finger*) dedo.
digital [dij'itəl] *a* digital.
digital computer *n* ordenador *m* digital.
dignified [dig'nəfīd] *a* grave, solemne; (*action*) decoroso.
dignify [dig'nəfī] *vt* dignificar.
dignitary [dig'nitärē] *n* dignatario/a.
dignity [dig'nitē] *n* dignidad *f*.
digress [digres'] *vi*: **to ~ from** apartarse de.
digression [digresh'ən] *n* digresión *f*.
digs [digz] *npl* (*Brit: col*) pensión *f*, alojamiento.
dike [dīk] *n* dique *m*.
dilapidated [dilap'ədātid] *a* desmoronado, ruinoso.
dilate [dīlāt'] *vt* dilatar ♦ *vi* dilatarse.
dilatory [dil'ətôrē] *a* (*person*) lento; (*action*) dilatorio.
dilemma [dilem'ə] *n* dilema *m*; **to be in a ~** estar en un dilema.
dilettante [dilitânt'] *n* diletante *m/f*.
diligence [dil'əjəns] *n* diligencia.
diligent [dil'ijənt] *a* diligente.
dill [dil] *n* eneldo.
dilly-dally [dil'ēdalē] *vi* (*hesitate*) vacilar; (*dawdle*) entretenerse.
dilute [dilōōt'] *vt* diluir.
dim [dim] *a* (*light*) débil; (*sight*) turbio; (*outline*) indistinto; (*stupid*) lerdo; (*room*) oscuro ♦ *vt* (*light*) bajar; **to take a ~ view of sth** tener una pobre opinión de algo; **to ~ one's lights** (*US AUT*) poner luces de cruce.
dime [dīm] *n* (*US*) moneda de diez centavos.
dimension [dimen'chən] *n* dimensión *f*.
-dimensional [dimen'chənl] *a suff*: **two~** de dos dimensiones.
dimensions [dimen'chənz] *npl* dimensiones *fpl*.
diminish [dimin'ish] *vt, vi* disminuir.
diminished [dimin'isht] *a*: **~ responsibility** (*LAW*) responsabilidad *f* disminuida.
diminutive [dimin'yətiv] *a* diminuto ♦ *n* (*LING*) diminutivo.
dimly [dim'lē] *ad* débilmente; (*not clearly*) indistintamente.
dimmer [dim'úr] *n* (*US AUT*) interruptor *m*.
dimple [dim'pəl] *n* hoyuelo.
dimwitted [dim'witid] *a* (*col*) lerdo, de pocas luces.

din [din] *n* estruendo, estrépito ♦ *vt*: **to ~ sth into sb** (*col*) meter algo en la cabeza a uno.

dine [dīn] *vi* cenar.

diner [dīn'ûr] *n* (*person: in restaurant*) comensal *m/f*; (*Brit RAIL*) = **dining car**; (*US*) restaurante económico.

dinghy [ding'ē] *n* bote *m*; (*also:* **rubber ~**) lancha (neumática).

dingy [din'jē] *a* (*room*) sombrío; (*dirty*) sucio; (*dull*) deslucido.

dining car [dīn'ing kár] *n* coche-comedor *m*.

dining room [dīn'ing rōōm] *n* comedor *m*.

dinner [din'ûr] *n* (*evening meal*) cena; (*lunch*) comida; (*public*) cena, banquete *m*; **~'s ready!** ¡la cena está servida!

dinner jacket *n* smoking *m*.

dinner party *n* cena.

dinner time *n* hora de cenar *or* comer.

dinosaur [dī'nəsôr] *n* dinosaurio.

dint [dint] *n*: **by ~ of (doing) sth** a fuerza de (hacer) algo.

diocese [dī'əsēs] *n* diócesis *f*.

dioxide [dīák'sīd] *n* bióxido; **carbon ~** bióxido de carbono.

dioxin [dīáks'in] *n* dioxina.

dip [dip] *n* (*slope*) pendiente *f*; (*in sea*) baño ♦ *vt* (*in water*) mojar; (*ladle etc*) meter; (*Brit AUT*): **to ~ one's lights** poner luces de cruce ♦ *vi* inclinarse hacia abajo.

diphtheria [dipthē'rēə] *n* difteria.

diphthong [dif'thông] *n* diptongo.

diploma [diplō'mə] *n* diploma *m*.

diplomacy [diplō'məsē] *n* diplomacia.

diplomat [dip'ləmat] *n* diplomático/a *m/f*.

diplomatic [dipləmat'ik] *a* diplomático; **to break off ~ relations** romper las relaciones diplomáticas.

diplomatic corps *n* cuerpo diplomático.

dipstick [dip'stik] *n* (*AUT*) varilla de nivel (del aceite).

dipswitch [dip'swich] *n* (*Brit AUT*) interruptor *m*.

dire [dī'ûr] *a* calamitoso.

direct [direkt'] *a* (*gen*) directo; (*manner, person*) franco ♦ *vt* dirigir; **can you ~ me to...?** ¿puede indicarme dónde está...?; **to ~ sb to do sth** mandar a uno hacer algo.

direct access *n* (*COMPUT*) acceso directo.

direct cost *n* costo directo.

direct current *n* corriente *f* continua.

direct debit *n* domiciliación *f* bancaria de recibos.

direction [direk'shən] *n* dirección *f*; **sense of ~** sentido de orientación; **~s** *npl* (*advice*) órdenes *fpl*, instrucciones *fpl*; (*to a place*) señas *fpl*; **in the ~ of** hacia, en dirección a; **~s for use** modo de empleo; **to ask for ~s** preguntar el camino.

directional [direk'shənəl] *a* direccional.

directive [direk'tiv] *n* orden *f*, instrucción *f*; **a government ~** una orden del gobierno.

directly [direkt'lē] *ad* (*in straight line*) directamente; (*at once*) en seguida.

direct mail *n* correspondencia directa.

direct mailshot *n* (*Brit*) promoción *f* por correspondencia directa.

directness [direkt'nis] *n* (*of person, speech*) franqueza.

director [direk'tûr] *n* director(a) *m/f*; **managing ~** director(a) *m/f* gerente.

Director of Public Prosecutions *n* (*Brit*) ≈ fiscal *m/f* oficial *or* gubernamental.

directory [direk'tûrē] *n* (*TEL*) guía (telefónica); (*street ~*) callejero; (*trade ~*) directorio de comercio; (*COMPUT*) directorio.

directory assistance, (*Brit*) **directory enquiries** *n* (*service*) (servicio de) información *f*.

dirt [dûrt] *n* suciedad *f*.

dirt-cheap [dûrt'chēp'] *a* baratísimo.

dirt road *n* (*US*) camino sin firme.

dirty [dûr'tē] *a* sucio; (*joke*) verde, colorado (*LAm*) ♦ *vt* ensuciar; (*stain*) manchar.

dirty trick *n* juego sucio.

disability [disəbil'ətē] *n* incapacidad *f*.

disability allowance *n* pensión *f* de invalidez.

disable [disā'bəl] *vt* (*subj: illness, accident*) dejar incapacitado; (*tank, gun*) inutilizar; (*LAW: disqualify*) incapacitar.

disabled [disā'bəld] *a* minusválido.

disabuse [disəbyōōz'] *vt*: **I ~d him of that idea** le saqué del error.

disadvantage [disədvan'tij] *n* desventaja, inconveniente *m*.

disadvantaged [disədvan'tijd] *a* (*person*) desventajado.

disadvantageous [disadvəntā'jəs] *a* desventajoso.

disaffected [disəfek'tid] *a* descontento; **to be ~ (to *o* towards)** estar descontento (de).

disaffection [disəfek'shən] *n* desafecto, descontento.

disagree [disəgrē'] *vi* (*differ*) discrepar; **to ~ (with)** no estar de acuerdo (con); **I ~ with you** no estoy de acuerdo contigo.

disagreeable [disəgrē'əbəl] *a* desagradable.

disagreement [disəgrē'mənt] *n* (*gen*) desacuerdo; (*quarrel*) riña; **to have a ~ with sb** estar en desacuerdo con uno.

disallow [disəlou'] *vt* (*goal*) anular; (*claim*) rechazar.

disappear [disəpi'ûr] *vi* desaparecer.

disappearance [disəpi'ûrəns] *n* desaparición *f*.

disappoint [disəpoint'] *vt* decepcionar; (*hopes*) defraudar.

disappointed [disəpoin'tid] *a* decepcionado.

disappointing [disəpoin'ting] *a* decepcionante.

disappointment [disəpoint'mənt] *n* decepción *f*.

disapproval [disəprōō'vəl] *n* desaprobación *f*.

disapprove [disəprōōv'] *vi:* **to ~ of** desaprobar.

disapproving [disəprōō'ving] *a* de desaprobación, desaprobador(a).

disarm [disârm'] *vt* desarmar.

disarmament [disâr'məmənt] *n* desarme *m.*

disarmament talks *npl* conversaciones *fpl* de *or* sobre desarme.

disarming [disârm'ing] *a* (*smile*) que desarma, encantador(a).

disarray [disərā'] *n:* **in ~** (*troops*) desorganizado; (*thoughts*) confuso; (*hair, clothes*) desarreglado; **to throw into ~** provocar el caos en.

disaster [dizas'tûr] *n* desastre *m.*

disaster area *n* zona de desastre.

disastrous [dizas'trəs] *a* desastroso.

disband [disband'] *vt* disolver ♦ *vi* desbandarse.

disbelief [disbilēf'] *n* incredulidad *f;* **in ~** con incredulidad.

disbelieve [disbilēv'] *vt* (*person, story*) poner en duda, no creer.

disc [disk] *n* disco; (*COMPUT*) = **disk.**

disc. *abbr* (*COMM*) = **discount.**

discard [diskârd'] *vt* (*old things*) tirar; (*fig*) descartar.

discern [disûrn'] *vt* percibir, discernir; (*understand*) comprender.

discernible [disûr'nəbəl] *a* perceptible.

discerning [disûr'ning] *a* perspicaz.

discharge *vt* [dischârj'] (*task, duty*) cumplir; (*ship etc*) descargar; (*patient*) dar de alta; (*employee*) despedir; (*soldier*) licenciar; (*defendant*) poner en libertad; (*settle: debt*) saldar ♦ *n* [dis'chârj] (*ELEC*) descarga; (*vaginal ~*) emisión *f* vaginal; (*dismissal*) despedida; (*of duty*) desempeño; (*of debt*) pago, descargo; (*of gas, chemicals*) escape *m.*

disciple [disī'pəl] *n* discípulo/a.

disciplinary [dis'əplənārē] *a:* **to take ~ action against sb** disciplinar a uno.

discipline [dis'əplin] *n* disciplina ♦ *vt* disciplinar; **to ~ o.s. to do sth** disciplinarse *or* obligarse a hacer algo.

disc jockey (DJ) [disk' jâkē] *n* pinchadiscos *m/f inv.*

disclaim [disklām'] *vt* negar.

disclaimer [disklām'ûr] *n* rectificación *f;* **to issue a ~** hacer una rectificación.

disclose [disklōz'] *vt* revelar.

disclosure [disklō'zhûr] *n* revelación *f.*

disco [dis'kō] *n abbr* = **discothèque.**

discoloration [diskulərā'shən] *n* (*US*) descoloramiento.

discolored [diskul'ûrd] *a* (*US*) descolorado.

discolouration [diskulərā'shən] *n* (*Brit*) = **discoloration.**

discoloured [diskul'ûrd] *a* (*Brit*) = **discolored.**

discomfort [diskum'fûrt] *n* incomodidad *f;* (*unease*) inquietud *f;* (*physical*) malestar *m.*

disconcert [diskənsûrt'] *vt* desconcertar.

disconnect [diskənekt'] *vt* (*gen*) separar; (*ELEC etc*) desconectar; (*supply*) cortar (el suministro) a.

disconsolate [diskân'səlit] *a* desconsolado.

discontent [diskəntent'] *n* descontento.

discontented [diskəntent'id] *a* descontento.

discontinue [diskəntin'yōō] *vt* interrumpir; (*payments*) suspender.

discord [dis'kôrd] *n* discordia; (*MUS*) disonancia.

discordant [diskôr'dənt] *a* disonante.

discothèque [dis'kōtek] *n* discoteca.

discount *n* [dis'kount] descuento ♦ *vt* [diskount'] descontar; (*report etc*) descartar; **at a ~** con descuento; **~ for cash** descuento por pago en efectivo; **to give sb a ~ on sth** hacer un descuento a uno en algo.

discount house *n* (*FINANCE*) banco de descuento; (*COMM: also:* **discount store**) ≈ tienda de descuentos.

discount rate *n* (*COMM*) tipo de descuento.

discount store *n* ≈ tienda de descuentos.

discourage [diskûr'ij] *vt* desalentar; (*oppose*) oponerse a; (*dissuade, deter*) desanimar, disuadir.

discouragement [diskûr'ijmənt] *n* (*dissuasion*) disuasión *f;* (*depression*) desánimo, desaliento; **to act as a ~ to** servir para disuadir.

discouraging [diskûr'ijing] *a* desalentador(a).

discourteous [diskûr'tēəs] *a* descortés.

discover [diskuv'ûr] *vt* descubrir.

discovery [diskuv'ûrē] *n* descubrimiento.

discredit [diskred'it] *vt* desacreditar.

discreet [diskrēt'] *a* (*tactful*) discreto; (*careful*) circunspecto, prudente.

discreetly [diskrēt'lē] *ad* discretamente.

discrepancy [diskrep'ənsē] *n* (*difference*) diferencia; (*disagreement*) discrepancia.

discretion [diskresh'ən] *n* (*tact*) discreción *f;* (*care*) prudencia, circunspección *f;* **use your own ~** haz lo que creas oportuno.

discretionary [diskresh'ənārē] *a* (*powers*) discrecional.

discriminate [diskrim'ənāt] *vi:* **to ~ between** distinguir entre; **to ~ against** discriminar contra.

discriminating [diskrim'ənāting] *a* entendido.

discrimination [diskrimənā'shən] *n* (*discernment*) perspicacia; (*bias*) discriminación *f;* **racial/sexual ~** discriminación racial/sexual.

discus [dis'kəs] *n* disco.

discuss [diskus'] *vt* (*gen*) discutir; (*a theme*) tratar.

discussion [diskush'ən] *n* discusión *f;* **under ~** en discusión.

disdain [disdān'] *n* desdén *m* ♦ *vt* desdeñar.

disease [dizēz'] *n* enfermedad *f*.
diseased [dizēzd'] *a* enfermo.
disembark [disembârk'] *vt, vi* desembarcar.
disembarkation [disembârkā'shən] *n* desembarque *m*.
disenchanted [disenchan'tid] *a*: ~ **(with)** desilusionado (con).
disenfranchise [disenfran'chīz] *vt* privar del derecho al voto; (*COMM*) privar de franquicias.
disengage [disengāj'] *vt* soltar; **to** ~ **the clutch** (*AUT*) desembragar.
disentangle [disentang'gəl] *vt* desenredar.
disfavor, (*Brit*) **disfavour** [disfā'vûr] *n* desaprobación *f*.
disfigure [disfig'yûr] *vt* desfigurar.
disgorge [disgôrj'] *vt* verter.
disgrace [disgrās'] *n* ignominia; (*downfall*) caída; (*shame*) vergüenza, escándalo ♦ *vt* deshonrar.
disgraceful [disgrās'fəl] *a* vergonzoso; (*behavior*) escandaloso.
disgruntled [disgrun'təld] *a* disgustado, descontento.
disguise [disgīz'] *n* disfraz *m* ♦ *vt* disfrazar; (*voice*) disimular; (*feelings etc*) ocultar; **in** ~ disfrazado; **to** ~ **o.s. as** disfrazarse de; **there's no disguising the fact that** ... no puede ocultarse el hecho de que....
disgust [disgust'] *n* repugnancia ♦ *vt* repugnar, dar asco a.
disgusting [disgus'ting] *a* repugnante, asqueroso.
dish [dish] *n* (*gen*) plato; **to do** *or* **wash the** ~**es** fregar los platos.
  dish out *vt* (*money, exam papers*) repartir; (*food*) servir; (*advice*) dar.
  dish up *vt* servir.
dishcloth [dish'klôth] *n* paño de cocina, bayeta.
dishearten [dis-hâr'tən] *vt* desalentar.
disheveled, (*Brit*) **dishevelled** [dishev'əld] *a* (*hair*) despeinado; (*clothes, appearance*) desarreglado.
dishonest [disân'ist] *a* (*person*) poco honrado, tramposo; (*means*) fraudulento.
dishonesty [disân'istē] *n* falta de honradez.
dishonor [disân'ûr] *n* (*US*) deshonra.
dishonorable [disân'ûrəbəl] *a* deshonroso.
dishonour [disân'ûr] *etc n* (*Brit*) = **dishonor** *etc*.
dish soap *n* (*US*) lavavajillas *m inv*.
dishtowel [dish'touəl] *n* trapo de fregar.
dishwasher [dish'wâshûr] *n* lavaplatos *m inv*; (*person*) friegaplatos *m/f inv*.
dishwashing liquid [dish'wâshing lik'wid] *n* (*US*) lavavajillas *m*.
disillusion [disilōo'zhən] *vt* desilusionar; **to become** ~**ed (with)** quedar desilusionado (con).
disillusionment [disilōo'zhənmənt] *n* desilusión *f*.
disincentive [disinsen'tiv] *n* desincentivo;

to act as a ~ **(to)** actuar de freno (a); **to be a** ~ **to** ser un freno a.
disinclined [disinklīnd'] *a*: **to be** ~ **to do sth** estar poco dispuesto a hacer algo.
disinfect [disinfekt'] *vt* desinfectar.
disinfectant [disinfek'tənt] *n* desinfectante *m*.
disinflation [disinflā'shən] *n* desinflación *f*.
disingenuous [disinjen'yōoəs] *a* poco sincero, doble.
disinherit [disinhär'it] *vt* desheredar.
disintegrate [disin'təgrāt] *vi* disgregarse, desintegrarse.
disinterested [disin'tristid] *a* desinteresado.
disjointed [disjoint'id] *a* inconexo.
disk [disk] *n* (*COMPUT*) disco, disquete *m*; **single-/double-sided** ~ disco de una cara/ dos caras.
disk drive *n* disc drive *m*.
diskette [disket'] *n* diskette *m*, disquete *m*, disco flexible.
disk operating system (DOS) *n* sistema *m* operativo de discos (DOS).
dislike [dislīk'] *n* antipatía, aversión *f* ♦ *vt* tener antipatía a; **to take a** ~ **to sb/sth** cogerle *or* agarrarle (*LAm*) antipatía a uno/algo; **I** ~ **the idea** no me gusta la idea.
dislocate [dis'lōkāt] *vt* dislocar; **he** ~**d his shoulder** se dislocó el hombro.
dislodge [dislâj'] *vt* sacar; (*enemy*) desalojar.
disloyal [disloi'əl] *a* desleal.
dismal [diz'məl] *a* (*dark*) sombrío; (*depressing*) triste; (*very bad*) fatal.
dismantle [disman'təl] *vt* desmontar, desarmar.
dismay [dismā'] *n* consternación *f* ♦ *vt* consternar; **much to my** ~ para gran consternación mía.
dismiss [dismis'] *vt* (*worker*) despedir; (*official*) destituir; (*idea, LAW*) rechazar; (*possibility*) descartar ♦ *vi* (*MIL*) romper filas.
dismissal [dismis'əl] *n* despedida; destitución *f*.
dismount [dismount'] *vi* apearse; (*rider*) desmontar.
disobedience [disəbē'dēəns] *n* desobediencia.
disobedient [disəbē'dēənt] *a* desobediente.
disobey [disəbā'] *vt* desobedecer; (*rule*) infringir.
disorder [disôr'dûr] *n* desorden *m*; (*rioting*) disturbio; (*MED*) trastorno; (*disease*) enfermedad *f*; **civil** ~ desorden *m* civil.
disorderly [disôr'dûrlē] *a* (*untidy*) desordenado; (*meeting*) alborotado; ~ **conduct** (*LAW*) conducta escandalosa.
disorganized [disôr'gənīzd] *a* desorganizado.
disorientated [disô'rēintātid] *a* desorientado.
disown [disōn'] *vt* desconocer.

disparaging [dispar'ijing] *a* despreciativo;
to be ~ about sth/sb menospreciar algo/a
uno.

disparate [dis'púrit] *a* dispar.

disparity [dispar'itē] *n* disparidad *f.*

dispassionate [dispash'ənit] *a* (*unbiased*)
imparcial; (*unemotional*) desapasionado.

dispatch [dispach'] *vt* enviar; (*kill*) despachar; (*deal with: business*) despachar ♦ *n*
(*sending*) envío; (*speed*) prontitud *f*;
(*PRESS*) informe *m*; (*MIL*) parte *m.*

dispatch department *n* departamento de
envíos.

dispatch rider *n* (*MIL*) correo.

dispel [dispel'] *vt* disipar, dispersar.

dispensary [dispen'sûrē] *n* dispensario,
farmacia.

dispensation [dispənsā'shən] *n* (*REL*) dis-
pensa.

dispense [dispens'] *vt* dispensar, repartir; (*medicine*) preparar.

dispense with *vt fus* (*make unnecessary*) prescindir de.

dispenser [dispen'sûr] *n* (*container*) distribuidor *m* automático.

dispensing chemist [dispen'sing kem'ist]
n (*Brit*) farmacia.

dispersal [dispûr'səl] *n* dispersión *f.*

disperse [dispûrs'] *vt* dispersar ♦ *vi* dispersarse.

dispirited [dispir'itid] *a* desanimado, des-
alentado.

displace [displās'] *vt* (*person*) desplazar;
(*replace*) reemplazar.

displaced person [displāst' pûr'sən] *n*
(*POL*) desplazado/a.

displacement [displās'mənt] *n* cambio de
sitio.

display [displā'] *n* (*exhibition*) exposición *f*;
(*COMPUT*) visualización *f*; (*MIL*) desfile *m*;
(*of feeling*) manifestación *f*; (*pej*) aparato,
pompa ♦ *vt* exponer; manifestar; (*ostenta-
tiously*) lucir; **on ~** (*exhibits*) expuesto,
exhibido; (*goods*) en el escaparate.

display advertising *n* publicidad *f*
gráfica.

displease [displēz'] *vt* (*offend*) ofender;
(*annoy*) fastidiar; **~d with** disgustado con.

displeasure [displezh'ûr] *n* disgusto.

disposable [dispō'zəbəl] *a* (*not reusable*)
desechable; **~ personal income** ingresos
mpl personales disponibles.

disposable diaper *n* (*US*) paño desechable.

disposal [dispō'zəl] *n* (*sale*) venta; (*of
house*) traspaso; (*by giving away*) donación
f; (*arrangement*) colocación *f*; (*of garbage*) destrucción *f*; **at one's ~** a la disposición de uno; **to put sth at sb's ~** poner
algo a disposición de uno.

disposed [dispōzd'] *a*: **~ to do** dispuesto a
hacer.

dispose of [dispōz' uv] *vt fus* (*time, money*) disponer de; (*unwanted goods*) desha-

cerse de; (*COMM: sell*) traspasar, vender;
(*throw away*) tirar.

disposition [dispəzish'ən] *n* disposición *f*;
(*temperament*) carácter *m.*

dispossess [dispəzes'] *vt*: **to ~ sb (of)** desposeer a uno (de).

disproportion [disprəpôr'shən] *n* desproporción *f.*

disproportionate [disprəpôr'shənit] *a* desproporcionado.

disprove [disprōōv'] *vt* refutar.

dispute [dispyōōt'] *n* disputa; (*verbal*) discusión *f*; (*also*: **industrial ~**) conflicto (laboral) ♦ *vt* (*argue*) disputar; (*question*)
cuestionar; **to be in** *o* **under ~** (*matter*)
estar en cuestión; (*territory*) estar en disputa.

disqualification [diskwâləfəkā'shən] *n* inha-
bilitación *f*; (*SPORT, from driving*) desca-
lificación *f.*

disqualify [diskwâl'əfī] *vt* (*SPORT*) descla-
sificar; **to ~ sb for sth/from doing sth**
incapacitar a uno para algo/hacer algo.

disquiet [diskwī'it] *n* preocupación *f*, inquietud *f.*

disquieting [diskwī'iting] *a* inquietante.

disregard [disrigárd'] *vt* desatender; (*ignore*) no hacer caso de ♦ *n* (*indifference*: *to
feelings, danger, money*): **~ (for)** indiferencia (a); **~ (of)** (*non-observance*: *of law,
rules*) violación *f* (de).

disrepair [disripär'] *n*: **to fall into ~**
(*building*) desmoronarse; (*street*) deteriorarse.

disreputable [disrep'yətəbəl] *a* (*person,
area*) de mala fama; (*behavior*) vergonzoso.

disrepute [disripyōōt'] *n* descrédito, ignominia; **to bring into ~** desacreditar.

disrespectful [disrispekt'fəl] *a* irrespetuoso.

disrupt [disrupt'] *vt* (*meeting, public
transport, conversation*) interrumpir;
(*plans*) desbaratar, alternar, trastornar.

disruption [disrup'shən] *n* trastorno; desba-
ratamiento; interrupción *f.*

disruptive [disrup'tiv] *a* (*influence*) disrupti-
vo; (*strike action*) perjudicial.

dissatisfaction [dissatisfak'shən] *n* disgusto,
descontento.

dissatisfied [dissat'isfīd] *a* insatisfecho.

dissect [disekt'] *vt* (*also fig*) disecar.

disseminate [disem'ənāt] *vt* divulgar, difundir.

dissent [disent'] *n* disensión *f.*

dissenter [disen'tûr] *n* (*REL, POL etc*) disidente *m/f.*

dissertation [disûrtā'shən] *n* (*UNIV*) tesina.

disservice [dissûr'vis] *n*: **to do sb a ~** perjudicar a alguien.

dissident [dis'idənt] *a, n* disidente *m/f.*

dissimilar [disim'ilûr] *a* distinto.

dissipate [dis'əpāt] *vt* disipar; (*waste*) desperdiciar.

dissipated [dis'əpātid] *a* disoluto.

dissipation [disəpā'shən] *n* disipación *f*; (*moral*) libertinaje *m*, vicio; (*waste*) derroche *m*.

dissociate [disō'shēāt] *vt* disociar; **to ~ o.s. from** disociarse de.

dissolute [dis'əlŏŏt] *a* disoluto.

dissolution [disəlŏŏ'shən] *n* (*of organization, marriage, POL*) disolución *f*.

dissolve [dizálv] *vt* (*gen, COMM*) disolver ♦ *vi* disolverse.

dissuade [diswād'] *vt*: **to ~ sb (from)** disuadir a uno (de).

distaff [dis'taf] *n*: **~ side** lado materno.

distance [dis'təns] *n* distancia; **in the ~** a lo lejos; **it's within walking ~** se puede ir andando.

distant [dis'tənt] *a* lejano; (*manner*) reservado, frío.

distaste [distāst'] *n* repugnancia.

distasteful [distāst'fəl] *a* repugnante, desagradable.

Dist. Atty. *abbr* (*US*) = **district attorney**.

distemper [distem'pûr] *n* (*of dogs*) moquillo.

distend [distend'] *vt* dilatar, hinchar ♦ *vi* dilatarse, hincharse.

distended [distend'id] *a* (*stomach*) hinchado.

distill, (*Brit*) **distil** [distil'] *vt* destilar.

distillery [distil'ûrē] *n* destilería.

distinct [distingkt'] *a* (*different*) distinto; (*clear*) claro; (*unmistakeable*) inequívoco; **as ~ from** a diferencia de.

distinction [distingk'shən] *n* distinción *f*; (*in exam*) sobresaliente *m*; **a writer of ~** un escritor destacado; **to draw a ~ between** hacer una distinción entre.

distinctive [distingk'tiv] *a* distintivo.

distinctly [distingkt'lē] *ad* claramente.

distinguish [disting'gwish] *vt* distinguir; **to ~ (between)** distinguir (entre).

distinguished [disting'gwisht] *a* (*eminent*) distinguido; (*career*) eminente; (*refined*) distinguido, de categoría.

distinguishing [disting'gwishing] *a* (*feature*) distintivo.

distort [distôrt'] *vt* torcer, retorcer; (*account, news*) desvirtuar, deformar.

distortion [distôr'shən] *n* deformación *f*; (*of sound*) distorsión *f*; (*of truth etc*) torcimiento; (*of facts*) falseamiento.

distr. *abbr* = **distribution; distributor**.

distract [distrakt'] *vt* distraer.

distracted [distrak'tid] *a* distraído.

distracting [distrak'ting] *a* que distrae la atención, molesto.

distraction [distrak'shən] *n* distracción *f*; (*confusion*) aturdimiento; (*amusement*) diversión *f*; **to drive sb to ~** (*distress, anxiety*) volver loco a uno.

distraught [distrôt'] *a* turbado, enloquecido.

distress [distres'] *n* (*anguish*) angustia;

(*want*) miseria; (*pain*) dolor *m*; (*danger*) peligro ♦ *vt* afligir; (*pain*) doler; **in ~** (*ship etc*) en peligro.

distressing [distres'ing] *a* angustioso; doloroso.

distress signal *n* señal *f* de socorro.

distribute [distrib'yŏŏt] *vt* (*gen*) distribuir; (*share out*) repartir.

distribution [distrəbyŏŏ'shən] *n* distribución *f*.

distribution cost *n* gastos *mpl* de distribución.

distributor [distrib'yətûr] *n* (*AUT*) distribuidor *m*; (*COMM*) distribuidora.

district [dis'trikt] *n* (*of country*) zona, región *f*; (*of town*) barrio; (*ADMIN*) comarca.

district attorney *n* (*US*) fiscal *m/f*.

district council *n* (*Brit*) municipio.

district manager *n* representante *m/f* regional.

district nurse *n* (*Brit*) enfermera que atiende a pacientes a domicilio.

distrust [distrust'] *n* desconfianza ♦ *vt* desconfiar de.

distrustful [distrust'fəl] *a* desconfiado.

disturb [distûrb'] *vt* (*person: bother, interrupt*) molestar; (*meeting*) interrumpir; (*disorganize*) desordenar; **sorry to ~ you** perdone la molestia.

disturbance [distûr'bəns] *n* (*political etc*) disturbio; (*violence*) alboroto; (*of mind*) trastorno; **to cause a ~** causar alboroto; **~ of the peace** alteración *f* del orden público.

disturbed [distûrbd'] *a* (*worried, upset*) preocupado, angustiado; **to be emotionally/ mentally ~** tener problemas emocionales/ ser un trastornado mental.

disturbing [distûrb'ing] *a* inquietante, perturbador(a).

disuse [disyŏŏs'] *n*: **to fall into ~** caer en desuso.

disused [disyŏŏzd'] *a* abandonado.

ditch [dich] *n* zanja; (*irrigation ~*) acequia ♦ *vt* (*col*) deshacerse de.

dither [dith'ûr] *vi* vacilar.

ditto [dit'ō] *ad* ídem, lo mismo.

div. *abbr* = **dividend**.

divan [divan'] *n* diván *m*.

divan bed *n* cama turca.

dive [dīv] *n* (*from board*) salto; (*underwater*) buceo; (*of submarine*) sumersión *f*; (*AVIAT*) picada ♦ *vi* saltar; bucear; sumergirse; picar.

diver [dī'vûr] *n* (*SPORT*) saltador(a) *m/f*; (*underwater*) buzo.

diverge [divûrj'] *vi* divergir.

divergent [divûr'jənt] *a* divergente.

diverse [divûrs'] *a* diversos/as, varios/as.

diversification [divûrsəfəkā'shən] *n* diversificación *f*.

diversify [divûr'səfī] *vt* diversificar.

diversion [divûr'zhən] *n* (*Brit AUT*) desviación *f*; (*distraction, MIL*) diversión *f*.

diversity [divûr'sitē] *n* diversidad *f*.

divert [divûrt'] *vt* (*train, plane, traffic*) desviar; (*amuse*) divertir.

divest [divest'] *vt*: **to ~ sb of sth** despojar a alguien de algo.

divide [divīd'] *vt* dividir; (*separate*) separar ♦ *vi* dividirse; (*road*) bifurcarse; **to ~ (between, among)** repartir *or* dividir (entre); **40 ~d by 5** 40 dividido por 5.
   divide out *vt*: **to ~ out (between, among)** (*candies, tasks etc*) repartir (entre).

divided [divīd'id] *a* (*country, couple*) dividido, separado; (*opinions*) en desacuerdo.

divided highway *n* (*US*) carretera de doble calzada.

dividend [div'idend] *n* dividendo; (*fig*) beneficio.

dividend cover *n* cobertura de dividendo.

dividers [divī'dûrz] *npl* compás *m* de puntas.

divine [divīn'] *a* divino ♦ *vt* (*future*) vaticinar; (*truth*) alumbrar; (*water, metal*) adivinar.

diving [dīv'ing] *n* (*SPORT*) salto; (*underwater*) buceo.

diving board [dīv'ing bōrd] *n* trampolín *m*.

diving suit *n* escafandra.

divinity [divin'ətē] *n* divinidad *f*; (*SCOL*) teología.

divisible [diviz'əbəl] *a* divisible.

division [divizh'ən] *n* (*also Brit SOCCER*) división *f*; (*sharing*) repartimiento; (*Brit POL*) votación *f*; **~ of labor** división *f* del trabajo.

divisive [divī'siv] *a* divisivo.

divorce [divôrs'] *n* divorcio ♦ *vt* divorciarse de.

divorced [divôrst'] *a* divorciado.

divorcee [divôrsē'] *n* divorciado/a.

divulge [divulj'] *vt* divulgar, revelar.

D.I.Y. *a, n abbr* (*Brit*) = **do-it-yourself.**

dizziness [diz'ēnis] *n* vértigo.

dizzy [diz'ē] *a* (*person*) mareado; (*height*) vertiginoso; **to feel ~** marearse; **I feel ~** estoy mareado.

DJ *n abbr* = **disc jockey.**

Djakarta [jəkâr'tə] *n* Yakarta.

DJIA *n abbr* (*US STOCK EXCHANGE*) = Dow Jones Industrial Average.

dl *abbr* (= *deciliter(s)*) dl.

DLit(t) *abbr* (= *Doctor of Literature, Doctor of Letters*) título universitario.

DLO *n abbr* (= *dead-letter office*) oficina de Correos que se encarga de las cartas que no llegan a su destino.

dm *abbr* (= *decimeter(s)*) dm.

DMus *abbr* (= *Doctor of Music*) título universitario.

DMZ *n abbr* (= *demilitarized zone*) zona desmilitarizada.

DNA *n abbr* = (*deoxyribonucleic acid*) ADN *m*.

do [dōō] *vb* (*pt* **did,** *pp* **done** [did, dun]) *vt,* *vi* (*gen*) hacer; (*speed*) ir a; (*visit: city, museum*) visitar, recorrer; (*THEATER*) representar ♦ *n* (*col: party*) fiesta, guateque *m*; (: *formal gathering*) reunión *f*, ceremonia; **he didn't laugh** no se rió; **she swims better than I ~** nada mejor que yo; **he laughed, didn't he?** se rió ¿no?; **that will ~!** ¡basta!; **to make ~ with** contentarse con; **~ you agree?** ¿está usted de acuerdo?; **I don't understand** no entiendo; **~ you speak English?** ¿habla (usted) inglés?; **you speak better than I ~** tú hablas mejor que yo; **so does he** él también; **DO come!** ¡venga, por favor!; **I DO wish I could ...** ojalá que pudiera ...; **but I DO like it!** pero, sí que *or* por supuesto que me gusta!; **what does he ~ for a living?** ¿a qué se dedica?; **what can I ~ for you?** (*in store*) ¿en qué puedo servirle?; **to ~ one's hair** (*comb*) peinarse; (*style*) arreglarse el pelo; **I'm going to ~ the washing-up** voy a fregar los platos; **we've done 200 km already** llevamos 200 km de viaje ya; **I'll ~ all I can** haré todo lo que pueda; **how ~ you like your steak done? — well done** ¿cómo te gusta el filete? — bien hecho; **will it ~?** ¿sirve?, ¿conviene?; **to ~ sb out of sth** pisar algo a uno; **to ~ well** prosperar, tener éxito; **he's ~ing well/badly at school** va bien/mal en la escuela; **it doesn't ~ to upset her** cuidado en ofenderle; **that'll ~!** (*in annoyance*) ¡basta ya!; **to ~ without sth** prescindir de algo; **what has that got to ~ with it?** ¿qué tiene que ver eso?; **what have you done with my slippers?** ¿qué has hecho con mis zapatillas?

do away with *vt fus* (*kill*) asesinar; (*suppress*) suprimir.

do up *vt* (*laces*) liar, atar; (*room*) renovar; **to ~ o.s. up** maquillarse.

do with *vt fus* (*with can, could: need*) no venirle mal; **I could ~ with some help/a drink** no me vendría mal un poco de ayuda/una bebida.

do. *abbr* = **ditto.**

DOA *abbr* = *dead on arrival.*

d.o.b. *abbr* = *date of birth.*

docile [dâs'əl] *a* dócil.

dock [dâk] *n* (*NAUT: wharf*) dársena, muelle *m*; (*LAW*) banquillo (de los acusados); **~s** *npl* muelles *mpl*, puerto *sg* ♦ *vi* (*enter ~*) atracar el muelle ♦ *vt* (*pay etc*) descontar.

dock dues *npl* derechos *mpl* de muelle.

docker [dâk'ûr] *n* trabajador *m* portuario, estibador *m*.

docket [dâk'it] *n* (*on parcel etc*) etiqueta.

dockyard [dâk'yârd] *n* astillero.

doctor [dâk'tûr] *n* médico; (*Ph.D. etc*) doctor(a) *m/f* ♦ *vt* (*fig*) arreglar, falsificar; (*drink etc*) adulterar.

doctorate [dâk'tûrit] *n* doctorado.

Doctor of Philosophy (Ph.D.) *n* Doctor

m (en Filosofía y Letras).

doctrinaire [dâktrənär'] *a* doctrinario.

doctrine [dák'trin] *n* doctrina.

document *n* [dák'yəmənt] documento ♦ *vt* [dák'yəment] documentar.

documentary [dákyəmen'tûrē] *a* documental ♦ *n* documental *m*.

documentation [dákyəməntā'shən] *n* documentación *f*.

DOD *n abbr* (*US*: = *Department of Defense*) Ministerio de Defensa.

doddering [dâd'ûring] *a*, **doddery** [dâd'ûrē] *a* chocho.

Dodecanese (Islands) [dōdekənəs' (i'ləndz)] *n(pl)* Dodecaneso *sg*.

dodge [dâj] *n* (*of body*) regate *m*; (*fig*) truco ♦ *vt* (*gen*) evadir; (*blow*) esquivar ♦ *vi* esquivarse, escabullirse; (*SPORT*) hacer una finta; **to ~ out of the way** echarse a un lado; **to ~ through the traffic** regatear por el tráfico.

dodgems [dâj'əmz] *npl* coches *mpl* de choque.

DOE *n abbr* (*US*) = *Department of Energy*; (*Brit*) = *Department of the Environment*.

doe [dō] *n* (*deer*) cierva, gama; (*rabbit*) coneja.

does [duz] *vb see* **do**.

doesn't [duz'nt] = **does not**.

dog [dôg] *n* perro ♦ *vt* seguir (de cerca); (*fig: memory etc*) perseguir; **to go to the ~s** (*person*) echarse a perder; (*nation etc*) ir a la ruina.

dog biscuit *n* galleta de perro.

dog collar *n* collar *m* de perro; (*fig*) cuello de cura.

dog-eared [dôg'ērd] *a* sobado.

dogfish [dôg'fish] *n* cazón *m*, perro marino.

dog food *n* comida para perros.

dogged [dôg'id] *a* tenaz, obstinado.

dogma [dôg'mə] *n* dogma *m*.

dogmatic [dôgmat'ik] *a* dogmático.

do-gooder [dōōgōōd'ûr] *n* (*col pej*): **to be a ~** ser una persona bien intencionada *or* un filantropista.

dogsbody [dôgz'bádē] *n* (*Brit*) burro de carga.

dog tag *n* (*US*) chapa de identidad.

doing [dōō'ing] *n*: **this is your ~** esto es obra tuya.

doings [dōō'ingz] *npl* (*events*) sucesos *mpl*; (*acts*) hechos *mpl*.

do-it-yourself [dōō'ityōōrself'] *n* bricolaje *m*.

do-it-yourselfer [dōō'ityōōrself'ûr] *n* bricolajista *m/f*.

doldrums [dōl'drəmz] *npl*: **to be in the ~** (*person*) estar abatido; (*business*) estar estancado.

dole [dōl] *n* (*Brit: payment*) subsidio de paro; **on the ~** parado.
  dole out *vt* repartir.

doleful [dōl'fəl] *a* triste, lúgubre.

doll [dâl] *n* muñeca.
  doll up *vt*: **to ~ o.s. up** ataviarse.

dollar [dâl'ûr] *n* dólar *m*.

dollar area *n* zona del dólar.

dolphin [dâl'fin] *n* delfín *m*.

domain [dōmān'] *n* (*fig*) campo, competencia; (*land*) dominios *mpl*.

dome [dōm] *n* (*ARCH*) cúpula; (*shape*) bóveda.

domestic [dəmes'tik] *a* (*animal, duty*) doméstico; (*flight, news, policy*) nacional.

domesticated [dəmes'tikātid] *a* domesticado; (*person: home-loving*) casero, hogareño.

domesticity [dōmestis'itē] *n* vida casera.

domestic servant *n* sirviente/a *m/f*.

domicile [dâm'isil] *n* domicilio.

dominant [dâm'ənənt] *a* dominante.

dominate [dâm'ənāt] *vt* dominar.

domination [dâmənā'shən] *n* dominación *f*.

domineering [dâmənēr'ing] *a* dominante.

Dominican Republic [dəmin'əkən ripub'lik] *n* República Dominicana.

dominion [dəmin'yən] *n* dominio.

domino, *pl* **~es** [dâm'ənō] *n* ficha de dominó.

dominoes [dâm'ənōz] *n* (*game*) dominó.

don [dân] *n* (*Brit*) catedrático/a.

donate [dō'nāt] *vt* donar.

donation [dōnā'shən] *n* donativo.

done [dun] *pp of* **do**.

donkey [dâng'kē] *n* burro.

donkey-work [dâng'kēwûrk] *n* (*Brit col*) trabajo pesado.

donor [dō'nûr] *n* donante *m/f*.

don't [dōnt] = **do not**.

donut [dō'nut] *n* (*US*) buñuelo.

doodle [dōōd'əl] *n* garabato ♦ *vi* pintar dibujitos *or* garabatos.

doom [dōōm] *n* (*fate*) suerte *f*; (*death*) muerte *f* ♦ *vt*: **to be ~ed to failure** ser condenado al fracaso.

doomsday [dōōmz'dā] *n* día *m* del juicio final.

door [dôr] *n* puerta; (*of car*) portezuela; (*entry*) entrada; **from ~ to ~** de puerta en puerta.

doorbell [dôr'bel] *n* timbre *m*.

door handle *n* tirador *m*; (*of car*) manija.

door knocker *n* aldaba.

doorman [dôr'man] *n* (*in hotel*) portero.

doormat [dôr'mat] *n* felpudo, estera.

doorstep [dôr'step] *n* peldaño.

door-to-door [dôr'tədôr'] *a*: **~ selling** venta a domicilio.

doorway [dôr'wā] *n* entrada, puerta; **in the ~** en la puerta.

dope [dōp] *n* (*col: person*) imbécil *m/f*; (: *information*) información *f*, informes *mpl*; (: *drugs*) drogas ♦ *vt* (*horse etc*) drogar.

dopey [dō'pē] *a* atontado.

dormant [dôr'mənt] *a* inactivo; (*latent*) latente.

dormer [dôr'mûr] *n* (*also*: ~ **window**) buhardilla.

dormitory [dôr'mitôrē] *n* (*US: for students*) residencia, colegio mayor; (*Brit*) dormitorio.

dormouse, *pl* **dormice** [dôr'mous, -mīs] *n* lirón *m*.

Dors *abbr* (*Brit*) = Dorset.

DOS [dōs] *n abbr* = **disk operating system.**

dosage [dō'sij] *n* (*on medicine bottle*) dosis *f inv*, dosificación *f*.

dose [dōs] *n* (*of medicine*) dosis *f inv*; **a** ~ **of flu** un ataque de gripe ♦ *vt*: **to** ~ **o.s. with** tomar una buena dosis de.

doss house [dâs' hous] *n* (*Brit*) pensión *f* de mala muerte.

dossier [dâs'ēā] *n*: ~ **(on)** expediente *m* (sobre).

DOT *n abbr* (*US*: = *Department of Transportation*) ≈ *Ministerio de Transportes, Turismo y Comunicaciones* (*Sp*).

dot [dât] *n* punto; ~**ted with** salpicado de; **on the** ~ en punto.

dot command *n* (*COMPUT*) instrucción *f* (precedida) de punto.

dote [dōt]: **to** ~ **on** *vt fus* adorar, idolatrar.

dot-matrix printer [dâtmāt'riks prin'tûr] *n* impresora matricial *or* de matriz.

dotted line [dât'id līn'] *n* línea de puntos; **to sign on the** ~ firmar.

dotty [dât'ē] *a* (*col*) disparatado, chiflado.

double [dub'əl] *a* doble ♦ *ad* (*twice*): **to cost** ~ costar el doble ♦ *n* (*gen*) doble *m* ♦ *vt* doblar; (*efforts*) redoblar ♦ *vi* doblarse; (*have two uses etc*); **to** ~ **as** hacer las veces de; **spelled with a** ~ **"s"** escrito con dos "eses"; **on the** ~ corriendo.

 double back *vi* (*person*) volver sobre sus pasos.

 double up *vi* (*bend over*) doblarse; (*share bedroom*) compartir.

double bass *n* contrabajo.

double bed *n* cama matrimonial.

double bend *n* (*Brit*) doble curva.

double-breasted [dub'əlbres'tid] *a* cruzado.

double-check [dub'əlchek'] *vt, vi* revisar de nuevo.

double cream *n* (*Brit*) nata enriquecida.

doublecross [dub'əlkrôs'] *vt* (*trick*) engañar; (*betray*) traicionar.

doubledecker [dubəldek'ûr] *n* autobús *m* de dos pisos.

double glazing [dub'əl glāz'ing] *n* (*Brit*) doble acristalamiento.

double indemnity [dub'əl indem'nitē] *n* doble indemnización *f*.

double-page [dub'əlpāj] *a*: ~ **spread** doble página.

double room *n* cuarto para dos.

doubles [dub'əlz] *n* (*TENNIS*) juego de dobles.

double time *n* tarifa doble.

doubly [dub'lē] *ad* doblemente.

doubt [dout] *n* duda ♦ *vt* dudar; (*suspect*) dudar de; **to** ~ **that** dudar que; **there is no** ~ **that** no cabe duda de que; **without (a)** ~ sin duda (alguna); **beyond** ~ fuera de duda; **I** ~ **it very much** lo dudo mucho.

doubtful [dout'fəl] *a* dudoso; (*person*) sospechoso; **to be** ~ **about sth** tener dudas sobre algo; **I'm a bit** ~ no estoy convencido.

doubtless [dout'lis] *ad* sin duda.

dough [dō] *n* masa, pasta; (*col: money*) pasta.

doughnut [dō'nut] *n* (*Brit*) buñuelo.

douse [dous] *vt* (*drench: with water*) mojar; (*extinguish: flames*) apagar.

dove [duv] *n* paloma.

dovetail [duv'tāl] *vi* (*fig*) encajar.

dowager [dou'əjûr] *n*: ~ **duchess** duquesa viuda.

dowdy [dou'dē] *a* desaliñado; (*inelegant*) poco elegante.

Dow Jones Average [dou'jōnz' av'ûrij], **Dow Jones Index** [dou'jōnz' in'deks] *n* (*US*) índice *m* Dow-Jones.

down [doun] *n* (*fluff*) pelusa; (*feathers*) plumón *m*, flojel *m*; (*hill*) loma ♦ *ad* (~*wards*) abajo, hacia abajo; (*on the ground*) por/en tierra ♦ *prep* abajo ♦ *vt* (*col: drink*) beberse, tragar(se); ~ **with X!** ¡abajo X!; ~ **there** allí abajo; ~ **here** aquí abajo; **I'll be** ~ **in a minute** ahora bajo; **England is two goals** ~ Inglaterra está perdiendo por dos tantos; **I've been** ~ **with flu** he estado con gripe; **the price of meat is** ~ ha bajado el precio de la carne; **I've got it** ~ **in my diary** lo he apuntado en mi agenda; **to pay $2** ~ dejar $2 de depósito; **he went** ~ **the hill** fue cuesta abajo; ~ **under** (*in Australia etc*) en Australia/Nueva Zelanda; **to** ~ **tools** (*Brit: fig*) declararse en huelga.

down-and-out [doun'ənout] *n* (*tramp*) vagabundo/a.

down-at-heel(s) [dounat·hēl(z)'] *a* venido a menos; (*appearance*) desaliñado.

downbeat [doun'bēt] *n* (*MUS*) compás *m* ♦ *a* (*gloomy*) pesimista.

downcast [doun'kast] *a* abatido.

downer [dou'nûr] *n* (*col: drug*) tranquilizante; **to be on a** ~ estar pasando un mal bache.

downfall [doun'fôl] *n* caída, ruina.

downgrade [doun'grād] *vt* (*job*) degradar; (*hotel*) bajar de categoría a.

downhearted [doun'hâr'tid] *a* desanimado.

downhill [doun'hil'] *ad*: **to go** ~ ir cuesta abajo; (*business*) estar en declive.

download [doun'lōd] *vt* (*COMPUT*) transferir, telecargar.

down-market [dounmâr'kit] *a* (*Brit*) para la sección popular del mercado.

down payment *n* entrada, pago al contado.

downplay |doun'plā| *vt* (*US*) quitar importancia a.

downpour |doun'pôr| *n* aguacero.

downright |doun'rīt| *a* (*nonsense, lie*) manifiesto; (*refusal*) terminante.

Down's syndrome |dounz' sin'drōm| *n* (*MED*) síndrome *m* de Down.

downstairs |doun'stärz'| *ad* (*below*) (en la casa de) abajo; (*motion*) escaleras abajo; **to come** (*or* go) ~ bajar la escalera.

downstream |doun'strēm'| *ad* aguas *or* río abajo.

downtime |doun'tīm| *n* (*COMM*) tiempo inactivo.

down-to-earth |dountōōúrth'| *a* práctico.

downtown |doun'toun'| *ad* en el centro de la ciudad.

downtrodden |doun'trádən| *a* oprimido.

downward |doun'wûrd| *ad* hacia abajo ♦ *a*: **a** ~ **trend** una tendencia descendente.

downwards |doun'wûrdz| *ad* hacia abajo; **face** ~ (*person*) boca abajo; (*object*) cara abajo.

dowry |dou'rē| *n* dote *f*.

doz. *abbr* = **dozen**.

doze |dōz| *vi* dormitar.

doze off *vi* quedarse medio dormido.

dozen |duz'ən| *n* docena; **a** ~ **books** una docena de libros; ~**s of** cantidad de; ~**s of times** cantidad de veces; **80 cents a** ~ 80 céntimos la docena.

DPh., D. Phil. *n abbr* (= *Doctor of Philosophy*) título universitario.

DPP *n abbr* (*Brit*) = **Director of Public Prosecutions.**

DPT *n abbr* (= *diphtheria, pertussis, tetanus*) vacuna trivalente.

DPW *n abbr* (*US*: = *Department of Public Works*) ≈ *Ministerio de Obras Públicas y Urbanismo* (*Sp*).

Dr, Dr. *abbr* (= *doctor*) Dr.

Dr. *abbr* (*in street names*) = **Drive**.

dr *abbr* (*COMM*) = **debtor**.

drab |drab| *a* gris, monótono.

draft |draft| *n* (*first copy: of document, report*) borrador *m*; (*COMM*) giro; (*US: call-up*) quinta; (: *of air*) corriente *f* de aire; (: *drink*) trago; (: *NAUT*) calado ♦ *vt* (*write roughly*) hacer un borrador de; **on** ~ (*US: beer*) de barril.

draftee |draftē'| *n* (*US MIL*) recluta *m/f*.

draftsman |drafts'mən| *n* (*US*) proyectista *m*, delineante *m*.

draftsmanship |drafts'mənship| *n* (*US: drawing*) dibujo lineal; (: *skill*) habilidad *f* para el dibujo.

drag |drag| *vt* arrastrar; (*river*) dragar, rastrear ♦ *vi* arrastrarse por el suelo ♦ *n* (*AVIAT: resistance*) resistencia aerodinámica; (*col*) lata; (*women's clothing*): **in** ~ vestido de travesti.

drag away *vt*: **to** ~ **away (from)** quitar arrastrando.

drag on *vi* ser interminable.

dragnet |drag'net| *n* (*NAUT*) rastra; (*fig*) emboscada.

dragon |drag'ən| *n* dragón *m*.

dragonfly |drag'ənflī| *n* libélula.

dragoon |drəgōōn'| *n* (*cavalryman*) dragón *m* ♦ *vt*: **to** ~ **sb into doing sth** forzar a uno a hacer algo.

drain |drān| *n* desaguadero; (*in street*) sumidero; (~ *cover*) rejilla del sumidero ♦ *vt* (*land, marshes*) desaguar; (*MED*) drenar; (*reservoir*) desecar; (*fig*) agotar ♦ *vi* escurrirse; **to be a** ~ **on** agotar; **to feel** ~**ed (of energy)** (*fig*) sentirse agotado.

drainage |drā'nij| *n* (*act*) desagüe *m*; (*MED, AGR*) drenaje *m*; (*sewage*) alcantarillado.

drainboard |drān'bôrd| *n* (*US*) escurridera, escurridor *m*.

draining board |drā'ning bōrd| *n* (*Brit*) = **drainboard.**

drainpipe |drān'pīp| *n* tubo de desagüe.

drake |drāk| *n* pato (macho).

dram |dram| *n* (*drink*) traguito, copita.

drama |drâm'ə| *n* (*art*) teatro; (*play*) drama *m*.

dramatic |drəmat'ik| *a* dramático.

dramatist |dram'ətist| *n* dramaturgo/a.

dramatize |dram'ətīz| *vt* (*events etc*) dramatizar; (*adapt: novel: for TV, cinema*) adaptar.

drank |drangk| *pt of* **drink**.

drape |drāp| *vt* cubrir.

draper |drā'pûr| *n* (*Brit*) pañero.

drapes |drāps| *npl* (*US*) cortinas *fpl*.

drastic |dras'tik| *a* (*measure, reduction*) severo; (*change*) radical.

draught |draft| *n* (*Brit: of air*) corriente *f* de aire; (: *drink*) trago; (: *NAUT*) calado; **on** ~ (*Brit: beer*) de barril.

draughtboard |draft'bôrd| *n* (*Brit*) tablero de damas.

draughts |drafts| *n* (*Brit*) juego de damas.

draughtsman |drafts'mən| *etc* (*Brit*) = **draftsman** *etc*.

draw |drô| *vb* (*pt* **drew**, *pp* **drawn** |drōō, drôn|) *vt* (*pull*) tirar; (*take out*) sacar; (*attract*) atraer; (*picture*) dibujar; (*money*) retirar; (*formulate: conclusion*): **to** ~ **(from)** sacar (de); (*comparison, distinction*): **to** ~ **(between)** hacer (entre) ♦ *vi* (*SPORT*) empatar ♦ *n* (*SPORT*) empate *m*; (*lottery*) sorteo; (*attraction*) atracción *f*; **to** ~ **near** *vi* acercarse.

draw back *vi*: **to** ~ **back (from)** echarse atrás (de).

draw in *vi* (*Brit: car*) aparcar; (: *train*) entrar en la estación.

draw on *vt* (*resources*) utilizar, servirse de; (*imagination, person*) recurrir a.

draw out *vi* (*lengthen*) alargarse.

draw up *vi* (*stop*) pararse ♦ *vt* (*document*) redactar; (*plans*) trazar.

drawback [drô'bak] n inconveniente m, desventaja.

drawbridge [drô'brij] n puente m levadizo.

drawee [drôē'] n girado.

drawer [drôr] n cajón m; [drô'ûr] (of check) librador(a) m/f.

drawing [drô'ing] n dibujo.

drawing board n tablero (de dibujante).

drawing pin n (Brit) chinche m.

drawing room n salón m.

drawl [drôl] n habla lenta y cansina.

drawn [drôn] pp of **draw ♦** a (haggard: with tiredness) ojeroso; (: with pain) maciento.

drawstring [drô'string] n apretadera.

dread [dred] n pavor m, terror m **♦** vt temer, tener miedo or pavor a.

dreadful [dred'fəl] a espantoso; **I feel ~!** (ill) ¡me siento fatal or malísimo!; (ashamed) ¡qué vergüenza!

dream [drēm] n sueño **♦** vt, vi (pt, pp **dreamed** or **dreamt** [dremt]) soñar; **to have a ~ about sb/sth** soñar con uno/algo; **sweet ~s!** ¡que sueñes con los ángeles!

dream up vt (reason, excuse) inventar; (plan, idea) idear.

dreamer [drē'mûr] n soñador(a) m/f.

dream world n mundo imaginario.

dreamy [drē'mē] a (person) soñador(a), distraído; (music) de sueño.

dreary [drēr'ē] a monótono, aburrido.

dredge [drej] vt dragar.

dredge up vt sacar con draga; (fig: unpleasant facts) pescar, sacar a luz.

dredger [drej'ûr] n (ship, machine) draga; (Brit CULIN) espolvoreador m.

dregs [dregz] npl heces fpl.

drench [drench] vt empapar; **~ed to the skin** calado hasta los huesos.

dress [dres] n vestido; (clothing) ropa **♦** vt vestir; (wound) vendar; (CULIN) aliñar; (store window) decorar, arreglar **♦** vi vestirse; **to ~ o.s., get ~ed** vestirse; **she ~es very well** se viste muy bien.

dress up vi vestirse de etiqueta; (in fancy dress) disfrazarse.

dress circle n (Brit) principal m.

dress designer n modisto/a.

dresser [dres'ûr] n (furniture) aparador m; (: US) cómoda con espejo; (THEATER) camarero/a.

dressing [dres'ing] n (MED) vendaje m; (CULIN) aliño.

dressing gown n (Brit) bata.

dressing room n (THEATER) camarín m; (SPORT) vestidor m.

dressing table n tocador m.

dressmaker [dres'mākûr] n modista, costurera.

dressmaking [dres'māking] n costura.

dress rehearsal n ensayo general.

dress shirt n camisa de frac.

dressy [dres'ē] a (col) elegante.

drew [drōō] pt of **draw**.

dribble [drib'əl] vi gotear, caer gota a gota; (baby) babear **♦** vt (ball) driblar, regatear.

dried [drīd] a (gen) seco; (fruit) paso; (milk) en polvo.

drier [drī'ûr] n = **dryer**.

drift [drift] n (of current etc) velocidad f; (of sand) montón m; (of snow) ventisquero; (meaning) significado **♦** vi (boat) ir a la deriva; (sand, snow) amontonarse; **to catch sb's ~** seguirle la corriente a uno; **to let things ~** dejar las cosas como están; **to ~ apart** (friends) seguir su camino; (lovers) disgustarse, romper.

drifter [drif'tûr] n vagabundo/a.

driftwood [drift'wŏŏd] n madera de deriva.

drill [dril] n taladro; (bit) broca; (of dentist) fresa; (for mining etc) perforadora, barrena; (MIL) instrucción f **♦** vt perforar, taladrar; (soldiers) ejercitar; (pupils: in grammar) dar práctica en gramática a **♦** vi (for oil) perforar.

drilling [dril'ing] n (for oil) perforación f.

drilling rig n (on land) torre f de perforación; (at sea) plataforma de perforación.

drily [drī'lē] ad secamente.

drink [dringk] n bebida **♦** vt, vi (pt **drank**, pp **drunk**) beber; **to have a ~** tomar algo; tomar una copa or un trago; **a ~ of water** un trago de agua; **to invite sb for ~s** invitar a uno a tomar unas copas; **there's food and ~ in the kitchen** hay de comer y de beber en la cocina; **would you like something to ~?** ¿quieres beber or tomar algo?

drink in vt (subj: person: fresh air) respirar; (story, sight) beberse.

drinkable [dring'kəbəl] a (not poisonous) potable; (palatable) aguantable.

drinker [dring'kûr] n bebedor(a) m/f.

drinking [dring'king] n (drunkenness) beber m.

drinking fountain n fuente f.

drinking water n agua potable.

drip [drip] n (act) goteo; (one ~) gota; (Brit: MED) gota a gota m; (sound: of water etc) goteo; (col: spineless person) soso/a **♦** vi gotear, caer gota a gota.

drip-dry [drip'drī] a (shirt) de lava y pon.

dripping [drip'ing] n (animal fat) pringue m **♦** a: **~ wet** calado.

drive [drīv] n paseo (en coche); (journey) viaje m (en coche); (also: **~way**) entrada; (street) calle; (energy) energía, vigor m; (PSYCH) impulso; (SPORT) ataque m; (COMPUT: also: **disk ~**) disc drive m **♦** vb (pt **drove**, pp **driven** [drōv, driv'ən]) vt (car) conducir, manejar (LAm); (nail) clavar; (push) empujar; (TECH: motor) impulsar **♦** vi (AUT: at controls) conducir; (: travel) pasearse en coche; **to go for a ~** dar una vuelta en coche; **it's 3 hours' ~ from New York** es un viaje de 3 horas desde Nueva York; **left-/right-hand ~**

conducción *f* a la izquierda/derecha; **front-/rear-wheel** ~ tracción *f* delantera/trasera; **sales** ~ promoción *f* de ventas; **to** ~ **sb mad** volverle loco a uno; **to** ~ **sb to (do) sth** empujar a uno a (hacer) algo; **he** ~**s a taxi** es taxista; **he** ~**s a Mercedes** tiene un Mercedes; **can you** ~? ¿sabes conducir *or* (*LAm*) manejar?; **to** ~ **at 50 km an hour** ir a 50km por hora.

drive at *vt fus* (*fig: intend, mean*) querer decir, insinuar.

drive on *vi* no parar, seguir adelante ♦ *vt* (*incite, encourage*) empujar.

drive-in [drīv'in] *a* (*esp US*): ~ **cinema** autocinema *m*.

drivel [driv'əl] *n* (*col*) tonterías *fpl*.

driven [driv'ən] *pp of* **drive**.

driver [drī'vûr] *n* conductor(a) *m/f*; (*of taxi, bus*) chofer *m*.

driver's license *n* (*US*) carnet *m or* permiso de conducir.

driveway [drīv'wā] *n* entrada.

driving [drī'ving] *n* conducir *m*, manejar *m* (*LAm*) ♦ *a* (*force*) impulsor(a).

driving instructor *n* instructor *m/f* de conducción.

driving lesson *n* clase *f* de conducción.

driving licence *n* (*Brit*) carnet *m or* permiso de conducir.

driving school *n* autoescuela.

driving test *n* examen *m* de conducción.

drizzle [driz'əl] *n* llovizna ♦ *vi* lloviznar.

droll [drōl] *a* gracioso.

dromedary [drâm'idārē] *n* dromedario.

drone [drōn] *vi* (*bee, aircraft, engine*) zumbar; (*also:* ~ **on**) murmurar sin interrupción ♦ *n* zumbido; (*male bee*) zángano.

drool [drōōl] *vi* babear; **to** ~ **over sb/sth** caérsele la baba por uno/algo.

droop [drōōp] *vi* (*fig*) decaer, desanimarse.

drop [drâp] *n* (*of water*) gota; (*fall: in price*) bajada; (*: in salary*) disminución *f* ♦ *vt* (*allow to fall*) dejar caer; (*voice, eyes, price*) bajar; (*set down from car*) dejar ♦ *vi* (*price, temperature*) bajar; (*wind*) calmarse, amainar; (*numbers, attendance*) disminuir; ~**s** *npl* (*MED*) gotas *fpl*; **cough** ~**s** pastillas *fpl* para la tos; **a** ~ **of 10%** una bajada del 10 por ciento; **to** ~ **anchor** echar el ancla; **to** ~ **sb a line** mandar unas líneas a uno.

drop in *vi* (*col: visit*): **to** ~ **in (on)** pasar por casa (de).

drop off *vi* (*sleep*) dormirse ♦ *vt* (*passenger*) bajar, dejar.

drop out *vi* (*withdraw*) retirarse.

droplet [drâp'lit] *n* gotita.

dropout [drâp'out] *n* (*from society*) marginado/a; (*from university*) estudiante *m/f* que ha abandonado el curso.

dropper [drâp'ûr] *n* (*MED*) cuentagotas *m inv*.

droppings [drâp'ingz] *npl* excremento *sg*.

dross [drôs] *n* (*coal, fig*) escoria.

drought [drout] *n* sequía.

drove [drōv] *pt of* **drive**.

drown [droun] *vt* (*also:* ~ **out:** *sound*) ahogar ♦ *vi* ahogarse.

drowse [drouz] *vi* estar medio dormido.

drowsy [drou'zē] *a* soñoliento; **to be** ~ tener sueño.

drudge [druj] *n* esclavo del trabajo.

drudgery [druj'ûrē] *n* trabajo pesado *or* monótono.

drug [drug] *n* (*MED*) medicamento, droga; (*narcotic*) droga ♦ *vt* drogar; **to be on** ~**s** drogarse; **he's on** ~**s** se droga.

drug addict *n* drogadicto/a.

druggist [drug'ist] *n* (*US*) farmacéutico/a.

drug peddler *n* vendedor(a) *m/f* de narcóticos.

drugstore [drug'stôr] *n* farmacia.

drug trafficker *n* narcotraficante *m/f*.

drum [drum] *n* tambor *m*; (*large*) bombo; (*for oil, gas*) bidón *m* ♦ *vi* tocar el tambor; (*with fingers*) tamborilear ♦ *vt*: **to** ~ **one's fingers on the table** tamborilear con los dedos sobre la mesa; ~**s** *npl* batería *sg*.

drum up *vt* (*enthusiasm, support*) movilizar, fomentar.

drummer [drum'ûr] *n* tambor *m*.

drumstick [drum'stik] *n* (*MUS*) palillo; (*chicken leg*) muslo (de pollo).

drunk [drungk] *pp of* **drink** ♦ *a* borracho ♦ *n* (*also:* ~**ard**) borracho/a; **to get** ~ emborracharse.

drunken [drung'kən] *a* borracho.

drunkenness [drung'kənnis] *n* embriaguez *f*.

dry [drī] *a* seco; (*day*) sin lluvia; (*climate*) árido, seco; (*humor*) agudo; (*uninteresting: lecture*) aburrido, pesado ♦ *vt* secar; (*tears*) enjugarse ♦ *vi* secarse; **on** ~ **land** en tierra firme; **to** ~ **one's hands/hair/eyes** secarse las manos/el pelo/las lágrimas.

dry up *vi* (*supply, imagination etc*) agotarse; (*in speech*) atascarse.

dry-clean [drī'klēn'] *vt* limpiar *or* lavar en seco; "~ **only**" (*on label*) "limpieza *or* lavado en seco (sólo)".

dry-cleaner's [drī'klē'nûrz] *n* tintorería.

dry-cleaning [drī'klē'ning] *n* lavado en seco.

dry dock *n* (*NAUT*) dique *m* seco.

dryer [drī'ûr] *n* (*for hair*) secador *m*; (*for clothes*) secadora.

dry goods *npl* (*COMM*) mercería *sg*.

dry goods store *n* (*US*) mercería.

dry ice *n* nieve *f* carbónica.

dryly [drī'lē] *ad* secamente.

dryness [drī'nis] *n* sequedad *f*.

dry rot *n* putrefacción *f* seca.

dry run *n* (*fig*) ensayo.

dry ski slope *n* pista artificial de esquí.

DSc *n abbr* (= *Doctor of Science*) título uni-

versitario.

DSS *n abbr* (*Brit*) = *Department of Social Security.*

DST *n abbr* (*US*: = *Daylight Saving Time*) *hora de verano.*

DT *n abbr* (*COMPUT*) = **data transmission.**

DTI *n abbr* (*Brit*) = *Department of Trade and Industry.*

DT's *n abbr* (*col*: = *delirium tremens*) delirium *m* tremens.

dual [dōō'əl] *a* doble.

dual carriageway *n* (*Brit*) carretera de doble calzada.

dual-control [dōō'əlkəntrōl'] *a* de doble mando.

dual nationality *n* doble nacionalidad *f.*

dual-purpose [dōō'əlpûr'pəs] *a* de doble uso.

dubbed [dubd] *a* (*CINEMA*) doblado.

dubious [dōō'bēəs] *a* indeciso; (*reputation, company*) dudoso; (*character*) sospechoso; **I'm very ~ about it** tengo mis grandes dudas sobre ello.

Dublin [dub'lin] *n* Dublín.

Dubliner [dub'linûr] *n* dublinés/esa *m/f.*

duchess [duch'is] *n* duquesa.

duck [duk] *n* pato ♦ *vi* agacharse ♦ *vt* (*plunge in water*) zambullir.

duckling [duk'ling] *n* patito.

duct [dukt] *n* conducto, canal *m.*

dud [dud] *n* (*shell*) obús *m* que no estalla; (*object, tool*): **it's a ~** es una filfa ♦ *a*: **~ cheque** (*Brit*) cheque *m* sin fondos.

dude [dōōd] *n* (*US*) tipo, tío.

due [dōō] *a* (*proper*) debido; (*fitting*) conveniente, oportuno ♦ *ad*: **~ north** derecho al norte; **~s** *npl* (*for club, union*) cuota *sg*; (*in harbor*) derechos *mpl*; **in ~ course** a su debido tiempo; **~ to** debido a; **to be ~ to** deberse a; **the train is ~ to arrive at 8.00** el tren debe llegar a las ocho; **the rent's ~ on the 30th** hay que pagar el alquiler el día 30; **I am ~ 6 days' leave** se me debe 6 días de vacaciones; **she is ~ back tomorrow** ella debe volver mañana.

due date *n* fecha de vencimiento.

duel [dōō'əl] *n* duelo.

duet [dōōet'] *n* dúo.

duff [duf] *a* (*Brit*) sin valor.

duffel bag [duf'əl bag] *n* especie de talega que se cuelga al hombro.

duffel coat [duf'əl kōt] *n* trenca.

dug [dug] *pt, pp of* **dig.**

duke [dōōk] *n* duque *m.*

dull [dul] *a* (*light*) apagado; (*stupid*) torpe; (*boring*) pesado; (*sound, pain*) sordo; (*weather, day*) gris ♦ *vt* (*pain, grief*) aliviar; (*mind, senses*) entorpecer.

duly [dōō'lē] *ad* debidamente; (*on time*) a su debido tiempo.

dumb [dum] *a* mudo; (*stupid*) estúpido; **to be struck ~** (*fig*) quedar boquiabierto.

dumbbell [dum'bel] *n* (*SPORT*) pesa; (*fool*) bobo.

dumbfounded [dumfound'id] *a* pasmado.

dummy [dum'ē] *n* (*tailor's model*) maniquí *m*; (*Brit: for baby*) chupete *m* ♦ *a* falso, postizo; **~ run** ensayo.

dump [dump] *n* (*heap*) montón *m* de basura; (*place*) basurero, vaciadero; (*col*) casucha; (*MIL*) depósito; (*COMPUT*) copia vaciada ♦ *vt* (*put down*) dejar; (*get rid of*) deshacerse de; (*COMPUT*) vaciar; (*COMM: goods*) inundar el mercado de; **to be (down) in the ~s** (*col*) tener murria, estar deprimido.

dumping [dum'ping] *n* (*ECON*) dumping *m*; (*of garbage*): **"no ~"** "prohibido verter basura".

dumpling [dump'ling] *n* bola de masa hervida.

dumpy [dump'ē] *a* regordete/a.

dunce [duns] *n* zopenco.

dune [dōōn] *n* duna.

dung [dung] *n* estiércol *m.*

dungarees [dunggərēz'] *npl* mono *sg.*

dungeon [dun'jən] *n* calabozo.

dunk [dungk] *vt* mojar.

duo [dōō'ō] *n* (*gen, MUS*) dúo.

duodenal [dōōədē'nəl] *a* (*ulcer*) de duodeno.

duodenum [dōōədē'nəm] *n* duodeno.

dupe [dōōp] *n* (*victim*) víctima ♦ *vt* engañar.

duplex [dōōp'leks] *n* (*US: also*: **~ apartment**) dúplex *m.*

duplicate [dōō'plikit] *n* duplicado; (*copy of letter etc*) copia ♦ *a* (*copy*) duplicado ♦ *vt* [dōō'plikāt] duplicar; (*on machine*) multicopiar; **in ~** por duplicado.

duplicate key *n* duplicado de una llave.

duplicating machine [dōō'plikāting məshēn'], **duplicator** [doop'likātûr] *n* multicopista *m.*

duplicity [dōōplis'ətē] *n* doblez *f*, duplicidad *f.*

Dur *abbr* (*Brit*) = *Durham.*

durability [dōōrəbil'ətē] *n* durabilidad *f.*

durable [dōōr'əbəl] *a* duradero; **~ goods** (*US*) biens *mpl* de consumo duraderos.

duration [dōōrā'shən] *n* duración *f.*

duress [dōōres'] *n*: **under ~** por compulsión.

Durex [dōō'reks] ® *n* (*Brit*) preservativo.

during [dōōr'ing] *prep* durante.

dusk [dusk] *n* crepúsculo, anochecer *m.*

dusky [dus'kē] *a* oscuro; (*complexion*) moreno.

dust [dust] *n* polvo ♦ *vt* (*furniture*) desempolvar; (*cake etc*): **to ~ with** espolvorear de.

dust off *vt* (*also fig*) desempolvar, quitar el polvo de.

dustbin [dust'bin] *n* (*Brit*) cubo de la basura, balde *m* (*LAm*).

dustbin liner *n* bolsa de basura.

duster [dus'tûr] *n* paño, trapo; (*feather* ~) plumero.

dust jacket *n* sobrecubierta.

dustman [dust'man] *n* (*Brit*) basurero.

dustpan [dust'pan] *n* cogedor *m*.

dust storm *n* vendaval *m* de polvo.

dusty [dus'tē] *a* polvoriento.

Dutch [duch] *a* holandés/esa ♦ *n* (*LING*) holandés *m* ♦ *ad*: **to go** ~ pagar cada uno lo suyo; **the** ~ *npl* los holandeses.

Dutch auction *n* subasta a la rebaja.

Dutchman [duch'mən], **Dutchwoman** [duch'wōōmən] *n* holandés/esa *m/f.*

dutiful [dōō'tifəl] *a* (*child*) obediente; (*husband*) sumiso; (*employee*) cumplido.

duty [dōō'tē] *n* deber *m*; (*tax*) derechos *mpl* de aduana; (*MED: in hospital*) servicio, guardia; **on** ~ de servicio; (*at night etc*) de guardia; **off** ~ libre (de servicio); **to make it one's** ~ **to do sth** encargarse de hacer algo sin falta; **to pay** ~ **on sth** pagar los derechos sobre algo.

duty-free [dōō'tēfrē'] *a* libre de derechos de aduana; ~ **store** tienda libre de impuestos.

duty officer *n* (*MIL etc*) oficial *m/f* de servicio.

duvet [dōō'vā] *n* (*Brit*) edredón *m.*

DV *abbr* (= *Deo volente*) Dios mediante.

DVM *n abbr* (*US*: = *Doctor of Veterinary Medicine*) título universitario.

dwarf [dwôrf], *pl* **dwarves** [dwôrvz] *n* enano ♦ *vt* empequeñecer.

dwell [dwel], *pt*, *pp* **dwelt** [dwelt] *vi* morar.

   dwell on *vt fus* explayarse en.

dweller [dwel'ûr] *n* habitante *m*; **city** ~ habitante *m* de la ciudad.

dwelling [dwel'ing] *n* vivienda.

dwelt [dwelt] *pt*, *pp of* **dwell**.

dwindle [dwin'dəl] *vi* menguar, disminuir.

dwindling [dwin'dling] *a* (*strength, interest*) menguante; (*resources, supplies*) disminuyente.

dye [dī] *n* tinte *m* ♦ *vt* teñir; **hair** ~ tinte *m* para el pelo.

dying [dī'ing] *a* moribundo, agonizante; (*moments*) final; (*words*) último.

dyke [dīk] *n* (*Brit*) = **dike.**

dynamic [dīnam'ik] *a* dinámico.

dynamics [dīnam'iks] *n or npl* dinámica *sg.*

dynamite [dī'nəmīt] *n* dinamita ♦ *vt* dinamitar.

dynamo [dī'nəmō] *n* dinamo *f.*

dynasty [dī'nəstē] *n* dinastía.

dysentery [dis'əntärē] *n* disentería.

dyslexic [dislek'sik] *a, n* disléxico/a *m/f.*

dyspepsia [dispep'shə] *n* dispepsia.

dystrophy [dis'trəfē] *n* distrofia; **muscular** ~ distrofia muscular.

E

E, e [ē] *n* (*letter*) E, e *f*; (*MUS*) mi *m*; **E for Easy** E de Enrique.

E *abbr* (= *east*) E.

E111 *n abbr* (*also*: **form** ~) impreso E111.

ea. *abbr* = **each.**

E.A. *abbr* (*US*: = *educational age*) nivel escolar.

each [ēch] *a* cada *inv* ♦ *pron* cada uno; ~ **other** el uno al otro; **they hate** ~ **other** se odian (entre ellos *or* mutuamente); ~ **day** cada día; **they have 2 books** ~ tienen 2 libros por persona; **they cost $5** ~ cuestan cinco dólares cada uno; ~ **of us** cada uno de nosotros.

eager [ē'gûr] *a* (*gen*) impaciente; (*hopeful*) ilusionado; (*keen*) entusiasmado; (: *pupil*) apasionado; **to be** ~ **to do sth** tener muchas ganas de hacer algo, impacientarse por hacer algo; **to be** ~ **for** ansiar, anhelar.

eagerly [ē'gûrlē] *ad* con impaciencia; con ilusión; con entusiasmo.

eagerness [ē'gûrnis] *n* impaciencia; ilusión *f*; entusiasmo.

eagle [ē'gəl] *n* águila.

E and OE *abbr* = **errors and omissions excepted.**

ear [ēr] *n* oreja; (*sense of hearing*) oído; (*of corn*) espiga; **up to the** ~**s in debt** abrumado de deudas.

earache [ēr'āk] *n* dolor *m* de oídos.

eardrum [ēr'drum] *n* tímpano.

earl [ûrl] *n* conde *m.*

early [ûr'lē] *ad* (*gen*) temprano; (*ahead of time*) con tiempo, con anticipación ♦ *a* (*gen*) temprano; (*reply*) pronto; (*man*) primitivo; (*first: Christians, settlers*) primero; **to have an** ~ **night** acostarse temprano; **in the** ~ *or* ~ **in the spring/19th century** a principios de primavera/del siglo diecinueve; **you're** ~! ¡has llegado temprano *or* pronto!; ~ **in the morning/afternoon** a primeras horas de la mañana/tarde; **she's in her** ~ **forties** tiene poco más de cuarenta años; **at your earliest convenience** (*COMM*) con la mayor brevedad posible; **I can't come any earlier** no puedo llegar antes.

early retirement *n* jubilación *f* anticipada.

early warning system *n* sistema *m* de alerta inmediata.

earmark [ēr'mârk] *vt*: **to** ~ **for** reservar

para, destinar a.

earn [ûrn] *vt* (*gen*) ganar; (*interest*) devengar; (*praise*) merecerse; **to ~ one's living** ganarse la vida.

earned income [ûrnd' in'kum] *n* renta del trabajo.

earnest [ûr'nist] *a* serio, formal ♦ *n* (*also*: **~ money**) anticipo, señal *f*; **in ~** *ad* en serio.

earnings [ûr'ningz] *npl* (*personal*) sueldo *sg*, ingresos *mpl*; (*of company etc*) ganancias *fpl*.

earphones [ēr'fōnz] *npl* auriculares *mpl*.

earplugs [ēr'plugz] *npl* tapones *mpl* para los oídos.

earring [ēr'ring] *n* pendiente *m*, arete *m*.

earshot [ēr'shât] *n*: **out of/within ~** fuera del/al alcance del oído.

earth [ûrth] *n* (*gen*) tierra; (*Brit*: ELEC) cable *m* de toma de tierra ♦ *vt* (*Brit*: ELEC) conectar a tierra.

earthenware [ûr'thənwär] *n* loza (de barro).

earthly [ûrth'lē] *a* terrenal, mundano; **~ paradise** paraíso terrenal; **there is no ~ reason to think ...** no existe razón para pensar ....

earthquake [ûrth'kwāk] *n* terremoto.

earthworm [ûrth'wûrm] *n* lombriz *f*.

earthy [ûr'thē] *a* (*fig*: *uncomplicated*) sencillo; (: *coarse*) grosero.

earwig [ēr'wig] *n* tijereta.

ease [ēz] *n* facilidad *f*; (*comfort*) comodidad *f* ♦ *vt* (*task*) facilitar; (*pain*) aliviar; (*loosen*) soltar; (*relieve: pressure, tension*) aflojar; (*weight*) aligerar; (*help pass*): **to ~ sth in/out** meter/sacar algo con cuidado ♦ *vi* (*situation*) relajarse; **with ~** con facilidad; **to feel at ~/ill at ~** sentirse a gusto/a disgusto; **at ~!** (MIL) ¡descansen!

ease off, ease up *vi* (*work, business*) aflojar; (*person*) relajarse.

easel [ē'zəl] *n* caballete *m*.

easily [ē'zilē] *ad* fácilmente.

easiness [ē'zēnis] *n* facilidad *f*; (*of manners*) soltura.

east [ēst] *n* este *m*, oriente *m* ♦ *a* del este, oriental ♦ *ad* al este, hacia el este; **the E~** el Oriente; (POL) el Este.

Easter [ēs'tûr] *n* Pascua (de Resurrección).

Easter egg *n* huevo de Pascua.

Easter Island *n* Isla de Pascua.

easterly [ēs'tûrlē] *a* (*to the east*) al este; (*from the east*) del este.

Easter Monday *n* lunes *m* de Pascua.

eastern [ēs'tûrn] *a* del este, oriental; **E~ Europe** Europa del Este; **the E~ bloc** (POL) el bloque del Este.

Easter Sunday *n* Domingo de Resurrección.

East Germany *n* Alemania Oriental.

eastward(s) [ēst'wûrd(z)] *ad* hacia el este.

easy [ē'zē] *a* fácil; (*simple*) sencillo; (*life*)

holgado, cómodo; (*relaxed*) natural ♦ *ad*: **to take it** *or* **things ~** (*not worry*) no preocuparse; (*go slowly*) tomarlo con calma; (*rest*) descansar; **payment on ~ terms** (COMM) pago a plazos; **I'm ~** (*col*) me da igual, no me importa; **easier said than done** del dicho al hecho hay buen trecho.

easy chair *n* sillón *m*.

easy-going [ē'zēgō'ing] *a* acomodadizo.

eat, *pt* **ate**, *pp* **eaten** [ēt, āt, ē'tən] *vt* comer.

eat away *vt* (*subj*: *sea*) desgastar; (: *acid*) corroer.

eat into, eat away at *vt fus* corroer.

eat out *vi* comer fuera.

eat up *vt* (*meal etc*) comerse; **it ~s up electricity** devora la electricidad.

eatable [ē'təbəl] *a* comestible.

eau de Cologne [ō' də kəlōn'] *n* (agua de) Colonia.

eaves [ēvz] *npl* alero *sg*.

eavesdrop [ēvz'dráp] *vi*: **to ~ (on sb)** escuchar a escondidas (a uno).

ebb [eb] *n* reflujo ♦ *vi* bajar; (*fig: also*: **~ away**) decaer; **~ and flow** el flujo y reflujo; **to be at a low ~** (*fig: person*) estar decaído; (: *business*) ir lento.

ebb tide *n* marea menguante.

ebony [eb'ənē] *n* ébano *m*.

ebullient [ibul'yənt] *a* entusiasta, animado.

EC *n abbr* (= *European Community*) CE *f*.

eccentric [iksen'trik] *a*, *n* excéntrico/a.

ecclesiastical [iklēzēas'tikəl] *a* eclesiástico.

ECG *n abbr* (= *electrocardiogram*) E.C. *m*.

ECGD *n abbr* (= *Export Credits Guarantee Department*) *servicio de garantía financiera a la exportación*.

echo, **~es** [ek'ō] *n* eco *m* ♦ *vt* (*sound*) repetir ♦ *vi* resonar, hacer eco.

éclair [iklär'] *n* relámpago, petisú *m*.

eclipse [iklips'] *n* eclipse *m* ♦ *vt* eclipsar.

ECM *n abbr* (US: = *European Common Market*) MCE *m*.

ecologist [ikâl'əjist] *n* ecologista *m/f*; (*scientist*) ecólogo/a *m/f*.

ecology [ikâl'əjē] *n* ecología.

economic [ēkənâm'ik] *a* (*profitable*: *price*) económico; (: *business etc*) rentable.

economical [ēkənâm'ikəl] *a* económico.

economically [ēkənâm'iklē] *ad* económicamente.

economics [ēkənâm'iks] *n* economía ♦ *npl* (*financial aspects*) finanzas *fpl*.

economic warfare *n* guerra económica.

economist [ikân'əmist] *n* economista *m/f*.

economize [ikân'əmīz] *vi* economizar, ahorrar.

economy [ikân'əmē] *n* economía; **economies of scale** economías *fpl* de escala.

economy class *n* (AVIAT etc) clase *f* turista.

economy size *n* tamaño familiar.

ecosystem [ek'ōsistəm] *n* ecosistema *m*.

ECSC *n abbr* (= *European Coal & Steel*

Community) CECA *f*.

ecstasy [εk'stəsē] *n* éxtasis *m inv*.

ecstatic [εkstat'ik] *a* extático.

ECT *n abbr* = **electroconvulsive therapy**.

ECU *n abbr* (= *European Currency Unit*) ECU *m*.

Ecuador [εk'wədôr] *n* Ecuador *m*.

Ecuador(i)an [εk'wədôr(ē)ən] *a*, *n* ecuatoriano/a *m/f*.

ecumenical [εkyōōmen'ikəl] *a* ecuménico.

eczema [εk'səmə] *n* eczema *m*.

eddy [εd'ē] *n* remolino.

Eden [ē'dən] *n* Edén *m*.

edge [εj] *n* (*of knife etc*) filo; (*of object*) borde *m*; (*of lake etc*) orilla ♦ *vt* (*SEWING*) ribetear ♦ *vi*: **to ~ past** pasar con dificultad; **on ~** (*fig*) = **edgy; to ~ away from** alejarse poco a poco de; **to ~ forward** avanzar poco a poco; **to ~ up** subir lentamente.

edgeways [εj'wāz] *ad*: **he couldn't get a word in ~** no pudo meter baza.

edging [εj'ing] *n* (*SEWING*) ribete *m*; (*of path*) borde *m*.

edgy [εj'ē] *a* nervioso, inquieto.

edible [εd'əbəl] *a* comestible.

edict [ē'dikt] *n* edicto.

edifice [εd'əfis] *n* edificio.

edifying [εd'əfiing] *a* edificante.

Edinburgh [εd'ənbûrə] *n* Edimburgo.

edit [εd'it] *vt* (*be editor of*) dirigir; (*rewrite*) redactar; (*cut*) cortar; (*COMPUT*) editar.

edition [idish'ən] *n* (*gen*) edición *f*; (*number printed*) tirada.

editor [εd'itûr] *n* (*of newspaper*) director(a) *m/f*; (*of book*) redactor(a) *m/f*; (*film ~*) montador(a) *m/f*.

editorial [εditôr'ēəl] *a* editorial ♦ *n* editorial *m*; **~ staff** redacción *f*.

EDP *n abbr* (= *electronic data processing*) TED *m*.

EDT *n abbr* (*US*: = *Eastern Daylight Time*) hora de verano de Nueva York.

educate [εj'ōōkāt] *vt* (*gen*) educar; (*instruct*) instruir.

education [εjōōkā'shən] *n* educación *f*; (*schooling*) enseñanza; (*SCOL*: *subject etc*) pedagogía; **primary/secondary ~** primera/segunda enseñanza.

educational [εjōōkā'shənəl] *a* (*policy etc*) educacional; (*teaching*) docente; (*instructive*) educativo; **~ technology** tecnología educacional.

Edwardian [εdwôr'dēən] *a* eduardiano.

E.E. *abbr* = **electrical engineer**.

EEC *n abbr* (= *European Economic Community*) CEE *f*.

EEG *n abbr* = **electroencephalogram**.

eel [ēl] *n* anguila.

EENT *n abbr* (*US MED*) = *eye, ear, nose and throat*.

EEOC *n abbr* (*US*: = *Equal Employment Opportunities Commission*) comisión que investiga discriminación racial o sexual en el empleo.

eerie [ē'rē] *a* (*sound, experience*) espeluznante.

EET *n abbr* (= *Eastern European Time*) hora de Europa oriental.

efface [ifās'] *vt* borrar.

effect [ifεkt'] *n* efecto ♦ *vt* efectuar, llevar a cabo; **~s** *npl* (*property*) efectos *mpl*; **to take ~** (*law*) entrar en vigor *or* vigencia; (*drug*) surtir efecto; **in ~** en realidad; **to have an ~ on sb/sth** hacerle efecto a uno/afectar algo; **to put into ~** (*plan*) llevar a la práctica; **his letter is to the ~ that...** su carta especifica que....

effective [ifεk'tiv] *a* (*gen*) eficaz; (*striking*: *display, outfit*) impresionante; (*real*) efectivo; **to become ~** (*LAW*) entrar en vigor; **~ date** fecha de vigencia.

effectively [ifεk'tivlē] *ad* (*efficiently*) eficazmente; (*strikingly*) de manera impresionante; (*in reality*) en efecto.

effectiveness [ifεk'tivnis] *n* eficacia.

effeminate [ifεm'ənit] *a* afeminado.

effervescent [εfûrvεs'ənt] *a* efervescente.

efficacy [εf'ikəsē] *n* eficacia.

efficiency [ifish'ənsē] *n* (*gen*) eficiencia; (*of machine*) rendimiento.

efficient [ifish'ənt] *a* eficiente; (*remedy, product, system*) eficaz; (*machine, car*) de buen rendimiento.

effigy [εf'ijē] *n* efigie *f*.

effluent [εf'lōōənt] *n* desperdicios *mpl* fluviales.

effort [εf'ûrt] *n* esfuerzo; **to make an ~ to do sth** esforzarse por hacer algo.

effortless [εf'ûrtlis] *a* sin ningún esfuerzo.

effrontery [ifrun'tûrē] *n* descaro.

effusive [ifyōō'siv] *a* (*person, welcome, letter*) efusivo; (*thanks, apologies*) expansivo.

EFL *n abbr* (*SCOL*) = *English as a foreign language*.

EFT *n abbr* (*US*: = *electronic funds transfer*) transferencia electrónica de fondos.

EFTA [εf'tə] *n abbr* (= *European Free Trade Association*) AELC *f*.

e.g. *ad abbr* (= *exempli gratia*) p.ej.

egg [εg] *n* huevo; **hard-boiled/soft-boiled/poached ~** huevo duro/pasado por agua/escalfado; **scrambled ~s** huevos revueltos.

egg on *vt* incitar.

eggcup [εg'kup] *n* huevera.

eggnog [εg'nâg] *n* ponche *m* de huevo.

eggplant [εg'plant] *n* (*esp US*) berenjena.

eggshell [εg'shεl] *n* cáscara de huevo.

egg white *n* clara de huevo.

egg yolk *n* yema de huevo.

ego [ē'gō] *n* ego.

egotism [ē'gətisəm] *n* egoísmo.

egotist [ē'gətist] *n* egoísta *m/f*.

Egypt [ē'jipt] *n* Egipto.

Egyptian [ijip'shən] *a, n* egipcio/a *m/f.*
eiderdown [ī'dûrdoun] *n* edredón *m.*
eight [āt] *num* ocho.
eighteen [ā'tēn'] *num* diez y ocho, dieciocho.
eighth [ātth] *num* octavo.
eighth note *n* (*US MUS*) corchea.
eighty [ā'tē] *num* ochenta.
Eire [ār'ə] *n* Eire *m.*
either [ē'thûr] *a* cualquiera de los dos ...;
  (*both, each*) cada ♦ *pron:* ~ (**of them**) cualquiera (de los dos) ♦ *ad* tampoco ♦ *conj:* ~ **yes or no** o sí o no; **on** ~ **side** en ambos lados; **I don't like** ~ no me gusta ninguno de los dos; **no, I don't** ~ no, yo tampoco.
eject [ijekt'] *vt* echar; (*tenant*) desahuciar ♦ *vi* eyectarse.
ejector seat [ijek'tûr sēt] *n* asiento proyectable.
eke [ēk]: **to** ~ **out** *vt* (*money*) hacer que llegue.
EKG *n abbr* (*US*) = **electrocardiogram.**
el [el] *n abbr* (*US col*) = **elevated railroad.**
elaborate *a* [ilab'ûrit] (*design*) elaborado; (*pattern*) intrincado ♦ *vb* [ilab'ərāt] *vt* elaborar ♦ *vi* explicarse con muchos detalles.
elaborately [ilab'ûritlē] *ad* de manera complicada; (*decorated*) profusamente.
elaboration [ilabərā'shən] *n* elaboración *f.*
elapse [ilaps'] *vi* transcurrir.
elastic [ilas'tik] *a, n* elástico.
elastic band *n* (*Brit*) gomita.
elated [ilā'tid] *a*: **to be** ~ regocijarse.
elation [ilā'shən] *n* regocijo.
elbow [el'bō] *n* codo ♦ *vt*: **to** ~ **one's way through the crowd** abrirse paso a codazos por la muchedumbre.
elder [el'dûr] *a* mayor ♦ *n* (*tree*) saúco; (*person*) mayor; (*of tribe*) anciano.
elderly [el'dûrlē] *a* de edad, mayor ♦ *npl:* **the** ~ la gente mayor, los ancianos.
eldest [el'dist] *a, n* el/la mayor.
elect [ilekt'] *vt* elegir; (*choose*): **to** ~ **to do** optar por hacer ♦ *a*: **the president** ~ el presidente electo.
election [ilek'shən] *n* elección *f*; **to hold an** ~ convocar elecciones.
election campaign *n* campaña electoral.
electioneering [ilekshənē'ring] *n* campaña electoral.
elective [ēlek'tiv] *n* (*US*) asignatura discrecional.
elector [ilek'tûr] *n* elector(a) *m/f.*
electoral [ilek'tûrəl] *a* electoral.
electoral college *n* colegio electoral.
electoral roll *n* censo electoral.
electorate [ilek'tûrit] *n* electorado.
electric [ilek'trik] *a* eléctrico.
electrical [ilek'trikəl] *a* eléctrico.
electrical engineer *n* ingeniero/a electricista.
electrical failure *n* fallo eléctrico.

electric blanket *n* manta eléctrica.
electric chair *n* silla eléctrica.
electric current *n* corriente *f* eléctrica.
electric heater *n* estufa eléctrica.
electrician [ilektrish'ən] *n* electricista *m/f.*
electricity [ilektris'ətē] *n* electricidad *f*; **to switch on/off the** ~ conectar/desconectar la electricidad.
electric light *n* luz *f* eléctrica.
electric shock *n* choque *m* eléctrico.
electric stove *n* cocina eléctrica.
electrification [ilektrəfəkā'shən] *n* electrificación *f.*
electrify [ilek'trəfī] *vt* (*RAIL*) electrificar; (*fig: audience*) electrizar.
electro... [ilek'trō] *pref* electro....
electrocardiogram (EKG, (*Brit*) **ECG)** [ilektrōkâr'dēəgram] *n* electrocardiograma *m.*
electrocardiograph [ilektrōkâr'dēəgraf] *n* electrocardiógrafo.
electro-convulsive therapy (ECT) [ilek'trōkənvul'siv thär'əpē] *n* electroterapia.
electrocute [ilek'trəkyōōt] *vt* electrocutar.
electrode [ilek'trōd] *n* electrodo.
electroencephalogram (EEG) [ilektrōensef'ələgram] *n* electroencefalograma *m.*
electrolysis [ilektrál'isis] *n* electrólisis *f inv.*
electromagnetic [ilektrōmagnet'ik] *a* electromagnético.
electron [ilek'trân] *n* electrón *m.*
electronic [ilektrân'ik] *a* electrónico.
electronic data processing (EDP) *n* tratamiento electrónico de datos.
electronic mail *n* correo electrónico.
electronics [ilektrân'iks] *n* electrónica.
electron microscope *n* microscopio electrónico.
electroplated [ilek'trəplātid] *a* galvanizado.
electrotherapy [ilektrōthär'əpē] *n* electroterapia.
elegance [el'əgəns] *n* elegancia.
elegant [el'əgənt] *a* elegante.
elegy [el'ijē] *n* elegía.
element [el'əmənt] *n* (*gen*) elemento; (*of heater, kettle etc*) resistencia.
elementary [elimen'tûrē] *a* elemental; (*primitive*) rudimentario; (*school, education*) primario.
elephant [el'əfənt] *n* elefante *m.*
elevate [el'əvāt] *vt* (*gen*) elevar; (*in rank*) ascender.
elevated railroad [el'əvātid rāl'rōd] *n* (*US*) ferrocarril *m* urbano elevado.
elevation [eləvā'shən] *n* elevación *f*; (*rank*) ascenso; (*height*) altura.
elevator [el'əvātûr] *n* (*US*) ascensor *m.*
eleven [ilev'ən] *num* once.
elevenses [ilev'ənziz] *npl* (*Brit*) ≈ café *m* de media mañana.
eleventh [ilev'ənth] *a* undécimo; **at the** ~ **hour** (*fig*) a última hora.
elf, *pl* **elves** [elf, elvz] *n* duende *m.*

elicit [ilis'it] *vt*: **to ~ sth (from sb)** sacar(le) algo (a uno).

eligible [el'ijəbəl] *a* elegible; **to be ~ for a pension** llenar los requisitos para una pensión.

eliminate [əlim'ənāt] *vt* eliminar; (*cross out*) suprimir; (*a suspect, possibility*) descartar.

elimination [əlimənā'shən] *n* eliminación *f*; supresión *f*; **by process of ~** por proceso de eliminación.

elite [ilēt'] *n* élite *f*.

elitist [ilē'tist] *a* (*pej*) elitista.

elixir [ilik'sûr] *n* elixir *m*.

Elizabethan [ilizəbē'thən] *a* isabelino.

elm [elm] *n* olmo.

elocution [eləkyōō'shən] *n* elocución *f*.

elongated [ilông'gātid] *a* alargado, estirado.

elope [ilōp'] *vi* fugarse para casarse.

elopement [ilōp'mənt] *n* fuga.

eloquence [el'əkwəns] *n* elocuencia.

eloquent [el'əkwənt] *a* elocuente.

else [els] *ad*: **or ~** si no; **something ~** otra cosa; **somewhere ~** en otra parte; **everywhere ~** en todas partes menos aquí; **everyone ~** todos los demás; **nothing ~** nada más; **is there anything ~ I can do?** ¿puedo hacer algo más?; **where ~?** ¿dónde más?, ¿en qué otra parte?; **there was little ~ to do** apenas quedaba otra cosa que hacer; **nobody ~ spoke** no habló nadie más.

elsewhere [els'hwär] *ad* (*be*) en otra parte; (*go*) a otra parte.

ELT *n abbr* (*SCOL*) = *English Language Teaching*.

elucidate [ilōō'sidāt] *vt* aclarar, elucidar.

elude [ilōōd'] *vt* eludir; (*blow, pursuer*) esquivar.

elusive [ilōō'siv] *a* esquivo; (*answer*) difícil de encontrar; **he is very ~** no es fácil encontrarlo.

elves [elvz] *npl of* **elf**.

emaciated [imā'shēātid] *a* demacrado.

emanate [em'ənāt] *vi* emanar, proceder.

emancipate [iman'səpāt] *vt* emancipar.

emancipated [iman'səpātid] *a* liberado.

emancipation [imansəpā'shən] *n* emancipación *f*, liberación *f*.

emasculate [imas'kyəlāt] *vt* castrar; (*fig*) incapacitar, debilitar.

embalm [embám'] *vt* embalsamar.

embankment [embangk'mənt] *n* (*of railroad*) terraplén *m*; (*riverside*) dique *m*.

embargo, *pl* **~es** [embár'gō] *n* prohibición *f*; (*COMM, NAUT*) embargo; **to put an ~ on sth** embargar algo.

embark [embárk'] *vi* embarcarse ♦ *vt* embarcar; **to ~ on** (*journey*) comenzar, iniciar; (*fig*) emprender, lanzarse a.

embarkation [embárkā'shən] *n* (*people*) embarco; (*goods*) embarque *m*.

embarkation card *n* tarjeta de embarque.

embarrass [embar'əs] *vt* avergonzar; (*financially etc*) poner en un aprieto.

embarrassed [embar'əst] *a* azorado; **to be ~** sentirse azorado *or* violento.

embarrassing [embar'əsing] *a* (*situation*) violento; (*question*) embarazoso.

embarrassment [embar'əsmənt] *n* desconcierto, azoramiento; (*financial*) apuros *mpl*.

embassy [em'bəsē] *n* embajada; **the Spanish E~** la embajada española.

embed [embed'] *vt* (*jewel*) empotrar; (*teeth etc*) clavar.

embellish [embel'ish] *vt* embellecer; (*fig: story, truth*) adornar.

embers [em'bûrz] *npl* rescoldo *sg*, ascua *sg*.

embezzle [embez'əl] *vt* desfalcar, malversar.

embezzlement [embez'əlmənt] *n* desfalco, malversación *f*.

embezzler [embez'lûr] *n* malversador(a) *m/f*.

embitter [embit'ûr] *vt* (*person*) amargar; (*relationship*) envenenar.

embittered [embit'ûrd] *a* resentido, amargado.

emblem [em'bləm] *n* emblema *m*.

embody [embâd'ē] *vt* (*spirit*) encarnar; (*ideas*) expresar.

embolden [embōl'dən] *vt* envalentonar; (*TYP*) poner en negrita.

embolism [em'bəlizəm] *n* embolia.

emboss [embôs'] *vt* estampar en relieve; (*metal, leather*) repujar.

embossed [embôst'] *a* realzado; **~ with ...** con ... en relieve.

embrace [embrās'] *vt* abrazar, dar un abrazo a; (*include*) abarcar; (*adopt: idea*) adherirse a ♦ *vi* abrazarse ♦ *n* abrazo.

embroider [embroi'dûr] *vt* bordar; (*fig: story*) adornar, embellecer.

embroidery [embroi'dûrē] *n* bordado.

embroil [embroil'] *vt*: **to become ~ed (in sth)** enredarse en algo.

embryo [em'brēō] *n* (*also fig*) embrión *m*.

emcee [em'sē'] *n* presentador(a) *m/f*.

emend [imend'] *vt* (*text*) enmendar.

emerald [em'ûrəld] *n* esmeralda.

emerge [imûrj'] *vi* (*gen*) salir; (*arise*) surgir; **it ~s that** resulta que.

emergence [imûr'jəns] *n* (*of nation*) salida, surgimiento.

emergency [imûr'jənsē] *n* (*event*) emergencia; (*crisis*) crisis *f inv*; **in an ~** en caso de urgencia; **(to declare a) state of ~** (declarar) estado de emergencia *or* de excepción.

emergency cord *n* (*US*) timbre *m* de alarma.

emergency exit *n* salida de emergencia.

emergency flasher [imûr'jənsē flash'ûr] *n* (*US AUT*) señales *fpl* de emergencia.

emergency landing *n* aterrizaje *m* forzoso.

emergency lane *n* (*US*) andén *m*, arcén *m*.

emergency meeting *n* reunión *f* extraordinaria.

emergency service *n* servicio de urgencia *or* emergencia.

emergency stop *n* (*AUT*) parada en seco.

emergent [imûr'jənt] *a* (*nation*) en vías de desarrollo.

emery board [em'ûrē bōrd] *n* lima de uñas.

emetic [imet'ik] *n* emético.

emigrant [em'əgrənt] *n* emigrante *m/f*.

emigrate [em'əgrāt] *vi* emigrarse.

emigration [eməgrā'shən] *n* emigración *f*.

émigré [em'igrā] *n* emigrado/a.

eminence [em'ənəns] *n* eminencia; **to gain** *or* **win** ~ ganarse fama.

eminent [em'ənənt] *a* eminente.

eminently [em'ənəntlē] *ad* eminentemente.

emirate [əmē'rit] *n* emirato.

emission [imish'ən] *n* emisión *f*.

emit [imit'] *vt* emitir; (*smoke*) arrojar; (*smell*) despedir; (*sound*) producir.

emolument [imâl'yəmənt] *n* (*often pl*: *formal*) honorario.

emotion [imō'shən] *n* emoción *f*.

emotional [imō'shənəl] *a* (*person*) sentimental; (*scene*) conmovedor(a), emocionante.

emotionally [imō'shənəlē] *ad* (*behave*, *speak*) con emoción; (*be involved*) sentimentalmente.

emotive [imō'tiv] *a* emotivo.

empathy [em'pəthē] *n* empatía; **to feel** ~ **with sb** sentir empatía por uno.

emperor [em'pûrûr] *n* emperador *m*.

emphasis, *pl* **emphases** [em'fəsis, -sēz] *n* énfasis *m inv*; **to place** ~ **on sth** (*fig*) hacer hincapié en algo; **the** ~ **is on sport** se da mayor importancia al deporte.

emphasize [em'fəsīz] *vt* (*word, point*) subrayar, recalcar; (*feature*) hacer resaltar.

emphatic [əmfat'ik] *a* (*condemnation, denial*) enfático.

emphatically [əmfat'iklē] *ad* con énfasis.

emphysema [emfisē'mə] *n* (*MED*) enfisema *m*.

empire [em'pīûr] *n* imperio.

empirical [empir'ikəl] *a* empírico.

employ [emploi'] *vt* (*give job to*) emplear; (*make use of*: *thing, method*) emplear, usar; **he's** ~**ed in a bank** está empleado en un banco.

employee [emploi'ē] *n* empleado/a.

employer [emploi'ûr] *n* patrón/ona *m/f*; (*businessman*) empresario/a.

employment [emploi'mənt] *n* (*gen*) empleo; (*work*) trabajo; **full** ~ pleno empleo; **without** ~ sin empleo; **to find** ~ encontrar trabajo; **place of** ~ lugar *m* de empleo.

employment agency *n* agencia de colocaciones.

empower [empou'ûr] *vt*: **to** ~ **sb to do sth** autorizar a uno para hacer algo.

empress [em'pris] *n* emperatriz *f*.

emptiness [emp'tēnis] *n* (*gen*) vacío; (*of life etc*) vaciedad *f*.

empty [emp'tē] *a* vacío; (*street, area*) desierto; (*house*) desocupado; (*threat*) vano ♦ *n* (*bottle*) envase *m* ♦ *vt* vaciar; (*place*) dejar vacío ♦ *vi* vaciarse; (*house*) quedar desocupado; (*place*) quedar desierto; **to** ~ **into** (*river*) desembocar en.

empty-handed [emp'tēhan'did] *a* con las manos vacías.

empty-headed [emp'tēhed'id] *a* casquivano.

EMT *n abbr* = *emergency medical technician*.

emulate [em'yəlāt] *vt* emular.

emulsion [imul'shən] *n* emulsión *f*.

enable [enā'bəl] *vt*: **to** ~ **sb to do sth** (*allow*) permitir a uno hacer algo; (*prepare*) capacitar a uno para hacer algo.

enact [enakt'] *vt* (*law*) promulgar; (*play, scene*) representar; (*role*) hacer.

enamel [inam'əl] *n* esmalte *m*.

enamel paint *n* esmalte *m*.

enamored, (*Brit*) **enamoured** [enam'ûrd] *a*: **to be** ~ **of** (*person*) estar enamorado de; (*activity etc*) tener gran afición a; (*idea*) aferrarse a.

encampment [enkamp'mənt] *n* campamento.

encase [enkās'] *vt*: **to** ~ **in** (*contain*) encajar; (*cover*) cubrir.

encased [enkāst'] *a*: ~ **in** (*covered*) revestido de.

enchant [enchant'] *vt* encantar.

enchanting [enchan'ting] *a* encantador(a).

encircle [ensûr'kəl] *vt* (*gen*) rodear; (*waist*) ceñir.

encl. *abbr* (= *enclosed*) adj.

enclave [en'klāv] *n* enclave *m*.

enclose [enklōz'] *vt* (*land*) cercar; (*with letter etc*) adjuntar; (*in receptacle*): **to** ~ **(with)** encerrar (con); **please find** ~**d** le mandamos adjunto.

enclosure [enklō'zhûr] *n* cercado, recinto; (*COMM*) carta adjunta.

encoder [enkō'dûr] *n* (*COMPUT*) codificador *m*.

encompass [enkum'pəs] *vt* abarcar.

encore [âng'kôr] *excl* ¡otra!, ¡bis! ♦ *n* bis *m*.

encounter [enkoun'tûr] *n* encuentro ♦ *vt* encontrar, encontrarse con; (*difficulty*) tropezar con.

encourage [enkûr'ij] *vt* alentar, animar; (*growth*) estimular; **to** ~ **sb (to do sth)** animar a uno (a hacer algo).

encouragement [enkûr'ijmənt] *n* estímulo; (*of industry*) fomento.

encouraging [enkûr'ijing] *a* alentador(a).

encroach [enkrōch'] *vi*: **to ~ (up)on** (*gen*) invadir; (*time*) adueñarse de.

encrust [enkrust'] *vt* incrustar.

encrusted [enkrus'tid] *a*: **~ with** incrustado de.

encumber [enkum'bûr] *vt*: **to be ~ed with** (*carry*) estar cargado de; (*debts*) estar gravado de.

encyclop(a)edia [ensīkləpē'dēə] *n* enciclopedia.

end [end] *n* (*gen, also aim*) fin *m*; (*of table*) extremo; (*of line, rope etc*) cabo; (*of pointed object*) punta; (*of town*) barrio; (*of street*) final *m*; (SPORT) lado ♦ *vt* terminar, acabar; (*also*: **bring to an ~, put an ~ to**) acabar con ♦ *vi* terminar, acabar; **to ~ (with)** terminar (con); **in the ~** al fin, por fin, finalmente; **to be at an ~** llegar al final; **at the ~ of the day** (*fig*) al fin y al cabo, a fin de cuentas; **to this ~, with this ~ in view** con este propósito; **from ~ to ~** de punta a punta; **on ~** (*object*) de punta, de cabeza; **to stand on ~** (*hair*) erizarse; **for hours on ~** hora tras hora.

end up *vi*: **to ~ up in** terminar en; (*place*) ir a parar en.

endanger [endān'jûr] *vt* poner en peligro; **an ~ed species** (*of animal*) una especie en peligro de extinción.

endear [endēr'] *vt*: **to ~ o.s. to sb** ganarse la simpatía de uno.

endearing [endēr'ing] *a* simpático, atractivo.

endearment [endēr'mənt] *n* cariño, palabra cariñosa; **to whisper ~s** decir unas palabras cariñosas al oído; **term of ~** nombre *m* cariñoso.

endeavor, (*Brit*) **endeavour** [endev'ûr] *n* esfuerzo; (*attempt*) tentativa ♦ *vi*: **to ~ to do** esforzarse por hacer; (*try*) procurar hacer.

endemic [endem'ik] *a* (*poverty, disease*) endémico.

ending [en'ding] *n* fin *m*, conclusión *f*; (*of book*) desenlace *m*; (LING) terminación *f*.

endive [en'dīv] *n* (*curly*) escarola; (*smooth, flat*) endibia.

endless [end'lis] *a* interminable, inacabable; (*possibilities*) infinito.

endorse [endôrs'] *vt* (*check*) endosar; (*approve*) aprobar.

endorsee [endôrsē'] *n* portador(a) *m/f* de un efecto.

endorsement [endôrs'mənt] *n* (*approval*) aprobación *f*; (*signature*) endoso; (*Brit*: *on driver's license*) anotación *f* de una sanción.

endorser [endôrs'ûr] *n* avalista *m/f*.

endow [endou'] *vt* (*provide with money*) dotar; (*found*) fundar; **to be ~ed with** (*fig*) estar dotado de.

endowment [endou'mənt] *n* (*amount*) donación *f*.

endowment insurance *n* seguro mixto.

end product *n* (INDUSTRY) producto final; (*fig*) resultado.

end result *n* resultado.

endurable [endoo'rəbəl] *a* soportable, tolerable.

endurance [endoor'əns] *n* resistencia.

endurance test *n* prueba de resistencia.

endure [endoor'] *vt* (*bear*) aguantar, soportar; (*resist*) resistir ♦ *vi* (*last*) durar; (*resist*) resistir.

enduring [endoor'ing] *a* duradero.

end user *n* (COMPUT) usuario final.

enema [en'əmə] *n* (MED) enema.

enemy [en'əmē] *a, n* enemigo/a *m/f*; **to make an ~ of sb** enemistarse con uno.

energetic [enûrjet'ik] *a* enérgico.

energy [en'ûrjē] *n* energía.

energy crisis *n* crisis *f* energética.

energy-saving [en'ûrjēsāving] *a* (*policy*) para ahorrar energía; (*device*) que ahorra energía ♦ *n* ahorro de energía.

enervating [en'ûrvāting] *a* deprimente.

enforce [enfôrs'] *vt* (LAW) hacer cumplir.

enforced [enfôrst'] *a* forzoso, forzado.

enfranchise [enfran'chīz] *vt* (*give vote to*) conceder el derecho de voto a; (*set free*) emancipar.

engage [engāj'] *vt* (*attention*) llamar; (*in conversation*) abordar; (*worker, lawyer*) contratar; (*clutch*) embragar ♦ *vi* (TECH) engranar; **to ~ in** dedicarse a, ocuparse en; **to ~ sb in conversation** entablar conversación con uno.

engaged [engājd'] *a* (*Brit*: *busy, in use*) ocupado; (*betrothed*) prometido; **to get ~** prometerse; **he is ~ in research** se dedica a la investigación.

engaged tone *n* (*Brit* TEL) señal *f* de comunicando.

engagement [engāj'mənt] *n* (*appointment*) compromiso, cita; (*battle*) combate *m*; (*to marry*) compromiso; (*period*) noviazgo; **I have a previous ~** ya tengo un compromiso.

engagement ring *n* anillo de pedida.

engaging [engā'jing] *a* atractivo, simpático.

engender [enjen'dûr] *vt* engendrar.

engine [en'jən] *n* (AUT) motor *m*; (RAIL) locomotora.

engine driver *n* (*Brit*: *of train*) maquinista *m/f*.

engineer [enjənēr'] *n* ingeniero/a; (US RAIL) maquinista *m/f*; **civil/mechanical ~** ingeniero/a de caminos, canales y puertos/ industrial.

engineering [enjənēr'ing] *n* ingeniería ♦ *cpd* (*works, factory, worker etc*) de ingeniería.

engine failure, engine trouble *n* avería del motor.

England [ing'glənd] *n* Inglaterra.

English [ing'glish] a inglés/esa ♦ n (LING) el inglés; **the ~** npl los ingleses.
English Channel n: **the ~** el Canal de la Mancha.
Englishman [ing'glishmən], **Englishwoman** [ing'glishwoōmən] n inglés/esa m/f.
English-speaker [ing'glishspēkûr] n persona de habla inglesa.
English-speaking [ing'glishpē'king] a de habla inglesa.
engraving [engrā'ving] n grabado.
engrossed [engrōst'] a: **~ in** absorto en.
engulf [engulf'] vt sumergir, hundir.
enhance [enhans'] vt (gen) aumentar; (beauty) realzar; (position, reputation) mejorar.
enigma [ənig'mə] n enigma m.
enigmatic [enigmat'ik] a enigmático.
enjoy [enjoi'] vt (have: health, fortune) disfrutar de, gozar de; (food) comer con gusto; **I ~ doing...** me gusta hacer...; **to ~ o.s.** divertirse, pasarlo bien.
enjoyable [enjoi'əbəl] a (pleasant) agradable; (amusing) divertido.
enjoyment [enjoi'mənt] n (use) disfrute m; (joy) placer m.
enlarge [enlârj'] vt aumentar; (broaden) extender; (PHOT) ampliar ♦ vi: **to ~ on** (subject) tratar con más detalles.
enlarged [enlârjd'] a (edition) aumentado; (MED: organ, gland) dilatado.
enlargement [enlârj'mənt] n (PHOT) ampliación f.
enlighten [enlīt'ən] vt (inform) informar.
enlightened [enlīt'ənd] a iluminado; (tolerant) comprensivo.
enlightening [enlīt'əning] a informativo.
Enlightenment [enlīt'ənmənt] n (HISTORY): **the ~** la Ilustración, el Siglo de las Luces.
enlist [enlist'] vt alistar; (support) conseguir ♦ vi alistarse; **~ed man** (US: MIL) soldado raso.
enliven [enlī'vən] vt (people) animar; (events) avivar, animar.
enmity [en'mitē] n enemistad f.
ennoble [ennō'bəl] vt ennoblecer.
enormity [inôr'mitē] n enormidad f.
enormous [inôr'məs] a enorme.
enough [inuf'] a: **~ time/books** bastante tiempo/bastantes libros ♦ n: **have you got ~?** ¿tiene usted bastante? ♦ ad: **big ~** bastante grande; **he has not worked ~** no ha trabajado bastante; **(that's) ~!** ¡basta ya!, ¡ya está bien!; **that's ~, thanks** con eso basta, gracias; **will 5 be ~?** ¿bastará con 5?; **I've had ~** estoy harto; **he was kind ~ to lend me the money** tuvo la bondad or amabilidad de prestarme el dinero; **... which, funny ~ ...** ... lo que, por extraño que parezca... .
enquire [enkwī'ûr] vt, vi = **inquire.**
enrage [enrāj'] vt enfurecer.

enrich [enrich'] vt enriquecer.
enroll, (Brit) enrol [enrōl'] vt (members) inscribir; (SCOL) matricular ♦ vi inscribirse; (SCOL) matricularse.
enrol(l)ment [enrōl'mənt] n inscripción f; matriculación f.
en route [ôn rōōt'] ad durante el viaje; **~ for/from/to** camino de/de/a.
ensconce [enskâns'] vt: **to ~ o.s.** instalarse cómodamente, acomodarse.
ensemble [ânsâm'bəl] n (MUS) conjunto.
enshrine [enshrīn'] vt encerrar, englobar.
ensign [en'sən] n (flag) bandera.
enslave [enslāv'] vt esclavizar.
ensue [ensōō'] vi seguirse; (result) resultar.
ensuing [ensōō'ing] a (subsequent) siguiente; (resulting) consiguiente.
ensure [enshōōr'] vt asegurar.
ENT n abbr (= Ear, Nose and Throat) otorrinolaringología.
entail [entāl'] vt (imply) suponer; (result in) acarrear.
entangle [entang'gəl] vt (thread etc) enredar, enmarañar; **to become ~d in sth** (fig) enmarañarse en algo.
entanglement [entang'gəlmənt] n enredo.
enter [en'tûr] vt (room) entrar en; (club) hacerse socio de; (army, profession) alistarse en; (sb for a competition) inscribir; (write down) anotar, apuntar; (COMPUT) introducir ♦ vi entrar; **to ~ for** vt fus presentarse para; **to ~ into** vt fus (relations) establecer; (plans) formar parte de; (debate) tomar parte en; (negotiations) entablar; (agreement) llegar a, firmar; **to ~ (up)on** vt fus (Brit: career) emprender.
enteritis [entərī'tis] n enteritis f.
enterprise [en'tûrprīz] n empresa; (spirit) iniciativa; **free ~** la libre empresa; **private ~** la iniciativa privada.
enterprising [en'tûrprīzing] a emprendedor(a).
entertain [entûrtān'] vt (amuse) divertir; (receive: guest) recibir (en casa); (idea) abrigar.
entertainer [entûrtān'ûr] n artista m/f.
entertaining [entûrtā'ning] a divertido, entretenido ♦ n: **to do a lot of ~** dar muchas fiestas, tener muchos invitados.
entertainment [entûrtān'mənt] n (amusement) diversión f; (show) espectáculo; (party) fiesta.
entertainment allowance n (COMM) gastos mpl de representación.
enthralled [enthrôld'] a cautivado.
enthralling [enthrôl'ing] a cautivador(a).
enthuse [enthōōz'] vi: **to become ~d about or over** entusiasmarse por.
enthusiasm [enthōō'zēazəm] n entusiasmo.
enthusiast [enthōō'zēast] n entusiasta m/f.
enthusiastic [enthōōzēas'tik] a entusiasta; **to be ~ about sb/sth** estar entusiasmado con uno/algo.

entice [entīs'] *vt* tentar; (*seduce*) seducir.
entire [entī'ûr] *a* entero.
entirely [entīûr'lē] *ad* totalmente.
entirety [entīr'tē] *n*: **in its ~** en su totalidad.
entitle [entīt'əl] *vt*: **to ~ sb to sth** dar a uno derecho a algo.
entitled [entīt'əld] *a* (*book*) que se titula; **to be ~ to sth/to do sth** tener derecho a algo/a hacer algo.
entity [en'titē] *n* entidad *f*.
entourage [ântōōrâzh'] *n* séquito.
entrails [en'trālz] *npl* entrañas *fpl*; (*US*) asadura *sg*, menudos *mpl*.
entrance *n* [en'trəns] entrada ♦ *vt* [entrans'] encantar, hechizar; **to gain ~ to** (*university etc*) ingresar en.
entrance examination *n* (*to school*) examen *m* de ingreso.
entrance fee *n* cuota.
entrance ramp *n* (*US AUT*) rampa de acceso.
entrancing [entrans'ing] *a* encantador(a).
entrant [en'trənt] *n* (*in race, competition*) participante *m/f*; (*in exam*) candidato/a.
entreat [entrēt'] *vt* rogar, suplicar.
entrenched [entrencht'] *a*: **~ interests** intereses *mpl* creados.
entrepreneur [ântrəprənûr'] *n* empresario/a, capitalista *m/f*.
entrepreneurial [ântrəprənûr'ēəl] *a* empresarial.
entrust [entrust'] *vt*: **to ~ sth to sb** confiar algo a uno.
entry [en'trē] *n* entrada; (*permission to enter*) acceso; (*in register, diary, ship's log*) apunte *m*; (*in account book, ledger, list*) partida; **no ~** prohibido el paso; (*AUT*) dirección prohibida; **single/double ~ book-keeping** contabilidad *f* simple/por partida doble.
entry form *n* boleto de inscripción.
entry phone *n* (*Brit*) portero automático.
enumerate [inōō'mərāt] *vt* enumerar.
enunciate [inun'sēāt] *vt* pronunciar; (*principle etc*) enunciar.
envelop [envel'əp] *vt* envolver.
envelope [en'vəlōp] *n* sobre *m*.
enviable [en'vēəbəl] *a* envidiable.
envious [en'vēəs] *a* envidioso; (*look*) de envidia.
environment [envī'rənmənt] *n* medio ambiente; **Department of the E~** ministerio del medio ambiente.
environmental [envīrənmen'təl] *a* ambiental; **~ studies** (*in school etc*) ecología *sg*.
environmentalist [envīrənmen'təlist] *n* ecologista *m/f*.
environment-friendly [envī'rənmənt-frend'lē] *a* amigo del medio ambiente.
envisage [enviz'ij] *vt* (*foresee*) prever; (*imagine*) concebir.

envision [envizh'ən] *vt* imaginar.
envoy [en'voi] *n* enviado.
envy [en'vē] *n* envidia ♦ *vt* tener envidia a; **to ~ sb sth** envidiar algo a uno.
enzyme [en'zīm] *n* enzima.
eon [ē'ən] *n* (*US*) eón *m*.
EPA *n abbr* (*US*: = *Environmental Protection Agency*) Agencia del Medio Ambiente.
ephemeral [ifem'ûrəl] *a* efímero.
epic [ep'ik] *n* épica ♦ *a* épico.
epicenter, (*Brit*) **epicentre** [ep'isentûr] *n* epicentro.
epidemic [epidem'ik] *n* epidemia.
epigram [ep'igram] *n* epigrama *m*.
epilepsy [ep'əlepsē] *n* epilepsia.
epileptic [epəlep'tik] *a*, *n* epiléptico/a *m/f*.
epilogue [ep'əlôg] *n* epílogo.
episcopal [ipis'kəpəl] *a* episcopal.
episode [ep'isōd] *n* episodio.
epistle [ipis'əl] *n* epístola.
epitaph [ep'itaf] *n* epitafio.
epithet [ep'əthet] *n* epíteto.
epitome [ipit'əmē] *n* epítome *m*.
epitomize [ipit'əmīz] *vt* epitomar, resumir.
epoch [ep'ək] *n* época.
eponymous [epân'əməs] *a* epónimo.
equable [ek'wəbəl] *a* (*climate*) estable; (*character*) ecuánime.
equal [ē'kwəl] *a* (*gen*) igual; (*treatment*) equitativo ♦ *n* igual *m/f* ♦ *vt* ser igual a; (*fig*) igualar; **to be ~ to** (*task*) estar a la altura de; **the E~ Opportunities Commission** (*Brit*) comisión para la igualdad de la mujer en el trabajo.
equality [ikwâl'itē] *n* igualdad *f*.
equalize [ē'kwəlīz] *vt, vi* igualar; (*SPORT*) empatar.
equalizer [ē'kwəlīzûr] *n* igualada.
equally [ē'kwəlē] *ad* igualmente; (*share etc*) a partes iguales; **they are ~ clever** son iguales de inteligente.
equal(s) sign [ē'kwəl(z) sīn] *n* signo de igualdad.
equanimity [ēkwənim'itē] *n* ecuanimidad *f*.
equate [ikwāt'] *vt*: **to ~ sth with** equiparar algo con.
equation [ikwā'zhən] *n* (*MATH*) ecuación *f*.
equator [ikwā'tûr] *n* ecuador *m*.
equatorial [ēkwətôr'ēəl] *a* ecuatorial.
Equatorial Guinea *n* Guinea Ecuatorial.
equestrian [ikwes'trēən] *a* ecuestre ♦ *n* caballista *m/f*, jinete/a *m/f*.
equilibrium [ēkwəlib'rēəm] *n* equilibrio.
equinox [ē'kwənâks] *n* equinoccio.
equip [ikwip'] *vt* (*gen*) equipar; (*person*) proveer; **~ped with** (*machinery etc*) provisto de; **to be well ~ped** estar bien equipado; **he is well ~ped for the job** tiene las dotes necesarias para este puesto.
equipment [ikwip'mənt] *n* equipo; (*tools*) avíos *mpl*.
equitable [ek'witəbəl] *a* equitativo.
equities [ek'witēz] *npl* (*Brit COMM*) dere-

chos *mpl* sobre *or* en el activo.
equity [ek'witē] *n* (*fairness*) equidad *f*; (*ECON*: *of debtor*) valor *m* líquido.
equity capital *n* capital *m* social *or* en acciones.
equivalent [ikwiv'ələnt] *a*, *n* equivalente *m*; **to be ~ to** equivaler a.
equivocal [ikwiv'əkəl] *a* equívoco.
equivocate [ikwiv'əkāt] *vi* ser evasivo.
equivocation [ikwivəkā'shən] *n* evasión *f*, vacilación *f*.
ER *abbr* (*Brit*: = *Elizabeth Regina*) la reina Isabel.
ERA *n abbr* (*US POL*: = *Equal Rights Amendment*) enmienda sobre la igualdad de derechos de la mujer.
era [ē'rə] *n* era, época.
eradicate [irad'ikāt] *vt* erradicar, extirpar.
erase [irās'] *vt* (*also COMPUT*) borrar.
eraser [irā'sûr] *n* goma de borrar.
erect [irekt'] *a* erguido ♦ *vt* erigir, levantar; (*assemble*) montar.
erection [irek'shən] *n* (*of building*) construcción *f*; (*of machinery*) montaje *m*; (*structure*) edificio; (*MED*) erección *f*.
ergonomics [ûrgənám'iks] *n* ergonomía.
ERISA *n abbr* (*US*: = *Employee Retirement Income Security Act*) ley que regula pensiones de jubilados.
ermine [ûr'min] *n* armiño.
erode [irōd'] *vt* (*GEO*) erosionar; (*metal*) corroer, desgastar.
erosion [irō'zhən] *n* erosión *f*; desgaste *m*.
erotic [irât'ik] *a* erótico.
eroticism [irât'isizəm] *n* erotismo.
err [ûr] *vi* equivocarse; (*REL*) pecar.
errand [är'ənd] *n* recado, mandado (*LAm*); **to run ~s** hacer recados; **~ of mercy** acto caritativo.
errand boy *n* recadero.
erratic [irat'ik] *a* variable; (*results etc*) desigual, poco uniforme.
erroneous [irō'nēəs] *a* erróneo.
error [är'ûr] *n* error *m*, equivocación *f*; **typing/spelling ~** error *m* de mecanografía/ortografía; **in ~** por equivocación; **~s and omissions excepted** salvo error u omisión.
error message *n* (*COMPUT*) mensaje *m* de error.
erstwhile [ûrst'hwīl] *a* antiguo, previo.
erudite [är'yōōdit] *a* erudito.
erudition [äryōōdish'ən] *n* erudición *f*.
erupt [irupt'] *vi* entrar en erupción; (*MED*) hacer erupción; (*fig*) estallar.
eruption [irup'shən] *n* erupción *f*; (*fig*: *of anger, violence*) explosión *f*, estallido.
ESA *n abbr* (= *European Space Agency*) Agencia Espacial Europea.
escalate [es'kəlāt] *vi* extenderse, intensificarse; (*costs*) aumentar vertiginosamente.
escalation clause [eskəlā'shən klôz] *n*

cláusula de reajuste de los precios.
escalator [es'kəlātûr] *n* escalera móvil.
escapade [es'kəpād] *n* travesura.
escape [eskāp'] *n* (*gen*) fuga; (*from duties*) escapatoria; (*from chase*) evasión *f* ♦ *vi* (*gen*) escaparse; (*flee*) huir, evadirse; (*leak*) fugarse ♦ *vt* evitar, eludir; (*consequences*) escapar a; **to ~ from** (*place*) escaparse de; (*person*) escaparse a; (*clutches*) librarse de; **to ~ to** (*another place, freedom, safety*) huirse a; **to ~ notice** pasar desapercibido.
escape artist *n* escapólogo/a.
escape clause *n* (*fig*: *in agreement*) cláusula de excepción.
escape hatch *n* (*in submarine, space rocket*) escotilla de salvamento.
escape key *n* (*COMPUT*) tecla de escape.
escape route *n* ruta de escape.
escapism [eskā'pizəm] *n* escapismo.
escapist [eskā'pist] *a*, *n* escapista *m/f*.
escapologist [eskəpâl'əjist] *n* (*Brit*) = **escape artist**.
escarpment [eskârp'mənt] *n* escarpa.
eschew [eschōō'] *vt* evitar, abstenerse de.
escort *n* [es'kôrt] acompañante *m/f*; (*MIL*) escolta; (*NAUT*) convoy *m* ♦ *vt* [eskôrt'] acompañar; (*MIL, NAUT*) escoltar.
escort agency *n* servicio de azafatas.
Eskimo [es'kəmō] *a* esquimal ♦ *n* esquimal *m/f*; (*LING*) esquimal *m*.
ESL *n abbr* (*SCOL*) = *English as a Second Language*.
esophagus [isâf'əgəs] *n* (*US*) esófago.
esoteric [esətär'ik] *a* esotérico.
ESP *n abbr* = **extrasensory perception**.
esp. *abbr* = **especially**.
especially [espesh'əlē] *ad* (*gen*) especialmente; (*above all*) sobre todo; (*particularly*) en particular.
espionage [es'pēənâzh] *n* espionaje *m*.
esplanade [esplənād'] *n* (*by sea*) paseo marítimo.
espouse [espouz'] *vt* adherirse a.
Esq. *abbr* (= *Esquire*) D.
Esquire [es'kwiûr] *n*: **J. Brown, ~** Sr. D. J. Brown.
essay [es'ā] *n* (*SCOL*) ensayo.
essayist [es'āist] *n* ensayista *m/f*.
essence [es'əns] *n* esencia; **in ~** en lo esencial; **speed is of the ~** es esencial hacerlo con la mayor prontitud.
essential [əsen'chəl] *a* (*necessary*) imprescindible; (*basic*) esencial ♦ *n* (*often pl*) lo esencial; **it is ~ that** es imprescindible que.
essentially [əsen'chəlē] *ad* esencialmente.
EST *n abbr* (*US*: = *Eastern Standard Time*) hora de invierno de Nueva York.
est. *abbr* (= *established*) fundado; (= *estimated*) aprox.
establish [əstab'lish] *vt* establecer; (*prove*: *fact, identity*) comprobar, verificar;

(*prove*) demostrar; (*relations*) entablar.
established [əstab'lisht] *a* (*business*) de buena reputación; (*staff*) de plantilla.
establishment [əstab'lishmənt] *n* (*also business*) establecimiento; **the E~** la clase dirigente; **a teaching** ~ un centro de enseñanza.
estate [əstāt'] *n* (*land*) finca, hacienda; (*property*) propiedad *f*; (*inheritance*) herencia; (*POL*) estado; **housing** ~ (*Brit*) urbanización *f*; **industrial** ~ polígono industrial.
estate agent *n* (*Brit*) agente *m/f* inmobiliario/a.
estate car *n* (*Brit*) furgoneta.
esteem [əstēm'] *n*: **to hold sb in high** ~ estimar en mucho a uno ♦ *vt* estimar.
esthetic [esthet'ik] *a* (*US*) estético.
estimate *n* [es'təmit] estimación *f*, apreciación *f*; (*assessment*) tasa, cálculo; (*COMM*) presupuesto ♦ *vt* [es'təmāt] estimar; tasar, calcular; **to give sb an** ~ **of** presentar a uno un presupuesto de; **at a rough** ~ haciendo un cálculo aproximado.
estimation [estəmā'shən] *n* opinión *f*, juicio; (*esteem*) aprecio; **in my** ~ según mis cálculos.
estimator [es'təmātûr] *n* estimador(a) *m/f*.
Estonia [estō'nēə] *n* Estonia.
estranged [estrānjd'] *a* separado.
estrangement [estrānj'mənt] *n* alejamiento, distanciamiento.
estrogen [es'trəjən] *n* (*US*) estrógeno.
estuary [es'chōōárē] *n* estuario, ría.
ETA *n abbr* = *estimated time of arrival*.
et al. *abbr* (= *et alii: and others*) et al.
etc *abbr* (= *et cetera*) etc.
etch [ech] *vt* grabar al aguafuerte.
etching [ech'ing] *n* aguafuerte *m or f*.
ETD *n abbr* = *estimated time of departure*.
eternal [itûr'nəl] *a* eterno.
eternity [itûr'nitē] *n* eternidad *f*.
ether [ē'thûr] *n* éter *m*.
ethereal [ithēr'ēəl] *a* etéreo.
ethical [eth'ikəl] *a* ético; (*honest*) honrado.
ethics [eth'iks] *n* ética ♦ *npl* moralidad *f*.
Ethiopia [ēthēō'pēə] *n* Etiopía.
Ethiopian [ēthēō'pēən] *a, n* etíope *m/f*.
ethnic [eth'nik] *a* étnico.
ethos [ē'thás] *n* (*of culture, group*) sistema *m* de valores.
etiquette [et'əkit] *n* etiqueta.
ETV *n abbr* (*US*: = *Educational Television*) televisión escolar.
etymology [etəmál'əjē] *n* etimología.
eucalyptus [yōōkəlip'təs] *n* eucalipto.
Eucharist [yōō'kúrist] *n* Eucaristía.
eulogy [yōō'ləjē] *n* elogio, encomio.
eunuch [yōō'nək] *n* eunuco.
euphemism [yōō'fəmizəm] *n* eufemismo.
euphemistic [yōōfəmis'tik] *a* eufemístico.
euphoria [yōōfôr'ēə] *n* euforia.
Eurasia [yōōrā'zhə] *n* Eurasia.

Eurasian [yōōrā'zhən] *a, n* eurasiático/a *m/f*.
Euratom [yōōrat'əm] *n abbr* (= *European Atomic Energy Commission*) Euratom *m*.
Euro... [yōō'rō] *pref* Euro....
Eurocheque [yōō'rōchek] *n* (*Brit*) Eurocheque *m*.
Eurocrat [yōō'rəkrat] *n* eurócrata *m/f*.
Eurodollar [yōō'rōdâlûr] *n* eurodólar *m*.
Europe [yōō'rəp] *n* Europa.
European [yōōrəpē'ən] *a, n* europeo/a *m/f*.
European Court of Justice *n* Tribunal *m* de Justicia de las Comunidades Europeas.
European Economic Community *n* Comunidad *f* Económica Europea.
euthanasia [yōōthənā'zhə] *n* eutanasia.
evacuate [ivak'yōōāt] *vt* desocupar.
evacuation [ivakyōōā'shən] *n* evacuación *f*.
evade [ivād'] *vt* evadir, eludir.
evaluate [ival'yōōāt] *vt* evaluar; (*value*) tasar; (*evidence*) interpretar.
evangelical [ēvanjel'ikəl] *a* evangélico.
evangelist [ivan'jəlist] *n* evangelista *m*; (*preacher*) evangelizador(a) *m/f*.
evaporate [ivap'ərāt] *vi* evaporarse; (*fig*) desvanecerse ♦ *vt* evaporar.
evaporated milk [ivap'ərātid milk'] *n* leche *f* evaporada.
evaporation [ivapərā'shən] *n* evaporación *f*.
evasion [ivā'zhən] *n* evasiva, evasión *f*.
evasive [ivā'siv] *a* evasivo.
eve [ēv] *n*: **on the** ~ **of** en vísperas de.
even [ē'vən] *a* (*level*) llano; (*smooth*) liso; (*speed, temperature*) uniforme; (*number*) par; (*SPORT*) igual(es) ♦ *ad* hasta, incluso; ~ **if**, ~ **though** aunque + *subjun*; ~ **more** aun más; ~ **so** aun así; **not** ~ ni siquiera; ~ **he was there** hasta él estuvo allí; ~ **on Sundays** incluso los domingos; ~ **faster** aún más rápido; **to break** ~ cubrir los gastos; **to get** ~ **with sb** ajustar cuentas con uno; **to** ~ **out** *vi* nivelarse.
evening [ēv'ning] *n* tarde *f*; (*dusk*) atardecer *m*; (*night*) noche *f*; **in the** ~ por la tarde; **this** ~ esta tarde *or* noche; **tomorrow/yesterday** ~ mañana/ayer por la tarde *or* noche.
evening class *n* clase *f* nocturna.
evening dress *n* (*man's*) traje *m* de etiqueta; (*woman's*) traje *m* de noche.
evenly [ē'vənlē] *ad* (*distribute, space, spread*) con igualdad, igualmente; (*divide*) equitativamente.
evensong [ē'vənsông] *n* vísperas *fpl*.
event [ivent'] *n* suceso, acontecimiento; (*SPORT*) prueba; **in the** ~ **of** en caso de; **in the** ~ en realidad; **in the course of** ~s en el curso de los acontecimientos; **in any** ~ pase lo que pase.
eventful [ivent'fəl] *a* accidentado; (*game etc*) lleno de emoción.
eventual [iven'chōōəl] *a* final.
eventuality [ivenchōōal'itē] *n* eventualidad

f.

eventually [ivɛn'chōōəlē] *ad* (*finally*) finalmente; (*in time*) a la larga.

ever [ɛv'ûr] *ad* nunca, jamás; (*at all times*) siempre; **for ~** (para) siempre; **the best ~** lo nunca visto; **did you ~ meet him?** ¿llegaste a conocerle?; **have you ~ been there?** ¿has estado allí alguna vez?; **have you ~ seen it?** ¿lo ha visto usted alguna vez?; **better than ~** mejor que nunca; **thank you ~ so much** muchísimas gracias; **yours ~** (*in letters*) un abrazo de; **~ since** *ad* desde entonces ♦ *conj* después de que.

Everest [ɛv'ûrist] *n* (*also*: **Mount ~**) Everest *m.*

evergreen [ɛv'ûrgrēn] *n* árbol *m* de hoja perenne.

everlasting [ɛvûrlas'ting] *a* eterno, perpetuo.

every [ɛv'rē] *a* (*each*) cada; (*all*) todo; **~ day** cada día; **~ other car** cada dos coches; **~ now and then** de vez en cuando; **I have ~ confidence in him** confío completamente en él.

everybody [ɛv'rēbâdē] *pron* todos *pl*, todo el mundo; **~ knows about it** todo el mundo lo sabe; **~ else** todos los demás.

everyday [ɛv'rēdā] *a* (*daily*: *use*, *occurrence*, *experience*) diario, cotidiano; (*usual*: *expression*) corriente; (*common*) vulgar; (*routine*) rutinario.

everyone [ɛv'rēwun] = **everybody.**

everything [ɛv'rēthing] *pron* todo; **~ is ready** todo está dispuesto; **he did ~ possible** hizo todo lo posible.

everywhere [ɛv'rēhwär] *ad* (*be*) en todas partes; (*go*) a *or* por todas partes; **~ you go you meet...** en todas partes encontrarás....

evict [ivikt'] *vt* desahuciar.

eviction [ivik'shən] *n* desahucio.

eviction notice *n* orden *f* de desahucio *or* desalojo (*LAm*).

evidence [ɛv'idəns] *n* (*proof*) prueba; (*of witness*) testimonio; (*facts*) datos *mpl*, hechos *mpl*; **to give ~** prestar declaración, dar testimonio.

evident [ɛv'idənt] *a* evidente, manifiesto.

evidently [ɛv'idəntlē] *ad* naturalmente.

evil [ē'vəl] *a* malo; (*influence*) funesto; (*smell*) horrible ♦ *n* mal *m*, maldad *f.*

evildoer [ē'vəldōōûr] *n* malhechor(a) *m/f.*

evince [ivins'] *vt* mostrar, dar señales de.

evocative [ivák'ətiv] *a* sugestivo, evocador(a).

evoke [ivōk'] *vt* evocar; (*admiration*) provocar.

evolution [ɛvəlōō'shən] *n* evolución *f*, desarrollo.

evolve [iválv'] *vt* desarrollar ♦ *vi* evolucionar, desarrollarse.

ewe [yōō] *n* oveja.

ex- [ɛks] *pref* (*former*: *husband*, *president etc*) ex-; (*out of*): **the price ~works** precio de fábrica.

exacerbate [igzas'ûrbāt] *vt* (*pain*, *disease*) exacerbar; (*fig*: *relations*, *situation*) empeorar.

exact [igzakt'] *a* exacto ♦ *vt*: **to ~ sth (from)** exigir algo (de).

exacting [igzak'ting] *a* exigente; (*conditions*) arduo.

exactitude [igzakt'ətōōd] *n* exactitud *f.*

exactly [igzakt'lē] *ad* exactamente; (*time*) en punto; **~!** ¡exactamente!

exactness [igzakt'nis] *n* exactitud *f.*

exaggerate [igzaj'ərāt] *vt*, *vi* exagerar.

exaggerated [igzaj'ərātid] *a* exagerado.

exaggeration [igzajərā'shən] *n* exageración *f.*

exalt [igzôlt'] *vt* (*praise*) ensalzar; (*elevate*) elevar, exaltar.

exalted [igzôl'tid] *a* (*position*) exaltado; (*elated*) excitado.

exam [igzam'] *n abbr* (*SCOL*) = **examination.**

examination [igzamənā'shən] *n* (*gen*) examen *m*; (*LAW*) interrogación *f*; (*inquiry*) investigación *f*; **to take an ~** hacer un examen; **the matter is under ~** se está examinando el asunto.

examine [igzam'in] *vt* (*gen*) examinar; (*inspect*: *machine*, *premises*) inspeccionar; (*SCOL, LAW*: *person*) interrogar; (*at customs*: *baggage*, *passport*) registrar; (*MED*) hacer un reconocimiento médico de.

examiner [igzam'inûr] *n* inspector(a) *m/f.*

example [igzam'pəl] *n* ejemplo; **for ~** por ejemplo; **to set a good/bad ~** dar buen/mal ejemplo.

exasperate [igzas'pərāt] *vt* exasperar, irritar; **~d by** *or* **at** *or* **with** exasperado por *or* con.

exasperating [igzas'pərāting] *a* irritante.

exasperation [igzaspərā'shən] *n* exasperación *f*, irritación *f.*

excavate [ɛks'kəvāt] *vt* excavar.

excavation [ɛks'kəvā'shən] *n* excavación *f.*

excavator [ɛks'kəvātûr] *n* excavadora.

exceed [iksēd'] *vt* exceder; (*number*) pasar de; (*speed limit*) sobrepasar; (*limits*) rebasar; (*powers*) excederse en; (*hopes*) superar.

exceedingly [iksē'dinglē] *ad* sumamente, sobremanera.

excel [iksɛl'] *vi* sobresalir.

excellence [ɛk'sələns] *n* excelencia.

Excellency [ɛk'sɛlənsē] *n*: **His ~** Su Excelencia.

excellent [ɛk'sələnt] *a* excelente.

except [iksɛpt'] *prep* (*also*: **~ for**, **~ing**) excepto, salvo ♦ *vt* exceptuar, excluir; **~ if/when** excepto si/cuando; **~ that** salvo que.

exception [iksɛp'shən] *n* excepción *f*; **to**

take ~ to ofenderse por; **with the ~ of** a excepción de; **to make an ~** hacer una excepción.

exceptional [iksep'shənəl] *a* excepcional.

excerpt [ek'sûrpt] *n* extracto.

excess [ekses'] *n* exceso; **in ~ of** superior a; *see also* **excesses**.

excess baggage *n* exceso de equipaje.

excesses [ekses'iz] *npl* excesos *mpl*.

excess fare *n* suplemento.

excessive [ikses'iv] *a* excesivo.

excess supply *n* oferta excedentaria.

excess weight *n* exceso de peso.

exchange [ikschānj'] *n* cambio; (*of goods*) canje *m*; (*of ideas*) intercambio; (*also:* **telephone ~**) central *f* (telefónica) ♦ *vt:* **to ~ (for)** cambiar (por); **in ~ for** a cambio de; **foreign ~** (*COMM*) divisas *fpl*.

exchange control *n* control *m* de cambios.

exchange rate *n* tipo de cambio.

exchequer [eks'chekûr] *n:* **the ~** (*Brit*) la Hacienda del Fisco.

excisable [iksī'zəbəl] *a* taxable.

excise [ek'sīz] *n* impuestos *mpl* sobre el comercio exterior.

excitable [iksī'təbəl] *a* exaltado.

excite [iksīt'] *vt* (*stimulate*) estimular; (*anger*) provocar; (*move*) entusiasmar; **to get ~d** emocionarse.

excitement [iksīt'mənt] *n* emoción *f*.

exciting [iksī'ting] *a* emocionante.

excl. *abbr* = **excluding**; **exclusive (of)**.

exclaim [iksklām'] *vi* exclamar.

exclamation [ekskləmā'shən] *n* exclamación *f*.

exclamation mark *n* punto de admiración.

exclude [iksklōōd'] *vt* excluir; (*except*) exceptuar.

excluding [iksklōō'ding] *prep:* **~ tax** impuesto no incluido.

exclusion [iksklōō'zhən] *n* exclusión *f;* **to the ~ of** con exclusión de.

exclusion clause *n* cláusula de exclusión.

exclusive [iksklōō'siv] *a* exclusivo; (*club, district*) selecto; **~ of tax** excluyendo impuestos; **~ of postage/service** franqueo/ servicio no incluido; **from the 1st to the 13th March ~** del 1 al 13 de marzo exclusive.

exclusively [iksklōō'sivlē] *ad* únicamente.

excommunicate [ekskəmyōō'nəkāt] *vt* excomulgar.

excrement [eks'krəmənt] *n* excremento.

excrete [ikskrēt'] *vi* excretar.

excruciating [ikskrōō'shēāting] *a* (*pain*) agudísimo, atroz.

excursion [ikskûr'zhən] *n* excursión *f*.

excursion ticket *n* billete *m* de excursión.

excusable [ikskyōō'zəbəl] *a* perdonable.

excuse *n* [ikskyōōs'] disculpa, excusa; (*evasion*) pretexto ♦ *vt* [ikskyōōz'] disculpar,

perdonar; (*justify*) justificar; **to make ~s for sb** presentar disculpas por uno; **to ~ sb from doing sth** dispensar a uno de hacer algo; **to ~ o.s. (for (doing) sth)** pedir disculpas a uno (por (hacer) algo); **~ me!** ¡perdón!; **if you will ~ me** con su permiso.

ex-directory [eksdirek'tûrē] *a* (*Brit*): **~ (phone) number** número que no consta en la guía.

exec. [igzek'] *n abbr* = **executive**.

execrable [ek'səkrəbəl] *a* execrable, abominable; (*manners*) detestable.

execute [ek'səkyōōt] *vt* (*plan*) realizar; (*order*) cumplir; (*person*) ajusticiar, ejecutar.

execution [eksəkyōō'shən] *n* realización *f;* cumplimiento; ejecución *f*.

executioner [eksəkyōō'shənûr] *n* verdugo.

executive [igzek'yətiv] *n* (*COMM*) ejecutivo; (*POL*) poder *m* ejecutivo ♦ *a* (*secretary, car, plane*) ejecutivo; (*offices, suite*) de los ejecutivos; (*position, job, duties*) de ejecutivo.

executive director *n* director(a) *m/f* ejecutivo/a.

executor [igzek'yətûr] *n* albacea *m*, testamentario.

exemplary [igzem'plûrē] *a* ejemplar.

exemplify [igzem'pləfī] *vt* ejemplificar.

exempt [igzempt'] *a:* **~ from** exento de ♦ *vt:* **to ~ sb from** eximir a uno de.

exemption [igzemp'shən] *n* exención *f;* (*immunity*) inmunidad *f*.

exercise [ek'sûrsīz] *n* ejercicio ♦ *vt* ejercer; (*right*) valerse de; (*dog*) llevar de paseo ♦ *vi* hacer ejercicio(s).

exercise book *n* cuaderno.

exert [igzûrt'] *vt* ejercer; (*strength, force*) emplear; **to ~ o.s.** esforzarse.

exertion [igzûr'shən] *n* esfuerzo.

exfoliant [eksfō'lēənt] *n* exfoliante *m*.

ex gratia [eks grā'tēə] *a:* **~ payment** pago a título gracioso.

exhale [eks·hāl'] *vt* despedir ♦ *vi* espirar, exhalar.

exhaust [igzôst'] *n* (*pipe*) escape *m;* (*fumes*) gases *mpl* de escape ♦ *vt* agotar; **to ~ o.s.** agotarse.

exhausted [igzôs'tid] *a* agotado.

exhausting [igzôs'ting] *a:* **an ~ journey/ day** un viaje/día agotador.

exhaustion [igzôs'chən] *n* agotamiento; **nervous ~** postración *f* nerviosa.

exhaustive [igzôs'tiv] *a* exhaustivo.

exhibit [igzib'it] *n* (*ART*) obra expuesta; (*LAW*) objeto expuesto ♦ *vt* (*show: emotions*) manifestar; (: *courage, skill*) demostrar; (*paintings*) exponer.

exhibition [eksəbish'ən] *n* exposición *f*.

exhibitionist [eksəbish'ənist] *n* exhibicionista *m/f*.

exhibitor [igzib'ətûr] *n* expositor(a) *m/f*.

exhilarating [igzil'ərāting] *a* estimulante, tó-

nico.
exhilaration [igzilərā'shən] *n* júbilo.
exhort [igzórt'] *vt* exhortar.
exile [eg'zīl] *n* exilio; (*person*) exiliado/a ♦ *vt* desterrar, exiliar.
exist [igzist'] *vi* existir.
existence [igzis'təns] *n* existencia.
existentialism [egzisten'chəlizəm] *n* existencialismo.
existing [igzis'ting] *a* existente, actual.
exit [eg'zit] *n* salida ♦ *vi* (*THEATER*) hacer mutis; (*COMPUT*) salir (al sistema).
exit poll *n* (*POL*) sondeo de votos a posteriori.
exit ramp *n* (*US AUT*) vía de acceso.
exit visa *n* visado de salida.
exodus [ek'sədəs] *n* éxodo.
ex officio [eks əfish'ēō] *a, ad* ex oficio.
exonerate [igzân'ərāt] *vt*: **to ~ from** exculpar de.
exorbitant [igzôr'bətənt] *a* (*price, demands*) exorbitante, excesivo.
exorcize [ek'sôrsīz] *vt* exorcizar.
exotic [igzât'ik] *a* exótico.
exp. *abbr* = **expenses; expired; export; express**.
expand [ikspand'] *vt* ampliar; (*number*) aumentar ♦ *vi* (*trade etc*) expandirse; (*gas, metal*) dilatarse; **to ~ on** (*notes, story etc*) ampliar.
expanse [ikspans'] *n* extensión *f*.
expansion [ikspan'chən] *n* ampliación *f*; aumento; (*of trade*) expansión *f*.
expansionism [ikspan'chənizəm] *n* expansionismo.
expansionist [ikspan'chənist] *a* expansionista.
expatriate [ikspā'trēit] *n* expatriado/a.
expect [ikspekt'] *vt* (*gen*) esperar; (*count on*) contar con; (*suppose*) suponer ♦ *vi*: **to be ~ing** estar encinta; **to ~ to do sth** esperar hacer algo; **as ~ed** como era de esperar; **I ~ so** supongo que sí.
expectancy [ikspek'tənsē] *n* (*anticipation*) esperanza; **life ~** esperanza de vida.
expectantly [ikspek'təntlē] *ad* (*look, listen*) con expectación.
expectant mother [ikspek'tənt muth'ûr] *n* futura madre *f*.
expectation [ekspektā'shən] *n* esperanza, expectativa; **in ~ of** en espera de; **against** *or* **contrary to all ~(s)** en contra de todas las previsiones; **to come** *or* **live up to sb's ~s** resultar tan bueno como se esperaba; **to fall short of sb's ~s** no cumplir las esperanzas de uno, decepcionar a uno.
expedience [ikspē'dēəns], **expediency** [ikspē'dēənsē] *n* conveniencia.
expedient [ikspē'dēənt] *a* conveniente, oportuno ♦ *n* recurso, expediente *m*.
expedite [ek'spidīt] *vt* (*speed up*) acelerar; (: *progress*) facilitar.
expedition [ekspədish'ən] *n* expedición *f*.

expeditionary force [ekspədish'ənärē fôrs] *n* cuerpo expedicionario.
expel [ikspel'] *vt* arrojar; (*SCOL*) expulsar.
expend [ikspend'] *vt* gastar; (*use up*) consumir.
expendable [ikspen'dəbəl] *a* prescindible.
expenditure [ikspen'dichûr] *n* gastos *mpl*, desembolso; (*of time, effort*) gasto.
expense [ikspens'] *n* gasto, gastos *mpl*; (*high cost*) costa; **~s** *npl* (*COMM*) gastos *mpl*; **at the ~ of** a costa de; **to meet the ~ of** hacer frente a los gastos de.
expense account *n* cuenta de gastos.
expensive [ikspen'siv] *a* caro, costoso.
experience [ikspēr'ēəns] *n* experiencia ♦ *vt* experimentar; (*suffer*) sufrir; **to learn by ~** aprender por experiencia.
experienced [ikspēr'ēənst] *a* experimentado.
experiment *n* [ikspär'əmənt] experimento ♦ *vi* [ikspär'əment] hacer experimentos; **to perform** *or* **carry out an ~** realizar un experimento; **as an ~** como experimento; **to ~ with a new vaccine** experimentar con una vacuna nueva.
experimental [ikspärəmen'təl] *a* experimental; **the process is still at the ~ stage** el proceso está todavía en prueba.
expert [ek'spûrt] *a* experto, perito ♦ *n* experto/a, perito/a; (*specialist*) especialista *m/f*; **~ witness** (*LAW*) testigo pericial; **~ in** *or* **at doing sth** experto *or* perito en hacer algo; **an ~ on sth** un experto en algo.
expertise [ekspûrtēz'] *n* pericia.
expiration [ekspərā'shən] *n* (*gen*) expiración *f*, vencimiento.
expire [ikspī'ûr] *vi* (*gen*) caducar, vencerse.
expiry [ikspiûr'ē] *n* vencimiento.
explain [iksplān'] *vt* explicar; (*mystery*) aclarar.
explain away *vt* justificar.
explanation [eksplənā'shən] *n* explicación *f*; aclaración *f*; **to find an ~ for sth** encontrarle una explicación a algo.
explanatory [iksplan'ətôrē] *a* explicativo; aclaratorio.
explicable [eksplik'əbəl] *a* explicable.
explicit [iksplis'it] *a* explícito.
explicitly [iksplis'itlē] *ad* explícitamente.
explode [iksplōd'] *vi* estallar, explotar; (*with anger*) reventar ♦ *vt* volar, explotar; (*fig: theory*) desacreditar, refutar; **to ~ a myth** demoler un mito.
exploit *n* [eks'ploit] hazaña ♦ *vt* [iksploit'] explotar.
exploitation [eksploitā'shən] *n* explotación *f*.
exploration [eksplərā'shən] *n* exploración *f*.
exploratory [iksplôr'ətôrē] *a* (*fig: talks*) exploratorio, preliminar.
explore [iksplôr'] *vt* explorar; (*fig*) examinar, sondear.
explorer [iksplôr'ûr] *n* explorador(a) *m/f*.

explosion [iksplō'zhən] *n* explosión *f*.

explosive [iksplō'siv] *a*, *n* explosivo.

exponent [ekspō'nent] *n* partidario/a, intérprete *m/f*.

export *vt* [ikspôrt'] exportar ♦ *n* [eks'pôrt] exportación *f* ♦ *cpd* [eks'pôrt] de exportación.

exportation [ekspôrtā'shən] *n* exportación *f*.

export drive *n* campaña de exportación.

exporter [ekspôr'tûr] *n* exportador(a) *m/f*.

export license *n* licencia de exportación.

export manager *n* gerente *m/f* de exportación.

export trade *n* comercio exterior.

expose [ikspōz'] *vt* exponer; (*unmask*) desenmascarar.

exposé [ekspōzā'] *n* revelación *f*.

exposed [ikspōzd'] *a* expuesto; (*land, house*) desprotegido; (*ELEC*: *wire*) al aire; (*pipe, beam*) al descubierto.

exposition [ekspəzish'ən] *n* exposición *f*.

exposure [ikspō'zhûr] *n* exposición *f*; (*PHOT*: *speed*) velocidad *f* de obturación (: *shot*) fotografía; **to die from ~** (*MED*) morir de frío.

exposure meter *n* fotómetro.

expound [ikspound'] *vt* exponer; (*theory, text*) comentar; (*one's views*) explicar.

express [ikspres'] *a* (*definite*) expreso, explícito; (*Brit*: *letter etc*) urgente ♦ *n* (*train*) rápido ♦ *ad* (*send*) por correo extraordinario ♦ *vt* expresar; (*squeeze*) exprimir; **to send sth ~** enviar algo por correo urgente; **to ~ o.s.** expresarse.

expression [ikspresh'ən] *n* expresión *f*.

expressionism [ikspresh'ənizəm] *n* expresionismo.

expressive [ikspres'iv] *a* expresivo.

expressly [ikspres'lē] *ad* expresamente.

expressway [ikspres'wā] *n* (*urban freeway*) autopista.

expropriate [eksprōp'rēāt] *vt* expropiar.

expulsion [ikspul'shən] *n* expulsión *f*.

expurgate [eks'pûrgāt] *vt* expurgar.

exquisite [ekskwiz'it] *a* exquisito.

exquisitely [ekskwiz'itlē] *ad* exquisitamente.

ex-serviceman [ekssûr'vismən] *n* (*Brit*) ex-combatiente *m*.

ext. *abbr* (*TEL*) = **extension.**

extemporize [ikstem'pərīz] *vi* improvisar.

extend [ikstend'] *vt* (*visit, street*) prolongar; (*building*) ensanchar; (*thanks, friendship etc*) extender; (*COMM*: *credit*) prorrogar, alargar; (*deadline*) prorrogar ♦ *vi* (*land*) extenderse; **the contract ~s to/ for ...** el contrato se prolonga hasta/por ....

extension [iksten'chən] *n* extensión *f*; (*building*) ampliación *f*; (*TEL*: *line*) línea derivada; (: *telephone*) extensión *f*; (*of deadline*) prórroga; **~ 3718** extensión 3718.

extension cord *n* (*ELEC*) extensión *f*.

extensive [iksten'siv] *a* (*gen*) extenso; (*damage*) importante; (*knowledge*) amplio.

extensively [iksten'sivlē] *ad* (*altered, damaged etc*) extensamente; **he's traveled ~** ha viajado por muchos países.

extent [ikstent'] *n* (*breadth*) extensión *f*; (*scope*: *of knowledge, activities*) alcance *m*; (*degree*: *of damage, loss*) grado; **to some ~** hasta cierto punto; **to a certain ~** hasta cierto punto; **to a large ~** en gran parte; **to the ~ of...** hasta el punto de...; **to such an ~ that...** hasta tal punto que...; **to what ~?** ¿hasta qué punto?; **debts to the ~ of $5000** deudas por la cantidad de $5000.

extenuating [iksten'yōōāting] *a*: **~ circumstances** circunstancias *fpl* atenuantes.

exterior [ikstēr'ēûr] *a* exterior, externo ♦ *n* exterior *m*.

exterminate [ikstûr'mənāt] *vt* exterminar.

extermination [ikstûrmənā'shən] *n* exterminación *f*.

extern [eks'tûrn] *n* (*US MED*) externo/a.

external [ikstûr'nəl] *a* externo, exterior ♦ *n*: **the ~s** las apariencias; **~ affairs** asuntos *mpl* exteriores; **for ~ use only** (*MED*) para uso tópico.

externally [ikstûr'nəlē] *ad* por fuera.

extinct [ikstingkt'] *a* (*volcano*) extinguido; (*race*) extinto.

extinction [ikstingk'shən] *n* extinción *f*.

extinguish [iksting'gwish] *vt* extinguir, apagar.

extinguisher [iksting'gwishûr] *n* extintor *m*.

extoll, (*Brit*) **extol** [ikstōl'] *vt* (*merits, virtues*) ensalzar, alabar; (*person*) alabar, elogiar.

extort [ikstôrt'] *vt* sacar a la fuerza.

extortion [ikstôr'shən] *n* exacción *f*.

extortionate [ikstôr'shənit] *a* excesivo, exorbitante.

extra [eks'trə] *a* adicional ♦ *ad* (*in addition*) de más ♦ *n* (*addition*) extra *m*, suplemento; (*THEATER*) extra *m/f*, comparsa *m/f*; (*newspaper*) edición *f* extraordinaria; **wine will cost ~** el vino no está incluido (en el precio); **~ large sizes** tamaños grandes; *see also* **extras.**

extra... *pref* extra... .

extract *vt* [ikstrakt'] sacar; (*tooth*) extraer; (*confession*) arrancar, obtener ♦ *n* [eks'trakt] extracto.

extraction [ikstrak'shən] *n* extracción *f*; (*origin*) origen *m*.

extracurricular [ekstrəkərik'yəlûr] *a* (*SCOL*) extraescolar, extra-académico.

extradite [eks'trədīt] *vt* extraditar.

extradition [ekstrədish'ən] *n* extradición *f*.

extramarital [ekstrəmar'itəl] *a* extramatrimonial.

extramural [ekstrəmyōōr'əl] *a* extraescolar.

extraneous [ikstrā'nēəs] *a* extraño, ajeno.

extraordinary [ikstrôr'dənärē] *a* extraordinario; (*odd*) raro; **the ~ thing is that ...** la cosa más extraordinaria es que ....

extraordinary general meeting *n*
junta general extraordinaria.
extrapolation [ikstrapəlä'shən] *n* extrapola-
ción *f*.
extras [eks'trəz] *npl* (*additional expense*) extras *mpl*.
extrasensory perception (ESP)
[ekstrəsen'sûrē pûrsep'shən] *n* percepción *f*
extrasensorial.
extra time *n* (*SOCCER*) prórroga.
extravagance [ikstrav'əgəns] *n* (*excessive
spending*) derroche *m*; (*thing bought*) extravagancia.
extravagant [ikstrav'əgənt] *a* (*lavish*) pródigo; (*wasteful*) derrochador(a); (*price*)
exorbitante; (*praise*) excesivo.
extreme [ikstrēm'] *a* extremo; (*poverty etc*)
extremado; (*case*) excepcional ♦ *n* extremo; **the ~ left/right** (*POL*) la extrema
izquierda/derecha; **~s of temperature**
temperaturas extremas.
extremely [ikstrēm'lē] *ad* sumamente, ex-
tremadamente.
extremist [ikstrē'mist] *a, n* extremista *m/f*.
extremity [ikstrem'itē] *n* extremidad *f*,
punta; (*need*) apuro, necesidad *f*; **extremities** *npl* (*hands and feet*) extremidades *fpl*.
extricate [ek'strikāt] *vt*: **to ~ o.s. from** librarse de.
extrovert [ek'strōvûrt] *n* extrovertido/a.
exuberance [igzoo'būrəns] *n* exuberancia.
exuberant [igzoo'būrənt] *a* (*person*) eufórico; (*style*) exuberante.
exude [igzood'] *vt* rezumar, sudar.
exult [igzult'] *vi* regocijarse.
exultant [igzul'tənt] *a* (*person, smile*) rego-
cijado, jubiloso; (*shout, expression*) jubiloso.
exultation [egzultā'shən] *n* regocijo, júbilo;
in ~ en exultación.
eye [ī] *n* ojo ♦ *vt* mirar de soslayo, ojear; **to
keep an ~ on** vigilar; **as far as the ~ can
see** hasta donde alcanza la vista; **to have
an ~ for sth** tener mucha vista *or* buen ojo
para algo; **there's more to this than
meets the ~** esto tiene su miga.
eyeball [ī'bôl] *n* globo del ojo.
eyebath [ī'bath] *n* (*Brit*) = **eye cup.**
eyebrow [ī'brou] *n* ceja.
eyebrow pencil *n* lápiz *m* de cejas.
eye-catching [ī'kaching] *a* llamativo.
eye cup *n* (*US*) baño para ojos.
eyedrops [ī'drâps] *npl* gotas *fpl* para los
ojos.
eyelash [ī'lash] *n* pestaña.
eyelet [ī'lit] *n* ojete *m*.
eye-level [ī'levəl] *a* a la altura de los ojos.
eyelid [ī'lid] *n* párpado.
eyeliner [ī'līnûr] *n* lápiz *m* de ojos.
eye-opener [ī'ōpənûr] *n* revelación *f*, gran
sorpresa.
eyeshadow [ī'shadō] *n* sombreador *m* de
ojos.

eyesight [ī'sīt] *n* vista.
eyesore [ī'sôr] *n* monstruosidad *f*.
eyestrain [ī'strān] *n*: **to get ~** cansar la
vista *or* los ojos.
eye test *n* examen *m* de los ojos.
eyetooth, *pl* **eyeteeth** [ī'tooth, -tēth] *n*
colmillo; **to give one's eyeteeth for sth/to
do sth** (*col, fig*) dar un ojo de la cara por
algo/por hacer algo.
eyewash [ī'wâsh] *n* (*fig*) disparates *mpl*,
tonterías *fpl*.
eye witness *n* testigo *m/f* presencial.
eyrie [är'ē] *n* aguilera.

F

F [ef] *n* (*letter*) F, f *f*; (*MUS*) fa *m*; **F for Fox**
F de Francia.
F. *abbr* = **Fahrenheit.**
FA *n abbr* (*Brit*: = *Football Association*) ≈
AFE *f* (*Sp*).
FAA *n abbr* (*US*: = *Federal Aviation Administration*) *organismo de control y desarrollo
de la aviación civil*.
fable [fā'bəl] *n* fábula.
fabric [fab'rik] *n* tejido, tela.
fabricate [fab'rikāt] *vt* fabricar; (*fig*)
inventar.
fabrication [fabrikā'shən] *n* fabricación *f*;
(*fig*) invención *f*.
fabric ribbon *n* (*for typewriter*) cinta de
tela.
fabulous [fab'yələs] *a* fabuloso.
façade [fəsâd'] *n* fachada.
face [fās] *n* (*ANAT*) cara, rostro; (*of clock*)
esfera, cara (*LAm*); (*side, surface*) superficie *f*; (*in mine*) frente *m* de carbón ♦ *vt*
(*subj: person*) encararse con; (: *building*)
dar a; **~ down** (*person, card*) boca abajo;
to lose ~ desprestigiarse; **to save ~**
salvar las apariencias; **to make** *or* **pull a
~** hacer muecas; **in the ~ of** (*difficulties
etc*) en vista de, ante; **on the ~ of it** a primera vista; **~ to ~** cara a cara; **to ~ the
fact that ...** reconocer que ... .
face up to *vt fus* hacer frente a, arros-
trar.
facecloth [fās'klôth] *n* manopla.
face cream *n* crema (de belleza).
faceless [fās'lis] *a* (*fig*) anónimo.
face lift *n* estirado facial.
face powder *n* polvos *mpl* para la cara.
face-saving [fās'sāving] *a* para salvar las
apariencias.
facet [fas'it] *n* faceta.
facetious [fəsē'shəs] *a* chistoso.

facetiously [fəsē'shəslē] *ad* chistosamente.
face value [fās val'yōō] *n* (*of stamp*) valor *m* nominal; **to take sth at ~** (*fig*) tomar algo en sentido literal, aceptar las apariencias de algo.
facial [fā'shəl] *a* de la cara ♦ *n* (*also:* **beauty ~**) tratamiento facial, limpieza.
facile [fas'əl] *a* superficial.
facilitate [fəsil'ətāt] *vt* facilitar.
facility [fəsil'ətē] *n* facilidad *f*; **facilities** *npl* facilidades *fpl*; **credit ~** facilidades de crédito.
facing [fā'sing] *prep* frente a ♦ *a* de enfrente.
facsimile [faksim'əlē] *n* (*document*) facsímil(e) *m*; (*machine*) telefax *m*.
fact [fakt] *n* hecho; **in ~** en realidad; **to know for a ~ that** ... saber a ciencia cierta que ... .
fact-finding [fakt'fīnding] *a*: **a ~ tour/mission** un viaje/una misión de reconocimiento.
faction [fak'shən] *n* facción *f*.
factor [fak'tûr] *n* factor *m*; (*COMM: person*) agente *m/f* comisionado/a ♦ *vi* (*COMM*) comprar deudas; **safety ~** factor de seguridad.
factory [fak'tûrē] *n* fábrica.
factory farming *n* (*Brit*) cría industrial.
factory ship *n* buque *m* factoría.
factual [fak'chōōəl] *a* basado en los hechos.
faculty [fak'əltē] *n* facultad *f*; (*US: teaching staff*) personal *m* docente.
fad [fad] *n* novedad *f*, moda.
fade [fād] *vi* desteñirse; (*sound, hope*) desvanecerse; (*light*) apagarse; (*flower*) marchitarse.
fade away *vi* (*sound*) apagarse.
fade in *vt* (*TV, CINEMA*) fundir; (*RADIO: sound*) mezclar ♦ *vi* (*TV, CINEMA*) fundirse; (*RADIO*) oírse por encima.
fade out *vt* (*TV, CINEMA*) desvanecer; (*RADIO*) apagar, disminuir el volumen de ♦ *vi* (*TV, CINEMA*) desvanecerse; (*RADIO*) apagarse, dejarse de oír.
faded [fā'did] *a* (*clothes, color*) descolorado; (*flower*) marchito.
faeces [fē'sēz] *npl* (*Brit*) = **feces**.
fag [fag] *n* (*Brit col: cigarette*) pitillo (*Sp*), cigarro; (*US col: homosexual*) maricón *m*.
fag end *n* (*Brit col*) colilla.
Fahrenheit [far'ənhīt] *n* Fahrenheit *m*.
fail [fāl] *vt* (*candidate*) suspender; (*exam*) no aprobar; (*subj: memory etc*) fallar a ♦ *vi* suspender; (*be unsuccessful*) fracasar; (*strength, brakes, engine*) fallar; **to ~ to do sth** (*neglect*) dejar de hacer algo; (*be unable*) no poder hacer algo; **without ~** sin falta; **words ~ me!** ¡no sé qué decir!
failing [fā'ling] *n* falta, defecto ♦ *prep* a falta de; **~ that** de no ser posible eso.
failsafe [fāl'sāf] *a* (*device etc*) seguro contra todo riesgo.

failure [fāl'yûr] *n* fracaso; (*person*) fracasado/a; (*mechanical etc*) fallo; (*in exam*) suspenso; (*of crops*) pérdida, destrucción *f*; **it was a complete ~** fue un fracaso total.
faint [fānt] *a* débil; (*smell, breeze, trace*) tenue, apenas perceptible; (*recollection*) vago; (*mark*) apenas visible ♦ *n* desmayo ♦ *vi* desmayarse; **to feel ~** estar mareado, marearse.
faint-hearted [fānt'hâr'tid] *a* apocado.
faintly [fānt'lē] *ad* débilmente; (*vaguely*) vagamente.
faintness [fānt'nis] *n* debilidad *f*; vaguedad *f*.
fair [fâr] *a* justo; (*hair, person*) rubio; (*weather*) bueno; (*good enough*) suficiente; (*sizeable*) considerable ♦ *ad*: **to play ~** jugar limpio ♦ *n* feria; (*carnival*) parque *m* de atracciones; **it's not ~!** ¡no es justo!, ¡no hay derecho!; **~ play** juego limpio; **a ~ amount of** bastante; **~ wear and tear** desgaste *m* natural; **trade ~** feria de muestras.
fairground [fâr'ground] *n* parque *m* de atracciones.
fair-haired [fâr'hârd] *a* (*person*) rubio.
fairly [fâr'lē] *ad* (*justly*) con justicia; (*equally*) equitativamente; (*quite*) bastante; **I'm ~ sure** estoy bastante seguro.
fairness [fâr'nis] *n* justicia; (*impartiality*) imparcialidad *f*; **in all ~** a decir verdad.
fairy [fâr'ē] *n* hada.
fairy godmother *n* hada madrina.
fairyland [fâr'ēland] *n* el país de ensueño.
fairy lights *npl* bombillas *fpl* de colorines.
fairy tale *n* cuento de hadas.
faith [fāth] *n* fe *f*; (*trust*) confianza; (*sect*) religión *f*; **to have ~ in sb/sth** fiarse de uno/algo.
faithful [fāth'fəl] *a* fiel.
faithfully [fāth'fəlē] *ad* fielmente; **yours ~** (*Brit: in letters*) le saluda atentamente.
faith healer [fāth' hē'lûr] *n* curador(a) *m/f* por fe.
fake [fāk] *n* (*painting etc*) falsificación *f*; (*person*) impostor(a) *m/f* ♦ *a* falso ♦ *vt* fingir; (*painting etc*) falsificar.
falcon [fal'kən] *n* halcón *m*.
Falkland Islands [fôlk'lənd ī'ləndz] *npl* Islas *fpl* Malvinas.
fall [fôl] *n* caída; (*US*) otoño; (*decrease*) disminución *f* ♦ *vi, pt* **fell,** *pp* **fallen** caer(se); (*price*) bajar; **~s** *npl* (*waterfall*) cascada *sg*, salto *sg* de agua; **a ~ of snow** (*Brit*) una nevada; **to ~ flat** *vi* (*on one's face*) caerse (boca abajo); (*joke, story*) no hacer gracia; **to ~ short of sb's expectations** decepcionar a uno; **to ~ in love (with sb/sth)** enamorarse (de uno/algo).
fall apart *vi* despedazarse.
fall back *vi* retroceder.

fall back on *vt fus* (*remedy etc*) recurrir a; **to have sth to ~ back on** tener algo a que recurrir.

fall behind *vi* quedarse atrás; (*fig: with payments*) retrasarse.

fall down *vi* (*person*) caerse; (*building, hopes*) derrumbarse.

fall for *vt fus* (*trick*) tragar; (*person*) enamorarse de.

fall in *vi* (*roof*) hundirse; (*MIL*) alinearse.

fall in with *vt fus*: **to ~ in with sb's plans** acomodarse con los planes de uno.

fall off *vi* caerse; (*diminish*) disminuir.

fall out *vi* (*friends etc*) reñir; (*MIL*) romper filas.

fall over *vi* caer(se).

fall through *vi* (*plan, project*) fracasar.

fallacy [fal'əsē] *n* error *m*.

fallback position [fôl'bak pəzish'ən] *n* posición *f* de repliegue.

fallen [fôl'ən] *pp of* **fall**.

fallible [fal'əbəl] *a* falible.

falling [fôl'ing] *a*: **~ market** mercado en baja.

falling-off [fôl'ing·ôf'] *n* (*Brit: reduction*) disminución *f*.

Fallopian tube [fəlō'pēən tōōb] *n* (*ANAT*) trompa de Falopio.

fallout [fôl'out] *n* lluvia radioactiva.

fallout shelter *n* refugio antinuclear.

fallow [fal'ō] *a* (*land, field*) en barbecho.

false [fôls] *a* (*gen*) falso; (*teeth etc*) postizo; (*disloyal*) desleal, traidor(a); **under ~ pretenses** con engaños.

false alarm *n* falsa alarma.

falsehood [fôls'hōōd] *n* (*lie*) mentira; (*falseness*) falsedad *f*.

falsely [fôls'lē] *ad* falsamente.

false teeth *npl* dentadura *sg* postiza.

falsify [fôl'səfī] *vt* falsificar; (*figures*) contrahacer.

falter [fôl'tûr] *vi* vacilar.

fame [fām] *n* fama.

familiar [fəmil'yûr] *a* familiar; (*well-known*) conocido; (*tone*) de confianza; **to be ~ with** (*subject*) estar enterado de; **to make o.s. ~ with** familiarizarse con; **to be on ~ terms with** conocer bien.

familiarity [fəmilēar'ətē] *n* familiaridad *f*.

familiarize [fəmil'yərīz] *vt*: **to ~ o.s. with** familiarizarse con.

family [fam'lē] *n* familia.

family allowance *n* pensión *f* familiar.

family business *n* negocio familiar.

family doctor *n* médico/a de cabecera.

family life *n* vida doméstica *or* familiar.

family planning *n* planificación *f* familiar.

family planning clinic *n* clínica de planificación familiar.

family tree *n* árbol *m* genealógico.

famine [fam'in] *n* hambre *f*, hambruna.

famished [fam'isht] *a* hambriento; **I'm ~!** (*col*) ¡estoy muerto de hambre!, ¡tengo un hambre canina!

famous [fā'məs] *a* famoso, célebre.

famously [fā'məslē] *ad* (*get on*) estupendamente.

fan [fan] *n* abanico; (*ELEC*) ventilador *m*; (*person*) aficionado/a; (*SPORT*) hincha *m/f* ♦ *vt* abanicar; (*fire, quarrel*) atizar.

fan out *vi* desparramarse.

fanatic [fənat'ik] *n* fanático/a.

fanatical [fənat'ikəl] *a* fanático.

fan belt *n* correa de ventilador.

fancied [fan'sēd] *a* imaginario.

fanciful [fan'sifəl] *a* (*gen*) fantástico; (*imaginary*) fantasioso.

fancy [fan'sē] *n* (*whim*) capricho, antojo; (*imagination*) imaginación *f* ♦ *a* (*luxury*) de lujo; (*price*) exorbitado ♦ *vt* (*feel like, want*) tener ganas de; (*imagine*) imaginarse, figurarse; **to take a ~ to sb** tomar cariño a uno; **when the ~ takes him** cuando se le antoja; **it took** *or* **caught my ~** me cayó en gracia; **to ~ that...** imaginarse que...; **he fancies her** le gusta (ella) mucho.

fancy dress *n* disfraz *m*.

fancy-dress ball [fan'sēdres bôl'] *n* baile *m* de disfraces.

fancy goods *n* artículos *mpl* de fantasía.

fanfare [fan'fär] *n* fanfarria (de trompeta).

fanfold paper [fan'fōld pā'pûr] *n* papel *m* plegado en abanico *or* en acordeón.

fang [fang] *n* colmillo.

fan heater *n* (*Brit*) soplador *m* de aire caliente.

fanlight [fan'līt] *n* (montante *m* de) abanico.

fantasize [fan'təsīz] *vi* fantasear, hacerse ilusiones.

fantastic [fantas'tik] *a* fantástico.

fantasy [fan'təsē] *n* fantasía.

FAO *n abbr* (= *Food and Agriculture Organization*) OAA *f*.

far [fär] *a* (*distant*) lejano ♦ *ad* lejos; **the ~ left/right** (*POL*) la extrema izquierda/derecha; **~ away, ~ off** (a lo) lejos; **~ better** mucho mejor; **~ from** lejos de; **by ~ con mucho; it's by ~ the best** es con mucho el mejor; **go as ~ as the farm** vaya hasta la granja; **is it ~ to New York?** ¿a cuánto está Nueva York?; **it's not ~ (from here)** no está lejos (de aquí); **as ~ as I know** que yo sepa; **how ~ have you got with your work?** ¿hasta dónde has llegado en tu trabajo?

faraway [fär'əwā] *a* remoto; (*voice*) distraído; (*look*) ausente, perdido.

farce [färs] *n* farsa.

farcical [fär'sikəl] *a* absurdo.

fare [fär] *n* (*on trains, buses*) precio (del billete); (*in taxi: cost*) tarifa; (: *passenger*) pasajero; (*food*) comida; **half/full ~** medio pasaje *m*/pasaje *m* completo.

Far East *n*: **the ~** el Extremo *or* Lejano Oriente.

farewell [fär'wel'] *excl*, *n* adiós *m*.
far-fetched [fär'fecht'] *a* inverosímil.
farm [fârm] *n* granja, finca, estancia (*LAm*) ♦ *vt* cultivar.
   farm out *vt* (*work*): **to ~ out (to sb)** mandar hacer fuera (a uno).
farmer [fär'mûr] *n* granjero, estanciero (*LAm*).
farmhand [fârm'hand] *n* peón *m*.
farmhouse [fârm'hous] *n* granja, casa de hacienda (*LAm*).
farming [fär'ming] *n* (*gen*) agricultura; (*tilling*) cultivo; **sheep ~** cría de ovejas.
farm laborer *n* = **farmhand**.
farmland [fârm'land] *n* tierra de cultivo.
farm produce *n* productos *mpl* agrícolas.
farm worker *n* = **farmhand**.
farmyard [fârm'yârd] *n* corral *m*.
Faroe Islands [fe'rō ī'ləndz], **Faroes** [fer'ōz] *npl*: **the ~** las Islas Feroe.
far-reaching [fär'rē'ching] *a* (*reform*, *effect*) de gran alcance.
farsighted [fär'sī'tid] *a* présbita; (*fig*) previsor(a).
farsightedness [fär'sī'tidnis] *n* clarividencia, previsión *f*.
fart [fârt] (*col!*) *n* pedo (*!*) ♦ *vi* tirarse un pedo (*!*).
farther [fär'thûr] *ad* más lejos, más allá ♦ *a* más lejano.
farthest [fär'thist] *superlative of* **far**.
FAS *abbr* (= *free alongside ship*) franco al costado del buque.
fascinate [fas'ənāt] *vt* fascinar.
fascinating [fas'ənāting] *a* fascinante.
fascination [fasənā'shən] *n* fascinación *f*.
fascism [fash'izəm] *n* fascismo.
fascist [fash'ist] *a*, *n* fascista *m/f*.
fashion [fash'ən] *n* moda; (*manner*) manera ♦ *vt* formar; **in ~** a la moda; **out of ~** pasado de moda; **in the Greek ~** a la griega, al estilo griego; **after a ~** (*finish*, *manage* etc) en cierto modo.
fashionable [fash'ənəbəl] *a* de moda; (*writer*) de moda, popular; **it is ~ to do ...** está de moda hacer ....
fashion designer *n* modisto/a.
fashion show *n* desfile *m* de modelos.
fast [fast] *a* (*also PHOT: film*) rápido; (*dye*, *color*) sólido; (*clock*): **to be ~** estar adelantado ♦ *ad* rápidamente, de prisa; (*stuck*, *held*) firmemente ♦ *n* ayuno ♦ *vi* ayunar; **~ asleep** profundamente dormido; **in the ~ lane** (*AUT*) en el carril de adelantamiento; **my watch is 5 minutes ~** mi reloj está adelantado 5 minutos; **as ~ as I** etc **can** lo más rápido posible.
fasten [fas'ən] *vt* asegurar, sujetar; (*coat*, *belt*) abrochar ♦ *vi* cerrarse.
   fasten (up)on *vt fus* (*idea*) aferrarse a.
fastener [fas'ənûr] *n* cierre *m*; (*of door* etc) cerrojo; (*Brit*: *zip* **~**) cremallera.
fastening [fas'əning] *n* = **fastener**.

fast food *n* comida rápida, platos *mpl* preparados.
fastidious [fastid'ēəs] *a* (*fussy*) delicado; (*demanding*) exigente.
fat [fat] *a* gordo; (*meat*) con mucha grasa; (*greasy*) grasiento ♦ *n* grasa; (*on person*) carnes *fpl*; (*lard*) manteca; **to live off the ~ of the land** vivir a cuerpo de rey.
fatal [fāt'əl] *a* (*mistake*) fatal; (*injury*) mortal; (*consequence*) funesto.
fatalism [fāt'əlizəm] *n* fatalismo.
fatality [fātal'itē] *n* (*road death* etc) víctima *f*.
fatally [fāt'əlē] *ad*: **~ injured** herido a muerte.
fate [fāt] *n* destino, sino.
fated [fā'tid] *a* predestinado.
fateful [fāt'fəl] *a* fatídico.
father [fä'thûr] *n* padre *m*.
Father Christmas *n* (*Brit*) Papá *m* Noel.
fatherhood [fä'thûrhŏŏd] *n* paternidad *f*.
father-in-law [fä'thûrinlô] *n* suegro.
fatherland [fä'thûrland] *n* patria.
fatherly [fä'thûrlē] *a* paternal.
fathom [fath'əm] *n* braza ♦ *vt* (*unravel*) desentrañar; (*understand*) concebir.
fatigue [fətēg'] *n* fatiga, cansancio; **metal ~** fatiga del metal.
fatness [fat'nis] *n* gordura.
fatten [fat'ən] *vt*, *vi* engordar; **chocolate is ~ing** el chocolate engorda.
fatty [fat'ē] *a* (*food*) graso ♦ *n* (*fam*) gordito/a, gordinflón/ona *m/f*.
fatuous [fach'ōōəs] *a* fatuo, necio.
faucet [fô'sit] *n* (*US*) grifo, llave *f* (*LAm*).
fault [fôlt] *n* (*blame*) culpa; (*defect: in character*) defecto; (*in manufacture*) desperfecto; (*GEO*) falla ♦ *vt* criticar; **it's my ~** es culpa mía; **to find ~ with** criticar, poner peros a; **at ~** culpable.
faultless [fôlt'lis] *a* (*action*) intachable; (*person*) sin defectos.
faulty [fôl'tē] *a* defectuoso.
fauna [fôn'ə] *n* fauna.
faux pas [fō pä'] *n* plancha.
favor [fā'vûr] *n* favor *m*; (*approval*) aprobación *f* ♦ *vt* (*proposition*) estar a favor de, aprobar; (*person* etc) favorecer; (*assist*) ser propicio a; **to ask a ~ of** pedir un favor a; **to do sb a ~** hacer un favor a uno; **to find ~ with sb** (*subj: person*) caerle bien a uno; (: *suggestion*) tener buena acogida por parte de uno; **in ~ of** a favor de; **to be in ~ of sth/of doing sth** ser partidario *or* estar a favor de algo/de hacer algo.
favorable [fā'vûrəbəl] *a* favorable.
favorably [fā'vûrəblē] *ad* favorablemente.
favorite [fā'vûrit] *a*, *n* favorito, preferido.
favoritism [fā'vûritizəm] *n* favoritismo.
favour [fā'vûr] *etc* (*Brit*) = **favor** *etc*.
fawn [fôn] *n* cervato ♦ *a* (*also*: **~-colored**) color de cervato, leonado ♦ *vi*: **to ~ (up)on** adular.

fax [faks] *n* (*document*) facsímil(e) *m*; (*machine*) telefax *m* ♦ *vt* mandar *or* enviar por telefax.

fazed [fāzd] *a* (*fam*) pasmado.

FBI *n abbr* (*US*: = *Federal Bureau of Investigation*) ≈ BIC *f* (*Sp*).

FCA *n abbr* (*US*) = *Farm Credit Administration*.

FCC *n abbr* (*US*) = *Federal Communications Commission*.

FCO *n abbr* (*Brit*: = *Foreign and Commonwealth Office*) ≈ Min. de AA. EE.

FD *n abbr* (*US*) = **fire department**.

FDA *n abbr* (*US*: = *Food and Drug Administration*) *oficina que se ocupa del control de los productos alimentarios y farmacéuticos*.

FDIC *n abbr* (*US*) = *Federal Deposit Insurance Corporation*.

fear [fēr] *n* miedo, temor *m* ♦ *vt* temer; **for ~ of** por temor a; **~ of heights** vértigo; **to ~ for/that** temer por/que.

fearful [fēr'fəl] *a* temeroso, miedoso; (*awful*) terrible; **to be ~ of** (*frightened*) tener miedo de.

fearfully [fēr'fəlē] *ad* (*timidly*) con miedo; (*col: very*) terriblemente.

fearless [fēr'lis] *a* (*gen*) sin miedo *or* temor; (*bold*) audaz.

fearlessly [fēr'lislē] *ad* temerariamente.

fearlessness [fēr'lisnis] *n* temeridad *f*.

fearsome [fēr'səm] *a* (*opponent*) temible; (*sight*) espantoso.

feasibility [fēzəbil'ətē] *n* factibilidad *f*, viabilidad *f*.

feasibility study *n* estudio de factibilidad.

feasible [fē'zəbəl] *a* factible.

feast [fēst] *n* banquete *m*; (*REL*: *also*: **~ day**) fiesta ♦ *vi* banquetear.

feat [fēt] *n* hazaña.

feather [feth'ûr] *n* pluma ♦ *vt*: **to ~ one's nest** (*fig*) hacer su agosto, sacar tajada ♦ *cpd* (*mattress, bed, pillow*) de plumas.

featherweight [feth'ûrwāt] *n* (*BOXING*) peso pluma.

feature [fē'chûr] *n* (*gen*) característica; (*ANAT*) rasgo; (*article*) artículo de fondo ♦ *vt* (*subj: film*) presentar ♦ *vi* figurar; **~s** *npl* (*of face*) facciones *fpl*; **a (special) ~ on sth/sb** un artículo de fondo sobre algo/uno; **it ~d prominently in ...** tuvo un papel destacado en ....

feature film *n* largometraje *m*.

Feb. *abbr* (= *February*) feb.

February [feb'yəwärē] *n* febrero.

feces [fē'sēz] *npl* excremento *sg*, heces *fpl*.

feckless [fek'lis] *a* irresponsable, irreflexivo.

Fed *abbr* (*US*) = **federal, federation**.

fed [fed] *pt, pp of* **feed**.

Fed. *n abbr* (*US col*) = *Federal Reserve Board*.

federal [fed'ûrəl] *a* federal.

Federal Republic of Germany *n* Repú-

blica Federal de Alemania.

federation [fedərā'shən] *n* federación *f*.

fedora [fədôr'ə] *n* (*US*) sombrero flexible *or* tirolés.

fed-up [fedup'] *a*: **to be ~ (with)** estar harto (de).

fee [fē] *n* (*professional*) derechos *mpl*, honorarios *mpl*; (*of school*) matrícula; (*entrance ~, membership ~*) cuota; **for a small ~** por poco dinero.

feeble [fē'bəl] *a* débil.

feeble-minded [fē'bəlmindid] *a* imbécil.

feed [fēd] *n* (*gen, of baby*) comida; (*of animal*) pienso; (*on printer*) dispositivo de alimentación ♦ *vt* (*pt, pp* **fed**) (*gen*) alimentar; (*Brit*: *baby*: *breastfeed*) dar el pecho a; (*animal*) dar de comer a ♦ *vi* (*baby, animal*) comer.

feed back *vt* (*results*) pasar.

feed in *vt* (*COMPUT*) introducir.

feed into *vt* (*data, information*) suministrar a; **to ~ sth into a machine** introducir algo en una máquina.

feed on *vt fus* alimentarse de.

feedback [fēd'bak] *n* (*from person*) reacción *f*; (*TEC*) feedback *m*.

feeder [fē'dûr] *n* (*bib*) babero.

feeding bottle [fē'ding bât'əl] *n* (*Brit*) biberón *m*.

feel [fēl] *n* (*sensation*) sensación *f*; (*sense of touch*) tacto ♦ *vt* (*pt, pp* **felt**) tocar; (*cold, pain etc*) sentir; (*think, believe*) creer; **to get the ~ of sth** (*fig*) acostumbrarse a algo; **to ~ hungry/cold** tener hambre/frío; **to ~ lonely/better** sentirse solo/mejor; **I don't ~ well** no me siento bien; **it ~s soft** es suave al tacto; **it ~s colder out here** se siente más frío aquí fuera; **to ~ like** (*want*) tener ganas de; **I'm still ~ing my way** (*fig*) aún me voy orientando; **I ~ that you ought to do it** creo que debes hacerlo; **to ~ around** tantear.

feeler [fē'lûr] *n* (*of insect*) antena; **to put out ~s** (*fig*) sondear.

feeling [fē'ling] *n* (*physical*) sensación *f*; (*foreboding*) presentimiento; (*impression*) impresión *f*; (*emotion*) sentimiento; **what are your ~s about the matter?** ¿qué opinas tú del asunto?; **to hurt sb's ~s** ofenderle a uno; **~s ran high about it** causó mucha controversia; **I got the ~ that ...** me dio la impresión de que ...; **there was a general ~ that ...** la opinión general fue que ....

feet [fēt] *npl of* **foot**.

feign [fān] *vt* fingir.

feigned [fānd] *a* fingido.

feline [fē'līn] *a* felino.

fell [fel] *pt of* **fall** ♦ *vt* (*tree*) talar ♦ *a*: **with one ~ blow** con un golpe feroz; **in one ~ swoop** de un solo golpe.

fellow [fel'ō] *n* tipo, tío (*Sp*); (*of learned society*) socio/a; (*UNIV*) miembro *de la junta* *de gobierno de un colegio* ♦ *cpd:* ~ **students** compañeros/as *m/fpl* de curso, condiscípulos/as *m/fpl.*

fellow citizen *n* conciudadano/a.

fellow countryman *n* compatriota *m.*

fellow feeling *n* compañerismo.

fellow men *npl* semejantes *mpl.*

fellowship [fel'ōship] *n* compañerismo; (*grant*) beca.

fellow traveler *n* compañero/a de viaje; (*POL: with communists*) simpatizante *m/f.*

fellow worker *n* colega *m/f.*

felon [fel'ən] *n* criminal *m/f.*

felony [fel'ənē] *n* crimen *m.*

felt [felt] *pt, pp* of **feel** ♦ *n* fieltro.

felt-tip pen [felt'tip pen'] *n* rotulador *m.*

female [fē'māl] *n* (*woman*) mujer *f;* (*ZOOL*) hembra ♦ *a* femenino.

feminine [fem'ənin] *a* femenino.

femininity [femənin'ətē] *n* feminidad *f.*

feminism [fem'ənizəm] *n* feminismo.

feminist [fem'ənist] *n* feminista.

fence [fens] *n* valla, cerca; (*RACING*) valla ♦ *vt* (*also:* ~ **in**) cercar ♦ *vi* hacer esgrima; **to sit on the** ~ (*fig*) nadar entre dos aguas.

fence in *vt* cercar.

fence off *vt* separar con cerca.

fencing [fen'sing] *n* esgrima.

fend [fend] *vi:* **to** ~ **for o.s.** valerse por sí mismo.

fend off *vt* (*attack, attacker*) rechazar, repeler; (*blow*) desviar; (*awkward question*) evadir.

fender [fen'dûr] *n* guardafuego; (*US: AUT*) parachoques *m inv;* (: *RAIL*) trompa.

fennel [fen'əl] *n* hinojo.

FEPC *n abbr* (*US*) = *Fair Employment Practices Committee.*

FERC *n abbr* (*US*) = *Federal Energy Regulatory Commission.*

ferment *vi* [fûrment'] fermentar ♦ *n* [fûr'ment] (*fig*) agitación *f.*

fermentation [fûrmentā'shən] *n* fermentación *f.*

fern [fûrn] *n* helecho.

ferocious [fərō'shəs] *a* feroz.

ferociously [fərō'shəslē] *ad* ferozmente, con ferocidad.

ferocity [fərâs'itē] *n* ferocidad *f.*

ferret [fär'it] *n* hurón *m.*

ferret around *vi* buscar.

ferret out *vt* (*secret, truth*) desentrañar.

Ferris wheel [fär'is wēl] *n* (*at fair*) noria.

ferry [fär'ē] *n* (*small*) barca (de pasaje), balsa; (*large: also:* ~**boat**) transbordador *m,* ferry *m* ♦ *vt* transportar; **to** ~ **sth/sb across** *or* **over** transportar algo/a uno a la otra orilla; **to** ~ **sb to and fro** llevar a uno de un lado para otro.

ferryman [fär'ēmən] *n* barquero.

fertile [fûr'təl] *a* fértil; (*BIOL*) fecundo.

fertility [fûrtil'ətē] *n* fertilidad *f;* fecundidad

f.

fertility drug *n* medicamento contra la infertilidad.

fertilization [fûrtələzā'shən] *n* fertilización *f.*

fertilize [fûr'təlīz] *vt* fertilizar; (*BIOL*) fecundar; (*AGR*) abonar.

fertilizer [fûr'təlīzûr] *n* abono, fertilizante *m.*

fervent [fûr'vənt] *a* (*admirer*) entusiasta; (*hope*) ferviente.

fervor, (*Brit*) **fervour** [fûr'vûr] *n* fervor *m,* ardor *m.*

fester [fes'tûr] *vi* ulcerarse.

festival [fes'təvəl] *n* (*REL*) fiesta; (*ART, MUS*) festival *m.*

festive [fes'tiv] *a* festivo; **the** ~ **season** (*Brit: Christmas*) las Navidades.

festivities [festiv'itēz] *npl* fiestas *fpl.*

festoon [festōōn'] *vt:* **to** ~ **with** festonear *or* engalanar de.

FET *n abbr* (*US*) = *Federal Excise Tax.*

fetal [fēt'l] *a* fetal.

fetch [fech] *vt* ir a buscar; (*Brit: sell for*) venderse por.

fetching [fech'ing] *a* atractivo.

fête [fet] *n* fiesta.

fetid [fet'id] *a* fétido.

fetish [fet'ish] *n* fetiche *m.*

fetter [fet'ûr] *vt* (*person*) encadenar, poner en grillos; (*horse*) trabar; (*fig*) poner trabas a.

fetters [fet'ûrz] *npl* grillos *mpl.*

fettle [fet'əl] *n:* **in fine** ~ en buenas condiciones.

fetus [fē'təs] *n* feto.

feud [fyōōd] *n* (*hostility*) enemistad *f;* (*quarrel*) disputa; **a family** ~ una pelea familiar.

feudal [fyōōd'əl] *a* feudal.

feudalism [fyōō'dəlizəm] *n* feudalismo.

fever [fē'vûr] *n* fiebre *f;* **he has a** ~ tiene fiebre.

feverish [fē'vûrish] *a* febril.

feverishly [fē'vûrishlē] *ad* febrilmente.

few [fyōō] *a* (*not many*) pocos; (*some*) algunos, unos ♦ *pron* algunos; **a** ~ *a* unos pocos; ~ **people** poca gente; **a good** ~, **quite a** ~ bastantes; **in** *or* **over the next** ~ **days** en los próximos días; **every** ~ **weeks** cada 2 o 3 semanas; **a** ~ **more days** unos días más.

fewer [fyōō'ûr] *a* menos.

fewest [fyōō'ist] *a* los/las menos.

FFA *n abbr* = *Future Farmers of America.*

FHA *n abbr* (*US:* = *Federal Housing Association*) *oficina federal de la vivienda.*

fiancé [fēânsā'] *n* novio, prometido.

fiancée [fēânsā'] *n* novia, prometida.

fiasco [fēas'kō] *n* fiasco.

fib [fib] *n* mentirilla ♦ *vi* decir mentirillas.

fiber, (*Brit*) **fibre** [fī'bûr] *n* fibra.

fiberboard, (*Brit*) **fibreboard** [fī'bûrbôrd] *n* fibra vulcanizada.

fiberglass, (Brit) **fibreglass** [fī'bûrglas] n fibra de vidrio.

fibrositis [fībrəsī'tis] n fibrositis f inv.

FIC n abbr (US) = Federal Information Centers.

FICA n abbr (US) = Federal Insurance Contributions Act.

fickle [fik'əl] a inconstante.

fiction [fik'shən] n (gen) ficción f.

fictional [fik'shənəl] a novelesco.

fictionalize [fik'shənəlīz] vt novelar.

fictitious [fiktish'əs] a ficticio.

fiddle [fid'əl] n (MUS) violín m; (cheating) trampa ♦ vt (Brit: accounts) falsificar; **to work a ~** hacer trampa.
    fiddle with vt fus jugar con.

fiddler [fid'lûr] n violinista m/f.

fiddly [fid'lē] a (task) delicado, mañoso; (object) cargado.

fidelity [fidel'itē] n fidelidad f.

fidget [fij'it] vi inquietarse.

fidgety [fij'itē] a nervioso.

fiduciary [fidōō'shēârē] n fiduciario/a.

field [fēld] n (gen, COMPUT) campo; (fig) campo, esfera; (SPORT) campo, cancha (LAm); (competitors) competidores mpl ♦ cpd: **to have a ~ day** (fig) sacar el máximo provecho; **to lead the ~** (SPORT, COMM) llevar la delantera; **to give sth a year's trial in the ~** (fig) sacar algo al mercado a prueba por un año; **my particular ~** mi especialidad.

field glasses npl gemelos mpl.

field marshal n mariscal m.

fieldwork [fēld'wûrk] n (ARCHEOLOGY, GEO) trabajo de campo.

fiend [fēnd] n demonio.

fiendish [fēn'dish] a diabólico.

fierce [fērs] a feroz; (wind, attack) violento; (heat) intenso; (fighting, enemy) encarnizado.

fiercely [fērs'lē] ad con ferocidad; violentamente; intensamente; encarnizadamente.

fierceness [fērs'nis] n ferocidad f; violencia; intensidad f; encarnizamiento.

fiery [fī'ûrē] a (burning) ardiente; (temperament) apasionado.

FIFA [fē'fa] n abbr (= Fédération Internationale de Football Association) FIFA f.

fifteen [fif'tēn'] num quince.

fifth [fifth] num quinto.

fiftieth [fif'tēith] num quincuagésimo.

fifty [fif'tē] num cincuenta; **the fifties** los años cincuenta; **to be in one's fifties** andar por los cincuenta.

fifty-fifty [fif'tēfif'tē] ad: **to go ~ with sb** ir a medias con uno ♦ a: **we have a ~ chance of success** tenemos un cincuenta por ciento de posibilidades de tener éxito.

fig [fig] n higo.

fight [fīt] n (gen) pelea; (MIL) combate m; (struggle) lucha ♦ vb (pt, pp **fought**) vt luchar contra; (cancer, alcoholism) comba-

tir; (LAW): **to ~ a case** defenderse; (quarrel): **to ~ (with sb)** pelear (con uno) ♦ vi pelear, luchar; (fig): **to ~ (for/against)** luchar por/contra.
    fight back vi defenderse; (after illness) recuperarse ♦ vt (tears) contener.
    fight down vt (anger, anxiety, urge) reprimir.
    fight off vt (attack, attacker) rechazar; (disease, sleep, urge) luchar contra.
    fight out vt: **to ~ it out** luchar hasta resolverlo.

fighter [fī'tûr] n combatiente m/f; (fig) luchador(a) m/f; (plane) caza m.

fighter-bomber [fī'tûrbâm'ûr] n cazabombardero.

fighter pilot n piloto de caza.

fighting [fī'ting] n (gen) el luchar; (battle) combate m; (in streets) disturbios mpl.

figment [fig'mənt] n: **a ~ of the imagination** una quimera.

figurative [fig'yûrətiv] a (meaning) figurado; (ART) figurativo.

figure [fig'yûr] n (DRAWING, GEOM) figura, dibujo; (number, cipher) cifra; (person) figura; (body, outline) talle m, tipo ♦ vt (esp US: think, calculate) calcular, imaginarse ♦ vi (appear) figurar; (esp US: make sense) ser lógico; **~ of speech** (LING) figura retórica; **public ~** personaje m.
    figure on vt fus (US) contar con.
    figure out vt (understand) comprender.

figurehead [fig'yûrhed] n (fig) testaferro.

figure skating n patinaje m de figuras.

Fiji (Islands) [fē'jē (ī'ləndz)] n(pl) (Islas fpl de) Fiji fpl.

filament [fil'əmənt] n (ELEC) filamento.

filch [filch] vt (col: steal) hurtar, robar.

file [fīl] n (tool) lima; (for nails) lima de uñas; (dossier) expediente m; (folder) carpeta; (in cabinet) archivo; (COMPUT) fichero; (row) fila ♦ vt limar; (papers) clasificar; (LAW: claim) presentar; (store) archivar; **to open/close a ~** (COMPUT) abrir/cerrar un fichero; **to ~ in/out** vi entrar/salir en fila; **to ~ a suit against sb** entablar pleito contra uno; **to ~ past** desfilar ante.

file name n (COMPUT) nombre m de fichero.

filibuster [fil'əbustûr] (esp US: POL) n filibustero/a ♦ vi ser un(a) filibustero/a.

filing [fī'ling] n: **to do the ~** llevar los archivos.

filing cabinet n fichero, archivo.

filing clerk n oficinista m/f.

fill [fil] vt llenar; (tooth) empastar; (vacancy) cubrir ♦ n: **to eat one's ~** llenarse; **we've already ~ed that vacancy** ya hemos cubierto esa vacante; **~ed with admiration (for)** lleno de admiración (por).
    fill in vt rellenar; (details, report) completar; **to ~ sb in on sth** (col) poner a uno

al corriente *or* al día sobre algo.
fill out *vt* (*form, receipt*) rellenar.
fill up *vt* llenar (hasta el borde) ♦ *vi* (*AUT*) poner gasolina.
fillet [filā'] *n* filete *m*.
fillet steak *n* filete *m* de ternera.
filling [fil'ing] *n* (*CULIN*) relleno; (*for tooth*) empaste *m*.
filling station *n* estación *f* de servicio.
fillip [fil'əp] *n* estímulo.
filly [fil'ē] *n* potra.
film [film] *n* película ♦ *vt* (*scene*) filmar ♦ *vi* rodar (una película).
film script *n* guión *m*.
film star *n* astro, estrella de cine.
filmstrip [film'strip] *n* tira de película.
film studio *n* estudio de cine.
filter [fil'tûr] *n* filtro ♦ *vt* filtrar.
filter in, filter through *vi* filtrarse.
filter coffee *n* café *m* (molido) para filtrar.
filter lane *n* (*Brit*) carril *m* de selección.
filter-tipped [fil'tûrtipt] *a* con filtro.
filth [filth] *n* suciedad *f*.
filthy [fil'thē] *a* sucio; (*language*) obsceno.
fin [fin] *n* (*gen*) aleta.
fin. *abbr* = **finance**.
final [fi'nəl] *a* (*last*) final, último; (*definitive*) definitivo, terminante ♦ *n* (*SPORT*) final *f*; **~s** *npl* (*SCOL*) examen *m* de fin de curso; **~ demand** (*on invoice etc*) último aviso; **~ dividend** dividendo final.
finale [final'ē] *n* final *m*.
finalist [fi'nəlist] *n* (*SPORT*) finalista *m/f*.
finality [final'itē] *n* finalidad *f*; **with an air of ~** en tono resuelto, de modo terminante.
finalize [fi'nəliz] *vt* concluir, completar.
finally [fi'nəlē] *ad* (*lastly*) por último, finalmente; (*eventually*) por fin; (*irrevocably*) de modo definitivo; (*once and for all*) definitivamente.
finance [fi'nans] *n* (*money, funds*) fondos *mpl*; **~s** *npl* finanzas *fpl* ♦ *cpd* (*page, section, company*) financiero ♦ *vt* [finans'] financiar.
financial [finan'chəl] *a* financiero.
financially [finan'chəlē] *ad* económicamente.
financial management *n* gestión *f* financiera.
financial statement *n* estado financiero.
financial year *n* ejercicio (financiero).
financier [finansiûr'] *n* financiero/a.
find [find] *vt* (*pt, pp* **found** [found]) (*gen*) encontrar, hallar; (*come upon*) descubrir ♦ *n* hallazgo; descubrimiento; **to ~ sb guilty** (*LAW*) declarar culpable a uno; **to ~ (some) difficulty in doing sth** encontrar dificultad en hacer algo.
  find out *vt* averiguar; (*truth, secret*) descubrir ♦ *vi*: **to ~ out about** enterarse de.
findings [fin'dingz] *npl* (*LAW*) veredicto *sg*, fallo *sg*; (*of report*) recomendaciones *fpl*.
fine [fin] *a* (*delicate*) fino; (*beautiful*)

hermoso ♦ *ad* (*well*) bien ♦ *n* (*LAW*) multa ♦ *vt* (*LAW*) multar; **the weather is ~** hace buen tiempo; **he's ~** está muy bien; **you're doing ~** lo estás haciendo muy bien; **to cut it ~** (*of time, money*) calcular muy justo; **to get a ~ for (doing) sth** recibir una multa por (hacer) algo.
fine arts *npl* bellas artes *fpl*.
finely [fin'lē] *ad* (*splendidly*) con elegancia; (*chop*) en trozos pequeños, fino; (*adjust*) con precisión.
fineness [fin'nis] *n* (*of cloth*) finura; (*of idea*) sutilidad *f*.
finery [fi'nûrē] *n* adornos *mpl*.
finesse [fines'] *n* sutileza.
fine-tooth comb [fin'tōōth kōm] *n*: **to go through sth with a ~** revisar algo a fondo.
finger [fing'gûr] *n* dedo ♦ *vt* (*touch*) manosear; (*MUS*) puntear; **little/index ~** (dedo) meñique *m*/índice *m*.
fingernail [fing'gûrnāl] *n* uña.
fingerprint [fing'gûrprint] *n* huella dactilar ♦ *vt* tomar las huellas dactilares de.
fingertip [fing'gûrtip] *n* yema del dedo; **to have sth at one's ~s** saberse algo al dedillo.
finicky [fin'ikē] *a* (*fussy*) delicado.
finish [fin'ish] *n* (*end*) fin *m*; (*SPORT*) meta; (*polish etc*) acabado ♦ *vt, vi* terminar; **to ~ doing sth** acabar de hacer algo; **to ~ first/second/third** (*SPORT*) llegar el primero/segundo/tercero; **I've ~ed with the paper** he terminado con el periódico; **she's ~ed with him** ha roto *or* acabado con él.
  finish off *vt* acabar, terminar; (*kill*) rematar.
  finish up *vt* acabar, terminar ♦ *vi* ir a parar, terminar.
finished [fin'isht] *a* (*product*) acabado; (*performance*) pulido; (*col: tired*) rendido, hecho polvo.
finishing [fin'ishing] *a*: **~ touches** toque *m* final.
finishing line [fin'ishing lin] *n* línea de llegada *or* meta.
finishing school [fin'ishing skōōl] *n* academia para señoritas.
finite [fi'nit] *a* finito.
Finland [fin'lənd] *n* Finlandia.
Finn [fin] *n* finlandés/esa *m/f*.
Finnish [fin'ish] *a* finlandés/esa ♦ *n* (*LING*) finlandés *m*.
fiord [fyôrd] *n* fiordo.
fir [fûr] *n* abeto.
fire [fi'ûr] *n* fuego; (*accidental, damaging*) incendio ♦ *vt* (*gun*) disparar; (*set fire to*) incendiar; (*excite*) exaltar; (*interest*) despertar; (*dismiss*) despedir ♦ *vi* encenderse; (*AUT: subj: engine*) encender; **on ~** ardiendo, en llamas; **to be on ~** estar ardiendo; **to catch ~** encenderse; **to set ~ to sth, set sth on ~** prender fuego a algo; **insured against ~** asegurado contra

incendios; **to be/come under** ~ estar/caer bajo fuego.

fire alarm *n* alarma de incendios.

firearm [fiûr'ârm] *n* arma de fuego.

fire department, (*Brit*) **fire brigade** *n* (cuerpo de) bomberos *mpl*.

fire drill *n* simulacro de incendio.

fire engine *n* coche *m* de bomberos.

fire escape *n* escalera de incendios.

fire extinguisher *n* extintor *m* (de fuego).

fire hazard *n* = **fire risk**.

fire hydrant *n* boca de incendios.

fire insurance *n* seguro contra incendios.

fireman [fiûr'mən] *n* bombero.

fireplace [fiûr'plās] *n* chimenea.

fireplug [fiûr'plug] *n* (*US*) boca de incendios.

fireproof [fiûr'prōōf] *a* a prueba de fuego; (*material*) incombustible.

fire regulations *npl* reglamentos *mpl* contra incendios.

fire risk *n* peligro de incendio.

firescreen [fiûr'skrēn] *n* pantalla refractaria.

fireside [fiûr'sīd] *n*: **by the** ~ al lado de la chimenea.

fire station *n* parque *m* de bomberos.

firewood [fiûr'wōōd] *n* leña.

fireworks [fiûr'wûrks] *npl* fuegos *mpl* artificiales.

firing [fiûr'ing] *n* (*MIL*) disparos *mpl*, tiroteo.

firing line *n* línea de fuego; **to be on the** ~ (*fig: liable to be criticized*) estar en la línea de fuego.

firing squad *n* pelotón *m* de ejecución.

firm [fûrm] *a* firme; (*offer, decision*) en firme ♦ *n* firma, empresa; **to be a** ~ **believer in sth** ser un partidario convencido de algo; **to stand** ~ *or* **take a** ~ **stand over sth** (*fig*) mantenerse firme ante algo.

firmly [fûrm'lē] *ad* firmemente.

firmness [fûrm'nis] *n* firmeza.

first [fûrst] *a* primero ♦ *ad* (*before others*) primero; (*when listing reasons etc*) en primer lugar, primeramente ♦ *n* (*person: in race*) primero/a; (*AUT: also:* ~ **gear**) primera; **at** ~ al principio; ~ **of all** ante todo; **the** ~ **of January** el uno *or* primero de enero; **in the** ~ **instance** en primer lugar; **I'll do it** ~ **thing tomorrow** lo haré mañana a primera hora; **for the** ~ **time** por primera vez; **head** ~ de cabeza; **from the (very)** ~ desde el principio.

first aid *n* primera ayuda, primeros auxilios *mpl*.

first aid kit *n* botiquín *m*.

first aid station, (*Brit*) **first aid post** *n* puesto de auxilio.

first-class [fûrst'klas'] *a* de primera clase; ~ **ticket** (*RAIL etc*) billete *m* *or* boleto (*LAm*) de primera clase; ~ **mail** correo de primera.

first-hand [fûrst'hand'] *a* de primera mano.

first lady *n* (*esp US*) primera dama.

firstly [fûrst'lē] *ad* en primer lugar.

first name *n* nombre *m* de pila.

first night *n* estreno.

first-rate [fûrst'rāt'] *a* de primera clase.

fir tree *n* abeto.

fiscal [fis'kəl] *a* fiscal; ~ **year** año fiscal, ejercicio.

fish [fish] *n*, *pl inv* pez *m*; (*food*) pescado ♦ *vt*, *vi* pescar; **to go** ~**ing** ir de pesca.

fish out *vt* (*from water, box etc*) sacar.

fishbone [fish'bōn] *n* espina.

fisherman [fish'ûrmən] *n* pescador *m*.

fishery [fish'ûrē] *n* pesquería.

fish factory *n* fábrica de elaboración de pescado.

fish farm *n* piscifactoría.

fish fingers *npl* (*Brit*) croquetas *fpl* de pescado.

fishing boat [fish'ing bōt] *n* barca de pesca.

fishing industry *n* industria pesquera.

fishing line *n* sedal *m*.

fishing net *n* red *f* de pesca.

fishing rod *n* caña (de pescar).

fishing tackle *n* aparejo (de pescar).

fish market *n* mercado de pescado.

fishmonger [fish'munggûr] *n* pescadero/a.

fishmonger's (shop) *n* pescadería.

fishseller [fish'selûr] *n* (*US*) pescadero(a).

fish slice *n* paleta para pescado.

fish sticks *npl* (*US*) croquetas *fpl* de pescado.

fishstore [fish'stôr] *n* (*US*) pescadería.

fishy [fish'ē] *a* (*fig*) sospechoso.

fission [fish'ən] *n* fisión *f*; **atomic/nuclear** ~ fisión *f* atómica/nuclear.

fissure [fish'ûr] *n* fisura.

fist [fist] *n* puño.

fistfight [fist'fīt] *n* lucha a puñetazos.

fit [fit] *a* (*MED, SPORT*) en (buena) forma; (*proper*) adecuado, apropiado ♦ *vt* (*subj: clothes*) sentar bien a; (*try on: clothes*) probar; (*match: facts*) cuadrar *or* corresponder *or* coincidir con; (*description*) estar de acuerdo con; (*accommodate*) ajustar, adaptar ♦ *vi* (*clothes*) entallar; (*in space, gap*) caber; (*facts*) coincidir ♦ *n* (*MED*) ataque *m*; (*outburst*) arranque *m*; ~ **to** apto para; ~ **for** apropiado para, **do as you think** *or* **see** ~ haz lo que te parezca (mejor); **to keep** ~ mantenerse en forma; **to be** ~ **for work** (*after illness*) estar apto para trabajar; ~ **of coughing** acceso de tos; ~ **of anger/enthusiasm** arranque de cólera/entusiasmo; **to have** *or* **suffer a** ~ tener un ataque *or* acceso; **this dress is a good** ~ este vestido me sienta bien; **by** ~**s and starts** a rachas.

fit in *vi* (*gen*) encajarse; (*fig: person*) llevarse bien (con todos) ♦ *vt* (*object*) acomodar; (*fig: appointment, visitor*) incluir; **to** ~ **in with sb's plans** acomodarse a los pla-

nes de uno.
fit out *vt* (*Brit: also:* **fit up**) equipar.
fitful |fit'fəl| *a* espasmódico, intermitente.
fitfully |fit'fəlē| *ad* irregularmente; **to sleep**
~ dormir inquieto.
fitment |fit'mənt| *n* (*Brit*) mueble *m*.
fitness |fit'nis| *n* (*MED*) salud *f*; (*of remark*)
conveniencia.
fitness activity *n* (*US*) ejercicios *mpl*
para mantenerse en forma.
fitted carpet |fit'id kâr'pit| *n* (*Brit*) moque-
ta.
fitted kitchen |fit'id kich'ən| *n* (*Brit*) coci-
na amueblada.
fitter |fit'ûr| *n* ajustador(a) *m/f*.
fitting |fit'ing| *a* apropiado ♦ *n* (*of dress*)
prueba; *see also* **fittings.**
fitting room *n* (*in shop*) probador *m*.
fittings |fit'ingz| *npl* instalaciones *fpl*.
five |fīv| *num* cinco; **she is** ~ **(years old)** tie-
ne cinco años (de edad); **it costs** ~ **dollars**
cuesta cinco dólares; **it's** ~ **(o'clock)** son
las cinco.
five-day week |fīv'dā wēk'| *n* semana in-
glesa.
fix |fiks| *vt* (*secure*) fijar, asegurar; (*mend*)
arreglar; (*make ready: meal, drink*) preparar; (*castrate*) castrar ♦ *n:* **to be in a** ~
estar en un aprieto; **to** ~ **sth in one's**
mind fijar algo en la memoria.
fix on *vt* (*decide on*) fijar.
fix up *vt* (*arrange: date, meeting*) arreglar; **to** ~ **sb up with sth** proveer a uno
de algo.
fixation |fiksā'shən| *n* (*PSYCH, fig*) obsesión
f.
fixative |fiks'ətiv| *n* fijador *m*.
fixed |fikst| *a* (*prices etc*) fijo; **how are you**
~ **for money?** (*col*) ¿qué tal andas de dinero?
fixed assets *npl* activo *sg* fijo.
fixed charge *n* gasto fijo.
fixed-price contract |fikst'prīs' kän'trakt|
n contrato a precio fijo.
fixture |fiks'chûr| *n* (*SPORT*) encuentro; ~**s**
npl instalaciones *fpl* fijas.
fizz |fiz| *vi* burbujear.
fizzle out |fiz'əl out| *vi* apagarse; (*enthu-
siasm, interest*) morirse; (*plan*) fracasar.
fizzy |fiz'ē| *a* (*drink*) gaseoso.
fjord |fyôrd| *n* = **fiord.**
FL (*US MAIL*) = *Florida.*
Fla. *abbr* (*US*) = *Florida.*
flabbergasted |flab'ûrgastid| *a* pasmado.
flabby |flab'ē| *a* flojo (de carnes); (*skin*)
fofo.
flag |flag| *n* bandera; (*stone*) losa ♦ *vi* de-
caer; ~ **of convenience** pabellón *m* de
conveniencia.
flag down *vt:* **to** ~ **sb down** hacer señas a uno para que pare.
flagpole |flag'pōl| *n* asta de bandera.
flagrant |flāg'rənt| *a* flagrante.

flagship |flag'ship| *n* buque *m* insignia *or*
almirante.
flagstone |flag'stōn| *n* losa.
flag stop *n* (*US*) parada a petición.
flair |flâr| *n* aptitud *f* especial.
flak |flak| *n* (*MIL*) fuego antiaéreo; (*col: crit-
icism*) lluvia de críticas.
flake |flāk| *n* (*of rust, paint*) escama; (*of
snow, soap powder*) copo ♦ *vi* (*also:* ~ **off**)
(*paint*) descoharse; (*skin*) descamarse.
flaky |flā'kē| *a* (*paintwork*) desconchado;
(*skin*) escamoso.
flaky pastry *n* (*Brit CULIN*) hojaldre *m*.
flamboyant |flamboi'ənt| *a* (*dress*) vistoso;
(*person*) extravagante.
flame |flām| *n* llama; **to burst into** ~**s**
incendiarse; **old** ~ (*col*) antiguo amor *m/f*.
flamingo |fləming'gō| *n* flamenco.
flammable |flam'əbəl| *a* inflamable.
flan |flan| *n* tarta.
flank |flangk| *n* flanco; (*of person*) costado ♦
vt flanquear.
flannel |flan'əl| *n* (*Brit: also:* **face** ~) mano-
pla; (*fabric*) franela; ~**s** *npl* pantalones
mpl de franela.
flannelette |flanəlet'| *n* franela de algodón.
flap |flap| *n* (*of pocket, envelope*) solapa; (*of
table*) hoja (plegadiza); (*wing movement*)
aletazo; (*AVIAT*) flap *m* ♦ *vt* (*wings*) ale-
tear ♦ *vi* (*sail, flag*) ondear.
flapjack |flap'jak| *n* (*US*) torta, panqueque
m (*LAm*).
flare |flâr| *n* llamarada; (*MIL*) bengala; (*in
skirt etc*) vuelo.
flare up *vi* encenderse; (*fig: person*)
encolerizarse; (: *revolt*) estallar.
flash |flash| *n* relámpago; (*also:* **news** ~)
noticias *fpl* de última hora; (*PHOT*) flash *m*
♦ *vt* (*light, headlights*) encender y apagar;
(*torch*) encender ♦ *vi* brillar; **in a** ~ en un
santiamén; ~ **of inspiration** ráfaga de
inspiración; **to** ~ **sth about** (*fig, col:
flaunt*) ostentar algo, presumir con algo; **he**
~**ed by** *or* **past** pasó como un rayo.
flashback |flash'bak| *n* flashback *m*.
flashbulb |flash'bulb| *n* bombilla fusible.
flash card *n* (*SCOL*) tarjeta, carta.
flash cube *n* cubo *m* de flash.
flashlight |flash'līt| *n* (*US: torch*) linterna.
flash point *n* punto de inflamación; (*fig*)
punto de indignación.
flashy |flash'ē| *a* (*pej*) ostentoso.
flask |flask| *n* frasco; (*also:* **vacuum** ~)
termo(s) *m*.
flat |flat| *a* llano; (*smooth*) liso; (*tire*) des-
inflado; (*Brit: battery*) descargado; (*beer*)
muerto; (*MUS: instrument*) desafinado ♦ *n*
(*Brit: apartment*) piso (*Sp*), departamento
(*LAm*), apartamento; (*AUT*) pinchazo;
(*MUS*) bemol *m*; **(to work)** ~ **out** (*trabajar*) a toda mecha; ~ **rate of pay** sueldo
fijo.
flatfooted |flat'foõtid| *a* de pies planos.

flatly [flat'lē] *ad* terminantemente, de plano.

flatmate [flat'māt] *n* (*Brit*) compañero/a de piso.

flatness [flat'nis] *n* (*of land*) llanura, lo llano.

flatten [flat'ən] *vt* (*also:* ~ **out**) allanar; (*smooth out*) alisar; (*house, city*) arrasar.

flatter [flat'ûr] *vt* adular, halagar; (*show to advantage*) favorecer.

flatterer [flat'ûrûr] *n* adulador(a) *m/f*.

flattering [flat'ûring] *a* halagüeño; (*clothes etc*) que favorece, favorecedor(a).

flattery [flat'ûrē] *n* adulación *f*.

flatulence [flach'ələns] *n* flatulencia.

flaunt [flônt] *vt* ostentar, lucir.

flavor [flā'vûr] (*US*) *n* sabor *m*, gusto ♦ *vt* sazonar, condimentar; **strawberry** ~**ed** con sabor a fresa.

flavoring [flā'vûring] *n* (*in product*) aromatizante *m*.

flavour [flā'vûr] *etc* (*Brit*) = **flavor** *etc*.

flaw [flô] *n* defecto.

flawless [flô'lis] *a* intachable.

flax [flaks] *n* lino.

flaxen [flak'sən] *a* rubio.

flea [flē] *n* pulga.

flea market *n* rastro, mercadillo.

fleck [flek] *n* (*mark, mud, paint*) mota; (*color, pattern*) punto; (*of dust*) partícula ♦ *vt* (*with blood, mud etc*) salpicar; **brown** ~**ed with white** marrón con puntos blancos.

fledg(e)ling [flej'ling] *n* (*fig*) novato/a, principiante *m/f*.

flee [flē] *pt, pp* **fled** [fled] *vt* huir de, abandonar ♦ *vi* huir, fugarse.

fleece [flēs] *n* vellón *m*; (*wool*) lana ♦ *vt* (*col*) pelar.

fleecy [flē'sē] *a* (*blanket*) lanoso, lanudo; (*cloud*) aborregado.

fleet [flēt] *n* flota; (*of cars, trucks etc*) escuadra.

fleeting [flē'ting] *a* fugaz.

Flemish [flem'ish] *a* flamenco ♦ *n* (*LING*) flamenco; **the** ~ los flamencos.

flesh [flesh] *n* carne *f*; (*of fruit*) pulpa; **of** ~ **and blood** de carne y hueso.

flesh wound *n* herida superficial.

flew [floo] *pt of* **fly**.

flex [fleks] *n* cordón *m* ♦ *vt* (*muscles*) tensar.

flexibility [fleksəbil'ətē] *n* flexibilidad *f*.

flexible [flek'səbəl] *a* (*gen, disk*) flexible; ~ **working hours** horario *sg* flexible.

flick [flik] *n* golpecito; (*with finger*) capirotazo; (*col: movie*) película ♦ *vt* dar un golpecito a.

flick off *vt* quitar con el dedo.

flick through *vt fus* hojear.

flicker [flik'ûr] *vi* (*light*) parpadear; (*flame*) vacilar ♦ *n* parpadeo.

flick knife *n* (*Brit*) navaja de muelle.

flier [flī'ûr] *n* aviador(a) *m/f*.

flies [flīz] *npl of* **fly**.

flight [flīt] *n* vuelo; (*escape*) huida, fuga;

(*also:* ~ **of steps**) tramo (de escaleras); **to take** ~ huir, darse a la fuga; **to put to** ~ ahuyentar; **how long does the** ~ **take?** ¿cuánto dura el vuelo?

flight attendant *n* tripulante *m/f* auxiliar.

flight deck *n* (*AVIAT*) cabina de mandos.

flight recorder *n* registrador *m* de vuelo.

flighty [flī'tē] *a* frívolo; caprichoso.

flimsy [flim'zē] *a* (*thin*) muy ligero; (*excuse*) flojo.

flinch [flinch] *vi* encogerse.

fling [fling] *vt* (*pt, pp* **flung** [flung]) arrojar ♦ *n* (*love affair*) aventura amorosa.

flint [flint] *n* pedernal *m*; (*in lighter*) piedra.

flip [flip] *vt*: **to** ~ **a coin** echar a cara o cruz.

flip over *vt* dar la vuelta a.

flip through *vt fus* (*book, records*) hojear, repasar.

flippancy [flip'ənsē] *n* ligereza.

flippant [flip'ənt] *a* poco serio.

flipper [flip'ûr] *n* (*of seal etc, for swimming*) aleta.

flip side *n* (*of record*) cara B.

flirt [flûrt] *vi* coquetear, flirtear ♦ *n* coqueta *f*.

flirtation [flûrtā'shən] *n* coqueteo, flirteo.

flit [flit] *vi* revolotear.

float [flōt] *n* flotador *m*; (*in procession*) carroza; (*sum of money*) reserva ♦ *vi* (*also* COMM: *currency*) flotar; (*bather*) hacer la plancha ♦ *vt* (*gen*) hacer flotar; (*company*) lanzar; **to** ~ **an idea** propagar una idea.

floating [flō'ting] *a*: ~ **vote** voto indeciso; ~ **voter** votante *m/f* indeciso/a.

flock [flâk] *n* (*of sheep*) rebaño; (*of birds*) bandada; (*of people*) multitud *f*.

floe [flō] *n*: **ice** ~ témpano de hielo.

flog [flâg] *vt* azotar.

flood [flud] *n* inundación *f*; (*of words, tears etc*) torrente *m* ♦ *vt* (*also* AUT: *carburetor*) inundar; **to** ~ **the market** (COMM) inundar el mercado.

flooding [flud'ing] *n* inundación *f*.

floodlight [flud'līt] *n* foco ♦ *vt* (*irg: like* **light**) iluminar con focos.

floodlit [flud'lit] *pt, pp of* **floodlight** ♦ *a* iluminado.

flood tide *n* pleamar *f*.

floor [flôr] *n* suelo; (*story*) piso; (*of sea, valley*) fondo; (*dance* ~) pista ♦ *vt* (*fig: baffle*) dejar sin respuesta, confundir; (*: silence*) dejar sin réplica posible; (*US* AUT) pisar el acelerador; **first** ~ (*US*), **ground** ~ (*Brit*) planta baja; **second** ~ (*US*), **first** ~ (*Brit*) primer piso; **top** ~ último piso; **to have the** ~ (*speaker*) tener la palabra.

floorboard [flôr'bôrd] *n* tabla.

flooring [flôr'ing] *n* suelo; (*material*) solería.

floor lamp *n* (*US*) lámpara de pie.

floor show *n* cabaret *m*.

floorwalker [flôr'wôkûr] *n* (*US* COMM) vigilante *m/f*.

flop [flâp] *n* fracaso ♦ *vi* (*fail*) fracasar.
flophouse [flâp'hous] *n* (*US*) pensión *f* de mala muerte.
floppy [flâp'ē] *a* flojo ♦ *n* = **floppy disk**.
floppy disk *n* (*COMPUT*) floppy *m*, floppy-disk *m*, disco flexible.
flora [flôr'ə] *n* flora.
floral [flôr'əl] *a* floral.
Florence [flâr'əns] *n* Florencia.
Florentine [flôr'əntēn] *a*, *n* florentino/a *m/f*.
florid [flôr'id] *a* (*style*) florido.
florist [flôr'ist] *n* florista *m/f*; ~'s (shop) *n* florería.
flotation [flōtā'shən] *n* (*of shares*) emisión *f*; (*of company*) lanzamiento.
flounce [flouns] *n* volante *m*.
   flounce in *vi* entrar con gesto exagerado.
   flounce out *vi* salir enfadado.
flounder [floun'dûr] *vi* tropezar ♦ *n* (*ZOOL*) platija.
flour [flou'ûr] *n* harina.
flourish [flûr'ish] *vi* florecer ♦ *n* ademán *m*, movimiento (ostentoso).
flourishing [flûr'ishing] *a* floreciente.
flout [flout] *vt* burlarse de; (*order*) no hacer caso de, hacer caso omiso de.
flow [flō] *n* (*movement*) flujo; (*direction*) curso; (*of river, tide, also ELEC*) corriente *f* ♦ *vi* correr, fluir.
flow chart *n* organigrama *m*.
flow diagram *n* organigrama *m*.
flower [flou'ûr] *n* flor *f* ♦ *vi* florecer; **in ~** en flor.
flower bed *n* macizo.
flowerpot [flou'ûrpát] *n* tiesto.
flowery [flou'ûrē] *a* florido.
flowing [flō'ing] *a* (*hair, clothes*) suelto; (*style*) fluido.
flown [flōn] *pp of* **fly**.
flu [flōō] *n* gripe *f*.
fluctuate [fluk'chōōāt] *vi* fluctuar.
fluctuation [flukchōōā'shən] *n* fluctuación *f*.
flue [flōō] *n* humero.
fluency [flōō'ənsē] *n* fluidez *f*.
fluent [flōō'ənt] *a* (*speech*) elocuente; **he speaks ~ French, he's ~ in French** domina el francés.
fluently [flōō'əntlē] *ad* con fluidez.
fluff [fluf] *n* pelusa.
fluffy [fluf'ē] *a* velloso.
fluid [flōō'id] *a*, *n* fluido, líquido; (*in diet*) líquido.
fluke [flōōk] *n* (*col*) chiripa.
flummox [flum'əks] *vt* desconcertar.
flung [flung] *pt, pp of* **fling**.
flunky [flung'kē] *n* lacayo.
fluorescent [flōōəres'ənt] *a* fluorescente.
fluoride [flōō'ərīd] *n* fluoruro.
fluoride toothpaste *n* pasta de dientes con flúor.
flurry [flûr'ē] *n* (*of snow*) temporal *m*; (*haste*) agitación *f*; ~ **of activity** frenesí *m*

de actividad.

flush [flush] *n* (*on face*) rubor *m*; (*fig: of youth, beauty*) resplandor *m* ♦ *vt* limpiar con agua; (*also:* ~ **out**) (*game, birds*) levantar; (*fig: criminal*) poner al descubierto ♦ *vi* ruborizarse ♦ *a:* ~ **with** a ras de; **to ~ the toilet** hacer funcionar el WC.
flushed [flusht] *a* ruborizado.
fluster [flus'tûr] *n* aturdimiento ♦ *vt* aturdir.
flustered [flus'tûrd] *a* aturdido.
flute [flōōt] *n* flauta.
flutter [flut'ûr] *n* (*of wings*) revoloteo, aleteo; (*Brit: fam: bet*) apuesta ♦ *vi* revolotear; **to be in a ~** estar nervioso.
flux [fluks] *n* flujo; **in a state of ~** cambiando continuamente.
fly [flī] *n* (*insect*) mosca; (*on pants: also:* **flies**) bragueta ♦ *vb* (*pt* **flew**, *pp* **flown**) *vt* (*plane*) pilot(e)ar; (*cargo*) transportar (en avión); (*distances*) recorrer (en avión) ♦ *vi* volar; (*passengers*) ir en avión; (*escape*) evadirse; (*flag*) ondear.
fly away *vi* (*bird, insect*) volarse.
fly in *vi* (*person*) llegar en avión; (*plane*) aterrizar; **he flew in from Bilbao** llegó en avión desde Bilbao.
fly off *vi* volarse.
fly out *vi* irse en avión.
fly-fishing [flī'fishing] *n* pesca con mosca.
flying [flī'ing] *n* (*activity*) (el) volar ♦ *a:* ~ **visit** visita relámpago; **with ~ colors** con lucimiento.
flying buttress *n* arbotante *m*.
flying saucer *n* platillo volante.
flying squad *n* (*MIL etc*) brigada móvil.
flying start *n:* **to get off to a ~** empezar con buen pie.
flyleaf, *pl* **flyleaves** [flī'lēf, lēvz] *n* (hoja de) guarda.
flyover [flī'ōvûr] *n* (*US*) desfile *m* aéreo; (*Brit: bridge*) paso superior *or* a desnivel.
flypast [flī'past] *n* desfile *m* aéreo.
flysheet [flī'shēt] *n* (*for tent*) doble techo.
flyswatter [flī'swâtûr] *n* matamoscas *m inv*.
flywheel [flī'hwēl] *n* volante *m* mecánico.
FM *abbr* (*RADIO*: = *frequency modulation*) FM; (*Brit MIL*) = **field marshal**.
FMB *n abbr* (*US*) = *Federal Maritime Board*.
FMCS *n abbr* (*US*: = *Federal Mediation and Conciliation Services*) organismo de conciliación en conflictos laborales.
foal [fōl] *n* potro.
foam [fōm] *n* espuma ♦ *vi* echar espuma.
foam rubber *n* espuma de caucho.
FOB *abbr* (= *free on board*) f.a.b.
fob [fâb] *n* (*also:* **watch ~**) leontina ♦ *vt:* **to ~ sb off with sth** deshacerse de uno con algo.
foc *abbr* (*Brit:* = *free of charge*) gratis.
focal [fō'kəl] *a* focal; ~ **point** punto focal; (*fig*) centro de atención.
focus [fō'kəs] (*pl:* ~**es**) *n* foco ♦ *vt* (*field*

glasses etc) enfocar ♦ *vi*: **to ~ (on)** enfocar (a); (*issue etc*) centrarse en; **in/out of ~** enfocado/desenfocado.

fodder [fåd'ûr] *n* pienso.

FOE *n abbr* (= *Friends of the Earth*) Amigos *mpl* de la Tierra; (*US*: = *Fraternal Order of Eagles*) organización benéfica.

foe [fō] *n* enemigo.

foetus [fē'təs] *n* (*Brit*) = **fetus.**

fog [fóg] *n* niebla.

  fog up *vi* (*windows*) empañarse.

fogbound [fóg'bound] *a* inmovilizado por la niebla.

foggy [fóg'ē] *a*: **it's ~** hay niebla, está brumoso.

fog light *n* (*AUT*) faro antiniebla.

foible [foi'bəl] *n* manía.

foil [foil] *vt* frustrar ♦ *n* hoja; (*kitchen ~*) papel *m* (de) aluminio; (*FENCING*) florete *m*.

foist [foist] *vt*: **to ~ sth on sb** colarle algo a uno.

fold [fōld] *n* (*bend, crease*) pliegue *m*; (*AGR*) redil *m* ♦ *vt* doblar; (*map etc*) plegar; **to ~ one's arms** cruzarse de brazos.

  fold up *vi* plegarse, doblarse; (*business*) quebrar.

folder [fōl'dûr] *n* (*for papers*) carpeta; (*binder*) carpeta de anillas; (*brochure*) folleto.

folding [fōl'ding] *a* (*chair, bed*) plegable.

foliage [fō'lēij] *n* follaje *m*.

folio [fō'lēō] *n* folio.

folk [fōk] *npl* gente *f* ♦ *a* popular, folklórico; **~s** *npl* familia, parientes *mpl*.

folklore [fōk'lôr] *n* folklore *m*.

folk music *n* música folk (lórica).

folk singer *n* cantante *m/f* de canciones folklóricas.

folk song *n* canción *f* popular *or* folklórica.

follow [fâl'ō] *vt* seguir ♦ *vi* seguir; (*result*) resultar; **he ~ed suit** hizo lo mismo; **to ~ sb's advice** seguir el consejo de uno; **I don't quite ~** you no le sigo (la pista); **to ~ in sb's footsteps** seguirle los pasos a uno; **it doesn't ~ that ...** no se puede concluir que ....

  follow on *vi* seguir; (*continue*): **to ~ on from** continuar.

  follow out *vt* (*implement: idea, plan*) realizar, llevar a cabo.

  follow through *vt* llevar hasta el fin ♦ *vi* (*SPORT*) dar el remate.

  follow up *vt* (*letter, offer*) responder a; (*case*) investigar.

follower [fâl'ōûr] *n* seguidor(a) *m/f*; (*POL*) partidario/a.

following [fâl'ōing] *a* siguiente ♦ *n* afición *f*, partidarios *mpl*.

follow-up [fâl'ōup] *n* seguimiento.

follow-up letter *n* carta recordatoria.

folly [fâl'ē] *n* locura.

fond [fând] *a* (*loving*) cariñoso; **to be ~ of**

sb tener cariño a uno; **she's ~ of swimming** tiene afición a la natación, a ella le gusta nadar.

fondle [fân'dəl] *vt* acariciar.

fondly [fând'lē] *ad* (*lovingly*) con cariño; **he ~ believed that ...** creía inocentemente que ....

fondness [fân'dnis] *n* (*for things*) afición *f*; (*for people*) cariño.

font [fânt] *n* pila bautismal.

food [fōōd] *n* comida.

food mixer *n* batidora.

food poisoning *n* botulismo.

food processor [fōōd prås'esûr] *n* robot *m* de cocina.

foodstuffs [fōōd'stufs] *npl* comestibles *mpl*.

fool [fōōl] *n* tonto/a; (*CULIN*) puré *m* de frutas con nata ♦ *vt* engañar; **to make a ~ of o.s.** ponerse en ridículo; **you can't ~ me** a mí no me engañas.

  fool about *vi* (*Brit*) = **fool around.**

  fool around *vi* bromear; (*waste time*) perder el tiempo.

foolhardy [fōōl'hârdē] *a* temerario.

foolish [fōō'lish] *a* tonto; (*careless*) imprudente.

foolishly [fōō'lishlē] *ad* tontamente, neciamente.

foolproof [fōōl'prōōf] *a* (*plan etc*) infalible.

foolscap [fōōlz'kap] *n* papel *m* folio.

foot [fōōt], *pl* **feet** [fēt] *n* (*gen, also: of page, stairs etc*) pie *m*; (*measure*) pie *m* (= *304 mm*); (*of animal, table*) pata ♦ *vt* (*bill*) pagar; **on ~** a pie; **to find one's feet** acostumbrarse; **to put one's ~ down** (*say no*) plantarse; (*Brit AUT*) pisar el acelerador.

footage [fōōt'ij] *n* (*CINEMA*) imágenes *fpl*.

foot-and-mouth (disease) [fōōt'-ənmouth' (dizēz'] *n* fiebre *f* aftosa.

football [fōōt'bôl] *n* balón *m*; (*game*) fútbol *m*.

footballer [fōōt'bôlûr] *n* (*Brit*) = **football player.**

football game *n* partido de fútbol.

football player *n* futbolista *m/f*, jugador(a) *m/f* de fútbol.

footbrake [fōōt'brāk] *n* freno de pie.

footbridge [fōōt'brij] *n* puente *m* para peatones.

foothills [fōōt'hilz] *npl* estribaciones *fpl*.

foothold [fōōt'hōld] *n* pie *m* firme.

footing [fōōt'ing] *n* (*fig*) posición *f*; **to lose one's ~** perder el pie; **on an equal ~** en pie de igualdad.

footlights [fōōt'lits] *npl* candilejas *fpl*.

footman [fōōt'mən] *n* lacayo.

footnote [fōōt'nōt] *n* nota (de pie de página).

footpath [fōōt'path] *n* sendero.

footprint [fōōt'print] *n* huella, pisada.

footrest [fōōt'rest] *n* apoyapiés *m inv*.

footsore [fōōt'sôr] *a* con los pies doloridos.

footstep [fōōt'step] *n* paso.

footwear |foŏt'weùr| *n* calzado.

FOR *abbr* (= *free on rail*) franco (puesto sobre) vagón.

for |fôr| *prep* (*gen*) para; (*as, in exchange for, because of*) por; (*during*) durante; (*in spite of*) a pesar de ♦ *conj* pues, ya que; **it was sold ~ 100 pesetas** se vendió por 100 pesetas; **what ~?** ¿para qué?; **what's this button ~?** ¿para qué sirve este botón?; **he was away ~ 2 years** estuvo fuera 2 años; **I haven't seen him ~ 3 days** hace 3 días que no le veo; **he went ~ the paper** fue a buscar el periódico; **the train ~ New York** el tren de Nueva York; **is this ~ me?** ¿es para mí esto?; **it's time ~ lunch** es la hora de comer; **G ~ George** G de Gerona.

forage |fôr'ij| *n* forraje *m*.

foray |fôr'ā| *n* incursión *f*.

forbid, *pt* **forbad(e)**, *pp* **forbidden** |fûrbid', fûrbād', fûrbid'ɔn| *vt* prohibir; **to ~ sb to do sth** prohibir a uno hacer algo.

forbidding |fûrbid'ing| *a* (*landscape*) inhóspito; (*severe*) severo.

force |fôrs| *n* fuerza ♦ *vt* forzar; **to ~ o.s. to do** hacer un esfuerzo por hacer; **the Armed F~s** *npl* las Fuerzas Armadas; **sales ~** (*COMM*) personal *m* de ventas; **a ~ 5 wind** un viento fuerza 5; **to join ~s** unir fuerzas; **in ~** (*law etc*) en vigor; **to ~ sb to do sth** obligar a uno a hacer algo.

force back *vt* (*crowd, enemy*) hacer retroceder; (*tears*) reprimir.

force down *vt* (*food*) comer sin gusto.

forced |fôrst| *a* (*smile*) forzado; (*landing*) forzoso.

force-feed |fôrs'fēd| *vt* (*animal, prisoner*) alimentar a la fuerza.

forceful |fôrs'fɔl| *a* enérgico.

forceps |fôr'sɔps| *npl* fórceps *m inv*.

forcible |fôr'sɔbɔl| *a* (*violent*) a la fuerza; (*telling*) convincente.

forcibly |fôr'sɔblē| *ad* a la fuerza.

ford |fôrd| *n* vado ♦ *vt* vadear.

fore |fôr| *n*: **to bring to the ~** sacar a la luz pública; **to come to the ~** hacerse notar.

forearm |fôr'ârm| *n* antebrazo.

forebear |fôr'beùr| *n* antepasado.

foreboding |fôrbō'ding| *n* presentimiento.

forecast |fôr'kast| *n* pronóstico ♦ *vt* (*irg*: *like* **cast**) pronosticar; **weather ~** previsión *f* meteorológica.

foreclose |fôrklōz'| *vt* (*LAW*: *also*: **~ on**) extinguir el derecho de redimir.

foreclosure |fôrklō'zhùr| *n* apertura de un juicio hipotecario.

forecourt |fôr'kôrt| *n* (*of gas station*) patio.

forefathers |fôr'fâthùrz| *npl* antepasados *mpl*.

forefinger |fôr'finggûr| *n* (dedo) índice *m*.

forefront |fôr'frunt| *n*: **in the ~ of** en la vanguardia de.

forego, *pt* **forewent**, *pp* **foregone** |fôrgō', -went', -gôn'| *vt* = **forgo**.

foregoing |fôrgō'ing| *a* anterior, precedente.

foregone |fôrgôn'| *pp of* **forego** ♦ *a*: **it's a ~ conclusion** es una conclusión inevitable.

foreground |fôr'ground| *n* primer plano.

forehand |fôr'hand| *n* (*TENNIS*) golpe *m* derecho *or* directo.

forehead |fôr'hed| *n* frente *f*.

foreign |fôr'in| *a* extranjero; (*trade*) exterior.

foreign currency *n* divisas *fpl*.

foreigner |fôr'ɔnûr| *n* extranjero/a.

foreign exchange *n* (*system*) cambio de divisas; (*money*) divisas *fpl*, moneda extranjera.

foreign investment *n* inversión *f* en el extranjero; (*money, stock*) inversiones *fpl* extranjeras.

Foreign Office *n* (*Brit*) Ministerio de Asuntos Exteriores.

Foreign Secretary *n* (*Brit*) Ministro de Asuntos Exteriores.

foreleg |fôr'leg| *n* pata delantera.

foreman |fôr'mɔn| *n* capataz *m*; (*in construction*) maestro de obras; (*LAW*: *of jury*) presidente *m/f*.

foremost |fôr'mōst| *a* principal ♦ *ad*: **first and ~** ante todo, antes que nada.

forename |fôr'nām| *n* nombre *m* (de pila).

forensic |fɔren'sik| *a* forense; **~ scientist** forense *m/f*.

forerunner |fôr'runûr| *n* precursor(a) *m/f*.

foresee, *pt* **foresaw**, *pp* **foreseen** |fôrsē', -sô', -sēn'| *vt* prever.

foreseeable |fôrsē'ɔbɔl| *a* previsible.

foreshadow |fôrshad'ō| *vt* prefigurar, anunciar.

foreshore |fôr'shôr| *n* playa.

foreshorten |fôrshôr'tɔn| *vt* (*figure, scene*) escorzar.

foresight |fôr'sīt| *n* previsión *f*.

foreskin |fôr'skin| *n* (*ANAT*) prepucio.

forest |fôr'ist| *n* bosque *m*.

forestall |fôrstôl'| *vt* prevenir.

forestry |fôr'istrē| *n* silvicultura.

foretaste |fôr'tāst| *n* anticipo.

foretell, *pt*, *pp* **foretold** |fôrtel', -tōld'| *vt* predecir, pronosticar.

forethought |fôr'thôt| *n* previsión *f*.

forever |fôrev'ùr| *ad* para siempre.

forewarn |fôrwôrn'| *vt* avisar, advertir.

forewent |fôrwent'| *pt of* **forego**.

foreword |fôr'wûrd| *n* prefacio.

forfeit |fôr'fit| *n* (*in game*) prenda ♦ *vt* perder (derecho a).

forgave |fûrgāv'| *pt of* **forgive**.

forge |fôrj| *n* fragua; (*smithy*) herrería ♦ *vt* (*signature*: *Brit*: *money*) falsificar; (*metal*) forjar.

forge ahead *vi* avanzar constantemente.

forger |fôr'jûr| *n* falsificador(a) *m/f*.

forgery |fôr'jûrē| *n* falsificación *f*.

forget, *pt* **forgot**, *pp* **forgotten** |fûrget', -gât',

-gát'ən] *vt* olvidar ♦ *vi* olvidarse.
forgetful [fûrget'fəl] *a* olvidadizo.
forget-me-not [fûrget'mēnât] *n* nomeolvides *f inv*.
forgive, *pt* **forgave,** *pp* **forgiven** [fûrgiv', -gāv', -giv'ən] *vt* perdonar; **to ~ sb for sth/for doing sth** perdonar algo a uno/a uno por haber hecho algo.
forgiveness [fûrgiv'nis] *n* perdón *m*.
forgiving [fûrgiv'ing] *a* compasivo.
forgo, *pt* **forwent,** *pp* **forgone** [fôrgō', -went', -gôn'] *vt* (*give up*) renunciar a; (*go without*) privarse de.
forgot [fûrgât'] *pt of* **forget.**
forgotten [fûrgât'ən] *pp of* **forget.**
fork [fôrk] *n* (*for eating*) tenedor *m*; (*for gardening*) horca; (*of roads*) bifurcación *f*; (*in tree*) horcadura ♦ *vi* (*road*) bifurcarse.
fork out *vt* (*col: pay*) desembolsar.
forked [fôrkt] *a* (*lightning*) en zigzag.
forklift truck [fôrk'lift truk'] *n* máquina elevadora.
forlorn [fôrlôrn'] *a* (*person*) triste, melancólico; (*deserted: cottage*) abandonado; (*desperate: attempt*) desesperado.
form [fôrm] *n* forma; (*Brit SCOL*) clase *f*; (*document*) formulario ♦ *vt* formar; **in the ~ of** en forma de; **in top ~** en plena forma; **to be in good ~** (*SPORT, fig*) estar en plena forma; **to ~ part of sth** formar parte de algo; **to ~ a circle/a line** hacer una curva/una cola.
formal [fôr'məl] *a* (*offer, receipt*) por escrito; (*person etc*) correcto; (*occasion, dinner*) ceremonioso; **~ dress** traje *m* de vestir; (*evening dress*) traje *m* de etiqueta.
formalities [fôrmal'itēz] *npl* formalidades *fpl*.
formality [fôrmal'itē] *n* ceremonia.
formalize [fôr'məliz] *vt* formalizar.
formally [fôr'məlē] *ad* oficialmente.
format [fôr'mat] *n* formato ♦ *vt* (*COMPUT*) formatear.
formation [fôrmā'shən] *n* formación *f*.
formative [fôr'mətiv] *a* (*years*) formativo.
format line *n* (*COMPUT*) línea de formato.
former [fôr'mûr] *a* anterior; (*earlier*) antiguo; (*ex*) ex; **the ~ ... the latter ...** aquél ... éste ...; **the ~ president** el antiguo *or* ex presidente.
formerly [fôr'mûrlē] *ad* antiguamente.
form feed *n* (*on printer*) salto de página.
Formica [fôrmī'kə] ® *n* Formica ®.
formidable [fôr'midəbəl] *a* formidable.
formula [fôr'myələ] *n* fórmula; **F~ One** (*AUT*) Fórmula Uno.
formulate [fôr'myəlāt] *vt* formular.
fornicate [fôr'nikāt] *vi* fornicar.
forsake, *pt* **forsook,** *pp* **forsaken** [fôrsāk', -sŏōk', -sā'kən] *vt* (*gen*) abandonar; (*plan*) renunciar a.
fort [fôrt] *n* fuerte *m;* **to hold the ~** (*fig*) quedarse a cargo.

forte [fôr'tā] *n* fuerte *m*.
forth [fôrth] *ad:* **back and ~** de acá para allá; **and so ~** y así sucesivamente.
forthcoming [fôrth'kum'ing] *a* próximo, venidero; (*character*) comunicativo.
forthright [fôrth'rīt] *a* franco.
forthwith [fôrthwith'] *ad* en el acto, acto seguido.
fortification [fôrtəfəkā'shən] *n* fortificación *f*.
fortified wine [fôr'təfid wīn'] *n* vino encabezado.
fortify [fôr'təfī] *vt* fortalecer.
fortitude [fôr'tətŏōd] *n* fortaleza.
fortnight [fôrt'nīt] *n* (*Brit*) quincena; **it's a ~ since ...** hace quince días que ....
fortnightly [fôrt'nitlē] (*Brit*) *a* quincenal ♦ *ad* quincenalmente.
FORTRAN [fôr'tran] *n* FORTRAN *m*.
fortress [fôr'tris] *n* fortaleza.
fortuitous [fôrtōō'itəs] *a* fortuito.
fortunate [fôr'chənit] *a:* **it is ~ that...** (es una) suerte que....
fortunately [fôr'chənitlē] *ad* afortunadamente.
fortune [fôr'chən] *n* suerte *f*; (*wealth*) fortuna; **to make a ~** hacer un dineral.
fortuneteller [fôr'chəntelûr] *n* adivino/a.
forty [fôr'tē] *num* cuarenta.
forum [fôr'əm] *n* (*also fig*) foro.
forward [fôr'wûrd] *a* (*movement, position*) avanzado; (*front*) delantero; (*not shy*) atrevido ♦ *n* (*SPORT*) delantero ♦ *vt* (*letter*) remitir; (*career*) promocionar; **to move ~** avanzar; **"please ~"** "remítase al destinatario".
forward(s) [fôr'wûrdz] *ad* (hacia) adelante.
forwent [fôrwent'] *pt of* **forgo.**
fossil [fâs'əl] *n* fósil *m*; **~ fuel** hidrocarburo.
foster [fôs'tûr] *vt* fomentar.
foster brother *n* hermano de leche.
foster child *n* hijo/a adoptivo/a.
foster mother *n* madre *f* adoptiva.
fought [fôt] *pt, pp of* **fight.**
foul [foul] *a* (*gen*) sucio, puerco; (*weather, smell etc*) asqueroso ♦ *n* (*SPORT*) falta ♦ *vt* (*dirty*) ensuciar; (*block*) atascar; (*entangle: anchor, propeller*) atascar, enredarse en; (*player*) cometer una falta contra.
foul play *n* (*SPORT*) mala jugada; (*LAW*) muerte *f* violenta.
found [found] *pt, pp of* **find** ♦ *vt* (*establish*) fundar.
foundation [foundā'shən] *n* (*act*) fundación *f*; (*basis*) base *f*; (*also:* **~ cream**) crema base.
foundations [foundā'shənz] *npl* (*of building*) cimientos *mpl*; **to lay the ~** poner los cimientos.
foundation stone *n:* **to lay the ~** poner la primera piedra.
founder [foun'dûr] *n* fundador(a) *m/f* ♦ *vi*

hundirse.
founding [foun'ding] *a*: ~ **fathers** (*esp US*) fundadores *mpl*, próceres *mpl*; ~ **member** miembro fundador.
foundry [foun'drē] *n* fundición *f*.
fountain [foun'tin] *n* fuente *f*.
fountain pen *n* (pluma) estilográfica, (*LAm*) plumafuente *f*.
four [fôr] *num* cuatro; **on all** ~**s** a gatas.
four-footed [fôr'fŏŏtid] *a* cuadrúpedo.
four-poster [fôr'pōs'tûr] *n* (*also*: ~ **bed**) cama de columnas.
foursome [fôr'səm] *n* grupo de cuatro personas.
fourteen [fôr'tēn'] *num* catorce.
fourteenth [fôr'tēnth'] *num* decimocuarto.
fourth [fôrth] *num* cuarto ♦ *n* (*AUT*: *also*: ~ **gear**) cuarta (velocidad).
four-wheel drive [fôr'hwēl drīv] *n* tracción *f* a las cuatro ruedas.
fowl [foul] *n* ave *f* (de corral).
fox [fåks] *n* zorro ♦ *vt* confundir.
fox fur *n* piel *f* de zorro.
foxglove [fåks'gluv] *n* (*BOT*) dedalera.
fox hunting *n* caza de zorros.
foxtrot [fåks'tråt] *n* fox *m*.
foyer [foi'ûr] *n* vestíbulo.
FP *n* *abbr* (*US*) = **fireplug**; (*Brit*) = former pupil.
Fr. *abbr* (*REL*) (= *Father*) P.; (= *friar*) Fr.
fr. *abbr* (= *franc*) f.
fracas [frä'kəs] *n* gresca, refriega.
fraction [frak'shən] *n* fracción *f*.
fractionally [frak'shənəlē] *ad* ligeramente.
fractious [frak'shəs] *a* (*person*, *mood*) malhumorado.
fracture [frak'chûr] *n* fractura ♦ *vt* fracturar.
fragile [fraj'əl] *a* frágil.
fragment [frag'mənt] *n* fragmento.
fragmentary [frag'məntärē] *a* fragmentario.
fragrance [frä'grəns] *n* fragancia.
fragrant [frā'grənt] *a* fragante, oloroso.
frail [frāl] *a* (*fragile*) frágil, quebradizo; (*weak*) delicado.
frame [frām] *n* (*TECH*) armazón *f*; (*of picture*, *door etc*) marco; (*of spectacles*: *also*: ~**s**) montura ♦ *vt* encuadrar; (*picture*) enmarcar; (*reply*) formular; **to** ~ **sb** (*col*) inculpar por engaños a uno.
frame of mind *n* estado de ánimo.
framework [frām'wûrk] *n* marco.
France [frans] *n* Francia.
franchise [fran'chīz] *n* (*POL*) derecho de votar, sufragio; (*COMM*) licencia, concesión *f*.
franchisee [franchīzē'] *n* concesionario/a.
franchiser [fran'chīzûr] *n* compañía concesionaria.
frank [frangk] *a* franco ♦ *vt* (*letter*) franquear.
frankfurter [frangk'fûrtûr] *n* salchicha de Frankfurt.
frankincense [frang'kinsens] *n* incienso.

frankly [frangk'lē] *ad* francamente.
frankness [frangk'nis] *n* franquezɪ.
frantic [fran'tik] *a* (*desperate*: *need*, *desire*) desesperado; (: *search*) frenético; (: *person*) desquiciado.
fraternal [frətûr'nəl] *a* fraterno.
fraternity [frətûr'nitē] *n* (*club*) fraternidad *f*; (*US*) club *m* de estudiantes; (*guild*) cofradía.
fraternization [fratûrnəzā'shən] *n* fraternización *f*.
fraternize [frat'ûrnīz] *vi* confraternizar.
fraud [frôd] *n* fraude *m*; (*person*) impostor(a) *m/f*.
fraudulent [frô'jələnt] *a* fraudulento.
fraught [frôt] *a* (*tense*) tenso; ~ **with** cargado de.
fray [frā] *n* combate *m*, lucha, refriega ♦ *vi* deshilacharse; **tempers were** ~**ed** el ambiente se ponía tenso.
FRB *n* *abbr* (*US*) = *Federal Reserve Board*.
freak [frēk] *n* (*person*) fenómeno; (*event*) suceso anormal; (*col*: *enthusiast*) adicto/a ♦ *a* (*storm*, *conditions*) anormal; **health** ~ (*col*) maniático/a en cuestión de salud.
freak out *vi* (*col*: *on drugs*) tener un viaje.
freakish [frēk'ish] *a* (*result*, *appearance*) inesperado, extravagante; (*weather*) cambiadizo.
freckle [frek'əl] *n* peca.
freckled [frek'əld] *a* pecoso, lleno de pecas.
free [frē] *a* (*person*: *at liberty*) libre; (*not fixed*) suelto; (*gratis*) gratuito; (*unoccupied*) desocupado; (*liberal*) generoso ♦ *vt* (*prisoner etc*) poner en libertad; (*jammed object*) soltar; **to give sb a** ~ **hand** darle campo libre a uno; ~ **and easy** despreocupado; **is this seat** ~? ¿está libre este asiento?; ~ **of tax** libre de impuestos; **admission** ~ entrada libre; ~ (**of charge**), **for** ~ *ad* gratis.
-free *a*: **additive**~ sin aditivos; **tax**~ libre de impuestos.
freebie [frē'bē] *n* (*col*): **it's a** ~ es gratis.
freedom [frē'dəm] *n* libertad *f*; ~ **of association** libertad *f* de asociación.
freedom fighter *n* libertador(a).
free enterprise *n* libre empresa.
free-for-all [frē'fûrôl'] *n* riña general.
free gift *n* obsequio.
freehold [frē'hōld] *n* feudo franco alodio.
free kick *n* tiro libre.
freelance [frē'lans] *a*, *ad* por cuenta propia; ~ **work** trabajo independiente.
freely [frē'lē] *ad* libremente; (*liberally*) generosamente.
freemason [frē'māsən] *n* francmasón *m*.
freemasonry [frē'māsənrē] *n* (*franc*)masonería.
free-range [frē'rānj] *a* (*Brit*: *hen*, *eggs*) de granja.
free sample *n* muestra gratuita.

freesia |frē'zhēə| n fresia.
free speech n libertad f de expresión.
freestyle wrestling |frē'stīl rēs'ling| n lucha libre.
free trade n libre comercio.
freeway |frē'wā| n (US) autopista.
freewheel |frē'hwēl'| vi ir en punto muerto.
freewheeling |frē'hwē'ling| a libre, espontáneo; (careless) irresponsable.
free will n libre albedrío; **of one's own ~** por su propia voluntad.
freeze |frēz| vb (pt **froze**, pp **frozen** |frōz, frō'zən|) vi helarse, congelarse ♦ vt helar; (prices, food, salaries) congelar ♦ n helada; congelación f.
  freeze over vi (lake, river) helarse, congelarse; (window, windshield) cubrirse de escarcha.
  freeze up vi helarse, congelarse.
freeze-dried |frēz'drīd'| a liofilizado.
freezer |frē'zûr| n congelador m, congeladora (LAm).
freezing |frē'zing| a helado.
freezing point n punto de congelación; **3 degrees below ~** tres grados bajo cero.
freight |frāt| n (goods) carga; (money charged) flete m; **~ forward** contra reembolso del flete, flete debido; **~ free** franco de porte; **~ inward** flete sobre compras; **~ paid** porte m pagado.
freight car n vagón m de mercancías.
freighter |frā'tûr| n nave f de mercancías.
freight forwarder |frāt fôr'wûrdûr| n agente m expedidor.
freight train n (US) tren m de mercancías.
French |french| a francés/esa ♦ n (LING) francés m; **the ~** npl los franceses.
French bean n judía verde.
French Canadian a, n francocanadiense m/f.
French dressing n (CULIN) vinagreta.
French fries, (Brit) **French fried (potatoes)** npl patatas fpl or papas fpl (LAm) fritas.
French Guiana |french gēan'ə| n la Guayana Francesa.
Frenchman |french'mən| n francés m.
French Riviera n: **the ~** la Riviera, la Costa Azul.
French window n puertaventana.
Frenchwoman |french'woomən| n francesa.
frenetic |frənet'ik| a frenético.
frenzy |fren'zē| n frenesí m.
frequency |frē'kwənsē| n frecuencia.
frequency modulation (FM) n frecuencia modulada.
frequent a |frē'kwint| frecuente ♦ vt |frikwent'| frecuentar.
frequently |frē'kwintlē| ad frecuentemente, a menudo.
fresco |fres'kō| n fresco.

fresh |fresh| a (gen) fresco; (new) nuevo; (water) dulce; **to make a ~ start** empezar de nuevo.
freshen |fresh'ən| vi (wind, air) soplar más recio.
  freshen up vi (person) refrescarse.
freshener |fresh'ənûr| n: **air ~** ambientador m; **skin ~** tónico.
fresher |fresh'ûr| n (Brit SCOL: col) = **freshman**.
freshly |fresh'lē| ad: **~ painted/arrived** recién pintado/llegado.
freshman |fresh'mən| n (US: SCOL) estudiante m/f de primer año.
freshness |fresh'nis| n frescura.
freshwater |fresh'wôtûr| a (fish) de agua dulce.
fret |fret| vi inquietarse.
fretful |fret'fəl| a (child) quejumbroso.
Freudian |froi'dēən| a freudiano; **~ slip** lapsus m.
FRG n abbr (= Federal Republic of Germany) RFA f.
Fri. abbr (= Friday) vier.
friar |frī'ûr| n fraile m; (before name) fray.
friction |frik'shən| n fricción f.
friction feed n (on printer) avance m por fricción.
Friday |frī'dā| n viernes m inv.
fridge |frij| n (Brit) nevera, frigo, refrigeradora (LAm).
fried |frīd| pt, pp of **fry** ♦ a: **~ egg** huevo frito, (LAm) huevo estrellado.
friend |frend| n amigo/a.
friendliness |frend'lēnis| n simpatía.
friendly |frend'lē| a simpático.
friendly society n (Brit) sociedad f de beneficiencia.
friendship |frend'ship| n amistad f.
frieze |frēz| n friso.
frigate |frig'it| n fragata.
fright |frīt| n susto; **to take ~** asustarse.
frighten |frīt'ən| vt asustar.
  frighten away, **frighten off** vt (birds, children etc) espantar, ahuyentar.
frightened |frīt'ənd| a asustado.
frightening |frīt'ning| a espantoso.
frightful |frīt'fəl| a espantoso, horrible.
frightfully |frīt'fəlē| ad terriblemente; **I'm ~ sorry** lo siento muchísimo.
frigid |frij'id| a (MED) frígido, frío.
frigidity |frijid'itē| n frialdad f; (MED) frigidez f.
frill |fril| n volante m; **without ~s** (fig) sin adornos.
fringe |frinj| n (Brit: of hair) flequillo; (edge: of forest etc) borde m, margen m.
fringe benefits npl ventajas fpl complementarias.
fringe theatre n (Brit) teatro experimental.
frisk |frisk| vt cachear, registrar.
frisky |fris'kē| a juguetón/ona.

fritter [frit'ûr] *n* buñuelo.
  fritter away *vt* desperdiciar.
frivolity [frəvál'itē] *n* frivolidad *f*.
frivolous [friv'ələs] *a* frívolo.
frizzy [friz'ē] *a* rizado.
fro [frō] *see* **to**.
frock [frák] *n* vestido.
frog [frôg] *n* rana; **to have a ~ in one's throat** tener carraspera.
frogman [frôg'man] *n* hombre-rana *m*.
frogmarch [frôg'märch] *vt* (*Brit*): **to ~ sb in/out** hacer entrar/salir a uno a la fuerza.
frolic [frál'ik] *vi* juguetear.
from [frum] *prep* de; **where is he ~?** ¿de dónde es?; **where has he come ~?** ¿de dónde ha venido?; **a telephone call ~ Mr Smith** una llamada de parte del Sr. Smith; **prices range ~ $10 to $50** los precios varían entre 10 y 50 dólares; **~ Friday** a partir del viernes; **~ what he says** por lo que dice.
frond [fránd] *n* fronda.
front [frunt] *n* (*foremost part*) parte *f* delantera; (*of house*) fachada; (*promenade*: *also*: **sea ~**) paseo marítimo; (*MIL*, *POL*, *METEOROLOGY*) frente *m*; (*fig*: *appearances*) apariencias *fpl* ♦ *a* (*wheel*, *leg*) delantero; (*row*, *line*) primero ♦ *vi*: **to ~ onto sth** dar a algo; **in ~ (of)** delante (de).
frontage [frun'tij] *n* (*of building*) fachada.
frontal [frun'təl] *a* frontal.
front bench *n* (*Brit POL*) los dirigentes del partido del gobierno o de la oposición.
front desk *n* (*US*) recepción *f*.
front door *n* puerta principal.
frontier [fruntēûr'] *n* frontera.
frontispiece [frun'tispēs] *n* portada.
front page *n* primera plana.
front room *n* salón *m*, sala.
front runner *n* favorito/a.
front-wheel drive [frunt'hwēl drīv] *n* tracción *f* delantera.
frost [frôst] *n* (*gen*) helada; (*also*: **hoar~**) escarcha ♦ *vt* (*US CULIN*) escarchar.
frostbite [frôst'bīt] *n* congelación *f*.
frosted [frôs'tid] *a* (*glass*) deslustrado; (*esp US*: *cake*) escarchado.
frosting [frôs'ting] *n* (*esp US*: *on cake*) escarcha.
frosty [frôs'tē] *a* (*surface*) cubierto de escarcha; (*welcome etc*) glacial.
froth [frôth] *n* espuma.
frothy [frôth'ē] *a* espumoso.
frown [froun] *vi* fruncir el ceño ♦ *n*: **with a ~** frunciendo el entrecejo.
  frown on *vt fus* desaprobar.
froze [frōz] *pt of* **freeze**.
frozen [frō'zən] *pp of* **freeze** ♦ *a* (*food*) congelado; (*COMM*): **~ assets** activos *mpl* congelados *or* bloqueados.
FRS *n* (*US*: = *Federal Reserve System*) *banco central de los EE. UU.*
frugal [frōō'gəl] *a* (*person*) frugal.

fruit [frōōt] *n* (*pl inv*) fruta.
fruiterer [frōōt'ərûr] *n* frutero/a; **~'s (shop)** frutería.
fruitful [frōōt'fəl] *a* provechoso.
fruition [frōōish'ən] *n*: **to come to ~** realizarse.
fruit juice *n* zumo *or* jugo (*LAm*) de fruta.
fruitless [frōōt'lis] *a* (*fig*) infructuoso, inútil.
fruit machine *n* (*Brit*) máquina tragaperras.
fruit salad *n* macedonia *or* ensalada (*LAm*) de frutas.
frump [frump] *n* espantajo, adefesio.
frustrate [frus'trāt] *vt* frustrar.
frustrated [frus'trātid] *a* frustrado.
frustrating [frus'trāting] *a* (*job*, *day*) frustrante.
frustration [frustrā'shən] *n* frustración *f*.
fry, *pt*, *pp* **fried** [frī, -d] *vt* freír ♦ *n*: **small ~** gente *f* menuda.
frying pan [frī'ing pan] *n* sartén *f*.
FSLIC *n abbr* (*US*) = *Federal Savings and Loan Insurance Corporation.*
FT *n abbr* (*Brit*: = *Financial Times*) *periódico financiero*; **the ~ index** el índice de valores del *Financial Times*.
ft. *abbr* = **foot**, **feet**.
FTC *n abbr* (*US*) = *Federal Trade Commission.*
fuchsia [fyōō'shə] *n* fucsia.
fuck [fuk] (*col!*) *vt* joder (*Sp!*), coger (*LAm*) ♦ *vi* joder (*Sp!*), coger (*LAm*!); **~ off!** ¡vete a la mierda! (*!*).
fuddled [fud'əld] *a* (*muddled*) confuso, aturdido; (*col*: *tipsy*) borracho.
fuddy-duddy [fud'ēdudē] (*pej*) *n* carcamal *m*, carroza *m/f* ♦ *a* chapado a la antigua.
fudge [fuj] *n* (*CULIN*) caramelo blando ♦ *vt* (*issue*, *problem*) rehuir, esquivar.
fuel [fyōō'əl] *n* (*for heating*) combustible *m*; (*coal*) carbón *m*; (*wood*) leña; (*for engine*) carburante *m* ♦ *vt* (*furnace etc*) alimentar; (*aircraft*, *ship etc*) repostar.
fuel oil *n* fuel oil *m*.
fuel pump *n* (*AUT*) surtidor *m* de gasolina.
fuel tank *n* depósito de combustible.
fug [fug] *n* (*Brit*) aire *m* viciado.
fugitive [fyōō'jətiv] *n* (*from prison*) fugitivo/a.
fulfill, (*Brit*) **fulfil** [fōōlfil'] *vt* (*function*) cumplir con; (*condition*) satisfacer; (*wish*, *desire*) realizar.
fulfilled [fōōlfild'] *a* (*person*) satisfecho.
fulfil(l)ment [fulfil'mənt] *n* satisfacción *f*; realización *f*.
full [fōōl] *a* lleno; (*fig*) pleno; (*complete*) completo; (*information*) detallado; (*price*) íntegro, sin descuento ♦ *ad*: **~ well** perfectamente; **we're ~ for July** estamos completos para julio; **I'm ~** no puedo más; **~ employment** pleno empleo; **~ name** nombre *m* y apellidos; **a ~ two hours** dos horas completas; **at ~ speed** a máxima ve-

locidad; **in** ~ (*reproduce, quote*) íntegramente; **to write sth in** ~ escribir algo por extenso; **to pay in** ~ pagar la deuda entera.

fullback [fŏŏl'bak] *n* (*SOCCER*) defensa *m*; (*RUGBY*) zaguero.

full-blooded [fŏŏl'blud'id] *a* (*vigorous: attack*) vigoroso; (*pure*) puro.

full-cream [fŏŏl'krēm] *a*: ~ **milk** (*Brit*) leche *f* cremosa.

full-fledged [fŏŏl'flejd'] *a* (*US: teacher, lawyer*) diplomado; (: *bird*) con todas sus plumas, capaz de volar; (: *fig*) con pleno derecho.

full-grown [fŏŏl'grōn'] *a* maduro.

full-length [fŏŏl'lengkth'] *a* (*portrait*) de cuerpo entero; (*film*) de largometraje.

full moon *n* luna llena, plenilunio.

fullness [fŏŏl'nis] *n* plenitud *f*, amplitud *f*.

full-scale [fŏŏl'skāl'] *a* (*attack, war, search, retreat*) en gran escala; (*plan, model*) de tamaño natural.

full stop *n* (*Brit*) punto.

full-time [fŏŏl'tīm] *a* (*work*) de tiempo completo ♦ *ad*: **to work** ~ trabajar a tiempo completo.

fully [fŏŏl'ē] *ad* completamente; (*at least*) al menos.

fully-fledged [fŏŏl'ēflejd'] *a* (*Brit*) = **full-fledged**.

fully-paid [fŏŏl'ēpād'] *a*: ~ **share** acción *f* liberada.

fulsome [fŏŏl'səm] *a* (*pej: praise, gratitude*) excesivo, exagerado; (: *manner*) obsequioso.

fumble with [fum'bəl with] *vt fus* manosear.

fume [fyŏŏm] *vi* humear, echar humo.

fumes [fyŏŏmz] *npl* humo *sg*, gases *mpl*.

fumigate [fyŏŏ'məgāt] *vt* fumigar.

fun [fun] *n* (*amusement*) diversión *f*; (*joy*) alegría; **to have** ~ divertirse; **for** ~ en broma; **to make** ~ **of** burlarse de.

function [fungk'shən] *n* función *f* ♦ *vi* funcionar; **to** ~ **as** hacer (las veces) de.

functional [fungk'shənəl] *a* funcional.

function key *n* (*COMPUT*) tecla de función.

fund [fund] *n* fondo; (*reserve*) reserva; ~**s** *npl* fondos *mpl*.

fundamental [fundəmen'təl] *a* fundamental ♦ *n*: ~**s** fundamentos *mpl*.

fundamentalist [fundəmen'təlist] *n* fundamentalista *m/f*.

fundamentally [fundəmen'təlē] *ad* fundamentalmente.

fund-raising [fund'rāzing] *n* recaudación *f* de fondos.

funeral [fyŏŏ'nûrəl] *n* (*burial*) entierro; (*ceremony*) funerales *mpl*.

funeral director *n* director *m* de pompas fúnebres.

funeral parlour *n* (*Brit*) funeraria.

funeral service *n* misa de difuntos.

funereal [fyŏŏnē'rēəl] *a* fúnebre, funéreo.

funfair [fun'fär] *n* (*Brit*) parque *m* de atracciones.

fungus, pl fungi [fung'gəs, -jī] *n* hongo.

funicular [fyŏŏnik'yəlûr] *n* (*also:* ~ **railway**) funicular *m*.

funnel [fun'əl] *n* embudo; (*of ship*) chimenea.

funnily [fun'ilē] *ad* de modo divertido, graciosamente; (*oddly*) de una manera rara.

funny [fun'ē] *a* gracioso, divertido; (*strange*) curioso, raro; ~ **enough** aunque parezca extraño.

funny bone *n* hueso de la alegría.

fur [fûr] *n* piel *f*; (*Brit: on tongue etc*) sarro.

fur coat *n* abrigo de pieles.

furious [fyŏŏr'ēəs] *a* furioso; (*effort, argument*) violento; **to be** ~ **with sb** estar furioso con uno.

furiously [fyŏŏr'ēəslē] *ad* con furia.

furl [fûrl] *vt* (*sail*) aferrar.

furlong [fûr'lông] *n* octava parte de una milla.

furlough [fûr'lō] *n* (*MIL, US*) permiso.

furnace [fûr'nis] *n* horno.

furnish [fûr'nish] *vt* amueblar; (*supply*) suministrar; (*information*) facilitar.

furnished [fûr'nisht] *a*: ~ **apartment** piso amueblado.

furnishings [fûr'nishingz] *npl* muebles *mpl*.

furniture [fûr'nichûr] *n* muebles *mpl*; **piece of** ~ mueble *m*.

furniture mover *n* compañía de mudanzas.

furniture polish *n* cera de lustrar.

furore [fyŏŏr'ôr] *n* (*protests*) escándalo.

furrier [fûr'ēûr] *n* peletero/a.

furrow [fûr'ō] *n* surco ♦ *vt* (*forehead*) arrugar.

furry [fûr'ē] *a* (*toy*) peludo.

further [fûr'thûr] *a* (*new*) nuevo, adicional; (*place*) más lejano ♦ *ad* más lejos; (*more*) más; (*moreover*) además ♦ *vt* promover, adelantar; **how much** ~ **is it?** ¿a qué distancia queda?; ~ **to your letter of** ... (*Brit COMM*) con referencia a su carta de ...; **to** ~ **one's interests** fomentar sus intereses.

further education *n* educación *f* superior.

furthermore [fûr'thûrmôr] *ad* además.

furthermost [fûr'thûrmōst] *a* más lejano.

furthest [fûr'thist] *superlative of* **far**.

furtive [fûr'tiv] *a* furtivo.

furtively [fûr'tivlē] *ad* furtivamente, a escondidas.

fury [fyŏŏr'ē] *n* furia.

fuse [fyŏŏz] *n* fusible *m*; (*Brit: for bomb etc*) mecha ♦ *vt* (*metal*) fundir; (*fig*) fusionar ♦ *vi* fundirse; fusionarse; (*Brit: ELEC*): **to** ~ **the lights** fundir los plomos; **a** ~ **has blown** se ha fundido un fusible.

fuse box *n* caja de fusibles.

fuselage [fyŏŏ'sələzh] *n* fuselaje *m*.

fuse wire *n* hilo fusible.

fusillade [fyōōs'əläd] *n* descarga cerrada; (*fig*) lluvia.
fusion [fyōō'zhən] *n* fusión *f.*
fuss [fus] *n* (*noise*) bulla; (*dispute*) lío; (*complaining*) protesta ♦ *vi* preocuparse (por pequeñeces) ♦ *vt* (*person*) molestar; **to make a ~** armar un lío *or* jaleo.
fuss over *vt fus* (*person*) consentir (a).
fussy [fus'ē] *a* (*person*) exigente; **I'm not ~** (*col*) me da igual.
futile [fyōō'təl] *a* vano.
futility [fyōōtil'ətē] *n* inutilidad *f.*
future [fyōō'chûr] *a* (*gen*) futuro; (*coming*) venidero ♦ *n* futuro, porvenir; **in the ~** de ahora en adelante.
futures [fyōō'chûrz] *npl* (*COMM*) operaciones *fpl* a término.
futuristic [fyōōchəris'tik] *a* futurístico.
fuze [fyōōz] *n* (*US: for bomb etc*) mecha.
fuzzy [fuz'ē] *a* (*PHOT*) borroso; (*hair*) muy rizado.
fwd. *abbr* = **forward.**
fwy *abbr* (*US*) = **freeway.**
FY *abbr* = **fiscal year.**
FYI *abbr* = *for your information.*

G

G, g [jē] *n* (*letter*) G, g *f;* **G** (*MUS*) sol *m;* **G for George** G de Gerona.
G *n abbr* (*US CINEMA*: = *general audience*) todos los públicos; (*Brit SCOL*: = *good*) N.
g. *abbr* (= *gram(s), gravity*) g.
GA *abbr* (*US MAIL*) = *Georgia.*
gab [gab] *n*: **to have the gift of the ~** (*col*) tener mucha labia.
gabble [gab'əl] *vi* hablar atropelladamente.
gaberdine [gab'ûrdēn] *n* gabardina.
gable [gā'bəl] *n* aguilón *m.*
Gabon [gā'bən] *n* Gabón *m.*
gad about [gad əbout'] *vi* (*col*) moverse mucho.
gadget [gaj'it] *n* aparato.
gadgetry [gaj'itrē] *n* chismes *mpl.*
Gaelic [gā'lik] *a, n* (*LING*) gaélico.
gaffe [gaf] *n* plancha, patinazo, metedura de pata.
gag [gag] *n* (*on mouth*) mordaza; (*joke*) chiste *m* ♦ *vt* amordazar.
gaga [gâ'gâ] *a*: **to go ~** (*senile*) chochear; (*ecstatic*) cáersele a uno la baba.
gage [gāj] *n, vt* (*US*) = **gauge.**
gaiety [gā'ətē] *n* alegría.
gaily [gā'lē] *ad* alegremente.
gain [gān] *n* ganancia ♦ *vt* ganar ♦ *vi*

(*watch*) adelantarse; **to ~ by sth** sacar provecho de algo; **to ~ ground** ganar terreno; **to ~ 3 lbs (in weight)** engordar 3 libras.
gain (up)on *vt fus* ganar terreno a.
gainful [gān'fəl] *a* (*employment*) remunerado.
gait [gāt] *n* (modo de) andar *m.*
gala [gā'lə] *n* fiesta; **swimming ~** gala de natación.
Galapagos Islands [gəlâ'pəgōs i'ləndz] *npl*: **the ~** las Islas Galápagos.
galaxy [gal'əksē] *n* galaxia.
gale [gāl] *n* (*wind*) vendaval *m;* **~ force 10** vendaval de fuerza 10.
gall [gôl] *n* (*ANAT*) bilis *f*, hiel *f*; (*fig: impudence*) descaro, caradura ♦ *vt* molestar.
gal(l). *abbr* = **gallon(s).**
gallant [gal'ənt] *a* valiente; [gəlânt'] (*towards ladies*) atento.
gallantry [gal'əntrē] *n* valor *m*, valentía; (*courtesy*) cortesía.
gallbladder [gôl'bladûr] *n* vesícula biliar.
galleon [gal'ēən] *n* galeón *m.*
gallery [gal'ûrē] *n* (*also THEATER*) galería; (*for spectators*) tribuna; (*also:* **art ~**: *government owned*) pinacoteca *or* galería de arte; (: *private*) colección *f* (de cuadros).
galley [gal'ē] *n* (*ship's kitchen*) cocina; (*ship*) galera.
galley proof *n* (*TYP*) prueba de galera, galerada.
Gallic [gal'ik] *a* galo, galicano.
gallon [gal'ən] *n* galón *m* (= *8 pints;* *US* = *3,785 litros, Brit* = *4,546 litros*).
gallop [gal'əp] *n* galope *m* ♦ *vi* galopar; **~ing inflation** inflación *f* galopante.
gallows [gal'ōz] *n* horca.
gallstone [gôl'stōn] *n* cálculo biliario.
galore [gəlôr'] *ad* en cantidad, en abundancia.
galvanize [gal'vənīz] *vt* (*metal*) galvanizar; (*fig*): **to ~ sb into action** animar a uno para que haga algo.
Gambia [gam'bēə] *n* Gambia.
gambit [gam'bit] *n* (*fig*): **opening ~** estrategia inicial.
gamble [gam'bəl] *n* (*risk*) riesgo; (*bet*) apuesta ♦ *vt*: **to ~ on** apostar a; (*fig*) confiar en que ♦ *vi* jugar; (*COMM*) especular; **to ~ on the Stock Exchange** jugar a la bolsa.
gambler [gam'blûr] *n* jugador(a) *m/f.*
gambling [gam'bling] *n* el juego.
gambol [gam'bəl] *vi* brincar, juguetear.
game [gām] *n* (*gen*) juego; (*match*) partido; (*of cards*) partida; (*HUNTING*) caza ♦ *a* valiente; (*ready*): **to be ~ for anything** atreverse a todo; **~s** (*SCOL*) el deporte; **big ~** caza mayor.
game bird *n* ave *f* de caza.
gamekeeper [gām'kēpûr] *n* guardabosques

m inv.

gamely [gām'lē] *ad* bravamente.

game reserve *n* coto de caza.

gamesmanship [gāmz'mənship] *n* habilidad *f*.

gammon [gam'ən] *n (bacon)* tocino ahumado; *(ham)* jamón *m* ahumado.

gamut [gam'ət] *n (MUS)* gama; **to run the (whole) ~ of emotions** *(fig)* pasar por toda la gama de emociones.

gander [gan'dûr] *n* ganso.

gang [gang] *n* pandilla; *(of workmen)* brigada ♦ *vi:* **to ~ up on sb** conspirar contra uno.

Ganges [gan'jēz] *n:* **the ~** el Ganges.

gangling [gang'gling] *a* larguirucho.

gangplank [gang'plangk] *n* plancha.

gangrene [gang'grēn] *n* gangrena.

gangster [gang'stûr] *n* gángster *m*.

gangway [gang'wā] *n (on ship)* pasarela; *(Brit: in theater, bus etc)* pasillo.

gantry [gan'trē] *n (for crane, railway signal)* pórtico; *(for rocket)* torre *f* de lanzamiento.

GAO *n abbr (US: = General Accounting Office)* tribunal de cuentas.

gaol [jāl] *n, vt (Brit)* = **jail**.

gap [gap] *n* vacío, hueco *(LAm)*; *(in trees, traffic)* claro; *(in time)* intervalo.

gape [gāp] *vi* mirar boquiabierto.

gaping [gā'ping] *a (hole)* muy abierto.

garage [gərázh'] *n* garaje *m*.

garb [gârb] *n* atuendo.

garbage [gâr'bij] *n (US)* basura; *(nonsense)* tonterías *fpl; (fig: movie, book etc)* basura.

garbage can *n (US)* cubo *or* balde *m or* bote *m (LAm)* de la basura.

garbage disposal unit *n* triturador *m* (de basura).

garbage dump *n (US)* vertedero.

garbageman [gâr'bijmən] *n* basurero.

garbage truck *n* camión *m* de la basura.

garbled [gâr'bəld] *a (account, explanation)* confuso.

garden [gâr'dən] *n* jardín *m;* **~s** *npl (public)* parque *m,* jardines *mpl; (private)* huertos *mpl.*

garden center *n* viveros *mpl.*

gardener [gârd'nûr] *n* jardinero/a.

gardening [gâr'dəning] *n* jardinería.

garden party *n* recepción *f* al aire libre.

gargle [gâr'gəl] *vi* hacer gárgaras, gargarear *(LAm)*.

gargoyle [gâr'goil] *n* gárgola.

garish [gär'ish] *a* chillón/ona.

garland [gâr'lənd] *n* guirnalda.

garlic [gâr'lik] *n* ajo.

garment [gâr'mənt] *n* prenda (de vestir).

garner [gâr'nûr] *vt* acumular.

garnish [gâr'nish] *vt* adornar; *(CULIN)* aderezar.

garret [gar'it] *n* desván *m,* guardilla.

garrison [gar'isən] *n* guarnición *f* ♦ *vt*

guarnecer.

garrulous [gar'ələs] *a* charlatán/ana.

garter [gâr'tûr] *n (US)* liga.

garter belt *n (US)* portaligas *m inv.*

gas [gas] *n* gas *m; (US: gasoline)* gasolina ♦ *vt* asfixiar con gas.

gas can *n (US)* bidón *m* de gasolina.

gas chamber *n* cámara de gas.

Gascony [gas'kənē] *n* Gascuña.

gas cylinder *n* bombona de gas.

gaseous [gas'ēəs] *a* gaseoso.

gash [gash] *n* raja; *(on face)* cuchillada ♦ *vt* rajar; *(with knife)* acuchillar.

gasket [gas'kit] *n (AUT)* junta de culata.

gas mask *n* careta antigás.

gas meter *n* contador *m* de gas.

gasoline [gasəlēn'] *n (US)* gasolina.

gasp [gasp] *n* grito sofocado ♦ *vi (pant)* jadear.

gasp out *vt (say)* decir con voz entrecortada.

gas pedal *n (esp US)* acelerador *m.*

gas pump *n (US) (in car)* bomba de gasolina; *(in gas station)* surtidor *m* de gasolina.

gas ring *n* hornillo de gas.

gas station *n (US)* gasolinera.

gas stove *n* cocina de gas.

gassy [gas'ē] *a* gaseoso.

gas tank *n (US AUT)* depósito (de gasolina).

gas tap *n* llave *f* del gas.

gastric [gas'trik] *a* gástrico.

gastric ulcer *n* úlcera gástrica.

gastroenteritis [gastrōentərī'tis] *n* gastroenteritis *f.*

gasworks [gas'wûrks] *nsg or npl* fábrica de gas.

gate [gāt] *n (also at airport)* puerta; *(RAIL: at grade crossing)* barrera; *(of castle, town)* reja, puerta.

gateau, *pl* **~x** [gatō', -z] *n (Brit)* torta, pastel *m.*

gate-crash [gāt'krash] *vt* colarse en.

gate-crasher [gāt'krashûr] *n* advenedizo/a, intruso/a.

gateway [gāt'wā] *n* puerta.

gather [gath'ûr] *vt (flowers, fruit)* coger *(Sp),* recoger *(LAm); (assemble)* reunir; *(pick up)* recoger; *(SEWING)* fruncir; *(understand)* entender ♦ *vi (assemble)* reunirse; *(dust)* acumularse; *(clouds)* cerrarse; **to ~ speed** ganar velocidad; **to ~ (from/that)** tener entendido (por/que); **as far as I can ~** por lo que tengo entendido.

gathering [gath'ûring] *n* reunión *f,* asamblea.

GATT [gat] *n abbr (= General Agreement on Tariffs and Trade)* GATT *m.*

gauche [gōsh] *a* torpe.

gaudy [gô'dē] *a* chillón/ona.

gauge [gāj] *n* calibre *m; (RAIL)* entrevía; *(instrument)* indicador *m* ♦ *vt* medir; *(fig:*

sb's capabilities, character) estimar, juzgar; **gas** ~ indicador *m* del nivel de gasolina; **to ~ the right moment** elegir el momento (oportuno).

Gaul |gól| *n* Galia.

gaunt |gônt| *a* descarnado; (*grim, desolate*) desolado.

gauntlet |gônt'lit| *n* (*fig*): **to run the ~ of sth** desafiar algo; **to throw down the ~** arrojar el guante.

gauze |gôz| *n* gasa.

gave |gãv| *pt of* **give**.

gawk |gôk| *vi* papar moscas.

gawky |gô'kē| *a* desgarbado.

gay |gã| *a* (*person*) alegre; (*color*) vivo; (*homosexual*) gay.

gaze |gãz| *n* mirada fija ♦ *vi:* **to ~ at sth** mirar algo fijamente.

gazelle |gəzcl'| *n* gacela.

gazette |gəzct'| *n* (*newspaper*) gaceta; (*official publication*) boletín *m* oficial.

gazetteer |gazitēr'| *n* diccionario geográfico.

GB *abbr* (= *Great Britain*) G.B.

GCE *n abbr* (*Brit:* = *General Certificate of Education*) ≈ certificado de BUP (*Sp*) *or* bachillerato.

GCSE *n abbr* (*Brit:* = *General Certificate of Secondary Education*) ≈ certificado de BUP (*Sp*) *or* bachillerato.

Gdns. *abbr* (= *Gardens*) jdns.

GDP *n abbr* (= *gross domestic product*) PIB *m*.

GDR *n abbr* (= *German Democratic Republic*) RDA *f*.

gear |gēr| *n* equipo, herramientas *fpl*; (*TECH*) engranaje *m*; (*AUT*) velocidad *f*, marcha ♦ *vt* (*fig: adapt*): **to ~ sth to** adaptar *or* ajustar algo a; **high** *or* (*Brit*) **top/low** ~ cuarta/primera velocidad; **in** ~ en marcha; **our service is ~ed to meet the needs of the disabled** nuestro servicio está destinado a responder a las necesidades de los minusválidos.

gear up *vi* hacer preparativos.

gear box *n* caja de cambios.

gear shift, (*Brit*) **gear lever** *n* palanca de cambio.

gear wheel *n* rueda dentada.

GED *n abbr* (*US SCOL*) = *general educational development*.

geese |gēs| *npl of* **goose**.

Geiger counter |gĩ'gŭr koun'tûr| *n* contador *m* Geiger.

gel |jel| *n* gel *m*.

gelatin(e) |jel'atin| *n* gelatina.

gelignite |jel'ignĩt| *n* gelignita.

gem |jem| *n* joya.

Gemini |jem'ənĩ| *n* Géminis *m*.

gen |jen| *n* (*Brit col*): **to give sb the ~ on sth** poner a uno al corriente de algo.

Gen. *abbr* (*MIL:* = *General*) Gen., Gral.

gen. *abbr* (= *general*) grl.; = **generally**.

gender |jen'dûr| *n* género.

gene |jēn| *n* gen(e) *m*.

genealogy |jēnēál'ajē| *n* genealogía.

general |jen'ûrəl| *n* general *m* ♦ *a* general; **in** ~ en general; ~ **audit** comprobación *f* general de cuentas; **the ~ public** el gran público.

general anesthetic *n* anestesia general.

general delivery *n* (*US*) lista de correos.

general election *n* elecciones *fpl* generales.

generalization |jcnûrələzã'shən| *n* generalización *f*.

generalize |jen'ûrəlĩz| *vi* generalizar.

generally |jen'ûrəlē| *ad* generalmente, en general.

general manager *n* director(a) *m/f* general.

general practitioner (GP) *n* médico/a general.

general strike *n* huelga general.

generate |jen'ərãt| *vt* (*ELEC*) generar; (*fig*) producir.

generation |jenərã'shən| *n* (*of electricity etc*) generación *f;* **first/second/third/fourth** ~ (*of computer*) primera/segunda/tercera/cuarta generación.

generator |jen'ərãtûr| *n* generador *m*.

generic |jənär'ik| *a* genérico.

generosity |jenərãs'ətē| *n* generosidad *f*.

generous |jen'ûrəs| *a* generoso; (*copious*) abundante.

generously |jen'ûrəslē| *ad* generosamente; abundantemente.

genesis |jen'əsis| *n* génesis *f*.

genetic |jinet'ik| *a* genético; ~ **engineering** selección *f* genética.

genetics |jənet'iks| *n* genética.

Geneva |jənē'va| *n* Ginebra.

genial |jē'nēəl| *a* afable, simpático.

genitals |jen'itəlz| *npl* (órganos *mpl*) genitales *mpl*.

genitive |jen'ətiv| *n* genitivo.

genius |jēn'yəs| *n* genio.

Genoa |jen'əwə| *n* Génova.

genocide |jen'əsĩd| *n* genocidio.

genteel |jentēl'| *a* fino, elegante.

Gentile |jen'tĩl| *n* gentil *m/f*.

gentle |jen'təl| *a* (*sweet*) amable, dulce; (*touch etc*) ligero, suave.

gentleman |jen'təlmən| *n* señor *m*; (*well-bred man*) caballero; ~**'s agreement** acuerdo entre caballeros.

gentlemanly |jen'təlmənlē| *a* caballeroso, cortés.

gentleness |jen'təlnis| *n* dulzura; (*of touch*) suavidad *f*.

gently |jen'tlē| *ad* suavemente.

gentry |jen'trē| *npl* aristocracia *sg*.

genuine |jen'yōōin| *a* auténtico; (*person*) sincero.

genuinely |jen'yōōinlē| *ad* sinceramente.

geographer |jēág'rəfûr| *n* geográfo/a.

geographic(al) |jēəgraf'ik(əl)| *a* geográfico.

geography [jēăg'rəfē] n geografía.
geological [jēəlăj'ikəl] a geológico.
geologist [jēăl'əjist] n geólogo/a.
geology [jēăl'əjē] n geología.
geometric(al) [jēəmet'rik(əl)] a geométrico.
geometry [jēăm'ətrē] n geometría.
geranium [jərā'nēəm] n geranio.
geriatric [jărēăt'rik] a, n geriátrico/a m/f.
germ [jûrm] n (microbe) microbio, bacteria; (seed, fig) germen m.
German [jûr'mən] a alemán/ana ♦ n alemán/ana m/f; (LING) alemán m.
German Democratic Republic n República Democrática Alemana.
German measles n rubéola.
German shepherd n (dog) pastor m alemán.
Germany [jûr'mənē] n Alemania; **East/West** ~ Alemania Oriental or Democrática/Occidental or Federal.
germination [jûrmənā'shən] n germinación f.
germ warfare n guerra bacteriológica.
gesticulate [jestik'yəlāt] vi gesticular.
gesticulation [jestikyəlā'shən] n gesticulación f.
gesture [jes'chûr] n gesto; **as a ~ of friendship** en señal de amistad.
get, pt, pp **got**, (US) pp **gotten** [get, gât, gât'ən] vt (obtain) obtener; (receive) recibir; (achieve) conseguir; (find) encontrar; (catch) coger (Sp), agarrar (LAm); (fetch) traer, ir a buscar; (take, move) llevar; (understand) entender; (col: annoy) molestar; (: thrill) chiflar ♦ vi (become) hacerse, volverse; **to ~ old** hacerse viejo, envejecer; **to ~ to** (place) llegar a; **he got under the fence** pasó por debajo de la barrera; **to ~ ready/washed** prepararse/lavarse; **to ~ sb to do sth** hacer que uno haga algo; **I've got to do it** tengo que hacerlo; **to ~ sth for sb** conseguir algo para uno; **to ~ sth out of sth** sacar algo de algo; **to ~ sth done** (do) hacer algo; (have done) mandar hacer algo; **to ~ sth/sb ready** preparar algo/a uno; **to ~ one's hair cut** cortarse el pelo; **~ me Mr. Jones, please** (TEL) póngame or (LAm) comuníqueme con el Sr. Jones, por favor; **can I ~ you a drink?** ¿quieres algo de beber?; **you've got to tell the police** tienes que denunciarlo a la policía; **to ~ used to sth** acostumbrarse a algo; **let's ~ going** or **started** vámonos.
get about vi (Brit) = **get around.**
get across vt (message, meaning) lograr comunicar ♦ vi: **to ~ across to sb** lograr hacer que uno comprenda.
get along vi (depart) marcharse; (manage) arreglárselas; (agree): **to ~ along (with)** entenderse (con); **how are you ~ting along?** ¿qué tal estás?, ¿cómo te va? (LAm).

get around vi salir mucho; (travel) viajar mucho; (news) divulgarse ♦ vt fus rodear; (fig: person) engatusar; **to ~ around to doing sth** llegar a hacer algo.
get at vt fus (attack) atacar; (reach) llegar a; (the truth) descubrir; **what are you ~ting at?** ¿qué insinúas?
get away vi marcharse; (on vacation) irse de vacaciones; (escape) escaparse.
get away with vt fus hacer impunemente.
get back vi (return) volver ♦ vt recobrar.
get back at vt fus (col): **to ~ back at sb (for sth)** vengarse de uno (por algo).
get by vi (pass) lograr pasar; (manage) arreglárselas; **I can ~ by in Dutch** me defiendo en holandés.
get down vi bajarse ♦ vt (object) bajar; (depress) deprimir.
get down to vt fus (work) ponerse a (hacer); **to ~ down to business** ponerse a trabajar en serio.
get in vi (train) llegar; (arrive home) volver a casa, regresar ♦ vt (bring in: harvest) recoger; (: coal, shopping, supplies) comprar, traer; (insert) lograr meter en.
get into vt fus (vehicle) subir a; (house) entrar en; (clothes) ponerse.
get off vi (from train etc) bajar; (depart: person, car) marcharse ♦ vt (send off) mandar; (have as leave: day, time) tener libre ♦ vt fus (train, bus) bajar de; **to ~ off to a good start** (fig) empezar muy bien or con buen pie.
get on vi (in exam etc) tener éxito ♦ vt fus (horse) subir.
get on to vt fus (Brit: deal with) ocuparse de; (: col: contact: on phone etc) hablar con.
get out vi salir; (of vehicle) bajar; (news) saberse, difundirse ♦ vt (take out: money from bank etc) sacar.
get out of vt fus (duty etc) escaparse de ♦ vt (extract: confession, words) sacar de; (gain from: pleasure, benefit) ganar de.
get over vt fus (illness) recobrarse de ♦ vt (communicate: idea etc) comunicar; **let's ~ it over (with)** acabemos de una vez.
get round vt fus = **get around.**
get through vt fus (finish: work) acabar con; (: book) terminar, acabar ♦ vi (TEL) lograr comunicarse.
get through to vt fus (TEL) comunicar con.
get together vi reunirse.
get up vi (rise) levantarse ♦ vt fus levantar; **to ~ up enthusiasm for sth** cobrar entusiasmo por algo.
get up to vt fus (reach) llegar a; (Brit: prank etc) hacer.
getaway [get'əwā] n fuga, escape m.

getaway car *n*: **the thieves'** ~ el coche en que los ladrones huyeron.

get-together [get'təgeᵗʰûr] *n* reunión *f*; (*party*) fiesta.

get-up [get'up] *n* (*col*: *outfit*) atavío, atuendo.

get-well card [getwel' kârd] *n* tarjeta que se envía a uno que está enfermo deseándole que se mejore.

geyser [gī'zûr] *n* (GEO) géiser *m*.

Ghana [gân'ə] *n* Ghana.

Ghanaian [gənā'ēən] *a, n* ghaneano/a *m/f*.

ghastly [gast'lē] *a* horrible; (*pale*) pálido.

gherkin [gûr'kin] *n* pepinillo.

ghetto [get'ō] *n* ghetto.

ghost [gōst] *n* fantasma *m* ♦ *vt* (*book*) escribir por otro.

ghostly [gōst'lē] *a* fantasmal.

ghost story *n* cuento de fantasmas.

ghostwriter [gōst'rītûr] *n* negro/a.

ghoul [gōōl] *n* demonio necrófago.

GHQ *n abbr* (MIL: = *general headquarters*) E.M.

GI *n abbr* (*US col*: = *government issue*) soldado del ejército norteamericano.

giant [jī'ənt] *n* gigante *m/f* ♦ *a* gigantesco, gigante; ~ **(size) packet** paquete *m* (de tamaño) gigante *or* familiar.

gibber [jib'ûr] *vi* (*monkey*) farfullar; (*idiot*) hablar de una manera ininteligible.

gibberish [jib'ûrish] *n* galimatías *m*.

gibe [jīb] *n* mofa.

giblets [jib'lits] *npl* menudillos *mpl*.

Gibraltar [jibrôl'tûr] *n* Gibraltar *m*.

giddiness [gid'ēnis] *n* vértigo.

giddy [gid'ē] *a* (*dizzy*) mareado; (*height, speed*) vertiginoso; **it makes me** ~ me marea; **I feel** ~ me siento mareado.

gift [gift] *n* (*gen*) regalo; (COMM: *also*: **free** ~) obsequio; (*ability*) talento; **to have a** ~ **for sth** tener talento para algo.

gift certificate *n* (*US*) vale-regalo *m*.

gifted [gif'tid] *a* dotado.

gift token *n* (*Brit*) vale-regalo *m*.

gig [gig] *n* (*col*: *concert*) función *f*.

gigantic [jīgan'tik] *a* gigantesco.

giggle [gig'əl] *vi* reírse tontamente ♦ *n* risilla.

GIGO [gīg'ō] *abbr* (COMPUT: *col*) = *garbage in, garbage out*.

gill [jil] *n* (*measure*) = *0.25 pints* (*US* = *0.118 l, Brit* = *0.148 l*).

gills [gilz] *npl* (*of fish*) branquias *fpl*, agallas *fpl*.

gilt [gilt] *a, n* dorado.

gilt-edged [gilt'ejd] *a* (COMM: *stocks, securities*) de máxima garantía.

gimlet [gim'lit] *n* barrena de mano.

gimmick [gim'ik] *n* truco; **sales** ~ truco de promoción.

gimmicky [gim'ikē] *a* truquero.

gin [jin] *n* (*liquor*) ginebra.

ginger [jin'jûr] *n* jengibre *m*.

ginger ale, ginger beer *n* gaseosa de jengibre.

gingerbread [jin'jûrbred] *n* pan *m* de jengibre.

ginger-haired [jin'jûrhärd] *a* pelirrojo.

gingerly [jin'jûrlē] *ad* con pies de plomo.

gipsy [jip'sē] *n* = **gypsy**.

giraffe [jəraf'] *n* jirafa.

girder [gûr'dûr] *n* viga.

girdle [gûr'dəl] *n* (*corset*) faja ♦ *vt* ceñir.

girl [gûrl] *n* (*small*) niña; (*young woman*) chica, joven *f*, muchacha; **an American** ~ una (chica) norteamericana.

girl Friday *n* empleada de confianza.

girlfriend [gûrl'frend] *n* (*of girl*) amiga; (*of boy*) novia.

Girl Guide *n* (*Brit*) = **Girl Scout**.

girlish [gûr'lish] *a* de niña.

Girl Scout *n* (*US*) exploradora.

giro [jī'rō] *n* (*Brit*: *bank* ~) giro bancario; (: *post office* ~) giro postal.

girth [gûrth] *n* circunferencia; (*of saddle*) cincha.

gist [jist] *n* lo esencial.

give [giv] *vb* (*pt* **gave**, *pp* **given** [gāv, giv'ən]) *vt* dar; (*deliver*) entregar; (*as gift*) regalar ♦ *vi* (*break*) romperse; (*stretch*: *fabric*) dar de sí; **to** ~ **sb sth**, ~ **sth to sb** darle algo a uno; **how much did you** ~ **for it?** ¿cuánto pagaste por él?; **12 o'clock**, ~ **or take a few minutes** más o menos las doce; ~ **them my regards** mándales saludos de mi parte; **I can** ~ **you 10 minutes** le puedo conceder 10 minutos; **to** ~ **way** (*Brit AUT*) ceder el paso; **to** ~ **way to despair** ceder a la desesperación.

give away *vt* (*give free*) regalar; (*betray*) traicionar; (*disclose*) revelar.

give back *vt* devolver.

give in *vi* ceder ♦ *vt* entregar.

give off *vt* despedir.

give out *vt* distribuir ♦ *vi* (*be exhausted*: *supplies*) agotarse; (*fail*: *engine*) averiarse; (*strength*) fallar.

give up *vi* rendirse, darse por vencido ♦ *vt* renunciar a; **to** ~ **up smoking** dejar de fumar; **to** ~ **o.s. up** entregarse.

give-and-take [giv'əntāk'] *n* (*col*) toma y daca *m*.

giveaway [giv'əwā] *n* (*col*): **her expression was a** ~ su expresión la delataba; **the exam was a** ~! ¡el examen estaba tirado! ♦ *cpd*: ~ **prices** precios *mpl* de regalo.

given [giv'ən] *pp of* **give** ♦ *a* (*fixed*: *time, amount*) determinado, fijo ♦ *conj*: ~ **(that)** ... dado (que) ...; ~ **the circumstances** ... dadas las circunstancias....

glacial [glā'shəl] *a* glacial.

glacier [glā'shûr] *n* glaciar *m*.

glad [glad] *a* contento; **to be** ~ **about sth/ that** alegrarse de algo/de que; **I was** ~ **of his help** agradecí su ayuda.

gladden [glad'ən] *vt* alegrar.

glade [glād] *n* claro.

gladiator [glad'ēātûr] *n* gladiador *m*.

gladioli [gladēō'lē] *npl* gladíolos *mpl*.

gladly [glad'lē] *ad* con mucho gusto.

glamor [glam'ûr] *n* encanto, atractivo, hechizo.

glamorous [glam'ûrəs] *a* encantador(a), atractivo.

glamour [glam'ûr] *n* (*Brit*) = **glamor**.

glance [glans] *n* ojeada, mirada ♦ *vi:* **to ~ at** echar una ojeada a.

glance off *vt fus* (*bullet*) rebotar en.

glancing [glan'sing] *a* (*blow*) oblicuo.

gland [gland] *n* glándula.

glandular [glan'jəlûr] *a:* **~ fever** (*Brit*) fiebre *f* glandular.

glare [glär] *n* deslumbramiento, brillo ♦ *vi* deslumbrar; **to ~ at** mirar ferozmente a.

glaring [glär'ing] *a* (*mistake*) manifiesto.

glass [glas] *n* vidrio, cristal *m*; (*for drinking*) vaso; (: *with stem*) copa; (*also:* **looking ~**) espejo.

glass-blowing [glas'blōing] *n* soplado de vidrio.

glasses [glas'iz] *npl* gafas *fpl*, anteojos *mpl* (*LAm*).

glass fiber, (*Brit*) **glass fibre** *n* fibra de vidrio.

glasshouse [glas'hous] *n* (*Brit*) invernadero.

glassware [glas'wär] *n* cristalería.

glassy [glas'ē] *a* (*eyes*) vidrioso.

glaze [glāz] *vt* (*window*) poner cristales a; (*pottery*) barnizar; (*CULIN*) glasear ♦ *n* barniz *m*; (*CULIN*) vidriado.

glazed [glāzd] *a* (*eye*) vidrioso; (*pottery*) barnizado.

glazier [glā'zhûr] *n* vidriero/a.

gleam [glēm] *n* destello ♦ *vi* brillar; **a ~ of hope** un rayo de esperanza.

gleaming [glē'ming] *a* reluciente.

glean [glēn] *vt* (*gather: information*) recoger.

glee [glē] *n* alegría, regocijo.

gleeful [glē'fəl] *a* alegre.

glen [glen] *n* cañada.

glib [glib] *a* (*person*) de mucha labia; (*comment*) fácil.

glibly [glib'lē] *ad* (*explain*) con mucha labia.

glide [glīd] *vi* deslizarse; (*AVIAT, birds*) planear.

glider [glī'dûr] *n* (*AVIAT*) planeador *m*.

gliding [glī'ding] *n* (*AVIAT*) vuelo sin motor.

glimmer [glim'ûr] *n* luz *f* tenue.

glimpse [glimps] *n* vislumbre *m* ♦ *vt* vislumbrar, entrever; **to catch a ~ of** vislumbrar.

glint [glint] *n* destello; (*in the eye*) chispa ♦ *vi* centellear.

glisten [glis'ən] *vi* relucir, brillar.

glitter [glit'ûr] *vi* relucir, brillar ♦ *n* brillo.

glittering [glit'ûring] *a* reluciente, brillante.

glitz [glits] *n* (*col*) brillo, resplandor *m*.

gloat [glōt] *vi:* **to ~ over** (*money*) recrearse en; (*sb's misfortune*) saborear.

global [glō'bəl] *a* (*world-wide*) mundial; (*comprehensive*) global.

globe [glōb] *n* globo, esfera.

globetrotter [glōb'trätûr] *n* trotamundos *m inv*.

globule [gläb'yōōl] *n* glóbulo.

gloom [glōōm] *n* tinieblas *fpl*, oscuridad *f*; (*sadness*) tristeza, melancolía.

gloomily [glōō'milē] *ad* tristemente; de moda pesimista.

gloomy [glōō'mē] *a* (*dark*) oscuro; (*sad*) triste; (*pessimistic*) pesimista; **to feel ~** sentirse pesimista.

glorification [glôrəfəkā'shən] *n* glorificación *f*.

glorify [glôr'əfī] *vt* glorificar; (*God*) alabar, ensalzar.

glorious [glôr'ēəs] *a* glorioso.

glory [glôr'ē] *n* gloria.

glory hole *n* (*col*) trastero.

Glos *abbr* (*Brit*) = *Gloucestershire*.

gloss [glós] *n* (*shine*) brillo; (*also:* **~ paint**) pintura de aceite.

gloss over *vt fus* encubrir.

glossary [glâs'ûrē] *n* glosario.

glossy [glâs'ē] *a* lustroso.

glove [gluv] *n* guante *m*.

glove compartment *n* (*AUT*) guantera.

glow [glō] *vi* (*shine*) brillar ♦ *n* brillo.

glower [glou'ûr] *vi:* **to ~ at** mirar con ceño.

glowing [glō'ing] *a* (*fire*) vivo; (*complexion*) encendido; (*fig: report, description*) entusiasta.

glow-worm [glō'wûrm] *n* luciérnaga.

glucose [glōō'kōs] *n* glucosa.

glue [glōō] *n* goma (de pegar), cemento (*LAm*) ♦ *vt* pegar.

glue-sniffing [glōō'snifing] *n* inhalación *f* del vapor del cemento.

glum [glum] *a* (*mood*) abatido; (*person, tone*) melancólico.

glut [glut] *n* superabundancia.

glutinous [glōōt'ənəs] *a* glutinoso.

glutton [glut'ən] *n* glotón/ona *m/f*; **~ for punishment** masoquista *m/f*.

gluttony [glut'ənē] *n* gula, glotonería.

glycerin(e) [glis'ûrin] *n* glicerina.

gm *abbr* (= *gram*) g.

GMAT *n abbr* (*US:* = *Graduate Management Admissions Test*) examen de admisión en el segundo ciclo de la enseñanza superior.

GMT *abbr* (= *Greenwich Mean Time*) GMT.

gnarled [nârld] *a* nudoso.

gnash [nash] *vt:* **to ~ one's teeth** rechinar los dientes.

gnat [nat] *n* mosquito.

gnaw [nó] *vt* roer.

gnome [nōm] *n* gnomo.

GNP *n abbr* (= *gross national product*) PNB

m.

go [gō] vb (pt **went**, pp **gone** [wɛnt, gón]) vi ir; (travel) viajar; (depart) irse, marcharse; (work) funcionar, marchar; (be sold) venderse; (time) pasar; (become) ponerse; (break etc) estropearse, romperse; (fit, suit): **to ~ with** hacer juego con ♦ n (pl **~es**): **to have a ~ (at)** probar suerte (con); **I'll have a ~ at it** lo intentaré; **to be on the ~** no parar; **to ~ by car/on foot** ir en coche/a pie; **he's ~ing to do it** va a hacerlo; **to ~ for a walk** ir de paseo; **to ~ dancing** ir a bailar; **to ~ looking for sth/sb** ir a buscar algo/a uno; **to make sth ~, get sth ~ing** poner algo en marcha; **my voice has gone** he perdido la voz; **the cake is all gone** se acabó la torta; **the money will ~ towards our vacation** el dinero será un aporte para las vacaciones; **how did it ~?** ¿qué tal salió or resultó?, ¿cómo ha ido?; **the meeting went well** la reunión salió bien; **to ~ and see sb**, **~ to see sb** ir a ver a uno; **to ~ to sleep** dormirse; **I'll take whatever is ~ing** acepto lo que haya; ... **to ~** (US: food) ... para llevar; **to ~ around the back** pasar por detrás.

go about vt fus: **how do I ~ about this?** ¿cómo me las arreglo para hacer esto?; **to ~ about one's business** ocuparse en sus asuntos.

go after vt fus (pursue) perseguir; (job, record etc) andar tras.

go against vt fus (be unfavorable to: results) ir en contra de; (be contrary to: principles) ser contrario a.

go ahead vi seguir adelante.

go along vi ir ♦ vt fus bordear.

go along with vt fus (accompany) acompañar; (agree with: idea) estar de acuerdo con.

go around vi (circulate: news, rumor) correr; (suffice) alcanzar, bastar; (revolve) girar, dar vueltas; (wander around) andar (de un sitio para otro); (visit): **to ~ around (to sb's)** pasar a ver (a uno); (make a detour): **to ~ around (by)** dar la vuelta (por).

go away vi irse, marcharse.

go back vi volver.

go back on vt fus (promise) faltar a.

go by vi (years, time) pasar ♦ vt fus guiarse por.

go down vi bajar; (ship) hundirse; (sun) ponerse ♦ vt fus bajar por; **that should ~ down well with him** eso le va a gustar.

go for vt fus (fetch) ir por; (like) gustar; (attack) atacar.

go in vi entrar.

go in for vt fus (competition) presentarse a.

go into vt fus entrar en; (investigate) investigar; (embark on) dedicarse a.

go off vi irse, marcharse; (food) pasarse; (lights etc) apagarse; (explode) estallar; (event) realizarse ♦ vt fus dejar de gustar; **the party went off well** la fiesta salió bien.

go on vi (continue) seguir, continuar; (lights) encenderse; (happen) pasar, ocurrir; (be guided by: evidence etc) partir de; **to ~ on doing sth** seguir haciendo algo; **what's ~ing on here?** ¿qué pasa aquí?

go on at vt fus (nag) reñir.

go out vi salir; (fire, light) apagarse; (ebb: tide) bajar, menguar; **to ~ out with sb** salir con uno.

go over vi (ship) zozobrar ♦ vt fus (check) revisar; **to ~ over sth in one's mind** repasar algo mentalmente.

go round vi (Brit) = **go around**.

go through vt fus (town etc) atravesar; (search through) revisar; (perform: ceremony) realizar; (examine: list, book) repasar.

go through with vt fus (plan, crime) llevar a cabo; **I couldn't ~ through with it** no pude llevarlo a cabo.

go together vi (Brit: harmonize: people etc) entenderse.

go under vi (sink: ship, person) hundirse; (fig: business, firm) quebrar.

go up vi subir; **to ~ up in flames** estallar en llamas.

go without vt fus pasarse sin.

goad [gōd] vt aguijonear.

go-ahead [gō'əhɛd] a emprendedor(a) ♦ n luz f verde; **to give sth/sb the ~** autorizar algo/a uno.

goal [gōl] n meta; (score) gol m.

goalkeeper [gōl'kēpûr] n portero.

goal post n poste m (de la portería).

goat [gōt] n cabra f.

gobble [gâb'əl] vt (also: **~ down**, **~ up**) engullirse.

gobbledygook [gâb'əldēgōōk] n jerga burocrática.

go-between [gō'bitwēn] n medianero/a, intermediario/a.

Gobi Desert [gō'bē dez'ûrt] n Desierto de Gobi.

goblet [gâb'lit] n copa.

goblin [gâb'lin] n duende m.

go-cart [gō'kârt] n = **go-kart**.

god [gâd] n dios m; **G~** n Dios m.

godchild [gâd'chīld] n ahijado/a.

goddamn [gâd'dam'] (US col!): **this ~...** este condenado or puñetero...(!)

goddess [gâd'is] n diosa.

godfather [gâd'fâthûr] n padrino.

godforsaken [gâd'fûrsā'kən] a olvidado de Dios.

godmother [gâd'muthûr] n madrina.

godparents [gâd'pärənts] npl: **the ~** los padrinos.

godsend |gâd'send| *n* don *m* del cielo.
godson |gâd'sun| *n* ahijado.
goes |gōz| *vb see* go.
gofer |gō'fûr| *n* (*col*) burro de carga.
go-getter |gō'get'ûr| *n* ambicioso/a.
goggle |gâg'əl| *vi:* **to ~ (at)** mirar con ojos desorbitados.
goggles |gâg'əlz| *npl* (*AUT*) anteojos *mpl*; (*diver's*) gafas *fpl* submarinas.
going |gō'ing| *n* (*conditions*) estado del terreno ♦ *a:* **the ~ rate** la tarifa corriente *or* en vigor; **it was slow ~** íbamos a paso lento.
goings-on |gō'ingzân'| *npl* (*col*) tejemanejes *mpl*.
go-kart |gō'kârt| *n* kart *m*.
gold |gōld| *n* oro ♦ *a* (*reserves*) de oro.
golden |gōl'dən| *a* (*made of gold*) de oro; (~ *in color*) dorado.
Golden Age *n* Siglo de Oro.
golden rule *n* regla de oro.
goldfish |gōld'fish| *n* pez *m* de colores.
gold leaf *n* oro en hojas, pan *m* de oro.
gold medal *n* (*SPORT*) medalla de oro.
goldmine |gōld'mīn| *n* mina de oro.
gold-plated |gōldplā'tid| *a* chapado en oro.
goldsmith |gōld'smith| *n* orfebre *m/f*.
gold standard *n* patrón *m* oro.
golf |gâlf| *n* golf *m*.
golf ball *n* (*for game*) pelota de golf; (*Brit: on typewriter*) esfera impresora.
golf club *n* club *m* de golf; (*stick*) palo (de golf).
golf course *n* campo de golf.
golfer |gâl'fûr| *n* jugador(a) *m/f* de golf.
gondola |gân'dələ| *n* góndola.
gondolier |gândəliûr'| *n* gondolero.
gone |gón| *pp of* go.
gong |góng| *n* gong *m*.
gonorrhea |gânərē'ə| *n* gonorrea.
good |gōod| *a* bueno; (*kind*) bueno, amable; (*well-behaved*) educado ♦ *n* bien *m*, provecho; **~!** ¡qué bien!; **to be ~ at** tener aptitud para; **to be ~ for** servir para; **it's ~ for you** te hace bien; **would you be ~ enough to...?** ¿podría hacerme el favor de...?, ¿sería tan amable de...?; **that's very ~ of you** es usted muy amable; **to feel ~** sentirse bien; **it's ~ to see you** me alegro de verte; **a ~ deal (of)** mucho; **a ~ many** muchos; **to make ~** reparar; **it's no ~ complaining** no vale la pena (de) quejarse; **is this any ~?** (*will it do?*) ¿sirve esto?; (*what's it like?*) ¿qué tal es esto?; **it's a ~ thing you were there** menos mal que tú estabas allí; **for ~** (*for ever*) para siempre, definitivamente; **~ morning/afternoon** ¡buenos días/buenas tardes!; **~ evening!** ¡buenas noches!; **~ night!** ¡buenas noches!; **he's up to no ~** está tramitando algo; **for the common ~** para el bien común; *see also* goods.
goodbye |gōodbī'| *excl* ¡adiós!; **to say ~**

(to) (*person*) despedirse (de).
good faith *n* buena fe *f*.
good-for-nothing |gōod'fərnuth'ing| *n* gandul(a) *m/f*, vago/a.
Good Friday *n* Viernes *m* Santo.
good-humored |gōod'hyōō'mûrd| *a* (*person*) afable, de buen humor; (*remark, joke*) bien intencionado.
good-looking |gōod'lōōk'ing| *a* guapo.
good-natured |gōod'nā'chûrd| *a* (*person*) amable, simpático; (*discussion*) de tono amistoso.
goodness |gōod'nis| *n* (*of person*) bondad *f*; **for ~ sake!** ¡por Dios!; **~ gracious!** ¡Dios mío!
goods |gōodz| *npl* bienes *mpl*; (*COMM etc*) géneros *mpl*, mercancías *fpl*, artículos *mpl*; **all his ~ and chattels** todos sus bienes.
goods train *n* (*Brit*) tren *m* de mercancías.
goodwill |gōod'wil'| *n* buena voluntad *f*; (*COMM*) crédito, clientela.
goody-goody |gōod'ēgōod'ē| *n* (*pej*) santurrón/ona *m/f*.
goof |gōof| *vi* (*US: col*) tirarse una plancha.
goose, *pl* **geese** |gōos, gēs| *n* ganso, oca.
gooseberry |gōos'bärē| *n* grosella espinosa.
gooseflesh |gōos'flesh| *n*, **goosepimples** |gōos'pimpəlz| *npl* carne *f* de gallina.
goose step *n* (*MIL*) paso de ganso.
GOP *n abbr* (*US POL: col* = *Grand Old Party*) Partido Republicano.
gore |gôr| *vt* cornear ♦ *n* sangre *f*.
gorge |gôrj| *n* barranco ♦ *vr:* **to ~ o.s. (on)** atracarse (de).
gorgeous |gôr'jəs| *a* magnífico, maravilloso.
gorilla |gəril'ə| *n* gorila *m*.
gorse |gôrs| *n* aulaga.
gory |gôr'ē| *a* sangriento.
go-slow |gō'slō'| *n* (*Brit*) huelga de manos caídas.
gospel |gâs'pəl| *n* evangelio.
gossamer |gâs'əmûr| *n* gasa sutil.
gossip |gâs'əp| *n* (*scandal*) chismorreo, chismes *mpl*; (*chat*) charla; (*scandalmonger*) chismoso/a; (*talker*) hablador(a) *m/f* ♦ *vi* chismear; **a piece of ~** un chisme, un cotilleo.
gossip column *n* notas *fpl* de sociedad, páginas *fpl* sociales.
got |gât| *pt, pp of* get.
Gothic |gâth'ik| *a* gótico.
gotten |gât'ən| (*US*) *pp of* get.
gouge |gouj| *vt* (*also:* ~ **out**: *hole etc*) excavar; (: *initials*) grabar; **to ~ sb's eyes out** sacar *or* arrancar los ojos a uno.
goulash |gōō'lâsh| *n* g(o)ulash *m*.
gourd |gôrd| *n* calabaza.
gourmet |gōōrmā'| *n* gastrónomo/a *m/f*.
gout |gout| *n* gota.
govern |guv'ûrn| *vt* (*gen*) gobernar; (*dominate*) dominar.

governess [guv'ûrnis] *n* institutriz *f*.
governing [guv'ûrning] *a* (*POL*) de gobierno, gubernamental; ~ **body** consejo de administración.
government [guv'ûrnmənt] *n* gobierno; **local** ~ administración *f* local.
governmental [guvûrnmen'təl] *a* gubernamental.
government stock *n* reservas *fpl* del Estado.
governor [guv'ûrnûr] *n* gobernador(a) *m/f*; (*Brit*: *of jail*) director(a) *m/f*.
Govt. *abbr* (= *Government*) gobno.
gown [goun] *n* traje *m*; (*academic*; *Brit*: *of judge*) toga.
GP *n abbr* = **general practitioner.**
GPO *n abbr* (*US*) = *Government Printing Office.*
gr. *abbr* (*COMM*: = *gross*) bto.
grab [grab] *vt* coger (*Sp*) *or* agarrar (*LAm*), arrebatar; **to** ~ **at** tratar de coger *or* agarrar.
grace [grās] *n* (*REL*) gracia; (*gracefulness*) elegancia, gracia; (*graciousness*) cortesía, gracia ♦ *vt* (*favor*) honrar; (*adorn*) adornar; **5 days'** ~ un plazo de 5 días; **to say** ~ bendecir la mesa; **his sense of humor is his saving** ~ su sentido del humor es su mérito.
graceful [grās'fəl] *a* elegante, gracioso.
gracious [grā'shəs] *a* amable ♦ *excl*: **good** ~! ¡Dios mío!
grade [grād] *n* (*quality*) clase *f*, calidad *f*; (*in hierarchy*) grado; (*US*: *SCOL*) año; (: *mark*) nota; (: *gradient*) pendiente *f*, cuesta ♦ *vt* clasificar; **to make the** ~ (*fig*) llegar al *or* alcanzar el nivel necesario.
grade crossing *n* (*US*) paso a nivel.
grade school *n* (*US*) escuela primaria.
gradient [grā'dēənt] *n* pendiente *f*.
gradual [graj'ōōəl] *a* paulatino.
gradually [graj'ōōəlē] *ad* paulatinamente.
graduate *n* [graj'ōōit] graduado/a, licenciado/a; (*US*: *SCOL*) bachiller *m/f* ♦ *vi* [graj'ōōāt] graduarse, licenciarse.
graduated pension [graj'ōōātid pen'shən] *n* pensión *f* escalonada.
graduation [grajōōā'shən] *n* graduación *f*; . (*US SCOL*) entrega del bachillerato.
graffiti [grəfē'tē] *npl* pintada *sg*.
graft [graft] *n* (*AGR*, *MED*) injerto; (*bribery*) corrupción *f* ♦ *vt* injertar; **hard** ~ (*Brit col*) trabajo duro.
grain [grān] *n* (*single particle*) grano; (*no pl*: *cereals*) cereales *mpl*; (*US*) trigo; (*in wood*) fibra.
gram [gram] *n* (*US*) gramo.
grammar [gram'ûr] *n* gramática.
grammatical [grəmat'ikəl] *a* gramatical.
gramme [gram] *n* (*Brit*) = **gram.**
granary [grā'nûrē] *n* granero, troj *f*.
grand [grand] *a* magnífico, imponente ♦ *n* (*US*: *col*) mil dólares *mpl*.

grandchildren [gran'childrən] *npl* nietos *mpl*.
granddad [gran'dad] *n* abuelito.
granddaughter [gran'dôtûr] *n* nieta.
grandeur [gran'jûr] *n* magnificencia, lo grandioso; (*of occasion*, *scenery etc*) lo imponente; (*of style*) lo elevado.
grandfather [gran'fâthûr] *n* abuelo.
grandiose [gran'dēōs] *a* grandioso; (*pej*) pomposo.
grand jury *n* (*US*) jurado de acusación.
grandma [gran'mə] *n* abuelita.
grandmother [gran'muthûr] *n* abuela.
grandpa [gran'pə] *n* = **granddad.**
grandparents [gran'pärənts] *npl* abuelos *mpl*.
grand piano *n* piano de cola.
Grand Prix [grand prē'] *n* (*AUT*) Grand Prix *m*.
grandson [gran'sun] *n* nieto.
grandstand [gran'stand] *n* (*SPORT*) tribuna.
grand total *n* suma total, total *m*.
granite [gran'it] *n* granito.
granny [gran'ē] *n* abuelita, yaya.
grant [grant] *vt* (*concede*) conceder; (*admit*): **to** ~ **(that)** reconocer (que) ♦ *n* (*SCOL*) beca; **to take sth for** ~**ed** dar algo por sentado.
granulated sugar [gran'yəlātid shōōg'ûr] *n* (*Brit*) azúcar *m* blanquilla *or* granulada.
granule [gran'yōōl] *n* gránulo.
grape [grāp] *n* uva; **sour** ~**s** (*fig*) envidia *sg*; **a bunch of** ~**s** un racimo de uvas.
grapefruit [grāp'frōōt] *n* pomelo, toronja (*LAm*).
grape juice *n* zumo (*Sp*) *or* jugo (*LAm*) de uva.
grapevine [grāp'vīn] *n* vid *f*, parra; **I heard it on the** ~ (*fig*) me enteré, me lo contaron.
graph [graf] *n* gráfica.
graphic [graf'ik] *a* gráfico.
graphic designer *n* diseñador(a) *m/f* gráfico/a.
graphics [graf'iks] *n* (*art*, *process*) artes *fpl* gráficas ♦ *npl* (*drawings*: *also COMPUT*) gráficos *mpl*.
graphite [graf'īt] *n* grafito.
graph paper *n* papel *m* cuadriculado.
grapple [grap'əl] *vi*: **to** ~ **with a problem** enfrentar un problema.
grappling iron [grap'ling ī'ûrn] *n* (*NAUT*) rezón *m*.
grasp [grasp] *vt* agarrar, asir; (*understand*) comprender ♦ *n* (*grip*) asimiento; (*reach*) alcance *m*; (*understanding*) comprensión *f*; **to have a good** ~ **of** (*subject*) dominar.
grasp at *vt fus* (*rope etc*) tratar de asir; (*fig*: *opportunity*) aprovechar.
grasping [gras'ping] *a* avaro.
grass [gras] *n* hierba; (*lawn*) césped *m*; (*pasture*) pasto; (*Brit*: *col*: *informer*) delator(a) *m/f*, denunciador(a) *m/f*.

grasshopper [gras'hắpûr] *n* saltamontes *m inv*.

grassland [gras'land] *n* pradera, pampa (*LAm*).

grass roots *a* popular ♦ *npl* (*POL*) base *fsg* popular.

grass snake *n* culebra.

grassy [gras'ē] *a* cubierto de hierba.

grate [grāt] *n* parrilla ♦ *vi* chirriar ♦ *vt* (*CULIN*) rallar.

grateful [grāt'fəl] *a* agradecido.

gratefully [grāt'fəlē] *ad* con agradecimiento.

grater [grā'tûr] *n* rallador *m*.

gratification [gratəfəkā'shən] *n* satisfacción *f*.

gratify [grat'əfī] *vt* complacer; (*whim*) satisfacer.

gratifying [grat'əfīing] *a* grato.

grating [grā'ting] *n* (*iron bars*) rejilla ♦ *a* (*noise*) áspero.

gratitude [grat'ətōod] *n* agradecimiento.

gratuitous [grətōo'itəs] *a* gratuito, caprichoso.

gratuity [grətōo'itē] *n* gratificación *f*.

grave [grāv] *n* tumba ♦ *a* serio, grave.

gravedigger [grāv'digûr] *n* sepulturero.

gravel [grav'əl] *n* grava.

gravely [grāv'lē] *ad* seriamente; ~ **ill** muy grave.

gravestone [grāv'stōn] *n* lápida.

graveyard [grāv'yârd] *n* cementerio, camposanto.

gravitate [grav'ətāt] *vi* gravitar.

gravitation [gravitā'shən] *n* gravitación *f*.

gravity [grav'itē] *n* gravedad *f*; (*seriousness*) seriedad *f*.

gravy [grā'vē] *n* salsa de carne.

gravy boat *n* salsera.

gravy train *n* (*esp US*: *col*): **to get on the** ~ coger un chollo.

gray [grā] *a* (*US*) gris; **to go** ~ salirle canas.

gray-haired [grā'hârd] *a* canoso.

grayhound [grā'hound] *n* galgo.

graze [grāz] *vi* pacer ♦ *vt* (*touch lightly*) rozar; (*scrape*) raspar ♦ *n* (*MED*) abrasión *f*.

grazing [grā'zing] *n* (*for livestock*) pastoreo.

grease [grēs] *n* (*fat*) grasa; (*lubricant*) lubricante *m* ♦ *vt* engrasar; **to** ~ **the skids** (*US*: *fig*) engrasar el mecanismo.

grease gun *n* engrasadora a presión.

greasepaint [grēs'pānt] *n* maquillaje *m*.

greaseproof [grēs'prōof] *a* a prueba de grasa; (*Brit*: *paper*) apergaminado.

greasy [grē'sē] *a* (*hands, clothes*) grasiento; (*road, surface*) resbaladizo.

great [grāt] *a* grande; (*col*) magnífico, estupendo; (*pain, heat*) intenso; **we had a** ~ **time** lo pasamos muy bien; **they're** ~ **friends** son íntimos *or* muy amigos; **the** ~ **thing is that** ... lo importante es que ...; **it was** ~! ¡fue estupendo!

Great Barrier Reef *n* Gran Barrera de Coral.

Great Britain *n* Gran Bretaña.

greater [grā'tûr] *a* mayor; **G~ London** el Gran Londres.

greatest [grā'tist] *a* el/la mayor.

great-grandchild, *pl* **-children** [grāt'gran'chīld, -children] *n* bisnieto/a.

great-grandfather [grāt'gran'fâthûr] *n* bisabuelo.

great-grandmother [grāt'gran'muthûr] *n* bisabuela.

Great Lakes *npl*: **the** ~ los Grandes Lagos.

greatly [grāt'lē] *ad* sumamente, mucho, muy.

greatness [grāt'nis] *n* grandeza.

Greece [grēs] *n* Grecia.

greed [grēd] *n* (*also*: ~**iness**) codicia, avaricia; (*for food*) gula.

greedily [grē'dilē] *ad* con avidez.

greedy [grē'dē] *a* avaro; (*for food*) glotón/ona.

Greek [grēk] *a* griego ♦ *n* griego/a; (*LING*) griego; **ancient/modern** ~ griego antiguo/moderno.

green [grēn] *a* verde; (*inexperienced*) novato; (*POL*) verde ♦ *n* verde *m*; (*stretch of grass*) césped *m*; (*of golf course*) campo, "green" *m*; **the G~s** (*POL*) los verdes *mpl*; ~**s** *npl* verduras *fpl*; **to have a** ~ **thumb** *or* (*Brit*) ~ **fingers** (*fig*) tener habilidad para la jardinería.

greenback [grēn'bak] *n* (*US*: *col*: *dollar bill*) billete de un dólar.

green bean *n* judía verde.

green belt *n* zona verde.

green card *n* (*US*: *ADMIN*) tarjeta verde; (*Brit*: *AUT*) carta verde.

greenery [grē'nûrē] *n* verdura, plantas *fpl* verdes.

greenfly [grēn'flī] *n* pulgón *m*.

greengage [grēn'gāj] *n* claudia.

greengrocer [grēn'grōsûr] *n* (*Brit*) verdulero/a.

greenhouse [grēn'hous] *n* invernadero.

greenhouse effect *n* efecto de invernadero.

greenish [grē'nish] *a* verdoso.

Greenland [grēn'lənd] *n* Groenlandia.

Greenlander [grēn'ləndûr] *n* groenlandés/esa *m/f*.

green light *n* luz *f* verde.

green pepper *n* pimiento verde.

greet [grēt] *vt* saludar; (*welcome*) dar la bienvenida a.

greeting [grē'ting] *n* (*gen*) saludo; (*welcome*) bienvenida; ~**s** recuerdos *mpl*, saludos *mpl*; **season's** ~**s** Felices Pascuas.

greeting(s) card [grē'ting(z) kârd] *n* tarjeta de felicitación.

gregarious [grigär'ēəs] *a* gregario.

grenade [grinād'] *n* (*also*: **hand** ~) granada.

grew [grōō] *pt of* **grow**.
grey [grā] *etc* (*Brit*) = **gray** *etc.*
grid [grid] *n* reja; (*ELEC*) red *f.*
griddle [grid'əl] *n* (*esp US*) plancha.
gridiron [grid'iûrn] *n* (*CULIN*) parrilla.
grief [grēf] *n* dolor *m*, pena; **to come to ~** (*plan*) fracasar, ir al traste; (*person*) acabar mal, desgraciarse.
grievance [grē'vəns] *n* (*cause for complaint*) motivo de queja, agravio.
grieve [grēv] *vi* afligirse, acongojarse ♦ *vt* dar pena a; **to ~ for** llorar por; **to ~ for sb** (*dead person*) llorar la pérdida de uno.
grievous [grē'vəs] *a* grave; (*loss*) cruel; **~ bodily harm** (*LAW*) daños *mpl* corporales graves.
grill [gril] *n* (*on stove*) parrilla ♦ *vt* asar a la parrilla; (*question*) interrogar; **~ed meat** carne *f* (asada) a la parrilla *or* plancha.
grille [gril] *n* reja.
grim [grim] *a* (*place*) sombrío; (*person*) ceñudo.
grimace [grim'əs] *n* mueca ♦ *vi* hacer muecas.
grime [grīm] *n* mugre *f.*
grimly [grim'lē] *ad* (*say*) sombríamente.
grimy [grī'mē] *a* mugriento.
grin [grin] *n* sonrisa abierta ♦ *vi*: **to ~ (at)** sonreír abiertamente (a).
grind [grīnd] *vb* (*pt, pp* **ground** [ground]) *vt* (*coffee, pepper etc*) moler; (*US: meat*) picar; (*make sharp*) afilar; (*polish: gem, lens*) esmerilar ♦ *vi* (*car gears*) rechinar ♦ *n*: **the daily ~** (*col*) la rutina diaria; **to ~ one's teeth** hacer rechinar los dientes; **to ~ to a halt** (*vehicle*) pararse con gran estruendo de frenos; (*fig: talks, scheme*) pararse en seco; (*work, production*) interrumpirse.
grinder [grīn'dûr] *n* (*machine: for coffee*) molinillo; (*US: for meat*) picadora de carne.
grindstone [grīnd'stōn] *n*: **to keep one's nose to the ~** batir el yunque.
grip [grip] *n* (*hold*) asimiento; (*of hands*) apretón *m*; (*handle*) asidero; (*of racquet etc*) mango; (*understanding*) comprensión *f* ♦ *vt* agarrar; **to come to ~s with** enfrentarse con; **to lose one's ~** írsele de las manos; (*fig*) perder el control.
gripe [grīp] *n* (*col: complaint*) queja ♦ *vi* (*col: complain*): **to ~ (about)** quejarse (de); **~s** *npl* retortijones *mpl.*
gripping [grip'ing] *a* absorbente.
grisly [griz'lē] *a* horripilante, horrible.
gristle [gris'əl] *n* cartílago.
grit [grit] *n* gravilla; (*courage*) valor *m* ♦ *vt* (*Brit: road*) poner gravilla en; **I've got a piece of ~ in my eye** tengo una arenilla en el ojo; **to ~ one's teeth** apretar los dientes.
grits [grits] *npl* (*US*) maíz *msg* a medio moler.

grizzle [griz'əl] *vi* (*cry*) lloriquear.
grizzly [griz'lē] *n* (*also*: **~ bear**) oso pardo.
groan [grōn] *n* gemido, quejido ♦ *vi* gemir, quejarse.
grocer [grō'sûr] *n* tendero (de ultramarinos); **~'s (shop)** *n* tienda de ultramarinos *or* de abarrotes (*LAm*).
groceries [grō'sûrēz] *npl* comestibles *mpl.*
grocery [grō'sûrē] *n* (*also*: **~ store**) tienda de ultramarinos.
grog [grâg] *n* grog *m.*
groggy [grâg'ē] *a* atontado.
groin [groin] *n* ingle *f.*
groom [grōōm] *n* mozo/a de cuadra; (*also*: **bride~**) novio ♦ *vt* (*horse*) almohazar; **well-~ed** acicalado.
groove [grōōv] *n* ranura, surco.
grope [grōp] *vi* ir a tientas; **to ~ for** buscar a tientas.
grosgrain [grō'grān] *n* grogrén *m*, cordellate *m.*
gross [grōs] *a* grueso; (*COMM*) bruto ♦ *vt* (*COMM*) recaudar en bruto.
gross domestic product (GDP) *n* producto interno bruto (PIB).
gross income *n* ingresos *mpl* brutos.
grossly [grōs'lē] *ad* (*greatly*) enormemente.
gross national product (GNP) *n* producto nacional bruto (PNB).
gross profit *n* beneficios *mpl* brutos.
gross sales *npl* ventas *fpl* brutas.
grotesque [grōtesk'] *a* grotesco.
grotto [grât'ō] *n* gruta.
grotty [grât'ē] *a* asqueroso.
grouch [grouch] *vi* (*col*) refunfuñar ♦ *n* (*col: person*) refunfuñón/ona *m/f.*
ground [ground] *pt, pp of* **grind** ♦ *n* suelo, tierra; (*SPORT*) campo, terreno; (*reason: gen pl*) causa, razón *f*; (*US: also*: **~ wire**) cable *m* de toma de tierra ♦ *vt* (*plane*) mantener en tierra; (*US: ELEC*) conectar a tierra ♦ *vi* (*ship*) varar, encallar ♦ *a* (*coffee etc*) molido; (*US: meat*) picado; **~s** *npl* (*of coffee etc*) poso *sg*; (*gardens etc*) jardines *mpl*, parque *m*; **on the ~** en el suelo; **common ~** terreno común; **to gain/lose ~** ganar/perder terreno; **to the ~** al suelo; **below ~** debajo de la tierra, bajo tierra; **he covered a lot of ~ in his lecture** abarcó mucho en la clase.
ground cloth *n* (*US*) tela impermeable.
ground control *n* (*AVIAT, SPACE*) control *m* desde tierra.
ground floor *n* (*Brit*) planta baja.
grounding [groun'ding] *n* (*in education*) conocimientos *mpl* básicos.
groundkeeper [ground'kēpûr] *n* = **groundskeeper**.
groundless [ground'lis] *a* infundado, sin fundamento.
groundnut [ground'nut] *n* cacahuete *m.*
ground rent *n* renta sobre el terreno.
groundsheet [ground'shēt] *n* (*Brit*) =

ground cloth.

groundskeeper [groundz'kēpŭr] *n* (*US SPORT*) encargado de pista de deportes.

groundsman [groundz'mən] *n* (*Brit*) = **groundskeeper.**

ground staff *n* (*Brit*) personal *m* de tierra.

ground swell *n* mar *m or f* de fondo; (*fig*) marejada.

ground-to-ground [ground'təground'] *a*: ~ **missile** proyectil *m* tierra-tierra.

groundwork [ground'wûrk] *n* preparación *f*.

group [grōōp] *n* grupo; (*MUS*: *pop* ~) conjunto, grupo ♦ (*vb*: *also*: ~ **together**) *vt* agrupar ♦ *vi* agruparse.

grouse [grous] *n* (*pl inv*) (*bird*) urogallo ♦ *vi* (*complain*) quejarse.

grove [grōv] *n* arboleda.

grovel [gruv'əl] *vi* (*fig*) arrastrarse.

grow, *pt* **grew,** *pp* **grown** [grō, grōō, grōn] *vi* crecer; (*increase*) aumentarse; (*expand*) desarrollarse; (*become*) volverse ♦ *vt* cultivar; (*hair, beard*) dejar crecer; **to ~ rich/ weak** enriquecerse/debilitarse; **to ~ tired of waiting** cansarse de esperar.

grow apart *vi* (*fig*) alejarse uno del otro.

grow away from *vt fus* (*fig*) alejarse de.

grow on *vt fus*: **that painting is ~ing on me** ese cuadro me gusta cada vez más.

grow out of *vt fus* (*clothes*): **I've grown out of this shirt** esta camisa se me queda pequeña; (*habit*) perder.

grow up *vi* crecer, hacerse hombre/ mujer.

grower [grō'ûr] *n* (*AGR*) cultivador(a) *m/f*, productor(a) *m/f*.

growing [grō'ing] *a* creciente; ~ **pains** (*also fig*) dificultades *fpl* de desarrollo.

growl [groul] *vi* gruñir.

grown [grōn] *pp of* **grow.**

grown-up [grōn'up'] *n* adulto/a, mayor *m/f*.

growth [grōth] *n* crecimiento, desarrollo; (*what has grown*) brote *m*; (*MED*) tumor *m*.

growth rate *n* tasa de crecimiento.

grub [grub] *n* gusano; (*col: food*) comida.

grubby [grub'ē] *a* sucio, mugriento.

grudge [gruj] *n* rencor ♦ *vt*: **to ~ sb sth** dar algo a uno de mala gana; **he ~s (giving) the money** da el dinero de mala gana.

grudgingly [gruj'inglē] *ad* de mala gana.

grueling, (*Brit*) **gruelling** [grōō'əling] *a* penoso, duro.

gruesome [grōō'səm] *a* horrible.

gruff [gruf] *a* (*voice*) ronco; (*manner*) brusco.

grumble [grum'bəl] *vi* refunfuñar, quejarse.

grumpy [grum'pē] *a* gruñón/ona.

grunt [grunt] *vi* gruñir ♦ *n* gruñido.

GSA *n abbr* (*US*) = *General Services Administration.*

G-string [jē'string] *n* taparrabo.

GSUSA *n abbr* = *Girl Scouts of the United States of America.*

GT *abbr* (*AUT*: = *gran turismo*) GT.

GU *abbr* (*US MAIL*) = *Guam.*

guarantee [garəntē'] *n* garantía ♦ *vt* garantizar; **he can't ~ (that) he'll come** no está seguro de poder venir.

guarantor [gar'əntôr] *n* garante *m/f*, fiador(a) *m/f*.

guard [gârd] *n* guardia; (*Brit RAIL*) jefe *m* de tren; (*safety device: on machine*) salvaguardia, resguardo; (*protection*) protección *f*; (*Brit: fire*~) pantalla ♦ *vt* guardar; **to ~ (against or from)** proteger (de); **to be on one's ~** (*fig*) estar en guardia.

guard against *vi*: **to ~ against doing sth** guardarse de hacer algo.

guard dog *n* perro guardián.

guarded [gâr'did] *a* (*fig*) cauteloso.

guardian [gâr'dēən] *n* guardián/ana *m/f*; (*of minor*) tutor(a) *m/f*.

guardrail [gârd'rāl] *n* pretil *m*.

guard's van [gârdz' van] *n* (*Brit RAIL*) furgón *m*.

Guatemala [gwâtəmâl'ə] *n* Guatemala.

Guatemalan [gwâtəmâl'ən] *a, n* guatemalteco/a *m/f*.

guerrilla [gəril'ə] *n* guerrillero/a.

guerrilla warfare *n* guerra de guerrillas.

guess [ges] *vi, vt* (*gen*) adivinar; (*suppose*) suponer ♦ *n* suposición *f*, conjetura; **I ~ you're right** (*esp US*) supongo que tienes razón; **to keep sb ~ing** mantener a uno a la expectativa; **to take a ~** tratar de adivinar; **my ~ is that ...** yo creo que ... .

guesstimate [ges'təmit] *n* conjetura.

guesswork [ges'wûrk] *n* conjeturas *fpl*; **I got the answer by ~** acerté a ojo de buen cubero.

guest [gest] *n* invitado/a; (*in hotel*) huésped(a) *m/f*; **be my ~** (*col*) estás en tu casa.

guest book *n* libro de visitas.

guesthouse [gest'hous] *n* casa de huéspedes, pensión *f*.

guest room *n* cuarto de huéspedes.

guffaw [gufô'] *n* carcajada ♦ *vi* reírse a carcajadas.

guidance [gīd'əns] *n* (*gen*) dirección *f*; (*advice*) consejos *mpl*; **marriage/vocational ~** orientación *f* matrimonial/profesional.

guide [gīd] *n* (*person*) guía *m/f*; (*book, fig*) guía *f*; (*Brit: also: girl* ~) exploradora ♦ *vt* guiar; **to be ~d by sb/sth** dejarse guiar por uno/algo.

guidebook [gīd'bŏŏk] *n* guía.

guided missile [gīd'id mis'əl] *n* misil *m* teledirigido.

guide dog *n* perro guía.

guided tour [gīd'id tŏŏr] *n* visita acompañada.

guidelines |gīd'līnz| *npl* (*fig*) directiva *sg*.
guild |gild| *n* gremio.
guile |gīl| *n* astucia.
guileless |gīl'lis| *a* cándido.
guillotine |gil'ətēn| *n* guillotina.
guilt |gilt| *n* culpabilidad *f*.
guilty |gil'tē| *a* culpable; **to feel ~ (about)** sentirse culpable (por); **to plead ~/not ~** declararse culpable/inocente.
Guinea |gin'ē| *n*: **Republic of ~** República de Guinea.
guinea pig *n* cobayo.
guise |gīz| *n*: **in** *or* **under the ~ of** bajo capa de.
guitar |gitár'| *n* guitarra.
guitarist |gitár'ist| *n* guitarrista *m/f*.
gulch |gulch| *n* (*US*) barranco.
gulf |gulf| *n* golfo; (*abyss*) abismo.
Gulf States *npl*: **the ~** los países del Golfo.
Gulf Stream *n*: **the ~** la Corriente del Golfo.
gull |gul| *n* gaviota.
gullet |gul'it| *n* esófago.
gullibility |guləbil'ətē| *n* credulidad *f*.
gullible |gul'əbəl| *a* crédulo.
gully |gul'ē| *n* barranco.
gulp |gulp| *vi* tragar saliva ♦ *vt* (*also*: **~ down**) tragarse ♦ *n* (*of liquid*) trago, sorbo; (*of food*) bocado; **in one ~** de un trago.
gum |gum| *n* (*ANAT*) encía; (*glue*) goma, cemento (*LAm*); (*sweet*) caramelo de goma; (*also*: **chewing-~**) chicle *m* ♦ *vt* pegar con goma.
gum up *vt*: **to ~ up the works** (*col*) meter un palo en la rueda.
gumboots |gum'bōōts| *npl* (*Brit*) botas *fpl* de goma.
gum tree *n* árbol *m* gomero.
gun |gun| *n* (*small*) pistola, revólver *m*; (*shotgun*) escopeta; (*rifle*) fusil *m*; (*cannon*) cañón *m* ♦ *vt* (*also*: **~ down**) asesinar; **to stick to one's ~s** (*fig*) mantenerse firme, aferrarse.
gunboat |gun'bōt| *n* cañonero.
gun dog *n* perro de caza.
gunfire |gun'fiūr| *n* disparos *mpl*.
gung-ho |gung'hō'| *a* (*col*) fogoso.
gunk |gungk| *n* (*col*) sustancia pegajosa *or* viscosa.
gunman |gun'mən| *n* pistolero.
gunner |gun'ûr| *n* artillero.
gunpoint |gun'point| *n*: **at ~** a mano armada.
gunpowder |gun'poudûr| *n* pólvora.
gunrunner |gun'runûr| *n* traficante *m/f* de armas.
gunrunning |gun'runing| *n* contrabando de armas.
gunshot |gun'shât| *n* escopetazo.
gunsmith |gun'smith| *n* armero.
gurgle |gûr'gəl| *vi* gorgotear.

guru |gōō'rōō| *n* guru *m*.
gush |gush| *vi* chorrear; (*fig*) deshacerse en efusiones.
gusset |gus'it| *n* (*in tights, pants*) escudete *m*.
gust |gust| *n* (*of wind*) ráfaga.
gusto |gus'tō| *n* entusiasmo.
gut |gut| *n* intestino; (*MUS etc*) cuerda de tripa ♦ *vt* (*poultry, fish*) destripar; (*building*): **the blaze ~ted the entire building** el fuego destruyó el edificio entero.
gut reaction *n* reacción *f* instintiva.
guts |guts| *npl* (*courage*) valor *m*; (*col: innards: of people, animals*) tripas *fpl*; **to hate sb's ~** echar a uno (a muerte).
gutter |gut'ûr| *n* (*of roof*) canalón *m*; (*in street*) arroyo.
guttural |gut'ûrəl| *a* gutural.
guy |gī| *n* (*also*: **~rope**) cuerda; (*col: man*) tío (*Sp*), tipo.
Guyana |gēân'ə| *n* Guayana.
guzzle |guz'əl| *vi* tragar ♦ *vt* engullir.
gym |jim| *n* (*also*: **gymnasium**) gimnasio; (*also*: **gymnastics**) gimnasia.
gymkhana |jimkä'nə| *n* gincana.
gymnast |jim'nast| *n* gimnasta *m/f*.
gymnastics |jimnas'tiks| *n* gimnasia.
gym shoes *npl* zapatillas *fpl* deportivas.
gym slip *n* (*Brit*) túnica de colegiala.
gynecologist, (*Brit*) **gynaecologist** |gīnəkâl'əjist| *n* ginecólogo/a.
gynecology, (*Brit*) **gynaecology** |gīnəkâl'əjē| *n* ginecología.
gypsy |jip'sē| *n* gitano/a.
gyrate |jī'rāt| *vi* girar.
gyroscope |jī'rəskōp| *n* giroscopio.

H

H, h |āch| *n* (*letter*) H, h *f*; **H for How** H de Historia.
habeas corpus |hā'bēəs kôr'pəs| *n* (*LAW*) hábeas corpus *m*.
haberdashery |hab'ûrdashûrē| *n* (*US: men's clothing*) prendas *fpl* de caballero; (*Brit*) mercería.
habit |hab'it| *n* hábito, costumbre *f*; **to get out of/into the ~ of doing sth** perder la costumbre de/acostumbrarse a hacer algo.
habitable |hab'itəbəl| *a* habitable.
habitat |hab'itat| *n* hábitat *m*.
habitation |habitä'shən| *n* habitación *f*.
habitual |həbich'ōōəl| *a* acostumbrado, habitual; (*drinker, liar*) empedernido.
habitually |həbich'ōōəlē| *ad* por costumbre.
hack |hak| *vt* (*cut*) cortar; (*slice*) tajar ♦ *vt*

corte *m*; (*ax blow*) hachazo; (*pej: writer*) escritor(a) *m/f* a sueldo; (*old horse*) jamelgo.

hacker [hak'úr] *n* (COMPUT) pirata *m* informático.

hackles [hak'əlz] *npl*: **to make sb's ~ rise** (*fig*) poner los pelos de punto a uno.

hackney cab [hak'nē kab] *n* coche *m* de alquiler.

hackneyed [hak'nēd] *a* trillado, gastado.

had [had] *pt, pp of* **have**.

haddock, *pl* ~ *or* ~s [had'ək] *n especie de merluza*.

hadn't [had'ənt] = **had not**.

haematology [hēmətâl'əjē] *n* (*Brit*) = **hematology**.

haemoglobin [hē'məglōbin] *n* (*Brit*) = **hemoglobin**.

haemophilia [hēməfil'ēə] *n* (*Brit*) = **hemophilia**.

haemorrhage [hem'ûrij] *n* (*Brit*) = **hemorrhage**.

haemorrhoids [hem'əroidz] *npl* (*Brit*) = **hemorrhoids**.

hag [hag] *n* (*ugly*) vieja fea, tarasca; (*nasty*) bruja; (*witch*) hechicera.

haggard [hag'ûrd] *a* ojeroso.

haggis [hag'is] *n* (*Scottish*) estómago de cordero relleno.

haggle [hag'əl] *vi* (*argue*) discutir; (*bargain*) regatear.

haggling [hag'ling] *n* regateo.

Hague [hāg] *n*: **The ~** La Haya.

hail [hāl] *n* (*weather*) granizo ♦ *vt* saludar; (*call*) llamar a ♦ *vi* granizar; **to ~ (as)** aclamar (como), celebrar (como); **he ~s from Scotland** es natural de Escocia.

hailstone [hāl'stōn] *n* (piedra de) granizo.

hailstorm [hāl'stôrm] *n* granizada.

hair [här] *n* (*gen*) pelo, cabellos *mpl*; (*one ~*) pelo, cabello; (*head of ~*) pelo, cabellera; (*on legs etc*) vello; **to do one's ~** arreglarse el pelo; **gray ~** canas *fpl*.

hairbrush [här'brush] *n* cepillo (para el pelo).

haircut [här'kut] *n* corte *m* (de pelo).

hairdo [här'dōō] *n* peinado.

hairdresser [här'dresûr] *n* peluquero/a; ~'s peluquería.

hair dryer *n* secador *m* de pelo.

-haired [härd] *a suff*: **fair/long~** de pelo rubio *or* güero/de pelo largo.

hair gel *n* gel *m* para el pelo.

hairgrip [här'grip] *n* (*Brit*) horquilla.

hairline [här'līn] *n* nacimiento del pelo.

hairline fracture *n* fractura fina.

hairnet [här'net] *n* redecilla.

hair oil *n* brillantina.

hairpiece [här'pēs] *n* (*for men*) tupé *m*; (*for women*) peluca.

hairpin [här'pin] *n* horquilla.

hairpin curve, (*Brit*) **hairpin bend** *n* curva de horquilla.

hair-raising [här'rāzing] *a* espeluznante.

hair remover *n* depilatorio.

hair's breadth *n*: **by a ~** por un pelo.

hair spray *n* laca.

hairstyle [här'stīl] *n* peinado.

hairy [här'ē] *a* peludo, velludo.

Haiti [hā'tē] *n* Haití *m*.

hake [hāk] *n* merluza.

halcyon [hal'sēən] *a* feliz.

hale [hāl] *a*: **~ and hearty** robusto.

half [haf] *n* (*pl* **halves** [havz]) mitad *f*; (SPORT: *of match*) tiempo; (: *of field*) campo ♦ *a* medio ♦ *ad* medio, a medias; **~ an hour** media hora; **two and a ~** dos y media; **~ a dozen** media docena; **~ a pound** media libra, ≈ 250 gr.; **to cut sth in ~** cortar algo por la mitad; **to go halves (with sb)** ir a medias (con uno); **~empty/ closed** medio vacío/entreabierto; **~ asleep** medio dormido; **~ after 3** las 3 y media.

halfback [haf'bak] *n* (SPORT) medio.

half-baked [haf'bākt'] *a* (*col: idea, scheme*) mal concebido *or* pensado.

half-breed [haf'brēd] *n* = **half-caste**.

half-brother [haf'bruth̸ûr] *n* medio hermano.

half-caste [haf'kast] *n* mestizo/a.

half-hearted [haf'hâr'tid] *a* indiferente, poco entusiasta.

half-hour [haf'our'] *n* media hora.

half-mast [haf'mast'] *n*: **at ~** (*flag*) a media asta.

half note *n* (US: MUS) blanca.

halfpenny [hā'pənē] *n* (*Brit*) medio penique *m*.

half-price [haf'prîs'] *a* a mitad de precio.

half term *n* (*Brit* SCOL) vacaciones de mediados del trimestre.

half-time [haf'tīm'] *n* descanso.

halfway [haf'wā'] *ad* a medio camino; **to meet sb ~** (*fig*) llegar a un acuerdo con uno.

half-yearly [haf'yēr'lē] *ad* semestralmente ♦ *a* semestral.

halibut [hal'əbət] *n*, *pl inv* halibut *m*.

halitosis [halitō'sis] *n* halitosis *f*.

hall [hôl] *n* (*for concerts*) sala; (*entrance way*) entrada, vestíbulo.

hallmark [hôl'mârk] *n* (*mark*) contraste *m*; (*seal*) sello.

hallo [həlō'] *excl* (*Brit*) = **hello**.

hall of residence *n* (*Brit*) colegio mayor.

Hallowe'en [haləwēn'] *n* víspera de Todos los Santos.

hallucination [həlōōsənā'shən] *n* alucinación *f*.

hallway [hôl'wā] *n* vestíbulo.

halo [hā'lō] *n* (*of saint*) aureola.

halt [hôlt] *n* (*stop*) alto, parada; (*Brit* RAIL) apeadero ♦ *vt* parar ♦ *vi* pararse; (*process*) interrumpirse; **to call a ~ (to sth)** (*fig*) poner fin (a algo).

halter [hôl'tûr] *n* (*for horse*) cabestro.

halterneck [hôl'túrnɛk] *a* de espalda escotada.

halve [hav] *vt* partir por la mitad.

halves [havz] *pl of* **half.**

ham [ham] *n* jamón *m* (cocido); (*col: also:* **radio** ~) radioaficionado/a *m/f*; (: *also:* ~ **actor**) comicastro.

hamburger [ham'bûrgûr] *n* hamburguesa.

ham-handed [ham'handid] *a* torpe, desmañado.

hamlet [ham'lit] *n* aldea.

hammer [ham'ûr] *n* martillo ♦ *vt* (*nail*) clavar; **to** ~ **a point home to sb** remacharle un punto a uno.

hammer out *vt* (*metal*) forjar a martillo; (*fig: solution, agreement*) elaborar con trabajos.

hammock [ham'ək] *n* hamaca.

hamper [ham'pûr] *vt* estorbar ♦ *n* cesto.

hamster [ham'stûr] *n* hámster *m*.

hand [hand] *n* mano *f*; (*of clock*) aguja; (*writing*) letra; (*worker*) obrero; (*measurement: of horse*) palmo ♦ *vt* (*give*) dar, pasar; (*deliver*) entregar; **to give sb a** ~ echar una mano a uno, ayudar a uno; **to force sb's** ~ forzarle la mano a uno; **at** ~ (*information etc*) a (la) mano; **in** ~ entre manos; **we have the matter in** ~ tenemos el asunto entre manos; **to have in one's** ~ (*knife, victory*) tener en la mano; **to have a free** ~ tener carta blanca; **on** ~ (*person, services*) a mano, al alcance; **on the one** ~ ..., **on the other** ~ ... por una parte ... por otra (parte) ....

hand around *vt* (*chocolates etc*) ofrecer; (*information, papers*) pasar (de mano en mano).

hand down *vt* pasar, bajar; (*tradition*) transmitir; (*heirloom*) dejar en herencia; (*US: sentence, verdict*) imponer.

hand in *vt* entregar.

hand out *vt* (*leaflets, advice*) repartir, distribuir.

hand over *vt* (*deliver*) entregar; (*surrender*) ceder.

hand round *vt* (*Brit*) = **hand around.**

handbag [hand'bag] *n* bolso, cartera (*LAm*).

handball [hand'bôl] *n* balonmano.

hand basin *n* lavabo.

handbook [hand'bo͞ok] *n* manual *m*.

handbrake [hand'brāk] *n* freno de mano.

hand cream *n* crema para las manos.

handcuffs [hand'kufs] *npl* esposas *fpl*.

handful [hand'fo͞ol] *n* puñado.

handicap [han'dēkap] *n* desventaja; (*SPORT*) hándicap *m* ♦ *vt* estorbar.

handicapped [han'dēkapt] *a*: **to be mentally** ~ ser deficiente *m/f* (mental); **to be physically** ~ ser minusválido/a (físico/a).

handicraft [han'dēkraft] *n* artesanía.

handiwork [han'dēwûrk] *n* manualidad(es) *f(pl)*; (*fig*) obra; **this looks like his** ~ (*pej*) es obra de él, parece.

handkerchief [hang'kúrchif] *n* pañuelo.

handle [han'dəl] *n* (*of door etc*) manija; (*of cup etc*) asa; (*of knife etc*) mango; (*for winding*) manivela ♦ *vt* (*touch*) tocar; (*deal with*) encargarse de; (*treat: people*) manejar; **"**~ **with care"** ''(manéjese) con cuidado''; **to fly off the** ~ perder los estribos.

handlebar(s) [han'dəlbár(z)] *n(pl)* manillar *msg*.

handling charges [han'dling châr'jəz] *npl* gastos *mpl* de tramitación.

hand luggage *n* equipaje *m* de mano.

handmade [hand'mād'] *a* hecho a mano.

handout [hand'out] *n* (*distribution*) repartición *f*; (*charity*) limosna; (*leaflet*) folleto, octavilla; (*press* ~) nota.

hand-picked [hand'pikt'] *a* (*produce*) escogido a mano; (*staff etc*) seleccionado cuidadosamente.

handrail [hand'rāl] *n* (*on staircase etc*) pasamanos *m inv*, barandilla.

handshake [hand'shāk] *n* apretón *m* de manos; (*COMPUT*) coloquio.

handsome [han'səm] *a* guapo.

hands-on [handz'ân] *a*: ~ **experience** (*COMPUT*) experiencia práctica.

handstand [hand'stand] *n* voltereta, salto mortal.

hand-to-mouth [hand'təmouth'] *a* (*existence*) precario.

handwriting [hand'rīting] *n* letra.

handwritten [hand'ritən] *a* escrito a mano, manuscrito.

handy [han'dē] *a* (*close at hand*) a la mano; (*useful: machine, tool etc*) práctico; (*skilful*) hábil, diestro; **to come in** ~ venir bien.

handyman [hand'dēman] *n* manitas *m inv*.

hang, *pt, pp* **hung** [hang, hung] *vt* colgar; (*head*) bajar; (*criminal: pt, pp* **hanged**) ahorcar; **to get the** ~ **of sth** (*col*) lograr dominar algo.

hang around *vi* haraganear.

hang back *vi* (*hesitate*): **to** ~ **back (from doing)** vacilar (en hacer).

hang on *vi* (*wait*) esperar ♦ *vt fus* (*depend on: decision etc*) depender de; **to** ~ **on to** (*keep hold of*) agarrarse *or* aferrarse a; (*keep*) guardar, quedarse con.

hang out *vt* (*washing*) tender, colgar ♦ *vi* (*col: live*) vivir, radicarse; **to** ~ **out of sth** colgar fuera de algo.

hang together *vi* (*cohere: argument etc*) sostenerse.

hang up *vt* (*coat*) colgar ♦ *vi* (*TEL*) colgar; **to** ~ **up on sb** colgarle a uno.

hangar [hang'ûr] *n* hangar *m*.

hangdog [hang'dôg] *a* (*guilty: look, expression*) avergonzado.

hanger [hang'ûr] *n* percha.

hanger-on [hang'ûrân'] *n* parásito.

hang-gliding [hang'glīding] *n* vuelo libre.

hanging [hang'ing] *n* (*execution*) ejecución *f* (en la horca).
hangman [hang'mən] *n* verdugo.
hangover [hang'ōvûr] *n* (*after drinking*) resaca.
hang-up [hang'up] *n* complejo.
hanker [hang'kûr] *vi*: **to ~ after** (*miss*) echar de menos; (*long for*) añorar.
hankie, hanky [hang'kē] *n abbr* = **handkerchief**.
hanky-panky [hang'kēpang'kē] *n* (*col*) trucos *mpl*, trampas *fpl*.
Hants *abbr* (*Brit*) = *Hampshire*.
haphazard [haphaz'ûrd] *a* fortuito.
hapless [hap'lis] *a* desventurado.
happen [hap'ən] *vi* suceder, ocurrir; (*take place*) tener lugar, realizarse; **as it ~s** da la casualidad de que; **what's ~ing?** ¿qué pasa?
happen (up)on *vt fus* tropezar *or* dar con.
happening [hap'əning] *n* suceso, acontecimiento.
happily [hap'ilē] *ad* (*luckily*) afortunadamente; (*cheerfully*) alegremente.
happiness [hap'ēnis] *n* (*contentment*) felicidad *f*; (*joy*) alegría.
happy [hap'ē] *a* feliz; (*cheerful*) alegre; **to be ~ (with)** estar contento (con); **yes, I'd be ~ to** sí, con mucho gusto; **H~ Christmas/New Year!** ¡Feliz Navidad!/¡Feliz Año Nuevo!; **~ birthday!** ¡felicidades!, ¡feliz cumpleaños!
happy-go-lucky [hap'ēgōluk'ē] *a* despreocupado.
harangue [hərang'] *vt* arengar.
harass [həras'] *vt* acosar, hostigar.
harassed [hərast'] *a* agobiado, presionado.
harassment [həras'mənt] *n* persecución *f*; (*worry*) preocupación *f*.
harbor [hâr'bûr] *n* puerto ♦ *vt* (*hope etc*) abrigar; (*hide*) dar abrigo a; (*retain*: *grudge etc*) guardar.
harbor dues *npl* derechos *mpl* portuarios.
harbour [hâr'bûr] *etc* (*Brit*) = **harbor** *etc*.
hard [hârd] *a* duro; (*difficult*) difícil; (*person*) severo ♦ *ad* (*work*) mucho, duro; (*think*) profundamente; **to look ~ at sb/sth** clavar los ojos en alguien/algo; **to try ~** esforzarse; **no ~ feelings!** ¡sin rencor(es)!; **to be ~ of hearing** ser duro de oído; **to be ~ on sb** ser muy duro con uno; **I find it ~ to believe that ...** me cuesta trabajo creer que ....
hard-and-fast [hârd'ənfast] *a* rígido, definitivo.
hardback [hârd'bak] *n* libro de tapas duras.
hard cash *n* dinero contante.
hard copy *n* (*COMPUT*) copia impresa.
hard-core [hârd'kôr'] *a* (*pornography*) duro; (*supporters*) incondicional.
hard court *n* (*TENNIS*) cancha (de tenis) de cemento.

hard disk *n* (*COMPUT*) disco duro *or* rígido.
harden [hâr'dən] *vt* endurecer; (*steel*) templar; (*fig*) curtir; (*: determination*) fortalecer ♦ *vi* (*substance*) endurecerse.
hardened [hâr'dənd] *a* (*criminal*) empedernido; **to be ~ to sth** estar acostumbrado a algo.
hard-headed [hârd'hed'id] *a* poco sentimental, realista.
hard-hearted [hârd'hâr'tid] *a* duro de corazón.
hard labor *n* trabajos *mpl* forzados.
hardliner [hârdlī'nûr] *n* partidario/a de la línea dura.
hardly [hârd'lē] *ad* (*scarcely*) apenas; **that can ~ be true** eso difícilmente puede ser cierto; **~ ever** casi nunca; **I can ~ believe it** apenas me lo puedo creer.
hardness [hârd'nis] *n* dureza.
hard sell *n* publicidad *f* agresiva; **~ techniques** técnicas *fpl* agresivas de venta.
hardship [hârd'ship] *n* (*troubles*) penas *fpl*; (*financial*) apuro.
hard shoulder *n* (*Brit AUT*) andén *m*, arcén *m*.
hard up *a* (*col*) sin un duro (*Sp*) *or* plata (*LAm*).
hardware [hârd'wär] *n* ferretería; (*COMPUT*) hardware *m*.
hardware dealer *n* (*US*) ferretero/a.
hardware store *n* ferretería.
hard-wearing [hârd'wär'ing] *a* resistente, duradero; (*shoes*) resistente.
hard-working [hârd'wûr'king] *a* trabajador(a).
hardy [hâr'dē] *a* fuerte; (*plant*) resistente.
hare [här] *n* liebre *f*.
harebrained [här'brānd] *a* casquivano.
harelip [här'lip] *n* labio leporino.
harem [här'əm] *n* harén *m*.
haricot (bean) [har'ikō (bēn)] *n* alubia.
hark back [hârk bak] *vi*: **to ~ to** (*former days, earlier occasion*) recordar.
harm [hârm] *n* daño, mal *m* ♦ *vt* (*person*) hacer daño a; (*health, interests*) perjudicar; (*thing*) dañar; **out of ~'s way** a salvo; **there's no ~ in trying** nada se pierde con intentar.
harmful [hârm'fəl] *a* (*gen*) dañino; (*reputation*) perjudicial.
harmless [hârm'lis] *a* (*person*) inofensivo; (*drugs*) inocuo.
harmonica [hârmân'ikə] *n* armónica.
harmonious [hârmō'nēəs] *a* armonioso.
harmonize [hâr'mənīz] *vt, vi* armonizar.
harmony [hâr'mənē] *n* armonía.
harness [hâr'nis] *n* arreos *mpl* ♦ *vt* (*horse*) enjaezar; (*resources*) aprovechar.
harp [hârp] *n* arpa ♦ *vi*: **to ~ on (about)** machacar (con).
harpoon [hârpōōn'] *n* arpón *m*.
harrow [har'ō] *n* grada ♦ *vt* gradar.
harrowing [har'ōing] *a* angustioso.

harry [har'ē] *vt* (*MIL*) acosar; (*person*) hostigar.

harsh [hârsh] *a* (*cruel*) duro, cruel; (*severe*) severo; (*words*) hosco; (*color*) chillón/ona; (*contrast*) violento.

harshly [hârsh'lē] *ad* (*say*) con aspereza; (*treat*) con mucha dureza.

harshness [hârsh'nis] *n* dureza.

harvest [hâr'vist] *n* cosecha; (*of grapes*) vendimia ♦ *vt, vi* cosechar.

harvester [hâr'vistûr] *n* (*machine*) cosechadora; (*person*) segador(a) *m/f*; **combine** ~ segadora trilladora.

has [haz] *vb see* **have**.

has-been [haz'bin] *n* (*col: person*) persona acabada; (: *thing*) vieja gloria.

hash [hash] *n* (*CULIN*) picadillo; (*fig: mess*) lío.

hashish [hash'ēsh] *n* hachís *m*, hachich *m*.

hasn't [haz'ənt] = **has not**.

hassle [has'əl] *n* (*col*) lío, problema *m* ♦ *vt* molestar.

haste [hāst] *n* prisa.

hasten [hā'sən] *vt* acelerar ♦ *vi* darse prisa; **I** ~ **to add that...** me apresuro a añadir que ....

hastily [hās'tilē] *ad* de prisa.

hasty [hās'tē] *a* apresurado.

hat [hat] *n* sombrero.

hatbox [hat'bâks] *n* sombrerera.

hatch [hach] *n* (*NAUT: also:* ~**way**) escotilla ♦ *vi* salir del cascarón ♦ *vt* incubar; (*fig: scheme, plot*) idear, tramar.

hatchback [hach'bak] *n* (*AUT*) tres *or* cinco puertas *m*.

hatchet [hach'it] *n* hacha.

hate [hāt] *vt* odiar, aborrecer ♦ *n* odio; **I** ~ **to trouble you, but** ... siento *or* lamento molestarle, pero ....

hateful [hāt'fəl] *a* odioso.

hatred [hā'trid] *n* odio.

hat trick *n*: **to score a** ~ (*SPORT*) marcar tres tantos (*or* triunfos) seguidos.

haughtily [hô'tilē] *ad* con arrogancia.

haughty [hô'tē] *a* altanero, arrogante.

haul [hôl] *vt* tirar; (*by truck*) transportar ♦ *n* (*of fish*) redada; (*of stolen goods etc*) botín *m*.

haulage [hô'lij] *n* transporte *m*; (*costs*) gastos *mpl* de transporte.

haulage contractor *n* (*company*) empresa de transportes; (*person*) transportista *m/f*.

hauler [hôl'ûr], (*Brit*) **haulier** [hôl'ēûr] *n* transportista *m/f*.

haunch [hônch] *n* anca; (*of meat*) pierna.

haunt [hônt] *vt* (*subj: ghost*) aparecer en; (*frequent*) frecuentar; (*obsess*) obsesionar ♦ *n* guarida.

haunted [hôn'tid] *a* (*castle etc*) embrujado; (*look*) de angustia.

haunting [hôn'ting] *a* (*sight, music*) evocativo.

Havana [həvan'ə] *n* la Havana.

have, *pt, pp* **had** [hav, had] *vt* (*gen*) tener; (*possess*) poseer; (*meal, shower*) tomar ♦ *auxiliary vb*: **to** ~ **arrived** haber llegado; **to** ~ **eaten** haber comido; **to** ~ **breakfast/lunch/dinner** tomar el desayuno/el almuerzo/la cena; **I'll** ~ **a coffee** tomaré un café; **to** ~ **an operation** operarse; **to** ~ **a party** dar una fiesta; **to** ~ **sth done** hacer hacer algo; **she has to do it** tiene que hacerlo; **to** ~ **a cold/flu** estar constipado/con gripe; **I had better leave** más vale que me marche; **I won't** ~ **it** no lo tolero; **let me** ~ **a try** déjame que lo intente; **rumor has it (that)** ... corre la voz de que ...; **he has gone** se ha ido; **to** ~ **it out with sb** ajustar cuentas con uno; **to** ~ **a baby** parir, dar a luz; *see also* **haves**.

have in *vt*: **to** ~ **it in for sb** (*col*) tenerla tomada con uno.

have on *vt*: **do you** ~ **anything on for tomorrow?** ¿tienes compromiso para mañana?; **I don't** ~ **any money on me** no llevo dinero; **to** ~ **sb on** (*Brit col*) tomarle el pelo a uno.

haven [hā'vən] *n* puerto; (*fig*) refugio.

haven't [hav'ənt] = **have not**.

haversack [hav'ûrsak] *n* mochila.

haves [havz] *npl*: **the** ~ **and the have-nots** los ricos y los pobres.

havoc [hav'ək] *n* estragos *mpl*.

Hawaii [həwī'yē] *n* (*Islas fpl*) Hawai *m*.

Hawaiian [həwī'ən] *a, n* hawaiano/a *m/f*.

hawk [hôk] *n* halcón *m* ♦ *vt* (*goods for sale*) pregonar.

hawthorn [hô'thôrn] *n* espino.

hay [hā] *n* heno.

hay fever *n* fiebre *f* del heno.

haystack [hā'stak] *n* almiar *m*.

haywire [hā'wīur] *a* (*col*): **to go** ~ (*person*) volverse loco; (*plan*) embrollarse.

hazard [haz'ûrd] *n* riesgo; (*danger*) peligro ♦ *vt* (*remark*) aventurar; (*one's life*) arriesgar; **to be a health** ~ ser peligroso para la salud; **to** ~ **a guess** atreverse a hacer una respuesta.

hazardous [haz'ûrdəs] *a* (*dangerous*) peligroso; (*risky*) arriesgado.

hazardous pay *n* (*US*) prima por trabajos peligrosos.

hazard warning lights *npl* (*Brit AUT*) señales *fpl* de emergencia.

haze [hāz] *n* neblina.

hazel [hā'zəl] *n* (*tree*) avellano ♦ *a* (*eyes*) color *m* de avellano.

hazelnut [hā'zəlnut] *n* avellana.

hazy [hā'zē] *a* (*weather*) brumoso; (*idea*) vago.

H-bomb [āch'bâm] *n* bomba H.

h & c *abbr* (*Brit*) = *hot and cold (water)*.

HE *abbr* = **high explosive**; (*REL. DIPLOMACY*): = *His (or Her) Excellency*) S. Exc.ª.

he [hē] *pron* él; ~ **who...** él que..., quien... .

head [hed] *n* cabeza; (*leader*) jefe/a *m/f*; (*COMPUT*) cabeza (grabadora) ♦ *vt* (*list*) encabezar; (*group*) capitanear; ~**s (or tails)** cara (o cruz); ~ **first** de cabeza; ~ **over heels** patas arriba; ~ **over heels in love** perdidamente enamorado; **it's on your** ~**!** ¡allá tú!; **they went over my** ~ **to the manager** fueron directamente al gerente sin hacerme caso; **it was above** *or* **over their** ~**s** no alcanzaron a entenderlo; **to come to a** ~ (*fig: situation etc*) llegar a un punto crítico; **to have a** ~ **for business** tener talento para los negocios; **to have no** ~ **for heights** (*Brit*) no resistir las alturas; **to lose/keep one's** ~ perder la cabeza/ mantener la calma; **to sit at the** ~ **of the table** sentarse a la cabecera; **to** ~ **the ball** cabecear (la pelota).

head for *vt fus* dirigirse a.

head off *vt* (*threat, danger*) desviar.

headache [hed'āk] *n* dolor *m* de cabeza; **to have a** ~ tener dolor de cabeza.

headcheese [hed'chēz] *n* carne *f* en gelatina.

headdress [hed'dres] *n* (*of bride, Indian*) tocado.

header [hed'ûr] *n* (*Brit col: SOCCER*) cabezazo; (: *fall*) caída de cabeza.

headhunter [hed'huntûr] *n* (*fig*) cazaejecutivos *m inv*.

heading [hed'ing] *n* título.

headlamp [hed'lamp] *n* (*Brit*) = **headlight**.

headland [hed'land] *n* promontorio.

headlight [hed'līt] *n* faro.

headline [hed'līn] *n* titular *m*; **to make the** ~**s** salir en primera plana.

headlong [hed'lông] *ad* (*fall*) de cabeza; (*rush*) precipitadamente.

headmaster/mistress [hed'mas'tûr/ mis'tris] *n* (*Brit*) director(a) *m/f* (de escuela).

head office *n* oficina central, central *f*.

head-on [hed'ân'] *a* (*collision*) de frente.

headphones [hed'fōnz] *npl* auriculares *mpl*.

headquarters (HQ) [hed'kwôrtûrz] *npl* sede *f* central; (*MIL*) cuartel *m* general.

headrest [hed'rest] *n* reposa-cabezas *m inv*.

headroom [hed'rōōm] *n* (*in car*) altura interior; (*under bridge*) (límite *m* de) altura.

headscarf [hed'skárf] *n* pañuelo.

headset [hed'set] *n* casco auricular.

headstone [hed'stōn] *n* lápida mortuoria.

headstrong [hed'strông] *a* testarudo.

head waiter *n* maître *m*.

headway [hed'wā] *n*: **to make** ~ (*fig*) hacer progresos.

headwind [hed'wind] *n* viento contrario.

heady [hed'ē] *a* (*experience, period*) apasionante; (*wine*) cabezón.

heal [hēl] *vt* curar ♦ *vi* cicatrizarse.

health [helth] *n* salud *f*.

health benefit *n* (*US*) subsidio de enfermedad.

health center *n* ambulatorio, centro médico.

health food(s) *n(pl)* alimentos *mpl* orgánicos.

health food store *n* tienda de alimentos orgánicos.

health hazard *n* riesgo para la salud.

Health Service *n* (*Brit*) servicio de salud pública, ≈ Insalud *m* (*Sp*).

healthy [hel'thē] *a* (*gen*) sano; (*economy, bank balance*) saludable.

heap [hēp] *n* montón *m* ♦ *vt* amontonar; (*plate*) colmar; ~**s (of)** (*col: lots*) montones (de); **to** ~ **favors/praise/gifts** *etc* **on sb** colmar a uno de favores/elogios/regalos *etc*.

hear, *pt, pp* **heard** [hēr, hûrd] *vt* oír; (*perceive*) sentir; (*listen to*) escuchar; (*lecture*) asistir a; (*LAW: case*) ver ♦ *vi* oír; **to** ~ **about** oír hablar de; **to** ~ **from sb** tener noticias de alguien; **I've never heard of that book** nunca he oído de ese libro.

hear out *vt*: **to** ~ **sb out** dejar que uno termine de hablar.

hearing [hē'ring] *n* (*sense*) oído; (*LAW*) vista; **to give sb a** ~ dar a uno la oportunidad de hablar, escuchar a uno.

hearing aid *n* audífono.

hearsay [hēr'sā] *n* rumores *mpl*, hablillas *fpl*.

hearse [hûrs] *n* coche *m* fúnebre.

heart [hárt] *n* corazón *m*; ~**s** *npl* (*CARDS*) corazones *mpl*; **at** ~ en el fondo; **by** ~ (*learn, know*) de memoria; **to have a weak** ~ tener el corazón débil; **to set one's** ~ **on sth/on doing sth** anhelar algo/ hacer algo; **I did not have the** ~ **to tell her** no tuve valor para decírselo; **to take** ~ cobrar ánimos; **the** ~ **of the matter** lo esencial *or* el meollo del asunto.

heart attack *n* infarto (de miocardio).

heartbeat [hárt'bēt] *n* latido (del corazón).

heartbreak [hárt'brāk] *n* angustia, congoja.

heartbreaking [hárt'brāking] *a* desgarrador(a).

heartbroken [hárt'brōkən] *a*: **she was** ~ **about it** le partió el corazón.

heartburn [hárt'bûrn] *n* acedía.

-hearted [-hár'tid] *a suff*: **a kind**~ **person** una persona bondadosa.

heartening [hár'təning] *a* alentador(a).

heart failure *n* (*MED*) fallo de corazón, colapso cardíaco.

heartfelt [hárt'felt] *a* (*cordial*) cordial; (*deeply felt*) más sentido.

hearth [hárth] *n* (*gen*) hogar *m*; (*fireplace*) chimenea.

heartily [hár'təlē] *ad* sinceramente, cordialmente; (*laugh*) a carcajadas; (*eat*) con buen apetito; **to be** ~ **sick of** estar completamente harto de.

heartland [hârt'land] *n* zona interior *or* central; (*fig*) corazón *m*.
heartless [hârt'lis] *a* cruel.
heart-to-heart [hârt'təhârt'] *n* (*also:* ~ **talk**) conversación *f* íntima.
heart transplant *n* transplante *m* de corazón.
hearty [hâr'tē] *a* cordial.
heat [hēt] *n* (*gen*) calor *m*; (*SPORT: also:* **qualifying** ~) prueba eliminatoria; (*ZOOL*): **in** *or* **on** ~ en celo ♦ *vt* calentar.
heat up *vi* (*gen*) calentarse; (*col: situation*) ponerse difícil *or* apurado; (*: party*) animarse.
heated [hē'tid] *a* caliente; (*fig*) acalorado.
heater [hē'tûr] *n* calentador *m*.
heath [hēth] *n* (*Brit*) brezal *m*.
heathen [hē'thən] *a, n* pagano/a *m/f*.
heather [heth'ûr] *n* brezo.
heating [hē'ting] *n* calefacción *f*.
heat-resistant [hēt'rizistənt] *a* refractario.
heatstroke [hēt'strōk] *n* insolación *f*.
heat wave *n* ola de calor.
heave [hēv] *vt* (*pull*) tirar; (*push*) empujar con esfuerzo; (*lift*) levantar (con esfuerzo) ♦ *vi* (*water*) subir y bajar ♦ *n* tirón *m*; empujón *m*; (*effort*) esfuerzo; (*throw*) echada; **to** ~ **a sigh** dar *or* echar un suspiro, suspirar.
heave to *vi* (*NAUT*) ponerse al pairo.
heaven [hev'ən] *n* cielo; (*REL*) paraíso; **thank** ~! ¡gracias a Dios!; **for** ~'**s sake!** (*pleading*) ¡por el amor de Dios!, ¡por lo que más quiera!; (*protesting*) ¡por Dios!; **to be in seventh** ~ estar loco de contento.
heavenly [hev'ənlē] *a* celestial; (*REL*) divino.
heavenly body *n* cuerpo celeste.
heavily [hev'ilē] *ad* pesadamente; (*drink, smoke*) con exceso; (*sleep, sigh*) profundamente.
heavy [hev'ē] *a* pesado; (*work*) duro; (*sea, rain, meal*) fuerte; (*drinker, smoker*) gran; (*eater*) comilón/ona.
heavy cream *n* (*US*) nata enriquecida.
heavy-duty [hev'ēdoo'tē] *a* resistente.
heavy goods vehicle (HGV) *n* (*Brit*) vehículo pesado.
heavy-handed [hev'ēhan'did] *a* (*clumsy, tactless*) torpe.
heavy industry *n* industria pesada.
heavy-set [hev'ēset] *a* (*US*) fornido.
heavy user *n* consumidor *m* intensivo.
heavyweight [hev'ēwāt] *n* (*SPORT*) peso pesado.
Hebrew [hē'brōō] *a, n* (*LING*) hebreo.
heckle [hek'əl] *vt* interrumpir.
heckler [hek'lûr] *n* el/la que interrumpe a un orador.
hectic [hek'tik] *a* agitado; (*busy*) ocupado.
hector [hek'tûr] *vt* intimidar con bravatas.
he'd [hēd] = **he would; he had.**
hedge [hej] *n* seto ♦ *vt* cercar (con un seto)

♦ *vi* contestar con evasivas; **as a** ~ **against inflation** como protección contra la inflación; **to** ~ **one's bets** (*fig*) cubrirse.
hedgehog [hej'hôg] *n* erizo.
hedgerow [hej'rō] *n* seto vivo.
hedonism [hēd'ənizəm] *n* hedonismo.
heed [hēd] *vt* (*also:* **take** ~ **of**) (*pay attention*) hacer caso de; (*bear in mind*) tener en cuenta; **to pay (no)** ~ **to, take (no)** ~ **of** (no) hacer caso a, (no) tener en cuenta.
heedless [hēd'lis] *a* desatento.
heel [hēl] *n* talón *m* ♦ *vt* (*shoe*) poner tacón a; **to take to one's** ~**s** (*col*) echar a correr; **to bring to** ~ meter en cintura.
hefty [hef'tē] *a* (*person*) fornido; (*piece*) grande; (*price*) gordo.
heifer [hef'ûr] *n* novilla, ternera.
height [hīt] *n* (*of person*) talle *m*; (*of building*) altura; (*high ground*) cerro; (*altitude*) altitud *f*; **what** ~ **are you?** ¿cuánto mides?; **of average** ~ de estatura mediana; **to be afraid of** ~**s** tener miedo a las alturas; **it's the** ~ **of fashion** es el último grito en moda.
heighten [hīt'ən] *vt* elevar; (*fig*) aumentar.
heinous [hā'nəs] *a* atroz, nefasto.
heir [är] *n* heredero.
heir apparent *n* presunto heredero.
heiress [är'is] *n* heredera.
heirloom [är'loom] *n* reliquia de familia.
heist [hīst] *n* (*col: hold-up*) atraco armado.
held [held] *pt, pp.* of **hold.**
helicopter [hel'əkáptûr] *n* helicóptero.
heliport [hel'əpôrt] *n* (*AVIAT*) helipuerto.
helium [hē'lēəm] *n* helio.
hell [hel] *n* infierno; **oh** ~! (*col*) ¡demonios!, ¡caramba!
he'll [hēl] = **he will, he shall.**
hellish [hel'ish] *a* infernal; (*col*) horrible.
hello [helō'] *excl* ¡hola!; (*surprise*) ¡caramba!
hell's angel [helz ān'jəl] *n* angel *m* del infierno.
helm [helm] *n* (*NAUT*) timón *m*.
helmet [hel'mit] *n* casco.
helmsman [helmz'mən] *n* timonel *m*.
help [help] *n* ayuda; (*charwoman*) criada, asistenta ♦ *vt* ayudar; ~! ¡socorro!; **with the** ~ **of** con la ayuda de; "~ **wanted**" (*US*) "ofertas de trabajo"; **can I** ~ **you?** (*in shop*) ¿qué desea?; **to be of** ~ **to sb** servir a uno; **to** ~ **sb (to) do sth** echarle una mano *or* ayudar a uno a hacer algo; ~ **yourself** sírvete; **he can't** ~ **it** no es culpa suya.
helper [hel'pûr] *n* ayudante *m/f*.
helpful [help'fəl] *a* útil; (*person*) servicial.
helping [hel'ping] *n* ración *f*.
helpless [help'lis] *a* (*incapable*) incapaz; (*defenseless*) indefenso.
Helsinki [hel'singkē] *n* Helsinki *m*.
helter-skelter [hel'tûrskel'tûr] *n* (*in funfair*)

tobogán m.

hem [hɛm] n dobladillo ♦ vt poner or coser el dobladillo a.
  hem in vt cercar; **to feel ~med in** (fig) sentirse acosado.

he-man [hē'man] n macho.

hematology [hēmətâl'əjē] n (US) hematología.

hemisphere [hɛm'isfēr] n hemisferio.

hemline [hɛm'lĭn] n bajo (del vestido).

hemlock [hɛm'lâk] n cicuta.

hemoglobin [hē'məglōbĭn] n (US) hemoglobina.

hemophilia [hēməfĭl'ēə] n (US) hemofilia.

hemorrhage [hɛm'ûrij] n (US) hemorragia.

hemorrhoids [hɛm'əroidz] npl (US) hemorroides fpl, almorranas fpl.

hemp [hɛmp] n cáñamo.

hen [hɛn] n gallina; (female bird) hembra.

hence [hɛns] ad (therefore) por lo tanto; **2 years ~** de aquí a 2 años.

henceforth [hɛns'fôrth] ad de hoy en adelante.

henchman [hɛnch'mən] n (pej) secuaz m.

henna [hɛn'ə] n alheña.

hen party n (col) reunión f de mujeres.

henpecked [hɛn'pɛkt] a: **to be ~** ser un calzonazos.

hepatitis [hɛpətī'tis] n hepatitis f inv.

her [hûr] pron (direct) la; (indirect) le; (stressed, after prep) ella ♦ a su; see also **me, my.**

herald [hăr'əld] n (forerunner) precursor(a) m/f ♦ vt anunciar.

heraldic [hiral'dik] a heráldico.

heraldry [hăr'əldrē] n heráldica.

herb [ûrb] n hierba.

herbaceous [hûrbā'shəs] a herbáceo.

herbal [hûr'bəl] a herbario.

herbicide [hûr'bisĭd] n herbicida m.

herd [hûrd] n rebaño; (of wild animals, swine) piara ♦ vt (drive, gather: animals) llevar en manada; (: people) reunir.
  herd together vt agrupar, reunir ♦ vi apiñarse, agruparse.

here [hēr] ad aquí; ~! (present) ¡presente!; **~ is/are** aquí está/están; **~ she is** aquí está; **come ~!** ¡ven aquí or acá!; **~ and there** aquí y allá.

hereabouts [hē'rəbouts] ad por aquí (cerca).

hereafter [hēraf'tûr] ad en el futuro ♦ n: **the ~** el más allá.

hereby [hērbī'] ad (in letter) por la presente.

hereditary [hərɛd'itărē] a hereditario.

heredity [hərɛd'itē] n herencia.

heresy [hăr'isē] n herejía.

heretic [hăr'itik] n hereje m/f.

heretical [hərɛt'ikəl] a herético.

herewith [hērwith'] ad: **I send you ~** ... le mando adjunto ....

heritage [hăr'itij] n (gen) herencia; (fig) patrimonio; **our national ~** nuestro patrimonio nacional.

hermetically [hûrmɛt'iklē] ad: **~ sealed** cerrado or tapado herméticamente.

hermit [hûr'mit] n ermitaño/a.

hernia [hûr'nēə] n hernia.

hero, pl **~es** [hē'rō] n héroe m; (in book, film) protagonista m.

heroic [hirō'ik] a heroico.

heroin [hăr'ōin] n heroína.

heroin addict n heroinómano/a, adicto/a a la heroína.

heroine [hăr'ōin] n heroína; (in book, film) protagonista.

heroism [hăr'ōizəm] n heroísmo.

heron [hăr'ən] n garza.

hero worship n adulación f.

herring [hăr'ing] n arenque m.

hers [hûrz] pron (el) suyo/(la) suya etc; **a friend of ~** un amigo suyo; **this is ~** esto es suyo or de ella; see also **mine.**

herself [hûrsɛlf'] pron (reflexive) se; (emphatic) ella misma; (after prep) sí (misma); see also **oneself.**

Herts abbr (Brit) = Hertfordshire.

he's [hēz] = **he is; he has.**

hesitant [hɛz'ətənt] a vacilante; **to be ~ about doing sth** no decidirse a hacer algo.

hesitate [hɛz'ətāt] vi vacilar; **don't ~ to ask (me)** no vaciles en or no dejes de pedírmelo.

hesitation [hɛzətā'shən] n indecisión f; **I have no ~ in saying (that)** ... no tengo el menor reparo en afirmar que ....

hessian [hɛsh'ən] n arpillera.

heterogeneous [hɛtûrəjē'nēəs] a heterogéneo.

heterosexual [hɛtûrəsɛk'shōōəl] a, n heterosexual m/f.

het up [hɛt up] a (col) agitado, nervioso.

hew [hyōō] vt cortar (con hacha).

hex [hɛks] (US) n maleficio, mal m de ojo ♦ vt embrujar.

hexagon [hɛk'səgən] n (h)exágono.

hexagonal [hɛksag'ənəl] a hexagonal.

hey [hā] excl ¡oye!

heyday [hā'dā] n: **the ~ of** el apogeo de.

HF n abbr = high frequency.

HGV n abbr (Brit) = **heavy goods vehicle.**

HI abbr (US MAIL) = Hawaii.

hi [hī] excl ¡hola!

hiatus [hiā'təs] n vacío, interrupción f; (LING) hiato.

hibernate [hī'bûrnāt] vi invernar.

hibernation [hībûrnā'shən] n hibernación f.

hiccough, hiccup [hik'up] vi hipar; **~s** npl hipo sg.

hick [hik] n (US) palurdo, rústico.

hid [hid] pt of **hide.**

hidden [hid'ən] pp of **hide** ♦ a: **there are no ~ extras** no hay gastos extra.

hide [hīd] n (skin) piel f ♦ vb (pt **hid,** pp

hidden [hid, hid'ən]) *vt* esconder, ocultar; (*feelings, truth*) encubrir, ocultar ♦ *vi*: **to ~ (from sb)** esconderse *or* ocultarse (de uno).

hide-and-seek [hĭd'ənsēk'] *n* escondite *m*.

hideaway [hĭd'əwā] *n* escondite *m*.

hideous [hĭd'ēəs] *a* horrible.

hideously [hĭd'ēəslē] *ad* horriblemente.

hide-out [hĭd'out] *n* escondite *m*, refugio.

hiding [hī'ding] *n* (*beating*) paliza; **to be in ~** (*concealed*) estar escondido.

hiding place *n* escondrijo.

hierarchy [hī'ərärkē] *n* jerarquía.

hieroglyphic [hīûrəglif'ik] *a* jeroglífico ♦ *n*: **~s** jeroglíficos *mpl*.

hi-fi [hī'fī'] *abbr* (= *high fidelity*) *n* estéreo, hifi *m* ♦ *a* de alta fidelidad.

higgledy-piggledy [hig'əldēpig'əldē] *ad* en desorden.

high [hī] *a* alto; (*speed, number*) grande; (*price*) elevado; (*wind*) fuerte; (*voice*) agudo; (*col: on drugs*) drogado; (: *on drink*) borracho; (*CULIN: meat, game*) manido; (: *spoiled*) estropeado ♦ *ad* alto, a gran altura ♦ *n*: **exports have reached a new ~** las exportaciones han alcanzado un niveles inusitados; **it is 20 m ~** tiene 20 m de altura; **~ in the air** en las alturas; **to pay a ~ price for sth** pagar algo muy caro.

highball [hī'bôl] *n* (*US: drink*) whisky *m* soda.

highboy [hī'boi] *n* (*US*) cómoda alta.

highbrow [hī'brou] *a* culto.

highchair [hī'chär] *n* silla alta.

high-class [hī'klas'] *a* (*neighborhood*) de alta sociedad; (*hotel*) de lujo; (*person*) distinguido, de categoría; (*food*) de alta categoría.

high court *n* (*LAW*) tribunal *m* supremo.

higher [hī'ûr] *a* (*form of life, study etc*) superior ♦ *ad* más alto.

higher education *n* educación *f* or enseñanza superior.

high explosive *n* explosivo de gran potencia.

high finance *n* altas finanzas *fpl*.

high-flier [hī'flī'ûr] *n* ambicioso/a.

high-handed [hī'han'did] *a* despótico.

high-heeled [hī'hēld] *a* de tacón alto.

highjack [hī'jak] = **hijack**.

high jump *n* (*SPORT*) salto de altura.

highlands [hī'ləndz] *npl* tierras *fpl* altas.

high-level [hī'levəl] *a* (*talks etc*) de alto nivel; **~ language** (*COMPUT*) lenguaje *m* de alto nivel.

highlight [hī'līt] *n* (*fig: of event*) punto culminante ♦ *vt* subrayar.

highly [hī'lē] *ad* sumamente; **~ paid** muy bien pagado; **to speak ~ of** hablar muy bien de.

highly-strung [hī'lēstrung'] *a* (*Brit*) = **high-strung**.

High Mass *n* misa mayor.

highness [hī'nis] *n* altura; **Her** *or* **His H~** Su Alteza.

high-pitched [hī'picht'] *a* agudo.

high-powered [hī'pou'ûrd] *a* (*engine*) de gran potencia; (*fig: person*) importante.

high-pressure [hī'presh'ûr] *a* de alta presión; (*fig: salesman etc*) enérgico.

high-rise building [hī'rīz bil'ding] *n* torre *f* de pisos.

high school *n* centro de enseñanza secundaria, ≈ Instituto Nacional de Bachillerato (*Sp*).

high season *n* temporada alta.

high-speed [hī'spēd] *a* de alta velocidad.

high-spirited [hī'spir'itid] *a* animado.

high spirits *npl* ánimos *mpl*.

high street *n* (*Brit*) calle *f* mayor.

high-strung [hī'strung'] *a* (*US*) hipertenso.

high tide *n* marea alta.

highway [hī'wā] *n* carretera; **divided ~** (*US*) carretera de doble calzada; **it's ~ robbery!** ¡es una extorsión!

Highway Code *n* (*Brit*) código de la circulación.

highwayman [hī'wāmən] *n* salteador *m* de caminos.

hijack [hī'jak] *vt* secuestrar ♦ *n* (*also*: **~ing**) secuestro.

hijacker [hī'jakûr] *n* secuestrador(a) *m/f*.

hike [hīk] *vi* (*go walking*) ir de excursión (a pie); (*trek*) caminar ♦ *n* caminata; (*col: in prices etc*) aumento.

hike up *vt* (*raise*) aumentar.

hiker [hī'kûr] *n* excursionista *m/f*.

hilarious [hilâr'ēəs] *a* divertidísimo.

hilarity [hilar'itē] *n* (*laughter*) risas *fpl*, carcajadas *fpl*.

hill [hil] *n* colina; (*high*) montaña; (*slope*) cuesta.

hillbilly [hil'bilē] *n* (*US*) rústico/a montañés/ esa; (*pej*) palurdo/a.

hillock [hil'ək] *n* montecillo, altozano.

hillside [hil'sīd] *n* ladera.

hilltop [hil'táp] *n* cumbre *f*.

hilly [hil'ē] *a* montañoso; (*uneven*) accidentado.

hilt [hilt] *n* (*of sword*) empuñadura; **to the ~** (*fig: support*) incondicionalmente; **to be in debt up to the ~** estar agobiado de deudas.

him [him] *pron* (*direct*) le, lo; (*indirect*) le; (*stressed, after prep*) él; *see also* **me**.

Himalayas [himəlā'əz] *npl*: **the ~** los montes Himalaya, el Himalaya.

himself [himself'] *pron* (*reflexive*) se; (*emphatic*) él mismo; (*after prep*) sí (mismo); *see also* **oneself**.

hind [hīnd] *a* posterior ♦ *n* cierva.

hinder [hin'dûr] *vt* estorbar, impedir.

hindquarters [hīnd'kwôrtûrz] *npl* (*ZOOL*) cuartos *mpl* traseros.

hindrance [hin'drəns] *n* estorbo, obstáculo.

hindsight [hīnd'sīt] *n* percepción *f* tardía *or*

retrospectiva; **with the benefit of** ~ con la perspectiva del tiempo transcurrido.

Hindu [hin'dōō] *n* hindú *m/f*.

hinge [hinj] *n* bisagra, gozne *m* ♦ *vi* (*fig*): **to** ~ **on** depender de.

hint [hint] *n* indirecta; (*advice*) consejo ♦ *vt*: **to** ~ **that** insinuar que ♦ *vi*: **to** ~ **at** referirse indirectamente a; **to drop a** ~ soltar *or* tirar una indirecta; **give me a** ~ dame una pista.

hip [hip] *n* cadera; (*BOT*) escaramujo.

hip flask *n* frasco.

hippie [hip'ē] *n* hippie *m/f*, jipi *m/f*.

hip pocket *n* bolsillo de atrás.

hippopotamus, *pl* ~**es** *or* **hippopotami** [hipəpât'əməs, -pât'əmī] hipopótamo.

hippy [hip'ē] *n* = **hippie**.

hire [hīūr] *vt* (*worker*) contratar; (*Brit: car, equipment*) alquilar ♦ *n* (*Brit*) alquiler *m*; **for** ~ se alquila; (*taxi*) libre; **on** ~ de alquiler.

hire out *vt* (*Brit*) alquilar, arrendar.

hire(d) car *n* (*Brit*) coche de alquiler.

hire purchase (HP) *n* (*Brit*) compra a plazos.

his [hiz] *pron* (el) suyo/(la) suya *etc* ♦ *a* su; **this is** ~ esto es suyo *or* de él; *see also* **my, mine**.

Hispanic [hispan'ik] *a* hispánico.

hiss [his] *vi* silbar; (*in protest*) sisear ♦ *n* silbido; siseo.

histogram [his'təgram] *n* histograma *m*.

historian [histôr'ēən] *n* historiador(a) *m/f*.

historic(al) [histôr'ik(əl)] *a* histórico.

history [his'tûrē] *n* historia; **there's a long** ~ **of that illness in his family** esa enfermedad corre en su familia.

histrionics [histrēán'iks] *npl* histrionismo.

hit [hit] *vt* (*pt, pp* **hit**) (*strike*) golpear, pegar; (*reach: target*) alcanzar; (*collide with: car*) chocar contra; (*fig: affect*) afectar ♦ *n* golpe *m*; (*success*) éxito; **to** ~ **the headlines** salir en primera plana; **to** ~ **the road** (*col*) largarse; **to** ~ **it off with sb** llevarse bien con uno.

hit back *vi* defenderse; (*fig*) devolver golpe por golpe.

hit out at *vt fus* asestar un golpe a; (*fig*) atacar.

hit (up)on *vt fus* (*answer*) dar con; (*solution*) hallar, encontrar.

hit-and-run driver [hit'ənrun' drī'vûr] *n* conductor(a) que atropella y huye.

hitch [hich] *vt* (*fasten*) atar, amarrar; (*also:* ~ **up**) remangar ♦ *n* (*difficulty*) dificultad *f*; **to** ~ **a ride** hacer autostop; **technical** ~ problema *m* técnico.

hitch up *vt* (*horse, cart*) enganchar, uncir.

hitchhike [hich'hīk] *vi* hacer autostop.

hitchhiker [hich'hīkûr] *n* autostopista *m/f*.

hi-tech [hī'tek'] *a* de alta tecnología.

hitherto [hith'ûrtōō] *ad* hasta ahora, hasta aquí.

hit man *n* asesino a sueldo.

hit-or-miss [hit'ərmis'] *a*: **it's** ~ **whether ...** está a la buena de Dios si ... .

hit parade *n*: **the** ~ los cuarenta principales.

hive [hīv] *n* colmena; **the shop was a** ~ **of activity** (*fig*) la tienda era una colmena humana.

hive off *vt* (*col: separate*) separar; (: *privatize*) privatizar.

hl *abbr* (= *hectoliter*) hl.

HM *abbr* (= *His* (*or Her*) *Majesty*) S.M.

HMG *abbr* (*Brit*) = *His* (*or Her*) *Majesty's Government*.

HMO *n abbr* (*US:* = *health maintenance organization*) seguro médico global.

HMS *abbr* (*Brit*) = *His* (*or Her*) *Majesty's Ship*.

hoard [hôrd] *n* (*treasure*) tesoro; (*stockpile*) provisión *f* ♦ *vt* acumular.

hoarding [hôr'ding] *n* (*for posters*) cartelera.

hoarfrost [hôr'frâst] *n* escarcha.

hoarse [hôrs] *a* ronco.

hoax [hōks] *n* trampa.

hob [hâb] *n* quemador *m*.

hobble [hâb'əl] *vi* cojear.

hobby [hâb'ē] *n* pasatiempo, afición *f*.

hobbyhorse [hâb'ēhôrs] *n* (*fig*) tema, manía.

hobnob [hâb'nâb] *vi*: **to** ~ (**with**) alternar (con).

hobo [hō'bō] *n* (*US*) vagabundo.

hock [hâk] *n* (*of animal, CULIN*) corvejón *m*; (*col*): **to be in** ~ (*person*) estar empeñado *or* endeudado; (*object*) estar empeñado.

hockey [hâk'ē] *n* hockey *m*.

hocus-pocus [hō'kəspō'kəs] *n* (*trickery*) juego de manos; (*words: of magician*) jerigonza.

hodge-podge [hâj'pâj] *n* mezcolanza.

hoe [hō] *n* azadón *m* ♦ *vt* azadonar.

hog [hôg] *n* cerdo, puerco ♦ *vt* (*fig*) acaparar; **to go the whole** ~ echar el todo por el todo.

hoist [hoist] *n* (*crane*) grúa ♦ *vt* levantar, alzar.

hold [hōld] *vb* (*pt, pp* **held** [held]) *vt* tener; (*contain*) contener; (*keep back*) retener; (*believe*) sostener; (*take* ~ *of*) coger (*Sp*), agarrar (*LAm*); (*take weight*) soportar; (*meeting*) celebrar ♦ *vi* (*withstand pressure*) resistir; (*be valid*) valer; (*stick*) pegarse ♦ *n* (*grasp*) asimiento; (*fig*) dominio; (*WRESTLING*) presa; (*NAUT*) bodega; ~ **the line!** (*TEL*) ¡no cuelgue!; **to** ~ **one's own** (*fig*) defenderse; **to** ~ **office** (*POL*) ocupar un cargo; **to** ~ **firm** *or* **fast** mantenerse firme; **he** ~**s the view that ...** opina *or* es su opinión que ...; **to** ~ **sb responsible for sth** culpar *or* echarle la culpa a uno de algo; **where can I get ~ of ...?** ¿dónde puedo encontrar (a) ...?; **to catch** or **get (a) ~ of** agarrarse or asirse de.

hold back vt retener; (secret) ocultar; **to ~ sb back from doing sth** impedir a uno hacer algo, impedir que uno haga algo.

hold down vt (person) sujetar; (job) mantener.

hold forth vi perorar.

hold off vt (enemy) rechazar ♦ vi: **if the rain ~s off** si no llueve.

hold on vi agarrarse bien; (wait) esperar.

hold on to vt fus agarrarse a; (keep) guardar.

hold out vt ofrecer ♦ vi (resist) resistir; **to ~ out (against)** resistir (a), sobrevivir.

hold over vt (meeting etc) aplazar.

hold up vt (raise) levantar; (support) apoyar; (delay) retrasar; (: traffic) demorar; (rob: bank) asaltar, atracar.

holdall [hōld'ôl] n (Brit) bolsa.

holder [hōl'dûr] n (of ticket, record) poseedor(a) m/f; (of passport, post, office, title etc) titular m/f.

holding [hōl'ding] n (share) interés m.

holding company n holding m.

holdup [hōld'up] n (robbery) atraco; (delay) retraso; (in traffic) embotellamiento.

hole [hōl] n agujero ♦ vt agujerear; **~ in the heart** (MED) boquete m en el corazón; **to pick ~s in** (fig) encontrar defectos en; **the ship was ~d** se abrió una vía de agua en el barco.

hole up vi esconderse.

holiday [hál'idā] n (day off) (día m de) fiesta, día m feriado; (from work) día m de asueto; (Brit: vacation) vacaciones fpl; **on ~** de vacaciones; **to be on ~** estar de vacaciones.

holiday camp n (Brit) colonia or centro vacacional; (: for children) colonia veraniega infantil.

holidaymaker [hál'idāmākûr] n (Brit) turista m/f.

holiday pay n (Brit) paga de las vacaciones.

holiday resort n centro turístico.

holiday season n (US) Las Navidades; (Brit) temporada de las vacaciones; **the ~ is from ... to ...** la época de vacaciones es de ... a ... .

holiness [hō'lēnis] n santidad f.

Holland [hál'ənd] n Holanda.

hollow [hál'ō] a hueco; (fig) vacío; (eyes) hundido; (sound) sordo ♦ n (gen) hueco; (in ground) hoyo ♦ vt: **to ~ out** ahuecar.

holly [hál'ē] n acebo.

hollyhock [hál'ēhâk] n malva loca.

holocaust [hál'əkôst] n holocausto.

holster [hōl'stûr] n pistolera.

holy [hō'lē] a (gen) santo, sagrado; (water)

bendito; **the H~ Father** el Santo Padre.

Holy Communion n Sagrada Comunión f.

Holy Ghost, Holy Spirit n Espíritu m Santo.

homage [hám'ij] n homenaje m; **to pay ~ to** rendir homenaje a.

home [hōm] n casa; (country) patria; (institution) asilo; (COMPUT) punto inicial or de partida ♦ a (domestic) casero, de casa; (ECON, POL) nacional; (SPORT: team) de casa; (: match, win) en casa ♦ ad (direction) a casa; **at ~** en casa; **to go/come ~** ir/volver a casa; **make yourself at ~** ¡estás en tu casa!; **it's near my ~** está cerca de mi casa.

home in on vt fus (missiles) dirigirse hacia.

home address n domicilio.

home-brew [hōm'broo'] n cerveza etc casera.

homecoming [hōm'kuming] n regreso (al hogar).

home computer n ordenador m doméstico.

home economics n economía doméstica.

home-grown [hōm'grōn'] a de cosecha propia.

home key n (COMPUT) tecla home.

homeland [hōm'land] n tierra natal.

homeless [hōm'lis] a sin hogar, sin casa ♦ npl: **the ~** las personas sin hogar.

home loan n préstamo para la vivienda.

homely [hōm'lē] a (domestic) casero; (simple) sencillo.

home-made [hōm'mād'] a hecho en casa.

Home Office n (Brit) Ministerio del Interior.

homeopath [hō'mēəpath] n homeópata m/f.

homeopathic [hōmēəpath'ik] a homeopático.

homeopathy [hōmēâp'əthē] n homeopatía.

home rule n autonomía.

Home Secretary n (Brit) Ministro del Interior.

homesick [hōm'sik] a: **to be ~** tener morriña, tener nostalgia.

homestead [hōm'sted] n hacienda.

home town n ciudad f natal.

homeward [hōm'wûrd] a (journey) de vuelta.

homeward(s) [hōm'wûrd(z)] ad hacia casa.

homework [hōm'wûrk] n deberes mpl.

homicidal [hámisīd'əl] a homicida.

homicide [hám'isīd] n (US) homicidio.

homily [hám'ilē] n homilía.

homing [hō'ming] a (device, missile) buscador(a), cazador(a); **~ pigeon** paloma mensajera.

homoeopathy [hōmēâp'əthē] etc (Brit) = **homeopathy** etc.

homogeneous [hōməjē'nēəs] a homogéneo.

homogenize [həmâj'ənīz] vt homogeneizar.

homosexual [hōməsek'shōōəl] a, n homosexual *m/f*.

Hon. *abbr* (= honorable, honorary) en títulos.

Honduras [hundōō'rəs] *n* Honduras *fpl*.

hone [hōn] *vt* (*sharpen*) afilar; (*fig*) perfeccionar.

honest [ân'ist] *a* honrado; (*sincere*) franco, sincero; **to be quite ~ with you** ... para serte franco ....

honestly [ân'istlē] *ad* honradamente; francamente.

honesty [ân'istē] *n* honradez *f*.

honey [hun'ē] *n* miel *f*; (*US col*) guapa, linda.

honeycomb [hun'ēkōm] *n* panal *m*; (*fig*) laberinto.

honeymoon [hun'ēmōōn] *n* luna de miel.

honeysuckle [hun'ēsukəl] *n* madreselva.

Hong Kong [hâng' kông'] *n* Hong-Kong *m*.

honk [hângk] *vi* (*AUT*) tocar la bocina.

Honolulu [hánəlōō'lōō] *n* Honolulú *m*.

honor [ân'ûr] (*US*) *vt* honrar ♦ *n* honor *m*, honra; **in ~ of** en honor de; **it's a great ~** es un gran honor.

honorable [ân'úrəbəl] *a* honrado, honorable.

honorary [ân'ərārē] *a* no remunerado; (*duty, title*) honorario.

honor-bound [ân'ûrbound'] *a* moralmente obligado.

honors degree *n* (*UNIV*) título de licenciado de categoría superior.

honour [ân'ûr] *etc* (*Brit*) = **honor** *etc*.

Hons. *abbr* (*UNIV*) = **honors degree**.

hood [hōōd] *n* capucha; (*US AUT*) capó *m*; (*Brit AUT*) capota; (*US col*) matón *m*.

hooded [hōōd'id] *a* (*robber*) encapuchado.

hoodlum [hōōd'ləm] *n* matón *m*.

hoodwink [hōōd'wingk] *vt* (*Brit*) timar.

hoof, *pl* **~s** *or* **hooves** [hōōf, hōōvz] *n* pezuña.

hook [hōōk] *n* gancho; (*on dress*) corchete *m*, broche *m*; (*for fishing*) anzuelo ♦ *vt* enganchar; **~s and eyes** corchetes *mpl*, macho y hembra *m*; **by ~ or by crook** por las buenas o por las malas; **to be ~ed on** (*col*) ser adicto a; **to be ~ed on drugs** estar colgado.
 hook up *vt* (*RADIO. TV*) transmitir en cadena.

hooker [hōōk'ûr] *n* (*col*) puta.

hooky [hōōk'ē] *n*: **to play ~** hacer novillos.

hooligan [hōō'ligən] *n* gamberro.

hooliganism [hōō'ligənizəm] *n* gamberrismo.

hoop [hōōp] *n* aro.

hoot [hōōt] *vi* (*owl*) ulular; (*siren*) sonar la sirena; (*Brit AUT*) tocar la bocina ♦ *n* bocinazo, toque *m* de sirena; **to ~ with laughter** morirse de risa.

hooter [hōō'tûr] *n* (*NAUT*) sirena; (*factory ~*) silbato; (*Brit AUT*) bocina.

hoover [hōō'vûr] ® (*Brit*) *n* aspiradora ♦ *vt* pasar la aspiradora por.

hooves [hōōvz] *pl of* **hoof.**

hop [hâp] *vi* saltar, brincar; (*on one foot*) saltar con un pie ♦ *n* salto, brinco; *see also* **hops.**

hope [hōp] *vt, vi* esperar ♦ *n* esperanza; **I ~ so/not** espero que sí/no.

hopeful [hōp'fəl] *a* (*person*) optimista; (*situation*) prometedor(a); **I'm ~ that she'll manage to come** confío en que podrá venir.

hopefully [hōp'fəlē] *ad* con optimismo, con esperanza.

hopeless [hōp'lis] *a* desesperado.

hopelessly [hōp'lislē] *ad* (*live etc*) sin esperanzas; **I'm ~ confused/lost** estoy totalmente despistado/perdido.

hopper [hâp'ûr] *n* (*chute*) tolva.

hops [hâps] *npl* lúpulo *sg*.

horde [hôrd] *n* horda.

horizon [hərī'zən] *n* horizonte *m*.

horizontal [hôrizân'təl] *a* horizontal.

hormone [hôr'mōn] *n* hormona.

horn [hôrn] *n* cuerno; (*MUS: also:* **French ~**) trompa; (*AUT*) bocina, claxón *m* (*LAm*); **English ~** corno inglés.

horned [hôrnd] *a* con cuernos.

hornet [hôr'nit] *n* avispón *m*.

horny [hôr'nē] *a* (*material*) córneo; (*hands*) calloso; (*col*) cachondo.

horoscope [hôr'əskōp] *n* horóscopo.

horrendous [hôrɛn'dəs] *a* horrendo.

horrible [hôr'əbəl] *a* horrible.

horribly [hôr'əblē] *ad* horriblemente.

horrid [hôr'id] *a* horrible, horroroso.

horridly [hôr'idlē] *ad* (*behave*) tremendamente mal.

horrific [hôrif'ik] *a* (*accident*) horroroso; (*film*) horripilante.

horrify [hôr'əfī] *vt* horrorizar.

horrifying [hôr'əfīing] *a* horroroso.

horror [hôr'ûr] *n* horror *m*.

horror film *n* película de horror.

horror-struck [hôr'ûrstruk], **horror-stricken** [hôr'ûrstrikən] *a* horrorizado.

hors d'œuvre [ôr dûrv'] *n* entremeses *mpl*.

horse [hôrs] *n* caballo.

horseback [hôrs'bak] *n*: **on ~** a caballo; **to go ~ riding** (*US*) montar, cabalgar.

horsebox [hôrs'bâks] *n* (*Brit*) = **horse trailer.**

horse chestnut *n* (*tree*) castaño de Indias.

horsedrawn [hôrs'drôn] *a* de tracción animal.

horsefly [hôrs'flī] *n* tábano.

horseman [hôrs'mən] *n* jinete *m*.

horsemanship [hôrs'mənship] *n* equitación *f*, manejo del caballo.

horseplay [hôrs'plā] *n* payasadas *fpl*.

horsepower (hp) [hôrs'pouûr] *n* caballo (de fuerza), potencia en caballos.

horse racing *n* carreras *fpl* de caballos.

horseradish [hôrs'radish] *n* rábano picante.

horseshoe [hôrs'shōō] *n* herradura.
horse show *n* concurso hípico.
horse-trader [hôrs'trādûr] *n* chalán/ana *m/f.*
horse trailer *n* (*US*) remolque *m* para caballerías.
horsewhip [hôrs'hwip] *vt* azotar.
horsewoman [hôrs'wōōmən] *n* jineta, caballista.
horsey [hôr'sē] *a* (*col: person*) aficionado a los caballos.
horticulture [hôr'təkulchûr] *n* horticultura.
hose [hōz] *n* (*also: Brit:* ~**pipe**) manguera.
hose down *vt* regar con manguera.
hosiery [hō'zhûrē] *n* calcetería.
hospice [hás'pis] *n* hospicio.
hospitable [hâspit'əbəl] *a* hospitalario.
hospital [hâs'pitəl] *n* hospital *m.*
hospitality [hâspətal'itē] *n* hospitalidad *f.*
hospitalize [hás'pitəlīz] *vt* hospitalizar.
host [hōst] *n* anfitrión *m*; (*TV, RADIO*) presentador(a) *m/f*; (*of inn etc*) mesonero; (*REL*) hostia; (*large number*): **a** ~ **of** multitud de.
hostage [hás'tij] *n* rehén *m.*
hostel [hás'təl] *n* hostal *m*; (*for students, nurses etc*) residencia; (*also:* **youth** ~) albergue *m* juvenil; (*for homeless people*) hospicio.
hosteling [hás'təling] *n*: **to go (youth)** ~ viajar de alberguista.
hostess [hōs'tis] *n* anfitriona; (*Brit:* **air** ~) azafata; (*in night-club*) señorita de compañía.
hostile [hás'təl] *a* hostil.
hostility [hâstil'ətē] *n* hostilidad *f.*
hot [hât] *a* caliente; (*weather*) caluroso, de calor; (*as opposed to only warm*) muy caliente; (*spicy*) picante; (*fig*) ardiente, acalorado; **to be** ~ (*person*) tener calor; (*object*) estar caliente; (*weather*) hacer calor.
hot up *vi* (*Brit col: situation*) ponerse difícil *or* apurado; (: *party*) animarse ♦ *vt* (*col: pace*) apretar; (: *engine*) aumentar la potencia de.
hot air *n* (*col*) palabras *fpl* huecas.
hot-air balloon [hátâr' bələōōn'] *n* (*AVIAT*) globo de aire caliente.
hotbed [hât'bed] *n* (*fig*) semillero.
hot-blooded [hât'blud'id] *a* impetuoso.
hotchpotch [hâch'pâch] *n* (*Brit*) = **hodgepodge.**
hot dog *n* perro caliente.
hotel [hōtel'] *n* hotel *m.*
hotelier [ōtelyā'] *n* hotelero.
hotel industry *n* industria hotelera.
hotel room *n* habitación *f.*
hotfoot [hât'fōōt] *ad* a toda prisa.
hotheaded [hât'hedid] *a* exaltado.
hothouse [hât'hous] *n* invernadero.
hot line [hât lin] *n* (*POL*) teléfono rojo, línea directa.

hotly [hât'lē] *ad* con pasión, apasionadamente.
hotplate [hât'plāt] *n* (*on stove*) hornillo.
hotpot [hât'pât] *n* (*Brit CULIN*) estofado.
hot seat *n* primera fila.
hot spot *n* (*trouble spot*) punto caliente; (*night club etc*) lugar *m* popular.
hot spring *n* terma, fuente *f* de aguas termales.
hot-tempered [hât'tem'pûrd] *a* de mal genio *or* carácter.
hot-water bottle [hâtwôt'ûr bâtəl] *n* bolsa de agua caliente.
hound [hound] *vt* acosar ♦ *n* perro de caza.
hour [ou'ûr] *n* hora; **at 30 miles an** ~ a 30 millas por hora; **lunch** ~ la hora del almuerzo *or* de comer; **to pay sb by the** ~ pagar a uno por hora.
hourly [ouûr'lē] *a* (de) cada hora; (*rate*) por hora ♦ *ad* cada hora.
house *n* [hous] (*pl* ~**s** [houz'iz]) (*also firm*) casa; (*POL*) cámara; (*THEATER*) sala ♦ *vt* [houz] (*person*) alojar; **at/to my** ~ en/a mi casa; **on the** ~ (*fig*) la casa invita.
house arrest *n* arresto domiciliario.
houseboat [hous'bōt] *n* casa flotante.
housebound [hous'bound] *a* confinado en casa.
housebreaking [hous'brāking] *n* allanamiento de morada.
house-broken [hous'brōkən] *a* (*US: animal*) domesticado.
housecoat [hous'kōt] *n* bata.
household [hous'hōld] *n* familia.
householder [hous'hōldûr] *n* propietario/a; (*head of house*) cabeza de familia, jefe *m* de familia.
house hunting *n*: **to go** ~ ir buscando casa.
housekeeper [hous'kēpûr] *n* ama de llaves.
housekeeping [hous'kēping] *n* (*work*) trabajos *mpl* domésticos; (*COMPUT*) gestión *f* interna; (*also:* ~ **money**) dinero para gastos domésticos.
houseman [hous'mən] *n* (*Brit MED*) médico recién titulado que vive en el hospital.
house plant *n* planta de interior.
house-proud [hous'proud] *a* preocupado por el embellecimiento de la casa.
house-to-house [houstəhous'] *a* (*collection*) de casa en casa; (*search*) casa por casa.
house-trained [hous'trānd] *a* (*Brit*) = **house-broken.**
house-warming [hous'wôrming] *n* (*also:* ~ **party**) fiesta de estreno de una casa.
housewife [hous'wīf] *n* ama de casa.
housework [hous'wûrk] *n* faenas *fpl* (de la casa).
housing [hou'zing] *n* (*act*) alojamiento; (*houses*) viviendas *fpl* ♦ *cpd* (*problem, shortage*) de (la) vivienda.
housing association *n* asociación *f* de la

vivienda.

housing conditions *npl* condiciones *fpl* de habitabilidad.

housing development, (*Brit*) **housing estate** *n* urbanización *f.*

hovel [huv'əl] *n* casucha.

hover [huv'ûr] *vi* flotar (en el aire); (*helicopter*) cernerse; **to ~ on the brink of disaster** estar en el borde mismo del desastre.

hovercraft [huv'ûrkraft] *n* aerodeslizador *m.*

hoverport [huv'ûrpôrt] *n* puerto de aerodeslizadores.

how [hou] *ad* cómo; **~ are you?** ¿cómo está usted?, ¿cómo estás?; **~ do you do?** ¿cómo está usted?, ¿qué tal estás?; **~ far is it to ...?** ¿qué distancia hay de aquí a ...?; **~ long have you been here?** ¿cuánto tiempo hace que estás aquí?; **~ lovely!** ¡qué bonito!; **~ many/much?** ¿cuántos/cuánto?; **~ old are you?** ¿cuántos años tienes?; **~ is school?** ¿qué tal la escuela?; **~ about a drink?** ¿te gustaría algo de beber?, ¿qué te parece una copa?

however [houev'ûr] *ad* de cualquier manera; (+ *adjective*) por muy ... que; (*in questions*) cómo ♦ *conj* sin embargo, no obstante.

howitzer [hou'itsûr] *n* (*MIL*) obús *m.*

howl [houl] *n* aullido ♦ *vi* aullar.

howler [hou'lûr] *n* plancha, falta garrafal.

HP *n abbr* = **hire purchase.**

hp *abbr* = **horsepower.**

HQ *n abbr* = **headquarters.**

HR *n abbr* (*US*) = *House of Representatives.*

HRH *abbr* (= *His (or Her) Royal Highness*) S.A.R.

hr(s) *abbr* (= *hour(s)*) hr.

HS *abbr* (*US*) = **high school.**

HST *abbr* (*US*: = *Hawaiian Standard Time*) hora de Hawai.

hub [hub] *n* (*of wheel*) centro.

hubbub [hub'ub] *n* barahúnda, barullo.

hubcap [hub'kap] *n* tapacubos *m inv.*

HUD *n abbr* (*US*: = *Department of Housing and Urban Development*) ministerio de la vivienda y urbanismo.

huddle [hud'əl] *vi*: **to ~ together** amontonarse.

hue [hyōō] *n* color *m*, matiz *m*; **~ and cry** *n* alarma.

huff [huf] *n*: **in a ~** enojado.

hug [hug] *vt* abrazar ♦ *n* abrazo.

huge [hyōōj] *a* enorme.

hulk [hulk] *n* (*ship*) barco viejo; (*person, building etc*) mole *f.*

hulking [hul'king] *a* pesado.

hull [hul] *n* (*of ship*) casco.

hullabaloo [huləbəlōō'] *n* (*col: noise*) algarabía, jaleo.

hullo [həlō'] *excl* (*Brit*) = **hello.**

hum [hum] *vt* tararear, canturrear ♦ *vi* tararear, canturrear; (*insect*) zumbar ♦ *n* (*also ELEC*) zumbido; (*of traffic, machines*)

zumbido, ronroneo; (*of voices etc*) murmullo.

human [hyōō'mən] *a* humano ♦ *n* (*also*: **~ being**) ser *m* humano.

humane [hyōōmān'] *a* humano, humanitario.

humanism [hyōō'mənizəm] *n* humanismo.

humanitarian [hyōōmanitär'ēən] *a* humanitario.

humanity [hyōōman'itē] *n* humanidad *f.*

humanly [hyōō'mənlē] *ad* humanamente.

humanoid [hyōō'mənoid] *a, n* humanoide *m/f.*

human relations *npl* relaciones *fpl* humanas.

humble [hum'bəl] *a* humilde ♦ *vt* humillar.

humbly [hum'blē] *ad* humildemente.

humbug [hum'bug] *n* tonterías *fpl*; (*Brit: sweet*) caramelo de menta.

humdrum [hum'drum] *a* (*boring*) monótono, aburrido; (*routine*) rutinario.

humid [hyōō'mid] *a* húmedo.

humidifier [hyōōmid'əfīûr] *n* humedecedor *m.*

humidity [hyōōmid'ətē] *n* humedad *f.*

humiliate [hyōōmil'ēāt] *vt* humillar.

humiliation [hyōōmilēā'shən] *n* humillación *f.*

humility [hyōōmil'ətē] *n* humildad *f.*

humor [hyōō'mûr] (*US*) *n* humorismo, sentido del humor; (*mood*) humor *m* ♦ *vt* (*person*) complacer; **sense of ~** sentido del humor; **to be in a good/bad ~** estar de buen/mal humor.

humorist [hyōō'mûrist] *n* humorista *m/f.*

humorless [hyōō'mûrlis] *a* arisco.

humorous [hyōō'mûrəs] *a* gracioso, divertido.

humour [hyōō'mûr] *etc* (*Brit*) = **humor** *etc.*

hump [hump] *n* (*in ground*) montículo; (*camel's*) giba.

humus [hyōō'məs] *n* (*BIO*) humus *m.*

hunch [hunch] *n* (*premonition*) presentimiento; **I have a ~ that** tengo una corazonada *or* un presentimiento de que.

hunchback [hunch'bak] *n* joroba *m/f.*

hunched [huncht] *a* jorobado.

hundred [hun'drid] *num* ciento; (*before n*) cien; **about a ~ people** unas cien personas, alrededor de cien personas; **~s of** centenares de; **~s of people** centenares de personas; **I'm a ~ percent sure** estoy completamente seguro.

hundredweight [hun'dridwāt] *n* (*US*) = *45.3 kg; 100 lb*; (*Brit*) = *50.8 kg; 112 lb.*

hung [hung] *pt, pp of* **hang.**

Hungarian [hunggär'ēən] *a, n* húngaro/a *m/f* ♦ *n* (*LING*) húngaro.

Hungary [hung'gûrē] *n* Hungría.

hunger [hung'gûr] *n* hambre *f* ♦ *vi*: **to ~ for** (*fig*) tener hambre de, anhelar.

hunger strike *n* huelga de hambre.

hungrily [hung'grilē] *ad* ávidamente, con ganas.

hungry [hung'grē] *a* hambriento; **to be ~** tener hambre; **~ for** (*fig*) sediento de.

hunk [hungk] *n* (*of bread etc*) trozo, pedazo.

hunt [hunt] *vt* (*seek*) buscar; (*SPORT*) cazar ♦ *vi* cazar ♦ *n* caza, cacería.
  hunt down *vt* acorralar, seguir la pista a.

hunter [hun'tûr] *n* cazador(a) *m/f*; (*horse*) caballo de caza.

hunting [hun'ting] *n* caza.

hurdle [hûr'dəl] *n* (*SPORT*) valla; (*fig*) obstáculo.

hurl [hûrl] *vt* lanzar, arrojar.

hurrah [hərá'], **hurray** [hərā'] *n* ¡viva!, ¡vítor!

hurricane [hûr'əkān] *n* huracán *m*.

hurried [hûr'ēd] *a* (*fast*) apresurado; (*rushed*) hecho de prisa.

hurriedly [hûr'ēdlē] *ad* con prisa, apresuradamente.

hurry [hûr'ē] *n* prisa ♦ *vb* (*also:* **~ up**) *vi* apresurarse, darse prisa ♦ *vt* (*person*) dar prisa a; (*work*) apresurar, hacer de prisa; **to be in a ~** tener prisa; **to ~ back/home** darse prisa para volver/volver a casa.
  hurry along *vi* pasar de prisa.
  hurry away, **hurry off** *vi* irse corriendo.
  hurry on *vi*: **to ~ on to say** apresurarse a decir.
  hurry up *vi* darse prisa.

hurt [hûrt] *vb* (*pt, pp* **hurt**) *vt* hacer daño a; (*business, interests etc*) perjudicar ♦ *vi* doler ♦ *a* lastimado; **I ~ my arm** me lastimé el brazo; **where does it ~?** ¿dónde te duele?

hurtful [hûrt'fəl] *a* (*remark etc*) dañoso.

hurtle [hûr'təl] *vi*: **to ~ past** pasar como un rayo.

husband [huz'bənd] *n* marido.

hush [hush] *n* silencio ♦ *vt* hacer callar; (*cover up*) encubrir; **~!** ¡chitón!, ¡cállate!
  hush up *vt* (*fact*) encubrir, callar.

hushed [husht] *a* (*voice*) bajo.

hush-hush [hush'hush] *a* (*col*) muy secreto.

husk [husk] *n* (*of wheat*) cáscara.

husky [hus'kē] *a* ronco; (*burly*) fornido ♦ *n* perro esquimal.

hustings [hus'tingz] *npl* (*Brit POL*) mítin *msg* preelectoral.

hustle [hus'əl] *vt* (*push*) empujar; (*hurry*) dar prisa a; (*US: col: girl*) enrollarse con ♦ *n* bullicio, actividad *f* febril; **~ and bustle** *n* vaivén *m*.

hut [hut] *n* cabaña; (*shed*) cobertizo.

hutch [huch] *n* conejera.

hyacinth [hī'əsinth] *n* jacinto.

hybrid [hī'brid] *a, n* híbrido.

hydrant [hī'drənt] *n* (*also:* **fire ~**) boca de incendios.

hydraulic [hīdrô'lik] *a* hidráulico.

hydraulics [hīdrô'liks] *n* hidráulica.

hydrochloric [hīdrəklôr'ik] *a*: **~ acid** ácido clorhídrico.

hydroelectric [hīdrōilek'trik] *a* hidroeléctrico.

hydrofoil [hī'drəfoil] *n* aerodeslizador *m*.

hydrogen [hī'drəjən] *n* hidrógeno.

hydrogen bomb *n* bomba de hidrógeno.

hydrophobia [hīdrəfō'bēə] *n* hidrofobia.

hydroplane [hī'drəplān] *n* hidroplano, hidroavión *m*.

hyena [hīē'nə] *n* hiena.

hygiene [hī'jēn] *n* higiene *f*.

hygienic [hījēen'ik] *a* higiénico.

hymn [him] *n* himno.

hype [hīp] *n* (*col*) bombardeo publicitario, superchería.

hyperactive [hīpûrak'tiv] *a* hiperactivo.

hypermarket [hī'pûrmârkit] *n* hipermercado.

hypertension [hīpûrten'chən] *n* hipertensión *f*.

hyphen [hī'fən] *n* guión *m*.

hypnosis [hipnō'sis] *n* hipnosis *f*.

hypnotic [hipnát'ik] *a* hipnótico.

hypnotism [hip'nətizəm] *n* hipnotismo.

hypnotist [hip'nətist] *n* hipnotista *m/f*.

hypnotize [hip'nətīz] *vt* hipnotizar.

hypoallergenic [hīpōalûrjen'ik] *a* hipoalérgeno.

hypochondriac [hīpəkân'drēak] *n* hipocondríaco/a.

hypocrisy [hipák'rəsē] *n* hipocresía.

hypocrite [hip'əkrit] *n* hipócrita *m/f*.

hypocritical [hipəkrit'ikəl] *a* hipócrita.

hypodermic [hīpədûr'mik] *a* hipodérmico ♦ *n* (*syringe*) aguja hipodérmica.

hypothermia [hīpōthûr'mēə] *n* hipotermia.

hypothesis, *pl* **hypotheses** [hīpáth'əsis, -sēz] *n* hipótesis *f inv*.

hypothetical [hīpəthet'ikəl] *a* hipotético.

hysterectomy [histərek'təmē] *n* histerectomía.

hysteria [histē'rēə] *n* histeria.

hysterical [histär'ikəl] *a* histérico.

hysterics [histär'iks] *npl* histeria *sg*, histerismo *sg*; **to have ~** ponerse histérico.

Hz *abbr* (= *Hertz*) Hz.

I, i [ī] *n* (*letter*) I, i *f*; **I for Item** I de Inés, I de Israel.

I [ī] *pron* yo ♦ *abbr* = **island; isle;** (*US*) = **interstate (highway).**

IA *abbr* (*US MAIL*) = *Iowa.*

IAEA *n abbr* = **International Atomic Energy**

Agency.
IBA *n abbr* (*Brit*: = *Independent Broadcasting Authority*) *entidad que controla los medios privados de televisión y radio.*
Iberian [ībēr'ēən] *a* ibero, ibérico.
Iberian Peninsula *n*: **the ~** la Península Ibérica.
IBEW *n abbr* (*US*: = *International Brotherhood of Electrical Workers*) *sindicato internacional de electricistas.*
ib(id). *abbr* (= *ibidem: from the same source*) ibídem.
i/c *abbr* (*Brit*) = *in charge.*
ICBM *n abbr* = **intercontinental ballistic missile.**
ICC *n abbr* (= *International Chamber of Commerce*) CCI *f*; (*US*) = *Interstate Commerce Commission.*
ice [īs] *n* hielo ♦ *vt* (*cake*) alcorzar ♦ *vi* (*also*: **~ over, ~ up**) helarse; **to keep sth on ~** (*fig*: *plan, project*) tener algo en reserva.
ice age *n* período glaciar.
ice ax *n* piqueta (de alpinista).
iceberg [īs'bûrg] *n* iceberg *m*; **the tip of the ~** (*also fig*) lo de menos.
icebox [īs'bāks] *n* (*US*) nevera, refrigeradora (*LAm*); (*Brit*) congelador *m*.
icebreaker [īs'brākûr] *n* rompehielos *m inv.*
ice bucket *n* cubo para el hielo.
ice-cold [īs'kōld'] *a* helado.
ice cream *n* helado.
ice-cream soda [īs'krēm sō'də] *n* soda mezclada con helado.
ice cube *n* cubito de hielo.
iced [īst] *a* (*drink*) con hielo; (*cake*) escarchado.
ice hockey *n* hockey *m* sobre hielo.
Iceland [īs'lənd] *n* Islandia.
Icelander [īs'landûr] *n* islandés/esa *m/f.*
Icelandic [īslan'dik] *a* islandés/esa ♦ *n* (*LING*) islandés *m.*
ice lolly [īs lāl'ē] *n* (*Brit*) polo helado.
ice pick *n* piolet *m.*
ice rink *n* pista de hielo.
ice-skate [īs'skāt] *n* patín *m* de hielo ♦ *vi* patinar sobre hielo.
ice-skating [īs'skāting] *n* patinaje *m* sobre hielo.
icicle [ī'sikəl] *n* carámbano.
icing [ī'sing] *n* (*CULIN*) alcorza; (*AVIAT etc*) formación *f* de hielo.
icing sugar *n* (*Brit*) azúcar *m* glas(eado).
ICJ *n abbr* = **International Court of Justice.**
icon [ī'kân] *n* ícono; (*COMPUT*) símbolo gráfico.
ICR *n abbr* (*US*) = *Institute for Cancer Research.*
ICU *n abbr* (= *intensive care unit*) UVI *f.*
icy [ī'sē] *a* (*road*) helado; (*fig*) glacial.
ID *abbr* (*US MAIL*) = *Idaho.*
I'd [īd] = **I would; I had.**
Ida. *abbr* (*US*) = *Idaho.*

ID card *n* (= *identity card*) DNI *m.*
idea [īdē'ə] *n* idea; **good ~!** ¡buena idea!; **to have an ~ that ...** tener la impresión de que ...; **I haven't the faintest ~** no tengo ni (la más remota) idea.
ideal [īdē'əl] *n* ideal *m* ♦ *a* ideal.
idealism [īdē'əlizəm] *n* idealismo.
idealist [īdē'əlist] *n* idealista *m/f.*
ideally [īdē'əlē] *ad* perfectamente; **~, the book should have ...** idealmente, el libro debería tener ....
identical [īden'tikəl] *a* idéntico.
identification [īdentəfəkā'shən] *n* identificación *f*; **means of ~** documentos *mpl* personales.
identification papers *npl* (*US*) documentos *mpl* (de identidad), documentación *fsg.*
identify [īden'təfī] *vt* identificar ♦ *vi*: **to ~ with** identificarse con.
Identikit [īden'təkit] ® *n* (*Brit*): **~ (picture)** retrato-robot *m.*
identity [īden'titē] *n* identidad *f.*
identity card *n* (*Brit*) carnet *m* de identidad.
identity papers *npl* documentos *mpl* (de identidad), documentación *fsg.*
identity parade *n* (*Brit*) identificación *f* de acusados.
ideological [īdēəláj'ikəl] *a* ideológico.
ideology [īdēál'əjē] *n* ideología.
idiocy [id'ēəsē] *n* idiotez *f*; (*stupid act*) estupidez *f.*
idiom [id'ēəm] *n* modismo; (*style of speaking*) lenguaje *m.*
idiomatic [īdēəmat'ik] *a* idiomático.
idiosyncrasy [idēəsing'krəsē] *n* idiosincrasia.
idiot [id'ēət] *n* (*gen*) idiota *m/f*; (*fool*) tonto/a.
idiotic [īdēât'ik] *a* idiota; tonto.
idle [ī'dəl] *a* (*lazy*) holgazán/ana; (*unemployed*) parado, desocupado; (*talk*) frívolo ♦ *vi* (*machine*) funcionar or marchar en vacío; **~ capacity** (*COMM*) capacidad *f* sin utilizar; **~ money** (*COMM*) capital *m* improductivo; **~ time** (*COMM*) tiempo de paro.
idle away *vt*: **to ~ away one's time** malgastar or desperdiciar el tiempo.
idleness [ī'dəlnis] *n* holgazanería; paro, desocupación *f.*
idler [īd'lûr] *n* holgazán/ana *m/f*, vago/a.
idol [ī'dəl] *n* ídolo.
idolize [ī'dəlīz] *vt* idolatrar.
idyllic [īdil'ik] *a* idílico.
i.e. *abbr* (= *id est: that is*) esto es.
if [if] *conj so* ♦ *n*: **there are a lot of ~s and buts** hay muchas dudas sin resolver; **(even) ~** aunque, si bien; **I'd be pleased ~ you could do it** yo estaría contento si pudieras hacerlo; **~ necessary** si es necesario; **~ only** si solamente; **as ~** como si.
igloo [ig'lōō] *n* iglú *m.*

ignite [ignīt'] *vt* (*set fire to*) encender ♦ *vi* encenderse.

ignition [ignish'ən] *n* (*AUT*) encendido; **to switch on/off the ~** arrancar/apagar el motor.

ignition key *n* (*AUT*) llave *f* de contacto.

ignoble [ignō'bəl] *a* innoble, vil.

ignominious [ignəmin'ēəs] *a* ignominioso, vergonzoso.

ignoramus [ignərā'məs] *n* ignorante *m/f*, inculto/a.

ignorance [ig'nûrəns] *n* ignorancia; **to keep sb in ~ of sth** ocultarle algo a uno.

ignorant [ig'nûrənt] *a* ignorante; **to be ~ of** (*subject*) desconocer; (*events*) ignorar.

ignore [ignôr'] *vt* (*person*) no hacer caso de; (*fact*) pasar por alto.

ikon [ī'kân] *n* = **icon**.

IL *abbr* (*US MAIL*) = *Illinois*.

ILA *n abbr* (*US:* = *International Longshoremen's Association*) *sindicato internacional de trabajadores portuarios*.

ILGWU *n abbr* (*US:* = *International Ladies' Garment Workers Union*) *sindicato de empleados del ramo de las prendas de vestir femeninas*.

Ill. *abbr* (*US*) = *Illinois*.

ill [il] *a* enfermo, malo ♦ *n* mal *m*; (*fig*) infortunio ♦ *ad* mal; **to take** *or* **be taken ~** caer *or* ponerse enfermo; **to feel ~ (with)** encontrarse mal (de); **to speak/think ~ of sb** hablar/pensar mal de uno; *see also* **ills.**

I'll [īl] = **I will, I shall.**

ill-advised [il'advīzd'] *a* poco recomendable; **he was ~ to go** se equivocaba al ir.

ill-at-ease [il'ətēz'] *a* incómodo.

ill-considered [il'kənsid'ûrd] *a* (*plan*) poco pensado.

ill-disposed [il'dispōzd'] *a*: **to be ~ towards sb/sth** estar maldispuesto hacia uno/algo.

illegal [ilē'gəl] *a* ilegal.

illegible [ilej'əbəl] *a* ilegible.

illegitimate [ilijit'əmit] *a* ilegítimo.

ill-fated [il'fā'tid] *a* malogrado.

ill-favored, (*Brit*) **ill-favoured** [il'fā'vûrd] *a* mal parecido.

ill feeling *n* (*Brit*) rencor *m*.

ill-gotten [il'gât'ən] *a* (*gains etc*) mal adquirido.

illicit [ilis'it] *a* ilícito.

ill-informed [il'infôrmd'] *a* (*judgement*) erróneo; (*person*) mal informado.

illiterate [ilit'ûrit] *a* analfabeto.

ill-mannered [il'man'ûrd] *a* mal educado.

illness [il'nis] *n* enfermedad *f*.

illogical [ilâj'ikəl] *a* ilógico.

ills [ilz] *npl* males *mpl*.

ill-suited [il'sōō'tid] *a* (*couple*) incompatible; **he is ~ to the job** no es la persona indicada para el trabajo.

ill-timed [il'tīmd] *a* inoportuno.

ill-treat [il'trēt] *vt* maltratar.

ill-treatment [il'trēt'mənt] *n* malos tratos *mpl*.

illuminate [ilōō'mənāt] *vt* (*room, street*) iluminar, alumbrar; (*subject*) aclarar; **~d sign** letrero luminoso.

illuminating [ilōō'mənāting] *a* revelador(a).

illumination [ilōōmənā'shən] *n* alumbrado; **~s** *npl* luminarias *fpl*, luces *fpl*.

illusion [ilōō'zhən] *n* ilusión *f*; **to be under the ~ that...** estar convencido de que ....

illusive [ilōō'siv], **illusory** [ilōō'sərē] *a* ilusorio.

illustrate [il'əstrāt] *vt* ilustrar.

illustration [iləstrā'shən] *n* (*example*) ejemplo, ilustración *f*; (*in book*) lámina.

illustrator [il'əstrātûr] *n* ilustrador(a) *m/f*.

illustrious [ilus'trēəs] *a* ilustre.

ill will *n* rencor *m*.

ILO *n abbr* (= *International Labour Organization*) OIT *f*.

ILWU *n abbr* (*US:* = *International Longshoremen's and Warehousemen's Union*) *sindicato internacional de trabajadores portuarios y almacenistas*.

I'm [īm] = **I am.**

image [im'ij] *n* imagen *f*.

imagery [im'ijrē] *n* imágenes *fpl*.

imaginable [imaj'ənəbəl] *a* imaginable.

imaginary [imaj'ənärē] *a* imaginario.

imagination [imajənā'shən] *n* imaginación *f*; (*inventiveness*) inventiva; (*illusion*) fantasía.

imaginative [imaj'ənətiv] *a* imaginativo.

imagine [imaj'in] *vt* imaginarse; (*suppose*) suponer.

imbalance [imbal'əns] *n* desequilibrio.

imbecile [im'bəsil] *n* imbécil *m/f*.

imbue [imbyōō'] *vt*: **to ~ sth with** imbuir algo de.

IMF *n abbr* = **International Monetary Fund.**

imitate [im'ətāt] *vt* imitar.

imitation [imətā'shən] *n* imitación *f*; (*copy*) copia; (*pej*) remedo.

imitator [im'ətātûr] *n* imitador(a) *m/f*.

immaculate [imak'yəlit] *a* perfectamente limpio; (*REL*) inmaculado.

immaterial [imətē'rēəl] *a* incorpóreo; **it is ~ whether...** no importa si... .

immature [imətōōr'] *a* (*person*) inmaduro; (*of one's youth*) joven.

immaturity [imətōō'ritē] *n* inmadurez *f*.

immeasurable [imezh'ûrəbəl] *a* inconmensurable.

immediacy [imē'dēəsē] *n* urgencia, proximidad *f*.

immediate [imē'dēit] *a* inmediato; (*pressing*) urgente, apremiante; **in the ~ future** en el futuro próximo.

immediately [imē'dēitlē] *ad* (*at once*) en seguida; **~ next to** muy junto a.

immense [imens'] *a* inmenso, enorme.

immensely [imens'lē] *ad* enormemente.

immensity [imen'sitē] *n* (*of size, differ-*

ence) inmensidad *f; (of problem)* enormidad *f.*

immerse [imûrs'] *vt (submerge)* sumergir; **to be ~d in** *(fig)* estar absorto en.

immersion heater [imûr'zhən hē'tûr] *n* calentador *m* de inmersión.

immigrant [im'əgrənt] *n* inmigrante *m/f.*

immigrate [im'əgrāt] *vi* inmigrar.

immigration [iməgrā'shən] *n* inmigración *f.*

immigration authorities *npl* servicio *sg* de inmigración.

immigration laws *npl* leyes *fpl* inmigratorias.

imminent [im'ənənt] *a* inminente.

immobile [imō'bəl] *a* inmóvil.

immobilize [imō'bəlīz] *vt* inmovilizar.

immoderate [imâd'ûrit] *a (person)* desmesurado; *(opinion, reaction, demand)* excesivo.

immodest [imâd'ist] *a (indecent)* desvergonzado, impúdico; *(boasting)* jactancioso.

immoral [imôr'əl] *a* inmoral.

immorality [imэral'itē] *n* inmoralidad *f.*

immortal [imôr'təl] *a* inmortal.

immortality [imôrtal'itē] *n* inmortalidad *f.*

immortalize [imôr'təlīz] *vt* inmortalizar.

immovable [imōō'vəbəl] *a (object)* imposible de mover; *(person)* inconmovible.

immune [imyōōn'] *a:* ~ **(to)** inmune (contra).

immunity [imyōō'nitē] *n (MED, of diplomat)* inmunidad *f; (COMM)* exención *f.*

immunization [imyōōnəzā'shən] *n* inmunización *f.*

immunize [im'yənīz] *vt* inmunizar.

imp [imp] *n (small devil, also fig: child)* diablillo.

impact [im'pakt] *n (gen)* impacto.

impair [impär'] *vt* perjudicar.

impale [impāl'] *vt (with sword)* atravesar.

impart [impárt'] *vt* comunicar; *(make known)* participar; *(bestow)* otorgar.

impartial [impár'shəl] *a* imparcial.

impartiality [impárshēal'itē] *n* imparcialidad *f.*

impassable [impas'əbəl] *a (barrier)* infranqueable; *(river, road)* intransitable.

impasse [im'pas] *n* callejón *m* sin salida; **to reach an** ~ alcanzar un punto muerto.

impassioned [impash'ənd] *a* apasionado, exaltado.

impassive [impas'iv] *a* impasible.

impatience [impā'shəns] *n* impaciencia.

impatient [impā'shənt] *a* impaciente; **to get** *or* **grow** ~ impacientarse.

impatiently [impā'shəntlē] *ad* con impaciencia.

impeachment [impēch'mənt] *n* denuncia, acusación *f.*

impeccable [impek'əbəl] *a* impecable.

impecunious [impəkyōō'nēəs] *a* sin dinero.

impede [impēd'] *vt* estorbar, dificultar.

impediment [imped'əmənt] *n* obstáculo, estorbo; *(also:* **speech** ~) defecto (del habla).

impel [impel'] *vt (force):* **to** ~ **sb (to do sth)** obligar a uno (a hacer algo).

impending [impen'ding] *a (near)* próximo.

impenetrable [impen'itrəbəl] *a (jungle, fortress)* impenetrable; *(unfathomable)* insondable.

imperative [impär'ətiv] *a (tone)* imperioso; *(necessary)* imprescindible ♦ *n (LING)* imperativo.

imperceptible [impûrsep'təbəl] *a* imperceptible, insensible.

imperfect [impûr'fikt] *a* imperfecto; *(goods etc)* defectuoso.

imperfection [impûrfek'shən] *n (blemish)* desperfecto; *(fault, flaw)* defecto.

imperial [impēr'ēəl] *a* imperial.

imperialism [impēr'ēəlizəm] *n* imperialismo.

imperil [impär'əl] *vt* poner en peligro.

imperious [impēr'ēəs] *a* señorial, apremiante.

impersonal [impûr'sənəl] *a* impersonal.

impersonate [impûr'sənāt] *vt* hacerse pasar por.

impersonation [impûrsənā'shən] *n* imitación *f.*

impersonator [impûr'sənātûr] *n (THEATER etc)* imitador(a) *m/f.*

impertinence [impûr'tənəns] *n* descaro.

impertinent [impûr'tənənt] *a* impertinente, insolente.

imperturbable [impûrtûr'bəbəl] *a* imperturbable, impasible.

impervious [impûr'vēəs] *a* impermeable; *(fig):* ~ **to** insensible a.

impetuous [impech'ōōəs] *a* impetuoso.

impetus [im'pitəs] *n* ímpetu *m; (fig)* impulso.

impinge [impinj'] : **to** ~ **on** *vt fus (affect)* afectar a.

impish [imp'ish] *a* travieso.

implacable [implak'əbəl] *a* implacable.

implant [implant'] *vt (MED)* injertar, implantar; *(fig: idea, principle)* inculcar.

implausible [implô'zəbəl] *a* implausible.

implement *n* [im'pləmənt] instrumento, herramienta ♦ *vt* [im'pləmənt] hacer efectivo; *(carry out)* realizar.

implicate [im'plikāt] *vt (compromise)* comprometer; *(involve)* enredar; **to** ~ **sb in sth** comprometer a uno en algo.

implication [implikā'shən] *n* consecuencia; **by** ~ indirectamente.

implicit [implis'it] *a (gen)* implícito; *(complete)* absoluto.

implicitly [implis'itlē] *ad* implícitamente.

implore [implôr'] *vt (person)* suplicar.

imploring [implôr'ing] *a* de súplica.

imply [implī'] *vt (involve)* implicar; *(mean)* significar; *(hint)* dar a entender.

impolite [impəlīt'] *a* mal educado.
impolitic [impâl'itik] *a* poco político.
imponderable [impân'dûrəbəl] *a* imponderable.
import *vt* [impôrt'] importar ♦ [im'pôrt] *n* (*COMM*) importación *f*; (*meaning*) significado, sentido ♦ *cpd* (*duty, license etc*) de importación.
importance [impôr'təns] *n* importancia; **to be of great/little** ~ tener mucha/poca importancia.
important [impôr'tənt] *a* importante; **it's not** ~ no importa, no tiene importancia; **it is** ~ **that** es importante que.
importantly [impôr'təntlē] *ad* (*pej*) dándose importancia; **but, more** ~ ... pero, lo más importante es ....
import duty [im'pôrt dōō'tē] *n* derechos *mpl* de importación.
imported [impôr'tid] *a* importado.
importer [impôr'tûr] *n* importador(a) *m/f*.
import license *n* licencia de importación.
impose [impōz'] *vt* imponer ♦ *vi*: **to** ~ **on sb** abusar de uno.
imposing [impō'zing] *a* imponente, impresionante.
imposition [impəzish'ən] *n* (*of tax etc*) imposición *f*; **to be an** ~ (*on person*) molestar.
impossibility [impâsəbil'itē] *n* imposibilidad *f*.
impossible [impâs'əbəl] *a* imposible; (*person*) insoportable; **it is** ~ **for me to leave now** me es imposible salir ahora.
impossibly [impâs'əblē] *ad* imposiblemente.
impostor [impâs'tûr] *n* impostor(a) *m/f*.
impotence [im'pətəns] *n* impotencia.
impotent [im'pətənt] *a* impotente.
impound [impound'] *vt* embargar.
impoverished [impâv'ûrisht] *a* necesitado; (*land*) agotado.
impracticable [imprak'tikəbəl] *a* no factible, irrealizable.
impractical [imprak'tikəl] *a* (*person*) poco práctico.
imprecise [imprisīs'] *a* impreciso.
impregnable [impreg'nəbəl] *a* invulnerable; (*castle*) inexpugnable.
impregnate [impreg'nāt] *vt* (*gen*) impregnar; (*soak*) empapar; (*fertilize*) fecundar.
impresario [imprəsâ'rēō] *n* empresario/a.
impress [impres'] *vt* impresionar; (*mark*) estampar ♦ *vi* hacer buena impresión; **to** ~ **sth on sb** convencer a uno de la importancia de algo.
impression [impresh'ən] *n* impresión *f*; (*footprint etc*) huella; (*print run*) edición *f*; **to be under the** ~ **that** tener la impresión de que; **to make a good/bad** ~ **on sb** causar buena/mala impresión a uno.
impressionable [impresh'ənəbəl] *a* impresionable.

impressionist [impresh'ənist] *n* impresionista *m/f*.
impressive [impres'iv] *a* impresionante.
imprint [im'print] *n* (*PUBLISHING*) pie *m* de imprenta; (*fig*) sello.
imprison [impriz'ən] *vt* encarcelar.
imprisonment [impriz'ənmənt] *n* encarcelamiento; (*term of* ~) cárcel *f*; **life** ~ cadena perpetua.
improbable [impráb'əbəl] *a* improbable, inverosímil.
impromptu [imprâmp'tōō] *a* improvisado ♦ *ad* de improviso.
improper [imprâp'ûr] *a* (*incorrect*) impropio; (*unseemly*) indecoroso; (*indecent*) indecente.
impropriety [imprəprī'ətē] *n* falta de decoro; (*indecency*) indecencia; (*of language*) impropiedad *f*.
improve [improōv'] *vt* mejorar; (*foreign language*) perfeccionar ♦ *vi* mejorarse; (*pupils*) hacer progresos.
improve (up)on *vt fus* (*offer*) mejorar.
improvement [improōv'mənt] *n* mejoramiento; perfección *f*; progreso; **to make** ~**s to** mejorar.
improvise [im'prəvīz] *vt, vi* improvisar.
imprudence [improōd'əns] *n* imprudencia.
imprudent [improōd'ənt] *a* imprudente.
impudent [im'pyədənt] *a* descarado, insolente.
impugn [impyoōn'] *vt* impugnar.
impulse [im'puls] *n* impulso; **to act on** ~ obrar sin reflexión.
impulse buying [im'puls bī'ing] *n* compra impulsiva.
impulsive [impul'siv] *a* irreflexivo.
impunity [impyoō'nitē] *n*: **with** ~ impunemente.
impure [impyoōr'] *a* (*adulterated*) adulterado; (*morally*) impuro.
impurity [impyoōr'itē] *n* impureza.
IN *abbr* (*US MAIL*) = Indiana.
in [in] *prep* en; (*within*) dentro de; (*with time: during, within*): ~ **2 days** en 2 días; (: *after*): ~ **2 weeks** dentro de 2 semanas; (*with town, country*): **it's** ~ **France** está en Francia ♦ *ad* dentro, adentro; (*fashionable*) de moda; **is he** ~**?** ¿está en casa?; ~ **the United States** en los Estados Unidos; ~ **1986** en 1986; ~ **May** en mayo; ~ **spring/autumn** en primavera/otoño; ~ **the morning** por la mañana; ~ **the country** en el campo; ~ **the distance** a lo lejos; ~ **town** en la ciudad; ~ **the sun** al sol, bajo el sol; ~ **the rain** bajo la lluvia; ~ **French** en francés; ~ **writing** por escrito; ~ **person** en persona; ~ **here/there** aquí/allí (dentro); **1** ~ **10** uno sobre 10, uno de cada 10; ~ **hundreds** por centenares; **the best pupil** ~ **the class** el mejor alumno de la clase; **written** ~ **pencil** escrito con lápiz; **to pay** ~ **dollars** pagar en dólares; **a**

rise ~ **prices** un aumento de precios; **once ~ a hundred years** una vez al siglo; ~ **saying this** al decir esto; **their party is ~** su partido ha llegado al poder; **to be ~ publishing** dedicarse a la publicación de libros; ~ **that** ya que; ~ **all** en total; **to ask sb ~** invitar a uno a entrar; **to run/limp ~** entrar corriendo/cojeando; **the ~s and outs** los pormenores.

in., ins *abbr* = **inch(es).**

inability [inəbil'ətē] *n* incapacidad *f*; ~ **to pay** incapacidad de pagar.

inaccessible [inakses'əbəl] *a* inaccesible.

inaccuracy [inak'yūrəsē] *n* inexactitud *f*.

inaccurate [inak'yûrit] *a* inexacto, incorrecto.

inaction [inak'shən] *n* inacción *f*.

inactive [inak'tiv] *a* inactivo.

inactivity [inaktiv'itē] *n* inactividad *f*.

inadequacy [inad'əkwəsē] *n* insuficiencia; incapacidad *f*.

inadequate [inad'əkwit] *a* (*insufficient*) insuficiente; (*unsuitable*) inadecuado; (*person*) incapaz.

inadmissible [inədmis'əbəl] *a* improcedente, inadmisible.

inadvertent [inədvûr'tənt] *a* descuidado, involuntario.

inadvertently [inədvûr'təntlē] *ad* por descuido.

inadvisable [inədvī'zəbəl] *a* poco aconsejable.

inane [inān'] *a* necio, fatuo.

inanimate [inan'əmit] *a* inanimado.

inapplicable [inap'likəbəl] *a* inaplicable.

inappropriate [inəprō'prēit] *a* inadecuado.

inapt [inapt'] *a* impropio.

inaptitude [inap'tətōōd] *n* incapacidad *f*.

inarticulate [inârtik'yəlit] *a* (*person*) incapaz de expresarse; (*speech*) mal pronunciado.

inartistic [inârtis'tik] *a* antiestético.

inasmuch as [inəzmuch' az] *ad* puesto que, ya que.

inattention [inətən'chən] *n* desatención *f*.

inattentive [inətən'tiv] *a* distraído.

inaudible [inô'dəbəl] *a* inaudible.

inaugural [inô'gyûrəl] *a* (*speech*) de apertura.

inaugurate [inô'gyərāt] *vt* inaugurar.

inauguration [inôgyərā'shən] *n* ceremonia de apertura.

inauspicious [inôspish'əs] *a* poco propicio, inoportuno.

in-between [in'bitwēn'] *a* intermedio.

inborn [in'bôrn] *a* (*feeling*) innato.

inbred [in'bred] *a* innato; (*family*) consanguíneo.

inbreeding [in'brēding] *n* endogamia.

Inc. *abbr* = **incorporated.**

Inca [ing'kə] *a* (*also*: ~**n**) incaico, de los incas ♦ *n* inca *m/f*.

incalculable [inkal'kyələbəl] *a* incalculable.

incapability [inkāpəbil'ətē] *n* incapacidad *f*.

incapable [inkā'pəbəl] *a*: ~ **(of doing sth)** incapaz (de hacer algo).

incapacitate [inkəpas'ətāt] *vt*: **to ~ sb** incapacitar a uno.

incapacitated [inkəpas'ətātid] *a* incapacitado.

incapacity [inkəpas'itē] *n* (*inability*) incapacidad *f*.

incarcerate [inkâr'sûrit] *vt* encarcelar.

incarnate *a* [inkâr'nit] en persona ♦ *vt* [inkâr'nāt] encarnar.

incarnation [inkârnā'shən] *n* encarnación *f*.

incendiary [insen'dēārē] *a* incendiario ♦ *n* (*bomb*) bomba incendiaria.

incense *n* [in'sens] incienso ♦ *vt* [insens'] (*anger*) indignar, encolerizar.

incentive [insen'tiv] *n* incentivo, estímulo.

incentive bonus *n* incentivo de bonificación extra.

incentive scheme *n* plan *m* de incentivos.

inception [insep'shən] *n* comienzo, principio.

incessant [inses'ənt] *a* incesante, continuo.

incessantly [inses'əntlē] *ad* constantemente.

incest [in'sest] *n* incesto.

inch [inch] *n* pulgada; **to be within an ~ of** estar a dos dedos de; **he didn't give an ~** no dio concesión alguna; **a few ~es** unas pulgadas.

inch forward *vi* avanzar palmo a palmo.

incidence [in'sidəns] *n* (*of crime, disease*) incidencia.

incident [in'sidənt] *n* incidente *m*; (*in book*) episodio.

incidental [insiden'təl] *a* circunstancial, accesorio; (*unplanned*) fortuito; ~ **to** relacionado con; ~ **expenses** gastos *mpl* imprevistos.

incidentally [insiden'təlē] *ad* (*by the way*) a propósito.

incidental music *n* música de fondo.

incinerate [insin'ərāt] *vt* incinerar, quemar.

incinerator [insin'ərātûr] *n* incinerador *m*.

incipient [insip'ēənt] *a* incipiente.

incision [insizh'ən] *n* incisión *f*.

incisive [insī'siv] *a* (*mind*) penetrante; (*remark etc*) incisivo.

incisor [insī'zûr] *n* incisivo.

incite [insīt'] *vt* provocar.

incl. *abbr* = **including; inclusive (of).**

inclement [inklem'ənt] *a* inclemente.

inclination [inklənā'shən] *n* (*tendency*) tendencia, inclinación *f*.

incline *n* [in'klīn] pendiente *f*, cuesta ♦ *vb* [inklīn'] *vt* (*slope*) inclinar; (*head*) poner de lado ♦ *vi* inclinarse; **to be ~d to** (*tend*) ser propenso a; (*be willing*) estar dispuesto a.

include [inklōōd'] *vt* incluir, comprender; (*in letter*) adjuntar; **the tip is/is not ~d** la propina está/no está incluida.

including [inklōōd'ing] *prep* incluso, inclusive; ~ **tip** propina incluida.

inclusion |inklōō'zhən| *n* inclusión *f*.
inclusive |inklōō'siv| *a* inclusivo ♦ *ad* inclusive; ~ **of tax** incluidos los impuestos; **$50,** ~ **of all surcharges** 50 dólares, incluidos todos los sobreimpuestos.
incognito |inkágnē'itō| *ad* de incógnito.
incoherent |inkōhē'rənt| *a* incoherente.
income |in'kum| *n* (*personal*) ingresos *mpl*; (*from property etc*) renta; (*profit*) rédito; **gross/net** ~ ingresos *mpl* brutos/netos; ~ **and expenditure account** cuenta de gastos e ingresos.
income bracket *n* categoría económica.
income support *n* (*Brit*) *subsidio estatal para personas con un nivel de ingresos muy bajo.*
income tax *n* impuesto sobre la renta.
income tax inspector *n* inspector(a) *m/f* fiscal.
income tax return *n* registro fiscal.
incoming |in'kuming| *a* (*passengers*) de llegada; (*government, tenant*) entrante; ~ **flight** vuelo entrante.
incommunicado |inkəmyōōnəká'dō| *a*: **to hold sb** ~ mantener incomunicado a uno.
incomparable |inkâm'pûrəbəl| *a* incomparable, sin par.
incompatible |inkəmpat'əbəl| *a* incompatible.
incompetence |inkâm'pitəns| *n* incompetencia.
incompetent |inkâm'pitənt| *a* incompetente.
incomplete |inkəmplēt'| *a* incompleto; (*unfinished*) sin terminar.
incomprehensible |inkâmprihcn'səbəl| *a* incomprensible.
inconceivable |inkənsē'vəbəl| *a* inconcebible.
inconclusive |inkənklōō'siv| *a* sin resultado (definitivo); (*argument*) poco convincente.
incongruity |inkânggrōō'itē| *n* incongruencia.
incongruous |inkâng'grōōəs| *a* discordante.
inconsequential |inkânsəkwen'chəl| *a* intranscendente.
inconsiderable |inkənsid'ûrəbəl| *a* insignificante.
inconsiderate |inkənsid'ûrit| *a* desconsiderado; **how** ~ **of him!** ¡qué falta de consideración (de su parte)!
inconsistency |inkənsis'tənsē| *n* inconsecuencia; (*of actions etc*) incompatibilidad *f*, falta de lógica; (*of work*) carácter *m* desigual, inconsistencia; (*of statement etc*) contradicción *f*, anomalía.
inconsistent |inkənsis'tənt| *a* inconsecuente; ~ **with** que no concuerda con.
inconsolable |inkənsō'ləbəl| *a* inconsolable.
inconspicuous |inkənspik'yōōəs| *a* (*discreet*) discreto; (*person*) que llama poco la atención.
inconstancy |inkân'stənsē| *n* inconstancia.

inconstant |inkân'stənt| *a* inconstante.
incontinence |inkân'tənəns| *n* incontinencia.
incontinent |inkân'tənənt| *a* incontinente.
incontrovertible |inkântrəvûr'təbəl| *a* incontrovertible.
inconvenience |inkənvēn'yəns| *n* (*gen*) inconvenientes *mpl*; (*trouble*) molestia, incomodidad *f* ♦ *vt* incomodar; **to put sb to great** ~ causar mucha molestia a uno; **don't** ~ **yourself** no te molestes.
inconvenient |inkənvēn'yənt| *a* incómodo, poco práctico; (*time, place*) inoportuno; **that time is very** ~ **for me** esa hora no me es muy inconveniente.
incorporate |inkôr'pûrāt| *vt* incorporar; (*contain*) comprender; (*add*) agregar.
incorporated |inkôr'pərātid| *a*: ~ **company** (*US: abbr* **Inc.**) ≈ Sociedad *f* Anónima (S.A.).
incorrect |inkərekt'| *a* incorrecto.
incorrigible |inkôr'ijəbəl| *a* incorregible.
incorruptible |inkərup'təbəl| *a* incorruptible.
increase *n* |in'krēs| aumento ♦ *vb* |inkrēs'| *vi* aumentarse; (*grow*) crecer; (*price*) subir ♦ *vt* aumentar; **an** ~ **of 5%** un aumento de 5%; **to be on the** ~ estar *or* ir en aumento.
increasing |inkrēs'ing| *a* (*number*) creciente, que va en aumento.
increasingly |inkrēs'inglē| *ad* de más en más, cada vez más.
incredible |inkred'əbəl| *a* increíble.
incredibly |inkred'əblē| *ad* increíblemente.
incredulity |inkridōō'litē| *n* incredulidad *f*.
incredulous |inkrej'ələs| *a* incrédulo.
increment |in'krəmənt| *n* aumento, incremento.
incriminate |inkrim'ənāt| *vt* incriminar.
incriminating |inkrim'ənāting| *a* incriminador(a).
incrust |inkrust'| *vt* = **encrust.**
incubate |in'kyəbāt| *vt* (*eggs*) incubar, empollar ♦ *vi* (*egg, disease*) incubar.
incubation |inkyəbā'shən| *n* incubación *f*.
incubation period *n* período de incubación.
incubator |in'kyəbātûr| *n* incubadora.
inculcate |in'kulkāt| *vt*: **to** ~ **sth in sb** inculcar algo en uno.
incumbent |inkum'bənt| *n* ocupante *m/f* ♦ *a*: **it is** ~ **on him to...** le incumbe... .
incur |inkûr'| *vt* (*expenses*) incurrir en; (*loss*) sufrir.
incurable |inkyōōr'əbəl| *a* incurable.
incursion |inkûr'zhən| *n* incursión *f*.
Ind. *abbr* (*US*) = *Indiana.*
indebted |indet'id| *a*: **to be** ~ **to sb** estar agradecido a uno.
indecency |indē'sənsē| *n* indecencia.
indecent |indē'sənt| *a* indecente.
indecent assault *n* (*Brit*) atentado contra

el pudor.
indecent exposure n exhibicionismo.
indecipherable [indisī'fûrəbəl] a indescifrable.
indecision [indisizh'ən] n indecisión f.
indecisive [indisī'siv] a indeciso; (discussion) no resuelto, inconcluyente.
indeed [indēd'] ad efectivamente, en realidad; **yes ~!** ¡claro que sí!
indefatigable [indifat'əgəbəl] a incansable, infatigable.
indefensible [indifen'səbəl] a (conduct) injustificable.
indefinable [indifī'nəbəl] a indefinible.
indefinite [indef'ənit] a indefinido; (uncertain) incierto.
indefinitely [indef'ənitlē] ad (wait) indefinidamente.
indelible [indel'əbəl] a imborrable.
indelicate [indel'əkit] a (tactless) indiscreto, inoportuno; (not polite) indelicado.
indemnify [indem'nəfī] vt indemnizar, resarcir.
indemnity [indem'nitē] n (insurance) indemnidad f; (compensation) indemnización f.
indent [indent'] vt (text) sangrar.
indentation [indentā'shən] n mella; (TYP) sangría.
independence [indipen'dəns] n independencia.
independent [indipen'dənt] a independiente; **to become ~** independizarse.
indescribable [indiskrī'bəbəl] a indescriptible.
indestructible [indistruk'təbəl] a indestructible.
indeterminate [inditûr'mənit] a indeterminado.
index [in'deks] n (pl: **~es**: in book) índice m; (: in library etc) catálogo; (pl: **indices** [in'disēz]: ratio, sign) exponente m.
index card n ficha.
indexed [in'dekst] a (US) indexado.
index finger n índice m.
index-linked [in'dekslingkt'] a (Brit) = **indexed**.
India [in'dēə] n la India.
Indian [in'dēən] a, n indio/a m/f; (American ~) indio/a m/f de América, amerindio/a m/f.
Indian Ocean n: **the ~** el Océano Índico, el Mar de las Indias.
Indian summer n (fig) veranillo de San Martín.
indicate [in'dikāt] vt indicar ♦ vi (Brit AUT): **to ~ left/right** indicar a la izquierda/a la derecha.
indication [indikā'shən] n indicio, señal f.
indicative [indik'ətiv] a: **to be ~ of sth** indicar algo ♦ n (LING) indicativo.
indicator [in'dikātûr] n (gen) indicador m.
indices [in'disēz] npl of **index**.
indict [indīt'] vt acusar.

indictable [indīt'əbəl] a: **~ offense** delito procesable.
indictment [indīt'mənt] n acusación f.
indifference [indif'ûrəns] n indiferencia.
indifferent [indif'ûrənt] a indiferente; (poor) regular.
indigenous [indij'ənəs] a indígena.
indigestible [indijes'təbəl] a indigesto.
indigestion [indijes'chən] n indigestión f.
indignant [indig'nənt] a: **to be ~ about sth** indignarse por algo.
indignation [indignā'shən] n indignación f.
indignity [indig'nitē] n indignidad f.
indigo [in'dəgō] a (color) de color añil ♦ n añil m.
indirect [indirekt'] a indirecto.
indirectly [indirekt'lē] ad indirectamente.
indiscernible [indisûr'nəbəl] a imperceptible.
indiscreet [indiskrēt'] a indiscreto, imprudente.
indiscretion [indiskresh'ən] n indiscreción f, imprudencia.
indiscriminate [indiskrim'ənit] a indiscriminado.
indispensable [indispen'səbəl] a indispensable, imprescindible.
indisposed [indispōzd'] a (unwell) indispuesto.
indisposition [indispəzish'ən] n indisposición f.
indisputable [indispyōō'təbəl] a incontestable.
indistinct [indistingkt'] a indistinto.
indistinguishable [indisting'gwishəbəl] a indistinguible.
individual [indəvij'ōōəl] n individuo ♦ a individual; (personal) personal; (for/of one only) particular.
individualist [indəvij'ōōəlist] n individualista m/f.
individuality [indəvijōōal'itē] n individualidad f.
individually [indəvij'ōōəlē] ad individualmente; particularmente.
indivisible [indəviz'əbəl] a indivisible.
Indo-China [in'dōchī'nə] n Indochina.
indoctrinate [indāk'trənāt] vt adoctrinar.
indoctrination [indāktrənā'shən] n adoctrinamiento.
indolence [in'dələns] n indolencia.
indolent [in'dələnt] a indolente, perezoso.
Indonesia [indənē'zhə] n Indonesia.
Indonesian [indənē'zhən] a, n indonesio/a m/f.
indoor [in'dôr] a (swimming pool) cubierto; (plant) de interior; (sport) bajo cubierta.
indoors [indôrz'] ad dentro; (at home) en casa.
indubitable [indōō'bitəbəl] a indudable.
indubitably [indōō'bitəblē] ad indudablemente.
induce [indōōs'] vt inducir, persuadir;

(*bring about*) producir; **to ~ sb to do sth** persuadir a uno a que haga algo.

inducement [indōōs'mənt] *n* (*incentive*) incentivo, aliciente *m*.

induct [indukt'] *vt* iniciar; (*in job, rank, position*) instalar.

induction [induk'shən] *n* (*MED: of birth*) inducción *f*.

induction course *n* (*Brit*) curso de inducción.

indulge [indulj'] *vt* (*whim*) satisfacer; (*person*) complacer; (*child*) mimar ♦ *vi*: **to ~ in** darse el gusto de.

indulgence [indul'jəns] *n* vicio.

indulgent [indul'jənt] *a* indulgente.

industrial [indus'trēəl] *a* industrial.

industrial action *n* huelga.

industrial estate *n* (*Brit*) = **industrial park**.

industrial goods *npl* bienes *mpl* de producción.

industrialist [indus'trēəlist] *n* industrial *m/f*.

industrialize [indus'trēəlīz] *vt* industrializar.

industrial park *n* (*US*) polígono *or* zona (*LAm*) industrial.

industrial relations *npl* relaciones *fpl* empresariales.

industrial tribunal *n* magistratura del trabajo, tribunal *m* laboral.

industrial unrest *n* agitación *f* obrera.

industrious [indus'trēəs] *a* (*gen*) trabajador(a); (*student*) aplicado.

industry [in'dəstrē] *n* industria; (*diligence*) aplicación *f*.

inebriated [inēb'rēātid] *a* borracho.

inedible [ined'əbəl] *a* incomestible, incomible; (*plant etc*) no comestible.

ineffective [inifek'tiv], **ineffectual** [inefek'chōōəl] *a* ineficaz, inútil.

inefficiency [inifish'ənsē] *n* ineficacia.

inefficient [inifish'ənt] *a* ineficaz, ineficiente.

inelegant [inel'əgənt] *a* poco elegante.

ineligible [inel'ijəbəl] *a* inelegible.

inept [inept'] *a* incompetente, incapaz.

ineptitude [inep'tətōōd] *n* incapacidad *f*, ineptitud *f*.

inequality [inikwâl'itē] *n* desigualdad *f*.

inequitable [inek'witəbəl] *a* injusto.

ineradicable [inirad'ikəbəl] *a* inextirpable.

inert [inûrt'] *a* inerte, inactivo; (*immobile*) inmóvil.

inertia [inûr'shə] *n* inercia; (*laziness*) pereza.

inertia-reel seat-belt [inûr'shərēl sēt'belt] *n* cinturón *m* de seguridad de inercia.

inescapable [inəskā'pəbəl] *a* ineludible, inevitable.

inessential [inisen'chəl] *a* no esencial.

inestimable [ines'təməbəl] *a* inestimable.

inevitability [inevitəbil'ətē] *n* inevitabilidad *f*.

inevitable [inev'itəbəl] *a* inevitable; (*nec-essary*) forzoso.

inevitably [inev'itəblē] *ad* inevitablemente; **as ~ happens** ... como siempre pasa ....

inexact [in'igzakt'] *a* inexacto.

inexcusable [inikskyōō'zəbəl] *a* imperdonable.

inexhaustible [inigzôs'təbəl] *a* inagotable.

inexorable [inek'sûrəbəl] *a* inexorable, implacable.

inexpensive [inikspen'siv] *a* económico.

inexperience [inikspēr'ēəns] *n* falta de experiencia.

inexperienced [inikspēr'ēənst] *a* inexperto; **to be ~ in sth** no tener experiencia en algo.

inexplicable [ineks'plikəbəl] *a* inexplicable.

inexpressible [inikspres'əbəl] *a* inexpresable.

inextricable [ineks'trikəbəl] *a* inseparable.

inextricably [ineks'trikəblē] *ad* indisolublemente.

infallibility [infaləbil'ətē] *n* infalibilidad *f*.

infallible [infal'əbəl] *a* infalible.

infamous [in'fəməs] *a* infame.

infamy [in'fəmē] *n* infamia.

infancy [in'fənsē] *n* infancia.

infant [in'fənt] *n* niño/a.

infantile [in'fəntīl] *a* infantil; (*pej*) aniñado.

infant mortality *n* mortandad *f* infantil.

infantry [in'fəntrē] *n* infantería.

infantryman [in'fəntrēmən] *n* soldado de infantería.

infant school *n* (*Brit*) escuela de párvulos.

infatuated [infach'ōōātid] *a*: **~ with** (*in love*) loco por; **to become ~ (with sb)** enamoriscarse, encapricharse (con uno).

infatuation [infachōōā'shən] *n* enamoramiento.

infect [infekt'] *vt* (*wound*) infectar; (*person*) contagiar; (*fig: pej*) corromper; **~ed with** (*illness*) contagiado de; **to become ~ed** (*wound*) infectarse.

infection [infek'shən] *n* infección *f*; (*fig*) contagio.

infectious [infek'shəs] *a* contagioso; (*also fig*) infeccioso.

infer [infûr'] *vt* deducir, inferir; **to ~ (from)** inferir (de), deducir (de).

inference [in'fûrəns] *n* deducción *f*, inferencia.

inferior [infē'rēûr] *a*, *n* inferior *m/f*; **to feel ~** sentirse inferior.

inferiority [infērēôr'itē] *n* inferioridad *f*.

inferiority complex *n* complejo de inferioridad.

infernal [infûr'nəl] *a* infernal.

inferno [infûr'nō] *n* infierno; (*fig*) hoguera.

infertile [infûr'təl] *a* estéril; (*person*) infecundo.

infertility [infûrtil'ətē] *n* esterilidad *f*; infecundidad *f*.

infest [infest'] *vt* infestar.

infested [infes'tid] *a*: ~ **(with)** plagado (de).

infidel [in'fidəl] *n* infiel *m/f*.

infidelity [infidel'itē] *n* infidelidad *f*.

infighting [in'fīting] *n* (*fig*) lucha(s) *f(pl)* interna(s).

infiltrate [infil'trāt] *vt* (*troops etc*) infiltrarse en ♦ *vi* infiltrarse.

infinite [in'fənit] *a* infinito; **an ~ amount of money/time** un sinfín de dinero/tiempo.

infinitely [in'fənitlē] *ad* infinitamente.

infinitesimal [infinites'əməl] *a* infinitésimo.

infinitive [infin'ətiv] *n* infinitivo.

infinity [infin'ətē] *n* (*also* MATH) infinito; (*an* ~) infinidad *f*.

infirm [infûrm'] *a* enfermo, débil.

infirmary [infûr'mûrē] *n* hospital *m*.

infirmity [infûr'mitē] *n* debilidad *f*; (*illness*) enfermedad *f*, achaque *m*.

inflame [inflām'] inflamar.

inflamed [inflāmd'] *a*: **to become ~** inflamarse.

inflammable [inflam'əbəl] *a* inflamable; (*situation etc*) explosivo.

inflammation [infləmā'shən] *n* inflamación *f*.

inflammatory [inflam'ətôrē] *a* (*speech*) incendiario.

inflatable [inflā'təbəl] *a* inflable.

inflate [inflāt'] *vt* (*tire, balloon*) inflar; (*fig*) hinchar.

inflated [inflā'tid] *a* (*tire etc*) inflado; (*price, self-esteem etc*) exagerado.

inflation [inflā'shən] *n* (ECON) inflación *f*.

inflationary [inflā'shənärē] *a* inflacionario.

inflationary spiral *n* espiral *f* inflacionista.

inflection [inflek'shən] *n* inflexión *f*.

inflexible [inflek'səbəl] *a* inflexible.

inflict [inflikt'] *vt*: **to ~ on** infligir en; (*tax etc*) imponer a.

infliction [inflik'shən] *n* imposición *f*.

in-flight [in'flīt] *a* durante el vuelo.

inflow [in'flō] *n* afluencia.

influence [in'flooəns] *n* influencia ♦ *vt* influir en, influenciar; (*persuade*) sugestionar; **under the ~ of alcohol** en estado de embriaguez.

influential [inflooen'chəl] *a* influyente.

influenza [inflooen'zə] *n* gripe *f*.

influx [in'fluks] *n* afluencia.

inform [infôrm'] *vt*: **to ~ sb of sth** informar a uno sobre *or* de algo; (*warn*) avisar a uno de algo; (*communicate*) comunicar algo a uno ♦ *vi* : **to ~ on sb** delatar a uno.

informal [infôr'məl] *a* (*manner, tone*) desenfadado; (*dress, interview, occasion*) informal.

informality [infôrmal'itē] *n* falta de ceremonia; (*intimacy*) intimidad *f*; (*familiarity*) familiaridad *f*; (*ease*) afabilidad *f*.

informally [infôr'məlē] *ad* sin ceremonia;

(*invite*) informalmente.

informant [infôr'mənt] *n* informante *m/f*.

information [infûrmā'shən] *n* información *f*; (*news*) noticias *fpl*; (*knowledge*) conocimientos *mpl*; (LAW) delación *f*; **a piece of ~** un dato; **for your ~** para que se informe usted, para su información.

information bureau *n* oficina de informaciones.

information desk *n* mesa de informes.

information processing *n* procesamiento de datos.

information retrieval *n* recuperación *f* de la información.

information science *n* gestión *f* de la información.

information technology *n* informática.

informative [infôr'mətiv] *a* informativo.

informed [infôrmd'] *a* (*observer*) informado, al corriente; **an ~ guess** una opinión bien fundamentada.

informer [infôr'mûr] *n* delator(a) *m/f*; (*also*: **police ~**) soplón/ona *m/f*.

infra dig [in'frə dig] *a abbr* (*col*: = *infra dignitatem*) denigrante.

infra-red [in'frəred'] *a* infrarrojo.

infrastructure [in'frəstruk'chûr] *n* (*of system etc*, ECON) infraestructura.

infrequent [infrē'kwint] *a* infrecuente.

infringe [infrinj'] *vt* infringir, violar ♦ *vi*: **to ~ on** abusar de.

infringement [infrinj'mənt] *n* infracción *f*; (*of rights*) usurpación *f*.

infuriate [infyoor'ēāt] *vt*: **to become ~d** ponerse furioso.

infuriating [infyoor'ēāting] *a*: **I find it ~** me saca de quicio.

infuse [infyooz'] *vt* (*with courage, enthusiasm*): **to ~ sb with sth** infundir a uno con algo.

infusion [infyoo'zhən] *n* (*tea etc*) infusión *f*.

ingenious [injēn'yəs] *a* ingenioso.

ingenuity [injənoo'itē] *n* ingeniosidad *f*.

ingenuous [injen'yooəs] *a* ingenuo.

ingot [ing'gət] *n* lingote *m*, barra.

ingrained [ingrānd'] *a* arraigado.

ingratiate [ingrā'shēāt] *vt*: **to ~ o.s. with** congraciarse con.

ingratiating [ingrā'shēāting] *a* (*smile, speech*) insinuante; (*person*) zalamero, congraciador(a).

ingratitude [ingrat'ətood] *n* ingratitud *f*.

ingredient [ingrē'dēənt] *n* ingrediente *m*.

ingrowing [in'grōing] *a*: **~ (toe)nail** uña encarnada.

inhabit [inhab'it] *vt* vivir en; (*occupy*) ocupar.

inhabitable [inhab'itəbəl] *a* habitable.

inhabitant [inhab'ətənt] *n* habitante *m/f*.

inhale [inhāl'] *vt* inhalar ♦ *vi* (*in smoking*) tragar.

inherent [inhär'ent] *a*: **~ in** *or* **to** inherente a.

inherently [inhär'entlē] *ad* esencialmente.
inherit [inhär'it] *vt* heredar.
inheritance [inhär'itəns] *n* herencia; (*fig*) patrimonio.
inheritance tax *n* derechos *mpl* de sucesión.
inhibit [inhib'it] *vt* inhibir, impedir; **to ~ sb from doing sth** impedir a uno hacer algo.
inhibited [inhib'itid] *a* (*person*) cohibido.
inhibition [inibish'ən] *n* cohibición *f*.
inhospitable [inhåspit'əbəl] *a* (*person*) inhospitalario; (*place*) inhóspito.
inhuman [inhyoo'mən] *a* inhumano.
inhumane [inhyoomān'] *a* inhumano.
inimitable [inim'itəbəl] *a* inimitable.
iniquity [inik'witē] *n* iniquidad *f*; (*injustice*) injusticia.
initial [inish'əl] *a* inicial; (*first*) primero ♦ *n* inicial *f* ♦ *vt* firmar con las iniciales; **~s** *npl* iniciales *fpl*; (*abbreviation*) siglas *fpl*.
initialize [inish'əliz] *vt* (*COMPUT*) inicializar.
initially [inish'əlē] *ad* al principio.
initiate [inish'ēāt] *vt* (*start*) iniciar; **to ~ sb into a secret** iniciar a uno en un secreto; **to ~ proceedings against sb** (*LAW*) entablar una demanda contra uno.
initiation [inishēā'shən] *n* (*into secret etc*) iniciación *f*; (*beginning*) comienzo.
initiative [inish'ēətiv] *n* iniciativa; **to take the ~** tomar la iniciativa.
inject [injekt'] *vt* inyectar; (*money, enthusiasm*) aportar.
injection [injek'shən] *n* inyección *f*; **to have an ~** hacerse inyectar.
injudicious [injoodish'əs] *a* imprudente, indiscreto.
injunction [injungk'shən] *n* entredicho, interdicto.
injure [in'jûr] *vt* herir; (*hurt*) lastimar; (*fig: reputation etc*) perjudicar; (*feelings*) herir; **to ~ o.s** hacerse daño, lastimarse.
injured [in'jûrd] *a* (*also fig*) herido; **~ party** (*LAW*) parte *f* perjudicada.
injurious [injoor'ēəs] *a*: **~ (to)** perjudicial (a).
injury [in'jûrē] *n* herida, lesión *f*; (*wrong*) perjuicio, daño; **to escape without ~** salir ileso.
injury time *n* (*SPORT*) descuento.
injustice [injus'tis] *n* injusticia; **you do me an ~** usted es injusto conmigo.
ink [ingk] *n* tinta.
ink-jet printer [ingk'jet prin'tûr] *n* impresora de chorro de tinta.
inkling [ingk'ling] *n* sospecha; (*idea*) idea.
inkpad [ingk'pad] *n* almohadilla.
inlaid [in'lād] *a* (*wood*) taraceado; (*tiles*) entarimado.
inland [in'land] *a* interior; (*town*) del interior ♦ *ad* tierra adentro.
Inland Revenue *n* (*Brit*) Hacienda.
in-laws [in'lôz] *npl* suegros *mpl*.
inlet [in'let] *n* (*GEO*) ensenada, cala; (*TECH*)

admisión *f*, entrada.
inmate [in'māt] *n* (*in prison*) preso/a; presidiario/a; (*in asylum*) internado/a.
inmost [in'mōst] *a* más íntimo, más secreto.
inn [in] *n* posada, mesón *m*.
innards [in'ûrdz] *npl* (*col*) tripas *fpl*.
innate [ināt'] *a* innato.
inner [in'ûr] *a* interior, interno.
inner city *n* barrios deprimidos del centro de una ciudad.
innermost [in'ûrmōst] *a* más íntimo, más secreto.
inner tube *n* (*of tire*) cámara, llanta (*LAm*).
innings [in'ingz] *n* (*SPORT*) entrada, turno.
innocence [in'əsəns] *n* inocencia.
innocent [in'əsənt] *a* inocente.
innocuous [inâk'yōōəs] *a* inocuo.
innovation [inəvā'shən] *n* novedad *f*.
innuendo, ~es [inyōōen'dō] *n* indirecta.
Innuit [in'ōōwit] *n* esquimal *m/f* ♦ *a* esquimal.
innumerable [inōō'mûrəbəl] *a* innumerable.
inoculate [inâk'yəlāt] *vt*: **to ~ sb with sth/against sth** inocular or vacunar a uno con algo/contra algo.
inoculation [inâkyəlā'shən] *n* inoculación *f*.
inoffensive [inəfen'siv] *a* inofensivo.
inopportune [inâpûrtōōn'] *a* inoportuno.
inordinate [inôr'dənit] *a* excesivo, desmesurado.
inordinately [inôr'dənitlē] *ad* excesivamente, desmesuradamente.
inorganic [inôrgan'ik] *a* inorgánico.
inpatient [in'pāshənt] *n* paciente *m/f* interno/a.
input [in'pōōt] *n* (*ELEC*) entrada; (*COMPUT*) entrada de datos ♦ *vt* (*COMPUT*) introducir, entrar.
inquest [in'kwest] *n* (*coroner's*) encuesta judicial.
inquire [inkwiûr'] *vi* preguntar ♦ *vt*: **to ~ when/where/whether** preguntar cuándo/dónde/si; **to ~ about** (*person*) preguntar por; (*fact*) informarse de.
inquire into *vt fus*: **to ~ into sth** investigar or indagar algo.
inquiring [inkwiûr'ing] *a* (*mind*) penetrante; (*look*) interrogativo.
inquiry [inkwiûr'ē] *n* pregunta; (*LAW*) investigación *f*, pesquisa; (*commission*) comisión *f* investigadora; **to hold an ~ into sth** montar una investigación sobre algo.
inquiry desk *n* (*Brit*) mesa de informes.
inquiry office *n* (*Brit*) oficina de informaciones.
inquisition [inkwizish'ən] *n* inquisición *f*.
inquisitive [inkwiz'ətiv] *a* (*mind*) inquisitivo; (*person*) fisgón/ona.
inroad [in'rōd] *n* incursión *f*; (*fig*) invasión *f*; **to make ~s into** (*time*) ocupar parte de; (*savings, supplies*) agotar parte de.
insane [insān'] *a* loco; (*MED*) demente.
insanitary [insan'itärē] *a* insalubre.

insanity |insan'itē| *n* demencia, locura.
insatiable |insā'shəbəl| *a* insaciable.
inscribe |inskrīb'| *vt* inscribir; (*book etc*):
to ~ (to sb) dedicar (a uno).
inscription |inskrip'shən| *n* (*gen*) ins-
cripción *f*; (*in book*) dedicatoria.
inscrutable |inskrōō'təbəl| *a* inescrutable,
insondable.
inseam measurement |insēm' mēzh'-
ûrmənt| *n* (*US*) medida de pernera.
insect |in'sekt| *n* insecto.
insect bite *n* picadura.
insecticide |insek'tisīd| *n* insecticida *m*.
insect repellent *n* loción *f* contra los
insectos.
insecure |insikyōor'| *a* inseguro.
insecurity |insikyōor'itē| *n* inseguridad *f*.
insemination |insemənā'shən| *n*: **artificial
~** inseminación *f* artificial.
insensible |insen'səbəl| *a* inconsciente;
(*unconscious*) sin conocimiento.
insensitive |insen'sətiv| *a* insensible.
insensitivity |insensətiv'itē| *n* insensibilidad
f.
inseparable |insep'ûrəbəl| *a* inseparable;
they were ~ friends los unía una estrecha
amistad.
insert *vt* |insûrt'| (*into sth*) introducir;
(*COMPUT*) insertar ♦ *n* |in'sûrt| encarte *m*.
insertion |insûr'shən| *n* inserción *f*.
in-service |in'sûr'vis| *a* (*training, course*) en
el trabajo, a cargo de la empresa.
inshore |in'shôr| *a*: **~ fishing** pesca *f* coste-
ra ♦ *ad* (*fish*) a lo largo de la costa;
(*move*) hacia la orilla.
inside |in'sīd'| *n* interior *m*; (*lining*) forro;
(*of road: US, Europe etc*) lado derecho; (:
Brit) lado izquierdo ♦ *a* interior, interno;
(*information*) confidencial ♦ *ad* (*within*)
(por) dentro; (*with movement*) hacia dentro; (*fam: in prison*) en la cárcel ♦ *prep*
dentro de; (*of time*): ~ **10 minutes** en menos de 10 minutos; ~s *npl* (*col*) tripas *fpl*;
~ **out** *ad* (*turn*) al revés; (*know*) a fondo.
inside forward *n* (*SPORT*) interior *m*.
inside information *n* información *f*
confidencial.
inside lane *n* (*AUT: in US*, Europe) carril
m derecho; (: *in Britain*) carril *m*
izquierdo.
inside leg measurement *n* (*Brit*) = **in-
seam measurement.**
insider |insī'dûr| *n* enterado/a.
insider dealing *n* delito de iniciados.
inside story *n* historia íntima.
insidious |insid'ēəs| *a* insidioso.
insight |in'sīt| *n* perspicacia, percepción *f*;
to gain *or* **get an ~ into sth** formarse una
idea de algo.
insignia |insig'nēə| *npl* insignias *fpl.*
insignificant |insignif'ikənt| *a* insignificante.
insincere |insinsēr'| *a* poco sincero.
insincerity |insinsär'itē| *n* falta de sinceri-

dad, doblez *f.*
insinuate |insin'yōoāt| *vt* insinuar.
insinuation |insinyōoā'shən| *n* insinuación *f.*
insipid |insip'id| *a* soso, insulso.
insist |insist'| *vi* insistir; **to ~ on doing**
empeñarse en hacer; **to ~ that** insistir en
que; (*claim*) exigir que.
insistence |insis'təns| *n* insistencia;
(*stubbornness*) empeño.
insistent |insis'tənt| *a* insistente; empeñado.
insole |in'sōl| *n* plantilla.
insolence |in'sələns| *n* insolencia, descaro.
insolent |in'sələnt| *a* insolente, descarado.
insoluble |insâl'yəbəl| *a* insoluble.
insolvency |insâl'vənsē| *n* insolvencia.
insolvent |insâl'vənt| *a* insolvente.
insomnia |insâm'nēə| *n* insomnio.
insomniac |insâm'nēak| *n* insomne *m/f.*
inspect |inspekt'| *vt* inspeccionar, exami-
nar; (*troops*) pasar revista a.
inspection |inspek'shən| *n* inspección *f*, exa-
men *m*.
inspector |inspek'tûr| *n* inspector(a) *m/f*;
(*Brit: on buses, trains*) revisor(a) *m/f*.
inspiration |insporā'shən| *n* inspiración *f.*
inspire |inspīur'| *vt* inspirar; **to ~ sb (to do
sth)** inspirar a uno (a hacer algo).
inspired |inspīurd'| *a* (*writer, book etc*) ins-
pirado, genial, iluminado; **in an ~ moment**
en un momento de inspiración.
inspiring |inspīur'ing| *a* inspirador(a).
inst. *abbr* (*Brit COMM*: = *instant, of the
present month*) cte.
instability |instəbil'ətē| *n* inestabilidad *f.*
install |instôl'| *vt* instalar.
installation |instəlā'shən| *n* instalación *f.*
installment, (*Brit*) **instalment** |instôl'mənt|
n plazo; (*of story*) entrega; (*of TV serial
etc*) capítulo; **in ~s** (*pay, receive*) a plazos; **to pay in ~s** pagar a plazos *or* por
abonos.
installment plan *n* (*US*) compra a plazos.
instance |in'stəns| *n* ejemplo, caso; **for ~**
por ejemplo; **in the first ~** en primer lugar; **in that ~** en ese caso.
instant |in'stənt| *n* instante *m*, momento ♦ *a*
inmediato; (*coffee*) instantáneo.
instantaneous |instəntā'nēəs| *a* instantá-
neo.
instantly |in'stəntlē| *ad* en seguida.
instant replay *n* (*US TV*) repetición *f* de
jugada.
instead |insted'| *ad* en cambio; ~ **of** en lu-
gar de, en vez de.
instep |in'step| *n* empeine *m*.
instigate |in'stəgāt| *vt* (*rebellion, strike,
crime*) instigar; (*new ideas etc*) fomentar.
instigation |instəgā'shən| *n* instigación *f*; **at
sb's ~** a instigación de uno.
instill, (*Brit*) **instil** |instil'| *vt*: **to ~ into**
inculcar a.
instinct |in'stingkt| *n* instinto.
instinctive |instingk'tiv| *a* instintivo.

instinctively [instingk'tivlē] *ad* por instinto.
institute [in'stitōōt] *n* instituto; (*professional body*) colegio ♦ *vt* (*begin*) iniciar, empezar; (*proceedings*) entablar.
institution [institōō'shən] *n* institución *f*; (*beginning*) iniciación *f*; (*MED: home*) asilo; (*asylum*) manicomio; (*custom*) costumbre *f* arraigada.
institutional [institōō'shənəl] *a* institucional.
instruct [instrukt'] *vt*: **to ~ sb in sth** instruir a uno en *or* sobre algo; **to ~ sb to do sth** dar instrucciones a uno de hacer algo.
instruction [instruk'shən] *n* (*teaching*) instrucción *f*; **~s** *npl* órdenes *fpl*; **~s (for use)** modo *sg* de empleo.
instruction book *n* manual *m*.
instructive [instruk'tiv] *a* instructivo.
instructor [instruk'tûr] *n* instructor(a) *m/f*; (*US UNIV*) profesor(a) *m/f*.
instrument [in'strəmənt] *n* instrumento.
instrumental [instrəmen'təl] *a* (*MUS*) instrumental; **to be ~ in** ser (el) artífice de; **to be ~ in sth/in doing sth** ser responsable de algo/de hacer algo.
instrumentalist [instrəmen'təlist] *n* instrumentalista *m/f*.
instrument panel *n* tablero (de instrumentos).
insubordinate [insəbôr'dənit] *a* insubordinado.
insubordination [insəbôrdənā'shən] *n* insubordinación *f*.
insufferable [insuf'ûrəbəl] *a* insoportable.
insufficient [insəfish'ənt] *a* insuficiente.
insufficiently [insəfish'əntlē] *ad* insuficientemente.
insular [in'səlûr] *a* insular; (*outlook*) estrecho de miras.
insularity [insəlar'itē] *n* insularidad *f*.
insulate [in'səlāt] *vt* aislar.
insulating tape [in'səlāting tāp] *n* cinta aislante.
insulation [insəlā'shən] *n* aislamiento.
insulator [in'səlātûr] *n* aistante *m*.
insulin [in'səlin] *n* insulina.
insult *n* [in'sult] insulto; (*offence*) ofensa ♦ *vt* [insult'] insultar; ofender.
insulting [insul'ting] *a* insultante; ofensivo.
insuperable [insōō'pûrəbəl] *a* insuperable.
insurance [inshûr'əns] *n* seguro; **fire/life ~** seguro sobre la vida/contra incendios; **to take out ~ (against)** hacerse un seguro (contra).
insurance agent *n* agente *m/f* de seguros.
insurance broker *n* corredor(a) *m/f* or agente *m/f* de seguros.
insurance policy *n* póliza (de seguros).
insurance premium *n* prima de seguros.
insure [inshōōr'] *vt* asegurar; **to ~ sb** *or* **sb's life** asegurar la vida de uno; **to ~ (against)** asegurar (contra); **to be ~d for $5000** tener un seguro de 5000 dólares.

insured [inshōōrd'] *n*: **the ~** el/la asegurado/a.
insurer [inshōō'rûr] *n* asegurador(a).
insurgent [insûr'jənt] *a*, *n* insurgente *m/f*, insurrecto/a *m/f*.
insurmountable [insûrmoun'təbəl] *a* insuperable.
insurrection [insərek'shən] *n* insurrección *f*.
intact [intakt'] *a* íntegro; (*untouched*) intacto.
intake [in'tāk] *n* (*TECH*) entrada, toma; (: *pipe*) tubo de admisión; (*of food*) ingestión *f*; (*Brit SCOL*): **an ~ of 200 a year** 200 matriculados al año.
intangible [intan'jəbəl] *a* intangible.
integer [in'tijûr] *n* (*número*) entero.
integral [in'təgrəl] *a* (*whole*) íntegro; (*part*) integrante.
integrate [in'təgrāt] *vt* integrar ♦ *vi* integrarse.
integrated circuit [in'təgrātid sûr'kit] *n* (*COMPUT*) circuito integrado.
integration [intəgrā'shən] *n* integración *f*; **racial ~** integración de razas.
integrity [integ'ritē] *n* honradez *f*, rectitud *f*; (*COMPUT*) integridad *f*.
intellect [in'təlekt] *n* intelecto.
intellectual [intəlek'chōōəl] *a*, *n* intelectual *m/f*.
intelligence [intel'ijəns] *n* inteligencia.
intelligence quotient (IQ) *n* cociente *m* de inteligencia.
Intelligence Service *n* Servicio de Inteligencia.
intelligence test *n* prueba de inteligencia.
intelligent [intel'ijənt] *a* inteligente.
intelligently [intel'ijəntlē] *ad* inteligentemente.
intelligentsia [intel'əjənt'sēə] *n* intelectualidad *f*.
intelligible [intel'ijəbəl] *a* inteligible, comprensible.
intemperate [intem'pûrit] *a* inmoderado.
intend [intend'] *vt* (*gift etc*): **to ~ sth for** destinar algo a; **to ~ to do sth** tener intención de *or* pensar hacer algo.
intended [inten'did] *a* (*effect*) deseado.
intense [intens'] *a* intenso; (*person*) nervioso.
intensely [intens'lē] *ad* intensamente; (*very*) sumamente.
intensify [inten'səfī] *vt* intensificar; (*increase*) aumentar.
intensity [inten'sitē] *n* (*gen*) intensidad *f*.
intensive [inten'siv] *a* intensivo.
intensive care *n*: **to be in ~** estar bajo cuidados intensivos; **~ unit** *n* unidad *f* de vigilancia intensiva.
intensively [inten'sivlē] *ad* intensivamente.
intent [intent'] *n* propósito ♦ *a* (*absorbed*) absorto; (*attentive*) atento; **to all ~s and purposes** prácticamente; **to be ~ on doing sth** estar resuelto *or* decidido a ha-

cer algo.

intention [inten'chən] *n* intención *f*, propósito.

intentional [inten'chənəl] *a* deliberado.

intentionally [inten'chənəlē] *ad* a propósito.

intently [intent'lē] *ad* atentamente, fijamente.

inter [intûr'] *vt* enterrar.

inter- [in'tûr] *pref* inter-.

interact [intûrakt'] *vi* influirse mutuamente.

interaction [intûrak'shən] *n* interacción *f*, acción *f* recíproca.

interactive [intûrak'tiv] *a* (*also* COMPUT) interactivo.

intercede [intûrsēd'] *vi*: **to ~ (with)** interceder (con); **to ~ with sb/on behalf of sb** interceder con uno/en nombre de uno.

intercept [intûrsept'] *vt* interceptar; (*stop*) detener.

interception [intûrsep'shən] *n* interceptación *f*; detención *f*.

interchange *n* [in'tûrchānj] intercambio; (*on freeway*) intersección *f* ♦ *vt* [intûrchānj'] intercambiar.

interchangeable [intûrchān'jəbəl] *a* intercambiable.

intercity [in'tûrsitē] *a*: **~ (train)** (tren *m*) interurbano.

intercom [in'tûrkâm] *n* interfono.

interconnect [intûrkənekt'] *vi* (*rooms*) conectarse.

intercontinental [intûrkântənen'təl] *a* intercontinental.

intercourse [in'tûrkôrs] *n* (*sexual ~*) relaciones *fpl* sexuales, contacto sexual; (*social*) trato.

interdependence [intûrdipen'dəns] *n* interdependencia.

interdependent [intûrdipen'dənt] *a* interdependiente.

interest [in'trist] *n* (*also* COMM) interés *m* ♦ *vt* interesar; **compound/simple ~** interés compuesto/simple; **business ~s** negocios *mpl*; **American ~s in the Middle East** los intereses norteamericanos en el Medio Oriente.

interested [in'tristid] *a* interesado; **to be ~ in** interesarse por.

interest-free [in'tristfrē] *a* libre *or* franco de interés.

interesting [in'tristing] *a* interesante.

interest rate *n* tipo *or* tasa de interés.

interface [in'tûrfās] *n* (COMPUT) junción *f*, interface *m*.

interfere [intûrfēr'] *vi*: **to ~ in** (*quarrel, other people's business*) entrometerse en; **to ~ with** (*hinder*) estorbar; (*damage*) estropear; (*radio*) interferir con.

interference [intûrfēr'əns] *n* (*gen*) intromisión *f*; (RADIO, TV) interferencia.

interfering [intûrfēr'ing] *a* entrometido.

interim [in'tûrim] *a*: **~ dividend** dividendo parcial ♦ *n*: **in the ~** en el ínterin.

interior [intē'rēûr] *n* interior *m* ♦ *a* interior.

interior decorator, interior designer *n* interiorista *m/f*.

interjection [intûrjek'shən] *n* interyección *f*.

interlock [intûrlâk'] *vi* entrelazarse; (*wheels etc*) endentarse.

interloper [intûrlō'pûr] *n* intruso/a.

interlude [in'tûrlōōd] *n* intervalo; (*rest*) descanso; (THEATER) intermedio.

intermarriage [intûrmar'ij] *n* endogamia.

intermarry [intûrmar'ē] *vi* casarse (entre parientes).

intermediary [intûrmē'dēârē] *n* intermediario/a.

intermediate [intûrmē'dēit] *a* intermedio.

interminable [intûr'mənəbəl] *a* inacabable.

intermission [intûrmish'ən] *n* (THEATER) descanso.

intermittent [intûrmit'ənt] *a* intermitente.

intermittently [intûrmit'əntlē] *ad* intermitentemente.

intern *vt* [intûrn'] internar; (*enclose*) encerrar ♦ *n* [in'tûrn] (US) interno/a.

internal [intûr'nəl] *a* interno, interior; **~ injuries** heridas *fpl or* lesiones *fpl* internas.

internally [intûr'nəlē] *ad* interiormente; **"not to be taken ~"** "uso externo".

Internal Revenue Service (IRS) *n* (US) Hacienda.

international [intûrnash'ənəl] *a* internacional; **~ (game)** partido internacional; **~ (player)** jugador(a) *m/f* internacional.

International Atomic Energy Agency (IAEA) *n* Organismo Internacional de Energía Atómica.

International Chamber of Commerce (ICC) *n* Cámara de Comercio Internacional (CCI *f*).

International Court of Justice (ICJ) *n* Corte *f* Internacional de Justicia (CIJ *f*).

international date line *n* línea de cambio de fecha.

internationally [intûrnash'ənəlē] *ad* internacionalmente.

International Monetary Fund (IMF) *n* Fondo Monetario Internacional (FMI *m*).

internecine [intûrnē'sīn] *a* internecino.

internee [intûrnē'] *n* internado/a.

internment [intûrn'mənt] *n* internamiento.

interplanetary [intûrplan'itārē] *a* interplanetario.

interplay [in'tûrplā] *n* interacción *f*.

Interpol [in'tûrpōl] *n* Interpol *f*.

interpret [intûrprit'] *vt* interpretar; (*translate*) traducir; (*understand*) entender ♦ *vi* hacer de intérprete.

interpretation [intûrpritā'shən] *n* interpretación *f*; traducción *f*; entendimiento.

interpreter [intûr'pritûr] *n* intérprete *m/f*.

interrelated [intərilā'tid] *a* interrelacionado.

interrogate [intär'əgāt] *vt* interrogar.

interrogation [intärəgā'shən] *n* interrogatorio.

interrogative [intərág'ətiv] *a* interrogativo.
interrupt [intərupt'] *vt, vi* interrumpir.
interruption [intərup'shən] *n* interrupción *f*.
intersect [intûrsekt'] *vt* cruzar ♦ *vi* (*roads*) cruzarse.
intersection [intûrsek'shən] *n* intersección *f*; (*of roads*) cruce *m*.
intersperse [intûrspûrs'] *vt*: **to ~ with** salpicar de.
interstate (highway) [in'tûrstât (hī'wā)] *n* (*US*) autopista.
intertwine [intûrtwīn'] *vt* entrelazar ♦ *vi* entrelazarse.
interval [in'tûrvəl] *n* intervalo; (*Brit*: THEATER, SPORT) descanso; **at ~s** a ratos, de vez en cuando; **sunny ~s** (*METEOROLOGY*) claros *mpl*.
intervene [intûrvēn'] *vi* intervenir; (*take part*) participar; (*occur*) sobrevenir.
intervening [intûrvēn'ing] *a* intermedio.
intervention [intûrven'chən] *n* intervención *f*.
interview [in'tûrvyōō] *n* (*RADIO, TV etc*) entrevista ♦ *vt* entrevistarse con.
interviewee [in'tûrvyōōē'] *n* entrevistado/a.
interviewer [in'tûrvyōōûr] *n* entrevistador(a) *m/f*.
intestate [intes'tāt] *a* intestado.
intestinal [intes'tənəl] *a* intestinal.
intestine [intes'tin] *n*: **large/small ~** intestino grueso/delgado.
intimacy [in'təməsē] *n* intimidad *f*; (*relations*) relaciones *fpl* íntimas.
intimate *a* [in'təmit] íntimo; (*friendship*) estrecho; (*knowledge*) profundo ♦ *vt* [in'təmāt] (*announce*) dar a entender.
intimately [in'təmitlē] *ad* íntimamente.
intimidate [intim'idāt] *vt* intimidar, amedrentar.
intimidation [intimidā'shən] *n* intimidación *f*.
into [in'tōō] *prep* (*gen*) en; (*towards*) a; (*inside*) hacia el interior de; **~ 3 pieces/ French** en 3 pedazos/al francés; **to change pounds ~ dollars** cambiar libras por dólares.
intolerable [intál'ûrəbəl] *a* intolerable, insoportable.
intolerance [intál'ûrəns] *n* intolerancia.
intolerant [intál'ûrənt] *a*: **~ (of)** intolerante (con *or* para).
intonation [intōnā'shən] *n* entonación *f*.
intoxicate [inták'sikāt] *vt* embriagar.
intoxicated [inták'sikātid] *a* embriagado.
intoxication [intáksikā'shən] *n* embriaguez *f*.
intractable [intrak'təbəl] *a* (*person*) intratable; (*problem*) insoluble; (*illness*) incurable.
intransigence [intran'sijəns] *n* intransigencia.
intransigent [intran'sijənt] *a* intransigente.
intransitive [intran'sətiv] *a* intransitivo.

intravenous [intrəvē'nəs] *a* intravenoso.
in-tray [in'trā] *n* bandeja de entrada.
intrepid [intrep'id] *a* intrépido.
intricacy [in'trəkəsē] *n* complejidad *f*.
intricate [in'trəkit] *a* intrincado; (*plot, problem*) complejo.
intrigue [intrēg'] *n* intriga ♦ *vt* fascinar ♦ *vi* andar en intrigas.
intriguing [intrē'ging] *a* fascinante.
intrinsic [intrin'sik] *a* intrínseco.
introduce [intrədōōs'] *vt* introducir, meter; (*POL*: *bill, law*) presentar; **to ~ sb (to sb)** presentar uno (a otro); **to ~ sb to** (*pastime, technique*) introducir a uno a; **may I ~ ...?** permítame presentarle a ....
introduction [intrəduk'shən] *n* introducción *f*; (*of person*) presentación *f*; **a letter of ~** una carta de recomendación.
introductory [intrəduk'tûrē] *a* introductorio; **an ~ offer** una oferta introductoria; **~ remarks** comentarios *mpl* introductorios.
introspection [intrəspek'shən] *n* introspección *f*.
introspective [intrəspek'tiv] *a* introspectivo.
introvert [in'trəvûrt] *a, n* introvertido/a *m/f*.
intrude [intrōōd'] *vi* (*person*) entrometerse; **to ~ on** estorbar.
intruder [intrōō'dûr] *n* intruso/a.
intrusion [intrōō'zhən] *n* invasión *f*.
intrusive [intrōō'siv] *a* intruso.
intuition [intōōish'ən] *n* intuición *f*.
intuitive [intōō'ətiv] *a* intuitivo.
intuitively [intōō'ətivlē] *ad* por intuición, intuitivamente.
inundate [in'undāt] *vt*: **to ~ with** inundar de.
inure [inyōōr'] *vt*: **to ~ (to)** acostumbrar *or* habituar (a).
invade [invād'] *vt* invadir.
invader [invā'dûr] *n* invasor(a) *m/f*.
invalid *n* [in'vəlid] minusválido/a ♦ *a* [inval'id] (*not valid*) inválido, nulo.
invalidate [inval'idāt] *vt* invalidar, anular.
invalid chair *n* (*Brit*) sillón *m* para inválidos.
invaluable [inval'yōōəbəl] *a* inestimable.
invariable [invār'ēəbəl] *a* invariable.
invariably [invār'ēəblē] *ad* sin excepción, siempre; **she is ~ late** siempre llega tarde.
invasion [invā'zhən] *n* invasión *f*.
invective [invek'tiv] *n* invectiva.
inveigle [invē'gəl] *vt*: **to ~ sb into (doing) sth** embaucar *or* engatusar a uno para (que haga) algo.
invent [invent'] *vt* inventar.
invention [inven'chən] *n* invento; (*inventiveness*) inventiva; (*lie*) ficción *f*, mentira.
inventive [inven'tiv] *a* inventivo.
inventiveness [inven'tivnis] *n* ingenio, inventiva.
inventor [inven'tûr] *n* inventor(a) *m/f*.

inventory |in'vəntôrē] *n* inventario.
inventory control *n* control *m* del inventario.
inverse |invûrs'] *a*, *n* inverso; **in ~ proportion (to)** en proporción inversa (a).
inversely |invûrs'lē] *ad* a la inversa.
invert |invûrt'] *vt* invertir.
invertebrate |invûr'təbrit] *n* invertebrado.
inverted commas |invûr'tid kâm'əz] *npl* (*Brit*) comillas *fpl*.
invest |invest'] *vt* invertir; (*fig: time, effort*) dedicar ♦ *vi* invertir; **to ~ sb with sth** investir a uno con algo.
investigate |inves'təgāt] *vt* investigar; (*study*) estudiar, examinar.
investigation |investəgāshən] *n* investigación *f*, pesquisa; examen *m*.
investigative journalism |inves'təgātiv jûr'nəlizəm] *n* periodismo investigador.
investigator |inves'təgātūr] *n* investigador(a) *m/f*; **private ~** investigador(a) *m/f* privado/a.
investiture |inves'tichûr] *n* investidura.
investment |invest'mənt] *n* inversión *f*.
investment grant *n* subvención *f* para la inversión.
investment income *n* ingresos *mpl* procedentes de inversiones.
investment portfolio *n* portafolio de inversiones.
investment trust *n* (*Brit*) compañía inversionista, sociedad *f* de cartera.
investor |inves'tûr] *n* inversionista *m/f*.
inveterate |invet'ûrit] *a* empedernido.
invidious |invid'ēəs] *a* odioso.
invigilator |invij'əlātûr] *n* (*Brit*) celador(a) *m/f*.
invigorating |invig'ərāting] *a* vigorizante.
invincible |invin'səbəl] *a* invencible.
inviolate |invī'əlit] *a* inviolado.
invisible |inviz'əbəl] *a* invisible.
invisible ink *n* tinta simpática.
invisible mending *n* puntada invisible.
invitation |invitā'shən] *n* invitación *f*; **at sb's ~** a invitación de uno; **by ~ only** solamente por invitación.
invite |invīt'] *vt* invitar; (*opinions etc*) solicitar, pedir; (*trouble*) buscarse; **to ~ sb (to do)** invitar a uno (a hacer); **to ~ sb to dinner** invitar a uno a cenar.
invite out *vt* invitar a salir.
invite over *vt* invitar a casa.
inviting |invī'ting] *a* atractivo; (*look*) provocativo; (*food*) apetitoso.
invoice |in'vois] *n* factura ♦ *vt* facturar; **to ~ sb for goods** facturar a uno por mercancías.
invoicing |in'voising] *n* facturación *f*.
invoke |invōk'] *vt* invocar; (*aid*) pedir; (*law*) recurrir a.
involuntary |invâl'əntärē] *a* involuntario.
involve |invâlv'] *vt* (*entail*) suponer, implicar; **to ~ sb (in)** comprometer a uno

(*con*).
involved |invâlvd'] *a* complicado; **to be/become ~ in sth** estar comprometido *or* involucrado/involucrarse en algo.
involvement |invâlv'mənt] *n* (*gen*) enredo; (*obligation*) compromiso; (*difficulty*) apuro.
invulnerable |invul'nûrəbəl] *a* invulnerable.
inward |in'wûrd] *a* (*movement*) interior, interno; (*thought, feeling*) íntimo.
inwardly |in'wûrdlē] *ad* (*feel, think etc*) para sí, para dentro.
inward(s) |in'wûrd(z)] *ad* hacia dentro.
I/O *abbr* (*COMPUT* = *input/output*) E/S; **~ error** error *m* de E/S.
IOC *n abbr* (= *International Olympic Committee*) COI *m*.
iodine |ī'ədīn] *n* yodo.
ion |ī'ən] *n* ion *m*.
Ionian Sea |īō'nēən sē] *n*: **the ~** el Mar Jónico.
iota |īō'tə] *n* (*fig*) jota, ápice *m*.
IOU *n abbr* (= *I owe you*) pagaré *m*.
IOW *abbr* (*Brit*) = *Isle of Wight*.
IPA *n abbr* = *International Phonetic Alphabet*.
IQ *n abbr* (= *intelligence quotient*) C.I. *m*.
IRA *n abbr* (*US*) = *individual retirement account*; (= *Irish Republican Army*) IRA *m*.
Iran |iran'] *n* Irán *m*.
Iranian |irā'nēən] *a* iraní ♦ *n* iraní *m/f*; (*LING*) iraní *m*.
Iraq |irak'] *n* Irak *m*.
Iraqi |irâk'ē] *a*, *n* irakí *m/f*.
irascible |iras'əbəl] *a* irascible.
irate |irāt'] *a* enojado, airado.
Ireland |īûr'lənd] *n* Irlanda; **Republic of ~** República de Irlanda.
iris, **~es** |ī'ris, -iz] *n* (*ANAT*) iris *m*; (*BOT*) lirio.
Irish |ī'rish] *a* irlandés/esa ♦ *n* (*LING*) irlandés *m*; **the ~** *npl* los irlandeses.
Irishman |ī'rishmən] *n* irlandés *m*.
Irish Sea *n*: **the ~** el Mar de Irlanda.
Irishwoman |ī'rishwōōmən] *n* irlandesa.
irk |ûrk] *vt* fastidiar.
irksome |ûrk'səm] *a* fastidioso.
IRO *n abbr* (*US*) = *International Refugee Organization*.
iron |ī'ûrn] *n* hierro; (*for clothes*) plancha ♦ *a* de hierro ♦ *vt* (*clothes*) planchar; **~s** *npl* (*chains*) grillos *mpl*.
iron out *vt* (*crease*) quitar; (*fig*) allanar.
Iron Curtain *n*: **the ~** el Telón de Acero.
iron foundry *n* fundición *f*, fundidora.
ironic(al) |īrân'ik(əl)] *a* irónico.
ironically |īrân'iklē] *ad* irónicamente.
ironing |ī'ûrning] *n* (*act*) planchado; (*ironed clothes*) ropa planchada; (*to be ironed*) ropa por planchar.
ironing board *n* tabla de planchar.
iron lung *n* (*MED*) pulmón *m* de acero.
ironmonger |ī'ûrnmunggûr] *n* (*Brit*)

ferretero/a; ~'s **(shop)** ferretería, quincallería.
iron ore |i'ûrn ôr| n mineral m de hierro.
ironworks |i'ûrnwûrks| n fundición f.
irony |i'rənē| n ironía; **the ~ of it is that...**
lo irónico es que... .
irrational |irash'ənəl| a irracional.
irreconcilable |irek'ənsīləbəl| a inconcilia-
ble; (enemies) irreconciliable.
irredeemable |iridē'məbəl| a irredimible.
irrefutable |irifyōō'təbəl| a irrefutable.
irregular |ireg'yəlûr| a irregular; (surface)
desigual.
irregularity |iregyəlar'itē| n irregularidad f;
desigualdad f.
irrelevance |irel'əvəns| n impertinencia.
irrelevant |irel'əvənt| a fuera de lugar, in-
oportuno.
irreligious |irilij'əs| a irreligioso.
irreparable |irep'ûrəbəl| a irreparable.
irreplaceable |iriplā'səbəl| a irremplazable.
irrepressible |iripres'əbəl| a incontenible.
irreproachable |iriprō'chəbəl| a irreprocha-
ble.
irresistible |irizis'təbəl| a irresistible.
irresolute |irez'olōōt| a indeciso.
irrespective |irispek'tiv|: **~ of** prep sin te-
ner en cuenta, no importa.
irresponsibility |irispânsəbil'ətē| n
irresponsabilidad f.
irresponsible |irispân'səbəl| a (act) irres-
ponsable; (person) poco serio.
irretrievable |iritrē'vəbəl| a (object) irrecu-
perable; (loss, damage) irremediable, irreparable.
irretrievably |iritrē'vəblē| ad irremisible-
mente.
irreverence |irev'ûrəns| n irreverencia.
irreverent |irev'ûrənt| a irreverente,
irrespetuoso.
irrevocable |irev'əkəbəl| a irrevocable.
irrigate |ir'igāt| vt regar.
irrigation |irigā'shən| n riego.
irritability |iritəbil'ətē| n irritabilidad f.
irritable |ir'itəbəl| a (person: temperament)
de (mal) carácter; (: mood) de mal humor.
irritant |ir'ətənt| n agente m irritante.
irritate |ir'ətāt| vt fastidiar; (MED) picar.
irritating |ir'ətāting| a fastidioso.
irritation |iritā'shən| n fastidio; picazón f,
picor m.
IRS n abbr (US) = **Internal Revenue
Service.**
is |iz| vb see **be.**
ISBN n abbr (= International Standard Book
Number) ISBN m.
Islam |iz'lâm| n Islam m.
island |i'lənd| n isla; (also: **traffic ~)** isle-
ta.
islander |i'ləndûr| n isleño/a.
isle |īl| n isla.
isn't |iz'ənt| = **is not.**

isobar |ī'sōbâr| n isobara.
isolate |ī'səlāt| vt aislar.
isolated |ī'səlātid| a aislado.
isolation |īsəlā'shən| n aislamiento.
isolationism |īsəlā'shənizəm| n aislacio-
nismo.
isolation ward n pabellón m de aislamiento.
isotope |ī'sətōp| n isótopo.
Israel |iz'rāəl| n Israel m.
Israeli |izrā'lē| a, n israelí m/f.
issue |ish'ōō| n cuestión f, asunto; (out-
come) resultado; (of banknotes etc) emisión f; (of newspaper etc) número; (offspring) sucesión f, descendencia ♦ vt (rations, equipment) distribuir, repartir;
(orders) dar; (certificate, passport) expedir; (decree) promulgar; (magazine) publicar; (checks) extender; (banknotes,
stamps) emitir ♦ vi: **to ~ (from)** derivar
(de), brotar (de); **at ~** en cuestión; **to
take ~ with sb (over)** estar en desacuerdo
con uno (sobre); **to avoid the ~** andar con
rodeos; **to confuse** or **obscure the ~**
confundir las cosas; **to make an ~ of sth**
hacer hincapié en algo; **to ~ sth to sb** entregar algo a uno.
Istanbul |istambōō'l| n Estambul m.
isthmus |is'məs| n istmo.
IT n abbr = **information technology.**
it |it| pron (subject) él/ella; (direct object)
lo/la; (indirect object) le; (impersonal)
ello; (after prep) él/ella/ello; **of/from ~** de
él; **about ~** sobre él; **out of ~** desde él; **in
~** en él; **to ~** a él; **at ~** en/a él; **in front
of/behind ~** delante de/detrás de él; **above
~, over ~** por encima de él, sobre él; **below ~, under ~** debajo de él; **~'s 6
o'clock** son las seis; **~'s 2 hours on the
train** son dos horas en el tren; **~'s raining**
llueve, está lloviendo; **where is ~?** ¿dónde
está?; **what is ~?** ¿qué pasa?; **who is ~?**
¿quién es?; **~'s me** soy yo; **he's proud of
~** le enorgullece; **he agreed to ~** está de
acuerdo (con ello).
Italian |ital'yən| a, n italiano/a m/f ♦ n
(LING) italiano.
italic |ital'ik| a cursivo; **~s** npl cursiva sg.
Italy |it'əlē| n Italia.
itch |ich| n picazón f; (fig) prurito ♦ vi (per-
son) sentir or tener comezón; (part of
body) picar; **to be ~ing to do sth** rabiar
por hacer algo.
itching |ich'ing| n picazón f, comezón f.
itchy |ich'ē| a: **to be ~** picar.
it'd |it'əd| = **it would; it had.**
item |ī'təm| n artículo; (on agenda) asunto
(a tratar); (in program) número; (also:
news ~) noticia; **~s of clothing** prendas
fpl de vestir.
itemize |ī'təmīz| vt detallar.
itinerant |itin'ûrənt| a ambulante.
itinerary |ītin'ərärē| n itinerario.

it'll [it'əl] = **it will, it shall.**

its [its] *a* su.

it's [its] = **it is; it has.**

itself [itself'] *pron* (*reflexive*) sí mismo/a; (*emphatic*) él mismo/ella misma.

ITV *n abbr* (*Brit* = *Independent Television*) cadena de television comercial independiente del Estado.

IUD *n abbr* (= *intra-uterine device*) DIU *m*.

I.V. *n* (*US MED*) gota a gota *m*.

I've [īv] = **I have.**

ivory [ī'vûrē] *n* marfil *m*.

Ivory Coast *n*: **the ~** la Costa de Marfil.

ivory tower *n* (*fig*) torre *f* de marfil.

ivy [ī'vē] *n* hiedra.

Ivy League *n* (*US*) grupo de famosas universidades en el noreste de los Estados Unidos.

J

J, j [jā] *n* (*letter*) J, j *f*; **J for Jig** J de José.

JA *n abbr* = **judge advocate.**

J/A *abbr* = **joint account.**

jab [jab] *vt* (*elbow*) dar un codazo a; (*punch*) dar un golpe rápido a ♦ *vi*: **to ~ at** intentar golpear a; **to ~ sth into sth** clavar algo en algo ♦ *n* codazo; golpe *m* (rápido); (*MED col*) pinchazo.

jabber [jab'ûr] *vi, vt* farfullar.

jack [jak] *n* (*AUT*) gato; (*CARDS*) sota; (*Brit BOWLS*) boliche *m*.

jack in *vt* (*col*) dejar.

jack up *vt* (*AUT*) alzar con gato.

jackal [jak'əl] *n* (*ZOOL*) chacal *m*.

jackass [jak'as] *n* (*also fig*) asno, burro.

jackdaw [jak'dô] *n* grajo/a, chova.

jacket [jak'it] *n* chaqueta, americana; (*of boiler etc*) camisa; (*of book*) sobrecubierta.

jack-in-the-box [jak'inthəbáks] *n* caja sorpresa, caja de resorte.

jackknife [jak'nīf] *vi* colear.

jack-of-all-trades [jak'əvôltrādz'] *n* factótum *m*.

jack (plug) [jak (plug)] *n* (*ELEC*) enchufe *m* de clavija.

jackpot [jak'pát] *n* premio gordo.

jacuzzi [jəkoo'zē] ® *n* jacuzzi *m* ®.

jade [jād] *n* (*stone*) jade *m*.

jaded [jā'did] *a* (*tired*) cansado; (*fed up*) hastiado.

jagged [jag'id] *a* dentado.

jaguar [jag'wâr] *n* jaguar *m*.

jail [jāl] *n* cárcel *f* ♦ *vt* encarcelar.

jailbird [jāl'bûrd] *n* presidiario/a *or* preso/a reincidente.

jailbreak [jāl'brāk] *n* fuga *or* evasión *f* (de la cárcel).

jailer [jā'lûr] *n* carcelero/a.

jalopy [jəláp'ē] *n* (*col*) cacharro, armatoste *m*.

jam [jam] *n* mermelada; (*also*: **traffic ~**) embotellamiento; (*difficulty*) apuro ♦ *vt* (*passage etc*) obstruir; (*mechanism, drawer etc*) atascar; (*RADIO*) interferir ♦ *vi* atascarse, trabarse; **to get sb out of a ~** sacar a uno del paso *or* de un apuro; **to ~ sth into sth** meter algo a la fuerza en algo; **the telephone lines are ~med** las líneas están ocupadas.

Jamaica [jəmā'kə] *n* Jamaica.

Jamaican [jəmā'kən] *a, n* jamaicano/a *m/f*.

jamb [jam] *n* jamba.

jamboree [jambərē'] *n* congreso de niños exploradores.

jam-packed [jam'pakt'] *a*: **~ (with)** atestado (de).

jam session *n* concierto improvisado de jazz/rock *etc*.

Jan. *abbr* (= *January*) ene.

jangle [jang'gəl] *vi* sonar (de manera) discordante.

janitor [jan'itûr] *n* (*caretaker*) portero, conserje *m*.

January [jan'yoowārē] *n* enero.

Japan [jəpan'] *n* (el) Japón.

Japanese [japənēz'] *a* japonés/esa ♦ *n* (*pl inv*) japonés/esa *m/f*; (*LING*) japonés *m*.

jar [jâr] *n* (*glass*: *large*) jarra; (*: small*) tarro ♦ *vi* (*sound*) chirriar; (*colors*) desentonar.

jargon [jâr'gən] *n* jerga.

jarring [jâr'ing] *a* (*sound, color*) discordante, desafinado, chocante.

Jas. *abbr* = *James*.

jasmin(e) [jaz'min] *n* jazmín *m*.

jaundice [jôn'dis] *n* ictericia.

jaundiced [jôn'dist] *a* (*fig*: *embittered*) amargado; (*: disillusioned*) desilusionado.

jaunt [jônt] *n* excursión *f*.

jaunty [jôn'tē] *a* alegre, desenvuelto.

Java [jâv'ə] *n* Java.

javelin [jav'lin] *n* jabalina.

jaw [jô] *n* mandíbula; **~s** *npl* (*TECH*: *of vise etc*) mordaza *sg*.

jawbone [jô'bōn] *n* mandíbula, quijada.

jay [jā] *n* (*ZOOL*) arrendajo.

jaywalker [jā'wôkûr] *n* peatón/ona *m/f* imprudente.

jazz [jaz] *n* jazz *m*.

jazz up *vt* (*liven up*) animar, avivar.

jazz band *n* orquesta de jazz.

jazzy [jaz'ē] *a* de colores llamativos.

JCC *n abbr* (*US*) = *Junior Chamber of Commerce.*

JCS *n abbr* (*US*) = *Joint Chiefs of Staff.*

JD *n abbr* (*US*: = *Doctor of Laws*) título universitario; (: = *Justice Department*) Ministerio de Justicia.

jealous [jel'əs] *a* (*gen*) celoso; (*envious*) envidioso; **to be ~** tener celos.
jealously [jel'əslē] *ad* (*enviously*) envidiosamente; (*watchfully*) vigilantemente, celosamente.
jealousy [jel'əsē] *n* celos *mpl*; envidia.
jeans [jēnz] *npl* (pantalones *mpl*) vaqueros *mpl or* tejanos *mpl*.
jeep [jēp] *n* jeep *m*.
jeer [jēr] *vi*: **to ~ (at)** (*boo*) abuchear; (*mock*) mofarse (de).
jeering [jē'ring] *a* (*crowd*) insolente, ofensivo ♦ *n* protestas *fpl*, burlas *fpl*.
jelly [jel'ē] *n* jalea, gelatina.
jellyfish [jel'ēfish] *n* medusa.
jemmy [jem'ē] *n* palanqueta.
jeopardize [jep'ûrdīz] *vt* arriesgar, poner en peligro.
jeopardy [jep'ûrdē] *n*: **to be in ~** estar en peligro.
jerk [jûrk] *n* (*jolt*) sacudida; (*wrench*) tirón *m*; (*US col*) pesado/a ♦ *vt* dar una sacudida a; tirar bruscamente de ♦ *vi* (*vehicle*) traquetear.
jerkin [jûr'kin] *n* chaleco.
jerky [jûr'kē] *a* espasmódico.
jerry-built [jär'ēbilt] *a* mal construido.
jerry can [jär'ē kan] *n* bidón *m*.
jersey [jûr'zē] *n* jersey *m*; (*fabric*) tejido de punto.
Jerusalem [jərōō'sələm] *n* Jerusalén *m*.
jest [jest] *n* broma.
jester [jes'tûr] *n* bufón *m*.
Jesus [jē'səs] *n* Jesús *m*; **~ Christ** Jesucristo.
jet [jet] *n* (*of gas, liquid*) chorro; (*AVIAT*) avión *m* a reacción.
jet-black [jet'blak'] *a* negro como el azabache.
jet engine *n* motor *m* a reacción.
jet lag *n* desorientación *f* después de un largo vuelo.
jetsam [jet'səm] *n* echazón *f*.
jettison [jet'əsən] *vt* desechar.
jetty [jet'ē] *n* muelle *m*, embarcadero.
Jew [jōō] *n* judío.
jewel [jōō'əl] *n* joya; (*in watch*) rubí *m*.
jeweler, (*Brit*) **jeweller** [jōō'əlûr] *n* joyero/a; **~'s (shop)** (*Brit*) joyería.
jewelry, (*Brit*) **jewellery** [jōō'əlrē] *n* joyas *fpl*, alhajas *fpl*; **~ store** (*US*) joyería.
Jewess [jōō'is] *n* judía.
Jewish [jōō'ish] *a* judío.
JFK *n abbr* (*US*) = *John Fitzgerald Kennedy International Airport.*
jib [jib] *vi* (*horse*) plantarse; **to ~ at doing sth** resistirse a hacer algo.
jibe [jīb] *n* mofa.
jiffy [jif'ē] *n* (*col*): **in a ~** en un santiamén.
jig [jig] *n* (*dance, tune*) giga.
jigsaw [jig'sô] *n* (*also*: **~ puzzle**) rompecabezas *m inv*; (*tool*) sierra de vaivén.
jilt [jilt] *vt* dejar plantado a.

jingle [jing'gəl] *n* (*advert*) musiquilla ♦ *vi* tintinear.
jingoism [jing'gōizəm] *n* patriotería, jingoísmo.
jinx [jingks] *n*: **there's a ~ on it** está gafado.
jitters [jit'ûrz] *npl* (*col*): **to get the ~** ponerse nervioso.
jittery [jit'ûrē] *a* (*col*) muy inquieto, nervioso.
jiujitsu [jōōjit'sōō] *n* ju-jitsu *m*.
job [jâb] *n* trabajo; (*task*) tarea; (*duty*) deber *m*; (*post*) empleo; (*fam*: *difficulty*) dificultad *f*; **it's a good ~ that...** menos mal que...; **just the ~!** ¡estupendo!; **a part-time/full-time ~** un trabajo de medio tiempo/tiempo completo; **that's not my ~** eso no me incumbe *or* toca a mí; **he's only doing his ~** está cumpliendo nada más.
job centre *n* (*Brit*) oficina estatal de colocaciones.
job creation scheme *n* (*Brit*) plan *m* de creación de puestos de trabajo.
job description *n* descripción *f* del puesto de trabajo.
jobless [jâb'lis] *a* sin trabajo.
job lot *n* lote *m* de mercancías, saldo.
job satisfaction *n* satisfacción *f* en el trabajo.
job security *n* garantía de trabajo.
job specification *n* especificación *f* del trabajo, profesiograma *m*.
jockey [jâk'ē] *n* jockey *m/f* ♦ *vi*: **to ~ for position** maniobrar para conseguir una posición.
jocular [jâk'yəlûr] *a* (*humorous*) gracioso; (*merry*) alegre.
jodhpurs [jâd'pûrz] *npl* pantalón *msg* de montar.
jog [jâg] *vt* empujar (ligeramente) ♦ *vi* (*run*) hacer footing; **to ~ along** ir tirando; **to ~ sb's memory** refrescar la memoria a uno.
jogger [jâg'ûr] *n* corredor(a) *m/f*.
jogging [jâg'ing] *n* footing *m*.
john [jân] *n* (*US col*) servicios *mpl*.
join [join] *vt* (*things*) juntar, unir; (*become member of*: *club*) hacerse socio de; (*POL*: *party*) afiliarse a; (*meet*: *people*) reunirse con; (*fig*) juntarse con ♦ *vi* (*roads*) empalmar; (*rivers*) confluir ♦ *n* juntura; **will you ~ us for dinner?** ¿nos acompañas a cenar?; **I'll ~ you later** te encontraré luego; **to ~ forces (with)** aliarse (con).
join in *vi* tomar parte, participar ♦ *vt fus* tomar parte *or* participar en.
join up *vi* unirse; (*MIL*) alistarse.
joiner [joi'nûr] *n* carpintero/a.
joinery [joi'nûrē] *n* carpintería.
joint [joint] *n* (*TECH*) juntura, unión *f*; (*ANAT*) articulación *f*; (*Brit CULIN*) pieza de carne (para asar); (*col*: *place*) garito ♦ *a* (*common*) común; (*combined*) combinado; (*responsibility*) compartido; (*committee*) mixto.

joint account n (with bank etc) cuenta común.

jointly [joint'lē] ad (gen) en común; (collectively) colectivamente; (together) conjuntamente.

joint owners npl copropietarios mpl.

joint ownership n copropiedad f, propiedad f común.

joint-stock bank [joint'stâk' bangk] n banco por acciones.

joint-stock company [joint'stâk' kum'pənē] n sociedad f anónima.

joint venture n sociedad f conjunta.

joist [joist] n viga.

joke [jōk] n chiste m; (also: **practical ~**) broma ♦ vi bromear; **to play a ~ on** gastar una broma a.

joker [jō'kûr] n chistoso/a, bromista m/f; (CARDS) comodín m.

joking [jō'king] n bromas fpl.

jokingly [jō'kinglē] ad en broma.

jollity [jâl'itē] n alegría.

jolly [jâl'ē] a (merry) alegre; (Brit: enjoyable) divertido ♦ ad (col) muy, terriblemente; **~ good!** (Brit) ¡estupendo!

jolt [jōlt] n (shake) sacudida; (blow) golpe m; (shock) susto ♦ vt sacudir; asustar.

Jordan [jôr'dun] n (country) Jordania; (river) Jordán m.

joss stick [jâs stik] n pebete m.

jostle [jâs'əl] vt dar empellones a, codear.

jot [jât] n: **not one ~** ni jota, ni pizca.

jot down vt apuntar.

jotter [jât'ûr] n (Brit) bloc m.

journal [jûr'nəl] n (paper) periódico; (magazine) revista; (diary) diario.

journalese [jûrnəlēz'] n (pej) lenguaje m periodístico.

journalism [jûr'nəlizəm] n periodismo.

journalist [jûr'nəlist] n periodista m/f, reportero/a.

journey [jûr'nē] n viaje m; (distance covered) trayecto ♦ vi viajar; **return ~** viaje de regreso; **a 5-hour ~** un viaje de 5 horas.

jovial [jō'vēəl] a risueño, alegre.

jowl [joul] n quijada.

joy [joi] n alegría.

joyful [joi'fəl] a alegre.

joyfully [joi'fəlē] ad alegremente.

joyous [joi'əs] a alegre.

joy ride n (illegal) paseo en coche robado.

joystick [joi'stik] n (AVIAT) palanca de mando; (COMPUT) palanca de control.

JP n abbr = **Justice of the Peace.**

Jr. abbr = **junior.**

JTPA n abbr (US: = Job Training Partnership Act) programa gubernamental de formación profesional.

jubilant [jōō'bələnt] a jubiloso.

jubilation [jōōbəlā'shən] n júbilo.

jubilee [jōō'bəlē] n aniversario; **silver ~** vigésimo quinto aniversario.

judge [juj] n juez m/f ♦ vt juzgar; (esti-

mate) considerar; (: weight, size etc) calcular ♦ vi: **judging** or **to ~ by his expression** a juzgar por su expresión; **as far as I can ~** por lo que puedo entender, a mi entender; **I ~d it necessary to inform him** lo consideré necesario informarle.

judge advocate n (MIL) auditor m de guerra.

judg(e)ment [juj'mənt] n juicio; (punishment) sentencia, fallo; **to pass ~ (on)** (LAW) pronunciar or dictar sentencia (sobre); (fig) emitir un juicio crítico or dictaminar (sobre); **in my ~** a mi criterio.

judicial [jōōdish'əl] a judicial.

judiciary [jōōdish'ēärē] n poder m judicial, magistratura.

judicious [jōōdish'əs] a juicioso.

judo [jōō'dō] n judo.

jug [jug] n jarro.

juggernaut [jug'ûrnôt] n (huge truck) camionazo m.

juggle [jug'əl] vi hacer juegos malabares.

juggler [jug'lûr] n malabarista m/f.

Jugoslav [yōō'gōslâv] etc = **Yugoslav** etc.

jugular [jug'yəlûr] a: **~ vein** vena yugular.

juice [jōōs] n zumo, jugo (esp LAm); (of meat) jugo; (col: gas): **we've run out of ~** se nos acabó la gasolina.

juiciness [jōō'sēnis] n jugosidad f.

juicy [jōō'sē] a jugoso.

jujitsu [jōōjit'sōō] n = **juijitsu.**

jukebox [jōōk'bâks] n tocadiscos m inv tragaperras.

Jul. abbr (= July) jul.

July [jʊlī'] n julio; **the first of ~** el primero de julio; **during ~** en el mes de julio; **in ~ of next year** en julio del año que viene.

jumble [jum'bəl] n revoltijo ♦ vt (also: **~ together, ~ up**: mix up) revolver; (: disarrange) mezclar.

jumble sale n (Brit) venta de objetos usados con fines benéficos.

jumbo (jet) [jum'bō (jet)] n jumbo.

jump [jump] vi saltar, dar saltos; (start) asustarse, sobresaltarse; (increase) aumentar ♦ vt saltar ♦ n salto; (fence) obstáculo; (increase) aumento.

jump around vi dar saltos, brincar.

jump at vt fus (fig) apresurarse a aprovechar; **he ~ed at the offer** se apresuró a aceptar la oferta.

jump down vi bajar de un salto, saltar a tierra.

jump up vi levantarse de un salto.

jumped-up [jumpt'up] a (Brit pej) engreído.

jumper [jum'pûr] n (US: pinafore dress) mandil m; (Brit: pullover) suéter m, jersey m; (SPORT) saltador(a) m/f.

jumper cables, (Brit) **jump leads** npl cables mpl puente de batería.

jump rope n (US) saltar m a la comba.

jump suit n mono.

jumpy [jum'pē] *a* nervioso.
Jun. *abbr* = **junior**; (= *June*) jun.
junction [jungk'shən] *n* (*of roads*) cruce *m*; (*RAIL*) empalme *m*.
juncture [jungk'chûr] *n*: **at this ~** en este momento, en esta coyuntura.
June [jōōn] *n* junio.
jungle [jung'gəl] *n* selva, jungla.
junior [jōōn'yûr] *a* (*in age*) menor, más joven; (*competition*) juvenil; (*position*) subalterno ♦ *n* menor *m/f*, joven *m/f*; **he's ~ to me** es menor que yo.
junior executive *n* ejecutivo/a subalterno/a.
junior high school *n* (*US*) instituto de enseñanza media.
junior school *n* (*Brit*) escuela primaria.
junk [jungk] *n* (*cheap goods*) baratijas *fpl*; (*trash*) trastos *mpl* viejos; (*rubbish*) basura; (*ship*) junco ♦ *vt* (*col*) desechar.
junk dealer *n* vendedor(a) *m/f* de objetos usados.
junket [jung'kit] *n* (*CULIN*) dulce de leche cuajada; (*col*): **to go on a ~**, **go ~ing** viajar a costo ajeno *or* del erario público.
junk foods *npl* alimentos preparados y envasados de escaso valor nutritivo.
junkie [jung'kē] *n* (*col*) yonqui *m/f*, heroinómano/a.
junk room *n* trastero.
junk shop *n* tienda de objetos usados.
junkyard [jungk'yârd] *n* depósito de chatarra.
junta [hōōn'tə] *n* junta militar.
Jupiter [jōō'pitûr] *n* (*MYTHOLOGY*, *ASTRO*) Júpiter *m*.
jurisdiction [jōōrisdik'shən] *n* jurisdicción *f*; **it falls** *or* **comes within/outside our ~** es/no es de nuestra competencia.
jurisprudence [jōōrisprōōd'əns] *n* jurisprudencia.
juror [jōō'rûr] *n* jurado.
jury [jōō'rē] *n* jurado.
jury box *n* tribuna del jurado.
juryman [jōōr'ēmən] *n* miembro del jurado.
just [just] *a* justo ♦ *ad* (*exactly*) exactamente; (*only*) sólo, solamente; **he's ~ done it/left** acaba de hacerlo/irse; **I've ~ seen him** acabo de verle; **~ right** perfecto, perfectamente; **~ two o'clock** las dos en punto; **she's ~ as clever as you** es tan lista como tú; **~ as well that...** menos mal que...; **it's ~ as well you didn't go** menos mal que no fuiste; **it's ~ as good (as)** es igual (que), es tan bueno (como); **~ as he was leaving** en el momento en que se marchaba; **we were ~ going** ya nos íbamos; **I was ~ about to phone** estaba a punto de llamar; **~ before/enough** justo antes/lo suficiente; **~ here** aquí mismo; **he ~ missed** falló por poco; **~ listen to this** escucha esto un momento; **~ ask someone the way** simplemente pregúntale a uno por

dónde se va; **not ~ now** ahora no.
justice [jus'tis] *n* justicia; **this photo doesn't do you ~** esta foto no te favorece.
Justice of the Peace (JP) *n* juez *m/f* de paz.
justifiable [jus'tifiəbəl] *a* justificable, justificado.
justifiably [jus'təfiəblē] *ad* justificadamente, con razón.
justification [justəfəkā'shən] *n* justificación *f*.
justify [jus'təfī] *vt* justificar; (*text*) alinear, justificar; **to be justified in doing sth** tener motivo para *or* razón al hacer algo.
justly [just'lē] *ad* (*gen*) justamente; (*with reason*) con razón.
justness [just'nis] *n* justicia.
jut [jut] *vi* (*also*: **~ out**) sobresalir.
jute [jōōt] *n* yute *m*.
juvenile [jōō'vənəl] *a* juvenil; (*court*) de menores ♦ *n* joven *m/f*, menor *m/f* de edad.
juvenile delinquency *n* delincuencia juvenil.
juvenile delinquent *n* delincuente *m/f* juvenil.
juxtapose [jukstəpōz'] *vt* yuxtaponer.
juxtaposition [jukstəpəzish'ən] *n* yuxtaposición *f*.

K

K, k [kā] *n* (*letter*) K, k *f*; **K for King** K de Kilo.
K [kā] *abbr* (= *one thousand*) K; = **kilobyte**.
kaftan [kaf'tən] *n* caftán *m*.
Kalahari Desert [kâləhâr'ē dez'ûrt] *n* desierto de Kalahari.
kale [kāl] *n* col *f* rizada.
kaleidoscope [kəlī'dəskōp] *n* calidoscopio.
Kampala [kâmpâl'ə] *n* Kampala.
Kampuchea [kampōōchē'ə] *n* Kampuchea.
kangaroo [kanggərōō'] *n* canguro.
Kans. *abbr* (*US*) = **Kansas**.
kaput [kəpōōt'] *a* (*col*) roto, estropeado.
karate [kərá'tē] *n* karate *m*.
Kashmir [kazh'mēr] *n* Cachemira.
kayak [kī'ak] *n* kayak *m*.
kd *abbr* (*US*: = *knocked down*) desmontado.
kebab [kəbáb'] *n* pincho moruno, brocheta.
keel [kēl] *n* quilla; **on an even ~** (*fig*) en equilibrio.
  keel over *vi* (*NAUT*) zozobrar, volcarse; (*person*) desplomarse.
keen [kēn] *a* (*interest*, *desire*) grande, vivo; (*eye*, *intelligence*) agudo; (*competition*) intenso; (*edge*) afilado; (*Brit*: *eager*)

entusiasta; **to be ~ to do** *or* **on doing sth** tener muchas ganas de hacer algo; **to be ~ on sth/sb** interesarse por algo/uno; **I'm not ~ on going** no tengo ganas de ir.

keenly [kēn'lē] *ad* (*enthusiastically*) con entusiasmo; (*acutely*) vivamente; (*intensely*) intensamente.

keenness [kēn'nis] *n* (*eagerness*) entusiasmo, interés *m*.

keep [kēp] *vb* (*pt, pp* **kept** [kept]) *vt* (*retain, preserve*) guardar; (*hold back*) quedarse con; (*shop*) ser propietario de; (*feed: family etc*) mantener; (*promise*) cumplir; (*chickens, bees etc*) criar ♦ *vi* (*food*) conservarse; (*remain*) seguir, continuar ♦ *n* (*of castle*) torreón *m*; (*food etc*) comida, subsistencia; **to ~ doing sth** seguir haciendo algo; **to ~ sb from doing sth** impedir a uno hacer algo; **to ~ sth from happening** impedir que algo ocurra; **to ~ sb happy** hacer a uno feliz; **to ~ sb waiting** hacer esperar a uno; **to ~ a place tidy** mantener un lugar limpio; **to ~ sth to o.s.** guardar algo para sí mismo; **to ~ time** (*clock*) mantener la hora exacta; **~ the change** quédese con la vuelta; **to ~ an appointment** guardar cita; **to ~ a record** *or* **note of sth** tomar nota de *or* apuntar algo; *see also* **keeps.**

keep away *vt*: **to ~ sth/sb away from sb** mantener algo/a uno aparte de uno ♦ *vi*: **to ~ away (from)** mantenerse aparte (de).

keep back *vt* (*crowd, tears, money*) contener, reprimir; (*conceal: information*): **to ~ sth back from sb** ocultar algo a uno ♦ *vi* hacerse a un lado.

keep down *vt* (*control: prices, spending*) controlar; (*retain: food*) retener ♦ *vi* seguir agachado, no levantar la cabeza.

keep in *vt* (*invalid, child*) impedir que salga, no dejar salir ♦ *vi* (*col*): **to ~ in with sb** congraciarse con uno.

keep off *vt* (*dog, person*) mantener a distancia ♦ *vi* evitar; **~ your hands off!** ¡no toques!; **"~ off the grass"** "prohibido pisar el césped".

keep on *vi* seguir, continuar.

keep out *vi* (*stay out*) permanecer fuera; **"~ out"** "prohibida la entrada".

keep up *vt* mantener, conservar ♦ *vi* no retrasarse; (*fig: in comprehension*) seguir (la corriente); **to ~ up with** (*pace*) ir al paso de; (*level*) mantenerse a la altura de; **to ~ up with sb** seguir el ritmo a uno; (*fig*) seguir a uno.

keeper [kē'pûr] *n* guardián/ana *m/f*.

keep-fit [kēp'fit'] *n* gimnasia (para mantenerse en forma).

keeping [kē'ping] *n* (*care*) cuidado; **in ~ with** de acuerdo con.

keeps [kēps] *n*: **for ~** (*col*) para siempre.

keepsake [kēp'sāk] *n* recuerdo.

keg [keg] *n* barrilete *m*, barril *m*.

Ken. *abbr* (*US*) = *Kentucky.*

kennel [ken'əl] *n* perrera; **~s** *npl* perreras *fpl.*

Kenya [ken'yə] *n* Kenia.

Kenyan [ken'yən] *a, n* keniano/a *m/f.*

kept [kept] *pt, pp of* **keep.**

kerb [kûrb] *n* (*Brit*) bordillo.

kernel [kûr'nəl] *n* (*nut*) fruta; (*fig*) meollo.

kerosene [kär'əsēn] *n* keroseno.

kestrel [kes'trəl] *n* cernícalo.

ketchup [kech'əp] *n* salsa de tomate, catsup *m.*

kettle [ket'əl] *n* hervidor *m*, olla.

kettle drum *n* (*MUS*) timbal *m.*

key [kē] *n* (*gen*) llave *f*; (*MUS*) tono; (*of piano, typewriter*) tecla; (*on map*) clave *f* ♦ *cpd* (*vital: position, industry etc*) clave ♦ *vt* (*also:* **~ in**) teclear.

keyboard [kē'bôrd] *n* teclado ♦ *vt* (*text*) teclear.

keyed up [kēd up] *a* (*person*) nervioso; **to be (all) ~** estar nervioso *or* emocionado.

keyhole [kē'hōl] *n* ojo (de la cerradura).

key man *n* hombre *m* clave.

keynote [kē'nōt] *n* (*MUS*) tónica; (*fig*) idea fundamental.

keynote speech *n* discurso de apertura.

keypad [kē'pad] *n* teclado numérico.

key ring *n* llavero.

keystone [kē'stōn] *n* piedra clave.

keystroke [kē'strōk] *n* pulsación *f* (de una tecla).

kg *abbr* (= *kilogram*) kg.

KGB *n abbr* KGB *f.*

khaki [kak'ē] *n* caqui *m.*

kibbutz [kibōōts', -ēm] *n* kibutz *m.*

kick [kik] *vt* (*person*) dar una patada a; (*ball*) dar un puntapié a ♦ *vi* (*horse*) dar coces ♦ *n* patada; puntapié *m*; (*of rifle*) culetazo; (*col: thrill*): **he does it for ~s** lo hace por pura diversión.

kick around *vt* (*idea*) dar vueltas a; (*person*) tratar a patadas a.

kick off *vi* (*SPORT*) hacer el saque inicial.

kick-start [kik'stârt] *n* (*also:* **~er**) (pedal *m* de) arranque *m.*

kid [kid] *n* (*col: child*) chiquillo/a; (*animal*) cabrito; (*leather*) cabritilla ♦ *vi* (*col*) bromear.

kidnap [kid'nap] *vt* secuestrar.

kidnap(p)er [kid'napûr] *n* secuestrador(a) *m/f.*

kidnap(p)ing [kid'naping] *n* secuestro.

kidney [kid'nē] *n* riñón *m.*

kidney bean *n* judía, alubia.

kidney machine *n* riñón *m* artificial.

Kilimanjaro [kiləmənjár'ō] *n* Kilimanjaro.

kill [kil] *vt* matar; (*murder*) asesinar; (*fig: story*) suprimir; (: *rumor*) acabar con ♦ *n* matanza; **to ~ time** matar el tiempo.

kill off *vt* exterminar, terminar con; (*fig*) echar por tierra.

killer [kil'ûr] *n* asesino/a.
killing [kil'ing] *n* (*one*) asesinato; (*several*) matanza; (*COMM*): **to make a ~** tener un gran éxito financiero.
killjoy [kil'joi] *n* aguafiestas *m/f inv*.
kiln [kiln] *n* horno.
kilo [kē'lō] *n* (*abbr*: = *kilogram(me)*) kilo.
kilobyte [kil'əbīt] *n* (*COMPUT*) kilobyte *m*, kiloocteto.
kilogram, (*Brit*) **kilogramme** [kil'əgram] *n* kilogramo.
kilometer, (*Brit*) **kilometre** [kil'əmētûr] *n* kilómetro.
kilowatt [kil'əwât] *n* kilovatio.
kilt [kilt] *n* falda escocesa.
kilter [kil'tûr] *n*: **out of ~** desbaratado.
kimono [kimō'nō] *n* quimono.
kin [kin] *n* parientes *mpl*.
kind [kīnd] *a* (*treatment*) bueno, cariñoso; (*person, act, word*) amable, atento ♦ *n* clase *f*, especie *f*; (*species*) género; **in ~** (*COMM*) en especie; **a ~ of** una especie de; **to be two of a ~** ser tal para cual; **would you be ~ enough to ...?, would you be so ~ as to ...?** ¿me hace el favor de ...?; **it's very ~ of you (to do)** le agradezco mucho (el que haya hecho).
kindergarten [kin'dûrgârtən] *n* jardín *m* de infantes.
kind-hearted [kīnd'hârtid] *a* bondadoso, de buen corazón.
kindle [kin'dəl] *vt* encender.
kindliness [kīnd'lēnis] *n* bondad *f*, amabilidad *f*.
kindling [kind'ling] *n* leña (menuda).
kindly [kīnd'lē] *a* bondadoso; (*gentle*) cariñoso ♦ *ad* bondadosamente, amablemente; **will you ~...** sea usted tan amable de... .
kindness [kīnd'nis] *n* bondad *f*, amabilidad *f*.
kindred [kin'drid] *n* familia, parientes *mpl* ♦ *a*: **~ spirits** almas *fpl* gemelas.
kinetic [kinɛt'ik] *a* cinético.
king [king] *n* rey *m*.
kingdom [king'dəm] *n* reino.
kingfisher [king'fishûr] *n* martín *m* pescador.
kingpin [king'pin] *n* (*TECH*) perno real *or* pinzote; (*fig*) persona clave.
king-size(d) [king'sīz(d)] *a* de tamaño gigante; (*cigarette*) extra largo.
kink [kingk] *n* (*in rope etc*) enroscadura; (*in hair*) rizo; (*fig: emotional, psychological*) trauma *m*, manía.
kinky [king'kē] *a* (*pej*) perverso.
kinship [kin'ship] *n* parentesco, afinidad *f*.
kinsman [kinz'mən] *n* pariente *m*.
kinswoman [kinz'wōōmən] *n* parienta.
kiosk [kēásk'] *n* quiosco, (*Brit TEL*) cabina; **newspaper ~** quiosco, kiosco.
kipper [kip'ûr] *n* arenque *m* ahumado.
kiss [kis] *n* beso ♦ *vt* besar; **~ of life** (*Brit: artificial respiration*) respiración *f* artificial; **to ~ sb goodbye** dar un beso de despedida a uno; **to ~ (each other)** besarse.
kit [kit] *n* avíos *mpl*; (*equipment*) equipo; (*set of tools etc*) (caja de) herramientas *fpl*; (*assembly ~*) juego de armar; **tool ~** juego *or* estuche *m* de herramientas.
kit out *vt* (*Brit*) equipar.
kitbag [kit'bag] *n* (*MIL*) petate *m*.
kitchen [kich'ən] *n* cocina.
kitchen garden *n* huerto.
kitchen sink *n* fregadero.
kitchen unit *n* mueble *m* de cocina.
kitchenware [kich'ənwär] *n* batería de cocina.
kite [kīt] *n* (*toy*) cometa.
kith [kith] *n*: **~ and kin** parientes *mpl* y allegados.
kitten [kit'ən] *n* gatito/a.
kitty [kit'ē] *n* (*pool of money*) fondo común; (*CARDS*) puesta.
KKK *n abbr* (*US*) = *Ku Klux Klan*.
Kleenex [klē'nɛks] ® *n* pañuelo de papel.
kleptomaniac [klɛptəmā'nēak] *n* cleptómano/a.
km *abbr* (= *kilometer*) km.
km/h *abbr* (= *kilometers per hour*) km/h.
knack [nak] *n*: **to have the ~ of doing sth** tener el don de hacer algo.
knapsack [nap'sak] *n* mochila.
knead [nēd] *vt* amasar.
knee [nē] *n* rodilla.
kneecap [nē'kap] *n* rótula.
knee-deep [nē'dēp] *a*: **the water was ~** el agua llegaba hasta la rodilla.
kneel [nēl], *pt, pp* **knelt** [nēl, nɛlt] *vi* (*also*: **~ down**) arrodillarse.
kneepad [nē'pad] *n* rodillera.
knell [nɛl] *n* toque *m* de difuntos.
knelt [nɛlt] *pt, pp of* **kneel**.
knew [nōō] *pt of* **know**.
knickers [nik'ûrz] *npl* (*Brit*) bragas *fpl*.
knick-knack [nik'nak] *n* chuchería, baratija.
knife [nīf] (*pl* **knives**) *n* cuchillo ♦ *vt* acuchillar; **~, fork and spoon** cubiertos *mpl*.
knight [nīt] *n* caballero; (*CHESS*) caballo.
knighthood [nīt'hōōd] *n* (*Brit: title*): **to get a ~** recibir el título de *Sir*.
knit [nit] *vt* tejer, tricotar; (*brows*) fruncir; (*fig*): **to ~ together** unir, juntar ♦ *vi* tejer, tricotar; (*bones*) soldarse.
knitted [nit'id] *a* tejido.
knitting [nit'ing] *n* labor *f* de punto.
knitting machine *n* máquina de calcetar *or* tricotar.
knitting needle *n* aguja de tejer.
knitting pattern *n* patrón *m* para tricotar.
knitwear [nit'wär] *n* prendas *fpl* de punto.
knives [nīvz] *npl of* **knife**.
knob [nâb] *n* (*of door*) tirador *m*; (*of stick*) puño; (*lump*) bulto; (*fig*): **a ~ of butter**

(*Brit*) un pedazo de mantequilla.

knobby, [nâb'ē] (*Brit*) **knobbly** [nâb'lē] *a* (*wood, surface*) nudoso; (*knee*) huesudo.

knock [nâk] *vt* (*strike*) golpear; (*bump into*) chocar contra; (*fig: col*) criticar ♦ *vi* (*at door etc*): **to ~ at/on** llamar a ♦ *n* golpe *m*; (*on door*) llamada; **he ~ed at the door** llamó a la puerta.

knock down *vt* (*pedestrian*) atropellar; (*price*) rebajar.

knock off *vi* (*col: finish*) salir del trabajo ♦ *vt* (*col: steal*) birlar; (*strike off*) quitar; (*fig: from price, record*): **to ~ off $10** rebajar en $10.

knock out *vt* dejar sin sentido; (*BOXING*) poner fuera de combate, dejar K.O.; (*stop*) estropear, dejar fuera de servicio.

knock over *vt* (*object*) derribar, tirar; (*pedestrian*) atropellar.

knockdown [nâk'doun] *a* (*Brit: price*) de regalo.

knocker [nâk'ûr] *n* (*on door*) aldaba.

knock-for-knock [nâk'fûrnâk'] *a* (*Brit*): **~ agreement** acuerdo de pago respectivo.

knocking [nâk'ing] *n* golpes *mpl*, golpeteo.

knock-kneed [nâk'nēd] *a* patizambo.

knock-on effect [nâk'ân ifekt'] *n* repercusión *f*.

knockout [nâk'out] *n* (*BOXING*) K.O. *m*, knockout *m*.

knock-up [nâk'up] *n* (*Brit TENNIS*) peloteo.

knot [nât] *n* (*gen*) nudo ♦ *vt* anudar; **to tie a ~** anudar, atar.

knotted [nât'id] *a* anudado.

knotty [nât'ē] *a* (*fig*) complicado.

know [nō] *vb* (*pt* **knew**, *pp* **known** [nōō, nōn]) *vt* (*gen*) saber; (*person, author, place*) conocer ♦ *vi*: **as far as I ~ ...** que yo sepa ...; **yes, I ~** sí, ya lo sé; **I don't ~** no lo sé; **to ~ how to do** saber hacer; **to ~ how to swim** saber nadar; **to ~ about** *or* **of sb/sth** saber de uno/algo; **to get to ~ sth** enterarse de algo; **I ~ nothing about it** no sé nada de eso; **I don't ~ him** no lo *or* le conozco; **to ~ right from wrong** saber distinguir el bien del mal.

know-all [nō'ôl] *n* (*Brit pej*) = **know-it-all.**

know-how [nō'hou] *n* conocimientos *mpl*.

knowing [nō'ing] *a* (*look etc*) de complicidad.

knowingly [nō'inglē] *ad* (*purposely*) adrede; (*smile, look*) con complicidad.

know-it-all [nō'itôl] *n* (*US*) sabelotodo *m/f inv*, sabihondo/a.

knowledge [nâl'ij] *n* (*gen*) conocimiento; (*learning*) saber *m*, conocimientos *mpl*; **to have no ~ of** no saber nada de; **with my ~** con mis conocimientos, sabiéndolo; **to (the best of) my ~** a mi entender, que yo sepa; **not to my ~** que yo sepa, no; **it is common ~ that ...** es del dominio público que ...; **it has come to my ~ that ...** me he enterado de que ...; **to have a working**

~ of Spanish manejárselas con el español.

knowledgeable [nâl'ijəbəl] *a* entendido, erudito.

known [nōn] *pp of* **know** ♦ *a* (*thief, facts*) conocido; (*expert*) reconocido.

knuckle [nuk'əl] *n* nudillo.

knuckle under *vi* someterse.

knuckle-duster [nuk'əldustûr] *n* puño de hierro.

knucklehead [nuk'elhed] *n* (*US*) tonto/a.

KO *abbr n* (= *knockout*) K.O. *m* ♦ *vt* (= *knock out*) dejar K.O.

koala [kōâl'ə] *n* (*also*: **~ bear**) koala *m*.

kook [kōōk] *n* (*US col*) majareta *m/f*, excéntrico/a.

Koran [kôrân'] *n* Corán *m*.

Korea [kôrē'ə] *n* Corea; **North/South ~** Corea del Norte/Sur.

Korean [kôrē'ən] *a, n* coreano/a *m/f*.

kosher [kō'shûr] *a* autorizado por la ley judía.

kowtow [kou'tou] *vi*: **to ~ to sb** humillarse ante uno.

KS *abbr* (*US MAIL*) = *Kansas.*

Kuala Lumpur [kōōâ'lə lōōm'pōōr] *n* Kuala Lumpur *m*.

kudos [kyōō'dōs] *n* gloria, méritos *mpl*.

Kuwait [kōōwât'] *n* Kuwait *m*.

Kuwaiti [kōōât'ē] *a, n* Kuwaití *m/f*.

kW *abbr* (= *kilowatt*) Kv.

KY *abbr* (*US MAIL*) = *Kentucky.*

L

L, l [el] *n* (*letter*) L, l *f*; **L for Love** L de Lorenzo.

L *abbr* (*on maps etc*) = **lake; large;** (= *left*) izq.; (*Brit AUT*: = *learner*) L.

l. *abbr* = **liter.**

LA *n abbr* (*US*) = *Los Angeles* ♦ *abbr* (*US MAIL*) = *Louisiana.*

La. *abbr* (*US*) = *Louisiana.*

lab [lab] *n abbr* = **laboratory.**

Lab. *abbr* (*Canada*) = *Labrador.*

label [lā'bəl] *n* etiqueta; (*brand: of record*) sello (discográfico) ♦ *vt* poner etiqueta a.

labor [lā'bûr] (*US*) *n* (*task*) trabajo; (*~ force*) mano *f* de obra; (*workers*) trabajadores *mpl*; (*MED*) (dolores *mpl* de) parto ♦ *vi*: **to ~ (at)** trabajar (en) ♦ *vt* insistir en; **hard ~** trabajos *mpl* forzados; **to be in ~** estar de parto.

laboratory [lab'rətôrē] *n* laboratorio.

labor cost *n* costo de la mano de obra.

Labor Day *n* (*US*) día *m* del trabajador.

labor dispute *n* conflicto laboral.

labored [lā'bûrd] *a* (*breathing*) fatigoso; (*style*) forzado, pesado.

laborer [lā'bûrûr] *n* peón *m*; (*on farm*) peón *m*, obrero; (*day* ~) jornalero.

labor force *n* mano *f* de obra.

labor-intensive [lā'bûrintensiv] *a* intensivo en mano de obra.

laborious [ləbôr'ēəs] *a* penoso.

laboriously [ləbôr'ēəslē] *ad* penosamente.

labor relations *npl* relaciones *fpl* laborales.

labor-saving [lā'bûrsā'ving] *a* que ahorra trabajo.

labor union *n* (*US*) sindicato.

labor unrest *n* (*US*) conflictividad *f* laboral.

Labour [lā'bûr] *n* (*Brit POL: also:* **the ~ Party**) el partido laborista, los laboristas.

labour [lā'bûr] *etc* (*Brit*) = **labor** *etc*.

laburnum [ləbûr'nəm] *n* codeso.

labyrinth [lab'ûrinth] *n* laberinto.

lace [lās] *n* encaje *m*; (*of shoe etc*) cordón *m* ♦ *vt* (*shoes: also:* ~ **up**) atarse; (*drink: fortify with spirits*) echar licor a.

lacemaking [lās'māking] *n* obra de encaje.

lacerate [las'ərāt] *vt* lacerar.

laceration [lasərā'shən] *n* laceración *f*.

lace-up [lās'up] *a* (*shoes etc*) con cordones.

lack [lak] *n* (*absence*) falta, carencia; (*scarcity*) escasez *f* ♦ *vt* faltarle a uno, carecer de; **through** *or* **for** ~ **of** por falta de; **to be ~ing** faltar, no haber.

lackadaisical [lakədā'zikəl] *a* (*careless*) descuidado; (*indifferent*) indiferente.

lackey [lak'ē] *n* (*also fig*) lacayo.

lackluster, (*Brit*) **lacklustre** [lak'lustûr] *a* (*surface*) deslustrado, deslucido; (*style*) inexpresivo; (*eyes*) apagado.

laconic [ləkân'ik] *a* lacónico.

lacquer [lak'ûr] *n* laca; **hair** ~ (*Brit*) laca para el pelo.

lacrosse [ləkrôs'] *n* lacrosse *f*.

lacy [lā'sē] *a* (*like lace*) parecido al encaje.

lad [lad] *n* muchacho, chico; (*in stable etc*) mozo.

ladder [lad'ûr] *n* escalera (de mano); (*Brit: in tights*) carrera ♦ *vt* (*Brit: tights*) hacer una carrera en.

laden [lā'dən] *a:* ~ (**with**) cargado (de); **fully** ~ (*truck, ship*) cargado hasta el tope.

ladle [lā'dəl] *n* cucharón *m*.

lady [lā'dē] *n* señora; (*distinguished, noble*) dama; **young** ~ señorita; **the ladies' (room)** los servicios de señoras.

ladybug [lā'debug] *n* (*US*) mariquita.

lady doctor *n* médica, doctora.

lady-in-waiting [lā'dēinwā'ting] *n* dama de honor.

ladykiller [lā'dēkilûr] *n* ladrón *m* de corazones.

ladylike [lā'dēlīk] *a* fino.

lag [lag] *vi* (*also:* ~ **behind**) retrasarse, quedarse atrás ♦ *vt* (*pipes*) revestir.

lager [lâ'gûr] *n* cerveza (rubia).

lagging [lag'ing] *n* revestimiento.

lagoon [ləgōōn'] *n* laguna.

Lagos [lāg'ōs] *n* Lagos *m*.

laid [lād] *pt, pp* of **lay**.

laid-back [lād'bak'] *a* (*col*) tranquilo, relajado.

laid up *a:* **to be** ~ (*person*) tener que guardar cama.

lain [lān] *pp* of **lie**.

lair [lär] *n* guarida.

laissez-faire [lesâfär'] *n* laissez-faire *m*.

laity [lā'itē] *n* laicado *m*.

lake [lāk] *n* lago.

lamb [lam] *n* cordero; (*meat*) carne *f* de cordero.

lamb chop *n* chuleta de cordero.

lambswool [lamz'wōōl] *n* lana de cordero.

lame [lām] *a* cojo; (*weak*) débil, poco convincente; ~ **duck** (*fig: person*) inútil *m/f*; (*: firm*) empresa en quiebra.

lamely [lām'lē] *ad* (*fig*) sin convicción.

lament [ləment'] *n* lamento ♦ *vt* lamentarse de.

lamentable [ləmen'təbəl] *a* lamentable.

lamentation [ləməntā'shən] *n* lamento.

laminated [lam'ənātid] *a* laminado.

lamp [lamp] *n* lámpara.

lamplight [lamp'līt] *n:* **by** ~ a la luz de la lámpara.

lampoon [lampōōn'] *vt* satirizar.

lamppost [lamp'pōst] *n* (poste *m* de) farol *m*.

lampshade [lamp'shād] *n* pantalla.

lance [lans] *n* lanza ♦ *vt* (*MED*) abrir con lanceta.

lance corporal *n* ≈ soldado de primera clase.

lancet [lan'sit] *n* (*MED*) lanceta.

Lancs [langks] *abbr* (*Brit*) = Lancashire.

land [land] *n* tierra; (*country*) país *m*; (*piece of* ~) terreno; (*estate*) tierras *fpl*, finca; (*AGR*) campo ♦ *vi* (*from ship*) desembarcar; (*AVIAT*) aterrizar; (*fig: fall*) caer ♦ *vt* (*obtain*) conseguir; (*passengers, goods*) desembarcar; **to go/travel by** ~ ir/viajar por tierra; **to own** ~ ser dueño de tierras; **to** ~ **on one's feet** caer de pie; (*fig: to be lucky*) salir adelante.

land up *vi:* **to** ~ **up in/at** ir a parar a/en.

landing [lan'ding] *n* desembarco; aterrizaje *m*; (*of staircase*) rellano.

landing card *n* (*Brit*) tarjeta de desembarque.

landing craft *n* barca de desembarco.

landing gear *n* (*AVIAT*) tren *m* de aterrizaje.

landing strip *n* pista de aterrizaje.

landlady [land'lādē] *n* (*of boarding house*) patrona; (*owner*) dueña.

landlocked [land'lâkt] *a* cercado de tierra.

landlord [land'lôrd] *n* propietario; (*Brit: of*

pub etc) patrón *m*.

landlubber [land'lubûr] *n* marinero de agua dulce.

landmark [land'márk] *n* lugar *m* conocido; **to be a ~** (*fig*) hacer época.

landowner [land'ōnûr] *n* terrateniente *m/f*.

landscape [land'skāp] *n* paisaje *m*.

landscape architecture *n* arquitectura paisajista.

landscaped [land'skāpt] *a* reformado artísticamente.

landscape gardener *n* diseñador(a) *m/f* de paisajes.

landscape gardening *n* jardinería paisajista.

landscape painting *n* (*ART*) paisaje *m*.

landslide [land'slīd] *n* (*GEO*) corrimiento de tierras; (*fig*: *POL*) victoria arrolladora.

lane [lān] *n* (*in country*) camino; (*in town*) callejón *m*; (*AUT*) carril *m*; (*in race*) calle *f*; (*for air or sea traffic*) ruta; **shipping ~** ruta marina.

language [lang'gwij] *n* lenguaje *m*; (*national tongue*) idioma *m*, lengua; **bad ~** palabrotas *fpl*.

language laboratory *n* laboratorio de idiomas.

language studies *npl* estudios *mpl* filológicos.

languid [lang'gwid] *a* lánguido.

languish [lang'gwish] *vi* languidecer.

languor [lang'gûr] *n* languidez *f*.

languorous [lang'gûrəs] *a* lánguido.

lank [langk] *a* (*hair*) lacio.

lanky [lang'kē] *a* larguirucho.

lanolin [lan'əlin] *n* lanolina.

lantern [lan'tûrn] *n* linterna, farol *m*.

Laos [lâ'ōs] *n* Laos *m*.

lap [lap] *n* (*of track*) vuelta; (*of body*): **to sit on sb's ~** sentarse en las rodillas de uno ♦ *vt* (*also*: **~ up**) beber a lengüetadas ♦ *vi* (*waves*) chapotear.

lap up *vt* beber a lengüetadas; (*fig*: *compliments, attention*) disfrutar; (*lies etc*) tragarse.

La Paz [lá pâs'] *n* La Paz.

lapdog [lap'dôg] *n* perro faldero.

lapel [ləpel'] *n* solapa.

Lapland [lap'lənd] *n* Laponia.

Laplander [lap'landûr] *n* lapón/ona *m/f*.

lapse [laps] *n* (*fault*) error *m*, fallo; (*moral*) desliz *m* ♦ *vi* (*expire*) caducar; (*morally*) cometer un desliz; (*time*) pasar, transcurrir; **to ~ into bad habits** volver a las andadas; **~ of time** lapso, período; **a ~ of memory** un fallo de memoria.

laptop [lap'tâp] *n* (*also*: **~ computer**) ordenador *m* portátil.

larceny [lâr'sənē] *n* latrocinio.

lard [lârd] *n* manteca (de cerdo).

larder [lâr'dûr] *n* despensa.

large [lârj] *a* grande ♦ *ad*: **by and ~** en general, en términos generales; **at ~** (*free*)

en libertad; (*generally*) en general; **to make ~(r)** hacer mayor *or* más extenso; **a ~ number of people** una gran cantidad de personas; **on a ~ scale** en gran escala.

largely [lârj'lē] *ad* en gran parte.

large-scale [lârj'skāl] *a* (*map, drawing*) en gran escala; (*reforms, business activities*) importante.

largesse [lârjes'] *n* generosidad *f*.

lark [lârk] *n* (*bird*) alondra; (*Brit*: *joke*) broma.

lark about *vi* bromear, hacer el tonto.

larva, *pl* **larvae** [lâr'və, -ē] *n* larva.

laryngitis [larənjī'tis] *n* laringitis *f*.

larynx [lar'ingks] *n* laringe *f*.

lascivious [ləsiv'ēəs] *a* lascivo.

laser [lā'zûr] *n* láser *m*.

laser beam [lā'zûr bēm] *n* rayo láser.

laser printer *n* impresora (por) láser.

lash [lash] *n* latigazo; (*punishment*) azote *m*; (*also*: **eyelash**) pestaña ♦ *vt* azotar; (*tie*) atar.

lash down *vt* sujetar con cuerdas ♦ *vi* (*rain*) caer a trombas.

lash out *vi* (*Brit*: *col*: *spend*) gastar a la loca; **to ~ out** *at or* **against sb** lanzar invectivas contra uno.

lashing [lash'ing] *n* (*beating*) azotaina, flagelación *f*.

lass [las] *n* (*Brit*) chica.

lassitude [las'ətōōd] *n* lasitud *f*.

lasso [las'ō] *n* lazo ♦ *vt* coger con lazo.

last [last] *a* (*gen*) último; (*final*) último, final ♦ *ad* por último ♦ *vi* (*endure*) durar; (*continue*) continuar, seguir; **~ night** anoche; **~ week** la semana pasada; **at ~** por fin; **next to (the) ~** penúltimo; **~ time** la última vez; **it ~s (for) 2 hours** dura dos horas.

last-ditch [last'dich'] *a* (*attempt*) de último recurso, último, desesperado.

lasting [las'ting] *a* duradero.

lastly [last'lē] *ad* por último, finalmente.

last-minute [last'min'it] *a* de última hora.

latch [lach] *n* picaporte *m*, pestillo.

latch on to *vt fus* (*cling to*: *person*) pegarse a; (: *idea*) agarrarse de.

latchkey [lach'kē] *n* llavín *m*.

latchkey child *n* niño cuyos padres trabajan.

late [lāt] *a* (*not on time*) tarde, atrasado; (*towards end of period, life*) tardío; (*hour*) avanzado; (*dead*) fallecido ♦ *ad* tarde; (*behind time, schedule*) con retraso; **to be (10 minutes) ~** llegar con (diez minutos de) retraso; **to be ~ with** estar atrasado con; **~ delivery** entrega tardía; **~ in life** a una edad avanzada; **of ~** últimamente; **in ~ May** hacia fines de mayo; **the ~ Mr X** el difunto Sr X; **to work ~** trabajar hasta tarde.

latecomer [lāt'kumûr] *n* recién llegado/a.

lately [lāt'lē] *ad* últimamente.

lateness [lāt'nis] *n* (*of person*) demora; (*of*

event) tardanza.

latent [lā'tənt] *a* latente; ~ **defect** defecto latente.

later [lā'tûr] *a* (*date etc*) posterior; (*version etc*) más reciente ♦ *ad* más tarde, después; ~ **on today** hoy más tarde.

lateral [lat'ûrəl] *a* lateral.

latest [lā'tist] *a* último; **at the** ~ a más tardar.

latex [lā'tɛks] *n* látex *m*.

lathe [lātʰ] *n* torno.

lather [latʰ'ûr] *n* espuma (de jabón) ♦ *vt* enjabonar.

Latin [lat'in] *n* latín *m* ♦ *a* latino.

Latin America *n* América Latina, Latinoamérica.

Latin American *a, n* latinoamericano/a *m/f*.

latitude [lat'ətōōd] *n* latitud *f*; (*fig: freedom*) latitud *f*, libertad *f*.

latrine [lətrēn'] *n* letrina.

latter [lat'ûr] *a* último; (*of two*) segundo ♦ *n*: **the** ~ el último, éste.

latter-day [lat'ûrdā] *a* moderno.

latterly [lat'ûrlē] *ad* últimamente.

lattice [lat'is] *n* enrejado.

lattice window [lat'is win'dō] *n* ventana enrejada *or* de celosía.

lattice work *n* enrejado.

Latvia [lat'vēə] *n* Letonia, Latvia.

laudable [lô'dəbəl] *a* loable.

laugh [laf] *n* risa; (*loud*) carcajada ♦ *vi* reírse, reír; reírse a carcajadas.
  laugh at *vt fus* reírse de.
  laugh off *vt* tomar a risa.

laughable [laf'əbəl] *a* ridículo.

laughing [laf'ing] *a* risueño ♦ *n*: **it's no** ~ **matter** no es cosa de risa.

laughing gas *n* gas *m* hilarante.

laughing stock *n*: **to be the** ~ **of the town** ser el hazmerreír de la ciudad.

laughter [laf'tûr] *n* risa.

launch [lônch] *n* (*boat*) lancha; *see also* **launching** ♦ *vt* (*ship, rocket, plan*) lanzar.
  launch forth *vi*: **to** ~ **forth (into)** lanzarse a *or* en, emprender.
  launch out *vi* = **launch forth**.

launching [lôn'ching] *n* (*of rocket etc*) lanzamiento; (*inauguration*) estreno.

launch(ing) pad *n* plataforma de lanzamiento.

launder [lôn'dûr] *vt* lavar.

launderette [lôndəret'] *n* (*Brit*) lavandería (automática).

laundromat [lôn'drəmat] *n* (*US*) lavandería (automática).

laundry [lôn'drē] *n* lavandería; (*clothes*) ropa sucia; **to do the** ~ hacer la colada.

laureate [lô'rēit] *a see* **poet**.

laurel [lôr'əl] *n* laurel *m*; **to rest on one's** ~**s** dormirse en *or* sobre los laureles.

lava [láv'ə] *n* lava.

lavatory [lav'ətôrē] *n* wáter *m*; **lavatories** *npl* servicios *mpl*, aseos *mpl*, sanitarios *mpl* (*LAm*).

lavender [lav'əndûr] *n* lavanda.

lavish [lav'ish] *a* abundante; (*giving freely*): ~ **with** pródigo en ♦ *vt*: **to** ~ **sth on sb** colmar a uno de algo.

lavishly [lav'ishlē] *ad* (*give, spend*) generosamente, liberalmente; (*furnished*) lujosamente.

law [lô] *n* ley *f*; (*study*) derecho; (*of game*) regla; **against the** ~ contra la ley; **to study** ~ estudiar derecho.

law-abiding [lô'əbīding] *a* respetuoso de la ley.

law and order *n* orden *m* público.

lawbreaker [lô'brākûr] *n* infractor(a) *m/f* de la ley.

law court *n* (*Brit*) tribunal *m* (de justicia).

lawful [lô'fəl] *a* legítimo, lícito.

lawfully [lô'fəlē] *ad* legalmente.

lawless [lô'lis] *a* (*act*) ilegal; (*person*) rebelde; (*country*) ingobernable.

lawmaker [lô'mākûr] *n* legislador(a) *m/f*.

lawn [lôn] *n* césped *m*.

lawnmower [lôn'mōûr] *n* cortacésped *m*.

lawn tennis *n* tenis *m* sobre hierba.

law school *n* (*US*) facultad *f* de derecho.

law student [lô' stōōd'ənt] *n* estudiante *m/f* de derecho.

lawsuit [lô'sōōt] *n* pleito; **to bring a** ~ **against** levantar pleito contra.

lawyer [lô'yûr] *n* abogado/a; (*for sales, wills etc*) notario/a.

lax [laks] *a* (*discipline*) relajado; (*person*) negligente.

laxative [lak'sətiv] *n* laxante *m*.

laxity [lak'sitē] *n* flojedad *f*; (*moral*) relajamiento; (*negligence*) negligencia.

lay [lā] *pt of* **lie** ♦ *a* laico; (*not expert*) lego ♦ *vt* (*pt, pp* **laid** [lād]) (*place*) colocar; (*eggs, Brit: table*) poner; (*trap*) tender; **to** ~ **the facts/one's proposals before sb** presentar los hechos/sus propuestas a uno.
  lay aside, lay by *vt* dejar a un lado.
  lay down *vt* (*pen etc*) dejar; (*arms*) rendir; (*policy*) asentar; **to** ~ **down the law** imponer las normas.
  lay in *vt* abastecerse de.
  lay into *vt fus* (*col: attack, scold*) arremeterse contra.
  lay off *vt* (*workers*) despedir.
  lay on *vt* (*Brit*) (*water, gas*) instalar; (*meal, facilities*) proveer.
  lay out *vt* (*plan*) trazar; (*display*) disponer; (*spend*) gastar.
  lay up *vt* (*store*) guardar; (*ship*) desarmar; (*subj: illness*) obligar a guardar cama.

layabout [lā'əbout] *n* (*Brit*) vago/a.

lay-by [lā'bī] *n* (*Brit AUT*) apartadero.

lay days *npl* días *mpl* de detención *or* inactividad.

layer [lā'ûr] *n* capa.

layette [lā'et'] *n* ajuar *m* (de niño).

layman [lā'mən] *n* lego.

layoff [lā'ôf] *n* despido, paro forzoso.

layout [lā'out] *n* (*design*) plan *m*, trazado; (*disposition*) disposición *f*; (*PRESS*) composición *f*.

layover [lā'ōvûr] *n* (*US*) parada intermedia; (: *AVIAT*) escala.

laze [lāz] *vi* no hacer nada; (*pej*) holgazanear.

lazily [lā'zilē] *ad* perezosamente.

laziness [lā'zēnis] *n* pereza.

lazy [lā'zē] *a* perezoso, vago.

LB *abbr* (*Canada*) = *Labrador*.

lb. *abbr* = **pound** (*weight*).

LC *n abbr* (*US*) = *Library of Congress*.

lc *abbr* (*TYP*: = *lower case*) min.

L/C *abbr* = **letter of credit.**

LCD *n abbr see* **liquid crystal display.**

LDS *n abbr* (= *Latter-day Saints*) Iglesia de Jesucristo de los Santos de los últimos días.

lead [lēd] *n* (*front position*) delantera; (*distance, time ahead*) ventaja; (*clue*) pista; (*ELEC*) cable *m*; (*Brit: for dog*) correa; (*THEATER*) papel *m* principal; [led] (*metal*) plomo; (*in pencil*) mina ♦ *vb* (*pt, pp* **led** [led]) *vt* conducir; (*life*) llevar; (*be leader of*) dirigir; (*SPORT*) ir en cabeza de; (*orchestra: US*) dirigir; (: *Brit*) ser el primer violín en ♦ *vi* ir primero; **to be in the ~** (*SPORT*) llevar la delantera; (*fig*) ir a la cabeza; **to take the ~** (*SPORT*) tomar la delantera; (*fig*) tomar la iniciativa; **to ~ sb to believe that ...** hacer creer a uno que ...; **to ~ sb to do sth** llevar a uno a hacer algo.

lead astray *vt* llevar por mal camino.

lead away *vt* llevar.

lead back *vt* hacer volver.

lead off *vt* llevar ♦ *vi* (*in game*) abrir.

lead on *vt* (*tease*) engañar; **to ~ sb on to** (*induce*) incitar a uno a.

lead to *vt fus* producir, provocar.

lead up to *vt fus* conducir a.

leaded [led'id] *a*: **~ windows** ventanas *fpl* emplomadas.

leaden [led'ən] *a* (*sky, sea*) plomizo; (*heavy: footsteps*) pesado.

leader [lē'dûr] *n* jefe/a *m/f*, líder *m*; (*of union etc*) dirigente *m/f*; (*of orchestra: US*) director(a) *m/f*; (: *Brit*) primer violín *m*; (*guide*) guía *m/f*; (*Brit: of newspaper*) artículo de fondo; **they are ~s in their field** (*fig*) llevan la delantera en su especialidad.

leadership [lē'dûrship] *n* dirección *f*; **qualities of ~** iniciativa *sg*; **under the ~ of ...** bajo la dirección de ..., al mando de ....

lead-free [ledfrē'] *a* sin plomo.

leading [lē'ding] *a* (*main*) principal; (*outstanding*) destacado; (*first*) primero; (*front*) delantero; **a ~ question** una pregunta tendenciosa.

leading lady *n* (*THEATER*) primera actriz *f*.

leading light *n* (*fig: person*) figura principal.

leading man *n* (*THEATER*) primer actor *m*.

leading role *n* papel *m* principal.

lead pencil [led pen'səl] *n* lápiz *m*.

lead poisoning [led' poi'zəning] *n* envenenamiento plúmbico.

lead time *n* (*COMM*) plazo de entrega.

lead weight [led wāt] *n* peso de plomo.

leaf, *pl* **leaves** [lēf, lēvz] *n* hoja; **to turn over a new ~** (*fig*) volver la hoja, hacer borrón y cuenta nueva; **to take a ~ out of sb's book** (*fig*) seguir el ejemplo de uno.

leaf through *vt fus* (*book*) hojear.

leaflet [lēf'lit] *n* folleto.

leafy [lē'fē] *a* frondoso.

league [lēg] *n* sociedad *f*; (*SPORTS*) liga; **to be in ~ with** estar de manga con.

leak [lēk] *n* (*of liquid, gas*) escape *m*, fuga; (*in pipe*) agujero; (*in roof*) gotera; (*fig: of information, in security*) filtración *f* ♦ *vi* (*shoes, ship*) hacer agua; (*pipe*) tener (un) escape; (*roof*) gotear; (*also: ~ out: liquid, gas*) escaparse, fugarse; (*fig: news*) divulgarse ♦ *vt* (*gen*) dejar escapar; (*fig: information*) filtrarse.

leakage [lē'kij] *n* (*of water, gas etc*) goteo, filtración *f*.

leaky [lē'kē] *a* (*pipe, bucket, roof*) que tiene goteras; (*shoe*) que deja entrar el agua; (*boat*) que hace agua.

lean [lēn] *a* (*thin*) flaco; (*meat*) magro ♦ *vb* (*pt, pp* **leaned** *or* **leant** [lent]) *vt*: **to ~ sth on sth** apoyar algo en algo ♦ *vi* (*slope*) inclinarse; (*rest*): **to ~ against** apoyarse contra; **to ~ on** apoyarse en.

lean back *vi* inclinarse hacia atrás.

lean forward *vi* inclinarse hacia adelante.

lean out *vi*: **to ~ out (of)** asomarse (de).

lean over *vi* inclinarse.

leaning [lē'ning] *a* inclinado ♦ *n*: **~ (towards)** inclinación *f* (hacia); **the L~ Tower of Pisa** la Torre Inclinada de Pisa.

leant [lent] *pt, pp of* **lean.**

lean-to [lēn'tōō] *n* (*roof*) tejado de una sola agua; (*building*) cobertizo.

leap [lēp] *n* salto ♦ *vi* (*pt, pp* **leaped** *or* **leapt** [lept]) saltar; **to ~ at an offer** apresurarse a aceptar una oferta.

leap up *vi* (*person*) saltar.

leapfrog [lēp'frâg] *n* pídola ♦ *vi*: **to ~ over sb/sth** saltar por encima de uno/algo.

leapt [lept] *pt, pp of* **leap.**

leap year *n* año bisiesto.

learn, *pt, pp* **learned** *or* **learnt** [lûrn, -t] *vt* (*gen*) aprender; (*come to know of*) enterarse de ♦ *vi* aprender; **to ~ how to do sth** aprender a hacer algo; **to ~ that ...**

enterarse *or* informarse de que ...; **to ~ about sth** (*SCOL*) hacer clase de algo; (*hear*) enterarse *or* informarse de algo; **we were sorry to ~ that ...** nos dio tristeza saber que ....

learned [lûr'nid] *a* erudito.

learner [lûr'nûr] *n* principiante *m/f*; (*Brit: also:* **~ driver**) aprendiz(a) *m/f*.

learning [lûr'ning] *n* saber *m*, conocimientos *mpl*.

learnt [lûrnt] *pp of* **learn**.

lease [lēs] *n* arriendo ♦ *vt* arrendar; **on ~** en arriendo.

lease back *vt* (*Brit*) subarrendar.

leasehold [lēs'hōld] *n* (*contract*) derechos *mpl* de arrendamiento ♦ *a* arrendado.

leash [lēsh] *n* correa.

least [lēst] *a* (*slightest*) menor, más pequeño; (*smallest amount of*) mínimo ♦ *ad* menos ♦ *n*: **the ~** lo menos; **the ~ expensive car** el coche menos costoso; **at ~** por lo menos, al menos; **not in the ~** en absoluto.

leather [leth'ûr] *n* cuero ♦ *cpd*: **~ goods** artículos *mpl* de cuero.

leathery [leth'ûrē] *a* (*skin*) curtido.

leave [lēv] *vb* (*pt, pp* **left** [left]) *vt* dejar; (*go away from*) abandonar ♦ *vi* irse; (*train*) salir ♦ *n* permiso; **to ~ school** salir del colegio; **~ it to me!** ¡yo me encargo!; **he's already left for the airport** ya se ha marchado al aeropuerto; **to be left** quedar, sobrar; **there's some milk left over** sobra *or* queda algo de leche; **on ~** de permiso; **to take one's ~ of** despedirse de; **on ~ of absence** con permiso de ausentarse.

leave behind *vt* (*on purpose*) dejar (atrás); (*accidentally*) olvidar.

leave off *vt* (*lid*) no reemplazar; (*switch*) no encender.

leave on *vt* (*lid*) dejar puesto; (*light, heater, stove*) dejar encendido.

leave out *vt* omitir.

leave over *vt* (*Brit: postpone*) dejar.

leave of absence *n* permiso de ausentarse.

leaves [lēvz] *pl of* **leaf**.

leavetaking [lēv'tāking] *n* despedida.

Lebanon [leb'ənən] *n*: **the ~** el Líbano.

lecherous [lech'ûrəs] *a* lascivo.

lectern [lek'tûrn] *n* atril *m*.

lecture [lek'chûr] *n* conferencia, (*SCOL*) clase *f* ♦ *vi* dar una clase ♦ *vt* (*scold*) sermonear; (*reprove*) echar una reprimenda a; **to give a ~ on** dar una conferencia sobre.

lecture hall *n* aula, sala de conferencias.

lecturer [lek'chûrûr] *n* conferenciante *m/f*; (*at university*) profesor(a) *m/f*.

LED *n abbr* (= *light-emitting diode*) LED *m*.

led [led] *pt, pp of* **lead**.

ledge [lej] *n* (*of window, on wall*) repisa, reborde *m*; (*of mountain*) saliente *m*.

ledger [lej'ûr] *n* libro mayor.

lee [lē] *n* sotavento; **in the ~ of** al abrigo de.

leech [lēch] *n* sanguijuela.

leek [lēk] *n* puerro.

leer [lēr] *vi*: **to ~ at sb** mirar de manera lasciva a uno.

leeward [lē'wûrd] *a* (*NAUT*) de sotavento ♦ *n* (*NAUT*) sotavento; **to ~** a sotavento.

leeway [lē'wā] *n* (*fig*): **to have some ~** tener cierta libertad de acción.

left [left] *pt, pp of* **leave** ♦ *a* izquierdo ♦ *n* izquierda ♦ *ad* a la izquierda; **on** *or* **to the ~** a la izquierda; **the L~** (*POL*) la izquierda.

left-hand drive [left'hand' drīv] *n* conducción *f* a la izquierda.

left-handed [left'han'did] *a* zurdo; **~ scissors** tijeras *fpl* zurdas *or* para zurdos.

left-hand side [left'hand' sīd] *n* la izquierda.

leftist [lef'tist] *a* (*POL*) izquierdista.

left-luggage (office) [leftlug'ij (ôf'is)] *n* (*Brit*) consigna.

leftovers [left'ōvûrz] *npl* sobras *fpl*.

left-wing [left'wing] *a* (*POL*) de izquierda, izquierdista.

left-winger [left'wingûr] *n* (*POL*) izquierdista *m/f*.

leg [leg] *n* pierna; (*of animal*) pata; (*of chair*) pie *m*; (*CULIN: of meat*) pierna; (*of journey*) etapa; **lst/2nd ~** (*SPORT*) partido de ida/de vuelta; **to pull sb's ~** bromear con uno; **to stretch one's ~s** dar una vuelta.

legacy [leg'əsē] *n* herencia; (*fig*) herencia, patrimonio.

legal [lē'gəl] *a* (*permitted by law*) lícito; (*of law*) legal; (*inquiry etc*) jurídico; **to take ~ action** *or* **proceedings against sb** entablar *or* levantar pleito contra uno.

legal adviser *n* asesor(a) *m/f* jurídico/a.

legal holiday *n* (*US*) fiesta oficial.

legality [lēgal'itē] *n* legalidad *f*.

legalize [lē'gəlīz] *vt* legalizar.

legally [lē'gəlē] *ad* legalmente; **~ binding** con fuerza legal.

legal tender *n* moneda de curso legal.

legatee [legətē'] *n* legatario/a.

legation [ligā'shən] *n* legación *f*.

legend [lej'ənd] *n* leyenda.

legendary [lej'əndärē] *a* legendario.

-legged [leg'id] *suff*: **two~** (*table etc*) de dos patas.

leggings [leg'ingz] *npl* polainas *fpl*.

legibility [lejəbil'ətē] *n* legibilidad *f*.

legible [lej'əbəl] *a* legible.

legibly [lej'əblē] *ad* legiblemente.

legion [lē'jən] *n* legión *f*.

legionnaire [lējənär'] *n* legionario.

legionnaire's disease *n* enfermedad *f* del legionario.

legislation [lejislā'shən] *n* legislación *f*; **a piece of ~** (*bill*) un proyecto de ley; (*act*) una ley.

legislative [lej'islātiv] *a* legislativo.

legislator [lej'islātûr] *n* legislador(a) *m/f*.

legislature [lej'islāchûr] *n* cuerpo legislativo.

legitimacy [lijit'əməsē] *n* legitimidad *f*.

legitimate [lijit'əmit] *a* legítimo.

legitimize [lijit'əmīz] *vt* legitimar.

leg-room [leg'rōōm] *n* espacio para las piernas.

leg warmers [leg wôr'mûrz] *npl* calientapiernas *mpl*.

Leics *abbr* (*Brit*) = *Leicestershire*.

leisure [lē'zhûr] *n* ocio, tiempo libre; **at ~** con tranquilidad.

leisurely [lē'zhûrlē] *a* sin prisa; lento.

leisure suit *n* conjunto tipo chandal.

lemon [lem'ən] *n* limón *m*.

lemonade [lemənād'] *n* (*fruit juice*) limonada; (*fizzy*) gaseosa.

lemon cheese, lemon curd *n* queso de limón.

lemon juice *n* zumo de limón.

lemon tea *n* té *m* con limón.

lend, *pt, pp* **lent** [lend, lent] *vt*: **to ~ sth to sb** prestar algo a uno.

lender [len'dûr] *n* prestador(a) *m/f*.

lending library [len'ding lī'brārē] *n* biblioteca circulante.

length [lengkth] *n* (*size*) largo, longitud *f*; (*section*: *of road, pipe*) tramo; (: *of rope etc*) largo; **at ~** (*at last*) por fin, finalmente; (*lengthily*) largamente; **it is 2 meters in ~** tiene dos metros de largo; **what ~ is it?** ¿cuánto tiene de largo?; **to fall full ~** (*Brit*) caer de bruces; **to go to any ~(s) to do sth** ser capaz de hacer cualquier cosa para hacer algo.

lengthen [lengk'thən] *vt* alargar ♦ *vi* alargarse.

lengthwise [length'wīz] *ad* a lo largo.

lengthy [lengk'thē] *a* largo, extenso; (*meeting*) prolongado.

lenient [lē'nēənt] *a* indulgente.

lens [lenz] *n* (*of spectacles*) lente *f*; (*of camera*) objetivo.

Lent [lent] *n* Cuaresma.

lent [lent] *pt, pp of* **lend**.

lentil [len'təl] *n* lenteja.

Leo [lē'ō] *n* Leo.

leopard [lep'ûrd] *n* leopardo.

leotard [lē'ətârd] *n* leotardo.

leper [lep'ûr] *n* leproso/a.

leper colony *n* colonia de leprosos.

leprosy [lep'rəsē] *n* lepra.

lesbian [lez'bēən] *a* lesbiano ♦ *n* lesbiana.

lesion [lē'zhən] *n* (*MED*) lesión *f*.

Lesotho [lisōō'tōō] *n* Lesotho.

less [les] *a* (*in size, degree etc*) menor; (*in quantity*) menos ♦ *pron, ad* menos; **~ than half** menos de la mitad; **~ than $1/a kilo/3 meters** menos de un dólar/un kilo/tres metros; **~ than ever** menos que nunca; **~ 5%** menos el cinco por ciento; **~ and ~** cada

vez menos; **the ~ he works...** cuanto menos trabaja ....

lessee [lesē'] *n* inquilino/a, arrendatario/a.

lessen [les'ən] *vi* disminuir, reducirse ♦ *vt* disminuir, reducir.

lesser [les'ûr] *a* menor; **to a ~ extent** *or* **degree** en menor grado.

lesson [les'ən] *n* clase *f*; **an English ~** una clase de inglés; **to give ~s in** dar clases de; **it taught him a ~** (*fig*) le sirvió de lección.

lessor [les'ôr] *n* arrendador(a) *m/f*.

lest [lest] *conj*: **~ it happen** para que no pase.

let, *pt, pp* **let** [let] *vt* (*allow*) dejar, permitir; (*Brit: lease*) alquilar; **to ~ sb do sth** dejar que uno haga algo; **to ~ sb have sth** dar algo a uno; **to ~ sb know sth** comunicar algo a uno; **~'s go** ¡vamos!; **~ him come** que venga; **"to ~"** (*Brit*) "se alquila".

let down *vt* (*lower*) bajar; (*dress*) alargar; (*tire*) desinflar; (*hair*) soltar; (*disappoint*) defraudar.

let go *vi* soltar; (*fig*) dejarse ir ♦ *vt* soltar.

let in *vt* dejar entrar; (*visitor etc*) hacer pasar; **what have you ~ yourself in for?** ¿en qué te has metido?

let off *vt* dejar escapar; (*firework etc*) disparar; (*bomb*) accionar; (*passenger*) dejar, bajar; **to ~ off steam** (*fig, col*) desahogarse, desfogarse.

let on *vi*: **to ~ on that ...** revelar que ...

let out *vt* dejar salir; (*dress*) ensanchar; (*Brit: rent out*) alquilar.

let up *vi* amainar, disminuir.

letdown [let'doun] *n* (*disappointment*) decepción *f*.

lethal [lē'thəl] *a* (*weapon*) mortífero; (*poison, wound*) mortal.

lethargic [ləthâr'jik] *a* aletargado.

lethargy [leth'ûrjē] *n* letargo.

letter [let'ûr] *n* (*of alphabet*) letra; (*correspondence*) carta; **~s** *npl* (*literature, learning*) letras *fpl*; **~s to the editor** (*sección f de*) cartas *fpl* al director; **small/capital ~** minúscula/mayúscula; **cover ~** carta adjunta.

letter bomb *n* carta-bomba.

letterbox [let'ûrbåks] *n* (*Brit*) buzón *m*.

letterhead [let'ûrhed] *n* membrete *m*, encabezamiento.

lettering [let'ûring] *n* letras *fpl*.

letter of credit *n* carta de crédito; **documentary ~** carta de crédito documentaria; **irrevocable ~** carta de crédito irrevocable.

letter-opener [let'ûrōpənûr] *n* abrecartas *m inv*.

letterpress [let'ûrpres] *n* (*method*) prensa de copiar; (*printed page*) impresión *f* tipográfica.

letter quality *n* calidad *f* de correspondencia.

letters patent *npl* letra *sg* de patente.

lettuce [let'is] *n* lechuga.

letup [let'up] *n* descanso, tregua.

leukemia, (*Brit*) **leukaemia** [lo͞oke͞'me͞ə] *n* leucemia.

level [lev'əl] *a* (*flat*) llano; (*flattened*) nivelado; (*uniform*) igual ♦ *ad* a nivel ♦ *n* nivel *m* ♦ *vt* nivelar, allanar; (*gun*) apuntar; (*accusation*): **to ~ (against)** levantar (contra) ♦ *vi* (*col*): **to ~ with sb** ser franco con uno; **to be ~ with** estar a nivel de; **a ~ spoonful** (*CULIN*) una cucharada rasa; **to draw ~ with** (*Brit*: *team*) igualar; (*runner, car*) alcanzar a; **"A" ~s** *npl* (*Brit*) ≈ Bachillerato Superior *sg*, B.U.P. *msg*; **"O" ~s** *npl* (*Brit*) ≈ bachillerato *sg* elemental, octavo *sg* de básica; **on the ~** (*fig: honest*) en serio; **talks at ministerial ~** charlas *fpl* a nivel ministerial.

level off *or* **out** *vi* (*prices etc*) estabilizarse; (*ground*) nivelarse; (*aircraft*) ponerse en una trayectoria horizontal.

level crossing *n* (*Brit*) paso a nivel.

levelheaded [lev'əlhed'id] *a* sensato.

leveling, (*Brit*) **levelling** [lev'əling] *a* (*process, effect*) de nivelación ♦ *n* igualación *f*, allanamiento.

lever [lev'ûr] *n* palanca ♦ *vt*: **to ~ up** levantar con palanca.

leverage [lev'úrij] *n* (*fig: influence*) influencia.

levity [lev'itē] *n* frivolidad *f*, informalidad *f*.

levy [lev'ē] *n* impuesto ♦ *vt* exigir, recaudar.

lewd [lo͞od] *a* lascivo; obsceno, colorado (*LAm*).

LF *n abbr* (= *low frequency*) baja frecuencia.

LI *abbr* (*US*) = *Long Island*.

liabilities [liəbil'ətēz] *npl* obligaciones *fpl*; pasivo *sg*.

liability [liəbil'ətē] *n* responsabilidad *f*; (*handicap*) desventaja.

liability insurance *n* (*US*) seguro contra terceros.

liable [li'əbəl] *a* (*subject*): **~ to** sujeto a; (*responsible*): **~ for** responsable de; (*likely*): **~ to do** propenso a hacer; **to be ~ to a fine** ser expuesto a una multa.

liaise [lēāz'] *vi* (*Brit*): **to ~ (with)** colaborar (con); **to ~ with sb** mantener informado a uno.

liaison [lēā'zân] *n* (*coordination*) enlace *m*; (*affair*) relación *f*.

liar [li'ûr] *n* mentiroso/a.

libel [li'bəl] *n* calumnia ♦ *vt* calumniar.

libel(l)ous [li'bələs] *a* difamatorio, calumnioso.

liberal [lib'ûrəl] *a* (*gen*) liberal; (*generous*): **~ with** generoso con ♦ *n*: **L~** (*POL*) liberal *m/f*.

liberality [libəral'itē] *n* (*generosity*) liberalidad *f*, generosidad *f*.

liberalize [lib'ûrəlīz] *vt* liberalizar.

liberally [lib'ûrəlē] *ad* liberalmente.

liberal-minded [lib'ûrəlmīn'did] *a* de miras anchas.

liberate [lib'ərāt] *vt* liberar.

liberation [libərā'shən] *n* liberación *f*.

Liberia [lībē'rēə] *n* Liberia.

Liberian [lībē'rēən] *a, n* liberiano/a *m/f*.

liberty [lib'ûrtē] *n* libertad *f*; **to be at ~ to do** estar libre para hacer; **to take the ~ of doing sth** tomarse la libertad de hacer algo.

libido [libē'dō] *n* libido.

Libra [lēb'rə] *n* Libra.

librarian [lībrär'ēən] *n* bibliotecario/a.

library [li'brärē] *n* biblioteca.

library book *n* libro de la biblioteca.

libretto [libret'ō] *n* libreto.

Libya [lib'ēə] *n* Libia.

Libyan [lib'ēən] *a, n* libio/a *m/f*.

lice [līs] *pl of* **louse**.

licence [lī'səns] *n* (*Brit*) = **license**.

license [lī'səns] *n* (*US*) licencia; (*permit*) permiso; (*also*: **driver's ~**, (*Brit*) **driving licence**) carnet *m* de conducir; (*excessive freedom*) libertad *f* ♦ *vt* autorizar, dar permiso a; (*car*) sacar la patente *or* la matrícula de; **import ~** licencia *or* permiso de importación; **produced under ~** elaborado bajo licencia.

licensed [lī'sənst] *a* (*for alcohol*) autorizado para vender bebidas alcohólicas.

license plate *n* placa (de matrícula).

licentious [līsen'chəs] *a* licencioso.

lichen [lī'kən] *n* liquen *m*.

lick [lik] *vt* lamer; (*col: defeat*) dar una paliza a ♦ *n* lamedura; **a ~ of paint** una mano de pintura.

licorice [lik'ûris] *n* (*US*) regaliz *m*.

lid [lid] *n* (*of box, case*) tapa; (*of pan*) cobertera; **to take the ~ off sth** (*fig*) exponer algo a la luz pública.

lido [lē'dō] *n* (*Brit*) piscina, alberca (*LAm*).

lie [lī] *n* mentira ♦ *vi* mentir; (*pt lay, pp lain* [lā, lān]) (*rest*) estar echado, estar acostado; (*of object: be situated*) estar, encontrarse; (*to tell ~s*) mentir; **to ~ low** (*fig*) mantenerse a escondidas.

lie around *vi* (*things*) estar tirado; (*people*) estar acostado *or* tumbado.

lie back *vi* recostarse.

lie down *vi* acostarse.

lie up *vi* (*Brit*: *hide*) esconderse.

Liechtenstein [lēch'tenstīn] *n* Liechtenstein *m*.

lie detector *n* detector *m* de mentiras.

lieu [lo͞o]: **in ~ of** *prep* en lugar de.

Lieut *abbr* = **lieutenant**.

lieutenant [lo͞oten'ənt] *n* (*MIL*) teniente *m*.

lieutenant colonel *n* teniente *m* colonel.

life, *pl* **lives** [līf, līvz] *n* vida; (*way of ~*) modo de vivir; (*of license etc*) vigencia; **to be sent to prison for ~** ser condenado a reclusión *or* cadena perpetua; **country/city** ~ la vida del campo/de la ciudad; **true to** ~ fiel a la realidad; **to paint from** ~ pintar del natural; **to put** *or* **breathe new** ~ **into** (*person*) reanimar; (*project, area etc*) infundir nueva vida a.

life annuity *n* anualidad *f* vitalicia.

life belt *n* cinturón *m* salvavidas.

lifeblood [līf'blud] *n* (*fig*) alma, nervio.

lifeboat [līf'bōt] *n* lancha de socorro.

lifebuoy [līf'boi] *n* boya *or* guindola salvavidas.

life expectancy *n* esperanza de vida.

lifeguard [līf'gârd] *n* vigilante *m/f*.

life imprisonment *n* cadena perpetua.

life insurance *n* (*Brit*) seguro de vida.

life jacket *n* chaleco salvavidas.

lifeless [līf'lis] *a* sin vida; (*dull*) soso.

lifelike [līf'līk] *a* natural.

lifeline [līf'līn] *n* (*fig*) cordón *m* umbilical.

lifelong [līf'lông] *a* de toda la vida.

life preserver [līf prēzûrv'ûr] *n* (*US*) cinturón *m* salvavidas.

lifesaver [līf'sāvûr] *n* socorrista *m/f*.

life sentence [līf sen'təns] *n* cadena perpetua.

life-sized [līf'sīzd] *a* de tamaño natural.

life span *n* vida.

lifestyle [līf'stīl] *n* estilo de vida.

life support system *n* (*MED*) sistema *m* de respiración asistida.

lifetime [līf'tīm] *n*: **in his** ~ durante su vida; **once in a** ~ una vez en la vida; **the chance of a** ~ una oportunidad única.

lift [lift] *vt* levantar; (*copy*) plagiar ♦ *vi* (*fog*) disiparse ♦ *n* (*Brit: elevator*) ascensor *m*; **to give sb a** ~ llevar a uno en el coche.

lift off *vt* levantar, quitar ♦ *vi* (*rocket, helicopter*) despegar.

lift out *vt* sacar; (*troops, evacuees etc*) evacuar.

lift up *vt* levantar.

lift-off [lift'ôf] *n* despegue *m*.

ligament [lig'əmənt] *n* ligamento.

light [līt] *n* luz *f*; (*flame*) lumbre *f*; (*lamp*) luz *f*, lámpara; (*daylight*) luz *f* del día; (*headlight*) faro; (*rear* ~) luz *f* trasera; (*for cigarette etc*): **have you got a** ~? ¿tienes fuego? ♦ *vt* (*pt, pp* **lighted** *or* **lit** [lit]) (*candle, cigarette, fire*) encender; (*room*) alumbrar ♦ *a* (*color*) claro; (*not heavy, also fig*) ligero; (*room*) alumbrado ♦ *ad* (*travel*) con poco equipaje; **to turn the** ~ **on/off** encender/apagar la luz; **in the** ~ **of** a la luz de; **to come to** ~ salir a luz; **to cast** *or* **shed** ~ **on** arrojar luz sobre; **to make** ~ **of sth** (*fig*) hacer poco caso de algo.

light up *vi* (*smoke*) encender un cigarrillo; (*face*) iluminarse ♦ *vt* (*illuminate*) iluminar, alumbrar.

light bulb *n* bombilla, foco (*LAm*).

lighten [līt'ən] *vi* (*grow light*) clarear ♦ *vt* (*give light to*) iluminar; (*make lighter*) aclarar; (*make less heavy*) aligerar.

lighter [lī'tûr] *n* (*also:* **cigarette** ~) encendedor *m*, mechero.

lighter fluid *n* bencina.

light-fingered [līt'fing'gûrd] *a* largo de manos.

light-headed [līt'hed'id] *a* (*dizzy*) mareado; (*excited*) exaltado; (*by nature*) casquivano.

lighthearted [līt'hâr'tid] *a* alegre.

lighthouse [līt'hous] *n* faro.

lighting [lī'ting] *n* (*act*) iluminación *f*; (*system*) alumbrado.

lightly [līt'lē] *ad* ligeramente; (*not seriously*) con poca seriedad; **to get off** ~ ser castigado con poca severidad.

light meter *n* (*PHOT*) fotómetro.

lightness [līt'nis] *n* claridad *f*; (*in weight*) ligereza.

lightning [līt'ning] *n* relámpago, rayo.

lightning rod [līt'ning rod], (*Brit*) **lightning conductor** *n* pararrayos *m inv*.

lightning strike *n* (*Brit*) huelga relámpago.

light pen *n* fotoestilo, lápiz *m* óptico *or* luminoso.

lightweight [līt'wāt] *a* (*suit*) ligero ♦ *n* (*BOXING*) peso ligero.

light-year [līt'yēr] *n* año luz.

like [līk] *vt* (*person*) querer a; (*thing*): **I** ~ **swimming/apples** me gusta nadar/me gustan las manzanas ♦ *prep* como ♦ *a* parecido, semejante ♦ *n*: **the** ~ semejante *m/f*; **his** ~**s and dislikes** sus gustos y aversiones; **I would** ~, **I'd** ~ me gustaría; (*for purchase*) quisiera; **would you** ~ **a coffee?** ¿te apetece un café?; **to be** *or* **look** ~ **sb/ sth** parecerse a uno/algo; **that's just** ~ **him** es muy de él, es característico de él; **do it** ~ **this** hazlo así; **it is nothing** ~... no tiene parecido alguno con...; **what's he** ~? ¿cómo es (él)?; **what's the weather** ~? ¿qué tiempo hace?; **something** ~ **that** algo así *or* por el estilo; **I feel** ~ **a drink** me apetece algo de beber; **if you** ~ si quieres.

likeable [lī'kəbəl] *a* simpático, agradable.

likelihood [līk'lēhood] *n* probabilidad *f*; **in all** ~ según todas las probabilidades.

likely [līk'lē] *a* probable; **he's** ~ **to leave** es probable que se vaya; **not** ~! ¡ni hablar!

like-minded [līk'mīn'did] *a* de la misma opinión.

liken [lī'kən] *vt*: **to** ~ **to** comparar con.

likeness [līk'nis] *n* (*similarity*) semejanza, parecido.

likewise [līk'wīz] *ad* igualmente.

liking [lī'king] *n*: ~ **(for)** (*person*) cariño (a); (*thing*) afición (a); **to take a** ~ **to sb** tomar cariño a uno; **to be to sb's** ~ ser del gusto de uno.

lilac [lī'lək] *n* lila ♦ *a* (*color*) de color lila.

lilt [lilt] *n* deje *m*.
lilting [lil'ting] *a* melodioso.
lily [lil'ē] *n* lirio, azucena.
lily of the valley *n* lirio de los valles.
Lima [lē'mə] *n* Lima.
limb [lim] *n* miembro; (*of tree*) rama; **to be out on a** ~ (*fig*) estar aislado.
limber [lim'bûr]: **to** ~ **up** *vi* (*fig*) entrenarse; (*SPORT*) desentumecerse.
limbo [lim'bō] *n*: **to be in** ~ (*fig*) quedar a la expectativa.
lime [līm] *n* (*tree*) limero; (*fruit*) lima; (*GEO*) cal *f*.
lime juice *n* zumo (*Sp*) *or* jugo de lima.
limelight [līm'līt] *n*: **to be in the** ~ (*fig*) ser el centro de atención.
limerick [lim'ûrik] *n* quintilla humorística.
limestone [līm'stōn] *n* piedra caliza.
limit [lim'it] *n* límite *m* ♦ *vt* limitar; **weight/speed** ~ peso máximo/velocidad *f* máxima; **within** ~s entre límites.
limitation [limitā'shən] *n* limitación *f*.
limited [lim'itid] *a* limitado; **to be** ~ **to** limitarse a; ~ **edition** tirada limitada.
limited (liability) company (Ltd) *n* (*Brit*) sociedad *f* anónima (SA).
limitless [lim'itlis] *a* sin límites.
limousine [lim'əzēn] *n* limusina.
limp [limp] *n*: **to have a** ~ tener cojera ♦ *vi* cojear ♦ *a* flojo.
limpet [lim'pit] *n* lapa.
limpid [lim'pid] *a* (*poetic*) límpido, cristalino.
limply [limp'lē] *ad* desmayadamente; **to say** ~ decir débilmente.
linchpin [linch'pin] *n* pezonera; (*fig*) eje *m*.
Lincs [lingks] *abbr* (*Brit*) = Lincolnshire.
line [līn] *n* (*also COMM*) línea; (*straight* ~) raya; (*rope*) cuerda; (*for fishing*) sedal *m*; (*wire*) hilo; (*row, series*) fila, hilera; (*of writing*) renglón *m*; (*on face*) arruga; (*speciality*) rama ♦ *vt* (*SEWING*): **to** ~ **(with)** forrar (de); **to** ~ **the streets** ocupar las aceras; **in** ~ **with** de acuerdo con; **she's in** ~ **for promotion** (*fig*) tiene muchas posibilidades de que la asciendan; **to bring sth into** ~ **with sth** poner algo de acuerdo con algo; **to cut in** ~ (*US*) colarse; ~ **of research/business** campo de investigación/comercio; **to take the** ~ **that ...** ser de la opinión que ...; **hold the** ~ **please** (*TEL*) no cuelgue usted, por favor; **to draw the** ~ **at doing sth** negarse a hacer algo; no permitir que se haga algo; **on the right** ~s por buen camino; **a new** ~ **in cosmetics** una nueva línea en cosméticos; *see also* **lines**.
 line up *vi* hacer cola ♦ *vt* alinear, poner en fila; **to have sth** ~d **up** tener algo arreglado.
linear [lin'êûr] *a* lineal.
lined [līnd] *a* (*face*) arrugado; (*paper*) rayado; (*clothes*) forrado.
line editing *n* (*COMPUT*) corrección *f* por

líneas.
line feed *n* (*COMPUT*) avance *m* de línea.
linen [lin'ən] *n* ropa blanca; (*cloth*) lino.
line printer *n* impresora de línea.
liner [lī'nûr] *n* vapor *m* de línea, transatlántico; **trash can** ~ bolsa de la basura.
lines [līnz] *npl* (*RAIL*) vía *sg*, raíles *mpl*.
linesman [līnz'mən] *n* (*SPORT*) juez *m* de línea.
lineup [līn'up] *n* alineación *f*; (*US*) identificación *f* de acusados.
linger [ling'gûr] *vi* retrasarse, tardar en marcharse; (*smell, tradition*) persistir.
lingerie [lân'jərā] *n* ropa interior *or* íntima (*LAm*) (de mujer).
lingering [ling'gûring] *a* persistente; (*death*) lento.
lingo, *pl* ~**es** [ling'gō] *n* (*pej*) jerga.
linguist [ling'gwist] *n* lingüista *m/f*.
linguistic [linggwis'tik] *a* lingüístico.
linguistics [linggwis'tiks] *n* lingüística.
liniment [lin'əmənt] *n* linimento.
lining [lī'ning] *n* forro; (*TECH*) revestimiento; (*of brake*) guarnición *f*.
link [lingk] *n* (*of a chain*) eslabón *m*; (*connection*) conexión *f*; (*bond*) vínculo, lazo ♦ *vt* vincular, unir; **rail** ~ línea de ferrocarril, servicio de trenes.
 link up *vt* acoplar ♦ *vi* unirse.
links [lingks] *npl* (*GOLF*) campo *sg* de golf.
linkup [lingk'up] *n* (*gen*) unión *f*; (*meeting*) encuentro, reunión *f*; (*of roads*) empalme *m*; (*of spaceships*) acoplamiento; (*RADIO, TV*) enlace *m*.
linoleum [linō'lēəm] *n* linóleo.
linseed oil [lin'sēd oil] *n* aceite *m* de linaza.
lint [lint] *n* gasa.
lintel [lin'təl] *n* dintel *m*.
lion [lī'ən] *n* león *m*.
lioness [lī'ənis] *n* leona.
lip [lip] *n* labio; (*of jug*) pico; (*of cup etc*) borde *m*.
lip-read [lip'rēd] *vi* leer los labios.
lip salve [lip sav] *n* crema protectora para labios.
lip service *n*: **to pay** ~ **to sth** alabar algo pero sin hacer nada.
lipstick [lip'stik] *n* lápiz *m* de labios, carmín *m*.
liquefy [lik'wəfī] *vt* licuar ♦ *vi* licuarse.
liqueur [lik'ûr] *n* licor *m*.
liquid [lik'wid] *a*, *n* líquido.
liquidate [lik'widāt] *vt* liquidar.
liquidation [likwidā'shən] *n* liquidación *f*; **to go into** ~ entrar en liquidación.
liquid crystal display (LCD) *n* pantalla de cristal líquido.
liquidity [likwid'itē] *n* (*COMM*) liquidez *f*.
liquidize [lik'widīz] *vt* (*CULIN*) licuar.
liquidizer [lik'widīzûr] *n* (*Brit CULIN*) licuadora.
Liquid Paper *n* ® Tipp-Ex *m* ®.
liquor [lik'ûr] *n* licor *m*, bebidas *fpl* alcohóli-

cas.

liquorice |lik'úris| n (Brit) regaliz m.
liquor store n (US) bodega, tienda de vinos y bebidas alcohólicas.
Lisbon |liz'bən| n Lisboa.
lisp |lisp| n ceceo.
lissom |lis'əm| a ágil.
list |list| n lista; (of ship) inclinación f ♦ vt (write down) hacer una lista de; (enumerate) catalogar; (COMPUT) listar ♦ vi (ship) inclinarse; **shopping** ~ lista de las compras; see also **lists**.
listed company |lis'tid kum'pənē| n compañía cotizable.
listen |lis'ən| vi escuchar, oír; (pay attention) atender.
listener |lis'ənûr| n oyente m/f.
listing |lis'ting| n (COMPUT) listado.
listless |list'lis| a apático, indiferente.
listlessly |list'lislē| ad con indiferencia.
listlessness |list'lisnis| n indiferencia, apatía.
list price n precio corriente or de tarifa.
lists |lists| npl (HISTORY) liza sg; **to enter the ~ (against sb/sth)** salir a la palestra (contra uno/algo).
lit |lit| pt, pp of **light**.
litany |lit'ənē| n letanía.
liter |lē'tûr| n (US) litro.
literacy |lit'ûrəsē| n capacidad f de leer y escribir; ~ **campaign** campaña de alfabetización.
literal |lit'ûrəl| a literal.
literally |lit'ûrəlē| ad literalmente.
literary |lit'ərärē| a literario.
literate |lit'ûrit| a que sabe leer y escribir; (fig) culto.
literature |lit'ûrəchûr| n literatura; (brochures etc) folletos mpl.
lithe |lithִ| a ágil.
litho(graph) |lith'ō(graf)| n litografía.
lithography |lithâg'rəfē| n litografía.
Lithuania |lithōōā'nēə| n Lituania.
litigate |lit'əgāt| vi litigar.
litigation |litəgā'shən| n litigio.
litmus paper |lit'məs pā'pûr| n papel m de tornasol.
litre |lē'tûr| n (Brit) = **liter**.
litter |lit'ûr| n (rubbish) basura; (paper) papel m tirado; (young animals) camada, cría.
litter bin n (Brit) papelera.
litterbug |lit'ûrbug| n persona que tira papeles usados en la vía pública.
littered |lit'ûrd| a: ~ **with** lleno de.
little |lit'əl| a (small) pequeño; (not much) poco; (often translated by suffix, eg): ~ **house** casita ♦ ad poco; **a** ~ un poco (de); ~ **by** ~ poco a poco; ~ **finger** (dedo) meñique m; **for a** ~ **while** por un rato; **with** ~ **difficulty** sin problema or dificultad; **as** ~ **as possible** lo menos posible.
liturgy |lit'ûrjē| n liturgia.

live vb |liv| vi vivir ♦ vt (a life) llevar; (experience) vivir ♦ a |līv| (animal) vivo; (wire) conectado; (broadcast) en directo; (issue) de actualidad; (unexploded) sin explotar; **to** ~ **in Chicago** vivir en Chicago; **to** ~ **together** vivir juntos; **to** ~ **off-campus** ser externo.
live down vt hacer olvidar.
live off vt fus (land, fish etc) vivir de; (pej: parents etc) vivir a costa de.
live on vt fus (food) vivirse de, alimentarse de; **to** ~ **on $150 a week** vivir con 150 dólares por semana.
live out vi (Brit: students) ser externo ♦ vt: **to** ~ **out one's days** or **life** acabar la vida.
live up vt: **to** ~ **it up** (col) vivir la gran vida.
live up to vt fus (fulfil) cumplir con; (justify) justificar.
livelihood |līv'lēhōōd| n sustento.
liveliness |līv'lēnis| n viveza.
lively |līv'lē| a (gen) vivo; (talk) animado; (pace) rápido; (party, tune) alegre.
liven up |lī'vən up'| vt (discussion, evening) animar.
liver |liv'ûr| n hígado.
liverish |liv'ûrish| a (Brit): **to feel** ~ sentirse or estar mal del hígado.
livery |liv'ûrē| n librea.
lives |līvz| npl of **life**.
livestock |līv'stâk| n ganado.
livid |liv'id| a lívido; (furious) furioso.
living |liv'ing| a (alive) vivo ♦ n: **to earn** or **make a** ~ ganarse la vida; **cost of** ~ coste m de la vida; **in** ~ **memory** que se recuerde or recuerda.
living conditions npl condiciones fpl de vida.
living expenses npl gastos mpl de mantenimiento.
living room n sala (de estar).
living standards npl nivel msg de vida.
living wage n sueldo suficiente para vivir.
lizard |liz'ûrd| n lagartija.
llama |lâm'ə| n llama.
LLB n abbr (= Bachelor of Laws) Ldo./a. en Dcho.
LLD n abbr (= Doctor of Laws) Dr(a). en Dcho.
load |lōd| n (gen) carga; (weight) peso ♦ vt (COMPUT) cargar; (also: ~ **up**): **to** ~ **(with)** cargar (con or de); **a** ~ **of**, ~**s of** (fig) (gran) cantidad de, montones de.
loaded |lō'did| a (dice) cargado; (question) intencionado; (col: rich) forrado (de dinero).
loading |lō'ding| n (COMM) sobreprima.
loading dock n (US) área de carga y descarga.
loaf, pl **loaves** |lōf, lōvz| n (barra de) pan m ♦ vi (also: ~ **around**) holgazanear.
loafer |lō'fûr| n vago/a.

loam [lōm] *n* marga.
loan [lōn] *n* préstamo; (*COMM*) empréstito ♦ *vt* prestar; **on** ~ prestado; **to raise a** ~ (*Brit: money*) procurar un empréstito.
loan account *n* cuenta de crédito.
loan capital *n* empréstito.
loath [lōth] *a*: **to be** ~ **to do sth** estar poco dispuesto a hacer algo.
loathe [lōth] *vt* aborrecer; (*person*) odiar.
loathing [lō'thing] *n* aversión *f*; odio.
loathsome [lōth'səm] *a* asqueroso, repugnante; (*person*) odioso.
loaves [lōvz] *pl* of **loaf**.
lob [lâb] *vt* (*ball*) volear por alto.
lobby [lâb'ē] *n* vestíbulo, sala de espera; (*POL: pressure group*) grupo de presión ♦ *vt* presionar.
lobbyist [lâb'ēist] *n* cabildero/a.
lobe [lōb] *n* lóbulo.
lobster [lâb'stûr] *n* langosta.
lobster pot *n* nasa, langostera.
local [lō'kəl] *a* local ♦ *n* (*Brit: pub*) bar *m*; **the** ~**s** *npl* los vecinos, los del lugar.
local anesthetic *n* (*MED*) anestesia local.
local authority *n* (*Brit*) municipio, ayuntamiento (*Sp*).
local call *n* (*TEL*) llamada local.
local government *n* gobierno municipal.
locality [lōkal'itē] *n* localidad *f*.
localize [lō'kəlīz] *vt* localizar.
locally [lō'kəlē] *ad* en la vecindad.
locate [lō'kāt] *vt* (*find*) localizar; (*situate*) colocar.
location [lōkā'shən] *n* situación *f*; **on** ~ (*CINEMA*) en exteriores, fuera del estudio.
loch [lâk] *n* lago.
lock [lâk] *n* (*of door, box*) cerradura; (*of canal*) esclusa; (*of hair*) mechón *m* ♦ *vt* (*with key*) cerrar con llave; (*immobilize*) inmovilizar ♦ *vi* (*door etc*) cerrarse con llave; (*wheels*) trabarse; ~ **stock and barrel** (*fig*) por completo *or* entero.
lock away *vt* (*valuables*) guardar bajo llave; (*criminal*) encerrar.
lock out *vt*: **the workers were** ~**ed out** los trabajadores tuvieron que enfrentarse con un cierre patronal.
lock up *vi* echar la llave.
locker [lâk'ûr] *n* casillero.
locker room *n* (*US SPORT*) vestuario.
locket [lâk'it] *n* medallón *m*.
lockout [lâk'out] *n* (*INDUSTRY*) paro *or* cierre *m* patronal, lockout *m*.
locksmith [lâk'smith] *n* cerrajero/a.
lock-up [lâk'up] *n* (*prison*) cárcel *f*; (*cell*) jaula.
lock-up stall *n* (*US AUT*) jaula, cochera.
locomotive [lōkəmō'tiv] *n* locomotora.
locum tenens [lō'kəm tē'nenz] *n* (*MED*) (médico/a) interino/a.
locust [lō'kəst] *n* langosta.
lodge [lâj] *n* (*FREEMASONRY*) logia; (*Brit*) portería; (: *porter's*) casa del guarda ♦ *vi*

(*person*): **to** ~ (**with**) alojarse (en casa de) ♦ *vt* (*complaint*) presentar.
lodger [lâj'ûr] *n* huésped(a) *m/f*.
lodgings [lâj'ingz] *npl* alojamiento *sg*; (*house*) casa *sg* de huéspedes.
loft [lôft] *n* desván *m*.
lofty [lôf'tē] *a* alto; (*haughty*) orgulloso; (*sentiments, aims*) elevado, noble.
log [lôg] *n* (*of wood*) leño, tronco; (*book*) = **logbook** ♦ *n abbr* (= *logarithm*) log. ♦ *vt* anotar, registrar.
log in, log on *vi* (*COMPUT*) iniciar la (*or* una) sesión.
log off, log out *vi* (*COMPUT*) finalizar la (*or* una) sesión.
logarithm [lôg'ərithəm] *n* logaritmo.
logbook [lôg'book] *n* (*NAUT*) diario de a bordo; (*AVIAT*) libro de vuelo; (*of car*) documentación *f* (del coche).
log cabin *n* cabaña de troncos.
log fire *n* fuego de leña.
loggerheads [lôg'ûrhedz] *npl*: **at** ~ (**with**) de pique (con).
logic [lâj'ik] *n* lógica.
logical [lâj'ikəl] *a* lógico.
logically [lâj'iklē] *ad* lógicamente.
logistics [lōjis'tiks] *n* logística.
logo [lō'gō] *n* logotipo.
loin [loin] *n* (*CULIN*) lomo, solomillo; ~**s** *npl* lomos *mpl*.
loincloth [loin'klôth] *n* taparrabo.
loiter [loi'tûr] *vi* vagar; (*pej*) merodear.
loll [lâl] *vi* repantigarse.
lollipop [lâl'ēpâp] *n* pirulí *m*; (*iced*) polo.
London [lun'dən] *n* Londres *m*.
Londoner [lun'dənûr] *n* londinense *m/f*.
lone [lōn] *a* solitario.
loneliness [lōn'lēnis] *n* soledad *f*, aislamiento.
lonely [lōn'lē] *a* solitario, solo.
loner [lō'nûr] *n* solitario/a.
lonesome [lōn'səm] *a* (*esp US*) = **lonely**.
long [lông] *a* largo ♦ *ad* mucho tiempo, largamente ♦ *vi*: **to** ~ **for sth** anhelar algo ♦ *n*: **the** ~ **and the short of it is that ...** (*fig*) en resumidas cuentas *or* concretamente, es que ...; **in the** ~ **run** a la larga; **so** *or* **as** ~ **as** mientras, con tal de que; **don't be** ~! ¡no tardes!, ¡vuelve pronto!; **how** ~ **is the street?** ¿cuánto tiene la calle de largo?; **how** ~ **is the lesson?** ¿cuánto dura la clase?; **6 meters** ~ que mide 6 metros, de 6 metros de largo; **6 months** ~ que dura 6 meses, de 6 meses de duración; **all night** ~ toda la noche; ~ **ago** hace mucho (tiempo); **he no** ~**er comes** ya no viene; ~ **before** mucho antes; **before** ~ (+ *future*) dentro de poco; (+ *past*) poco tiempo después; **at** ~ **last** al fin, por fin; **I won't be** ~ termino pronto.
long-distance [lông'dis'təns] *a* (*race*) de larga distancia; (*call*) interurbano.
longevity [lânjev'itē] *n* longevidad *f*.

long-haired [lông'härd] a de pelo largo.
longhand [lông'hand] n escritura (corriente).
longing [lông'ing] n anhelo, ansia; (nostalgia) nostalgia ♦ a anhelante.
longingly [lông'inglē] ad con ansia.
longitude [lán'jətōod] n longitud f.
long jump n salto de longitud.
long-lost [lông'lôst] a desaparecido hace mucho tiempo.
long-playing record (LP) [lông'plā'ing rck'ûrd] n elepé m, disco de larga duración.
long-range [lông'rānj] a de gran alcance; (weather forecast) de larga proyección.
longshoreman [lông'shôrmən] n (US) estibador m.
long-sighted [lông'sītid] a présbita.
long-standing [lông'stan'ding] a de mucho tiempo.
long-suffering [lông'suf'ûring] a sufrido.
long-term [lông'tûrm'] a a largo plazo.
long wave n onda larga.
long-winded [lông'win'did] a prolijo.
loo [lōo] n (Brit: col) wáter m.
loofah [lōo'fə] n (Brit: sponge) esponja de lufa.
look [lōok] vi mirar; (seem) parecer; (building etc): **to ~ south/on to the sea** dar al sur/al mar ♦ n mirada; (glance) vistazo; (appearance) aire m, aspecto; **~s** npl físico sg, belleza sg; **to ~ ahead** mirar hacia delante; **it ~s about 4 meters long** yo calculo que tiene unos 4 metros de largo; **it ~s all right to me** me parece que está bien; **to have a ~ at sth** echar un vistazo a algo.
look after vt fus cuidar.
look around vi echar una mirada alrededor; **to ~ around for sth** buscar algo.
look at vt fus mirar; (consider) considerar.
look back vi mirar hacia atrás; **to ~ back at sb/sth** mirar hacia atrás algo/a uno; **to ~ back on** (event, period) recordar.
look down on vt fus (fig) despreciar, mirar con desprecio.
look for vt fus buscar.
look forward to vt fus esperar con ilusión; (in letters): **we ~ forward to hearing from you** quedamos a la espera de sus gratas noticias; **I'm not ~ing forward to it** no tengo ganas de eso, no me hace ilusión.
look in vi: **to ~ in on sb** (visit) pasar por casa de uno.
look into vt fus investigar.
look on vi mirar (como espectador).
look out vi (beware): **to ~ out (for)** tener cuidado (de).
look out for vt fus (seek) buscar; (await) esperar.
look over vt (essay) revisar; (town, building) inspeccionar, registrar; (person)

examinar.
look round vi = look around.
look through vt fus (papers, book) hojear; (briefly) echar un vistazo a; (telescope) mirar por.
look to vt fus ocuparse de; (rely on) contar con.
look up vi mirar hacia arriba; (improve) mejorar ♦ vt (word) buscar; (friend) visitar.
look up to vt fus admirar.
lookout [lōok'out] n (tower etc) puesto de observación; (person) vigía m/f; **to be on the ~ for sth** estar al acecho de algo.
look-up table [lōok'up tā'bəl] n (COMPUT) tabla de consulta.
LOOM n abbr (US: = Loyal Order of Moose) asociación benéfica.
loom [lōom] n telar m ♦ vi (threaten) amenazar.
loony [lōo'nē] a, n (col) loco/a m/f.
loop [lōop] n lazo; (bend) vuelta, recodo; (COMPUT) bucle m.
loophole [lōop'hōl] n escapatoria.
loose [lōos] a (gen) suelto; (not tight) flojo; (wobbly etc) movedizo; (clothes) ancho; (morals, discipline) relajado ♦ vt (free) soltar; (slacken) aflojar; **~ connection** (ELEC) rotura; **to be at ~ ends** or (Brit) **at a ~ end** no saber qué hacer; **to tie up ~ ends** (fig) no dejar cabo suelto.
loose change n cambio.
loose chippings npl (Brit: on road) gravilla sg suelta.
loose-fitting [lōos'fit'ing] a suelto.
loose-leaf [lōos'lēf] a: **~ binder** or **folder** carpeta de hojas sueltas or insertables.
loosely [lōos'lē] ad libremente, aproximadamente.
loosen [lōo'sən] vt (free) soltar; (untie) desatar; (slacken) aflojar.
loosen up vi (before game) desentumecerse; (col: relax) soltarse, relajarse.
looseness [lōos'nis] n soltura; flojedad f.
loot [lōot] n botín m ♦ vt saquear.
looter [lōo'tûr] n saqueador(a) m/f.
looting [lōo'ting] n pillaje m.
lop [láp]: **to ~ off** vt cortar; (branches) podar.
lopsided [láp'sídid] a desequilibrado.
lord [lôrd] n señor m; **L~ Smith** Lord Smith; **the L~** el Señor; **the (House of) L~s** (Brit) la Cámara de los Lores.
lordly [lôrd'lē] a señorial.
lore [lôr] n saber m popular, tradiciones fpl.
lorry [lôr'ē] n (Brit) camión m.
lorry driver n (Brit) camionero/a.
lose, pt, pp **lost** [lōoz, lôst] vt perder ♦ vi perder, ser vencido; **to ~ (time)** (clock) atrasarse; **to ~ no time (in doing sth)** no tardar (en hacer algo); **to get lost** (object) extraviarse; (person) perderse.
lose out vi salir perdiendo.

loser [lōō'zûr] *n* perdedor(a) *m/f*; **to be a bad ~** no saber perder.

losing [lōō'zing] *a* (*team etc*) vencido, perdedor(a).

loss [lôs] *n* pérdida; **heavy ~es** (*MIL*) grandes pérdidas *fpl*; **to be at a ~** no saber qué hacer; **to be a dead ~** ser completamente inútil; **to cut one's ~es** cortar por lo sano; **to sell sth at a ~** vender algo con pérdida.

loss leader *n* (*COMM*) artículo de promoción.

lost [lôst] *pt, pp of* **lose** ♦ *a* perdido; **~ in thought** absorto, ensimismado.

lost and found *n* (*US*) objetos *mpl* perdidos, departamento de objetos perdidos.

lost cause *n* causa perdida.

lost property, lost property office *or* **department** *n* (*Brit*) = **lost and found**.

lot [lât] *n* (*at auctions*) lote *m*; (*destiny*) suerte *f*; (*US: plot of land*) terreno; **the ~** el todo, todos *mpl*, todas *fpl*; **a ~ of** mucho, bastante; **a ~ of, ~s of** mucho(s)/a(s) (*pl*); **I read a ~** leo bastante; **to draw ~s (for sth)** echar suertes (para decidir algo).

lotion [lō'shən] *n* loción *f*.

lottery [lât'ûrē] *n* lotería.

loud [loud] *a* (*voice, sound*) fuerte; (*laugh, shout*) estrepitoso; (*gaudy*) chillón/ona ♦ *ad* (*speak etc*) fuerte; **out ~** en voz alta.

loudly [loud'lē] *ad* (*noisily*) fuerte; (*aloud*) en alta voz.

loudness [loud'nis] *n* (*of sound etc*) fuerza.

loudspeaker [loud'spēkûr] *n* altavoz *m*.

lounge [lounj] *n* salón *m*, sala (de estar); (*of hotel*) salón *m*; (*of airport*) sala (de embarque) ♦ *vi* (*also: ~ around*) holgazanear, no hacer nada.

lounge bar *n* (*Brit*) salón *m*.

lounge suit *n* (*Brit*) traje *m* de calle.

louse, *pl* **lice** [lous, līs] *n* piojo.

louse up *vt* (*col*) echar a perder.

lousy [lou'zē] *a* (*fig*) vil, asqueroso.

lout [lout] *n* gamberro/a.

louver, (*Brit***) louvre** [lōō'vûr] *a*: **~ door** puerta de rejilla; **~ window** ventana de libro.

lovable [luv'əbəl] *a* amable, simpático.

love [luv] *n* amor *m* ♦ *vt* amar, querer; **to send one's ~ to sb** dar sus recuerdos a uno; **~ from Anne** (*in letter*) con cariño de Anne; **I ~ to read** me encanta leer; **to be in ~ with** estar enamorado de; **to make ~** hacer el amor; **for the ~ of** por amor de; "**15 ~**" (*TENNIS*) "15 a cero"; **I ~ paella** me encanta la paella; **I'd ~ to come** me gustaría muchísimo venir.

love affair *n* aventura sentimental.

love letter *n* carta de amor.

love life *n* vida sentimental.

lovely [luv'lē] *a* (*delightful*) precioso, encantador(a); (*beautiful*) hermoso; **we had a ~ time** lo pasamos estupendo.

lovemaking [luv'māking] *n* relaciones *fpl* sexuales.

lover [luv'ûr] *n* amante *m/f*; (*amateur*): **a ~ of** un(a) aficionado/a *or* un(a) amante de.

lovesick [luv'sik] *a* enfermo de amor, amartelado.

lovesong [luv'sông] *n* canción *f* de amor.

loving [luv'ing] *a* amoroso, cariñoso.

lovingly [luv'inglē] *ad* amorosamente, cariñosamente.

low [lō] *a, ad* bajo ♦ *n* (*METEOROLOGY*) área de baja presión ♦ *vi* (*cow*) mugir; **to feel ~** sentirse deprimido; **to turn (down) ~** bajar; **to reach a new** *or* **an all-time ~** llegar a su punto más bajo.

low-beam [lō'bēm] *a*: **~ headlights** luces *fpl* de cruce.

lowbrow [lō'brou] *a* (*person*) de poca cultura.

low-calorie [lō'kal'ûrē] *a* de bajo contenido calorífico.

low-cut [lō'kut] *a* (*dress*) escotado.

lowdown [lō'doun] *n* (*col*): **he gave me the ~ on it** me puso al corriente ♦ *a* (*mean*) vil, bajo.

lower *vt* [lō'ûr] bajar; (*US AUT: lights*) poner luces de cruce; (*reduce: price*) reducir, rebajar; (: *resistance*) debilitar: **to ~ o.s. to** (*fig*) rebajarse a ♦ *vi* [lou'ûr]: **to ~ (at sb)** fulminar a uno con la mirada.

lower case *n* (*TYP*) minúscula.

lowering [lou'ûring] *a* (*sky*) amenazador(a).

low-fat [lō'fat'] *a* (*milk, yogurt*) desnatado; (*diet*) bajo en calorías.

low-key [lō'kē'] *a* de mínima intensidad; (*operation*) de poco perfil.

lowland [lō'lənd] *n* tierra baja.

low-level [lō'levəl] *a* de bajo nivel; (*flying*) a poca altura.

lowly [lō'lē] *a* humilde.

low-lying [lō'lī'ing] *a* bajo.

loyal [loi'əl] *a* leal.

loyalist [loi'əlist] *n* legitimista *m/f*.

loyally [loi'əlē] *ad* lealmente.

loyalty [loi'əltē] *n* lealtad *f*.

lozenge [lâz'inj] *n* (*MED*) pastilla.

LP *n abbr* = **long-playing record**.

L-plates [el plāts] *npl* (*Brit*) placas *fpl* de aprendiz de conductor.

LPN *n abbr* (*US*: = *Licensed Practical Nurse*) enfermero/a practicante.

LSAT *n abbr* (*US*) = *Law School Admissions Test*.

LSD *n abbr* (= *lysergic acid diethylamide*) LSD *f*.

LSE *n abbr* = *London School of Economics*.

LST *n abbr* (*US*) = *local standard time*.

Ltd *abbr* (*Brit*: = *limited company*) S.A.

lubricant [lōōb'rikənt] *n* lubricante *m*.

lubricate [lōōb'rikāt] *vt* lubricar, engrasar.

lubrication [lōōbrikā'shən] *n* lubricación *f*.

lucid [lōō'sid] *a* lúcido.

lucidity [lōōsid'itē] *n* lucidez *f*.
lucidly [lōō'sidlē] *ad* lúcidamente.
luck [luk] *n* suerte *f*; **good/bad** ~ buena/ mala suerte; **good** ~! ¡(que tengas) suerte!; **to be in** ~ estar de *or* con suerte; **to be out of** ~ tener mala suerte.
luckily [luk'ilē] *ad* afortunadamente.
lucky [luk'ē] *a* afortunado.
lucrative [lōō'krətiv] *a* lucrativo.
ludicrous [lōō'dəkrəs] *a* absurdo.
luffa [luf'ə] *n* (*US: sponge*) esponja de lufa.
lug [lug] *vt* (*drag*) arrastrar.
luggage [lug'ij] *n* equipaje *m*.
luggage car *n* (*US*) furgón *m or* vagón *m* de equipaje.
luggage checkroom *n* (*US*) consigna.
luggage rack *n* (*in train*) rejilla, redecilla; (*on car*) baca, portaequipajes *m inv*.
lugubrious [lōōgōō'brēəs] *a* lúgubre.
lukewarm [lōōk'wôrm'] *a* tibio, templado.
lull [lul] *n* tregua ♦ *vt* (*child*) acunar; (*person, fear*) calmar.
lullaby [lul'əbī] *n* nana.
lumbago [lumbā'gō] *n* lumbago.
lumber [lum'bûr] *n* (*junk*) trastos *mpl* viejos; (*wood*) maderos *mpl* ♦ *vt* (*Brit col*): **to** ~ **sb with sth/sb** hacer que uno cargue con algo/uno ♦ *vi* (*also:* ~ **about,** ~ **along**) moverse pesadamente.
lumberjack [lum'bûrjak] *n* maderero.
lumberyard [lum'bûryârd] *n* (*US*) almacén *m* de madera.
luminous [lōō'minəs] *a* luminoso.
lump [lump] *n* terrón *m*; (*fragment*) trozo; (*in sauce*) grumo; (*in throat*) nudo; (*swelling*) bulto ♦ *vt* (*also:* ~ **together**) juntar.
lump sum *n* suma global.
lumpy [lum'pē] *a* (*sauce*) lleno de grumos.
lunacy [lōō'nəsē] *n* locura.
lunar [lōō'nûr] *a* lunar.
lunatic [lōō'nətik] *a, n* loco/a *m/f*; **the** ~ **fringe** la corriente extremista.
lunatic asylum *n* manicomio.
lunch [lunch] *n* almuerzo, comida ♦ *vi* almorzar; **to invite sb to** *or* **for** ~ invitar a uno a almorzar.
lunch break, lunch hour *n* hora del almuerzo.
luncheon [lun'chən] *n* almuerzo.
luncheon meat *n tipo de fiambre*.
lunchtime [lunch'tīm] *n* hora del almuerzo *or* de comer.
lung [lung] *n* pulmón *m*.
lung cancer *n* cáncer *m* del pulmón.
lunge [lunj] *vi* (*also:* ~ **forward**) abalanzarse; **to** ~ **at** arremeter contra.
lupin [lōō'pin] *n* altramuz *m*.
lurch [lûrch] *vi* dar sacudidas ♦ *n* sacudida; **to leave sb in the** ~ dejar a uno plantado.
lure [lōōr] *n* (*bait*) cebo; (*decoy*) señuelo ♦ *vt* convencer con engaños.
lurid [lōō'rid] *a* (*color*) chillón/ona; (*account*) sensacional; (*detail*) horripilante.

lurk [lûrk] *vi* (*hide*) esconderse; (*wait*) estar al acecho.
luscious [lush'əs] *a* delicioso.
lush [lush] *a* exuberante.
lust [lust] *n* lujuria; (*greed*) codicia.
lust after *vt fus* codiciar.
luster [lus'tûr] *n* (*US*) lustre *m*, brillo.
lustful [lust'fəl] *a* lascivo, lujurioso.
lustre [lus'tûr] *n* (*Brit*) = **luster.**
lustrous [lus'trəs] *a* brillante.
lusty [lus'tē] *a* robusto, fuerte.
lute [lōōt] *n* laúd *m*.
Luxembourg [luk'səmbûrg] *n* Luxemburgo.
luxuriant [lōōgzhōōr'ēənt] *a* exuberante.
luxurious [lōōgzhōōr'ēəs] *a* lujoso.
luxury [luk'shûrē] *n* lujo ♦ *cpd* de lujo.
luxury tax *n* impuesto de lujo.
LW *abbr* (*RADIO*) = **long wave.**
lying [lī'ing] *n* mentiras *fpl* ♦ *a* (*statement, story*) mentiroso, falso; (*person*) mentiroso.
lynch [linch] *vt* linchar.
lynx [lingks] *n* lince *m*.
Lyons [lī'ənz] *n* Lyón *m*.
lyre [lī'ûr] *n* lira.
lyric [lir'ik] *a* lírico; ~**s** *npl* (*of song*) letra *sg*.
lyrical [lir'ikəl] *a* lírico.

M

M, m [em] *n* (*letter*) M, m *f*; **M for Mike** M de Madrid.
M *n abbr* = **million(s)**; (= *medium*) M; (*Brit:* = *motorway*): **the M8** ≈ la A8.
m *abbr* (= *meter*) m.; = **mile(s).**
MA *n abbr* (*US*) = *Military Academy*; = **Master of Arts** ♦ *abbr* (*US MAIL*) = *Massachusetts.*
mac [mak] *n* (*Brit*) impermeable *m*.
macabre [məkâ'brə] *a* macabro.
macaroni [makərō'nē] *n* macarrones *mpl*.
macaroon [makərōōn'] *n* macarrón *m*, mostachón *m*.
mace [mās] *n* (*weapon, ceremonial*) maza; (*spice*) macis *f*.
machinations [makənā'shənz] *npl* intrigas *fpl*, manipulaciones *fpl*.
machine [məshēn'] *n* máquina ♦ *vt* (*TECH*) trabajar a máquina; (*Brit: dress etc*) coser a máquina.
machine code *n* (*COMPUT*) código máquina.
machine gun *n* ametralladora.
machine language *n* (*COMPUT*) lenguaje *m* máquina.
machine readable *a* (*COMPUT*) legible

por máquina.

machinery [məshē'nûrē] *n* maquinaria; (*fig*) mecanismo.

machine shop *n* taller *m* de máquinas.

machine tool *n* máquina herramienta.

machine translation *n* traducción *f* automática.

machine washable *a* lavable en la lavadora.

machinist [məshē'nist] *n* operario/a *m/f* (de máquina).

macho [mách'ō] *a* macho.

mackerel [mak'ûrəl] *n, pl inv* caballa.

mackintosh [mak'intâsh] *n* (*Brit*) impermeable *m*.

macro... [mak'rō] *pref* macro....

macroeconomics [makrōēkənâm'iks] *n* macroeconomía.

mad [mad] *a* loco; (*idea*) disparatado; (*angry*) furioso; ~ **(at** *or* **with sb)** furioso con uno; **to be** ~ **(keen) about** *or* **on sth** estar loco por algo; **to go** ~ volverse loco, enloquecer(se).

madam [mad'əm] *n* señora; **can I help you** ~? ¿le puedo ayudar, señora?; **M~ Chairman** señora presidenta.

madden [mad'ən] *vt* volver loco.

maddening [mad'əning] *a* enloquecedor(a).

made [mād] *pt, pp of* **make.**

Madeira [mədē'rə] *n* (*GEO*) Madera; (*wine*) vino de Madera, madera *m.*

made-to-measure [mād'təmezh'ûr] *a* (*Brit*) hecho a la medida.

made-to-order [mād'tōōôr'dûr] *a* (*US*) hecho a la medida.

made-up [mād'up'] *a* (*story*) ficticio.

madly [mad'lē] *ad* locamente.

madman [mad'man] *n* loco.

madness [mad'nis] *n* locura.

Madonna [mədân'ə] *n* Virgen *f.*

Madrid [mədrid'] *n* Madrid *m.*

madrigal [mad'rəgəl] *n* madrigal *m.*

Mafia [máf'ēə] *n* Mafia.

magazine [magəzēn'] *n* revista; (*MIL*: *store*) almacén *m*; (*of firearm*) recámara.

maggot [mag'ət] *n* gusano.

magic [maj'ik] *n* magia ♦ *a* mágico.

magical [maj'ikəl] *a* mágico.

magician [məjish'ən] *n* mago/a; (*conjurer*) prestidigitador(a) *m/f.*

magistrate [maj'istrāt] *n* juez *m/f* (municipal).

magnanimity [magnənim'itē] *n* magnanimidad *f.*

magnanimous [magnan'əməs] *a* magnánimo.

magnate [mag'nāt] *n* magnate *m/f.*

magnesium [magnē'zēəm] *n* magnesio.

magnet [mag'nit] *n* imán *m.*

magnetic [magnet'ik] *a* magnético.

magnetic disk *n* (*COMPUT*) disco magnético.

magnetic tape *n* cinta magnética.

magnetism [mag'nitizəm] *n* magnetismo.

magnification [magnəfəkā'shən] *n* aumento.

magnificence [magnif'isəns] *n* magnificencia.

magnificent [magnif'əsənt] *a* magnífico.

magnificently [magnif'əsəntlē] *ad* magníficamente.

magnify [mag'nəfī] *vt* aumentar; (*fig*) exagerar.

magnifying glass [mag'nəfiing glas] *n* lupa.

magnitude [mag'nətōōd] *n* magnitud *f.*

magnolia [magnōl'yə] *n* magnolia.

magpie [mag'pī] *n* urraca.

maharajah [máhərâ'jə] *n* maharajá *m.*

mahogany [məhâg'ənē] *n* caoba ♦ *cpd* de caoba.

maid [mād] *n* criada; **old** ~ (*pej*) solterona.

maiden [mād'ən] *n* doncella ♦ *a* (*aunt etc*) solterona; (*speech, voyage*) inaugural.

maiden name *n* nombre *m* de soltera.

mail [māl] *n* correo; (*letters*) cartas *fpl* ♦ *vt* (*post*) echar al correo; (*send*) mandar por correo; **by** ~ por correo; **by return** ~ (*US*) a vuelta de correo.

mailbox [māl'bâks] *n* (*US: for letters etc*; *COMPUT*) buzón *m.*

mailing [mā'ling] *n* correo instantáneo.

mailing list [mā'ling list] *n* lista de direcciones.

mailman [māl'man] *n* (*US*) cartero.

mail order *n* pedido postal; (*business*) venta por correo ♦ *a*: ~ **firm** *or* **house** casa de venta por correo.

mailtrain [māl'trān] *n* tren *m* correo.

mail truck, (*Brit*) **mail van** *n* (*AUT*) camioneta de correos *or* de reparto.

maim [mām] *vt* mutilar, lisiar.

main [mān] *a* principal, mayor ♦ *n* (*pipe*) cañería maestra; (*US*) red *f* eléctrica; **the** ~**s** (*Brit ELEC*) la red eléctrica; **in the** ~ en general.

main course *n* (*CULIN*) plato principal.

mainframe [mān'frām] *n* (*also*: ~ **computer**) computador *m or* ordenador *m* central.

mainland [mān'lənd] *n* continente *m.*

main line *n* línea de largo recorrido.

mainly [mān'lē] *ad* principalmente, en su mayoría.

main road *n* carretera principal.

mainstay [mān'stā] *n* (*fig*) pilar *m.*

mainstream [mān'strēm] *n* (*fig*) corriente *f* principal.

main street *n* calle *f* mayor.

maintain [māntān'] *vt* mantener; (*affirm*) sostener; **to** ~ **that ...** mantener *or* sostener que ... .

maintenance [mān'tənəns] *n* mantenimiento; (*alimony*) pensión *f* alimenticia.

maintenance contract *n* contrato de mantenimiento.

maintenance order *n* (*LAW*) obligación *f*

de pagar una pensión alimenticia al cónyuge.

maisonette [māzənet'] *n* (*Brit*) apartamento de dos pisos.

maize [māz] *n* maíz *m*, choclo (*LAm*).

Maj. *abbr* (*MIL*) = **major**.

majestic [məjes'tik] *a* majestuoso.

majesty [maj'istē] *n* majestad *f*.

major [mā'jûr] *n* (*MIL*) comandante *m* ♦ *a* principal; (*MUS*) mayor ♦ *vi* (*US UNIV*): **to ~ (in)** especializarse en; **a ~ operation** una operación *or* intervención de gran importancia.

Majorca [məyôr'kə] *n* Mallorca.

major general *n* (*MIL*) general *m* de división.

majority [məjór'itē] *n* mayoría ♦ *cpd* (*verdict*) mayoritario.

majority holding *n* (*COMM*): **to have a ~** tener un interés mayoritario.

make [māk] *vt* (*pt, pp* **made** [mād]) hacer; (*manufacture*) hacer, fabricar; (*cause to be*): **to ~ sb sad** hacer *or* poner triste a uno; (*force*): **to ~ sb do sth** obligar a uno a hacer algo; (*equal*): **2 and 2 ~ 4** 2 y 2 son 4 ♦ *n* marca; **to ~ a fool of sb** poner a uno en ridículo; **to ~ a profit/loss** obtener ganancias/sufrir pérdidas; **to ~ a profit of $500** sacar una ganancia de 500 dólares; **to ~ it** (*arrive*) llegar; (*achieve sth*) tener éxito; **what time do you ~ it?** ¿qué hora tienes?; **to ~ do with** contentarse con.

make for *vt fus* (*place*) dirigirse a.

make off *vi* largarse.

make out *vt* (*decipher*) descifrar; (*understand*) entender; (*see*) distinguir; (*write: cheque*) extender; **to ~ out (that)** (*claim, imply*) dar a entender (que); **to ~ out a case for sth** presentar una defensa de algo.

make over *vt* (*assign*): **to ~ over (to)** ceder *or* traspasar (a).

make up *vt* (*invent*) inventar; (*parcel*) hacer ♦ *vi* reconciliarse; (*with cosmetics*) maquillarse; **to be made up of** estar compuesto de.

make up for *vt fus* compensar.

make-believe [māk'bilēv] *n* ficción *f*, invención *f*.

maker [mā'kûr] *n* fabricante *m/f*.

makeshift [māk'shift] *a* improvisado.

make-up [māk'up] *n* maquillaje *m*.

make-up bag *n* bolsita del maquillaje *or* de los cosméticos.

make-up remover *n* desmaquillador *m*.

making [mā'king] *n* (*fig*): **in the ~** en vías de formación; **to have the ~s of** (*person*) tener madera de.

maladjusted [maləjus'tid] *a* inadaptado.

maladroit [malədroit'] *a* torpe.

malaise [malāz'] *n* malestar *m*.

malaria [məlär'ēə] *n* malaria.

Malawi [mə'lâwē] *n* Malawi *m*.

Malay [məlā'] *a* malayo ♦ *n* (*person*) malayo/a; (*LING*) malayo.

Malaya [məlā'yə] *n* Malaya, Malaca.

Malayan [məlā'yən] *a, n* = **Malay**.

Malaysia [məlā'zhə] *n* Malasia.

Malaysian [məlā'zhən] *a, n* malasio/a *m/f*.

Maldive Islands [maldiv' i'ləndz], **Maldives** [mal'dīvz] *npl*: **the ~** las Maldivas.

male [māl] *n* (*BIOL, ELEC*) macho ♦ *a* (*sex, attitude*) masculino; (*child etc*) varón.

male chauvinist (pig) [māl' shōvənist (pig')] *n* machista *m*.

male nurse *n* enfermero.

malevolence [məlev'ələns] *n* malevolencia.

malevolent [məlev'ələnt] *a* malévolo.

malfunction [malfungk'shən] *n* mal funcionamiento.

malice [mal'is] *n* (*ill will*) malicia; (*rancor*) rencor *m*.

malicious [məlish'əs] *a* malicioso; rencoroso.

maliciously [məlish'əslē] *ad* con malevolencia, con malicia; rencorosamente.

malign [məlīn'] *vt* difamar, calumniar ♦ *a* maligno.

malignant [məlig'nənt] *a* (*MED*) maligno.

malinger [məling'gûr] *vi* fingirse enfermo.

malingerer [məling'gûrûr] *n* enfermo/a fingido/a.

mall [môl] *n* (*also:* **shopping ~**) centro comercial.

malleable [mal'ēəbəl] *a* maleable.

mallet [mal'it] *n* mazo.

malnutrition [malnōōtrish'ən] *n* desnutrición *f*.

malpractice [malprak'tis] *n* negligencia profesional.

malt [môlt] *n* malta.

Malta [môl'tə] *n* Malta.

Maltese [môltēz'] *a* maltés/esa ♦ *n, pl inv* maltés/esa *m/f*; (*LING*) maltés *m*.

maltreat [maltrēt'] *vt* maltratar.

mammal [mam'əl] *n* mamífero.

mammoth [mam'əth] *n* mamut *m* ♦ *a* gigantesco.

man, *pl* **men** [man, men] *n* hombre *m*; (*CHESS*) pieza ♦ *vt* (*NAUT*) tripular; (*MIL*) guarnecer; **an old ~** un viejo; **~ and wife** marido y mujer.

Man. *abbr* (*Canada*) = *Manitoba*.

manacle [man'əkəl] *n* esposa, manilla; **~s** *npl* grillos *mpl*.

manage [man'ij] *vi* arreglárselas, ir tirando ♦ *vt* (*be in charge of*) dirigir; (*person etc*) manejar; **to ~ to do sth** alcanzar a *or* conseguir hacer algo; **to ~ without sth/sb** prescindir de algo/uno.

manageable [man'ijəbəl] *a* manejable.

management [man'ijmənt] *n* dirección *f*, administración *f*; **"under new ~"** "bajo nueva dirección".

management accounting *n* contabilidad *f* de gestión.

management consultant *n* consultor(a) *m/f* en dirección de empresas, asesor(a) *m/f* administrativo/a.

manager [man'ijûr] *n* director *m*; (*SPORT*) entrenador *m*; **sales ~** jefe/a *m/f* de ventas.

manageress [man'ijûris] *n* directora; (*SPORT*) entrenadora.

managerial [manijē'rēəl] *a* directivo.

managing director [man'ijing direk'tûr] *n* director(a) *m/f* general.

mandarin [man'dûrin] *n* (*also:* **~ orange**) mandarina; (*person*) mandarín *m*.

mandate [man'dāt] *n* mandato.

mandatory [man'dətôrē] *a* obligatorio.

mandolin(e) [man'dəlin] *n* mandolina.

mane [mān] *n* (*of horse*) crin *f*; (*of lion*) melena.

maneuver [mənōō'vûr] (*US*) *vt, vi* maniobrar ♦ *n* maniobra; **to ~ sb into doing sth** manipular a uno para que haga algo.

maneuvrable [mənōō'vrəbəl] *a* (*car etc*) manejable.

manful [man'fəl] *a* resuelto.

manfully [man'fəlē] *ad* resueltamente.

mangle [mang'gəl] *vt* mutilar, destrozar ♦ *n* rodillo.

mango, ~**es** [mang'gō] *n* mango.

mangrove [mang'grōv] *n* mangle *m*.

mangy [mān'jē] *a* roñoso; (*MED*) sarnoso.

manhandle [man'handəl] *vt* maltratar; (*move by hand: goods*) manipular.

manhole [man'hōl] *n* pozo de visita.

manhood [man'hōōd] *n* edad *f* viril; virilidad *f*.

man-hour [man'ouûr] *n* hora-hombre *f*.

manhunt [man'hunt] *n* caza de hombre.

mania [mā'nēə] *n* manía.

maniac [mā'nēak] *n* maníaco/a; (*fig*) maniático.

manic [man'ik] *a* (*behavior, activity*) frenético.

manic-depressive [man'ikdipres'iv] *a, n* maniacodepresivo/a *m/f*.

manicure [man'əkyōōr] *n* manicura.

manicure set *n* estuche *m* de manicura.

manifest [man'əfest] *vt* manifestar, mostrar ♦ *a* manifiesto ♦ *n* manifiesto.

manifestation [manəfestā'shən] *n* manifestación *f*.

manifestly [man'əfestlē] *ad* evidentemente.

manifesto [manəfes'tō] *n* manifiesto.

manifold [man'əfōld] *a* múltiples ♦ *n* (*AUT etc*): **exhaust ~** colector *m* de escape.

Manila [mənil'ə] *n* Manila.

manil(l)a *n* (*paper, envelope*) manila.

manipulate [mənip'yəlāt] *vt* manipular.

manipulation [mənipyəlā'shən] *n* manipulación *f*, manejo.

mankind [man'kīnd'] *n* humanidad *f*, género humano.

manliness [man'lēnis] *n* virilidad *f*, hombradía.

manly [man'lē] *a* varonil.

man-made [man'mād] *a* artificial.

manna [man'ə] *n* maná *m*.

mannequin [man'əkin] *n* (*dummy*) maniquí *m*; (*fashion model*) modelo *f*.

manner [man'ûr] *n* manera, modo; (*behavior*) conducta, manera de ser; (*type*) clase *f*; ~**s** *npl* modales *mpl*, educación *fsg*; (**good**) ~**s** educación *fsg*, (**buenos**) modales *mpl*; **bad** ~**s** falta *sg* de educación, pocos modales *mpl*; **all ~ of** toda clase *or* suerte de.

mannerism [man'ərizəm] *n* hábito, peculiaridad *f*.

mannerly [man'ûrlē] *a* bien educado, formal.

manoeuvre [mənōō'vûr] *etc* (*Brit*) = **maneuver** *etc*.

manor [man'ûr] *n* (*also:* ~ **house**) casa solariega.

manpower [man'pouûr] *n* mano *f* de obra.

manservant [man'sûrvənt] *n* criado.

mansion [man'chən] *n* palacio, casa grande.

manslaughter [man'slôtûr] *n* homicidio no premeditado.

mantelpiece [man'təlpēs] *n* repisa, chimenea.

mantle [man'təl] *n* manto; (*fig*) capa.

man-to-man [man'təman'] *a* entre hombres.

manual [man'yōōəl] *a* manual ♦ *n* manual *m*; ~ **worker** obrero, trabajador *m* de camisa azul.

manufacture [manyəfak'chûr] *vt* fabricar ♦ *n* fabricación *f*.

manufactured goods [manyəfak'chûrd gōōdz] *npl* manufacturas *fpl*, bienes *mpl* manufacturados.

manufacturer [manyəfak'chûrûr] *n* fabricante *m/f*.

manufacturing industries [manyəfak'chûring in'dəstrēz] *npl* industrias *fpl* de manufactura.

manure [mənōōr'] *n* estiércol *m*, abono.

manuscript [man'yəskript] *n* manuscrito.

Manx [mangks] *a* de la Isla de Man.

many [men'ē] *a* muchos/as ♦ *pron* muchos/as; **a great ~** muchísimos, buen número de; **~ a time** muchas veces; **too ~ difficulties** demasiadas dificultades; **twice as ~** el doble; **how ~?** ¿cuántos?

map [map] *n* mapa *m* ♦ *vt* trazar el mapa de.

map out *vt* (*fig: career, vacation, essay*) proyectar, planear.

maple [mā'pəl] *n* arce *m*, maple *m* (*LAm*).

mar [mar] *vt* estropear.

Mar. *abbr* (= *March*) mar.

marathon [mar'əthân] *n* maratón *m* ♦ *a*: **a ~ session** una sesión larguísima *or* interminable.

marathon runner *n* corredor(a) *m/f* de maratones.

marauder |mərṓd'ûr| *n* merodeador(a) *m/f*, intruso/a.

marble |mär'bəl| *n* mármol *m*; (*toy*) canica.

March |märch| *n* marzo.

march |märch| *vi* (*MIL*) marchar; (*fig*) caminar con resolución ♦ *n* marcha; (*demonstration*) manifestación *f*.

marcher |mär'chûr| *n* manifestante *m/f*.

marching |mär'ching| *n*: **to give sb his ~ orders** (*fig*) mandar a paseo a uno; (*employee*) poner de patitas en la calle a uno.

march-past |märch'past| *n* desfile *m*.

mare |mär| *n* yegua.

margarine |mär'jûrin| *n* margarina.

marg(e) |märj| *n* *abbr* = **margarine**.

margin |mär'jin| *n* margen *m*.

marginal |mär'jinəl| *a* marginal.

marginally |mär'jinəlē| *ad* ligeramente.

marginal seat *n* (*POL*) circunscripción *f* políticamente indefinida.

marigold |mar'əgōld| *n* caléndula.

marijuana |marəwä'nə| *n* marijuana.

marina |mərē'nə| *n* marina.

marinade |mar'ənād| *n* adobo.

marinate |mar'ənāt| *vt* adobar.

marine |mərēn'| *a* marino ♦ *n* soldado de marina.

marine insurance *n* seguro marítimo.

mariner |mar'inûr| *n* marinero, marino.

marionette |marēənet'| *n* marioneta, títere *m*.

marital |mar'itəl| *a* matrimonial; **~ status** estado civil.

maritime |mar'itīm| *a* marítimo.

marjoram |mär'jûrəm| *n* mejorana.

mark |märk| *n* marca, señal *f*; (*imprint*) huella; (*stain*) mancha; (*SCOL*) nota; (*currency*) marco ♦ *vt* (*also SPORT: player*) marcar; (*stain*) manchar; (*Brit SCOL*) calificar, corregir; **puntuation: ~s** signos *mpl* de puntuación; **to be quick off the ~** (*fig*) ser listo; **up to the ~** (*in efficiency*) a la altura de las circunstancias; **to ~ time** marcar el paso.

mark down *vt* (*reduce: prices, goods*) rebajar.

mark off *vt* (*tick*) indicar, señalar.

mark out *vt* trazar.

mark up *vt* (*price*) aumentar.

marked |märkt| *a* marcado, acusado.

markedly |mär'kidlē| *ad* marcadamente, apreciablemente.

marker |mär'kûr| *n* (*sign*) marcador *m*; (*bookmark*) registro.

market |mär'kit| *n* mercado ♦ *vt* (*COMM*) comercializar; (*promote*) publicitar; **open ~** mercado libre; **to be on the ~** estar en venta; **to play the ~** jugar a la bolsa.

marketable |mär'kitəbəl| *a* comerciable.

market analysis *n* análisis *m* del mercado.

market day *n* día *m* de mercado.

market demand *n* demanda de mercado.

market forces *npl* tendencias *fpl* del mercado.

market garden *n* (*Brit*) huerto.

marketing |mär'kiting| *n* márketing *m*, mercadotecnia.

marketing manager *n* director *m* de marketing.

market leader *n* líder *m* de ventas.

marketplace |mär'kitplās| *n* mercado.

market price *n* precio de mercado.

market research *n* (*COMM*) investigación *f* de mercados.

market value *n* valor *m* en el mercado.

marking |mär'king| *n* (*on animal*) pinta; (*on road*) señal *f*.

marking ink *n* tinta indeleble *or* de marcar.

marksman |märks'mən| *n* tirador *m*.

marksmanship |märks'mənship| *n* puntería.

mark-up |märk'up| *n* (*COMM: margin*) margen *m* de beneficio; (: *increase*) aumento.

marmalade |mär'məlād| *n* mermelada de naranja.

maroon |mərōōn'| *vt*: **to be ~ed** (*shipwrecked*) naufragarse; (*fig*) quedar abandonado ♦ *a* marrón *inv*.

marquee |märkē'| *n* entoldado.

marquess, marquis |mär'kwis| *n* marqués *m*.

Marrakech, Marrakesh |mär'əkesh| *n* Marrakech *m*.

marriage |mar'ij| *n* (*state*) matrimonio; (*wedding*) boda; (*act*) casamiento.

marriage bureau *n* (*Brit*) agencia matrimonial.

marriage certificate *n* partida de casamiento.

marriage counseling, (*Brit*) **marriage guidance** *n* orientación *f* matrimonial.

married |mar'ēd| *a* casado; (*life, love*) conyugal.

marrow |mar'ō| *n* médula; (*vegetable*) calabacín *m*.

marry |mar'ē| *vt* casarse con; (*subj: father, priest etc*) casar ♦ *vi* (*also*: **get married**) casarse.

Mars |märz| *n* Marte *m*.

Marseilles |märsā'| *n* Marsella.

marsh |märsh| *n* pantano; (*salt ~*) marisma.

marshal |mär'shəl| *n* (*MIL*) mariscal *m*; (*at parade*) oficial *m*; (*US: of police, fire department*) jefe/a *m/f* ♦ *vt* (*facts*) ordenar; (*soldiers*) formar.

marshalling yard |mär'shəling yärd| *n* (*Brit RAIL*) estación *f* clasificadora.

marshmallow |märsh'melō| *n* (*BOT*) malvavisco; (*sweet*) bombón *m* de merengue blando.

marshy |mär'shē| *a* pantanoso.

marsupial |märsōō'pēəl| *a, n* marsupial *m*.

martial [mâr'shəl] *a* marcial.
martial law *n* ley *f* marcial.
martin [mâr'tən] *n* (*also:* **house** ~) avión *m*.
martyr [mâr'tûr] *n* mártir *m/f* ♦ *vt* martirizar.
martyrdom [mâr'tûrdəm] *n* martirio.
marvel [mâr'vəl] *n* maravilla, prodigio ♦ *vi:* **to** ~ **(at)** maravillarse (de).
marvelous, (*Brit*) **marvellous** [mâr'vələs] *a* maravilloso.
marvel(l)ously [mâr'vələslē] *ad* maravillosamente.
Marxism [mârk'sizəm] *n* marxismo.
Marxist [mârk'ksist] *a,* *n* marxista *m/f.*
marzipan [mâr'zəpan] *n* mazapán *m.*
mascara [maskar'ə] *n* rimel *m.*
mascot [mas'kət] *n* mascota.
masculine [mas'kyəlin] *a* masculino.
masculinity [maskyəlin'itē] *n* masculinidad *f.*
MASH [mash] *n* *abbr* (*US*) = *mobile army surgical hospital.*
mash [mash] *n* (*mix*) mezcla; (*CULIN*) puré *m*; (*pulp*) amasijo.
mashed potatoes [masht pətā'tōz] *npl* puré *m* de patatas *or* papas (*LAm*).
mask [mask] *n* (*also ELEC*) máscara ♦ *vt* enmascarar.
masochism [mas'əkizəm] *n* masoquismo.
masochist [mas'əkist] *n* masoquista *m/f.*
mason [mā'sən] *n* (*also:* **stone~**) albañil *m*; (*also:* **free~**) masón *m.*
masonic [məsán'ik] *a* masónico.
masonry [mā'sənrē] *n* masonería; (*building*) mampostería.
masquerade [maskərād'] *n* baile *m* de máscaras; (*fig*) mascarada ♦ *vi:* **to** ~ **as** disfrazarse de, hacerse pasar por.
mass [mas] *n* (*people*) muchedumbre *f*; (*PHYSICS*) masa; (*REL*) misa; (*great quantity*) montón *m* ♦ *vi* reunirse; (*MIL*) concentrarse; **the ~es** las masas; **to go to** ~ oír misa.
Mass. *abbr* (*US*) = *Massachusetts.*
massacre [mas'əkûr] *n* masacre *f* ♦ *vt* masacrar.
massage [məsâzh'] *n* masaje *m* ♦ *vt* dar masaje a.
masseur [masûr'] *n* masajista *m.*
masseuse [məsōōs'] *n* masajista *f.*
massive [mas'iv] *a* enorme; (*support, intervention*) masivo.
mass media [mas mē'dēə] *npl* medios *mpl* de comunicación masiva.
mass meeting *n* (*of everyone concerned*) reunión *f* en masa; (*huge*) mitin *m.*
mass-produce [mas'prədōōs'] *vt* fabricar en serie.
mass production *n* fabricación *f* or producción *f* en serie.
mast [mast] *n* (*NAUT*) mástil *m*; (*RADIO etc*) torre *f*, antena.

master [mas'tûr] *n* maestro; (*in secondary school*) profesor *m*; (*title for boys*): **M~ X** Señorito X ♦ *vt* dominar; (*learn*) aprender a fondo.
master disk *n* (*COMPUT*) disco maestro.
masterful [mas'tûrfəl] *a* magistral, dominante.
master key *n* llave *f* maestra.
masterly [mas'tûrlē] *a* magistral.
mastermind [mas'tûrmīnd] *n* inteligencia superior ♦ *vt* dirigir, planear.
Master of Arts (MA) *n* licenciatura superior en Letras.
Master of Ceremonies *n* encargado de protocolo.
Master of Science (MSc) *n* licenciatura superior en Ciencias.
masterpiece [mas'tûrpēs] *n* obra maestra.
master plan *n* plan *m* rector.
masterstroke [mas'tûrstrōk] *n* golpe *m* maestro.
mastery [mas'tûrē] *n* maestría.
mastiff [mas'tif] *n* mastín *m.*
masturbate [mas'tûrbāt] *vi* masturbarse.
masturbation [mastûrbā'shən] *n* masturbación *f.*
mat [mat] *n* estera; (*also:* **door~**) felpudo ♦ *a* = **matt.**
match [mach] *n* cerilla, fósforo; (*game*) partido; (*fig*) igual *m/f* ♦ *vt* emparejar; (*go well with*) hacer juego con; (*equal*) igualar ♦ *vi* hacer juego; **to be a good** ~ hacer buena pareja.
matchbox [mach'bâks] *n* caja de cerillas.
matching [mach'ing] *a* que hace juego.
matchless [mach'lis] *a* sin par, incomparable.
matchmaker [mach'mākûr] *n* casamentero.
mate [māt] *n* (*work~*) colega *m/f*; (*col: friend*) amigo/a; (*animal*) macho/hembra; (*in merchant navy*) segundo de a bordo ♦ *vi* acoplarse, parearse ♦ *vt* acoplar, parear.
material [mətē'rēəl] *n* (*substance*) materia; (*equipment*) material *m*; (*cloth*) tela, tejido ♦ *a* material; (*important*) esencial; **~s** *npl* materiales *mpl*; (*equipment etc*) artículos *mpl.*
materialistic [mətērēəlis'tik] *a* materialista.
materialize [mətēr'ēəlīz] *vi* materializarse.
materially [mətēr'ēəlē] *ad* materialmente.
maternal [mətûr'nəl] *a* maternal; ~ **grandmother** abuela materna.
maternity [mətûr'nitē] *n* maternidad *f.*
maternity benefit *n* subsidio de maternidad.
maternity dress *n* vestido premamá.
maternity hospital *n* hospital *m* de maternidad.
maternity leave *n* licencia por maternidad.
math [math] *n* *abbr* (*US:* = *mathematics*) matemáticas *fpl.*
mathematical [mathəmat'ikəl] *a* matemáti-

co.

mathematically [mathəmat'ikəlē] *ad* matemáticamente.

mathematician [mathəmətish'ən] *n* matemático.

mathematics [mathəmat'iks] *n* matemáticas *fpl*.

maths [maths] *n abbr* (*Brit*: = *mathematics*) matemáticas *fpl*.

matinée [matənā'] *n* función *f* de la tarde.

mating [mā'ting] *n* aparejamiento.

mating call *n* llamada del macho.

mating season *n* época de celo.

matins [mat'ənz] *n* maitines *mpl*.

matriarchal [mātrēār'kəl] *a* matriarcal.

matrices [māt'risēz] *pl of* **matrix**.

matriculation [mətrikyəlā'shən] *n* matriculación *f*.

matrimonial [matrəmō'nēəl] *a* matrimonial.

matrimony [mat'rəmōnē] *n* matrimonio.

matrix, *pl* **matrices** [mā'triks, māt'risēz] *n* matriz *f*.

matron [mā'trən] *n* (*in hospital*) enfermera jefe; (*in school*) ama de llaves.

matronly [mā'trənlē] *a* de matrona; (*fig: figure*) corpulento.

matt [mat] *a* mate.

matted [mat'id] *a* enmarañado.

matter [mat'ûr] *n* cuestión *f*, asunto; (*PHYSICS*) sustancia, materia; (*content*) contenido; (*MED: pus*) pus *m* ♦ *vi* importar; **it doesn't** ~ no importa; **what's the** ~? ¿qué pasa?; **no** ~ **what** pase lo que pase; **as a** ~ **of course** por rutina; **as a** ~ **of fact** en realidad; **printed** ~ impresos *mpl*; **reading** ~ algo para leer, libros *mpl*.

matter-of-fact [mat'ûrəvfakt'] *a* prosaico, práctico.

mattress [mat'ris] *n* colchón *m*.

mature [mətōōr'] *a* maduro ♦ *vi* madurar.

maturity [mətōō'ritē] *n* madurez *f*.

maudlin [môd'lin] *a* llorón/ona.

maul [môl] *vt* magullar.

Mauritania [môritā'nēə] *n* Mauritania.

Mauritius [môrish'ēəs] *n* Mauricio.

mausoleum [môsəlē'əm] *n* mausoleo.

mauve [mōv] *a* de color malva *or* guinda (*LAm*).

maverick [mav'ûrik] *n* (*fig*) inconformista *m/f*, persona independiente.

mawkish [môk'ish] *a* empalagoso.

max. *abbr* = **maximum**.

maxim [mak'sim] *n* máxima.

maxima [mak'səmə] *pl of* **maximum**.

maximize [mak'səmīz] *vt* (*profits etc*) llevar al máximo; (*chances*) maximizar.

maximum [mak'səməm] *a* máximo ♦ *n* (*pl* **maxima** [mak'səmə]) máximo.

May [mā] *n* mayo.

may [mā] *vi* (*conditional*: **might**) (*indicating possibility*): **he** ~ **come** puede que venga; (*be allowed to*): ~ **I smoke?** ¿puedo fumar?; (*wishes*): ~ **God bless you!** ¡que

Dios le bendiga!; ~ **I sit here?** ¿me puedo sentar aquí?

maybe [mā'bē] *ad* quizá(s); ~ **not** quizás no.

May Day *n* el primero de Mayo.

mayday [mā'dā] *n* S.O.S. *m*.

mayhem [mā'hem] *n* caos *m* total.

mayonnaise [māənāz'] *n* mayonesa.

mayor [mā'ûr] *n* alcalde *m*.

mayoress [mā'ûris] *n* alcaldesa.

maypole [mā'pōl] *n* mayo.

maze [māz] *n* laberinto.

MB *abbr* (*COMPUT*) = **megabyte**; (*Canada*) = *Manitoba*.

MBA *n abbr* (= *Master of Business Administration*) título universitario.

MBBS, MBChB *n abbr* (*Brit*: = *Bachelor of Medicine and Surgery*) título universitario.

MC *n abbr* (= *master of ceremonies*) e.p.; (*US*: = *Member of Congress*) diputado del Congreso de los Estados Unidos.

MCAT *n abbr* (*US*) = *Medical College Admissions Test*.

MCP *n abbr* (*Brit col*) = **male chauvinist pig**.

MD *n abbr* (= *Doctor of Medicine*) título universitario; (*COMM*) = **managing director** ♦ *abbr* (*US MAIL*) = *Maryland*.

ME *abbr* (*US MAIL*) = *Maine* ♦ *n abbr* (*US MED*) = *medical examiner*; (*MED*) = *myalgic encephalomyelitis*.

me [mē] *pron* (*direct*) me; (*stressed, after pronoun*) mí; **can you hear** ~? ¿me oyes?; **he heard ME!** me oyó a mí; **it's** ~ soy yo; **give them to** ~ dámelos; **with/without** ~ conmigo/sin mí; **it's for** ~ es para mí.

meadow [med'ō] *n* prado, pradera.

meager, (*Brit*) **meagre** [mē'gûr] *a* escaso, pobre.

meal [mēl] *n* comida; (*flour*) harina; **to go out for a** ~ salir a comer.

meal ticket *n* (*US*) vale *m* de comida.

mealtime [mēl'tīm] *n* hora de comer.

mealy-mouthed [mē'lēmouthd] *a*: **to be** ~ nunca decir las cosas claras.

mean [mēn] *a* (*with money*) tacaño; (*unkind*) mezquino, malo; (*average*) medio; (*US: vicious: animal*) resabiado; (: *person*) malicioso ♦ *vt* (*pt*, *pp* **meant** [ment]) (*signify*) querer decir, significar; (*intend*): **to** ~ **to do sth** pensar *or* pretender hacer algo ♦ *n* medio, término medio; **do you** ~ **it?** ¿lo dices en serio?; **what do you** ~? ¿qué quiere decir?; **to be meant for sb/sth** ser para uno/algo; *see also* **means**.

meander [mēan'dûr] *vi* (*river*) serpentear; (*person*) vagar.

meaning [mē'ning] *n* significado, sentido.

meaningful [mē'ningfəl] *a* significativo.

meaningless [mē'ninglis] *a* sin sentido.

meanness [mēn'nis] *n* (*with money*) tacañería; (*unkindness*) maldad *f*, mezquindad *f.*

means [mēnz] *npl* medio *sg*, manera *sg*; (*resource*) recursos *mpl*, medios *mpl*; **by ~ of** mediante, por medio de; **by all ~!** ¡naturalmente!, ¡claro que sí!

means test *n* control *m* de los recursos económicos.

meant [ment] *pt, pp of* **mean**.

meantime [mēn'tīm] *ad* (*also:* **in the meantime**) mientras tanto.

meanwhile [mēn'wīl] *ad* mientras tanto.

measles [mē'zəlz] *n* sarampión *m*.

measly [mēz'lē] *a* (*col*) miserable.

measurable [mezh'ûrəbəl] *a* mensurable, que se puede medir.

measure [mezh'ûr] *vt* medir; (*for clothes etc*) tomar las medidas a ♦ *vi* medir ♦ *n* medida; (*ruler*) regla; **a liter ~** una medida de un litro; **some ~ of success** cierto éxito; **to take ~s to do sth** tomar medidas para hacer algo.

measure up *vi:* **to ~ up (to)** mostrarse capaz (de).

measured [mezh'ûrd] *a* moderado; (*tone*) mesurado.

measurement [mezh'ûrmənt] *n* (*measure*) medida; (*act*) medición *f*; **to take sb's ~s** tomar las medidas a uno.

meat [mēt] *n* carne *f*; **cold ~s** (*Brit*) fiambres *mpl*; **crab ~** carne *f* de cangrejo.

meatball [mēt'bôl] *n* albóndiga.

meat pie *n* pastel *m* de carne.

meaty [mē'tē] *a* carnoso; (*fig*) sustancioso.

Mecca [mek'ə] *n* (*city*) la Meca; (*fig*) Meca.

mechanic [məkan'ik] *n* mecánico/a.

mechanical [məkan'ikəl] *a* mecánico.

mechanical engineering *n* (*science*) ingeniería mecánica; (*industry*) construcción *f* mecánica.

mechanical pencil *n* (*US*) lapicero.

mechanics [məkan'iks] *n* mecánica ♦ *npl* mecanismo *sg*.

mechanism [mek'ənizəm] *n* mecanismo.

mechanization [mekənizā'shən] *n* mecanización *f*.

mechanize [mek'ənīz] *vt* mecanizar; (*factory etc*) automatizar, reconvertir.

MEd *n abbr* (= *Master of Education*) título universitario.

medal [med'əl] *n* medalla.

medallion [mədal'yən] *n* medallón *m*.

medalist, (*Brit*) **medallist** [med'əlist] *n* (*SPORT*) ganador(a) *m/f*.

meddle [med'əl] *vi:* **to ~ in** entrometerse en; **to ~ with sth** manosear algo.

meddlesome [med'əlsəm], **meddling** [med'ling] *a* (*interfering*) entrometido; (*touching things*) curioso.

media [mē'dēə] *npl* medios *mpl* de comunicación.

mediaeval [mēdēē'vəl] *a* = **medieval**.

median [mē'dēən] *n* (*US: also:* **~ strip**) faja intermedia, mediana.

media research *n* investigación *f* de los medios de publicidad.

mediate [mē'dēāt] *vi* mediar.

mediation [mēdēā'shən] *n* mediación *f*.

mediator [mē'dēātûr] *n* intermediario/a, mediador(a) *m/f*.

Medicaid [med'ikād] *n* (*US*) *programa de ayuda médica*.

medical [med'ikəl] *a* médico ♦ *n* (*also:* **~ examination**) reconocimiento médico.

medical certificate *n* certificado *m* médico.

medical examiner *n* (*US*) médico/a forense.

Medicare [med'əkär] *n* (*US*) *seguro médico del Estado*.

medicated [med'ikātid] *a* medicinal.

medication [medikā'shən] *n* (*drugs etc*) medicación *f*.

medicinal [mədis'ənəl] *a* medicinal.

medicine [med'isin] *n* medicina; (*drug*) medicamento.

medicine chest *n* botiquín *m*.

medicine man *n* hechicero.

medieval, mediaeval [mēdēē'vəl] *a* medieval.

mediocre [mē'dēōkûr] *a* mediocre.

mediocrity [mēdēák'ritē] *n* mediocridad *f*.

meditate [med'ətāt] *vi* meditar.

meditation [meditā'shən] *n* meditación *f*.

Mediterranean [meditərā'nēən] *a* mediterráneo; **the ~ (Sea)** el (Mar *m*) Mediterráneo.

medium [mē'dēəm] *a* mediano, regular ♦ *n* (*pl* **media:** *means*) medio; (*pl* **mediums:** *person*) médium *m/f*; **happy ~** justo medio.

medium-sized [mē'dēəmsīzd] *a* (*tin etc*) regular; (*clothes*) de tamaño mediano.

medium wave *n* onda media.

medley [med'lē] *n* mezcla; (*MUS*) popurrí *m*.

meek [mēk] *a* manso, sumiso.

meekly [mēk'lē] *ad* mansamente, dócilmente.

meet [mēt] *vb* (*pt, pp* **met** [met]) *vt* encontrar; (*accidentally*) encontrarse con, tropezar con; (*by arrangement*) reunirse con; (*for the first time*) conocer; (*go and fetch*) ir a buscar; (*opponent*) enfrentarse con; (*obligations*) cumplir; (*bill, expenses*) pagar, costear ♦ *vi* encontrarse; (*in session*) reunirse; (*join: objects*) unirse; (*get to know*) conocerse ♦ *n* (*Brit: HUNTING*) cacería; (*US: SPORT*) encuentro; **pleased to ~ you!** ¡encantado de conocerle!, ¡mucho gusto!

meet up *vi:* **to ~ up with sb** reunirse con uno.

meet with *vt fus* reunirse con; (*difficulty*) tropezar con.

meeting [mē'ting] *n* (*also SPORT:* **rally**) encuentro; (*arranged*) cita, compromiso (*LAm*); (*formal session, business meet*) reunión *f*; (*POL*) mitin *m*; **to call a ~** convocar *or* llamar una reunión.

meeting place *n* lugar *m* de reunión *or* encuentro.

megabyte [mɛg'əbīt] *n* (*COMPUT*) megabyte *m*, megaocteto.

megalomaniac [mɛgəlōmā'nēak] *a*, *n* megalómano/a *m/f*.

megaphone [mɛg'əfōn] *n* megáfono.

melancholy [mɛl'ənkâlē] *n* melancolía ♦ *a* melancólico.

melee [mā'lā] *n* refriega.

mellow [mɛl'ō] *a* (*wine*) añejo; (*sound, color*) suave; (*fruit*) maduro ♦ *vi* (*person*) madurar.

melodious [məlō'dēəs] *a* melodioso.

melodrama [mɛl'ədrâmə] *n* melodrama *m*.

melodramatic [mɛlədrəmat'ik] *a* melodramático.

melody [mɛl'ədē] *n* melodía.

melon [mɛl'ən] *n* melón *m*.

melt [mɛlt] *vi* (*metal*) fundirse; (*snow*) derretirse; (*fig*) ablandarse ♦ *vt* (*also:* ~ **down**) fundir; **~ed butter** mantequilla derretida.

melt away *vi* desvanecerse.

meltdown [mɛlt'doun] *n* (*in nuclear reactor*) fusión *f* (de un reactor nuclear).

melting point [mɛlt'ing point] *n* punto de fusión.

melting pot [mɛlt'ing pât] *n* (*fig*) crisol *m*; **to be in the ~** estar sobre el tapete.

member [mɛm'bûr] *n* (*of political party*) miembro; (*of club*) socio/a; **M~ of Congress (MC)** (*US*) diputado/a del Congreso; **M~ of the House of Representatives (MHR)** (*US*) diputado/a del Congreso de los Estados Unidos; **M~ of Parliament (MP)** (*Brit*) diputado/a; **M~ of the European Parliament (MEP)** (*Brit*) eurodiputado/a.

membership [mɛm'bûrship] *n* (*members*) número de miembros; **to seek ~ of** pedir el ingreso a.

membership card *n* carnet *m* de socio.

membrane [mɛm'brān] *n* membrana.

memento [məmɛn'tō] *n* recuerdo.

memo [mɛm'ō] *n* *abbr* (= *memorandum*) memo.

memoirs [mɛm'wârz] *npl* memorias *fpl*.

memo pad *n* agenda.

memorable [mɛm'ûrəbəl] *a* memorable.

memorandum, *pl* memoranda [mɛmə-ran'dəm, -də] *n* apunte *m*, nota; (*POL*) memorándum *m*.

memorial [məmō'rēəl] *n* monumento conmemorativo ♦ *a* conmemorativo.

memorial day *n* día *m* de conmemoración de los difuntos de guerra.

memorize [mɛm'ərīz] *vt* aprender de memoria.

memory [mɛm'ûrē] *n* memoria; (*recollection*) recuerdo; (*COMPUT*) memoria; **to have a good/bad ~** tener buena/mala memoria; **loss of ~** pérdida de memoria.

men [mɛn] *pl of* **man**.

menace [mɛn'is] *n* amenaza; (*col: nuisance*) lata ♦ *vt* amenazar; **a public ~** un peligro para la humanidad.

menacing [mɛn'ising] *a* amenazador(a).

menacingly [mɛn'isinglē] *ad* amenazadoramente.

menagerie [mənaj'ûrē] *n* casa de fieras.

mend [mɛnd] *vt* reparar, arreglar; (*darn*) zurcir ♦ *vi* reponerse ♦ *n* (*gen*) remiendo; (*darn*) zurcido; **to be on the ~** ir mejorando.

mending [mɛnd'ing] *n* reparación *f*; (*clothes*) ropa por remendar.

menial [mē'nēəl] *a* doméstico; (*pej*) bajo.

meningitis [mɛninji'tis] *n* meningitis *f*.

menopause [mɛn'əpóz] *n* menopausia.

menstrual [mɛn'strōōəl] *a* menstrual.

menstruate [mɛn'strōōāt] *vi* menstruar.

menstruation [mɛnstrōōā'shən] *n* menstruación *f*.

mental [mɛn'təl] *a* mental; **~ illness** enfermedad *f* mental.

mentality [mɛntal'itē] *n* mentalidad *f*.

mentally [mɛn'təlē] *ad*: **to be ~ handicapped** ser un retrasado mental.

menthol [mɛn'thôl] *n* mentol *m*.

mention [mɛn'chən] *n* mención *f* ♦ *vt* mencionar; (*speak of*) hablar de; **don't ~ it!** ¡de nada!; **I need hardly ~ that ...** huelga decir que ...; **not to ~, without ~ing** sin contar.

mentor [mɛn'tûr] *n* mentor *m*.

menu [mɛn'yōō] *n* (*set ~*) menú *m*; (*printed*) carta; (*COMPUT*) menú *m*.

menu-driven [mɛn'yōōdriv'ən] *a* (*COMPUT*) guiado por menú.

meow [mēou'] *vi* maullar.

MEP *n abbr* = **Member of the European Parliament**.

mercantile [mûr'kəntil] *a* mercantil.

mercenary [mûr'sənɛrē] *a*, *n* mercenario.

merchandise [mûr'chəndīs] *n* mercancías *fpl*.

merchandiser [mûr'chəndīzûr] *n* comerciante *m/f*, tratante *m*.

merchant [mûr'chənt] *n* comerciante *m/f*.

merchant bank *n* (*Brit*) banco comercial.

merchantman [mûr'chəntmən] *n* buque *m* mercante.

merchant marine, (*Brit*) **merchant navy** *n* marina mercante.

merciful [mûr'sifəl] *a* compasivo.

mercifully [mûr'sifəlē] *ad* con compasión; (*fortunately*) afortunadamente.

merciless [mûr'silis] *a* despiadado.

mercilessly [mûr'silislē] *ad* despiadadamente, sin piedad.

mercurial [mûrkyōō'rēəl] *a* veleidoso, voluble.

mercury [mûrk'yûrē] *n* mercurio.

mercy [mûr'sē] *n* compasión *f*; (*REL*) mise-

ricordia; **at the** ~ **of** a la merced de.
mercy killing n eutanasia.
mere |mēr| a simple, mero.
merely |mēr'lē| ad simplemente, sólo.
merge |mûrj| vt (join) unir; (mix) mezclar; (fuse) fundir; (COMPUT: files, text) intercalar ♦ vi unirse; (COMM) fusionarse.
merger |mûr'jûr| n (COMM) fusión f.
meridian |mərid'ēən| n meridiano.
meringue |mərang'| n merengue m.
merit |mär'it| n mérito ♦ vt merecer.
meritocracy |märitâk'rəsē| n meritocracia.
mermaid |mûr'mād| n sirena.
merrily |mär'ilē| ad alegremente.
merriment |mär'imənt| n alegría.
merry |mär'ē| a alegre; **M~ Christmas!** ¡Felices Pascuas!
merry-go-round |mär'ēgōround| n tiovivo.
mesh |mesh| n malla; (TECH) engranaje m ♦ vi (gears) engranar; **wire** ~ tela metálica.
mesmerize |mez'mərīz| vt hipnotizar.
mess |mes| n confusión f; (of objects) revoltijo; (tangle) lío; (MIL) comedor m; **to be (in) a** ~ (room) estar revuelto; **to be/ get o.s. in a** ~ estar/meterse en un lío.
mess about vi (Brit) = **mess around.**
mess around vi (col) perder el tiempo; (pass the time) entretenerse.
mess around with vt fus (col: play with) divertirse con; (: handle) manosear.
mess up vt (disarrange) desordenar; (spoil) estropear; (dirty) ensuciar.
message |mes'ij| n recado, mensaje m; **to get the** ~ (fig, col) caer en la cuenta.
message switching n (COMPUT) conmutación f de mensajes.
messenger |mes'injûr| n mensajero/a.
Messiah |misī'ə| n Mesías m.
Messrs |mes'ûrz| abbr (on letters: = Messieurs) Sres.
messy |mes'ē| a (dirty) sucio; (untidy) desordenado; (confused: situation etc) confuso.
Met |met| n abbr (US) = Metropolitan Opera.
met |met| pt, pp of **meet** ♦ a abbr (Brit) = **meteorological.**
metabolism |mətab'əlizəm| n metabolismo.
metal |met'əl| n metal m.
metallic |mital'ik| a metálico.
metallurgy |met'əlûrjē| n metalurgia.
metalwork |met'əlwûrk| n (craft) metalistería.
metamorphosis, pl **metamorphoses** |metəmôr'fəsis, -sēz| n metamorfosis f inv.
metaphor |met'əfôr| n metáfora.
metaphorical |metəfôr'ikəl| a metafórico.
metaphysics |metəfiz'iks| n metafísica.
mete |mēt| **to** ~ **out** vt fus (punishment) imponer.
meteor |mē'tēôr| n meteoro.
meteoric |mētēôr'ik| a (fig) rápido, meteórico.

meteorite |mē'tēərīt| n meteorito.
meteorological |mētēûrəlâj'ikəl| a meteorológico.
meteorology |mētēərâl'əjē| n meteorología.
meter |mē'tûr| n (instrument) contador m; (US: unit) metro ♦ vt (US MAIL) franquear; **parking** ~ parquímetro.
methane |meth'ān| n metano.
method |meth'əd| n método; ~ **of payment** método de pagar.
methodical |məthâd'ikəl| a metódico.
Methodist |meth'ədist| a, n metodista m/f.
methodology |methədâl'əjē| n metodología.
meths |meths|, **methylated spirit(s)** |meth'-əlātid spir'it(s)| n (Brit) alcohol m metilado or desnaturalizado.
meticulous |mətik'yələs| a meticuloso.
metre |mē'tûr| n (Brit: unit) metro.
metric |met'rik| a métrico; **to go** ~ pasar al sistema métrico.
metrication |metrikā'shən| n conversión f al sistema métrico.
metric system n sistema m métrico.
metric ton n tonelada métrica.
metronome |met'rənōm| n metrónomo.
metropolis |miträp'əlis| n metrópoli f.
metropolitan |metrəpâl'itən| a metropolitano.
Metropolitan Police n (Brit): **the** ~ la policía londinense.
mettle |met'əl| n valor m, ánimo.
mew |myōō| vi (cat) maullar.
mews |myōōz| (Brit) n: ~ **cottage** casa acondicionada en antiguos establos o cocheras; ~ **flat** piso en antiguos establos o cocheras.
Mexican |mek'səkən| a, n mejicano/a m/f, mexicano/a m/f (LAm).
Mexico |mek'səkō| n Méjico, México (LAm).
Mexico City n Ciudad f de Méjico or México (LAm).
mezzanine |mez'ənēn| n entresuelo.
MFA n abbr (US: = Master of Fine Arts) título universitario.
mfr abbr (= manufacturer) fab.
mg abbr (= milligram) mg.
Mgr abbr (= Monseigneur, Monsignor) Mons.
mgr abbr = **manager.**
MHR n abbr = **Member of the House of Representatives.**
MHz abbr (= megahertz) MHz.
MI abbr (US MAIL) = Michigan.
MI5 n abbr (Brit: = Military Intelligence 5) servicio de contraespionaje del gobierno británico.
MI6 n abbr (Brit: = Military Intelligence 6) servicio de inteligencia del gobierno británico.
MIA abbr (= missing in action) desaparecido.

mice [mīs] *pl of* **mouse.**
Mich. *abbr* (*US*) = *Michigan.*
micro... [mī'krō] *pref* micro....
microbe [mī'krōb] *n* microbio.
microbiology [mīkrōbīάl'əjē] *n* microbiología.
microchip [mī'krəchip] *n* microplaqueta.
micro(computer) [mīkrō(kəmpyōō'tûr)] *n* microordenador *m*, microcomputador *m*.
microcosm [mī'krəkâzəm] *n* microcosmo.
microeconomics [mīkrōēkənâm'iks] *n* microeconomía.
microfiche [mī'krōfēsh] *n* microficha.
microfilm [mī'krəfilm] *n* microfilm *m*.
micrometer [mīkrâm'itûr] *n* micrómetro.
microphone [mī'krəfōn] *n* micrófono.
microprocessor [mīkrōprâs'esûr] *n* microprocesador *m*.
microscope [mī'krəskōp] *n* microscopio; **under the ~** bajo el microscopio.
microscopic [mī'krəskâp'ik] *a* microscópico.
microwave [mī'krōwāv] *n* (*also*: **~ oven**) horno microondas.
mid [mid] *a*: **in ~ May** a mediados de mayo; **in ~ afternoon** a media tarde; **in ~ air** en el aire; **he's in his ~ thirties** tiene unos treinta y cinco años.
midday [mid'dā] *n* mediodía *m*.
middle [mid'əl] *n* medio, centro; (*waist*) cintura ♦ *a* de en medio; **in the ~ of the night** en plena noche; **I'm in the ~ of reading it** lo estoy leyendo ahora mismo.
middle-aged [mid'əlājd'] *a* de mediana edad.
Middle Ages *npl*: **the ~** la Edad *sg* Media.
middle class *n*: **the ~(es)** la clase media ♦ *a* (*also*: **middle-class**) de clase media.
Middle East *n* Oriente *m* Medio.
middleman [mid'əlman] *n* intermediario.
middle management *n* dirección *f* de nivel medio.
middle name *n* nombre *m* segundo.
middle-of-the-road [mid'ələvΐhərōd'] *a* moderado, centrista.
middleweight [mid'əlwāt] *n* (*BOXING*) peso medio.
middling [mid'ling] *a* mediano.
Middx *abbr* (*Brit*) = *Middlesex.*
midge [mij] *n* mosca.
midget [mij'it] *n* enano/a.
midnight [mid'nīt] *n* medianoche *f*; **at ~** a medianoche.
midriff [mid'rif] *n* diafragma *m*.
midst [midst] *n*: **in the ~ of** entre, en medio de.
midsummer [mid'sum'ûr] *n*: **a ~ day** un día de pleno verano.
Midsummer's Day *n* Día *m* de San Juan.
midway [mid'wā] *a, ad*: **~ (between)** a mitad de camino *or* a medio camino (entre).
midweek [mid'wēk] *ad* entre semana.

midwife, *pl* **midwives** [mid'wīf, mid'wīvz] *n* comadrona, partera.
midwifery [mid'wīfûrē] *n* partería.
midwinter [mid'win'tûr] *n*: **in ~** en pleno invierno.
might [mīt] *vb see* **may** ♦ **he ~ be there** podría estar allí, puede que esté allí; **I ~ as well go** más vale que vaya; **you ~ like to try** podría intentar ♦ *n* fuerza, poder *m*.
mightily [mī'təlē] *ad* fuertemente, poderosamente; **I was ~ surprised** me sorprendí enormemente.
mightn't = **might not.**
mighty [mī'tē] *a* fuerte, poderoso.
migraine [mī'grān] *n* jaqueca.
migrant [mī'grənt] *a, n* (*bird*) migratorio/a *m/f*; (*worker*) emigrante *m/f*.
migrate [mī'grāt] *vi* emigrar.
migration [mīgrā'shən] *n* emigración *f*.
mike [mīk] *n abbr* (= *microphone*) micro.
Milan [milan'] *n* Milán *m*.
mild [mīld] *a* (*person*) apacible; (*climate*) templado; (*slight*) ligero; (*taste*) suave; (*illness*) leve.
mildew [mil'dōō] *n* moho.
mildly [mīld'lē] *ad* ligeramente; suavemente; **to put it ~** para no decir más.
mildness [mīld'nis] *n* suavidad *f*; (*of illness*) levedad *f*.
mile [mīl] *n* milla; **to do 20 ~s per gallon** hacer 20 millas por galón.
mileage [mī'lij] *n* número de millas; (*AUT*) kilometraje *m*.
mileage allowance *n* ≈ asignación *f* por kilometraje.
mileometer [mīlâm'itûr] *n* cuentakilómetros *m inv.*
milestone [mīl'stōn] *n* mojón *m*.
milieu [mēlyōō'] *n* (medio) ambiente *m*.
militant [mil'ətənt] *a, n* militante *m/f*.
militarism [mil'itərizəm] *n* militarismo.
militaristic [militəris'tik] *a* militarista.
military [mil'itārē] *a* militar.
militate [mil'ətāt] *vi*: **to ~ against** militar en contra de.
militia [milish'ə] *n* milicia.
milk [milk] *n* leche *f* ♦ *vt* (*cow*) ordeñar; (*fig*) chupar.
milk chocolate *n* chocolate *m* con leche.
milk float *n* (*Brit*) carro de la leche.
milking [mil'king] *n* ordeño.
milkman [milk'man] *n* lechero.
milk shake *n* batido, malteada (*LAm*).
milk tooth *n* diente *m* de leche.
milk truck *n* (*US*) carro de la leche.
milky [mil'kē] *a* lechoso.
Milky Way *n* Vía Láctea.
mill [mil] *n* (*windmill etc*) molino; (*coffee* **~**) molinillo; (*factory*) fábrica; (*spinning* **~**) hilandería ♦ *vt* moler ♦ *vi* (*also*: **~ around**) arremolinarse.
milled [mild] (*grain*) molido; (*coin, edge*) acordonado.

millennium, *pl* ~s *or* **millennia** [milen'ēəm, milen'ēə] *n* milenio, milenario.
miller [mil'ûr] *n* molinero.
millet [mil'it] *n* mijo.
milli... [mil'ə] *pref* mili... .
milligram(me) [mil'əgram] *n* miligramo.
milliliter, (*Brit*) **millilitre** [mil'əlētûr] *n* mililitro.
millimeter, (*Brit*) **millimetre** [mil'əmētûr] *n* milímetro.
milliner [mil'inûr] *n* sombrerero/a.
millinery [mil'ənārē] *n* sombrerería.
million [mil'yən] *n* millón *m*; **a** ~ **times** un millón de veces.
millionaire [milyənär'] *n* millonario/a.
millipede [mil'əpēd] *n* milpiés *m inv*.
millstone [mil'stōn] *n* piedra de molino.
millwheel [mil'wēl] *n* rueda de molino.
milometer [mī'lōmētûr] *n* (*Brit*) cuentakilómetros *m inv*.
mime [mīm] *n* mímica; (*actor*) mimo/a ♦ *vt* remedar ♦ *vi* actuar de mimo.
mimic [mim'ik] *n* imitador(a) *m/f* ♦ *a* mímico ♦ *vt* remedar, imitar.
mimicry [mim'ikrē] *n* imitación *f*.
Min. *abbr* (*Brit POL*: = *Ministry*) Min.
min. *abbr* (= *minute(s)*) m.; = **minimum.**
minaret [minəret'] *n* alminar *m*.
mince [mins] *vt* picar ♦ *vi* (*in walking*) andar con pasos menudos ♦ *n* (*CULIN*) carne *f* picada, picadillo.
mincemeat [mins'mēt] *n* conserva de fruta picada.
mince pie *n* empanadilla rellena de fruta picada.
mincer [min'sûr] *n* picadora de carne.
mincing [min'sing] *a* afectado.
mind [mīnd] *n* (*gen*) mente *f*; (*contrasted with matter*) espíritu *m* ♦ *vt* (*attend to, look after*) ocuparse de, cuidar; (*be careful of*) tener cuidado con; (*object to*): **I don't** ~ **the noise** no me molesta el ruido; **it is on my** ~ me preocupa; **to my** ~ a mi parecer *or* juicio; **to change one's** ~ cambiar de idea *or* de parecer; **to bring** *or* **call sth to** ~ recordar algo; **to have sth/ sb in** ~ tener algo/a uno en mente; **to be out of one's** ~ estar fuera de juicio; **to bear sth in** ~ tomar *or* tener algo en cuenta; **to make up one's** ~ decidirse; **it went right out of my** ~ se me fue por completo (de la cabeza); **to be of two** ~s **about sth** estar indeciso *or* dudar ante algo; **I don't** ~ me es igual; ~ **you, ...** te advierto que ...; **never** ~! ¡es igual!, ¡no importa!; (*don't worry*) ¡no te preocupes!
-minded [-mīn'did] *a*: **fair**~ imparcial; **an industrially**~ **nation** una nación que se dedica *or* se orienta a la industria.
minder [mīnd'ûr] *n* guardaespaldas *m inv*.
mindful [mīnd'fəl] *a*: ~ **of** consciente de.
mindless [mīnd'lis] *a* (*violence, crime*) sin motivo; (*work*) de autómata.

mine [mīn] *pron* (el) mío/(la) mía *etc*; **a friend of** ~ un(a) amigo/a mío/mía *a*: **this book is** ~ este libro es mío ♦ *n* mina ♦ *vt* (*coal*) extraer; (*ship, beach*) minar.
mine detector *n* detector *m* de minas.
minefield [mīn'fēld] *n* campo de minas.
miner [mīn'ûr] *n* minero/a.
mineral [min'ûrəl] *a* mineral ♦ *n* mineral *m*; ~**s** *npl* (*Brit*: *soft drinks*) agua *sg* mineral, gaseosa *sg*.
mineral water *n* agua mineral.
minesweeper [mīn'swēpûr] *n* dragaminas *m inv*.
mingle [ming'gəl] *vi*: **to** ~ **with** mezclarse con.
mingy [min'jē] *a* (*col*) tacaño.
mini... [min'ē] *pref* mini..., micro....
miniature [min'ēəchûr] *a* (en) miniatura ♦ *n* miniatura.
minibus [min'ēbus] *n* microbús *m*.
minicab [min'ēkab] *n* microtaxi *m*.
minicomputer [min'ēkəmpyōōtûr] *n* minicomputador *m*.
minim [min'əm] *n* (*Brit MUS*) blanca.
minimal [min'əməl] *a* mínimo.
minimize [min'əmīz] *vt* minimizar.
minimum [min'əməm] *n* (*pl* **minima** [min'əmə]) mínimo ♦ *a* mínimo; **to reduce to a** ~ reducir algo al mínimo; ~ **wage** salario mínimo.
minimum lending rate (MLR) *n* tipo de interés mínimo.
mining [mī'ning] *n* explotación *f* minera ♦ *a* minero.
minion [min'yən] *n* secuaz *m*.
miniskirt [min'ēskûrt] *n* minifalda.
minister [min'istûr] *n* (*Brit POL*) ministro/a; (*REL*) pastor *m* ♦ *vi*: **to** ~ **to** atender a.
ministerial [ministēr'ēəl] *a* (*Brit POL*) ministerial.
ministry [min'istrē] *n* (*REL*) sacerdocio; (*Brit POL*) ministerio.
mink [mingk] *n* visón *m*.
mink coat *n* abrigo de visón.
Minn. *abbr* (*US*) = *Minnesota*.
minnow [min'ō] *n* pececillo (de agua dulce).
minor [mī'nûr] *a* (*unimportant*) secundario; (*MUS*) menor ♦ *n* (*LAW*) menor *m/f* de edad; (*US UNIV*) asignatura secundaria.
Minorca [minôr'kə] *n* Menorca.
minority [minôr'itē] *n* minoría; **to be in a** ~ estar en la minoría, ser minoría (*LAm*).
minority interest *n* participación *f* minoritaria.
minster [min'stûr] *n* catedral *f*.
minstrel [min'strəl] *n* juglar *m*.
mint [mint] *n* (*plant*) menta, hierbabuena; (*sweet*) caramelo de menta ♦ *vt* (*coins*) acuñar; **the (US) M**~, (*Brit*) **the (Royal) M**~ la Casa de la Moneda; **in** ~ **condition** en perfecto estado.
mint sauce *n* salsa de menta.

minuet [minyo͞oet'] n minué m.
minus [mī'nəs] n (also: ~ **sign**) signo de menos ♦ prep menos.
minuscule [min'əskyo͞ol] a minúsculo.
minute n [min'it] minuto; (fig) momento; ~**s** npl actas fpl ♦ a [minōot'] diminuto; (search) minucioso; **it is 5 ~s past 3** son las 3 y 5 (minutos); **at the last ~** a última hora; **wait a ~!** ¡espera un momento!; **up to the ~** de última hora; **in ~ detail** en detalle minucioso.
minute book n libro de actas.
minute hand n minutero.
minutely [mīnōot'lē] ad (by a small amount) por muy poco; (in detail) detalladamente, minuciosamente.
miracle [mir'əkəl] n milagro.
miracle play n auto, milagro.
miraculous [mirak'yələs] a milagroso.
miraculously [mirak'yələslē] ad milagrosamente.
mirage [mirázh'] n espejismo.
mire [mī'ûr] n fango, lodo.
mirror [mir'ûr] n espejo; (in car) retrovisor m ♦ vt reflejar.
mirror image n reflejo inverso.
mirth [mûrth] n alegría; (laughter) risa, risas fpl.
misadventure [misədven'chûr] n desgracia, accidente m; **death by ~** muerte f accidental.
misanthropist [misan'thrəpist] n misántropo/a.
misapply [misəplī'] vt emplear mal.
misapprehension [misaprihen'chən] n equivocación f.
misappropriate [misəprō'prēāt] vt (funds) malversar.
misappropriation [misəprōprēā'shən] n malversación f, desfalco.
misbehave [misbihāv'] vi portarse mal.
misbehavior, (Brit) **misbehaviour** [misbihāv'yûr] n mala conducta.
misc. abbr = **miscellaneous**.
miscalculate [miskal'kyəlāt] vt calcular mal.
miscalculation [miskalkyəlā'shən] n error m (de cálculo).
miscarriage [miskar'ij] n (MED) aborto; ~ **of justice** error m judicial.
miscarry [miskar'ē] vi (MED) abortar; (fail: plans) fracasar, malograrse.
miscellaneous [misəlā'nēəs] a varios/as, diversos/as; ~ **expenses** diversos gastos.
miscellany [mis'əlānē] n miscelánea.
mischance [mischans'] n desgracia, mala suerte f; **by (some) ~** por (alguna) desgracia.
mischief [mis'chif] n (naughtiness) travesura; (harm) mal m, daño; (maliciousness) malicia.
mischievous [mis'chəvəs] a travieso; dañoso; (playful) malicioso.

mischievously [mis'chəvəslē] ad por travesura; maliciosamente.
misconception [miskənsep'shən] n concepto erróneo; equivocación f.
misconduct [miskán'dukt] n mala conducta; **professional ~** falta profesional.
miscount [miskount'] vt, vi contar mal.
misconstrue [miskənstro͞o'] vt interpretar mal.
misdeed [misdēd'] n (old) fechoría, delito.
misdemeanor, (Brit) **misdemeanour** [misdimē'nûr] n delito, ofensa.
misdirect [misdirekt'] vt (person) informar mal; (letter) poner señas incorrectas en.
miser [mī'zûr] n avaro/a.
miserable [miz'ûrəbəl] a (unhappy) triste, desgraciado; (wretched) miserable; **to feel ~** sentirse triste.
miserably [miz'ûrəblē] ad (smile, answer) tristemente; (fail) rotundamente; **to pay ~** pagar una miseria.
miserly [mī'zûrlē] a avariento, tacaño.
misery [miz'ûrē] n (unhappiness) tristeza; (wretchedness) miseria, desdicha.
misfire [misfīr'] vi fallar.
misfit [mis'fit] n (person) inadaptado/a.
misfortune [misfôr'chən] n desgracia.
misgiving(s) [misgiv'ing(z)] n(pl) (mistrust) recelo; (apprehension) presentimiento; **to have ~s about sth** tener dudas sobre algo.
misguided [misgī'did] a equivocado.
mishandle [mis·han'dəl] vt (treat roughly) maltratar; (mismanage) manejar mal.
mishap [mis'hap] n desgracia, contratiempo.
mishear [mis·hiûr'] vt, vi (irg: like **hear**) oír mal.
mishmash [mish'mash] n (col) revoltijo.
misinform [misinfôrm'] vt informar mal.
misinterpret [misintûr'prit] vt interpretar mal.
misinterpretation [misintûrpritā'shən] n mala interpretación f.
misjudge [misjuj'] vt juzgar mal.
mislay [mislā'] vt (irg: like **lay**) extraviar, perder.
mislead [mislēd'] vt (irg: like **lead**) llevar a conclusiones erróneas.
misleading [mislē'ding] a engañoso.
misled [misled'] pt, pp of **mislead**.
mismanage [misman'ij] vt administrar mal.
mismanagement [misman'ijmənt] n mala administración f.
misnomer [misnō'mûr] n término inapropiado o equivocado.
misogynist [misâj'ənist] n misógino.
misplace [misplās'] vt (lose) extraviar; ~**d** (trust etc) inmerecido.
misprint [mis'print] n errata, error m de imprenta.
mispronounce [misprənouns'] vt pronunciar mal.

misquote [miskwōt'] *vt* citar incorrectamente.

misread [misrēd'] *vt* (*irg: like* **read**) leer mal.

misrepresent [misreprizent'] *vt* falsificar.

misrepresentation [misreprizentā'shən] *n* (*LAW*) falsa declaración *f*.

Miss. *abbr* (*US*) = *Mississippi.*

Miss [mis] *n* Señorita; **Dear ~ Smith** Estimada Señorita Smith.

miss [mis] *vt* (*train etc*) perder; (*shot*) errar, fallar; (*appointment, class*) faltar a; (*escape, avoid*) evitar; (*notice loss of: money etc*) notar la falta de; (*regret the absence of*): **I ~ him** (yo) le echo de menos *or* a faltar ♦ *vi* fallar ♦ *n* (*shot*) tiro fallido *or* perdido; **the bus just ~ed the wall** por poco el autobús se estrelló contra el muro; **you're ~ing the point** no caes, no te entra.

miss out *vt* (*Brit*) omitir.

miss out on *vt fus* (*fun, party, opportunity*) perder.

missal [mis'əl] *n* misal *m*.

misshapen [mis-shā'pən] *a* deforme.

missile [mis'əl] *n* (*AVIAT*) misil *m*; (*object thrown*) proyectil *m*.

missile base *n* base *f* de misiles.

missile launcher [mis'əl lônch'ûr] *n* dispositivo de lanzamiento de proyectiles *or* misiles.

missing [mis'ing] *a* (*pupil*) ausente; (*thing*) perdido; (*MIL*) desaparecido; **to be ~** faltar; **~ person** desaparecido/a.

mission [mish'ən] *n* misión *f*; **on a ~ for sb** en una misión para uno.

missionary [mish'ənärē] *n* misionero/a.

misspell [misspel'] *vt* (*irg: like* **spell**) escribir mal.

misspent [misspent'] *a*: **his ~ youth** su juventud disipada.

mist [mist] *n* (*light*) neblina; (*heavy*) niebla; (*at sea*) bruma ♦ *vi* (*also: ~ over, ~ up: weather*) nublarse; (: *Brit: windows*) empañarse.

mistake [mistāk'] *n* error *m* ♦ *vt* (*irg: like* **take**) entender mal; **by ~** por equivocación; **to make a ~** (*about sb/sth*) equivocarse; (*in writing, calculating etc*) cometer un error; **to ~ A for B** confundir A con B.

mistaken [mistā'kən] *pp of* **mistake** ♦ *a* (*idea etc*) equivocado; **to be ~** equivocarse, engañarse; **~ identity** identificación *f* errónea.

mistakenly [mistā'kənlē] *ad* erróneamente.

mister [mis'tûr] *n* (*col*) señor *m*; *see* **Mr.**

mistletoe [mis'əltō] *n* muérdago.

mistook [mistook'] *pt of* **mistake.**

mistranslation [mistranzlā'shən] *n* mala traducción *f*.

mistreat [mistrēt'] *vt* maltratar, tratar mal.

mistress [mis'tris] *n* (*lover*) amante *f*; (*of house*) señora (de la casa); (*Brit: in primary school*) maestra; (*in secondary school*) profesora; *see* **Mrs.**

mistrust [mistrust'] *vt* desconfiar de ♦ *n*: **~ (of)** desconfianza (de).

mistrustful [mistrust'fəl] *a*: **~ (of)** desconfiado (de), receloso (de).

misty [mis'tē] *a* nebuloso, brumoso; (*day*) de niebla; (*glasses*) empañado.

misty-eyed [mis'tēīd'] *a* sentimental.

misunderstand [misundûrstand'] *vt, vi* (*irg: like* **understand**) entender mal.

misunderstanding [misundûrstan'ding] *n* malentendido.

misunderstood [misundûrstood'] *pt, pp of* **misunderstand** ♦ *a* (*person*) incomprendido.

misuse *n* [misyoos'] mal uso; (*of power*) abuso ♦ *vt* [misyooz'] abusar de; (*funds*) malversar.

MIT *n abbr* (*US*) = *Massachusetts Institute of Technology.*

mite [mīt] *n* (*small quantity*) pizca.

miter, (*Brit*) **mitre** [mī'tûr] *n* mitra.

mitigate [mit'əgāt] *vt* mitigar; **mitigating circumstances** circunstancias *fpl* mitigantes.

mitigation [mitəgā'shən] *n* mitigación *f*, alivio.

mitt(en) [mit'(ən)] *n* manopla.

mix [miks] *vt* (*gen*) mezclar; (*combine*) unir ♦ *vi* mezclarse; (*people*) llevarse bien ♦ *n* mezcla; **to ~ sth with sth** mezclar algo con algo; **to ~ business with pleasure** combinar los negocios con el placer; **cake ~** mezcla de ingredientes de pastelería.

mix in *vt* (*eggs etc*) añadir.

mix up *vt* mezclar; (*confuse*) confundir; **to be ~ed up in sth** estar metido en algo.

mixed [mikst] *a* (*assorted*) variado, surtido; (*school etc*) mixto.

mixed doubles *n* (*SPORT*) mixtos *mpl*.

mixed economy *n* economía mixta.

mixed grill *n* parrillada mixta.

mixed-up [mikst'up] *a* (*confused*) confuso, revuelto.

mixer [mik'sûr] *n* (*for food*) licuadora; (*person*): **he's a good ~** tiene don de gentes.

mixture [miks'chûr] *n* mezcla.

mix-up [miks'up] *n* confusión *f*.

Mk *abbr* (*Brit TECH:* = *mark*) Mk.

mk *abbr* = **mark** (*currency*).

mkt *abbr* = **market.**

MLitt *n abbr* (= *Master of Literature, Master of Letters*) título universitario.

MLR *n abbr* (*Brit*) = **minimum lending rate.**

mm *abbr* (= *millimeter*) mm.

MN *abbr* (*US MAIL*) = *Minnesota*; (*Brit*) = **Merchant Navy.**

MO *n abbr* (*MED*) = *medical officer*; (*US col*) = **modus operandi** ♦ *abbr* (*US MAIL*) = *Missouri.*

mo *abbr* (= *month*) m.

m.o. *abbr* (= *money order*) g/.

moan [mōn] n gemido ♦ vi gemir; (col:
complain): **to ~ (about)** quejarse (de).
moaning [mō'ning] n gemidos mpl; quejas
fpl, protestas fpl.
moat [mōt] n foso.
mob [mâb] n multitud f; (pej): **the ~** el populacho ♦ vt acosar.
mobile [mō'bəl] a móvil ♦ n móvil m.
mobile home n caravana, remolque m.
mobility [mōbil'ətē] n movilidad f; (of applicant) disposición f a mudarse de casa; **~
of labor** movilidad f de la mano de obra.
mobilize [mō'bəliz] vt movilizar.
moccasin [mâk'əsin] n mocasín m.
mock [mâk] vt (make ridiculous) ridiculizar; (laugh at) burlarse de ♦ a fingido.
mockery [mâk'ûrē] n burla; **to make a ~
of** desprestigiar.
mocking [mâk'ing] a (tone) burlón/ona.
mockingbird [mâk'ingbûrd] n sinsonte m,
zenzontle (LAm).
mock-up [mâk'up] n maqueta.
mod cons [mâd kânz] npl abbr (Brit) (=
modern conveniences) see **convenience.**
mode [mōd] n modo; (of transport) medio;
(COMPUT) modo, modalidad f.
model [mâd'əl] n (gen) modelo; (ARCH) maqueta; (person: for fashion, ART) modelo
m/f ♦ a modelo inv ♦ vt modelar ♦ vi ser
modelo; **~ railway** ferrocarril m de juguete; **to ~ clothes** pasar modelos, ser modelo; **to ~ on** crear a imitación de.
model apartment n (US) piso modelo.
modeling, (Brit) **modelling** [mâd'əling] n
(modelmaking) modelado.
modeling clay [mâd'ling klā] n plastilina
®.
modem [mō'dcm] n modem m.
moderate [mâd'ûrit] a, n moderado/a m/f ♦
(vb: [mâd'ərāt]) vi moderarse, calmarse ♦
vt moderar.
moderately [mâd'ûritlē] ad (act) con moderación; (expensive, difficult) medianamente; (pleased, happy) bastante.
moderation [mâdərā'shən] n moderación f;
in ~ con moderación.
modern [mâd'ûrn] a moderno; **~ languages**
lenguas fpl vivas.
modernity [mâdûr'nitē] n modernidad f.
modernization [mâdûrnəzā'shən] n moder-
nización f.
modernize [mâd'ûrnīz] vt modernizar.
modest [mâd'ist] a modesto.
modestly [mâd'istlē] ad modestamente.
modesty [mâd'istē] n modestia.
modicum [mâd'əkəm] n: **a ~ of** un mínimo
de.
modification [mâdəfəkā'shən] n modificación f; **to make ~s** hacer cambios or mo-
dificaciones.
modify [mâd'əfī] vt modificar.
modular [mâj'ələr] a (filing, unit) modular.
modulate [mâj'əlāt] vt modular.

modulation [mâjəlā'shən] n modulación f.
module [mâj'ōōl] n (unit, component,
SPACE) módulo.
modus operandi [mō'dəs âpəran'dī] n manera de actuar.
Mogadishu [mâgədish'ōō] n Mogadisio.
mogul [mō'gəl] n (fig) magnate m.
mohair [mō'här] n mohair m.
Mohammed [mōham'id] n Mahoma m.
moist [moist] a húmedo.
moisten [mois'ən] vt humedecer.
moisture [mois'chûr] n humedad f.
moisturize [mois'chərīz] vt (skin) hidratar.
moisturizer [mois'chərīzûr] n crema hidratante.
molar [mō'lûr] n muela.
molasses [məlas'iz] n melaza.
mold [mōld] (US) n molde m; (mildew)
moho ♦ vt moldear; (fig) formar.
molder [mōl'dûr] vi (decay) decaer.
molding [mōl'ding] n (ARCH) moldura.
moldy [mōl'dē] a enmohecido.
mole [mōl] n (animal) topo; (spot) lunar m.
molecular [məlek'yəlûr] a molecular.
molecule [mâl'əkyōōl] n molécula.
molest [məlest'] vt importunar.
mollusk, (Brit) **mollusc** [mâl'əsk] n molusco.
mollycoddle [mâl'ēkâdəl] vt mimar.
molt [mōlt] vi (US) mudar (la piel/las plumas).
molten [mōl'tən] a fundido; (lava) líquido.
mom [mâm] n (US) mamá.
moment [mō'mənt] n momento; **at** or **for
the ~** de momento, por el momento, por
ahora; **in a ~** dentro de un momento, luego.
momentarily [mōməntar'ilē] ad momentá-
neamente; (US: very soon) de un momento
a otro.
momentary [mō'məntärē] a momentáneo.
momentous [mōmen'təs] a trascendental,
importante.
momentum [mōmen'təm] n momento; (fig)
ímpetu m; **to gather ~** cobrar velocidad.
mommy [mâm'ē] n (US) mamá.
Mon. abbr (= Monday) lun.
Monaco [mân'əkō] n Mónaco.
monarch [mân'ûrk] n monarca m/f.
monarchist [mân'ûrkist] n monárquico/a.
monarchy [mân'ûrkē] n monarquía.
monastery [mân'əstärē] n monasterio.
monastic [mənas'tik] a monástico.
Monday [mun'dā] n lunes m inv.
Monegasque [mânəgask'] a, n monegasco/
a m/f.
monetarist [mân'itärist] n monetarista m.
monetary [mân'itärē] a monetario.
monetary policy n política monetaria.
money [mun'ē] n dinero; **to make ~** ganar
dinero; **I've got no ~ left** no me queda dinero.
moneyed [mun'ēd] a adinerado.

moneylender [mun'ēlendûr] *n* prestamista *m/f*.

moneymaking [mun'ēmāking] *a* rentable.

money market *n* mercado monetario.

money order *n* giro.

money-spinner [mun'ēspinûr] *n* (*col: person, idea, business*) fuente *f* de ganancias.

money supply *n* oferta monetaria, medio circulante, volumen *m* monetario.

Mongol [máng'gəl] *n* mongol(a) *m/f*; (*LING*) mongol *m*.

mongol [máng'gəl] *a, n* (*MED*) mongólico.

Mongolia [mánggō'lēə] *n* Mongolia.

Mongolian [mánggō'lēən] *a* mongol(a) ♦ *n* mongol(a) *m/f*; (*LING*) mongol *m*.

mongoose [máng'gōōs] *n* mangosta.

mongrel [mung'grəl] *n* (*dog*) perro mestizo.

monitor [mán'itûr] *n* (*SCOL*) monitor *m*; (*TV, COMPUT*) monitor *m* ♦ *vt* controlar; (*foreign station*) escuchar, oír.

monk [mungk] *n* monje *m*.

monkey [mung'kē] *n* mono.

monkey business *n* travesuras *fpl*.

monkey nut *n* (*Brit*) cacahuete *m*, maní (*LAm*).

monkey wrench *n* llave *f* inglesa.

mono [mán'ō] *a* (*broadcast etc*) mono *inv*.

mono... [mán'ō] *pref* mono ... .

monochrome [mán'əkrōm] *a* monocromo.

monocle [mán'əkəl] *n* monóculo.

monogram [mán'əgram] *n* monograma *m*.

monolith [mán'əlith] *n* monolito.

monolithic [mánəlith'ik] *a* monolítico.

monolog(ue) [mán'əlóg] *n* monólogo.

mononucleosis [mánōnōōklēō'sis] *n* (*US*) fiebre *f* glandular.

monoplane [mán'əplān] *n* monoplano.

monopolist [mənáp'əlist] *n* monopolista *m/f*.

monopolize [mənáp'əlīz] *vt* monopolizar.

monopoly [mənáp'əlē] *n* monopolio; **Monopolies and Mergers Commission** (*Brit*) *comisión reguladora de monopolios y fusiones*.

monorail [mán'ərāl] *n* monocarril *m*, monorriel *m*.

monosodium glutamate [mánəsō'dēəm glōō'təmāt] *n* glutamato monosódico.

monosyllabic [mánəsilab'ik] *a* monosílabo.

monosyllable [mán'əsiləbəl] *n* monosílabo.

monotone [mán'ətōn] *n* voz *f* (*or* tono) monocorde.

monotonous [mənát'ənəs] *a* monótono.

monotony [mənát'ənē] *n* monotonía.

monoxide [mənák'sīd] *n*: **carbon ~** monóxido de carbono.

monseigneur, monsignor [mánsēn'yûr] *n* monseñor *m*.

monsoon [mánsōōn'] *n* monzón *m/f*.

monster [mán'stûr] *n* monstruo.

monstrosity [mánstrâs'ətē] *n* monstruosidad *f*.

monstrous [mán'strəs] *a* (*huge*) enorme;

(*atrocious*) monstruoso.

Mont. *abbr* (*US*) = *Montana*.

montage [mántázh'] *n* montaje *m*.

Mont Blanc [mánt blangk'] *n* el monte Blanco.

month [munth] *n* mes *m*; **300 dollars a ~** 300 dólares al mes; **every ~** cada mes.

monthly [munth'lē] *a* mensual ♦ *ad* mensualmente ♦ *n* (*magazine*) revista mensual; **twice ~** dos veces por mes *or* mensuales; **~ installment** mensualidad *f*.

monument [mán'yəmənt] *n* monumento.

monumental [mányəmen'təl] *a* monumental.

moo [mōō] *vi* mugir.

mood [mōōd] *n* humor *m*; **to be in a good/bad ~** estar de buen/mal humor.

moodily [mōō'dilē] *ad* malhumoradamente.

moodiness [mōō'dēnis] *n* humor *m* cambiante; mal humor *m*.

moody [mōō'dē] *a* (*variable*) de humor variable; (*sullen*) malhumorado.

moon [mōōn] *n* luna.

moonbeam [mōōn'bēm] *n* rayo de luna.

moon landing *n* alunizaje *m*.

moonless [mōōn'lis] *a* sin luna.

moonlight [mōōn'līt] *n* luz *f* de la luna ♦ *vi* tener un pluriempleo.

moonlighting [mōōn'līting] *n* pluriempleo.

moonlit [mōōn'lit] *a*: **a ~ night** una noche de luna.

moonshot [mōōn'shât] *n* lanzamiento de una astronave a la luna.

moonstruck [mōōn'struk] *a* chiflado.

Moor [mōōr] *n* moro/a.

moor [mōōr] *n* páramo ♦ *vt* (*ship*) amarrar ♦ *vi* echar las amarras.

moorings [mōōr'ingz] *npl* (*chains*) amarras *fpl*; (*place*) amarradero *sg*.

Moorish [mōō'rish] *a* moro; (*architecture*) árabe, morisco.

moorland [mōōr'land] *n* páramo, brezal *m*.

moose [mōōs] *n, pl inv* alce *m*.

moot [mōōt] *vt* proponer para la discusión, sugerir ♦ *a*: **~ point** punto discutible.

mop [máp] *n* fregona; (*of hair*) greña, melena ♦ *vt* fregar.

mop up *vt* limpiar.

mope [mōp] *vi* estar deprimido.

mope around *vi* andar abatido.

moquette [mōket'] *n* moqueta.

moral [mór'əl] *a* moral ♦ *n* moraleja; **~s** *npl* moralidad *f*, moral *f*.

morale [məral'] *n* moral *f*.

morality [məral'itē] *n* moralidad *f*.

moralize [mór'əlīz] *vi*: **to ~ (about)** moralizar (sobre).

morally [mór'əlē] *ad* moralmente.

morass [məras'] *n* pantano.

moratorium [mórətôr'ēəm] *n* moratoria.

morbid [mór'bid] *a* (*interest*) morboso; (*MED*) mórbido.

more [mór] *a, ad* más ♦ *pron*: **and what's**

~ ... y además ...; **many/much** ~ muchos/mucho más; **is there any** ~**?** ¿hay más?; **once** ~ otra vez, una vez más; **I want** ~ quiero más; ~ **dangerous than** más peligroso que; ~ **or less** más o menos; ~ **than ever** más que nunca; ~ **and** ~ cada vez más; **no** ~, **not any** ~ ya no.

moreover [môrō'vûr] *ad* además, por otra parte.

morgue [môrg] *n* depósito de cadáveres.

MORI [mō'rē] *n abbr* (*Brit*) = *Market and Opinion Research Institute.*

moribund [môr'əbund] *a* moribundo.

Mormon [môr'mən] *n* mormón/ona *m/f.*

morning [môr'ning] *n* (*gen*) mañana; (*early* ~) madrugada; **in the** ~ por la mañana; **7 o'clock in the** ~ las 7 de la mañana; **this** ~ esta mañana.

morning sickness *n* (*MED*) náuseas *fpl* del embarazo.

Moroccan [mərák'ən] *a, n* marroquí *m/f.*

Morocco [mərák'ō] *n* Marruecos *m.*

moron [môr'ân] *n* imbécil *m/f.*

morose [mərōs'] *a* hosco, malhumorado.

morphine [môr'fēn] *n* morfina.

Morse [môrs] *n* (*also:* ~ **code**) (código) morse.

morsel [môr'səl] *n* (*of food*) bocado.

mortal [môr'təl] *a, n* mortal *m.*

mortality [môrtal'itē] *n* mortalidad *f.*

mortality rate *n* tasa de mortalidad.

mortally [môr'təlē] *ad* mortalmente.

mortar [môr'tûr] *n* argamasa; (*implement*) mortero.

mortgage [môr'gij] *n* hipoteca ♦ *vt* hipotecar; **to take out a** ~ sacar una hipoteca.

mortgage company *n* (*US*) ≈ banco hipotecario.

mortgagee [môrgəjē'] *n* acreedor(a) *m/f* hipotecario/a.

mortgager [môr'gəjûr] *n* deudor(a) *m/f* hipotecario/a.

mortice [môr'tis] = **mortise.**

mortician [môrtish'ən] *n* (*US*) director(a) *m/f* de pompas fúnebres.

mortification [môrtəfəkā'shən] *n* mortificación *f,* humillación *f.*

mortified [môr'təfīd] *a:* **I was** ~ me dio muchísima vergüenza.

mortise (lock) [môr'tis (lâk)] *n* cerradura de muesca.

mortuary [môr'chōōärē] *n* (*US*) funeraria; (*Brit*) depósito de cadáveres.

mosaic [mōzā'ik] *n* mosaico.

Moscow [más'kou] *n* Moscú *m.*

Moslem [máz'ləm] *a, n* = **Muslim.**

mosque [mâsk] *n* mezquita.

mosquito, ~**es** [məskē'tō] *n* mosquito, zancudo.

moss [môs] *n* musgo.

mossy [môs'ē] *a* musgoso, cubierto de musgo.

most [mōst] *a* la mayor parte de, la mayoría de ♦ *pron* la mayor parte, la mayoría ♦ *ad* el más; (*very*) muy; **the** ~ (*also:* + *adjective*) el más; ~ **of them** la mayor parte de ellos; **at the (very)** ~ a lo sumo, todo lo más; **to make the** ~ **of** aprovechar (al máximo); **a** ~ **interesting book** un libro interesantísimo.

mostly [mōst'lē] *ad* en su mayor parte, principalmente.

MOT *n abbr* (*Brit* = *Ministry of Transport*): **the** ~ (**test**) inspección (*anual*) obligatoria de coches y camiones.

motel [mōtel'] *n* motel *m.*

moth [môth] *n* mariposa nocturna; (*clothes* ~) polilla.

mothball [môth'bôl] *n* bola de naftalina.

moth-eaten [môth'ētən] *a* apolillado.

mother [muŧh'úr] *n* madre *f* ♦ *a* materno ♦ *vt* (*care for*) cuidar (como a una madre).

mother board *n* (*COMPUT*) placa madre.

motherhood [muŧh'úrhōōd] *n* maternidad *f.*

mother-in-law [muŧh'úrinlô] *n* suegra.

motherly [muŧh'úrlē] *a* maternal.

mother-of-pearl [muŧh'úrəvpûrl'] *n* nácar *m.*

mother's help *n* niñera.

mother-to-be [muŧh'úrtəbē'] *n* futura madre.

mother tongue *n* lengua materna.

mothproof [môth'prōōf] *a* a prueba de polillas.

motif [mōtēf'] *n* motivo; (*theme*) tema *m.*

motion [mō'shən] *n* movimiento; (*gesture*) ademán *m,* señal *f;* (*at meeting*) moción *f;* (*Brit: also:* **bowel** ~) evacuación *f* intestinal ♦ *vt, vi:* **to** ~ (**to**) **sb to do sth** hacer señas a uno para que haga algo; **to be in** ~ (*vehicle*) estar en movimiento; **to set in** ~ poner en marcha; **to go through the** ~**s of doing sth** (*fig*) hacer algo mecánicamente *or* sin convicción.

motionless [mō'shənlis] *a* inmóvil.

motion picture *n* película.

motivate [mō'təvāt] *vt* (*act, decision*) provocar; (*person*) motivar.

motivated [mō'təvātid] *a* motivado.

motivation [mōtəvā'shən] *n* motivación *f.*

motivational research [mōtəvā'shənəl rē'sûrch] *n* estudios *mpl* de motivación.

motive [mō'tiv] *n* motivo; **from the best** ~**s** de los mejores motivos.

motley [mât'lē] *a* variado.

motor [mō'tûr] *n* motor *m;* (*Brit: col: vehicle*) coche *m,* carro (*LAm*), automóvil *m* ♦ *a* motor (*f:* motora, motriz).

motorbike [mō'tûrbīk] *n* moto *f.*

motorboat [mō'tûrbōt] *n* lancha motora.

motorcar [mō'tûrkâr] *n* (*Brit*) coche *m,* carro (*LAm*), automóvil *m.*

motorcoach [mō'tûrkōch] *n* autocar *m,* autobús *m,* camión *m* (*LAm*).

motorcycle [mō'tûrsī'kəl] *n* motocicleta.

motorcycle racing n motociclismo.
motorcyclist [mō'tûrsĭklist] n motociclista m/f.
motoring [mō'tûring] n (Brit) automovilismo ♦ a (: accident) de tráfico or tránsito (LAm); (: offense) de carretera.
motorist [mō'tûrist] n conductor(a) m/f, automovilista m/f.
motorize [mō'tərīz] vt motorizar.
motor oil n aceite m para motores.
motor racing n (Brit) carreras fpl de coches, automovilismo.
motor scooter n moto f.
motor vehicle n automóvil m.
motorway [mō'tûrwā] n (Brit) autopista.
mottled [mát'əld] a abigarrado, multicolor.
motto, ~es [mát'ō] n lema m; (watchword) consigna.
mould [mōld] etc (Brit) = **mold** etc.
moult [mōlt] vi (Brit) = **molt**.
mound [mound] n montón m, montículo.
mount [mount] n monte m; (horse) montura; (for jewel etc) engarce m; (for picture) marco ♦ vt montar, subir a; (stairs) subir; (exhibition) montar; (attack) lanzar; (picture, stamp) pegar, fijar ♦ vi (also: ~ up) subirse, montarse.
mountain [moun'tən] n montaña ♦ cpd de montaña; **to make a ~ out of a molehill** hacerse de todo una montaña.
mountaineer [mountənēr'] n alpinista m/f, andinista m/f (LAm).
mountaineering [mountənē'ring] n alpinismo, andinismo (LAm).
mountainous [moun'tənəs] a montañoso.
mountain rescue team n equipo de rescate de montaña.
mountainside [moun'tənsīd] n ladera de la montaña.
mounted [moun'tid] a montado.
Mount Everest [mount ev'ûrist] n Monte m Everest.
mourn [mōrn] vt llorar, lamentar ♦ vi: **to ~ for** llorar la muerte de, lamentarse por.
mourner [mōr'nûr] n doliente m/f.
mournful [mōrn'fəl] a triste, lúgubre.
mourning [mōr'ning] n luto ♦ cpd (dress) de luto; **in ~** de luto.
mouse, pl mice [mous, mīs] n (also COMPUT) ratón m.
mousetrap [mous'trap] n ratonera.
mousse [mōōs] n (CULIN) crema batida; (for hair) espuma (moldeadora).
moustache [məstash'] n (Brit) = **mustache**.
mousy [mou'sē] a (person) tímido; (hair) pardusco.
mouth, pl mouths [mouth, -t͡hz] n boca; (of river) desembocadura.
mouthful [mouth'fōōl] n bocado.
mouth organ n armónica.
mouthpiece [mouth'pēs] n (of musical instrument) boquilla; (TEL) micrófono;

(spokesman) portavoz m/f.
mouth-to-mouth [mouth'təmouth'] a: ~ **resuscitation** boca a boca m.
mouthwash [mouth'wôsh] n enjuague m bucal.
mouth-watering [mouth'wôtûring] a apetitoso.
movable [mōō'vəbəl] a movible.
move [mōōv] n (movement) movimiento; (in game) jugada; (: turn to play) turno; (change of house) mudanza ♦ vt mover; (emotionally) conmover; (POL: resolution etc) proponer ♦ vi (gen) moverse; (traffic) circular; (also: Brit: ~ **house**) trasladarse, mudarse; **to ~ sb to do sth** mover a uno a hacer algo; **to ~d** estar conmovido; **to get a ~ on** darse prisa; **to ~ like a bat out of hell** (col) correr como un loco.
move around vi moverse; (travel) viajar.
move along vi avanzar, adelantarse.
move away vi alejarse.
move back vi retroceder.
move down vt (demote) degradar.
move forward vi avanzar ♦ vt adelantar.
move in vi (to a house) instalarse.
move off vi ponerse en camino.
move on vi seguir viaje ♦ vt (onlookers) hacer circular.
move out vi (of house) mudarse.
move over vi apartarse.
move up vi subir; (employee) ser ascendido.
movement [mōōv'mənt] n movimiento; (TECH) mecanismo; ~ **(of the bowels)** (MED) evacuación f.
mover [mōō'vûr] n proponente m/f; (US) agente m de mudanzas.
movie [mōō'vē] n película; **to go to the ~s** ir al cine.
movie camera n cámara cinematográfica.
moviegoer [mōō'vēgôûr] n (US) aficionado/a al cine.
movie projector n proyector m de películas.
movie theater n (US) cine m.
moving [mōō'ving] a (emotional) conmovedor(a); (that moves) móvil; (instigating) motor(a).
moving van n (US) camión m de mudanzas.
mow, pt mowed, pp mowed or mown [mō, -n] vt (grass) cortar; (grain: also: ~ **down**) segar; (shoot) acribillar.
mower [mō'ûr] n (also: **lawn~**) cortacéspedes m inv.
Mozambique [mōzambēk'] n Mozambique m.
MP n abbr (= Military Police) PM; (= Member of Parliament) Dip.; (Canada) = Mounted Police.
mpg n abbr (= miles per gallon) millas por

galón.

mph *abbr = miles per hour* (*60 mph = 96 km/h.*).

MPhil *n abbr* (= *Master of Philosophy*) *título universitario.*

Mr, Mr. [mis'tûr] *n:* ~ **Smith** (el) Sr. Smith.

Mrs, Mrs. [mis'iz] *n:* ~ **Smith** (la) Sra. de Smith.

MS *n abbr* (= *manuscript*) MS; = **multiple sclerosis;** (*US:* = *Master of Science*) *título universitario* ♦ *abbr* (*US MAIL*) = *Mississippi.*

Ms, Ms. [miz] *n* (= *Miss or Mrs*): ~ **Smith** (la) Sa. Smith.

MSA *n abbr* (*US:* = *Master of Science in Agriculture*) *título universitario.*

MSc *abbr* = **Master of Science.**

MSG *n abbr* = **monosodium glutamate.**

MSS *n abbr* (= *manuscripts*) MSS.

MST *abbr* (*US:* = *Mountain Standard Time*) *hora de invierno de las Montañas Rocosas.*

MSW *n abbr* (*US:* = *Master of Social Work*) *título universitario.*

MT *n abbr* (= *machine translation*) traducción *f* automática ♦ *abbr* (*US MAIL*) = *Montana.*

Mt *abbr* (*GEO:* = *mount*) m.

much [much] *a* mucho ♦ *ad, n, pron* mucho; (*before pp*) muy; **how** ~ **is it?** ¿cuánto es?, ¿cuánto cuesta?; **too** ~ demasiado; **so** ~ tanto; **it's not** ~ no es mucho; **as** ~ **as** tanto como; **however** ~ **he tries** por mucho que se esfuerce; **I like it very/so** ~ me gusta mucho/tanto; **thank you very** ~ muchas gracias, muy agradecido.

muck [muk] *n* (*dirt*) suciedad *f;* (*fig*) porquería.

    muck about *or* **around** *vi* (*Brit: col*) = **mess around.**

    muck in *vi* (*Brit: col*) compartir el trabajo.

    muck out *vt* (*stable*) limpiar.

    muck up *vt* (*col: dirty*) ensuciar; (: *spoil*) echar a perder; (: *ruin*) arruinar, estropear.

muckraking [muk'rāk'ing] (*fig col*) *n* amarillismo ♦ *a* especializado en escándalos.

mucky [muk'ē] *a* (*dirty*) sucio.

mucus [myōō'kəs] *n* moco.

mud [mud] *n* barro, lodo.

muddle [mud'əl] *n* desorden *m*, confusión *f;* (*mix-up*) embrollo, lío ♦ *vt* (*also:* ~ **up**) embrollar, confundir.

    muddle along *vi* arreglárselas de alguna manera.

    muddle through *vi* salir del paso.

muddle-headed [mud'əlhedid] *a* (*person*) despistado, confuso.

muddy [mud'ē] *a* fangoso, cubierto de lodo.

mudguard [mud'gârd] *n* guardabarros *m inv.*

mudpack [mud'pak] *n* mascarilla.

mudslinging [mud'slinging] *n* injurias *fpl,*

difamación *f.*

muff [muf] *n* manguito ♦ *vt* (*chance*) desperdiciar; (*lines*) estropear; (*shot, catch etc*) fallar; **to** ~ **it** fracasar.

muffin [muf'in] *n* (*US*) *una especie de pan dulce,* ≈ *bollo;* (*Brit*) mollete *m.*

muffle [muf'əl] *vt* (*sound*) amortiguar; (*against cold*) embozar.

muffled [muf'əld] *a* sordo, apagado.

muffler [muf'lûr] *n* (*scarf*) bufanda; (*US AUT*) silenciador *m;* (*on motorbike*) silenciador *m,* mofle *m.*

mufti [muf'tē] *n:* **in** ~ (vestido) de paisano.

mug [mug] *n* (*cup*) taza grande (*sin platillo*); (*for beer*) jarra; (*col: face*) jeta; (: *fool*) bobo ♦ *vt* (*assault*) asaltar.

    mug up *vt* (*Brit: col: also:* ~ **up on**) empollar.

mugger [mug'ûr] *n* asaltador(a) *m/f.*

mugging [mug'ing] *n* ataque *m or* asalto callejero.

muggy [mug'ē] *a* bochornoso.

mulatto, es [məlat'ō] *n* mulato/a.

mulberry [mul'bärē] *n* (*fruit*) mora; (*tree*) morera, moral *m.*

mule [myōōl] *n* mula.

mull [mul]: **to** ~ **over** *vt* meditar sobre.

mulled [muld] *a:* ~ **wine** vino caliente.

mullioned [mul'yənd] *a* (*windows*) dividido por parteluces.

multi... [mul'tē] *pref* multi....

multi-access [multēak'ses] *a* (*COMPUT*) multiacceso, de acceso múltiple.

multicolored, (*Brit*) **multicoloured** [mul'tikulûrd] *a* multicolor.

multifarious [multəfär'ēəs] *a* múltiple, vario.

multilateral [multilat'ûrəl] *a* (*POL*) multilateral.

multilevel [multilev'əl] *a* (*US: building, car park*) de muchos pisos.

multimillionaire [multēmilyənär'] *n* multimillonario/a.

multinational [multənash'ənəl] *n* multinacional *m,* transnacional *m* ♦ *a* multinacional.

multiple [mul'təpəl] *a* múltiple ♦ *n* múltiplo; (*Brit: also:* ~ **store**) (cadena de) grandes almacenes *mpl.*

multiple choice *n* examen *m* de tipo selección múltiple.

multiple crash *n* colisión *f* en cadena.

multiple sclerosis [mul'təpəl sklirō'sis] *n* esclerosis *f* múltiple.

multiplication [multəpləkā'shən] *n* multiplicación *f.*

multiplication table *n* tabla de multiplicar.

multiplicity [multəplis'ətē] *n* multiplicidad *f.*

multiply [mul'təplī] *vt* multiplicar ♦ *vi* multiplicarse.

multiracial [multērā'shəl] *a* multirracial.

multistorey |multēstór'ē| *a* (*Brit*) = **multi-level**.

multistrike ribbon |multistrīk' rib'ən| *n* (*COMPUT*: *on printer*) cinta de múltiples impactos.

multi-tasking |multētas'king| *n* (*COMPUT*) ejecución *f* de tareas múltiples, multitarea.

multitude |mul'tətōōd| *n* multitud *f*.

mum |mum| (*Brit*) *n* mamá ♦ *a*: **to keep ~ (about sth)** no decir ni mu (de algo).

mumble |mum'bəl| *vt* decir entre dientes ♦ *vi* hablar entre dientes, musitar.

mummify |mum'əfī| *vt* momificar.

mummy |mum'ē| *n* (*Brit*: *mother*) mamá; (*embalmed*) momia.

mumps |mumps| *n* paperas *fpl*.

munch |munch| *vt*, *vi* mascar.

mundane |mundān'| *a* mundano.

municipal |myōōnis'əpəl| *a* municipal.

municipality |myōōnisəpal'itē| *n* municipio.

munificence |myōōnif'əsəns| *n* munificencia.

munitions |myōōnish'ənz| *npl* municiones *fpl*.

mural |myōōr'əl| *n* (pintura) mural *m*.

murder |mûr'dûr| *n* asesinato; (*in law*) homicidio ♦ *vt* asesinar, matar; **to commit ~** cometer un asesinato *or* homicidio.

murderer |mûr'dûrûr| *n* asesino.

murderess |mûr'dûris| *n* asesina.

murderous |mûr'dûrəs| *a* homicida.

murk |mûrk| *n* oscuridad *f*, tinieblas *fpl*.

murky |mûr'kē| *a* (*water*, *past*) turbio; (*room*) sombrío.

murmur |mûr'mûr| *n* murmullo ♦ *vt*, *vi* murmurar; **heart ~** soplo cardíaco.

MusB(ac) *n abbr* (= *Bachelor of Music*) título universitario.

muscle |mus'əl| *n* músculo.

muscle in *vi* entrometerse.

muscular |mus'kyəlûr| *a* muscular; (*person*) musculoso.

MusD(oc) *n abbr* (= *Doctor of Music*) título universitario.

muse |myōōz| *vi* meditar ♦ *n* musa.

museum |myōōzē'əm| *n* museo.

mush |mush| *n* gachas *fpl*.

mushroom |mush'rōōm| *n* (*gen*) seta, hongo; (*small*) champiñón *m* ♦ *vi* (*fig*) crecer de la noche a la mañana.

mushy |mush'ē| *a* triturado; (*pej*) sensiblero.

music |myōō'zik| *n* música.

musical |myōō'zikəl| *a* melodioso; (*person*) musical ♦ *n* (*show*) comedia musical.

musical instrument *n* instrumento musical.

musically |myōō'ziklē| *ad* melodiosamente, armoniosamente.

music box *n* caja de música.

music hall *n* teatro de variedades.

musician |myōōzish'ən| *n* músico/a.

music stand *n* atril *m*.

musk |musk| *n* (perfume *m* de) almizcle *m*.

musket |mus'kit| *n* mosquete *m*.

musk rat *n* ratón *m* almizclero.

musk rose *n* (*BOT*) rosa almizcleña.

Muslim |muz'lim| *a*, *n* musulmán/ana *m/f*.

muslin |muz'lin| *n* muselina.

musquash |mus'kwåsh| *n* (*fur*) piel *f* del ratón almizclero.

muss |mus| *vt* (*col*: *hair*) despeinar; (: *dress*) arrugar.

mussel |mus'əl| *n* mejillón *m*.

must |must| *auxiliary vb* (*obligation*): **I ~ do it** debo hacerlo, tengo que hacerlo; (*probability*): **he ~ be there by now** ya debe (de) estar allí ♦ *n*: **it's a ~** es imprescindible.

mustache |məstash'| *n* (*US*) bigote *m*.

mustard |mus'tûrd| *n* mostaza.

mustard gas *n* gas *m* mostaza.

muster |mus'tûr| *vt* juntar, reunir; (*also*: **~ up**: *strength*, *courage*) cobrar.

mustiness |mus'tēnis| *n* olor *m* a cerrado.

mustn't |mus'ənt| = **must not**.

musty |mus'tē| *a* mohoso, que huele a humedad.

mutant |myōō'tənt| *a*, *n* mutante *m*.

mutate |myōō'tāt| *vi* sufrir mutación, transformarse.

mutation |myōōtā'shən| *n* mutación *f*.

mute |myōōt| *a*, *n* mudo/a *m/f*.

muted |myōō'tid| *a* (*noise*) sordo; (*criticism*) callado.

mutilate |myōō'təlāt| *vt* mutilar.

mutilation |myōōtəlā'shən| *n* mutilación *f*.

mutinous |myōō'tənəs| *a* (*troops*) amotinado; (*attitude*) rebelde.

mutiny |myōō'tənē| *n* motín *m* ♦ *vi* amotinarse.

mutter |mut'ûr| *vt*, *vi* murmurar.

mutton |mut'ən| *n* carne *f* de cordero.

mutual |myōō'chōōəl| *a* mutuo; (*friend*) común.

mutual fund *n* (*US*) bono fiduciario.

mutually |myōō'chōōəlē| *ad* mutuamente.

muzzle |muz'əl| *n* hocico; (*protective device*) bozal *m*; (*of gun*) boca ♦ *vt* amordazar; (*dog*) poner un bozal a.

MVP *n abbr* (*US SPORT*) = *most valuable player*.

MW *abbr* (= *medium wave*) onda media.

my |mī| *a* mi(s); **~ house/brother/sisters** mi casa/hermano/mis hermanas; **I've washed ~ hair/cut ~ finger** me he lavado el pelo/cortado un dedo; **is this ~ pen or yours?** ¿es este bolígrafo mío o tuyo?

myopic |mīáp'ik| *a* miope.

myriad |mir'ēəd| *n* (*of people*, *things*) miríada.

myrrh |mûr| *n* mirra.

myself |mīself'| *pron* (*reflexive*) me; (*emphatic*) yo mismo; (*after prep*) mí (mismo); *see also* **oneself**.

mysterious |mistēr'ēəs| *a* misterioso.

mysteriously [mistēr'ēəslē] *ad* misteriosamente.
mystery [mis'tûrē] *n* misterio.
mystery play *n* auto, misterio.
mystic [mis'tik] *a, n* místico/a *m/f.*
mystical [mis'tikəl] *a* místico.
mysticism [mis'tisizəm] *n* misticismo.
mystification [mistəfəkā'shən] *n* perplejidad *f;* desconcierto.
mystify [mis'təfī] *vt (perplex)* dejar perplejo; *(disconcert)* desconcertar.
mystique [mistēk'] *n* misterio.
myth [mith] *n* mito.
mythical [mith'ikəl] *a* mítico.
mythological [mithəlâj'ikəl] *a* mitológico.
mythology [mithâl'əjē] *n* mitología.

N

N, n [en] *n (letter)* N, n *f;* **N for Nan** N de Navarra.
N *abbr (= North)* N.
NA *n abbr (US: = Narcotics Anonymous) organización de ayuda a los drogadictos; (US) = National Academy.*
n/a *abbr (= not applicable)* no interesa; *(COMM etc) = no account.*
NAACP *n abbr (US) = National Association for the Advancement of Colored People.*
nab [nab] *vt (col: grab)* coger *(Sp),* agarrar *(LAm);* (: *criminal)* pillar.
NACU *n abbr (US) = National Association of Colleges and Universities.*
nadir [nā'dûr] *n (ASTRO)* nadir *m; (fig)* punto más bajo.
nag [nag] *n (pej: horse)* rocín *m ♦ vt (scold)* regañar; *(annoy)* fastidiar.
nagging [nag'ing] *a (doubt)* persistente; *(pain)* continuo ♦ *n* quejas *fpl.*
nail [nāl] *n (human)* uña; *(metal)* clavo ♦ *vt* clavar; *(fig: catch)* coger *(Sp),* pillar; **to pay cash on the ~** *(Brit)* pagar al contado; **to ~ sb down to a date/price** hacer comprometerse a uno a una fecha.un precio.
nailbrush [nāl'brush] *n* cepillo para las uñas.
nailfile [nāl'fīl] *n* lima para las uñas.
nail polish *n* esmalte *m* or laca para las uñas.
nail scissors *npl* tijeras *fpl* para las uñas.
nail varnish *n (Brit) =* **nail polish.**
Nairobi [nīrō'bē] *n* Nairobi *m.*
naïve [nīēv'] *a* ingenuo.
naïvely [nīēv'lē] *ad* ingenuamente.
naïveté [nīēvtā'] *n* ingenuidad *f,* candidez *f.*

naked [nā'kid] *a (nude)* desnudo; *(flame)* expuesto al aire; **with the ~ eye** a simple vista.
NAM *n abbr (US) = National Association of Manufacturers.*
name [nām] *n (gen)* nombre *m; (surname)* apellido; *(reputation)* fama, renombre *m ♦ vt (child)* poner nombre a; *(appoint)* nombrar; **by ~** de nombre; **in the ~ of** en nombre de; **what's your ~?** ¿cómo se llama usted?; **my ~ is Peter** me llamo Pedro; **to give one's ~ and address** dar sus señas; **to take sb's ~ and address** apuntar las señas de uno; **to make a ~ for o.s.** hacerse famoso; **to get (o.s.) a bad ~** hacerse una mala reputación.
name-drop [nām'drâp] *vi:* **he's always ~ping** siempre está presumiendo de la gente que conoce.
nameless [nām'lis] *a* anónimo, sin nombre.
namely [nām'lē] *ad* a saber.
nameplate [nām'plāt] *n (on door etc)* placa.
namesake [nām'sāk] *n* tocayo/a.
nanny [nan'ē] *n* niñera.
nap [nap] *n (sleep)* sueñecito, siesta; **to be caught ~ping** estar desprevenido.
NAPA *n abbr (US: = National Association of Performing Artists)* sindicato *de trabajadores del espectáculo.*
napalm [nā'pâm] *n* napalm *m.*
nape [nāp] *n:* **~ of the neck** nuca, cogote *m.*
napkin [nap'kin] *n (also:* **table ~)** servilleta.
Naples [nā'pəlz] *n* Nápoles.
nappy [nap'ē] *n (Brit)* pañal *m.*
narcissism [nâr'sisizəm] *n* narcisismo.
narcissus, *pl* **narcissi** [nârsis'əs, -ē] *n* narciso.
narcotic [nârkât'ik] *a, n* narcótico.
narrate [nar'āt] *vt* narrar, contar.
narration [narā'shən] *n* narración *f,* relato.
narrative [nar'ətiv] *n* narrativa ♦ *a* narrativo.
narrator [nar'ātûr] *n* narrador(a) *m/f.*
narrow [nar'ō] *a* estrecho, angosto; *(resources, means)* escaso ♦ *vi* estrecharse, angostarse; *(diminish)* reducirse; **to have a ~ escape** escaparse por los pelos; **to ~ sth down** reducir algo.
narrow gauge *a (RAIL)* de vía estrecha.
narrowly [nar'ōlē] *ad (miss)* por poco.
narrow-minded [nar'ōmīn'did] *a* de miras estrechas.
narrow-mindedness [nar'ōmīn'didnis] *n* estrechez *f* de miras.
NAS *n abbr (US) = National Academy of Sciences.*
NASA [nas'ə] *n abbr (US: = National Aeronautics and Space Administration)* NASA *f.*
nasal [nā'zəl] *a* nasal.

Nassau [nas'ô] *n* (*in Bahamas*) Nassau *m*.
nastily [nas'tilē] *ad* (*unpleasantly*) de mala manera; (*spitefully*) con rencor.
nastiness [nas'tēnis] *n* (*malice*) malevolencia; (*rudeness*) grosería; (*of person, remark*) maldad *f*; (*spitefulness*) rencor *m*.
nasturtium [nəstûr'shəm] *n* capuchina.
nasty [nas'tē] *a* (*remark*) feo; (*person*) antipático; (*revolting: taste, smell*) asqueroso; (*wound, disease etc*) peligroso, grave; **to turn ~** (*situation*) ponerse feo; (*weather*) volverse malo; (*person*) ponerse negro.
NAS/UWT *n abbr* (*Brit*: = *National Association of Schoolmasters/Union of Women Teachers*) sindicato de profesores.
nation [nā'shən] *n* nación *f*.
national [nash'ənəl] *a, n* nacional *m/f*.
national anthem *n* himno nacional.
national debt *n* deuda pública.
national dress *n* vestido nacional.
National Forest Service *n* (*US*) ≈ la Comisión del Patrimonio Forestal.
National Guard *n* (*US*) Guardia Nacional.
National Health Service (NHS) *n* (*Brit*) servicio nacional de sanidad, ≈ INSALUD *m* (*Sp*).
National Insurance *n* (*Brit*) seguro social nacional.
nationalism [nash'ənəlizəm] *n* nacionalismo.
nationalist [nash'nəlist] *a, n* nacionalista *m/f*.
nationality [nashənal'ətē] *n* nacionalidad *f*.
nationalization [nashnələzā'shən] *n* nacionalización *f*.
nationalize [nash'nəlīz] *vt* nacionalizar; **~d industry** industria nacionalizada.
nationally [nash'nəlē] *ad* (*nationwide*) en escala nacional; (*as a nation*) nacionalmente, como nación.
national park *n* reserva natural.
national press *n* prensa nacional.
national service *n* (*MIL*) servicio militar.
National Weather Service *n* (*US*) *estación meteorológica estatal*.
nationwide [nā'shənwīd'] *a* en escala *or* a nivel nacional.
native [nā'tiv] *n* (*local inhabitant*) natural *m/f*, nacional *m/f*; (*in colonies*) indígena *m/f*, nativo/a ♦ *a* (*indigenous*) indígena; (*country*) natal; (*innate*) natural, innato; **a ~ of Russia** un(a) natural de Rusia; **~ language** lengua materna; **a ~ speaker of French** un hablante nativo de francés.
Nativity [nətiv'ətē] *n*: **the ~** Navidad *f*.
NATO [nā'tō] *n abbr* (= *North Atlantic Treaty Organization*) OTAN *f*.
natter [nat'ûr] *vi* (*Brit*) charlar ♦ *n*: **to have a ~** cotillear.
natural [nach'ûrəl] *a* natural; **death from ~ causes** (*LAW*) muerte *f* de causas naturales.
natural childbirth *n* parto natural.

natural gas *n* gas *m* natural.
naturalist [nach'ûrəlist] *n* naturalista *m/f*.
naturalization [nachûrələzā'shən] *n* naturalización *f*.
naturalize [nach'ûrəlīz] *vt*: **to become ~d** (*person*) naturalizarse; (*plant*) aclimatarse.
naturally [nach'ûrəlē] *ad* (*speak etc*) naturalmente; (*of course*) desde luego, por supuesto; (*instinctively*) por instinto, por naturaleza.
naturalness [nach'ûrəlnis] *n* naturalidad *f*.
natural resources *npl* recursos *mpl* naturales.
natural wastage *n* (*INDUSTRY*) desgaste *m* natural.
nature [nā'chûr] *n* naturaleza; (*group, sort*) género, clase *f*; (*character*) carácter *m*, genio; **by ~** por *or* de naturaleza; **documents of a confidential ~** documentos *mpl* de tipo confidencial.
-natured [nā'chûrd] *suff*: **ill~** malhumorado.
nature reserve *n* (*Brit*) reserva natural.
nature trail *n* camino forestal educativo.
naturist [nā'chûrist] *n* naturista *m/f*.
naught [nôt] = **nought**.
naughtily [nôt'ilē] *ad* (*behave*) mal; (*say*) con malicia.
naughtiness [nôt'ēnis] *n* travesuras *fpl*.
naughty [nôt'ē] *a* (*child*) travieso; (*story, film*) verde, escabroso, colorado (*LAm*).
nausea [nô'zēə] *n* náusea.
nauseate [nô'zēāt] *vt* dar náuseas a; (*fig*) dar asco a.
nauseating [nô'zēāting] *a* nauseabundo; (*fig*) asqueroso, repugnante.
nauseous [nô'shəs] *a* (*MED, fig*) nauseabundo.
nautical [nô'tikəl] *a* náutico, marítimo; **~ mile** milla marina.
naval [nā'vəl] *a* naval, de marina.
naval officer *n* oficial *m/f* de marina.
nave [nāv] *n* nave *f*.
navel [nā'vəl] *n* ombligo.
navigable [nav'əgəbəl] *a* navegable.
navigate [nav'əgāt] *vt* gobernar ♦ *vi* (*also AUT*) navegar.
navigation [navəgā'shən] *n* (*action*) navegación *f*; (*science*) náutica.
navigator [nav'əgātûr] *n* navegador(a) *m/f*, navegante *m/f*.
navvy [nav'ē] *n* (*Brit*) peón *m* caminero.
navy [nā'vē] *n* marina de guerra; (*ships*) armada, flota.
navy (blue) *a* azul marino.
Nazareth [naz'ûrith] *n* Nazaret *m*.
Nazi [nât'sē] *a, n* nazi *m/f*.
NB *abbr* (= *nota bene*) nótese; (*Canada*) = *New Brunswick*.
NBA *n abbr* (*US*) = *National Basketball Association, National Boxing Association*.
NBC *n abbr* (*US*: = *National Broadcasting Company*) *cadena de televisión*.

NBS *n abbr* (*US:* = *National Bureau of Standards*) ≈ Oficina Nacional de Normas.

NC *abbr* (*COMM etc*) = *no charge;* (*US MAIL*) = *North Carolina.*

NCC *n abbr* (*US*) = *National Council of Churches.*

NCO *n abbr* = **non-commissioned officer.**

ND *abbr* (*US MAIL*) = *North Dakota.*

N.Dak. *abbr* (*US*) = *North Dakota.*

N.E. *abbr* (*US MAIL*) = *Nebraska, New England.*

NEA *n abbr* (*US*) = *National Education Association.*

Neapolitan [nēəpâl'ətən] *a, n* napolitano/a *m/f.*

neaptide [nēp'tīd'] *n* marea muerta.

near [nēr] *a* (*place, relation*) cercano; (*time*) próximo ♦ *ad* cerca ♦ *prep* (*also:* ~ **to**: *space*) cerca de, junto a; (: *time*) cerca de ♦ *vt* acercarse a, aproximarse a; ~ **here/there** cerca de aquí/de allí; **$25,000 or** ~**est offer** 25,000 dólares o precio a discutir; **in the** ~ **future** en fecha próxima; **the building is** ~**ing completion** el edificio está por terminarse.

nearby [nēr'bī'] *a* cercano, próximo ♦ *ad* cerca.

nearly [nēr'lē] *ad* casi, por poco; **I** ~ **fell** por poco me caigo; **not** ~ ni mucho menos, ni con mucho.

near miss *n* tiro cercano.

nearness [nēr'nis] *n* cercanía, proximidad *f.*

nearside [nēr'sīd] *n* (*AUT*: *right-hand drive*) lado izquierdo (: *left-hand drive*) lado derecho.

near-sighted [nēr'sītid] *a* miope, corto de vista.

neat [nēt] *a* (*place*) ordenado, bien cuidado; (*person*) pulcro; (*plan*) ingenioso; (*spirits*) solo; (*col*) magnífico, estupendo.

neatly [nēt'lē] *ad* (*tidily*) con esmero; (*skilfully*) ingeniosamente.

neatness [nēt'nis] *n* (*tidiness*) orden *m*; (*skilfulness*) destreza, habilidad *f.*

Nebr. *abbr* (*US*) = *Nebraska.*

nebulous [neb'yələs] *a* (*fig*) vago, confuso.

necessarily [nesəsär'ilē] *ad* necesariamente; **not** ~ no necesariamente.

necessary [nes'isärē] *a* necesario, preciso; **he did all that was** ~ hizo todo lo necesario; **if** ~ si es necesario.

necessitate [nəses'ətāt] *vt* necesitar, exigir.

necessity [nəses'itē] *n* necesidad *f*; **necessities** *npl* artículos *mpl* de primera necesidad; **in case of** ~ en caso de urgencia.

neck [nek] *n* (*ANAT*) cuello; (*of animal*) pescuezo ♦ *vi* besuquearse; ~ **and** ~ parejos; **to stick one's** ~ **out** (*col*) arriesgarse.

necklace [nek'lis] *n* collar *m.*

neckline [nek'līn] *n* escote *m.*

necktie [nek'tī] *n* (*US*) corbata.

nectar [nek'tûr] *n* néctar *m.*

nectarine [nektərēn'] *n* nectarina.

née [nā] *a*: ~ **Scott** de soltera Scott.

need [nēd] *n* (*lack*) escasez *f*, falta; (*necessity*) necesidad *f* ♦ *vt* (*require*) necesitar; **in case of** ~ en caso de necesidad; **there's no** ~ **for ...** no hace(n) falta ...; **to be in** ~ **of, have** ~ **of** necesitar; **10 will meet my immediate** ~**s** 10 satisfacerán mis necesidades más premiantes; **the** ~**s of industry** las necesidades de la industria; **I** ~ **it** lo necesito; **a signature is** ~**ed** se requiere una firma; **I** ~ **to do it** tengo que *or* debo hacerlo; **you don't** ~ **to go** no hace falta que vayas.

needle [nē'dəl] *n* aguja ♦ *vt* (*fig: col*) picar, fastidiar.

needless [nēd'lis] *a* innecesario, inútil; ~ **to say** huelga decir que.

needlessly [nēd'lislē] *ad* innecesariamente, inútilmente.

needlework [nēd'əlwûrk] *n* (*activity*) costura, labor *f* de aguja.

needn't [nēd'ənt] = **need not.**

needy [nē'dē] *a* necesitado.

negation [nigā'shən] *n* negación *f.*

negative [neg'ətiv] *n* (*PHOT*) negativo; (*answer*) negativa; (*LING*) negación *f* ♦ *a* negativo.

negative cash flow *n* flujo negativo de efectivo.

neglect [niglekt'] *vt* (*one's duty*) faltar a, no cumplir con; (*child*) descuidar, desatender ♦ *n* (*state*) abandono; (*personal*) dejadez *f*; (*of duty*) incumplimiento; **to** ~ **to do sth** olvidarse de hacer algo.

neglected [niglek'tid] *a* abandonado.

neglectful [niglekt'fəl] *a* negligente; **to be** ~ **of sb/sth** descuidarse de algo.

negligee [neg'ləzhā] *n* (*nightdress*) salto de cama.

negligence [neg'lijəns] *n* negligencia, descuido.

negligent [neg'lijənt] *a* (*careless*) descuidado, negligente; (*forgetful*) olvidadizo.

negligently [neg'lijəntlē] *ad* con descuido, negligentemente.

negligible [neg'lijəbəl] *a* insignificante, despreciable.

negotiable [nigō'shəbəl] *a* (*check*) negociable; **not** ~ (*check*) no trasmisible.

negotiate [nigō'shēāt] *vt* (*treaty, loan*) negociar; (*obstacle*) franquear; (*curve in road*) tomar ♦ *vi*: **to** ~ **(with)** negociar (con); **to** ~ **with sb for sth** tratar *or* negociar con uno por algo.

negotiation [nigōshēā'shən] *n* negociación *f*, gestión *f*; **to enter into** ~**s with sb** entrar en negociaciones con uno.

negotiator [nigō'shēātûr] *n* negociador(a) *m/f.*

Negress [nēg'ris] *n* negra.

Negro [nēg'rō] *a, n* negro.

neigh [nā] *n* relincho ♦ *vi* relinchar.

neighbor [nā'bûr] *n* (*US*) vecino/a.

neighborhood [nā'bûrhŏŏd] *n* (*place*) vecindad *f*, barrio; (*people*) vecindario.
neighboring [nā'bûring] *a* vecino.
neighborly [nā'bûrlē] *a* amigable, sociable.
neighbour [nā'bûr] *etc* (*Brit*) = **neighbor** *etc*.
neither [nē'thûr] *a* ni ♦ *conj*: **I** didn't move and ~ did John no me he movido, ni Juan tampoco ♦ *pron* ninguno; ~ is true ninguno/a de los/las dos es cierto/a ♦ *ad*: ~ good nor bad ni bueno ni malo.
neo... [nē'ō] *pref* neo....
neolithic [nēəlith'ik] *a* neolítico.
neologism [nēăl'əjizəm] *n* neologismo.
neon [nē'än] *n* neón *m*.
neon light *n* lámpara de neón.
Nepal [nəpôl'] *n* Nepal *m*.
nephew [nef'yōō] *n* sobrino.
nepotism [nep'ətizəm] *n* nepotismo.
nerve [nûrv] *n* (*ANAT*) nervio; (*courage*) valor *m*; (*impudence*) descaro, frescura; **a fit of** ~**s** un ataque de nervios; **to lose one's** ~ (*self-confidence*) perder el valor.
nerve center *n* (*ANAT*) centro nervioso; (*fig*) punto neurálgico.
nerve gas *n* gas *m* nervino.
nerve-racking [nûrv'raking] *a* angustioso.
nervous [nûr'vəs] *a* (*anxious, ANAT*) nervioso; (*timid*) tímido, miedoso.
nervous breakdown *n* crisis *f* nerviosa.
nervously [nûr'vəslē] *ad* nerviosamente; tímidamente.
nervousness [nûr'vəsnis] *n* nerviosidad *f*, nerviosismo; timidez *f*.
nest [nest] *n* (*of bird*) nido ♦ *vi* anidar.
nest egg *n* (*fig*) ahorros *mpl*.
nestle [nes'əl] *vi*: **to** ~ **down** acurrucarse.
nestling [nest'ling] *n* pajarito.
NET *n abbr* (*US*) = *National Educational Television*.
net [net] *n* (*gen*) red *f*; (*fabric*) tul *m* ♦ *a* (*COMM*) neto, líquido; (*weight, price, salary*) neto ♦ *vt* coger (*Sp*) *or* agarrar (*LAm*) con red; (*money: subj: person*) cobrar; (: *deal, sale*) conseguir; ~ **of tax** neto; **he earns $10,000** ~ **per year** gana 10,000 dólares netos por año.
netball [net'bôl] *n* básquet *m*.
net curtain *n* (*Brit*) visillo.
Netherlands [netħ'ûrləndz] *npl*: **the** ~ los Países Bajos.
net income *n* renta neta.
net loss *n* pérdida neta.
net profit *n* beneficio neto.
nett [net] *a* = **net**.
netting [net'ing] *n* red *f*, redes *fpl*.
nettle [net'əl] *n* ortiga.
network [net'wûrk] *n* red *f* ♦ *vt* (*RADIO, TV*) difundir por la red de emisores; (*COMPUT*) conectar a la red; **local area** ~ red local.
neuralgia [nōōral'jə] *n* neuralgia.
neurosis, pl -ses [nōōrō'sis, -sēz] *n* neurosis

f inv.
neurotic [nōōrât'ik] *a*, *n* neurótico/a *m/f*.
neuter [nōō'tûr] *a* (*LING*) neutro ♦ *vt* castrar, capar.
neutral [nōō'trəl] *a* (*person*) neutral; (*color etc, ELEC*) neutro ♦ *n* (*AUT*) punto muerto.
neutrality [nōōtral'itē] *n* neutralidad *f*.
neutralize [nōō'trəliz] *vt* neutralizar.
neutron [nōō'trân] *n* neutrón *m*.
neutron bomb [nōō'trân bâm] *n* bomba de neutrones.
Nev. *abbr* (*US*) = *Nevada*.
never [nev'ûr] *ad* nunca, jamás; **I** ~ **went** no fui nunca; ~ **in my life** jamás en la vida; *see also* **mind**.
never-ending [nev'ûren'ding] *a* interminable, sin fin.
nevertheless [nevûrħəles'] *ad* sin embargo, no obstante.
new [nōō] *a* nuevo; (*recent*) reciente; **as good as** ~ como nuevo.
newborn [nōō'bôrn] *a* recién nacido.
newcomer [nōō'kumûr] *n* recién venido *or* llegado.
newfangled [nōō'fang'gəld] *a* (*pej*) modernísimo.
newfound [nōō'found] *a* (*friend*) nuevo; (*enthusiasm*) recién adquirido.
New Guinea *n* Nueva Guinea.
newly [nōō'lē] *ad* nuevamente, recién.
newlyweds [nōō'lēwedz] *npl* recién casados.
new moon *n* luna nueva.
newness [nōō'nis] *n* novedad *f*; (*fig*) inexperiencia.
news [nōōz] *n* noticias *fpl*; **the** ~ (*RADIO, TV*) las noticias *fpl*, telediario; **good/bad** ~ buenas/malas noticias *fpl*; **financial** ~ noticias *fpl* financieras.
news agency *n* agencia de noticias.
newsagent [nōōz'ājənt] *n* (*Brit*) vendedor(a) *m/f* de periódicos.
news bulletin *n* (*RADIO, TV*) noticiario.
newscaster [nōōz'kastûr] *n* presentador(a) *m/f*, locutor(a) *m/f*.
news dealer *n* (*US*) vendedor(a) *m/f* de periódicos.
news flash *n* noticia de última hora.
news item *n* una noticia.
newsletter [nōōz'letûr] *n* hoja informativa, boletín *m*.
newspaper [nōōz'pāpûr] *n* periódico, diario; **daily** ~ diario; **weekly** ~ periódico semanal.
newsprint [nōōz'print] *n* papel *m* de periódico.
newsreader [nōōz'rēdûr] *n* (*Brit*) = **newscaster**.
newsreel [nōōz'rēl] *n* noticiario.
newsroom [nōōz'rōōm] *n* (*PRESS, RADIO, TV*) sala de redacción.
newsstand [nōōz'stand] *n* quiosco *or* puesto de periódicos.

newt [nōōt] n tritón m.
New Year n Año Nuevo; **Happy ~!** ¡Feliz Año Nuevo!; **to wish sb a happy ~** desear a uno un feliz año nuevo.
New Year's Day n Día m de Año Nuevo.
New Year's Eve n Nochevieja.
New York [nōō yôrk] n Nueva York.
New Zealand [nōō zē'lənd] n Nueva Zeland(i)a ♦ a neozelandés/esa.
New Zealander [nōō zē'ləndûr] n neozelandés/esa m/f.
next [nɛkst] a (house, room) vecino; (meeting) próximo; (page) siguiente ♦ ad después; **the ~ day** al día siguiente; **~ time** la próxima vez; **~ year** el año próximo or que viene; **~ month** el mes que viene or entrante; **the week after ~** no la semana que viene sino la otra; **"turn to the ~ page"** "vuelva a la página siguiente"; **you're ~** le toca; **~ to** prep junto a, al lado de; **~ to nothing** casi nada; **~ to the last** el penúltimo.
next door ad en la casa de al lado ♦ a vecino, de al lado.
next-of-kin [nɛkst'əvkin'] n pariente(s) m(pl) más cercano(s).
NF n abbr (Brit POL: = National Front) partido político de la extrema derecha ♦ abbr (Canada) = Newfoundland.
NFL n abbr (US) = National Football League.
Nfld. abbr (Canada) = Newfoundland.
NG abbr (US) = **National Guard.**
NGO n abbr (US: = non-governmental organization) organización no-gubernamental.
NH abbr (US MAIL) = New Hampshire.
NHL n abbr (US) = National Hockey League.
NHS n abbr = **National Health Service.**
NI abbr = **Northern Ireland**; (Brit) = **National Insurance.**
nib [nib] n plumilla.
nibble [nib'əl] vt mordisquear, mordiscar.
Nicaragua [nikərãg'wə] n Nicaragua.
Nicaraguan [nikərãg'wən] a, n nicaragüense m/f, nicaragüeño/a m/f.
Nice [nēs] n Niza.
nice [nīs] a (likeable) simpático; (kind) amable; (pleasant) agradable; (attractive) bonito, mono; (distinction) fino; (taste, smell, meal) rico.
nice-looking [nīs'lōōk'ing] a guapo.
nicely [nīs'lē] ad amablemente; bien; **that will do ~** perfecto.
niceties [nī'sətēz] npl detalles mpl.
niche [nich] n (ARCH) nicho, hornacina.
nick [nik] n (wound) rasguño; (cut, indentation) mella, muesca ♦ vt (cut) cortar; (col) birlar, robar; (: Brit: arrest) pillar; **in the ~ of time** justo a tiempo; **to ~ o.s.** cortarse.
nickel [nik'əl] n níquel m; (US) moneda de 5 centavos.

nickname [nik'nām] n apodo, mote m ♦ vt apodar.
Nicosia [nikōsē'ə] n Nicosía.
nicotine [nik'ətēn] n nicotina.
niece [nēs] n sobrina.
nifty [nif'tē] a (col: car, jacket) elegante; (: gadget, tool) diestro.
Niger [nī'jûr] n (country, river) Níger m.
Nigeria [nījē'rēə] n Nigeria.
Nigerian [nījē'rēən] a, n nigeriano/a m/f.
niggardly [nig'ûrdlē] a (person) avaro, tacaño, avariento; (allowance, amount) miserable.
nigger [nig'ûr] n (col!: highly offensive) negro/a.
niggle [nig'əl] vt preocupar ♦ vi (complain) quejarse; (fuss) preocuparse por minucias.
niggling [nig'ling] a (detail: trifling) nimio, insignificante; (annoying) molesto; (doubt, pain) constante.
night [nīt] n (gen) noche f; (evening) tarde f; **last ~** anoche; **the ~ before last** anteanoche; **at ~, by ~** de noche, por la noche; **in the ~, during the ~** durante la noche.
nightcap [nīt'kap] n (drink) bebida que se toma antes de acostarse.
nightclub [nīt'klub] n cabaret m.
nightdress [nīt'drɛs] n (Brit) camisón m.
nightfall [nīt'fôl] n anochecer m.
nightgown [nīt'goun], **nightie** [nī'tē] n camisón m.
nightingale [nī'təngāl] n ruiseñor m.
night life n vida nocturna.
nightly [nīt'lē] a de todas las noches ♦ ad todas las noches, cada noche.
nightmare [nīt'mär] n pesadilla.
night owl n (fig) trasnochador(a) m/f, madrugador(a) m/f (LAm).
night porter n guardián m nocturno.
night safe n caja fuerte.
night school n clase(s) f(pl) nocturna(s).
nightshade [nīt'shād] n: **deadly ~** (BOT) belladona.
night shift n turno nocturno or de noche.
nightstick [nīt'stik] n (US) porra.
night-time [nīt'tīm] n noche f.
night watchman n vigilante m nocturno, sereno.
NIH n abbr (US) = National Institutes of Health.
nihilism [nē'əlizəm] n nihilismo.
nil [nil] n cero, nada.
Nile [nīl] n: **the ~** el Nilo.
nimble [nim'bəl] a (agile) ágil, ligero; (skilful) diestro.
nimbly [nim'blē] ad ágilmente; con destreza.
nine [nīn] num nueve.
nineteen [nīn'tēn'] num diecinueve, diez y nueve.
nineteenth [nīn'tēnth'] num decimonoveno, decimonono.
ninety [nīn'tē] num noventa.

ninth [nīnth] *num* noveno.

nip [nip] *vt* (*pinch*) pellizcar; (*bite*) morder ♦ (*Brit col*): **to ~ out/down/up** salir/bajar/subir un momento ♦ *n* (*drink*) trago.

nipple [nip'əl] *n* (ANAT) pezón *m*; (*of bottle*) tetilla; (TECH) boquilla, manguito.

nippy [nip'ē] *a* (*taste*) picante; (*Brit: person*) ágil; **it's a very ~ car** (*Brit*) es un coche muy potente para el tamaño que tiene.

nit [nit] *n* (*of louse*) liendre *f*; (*col: idiot*) imbécil *m/f*.

nit-pick [nit'pik] *vi* (*col*) buscar pelos en la sopa.

nitrogen [nī'trəjən] *n* nitrógeno.

nitroglycerin(e) [nītrəglis'ûrin] *n* nitroglicerina.

nitty-gritty [nit'ēgrit'ē] *n* (*col*): **to get down to the ~** ir al grano.

nitwit [nit'wit] *n* cretino/a.

NJ *abbr* (US MAIL) = New Jersey.

NLF *n abbr* (= *National Liberation Front*) FLN *m*.

NLQ *abbr* (= *near letter quality*) calidad *f* correspondencia.

NLRB *n abbr* (US: = *National Labor Relations Board*) *organismo de protección al trabajador*.

NM *abbr* (US MAIL) = New Mexico.

N.Mex. *abbr* = New Mexico.

no [nō] *ad* no ♦ *a* ninguno, no ... alguno ♦ *n* no; **I won't take ~ for an answer** no hay pero que valga.

no. *abbr* (= *number*) nº., núm.

nobble [nâb'əl] *vt* (*Brit col: bribe*) sobornar; (: *catch*) pescar; (: RACING) drogar.

Nobel prize [nō'bel priz'] *n* premio Nobel.

nobility [nōbil'ətē] *n* nobleza.

noble [nō'bəl] *a* (*person*) noble; (*title*) de nobleza.

nobleman [nō'bəlmən] *n* noble *m*.

nobly [nō'blē] *ad* (*selflessly*) noblemente.

nobody [nō'bâdē] *pron* nadie.

no-claims bonus [nō'klāmz bō'nəs] *n* (*Brit*) = **no-claims discount**.

no-claims discount [nō'klāmz dis'kount] *n* (US) bonificación *f* por carencia de reclamaciones.

nocturnal [nâktûr'nəl] *a* nocturno.

nod [nâd] *vi* saludar con la cabeza; (*in agreement*) decir que sí con la cabeza ♦ *vt*: **to ~ one's head** inclinar la cabeza ♦ *n* inclinación *f* de cabeza; **they ~ded their agreement** asintieron con la cabeza.
nod off *vi* cabecear.

no-fault [nō'fôlt'] *a* (US): **~ agreement** acuerdo de pago respectivo.

noise [noiz] *n* ruido; (*din*) escándalo, estrépito.

noisily [noi'zilē] *ad* ruidosamente, estrepitosamente.

noisy [noi'zē] *a* (*gen*) ruidoso; (*child*) escandaloso.

nomad [nō'mad] *n* nómada *m/f*.

nomadic [nōmad'ik] *a* nómada.

no man's land *n* tierra de nadie.

nominal [nâm'ənəl] *a* nominal.

nominate [nâm'ənāt] *vt* (*propose*) proponer; (*appoint*) nombrar.

nomination [nâmənā'shən] *n* propuesta; nombramiento.

nominee [nâmənē'] *n* candidato/a.

non... [nân] *pref* no, des..., in....

nonalcoholic [nânalkəhôl'ik] *a* no alcohólico.

nonaligned [nânəlīnd'] *a* no alineado.

nonarrival [nânərī'vəl] *n* falta de llegada.

nonce word [nâns'wûrd] *n* hápax *m*.

nonchalant [nânshəlânt'] *a* indiferente.

noncommissioned [nânkəmish'ənd] *a*: **~ officer** suboficial *m/f*.

noncommittal [nânkəmit'əl] *a* (*reserved*) reservado; (*uncommitted*) evasivo.

nonconformist [nânkənfôr'mist] *a* (*attitude*) heterodoxo; (*person*) inconformista *m/f* ♦ *n* inconforme *m/f*; (*Brit* REL) no conformista *m/f*.

noncontributory [nânkəntrib'yətôrē] *a*: **~ pension plan** *or* (*Brit*) **scheme** fondo de pensiones no contributivo.

noncooperation [nânkōâpərā'shən] *n* no cooperación *f*.

nondescript [nân'diskript] *a* soso.

none [nun] *pron* ninguno/a ♦ *ad* de ninguna manera; **~ of you** ninguno de vosotros; **I've ~ left** no me queda ninguno/a; **he's ~ the worse for it** no le ha hecho ningún mal; **I have ~** no tengo ninguno; **~ at all** (*not one*) ni uno.

nonentity [nânen'titē] *n* cero a la izquierda, nulidad *f*.

nonessential [nânəsen'chəl] *a* no esencial ♦ *n*: **~s** cosas *fpl* secundarias *or* sin importancia.

nonetheless [nun'thəles'] *ad* sin embargo, no obstante, aún así.

nonexecutive [nânigzek'yətiv] *a*: **~ director** director *m* no ejecutivo.

nonexistent [nânigzis'tənt] *a* inexistente.

nonfiction [nânfik'shən] *n* literatura no novelesca.

nonintervention [nânintûrven'chən] *n* no intervención *f*.

non obst. *abbr* (= *non obstante: notwithstanding*) no obstante.

nonpayment [nânpā'mənt] *n* falta de pago.

nonplussed [nânplust'] *a* perplejo.

nonprofit-making [nânprâf'itmāking] *a* de misión no comercial.

nonsense [nân'sens] *n* tonterías *fpl*, disparates *fpl*; **~!** ¡qué tonterías!; **it is ~ to say that ...** es absurdo decir que ....

nonskid [nânskid'] *a* antideslizante.

nonsmoker [nânsmō'kûr] *n* no fumador(a) *m/f*.

nonstick [nânstik'] *a* (*pan, surface*) antiadherente.

nonstop [nân'stâp'] *a* continuo; (*RAIL*) directo ♦ *ad* sin parar.

nontaxable [nântak'səbəl] *a*: ~ **income** renta no imponible.

nonvolatile [nânvâl'ətəl] *a*: ~ **memory** (*COMPUT*) memoria permanente.

nonvoting [nânvō'ting] *a*: ~ **shares** acciones *fpl* sin derecho a voto.

nonwhite [nânwīt'] *a* de color ♦ *n* (*person*) persona de color.

noodles [nōō'dəlz] *npl* tallarines *mpl*.

nook [nōōk] *n* rincón *m*; ~**s and crannies** escondrijos *mpl*.

noon [nōōn] *n* mediodía *m*.

no-one [nō'wun] *pron* = **nobody**.

noose [nōōs] *n* lazo corredizo.

nor [nôr] *conj* = **neither** ♦ *ad see* **neither**.

Norf *abbr* (*Brit*) = *Norfolk*.

norm [nôrm] *n* norma.

normal [nôr'məl] *a* normal; **to return to** ~ volver a la normalidad.

normality [nôrmal'itē] *n* normalidad *f*.

normally [nôr'məlē] *ad* normalmente.

Normandy [nôr'məndē] *n* Normandía.

north [nôrth] *n* norte *m* ♦ *a* del norte, norteño ♦ *ad* al *or* hacia el norte.

North Africa *n* África del Norte.

North African *a*, *n* norteafricano/a *m/f*.

North America *n* América del Norte.

North American *a*, *n* norteamericano/a *m/f*.

Northants [nôrthants'] *abbr* (*Brit*) = *Northamptonshire*.

norrthbound [nôrth'bound'] *a* (*traffic*) que se dirige al norte; (*lane*) de dirección norte.

Northd *abbr* (*Brit*) = *Northumberland*.

northeast [nôrthēst'] *n* nor(d)este *m*.

northerly [nôr'thûrlē] *a* (*point, direction*) hacia el norte, septentrional; (*wind*) del norte.

northern [nôr'thûrn] *a* norteño, del norte.

Northern Ireland *n* Irlanda del Norte.

North Korea *n* Corea del Norte.

North Pole *n*: **the** ~ el Polo Norte.

North Sea *n*: **the** ~ el Mar del Norte.

North Sea oil *n* petróleo del Mar del Norte.

northward(s) [nôrth'wûrd(z)] *ad* hacia el norte.

northwest [nôrthwest'] *n* nor(d)oeste *m*.

Norway [nôr'wā] *n* Noruega.

Norwegian [nôrwē'jən] *a*, *n* noruego/a *m/f*; (*LING*) noruego.

nos. *abbr* (= *numbers*) núms.

nose [nōz] *n* (*ANAT*) nariz *f*; (*ZOOL*) hocico; (*sense of smell*) olfato ♦ *vi* (*also*: ~ **one's way**) avanzar con cuidado; **to pay through the** ~ **(for sth)** (*col*) pagar un dineral (por algo).

    nose around *vi* curiosear.

nosebleed [nōz'blēd] *n* hemorragia nasal.

nosedive [nōz'dīv] *n* picado vertical.

nose drops *npl* gotas *fpl* para la nariz.

nosey [nō'zē] *a* curioso, fisgón(ona).

nostalgia [nəstal'jə] *n* nostalgia.

nostalgic [nəstal'jik] *a* nostálgico.

nostril [nâs'trəl] *n* ventana de la nariz.

nosy [nō'zē] *a* = **nosey**.

not [nât] *ad* no; ~ **at all** no ... en absoluto; ~ **that**... no es que...; **it's too late, isn't it?** es demasiado tarde, ¿verdad?; ~ **yet** todavía no; ~ **now** ahora no; **why** ~? ¿por qué no?; **I hope** ~ espero que no; ~ **at all** no ... nada; (*after thanks*) de nada.

notable [nō'təbəl] *a* notable.

notably [nō'təblē] *ad* especialmente; (*in particular*) sobre todo.

notary [nō'tûrē] *n* (*also*: ~ **public**) notario/a.

notation [nōtā'shən] *n* notación *f*.

notch [nâch] *n* muesca, corte *m* ♦ *vt* (*also*: ~ **up**: *score, victory*) apuntarse.

note [nōt] *n* (*MUS, record, letter*) nota; (*banknote*) billete *m*; (*tone*) tono ♦ *vt* (*observe*) notar, observar; (*write down*) apuntar, anotar; **delivery** ~ nota de entrega; **to compare** ~**s** (*fig*) cambiar impresiones; **of** ~ conocido, destacado; **to take** ~ prestar atención a; **just a quick** ~ **to let you know that** ... sólo unas líneas para informarte que ....

notebook [nōt'bōōk] *n* libreta, cuaderno; (*for shorthand*) libreta.

notecase [nōt'kās] *n* (*Brit*) cartera, billetero.

noted [nō'tid] *a* célebre, conocido.

notepad [nōt'pad] *n* bloc *m*.

notepaper [nōt'pāpûr] *n* papel *m* para cartas.

noteworthy [nōt'wûrthē] *a* notable, digno de atención.

nothing [nuth'ing] *n* nada; (*zero*) cero; **he does** ~ no hace nada; ~ **new** nada nuevo; **for** ~ (*free*) gratis, sin pago; (*in vain*) en balde; ~ **at all** nada en absoluto.

notice [nō'tis] *n* (*announcement*) anuncio; (*dismissal*) despido; (*resignation*) dimisión *f*; (*review*: *of play etc*) reseña ♦ *vt* (*observe*) notar, observar; **to take** ~ **of** tomar nota de, prestar atención a; **at short** ~ a última hora, a corto plazo, con poca anticipación; **without** ~ sin aviso; **advance** ~ previo aviso; **until further** ~ hasta nuevo aviso; **to give sb** ~ **of sth** avisar a uno de algo; **to give** ~, **hand in one's** ~ dimitir, renunciar; **it has come to my** ~ **that** ... he llegado a saber que ...; **to escape** *or* **avoid** ~ pasar inadvertido.

noticeable [nō'tisəbəl] *a* evidente, obvio.

notice board *n* (*Brit*) tablón *m* de anuncios.

notification [nōtəfəkā'shən] *n* aviso; (*announcement*) anuncio.

notify [nō'təfī] *vt*: **to** ~ **sb (of sth)** comunicar (algo) a uno.

notion [nō'shən] *n* noción *f*, concepto; (*opinion*) opinión *f*.

notions [nō'shənz] *npl* (*US*) mercería.

notoriety [nōtərī'ətē] *n* notoriedad *f*, mala fama.

notorious [nōtôr'ēəs] *a* notorio, célebre.

notoriously [nōtôr'ēəslē] *ad* notoriamente.

Notts [nâts] *abbr* (*Brit*) = Nottinghamshire.

notwithstanding [nâtwithstan'ding] *ad* no obstante, sin embargo; ~ **this** a pesar de esto.

nougat [nōō'gət] *n* turrón *m*.

nought [nôt] *n* cero.

noun [noun] *n* nombre *m*, sustantivo.

nourish [nûr'ish] *vt* nutrir, alimentar; (*fig*) fomentar, nutrir.

nourishing [nûr'ishing] *a* nutritivo, rico.

nourishment [nûr'ishmənt] *n* alimento, sustento.

Nov. *abbr* (= *November*) nov.

novel [nâv'əl] *n* novela ♦ *a* (*new*) nuevo, original; (*unexpected*) insólito.

novelist [nâv'əlist] *n* novelista *m/f*.

novelty [nâv'əltē] *n* novedad *f*.

November [nōvem'bûr] *n* noviembre *m*.

novice [nâv'is] *n* principiante *m/f*, novato/a; (*REL*) novicio/a.

NOW [nou] *n abbr* (*US*) = *National Organization for Women*.

now [nou] *ad* (*at the present time*) ahora; (*these days*) actualmente, hoy día ♦ *conj*: ~ (*that*) ya que, ahora que; **right** ~ ahora mismo; **by** ~ ya; ~ **and then**, ~ **and again** de vez en cuando; **from** ~ **on** de ahora en adelante; **between** ~ **and Monday** entre hoy y el lunes; **in 3 days from** ~ de hoy en 3 días; **that's all for** ~ eso es todo por ahora.

nowadays [nou'ədāz] *ad* hoy (en) día, actualmente.

nowhere [nō'wär] *ad* (*direction*) a ninguna parte; (*location*) en ninguna parte; ~ **else** en *or* a ninguna otra parte.

noxious [nâk'shəs] *a* nocivo.

nozzle [nâz'əl] *n* boquilla.

NP *n abbr* = **notary public.**

NS *abbr* (*Canada*) = Nova Scotia.

NSC *n abbr* (*US*) = *National Security Council.*

NSF *n abbr* (*US*) = *National Science Foundation.*

NSW *abbr* (*Australia*) = New South Wales.

NT *n abbr* = New Testament.

nth [enth] *a*: **for the** ~ **time** (*col*) por enésima vez.

nuance [nōō'ânts] *n* matiz *m*.

nubile [nōō'bil] *a* núbil.

nuclear [nōō'klēûr] *a* nuclear.

nuclear disarmament *n* desarme *m* nuclear.

nucleus, *pl* **nuclei** [nōō'klēəs, nōō'klēī] *n* núcleo.

nude [nōōd] *a, n* desnudo/a *m/f*; **in the** ~ desnudo.

nudge [nuj] *vt* dar un codazo a.

nudist [nōō'dist] *n* nudista *m/f*.

nudist colony *n* colonia de desnudistas.

nudity [nōō'ditē] *n* desnudez *f*.

nugget [nug'it] *n* pepita.

nuisance [nōō'səns] *n* molestia, fastidio; (*person*) pesado, latoso; **what a** ~! ¡qué lata!

nuke [nōōk] (*col*) *n* bomba atómica ♦ *vt* atacar con arma nuclear.

null [nul] *a*: ~ **and void** nulo y sin efecto.

nullify [nul'əfī] *vt* anular, invalidar.

numb [num] *a* entumecido; (*fig*) insensible ♦ *vt* quitar la sensación a, entumecer, entorpecer; **to be** ~ **with cold** estar entumecido de frío; ~ **with fear** paralizado de miedo; ~ **with grief** paralizado de dolor.

number [num'bûr] *n* número; (*numeral*) número, cifra ♦ *vt* (*pages etc*) numerar, poner número a; (*amount to*) sumar, ascender a; **reference** ~ número de referencia; **telephone** ~ número de teléfono; **wrong** ~ (*TEL*) número equivocado; **opposite** ~ (*Brit: person*) homólogo/a; **to be** ~**ed among** figurar entre; **a** ~ **of** varios, algunos; **they were ten in** ~ eran diez.

numbered account [num'bûrd əkount'] *n* (*in bank*) cuenta numerada.

number plate *n* (*Brit*) matrícula, placa.

Number Ten *n* (*Brit: 10 Downing Street*) *residencia del primer ministro.*

numbness [num'nis] *n* insensibilidad *f*, parálisis *f inv*; (*due to cold*) entumecimiento.

numbskull [num'skul] *n* imbécil *m/f*, majadero/a.

numeral [nōō'mûrəl] *n* número, cifra.

numerical [nōōmär'ikəl] *a* numérico.

numerous [nōō'mûrəs] *a* numeroso, muchos.

nun [nun] *n* monja, religiosa.

nuptial [nup'shəl] *a* nupcial.

nurse [nûrs] *n* enfermero/a; (*Brit: nanny*) niñera ♦ *vt* (*patient*) cuidar, atender; (*baby: US*) criar, amamantar; (: *Brit*) mecer; **male** ~ enfermero.

nursery [nûr'sûrē] *n* (*institution*) guardería infantil; (*room*) cuarto de los niños; (*for plants*) criadero, semillero.

nursery rhyme *n* canción *f* infantil.

nursery school *n* parvulario, escuela de párvulos.

nursery slope *n* (*Brit SKI*) cuesta para principiantes.

nursing [nûrs'ing] *n* (*profession*) profesión *f* de enfermera; (*care*) asistencia, cuidado ♦ *a* (*mother*) lactante.

nursing home *n* clínica de reposo.

nurture [nûr'chûr] *vt* (*child, plant*) alimentar, nutrir.

nut [nut] *n* (*TECH*) tuerca; (*BOT*) nuez *f* ♦ *a* (*chocolate etc*) con nueces ♦ *excl* ~**s!** (*US*)

¡narices!

nutcracker [nut'krakûr] *n* cascanueces *m* *inv*.

nutmeg [nut'meg] *n* nuez *f* moscada.

nutrient [nōō'trēənt] *a* nutritivo ♦ *n* nutrimento.

nutrition [nōōtrish'ən] *n* nutrición *f*, alimentación *f*.

nutritionist [nōōtrish'ənist] *n* dietista *m/f*.

nutritious [nōōtrish'əs] *a* nutritivo.

nuts [nuts] *a* (*col*) chiflado.

nutshell [nut'shel] *n* cáscara de nuez; **in a ~** en resumidas cuentas.

nuzzle [nuz'əl] *vi*: **to ~ up to** arrimarse a.

NV *abbr* (*US MAIL*) = *Nevada*.

NWT *abbr* (*Canada*) = *Northwest Territories*.

NY *abbr* (*US MAIL*) = *New York*.

NYC *abbr* (*US MAIL*) = *New York City*.

nylon [nī'lân] *n* nilón *m* ♦ *a* de nilón.

nymph [nimf] *n* ninfa.

nymphomaniac [nimfəmā'nēak] *a, n* ninfómana.

NYSE *n abbr* (*US*) = *New York Stock Exchange*.

NZ *abbr* = **New Zealand**.

O

O, o [ō] (*letter*) O, o *f*; **O for Oboe** O de Oviedo.

oaf [ōf] *n* zoquete *m/f*.

oak [ōk] *n* roble *m* ♦ *a* de roble.

OAP *abbr* = **old-age pensioner**.

oar [ôr] *n* remo; **to put** *or* **shove one's ~ in** (*fig: col*) entrometerse.

oarlock [ôr'lâk] *n* (*US*) chumacera.

OAS *n abbr* (= *Organization of American States*) OEA *f*.

oasis, *pl* **oases** [ōā'sis, ōā'sēz] *n* oasis *m inv*.

oath [ōth] *n* juramento; (*swear word*) palabrota; **under ~** bajo juramento.

oatmeal [ōt'mēl] *n* harina de avena.

oats [ōts] *n* avena.

OAU *n abbr* (= *Organization of African Unity*) OUA *f*.

obdurate [âb'dyərit] *a* (*stubborn*) terco, obstinado; (*sinner*) empedernido; (*unyielding*) inflexible, firme.

obedience [ōbē'dēəns] *n* obediencia; **in ~ to** de acuerdo con.

obedient [ōbē'dēənt] *a* obediente.

obelisk [âb'əlisk] *n* obelisco.

obesity [ōbē'sitē] *n* obesidad *f*.

obey [ōbā'] *vt* obedecer; (*instructions, regulations*) cumplir.

obituary [ōbich'ōōārē] *n* necrología.

object *n* [âb'jikt] (*gen*) objeto; (*purpose*) objeto, propósito; (*LING*) complemento ♦ *vi* [əbjekt']: **to ~ to** (*attitude*) protestar contra; (*proposal*) oponerse a; **expense is no ~** no importan los gastos; **I ~!** ¡yo protesto!; **to ~ that** objetar que.

objection [əbjek'shən] *n* protesta; **I have no ~ to...** no tengo inconveniente en que....

objectionable [əbjek'shənəbəl] *a* (*gen*) desagradable; (*conduct*) censurable.

objective [əbjek'tiv] *a, n* objetivo.

objectively [əbjek'tivlē] *ad* objetivamente.

objectivity [âbjektiv'ətē] *n* objetividad *f*.

object lesson *n* (*fig*) (buen) ejemplo.

objector [əbjek'tûr] *n* objetor(a) *m/f*.

obligation [âbligā'shən] *n* obligación *f*; (*debt*) deber *m*; **"without ~"** "sin compromiso"; **to be under an ~ to sb/to do sth** estar comprometido con uno/a hacer algo.

obligatory [əblig'ətôrē] *a* obligatorio.

oblige [əblīj'] *vt* (*do a favor for*) complacer, hacer un favor a; **to ~ sb to do sth** forzar *or* obligar a uno a hacer algo; **to be ~d to sb for sth** estarle agradecido a uno por algo; **anything to ~!** (*col*) todo sea por complacerte.

obliging [əblī'jing] *a* servicial, atento.

oblique [əblēk'] *a* oblicuo; (*allusion*) indirecto ♦ *n* (*TYP*) oblicua.

obliterate [əblit'ərāt] *vt* borrar.

oblivion [əbliv'ēən] *n* olvido.

oblivious [əbliv'ēəs] *a*: **~ of** inconsciente de.

oblong [âb'lông] *a* oblongo, rectangular ♦ *n* rectángulo.

obnoxious [əbnâk'shəs] *a* odioso, detestable; (*smell*) nauseabundo.

o.b.o. *abbr* (*US*: = *or best offer*: *in classified ads*) abierto ofertas.

oboe [ō'bō] *n* oboe *m*.

obscene [əbsēn'] *a* obsceno.

obscenity [əbsen'itē] *n* obscenidad *f*.

obscure [əbskyōōr'] *a* oscuro ♦ *vt* oscurecer; (*hide: sun*) esconder.

obscurity [əbskyōōr'itē] *n* oscuridad *f*; (*obscure point*) punto oscuro; **to rise from ~** salir de la nada.

obsequious [əbsē'kwēəs] *a* obsequioso.

observable [əbzûr'vəbəl] *a* observable, perceptible.

observance [əbzûr'vəns] *n* observancia, cumplimiento; (*ritual*) práctica; **religious ~s** prácticas *fpl* religiosas.

observant [əbzûr'vənt] *a* observador(a).

observation [âbzûrvā'shən] *n* observación *f*; (*by police etc*) vigilancia; (*MED*) examen *m*.

observation post *n* (*MIL*) puesto de observación.

observatory [əbzûr'vətôrē] *n* observatorio.

observe [əbzûrv'] *vt* (*gen*) observar; (*rule*) cumplir.

observer [əbzûr'vûr] *n* observador(a) *m/f*.

obsess [əbses'] *vt* obsesionar; **to be ~ed by** *or* **with sb/sth** estar obsesionado por uno/ algo.

obsession [əbsesh'ən] *n* obsesión *f*, idea fija.

obsessive [əbses'iv] *a* obsesivo; obsesionante.

obsolescence [ábsəles'əns] *n* obsolescencia.

obsolescent [ábsəles'ənt] *a* que está cayendo en desuso.

obsolete [ábsəlēt'] *a* (que está) en desuso.

obstacle [âb'stəkəl] *n* obstáculo; (*nuisance*) estorbo.

obstacle race *n* carrera de obstáculos.

obstetrician [ábstətrish'ən] *n* obstétrico/a.

obstetrics [əbstet'riks] *n* obstetricia.

obstinacy [âb'stənəsē] *n* obstinación *f*, terquedad *f*; tenacidad *f*.

obstinate [âb'stənit] *a* terco; (*determined*) tenaz.

obstinately [âb'stənitlē] *ad* obstinadamente, tercamente.

obstreperous [əbstrep'ûrəs] *a* ruidoso; (*unruly*) revoltoso.

obstruct [əbstrukt'] *vt* (*block*) obstruir; (*hinder*) estorbar, obstaculizar.

obstruction [əbstruk'shən] *n* obstrucción *f*; estorbo, obstáculo.

obstructive [əbstruk'tiv] *a* obstruccionista; **stop being ~!** ¡deja de poner peros!

obtain [əbtān'] *vt* (*get*) obtener; (*achieve*) conseguir; **to ~ sth (for o.s.)** conseguir *or* adquirir algo.

obtainable [əbtān'əbəl] *a* asequible.

obtrusive [əbtrōō'siv] *a* (*person*) importuno, entrometido; (*building etc*) demasiado visible.

obtuse [əbtōōs'] *a* obtuso.

obverse [âb'vûrs] *n* (*of medal*) anverso; (*fig*) complemento.

obviate [âb'vēāt] *vt* obviar, evitar.

obvious [âb'vēəs] *a* (*clear*) obvio, evidente; (*unsubtle*) poco sutil; **it's ~ that** ... está claro que ..., es evidente que ....

obviously [âb'vēəslē] *ad* evidentemente, naturalmente; **~ not!** ¡por supuesto que no!; **he was ~ not drunk** era evidente que no estaba borracho; **he was not ~ drunk** no se le notaba lo borracho.

OCAS *n abbr* (= *Organization of Central American States*) ODECA *f*.

occasion [əkā'zhən] *n* oportunidad *f*, ocasión *f*; (*event*) acontecimiento ♦ *vt* ocasionar, causar; **on that ~** esa vez, en aquella ocasión; **to rise to the ~** ponerse a la altura de las circunstancias.

occasional [əkā'zhənəl] *a* poco frecuente, ocasional; **~ worker** (*US*) jornalero temporero.

occasionally [əkā'zhənəlē] *ad* de vez en cuando; **very ~** muy de tarde en tarde, en muy contadas ocasiones.

occasional table *n* mesita.

occult [əkult'] *a* (*gen*) oculto.

occupancy [âk'yəpənsē] *n* ocupación *f*.

occupant [âk'yəpənt] *n* (*of house*) inquilino/ a; (*of boat, car*) ocupante *m/f*.

occupation [âkyəpā'shən] *n* (*of house*) tenencia; (*job*) trabajo; (: *calling*) oficio.

occupational accident *n* accidente *m* laboral.

occupational hazard *n* riesgo profesional.

occupational pension plan *n* plan *m* profesional de jubilación.

occupational therapy *n* reeducación *f* terapéutica.

occupied [âk'yəpīd] *a*: **to be ~** (*US TEL*) estar comunicando.

occupier [âk'yəpīûr] *n* inquilino/a.

occupy [âk'yəpī] *vt* (*seat, post, time*) ocupar; (*house*) habitar; **to ~ o.s. with** *or* **by doing** (*as job*) dedicarse a hacer; (*to pass time*) pasar el tiempo haciendo; **to be occupied with sth/in doing sth** estar ocupado con algo/haciendo algo.

occur [əkûr'] *vi* pasar, suceder; **to ~ to sb** ocurrírsele a uno.

occurrence [əkûr'əns] *n* acontecimiento.

ocean [ō'shən] *n* océano; **~s of** (*col*) la mar de.

ocean bed *n* fondo del océano.

ocean-going [ō'shəngōing] *a* de alta mar.

Oceania [ōshēan'ēə] *n* Oceanía.

ocean liner *n* buque *m* transoceánico.

ocher, (*Brit*) **ochre** [ō'kûr] *n* ocre *m*.

OCR *n abbr* = **optical character recognition/reader.**

o'clock [əklâk'] *ad*: **it is 5 ~** son las 5.

Oct. *abbr* (= *October*) oct.

octagonal [âktag'ənəl] *a* octagonal.

octane [âk'tān] *n* octano; **high ~ gas** *or* (*Brit*) **petrol** gasolina de alto octanaje.

octave [âk'tiv] *n* octava.

October [âktō'bûr] *n* octubre *m*.

octogenarian [âktəjənär'ēən] *n* octogenario/a.

octopus [âk'təpəs] *n* pulpo.

oculist [âk'yəlist] *n* oculista *m/f*.

odd [âd] *a* (*strange*) extraño, raro; (*number*) impar; (*left over*) sobrante, suelto; **60-~** 60 y pico; **at ~ times** de vez en cuando; **to be the ~ one out** estar de más; *see also* **odds.**

oddball [âd'bôl] *n* (*col*) bicho raro.

oddity [âd'itē] *n* rareza; (*person*) excéntrico/a.

odd-job man [âdjâb' man] *n* hombre *m* que hace de todo.

odd jobs *npl* bricolaje *m*.

oddly [âd'lē] *ad* curiosamente, extrañamente.

odds [âdz] *npl* (*in betting*) puntos *mpl* de ventaja; **it makes no ~** da lo mismo; **at ~** reñidos/as; **to succeed against all the ~**

tener éxito a pesar de todas las desventajas; **~ and ends** minucias *fpl*.

ode [ōd] *n* oda.

odious [ō'dēəs] *a* odioso.

odometer [ōdâm'itûr] *n* (*US*) cuentakilómetros *m inv*.

odor [ō'dûr] *n* (*US*) olor *m*; (*perfume*) perfume *m*.

odorless [ō'dûrlis] *a* sin olor.

odour [ō'dûr] *etc* (*Brit*) = **odor** *etc*.

OECD *n abbr* (= *Organization for Economic Co-operation and Development*) OCDE *f*.

oesophagus [isâf'əgəs] *n* (*Brit*) = **esophagus**.

oestrogen [es'trəjən] *n* (*Brit*) = **estrogen**.

of [uv] *prep* de; **a friend ~ ours** un amigo nuestro; **3 ~ them** 3 de ellos; **the 4th ~ July** el 4 de julio; **a boy ~ 10** un niño de 10 años; **a kilo ~ flour** un kilo de harina; **a quarter ~ 4** (*US*) las 4 menos cuarto; **made ~ wood** hecho de madera; **that was very kind ~ you** fue muy amable de su parte.

off [ôf] *a, ad* (*engine*) desconectado; (*light*) apagado; (*tap*) cerrado; (*Brit: food: bad*) pasado, malo; (: *milk*) cortado; (*cancelled*) cancelado; (*removed*): **the lid was ~** la tapadera no estaba puesta ♦ *prep* de; **to be ~** (*to leave*) irse, marcharse; **to be ~ sick** estar enfermo *or* de baja; **to be ~ in one's calculations** equivocarse (en sus cálculos); **a day ~** un día libre *or* sin trabajar; **to have an ~ day** tener un día malo; **he had his coat ~** se había quitado el abrigo; **10% ~** (*COMM*) (con el) 10% de descuento; **it's a long way ~** está muy lejos; **5 km ~ (the road)** a 5 km (de la carretera); **~ the coast** frente a la costa; **I'm ~ meat** (*no longer eat/like it*) paso de la carne; **on the ~ chance** por si acaso; **~ and on** de vez en cuando; **I must be ~** tengo que irme; **to be well/badly ~** andar bien/mal de dinero; **that's a bit ~, isn't it!** (*fig, col*) ¡mal hecho!

offal [ôf'əl] *n* (*CULIN*) menudencias *fpl*.

off-center, (*Brit*) **off-centre** [ôf'sen'tûr] *a* descentrado, ladeado.

off-colour [ôf'kul'ûr] *a* (*Brit: ill*) indispuesto; **to feel ~** sentirse *or* estar mal.

offence [əfens'] *n* (*Brit*) = **offense**.

offend [əfend'] *vt* (*person*) ofender ♦ *vi*: **to ~ against** (*law, rule*) infringir.

offender [əfen'dûr] *n* delincuente *m/f*; (*against regulations*) infractor(a) *m/f*.

offense [əfens'] *n* (*US*) (*crime*) delito; (*insult*) ofensa; **to take ~ at** ofenderse por; **to commit an ~** cometer un delito.

offensive [əfen'siv] *a* ofensivo; (*smell etc*) repugnante ♦ *n* (*MIL*) ofensiva.

offer [ôf'ûr] *n* (*gen*) oferta, ofrecimiento; (*proposal*) propuesta ♦ *vt* ofrecer; (*opportunity*) facilitar; **"on ~"** (*COMM*) "en oferta"; **to make an ~ for sth** hacer

una oferta por algo; **to ~ sth to sb, ~ sb sth** ofrecer algo a uno; **to ~ to do sth** ofrecerse *or* brindarse a hacer algo.

offering [ôf'ûring] *n* ofrenda.

offertory [ôf'ûrtôrē] *n* (*REL*) ofertorio.

offhand [ôf'hand'] *a* informal ♦ *ad* de improviso; **I can't tell you ~** no te lo puedo decir así de improviso *or* así nomás.

office [ôf'is] *n* (*place*) oficina; (*room*) despacho; (*position*) cargo, oficio; **doctor's ~** (*US*) consultorio; **to take ~** entrar en funciones; **through his good ~s** gracias a sus buenos oficios.

office automation *n* ofimática, buromática.

office bearer *n* (*Brit*) = **office holder**.

office building, (*Brit*) **office block** *n* bloque *m* de oficinas.

office boy *n* ordenanza *m*.

office holder *n* (*US: of club etc*) titular *m/f* (de una cartera).

office hours *npl* horas *fpl* de oficina; (*US MED*) horas *fpl* de consulta.

office manager *n* jefe/a *m/f* de oficina.

officer [ôf'isûr] *n* (*MIL etc*) oficial *m/f*; (*of organization*) director(a) *m/f*; (*of club etc*) titular *m/f* (de una cartera); (*also*: **police ~**) agente *m/f* de policía.

office work *n* trabajo de oficina.

office worker *n* oficinista *m/f*.

official [əfish'əl] *a* (*authorized*) oficial, autorizado; (*strike*) oficial ♦ *n* funcionario, oficial *m*.

officialdom [əfish'əldəm] *n* burocracia.

officially [əfish'əlē] *ad* oficialmente.

officiate [əfish'ēāt] *vi* (*also REL*) oficiar; **to ~ as Mayor** ejercer las funciones de alcalde; **to ~ at a marriage** celebrar una boda.

officious [əfish'əs] *a* oficioso.

offing [ôf'ing] *n*: **in the ~** (*fig*) en perspectiva.

off-key [ôfkē'] *a* desafinado ♦ *ad* desentonadamente, fuera de tono.

off-limits [ôf'lim'its] *a* (*US*) prohibido el paso.

off line *a, ad* (*COMPUT*) fuera de línea; (*switched off*) desconectado.

off-load [ôf'lōd'] *vt* descargar, desembarcar.

off-peak [ôf'pēk'] *a* (*holiday*) de temporada baja; (*electricity*) de banda económica.

off-putting [ôf'pŏŏt'ing] *a* (*Brit: person*) poco amable, difícil; (*behavior*) chocante.

off ramp *n* (*US*) vía de acceso.

off-season [ôf'sēzən] *a, ad* fuera de temporada.

offset *vt* [ôfset'] (*irg: like set*) (*counteract*) contrarrestar, compensar ♦ *n* [ôf'set] (*also*: **~ printing**) offset *m*.

offshoot [ôf'shŏŏt] *n* (*BOT*) vástago; (*fig*) ramificación *f*.

offshore [ôf'shôr] *a* (*breeze, island*) costero; (*fishing*) de bajura; ~ **oilfield** campo petrolífero submarino.

offside n [ôf'sïd] (*AUT: with left-hand drive*) lado izquierdo; (: *with right-hand drive*) lado derecho ♦ a [ôf'sïd'] (*SPORT*) fuera de juego; (*AUT*) del lado derecho; del lado izquierdo.

offspring [ôf'spring] n descendencia.

offstage [ôf'stäj'] ad entre bastidores.

off-the-cuff [ôf'thəkuf'] a espontáneo.

off-the-job [ôf'thəjâb'] a: ~ **training** formación f fuera del trabajo.

off-the-peg [ôf'thəpeg'] ad (*Brit*) = **off-the-rack.**

off-the-rack [ôf'thərak'] ad (*US*) confeccionado.

off-the-wall [ôf'thəwôl'] a desquiciado.

off-white [ôf'wït] a blanco grisáceo.

off-year [ôf'yēr] a: ~ **election** elección f parcial.

often [ôf'ən] ad a menudo, con frecuencia; **how** ~ **do you go?** ¿cada cuánto vas?

ogle [ō'gəl] vt comerse con los ojos a.

ogre [ō'gûr] n ogro.

OH abbr (*US MAIL*) = Ohio.

oh [ō] excl ¡ah!

OHMS abbr (*Brit*) On His (or Her) Majesty's Service.

oil [oil] n aceite m; (*petroleum*) petróleo ♦ vt (*machine*) engrasar; **fried in** ~ frito en aceite.

oilcan [oil'kan] n lata de aceite.

oilfield [oil'fēld] n campo petrolífero.

oil filter n (*AUT*) filtro de aceite.

oil-fired [oil'fiûrd] a que quema aceite combustible.

oil gauge n indicador m del aceite.

oil industry n industria petrolífera.

oil level n nivel m del aceite.

oil painting n pintura al óleo.

oil pan n (*US AUT*) cárter m.

oil refinery n refinería de petróleo.

oil rig n torre f de perforación.

oilskins [oil'skinz] npl impermeable msg, chubasquero sg.

oil tanker n petrolero.

oil well n pozo (de petróleo).

oily [oi'lē] a aceitoso; (*food*) grasiento.

ointment [oint'mənt] n ungüento.

OJT n abbr (*US:* = *on-the-job training*) aprendizaje en el trabajo.

OK abbr (*US MAIL*) = Oklahoma.

O.K., okay [ōkā'] excl O.K., ¡está bien!, ¡vale! ♦ a bien ♦ n: **to give sth one's** ~ dar el visto bueno a or aprobar algo ♦ vt dar el visto bueno a; **it's** ~ **with** or **by me** estoy de acuerdo, me parece bien; **are you** ~ **for money?** ¿andas or vas bien de dinero?

Okla. abbr (*US*) = Oklahoma.

old [ōld] a viejo; (*former*) antiguo; **how** ~ **are you?** ¿cuántos años tienes?, ¿qué edad tienes?; **he's 10 years** ~ tiene 10 años; ~**er**

brother hermano mayor; **any** ~ **thing will do** sirve cualquier cosa.

old age n vejez f.

old-age pension [ōld'āj pen'chən] n (*Brit*) jubilación f, pensión f.

old-age pensioner (OAP) [ōld'āj pen'chənûr] n (*Brit*) jubilado/a.

olden [ōl'dən] a antiguo.

old-fashioned [ōld'fash'ənd] a anticuado, pasado de moda.

old maid n solterona.

old-time [ōld'tïm'] a antiguo, de antaño.

old-timer [ōld'tï'mûr] n veterano/a, anciano/a.

old wives' tale n cuento de viejas, patraña.

olive [âl'iv] n (*fruit*) aceituna; (*tree*) olivo ♦ a (*also:* ~**-green**) verde oliva inv.

olive branch n (*fig*): **to offer an** ~ **to sb** ofrecer hacer las paces con uno.

olive oil n aceite m de oliva.

Olympic [ōlim'pik] a olímpico; **the** ~ **Games, the** ~**s** npl las Olimpíadas.

O & M n abbr = organization and method.

Oman [ō'mân] n Omán m.

OMB n abbr (*US:* = *Office of Management and Budget*) servicio que asesora al presidente en materia presupuestaria.

omelet(te) [âm'lit] n tortilla (*Sp*), tortilla de huevo (*LAm*).

omen [ō'mən] n presagio.

ominous [âm'ənəs] a de mal agüero, amenazador(a).

omission [ōmish'ən] n omisión f; (*error*) descuido.

omit [ōmit'] vt omitir; (*by mistake*) olvidar, descuidar; **to** ~ **to do sth** olvidarse or dejar de hacer algo.

omnivorous [âmniv'ûrəs] a omnívoro.

ON abbr (*Canada*) = Ontario.

on [ân] prep en, sobre ♦ ad (*machine*) conectado; (*light, radio*) encendido; (*tap*) abierto; **is the meeting still** ~? ¿todavía hay reunión?; **when is this movie** ~? ¿cuándo van a poner esta película?; ~ **the wall** en la pared, colgado de la pared; ~ **television** en la televisión; ~ **foot** a pie; ~ **horseback** a caballo; ~ **the Continent** en Europa; ~ **seeing this** al ver esto; ~ **arrival** al llegar; ~ **the left** a la izquierda; ~ **Friday** el viernes; **to be** ~ **vacation** estar de vacaciones; **I haven't any money** ~ **me** no llevo dinero encima; **we're** ~ **irregular verbs** estamos con los verbos irregulares; **this round's** ~ **me** esta ronda la pago yo, invito yo; **a book** ~ **physics** un libro de or sobre física; **to have one's coat** ~ tener el abrigo puesto; **to go** ~ seguir adelante; **I'm** ~ **to sth** creo haber encontrado algo; **it's not** ~! ¡eso no se hace!; **from that day** ~ de aquel día en adelante; **my father's always** ~ **me** or (*Brit*) ~ **at me to get a job** (*col*) mi padre siempre me está dando la lata que coja un empleo.

once [wuns] *ad* una vez; (*formerly*) antiguamente ♦ *conj* una vez que; ~ **he had left/it was done** una vez que se había marchado/se hizo; **at** ~ en seguida, inmediatamente; (*simultaneously*) a la vez; ~ **a week** una vez por semana; ~ **more** otra vez; ~ **and for all** de una vez por todas; ~ **upon a time** érase una vez; **I knew him** ~ le conocía hace tiempo.

oncoming [ân'kuming] *a* (*traffic*) que viene de frente.

one [wun] *num* un, uno, una ♦ *pron* uno; (*impersonal*) se ♦ *a* (*sole*) único; (*same*) mismo; **this** ~ éste/a; **that** ~ ése/a, aquél; **which** ~ **do you want?** ¿cuál quieres?; ~ **by** ~ uno por uno; ~ **never knows** nunca se sabe; ~ **another** el uno al otro; **it's** ~ **(o'clock)** es la una; **to be** ~ **up on sb** llevar ventaja a uno; **to be at** ~ **(with sb)** estar completamente de acuerdo (con uno).

one-armed bandit [wun'ârmd ban'dit] *n* máquina tragaperras.

one-day excursion [wun'dā ikskûr'zhən] *n* (*US*) billete *m* de ida y vuelta en un día.

one-man [wun'man] *a* (*business*) individual.

one-man band *n* hombre-orquesta *m*.

one-off [wun'ôf] *n* (*Brit col*) artículo fuera de serie.

one-piece [wun'pēs] *a* (*bathing suit*) de una pieza.

onerous [ân'ûrəs] *a* (*task, duty*) pesado; (*responsibility*) oneroso.

oneself [wunself'] *pron* uno mismo; (*after prep, also emphatic*) sí (mismo/a); **to do sth by** ~ hacer algo solo *or* por sí solo.

one-shot [wun'shât] *n* (*US: col*) artículo fuera de serie.

one-sided [wun'sīdid] *a* (*argument*) parcial; (*decision, view*) unilateral; (*game, contest*) desigual.

one-time [wun'tīm] *a* antiguo, ex-.

one-to-one [wun'təwun'] *a* (*relationship*) exacto.

one-upmanship [wunup'mənship] *n*: **the art of** ~ el arte de quedar siempre por encima.

one-way [wun'wā'] *a* (*street, traffic*) de dirección única; (*ticket*) sencillo.

ongoing [ân'gōing] *a* continuo.

onion [un'yən] *n* cebolla.

on line *a, ad* (*COMPUT*) en línea; (*switched on*) conectado.

onlooker [ân'lo͞okûr] *n* espectador(a) *m/f*.

only [ōn'lē] *ad* solamente, sólo ♦ *a* único, solo ♦ *conj* solamente que, pero; **an** ~ **child** un hijo único; **not** ~ ... **but also...** no sólo ... sino también...; **I'd be** ~ **too pleased to help** encantado de servir(les); **I saw her** ~ **yesterday** le vi ayer mismo; **I would come,** ~ **I'm very busy** iría, sólo *or* salvo que estoy muy atareado.

ono *abbr* (= *or nearest offer*: *in classified ads*) abierto ofertas.

on ramp *n* rampa de acceso.

onset [ân'set] *n* comienzo.

onshore [ân'shôr'] *a* (*wind*) que sopla del mar hacia la tierra.

onslaught [ân'slôt] *n* ataque *m*, embestida.

Ont. *abbr* (*Canada*) = *Ontario*.

on-the-job [ânth̩əjâb'] *a*: ~ **training** formación *f* en el trabajo *or* sobre la práctica.

onto [ân'to͞o] *prep* = **on to**.

onus [ō'nəs] *n* responsabilidad *f*; **the** ~ **is upon him to prove it** le incumbe a él demostrarlo.

onward(s) [ân'wûrd(z)] *ad* (*move*) (hacia) adelante.

onyx [ân'iks] *n* ónice *m*, onyx *m*.

ooze [o͞oz] *vi* rezumar.

opal [ō'pəl] *n* ópalo.

opaque [ōpāk'] *a* opaco.

OPEC [ō'pek] *n abbr* (= *Organization of Petroleum-Exporting Countries*) OPEP *f*.

open [ō'pən] *a* abierto; (*car*) descubierto; (*road, view*) despejado; (*meeting*) público; (*admiration*) manifiesto ♦ *vt* abrir ♦ *vi* (*flower, eyes, door, debate*) abrirse; (*book etc: commence*) comenzar; **in the** ~ **(air)** al aire libre; ~ **ticket** billete *m* sin fecha; ~ **ground** (*among trees*) claro; (*waste ground*) solar *m;* **to have an** ~ **mind (on sth)** estar sin decidirse aún (sobre algo); **to** ~ **a bank account** abrir una cuenta en el banco.

open on to *vt fus* (*subj: room, door*) dar a.

open out *vt* abrir ♦ *vi* (*person*) abrirse.

open up *vt* abrir; (*blocked road*) despejar ♦ *vi* abrirse, empezar.

open-and-shut [ō'pənənshut'] *a*: ~ **case** caso claro *or* evidente.

open day *n* (*Brit*) jornada de acceso público.

open-ended [ō'pənen'did] *a* (*fig*) indefinido, sin definir.

opener [ō'pənûr] *n* (*also:* **can** ~) abrelatas *m inv*.

open-heart surgery [ō'pənhârt sûr'jûrē] *n* cirugía a corazón abierto.

open house *n* jornada de acceso público.

opening [ō'pəning] *n* abertura, comienzo; (*opportunity*) oportunidad *f*; (*job*) puesto vacante, vacante *f*.

opening night *n* estreno.

openly [ō'pənlē] *ad* abiertamente.

open-minded [ō'pənmīn'did] *a* imparcial.

open-necked [ō'pənnekt'] *a* sin corbata.

openness [ō'pənnis] *n* (*frankness*) franqueza.

open-plan [ō'pənplan'] *a*: ~ **office** gran oficina sin particiones.

open return *n* vuelta con fecha abierta.

open shop *n empresa que contrata a mano de obra no afiliada a ningún sindica-*

to.

Open University n (*Brit*) ≈ Universidad *f* Nacional de Enseñanza a Distancia, UNED *f*.

opera [âp'rə] n ópera.

opera glasses *npl* gemelos *mpl*.

opera house n teatro de la ópera.

opera singer n cantante *m/f* de ópera.

operate [âp'ərāt] *vt* (*machine*) hacer funcionar; (*company*) dirigir ♦ *vi* funcionar; (*drug*) hacer efecto; **to ~ on sb** (*MED*) operar a uno.

operatic [âpərat'ik] *a* de ópera.

operating costs [âp'ərāting kôsts] *npl* gastos *mpl* operacionales.

operating profit n beneficio de explotación.

operating room n (*US*) sala de operaciones.

operating table n mesa de operaciones.

operating theatre n (*Brit*) sala de operaciones.

operation [âpərā'shən] n (*gen*) operación *f*; (*of machine*) funcionamiento; **to be in ~** estar funcionando *or* en funcionamiento; **to have an ~** (*MED*) ser operado; **to have an ~ for** operarse de; **the company's ~s during the year** las actividades de la compañía durante el año.

operational [âpərā'shənəl] *a* operacional, en buen estado; (*COMM*) en condiciones de servicio; (*ready for use or action*) en condiciones de funcionar; **when the service is fully ~** cuando el servicio esté en pleno funcionamiento.

operative [âp'ûrətiv] *a* (*measure*) en vigor; **the ~ word** la palabra clave.

operator [âp'ərātûr] n (*of machine*) maquinista *m/f*, operario/a; (*TEL*) operador(a) *m/f*, telefonista *m/f*.

operetta [âpəret'ə] n opereta; (*in Spain*) zarzuela.

ophthalmic [âfthal'mik] *a* oftálmico.

ophthalmologist [âfthalmâl'əjist] n oftalmólogo/a.

opinion [əpin'yən] n (*gen*) opinión *f*; **in my ~** en mi opinión, a mi juicio; **to seek a second ~** pedir una segunda opinión.

opinionated [əpin'yənātid] *a* testarudo.

opinion poll n encuesta, sondeo.

opium [ō'pēəm] n opio.

opponent [əpō'nənt] n adversario/a, contrincante *m/f*.

opportune [âpûrtōōn'] *a* oportuno.

opportunism [âpûrtōō'nizəm] n oportunismo.

opportunist [âpûrtōō'nist] n oportunista *m/f*.

opportunity [âpûrtyōō'nitē] n oportunidad *f*; **to take the ~ to do** *or* **of doing** aprovechar la ocasión para hacer.

oppose [əpōz'] *vt* oponerse a; **to be ~d to sth** oponerse a algo; **as ~d to** a diferencia

de.

opposing [əpōz'ing] *a* (*side*) opuesto, contrario.

opposite [âp'əzit] *a* opuesto, contrario a; (*house etc*) de enfrente ♦ *ad* en frente ♦ *prep* en frente de, frente a ♦ *n* lo contrario; **the ~ sex** el otro sexo, el sexo opuesto.

opposite number n (*Brit*) homólogo/a.

opposition [âpəzish'ən] n oposición *f*.

oppress [əpres'] *vt* oprimir.

oppression [əpresh'ən] n opresión *f*.

oppressive [əpres'iv] *a* opresivo.

opprobrium [əprō'brēəm] n (*formal*) oprobio.

opt [âpt] *vi*: **to ~ for** optar por; **to ~ to do** optar por hacer; **to ~ out of** optar por no hacer.

optical [âp'tikəl] *a* óptico.

optical character recognition/reader (OCR) n reconocimiento/lector *m* óptico de caracteres.

optical fiber, (*Brit*) **optical fibre** n fibra óptica.

optician [âptish'ən] n óptico *m/f*.

optics [âp'tiks] n óptica.

optimism [âp'təmizəm] n optimismo.

optimist [âp'təmist] n optimista *m/f*.

optimistic [âptəmis'tik] *a* optimista.

optimum [âp'təməm] *a* óptimo.

option [âp'shən] n opción *f*; **to keep one's ~s open** (*fig*) mantener las opciones abiertas; **I have no ~** no tengo más *or* otro remedio; **~s** (*US*) opciones *fpl* extras.

optional [âp'shənəl] *a* facultativo, discrecional; **~ extras** (*Brit*) opciones *fpl* extras.

opulence [âp'yələns] n opulencia.

opulent [âp'yələnt] *a* opulento.

OR *abbr* (*US MAIL*) = *Oregon*.

or [ôr] *conj* o; (*before o, ho*) u; (*with negative*): **he hasn't seen ~ heard anything** no ha visto ni oído nada; **~ else** si no; **let me go ~ I'll scream!** ¡suélteme, o me pongo a gritar!

oracle [ôr'əkəl] n oráculo.

oral [ôr'əl] *a* oral ♦ n examen *m* oral.

orange [ôr'inj] n (*fruit*) naranja ♦ *a* color naranja.

orangeade [ôrinjād'] n naranjada, refresco de naranja.

orange juice n zumo *or* jugo (*LAm*) de naranja.

orang-outang, orang-utan [ôrang'ōōtang] n orangután *m*.

oration [ôrā'shən] n discurso solemne; **funeral ~** oración *f* fúnebre.

orator [ôr'ətûr] n orador(a) *m/f*.

oratorio [ôrətôr'ēō] n oratorio.

orbit [ôr'bit] n órbita ♦ *vt*, *vi* orbitar; **to be in/go into ~ (around)** estar en/entrar en órbita (alrededor de).

orchard [ôr'chûrd] n huerto; **apple ~** manzanar *m*, manzanal *m*.

orchestra [ôr'kistrə] n orquesta; (*US: seat-*

ing) platea.
orchestral |ôrkɛs'trəl| *a* de orquesta.
orchestrate |ôr'kistrāt| *vt* (*MUS*, *fig*) orquestar.
orchid |ôr'kid| *n* orquídea.
ordain |ôrdān'| *vt* (*REL*) ordenar, decretar; (*decide*) mandar.
ordeal |ôrdēl'| *n* experiencia horrorosa.
order |ôr'dûr| *n* orden *m*; (*command*) orden *f*; (*type*, *kind*) clase *f*; (*state*) estado; (*COMM*) pedido, encargo ♦ *vt* (*also*: **put in** ~) arreglar, poner en orden; (*COMM*) encargar, pedir; (*command*) mandar, ordenar; **in** ~ (*gen*) en orden; (*of document*) en regla; **in (working)** ~ en funcionamiento; **a machine in working** ~ una máquina en funcionamiento; **to be out of** ~ (*machine*, *toilets*) estar estropeado *or* descompuesto (*LAm*); **in** ~ **to do** para hacer; **on** ~ (*COMM*) pedido; **to be on** ~ estar pedido; **to be under** ~**s to do sth** estar bajo órdenes de hacer algo; **a point of** ~ una cuestión de procedimiento; **to place an** ~ **for sth with sb** hacer un pedido de algo a uno; **made to** ~ hecho a la medida; **his income is on** *or* (*Brit*) **of the** ~ **of $40,000 per year** sus ingresos son del orden de 40 mil dólares al año; **to the** ~ **of** (*BANKING*) a la orden de; **to** ~ **sb to do sth** mandar a uno hacer algo.
order book *n* cartera de pedidos.
order form *n* hoja de pedido.
orderly |ôr'dûrlē| *n* (*MIL*) ordenanza *m*; (*MED*) enfermero/a (auxiliar) ♦ *a* ordenado.
order number *n* número de pedido.
ordinal |ôr'dənəl| *a* ordinal.
ordinarily |ôrdənâr'ilē| *ad* por lo común.
ordinary |ôr'dənârē| *a* corriente, normal; (*pej*) común y corriente; **out of the** ~ fuera de lo común, extraordinario.
ordinary seaman *n* (*Brit*) marinero.
ordinary shares *npl* acciones *fpl* ordinarias.
ordination |ôrdənā'shən| *n* ordenación *f*.
ordnance |ôrd'nəns| *n* (*MIL*: *unit*) artillería.
ordnance factory *n* fábrica de artillería.
Ore. *abbr* (*US*) = Oregon.
ore |ôr| *n* mineral *m*.
organ |ôr'gən| *n* órgano.
organic |ôrgan'ik| *a* orgánico.
organism |ôr'gənizəm| *n* organismo.
organist |ôr'gənist| *n* organista *m/f*.
organization |ôrgənəzā'shən| *n* organización *f*.
organization chart *n* organigrama *m*.
organize |ôr'gəniz| *vt* organizar; **to get** ~**d** organizarse.
organizer |ôr'gənizûr| *n* organizador(a) *m/f*.
orgasm |ôr'gazəm| *n* orgasmo.
orgy |ôr'jē| *n* orgía.
Orient |ôr'ēənt| *n* Oriente *m*.
oriental |ôrēɛn'təl| *a* oriental.
orientate |ôr'ēɛntāt| *vt* orientar.

origin |ôr'ijin| *n* origen *m*; (*point of departure*) procedencia.
original |ərij'ənəl| *a* original; (*first*) primero; (*earlier*) primitivo ♦ *n* original *m*.
originality |ərijənal'itē| *n* originalidad *f*.
originally |ərij'ənəlē| *ad* (*at first*) al principio; (*with originality*) con originalidad.
originate |ərij'ənāt| *vi*: **to** ~ **from, to** ~ **in** surgir de, tener su origen en.
originator |ərij'inātûr| *n* inventor(a) *m/f*, autor(a) *m/f*.
ornament |ôr'nəmənt| *n* adorno; (*trinket*) chuchería.
ornamental |ôrnəmɛn'təl| *a* decorativo, de adorno.
ornamentation |ôrnəməntā'shən| *n* ornamentación *f*.
ornate |ôrnāt'| *a* muy ornado, vistoso.
ornithologist |ôrnəthál'əjist| *n* ornitólogo/a.
ornithology |ôrnəthál'əjē| *n* ornitología.
orphan |ôr'fən| *n* huérfano/a ♦ *vt*: **to be** ~**ed** quedar huérfano/a.
orphanage |ôr'fənij| *n* orfanato.
orthodox |ôr'thədâks| *a* ortodoxo.
orthodoxy |ôr'thədâksē| *n* ortodoxia.
orthopaedic |ôrthəpē'dik| *etc* = **orthopedic** *etc*.
orthopedic |ôrthəpē'dik| *a* ortopédico.
orthopedics |ôrthəpē'diks| *n* ortopedia.
O/S *abbr* = **out of stock**.
oscillate |âs'əlāt| *vi* oscilar; (*person*) vacilar.
oscillation |âsəlā'shən| *n* oscilación *f*; (*of prices*) fluctuación *f*.
OSHA *n abbr* (*US*: = *Occupational Safety and Health Administration*) oficina de la higiene y la seguridad en el trabajo.
Oslo |âz'lō| *n* Oslo.
ostensible |âstɛn'səbəl| *a* aparente, pretendido.
ostensibly |âstɛn'səblē| *ad* aparentemente.
ostentatious |âstɛntā'shəs| *a* pretencioso, aparatoso; (*person*) ostentativo.
osteopath |âs'tēəpath| *n* osteópata *m/f*.
ostracize |âs'trəsiz| *vt* hacer el vacío a.
ostrich |ôs'trich| *n* avestruz *m*.
OT *n abbr* (= *Old Testament*) A.T. *m*.
OTB *n abbr* (*US*: = *off-track betting*) apuestas hechas fuera del hipódromo.
O.T.E. *abbr* (*Brit*: = *on-target earnings*) beneficios según objetivos.
other |uth'ûr| *a* otro ♦ *pron*: **the** ~ (*one*) el/la otro/a; ~**s** (~ *people*) otros; ~ **than** (*apart from*) aparte de; **the** ~ **day** el otro día; **some** ~ **people have still to arrive** quedan por llegar otros; **some actor or** ~ (*Brit*) algún actor; **somebody or** ~ alguien, alguno; **the car was none** ~ **than Roberta's** fíjate que el coche era de Roberta.
otherwise |uth'ûrwiz| *ad*, *conj* de otra manera; (*if not*) si no; **an** ~ **good piece of work** un trabajo que, eso aparte, es bueno.

OTT *abbr* (*col*) = **over the top;** *see* **top.**

otter [ât'ûr] *n* nutria.

ouch [ouch] *excl* ¡ay!

ought, *pt* **ought** [ôt] *auxiliary vb:* **I ~ to do it** debería hacerlo; **this ~ to have been corrected** esto debiera de haberse corregido; **he ~ to win** (*probability*) debe *or* debiera ganar; **you ~ to go and see it** vale la pena ir a verlo.

ounce [ouns] *n* onza (*28.35g; 16 in a pound*).

our [ou'ûr] *a* nuestro; *see also* **my.**

ours [ou'ûrz] *pron* (el) nuestro/(la) nuestra *etc; see also* **mine.**

ourselves [ouûrselvz'] *pron pl* (*reflexive, after prep*) nosotros; (*emphatic*) nosotros mismos; **we did it (all) by ~** lo hicimos nosotros mismos *or* solos; *see also* **oneself.**

oust [oust] *vt* desalojar.

out [out] *ad* fuera, afuera; (*not at home*) fuera (de casa); (*light, fire*) apagado; (*on strike*) en huelga; **~ there** allí (fuera); **he's ~** (*absent*) no está, ha salido; **to be ~ in one's calculations** (*Brit*) equivocarse (en sus cálculos); **to run ~** salir corriendo; **~ loud** en alta voz; **~ of** *prep* (*outside*) fuera de; (*because of: anger etc*) por; **to look ~ of the window** mirar por la ventana; **to drink ~ of a cup** beber de una taza; **made ~ of wood** de madera; **~ of gas** sin gasolina; "**~ of order**" "no funciona"; **it's ~ of stock** (*COMM*) está agotado; **to be ~ and about again** estar repuesto y levantado; **the journey ~** el viaje de ida; **the boat was 10 km ~** el barco estaba a diez kilómetros de la costa; **before the week was ~** antes del fin de la semana; **he's ~ for all he can get** busca sus propios fines, anda detrás de lo suyo.

out-and-out [out'əndout'] *a* (*liar, thief etc*) redomado, empedernido.

outback [out'bak] *n* interior *m*.

outbid [outbid'] *vt* pujar más alto que, sobrepujar.

outboard [out'bôrd] *a:* **~ motor** (motor *m*) fuera borda *m*.

outbreak [out'brāk] *n* (*of war*) comienzo; (*of disease*) epidemia; (*of violence etc*) ola.

outbuilding [out'bilding] *n* dependencia; (*shed*) cobertizo.

outburst [out'bûrst] *n* explosión *f*, arranque *m*.

outcast [out'kast] *n* paria *m/f*.

outclass [outklas'] *vt* aventajar, superar.

outcome [out'kum] *n* resultado.

outcrop [out'krâp] *n* (*of rock*) afloramiento.

outcry [out'krī] *n* protestas *fpl*.

outdated [outdā'tid] *a* anticuado, fuera de moda.

outdistance [outdis'təns] *vt* dejar atrás.

outdo [outdoo'] *vt* (*irg: like* **do**) superar; **to ~ o.s.** lucirse.

outdoor [out'dôr] *a* al aire libre.

outdoors [outdôrz'] *ad* al aire libre.

outer [out'ûr] *a* exterior, externo.

outer space *n* espacio exterior.

outfit [out'fit] *n* equipo; (*clothes*) traje *m*; (*col: organization*) grupo, organización *f*.

outfitter's [out'fittûrz] *n* sastrería.

outgoing [out'gōing] *a* (*president, tenant*) saliente; (*means of transport*) que sale; (*character*) extrovertido.

outgoings [out'gōingz] *npl* (*Brit*) gastos *mpl*.

outgrow [outgrō'] *vt*: (*irg: like* **grow**) **he has ~n his clothes** su ropa le queda pequeña ya.

outhouse [out'hous] *n* (*US*) retrete *m* fuera de la casa; (*Brit*) dependencia.

outing [ou'ting] *n* excursión *f*, paseo.

outlandish [outlan'dish] *a* estrafalario.

outlast [outlast'] *vt* durar más tiempo que, sobrevivir a.

outlaw [out'lô] *n* proscrito/a ♦ *vt* (*person*) declarar fuera de la ley; (*practice*) declarar ilegal.

outlay [out'lā] *n* inversión *f*.

outlet [out'let] *n* salida; (*of pipe*) desagüe *m*; (*US ELEC*) toma de corriente; (*for emotion*) desahogo; (*also:* **retail ~**) punto de venta.

outline [out'līn] *n* (*shape*) contorno, perfil *m*; **in ~** (*fig*) a grandes rasgos.

outlive [outliv'] *vt* sobrevivir a.

outlook [out'look] *n* perspectiva; (*opinion*) punto de vista.

outlying [out'līing] *a* remoto, aislado.

outmaneuver, (*Brit*) **outmanoeuvre** [outmənoo'vûr] *vt* (*MIL, fig*) superar en la estrategia, superar a.

outmoded [outmō'did] *a* anticuado, pasado de moda.

outnumber [outnum'bûr] *vt* exceder en número.

out of bounds *a:* **it's ~** está prohibido el paso.

out-of-date [outəvdāt'] *a* (*passport*) caducado, vencido; (*theory, idea*) anticuado; (*clothes, customs*) pasado de moda.

out-of-doors [outəvdôrz'] *ad* al aire libre.

out-of-the-way [outəvthəwā'] *a* (*remote*) apartado; (*unusual*) poco común *or* corriente.

outpatient [out'pāshənt] *n* paciente *m/f* externo/a.

outpost [out'pōst] *n* puesto avanzado.

output [out'poot] *n* (volumen *m* de) producción *f*, rendimiento; (*COMPUT*) salida ♦ *vt* (*COMPUT: to power*) imprimir.

outrage [out'rāj] *n* (*scandal*) escándalo; (*atrocity*) atrocidad *f* ♦ *vt* ultrajar.

outrageous [outrā'jəs] *a* monstruoso; (*clothes*) extravagante, escandaloso.

outright *ad* [out'rīt'] (*win*) de manera absoluta; (*be killed*) en el acto; (*completely*) completamente ♦ *a* [out'rīt] completo.

outrun [outrun'] *vt* (*irg: like* **run**) correr

más aprisa que, dejar atrás.

outset [out'set] *n* principio.

outshine [outshīn'] *vt* (irg: *like* **shine**) (*fig*) eclipsar, brillar más que.

outside [out'sīd'] *n* exterior *m* ♦ *a* exterior, externo ♦ *ad* fuera ♦ *prep* fuera de; (*beyond*) más allá de; **at the ~** (*fig*) a lo sumo; **an ~ chance** una posibilidad remota; **~ left/right** (*SOCCER*) extremo izquierdo/derecho.

outside broadcast *n* (*RADIO*, *TV*) emisión *f* exterior.

outside contractor *n* contratista *m/f* independiente.

outside line *n* (*TEL*) línea (exterior).

outsider [outsī'dûr] *n* (*stranger*) extraño, forastero.

outsize [out'sīz] *a* (*Brit: clothes*) de talla grande.

outskirts [out'skûrts] *npl* alrededores *mpl*, afueras *fpl*.

outsmart [outsmârt'] *vt* ser más listo que.

outspoken [out'spō'kən] *a* muy franco.

outspread [out'spred] *a* extendido; (*wings*) desplegado.

outstanding [outstan'ding] *a* excepcional, destacado; (*unfinished*) pendiente.

outstretched [outstrecht'] *a* (*hand*) extendido.

outstrip [outstrip'] *vt* (*competitors, demand, also fig*) dejar atrás, aventajar.

out-tray [out'trā] *n* bandeja de salida.

outvote [outvōt'] *vt*: **it was ~d (by ...)** fue rechazado en el voto (por ...).

outward [out'wûrd] *a* (*sign, appearances*) externo; (*journey*) de ida.

outwardly [out'wûrdlē] *ad* por fuera.

outweigh [outwā'] *vt* pesar más que.

outwit [outwit'] *vt* ser más listo que.

outworn [outwôrn'] *a* (*expression*) cansado.

oval [ō'vəl] *a* ovalado ♦ *n* óvalo.

ovary [ō'vûrē] *n* ovario.

ovation [ōvā'shən] *n* ovación *f*.

oven [uv'ən] *n* horno.

ovenproof [uv'ənprōōf] *a* resistente al horno.

oven-ready [uv'ənred'ē] *a* listo para el horno.

ovenware [uv'ənwär] *n* artículos *mpl* para el horno.

over [ō'vûr] *ad* encima, por encima ♦ *a* (*or ad*) (*finished*) terminado; (*surplus*) de sobra; (*excessively*) demasiado ♦ *prep* (por) encima de; (*above*) sobre; (*on the other side of*) al otro lado de; (*more than*) más de; (*during*) durante; **~ here** (por) aquí; **~ there** (por) allí *or* allá; **all ~** (*everywhere*) por todas partes; **~ and ~ (again)** una y otra vez; **~ and above** además de; **to ask sb ~** invitar a uno a casa; **to bend ~** inclinarse; **the world ~** en todo el mundo, en el mundo entero.

over... [ō'vûr] *pref* sobre..., super....

overact [ōvûrakt'] *vi* (*THEATER*) exagerar el papel.

overall *a* [ō'vûrôl] (*length*) total; (*study*) de conjunto ♦ *ad* [ōvûrôl'] en conjunto ♦ *n* [ō'vûrôl] (*Brit*) guardapolvo; **~s** *npl* mono *sg*, overol *msg* (*LAm*).

overanxious [ōvûrangk'shəs] *a* demasiado preocupado *or* ansioso.

overawe [ōvûrô'] *vt* impresionar.

overbalance [ōvûrbal'əns] *vi* perder el equilibrio.

overbearing [ōvûrbär'ing] *a* autoritario, imperioso.

overboard [ō'vûrbôrd] *ad* (*NAUT*) por la borda; **to go ~ for sth** (*fig*) enloquecerse por algo.

overbook [ō'vûrbōōk'] *vt* sobrereservar, reservar con exceso.

overcapitalize [ōvûrkap'itəlīz] *vi* sobrecapitalizar.

overcast [ō'vûrkast] *a* encapotado.

overcharge [ōvûrchârj'] *vt*: **to ~ sb** cobrar un precio excesivo a uno.

overcoat [ō'vûrkōt] *n* abrigo, sobretodo.

overcome [ōvûrkum'] *vt* (irg: *like* **come**) (*gen*) vencer; (*difficulty*) superar; **she was quite ~ by the occasion** la ocasión le conmovió mucho *or* le vino en grande.

overconfident [ōvûrkán'fidənt] *a* demasiado confiado.

overcrowded [ōvûrkrou'did] *a* atestado de gente; (*city, country*) superpoblado.

overcrowding [ōvûrkrou'ding] *n* (*in town, country*) superpoblación *f*; (*in bus etc*) hacinamiento, apiñamiento.

overdo [ōvûrdōō'] *vt* (irg: *like* **do**) exagerar; (*overcook*) cocer demasiado; **to ~ it, to ~ things** (*work too hard*) trabajar demasiado.

overdose [ō'vûrdōs] *n* sobredosis *f inv*.

overdraft [ō'vûrdraft] *n* saldo deudor.

overdrawn [ōvûrdrôn'] *a* (*account*) en descubierto.

overdrive [ō'vûrdrīv] *n* (*AUT*) sobremarcha, superdirecta.

overdue [ōvûrdōō'] *a* retrasado; (*recognition*) tardío; (*bill*) vencido y no pagado; **that change was long ~** ese cambio tenía que hacerse hace tiempo.

overenthusiastic [ōvûrenthōōzēas'tik] *a* demasiado entusiasta.

overestimate [ōvûres'təmāt] *vt* sobreestimar.

overexcited [ōvûriksī'tid] *a* sobreexcitado.

overexertion [ōvûrigzûr'shən] *n* agotamiento, fatiga.

overexpose [ōvûrikspōz'] *vt* (*PHOT*) sobreexponer.

overflow *vi* [ōvûrflō'] desbordarse ♦ *n* [ō'vûrflō] (*excess*) exceso; (*of river*) desbordamiento; (*also: ~ pipe*) (cañería de) desagüe *m*.

overfly [ōvûrflī'] *vt* (irg: *like* **fly**) sobrevolar.

overgenerous [ōvûrjen'ûrəs] *a* demasiado generoso.

overgrown [ōvûrgrōn'] *a* (*garden*) cubierto de hierba; **he's just an ~ schoolboy** es un niño en grande.

overhang [ōvûrhang'] (*irg: like* **hang**) *vt* sobresalir por encima de ♦ *vi* sobresalir.

overhaul *vt* [ōvûrhól'] revisar, repasar ♦ *n* [ō'vûrhól] revisión *f*.

overhead *ad* [ō'vûrhed'] por arriba *or* encima ♦ [ō'vûrhed] *a* (*cable*) aéreo; (*railway*) elevado, aéreo ♦ *n* (*US*) gastos *mpl* generales.

overheads [ō'vûrhedz] *npl* (*Brit*) gastos *mpl* generales.

overhear [ōvûrhiûr'] *vt* (*irg: like* **hear**) oír por casualidad.

overheat [ōvûrhēt'] *vi* (*engine*) recalentarse.

overjoyed [ōvûrjoid'] *a* encantado, lleno de alegría.

overkill [ō'vûrkil] *n* (MIL *fig*) capacidad *f* excesiva de destrucción.

overland [ō'vûrland] *a, ad* por tierra.

overlap *vi* [ōvûrlap'] traslaparse ♦ *n* [ō'vûrlap] traslapo.

overleaf [ō'vûrlēf] *ad* al dorso.

overload [ōvûrlōd'] *vt* sobrecargar.

overlook [ōvûrlŏŏk'] *vt* (*have view of*) dar a, tener vistas a; (*miss*) pasar por alto; (*forgive*) hacer la vista gorda a.

overlord [ō'vûrlórd] *n* señor *m*.

overmanning [ōvûrman'ing] *n* empleo de más personal de lo necesario.

overnight *ad* [ōvûrnīt'] durante la noche; (*fig*) de la noche a la mañana ♦ *a* [ō'vûrnīt] de noche; **to stay ~** pasar la noche.

overnight bag *n* fin *m* de semana, neceser *m* de viaje.

overnight stay *n* estancia de una noche.

overpass [ō'vûrpas] *n* (*US*) paso superior *or* a desnivel.

overpay [ōvûrpā'] *vt*: **to ~ sb by $50** pagar 50 dólares de más a uno.

overpower [ōvûrpou'ûr] *vt* dominar; (*fig*) embargar.

overpowering [ōvûrpou'ûring] *a* (*heat*) agobiante; (*smell*) penetrante.

overproduction [ōvûrprəduk'shən] *n* superproducción *f*.

overrate [ōvərrāt'] *vt* sobreestimar.

overreach [ōvərēch'] *vt*: **to ~ o.s.** ir demasiado lejos, pasarse.

override [ōvərīd'] *vt* (*irg: like* **ride**) (*order, objection*) no hacer caso de.

overriding [ōvərīd'ing] *a* predominante.

overrule [ōvərōōl'] *vt* (*decision*) anular; (*claim*) denegar.

overrun [ō'vərun] *vt* (*irg: like* **run**) (MIL: *country*) invadir; (*time limit*) rebasar, exceder ♦ *vi* rebasar el límite previsto; **the town is ~ with tourists** el pueblo está inundado de turistas.

overseas *ad* [ō'vûrsēz'] en ultramar; (*abroad*) en el extranjero ♦ *a* [ō'vûrsēz] (*trade*) exterior; (*visitor*) extranjero.

overseer [ō'vûrsēûr] *n* (*in factory*) superintendente *m/f*; (*foreman*) capataz *m*.

overshadow [ōvûrshad'ō] *vt* (*fig*) eclipsar.

overshoot [ōvûrshōōt'] *vt* (*irg: like* **shoot**) excederse.

oversight [ō'vûrsīt] *n* descuido; **due to an ~** a causa de un descuido *or* una equivocación.

oversimplify [ōvûrsim'pləfī] *vt* simplificar demasiado.

oversize [ō'vûrsīz] *a* (*US: clothes*) de talla grande.

oversleep [ōvûrslēp'] *vi* (*irg: like* **sleep**) quedarse dormido.

overspend [ōvûrspend'] *vi* gastar más de la cuenta; **we have overspent by 5 dollars** hemos excedido el presupuesto en 5 dólares.

overspill [ō'vûrspil] *n* exceso de población.

overstaffed [ō'vûrstaft] *a*: **to be ~** tener una plantilla excesiva.

overstate [ōvûrstāt'] *vt* exagerar.

overstatement [ōvûrstāt'mənt] *n* exageración *f*.

overstay [ōvûrstā'] *vt*: **to ~ one's welcome** quedarse más de la cuenta.

overstep [ōvûrstep'] *vt*: **to ~ the mark** *or* **the limits** pasarse de la raya.

overstock [ōvûrsták'] *vt* abarrotar.

overstrike [ōvûrstrīk] *n* (*on printer*) superposición *f* ♦ *vt* (*irg: like* **strike**) superponer.

oversubscribed [ōvûrsəbskrībd'] *a* suscrito en exceso.

overt [ōvûrt'] *a* abierto.

overtake [ōvûrtāk'] *vt* (*irg: like* **take**) sobrepasar; (*Brit* AUT) adelantar.

overtax [ōvûrtaks'] *vt* (ECON) exigir contribuciones *fpl* excesivas *or* impuestos *mpl* excesivos a; (*fig: strength, patience*) agotar, abusar de; **to ~ o.s.** fatigarse demasiado.

overthrow [ōvûrthrō'] *vt* (*irg: like* **throw**) (*government*) derrocar.

overtime [ō'vûrtīm] *n* horas *fpl* extraordinarias; (*US SPORT*) prórroga; **to do** *or* **work ~** hacer *or* trabajar horas extraordinarias *or* extras.

overtime ban *n* prohibición *f* de (hacer) horas extraordinarias.

overtone [ō'vûrtōn] *n* (*fig*) tono.

overture [ō'vûrchûr] *n* (MUS) obertura; (*fig*) propuesta.

overturn [ōvûrtûrn'] *vt, vi* volcar.

overweight [ōvûrwāt'] *a* demasiado gordo *or* pesado.

overwhelm [ōvûrwelm'] *vt* aplastar.

overwhelming [ōvûrwel'ming] *a* (*victory, defeat*) arrollador(a); (*desire*) irresistible; **one's ~ impression is of heat** lo que más impresiona es el calor.

overwhelmingly [ōvûrwel'minglē] *ad* abrumadoramente.
overwork [ōvûrwûrk'] *n* trabajo excesivo ♦ *vt* hacer trabajar demasiado ♦ *vi* trabajar demasiado.
overwrite [ōvərīt'] *vt* (*irg: like* write) (*COMPUT*) sobreescribir.
overwrought [ō'vərôt'] *a* sobreexcitado.
ovulation [ăvyəlā'shən] *n* ovulación *f*.
owe [ō] *vt* deber; **to ~ sb sth, to ~ sth to sb** deber algo a uno.
owing to [ō'ing tōō] *prep* debido a, por causa de.
owl [oul] *n* búho, lechuza.
own [ōn] *vt* tener, poseer ♦ *vi* (*Brit*): **to ~ to sth/to having done sth** confesar *or* reconocer algo/haber hecho algo ♦ *a* propio; **a room of my ~** una habitación propia; **on one's ~** solo, a solas; **can I have it for my (very) ~?** ¿puedo quedarme con él?; **to come into one's ~** justificarse.
own up *vi* confesar.
own brand *n* (*COMM*) marca propia.
owner [ō'nûr] *n* dueño/a.
owner-occupier [ō'nûr ăk'yəpīûr] *n* ocupante propietario/a *m/f*.
ownership [ō'nûrship] *n* posesión *f*; **it's under new ~** está bajo nueva dirección.
ox, *pl* **oxen** [ăks, ăk'sən] *n* buey *m*.
Oxfam [ăks'fam] *n abbr* (*Brit*: = *Oxford Committee for Famine Relief*) OXFAM.
oxide [ăk'sīd] *n* óxido.
oxtail [ăks'tāl] *n*: **~ soup** sopa de rabo de buey.
oxyacetylene [ăksēəset'əlin] *a* oxiacetilénico; **~ burner, ~ torch** soplete *m* oxiacetilénico.
oxygen [ăk'sijən] *n* oxígeno.
oxygen mask *n* máscara de oxígeno.
oxygen tent *n* tienda de oxígeno.
oyster [ois'tûr] *n* ostra.
oz. *abbr* = **ounce(s)**.
ozone [ō'zōn] *n* ozono; **~ friendly** amigo del ozono; **~ layer** capa de ozono.

P

P, p [pē] *n* (*letter*) P, p *f*; **P for Peter** P de París.
P *abbr* = **president, prince**.
p *abbr* (= *page*) pág.; (*Brit*) = **penny, pence**.
PA *n abbr* = **personal assistant, public address system** ♦ *abbr* (*US MAIL*) = *Pennsylvania*.
pa [pâ] *n* (*col*) papá *m*.

p.a. *abbr* = **per annum**.
PAC *n abbr* (*US*) = *political action committee*.
pace [pās] *n* paso; (*rhythm*) ritmo ♦ *vi*: **to ~ up and down** pasearse de un lado a otro; **to keep ~ with** llevar el mismo paso que; (*events*) mantenerse a la altura de *or* al corriente de; **to set the ~** (*running*) marcar el paso; (*fig*) dar la pauta; **to put sb through his ~s** (*fig*) poner a uno a prueba.
pacemaker [pās'mākûr] *n* (*MED*) regulador *m* cardíaco, marcapasos *m inv*.
pacific [pəsif'ik] *a* pacífico ♦ *n*: **the P~ (Ocean)** el (Océano) Pacífico.
pacification [pasəfəkā'shən] *n* pacificación *f*.
pacifier [pas'əfīûr] *n* (*US: for baby*) chupete *m*.
pacifism [pas'əfizəm] *n* pacifismo.
pacifist [pas'əfist] *n* pacifista *m/f*.
pacify [pas'əfī] *vt* (*soothe*) apaciguar; (*country*) pacificar.
pack [pak] *n* (*packet*) paquete *m*; (*COMM*) embalaje *m*; (*of hounds*) jauría; (*of wolves*) manada; (*of thieves etc*) manada, bando; (*of cards*) baraja; (*bundle*) fardo; (*of cigarettes*) paquete *m*, cajetilla ♦ *vt* (*wrap*) empaquetar; (*fill*) llenar; (*in suitcase etc*) meter, poner; (*cram*) llenar, atestar; (*fig: meeting etc*) llenar de partidarios; (*COMPUT*) comprimir; **to ~** (*one's bags*) hacer la maleta; **to ~ sb off** despachar a uno; **the place was ~ed** el local estaba lleno hasta el tope; **to send sb ~ing** (*col*) echar *or* despedir a uno.
pack in *vt* (*col*) dejar ♦ *vi* (*Brit: break down: watch, car*) estropearse; **~ it in!** ¡para!, ¡basta ya!
pack up *vt* (*belongings, clothes*) recoger; (*goods, presents*) empaquetar, envolver ♦ *vi* (*Brit: col: machine*) estropearse; (*person*) irse.
package [pak'ij] *n* paquete *m*; (*bulky*) bulto; (*also: ~ deal*) acuerdo global ♦ *vt* (*COMM: goods*) envasar, embalar.
package bomb *n* (*US*) paquete *m* bomba.
package holiday *n* (*Brit*) viaje *m* todo comprendido.
package tour *n* viaje *m* organizado.
packaging [pak'ijing] *n* envase *m*.
packed lunch [pakt lunch] *n* (*Brit*) almuerzo frío, merienda.
packer [pak'ûr] *n* (*person*) empacador(a) *m/f*.
packet [pak'it] *n* paquete *m*.
packet switching [pak'it swich'ing] *n* (*COMPUT*) conmutación *f* por paquetes.
packhorse [pak'hôrs] *n* caballo de carga.
pack ice [pak īs] *n* banco de hielo.
packing [pak'ing] *n* embalaje *m*.
packing case *n* cajón *m* de embalaje.
pact [pakt] *n* pacto.

pad |pad| n (*of paper*) bloc m; (*cushion*) cojinete m; (*launching* ~) plataforma (de lanzamiento); (*col: apartment*) casa ♦ vt rellenar.

padding |pad'ing| n relleno; (*fig*) paja.

paddle |pad'əl| n (*oar*) canalete m; (*US: for table tennis*) raqueta ♦ vt impulsar con canalete ♦ vi (*with feet*) chapotear.

paddle steamer n vapor m de ruedas.

paddling pool |pad'ling pōōl| n (*Brit*) estanque m de juegos.

paddock |pad'ək| n corral m.

paddy |pad'ē| n arrozal m.

padlock |pad'lâk| n candado ♦ vt cerrar con candado.

paediatrics |pēdēat'riks| n (*Brit*) = **pediatrics**.

paediatrician |pēdēətrish'ən| n (*Brit*) = **pediatrician**.

pagan |pā'gən| a, n pagano/a m/f.

page |pāj| n (*of book*) página; (*of newspaper*) plana; (*also:* ~ **boy**) paje m ♦ vt (*in hotel etc*) llamar por altavoz a.

pageant |paj'ənt| n (*procession*) desfile m; (*show*) espectáculo.

pageantry |paj'əntrē| n pompa.

page break n límite m de la página.

pager |pā'jûr| n localizador m personal.

paginate |paj'ənāt| vt paginar.

pagination |pajənā'shən| n paginación f.

pagoda |pəgō'də| n pagoda.

paid |pād| pt, pp of **pay** ♦ a (*work*) remunerado; (*official*) asalariado; **to put** ~ **to** (*Brit*) acabar con.

paid-up |pād'up| a (*member*) con sus cuotas pagadas or al día; (*share*) liberado; ~ **capital** capital m desembolsado.

pail |pāl| n cubo, balde m.

pain |pān| n dolor m; **to be in** ~ sufrir; **on** ~ **of death** so or bajo pena de muerte; *see also* **pains**.

pained |pānd| a (*expression*) afligido.

painful |pān'fəl| a doloroso; (*difficult*) penoso; (*disagreeable*) desagradable.

painfully |pān'fəlē| ad (*fig: very*) terriblemente.

painkiller |pān'kilûr| n analgésico.

painless |pān'lis| a que no causa dolor; (*method*) fácil.

pains |pānz| npl (*efforts*) esfuerzos mpl; **to take** ~ **to do sth** tomarse trabajo en hacer algo.

painstaking |pānz'tāking| a (*person*) concienzudo, esmerado.

paint |pānt| n pintura ♦ vt pintar; **a can of** ~ una lata de pintura; **to** ~ **the door blue** pintar la puerta de azul.

paintbox |pānt'bâks| n caja de pinturas.

paintbrush |pānt'brush| n (*artist's*) pincel m; (*decorator's*) brocha.

painter |pān'tûr| n pintor(a) m/f.

painting |pān'ting| n pintura.

paintwork |pānt'wûrk| n pintura.

pair |pär| n (*of shoes, gloves etc*) par m; (*of people*) pareja; **a** ~ **of scissors** unas tijeras; **a** ~ **of pants** unos pantalones, un pantalón.

pair off vi: **to** ~ **off (with sb)** hacer pareja (con uno).

pajamas |pəjâm'əz| npl (*US*) pijama m; **a pair of** ~ un pijama.

Pakistan |pak'istan| n Paquistán m.

Pakistani |pak'əstan'ē| a, n paquistaní m/f.

PAL |pal| n abbr (*TV*) = *phase alternation line*.

pal |pal| n (*col*) compinche m/f, compañero/a.

palace |pal'is| n palacio.

palatable |pal'ətəbəl| a sabroso; (*acceptable*) aceptable.

palate |pal'it| n paladar m.

palatial |pəlā'shəl| a (*surroundings, residence*) suntuoso, espléndido.

palaver |pəlav'ûr| n (*US: chatter*) palabrería; (*Brit: fuss*) lío.

pale |pāl| a (*gen*) pálido; (*color*) claro ♦ n: **to be beyond the** ~ pasarse de la raya ♦ vi palidecer; **to grow** or **turn** ~ palidecer; **to** ~ **into insignificance (beside)** no poderse comparar (con).

paleness |pāl'nis| n palidez f.

Palestine |pal'istīn| n Palestina.

Palestinian |palistin'ēən| a, n palestino/a m/f.

palette |pal'it| n paleta.

paling |pā'ling| n (*stake*) estaca; (*fence*) valla.

palisade |palisād'| n palizada.

pall |pôl| n (*of smoke*) capa (de humo) ♦ vi perder el sabor.

pallbearer |pôl'bärûr| n portador m del féretro.

pallet |pal'it| n (*for goods*) paleta.

palletization |palitəzā'shən| n paletización f.

palliative |pal'ēātiv| n paliativo.

pallid |pal'id| a pálido.

pallor |pal'ûr| n palidez f.

pally |pal'ē| a (*col*): **to be very** ~ **with sb** ser muy amigo de uno.

palm |pâm| n (*ANAT*) palma; (*also:* ~ **tree**) palmera, palma ♦ vt: **to** ~ **sth off on sb** (*col*) encajar algo a uno.

palmist |pâm'ist| n quiromántico/a, palmista m/f.

Palm Sunday n Domingo de Ramos.

palpable |pal'pəbəl| a palpable.

palpably |pal'pəblē| ad obviamente.

palpitation |palpitā'shən| n palpitación f; **to have** ~**s** tener vahidos or palpitaciones.

paltry |pôl'trē| a (*amount etc*) miserable; (*insignificant: person*) insignificante.

pamper |pam'pûr| vt mimar.

pamphlet |pam'flit| n folleto; (*political: handed out in street*) panfleto.

pan |pan| n (*also:* **sauce**~) cacerola, cazuela, olla; (also: **frying ~**) sartén m; (of lavatory) taza ♦ vi (CINEMA) tomar panorámicas; **to ~ for gold** cribar oro ♦ vt (criticize) criticar duramente a, dar una paliza a.

pan- [pan] pref pan-.

panacea [panəse'ə] n panacea.

panache [pənash'] n bríos mpl, orgullo, brillantez f.

Panama [pan'əmâ] n Panamá m.

Panama Canal n el Canal de Panamá.

pancake [pan'kāk] n panqueque m.

Pancake Day n martes m de carnaval.

pancreas [pan'krēəs] n páncreas m.

panda [pan'də] n panda m.

pandemonium [pandəmō'nēəm] n (noise): **there was ~** se armó un tremendo jaleo; (mess) caos m.

pander [pan'dûr] vi: **to ~ to** complacer a.

pane [pān] n cristal m.

panel [pan'əl] n (of wood) panel m; (of cloth) paño; (RADIO, TV) panel m de invitados.

panel game n (TV) programa m concurso para equipos.

paneling, (Brit) **panelling** [pan'əling] n paneles mpl.

panelist, (Brit) **panellist** [pan'əlist] n miembro del jurado.

pang [pang] n: **~s of conscience** remordimiento sg; **~s of hunger** dolores mpl del hambre.

panic [pan'ik] n (terror m) pánico ♦ vi dejarse llevar por el pánico.

panicky [pan'ikē] a (person) asustadizo.

panic-stricken [pan'ikstrikən] a preso de pánico.

pannier [pan'yûr] n (on bicycle) cartera; (on mule etc) alforja.

panorama [panəram'ə] n panorama m.

panoramic [panəram'ik] a panorámico.

pansy [pan'zē] n (BOT) pensamiento; (col: pej) maricón m.

pant [pant] vi jadear.

panther [pan'thûr] n pantera.

panties [pan'tēz] npl bragas fpl, pantis mpl.

pantomime [pan'təmīm] n (Brit) representación f musical navideña.

pantry [pan'trē] n despensa.

pants [pants] n (US: trousers) pantalones mpl; (Brit: underwear: woman's) bragas fpl; (: man's) calzoncillos mpl.

pants press n (US) prensa para pantalones.

pantsuit [pant'sōōt] n traje m de chaqueta y pantalón.

pantyhose [pan'tēhōz] n (US) pantimedias fpl.

papal [pā'pəl] a papal.

paper [pā'pûr] n papel m; (also: **news~**) periódico, diario; (study, article) artículo; (exam) examen m ♦ a de papel ♦ vt empapelar; (identity) **~s** npl papeles mpl, docu-

mentos mpl; **useless ~s** papeleo; **a piece of ~** (odd bit) un pedazo de papel (suelto); (sheet) una hoja de papel; **to put sth down on ~** poner algo por escrito.

paper advance n (on printer) avance m de papel.

paperback [pā'pûrbak] n libro de bolsillo.

paper bag n bolsa de papel.

paperboy [pā'pûrboi] n (selling) vendedor m de periódicos; (delivering) repartidor m de periódicos.

paper clip n clip m.

paper hankie n (Brit) pañuelo de papel.

paper money n papel m moneda.

paper profit n beneficio no realizado.

paperweight [pā'pûrwāt] n pisapapeles m inv.

paperwork [pā'pûrwûrk] n trabajo administrativo; (pej) papeleo.

papier-mâché [pā'pûrməshā'] n cartón m piedra.

paprika [paprē'kə] n pimienta húngara or roja.

Pap test [pap test] n (MED) frotis m (cervical).

papyrus [pəpī'rəs] n papiro.

par [pâr] n par f; (GOLF) par m ♦ a a la par; **to be on a ~ with** estar a la par con; **at ~** a la par; **to be above/below ~** estar sobre/bajo la par; **to feel under ~** sentirse en baja forma.

parable [par'əbəl] n parábola.

parachute [par'əshōōt] n paracaídas m inv ♦ vi lanzarse en paracaídas.

parachutist [par'əshōōtist] n paracaidista m/f.

parade [pərād'] n desfile m ♦ vt (gen) recorrer, desfilar por; (show off) hacer alarde de ♦ vi desfilar; (MIL) pasar revista.

parade ground n plaza de armas.

paradise [par'ədīs] n paraíso.

paradox [par'ədâks] n paradoja.

paradoxical [parədâk'sikəl] a paradójico.

paradoxically [parədâk'siklē] ad paradójicamente.

paraffin [par'əfin] n (Brit): **~ (oil)** parafina.

paragon [par'əgân] n modelo.

paragraph [par'əgraf] n párrafo; **to begin a new ~** empezar un nuevo párrafo.

Paraguay [par'əgwā] n Paraguay m.

Paraguayan [parəgwā'ən] a, n paraguayo/a m/f, paraguayano/a m/f.

parakeet [par'əkēt] n (US) periquito.

parallel [par'əlel] a: **~ (with/to)** en paralelo (con/a); (fig) semejante (a) ♦ n (line) paralela; (fig, GEO) paralelo.

paralysis [pəral'isis] n parálisis f inv.

paralytic [parəlit'ik] a paralítico.

paralyze [par'əlīz] vt paralizar.

paramedic [parəmed'ik] n (US) ambulanciero/a.

parameter [pəram'itûr] n parámetro.

paramilitary [parəmil'itārē] a (organization,

operations) paramilitar.

paramount [par'əmount] *a:* **of ~ importance** de suma importancia.

paranoia [parənoi'ə] *n* paranoia.

paranoid [par'ənoid] *a* (*person, feeling*) paranoico.

paranormal [parənôr'məl] *a* paranormal.

parapet [par'əpit] *n* parapeto.

paraphernalia [parəfûrnāl'yə] *n* (*gear*) avíos *mpl.*

paraphrase [par'əfrāz] *vt* parafrasear.

paraplegic [parəplē'jik] *n* parapléjico/a.

parapsychology [parəsīkál'əjē] *n* parasicología.

parasite [par'əsīt] *n* parásito/a.

parasol [par'əsôl] *n* sombrilla, quitasol *m.*

paratrooper [par'ətrŌŌpûr] *n* paracaidista *m/f.*

parcel [pâr'səl] *n* paquete *m* ♦ *vt* empaquetar, embalar; **to be part and ~ of** ser íntegro a.

parcel out *vt* parcelar, repartir.

parcel bomb *n* (*Brit*) paquete *m* bomba.

parcel post *n* servicio de paquetes postales.

parch [pârch] *vt* secar, resecar.

parched [pârcht] *a* (*person*) muerto de sed.

parchment [pârch'mənt] *n* pergamino.

pardon [pâr'dən] *n* perdón *m;* (*LAW*) indulto ♦ *vt* perdonar; indultar; **~ me!, I beg your ~!** ¡perdone usted!; **(I beg your) ~?,** (*US*) **~ me?** ¿cómo?

pare [pär] *vt* (*nails*) cortar; (*fruit etc*) pelar.

parent [pär'ənt] *n:* **~s** *npl* padres *mpl.*

parentage [pär'əntij] *n* familia, linaje *m;* **of unknown ~** de padres desconocidos.

parental [pəren'təl] *a* paternal/maternal.

parent company *n* casa matriz.

parenthesis, *pl* **parentheses** [pəren'thəsis, -thəsēz] *n* paréntesis *m inv;* **in parentheses** entre paréntesis.

parenthood [pär'ənt·hŌŌd] *n* el ser padre o madre.

parent ship *n* buque *m* nodriza.

Paris [par'is] *n* París *m.*

parish [par'ish] *n* parroquia.

parish council *n* concejo parroquial.

parishioner [pərish'ənûr] *n* feligrés/esa *m/f.*

Parisian [pərizh'ən] *a, n* parisino/a *m/f,* parisiense *m/f.*

parity [par'itē] *n* paridad *f,* igualdad *f.*

park [pârk] *n* parque *m,* jardín *m* público ♦ *vt* aparcar, estacionar ♦ *vi* aparcar, estacionarse.

parka [pâr'kə] *n* *chaquetón acolchado con capucha.*

parking [pâr'king] *n* aparcamiento, estacionamiento; **"no ~"** "prohibido aparcar *or* estacionarse".

parking lights *npl* luces *fpl* de estacionamiento.

parking lot *n* (*US*) parking *m,*

aparcamiento.

parking meter *n* parquímetro.

parking place *n* sitio para aparcar, aparcamiento.

parking ticket *n* multa de aparcamiento.

parking violation, (*Brit*) **parking offence** *n* ofensa por aparcamiento indebido.

parkway [pârk'wā] *n* (*US*) alameda.

parlance [pâr'ləns] *n* lenguaje *m;* **in common/modern ~** en lenguaje corriente/moderno.

parliament [pâr'ləmənt] *n* parlamento; (*Spanish*) Cortes *fpl.*

parliamentary [pârləmen'tûrē] *a* parlamentario.

parlor, (*Brit*) **parlour** [pâr'lûr] *n* sala de recibo, salón *m,* living *m* (*LAm*).

parlous [pâr'ləs] *a* peligroso, alarmante.

Parmesan [pâr'məzân] *n* (*also:* **~ cheese**) queso parmesano.

parochial [pərō'kēəl] *a* parroquial; (*pej*) de miras estrechas.

parody [par'ədē] *n* parodia ♦ *vt* parodiar.

parole [pərōl'] *n:* **on ~** libre bajo palabra.

paroxysm [par'əksizəm] *n* (*MED*) paroxismo, ataque *m;* (*of anger, laughter, coughing*) ataque *m;* (*of grief*) crisis *f.*

parquet [pârkā'] *n:* **~ floor(ing)** parquet *m.*

parrot [par'ət] *n* loro, papagayo.

parrot fashion *ad* mecánicamente.

parry [par'ē] *vt* parar.

parsimonious [pârsəmō'nēəs] *a* tacaño.

parsley [pârs'lē] *n* perejil *m.*

parsnip [pârs'nip] *n* chirivía.

parson [pâr'sən] *n* cura *m.*

part [pârt] *n* (*gen, MUS*) parte *f;* (*bit*) trozo; (*of machine*) pieza; (*THEATER etc*) papel *m;* (*of serial*) entrega; (*US: in hair*) raya ♦ *ad* = **partly** ♦ *vt* separar; (*break*) partir ♦ *vi* (*people*) separarse; (*roads*) bifurcarse; (*crowd*) apartarse; (*break*) romperse; **to take ~ in** participar *or* tomar parte en; **to take sb's ~** defender a uno; **for my ~** por mi parte; **for the most ~** en su mayor parte; (*people*) en su mayoría; **for the better ~ of the day** durante la mayor parte del día; **~ of speech** (*LING*) parte *f* de la oración.

part with *vt fus* ceder, entregar; (*money*) pagar; (*get rid of*) deshacerse de.

partake [pârtāk'] *vi* (*irg: like* **take**) (*formal*): **to ~ of sth** tomar algo.

part exchange *n* (*Brit*): **in ~** como parte del pago.

partial [pâr'shəl] *a* parcial; **to be ~ to** ser aficionado a.

partially [pâr'shəlē] *ad* en parte, parcialmente.

participant [pârtis'əpənt] *n* (*in competition*) concursante *m/f.*

participate [pârtis'əpāt] *vi:* **to ~ in** participar en.

participation [pârtisəpā'shən] *n* participación f.

participle [pâr'tisipəl] n participio.

particle [pâr'tikəl] n partícula; (of dust) grano; (fig) pizca.

particleboard [pâr'tikəlbôrd] n (US) madera aglomerada.

particular [pûrtik'yəlûr] a (special) particular; (concrete) concreto; (given) determinado; (detailed) detallado, minucioso; (fussy) quisquilloso, exigente; ~s npl (information) datos mpl, detalles mpl; (details) pormenores mpl; in ~ en particular; to be very ~ about ser muy exigente en cuanto a; I'm not ~ me es or da igual.

particularly [pûrtik'yəlûrlē] ad especialmente, en particular.

parting [pâr'ting] n (act of) separación f; (farewell) despedida; (Brit: in hair) raya ♦ a de despedida; ~ shot (fig) golpe m final.

partisan [pâr'tizən] a, n partidario/a m/f.

partition [pârtish'ən] n (POL) división f; (wall) tabique m ♦ vt dividir; dividir con tabique.

partly [pârt'lē] ad en parte.

partner [pârt'nûr] n (COMM) socio/a; (SPORT, at dance) pareja; (spouse) cónyuge m/f; (friend etc) compañero/a ♦ vt acompañar.

partnership [pârt'nûrship] n (gen) asociación f; (COMM) sociedad f; to go into ~ (with), form a ~ (with) asociarse (con).

part payment n pago parcial, abono.

partridge [pâr'trij] n perdiz f.

part-time [pârt'tīm] a, ad a tiempo parcial.

part-timer [pârttī'mûr] n trabajador(a) m/f a tiempo partido.

party [pâr'tē] n (POL) partido; (celebration) fiesta; (group) grupo; (LAW) parte f, interesado ♦ a (POL) de partido; (dress etc) de fiesta, de gala; to have or give or throw a ~ organizar una fiesta; dinner ~ cena; to be a ~ to a crime ser cómplice m/f de un crimen.

party line n (POL) línea política del partido; (TEL) línea compartida.

par value n (of share, bond) valor m a la par.

pass [pas] vt (time, object) pasar; (place) pasar por; (exam, law) aprobar; (overtake, surpass) rebasar; (approve) aprobar; (AUT) adelantar a ♦ vi pasar; (SCOL) aprobar, ser aprobado ♦ n (permit) permiso; (membership card) carnet m; (in mountains) puerto, desfiladero; (SPORT) pase m; to get a ~ in aprobar en; to ~ sth through sth pasar algo por algo; to ~ the time of day with sb pasar el rato con uno; to make a ~ at sb (col) hacer proposiciones a uno.

pass away vi fallecer.

pass by vi pasar ♦ vt (ignore) pasar por alto.

pass down vt (customs, inheritance) pa-

sar, transmitir.

pass for vt fus pasar por; she could ~ for twenty-five se podría creer que sólo tiene 25 años.

pass on vi (die) fallecer, morir ♦ vt (hand on): to ~ on (to) transmitir (a); (cold, illness) pegar (a); (benefits) dar (a); (price rises) pasar (a).

pass out vi desmayarse ♦ vt (information, papers) pasar (de mano en mano); (chocolates etc) ofrecer.

pass over vi (die) fallecer ♦ vt omitir, pasar por alto.

pass up vt (opportunity) dejar pasar, no aprovechar.

passable [pas'əbəl] a (road) transitable; (tolerable) pasable.

passably [pas'əblē] ad pasablemente (bien).

passage [pas'ij] n pasillo; (act of passing) tránsito; (fare, in book) pasaje m; (by boat) travesía.

passageway [pas'ijwā] n (in house) pasillo, corredor m; (between buildings etc) pasaje m, pasadizo.

passbook [pas'book] n libreta de banco.

passenger [pas'injûr] n pasajero/a, viajero/a.

passer-by [pasûrbī'] n transeúnte m/f.

passing [pas'ing] a (fleeting) pasajero; in ~ de paso.

passing place n (Brit AUT) apartadero.

passion [pash'ən] n pasión f.

passionate [pash'ənit] a apasionado.

passionately [pash'ənitlē] ad apasionadamente, con pasión.

passive [pas'iv] a (also LING) pasivo.

passkey [pas'kē] n llave f maestra.

Passover [pas'ōvûr] n Pascua (de los judíos).

passport [pas'pôrt] n pasaporte m.

passport control n control m de pasaporte.

password [pas'wûrd] n (also COMPUT) contraseña.

past [past] prep (further than) más allá de; (later than) después de ♦ a pasado; (president etc) antiguo ♦ n (time) pasado; (of person) antecedentes mpl; quarter/half ~ four las cuatro y cuarto/media; he's ~ forty tiene más de cuarenta años; I'm ~ caring ya no me importa; to be ~ one's prime (person) ser acabado; for the ~ few/3 days durante los últimos días/últimos 3 días; to run ~ pasar a la carrera por; in the ~ en el pasado, antes.

pasta [pâs'tə] n pasta.

paste [pāst] n (gen) pasta; (glue) engrudo ♦ vt (stick) pegar; (glue) engomar; **tomato** ~ puré m de tomate.

pastel [pastel'] a pastel; (painting) al pastel.

pasteurized [pas'chərīzd] a pasteurizado.

pastille [pastēl'] n pastilla.

pastime [pas'tīm] n pasatiempo.

pastor [pas'tûr] *n* pastor *m*.
pastoral [pas'tûrəl] *a* pastoral.
pastry [pās'trē] *n* (*dough*) pasta; (*cake*) pastel *m*.
pasture [pas'chûr] *n* (*grass*) pasto.
pasty *a* [pās'tē] pastoso; (*complexion*) pálido ♦ *n* [pas'tē] (*Brit*) empanada.
pat [pat] *n* dar una palmadita a; (*dog etc*) acariciar ♦ *n* (*of butter*) porción *f* ♦ *a*: **he has it down** ~ se lo sabe de memoria *or* al dedillo; **to give sb/o.s. a** ~ **on the back** (*fig*) felicitar a uno/felicitarse.
patch [pach] *n* (*of material*) parche *m*; (*mended part*) remiendo; (*of land*) terreno; (*COMPUT*) ajuste *m* ♦ *vt* (*clothes*) remendar.
   patch up *vt* (*mend temporarily*) reparar; **to** ~ **up a quarrel** hacer las paces.
patchwork [pach'wûrk] *n* labor *f* de retazos.
patchy [pach'ē] *a* desigual.
pate [pāt] *n*: **bald** ~ calva.
pâté [pätā'] *n* paté *m*.
patent [pat'ənt] *n* patente *f* ♦ *vt* patentar ♦ *a* patente, evidente.
patent leather *n* charol *m*.
patently [pat'əntlē] *ad* evidentemente.
patent medicine *n* medicina de patente.
patent office *n* oficina de patentes y marcas.
patent rights *npl* derechos *mpl* de patente.
paternal [pətûr'nəl] *a* paternal; (*relation*) paterno.
paternalistic [pətûrnəlis'tik] *a* paternalista.
paternity [pətûr'nitē] *n* paternidad *f*.
paternity suit *n* (*LAW*) caso de paternidad.
path [path] *n* camino, sendero; (*trail, track*) pista; (*of missile*) trayectoria.
pathetic [pəthet'ik] *a* (*pitiful*) patético, lastimoso; (*very bad*) malísimo; (*moving*) conmovedor(a).
pathetically [pəthet'iklē] *ad* patéticamente; (*very badly*) malísimamente mal.
pathological [pathəláj'ikəl] *a* patológico.
pathologist [pəthál'əjist] *n* patólogo/a.
pathology [pəthál'əjē] *n* patología.
pathos [pā'thâs] *n* patetismo.
pathway [path'wā] *n* sendero, vereda.
patience [pā'shəns] *n* paciencia; (*Brit CARDS*) solitario; **to lose one's** ~ perder la paciencia.
patient [pā'shənt] *n* paciente *m/f* ♦ *a* paciente, sufrido; **to be** ~ **with sb** tener paciencia con uno.
patiently [pā'shəntlē] *ad* pacientemente, con paciencia.
patio [pat'ēō] *n* patio.
patriot [pā'trēət] *n* patriota *m/f*.
patriotic [pātrēât'ik] *a* patriótico.
patriotism [pā'trēətizəm] *n* patriotismo.
patrol [pətrōl'] *n* patrulla ♦ *vt* patrullar por;

to be on ~ patrullar, estar de patrulla.
patrol boat *n* patrullero, patrullera.
patrol car *n* coche *m* patrulla.
patrolman [pətrōl'mən] *n* (*US*) policía *m*.
patron [pā'trən] *n* (*in shop*) cliente *m/f*; (*of charity*) patrocinador(a) *m/f*; ~ **of the arts** mecenas *m*.
patronage [pā'trənij] *n* patrocinio, protección *f*.
patronize [pā'trənīz] *vt* (*shop*) ser cliente de; (*look down on*) condescender con.
patronizing [pā'trənīzing] *a* condescendiente.
patron saint *n* santo/a patrono/a.
patter [pat'ûr] *n* golpeteo; (*sales talk*) labia ♦ *vi* (*rain*) tamborilear.
pattern [pat'ûrn] *n* (*SEWING*) patrón *m*; (*design*) dibujo; (*behavior, events*) esquema *m*; ~ **of events** curso de los hechos; **behavior** ~**s** modelos *mpl* de comportamiento.
patterned [pat'ûrnd] *a* (*material*) con diseño *or* dibujo.
paucity [pô'sitē] *n* escasez *f*.
paunch [pônch] *n* panza, barriga.
pauper [pô'pûr] *n* pobre *m/f*.
pause [pôz] *n* pausa; (*interval*) intervalo ♦ *vi* hacer una pausa; **to** ~ **for breath** detenerse para tomar aliento.
pave [pāv] *vt* pavimentar; **to** ~ **the way for** preparar el terreno para.
pavement [pāv'mənt] *n* (*US*) calzada, pavimento; (*Brit*) acera, vereda (*LAm*).
pavilion [pəvil'yən] *n* pabellón *m*; (*SPORT*) vestuarios *mpl*.
paving [pā'ving] *n* pavimento, enlosado.
paving stone *n* losa.
paw [pô] *n* pata; (*claw*) garra ♦ *vt* (*animal*) tocar con la pata; (*pej: touch*) tocar, manosear.
pawn [pôn] *n* (*CHESS*) peón *m*; (*fig*) instrumento ♦ *vt* empeñar.
pawnbroker [pôn'brōkûr] *n* prestamista *m/f*.
pawnshop [pôn'shâp] *n* monte *m* de piedad.
pay [pā] *n* paga; (*wage etc*) sueldo, salario ♦ (*vb: pt, pp* **paid**) *vt* pagar; (*visit*) hacer; (*respect*) ofrecer ♦ *vi* pagar; (*be profitable*) rendir, compensar, ser rentable; **to be in sb's** ~ estar al servicio de uno; **to** ~ **attention (to)** prestar atención (a); **I paid $5 for that record** pagué 5 dólares por ese disco; **how much did you** ~ **for it?** ¿cuánto pagaste por él?; **to** ~ **one's way** (*contribute one's share*) pagar su parte; (*remain solvent: company*) ser solvente; **to** ~ **dividends** (*COMM*) pagar dividendos; (*fig*) compensar; **it won't** ~ **you to do that** no te merece la pena hacer eso.
   pay back *vt* (*money*) reembolsar; (*person*) pagar.
   pay for *vt fus* pagar.
   pay in *vt* ingresar.

pay off vt liquidar; (person) pagar; (debts) liquidar, saldar; (creditor) cancelar, redimir; (workers) despedir; (mortgage) cancelar, redimir ♦ vi (scheme, decision) dar resultado; **to ~ sth off in installments** pagar algo a plazos.

pay out vt (rope) ir dando; (money) gastar, desembolsar.

pay up vt pagar (de mala gana).

payable [pā'əbəl] a pagadero; **to make a check ~ to sb** extender un cheque a favor de uno.

pay day n día m de paga.

PAYE n abbr (Brit: = pay as you earn) sistema de contribuciones personales.

payee [pāē'] n portador(a) m/f.

pay envelope n (US) sobre m (de paga).

paying [pā'ing] a: **~ guest** huésped(a) m/f que paga.

payload [pā'lōd] n carga útil.

payment [pā'mənt] n pago; **advance ~** (part sum) anticipo, adelanto; (total sum) saldo; **monthly ~** mensualidad f; **deferred ~, ~ by installments** pago a plazos or diferido; **on ~ of $5** mediante pago de or pagando $5; **in ~ for** (goods, sum owed) en pago de.

pay packet n (Brit) sobre m (de paga).

pay phone n teléfono público.

payroll [pā'rōl] n nómina; **to be on a firm's ~** estar en la nómina de una compañía.

pay slip n recibo de sueldo.

pay station n (US) teléfono público.

PBS n abbr (US: = Public Broadcasting System) agrupación de ayuda a la realización de emisiones para la TV pública.

PBX n abbr (US) = private branch (telephone) exchange.

PC n abbr = **personal computer**; (Brit) = **police constable**.

pc abbr = **percent; postcard**.

p/c abbr = **petty cash**.

PCB n abbr = **printed circuit board**.

PD n abbr (US) = **police department**.

pd abbr = **paid**.

PDT n abbr (US: = Pacific Daylight Time) hora de verano del Pacífico.

PE n abbr (= physical education) ed. física.

pea [pē] n guisante m, chícharo (LAm), arveja (LAm).

peace [pēs] n paz f; (calm) paz f, tranquilidad f; **to be at ~ with sb/sth** estar en paz con uno/algo; **to keep the ~** (policeman) mantener el orden; (citizen) guardar el orden.

peaceable [pē'səbəl] a pacífico.

peaceably [pē'səblē] ad pacíficamente.

Peace Corps n (US) organización que envía jóvenes voluntarios a trabajar y enseñar en el Tercer Mundo.

peaceful [pēs'fəl] a (gentle) pacífico; (calm) tranquilo, sosegado.

peacekeeping [pēs'kēping] a de pacifica-

ción.

peace offering n (fig) prenda de paz.

peacetime [pēs'tīm] n: **in ~** en tiempo de paz.

peach [pēch] n melocotón m, durazno (LAm).

peacock [pē'kâk] n pavo real.

peak [pēk] n (of mountain: top) cumbre f, cima; (: point) pico; (of cap) visera; (fig) cumbre f.

peaked [pē'kid] (US) pálido, paliducho; **I'm feeling a bit ~** me encuentro malucho, no me encuentro bien.

peak-hour [pēk'ouûr] a (traffic etc) de horas punta.

peak hours npl, **peak period** n horas fpl punta.

peaky [pē'kē] a (Brit) = **peaked**.

peal [pēl] n (of bells) repique m; **~ of laughter** carcajada.

peanut [pē'nut] n cacahuete m, maní m (LAm).

peanut butter n manteca de cacahuete.

peanut oil n (US) aceite m de cacahuete.

pear [pär] n pera.

pearl [pûrl] n perla.

peasant [pez'ənt] n campesino/a.

peat [pēt] n turba.

pebble [peb'əl] n guijarro.

peck [pek] vt (also: **~ at**) picotear; (food) comer sin ganas ♦ n picotazo; (kiss) besito.

pecking order [pek'ing ôrdûr] n orden m de jerarquía.

peckish [pek'ish] a (Brit col): **I feel ~** tengo ganas de picar algo.

peculiar [pikyōōl'yûr] a (odd) extraño, raro; (typical) propio, característico; (particular: importance, qualities) particular; **~ to** propio de.

peculiarity [pikyōōlēar'itē] n peculiaridad f, característica.

peculiarly [pikyōōl'yûrlē] ad extrañamente; particularmente.

pedal [ped'əl] n pedal m ♦ vi pedalear.

pedal bin n (Brit) cubo de la basura con pedal.

pedant [ped'ənt] n pedante m/f.

pedantic [pədan'tik] a pedante.

pedantry [ped'əntrē] n pedantería.

peddle [ped'əl] vt (goods) ir vendiendo or vender de puerta en puerta; (drugs) traficar; (gossip) divulgar.

peddler [ped'lûr] n vendedor(a) m/f ambulante.

pedestal [ped'istəl] n pedestal m.

pedestrian [pədes'trēən] n peatón/ona m/f ♦ a pedestre.

pedestrian crossing n paso de peatones.

pedestrian precinct n (Brit) zona reservada para peatones.

pediatrician [pēdēətrish'ən] n (US) pediatra m/f.

pediatrics [pēdēat'riks] n (US) pediatría.

pediatrist [pēdēat'rist] *n* (*US*) pedicuro/a.

pedigree [ped'əgrē] *n* genealogía; (*of animal*) raza ♦ *cpd* (*animal*) de raza, de casta.

pedlar [ped'lûr] *n* (*Brit*) = **peddler**.

pee [pē] *vi* (*col*) mear.

peek [pēk] *vi* mirar a hurtadillas; (*COMPUT*) inspeccionar.

peel [pēl] *n* piel *f*; (*of orange, lemon*) cáscara; (: *removed*) peladuras *fpl* ♦ *vt* pelar ♦ *vi* (*paint etc*) desconcharse; (*wallpaper*) despegarse, desprenderse.

peel back *vt* pelar.

peeler [pē'lûr] *n*: **potato** ~ mondador *m or* pelador *m* de patatas, pelapatatas *m inv*.

peep [pēp] *n* (*look*) mirada furtiva; (*sound*) pío ♦ *vi* piar.

peep out *vi* asomar la cabeza.

peephole [pēp'hōl] *n* mirilla.

peer [pēr] *vi*: **to** ~ **at** escudriñar ♦ *n* (*noble*) par *m*; (*equal*) igual *m*.

peerage [pē'rij] *n* nobleza.

peerless [pēr'lis] *a* sin par, incomparable, sin igual.

peeved [pēvd] *a* enojado.

peevish [pē'vish] *a* malhumorado.

peevishness [pē'vishnis] *n* mal humor *m*.

peg [peg] *n* clavija; (*for coat etc*) gancho, colgadero; (*Brit: also:* **clothes** ~) pinza; (*tent* ~) estaca ♦ *vt* (*clothes*) tender; (*groundcloth*) enclavijar, fijar con estacas; (*fig: wages, prices*) fijar.

PEI *abbr* (*Canada*) = *Prince Edward Island.*

pejorative [pijôr'ətiv] *a* peyorativo.

Pekin [pē'kin], **Peking** [pēking'] *n* Pekín *m*.

pekinese [pēkənēz'] *n* pequinés/esa *m/f.*

pelican [pel'ikən] *n* pelícano.

pelican crossing *n* (*Brit AUT*) paso de peatones señalizado.

pellet [pel'it] *n* bolita; (*bullet*) perdigón *m*.

pell-mell [pel'mel'] *ad* en tropel.

pelmet [pel'mit] *n* galería.

pelt [pelt] *vt*: **to** ~ **sb with sth** arrojarle algo a uno ♦ *vi* (*rain: also:* ~ **down**) llover a cántaros ♦ *n* pellejo.

pelvis [pel'vis] *n* pelvis *f.*

pen [pen] *n* pluma; (*for sheep*) redil *m*; (*US col: prison*) cárcel *f*, chirona; **to put** ~ **to paper** tomar la pluma.

penal [pē'nəl] *a* penal; ~ **servitude** trabajos *mpl* forzados.

penalize [pē'nəlīz] *vt* (*punish*; *SPORT*) castigar.

penalty [pen'əltē] *n* (*gen*) pena; (*fine*) multa; (*SPORT*) castigo; ~ **(kick)** (*SOCCER*) penalty *m*.

penalty clause *n* cláusula penal.

penance [pen'əns] *n* penitencia.

pence [pens] (*Brit*) *pl of* **penny**.

penchant [pen'chənt] *n* predilección *f*, inclinación *f.*

pencil [pen'səl] *n* lápiz *m*, lapicero (*LAm*) ♦ *vt* (*also:* ~ **in**) escribir con lápiz.

pencil case *n* estuche *m*.

pencil sharpener *n* sacapuntas *m inv.*

pendant [pen'dənt] *n* pendiente *m*.

pending [pen'ding] *prep* antes de ♦ *a* pendiente; ~ **the arrival of** ... hasta que llegue ..., hasta llegar ... .

pendulum [pen'jələm] *n* péndulo.

penetrate [pen'itrāt] *vt* penetrar.

penetrating [pen'itrāting] *a* penetrante.

penetration [penitrā'shən] *n* penetración *f.*

pen friend *n* amigo/a por correspondencia.

penguin [peng'gwin] *n* pingüino.

penicillin [penisil'in] *n* penicilina.

peninsula [pənin'sələ] *n* península.

penis [pē'nis] *n* pene *m*.

penitence [pen'itəns] *n* penitencia.

penitent [pen'itənt] *a* arrepentido; (*REL*) penitente.

penitentiary [peniten'chûrē] *n* (*US*) cárcel *f*, presidio.

penknife [pen'nīf] *n* navaja.

Penn., Penna. *abbr* (*US*) = *Pennsylvania.*

pen name *n* [pen' nām] *n* seudónimo.

pennant [pen'ənt] *n* banderola; banderín *m*.

penniless [pen'ēlis] *a* sin dinero.

Pennines [pen'īnz] *npl* (Montes *mpl*) Peninos *mpl.*

penny, *pl* **pennies** *or* (*Brit*) **pence** [pen'ē, pen'ēz, pens] *n* penique *m*; (*US*) centavo.

penpal [pen'pal] *n* amigo/a por correspondencia.

pension [pen'chən] *n* (*allowance, state payment*) pensión *f*; (*old-age*) jubilación *f.*

pension off *vt* jubilar.

pensioner [pen'chənûr] *n* (*Brit*) jubilado/a.

pension fund *n* fondo de pensiones.

pensive [pen'siv] *a* pensativo; (*withdrawn*) preocupado.

pentagon [pen'təgân] *n* pentágono.

Pentecost [pen'təkôst] *n* Pentecostés *m*.

penthouse [pent'hous] *n* ático de lujo.

pent-up [pent'up'] *a* (*feelings*) reprimido.

penultimate [pinul'təmit] *a* penúltimo.

penury [pen'yûrē] *n* miseria, pobreza.

people [pē'pəl] *npl* gente *f*; (*citizens*) pueblo *sg*, ciudadanos *mpl* ♦ *n* (*nation, race*) pueblo, nación *f* ♦ *vt* poblar; **several** ~ **came** vinieron varias personas; ~ **say that...** dice la gente que...; **old/young** ~ los ancianos/jóvenes; ~ **at large** la gente en general; **a man of the** ~ un hombre del pueblo.

pep [pep] *n* (*col*) energía.

pep up *vt* animar.

pepper [pep'ûr] *n* (*spice*) pimienta; (*vegetable*) pimiento ♦ *vt* (*fig*) salpicar.

pepper mill *n* molinillo de pimienta.

peppermint [pep'ûrmint] *n* menta; (*sweet*) pastilla de menta.

pepperpot [pep'ûrpât] *n* pimentero.

pepper shaker [pep'ûr shā'kûr] *n* (*US*) pimentero.

pep talk *n* (*col*): **to give sb a** ~ darle a

uno una inyección de ánimo.

per |pûr| *prep* por; ~ **day/person** por día/persona; **as** ~ **your instructions** de acuerdo con sus instrucciones.

per annum *ad* al año.

per capita *a*, *ad* per cápita.

perceive [pûrsēv'] *vt* percibir; *(realize)* darse cuenta de.

percent, *(Brit)* **per cent** [pûrsent'] *n* por ciento; **a 20** ~ **discount** un descuento de 20 por ciento.

percentage [pûrsen'tij] *n* porcentaje *m;* **to get a** ~ **on all sales** percibir un tanto por ciento sobre todas las ventas; **on a** ~ **basis** sobre una base de porcentaje.

perception [pûrsep'shən] *n* percepción *f;* *(insight)* perspicacia.

perceptible [pûrsep'təbəl] *a* perceptible; *(notable)* sensible.

perceptive [pûrsep'tiv] *a* perspicaz.

perch [pûrch] *n (fish)* perca; *(for bird)* percha ♦ *vi* posarse.

percolate [pûr'kəlāt] *vt (coffee)* filtrar, colar ♦ *vi (coffee, fig)* filtrarse, colarse.

percolator [pûr'kəlātûr] *n* cafetera de filtro.

percussion [pûrkush'ən] *n* percusión *f.*

percussionist [pûrkush'ənist] *n* percusionista *m/f.*

peremptory [pəremp'tûrē] *a* perentorio.

perennial [pəren'ēəl] *a* perenne.

perfect *a* [pûr'fikt] perfecto ♦ *n (also:* ~ **tense)** perfecto ♦ *vt* [pûrfekt'] perfeccionar; **he's a** ~ **stranger to me** no le conozco de nada, me es completamente desconocido.

perfection [pûrfek'shən] *n* perfección *f.*

perfectionist [pûrfek'shənist] *n* perfeccionista *m/f.*

perfectly [pûr'fiktlē] *ad* perfectamente; **I'm** ~ **happy with the situation** estoy muy contento con la situación; **you know** ~ **well** lo sabes muy bien *or* perfectamente.

perforate [pûr'fûrāt] *vt* perforar.

perforated ulcer [pûr'fûrātid ul'sûr] *n* úlcera perforada.

perforation [pûrfərā'shən] *n* perforación *f.*

perform [pûrfôrm'] *vt (carry out)* realizar, llevar a cabo; *(THEATER)* representar; *(piece of music)* interpretar ♦ *vi (THEATER)* actuar; *(TECH)* funcionar.

performance [pûrfôr'məns] *n (of task)* realización *f;* *(of a play)* representación *f;* *(of player etc)* actuación *f;* *(of car, engine)* rendimiento; *(of function)* desempeño.

performer [pûrfôr'mûr] *n (actor)* actor *m,* actriz *f;* *(MUS)* intérprete *m/f.*

performing [pûrfôr'ming] *a (animal)* amaestrado.

perfume [pûr'fyōōm] *n* perfume *m.*

perfunctory [pûrfungk'tûrē] *a* superficial.

perhaps [pûrhaps'] *ad* quizá(s), tal vez; ~ **so/not** puede que sí/no.

peril [pär'əl] *n* peligro, riesgo.

perilous [pär'ələs] *a* peligroso.

perilously [pär'ələslē] *ad:* **they came** ~ **close to being caught** por poco les cogen *or* agarran.

perimeter [pərim'itûr] *n* perímetro.

period [pēr'ēəd] *n* período; *(HISTORY)* época; *(SCOL)* clase *f;* *(punctuation)* punto; *(MED)* regla; *(US SPORT)* tiempo ♦ *a (costume, furniture)* de época; **for a** ~ **of three weeks** durante (un período de) tres semanas; **the holiday** ~ el período de vacaciones.

periodic [pērēād'ik] *a* periódico.

periodical [pērēād'ikəl] *a, n* periódico *m.*

periodically [pērēād'iklē] *ad* de vez en cuando, cada cierto tiempo.

peripatetic [päripətet'ik] *a (salesman)* ambulante; *(teacher)* peripatético.

peripheral [pərif'ûrəl] *a* periférico ♦ *n (COMPUT)* periférico, unidad *f* periférica.

periphery [pərif'ûrē] *n* periferia.

periscope [pär'iskōp] *n* periscopio.

perish [pär'ish] *vi* perecer; *(decay)* echarse a perder.

perishable [pär'ishəbəl] *a* perecedero.

perishables [pär'ishəbəlz] *npl* productos *mpl* perecederos.

peritonitis [päritənī'tis] *n* peritonitis *f.*

perjure [pûr'jûr] *vt:* **to** ~ **o.s.** perjurarse.

perjury [pûr'jûrē] *n (LAW)* perjurio.

perk [pûrk] *n* extra *m.*

perk up *vi (cheer up)* animarse.

perky [pûr'kē] *a* alegre, despabilado.

perm [pûrm] *n* permanente *f* ♦ *vt:* **to have one's hair** ~**ed** hacerse una permanente.

permanence [pûr'mənəns] *n* permanencia.

permanent [pûr'mənənt] *a* permanente; *(job, position)* fijo; *(dye, ink)* indeleble; ~ **address** domicilio permanente; **I'm not** ~ **here** no trabajo fijo aquí.

permanently [pûr'mənəntlē] *ad (lastingly)* para siempre, de modo definitivo; *(all the time)* permanentemente.

permeate [pûr'mēāt] *vi* penetrar, trascender ♦ *vt* penetrar, trascender a.

permissible [pûrmis'əbəl] *a* permisible, lícito.

permission [pûrmish'ən] *n* permiso; **to give sb** ~ **to do sth** autorizar a uno para que haga algo; **with your** ~ con su permiso.

permissive [pûrmis'iv] *a* permisivo.

permit *n* [pûr'mit] permiso, licencia; *(entrance pass)* pase *m* ♦ *vt* [pûrmit'] permitir; *(accept)* tolerar ♦ *vi:* **weather** ~**ting** si el tiempo lo permite; **fishing** ~ permiso de pesca; **building/export** ~ licencia *or* permiso de construcción/exportación.

permutation [pûrmyətā'shən] *n* permutación *f.*

pernicious [pûrnish'əs] *a* nocivo; *(MED)* pernicioso.

pernickety [pûrnik'ətē] *a (Brit)* = **persnickety.**

perpendicular [pûrpəndik'yələr] *a* per-

pendicular.
perpetrate [pûr'pitrāt] *vt* cometer.
perpetual [pûrpech'ōōəl] *a* perpetuo.
perpetually [pûrpech'ōōəlē] *ad* (*eternally*) perpetuamente; (*continuously*) constantemente, continuamente.
perpetuate [pûrpech'ōōāt] *vt* perpetuar.
perpetuity [pûrpətōō'itē] *n*: **in** ~ para siempre.
perplex [pûrplɛks'] *vt* dejar perplejo.
perplexed [pûrplɛkst'] *a* perplejo, confuso.
perplexing [pûrplɛk'sing] *a* que causa perplejidad.
perplexity [pûrplɛk'sitē] *n* perplejidad *f*, confusión *f*.
perquisites [pûr'kwizits] *npl* (*also*: **perks**) gajes y emolumentos *mpl*.
persecute [pûr'səkyōōt] *vt* (*pursue*) perseguir; (*harass*) acosar.
persecution [pûrsəkyōō'shən] *n* persecución *f*.
perseverance [pûrsəvēr'əns] *n* perseverancia.
persevere [pûrsəvēr'] *vi* persistir.
Persia [pûr'zhə] *n* Persia.
Persian [pûr'zhən] *a*, *n* persa *m/f* ♦ *n* (*LING*) persa *m*; **the** ~ **Gulf** el Golfo Pérsico.
persist [pûrsist'] *vi*: **to** ~ (**in doing sth**) persistir (en hacer algo).
persistence [pûrsis'təns] *n* empeño.
persistent [pûrsis'tənt] *a* (*lateness, rain*) persistente; (*determined*) porfiado; (*continuing*) constante.
persistently [pûrsis'təntlē] *ad* persistentemente; (*continually*) constantemente.
persnickety [pûrsnik'ətē] *a* (*US col: person*) quisquilloso; (: *task*) delicado.
person [pûr'sən] *n* persona; **in** ~ en persona; **on** *or* **about one's** ~ (*weapon, money*) encima; **a** ~ **to** ~ **call** (*TEL*) una llamada (de) persona a persona.
personable [pûr'sənəbəl] *a* atractivo.
personal [pûr'sənəl] *a* personal, individual; (*visit*) en persona; (*Brit TEL*) persona a persona.
personal allowance *n* desgravación *f* personal.
personal assistant (PA) *n* ayudante *m/f* personal.
personal belongings *npl* efectos *mpl* personales.
personal column *n* anuncios *mpl* personales.
personal computer (PC) *n* computador *m* personal.
personal effects *npl* efectos *mpl* personales.
personality [pûrsənal'itē] *n* personalidad *f*.
personal loan *n* préstamo personal.
personally [pûr'sənəlē] *ad* personalmente.
personal organizer *n* organizador *m* personal.
personal property *n* bienes *mpl* muebles.

personification [pûrsânəfəkā'shən] *n* personificación *f*.
personify [pûrsân'əfī] *vt* encarnar.
personnel [pûrsənel'] *n* personal *m*.
personnel department *n* departamento de personal.
personnel management *n* gestión *f* de personal.
personnel manager *n* jefe *m* de personal.
perspective [pûrspɛk'tiv] *n* perspectiva; **to get sth into** ~ ver algo en perspectiva *or* como es.
Perspex [pûr'spɛks] ® *n* (*Brit*) vidrio acrílico.
perspiration [pûrspərā'shən] *n* transpiración *f*, sudor *m*.
perspire [pûrspīr'] *vi* transpirar, sudar.
persuade [pûrswād'] *vt*: **to** ~ **sb to do sth** persuadir a uno para que haga algo; **to** ~ **sb of sth/that** persuadir *or* convencer a uno de algo/de que; **I am** ~d **that** ... estoy convencido de que ... .
persuasion [pûrswā'zhən] *n* persuasión *f*; (*persuasiveness*) persuasiva; (*creed*) creencia.
persuasive [pûrswā'siv] *a* persuasivo.
persuasively [pûrswā'sivlē] *ad* de modo persuasivo.
pert [pûrt] *a* impertinente, fresco, atrevido.
pertaining [pûrtān'ing]: ~ **to** *prep* relacionado con.
pertinent [pûr'tənənt] *a* pertinente, a propósito.
perturb [pûrtûrb'] *vt* perturbar.
perturbing [pûrtûrb'ing] *a* inquietante, perturbador(a).
Peru [pərōō'] *n* el Perú.
perusal [pərōō'zəl] *n* examen *m*.
peruse [pərōōz'] *vt* leer con detención, examinar.
Peruvian [pərōō'vēən] *a*, *n* peruano/a *m/f*.
pervade [pûrvād'] *vt* impregnar, infundirse en.
pervasive [pûrvā'siv] *a* (*smell*) penetrante; (*influence*) muy extendido; (*gloom, feelings, ideas*) reinante.
perverse [pûrvûrs'] *a* perverso; (*stubborn*) terco; (*wayward*) travieso.
perversely [pûrvûrs'lē] *ad* perversamente; tercamente; traviesamente.
perverseness [pûrvûrs'nis] *n* perversidad *f*; terquedad *f*; travesura.
perversion [pûrvûr'zhən] *n* perversión *f*.
pervert *n* [pûr'vûrt] pervertido/a ♦ *vt* [pûrvûrt'] pervertir.
pessary [pɛs'ərē] *n* pesario.
pessimism [pɛs'əmizəm] *n* pesimismo.
pessimist [pɛs'əmist] *n* pesimista *m/f*.
pessimistic [pɛsəmis'tik] *a* pesimista.
pest [pɛst] *n* (*insect*) insecto nocivo; (*fig*) lata, molestia; ~**s** *npl* plaga.
pest control *n* control *m* de plagas.

pester [pɛs'tûr] *vt* molestar, acosar.
pesticide [pɛs'tisīd] *n* pesticida *m*.
pestilent [pɛs'tələnt], **pestilential** [pɛstilɛn'shəl] *a* (*col*: *exasperating*) condenado.
pestle [pɛs'əl] *n* mano *f* de mortero *or* de almirez.
pet [pɛt] *n* animal *m* doméstico; (*favorite*) favorito/a ♦ *vt* acariciar ♦ *vi* (*col*) besuquearse ♦ *cpd*: **my ~ aversion** mi manía.
petal [pɛt'əl] *n* pétalo.
pet door *n* (*US*) gatera.
peter [pē'tûr]: **to ~ out** *vi* agotarse, acabarse.
petite [pətēt'] *a* chiquita.
petition [pətish'ən] *n* petición *f* ♦ *vt* presentar una petición a ♦ *vi*: **to ~ for divorce** pedir el divorcio.
pet name *n* nombre *m* cariñoso, apodo.
petrified [pɛt'rəfīd] *a* (*fig*) pasmado, horrorizado.
petrochemical [pɛtrōkem'ikəl] *a* petroquímico.
petrodollars [pɛtrōdál'ûrz] *npl* petrodólares *mpl*.
petrol [pɛt'rəl] *n* (*Brit*) gasolina; (*for lighter*) bencina; **two/four-star ~** (*Brit*) gasolina normal/súper.
petrol can *n* (*Brit*) bidón *m* de gasolina.
petrol engine *n* (*Brit*) motor *m* de gasolina.
petroleum [pətrō'lēəm] *n* petróleo.
petroleum jelly *n* jalea de petróleo.
petrol pump *n* (*Brit*) (*in car*) bomba de gasolina; (*in garage*) surtidor *m* de gasolina.
petrol station *n* (*Brit*) gasolinera.
petrol tank *n* (*Brit*) depósito (de gasolina).
petticoat [pɛt'ēkōt] *n* enaguas *fpl*.
pettifogging [pɛt'ēfáging] *a* quisquilloso.
pettiness [pɛt'ēnis] *n* mezquindad *f*.
petty [pɛt'ē] *a* (*mean*) mezquino; (*unimportant*) insignificante.
petty cash *n* dinero para gastos menores.
petty cash book *n* libro de caja auxiliar.
petty officer *n* contramaestre *m*.
petulant [pɛch'ələnt] *a* malhumorado.
pew [pyōō] *n* banco.
pewter [pyōō'tûr] *n* peltre *m*.
Pfc *abbr* (*US MIL*) = *private first class*.
PG *n abbr* (*CINEMA*) = *parental guidance*.
PGA *n abbr* = *Professional Golfers' Association*.
PH *n abbr* (*US MIL*: = *Purple Heart*) decoración otorgada a los heridos de guerra.
pH *n abbr* (= *pH value*) pH.
p&h *abbr* (*US*: = *postage and handling*) gastos de envío.
PHA *n abbr* (*US*) = *Public Housing Administration*.
phallic [fal'ik] *a* fálico.
phantom [fan'təm] *n* fantasma *m*.
Pharaoh [fär'ō] *n* Faraón *m*.

pharmaceutical [fârməsōō'tikəl] *a* farmacéutico.
pharmacist [fâr'məsist] *n* farmacéutico.
pharmacy [fâr'məsē] *n* (*US*) farmacia.
phase [fāz] *n* fase *f* ♦ *vt*: **to ~ sth in/out** introducir/retirar algo por etapas; **~d withdrawal** retirada progresiva.
Ph.D. *abbr* = **Doctor of Philosophy.**
pheasant [fez'ənt] *n* faisán *m*.
phenomenal [finâm'ənəl] *a* fenomenal.
phenomenally [finâm'ənəlē] *ad* fenomenalmente, de modo fenomenal.
phenomenon, *pl* **phenomena** [finâm'ənân, -nə] *n* fenómeno.
phial [fī'əl] *n* ampolla.
philanderer [filan'dûrûr] *n* donjuan *m*.
philanthropic [filənthrəp'ik] *a* filantrópico.
philanthropist [filan'thrəpist] *n* filántropo/a.
philatelist [filat'əlist] *n* filatelista *m/f*.
philately [filat'əlē] *n* filatelia.
Philippines [fil'ipēnz] *npl*: **the ~** las (Islas) Filipinas.
philosopher [filâs'əfûr] *n* filósofo/a.
philosophical [filəsâf'ikəl] *a* filosófico.
philosophy [filâs'əfē] *n* filosofía.
phlegm [flem] *n* flema.
phlegmatic [flegmat'ik] *a* flemático.
phobia [fō'bēə] *n* fobia.
phone [fōn] *n* teléfono ♦ *vt* telefonear, llamar por teléfono; **to be on the ~** tener teléfono; (*be calling*) estar hablando por teléfono.
  phone back *vt, vi* volver a llamar.
phone book *n* guía telefónica.
phone booth, (*Brit*) **phone box** *n* cabina telefónica.
phone call *n* llamada (telefónica).
phone-in [fōn'in] *n* (*Brit RADIO, TV*) programa de radio o televisión en el que el público puede llamar por teléfono.
phonetics [fənet'iks] *n* fonética.
phon(e)y [fō'nē] *a* falso ♦ *n* (*person*) farsante *m/f*.
phonograph [fō'nəgraf] *n* (*US*) fonógrafo, tocadiscos *m inv*.
phonology [fənâl'əjē] *n* fonología.
phosphate [fâs'fāt] *n* fosfato.
phosphorus [fâs'fûrəs] *n* fósforo.
photo [fō'tō] *n* foto *f*.
photo... [fō'tō] *pref* foto... .
photocopier [fō'təkâpēûr] *n* fotocopiadora.
photocopy [fō'təkâpē] *n* fotocopia ♦ *vt* fotocopiar.
photoelectric [fōtōilek'trik] *a*: **~ cell** célula fotoeléctrica.
photo finish *n* resultado comprobado por fotocontrol.
photogenic [fōtəjen'ik] *a* fotogénico.
photograph [fō'təgraf] *n* fotografía ♦ *vt* fotografiar; **to take a ~ of sb** sacar una foto de uno.
photographer [fətâg'rəfûr] *n* fotógrafo.
photographic [fōtəgraf'ik] *a* fotográfico.

photography |fətåg'rəfē| n fotografía.
photostat |fō'təstat| ® n fotóstato.
photosynthesis |fōtəsin'thəsis| n fotosíntesis f.
phrase |frāz| n frase f ♦ vt (letter) expresar, redactar.
phrase book n libro de frases.
physical |fiz'ikəl| a físico; ~ **examination** reconocimiento médico; ~ **exercises** ejercicios mpl físicos ♦ n reconocimiento médico.
physical education n educación f física.
physically |fiz'iklē| ad físicamente.
physical training n gimnasia.
physician |fizish'ən| n médico/a.
physicist |fiz'əsist| n físico/a.
physics |fiz'iks| n física.
physiological |fizēəlåj'ikəl| a fisiológico.
physiology |fizēål'əjē| n fisiología.
physiotherapist |fizēōthär'əpist| n fisioterapeuta m/f.
physiotherapy |fizēōthär'əpē| n fisioterapia.
physique |fizēk'| n físico.
pianist |pēan'ist| n pianista m/f.
piano |pēan'ō| n piano.
piano accordion n (Brit) acordeón-piano m.
piccolo |pik'əlō| n (MUS) flautín m.
pick |pik| n (tool) pico, piqueta ♦ vt (select) elegir, escoger; (gather) coger (Sp), recoger (LAm); (lock) abrir con ganzúa; (scab, spot) rascar ♦ vi: **to ~ and choose** ser muy exigente; **take your** ~ escoja lo que quiera; **the ~ of** lo mejor de; **to ~ one's nose/teeth** hurgarse las narices/limpiarse los dientes; **to ~ pockets** ratear, ser carterista; **to ~ one's way through** andar a tientas, abrirse camino; **to ~ a fight with sb** buscar pelea con uno; **to ~ sb's brains** aprovecharse de los conocimientos de uno.
pick at vt fus: **to ~ at one's food** comer con poco apetito.
pick off vt (kill) matar de un tiro.
pick on vt fus (person) meterse con.
pick out vt escoger; (distinguish) identificar.
pick up vi (improve: sales) ir mejor; (: patient) reponerse; (: FINANCE) recobrarse ♦ vt (from floor) recoger; (buy) comprar; (find) encontrar; (learn) aprender; (RADIO, TV, TEL) captar; **to ~ up speed** acelerarse; **to ~ o.s. up** levantarse; **to ~ up where one left off** reempezar algo donde lo había dejado.
pickax, (Brit) **pickaxe** |pik'aks| n pico, zapapico.
picket |pik'it| n (in strike) piquete m ♦ vt piquetear; **to be on ~ duty** estar de piquete.
picketing |pik'iting| n organización f de piquetes.
picket line n piquete m.
pickings |pik'ingz| npl (pilferings): **there**

are good ~ to be had here se puede sacar buenas ganancias de aquí.
pickle |pik'əl| n (also: ~s: as condiment) escabeche m; (fig: mess) apuro ♦ vt encurtir; (in vinegar) envinagrar; **in a ~** en un lío, en apuros.
pick-me-up |pik'mēup| n tónico.
pickpocket |pik'påkit| n carterista m/f.
pickup |pik'up| n (small truck: also: ~ **truck**) furgoneta; (Brit: on record player) pickup m.
picnic |pik'nik| n picnic m, merienda ♦ vi merendar en el campo.
pictorial |piktôr'ēəl| a pictórico; (magazine etc) ilustrado.
picture |pik'chûr| n cuadro; (painting) pintura; (photograph) fotografía; (film) película; (TV) imagen f ♦ vt pintar; **the ~s** (Brit) el cine; **we get a good ~ here** captamos buena imagen aquí; **to take a ~ of sb/sth** hacer or sacar una foto a uno/de algo; **the garden is a ~ in June** el jardín es una preciosidad en junio; **the overall ~** la impresión en general; **to put sb in the ~** poner uno al corriente or al tanto.
picture book n libro de dibujos.
picturesque |pikchəresk'| a pintoresco.
piddling |pid'ling| a insignificante.
pidgin |pij'in| a: ~ **English** lengua franca basada en el inglés.
pie |pī| n pastel m; (open) tarta; (small: of meat) empanada.
piebald |pī'bôld| a pío.
piece |pēs| n pedazo, trozo; (of cake) trozo; (CHECKERS etc) pieza, ficha; (item): **a ~ of furniture/advice** un mueble/un consejo ♦ vt: **to ~ together** juntar; (TECH) armar; **to break into ~s** hacerse pedazos; **to take to ~s** desmontar; **a ~ of news** una noticia; **a 10¢ ~** una moneda de 10 centavos; **a six-~ band** un conjunto de seis (músicos); **in one ~** (object) de una sola pieza; ~ **by ~** pieza por or a pieza; **to speak one's ~** decir su parecer.
piecemeal |pēs'mēl| ad poco a poco.
piece rate n tarifa a destajo.
piecework |pēs'wûrk| n trabajo a destajo.
pie chart n gráfico de sectores or de tarta.
pie crust pastry n (US) pasta quebradiza.
pier |pēr| n muelle m, embarcadero.
pierce |pērs| vt penetrar en, perforar; **to have one's ears ~d** hacerse los agujeros de las orejas.
piercing |pērs'ing| a (cry) penetrante.
piety |pī'ətē| n piedad f.
pig |pig| n cerdo, puerco; (fig) cochino.
pigeon |pij'ən| n paloma; (as food) pichón m.
pigeonhole |pij'ənhōl| n casilla.
piggy bank |pig'ē bangk| n hucha (en forma de cerdito).
pigheaded |pig'hedid| a terco, testarudo.
piglet |pig'lit| n cerdito.

pigment [pig'mənt] *n* pigmento.

pigmentation [pigməntā'shən] *n* pigmentación *f*.

pigmy [pig'mē] *n* = **pygmy**.

pigskin [pig'skin] *n* piel *f* de cerdo.

pigsty [pig'stī] *n* pocilga.

pigtail [pig'tāl] *n* (*girl's*) trenza; (*Chinese*, *TAUR*) coleta.

pike [pīk] *n* (*spear*) pica; (*fish*) lucio.

pilchard [pil'chûrd] *n* sardina.

pile [pīl] *n* (*heap*) montón *m*; (*of carpet*) pelo ♦ (*vb*: *also*: ~ **up**) *vt* amontonar; (*fig*) acumular ♦ *vi* amontonarse; **in a** ~ en un montón; **to** ~ **into** (*car*) meterse en.

  pile on *vt*: **to** ~ **it on** (*col*) exagerar.

piles [pīlz] *npl* (*MED*) almorranas *fpl*, hemorroides *mpl*.

pile-up [pīl'up] *n* (*AUT*) accidente *m* múltiple.

pilfer [pil'fûr] *vt*, *vi* ratear, robar, sisar.

pilfering [pil'fûring] *n* ratería.

pilgrim [pil'grim] *n* peregrino/a.

pilgrimage [pil'grəmij] *n* peregrinación *f*, romería.

pill [pil] *n* píldora; **the** ~ la píldora; **to be on the** ~ tomar la píldora (anticonceptiva).

pillage [pil'ij] *vt* pillar, saquear.

pillar [pil'ûr] *n* (*gen*) pilar *m*; (*concrete*) columna.

pillar box *n* (*Brit*) buzón *m*.

pillion [pil'yən] *n* (*of motorcycle*) asiento trasero; **to ride** ~ ir en el asiento trasero.

pillion passenger *n* pasajero que va detrás.

pillory [pil'ûrē] *vt* poner en ridículo.

pillow [pil'ō] *n* almohada.

pillowcase [pil'ōkās] *n* funda (de almohada).

pillowslip [pil'ōslip] *n* = **pillowcase**.

pilot [pī'lət] *n* piloto *inv* ♦ *a* (*plan etc*) piloto ♦ *vt* pilotar; (*fig*) guiar, conducir.

pilot light *n* piloto.

pimento [pimen'tō] *n* pimentón *m*.

pimp [pimp] *n* chulo, cafiche *m* (*LAm*).

pimple [pim'pəl] *n* grano.

pimply [pim'plē] *a* lleno de granos.

PIN *n* (*COMPUT*, *BANKING*) número personal de identificación.

pin [pin] *n* alfiler *m*; (*ELEC*: *of plug*) clavija; (*TECH*) perno; (: *wooden*) clavija; (*Brit*: *drawing* ~) chincheta; (*in grenade*) percutor *m* ♦ *vt* prender (con alfiler); sujetar con perno; ~**s and needles** hormigueo *sg*; **to** ~ **sth on sb** (*fig*) acusar (falsamente) a uno de algo.

  pin down *vt* (*fig*): **there's something strange here, but I can't quite** ~ **it down** aquí hay algo raro pero no puedo precisar qué es; **to** ~ **sb down** hacer que uno concrete.

pinafore [pin'əfôr] *n* delantal *m*.

pinafore dress *n* (*Brit*) mandil *m*.

pinball [pin'bôl] *n* (*also*: ~ **machine**) millón *m*, fliper *m*.

pincers [pin'sûrz] *npl* pinzas *fpl*, tenazas *fpl*.

pinch [pinch] *n* pellizco; (*of salt etc*) pizca ♦ *vt* pellizcar; (*col*: *steal*) birlar ♦ *vi* (*shoe*) apretar; **at a** ~ en caso de apuro; **to feel the** ~ (*fig*) pasar apuros *or* estrechos.

pinched [pincht] *a* (*drawn*) cansado; ~ **with cold** transido de frío; ~ **for money/ space** mal *or* falto de dinero/espacio *or* sitio.

pincushion [pin'kŏŏshən] *n* acerico.

pine [pīn] *n* (*also*: ~ **tree**) pino ♦ *vi*: **to** ~ **for** suspirar por.

  pine away *vi* morirse de pena.

pineapple [pīn'apəl] *n* piña, ananás *m*.

pine nut *n* piña, piñón *m*.

ping [ping] *n* (*noise*) sonido agudo.

ping-pong [ping'pông] *n* pingpong *m*.

pink [pingk] *a* rosado, color de rosa ♦ *n* (*color*) rosa; (*BOT*) clavel *m*, clavellina.

pinking shears [ping'king shirz] *npl* tijeras *fpl* dentadas.

pin money *n* dinero para gastos extra.

pinnacle [pin'əkəl] *n* cumbre *f*.

pinpoint [pin'point] *vt* precisar.

pinstripe [pin'strīp] *a*: ~ **suit** traje *m* a rayas.

pint [pīnt] *n* pinta (*US* = 0.47 *l*; *Brit* = 0.57 *l*).

pin-up [pin'up] *n* fotografía de mujer desnuda.

pinwheel [pin'wēl] *n* (*US*) rueda catalina.

pioneer [pīənēr'] *n* pionero/a ♦ *vt* promover.

pious [pī'əs] *a* piadoso, devoto.

pip [pip] *n* (*seed*) pepita; **the** ~**s** (*Brit TEL*) la señal.

pipe [pīp] *n* tubo, caño; (*for smoking*) pipa ♦ *vt* conducir en cañerías; ~**s** *npl* (*gen*) cañería *sg*; (*also*: **bag**~**s**) gaita *sg*.

  pipe down *vi* (*col*) callarse.

pipe cleaner *n* limpiapipas *m inv*.

piped music [pīpt myōō'zik] *n* música ambiental.

pipe dream *n* sueño imposible.

pipeline [pīp'līn] *n* tubería, cañería; (*for oil*) oleoducto; (*for natural gas*) gasoducto; **it is in the** ~ (*fig*) está en trámite.

piper [pī'pûr] *n* (*gen*) flautista *m/f*; (*with bagpipes*) gaitero/a.

pipe tobacco *n* tabaco de pipa.

piping [pī'ping] *ad*: **to be** ~ **hot** estar que quema.

piquant [pē'kənt] *a* picante.

pique [pēk] *n* pique *m*, resentimiento.

pirate [pī'rət] *n* pirata *m/f* ♦ *vt* (*record*, *video*, *book*) hacer una copia pirata de.

pirated [pī'ritid] *a* (*book*, *record etc*) pirata *inv*.

pirate radio *n* (*Brit*) emisora pirata.

pirouette [pirōōet'] *n* pirueta ♦ *vi* piruetear.

Pisces [pī'sēz] *n* Piscis *m*.

piss [pis] *vi* (*col*) mear.

pissed [pist] a (Brit: col: drunk) borracho.
pistol [pis'təl] n pistola.
piston [pis'tən] n pistón m, émbolo.
pit [pit] n hoyo; (also: **coal** ~) mina; (in garage) foso de inspección; (also: **orchestra** ~) platea; (quarry) cantera; (US: of fruit) hueso ♦ vt (subj: chickenpox) picar; (: rust) comer; (US: fruit) deshuesar; **to ~ A against B** oponer A a B; **~s** npl (AUT) box msg; **~ted with** (chickenpox) picado de.
pitapat [pit'əpat] ad; **to go ~** (heart) latir rápidamente; (rain) golpetear.
pitch [pich] n (throw) lanzamiento; (MUS) tono; (Brit SPORT) campo, terreno; (tar) brea; (fig: degree) nivel m, grado ♦ vt (throw) arrojar, lanzar ♦ vi (fall) caer(se); (NAUT) cabecear; **I can't keep working at this ~** no puedo seguir trabajando a este ritmo; **at its (highest) ~** en su punto máximo; **his anger reached such a ~ that ...** su ira or cólera llegó a tal extremo que ...; **to ~ a tent** montar una tienda (de campaña).
pitch-black [pich'blak'] a negro como boca de lobo.
pitched battle [picht bat'əl] n batalla campal.
pitcher [pich'ûr] n cántaro, jarro.
pitchfork [pich'fôrk] n horca.
piteous [pit'ēəs] a lastimoso.
pitfall [pit'fôl] n riesgo.
pith [pith] n (of orange) médula; (fig) meollo.
pithy [pith'ē] a jugoso.
pitiful [pit'ifəl] a (touching) lastimoso, conmovedor(a); (contemptible) lamentable, miserable.
pitifully [pit'ifəlē] ad: **it's ~ obvious** es tan evidente que da pena.
pitiless [pit'ilis] a despiadado, implacable.
pitilessly [pit'ilislē] ad despiadadamente, implacablemente.
pittance [pit'əns] n miseria.
pity [pit'ē] n (compassion) compasión f, piedad f; (shame) lástima ♦ vt compadecer(se de); **to have** or **take ~ on sb** compadecerse de uno; **what a ~!** ¡qué pena!; **it is a ~ that you can't come** ¡qué pena que no puedas venir!
pitying [pit'ēing] a compasivo, de lástima.
pivot [piv'ət] n eje m ♦ vi: **to ~ on** girar sobre; (fig) depender de.
pixel [pik'səl] n (COMPUT) pixel m, punto.
pixie [pik'sē] n duendecillo.
pizza [pēt'sə] n pizza.
P&L abbr = profit and loss.
placard [plak'ârd] n (in march etc) pancarta.
placate [plā'kāt] vt apaciguar.
place [plās] n lugar m, sitio; (rank) rango; (seat) plaza, asiento; (post) puesto; (in street names) plaza; (home): **at/to his ~** en/a su casa ♦ vt (object) poner, colocar;

(identify) reconocer; (find a post for) dar un puesto a, colocar; (goods) vender; **to take ~** tener lugar; **to be ~d** (in race, exam) colocarse; **out of ~** (not suitable) fuera de lugar; **in the first ~** (first of all) en primer lugar; **to change ~s with sb** cambiarse de sitio con uno; **from ~ to ~** de un sitio a or para otro; **all over the ~** por todas partes; **he's going ~s** (fig, col) llegará lejos; **I feel rather out of ~ here** me encuentro algo desplazado; **to put sb in his ~** (fig) poner a uno en su lugar; **it is not my ~ to do it** no me incumbe a mí hacerlo; **to ~ an order with sb (for)** hacer un pedido a uno (de); **we are better ~d than a month ago** estamos en mejor posición que hace un mes.
placebo [pləsē'bō] n placebo.
place mat n (wooden etc) salvamanteles m inv; (in linen etc) mantel m individual.
placement [plās'mənt] n colocación f.
place name n topónimo.
placenta [pləsen'tə] n placenta.
placid [plas'id] a apacible.
placidity [pləsid'itē] n apacibilidad f, placidez f.
plagiarism [plā'jərizəm] n plagio.
plagiarist [plā'jərist] n plagiario/a.
plagiarize [plā'jərīz] vt plagiar.
plague [plāg] n plaga; (MED) peste f ♦ vt (fig) acosar, atormentar; **to ~ sb with questions** acribillar a uno con preguntas.
plaice [plās] n, pl inv platija.
plaid [plad] n (material) tartán m.
plain [plān] a (clear) claro, evidente; (simple) sencillo; (frank) franco, abierto; (not handsome) poco atractivo; (pure) natural, puro ♦ ad claramente ♦ n llano, llanura; **in ~ clothes** (police) vestido de paisano; **to make sth ~ to sb** poner algo de manifiesto para uno.
plain chocolate n chocolate m oscuro or amargo.
plainly [plān'lē] ad claramente, evidentemente; (frankly) francamente.
plainness [plān'nis] n (clarity) claridad f; (simplicity) sencillez f; (of face) falta de atractivo.
plaintiff [plān'tif] n demandante m/f.
plaintive [plān'tiv] a (cry, voice) lastimero, quejumbroso; (look) que da lástima.
plait [plat] n trenza ♦ vt trenzar.
plan [plan] n (drawing) plano; (scheme) plan m, proyecto ♦ vt (think) pensar; (prepare) proyectar, planificar; (intend) pensar, tener la intención de ♦ vi hacer proyectos; **have you any ~s for today?** ¿piensas hacer algo hoy?; **to ~ to do** pensar hacer; **how long do you ~ to stay?** ¿cuánto tiempo piensas quedarte?; **to ~ (for)** planear, proyectar.
plan out vt planear detalladamente.
plane [plān] n (AVIAT) avión m; (tree) plá-

tano; (*tool*) cepillo; (*MATH*) plano.

planet [plan'it] *n* planeta *m*.

planetarium [planitär'ēəm] *n* planetario.

planetary [plan'itärē] *a* planetario.

plank [plangk] *n* tabla.

plankton [plangk'tən] *n* plancton *m*.

planner [plan'ûr] *n* planificador(a) *m/f*; (*chart*) diagrama *m* de planificación; **city ~** urbanista *m/f*.

planning [plan'ing] *n* (*POL, ECON*) planificación *f*; **family ~** planificación familiar.

planning committee *n* (*in local government*) comité *m* de planificación.

plant [plant] *n* planta; (*machinery*) maquinaria; (*factory*) fábrica ♦ *vt* plantar; (*field*) sembrar; (*bomb*) colocar.

plantain [plan'tin] *n* llantén *m*.

plantation [plantā'shən] *n* plantación *f*; (*estate*) hacienda.

planter [plan'tûr] *n* hacendado.

plant pot *n* maceta, tiesto.

plaque [plak] *n* placa.

plasma [plaz'mə] *n* plasma *m*.

plaster [plas'tûr] *n* (*for walls*) yeso; (*also:* **~ of Paris**) yeso mate; (*Brit: also:* **sticking ~**) tirita, esparadrapo ♦ *vt* enyesar; (*cover*): **to ~ with** llenar *or* cubrir de; **to be ~ed with mud** estar cubierto de barro.

plaster cast *n* (*MED*) escayola; (*model, statue*) vaciado de yeso.

plastered [plas'tûrd] *a* (*col*) borracho.

plasterer [plas'tərûr] *n* yesero.

plastic [plas'tik] *n* plástico ♦ *a* de plástico.

plastic bag *n* bolsa de plástico.

plasticine [plas'tisēn] ® *n* (*Brit*) plastilina ®.

plastic surgery *n* cirujía plástica.

plate [plāt] *n* (*dish*) plato; (*metal, in book*) lámina; (*PHOT*) placa; (*on door*) placa; (*AUT: license* ~) matrícula.

plateau, ~s *or* ~x [platō', -z] *n* meseta, altiplanicie *f*.

plateful [plāt'fəl] *n* plato.

plate glass *n* vidrio *or* cristal *m* cilindrado.

platen [plat'ən] *n* (*on typewriter, printer*) rodillo.

platform [plat'fôrm] *n* (*RAIL*) andén *m*; (*stage*) plataforma; (*at meeting*) tribuna; (*POL*) programa *m* (electoral); **the train leaves from ~ 7** el tren sale del andén número 7.

platinum [plat'ənəm] *n* platino.

platitude [plat'ətōōd] *n* lugar *m* común, tópico.

platonic [plətân'ik] *a* platónico.

platoon [plətōōn'] *n* pelotón *m*.

platter [plat'ûr] *n* fuente *f*.

plaudits [plô'dits] *npl* aplausos *mpl*.

plausibility [plôzəbil'ətē] *n* verosimilitud *f*, credibilidad *f*.

plausible [plô'zəbəl] *a* verosímil; (*person*) convincente.

play [plā] *n* (*gen*) juego; (*THEATER*) obra, comedia ♦ *vt* (*game*) jugar; (*instrument*) tocar; (*THEATER*) representar; (: *part*) hacer el papel de; (*fig*) desempeñar ♦ *vi* jugar; (*frolic*) juguetear; **to ~ it safe** ir a lo seguro; **to bring** *or* **call into ~** poner en juego; **to ~ a trick on sb** gastar una broma a uno; **they're ~ing soldiers** están jugando a (los) soldados; **to ~ for time** (*fig*) tratar de ganar tiempo; **to ~ into sb's hands** (*fig*) hacerle el juego a uno; **a smile ~ed on his lips** una sonrisa le bailaba en los labios.

play around *vi* (*person*) hacer el tonto; **to ~ around with** (*fiddle with*) juguetear con; (*idea*) darle vueltas a.

play along *vi*: **to ~ along with** (*fig: person*) seguirle el juego a; (: *plan, idea*) seguir el juego a.

play back *vt* repasar.

play down *vt* quitar importancia a.

play on *vt fus* (*sb's feelings, credulity*) aprovecharse de; **to ~ on sb's nerves** atacarle los nervios a uno.

play up *vi* (*Brit*) = **act up**.

playact [plā'akt] *vi* (*fig*) hacer comedia *or* teatro.

play-acting [plā'akting] *n* teatro.

playboy [plā'boi] *n* playboy *m*.

player [plā'ûr] *n* jugador(a) *m/f*; (*THEATER*) actor *m*, actriz *f*; (*MUS*) músico/a.

playful [plā'fəl] *a* juguetón/ona.

playground [plā'ground] *n* (*in school*) patio de recreo.

playgroup [plā'grōōp] *n* jardín *m* de niños.

playing card [plā'ing kârd] *n* naipe *m*, carta.

playing field *n* campo de deportes.

playmate [plā'māt] *n* compañero/a de juego.

play-off [plā'ôf] *n* (*SPORT*) (partido de) desempate *m*.

playpen [plā'pen] *n* corral *m*.

playroom [plā'rōōm] *n* cuarto de juego.

plaything [plā'thing] *n* juguete *m*.

playtime [plā'tīm] *n* (*SCOL*) (hora de) recreo.

playwright [plā'rīt] *n* dramaturgo/a.

plc (*Brit*) *abbr* (= *public limited company*) S.A.

plea [plē] *n* (*request*) súplica, petición *f*; (*excuse*) pretexto, disculpa; (*LAW*) alegato, defensa.

plead [plēd] *vt* (*LAW*): **to ~ sb's case** defender a alguien; (*give as excuse*) poner como pretexto ♦ *vi* (*LAW*) declararse; (*beg*): **to ~ with sb** suplicar *or* rogar a uno; **to ~ guilty/not guilty** (*defendant*) declararse culpable/inocente; **to ~ for sth** (*beg for*) suplicar algo.

pleasant [plez'ənt] *a* agradable.

pleasantly [plez'əntlē] *ad* agradablemente.

pleasantness [plez'əntnis] *n* (*of person*) simpatía, amabilidad *f*; (*of place*) lo agradable.

pleasantries [plez'əntrēz] *npl* (*polite re-marks*) cortesías *fpl*; **to exchange ~** ha-blar en forma amena.

please [plēz] *vt* (*give pleasure to*) dar gusto a, agradar ♦ *vi* (*think fit*): **do as you ~** haz lo que quieras *or* lo que te dé la gana; **to ~ o.s.** hacer lo que le parezca; **~!** ¡por favor!; **~ yourself!** ¡haz lo que quieras!, ¡como quieras!; **~ don't cry!** ¡no llores! te lo ruego.

pleased [plēzd] *a* (*happy*) alegre, contento; (*satisfied*): **~ (with)** satisfecho (de); **~ to meet you** (*col*) ¡encantado!, ¡tanto *or* mu-cho gusto!; **to be ~ (about sth)** alegrarse (de algo); **we are ~ to inform you that ...** tenemos el gusto de comunicarle que ....

pleasing [plē'zing] *a* agradable, grato.

pleasurable [plezh'ûrəblē] *a* agradable, gra-to.

pleasurably [plezh'ûrəblē] *ad* agradable-mente, gratamente.

pleasure [plezh'ûr] *n* placer *m*, gusto; (*will*) voluntad *f* ♦ *cpd* de recreo; **"it's a ~"** "el gusto es mío"; **it's a ~ to see him** da gus-to verle; **it's a ~ to inform you that ...** tengo el gran placer de comunicarles que ...; **with ~** con mucho *or* todo gusto; **is this trip for business or ~?** ¿este viaje es de negocios o de placer?

pleasure-seeking [plezh'ûrsēking] *a* hedo-nista.

pleasure steamer *n* (*Brit*) vapor *m* de recreo.

pleat [plēt] *n* pliegue *m*.

pleb [pleb] *n*: **the ~s** la gente baja, la plebe.

plebeian [pləbē'ən] *n* plebeyo/a ♦ *a* plebeyo; (*pej*) ordinario.

plebiscite [pleb'isit] *n* plebiscito.

plectrum [plek'trəm] *n* plectro.

pledge [plej] *n* (*object*) prenda; (*promise*) promesa, voto ♦ *vt* (*pawn*) empeñar; (*promise*) prometer; **to ~ support for sb** prometer su apoyo a uno; **to ~ sb to se-crecy** hacer a uno jurar guardar un secre-to.

plenary [plē'nûrē] *a*: **in ~ session** en sesión plenaria.

plentiful [plen'tifəl] *a* copioso, abundante.

plenty [plen'tē] *n* abundancia; **~ of** mucho(s)/a(s); **we've got ~ of time to get there** tenemos tiempo de sobra para llegar.

plethora [pleth'ərə] *n* plétora.

pleurisy [ploor'isē] *n* pleuresía.

Plexiglas [pleks'iglas] ® *n* (*US*) plexiglás *m* ®.

pliability [pliəbil'ətē] *n* flexibilidad *f*.

pliable [pli'əbəl] *a* flexible.

pliers [pli'ûrz] *npl* alicates *mpl*, tenazas *fpl*.

plight [plit] *n* condición *f* or situación *f* difí-cil.

plimsolls [plim'səlz] *npl* (*Brit*) zapatos *mpl*

de tenis.

plinth [plinth] *n* plinto.

PLO *n abbr* (= *Palestine Liberation Organi-zation*) OLP *f*.

plod [plåd] *vi* caminar con paso pesado; (*fig*) trabajar laboriosamente.

plodder [plåd'ûr] *n* trabajador(a) diligente pero lento/a.

plodding [plåd'ing] *a* (*student*) empo-llón(ona); (*worker*) más aplicado que bri-llante.

plonk [plångk] *n* (*Brit col: wine*) vino pe-león.

plot [plåt] *n* (*scheme*) complot *m*, conjura; (*of story, play*) argumento; (*of land*) terre-no ♦ *vt* (*mark out*) trazar; (*conspire*) tra-mar, urdir ♦ *vi* conspirar.

plotter [plåt'ûr] *n* (*instrument*) trazador *m* (de gráficos); (*COMPUT*) trazador *m*.

plotting [plåt'ing] *n* conspiración *f*, intrigas *fpl*.

plough [plou] *etc* (*Brit*) = **plow** *etc*.

plow [plou] (*US*) *n* arado ♦ *vt* (*earth*) arar.
   plow back *vt* (*COMM*) reinvertir.
   plow through *vt fus* (*crowd*) abrirse paso a la fuerza por.

plowing [plou'ing] *n* labranza.

plowman [plou'mən] *n*: **~'s lunch** pan *m* con queso.

plowshare [plou'shär] *n* reja del arado.

ploy [ploi] *n* truco, estratagema.

pluck [pluk] *vt* (*fruit*) coger (*Sp*), recoger (*LAm*); (*musical instrument*) puntear; (*bird*) desplumar ♦ *n* valor *m*, ánimo; **to ~ up courage** hacer de tripas corazón; **to ~ one's eyebrows** depilarse las cejas.

plucky [pluk'ē] *a* valiente.

plug [plug] *n* tapón *m*; (*ELEC*) enchufe *m*, clavija; (*AUT: also:* **spark ~**) bujía ♦ *vt* (*hole*) tapar; (*col: advertise*) dar publici-dad a; **to give sb/sth a ~** dar publicidad a uno/algo; **to ~ a cord into a socket** enchu-far un hilo en una toma.
   plug in *vt, vi* (*ELEC*) enchufar.

plughole [plug'hōl] *n* desagüe *m*, desagua-dero.

plum [plum] *n* (*fruit*) ciruela ♦ *a* (*col: job*) chollo.

plumage [ploō'mij] *n* plumaje *m*.

plumb [plum] *a* vertical ♦ *n* plomo ♦ *ad* (*exactly*) exactamente, en punto ♦ *vt* sondar; (*fig*) sondear.
   plumb in *vt* (*washing machine*) co-nectar.

plumber [plum'ûr] *n* fontanero/a, plomero/a.

plumbing [plum'ing] *n* (*trade*) fontanería; (*piping*) cañería.

plume [ploōm] *n* (*gen*) pluma; (*on helmet*) penacho.

plummet [plum'it] *vi*: **to ~ (down)** caer a plomo.

plump [plump] *a* rechoncho, rollizo ♦ *vt*: **to ~ sth (down) on** dejar caer algo en.

plump up *vt* hinchar.
plumpness |plump'nis| *n* gordura.
plunder |plun'dûr| *n* pillaje *m*; (*loot*) botín *m* ♦ *vt* pillar, saquear.
plunge |plunj| *n* zambullida ♦ *vt* sumergir, hundir ♦ *vi* (*fall*) caer; (*dive*) saltar; (*person*) arrojarse; (*sink*) hundirse; **to take the ~** lanzarse; **to ~ a room into darkness** dejar una habitación a oscuras.
plunger |plun'jûr| *n* émbolo; (*for drain*) desatascador *m*.
plunging |plun'jing| *a* (*neckline*) escotado.
pluperfect |plōōpúr'fikt| *n* pluscuamperfecto.
plural |plŏŏr'əl| *n* plural *m*.
plus |plus| *n* (*also*: **~ sign**) signo más; (*fig*) punto a favor ♦ *a*: **a ~ factor** (*fig*) un plus ♦ *prep* más, y, además de; **ten/twenty ~** más de diez/veinte.
plush |plush| *a* de felpa.
plutonium |plōōtō'nēəm| *n* plutonio.
ply |plī| *vt* (*a trade*) ejercer ♦ *vi* (*ship*) ir y venir; **three ~** (*wool*) de tres cabos; **to ~ sb with drink** insistir en ofrecer a alguien muchas copas.
plywood |plī'wŏŏd| *n* madera contrachapada.
PM *abbr* = **Prime Minister**.
p.m. *ad abbr* (= *post meridiem*) de la tarde *or* noche.
pneumatic |nŏŏmat'ik| *a* neumático.
pneumatic drill *n* taladro neumático.
pneumonia |nyŏŏmōn'yə| *n* pulmonía.
PO *n abbr* (= *Post Office*) Correos *mpl*; (*NAUT*) = **petty officer**.
po (*Brit*) *abbr* = **postal order**.
poach |pōch| *vt* (*cook*) escalfar; (*steal*) cazar/pescar en vedado ♦ *vi* cazar/pescar en vedado.
poached |pōcht| *a* (*egg*) escalfado.
poacher |pō'chûr| *n* cazador(a) *m/f* furtivo/a.
poaching |pō'ching| *n* caza/pesca furtiva.
PO Box *n abbr* = **Post Office Box**.
pocket |pâk'it| *n* bolsillo; (*of air, GEO, fig*) bolsa; (*BILLIARDS*) tronera ♦ *vt* meter en el bolsillo; (*steal*) embolsar; (*BILLIARDS*) entronerar; **breast ~** bolsillo de pecho; **~ of resistance** foco de resistencia; **~ of warm air** bolsa de aire caliente.
pocketbook |pâk'itbŏŏk| *n* (*US: wallet*) cartera; (: *handbag*) bolso.
pocketful |pâk'itfŏŏl| *n* bolsillo.
pocket knife *n* navaja.
pocket money *n* dinero de bolsillo.
pockmarked |pâk'mârkt| *a* (*face*) picado de viruelas.
pod |pâd| *n* vaina.
podgy |pâj'ē| *a* gordinflón/ona.
podiatrist |pədĭ'ətrist| *n* (*US*) pedicuro/a.
podiatry |pədĭ'ətrē| *n* (*US*) pedicura.
podium |pō'dēəm| *n* podio.
POE *n abbr* = *port of embarkation, port of*

entry.
poem |pō'əm| *n* poema *m*.
poet |pō'it| *n* poeta *m/f*.
poetic |pōet'ik| *a* poético.
poet laureate |pō'it lō'rēit| *n* poeta *m* laureado.
poetry |pō'itrē| *n* poesía.
poignant |poin'yənt| *a* conmovedor(a).
poignantly |poin'yəntlē| *ad* de modo conmovedor.
point |point| *n* punto; (*tip*) punta; (*purpose*) fin *m*, propósito; (*Brit ELEC: also:* **power ~**) toma de corriente, enchufe *m*; (*use*) utilidad *f*; (*significant part*) lo significativo; (*place*) punto, lugar *m*; (*also:* **decimal ~**): **2 ~ 3 (2.3)** dos coma tres (2,3) ♦ *vt* (*gun etc*): **to ~ sth at sb** apuntar algo a uno ♦ *vi* señalar con el dedo; **~s** *npl* (*AUT*) contactos *mpl*; (*RAIL*) agujas *fpl*; **to be on the ~ of doing sth** estar a punto de hacer algo; **to make a ~ of doing sth** poner empeño en hacer algo; **to get the ~** comprender; **to come to the ~** ir al meollo; **there's no ~ (in doing)** no tiene sentido (hacer); **~ of departure** (*also fig*) punto de partida; **~ of order** cuestión *f* de procedimiento; **~ of sale** (*COMM*) lugar *m* de venta; **~-of-sale advertising** publicidad *f* en el punto de venta; **the train stops at Boston and all ~s south** el tren para en Boston, y en todas las estaciones al sur; **when it comes to the ~** en el momento de la verdad; **in ~ of fact** en realidad; **that's the whole ~!** ¡eso es!, ¡ahí está!; **to be beside the ~** no venir al caso; **you've got a ~ there!** ¡tienes razón!.
point out *vt* señalar.
point to *vt fus* indicar con el dedo; (*fig*) indicar, señalar.
point-blank |point'blangk'| *ad* (*also:* **at ~ range**) a quemarropa.
pointed |poin'tid| *a* (*shape*) puntiagudo, afilado; (*remark*) intencionado.
pointedly |poin'tidlē| *ad* intencionadamente.
pointer |poin'tûr| *n* (*stick*) puntero; (*needle*) aguja, indicador *m*; (*clue*) indicación *f*, pista; (*advice*) consejo.
pointless |point'lis| *a* sin sentido.
pointlessly |point'lislē| *ad* inútilmente, sin motivo.
point of view *n* punto de vista.
poise |poiz| *n* (*of head, body*) porte *m*; (*calmness*) aplomo, elegancia.
poised |poizd| *a* (*in temperament*) sereno.
poison |poi'zən| *n* veneno ♦ *vt* envenenar.
poisoning |poi'zəning| *n* envenenamiento.
poisonous |poi'zənəs| *a* venenoso; (*fumes etc*) tóxico; (*fig: ideas, literature*) pernicioso; (: *rumors, individual*) nefasto.
poke |pōk| *vt* (*fire*) hurgar, atizar; (*jab with finger, stick etc*) empujar; (*COMPUT*) almacenar; (*put*): **to ~ sth in(to)** introducir algo en ♦ *n* (*jab*) empujón *m*; (*with*

elbow) codazo; **to ~ one's head out of the window** asomar la cabeza por la ventana; **to ~ fun at sb** ridiculizar a uno; **to give the fire a ~** atizar el fuego.
poke around *vi* fisgonear.
poker [pō'kûr] *n* atizador *m*; (*CARDS*) póker *m*.
poker-faced [pō'kúrfāst'] *a* de cara impasible.
poky [pō'kē] *a* estrecho.
Poland [pō'lənd] *n* Polonia.
polar [pō'lûr] *a* polar.
polar bear *n* oso polar.
polarization [pōlûrəzā'shən] *n* polarización *f*.
polarize [pō'lərīz] *vt* polarizar.
Pole [pōl] *n* polaco/a.
pole [pōl] *n* palo; (*GEO*) polo; (*TEL*) poste *m*; (*flag ~*) asta; (*tent ~*) mástil *m*.
pole bean *n* (*US*) judía trepadora.
polecat [pōl'kat] *n* (*US: skunk*) mofeta; (*Brit*) turón *m*.
Pol. Econ. [pâl'ēkân] *n abbr* = *political economy*.
polemic [pəlem'ik] *n* polémica.
polemicist [pōlem'isist] *n* polemista *m/f*.
pole star *n* estrella polar.
pole vault *n* salto con pértiga.
police [pəlēs'] *n* policía ♦ *vt* (*streets, city, frontier*) vigilar.
police captain *n* (*US*) subjefe/a *m/f*.
police car *n* coche-patrulla *m*.
police constable *n* (*Brit*) guardia *m*, policía *m*.
police department *n* (*US*) policía.
police force *n* cuerpo de policía.
policeman [pəlēs'mən] *n* guardia *m*, policía *m*.
police officer *n* guardia *m*, policía *m*.
police record *n*: **to have a ~** tener antecedentes penales.
police state *n* estado policial.
police station *n* comisaría.
policewoman [pəlēs'wŏŏmən] *n* mujer *f* policía.
policy [pâl'isē] *n* política; (*also:* **insurance ~**) póliza; (*of newspaper, company*) política; **it is our ~ to do that** tenemos por norma hacer eso; **to take out a ~** sacar una póliza.
policy holder *n* asegurado/a.
polio [pō'lēō] *n* polio *f*.
Polish [pō'lish] *a* polaco ♦ *n* (*LING*) polaco.
polish [pâl'ish] *n* (*for shoes*) betún *m*; (*for floor*) cera (de lustrar); (*for nails*) esmalte *m*; (*shine*) brillo, lustre *m*; (*fig: refinement*) cultura ♦ *vt* (*shoes*) limpiar; (*make shiny*) pulir, sacar brillo a; (*fig: improve*) perfeccionar.
polish off *vt* (*work*) terminar; (*food*) despachar.
polished [pâl'isht] *a* (*fig: person*) elegante.
polite [pəlīt'] *a* cortés, atento; (*formal*) co-

rrecto; **it's not ~ to do that** es de mala educación hacer eso.
politely [pəlīt'lē] *ad* cortésmente.
politeness [pəlīt'nis] *n* cortesía.
politic [pâl'itik] *a* prudente.
political [pəlit'ikəl] *a* político.
political asylum *n* asilo político.
politically [pəlit'iklē] *ad* políticamente.
politician [pâlitish'ən] *n* político/a.
politics [pâl'itiks] *n* política.
polka [pōl'kə] *n* polca.
polka dot *n* lunar *m*.
poll [pōl] *n* (*votes*) votación *f*, votos *mpl*; (*also:* **opinion ~**) sondeo, encuesta ♦ *vt* (*votes*) obtener; (*in opinion ~*) sondear; **to go to the ~s** (*voters*) votar; (*government*) acudir a las urnas.
pollen [pâl'ən] *n* polen *m*.
pollen count *n* índice *m* de polen.
pollination [pâlənā'shən] *n* polinización *f*.
polling [pō'ling] *n* (*Brit POL*) votación *f*; (*TEL*) interrogación *f*.
pollute [pəlōōt'] *vt* contaminar.
pollution [pəlōō'shən] *n* polución *f*, contaminación *f* del medio ambiente.
polo [pō'lō] *n* (*sport*) polo.
poloneck [pō'lōnek] *a* de cuello vuelto ♦ *n* (*sweater*) suéter *m* de cuello vuelto.
poly [pâl'ē] *n abbr* (*Brit*) = **polytechnic**.
poly... [pâl'ē] *pref* poli....
polyester [pâlēes'tûr] *n* poliéster *m*.
polyethylene [pâlēeth'əlēn] *n* (*US*) politeno.
polygamy [pəlig'əmē] *n* poligamia.
polymath [pâl'ēmath] *n* erudito/a.
Polynesia [pâlinē'zhə] *n* Polinesia.
Polynesian [pâlənē'zhən] *a, n* polinesio/a *m/f*.
polyp [pâl'ip] *n* (*MED*) pólipo.
polystyrene [pâlēstī'rēn] *n* poliestireno.
polytechnic [pâlētek'nik] *n* ≈ escuela de formación profesional.
polythene [pâl'əthēn] *n* (*Brit*) politeno.
polythene bag *n* bolsa de plástico.
polyurethane [pâlēyŏŏr'əthān] *n* poliuretano.
pomegranate [pâm'əgranit] *n* granada.
pommel [pum'əl] *n* pomo ♦ *vt* = **pummel**.
pomp [pâmp] *n* pompa.
pompom [pâm'pâm], **pompon** [pâm'pân] *n* borla.
pompous [pâm'pəs] *a* pomposo; (*person*) presumido.
pond [pând] *n* (*natural*) charca; (*artificial*) estanque *m*.
ponder [pân'dûr] *vt* meditar.
ponderous [pân'dûrəs] *a* pesado.
pong [pông] *n* (*Brit col*) mal olor *m* ♦ *vi* (*Brit col*) apestar.
pontiff [pân'tif] *n* pontífice *m*.
pontificate [pântif'ikāt] *vi* (*fig*): **to ~ (about)** pontificar (sobre).
pontoon [pântōōn'] *n* pontón *m*; (*Brit: card*

game) veintiuna.
pony [pō'nē] *n* poney *m*, jaca, potro (*LAm*).
ponytail [pō'nētāl] *n* cola de caballo.
pony trekking [pō'nē trek'ing] *n* (*Brit*) excursión *f* a caballo.
poodle [pōō'dəl] *n* caniche *m*.
pooh-pooh [pōōpōō'] *vt* desdeñar.
pool [pōōl] *n* (*natural*) charca; (*pond*) estanque *m*; (*also:* **swimming ~**) piscina, alberca (*LAm*); (*billiards*) chapolín; (*COMM: consortium*) consorcio; (: *US: monopoly trust*) trust *m* ♦ *vt* juntar; **typing ~** servicio de mecanografía; (**football**) **~s** *npl* quinielas *fpl*.
pooped [pōōpt] *a* (*US col*) hecho polvo.
poor [pōōr] *a* pobre; (*bad*) de mala calidad ♦ *npl*: **the ~** los pobres.
poorly [pōōr'lē] *a* mal, enfermo.
pop [páp] *n* ¡pum!; (*sound*) ruido seco; (*MUS*) (música) pop *m*; (*US col: father*) papá *m*; (*col: drink*) gaseosa ♦ *vt* (*burst*) hacer reventar ♦ *vi* reventar; (*cork*) saltar; **she ~ped her head out (of the window)** asomó de repente la cabeza (por la ventana).
pop in *vi* entrar un momento.
pop out *vi* salir un momento.
pop up *vi* aparecer inesperadamente.
pop concert *n* concierto pop.
popcorn [páp'kórn] *n* palomitas *fpl*.
pope [pōp] *n* papa *m*.
poplar [páp'lûr] *n* álamo.
poplin [páp'lin] *n* popelina.
poppy [páp'ē] *n* amapola.
poppycock [páp'ēkâk] *n* (*col*) tonterías *fpl*.
popsicle [páp'sikəl] *n* (*US*) ʟolo.
populace [páp'yələs] *n* pueblo, plebe *f*.
popular [páp'yəlûr] *a* popular; **a ~ song** una canción popular; **to be ~ (with)** (*person*) caer bien (a); (*decision*) ser popular (entre).
popularity [pâpyəlar'itē] *n* popularidad *f*.
popularize [páp'yələrīz] *vt* popularizar; (*disseminate*) vulgarizar.
populate [páp'yəlāt] *vt* poblar.
population [pápyəlā'shən] *n* población *f*.
population explosion ♦ *n* explosión *f* demográfica.
populous [páp'yələs] *a* populoso.
porcelain [pôr'səlin] *n* porcelana.
porch [pôrch] *n* pórtico, entrada.
porcupine [pôr'kyəpīn] *n* puerco *m* espín.
pore [pôr] *n* poro ♦ *vi*: **to ~ over** engolfarse en.
pork [pôrk] *n* carne *f* de cerdo *or* chancho (*LAm*).
pork chop *n* chuleta de cerdo.
pornographic [pôrnəgraf'ik] *a* pornográfico.
pornography [pôrná'grəfē] *n* pornografía.
porous [pôr'əs] *a* poroso.
porpoise [pôr'pəs] *n* marsopa.
porridge [pôr'ij] *n* gachas *fpl* de avena.
port [pôrt] *n* (*harbor*) puerto; (*NAUT*: left

side) babor *m*; (*wine*) vino de Oporto; (*COMPUT*) puerta, puerto, port *m;* **~ of call** puerto de escala.
portable [pôr'təbəl] *a* portátil; **~ crib** (*US*) cuna portátil.
portal [pôr'təl] *n* puerta (grande), portalón *m*.
port authorities *npl* autoridades *fpl* portuarias.
portcullis [pôrtkul'is] *n* rastrillo.
portend [pôrtend'] *vt* presagiar, anunciar.
portent [pôr'tent] *n* presagio, augurio.
porter [pôr'tûr] *n* (*for luggage*) maletero; (*doorkeeper*) portero/a, conserje *m/f*; (*US RAIL*) mozo de los coches-cama.
portfolio [pôrtfō'lēō] *n* (*case, of artist*) cartera, carpeta; (*POL, FINANCE*) cartera.
porthole [pôrt'hōl] *n* portilla.
portico [pôr'tikō] *n* pórtico.
portion [pôr'shən] *n* porción *f*; (*helping*) ración *f*.
portly [pôrt'lē] *a* corpulento.
portrait [pôr'trit] *n* retrato.
portray [pôrtrā'] *vt* retratar; (*in writing*) representar.
portrayal [pôrtrā'əl] *n* representación *f*.
Portugal [pôr'chəgəl] *n* Portugal *m*.
Portuguese [pôrchəgēz'] *a* portugués/esa ♦ *n*, *pl inv* portugués/esa *m/f*; (*LING*) portugués *m*.
Portuguese man-of-war *n* (*jellyfish*) especie *f* de medusa.
pose [pōz] *n* postura, actitud *f*; (*pej*) afectación *f*, pose *f* ♦ *vi* posar; (*pretend*): **to ~ as** hacerse pasar por ♦ *vt* (*question*) plantear; **to strike a ~** tomar *or* adoptar una pose *or* actitud.
poser [pō'zûr] *n* problema *m*/pregunta difícil; (*person*) = **poseur**.
poseur [pōzir'] *n* presumido/a, persona afectada.
posh [pásh] *a* (*col*) elegante, de lujo ♦ *ad* (*col*): **to talk ~** hablar con acento afectado.
position [pəzish'ən] *n* posición *f*; (*job*) puesto ♦ *vt* colocar; **to be in a ~ to do sth** estar en condiciones de hacer algo.
positive [páz'ətiv] *a* positivo; (*certain*) seguro; (*definite*) definitivo; **we look forward to a ~ reply** (*COMM*) esperamos ansiosamente su respuesta en firme; **he's a ~ nuisance** es un auténtico pelmazo; **~ cash flow** (*COMM*) flujo positivo de efectivo.
positively [páz'ətivlē] *ad* (*affirmatively, enthusiastically*) de forma positiva; (*col: really*) absolutamente.
posse [pás'ē] *n* (*US*) pelotón *m*.
possess [pəzes'] *vt* poseer; **like one ~ed** como un poseído; **whatever can have ~ed you?** ¿cómo se te ocurrió?
possessed [pəzest'] *a* poseso, poseído.
possession [pəzesh'ən] *n* posesión *f*; **to take ~ of sth** tomar posesión de algo.

possessive [pəzes'iv] *a* posesivo.
possessively [pəzes'ivlē] *ad* de modo posesivo.
possessor [pəzes'ûr] *n* poseedor(a) *m/f*, dueño/a.
possibility [pâsəbil'ətē] *n* posibilidad *f*; **he's a ~ for the part** es uno de los posibles para el papel.
possible [pâs'əbəl] *a* posible; **as big as ~** lo más grande posible; **it is ~ to do it** es posible hacerlo; **as far as ~** en la medida de lo posible; **a ~ candidate** un(a) posible candidato/a.
possibly [pâs'əblē] *ad* (*perhaps*) posiblemente, tal vez; **I cannot ~ come** me es imposible venir; **could you ~ ...?** ¿podrías ...?
post [pōst] *n* (*Brit: letters, delivery*) correo; (*job, situation*) puesto; (*trading ~*) factoría; (*pole*) poste *m* ♦ *vt* (*Brit: send by ~*) echar al correo; (*MIL*) apostar; (*bills*) fijar, pegar; (*appoint*): **to ~ to** enviar a; **by ~** (*Brit*) por correo; **by return of ~** (*Brit*) a vuelta de correo; **to keep sb ~ed** tener a uno al corriente.
post... [pōst] *pref* post..., pos...; **~ 1950** pos(t) 1950.
postage [pōs'tij] *n* porte *m*, franqueo.
postage stamp *n* sello (de correo).
postal [pōs'təl] *a* postal, de correos.
postal order *n* (*Brit*) giro postal.
postal vote *n* (*Brit*) voto postal.
postbag [pōst'bag] *n* (*Brit*) correspondencia, cartas *fpl.*
postbox [pōst'bâks] *n* (*Brit*) buzón *m.*
postcard [pōst'kârd] *n* tarjeta postal.
postcode [pōst'kōd] *n* (*Brit*) código *or* clave *f* postal.
postdate [pōst'dāt] *vt* (*check*) poner fecha adelantada a.
poster [pōs'tûr] *n* cartel *m.*
posterior [pâstēr'ēûr] *n* (*col*) culo, trasero.
posterity [pâstär'itē] *n* posteridad *f.*
poster paint *n* pintura al agua.
post-free [pōst'frē'] *a* (*Brit*) libre de franqueo.
postgraduate [pōstgraj'ōōit] *n* posgraduado/a.
posthumous [pâs'chəməs] *a* póstumo.
posthumously [pâs'chəməslē] *ad* póstumamente, con carácter póstumo.
postman [pōst'mən] *n* cartero.
postmark [pōst'mârk] *n* matasellos *m inv.*
postmaster [pōst'mastûr] *n* administrador *m* de correos.
Postmaster General *n* director *m* general de correos.
postmistress [pōst'mistris] *n* administradora de correos.
post-mortem [pōstmôr'təm] *n* autopsia.
postnatal [pōstnāt'əl] *a* postnatal, postparto.
post office *n* (*building*) (oficina de) correos *m*; (*organization*): **the P~ O~** Administración *f* General de Correos.
Post Office Box (PO Box) *n* apartado postal, casilla de correos (*LAm*).
post-paid [pōst'pād'] *a* porte pagado.
postpone [pōstpōn'] *vt* aplazar.
postponement [pōstpōn'mənt] *n* aplazamiento.
postscript [pōst'skript] *n* posdata.
postulate [pâs'chəlāt] *vt* postular.
posture [pâs'chûr] *n* postura, actitud *f.*
post-viral syndrome [pōst'vī'rəl sin'drōm] *n* síndrome *m* post-vírico.
postwar [pōst'wôr'] *a* de la posguerra.
posy [pō'zē] *n* ramillete *m* (de flores).
pot [pât] *n* (*for cooking*) olla; (*for flowers*) maceta; (*for jam*) tarro, pote *m*; (*piece of pottery*) cacharro; (*Brit col: marijuana*) costo ♦ *vt* (*plant*) poner en tiesto; (*conserve*) conservar; **~s of** (*Brit col*) montones de; **to go to ~** (*col: work, performance*) irse al traste.
potash [pât'ash] *n* potasa.
potassium [pətas'ēəm] *n* potasio.
potato, **~es** [pətā'tō, -z] *n* patata, papa (*LAm*).
potato chips, (*Brit*) **potato crisps** *npl* patatas *fpl or* papas *fpl* (*LAm*) fritas.
potato peeler [pətā'tō pē'lûr] *n* pelapatatas *m inv.*
potbellied [pât'belēd] *a* (*from overeating*) barrigón/ona; (*from malnutrition*) con el vientre hinchado.
potency [pōt'ənsē] *n* potencia.
potent [pōt'ənt] *a* potente, poderoso; (*drink*) fuerte.
potentate [pōt'əntāt] potentado.
potential [pəten'chəl] *a* potencial, posible ♦ *n* potencial *m*; **to have ~** mostrar gran potencial.
potentially [pəten'chəlē] *ad* en potencia.
pothole [pât'hōl] *n* (*in road*) bache *m*; (*Brit: underground*) gruta.
potholer [pât'hōlûr] *n* (*Brit*) espeleólogo/a.
potion [pō'shən] *n* poción *f*, pócima.
potluck [pât'luk] *n*: **to take ~** tomar lo que haya.
pot roast *n* carne *f* asada.
potshot [pât'shât] *n*: **to take a ~ at sth** tirar a algo sin apuntar.
potted [pât'id] *a* (*food*) en conserva; (*plant*) en tiesto *or* maceta; (*fig: shortened*) resumido.
potter [pât'ûr] *n* alfarero/a ♦ *vi* (*Brit*): **to ~ around**, **~ about** ocuparse en fruslerías; **to ~ around the house** ir de aquí para allá sin hacer nada de provecho; **~'s wheel** torno de alfarero.
pottery [pât'ûrē] *n* cerámica, alfarería; **a piece of ~** un artículo de cerámica.
potty [pât'ē] *n* orinal *m* de niño.
potty-trained [pât'ētrānd] *a* que ya no necesita pañales.

pouch [pouch] *n* (*ZOOL*) bolsa; (*for tobacco*) petaca.

pouf(fe) [pōōf] *n* (*stool*) puf *m*.

poultry [pōl'trē] *n* aves *fpl* de corral; (*dead*) pollos *mpl*.

poultry farm *n* granja avícola.

poultry farmer *n* avicultor(a) *m/f*.

pounce [pouns] *vi*: **to ~ on** precipitarse sobre ♦ *n* salto, ataque *m*.

pound [pound] *n* libra; (*for dogs*) corral *m*; (*for cars*) depósito ♦ *vt* (*beat*) golpear; (*crush*) machacar ♦ *vi* (*beat*) dar golpes; **half a ~** media libra; **a one ~ note** un billete de una libra.

pounding [poun'ding] *n*: **to take a ~** (*team*) sufrir terriblemente.

pound sterling *n* (libra) esterlina.

pour [pòr] *vt* echar; (*tea*) servir ♦ *vi* correr, fluir; (*rain*) llover a cántaros.

pour away, pour off *vt* vaciar, verter.

pour in *vi* (*people*) entrar en tropel; **to come ~ing in** (*water*) entrar a raudales; (*letters*) llegar a montones; (*cars, people*) llegar en tropel.

pour out *vi* (*people*) salir en tropel ♦ *vt* (*drink*) echar, servir.

pouring [pòr'ing] *a*: **~ rain** lluvia torrencial.

pout [pout] *vi* hacer pucheros.

poverty [pàv'ûrtē] *n* pobreza, miseria; (*fig*) falta, escasez *f*.

poverty-stricken [páv'ûrtēstrikən] *a* necesitado.

POW *n abbr* = **prisoner of war.**

powder [pou'dúr] *n* polvo; (*face ~*) polvos *mpl*; (*gun~*) pólvora ♦ *vt* polvorear; **to ~ one's face** ponerse polvos; **to ~ one's nose** empolvarse la nariz, ponerse polvos; (*euphemism*) ir a los servicios *or* al cuarto de baño.

powder compact *n* polvera.

powdered milk [pou'dûrd milk'] *n* leche *f* en polvo.

powdered sugar [pou'dûrd shōōg'ûr] *n* (*US*) azúcar *m* extrafino.

powder puff *n* borla.

powder room *n* aseos *mpl*.

powdery [pou'dûrē] *a* polvoriento.

power [pou'ûr] *n* poder *m*; (*strength*) fuerza; (*nation*) potencia; (*drive*) empuje *m*; (*TECH*) potencia; (*ELEC*) fuerza, energía ♦ *vt* impulsar; **to be in ~** (*POL*) estar en el poder; **to do all in one's ~ to help sb** hacer todo lo posible por ayudar a uno; **the world ~s** las potencias mundiales.

power cut *n* apagón *m*.

power-driven [pou'ûrdrivən] *a* mecánico; (*ELEC*) eléctrico.

powered [pou'ûrd] *a*: **~ by** impulsado por; **nuclear-~ submarine** submarino nuclear.

power failure *n* = **power cut.**

powerful [pou'ûrfəl] *a* poderoso; (*engine*) potente; (*strong*) fuerte; (*play, speech*) conmovedor(a).

powerhouse [pou'ûrhous] *n* (*fig: person*) fuerza motriz; **a ~ of ideas** una cantera de ideas.

powerless [pou'ûrlis] *a* impotente, ineficaz.

power line *n* línea de conducción eléctrica.

power outage [pou'ûr out'ij] *n* (*US*) apagón *m*.

power shovel *n* excavadora.

power station *n* central *f* eléctrica.

power steering *n* (*AUT*) dirección *f* asistida.

powwow [pou'wou] *n* conferencia ♦ *vi* conferenciar.

pp *abbr* (= *per procurationem*: *by proxy*) p.p.

p & p *abbr* (*Brit*: = *postage and packing*) gastos de envío.

PPS *abbr* (= *post postscriptum*) posdata adicional.

PQ *abbr* (*Canada*) = *Province of Quebec.*

PR *n abbr* = **proportional representation**; (= *public relations*) relaciones *fpl* públicas ♦ *abbr* (*US MAIL*) = *Puerto Rico.*

Pr. *abbr* (= *prince*) P.

practicability [praktikəbil'ətē] *n* factibilidad *f*.

practicable [prak'tikəbəl] *a* (*scheme*) factible.

practical [prak'tikəl] *a* práctico.

practicality [praktikal'itē] *n* (*of situation etc*) factibilidad *f*.

practical joke *n* broma pesada.

practically [prak'tiklē] *ad* (*almost*) casi.

practice [prak'tis] *n* (*habit*) costumbre *f*; (*exercise*) práctica, ejercicio; (*training*) adiestramiento; (*MED*) clientela ♦ *vt* (*US*) (*carry out*) practicar; (*profession*) ejercer; (*train at*) practicar ♦ *vi* (*US*) ejercer; (*train*) practicar; **in ~** (*in reality*) en la práctica; **out of ~** desentrenado; **to put sth into ~** poner algo en práctica; **it's common ~** es práctica regular; **target ~** práctica de tiro; **he has a small ~** (*doctor*) tiene pocos pacientes; **to set up in ~ as** establecerse como.

practiced [prak'tist] *a* (*person*) experto; (*performance*) bien ensayado; (*liar*) consumado; **with a ~ eye** con ojo experto.

practice test *n* (*SCOL*) examen *m* de prueba.

practicing [prak'tising] *a* (*Christian etc*) practicante; (*lawyer*) que ejerce; (*homosexual*) activo.

practise [prak'tis] *vt, vi* (*Brit*) = **practice.**

practitioner [praktish'ənûr] *n* practicante *m/f*; (*MED*) médico/a.

pragmatic [pragmat'ik] *a* pragmático.

pragmatism [prag'mətizəm] *n* pragmatismo.

pragmatist [prag'mətist] *n* pragmatista *m/f*.

Prague |prág| n Praga.
prairie |prär'ē| n (US) llanura.
praise |präz| n alabanza(s) f(pl), elogio(s) m(pl).
praiseworthy |prāz'wûrthē| a loable.
pram |pram| n (Brit) cochecito de niño.
prance |prans| vi (horse) hacer cabriolas.
prank |prangk| n travesura.
prattle |prat'əl| vi parlotear; (child) balbucear.
prawn |prôn| n gamba.
pray |prā| vi rezar; **to ~ for forgiveness** pedir perdón.
prayer |prär| n oración f, rezo; (entreaty) ruego, súplica.
prayer book n devocionario, misal m.
pre- |prē| pref pre..., ante-; **~1970** pre 1970.
preach |prēch| vi predicar.
preacher |prē'chûr| n predicador(a) m/f; (minister) pastor(a) m/f.
preamble |prē'ambəl| n preámbulo.
prearrange |prēərānj'| vt organizar or acordar de antemano.
prearrangement |prēərānj'mənt| n: **by ~** por previo acuerdo.
precarious |prikär'ēəs| a precario.
precariously |prikär'ēəslē| ad precariamente.
precaution |prikô'shən| n precaución f.
precautionary |prikô'shənärē| a (measure) de precaución, precautorio.
precede |prisēd'| vt, vi preceder.
precedence |pres'idəns| n precedencia; (priority) prioridad f.
precedent |pres'idənt| n precedente m; **to establish** or **set a ~** sentar un precedente.
preceding |prisē'ding| a precedente.
precept |prē'sept| n precepto.
precinct |prē'singkt| n recinto; (US: district) distrito, barrio; (: of policeman) ronda; **~s** npl contornos mpl; **pedestrian ~** (Brit) zona peatonal; **shopping ~** (Brit) centro comercial.
precious |presh'əs| a precioso; (stylized) afectado ♦ ad (col): **~ little/few** muy poco/pocos.
precipice |pres'əpis| n precipicio.
precipitate a |prisip'itit| (hasty) precipitado ♦ vt |prisip'itāt| (hasten) acelerar; (bring about) provocar.
precipitation |prisipitā'shən| n precipitación f.
precipitous |prisip'itəs| a (steep) escarpado; (hasty) precipitado.
précis |prā'sē| n resumen m.
precise |prisīs'| a preciso, exacto; (person) escrupuloso.
precisely |prisīs'lē| ad exactamente, precisamente.
precision |prisizh'ən| n precisión f.
preclude |priklōōd'| vt excluir.
precocious |prikō'shəs| a precoz.
preconceived |prēkənsēvd'| a (idea) pre-

concebido.
preconception |prēkənsep'shən| n (idea) idea preconcebida.
precondition |prēkəndish'ən| n condición f previa.
precursor |prikûr'sûr| n precursor(a) m/f.
predate |prēdāt'| vt (precede) preceder.
predator |pred'ətûr| n animal m de rapiña.
predatory |pred'ətôrē| a (animal) rapaz, de rapiña; (person) agresivo, depredador(a).
predecessor |pred'isesûr| n antecesor(a) m/f.
predestination |prēdestinā'shən| n predestinación f.
predestine |prēdes'tin| vt predestinar.
predetermine |prēditûr'min| vt predeterminar.
predicament |pridik'əmənt| n apuro.
predicate |pred'əkit| n predicado.
predict |pridikt'| vt pronosticar.
predictable |pridikt'əbəl| a previsible.
predictably |pridikt'əblē| ad (behave, react) de forma previsible; **~ she didn't arrive** como era de esperar, no llegó.
prediction |pridik'shən| n pronóstico.
predispose |prēdispōz'| vt predisponer.
predominance |pridâm'ənəns| n predominio.
predominant |pridâm'ənənt| a predominante.
predominantly |pridâm'ənəntlē| ad en su mayoría.
predominate |pridâm'ənāt| vi predominar.
pre-eminent |prēem'ənənt| a preeminente.
pre-empt |prēempt'| vt adelantarse a.
pre-emptive |prēemp'tiv| a: **~ strike** ataque m preventivo.
preen |prēn| vt: **to ~ itself** (bird) limpiarse (las plumas); **to ~ o.s.** pavonearse.
prefab |prē'fab'| n casa prefabricada.
prefabricated |prēfab'rikātid| a prefabricado.
preface |pref'is| n prefacio.
prefect |prē'fekt| n (Brit: in school) monitor(a) m/f.
prefer |prifûr'| vt preferir; (LAW: charges, complaint) presentar; (: action) entablar; **to ~ coffee to tea** preferir el café al té.
preferable |pref'ûrəbəl| a preferible.
preferably |prifûr'əblē| ad de preferencia.
preference |pref'ûrəns| n preferencia; (priority) prioridad f; **in ~ to sth** antes que algo.
preference shares npl (Brit) = **preferred stock**.
preferential |prefəren'chəl| a preferente.
preferred stock |prifûrd' sták| acciones fpl privilegiadas.
prefix |prē'fiks| n prefijo.
pregnancy |preg'nansē| n embarazo.
pregnant |preg'nənt| a embarazada; **3 months ~** tres meses embarazada or

encinta; ~ **with meaning** cargado de significado.

prehistoric [prēhistôr'ik] *a* prehistórico.

prehistory [prēhis'tûrē] *n* prehistoria.

prejudge [prējuj'] *vt* prejuzgar.

prejudice [prej'ədis] *n* (*bias*) prejuicio; (*harm*) perjuicio ♦ *vt* (*bias*) predisponer; (*harm*) perjudicar; **to ~ sb in favor of/against** (*bias*) predisponer a uno a favor de/en contra de.

prejudiced [prej'ədist] *a* (*person*) predispuesto; (*view*) parcial, interesado; **to be ~ against sb/sth** estar predispuesto en contra de uno/algo.

prelate [prel'it] *n* prelado.

preliminaries [prilim'ənärēz] *npl* preliminares *mpl*, preparativos *mpl*.

preliminary [prilim'ənärē] *a* preliminar.

prelude [prā'lōōd] *n* preludio.

premarital [prēmar'itəl] *a* premarital.

premature [prēməchōōr'] *a* (*arrival etc*) prematuro; **you are being a little ~** te has adelantado.

prematurely [prēmətōōr'lē] *ad* prematuramente, antes de tiempo.

premeditate [primed'ətāt] *vt* premeditar.

premeditated [primed'ətātid] *a* premeditado.

premeditation [primeditā'shən] *n* premeditación *f*.

premenstrual [prēmen'strōōəl] *a* premenstrual.

premenstrual tension *n* (*MED*) tensión *f* premenstrual.

premier [primyēr'] *a* primero, principal ♦ *n* (*POL*) primer(a) ministro/a.

première [primyēr'] *n* estreno.

premise [prem'is] *n* premisa.

premises [prem'isiz] *npl* local *msg*; **on the ~** en el lugar mismo; **business ~** locales *mpl* comerciales.

premium [prē'mēəm] *n* premio; (*COMM*) prima; **to be at a ~** ser muy solicitado; **to sell at a ~** (*shares*) vender caro.

premium bond *n* (*Brit*) bono del estado que participa en un sorteo nacional.

premium deal *n* (*COMM*) oferta extraordinaria.

premium gasoline *n* (*US*) (gasolina) súper *m*.

premonition [premənish'ən] *n* presentimiento.

prenatal [prēnāt'l] *a* (*US*) antenatal, prenatal.

prenatal clinic *n* (*US*) clínica prenatal.

preoccupation [prēākyəpā'shən] *n* preocupación *f*.

preoccupied [prēāk'yəpīd] *a* (*worried*) preocupado; (*absorbed*) ensimismado.

prep [prep] *a abbr*: ~ **school** = **preparatory school**.

prepaid [prēpād'] *a* porte pagado; ~ **envelope** sobre *m* de porte pagado.

preparation [prepərā'shən] *n* preparación *f*; ~**s** *npl* preparativos *mpl*; **in ~ for sth** en preparación para algo.

preparatory [pripar'ətôrē] *a* preparatorio, preliminar; ~ **to sth/to doing sth** como preparación para algo/para hacer algo.

preparatory school *n* (*US*) colegio privado; (*Brit*) escuela preparatoria.

prepare [pripär'] *vt* preparar, disponer ♦ *vi*: **to ~ for** prepararse *or* disponerse para; (*make preparations*) hacer preparativos para.

prepared [pripärd'] *a* (*willing*): **to be ~ to help sb** estar dispuesto a ayudar a uno.

preponderance [pripân'dûrəns] *n* preponderancia, predominio.

preposition [prepəzish'ən] *n* preposición *f*.

prepossessing [prēpəzes'ing] *a* agradable, atractivo.

preposterous [pripâs'tûrəs] *a* absurdo, ridículo.

prerecorded [prērikôr'did] *a*: ~ **broadcast** programa *m* grabado de antemano; ~ **cassette** cassette *f* pregrabada.

prerequisite [prirek'wizit] *n* requisito previo.

prerogative [prərâg'ətiv] *n* prerrogativa.

Presbyterian [prezbitēr'ēən] *a, n* presbiteriano/a *m/f*.

presbytery [prez'bitärē] *n* casa parroquial.

preschool [prē'skōōl'] *a* (*child, age*) preescolar.

prescribe [priskrīb'] *vt* prescribir; (*MED*) recetar.

prescription [priskrip'shən] *n* (*MED*) receta; **to fill a ~** preparar una receta.

prescriptive [priskrip'tiv] *a* normativo.

presence [prez'əns] *n* presencia; (*attendance*) asistencia.

presence of mind *n* aplomo.

present *a* [prez'ənt] (*in attendance*) presente; (*current*) actual ♦ *n* (*gift*) regalo; (*actuality*) actualidad *f*, presente *m* ♦ *vt* [prizent'] (*introduce*) presentar; (*expound*) exponer; (*give*) presentar, dar, ofrecer; (*THEATER*) representar; **to be ~ at** asistir a, estar presente en; **those ~** los presentes; **to give sb a ~, make sb a ~ of sth** regalar algo a uno; **at ~** actualmente; **to ~ o.s. for an interview** presentarse a una entrevista; **may I ~ Miss Clark** permítame presentarle *or* le presento a la Srta Clark.

presentable [prizen'təbəl] *a*: **to make o.s. ~** arreglarse.

presentation [prezəntā'shən] *n* presentación *f*; (*gift*) obsequio; (*of case*) exposición *f*; (*THEATER*) representación *f*; **on ~ of the voucher** al presentar el vale.

present-day [prez'əntdā'] *a* actual.

presenter [prizen'tûr] *n* (*RADIO, TV*) locutor(a) *m/f*.

presently [prez'əntlē] *ad* (*soon*) dentro de

poco; (*US: now*) ahora.
present participle *n* participio (de) presente.
present tense *n* (tiempo) presente *m*.
preservation [prezûrvā'shən] *n* conservación *f*.
preservative [prizûr'vətiv] *n* preservativo.
preserve [prizûrv'] *vt* (*keep safe*) preservar, proteger; (*maintain*) mantener; (*food*) conservar; (*in salt*) salar ♦ *n* (*for game*) coto, vedado; (*often pl: jam*) conserva, confitura.
preshrunk [prē'shrungk'] *a* inencogible.
preside [prizīd'] *vi* presidir.
presidency [prez'idənsē] *n* presidencia.
president [prez'idənt] *n* presidente *m/f*; (*US: of company*) director(a) *m/f*, gerente *m/f*.
presidential [prezidən'chəl] *a* presidencial.
press [pres] *n* (*tool, machine, newspapers*) prensa; (*printer's*) imprenta; (*of hand*) apretón *m* ♦ *vt* (*push*) empujar; (*squeeze*) apretar; (*grapes*) pisar; (*clothes: iron*) planchar; (*pressure*) presionar; (*doorbell*) apretar, pulsar, tocar; (*insist*): **to ~ sth on sb** insistir en que uno acepte algo ♦ *vi* (*squeeze*) apretar; (*pressurize*) ejercer presión; **to go to ~** (*newspaper*) entrar en prensa; **to be in the ~** (*being printed*) estar en prensa; (*in the newspapers*) aparecer en la prensa; **we are ~ed for time** tenemos poco tiempo; **to ~ sb to do** *or* **into doing sth** (*urge, entreat*) presionar a uno para que haga algo; **to ~ sb for an answer** insistir a uno para que conteste; **to ~ charges against sb** (*LAW*) formular acusaciones contra. uno.
press on *vi* avanzar; (*hurry*) apretar el paso.
press agency *n* agencia de prensa.
press clipping *n* = **press cutting**.
press conference *n* rueda de prensa.
press cutting *n* recorte *m* (de periódico).
pressing [pres'ing] *a* apremiante.
pressman [pres'mən] *n* (*US*) tipógrafo; (*Brit*) periodista *m*.
press release *n* comunicado de prensa.
press stud *n* (*Brit*) botón *m* de presión.
press-up [pres'up] *n* (*Brit*) plancha.
pressure [presh'ûr] *n* presión *f*; (*urgency*) apremio, urgencia; (*influence*) influencia; **high/low ~** alta/baja presión; **to put ~ on sb** presionar a uno, hacer presión sobre uno.
pressure cooker *n* olla a presión.
pressure gauge *n* manómetro.
pressure group *n* grupo de presión.
pressurize [presh'ərīz] *vt* presurizar; **to ~ sb (into doing sth)** presionar a uno (para que haga algo).
pressurized [presh'ərīzd] *a* (*container*) a presión.
prestige [prestēzh'] *n* prestigio.

prestigious [prestij'əs] *a* prestigioso.
presumably [prizōō'məblē] *ad* es de suponer que, cabe presumir que; **~ he did it** lo más probable es que lo hiciera.
presume [prizōōm'] *vt* presumir, suponer; **to ~ to do** (*dare*) atreverse a hacer.
presumption [prizump'shən] *n* suposición *f*; (*pretension*) presunción *f*.
presumptuous [prizump'chōōəs] *a* presumido.
presuppose [prēsəpōz'] *vt* presuponer.
presupposition [prēsupəzish'ən] *n* presuposición *f*.
pre-tax [prē'taks'] *a* anterior al impuesto.
pretence [pritens'] *n* (*Brit*) = **pretense**.
pretend [pritend'] *vt* (*feign*) fingir ♦ *vi* (*feign*) fingir; (*claim*): **to ~ to sth** pretender a algo.
pretense [pritens'] *n* (*US: claim*) pretensión *f*; (: *pretext*) pretexto; (: *make-believe*) fingimiento; **on** *or* **under the ~ of doing sth** bajo *or* con el pretexto de hacer algo; **she is devoid of all ~** es siempre franca.
pretension [priten'chən] *n* (*claim*) pretensión *f*; **to have no ~s to sth/to being sth** no engañarse en cuanto a algo/a ser algo.
pretentious [priten'chəs] *a* presumido; (*ostentatious*) ostenso, aparatoso.
pretext [prē'tekst] *n* pretexto; **on** *or* **under the ~ of doing sth** so pretexto de hacer algo.
prettily [prit'ilē] *ad* encantadoramente, con gracia.
pretty [prit'ē] *a* (*gen*) bonito, lindo (*LAm*) ♦ *ad* bastante.
prevail [privāl'] *vi* (*gain mastery*) prevalecer; (*be current*) predominar; (*persuade*): **to ~ (up)on sb to do sth** persuadir a uno para que haga algo.
prevailing [privā'ling] *a* (*dominant*) predominante.
prevalent [prev'ələnt] *a* (*dominant*) dominante; (*widespread*) extendido; (*fashionable*) de moda.
prevarication [privarikā'shən] *n* tergiversación *f*, evasivas *fpl*.
prevent [privent'] *vt*: **to ~ (sb) from doing sth** impedir (a uno) hacer algo.
preventable [privent'əbəl] *a* evitable.
preventative [priven'tətiv] *a* preventivo.
prevention [priven'chən] *n* prevención *f*.
preventive [priven'tiv] *a* preventivo.
preview [prē'vyōō] *n* (*of movie*) preestreno.
previous [prē'vēəs] *a* previo, anterior; **he has no ~ experience in that field** no tiene antecedentes en esa rama; **I have a ~ engagement** tengo un compromiso anterior.
previously [prē'vēəslē] *ad* antes.
prewar [prē'wôr'] *a* antes de la guerra.
prey [prā] *n* presa ♦ *vi*: **to ~ on** vivir a costa de; (*feed on*) alimentarse de; **it was ~ing on his mind** le quitaba el sueño.

price [prīs] *n* precio; (*BETTING*: *odds*) puntos *mpl* de ventaja ♦ *vt* (*goods*) fijar el precio de; **to go up** *or* **rise in** ~ subir de precio; **what is the** ~ **of ...?** ¿qué precio tiene ...?; **to put a** ~ **on sth** poner precio a algo; **he regained his freedom, but at a** ~ recobró su libertad, pero le había costado caro; **to be** ~**d out of the market** (*article*) no encontrar comprador por ese precio; (*nation*) no ser competitivo.

price control *n* control *m* de precios.

price-cutting [prīs'kuting] *n* reducción *f* de precios.

priceless [prīs'lis] *a* que no tiene precio; (*col: amusing*) divertidísimo.

price list *n* tarifa.

price range *n* gama de precios; **it's within my** ~ está al alcance de mi bolsillo.

price tag *n* etiqueta.

price war *n* guerra de precios.

pricey [prī'sē] *a* (*Brit col*) caro.

prick [prik] *n* pinchazo; (*with pin*) alfilerazo; (*sting*) picadura ♦ *vt* pinchar; picar; **to** ~ **up one's ears** aguzar el oído.

prickle [prik'əl] *n* (*sensation*) picor *m*; (*BOT*) espina; (*ZOOL*) púa.

prickly [prik'lē] *a* espinoso; (*fig: person*) malhumorado; (: *touchy*) quisquilloso.

prickly heat *n* sarpullido causado por exceso de calor.

prickly pear *n* chumbo.

pride [prīd] *n* orgullo; (*pej*) soberbia ♦ *vt*: **to** ~ **o.s.** enorgullecerse de; **to take (a)** ~ **in** enorgullecerse de; **her** ~ **and joy** su orgullo; **to have** ~ **of place** (*Brit*) tener prioridad.

priest [prēst] *n* sacerdote *m*.

priestess [prēs'tis] *n* sacerdotisa.

priesthood [prēst'hood] *n* (*practice*) sacerdocio; (*priests*) clero.

prig [prig] *n* gazmoño/a.

prim [prim] *a* (*demure*) remilgado; (*prudish*) gazmoño.

prima donna [prē'mə dän'ə] *n* primadonna, diva.

prima facie [prē'mə fā'sē] *a*: **to have a** ~ **case** (*LAW*) tener razón a primera vista.

primarily [prīmär'ilē] *ad* (*above all*) ante todo, primordialmente.

primary [prī'märē] *a* primario; (*first in importance*) principal ♦ *n* (*US: also:* ~ **election**) (elección *f*) primaria.

primary color *n* color *m* primario.

primary education *n* enseñanza primaria.

primary products *npl* productos *mpl* primarios.

primary school *n* (*Brit*) escuela primaria.

primate *n* [prī'mit] (*REL*) primado; [prī'māt] (*ZOOL*) primate *m*.

prime [prīm] *a* primero, principal; (*basic*) fundamental; (*excellent*) selecto, de primera clase ♦ *n*: **in the** ~ **of life** en la flor de la vida ♦ *vt* (*gun, pump*) cebar; (*fig*) preparar.

Prime Minister (PM) *n* primer(a) ministro/a.

primer [prī'mûr] *n* (*book*) texto elemental; (*paint*) pintura de base, imprimación *f*.

prime time *n* (*RADIO, TV*) tiempo preferencial.

primeval [prīmē'vəl] *a* primitivo.

primitive [prim'ətiv] *a* primitivo; (*crude*) rudimentario; (*uncivilized*) inculto.

primly [prim'lē] *ad* remilgadamente; con gazmoñería.

primrose [prim'rōz] *n* primavera, prímula.

primus (stove) [prī'məs (stōv)] ® *n* (*Brit*) hornillo de camping.

prince [prins] *n* príncipe *m*.

prince charming *n* príncipe *m* azul.

princess [prin'sis] *n* princesa.

principal [prin'səpəl] *a* principal, mayor ♦ *n* director(a) *m/f*; (*in play*) protagonista principal *m/f*; (*COMM*) capital *m*, principal *m*.

principality [prinsəpal'itē] *n* principado.

principle [prin'səpəl] *n* principio; **in** ~ en principio; **on** ~ por principio.

print [print] *n* (*impression*) marca, impresión *f*; huella; (*letters*) letra de molde; (*fabric*) estampado; (*ART*) grabado; (*PHOT*) impresión *f* ♦ *vt* (*gen*) imprimir; (*on mind*) grabar; (*write in capitals*) escribir en letras de molde; **out of** ~ agotado.

print out *vt* (*COMPUT*) imprimir.

printed circuit [prin'tid sûr'kit] *n* circuito impreso.

printed circuit board (PCB) *n* tarjeta de circuito impreso (TCI).

printed matter *n* impresos *mpl*.

printer [prin'tûr] *n* (*person*) impresor(a) *m/f*; (*machine*) impresora.

printhead [print'hed] *n* cabeza impresora.

printing [prin'ting] *n* (*art*) imprenta; (*act*) impresión *f*; (*quantity*) tirada.

printing press *n* prensa.

print-out [print'out] *n* (*COMPUT*) printout *m*.

print shop *n* imprenta.

print wheel *n* rueda impresora.

prior [prī'ûr] *a* anterior, previo ♦ *n* prior *m*; ~ **to doing** antes de *or* hasta hacer; **without** ~ **notice** sin previo aviso; **to have a** ~ **claim to sth** tener prioridad en algo.

prioress [prī'ûris] *n* priora.

priority [prīôr'itē] *n* prioridad *f*; **to have** *or* **take** ~ **over sth** tener prioridad sobre algo.

priory [prī'ərē] *n* priorato.

prise [prīz] *vt* (*Brit*) = **prize**.

prism [priz'əm] *n* prisma *m*.

prison [priz'ən] *n* cárcel *f*, prisión *f* ♦ *cpd* carcelario.

prison camp *n* campamento para prisioneros.

prisoner [priz'ənûr] *n* (*in prison*) preso/a;

(*under arrest*) detenido/a; (*in dock*) acusado/a; **the ~ at the bar** el/la acusado/a; **to take sb ~** hacer *or* tomar prisionero a uno.

prisoner of war *n* prisionero/a *or* preso/a de guerra.

prison warden *n* (*US*) director(a) *m/f* de prisión.

prissy [pris'ē] *a* remilgado.

pristine [pris'tēn] *a* pristino.

privacy [prī'vəsē] *n* (*seclusion*) soledad *f*; (*intimacy*) intimidad *f*; **in the strictest ~** de máxima confianza.

private [prī'vit] *a* (*personal*) particular; (*confidential*) secreto, confidencial; (*intimate*) privado, íntimo; (*sitting etc*) a puertas cerradas ♦ *n* soldado raso; "~" (*on envelope*) "confidencial"; (*on door*) "privado"; **in ~** en privado; **in (his) ~ life** en su vida privada; **to be in ~ practice** tener consultorio particular.

private enterprise *n* la empresa privada.

private eye *n* detective *m/f* privado/a.

private hearing *n* (*LAW*) vista a puertas cerradas.

private limited company *n* (*Brit*) sociedad *f* de responsabilidad limitada.

privately [prī'vitlē] *ad* en privado; (*in o.s.*) en secreto.

private parts *npl* partes *fpl* privadas *or* pudendas.

private practice *n*: **to be in ~** ser médico/a (*or* dentista *m/f*) particular.

private property *n* propiedad *f* privada.

private school *n* colegio privado.

privation [prīvā'shən] *n* (*state*) privación *f*; (*hardship*) privación *f*, estrechez *f*.

privatize [prī'vətīz] *vt* privatizar.

privet [priv'it] *n* alheña.

privilege [priv'əlij] *n* privilegio; (*prerogative*) prerrogativa.

privileged [priv'əlijd] *a* privilegiado; **to be ~ to do sth** gozar del privilegio de hacer algo.

privy [priv'ē] *a*: **to be ~ to** estar enterado de.

privy council *n* consejo del estado.

prize [prīz] *n* premio ♦ *a* (*first class*) de primera clase ♦ *vt* apreciar, estimar; **to ~ open** abrir con palanca.

prize fighter *n* boxeador *m* profesional.

prize fighting *n* boxeo *m* profesional.

prize-giving [prīz'giving] *n* distribución *f* de premios.

prize money *n* (*SPORT*) bolsa.

prizewinner [prīz'winûr] *n* premiado/a.

prizewinning [prīz'wining] *a* (*novel, essay*) premiado.

PRO *n abbr* = **public relations officer.**

pro [prō] *n* (*SPORT*) profesional *m/f*; **the ~s and cons** los pros y los contras.

pro- [prō] *pref* (*in favor of*) pro, en pro de; **~Soviet** pro-soviético.

probability [prâbəbil'ətē] *n* probabilidad *f*; **in all ~** lo más probable.

probable [prâb'əbəl] *a* probable; **it is ~/ hardly ~ that** es probable/poco probable que.

probably [prâb'əblē] *ad* probablemente.

probate [prō'bāt] *n* (*LAW*) legalización *f* de un testamento.

probation [prəbā'shən] *n*: **on ~** (*employee*) a prueba; (*LAW*) en libertad condicional.

probationary [prəbā'shənärē] *a*: **~ period** período de prueba.

probationer [prəbā'shənûr] *n* (*LAW*) persona en libertad condicional; (*nurse*) ≈ aprendiz *m/f* de ATS (*Sp*), aprendiz de enfermero.

probation officer *n* oficial a cargo de los presos en libertad condicional.

probe [prōb] *n* (*MED, SPACE*) sonda; (*enquiry*) encuesta, investigación *f* ♦ *vt* sondar; (*investigate*) investigar.

probity [prō'bitē] *n* probidad *f*.

problem [prâb'ləm] *n* problema *m*; **what's the ~?** ¿cuál es el problema?, ¿qué pasa?; **no ~!** ¡por supuesto!; **to have ~s with the car** tener problemas con el coche.

problematic(al) [prâbləmət'ik(əl)] *a* problemático.

procedural [prəsē'jûrəl] *a* de procedimiento; (*LAW*) procesal.

procedure [prəsē'jûr] *n* procedimiento; (*bureaucratic*) trámites *mpl*; **cashing a check is a simple ~** cobrar un cheque es un trámite sencillo.

proceed [prəsēd'] *vi* proceder; (*continue*): **to ~ (with)** continuar *or* seguir (con); **to ~ against sb** (*LAW*) proceder contra uno; **I am not sure how to ~** no sé cómo proceder; *see also* **proceeds.**

proceedings [prəsē'dingz] *npl* acto *sg*, actos *mpl*; (*LAW*) proceso *sg*; (*meeting*) función *fsg*; (*records*) actas *fpl*.

proceeds [prō'sēds] *npl* ganancias *fpl*, ingresos *mpl*.

process [prâs'es] *n* proceso; (*method*) método, sistema *m*; (*proceeding*) procedimiento ♦ *vt* tratar, elaborar ♦ *vi* [prâses'] (*Brit formal*: *go in procession*) desfilar; **in ~** en curso; **we are in the ~ of moving to ...** estamos en vías de mudarnos a ....

process cheese [prâs'es chēz'], (*Brit*) **processed cheese** *n* queso procesado.

processing [prâs'esing] *n* elaboración *f*.

procession [prəsesh'ən] *n* desfile *m*; **funeral ~** cortejo fúnebre.

proclaim [prəklām'] *vt* proclamar; (*announce*) anunciar.

proclamation [prâkləmā'shən] *n* proclamación *f*; (*written*) proclama.

proclivity [prōkliv'ətē] *n* propensión *f*, inclinación *f*.

procrastinate [prōkras'tənāt] *vi* demorarse.

procrastination [prōkrastənā'shən] *n* dilación *f*.

procreation [prōkrēā'shən] *n* procreación *f*.

proctor [prâk'tûr] (*US*) *n* celador(a) *m/f* ♦ *vt*, *vi* vigilar.

procure [prəkyōōr'] *vt* conseguir, obtener.

procurement [prəkyōōr'mənt] *n* obtención *f*.

prod [prâd] *vt* (*push*) empujar; (*with elbow*) dar un codazo a ♦ *n* empuje *m*; codazo.

prodigal [prâd'əgəl] *a* pródigo.

prodigious [prədij'əs] *a* prodigioso.

prodigy [prâd'əjē] *n* prodigio.

produce *n* [prō'dōōs] (*AGR*) productos *mpl* agrícolas ♦ *vt* [prədōōs'] producir; (*yield*) rendir; (*bring*) sacar; (*show*) presentar, mostrar; (*proof of identity*) enseñar, presentar; (*THEATER*) presentar, poner en escena; (*offspring*) dar a luz.

produce dealer *n* (*US*) verdulero/a.

producer [prədōō'sûr] *n* (*THEATER*) director(a) *m/f*; (*AGR*, *CINEMA*) productor(a) *m/f*.

product [prâd'əkt] *n* producto.

production [prəduk'shən] *n* (*act*) producción *f*; (*THEATER*) representación *f*, obra; **to put into** ~ lanzar a la producción.

production agreement *n* (*US*) acuerdo de productividad.

production control *n* control *m* de producción.

production line *n* línea de producción.

production manager *n* jefe/jefa *m/f* de producción.

productive [prəduk'tiv] *a* productivo.

productivity [prâdəktiv'ətē] *n* productividad *f*.

productivity agreement *n* (*Brit*) acuerdo de productividad.

productivity bonus *n* bono de productividad.

Prof. [prâf] *abbr* (= *professor*) Prof.

profane [prəfān'] *a* profano.

profess [prəfes'] *vt* profesar; **I do not** ~ **to be an expert** no pretendo ser experto.

professed [prəfest'] *a* (*self-declared*) declarado.

profession [prəfesh'ən] *n* profesión *f*.

professional [prəfesh'ənəl] *n* profesional *m/f* ♦ *a* profesional; (*by profession*) de profesión; **to seek** ~ **advice** buscar un consejo profesional.

professionalism [prəfesh'ənəlizəm] *n* profesionalismo.

professionally [prəfesh'ənəlē] *ad*: **I only know him** ~ sólo le conozco por nuestra relación de trabajo.

professor [prəfes'ûr] *n* (*US*) profesor(a) *m/f*; (*Brit*) catedrático/a.

professorship [prəfes'ûrship] *n* cátedra.

proffer [prâf'ûr] *vt* ofrecer.

proficiency [prəfish'ənsē] *n* capacidad *f*, habilidad *f*.

proficiency test *n* prueba de capacitación.

proficient [prəfish'ənt] *a* experto, hábil.

profile [prō'fīl] *n* perfil *m*; **to keep a high/ low** ~ tratar de llamar la atención/pasar inadvertido.

profit [prâf'it] *n* (*COMM*) ganancia; (*fig*) provecho ♦ *vi*: **to** ~ **by** *or* **from** aprovechar *or* sacar provecho de; ~ **and loss statement** cuenta de ganancias y pérdidas; **to sell sth at a** ~ vender algo con ganancia.

profitability [prâfitəbil'ətē] *n* rentabilidad *f*.

profitable [prâf'itəbəl] *a* (*ECON*) rentable; (*beneficial*) provechoso, útil.

profitably [prâf'itəblē] *ad* rentablemente; provechosamente.

profit center *n* centro de beneficios.

profiteering [prâfitēr'ing] *n* (*pej*) explotación *f*.

profit-making [prâf'itmāking] *a* rentable.

profit margin *n* margen *m* de ganancia.

profit sharing [prâf'it shä'ring] *n* participación *f* de empleados en los beneficios.

profits tax *n* impuesto sobre los beneficios.

profligate [prâf'ləgit] *a* (*dissolute: behavior, act*) disoluto; (*: person*) libertino; (*extravagant*): **he's very** ~ **with his money** es muy derrochador.

pro forma [prō fôr'mə] *a*: ~ **invoice** factura pro-forma.

profound [prəfound'] *a* profundo.

profoundly [prəfound'lē] *ad* profundamente.

profusely [prəfyōōs'lē] *ad* profusamente.

profusion [prəfyōō'zhən] *n* profusión *f*, abundancia.

progeny [prâj'ənē] *n* progenie *f*.

program (*US*) *n* [prō'grəm] programa *m* ♦ *vt* [prō'gram] programar.

programer [prō'gramûr] *n* programador(a) *m/f*.

programing [prō'graming] *n* programación *f*.

programing language *n* lenguaje *m* de programación.

programme [prō'gram] *etc* (*Brit*) = **program** *etc*.

progress *n* [prâg'res] progreso; (*development*) desarrollo ♦ *vi* [prəgres'] progresar, avanzar; desarrollarse; **in** ~ (*meeting, work etc*) en curso; **as the match** ~**ed** en el curso del partido.

progression [prəgresh'ən] *n* progresión *f*.

progressive [prəgres'iv] *a* progresivo; (*person*) progresista.

progressively [prəgres'ivlē] *ad* progresivamente, poco a poco.

progress report *n* (*MED*) informe *m* sobre el estado; (*ADMIN*) informe *m* sobre el progreso.

prohibit [prōhib'it] *vt* prohibir; **to** ~ **sb from doing sth** prohibir a uno hacer algo; **"smoking** ~**ed"** "prohibido fumar".

prohibition [prōəbish'ən] *n* (*US*) prohibición *f*.

prohibitive [prōhib'ətiv] *a* (*price etc*) prohibitivo.

project *n* [práj'ekt] proyecto; (*SCOL. UNIV*: *research*) trabajo, proyecto ♦ (*vb*: [prəjekt']) *vt* proyectar ♦ *vi* (*stick out*) salir, sobresalir.

projectile [prəjek'təl] *n* proyectil *m*.

projection [prəjek'shən] *n* proyección *f*; (*overhang*) saliente *m*.

projectionist [prəjek'shənist] *n* (*CINE*) operador(a) *m/f* de cine.

projection room *n* (*CINE*) cabina de proyección.

projector [prəjek'tûr] *n* proyector *m*.

proletarian [prōlitär'ēən] *a* proletario.

proletariat [prōlitär'ēət] *n* proletariado.

proliferate [prōlif'ərāt] *vi* proliferar, multiplicarse.

proliferation [prōlifərā'shən] *n* proliferación *f*.

prolific [prōlif'ik] *a* prolífico.

prolog(ue) [prō'lôg] *n* prólogo.

prolong [prəlông'] *vt* prolongar, extender.

prom [prám] *n abbr* = **promenade**; (*Brit*) **promenade concert** ♦ *n* (*US*: *ball*) baile *m* de gala.

promenade [prámənād'] *n* (*by sea*) paseo marítimo ♦ *vi* (*stroll*) pasearse.

promenade concert *n* (*Brit*) concierto (en que parte del público permanece de pie).

promenade deck *n* cubierta de paseo.

prominence [prám'ənəns] *n* (*fig*) importancia.

prominent [prám'ənənt] *a* (*standing out*) saliente; (*important*) eminente, importante; **he is ~ in the field of** ... tiene fama en el campo de ....

prominently [prám'ənəntlē] *ad* (*display, set*) muy a la vista; **he figured ~ in the case** desempeñó un papel importante en el juicio.

promiscuity [prámiskyōō'itē] *n* promiscuidad *f*.

promiscuous [prəmis'kyōōəs] *a* (*sexually*) promiscuo.

promise [prám'is] *n* promesa ♦ *vt*, *vi* prometer; **to make sb a ~** prometer algo a uno; **a young man of ~** un joven con futuro; **to ~ (sb) to do sth** prometer (a uno) hacer algo; **to ~ well** ser muy prometedor.

promising [prám'ising] *a* prometedor(a).

promissory note [prám'isôrē nōt] *n* pagaré *m*.

promontory [prám'əntôrē] *n* promontorio.

promote [prəmōt'] *vt* promover; (*new product*) dar publicidad a, lanzar; (*MIL*) ascender; **the team was ~d to the second division** (*Brit SOCCER*) el equipo fue ascendido a la segunda división.

promoter [prəmō'tûr] *n* (*of sporting event*) promotor(a) *m/f*; (*of company, business*) patrocinador(a) *m/f*.

promotion [prəmō'shən] *n* (*gen*) promoción *f*; (*MIL*) ascenso.

prompt [prámpt] *a* pronto ♦ *ad*: **at 6 o'clock ~** a las seis en punto ♦ *n* (*COMPUT*) aviso, guía ♦ *vt* (*urge*) mover, incitar; (*THEATER*) apuntar; **to ~ sb to do sth** instar a uno a hacer algo; **to be ~ to do sth** no tardar en hacer algo; **they're very ~** (*punctual*) son muy puntuales.

prompter [prámp'tûr] *n* (*THEATER*) apuntador(a) *m/f*.

promptly [prámpt'lē] *ad* (*punctually*) puntualmente; (*rapidly*) rápidamente.

promptness [prámpt'nis] *n* puntualidad *f*; rapidez *f*.

promulgate [prám'əlgāt] *vt* promulgar.

prone [prōn] *a* (*lying*) postrado; **~ to** propenso a.

prong [prông] *n* diente *m*, punta.

pronoun [prō'noun] *n* pronombre *m*.

pronounce [prənouns'] *vt* pronunciar; (*declare*) declarar ♦ *vi*: **to ~ (up)on** pronunciarse sobre; **they ~d him unfit to drive** le declararon incapaz de conducir.

pronounced [prənounst'] *a* (*marked*) marcado.

pronouncement [prənouns'mənt] *n* declaración *f*.

pronunciation [prənunsēā'shən] *n* pronunciación *f*.

proof [prōōf] *n* prueba; **35° ~** graduación *f* del 35 por 100 ♦ *a*: **~ against** a prueba de.

proofreader [prōōf'rēdûr] *n* corrector(a) *m/f* de pruebas.

Prop. *abbr* (*COMM*) = **proprietor**.

prop [práp] *n* apoyo; (*fig*) sostén *m* ♦ *vt* (*also*: **~ up**) apoyar; (*lean*): **to ~ sth against** apoyar algo contra.

propaganda [prápəgan'də] *n* propaganda.

propagate [práp'əgāt] *vt* propagar.

propagation [prápəgā'shən] *n* propagación *f*.

propel [prəpel'] *vt* impulsar, propulsar.

propeller [prəpel'ûr] *n* hélice *f*.

propensity [prəpen'sitē] *n* propensión *f*.

proper [práp'ûr] *a* (*suited, right*) propio; (*exact*) justo; (*apt*) apropiado, conveniente; (*timely*) oportuno; (*seemly*) correcto, decente; (*authentic*) verdadero; (*col: real*) auténtico; **to go through the ~ channels** (*ADMIN*) ir por la vía oficial.

properly [práp'ûrlē] *ad* (*adequately*) correctamente; (*decently*) decentemente.

proper noun *n* nombre *m* propio.

properties [práp'ûrtēz] *npl* (*THEATER*) accesorios *mpl*.

property [práp'ûrtē] *n* propiedad *f*; (*estate*) finca; **lost ~** objetos *mpl* perdidos; **personal ~** bienes *mpl* muebles.

property developer *n* promotor(a) *m/f* de construcciones.

property owner *n* dueño/a de propiedades.

property tax *n* impuesto sobre la propiedad.

prophecy [práf'isē] *n* profecía.

prophesy [práf'isī] *vt* profetizar; *(fig)* predecir.

prophet [práf'it] *n* profeta *m/f*.

prophetic [prəfet'ik] *a* profético.

prophylactic [prōfəlak'tik] *n* preservativo.

proportion [prəpôr'shən] *n* proporción *f*; *(share)* parte *f*; **to be in/out of ~ to** *or* **with sth** estar en/no guardar proporción con algo; **to see sth in ~** *(fig)* ver algo en su justa medida.

proportional [prəpôr'shənəl] *a* proporcional.

proportionally [prəpôr'shənəlē] *ad* proporcionalmente, en proporción.

proportional representation (PR) *n* *(POL)* representación *f* proporcional.

proportional spacing *n* *(on printer)* espaciado proporcional.

proportionate [prəpôr'shənit] *a* proporcionado.

proportionately [prəpôr'shənitlē] *ad* proporcionadamente, en proporción.

proportioned [prəpôr'shənd] *a* proporcionado.

proposal [prəpō'zəl] *n* propuesta; *(offer of marriage)* oferta de matrimonio; *(plan)* proyecto; *(suggestion)* sugerencia.

propose [prəpōz'] *vt* proponer; *(have in mind)*: **to ~ sth/to do** *or* **doing sth** proponer algo/proponerse a hacer algo ♦ *vi* declararse.

proposer [prəpō'zûr] *n* *(of motion)* proponente *m/f*.

proposition [prápəzish'ən] *n* propuesta, proposición *f*; **to make sb a ~** proponer algo a uno.

propound [prəpound'] *vt* *(theory)* exponer.

proprietary [prəprī'itârē] *a* *(COMM)*: **~ article** artículo de marca; **~ brand** marca comercial.

proprietor [prəprī'ətûr] *n* propietario/a, dueño/a.

propriety [prəprī'ətē] *n* decoro.

propulsion [prəpul'shən] *n* propulsión *f*.

pro rata [prō ra'tə] *ad* a prorrata.

prosaic [prōzā'ik] *a* prosaico.

Pros. Atty. *abbr* *(US)* = *prosecuting attorney*.

proscribe [prōskrīb'] *vt* proscribir.

prose [prōz] *n* prosa; *(Brit SCOL)* traducción *f* inversa.

prosecute [prás'əkyōōt] *vt* *(LAW)* procesar; **"trespassers will be ~d"** *(LAW)* ''se procesará a los intrusos''.

prosecution [prásəkyōō'shən] *n* proceso, causa; *(accusing side)* acusación *f*.

prosecutor [prás'əkyōōtûr] *n* acusador(a) *m/f*; *(also:* **public ~)** fiscal *m*.

prospect *n* [prás'pekt] *(view)* vista; *(chance)* posibilidad *f*; *(outlook)* perspecti-

va; *(hope)* esperanza ♦ *(vb:* [práspekt']) *vt* explorar ♦ *vi* buscar; **~s** *npl* *(for work etc)* perspectivas *fpl*; **to be faced with the ~ of** tener que enfrentarse a la posibilidad de que ...; **we were faced with the ~ of leaving early** se nos planteó la posibilidad de marcharnos pronto; **there is every ~ of an early victory** hay buenas perspectivas de una pronta victoria.

prospecting [prás'pekting] *n* prospección *f*.

prospective [prəspek'tiv] *a* *(possible)* probable, eventual; *(certain)* futuro; *(buyer)* presunto; *(legislation, son-in-law)* futuro.

prospector [prás'pektûr] *n* explorador(a) *m/f*; **gold ~** buscador *m* de oro.

prospectus [prəspek'təs] *n* prospecto.

prosper [prás'pûr] *vi* prosperar.

prosperity [práspär'itē] *n* prosperidad *f*.

prosperous [prás'pûrəs] *a* próspero.

prostate [prás'tāt] *n* *(also:* **~ gland)** próstata.

prostitute [prás'titōōt] *n* prostituta; **male ~** prostituto.

prostitution [prástitōō'shən] *n* prostitución *f*.

prostrate [prás'trāt] *a* postrado; *(fig)* abatido ♦ *vt*: **to ~ o.s.** *(before sb)* prosternarse; *(on the floor, fig)* prostrarse.

protagonist [prōtag'ənist] *n* protagonista *m/f*.

protect [prətekt'] *vt* proteger.

protection [prətek'shən] *n* protección *f*; **to be under sb's ~** estar amparado por uno.

protectionism [prətek'shənizəm] *n* proteccionismo.

protection racket *n* chantaje *m*.

protective [prətek'tiv] *a* protector(a); **~ cream** crema protectora; **~ custody** *(LAW)* detención *f* preventiva.

protector [prətek'tûr] *n* protector(a) *m/f*.

protégé [prō'təzhā'] *n* protegido/a.

protein [prō'tēn] *n* proteína.

pro tem [prō tem] *ad abbr* (= *pro tempore: for the time being)* provisionalmente.

protest *n* [prō'test] protesta ♦ *(vb:* [prōtest']) *vi* protestar ♦ *vt* *(affirm)* afirmar, declarar; **to do sth under ~** hacer algo bajo protesta; **to ~ against/about** protestar en contra de/por.

Protestant [prát'istənt] *a*, *n* protestante *m/f*.

protester, protestor [prətes'tûr] *n* *(in demonstration)* manifestante *m/f*.

protest march *n* manifestación *f* *or* marcha (de protesta).

protocol [prō'təkôl] *n* protocolo.

prototype [prō'tətīp] *n* prototipo.

protracted [prōtrak'tid] *a* prolongado.

protractor [prōtrak'tûr] *n* *(GEOM)* transportador *m*.

protrude [prōtrōōd'] *vi* salir, sobresalir.

protuberance [prōtōō'bûrəns] *n* protuberancia.

proud [proud] *a* orgulloso; *(pej)* soberbio,

altanero ♦ *ad*: **to do sb** ~ tratar a uno a
cuerpo de rey; **to do o.s.** ~ no privarse de
nada; **to be** ~ **to do sth** estar orgulloso de
hacer algo.
proudly [proud'lē] *ad* orgullosamente, con
orgullo; (*pej*) con soberbia, con altanería.
prove [proov'] *vt* probar; (*verify*) comprobar; (*show*) demostrar ♦ *vi*: **to** ~ **correct**
resultar correcto; **to** ~ **o.s.** ponerse a
prueba; **he was** ~**d right in the end** al
final *or* por fin se le dio la razón.
proverb [prǎv'ûrb] *n* refrán *m*.
proverbial [prəvûr'bēəl] *a* proverbial.
proverbially [prəvûr'bēəlē] *ad* pro-
verbialmente.
provide [prəvīd'] *vt* proporcionar, dar; **to** ~
sb with sth proveer a uno de algo; **to be**
~**d with** ser provisto de.
provide for *vt fus* (*person*) mantener a;
(*problem etc*) tener en cuenta.
provided [prəvī'did] *conj*: ~ (**that**) con tal
de que, a condición de que.
Providence [prǎv'idəns] *n* Divina Providencia.
providing [prəvī'ding] *conj* a condición de
que, con tal de que.
province [prǎv'ins] *n* provincia; (*fig*) esfera.
provincial [prəvin'chəl] *a* provincial; (*pej*)
provinciano.
provision [prəvizh'ən] *n* provisión *f*;
(*supply*) suministro, abastecimiento; ~**s**
npl provisiones *fpl*, víveres *mpl*; **to make**
~ **for** (*one's family, future*) atender las necesidades de.
provisional [prəvizh'ənəl] *a* provisional;
(*temporary*) interino ♦ *n*: **P~** (*Irish POL*)
Provisional *m* (*miembro de la tendencia
activista del IRA*).
provisional licence *n* (*Brit AUT*) carnet
m (de conducir) provisional.
proviso [prəvī'zō] *n* condición *f*, estipulación
f; **with the** ~ **that** a condición de que.
Provo [prō'vō] *n abbr* (*Irish POL*) = **Provisional**.
provocation [prǎvəkā'shən] *n* provocación
f.
provocative [prəvǎk'ətiv] *a* provocativo.
provoke [prəvōk'] *vt* (*arouse*) provocar,
incitar; (*cause*) causar, producir; (*anger*)
enojar; **to** ~ **sb to sth/to do** *or* **into doing**
sth provocar a uno a algo/a hacer algo.
provoking [prəvōk'ing] *a* provocador(a).
provost [prǎv'əst] *n* (*of university*)
rector(a) *m/f*; (*Scottish*) alcalde(sa) *m/f*.
prow [prou] *n* proa.
prowess [prou'is] *n* (*skill*) destreza, habilidad *f*; (*courage*) valor *m*; **his** ~ **as a football player** (*skill*) su habilidad como
futbolista.
prowl [proul] *vi* (*also*: ~ **about**, ~ **around**)
merodear ♦ *n*: **on the** ~ de merodeo, mero-
deando.
prowler [prou'lûr] *n* merodeador(a) *m/f*.

proximity [prǎksim'itē] *n* proximidad *f*.
proxy [prǎk'sē] *n* poder *m*; (*person*)
apoderado/a; **by** ~ por poderes.
prude [prood] *n* gazmoño/a, mojigato/a.
prudence [prood'əns] *n* prudencia.
prudent [prood'ənt] *a* prudente.
prudently [prood'əntlē] *ad* prudentemente,
con prudencia.
prudish [prood'ish] *a* gazmoño.
prudishness [prood'ishnis] *n* gazmoñería,
ñoñería.
prune [proon] *n* ciruela pasa ♦ *vt* podar.
pruning shears [proon'ing shirz] *npl* podadera *sg*.
pry [prī] *vi*: **to** ~ **into** entrometerse en.
PS *abbr* (= *postscript*) P.D.
psalm [sǎm] *n* salmo.
PSAT *n abbr* (*US*) = *Preliminary Scholastic
Aptitude Test*.
pseudo... [soo'dō] *pref* seudo....
pseudonym [soo'dənim] *n* seudónimo.
PST *n abbr* (*US*: = *Pacific Standard Time*)
hora de invierno del Pacífico.
psyche [sī'kē] *n* psique *f*.
psychiatric [sīkēat'rik] *a* psiquiátrico.
psychiatrist [sikī'ətrist] *n* psiquiatra *m/f*.
psychiatry [sikī'ətrē] *n* psiquiatría.
psychic [sī'kik] *a* (*also*: ~**al**) psíquico.
psychoanalyze [sīkōan'əlīz] *vt* psicoanali-
zar.
psychoanalysis, *pl* **psychoanalyses**
[sīkōənal'isis, -sēz] *n* psicoanálisis *m inv*.
psychoanalyst [sīkōan'əlist] *n* psicoanalista
m/f.
psychological [sīkəlǎj'ikəl] *a* psicológico.
psychologically [sīkəlǎj'iklē] *ad* psicológi-
camente.
psychologist [sīkǎl'əjist] *n* psicólogo/a.
psychology [sīkǎl'əjē] *n* psicología.
psychopath [sī'kəpath] *n* psicópata *m/f*.
psychosis, *pl* **psychoses** [sīkō'sis, -sēz] *n*
psicosis *f inv*.
psychosomatic [sīkōsōmat'ik] *a* psicoso-
mático.
psychotherapy [sīkōthär'əpē] *n* psicoterapia.
psychotic [sīkǎt'ik] *a*, *n* psicótico/a.
PT *n abbr* (*Brit*: = *Physical Training*) Ed.
Fís.
pt *abbr* = **pint(s), point(s)**.
PTA *n abbr* = *Parent-Teacher Association*)
≈ Asociación *f* de Padres de Alumnos.
PTO *abbr* (= *please turn over*) sigue.
PTV *n abbr* (*US*) = *pay television, public
television*.
pub [pub] *n* (*Brit*) pub *m*, taberna.
puberty [pyoo'bûrtē] *n* pubertad *f*.
pubic [pyoo'bik] *a* púbico.
public [pub'lik] *a*, *n* público; **in** ~ en público; **to make sth** ~ revelar *or* anunciar
algo; **to be** ~ **knowledge** ser del dominio
público; **to go** ~ (*COMM*) proceder a la
venta pública de acciones.

public address system (PA) *n* megafonía, sistema *m* de altavoces.
publican [pub'likən] *n* (*Brit*) tabernero/a.
publication [publikā'shən] *n* publicación *f*.
public company *n* sociedad *f* anónima.
public convenience *n* (*Brit*) aseos *mpl* públicos, sanitarios *mpl* (*LAm*).
public holiday *n* (*Brit*) día *m* de fiesta, (día) feriado (*LAm*).
public house *n* (*Brit*) bar *m*, pub *m*.
public housing unit (*US*) *n* vivienda *municipal de alquiler*.
publicity [publis'ətē] *n* publicidad *f*.
publicize [pub'ləsīz] *vt* publicitar; (*advertise*) hacer propaganda para.
public limited company (plc) *n* sociedad *f* anónima (S.A.).
publicly [pub'liklē] *ad* públicamente, en público.
public opinion *n* opinión *f* pública.
public ownership *n* propiedad *f* pública; **to be taken into** ~ ser nacionalizado.
Public Prosecutor *n* Fiscal *m* del Estado.
public relations (PR) *n* relaciones *fpl* públicas.
public relations officer *n* encargado/a de relaciones públicas.
public school *n* (*US*) escuela pública; (*Brit*) colegio privado.
public sector *n* sector *m* público.
public service vehicle *n* (*Brit*) vehículo de servicio público.
public-spirited [pub'likspir'itid] *a* cívico.
public transport *n* (*Brit*) = **public transportation**.
public transportation *n* (*US*) transporte *m* público.
public utility *n* servicio público.
public works *npl* obras *fpl* públicas.
publish [pub'lish] *vt* publicar.
publisher [pub'lishûr] *n* (*person*) editor(a) *m/f*; (*firm*) editorial *f*.
publishing [pub'lishing] *n* (*industry*) industria del libro.
publishing company *n* (casa) editorial *f*.
puce [pyoos] *a* de color pardo rojizo.
puck [puk] *n* (*ICE HOCKEY*) puck *m*.
pucker [puk'ûr] *vt* (*pleat*) arrugar; (*brow etc*) fruncir.
pudding [pood'ing] *n* pudín *m*; **rice** ~ arroz *m* con leche.
puddle [pud'əl] *n* charco.
pudgy [puj'ē] *a* gordinflón/ona.
puerile [pyoo'ûrəl] *a* pueril.
Puerto Rican [pwär'tō rē'kən] *a*, *n* puertorriqueño/a *m/f*.
Puerto Rico [pwär'tō rē'kō] *n* Puerto Rico.
puff [puf] *n* soplo; (*of smoke*) bocanada; (*of breathing, engine*) resoplido; (*powder* ~) borla ♦ *vt*: **to** ~ **one's pipe** dar chupadas a la pipa; (*also*: ~ **out**: *sails, cheeks*) hinchar, inflar (*LAm*) ♦ *vi* (*gen*) soplar; (*pant*) jadear; **to** ~ **out smoke** echar

humo.
puffed [puft] *a* (*col*: *out of breath*) sin aliento.
puffin [puf'in] *n* frailecillo.
puff paste, (*Brit*) **puff pastry** *n* hojaldre *m*.
puffy [puf'ē] *a* hinchado.
pull [pool] *n* (*tug*): **to give sth a** ~ dar un tirón a algo; (*fig*: *advantage*) ventaja; (: *influence*) influencia ♦ *vt* tirar de; (*haul*) tirar, arrastrar; (*strain*): **to** ~ **a muscle** sufrir un tirón ♦ *vi* tirar; **to** ~ **to pieces** hacer pedazos; **to** ~ **one's punches** andarse con rodeos; **to** ~ **one's weight** hacer su parte; **to** ~ **o.s. together** tranquilizarse; **to** ~ **sb's leg** tomar el pelo a uno; **to** ~ **strings (for sb)** enchufar (a uno).
pull apart *vt* (*take apart*) desmontar.
pull around *vt* (*handle roughly*: *object*) manosear; (: *person*) maltratar.
pull down *vt* (*house*) derribar.
pull in *vi* (*AUT*: *at the curb*) parar (junto a la acera); (*RAIL*) llegar.
pull off *vt* (*deal etc*) cerrar.
pull out *vi* irse, marcharse; (*AUT*: *from curb*) salir ♦ *vt* sacar, arrancar.
pull over *vi* (*AUT*) hacerse a un lado.
pull through *vi* salvarse; (*MED*) recobrar la salud.
pull up *vi* (*stop*) parar ♦ *vt* (*uproot*) arrancar, desarraigar; (*stop*) parar.
pulley [pool'ē] *n* polea.
Pullman [pool'mən] *n* (*US*) litera.
pull-out [pool'out] *n* suplemento ♦ *cpd* (*pages, magazine*) separable.
pullover [pool'ōvûr] *n* jersey *m*, suéter *m*.
pulp [pulp] *n* (*of fruit*) pulpa; (*for paper*) pasta; (*pej*: *also*: ~ **magazines** *etc*) prensa amarilla; **to reduce sth to** ~ hacer algo papilla.
pulpit [pool'pit] *n* púlpito.
pulsate [pul'sāt] *vi* pulsar, latir.
pulse [puls] *n* (*ANAT*) pulso; (*of music, engine*) pulsación *f*; (*BOT*) legumbre *f*; **to feel** *or* **take sb's** ~ tomar el pulso a uno.
pulverize [pul'vərīz] *vt* pulverizar; (*fig*) hacer polvo.
puma [pyoo'mə] *n* puma.
pumice (stone) [pum'is (stōn)] *n* piedra pómez.
pummel [pum'əl] *vt* aporrear.
pump [pump] *n* bomba; (*shoe*) zapato de tenis ♦ *vt* sacar con una bomba; (*fig*: *col*) (son)sacar; **to** ~ **sb for information** (son)sacarle informes a uno.
pump up *vt* inflar.
pumpkin [pump'kin] *n* calabaza.
pun [pun] *n* juego de palabras.
punch [punch] *n* (*blow*) golpe *m*, puñetazo; (*tool*) punzón *m*; (*for paper*) perforadora; (*for tickets*) taladro; (*drink*) ponche *m* ♦ *vt* (*hit*): **to** ~ **sb/sth** dar un puñetazo *or* golpear a uno/algo; (*make a hole in*)

punzar; perforar.

punch in *vi* (*US*) fichar, picar.

punch out *vi* (*US*) fichar *or* picar la salida.

punch-drunk [punch'drungk] *a* grogui, sonado.

punch(ed) card *n* tarjeta perforada.

punch line *n* (*of joke*) remate *m*.

punch-up [punch'up] *n* (*Brit col*) riña.

punctual [pungk'chōōəl] *a* puntual.

punctuality [pungkchōōal'itē] *n* puntualidad *f*.

punctually [pungk'chōōəlē] *ad*: **it will start ~ at 6** empezará a las 6 en punto.

punctuate [pungk'chōōāt] *vt* puntuar; (*fig*) interrumpir.

punctuation [pungkchōōā'shən] *n* puntuación *f*.

punctuation mark *n* signo de puntuación.

puncture [pungk'chûr] *n* pinchazo ♦ *vt* pinchar; **to have a ~** tener un pinchazo.

pundit [pun'dit] *n* experto/a.

pungent [pun'jənt] *a* acre.

punish [pun'ish] *vt* castigar; **to ~ sb for sth/for doing sth** castigar a uno por algo/ por haber hecho algo.

punishable [pun'ishəbəl] *a* punible, castigable.

punishing [pun'ishing] *a* (*fig: exhausting*) agotador(a).

punishment [pun'ishmənt] *n* castigo; (*fig, col*): **to take a lot of ~** (*boxer*) recibir una paliza; (*car*) ser maltratado.

punitive [pyōō'nətiv] *a* punitivo.

punk [pungk] *n* (*also: ~ rocker*) punki *m/f*; (*also: ~ rock*) música punk; (*US col: hoodlum*) matón *m*.

punt [punt] *n* (*boat*) batea.

puny [pyōō'nē] *a* débil.

pup [pup] *n* cachorro.

pupil [pyōō'pəl] *n* alumno/a.

puppet [pup'it] *n* títere *m*.

puppet government *n* gobierno títere.

puppy [pup'ē] *n* cachorro, perrito.

purchase [pûr'chis] *n* compra; (*grip*) agarre *m*, asidero ♦ *vt* comprar.

purchase order *n* decreto de compra.

purchase price *n* precio de compra.

purchaser [pûr'chisûr] *n* comprador(a) *m/f*.

purchasing power [pûr'chising pouûr] *n* poder *m* adquisitivo.

pure [pyōōr] *a* puro; **a ~ wool jumper** un jersey de pura lana; **it's laziness, ~ and simple** es pura vagancia.

purebred [pyōōr'bred'] *a* de pura sangre.

purée [pyōōrā'] *n* puré *m*.

purely [pyōōr'lē] *ad* puramente.

purgatory [pûr'gətôrē] *n* purgatorio.

purge [pûrj] *n* (*MED*, *POL*) purga ♦ *vt* purgar.

purification [pyōōrəfəkā'shən] *n* purificación *f*, depuración *f*.

purify [pyōōr'əfi] *vt* purificar, depurar.

purist [pyōōr'ist] *n* purista *m/f*.

puritan [pyōōr'itən] *n* puritano/a.

puritanical [pyōōritan'ikəl] *a* puritano.

purity [pyōōr'itē] *n* pureza.

purl [pûrl] *n* punto del revés.

purloin [pûrloin'] *vt* hurtar, robar.

purple [pûr'pəl] *a* purpúreo, morado.

purport [pərpôrt'] *vi*: **to ~ to be/do** dar a entender que es/hace.

purpose [pûr'pəs] *n* propósito; **on ~** a propósito, adrede; **to no ~** para nada, en vano; **for teaching ~s** con fines pedagógicos; **for the ~s of this meeting** para los fines de esta reunión.

purpose-built [pûr'pəsbilt'] *a* (*Brit*) construido especialmente.

purposeful [pûr'pəsfəl] *a* resuelto, determinado.

purposely [pûr'pəslē] *ad* a propósito, adrede.

purr [pûr] *n* ronroneo ♦ *vi* ronronear.

purse [pûrs] *n* (*US*) bolso; (*Brit*) monedero; ♦ *vt* fruncir.

purser [pûr'sûr] *n* (*NAUT*) comisario/a.

purse snatcher [pûrs snach'ûr] *n* (*US*) tironista *m/f*.

pursue [pûrsōō'] *vt* seguir; (*harass*) perseguir; (*profession*) ejercer; (*pleasures*) buscar; (*inquiry, matter*) seguir.

pursuer [pûrsōō'ûr] *n* perseguidor(a) *m/f*.

pursuit [pûrsōōt'] *n* (*chase*) caza; (*of pleasure etc*) busca; (*occupation*) actividad *f*; **in (the) ~ of sth** en busca de algo.

purveyor [pûrvā'ûr] *n* proveedor(a) *m/f*.

pus [pus] *n* pus *m*.

push [pōōsh] *n* empuje *m*, empujón *m*; (*MIL*) ataque *m*; (*drive*) empuje *m* ♦ *vt* empujar; (*button*) apretar; (*promote*) promover; (*fig: press, advance: views*) avanzar; (*thrust*): **to ~ sth (into)** meter algo a la fuerza (en) ♦ *vi* empujar; (*fig*) hacer esfuerzos; **at a ~** (*col*) a duras penas; **she is ~ing 50** (*col*) raya en los 50; **to be ~ed for time/money** andar justo de tiempo/escaso de dinero; **to ~ a door open/shut** abrir/cerrar una puerta empujándola; **to ~ for** (*better pay, conditions*) reivindicar; **"~"** (*on door*) "empujar"; (*on bell*) "pulse".

push aside *vt* apartar con la mano.

push in *vi* colarse.

push off *vi* (*col*) largarse.

push on *vi* (*continue*) seguir adelante.

push through *vt* (*measure*) despachar.

push up *vt* (*total, prices*) hacer subir.

push-button [pōōsh'butən] *a* de mando de botón.

pushchair [pōōsh'chär] *n* (*Brit*) sillita de ruedas.

pusher [pōōsh'ûr] *n* (*drug ~*) traficante *m/f* de drogas.

pushover [pōōsh'ōvûr] *n* (*col*): **it's a ~** está tirado.

push-up [pǒǒsh'up] *n* plancha.
pushy [pǒǒsh'ē] *a* (*pej*) agresivo.
pussycat [pǒǒs'ēkat] *n* minino.
put [pǒǒt], *pt*, *pp* **put** *vt* (*place*) poner, colocar; (*~ into*) meter; (*express, say*) expresar; (*a question*) hacer; (*estimate*) calcular; (*cause to be*): **to ~ sb in a good/bad mood** poner a uno de buen/mal humor; **to ~ a lot of time into sth** dedicar mucho tiempo a algo; **to ~ money on a horse** jugarse dinero a un caballo; **to ~ money into a company** invertir dinero en una compañía; **to ~ sb to a lot of trouble** causar mucha molestia a uno; **we ~ the children to bed** acostamos a los niños; **how shall I ~ it?** ¿cómo puedo explicarlo *or* decirlo?; **to stay ~** no moverse.
  put about *vi* (*NAUT*) virar ♦ *vt* (*rumor*) diseminar.
  put across *vt* (*ideas etc*) comunicar.
  put aside *vt* (*lay down: book etc*) dejar *or* poner a un lado; (*save*) ahorrar; (*in store*) guardar.
  put away *vt* (*store*) guardar.
  put back *vt* (*replace*) devolver a su lugar; (*postpone*) posponer; (*set back: watch, clock*) retrasar; **this will ~ us back 10 years** esto nos retrasará 10 años.
  put down *vt* (*on ground*) poner en el suelo; (*in writing*) apuntar; (*suppress: revolt etc*) sofocar; (*attribute*) atribuir; **~ me down for $15** apúntame por 15 dólares.
  put forward *vt* (*ideas*) presentar, proponer; (*date*) adelantar.
  put in *vt* (*application, complaint*) presentar.
  put in for *vt fus* (*job*) solicitar; (*promotion*) pedir.
  put off *vt* (*postpone*) aplazar; (*discourage*) desanimar.
  put on *vt* (*clothes, lipstick etc*) ponerse; (*light etc*) encender; (*play etc*) presentar; (*weight*) ganar; (*brake*) echar; (*assume: accent, manner*) afectar, fingir; (*airs*) adoptar, darse; (*concert, exhibition etc*) montar; (*extra bus, train etc*) poner; (*col: kid: esp US*) tomar el pelo a; (*inform, indicate*): **to ~ sb on to sb/sth** informar a uno de uno/algo.
  put out *vt* (*fire, light*) apagar; (*one's hand*) alargar; (*news, rumor*) hacer circular; (*tongue etc*) sacar; (*person: inconvenience*) molestar, fastidiar; (*dislocate: shoulder, vertebra, knee*) dislocar(se) ♦ *vi* (*NAUT*): **to ~ out to sea** hacerse a la mar; **to ~ out from New York** salir de Nueva York.
  put through *vt* (*call*) poner; **~ me through to Miss Blair** póngame *or* comuníqueme con (*LAm*) la Señorita Blair.
  put together *vt* unir, reunir; (*assemble: furniture*) armar, montar; (*meal*) confeccionar.
  put up *vt* (*raise*) levantar, alzar; (*hang*) colgar; (*build*) construir; (*increase*) aumentar; (*accommodate*) alojar; (*incite*): **to ~ sb up to doing sth** instar *or* incitar a uno a hacer algo; **to ~ sth up for sale** exponer algo a la venta.
  put upon *vt fus*: **to be ~ upon** (*imposed upon*) dejarse explotar.
  put up with *vt fus* aguantar.
putrid [pyǒǒ'trid] *a* podrido.
putsch [pǒǒch] *n* golpe *m* de estado.
putt [put] *vt* hacer un putt ♦ *n* putt *m*, golpe *m* corto.
putter [put'ûr] *n* putter *m* ♦ *vi* (*US*): **to ~ around** ocuparse en fruslerías; **to ~ around the house** ir de aquí para allá sin hacer nada de provecho.
putting green [put'ing grēn] *n* green *m*, minigolf *m*.
putty [put'ē] *n* masilla.
put-up [pǒǒt'up] *a*: **~ job** (*Brit*) estafa.
puzzle [puz'əl] *n* (*riddle*) acertijo; (*jigsaw*) rompecabezas *m inv*; (*also*: **crossword ~**) crucigrama *m*; (*mystery*) misterio ♦ *vt* dejar perplejo, confundir ♦ *vi*: **to ~ about** quebrar la cabeza por; **to ~ over** (*sb's actions*) quebrarse la cabeza por; (*mystery, problem*) devanarse los sesos sobre; **to be ~d about sth** no llegar a entender algo.
puzzling [puz'ling] *a* (*question*) misterioso, extraño; (*attitude, set of instructions*) extraño.
PVC *n abbr* (= *polyvinyl chloride*) P.V.C. *m*.
PVS *n abbr* (= *post-viral syndrome*) síndrome *m* post-vírico.
Pvt. *abbr* (*US MIL*) = **private.**
PW *n abbr* (*US*) = **prisoner of war.**
pw *abbr* (= *per week*) por semana.
PX *n abbr* (*US*: = *post exchange*) economato militar.
pygmy [pig'mē] *n* pigmeo/a.
pyjamas [pəjâm'əz] *npl* (*Brit*) = **pajamas.**
pylon [pī'lân] *n* torre *f* de conducción eléctrica.
pyramid [pir'əmid] *n* pirámide *f*.
Pyrenean [pirənē'ən] *a* pirenaico.
Pyrenees [pir'ənēz] *npl*: **the ~** los Pirineos.
python [pī'thân] *n* pitón *m*.

Q

Q, q [kyōō] *n* (*letter*) Q, q *f*; **Q for Queen** Q de Quebec.
Qatar [kətâr'] *n* Qatar *m*.
QC *n abbr* (= *Queen's Council*) título conce-

dido a determinados abogados.
QED *abbr* (= *quod erat demonstrandum*)
Q.E.D.
QM *n abbr* = **quartermaster.**
q.t. *n abbr* (*col*: = *quiet*): **on the ~** a hurtadillas.
qty *abbr* (= *quantity*) ctdad.
quack [kwak] *n* (*of duck*) graznido; (*pej*:
doctor) curandero/a, matasanos *m inv* ♦ *vi*
graznar.
quad [kwád] *abbr* = **quadrangle, quadruple,
quadruplet.**
quadrangle [kwâd'ranggəl] *n* (*courtyard*:
abbr: **quad**) patio.
quadruple [kwâdrōō'pəl] *vt, vi* cuadrupli-
car.
quadruplet [kwâdru'plit] *n* cuatrillizo.
quagmire [kwag'mīūr] *n* lodazal *m*, cenegal
m.
quail [kwāl] *n* (*bird*) codorniz *f* ♦ *vi* amedrentarse.
quaint [kwānt] *a* extraño; (*picturesque*)
pintoresco.
quaintly [kwānt'lē] *ad* extrañamente; pinto-
rescamente.
quaintness [kwānt'nis] *n* lo pintoresco, ti-
pismo.
quake [kwāk] *vi* temblar ♦ *n abbr* =
earthquake.
Quaker [kwā'kûr] *n* cuáquero/a.
qualification [kwâləfəkā'shən] *n* (*reservation*) reserva; (*modification*) modificación
f; (*act*) calificación *f*; (*paper* ~) título;
what are your ~s? ¿qué títulos tienes?
qualified [kwâl'əfīd] *a* (*trained*) cualificado;
(*fit*) capacitado; (*limited*) limitado; (*professionally*) titulado; **~ for/to do sth** capacitado para/para hacer algo; **he's not ~ for
the job** no está capacitado para ese trabajo; **it was a ~ success** fue un éxito relativo.
qualify [kwâl'əfī] *vt* (*LING*) calificar a; (*ca-
pacitate*) capacitar; (*modify*) modificar;
(*limit*) moderar ♦ *vi* (*SPORT*) clasificarse;
to ~ (as) calificarse (de), graduarse (en);
to ~ (for) reunir los requisitos (para); **to
~ as an engineer** sacar el título de ingeniero.
qualifying [kwâl'əfīing] *a* (*exam, round*) eliminatorio.
qualitative [kwâl'itātiv] *a* cualitativo.
quality [kwâl'itē] *n* calidad *f*; (*moral*) cualidad *f*; **of good/poor ~** de buena *or* alta/
poca calidad.
quality control *n* control *m* de calidad.
qualm [kwâm] *n* escrúpulo; **to have ~s
about sth** sentir escrúpulos por algo.
quandary [kwán'drē] *n*: **to be in a ~** tener
dudas.
quantitative [kwán'titātiv] *a* cuantitativo.
quantity [kwán'titē] *n* cantidad *f*; **in ~** en
grandes cantidades.
quarantine [kwôr'əntēn] *n* cuarentena.

quarrel [kwôr'əl] *n* riña, pelea ♦ *vi* reñir, pelearse; **to have a ~ with sb** reñir *or* pelearse con uno; **I can't ~ with that** no le
encuentro pegas.
quarrelsome [kwôr'əlsəm] *a* pendenciero.
quarry [kwôr'ē] *n* (*for stone*) cantera; (*animal*) presa.
quart [kwôrt] *n cuarto de galón = 1.136 l.*
quarter [kwôr'tûr] *n* cuarto, cuarta parte *f*;
(*of year*) trimestre *m*; (*district*) barrio;
(*US, Canada*: *25 cents*) cuarto de dólar ♦ *vt*
dividir en cuartos; (*MIL*: *lodge*) alojar; **~s**
npl (*barracks*) cuartel *m*; (*living* ~s) alojamiento *sg*; **a ~ of an hour** un cuarto de
hora; **to pay by the ~** pagar trimestralmente *or* cada 3 meses; **it's a ~ of** *or*
(*Brit*) **to 3** son las 3 menos cuarto; **it's a ~
after** *or* (*Brit*) **past 3** son las 3 y cuarto;
from all ~s de todas partes; **at close ~s**
de cerca.
quarter-deck [kwôr'tûrdek] *n* (*NAUT*) alcázar *m*.
quarter final *n* cuarto de final.
quarterly [kwôr'tûrlē] *a* trimestral ♦ *ad*
cada 3 meses, trimestralmente.
quartermaster [kwôr'tûrmastûr] *n* (*MIL*)
comisario, intendente *m* militar.
quarter note *n* (*US MUS*) negra.
quartet(te) [kwôrtet'] *n* cuarteto.
quarto [kwôr'tō] *n* tamaño holandés ♦ *a* de
tamaño holandés.
quartz [kwôrts] *n* cuarzo.
quash [kwâsh] *vt* (*verdict*) anular.
quasi- [kwā'zi] *pref* cuasi.
quaver [kwā'vûr] *n* (*Brit MUS*) corchea ♦ *vi*
temblar.
quay [kē] *n* (*also*: ~**side**) muelle *m*.
Que. *abbr* (*Canada*) = *Quebec*.
queasiness [kwē'zēnis] *n* malestar *m*, náuseas *fpl*.
queasy [kwē'zē] *a*: **to feel ~** tener náuseas.
Quebec [kwibek'] *n* Quebec *m*.
queen [kwēn] *n* reina; (*CARDS etc*) dama.
queen mother *n* reina madre.
queer [kwēr] *a* (*odd*) raro, extraño ♦ *n* (*pej*:
col) maricón *m*.
quell [kwel] *vt* calmar; (*put down*) sofocar.
quench [kwench] *vt* (*flames*) apagar; **to ~
one's thirst** apagar la sed.
querulous [kwär'ələs] *a* (*person, voice*) quejumbroso.
query [kwiûr'ē] *n* (*question*) pregunta;
(*doubt*) duda ♦ *vt* preguntar; (*disagree
with, dispute*) no estar conforme con, dudar
de.
quest [kwest] *n* busca, búsqueda.
question [kwes'chən] *n* pregunta; (*matter*)
asunto, cuestión *f* ♦ *vt* (*doubt*) dudar de;
(*interrogate*) interrogar, hacer preguntas
a; **to ask sb a ~, put a ~ to sb** hacer
una pregunta a uno; **the ~ is ...** el asunto
es ...; **to bring** *or* **call sth into ~** poner
algo en (tela de) duda; **beyond ~** fuera de

toda duda; **it's out of the** ~ imposible, ni hablar.
questionable [kwes'chənəbəl] *a* discutible; (*doubtful*) dudoso.
questioner [kwes'chənûr] *n* interrogador(a) *m/f*.
questioning [kwes'chəning] *a* interrogativo ♦ *n* preguntas *fpl*; (*by police etc*) interrogatorio.
question mark *n* punto de interrogación.
questionnaire [kweschənâr'] *n* cuestionario.
queue [kyōō] *n* cola ♦ *vi* hacer cola; **to jump the** ~ salirse de su turno, colarse.
quibble [kwib'əl] *vi* sutilizar.
quick [kwik] *a* rápido; (*temper*) vivo; (*agile*) ágil; (*mind*) listo; (*eye*) agudo; (*ear*) fino ♦ *n*: **cut to the** ~ (*fig*) herido en lo vivo; **be** ~**!** ¡date prisa!; **to be** ~ **to act** obrar con prontitud; **she was** ~ **to see that** se dio cuenta de eso en seguida.
quicken [kwik'ən] *vt* apresurar ♦ *vi* apresurarse, darse prisa.
quickly [kwik'lē] *ad* rápidamente, de prisa; **we must act** ~ tenemos que actuar cuanto antes.
quickness [kwik'nis] *n* rapidez *f*; (*of temper*) viveza; (*agility*) agilidad *f*; (*of mind, eye etc*) agudeza.
quicksand [kwik'sand] *n* arenas *fpl* movedizas.
quickstep [kwik'step] *n* baile de ritmo rápido.
quick-tempered [kwik'tempûrd] *a* de genio vivo.
quick-witted [kwik'wit'id] *a* listo, despabilado.
quid [kwid] *n*, *pl inv* (*Brit col*) libra.
quid pro quo [kwid' prō kwō'] *n* quid pro quo *m*, compensación *f*.
quiet [kwī'it] *a* (*not busy: day*) tranquilo; (*silent*) callado; (*reserved*) reservado; (*discreet*) discreto; (*not noisy: engine*) silencioso ♦ *n* silencio, tranquilidad *f* ♦ *vb* (*US: also* ~ **down**) *vi* (*grow calm*) calmarse; (*grow silent*) callarse ♦ *vt* calmar; hacer callar; **keep** ~**!** ¡cállate!, ¡silencio!; **business is** ~ **at this time of year** hay poco movimiento en esta época.
quieten [kwī'itən] (*Brit: also* ~ **down**) *vi*, *vt* = **quiet**.
quietly [kwī'itlē] *ad* tranquilamente; (*silently*) silenciosamente.
quietness [kwī'itnis] *n* (*silence*) silencio; (*calm*) tranquilidad *f*.
quill [kwil] *n* (*of porcupine*) púa; (*pen*) pluma.
quilt [kwilt] *n* (*Brit*) edredón *m*.
quilting [kwil'ting] *n* acolchado, guateado.
quin [kwin] *n abbr* = **quintuplet**.
quince [kwins] *n* membrillo.
quinine [kwī'nīn] *n* quinina.
quintet(te) [kwintet'] *n* quinteto.

quintuplet [kwintu'plit] *n* quintillizo.
quip [kwip] *n* ocurrencia ♦ *vi* decir sarcásticamente.
quire [kwiûr] *n* mano *f* de papel.
quirk [kwûrk] *n* peculiaridad *f*; **by some** ~ **of fate** por algún capricho del destino.
quit, *pt*, *pp* **quit** *or* **quitted** [kwit] *vt* dejar, abandonar; (*premises*) desocupar; (*COMPUT*) abandonar ♦ *vi* (*give up*) renunciar; (*go away*) irse; (*resign*) dimitir; ~ **stalling!** (*US col*) ¡déjate de evasivas!
quite [kwit] *ad* (*rather*) bastante; (*entirely*) completamente; ~ **a few of them** un buen número de ellos; ~ (**so**)! ¡así es!, ¡exactamente!; ~ **new** completamente nuevo; **that's not** ~ **right** eso no está del todo bien; **not** ~ **as many as last time** no tantos como la última vez; **she's** ~ **pretty** es bastante guapa.
Quito [kē'tō] *n* Quito.
quits [kwits] *a*: ~ (**with**) en paz (con); **let's call it** ~ dejémoslo en tablas.
quiver [kwiv'ûr] *vi* estremecerse ♦ *n* (*for arrows*) carcaj *m*.
quiz [kwiz] *n* (*game*) concurso; (: *TV, RADIO*) programa-concurso; (*questioning*) interrogatorio ♦ *vt* interrogar.
quizzical [kwiz'ikəl] *a* burlón(ona).
quoits [kwoits] *npl* juego de aros.
quorum [kwôr'əm] *n* quórum *m*.
quota [kwō'tə] *n* cuota.
quotation [kwōtā'shən] *n* cita; (*estimate*) presupuesto.
quotation marks *npl* comillas *fpl*.
quote [kwōt] *n* cita ♦ *vt* (*sentence*) citar; (*COMM: sum, figure*) cotizar ♦ *vi*: **to** ~ **from** citar de; ~**s** *npl* (*inverted commas*) comillas *fpl*; **in** ~**s** entre comillas; **the figure** ~**d for the repairs** la cifra estimada por las reparaciones; ~ ... **unquote** (*in dictation*) comillas iniciales ... finales.
quotient [kwō'shənt] *n* cociente *m*.
qv *n abbr* (= *quod vide: which see*) q.v.
qwerty keyboard [kwûr'tē kē'bôrd] *n* (*Brit*) teclado QWERTY.

R

R, r [âr] *n* (*letter*) R, r *f*; **R for Roger** R de Ramón.
R *abbr* (= *right*) dcha.; (= *river*) R.; (= *Réaumur (scale)*) R; (*US CINEMA*: = *restricted*) sólo mayores; (*US POL*) = **republican**; (*Brit*: = *Rex, Regina*) R.
RA *abbr* = *rear admiral*.
RAAF *n abbr* = *Royal Australian Air Force*.

Rabat [râbât'] *n* Rabat *m*.
rabbi [rab'ī] *n* rabino.
rabbit [rab'it] *n* conejo.
rabbit hutch *n* conejera.
rabble [rab'əl] *n* (*pej*) chusma, populacho.
rabies [rā'bēz] *n* rabia.
RAC *n abbr* (*Brit*: = *Royal Automobile Club*) ≈ RACE *m* (*Sp*).
raccoon [rakōōn'] *n* mapache *m*.
race [rās] *n* carrera; (*species*) raza ♦ *vt* (*horse*) hacer correr; (*person*) competir contra; (*engine*) acelerar ♦ *vi* (*compete*) competir; (*run*) correr; (*pulse*) latir a ritmo acelerado; **the arms** ~ la carrera armamentista; **the human** ~ el género humano; **he** ~**d across the road** cruzó corriendo la carretera; **to** ~ **in/out** entrar/salir corriendo.
race car *n* (*US*) coche *m* de carreras.
race car driver *n* (*US*) corredor(a) *m/f* de coches.
racecourse [rās'kôrs] *n* hipódromo.
racehorse [rās'hôrs] *n* caballo de carreras.
race meeting *n* concurso hípico.
race relations *npl* relaciones *fpl* entre las razas.
racetrack [rās'trak] *n* hipódromo; (*for cars*) autódromo.
racial [rā'shəl] *a* racial.
racial discrimination *n* discriminación *f* racial.
racial integration *n* integración *f* racial.
racialism [rā'shəlizəm] *n* racismo.
racialist [rā'shəlist] *a, n* racista *m/f*.
racing [rā'sing] *n* carreras *fpl*.
racing car *n* (*Brit*) = **race car**.
racing driver *n* (*Brit*) = **race car driver**.
racism [rā'sizəm] *n* racismo.
racist [rā'sist] *a, n* racista *m/f*.
rack [rak] *n* (*also*: **luggage** ~) rejilla; (*shelf*) estante *m*; (*also*: **roof** ~) baca, portaequipajes *m inv*; (*clothes* ~) percha ♦ *vt* (*cause pain to*) atormentar; **to go to** ~ **and ruin** (*building*) echarse a perder, venirse abajo; (*business*) arruinarse; **to** ~ **one's brains** devanarse los sesos.
　rack up *vt* conseguir, ganar.
rack-and-pinion [rak'əndpin'yən] *n* (*TECH*) cremallera y piñón.
racket [rak'it] *n* (*for tennis*) raqueta; (*noise*) ruido, estrépito; (*swindle*) estafa, timo.
racketeer [rakitēr'] *n* (*esp US*) estafador(a) *m/f*.
racoon [rakōōn'] *n* = **raccoon**.
racquet [rak'it] *n* raqueta.
racy [rā'sē] *a* picante, salado.
radar [rā'dâr] *n* radar *m*.
radar trap *n* trampa radar.
radial [rā'dēəl] *a* (*tire*: *also*: ~**-ply**) radial.
radiance [rā'dēəns] *n* brillantez *f*, resplandor *m*.
radiant [rā'dēənt] *a* brillante, resplande-

ciente.
radiate [rā'dēāt] *vt* (*heat*) radiar, irradiar ♦ *vi* (*lines*) extenderse.
radiation [rādēā'shən] *n* radiación *f*.
radiation sickness *n* enfermedad *f* de radiación.
radiator [rā'dēātûr] *n* (*AUT*) radiador *m*.
radiator cap *n* tapón *m* de radiador.
radiator grill *n* (*AUT*) rejilla del radiador.
radical [rad'ikəl] *a* radical.
radically *ad* radicalmente.
radii [rā'dēī] *npl of* **radius**.
radio [rā'dēō] *n* radio *f* ♦ *vi*: **to** ~ **to sb** mandar un mensaje por radio a uno ♦ *vt* (*information*) radiar, transmitir por radio; (*one's position*) indicar por radio; (*person*) llamar por radio; **on the** ~ por radio.
radioactive [rādēōak'tiv] *a* radioactivo.
radioactivity [rādēōaktiv'ətē] *n* radioactividad *f*.
radio announcer *n* locutor(a) *m/f* de radio.
radio-controlled [rā'dēōkəntrōld'] *a* teledirigido.
radiographer [rādēāg'rəfûr] *n* radiógrafo/a.
radiography [rādēāg'rəfē] *n* radiografía.
radiology [rādēâl'əjē] *n* radiología.
radio station *n* emisora.
radio taxi *n* radio taxi *m*.
radiotelephone [rādēōtel'əfōn] *n* radioteléfono.
radiotelescope *n* radiotelescopio.
radiotherapist [rādēōthär'əpist] *n* radioterapeuta *m/f*.
radiotherapy [rādēōthär'əpē] *n* radioterapia.
radish [rad'ish] *n* rábano.
radium [rā'dēəm] *n* radio.
radius, *pl* **radii** [rā'dēəs, -ēī] *n* radio; **within a** ~ **of 50 miles** en un radio de 50 millas.
RAF *n abbr* = **Royal Air Force**.
raffia [raf'ēə] *n* rafia.
raffle [raf'əl] *n* rifa, sorteo ♦ *vt* (*object*) rifar.
raft [raft] *n* (*craft*) balsa; (*also*: **life** ~) balsa salvavidas.
rafter [raf'tûr] *n* viga.
rag [rag] *n* (*piece of cloth*) trapo; (*torn cloth*) harapo; (*pej*: *newspaper*) periodicucho; (*Brit*: *for charity*) actividades estudiantiles benéficas; ~**s** *npl* harapos *mpl*; **in** ~**s** en harapos, hecho jirones.
rag-and-bone man [ragənbōn' man] *n* (*Brit*) = **ragman**.
rag doll *n* muñeca de trapo.
rage [rāj] *n* (*fury*) rabia, furor *m* ♦ *vi* (*person*) rabiar, estar furioso; (*storm*) bramar; **to fly into a** ~ montar en cólera; **it's all the** ~ es lo último.
ragged [rag'id] *a* (*edge*) desigual, mellado; (*cuff*) roto; (*appearance*) andrajoso, harapiento; ~ **left/right** (*text*) margen *m* izquierdo/derecho irregular.

raging [rā'jing] a furioso; **in a ~ temper** de un humor terrible, furioso.
ragman [rag'man] n trapero.
rag trade n: **the ~** (col) la industria de la confección.
raid [rād] n (MIL) incursión f; (criminal) asalto; (by police) redada ♦ vt invadir, atacar; asaltar.
raider [rā'dûr] n invasor(a) m/f.
rail [rāl] n (on stair) barandilla, pasamanos m inv; (on bridge, balcony) pretil m; (of ship) barandilla; (for train) riel m, carril m; **~s** npl vía sg; **by ~** por ferrocarril, en tren.
railing(s) [rā'ling(z)] n(pl) verja sg, enrejado sg.
railroad [rāl'rōd] n (US) ferrocarril m, vía férrea.
railroader [rāl'rōdûr] n (US) ferroviario.
railroad line n línea de ferrocarril.
railroad station n estación de ferrocarril.
railway [rāl'wā] etc (Brit) = **railroad** etc.
railway engine n (Brit) (máquina) locomotora.
railwayman [rāl'wāmən] n (Brit) = **railroader**.
rain [rān] n lluvia ♦ vi llover; **in the ~** bajo la lluvia; **it's ~ing** llueve, está lloviendo; **it's ~ing cats and dogs** está lloviendo a cántaros or a mares.
rainbow [rān'bō] n arco iris.
raincoat [rān'kōt] n impermeable m.
raindrop [rān'dräp] n gota de lluvia.
rainfall [rān'fôl] n lluvia.
rainforest [rān'fôrist] n (also: **tropical ~**) selva tropical.
rainproof [rān'prōof] a impermeable, a prueba de lluvia.
rainstorm [rān'stôrm] n temporal m (de lluvia).
rainwater [rān'wôtûr] n agua llovediza or de lluvia.
rainy [rā'nē] a lluvioso.
raise [rāz] n aumento ♦ vt (lift) levantar; (build) erigir, edificar; (increase) aumentar; (doubts) suscitar; (a question) plantear; (cattle, family) criar; (crop) cultivar; (army) reclutar; (funds) reunir; (money) obtener; (Brit: end: embargo) levantar; **to ~ one's voice** alzar la voz; **to ~ one's glass to sb/sth** brindar por uno/algo; **to ~ a laugh/a smile** provocar risa/una sonrisa; **to ~ sb's hopes** dar esperanzas a uno.
raisin [rā'zin] n pasa.
rake [rāk] n (tool) rastrillo; (person) libertino ♦ vt (garden) rastrillar; (fire) hurgar; (with machine gun) barrer.
 rake in vt reunir.
rake-off [rāk'ôf] n (col) comisión f, tajada.
rakish [rā'kish] a (dissolute) libertino; **at a ~ angle** (hat) echado a un lado, de lado.
rally [ral'ē] n (POL etc) reunión f, mitin m;

(AUT) rallye m; (TENNIS) peloteo ♦ vt reunir ♦ vi reunirse; (sick person, Stock Exchange) recuperarse.
rally around vt fus (fig) dar apoyo a.
rallying point [ral'ēing point] n (POL, MIL) punto de reunión.
RAM [ram] n abbr (= random access memory) RAM f.
ram [ram] n carnero; (TECH) pisón m ♦ vt (crash into) dar contra, chocar con; (tread down) apisonar.
ramble [ram'bəl] n caminata, excursión f en el campo ♦ vi (pej: also: ~ **on**) divagar.
rambler [ram'blûr] n excursionista m/f; (BOT) trepadora.
rambling [ram'bling] a (speech) inconexo; (BOT) trepador(a); (house) laberíntico.
rambunctious [rambungk'shəs] a (person) bullicioso.
ramification [raməfəkā'shən] n ramificación f.
ramp [ramp] n rampa; **on/off ~** n (US AUT) vía de acceso/salida; "**~**" (Brit AUT) "rampa".
rampage [ram'pāj] n: **to be on the ~** desmandarse.
rampant [ram'pənt] a (disease etc): **to be ~** estar extendiéndose mucho.
rampart [ram'pârt] n terraplén m; (wall) muralla.
ramshackle [ram'shakəl] a destartalado.
ran [ran] pt of **run**.
ranch [ranch] n (US) hacienda, estancia.
rancher [ran'chûr] n ganadero.
rancid [ran'sid] a rancio.
rancor, (Brit) **rancour** [rang'kûr] n rencor m.
random [ran'dəm] a fortuito, sin orden; (COMPUT, MATH) aleatorio ♦ n: **at ~** al azar.
random access n (COMPUT) acceso aleatorio.
randy [ran'dē] a (Brit col) cachondo.
rang [rang] pt of **ring**.
range [rānj] n (of mountains) cadena de montañas, cordillera; (of missile) alcance m; (of voice) registro; (series) serie f; (of products) surtido; (MIL: also: **shooting ~**) campo de tiro; (also: **kitchen ~**) fogón m ♦ vt (place) colocar; (arrange) arreglar ♦ vi: **to ~ over** (wander) recorrer; (extend) extenderse por; **within (firing) ~** a tiro; **do you have anything else in this price ~?** ¿tiene algo más de esta gama de precios?; **intermediate-/short-~ missile** proyectil m de medio/corto alcance; **to ~ from ... to...** oscilar entre ... y...; **~d left/right** (Brit: text) alineado a la izquierda/derecha.
ranger [rān'jûr] n guardabosques m inv.
Rangoon [ranggōon'] n Rangún m.
rangy [rān'jē] a alto y delgado.
rank [rangk] n (row) fila; (MIL) rango; (status) categoría; (Brit: also: **taxi ~**) parada

♦ *vi*: **to ~ among** figurar entre ♦ *a* (*stinking*) fétido, rancio; (*hypocrisy, injustice etc*) manifiesto; **the ~ and file** (*fig*) la base; **to close ~ s** (*MIL*) apretar las filas, cerrar filas; (*fig*) hacer un frente común; **I ~ him 6th** yo le pongo en sexto lugar.

rankle [rang'kəl] *vi* (*insult*) doler.

ransack [ran'sak] *vt* (*search*) registrar; (*plunder*) saquear.

ransom [ran'səm] *n* rescate *m* ♦ *vt* rescatar; **to hold sb to ~** (*fig*) poner a uno entre la espada y la pared.

rant [rant] *vi* divagar, desvariar.

ranting [ran'ting] *n* desvaríos *mpl*.

rap [rap] *vt* golpear, dar un golpecito en ♦ *n* **to take the ~** pagar el gato.

rape [rāp] *n* violación *f*; (*BOT*) colza ♦ *vt* violar.

rape(seed) oil [rāp'(sēd) oil] *n* aceite *m* de colza.

rapid [rap'id] *a* rápido.

rapidity [rəpid'itē] *n* rapidez *f*.

rapidly [rap'idlē] *ad* rápidamente.

rapids [rap'idz] *npl* (*GEO*) rápidos *mpl*.

rapier [rā'pēūr] *n* estoque *m*.

rapist [rā'pist] *n* violador *m*.

rapport [rapôr'] *n* simpatía.

rapprochement [raprōchmônt'] *n* acercamiento.

rapt [rapt] *a* (*attention*) profundo; **to be ~ in contemplation** estar ensimismado.

rapture [rap'chūr] *n* éxtasis *m*.

rapturous [rap'chūrəs] *a* extático; (*applause*) entusiasta.

rare [rär] *a* raro, poco común; (*CULIN: steak*) poco hecho; **it is ~ to find that ...** es raro descubrir que ....

rarefied [rär'əfīd] *a* (*air, atmosphere*) enrarecido.

rarely [reūr'lē] *ad* rara vez, pocas veces.

raring [rär'ing] *a*: **to be ~ to go** (*col*) tener muchas ganas de empezar.

rarity [rär'itē] *n* rareza.

rascal [ras'kəl] *n* pillo/a, pícaro/a.

rash [rash] *a* imprudente, precipitado ♦ *n* (*MED*) salpullido, erupción *f* (cutánea); **to come out in a ~** salirle salpullido a uno.

rasher [rash'ûr] *n* lonja.

rashly [rash'lē] *ad* imprudentemente, precipitadamente.

rashness [rash'nis] *n* imprudencia, precipitación *f*.

rasp [rasp] *n* (*tool*) escofina ♦ *vt* (*speak: also*: **~ out**) decir con voz áspera.

raspberry [raz'bärē] *n* frambuesa.

rasping [ras'ping] *a*: **a ~ noise** un ruido áspero.

rat [rat] *n* rata.

ratchet [rach'it] *n* (*TECH*) trinquete *m*.

rate [rāt] *n* (*ratio*) razón *f*; (*percentage*) tanto por ciento; (*price*) precio; (: *of hotel*) tarifa; (*of interest*) tipo; (*speed*) velocidad *f* ♦ *vt* (*value*) tasar; (*estimate*) estimar; **to**

~ as ser considerado como; **~s** *npl* (*Brit*) impuesto *sg* municipal; (*fees*) tarifa *sg*; **failure ~** porcentaje *m* de fallos; **pulse ~** pulsaciones *fpl* por minuto; **~ of pay** tipos *mpl* de sueldo; **at a ~ of 60 kph** a una velocidad de 60 kph; **~ of growth** ritmo de crecimiento; **~ of return** (*COMM*) tasa de rendimiento; **bank ~** tipo *or* tasa de interés bancario; **at any ~** de todas formas, de todos modos; **to ~ sb/sth highly** tener a uno/algo en alta estima.

rather [rath'ûr] *ad* antes, más bien; (*somewhat*) algo, un poco; (*to some extent*) un poco; **it's ~ expensive** es algo caro; (*too much*) es demasiado caro; **there's ~ a lot** (*Brit*) hay bastante; **I would** *or* **I'd ~ go** preferiría ir; **I'd ~ not** prefiero que no; **or ~** (*more accurately*) o mejor dicho.

ratification [ratəfəkā'shən] *n* ratificación *f*.

ratify [rat'əfī] *vt* ratificar.

rating [rā'ting] *n* (*appraisal*) tasación *f*; (*standing*) posición *f*; (*Brit NAUT: sailor*) marinero; **~s** *npl* (*RADIO, TV*) clasificación *f*.

ratio [rā'shō] *n* razón *f*; **in the ~ of 100 to 1** a razón de *or* en la proporción de 100 a 1.

ration [rash'ən] *n* ración *f*; **~s** *npl* víveres *mpl* ♦ *vt* racionar.

rational [rash'ənəl] *a* racional; (*solution, reasoning*) lógico, razonable; (*person*) cuerdo, sensato.

rationale [rashənal'] *n* razón *f* fundamental.

rationalism [rash'ənəlizəm] *n* racionalismo.

rationalization [rashənələzā'shən] *n* racionalización *f*.

rationalize [rash'ənəlīz] *vt* (*reorganize: industry*) reconvertir, reorganizar.

rationally [rash'ənəlē] *ad* racionalmente; (*logically*) lógicamente.

rationing [rash'əning] *n* racionamiento.

rat race *n* lucha incesante por la supervivencia.

rattan [ratan'] *n* rota, caña de Indias.

rattle [rat'əl] *n* golpeteo; (*of train etc*) traqueteo; (*object: of baby*) sonaja, sonajero; (: *of sports fan*) matraca ♦ *vi* sonar, golpear; traquetear; (*small objects*) castañetear ♦ *vt* hacer sonar agitando; (*col: disconcert*) desconcertar.

rattlesnake [rat'əlsnāk] *n* serpiente *f* de cascabel.

ratty [rat'ē] *a* (*col: US*) andrajoso; (: *Brit*) furioso; **to get ~** ponerse de malas.

raucous [rô'kəs] *a* estridente, ronco.

raucously [rô'kəslē] *ad* de modo estridente, roncamente.

ravage [rav'ij] *vt* hacer estragos en, destrozar; **~s** *npl* estragos *mpl*.

rave [rāv] *vi* (*in anger*) encolerizarse; (*with enthusiasm*) entusiasmarse; (*MED*) delirar, desvariar ♦ *cpd*: **~ review** reseña entusiasta.

raven [rā'vən] *n* cuervo.

ravenous [rav'ənəs] *a* famélico.
ravine [rəvēn'] *n* barranco.
raving [rā'ving] *a*: ~ **lunatic** loco de atar.
ravings [rā'vingz] *npl* divagaciones *fpl*, desvaríos *mpl*.
ravioli [ravēō'lē] *n* ravioles *mpl*, ravioli *mpl*.
ravish [rav'ish] *vt* (*charm*) encantar, embelesar; (*rape*) violar.
ravishing [rav'ishing] *a* encantador(a).
raw [rô] *a* (*uncooked*) crudo; (*not processed*) bruto; (*sore*) vivo; (*inexperienced*) novato, inexperto.
Rawalpindi [râwəlpin'dē] *n* Rawalpindi *m*.
raw data *n* (*COMPUT*) datos *mpl* en bruto.
raw deal *n* (*col: bad deal*) mala pasada *or* jugada; (: *harsh treatment*) injusticia.
raw material *n* materia prima.
ray [rā] *n* rayo; ~ **of hope** (rayo de) esperanza.
rayon [rā'ân] *n* rayón *m*.
raze [rāz] *vt* (*also*: ~ **to the ground**) arrasar, asolar.
razor [rā'zûr] *n* (*open*) navaja; (*safety* ~) máquina de afeitar.
razor blade *n* hoja de afeitar.
razzmatazz [raz'mətaz] *n* (*col*) animación *f*, bullicio.
R & B *n abbr* = *rhythm and blues.*
RC *abbr* = **Roman Catholic.**
RCAF *n abbr* = *Royal Canadian Air Force.*
RCMP *n abbr* = *Royal Canadian Mounted Police.*
RCN *n abbr* = *Royal Canadian Navy.*
RD *abbr* (*US MAIL*) = *rural delivery.*
Rd *abbr* = *road.*
R & D *n abbr* (= *research and development*) investigación *f* y desarrollo.
re [rā] *prep* con referencia a.
re... [rā] *pref* re....
reach [rēch] *n* alcance *m*; (*BOXING*) envergadura; (*of river etc*) extensión *f* entre dos recodos ♦ *vt* alcanzar, llegar a; (*achieve*) lograr ♦ *vi* extenderse; (*stretch out hand*: *also*: ~ **down**, ~ **over**, ~ **across** *etc*) tender la mano; **within** ~ al alcance (de la mano); **out of** ~ fuera del alcance; **to** ~ **out for sth** alargar *or* tender la mano para tomar algo; **can I** ~ **you at your hotel?** ¿puedo ponerme en contacto contigo en tu hotel?; **to** ~ **sb by phone** comunicarse con uno por teléfono.
react [rēakt'] *vi* reaccionar.
reaction [rēak'shən] *n* reacción *f*.
reactionary [rēak'shənärē] *a, n* reaccionario/a *m/f*.
reactor [rēak'tûr] *n* reactor *m*.
read, *pt, pp* **read** [rēd, red] *vi* leer ♦ *vt* leer; (*understand*) entender; (*study*) estudiar; **to take sth as read** (*fig*) dar algo por sentado; **do you** ~ **me?** (*TEL*) ¿me escucha?; **to** ~ **between the lines** leer entre líneas.
read out *vt*: ~ **out aloud** leer en alta voz.

read over *vt* repasar.
read through *vt* (*quickly*) leer rápidamente, echar un vistazo a; (*thoroughly*) leer con cuidado *or* detenidamente.
read up on *vt fus* estudiar.
readable [rē'dəbəl] *a* (*writing*) legible; (*book*) que merece leerse.
reader [rē'dûr] *n* lector(a) *m/f*; (*book*) libro de lecturas; (*Brit: at university*) profesor(a) *m/f*.
readership [rē'dûrship] *n* (*of paper etc*) número de lectores.
readily [red'əlē] *ad* (*willingly*) de buena gana; (*easily*) fácilmente; (*quickly*) en seguida.
readiness [red'ēnis] *n* buena voluntad; (*preparedness*) preparación *f*; **in** ~ (*prepared*) listo, preparado.
reading [rēd'ing] *n* lectura; (*understanding*) comprensión *f*; (*on instrument*) indicación *f*.
reading lamp *n* lámpara portátil.
reading room *n* sala de lectura.
readjust [rēəjust'] *vt* reajustar ♦ *vi* (*person*): **to** ~ **to** reajustarse a.
readjustment [rēəjust'mənt] *n* reajuste *m*.
ready [red'ē] *a* listo, preparado; (*willing*) dispuesto; (*available*) disponible ♦ *n*: **at the** ~ (*MIL*) listo para tirar; ~ **for use** listo para usar; **to be** ~ **to do sth** estar listo para hacer algo; **to get** ~ *vi* prepararse ♦ *vt* preparar.
ready cash *n* (dinero) efectivo, dinero contante.
ready-made [red'ēmād'] *a* confeccionado.
ready-to-wear [red'ētəwär'] *a* confeccionado.
reaffirm [rēəfurm'] *vt* reafirmar.
reagent [rēā'jənt] *n* reactivo.
real [rēl] *a* verdadero, auténtico; **in** ~ **terms** en términos reales; **in** ~ **life** en la vida real, en la realidad.
real estate *n* bienes *mpl* raíces.
real estate agent *n* agente *m/f* inmobiliario(a).
real estate office *n* agencia inmobiliaria.
realism [rē'əlizəm] *n* (*also ART*) realismo.
realist [rē'əlist] *n* realista *m/f*.
realistic [rēəlis'tik] *a* realista.
realistically [rēəlis'tiklē] *ad* de modo realista.
reality [rēal'itē] *n* realidad *f*; **in** ~ en realidad.
realization [rēələzā'shən] *n* comprensión *f*; (*of a project*; *COMM: of assets*) realización *f*.
realize [rē'əliz] *vt* (*understand*) darse cuenta de; (*a project*; *COMM: asset*) realizar; **I** ~ **that ...** comprendo *or* entiendo que ....
really [rē'əlē] *ad* realmente; ~**?** ¿de veras?
realm [relm] *n* reino; (*fig*) esfera.
real time *n* (*COMPUT*) tiempo real.
realtor [rē'əltûr] *n* (*US*) corredor(a) *m/f* de

bienes raíces.

ream [rēm] *n* resma; **~s** (*fig, col*) montones *mpl*.

reap [rēp] *vt* segar; (*fig*) cosechar, recoger.

reaper [rē'pûr] *n* segador(a) *m/f*.

reappear [rēəpi'ûr] *vi* reaparecer.

reappearance [rēəpēr'əns] *n* reaparición *f*.

reapply [rēəpli'] *vi* volver a presentarse, hacer *or* presentar nueva solicitud.

reappoint [rēəpoint'] *vt* volver a nombrar.

reappraisal [rēəprā'zəl] *n* revaluación *f*.

rear [rēr] *a* trasero ♦ *n* parte *f* trasera ♦ *vt* (*cattle, family*) criar ♦ *vi* (*also*: ~ up) (*animal*) encabritarse.

rear-engined [rēr'en'jənd] *a* (AUT) con motor trasero.

rearguard [rēr'gârd] *n* retaguardia.

rearm [rēârm'] *vt* rearmar ♦ *vi* rearmarse.

rearmament [rēârm'əmənt] *n* rearme *m*.

rearrange [rēərānj'] *vt* ordenar *or* arreglar de nuevo.

rear-view [rēr'vyōō']: ~ **mirror** *n* (AUT) espejo retrovisor.

reason [rē'zən] *n* razón *f* ♦ *vi*: **to ~ with sb** tratar de una uno entre en razón; **it stands to ~ that** es lógico que; **the ~ for/why** la causa de/la razón por la cual; **she claims with good ~ that she's underpaid** dice con razón que está mal pagada; **all the more ~ why you should not sell it** razón de más para que no lo vendas.

reasonable [rē'zənəbəl] *a* razonable; (*sensible*) sensato.

reasonably [rē'zənəblē] *ad* razonablemente; **a ~ accurate report** un informe bastante exacto.

reasoned [rē'zənd] *a* (*argument*) razonado.

reasoning [rē'zəning] *n* razonamiento, argumentos *mpl*.

reassemble [rēəsem'bəl] *vt* volver a reunir; (*machine*) montar de nuevo ♦ *vi* volver a reunirse.

reassert [rēəsûrt'] *vt* reafirmar, reiterar.

reassurance [rēəshōōr'əns] *n* consuelo.

reassure [rēəshōōr'] *vt* tranquilizar, alentar; **to ~ sb that** tranquilizar a uno asegurándole que.

reassuring [rēəshōōr'ing] *a* alentador(a).

reawakening [rēəwā'kəning] *n* despertar *m*.

rebate [rē'bāt] *n* (*on product*) rebaja; (*on tax etc*) descuento; (*repayment*) reembolso.

rebel *n* [reb'əl] rebelde *m/f* ♦ *vi* [ribel'] rebelarse, sublevarse.

rebellion [ribel'yən] *n* rebelión *f*, sublevación *f*.

rebellious [ribel'yəs] *a* rebelde; (*child*) revoltoso.

rebirth [rēbûrth'] *n* renacimiento.

rebound *vi* [ribound'] (*ball*) rebotar ♦ *n* [rē'bound] rebote *m*.

rebuff [ribuf'] *n* desaire *m*, rechazo ♦ *vt* rechazar.

rebuild [rēbild'] *vt* (*irg*: *like* **build**) reconstruir.

rebuilding [rēbil'ding] *n* reconstrucción *f*.

rebuke [ribyōōk'] *n* reprimenda ♦ *vt* reprender.

rebut [ribut'] *vt* rebatir.

recalcitrant [rikal'sitrənt] *a* reacio.

recall *vt* [rikôl'] (*remember*) recordar; (*ambassador etc*) retirar; (COMPUT) volver a llamar ♦ *n* [rē'kôl] recuerdo.

recant [rikant'] *vi* retractarse.

recap [rē'kap] *vt, vi* recapitular.

recapitulate [rēkəpich'əlāt] *vt, vi* = **recap**.

recapture [rēkap'chûr] *vt* (*town*) reconquistar; (*atmosphere*) hacer revivir.

recd., rec'd *abbr* (= *received*) rbdo.

recede [risēd'] *vi* retroceder.

receding [risē'ding] *a* (*forehead, chin*) huidizo; ~ **hairline** entradas *fpl*.

receipt [risēt'] *n* (*document*) recibo; (*act of receiving*) recepción *f*; **~s** *npl* (COMM) ingresos *mpl*; **to acknowledge ~ of** acusar recibo de; **we are in ~ of** ... obra en nuestro poder ... .

receivable [risē'vəbəl] *a* (COMM) a cobrar.

receive [risēv'] *vt* recibir; (*guest*) acoger; (*wound*) sufrir; **"~ed with thanks"** (COMM) "recibí".

receiver [risē'vûr] *n* (TEL) auricular *m*; (RADIO) receptor *m*; (*of stolen goods*) perista *m/f*; (LAW) administrador *m* jurídico.

recent [rē'sənt] *a* reciente; **in ~ years** en los últimos años.

recently [rē'səntlē] *ad* recientemente; ~ **arrived** recién llegado; **until ~** hasta hace poco.

receptacle [risep'təkəl] *n* receptáculo.

reception [risep'shən] *n* (*in building, office etc*) recepción *f*; (*welcome*) acogida.

reception center *n* centro de recepción.

reception desk *n* recepción *f*.

receptionist [risep'shənist] *n* recepcionista *m/f*.

receptive [risep'tiv] *a* receptivo.

recess [rē'ses] *n* (*in room*) hueco; (*for bed*) nicho; (*secret place*) escondrijo; (POL *etc*: *holiday*) clausura; (US LAW: *short break*) descanso; (SCOL: *esp* US) recreo.

recession [risesh'ən] *n* recesión *f*, depresión *f*.

recharge [rēchârj'] *vt* (*battery*) recargar.

rechargeable [rēchâr'jəbəl] *a* recargable.

recipe [res'əpē] *n* receta.

recipient [risip'ēənt] *n* recibidor(a) *m/f*; (*of letter*) destinatario/a.

reciprocal [risip'rəkəl] *a* recíproco.

reciprocate [risip'rəkāt] *vt* devolver, corresponder a ♦ *vi* corresponder.

recital [risit'əl] *n* (MUS) recital *m*.

recitation [resitā'shən] *n* (*of poetry*) recitado; (*of complaints etc*) enumeración *f*, relación *f*.

recite [risīt'] *vt* (*poem*) recitar; (*complaints etc*) enumerar.

reckless [rek'lis] *a* temerario, imprudente; (*speed*) peligroso.

recklessly [rek'lislē] *ad* imprudentemente; de modo peligroso.

recklessness [rek'lisnis] *n* temeridad *f*, imprudencia.

reckon [rek'ən] *vt* (*count*) contar; (*consider*) considerar ♦ *vi*: **to ~ without sb/sth** dejar de contar con uno/algo; **he is somebody to be ~ed with** no se le puede descartar; **I ~ that...** me parece que..., creo que ....
reckon on *vt fus* contar con.

reckoning [rek'əning] *n* (*calculation*) cálculo.

reclaim [riklām'] *vt* (*land*) recuperar; (: *from sea*) rescatar; (*demand back*) reclamar.

reclamation [rekləmā'shən] *n* recuperación *f*; rescate *m*.

recline [riklīn'] *vi* reclinarse.

reclining [riklīn'ing] *a* (*seat*) reclinable.

recluse [rek'lōōs] *n* recluso/a.

recognition [rekəgnish'ən] *n* reconocimiento; **transformed beyond ~** irreconocible; **in ~ of** en reconocimiento de.

recognizable [rekəgnī'zəbəl] *a*: **~ (by)** reconocible (por).

recognize [rek'əgnīz] *vt* reconocer, conocer; **to ~ (by/as)** reconocer (por/como).

recoil [rikoil'] *vi* (*person*): **to ~ from doing sth** retraerse de hacer algo ♦ *n* (*of gun*) retroceso.

recollect [rekəlekt'] *vt* recordar, acordarse de.

recollection [rekəlek'shən] *n* recuerdo; **to the best of my ~** que yo recuerde.

recommend [rekəmend'] *vt* recomendar; **she has a lot to ~ her** tiene mucho a su favor.

recommendation [rekəmendā'shən] *n* recomendación *f*.

recommended retail price (RRP) [rekəmen'did rē'tāl prīs] *n* (*Brit*) precio recomendado de venta al público.

recompense [rek'əmpens] *vt* recompensar ♦ *n* recompensa.

reconcilable [rek'ənsīləbəl] *a* (re)conciliable.

reconcile [rek'ənsīl] *vt* (*two people*) reconciliar; (*two facts*) compaginar; **to ~ o.s. to sth** resignarse *or* conformarse a algo.

reconciliation [rekənsilēā'shən] *n* reconciliación *f*.

recondite [rek'əndīt] *a* recóndito.

recondition [rēkəndi'shən] *vt* (*machine*) reparar, reponer.

reconditioned [rēkəndi'shənd] *a* renovado, reparado.

reconnaissance [rikân'isəns] *n* (*MIL*) reconocimiento.

reconnoiter, (*Brit*) **reconnoitre** [rēkənoi'tûr] *vt, vi* (*MIL*) reconocer.

reconsider [rēkənsid'ûr] *vt* repensar.

reconstitute [rēkán'stitōōt] *vt* reconstituir.

reconstruct [rēkənstrukt'] *vt* reconstruir.

reconstruction [rēkənstruk'shən] *n* reconstrucción *f*.

record *n* [rek'ûrd] (*MUS*) disco; (*of meeting etc*) relación *f*; (*register*) registro, partida; (*file*) archivo; (*also*: **police** *or* **criminal ~**) antecedentes *mpl* penales; (*written*) expediente *m*; (*SPORT*) récord *m*; (*COMPUT*) registro ♦ *vt* [rikôrd'] (*set down, also COMPUT*) registrar; (*relate*) hacer constar; (*MUS: song etc*) grabar; **in ~ time** en un tiempo récord; **public ~s** archivos *mpl* nacionales; **he is on ~ as saying that ...** hay pruebas de que ha dicho públicamente que ...; **Spain's excellent ~** el excelente historial de España; **off the ~** *a* no oficial ♦ *ad* confidencialmente.

record card *n* (*in file*) ficha.

recorded delivery letter [rikôr'did diliv'ûrē let'ûr] *n* (*Brit MAIL*) carta de entrega recordada.

recorded music *n* música grabada.

recorder [rikôr'dûr] *n* (*MUS*) flauta de pico; (*TECH*) contador *m*.

record holder *n* (*SPORT*) actual poseedor(a) *m/f* del récord.

recording [rikôr'ding] *n* (*MUS*) grabación *f*.

recording studio *n* estudio de grabación.

record library *n* discoteca.

record player *n* tocadiscos *m inv*.

recount [rikount'] *vt* contar.

re-count *n* [rē'kount] (*POL: of votes*) segundo escrutinio, recuento ♦ *vt* [rēkount'] volver a contar.

recoup [rikōōp'] *vt*: **to ~ one's losses** recuperar las pérdidas.

recourse [rē'kôrs] *n* recurso; **to have ~ to** recurrir a.

recover [rikuv'ûr] *vt* recuperar; (*rescue*) rescatar ♦ *vi* (*from illness, shock*) recuperarse; (*country*) recuperar.

recovery [rikuv'ûrē] *n* recuperación *f*; rescate *m*; (*MED*): **to make a ~** restablecerse.

re-create [rēkrēāt'] *vt* recrear.

recreation [rekrēā'shən] *n* recreación *f*; (*amusement*) recreo.

recreational [rekrēā'shənəl] *a* de recreo.

recreational vehicle *n* (*US*) caravana *or* roulotte *f* pequeña.

recreation center *n* centro de recreo.

recrimination [rikrimənā'shən] *n* recriminación *f*.

recruit [rikrōōt'] *n* recluta *m/f* ♦ *vt* reclutar; (*staff*) contratar.

recruiting office [rikrōōt'ing ôf'is] *n* caja de reclutas.

recruitment [rikrōōt'mənt] *n* reclutamiento.

rectangle [rek'tanggəl] *n* rectángulo.

rectangular |rektang'gyəlûr| *a* rectangular.
rectify |rck'təfī| *vt* rectificar.
rector |rck'tûr| *n* (*REL*) párroco; (*SCOL*) rector(a) *m/f*.
rectory |rck'tûrč| *n* casa del párroco.
rectum |rck'təm| *n* (*ANAT*) recto.
recuperate |rikoō'pərāt| *vi* reponerse, restablecerse.
recur |rikûr'| *vi* repetirse; (*pain, illness*) producirse de nuevo.
recurrence |rikûr'əns| *n* repetición *f*.
recurrent |rikûr'ənt| *a* repetido.
recycle |rēsi'kəl| *vt* (*waste, paper etc*) reciclar.
red |red| *n* rojo ♦ *a* rojo; **to be in the ~** (*account*) estar en números rojos; (*business*) tener un saldo negativo; **to give sb the ~ carpet treatment** recibir a uno con todos los honores.
Red Cross *n* Cruz *f* Roja.
redcurrant |red'kur'ənt| *n* grosella.
redden |red'ən| *vt* enrojecer ♦ *vi* enrojecerse.
reddish |red'ish| *a* (*hair*) rojizo.
redecorate |rēdek'ərāt| pintar de nuevo; volver a decorar.
redecoration |rēdekərā'shən| *n* renovación *f*.
redeem |ridēm'| *vt* (*sth in pawn*) desempeñar; (*fig, also REL*) rescatar.
redeemable |ridē'məbəl| *a* reembolsable.
redeeming |ridē'ming| *a*: **~ feature** rasgo bueno *or* favorable.
redeploy |rēdiploi'| *vt* (*resources*) disponer de nuevo.
redeployment |rēdiploi'mənt| *n* redistribución *f*.
redevelop |rēdivel'əp| *vt* reorganizar.
redevelopment |rēdivel'əpmənt| *n* reorganización *f*.
red-haired |red'hârd| *a* pelirrojo.
red-handed |red'han'did| *a*: **to be caught ~** cogerse (*Sp*) *or* pillarse (*LAm*) con las manos en la masa.
redhead |red'hed| *n* pelirrojo/a.
red herring *n* (*fig*) pista falsa.
red-hot |red'hât'| *a* candente.
redirect |rēdərekt'| *vt* (*mail*) reexpedir.
rediscover |rēdiskuv'ûr| *vt* redescubrir.
rediscovery |rēdiskuv'ûrē| *n* redescubrimiento.
redistribute |rēdistrib'yoōt| *vt* redistribuir, hacer una nueva distribución de.
red-letter day |red'let'ûr dā| *n* día *m* señalado, día *m* especial.
red light *n*: **to go through a ~** (*AUT*) pasar la luz roja.
red-light district |red'līt dis'trikt| *n* zona de tolerancia.
redness |red'nis| *n* rojez *f*.
redo |rēdoō'| *vt* (*irg: like* **do**) rehacer.
redolent |red'ələnt| *a*: **~ of** (*smell*) oliente *or* con fragancia a; **to be ~ of** (*fig*) re-

cordar.
redouble |rēdub'əl| *vt*: **to ~ one's efforts** intensificar los esfuerzos.
redraft |rēdraft'| *vt* volver a redactar.
redress |ridres'| *n* reparación *f* ♦ *vt* reparar, corregir; **to ~ the balance** restablecer el equilibrio.
Red Sea *n*: **the ~** el mar Rojo.
redskin |red'skin| *n* piel roja *m/f*.
red tape *n* (*fig*) trámites *mpl*, papeleo (*col*).
reduce |ridoōs'| *vt* reducir; (*lower*) rebajar; **to ~ sth by/to** reducir algo en/a; **to ~ sb to silence/despair/tears** reducir a uno al silencio/a la desesperación/a las lágrimas; **'~d speed ahead'** (*AUT*) 'reduzca la velocidad'.
reduced |ridoōst'| *a* (*decreased*) reducido, rebajado; **at a ~ price** con rebaja *or* descuento; **"greatly ~ prices"** "grandes rebajas".
reduction |riduk'shən| *n* reducción *f*; (*of price*) rebaja; (*discount*) descuento.
redundancy |ridun'dənsē| *n* redundancia; (*Brit*) desempleo; **compulsory ~** despido; **voluntary ~** dimisión *f*.
redundancy payment *n* (*Brit*) indemnización *f* por desempleo.
redundant |ridun'dənt| *a* (*Brit*) (*worker*) parado, sin trabajo; (*detail, object*) superfluo; **to be made ~** quedar(se) sin trabajo, perder su empleo.
reed |rēd| *n* (*BOT*) junco, caña; (*MUS: of clarinet etc*) lengüeta.
reedy |rē'dē| *a* (*voice, instrument*) aflautado.
reef |rēf| *n* (*at sea*) arrecife *m*.
reek |rēk| *vi*: **to ~ (of)** oler *or* heder (a).
reel |rēl| *n* carrete *m*, bobina; (*of film*) rollo ♦ *vt* (*TECH*) devanar; (*also*: **~ in**) sacar ♦ *vi* (*sway*) tambalear(se); **my head is ~ing** me da vueltas la cabeza.
reel off *vt* recitar de memoria.
re-election |rēilek'shən| *n* reelección *f*.
re-enter |rēen'tûr| *vt* reingresar en, volver a entrar en.
re-entry |rēen'trē| *n* reingreso, reentrada.
re-examine |rēigzam'in| *vt* reexaminar.
re-export *vt* |rēekspôrt'| reexportar ♦ *n* |rēeks'pôrt| reexportación *f*.
ref |ref| *n abbr* (*col*) = **referee**.
ref. *abbr* (*COMM*: = *with reference to*) Ref.
refectory |rifek'tûrē| *n* comedor *m*.
refer |rifûr'| *vt* (*send*) remitir; (*ascribe*) referir a, relacionar con ♦ *vi*: **to ~ to** (*allude to*) referirse a, aludir a; (*apply to*) relacionarse con; (*consult*) remitirse a; **he ~red me to the manager** me envió al gerente.
referee |refərē'| *n* árbitro; (*Brit: for job application*) persona que recomienda a otro ♦ *vt* (*match*) arbitrar en.
reference |ref'ûrəns| *n* (*mention, in book*) referencia; (*sending*) remisión *f*; (*rel-*

evance) relación *f*; (*for job application: letter*) carta de recomendación; **with ~ to** con referencia a; (*COMM: in letter*) me remito a.

reference book *n* libro de consulta.

reference number *n* número de referencia.

referendum, *pl* **referenda** [refərɛn'dəm, -də] *n* referéndum *m inv*.

refill *vt* [rē'fil'] rellenar ♦ *n* [rē'fil] repuesto, recambio.

refine [rifin'] *vt* (*sugar, oil*) refinar.

refined [rifind'] *a* (*person, taste*) refinado, culto.

refinement [rifin'mənt] *n* (*of person*) cultura, educación *f*.

refinery [rifi'nûrē] *n* refinería.

refit (*NAUT*) *n* [rē'fit] equipamiento ♦ *vt* [rēfit'] reparar.

reflate [riflāt'] *vt* (*economy*) reflacionar.

reflation [riflā'shən] *n* reflación *f*.

reflationary [riflā'shənârē] *a* reflacionario.

reflect [riflɛkt'] *vt* (*light, image*) reflejar ♦ *vi* (*think*) reflexionar, pensar; **it ~s badly/ well on him** le perjudica/le hace honor.

reflection [riflɛk'shən] *n* (*act*) reflexión *f*; (*image*) reflejo; (*discredit*) crítica; **on ~** pensándolo bien.

reflector [riflɛk'tûr] *n* (*AUT*) captafaros *m inv*; (*telescope*) reflector *m*.

reflex [rē'flɛks] *a, n* reflejo.

reflexive [riflɛk'siv] *a* (*LING*) reflexivo.

reforest [rēfôr'ist] *vt* repoblar de árboles.

reform [rifôrm'] *n* reforma ♦ *vt* reformar.

reformat [rēfôr'mat] *vt* (*COMPUT*) recomponer.

Reformation [rɛfûrmā'shən] *n*: **the ~** la Reforma.

reformatory [rifôr'mətôrē] *n* reformatorio.

reformer [rifôr'mûr] *n* reformador(a) *m/f*.

refrain [rifrān'] *vi*: **to ~ from doing** abstenerse de hacer ♦ *n* (*MUS etc*) estribillo.

refresh [rifresh'] *vt* refrescar.

refresher course [rifresh'ûr kôrs] *n* curso de repaso.

refreshing [rifresh'ing] *a* (*drink*) refrescante; (*sleep*) reparador; (*change etc*) estimulante; (*idea, point of view*) estimulante, interesante.

refreshments [rifresh'mənts] *npl* (*drinks*) refrescos *mpl*.

refreshment stand *n* puesto de refrescos.

refrigeration [rifrijərā'shən] *n* refrigeración *f*.

refrigerator [rifrij'ərātûr] *n* nevera, refrigeradora (*LAm*).

refuel [rēfyōō'əl] *vi* repostar (combustible).

refueling, (*Brit*) **refuelling** [rēfyōō'əling] *n* reabastecimiento de combustible.

refuge [ref'yōōj] *n* refugio, asilo; **to take ~ in** refugiarse en.

refugee [refyōōjē'] *n* refugiado/a.

refugee camp *n* campamento para refu-

giados.

refund *n* [rē'fund] reembolso ♦ *vt* [rifund'] devolver, reembolsar.

refurbish [rēfûr'bish] *vt* restaurar, renovar.

refurnish [rēfûr'nish] *vt* amueblar de nuevo.

refusal [rifyōō'zəl] *n* negativa; **first ~** primera opción; **to have first ~ on sth** tener la primera opción a algo.

refuse *n* [ref'yōōs] basura ♦ (*vb*: [rifyōōz']) *vt* (*reject*) rehusar; (*say no to*) negarse a ♦ *vi* negarse; (*horse*) rehusar; **to ~ to do sth** negarse a *or* rehusar hacer algo.

refuse collection *n* (*Brit*) recolección *f* de basuras.

refuse disposal *n* (*Brit*) eliminación *f* de basuras.

refute [rifyōōt'] *vt* refutar, rebatir.

regain [rigān'] *vt* recobrar, recuperar.

regal [rē'gəl] *a* regio, real.

regale [rigāl'] *vt* agasajar, entretener.

regalia [rigā'lēə] *n* insignias *fpl*.

regard [rigárd'] *n* (*gaze*) mirada; (*aspect*) respecto; (*esteem*) respeto, consideración *f* ♦ *vt* (*consider*) considerar; (*look at*) mirar; **to give one's ~s to** saludar de su parte a; **"(kind) ~s"** "muy atentamente"; **"with kindest ~s"** "con muchos recuerdos"; **~s to María, please give my ~s to María** recuerdos a María, dele recuerdos a María de mi parte; **~ing, as ~s, with ~ to** con respecto a, en cuanto a.

regarding [rigár'ding] *prep* con respecto a, en cuanto a.

regardless [rigárd'lis] *ad* a pesar de todo; **~ of** sin reparar en.

regatta [rigát'ə] *n* regata.

regency [rē'jənsē] *n* regencia.

regenerate [rējen'ûrāt] *vt* regenerar.

regent [rē'jənt] *n* regente *m/f*.

régime [rāzhēm'] *n* régimen *m*.

regiment *n* [rej'əmənt] regimiento ♦ *vt* [rej'əment] reglamentar.

regimental [rejəmɛn'təl] *a* militar.

regimentation [rejəməntā'shən] *n* regimentación *f*.

region [rē'jən] *n* región *f*; **in the ~ of** (*fig*) alrededor de.

regional [rē'jənəl] *a* regional.

regional development *n* desarrollo regional.

register [rej'istûr] *n* registro ♦ *vt* registrar; (*birth*) declarar; (*letter*) certificar; (*subj: instrument*) marcar, indicar ♦ *vi* (*at hotel*) registrarse; (*sign on*) inscribirse; (*make impression*) producir impresión; **to ~ a protest** presentar una queja; **to ~ for a course** matricularse *or* inscribirse en un curso.

registered [rej'istûrd] *a* (*design*) registrado; (*letter*) certificado; (*student*) matriculado; (*voter*) registrado.

registered company *n* sociedad *f* legalmente constituida.

registered nurse n (US) enfermero/a calificado/a.

registered office n (Brit) domicilio social.

registered trademark n marca registrada.

registrar [rej'istrár] n secretario/a (del registro civil).

registration [rejisträ'shən] n (act) declaración f; (AUT: also: ~ **number**) matrícula.

registry [rej'istrē] n registro.

registry office [rej'istrē ófis] n (Brit) registro civil; **to get married in a** ~ casarse por lo civil.

regret [rigret'] n sentimiento, pesar m; (remorse) remordimiento ♦ vt sentir, lamentar; (repent of) arrepentirse de; **we ~ to inform you that ...** sentimos informarle que ....

regretful [rigret'fəl] a pesaroso, arrepentido.

regretfully [rigret'fəlē] ad con pesar, sentidamente.

regrettable [rigret'əbəl] a lamentable; (loss) sensible.

regrettably [rigret'əblē] ad desgraciadamente.

regroup [rēgrōōp'] vt reagrupar ♦ vi reagruparse.

regt abbr = **regiment**.

regular [reg'yəlûr] a regular; (soldier) profesional; (col: intensive) verdadero; (listener, reader) asiduo, habitual ♦ n (client etc) cliente/a m/f habitual; (US: ~ **gas**) gasolina normal.

regularity [regyəlar'itē] n regularidad f.

regularly [reg'yəlûrlē] ad con regularidad.

regulate [reg'yəlāt] vt (gen) controlar; (TECH) regular, ajustar.

regulation [regyəlā'shən] n (rule) regla, reglamento; (adjustment) regulación f.

rehabilitation [rēhəbilätä'shən] n rehabilitación f.

rehash [rēhash'] vt (col) hacer un refrito de.

rehearsal [rihûr'səl] n ensayo; **dress** ~ ensayo general or final.

rehearse [rihûrs'] vt ensayar.

rehouse [rēhouz'] vt dar nueva vivienda a.

reign [rān] n reinado; (fig) predominio ♦ vi reinar; (fig) imperar.

reigning [rā'ning] a (monarch) reinante, actual; (predominant) imperante.

reimburse [rēimbûrs'] vt reembolsar.

rein [rān] n (for horse) rienda; **to give sb free** ~ dar rienda suelta a uno.

reincarnation [rēinkârnä'shən] n reencarnación f.

reindeer [rān'dēr] n, pl inv reno.

reinforce [rēinfôrs'] vt reforzar.

reinforced concrete [rēinfôrst' kán'krēt] n hormigón armado.

reinforcement [rēinfôrs'mənt] n (action) refuerzo; **~s** npl (MIL) refuerzos mpl.

reinstate [rēinstāt'] vt (worker) reintegrar (a su puesto).

reinstatement [rēinstät'mənt] n reintegración f.

reissue [rēish'ōō] vt (record, book) reeditar.

reiterate [rēit'ərāt] vt reiterar, repetir.

reject n [rē'jekt] (thing) desecho ♦ vt [rijekt'] rechazar; (proposition, offer etc) descartar.

rejection [rijek'shən] n rechazo.

rejoice [rijois'] vi: **to** ~ **at** or **over** regocijarse or alegrarse de.

rejoinder [rijoin'dûr] n (retort) réplica.

rejuvenate [rijōō'vənāt] vt rejuvenecer.

rekindle [rēkin'dəl] vt reencender; (fig) despertar.

relapse [rilaps'] n (MED) recaída; (into crime) reincidencia.

relate [rilāt'] vt (tell) contar, relatar; (connect) relacionar ♦ vi relacionarse; **to** ~ **to** (connect) relacionarse or tener que ver con.

related [rilā'tid] a afín; (person) emparentado; ~ **to** con referencia a, relacionado con.

relating [rilā'ting]: ~ **to** prep referente a.

relation [rilā'shən] n (person) pariente m/f; (link) relación f; **in** ~ **to** en relación con, en lo que se refiere a; **to bear a** ~ **to** guardar relación con; **diplomatic/international** ~**s** relaciones fpl diplomáticas/internacionales.

relationship [rilā'shənship] n relación f; (personal) relaciones fpl; (also: **family** ~) parentesco.

relative [rel'ətiv] n pariente m/f, familiar m/f ♦ a relativo.

relatively [rel'ətivlē] ad (fairly, rather) relativamente.

relative pronoun n pronombre m relativo.

relax [rilaks'] vi descansar; (quiet down) relajarse ♦ vt relajar; (mind, person) descansar; ~! (calm down) ¡tranquilo!

relaxation [rēlaksä'shən] n (rest) descanso; (easing) relajación f, relajamiento m; (amusement) recreo; (entertainment) diversión f.

relaxed [rilakst'] a relajado; (tranquil) tranquilo.

relaxing [rilaks'ing] a relajante.

relay n [rē'lā] (race) carrera de relevos ♦ vt [rēlā'] (RADIO, TV, pass on) retransmitir.

release [rilēs'] n (liberation) liberación f; (discharge) puesta en libertad f; (of gas etc) escape m; (of movie etc) estreno ♦ vt (prisoner) poner en libertad; (movie) estrenar; (book) publicar; (piece of news) difundir; (gas etc) despedir, arrojar; (free: from wreckage etc) soltar; (TECH: catch, spring etc) desenganchar; (let go) soltar, aflojar.

relegate [rel'əgāt] vt relegar; (SPORT): **to be** ~**d to** bajar a.

relent [rilent'] vi ablandarse; (let up) descansar.

relentless [rilent'lis] a implacable.

relentlessly [rilent'lislē] *ad* implacablemente.

relevance [rel'əvəns] *n* relación *f*.

relevant [rel'əvənt] *a* (*fact*) pertinente; ~ **to** relacionado con.

reliability [rilīəbil'ətē] *n* fiabilidad *f*; seguridad *f*; veracidad *f*.

reliable [rilī'əbəl] *a* (*person, firm*) de confianza, de fiar; (*method, machine*) seguro; (*source*) fidedigno.

reliably [rilī'əblē] *ad*: **to be ~ informed that...** saber de fuente fidedigna que... .

reliance [rilī'əns] *n*: ~ (**on**) dependencia (de).

reliant [rilī'ənt] *a*: **to be ~ on sth/sb** confiar en algo/uno.

relic [rel'ik] *n* (*REL*) reliquia; (*of the past*) vestigio.

relief [rilēf'] *n* (*from pain, anxiety*) alivio, desahogo; (*help, supplies*) socorro, ayuda; (*ART, GEO*) relieve *m*; **by way of ~** a modo de diversión.

relief road *n* (*Brit*) carretera de desgestionamiento.

relieve [rilēv'] *vt* (*pain, patient*) aliviar; (*bring help to*) ayudar, socorrer; (*burden*) aligerar; (*take over from: gen*) sustituir a; (*: guard*) relevar; **to ~ sb of sth** quitar algo a uno; **to ~ sb of his command** (*MIL*) relevar a uno de su mando; **to ~ o.s.** hacer sus necesidades; **I am ~d to hear you are better** me tranquiliza saber que estás *or* te encuentras mejor.

religion [rilij'ən] *n* religión *f*.

religious [rilij'əs] *a* religioso.

religiously [rilij'əslē] *ad* religiosamente; (*conscientiously*) puntualmente, fielmente.

reline [rēlīn'] *vt* (*brakes*) poner nueva guarnición a.

relinquish [riling'kwish] *vt* abandonar; (*plan, habit*) renunciar a.

relish [rel'ish] *n* (*CULIN*) salsa; (*enjoyment*) entusiasmo; (*flavor*) sabor *m*, gusto ♦ *vt* (*food etc*) saborear; **to ~ doing** gustar mucho de hacer.

relive [rēliv'] *vt* vivir de nuevo, volver a vivir.

relocate [rēlō'kāt] *vt* cambiar de lugar, mudar ♦ *vi* mudarse.

reluctance [riluk'təns] *n* renuencia.

reluctant [riluk'tənt] *a* renuente; **to be ~ to do sth** resistirse a hacer algo.

reluctantly [riluk'təntlē] *ad* de mala gana.

rely [rilī']: **to ~ on** *vt fus* confiar en, fiarse de; (*be dependent on*) depender de; **you can ~ on my discretion** puedes contar con mi discreción.

remain [rimān'] *vi* (*survive*) quedar; (*be left*) sobrar; (*continue*) quedar(se), permanecer; **to ~ silent** permanecer callado.

remainder [rimān'dûr] *n* resto.

remaining [rimā'ning] *a* sobrante.

remains [rimānz'] *npl* restos *mpl*.

remand [rimand'] *n*: **on ~** detenido (bajo custodia) ♦ *vt*: **to ~ in custody** mantener bajo custodia.

remark [rimârk'] *n* comentario ♦ *vt* comentar; **to ~ on sth** hacer observaciones sobre algo.

remarkable [rimâr'kəbəl] *a* notable; (*outstanding*) extraordinario.

remarkably [rimâr'kəblē] *ad* extraordinariamente.

remarry [rēmar'ē] *vi* casarse por segunda vez, volver a casarse.

remedial [rimē'dēəl] *a*: ~ **education** educación *f* de los niños atrasados.

remedy [rem'idē] *n* remedio ♦ *vt* remediar, curar.

remember [rimem'bûr] *vt* recordar, acordarse de; (*bear in mind*) tener presente; **I ~ seeing it, I ~ having seen it** recuerdo haberlo visto; **she ~ed doing it** se acordó de hacerlo; ~ **me to your wife and children!** ¡déle recuerdos a su familia!

remembrance [rimem'brəns] *n* (*memory, souvenir*) recuerdo; **in ~ of** en conmemoración de.

remind [rimīnd'] *vt*: **to ~ sb to do sth** recordar a uno que haga algo; **to ~ sb of sth** recordar algo a uno; **she ~s me of her mother** me recuerda a su madre; **that ~s me!** ¡a propósito!

reminder [rimīnd'ûr] *n* notificación *f*; (*memento*) recuerdo.

reminisce [remənis'] *vi* recordar (viejas historias).

reminiscences [remənis'ənsiz] *npl* reminiscencias *fpl*, recuerdos *mpl*.

reminiscent [remənis'ənt] *a*: **to be ~ of sth** recordar algo.

remiss [rimis'] *a* descuidado; **it was ~ of me** fue un descuido de mi parte.

remission [rimish'ən] *n* remisión *f*; (*of sentence*) disminución *f* de pena.

remit [rimit'] *vt* (*send: money*) remitir, enviar.

remittance [rimit'əns] *n* remesa, envío.

remnant [rem'nənt] *n* resto; (*of cloth*) retazo; ~**s** *npl* (*COMM*) restos de serie.

remonstrate [rimân'strāt] *vi* protestar.

remorse [rimôrs'] *n* remordimientos *mpl*.

remorseful [rimôrs'fəl] *a* arrepentido.

remorseless [rimôrs'lis] *a* (*fig*) implacable, inexorable.

remorselessly [rimôrs'lislē] *ad* implacablemente, inexorablemente.

remote [rimōt'] *a* (*distant*) lejano; (*person*) distante; (*COMPUT*) remoto; **there is a ~ possibility that ...** hay una posibilidad remota de que ....

remote control *n* telecontrol *m*.

remote-controlled [rimōt'kəntrōld'] *a* teledirigido.

remotely [rimōt'lē] *ad* remotamente; (*slightly*) levemente.

remoteness [rimōt'nis] *n* alejamiento; distancia.

remould [rē'mōld] *n* (*Brit: tire*) neumático *or* llanta (*LAm*) recauchutado/a.

removable [rimōō'vəbəl] *a* (*detachable*) separable.

removal [rimōō'vəl] *n* (*taking away*) el quitar; (*Brit: from house*) mudanza; (*from office: dismissal*) destitución *f*; (*MED*) extirpación *f*.

removal van *n* (*Brit*) camión *m* de mudanzas.

remove [rimōō'v] *vt* quitar; (*employee*) destituir; (*name: from list*) tachar, borrar; (*doubt*) disipar; (*TECH*) retirar, separar; (*MED*) extirpar; **first cousin once ~d** (*parent's cousin*) tío/a segundo/a; (*cousin's child*) sobrino/a segundo/a.

remover [rimōō'vûr] *n*: **make-up ~** desmaquilladora; **~s** *npl* (*Brit: company*) agencia de mudanzas.

remunerate [rimyōō'nərāt] *vt* remunerar.

remuneration [rimyōōnərā'shən] *n* remuneración *f*.

Renaissance [ren'isâns] *n*: **the ~** el Renacimiento.

rename [rēnām'] *vt* poner nuevo nombre a.

render [ren'dûr] *vt* (*thanks*) dar; (*aid*) proporcionar; (*honor*) dar, conceder; (*assistance*) dar, prestar; **to ~ sth + a** volver algo + *a*.

rendering [ren'dûring] *n* (*MUS etc*) interpretación *f*.

rendezvous [rân'dāvōō] *n* cita ♦ *vi* reunirse, encontrarse; (*spaceship*) efectuar una reunión espacial.

rendition [rendish'ən] *n* (*MUS*) interpretación *f*.

renegade [ren'əgād] *n* renegado/a.

renew [rinōō'] *vt* renovar; (*resume*) reanudar; (*extend date*) prorrogar; (*negotiations*) volver a.

renewable [rinōō'əbəl] *a* renovable.

renewal [rinōō'əl] *n* renovación *f*; reanudación *f*; prórroga.

renounce [rinouns'] *vt* renunciar a; (*right, inheritance*) renunciar.

renovate [ren'əvāt] *vt* renovar.

renovation [renəvā'shən] *n* renovación *f*.

renown [rinoun'] *n* renombre *m*.

renowned [rinound'] *a* renombrado.

rent [rent] *n* alquiler *m*; (*for house*) arriendo, renta; **"for ~"** "se alquila" ♦ *vt* (*also: ~ out*) alquilar.

rental [ren'təl] *n* (*for television, car*) alquiler *m*.

rental car *n* coche *m* de alquiler.

rental fee *n* tarifa de alquiler.

renunciation [rinunsēā'shən] *n* renuncia.

reopen [rēō'pən] *vt* volver a abrir, reabrir.

reorder [rēôr'dûr] *vt* volver a pedir, repetir el pedido de; (*rearrange*) volver a ordenar *or* arreglar.

reorganization [rēôrgənəzā'shən] *n* reorganización *f*.

reorganize [rēôr'gənīz] *vt* reorganizar.

rep [rep] *n abbr* ('COMM) = **representative**; (*THEATER*) = **repertory.**

Rep. *abbr* (*US POL*) = **representative, republican.**

repair [ripär'] *n* reparación *f*, compostura; (*patch*) remiendo ♦ *vt* reparar, componer; (*shoes*) remendar; **in good/bad ~** en buen/mal estado; **under ~** en obras.

repair kit *n* caja de herramientas.

repair man *n* mecánico.

repair shop *n* taller *m* de reparaciones.

repartee [repûrtē'] *n* réplicas *fpl* agudas.

repast [ripast'] *n* (*formal*) comida.

repatriate [rēpā'trēāt] *vt* repatriar.

repay [ripā'] *vt* (*irg: like* **pay**) (*money*) devolver, reembolsar; (*person*) pagar; (*debt*) liquidar; (*sb's efforts*) devolver, corresponder a.

repayment [ripā'mənt] *n* reembolso, devolución *f*; (*sum of money*) recompensa.

repeal [ripēl'] *n* revocación *f* ♦ *vt* revocar.

repeat [ripēt'] *n* (*RADIO, TV*) reposición *f* ♦ *vt* repetir ♦ *vi* repetirse.

repeatedly [ripēt'idlē] *ad* repetidas veces.

repeat order *n* (*COMM*): **to place a ~ for** renovar un pedido de.

repel [ripel'] *vt* repugnar.

repellent [ripel'ənt] *a* repugnante ♦ *n*: **insect ~** crema/loción *f* anti-insectos.

repent [ripent'] *vi*: **to ~ (of)** arrepentirse (de).

repentance [ripen'təns] *n* arrepentimiento.

repercussion [rēpûrkush'ən] *n* (*consequence*) repercusión *f*; **to have ~s** repercutir.

repertoire [rep'ûrtwâr] *n* repertorio.

repertory [rep'ûrtôrē] *n* (*also:* **~ theater**) teatro de repertorio.

repertory company *n* compañía de repertorio.

repetition [repitish'ən] *n* repetición *f*.

repetitious [repitish'əs] *a* repetidor(a), que se repite.

repetitive [ripet'ətiv] *a* (*movement, work*) reiterativo; (*speech*) lleno de repeticiones.

rephrase [rēfrāz'] *vt* decir *or* formular de otro modo.

replace [riplās'] *vt* (*put back*) devolver a su sitio; (*take the place of*) reemplazar, sustituir.

replacement [riplās'mənt] *n* reemplazo; (*act*) reposición *f*; (*thing*) recambio; (*person*) suplente *m/f*.

replacement cost *n* costo de sustitución.

replacement part *n* repuesto.

replacement value *n* valor *m* de sustitución.

replay [rēplā'] *n* (*SPORT*) desempate *m*; (*TV: playback*) repetición *f*.

replenish [riplen'ish] *vt* (*tank etc*) rellenar;

(*stock etc*) reponer; (*with fuel*) repostar.
replete |riplēt'| *a* repleto, lleno.
replica |rep'lǝkǝ| *n* copia, reproducción *f*.
reply |riplī'| *n* respuesta, contestación *f* ♦ *vi* contestar, responder; **in ~ en** respuesta.
report |ripôrt'| *n* informe *m*; (*PRESS etc*) reportaje *m*; (*Brit: also:* **school ~**) nota; (*of gun*) estallido ♦ *vt* informar sobre; (*PRESS etc*) hacer un reportaje sobre; (*notify: accident, culprit*) denunciar ♦ *vi* (*make a report*) presentar un informe; (*present o.s.*): **to ~ (to sb)** presentarse (ante uno); **annual ~** (*COMM*) informe *m* anual; **to ~ (on)** hacer un informe (sobre); **it is ~ed from Berlin that ...** se informa desde Berlín que ....
report card *n* (*US, Scottish*) cartilla escolar.
reportedly |ripôr'tidlē| *ad* según se dice, según se informe.
reporter |ripôr'tûr| *n* (*PRESS*) periodista *m/f*; (*RADIO, TV*) locutor(a) *m/f*.
repose |ripōz'| *n*: **in ~** (*face, mouth*) en reposo.
repossess |rēpǝzɛs'| *vt* recobrar.
reprehensible |reprihɛn'sǝbǝl| *a* reprensible, censurable.
represent |reprizɛnt'| *vt* representar; (*COMM*) ser agente de.
representation |reprizɛntā'shǝn| *n* representación *f*; (*petition*) petición *f*; **~s** *npl* (*protest*) quejas *fpl*.
representative |reprizen'tǝtiv| *n* (*US POL*) representante *m/f*, diputado/a; (*COMM*) representante *m/f* ♦ *a*: **~ (of)** representativo (de).
repress |riprɛs'| *vt* reprimir.
repression |riprɛsh'ǝn| *n* represión *f*.
repressive |riprɛs'iv| *a* represivo.
reprieve |riprēv'| *n* (*LAW*) indulto; (*fig*) alivio ♦ *vt* indultar; (*fig*) salvar.
reprimand |rep'rǝmand| *n* reprimenda ♦ *vt* reprender.
reprint *n* |rē'print| reimpresión *f*, reedición *f* ♦ *vt* |rēprint'| reimprimir.
reprisal |riprī'zǝl| *n* represalia; **to take ~s** tomar represalias.
reproach |riprōch'| *n* reproche *m* ♦ *vt*: **to ~ sb with sth** reprochar algo a uno; **beyond ~** intachable.
reproachful |riprōch'fǝl| *a* de reproche, de acusación.
reproduce |rēprǝdōōs'| *vt* reproducir ♦ *vi* reproducirse.
reproduction |rēprǝduk'shǝn| *n* reproducción *f*.
reproductive |rēprǝduk'tiv| *a* reproductor(a).
reproof |riprōōf'| *n* reproche *m*.
reprove |riprōōv'| *vt*: **to ~ sb for sth** reprochar algo a uno.
reptile |rep'til| *n* reptil *m*.
republic |ripub'lik| *n* república.

republican |ripub'likǝn| *a, n* republicano/a *m/f*.
repudiate |ripyōō'dēāt| *vt* (*accusation*) rechazar; (*obligation*) desconocer.
repudiation |ripyōōdēā'shǝn| *n* incumplimiento.
repugnance |ripug'nǝns| *n* repugnancia.
repugnant |ripug'nǝnt| *a* repugnante.
repulse |ripuls'| *vt* rechazar.
repulsion |ripul'shǝn| *n* repulsión *f*, repugnancia.
repulsive |ripul'siv| *a* repulsivo.
repurchase |rēpûr'chis| *vt* volver a comprar, readquirir.
reputable |rep'yǝtǝbǝl| *a* (*make etc*) de renombre.
reputation |repyǝtā'shǝn| *n* reputación *f;* **he has a ~ for being awkward** tiene fama de difícil.
repute |ripyōōt'| *n* reputación *f*, fama.
reputed |ripyōō'tid| *a* supuesto; **to be ~ to be rich/intelligent** *etc* tener fama de rico/inteligente *etc*.
reputedly |ripyōō'tidlē| *ad* según dicen *or* se dice.
request |rikwɛst'| *n* solicitud *f*, petición *f* ♦ *vt*: **to ~ sth of** *or* **from sb** solicitar algo a uno; **at the ~ of** a petición de; **"you are ~ed not to smoke"** "se ruega no fumar".
request stop *n* (*Brit*) parada a petición.
requiem |rɛk'wēǝm| *n* réquiem *m*.
require |rikwiûr'| *vt* (*need: subj: person*) necesitar, tener necesidad de; (*: thing, situation*) exigir; (*want*) pedir; (*demand*) insistir en que; **to ~ sb to do sth/sth of sb** exigir que uno haga algo; **what qualifications are ~d?** ¿qué títulos se requieren?; **~d by law** requerido por la ley.
requirement |rikwiûr'mǝnt| *n* requisito; (*need*) necesidad *f*.
requisite |rɛk'wizit| *n* requisito ♦ *a* necesario, requerido.
requisition |rɛkwizish'ǝn| *n*: **~ (for)** solicitud *f* (de) ♦ *vt* (*MIL*) requisar.
reroute |rērout'| *vt* desviar.
resale |rē'sāl| *n* reventa.
resale price maintenance |rē'sāl prīs mān'tǝnǝns| *n* mantenimiento del precio de venta.
rescind |risind'| *vt* (*LAW*) abrogar; (*contract, order etc*) anular.
rescue |rɛs'kyōō| *n* rescate *m* ♦ *vt* rescatar; **to come/go to sb's ~** ir en auxilio de uno, socorrer a uno; **to ~ from** librar de.
rescue party *n* expedición *f* de salvamento.
rescuer |rɛs'kyōōûr| *n* salvador(a) *m/f*.
research |risûrch'| *n* investigaciones *fpl* ♦ *vt* investigar; **a piece of ~** un trabajo de investigación; **to ~ (into sth)** investigar (algo).
research and development (R & D) *n* investigación *f* y desarrollo.

researcher [risûr'chûr] *n* investigador(a) *m/f*.

research work *n* investigación *f*.

resell [rēsel'] *vt* revender.

resemblance [rizem'bləns] *n* parecido; **to bear a strong ~ to** parecerse mucho a.

resemble [rizem'bəl] *vt* parecerse a.

resent [rizent'] *vt* resentirse de.

resentful [rizent'fəl] *a* resentido.

resentment [rizent'mənt] *n* resentimiento.

reservation [rezûrvā'shən] *n* reserva; (*booking*) reservación *f*; (*Brit: also*: **central ~**) faja intermedia; **with ~s** con reservas.

reservation desk *n* (*US: in hotel*) recepción *f*.

reserve [rizûrv'] *n* reserva; (*SPORT*) suplente *m/f* ♦ *vt* (*seats etc*) reservar; **~s** *npl* (*MIL*) reserva *sg*; **in ~** en reserva.

reserve currency *n* divisa de reserva.

reserved [rizûrvd'] *a* reservado.

reserve price *n* (*Brit*) precio mínimo.

reservist [rizûr'vist] *n* (*MIL*) reservista *m*.

reservoir [rez'ûrvwâr] *n* (*artificial lake*) embalse *m*, represa (*LAm*); (*small*) depósito.

reset [rēset'] *vt* (*COMPUT*) reinicializar.

reshape [rēshāp'] *vt* (*policy*) reformar, rehacer.

reshuffle [rēshuf'əl] *n*: **Cabinet ~** (*Brit POL*) remodelación *f* del gabinete.

reside [rizīd'] *vi* residir, vivir.

residence [rez'idəns] *n* residencia; (*formal: home*) domicilio; (*length of stay*) permanencia; **in ~** (*queen etc*) en residencia; (*doctor*) residente; **to take up ~** instalarse.

resident [rez'idənt] *n* vecino/a; (*in hotel*) huésped/a *m/f* ♦ *a* (*population*) permanente; (*COMPUT*) residente.

residential [rezident'chəl] *a* residencial.

residue [rez'idoo] *n* resto, residuo.

resign [rizīn'] *vt* (*gen*) renunciar a ♦ *vi*: **to ~ (from)** dimitir (de), renunciar (a); **to ~ o.s. to** (*endure*) resignarse a.

resignation [rezignā'shən] *n* dimisión *f*; (*state of mind*) resignación *f*; **to tender one's ~** presentar la dimisión.

resigned [rizīnd'] *a* resignado.

resilience [rizil'yəns] *n* (*of material*) elasticidad *f*; (*of person*) resistencia.

resilient [rizil'yənt] *a* (*person*) resistente.

resin [rez'in] *n* resina.

resist [rizist'] *vt* resistir, oponerse a.

resistance [rizis'təns] *n* resistencia.

resistant [rizis'tənt] *a*: **~ (to)** resistente (a).

resolute [rez'əloot] *a* resuelto.

resolutely [rez'əlootlē] *ad* resueltamente.

resolution [rezəloo'shən] *n* (*gen*) resolución *f*; (*purpose*) propósito; (*COMPUT*) definición *f*; **to make a ~** tomar una resolución.

resolve [rizâlv'] *n* (*determination*) resolución *f*; (*purpose*) propósito ♦ *vt* resolver ♦

vi resolverse; **to ~ to do** resolver hacer.

resolved [rizâlvd'] *a* resuelto.

resonance [rez'ənəns] *n* resonancia.

resonant [rez'ənənt] *a* resonante.

resort [rizôrt'] *n* (*town*) centro turístico; (*recourse*) recurso ♦ *vi*: **to ~ to** recurrir a; **in the last ~** como último recurso; **seaside/winter sports ~** playa, estación *f* balnearia/centro de deportes de invierno.

resound [rizound'] *vi*: **to ~ (with)** resonar (con).

resounding [rizoun'ding] *a* sonoro; (*fig*) clamoroso.

resource [rē'sôrs] *n* recurso; **~s** *npl* recursos *mpl*; **natural ~s** recursos *mpl* naturales; **to leave sb to his/her own ~s** (*fig*) abandonar a uno/a a sus propios recursos.

resourceful [risôrs'fəl] *a* despabilado, ingenioso.

resourcefulness [risôrs'fəlnis] *n* inventiva, iniciativa.

respect [rispekt'] *n* (*consideration*) respeto; (*relation*) respecto; **~s** *npl* recuerdos *mpl*, saludos *mpl* ♦ *vt* respetar; **with ~ to** con respecto a; **in this ~** en cuanto a eso; **to have** *or* **show ~ for** tener *or* mostrar respeto a; **out of ~ for** por respeto a; **in some ~s** en algunos aspectos; **with due ~ I still think you're wrong** con el respeto debido, sigo creyendo que está equivocado.

respectability [rispektəbil'ətē] *n* respetabilidad *f*.

respectable [rispek'təbəl] *a* respetable; (*quite big: amount etc*) apreciable; (*passable*) tolerable; (*quite good: player, result etc*) bastante bueno.

respected [rispek'tid] *a* respetado, estimado.

respectful [rispek'fəl] *a* respetuoso.

respectfully [rispek'fəlē] *ad* respetuosamente; **Yours ~** Le saluda atentamente.

respecting [rispek'ting] *prep* (con) respecto a, en cuanto a.

respective [rispek'tiv] *a* respectivo.

respectively [rispek'tivlē] *ad* respectivamente.

respiration [respərā'shən] *n* respiración *f*.

respiratory [res'pûrətôrē] *a* respiratorio.

respite [res'pit] *n* respiro; (*LAW*) prórroga.

resplendent [risplen'dənt] *a* resplandeciente.

respond [rispând'] *vi* responder; (*react*) reaccionar.

respondent [rispân'dənt] *n* (*LAW*) acusado/a.

response [rispâns'] *n* respuesta; (*reaction*) reacción *f*; **in ~ to** como respuesta a.

responsibility [rispânsəbil'ətē] *n* responsabilidad *f*; **to take ~ for sth/sb** admitir responsabilidad por algo/uno.

responsible [rispân'səbəl] *a* (*liable*): **~ (for)** responsable (de); (*character*) serio, formal; (*job*) de confianza; **to be ~ to sb**

(for sth) ser responsable ante uno (de algo).

responsibly [rispán'səblē] *ad* con seriedad.

responsive [rispán'siv] *a* sensible.

rest [rest] *n* descanso, reposo; (*MUS*) pausa, silencio; (*support*) apoyo; (*remainder*) resto ♦ *vi* descansar; **to have a ~** echarse una siesta; (*be supported*): **to ~ on** posar(se) en ♦ *vt* (*lean*): **to ~ sth on/against** apoyar algo en *or* sobre/contra; **the ~ of them** (*people*, *objects*) los demás; **to set sb's mind at ~** tranquilizar a uno; **to ~ one's eyes** *or* **gaze on** fijar la mirada en; **it ~s with him** depende de él; **~ assured that ...** téngalo por seguro que ....

rest area *n* (*US AUT*) apartadero.

restaurant [res'túrənt] *n* restorán *m*, restaurante *m*.

restaurant car *n* (*Brit*) coche-comedor *m*.

restaurant owner *n* dueño/a *or* propietario/a de un restaurante.

rest cure *n* cura de reposo.

restful [rest'fəl] *a* descansado, tranquilo.

rest home *n* residencia para jubilados.

restitution [restitoo'shən] *n*: **to make ~ to sb for sth** indemnizar a uno por algo.

restive [res'tiv] *a* inquieto; (*horse*) rebelón/ona.

restless [rest'lis] *a* inquieto; **to get ~** impacientarse.

restlessly [rest'lislē] *ad* inquietamente, con inquietud *f*.

restlessness [rest'lisnis] *n* inquietud *f*.

restock [rēstâk'] *vt* reaprovisionar.

restoration [restərā'shən] *n* restauración *f*.

restorative [ristôr'ətiv] *a* reconstituyente, fortalecedor(a) ♦ *n* reconstituyente *m*.

restore [ristôr'] *vt* (*building*) restaurar; (*sth stolen*) devolver; (*health*) restablecer.

restorer [ristôr'ûr] *n* (*ART etc*) restaurador(a) *m/f*.

restrain [ristrān'] *vt* (*feeling*) contener, refrenar; (*person*): **to ~ (from doing)** disuadir (de hacer).

restrained [ristrānd'] *a* (*style*) reservado.

restraint [ristrānt'] *n* (*restriction*) freno, control *m*; (*of style*) reserva; **wage ~** control *m* de sueldos.

restrict [ristrikt'] *vt* restringir, limitar.

restricted [ristrik'tid] *a* restringido, limitado.

restriction [ristrik'shən] *n* restricción *f*, limitación *f*.

restrictive [ristrik'tiv] *a* restrictivo.

restrictive practices *npl* (*INDUSTRY*) prácticas *fpl* restrictivas.

rest room *n* (*US*) aseos *mpl*.

restructure [rēstruk'chûr] *vt* reestructurar.

rest stop *n* (*US AUT*) apartadero.

result [rizult'] *n* resultado ♦ *vi*: **to ~ in** terminar en, tener por resultado; **as a ~ of** a *or* como consecuencia de; **to ~ (from)** resultar (de).

resultant [rizul'tənt] *a* resultante.

resume [rēzoom'] *vt* (*work*, *journey*) reanudar; (*sum up*) resumir ♦ *vi* (*meeting*) continuar.

résumé [rez'oomā'] *n* resumen *m*; (*US*) curriculum *m* (vitae).

resumption [rizump'shən] *n* reanudación *f*.

resurgence [risûr'jəns] *n* resurgimiento.

resurrection [rezərek'shən] *n* resurrección *f*.

resuscitate [risus'ətāt] *vt* (*MED*) resucitar.

resuscitation [risusətā'shən] *n* resucitación *f*.

retail [rē'tāl] *n* venta al por menor ♦ *cpd* al por menor ♦ *vt* vender al por menor *or* al detalle ♦ *vi*: **to ~ at** (*COMM*) tener precio al público de.

retailer [rē'tālûr] *n* detallista *m/f*.

retail outlet *n* punto de venta.

retail price *n* precio de venta al público, precio al detalle *or* al por menor.

retail price index *n* índice *m* de precios al por menor.

retain [ritān'] *vt* (*keep*) retener, conservar; (*employ*) contratar.

retainer [ritā'nûr] *n* (*servant*) criado; (*fee*) anticipo.

retaliate [rital'ēāt] *vi*: **to ~ (against)** tomar represalias (contra).

retaliation [ritalēā'shən] *n* represalias *fpl*; **in ~ for** como represalia por.

retaliatory [rital'ēətôrē] *a* de represalia.

retarded [ritâr'did] *a* retrasado.

retch [rech] *vi* darle a uno arcadas.

retentive [riten'tiv] *a* (*memory*) retentivo.

rethink [rēthingk'] *vt* repensar.

reticence [ret'isəns] *n* reticencia, reserva.

reticent [ret'isənt] *a* reservado.

retina [ret'ənə] *n* retina.

retinue [ret'ənoo] *n* séquito, comitiva.

retire [ritiûr'] *vi* (*give up work*) jubilarse; (*withdraw*) retirarse; (*go to bed*) acostarse.

retired [ritiûrd'] *a* (*person*) jubilado.

retirement [ritiûr'mənt] *n* (*state*) retiro; (*act*) jubilación *f*; **early ~** jubilación *f* temprana.

retiring [ritiûr'ing] *a* (*departing*: *chairman*) saliente; (*shy*) retraído.

retort [ritôrt'] *n* (*reply*) réplica ♦ *vi* contestar.

retrace [rētrās'] *vt*: **to ~ one's steps** volver sobre sus pasos, desandar lo andado.

retract [ritrakt'] *vt* (*statement*) retirar; (*claws*) retraer; (*landing gear*, *aerial*) replegar ♦ *vi* retractarse.

retractable [ritrakt'əbəl] *a* replegable.

retrain [rētrān'] *vt* reciclar.

retraining [rētrā'ning] *n* readaptación *f* profesional.

retread [rē'tred] *n* neumático *or* llanta (*LAm*) recauchutado/a.

retreat [ritrēt'] *n* (*place*) retiro; (*MIL*) reti-

rada ♦ *vi* retirarse; (*flood*) bajar; **to beat a hasty ~** (*fig*) retirarse en desorden.
retrial [rētrīl'] *n* nuevo proceso.
retribution [retrəbyōō'shən] *n* desquite *m*.
retrieval [ritrē'vəl] *n* recuperación *f*; **information ~** recuperación *f* de datos.
retrieve [ritrēv'] *vt* recobrar; (*situation, honor*) salvar; (*COMPUT*) recuperar; (*error*) reparar.
retriever [ritrē'vûr] *n* perro cobrador.
retroactive [retrōak'tiv] *a* retroactivo.
retrograde [ret'rəgrād] *a* retrógrado.
retrospect [ret'rəspekt] *n*: **in ~** retrospectivamente.
retrospective [retrəspek'tiv] *a* retrospectivo; (*law*) retroactivo ♦ *n* exposición *f* retrospectiva.
return [ritûrn'] *n* (*going or coming back*) vuelta, regreso; (*of sth stolen etc*) devolución *f*; (*recompense*) recompensa; (*FINANCE: from land, shares*) ganancia, ingresos *mpl*; (*COMM: of merchandise*) devolución *f* ♦ *cpd* (*journey*) de regreso; (*ticket*) de ida y vuelta; (*match*) de desquite ♦ *vi* (*person etc: come or go back*) volver, regresar; (*symptoms etc*) reaparecer ♦ *vt* devolver; (*favor, love etc*) corresponder a; (*verdict*) pronunciar; (*POL: candidate*) elegir; **~s** *npl* (*COMM*) ingresos *mpl*; **tax ~** declaración *f* sobre la renta; **in ~ (for)** en cambio (de); **by ~ mail** a vuelta de correo; **many happy ~s (of the day)!** ¡feliz cumpleaños!
returnable [ritûr'nəbəl] *a*: **~ bottle** envase *m* retornable.
return key *n* (*COMPUT*) tecla de retorno.
reunion [rēyōōn'yən] *n* reunión *f*.
reunite [rēyōōnīt'] *vt* reunir; (*reconcile*) reconciliar.
rev [rev] *n abbr* (*AUT*: = *revolution*) revolución *f* ♦ (*vb: also:* **~ up**) *vt* girar ♦ *vi* (*engine*) girarse; (*driver*) girar el motor.
revaluation [rēval'yōōāshən] *n* revalorización *f*.
revamp [rēvamp'] *vt* (*house, company*) renovar.
Rev(d). *abbr* (= *reverend*) R., Rvdo.
reveal [rivēl'] *vt* (*make known*) revelar.
revealing [rivē'ling] *a* revelador(a).
reveille [rev'əlē] *n* (*MIL*) diana.
revel [rev'əl] *vi*: **to ~ in sth/in doing sth** gozar de algo/con hacer algo.
revelation [revəlā'shən] *n* revelación *f*.
reveler, (*Brit*) **reveller** [rev'əlûr] *n* jaranero, juergista *m/f*.
revelry [rev'əlrē] *n* jarana, juerga.
revenge [rivenj'] *n* venganza; (*in sport*) revancha; **to take ~ on** vengarse de; **to get one's ~ (for sth)** vengarse (de algo).
revengeful [rivenj'fəl] *a* vengativo.
revenue [rev'ənōō] *n* ingresos *mpl*, rentas *fpl*.
revenue account *n* cuenta de ingresos

presupuestarios.
revenue expenditure *n* gasto corriente.
reverberate [rivûr'bərāt] *vi* (*sound*) resonar, retumbar.
reverberation [rivûrbərā'shən] *n* retumbo, eco.
revere [rivēr'] *vt* reverenciar, venerar.
reverence [rev'ûrəns] *n* reverencia.
Reverend [rev'ûrənd] *a* (*in titles*): **the ~ John Smith** (*Anglican*) el Reverendo John Smith; (*Catholic*) el Padre John Smith; (*Protestant*) el Pastor John Smith.
reverent [rev'ûrənt] *a* reverente.
reverie [rev'ûrē] *n* ensueño.
reversal [rivûr'səl] *n* (*of order*) inversión *f*; (*of policy*) cambio de rumbo; (*of decision*) revocación *f*.
reverse [rivûrs'] *n* (*opposite*) contrario; (*back: of cloth*) revés *m*; (: *of coin*) reverso; (: *of paper*) dorso; (*AUT: also:* **~ gear**) marcha atrás ♦ *a* (*order*) inverso; (*direction*) contrario ♦ *vt* (*decision, AUT*) dar marcha atrás a; (*position, function*) invertir ♦ *vi* (*Brit AUT*) poner en marcha atrás; **in ~ order** en orden inverso; **the ~** lo contrario; **to go into ~** dar marcha atrás.
reverse-charge call [rivûrs'chärj kôl] *n* (*Brit*) llamada a cobro revertido.
reverse video *n* vídeo inverso.
reversible [rivûr'səbəl] *a* (*garment, procedure*) reversible.
reversing lights [rivûr'sing līts] *npl* (*Brit AUT*) luces *fpl* de marcha atrás.
revert [rivûrt'] *vi*: **to ~ to** volver *or* revertir a.
review [rivyōō'] *n* (*magazine, MIL*) revista; (*of book, movie*) reseña; (*US: examination*) repaso, examen *m* ♦ *vt* (*US: subject at school*) repasar, examinar; (*MIL*) pasar revista a; (*book, movie*) reseñar; **to come under ~** ser examinado.
reviewer [rivyōō'ûr] *n* crítico/a.
revile [rivīl'] *vt* injuriar, vilipendiar.
revise [rivīz'] *vt* (*manuscript*) corregir; (*opinion*) modificar; (*Brit: study: subject*) repasar; (*look over*) revisar; **~d edition** edición *f* corregida.
revision [rivizh'ən] *n* corrección *f*; modificación *f*; (*revised version*) repaso, revisión *f*.
revisit [rēviz'it] *vt* volver a visitar.
revitalize [rēvī'təlīz] *vt* revivificar.
revival [rivī'vəl] *n* (*recovery*) reanimación *f*; (*POL*) resurgimiento; (*of interest*) renacimiento; (*THEATER*) reestreno; (*of faith*) despertar *m*.
revive [rivīv'] *vt* resucitar; (*custom*) restablecer; (*hope, courage*) reanimar; (*play*) reestrenar ♦ *vi* (*person*) volver en sí; (*from tiredness*) reponerse; (*business*) reactivarse.
revoke [rivōk'] *vt* revocar.
revolt [rivōlt'] *n* rebelión *f* ♦ *vi* rebelarse,

sublevarse ♦ *vt* dar asco a, repugnar; **to ~ (against sb/sth)** rebelarse (contra uno/ algo).

revolting [rivōl'ting] *a* asqueroso, repugnante.

revolution [revəlōō'shən] *n* revolución *f*.

revolutionary [revəlōō'shənãrē] *a*, *n* revolucionario/a *m/f*.

revolutionize [revəlōō'shəniz] *vt* revolucionar.

revolve [rivâlv'] *vi* dar vueltas, girar.

revolver [rivâl'vûr] *n* revólver *m*.

revolving [rivâl'ving] *a* (*chair, door etc*) giratorio.

revolving credit [rivâl'ving kred'it] *n* crédito rotativo *or* renovable.

revue [rivyōō'] *n* (*THEATER*) revista.

revulsion [rivul'shən] *n* asco, repugnancia.

reward [riwôrd'] *n* premio, recompensa ♦ *vt*: **to ~ (for)** recompensar *or* premiar (por).

rewarding [riwôrd'ing] *a* (*fig*) valioso; **financially ~** económicamente provechoso.

rewind [rēwind'] *vt* (*watch*) dar cuerda a; (*wool etc*) devanar.

rewire [rēwiûr'] *vt* (*house*) renovar la instalación eléctrica de.

reword [rēwûrd'] *vt* expresar en otras palabras.

rewrite [rērit'] *vt* (*irg: like* **write**) reescribir.

Reykjavik [rā'kyəvik] *n* Reykjavik *m*.

RFD *abbr* (*US MAIL*) = *rural free delivery*.

Rh *abbr* (= *rhesus*) Rh *m*.

rhapsody [rap'sədē] *n* (*MUS*) rapsodia; (*fig*): **to go into rhapsodies over** extasiarse por.

Rh factor *n* (*MED*) factor *m* rhesus.

rhetoric [ret'ûrik] *n* retórica.

rhetorical [ritôr'ikəl] *a* retórico.

rheumatic [rōōmat'ik] *a* reumático.

rheumatism [rōō'mətizəm] *n* reumatismo, reúma.

rheumatoid arthritis [rōō'mətoid ârthri'tis] *n* reúma *m* articular.

Rhine [rin] *n*: **the ~** el (río) Rin.

rhinestone [rin'stōn] *n* diamante *m* de imitación.

rhinoceros [rinâs'ûrəs] *n* rinoceronte *m*.

Rhodes [rōdz] *n* Rodas *f*.

rhododendron [rōdədən'drən] *n* rododendro.

Rhone [rōn] *n*: **the ~** el (río) Ródano.

rhubarb [rōō'bârb] *n* ruibarbo.

rhyme [rim] *n* rima; (*verse*) poesía ♦ *vi*: **to ~ (with)** rimar (con); **without ~ or reason** sin ton ni son.

rhythm [rith'əm] *n* ritmo.

rhythmic(al) [rith'mik(əl)] *a* rítmico.

rhythmically [rith'miklē] *ad* rítmicamente.

RI *abbr* (*US MAIL*) = *Rhode Island*.

rib [rib] *n* (*ANAT*) costilla ♦ *vt* (*mock*) tomar el pelo a.

ribald [rib'əld] *a* escabroso.

ribbon [rib'ən] *n* cinta; **in ~s** (*torn*) hecho trizas.

rice [ris] *n* arroz *m*.

ricefield [ris'fēld] *n* arrozal *m*.

rice paddy *n* (*US*) arrozal *m*.

rice pudding *n* arroz *m* con leche.

rich [rich] *a* rico; (*soil*) fértil; (*food*) pesado; (: *sweet*) empalagoso; **the ~** *npl* los ricos; **~es** *npl* riqueza *sg*; **to be ~ in sth** abundar en algo.

richly [rich'lē] *ad* ricamente.

richness [rich'nis] *n* riqueza; fertilidad *f*.

rickets [rik'its] *n* raquitismo.

rickety [rik'ətē] *a* (*old*) desvencijado; (*shaky*) tambaleante.

rickshaw [rik'shô] *n* carro de culi.

ricochet [rikəshā'] *n* rebote *m* ♦ *vi* rebotar.

rid [rid], *pt, pp* **rid** [rid] *vt*: **to ~ sb of sth** librar a uno de algo; **to get ~ of** deshacerse *or* desembarazarse de.

riddance [rid'əns] *n*: **good ~!** ¡y adiós muy buenas!

ridden [rid'ən] *pp of* **ride**.

riddle [rid'əl] *n* (*conundrum*) acertijo; (*mystery*) enigma *m*, misterio ♦ *vt*: **to be ~d with** ser lleno *o* plagado de.

ride [rid] *n* paseo; (*distance covered*) viaje *m*, recorrido ♦ *vb* (*pt* **rode**, *pp* **ridden** [rōd, rid'ən]) *vi* (*horse: as sport*) montar; (*go somewhere: on horse, bicycle*) dar un paseo, pasearse; (*journey: on bicycle, motorcycle, bus*) viajar ♦ *vt* (*a horse*) montar a; (*distance*) viajar; **to ~ a bicycle** andar en bicicleta; **to ~ at anchor** (*NAUT*) estar fondeado; **can you ~ a bike?** ¿sabes montar en bici(cleta)?; **to give sb a ~** (*to work etc*) llevar a uno en el coche; **to go for a ~** dar un paseo; **to take sb for a ~** (*fig*) engañar a uno.
ride out *vt*: **to ~ out the storm** (*fig*) capear el temporal.

rider [ri'dûr] *n* (*on horse*) jinete *m*; (*on bicycle*) ciclista *m/f*; (*on motorcycle*) motociclista *m/f*.

ridge [rij] *n* (*of hill*) cresta; (*of roof*) caballete *m*; (*wrinkle*) arruga.

ridicule [rid'əkyōōl] *n* irrisión *f*, burla ♦ *vt* poner en ridículo, burlarse de; **to hold sth/sb up to ~** poner algo/a uno en ridículo.

ridiculous [ridik'yələs] *a* ridículo.

ridiculously [ridik'yələslē] *ad* ridículamente, de modo ridículo.

riding [ri'ding] *n* equitación *f*; **I like ~** me gusta montar a caballo.

riding habit *n* traje *m* de montar.

riding school *n* escuela de equitación.

rife [rif] *a*: **to be ~** ser muy común; **to be ~ with** abundar en.

riffraff [rif'raf] *n* chusma, gentuza.

rifle [ri'fəl] *n* rifle *m*, fusil *m* ♦ *vt* saquear.
rifle through *vt fus* saquear.

rifle range *n* campo de tiro; (*at fair*) tiro al blanco.

rift |rift| *n* (*fig: between friends*) desavenencia; (*: in party*) escisión *f*.

rig |rig| *n* (*also*: **oil ~**: *on land*) torre *f* de perforación; (*: at sea*) plataforma petrolera ♦ *vt* (*election etc*) amañar los resultados de.

rig up *vt* improvisar.

rigging |rig'ing| *n* (NAUT) aparejo.

right |rīt| *a* (*true, correct*) correcto, exacto; (*suitable*) indicado, debido; (*proper*) apropiado, propio; (*just*) justo; (*morally good*) bueno; (*not left*) derecho ♦ *n* (*title, claim*) derecho; (*not left*) derecha ♦ *ad* (*correctly*) bien, correctamente; (*straight*) derecho, directamente; (*not on the left*) a la derecha; (*to the ~*) hacia la derecha ♦ *vt* enderezar ♦ *excl* ¡bueno!, ¡está bien!; **to be ~** (*person*) tener razón; **to be ~ on time** llegar en punto; **to get sth ~** acertar en algo; **you did the ~ thing** hiciste bien; **let's get it ~ this time!** ¡a ver si esta vez nos sale bien!; **the ~ time** la hora exacta; (*fig*) el momento oportuno; **by ~s** en justicia; **~ and wrong** el bien y el mal; **film ~s** derechos *mpl* de la película; **on the ~** a la derecha; **to be in the ~** tener razón; **~ now** ahora mismo; **~ before/after** inmediatamente antes/después; **~ in the middle** exactamente en el centro; **~ away** en seguida; **~ off the bat** (*US*) en seguida; **to go ~ to the end of sth** llegar hasta el final de algo; **~, who's next?** bueno, ¿quién sigue?; **all ~!** ¡vale!; **I'm/I feel all ~ now** ya estoy bien.

right angle *n* ángulo recto.

righteous |rī'chəs| *a* justado, honrado; (*anger*) justificado.

righteousness |rī'chəsnis| *n* justicia.

rightful |rīt'fəl| *a* (*heir*) legítimo.

right-hand |rīt'hand| *a* (*drive, turn*) por la derecha.

right-handed |rīt'handid| *a* (*person*) que usa la mano derecha.

right-hand man |rīt'hand' man| *n* brazo derecho.

right-hand side |rīt'hand' sīd| *n* derecha.

rightly |rīt'lē| *ad* correctamente, debidamente; (*with reason*) con razón; **if I remember ~** si me acuerdo bien.

right-minded |rīt'mīndid| *a* (*sensible*) sensato; (*decent*) honrado.

right of way *n* (*on path etc*) derecho de paso; (AUT) prioridad *f* de paso.

rights issue *n* (STOCK EXCHANGE) emisión *f* gratuita de acciones.

right-wing |rīt'wing'| *a* (POL) derechista.

right-winger |rīt'wing'ûr| *n* (POL) derechista *m/f*; (*Brit* SPORT) extremo derecha.

rigid |rij'id| *a* rígido; (*person, ideas*) inflexible.

rigidity |rijid'itē| *n* rigidez *f*; inflexibilidad *f*.

rigidly |rij'idlē| *ad* rígidamente; (*inflexibly*) inflexiblemente.

rigmarole |rig'mərōl| *n* galimatías *m inv.*

rigor, (*Brit*) **rigour** |rig'ûr| *n* rigor *m*, severidad *f*.

rigor mortis |rig'ûr môr'tis| *n* rigidez *f* cadavérica.

rigorous |rig'ûrəs| *a* riguroso.

rigorously |rig'ûrəslē| *ad* rigurosamente.

rig-out |rig'out| *n* (*Brit col*) atuendo.

rile |rīl| *vt* irritar.

rim |rim| *n* borde *m*; (*of spectacles*) montura, aro; (*of wheel*) llanta.

rimless |rim'lis| *a* (*spectacles*) sin aros.

rimmed |rimd| *a*: **~ with** con un borde de, bordeado de.

rind |rīnd| *n* (*of bacon*) corteza; (*of lemon etc*) cáscara; (*of cheese*) costra.

ring |ring| *n* (*of metal*) aro; (*on finger*) anillo; (*of people*) corro; (*of objects*) círculo; (*gang*) banda; (*for boxing*) cuadrilátero; (*of circus*) pista; (*bull ~*) ruedo, plaza; (*sound of bell*) toque *m*; (*telephone call*) llamada ♦ *vb* (*pt* **rang**, *pp* **rung** |rang, rung|) *vi* (*on telephone*) llamar por teléfono; (*large bell*) repicar; (*also*: **~ out**: *voice, words*) sonar; (*ears*) zumbar ♦ *vt* (*Brit* TEL: *also*: **~ up**) llamar; (*bell etc*) hacer sonar; (*doorbell*) tocar; **that has the ~ of truth about it** eso suena a verdad; **to give sb a ~** (*Brit* TEL) llamar por teléfono a uno, dar un telefonazo a uno; **the name doesn't ~ a bell (with me)** el nombre no me suena; **to ~ sb (up)** (*Brit*) llamar a uno.

ring back *vt, vi* (*Brit* TEL) devolver la llamada.

ring off *vi* (*Brit* TEL) colgar, cortar la comunicación.

ring binder *n* carpeta.

ring finger *n* (dedo) anular *m*.

ringing |ring'ing| *n* (*of bell*) toque *m*, tañido; (*louder: of large bell*) repique *m*; (*of telephone*) sonar *m*; (*in ears*) zumbido.

ringing tone *n* (TEL) tono de llamada.

ringleader |ring'lēdûr| *n* (*of gang*) cabecilla *m/f.*

ringlets |ring'lits| *npl* rizos *mpl*, bucles *mpl*.

ring road *n* (*Brit*) carretera periférica *or* de circunvalación.

rink |ringk| *n* (*also*: **ice ~**) pista de hielo; (*for roller-skating*) pista de patinaje.

rinse |rins| *n* (*of dishes*) enjuague *m*; (*of clothes*) aclarado; (*of hair*) reflejo ♦ *vt* enjuagar; aclarar; dar reflejos a.

Rio (de Janeiro) |rē'ō (dē zhəner'ō)| *n* Río de Janeiro.

riot |rī'ət| *n* motín *m*, disturbio ♦ *vi* amotinarse; **to run ~** desmandarse.

rioter |rī'ətûr| *n* amotinado/a.

riotous |rī'ətəs| *a* alborotado; (*party*) bullicioso; (*uncontrolled*) desenfrenado.

riotously |rī'ətəslē| *ad* bulliciosamente.

riot police *n* policía antidisturbios.

RIP *abbr* (= *rest in peace*) q.e.p.d.

rip [rip] *n* rasgón *m*, rasgadura ♦ *vt* rasgar, desgarrar ♦ *vi* correr.

rip up *vt* hacer pedazos.

ripcord [rip'kôrd] *n* cabo de desgarre.

ripe [rīp] *a* (*fruit*) maduro.

ripen [rī'pən] *vt* madurar ♦ *vi* madurarse.

ripeness [rīp'nis] *n* madurez *f*.

rip-off [rip'ôf] *n* (*col*): **it's a ~!** ¡es una estafa!, ¡es un timo!

riposte [ripōst'] *n* respuesta aguda, réplica.

ripple [rip'əl] *n* onda, rizo; (*sound*) murmullo ♦ *vi* rizarse ♦ *vt* rizar.

rise [rīz] *n* (*slope*) cuesta, pendiente *f*; (*hill*) altura; (*increase: in wages*: Brit) aumento; (: *in prices, temperature*) subida, alza; (*fig: to power etc*) ascenso; (: *ascendancy*) auge *m* ♦ *vi* (*pt* **rose**, *pp* **risen** [rōz, riz'ən]) (*gen*) elevarse; (*prices*) subir; (*waters*) crecer; (*river*) nacer; (*sun*) salir; (*person: from bed etc*) levantarse; (*also:* ~ **up**: *rebel*) sublevarse; (*in rank*) ascender; ~ **to power** ascenso al poder; **to give ~ to** dar lugar *or* origen a; **to ~ to the occasion** ponerse a la altura de las circunstancias.

rising [rī'zing] *a* (*increasing: number*) creciente; (: *prices*) en aumento *or* alza; (*tide*) creciente; (*sun, moon*) naciente ♦ *n* (*uprising*) sublevación *f*.

rising damp *n* (Brit) humedad *f* de paredes.

risk [risk] *n* riesgo, peligro ♦ *vt* (*gen*) arriesgar; (*dare*) atreverse a; **to take** *or* **run the ~ of doing** correr el riesgo de hacer; **at ~** en peligro; **at one's own ~** bajo su propia responsabilidad; **fire/health/ security ~** peligro de incendio/para la salud/para la seguridad.

risk capital *n* capital *m* de riesgo.

risky [ris'kē] *a* arriesgado, peligroso.

risqué [riskā'] *a* (*joke*) subido de color.

rissole [ris'âl] *n* croqueta.

rite [rīt] *n* rito; **last ~s** últimos sacramentos *mpl*.

ritual [rich'ōōəl] *a* ritual ♦ *n* ritual *m*, rito.

rival [rī'vəl] *n* rival *m/f*; (*in business*) competidor(a) *m/f* ♦ *a* rival, opuesto ♦ *vt* competir con.

rivalry [rī'vəlrē] *n* rivalidad *f*, competencia.

river [riv'ûr] *n* río ♦ *cpd* (*port, traffic*) de río, del río; **up/down ~** río arriba/abajo.

riverbank [riv'ûrbangk] *n* orilla (del río).

riverbed [riv'ûrbed] *n* lecho, cauce *m*.

rivet [riv'it] *n* roblón *m*, remache *m* ♦ *vt* remachar; (*fig*) captar.

riveting [riv'iting] *a* (*fig*) fascinante.

Riviera [rivēār'ə] *n*: **the (French) ~** la Costa Azul (francesa), la Riviera (francesa); **the Italian ~** la Riviera italiana.

Riyadh [rēyâd'] *n* Riyadh *m*.

RN *n abbr* (US) = **registered nurse**; (Brit)

= **Royal Navy**.

RNA *n abbr* (= *ribonucleic acid*) ARN *m*, RNA *m*.

road [rōd] *n* (*gen*) camino; (*highway etc*) carretera; (*in town*) calle *f*; **major/minor ~** carretera general/secundaria; **main ~** carretera; **it takes 4 hours by ~** se tarda 4 horas por carretera; **on the ~ to success** en camino del éxito.

roadblock [rōd'blâk] *n* barricada.

road haulage *n* transporte *m* por carretera.

road hog *n* loco/a del volante.

road map *n* mapa *m* de carreteras.

road safety *n* seguridad *f* vial.

roadside [rōd'sīd] *n* borde *m* (del camino) ♦ *cpd* al lado de la carretera; **by the ~** al borde del camino.

road sign *n* señal *f* de tráfico.

roadsweeper [rōd'swēpûr] *n* (Brit: *person*) barrendero/a.

road transport *n* = **road haulage**.

road user *n* usuario/a de la vía pública.

roadway [rōd'wā] *n* calzada.

roadworthy [rōd'wûrthē] *a* (*car*) en buen estado para circular.

roam [rōm] *vi* vagar ♦ *vt* vagar por.

roar [rôr] *n* (*of animal*) rugido, bramido; (*of crowd*) rugido; (*of vehicle, storm*) estruendo; (*of laughter*) carcajada ♦ *vi* rugir, bramar; hacer estruendo; **to ~ with laughter** reírse a carcajadas.

roaring [rôr'ing] *a*: **a ~ success** un tremendo éxito; **to do a ~ trade** hacer buen negocio.

roast [rōst] *n* carne *f* asada, asado ♦ *vt* (*meat*) asar; (*coffee*) tostar.

roast beef *n* rosbif *m*.

rob [râb] *vt* robar; **to ~ sb of sth** robar algo a uno; (*fig: deprive*) quitar algo a uno.

robber [râb'ûr] *n* ladrón/ona *m/f*.

robbery [râb'ûrē] *n* robo.

robe [rōb] *n* (*for ceremony etc*) toga; (*also:* **bath ~**) bata.

robin [râb'in] *n* petirrojo.

robot [rō'bət] *n* robot *m*.

robotics [rōbât'iks] *n* robótica.

robust [rōbust'] *a* robusto, fuerte.

rock [râk] *n* (*gen*) roca; (*boulder*) peña, peñasco; (*Brit: candy*) ≈ pirulí *m* ♦ *vt* (*swing gently: cradle*) balancear, mecer; (: *child*) arrullar; (*shake*) sacudir ♦ *vi* mecerse, balancearse; sacudirse; **on the ~s** (*drink*) con hielo; (*marriage etc*) en ruinas; **to ~ the boat** (*fig*) causar perturbaciones.

rock and roll *n* rocanrol *m*.

rock-bottom [râk'bât'am] *a* (*fig*) por los suelos; **to reach** *or* **touch ~** (*price*) estar por los suelos; (*person*) tocar fondo.

rock climber *n* escalador(a) *m/f*.

rock climbing *n* (SPORT) escalada.

rockery [râk'ûrē] *n* cuadro alpino.

rocket [râk'it] *n* cohete *m* ♦ *vi* (*prices*) ir

por las nubes.

rocket launcher [råk'it lônch'ûr] *n* lanzacohetes *m inv*.

rock face *n* pared *f* de roca.

rock garden *n* cuadro alpino.

rocking chair [råk'ing chär] *n* mecedora.

rocking horse [råk'ing hôrs] *n* caballo de balancín.

rocky [råk'ē] *a* (*gen*) rocoso; (*unsteady: table*) débil.

Rocky Mountains *npl*: **the ~** las Montañas Rocosas.

rococo [rəkō'kō] *a* rococó *inv* ♦ *n* rococó.

rod [råd] *n* vara, varilla; (*TECH*) barra; (*also*: **fishing ~**) caña.

rode [rōd] *pt of* **ride**.

rodent [rō'dənt] *n* roedor *m*.

rodeo [rō'dēō] *n* rodeo.

roe [rō] *n* (*species: also*: **~ deer**) corzo; (*of fish*): **hard/soft ~** hueva/lecha.

rogue [rōg] *n* pícaro, pillo.

roguish [rō'gish] *a* (*child*) travieso; (*smile etc*) pícaro.

ROI *abbr* (= *return on investment*) beneficios por inversión.

role [rōl] *n* papel *m*, rol *m*.

roll [rōl] *n* rollo; (*of bank notes*) fajo; (*also*: **bread ~**) panecillo; (*register*) lista, nómina; (*sound: of drums etc*) redoble *m*; (*movement: of ship*) balanceo ♦ *vt* hacer rodar; (*also*: **~ up**: *string*) enrollar; (: *sleeves*) arremangar; (*cigarettes*) liar; (*also*: **~ out**: *pastry*) aplanar ♦ *vi* (*gen*) rodar; (*drum*) redoblar; (*in walking*) bambolearse; (*ship*) balancearse; **cheese ~** panecillo de queso.

   roll around *vi* (*person*) revolcarse.

   roll by *vi* (*time*) pasar.

   roll in *vi* (*mail, cash*) entrar a raudales.

   roll over *vi* dar una vuelta.

   roll up *vi* (*col: arrive*) presentarse, aparecer ♦ *vt* (*carpet, cloth, map*) arrollar; (*sleeves*) arremangar; **to ~ o.s. up into a ball** acurrucarse, hacerse un ovillo.

roll call *n*: **to take a ~** pasar lista.

roller [rō'lûr] *n* rodillo; (*wheel*) rueda.

roller coaster *n* montaña rusa.

roller skates *npl* patines *mpl* de rueda.

rollicking [rål'iking] *a*: **we had a ~ time** nos divertimos una barbaridad.

rolling [rō'ling] *a* (*landscape*) ondulado.

rolling mill *n* taller *m* de laminación.

rolling pin *n* rodillo (de cocina).

rolling stock *n* (*RAIL*) material *m* rodante.

ROM [råm] *n abbr* (= *read only memory*) (memoria) ROM *f*.

romaine (lettuce) [rōmān' (let'is)] *n* (*US*) lechuga cos.

Roman [rō'mən] *a*, *n* romano/a *m/f*.

Roman Catholic *a*, *n* católico/a *m/f* (romano/a).

romance [rōmans'] *n* (*love affair*) amor *m*; (*charm*) lo romántico; (*novel*) novela de

amor.

romanesque [rōmənesk'] *a* románico.

Romania [rōmā'nēə] *n* = **Rumania**.

Romanian [rəmā'nēən] *a*, *n* = **Rumanian**.

Roman numeral *n* número romano.

romantic [rōman'tik] *a* romántico.

romanticism [rōman'tisizəm] *n* romanticismo.

Romany [rōm'ənē] *a* gitano ♦ *n* (*person*) gitano/a; (*LING*) lengua gitana, caló (*Sp*).

Rome [rōm] *n* Roma.

romp [rämp] *n* retozo, juego ♦ *vi* (*also*: **~ around**) jugar, brincar; **to ~ home** (*horse*) ganar fácilmente.

rompers [råm'pûrz] *npl* pelele *m*.

roof [rōōf] *n* (*gen*) techo; (*of house*) techo, tejado; (*of car*) baca ♦ *vt* techar, poner techo a; **~ of the mouth** paladar *m*.

roofing [rōō'fing] *n* techumbre *f*.

roof rack *n* (*AUT*) baca, portaequipajes *m inv*.

rook [rōōk] *n* (*bird*) graja; (*CHESS*) torre *f*.

room [rōōm] *n* (*in house*) cuarto, habitación *f*, pieza (*esp LAm*); (*also*: **bed~**) dormitorio; (*in school etc*) sala; (*space*) sitio, cabida; **~s** *npl* (*lodging*) alojamiento *sg*; **"~s for rent"**, (*Brit*) **"~s to let"** "se alquilan pisos *or* cuartos"; **~ and board** casa y comida; **single/double ~** habitación individual/doble *or* para dos personas; **is there ~ for this?** ¿cabe esto?; **to make ~ for sb** hacer lugar para uno; **there is ~ for improvement** podría mejorarse.

roominess [rōō'mēnis] *n* amplitud *f*, espaciosidad *f*.

rooming house [rōō'ming hous] *n* (*US*) pensión *f*.

roommate [rōōm'māt] *n* compañero/a de cuarto *or* piso.

room service *n* servicio de habitaciones.

room temperature *n* temperatura ambiente.

roomy [rōō'mē] *a* espacioso.

roost [rōōst] *n* percha ♦ *vi* pasar la noche.

rooster [rōōs'tûr] *n* gallo.

root [rōōt] *n* (*BOT, MATH*) raíz *f* ♦ *vi* (*plant, belief*) arriesgarse; **to take ~** (*plant*) echar raíces; (*idea*) arraigar(se); **the ~ of the problem is that ...** el fondo *or* lo fundamental del problema es que ....

   root around *vi* (*fig*) andar buscando.

   root for *vt fus* apoyar a.

   root out *vt* desarraigar.

rooted [rōō'tid] *a* enraizado; (*opinions etc*) arraigado.

rope [rōp] *n* cuerda; (*NAUT*) cable *m* ♦ *vt* (*box*) atar *or* amarrar con (una) cuerda; (*climbers: also*: **~ together**) encordarse; **to jump** *or* **skip ~** (*US*) saltar a la comba; **to ~ sb in** (*fig*) persuadir a uno a tomar parte; **to know the ~s** (*fig*) conocer los trucos (del oficio).

rope ladder *n* escala de cuerda.

rosary [rō'zûrē] *n* rosario.
rose [rōz] *pt of* **rise** ♦ *n* rosa; (*also:* ~**bush**) rosal *m*; (*on watering can*) roseta ♦ *a* color de rosa.
rosé [rōzā'] *n* vino rosado, clarete *m*.
rosebed [rōz'bed] *n* rosaleda.
rosebud [rōz'bud] *n* capullo de rosa.
rosebush [rōz'boosh] *n* rosal *m*.
rosemary [rōz'mārē] *n* romero.
rosette [rōzet'] *n* rosetón *m*.
roster [râs'tûr] *n*: **duty** ~ lista de deberes.
rostrum [râs'trəm] *n* tribuna.
rosy [rō'zē] *a* rosado, sonrosado; **the future looks** ~ el futuro parece prometedor.
rot [rât] *n* (*decay*) putrefacción *f*, podredumbre *f*; (*fig: pej*) tonterías *fpl* ♦ *vt, vi* pudrirse, corromperse; **it has** ~**ted** está podrido; **to stop the** ~ (*Brit: fig*) poner fin a las pérdidas.
rota [rō'tə] *n* lista (de tandas).
rotary [rō'tûrē] *a* rotativo.
rotate [rō'tāt] *vt* (*revolve*) hacer girar, dar vueltas a; (*crops*) cultivar en rotación; (*jobs*) alternar ♦ *vi* (*revolve*) girar, dar vueltas.
rotating [rō'tāting] *a* (*movement*) rotativo.
rotation [rōtā'shən] *n* rotación *f*; **in** ~ por turno.
rote [rōt] *n*: **by** ~ de memoria.
rotor [rō'tûr] *n* rotor *m*.
rotten [rât'ən] *a* (*decayed*) podrido; (: *wood*) carcomido; (*fig*) corrompido; (*col: bad*) pésimo; **to feel** ~ (*ill*) sentirse muy mal; ~ **to the core** completamente podrido.
rotund [rōtund'] *a* rotundo.
rouge [roozh] *n* colorete *m*.
rough [ruf] *a* (*skin, surface*) áspero; (*terrain*) quebrado; (*road*) desigual; (*voice*) bronco; (*person, manner: coarse*) tosco, grosero; (*weather*) borrascoso; (*treatment*) brutal; (*sea*) bravo; (*cloth*) basto; (*plan*) preliminar; (*guess*) aproximado; (*violent*) violento ♦ *n* (*GOLF*): **in the** ~ en las hierbas altas; **to** ~ **it** vivir sin comodidades; **the sea is** ~ **today** el mar está agitado hoy; **to have a** ~ **time (of it)** pasar una mala temporada; ~ **estimate** cálculo aproximado.
roughage [ruf'ij] *n* fibra(s) *f(pl)*, forraje *m*.
rough-and-ready [ruf'ənred'ē] *a* improvisado, tosco.
rough-and-tumble [ruf'əntum'bəl] *n* pelea.
roughcast [ruf'kast] *n* mezcla gruesa.
rough copy, rough draft *n* borrador *m*.
roughen [ruf'ən] *vt* (*a surface*) poner áspero.
roughly [ruf'lē] *ad* (*handle*) torpemente; (*make*) toscamente; (*approximately*) aproximadamente; ~ **speaking** más o menos.
roughness [ruf'nis] *n* aspereza; tosquedad *f*; brutalidad *f*.

roughshod [ruf'shâd'] *ad*: **to ride** ~ **over** (*person*) pisotear a; (*objections*) hacer caso omiso de.
rough work *n* (*SCOL etc*) borrador *m*.
roulette [roolet'] *n* ruleta.
Roumania [roomā'nēə] *n* = **Rumania**.
round [round] *a* redondo ♦ *n* círculo; (*Brit: of toast*) rodaja; (*of policeman*) ronda; (*of milkman*) recorrido; (*of doctor*) visitas *fpl*; (*game: of cards, in competition*) partida; (*of ammunition*) cartucho; (*BOXING*) asalto; (*of talks*) ronda ♦ *vt* (*corner*) doblar ♦ *prep* alrededor de ♦ *ad*: **all the year** ~ durante todo el año; **she arrived** ~ (**about**) **noon** (*Brit*) llegó alrededor del mediodía; **in** ~ **figures** en cifras redondas; **to go the** ~**s** (*story*) divulgarse; **a** ~ **of applause** una salva de aplausos; **a** ~ **of drinks/sandwiches** una ronda de bebidas/bocadillos; **the daily** ~ la rutina cotidiana; *see also* **around**.
round off *vt* (*speech etc*) acabar, poner término a.
round up *vt* (*cattle*) acorralar; (*people*) reunir; (*prices*) redondear.
roundabout [round'əbout] *n* (*Brit: AUT*) glorieta, redondel *m*; (: *at fair*) tiovivo ♦ *a* (*route, means*) indirecto.
rounded [roun'did] *a* redondeado, redondo.
rounders [roun'dûrz] *n* (*Brit: game*) *juego similar al béisbol.*
roundly [round'lē] *ad* (*fig*) rotundamente.
round-shouldered [round'shōldûrd] *a* cargado de espaldas.
round trip *n* viaje *m* de ida y vuelta.
round-trip ticket [round'trip tik'it] *n* billete *m* de ida y vuelta.
roundup [round'up] *n* rodeo; (*of criminals*) redada; **a** ~ **of the latest news** un resumen de las últimas noticias.
rouse [rouz] *vt* (*wake up*) despertar; (*stir up*) suscitar.
rousing [rou'zing] *a* (*applause*) caluroso; (*speech*) conmovedor(a).
rout [rout] *n* (*MIL*) derrota; (*flight*) fuga ♦ *vt* derrotar.
route [root] *n* ruta, camino; (*of bus*) recorrido; (*of shipping*) rumbo, derrota; **the best** ~ **to New York** el mejor camino *or* la mejor ruta para ir a Nueva York; **en** ~ **from** ... **to** en el viaje de ... a; **en** ~ **for** rumbo a, con destino en.
routine [rootēn'] *a* (*work*) rutinario ♦ *n* rutina; (*THEATER*) número; (*COMPUT*) rutina; ~ **procedure** trámite *m* rutinario.
rover [rō'vûr] *n* vagabundo/a.
roving [rō'ving] *a* (*wandering*) errante; (*salesman*) ambulante; (*reporter*) volante.
row *n* [rō] (*line*) fila, hilera; (*KNITTING*) pasada; [rou] (*noise*) escándalo; (*dispute*) bronca, pelea; (*fuss*) jaleo; (*scolding*) regaño ♦ *vi* [rō] (*in boat*) remar; [rou] reñir(se) ♦ *vt* [rō] (*boat*) conducir remando;

4 days in a ~ 4 días seguidos; **to make a ~** armar un lío; **to have a ~** pelearse, reñir.

rowboat [rō'bōt] *n* (*US*) bote *m* de remos.

rowdy [rou'dē] *a* (*person: noisy*) ruidoso; (: *quarrelsome*) pendenciero; (*occasion*) alborotado ♦ *n* pendenciero.

rowdyism [rou'dēizəm] *n* pendencias *fpl*.

row houses *npl* (*US*) casas *fpl* adosadas.

rowing [rō'ing] *n* remo.

rowing boat *n* (*Brit*) bote *m* or barco de remos.

rowlock [rō'lák] *n* (*Brit*) chumacera.

royal [roi'əl] *a* real.

Royal Air Force (RAF) *n* Fuerzas Aéreas Británicas *fpl*.

royal blue *n* azul *m* marino.

royalist [roi'əlist] *a, n* monárquico/a *m/f*.

Royal Navy (RN) *n* (*Brit*) Marina Británica.

royalty [roi'əltē] *n* (*royal persons*) (miembros *mpl* de la) familia real; (*payment to author*) derechos *mpl* de autor.

RP *n abbr* (*Brit*: = *received pronunciation*) *pronunciación estándar del inglés.*

rpm *abbr* (= *revs per minute*) r.p.m.

RR *abbr* (*US*) = **railroad.**

RRP *n abbr* (*Brit*) = **recommended retail price.**

R & R *n abbr* (*US MIL*) = *rest and recreation.*

R.S.V.P. *abbr* (= *répondez s'il vous plaît*) SRC.

Rt. Hon. *abbr* (*Brit*: = *Right Honourable*) *título honorífico de diputado.*

Rt. Rev. *abbr* (= *Right Reverend*) Rvdo.

rub [rub] *vt* (*gen*) frotar; (*hard*) restregar ♦ *n* (*gen*) frotamiento; (*touch*) roce *m*; **to ~ sb the wrong way** or (*Brit*) **~ sb up** entrarle uno por mal ojo.

rub down *vt* (*body*) secar frotando; (*horse*) almohazar.

rub in *vt* (*ointment*) frotar.

rub off *vt* borrarse ♦ *vi* quitarse (frotando); **to ~ off on sb** influir en uno, pegársele a uno.

rub out *vt* borrar ♦ *vi* borrarse.

rubber [rub'ûr] *n* caucho, goma; (*Brit*: *eraser*) goma de borrar.

rubber band *n* goma, gomita.

rubber plant *n* ficus *m*.

rubber stamp *n* sello (de caucho) ♦ *vt*: **rubber-stamp** (*fig*) aprobar maquinalmente.

rubbery [rub'ûrē] *a* elástico, parecido a la goma.

rubbing alcohol [rub'ing al'kəhôl] *n* (*US*) alcohol *m*.

rubbish [rub'ish] *n* (*waste*) desperdicios *mpl*; (*Brit*: *from household*) basura; (*fig*: *pej*) tonterías *fpl*; (*trash*) pacotilla ♦ *vt* (*Brit*: *col*) poner por los suelos; **what you've just said is ~** lo que acabas de de-

cir es una tontería.

rubbish bin *n* (*Brit*) cubo or bote *m* (*LAm*) de la basura.

rubbish dump *n* (*Brit*: *in town*) vertedero, basurero.

rubbishy [rub'ishē] *a* (*Brit*) de mala calidad, de pacotilla.

rubble [rub'əl] *n* escombros *mpl*.

ruble [rōō'bəl] *n* rublo.

ruby [rōō'bē] *n* rubí *m*.

RUC *n abbr* (= *Royal Ulster Constabulary*) *fuerza de policía en Irlanda del Norte.*

rucksack [ruk'sak] *n* mochila.

rudder [rud'ûr] *n* timón *m*.

ruddy [rud'ē] *a* (*face*) rubicundo.

rude [rōōd] *a* (*impolite*: *person*) grosero; (: *word, manners*) rudo, grosero; (*indecent*) indecente; **to be ~ to sb** ser grosero con uno.

rudeness [rōōd'nis] *n* grosería, tosquedad *f*.

rudiment [rōō'dəmənt] *n* rudimento.

rudimentary [rōōdəmən'tûrē] *a* rudimentario.

rueful [rōō'fəl] *a* arrepentido.

ruffian [ruf'ēən] *n* matón *m*, criminal *m*.

ruffle [ruf'əl] *vt* (*hair*) despeinar; (*clothes*) arrugar; (*fig*: *person*) agitar.

rug [rug] *n* alfombra.

rugby [rug'bē] *n* (*also*: ~ **football**) rugby *m*.

rugged [rug'id] *a* (*landscape*) accidentado; (*features*) robusto.

ruin [rōō'in] *n* ruina ♦ *vt* arruinar; (*spoil*) estropear; **~s** *npl* ruinas *fpl*, restos *mpl*; **in ~s** en ruinas.

ruinous [rōō'inəs] *a* ruinoso.

rule [rōōl] *n* (*norm*) norma, costumbre *f*; (*regulation*) regla; (*government*) dominio; (*ruler*) metro; (*dominion etc*): **under British ~** bajo el dominio británico ♦ *vt* (*country, person*) gobernar; (*decide*) disponer; (*draw lines*) trazar ♦ *vt* gobernar; (*LAW*) fallar; **to ~ against/in favor of/on** fallar en contra de/a favor de/sobre; **to ~ that ...** (*umpire, judge*) fallar que ...; **it's against the ~s** está prohibido; **as a ~** por regla general, generalmente; **by ~ of thumb** por experiencia; **majority ~** (*POL*) gobierno mayoritario; **the ~s of the road** el código de la circulación.

rule out *vt* excluir.

ruled [rōōld] *a* (*paper*) rayado.

ruler [rōō'lûr] *n* (*sovereign*) soberano; (*for measuring*) regla.

ruling [rōō'ling] *a* (*party*) gobernante; (*class*) dirigente ♦ *n* (*LAW*) fallo, decisión *f*.

rum [rum] *n* ron *m*.

Rumania [rōōmā'nēə] *n* Rumanía.

Rumanian [rōōmā'nēən] *a, n* rumano/a *m/f*.

rumble [rum'bəl] *n* retumbo, ruido sordo; (*of thunder*) redoble *m* ♦ *vi* retumbar, hacer un ruido sordo; (*stomach, pipe*) sonar.

rummage [rum'ij] *vi* revolverlo todo.

rummage sale n (US) venta de objetos usados con fines benéficos.

rumor, (Brit) **rumour** [roō'mûr] n rumor m ♦ vt: **it is ~ed that...** se rumorea que... .

rump [rump] n (of animal) ancas fpl, grupa.

rumple [rum'pəl] vt (clothes) arrugar; (hair) despeinar.

rump steak n filete m de lomo.

rumpus [rum'pəs] n (col) lío, jaleo; (quarrel) pelea, riña; **to kick up a ~** armar un follón or armar bronca.

run [run] n (SPORT) carrera; (trip) paseo, excursión f; (distance traveled) trayecto; (series) serie f; (THEATER) temporada; (SKI) pista; (in tights, stockings) carrera ♦ vb (pt **ran**, pp **run** [ran, run]) vt (operate: business) dirigir; (: competition, course) organizar; (: hotel, house) administrar, llevar; (COMPUT: program) ejecutar; (to pass: hand) pasar; (tights) hacer una carrera en; (bath): **to ~ a bath** llenar la bañera ♦ vi (gen) correr; (work: machine) funcionar, marchar; (bus, train: operate) circular, ir; (: travel) ir; (continue: play) seguir; (: contract) ser válido; (flow: river, bath) fluir; (colors, washing) desteñirse; (in election) ser candidato; **to go for a ~** dar una vuelta; **to make a ~ for it** echar(se) a correr, escapar(se), huir; **to have the ~ of sb's house** tener el libre uso de la casa de uno; **a ~ of luck** una racha de suerte; **there was a ~ on** (meat, tickets) hubo mucha demanda de; **in the long ~** a la larga; **on the ~** en fuga; **I'll ~ you to the station** te llevaré a la estación en coche; **to ~ a risk** correr un riesgo; **to ~ a stoplight** (US) saltarse el semáforo en rojo; **to ~ errands** hacer or llevar recados; **it's very cheap to ~** es muy económico; **to ~ for Congress** (US) presentarse como candidato a las elecciones al Congreso; **to ~ for the bus** correr tras el autobús; **we shall have to ~ for it** tendremos que escapar; **the train ~s between Boston and New York** el tren circula entre Boston y Nueva York; **the bus ~s every 20 minutes** hay salidas de bus cada 20 minutos; **to ~ on gasoline/on diesel/off batteries** funcionar con gasolina/gasoil/baterías; **the car ran into the lamppost** el coche chocó contra el farol.

run about (Brit) = **run around**.

run across vt fus (find) dar or topar con.

run around vi (children) correr por todos lados.

run away vi huir.

run down vi (clock) parar ♦ vt (reduce: production) ir reduciendo; (factory) restringir la producción de; (AUT) atropellar; (criticize) criticar; **to be ~ down** (person: tired) encontrarse agotado.

run in vt (Brit: car) rodar.

run into vt fus (meet: person, trouble)

tropezar con; (collide with) chocar con; **to ~ into debt** contraer deudas, endeudarse.

run off vt (water) dejar correr ♦ vi huir corriendo.

run out vi (person) salir corriendo; (liquid) irse; (lease) caducar, vencer; (money) acabarse.

run out of vt fus quedar sin; **I've ~ out of gas** se me acabó la gasolina.

run over vt (AUT) atropellar ♦ vt fus (revise) repasar.

run through vt fus (instructions) repasar.

run up vt (debt) incurrir en; **to ~ up against** (difficulties) tropezar con.

runaway [run'əwā] a (horse) desbocado; (truck) sin frenos; (person) fugitivo.

rundown [run'doun] n (Brit: of industry etc) cierre m gradual.

rung [rung] pp of **ring** ♦ n (of ladder) escalón m, peldaño.

run-in [run'in] n (col) altercado.

runner [run'ûr] n (in race: person) corredor(a) m/f; (: horse) caballo; (on sleigh) patín m; (wheel) ruedecilla.

runner bean n (Brit) judía escarlata.

runner-up [runûrup'] n subcampeón/ona m/f.

running [run'ing] n (sport) atletismo; (race) carrera ♦ a (costs, water) corriente; (commentary) continuo; **to be in/out of the ~ for sth** tener/no tener posibilidades de ganar algo; **6 days ~** 6 días seguidos.

running costs npl (of business) gastos mpl (de operación); (of car) gastos mpl corrientes.

running head n (TYP, WORD PROCESSING) encabezamiento normal.

running mate n (US POL) candidato/a a la vice-presidencia.

runny [run'ē] a derretido.

run-off [run'ôf] n (in contest, election) desempate m; (extra race) carrera de desempate.

run-of-the-mill [runəvthəmil'] a común y corriente.

runt [runt] n (also pej) redrojo, enano.

run-up [run'up] n (Brit): **~ to** (election etc) período previo a.

runway [run'wā] n (AVIAT) pista de aterrizaje.

rupee [roō'pē] n rupia.

rupture [rup'chûr] n (MED) hernia ♦ vt: **to ~ o.s.** causarse una hernia.

rural [roōr'əl] a rural.

ruse [roōz] n ardid m.

rush [rush] n ímpetu m; (hurry) prisa, apuro (LAm); (COMM) demanda repentina; (BOT) junco; (current) corriente f fuerte, ráfaga ♦ vt apresurar; (work) hacer de prisa; (attack: town etc) asaltar ♦ vi correr, precipitarse; **gold ~** fiebre f del oro; **we've had a ~ of orders** ha habido una gran demanda; **I'm in a ~ (to do)** tengo prisa *or* apuro (*LAm*) (por hacer); **is there any ~ for this?** ¿te corre prisa esto?; **to ~ sth off** hacer algo de prisa.

rush through *vt fus* (*meal*) comer de prisa; (*book*) leer de prisa; (*work*) hacer de prisa; (*town*) atravesar a toda velocidad; (*COMM: order*) despachar rápidamente.

rush hour *n* horas *fpl* punta.

rush job *n* (*urgent*) trabajo urgente.

rusk [rusk] *n* bizcocho tostado.

Russia [rush'ə] *n* Rusia.

Russian [rush'ən] *a* ruso ♦ *n* ruso/a; (*LING*) ruso.

rust [rust] *n* herrumbre *f*, moho ♦ *vi* oxidarse.

rustic [rus'tik] *a* rústico.

rustle [rus'əl] *vi* susurrar ♦ *vt* (*paper*) hacer crujir; (*US: cattle*) hurtar, robar.

rustproof [rust'prōōf] *a* inoxidable.

rusty [rus'tē] *a* oxidado, mohoso.

rut [rut] *n* surco; (*ZOOL*) celo; **to be in a ~** ser esclavo de la rutina.

rutabaga [rōōtəbā'gə] *n* (*US*) naba.

ruthless [rōōth'lis] *a* despiadado.

RV *abbr* (= *revised version*) traducción inglesa de la Biblia de 1855 ♦ *n abbr* (*US*) = **recreational vehicle.**

rye [rī] *n* centeno.

rye bread *n* pan de centeno.

S

S, s [es] *n* (*letter*) S, s *f*; **S for Sugar** S de sábado.

S *abbr* (= *Saint*) Sto./a.; (*US SCOL: grade: = satisfactory*) suficiente; (= *south*) S; = **small.**

SA *n abbr* = **South Africa, South America.**

sabbath [sab'əth] *n* domingo; (*Jewish*) sábado.

sabbatical [səbat'ikəl] *a:* **~ year** año de licencia.

saber, (*Brit*) **sabre** [sā'bûr] *n* sable *m*.

saber rattling [sā'bûr rat'ling] *n* patriotería, jingoísmo.

sabotage [sab'ətâzh] *n* sabotaje *m* ♦ *vt* sabotear.

saccharin(e) [sak'ûrin] *n* sacarina.

sachet [sashā'] *n* sobrecito.

sack [sak] *n* (*bag*) saco, costal *m* ♦ *vt* (*dismiss*) despedir; (*plunder*) saquear; **to get the ~** ser despedido.

sackful [sak'fəl] *n* saco.

sacking [sak'ing] *n* (*material*) arpillera.

sacrament [sak'rəmənt] *n* sacramento.

sacred [sā'krid] *a* sagrado, santo.

sacrifice [sak'rəfis] *n* sacrificio ♦ *vt* sacrificar; **to make ~s (for sb)** sacrificarse (a favor de uno), privarse (para uno).

sacrilege [sak'rəlij] *n* sacrilegio.

sacrosanct [sak'rōsangkt] *a* sacrosanto.

sad [sad] *a* (*unhappy*) triste; (*deplorable*) lamentable.

sadden [sad'ən] *vt* entristecer.

saddle [sad'əl] *n* silla (de montar); (*of cycle*) sillín *m* ♦ *vt* (*horse*) ensillar; **to ~ sb with sth** (*col: task, bill, name*) cargar a uno con algo; (: *responsibility*) gravar a uno con algo; **to be ~d with sth** (*col*) quedar cargado con algo.

saddlebag [sad'əlbag] *n* alforja.

sadism [sā'dizəm] *n* sadismo.

sadist [sā'dist] *n* sádico/a.

sadistic [sədis'tik] *a* sádico.

sadly [sad'lē] *ad* tristemente; (*regrettably*) desgraciadamente; **~ lacking (in)** muy deficiente (en).

sadness [sad'nis] *n* tristeza.

sae *abbr* (*Brit*) = **stamped addressed envelope.**

safari [səfâ'rē] *n* safari *m*.

safari park *n* parque *m* aventura.

safe [sāf] *a* (*out of danger*) fuera de peligro; (*not dangerous, sure*) seguro; (*unharmed*) ileso; (*trustworthy*) digno de confianza ♦ *n* caja de caudales, caja fuerte; **~ and sound** sano y salvo; **(just) to be on the ~ side** para mayor seguridad; **~ journey!** ¡buen viaje!; **it is ~ to say that ...** se puede decir con confianza que ....

safe-breaker [sāf'brākûr] *n* (*Brit*) = **safe-cracker.**

safe-conduct [sāf'kân'dukt] *n* salvoconducto.

safe-cracker [sāf'krakûr] *n* (*US*) ladrón/ona *m/f* de cajas fuertes.

safe-deposit [sāf'dipâzit] *n* (*vault*) cámara acorazada; (*box*) caja de seguridad *or* de caudales.

safeguard [sāf'gârd] *n* protección *f*, garantía ♦ *vt* proteger, defender.

safekeeping [sāfkē'ping] *n* custodia.

safely [sāf'lē] *ad* seguramente, con seguridad; (*without mishap*) sin peligro; **I can ~ say** puedo decir *or* afirmar con toda seguridad.

safeness [sāf'nis] *n* seguridad *f*.

safe sex *n* sexo seguro.

safety [sāf'tē] *n* seguridad *f* ♦ *cpd* de seguridad; **road ~** seguridad *f* en carretera; **~ first!** ¡precaución!

safety belt *n* cinturón *m* (de seguridad).

safety curtain *n* telón *m* de seguridad.

safety net *n* red *f* (de seguridad).

safety pin *n* imperdible *m*, seguro (*LAm*).

safety valve *n* válvula de seguridad *or* de escape.

saffron [saf'rən] n azafrán m.
sag [sag] vi aflojarse.
saga [sâg'ə] n (HISTORY) saga; (fig) epopeya.
sage [sāj] n (herb) salvia; (man) sabio.
Sagittarius [sajitär'ēəs] n Sagitario.
sago [sā'gō] n sagú m.
Sahara [səhar'ə] n: **the ~ (Desert)** el Sáhara.
Sahel [sâhel] n Sahel m.
said [sed] pt, pp of **say**.
Saigon [sīgân'] n Saigón m.
sail [sāl] n (on boat) vela ♦ vt (boat) gobernar ♦ vi (travel: ship) navegar; (: passenger) pasear en barco; (set off: also: **to set ~**) zarpar; **to go for a ~** dar un paseo en barco; **they ~ed into Copenhagen** arribaron a Copenhague.
sail through vt fus (exam) aprobar fácilmente.
sailboat [sāl'bōt] n (US) velero, barco de vela.
sailing [sā'ling] n (SPORT) balandrismo; **to go ~** salir en balandro.
sailing ship n barco de vela.
sailor [sā'lûr] n marinero, marino.
saint [sānt] n santo; **S~ John** San Juan.
saintliness [sānt'lēnis] n santidad f.
saintly [sānt'lē] a santo.
sake [sāk] n: **for the ~ of** por; **for the ~ of argument** digamos, es un decir; **art for art's ~** el arte por el arte.
salad [sal'əd] n ensalada; **tomato ~** ensalada de tomate.
salad bowl n ensaladera.
salad cream n (Brit) mayonesa.
salad dressing n aliño, mayonesa.
salad oil n aceite m para ensalada.
salami [səlâ'mē] n salami m, salchichón m.
salaried [sal'ûrēd] a asalariado.
salary [sal'ûrē] n sueldo.
salary scale n escala salarial.
sale [sāl] n venta; (at reduced prices) liquidación f, saldo; **"for ~"** "se vende"; **on ~** en venta; **on ~ or return** (goods) venta por reposición; **liquidation ~** liquidación f; **~ and lease back** venta y arrendamiento al vendedor.
saleroom [sāl'rōōm] n (Brit) = **salesroom**.
sales assistant n (Brit) dependiente/a m/f.
sales campaign n campaña de venta.
sales clerk n (US) dependiente/a m/f.
sales conference n conferencia de ventas.
sales drive n promoción f de ventas.
sales figures npl cifras fpl de ventas.
sales force n personal m de ventas.
salesman [sālz'mən] n vendedor m; (in store) dependiente m; (representative) viajante m.
sales manager n gerente m/f de ventas.
salesmanship [sālz'mənship] n arte m de vender.

sales meeting n reunión f de ventas.
salesroom [sālz'rōōm] n (US) sala de subastas.
sales slip n recibo.
sales tax n (US) impuesto sobre la venta.
saleswoman [sālz'wōōmən] n vendedora; (in store) dependienta; (representative) viajante f.
salient [sā'lēənt] a (features, points) sobresaliente.
saline [sā'lēn] a salino.
saliva [səli'və] n saliva.
sallow [sal'ō] a cetrino.
salmon [sam'ən] n (pl inv) salmón m.
salon [səlân'] n (hairdressing ~, beauty ~) salón m.
saloon [səlōōn'] n (US) bar m, taberna; (Brit AUT) (coche m de) turismo; (ship's lounge) cámara, salón m.
Salop [sal'əp] n abbr (Brit) = **Shropshire**.
SALT [sôlt] n abbr (= Strategic Arms Limitation Treaty) tratado SALT.
salt [sôlt] n sal f ♦ vt (also: **put ~ on**) poner sal en; **an old ~** un lobo de mar.
salt away vt (col: money) ahorrar.
saltcellar [sôlt'selûr] n (Brit) salero.
salt mine n mina de sal.
salt shaker [sôlt shā'kûr] n (US) salero.
saltwater [sôlt'wôtûr] a (fish etc) de agua salada, de mar.
salty [sôl'tē] a salado.
salubrious [səlōō'brēəs] a sano; (fig: district etc) atractivo.
salutary [sal'yətärē] a saludable.
salute [səlōōt'] n saludo; (of guns) salva ♦ vt saludar.
salvage [sal'vij] n (saving) salvamento, recuperación f; (things saved) objetos mpl salvados ♦ vt salvar.
salvage vessel n buque m de salvamento.
salvation [salvā'shən] n salvación f.
Salvation Army n Ejército de Salvación.
salve [sav] n (cream etc) ungüento, bálsamo.
salver [sal'vûr] n bandeja.
salvo [sal'vō] n (MIL) salva.
same [sām] a mismo ♦ pron: **the ~** el mismo/la misma; **the ~ book as** el mismo libro que; **on the ~ day** el mismo día; **at the ~ time** (at the ~ moment) al mismo tiempo; (yet) sin embargo; **all** or **just the ~** sin embargo, aun así; **they're one and the ~** (person) son la misma persona; (thing) son iguales; **to do the ~ (as sb)** hacer lo mismo (que otro); **and the ~ to you!** ¡igualmente!; **~ here!** ¡yo también!; **the ~ again** (Brit: in bar etc) otro igual.
sampan [sam'pan] n sampán m.
sample [sam'pəl] n muestra ♦ vt (food, wine) probar; **to take a ~** tomar una muestra; **free ~** muestra gratuita.
sanatorium, pl **-ria** [sanətôr'ēəm, -tôr'ēə] n (Brit) = **sanitarium**.

sanctify [sangk'təfī] *vt* santificar.
sanctimonious [sangktəmō'nēəs] *a* santurrón/ona.
sanction [sangk'shən] *n* sanción *f* ♦ *vt* sancionar; **to impose economic ~s on** *or* **against** imponer sanciones económicas a *or* contra.
sanctity [sangk'titē] *n* (*gen*) santidad *f*; (*inviolability*) inviolabilidad *f*.
sanctuary [sangk'chōōärē] *n* (*gen*) santuario; (*refuge*) asilo, refugio.
sand [sand] *n* arena; (*beach*) playa ♦ *vt* (*also*: ~ **down**: *wood etc*) lijar; (*road*) poner gravilla en.
sandal [san'dəl] *n* sandalia.
sandalwood [san'dəlwōōd] *n* sándalo.
sandbag [sand'bag] *n* saco de arena.
sandblast [sand'blast] *vt* limpiar con chorro de arena.
sandbox [sand'bâks] *n* (*US: for children*) cajón *m* de arena.
sand castle *n* castillo de arena.
sand dune *n* duna.
sandpaper [sand'pāpûr] *n* papel *m* de lija.
sandpit [sand'pit] *n* (*Brit*) = **sandbox**.
sands [sandz] *npl* playa *sg* de arena.
sandstone [sand'stōn] *n* piedra arenisca.
sandstorm [sand'stôrm] *n* tormenta de arena.
sandwich [sand'wich] *n* bocadillo (*Sp*), sandwich *m* (*LAm*) ♦ *vt* (*also*: ~ **in**) intercalar; **to be ~ed between** estar apretujado entre; **cheese/ham ~** sandwich *m* de queso/jamón.
sandwich board *n* cartelón *m*.
sandy [san'dē] *a* arenoso; (*color*) rojizo.
sane [sān] *a* cuerdo, sensato.
sang [sang] *pt of* **sing**.
sanitarium [sanitär'ēəm] *n* (*US*) sanatorio.
sanitary [san'itärē] *a* (*system, arrangements*) sanitario; (*clean*) higiénico.
sanitary napkin *n* paño higiénico, compresa.
sanitation [sanitā'shən] *n* (*in house*) servicios *mpl* higiénicos; (*in town*) servicio de desinfección.
sanitation department *n* (*US*) departamento de limpieza y recogida de basuras.
sanity [san'itē] *n* cordura; (*of judgment*) sensatez *f*.
sank [sangk] *pt of* **sink**.
San Marino [san mərē'nō] *n* San Marino.
Santa Claus [san'tə klôz] *n* San Nicolás *m*, Papá Noel *m*.
Santiago [santēâ'gō] *n* (*also*: ~ **de Chile**) Santiago (de Chile).
sap [sap] *n* (*of plants*) savia ♦ *vt* (*strength*) minar, agotar.
sapling [sap'ling] *n* árbol nuevo *or* joven.
sapphire [saf'īûr] *n* zafiro.
Saragossa [sarəgâs'ə] *n* Zaragoza.
sarcasm [sâr'kazəm] *n* sarcasmo.
sarcastic [sârkas'tik] *a* sarcástico; **to be ~**

ser sarcástico.
sarcophagus, *pl* **sarcophagi** [sârkâf'əgəs, -gī] *n* sarcófago.
sardine [sârdēn'] *n* sardina.
Sardinia [sârdin'ēə] *n* Cerdeña.
Sardinian [sârdin'ēən] *a, n* sardo/a *m/f*.
sardonic [sârdân'ik] *a* sardónico.
sari [sâ'rē] *n* sari *m*.
SAS *n abbr* (*Brit* MIL: = *Special Air Service*) *cuerpo del ejército británico encargado de misiones clandestinas.*
SASE *n abbr* (*US*) = **self-addressed stamped envelope.**
sash [sash] *n* faja.
Sask. *abbr* (*Canada*) = *Saskatchewan.*
sassy [sas'ē] *a* (*US*) fresco, descarado.
SAT *n abbr* (*US*) = *Scholastic Aptitude Test.*
sat [sat] *pt, pp of* **sit**.
Sat. *abbr* (= *Saturday*) sáb.
Satan [sā'tən] *n* Satanás *m*.
satanic [sətan'ik] *a* satánico.
satchel [sach'əl] *n* bolsa; (*child's*) cartera, mochila (*LAm*).
sated [sā'tid] *a* (*appetite, person*) saciado.
satellite [sat'əlīt] *n* satélite *m*.
satellite dish *n* (*TV*) antena parabólica.
satiate [sā'shēāt] *vt* saciar, hartar.
satin [sat'ən] *n* raso ♦ *a* de raso; **with a ~ finish** satinado.
satire [sat'īûr] *n* sátira.
satirical [sətir'ikəl] *a* satírico.
satirist [sat'ûrist] *n* (*writer etc*) escritor(a) *m/f* satírico/a; (*cartoonist*) caricaturista *m/f*.
satirize [sat'ərīz] *vt* satirizar.
satisfaction [satisfak'shən] *n* satisfacción *f*; **it gives me great ~** es para mí una gran satisfacción; **has it been done to your ~?** ¿se ha hecho a su satisfacción?
satisfactorily [satisfak'tərəlē] *ad* satisfactoriamente, de modo satisfactorio.
satisfactory [satisfak'tûrē] *a* satisfactorio.
satisfy [sat'isfī] *vt* satisfacer; (*pay*) liquidar; (*convince*) convencer; **to ~ the requirements** llenar los requisitos; **to ~ sb that** convencer a uno de que; **to ~ o.s. of sth** convencerse de algo.
satisfying [sat'isfīing] *a* satisfactorio.
saturate [sach'ûrāt] *vt*: **to ~ (with)** empapar *or* saturar (de).
saturation [sachərā'shən] *n* saturación *f*.
Saturday [sat'ûrdā] *n* sábado.
sauce [sôs] *n* salsa; (*sweet*) crema; (*fig: cheek*) frescura.
saucepan [sôs'pan] *n* cacerola, olla.
saucer [sô'sûr] *n* platillo.
saucily [sô'silē] *ad* con frescura, descaradamente.
sauciness [sô'sēnis] *n* frescura, descaro.
saucy [sôs'ē] *a* fresco, descarado.
Saudi Arabia [sou'dē ərâ'bēə] *n* Arabia Saudí *or* Saudita.
Saudi (Arabian) [sou'dē (ərā'bēən)] *a, n*

saudí *m/f*, saudita *m/f*.

sauna [sô'nə] *n* sauna.

saunter [sôn'tûr] *vi* deambular.

sausage [sô'sij] *n* salchicha; (*salami etc*) salchichón *m*.

sausage roll *n* empanadilla.

sauté [sôtã'] *a* (*CULIN*: *potatoes*) salteado; (: *onions*) dorado, rehogado ♦ *vt* saltear; dorar.

savage [sav'ij] *a* (*cruel, fierce*) feroz, furioso; (*primitive*) salvaje ♦ *n* salvaje *m/f* ♦ *vt* (*attack*) embestir.

savagely [sav'ijlē] *ad* con ferocidad, furiosamente; de modo salvaje.

savagery [sav'ijrē] *n* ferocidad *f*; salvajismo.

save [sāv] *vt* (*rescue*) salvar, rescatar; (*money, time*) ahorrar; (*set aside*) guardar; (*COMPUT*) salvar (y guardar); (*avoid: trouble*) evitar ♦ *vi* (*also:* ~ **up**) ahorrar ♦ *n* (*SPORT*) parada ♦ *prep* salvo, excepto; **to ~ face** salvar las apariencias; **God ~ the Queen!** ¡Dios guarde a la Reina!, ¡Viva la Reina!; **I ~d you a piece of cake** te he guardado un trozo de tarta; **it will ~ me an hour** con ello ganaré una hora.

saving [sā'ving] *n* (*on price etc*) economía ♦ *a*: **the ~ grace of** el único mérito de; **~s** *npl* ahorros *mpl*; **to make ~s** economizar.

savings account *n* cuenta de ahorros.

savings and loan association *n* (*US*) sociedad *f* inmobiliaria, cooperativa de construcciones.

savings bank *n* caja de ahorros.

savior, (*Brit*) **saviour** [sāv'yûr] *n* salvador(a) *m/f*.

savoir-faire [savwârfär'] *n* don *m* de gentes.

savor, (*Brit*) **savour** [sā'vûr] *n* sabor *m*, gusto ♦ *vt* saborear.

savo(u)ry [sā'vûrē] *a* sabroso; (*dish: not sweet*) salado.

savvy [sav'ē] *n* (*col*) conocimiento, experiencia.

saw [sô] *pt of* **see** ♦ *n* (*tool*) sierra ♦ *vt* (*pt* **sawed**, *pp* **sawed** *or* **sawn** [sôn]) serrar; **to ~ sth up** (a)serrar algo.

sawdust [sô'dust] *n* (a)serrín *m*.

sawed-off [sôd'ôf], (*Brit*) **sawn-off** [sôn'ôf] *a*: **~ shotgun** escopeta de cañones recortados.

sawmill [sô'mil] *n* aserradero.

sawn [sôn] (*Brit*) *pp of* **saw**.

saxophone [sak'səfōn] *n* saxófono.

say [sā] *n*: **to have one's ~** expresar su opinión; **to have a** *or* **some ~ in sth** tener voz *or* tener que ver en algo ♦ *vt*, *vi* (*pt*, *pp* **said** [sed]) decir; **to ~ yes/no** decir que sí/no; **my watch ~s 3 o'clock** mi reloj marca las tres; **that is to ~** es decir; **that goes without ~ing** ni que decir tiene; **she said (that) I was to give you this** me pidió que te diera esto; **I'd ~ it's worth about $100**

yo diría que vale unos 100 dólares; **~ after me** repite lo que yo diga; **shall we ~ Tuesday?** ¿quedamos en el martes?; **that doesn't ~ much for him** eso no dice nada a su favor; **when all is said and done** al fin y al cabo, a fin de cuentas; **there is something** *or* **a lot to be said for it** hay algo *or* mucho que decir a su favor.

saying [sā'ing] *n* dicho, refrán *m*.

say-so [sā'sō] *n* (*col*) autorización *f*.

SBA *n abbr* (*US*) = *Small Business Administration*.

SC *n abbr* (*US*) = **Supreme Court** ♦ *abbr* (*US MAIL*) = *South Carolina*.

s/c *abbr* = **self-contained.**

scab [skab] *n* costra; (*pej*) esquirol(a) *m/f*.

scaffold [skaf'əld] *n* (*for execution*) cadalso.

scaffolding [skaf'əlding] *n* andamio, andamiaje *m*.

scald [skôld] *n* escaldadura ♦ *vt* escaldar.

scalding [skôl'ding] *a* (*also:* ~ **hot**) hirviendo, que arde.

scale [skāl] *n* (*gen*, *MUS*) escala; (*of fish*) escama; (*of salaries, fees etc*) escalafón *m* ♦ *vt* (*mountain*) escalar; (*tree*) trepar; **~s** *npl* (*small*) balanza *sg*; (*large*) báscula *sg*; **on a large ~** en gran escala; **~ of charges** tarifa, lista de precios; **pay ~** escala salarial; **to draw sth to ~** dibujar algo a escala.

scale down *vt* reducir.

scale model *n* modelo a escala.

scallion [skal'yən] *n* (*US*) cebollita, chalote *m*.

scallop [skâl'əp] *n* (*ZOOL*) venera; (*SEWING*) festón *m*.

scalp [skalp] *n* cabellera ♦ *vt* escalpar.

scalpel [skal'pəl] *n* bisturí *m*.

scamper [skam'pûr] *vi*: **to ~ away**, **~ off** irse corriendo.

scampi [skam'pē] *npl* gambas *fpl*.

scan [skan] *vt* (*examine*) escudriñar; (*glance at quickly*) dar un vistazo a; (*TV, RADAR*) explorar, registrar ♦ *n* (*MED*) examen *m* ultrasónico.

scandal [skan'dəl] *n* escándalo; (*gossip*) chismes *mpl*.

scandalize [skan'dəlīz] *vt* escandalizar.

scandalous [skan'dələs] *a* escandaloso.

Scandinavia [skandənā'vēə] *n* Escandinavia.

Scandinavian [skandənā'vēən] *a*, *n* escandinavo/a *m/f*.

scanner [skan'ûr] *n* (*RADAR, MED*) escáner *m*.

scant [skant] *a* escaso.

scantily [skan'tilē] *ad*: **~ clad** *or* **dressed** ligeramente vestido.

scantiness [skan'tēnis] *n* escasez *f*, insuficiencia.

scanty [skan'tē] *a* (*meal*) insuficiente; (*clothes*) ligero.

scapegoat [skāp'gōt] *n* cabeza de turco,

chivo expiatorio.

scar [skär] *n* cicatriz *f* ♦ *vt* marcar con una cicatriz ♦ *vi* cicatrizarse.

scarce [skärs] *a* escaso.

scarcely [skärs'lē] *ad* apenas; ~ **anybody** casi nadie; **I can ~ believe it** casi no puedo creerlo.

scarceness [skärs'nis], **scarcity** [skär'sitē] *n* escasez *f*.

scarcity value *n* valor *m* de escasez.

scare [skär] *n* susto, sobresalto; (*panic*) pánico ♦ *vt* asustar, espantar; **to ~ sb stiff** dar a uno un susto de muerte; **bomb ~** amenaza de bomba.

  scare away, scare off *vt* espantar, ahuyentar.

scarecrow [skär'krō] *n* espantapájaros *m inv*.

scared [skärd] *a*: **to be ~** asustarse, estar asustado.

scaremonger [skär'munggûr] *n* alarmista *m/f*.

scarf, *pl* **scarves** [skärf, skärvz] *n* (*long*) bufanda; (*square*) pañuelo.

scarlet [skär'lit] *a* escarlata.

scarlet fever *n* escarlatina.

scarred [skärd] *a* lleno de cicatrices.

scarves [skärvz] *npl of* **scarf.**

scary [skär'ē] *a* (*col*) de miedo.

scathing [skā'thing] *a* mordaz; **to be ~ about sth** criticar algo duramente.

scatter [skat'ûr] *vt* (*spread*) esparcir, desparramar; (*put to flight*) dispersar ♦ *vi* desparramarse; dispersarse.

scatterbrained [skat'ûrbrānd] *a* ligero de cascos.

scavenge [skav'inj] *vi*: **to ~ (for)** (*person*) revolver entre la basura (para encontrar); **to ~ for food** (*hyenas etc*) nutrirse de carroña.

scavenger [skav'injûr] *n* (*person*) basurero/a; (*ZOOL: animal*) animal *m* de carroña; (: *bird*) ave *f* de carroña.

scenario [sinär'ēō] *n* (*THEATER*) argumento; (*CINEMA*) guión *m*; (*fig*) escenario.

scene [sēn] *n* (*THEATER, fig etc*) escena; (*of crime, accident*) escenario; (*sight, view*) vista, perspectiva; (*fuss*) escándalo; **the political ~ in Spain** el panorama político español; **behind the ~s** (*also fig*) entre bastidores; **to appear** *or* **come on the ~** (*also fig*) aparecer, presentarse; **to make a ~** (*col: fuss*) armar un escándalo.

scenery [sē'nûrē] *n* (*THEATER*) decorado; (*landscape*) paisaje *m*.

scenic [sē'nik] *a* (*picturesque*) pintoresco.

scent [sent] *n* perfume *m*, olor *m*; (*fig: track*) rastro, pista; (*sense of smell*) olfato ♦ *vt* perfumar; (*suspect*) presentir; **to put** *or* **throw sb off the ~** (*fig*) despistar a uno.

scepter, (*Brit*) **sceptre** [sep'tûr] *n* cetro.

sceptic [skep'tik] *etc* (*Brit*) = **skeptic** *etc*.

schedule [skej'ōōl, (*Brit*) shed'yōōl] *n* (*of*

trains) horario; (*of events*) programa *m*; (*list*) lista ♦ *vt* (*timetable*) establecer el horario de; (*visit*) fijar la hora de; **on ~** a la hora, sin retraso; **to be ahead of/behind ~** estar adelantado/en retraso; **we are working to a very tight ~** tenemos un programa de trabajo muy exigente; **everything went according to ~** todo sucedió según se había previsto; **the meeting is ~d for 7** *or* **to begin at 7** la reunión está fijada para las 7.

scheduled [skej'ōōld, (*Brit*) shed'yōōld] *a* (*date, time*) fijado; (*visit, event, bus, train*) programado; (*stop*) previsto; **~ flight** vuelo regular.

schematic [skēmat'ik] *a* (*diagram etc*) esquemático.

scheme [skēm] *n* (*plan*) plan *m*, proyecto; (*method*) esquema *m*; (*plot*) intriga; (*trick*) ardid *m*; (*arrangement*) disposición *f*; (*Brit: pension ~ etc*) sistema *m* ♦ *vt* proyectar ♦ *vi* (*plan*) hacer proyectos; (*intrigue*) intrigar; **color ~** combinación *f* de colores.

scheming [skēm'ing] *a* intrigante.

schism [skiz'əm] *n* cisma *m*.

schizophrenia [skitsəfrē'nēə] *n* esquizofrenia.

schizophrenic [skitsəfren'ik] *a* esquizofrénico.

scholar [skâl'ûr] *n* (*pupil*) alumno/a, estudiante *m/f*; (*learned person*) sabio/a, erudito/a.

scholarly [skâl'ûrlē] *a* erudito.

scholarship [skâl'ûrship] *n* erudición *f*; (*grant*) beca.

school [skōōl] *n* (*gen*) escuela, colegio; (*in university*) facultad *f*; (*of fish*) banco ♦ *vt* (*animal*) amaestrar; **to be at** *or* **go to ~** ir al colegio *or* a la escuela.

school age *n* edad *f* escolar.

school bag *n* bolso, cabás *m*.

schoolbook [skōōl'bōōk] *n* libro de texto.

schoolboy [skōōl'boi] *n* alumno.

schoolchild, *pl* **-children** [skōōl'chīld, -childrən] *n* alumno/a.

schooldays [skōōl'dāz] *npl* años *mpl* del colegio.

schoolgirl [skōōl'gûrl] *n* alumna.

schooling [skōō'ling] *n* enseñanza.

schoolmaster [skōōl'mastûr] *n* (*grade*) maestro; (*high*) profesor *m*.

schoolmistress [skōōl'mistris] *n* (*grade*) maestra; (*high*) profesora.

schoolroom [skōōl'rōōm] *n* clase *f*.

schoolteacher [skōōl'tēchûr] *n* (*grade*) maestro/a; (*high*) profesor(a) *m/f*.

schoolyard [skōōl'yârd] *n* patio (de recreo).

schooner [skōō'nûr] *n* (*ship*) goleta.

sciatica [sīat'ikə] *n* ciática.

science [sī'əns] *n* ciencia; **the ~s** las ciencias.

science fiction *n* ciencia-ficción *f*.

scientific [sīəntif'ik] *a* científico.

scientist [sī'əntist] *n* científico/a.

sci-fi [sī'fī'] *n abbr* (*col*) = **science fiction.**

scintillating [sin'təlāting] *a* (*wit, conversation, company*) brillante, chispeante, ingenioso.

scissors [siz'ûrz] *npl* tijeras *fpl*; **a pair of ~** unas tijeras.

scoff [skåf] *vi*: **to ~ at** (*mock*) mofarse (de).

scold [skōld] *vt* regañar.

scolding [skōld'ing] *n* riña, reprimenda.

scone [skōn] *n pastel de pan.*

scoop [skōōp] *n* cucharón *m*; (*for flour etc*) pala; (*PRESS*) exclusiva ♦ *vt* (*COMM: market*) adelantarse a; (: *profit*) sacar; (*COMM, PRESS: competitors*) adelantarse a.
  scoop out *vt* excavar.
  scoop up *vt* recoger.

scooter [skōō'tûr] *n* (*motorcycle*) moto *f*; (*toy*) patinete *m*.

scope [skōp] *n* (*of plan, undertaking*) ámbito; (*reach*) alcance *m*; (*of person*) competencia; (*opportunity*) libertad *f* (de acción); **there is plenty of ~ for improvement** (*Brit*) hay bastante campo para efectuar mejoras.

scorch [skôrch] *vt* (*clothes*) chamuscar; (*earth, grass*) quemar, secar.

scorcher [skôr'chûr] *n* (*col: hot day*) día *m* abrasador.

scorching [skôrch'ing] *a* abrasador(a).

score [skôr] *n* (*points etc*) puntuación *f*; (*MUS*) partitura; (*reckoning*) cuenta; (*twenty*) veintena ♦ *vt* (*goal, point*) ganar; (*mark, cut*) rayar ♦ *vi* marcar un tanto; (*SOCCER*) marcar un gol; (*keep score*) llevar el tanteo; **to keep (the) ~** tantear, llevar la cuenta (*LAm*); **to have an old ~ to settle with sb** (*fig*) tener cuentas pendientes con uno; **on that ~** en lo que se refiere a eso; **~s of people** (*fig*) muchísima gente, cantidad de gente; **to ~ 6 out of 10** obtener una puntuación de 6 sobre 10.
  score out *vt* tachar.

scoreboard [skôr'bôrd] *n* marcador *m*.

scorer [skôr'ûr] *n* marcador *m*; (*keeping score*) tanteador(a) *m/f*.

scorn [skôrn] *n* desprecio ♦ *vt* despreciar.

scornful [skôrn'fəl] *a* desdeñoso, despreciativo.

scornfully [skôrn'fəlē] *ad* desdeñosamente, con desprecio.

Scorpio [skôr'pēō] *n* Escorpión *m*.

scorpion [skôr'pēən] *n* alacrán *m*.

Scot [skåt] *n* escocés/esa *m/f*.

Scotch [skåch] *n* whisky *m* escocés.

scotch [skåch] *vt* (*rumor*) desmentir; (*plan*) abandonar.

Scotch tape ® *n* (*US*) cinta adhesiva, celo, scotch *m* ® (*LAm*).

scot-free [skåt'frē'] *ad*: **to get off ~** (*unpunished*) salir impune; (*unhurt*) salir ile-

so.

Scotland [skåt'lənd] *n* Escocia.

Scots [skåts] *a* escocés/esa.

Scotsman [skåts'mən] *n* escocés *m*.

Scotswoman [skåts'wŏŏmən] *n* escocesa.

Scottish [skåt'ish] *a* escocés/esa.

scoundrel [skoun'drəl] *n* canalla *m/f*, sinvergüenza *m/f*.

scour [skour] *vt* (*clean*) fregar, estregar; (*search*) recorrer, registrar.

scourer [skour'ûr] *n* (*pad*) estropajo; (*powder*) limpiador *m*, desgrasador *m*.

scourge [skûrj] *n* azote *m*.

scouring pad [skour'ing pad] *n* estropajo.

scout [skout] *n* (*MIL, also:* **boy ~**) explorador *m*.
  scout around *vi* reconocer el terreno.

scowl [skoul] *vi* fruncir el ceño; **to ~ at sb** mirar con ceño a uno.

scrabble [skrab'əl] *vi* (*claw*): **to ~ (at)** arañar ♦ *n*: **S~** ® Scrabble *m* ®; **to ~ around for sth** revolver todo buscando algo.

scraggy [skrag'ē] *a* flaco, descarnado.

scram [skram] *vi* (*col*) largarse.

scramble [skram'bəl] *n* (*climb*) subida (difícil); (*struggle*) pelea ♦ *vi*: **to ~ out/through** salir/abrirse paso con dificultad; **to ~ for** pelear por; **to go scrambling** (*SPORT*) hacer motocrós.

scrambled eggs [skram'bəld egz] *npl* huevos *mpl* revueltos.

scrap [skrap] *n* (*bit*) pedacito; (*fig*) pizca; (*fight*) riña, bronca; (*also:* **~ iron**) chatarra, hierro viejo ♦ *vt* (*discard*) desechar, descartar ♦ *vi* reñir, armar (una) bronca; **~s** *npl* (*waste*) sobras *fpl*, desperdicios *mpl*; **to sell sth for ~** vender algo como chatarra.

scrapbook [skrap'bŏŏk] *n* álbum *m* de recortes.

scrap dealer *n* chatarrero/a.

scrape [skrāp] *n* (*fig*) lío, apuro ♦ *vt* raspar; (*skin etc*) rasguñar; (~ *against*) rozar.
  scrape through *vi* (*succeed*) apenas lograr hacer algo; (*exam*) aprobar por los pelos.

scraper [skrā'pûr] *n* raspador *m*.

scrap heap *n* (*fig*): **on the ~** desperdiciado; **to throw sth on the ~** desechar *or* descartar algo.

scrap iron *n* chatarra.

scrap metal *n* chatarra, desecho de metal.

scrap paper *n* pedazos *mpl* de papel.

scrappy [skrap'ē] *a* (*poor*) pobre; (*bitty*) fragmentario.

scrap yard *n* depósito de chatarra; (*for cars*) cementerio de coches.

scratch [skrach] *n* rasguño; (*from claw*) arañazo ♦ *vt* (*record*) rayar; (*with claw, nail*) rasguñar, arañar; (*COMPUT*) borrar ♦ *vi* rascarse; **to start from ~** partir de cero.

scratchpad [skrach'pad] *n* (*US*) bloc *m*.
scrawl [skról] *n* garabatos *mpl* ♦ *vi* hacer garabatos.
scrawny [skró'nē] *a* (*person, neck*) flaco.
scream [skrēm] *n* chillido ♦ *vi* chillar; **it was a ~** (*fig, col*) fue para morirse de risa *or* muy divertido; **he's a ~** (*fig, col*) es muy divertido *or* de lo más gracioso; **to ~ at sb (to do sth)** gritarle a uno (para que haga algo).
scree [skrē] *n* cono de desmoronamiento.
screech [skrēch] *vi* chirriar.
screen [skrēn] *n* (*CINEMA, TV*) pantalla; (*movable*) biombo; (*wall*) tabique *m*; (*Brit: also:* **wind~**) parabrisas *m inv* ♦ *vt* (*conceal*) tapar; (*from the wind etc*) proteger; (*movie*) proyectar; (*fig: person: for security*) investigar a; (*: for illness*) hacer una exploración a.
screen editing *n* (*COMPUT*) corrección *f* en pantalla.
screening [skrē'ning] *n* (*of movie*) proyección *f*; (*for security*) investigación *f*; (*MED*) exploración *f*.
screen memory *n* (*COMPUT*) memoria de la pantalla.
screenplay [skrēn'plā] *n* guión *m*.
screen test *n* prueba de pantalla.
screw [skrōō] *n* tornillo; (*propeller*) hélice *f* ♦ *vt* atornillar; **to ~ sth to the wall** fijar algo a la pared con tornillos.
screw up *vt* (*paper, material etc*) arrugar; (*col: ruin*) estropear; **to ~ up one's eyes** arrugar el entrecejo; **to ~ up one's face** torcer *or* arrugar la cara.
screwball [skrōō'ból] *n* (*col*) chalado, tarado (*LAm*).
screwdriver [skrōō'drīvûr] *n* destornillador *m*.
screwy [skrōō'ē] *a* (*col*) chiflado.
scribble [skrib'əl] *n* garabatos *mpl* ♦ *vt* escribir con prisa; **to ~ sth down** garabatear algo.
script [skript] *n* (*CINEMA etc*) guión *m*; (*writing*) escritura, letra.
scripted [skrip'tid] *a* (*RADIO, TV*) escrito.
Scripture [skrip'chûr] *n* Sagrada Escritura.
scriptwriter [skript'rītûr] *n* guionista *m/f*.
scroll [skrōl] *n* rollo ♦ *vt* (*COMPUT*) desplazar.
scrotum [skrō'təm] *n* escroto.
scrounge [skrounj] (*col*) *vt*: **to ~ sth off** *or* **from sb** obtener algo de uno de gorra ♦ *vi*: **to ~ off sb** vivir a costa de uno.
scrounger [skrounj'ûr] *n* gorrón/ona *m/f*.
scrub [skrub] *n* (*clean*) fregado; (*land*) maleza ♦ *vt* fregar, restregar; (*reject*) cancelar, anular.
scrub brush *n* (*US*) cepillo para fregar.
scrubbing brush [skrub'ing brush] *n* (*Brit*) cepillo de fregar.
scruff [skruf] *n*: **by the ~ of the neck** por el pescuezo.

scruffy [skruf'ē] *a* desaliñado, piojoso.
scrum(mage) [skrum'(ij)] *n* (*RUGBY*) melée *f*.
scruple [skrōō'pəl] *n* escrúpulo; **to have no ~s about doing sth** no tener reparos en *or* escrúpulos acerca de hacer algo.
scrupulous [skrōō'pyələs] *a* escrupuloso.
scrupulously [skrōō'pyələslē] *ad* escrupulosamente; **to be ~ fair/honest** ser sumamente justo/honesto.
scrutinize [skrōō'tənīz] *vt* escudriñar; (*votes*) escrutar.
scrutiny [skrōō'tənē] *n* escrutinio, examen *m*; **under the ~ of sb** bajo la mirada *or* el escrutinio de uno.
scuba [skōō'bə] *n* escafandra autónoma.
scuba diving *n* buceo con escafandra autónoma.
scuff [skuf] *vt* (*shoes, floor*) rayar.
scuffle [skuf'əl] *n* refriega.
scullery [skul'ûrē] *n* trascocina.
sculptor [skulp'tûr] *n* escultor(a) *m/f*.
sculpture [skulp'chûr] *n* escultura.
scum [skum] *n* (*on liquid*) nata; (*pej: people*) canalla; (*fig*) heces *fpl*.
scurrilous [skûr'ələs] *a* difamatorio, calumnioso.
scurry [skûr'ē] *vi*: **to ~ off** escabullirse.
scurvy [skûr'vē] *n* escorbuto.
scuttle [skut'əl] *n* (*also:* **coal ~**) cubo, carbonera ♦ *vt* (*ship*) barrenar ♦ *vi* (*scamper*): **to ~ away, ~ off** escabullirse.
scythe [sīth] *n* guadaña.
SD *abbr* (*US MAIL*) = *South Dakota*.
S.Dak. *abbr* (*US*) = *South Dakota*.
SDI *n abbr* (= *Strategic Defense Initiative*) IDE *f*.
SDLP *n abbr* (*Brit POL*) = *Social Democratic and Labour Party*.
SDP *n abbr* (*Brit POL*) = *Social Democratic Party*.
sea [sē] *n* mar *m/f*; **by ~** (*travel*) en barco; **on the ~** (*boat*) en el mar; (*town*) junto al mar; **out to ~** *or* **at ~** en alta mar; **to go by ~** ir en barco; **heavy** *or* **rough ~s** mar *msg* agitado *or* picado; **by** *or* **beside the ~** (*vacation*) en la playa; (*village*) a orillas del mar; **a ~ of faces** una multitud de caras.
sea bed *n* fondo del mar.
sea bird *n* ave *f* marina.
seaboard [sē'bôrd] *n* litoral *m*.
sea breeze *n* brisa de mar.
seadog [sē'dóg'] *n* lobo de mar.
seafarer [sē'fârûr] *n* marinero.
seafaring [sē'fâring] *a* (*community*) marinero; (*life*) de marinero.
seafood [sē'fōōd] *n* mariscos *mpl*.
sea front *n* (*beach*) playa; (*prom*) paseo marítimo.
seagoing [sē'gōing] *a* (*ship*) de alta mar.
seagull [sē'gul] *n* gaviota.
seal [sēl] *n* (*animal*) foca; (*stamp*) sello ♦ *vt*

(*close*) cerrar; (: *with* ~) sellar; (*decide: sb's fate*) decidir; (: *bargain*) cerrar; ~ **of approval** sello de aprobación.
seal off *vt* obturar.
sea level *n* nivel *m* del mar.
sealing wax [sē'ling waks] *n* lacre *m*.
sea lion *n* león *m* marino.
sealskin [sēl'skin] *n* piel *f* de foca.
seam [sēm] *n* costura; (*of metal*) juntura; (*of coal*) veta, filón *m*; **the hall was bursting at the ~s** la sala rebosaba de gente.
seaman [sē'mən] *n* marinero.
seamanship [sē'mənship] *n* náutica.
seamless [sēm'lis] *a* sin costura(s).
seamy [sē'mē] *a* sórdido.
seance [sā'âns] *n* sesión *f* de espiritismo.
seaplane [sē'plān] *n* hidroavión *m*.
seaport [sē'pôrt] *n* puerto de mar.
search [sûrch] *n* (*for person, thing*) busca, búsqueda; (*of drawer, pockets*) registro; (*inspection*) reconocimiento ♦ *vt* (*look in*) buscar en; (*examine*) examinar; (*person, place*) registrar; (*COMPUT*) buscar ♦ *vi*: **to ~ for** buscar; **in ~ of** en busca de; "**~ and replace**" (*COMPUT*) "buscar y reemplazar".
search through *vt fus* registrar.
searcher [sûr'chûr] *n* buscador(a) *m/f*.
searching [sûr'ching] *a* (*question*) penetrante.
searchlight [sûrch'līt] *n* reflector *m*.
search party *n* pelotón *m* de salvamento.
search warrant *n* mandamiento de registro (judicial).
searing [sē'ring] *a* (*heat*) abrasador(a); (*pain*) agudo.
seashore [sē'shôr] *n* playa, orilla del mar; **on the ~** a la orilla del mar.
seasick [sē'sik] *a* mareado; **to be ~** marearse.
seaside [sē'sīd] *n* playa, orilla del mar.
seaside resort *n* playa.
season [sē'zən] *n* (*of year*) estación *f*; (*sporting etc*) temporada; (*gen*) época, período ♦ *vt* (*food*) sazonar; **to be in/out of ~** estar en sazón/fuera de temporada; **the busy ~** (*for stores, hotels etc*) la temporada alta; **the open ~** (*HUNTING*) la temporada de caza *or* de pesca.
seasonal [sē'zənəl] *a* estacional.
seasoned [sē'zənd] *a* (*wood*) curado; (*fig: worker, actor*) experimentado; (*troops*) aguerrido; **~ campaigner** veterano/a.
seasoning [sē'zəning] *n* condimento, aderezo.
season ticket *n* abono.
seat [sēt] *n* (*in bus, train: place*) asiento; (*chair*) silla; (*PARLIAMENT*) escaño; (*buttocks*) culo, trasero; (*center: of government etc*) sede *f* ♦ *vt* sentar; (*have room for*) tener cabida para; **are there any ~s left?** ¿quedan plazas?; **to take one's ~** sentarse, tomar asiento; **to be ~ed** estar

sentado, sentarse.
seat belt *n* cinturón *m* de seguridad.
seating [sē'ting] *n* asientos *mpl*.
seating arrangements *npl* arreglo *sg* de los asientos.
seating capacity [sē'ting kəpas'itē] *n* cabida, número de asientos.
SEATO [sē'tō] *n abbr* (= *Southeast Asia Treaty Organization*) OTASE *f*.
sea water *n* agua *m* del mar.
seaweed [sē'wēd] *n* alga marina.
seaworthy [sē'wûrthē] *a* en condiciones de navegar.
SEC *n abbr* (*US:* = *Securities and Exchange Commission*) comisión de operaciones bursátiles.
sec. *abbr* = **second(s)**.
secateurs [sek'ətûrz] *npl* podadera *sg*.
secede [sisēd'] *vi*: **to ~ (from)** separarse (de).
secluded [siklōō'did] *a* retirado.
seclusion [siklōō'zhən] *n* retiro.
second [sek'ənd] *a* segundo ♦ *ad* (*in race etc*) en segundo lugar ♦ *n* (*gen*) segundo; (*AUT: also:* ~ **gear**) segunda; (*COMM*) artículo con algún desperfecto; (*Brit SCOL: degree*) título universitario de segunda clase ♦ *vt* (*motion*) apoyar; [sikând'] (*employee*) trasladar temporalmente; ~ **floor** (*US*) primer piso; (*Brit*) segundo piso; **Charles the S~** Carlos Segundo; **to ask for a ~ opinion** (*MED*) pedir una segunda opinión; **just a ~!** ¡un momento!; **to have ~ thoughts** cambiar de opinión; **on ~ thought** *or* (*Brit*) **thoughts** pensándolo bien; ~ **mortgage** segunda hipoteca.
secondary [sek'əndärē] *a* secundario.
secondary education *n* segunda enseñanza.
secondary picket *n* piquete *m* secundario.
secondary school *n* escuela secundaria.
second-best [sek'əndbest'] *n* segundo.
second-class [sek'əndklas'] *a* de segunda clase ♦ *ad*: **to send sth ~** enviar algo por segunda clase; **to travel ~** viajar en segunda; ~ **citizen** ciudadano/a de segunda clase.
second cousin *n* primo/a segundo/a.
seconder [sek'əndûr] *n* el/la que apoya una moción.
secondhand [sek'əndhand'] *a* de segunda mano, usado ♦ *ad*: **to buy sth ~** comprar algo de segunda mano; **to hear sth ~** oír algo indirectamente.
second hand *n* (*on clock*) segundero.
second-in-command [sek'əndinkəmand'] *n* (*MIL*) segundo jefe *m*; (*ADMIN*) segundo/a, ayudante *m/f*.
secondly [sek'əndlē] *ad* en segundo lugar.
second-rate [sek'əndrāt'] *a* de segunda categoría.
secrecy [sē'krisē] *n* secreto.

secret [sē'krit] *a, n* secreto; **in ~** *ad* en secreto; **to keep sth ~ (from sb)** ocultarle algo (a uno); **to make no ~ of sth** no ocultar algo.

secret agent *n* agente *m/f* secreto/a, espía *m/f*.

secretarial [sekritär'ēəl] *a (course)* de secretariado; *(staff)* de secretaría; *(work, duties)* de secretaria.

secretariat [sekritär'ēət] *n* secretaría.

secretary [sek'ritärē] *n* secretario/a; **S~ of State** *(Brit POL)* Ministro (con cartera).

secretary pool *n (US)* servicio de mecanógrafos.

secrete [sikrēt'] *vt (MED, ANAT, BIO)* secretar; *(hide)* ocultar, esconder.

secretion [sikrē'shən] *n* secreción *f*.

secretive [sē'kritiv] *a* reservado, sigiloso.

secretly [sē'kritlē] *ad* en secreto.

sect [sekt] *n* secta.

sectarian [sektär'ēən] *a* sectario.

section [sek'shən] *n* sección *f*; *(part)* parte *f*; *(of document)* artículo; *(of opinion)* sector *m*; **business ~** *(PRESS)* sección *f* de economía.

sectional [sek'shənəl] *a (regional)* regional, local.

sector [sek'tûr] *n (gen, COMPUT)* sector *m*.

secular [sek'yəlûr] *a* secular, seglar.

secure [sikyōōr'] *a (free from anxiety)* seguro; *(firmly fixed)* firme, fijo ♦ *vt (fix)* asegurar, afianzar; *(get)* conseguir; *(COMM: loan)* garantizar; **to make sth ~** afianzar algo; **to ~ sth for sb** conseguir algo para uno.

secured creditor [sikyōōrd' kred'itûr] *n* acreedor(a) *m/f* con garantía.

securely [sikyōōr'lē] *ad* firmemente; **it is ~ fastened** está bien sujetado.

security [sikyōōr'itē] *n* seguridad *f*; *(for loan)* fianza; *(: object)* prenda; **securities** *npl (COMM)* valores *mpl*, títulos *mpl*; **~ of tenure** tenencia asegurada; **to increase/ tighten ~** aumentar/estrechar las medidas de seguridad; **job ~** trabajo asegurado.

security forces *npl* fuerzas *fpl* de seguridad.

security guard *n* guardia *m/f* de seguridad.

security risk *n* riesgo para la seguridad.

secy. *abbr* (= *secretary*) Srio/a.

sedan [sidan'] *n (US AUT)* sedán *m*.

sedate [sidāt'] *a* tranquilo ♦ *vt* tratar con sedantes.

sedation [sidā'shən] *n (MED)* sedación *f*; **to be under ~** estar bajo sedación.

sedative [sed'ətiv] *n* sedante *m*, sedativo.

sedentary [sed'əntärē] *a* sedentario.

sediment [sed'əmənt] *n* sedimento.

sedimentary [sedəmen'tûrē] *a (GEO)* sedimentario.

sedition [sidish'ən] *n* sedición *f*.

seduce [sidōōs'] *vt (gen)* seducir.

seduction [siduk'shən] *n* seducción *f*.

seductive [siduk'tiv] *a* seductor(a).

see [sē] *vb (pt* **saw,** *pp* **seen** [sô, sēn]) *vt (gen)* ver; *(understand)* ver, comprender; *(look at)* mirar ♦ *vi* ver ♦ *n* sede *f*; **to ~ sb to the door** acompañar a uno a la puerta; **to ~ that** *(ensure)* asegurar que; **~ you soon/later/tomorrow!** ¡hasta pronto/luego/ mañana!; **as far as I can ~** por lo visto or por lo que yo veo; **there was nobody to be ~n** no se veía a nadie; **let me ~** *(show me)* a ver; *(let me think)* vamos a ver; **to go and ~ sb** ir a ver a uno; **~ for yourself** míralo tú mismo; **I don't know what she ~s in him** no sé qué le encuentra.

see about *vt fus* atender a, encargarse de.

see off *vt* despedir.

see through *vt fus* penetrar (con la vista) ♦ *vt* llevar a cabo.

see to *vt fus* atender a, encargarse de.

seed [sēd] *n* semilla; *(in fruit)* pepita; *(fig)* germen *m*; *(TENNIS)* preseleccionado/a; **to go to ~** *(plant)* granar; *(fig)* descuidarse.

seedless [sēd'lis] *a* sin semillas or pepitas.

seedling [sēd'ling] *n* planta de semillero.

seedy [sē'dē] *a (shabby)* desaseado, raído.

seeing [sē'ing] *conj:* **~ (that)** visto que, en vista de que.

seek, *pt, pp* **sought** [sēk, sôt] *vt (gen)* buscar; *(post)* solicitar; **to ~ advice/help from sb** pedir consejos/solicitar ayuda a uno.

seek out *vt (person)* buscar.

seem [sēm] *vi* parecer; **there ~s to be...** parece que hay ...; **it ~s (that)** ... parece que ...; **what ~s to be the trouble?** ¿qué pasa?; **I did what ~ed best** hice lo que parecía mejor.

seemingly [sē'minglē] *ad* aparentemente, según parece.

seen [sēn] *pp* of **see.**

seep [sēp] *vi* filtrarse.

seer [sēr] *n* vidente *m/f*, profeta *m/f*.

seersucker [sēr'sukûr] *n* sirsaca.

seesaw [sē'sô] *n* balancín *m*, columpio.

seethe [sēth] *vi* hervir; **to ~ with anger** enfurecerse.

see-through [sē'thrōō] *a* transparente.

segment [seg'mənt] *n* segmento.

segregate [seg'rəgāt] *vt* segregar.

segregation [segrəgā'shən] *n* segregación *f*.

Seine [sān] *n* Sena *m*.

seismic [sīz'mik] *a* sísmico.

seize [sēz] *vt (grasp)* agarrar, asir; *(take possession of)* secuestrar; *(: territory)* apoderarse de; *(opportunity)* aprovecharse de.

seize up *vi (TECH)* agarrotarse.

seize (up)on *vt fus* valerse de.

seizure [sē'zhûr] *n (MED)* ataque *m*; *(LAW)* incautación *f*.

seldom [sel'dəm] *ad* rara vez.

select [silekt'] *a* selecto, escogido; *(hotel,*

restaurant, clubs) exclusivo ♦ *vt* escoger, elegir; (*SPORT*) seleccionar; **a ~ few** una minoría privilegiada.

selection [silɛk'shən] *n* selección *f*, elección *f*; (*COMM*) surtido.

selection committee *n* comisión *f* de nombramiento.

selective [silɛk'tiv] *a* selectivo.

self [self] *n* (*pl* **selves** [sɛlvz]) uno mismo ♦ *pref* auto ...; **the ~** el yo.

self-addressed [self'ədrɛst'] *a* (*US*): **~ stamped envelope (SASE)** *sobre con las propias señas de uno y con sello.*

self-adhesive [self'adhē'siv] *a* autoadhesivo, autoadherente.

self-appointed [self'əpoin'tid] *a* autonombrado.

self-assurance [self'əshoōr'əns] *n* confianza en sí mismo.

self-assured [self'əshoōrd'] *a* seguro de sí mismo.

self-catering [self'kā'tùring] *a* (*Brit*) sin pensión; **~ apartment** piso sin pensión.

self-centered [self'sɛn'tùrd] *a* egocéntrico.

self-cleaning [self'klē'ning] *a* autolimpiador.

self-colored [self'kul'ùrd] *a* de un color.

self-confessed [self'kənfɛst'] *a* (*alcoholic etc*) confeso.

self-confidence [self'kán'fidəns] *n* confianza en sí mismo.

self-confident [self'kán'fidənt] *a* seguro de sí (mismo), lleno de confianza en sí mismo.

self-conscious [self'kán'chəs] *a* cohibido.

self-contained [self'kəntānd'] *a* (*gen*) independiente; (*Brit: apartment*) con entrada particular.

self-control [self'kəntrōl'] *n* autodominio.

self-defeating [self'difē'ting] *a* contraproducente.

self-defense [self'difɛns'] *n* defensa propia.

self-discipline [self'dis'əplin] *n* autodisciplina.

self-employed [self'imploid'] *a* que trabaja por cuenta propia.

self-esteem [self'əstēm'] *n* amor *m* propio.

self-evident [self'ev'idənt] *a* patente.

self-explanatory [self'iksplan'ətôrē] *a* que no necesita explicación.

self-financing [self'finan'sing] *a* autofinanziado.

self-governing [self'guv'ùrning] *a* autónomo.

self-help [self'help'] *n* autosuficiencia, ayuda propia.

self-importance [self'impôr'təns] *n* presunción *f*, vanidad *f*.

self-important [self'impôr'tənt] *a* presumido.

self-indulgent [self'indul'jənt] *a* inmoderado.

self-inflicted [self'inflik'tid] *a* infligido a sí mismo.

self-interest [self'in'trist] *n* egoísmo.

selfish [sel'fish] *a* egoísta.

selfishly [sel'fishlē] *ad* con egoísmo, de modo egoísta.

selfishness [sel'fishnis] *n* egoísmo.

selflessly [self'lislē] *ad* desinteresadamente.

selfless [self'lis] *a* desinteresado.

self-made man [self'mād' man'] *n* hombre *m* que ha triunfado por sus propios esfuerzos.

self-pity [self'pit'ē] *n* lástima de sí mismo.

self-portrait [self'pôr'trit] *n* autorretrato.

self-possessed [self'pəzɛst'] *a* sereno, dueño de sí mismo.

self-preservation [self'prezûrvā'shən] *n* propia conservación *f*.

self-propelled [self'prəpeld'] *a* autopropulsado, automotor/triz.

self-raising [self'rā'zing] *a* (*Brit*) = **self-rising**.

self-reliant [self'rili'ənt] *a* independiente, autosuficiente.

self-respect [self'rispɛkt'] *n* amor *m* propio.

self-respecting [self'rispɛkt'ing] *a* que tiene amor propio.

self-righteous [self'rī'chəs] *a* santurrón/ona.

self-rising [self'rī'zing] *a* (*US*): **~ flour** harina con levadura.

self-sacrifice [self'sak'rəfis] *n* abnegación *f*.

self-same [self'sām] *a* mismo, mismísimo.

self-satisfied [self'sat'isfid] *a* satisfecho de sí mismo.

self-service [self'sûr'vis] *a* de autoservicio.

self-styled [self'stīld'] *a* supuesto, sedicente.

self-sufficient [self'səfish'ənt] *a* autosuficiente.

self-supporting [self'səpôrt'ing] *a* económicamente independiente.

self-taught [self'tôt'] *a* autodidacta.

self-test [self'test'] *n* (*COMPUT*) autocomprobación *f*.

sell, *pt*, *pp* **sold** [sel, sōld] *vt* vender ♦ *vi* venderse; **to ~ at** *or* **for $10** venderse a 10 dólares; **to ~ sb an idea** (*fig*) convencer a uno de una idea.

sell off *vt* liquidar.

sell out *vi* transigir, transar (*LAm*); **to ~ out (to sb/sth)** (*COMM*) vender su negocio (a uno/algo) ♦ *vt* agotar las existencias de, venderlo todo; **the tickets are all sold out** los billetes están agotados.

sell-by date [sel'bī dāt] *n* fecha de caducidad.

seller [sel'ùr] *n* vendedor(a) *m/f*; **~'s market** mercado de demanda.

selling price [sel'ing prīs] *n* precio de venta.

sellotape [sel'ətāp] ® *n* (*Brit*) cinta adhesiva, celo, scotch *m* ® (*LAm*).

sellout [sel'out] *n* traición *f*; **it was a ~** (*THEATER etc*) fue un éxito de taquilla.

selves [selvz] *npl of* **self**.

semantic [siman'tik] *a* semántico.
semaphore [sem'əfôr] *n* semáforo.
semblance [sem'bləns] *n* apariencia.
semen [sē'mən] *n* semen *m*.
semester [simes'tûr] *n* semestre *m*.
semi [sem'ē] *n* (*Brit*) = **semidetached house.**
semi... [sem'ē] *pref* semi..., medio....
semiannually [sem'ēan'yōōəlē] *ad* (*US*) semestralmente ♦ *a* semestral.
semicircle [sem'ēsûrkəl] *n* semicírculo.
semicircular [semēsûr'kyəlûr] *a* semicircular.
semicolon [sem'ēkōlən] *n* punto y coma.
semiconductor [semēkənduk'tûr] *n* semiconductor *m*.
semiconscious [semēkân'chəs] *a* semiconsciente.
semidetached (house) [semēditacht' (hous)] *n* (*Brit*) (casa) semiseparada.
semi-final [semēfi'nəl] *n* semi-final *m*.
seminar [sem'ənâr] *n* seminario.
seminary [sem'ənārē] *n* (*REL*) seminario.
semiprecious stone [semēpresh'əs stōn] *n* piedra semipreciosa.
semiquaver [sem'ēkwāvûr] *n* (*Brit*) semicorchea.
semiskilled [semēskild'] *a* (*work, worker*) semicalificado.
semitone [sem'ētōn] *n* semitono.
semi(trailer) [sem'ē(trā'lûr)] *n* (*US*) trailer *m*.
semolina [seməlē'nə] *n* sémola.
Sen., sen. *abbr* = **senator, senior.**
senate [sen'it] *n* senado.
senator [sen'ətûr] *n* senador(a) *m/f*.
send, *pt*, *pp* **sent** [send, sent] *vt* mandar, enviar; **to ~ by mail** mandar por correo; **to ~ sb for sth** mandar a uno a buscar algo; **to ~ word that ...** avisar *or* mandar decir que ...; **she ~s (you) her love** te manda *or* envía cariñosos recuerdos; **to ~ sb into fits of laughter** hacer reír a uno; **to ~ sth flying** echar a uno; **to ~ sb flying** tirar algo.
send away *vt* (*letter, goods*) despachar.
send away for *vt fus* pedir.
send back *vt* devolver.
send for *vt fus* mandar traer; (*by mail*) escribir pidiendo algo.
send in *vt* (*report, application, resignation*) mandar.
send off *vt* (*goods*) despachar.
send on *vt* (*letter*) mandar, expedir; (*luggage etc: in advance*) facturar.
send out *vt* (*invitation*) mandar; (*emit: light, heat*) emitir, difundir; (: *signal*) emitir.
send up *vt* (*person, price*) hacer subir.
sender [send'ûr] *n* remitente *m/f*.
send-off [send'ôf] *n*: **a good ~** una buena despedida.
Senegal [sen'əgâl] *n* Senegal *m*.
Senegalese [senəgəlēz'] *a, n* senegalés/esa

m/f.
senile [sē'nīl] *a* senil.
senility [sinil'ətē] *n* senilidad *f*.
senior [sēn'yûr] *a* (*older*) mayor, más viejo; (: *on staff*) más antiguo; (*of higher rank*) superior ♦ *n* mayor *m*; **P. Jones ~** P. Jones padre.
senior citizen *n* jubilado/a, anciano/a.
senior high school *n* (*US*) ≈ instituto de enseñanza media *or* de BUP (*Sp*).
seniority [sēnyôr'itē] *n* antigüedad *f*; (*in rank*) rango superior.
sensation [sensā'shən] *n* (*physical feeling, impression*) sensación *f*.
sensational [sensā'shənəl] *a* sensacional.
sense [sens] *n* (*faculty, meaning*) sentido; (*feeling*) sensación *f*; (*good ~*) sentido común, juicio ♦ *vt* sentir, percibir; **~ of humor** sentido del humor; **it makes ~** tiene sentido; **there is no ~ in (doing) that** no hay sentido en (hacer) eso; **to come to one's ~s** (*regain consciousness*) volver en sí, recobrar el sentido; **to take leave of one's ~s** perder el juicio.
senseless [sens'lis] *a* estúpido, insensato; (*unconscious*) sin conocimiento.
senselessly [sens'lislē] *ad* estúpidamente, insensatamente.
sensibility [sensəbil'ətē] *n* sensibilidad *f*; **sensibilities** *npl* delicadeza *sg*.
sensible [sen'səbəl] *a* sensato; (*reasonable*) razonable, lógico.
sensibly [sen'səblē] *ad* sensatamente; razonablemente, de modo lógico.
sensitive [sen'sətiv] *a* sensible; (*touchy*) susceptible; **he is very ~ about it** es muy susceptible acerca de eso.
sensitivity [sensətiv'ətē] *n* sensibilidad *f*; susceptibilidad *f*.
sensual [sen'shōōəl] *a* sensual.
sensuous [sen'shōōəs] *a* sensual.
sent [sent] *pt*, *pp* of **send**.
sentence [sen'təns] *n* (*LING*) frase *f*, oración *f*; (*LAW*) sentencia, fallo ♦ *vt*: **to ~ sb to death/to 5 years** condenar a uno a muerte/a 5 años de cárcel; **to pass ~ on sb** (*also fig*) sentenciar *or* condenar a uno.
sentiment [sen'təmənt] *n* sentimiento; (*opinion*) opinión *f*.
sentimental [sentəmen'təl] *a* sentimental.
sentimentality [sentəmental'itē] *n* sentimentalismo, sensiblería.
sentinel [sen'tənəl] *n* centinela *m*.
sentry [sen'trē] *n* centinela *m*.
sentry duty *n*: **to be on ~** estar de guardia, hacer guardia.
Seoul [sōl] *n* Seúl *m*.
separable [sep'ûrəbəl] *a* separable.
separate *a* [sep'rit] separado; (*distinct*) distinto ♦ (*vb*: [sep'ərāt]) *vt* separar; (*part*) dividir ♦ *vi* separarse; **~ from** separar *or* distinto de; **under ~ cover** (*COMM*) por separado; **to ~ into** dividir *or* separar en; **he**

is ~d from his wife, but not divorced está separado de su mujer, pero no (está) divorciado.

separately [sep'ritlē] *ad* por separado.

separates [sep'rits] *npl* (*clothes*) coordinados *mpl*.

separation [sepərā'shən] *n* separación *f*.

sepia [sē'pēə] *a* color sepia *inv*.

Sept. *abbr* (= *September*) sep.

September [septem'bûr] *n* se(p)tiembre *m*.

septic [sep'tik] *a* séptico; **to go ~** ponerse séptico.

septicemia, (*Brit*) **septicaemia** [septisē'mēə] *n* septicemia.

septic tank *n* fosa séptica.

sequel [sē'kwəl] *n* consecuencia, resultado; (*of story*) continuación *f*.

sequence [sē'kwins] *n* sucesión *f*, serie *f*; (*CINEMA*) secuencia; **in ~** en orden *or* serie.

sequential [sikwen'chəl] *a*: **~ access** (*COMPUT*) acceso en serie.

sequin [sē'kwin] *n* lentejuela.

Serbo-Croat [sûr'bōkrōat] *n* (*LING*) serbocroata *m*.

serenade [sərənād'] *n* serenata ♦ *vt* dar serenata a.

serene [sərēn'] *a* sereno, tranquilo.

serenely [sərēn'lē] *ad* serenamente, tranquilamente.

serenity [səren'itē] *n* serenidad *f*, tranquilidad *f*.

sergeant [sâr'jənt] *n* sargento.

sergeant major *n* sargento mayor.

serial [sēr'ēəl] *n* novela por entregas; (*TV*) telenovela.

serial access *n* (*COMPUT*) acceso en serie.

serial interface *n* (*COMPUT*) interface *m* en serie.

serialize [sēr'ēəlīz] *vt* publicar/televisar por entregas.

serial number *n* número de serie.

serial printer *n* (*COMPUT*) impresora en serie.

series [sēr'ēz] *n*, *pl inv* serie *f*.

serious [sēr'ēəs] *a* serio; (*grave*) grave; **are you ~ (about it)?** ¿lo dices en serio?

seriously [sēr'ēəslē] *ad* en serio; (*ill, wounded etc*) gravemente; **to take sth/sb ~** tomar algo/a uno en serio.

seriousness [sē'rēəsnis] *n* seriedad *f*; gravedad *f*.

sermon [sûr'mən] *n* sermón *m*.

serpent [sûr'pənt] *n* serpiente *f*.

serrated [sârā'tid] *a* serrado, dentellado.

serum [sēr'əm] *n* suero.

servant [sûr'vənt] *n* (*gen*) servidor(a) *m/f*; (*house ~*) criado/a.

serve [sûrv] *vt* servir; (*customer*) atender; (*subj: train*) pasar por; (*apprenticeship*) hacer; (*prison term*) cumplir ♦ *vi* (*servant, soldier etc*) servir; (*TENNIS*) sacar ♦ *n* (*TENNIS*) saque *m*; **it ~s him right** se lo

merece, se lo tiene merecido; **to ~ a summons on sb** entregar una citación a uno; **it ~s my purpose** me viene al caso; **are you being ~d?** (*Brit*) ¿le atienden?; **the power station ~s the entire region** la central eléctrica abastece a toda la región; **to ~ as/for/to do** servir de/para/para hacer; **to ~ on a committee/a jury** ser miembro de una comisión/un jurado.

serve up *vt* (*food*) servir.

service [sûr'vis] *n* (*gen*) servicio; (*REL*: *Catholic*) misa; (: *other*) oficio (religioso); (*AUT*) mantenimiento; (*of dishes*) juego ♦ *vt* (*car, washing machine*) mantener; (: *repair*) reparar; **the Armed S~s** las fuerzas armadas; **funeral ~** exequias *fpl*; **to hold a ~** celebrar un oficio religioso; **the essential ~s** los servicios esenciales; **medical/social ~s** servicios *mpl* médicos/ sociales; **the train ~ to New York** el servicio de tren para Nueva York; **to be of ~ to sb** ser útil a uno.

serviceable [sûr'visəbəl] *a* servible, utilizable.

service area *n* (*on motorway*) servicios *mpl*.

service charge *n* (*Brit*) servicio.

service industries *npl* industrias *fpl* del servicio.

serviceman [sûr'visman] *n* militar *m*.

service station *n* estación *f* de servicio.

servicing [sûr'vising] *n* (*of car*) revisión *f*; (*of washing machine etc*) servicio de reparaciones.

serviette [sûrvēet'] *n* (*Brit*) servilleta.

servile [sûr'vil] *a* servil.

serving cart [sûr'ving kârt] *n* (*US*) carrito.

session [sesh'ən] *n* (*sitting*) sesión *f*; **to be in ~** estar en sesión.

set [set] *n* juego; (*RADIO*) aparato; (*TV*) televisor *m*; (*of utensils*) batería; (*of cutlery*) cubierto; (*of books*) colección *f*; (*TENNIS*) set *m*; (*group of people*) grupo; (*CINEMA*) plató *m*; (*THEATER*) decorado; (*HAIRDRESSING*) marcado ♦ *a* (*fixed*) fijo; (*ready*) listo; (*resolved*) resuelto, decidido ♦ *vb*: *pt, pp* **set**) *vt* (*place*) poner, colocar; (*fix*) fijar; (*adjust*) ajustar, arreglar; (*decide: rules etc*) establecer, decidir; (*assign: task*) asignar; (: *assignment*) poner ♦ *vi* (*sun*) ponerse; (*jam, jelly*) cuajarse; (*concrete*) fraguar; **a ~ of false teeth** una dentadura postiza; **a ~ of dining-room furniture** muebles *mpl* de comedor; **~ in one's ways** con costumbres arraigadas; **a ~ phrase** una frase hecha; **to be all ~ to do sth** estar listo para hacer algo; **to be ~ on doing sth** estar empeñado en hacer algo; **a novel ~ in Valencia** una novela ambientada en Valencia; **to ~ to music** poner música a; **to ~ on fire** incendiar, poner fuego a; **to ~ free** poner en libertad; **to ~ the table** poner la mesa;

to ~ sth going poner algo en marcha; **to ~ sail** zarpar, hacerse a la vela.

set about vt fus: **to ~ about doing sth** ponerse a hacer algo.

set aside vt poner aparte, dejar de lado.

set back vt (progress): **to ~ back (by)** retrasar (por); **a house ~ back from the road** una casa apartada de la carretera.

set in vi (infection) declararse; (complications) comenzar; **the rain has ~ in for the day** parece que va a llover todo el día.

set off vi partir ♦ vt (bomb) hacer estallar; (cause to start) poner en marcha; (show up well) hacer resaltar.

set out vi: **to ~ out to do sth** proponerse hacer algo ♦ vt (arrange) disponer; (state) exponer; **to ~ out (from)** salir (de).

set up vt (organization) establecer.

setback [set'bak] n (hitch) revés m, contratiempo; (in health) recaída.

set menu n menú m.

set phrase n frase f hecha.

set square n (Brit) cartabón m.

settee [setē'] n sofá m.

setting [set'ing] n (scenery) marco; (of jewel) engaste m, montadura.

settle [set'əl] vt (argument, matter) resolver; (pay: bill, accounts) pagar, ajustar, liquidar; (colonize: land) colonizar; (MED: calm) calmar, sosegar ♦ vi (dust etc) depositarse; (weather) serenarse; (also: ~ down) instalarse; (calm down) tranquilizarse; **to ~ for sth** convenir en aceptar algo; **to ~ on sth** decidirse por algo; **that's ~d then** bueno, está arreglado; **to ~ one's stomach** asentar el estómago.

settle in vi instalarse.

settle up vi: **to ~ up with sb** ajustar cuentas con uno.

settlement [set'əlmənt] n (payment) liquidación f; (agreement) acuerdo, convenio; (village etc) pueblo; **in ~ of our account** (COMM) en pago or liquidación de nuestra cuenta.

settler [set'lûr] n colono/a, colonizador(a) m/f.

setup [set'up] n sistema m.

seven [sev'ən] num siete.

seventeen [sev'əntēn'] num diez y siete, diecisiete.

seventh [sev'ənth] a séptimo.

seventy [sev'əntē] num setenta.

sever [sev'ûr] vt cortar; (relations) romper.

several [sev'ûrəl] a, pron varios/as m/fpl, algunos/as m/fpl; **~ of us** varios de nosotros; **~ times** varias veces.

severance [sev'ûrəns] n (of relations) ruptura.

severance pay n pago or indemnización f de despedida.

severe [sivēr'] a severo; (serious) grave; (hard) duro; (pain) intenso.

severely [sivēr'lē] ad severamente;

(wounded, ill) de gravedad, gravemente.

severity [sivär'itē] n severidad f; gravedad f; intensidad f.

Seville [səvil'] n Sevilla.

sew [sō], pt **sewed**, pp **sewn** [sō, sōd, sōn] vt, vi coser.

sew up vt coser, zurcir.

sewage [sōō'ij] n (effluence) aguas fpl residuales; (system) alcantarillado.

sewer [sōō'ûr] n alcantarilla, cloaca.

sewing [sō'ing] n costura.

sewing machine n máquina de coser.

sewn [sōn] pp of **sew**.

sex [seks] n sexo; **the opposite ~** el sexo opuesto; **to have ~ with sb** tener relaciones (sexuales) con uno.

sex act n acto sexual, coito.

sexism [sek'sizəm] n sexismo

sexist [seks'ist] a, n sexista m/f.

sextant [seks'tənt] n sextante m.

sextet [sekstet'] n sexteto.

sexual [sek'shōōəl] a sexual; **~ assault** atentado contra el pudor; **~ intercourse** relaciones fpl sexuales.

sexually [sek'shōōəlē] ad sexualmente.

sexy [sek'sē] a sexy.

Seychelles [sāshel'] npl: **the ~** las Seychelles.

SF n abbr = **science fiction.**

SG n abbr (US: = Surgeon General) jefe del servicio federal de sanidad.

Sgt abbr (= sergeant) sgto.

shabbily [shab'ilē] ad (treat) muy mal; (dressed) pobremente.

shabbiness [shab'ēnis] n (of dress, person) aspecto desharrapado; (of building) mal estado.

shabby [shab'ē] a (person) desharrapado; (clothes) raído, gastado.

shack [shak] n choza, chabola.

shackle [shak'əl] vt encadenar; (fig): **to be ~d by sth** verse obstaculizado por algo.

shackles [shak'əlz] npl grillos mpl, grilletes mpl.

shade [shād] n sombra; (for lamp) pantalla; (for eyes) visera; (of color) matiz m, tonalidad f; (US: window ~) persiana ♦ vt dar sombra a; **~s** npl (sunglasses) gafas fpl de sol; **in the ~** a la sombra; (small quantity): **a ~ of** un poquito de; **a ~ smaller** un poquito menor.

shadow [shad'ō] n sombra ♦ vt (follow) seguir y vigilar; **without** or **beyond a ~ of doubt** sin lugar a dudas.

shadow cabinet n (Brit POL) gabinete paralelo formado por el partido de oposición.

shadowy [shad'ōē] a oscuro; (dim) indistinto.

shady [shā'dē] a sombreado; (fig: dishonest) sospechoso; (: deal) turbio.

shaft [shaft] n (of arrow, spear) astil m; (AUT, TECH) eje m, árbol m; (of mine) pozo; (*of elevator*) hueco, caja; (*of light*) rayo; **ventilator** ~ chimenea de ventilación.

shaggy [shag'ē] *a* peludo.

shake [shāk] *vb* (*pt* **shook**, *pp* **shaken** [shŏŏk, shā'kən]) *vt* sacudir; (*building*) hacer temblar; (*perturb*) inquietar, perturbar; (*weaken*) debilitar; (*alarm*) trastornar ♦ *vi* estremecerse; (*tremble*) temblar ♦ *n* (*movement*) sacudida; **to ~ one's head** (*in refusal*) negar con la cabeza; (*in dismay*) mover *or* menear la cabeza, incrédulo; **to ~ hands with sb** estrechar la mano a uno; **to ~ in one's shoes** (*fig*) temblar de aprensión, tener mieditis.

shake off *vt* sacudirse; (*fig*) deshacerse de.

shake up *vt* agitar.

shake-up [shāk'up] *n* reorganización *f*.

shakily [shā'kilē] *ad* (*reply*) con voz temblorosa *or* trémula; (*walk*) con paso vacilante; (*write*) con mano temblorosa.

shaky [shā'kē] *a* (*unstable*) inestable, poco firme; (*trembling*) tembloroso; (*health*) delicado; (*memory*) defectuoso; (*person: from illness*) temblando; (*premise etc*) incierto.

shale [shāl] *n* esquisto.

shall [shal] *auxiliary vb*: **I ~ go** iré.

shallot [shəlât'] *n* cebollita, chalote *m*.

shallow [shal'ō] *a* poco profundo; (*fig*) superficial.

shallows [shal'ōz] *npl* bajío *sg*, bajos *mpl*.

sham [sham] *n* fraude *m*, engaño ♦ *a* falso, fingido ♦ *vt* fingir, simular.

shambles [sham'bəlz] *n* desorden *m*, confusión *f*; **the economy is (in) a complete ~** la economía está en ruinas.

shame [shām] *n* vergüenza; (*pity*) lástima ♦ *vt* avergonzar; **it is a ~ that/to do es** una lástima que/hacer; **what a ~!** ¡qué lástima!; **to put sth/sb to ~** (*fig*) ridiculizar algo/a uno.

shamefaced [shām'fāst] *a* avergonzado.

shameful [shām'fəl] *a* vergonzoso.

shamefully [shām'fəlē] *ad* vergonzosamente.

shameless [shām'lis] *a* descarado.

shampoo [shampōō'] *n* champú *m* ♦ *vt* lavar con champú.

shampoo and set *n* lavado y marcado.

shamrock [sham'râk] *n* trébol *m*.

shandy [shan'dē] *n* mezcla de cerveza con gaseosa.

shan't [shant] = **shall not**.

shanty town [shan'tē toun] *n* barrio de chabolas.

SHAPE [shāp] *n abbr* (= *Supreme Headquarters Allied Powers, Europe*) cuartel general de las fuerzas aliadas en Europa.

shape [shāp] *n* forma ♦ *vt* formar, dar forma a; (*clay*) modelar; (*stone*) labrar; (*sb's ideas*) formar; (*sb's life*) determinar

♦ *vi* (*also:* ~ **up**) (*events*) desarrollarse; (*person*) formarse; **to take ~** tomar forma; **to get o.s. into ~** ponerse en forma *or* en condiciones; **in the ~ of a heart** en forma de corazón; **I can't bear gardening in any ~ or form** no aguanto la jardinería de ningún modo.

-shaped [shāpt] *suff* **heart~** en forma de corazón.

shapeless [shāp'lis] *a* informe, sin forma definida.

shapely [shāp'lē] *a* bien formado *or* proporcionado.

share [shär] *n* (*part*) parte *f*, porción *f*; (*contribution*) cuota; (*COMM*) acción *f* ♦ *vt* dividir; (*fig: have in common*) compartir; **to have a ~ in the profits** tener una proporción de las ganancias; **he has a 50% ~ in a new business venture** tiene una participación del 50% en un nuevo negocio; **to ~ in** participar en; **to ~ among** *or* **between** repartir entre.

share capital *n* (*COMM*) capital *m* en acciones *or* accionario.

share certificate *n* certificado *or* título de una acción.

shareholder [shär'hōldûr] *n* (*Brit*) accionista *m/f*.

share index *n* (*COMM*) índice *m* de la bolsa.

share issue *n* emisión *f* de acciones.

share price *n* (*COMM*) cotización *f*.

shark [shârk] *n* tiburón *m*.

sharp [shârp] *a* (*razor, knife*) afilado; (*point*) puntiagudo; (*outline*) definido; (*pain*) intenso; (*MUS*) desafinado; (*contrast*) marcado; (*voice*) agudo; (*curve, bend*) cerrado; (*person: quick-witted*) astuto; (: *dishonest*) poco escrupuloso ♦ *n* (*MUS*) sostenido ♦ *ad*: **at 2 o'clock ~** a las 2 en punto; **to be ~ with sb** hablar a uno con voz tajante; **turn ~ left** dobla fuertemente a la izquierda.

sharpen [shâr'pən] *vt* afilar; (*pencil*) sacar punta a; (*fig*) agudizar.

sharpener [shâr'pənûr] *n* (*gen*) afilador *m*; (*pencil ~*) sacapuntas *m inv*.

sharp-eyed [shârp'īd] *a* de vista aguda.

sharply [shârp'lē] *ad* (*abruptly*) bruscamente; (*clearly*) claramente; (*harshly*) severamente.

sharp-tempered [shârp'tempûrd] *a* de genio arisco.

sharp-witted [shârp'wit'id] *a* listo, despabilado.

shatter [shat'ûr] *vt* hacer añicos *or* pedazos; (*fig: ruin*) destruir, acabar con ♦ *vi* hacerse añicos.

shattered [shat'ûrd] *a* (*grief-stricken*) destrozado, deshecho; (*exhausted*) agotado, hecho polvo.

shattering [shat'ûring] *a* (*experience*) devastador(a), anonadante.

shatterproof [shat'úrpr͞oof] *a* inastillable.
shave [shāv] *vt* afeitar, rasurar ♦ *vi* afeitarse ♦ *n*: **to have a** ~ afeitarse.
shaven [shā'vən] *a* (*head*) rapado.
shaver [shā'vúr] *n* (*also*: **electric** ~) máquina de afeitar (eléctrica).
shaving [shā'ving] *n* (*action*) el afeitarse,
rasurado; ~**s** *npl* (*of wood etc*) virutas *fpl*.
shaving brush *n* brocha (de afeitar).
shaving cream *n* crema (de afeitar).
shaving soap *n* jabón *m* de afeitar.
shawl [shôl] *n* chal *m*.
she [shē] *pron* ella; **there** ~ **is** allí está; ~-
cat gata; *NB: for ships, countries follow
the gender of your translation.*
sheaf, *pl* **sheaves** [shēf, shēvz] *n* (*of corn*)
gavilla; (*of arrows*) haz *m*; (*of papers*)
fajo.
shear [shē'ûr] *vt* (*pt* ~**ed**, *pp* ~**ed** *or* **shorn**
[shôrn]) (*sheep*) esquilar, trasquilar.
  shear off *vi* romperse.
shears [shē'ûrz] *npl* (*for hedge*) tijeras *fpl*
de jardín.
sheath [shēth] *n* vaina; (*contraceptive*) preservativo.
sheath knife *n* cuchillo de monte.
sheaves [shēvz] *npl of* **sheaf**.
shed [shed] *n* cobertizo; (*INDUSTRY, RAIL*)
nave *f* ♦ *vt* (*pt, pp* **shed**) (*skin*) mudar;
(*tears*) derramar; **to** ~ **light on** (*problem,
mystery*) aclarar, arrojar luz sobre.
she'd [shēd] = **she had, she would.**
sheen [shēn] *n* brillo, lustre *m*.
sheep [shēp] *n* (*pl inv*) oveja.
sheepdog [shēp'dôg] *n* perro pastor.
sheep farmer *n* ganadero.
sheepish [shē'pish] *a* tímido, vergonzoso.
sheepskin [shēp'skin] *n* piel *f* de carnero.
sheepskin jacket *n* zamarra.
sheer [shēr] *a* (*utter*) puro, completo;
(*steep*) escarpado; (*material*) diáfano ♦ *ad*
verticalmente; **by** ~ **chance** de pura casualidad.
sheet [shēt] *n* (*on bed*) sábana; (*of paper*)
hoja; (*of glass, metal*) lámina.
sheet feed *n* (*on printer*) alimentador *m*
de papel.
sheet lightning *n* relámpago (difuso).
sheet metal *n* metal *m* en lámina.
sheet music *n* hojas *fpl* de partitura.
sheik(h) [shēk] *n* jeque *m*.
shelf, *pl* **shelves** [shelf, shelvz] *n* estante *m*.
shelf life *n* (*COMM*) periodo de conservación antes de la venta.
shell [shel] *n* (*on beach*) concha; (*of egg,
nut etc*) cáscara; (*explosive*) proyectil *m*,
obús *m*; (*of building*) armazón *m* ♦ *vt*
(*peas*) desenvainar; (*MIL*) bombardear.
  shell out *vi* (*col*): **to** ~ **out (for)** soltar
el dinero (para), desembolsar (para).
she'll [shēl] = **she will, she shall.**
shellfish [shel'fish] *n* (*pl inv*) crustáceo;
(*pl: as food*) mariscos *mpl*.

shelter [shel'tûr] *n* abrigo, refugio ♦ *vt* (*aid*)
amparar, proteger; (*give lodging to*) abrigar; (*hide*) esconder ♦ *vi* abrigarse, refugiarse; **to take** ~ **(from)** refugiarse *or* asi-
larse (de); **bus** ~ parada de autobús cubierta.
sheltered [shel'tûrd] *a* (*life*) protegido;
(*spot*) abrigado.
shelve [shelv] *vt* (*fig*) dar carpetazo a.
shelves [shelvz] *npl of* **shelf**.
shelving [shel'ving] *n* estantería.
shepherd [shep'ûrd] *n* pastor *m* ♦ *vt*
(*guide*) guiar, conducir.
shepherdess [shep'úrdis] *n* pastora.
shepherd's pie *n* pastel de carne y patatas.
sherbert [shûr'bûrt] *n* (*US: dessert*) sorbete
m; (*Brit: powder*) polvos *mpl* azucarados.
sherbet [shûr'bit] *n* sorbete *m*.
sheriff [shär'if] *n* (*US*) alguacil *m*.
sherry [shär'ē] *n* jerez *m*.
she's [shēz] = **she is, she has.**
Shetland [shet'lənd] *n* (*also*: **the** ~**s, the** ~
Isles) las Islas *fpl* de Zetlandia.
shield [shēld] *n* escudo; (*TECH*) blindaje *m*
♦ *vt*: **to** ~ **(from)** proteger (de).
shift [shift] *n* (*change*) cambio; (*at work*)
turno ♦ *vt* trasladar; (*remove*) quitar;
(*AUT*) cambiar ♦ *vi* moverse; (*change
place*) cambiar de sitio; **the wind has** ~**ed
to the south** el viento ha virado al sur; **a**
~ **in demand** (*COMM*) un desplazamiento
de la demanda.
shift key *n* (*on typewriter*) tecla de mayúsculas.
shiftless [shift'lis] *a* (*person*) vago.
shift work *n* trabajo por turno; **to do** ~
trabajar por turno.
shifty [shif'tē] *a* tramposo; (*eyes*) furtivo.
shilling [shil'ing] *n* (*Brit*) chelín *m* (= *12 old
pence; 20 in a pound*).
shilly-shally [shil'ēshalē] *vi* titubear, vacilar.
shimmer [shim'ûr] *n* reflejo trémulo ♦ *vi* relucir.
shimmering [shim'ûring] *a* reluciente;
(*haze*) trémulo; (*satin etc*) lustroso.
shin [shin] *n* espinilla ♦ *vi*: **to** ~ **up/down a
tree** trepar/bajar de un árbol.
shindig [shin'dig] *n* (*col*) fiesta, juerga.
shine [shīn] *n* brillo, lustre *m* ♦ *vi* (*vb*: *pt, pp*
shone [shōn]) *vi* brillar, relucir ♦ *vt*
(*shoes*) lustrar, sacar brillo a; **to** ~ **a
flashlight on sth** dirigir una linterna hacia
algo.
shingle [shing'gəl] *n* (*on beach*) guijarras
fpl.
shingles [shing'gəlz] *n* (*MED*) herpes *mpl* *or*
fpl.
shining [shī'ning] *a* (*surface, hair*) lustroso;
(*light*) brillante.
shiny [shī'nē] *a* brillante, lustroso.
ship [ship] *n* buque *m*, barco ♦ *vt* (*goods*)

embarcar; (*oars*) desarmar; (*send*) transportar *or* enviar por vía marítima; ~'s **manifest** manifiesto del buque; **on board** ~ a bordo.

shipbuilder [ship'bildúr] *n* constructor(a) *m/f* de buques.

shipbuilding [ship'bilding] *n* construcción *f* de barcos.

ship canal *n* canal *m* de navegación.

ship chandler [ship chan'dlúr] *n* proveedor *m* de efectos navales.

shipment [ship'mənt] *n* (*act*) embarque *m*; (*goods*) envío.

shipowner [ship'ōnúr] *n* naviero, armador *m*.

shipper [ship'úr] *n* exportador(a) *m/f*, empresa naviera.

shipping [ship'ing] *n* (*act*) embarque *m*; (*traffic*) buques *mpl*.

shipping agent *n* agente *m/f* marítimo/a.

shipping company *n* compañía naviera.

shipping lane *n* ruta de navegación.

shipping line *n* = **shipping company**.

shipshape [ship'shāp] *a* en buen orden.

shipwreck [ship'rek] *n* naufragio ♦ *vt*: **to be ~ed** naufragar.

shipyard [ship'yârd] *n* astillero.

shirk [shúrk] *vt* eludir, esquivar; (*obligations*) faltar a.

shirt [shúrt] *n* camisa; **in ~ sleeves** en mangas de camisa.

shit [shit] *excl* (*col!*) ¡mierda! (*!*).

shiver [shiv'úr] *vi* temblar, estremecerse; (*with cold*) tiritar.

shoal [shōl] *n* (*Brit: of fish*) banco.

shock [shâk] *n* (*impact*) choque *m*; (*ELEC*) descarga (eléctrica); (*emotional*) conmoción *f*; (*start*) sobresalto, susto; (*MED*) postración *f* nerviosa ♦ *vt* dar un susto a; (*offend*) escandalizar; **to get a ~** (*ELEC*) sentir una sacudida eléctrica; **to give sb a ~** dar un susto a uno; **to be suffering from ~** padecer una postración nerviosa; **it came as a ~ to hear that ...** me (*etc*) asombró descubrir que ....

shock absorber [shâk absôrb'úr] *n* amortiguador *m*.

shocking [shâk'ing] *a* (*awful: weather, handwriting*) espantoso, horrible; (*improper*) escandaloso; (*result*) inesperado.

shock therapy, shock treatment *n* (*MED*) tratamiento por electrochoque.

shod [shâd] *pt, pp of* **shoe** ♦ *a* calzado.

shoddiness [shâd'ēnis] *n* baja calidad *f*.

shoddy [shâd'ē] *a* de pacotilla.

shoe [shōō] *n* zapato; (*for horse*) herradura; (*brake* ~) zapata ♦ *vt* (*pt, pp* **shod** [shâd]) (*horse*) herrar.

shoe brush *n* cepillo para zapatos.

shoehorn [shōō'hôrn] *n* calzador *m*.

shoelace [shōō'lās] *n* cordón *m*.

shoemaker [shōō'mākúr] *n* zapatero/a.

shoe polish *n* betún *m*.

shoe shop *n* zapatería.

shoestring [shōō'string] *n* (*shoelace*) cordón *m*; (*fig*): **on a ~** con muy poco dinero, a lo barato.

shone [shōn] *pt, pp of* **shine**.

shoo [shōō] *excl* ¡fuera!; (*to animals*) ¡zape! ♦ *vt* (*also*: ~ **away,** ~ **off**) ahuyentar.

shook [shōōk] *pt of* **shake**.

shoot [shōōt] *n* (*on branch, seedling*) retoño, vástago; (*shooting party*) cacería; (*competition*) concurso de tiro; (*preserve*) coto de caza ♦ (*vb: pt, pp* **shot** [shât]) *vt* disparar; (*kill*) matar a tiros; (*execute*) fusilar; (*CINE: movie, scene*) rodar, filmar ♦ *vi* (*SOCCER*) chutar; **to ~ (at)** tirar (a); **to ~ past sb** pasar a uno como un rayo; **to shoot in/out** *vi* entrar corriendo/salir disparado.

shoot down *vt* (*plane*) derribar.

shoot up *vi* (*prices*) dispararse.

shooting [shōō'ting] *n* (*shots*) tiros *mpl*, tiroteo; (*HUNTING*) caza con escopeta; (*act: murder*) asesinato (a tiros); (*CINE*) rodaje *m*.

shooting star *n* estrella fugaz.

shop [shâp] *n* tienda; (*workshop*) taller *m* ♦ *vi* (*also*: **go ~ping**) ir de compras; **to talk ~** (*fig*) hablar del trabajo; **repair ~** taller *m* de reparaciones.

shop around *vi* comparar precios.

shop assistant *n* (*Brit*) dependiente/a *m/f*.

shop floor *n* (*fig*) taller *m*, fábrica.

shopkeeper [shâp'kēpúr] *n* tendero/a.

shoplift [shâp'lift] *vi* robar en las tiendas.

shoplifter [shâp'liftúr] *n* ratero/a.

shoplifting [shâp'lifting] *n* mechería.

shopper [shâp'úr] *n* comprador(a) *m/f*.

shopping [shâp'ing] *n* (*goods*) compras *fpl*.

shopping bag *n* bolsa (de compras).

shopping center *n* centro comercial.

shopping mall *n* galería comercial.

shop-soiled [shâp'soild] *a* (*Brit*) usado.

shop steward *n* (*INDUSTRY*) enlace *m/f*.

shop window *n* escaparate *m*, vidriera (*LAm*).

shopworn [shâp'wôrn] *a* (*US*) usado.

shore [shôr] *n* (*of sea, lake*) orilla ♦ *vt*: **to ~ (up)** reforzar; **on ~** en tierra.

shore leave *n* (*NAUT*) permiso para bajar a tierra.

shorn [shôrn] *pp of* **shear**.

short [shôrt] *a* (*not long*) corto; (*in time*) breve, de corta duración; (*person*) bajo; (*curt*) brusco, seco ♦ *vi* (*ELEC*) ponerse en cortocircuito ♦ *n* (*also*: ~ **film**) cortometraje *m*; (**a pair of**) ~**s** (unos) pantalones *mpl* cortos; **to be ~ of sth** estar falto de algo; **in ~** en pocas palabras; **a ~ time ago** hace poco (tiempo); **in the ~ term** a corto plazo; **to be in ~ supply** escasear, haber escasez de; **I'm ~ of time** me falta tiempo; **~ of doing...** fuera de hacer...; **everything**

~ **of**... todo menos...; **it is** ~ **for** es la forma abreviada de; **to cut** ~ (*speech*, *visit*) interrumpir, terminar inesperadamente; **to fall** ~ **of** no alcanzar; **to run** ~ **of sth** acabársele algo; **to stop** ~ parar en seco; **to stop** ~ **of** detenerse antes de.

shortage [shôr'tij] *n* escasez *f*, falta.

shortbread [shôrt'bred] *n* torta seca y quebradiza.

shortchange [shôrt'chānj'] *vt*: **to** ~ **sb** no dar el cambio completo a uno.

short-circuit [shôrtsûr'kit] *n* cortocircuito ♦ *vt* poner en cortocircuito ♦ *vi* ponerse en cortocircuito.

shortcoming [shôrt'kuming] *n* defecto, deficiencia.

short(crust) pastry [shôrt'(krust) pās'trē] *n* (*Brit*) pasta quebradiza.

shortcut [shôrt'kut] *n* atajo.

shorten [shôr'tən] *vt* acortar; (*visit*) interrumpir.

shortfall [shôrt'fôl] *n* déficit *m*, deficiencia.

shorthand [shôrt'hand] *n* taquigrafía; **to take sth down in** ~ escribir algo taquigráficamente.

shorthand notebook *n* cuaderno de taquigrafía.

shorthand typist *n* (*Brit*) taquimecanógrafo/a.

short list *n* (*for job*) lista de candidatos escogidos.

short-lived [shôrt'livd'] *a* efímero.

shortly [shôrt'lē] *ad* en breve, dentro de poco.

shortness [shôrt'nis] *n* (*of distance*) cortedad *f*; (*of time*) brevedad *f*; (*manner*) brusquedad *f*.

shortsighted [shôrt'sī'tid] *a* corto de vista, miope; (*fig*) imprudente.

short-sightedness [shôrt'sī'tidnis] *n* miopía, cortedad *f* de vista; (*fig*) falta de previsión, imprudencia.

short-staffed [shôrt'staft'] *a* falto de personal.

short story *n* cuento.

short-tempered [shôrt'tempûrd] *a* enojadizo.

short-term [shôrt'tûrm'] *a* (*effect*) a corto plazo.

short time *n*: **to work** ~, **be on** ~ (*INDUSTRY*) trabajar con sistema de horario reducido.

short-time working [shôrt'tīm wûr'king] *n* trabajo de horario reducido.

short wave *n* (*RADIO*) onda corta.

shot [shât] *pt*, *pp of* **shoot** ♦ *n* (*sound*) tiro, disparo; (*person*) tirador(a) *m/f*; (*try*) tentativa; (*injection*) inyección *f*; (*PHOT*) toma, fotografía; (*shotgun pellets*) perdigones *mpl*; **to fire a** ~ **at sb/sth** tirar *or* disparar contra uno/algo; **to have a** ~ **at (doing) sth** probar suerte con algo; **like a** ~ (*without any delay*) como un rayo; **a big**

~ (*col*) un pez gordo; **to get** ~ **of sth/sb** (*col*) deshacerse de algo/uno, quitarse algo/ a uno de encima.

shotgun [shât'gun] *n* escopeta.

should [shŏŏd] *auxiliary vb*: **I** ~ **go now** debo irme ahora; **he** ~ **be there now** debe de haber llegado (ya); ~ **he phone** ... si llamara ..., en caso de que llamase ....

shoulder [shōl'dûr] *n* hombro; (*Brit*: *of road*): **hard** ~ arcén *m* ♦ *vt* (*fig*) cargar con; **to look over one's** ~ mirar hacia atrás; **to rub** ~**s with sb** (*fig*) codearse con uno; **to give sb the cold** ~ (*fig*) dar de lado a uno.

shoulder blade *n* omóplato.

shoulder bag *n* bolso de bandolera.

shoulder strap *n* tirante *m*.

shouldn't [shŏŏd'ant] = **should not**.

shout [shout] *n* grito ♦ *vt* gritar ♦ *vi* gritar, dar voces.

shout down *vt* hundir a gritos.

shouting [shout'ing] *n* griterío.

shove [shuv] *n* empujón *m* ♦ *vt* empujar; (*col*: *put*): **to** ~ **sth in** meter algo a empellones; **he** ~**d me out of the way** me quitó de en medio de un empujón.

shove off *vi* (*NAUT*) alejarse del muelle; (*fig*: *col*) largarse.

shovel [shuv'əl] *n* pala; (*mechanical*) excavadora ♦ *vt* mover con pala.

show [shō] *n* (*of emotion*) demostración *f*; (*semblance*) apariencia; (*COMM*, *TECH*: *exhibition*) exhibición *f*, exposición *f*; (*THEATER*) función *f*, espectáculo; (*organization*) negocio, empresa ♦ *vb* (*pt* **showed**, *pp* **shown** [shōn]) *vt* mostrar, enseñar; (*courage etc*) mostrar, manifestar; (*exhibit*) exponer; (*film*) proyectar ♦ *vi* mostrarse; (*appear*) aparecer; **on** ~ (*exhibits etc*) expuesto; **to be on** ~ estar expuesto; **it's just for** ~ es para lucir nada más; **to ask for a** ~ **of hands** pedir una votación a mano alzada; **who's running the** ~ **here?** ¿quién manda aquí?; **to** ~ **a profit/loss** (*COMM*) arrojar un saldo positivo/negativo; **I have nothing to** ~ **for it** no saqué ningún provecho (de ello); **to** ~ **sb to his seat/to the door** acompañar a uno a su asiento/a la puerta; **as** ~**n in the illustration** como se ve en el grabado; **it just goes to** ~ **that** ... queda demostrado que ...; **it doesn't** ~ no se ve *or* nota.

show in *vt* (*person*) hacer pasar.

show off *vi* (*pej*) presumir ♦ *vt* (*display*) lucir; (*pej*) hacer gala de.

show out *vt*: **to** ~ **sb out** acompañar a uno a la puerta.

show up *vi* (*stand out*) destacar; (*col*: *turn up*) presentarse ♦ *vt* descubrir; (*unmask*) desenmascarar.

show business *n* el mundo del espectáculo.

showcase [shō'kās] *n* vitrina; (*fig*) escaparate *m*.

showdown [shō'doun] *n* crisis *f*, momento decisivo.

shower [shou'ûr] *n* (*rain*) chaparrón *m*, chubasco; (*of stones etc*) lluvia; (*also*: ~ **bath**) ducha ♦ *vi* llover ♦ *vt*: **to** ~ **sb with sth** colmar a uno de algo; **to have** *or* **take a** ~ ducharse.

shower cap *n* gorro de baño.

showerproof [shou'ûrprōōf] *a* impermeable.

showery [shou'ûrē] *a* (*weather*) lluvioso.

showground [shō'ground] *n* ferial *m*, real *m* (de la feria).

showing [shō'ing] *n* (*of movie*) proyección *f*.

show jumping [shō' jum'ping] *n* hipismo.

showman [shō'mən] *n* (*at fair, circus*) empresario; (*fig*) persona extrovertida, exhibicionista *m/f*.

showmanship [shō'mənship] *n* dotes *fpl* teatrales.

shown [shōn] *pp of* **show**.

show-off [shō'óf] *n* (*col: person*) presumido/a.

showpiece [shō'pēs] *n* (*of exhibition etc*) objeto cumbre; **that hospital is a** ~ ese hospital es un modelo del género.

showroom [shō'rōōm] *n* sala de muestras.

showy [shō'ē] *a* ostentoso.

shrank [shrangk] *pt of* **shrink**.

shrapnel [shrap'nəl] *n* metralla.

shred [shred] *n* (*gen pl*) triza, jirón *m*; (*fig: of truth, evidence*) pizca, chispa ♦ *vt* hacer trizas; (*documents*) triturar; (*CULIN*) desmenuzar.

shredder [shred'ûr] *n* (*vegetable shredder*) picadora; (*document shredder*) trituradora (de papel).

shrewd [shrōōd] *a* astuto.

shrewdly [shrōōd'lē] *ad* astutamente.

shrewdness [shrōōd'nis] *n* astucia.

shriek [shrēk] *n* chillido ♦ *vt, vi* chillar.

shrill [shril] *a* agudo, estridente.

shrimp [shrimp] *n* camarón *m*.

shrine [shrīn] *n* santuario, sepulcro.

shrink [shringk], *pt* **shrank**, *pp* **shrunk** [shringk, shrangk, shrungk] *vi* encogerse; (*be reduced*) reducirse ♦ *vt* encoger; **to** ~ **from (doing) sth** no atreverse a hacer algo.

shrink away *vi* retroceder, retirarse.

shrinkage [shringk'ij] *n* encogimiento; reducción *f*.

shrink-wrap [shringk'rap] *vt* empaquetar en envase termoretráctil.

shrivel [shriv'əl] (*also*: ~ **up**) *vt* (*dry*) secar; (*crease*) arrugar ♦ *vi* secarse; arrugarse.

shroud [shroud] *n* sudario ♦ *vt*: ~**ed in mystery** envuelto en el misterio.

Shrove Tuesday [shrōv tōōz'dā] *n* martes *m* de carnaval.

shrub [shrub] *n* arbusto.

shrubbery [shrub'ûrē] *n* arbustos *mpl*.

shrug [shrug] *n* encogimiento de hombros ♦ *vt, vi*: **to** ~ **(one's shoulders)** encogerse de hombros.

shrug off *vt* negar importancia a; (*cold, illness*) deshacerse de.

shrunk [shrungk] *pp of* **shrink**.

shrunken [shrungk'ən] *a* encogido.

shudder [shud'ûr] *n* estremecimiento, escalofrío ♦ *vi* estremecerse.

shuffle [shuf'əl] *vt* (*cards*) barajar; **to** ~ **(one's feet)** arrastrar los pies.

shun [shun] *vt* rehuir, esquivar.

shunt [shunt] *vt* (*RAIL*) maniobrar.

shut, *pt, pp* **shut** [shut] *vt* cerrar ♦ *vi* cerrarse.

shut down *vt, vi* cerrarse, parar; (*machine*) apagar.

shut off *vt* (*stop: power, water supply etc*) interrumpir, cortar; (: *engine*) parar.

shut out *vt* (*person*) excluir, dejar fuera; (*noise, cold*) no dejar entrar; (*block: view*) tapar; (: *memory*) tratar de olvidar.

shut up *vi* (*col: keep quiet*) callarse ♦ *vt* (*close*) cerrar; (*silence*) callar.

shutdown [shut'doun] *n* cierre *m*.

shutter [shut'ûr] *n* contraventana; (*PHOT*) obturador *m*.

shuttle [shut'əl] *n* lanzadera; (*also*: ~ **service**: *AVIAT*) puente *m* aéreo ♦ *vi* (*subj: vehicle, person*) ir y venir ♦ *vt* (*passengers*) transportar, trasladar (*LAm*).

shuttlecock [shut'əlkâk] *n* volante *m*.

shy [shī] *a* tímido ♦ *vi*: **to** ~ **away from doing sth** (*fig*) rehusar hacer algo; **to be** ~ **of doing sth** esquivar hacer algo.

shyly [shī'lē] *ad* tímidamente.

shyness [shī'nis] *n* timidez *f*.

Siam [sīam'] *n* Siam *m*.

Siamese [sīəmēz'] *a* siamés/esa ♦ *n* (*person*) siamés/esa *m/f*; (*LING*) siamés *m*; ~ **cat** gato siamés; ~ **twins** gemelos/as *m/fpl* siameses/as.

Siberia [sībē'rēə] *n* Siberia.

sibling [sib'ling] *n* (*formal*) hermano/a.

Sicilian [sisil'yən] *a, n* siciliano/a *m/f*.

Sicily [sis'ilē] *n* Sicilia.

sick [sik] *a* (*ill*) enfermo; (*nauseated*) mareado; (*humor*) negro; **to be** ~ (*Brit*) vomitar; **to feel** ~ estar mareado; **to feel** ~ **to one's stomach** sentirse mareado; **to be** ~ **of** (*fig*) estar harto de; **a** ~ **person** un(a) enfermo/a; **to be (off)** ~ estar ausente por enfermedad; **to take** ~ ponerse enfermo.

sick bay *n* enfermería.

sickbed [sik'bed] *n* lecho de enfermo.

sicken [sik'ən] *vt* dar asco a ♦ *vi* enfermar.

sickening [sik'əning] *a* (*fig*) asqueroso.

sickle [sik'əl] *n* hoz *f*.

sick leave *n* baja por enfermedad.

sick list *n*: **to be on the** ~ estar de baja.

sickly [sik'lē] *a* enfermizo; (*taste*) empalagoso.

sickness [sik'nis] *n* enfermedad *f*, mal *m*; (*vomiting*) náuseas *fpl*.

sickness benefit *n* (*Brit*) subsidio de enfermedad.

sick pay *n* subsidio de enfermedad.

sickroom [sik'rōōm] *n* cuarto del enfermo.

side [sīd] *n* (*gen*) lado; (*face, surface*) cara; (*of paper*) cara; (*slice of bread*) rebanada; (*of body*) costado; (*of animal*) ijar *m*, ijada; (*of lake*) orilla; (*part*) lado; (*aspect*) aspecto; (*team*: SPORT) equipo; (: POL *etc*) partido; (*of hill*) ladera ♦ *a* (*door, entrance*) de al lado ♦ *vi*: **to ~ with sb** tomar el partido de uno; **by the ~ of** al lado de; **~ by ~** juntos/as; **from all ~s** de todos lados; **to take ~s (with)** tomar partido (con); **~ of beef** flanco de vaca; **the right/wrong ~** el derecho/revés; **from ~ to ~** de un lado a otro.

sideboard [sīd'bôrd] *n* aparador *m*.

sideburns [sīd'bûrnz] *npl* patillas *fpl*.

sidecar [sīd'kär] *n* sidecar *m*.

side dish *n* entremés *m*.

side drum *n* (MUS) tamboril *m*.

side effect *n* efecto secundario.

sidekick [sīd'kik] *n* compinche *m*.

sidelight [sīd'līt] *n* (AUT) luz *f* lateral.

sideline [sīd'līn] *n* (SPORT) línea lateral; (*fig*) empleo suplementario.

sidelong [sīd'lông] *a* de soslayo; **to give a ~ glance at sth** mirar algo de reojo.

side plate *n* platito.

side road *n* (*Brit*) calle *f* lateral.

sidesaddle [sīd'sadəl] *ad* a mujeriegas, a la inglesa.

sideshow [sīd'shō] *n* (*stall*) caseta; (*fig*) atracción *f* secundaria.

sidestep [sīd'step] *vt* (*question*) eludir; (*problem*) esquivar ♦ *vi* (BOXING *etc*) dar un quiebro.

side street *n* calle *f* lateral.

sidetrack [sīd'trak] *vt* (*fig*) desviar (de su propósito).

sidewalk [sīd'wôk] *n* (US) acera.

sideways [sīd'wāz] *ad* de lado.

siding [sī'ding] *n* (RAIL) apartadero, vía muerta.

sidle [sī'dəl] *vi*: **to ~ up (to)** acercarse furtivamente (a).

SIDS *n abbr* (= *sudden infant death syndrome*) muerte *f* en la cuna.

siege [sēj] *n* cerco, sitio; **to lay ~ to** cercar, sitiar.

siege economy *n* economía de sitio *or* de asedio.

Sierra Leone [sēär'ə lēōn'] *n* Sierra Leona.

siesta [sēes'tə] *n* siesta.

sieve [siv] *n* colador *m* ♦ *vt* cribar.

sift [sift] *vt* cribar; (*fig*: *information*) escudriñar ♦ *vi*: **to ~ through** pasar por una criba; (*of information*) llegar a saberse.

sigh [sī] *n* suspiro ♦ *vi* suspirar.

sight [sīt] *n* (*faculty*) vista; (*spectacle*) espectáculo; (*on gun*) mira, alza ♦ *vt* ver, divisar; **in ~** a la vista; **out of ~** fuera de (la) vista; **on ~** a la vista; **at first ~** a primera vista; **to lose ~ of sth/sb** perder algo/a uno de vista; **to catch ~ of sth/sb** divisar algo/a uno; **I know her by ~** la conozco de vista; **to set one's ~s on (doing) sth** aspirar a *or* ambicionar (hacer) algo.

sighted [sī'tid] *a* que ve, de vista normal; **partially ~** de vista limitada.

sightseer [sīt'sēr] *n* excursionista *m/f*, turista *m/f*.

sightseeing [sīt'sēing] *n* excursionismo, turismo; **to go ~** visitar monumentos.

sign [sīn] *n* (*with hand*) señal *f*, seña; (*trace*) huella, rastro; (*notice*) letrero; (*written*) signo; (*road ~*) indicador *m*; (: *with instructions*) señal *f* de tráfico ♦ *vt* firmar; **as a ~ of** en señal de; **it's a good/bad ~** es buena/mala señal; **plus/minus ~** signo de más/de menos; **to ~ one's name** firmar.

sign away *vt* (*rights etc*) ceder.

sign off *vi* (RADIO, TV) cerrar el programa.

sign on *vi* (*as unemployed*) registrarse como desempleado; (*employee*) firmar un contrato ♦ *vt* (MIL) alistar; (*employee*) contratar; **to ~ on for a course** matricularse en un curso.

sign out *vi* firmar el registro (al salir).

sign over *vt*: **to ~ sth over to sb** traspasar algo a uno.

sign up *vi* (MIL) alistarse ♦ *vt* (*contract*) contratar.

signal [sig'nəl] *n* señal *f* ♦ *vi* (AUT) señalizar ♦ *vt* (*person*) hacer señas a uno; (*message*) transmitir; **the busy ~** (TEL) la señal de comunicando; **the ~ is very weak** (TV) no captamos bien la sintonía; **to ~ a left/right turn** (AUT) indicar que se va a doblar a la izquierda/derecha; **to ~ to sb (to do sth)** hacer señas a uno (para que haga algo).

signal box *n* (RAIL) garita de señales.

signalman [sig'nəlmən] *n* (RAIL) guardavía *m*.

signatory [sig'nətôrē] *n* firmante *m/f*.

signature [sig'nəchûr] *n* firma.

signature tune *n* sintonía de apertura de un programa.

signet ring [sig'nit ring] *n* anillo de sello.

significance [signif'əkəns] *n* significado; (*importance*) trascendencia; **that is of no ~** eso no tiene importancia.

significant [signif'ikənt] *a* significativo; trascendente; **it is ~ that ...** es significativo que ....

significantly [signif'ikəntlē] *ad* (*smile*) expresivamente; (*improve, increase*) sensiblemente; **and, ~ ...** y debe notarse que ....

signify [sig'nəfī] *vt* significar.

sign language *n* mímica, lenguaje *m* por

or de señas.
signpost [sīn'pōst] *n* indicador *m*.
silage [sī'lij] *n* ensilaje *m*.
silence [sī'ləns] *n* silencio ♦ *vt* hacer callar; (*guns*) reducir al silencio.
silencer [sī'lənsûr] *n* (*on gun*, *Brit* *AUT*) silenciador *m*.
silent [sī'lənt] *a* (*gen*) silencioso; (*not speaking*) callado; (*film*) mudo; **to keep** *or* **remain ~** guardar silencio.
silently [sī'ləntlē] *ad* silenciosamente, en silencio.
silent partner *n* (*COMM*) socio/a comanditario/a.
silhouette [silōōet'] *n* silueta; **~d against** destacado sobre *or* contra.
silicon [sil'ikən] *n* silicio.
silicon chip [sil'ikən chip] *n* plaqueta de silicio.
silicone [sil'əkōn] *n* silicona.
silk [silk] *n* seda ♦ *cpd* de seda.
silky [sil'kē] *a* sedoso.
sill [sil] *n* (*also*: **window~**) alféizar *m*; (*AUT*) umbral *m*.
silliness [sil'ēnis] *n* (*of person*) necedad *f*; (*of idea*) lo absurdo.
silly [sil'ē] *a* (*person*) tonto; (*idea*) absurdo; **to do sth ~** hacer una tontería.
silo [sī'lō] *n* silo.
silt [silt] *n* sedimento.
silver [sil'vûr] *n* plata; (*money*) moneda suelta ♦ *a* de plata, plateado.
silver paper (*Brit*) *n* papel *m* de plata.
silver plate *n* vajilla de plata.
silver-plated [sil'vûrplā'tid] *a* plateado.
silversmith [sil'vûrsmith] *n* platero/a.
silverware [sil'vûrwär] *n* plata.
silver wedding (anniversary) *n* bodas *fpl* de plata.
silvery [sil'vûrē] *a* plateado.
similar [sim'əlûr] *a*: **~ to** parecido *or* semejante a.
similarity [siməlar'itē] *n* parecido, semejanza.
similarly [sim'əlûrlē] *ad* del mismo modo; (*in a similar way*) de manera parecida; (*equally*) igualmente.
simile [sim'əlē] *n* símil *m*.
simmer [sim'ûr] *vi* hervir a fuego lento.
　simmer down *vi* (*fig*, *col*) calmarse, tranquilizarse.
simpering [sim'pûring] *a* afectado; (*foolish*) bobo.
simple [sim'pəl] *a* (*easy*) sencillo; (*foolish*, *COMM*) simple; **the ~ truth** la pura verdad.
simple interest *n* (*COMM*) interés *m* simple.
simple-minded [sim'pəlmīn'did] *a* simple, ingenuo.
simpleton [sim'pəltən] *n* inocentón/ona *m/f*.
simplicity [simplis'ətē] *n* sencillez *f*; (*foolishness*) ingenuidad *f*.

simplification [simpləfəkā'shən] *n* simplificación *f*.
simplify [sim'pləfī] *vt* simplificar.
simply [sim'plē] *ad* (*in a simple way: live*, *talk*) sencillamente; (*just*, *merely*) sólo.
simulate [sim'yəlāt] *vt* simular.
simulation [simyəlā'shən] *n* simulación *f*.
simultaneous [sīməltā'nēəs] *a* simultáneo.
simultaneously [sīməltā'nēəslē] *ad* simultáneamente, a la vez.
sin [sin] *n* pecado ♦ *vi* pecar.
since [sins] *ad* desde entonces, después ♦ *prep* desde ♦ *conj* (*time*) desde que; (*because*) ya que, puesto que; **~ then** desde entonces; **~ Monday** desde el lunes; (**ever**) **~ I arrived** desde que llegué.
sincere [sinsēr'] *a* sincero.
sincerely [sinsēr'lē] *ad* sinceramente; **~ yours** (*in letters*) le saluda atentamente; **yours ~** (*Brit: in letters*) le saluda (afectuosamente).
sincerity [sinsär'itē] *n* sinceridad *f*.
sinecure [sī'nəkyōōr] *n* chollo.
sinew [sin'yōō] *n* tendón *m*.
sinful [sin'fəl] *a* (*thought*) pecaminoso; (*person*) pecador(a).
sing, *pt* **sang**, *pp* **sung** [sing, sang, sung] *vt* cantar ♦ *vi* (*gen*) cantar; (*bird*) trinar; (*ears*) zumbar.
Singapore [sing'gəpôr] *n* Singapur *m*.
singe [sinj] *vt* chamuscar.
singer [sing'ûr] *n* cantante *m/f*.
Singhalese [singəlēz'] *a* = **Sinhalese**.
singing [sing'ing] *n* (*of person*, *bird*) canto; (*songs*) canciones *fpl*; (*in the ears*) zumbido; (*of kettle*) silbido.
single [sing'gəl] *a* único, solo; (*unmarried*) soltero; (*not double*) simple, sencillo ♦ *n* (*Brit: also*: **~ ticket**) billete *m* sencillo; (*record*) sencillo, single *m*; **~s** *npl* (*TENNIS*) individual *msg*; **not a ~ one was left** no quedaba ni uno; **every ~ day** todos los días (sin excepción).
　single out *vt* (*choose*) escoger; (*point out*) singularizar.
single bed *n* cama individual.
single-breasted [sing'gəlbres'tid] *a* (*jacket*, *suit*) recto.
single-density [sing'gəldensitē] *a* (*COMPUT: disk*) de densidad sencilla.
single-entry book-keeping [sing'gəlen'trē bōōk'kēping] *n* contabilidad *f* por partida simple.
single file *n*: **in ~** en fila de uno.
single-handed [sing'gəlhan'did] *ad* sin ayuda.
single-minded [sing'gəlmīn'did] *a* resuelto, firme.
single parent *n* (*mother*) madre *f* soltera; (*father*) padre *m* soltero.
single room *n* cuarto individual.
single-sided [sing'gəlsī'did] *a* (*COMPUT: disk*) de una cara.

single spacing *n* (*TYP*) interlineado simple.

singly [sing'glē] *ad* uno por uno.

singsong [sing'sông] *n* (*songs*): **to have a** ~ tener un concierto improvisado.

singular [sing'gyəlûr] *a* (*odd*) raro, extraño; (*LING*) singular ♦ *n* (*LING*) singular *m;* **in the feminine** ~ en femenino singular.

singularly [sing'gyəlûrlē] *ad* singularmente, extraordinariamente.

Sinhalese [sinhəlēz'] *a* singhalese.

sinister [sin'istûr] *a* siniestro.

sink [singk] *n* fregadero ♦ *vb* (*pt* **sank**, *pp* **sunk** [sangk, sungk]) *vt* (*ship*) hundir, echar a pique; (*foundations*) excavar; (*piles etc*): **to** ~ **sth into** hundir algo en ♦ *vi* (*gen*) hundirse; **he sank into a chair/the mud** se dejó caer en una silla/se hundió en el barro; **the shares** *or* **share prices have sunk to 3 dollars** las acciones han bajado a 3 dólares.

sink in *vi* (*fig*) penetrar, calar; **the news took a long time to** ~ **in** la noticia tardó mucho en hacerle (*or* hacerme *etc*) mella.

sinking fund [sing'king fund] *n* fondo de amortización.

sink unit *n* fregadero.

sinner [sin'ûr] *n* pecador(a) *m/f.*

sinuous [sin'yōōəs] *a* sinuoso.

sinus [sī'nəs] *n* (*ANAT*) seno.

sip [sip] *n* sorbo ♦ *vt* sorber, beber a sorbitos.

siphon [sī'fən] *n* sifón *m* ♦ *vt* (*also:* ~ **off**) (*funds*) desviar.

sir [sûr] *n* señor *m;* **S~ John Smith** el Señor John Smith; **yes** ~ sí, señor; **Dear S~** (*in letter*) Muy señor mío, Estimado Señor; **Dear S~s** Muy señores nuestros, Estimados Señores.

siren [sī'rən] *n* sirena.

sirloin [sûr'loin] *n* solomillo; ~ **steak** filete *m* de solomillo.

sisal [sī'səl] *n* pita, henequén *m* (*LAm*).

sissy [sis'ē] *n* (*col*) marica *m.*

sister [sis'tûr] *n* hermana; (*Brit: nurse*) enfermera jefe.

sister-in-law [sis'tûrinlô] *n* cuñada.

sister organization *n* organización *f* hermana.

sister ship *n* barco gemelo.

sit, *pt*, *pp* **sat** [sit, sat] *vi* sentarse; (*be sitting*) estar sentado; (*assembly*) reunirse; (*dress etc*) caer, sentar ♦ *vt* (*Brit: exam*) presentarse a; **that jacket ~s well** esa chaqueta sienta bien; **to** ~ **on a committee** ser miembro de una comisión *or* un comité.

sit about (*Brit*) = **sit around.**

sit around *vi* holgazanear.

sit back *vi* (*in seat*) recostarse.

sit down *vi* sentarse; **to be ~ting down** estar sentado.

sit in on *vt fus:* **to** ~ **in on a discussion** asistir a una discusión.

sit up *vi* incorporarse; (*not go to bed*) velar.

sitcom [sit'kâm] *n abbr* (= *situation comedy*) serie *f* cómica.

sit-down [sit'doun] *a:* ~ **strike** huelga de brazos caídos; **a** ~ **meal** una comida sentada.

site [sīt] *n* sitio; (*also:* **building** ~) solar *m* ♦ *vt* situar.

sit-in [sit'in] *n* (*demonstration*) ocupación *f.*

siting [sī'ting] *n* (*location*) situación *f*, emplazamiento.

sitter [sit'ûr] *n* (*baby~*) niñera *f.*

sitting [sit'ing] *n* (*of assembly etc*) sesión *f*; (*in canteen*) turno.

sitting member *n* (*POL*) titular *m/f* de un escaño.

sitting room *n* sala de estar.

situate [sich'ōōāt] *vt* situar.

situated [sich'ōōātid] *a* situado.

situation [sichōōā'shən] *n* situación *f.*

situation comedy *n* (*TV*, *RADIO*) serie *f* cómica.

six [siks] *num* seis.

sixteen [siks'tēn'] *num* diez y seis, dieciséis.

sixteenth note [siks'tēnth' nōt] (*US MUS*) semicorchea.

sixth [siksth] *a* sexto; **the upper/lower** ~ (*Brit SCOL*) el séptimo/sexto año.

sixty [siks'tē] *num* sesenta.

size [sīz] *n* (*gen*) tamaño; (*extent*) extensión *f*; (*of clothing*) talla; (*of shoes*) número; **I take** ~ **5 shoes** calzo el número cinco; **I take** ~ **14** mi talla es la 42; **I'd like the small/large** ~ (*of soap powder etc*) quisiera el tamaño pequeño/grande.

size up *vt* formarse una idea de.

sizeable [sī'zəbəl] *a* importante, considerable.

sizzle [siz'əl] *vi* crepitar.

SK *abbr* (*Canada*) = Saskatchewan.

skate [skāt] *n* patín *m*; (*fish: pl inv*) raya ♦ *vi* patinar.

skate around, skate over *vt fus* (*problem, issue*) pasar por alto.

skateboard [skāt'bôrd] *n* monopatín *m.*

skater [skā'tûr] *n* patinador(a) *m/f.*

skating [skā'ting] *n* patinaje *m*; **figure** ~ patinaje *m* de figuras.

skating rink *n* pista de patinaje.

skeleton [skel'itən] *n* esqueleto; (*TECH*) armazón *m*; (*outline*) esquema *m.*

skeleton key *n* llave *f* maestra.

skeleton staff *n* personal *m* reducido.

skeptic [skep'tik] *n* (*US*) escéptico/a.

skeptical [skep'tikəl] *a* (*US*) escéptico.

skepticism [skep'tisizəm] *n* (*US*) escepticismo.

sketch [skech] *n* (*drawing*) dibujo; (*outline*) esbozo, bosquejo; (*THEATER*) pieza corta ♦ *vt* dibujar; esbozar.

sketch book *n* libro de dibujos.

sketching [skech'ing] *n* dibujo.

sketch pad n bloc m de dibujo.
sketchy [skech'ē] a incompleto.
skewer [skyoō'ûr] n broqueta.
ski [skē] n esquí m ♦ vi esquiar.
ski boot n bota de esquí.
skid [skid] n patinazo ♦ vi patinar; **to go into a** ~ comenzar a patinar.
skid mark n señal f de patinazo.
skier [skē'ûr] n esquiador(a) m/f.
skiing [skē'ing] n esquí m; **to go** ~ practicar el esquí, (ir a) esquiar.
ski instructor n instructor(a) m/f de esquí.
ski jump n pista para salto de esquí.
skilful [skil'fəl] etc (Brit) = **skillful** etc.
ski lift n telesilla m, telesquí m.
skill [skil] n destreza, pericia; (technique) arte m, técnica; **there's a certain** ~ **to doing it** se necesita cierta habilidad para hacerlo.
skilled [skild] a hábil, diestro; (worker) cualificado.
skillet [skil'it] n sartén f pequeña.
skillful [skil'fəl] a (US) diestro, experto.
skillfully [skil'fəlē] ad hábilmente, con destreza.
skim [skim] vt (milk) desnatar; (glide over) rozar, rasar ♦ vi: **to** ~ **through** (book) hojear.
skimmed milk [skimd milk] n leche f desnatada or descremada.
skimp [skimp] vt (work) chapucear; (cloth etc) escatimar; **to** ~ **on** (material etc) economizar; (work) escatimar.
skimpy [skim'pē] a (meager) escaso; (skirt) muy corto.
skin [skin] n (gen) piel f; (complexion) cutis m; (of fruit, vegetable) piel f, cáscara, pellejo; (crust: on pudding, paint) nata ♦ vt (fruit etc) pelar; (animal) despellejar; **wet or soaked to the** ~ calado hasta los huesos.
skin-deep [skin'dēp'] a superficial.
skin diver n buceador(a) m/f.
skin diving n buceo.
skinflint [skin'flint] n tacaño/a, roñoso/a.
skinny [skin'ē] a flaco, magro.
skintight [skin'tīt] a (dress etc) muy ajustado.
skip [skip] n brinco, salto; (Brit: container) cuba ♦ vi brincar; (with rope) saltar a la comba ♦ vt (pass over) omitir, saltar.
ski pants npl pantalones mpl de esquí.
ski pole n bastón m de esquiar.
skipper [skip'ûr] n (NAUT, SPORT) capitán m.
skipping rope [skip'ing rōp] n (Brit) cuerda (de saltar).
ski resort n estación f de esquí.
skirmish [skûr'mish] n escaramuza.
skirt [skûrt] n falda, pollera (LAm) ♦ vt (surround) ceñir, rodear; (go around) ladear.
skirting board [skûr'ting bôrd] n (Brit) ro-

dapié m.
ski run n pista de esquí.
ski suit n traje m de esquiar.
skit [skit] n sátira, parodia.
ski tow n arrastre m (de esquí).
skittle [skit'əl] n bolo; ~**s** (game) boliche m.
skive [skīv] vi (Brit col) gandulear.
skulk [skulk] vi esconderse.
skull [skul] n calavera; (ANAT) cráneo.
skullcap [skul'kap] n (worn by Jews) casquete m; (worn by Pope) solideo.
skunk [skungk] n mofeta.
sky [skī] n cielo; **to praise sb to the skies** poner a uno por las nubes.
sky-blue [skī'blōō'] a (azul) celeste.
sky-high [skī'hī'] ad (throw) muy alto; **prices have gone** ~ los precios están por las nubes.
skylark [skī'lârk] n (bird) alondra.
skylight [skī'līt] n tragaluz m, claraboya.
skyline [skī'līn] n (horizon) horizonte m; (of city) perfil m.
skyscraper [skī'skrāpûr] n rascacielos m inv.
slab [slab] n (stone) bloque m; (of wood) tabla, plancha; (flat) losa; (of cake) trozo; (of meat, cheese) tajada, trozo.
slack [slak] a (loose) flojo; (slow) de poca actividad; (careless) descuidado; (COMM: market) poco activo; (: demand) débil; (period) bajo; **business is** ~ hay poco movimiento en el negocio.
slacken [slak'ən] (also: ~ **off**) vi aflojarse ♦ vt aflojar; (speed) disminuir.
slackness [slak'nis] n flojedad f; negligencia.
slacks [slaks] npl pantalones mpl.
slag [slag] n escoria, escombros mpl.
slag heap n escorial m, escombrera.
slain [slān] pp of **slay**.
slake [slāk] vt (one's thirst) apagar.
slalom [slâ'ləm] n eslálom m.
slam [slam] vt (door) cerrar de golpe; (throw) arrojar (violentamente); (criticize) vapulear, vituperar ♦ vi cerrarse de golpe.
slander [slan'dûr] n calumnia, difamación f ♦ vt calumniar, difamar.
slanderous [slan'dûrəs] a calumnioso, difamatorio.
slang [slang] n argot m; (jargon) jerga.
slant [slant] n sesgo, inclinación f; (fig) punto de vista; **to get a new** ~ **on sth** obtener un nuevo punto de vista sobre algo.
slanted [slan'tid], **slanting** [slan'ting] a inclinado.
slap [slap] n palmada; (in face) bofetada ♦ vt dar una palmada/bofetada a ♦ ad (directly) exactamente, directamente.
slapdash [slap'dash] a descuidado.
slapstick [slap'stik] n: ~ **comedy** comedia de golpe y porrazo.
slash [slash] vt acuchillar; (fig: prices) que-

mar ♦ n (US TYP) oblicua.

slat [slat] n (of wood, plastic) tablilla, listón m.

slate [slāt] n pizarra ♦ vt (Brit: fig: criticize) criticar duramente, dar una paliza a.

slaughter [slô'tûr] n (of animals) matanza; (of people) carnicería ♦ vt matar.

slaughterhouse [slô'tûrhous] n matadero.

Slav [slâv] a eslavo.

slave [slāv] n esclavo/a ♦ vi (also: ~ away) sudar tinta; **to ~ (away) at (doing) sth** sudar tinta en (hacer) algo.

slave labor n trabajo de esclavos.

slaver [slā'vûr] vi (dribble) babear.

slavery [slā'vûrē] n esclavitud f.

slavish [slā'vish] a (devotion) de esclavo; (imitation) servil.

slay, pt **slew**, pp **slain** [slā, slōō, slān] vt (literary) matar.

SLD n abbr (Brit POL) = Social and Liberal Democratic Party.

sleazy [slē'zē] a (fig: place) de mala fama.

sled [sled], (Brit) **sledge** [slej] n trineo.

sledgehammer [slej'hamûr] n mazo.

sleek [slēk] a (shiny) lustroso.

sleep [slēp] n sueño ♦ vb (pt, pp **slept** [slept]) vi dormir ♦ vt: **we can ~ 4** podemos alojar a 4, tenemos cabida para 4; **to go to ~** quedarse dormido; **to have a good night's ~** dormir toda la noche; **to put to ~** (patient) dormir; (animal: euphemism: kill) sacrificar; **to ~ lightly** tener el sueño ligero; **to ~ with sb** (euphemism) acostarse con uno.

sleep in vi (oversleep) dormir tarde.

sleeper [slē'pûr] n (person) durmiente m/f; (US: for baby) pijama m de niño; (Brit RAIL: on track) traviesa; (: train) coche-cama m.

sleepiness [slēp'ēnis] n somnolencia.

sleeping bag [slē'ping bag] n saco de dormir.

sleeping car n coche-cama m.

sleeping partner n (COMM) socio/a comanditario/a.

sleeping pill n somnífero.

sleepless [slēp'lis] a: **a ~ night** una noche en blanco.

sleeplessness [slēp'lisnis] n insomnio.

sleepwalker [slēp'wôkûr] n sonámbulo/a.

sleepy [slē'pē] a soñoliento; **to be** or **feel ~** tener sueño.

sleet [slēt] n nevisca.

sleeve [slēv] n manga; (TECH) manguito; (of record) funda.

sleeveless [slēv'lis] a (garment) sin mangas.

sleigh [slā] n trineo.

sleight [slīt] n: **~ of hand** escamoteo.

slender [slen'dûr] a delgado; (means) escaso.

slept [slept] pt, pp of **sleep.**

sleuth [slōōth] n (col) detective m/f.

slew [slōō] vi (Brit: veer) torcerse ♦ pt of **slay.**

slice [slīs] n (of meat) tajada; (of bread) rebanada; (of lemon) rodaja; (utensil) pala ♦ vt cortar, tajar; rebanar; **~d bread** pan m de molde.

slick [slik] a (skilful) hábil, diestro ♦ n (also: **oil ~**) capa de aceite.

slid [slid] pt, pp of **slide.**

slide [slīd] n (in playground) tobogán m; (PHOT) diapositiva; (microscope ~) portaobjetos m inv, plaquilla de vidrio; (Brit: also: **hair ~**) pasador m ♦ (vb: pt, pp **slid** [slid]) vt correr, deslizar ♦ vi (slip) resbalarse; (glide) deslizarse; **to let things ~** (fig) dejar que ruede la bola.

slide projector n (PHOT) proyector m de diapositivas.

slide rule n regla de cálculo.

sliding [slī'ding] a (door) corredizo; **~ roof** (AUT) techo de corredera.

sliding scale n escala móvil.

slight [slīt] a (slim) delgado; (frail) delicado; (pain etc) leve; (trifling) insignificante; (small) pequeño ♦ n desaire m ♦ vt (offend) ofender, desairar; **a ~ improvement** una ligera mejora; **not in the ~est** en absoluto; **there's not the ~est possibility** no hay la menor or más mínima posibilidad.

slightly [slīt'lē] ad ligeramente, un poco; **~ built** delgado, fino.

slim [slim] a delgado, esbelto ♦ vi adelgazar.

slime [slīm] n limo, cieno.

slimness [slim'nis] n delgadez f.

slimy [slī'mē] a limoso; (covered with mud) fangoso; (also fig: person) adulón, zalamero.

slimming [slim'ing] n adelgazamiento ♦ a (diet, pills) adelgazador(a), adelgazante.

sling [sling] n (MED) cabestrillo; (weapon) honda ♦ vt (pt, pp **slung** [slung]) tirar, arrojar; **to have one's arm in a ~** llevar el brazo en cabestrillo.

slingshot [sling'shât] n tirador m.

slink, pt, pp **slunk** [slingk, slungk] vi: **to ~ away**, **~ off** escabullirse.

slip [slip] n (slide) resbalón m; (mistake) descuido; (underskirt) combinación f; (of paper) papelito; (delivery ~) nota de entrega ♦ vt (slide) deslizar ♦ vi (slide) deslizarse; (stumble) resbalar(se); (decline) decaer; (move smoothly): **to ~ into/out of** (room etc) introducirse en/salirse de; **to let a chance ~ by** escapársele la oportunidad; **to ~ sth on/off** ponerse/quitarse algo; **to ~ on a jumper** ponerse un jersey or un suéter; **it ~ped from her hand** se le cayó de la mano; **to give sb the ~** eludir a uno; **a ~ of the tongue** un lapsus.

slip away vi escabullirse.

slip in vt meter ♦ vi meterse.

slip out vi (go out) salir (un momento).

slip-on [slip'án] *a* de quitaipón; (*shoes*) sin cordones.

slipped disc [slipt disk] *n* vértebra dislocada.

slipper [slip'ûr] *n* zapatilla, pantufla.

slippery [slip'ûrē] *a* resbaladizo.

slip road *n* (*Brit*) carretera de acceso.

slipshod [slip'shâd] *a* descuidado.

slipstream [slip'strēm] *n* viento de la hélice.

slip-up [slip'up] *n* (*error*) desliz *m*.

slipway [slip'wā] *n* grada, gradas *fpl*.

slit [slit] *n* raja; (*cut*) corte *m* ♦ *vt* (*pt, pp* **slit**) rajar, cortar; **to ~ sb's throat** cortarle el pescuezo a uno.

slither [slith̩'ûr] *vi* deslizarse.

sliver [sliv'ûr] *n* (*of glass, wood*) astilla; (*of cheese, sausage*) lonja, loncha.

slob [slâb] *n* (*col*) patán/ana *m/f*, palurdo/a.

slog [slâg] (*Brit*) *vi* sudar tinta ♦ *n*: **it was a ~** costó trabajo (hacerlo).

slogan [slō'gən] *n* eslogan *m*, lema *m*.

slop [slâp] *vi* (*also:* **~ over**) derramarse, desbordarse ♦ *vt* derramar, verter.

slope [slōp] *n* (*up*) cuesta, pendiente *f*; (*down*) declive *m*; (*side of mountain*) falda, vertiente *f* ♦ *vi*: **to ~ down** estar en declive; **to ~ up** inclinarse.

sloping [slō'ping] *a* en pendiente; en declive.

sloppily [slâp'ilē] *ad* descuidadamente; con descuido *or* desaliño.

sloppiness [slâp'ēnis] *n* descuido; desaliño.

sloppy [slâp'ē] *a* (*work*) descuidado; (*appearance*) desaliñado.

slosh [slâsh] *vi*: **to ~ around** chapotear.

slot [slât] *n* ranura; (*fig: in timetable, RADIO, TV*) hueco ♦ *vt*: **to ~ into** encajar en.

sloth [slôth] *n* (*vice*) pereza; (*ZOOL*) oso perezoso.

slot machine *n* (*for gambling*) máquina tragaperras; (*Brit: vending machine*) aparato vendedor, distribuidor *m* automático.

slouch [slouch] *vi*: **to ~ around** (*laze*) gandulear.

slovenly [sluv'ənlē] *a* (*dirty*) desaliñado, desaseado; (*careless*) descuidado.

slow [slō] *a* lento; (*watch*): **to be ~** estar atrasado ♦ *ad* lentamente, despacio ♦ *vt, vi* (*also:* **~ down**, **~ up**) retardar; **at a ~ speed** a una velocidad lenta; **business is ~** (*COMM*) hay poca actividad; **my watch is 20 minutes ~** mi reloj lleva 20 minutos de retraso; **bake for two hours in a ~ oven** cocer *or* asar 2 horas en el horno a fuego lento; **to be ~ to act/decide** tardar en obrar/decidir; **to go ~** (*driver*) conducir despacio; (*Brit: in industrial dispute*) trabajar a ritmo lento.

slow-acting [slō'ak'ting] *a* de efecto retardado.

slowdown [slō'doun] *n* (*US*) huelga de manos caídas.

slowly [slō'lē] *ad* lentamente, despacio; **to**

drive ~ conducir despacio; **~ but surely** paso a paso.

slow motion *n*: **in ~** a cámara lenta.

slow-moving [slō'mōo'ving] *a* lento.

slowpoke [slō'pōk] *n* (*US*) perezoso/a, vago/a.

sludge [sluj] *n* lodo, fango.

slue [slōo] *vi* (*US: veer*) torcerse.

slug [slug] *n* babosa; (*bullet*) posta.

sluggish [slug'ish] *a* (*slow*) lento; (*lazy*) perezoso; (*business, market, sales*) inactivo, moroso.

sluggishly [slug'ishlē] *ad* lentamente.

sluggishness [slug'ishnis] *n* lentitud *f*.

sluice [slōos] *n* (*gate*) esclusa; (*channel*) canal *m* ♦ *vt*: **to ~ down** *or* **out** regar.

slum [slum] *n* (*area*) barrio bajo, tugurios *mpl*.

slumber [slum'bûr] *n* sueño.

slump [slump] *n* (*economic*) depresión *f* ♦ *vi* hundirse; **the ~ in the price of copper** la baja repentina del precio del cobre; **he was ~ed over the wheel** se había desplomado encima del volante.

slung [slung] *pt, pp* of **sling**.

slunk [slungk] *pt, pp* of **slink**.

slur [slûr] *n* calumnia ♦ *vt* calumniar, difamar; (*word*) pronunciar indistintamente; **to cast a ~ on sb** manchar la reputación de uno, difamar a uno.

slurred [slûrd] *a* (*pronunciation*) mal articulado, borroso.

slush [slush] *n* nieve *f* a medio derretir.

slush fund *n* (*for bribes*) fondos *mpl* para sobornar.

slushy [slush'ē] *a* (*col: poetry etc*) sentimentaloide.

slut [slut] *n* marrana.

sly [slī] *a* (*clever*) astuto; (*nasty*) malicioso.

slyly [slī'lē] *ad* astutamente; taimadamente.

slyness [slī'nis] *n* astucia.

smack [smak] *n* (*slap*) manotada; (*blow*) golpe *m* ♦ *vt* dar una manotada a; golpear con la mano ♦ *vi*: **to ~ of** saber a, oler a ♦ *ad*: **it fell ~ in the middle** (*col*) cayó justo en medio.

smacker [smak'ûr] *n* (*col: kiss*) beso sonoro; (: *US: dollar bill*) billete *m* de un dólar; (: *Brit: pound note*) billete *m* de una libra.

small [smôl] *a* pequeño; (*in height*) bajo, chaparro (*LAm*); (*letter*) en minúscula ♦ *n*: **~ of the back** región *f* lumbar; **~ store-keeper** pequeño/a comerciante *m/f*; **to get** *or* **grow ~er** (*stain, town*) empequeñecer; (*debt, organization, numbers*) reducir, disminuir; **to make ~er** (*amount, income*) reducir; (*garden, object, garment*) achicar.

small change *n* suelto, cambio.

smallholding [smôl'hōlding] *n* (*Brit*) parcela, minifundio.

small hours *npl*: **in the ~** en las altas ho-

ras (de la noche).
smallish [smó'lish] *a* más bien pequeño.
small-minded [smól'mīn'did] *a* mezquino, de miras estrechas.
smallness [smól'nis] *n* pequeñez *f*.
smallpox [smól'páks] *n* viruela.
small print *n* letra pequeña *or* menuda.
small-scale [smól'skāl] *a* (*map, model*) en escala reducida; (*business, farming*) en pequeña escala.
small talk *n* cháchara.
small-time [smól'tīm'] *a* (*col*) de poca categoría *or* monta; **a ~ thief** un(a) ratero/a.
smart [smárt] *a* elegante; (*clever*) listo, inteligente; (*quick*) rápido, vivo ♦ *vi* escocer, picar; **the ~ set** la gente de buen tono; **to look ~** estar elegante; **my eyes are ~ing** me pican los ojos.
smart-ass [smárt'as] *n* (*US col*) sabelotodo/a, listillo/a.
smarten up [smár'tən up] *vi* arreglarse ♦ *vt* arreglar.
smartness [smárt'nis] *n* elegancia; (*cleverness*) inteligencia.
smash [smash] *n* (*also:* **~-up**) choque *m*; (*sound*) estrépito ♦ *vt* (*break*) hacer pedazos; (*car etc*) estrellar; (*SPORT: record*) batir ♦ *vi* hacerse pedazos; (*against wall etc*) estrellarse.
smash up *vt* (*car*) hacer pedazos; (*room*) destrozar.
smash hit *n* exitazo.
smattering [smat'úring] *n*: **a ~ of Spanish** algo de español.
smear [smē'úr] *n* mancha; (*MED*) frotis *m inv* (*cervical*); (*insult*) calumnia ♦ *vt* untar; (*fig*) calumniar, difamar; **his hands were ~ed with oil/ink** tenía las manos manchadas de aceite/tinta.
smear campaign *n* campaña de calumnias.
smell [smel] *n* olor *m*; (*sense*) olfato ♦ (*vb: pt, pp* **smelled** *or* (*Brit*) **smelt** [smelt]) *vt, vi* oler; **it ~s good/of garlic** huele bien/a ajo.
smelly [smel'ē] *a* maloliente.
smelt [smelt] *vt* (*ore*) fundir ♦ (*Brit*) *pt, pp of* **smell**.
smile [smīl] *n* sonrisa ♦ *vi* sonreír.
smiling [smī'ling] *a* sonriente, risueño.
smirk [smúrk] *n* sonrisa falsa *or* afectada.
smith [smith] *n* herrero.
smithy [smith'ē] *n* herrería.
smitten [smit'ən] *a*: **he's really ~ with her** está totalmente loco por ella.
smock [smák] *n* blusa; (*children's*) delantal *m*; (*US: overall*) guardapolvo.
smog [smág] *n* esmog *m*.
smoke [smōk] *n* humo ♦ *vi* fumar; (*chimney*) echar humo ♦ *vt* (*cigarettes*) fumar; **to go up in ~** (*house etc*) quemarse; (*fig*) irse todo en humo, fracasar; **do you ~?** ¿fumas?

smoked [smōkt] *a* (*bacon, glass*) ahumado.
smokeless fuel [smōk'lis fyōō'əl] *n* combustible *m* sin humo.
smoker [smō'kûr] *n* (*person*) fumador(a) *m/f*; (*RAIL*) coche *m* fumador.
smoke screen *n* cortina de humo.
smoking [smō'king] *n*: **"no ~"** "prohibido fumar"; **he's given up ~** ha dejado de fumar.
smoking car *n* departamento de fumadores.
smoky [smō'kē] *a* (*room*) lleno de humo.
smolder [smōl'dûr] *vi* (*US*) arder sin llama.
smooth [smōōth] *a* liso; (*sea*) tranquilo; (*flavor, movement*) suave; (*person: pej*) meloso ♦ *vt* alisar; (*also:* **~ out**) (*creases, difficulties*) allanar.
smooth over *vt*: **to ~ things over** (*fig*) limar las asperezas.
smoothly [smōōth'lē] *ad* (*easily*) fácilmente; **everything went ~** todo pasó sin novedad.
smoothness [smōōth'nis] *n* (*of skin, cloth*) tersura; (*of surface, flavor, movement*) suavidad *f*.
smother [smuth'ûr] *vt* sofocar; (*repress*) contener.
smoulder [smōl'dûr] *vi* (*Brit*) = **smolder**.
smudge [smuj] *n* mancha ♦ *vt* manchar.
smug [smug] *a* presumido.
smuggle [smug'əl] *vt* pasar de contrabando; **to ~ in/out** (*goods etc*) meter/sacar de contrabando.
smuggler [smug'lûr] *n* contrabandista *m/f*.
smuggling [smug'ling] *n* contrabando.
smugly [smug'lē] *ad* con suficiencia.
smugness [smug'nis] *n* suficiencia.
smut [smut] *n* (*grain of soot*) carbonilla, hollín *m*; (*mark*) tizne *m*; (*in conversation etc*) obscenidades *fpl*.
smutty [smut'ē] *a* (*fig*) verde, obsceno.
snack [snak] *n* bocado; **to have a ~** probarse un bocado.
snack bar *n* cafetería.
snag [snag] *n* problema *m*; **to run into** *or* **hit a ~** encontrar inconvenientes, dar con un obstáculo.
snail [snāl] *n* caracol *m*.
snake [snāk] *n* (*gen*) serpiente *f*; (*harmless*) culebra; (*poisonous*) víbora.
snap [snap] *n* (*sound*) chasquido; golpe *m* seco ♦ *a* (*decision*) instantáneo ♦ *vt* (*fingers etc*) castañetear; (*break*) quebrar ♦ *vi* (*break*) quebrarse; (*fig: person*) contestar bruscamente; **to ~ (at sb)** (*subj: person*) hablar con brusquedad (a uno); (: *dog*) intentar morder (a uno); **to ~ shut** cerrarse de golpe; **to ~ one's fingers at sth/sb** (*fig*) burlarse de algo/uno; **a cold ~** (*of weather*) una ola de frío.
snap off *vi* (*break*) partirse.
snap up *vt* agarrar.
snap fastener *n* botón *m* de presión.

snappy [snap'ē] *a* (*col*: *answer*) instantáneo; (*slogan*) conciso; **make it ~!** (*hurry up*) ¡date prisa!

snapshot [snap'shåt] *n* foto *f* (instantánea).

snare [snär] *n* trampa ♦ *vt* cazar con trampa; (*fig*) engañar.

snarl [snârl] *n* gruñido ♦ *vi* gruñir; **to get ~ed up** (*wool, plans*) enmarañarse, enredarse; (*traffic*) quedar atascado.

snatch [snach] *n* (*fig*) robo; **~es of trocitos** *mpl* de ♦ *vt* (~ *away*) arrebatar; (*grasp*) coger (*Sp*), agarrar; **~es of conversation** fragmentos *mpl* de conversación.

snatch up *vt* agarrar.

sneak [snēk] *vi*: **to ~ in/out** entrar/salir a hurtadillas ♦ *vt*: **to ~ a look at sth** mirar algo de reojo ♦ *n* (*fam*) soplón/ona *m/f*.

sneakers [snē'kûrz] *npl* (*US*) zapatos *mpl* de lona, zapatillas *fpl*.

sneaking [snē'king] *a*: **to have a ~ feeling/suspicion that** ... tener la (horrible) sensación/sospecha de que ....

sneaky [snē'kē] *a* furtivo.

sneer [snēr] *n* sonrisa de desprecio ♦ *vi* sonreír con desprecio; **to ~ at sth/sb** burlarse *or* mofarse de algo/uno.

sneeze [snēz] *n* estornudo ♦ *vi* estornudar.

snicker [snik'ûr] *n* risa disimulada ♦ *vi* reírse con disimulo.

snide [snīd] *a* (*col*: *sarcastic*) sarcástico.

sniff [snif] *vi* sorber (por la nariz) ♦ *vt* husmear, oler; (*glue, drug*) esnifar.

sniff at *vt fus*: **it's not to be ~ed at** no es de despreciar.

snigger [snig'ûr] *n* risa disimulada ♦ *vi* reírse con disimulo.

snip [snip] *n* (*piece*) recorte *m*; (*bargain*) ganga ♦ *vt* tijeretear.

sniper [snī'pûr] *n* francotirador(a) *m/f*.

snippet [snip'it] *n* retazo.

sniveling, (*Brit*) **snivelling** [sniv'əling] *a* llorón/ona.

snob [snåb] *n* (e)snob *m/f*.

snobbery [snåb'ûrē] *n* (e)snobismo.

snobbish [snåb'ish] *a* (e)snob.

snobbishness [snåb'ishnis] *n* (e)snobismo.

snooker [snōōk'ûr] *n* especie de billar.

snoop [snōōp] *vi*: **to ~ around** fisgonear.

snooper [snōō'pûr] *n* fisgón/ona *m/f*.

snooty [snōō'tē] *a* (e)snob.

snooze [snōōz] *n* siesta ♦ *vi* echar una siesta.

snore [snôr] *vi* roncar ♦ *n* ronquido.

snoring [snôr'ing] *n* ronquidos *mpl*.

snorkel [snôr'kəl] *n* (tubo) respirador *m*.

snort [snôrt] *n* bufido ♦ *vi* bufar ♦ *vt* (*col*: *drugs*) aspirar, esnifar.

snotty [snåt'ē] *a* (*col*) engreído.

snout [snout] *n* hocico, morro.

snow [snō] *n* nieve *f* ♦ *vi* nevar ♦ *vt*: **to be ~ed under with work** estar agobiado de trabajo.

snowball [snō'bôl] *n* bola de nieve ♦ *vi* ir aumentándose.

snow-blind [snō'blīnd] *a* cegado por la nieve.

snowbound [snō'bound] *a* bloqueado por la nieve.

snowcapped [snō'kapt] *a* (*peak*) cubierto de nieve, nevado.

snowdrift [snō'drift] *n* ventisquero.

snowdrop [snō'dråp] *n* campanilla.

snowfall [snō'fôl] *n* nevada.

snowflake [snō'flāk] *n* copo de nieve.

snowline [snō'līn] *n* límite *m* de las nieves perpetuas.

snowman [snō'man] *n* figura de nieve.

snowplow, (*Brit*) **snowplough** [snō'plou] *n* quitanieves *m inv*.

snowshoe [snō'shōō] *n* raqueta (de nieve).

snowstorm [snō'stôrm] *n* nevada, nevasca.

Snow White *n* Blancanieves *f*.

snowy [snō'ē] *a* de (mucha) nieve.

SNP *n abbr* (*Brit POL*) = *Scottish National Party*.

snub [snub] *vt*: **to ~ sb** desairar a uno ♦ *n* desaire *m*, repulsa.

snub-nosed [snub'nōzd] *a* chato.

snuff [snuf] *n* rapé *m* ♦ *vt* (*also*: ~ **out**: *candle*) apagar.

snuffbox [snuf'båks] *n* caja de rapé.

snug [snug] *a* (*cosy*) cómodo; (*fitted*) ajustado.

snuggle [snug'əl] *vi*: **to ~ down in bed** hacerse un ovillo en la cama; **to ~ up to sb** arrimarse *or* abrazarse a uno.

snugly [snug'lē] *ad* cómodamente; **it fits ~** (*object in pocket etc*) cabe perfectamente; (*garment*) ajusta perfectamente.

SO *abbr* (*BANKING*) = **standing order**.

so [sō] *ad* (*degree*) tan; (*manner: thus*) así, de este modo ♦ *conj* así que, por tanto; ~ **that** (*purpose*) para que, a fin de que; ~ (*result*) de modo que; ~ **do I** yo también; **if** ~ de ser así, si es así; **I hope** ~ espero que sí; **10 or** ~ 10 más o menos; ~ **far** hasta aquí; ~ **quickly** (*early*) tan pronto; (*fast*) tan rápidamente; **quite ~!** ¡así es!, ¡exacto!; **even** ~ sin embargo; ~ **to speak** por decirlo así, es un decir; ~ **it is!**, ~ **it does!** ¡es verdad!, ¡es cierto!; ~ **long!** ¡hasta luego!; ~ **many** tantos/as; ~ **much** *a*, *ad* tanto; **she didn't** ~ **much as send me a birthday card** no me mandó ni una tarjeta siquiera por mi cumpleaños; ~ **that's the reason!** ¡así que es por eso *or* por eso es!; ~ **(what)?** (*col*) ¿y qué?

soak [sōk] *vt* (*drench*) empapar; (*put in water*) remojar ♦ *vi* remojarse, estar a remojo.

soak in *vi* penetrar.

soak up *vt* absorber.

soaking [sō'king] *a* (*also*: ~ **wet**) calado *or* empapado (hasta los huesos en el tuétano).

so-and-so [sō'ənsō] *n* (*somebody*) fulano/a de tal.

soap · 322 · solidarity

soap [sōp] *n* jabón *m*.

soapflakes [sōp'flāks] *npl* jabón *msg* en escamas.

soap opera *n* (*TV*) telenovela; (*RADIO*) radionovela.

soap powder *n* jabón *m* en polvo.

soapsuds [sōp'sudz] *npl* espuma *sg*.

soapy [sō'pē] *a* jabonoso.

soar [sôr] *vi* (*on wings*) remontarse; (*building etc*) elevarse; (*price*) subir vertiginosamente; (*morale*) renacer.

soaring [sôr'ing] *a* (*flight*) planeador(a), que vuela; (*prices*) en alza *or* aumento; ~ **inflation** inflación *f* altísima *or* en aumento.

sob [sáb] *n* sollozo ♦ *vi* sollozar.

s.o.b. *n abbr* (*US col!* = *son of a bitch*) hijo de puta (*!*).

sober [sō'bûr] *a* (*moderate*) moderado; (*not drunk*) sobrio; (*color, style*) discreto.
sober up *vi* pasársele a uno la borrachera.

soberly [sō'bûrlē] *ad* sobriamente.

sobriety [səbrī'ətē] *n* (*not being drunk*) sobriedad *f*; (*seriousness, sedateness*) seriedad *f*, sensatez *f*.

Soc. *abbr* (= *society*) S.

so-called [sō'kōld'] *a* presunto, supuesto.

soccer [sák'ûr] *n* fútbol *m*.

soccer player *n* jugador(a) *m/f* de fútbol.

sociability [sōshəbil'ətē] *n* sociabilidad *f*.

sociable [sō'shəbəl] *a* sociable.

social [sō'shəl] *a* social ♦ *n* velada, fiesta.

social class *n* clase *f* social.

social climber *n* arribista *m/f*.

social club *n* club *m*.

Social Democrat *n* socialdemócrata *m/f*.

socialism [sō'shəlizəm] *n* socialismo.

socialist [sō'shəlist] *a, n* socialista *m/f*.

socialite [sō'shəlīt] *n* persona de la buena sociedad.

socialize [sō'shəlīz] *vi* hacer vida social; **to ~ with** (*colleagues*) salir con.

socially [sō'shəlē] *ad* socialmente.

social science(s) *n* ciencias *fpl* sociales.

social security *n* seguridad *f* social.

social welfare *n* asistencia social.

social work *n* asistencia social.

social worker *n* asistente/a *m/f* social.

socioeconomic [sōshēōēkənám'ik] *a* socioeconómico.

society [səsī'ətē] *n* sociedad *f*; (*club*) asociación *f*; (*also:* **high ~**) buena sociedad ♦ *cpd* (*party, column*) social, de sociedad.

sociological [sōsēəlâj'ikəl] *a* sociológico.

sociologist [sōsēál'əjist] *n* sociólogo/a.

sociology [sōsēál'əjē] *n* sociología.

sock [sák] *n* calcetín *m*, media (*LAm*); **to pull one's ~s up** (*fig*) hacer esfuerzos, despabilarse.

socket [sák'it] *n* (*ELEC*) enchufe *m*.

sod [sád] *n* (*of earth*) césped *m*; (*Brit: col!*) cabrón/ona *m/f* (*!*).

soda [sō'də] *n* (*CHEM*) sosa; (*also:* ~ **water**) soda; (*US: also:* ~ **pop**) gaseosa.

sodden [sád'ən] *a* empapado.

sodium [sō'dēəm] *n* sodio.

sodium chloride *n* cloruro sódico *or* de sodio.

sofa [sō'fə] *n* sofá *m*.

Sofia [sōfē'ə] *n* Sofía.

soft [sôft] *a* (*teacher, parent*) blando; (*gentle, not loud*) suave; (*stupid*) bobo; ~ **currency** divisa blanda *or* débil.

soft-boiled [sôft'boild'] *a* (*egg*) pasado (por agua).

soft copy *n* (*COMPUT*) copia transitoria.

soft drink *n* bebida no alcohólica.

soft drugs *npl* drogas *fpl* blandas.

soften [sôf'ən] *vt* ablandar; suavizar ♦ *vi* ablandarse; suavizarse.

softener [sôf'ənûr] *n* suavizador *m*.

softhearted [sôft'hár'tid] *a* bondadoso.

softly [sôft'lē] *ad* suavemente; (*gently*) delicadamente, con delicadeza.

softness [sôft'nis] *n* blandura; suavidad *f*.

soft sell *n* venta suave.

soft toy *n* juguete *m* de peluche.

software [sôft'wār] *n* (*COMPUT*) software *m*.

soft water *n* agua blanda.

soggy [ság'ē] *a* empapado.

soil [soil] *n* (*earth*) tierra, suelo ♦ *vt* ensuciar.

soiled [soild] *a* sucio, manchado.

sojourn [sō'jûrn] *n* (*formal*) estancia.

solace [sál'is] *n* consuelo.

solar [sō'lûr] *a* solar.

solarium, *pl* **solaria** [sōlär'ēəm, -ēə] *n* solario.

solar plexus [sō'lûr plek'səs] *n* (*ANAT*) plexo solar.

solar system *n* sistema *m* solar.

sold [sōld] *pt, pp of* **sell**.

solder [sád'ûr] *vt* soldar ♦ *n* soldadura.

soldier [sōl'jûr] *n* (*gen*) soldado; (*army man*) militar *m*; **toy ~** soldadito de plomo.

sold out *a* (*COMM*) agotado.

sole [sōl] *n* (*of foot*) planta; (*of shoe*) suela; (*fish: pl inv*) lenguado ♦ *a* único; **the ~ reason** la única razón.

solely [sōl'lē] *ad* únicamente, sólo, solamente; **I will hold you ~ responsible** le daré toda la responsabilidad.

solemn [sál'əm] *a* solemne.

sole trader *n* (*COMM*) comerciante *m/f* exclusivo/a.

solicit [səlis'it] *vt* (*request*) solicitar ♦ *vi* (*prostitute*) abordar, importunar.

solicitor [səlis'itûr] *n* (*Brit: for wills etc*) notario/a; (: *in court*) abogado/a.

solid [sál'id] *a* sólido; (*gold etc*) macizo; (*line*) continuo; (*vote*) unánime ♦ *n* sólido; **we waited 2 ~ hours** esperamos 2 horas enteras; **to be on ~ ground** estar en tierra firme; (*fig*) estar seguro.

solidarity [sálidar'itē] *n* solidaridad *f*.

solidify [səlid'əfī] *vi* solidificarse.
solidity [səlid'itē] *n* solidez *f*.
solidly [sál'idlē] *ad* sólidamente; (*fig*) unánimemente.
solid-state [sál'idstāt'] *a* (*ELEC*) estado sólido.
soliloquy [səlil'əkwē] *n* soliloquio.
solitaire [sál'itär] *n* (*game, gem*) solitario.
solitary [sál'itärē] *a* solitario, solo; (*isolated*) apartado, aislado; (*only*) único.
solitary confinement *n* incomunicación *f*; **to be in** ~ estar incomunicado.
solitude [sál'ətōōd] *n* soledad *f*.
solo [sō'lō] *n* solo.
soloist [sō'lōist] *n* solista *m/f*.
Solomon Islands [sál'əmən ī'ləndz] *npl*: **the** ~ las Islas Salomón.
solstice [sál'stis] *n* solsticio.
soluble [sál'yəbəl] *a* soluble.
solution [səlōō'shən] *n* solución *f*.
solve [sálv] *vt* resolver, solucionar.
solvency [sál'vənsē] *n* (*COMM*) solvencia.
solvent [sál'vənt] *a* (*COMM*) solvente ♦ *n* (*CHEM*) solvente *m*.
solvent abuse *n* abuso de los solventes.
Som. *abbr* (*Brit*) = *Somerset*.
Somali [sōmá'lē] *a*, *n* somalí *m/f*.
Somalia [sōmál'ēə] *n* Somalia.
somber, (*Brit*) **sombre** [sám'bûr] *a* sombrío.
some [sum] *a* (*a few*) algunos/as; (*certain*) algún/una; (*a certain number or amount*) *see phrases below*; (*unspecified*) algo de ♦ *pron* algunos/as; (*a bit*) algo ♦ *ad*: ~ **10 people** unas 10 personas; ~ **children came** vinieron algunos niños; ~ **people say that** ... hay quien dice que ...; **have** ~ **tea** tome té; **there's** ~ **milk in the fridge** hay leche en la nevera (*Sp*) or el frigo; ~ **(of it) was left** quedaba algo; **could I have** ~ **of that cheese?** ¿me sirve un poco del queso aquel?; **I've got** ~ (*books etc*) tengo algunos; (*milk, money etc*) tengo algo or un poco; **would you like** ~? ¿quieres algunos (*or* un poco)?; **after** ~ **time** pasado algún tiempo; **at** ~ **length** con mucho detalle; **in** ~ **form or other** en alguna que otra manera.
somebody [sum'bádē] *pron* alguien; ~ **or other** alguien.
someday [sum'dā] *ad* algún día.
somehow [sum'hou] *ad* de alguna manera; (*for some reason*) por una u otra razón.
someone [sum'wun] *pron* = **somebody**.
someplace [sum'plās] *ad* (*US*) = **somewhere**.
somersault [sum'ûrsôlt] *n* (*deliberate*) salto mortal; (*accidental*) vuelco ♦ *vi* dar un salto mortal; dar vuelcos.
something [sum'thing] *pron* algo ♦ *ad*: **he's** ~ **like me** es un poco como yo; ~ **to do** algo que hacer; **it's** ~ **of a problem** es bastante problemático.

sometime [sum'tīm] *ad* (*in future*) algún día, en algún momento; ~ **last month** durante el mes pasado; **I'll finish it** ~ lo terminaré un día de éstos.
sometimes [sum'tīmz] *ad* a veces.
somewhat [sum'wut] *ad* algo.
somewhere [sum'wär] *ad* (*be*) en alguna parte; (*go*) a alguna parte; ~ **else** (*be*) en otra parte; (*go*) a otra parte.
son [sun] *n* hijo.
sonar [sō'nâr] *n* sonar *m*.
sonata [sənât'ə] *n* sonata.
song [sông] *n* canción *f*.
songwriter [sông'rī'tûr] *n* compositor(a) *m/f* de canciones.
sonic [sân'ik] *a* (*boom*) sónico.
son-in-law [sun'inlô] *n* yerno.
sonnet [sân'it] *n* soneto.
sonny [sun'ē] *n* (*col*) hijo.
soon [sōōn] *ad* pronto, dentro de poco; ~ **afterwards** poco después; **very/quite** ~ muy/bastante pronto; **how** ~ **can you be ready?** ¿cuánto tardas en prepararte?; **it's too** ~ **to tell** es demasiado pronto para saber; **see you** ~! ¡hasta pronto!; *see also* **as**.
sooner [sōō'nûr] *ad* (*time*) antes, más temprano; **I would** ~ **do that** preferiría hacer eso; ~ **or later** tarde o temprano; **no** ~ **said than done** dicho y hecho; **the** ~ **the better** cuanto antes mejor; **no** ~ **had we left than** ... apenas nos habíamos marchado cuando ....
soot [sōōt] *n* hollín *m*.
soothe [sōōth] *vt* tranquilizar; (*pain*) aliviar.
soothing [sōō'thing] *a* (*ointment etc*) sedante; (*tone, words etc*) calmante, tranquilizante.
SOP *n abbr* = *standard operating procedure*.
sophisticated [səfis'tikātid] *a* sofisticado.
sophistication [səfis'tikā'shən] *n* sofisticación *f*.
sophomore [sáf'əmôr] *n* (*US*) estudiante *m/f* de segundo año.
soporific [sâpərif'ik] *a* soporífero.
sopping [sáp'ing] *a*: ~ (**wet**) empapado.
soprano [səpran'ō] *n* soprano *f*.
sorbet [sôrbā'] *n* sorbete *m*.
sorcerer [sôr'sərûr] *n* hechicero.
sordid [sôr'did] *a* (*place etc*) sórdido; (*motive etc*) mezquino.
sore [sôr] *a* (*painful*) doloroso, que duele; (*offended*) resentido ♦ *n* llaga; ~ **throat** dolor *m* de garganta; **my eyes are** ~, **I have** ~ **eyes** me duelen los ojos; **it's a** ~ **point** es un asunto delicado or espinoso.
sorely [sôr'lē] *ad*: **I am** ~ **tempted to** (**do it**) estoy muy tentado a (hacerlo).
soreness [sôr'nis] *n* dolor *m*.
sorrel [sôr'əl] *n* (*BOT*) acedera.
sorrow [sâr'ō] *n* pena, dolor *m*.
sorrowful [sâr'ōfəl] *a* afligido, triste.

sorrowfully [sår'ōfəlē] *ad* tristemente.
sorry [sår'ē] *a* (*regretful*) arrepentido;
(*condition, excuse*) lastimoso; (*sight, failure*) triste; ~! ¡perdón!, ¡perdone!; **to feel
~ for sb** tener lástima a uno; **I feel ~ for
him** me da lástima; **I'm ~ to hear that ...**
me da pena *or* tristeza saber que ...; **to be
~ about sth** lamentar algo.
sort [sôrt] *n* clase *f*, género, tipo; (*make: of
coffee, car etc*) marca ♦ *vt* (*also: ~ out:
papers*) clasificar; (: *problems*) arreglar,
solucionar; (*COMPUT*) clasificar; **what ~
do you want?** (*make*) ¿qué marca quieres?; **what ~ of car?** ¿qué tipo de coche?;
I shall do nothing of the ~ no haré eso
bajo ningún concepto; **it's ~ of awkward**
(*col*) es bastante difícil.
sortie [sôr'tē] *n* salida.
sorting office [sôr'ting ô'fis] *n* sala de batalla.
SOS [es'ō'es'] *n* SOS *m*.
so-so [sō'sō'] *ad* regular, así así.
soufflé [sōōflā'] *n* suflé *m*.
sought [sôt] *pt, pp* of **seek.**
sought-after [sôt'af'tûr] *a* solicitado, codi-
ciado.
soul [sōl] *n* alma *f*; **God rest his ~** Dios le
reciba en su seno *or* en su gloria; **I didn't
see a ~** no vi a nadie; **the poor ~ had nowhere to sleep** el pobre no tenía dónde
dormir.
soul-destroying [sōl'distroiing] *a* (*work*)
deprimente.
soulful [sōl'fəl] *a* lleno de sentimiento.
soulmate [sōl'māt] *n* compañero/a del alma.
soul-searching [sōl'sûrching] *n*: **after
much ~** después de pensarlo mucho, después de darle muchas vueltas.
sound [sound] *a* (*healthy*) sano; (*safe, not
damaged*) en buen estado; (*valid: argument, policy, claim*) válido; (: *move*)
acertado; (*dependable: person*) de fiar;
(*sensible*) sensato, razonable ♦ *ad*: **~
asleep** profundamente dormido ♦ *n* (*noise*)
sonido, ruido; (*GEO*) estrecho ♦ *vt* (*alarm*)
sonar; (*also: ~ out: opinions*) consultar,
sondear ♦ *vi* sonar, resonar; (*fig: seem*)
parecer; **to ~ like** sonar a; **to be of ~
mind** estar en su cabal juicio; **I don't like
the ~ of it** no me gusta nada; **it ~s as if
... parece que ...**
  sound off *vi* (*col*): **to ~ off (about)**
  (*give one's opinions*) despotricar (contra).
sound barrier *n* barrera del sonido.
sound effects *npl* efectos *mpl* sonoros.
sound engineer *n* ingeniero/a del sonido.
sounding [soun'ding] *n* (*NAUT etc*) sondeo.
sounding board *n* (*MUS*) tablero sonoro;
(*fig*) piedra de toque.
soundly [sound'lē] *ad* (*sleep*) profundamente; (*beat*) completamente.
soundproof [sound'prōōf] *a* insonorizado.
soundtrack [sound'trak] *n* (*of movie*)

banda sonora.
sound wave *n* (*PHYSICS*) onda sonora.
soup [sōōp] *n* (*thick*) sopa; (*thin*) caldo; **in
the ~** (*fig*) en apuros ♦ *vt* **to ~ up** (*col:
engine*) aumentar la potencia de.
soup kitchen *n* comedor *m* de beneficencia.
soup plate *n* plato sopero.
soupspoon [sōōp'spōōn] *n* cuchara sopera.
sour [sou'ûr] *a* agrio; (*milk*) cortado; **it's
just ~ grapes!** (*fig*) ¡están verdes!; **to go
or turn ~** (*milk*) cortarse; (*wine*) agriarse; (*fig: relationship, plans*) agriarse.
source [sôrs] *n* fuente *f*; **I have it from a reliable ~ that ...** sé de fuente fidedigna que
....
source language *n* (*COMPUT*) lenguaje *m*
original.
south [south] *n* sur *m* ♦ *a* del sur ♦ *ad* al
sur, hacia el sur; **(to the) ~ of** al sur de;
the S~ of France el Sur de Francia; **to
travel ~** viajar hacia el sur.
South Africa *n* África del Sur.
South African *a, n* sudafricano/a *m/f*.
South America *n* América del Sur, Sudamérica.
South American *a, n* sudamericano/a *m/
f*.
southbound [south'bound'] *a* (con) rumbo
al sur.
southeast [southēst'] *n* sudeste *m* ♦ *a*
(*counties etc*) (del) sudeste.
Southeast Asia *n* Sudeste *m* asiático.
southerly [suth'ûrlē] *a* sur; (*from the
south*) del sur.
southern [suth'ûrn] *a* del sur, meridional;
the ~ hemisphere el hemisferio sur.
South Korea *n* Corea del Sur.
South Pole *n* Polo Sur.
South Sea Islands *npl*: **the ~** Oceanía.
South Seas *npl*: **the ~** los Mares del Sur.
southward(s) [south'wûrd(z)] *ad* hacia el
sur.
southwest [southwest'] *n* suroeste *m*.
souvenir [sōōvənēr'] *n* recuerdo.
sovereign [sâv'rin] *a, n* soberano/a *m/f*.
sovereignty [sâv'rəntē] *n* soberanía.
soviet [sō'vēit] *a* soviético.
Soviet Union *n*: **the ~** la Unión Soviética.
sow *n* [sou] cerda, puerca ♦ *vt* [sō] (*pt ~ed,
pp ~n* [sōn]) (*gen*) sembrar; (*spread*)
esparcir.
soy [soi] *n* soja.
soya [soi'ə] (*Brit*) = **soy.**
soy bean *n* semilla de soja.
soy sauce *n* salsa de soja.
spa [spâ] *n* balneario.
space [spās] *n* espacio; (*room*) sitio ♦ *vt*
(*also: ~ out*) espaciar; **to clear a ~ for
sth** hacer sitio para algo; **in a confined ~**
en un espacio restringido; **in a short ~ of
time** en poco *or* un corto espacio de
tiempo; **(with)in the ~ of an hour/three**

generations en el espacio de una hora/tres generaciones.

space bar *n* (*on typewriter*) barra espaciadora.

spacecraft [spās'kraft] *n* nave *f* espacial, astronave *f*.

spaceman [spās'man] *n* astronauta *m*, cosmonauta *m*.

spaceship [spās'ship] *n* = **spacecraft**.

space shuttle *n* transbordador *m* espacial.

spacesuit [spās'sōōt] *n* traje *m* espacial.

spacewoman [spās'wōōmən] *n* astronauta, cosmonauta.

spacing [spā'sing] *n* espaciamiento.

spacious [spā'shəs] *a* amplio.

spade [spād] *n* (*tool*) pala, laya; ~s *npl* (*CARDS: British*) picos *mpl*; (: *Spanish*) espadas *fpl*.

spadework [spād'wûrk] *n* (*fig*) trabajo preliminar.

spaghetti [spəget'ē] *n* espaguetis *mpl*, fideos *mpl*.

Spain [spān] *n* España.

span [span] *pt* of **spin** ♦ *n* (*of bird*, *plane*) envergadura; (*of hand*) palmo; (*of arch*) luz *f*; (*in time*) lapso ♦ *vt* extenderse sobre, cruzar; (*fig*) abarcar.

Spaniard [span'yûrd] *n* español(a) *m/f*.

spaniel [span'yəl] *n* perro de aguas.

Spanish [span'ish] *a* español(a) ♦ *n* (*LING*) español *m*, castellano; **the** ~ *npl* (*people*) los españoles; ~ **omelette** tortilla española.

spank [spangk] *vt* zurrar.

spanner [span'ûr] *n* (*Brit*) llave *f* (inglesa).

spar [spär] *n* palo, verga ♦ *vi* (*BOXING*) entrenarse (en el boxeo).

spare [spär] *a* de reserva; (*surplus*) sobrante, de más ♦ *n* (*part*) pieza de repuesto ♦ *vt* (*do without*) pasarse sin; (*afford to give*) tener de sobra; (*refrain from hurting*) perdonar; (*details etc*) ahorrar; **to** ~ (*surplus*) sobrante, de sobra; **to** ~ **no expense** no escatimar gastos; **can you** ~ **(me) $10?** ¿puedes prestarme *or* darme 10 dólares?; **can you** ~ **the time?** ¿tienes tiempo?; **I've a few minutes to** ~ tengo unos minutos libres; **there is no time to** ~ no hay tiempo que perder.

spare part *n* pieza de repuesto.

spare room *n* cuarto para visitas.

spare time *n* ratos *mpl* de ocio, tiempo libre.

spare tire, (*Brit*) **spare tyre** *n* (*AUT*) neumático *or* llanta (*LAm*) de recambio.

spare wheel *n* (*AUT*) rueda de recambio.

sparing [spär'ing] *a*: **to be** ~ **with** ser parco en.

sparingly [spär'inglē] *ad* escasamente.

spark [spärk] *n* chispa; (*fig*) chispazo.

spark plug [spärk' plug] *n* bujía.

sparkle [spär'kəl] *n* centelleo, destello ♦ *vi* centellear; (*shine*) relucir, brillar.

sparkling [spär'kling] *a* centelleante; (*wine*) espumoso.

sparrow [spar'ō] *n* gorrión *m*.

sparse [spärs] *a* esparcido, escaso.

sparsely [spärs'lē] *ad* escasamente; **a** ~ **furnished room** un cuarto con pocos muebles.

spartan [spâr'tən] *a* (*fig*) espartano.

spasm [spaz'əm] *n* (*MED*) espasmo; (*fig*) arranque *m*, ataque *m*.

spasmodic [spazmâd'ik] *a* espasmódico.

spastic [spas'tik] *n* espástico/a.

spat [spat] *pt*, *pp* of **spit** ♦ *n* (*US*) riña.

spate [spāt] *n* (*fig*): ~ **of** torrente *m* de; **in** ~ (*river*) crecido.

spatial [spā'shəl] *a* espacial.

spatter [spat'ûr] *vt*: **to** ~ **with** salpicar de.

spatula [spach'ələ] *n* espátula.

spawn [spôn] *vt* (*pej*) engendrar ♦ *vi* desovar, frezar ♦ *n* huevas *fpl*.

SPCA *n abbr* (*US*) = *Society for the Prevention of Cruelty to Animals*.

SPCC *n abbr* (*US*) = *Society for the Prevention of Cruelty to Children*.

speak, *pt* **spoke**, *pp* **spoken** [spēk, spōk, spō'kən] *vt* (*language*) hablar; (*truth*) decir ♦ *vi* hablar; (*make a speech*) intervenir; **to** ~ **one's mind** hablar claro *or* con franqueza; **to** ~ **to sb/of** *or* **about sth** hablar con uno/de *or* sobre algo; **to** ~ **at a conference/in a debate** hablar en un congreso/un debate; **he has no money to** ~ **of** no tiene mucho dinero que digamos; ~**ing!** ¡al habla!; ~ **up!** ¡habla más alto!

speak for *vt fus*: **to** ~ **for sb** hablar por *or* en nombre de uno; **that picture is already spoken for** (*in shop*) ese cuadro está reservado.

speaker [spē'kûr] *n* (*in public*) orador(a) *m/f*; (*also*: **loud**~) altavoz *m*; (*for stereo etc*) bafle *m*; (*POL*): **the S**~ (*US*) él que preside la cámara de los representantes del Congreso; (*Brit*) el Presidente de la Cámara de los Comunes; **are you a Welsh** ~**?** ¿habla Ud galés?

speaking [spē'king] *a* hablante.

-speaking *suff* -hablante; **Spanish**~ **people** los hispanoparlantes.

spear [spi'ûr] *n* lanza; (*for fishing*) arpón *m* ♦ *vt* alancear; arponear.

spearhead [spēr'hed] *vt* (*attack etc*) encabezar ♦ *n* (*MIL*) punta de lanza; (*fig*) vanguardia.

spearmint [spēr'mint] *n* (*BOT etc*) menta verde.

special [spesh'əl] *a* especial; (*edition etc*) extraordinario; (*delivery*) urgente ♦ *n* (*train*) tren *m* especial: **on** ~ (**offer**) en oferta especial; **nothing** ~ nada de particular, nada extraordinario.

special agent *n* agente *m/f* especial.

special correspondent *n* corresponsal *m/f* especial.

special delivery *n* (*MAIL*): **by** ~ por entrega urgente.

specialist [spesh'əlist] *n* especialista *m/f*; **a heart** ~ (*MED*) un(a) especialista del corazón.

speciality [speshēal'ətē] *n* (*Brit*) = **specialty**.

specialize [spesh'əlīz] *vi*: **to** ~ **(in)** especializarse en.

specially [spesh'əlē] *ad* sobre todo, en particular.

special offer *n* (*COMM*) oferta especial, ganga.

special train *n* tren *m* especial.

specialty [spesh'əltē] *n* especialidad *f*.

species [spē'shēz] *n* especie *f*.

specific [spisif'ik] *a* específico.

specifically [spisif'iklē] *ad* (*explicitly*: *state*, *warn*) específicamente, expresamente; (*especially*: *design*, *intend*) especialmente.

specification [spesəfəkā'shən] *n* especificación *f*; ~**s** *npl* (*of car*, *machine*) especificación *fsg*; (*for building*) plan *msg* detallado.

specify [spes'əfī] *vt*, *vi* especificar, precisar; **unless otherwise specified** salvo indicaciones contrarias.

specimen [spes'əmən] *n* ejemplar *m*; (*MED*: *of urine*) espécimen *m*; (: *of blood*) muestra.

specimen copy *n* ejemplar *m* de muestra.

specimen signature *n* muestra de firma.

speck [spek] *n* grano, mota.

speckled [spek'əld] *a* moteado.

specs [speks] *npl* (*col*) gafas *fpl* (*Sp*), anteojos *mpl*.

spectacle [spek'təkəl] *n* espectáculo.

spectacles [spek'təkəlz] *npl* (*Brit*) gafas *fpl* (*Sp*), anteojos *mpl*.

spectacular [spektak'yəlûr] *a* espectacular; (*success*) impresionante.

spectator [spek'tātûr] *n* espectador(a) *m/f*.

specter, (*Brit*) **spectre** [spek'tûr] *n* espectro, fantasma *m*.

spectra [spek'trə] *npl* of **spectrum**.

spectrum, *pl* **spectra** [spek'trəm, -trə] *n* espectro.

speculate [spek'yəlāt] *vi* especular; (*try to guess*): **to** ~ **about** especular sobre.

speculation [spekyəlā'shən] *n* especulación *f*.

speculative [spek'yəlātiv] *a* especulativo.

speculator [spek'yəlātûr] *n* especulador(a) *m/f*.

sped [sped] *pt*, *pp* of **speed**.

speech [spēch] *n* (*faculty*) habla; (*formal talk*) discurso; (*words*) palabras *fpl*; (*manner of speaking*) forma de hablar; (*language*) idioma *m*, lenguaje *m*.

speech day *n* (*Brit SCOL*) ≈ reparto de premios.

speech impediment *n* defecto del habla.

speechless [spēch'lis] *a* mudo, estupฺfacto.

speech therapy *n* logopedia.

speed [spēd] *n* (*also*: *AUT*, *TECH*: *gear*) ve-

locidad *f*; (*haste*) prisa; (*promptness*) rapidez *f* ♦ *vi* (*pt*, *pp* **sped** [sped]) (*AUT*: *exceed* ~ *limit*) conducir con exceso de velocidad; **at full** *or* **top** ~ a máxima velocidad; **at a** ~ **of 70 km/h** a una velocidad de 70 km por hora; **five-**~ **transmission** una caja de cambios de 5 velocidades; **shorthand/ typing** ~ rapidez *f* en taquigrafía/ mecanografía; **the years sped by** los años pasaron volando.

speed up *vi* acelerarse ♦ *vt* acelerar.

speedboat [spēd'bōt] *n* lancha motora.

speedily [spē'dilē] *ad* rápido, rápidamente.

speeding [spē'ding] *n* (*AUT*) exceso de velocidad.

speed limit *n* límite *m* de velocidad, velocidad *f* máxima.

speedometer [spēdâm'itûr] *n* velocímetro.

speed trap *n* (*AUT*) control *m* de velocidades.

speedway [spēd'wā] *n* (*SPORT*) pista de carrera.

speedy [spē'dē] *a* (*fast*) veloz, rápido; (*prompt*) pronto.

spell [spel] *n* (*also*: **magic** ~) encanto, hechizo; (*period of time*) rato, período; (*turn*) turno ♦ *vt* (*pt*, *pp* ~**ed** *or* **spelt** [speld, spelt]) (*also*: ~ **out**) deletrear; (*fig*) anunciar, presagiar; **to cast a** ~ **on sb** hechizar a uno; **he can't** ~ no sabe escribir bien, sabe poco de ortografía; **can you** ~ **it for me?** ¿cómo se deletrea *or* se escribe?; **how do you** ~ **your name?** ¿cómo se escribe tu nombre?

spellbound [spel'bound] *a* embelesado, hechizado.

spelling [spel'ing] *n* ortografía.

spelling mistake *n* falta de ortografía.

spelt [spelt] *pt*, *pp* of **spell**.

spelunker [spēlung'kûr] *n* (*US*) espeleólogo/a.

spend, *pt*, *pp* **spent** [spend, spent] *vt* (*money*) gastar; (*time*) pasar; (*life*) dedicar; **to** ~ **time/money/effort on sth** gastar tiempo/dinero/energías en algo.

spending [spen'ding] *n*: **government** ~ gastos *mpl* del gobierno.

spending money *n* dinero para gastos.

spending power *n* poder *m* de compra *or* adquisitivo.

spendthrift [spend'thrift] *n* derrochador(a) *m/f*, pródigo/a.

spent [spent] *pt*, *pp* of **spend** ♦ *a* (*cartridge*, *bullets*, *match*) usado.

sperm [spûrm] *n* esperma.

sperm whale *n* cachalote *m*.

spew [spyōō] *vt* vomitar, arrojar.

sphere [sfēr] *n* esfera.

spherical [sfär'ikəl] *a* esférico.

sphinx [sfingks] *n* esfinge *f*.

spice [spīs] *n* especia ♦ *vt* especiar.

spiciness [spī'sēnis] *n* lo picante.

spicy [spī'sē] *a* picante.

spick-and-span [spik'ənspan'] *a* aseado, (bien) arreglado.
spider [spī'dûr] *n* araña.
spider's web *n* telaraña.
spiel [spēl] *n* (*col*) rollo.
spike [spīk] *n* (*point*) punta; (*ZOOL*) pincho, púa; (*BOT*) espiga; (*ELEC*) pico parásito ♦ *vt*: **to ~ a quote** cancelar una cita; **~s** *npl* (*SPORT*) zapatillas *fpl* con clavos.
spiky [spī'kē] *a* (*bush, branch*) cubierto de púas; (*animal*) erizado.
spill, *pt, pp* **spilt** *or* **~ed** [spil, spilt, spild] *vt* derramar, verter; (*blood*) derramar ♦ *vi* derramarse; **to ~ the beans** (*col*) descubrir el pastel.
  spill out *vi* derramarse, desparramarse.
  spill over *vi* desbordarse.
spin [spin] *n* (*revolution of wheel*) vuelta, revolución *f*; (*AVIAT*) barrena; (*trip in car*) paseo (en coche) ♦ *vb* (*pt* **spun, span**, *pp* **spun** [spun, span]) *vt* (*wool etc*) hilar; (*wheel*) girar ♦ *vi* girar, dar vueltas; **the car spun out of control** el coche se descontroló dando vueltas.
  spin out *vt* alargar, prolongar.
spinach [spin'ich] *n* espinaca; (*as food*) espinacas *fpl*.
spinal [spī'nəl] *a* espinal.
spinal column *n* columna vertebral.
spinal cord *n* médula espinal.
spindly [spind'lē] *a* (*leg*) zanquivano.
spin-dry [spindrī'] *vt* centrifugar.
spin-dryer [spindrī'ûr] *n* (*Brit*) secador *m* centrífugo.
spine [spīn] *n* espinazo, columna vertebral; (*thorn*) espina.
spine-chilling [spīn'chiling] *a* de terror.
spineless [spīn'lis] *a* (*fig*) débil, flojo.
spinet [spin'it] *n* espineta.
spinning [spin'ing] *n* (*of thread*) hilado; (*art*) hilandería.
spinning top *n* peonza.
spinning wheel *n* rueca, torno de hilar.
spin-off [spin'ôf] *n* derivado, producto secundario.
spinster [spin'stûr] *n* soltera; (*pej*) solterona.
spiral [spī'rəl] *n* espiral *f* ♦ *a* en espiral ♦ *vi* (*prices*) dispararse; **the inflationary ~** la espiral inflacionista.
spiral staircase *n* escalera de caracol.
spire [spī'ûr] *n* aguja, chapitel *m*.
spirit [spir'it] *n* (*soul*) alma *f*; (*ghost*) fantasma *m*; (*attitude*) espíritu *m*; (*courage*) valor *m*, ánimo; **~s** *npl* (*drink*) alcohol *msg*, bebidas *fpl* alcohólicas; **in good ~s** alegre, de buen ánimo; **Holy S~** Espíritu *m* Santo; **community ~, public ~** civismo.
spirit duplicator *n* copiadora al alcohol.
spirited [spir'itid] *a* enérgico, vigoroso.
spirit level *n* nivel *m* de aire.
spiritual [spir'ichōōəl] *a* espiritual ♦ *n* (*also:*

Negro ~) canción *f* religiosa, espiritual *m*.
spiritualism [spir'ichōōəlizəm] *n* espiritualismo.
spit [spit] *n* (*for roasting*) asador *m*, espetón *m*; (*spittle*) esputo, escupitajo; (*saliva*) saliva ♦ *vi* (*pt, pp* **spat** [spat]) escupir; (*sound*) chisporrotear.
spite [spīt] *n* rencor *m*, ojeriza ♦ *vt* causar pena a, mortificar; **in ~ of** a pesar de, pese a.
spiteful [spīt'fəl] *a* rencoroso, malévolo.
spitting [spit'ing] *n*: "**~ prohibited**" "se prohíbe escupir" ♦ *a*: **to be the ~ image of sb** ser la viva imagen de uno.
spittle [spit'əl] *n* saliva, baba.
splash [splash] *n* (*sound*) chapoteo; (*of color*) mancha ♦ *vt* salpicar de ♦ *vi* (*also:* **~ around**) chapotear; **to ~ paint on the floor** manchar el suelo de pintura.
splashdown [splash'doun] *n* amaraje *m*, amerizaje *m*.
spleen [splēn] *n* (*ANAT*) bazo.
splendid [splen'did] *a* espléndido.
splendidly [splen'didlē] *ad* espléndidamente; **everything went ~** todo fue a las mil maravillas.
splendor, (*Brit*) **splendour** [splen'dûr] *n* esplendor *m*; (*of achievement*) brillo, gloria.
splice [splīs] *vt* empalmar.
splint [splint] *n* tablilla.
splinter [splin'tûr] *n* (*of wood*) astilla; (*in finger*) espigón *m* ♦ *vi* astillarse, hacer astillas.
splinter group *n* grupo disidente, facción *f*.
split [split] *n* hendedura, raja; (*fig*) división *f*; (*POL*) escisión *f* ♦ (*vb: pt, pp* **split**) *vt* partir, rajar; (*party*) dividir; (*work, profits*) repartir ♦ *vi* (*divide*) dividirse, escindirse; **to ~ the difference** partir la diferencia; **to do the ~s** esparrancarse; **to ~ sth down the middle** (*also fig*) dividir algo en dos.
  split up *vi* (*couple*) separarse; (*meeting*) acabarse.
split-level [split'lev'əl] *a* (*house*) dúplex.
split peas *npl* guisantes *mpl* secos.
split personality *n* personalidad *f* desdoblada.
split second *n* fracción *f* de segundo.
splitting [split'ing] *a* (*headache*) horrible.
splutter [splut'ûr] *vi* = **sputter**.
spoil, *pt, pp* **~ed** *or* **spoilt** [spoil, spoild, spoilt] *vt* (*damage*) dañar; (*ruin*) estropear, echar a perder; (*child*) mimar, consentir; (*ballot paper*) invalidar ♦ *vi*: **to be ~ing for a fight** estar con ganas de lucha, andar con ganas de pelea.
spoiled [spoild] *a* (*US: food:* ·*bad*) pasado, malo; (*: milk*) cortado.
spoiler [spoi'lûr] *n* (*AUT*) spoiler *m*.
spoils [spoilz] *npl* despojo *sg*, botín *msg*.
spoilsport [spoil'spôrt] *n* aguafiestas *m inv*.

spoilt [spoilt] *pt, pp of* **spoil** ♦ *a* (*Brit*: *child*) mimado, consentido; (: *ballot paper*) invalidado.

spoke [spōk] *pt of* **speak** ♦ *n* rayo, radio.

spoken [spō'kən] *pp of* **speak**.

spokesman [spōks'mən], **spokeswoman** [spōks'wŏŏmən] *n* vocero *m/f*, portavoz *m/f*.

sponge [spunj] *n* esponja; (*CULIN*: *also*: ~ **cake**) bizcocho ♦ *vt* (*wash*) lavar con esponja ♦ *vi*: **to ~ off sb** vivir a costa de uno.

sponge bag *n* (*Brit*) esponjera.

sponge cake *n* bizcocho, pastel *m*.

sponger [spun'jûr] *n* gorrón/ona *m/f*.

spongy [spun'jē] *a* esponjoso.

sponsor [spân'sûr] *n* (*RADIO*, *TV*) patrocinador(a) *m/f*; (*for membership*) padrino/madrina; (*COMM*) fiador(a) *m/f* ♦ *vt* patrocinar; apadrinar; (*parliamentary bill*) apoyar, respaldar; (*idea etc*) presentar, promover; **I ~ed him at 25¢ a mile** (*in fundraising race*) me suscribí a darle 25 centavos la milla.

sponsorship [spân'sûrship] *n* patrocinio.

spontaneity [spântənē'itē] *n* espontaneidad *f*.

spontaneous [spântā'nēəs] *a* espontáneo.

spontaneously [spântā'nēəslē] *ad* espontáneamente.

spooky [spŏŏ'kē] *a* (*col*: *place*, *atmosphere*) espeluznante, horripilante.

spool [spŏŏl] *n* carrete *m*; (*of sewing machine*) canilla.

spoon [spŏŏn] *n* cuchara.

spoon-feed [spŏŏn'fēd] *vt* dar de comer con cuchara a; (*fig*) tratar como un niño a.

spoonful [spŏŏn'fŏŏl] *n* cucharada.

sporadic [spôrad'ik] *a* esporádico.

sport [spôrt] *n* deporte *m*; (*person*) buen(a) perdedor(a) *m/f*; (*amusement*) juego, diversión *f*; **indoor/outdoor ~s** deportes *mpl* en sala cubierta/al aire libre; **to say sth in ~** decir algo en broma.

sporting [spôr'ting] *a* deportivo; **to give sb a ~ chance** darle a uno su oportunidad.

sports car [spôrts kâr] *n* coche *m* sport.

sport(s) coat *n* (*US*) chaqueta deportiva.

sports field *n* campo de deportes, centro deportivo (*LAm*).

sports jacket *n* (*Brit*) chaqueta deportiva.

sportsman [spôrts'mən] *n* deportista *m*.

sportsmanship [spôrts'mənship] *n* deportividad *f*.

sports pages *npl* páginas *fpl* deportivas.

sportswear [spôrts'weûr] *n* trajes *mpl* de deporte *or* sport.

sportswoman [spôrts'wŏŏmən] *n* deportista.

sporty [spôr'tē] *a* deportivo.

spot [spât] *n* sitio, lugar *m*; (*dot: on pattern*) punto, mancha; (*pimple*) grano; (*also*: **advertising ~**) spot *m*; (*small amount*): **a ~ of** un poquito de ♦ *vt* (*no-*

tice) notar, observar ♦ *a* (*COMM*) inmediatamente efectivo; **on the ~** en el acto, acto seguido; (*in difficulty*) en un aprieto; **to do sth on the ~** hacer algo en el acto; **to put sb on the ~** poner a uno en un apuro; **to pay cash on the ~** (*US*) pagar al contado.

spot check *n* reconocimiento rápido.

spotless [spât'lis] *a* nítido, perfectamente limpio.

spotlessly [spât'lislē] *ad*: ~ **clean** limpísimo.

spotlight [spât'līt] *n* foco, reflector *m*; (*AUT*) faro auxiliar.

spot price *n* precio de entrega inmediata.

spotted [spât'id] *a* (*pattern*) de puntos.

spotty [spât'ē] *a* (*face*) con granos.

spouse [spous] *n* cónyuge *m/f*.

spout [spout] *n* (*of jug*) pico; (*pipe*) caño ♦ *vi* chorrear.

sprain [sprān] *n* torcedura ♦ *vt*: **to ~ one's ankle** torcerse el tobillo.

sprang [sprang] *pt of* **spring**.

sprawl [sprôl] *vi* tumbarse ♦ *n*: **urban ~** crecimiento urbano descontrolado; **to send sb ~ing** tirar a uno al suelo.

sprawling [sprôl'ing] *a* (*town*) desparramado.

spray [sprā] *n* rociada; (*of sea*) espuma; (*container*) atomizador *m*; (*of paint*) pistola rociadora; (*of flowers*) ramita ♦ *vt* rociar; (*crops*) regar ♦ *cpd* (*deodorant*) en atomizador.

spread [spred] *n* extensión *f*; (*of idea*) diseminación *f*; (*col: food*) comilona; (*PRESS*, *TYP*: *two pages*) plana ♦ *vb* (*pt, pp* **spread**) *vt* extender; diseminar; (*butter*) untar; (*wings, sails*) desplegar; (*scatter*) esparcir ♦ *vi* extenderse; diseminarse; untarse; desplegarse; esparcirse; **middle-age ~** gordura de la mediana edad; **repayments will be ~ over 18 months** los pagos se harán a lo largo de 18 meses.

spread-eagled [spred'ēgəld] *a*: **to be ~** estar despatarrado.

spreadsheet [spred'shēt] *n* (*COMPUT*) hoja de cálculo.

spree [sprē] *n*: **to go on a ~** ir de juerga.

sprightly [sprīt'lē] *a* vivo, enérgico.

spring [spring] *n* (*season*) primavera; (*leap*) salto, brinco; (*coiled metal*) resorte *m*; (*of water*) fuente *f*, manantial *m*; (*bounciness*) elasticidad *f* ♦ *vb* (*pt* **sprang**, *pp* **sprung** [sprang, sprung]) *vi* (*arise*) brotar, nacer; (*leap*) saltar, brincar ♦ *vt*: **to ~ a leak** (*pipe etc*) empezar a hacer agua; **he sprang the news on me** de repente me soltó la noticia; **in (the)** ~ en (la) primavera; **to walk with a ~ in one's step** andar dando saltos *or* brincos; **to ~ into action** lanzarse a la acción.

spring up *vi* (*problem*) surgir.

springboard [spring'bôrd] *n* trampolín *m*.

spring-clean [spring'klēn'] *n* (*also*: ~**ing**)

limpieza general.

spring onion *n* cebolleta.

springtime [spring'tīm] *n* primavera.

springy [spring'ē] *a* elástico; (*grass*) muelle.

sprinkle [spring'kəl] *vt* (*pour*) rociar; **to ~ water on, ~ with water** rociar *or* salpicar de agua.

sprinkler [spring'klûr] *n* (*for lawn*) rociadera; (*to put out fire*) aparato de rociadura automática.

sprinkling [spring'kling] *n* (*of water*) rociada; (*of salt, sugar*) un poco de.

sprint [sprint] *n* esprint *m* ♦ *vi* (*gen*) correr a toda velocidad; (*SPORT*) esprintar; **the 200 meters ~** el esprint de 200 metros.

sprinter [sprin'tûr] *n* esprínter *m/f*, corredor(a) *m/f*.

sprocket [språk'it] *n* (*on printer etc*) rueda de espigas.

sprocket feed *n* avance *m* por rueda de espigas.

sprout [sprout] *vi* brotar, retoñar ♦ *n:* **(Brussels) ~s** *npl* coles *fpl* de Bruselas.

spruce [sprōōs] *n* (*BOT*) pícea ♦ *a* aseado, pulcro.

spruce up *vt* (*tidy*) arreglar, acicalar; (*smarten up: room etc*) ordenar; **to ~ o.s up** arreglarse.

sprung [sprung] *pp of* **spring**.

spry [sprī] *a* ágil, activo.

SPUC *n abbr* (= *Society for the Protection of Unborn Children*) ≈ Federación *f* Española de Asociaciones Pro-vida.

spun [spun] *pt, pp of* **spin**.

spur [spûr] *n* espuela; (*fig*) estímulo, aguijón *m* ♦ *vt* (*also:* **~ on**) estimular, incitar; **on the ~ of the moment** de improviso.

spurious [spyōōr'ēəs] *a* falso.

spurn [spûrn] *vt* desdeñar, rechazar.

spurt [spûrt] *n* chorro; (*of energy*) arrebato ♦ *vi* chorrear; **to put in** *or* **on a ~** (*runner*) acelerar; (*fig: in work etc*) hacer un gran esfuerzo.

sputter [sput'ûr] *vi* chisporrotear; (*person*) balbucear.

spy [spī] *n* espía *m/f* ♦ *vi:* **to ~ on** espiar a ♦ *vt* (*see*) divisar, lograr ver ♦ *cpd* (*film, story*) de espionaje.

spying [spī'ing] *n* espionaje *m*.

Sq. *abbr* (*in address:* = *Square*) Plza.

sq. *abbr* (*MATH etc*) = **square**.

squabble [skwâb'əl] *n* riña, pelea ♦ *vi* reñir, pelear.

squad [skwâd] *n* (*MIL*) pelotón *m*; (*POLICE*) brigada; (*SPORT*) equipo.

squad car *n* (*POLICE*) coche-patrulla *m*.

squadron [skwâd'rən] *n* (*MIL*) escuadrón *m*; (*AVIAT, NAUT*) escuadra.

squalid [skwâl'id] *a* vil, miserable.

squall [skwôl] *n* (*storm*) chubasco; (*wind*) ráfaga.

squalor [skwâl'ûr] *n* miseria.

squander [skwân'dûr] *vt* (*money*) derrochar, despilfarrar; (*chances*) desperdiciar.

square [skwär] *n* cuadro; (*in town*) plaza; (*US: block*) manzana, cuadra (*LAm*) ♦ *a* cuadrado ♦ *vt* (*arrange*) arreglar; (*MATH*) cuadrar; (*reconcile*): **can you ~ it with your conscience?** ¿cómo lo justifica? ♦ *vi* cuadrar, conformarse; **all ~** igual(es); **a ~ meal** una comida decente; **2 meters ~** 2 metros en cuadro; **1 ~ meter** un metro cuadrado; **to get one's accounts ~** dejar las cuentas claras; **I'll ~ it with him** (*col*) yo lo arreglo con él; **we're back to ~ one** (*fig*) hemos vuelto al principio.

square bracket *n* (*TYP*) corchete *m*.

squarely [skwär'lē] *ad* (*fully*) de lleno; (*honestly, fairly*) honradamente, justamente.

square root *n* raíz *f* cuadrada.

squash [skwâsh] *n* (*vegetable*) calabaza; (*SPORT*) squash *m*, frontenis *m*; (*Brit: drink*): **lemon/orange ~** zumo (*Sp*) *or* jugo (*LAm*) de limón/naranja ♦ *vt* aplastar.

squat [skwât] *a* achaparrado ♦ *vi* agacharse, sentarse en cuclillas; (*on property*) ocupar ilegalmente.

squatter [skwât'ûr] *n* persona que ocupa ilegalmente una casa.

squawk [skwôk] *vi* graznar.

squeak [skwēk] *vi* (*hinge, wheel*) chirriar, rechinar; (*shoe, wood*) crujir ♦ *n* (*of hinge, wheel etc*) chirrido, rechinamiento; (*of shoes*) crujir *m*; (*of mouse etc*) chillido.

squeal [skwēl] *vi* chillar, dar gritos agudos.

squeamish [skwē'mish] *a* delicado, remilgado.

squeeze [skwēz] *n* presión *f*; (*of hand*) apretón *m*; (*COMM: credit ~*) restricción *f* ♦ *vt* (*lemon etc*) exprimir; (*hand, arm*) apretar; **a ~ of lemon** unas gotas de limón; **to ~ past/under sth** colarse al lado de/por debajo de algo.

squeeze out *vt* exprimir; (*fig*) excluir.

squeeze through *vi* abrirse paso con esfuerzos.

squelch [skwelch] *vi* chapotear.

squid [skwid] *n* calamar *m*.

squiggle [skwig'əl] *n* garabato.

squint [skwint] *vi* guiñar los ojos ♦ *n* (*MED*) estrabismo; **to ~ at sth** mirar algo entornando los ojos.

squirm [skwûrm] *vi* retorcerse, revolverse.

squirrel [skwûr'əl] *n* ardilla.

squirt [skwûrt] *vi* salir a chorros.

Sr *abbr* = **senior, sister** (*REL*).

Sri Lanka [srē lángk'ə] *n* Sri Lanka *m*.

SRO *abbr* (*US*) = *standing room only*.

SS *abbr* (= *steamship*) M.V.

SSA *n abbr* (*US:* = *Social Security Administration*) ≈ Seguro Social.

SST *n abbr* (*US*) = *supersonic transport*.

St *abbr* (= *saint*) Sto./a.; (= *street*) c/.

stab [stab] *n* (*with knife etc*) puñalada; (*of*

pain) pinchazo; **to have a ~ at (doing) sth** (*col*) intentar (hacer) algo ♦ *vt* apuñalar; **to ~ sb to death** matar a uno a puñaladas.

stabbing [stab'ing] *n*: **there's been a ~** han apuñalado a alguien ♦ *a* (*pain*) punzante.

stability [stəbil'ətē] *n* estabilidad *f*.

stabilization [stābiləzā'shən] *n* estabilización *f*.

stabilize [stā'bəlīz] *vt* estabilizar ♦ *vi* estabilizarse.

stabilizer [stā'bəlīzûr] *n* (*AVIAT*, *NAUT*) estabilizador *m*.

stable [stā'bəl] *a* estable ♦ *n* cuadra, caballeriza; **riding ~s** escuela hípica.

stableboy [stā'bəlboi] *n* mozo de cuadra.

staccato [stəká'tō] *a*, *ad* staccato.

stack [stak] *n* montón *m*, pila; (*col*) mar *f* ♦ *vt* amontonar, apilar.

stacker [stak'ûr] *n* (*for printer*) apiladora.

stadium [stā'dēəm] *n* estadio.

staff [staf] *n* (*work force*) personal *m*, plantilla; (*Brit SCOL*: *also*: **teaching ~**) cuerpo docente; (*stick*) bastón *m* ♦ *vt* proveer de personal; **to be ~ed by Asians/women** tener una plantilla asiática/femenina.

Staffs *abbr* (*Brit*) = Staffordshire.

stag [stag] *n* ciervo, venado; (*Brit STOCK EXCHANGE*) especulador *m* con nuevas emisiones.

stage [stāj] *n* escena; (*point*) etapa; (*platform*) plataforma; **the ~** el escenario, el teatro ♦ *vt* (*play*) poner en escena, representar; (*organize*) montar, organizar; (*fig: perform: recovery etc*) efectuar; **in ~s** por etapas; **in the early/final ~s** en las primeras/últimas etapas; **to go through a difficult ~** pasar una fase *or* etapa mala.

stagecoach [stāj'kōch] *n* diligencia.

stage door *n* entrada de artistas.

stagehand [stāj'hand] *n* tramoyista *m/f*.

stage-manage [stāj'man'ij] *vt* (*fig*) manipular.

stage manager *n* director(a) *m/f* de escena.

stagger [stag'ûr] *vi* tambalear ♦ *vt* (*amaze*) asombrar; (*hours*, *vacation*) escalonar.

staggering [stag'ûring] *a* (*amazing*) asombroso, pasmoso.

stagnant [stag'nənt] *a* estancado.

stagnate [stag'nāt] *vi* estancarse; (*fig: economy*, *mind*) quedarse estancado.

stagnation [stagnā'shən] *n* estancamiento.

stag party *n* despedida de soltero.

staid [stād] *a* (*clothes*) serio, formal.

stain [stān] *n* mancha; (*coloring*) tintura ♦ *vt* manchar; (*wood*) teñir.

stained glass window [stānd' glas win'dō] *n* vidriera de colores.

stainless [stān'lis] *a* (*steel*) inoxidable.

stain remover *n* quitamanchas *m inv*.

stair [stär] *n* (*step*) peldaño, escalón *m*; **~s** *npl* escaleras *fpl*.

staircase [stär'kās], **stairway** [stär'wā] *n* escalera.

stairwell [stär'wel] *n* hueco *or* caja de la escalera.

stake [stāk] *n* estaca, poste *m*; (*BETTING*) apuesta ♦ *vt* (*bet*) apostar; (*also*: **~ out**: *area*) estacar, cercar con estacas; **to be at ~** estar en juego; **to have a ~ in sth** tener interés en algo; **to ~ a claim to (sth)** presentar reclamación por *or* reclamar (algo).

stalactite [stəlak'tīt] *n* estalactita.

stalagmite [stəlag'mīt] *n* estalagmita.

stale [stāl] *a* (*bread*) duro; (*food*) pasado.

stalemate [stāl'māt] *n* tablas *fpl* (por ahogado); **to reach ~** (*fig*) estancarse.

stalk [stôk] *n* tallo, caña ♦ *vt* acechar, cazar al acecho; **to ~ off** irse airado.

stall [stôl] *n* (*in market*) puesto; (*in stable*) casilla (de establo) ♦ *vt* (*AUT*) parar ♦ *vi* (*AUT*) pararse; (*fig*) buscar evasivas; **~s** *npl* (*Brit: in cinema*, *theater*) butacas *fpl*; **a newspaper ~** (*Brit*) un quiosco (de periódicos); **a flower ~** un puesto de flores.

stallholder [stôl'hōldûr] *n* dueño/a de un puesto.

stallion [stal'yən] *n* semental *m*, garañón *m*.

stalwart [stôl'wûrt] *n* partidario/a incondicional.

stamen [stā'mən] *n* estambre *m*.

stamina [stam'inə] *n* resistencia.

stammer [stam'ûr] *n* tartamudeo, balbuceo ♦ *vi* tartamudear, balbucir.

stamp [stamp] *n* sello, estampilla (*LAm*); (*mark*, *also fig*) marca, huella; (*on document*) timbre *m* ♦ *vi* (*also*: **~ one's foot**) patear ♦ *vt* patear, golpear con el pie; (*letter*) poner sellos en; (*with rubber ~*) marcar con sello; **~ed addressed envelope (sae)** (*Brit*) sobre con las propias señas de uno y con sello.

stamp out *vt* (*fire*) apagar con el pie; (*crime*, *opposition*) acabar con.

stamp album *n* álbum *m* para sellos.

stamp collecting *n* filatelia.

stampede [stampēd'] *n* (*of cattle*) estampida.

stamp machine *n* máquina (expendedora) de sellos.

stance [stans] *n* postura.

stand [stand] *n* (*attitude*) posición *f*, postura; (*for taxis*) parada; (*music ~*) atril *m*; (*SPORT*) tribuna; (*at exhibition*) stand *m* ♦ *vb* (*pt*, *pp* **stood** [stood]) *vi* (*be*) estar, encontrarse; (*be on foot*) estar de pie; (*rise*) levantarse; (*remain*) quedar en pie ♦ *vt* (*place*) poner, colocar; (*tolerate*, *withstand*) aguantar, soportar; **to make a ~** resistir; (*fig*) mantener una postura firme; **to take a ~ on an issue** adoptar una actitud hacia una cuestión; **to ~ for parliament** (*Brit*) presentarse (como candidato) a las elecciones; **nothing ~s in our way** nada nos lo impide; **to ~ still** quedarse inmóvil; **to let sth ~ as it is** dejar algo como está;

as things ~ tal como están las cosas; **to ~ sb a drink/meal** invitar a uno a una copa/a comer; **the company will have to ~ the loss** la empresa tendrá que encargarse de las pérdidas; **I can't ~ him** no le aguanto, no le puedo ver; **to ~ guard** or **watch** (*MIL*) hacer guardia.

stand aside *vi* apartarse, mantenerse aparte.

stand by *vi* (*be ready*) estar listo ♦ *vt fus* (*opinion*) aferrarse a.

stand down *vi* (*withdraw*) ceder el puesto; (*MIL*, *LAW*) retirarse.

stand for *vt fus* (*signify*) significar; (*tolerate*) aguantar, permitir.

stand in for *vt fus* suplir a.

stand out *vi* (*be prominent*) destacarse.

stand up *vi* (*rise*) levantarse, ponerse de pie ♦ *vt* (*person*) dejar plantado.

stand up for *vt fus* defender.

stand up to *vt fus* hacer frente a.

stand-alone [stand'əlōn'] *a* (*COMPUT*) autónomo.

standard [stan'dûrd] *n* patrón *m*, norma; (*flag*) estandarte *m* ♦ *a* (*size etc*) normal, corriente, estándar; **~s** *npl* (*morals*) valores *mpl* morales; **the gold ~** (*COMM*) el patrón oro; **high/low ~** de alto/bajo nivel; **below** or **not up to ~** (*work*) de calidad inferior; **to be** or **come up to ~** satisfacer los requisitos; **to apply a double ~** aplicar un doble criterio.

standardization [standûrdəzā'shən] *n* normalización *f*.

standardize [stan'dûrdīz] *vt* estandarizar.

standard lamp *n* (*Brit*) lámpara de pie.

standard model *n* modelo standard.

standard of living *n* nivel *m* de vida.

standard practice *n* norma, práctica común.

standard rate *n* tasa de imposición.

standard time *n* hora legal.

stand-by [stand'bī] *n* (*alert*) alerta, aviso; **to be on ~** estar sobre aviso, estar preparado para salir; (*doctor*) estar listo para acudir.

stand-by generator *n* generador *m* de reserva.

stand-by passenger *n* (*AVIAT*) pasajero/a que está en la lista de espera.

stand-by ticket *n* (*AVIAT*) (billete *m*) standby *m*.

stand-in [stand'in] *n* suplente *m/f*; (*CINEMA*) doble *m/f*.

standing [stan'ding] *a* (*upright*) derecho; (*on foot*) de pie, en pie; (*permanent*: *committee*) permanente; (: *rule*) fijo; (: *army*) permanente, regular; (*grievance*) constante, viejo ♦ *n* reputación *f*; (*duration*): **of 6 months' ~** que lleva 6 meses; **of many years' ~** que lleva muchos años; **he was given a ~ ovation** le aplaudieron mucho (de a pie); **~ joke** motivo constante de bro-

ma; **a man of some ~** un hombre de posición or categoría; **"no ~"** (*US AUT*) prohibido estacionarse.

standing order *n* (*Brit*: *at bank*) giro bancario; **~ orders** *npl* (*MIL*) reglamento *sg* general.

standing room *n* sitio para estar de pie.

standoffish [standôf'ish] *a* reservado, poco afable.

standpat [stand'pat] *a* (*US*) inmovilista.

standpipe [stand'pīp] *n* tubo vertical.

standpoint [stand'point] *n* punto de vista.

standstill [stand'stil] *n*: **at a ~** paralizado, en paro; **to come to a ~** pararse, quedar paralizado.

stank [stangk] *pt of* **stink**.

staple [stā'pəl] *n* (*for papers*) grapa; (*product*) producto or artículo de primera necesidad ♦ *a* (*crop, industry, food etc*) básico ♦ *vt* engrapar.

stapler [stā'plûr] *n* grapadora.

star [stâr] *n* estrella; (*celebrity*) estrella, astro ♦ *vi*: **to ~ in** ser la estrella or el astro de; **four-~ hotel** hotel *m* de cuatro estrellas; **4-~ petrol** gasolina extra.

star attraction *n* atracción *f* principal.

starboard [stâr'bûrd] *n* estribor *m*.

starch [stârch] *n* almidón *m*.

starchy [stâr'chē] *a* (*food*) feculento.

stardom [stâr'dəm] *n* estrellato.

stare [stär] *n* mirada fija ♦ *vi*: **to ~ at** mirar fijo.

starfish [stâr'fish] *n* estrella de mar.

stark [stârk] *a* (*bleak*) severo, escueto; (*simplicity, color*) austero; (*reality, poverty, truth*) absoluto, puro ♦ *ad*: **~ naked** en cueros, en pelotas.

starlet [stâr'lit] *n* (*CINEMA*) actriz *f* principiante.

starling [stâr'ling] *n* estornino.

starry [stâr'ē] *a* estrellado.

starry-eyed [stâr'ēid] *a* (*gullible, innocent*) inocentón/ona, ingenuo; (*idealistic*) idealista; (*from wonder*) asombrado; (*from love*) enamoradísimo.

star-studded [stâr'studid] *a*: **a ~ cast** un elenco estelar.

start [stârt] *n* (*beginning*) principio, comienzo; (*departure*) salida; (*sudden movement*) salto, sobresalto; (*advantage*) ventaja ♦ *vt* empezar, comenzar; (*cause*) causar; (*found*: *business, newspaper*) establecer, fundar; (*engine*) poner en marcha ♦ *vi* (*begin*) comenzar, empezar; (*with fright*) asustarse, sobresaltarse; (*train etc*) salir; **to give sb a ~** dar un susto a uno; **at the ~** al principio; **for a ~** en primer lugar; **to make an early ~** ponerse en camino temprano; **the thieves had 3 hours' ~** los ladrones llevaban 3 horas de ventaja; **to ~ a fire** provocar un incendio; **to ~ doing** or **to do sth** empezar a hacer algo; **to ~ (off) with** (*firstly*) para empezar; (*at the be-*

ginning) al principio.

start off *vi* empezar, comenzar; (*leave*) salir, ponerse en camino.

start over *vi* (*US*) volver a empezar.

start up *vi* comenzar; (*car*) arrancarse ♦ *vt* comenzar; (*car*) arrancar.

starter [stâr'tûr] *n* (*AUT*) arranque *m*; (*SPORT*: *official*) juez *m/f* de salida; (: *runner*) corredor(a) *m/f*; (*Brit CULIN*) entrada; **for ~s** en primer lugar.

starting price [stâr'ting prīs] *n* (*COMM*) precio inicial.

starting point [stâr'ting point] *n* punto de partida.

startle [stâr'təl] *vt* asustar, sobrecoger.

startling [stârt'ling] *a* alarmante.

starvation [stârvā'shən] *n* hambre *f*; (*MED*) inanición *f*.

starvation wages *npl* sueldo *sg* de hambre.

starve [stârv] *vi* pasar hambre; (*to death*) morir de hambre ♦ *vt* hacer pasar hambre; (*fig*) privar; **I'm starving** estoy muerto de hambre.

state [stāt] *n* estado; (*pomp*): **in ~** con mucha ceremonia ♦ *vt* (*say, declare*) afirmar; (*a case*) presentar, exponer; **~ of emergency** estado de excepción *or* emergencia; **~ of mind** estado de ánimo; **to lie in ~** (*corpse*) estar de cuerpo presente; **to be in a ~** estar agitado.

State Department *n* (*US*) Ministerio de Relaciones Exteriores.

state highway *n* (*US AUT*) ≈ carretera nacional.

stateless [stāt'lis] *a* desnacionalizado.

stately [stāt'lē] *a* majestuoso, imponente.

statement [stāt'mənt] *n* afirmación *f*; (*LAW*) declaración *f*; (*COMM*) estado; **official ~** comunicado *m* oficial; **~ of account, bank ~** estado de cuenta.

state-of-the-art [stāt'əvthēârt] *a* (*technology etc*) de punta.

state-owned [stāt'ōnd'] *a* estatal, del estado.

States [stāts] *npl*: **the ~** los Estados Unidos.

statesman [stāts'mən] *n* estadista *m*.

statesmanship [stāts'mənship] *n* habilidad *f* política, arte *m* de gobernar.

static [stat'ik] *n* (*RADIO*) parásitos *mpl* ♦ *a* estático.

static electricity *n* estática.

station [stā'shən] *n* (*gen*) estación *f*; (*place*) puesto, sitio; (*RADIO*) emisora; (*rank*) posición *f* social ♦ *vt* colocar, situar; (*MIL*) apostar; **action ~s!** ¡a los puestos de combate!; **to be ~ed in** (*MIL*) estar estacionado en.

stationary [stā'shənārē] *a* estacionario, fijo.

stationer [stā'shənûr] *n* papelero/a.

stationer's (shop) *n* (*Brit*) papelería.

stationery [stā'shənārē] *n* (*writing paper*) papel *m* de escribir; (*writing materials*)

artículos *mpl* de escritorio.

station master *n* (*RAIL*) jefe *m* de estación.

station wagon *n* (*US*) furgoneta.

statistic [stətis'tik] *n* estadística.

statistical [stətis'tikəl] *a* estadístico.

statistics [stətis'tiks] *n* (*science*) estadística.

statue [stach'ōō] *n* estatua.

statuette [stachōōet'] *n* figurilla.

stature [stach'ûr] *n* estatura; (*fig*) talla.

status [stā'təs] *n* condición *f*, estado; (*reputation*) reputación *f*, estatus *m*; **the ~ quo** el statu quo.

status line *n* (*COMPUT*) línea de situación *or* de estado.

status symbol *n* símbolo de prestigio.

statute [stach'ōōt] *n* estatuto, ley *f*.

statute book *n* código de leyes.

statutory [stach'ōōtôrē] *a* estatutario; **~ meeting** junta ordinaria.

staunch [stônch] *a* leal, incondicional ♦ *vt* (*flow, blood*) restañar.

stave [stāv] *vt*: **to ~ off** (*attack*) rechazar; (*threat*) evitar.

stay [stā] *n* (*period of time*) estancia; (*LAW*): **~ of execution** aplazamiento de una sentencia ♦ *vi* (*remain*) quedar(se); (*as guest*) hospedarse; **to ~ put** seguir en el mismo sitio; **to ~ the night/5 days** pasar la noche/estar 5 días.

stay behind *vi* quedar atrás.

stay in *vi* (*at home*) quedarse en casa.

stay on *vi* quedarse.

stay out *vi* (*of house*) no volver a casa; (*strikers*) no volver al trabajo.

stay up *vi* (*at night*) velar, no acostarse.

staying power [stā'ing pou'ûr] *n* resistencia, aguante *m*.

STD *n abbr* (*Brit*: = *subscriber trunk dialling*) servicio de conferencias automáticas; (= *sexually transmitted disease*) enfermedad *f* venérea.

stead [sted] *n*: **in sb's ~** en lugar de uno.

steadfast [sted'fast] *a* firme, resuelto.

steadily [sted'ilē] *ad* (*firmly*) firmemente; (*unceasingly*) sin parar; (*fixedly*) fijamente; (*walk*) normalmente; (*drive*) a velocidad constante.

steady [sted'ē] *a* (*fixed*) firme, fijo; (*regular*) regular; (*boyfriend etc*) formal, fijo; (*person, character*) sensato, juicioso ♦ *vt* (*hold*) mantener firme; (*stabilize*) estabilizar; (*nerves*) calmar; **to ~ o.s. on** *or* **against sth** afirmarse en algo.

steak [stāk] *n* (*gen*) filete *m*; (*beef*) bistec *m*.

steal [stēl], *pt* **stole**, *pp* **stolen** [stēl, stōl, stō'lən] *vt, vi* robar.

steal away, steal off *vi* marcharse furtivamente, escabullirse.

stealth [stelth] *n*: **by ~** a escondidas, sigilosamente.

stealthy [stel'thē] *a* cauteloso, sigiloso.

steam [stēm] *n* vapor *m*; (*mist*) vaho, humo ♦ *vt* (*CULIN*) cocer al vapor ♦ *vi* echar vapor; (*ship*): **to ~ along** avanzar, ir avanzando; **under one's own ~** (*fig*) por sus propios medios *or* propias fuerzas; **to run out of ~** (*fig: person*) quedar(se) agotado; **to let off ~** (*fig*) desahogarse.

steam up *vi* (*window*) empañarse; **to get ~ed up about sth** (*fig*) volverse loco por algo.

steam engine *n* máquina de vapor.

steamer [stē'mûr] *n* (buque *m* de) vapor *m*; (*CULIN*) vaporera.

steam iron *n* plancha de vapor.

steamroller [stēm'rōlûr] *n* apisonadora.

steamship [stēm'ship] *n* (buque *m* de) vapor *m*.

steamy [stē'mē] *a* (*room*) lleno de vapor; (*window*) empañado.

steel [stēl] *n* acero ♦ *a* de acero.

steel band *n* banda de percusión del Caribe.

steel industry *n* industria siderúrgica.

steel mill *n* fábrica de acero.

steelworks [stēl'wûrks] *n* acería.

steely [stē'lē] *a* (*determination*) inflexible; (*gaze*) duro; (*eyes*) penetrante; **~ grey** gris *m* metálico.

steelyard [stēl'yârd] *n* romana.

steep [stēp] *a* escarpado, abrupto; (*stair*) empinado; (*price*) exorbitante, excesivo ♦ *vt* empapar, remojar.

steeple [stē'pəl] *n* aguja, campanario.

steeplechase [stē'pəlchās] *n* carrera de obstáculos.

steeplejack [stē'pəljak] *n* reparador(a) *m/f* de chimeneas *or* de campanarios.

steer [stēr] *vt* (*car*) conducir (*Sp*), manejar (*LAm*); (*person*) dirigir ♦ *vi* conducir; **to ~ clear of sb/sth** (*fig*) esquivar a uno/ evadir algo.

steering [stēr'ing] *n* (*AUT*) dirección *f*.

steering committee *n* comisión *f* directiva.

steering wheel *n* volante *m*.

stellar [stel'ûr] *a* estelar.

stem [stem] *n* (*of plant*) tallo; (*of glass*) pie *m*; (*of pipe*) cañón *m* ♦ *vt* detener; (*blood*) restañar.

stem from *vt fus* ser consecuencia de.

stench [stench] *n* hedor *m*.

stencil [sten'səl] *n* (*typed*) cliché *m*, clisé *m*; (*lettering*) plantilla ♦ *vt* hacer un cliché de.

stenographer [stənåg'rəfûr] *n* (*US*) taquígrafo/a.

step [step] *n* paso; (*sound*) paso, pisada; (*stair*) peldaño, escalón *m* ♦ *vi*: **to ~ forward** dar un paso adelante; **~ by ~** paso a paso; (*fig*) poco a poco; **to keep in ~ (with)** llevar el paso de; (*fig*) llevar el paso de, estar de acuerdo con; **to be in/out of ~ with** estar acorde con/estar en disonancia con; **to take ~s to solve a problem** tomar medidas para resolver un problema.

step down *vi* (*fig*) retirarse.

step in *vi* entrar; (*fig*) intervenir.

step off *vt fus* bajar de.

step on *vt fus* pisar.

step over *vt fus* pasar por encima de.

step up *vt* (*increase*) aumentar.

stepbrother [step'bruthûr] *n* hermanastro.

stepdaughter [step'dôtûr] *n* hijastra.

stepfather [step'fâthûr] *n* padrastro.

stepladder [step'ladûr] *n* escalera doble *or* de tijera.

stepmother [step'muthûr] *n* madrastra.

stepping stone [step'ingstōn] *n* pasadera.

stepsister [step'sistûr] *n* hermanastra.

stepson [step'sun] *n* hijastro.

stereo [stär'ēō] *n* estéreo ♦ *a* (*also*: **~phonic**) estéreo, estereofónico; **in ~** en estéreo.

stereotype [stär'ēətīp] *n* estereotipo ♦ *vt* estereotipar.

sterile [stär'əl] *a* estéril.

sterilization [stärələzə'shən] *n* esterilización *f*.

sterilize [stär'əlīz] *vt* esterilizar.

sterling [stûr'ling] *a* (*silver*) de ley ♦ *n* (*ECON*) (libras *fpl*) esterlinas *fpl*; **a pound ~** una libra esterlina; **he is of ~ character** tiene un carácter excelente.

stern [stûrn] *a* severo, austero ♦ *n* (*NAUT*) popa.

sternum [stûr'nəm] *n* esternón *m*.

steroid [stär'oid] *n* esteroide *m*.

stethoscope [steth'əskōp] *n* estetoscopio.

stew [stōō] *n* cocido, estofado, guisado (*LAm*) ♦ *vt*, *vi* estofar, guisar; (*fruit*) cocer; **~ed fruit** compota de fruta.

steward [stōō'ûrd] *n* (*Brit: gen*) camarero; (*shop ~*) enlace *m/f* sindical.

stewardess [stōō'ûrdis] *n* azafata.

stewing steak [stōō'ing stāk] *n* (*Brit*) = **stew meat**.

stew meat *n* (*US*) carne *f* de vaca.

stewpan [stōō'pan] *n* cazuela.

St. Ex. *abbr* = **stock exchange**.

stg *abbr* (= *sterling*) ester.

stick [stik] *n* palo; (*as weapon*) porra; (*walking ~*) bastón *m* ♦ *vb* (*pt, pp* **stuck** [stuk]) *vt* (*glue*) pegar; (*col: put*) meter; (: *tolerate*) aguantar, soportar ♦ *vi* pegarse; (*come to a stop*) quedarse parado; (*get jammed: door, lift*) atascarse; **to ~ to** (*word, principles*) atenerse a, ser fiel a; (*promise*) cumplir; **it stuck in my mind** se me quedó grabado; **to ~ sth into** clavar *or* hincar algo en.

stick around *vi* (*col*) quedarse.

stick out *vi* sobresalir ♦ *vt*: **to ~ it out** (*col*) aguantar.

stick up *vi* sobresalir.

stick up for *vt fus* defender.

sticker [stik'ûr] n (*label*) etiqueta engomada; (*with slogan*) pegatina.

sticking plaster [stik'ing plas'tûr] n (*Brit*) esparadrapo.

stickler [stik'lûr] n: **to be a ~ for** insistir mucho en.

stick-up [stik'up] n asalto, atraco.

sticky [stik'ē] a pegajoso; (*label*) engomado; (*fig*) difícil.

stiff [stif] a rígido, tieso; (*hard*) duro; (*difficult*) difícil; (*person*) inflexible; (*price*) exorbitante; **to have a ~ neck/ back** tener tortícolis/dolor de espalda; **the door's ~** la puerta está atrancada.

stiffen [stif'ən] vt hacer más rígido; (*limb*) entumecer ♦ vi endurecerse; (*grow stronger*) fortalecerse.

stiffness [stif'nis] n rigidez f, tiesura.

stifle [stī'fəl] vt ahogar, sofocar.

stifling [stīf'ling] a (*heat*) sofocante, bochornoso.

stigma, pl (*BOT, MED, REL*) ~**ta**, (*fig*) ~**s** [stig'mə, stigmâ'tə] n estigma m.

stile [stīl] n escalera (*para pasar una cerca*).

stiletto [stilet'ō] n (*Brit: also: ~ heel*) tacón m de aguja.

still [stil] a inmóvil, quieto; (*orange juice etc*) sin gas ♦ ad (*up to this time*) todavía; (*even*) aún; (*nonetheless*) sin embargo, aun así ♦ n (*CINEMA*) foto f fija; **keep ~!** ¡estate quieto!, ¡no te muevas!; **he ~ hasn't arrived** todavía no ha llegado.

stillborn [stil'bôrn] a nacido muerto.

still life n naturaleza muerta.

stilt [stilt] n zanco; (*pile*) pilar m, soporte m.

stilted [stil'tid] a afectado.

stimulant [stim'yələnt] n estimulante m.

stimulate [stim'yəlāt] vt estimular.

stimulating [stim'yəlāting] a estimulante.

stimulation [stimyəlā'shən] n estímulo.

stimulus, pl **-li** [stim'yələs, -lī] n estímulo, incentivo.

sting [sting] n (*wound*) picadura; (*pain*) escozor m, picazón m; (*col: confidence trick*) timo ♦ vb (*pt, pp* **stung** [stung]) vt picar ♦ vi picar, escocer; **my eyes are ~ing** los ojos me pican or escuecen.

stingy [stin'jē] a tacaño.

stink [stingk] n hedor m, tufo ♦ vi (*pt* **stank**, *pp* **stunk** [stangk, stungk]) heder, apestar.

stinking [sting'king] a hediondo, fétido; (*fig: col*) horrible.

stint [stint] n tarea, destajo; **to do one's ~ at sth** hacer su parte (de algo), hacer lo que corresponde (de algo) ♦ vi: **to ~ on** escatimar.

stipend [stī'pend] n salario, remuneración f.

stipulate [stip'yəlāt] vt estipular.

stipulation [stipyəlā'shən] n estipulación f.

stir [stûr] n (*fig: agitation*) conmoción f ♦ vt (*tea etc*) remover; (*fire*) atizar; (*move*) agitar; (*fig: emotions*) conmover ♦ vi mo-

verse; **to give sth a ~** remover algo; **to cause a ~** causar conmoción or sensación.

stir up vt excitar; (*trouble*) fomentar.

stirrup [stûr'əp] n estribo.

stitch [stich] n (*SEWING*) puntada; (*KNITTING*) punto; (*MED*) punto (de sutura); (*pain*) punzada ♦ vt coser; (*MED*) suturar.

stoat [stōt] n armiño.

stock [stâk] n (*COMM: reserves*) existencias fpl, stock m; (*: selection*) surtido; (*AGR*) ganado, ganadería; (*CULIN*) caldo; (*fig: lineage*) estirpe f, cepa; (*FINANCE*) capital m; (*: shares*) acciones fpl; (*RAIL: rolling ~*) material m rodante ♦ a (*COMM: goods, size*) normal, de serie; (*fig: reply etc*) clásico, trillado; (*: greeting*) acostumbrado ♦ vt (*have in ~*) tener existencias de; (*supply*) proveer, abastecer; **in ~** en existencia or almacén; **to have sth in ~** tener existencias de algo; **out of ~** agotado; **to take ~ of** (*fig*) asesorar, examinar; **~s** npl (*HISTORY: punishment*) cepo sg; **~s and shares** acciones y valores; **government ~** papel m del Estado.

stock up with vt fus abastecerse de.

stockbroker [stâk'brōkûr] n agente m/f or corredor(a) m/f de bolsa.

stock control n (*COMM*) control m de existencias.

stock cube n (*Brit*) pastilla or cubito de caldo.

stock exchange n bolsa.

stockholder [stâk'hōldûr] n (*US*) accionista m/f.

Stockholm [stâk'hōm] n Estocolmo.

stocking [stâk'ing] n media.

stock-in-trade [stâk'intrād'] n (*tools etc*) herramientas fpl; (*stock*) existencia de mercancías; (*fig*): **it's his ~** es su especialidad.

stockist [stâk'ist] n (*Brit*) distribuidor(a) m/f.

stock market n bolsa (de valores).

stock phrase n vieja frase f.

stockpile [stâk'pīl] n reserva ♦ vt acumular, almacenar.

stockroom [stâk'rōōm] n almacén m, depósito.

stocktaking [stâk'tāking] n (*Brit COMM*) inventario, balance m.

stocky [stâk'ē] a (*strong*) robusto; (*short*) achaparrado.

stodgy [stâj'ē] a indigesto, pesado.

stoical [stō'ikəl] a estoico.

stoke [stōk] vt atizar.

stole [stōl] pt of **steal** ♦ n estola.

stolen [stō'lən] pp of **steal**.

stolid [stâl'id] a (*person*) imperturbable, impasible.

stomach [stum'ək] n (*ANAT*) estómago; (*belly*) vientre m ♦ vt tragar, aguantar.

stomachache [stum'əkāk] n dolor m de

estómago.

stomach pump n bomba gástrica.

stomach ulcer n úlcera de estómago.

stomp [ståmp] vi: **to ~ in/out** entrar/salir con pasos ruidosos.

stone [stōn] n piedra; (in fruit) hueso; (Brit: weight) = 6.348kg; 14 pounds ♦ a de piedra ♦ vt apedrear; **within a ~'s throw of the station** a tiro de piedra or a dos pasos de la estación.

Stone Age n: **the ~** la Edad de Piedra.

stone-cold [stōn'kōld'] a helado.

stoned [stōnd] a (col: drunk) trompa, borracho, colocado.

stone-deaf [stōn'def'] a sordo como una tapia.

stonemason [stōn'māsən] n albañil m.

stonework [stōn'wûrk] n (art) cantería.

stony [stō'nē] a pedregoso; (glance) glacial.

stood [stŏŏd] pt, pp of **stand**.

stool [stōōl] n taburete m.

stool pigeon n (US: col: informer) delator(a) m/f, denunciador(a) m/f.

stoop [stōōp] vi ser cargado de espaldas; (bend) inclinarse, encorvarse; **to ~ to (doing) sth** rebajarse a (hacer) algo.

stop [ståp] n parada, alto; (in punctuation) punto ♦ vt parar, detener; (break off) suspender; (block) tapar, cerrar; (prevent) impedir; (tooth) empastar; (also: **put a ~ to**) poner término a ♦ vi pararse, detenerse; (end) acabarse; **to ~ doing sth** dejar de hacer algo; **to ~ sb (from) doing sth** impedir a uno hacer algo; **to ~ dead** pararse en seco; **~ it!** ¡basta ya!, ¡párate! (LAm).

stop by vi pasar por.

stop off vi interrumpir el viaje.

stop up vt (hole) tapar.

stopcock [ståp'kåk] n llave f de paso.

stopgap [ståp'gap] n interino; (person) sustituto/a; (measure) medida provisoria ♦ cpd (situation) provisional.

stoplights [ståp'līts] npl (AUT) luces fpl de detención.

stopover [ståp'ōvûr] n parada intermedia; (AVIAT) escala.

stoppage [ståp'ij] n (strike) paro; (temporary stop) interrupción f; (of pay) suspensión f; (blockage) obstrucción f.

stopper [ståp'ûr] n tapón m.

stop press n noticias fpl de última hora.

stopwatch [ståp'wåch] n cronómetro.

storage [stôr'ij] n almacenaje m; (COMPUT) almacenamiento.

storage capacity n espacio de almacenaje.

storage heater n calentador m, acumulador m.

store [stôr] n (stock) provisión f; (depot; Brit: large shop) almacén m; (US) tienda; (reserve) reserva, repuesto ♦ vt (gen, COMPUT) almacenar; (keep) guardar; (in filing

system) archivar; **~s** npl víveres mpl; **who knows what is in ~ for us** quién sabe lo que nos espera; **to set great/little ~ by sth** dar mucha/poca importancia a algo, valorar mucho/poco algo.

store up vt acumular.

storehouse [stôr'hous] n almacén m, depósito.

storekeeper [stôr'kēpûr] n tendero/a.

storeroom [stôr'rōōm] n despensa.

storey [stôr'ē] n (Brit) piso.

stork [stôrk] n cigüeña.

storm [stôrm] n tormenta; (wind) vendaval m; (fig) tempestad f ♦ vi (fig) rabiar ♦ vt tomar por asalto, asaltar; **to take a town by ~** (MIL) tomar una ciudad por asalto.

storm cloud n nubarrón m.

storm door n contrapuerta.

stormy [stôr'mē] a tempestuoso.

story [stôr'ē] n historia; (PRESS) artículo; (joke) cuento, chiste m; (plot) argumento; (lie) cuento; (US: floor) piso.

storybook [stôr'ēbŏŏk] n libro de cuentos.

storyteller [stôr'ētelûr] n cuentista m/f.

stout [stout] a (strong) sólido; (fat) gordo, corpulento ♦ n cerveza negra.

stove [stōv] n (for cooking) cocina; (for heating) estufa; **gas/electric ~** cocina de gas/eléctrica.

stow [stō] vt meter, poner; (NAUT) estibar.

stowaway [stō'əwā] n polizón/ona m/f.

straddle [strad'əl] vt montar a horcajadas.

straggle [strag'əl] vi (wander) vagar en desorden; (lag behind) rezagarse.

straggler [strag'lûr] n rezagado/a.

straggling [strag'ling], **straggly** [strag'lē] a (hair) desordenado.

straight [strāt] a (direct) recto, derecho; (plain, uncomplicated) sencillo; (frank) franco, directo; (in order) en orden; (continuous) continuo; (THEATER: part, play) serio; (person: conventional) recto, convencional; (: heterosexual) heterosexual; (drink) puro ♦ ad derecho, directamente; (drink) sin mezcla; **to put** or **get sth ~** dejar algo en claro; **10 ~ wins** 10 victorias seguidas; **to be (all) ~** (tidy) estar en orden; (clarified) estar claro; **I went ~ home** (me) fui directamente a casa; **~ away** (at once) en seguida.

straighten [strā'tən] vt (also: **~ out**) enderezar, poner derecho; **to ~ things out** poner las cosas en orden.

straight-faced [strāt'fāst] a serio ♦ ad sin mostrar emoción, impávido.

straightforward [strātfôr'wûrd] a (simple) sencillo; (honest) honrado, franco.

strain [strān] n (gen) tensión f; (TECH) esfuerzo; (MED) torcedura; (breed) raza; (lineage) linaje m; (of virus) variedad f ♦ vt (back etc) torcerse; (tire) cansar; (stretch) estirar; (filter) filtrar; (meaning) tergiversar ♦ vi esforzarse; **~s** npl (MUS) son *m*; **she's under a lot of** ~ está bajo mucha tensión.

strained [strānd] *a* (*muscle*) torcido; (*laugh*) forzado; (*relations*) tenso.

strainer [strā'nûr] *n* colador *m*.

strait [strāt] *n* (GEO) estrecho; **to be in dire** ~**s** (*fig*) estar en un gran aprieto.

straitjacket [strāt'jakit] *n* camisa de fuerza.

strait-laced [strāt'lāst] *a* mojigato, gazmoño.

strand [strand] *n* (*of thread*) hebra; (*of hair*) trenza; (*of rope*) ramal *m*.

stranded [stran'did] *a* (*person: without money*) desamparado; (: *without transport*) colgado.

strange [strānj] *a* (*not known*) desconocido; (*odd*) extraño, raro.

stranger [strān'jûr] *n* desconocido/a; (*from another area*) forastero/a; **I'm a** ~ **here** no soy de aquí.

strangle [strang'gəl] *vt* estrangular.

stranglehold [strang'gəlhōld] *n* (*fig*) dominio completo.

strangulation [stranggyəlā'shən] *n* estrangulación *f*.

strap [strap] *n* correa; (*of slip, dress*) tirante *m* ♦ *vt* atar con correa.

straphanging [strap'hanging] *n* viajar *m* de pie *or* parado (*LAm*).

strapless [strap'lis] *a* (*bra, dress*) sin tirantes.

strapping [strap'ing] *a* robusto, fornido.

Strasbourg [stras'bûrg] *n* Estrasburgo.

strata [strā'tə] *npl of* **stratum**.

stratagem [strat'əjəm] *n* estratagema.

strategic [strətē'jik] *a* estratégico.

strategy [strat'ijē] *n* estrategia.

stratum, *pl* **strata** [strā'təm, strā'tə] *n* estrato.

straw [strô] *n* paja; (*drinking* ~) caña, pajita; **that's the last** ~! ¡eso es el colmo!

strawberry [strô'bärē] *n* fresa, frutilla (*LAm*).

stray [strā] *a* (*animal*) extraviado; (*bullet*) perdido; (*scattered*) disperso ♦ *vi* extraviarse, perderse; (*wander: walker*) vagar, ir sin rumbo fijo; (: *speaker*) desvariar.

streak [strēk] *n* raya; (*fig: of madness etc*) vena ♦ *vt* rayar ♦ *vi*: **to** ~ **past** pasar como un rayo; **to have** ~**s in one's hair** tener vetas en el pelo; **a winning/losing** ~ una racha de buena/mala suerte.

streaky [strē'kē] *a* rayado.

stream [strēm] *n* riachuelo, arroyo; (*jet*) chorro; (*flow*) corriente *f*; (*of people*) oleada ♦ *vt* (*Brit SCOL*) dividir en grupos por habilidad ♦ *vi* correr, fluir; **to** ~ **in/out** (*people*) entrar/salir en tropel; **against the** ~ a contracorriente.

streamer [strē'mûr] *n* serpentina.

streamline [strēm'līn] *vt* aerodinamizar; (*fig*) racionalizar.

streamlined [strēm'līnd] *a* aerodinámico.

street [strēt] *n* calle *f* ♦ *a* callejero; **the back** ~**s** las callejuelas; **to walk the** ~**s** (*homeless*) estar sin vivienda; (*as prostitute*) ser de la vida.

streetcar [strēt'kâr] *n* (US) tranvía *m*.

streetlight [strēt'līt] *n* farol *m*.

street lighting *n* alumbrado público.

street market *n* mercado callejero.

street plan *n* plano callejero.

streetsweeper [strēt'swēp'ûr] *n* (US) barrendero/a.

streetwise [strēt'wīz] *a* (*col*) pícaro.

strength [strengkth] *n* fuerza; (*of girder, knot etc*) resistencia; (*of chemical solution*) potencia, proporción *f*; (*of wine*) graduación *f* de alcohol; **on the** ~ **of** a base de, en base a; **to be at full/below** ~ tener/no tener todo su complemento.

strengthen [strengk'thən] *vt* fortalecer, reforzar.

strenuous [stren'yōōəs] *a* (*tough*) arduo; (*energetic*) enérgico; (*opposition*) firme, tenaz; (*efforts*) intensivo.

stress [stres] *n* (*force, pressure*) presión *f*; (*mental strain*) estrés *m*; (*accent, emphasis*) énfasis *m*, acento; (LING, POETRY) acento; (TECH) tensión *f*, carga ♦ *vt* subrayar, recalcar; **to be under** ~ sufrir una tensión nerviosa; **to lay great** ~ **on sth** hacer hincapié en algo.

stressful [stres'fəl] *a* (*job*) que produce tensión nerviosa.

stretch [strech] *n* (*of sand etc*) trecho; (*of road*) tramo; (*of time*) período, tiempo ♦ *vi* estirarse; (*extend*): **to** ~ **to** *or* **as far as** extenderse hasta; (*be enough: money, food*): **to** ~ **to** alcanzar para, dar de sí para ♦ *vt* extender, estirar; (*make demands of*) exigir el máximo esfuerzo a; **to** ~ **one's legs** estirar las piernas.

stretch out *vi* tenderse ♦ *vt* (*arm etc*) extender; (*spread*) estirar.

stretcher [strech'ûr] *n* camilla.

stretcher-bearer [strech'ûrbärûr] *n* camillero/a.

stretch marks *npl* estrillas *fpl*.

strewn [strōōn] *a*: ~ **with** cubierto *or* sembrado de.

stricken [strik'ən] *a* (*person*) herido; (*city, industry etc*) condenado; ~ **with** (*arthritis, disease*) afligido por; **grief-**~ destrozado por el dolor.

strict [strikt] *a* (*order, rule etc*) estricto; (*discipline, ban*) severo; **in** ~ **confidence** en la más absoluta confianza.

strictly [strikt'lē] *ad* estrictamente; (*totally*) terminantemente; ~ **confidential** estrictamente confidencial; ~ **speaking** en (el) sentido estricto (de la palabra); ~ **between ourselves** ... entre nosotros ... .

stridden [strid'ən] *pp of* **stride**.

stride [strīd] *n* zancada, tranco ♦ *vi* (*pt* **strode**, *pp* **stridden** [strōd, strid'ən]) dar zancadas, andar a trancos; **to take in one's** ~ (*fig: changes etc*) tomar con calma.

strident [strīd'ənt] *a* estridente; (*color*) chillón/ona.

strife [strīf] *n* lucha.

strike [strīk] *n* huelga; (*of oil etc*) descubrimiento; (*attack*) ataque *m*; (*SPORT*) golpe *m* ♦ *vb* (*pt, pp* **struck** [struk]) *vt* golpear, pegar; (*oil etc*) descubrir; (*obstacle*) topar con; (*produce: coin, medal*) acuñar; (: *agreement, deal*) concertar ♦ *vi* declarar la huelga; (*attack: MIL etc*) atacar; (*clock*) dar la hora; **on** ~ (*workers*) en huelga; **to call a** ~ declarar una huelga; **to go on** *or* **come out on** ~ ponerse *or* declararse en huelga; **to** ~ **a match** encender un fósforo; **to** ~ **a balance** (*fig*) encontrar un equilibrio; **to** ~ **a bargain** cerrar un trato; **the clock struck 9 o'clock** el reloj dio las nueve.

strike back *vi* (*MIL*) contraatacar; (*fig*) devolver el golpe.

strike down *vt* derribar.

strike off *vt* (*from list*) tachar; (*doctor etc*) suspender.

strike out *vt* borrar, tachar.

strike up *vt* (*MUS*) empezar a tocar; (*conversation*) entablar; (*friendship*) trabar.

strikebreaker [strīk'brākûr] *n* rompehuelgas *m/f inv*.

striker [strī'kûr] *n* huelgista *m/f*; (*SPORT*) delantero.

striking [strī'king] *a* (*color*) llamativo; (*obvious*) notorio.

string [string] *n* (*gen*) cuerda; (*row*) hilera; (*COMPUT*) cadena ♦ *vt* (*pt, pp* **strung** [strung]): **to** ~ **together** ensartar; **to** ~ **out** extenderse; **to** ~ **sb along** (*fig*) jugar con uno; **the** ~**s** *npl* (*MUS*) los instrumentos de cuerda; **to pull** ~**s** (*fig*) mover palancas; **to get a job by pulling** ~**s** conseguir un trabajo por enchufe; **with no** ~**s attached** (*fig*) sin compromiso.

string bean *n* judía verde, habichuela.

string(ed) instrument [string(d)'-in'strəmənt] *n* (*MUS*) instrumento de cuerda.

stringent [strin'jənt] *a* riguroso, severo.

string quartet *n* cuarteto de cuerdas.

strip [strip] *n* tira; (*of land*) franja; (*of metal*) cinta, lámina ♦ *vt* desnudar; (*also:* ~ **down**: *machine*) desmontar ♦ *vi* desnudarse.

stripe [strīp] *n* raya; (*MIL*) galón *m*; **white with green** ~**s** blanco con rayas verdes.

striped [strīpt] *a* a rayas, rayado.

stripper [strip'ûr] *n* artista *m/f* de striptease.

striptease [strip'tēz] *n* striptease *m*.

strive, *pt* **strove**, *pp* **striven** [strīv, strōv, striv'ən] *vi*: **to** ~ **to do sth** esforzarse *or* luchar por hacer algo.

strode [strōd] *pt of* **stride**.

stroke [strōk] *n* (*blow*) golpe *m*; (*MED*) apoplejía; (*caress*) caricia; (*of pen*) trazo; (*SWIMMING: style*) estilo; (*of piston*) carrera ♦ *vt* acariciar; **at a** ~ de golpe; **a** ~ **of luck** un golpe de suerte; **two-**~ **engine** motor *m* de dos tiempos.

stroll [strōl] *n* paseo, vuelta ♦ *vi* dar un paseo *or* una vuelta; **to go for a** ~, **have** *or* **take a** ~ dar un paseo.

stroller [strō'lûr] *n* (*US: pushchair*) cochecito.

strong [strông] *a* fuerte; (*bleach, acid*) concentrado ♦ *ad*: **to be going** ~ (*company*) marchar bien; (*person*) conservarse bien; **they are 50** ~ son 50.

strong-arm [strông'ârm] *a* (*tactics, methods*) represivo.

strongbox [strông'bâks] *n* caja fuerte.

strong drink *n* bebida cargada *or* fuerte.

stronghold [strông'hōld] *n* fortaleza; (*fig*) baluarte *m*.

strong language *n* lenguaje *m* fuerte.

strongly [strông'lē] *ad* fuertemente, con fuerza; (*believe*) firmemente; **to feel** ~ **about sth** tener una opinión decidida de algo.

strongman [strông'man] *n* forzudo; (*fig*) hombre *m* robusto.

strongroom [strông'rōōm] *n* cámara acorazada.

strove [strōv] *pt of* **strive**.

struck [struk] *pt, pp of* **strike**.

structural [struk'chûrəl] *a* estructural.

structure [struk'chûr] *n* estructura; (*building*) construcción *f*.

struggle [strug'əl] *n* lucha ♦ *vi* luchar; **to** ~ **to do sth** esforzarse por hacer algo.

strum [strum] *vt* (*guitar*) rasguear.

strung [strung] *pt, pp of* **string**.

strut [strut] *n* puntal *m* ♦ *vi* pavonearse.

strychnine [strik'nīn] *n* estricnina.

stub [stub] *n* (*of ticket etc*) talón *m*; (*of cigarette*) colilla ♦ *vt*: **to** ~ **one's toe on sth** dar con el dedo del pie contra algo.

stub out *vt* (*cigarette*) apagar.

stubble [stub'əl] *n* rastrojo; (*on chin*) barba (incipiente).

stubborn [stub'ûrn] *a* terco, testarudo.

stucco [stuk'ō] *n* estuco.

stuck [stuk] *pt, pp of* **stick** ♦ *a* (*jammed*) atascado.

stuck-up [stuk'up'] *a* engreído, presumido.

stud [stud] *n* (*shirt* ~) corchete *m*; (*of boot*) taco; (*of horses*) caballeriza; (*also:* ~ **horse**) caballo semental ♦ *vt* (*fig*): ~**ded with** salpicado de.

student [stōō'dənt] *n* estudiante *m/f*; (*US: of school*) alumno/a ♦ *a* estudiantil; **a law/medical** ~ un(a) estudiante de derecho/medicina.

student driver *n* (*US AUT*) aprendiz(a) *m/f*.

studio [stoo'dēō] *n* estudio; (*artist's*) taller *m*.

studio apartment *n* estudio.

studious [stoo'dēəs] *a* estudioso; (*studied*) calculado.

studiously [stoo'dēəslē] *ad* (*carefully*) con esmero.

study [stud'ē] *n* estudio ♦ *vt* estudiar; (*examine*) examinar, investigar ♦ *vi* estudiar; **to make a ~ of sth** realizar una investigación de algo; **to ~ for an exam** preparar un examen.

stuff [stuf] *n* materia; (*cloth*) tela; (*substance*) material *m*, sustancia; (*things, belongings*) cosas *fpl* ♦ *vt* llenar; (*CULIN*) rellenar; (*animal*: *for exhibition*) disecar; **my nose is ~ed up** tengo la nariz tapada; **~ed toy** juguete *m or* muñeco de trapo.

stuffing [stuf'ing] *n* relleno.

stuffy [stuf'ē] *a* (*room*) mal ventilado; (*person*) de miras estrechas.

stumble [stum'bəl] *vi* tropezar, dar un traspié.

stumble across *vt fus* (*fig*) tropezar con.

stumbling block [stum'bling blâk] *n* tropiezo, obstáculo.

stump [stump] *n* (*of tree*) tocón *m*; (*of limb*) muñón *m* ♦ *vt*: **to be ~ed** quedar perplejo; **to be ~ed for an answer** no tener respuesta.

stun [stun] *vt* dejar sin sentido.

stung [stung] *pt, pp of* **sting**.

stunk [stungk] *pp of* **stink**.

stunning [stun'ing] *a* (*fig*) pasmoso.

stunt [stunt] *n* (*AVIAT*) vuelo acrobático; (*publicity ~*) truco publicitario.

stunted [stun'tid] *a* enano, achaparrado.

stuntman [stunt'mən] *n* especialista *m*.

stupefaction [stoopəfak'shən] *n* estupefacción *f*.

stupefy [stoo'pəfī] *vt* dejar estupefacto.

stupendous [stoopen'dəs] *a* estupendo, asombroso.

stupid [stoo'pid] *a* estúpido, tonto.

stupidity [stoopid'itē] *n* estupidez *f*.

stupor [stoo'pûr] *n* estupor *m*.

sturdy [stûr'dē] *a* robusto, fuerte.

stutter [stut'ûr] *n* tartamudeo ♦ *vi* tartamudear.

sty [stī] *n* (*for pigs*) pocilga.

stye [stī] *n* (*MED*) orzuelo.

style [stīl] *n* estilo; (*fashion*) moda; (*of dress etc*) hechura; (*hair ~*) corte *m*; **in the latest ~** en el último modelo.

stylish [stī'lish] *a* elegante, a la moda.

stylist [stī'list] *n* (*hair ~*) peluquero/a.

stylus [stī'ləs] *pl* **styli** *or* **styluses** [stī'ləs, -lē, ləsiz] *n* (*of record player*) aguja.

suave [swâv] *a* cortés, fino.

sub [sub] *n abbr* = **submarine, subscription**.

sub... [sub] *pref* sub....

subcommittee [sub'kəmitē] *n* subcomisión *f*.

subconscious [subkân'chəs] *a* subconsciente ♦ *n* subconsciente *m*.

subcontinent [subkân'tənənt] *n*: **the Indian ~** el subcontinente (de la India).

subcontract *n* [subkân'trakt] subcontrato ♦ *vt* [subkəntrakt'] subcontratar.

subcontractor [subkân'traktûr] *n* subcontratista *m/f*.

subdivide [subdivīd'] *vt* subdividir.

subdue [səbdoo'] *vt* sojuzgar; (*passions*) dominar.

subdued [səbdood'] *a* (*light*) tenue; (*person*) sumiso, manso.

subject *n* [sub'jikt] súbdito; (*SCOL*) tema *m*, materia ♦ *vt* [səbjekt']: **to ~ sb to sth** someter a uno a algo ♦ *a* [sub'jikt]: **to be ~ to** (*law*) estar sujeto a; **~ to confirmation in writing** sujeto a confirmación por escrito; **to change the ~** cambiar de tema.

subjective [səbjek'tiv] *a* subjetivo.

subject matter *n* materia; (*content*) contenido.

sub judice [sub joo'disē] *a* (*LAW*) pendiente de resolución.

subjugate [sub'jəgāt] *vt* subyugar, sojuzgar.

subjunctive [səbjungk'tiv] *a, n* subjuntivo.

sublease [sublēs'] *n* (*US*) subarriendo ♦ *vt* subarrendar.

sublet [sublet'] *vt, vi* subarrendar, realquilar.

sublime [səblīm'] *a* sublime.

subliminal [sublim'ənəl] *a* subliminal.

submachine gun [subməshēn' gun] *n* metralleta.

submarine [sub'mərēn] *n* submarino.

submerge [səbmûrj'] *vt* sumergir; (*flood*) inundar ♦ *vi* sumergirse.

submersion [səbmûr'zhən] *n* submersión *f*.

submission [səbmish'ən] *n* sumisión *f*; (*to committee etc*) ponencia.

submissive [səbmis'iv] *a* sumiso.

submit [səbmit'] *vt* someter; (*proposal, claim*) presentar ♦ *vi* someterse; **I ~ that ...** me permito sugerir que ....

subnormal [subnôr'məl] *a* subnormal.

subordinate [səbôr'dənit] *a, n* subordinado/a *m/f*.

subpoena [səpē'nə] (*LAW*) *n* citación *f* ♦ *vt* citar.

subroutine [subrootēn'] *n* (*COMPUT*) subrutina.

subscribe [səbskrīb'] *vi* suscribir; **to ~ to** (*opinion, fund*) suscribir, aprobar; (*newspaper*) suscribirse a.

subscribed capital [səbskrībd' kap'itəl] *n* capital *m* suscrito.

subscriber [səbskrīb'ûr] *n* (*to periodical, telephone*) abonado/a.

subscript [sub'skript] *n* (*TYP*) subíndice *m*.

subscription [səbskrip'shən] *n* (*to club*) abono; (*to magazine*) suscripción *f*; **to take out a ~ to** suscribir a, abonarse a.

subsequent [sub'səkwənt] *a* subsiguiente, posterior; ~ **to** posterior a.
subsequently [sub'səkwəntlē] *ad* posteriormente, más tarde.
subservient [səbsûr'vēənt] *a*: ~ **(to)** servil (a).
subside [səbsīd'] *vi* hundirse; (*flood*) bajar; (*wind*) amainar.
subsidence [səbsīd'əns] *n* hundimiento; (*in road*) socavón *m*.
subsidiary [səbsid'ēārē] *n* sucursal *f*, filial *f* ♦ *a* (*UNIV: subject*) secundario.
subsidize [sub'sidīz] *vt* subvencionar.
subsidy [sub'sidē] *n* subvención *f*.
subsist [səbsist'] *vi*: **to** ~ **on sth** sustentarse con algo.
subsistence [səbsis'təns] *n* subsistencia.
subsistence allowance *n* dietas *fpl*.
subsistence level *n* nivel *m* de subsistencia.
subsistence wage *n* sueldo de subsistencia.
substance [sub'stəns] *n* sustancia; (*fig*) esencia; **to lack** ~ (*argument*) ser poco convincente; (*accusation*) no tener fundamento; (*film, book*) tener poca profundidad.
substandard [substan'dûrd] *a* (*goods*) inferior; (*housing*) deficiente.
substantial [səbstan'chəl] *a* sustancial, sustancioso; (*fig*) importante.
substantially [səbstan'chəlē] *ad* sustancialmente; ~ **bigger** bastante más grande.
substantiate [səbstan'chēāt] *vt* comprobar.
substitute [sub'stitōōt] *n* (*person*) suplente *m/f*; (*thing*) sustituto ♦ *vt*: **to** ~ **A for B** sustituir B por A, reemplazar A por B.
substitute teacher *n* (*US*) profesor(a) *m/f* suplente.
substitution [substitōō'shən] *n* sustitución *f*.
subterfuge [sub'tûrfyōōj] *n* subterfugio.
subterranean [subtərā'nēən] *a* subterráneo.
subtitle [sub'tītəl] *n* subtítulo.
subtle [sut'əl] *a* sutil.
subtlety [sut'əltē] *n* sutileza.
subtly [sut'lē] *ad* sutilmente.
subtotal [subtō'təl] *n* subtotal *m*.
subtract [səbtrakt'] *vt* restar; sustraer.
subtraction [səbtrak'shən] *n* resta; sustracción *f*.
suburb [sub'ûrb] *n* suburbio; **the** ~**s** las afueras (de la ciudad).
suburban [səbûr'bən] *a* suburbano; (*train etc*) de cercanías.
suburbia [səbûr'bēə] *n* barrios *mpl* residenciales *or* satélites.
subversion [səbvûr'zhən] *n* subversión *f*.
subversive [səbvûr'siv] *a* subversivo.
subway [sub'wā] *n* (*US*) metro; (*Brit*) paso subterráneo *or* inferior.
subway station *n* (*US*) estación *f* de metro.
sub-zero [sub'zē'rō] *a*: ~ **temperatures**

temperaturas *fpl* por debajo del cero.
succeed [səksēd'] *vi* (*person*) tener éxito; (*plan*) salir bien ♦ *vt* suceder a; **to** ~ **in doing** lograr hacer.
succeeding [səksē'ding] *a* (*following*) sucesivo; ~ **generations** generaciones *fpl* futuras.
success [səkses'] *n* éxito; (*gain*) triunfo.
successful [səkses'fəl] *a* (*venture*) de éxito; **to be** ~ **(in doing)** lograr (hacer).
successfully [səkses'fəlē] *ad* con éxito.
succession [səksesh'ən] *n* (*series*) sucesión *f*, serie *f*; (*descendants*) descendencia; **in** ~ sucesivamente.
successive [səkses'iv] *a* sucesivo, consecutivo; **on 3** ~ **days** tres días seguidos.
successor [səkses'ûr] *n* sucesor(a) *m/f*.
succinct [səksingkt'] *a* sucinto.
succulent [suk'yələnt] *a* suculento ♦ *n* (*BOT*): ~**s** plantas *fpl* carnosas.
succumb [səkum'] *vi* sucumbir.
such [such] *a* tal, semejante; (*of that kind*): ~ **a book** tal libro; ~ **books** tales libros; (*so much*): ~ **courage** tanto valor ♦ *ad* tan; ~ **a long trip** un viaje tan largo; ~ **a lot of** tanto; ~ **as** (*like*) tal como; **a noise** ~ **as to** un ruido tal que; ~ **books as I have** cuantos libros tengo; **I said no** ~ **thing** no dije tal cosa; **it's** ~ **a long time since we saw each other** hace tanto tiempo que no nos vemos; ~ **a long time ago** hace tantísimo tiempo; **as** ~ *ad* como tal.
such-and-such [such'ənsuch] *a* tal o cual.
suchlike [such'līk] *pron* (*col*): **and** ~ y cosas por el estilo.
suck [suk] *vt* chupar; (*bottle*) sorber; (*breast*) mamar; (*subj: pump, machine*) aspirar.
sucker [suk'ûr] *n* (*BOT*) serpollo; (*ZOOL*) ventosa; (*col*) bobo, primo.
sucrose [sōō'krōs] *n* sucrosa.
suction [suk'shən] *n* succión *f*.
suction pump *n* bomba aspirante *or* de succión.
Sudan [sōōdan'] *n* Sudán *m*.
Sudanese [sōōdənēz'] *a*, *n* sudanés/esa *m/f*.
sudden [sud'ən] *a* (*rapid*) repentino, súbito; (*unexpected*) imprevisto; **all of a** ~ de repente.
suddenly [sud'ənlē] *ad* de repente.
suds [sudz] *npl* espuma *sg* de jabón.
sue [sōō] *vt* demandar; **to** ~ **(for)** demandar (por); **to** ~ **for divorce** solicitar *or* pedir el divorcio; **to** ~ **for damages** demandar por daños y perjuicios.
suede [swād] *n* ante *m*, gamuza (*LAm*).
suet [sōō'it] *n* sebo.
Suez Canal [sōōez' kənal'] *n* Canal *m* de Suez.
Suff. *abbr* (*Brit*) = *Suffolk*.
suffer [suf'ûr] *vt* sufrir, padecer; (*tolerate*) aguantar, soportar; (*undergo: loss*,

setback) experimentar ♦ *vi* sufrir, padecer; **to ~ from** sufrir, tener; **to ~ from the effects of alcohol/a fall** resentirse del alcohol/de una caída.

sufferance [suf'ûrəns] *n*: **he was only there on ~** estuvo allí sólo por tolerancia.

sufferer [suf'ûrûr] *n* víctima *f*; (*MED*) **~ from** enfermo/a de.

suffering [suf'ûring] *n* (*hardship, deprivation*) sufrimiento; (*pain*) dolor *m*.

suffice [səfīs'] *vi* bastar, ser suficiente.

sufficient [səfish'ənt] *a* suficiente, bastante.

sufficiently [səfish'əntlē] *ad* suficientemente, bastante.

suffix [suf'iks] *n* sufijo.

suffocate [suf'əkāt] *vi* ahogarse, asfixiarse.

suffocation [sufəkā'shən] *n* sofocación *f*, asfixia.

suffrage [suf'rij] *n* sufragio.

suffuse [səfyōōz'] *vt*: **to ~ (with)** (*color*) bañar (de); **her face was ~d with joy** su cara estaba llena de alegría.

sugar [shōōg'ûr] *n* azúcar *m* ♦ *vt* echar azúcar a, azucarar.

sugar beet *n* remolacha.

sugar bowl *n* azucarero.

sugar cane *n* caña de azúcar.

sugar-coated [shōōg'ûrkō'tid] *a* azucarado, garapiñado.

sugar lump *n* terrón *m* de azúcar.

sugar refinery *n* ingenio azucarero.

sugary [shōōg'ûrē] *a* azucarado.

suggest [səgjest'] *vt* sugerir; (*recommend*) aconsejar; **what do you ~ I do?** ¿qué sugieres que haga?; **this ~s that ...** esto hace pensar que ....

suggestion [səgjes'chən] *n* sugerencia; **there's no ~ of ...** no hay indicación *or* evidencia de ....

suggestive [səgjes'tiv] *a* sugestivo; (*pej*: *indecent*) indecente.

suicidal [sōōisīd'əl] *a* suicida; (*fig*) suicida, peligroso.

suicide [sōō'isīd] *n* suicidio; (*person*) suicida *m/f*; **to commit ~** suicidarse.

suicide attempt *n* intento de suicidio.

suit [sōōt] *n* (*man's*) traje *m*; (*woman's*) conjunto; (*LAW*) pleito; (*CARDS*) palo ♦ *vt* convenir; (*clothes*) sentar a, ir bien a; (*adapt*): **to ~ sth to** adaptar *or* ajustar algo a; **to be ~ed to sth** (*suitable for*) ser apto para algo; **well ~ed** (*couple*) hechos el uno para el otro; **to bring a ~ against sb** entablar demanda contra uno; **to follow ~** (*CARDS*) seguir el palo; (*fig*) seguir el ejemplo (de uno); **that ~s me** me va bien.

suitable [sōō'təbəl] *a* conveniente; (*apt*) indicado.

suitably [sōō'təblē] *ad* convenientemente; (*appropriately*) en forma debida.

suitcase [sōōt'kās] *n* maleta, valija (*LAm*).

suite [swēt] *n* (*of rooms, MUS*) suite *f*; (*furniture*): **bedroom/dining room ~** (*jue-*

go de) dormitorio/comedor *m*; **a three-piece ~** un tresillo.

suitor [sōō'tûr] *n* pretendiente *m*.

sulfate [sul'fāt] *n* sulfato; **copper ~** sulfato de cobre.

sulfur [sul'fûr] *n* azufre *m*.

sulk [sulk] *vi* estar de mal humor.

sulky [sul'kē] *a* malhumorado.

sullen [sul'ən] *a* hosco, malhumorado.

sulphate [sul'fāt] *n* (*Brit*) = **sulfate.**

sulphur [sul'fûr] *n* (*Brit*) = **sulfur.**

sultan [sul'tən] *n* sultán *m*.

sultana [sultan'ə] *n* (*fruit*) pasa de Esmirna.

sultry [sul'trē] *a* (*weather*) bochornoso; (*seductive*) seductor(a).

sum [sum] *n* suma; (*total*) total *m*.
  sum up *vt* resumir; (*evaluate rapidly*) evaluar ♦ *vi* hacer un resumen.

Sumatra [sōōmát'rə] *n* Sumatra.

summarize [sum'ərīz] *vt* resumir.

summary [sum'ûrē] *n* resumen *m* ♦ *a* (*justice*) sumario.

summer [sum'ûr] *n* verano ♦ *a* de verano; **in (the) ~** en (el) verano.

summer camp *n* (*US*) colonia veraniega infantil.

summerhouse [sum'ûrhous] *n* (*in garden*) cenador *m*, glorieta.

summertime [sum'ûrtīm] *n* (*season*) verano.

summer time *n* (*by clock*) hora de verano.

summery [sum'ûrē] *a* veraniego.

summing-up [sum'ingup'] *n* (*LAW*) resumen *m*.

summit [sum'it] *n* cima, cumbre *f*.

summit (conference) *n* (conferencia) cumbre *f*.

summon [sum'ən] *vt* (*person*) llamar; (*meeting*) convocar; **to ~ a witness** citar a un testigo.
  summon up *vt* (*courage*) armarse de.

summons [sum'ənz] *n* llamamiento, llamada ♦ *vt* citar, emplazar; **to serve a ~ on sb** citar a uno ante el juicio.

sump [sump] *n* (*Brit AUT*) cárter *m*.

sumptuous [sump'chōōəs] *a* suntuoso.

sun [sun] *n* sol *m*; **they have everything under the ~** no les falta nada, tienen de todo.

Sun. *abbr* (= *Sunday*) dom.

sunbathe [sun'bāth] *vi* tomar el sol.

sunbeam [sun'bēm] *n* rayo de sol.

sunbed [sun'bed] *n* cama solar.

sunburn [sun'bûrn] *n* (*painful*) quemadura del sol; (*tan*) bronceado.

sunburned [sun'bûrnd], (*Brit*) **sunburnt** [sun'bûrnt] *a* (*tanned*) bronceado; (*painfully*) quemado por el sol.

sundae [sun'dē] *n* *helado con frutas y nueces.*

Sunday [sun'dā] *n* domingo.

Sunday school *n* catequesis *f*.

sundial [sun'dīl] *n* reloj *m* de sol.

sundown [sun'doun] *n* anochecer *m*, puesta de sol.

sundries [sun'drēz] *npl* géneros *mpl* diversos.

sundry [sun'drē] *a* varios, diversos; **all and ~** todos sin excepción.

sunflower [sun'flouûr] *n* girasol *m*.

sung [sung] *pp of* **sing**.

sunglasses [sun'glasiz] *npl* gafas *fpl or* anteojos *mpl* de sol.

sunk [sungk] *pp of* **sink**.

sunken [sung'kən] *a* (*bath*) hundido.

sunlamp [sun'lamp] *n* lámpara solar ultravioleta.

sunlight [sun'līt] *n* luz *f* del sol.

sunlit [sun'lit] *a* iluminado por el sol.

sunny [sun'ē] *a* soleado; (*day*) de sol; (*fig*) alegre; **it is ~** hace sol.

sunrise [sun'rīz] *n* salida del sol.

sun roof *n* (*AUT*) techo corredizo; (*on building*) azotea, terraza.

sunset [sun'set] *n* puesta del sol.

sunshade [sun'shād] *n* (*over table*) sombrilla.

sunshine [sun'shīn] *n* sol *m*.

sunstroke [sun'strōk] *n* insolación *f*.

suntan [sun'tan] *n* bronceado.

suntan lotion *n* bronceador *m*.

suntanned [sun'tand] *a* bronceado.

super [sōō'pûr] *a* (*col*) bárbaro.

superannuation [sōōpúranyōōā'shən] *n* jubilación *f*.

superb [sōōpûrb'] *a* magnífico, espléndido.

supercilious [sōōpûrsil'ēəs] *a* (*disdainful*) desdeñoso; (*haughty*) altanero.

superficial [sōōpûrfish'əl] *a* superficial.

superfluous [sōōpûr'flōōəs] *a* superfluo, de sobra.

superhuman [sōōpûrhyōō'mən] *a* sobrehumano.

superimpose [sōōpúrimpōz'] *vt* sobreponer.

superintend [sōōpúrintend'] *vt* supervisar.

superintendent [sōōpúrinten'dənt] *n* director(a) *m/f*; (*police ~*) subjefe/a *m/f*.

superior [səpēr'ēûr] *a* superior; (*smug*: *person*) presumido, desdeñoso; (: *smile*, *air*) de suficiencia; (: *remark*) desdeñoso ♦ *n* superior *m*; **Mother S~** (*REL*) madre *f* superiora.

superiority [səpērēôr'itē] *n* superioridad *f*; desdén *m*.

superlative [səpûr'lətiv] *a*, *n* superlativo.

superman [sōō'púrman] *n* superhombre *m*.

supermarket [sōō'púrmârkit] *n* supermercado.

supernatural [sōōpúrnach'ûrəl] *a* sobrenatural.

superpower [sōō'púrpou'ûr] *n* (*POL*) superpotencia.

supersede [sōōpûrsēd'] *vt* suplantar.

supersonic [sōōpúrsân'ik] *a* supersónico.

superstition [sōōpûrstish'ən] *n* superstición *f*.

superstitious [sōōpûrstish'əs] *a* supersticioso.

superstore [sōō'púrstôr] *n* (*Brit*) hipermercado.

supertanker [sōō'púrtangkûr] *n* superpetrolero.

supertax [sōō'púrtaks] *n* sobretasa, sobreimpuesto.

supervise [sōō'púrvīz] *vt* supervisar.

supervision [sōōpúrvizh'ən] *n* supervisión *f*.

supervisor [sōō'púrvīzûr] *n* (*gen*, *UNIV*) supervisor(a) *m/f*.

supervisory [sōōpúrvī'zûrē] *a* de supervisión.

supine [sōō'pīn] *a* supino.

supper [sup'ûr] *n* cena; **to have ~** cenar.

supplant [səplant'] *vt* suplantar, reemplazar.

supple [sup'əl] *a* flexible.

supplement *n* [sup'ləmənt] suplemento ♦ *vt* [sup'ləmənt] suplir.

supplementary [supləmen'tûrē] *a* suplementario.

supplementary benefit *n* (*Brit*) subsidio adicional de la seguridad social.

supplier [səpli'ûr] *n* suministrador(a) *m/f*; (*COMM*) distribuidor(a) *m/f*.

supply [səpli'] *vt* (*provide*) suministrar; (*information*) facilitar; (*fill*: *need*, *want*) suplir, satisfacer; (*equip*): **to ~ (with)** proveer (de) ♦ *n* provisión *f*; (*of gas*, *water etc*) suministro ♦ *a* (*Brit*: *teacher etc*) suplente; **supplies** *npl* (*food*) víveres *mpl*; (*MIL*) pertrechos *mpl*; **office supplies** materiales *mpl* para oficina; **to be in short ~** escasear, haber escasez de; **the electricity/water/gas ~** el suministro de electricidad/agua/gas; **~ and demand** la oferta y la demanda.

support [səpôrt'] *n* (*moral*, *financial etc*) apoyo; (*TECH*) soporte *m* ♦ *vt* apoyar; (*financially*) mantener; (*uphold*) sostener; (*SPORT*: *team*) seguir; **they stopped work in ~ (of)** pararon de trabajar en apoyo (de); **to ~ o.s.** (*financially*) ganarse la vida.

support buying *n* compra proteccionista.

supporter [səpôr'tûr] *n* (*POL etc*) partidario/a; (*SPORT*) aficionado/a.

supporting [səpôr'ting] *a* (*THEATER*: *role*, *actor*) secundario.

suppose [səpōz'] *vt*, *vi* suponer; (*imagine*) imaginarse; **to be ~d to do sth** deber hacer algo; **I don't ~ she'll come** no creo que venga; **he's ~d to be an expert** se le supone un experto.

supposedly [səpō'zidlē] *ad* según cabe suponer.

supposing [səpō'zing] *conj* en caso de que; **always ~ (that) he comes** suponiendo que venga.

supposition [supəzish'ən] *n* suposición *f*.

suppository [səpâz'itôrē] *n* supositorio.
suppress [səpres'] *vt* suprimir; (*yawn*) ahogar.
suppression [səpresh'ən] *n* represión *f*.
supremacy [səprem'əsē] *n* supremacía.
supreme [səprēm'] *a* supremo.
Supreme Court *n* (*US*) Tribunal *m* Supremo, Corte *f* Suprema (*LAm*).
Supt. *abbr* (*POLICE*) = **superintendent.**
surcharge [sûr'chârj] *n* sobretasa, recargo.
sure [shōōr] *a* seguro; (*definite, convinced*) cierto; (*aim*) certero ♦ *ad* (*col: esp US*): **that ~ is pretty, that's ~ pretty** ¡qué bonito es!; **to be ~ of sth** estar seguro de algo; **to be ~ of o.s.** estar seguro de sí mismo; **to make ~ of sth/that** asegurarse de algo/asegurar que; **I'm not ~ how/why/when** no estoy seguro de cómo/por qué/cuándo; **~!** (*of course*) ¡claro!, ¡por supuesto!; **~ enough** efectivamente.
sure-footed [shōōr'fōōt'id] *a* de pie firme.
surely [shōōr'lē] *ad* (*certainly*) seguramente; **~ you don't mean that!** ¡no lo dices en serio!
surety [shōōr'ətē] *n* fianza; (*person*) fiador(a) *m/f*; **to go** *or* **stand ~ for sb** ser fiador de uno, salir garante por uno.
surf [sûrf] *n* olas *fpl*.
surface [sûr'fis] *n* superficie *f* ♦ *vt* (*road*) revestir ♦ *vi* salir a la superficie ♦ *cpd* (*MIL, NAUT*) de (la) superficie; **on the ~ it seems that ...** (*fig*) a primera vista parece que ... .
surface area *n* área de la superficie.
surface mail *n* vía terrestre.
surface-to-air missile [sûr'fistōōär' mis'əl] *n* proyectil *m* tierra-aire.
surfboard [sûrf'bôrd] *n* plancha (de surf).
surfeit [sûr'fit] *n*: **a ~ of** un exceso de.
surfer [sûrf'ûr] *n* súrfer *m/f*.
surfing [sûrf'ing] *n* surf *m*.
surge [sûrj] *n* oleada, oleaje *m*; (*ELEC*) sobretensión *f* transitoria ♦ *vi* avanzar a tropel; **to ~ forward** avanzar rápidamente.
surgeon [sûr'jən] *n* cirujano/a.
surgery [sûr'jûrē] *n* cirugía; (*Brit: room*) consultorio; **to undergo ~** operarse.
surgery hours *npl* (*Brit*) horas *fpl* de consulta.
surgical [sûr'jikəl] *a* quirúrgico.
surgical spirit *n* (*Brit*) alcohol *m*.
surly [sûr'lē] *a* hosco, malhumorado.
surmount [sûrmount'] *vt* superar, vencer.
surname [sûr'nām] *n* apellido.
surpass [sûrpas'] *vt* superar, exceder.
surplus [sûr'pləs] *n* excedente *m*; (*COMM*) superávit *m* ♦ *a* (*COMM*) excedente, sobrante; **to have a ~ of sth** tener un excedente de algo; **it is ~ to our requirements** nos sobra; **~ stock** saldos *mpl*.
surprise [sûrprīz'] *n* sorpresa ♦ *vt* sorprender; **to take by ~** (*person*) coger a uno desprevenido, sorprender a uno; (*MIL*:

town, fort) atacar por sorpresa.
surprising [sûrprī'zing] *a* sorprendente.
surprisingly [sûrprī'zinglē] *ad* (*easy, helpful*) de modo sorprendente; **(somewhat) ~, he agreed** para sorpresa de todos, aceptó.
surrealism [sərē'əlizəm] *n* surrealismo.
surrealist [sərē'əlist] *a, n* surrealista *m/f*.
surrender [səren'dûr] *n* rendición *f*, entrega ♦ *vi* rendirse, entregarse ♦ *vt* (*claim, right*) renunciar.
surrender value *n* valor *m* de rescate.
surreptitious [sûrəptish'əs] *a* subrepticio.
surrogate [sûr'əgit] *n* (*substitute*) sustituto/a ♦ *a*: **~ coffee** sucedáneo de café.
surrogate mother *n* madre *f* portadora.
surround [səround'] *vt* rodear, circundar; (*MIL etc*) cercar.
surrounding [səroun'ding] *a* circundante.
surroundings [səroun'dingz] *npl* alrededores *mpl*, cercanías *fpl*.
surtax [sûr'taks] *n* sobretasa, sobreimpuesto.
surveillance [sûrvā'ləns] *n* vigilancia.
survey *n* [sûr'vā] inspección *f*, reconocimiento; (*inquiry*) encuesta; (*comprehensive view: of situation etc*) vista de conjunto ♦ *vt* [sərvā'] examinar, inspeccionar; (*Brit SURVEYING: building*) inspeccionar; (: *land*) hacer un reconocimiento de, reconocer; (*look at*) mirar, contemplar; (*make inquiries about*) hacer una encuesta de; **to carry out a ~ of** inspeccionar, examinar.
surveyor [sûrvā'ûr] *n* agrimensor(a) *m/f*.
survival [sûrvī'vəl] *n* supervivencia.
survival course *n* curso de supervivencia.
survival kit *n* equipo de emergencia.
survive [sûrvīv'] *vi* sobrevivir; (*custom etc*) perdurar ♦ *vt* sobrevivir a.
survivor [sûrvī'vûr] *n* superviviente *m/f*.
susceptibility [səseptəbil'ətē] *n* (*to illness*) propensión *f*.
susceptible [səsep'təbəl] *a* (*easily influenced*) influenciable; (*to disease, illness*): **~ to** propenso a.
suspect *a, n* [sus'pekt] sospechoso/a *m/f* ♦ *vt* [səspekt'] sospechar.
suspend [səspend'] *vt* suspender.
suspended sentence [səspen'did sen'təns] *n* (*LAW*) libertad *f* condicional.
suspender belt [səspen'dûr belt] *n* (*Brit*) portaligas *m inv*.
suspenders [səspen'dûrz] *npl* (*US*) tirantes *mpl*; (*Brit*) ligas *fpl*.
suspense [səspens'] *n* incertidumbre *f*, duda; (*in film etc*) suspense *m*.
suspense account *n* cuenta en suspenso.
suspension [səspen'chən] *n* (*gen, AUT*) suspensión *f*; (*of driver's license*) privación *f*.
suspension bridge *n* puente *m* colgante.
suspension file *n* archivador *m* colgante.
suspicion [səspish'ən] *n* sospecha; (*distrust*) recelo; (*trace*) traza; **to be under ~** estar bajo sospecha; **arrested on ~ of murder**

detenido bajo sospecha de asesinato.

suspicious [səspish'əs] *a* (*suspecting*) receloso; (*causing suspicion*) sospechoso; **to be ~ of** *or* **about sb/sth** tener sospechas de uno/algo.

suss out [sus out] *vt* (*Brit col*) explorar.

sustain [səstān'] *vt* sostener, apoyar; (*suffer*) sufrir, padecer.

sustained [səstānd'] *a* (*effort*) sostenido.

sustenance [sus'tənəns] *n* sustento.

suture [sōō'chûr] *n* sutura.

SW *abbr* = **short wave**.

swab [swâb] *n* (*MED*) algodón *m*, frotis *m inv* ♦ *vt* (*NAUT*: *also*: **~ down**) limpiar, fregar.

swagger [swag'ûr] *vi* pavonearse.

swallow [swâl'ō] *n* (*bird*) golondrina; (*of food*) bocado; (*of drink*) trago ♦ *vt* tragar.

swallow up *vt* (*savings etc*) consumir.

swam [swam] *pt of* **swim**.

swamp [swâmp] *n* pantano, ciénaga ♦ *vt* abrumar, agobiar.

swampy [swâmp'ē] *a* pantanoso.

swan [swân] *n* cisne *m*.

swank [swangk] (*col*) *n* (*vanity, boastfulness*) fanfarronada ♦ *vi* fanfarronear, presumir.

swan song *n* (*fig*) canto del cisne.

swap [swâp] *n* canje *m*, trueque *m* ♦ *vt*: **to ~ (for)** canjear (por).

SWAPO [swâ'pō] *n abbr* (= *South-West Africa People's Organization*) SWAPO *m*.

swarm [swôrm] *n* (*of bees*) enjambre *m*; (*fig*) multitud *f* ♦ *vi* (*fig*) hormiguear, pulular.

swarthy [swôr'thē] *a* moreno.

swashbuckling [swâsh'bukling] *a* (*person*) aventurero; (*film*) de capa y espada.

swastika [swâs'tika] *n* esvástica, cruz *f* gamada.

swat [swât] *vt* aplastar.

swathe [swâth] *vt*: **to ~ in** (*blankets*) envolver en; (*bandages*) vendar en.

sway [swā] *vi* mecerse, balancearse ♦ *vt* (*influence*) mover, influir en ♦ *n* (*rule, power*): **~ (over)** dominio (sobre); **to hold ~ over sb** dominar a uno, mantener el dominio sobre uno.

Swaziland [swâ'zēland] *n* Swazilandia.

swear, *pt* **swore**, *pp* **sworn** [swe'ûr, swôr, swôrn] *vi* jurar ♦ *vt*: **to ~ an oath** prestar juramento, jurar; **to ~ to sth** declarar algo bajo juramento.

swear in *vt* tomar juramento (a).

swearword [swär'wûrd] *n* taco, palabrota.

sweat [swet] *n* sudor *m* ♦ *vi* sudar.

sweatband [swet'band] *n* (*SPORT*: *on head*) venda, banda; (: *on wrist*) muñequera.

sweater [swet'ûr] *n* suéter *m*.

sweatshirt [swet'shûrt] *n* sudadera.

sweatshop [swet'shâp] *n* fábrica donde se explota al obrero.

sweat suit *n* chandal *m*.

sweaty [swet'ē] *a* sudoroso.

Swede [swēd] *n* sueco/a.

swede [swēd] *n* (*Brit*) naba.

Sweden [swēd'ən] *n* Suecia.

Swedish [swē'dish] *a*, *n* (*LING*) sueco.

sweep [swēp] *n* (*act*) barrida; (*of arm*) manotazo *m*; (*curve*) curva, alcance *m*; (*also*: **chimney ~**) deshollinador(a) *m/f* ♦ *vb* (*pt*, *pp* **swept** [swept]) *vt* barrer; (*disease, fashion*) recorrer ♦ *vi* barrer.

sweep away *vt* barrer; (*rub out*) borrar.

sweep past *vi* pasar rápidamente; (*brush by*) rozar.

sweep up *vi* barrer.

sweeping [swē'ping] *a* (*gesture*) dramático; (*generalized*) generalizado; (*changes, reforms*) radical.

sweepstake [swēp'stāk] *n* lotería.

sweet [swēt] *n* (*candy*) dulce *m*, caramelo; (*Brit*: *pudding*) postre *m* ♦ *a* dulce; (*sugary*) azucarado; (*charming*: *person*) encantador(a); (: *smile, character*) dulce, amable, agradable ♦ *ad*: **to smell/taste ~** oler/saber dulce.

sweet and sour *a* agridulce.

sweetcorn [swēt'kôrn] *n* maíz *m*.

sweeten [swēt'ən] *vt* (*person*) endulzar; (*add sugar to*) poner azúcar a.

sweetener [swēt'ənûr] *n* (*CULIN*) dulcificante *m*.

sweetheart [swēt'hârt] *n* novio/a; (*in speech*) amor.

sweetness [swēt'nis] *n* (*gen*) dulzura.

sweet pea *n* guisante *m* de olor.

sweet potato *n* batata, camote *m* (*LAm*).

sweetshop [swēt'shâp] *n* (*Brit*) confitería, bombonería.

sweet-talk [swēt'tôk] *vt* (*US col*) enrollarse con.

swell [swel] *n* (*of sea*) marejada, oleaje *m* ♦ *a* (*US*: *col*: *excellent*) estupendo, fenomenal ♦ *vb* (*pt* **~ed**, *pp* **swollen** *or* **~ed** [swō'lən]) *vt* hinchar, inflar ♦ *vi* hincharse, inflarse.

swelling [swel'ing] *n* (*MED*) hinchazón *f*.

sweltering [swel'tûring] *a* sofocante, de mucho calor.

swept [swept] *pt*, *pp of* **sweep**.

swerve [swûrv] *n* esguince *m*; (*in car*) desvío brusco ♦ *vi* desviarse bruscamente.

swift [swift] *n* (*bird*) vencejo ♦ *a* rápido, veloz.

swiftly [swift'lē] *ad* rápidamente.

swiftness [swift'nis] *n* rapidez *f*, velocidad *f*.

swig [swig] *n* (*col*: *drink*) trago.

swill [swil] *n* bazofia ♦ *vt* lavar, limpiar con agua.

swim [swim] *n*: **to go for a ~** ir a nadar *or* a bañarse ♦ *vb* (*pt* **swam**, *pp* **swum** [swam, swum]) *vi* nadar; (*head, room*) dar vueltas ♦ *vt* pasar a nado; **to go ~ming** ir a nadar(se); **to ~ a length** nadar *or* hacer un

largo.
swimmer [swim'ûr] *n* nadador(a) *m/f*.
swimming [swim'ing] *n* natación *f*.
swimming cap *n* gorro de baño.
swimming costume *n* (*Brit*) = **swimsuit**.
swimming pool *n* piscina, alberca (*LAm*).
swimming trunks *npl* bañador *msg*.
swimsuit [swim'sōōt] *n* bañador *m*, traje *m* de baño.
swindle [swin'dəl] *n* estafa ♦ *vt* estafar.
swine [swīn] *n*, *pl inv* cerdos *mpl*, puercos *mpl*; (*col!*) canalla *m* (*!*).
swing [swing] *n* (*in playground*) columpio; (*movement*) balanceo, vaivén *m*; (*change of direction*) viraje *m*; (*rhythm*) ritmo; (*POL: in votes etc*): **there has been a ~ towards/away from the Republicans** ha habido un viraje en favor/en contra del Partido Republicano ♦ *vb* (*pt, pp* **swung** [swung]) *vt* balancear; (*on a ~*) columpiar; (*also*: **~ around**) voltear, girar ♦ *vi* balancearse, columpiarse; (*also*: **~ around**) dar media vuelta; **a ~ to the left** un movimiento hacia la izquierda; **to be in full ~** estar en plena marcha; **to get into the ~ of things** ponerse al corriente de las cosas *or* de la situación; **the road ~s south** la carretera gira hacia el sur.
swing bridge *n* puente *m* giratorio.
swing door *n* (*Brit*) puerta giratoria.
swingeing [swin'jing] *a* (*Brit*) abrumador(a).
swinging door [swing'ing dôr] *n* (*US*) puerta giratoria.
swipe [swīp] *n* golpe *m* fuerte ♦ *vt* (*hit*) golpear fuerte; (*col: steal*) guindar.
swirl [swûrl] *vi* arremolinarse.
swish [swish] *n* (*sound: of whip*) chasquido; (: *of skirts*) frufrú *m*; (: *of grass*) crujido ♦ *a* (*Brit: col: smart*) elegante ♦ *vi* chasquear.
Swiss [swis] *a, n* (*pl inv*) suizo/a *m/f*.
switch [swich] *n* (*for light, radio etc*) interruptor *m*; (*change*) cambio ♦ *vt* (*change*) cambiar de; (*invert: also*: **~ around, ~ over**) intercambiar.
switch off *vt* apagar; (*engine*) parar.
switch on *vt* (*AUT: ignition*) encender, prender (*LAm*); (*engine, machine*) arrancar; (*water supply*) conectar.
switchblade [swich'blād] *n* (*US*) navaja de muelle.
switchboard [swich'bôrd] *n* (*TEL*) centralita (de teléfonos), conmutador *m* (*LAm*).
switchtower [swich'touûr] *n* (*US RAIL*) garita de señales.
switchyard [swich'yârd] *n* (*US RAIL*) estación *f* clasificadora.
Switzerland [swit'sûrlənd] *n* Suiza.
swivel [swiv'əl] *vi* (*also*: **~ around**) girar.
swollen [swō'lən] *pp* of **swell**.

swoon [swōōn] *vi* desmayarse.
swoop [swōōp] *n* (*by police etc*) redada; (*of bird etc*) calada ♦ *vi* (*also*: **~ down**) calarse.
swop [swâp] = **swap**.
sword [sôrd] *n* espada.
swordfish [sôrd'fish] *n* pez *m* espada.
swore [swôr] *pt* of **swear**.
sworn [swôrn] *pp* of **swear**.
swot [swât] (*Brit*) *vt, vi* empollar ♦ *n* empollón/ona *m/f*.
swum [swum] *pp* of **swim**.
swung [swung] *pt, pp* of **swing**.
sycamore [sik'əmôr] *n* sicomoro.
sycophant [sik'əfənt] *n* adulador(a), pelotillero/a.
Sydney [sid'nē] *n* Sidney *m*.
syllable [sil'əbəl] *n* sílaba.
syllabus [sil'əbəs] *n* programa *m* de estudios; **on the ~** en el programa de estudios.
symbol [sim'bəl] *n* símbolo.
symbolic(al) [simbâl'ik(əl)] *a* simbólico; **to be ~ of sth** simbolizar algo.
symbolism [sim'bəlizəm] *n* simbolismo.
symbolize [sim'bəlīz] *vt* simbolizar.
symmetrical [simet'rikəl] *a* simétrico.
symmetry [sim'itrē] *n* simetría.
sympathetic [simpəthet'ik] *a* compasivo; (*understanding*) comprensivo; **to be ~ to a cause** (*well-disposed*) apoyar una causa; **to be ~ towards** (*person*) ser comprensivo con.
sympathize [sim'pəthīz] *vi*: **to ~ with sb** compadecerse de uno; (*understand*) comprender a uno.
sympathizer [sim'pəthīzûr] *n* (*POL*) simpatizante *m/f*.
sympathy [sim'pəthē] *n* (*pity*) compasión *f*; (*understanding*) comprensión *f*; **a letter of ~** un pésame; **with our deepest ~** nuestro más sentido pésame.
symphony [sim'fənē] *n* sinfonía.
symposium [simpō'zēəm] *n* simposio.
symptom [simp'təm] *n* síntoma *m*, indicio.
symptomatic [simptəmat'ik] *a*: **~ (of)** sintomático (de).
synagogue [sin'əgåg] *n* sinagoga.
synchromesh [sing'krəmesh] *n* cambio sincronizado de velocidades.
synchronize [sing'krəniz] *vt* sincronizar ♦ *vi*: **to ~ with** sincronizarse con.
syncopated [sing'kəpātid] *a* sincopado.
syndicate [sin'dəkit] *n* (*gen*) sindicato; (*PRESS*) agencia (de noticias).
syndrome [sin'drōm] *n* síndrome *m*.
synonym [sin'ənim] *n* sinónimo.
synonymous [sinân'əməs] *a*: **~ (with)** sinónimo (con).
synopsis, *pl* **synopses** [sinâp'sis, -sēz] *n* sinopsis *f inv*.
syntax [sin'taks] *n* sintaxis *f*.
syntax error *n* (*COMPUT*) error *m* sintáctico.

synthesis, *pl* **syntheses** [sin'thəsis, -sēz] *n* síntesis *f inv*.
synthesizer [sin'thisīzûr] *n* sintetizador *m*.
synthetic [sinthet'ik] *a* sintético ♦ *n* sintético.
syphilis [sif'əlis] *n* sífilis *f*.
syphon [sī'fən] = **siphon**.
Syria [sē'rēə] *n* Siria.
Syrian [sēr'ēən] *a, n* sirio/a *m/f*.
syringe [sərinj'] *n* jeringa.
syrup [sir'əp] *n* jarabe *m*, almíbar *m*.
system [sis'təm] *n* sistema *m*; (*ANAT*) organismo; **it was quite a shock to his** ~ fue un golpe para el organismo.
systematic [sistəmat'ik] *a* sistemático; metódico.
system disk *n* (*COMPUT*) disco del sistema.
systems analyst [sis'təmz an'əlist] *n* analista *m/f* de sistemas.

T

T, t [tē] *n* (*letter*) T, t *f*; **T for Tommy** T de Tarragona.
ta [tâ] *excl* (*Brit col*) ¡gracias!
tab [tab] *n abbr* = **tabulator** ♦ *n* lengüeta; (*label*) etiqueta; **to keep** ~**s on** (*fig*) vigilar.
tabby [tab'ē] *n* (*also:* ~ **cat**) gato atigrado.
tabernacle [tab'ûrnakəl] *n* tabernáculo.
table [tā'bəl] *n* mesa; (*chart: of statistics etc*) cuadro, gráfica, tabla; **to lay** *or* **set the** ~ poner la mesa; **to clear the** ~ quitar *or* levantar la mesa; ~ **of contents** índice *m* de materias.
tablecloth [tā'bəlklôth] *n* mantel *m*.
table d'hôte [tab'əl dōt'] *n* menú *m*.
table lamp *n* lámpara de mesa.
tableland [tā'bəlland] *n* meseta, altiplano (*LAm*).
tablemat [tā'bəlmat] *n* salvamanteles *m inv*.
tablespoon [tā'bəlspōōn] *n* cuchara grande; (*also:* ~**ful:** *as measurement*) cucharada.
tablet [tab'lit] *n* (*MED*) pastilla, comprimido; (*for writing*) bloc *m*; (*of stone*) lápida.
table talk *n* conversación *f* de sobremesa.
table tennis *n* ping-pong *m*, tenis *m* de mesa.
table wine *n* vino de mesa.
tabloid [tab'loid] *n* (*newspaper*) periódico popular sensacionalista; **the** ~**s** la prensa amarilla.
taboo [tabōō'] *a, n* tabú *m*.

tabulate [tab'yəlāt] *vt* disponer en tablas.
tabulator [tab'yəlātûr] *n* tabulador *m*.
tachograph [tak'əgraf] *n* tacógrafo.
tachometer [təkâm'ətûr] *n* taquímetro.
tacit [tas'it] *a* tácito.
tacitly [tas'itlē] *ad* tácitamente.
taciturn [tas'itûrn] *a* taciturno.
tack [tak] *n* (*nail*) tachuela; (*stitch*) hilván *m*; (*NAUT*) bordada ♦ *vt* (*nail*) clavar con tachuelas; (*Brit: stitch*) hilvanar ♦ *vi* virar; **to** ~ **sth on to (the end of) sth** (*of letter, book*) añadir algo a(l final de) algo.
tackle [tak'əl] *n* (*gear*) equipo; (*fishing* ~, *for lifting*) aparejo; (*FOOTBALL, SOCCER*) entrada, tackle *m*; (*RUGBY*) placaje *m* ♦ *vt* (*difficulty*) enfrentar; (*grapple with*) agarrar; (*SOCCER*) atajar, entrar; (*RUGBY*) placar.
tacky [tak'ē] *a* pegajoso; (*US: shabby*) destartalado.
tact [takt] *n* tacto, discreción *f*.
tactful [takt'fəl] *a* discreto, diplomático; **to be** ~ tener tacto, actuar discretamente.
tactfully [takt'fəlē] *ad* diplomáticamente, con tacto.
tactical [tak'tikəl] *a* táctico.
tactics [tak'tiks] *n, npl* táctica *sg*.
tactless [takt'lis] *a* indiscreto.
tactlessly [takt'lislē] *ad* indiscretamente, sin tacto.
tadpole [tad'pōl] *n* renacuajo.
taffy [taf'ē] *n* (*US*) melcocha.
tag [tag] *n* (*label*) etiqueta; **price/name** ~ etiqueta con el precio/con el nombre.
tag along *vi*: **to** ~ **along with sb** acompañar a uno.
tag question *n* pregunta coletilla.
Tahiti [təhē'tē] *n* Tahití *m*.
tail [tāl] *n* cola; (*ZOOL*) rabo; (*of shirt, coat*) faldón *m* ♦ *vt* (*follow*) vigilar a; **heads or** ~**s** cara o cruz; **to turn** ~ volver la espalda.
tail away, tail off *vi* (*in size, quality etc*) ir disminuyendo.
tailback [tāl'bak] *n* (*Brit AUT*) cola.
tail coat *n* frac *m*.
tail end *n* cola, parte *f* final.
tailgate [tāl'gāt] *n* (*AUT*) puerta trasera.
taillight [tāl'līt] *n* (*AUT*) luz *f* trasera.
tailor [tā'lûr] *n* sastre *m* ♦ *vt*: **to** ~ **sth (to)** confeccionar algo a medida (para); ~**'s (shop)** sastrería.
tailoring [tā'lûring] *n* (*cut*) corte *m*; (*craft*) sastrería.
tailor-made [tā'lûrmād] *a* (*also fig*) hecho a la medida.
tailwind [tāl'wind] *n* viento de cola.
taint [tānt] *vt* (*meat, food*) contaminar; (*fig: reputation*) manchar, tachar (*LAm*).
tainted [tānt'id] *a* (*water, air*) contaminado; (*fig*) manchado.
Taiwan [tī'wân'] *n* Taiwán *m*.
take [tāk] *vb* (*pt* **took,** *pp* **taken** [tōōk,

tā'kən]) *vt* tomar; (*grab*) coger (*Sp*), agarrar (*LAm*); (*gain: prize*) ganar; (*require: effort, courage*) exigir; (*support weight of*) aguantar; (*hold: passengers etc*) tener cabida para; (*accompany, bring, carry*) llevar; (*exam*) presentarse a; (*conduct: meeting*) presidir ♦ *vi* (*fire*) prender; (*dye*) agarrar, tomar ♦ *n* (*CINEMA*) toma; **to ~ sth from** (*drawer etc*) sacar algo de; (*person*) coger (*Sp*) algo a; **to ~ sb's hand** tomar de la mano a uno; **to ~ notes** tomar apuntes; **to be ~n ill** ponerse enfermo; ~ **the first on the left** toma la primera a la izquierda; **I only took Russian for one year** sólo estudié el ruso un año; **I took him for a doctor** le tenía por médico; **it won't ~ long** durará poco; **it will ~ at least 5 liters** tiene cabida para 5 litros como mínimo; **to be ~n with sb/sth** (*attracted*) tomarle cariño a uno/tomarle gusto a algo; **I ~ it that...** supongo que....

take after *vt fus* parecerse a.

take apart *vt* desmontar.

take away *vt* (*remove*) quitar; (*carry off*) llevar *vi*: **to ~ away from** quitar mérito a.

take back *vt* (*return*) devolver; (*one's words*) retractar.

take down *vt* (*building*) derribar; (*dismantle: scaffolding*) desmantelar; (*letter etc*) apuntar.

take in *vt* (*deceive*) engañar; (*understand*) entender; (*include*) abarcar; (*lodger*) acoger, recibir; (*orphan, stray dog*) recoger; (*SEWING*) achicar.

take off *vi* (*AVIAT*) despegar; (*leave*) salir, largarse ♦ *vt* (*remove*) quitar; (*imitate*) imitar.

take on *vt* (*work*) emprender; (*employee*) contratar; (*opponent*) desafiar.

take out *vt* sacar; (*remove*) quitar; **don't ~ it out on me!** ¡no te desquites conmigo!

take over *vt* (*business*) tomar posesión de ♦ *vi*: **to ~ over from sb** reemplazar a uno.

take to *vt fus* (*person*) coger cariño a (*Sp*), encariñarse con (*LAm*); (*activity*) aficionarse a; **to ~ to doing sth** entregarse a (hacer) algo.

take up *vt* (*a dress*) acortar; (*occupy: time, space*) ocupar; (*engage in: hobby etc*) dedicarse a; (*absorb: liquids*) absorber; (*accept: offer, challenge*) aceptar ♦ *vi*: **to ~ up with sb** hacerse amigo de uno.

take upon *vt*: **to ~ it upon o.s. to do sth** encargarse de hacer algo.

takeaway [tā'kəwā] *a* (*Brit: food*) para llevar.

take-home pay [tāk'hōm pā] *n* salario neto.

taken [tā'kən] *pp of* **take**.

takeoff [tāk'ôf] *n* (*AVIAT*) despegue *m*.

takeover [tāk'ōvûr] *n* (*COMM*) absorción *f*.

takeover bid *n* oferta pública de compra.

takings [tā'kingz] *npl* (*COMM*) ingresos *mpl*.

talc [talk] *n* (*also:* ~**um powder**) talco.

tale [tāl] *n* (*story*) cuento; (*account*) relación *f*; **to tell ~s** (*fig*) chismear.

talent [tal'ənt] *n* talento.

talented [tal'əntid] *a* talentoso, de talento.

talk [tôk] *n* charla; (*gossip*) habladurías *fpl*, chismes *mpl*; (*conversation*) conversación *f* ♦ *vi* (*speak*) hablar; (*chatter*) charlar; ~**s** *npl* (*POL etc*) conversaciones *fpl*; **to give a ~** dar una charla *or* conferencia; **to ~ about** hablar de; **to ~ sb into doing sth** convencer a uno para que haga algo; **to ~ sb out of doing sth** disuadir a uno de que haga algo; **to ~ shop** hablar del trabajo; ~**ing of movies, have you seen ...?** hablando de películas, ¿has visto ...?

talk over *vt* discutir.

talkative [tô'kətiv] *a* hablador(a).

talker [tô'kûr] *n* hablador(a) *m/f*.

talking point [tô'king point] *n* tema *m* de conversación.

talking-to [tô'kingtōō] *n*: **to give sb a good ~** echar una buena bronca a uno.

talk show *n* programa *m* de entrevistas.

tall [tôl] *a* alto; (*tree*) grande; **to be 6 feet ~** ≈ medir 1 metro 80, tener 1 metro 80 de alto; **how ~ are you?** ¿cuánto mides?

tallboy [tôl'boi] *n* (*Brit*) cómoda alta.

tallness [tôl'nis] *n* altura.

tall story *n* cuento chino.

tally [tal'ē] *n* cuenta ♦ *vi*: **to ~ (with)** corresponder (con); **to keep a ~ of sth** llevar la cuenta de algo.

talon [tal'ən] *n* garra.

tambourine [tam'bərēn] *n* pandereta.

tame [tām] *a* (*mild*) manso; (*tamed*) domesticado; (*fig: story, style*) mediocre; (: *person*) soso.

tameness [tām'nis] *n* mansedumbre *f*.

tamper [tam'pûr] *vi*: **to ~ with** entrometerse en.

tampon [tam'pân] *n* tampón *m*.

tan [tan] *n* (*also:* **sun~**) bronceado ♦ *vt* broncear ♦ *vi* ponerse moreno ♦ *a* (*color*) marrón; **to get a ~** broncearse, ponerse moreno.

tandem [tan'dəm] *n* tándem *m*.

tang [tang] *n* sabor *m* fuerte.

tangent [tan'jənt] *n* (*MATH*) tangente *f*; **to go off on a ~** (*fig*) salirse por la tangente.

tangerine [tanjərēn'] *n* mandarina.

tangible [tan'jəbəl] *a* tangible; **~ assets** bienes *mpl* tangibles.

Tangier [tanjiûr'] *n* Tánger *m*.

tangle [tang'gəl] *n* enredo ♦ *a*: **to get ~d up** enredarse.

tango [tang'gō] *n* tango.

tank [tangk] *n* (*water* ~) depósito, tanque *m*; (*for fish*) acuario; (*MIL*) tanque *m*.

tankard [tangk'ûrd] *n* bock *m*.

tanker [tangk'ûr] *n* (*ship*) petrolero; (*truck*) camión *m* cisterna.

tankful [tangk'fəl] *n*: **to get a ~ of gasoline** llenar el tanque de gasolina.

tanned [tand] *a* (*skin*) moreno, bronceado.

tannin [tan'in] *n* tanino.

tanning [tan'ing] *n* (*of leather*) curtido.

tantalizing [tan'təlīzing] *a* tentador(a).

tantamount [tan'təmount] *a*: **~ to** equivalente a.

tantrum [tan'trəm] *n* rabieta; **to throw a ~** coger una rabieta.

Tanzania [tanzənē'ə] *n* Tanzanía.

Tanzanian [tanzənē'ən] *a, n* tanzano/a *m/f*.

tap [tap] *n* (*on sink etc*) grifo, canilla (*LAm*); (*gentle blow*) golpecito; (*Brit: gas ~*) llave *f* ♦ *vt* (*table etc*) tamborilear; (*shoulder etc*) palmear; (*resources*) utilizar, explotar; (*telephone conversation*) interceptar, escuchar clandestinamente; **on ~** (*fig: resources*) a mano; **beer on ~** cerveza de barril.

tap-dancing [tap'dansing] *n* claqué *m*.

tape [tāp] *n* cinta; (*also:* **magnetic ~**) cinta magnética; (*Brit: sticky ~*) cinta adhesiva ♦ *vt* (*record*) grabar (en cinta); **on ~** (*song etc*) grabado (en cinta).

tape deck *n* tocacassettes *m inv*.

tape measure *n* cinta métrica, metro.

taper [tā'pûr] *n* cirio ♦ *vi* afilarse.

tape-record [tāp'rikôrd] *vt* grabar (en cinta).

tape recorder *n* grabadora.

tape recording *n* grabación *f*.

tapered [tā'pûrd], **tapering** [tā'pûring] *a* terminado en punta.

tapestry [tap'istrē] *n* (*object*) tapiz *m*; (*art*) tapicería.

tapeworm [tāp'wûrm'] *n* solitaria, tenia.

tapioca [tapēō'kə] *n* tapioca *m*.

tappet [tap'it] *n* varilla de levantamiento.

tar [târ] *n* alquitrán *m*, brea; **low/middle ~ cigarettes** cigarrillos con contenido bajo/medio de alquitrán.

tarantula [təran'chələ] *n* tarántula.

tardy [târ'dē] *a* (*late*) tardío; (*slow*) lento.

tare [tär] *n* (*COMM*) tara.

target [târ'git] *n* (*gen*) blanco; **to be on ~** (*project*) seguir el curso previsto.

target audience *n* público objetivo.

target market *n* (*COMM*) mercado objetivo.

target practice *n* tiro al blanco.

tariff [tar'if] *n* tarifa.

tariff barrier *n* (*COMM*) barrera arancelaria.

tarmac [târ'mak] *n* (*AVIAT*) pista (de aterrizaje); (*Brit: on road*) alquitranado.

tarn [târn] *n* lago pequeño de montaña.

tarnish [târ'nish] *vt* deslustrar.

tarpaulin [târpô'lin] *n* alquitranado.

tarragon [tar'əgən] *n* estragón *m*.

tarry [tar'ē] *vi* entretenerse, quedarse atrás.

tart [târt] *n* (*CULIN*) tarta; (*Brit col: pej: woman*) fulana ♦ *a* (*flavor*) agrio, ácido.

tart up *vt* (*Brit: room, building*) dar tono a.

tartan [târ'tən] *n* tartán *m*, escocés *m* ♦ *a* de tartán.

tartar [târ'tûr] *n* (*on teeth*) sarro.

tartar sauce *n* salsa tártara.

tartly [târt'lē] *ad* (*answer*) ásperamente.

task [task] *n* tarea; **to take to ~** reprender.

task force *n* (*MIL, POLICE*) grupo de operaciones.

taskmaster [task'mastûr] *n*: **he's a hard ~** es muy exigente.

Tasmania [tazmā'nēə] *n* Tasmania.

tassel [tas'əl] *n* borla.

taste [tāst] *n* sabor *m*, gusto; (*also:* **after~**) dejo; (*sip*) sorbo; (*fig: glimpse, idea*) muestra, idea ♦ *vt* probar ♦ *vi*: **to ~ of** *or* **like** (*fish etc*) saber a; **you can ~ the garlic (in it)** se nota el sabor a ajo; **can I have a ~ of this wine?** ¿puedo probar este vino?; **to have a ~ for sth** ser aficionado a algo; **in good/bad ~** de buen/mal gusto; **to be in bad** *or* **poor ~** ser de mal gusto.

taste bud *n* papila gustativa *or* del gusto.

tasteful [tāst'fəl] *a* de buen gusto.

tastefully [tāst'fəlē] *ad* elegantemente, con buen gusto.

tasteless [tāst'lis] *a* (*food*) soso; (*remark*) de mal gusto.

tastelessly [tāst'lislē] *ad* con mal gusto.

tastily [tās'tilē] *ad* sabrosamente.

tastiness [tās'tēnis] *n* (buen) sabor *m*, lo sabroso.

tasty [tās'tē] *a* sabroso, rico.

ta-ta [tátá'] *interj* (*Brit col*) hasta luego, adiós.

tatters [tat'ûrz] *npl*: **in ~** (*also:* **tattered**) hecho jirones.

tattoo [tatōō'] *n* tatuaje *m*; (*spectacle*) espectáculo militar ♦ *vt* tatuar.

tatty [tat'ē] *a* (*Brit col*) raído.

taught [tôt] *pt, pp of* **teach**.

taunt [tônt] *n* burla ♦ *vt* burlarse de.

Taurus [tôr'əs] *n* Tauro.

taut [tôt] *a* tirante, tenso.

tavern [tav'ûrn] *n* (*old*) posada, fonda.

tawdry [tô'drē] *a* de mal gusto.

tawny [tô'nē] *a* leonado.

tax [taks] *n* impuesto ♦ *vt* gravar (con un impuesto); (*fig: test*) poner a prueba; (: *patience*) agotar; **before/after ~** impuestos excluidos/incluidos; **free of ~** libre de impuestos.

taxable [tak'səbəl] *a* (*income*) imponible, sujeto a impuestos.

tax allowance *n* desgravación *f* fiscal.

taxation [taksā'shən] *n* impuestos *mpl*; **system of ~** sistema *m* tributario.

tax avoidance *n* evasión *f* de impuestos.

tax collector *n* recaudador(a) *m/f*.

tax disc *n* (*Brit AUT*) pegatina del impuesto

de circulación.

tax evasion *n* evasión *f* fiscal.

tax exemption *n* exención *f* de impuestos.

tax-free |taks'frē'| *a* libre de impuestos.

tax haven *n* paraíso fiscal.

taxi |tak'sē| *n* taxi *m* ♦ *vi* (*AVIAT*) rodar por la pista.

taxidermist |tak'sidûrmist| *n* taxidermista *m/f*.

taxi driver *n* taxista *m/f*.

taximeter |tak'simētûr| *n* taxímetro.

tax inspector *n* tasador(a) *m/f* de impuestos.

taxi rank *n* (*Brit*) = **taxi stand**.

taxi stand *n* parada de taxis.

tax payer *n* contribuyente *m/f*.

tax rebate *n* devolución *f* de impuestos, reembolso fiscal.

tax relief *n* desgravación *f* fiscal.

tax return *n* declaración *f* de ingresos.

tax shelter *n* protección *f* fiscal.

tax year *n* año fiscal.

TB *n abbr* = **tuberculosis**.

TD *n abbr* (*US*) = **Treasury Department**; (: *SOCCER*) = **touchdown**.

tea |tē| *n* té *m*; (*Brit*: *snack*) merienda; **high ~** (*Brit*) merienda-cena.

tea bag *n* bolsita de té.

tea break *n* (*Brit*) descanso para el té.

teach, *pt*, *pp* **taught** |tēch, tôt| *vt*: **to ~ sb sth**, **~ sth to sb** enseñar algo a uno ♦ *vi* enseñar; (*be a teacher*) ser profesor(a); **it taught him a lesson** (eso) le sirvió de escarmiento.

teacher |tē'chûr| *n* (*in secondary school*) profesor(a) *m/f*; (*in primary school*) maestro/a; **Spanish ~** profesor(a) *m/f* de español.

teacher training college *n* (*for primary schools*) escuela normal; (*for secondary schools*) centro de formación profesoral.

teach-in |tēch'in| *n* reunión tipo seminario con fines formativos o didácticos.

teaching |tē'ching| *n* enseñanza.

teaching aids *npl* ayudas *fpl* pedagógicas.

teaching hospital *n* hospital *m* con facultad de medicina.

tea cosy *n* cubretetera *m*.

teacup |tē'kup| *n* taza para el té.

teak |tēk| *n* (madera de) teca.

tea leaves *npl* hojas *fpl* de té.

team |tēm| *n* equipo; (*of animals*) pareja.

team up *vi* asociarse.

team spirit *n* espíritu *m* de equipo.

teamwork |tēm'wûrk| *n* trabajo en equipo.

tea party *n* té *m*.

teapot |tē'pât| *n* tetera.

tear *n* |tär| rasgón *m*, desgarrón *m*; |tēr| lágrima ♦ *vb* |tär| (*pt* **tore**, *pp* **torn** |tôr, tôrn|) *vt* romper, rasgar ♦ *vi* rasgarse; **in ~s** llorando; **to burst into ~s** deshacerse en lágrimas; **to ~ to pieces** *or* **to bits** *or* **to shreds** (*also fig*) hacer pedazos, destro-

zar.

tear along *vi* (*rush*) precipitarse.

tear apart *vt* (*also fig*) hacer pedazos.

tear away *vt*: **to ~ o.s. away (from sth)** arrancarse (de algo), dejar (algo).

tear out *vt* (*sheet of paper, check*) arrancar.

tear up *vt* (*sheet of paper etc*) romper.

teardrop |tēr'drâp| *n* lágrima.

tearful |tēr'fəl| *a* lloroso.

tear gas *n* gas *m* lacrimógeno.

tearoom |tē'rōōm| *n* salón *m* de té, cafetería.

tease |tēz| *n* bromista *m/f* ♦ *vt* tomar el pelo a; (*hair*) cardar.

tea set *n* servicio de té.

teashop |tē'shâp| *n* café *m*, cafetería.

teaspoon |tē'spōōn| *n* cucharita; (*also*: **~ful**: *as measurement*) cucharadita.

tea strainer *n* colador *m* de té.

teat |tēt| *n* (*of bottle*) boquilla, tetilla.

teatime |tē'tīm| *n* hora del té.

tea towel *n* (*Brit*) paño de cocina.

tea urn *n* tetera grande.

tech |tek| *n abbr* (*col*) = **technology**; **technical college**.

technical |tek'nikəl| *a* técnico.

technical college *n* centro de formación profesional.

technicality |teknikal'itē| *n* detalle *m* técnico; **on a legal ~** por una cuestión formal.

technically |tek'niklē| *ad* técnicamente.

technician |teknish'ən| *n* técnico/a.

technique |teknēk'| *n* técnica.

technocrat |tek'nəkrat| *n* tecnócrata *m/f*.

technological |teknəlâj'ikəl| *a* tecnológico.

technologist |teknâl'əjist| *n* tecnólogo/a.

technology |teknâl'əjē| *n* tecnología.

teddy (bear) |ted'ē (bär)| *n* osito de felpa.

tedious |tē'dēəs| *a* pesado, aburrido.

tediously |tē'dēəslē| *ad* aburridamente, de modo pesado.

tedium |tē'dēəm| *n* tedio.

tee |tē| *n* (*GOLF*) tee *m*.

teem |tēm| *vi*: **to ~ with** rebosar de.

teenage |tēn'āj| *a* (*fashions etc*) juvenil.

teenager |tēn'ājûr| *n* joven *m/f* (de 13 a 19 años).

teens |tēnz| *npl*: **to be in one's ~** ser adolescente.

tee shirt *n* = **T-shirt**.

teeter |tē'tûr| *vi* balancearse.

teeth |tēth| *npl* of **tooth**.

teethe |tēth| *vi* echar los dientes.

teething ring |tē'thing ring| *n* mordedor *m*.

teething troubles |tē'thing trub'əlz| *npl* (*fig*) dificultades *fpl* iniciales.

teetotal |tētōt'əl| *a* (*person*) abstemio.

teetotaler, (*Brit*) **teetotaller** |tētōt'əlûr| *n* (*person*) abstemio/a.

TEFL |tef'əl| *n abbr* = *Teaching of English as a Foreign Language*.

Teheran [teərân'] n Teherán m.

tel. abbr (= telephone) tel.

Tel Aviv [tel' əvēv'] n Tel Aviv m.

telecast [tel'əkast] vt, vi transmitir por televisión.

telecommunications [teləkəmyōōnikā'shənz] n telecomunicaciones fpl.

telegram [tel'əgram] n telegrama m.

telegraph [tel'əgraf] n telégrafo.

telegraphic [teləgraf'ik] a telegráfico.

telegraph pole n poste m telegráfico.

telegraph wire n hilo telegráfico.

telepathic [teləpath'ik] a telepático.

telepathy [təlep'əthē] n telepatía.

telephone [tel'əfōn] n teléfono ♦ vt llamar por teléfono, telefonear; **to be on the ~** (be speaking) estar hablando por teléfono.

telephone booth, (Brit) **telephone box** n cabina telefónica.

telephone call n llamada (telefónica).

telephone directory n guía (telefónica).

telephone exchange n central f telefónica.

telephone kiosk n (Brit) cabina telefónica.

telephone number n número de teléfono.

telephone operator n telefonista m/f.

telephonist [tel'əfōnist] n (Brit) telefonista m/f.

telephoto [teləfō'tō] a: ~ **lens** teleobjetivo.

teleprinter [tel'əprintûr] n teletipo, teleimpresora.

telescope [tel'əskōp] n telescopio.

telescopic [teliskâp'ik] a telescópico; (umbrella) plegable.

teletext [tel'ətekst] n (TEL) teletex(to) m.

telethon [tel'əthân] n maratón m televisivo.

televise [tel'əvīz] vt televisar.

television [tel'əvizhən] n televisión f; **to watch ~** mirar la televisión.

television licence n (Brit) impuesto de televisor.

television set n televisor m.

telex [tel'eks] n télex m; (machine) máquina télex ♦ vt (message) enviar por télex; (person) enviar un télex a ♦ vi enviar un télex.

tell, pt, pp **told**, [tel, tōld] vt decir; (relate: story) contar; (distinguish): **to ~ sth from** distinguir algo de ♦ vi (talk): **to ~ (of)** contar; (have effect) tener efecto; **to ~ sb to do sth** mandar a uno hacer algo; **to ~ sb about sth** explicar algo a uno; **can you ~ me the time?** ¿me puedes decir la hora?; **(I) ~ you what ...** fíjate ...; **I couldn't ~ them apart** no podía distinguirlos.

  tell off vt: **to ~ sb off** regañar a uno.

  tell on vt fus: **to ~ on sb** chivarse de uno.

teller [tel'ûr] n (in bank) cajero/a.

telling [tel'ing] a (remark, detail) revelador(a).

telltale [tel'tāl] a (sign) indicador(a).

telly [tel'ē] n (Brit col) tele f.

temerity [təmär'itē] n temeridad f.

temp [temp] n abbr (= temporary office worker) temporero/a ♦ vi trabajar de interino/a.

temper [tem'pûr] n (mood) humor m; (bad ~) (mal) genio; (fit of anger) ira; (of child) rabieta ♦ vt (moderate) moderar; **to be in a ~** estar furioso; **to lose one's ~** enfadarse, enojarse (LAm); **to keep one's ~** contenerse, no alterarse.

temperament [tem'pûrəmənt] n (nature) temperamento.

temperamental [tempûrəmen'təl] a temperamental.

temperance [tem'pûrəns] n moderación f; (in drinking) sobriedad f.

temperate [tem'pûrit] a moderado; (climate) templado.

temperature [tem'pûrəchûr] n temperatura; **to have** or **run a ~** tener fiebre.

tempered [tem'pûrd] a (steel) templado.

tempest [tem'pist] n tempestad f.

tempestuous [tempes'chōōəs] a (relationship, meeting) tempestuoso.

tempi [tem'pē] npl of **tempo**.

template [tem'plit] n plantilla.

temple [tem'pəl] n (building) templo; (ANAT) sien f.

templet [tem'plit] n = **template**.

tempo, pl ~s or **tempi** [tem'pō, tem'pē] n tempo; (fig: of life etc) ritmo.

temporal [tem'pûrəl] a temporal.

temporarily [tempərär'ilē] ad temporalmente.

temporary [tem'pərärē] a provisional, temporal; (passing) transitorio; (worker) temporero; ~ **teacher** (Brit) maestro/a interino/a.

tempt [tempt] vt tentar; **to ~ sb into doing sth** tentar or inducir a uno a hacer algo; **to be ~ed to do sth** (person) sentirse tentado de hacer algo.

temptation [temptā'shən] n tentación f.

tempting [temp'ting] a tentador(a).

ten [ten] num diez; **~s of thousands** decenas fpl de miles.

tenable [ten'əbəl] a sostenible.

tenacious [tənā'shəs] a tenaz.

tenaciously [tənā'shəslē] ad tenazmente.

tenacity [tənas'itē] n tenacidad f.

tenancy [ten'ənsē] n alquiler m; (of house) inquilinato.

tenant [ten'ənt] n (rent-payer) inquilino/a; (occupant) habitante m/f.

tend [tend] vt (sick etc) cuidar, atender; (cattle, machine) vigilar, cuidar ♦ vi: **to ~ to do sth** tener tendencia a hacer algo.

tendency [ten'dənsē] n tendencia.

tender [ten'dûr] a tierno, blando; (delicate) delicado; (sore) sensible; (affectionate) tierno, cariñoso ♦ n (COMM: offer) oferta; (money): **legal ~** moneda de curso legal ♦

vt ofrecer; **to put in a ~ (for)** hacer una oferta (para); **to ~ one's resignation** presentar la dimisión.

tenderize [ten'dərīz] *vt* (*CULIN*) ablandar.

tenderly [ten'dúrlē] *ad* tiernamente.

tenderness [ten'dúrnis] *n* ternura; (*of meat*) blandura.

tendon [ten'dən] *n* tendón *m*.

tendril [ten'dril] *n* zarcillo.

tenement [ten'əmənt] *n* casa *or* bloque *m* de pisos *or* vecinos (*Sp*).

Tenerife [tenərēf'] *n* Tenerife *m*.

tenet [ten'it] *n* principio.

Tenn. *abbr* (*US*) = *Tennessee.*

tenner [ten'ûr] *n* (*US*) (billete *m* de) diez dólares *mpl*; (*Brit*) (billete *m* de) diez libras *fpl*.

tennis [ten'is] *n* tenis *m*.

tennis ball *n* pelota de tenis.

tennis club *n* club *m* de tenis.

tennis court *n* cancha de tenis.

tennis elbow *n* (*MED*) sinovitis *f* del codo.

tennis match *n* partido de tenis.

tennis player *n* tenista *m/f*.

tennis racket *n* raqueta de tenis.

tennis shoes *npl* zapatillas *fpl* de tenis.

tenor [ten'ûr] *n* (*MUS*) tenor *m*.

tenpin bowling [ten'pin bō'ling] *n* bolos *mpl*, bolera.

tense [tens] *a* tenso; (*stretched*) tirante; (*stiff*) rígido, tieso; (*person*) nervioso ♦ *n* (*LING*) tiempo ♦ *vt* (*tighten: muscles*) tensar.

tensely [tens'lē] *ad* tensamente.

tenseness [tens'nis] *n* tirantez *f*, tensión *f*.

tension [ten'chən] *n* tensión *f*.

tent [tent] *n* tienda (de campaña), carpa (*LAm*).

tentacle [ten'təkəl] *n* tentáculo.

tentative [ten'tətiv] *a* (*person*) indeciso; (*provisional*) provisional.

tentatively [ten'tətivlē] *ad* con indecisión; (*provisionally*) provisionalmente.

tenterhooks [ten'tûrhōōks] *npl*: **on ~** sobre ascuas.

tenth [tenth] *a* décimo.

tent peg *n* clavija, estaca.

tent pole *n* mástil *m*.

tenuous [ten'yōōəs] *a* tenue.

tenure [ten'yûr] *n* posesión *f*, tenencia; **to have ~** tener posesión *or* título de propiedad.

tepid [tep'id] *a* tibio.

term [tûrm] *n* (*limit*) límite *m*; (*COMM*) plazo; (*word*) término; (*period*) período; (*SCOL*) trimestre *m* ♦ *vt* llamar; **~s** *npl* (*conditions*) condiciones *fpl*; (*COMM*) precio, tarifa; **in the short/long ~** a corto/largo plazo; **during his ~ of office** bajo su mandato; **to be on good ~s with sb** llevarse bien con uno; **to come to ~s with** (*problem*) adaptarse a; **in ~s of ...** en cuanto a ..., en términos de ....

terminal [tûr'mənəl] *a* terminal; (*disease*) mortal ♦ *n* (*ELEC*) borne *m*; (*COMPUT*) terminal *m*; (*also*: **air ~**) terminal *f*; (*Brit: also*: **coach ~**) (estación *f*) terminal *f*.

terminate [tûr'mənāt] *vt* terminar ♦ *vi*: **to ~ in** acabar por.

termination [tûrmənā'shən] *n* fin *m*; (*of contract*) terminación *f*; **~ of pregnancy** aborto.

termini [tûr'mənē] *npl of* **terminus.**

terminology [tûrmənâl'əjē] *n* terminología.

terminus, *pl* termini [tûr'mənəs, tûr'mənē] *n* término, (estación *f*) terminal *f*.

termite [tûr'mīt] *n* termita.

Ter(r). *abbr* = **terrace.**

terrace [tär'əs] *n* terraza; (*Brit: row of houses*) hilera de casas adosadas; **the ~s** (*Brit SPORT*) las gradas *fpl*.

terraced [tär'əst] *a* (*garden*) escalonado; (*house*) alineado, adosado.

terracotta [tärəkät'ə] *n* terracota.

terrain [tərān'] *n* terreno.

terrible [tär'əbəl] *a* terrible, horrible; (*fam*) malísimo.

terribly [tär'əblē] *ad* terriblemente; (*very badly*) malísimamente.

terrier [tär'ēûr] *n* terrier *m*.

terrific [tərif'ik] *a* fantástico, fenomenal; (*wonderful*) maravilloso.

terrify [tär'əfī] *vt* aterrorizar; **to be terrified** estar aterrado *or* aterrorizado.

terrifying [tär'əfīing] *a* aterrador(a).

territorial [täritôr'ēəl] *a* territorial.

territorial waters *npl* aguas *fpl* jurisdiccionales.

territory [tär'itôrē] *n* territorio.

terror [tär'úr] *n* terror *m*.

terrorism [tär'ərizəm] *n* terrorismo.

terrorist [tär'úrist] *n* terrorista *m/f*.

terrorize [tär'ərīz] *vt* aterrorizar.

terse [tûrs] *a* (*style*) conciso; (*reply*) brusco.

tertiary [tûr'shēärē] *a* terciario.

Terylene [tär'əlēn] ® *n* (*Brit*) terylene *m* ®.

TESL [tes'əl] *n abbr* = *Teaching of English as a Second Language.*

test [test] *n* (*trial, check*) prueba, ensayo; (: *of goods in factory*) control *m*; (*of courage etc*, *CHEM*) prueba; (*MED*) examen *m*; (*exam*) examen *m*, test *m*; (*also*: **driving ~**) examen *m* de conducir ♦ *vt* probar, poner a prueba; (*MED*) examinar; **to put sth to the ~** someter algo a prueba; **to ~ sth for sth** analizar algo en busca de algo.

testament [tes'təmənt] *n* testamento; **the Old/New T~** el Antiguo/Nuevo Testamento.

test ban *n* (*also*: **nuclear ~**) suspensión *f* de pruebas nucleares.

test case *n* (*JUR*) juicio que sienta precedente.

test flight *n* vuelo de ensayo.

testicle [tes'tikəl] *n* testículo.

testify [tes'təfī] *vi* (*LAW*) prestar declaración; **to ~ to sth** atestiguar algo.

testimonial [testimō'nēəl] *n* (*of character*) (carta de) recomendación *f*, testimonial *m*.

testimony [tes'təmōnē] *n* (*LAW*) testimonio, declaración *f*.

testing [tes'ting] *a* (*difficult: time*) duro.

testing ground *n* zona de pruebas.

test match *n* (*Brit CRICKET, RUGBY*) partido internacional.

test paper *n* examen *m*, test *m*.

test pilot *n* piloto/mujer piloto *m/f* de pruebas.

test tube *n* probeta.

test-tube baby [tes'tōōb bā'bē] *n* bebé *m* (de) probeta.

testy [tes'tē] *a* irritable.

tetanus [tet'ənəs] *n* tétano.

tetchy [tech'ē] *a* malhumorado, irritable.

tether [teth'ûr] *vt* atar (con una cuerda) ♦ *n*: **to be at the end of one's ~** (*Brit*) no aguantar más.

Tex. *abbr* (*US*) = *Texas*.

text [tekst] *n* texto.

textbook [tekst'bŏōk] *n* libro de texto.

textiles [teks'təlz] *npl* textiles *mpl*, tejidos *mpl*.

texture [teks'chûr] *n* textura.

TGIF *abbr* (*col*) = *thank God it's Friday*.

Thai [tī] *a*, *n* tailandés/esa *m/f*.

Thailand [tī'lənd] *n* Tailandia.

thalidomide [thəlid'əmīd] ® *n* talidomida ®.

Thames [temz] *n*: **the ~** el (río) Támesis.

than [than, then] *conj* que; (*with numerals*): **more ~ 10/once** más de 10/una vez; **I have more/less ~ you** tengo más/menos que tú; **it is better to phone ~ to write** es mejor llamar por teléfono que escribir; **no sooner did he leave ~ the phone rang** en cuanto se marchó, sonó el teléfono.

thank [thangk] *vt* dar las gracias a, agradecer; **~ you (very much)** muchas gracias; **~ heavens, ~ God!** ¡gracias a Dios!, ¡menos mal!

thankful [thangk'fəl] *a*: **~ for** agradecido (por).

thankfully [thangk'fəlē] *ad* (*gratefully*) con agradecimiento; (*with relief*) por suerte; **~ there were few victims** afortunadamente hubo pocas víctimas.

thankless [thangk'lis] *a* ingrato.

thanks [thangks] *npl* gracias *fpl* ♦ *excl* ¡gracias!; **~ to** *prep* gracias a.

Thanksgiving (Day) [thangksgiv'ing (dā)] *n* día *m* de Acción de Gracias.

that [that, thət] *conj* que ♦ *a* ese/esa; (*more remote*) aquel/aquella ♦ *pron* ése/ésa; aquél/aquélla; (*neuter*) eso; aquello; (*relative: subject*) que; (: *object*) que, el cual/la cual *etc*; (*with time*): **on the day ~ he came** el día que vino ♦ *ad*: **~ high** tan alto,

así de alto; **it's about ~ high** es más o menos así de alto; **~ one** ése/ésa; aquél/aquélla; **~ one over there** aquél/aquélla; **what's ~?** ¿qué es eso?; **who's ~?** ¿quién es?; **is ~ you?** ¿eres tú?; (*formal*) ¿es usted?; **~'s what he said** eso es lo que dijo; **all ~** todo eso; **I can't work ~ much** no puedo trabajar tanto; **at** *or* **with ~ she ...** con eso, ella ...; **do it like ~** hazlo así; **not ~ I know of** que yo sepa, no; **so ~, in order ~** para que + *subjun*.

thatched [thacht] *a* (*roof*) de paja; **~ cottage** casita con tejado de paja.

thaw [thô] *n* deshielo ♦ *vi* (*ice*) derretirse; (*food*) descongelarse ♦ *vt* (*food*) descongelar.

the [thə, thē] *def art* el/la; (*pl*) los/las; (*neuter*) lo; (*in titles*): **Richard ~ Second** Ricardo Segundo; **~ sooner ~ better** cuanto antes mejor; **~ more he works, ~ more he earns** cuanto más trabaja, más gana; **I haven't ~ time/money** no tengo tiempo/dinero; **100 pesetas to ~ dollar** 100 pesetas por dólar; **paid by ~ hour** pagado por hora; **do you know ~ Smiths?** ¿conoce a los Smith?

theater, (*Brit*) **theatre** [thē'ətûr] *n* teatro.

theatergoer [thē'ətûrgŏūr] *n* aficionado/a al teatro.

theatrical [thēat'rikəl] *a* teatral.

theft [theft] *n* robo.

their [thär] *a* su.

theirs [thärz] *pron* (el) suyo/(la) suya *etc*; *see also* **my, mine**.

them [them, thəm] *pron* (*direct*) los/las; (*indirect*) les; (*stressed, after prep*) ellos/ellas; **I see ~** los veo; **both of ~** ambos/as, los/las dos; **give me a few of ~** dame algunos/as; *see also* **me**.

theme [thēm] *n* tema *m*.

theme song *n* tema *m* (musical).

themselves [thəmselvz'] *pl pron* (*subject*) ellos mismos/ellas mismas; (*complement*) se; (*after prep*) sí (mismos/as); *see also* **oneself**.

then [then] *ad* (*at that time*) entonces; (*next*) pues; (*later*) luego, después; (*and also*) además ♦ *conj* (*therefore*) en ese caso, entonces ♦ *a*: **the ~ president** el entonces presidente; **from ~ on** desde entonces; **until ~** hasta entonces; **and ~ what?** y luego, ¿qué?; **what do you want me to do, ~?** ¿qué quiere que haga, entonces?

theologian [thēəlō'jən] *n* teólogo/a.

theological [thēəláj'ikəl] *a* teológico.

theology [thēál'əjē] *n* teología.

theorem [thēr'əm] *n* teorema *m*.

theoretical [thēəret'ikəl] *a* teórico.

theoretically [thēəret'ikəlē] *ad* teóricamente, en teoría.

theorize [thē'ərīz] *vi* teorizar.

theory [thiûr'ē] *n* teoría.

therapeutic(al) [thärəpyōō'tik(əl)] a terapéutico.

therapist [thär'əpist] n terapeuta m/f.

therapy [thär'əpē] n terapia.

there [thär] ad allí, allá, ahí; ~, ~! ¡cálmate!; **it's** ~ está ahí; ~**'s the bus** ahí or ya viene el autobús; ~ **is**, ~ **are** hay; ~ **he is** ahí está; **on/in** ~ allí encima/dentro; **back/down** ~ allá or allí atrás/abajo; **over** ~, **through** ~ por allí.

thereabouts [thär'əbouts] ad por ahí.

thereafter [thäraf'tûr] ad después.

thereby [thärbī'] ad así, de ese modo.

therefore [thär'fôr] ad por lo tanto.

there's [thärz] = **there is**; **there has**.

thereupon [thärəpân'] ad (at that point) en eso, en seguida.

thermal [thûr'məl] a termal.

thermal paper n papel m térmico.

thermal printer n termoimpresora.

thermodynamics [thûrmōdīnam'iks] n termodinámica.

thermometer [thûrmâm'itûr] n termómetro.

thermonuclear [thûrmōnōō'klēûr] a termonuclear.

Thermos [thûr'məs] ® n termo.

thermostat [thûr'məstat] n termostato.

thesaurus [thisôr'əs] n tesoro.

these [thēz] pl a estos/as ♦ pl pron éstos/as.

thesis, pl **theses** [thē'sis, -sēz] n tesis f inv.

they [thā] pl pron ellos/ellas; (stressed) ellos (mismos)/ellas (mismas); ~ **say that...** (it is said that) se dice que....

they'd [thād] = **they had**; **they would**.

they'll [thāl] = **they shall**, **they will**.

they're [thār] = **they are**.

they've [thāv] = **they have**.

thick [thik] a (wall, slice) grueso; (dense: liquid, smoke etc) espeso; (vegetation, beard) tupido; (stupid) torpe ♦ n: **in the** ~ **of the battle** en lo más reñido de la batalla; **it's 20 cm** ~ tiene 20 cm de espesor.

thicken [thik'ən] vi espesarse ♦ vt (sauce etc) espesar.

thicket [thik'it] n espesura.

thickly [thik'lē] ad (spread) en capa espesa; (cut) en rebanada gruesa; (populated) densamente.

thickness [thik'nis] n espesor m, grueso.

thickset [thik'set'] a (Brit) fornido.

thickskinned [thik'skind'] a (fig) insensible.

thief, pl **thieves** [thēf, thēvz] n ladrón/ona m/f.

thieving [thē'ving] n robo, hurto ♦ a ladrón/ona.

thigh [thī] n muslo.

thighbone [thī'bōn] n fémur m.

thimble [thim'bəl] n dedal m.

thin [thin] a delgado; (watery) aguado; (light) tenue; (hair) escaso; (fog) ligero; (crowd) disperso ♦ vt: **to** ~ **(down)** (sauce, paint) diluir ♦ vi (fog) aclararse; (also: ~

out: crowd) dispersarse; **his hair is** ~**ning** está perdiendo (el) pelo.

thing [thing] n cosa; (object) objeto, artículo; (contraption) chisme m; (mania) manía; ~**s** npl (belongings) efectos mpl (personales); **the best** ~ **would be to...** lo mejor sería...; **the main** ~ **is to ...** lo principal que hay que hacer es ...; **first** ~ **(in the morning)** a primera hora (de la mañana); **last** ~ **(at night)** a última hora (de la noche); **the** ~ **is ...** lo que pasa es que ...; **how are** ~**s?** ¿qué tal?; **she's got a** ~ **about mice** le da no sé qué de los ratones; **poor** ~! ¡pobre! m/f, ¡pobrecito/a!

think, pt, pp **thought** [thingk, thôt] vi pensar ♦ vt (imagine) imaginar; **what did you** ~ **of it?** ¿qué te parece?; **what did you** ~ **of them?** ¿qué te parecieron?; **to** ~ **about sth/sb** pensar en algo/ uno; **I'll** ~ **about it** lo pensaré; **to** ~ **of doing sth** pensar en hacer algo; **I** ~ **so/not** creo que sí/no; ~ **again!** ¡piénsalo bien!; **to** ~ **aloud** pensar en voz alta; **to** ~ **well of sb** tener buen concepto de uno.

think out vt (plan) elaborar, tramar; (solution) encontrar.

think over vt reflexionar sobre, meditar; **I'd like to** ~ **things over** me gustaría examinarlo detenidamente.

think through vt pensar bien.

think up vt imaginar.

thinking [thingk'ing] n: **to my (way of)** ~ a mi parecer.

think tank n gabinete m de estrategia.

thinly [thin'lē] ad (cut) en lonchas finas; (spread) en una ligera capa.

thinness [thin'is] n delgadez f.

third [thûrd] a (before nmsg: **tercer**) tercero ♦ n tercero/a; (fraction) tercio.

third degree a (burns) de tercer grado.

thirdly [thûrd'lē] ad en tercer lugar.

third party insurance n (Brit) seguro contra terceros.

third-rate [thûrd'rāt'] a (de calidad) mediocre.

Third World n: **the** ~ el Tercer Mundo ♦ cpd tercermundista.

thirst [thûrst] n sed f.

thirsty [thûrs'tē] a (person) sediento; **to be** ~ tener sed.

thirteen [thûr'tēn'] num trece.

thirteenth [thûr'tēnth'] a decimotercero ♦ n (in series) decimotercero/a; (fraction) decimotercio.

thirtieth [thûr'tēith] a trigésimo ♦ n (in series) trigésimo/a; (fraction) treintavo.

thirty [thûr'tē] num treinta.

this [this] a este/esta ♦ pron éste/ésta; (neuter) esto; ~ **is what he said** esto es lo que dijo; ~ **high** así de alto; ~ **way** por aquí; ~ **time** esta vez; ~ **time last year** hoy hace un año; **who is** ~? ¿quién es éste/ ésta? **what is** ~? ¿qué es esto?; ~ **is Mr**

Brown (*in introductions*) le presento al Sr Brown; (*in photo*) éste es el Sr Brown; (*on telephone*) el Sr Brown al habla; **they were talking of ~ and that** hablaban de esto y aquello.

thistle [this'əl] *n* cardo.

thong [thông] *n* correa.

thorn [thôrn] *n* espina.

thorny [thôr'nē] *a* espinoso.

thorough [thûr'ō] *a* (*search*) minucioso; (*knowledge, research*) profundo.

thoroughbred [thûr'ōbred] *a* (*horse*) de pura sangre.

thoroughfare [thûr'ōfär] *n* calle *f*.

thoroughly [thûr'ōlē] *ad* minuciosamente; profundamente, a fondo.

thoroughness [thûr'ōnis] *n* minuciosidad *f*.

those [thōz] *pl pron* ésos/ésas; (*more remote*) aquéllos/as ♦ *pl a* esos/esas; aquellos/as.

though [thō] *conj* aunque ♦ *ad* sin embargo, aún así; **even ~** aunque; **it's not so easy, ~** sin embargo no es tan fácil.

thought [thôt] *pt, pp of* **think** ♦ *n* pensamiento; (*opinion*) opinión *f*; (*intention*) intención *f*; **to give sth some ~** pensar algo detenidamente; **after much ~** pensándolo bien; **I've just had a ~** se me acaba de ocurrir una idea.

thoughtful [thôt'fəl] *a* pensativo; (*considerate*) atento.

thoughtfully [thôt'fəlē] *ad* pensativamente; atentamente.

thoughtless [thôt'lis] *a* desconsiderado.

thoughtlessly [thôt'lislē] *ad* impensadamente, insensatamente.

thousand [thou'zənd] *num* mil; **two ~** dos mil; **~s of** miles de.

thousandth [thou'zəndth] *num* milésimo.

thrash [thrash] *vt* apalear; (*defeat*) derrotar.

thrash about *vi* revolcarse.

thrash out *vt* discutir a fondo.

thrashing [thrash'ing] *n*: **to give sb a ~** dar una paliza a uno.

thread [thred] *n* hilo; (*of screw*) rosca ♦ *vt* (*needle*) enhebrar.

threadbare [thred'bär] *a* raído.

threat [thret] *n* amenaza; **to be under ~ of** estar amenazado.

threaten [thret'ən] *vi* amenazar ♦ *vt*: **to ~ sb with sth/to do** amenazar a uno con algo/con hacer.

threatening [thret'əning] *a* amenazador(a), amenazante.

three [thrē] *num* tres.

three-dimensional [thrē'dimen'chənəl] *a* tridimensional.

threefold [thrē'fōld] *ad*: **to increase ~** triplicar.

three-piece [thrē'pēs] : **~ suit** *n* traje *m* de tres piezas; **~ suite** *n* tresillo.

three-ply [thrē'plī] *a* (*wood*) de tres capas;

(*wool*) triple.

three-quarter [thrē'kwôr'tûr] *a*: **~ length sleeves** mangas *fpl* tres cuartos.

three-quarters [thrē'kwôr'tûrz] *npl* tres cuartas partes; **~ full** tres cuartas partes lleno.

thresh [thresh] *vt* (AGR) trillar.

threshing machine [thresh'ing məshēn'] *n* trilladora.

threshold [thresh'ōld] *n* umbral *m*; **to be on the ~ of** (*fig*) estar al borde de.

threshold agreement *n* convenio de nivel crítico.

threw [thrōō] *pt of* **throw**.

thrift [thrift] *n* economía.

thrifty [thrif'tē] *a* económico.

thrill [thril] *n* (*excitement*) emoción *f* ♦ *vt* emocionar; **to be ~ed** (*with gift etc*) estar encantado.

thriller [thril'ûr] *n* película/novela de suspense.

thrilling [thril'ing] *a* emocionante.

thrive, *pt* **thrived, throve**, *pp* **thrived, thriven** [thrīv, thrōv, thriv'ən] *vi* (*grow*) crecer; (*do well*) prosperar.

thriving [thrīv'ing] *a* próspero.

throat [thrōt] *n* garganta; **to have a sore ~** tener dolor de garganta.

throb [thrâb] *n* (*of heart*) latido; (*of engine*) vibración *f* ♦ *vi* latir; vibrar; (*with pain*) dar punzadas; **my head is ~bing** la cabeza me da punzadas.

throes [thrōz] *npl*: **in the ~ of** en medio de.

thrombosis [thrâmbō'sis] *n* trombosis *f*.

throne [thrōn] *n* trono.

throng [thrông] *n* multitud *f*, muchedumbre *f* ♦ *vt, vi* apiñarse, agolparse.

throttle [thrât'əl] *n* (AUT) acelerador *m* ♦ *vt* estrangular.

through [thrōō] *prep* por, a través de; (*time*) durante; (*by means of*) por medio de, mediante; (*owing to*) gracias a ♦ *a* (*ticket, train*) directo ♦ *ad* completamente, de parte a parte; de principio a fin; **(from) Monday ~ Friday** (US) de lunes a viernes; **to go ~ sb's papers** mirar entre los papeles de uno; **I am halfway ~ the book** voy por la mitad del libro; **the soldiers didn't let us ~** los soldados no nos dejaron pasar; **to put sb ~ to sb** (TEL) poner or pasar a uno con uno; **to get ~** (TEL) tener comunicación; (*have finished*) haber terminado; **"no ~ road"** "calle sin salida".

throughout [thrōōout'] *prep* (*place*) por todas partes de, por todo; (*time*) durante todo ♦ *ad* por or en todas partes.

throughput [thrōō'pŏŏt] *n* (*of goods, materials*) producción *f*; (COMPUT) capacidad *f* de procesamiento.

throve [thrōv] *pt of* **thrive**.

throw [thrō] *n* tiro; (SPORT) lanzamiento ♦ *vt* (*pt* **threw**, *pp* **thrown** [thrōō, thrōn]) tirar, echar; (SPORT) lanzar; (*rider*) derribar; (*fig*) desconcertar; **to ~ a party** dar una fiesta.

throw about *vt* (*Brit*) = **throw around.**

throw around *vt* (*litter etc*) tirar, esparcir.

throw away *vt* tirar.

throw off *vt* deshacerse de.

throw open *vt* (*doors, windows*) abrir de par en par; (*house, gardens etc*) abrir al público; (*competition, race*) abrir a todos.

throw out *vt* tirar.

throw together *vt* (*clothes*) amontonar; (*meal*) preparar a la carrera; (*essay*) hacer sin cuidado.

throw up *vi* vomitar.

throwaway [thrō'əwā] *a* para tirar, desechable.

throwback [thrō'bak] *n*: **it's a ~ to** (*fig*) eso nos lleva de nuevo a.

throw-in [thrō'in] *n* (*SPORT*) saque *m*.

thrown [thrōn] *pp of* **throw.**

thru [thrōō] (*US*) = **through.**

thrush [thrush] *n* zorzal *m*, tordo; (*MED*) afta.

thrust [thrust] *n* (*TECH*) empuje *m* ♦ *vt* (*pt, pp* **thrust**) empujar; (*push in*) introducir.

thrusting [thrust'ing] *a* (*person*) dinámico, con empuje.

thud [thud] *n* golpe *m* sordo.

thug [thug] *n* gamberro/a.

thumb [thum] *n* (*ANAT*) pulgar *m* ♦ *vt*: **to ~ (a ride)** hacer autostop; **to give sth/sb the ~s up** aprobar algo/a uno.

thumb through *vt fus* (*book*) hojear.

thumb index *n* índice *m* recortado.

thumbnail [thum'nāl] *n* uña del pulgar.

thumbnail sketch *n* esbozo.

thumbtack [thum'tak] *n* (*US*) chincheta, chinche *m* (*LAm*).

thump [thump] *n* golpe *m*; (*sound*) ruido seco *or* sordo ♦ *vt, vi* golpear.

thunder [thun'dûr] *n* trueno; (*of applause etc*) estruendo ♦ *vi* tronar; (*train etc*): **to ~ past** pasar como un trueno.

thunderbolt [thun'dûrbōlt] *n* rayo.

thunderclap [thun'dûrklap] *n* trueno.

thunderous [thun'dûrəs] *a* ensordecedor(a), estruendoso.

thunderstorm [thun'dûrstôrm] *n* tormenta.

thunderstruck [thun'dûrstruk] *a* pasmado.

thundery [thun'dûrē] *a* tormentoso.

Thur(s). *abbr* (= *Thursday*) juev.

Thursday [thûrz'dā] *n* jueves *m inv.*

thus [thus] *ad* así, de este modo.

thwart [thwôrt] *vt* frustrar.

thyme [tīm] *n* tomillo.

thyroid [thī'roid] *n* tiroides *m inv.*

tiara [tēar'ə] *n* tiara, diadema.

Tiber [tī'bûr] *n* Tíber *m.*

Tibet [tibet'] *n* el Tibet.

Tibetan [tibet'ən] *a* tibetano ♦ *n* tibetano/a; (*LING*) tibetano.

tibia [tib'ēə] *n* tibia.

tic [tik] *n* tic *m.*

tick [tik] *n* (*sound: of clock*) tictac *m*; (*mark*) palomita; (*ZOOL*) garrapata ♦ *vi* hacer tictac ♦ *vt* marcar; **to put a ~ against sth** marcar algo (con palmita).

tick off *vt* marcar; (*person*) reñir.

tick over *vi* (*engine*) girar en marcha lenta; (: *fig*) ir tirando.

ticker tape [tik'ûr tāp] *n* cinta perforada.

ticket [tik'it] *n* billete *m*, tíquet *m*, boleto (*LAm*); (*for cinema etc*) entrada, boleto (*LAm*); (*in shop: on goods*) etiqueta; (*US POL*) lista (de candidatos); **to get a parking ~** (*AUT*) ser multado por estacionamiento ilegal.

ticket agency *n* (*THEATER*) agencia de billetes.

ticket collector *n* (*Brit*) revisor(a) *m/f.*

ticket holder *n* poseedor(a) *m/f* de billete.

ticket inspector *n* (*Brit*) revisor(a) *m/f*, inspector(a) *m/f* de boletos (*LAm*).

ticket office *n* (*THEATER*) taquilla, boletería (*LAm*); (*RAIL*) despacho de billetes *or* boletos (*LAm*).

tickle [tik'əl] *vt* hacer cosquillas a.

ticklish [tik'lish] *a* (*person*) cosquilloso; (*which tickles: blanket*) que pica; (: *cough*) irritante.

tidal [tīd'əl] *a* de marea.

tidal wave *n* maremoto.

tidbit [tid'bit] *n* (*US*) (*food*) golosina; (*news*) pedazo.

tiddlywinks [tid'lēwingks] *n* juego infantil de habilidad con fichas de plástico.

tide [tīd] *n* marea; (*fig: of events*) curso, marcha ♦ *vt*: **to ~ sb over** *or* **through (until)** ayudarle a uno con medios (hasta); **high/low ~** marea alta/baja; **the ~ of public opinion** la tendencia de la opinión pública.

tidily [tī'dilē] *ad* bien, ordenadamente; **to arrange ~** ordenar; **to dress ~** vestir bien.

tidiness [tī'dēnis] *n* (*order*) orden *m*; (*cleanliness*) aseo.

tidy [tī'dē] *a* (*room*) ordenado; (*drawing, work*) limpio; (*person*) (bien) arreglado; (: *in character*) metódico; (*mind*) claro, metódico ♦ *vt* (*also: ~ up*) poner en orden.

tie [tī] *n* (*string etc*) atadura; (*US RAIL: on track*) traviesa; (*Brit: neck~*) corbata; (*fig: link*) vínculo, lazo; (*SPORT: draw*) empate *m* ♦ *vt* atar ♦ *vi* (*SPORT*) empatar; **family ~s** obligaciones *fpl* familiares; **cup ~** (*Brit SPORT: match*) partido de copa; **to ~ in a bow** hacer un lazo; **to ~ a knot in sth** hacer un nudo en algo.

tie down *vt* atar; (*fig*): **to ~ sb down to** obligar a uno a.

tie in *vi*: **to ~ in (with)** (*correspond*) concordar (con).

tie on *vt* (*Brit: label etc*) atar.

tie up *vt* (*parcel*) envolver; (*dog*) atar;

(*boat*) amarrar; (*arrangements*) concluir; **to be ~d up** (*busy*) estar ocupado.

tie-break(er) [tī'brāk(ûr)] *n* (*TENNIS*) tie-break *m*, muerte *f* rápida; (*in quiz*) punto decisivo.

tie-on [tī'án] *a* (*Brit*: *label*) para atar.

tie-pin [tī'pin] *n* (*Brit*) alfiler *m* de corbata.

tier [tēr] *n* grada; (*of cake*) piso.

tie tack *n* (*US*) alfiler *m* de corbata.

tiff [tif] *n* (*col*) pelea, riña.

tiger [tī'gûr] *n* tigre *m*.

tight [tīt] *a* (*rope*) tirante; (*money*) escaso; (*clothes*, *budget*) ajustado; (*schedule*) apretado; (*col: drunk*) borracho ♦ *ad* (*squeeze*) muy fuerte; (*shut*) herméticamente; **to be packed ~** (*suitcase*) estar completamente lleno; (*people*) estar apretados; **everybody hold ~!** ¡agárrense bien!

tighten [tīt'ən] *vt* (*rope*) estirar; (*screw*) apretar ♦ *vi* estirarse; apretarse.

tightfisted [tīt'fis'tid] *a* tacaño.

tightly [tīt'lē] *ad* (*grasp*) muy fuerte.

tightness [tīt'nis] *n* (*of rope*) tirantez *f*; (*of clothes*, *budget*) estrechez *f*, lo ajustado.

tightrope [tīt'rōp] *n* cuerda floja.

tightrope walker *n* equilibrista *m/f*, funambulista *m/f*.

tights [tīts] *npl* (*US*) traje *m* de malla; (*Brit*) pantimedias *fpl*.

tigress [tī'gris] *n* tigresa.

tilde [til'də] *n* tilde *f*.

tile [tīl] *n* (*on roof*) teja; (*on floor*) baldosa; (*on wall*) azulejo ♦ *vt* (*floor*) poner baldosas en; (*wall*) poner azulejos en.

tiled [tīld] *a* (*floor*) embaldosado; (*wall*, *bathroom*) cubierto de azulejos; (*roof*) tejado.

till [til] *n* caja (registradora) ♦ *vt* (*land*) cultivar ♦ *prep*, *conj* = **until**.

tiller [til'ûr] *n* (*NAUT*) caña del timón.

tilt [tilt] *vt* inclinar ♦ *vi* inclinarse ♦ *n* (*slope*) inclinación *f*; **to wear one's hat at a ~** llevar el sombrero echado a un lado *or* terciado; **(at) full ~** a toda velocidad *or* carrera.

timber [tim'bûr] *n* (*material*) madera; (*trees*) árboles *mpl*.

time [tīm] *n* tiempo; (*epoch: often pl*) época; (*by clock*) hora; (*moment*) momento; (*occasion*) vez *f*; (*MUS*) compás *m* ♦ *vt* calcular *or* medir el tiempo de; (*race*) cronometrar; (*remark etc*) elegir el momento para; **a long ~** mucho tiempo; **4 at a ~** 4 a la vez; **for the ~ being** de momento, por ahora; **at ~s** a veces, a ratos; **~ after ~**, **~ and again** repetidas veces, una y otra vez; **from ~ to ~** de vez en cuando; **in ~** (*soon enough*) a tiempo; (*after some time*) con el tiempo; (*MUS*) al compás; **in a week's ~** dentro de una semana; **in no ~** en un abrir y cerrar de ojos; **any ~** cuando sea; **on ~** a la hora; **to buy sth on ~** (*US*) comprar algo a plazos *or* en abonos;

to be 30 minutes behind/ahead of ~ llevar media hora de retraso/adelanto; **to take one's ~** hacer las cosas con calma; **he'll do it in his own ~** (*without being hurried*) lo hará sin prisa; (*out of working hours*) lo hará en su tiempo libre; **by the ~ he arrived** cuando llegó; **5 ~s 5** 5 por 5; **what ~ is it?** ¿qué hora es?; **to be behind the ~s** estar atrasado; **to carry 3 boxes at a ~** llevar 3 cajas a la vez; **to keep ~** llevar el ritmo *or* el compás; **to have a good ~** pasarlo bien, divertirse; **to ~ sth well/badly** poner algo en vigor en un momento oportuno/inoportuno; **the bomb was ~d to explode 5 minutes later** la bomba estaba sincronizada para explotar 5 minutos más tarde.

time-and-motion expert [tīm'ənmō'shən ek'spûrt] *n* experto/a en la ciencia de la producción.

time-and-motion study [tīm'ənmō'shən stu'dē] *n* estudio de desplazamientos y tiempos.

time bomb *n* bomba de efecto retardado.

time card *n* tarjeta de registro horario.

time clock *n* reloj *m* registrador.

time-consuming [tīm'kənsōōming] *a* que requiere mucho tiempo.

time-honored [tīm'ânûrd] *a* consagrado.

timekeeper [tīm'kēpûr] *n* (*SPORT*) cronómetro.

time lag *n* desfase *m*.

timeless [tīm'lis] *a* eterno.

time limit *n* (*gen*) limitación *f* de tiempo; (*COMM*) plazo.

timely [tīm'lē] *a* oportuno.

time off *n* tiempo libre.

timer [tī'mûr] *n* (**~ switch**) interruptor *m*; (*in kitchen*, *TECH*) reloj *m* automático.

timesaving [tīm'sāving] *a* que ahorra tiempo.

time scale *n* escala de tiempo.

time sharing [tīm' shä'ring] *n* (*COMPUT*) tiempo compartido.

time sheet *n* = **time card**.

time signal *n* señal *f* horaria.

time switch *n* (*Brit*) interruptor *m* (horario).

timetable [tīm'tābəl] *n* horario; (*schedule of events etc*) programa *m*, itinerario.

time warp *n* salto en el tiempo.

time zone *n* huso horario.

timid [tim'id] *a* tímido.

timidity [timid'itē] *n* timidez *f*.

timidly [tim'idlē] *ad* tímidamente.

timing [tī'ming] *n* (*SPORT*) cronometraje *m*; **the ~ of his resignation** el momento que eligió para dimitir.

timpani [tim'pənē] *npl* tímpanos *mpl*.

tin [tin] *n* estaño; (*also*: **~ plate**) hojalata; (*Brit*: *can*) lata.

tinfoil [tin'foil] *n* papel *m* de estaño.

tinge [tinj] *n* matiz *m* ♦ *vt*: **~d with** teñido

de.

tingle [ting'gəl] n hormigueo ♦ vi (cheeks, skin: from cold) sentir comezón; (: from bad circulation) sentir hormigueo.

tinker [tingk'ûr] n calderero/a; (gipsy) gitano/a.

tinker with vt fus jugar con, tocar.

tinkle [ting'kəl] vi tintinear.

tin mine n mina de estaño.

tinned [tind] a (Brit: food) en lata, en conserva.

tinny [tin'ē] a (sound, taste) metálico; (pej: car) poco sólido, de pacotilla.

tin opener n (Brit) abrelatas m inv.

tinsel [tin'səl] n oropel m.

tint [tint] n matiz m; (for hair) tinte m ♦ vt (hair) teñir.

tinted [tin'tid] a (hair) teñido; (glass) ahumado.

T-intersection [te'intərsek'shən] n cruce m en T.

tiny [tī'nē] a minúsculo, pequeñito.

tip [tip] n (end) punta; (gratuity) propina; (Brit: for rubbish) vertedero; (advice) consejo ♦ vt (waiter) dar una propina a; (tilt) inclinar; (empty: Brit: also: ~ out) vaciar, echar; (predict: winner) pronosticar; (: horse) recomendar.

tip off vt avisar, notificar.

tip over vt volcar ♦ vi volcarse.

tip-off [tip'ôf] n (hint) advertencia.

tipped [tipt] a (Brit: cigarette) con filtro.

Tipp-Ex [tip'eks] ® n (Brit) Tipp-Ex m ®.

tipple [tip'əl] n (Brit): his ~ is Cointreau bebe Cointreau.

tippy-toe [tip'ētō] n (US): on ~ de puntillas.

tipsy [tip'sē] a alegre, mareado.

tiptoe [tip'tō] n (Brit) = tippy-toe.

tiptop [tip'tâp] a: in ~ condition en perfectas condiciones.

tire [tīûr'] n (US) neumático, llanta (LAm) ♦ vt cansar ♦ vi (gen) cansarse; (become bored) aburrirse.

tire out vt agotar, rendir (LAm).

tired [tīûrd'] a cansado; to be ~ of sth estar harto de algo; to be/feel/look ~ estar/sentirse/parecer cansado.

tiredness [tīûrd'nis] n cansancio.

tireless [tīûr'lis] a incansable.

tirelessly [tīûr'lislē] ad incansablemente.

tire pressure n presión f de los neumáticos.

tiresome [tīûr'səm] a aburrido.

tiring [tīûr'ing] a cansado.

tissue [tish'ōō] n tejido; (paper handkerchief) pañuelo de papel, kleenex m ®.

tissue paper n papel m de seda.

tit [tit] n (bird) herrerillo común; to give ~ for tat dar ojo por ojo.

titbit [tit'bit] n (Brit) = tidbit.

titillate [tit'əlāt] vt estimular, excitar.

titillation [titəlā'shən] n estimulación f, excitación f.

titivate [tit'əvāt] vt emperejilar.

title [tīt'əl] n título; (LAW: right): ~ (to) derecho (a).

title deed n (LAW) título de propiedad.

title page n portada.

title role n papel m principal.

titter [tit'ûr] vi reírse entre dientes.

tittle-tattle [tit'əltatəl] n chismes mpl.

titular [tich'əlûr] a (in name only) nominal.

T-junction [tē'jung'kshən] n cruce m en T.

TM abbr (= trademark) marca de fábrica; = transcendental meditation.

TN abbr (US MAIL) = Tennessee.

TNT n abbr (= trinitrotoluene) TNT m.

to [tōō, tōō] prep a; (towards) hacia; (of time) a, hasta; (of hour) menos; (with vb: purpose, result) para; (of) de; (following another vb): to want/try ~ do querer/intentar hacer; the road ~ Philadelphia la carretera de Filadelfia; to count ~ 10 contar hasta diez; ~ the left/right a la izquierda/derecha; to give sth ~ sb darle algo a uno; give it ~ me dámelo; the key ~ the door la llave de la puerta; the main thing is ~... lo importante es...; to go ~ France/school ir a Francia/al colegio; a quarter ~ 5 las 5 menos cuarto; it's twenty-five ~ 3 son las 3 menos veinticinco; it belongs ~ him le pertenece a él; superior ~ the others superior a los otros; 8 apples ~ the kilo 8 manzanas por kilo; pull/push the door ~ tirar/empujar la puerta; to go ~ and fro ir y venir; I don't want ~ no quiero; I have things ~ do tengo cosas que hacer; ready ~ go listo para salir; he did it ~ help you lo hizo para ayudarte.

toad [tōd] n sapo.

toadstool [tōd'stōōl] n hongo venenoso.

toady [tō'dē] n pelotillero/a, lameculos m/f inv ♦ vi: to ~ to sb hacer la pelotilla a uno.

toast [tōst] n (CULIN: also: piece of ~) tostada; (drink, speech) brindis m inv ♦ vt (CULIN) tostar; (drink to) brindar.

toaster [tōs'tûr] n tostadora.

toastmaster [tōst'mastûr] n persona que propone brindis y anuncia a los oradores en un banquete.

toast rack n rejilla para tostadas.

tobacco [təbak'ō] n tabaco; pipe ~ tabaco de pipa.

tobacconist [təbak'ənist] n estanquero/a, tabaquero/a (LAm); ~'s (shop) (Brit) estanco, tabaquería (LAm).

tobacco plantation n plantación f de tabaco, tabacal m.

Tobago [tōbā'gō] n see Trinidad and Tobago.

toboggan [təbâg'ən] n tobogán m.

today [tədā'] ad, n (also fig) hoy m; what day is it ~? ¿qué día es hoy?; what date is it ~? ¿cuál es la fecha de hoy?; ~ **is the 4th of March** hoy es el 4 de marzo; ~'**s paper** el periódico de hoy; **two weeks from** ~ de hoy en 15 días, dentro de 15 días.

toddle [tád'əl] *vi* empezar a andar, dar los primeros pasos.

toddler [tád'lûr] *n* niño/a (que empieza a andar).

toddy [tád'ē] *n* caliente *m*.

to-do [tədōō'] *n* (*fuss*) lío.

toe [tō] *n* dedo (del pie); (*of shoe*) punta ♦ *vt*: **to** ~ **the line** (*fig*) conformarse; **big/ little** ~ dedo gordo/pequeño del pie.

toehold [tō'hōld] *n* punto de apoyo (para el pie).

toenail [tō'nāl] *n* uña del pie.

toffee [tôf'ē] *n* caramelo.

toffee apple *n* (*Brit*) pirulí *m*.

toga [tō'gə] *n* toga.

together [tōōgeth'ûr] *ad* juntos; (*at same time*) al mismo tiempo, a la vez; ~ **with** *prep* junto con.

togetherness [tōōgeth'ûrnis] *n* compañerismo.

toggle switch [tág'əl swich] *n* (*COMPUT*) conmutador *m* de palanca.

Togo [tō'gō] *n* Togo.

togs [tágz] *npl* (*col: clothes*) atuendo, ropa.

toil [toil] *n* trabajo duro, labor *f* ♦ *vi* esforzarse.

toilet [toi'lit] *n* (*Brit: lavatory*) servicios *mpl*, wáter *m*, sanitario (*LAm*) ♦ *cpd* (*bag, soap etc*) de aseo; **to go to the** ~ ir al excusado *or* al baño; *see also* **toilets.**

toilet bag *n* neceser *m*, bolsa de aseo.

toilet bowl *n* taza (de retrete).

toilet paper *n* papel *m* higiénico.

toiletries [toi'litrēz] *npl* artículos *mpl* de aseo; (*make-up etc*) artículos *mpl* de tocador.

toilet roll *n* rollo de papel higiénico.

toilets [toi'lits] *npl* (*Brit*) servicios *mpl*.

toilet soap *n* jabón *m* de tocador.

toilet water *n* (agua de) colonia.

token [tō'kən] *n* (*sign*) señal *f*, muestra; (*souvenir*) recuerdo; (*voucher*) vale *m*; (*disc*) ficha ♦ *cpd* (*fee, strike*) nominal, simbólico; **book/record** ~ (*Brit*) vale *m* para comprar libros/discos; **by the same** ~ (*fig*) por la misma razón.

Tokyo [tō'kēyō] *n* Tokio, Tokío.

told [tōld] *pt, pp of* **tell.**

tolerable [tál'ûrəbəl] *a* (*bearable*) soportable; (*fairly good*) pasable.

tolerably [tál'ûrəblē] *ad* (*good, comfortable*) medianamente.

tolerance [tál'ûrəns] *n* (*also: TECH*) tolerancia.

tolerant [tál'ûrənt] *a*: ~ **of** tolerante con.

tolerantly [tál'ûrəntlē] *ad* con tolerancia.

tolerate [tál'ərāt] *vt* tolerar.

toleration [tálərā'shən] *n* tolerancia.

toll [tōl] *n* (*of casualties*) número de víctimas; (*tax, charge*) peaje *m* ♦ *vi* (*bell*) doblar.

toll bridge *n* puente *m* de peaje.

toll-free [tōl'frē'] *ad* (*US TEL*): **to call** ~ llamar sin pagar.

toll road *n* carretera de peaje.

tomato, ~es [təmā'tō] *n* tomate *m*.

tomato paste *n* puré *m* de tomate.

tomato purée *n* puré *m* de tomate.

tomb [tōōm] *n* tumba.

tomboy [tám'boi] *n* marimacho.

tombstone [tōōm'stōn] *n* lápida.

tomcat [tám'kat] *n* gato.

tomorrow [təmôr'ō] *ad, n* (*also fig*) mañana; **the day after** ~ pasado mañana; ~ **morning** mañana por la mañana; **a week from** ~ de mañana en ocho (días).

ton [tun] *n* (*US: also:* **short** ~ = *907,18 kg; Brit* = *1016 kg*) tonelada.

tonal [tō'nəl] *a* tonal.

tone [tōn] *n* tono ♦ *vi* armonizar; **dial** (*US*) *or* **dialling** (*Brit*) ~ (*TEL*) señal *f* para marcar.

tone down *vt* (*criticism*) suavizar; (*color*) atenuar.

tone up *vt* (*muscles*) tonificar.

tone-deaf [tōn'def] *a* que no tiene oído musical.

toner [tō'nûr] *n* (*for photocopier*) virador *m*.

Tonga [tâng'gə] *n* Islas *fpl* Tonga.

tongs [tôngz] *npl* (*for coal*) tenazas *fpl*; (*Brit: for hair*) tenacillas *fpl*.

tongue [tung] *n* lengua; ~ **in cheek** *ad* irónicamente.

tongue-tied [tung'tīd] *a* (*fig*) mudo.

tongue twister [tung' twis'tûr] *n* trabalenguas *m inv*.

tonic [tán'ik] *n* (*MED*) tónico; (*MUS*) tónica; (*also:* ~ **water**) (agua) tónica.

tonight [tənīt'] *ad, n* esta noche; **I'll see you** ~ nos vemos esta noche.

tonnage [tun'ij] *n* (*NAUT*) tonelaje *m*.

tonsil [tán'səl] *n* amígdala; **to have one's** ~s **out** sacarse las amígdalas *or* anginas.

tonsillitis [tánsəlī'tis] *n* amigdalitis *f*; **to have** ~ tener amigdalitis.

too [tōō] *ad* (*excessively*) demasiado; (*very*) muy; (*also*) también; **it's** ~ **sweet** está demasiado dulce; **I'm not** ~ **sure about that** no estoy muy seguro de eso; **I went** ~ yo fui también; ~ **much** *ad, a* demasiado; ~ **many** *a* demasiados/as; ~ **bad!** ¡mala suerte!

took [tōōk] *pt of* **take.**

tool [tōōl] *n* herramienta; (*fig: person*) instrumento.

tool box *n* caja de herramientas.

tool kit *n* juego de herramientas.

tool shed *n* cobertizo (para herramientas).

toot [tōōt] *n* (*of horn*) bocinazo; (*of whistle*) silbido ♦ *vi* (*with car horn*) tocar la bocina.

tooth, pl teeth [tōōth, tēth] *n* (*ANAT, TECH*) diente *m*; (*molar*) muela; **to clean one's**

teeth lavarse los dientes; **to have a ~ pulled** or (*Brit*) **out** sacarse una muela; **by the skin of one's teeth** por un pelo.

toothache [tōōth'āk] *n* dolor *m* de muelas.

toothbrush [tōōth'brush] *n* cepillo de dientes.

toothpaste [tōōth'pāst] *n* pasta de dientes.

toothpick [tōōth'pik] *n* palillo.

tooth powder *n* polvos *mpl* dentífricos.

top [tåp] *n* (*of mountain*) cumbre *f*, cima; (*of head*) coronilla; (*of ladder*) lo alto; (*of cupboard, table*) superficie *f*; (*lid: of box, jar*) tapa; (: *of bottle*) tapón *m*; (*of list, table, line, page*) cabeza; (*toy*) peonza; (*DRESS: blouse etc*) blusa; (: *of pyjamas*) chaqueta; (*US AUT*) capota ♦ *a* de arriba; (*in rank*) principal, primero; (*best*) mejor ♦ *vt* (*exceed*) exceder; (*be first in*) encabezar; **on ~ of** sobre, encima de; **from ~ to bottom** de pies a cabeza; **at the ~ of the stairs** en lo alto de la escalera; **at the ~ of the street** al final de la calle; **at the ~ of one's voice** (*fig*) a voz en grito; **at ~ speed** a máxima velocidad; **a ~ surgeon** un cirujano eminente; **over the ~** (*col*) excesivo, desmesurado; **to go over the ~** pasarse (de la raya).

top off, (*Brit*) **top up** *vt* llenar.

topaz [tō'paz] *n* topacio.

topcoat [tåp'kōt] *n* sobretodo, abrigo.

topflight [tåp'flīt'] *a* de primera (categoría or clase).

top floor *n* último piso.

top hat *n* sombrero de copa.

top-heavy [tåp'hevē] *a* (*object*) descompensado en la parte superior.

topic [tåp'ik] *n* tema *m*.

topical [tåp'ikǝl] *a* (*current*) actual; (*US: local*) local.

topless [tåp'lis] *a* (*bather etc*) topless.

top-level [tåp'lev'ǝl] *a* (*talks*) al más alto nivel.

topmost [tåp'mōst] *a* más alto.

topography [tǝpåg'rǝfē] *n* topografía.

topping [tåp'ing] *n* (*CULIN*) cubierta.

topple [tåp'ǝl] *vt* volcar, derribar ♦ *vi* caerse.

top-ranking [tåp'rang'king] *a* de alto rango.

top-secret [tåp'sē'krit] *a* de alto secreto.

top-security [tåpsikyōō'ritē] *a* de máxima seguridad.

topsy-turvy [tåp'sētûr'vē] *a*, *ad* patas arriba.

top-up [tåp'up] *n* (*Brit*): **would you like a ~?** ¿quiere que se lo llene?

torch [tôrch] *n* antorcha; (*Brit: electric*) linterna.

tore [tôr] *pt of* **tear**.

torment *n* [tôr'ment] tormento ♦ *vt* [tôr'ment'] atormentar; (*fig: annoy*) fastidiar.

torn [tôrn] *pp of* **tear**.

tornado, **~es** [tôrnā'dō] *n* tornado.

torpedo, **~es** [tôrpē'dō] *n* torpedo.

torpedo boat *n* torpedero, lancha torpedera.

torpor [tôr'pûr] *n* letargo.

torrent [tôr'ǝnt] *n* torrente *m*.

torrential [tôren'chǝl] *a* torrencial.

torrid [tôr'id] *a* tórrido; (*fig*) apasionado.

torso [tôr'sō] *n* torso.

tortoise [tôr'tǝs] *n* tortuga.

tortoiseshell [tôr'tǝs·shel] *a* de carey.

tortuous [tôr'chōōǝs] *a* tortuoso.

torture [tôr'chûr] *n* tortura ♦ *vt* torturar; (*fig*) atormentar.

torturer [tôr'chûrûr] *n* torturador(a) *m/f*.

Tory [tôr'ē] *a*, *n* (*Brit POL*) conservador(a) *m/f*.

toss [tôs] *vt* tirar, echar; (*head*) sacudir ♦ *n* (*movement: of head etc*) sacudida; (*of coin*) tirada, echada (*LAm*); **to ~ a coin** echar a cara o cruz; **to ~ up for sth** jugar algo a cara o cruz; **to ~ and turn** (*in bed*) dar vueltas (en la cama); **to win/lose the ~** (*also SPORT*) ganar/perder (a cara o cruz).

tot [tåt] *n* (*child*) nene/a *m/f*; (*Brit: drink*) copita.

total [tōt'ǝl] *a* total, entero ♦ *n* total *m*, suma ♦ *vt* (*add up*) sumar; (*amount to*) ascender a; **grand ~** importe *m* total; **in ~** en total, en suma.

totalitarian [tōtalitär'ēǝn] *a* totalitario.

totality [tōtal'itē] *n* totalidad *f*.

total loss *n* siniestra total.

totally [tōt'ǝlē] *ad* totalmente.

tote [tōt] *vt* (*col*) acarrear, cargar con.

tote bag *n* bolsa, bolso.

totem pole [tō'tǝm pōl] *n* poste *m* totémico.

totter [tåt'ûr] *vi* tambalearse.

touch [tuch] *n* tacto; (*contact*) contacto; (*SOCCER*) fuera de juego ♦ *vt* tocar; (*emotionally*) conmover; **a ~ of** (*fig*) una pizca or un poquito de; **to get in ~ with sb** ponerse en contacto con uno; **I'll be in ~** le llamaré/escribiré; **to lose ~** (*friends*) perder contacto; **to be out of ~ with events** no estar al corriente (de los acontecimientos); **the personal ~** el toque personal; **to put the finishing ~es to sth** dar el último toque a algo; **no artist in the country can ~ him** no hay artista en todo el país que le iguale.

touch on *vt fus* (*topic*) aludir (brevemente) a.

touch up *vt* (*paint*) retocar.

touch-and-go [tuch'ǝngō'] *a* arriesgado.

touchdown [tuch'doun] *n* aterrizaje *m*; (*US FOOTBALL*) tanto.

touched [tucht] *a* conmovido; (*col*) chiflado.

touchiness [tuch'ēnis] *n* susceptibilidad *f*.

touching [tuch'ing] *a* conmovedor(a).

touchline [tuch'līn] *n* (*SPORT*) línea de banda.

touch-type [tuch'tīp] *vi* mecanografiar al

tacto.

touchy [tuch'ē] a (person) quisquilloso.

tough [tuf] a (meat) duro; (journey) penoso; (task, problem, situation) difícil; (resistant) resistente; (person) fuerte; (: pej) bruto ♦ n (gangster etc) gorila m; **they got ~ with the workers** fueron muy duros con los trabajadores.

toughen [tuf'ən] vt endurecer.

toughness [tuf'nis] n dureza; (resistance) resistencia; (strictness) inflexibilidad f.

toupée [tōōpā'] n peluca.

tour [tōōr] n viaje m, vuelta; (also: **package ~**) viaje m todo comprendido; (of town, museum) visita ♦ vt viajar por; **to go on a ~ of** (region, country) ir de viaje por; (museum, castle) dar una vuelta de; **to go on ~** partir or ir de gira.

touring [tōō'ring] n viajes mpl turísticos, turismo.

tourism [tōōr'izəm] n turismo.

tourist [tōōr'ist] n turista m/f ♦ cpd turístico; **the ~ trade** el turismo.

tourist office n oficina de turismo.

tournament [tōōr'nəmənt] n torneo.

tourniquet [tûr'nikit] n (MED) torniquete m.

tour operator n agente m/f or agencia de viajes.

tousled [tou'zəld] a (hair) despeinado.

tout [tout] vi: **to ~ for business** solicitar clientes ♦ n (Brit): **ticket ~** revendedor(a) m/f.

tow [tō] n: **to give sb a ~** (AUT) darle remolque or remolcar a uno ♦ vt remolcar; **"in** or (Brit) **on ~"** (AUT) "a remolque".

toward(s) [tôrd(z)] prep hacia; (of attitude) respecto a, con; (of purpose) para; **~ noon** alrededor de mediodía; **~ the end of the year** hacia finales de año; **to feel friendly ~ sb** sentir amistad hacia uno.

towel [tou'əl] n toalla; **to throw in the ~** (fig) darse por vencido, renunciar.

towel(l)ing [tou'əling] n (fabric) felpa.

towel rack, (Brit) **towel rail** n toallero.

tower [tou'ûr] n torre f ♦ vi (building, mountain) elevarse; **to ~ above or over sth/sb** dominar algo/destacarse sobre uno.

tower block n (Brit) rascacielos m inv.

towering [tou'ûring] a muy alto, imponente.

town [toun] n ciudad f; **to go to ~** ir a la ciudad; (fig) echar los bofes; **in the ~** en la ciudad; **to be out of ~** estar fuera de la ciudad.

town center n centro de la ciudad.

town clerk n secretario/a del Ayuntamiento.

town council n Ayuntamiento, consejo municipal.

town hall n ayuntamiento.

town house n (US) casa adosada.

town planner n (Brit) urbanista m/f.

town planning n (Brit) urbanismo.

townspeople [tounz'pēpəl] npl gente f de ciudad.

towpath [tō'path] n camino de sirga.

towrope [tō'rōp] n cable m de remolque.

tow truck n (US) camión m grúa.

toxic [tâk'sik] a tóxico.

toxin [tâk'sin] n toxina.

toy [toi] n juguete m.

toy with vt fus jugar con; (idea) acariciar.

toyshop [toi'shâp] n juguetería.

toy train n tren m de juguete.

trace [trās] n rastro ♦ vt (draw) trazar, delinear; (locate) encontrar; **there was no ~ of it** no había ningún indicio de eso.

trace element n oligoelemento.

trachea [trā'kēə] n (ANAT) tráquea.

tracing paper [trā'sing pā'pûr] n papel m de calco.

track [trak] n (mark) huella, pista; (path: gen) camino, senda; (: of bullet etc) trayectoria; (: of suspect, animal) pista, rastro; (RAIL) vía; (COMPUT, SPORT) pista; (on record) canción f ♦ vt seguir la pista de; **to keep ~ of** mantenerse al tanto de, seguir; **a 4-~ tape** una cinta de 4 pistas; **the first ~ on the record/tape** la primera canción en el disco/cassette; **to be on the right ~** (fig) ir por buen camino.

track down vt (person) localizar; (sth lost) encontrar.

track events npl (SPORT) pruebas fpl en pista.

tracking station [trak'ing stā'shən] n (SPACE) estación f de seguimiento.

track record n: **to have a good ~** (fig) tener (buenos) antecedentes.

tracksuit [trak'sōōt] n chandal m.

tract [trakt] n (GEO) región f; (pamphlet) folleto.

traction [trak'shən] n (AUT, power) tracción f; **in ~** (MED) en tracción.

tractor [trak'tûr] n tractor m.

tractor feed n (on printer) arrastre m de papel por tracción.

trade [trād] n comercio, negocio; (skill, job) oficio, empleo; (industry) industria ♦ vi negociar, comerciar; **foreign ~** comercio exterior.

trade in vt (old car etc) ofrecer como parte del pago.

trade barrier n barrera comercial.

trade deficit n déficit m comercial.

trade discount n descuento comercial.

trade fair n feria de muestras.

trade-in [trād'in] a: **~ price/value** precio/valor m de entrega or a cuenta.

trademark [trād'mârk] n marca de fábrica.

trade mission n misión f comercial.

trade name n marca registrada.

trade price n precio al detallista.

trader [trā'dûr] n comerciante m/f.

trade reference n referencia comercial.

trade secret n secreto profesional.
tradesman [trādz'mən] n (shopkeeper) tendero.
trade union n sindicato.
trade unionist [trād yōōn'yənist] n sindicalista m/f.
trade wind n viento alisio.
trading [trā'ding] n comercio.
trading account n cuenta de compraventa.
trading estate n (Brit) zona comercial.
trading stamp n cupón m, sello de prima.
tradition [trədish'ən] n tradición f.
traditional [trədish'ənəl] a tradicional.
traditionally [trədish'ənəlē] ad tradicionalmente.
traffic [traf'ik] n (gen, AUT) tráfico, circulación f, tránsito (LAm) ♦ vi: **to ~ in** (pej: liquor, drugs) traficar en; **air ~** tránsito aéreo.
traffic circle n (US) glorieta de tráfico.
traffic island n refugio, isleta.
traffic jam n embotellamiento, atasco.
trafficker [traf'ikûr] n traficante m/f.
traffic lights npl semáforo sg.
traffic offence n (Brit) = **traffic violation**.
traffic violation n infracción f de tránsito.
traffic warden n (Brit) guardia m/f de tráfico.
tragedy [traj'idē] n tragedia.
tragic [traj'ik] a trágico.
tragically [traj'iklē] ad trágicamente.
trail [trāl] n (tracks) rastro, pista; (path) camino, sendero; (dust, smoke) estela ♦ vt (drag) arrastrar; (follow) seguir la pista de; (follow closely) vigilar ♦ vi arrastrarse; **to be on sb's ~** seguir la pista de uno.
trail behind vi quedar a la zaga.
trail off vi (sound) desvanecerse; (interest, voice) desaparecer.
trailer [trā'lûr] n (AUT) remolque m; (Brit: caravan) caravana; (CINEMA) trailer m, avance m.
trailer park n (US) camping m para caravanas or remolques.
trail truck n (US) trailer m.
train [trān] n tren m; (of dress) cola; (series): **~ of events** curso de los acontecimientos ♦ vt (educate) formar; (teach skills to) adiestrar; (sportsman) entrenar; (dog) amaestrar; (point: gun etc): **to ~ on** apuntar a ♦ vi (SPORT) entrenarse; (be educated, learn a skill) formarse; **to go by ~** ir en tren; **one's ~ of thought** el razonamiento de uno; **to ~ sb to do sth** entrenar a uno a hacer algo.
train attendant n (US RAIL) empleado/a de coches-cama.
trained [trānd] a (worker) cualificado; (animal) amaestrado.
trainee [trānē'] n aprendiz(a) m/f.
trainer [trā'nûr] n (SPORT) entrenador(a)

m/f; (of animals) domador(a) m/f; **~s** npl (shoes) zapatillas fpl (de deporte).
training [trā'ning] n formación f; entrenamiento; **to be in ~** (SPORT) estar entrenando; (: fit) estar en forma.
training college n (gen) colegio de formación profesional; (for teachers) escuela normal.
training course n curso de formación.
training shoes npl zapatillas fpl (de deporte).
train station n estación f de ferrocarril.
traipse [trāps] vi andar penosamente.
trait [trāt] n rasgo.
traitor [trā'tûr] n traidor(a) m/f.
trajectory [trəjek'tûrē] n trayectoria, curso.
tram [tram] n (Brit: also: **~car**) tranvía m.
tramline [tram'līn] n carril m de tranvía.
tramp [tramp] n (person) vagabundo/a; (col: offensive: woman) puta ♦ vi andar con pasos pesados.
trample [tram'pəl] vt: **to ~ (underfoot)** pisotear.
trampoline [trampəlēn'] n trampolín m.
trance [trans] n trance m; **to go into a ~** entrar en trance.
tranquil [trang'kwil] a tranquilo.
tranquility, (Brit) tranquillity [trangkwil'itē] n tranquilidad f.
tranquilizer, (Brit) tranquillizer [trang'kwəlīzûr] n (MED) tranquilizante m.
trans- [trans] pref trans-, tras-.
transact [transakt'] vt (business) tramitar.
transaction [transak'shən] n transacción f, operación f; **cash ~s** comercio al contado.
transatlantic [transətlan'tik] a transatlántico.
transcend [transend'] vt rebasar.
transcendent [transen'dənt] a trascendente.
transcendental [transenden'təl] a: **~ meditation** meditación f transcendental.
transcribe [transkrīb'] vt transcribir, copiar.
transcript [tran'skript] n copia.
transcription [transkrip'shən] n transcripción f.
transept [tran'sept] n crucero.
transfer n [trans'fûr] transferencia; (SPORT) traspaso; (picture, design) calcomanía ♦ vt [transfûr'] trasladar, pasar; **to ~ the charges** (Brit TEL) llamar a cobro revertido; **by bank ~** por transferencia bancaria or giro bancario; **to ~ money from one account to another** transferir dinero de una cuenta a otra; **to ~ sth to sb's name** transferir algo al nombre de uno.
transferable [transfûr'əbəl] a: **not ~** intransferible.
transfix [transfiks'] vt traspasar; (fig): **~ed with fear** paralizado por el miedo.
transform [transfôrm'] vt transformar.
transformation [transfûrmā'shən] n trans-

formación *f*.

transformer [transfôr'mûr] *n* (*ELEC*) transformador *m*.

transfusion [transfyōō'zhən] *n* transfusión *f*.

transgress [transgres'] *vt* (*go beyond*) traspasar; (*violate*) violar, infringir.

tranship [tranship'] *vt* trasbordar.

transient [tran'shənt] *a* transitorio.

transistor [tranzis'tûr] *n* (*ELEC*) transistor *m*.

transistorized [tranzis'tərīzd] *a* (*circuit*) transistorizado.

transistor radio *n* transistor *m*.

transit [tran'sit] *n*: **in ~** en tránsito.

transit camp *n* campo de tránsito.

transition [tranzish'ən] *n* transición *f*.

transitional [tranzish'ənəl] *a* transitorio.

transition period *n* período de transición.

transitive [tran'sətiv] *a* (*LING*) transitivo.

transitively [tran'sətivlē] *ad* transitivamente.

transitory [tran'sitôrē] *a* transitorio.

transit visa *n* visado de tránsito.

translate [tranz'lāt] *vt*: **to ~ (from/into)** traducir (de/a).

translation [tranzlā'shən] *n* traducción *f*.

translator [tranzlā'tûr] *n* traductor(a) *m/f*.

translucent [translōō'sənt] *a* traslúcido.

transmission [transmish'ən] *n* transmisión *f*.

transmit [transmit'] *vt* transmitir.

transmitter [transmit'ûr] *n* transmisor *m*; (*station*) emisora.

transom [tran'səm] *n* (*US*) (montante *m* de) abanico.

transparency [transpär'ənsē] *n* (*PHOT*) diapositiva.

transparent [transpär'ənt] *a* transparente.

transpire [transpīur'] *vi* (*turn out*) resultar (ser); (*happen*) ocurrir, suceder; (*become known*): **it finally ~d that ...** por fin se supo que ....

transplant *vt* [transplant'] transplantar ♦ *n* [trans'plant] (*MED*) transplante *m*; **to have a heart ~** hacerse un transplante de corazón.

transport *n* [trans'pôrt] transporte *m* ♦ *vt* [transpôrt'] transportar.

transportable [transpôr'təbəl] *a* transportable.

transportation [transpûrtā'shən] *n* transporte *m*; (*of prisoners*) deportación *f*; **public ~** transporte *m* público.

transport café *n* (*Brit*) bar-restaurante *m* de carretera.

transpose [tranzpōz'] *vt* transponer.

transship [transship'] *vt* trasbordar.

transverse [transvûrs'] *a* transverso, transversal.

transvestite [transves'tīt] *n* travesti *m/f*.

trap [trap] *n* (*snare, trick*) trampa; (*carriage*) cabriolé *m* ♦ *vt* coger (*Sp*) *or* agarrar (*LAm*) en una trampa; (*immobilize*)

bloquear; (*jam*) atascar; **to set** *or* **lay a ~ (for sb)** poner(le) una trampa (a uno).

trap door *n* escotilla.

trapeze [trapēz'] *n* trapecio.

trapper [trap'ûr] *n* trampero, cazador *m*.

trappings [trap'ingz] *npl* adornos *mpl*.

trash [trash] *n* (*pej: goods*) pacotilla; (: *nonsense*) tonterías *fpl*; (*garbage*) basura ♦ *vt* (*col*) poner por los suelos.

trash can *n* (*US*) cubo *or* balde *m* (*LAm*) de la basura.

trash can liner *n* (*US*) bolsa de basura.

trashy [trash'ē] *a* malísimo.

trauma [trou'mə] *n* trauma *m*.

traumatic [trômat'ik] *a* (*PSYCH, fig*) traumático.

travel [trav'əl] *n* viaje *m* ♦ *vi* viajar ♦ *vt* (*distance*) recorrer; **this wine doesn't ~ well** este vino no se transporta bien.

travel agency *n* agencia de viajes.

travel agent *n* agente *m/f* de viajes.

travel brochure *n* folleto turístico.

traveler [trav'əlûr] *n* (*US*) viajero/a; (: *COMM*) viajante *m/f*.

traveler's check *n* cheque *m* de viajero.

traveling [trav'əling] (*US*) *n* los viajes, el viajar ♦ *a* (*circus, exhibition*) ambulante ♦ *cpd* (*bag, clock*) de viaje.

traveling expenses *npl* dietas *fpl*.

traveling salesman *n* viajante *m*.

traveller [trav'əlûr] *n* (*Brit*) = **traveler**.

traveller's cheque *n* (*Brit*) = **traveler's check**.

travelling [trav'əling] *etc* (*Brit*) = **traveling** *etc*.

travelog(ue) [trav'əlôg] *n* (*book*) relación *f* de viajes; (*film*) documental *m* de viajes; (*talk*) recuento de viajes.

travel sickness *n* mareo.

traverse [trav'ûrs] *vt* atravesar.

travesty [trav'istē] *n* parodia.

trawler [trô'lûr] *n* pesquero de arrastre.

tray [trā] *n* (*for carrying*) bandeja; (*on desk*) cajón *m*.

treacherous [trech'ûrəs] *a* traidor(a); **road conditions are ~** el estado de las carreteras es peligroso.

treachery [trech'ûrē] *n* traición *f*.

treacle [trē'kəl] *n* (*Brit*) melaza.

tread [tred] *n* (*step*) paso, pisada; (*sound*) ruido de pasos; (*of tire*) banda de rodadura ♦ *vi* (*pt* **trod**, *pp* **trodden** [trâd, trâd'ən]) pisar.

tread on *vt fus* pisar.

treas. *abbr* = **treasurer**.

treason [trē'zən] *n* traición *f*.

treasure [trezh'ûr] *n* tesoro ♦ *vt* (*value*) apreciar, valorar.

treasure hunt *n* caza al tesoro.

treasurer [trezh'ûrûr] *n* tesorero/a.

treasury [trezh'ûrē] *n*: **the T~ Department,** (*Brit*) **the T~** ≈ el Ministerio *or* la Secretaría de Hacienda.

treasury bill *n* bono del Tesoro.

treat [trēt] *n* (*present*) regalo; (*pleasure*) placer *m* ♦ *vt* tratar; (*consider*) considerar; **to give sb a ~** hacer un regalo a uno; **to ~ sb to sth** invitar a uno a algo; **to ~ sth as a joke** tomar algo a broma.

treatise [trē'tis] *n* tratado.

treatment [trēt'mənt] *n* tratamiento; **to have ~ for sth** recibir tratamiento por algo.

treaty [trē'tē] *n* tratado.

treble [treb'əl] *a* triple ♦ *vt* triplicar ♦ *vi* triplicarse.

treble clef *n* (*MUS*) clave *f* de sol.

tree [trē] *n* árbol *m*.

tree-lined [trē'līnd] *a* bordeado de árboles.

tree trunk *n* tronco de árbol.

trek [trek] *n* (*long journey*) expedición *f*; (*tiring walk*) caminata.

trellis [trel'is] *n* enrejado.

tremble [trem'bəl] *vi* temblar.

trembling [trem'bling] *n* temblor *m* ♦ *a* tembloroso.

tremendous [trimen'dəs] *a* tremendo; (*enormous*) enorme; (*excellent*) estupendo.

tremendously [trimen'dəslē] *ad* enormemente, sobremanera; **he enjoyed it ~** lo disfrutó de lo lindo.

tremor [trem'ûr] *n* temblor *m*; (*also:* **earth ~**) temblor *m* de tierra.

trench [trench] *n* zanja; (*MIL*) trinchera.

trench coat *n* trinchera.

trench warfare *n* guerra de trincheras.

trend [trend] *n* (*tendency*) tendencia; (*of events*) curso; (*fashion*) moda; **~ towards/away from sth** tendencia hacia/en contra de algo; **to set the ~** marcar la pauta.

trendy [tren'dē] *a* de moda.

trepidation [trepidā'shən] *n* inquietud *f*.

trespass [tres'pas] *vi*: **to ~ on** entrar sin permiso en; **"no ~ing"** "prohibido el paso".

trespasser [tres'pasûr] *n* intruso/a *m/f*; **"~s will be prosecuted"** "se procesará a los intrusos".

tress [tres] *n* trenza.

trestle [tres'əl] *n* caballete *m*.

trestle table *n* mesa de caballete.

tri- [trī] *pref* tri-.

trial [trīl] *n* (*LAW*) juicio, proceso; (*test: of machine etc*) prueba; (*hardship*) desgracia; **~s** *npl* (*ATHLETICS, of horses*) pruebas *fpl*; **to bring sb to ~ (for a crime)** llevar a uno a juicio (por un delito); **~ by jury** juicio ante jurado; **to be sent for ~** ser remitido al tribunal; **by ~ and error** a fuerza de probar.

trial balance *n* balance *m* de comprobación.

trial basis *n*: **on a ~** en concepto de prueba.

trial offer *n* oferta de prueba.

trial run *n* prueba.

triangle [trī'anggəl] *n* (*MATH, MUS*) triángulo; (*TECH*) cartabón *m*.

triangular [trīang'gyəlûr] *a* triangular.

tribal [trī'bəl] *a* tribal.

tribe [trīb] *n* tribu *f*.

tribesman [trībz'mən] *n* miembro de una tribu.

tribulation [tribyəlā'shən] *n* tribulación *f*.

tribunal [trībyōō'nəl] *n* tribunal *m*.

tributary [trib'yətärē] *n* (*river*) afluente *m*.

tribute [trib'yōōt] *n* homenaje *m*, tributo; **to pay ~ to** rendir homenaje a.

trice [trīs] *n*: **in a ~** en un santiamén.

trick [trik] *n* trampa; (*conjuring ~, deceit*) truco; (*prank*) broma; (*CARDS*) baza ♦ *vt* engañar; **it's a ~ of the light** es una ilusión óptica; **to play a ~ on sb** gastar una broma a uno; **that should do the ~** eso servirá; **to ~ sb out of sth** quitarle algo a uno con engaños; **to ~ sb into doing sth** hacer que uno haga algo con engaños.

trickery [trik'ûrē] *n* engaño.

trickle [trik'əl] *n* (*of water etc*) chorrito ♦ *vi* gotear.

trick question *n* pega.

trickster [trik'stûr] *n* estafador(a) *m/f*.

tricky [trik'ē] *a* difícil; (*problem*) delicado.

tricycle [trī'sikəl] *n* triciclo.

tried [trīd] *a* probado.

trifle [trī'fəl] *n* bagatela; (*CULIN*) dulce de bizcocho, gelatina, fruta y natillas ♦ *ad*: **a ~ long** un poquito largo ♦ *vi*: **to ~ with** jugar con.

trifling [trī'fling] *a* insignificante.

trigger [trig'ûr] *n* (*of gun*) gatillo.

trigger off *vt* desencadenar.

trigonometry [trigənám'ətrē] *n* trigonometría.

trilby [tril'bē] *n* (*Brit: also:* **~ hat**) sombrero flexible *or* tirolés.

trill [tril] *n* (*of bird*) gorjeo; (*MUS*) trino.

trillion [tril'yən] *n* (*US*) billón *m*.

trilogy [tril'əjē] *n* trilogía.

trim [trim] *a* (*elegant*) aseado; (*house, garden*) en buen estado; (*figure*): **to be ~** tener buen talle ♦ *n* (*haircut etc*) recorte *m* ♦ *vt* (*tidy*) arreglar; (*cut*) recortar; (*decorate*) adornar; (*NAUT: a sail*) orientar; **to keep in (good) ~** mantener en buen estado.

trimmings [trim'ingz] *npl* (*extras*) accesorios *mpl*; (*cuttings*) recortes *mpl*.

Trinidad and Tobago [trin'idad and tōbā'gō] *n* Trinidad *f* y Tobago.

Trinity [trin'itē] *n*: **the ~** la Trinidad.

trinket [tring'kit] *n* chuchería, baratija.

trio [trē'ō] *n* trío.

trip [trip] *n* viaje *m*; (*excursion*) excursión *f*; (*stumble*) traspié *m* ♦ *vi* (*stumble*) tropezar; (*go lightly*) andar a paso ligero; **on a ~** de viaje.

trip over *vt fus* tropezar con.

trip up *vi* tropezar, caerse ♦ *vt* hacer tropezar *or* caer; (*US*: *fig*: *with trick question*) hundir.

tripartite [trĭpâr'tīt] *a* (*agreement, talks*) tripartito.

tripe [trīp] *n* (*CULIN*) callos *mpl*; (*pej*: *rubbish*) bobadas *fpl*.

triple [trip'əl] *a* triple ♦ *ad*: ~ **the distance/the speed** 3 veces la distancia/la velocidad.

triplets [trip'lits] *npl* trillizos/as *m/fpl*.

triplicate [trip'ləkit] *n*: **in** ~ por triplicado.

tripod [trī'pâd] *n* trípode *m*.

Tripoli [trip'əlē] *n* Trípoli *m*.

tripwire [trip'wīər] *n* cuerda de trampa.

trite [trīt] *a* trillado.

triumph [trī'əmf] *n* triunfo ♦ *vi*: **to** ~ **(over)** vencer.

triumphal [trīum'fəl] *a* triunfal.

triumphant [trīum'fənt] *a* triunfante.

triumphantly [trīum'fəntlē] *ad* triunfalmente, en tono triunfal.

trivia [triv'ēə] *npl* trivialidades *fpl*.

trivial [triv'ēəl] *a* insignificante, trivial.

triviality [trivēal'ətē] *n* insignificancia, trivialidad *f*.

trivialize [triv'ēəlīz] *vt* minimizar, tratar con desprecio.

trod [trâd] *pt of* **tread.**

trodden [trâd'ən] *pp of* **tread.**

trolley bus [trâl'ē bus] *n* trolebús *m*.

trombone [trâmbōn'] *n* trombón *m*.

troop [trōōp] *n* grupo, banda.
   troop in *vi* entrar en tropel.
   troop out *vi* salir en tropel.

troop carrier *n* (*plane*) transporte *n* (militar); (*NAUT*: *also*: **troopship**) (buque *m* de) transporte *m*.

trooper [trōō'pûr] *n* (*MIL*) soldado (de caballería); (*US*: *policeman*) policía *m/f* estatal.

troopship [trōōp'ship] *n* (buque *m* de) transporte *m*.

trophy [trō'fē] *n* trofeo.

tropic [trâp'ik] *n* trópico; **the ~s** los trópicos, la zona tropical; **T~ of Cancer/Capricorn** trópico de Cáncer/Capricornio.

tropical [trâp'ikəl] *a* tropical.

trot [trât] *n* trote *m* ♦ *vi* trotar; **on the** ~ (*Brit fig*) seguidos/as.
   trot out *vt* (*excuse, reason*) sacar a luz; (*names, facts*) sacar a relucir.

trouble [trub'əl] *n* problema *m*, dificultad *f*; (*worry*) preocupación *f*; (*bother, effort*) molestia, esfuerzo; (*unrest*) inquietud *f*; (*with machine etc*) fallo, avería; (*MED*): **stomach** ~ problemas *mpl* gástricos ♦ *vt* molestar; (*worry*) preocupar, inquietar ♦ *vi*: **to** ~ **to do sth** molestarse en hacer algo; **~s** *npl* (*POL etc*) conflictos *mpl*; **to be in** ~ estar en un apuro; (*for doing wrong*) tener problemas; **to have** ~ **doing sth** tener dificultad en *or* para hacer algo; **to go to the** ~ **of doing sth** tomarse la molestia de hacer algo; **what's the** ~?

¿qué pasa?; **the** ~ **is** ... el problema es ..., lo que pasa es ...; **please don't** ~ **yourself** por favor no se moleste.

troubled [trub'əld] *a* (*person*) preocupado; (*epoch, life*) agitado.

trouble-free [trub'əlfrē] *a* sin problemas *or* dificultades.

troublemaker [trub'əlmākûr] *n* agitador(a) *m/f*.

troubleshooter [trub'əlshōōtûr] *n* (*in conflict*) conciliador(a) *m/f*.

troublesome [trub'əlsəm] *a* molesto, inoportuno.

trouble spot *n* centro de fricción, punto caliente.

trough [trôf] *n* (*also*: **drinking** ~) abrevadero; (*also*: **feeding** ~) comedero; (*channel*) canal *m*.

trounce [trouns] *vt* derrotar.

troupe [trōōp] *n* grupo.

trouser press [trou'zûr pres] *n* prensa para pantalones.

trousers [trou'zûrz] *npl* (*esp Brit*) pantalones *mpl*; **short** ~ pantalones *mpl* cortos.

trouser suit [trou'zûr sōōt] *n* (*Brit*) traje *m* de chaqueta y pantalón.

trousseau, *pl* ~**x** *or* ~**s** [trōō'sō, z] *n* ajuar *m*.

trout [trout] *n* (*pl inv*) trucha.

trowel [trou'əl] *n* paleta.

truant [trōō'ənt] *n*: **to play** ~ (*Brit*) hacer novillos.

truce [trōōs] *n* tregua.

truck [truk] *n* (*US*) camión *m*; (*RAIL*) vagón *m*.

truck driver *n* camionero/a.

trucker [truk'ûr] *n* (*esp US*) camionero/a, camionista *m/f*.

truck farm *n* (*US*) huerto de hortalizas.

truck farmer *n* (*US*) hortelano/a.

truck farming *n* (*US*) horticultura.

trucking [truk'ing] *n* (*esp US*) acarreo, transporte *m* en camión.

trucking company *n* (*US*) compañía de transporte por carretera.

truckload [truk'lōd] *n* camión *m* lleno.

truck stop *n* (*US*) restaurante *m* de carretera.

truculent [truk'yələnt] *a* agresivo.

trudge [truj] *vi* caminar penosamente.

true [trōō] *a* verdadero; (*accurate*) exacto; (*genuine*) auténtico; (*faithful*) fiel; (*wheel*) centrado; (*wall*) a plomo; (*beam*) alineado; ~ **to life** verídico; **to come** ~ realizarse, cumplirse.

truffle [truf'əl] *n* trufa.

truly [trōō'lē] *ad* realmente; (*faithfully*) fielmente; **yours** ~ (*in letter-writing*) atentamente.

trump [trump] *n* (*CARDS*) triunfo; **to turn up ~s** (*fig*) salir *or* resultar bien.

trump card *n* triunfo; (*fig*) baza.

trumped-up [trumpt'up'] *a* inventado.

trumpet [trum'pit] *n* trompeta.
truncated [trung'kātid] *a* truncado.
truncheon [trun'chən] *n* (*Brit*) porra.
trundle [trun'dəl] *vt, vi*: **to ~ along** rodar haciendo ruido.
trunk [trungk] *n* (*of tree, person*) tronco; (*of elephant*) trompa; (*case*) baúl *m*; (*US AUT*) maletero; *see also* **trunks**.
trunk road *n* (*Brit*) carretera principal.
trunks [trungks] *npl* (*also:* **swimming ~**) bañador *m*.
truss [trus] *n* (*MED*) braguero ♦ *vt*: **to ~ (up)** atar; (*CULIN*) espetar.
trust [trust] *n* confianza; (*COMM*) trust *m*; (*LAW*) fideicomiso ♦ *vt* (*rely on*) tener confianza en; (*entrust*): **to ~ sth to sb** confiar algo a uno; (*hope*): **to ~ (that)** esperar (que); **in ~** en fideicomiso; **you'll have to take it on ~** tienes que aceptarlo a ojos cerrados.
trust company *n* empresa de fideicomiso.
trusted [trus'tid] *a* de confianza, fiable, de fiar.
trustee [trustē'] *n* (*LAW*) fideicomisario.
trustful [trust'fəl] *a* confiado.
trust fund *n* fondo fiduciario *or* de fideicomiso.
trusting [trus'ting] *a* confiado.
trustworthy [trust'wûrᵺē] *a* digno de confianza, fiable, de fiar.
trusty [trus'tē] *a* fiel.
truth, **~s** [trōōth, trōōᵺz] *n* verdad *f*.
truthful [trōōth'fəl] *a* (*person*) sincero; (*account*) fidedigno.
truthfully [trōōth'fəlē] *ad* (*answer*) con sinceridad.
truthfulness [trōōth'fəlnis] *n* (*of account*) verdad *f*; (*of person*) sinceridad *f*.
try [trī] *n* tentativa, intento; (*RUGBY*) ensayo ♦ *vt* (*LAW*) juzgar, procesar; (*test: sth new*) probar, someter a prueba; (*attempt*) intentar; (*strain: patience*) hacer perder ♦ *vi* probar; **to give sth a ~** intentar hacer algo; **to ~ one's (very) best** *or* **hardest** poner todo su empeño, esmerarse; **to ~ to do sth** intentar hacer algo.
try on *vt* (*clothes*) probarse.
try out *vt* probar, poner a prueba.
trying [trī'ing] *a* cansado; (*person*) pesado.
tsar [zår] *n* zar *m*.
T-shirt [tē'shûrt] *n* camiseta.
T-square [tē'skwär] *n* regla en T.
TT *a abbr* (*Brit col*) = **teetotal** ♦ *abbr* (*US MAIL*) = *Trust Territory*.
tub [tub] *n* cubo (*Sp*), balde *m* (*LAm*); (*bath*) tina, bañera.
tuba [tōō'bə] *n* tuba.
tubby [tub'ē] *a* regordete.
tube [tōōb] *n* tubo; (*col: television*) tele *f*; (*Brit: subway*) metro; **to be down the ~s** estar en un apuro.
tubeless [tōōb'lis] *a* (*tire*) sin cámara.
tuber [tōō'bûr] *n* (*BOT*) tubérculo.

tuberculosis [tōōbûrkyəlō'sis] *n* tuberculosis *f inv*.
tube station [tōōb' stā'shən] *n* (*Brit*) estación *f* de metro.
tubing [tōō'bing] *n* tubería (*Sp*), cañería; **a piece of ~** un trozo de tubo.
tubular [tōō'byəlûr] *a* tubular.
TUC *n abbr* (*Brit*: = *Trades Union Congress*) *federación nacional de sindicatos*.
tuck [tuk] *n* (*SEWING*) pliegue *m* ♦ *vt* (*put*) poner.
tuck away *vt* esconder.
tuck in *vt* meter dentro; (*child*) arropar ♦ *vi* (*eat*) comer con apetito.
tuck up *vt* (*child*) arropar.
Tue(s). *abbr* (= *Tuesday*) mart.
Tuesday [tōōz'dā] *n* martes *m inv*; **on ~** el martes; **on ~s** los martes; **every ~** todos los martes; **every other ~** cada dos martes; **last/next ~** el martes pasado/próximo; **a week on ~**, **~ week** del martes en 8 días, del martes en una semana.
tuft [tuft] *n* mechón *m*; (*of grass etc*) manojo.
tug [tug] *n* (*ship*) remolcador *m* ♦ *vt* remolcar.
tug-of-war [tug'əvwôr'] *n* lucha de tiro de cuerda.
tuition [tōōish'ən] *n* (*US: school fees*) matrícula; (*Brit*) enseñanza; (: *private ~*) clases *fpl* particulares.
tulip [tōō'lip] *n* tulipán *m*.
tumble [tum'bəl] *n* (*fall*) caída ♦ *vi* caerse, tropezar; **to ~ to sth** (*col*) caer en la cuenta de algo.
tumbledown [tum'bəldoun] *a* destartalado.
tumble dryer *n* (*Brit*) secadora.
tumbler [tum'blûr] *n* vaso.
tummy [tum'ē] *n* (*col*) barriga, vientre *m*.
tumor, (*Brit*) **tumour** [tōō'mûr] *n* tumor *m*.
tumult [tōō'məlt] *n* tumulto.
tumultuous [tōōmul'chōōəs] *a* tumultuoso.
tuna [tōō'nə] *n* (*pl inv*) (*also:* **~ fish**) atún *m*.
tundra [tun'drə] *n* tundra.
tune [tōōn] *n* (*melody*) melodía ♦ *vt* (*MUS*) afinar; (*RADIO, TV, AUT*) sintonizar; **to be in/out of ~** (*instrument*) estar afinado/desafinado; (*singer*) cantar afinadamente/desafinar; **to be in/out of ~ with** (*fig*) armonizar/desentonar con; **to the ~ of** (*fig: amount*) por (la) cantidad de.
tune in *vi* (*RADIO, TV*): **to ~ in (to)** sintonizar (con).
tune up *vi* (*musician*) afinar (su instrumento).
tuneful [tōōn'fəl] *a* melodioso.
tuner [tōō'nûr] *n* (*radio set*) sintonizador *m*; **piano ~** afinador(a) *m/f* de pianos.
tungsten [tung'stən] *n* tungsteno.
tunic [tōō'nik] *n* túnica.
tuning [tōō'ning] *n* sintonización *f*; (*MUS*) afinación *f*.

tuning fork n diapasón m.

Tunis [tōō'nis] n Túnez m.

Tunisia [tōōnē'zhə] n Túnez m.

Tunisian [tōōnē'zhən] a, n tunecino/a m/f.

tunnel [tun'əl] n túnel m; (in mine) galería ♦ vi construir un túnel/una galería.

tunny [tun'ē] n atún m.

turban [tûr'bən] n turbante m.

turbid [tûr'bid] a turbio.

turbine [tûr'bīn] n turbina.

turboprop [tûr'bōprâp] n turbohélice m.

turbot [tûr'bət] n (pl inv) rodaballo.

turbulence [tûr'byələns] n (AVIAT) turbulencia.

turbulent [tûr'byələnt] a turbulento.

tureen [tərēn'] n sopera.

turf [tûrf] n césped m; (clod) tepe m ♦ vt cubrir con césped.

turf out vt (Brit: col) echar a la calle.

turgid [tûr'jid] a (prose) pesado.

Turin [tōō'rin] n Turín m.

Turk [tûrk] n turco/a.

Turkey [tûr'kē] n Turquía.

turkey [tûr'kē] n pavo.

Turkish [tûr'kish] a turco ♦ n (LING) turco.

Turkish bath n baño turco.

turmeric [tûr'mûrik] n cúrcuma.

turmoil [tûr'moil] n desorden m, alboroto.

turn [tûrn] n turno; (in road) curva; (THEATER) número; (MED) ataque m ♦ vt girar, volver; (collar, steak) dar la vuelta a; (shape: wood, metal) tornear; (change): **to ~ sth into** convertir algo en ♦ vi volver; (person: look back) volverse; (reverse direction) dar la vuelta; (milk) cortarse; (change) cambiar; (become): **to ~ into sth** convertirse or transformarse en algo; **a good ~** un favor; **it gave me quite a ~** me dio un susto; **"no left ~"** (AUT) "prohibido girar a la izquierda"; **it's your ~** te toca a ti; **in ~** por turnos; **to take ~s** turnarse; **at the ~ of the century** a finales de siglo; **to take a ~ for the worse** (situation, patient) empeorar; **they ~ed him against us** le pusieron en contra nuestra; **the car ~ed the corner** el coche dobló la esquina; **to ~ left** (AUT) torcer or girar a la izquierda; **she has no-one to ~ to** no tiene a quién recurrir.

turn around vi volverse; (rotate) girar.

turn away vi apartar la vista ♦ vt (reject: person, business) rechazar.

turn back vi volverse atrás.

turn down vt (refuse) rechazar; (reduce) bajar; (fold) doblar.

turn in vi (col: go to bed) acostarse ♦ vt (fold) doblar hacia dentro; (essay, report) entregar.

turn off vi (from road) desviarse ♦ vt (light, radio etc) apagar; (engine) parar.

turn on vt (light, radio etc) encender, prender (LAm); (engine) poner en marcha.

turn out vt (light, gas) apagar; (produce: goods, novel etc) producir ♦ vi (attend: troops) presentarse; (: doctor) atender; **to ~ out to be ...** resultar ser ....

turn over vi (person) volverse ♦ vt (mattress, card) dar la vuelta a; (page) volver.

turn round vi (Brit) = **turn around**.

turn to vt fus: **to ~ to sb** acudir a uno.

turn up vi (person) llegar, presentarse; (lost object) aparecer ♦ vt (radio) subir, poner más alto; (heat, gas) poner más fuerte.

turnabout [tûr'nəbout], **turnaround** [tûr'nəround] n (fig) giro total.

turncoat [tûrn'kōt] n renegado/a.

turned-up [tûrnd'up] a (nose) respingón/ona.

turning [tûr'ning] n (curve) curva; (Brit: side road) bocacalle f.

turning point n (fig) momento decisivo.

turnip [tûr'nip] n nabo.

turnkey system [tûrn'kē sis'təm] n (COMPUT) sistema m de seguridad.

turnout [tûrn'out] n asistencia, número de asistentes, público.

turnover [tûrn'ōvûr] n (COMM: amount of money) facturación f; (: of goods) movimiento; **there is a rapid ~ in staff** hay una rápida rotación de personal.

turnpike [tûrn'pīk] n (US) autopista de peaje.

turn signal n (US) indicador m (de dirección).

turnstile [tûrn'stīl] n torniquete m.

turntable [tûrn'tābəl] n plato.

turn-up [tûrn'up] n (Brit: on trousers) vuelta.

turpentine [tûr'pəntīn] n trementina.

turquoise [tûr'koiz] n (stone) turquesa ♦ a color turquesa.

turret [tûr'it] n torreón m.

turtle [tûr'təl] n galápago.

turtleneck (sweater) [tûr'təlnek (swet'ûr)] n (jersey m de) cuello cisne.

Tuscany [tus'kənē] n Toscana.

tusk [tusk] n colmillo.

tussle [tus'əl] n lucha, pelea.

tutor [tōō'tûr] n (US) preceptor(a) m/f; (Brit) profesor(a) m/f.

tutorial [tōōtôr'ēəl] n (SCOL) seminario.

tuxedo [tuksē'dō] n smóking m, esmoquin m.

TV [tēvē] n abbr (= television) tele f.

TVP n abbr = texturized vegetable protein.

twaddle [twâd'əl] n (col) tonterías fpl.

twang [twang] n (of instrument) punteado; (of voice) timbre m nasal.

tweak [twēk] vt (nose, ear) pellizcar; (hair) tirar.

tweed [twēd] n tweed m.

tweezers [twē'zûrz] npl pinzas fpl (de depilar).

twelfth [twelfth] num duodécimo.

Twelfth Night n (Día m de) Reyes mpl.
twelve [twelv] num doce; **at ~ o'clock**
(midday) a mediodía; (midnight) a medianoche.
twentieth [twen'tēith] num vigésimo.
twenty [twen'tē] num veinte.
twerp [twûrp] n (col) idiota m/f.
twice [twīs] ad dos veces; **~ as much** dos
veces más; **she is ~ your age** ella tiene
dos veces tu edad; **~ a week** dos veces a
la or por semana.
twiddle [twid'əl] vt, vi: **to ~ (with)** sth dar
vueltas a algo; **to ~ one's thumbs** (fig)
estar mano sobre mano.
twig [twig] n ramita ♦ vi (Brit: col) caer en
la cuenta.
twilight [twī'līt] n crepúsculo; (morning)
madrugada; **in the ~** en la media luz.
twill [twil] n sarga, estameña.
twin [twin] a, n gemelo/a m/f ♦ vt hermanar.
twin beds npl camas fpl gemelas.
twin-carburetor [twinkâr'bərātûr] a de dos
carburadores.
twine [twīn] n bramante m ♦ vi (plant)
enroscarse.
twin-engined [twin'enjənd] a bimotor; **~
aircraft** avión m bimotor.
twinge [twinj] n (of pain) punzada; (of
conscience) remordimiento.
twinkle [twing'kəl] n centelleo ♦ vi centellear; (eyes) parpadear.
twin town n ciudad f hermanada or geme-
la.
twirl [twûrl] n giro ♦ vt dar vueltas a ♦ vi piruetear.
twist [twist] n (action) torsión f; (in road,
coil) vuelta; (in wire, cord) doblez f; (in
story) giro ♦ vt torcer, retorcer; (roll
around) enrollar; (fig) deformar ♦ vi
serpentear; **to ~ one's ankle/wrist** (MED)
torcerse el tobillo/la muñeca.
twisted [twis'tid] a (wire, rope) trenzado,
enroscado; (ankle, wrist) torcido; (fig: logic, mind) retorcido.
twit [twit] n (col) tonto.
twitch [twich] n sacudida; (nervous) tic m
nervioso ♦ vi moverse nerviosamente.
two [tōō] num dos; **~ by ~, in ~s** de dos en
dos; **to put ~ and ~ together** (fig) atar
cabos.
two-door [tōō'dôr] a (AUT) de dos puertas.
two-faced [tōō'fāst] a (pej: person) falso.
twofold [tōō'fōld] ad: **to increase ~** dupli-
carse ♦ a (increase) doble; (reply) en dos
partes.
two-piece [tōō'pēs] n (also: **~ suit**) traje
m de dos piezas; (also: **~ swimsuit**) dos
piezas m inv, bikini m.
two-seater [tōō'sē'tûr] n (plane, car) avión
m/coche m de dos plazas.
twosome [tōō'səm] n (people) pareja.
two-stroke [tōō'strōk'] n (also: **~ engine**)
motor m de dos tiempos ♦ a de dos

tiempos.
two-tone [tōō'tōn'] a (color) bicolor, de dos
tonos.
two-way [tōō'wā'] a: **~ traffic** circulación f
de dos sentidos; **~ radio** radio f emisora y
receptora.
TX abbr (US MAIL) = Texas.
tycoon [tīkōōn'] n: **(business) ~** magnate
m/f.
type [tīp] n (category) tipo, género; (model)
modelo; (TYP) tipo, letra ♦ vt (letter etc)
escribir a máquina; **what ~ do you want?**
¿qué tipo quieres?; **in bold/italic ~** en
negrita/cursiva.
type-cast [tīp'kast] a (actor) encasillado.
typeface [tīp'fās] n tipo de letra.
typescript [tīp'skript] n texto mecanografiado.
typeset [tīp'set] vt (irg: like **set**) componer.
typesetter [tīp'setûr] n cajista m/f, compo-
sitor(a) m/f.
typewriter [tīp'rītûr] n máquina de escribir.
typewritten [tīp'ritən] a mecanografiado.
typhoid [tī'foid] n tifoidea.
typhoon [tīfōōn'] n tifón m.
typhus [tī'fəs] n tifus m.
typical [tip'ikəl] a típico.
typically [tip'ikəlē] ad típicamente.
typify [tip'əfī] vt tipificar.
typing [tī'ping] n mecanografía.
typing pool n (Brit) servicio de mecanógrafos.
typist [tī'pist] n mecanógrafo/a.
typography [tīpâg'rəfē] n tipografía.
tyranny [tēr'ənē] n tiranía.
tyrant [tī'rənt] n tirano/a.
tyre [tīûr'] n (Brit) = **tire**.
Tyrol [tīrōl'] n Tirol m.
Tyrolean [tīrō'lēən], **Tyrolese** [tirəlēz'] a
tirolés/esa.
Tyrrhenian Sea [tīrē'nēən sē'] n Mar m Ti-
rreno.
tzar [zâr] n = **tsar**.

U

U, u [yōō] n (letter) U, u f; **U for Uncle** U
de Uruguay.
U [yōō] n abbr (Brit CINEMA: = universal)
todos los públicos.
U-bend [yōō'bend] n (AUT, in pipe) recodo.
ubiquitous [yōōbik'witəs] a ubicuo.
UDA n abbr (Brit: = Ulster Defence Association) organización paramilitar protestante en Irlanda del Norte.
udder [ud'ûr] n ubre f.

UDI *n abbr* (*Brit POL*) = *unilateral declaration of independence.*

UDR *n abbr* (*Brit:* = *Ulster Defence Regiment*) *fuerza de seguridad de Irlanda del Norte.*

UEFA [yōōā'fa] *n abbr* (= *Union of European Football Associations*) U.E.F.A. *f.*

UFO [yōōefō'] *n abbr* = (*unidentified flying object*) OVNI *m.*

Uganda [yōōgan'də] *n* Uganda.

Ugandan [yōōgan'dən] *a* de Uganda.

ugh [u] *excl* ¡uf!

ugliness [ug'lēnis] *n* fealdad *f.*

ugly [ug'lē] *a* feo; (*dangerous*) peligroso.

UHF *abbr* (= *ultra-high frequency*) UHF *m.*

UHT *a abbr* (= *ultra heat treated*): ~ **milk** leche *f* uperizada.

UK *n abbr* (= *United Kingdom*) R.U.

ulcer [ul'sûr] *n* úlcera; **mouth** ~ úlcera oral.

Ulster [ul'stûr] *n* Ulster *m.*

ulterior [ultēr'ēûr] *a* ulterior; ~ **motive** segundas intenciones *fpl.*

ultimate [ul'təmit] *a* último, final; (*greatest*) mayor ♦ *n:* **the** ~ **in luxury** el colmo del lujo.

ultimately [ul'təmitlē] *ad* (*in the end*) por último, al final; (*fundamentally*) a *or* en fin de cuentas.

ultimatum, *pl* ~**s** *or* **ultimata** [ultimā'təm, -tə] *n* ultimátum *m.*

ultra- [ul'trə] *pref* ultra-.

ultralight [ultrəlīt'] *n* (avión *m*) ultraligero, avioneta.

ultrasonic [ultrəsân'ik] *a* ultrasónico.

ultrasound [ul'trəsound] *n* (*MED*) ultrasonido.

ultraviolet [ultrəvī'əlit] *a* ultravioleta.

umbilical cord [umbil'ikəl kôrd] *n* cordón *m* umbilical.

umbrage [um'brij] *n:* **to take** ~ **(at)** ofenderse (por).

umbrella [umbrel'ə] *n* paraguas *m inv*; **under the** ~ **of** (*fig*) bajo la protección de.

umpire [um'pīûr] *n* árbitro ♦ *vt* arbitrar.

umpteen [ump'tēn'] *num* enésimos/as; **for the** ~**th time** por enésima vez.

UMW *n abbr* (= *United Mineworkers of America*) sindicato de mineros.

UN *n abbr* (= *United Nations*) N.U. *fpl*, NN.UU. *fpl.*

un- [un-] *pref* in-; des-; no ...; poco ...; nada ...

unabashed [unəbasht'] *a* nada avergonzado.

unabated [unəbā'tid] *a:* **to continue** ~ seguir sin disminuir.

unable [unā'bəl] *a:* **to be** ~ **to do sth** no poder hacer algo; (*not know how to*) ser incapaz de hacer algo, no saber hacer algo.

unabridged [unəbrijd'] *a* íntegro.

unacceptable [unaksep'təbəl] *a* (*proposal, behavior, price*) inaceptable; **it's** ~ **that** no se puede aceptar que.

unaccompanied [unəkum'pənēd] *a* no acompañado; (*singing, song*) sin acompañamiento.

unaccountably [unəkount'əblē] *ad* inexplicablemente.

unaccounted [unəkoun'tid] *a:* **two passengers are** ~ **for** faltan dos pasajeros.

unaccustomed [unəkus'təmd] *a:* **to be** ~ **to** no estar acostumbrado a.

unacquainted [unəkwān'tid] *a:* **to be** ~ **with** (*facts*) desconocer, ignorar.

unadulterated [unədul'tərātid] *a* (*gen*) puro; (*wine*) sin mezcla.

unaffected [unəfek'tid] *a* (*person, behavior*) sin afectación, sencillo; (*emotionally*): **to be** ~ **by** no estar afectado por.

unafraid [unəfrād'] *a:* **to be** ~ no tener miedo.

unaided [unā'did] *a* sin ayuda, por sí solo.

unanimity [yōōnənim'itē] *n* unanimidad *f.*

unanimous [yōōnan'əməs] *a* unánime.

unanimously [yōōnan'əməslē] *ad* unánimemente.

unanswered [unan'sûrd] *a* (*question, letter*) sin contestar; (*criticism*) incontestado.

unappetizing [unap'itīzing] *a* poco apetitoso.

unappreciative [unəprē'shēətiv] *a* desagradecido.

unarmed [unârmd'] *a* (*person*) desarmado; (*combat*) sin armas.

unashamed [unəshāmd'] *a* desvergonzado.

unassisted [unəsis'tid] *a, ad* sin ayuda.

unassuming [unəsōō'ming] *a* modesto, sin pretensiones.

unattached [unətacht'] *a* (*person*) soltero; (*part etc*) suelto.

unattended [unəten'did] *a* (*car, luggage*) sin atender.

unattractive [unətrak'tiv] *a* poco atractivo.

unauthorized [unôth'ərīzd] *a* no autorizado.

unavailable [unəvā'ləbəl] *a* (*article, room, book*) indisponible; (*person*) ocupado.

unavoidable [unəvoi'dəbəl] *a* inevitable.

unavoidably [unəvoi'dəblē] *ad* (*detained*) por causas ajenas a su voluntad.

unaware [unəwär'] *a:* **to be** ~ **of** ignorar.

unawares [unəwärz'] *ad* de improviso.

unbalanced [unbal'ənst] *a* desequilibrado; (*mentally*) trastornado.

unbearable [unbär'əbəl] *a* insoportable.

unbeatable [unbē'təbəl] *a* (*gen*) invencible; (*price*) inmejorable.

unbeaten [unbēt'ən] *a* imbatido; (*team, army*) invicto; (*record*) no batido.

unbecoming [unbikum'ing] *a* (*unseemly: language, behavior*) indecoroso, impropio; (*unflattering: garment*) poco favorecedor(a).

unbeknown(st) [unbinōn(st)'] *ad:* ~ **to**

me sin saberlo yo.
unbelief |unbilēf'| *n* incredulidad *f.*
unbelievable |unbilē'vǝbǝl| *a* increíble.
unbelievingly |unbilē'vinglē| *ad* sin creer.
unbend |unbend'| (*irg: like* **bend**) *vi* (*fig: person*) relajarse ♦ *vt* (*wire*) enderezar.
unbending |unben'ding| *a* (*fig*) inflexible.
unbias(s)ed |unbī'ǝst| *a* imparcial.
unblemished |unblem'isht| *a* sin mancha.
unblock |unblâk'| *vt* (*pipe*) desatascar; (*road*) despejar.
unborn |unbôrn'| *a* que va a nacer.
unbounded |unboun'did| *a* ilimitado, sin límite.
unbreakable |unbrā'kǝbǝl| *a* irrompible.
unbridled |unbrī'dǝld| *a* (*fig*) desenfrenado.
unbroken |unbrō'kǝn| *a* (*seal*) intacto; (*series*) continuo; (*record*) no batido; (*spirit*) indómito.
unbuckle |unbuk'ǝl| *vt* desabrochar.
unburden |unbûr'dǝn| *vt:* **to ~ o.s.** desahogarse.
unbusinesslike |unbiz'nislīk| *a* (*trader*) poco metódico; (*transaction*) incorrecto; (*fig: person*) poco práctico.
unbutton |unbut'ǝn| *vt* desabrochar.
uncalled-for |unkôld'fôr| *a* gratuito, inmerecido.
uncanny |unkan'ē| *a* extraño, extraordinario.
unceasing |unsē'sing| *a* incesante.
unceremonious |unsãrǝmō'nēǝs| *a* (*abrupt, rude*) brusco, hosco.
uncertain |unsûr'tǝn| *a* incierto; (*indecisive*) indeciso; **it's ~ whether** no se sabe si; **in no ~ terms** sin dejar lugar a dudas.
uncertainty |unsûr'tǝntē| *n* incertidumbre *f.*
unchallenged |unchal'injd| *a* (*LAW etc*) incontestado; **to go ~** no encontrar respuesta.
unchanged |unchānjd'| *a* sin cambiar *or* alterar.
uncharitable |unchar'itǝbǝl| *a* (*remark, behavior*) demasiado duro.
uncharted |unchâr'tid| *a* inexplorado.
unchecked |unchekt'| *a* desenfrenado.
uncivil |unsiv'ǝl| *a* grosero.
uncivilized |unsiv'ilīzd| *a* (*gen*) inculto, poco civilizado; (*fig: behavior etc*) bárbaro.
uncle |ung'kǝl| *n* tío.
unclear |unkliûr'| *a* poco claro; **I'm still ~ about what I'm supposed to do** todavía no estoy muy seguro de lo que tengo que hacer.
uncoil |unkoil'| *vt* desenrollar ♦ *vi* desenrollarse.
uncomfortable |unkumf'tǝbǝl| *a* incómodo; (*uneasy*) inquieto.
uncomfortably |unkumf'tǝblē| *ad* (*uneasily: say*) con inquietud; (: *think*) con remordimiento *or* nerviosismo.
uncommitted |unkǝmit'id| *a* (*attitude, country*) no comprometido; **to remain ~ to**

(*policy, party*) no comprometerse a.
uncommon |unkâm'ǝn| *a* poco común, raro.
uncommunicative |unkǝmyōō'nikǝtiv| *a* poco comunicativo, reservado.
uncomplicated |unkâm'plikātid| *a* sin complicaciones.
uncompromising |unkâm'prǝmīzing| *a* intransigente.
unconcerned |unkǝnsûrnd'| *a* indiferente, despreocupado; **to be ~ about** ser indiferente a, no preocuparse de.
unconditional |unkǝndish'ǝnǝl| *a* incondicional.
uncongenial |unkǝnjēn'yǝl| *a* desagradable.
unconnected |unkǝnek'tid| *a* (*unrelated*): **to be ~ with** no estar relacionado con.
unconscious |unkân'chǝs| *a* sin sentido; (*unaware*) inconsciente ♦ *n:* **the ~** el inconsciente; **to knock sb ~** dejar a uno sin sentido.
unconsciously |unkân'chǝslē| *ad* inconscientemente.
unconsciousness |unkân'chǝsnis| *n* inconsciencia.
unconstitutional |unkânstitōō'shǝnǝl| *a* anti-constitucional.
uncontested |unkântes'tid| *a* (*champion*) incontestado; (*POL: seat*) ganado sin oposición.
uncontrollable |unkǝntrō'lǝbǝl| *a* (*temper*) indomable; (*laughter*) incontenible.
uncontrolled |unkǝntrōld'| *a* (*child, dog, emotion*) incontrolado; (*inflation, price rises*) desenfrenado.
unconventional |unkǝnven'chǝnǝl| *a* poco convencional.
unconvinced |unkǝnvinst'| *a:* **to be** *or* **remain ~** seguir sin convencerse.
unconvincing |unkǝnvin'sing| *a* poco convincente.
uncork |unkôrk'| *vt* descorchar, destapar.
uncorroborated |unkǝrâb'ǝrātid| *a* no confirmado.
uncouth |unkōōth'| *a* grosero, inculto.
uncover |unkuv'ûr| *vt* (*gen*) descubrir; (*take lid off*) destapar.
uncovered |unkuv'ûrd| *a:* **~ check** cheque *m* sin fondos.
undamaged |undam'ijd| *a* (*goods*) en buen estado; (*fig: reputation*) intacto, indemne.
undaunted |undôn'tid| *a:* **~ by** nada desanimado por.
undecided |undisī'did| *a* (*character*) indeciso; (*question*) no resuelto, pendiente.
undelivered |undiliv'ûrd| *a* no entregado al destinatario; **if ~ return to sender** en caso de no llegar a su destino devolver al remitente.
undeniable |undinī'ǝbǝl| *a* innegable.
undeniably |undinī'ǝblē| *ad* innegablemente.
under |un'dûr| *prep* debajo de; (*less than*)

menos de; (*according to*) según, de acuerdo con ♦ *ad* debajo, abajo; ~ **there** allí abajo; ~ **construction** en construcción; en obras; ~ **the circumstances** dadas las circunstancias; **in** ~ **2 hours** en menos de dos horas; ~ **anesthetic** bajo los efectos de la anestesia; ~ **discussion** en discusión, sobre el tapete.

under... *pref* sub....

underage [undârāj'] *a* menor de edad.

underarm [un'dûrârm] *n* axila, sobaco ♦ *cpd*: ~ **deodorant** desodorante *m* corporal.

undercapitalized [undûrkap'itəlīzd] *a* descapitalizado.

undercarriage [un'dûrkarij] *n* (*Brit AVIAT*) tren *m* de aterrizaje.

undercharge [undûrchârj'] *vt* cobrar de menos.

underclothes [un'dûrklōz] *npl* ropa *sg* interior *or* íntima (*LAm*).

undercoat [un'dûrkōt] *n* (*paint*) primera mano ♦ *vt* (*US AUT*) proteger contra la corrosión.

undercover [undûrkuv'ûr] *a* clandestino.

undercurrent [un'dûrkûrənt] *n* corriente *f* submarina; (*fig*) tendencia oculta.

undercut [un'dûrkut'] *vt* (*irg*: *like* **cut**) vender más barato que; fijar un precio más barato que.

underdeveloped [un'dûrdivcl'əpt] *a* subdesarrollado.

underdog [un'dûrdôg] *n* desvalido/a.

underdone [un'dûrdun'] *a* (*CULIN*) poco hecho.

underemployment [un'dûremploi'mənt] *n* subempleo.

underestimate [undûres'təmāt] *vt* subestimar.

underexposed [undûrikspōzd'] *a* (*PHOT*) subexpuesto.

underfed [undûrfed'] *a* subalimentado.

underfoot [undûrfoot'] *ad*: **it's wet** ~ el suelo está mojado.

undergo [undûrgō'] *vt* (*irg*: *like* **go**) sufrir; (*treatment*) recibir; **the car is** ~**ing repairs** están reparando el coche.

undergraduate [undûrgraj'ōoit] *n* estudiante *m/f* ♦ *cpd*: ~ **courses** cursos *mpl* de licenciatura.

underground [un'dûrground] *n* (*POL*) movimiento clandestino; (*Brit*: *railway*) metro ♦ *a* subterráneo.

undergrowth [un'dûrgrōth] *n* maleza.

underhand(ed) [un'dûrhan'd(id)] *a* (*fig*) socarrón.

underinsured [undûrinshoord'] *a* insuficientemente asegurado.

underlie [undûrlī'] *vt* (*irg*: *like* **lie**) (*fig*) ser la razón fundamental de; **the underlying cause** la causa fundamental.

underline [un'dûrlīn] *vt* subrayar.

underling [un'dûrling] *n* (*pej*) subalterno/a.

undermanning [un'dûrman'ing] *n* falta de

personal.

undermentioned [un'dûrmenchənd] *a* abajo citado.

undermine [un'dûrmīn] *vt* socavar, minar.

underneath [undûrnēth'] *ad* debajo ♦ *prep* debajo de, bajo.

undernourished [undûrnûr'isht] *a* desnutrido.

underpaid [undûrpād'] *a* mal pagado.

underpants [un'dûrpants] *npl* calzoncillos *mpl*.

underpass [un'dûrpas] *n* paso subterráneo.

underpin [undûrpin'] *vt* (*argument, case*) secundar, sostener.

underplay [undûrplā'] *vt* minimizar.

underpopulated [undûrpâp'yəlātid] *a* despoblado.

underprice [undûrprīs'] *vt* vender demasiado barato.

underpriced [undûrprīst'] *a* con precio demasiado bajo.

underprivileged [undûrpriv'əlijd] *a* desvalido.

underrate [undərāt'] *vt* menospreciar, subestimar.

underscore [undûrskôr'] *vt* subrayar, sostener.

underseal [un'dûrsēl] *vt* (*AUT*) proteger contra la corrosión.

undersecretary [un'dûrsek'ritārē] *n* subsecretario/a.

undersell [undûrsel'] *vt* (*competitors*) vender más barato que.

undershirt [un'dûrshûrt] *n* (*US*) camiseta.

undershorts [un'dûrshôrts] *npl* (*US*) calzoncillos *mpl*.

underside [un'dûrsīd] *n* parte *f* inferior, revés *m*.

undersigned [un'dûrsīnd'] *a, n*: **the** ~ el/la *etc* abajo firmante.

underskirt [un'dûrskûrt] *n* enaguas *fpl*.

understaffed [undûrstaft'] *a* falto de personal.

understand [undûrstand'] (*irg*: *like* **stand**) *vt, vi* entender, comprender; (*assume*) tener entendido; **to make o.s. understood** hacerse entender; **I** ~ **you have been absent** tengo entendido que (usted) ha estado ausente.

understandable [undûrstan'dəbəl] *a* comprensible.

understanding [undûrstan'ding] *a* comprensivo ♦ *n* comprensión *f*, entendimiento; (*agreement*) acuerdo; **to come to an** ~ **with sb** llegar a un acuerdo con uno; **on the** ~ **that** a condición de que (+ *subjun*).

understate [undûrstāt'] *vt* minimizar.

understatement [undûrstāt'mənt] *n* subestimación *f*; (*modesty*) modestia (excesiva).

understood [undûrstood'] *pt, pp of* **understand** ♦ *a* entendido; (*implied*): **it is** ~ **that** se sobreentiende que.

understudy [un'dûrstudē] n suplente m/f.
undertake [undûrtāk'] (irg: like **take**) vt emprender; **to ~ to do sth** comprometerse a hacer algo.
undertaker [un'dûrtākûr] n director(a) m/f de pompas fúnebres.
undertaking [un'dûrtāking] n empresa; (promise) promesa.
undertone [un'dûrtōn] n (of criticism) connotación f; (low voice): **in an ~** en voz baja.
undervalue [undûrval'yōō] vt (fig) subestimar, menospreciar; (COMM etc) valorizar por debajo de su precio.
underwater [un'dûrwôt'ûr] ad bajo el agua ♦ a submarino.
underwear [un'dûrwär] n ropa interior or íntima (LAm).
underweight [un'dûrwāt] a de peso insuficiente; (person) demasiado delgado.
underworld [un'dûrwûrld] n (of crime) hampa, inframundo.
underwrite [un'dərīt] (irg: like **write**) vt (COMM) suscribir; (INSURANCE) asegurar (contra riesgos).
underwriter [un'dərītûr] n (INSURANCE) asegurador/a m/f.
undeserving [undizûr'ving] a: **to be ~ of** no ser digno de.
undesirable [undizīûr'əbəl] a indeseable.
undeveloped [undivel'əpt] a (land, resources) sin explotar.
undies [un'dēz] npl (col) ropa sg interior or íntima (LAm).
undiluted [undilōō'tid] a (concentrate) concentrado.
undiplomatic [undipləmat'ik] a poco diplomático.
undischarged [undischârjd'] a: **~ bankrupt** (Brit) quebrado/a no rehabilitado/a.
undisciplined [undis'əplind] a indisciplinado.
undiscovered [undiskuv'ûrd] a no descubierto; (unknown) desconocido.
undisguised [undisgīzd'] a (dislike) no disfrazado; (amusement etc) franco, abierto.
undisputed [undispyōō'tid] a incontestable.
undistinguished [undisting'gwisht] a mediocre.
undisturbed [undistûrbd'] a (sleep) ininterrumpido; **to leave sth ~** dejar algo tranquilo.
undivided [undivī'did] a: **I want your ~ attention** quiero su completa atención.
undo [undōō'] vt (irg: like **do**) deshacer.
undoing [undōō'ing] n ruina, perdición f.
undone [undun'] pp of **undo** ♦ a: **to come ~** (clothes) desabrocharse; (parcel) desatarse.
undoubted [undou'tid] a indudable.
undoubtedly [undou'tidlē] ad indudablemente, sin duda.
undress [undres'] vi desnudarse.

undrinkable [undringk'əbəl] a (unpalatable) que no se puede beber; (poisonous) no potable.
undue [undōō'] a indebido, excesivo.
undulating [un'jəlāting] a ondulante.
unduly [undōō'lē] ad excesivamente, demasiado.
undying [undī'ing] a eterno.
unearned [unûrnd'] a (praise, respect) inmerecido; **~ income** ingresos mpl no ganados, renta no ganada or salarial.
unearth [unûrth'] vt desenterrar.
unearthly [unûrth'lē] a: **~ hour** (col) hora inverosímil or intempestiva.
unease [unēz'] n malestar m.
uneasy [unē'zē] a intranquilo; (worried) preocupado; **to feel ~ about doing sth** sentirse incómodo con la idea de hacer algo.
uneconomic(al) [unēkənâm'ik(əl)] a no económico.
uneducated [unej'ōōkātid] a ignorante, inculto.
unemployed [unemploid'] a parado, sin trabajo ♦ n: **the ~** los parados.
unemployment [unemploi'mənt] n paro, desempleo.
unemployment benefit n subsidio de paro.
unending [unen'ding] a interminable.
unenviable [unen'vēəbəl] a poco envidiable.
unequal [unēk'wəl] a (length, objects etc) desigual; (amounts) distinto; (division of labor) poco justo.
unequaled, (Brit) **unequalled** [unēk'wəld] a inigualado, sin par.
unequivocal [unikwiv'əkəl] a (answer) inequívoco, claro; (person) claro.
unerring [unûr'ing] a infalible.
UNESCO [yōōnes'kō] n abbr (= United Nations Educational, Scientific and Cultural Organization) UNESCO f.
unethical [uneth'ikəl] a (methods) inmoral; (doctor's behavior) que infringe la ética profesional.
uneven [unē'vən] a desigual; (road etc) quebrado.
uneventful [univent'fəl] a sin novedad.
unexceptional [uniksep'shənəl] a sin nada de extraordinario, corriente.
unexciting [uniksī'ting] a (news) sin interés; (film, evening) aburrido.
unexpected [unikspek'tid] a inesperado.
unexpectedly [unikspek'tidlē] ad inesperadamente.
unexplained [uniksplānd'] a inexplicado.
unexploded [uniksplō'did] a sin explotar.
unfailing [unfā'ling] a (support) indefectible; (energy) inagotable.
unfair [unfär'] a: **~ (to sb)** injusto (con uno); **it's ~ that ...** es injusto que ..., no es justo que ....
unfair dismissal n despido improcedente.

unfairly [unfär'lē] *ad* injustamente.

unfaithful [unfāth'fəl] *a* infiel.

unfamiliar [unfəmil'yûr] *a* extraño, desconocido; **to be ~ with sth** desconocer *or* ignorar algo.

unfashionable [unfash'ənəbəl] *a* (*clothes*) pasado *or* fuera de moda; (*district*) poco elegante.

unfasten [unfas'ən] *vt* desatar.

unfathomable [unfath'əm, 'əməbəl] *a* insondable.

unfavorable, (*Brit*) **unfavourable** [unfā'vûrəbəl] *a* desfavorable.

unfavorably [unfā'vûrablē] *ad*: **to look ~ upon** ver desfavorablemente.

unfeeling [unfē'ling] *a* insensible.

unfinished [unfin'isht] *a* inacabado, sin terminar.

unfit [unfit'] *a* (*ill*) indispuesto, enfermo; (*incompetent*) incapaz; **~ for work** no apto para trabajar.

unflagging [unflag'ing] *a* incansable.

unflappable [unflap'əbəl] *a* imperturbable.

unflattering [unflat'ûring] *a* (*dress, hairstyle*) poco halagüeño.

unflinching [unflin'ching] *a* impávido, resuelto.

unfold [unfōld'] *vt* desdoblar; (*fig*) revelar ♦ *vi* abrirse; revelarse.

unforeseeable [unfôrsē'əbəl] *a* imprevisible.

unforeseen [unfôrsēn'] *a* imprevisto.

unforgettable [unfûrget'əbəl] *a* inolvidable.

unforgivable [unfûrgiv'əbəl] *a* imperdonable.

unformatted [unfôr'matid] *a* (*disk, text*) sin formato.

unfortunate [unfôr'chənit] *a* desgraciado; (*event, remark*) inoportuno.

unfortunately [unfôr'chənitlē] *ad* desgraciadamente, por desgracia.

unfounded [unfoun'did] *a* infundado.

unfriendly [unfrend'lē] *a* antipático.

unfulfilled [unfʊʊlfild'] *a* (*ambition*) sin realizar; (*prophecy, promise, terms of contract*) incumplido; (*desire, person*) insatisfecho.

unfurl [unfûrl'] *vt* desplegar.

unfurnished [unfûr'nisht] *a* desamueblado.

ungainly [ungān'lē] *a* (*walk*) desgarbado.

ungodly [ungâd'lē] *a*: **at an ~ hour** a una hora inverosímil.

ungrateful [ungrāt'fəl] *a* ingrato.

unguarded [ungâr'did] *a* (*moment*) de descuido.

unhappily [unhap'ilē] *ad* (*unfortunately*) desgraciadamente.

unhappiness [unhap'ēnis] *n* tristeza.

unhappy [unhap'ē] *a* (*sad*) triste; (*unfortunate*) desgraciado; (*childhood*) infeliz; **~ with** (*arrangements etc*) poco contento con, descontento de.

unharmed [unhârmd'] *a* (*person*) ileso.

unhealthy [unhel'thē] *a* (*gen*) malsano; (*person*) enfermizo; (*interest*) morboso.

unheard-of [unhûrd'əv] *a* inaudito, sin precedente.

unhelpful [unhelp'fəl] *a* (*person*) poco servicial; (*advice*) inútil.

unhesitating [unhez'itāting] *a* (*loyalty*) automático; (*reply, offer*) resuelto, inmediato.

unhook [unhōōk'] *vt* desenganchar; (*from wall*) descolgar; (*undo*) desabrochar.

unhurt [unhûrt'] *a* ileso.

unhygienic [unhijēen'ik] *a* antihigiénico.

UNICEF [yōō'nisef] *n abbr* (= *United Nations International Children's Emergency Fund*) UNICEF *m*.

unicolor [yōōnəkul'ûr] *a* de un color.

unidentified [unīden'təfid] *a* no identificado; **~ flying object (UFO)** objeto volante no identificado.

unification [yōōnifikā'shən] *n* unificación *f*.

uniform [yōō'nəfôrm] *n* uniforme *m* ♦ *a* uniforme.

uniformity [yōōnəfôr'mitē] *n* uniformidad *f*.

unify [yōō'nəfī] *vt* unificar, unir.

unilateral [yōōnəlat'ûrəl] *a* unilateral.

unimaginable [unimaj'ənəbəl] *a* inconcebible, inimaginable.

unimaginative [unimaj'ənətiv] *a* falto de imaginación.

unimpaired [unimpärd'] *a* (*unharmed*) intacto; (*not lessened*) no disminuido; (*unaltered*) inalterado.

unimportant [unimpôr'tənt] *a* sin importancia.

unimpressed [unimprest'] *a* poco impresionado.

uninhabited [uninhab'itid] *a* desierto; (*country*) despoblado; (*house*) deshabitado, desocupado.

uninhibited [uninhib'itid] *a* nada cohibido, desinhibido.

uninjured [unin'jûrd] *a* (*person*) ileso.

unintelligent [unintel'ijənt] *a* poco inteligente.

unintentional [uninten'chənəl] *a* involuntario.

unintentionally [uninten'chənəlē] *ad* sin querer.

uninvited [uninvī'tid] *a* (*guest*) sin invitación.

uninviting [uninvī'ting] *a* (*place, offer*) poco atractivo; (*food*) poco apetitoso.

union [yōōn'yən] *n* unión *f*; (*also*: **trade ~**) sindicato ♦ *cpd* sindical; **the U~** (*US*) la Unión.

union card *n* carnet *m* de sindicato.

unionize [yōōn'yənīz] *vt* sindicalizar.

Union Jack *n* bandera del Reino Unido.

Union of Soviet Socialist Republics (USSR) *n* Unión *f* de Repúblicas Socialistas Soviéticas.

union shop *n* (*US*) *taller de afiliación*

sindical obligatoria.

unique [yōōnēk'] *a* único.

unisex [yōō'niseks] *a* unisex.

unison [yōō'nisən] *n*: **in** ~ en armonía.

unissued capital [unish'ōōd kap'itəl] *n* capital *m* no emitido.

unit [yōō'nit] *n* unidad *f*; (*team, squad*) grupo; **kitchen** ~ módulo de cocina; **production** ~ taller *m* de fabricación; **sink** ~ fregadero.

unit cost *n* costo unitario.

unite [yōōnīt'] *vt* unir ♦ *vi* unirse.

united [yōōnī'tid] *a* unido.

United Arab Emirates *npl* Emiratos *mpl* Árabes Unidos.

United Kingdom (UK) *n* Reino Unido.

United Nations (Organization) (UN, UNO) *n* Naciones Unidas *fpl* (ONU *f*).

United States (of America) (US, USA) *n* Estados Unidos *mpl* (de América) (EE.UU. *mpl*).

unit price *n* precio unitario.

unit trust *n* (*Brit*) bono fiduciario.

unity [yōō'nitē] *n* unidad *f*.

Univ. *abbr* = **university.**

universal [yōōnəvûr'səl] *a* universal.

universally [yōōnəvûr'səlē] *ad* universalmente.

universe [yōō'nəvûrs] *n* universo.

university [yōōnəvûr'sitē] *n* universidad *f* ♦ *cpd* (*student, professor, education, degree*) universitario; (*year*) académico, universitario; **to be at/go to the** ~ estudiar en/ir a la universidad.

unjust [unjust'] *a* injusto.

unjustifiable [unjus'tifiəbəl] *a* injustificable.

unjustified [unjus'təfid] *a* (*text*) no alineado *or* justificado.

unkempt [unkempt'] *a* descuidado; (*hair*) despeinado.

unkind [unkīnd'] *a* poco amable; (*comment etc*) cruel.

unkindly [unkīnd'lē] *ad* (*speak*) severamente; (*treat*) cruelmente, mal.

unknown [unnōn'] *a* desconocido ♦ *ad*: ~ **to me** sin saberlo yo; ~ **quantity** (*MATH, fig*) incógnita.

unladen [unlā'dən] *a* (*weight*) vacío, sin cargamento.

unlawful [unlô'fəl] *a* ilegal, ilícito.

unleaded [unled'id] *a* sin plomo.

unleash [unlēsh'] *vt* desatar.

unleavened [unlev'ənd] *a* ácimo, sin levadura.

unless [unles'] *conj* a menos que; ~ **he comes** a menos que venga; ~ **otherwise stated** salvo indicación contraria; ~ **I am mistaken** si no mi equivoco.

unlicensed [unlī'sənst] *a* (*Brit*: *to sell alcohol*) no autorizado.

unlike [unlīk'] *a* distinto ♦ *prep* a diferencia de.

unlikelihood [unlīk'lēhōōd] *n* improbabili-

dad *f*.

unlikely [unlīk'lē] *a* improbable.

unlimited [unlim'itid] *a* ilimitado; ~ **liability** responsabilidad *f* ilimitada.

unlisted [unlis'tid] *a* (*US TEL*) que no consta en la guía; ~ **company** empresa sin cotización en bolsa.

unlit [unlit'] *a* (*room*) oscuro, sin luz.

unload [unlōd'] *vt* descargar.

unlock [unlâk'] *vt* abrir (con llave).

unlucky [unluk'ē] *a* desgraciado; (*object, number*) que da mala suerte; **to be** ~ (*person*) tener mala suerte.

unmanageable [unman'ijəbəl] *a* (*unwieldy*: *tool, vehicle*) difícil de manejar; (: *situation*) incontrolable.

unmanned [unmand'] *a* (*spacecraft*) sin tripulación.

unmannerly [unman'ûrlē] *a* mal educado, descortés.

unmarked [unmârkt'] *a* (*unstained*) sin mancha; ~ **police car** vehículo policial camuflado.

unmarried [unmar'ēd] *a* soltero.

unmask [unmask'] *vt* desenmascarar.

unmatched [unmacht'] *a* incomparable.

unmentionable [unmen'chənəbəl] *a* (*topic, vice*) indecible; (*word*) que no se debe decir.

unmerciful [unmûr'sifəl] *a* despiadado.

unmistakable [unmistā'kəbəl] *a* inconfundible.

unmistakably [unmistā'kəblē] *ad* de modo inconfundible.

unmitigated [unmit'əgātid] *a* rematado, absoluto.

unnamed [unnāmd'] *a* (*nameless*) sin nombre; (*anonymous*) anónimo.

unnatural [unnach'ûrəl] *a* (*gen*) antinatural; (*manner*) afectado; (*habit*) perverso.

unnecessary [unnes'isärē] *a* innecesario, inútil.

unnerve [unnûrv'] *vt* (*subj*: *accident*) poner nervioso; (: *hostile attitude*) acobardar; (: *long wait, interview*) intimidar.

unnoticed [unnō'tist] *a*: **to go** *or* **pass** ~ pasar desapercibido.

UNO [ōō'nō] *n abbr* = (*United Nations Organization*) ONU *f*.

unobservant [unəbzûr'vənt] *a*: **to be** ~ ser poco observador, ser distraído.

unobtainable [unəbtā'nəbəl] *a* inconseguible; (*TEL*) inexistente.

unobtrusive [unəbtrōō'siv] *a* discreto.

unoccupied [unâk'yəpīd] *a* (*house etc*) libre, desocupado.

unofficial [unəfish'əl] *a* no oficial; ~ **strike** huelga no oficial.

unopened [unō'pənd] *a* (*letter, present*) sin abrir.

unopposed [unəpōzd'] *a* (*enter, be elected*) sin oposición.

unorthodox [unôr'thədâks] *a* poco ortodoxo.

unpack [unpak'] *vi* deshacer las maletas, desempacar (*LAm*).

unpaid [unpād'] *a* (*bill, debt*) sin pagar, impagado; (*COMM*) pendiente; (*vacation*) sin sueldo; (*work*) sin pago, voluntario.

unpalatable [unpal'ətəbəl] *a* (*truth*) desagradable.

unparalleled [unpar'əleld] *a* (*unequalled*) sin par; (*unique*) sin precedentes.

unpatriotic [unpātrēăt'ik] *a* (*person*) poco patriota; (*speech, attitude*) antipatriótico.

unplanned [unpland'] *a* (*visit*) imprevisto; (*baby*) no planeado.

unpleasant [unplez'ənt] *a* (*disagreeable*) desagradable; (*person, manner*) antipático.

unplug [unplug'] *vt* desenchufar, desconectar.

unpolluted [unpəlōō'tid] *a* impoluto, no contaminado.

unpopular [unpáp'yəlûr] *a* poco popular; **to be ~ with sb** (*person, law*) no ser popular con uno; **to make o.s. ~ (with)** hacerse impopular (con).

unprecedented [unpres'identid] *a* sin precedentes.

unpredictable [unpridik'təbəl] *a* imprevisible.

unprejudiced [unprej'ədist] *a* (*not biased*) imparcial; (*having no prejudices*) sin prejuicio.

unprepared [unpripärd'] *a* (*person*) desprevenido; (*speech*) improvisado.

unprepossessing [unprēpəzes'ing] *a* poco atractivo.

unprincipled [unprin'səpəld] *a* sin escrúpulos.

unproductive [unprəduk'tiv] *a* improductivo; (*discussion*) infructuoso.

unprofessional [unprəfesh'ənəl] *a* indigno de su profesión; **~ conduct** negligencia.

unprofitable [unpráf'itəbəl] *a* poco provechoso, no rentable.

unprovoked [unprəvōkt'] *a* no provocado.

unpunished [unpun'isht] *a*: **to go ~** quedar sin castigo, salir impune.

unqualified [unkwál'əfīd] *a* sin título, no cualificado; (*success*) total, incondicional.

unquestionably [unkwes'chənəblē] *ad* indiscutiblemente.

unquestioning [unkwes'chəning] *a* (*obedience, acceptance*) incondicional.

unravel [unrav'əl] *vt* desenmarañar.

unreal [unrēl'] *a* irreal.

unrealistic [unrēəlis'tik] *a* poco realista.

unreasonable [unrē'zənəbəl] *a* irrazonable; **to make ~ demands on sb** hacer demandas excesivas a uno.

unrecognizable [unrek'əgnīzəbəl] *a* irreconocible.

unrecognized [unrek'əgnīzd] *a* (*talent, genius*) desapercibido; (*POL: regime*) no reconocido.

unrecorded [unrikôr'did] *a* no registrado.

unrefined [unrifīnd'] *a* (*sugar, petroleum*) sin refinar.

unrehearsed [unrihûrst'] *a* (*THEATER etc*) improvisado; (*spontaneous*) espontáneo.

unrelated [unrilā'tid] *a* sin relación; (*family*) no emparentado.

unrelenting [unrilen'ting] *a* implacable.

unreliable [unrili'əbəl] *a* (*person*) informal; (*machine*) poco fiable.

unrelieved [unrilēvd'] *a* (*monotony*) constante.

unremitting [unrimit'ing] *a* constante.

unrepeatable [unripē'təbəl] *a* irrepetible.

unrepentant [unripen'tənt] *a* (*smoker, sinner*) impenitente; **to be ~ about sth** no arrepentirse de algo.

unrepresentative [unreprizen'tətiv] *a* (*untypical*) poco representativo.

unreserved [unrizûrvd'] *a* (*seat*) no reservado; (*approval, admiration*) total.

unreservedly [unrizûr'vidlē] *ad* sin reserva.

unresponsive [unrispân'siv] *a* insensible.

unrest [unrest'] *n* inquietud *f*, malestar *m*; (*POL*) disturbios *mpl*.

unrestricted [unristrik'tid] *a* (*power, time*) sin restricción; (*access*) libre.

unrewarded [unriwôr'did] *a* sin recompensa.

unripe [unrīp'] *a* verde, inmaduro.

unrivaled, (*Brit*) **unrivalled** [unrī'vəld] *a* incomparable, sin par.

unroll [unrōl'] *vt* desenrollar.

unruffled [unruf'əld] *a* (*person*) imperturbable, ecuánime; (*hair*) liso.

unruly [unrōō'lē] *a* indisciplinado.

unsafe [unsāf'] *a* (*journey*) peligroso; (*car etc*) inseguro; (*method*) arriesgado; **~ to drink/eat** no apto para el consumo humano.

unsaid [unsed'] *a*: **to leave sth ~** dejar algo sin decir.

unsalable, (*Brit*) **unsaleable** [unsā'ləbəl] *a* invendible.

unsatisfactory [unsatisfak'tûrē] *a* poco satisfactorio.

unsatisfied [unsat'isfīd] *a* (*desire, need etc*) insatisfecho.

unsavory, (*Brit*) **unsavoury** [unsā'vûrē] *a* (*fig*) repugnante.

unscathed [unskāt͟hd'] *a* ileso.

unscientific [unsiəntif'ik] *a* poco científico.

unscrew [unskrōō'] *vt* destornillar.

unscrupulous [unskrōō'pyələs] *a* sin escrúpulos.

unsecured [unsikyōōrd'] *a*: **~ creditor** acreedor(a) *m/f* común.

unseen [unsēn'] *a* (*person, danger*) oculto.

unselfish [unsel'fish] *a* generoso, poco egoísta; (*act*) desinteresado.

unsettled [unset'əld] *a* inquieto; (*situation*) inestable; (*weather*) variable.

unsettling [unset'ling] *a* perturbador(a), inquietante.

unshak(e)able [unshā'kəbəl] *a* inquebrantable.

unshaven [unshā'vən] *a* sin afeitar.

unsightly [unsīt'lē] *a* feo.

unskilled [unskild'] *a:* ~ **workers** mano *f* de obra no cualificada.

unsociable [unsō'shəbəl] *a* (*person*) poco sociable, huraño; (*behavior*) insociable.

unsocial [unsō'shəl] *a:* ~ **hours** horario nocturno.

unsold [unsōld'] *a* sin vender.

unsolicited [unsəlis'itid] *a* no solicitado.

unsophisticated [unsəfis'tikātid] *a* (*person*) sencillo, ingenuo; (*method*) poco sofisticado.

unsound [unsound'] *a* (*health*) malo; (*in construction: floor, foundations*) defectuoso; (*policy, advice, judgment*) erróneo; (*investment*) poco seguro.

unspeakable [unspē'kəbəl] *a* indecible; (*awful*) incalificable.

unspoken [unspō'kən] *a* (*words*) sobreentendido; (*agreement, approval*) tácito.

unstable [unstā'bəl] *a* inestable.

unsteady [unsted'ē] *a* inestable.

unstinting [unstin'ting] *a* (*support etc*) pródigo.

unstuck [unstuk'] *a:* **to come** ~ despegarse; (*fig*) fracasar.

unsubstantiated [unsəbstan'chēātid] *a* (*rumor, accusation*) no comprobado.

unsuccessful [unsəkses'fəl] *a* (*attempt*) infructuoso; (*writer, proposal*) sin éxito; **to be** ~ (*in attempting sth*) no tener éxito, fracasar.

unsuccessfully [unsəkses'fəlē] *ad* en vano, sin éxito.

unsuitable [unsōō'təbəl] *a* inconveniente, inapropiado; (*time*) inoportuno.

unsuited [unsōō'tid] *a:* **to be** ~ **for** *or* **to** ser poco apto para.

unsupported [unsəpôr'tid] *a* (*claim*) sin fundamento; (*theory*) sin base firme.

unsure [unshōōr'] *a* inseguro, poco seguro; **to be** ~ **of o.s.** estar poco seguro de sí mismo.

unsuspecting [unsəspek'ting] *a* confiado.

unsweetened [unswēt'ənd] *a* sin azúcar.

unsympathetic [unsimpəthet'ik] *a* (*attitude*) poco comprensivo; (*person*) sin compasión; ~ **(to)** indiferente(a).

untangle [untang'gəl] *vt* desenredar.

untapped [untapt'] *a* (*resources*) sin explotar.

untaxed [untakst'] *a* (*goods*) libre de impuestos; (*income*) antes de impuestos.

unthinkable [unthingk'əbəl] *a* inconcebible, impensable.

untidy [untī'dē] *a* (*room*) desordenado, en desorden; (*appearance*) desaliñado.

untie [untī'] *vt* desatar.

until [until'] *prep* hasta ♦ *conj* hasta que; ~ **he comes** hasta que venga; ~ **now** hasta

ahora; ~ **then** hasta entonces; **from morning** ~ **night** de la mañana a la noche.

untimely [untīm'lē] *a* inoportuno; (*death*) prematuro.

untold [untōld'] *a* (*story*) nunca contado; (*suffering*) indecible; (*wealth*) incalculable.

untouched [untucht'] *a* (*not used etc*) intacto, sin tocar; (*safe: person*) indemne, ileso; (*unaffected*): ~ **by** insensible a.

untoward [untôrd'] *a* (*behavior*) impropio; (*event*) adverso.

untrammeled, (*Brit*) **untrammelled** [untram'əld] *a* ilimitado.

untranslatable [untranz'lātəbəl] *a* intraducible.

untried [untrīd'] *a* (*plan*) no probado.

untrue [untrōō'] *a* (*statement*) falso.

untrustworthy [untrust'wûr#ē] *a* (*person*) poco fiable.

unusable [unyōō'zəbəl] *a* inservible.

unused [unyōōzd'] *a* sin usar, nuevo; [unyōōst']: **to be** ~ **to (doing) sth** no estar acostumbrado a (hacer) algo.

unusual [unyōō'zhōōəl] *a* insólito, poco común.

unusually [unyōō'zhōōəlē] *ad:* **he arrived** ~ **early** llegó más temprano que de costumbre.

unveil [unvāl'] *vt* (*statue*) descubrir.

unwanted [unwôn'tid] *a* (*person, effect*) no deseado.

unwarranted [unwôr'əntid] *a* injustificado.

unwary [unwār'ē] *a* imprudente, incauto.

unwavering [unwā'vûring] *a* inquebrantable.

unwelcome [unwel'kəm] *a* (*at a bad time*) inoportuno, molesto; **to feel** ~ sentirse incómodo.

unwell [unwel'] *a:* **to feel** ~ estar indispuesto, sentirse mal.

unwieldy [unwēl'dē] *a* difícil de manejar.

unwilling [unwil'ing] *a:* **to be** ~ **to do sth** estar poco dispuesto a hacer algo.

unwillingly [unwil'inglē] *ad* de mala gana.

unwind [unwīnd'] (*irg: like* **wind**) *vt* desenvolver ♦ *vi* (*relax*) relajarse.

unwise [unwīz'] *a* imprudente.

unwitting [unwit'ing] *a* inconsciente.

unworkable [unwûr'kəbəl] *a* (*plan*) impráctico.

unworthy [unwûr'#ē] *a* indigno; **to be** ~ **of sth/to do sth** ser indigno de algo/de hacer algo.

unwrap [unrap'] *vt* desenvolver.

unwritten [unrit'ən] *a* (*agreement*) tácito; (*rules, law*) no escrito.

unzip [unzip'] *vt* abrir la cremallera de.

up [up] *prep:* **to go/be** ~ **sth** subir/estar encima de algo ♦ *ad* hacia arriba, arriba ♦ *vi* (*col*): **she** ~**ped and left** se levantó y se marchó ♦ *vt* (*col: price*) subir, aumentar; **when the year was** ~ (*finished*) al terminarse el año; **what's** ~? (*col: wrong*) ¿qué pasa?; ~ **there** allí arriba; ~ **above** encima, allí arriba; **"this side ~"** "este lado hacia arriba"; **to be** ~ (out of bed) estar levantado; (installed, built etc) estar construido; (tent) estar levantado; (curtains, paper etc) estar colocado; **to be** ~ **(by)** (in price, value) haber alzado (en); **prices are** ~ **from last year** los precios han subido desde el año pasado; **it is** ~ **to you** usted decide/tú decides; **what is he** ~ **to?** ¿qué es lo que quiere?, ¿qué está tramando?; **he is not** ~ **to it** no es capaz de hacerlo; **I don't feel** ~ **to it** no me encuentro con ánimos para ello; **to stop halfway** ~ pararse a la mitad del camino or de la subida; **time's** ~ se acabó el tiempo; **what's** ~ **with him?** ¿qué le pasa (a él)?; **to live/go** ~ **North** vivir en el norte/ir al norte; **~s and downs** npl (fig) altibajos mpl.

up-and-coming [upənkum'ing] a prometedor(a).

upbeat [up'bēt] n (MUS) tiempo no acentuado; (in economy, prosperity) aumento ♦ a (col) optimista, animado.

upbraid [upbrād'] vt censurar, reprender.

upbringing [up'bringing] n educación f.

update [updāt'] vt poner al día.

upend [upend'] vt poner vertical.

upgrade [upgrād'] vt ascender; (COMPUT) modernizar.

upheaval [uphē'vəl] n trastornos mpl; (POL) agitación f.

uphill [up'hil'] a (fig: task) penoso, difícil ♦ ad [uphil']: **to go** ~ ir cuesta arriba.

uphold [uphōld'] (irg: like hold) vt sostener.

upholstery [uphōl'stûrē] n tapicería.

UPI n abbr (US) = United Press International.

upkeep [up'kēp] n mantenimiento.

upmarket [upmár'kit] a (Brit: product) de primera calidad.

upon [əpän'] prep sobre.

upper [up'ûr] a superior, de arriba ♦ n (of shoe: also: ~s) pala.

upper case n (TYP) mayúsculas fpl.

upper-class [up'ûrklas'] a (district, people, accent) de clase alta; (attitude) altivo.

upper hand n: **to have the** ~ tener la sartén por el mango, llevar la delantera.

uppermost [up'ûrmōst] a el más alto; **what was** ~ **in my mind** lo que me preocupaba más.

Upper Volta [up'ûr vōl'tə] n Alto Volta m.

upright [up'rīt] a vertical; (fig) honrado.

uprising [up'rīzing] n sublevación f.

uproar [up'rôr] n tumulto, escándalo.

uproot [uprōōt'] vt desarraigar.

upset n [up'set] (to plan etc) revés m, contratiempo; (MED) trastorno ♦ vt [upset'] (irg: like set) (glass etc) volcar; (spill) derramar; (plan) alterar; (person) molestar,

perturbar ♦ a [upset'] preocupado, perturbado; (stomach) revuelto; **to have an** ~ **stomach** tener el estómago revuelto; **to get** ~ ofenderse, llevarse un disgusto.

upset price n (US, Scottish) precio mínimo or de reserva.

upsetting [upset'ing] a (worrying) inquietante; (offending) ofensivo; (annoying) molesto.

upshot [up'shät] n resultado.

upside-down [up'sīddoun'] ad al revés.

upstairs [up'stärz] ad arriba ♦ a (room) de arriba ♦ n el piso superior.

upstart [up'stärt] n advenedizo.

upstream [up'strēm] ad río arriba.

upsurge [up'sûrj] n (of enthusiasm etc) arrebato.

uptake [up'tāk] n: **he is quick/slow on the** ~ es muy listo/torpe.

uptight [up'tīt'] a tenso, nervioso.

up-to-date [up'tədāt'] a moderno, actual; **to bring sb** ~ **(on sth)** poner a uno al corriente/tanto (de algo).

upturn [up'tûrn] n (in luck) mejora; (COMM: in market) resurgimiento económico; (: in value of currency) aumento.

upturned [uptûrnd'] a: ~ **nose** nariz f respingona.

upward [up'wûrd] a ascendente.

upward(s) [up'wûrd(z)] ad hacia arriba.

URA n abbr (US) = Urban Renewal Administration.

Ural Mountains [yōōr'əl moun'tənz] npl: **the** ~ (also: **the Urals**) los Montes Urales.

uranium [yōōrā'nēəm] n uranio.

Uranus [yōōr'ānəs] n (ASTRO) Urano.

urban [ûr'bən] a urbano.

urbane [ûrbān'] a cortés, urbano.

urbanization [ûrbənəzā'shən] n urbanización f.

urchin [ûr'chin] n pilluelo, golfillo.

urge [ûrj] n (force) impulso; (desire) deseo ♦ vt: **to** ~ **sb to do sth** animar a uno a hacer algo.

urge on vt animar.

urgency [ûr'jənsē] n urgencia.

urgent [ûr'jənt] a (earnest, persistent: plea) insistente; (: tone) urgente.

urgently [ûr'jəntlē] ad con urgencia, urgentemente.

urinal [yōōr'ənəl] n (room) urinario; (vessel) orinal m.

urinate [yōōr'ənāt] vi orinar.

urine [yōōr'in] n orina, orines mpl.

urn [ûrn] n urna; (also: **tea** ~) cacharro metálico grande para hacer té.

Uruguay [yōō'rəgwā] n el Uruguay.

Uruguayan [yōōrəgwā'ən] a, n uruguayo/a m/f.

US n abbr (= United States) EE.UU.

us [us] pron nos; (after prep) nosotros/as; (col: me): **give** ~ **a kiss** dame un beso; see also **me**.

USA n abbr see **United States of America**; (MIL) = United States Army.
usable [yōō'zəbəl] a utilizable.
USAF n abbr = United States Air Force.
usage [yōō'sij] n (LING) uso; (utilization) utilización f.
USCG n abbr = United States Coast Guard.
USDA n abbr = United States Department of Agriculture.
USDI n abbr = United States Department of the Interior.
use n [yōōs] uso, empleo; (usefulness) utilidad f ♦ vt [yōōz] usar, emplear; **in** ~ en uso; **out of** ~ en desuso; **to be of** ~ servir; **ready to** ~ listo (para ser usado); **to make** ~ **of sth** aprovecharse or servirse de algo; **it's no** ~ (pointless) es inútil; (not useful) no sirve; **what's this** ~**d for?** ¿para qué sirve esto?; [yōōst]: **to be** ~**d to** estar acostumbrado a (Sp), acostumbrar; **to get** ~**d to** acostumbrarse a; **she** ~**d to do it** (ella) solía or acostumbraba hacerlo.
 use up vt agotar.
used [yōōzd] a (car) usado.
useful [yōōs'fəl] a útil; **to come in** ~ ser útil.
usefulness [yōōs'fəlnis] n utilidad.
useless [yōōs'lis] a inútil; (unusable: object) inservible.
uselessly [yōōs'lislē] ad inútilmente, en vano.
uselessness [yōōs'lisnis] n inutilidad f.
user [yōō'zûr] n usuario/a; (of gas, electricity etc) consumidor(a) m/f.
user-friendly [yōō'zûrfrend'lē] a (COMPUT) amistoso, fácil de utilizar.
USES n abbr = United States Employment Service.
usher [ush'ûr] n (at wedding) ujier m; (in cinema etc) acomodador m ♦ vt: **to** ~ **sb in** (into room) hacer pasar a uno; **it** ~**ed in a new era** (fig) anunció una nueva era.
usherette [ushəret'] n (in cinema) acomodadora.
USIA n abbr = United States Information Agency.
USM n abbr = United States Mail; United States Mint.
USN n abbr = United States Navy.
USPHS n abbr = United States Public Health Service.
USPS n abbr = United States Postal Service.
USS abbr = United States Ship.
USSR n abbr: **the** ~ la U.R.S.S.
usu. abbr = usually.
usual [yōō'zhōōəl] a normal, corriente; **as** ~ como de costumbre, como siempre.
usually [yōō'zhōōəlē] ad normalmente.
usurer [yōō'zhûrûr] n usurero.
usurp [yōōsûrp'] vt usurpar.
usury [yōō'zhûrē] n usura.
UT abbr (US MAIL) = Utah.

utensil [yōōten'səl] n utensilio; **kitchen** ~**s** batería de cocina.
uterus [yōō'tûrəs] n útero.
utilitarian [yōōtilitär'ēən] a utilitario.
utility [yōōtil'itē] n utilidad f.
utility room n lavadero.
utilization [yōōtəliza'shən] n utilización f.
utilize [yōō'təliz] vt utilizar.
utmost [ut'mōst] a mayor ♦ n: **to do one's** ~ hacer todo lo posible; **it is of the** ~ **importance that** ... es de la mayor importancia que ....
utter [ut'ûr] a total, completo ♦ vt pronunciar, proferir.
utterance [ut'ûrəns] n palabras fpl, declaración f.
utterly [ut'ûrlē] ad completamente, totalmente.
U-turn [yōō'tûrn] n viraje m or vuelta en U.

V

V, v [vē] (letter) V, v f; **V for Victor** V de Valencia.
v. abbr (= verse) vers.º (= vide: see) V, vid., vide; (= versus) vs.; = **volt.**
VA abbr (US MAIL) = Virginia.
vac [vak] n abbr (Brit col) = **vacation.**
vacancy [vā'kənsē] n (Brit: job) vacante f; (room) cuarto libre; **have you any vacancies?** ¿tiene or hay alguna habitación or algún cuarto libre?
vacant [vā'kənt] a (expression) distraído.
vacant lot n (US) solar m.
vacate [vā'kāt] vt (house) desocupar; (job) dejar (vacante).
vacation [vākā'shən] n vacaciones fpl ; **on** ~ de vacaciones; **to take a** ~ (esp US) tomarse unas vacaciones.
vacation course n curso de vacaciones.
vacationer [vākā'shənûr], **vacationist** [vākā'shənist] n (US) turista m/f.
vacation pay n (US) paga de las vacaciones.
vacation resort n (US) centro turístico.
vacation season n (US) temporada de las vacaciones.
vaccinate [vak'sənāt] vt vacunar.
vaccination [vak'sonā'shən] n vacunación f.
vaccine [vaksēn'] n vacuna.
vacuum [vak'yōōm] n vacío ♦ vt (US) pasar la aspiradora por.
vacuum bottle n (US) termo.
vacuum cleaner n aspiradora.
vacuum flask n (Brit) termo.

vacuum-packed [vak'yōōmpakt'] *a* envasado al vacío.

vagabond [vag'əbând] *n* vagabundo/a.

vagary [vā'gûrē] *n* capricho.

vagina [vəjī'nə] *n* vagina.

vagrancy [vā'grənsē] *n* vagabundeo.

vagrant [vā'grənt] *n* vagabundo/a.

vague [vāg] *a* vago; (*blurred: memory*) borroso; (*uncertain*) incierto, impreciso; (*person*) distraído; **I haven't the ~st idea** no tengo la más remota idea.

vaguely [vāg'lē] *ad* vagamente.

vagueness [vāg'nis] *n* vaguedad *f*; imprecisión *f*; (*absent-mindedness*) despiste *m*.

vain [vān] *a* (*conceited*) presumido; (*useless*) vano, inútil; **in ~** en vano.

vainly [vān'lē] *ad* (*to no effect*) en vano; (*conceitedly*) vanidosamente.

valance [val'əns] *n* (*for bed*) volante alrededor de la colcha que cuelga hasta el suelo.

valedictory [validik'tûrē] *a* de despedida.

valentine [val'əntīn] *n* (*also:* **~ card**) tarjeta del Día de los Enamorados.

valet [valā'] *n* ayuda *m* de cámara.

valet service *n* (*for clothes*) planchado.

valiant [val'yənt] *a* valiente.

valiantly [val'yəntlē] *ad* valientemente, con valor.

valid [val'id] *a* válido; (*ticket*) valedero; (*law*) vigente.

validate [val'idāt] *vt* (*contract, document*) convalidar; (*argument, claim*) dar validez a.

validity [vəlid'itē] *n* validez *f*; vigencia.

valise [vəlēs'] *n* maletín *m*.

valley [val'ē] *n* valle *m*.

valor, (*Brit*) **valour** [val'ûr] *n* valor *m*, valentía.

valuable [val'yōōəbəl] *a* (*jewel*) de valor; (*time*) valioso; **~s** *npl* objetos *mpl* de valor.

valuation [valyōōā'shən] *n* tasación *f*, valuación *f*.

value [val'yōō] *n* valor *m*; (*importance*) importancia ♦ *vt* (*fix price of*) tasar, valorar; (*esteem*) apreciar; **~s** *npl* (*moral*) valores *mpl* morales; **to lose (in) ~** (*currency*) bajar; (*property*) desvalorizarse; **to gain (in) ~** (*currency*) subir; (*property*) valorizarse; **you get good ~ (for money) in that store** los precios son muy buenos en esa tienda; **to be of great ~ to sb** ser de gran valor para uno; **it is ~d at $8** está valorado en ocho dólares.

value added tax (VAT) *n* (*Brit*) impuesto sobre el valor añadido (IVA *m*).

valued [val'yōōd] *a* (*appreciated*) apreciado.

valueless [val'yōōlis] *a* sin valor.

valuer [val'yōōûr] *n* tasador(a) *m/f*.

valve [valv] *n* (*ANAT, TECH*) válvula.

vampire [vam'pīûr] *n* vampiro/vampiresa *m/f*.

van [van] *n* (*AUT*) furgoneta, camioneta

(*LAm*); (*Brit RAIL*) furgón *m* (de equipajes).

vandal [van'dəl] *n* vándalo/a.

vandalism [van'dəlizəm] *n* vandalismo.

vandalize [van'dəlīz] *vt* dañar, destruir, destrozar.

vanguard [van'gârd] *n* vanguardia.

vanilla [vənil'ə] *n* vainilla.

vanish [van'ish] *vi* desaparecer, esfumarse.

vanity [van'itē] *n* vanidad *f*.

vanity case *n* neceser *m*.

vantage point [van'tij point] *n* posición *f* ventajosa.

vapor [vā'pûr] *n* (*US*) vapor *m*; (*on breath, window*) vaho.

vaporize [vā'pərīz] *vt* vaporizar ♦ *vi* vaporizarse.

vapor trail *n* (*AVIAT*) estela.

vapour [vā'pûr] *etc* (*Brit*) = **vapor** *etc*.

variable [vär'ēəbəl] *a* variable ♦ *n* variable *f*.

variance [vär'ēəns] *n*: **to be at ~ (with)** estar en desacuerdo (con), no cuadrar (con).

variant [vär'ēənt] *n* variante *f*.

variation [värēā'shən] *n* variación *f*.

varicose [var'əkōs] *a*: **~ veins** varices *fpl*.

varied [vär'ēd] *a* variado.

variety [vərī'ətē] *n* variedad *f*, diversidad *f*; (*quantity*) surtido; **for a ~ of reasons** por varias *or* diversas razones.

variety show *n* espectáculo de variedades.

various [vär'ēəs] *a* varios/as, diversos/as; **at ~ times** (*different*) en distintos momentos; (*several*) varias veces.

varnish [vâr'nish] *n* (*gen*) barniz *m*; (*nail ~*) esmalte *m* ♦ *vt* (*gen*) barnizar; (*nails*) pintar (con esmalte).

vary [vär'ē] *vt* variar; (*change*) cambiar ♦ *vi* variar; (*disagree*) discrepar; **to ~ with** *or* **according to** variar según *or* de acuerdo con.

varying [vär'ēing] *a* diversos/as.

vase [vās] *n* florero.

vasectomy [vasek'təmē] *n* vasectomía.

Vaseline [vas'əlēn] ® *n* vaselina ®.

vast [vast] *a* enorme; (*success*) abrumador(a), arrollador(a).

vastly [vast'lē] *ad* enormemente.

vastness [vast'nis] *n* inmensidad *f*.

VAT [vat] *n abbr* (= *value added tax*) IVA *m*.

vat [vat] *n* tina, tinaja.

Vatican [vat'ikən] *n*: **the ~** el Vaticano.

vaudeville [vôd'vil] *n* (*US*) vodevil *m*, vaudeville *m*.

vault [vôlt] *n* (*of roof*) bóveda; (*tomb*) tumba; (*in bank*) cámara acorazada ♦ *vt* (*also:* **~ over**) saltar (por encima de).

vaunted [vôn'tid] *a*: **much ~** cacareado, alardeado.

VC *n abbr* = **vice-chairman**.

VCR *n abbr* = **video cassette recorder**.

VD *n abbr* = **venereal disease**.
VDU *n abbr* = **visual display unit**.
veal [vēl] *n* ternera.
veer [vēr] *vi* (*ship*) virar.
vegan [vē'gən] *n* vegetariano/a *m/f* estricto/
a.
vegetable [vej'təbəl] *n* (*BOT*) vegetal *m*;
(*edible plant*) legumbre *f*, hortaliza ♦ *a* vegetal; ~**s** *npl* (*cooked*) verduras *fpl*.
vegetable garden *n* huerta, huerto.
vegetarian [vejitär'ēən] *a, n* vegetariano/a
m/f.
vegetate [vej'itāt] *vi* vegetar.
vegetation [vejitā'shən] *n* vegetación *f*.
vehemence [vē'əməns] *n* vehemencia; violencia.
vehement [vē'əmənt] *a* vehemente, apasionado; (*dislike, hatred*) violento.
vehicle [vē'ikəl] *n* vehículo; (*fig*) vehículo,
medio.
vehicular [vēhik'yəlûr] *a*: ~ **traffic** circulación *f* rodada.
veil [vāl] *n* velo ♦ *vt* velar; **under a** ~ **of secrecy** (*fig*) en el mayor secreto.
veiled [vāld] *a* (*also fig*) disimulado, velado.
vein [vān] *n* vena; (*of ore etc*) veta.
vellum [vel'əm] *n* (*writing paper*) papel *m*
vitela.
velocity [vəlâs'itē] *n* velocidad *f*.
velvet [vel'vit] *n* terciopelo ♦ *a* aterciopelado.
vendetta [vendet'ə] *n* vendetta.
vending machine [ven'ding məshēn'] *n*
distribuidor *m* automático.
vendor [ven'dûr] *n* vendedor(a) *m/f*; **street**
~ vendedor(a) *m/f* callejero/a.
veneer [vənēr'] *n* chapa, enchapado; (*fig*)
barniz *m*.
venereal [vənēr'ēəl] *a*: ~ **disease (VD)**
enfermedad *f* venérea.
Venetian blind [vənē'shən blīnd] *n* persiana.
Venezuela [venizwā'lə] *n* Venezuela.
Venezuelan [venizwā'lən] *a, n* venezolano/a
m/f.
vengeance [ven'jəns] *n* venganza; **with a** ~
(*fig*) con creces.
vengeful [venj'fəl] *a* vengativo.
Venice [ven'is] *n* Venecia.
venison [ven'isən] *n* carne *f* de venado.
venom [ven'əm] *n* veneno.
venomous [ven'əməs] *a* venenoso.
venomously [ven'əməslē] *ad* con odio.
vent [vent] *n* (*opening*) abertura; (*air-hole*)
respiradero; (*in wall*) rejilla (de ventilación) ♦ *vt* (*fig: feelings*) desahogar.
ventilate [ven'təlāt] *vt* ventilar.
ventilation [ventəlā'shən] *n* ventilación *f*.
ventilation shaft *n* pozo de ventilación.
ventilator [ven'təlātûr] *n* ventilador *m*.
ventriloquist [ventril'əkwist] *n* ventrílocuo/
a.
venture [ven'chûr] *n* empresa ♦ *vt* arries-

gar; (*opinion*) ofrecer ♦ *vi* arriesgarse,
lanzarse; **a business** ~ una empresa comercial; **to** ~ **to do sth** aventurarse a hacer algo.
venture capital *n* capital *m* arriesgado.
venue [ven'yōō] *n* lugar *m*; (*meeting place*)
lugar *m* de reunión.
Venus [vē'nəs] *n* (*ASTRO*) Venus *m*.
veracity [vəras'itē] *n* veracidad *f*.
veranda(h) [vəran'də] *n* terraza; (*with
glass*) galería.
verb [vûrb] *n* verbo.
verbal [vûr'bəl] *a* verbal.
verbally [vûr'bəlē] *ad* verbalmente, de palabra.
verbatim [vûrbā'tim] *a, ad* al pie de la letra, palabra por palabra.
verbose [vûrbōs'] *a* prolijo.
verdict [vûr'dikt] *n* veredicto, fallo; (*fig:
opinion*) opinión *f*, juicio; ~ **of guilty/not
guilty** veredicto de culpabilidad/inocencia.
verge [vûrj] *n* (*Brit*) borde *m*; **to be on the**
~ **of doing sth** estar a punto de hacer
algo.
verge on *vt fus* rayar en.
verger [vûr'jûr] *n* sacristán *m*.
verification [värəfəkā'shən] *n* comprobación
f, verificación *f*.
verify [vär'əfī] *vt* comprobar, verificar;
(*COMPUT*) verificar; (*prove the truth of*)
confirmar.
veritable [vär'itəbəl] *a* verdadero, auténtico.
vermin [vûr'min] *npl* (*animals*) bichos *mpl*;
(*insects, fig*) sabandijas *fpl*.
vermouth [vûrmōōth'] *n* vermut *m*.
vernacular [vûrnak'yəlûr] *n* vernáculo.
versatile [vûr'sətəl] *a* (*person*) polifacético;
(*machine, tool etc*) versátil.
versatility [vûrsətil'itē] *n* versatilidad *f*.
verse [vûrs] *n* versos *mpl*, poesía; (*stanza*)
estrofa; (*in bible*) versículo; **in** ~ en verso.
versed [vûrst] *a*: (**well-**)~ **in** versado en.
version [vûr'zhən] *n* versión *f*.
versus [vûr'səs] *prep* contra.
vertebra, *pl* ~e [vûr'təbrə, -brē] *n* vértebra.
vertebrate [vûr'təbrāt] *n* vertebrado.
vertical [vûr'tikəl] *a* vertical.
vertically [vûr'tiklē] *ad* verticalmente.
vertigo [vûr'təgō] *n* vértigo; **to suffer from**
~ tener vértigo.
verve [vûrv] *n* brío.
very [vär'ē] *ad* muy ♦ *a*: **the** ~ **book which**
el mismo libro que; **the** ~ **last** el último
(de todos); **at the** ~ **least** al menos; ~
much muchísimo; ~ **well/little** muy bien/
poco; ~ **high frequency** (*RADIO*) frecuencia muy alta; **it's** ~ **cold** hace mucho
frío; **the** ~ **thought (of it) alarms me** con
sólo pensarlo me entra miedo.
vespers [ves'pûrz] *npl* vísperas *fpl*.
vessel [ves'əl] *n* (*ANAT*) vaso; (*ship*) barco;
(*container*) vasija.
vest [vest] *n* (*US: waistcoat*) chaleco; (*Brit*

camiseta.
vested interests [ves'tid in'trists] *npl*
  (*COMM*) intereses *mpl* creados.
vestibule [ves'təbyōōl] *n* vestíbulo.
vestige [ves'tij] *n* vestigio, rastro.
vestry [ves'trē] *n* sacristía.
Vesuvius [vəsōō'vēəs] *n* Vesubio.
vet [vet] *n abbr =* **veterinary surgeon** ♦ *vt*
  repasar, revisar; **to ~ sb for a job** investigar a uno para un trabajo.
veteran [vet'ûrən] *n* veterano/a; (*MIL*) ex-
  combatiente *m* ♦ *a*: **she is a ~ campaigner
  for ...** es una veterana de la campaña de
  ....
veteran car *n* coche *m* antiguo.
veterinarian [vetûrənär'ēən] *n* (*US*)
  veterinario/a.
veterinary [vet'ûrənärē] *a* veterinario.
veterinary surgeon *n* (*Brit*) veterinario/
  a.
veto [vē'tō] *n* (*pl ~es*) veto ♦ *vt* prohibir,
  vedar; **to put a ~ on** vetar.
vex [veks] *vt* (*irritate*) fastidiar; (*make
  impatient*) impacientar.
vexed [vekst] *a* (*question*) controvertido.
vexing [vek'sing] *a* molesto, engorroso.
VFD *n abbr* (*US*) = *voluntary fire department.*
VHF *abbr* (= *very high frequency*) VHF *m.*
VI *abbr* (*US MAIL*) = *Virgin Islands.*
via [vī'ə] *prep* por, por vía de.
viability [vīəbil'ətē] *n* viabilidad *f.*
viable [vī'əbəl] *a* viable.
viaduct [vī'ədukt] *n* viaducto.
vibrant [vī'brənt] *a* (*lively*, *bright*) vivo;
  (*full of emotion: voice*) vibrante; (*color*)
  fuerte.
vibrate [vī'brāt] *vi* vibrar.
vibration [vībrā'shən] *n* vibración *f.*
vicar [vik'ûr] *n* párroco.
vicarage [vik'ûrij] *n* parroquia.
vicarious [vīkär'ēəs] *a* indirecto; (*responsibility*) delegado.
vice [vīs] *n* (*evil*) vicio; (*TECH*) torno de
  banco.
vice- *pref* vice... .
vice-chairman [vīs'chär'mən] *n* vicepresidente *m.*
vice-chancellor [vīs'chan'səlûr] *n* (*UNIV*)
  rector(a) *m/f.*
vice-president [vīs'prez'idənt] *n* vice-
  presidente/a *m/f.*
vice-principal [vīs'prin'səpəl] *n* (*US SCOL*)
  subdirector(a) *m/f.*
vice versa [vīs'vûr'sə] *ad* viceversa.
vicinity [visin'ətē] *n* (*area*) vecindad *f*;
  (*nearness*) proximidad *f*; **in the ~ (of)**
  cercano (a).
vicious [vish'əs] *a* (*remark*) malicioso;
  (*blow*) fuerte; **a ~ circle** un círculo vicioso.
viciousness [vish'əsnis] *n* brutalidad *f.*
vicissitudes [visis'ətōōdz] *npl* vicisitudes
  fpl, peripecias *fpl.*

victim [vik'tim] *n* víctima; **to be the ~ of**
  ser víctima de.
victimization [viktiməzā'shən] *n* persecución *f*; (*of striker etc*) represalias *fpl.*
victimize [vik'təmīz] *vt* (*strikers etc*) tomar
  represalias contra.
victor [vik'tûr] *n* vencedor(a) *m/f.*
Victorian [viktôr'ēən] *a* victoriano.
victorious [viktôr'ēəs] *a* vencedor(a).
victory [vik'tûrē] *n* victoria; **to win a ~
  over sb** obtener una victoria sobre uno.
video [vid'ēō] *cpd* vídeo ♦ *n* (~ *film*) videofilm *m*; (*also*: ~ **cassette**) videocassette *f*; (*also*: ~ **cassette recorder**) videograbadora, vídeo.
video cassette *n* videocassette *f.*
video cassette recorder *n* videograbadora, vídeo.
video recording *n* videograbación *f.*
video tape *n* cinta de vídeo.
videotex [vid'ēōteks] *n* videodatos *mpl.*
vie [vī] *vi*: **to ~ with** competir con.
Vienna [vēen'ə] *n* Viena.
Viennese [vēənēz'] *a, n* vienés/esa *m/f.*
Vietnam, Viet Nam [vēetnâm'] *n* Vietnam
  m.
Vietnamese [vēetnâmēz'] *a* vietnamita ♦ *n*
  (*pl inv*) vietnamita *m/f*; (*LING*) vietnamita
  m.
view [vyōō] *n* vista, perspectiva; (*landscape*) paisaje *m*; (*opinion*) opinión *f*, criterio ♦ *vt* (*look at*) mirar; (*examine*) examinar; **on ~** (*in museum etc*) expuesto; **in
  full ~ of sb** a la vista *or* a plena vista de
  uno; **to be within ~ (of sth)** estar a la
  vista (de algo); **an overall ~ of the situation** una visión de conjunto de la situación;
  in ~ of the fact that en vista del hecho de
  que; **to take** *or* **hold the ~ that ...** opinar
  or pensar que ...; **with a ~ to doing sth**
  con miras *or* vistas a hacer algo.
viewdata [vyōō'dātə] *n* (*Brit*) vídeodatos
  mpl.
viewer [vyōō'ûr] *n* (*small projector*) visiona-
  dora; (*TV*) televidente *m/f.*
viewfinder [vyōō'fīndûr] *n* visor *m* de imagen.
viewpoint [vyōō'point] *n* punto de vista.
vigil [vij'əl] *n* vigilia; **to keep ~** velar.
vigilance [vij'ələns] *n* vigilancia.
vigilance committee *n* (*US*) comité *m*
  de autodefensa.
vigilant [vij'ələnt] *a* vigilante.
vigilantly [vij'ələntlē] *ad* vigilantemente.
vigor [vig'ûr] *n* (*US*) energía, vigor *m.*
vigorous [vig'ûrəs] *a* enérgico, vigoroso.
vigorously [vig'ûrəslē] *ad* enérgicamente,
  vigorosamente.
vigour [vig'ûr] *n* (*Brit*) = **vigor.**
vile [vīl] *a* (*action*) vil, infame; (*smell*)
  asqueroso.
vilify [vil'əfī] *vt* denigrar, vilipendiar.
villa [vil'ə] *n* (*country house*) casa de

campo; (*suburban house*) chalet *m*.
village |vil'ij| *n* aldea.
villager |vil'ijür| *n* aldeano/a.
villain |vil'in| *n* (*scoundrel*) malvado/a; (*criminal*) maleante *m/f*.
VIN *n abbr* (*US*) = *vehicle identification number*.
vindicate |vin'dikāt| *vt* vindicar, justificar.
vindication |vindikā'shən| *n*: **in ~ of** en justificación de.
vindictive |vindik'tiv| *a* vengativo.
vine |vīn| *n* vid *f*.
vinegar |vin'əgûr| *n* vinagre *m*.
vine-growing |vīn'grōing| *a* (*region*) viticultor(a).
vineyard |vin'yûrd| *n* viña, viñedo.
vintage |vin'tij| *n* (*year*) vendimia, cosecha; **the 1970 ~** la cosecha de 1970.
vintage car *n* coche *m* antiguo *or* de época.
vintage wine *n* vino añejo.
vintage year *n*: **it's been a ~ for plays** ha sido un año destacado en lo que a teatro se refiere.
vinyl |vī'nil| *n* vinilo.
viola |vēō'lə| *n* (*MUS*) viola.
violate |vī'əlāt| *vt* violar.
violation |vīəlā'shən| *n* violación *f*; **in ~ of sth** en violación de algo.
violence |vī'ələns| *n* violencia; **acts of ~** actos *mpl* de violencia.
violent |vī'ələnt| *a* (*gen*) violento; (*pain*) intenso; **a ~ dislike of sb/sth** una profunda antipatía *or* manía a uno/algo.
violently |vī'ələntlē| *ad* (*severely*: *ill*, *angry*) muy.
violet |vī'əlit| *a* violado, violeta ♦ *n* (*plant*) violeta.
violin |vīəlin'| *n* violín *m*.
violinist |vīəlin'ist| *n* violinista *m/f*.
VIP *n abbr* (= *very important person*) VIP *m*.
viper |vī'pûr| *n* víbora.
virgin |vûr'jin| *n* virgen *m/f* ♦ *a* virgen; **the Blessed V~** la Santísima Virgen.
virginity |vûrjin'ətē| *n* virginidad *f*.
Virgo |vûr'gō| *n* Virgo.
virile |vir'əl| *a* viril.
virility |vəril'ətē| *n* virilidad *f*.
virtual |vûr'chōōəl| *a* virtual.
virtually |vûr'chōōəlē| *ad* (*almost*) virtualmente; **it is ~ impossible** es prácticamente imposible.
virtue |vûr'chōō| *n* virtud *f*; **by ~ of** en virtud de.
virtuoso |vûrchōōō'sō| *n* virtuoso.
virtuous |vûr'chōōəs| *a* virtuoso.
virulence |vir'yələns| *n* virulencia.
virulent |vir'yələnt| *a* virulento, violento.
virus |vī'rəs| *n* (*also*: *COMPUT*) virus *m*.
visa |vē'zə| *n* visado, visa (*LAm*).
vis-à-vis |vēzàvē'| *prep* con respecto a.
viscount |vī'kount| *n* vizconde *m*.

viscous |vis'kəs| *a* viscoso.
vise |vīs| *n* (*US TECH*) torno de banco.
visibility |vizəbil'ətē| *n* visibilidad *f*.
visible |viz'əbəl| *a* visible; **~ exports/imports** exportaciones *fpl*/importaciones *fpl* visibles.
visibly |viz'əblē| *ad* visiblemente.
vision |vizh'ən| *n* (*sight*) vista; (*foresight*, *in dream*) visión *f*.
visionary |vizh'ənärē| *n* visionario/a.
visit |viz'it| *n* visita ♦ *vt* (*person*) visitar, hacer una visita a; (*place*) ir a, (ir a) conocer; **to pay a ~ to** (*person*) visitar a; **on a private/official ~** en visita privada/oficial.
visiting |viz'iting| *a* (*speaker*, *professor*) invitado; (*team*) visitante.
visiting card *n* tarjeta de visita.
visiting hours *npl* (*in hospital etc*) horas *fpl* de visita.
visitor |viz'itûr| *n* (*gen*) visitante *m/f*; (*to one's house*) invitado/a; (*tourist*) turista *m/f*; (*tourist*) excursionista *m/f*; **to have ~s** (*at home*) tener visita.
visitors' book *n* (*Brit*) libro de visitas.
visor |vī'zûr| *n* visera.
VISTA |vis'tə| *n abbr* (= *Volunteers In Service to America*) programa de ayuda voluntaria a los necesitados.
vista |vis'tə| *n* vista, panorama.
visual |vizh'ōōəl| *a* visual.
visual aid *n* medio visual.
visual display unit (VDU) *n* unidad *f* de despliegue visual, monitor *m*.
visualize |vizh'ōōəlīz| *vt* imaginarse; (*foresee*) prever.
visually |vizh'ōōəlē| *ad*: **~ handicapped** con visión deficiente.
vital |vīt'əl| *a* (*essential*) esencial, imprescindible; (*crucial*) crítico; (*person*) enérgico, vivo; (*of life*) vital; **of ~ importance (to sb/sth)** de suma importancia (para uno/algo).
vitality |vītal'itē| *n* energía, vitalidad *f*.
vitally |vī'təlē| *ad*: **~ important** de primera importancia.
vital statistics *npl* (*of population*) estadísticas *fpl* demográficas; (*col*: *woman's*) medidas *fpl* vitales.
vitamin |vī'təmin| *n* vitamina.
vitamin pill *n* pastilla de vitaminas.
vitreous |vit'rēəs| *a* (*china*, *enamel*) vítreo.
vitriolic |vitrēāl'ik| *a* mordaz.
viva |vē'və| *n* (*also*: **~ voce**) examen *m* oral.
vivacious |vivā'shəs| *a* vivaz, alegre.
vivacity |vivas'itē| *n* vivacidad *f*.
vivid |viv'id| *a* (*account*) gráfico; (*light*) intenso; (*imagination*) vivo.
vividly |viv'idlē| *ad* (*describe*) gráficamente; (*remember*) como si fuera hoy.
vivisection |vivisek'shən| *n* vivisección *f*.
vixen |vik'sən| *n* (*ZOOL*) zorra, raposa; (*pej*: *woman*) arpía, bruja.
viz *abbr* (= *videlicet*: *namely*) v.gr.

VLF *abbr* = *very low frequency.*
V-neck [vē'nɛk] *n* cuello de pico.
VOA *n abbr* (= *Voice of America*) Voz *f* de América.
vocabulary [vōkab'yəlärē] *n* vocabulario.
vocal [vō'kəl] *a* vocal; (*articulate*) elocuente.
vocal cords *npl* cuerdas *fpl* vocales.
vocalist [vō'kəlist] *n* cantante *m/f.*
vocation [vōkā'shən] *n* vocación *f.*
vocational [vōkā'shənəl] *a* vocacional; ~ **guidance** orientación *f* profesional; ~ **training** formación *f* profesional.
vociferous [vōsif'ûrəs] *a* vociferante.
vociferously [vōsif'ûrəslē] *ad* a gritos, clamorosamente.
vodka [vâd'kə] *n* vodka *m.*
vogue [vōg] *n* boga, moda; **to be in ~, be the ~** estar de moda *or* en boga.
voice [vois] *n* voz *f* ♦ *vt* (*opinion*) expresar; **in a loud/soft ~** en voz alta/baja; **to give ~ to** expresar.
void [void] *n* vacío; (*hole*) hueco ♦ *a* (*invalid*) nulo, inválido; (*empty*): ~ **of** carente *or* desprovisto de.
voile [voil] *n* gasa.
vol. *abbr* (= *volume*) t.
volatile [vâl'ətəl] *a* volátil; (*COMPUT: memory*) no permanente.
volcanic [vâlkan'ik] *a* volcánico.
volcano, ~es [vâlkā'nō] *n* volcán *m.*
volition [vōlish'ən] *n*: **of one's own ~** de su propia voluntad.
volley [vâl'ē] *n* (*of gunfire*) descarga; (*of stones etc*) lluvia; (*TENNIS etc*) volea.
volleyball [vâl'ēbôl] *n* vol(e)ibol *m.*
volt [vōlt] *n* voltio.
voltage [vōl'tij] *n* voltaje *m*; **high/low ~** alto/bajo voltaje, alta/baja tensión.
volte-face [vōltfâs'] *n* viraje *m.*
voluble [vâl'yəbəl] *a* locuaz, hablador(a).
volume [vâl'yoom] *n* (*of tank*) volumen *m*; (*book*) tomo; ~ **one/two** (*of book*) tomo primero/segundo; **~s** *npl* (*great quantities*) cantidad *fsg*; **his expression spoke ~s** su expresión (lo) decía todo.
volume control *n* (*RADIO, TV*) (botón *m* del) volumen *m.*
volume discount *n* (*COMM*) descuento por volumen de compras.
voluminous [vəloo'minəs] *a* (*large*) voluminoso; (*prolific*) prolífico.
voluntarily [vâləntär'ilē] *ad* libremente, voluntariamente.
voluntary [vâl'əntärē] *a* voluntario, espontáneo.
voluntary liquidation *n* (*COMM*) liquidación *f* voluntaria.
voluntary redundancy *n* (*Brit*) despido voluntario.
volunteer [vâləntēr'] *n* voluntario/a ♦ *vi* ofrecerse (de voluntario); **to ~ to do** ofrecerse a hacer.

voluptuous [vəlup'chooəs] *a* voluptuoso.
vomit [vâm'it] *n* vómito ♦ *vt, vi* vomitar.
vote [vōt] *n* voto; (*votes cast*) votación *f*; (*right to* ~) derecho de votar; (*franchise*) sufragio ♦ *vt* (*chairman*) elegir ♦ *vi* votar, ir a votar; ~ **of thanks** voto de gracias; **to put sth to a ~, to take a ~ on sth** someter algo a voto; ~ **for** *or* **in favor of/against** voto a favor de/en contra de; **to ~ to do sth** votar por hacer algo; **he was ~d secretary** fue elegido secretario por votación; **to pass a ~ of confidence/no confidence** aprobar un voto de confianza/de censura.
voter [vō'tûr] *n* votante *m/f.*
voting [vō'ting] *n* votación *f.*
voting right *n* derecho a voto.
vouch [vouch]: **to ~ for** *vt fus* garantizar, responder de.
voucher [vou'chûr] *n* (*for meal, gasoline*) vale *m*; **luncheon/travel ~** vale *m* de comida/de viaje.
vow [vou] *n* voto ♦ *vi* hacer voto; **to take** *or* **make a ~ to do sth** jurar hacer algo, comprometerse a hacer algo.
vowel [vou'əl] *n* vocal *f.*
voyage [voi'ij] *n* (*journey*) viaje *m*; (*crossing*) travesía.
VP *n abbr* (= *vice-president*) V.P.
vs *abbr* (= *versus*) vs.
VSO *n abbr* (*Brit*: = *Voluntary Service Overseas*) organización que envía jóvenes voluntarios a trabajar y enseñar en los países del Tercer Mundo.
VT *abbr* (*US MAIL*) = *Vermont.*
VTR *n abbr* (= *video tape recorder*) videograbadora.
vulgar [vul'gûr] *a* (*rude*) ordinario, grosero; (*in bad taste*) de mal gusto.
vulgarity [vulgar'itē] *n* grosería; mal gusto.
vulnerability [vulnûrəbil'ətē] *n* vulnerabilidad *f.*
vulnerable [vul'nûrəbəl] *a* vulnerable.
vulture [vul'chûr] *n* buitre *m.*

W

W, w [dub'əlyoo] *n* (*letter*) W, w *f*; **W for William** W de Washington.
W *abbr* (= *west*) O; (*ELEC*: = *watt*) v.
WA *abbr* (*US MAIL*) = *Washington.*
wad [wâd] *n* (*of cotton wool, paper*) bolita; (*of banknotes etc*) fajo.
wadding [wâd'ing] *n* relleno.
waddle [wâd'əl] *vi* anadear.

wade [wād] *vi*: **to ~ through** caminar por el agua; (*fig*: *a book*) leer con dificultad.
wading pool [wād'ing pool] *n* (*US*) piscina para niños.
wafer [wā'fûr] *n* (*cookie*) galleta, barquillo; (*REL*) oblea; (*COMPUT*) oblea, microplaqueta.
wafer-thin [wā'fûrthin'] *a* finísimo.
waffle [wâf'əl] *n* (*CULIN*) gofre *m* ♦ *vi* dar el rollo.
waffle iron *n* molde *m* para hacer gofres.
waft [waft] *vt* llevar por el aire ♦ *vi* flotar.
wag [wag] *vt* menear, agitar ♦ *vi* moverse, menearse; **the dog ~ged its tail** el perro meneó la cola.
wage [wāj] *n* (*also:* **~s**) sueldo, salario ♦ *vt*: **to ~ war** hacer la guerra; **a day's ~** un día de salario.
wage claim *n* reivindicación *f* salarial.
wage differential *n* diferencia salarial.
wage earner *n* asalariado/a.
wage freeze *n* congelación *f* de los salarios.
wage packet *n* (*Brit*) sobre *m* de paga.
wager [wā'jûr] *n* apuesta ♦ *vt* apostar.
waggle [wag'əl] *vt* menear, mover.
wag(g)on [wag'ən] *n* (*horse-drawn*) carro; (*Brit RAIL*) vagón *m*.
wail [wāl] *n* gemido ♦ *vi* gemir.
waist [wāst] *n* cintura, talle *m*.
waistcoat [wāst'kōt] *n* (*Brit*) chaleco.
waistline [wāst'līn] *n* talle *m*.
wait [wāt] *n* espera; (*interval*) pausa ♦ *vi* esperar; **to lie in ~ for** acechar a; **I can't ~ to** (*fig*) estoy deseando; **to ~ for** esperar (a); **to keep sb ~ing** hacer esperar a uno; **~ a moment!** ¡un momento!, ¡un momentito! (*LAm*); **"repairs while you ~"** "reparaciones en el acto".
wait behind *vi* quedarse.
wait on *vt fus* servir a.
wait up *vi* quedarse levantado.
waiter [wā'tûr] *n* camarero.
waiting list [wā'ting list] *n* lista de espera.
waiting room *n* sala de espera.
waitress [wā'tris] *n* camarera.
waive [wāv] *vt* suspender.
waiver [wā'vûr] *n* renuncia.
wake [wāk] *vb* (*pt* **woke** *or* **waked**, *pp* **woken** *or* **waked** [wōk, wō'kən]) *vt* (*also:* **~ up**) despertar ♦ *vi* (*also:* **~ up**) despertarse ♦ *n* (*for dead person*) vela, velatorio; (*NAUT*) estela; **to ~ up to sth** (*fig*) darse cuenta de algo; **in the ~ of** tras, después de; **to follow in sb's ~** (*fig*) seguir las huellas de uno.
waken [wā'kən] *vt, vi* = **wake**.
Wales [wālz] *n* País *m* de Gales.
walk [wôk] *n* (*stroll*) paseo; (*hike*) excursión *f* a pie, caminata; (*gait*) paso, andar *m*; (*in park etc*) paseo, alameda ♦ *vi* andar, caminar; (*for pleasure, exercise*) pasearse ♦ *vt* (*distance*) recorrer a pie,

andar; (*dog*) pasear; **to go for a ~** ir de paseo; **10 minutes' ~ from here** a 10 minutos de aquí andando; **people from all ~s of life** gente de todas las esferas; **to ~ in one's sleep** ser sonámbulo/a; **I'll ~ you home** te acompañaré a casa.
walk out *vi* (*go out*) salir; (*as protest*) salirse; (*strike*) declararse en huelga; **to ~ out on sb** abandonar a uno.
walker [wôk'ûr] *n* (*person*) paseante *m/f*, caminante *m/f*.
walkie-talkie [wô'kētô'kē] *n* transmisorreceptor *m* portátil.
walking [wô'king] *n* el andar; **it's within ~ distance** se puede ir andando *or* a pie.
walking shoes *npl* zapatos *mpl* para andar.
walking stick *n* bastón *m*.
walk-on [wôk'ân] *a* (*THEATER*: *part*) de comparsa.
walkout [wôk'out] *n* (*of workers*) huelga.
walkover [wôk'ōvûr] *n* (*col*) pan *m* comido.
walkway [wôk'wā] *n* paseo.
wall [wôl] *n* pared *f*; (*exterior*) muro; (*city ~ etc*) muralla; **to go to the ~** (*fig*: *firm etc*) quebrar, ir a la bancarrota.
wall in *vt* (*garden etc*) cercar con una tapia.
walled [wôld] *a* (*city*) amurallado; (*garden*) con tapia.
wallet [wâl'it] *n* cartera, billetera (*LAm*).
wallflower [wôl'flouûr] *n* alhelí *m*; **to be a ~** (*fig*) comer pavo.
wall hanging *n* tapiz *m*.
wallop [wâl'əp] *vt* (*col*) zurrar.
wallow [wâl'ō] *vi* revolcarse; **to ~ in one's grief** sumirse en su pena.
wallpaper [wôl'pāpûr] *n* papel *m* pintado.
wall-to-wall [wôl'təwôl'] *a*: **~ carpeting** moqueta.
wally [wā'lē] *n* (*Brit*: *col*) palurdo/a, majadero/a.
walnut [wôl'nut] *n* nuez *f*; (*tree*) nogal *m*.
walrus, *pl* ~ *or* **~es**, [wôl'rəs] *n* morsa.
waltz [wôlts] *n* vals *m* ♦ *vi* bailar el vals.
wan [wân] *a* pálido.
wand [wând] *n* (*also:* **magic ~**) varita (mágica).
wander [wân'dûr] *vi* (*person*) vagar; deambular; (*thoughts*) divagar; (*get lost*) extraviarse ♦ *vt* recorrer, vagar por.
wanderer [wân'dûrûr] *n* vagabundo/a.
wandering [wân'dûring] *a* (*tribe*) nómada; (*minstrel, actor*) ambulante; (*path, river*) sinuoso; (*glance, mind*) distraído.
wane [wān] *vi* menguar.
wangle [wang'gəl] (*col*) *vt*: **to ~ sth** agenciarse *or* conseguir algo ♦ *n* chanchullo.
want [wônt] *vt* (*wish for*) querer, desear; (*need*) necesitar; (*lack*) carecer de ♦ *n* (*poverty*) pobreza; **for ~ of** por falta de; **~s** *npl* (*needs*) necesidades *fpl*; **to ~ to do**

querer hacer; **to ~ sb to do sth** querer que uno haga algo; **you're ~ed on the phone** te llaman al teléfono; **to be in ~** estar necesitado; **"cook ~ed"** "se busca cocinero/a".

want ads *npl* (*US*) anuncios *mpl* por palabras.

wanting [wón'ting] *a*: **to be ~ (in)** estar falto (de); **to be found ~** no estar a la altura de las circunstancias.

wanton [wân'tən] *a* (*playful*) juguetón/ona; (*licentious*) lascivo.

war [wôr] *n* guerra; **to make ~** hacer la guerra.

warble [wôr'bəl] *n* (*of bird*) trino, gorjeo ♦ *vi* (*bird*) trinar.

war cry *n* grito de guerra.

ward [wôrd] *n* (*in hospital*) sala; (*LAW: child*) pupilo/a.

ward off *vt* desviar, parar; (*attack*) rechazar.

warden [wôr'dən] *n* (*of park, game reserve*) guardián/ana *m/f*; (*Brit: of institution*) director(a) *m/f*; (*Brit: also*: **traffic ~**) guardia *m/f*.

warder [wôr'dûr] *n* (*Brit*) guardián/ana *m/f*, carcelero/a.

wardrobe [wôrd'rōb] *n* armario, guardarropa, ropero (*esp LAm*).

warehouse [wär'hous] *n* almacén *m*, depósito.

wares [wärz] *npl* mercancías *fpl*.

warfare [wôr'fär] *n* guerra.

war game *n* juego de estrategia militar.

warhead [wôr'hed] *n* cabeza armada; **nuclear ~s** cabezas *fpl* armadas.

warily [wär'ilē] *ad* con cautela, cautelosamente.

warlike [wôr'līk] *a* guerrero.

warm [wôrm] *a* caliente; (*person, greeting, heart*) afectuoso, cariñoso; (*supporter*) entusiasta; (*thanks, congratulations, apologies*) efusivo; (*clothes etc*) que abriga; (*welcome, day*) caluroso; **it's ~** hace calor; **I'm ~** tengo calor; **to keep sth ~** mantener algo caliente.

warm up *vi* (*room*) calentarse; (*person*) entrar en calor; (*athlete*) hacer ejercicios de calentamiento; (*discussion*) acalorarse ♦ *vt* calentar.

warm-blooded [wôrm'blud'id] *a* de sangre caliente.

war memorial *n* monumento a los caídos.

warm-hearted [wôrm'hâr'tid] *a* afectuoso.

warmly [wôrm'lē] *ad* afectuosamente.

warmonger [wôr'munggûr] *n* belicista *m/f*.

warmongering [wôr'munggûring] *n* belicismo.

warmth [wôrmth] *n* calor *m*.

warm-up [wôrm'up] *n* (*SPORT*) ejercicios *mpl* de calentamiento.

warn [wôrn] *vt* avisar, advertir; (*SOCCER*) amonestar; **to ~ sb not to do sth** *or*

against doing sth aconsejar a uno que no haga algo.

warning [wôr'ning] *n* aviso, advertencia; **gale ~** (*METEOROLOGY*) aviso de vendaval; **without (any) ~** sin aviso *or* avisar.

warning light *n* luz *f* de advertencia.

warning triangle *n* (*AUT*) triángulo señalizador.

warp [wôrp] *vi* (*wood*) combarse.

warpath [wôr'path] *n*: **to be on the ~** (*fig*) estar en pie de guerra.

warped [wôrpt] *a* (*wood*) alabeado; (*fig: character, sense of humor etc*) pervertido.

warrant [wôr'ənt] *n* (*LAW: to arrest*) orden *f* de detención; (: *to search*) mandamiento de registro ♦ *vt* (*justify, merit*) merecer.

warrant officer *n* (*MIL*) brigada *m*; (*NAUT*) contramaestre *m*.

warranty [wôr'əntē] *n* garantía; **under ~** (*COMM*) bajo garantía.

warren [wôr'ən] *n* (*of rabbits*) madriguera; (*fig*) laberinto.

warring [wô'ring] *a* (*interests etc*) opuesto; (*nations*) en guerra.

warrior [wôr'ēûr] *n* guerrero/a.

Warsaw [wôr'sô] *n* Varsovia.

warship [wôr'ship] *n* buque *m* o barco de guerra.

wart [wôrt] *n* verruga.

wartime [wôr'tīm] *n*: **in ~** en tiempos de guerra, en la guerra.

wary [wär'ē] *a* cauteloso; **to be ~ about** *or* **of doing sth** tener cuidado con hacer algo.

was [wuz] *pt of* **be**.

Wash. *abbr* (*US*) = *Washington*.

wash [wâsh] *vt* lavar; (*sweep, carry: sea etc*) llevar ♦ *vi* lavarse ♦ *n* (*clothes etc*) lavado; (*bath*) baño; (*of ship*) estela; **he was ~ed overboard** fue arrastrado del barco por las olas.

wash away *vt* (*stain*) quitar lavando; (*subj: river etc*) llevarse; (*fig*) limpiar.

wash down *vt* lavar.

wash off *vt* quitar lavando.

wash up *vi* (*US*) lavarse; (*Brit: dishes*) fregar los platos.

washable [wâsh'əbəl] *a* lavable.

wash bag *n* (*US*) esponjera.

washbasin [wâshbās'ən] *n* (*Brit*) = **washbowl**.

washbowl [wâsh'bōl] *n* (*US*) lavabo.

washcloth [wâsh'klôth] *n* (*US*) manopla.

washer [wâsh'ûr] *n* (*TECH*) arandela.

washing [wâsh'ing] *n* (*dirty*) ropa sucia; (*clean*) colada.

washing line *n* (*Brit*) cuerda de (colgar) la ropa.

washing machine *n* lavadora.

washing powder *n* (*Brit*) detergente *m* (en polvo).

Washington [wâsh'ingtən] *n* (*city, state*) Washington *m*.

washing-up [wâsh'ingup'] *n* (*Brit*) fregado,

platos *mpl* (para fregar).

washing-up liquid *n* (*Brit*) (detergente *m*) lavavajillas *m inv.*

wash-out [wâsh'out] *n* (*col*) fracaso.

washroom [wâsh'rōōm] *n* servicios *mpl.*

wasn't [wuz'ənt] = **was not.**

Wasp, WASP [wâsp] *n abbr* (*US:* = *White Anglo-Saxon Protestant) sobrenombre que se da a los americanos de origen anglosajón, acomodados y de tendencia conservadora.*

wasp [wâsp] *n* avispa.

waspish [wâs'pish] *a* (*character*) irascible; (*comment*) mordaz, punzante.

wastage [wās'tij] *n* desgaste *m*; (*loss*) pérdida; **natural ~** (*Brit*) desgaste natural.

waste [wāst] *n* derroche *m*, despilfarro; (*misuse*) desgaste *m*; (*of time*) pérdida; (*food*) sobras *fpl*; (*rubbish*) basura, desperdicios *mpl* ♦ *a* (*material*) de desecho; (*left over*) sobrante; (*energy, heat*) desperdiciado; (*land, ground: in city*) sin construir; (: *in country*) baldío ♦ *vt* (*squander*) malgastar, derrochar; (*time*) perder; (*opportunity*) desperdiciar; **~s** *npl* (*Brit: area of land*) tierras *fpl* baldías; **to lay ~** devastar, arrasar; **it's a ~ of money** es dinero perdido; **to go to ~** desperdiciarse.

waste away *vi* consumirse.

wastebin [wāst'bin] *n* (*Brit*) cubo *or* (*LAm*) bote *m* de la basura.

wasteful [wāst'fəl] *a* derrochador(a); (*process*) antieconómico.

wastefully [wāst'fəlē] *ad* derrochadoramente; antieconómicamente.

waste ground *n* (*Brit*) terreno baldío.

wasteland [wāst'land] *n* (*urban*) descampados *mpl.*

wastepaper basket [wāst'pāpûr bas'kit] *n* papelera.

waste products *npl* (*INDUSTRY*) residuos *mpl.*

watch [wâch] *n* reloj *m*; (*vigil*) vigilia; (*vigilance*) vigilancia; (*MIL: guard*) centinela *m*; (*NAUT: spell of duty*) guardia ♦ *vt* (*look at*) mirar, observar; (: *match, program*) ver; (*spy on, guard*) vigilar; (*be careful of*) cuidarse de, tener cuidado de ♦ *vi* ver, mirar; (*keep guard*) montar guardia; **to keep a close ~ on sth/sb** vigilar algo/a uno de cerca; **~ how you drive/what you're doing** ten cuidado al conducir/con lo que haces.

watch out *vi* cuidarse, tener cuidado.

watch band *n* (*US*) pulsera (de reloj).

watchdog [wâch'dôg] *n* perro guardián; (*fig*) autoridad *f* protectora.

watchful [wâch'fəl] *a* vigilante, sobre aviso.

watchfully [wâch'fəlē] *ad* vigilantemente.

watchmaker [wâch'mākûr] *n* relojero/a.

watchman [wâch'mən] *n* guardián *m*; (*also:* **night ~**) sereno, vigilante *m* (*LAm*); (*in factory*) vigilante *m* nocturno.

watch stem *n* (*US*) cuerda.

watch strap *n* pulsera (de reloj).

watchword [wâch'wûrd] *n* consigna, contraseña.

water [wô'tûr] *n* agua ♦ *vt* (*plant*) regar ♦ *vi* (*eyes*) llorar; **I'd like a drink of ~** quisiera un vaso de agua; **in British ~s** en aguas británicas; **to pass ~** hacer aguas; **to make sb's mouth ~** hacerle la boca agua a uno; **to be in ~ over one's head** (*US: swimmer*) perder pie; (*fig*) estar perdido.

water down *vt* (*milk etc*) aguar.

water closet *n* wáter *m.*

watercolor, (*Brit*) **watercolour** [wô'tûrkulûr] *n* acuarela.

water-cooled [wô'tûrkōōld] *a* refrigerado (por agua).

watercress [wô'tûrkres] *n* berro.

waterfall [wô'tûrfôl] *n* cascada, salto de agua.

waterfront [wô'tûrfrunt] *n* (*seafront*) parte *f* que da al mar; (*at docks*) muelles *mpl.*

water heater *n* calentador *m* de agua.

water hole *n* abrevadero.

watering can [wô'tûring kan] *n* regadera.

water level *n* nivel *m* del agua.

water lily *n* nenúfar *m.*

waterline [wô'tûrlīn] *n* (*NAUT*) línea de flotación.

waterlogged [wô'tûrlôgd] *a* (*boat*) anegado; (*ground*) inundado.

water main *n* cañería del agua.

watermark [wô'tûrmârk] *n* (*on paper*) filigrana.

watermelon [wô'tûrmelən] *n* sandía.

water polo *n* polo acuático.

waterproof [wô'tûrprōōf] *a* impermeable.

water-repellent [wô'tərîpel'ənt] *a* hidrófugo.

watershed [wô'tûrshed] *n* (*GEO*) cuenca; (*fig*) momento crítico.

water-skiing [wô'tûrskēing] *n* esquí *m* acuático.

water softener *n* ablandador *m* de agua.

water tank *n* depósito de agua.

watertight [wô'tûrtīt] *a* hermético.

water vapor *n* vapor *m* de agua.

waterway [wô'tûrwā] *n* vía fluvial *or* navegable.

waterworks [wô'tûrwûrks] *npl* central *fsg* depuradora.

watery [wô'tûrē] *a* (*color*) desvaído; (*coffee*) aguado; (*eyes*) lloroso.

WATS [wâts] *n abbr* (*US*) = *Wide Area Telecommunications Service.*

watt [wât] *n* vatio.

wattage [wât'ij] *n* potencia en vatios.

wattle [wât'əl] *n* zarzo.

wave [wāv] *n* ola; (*of hand*) señal *f* con la mano; (*RADIO, in hair*) onda; (*fig: of enthusiasm, strikes*) oleada ♦ *vi* agitar la mano; (*flag*) ondear ♦ *vt* (*handkerchief,* *gun*) agitar; **short/medium/long** ~ (*RA-DIO*) onda corta/media/larga; **the new** ~ (*CINEMA, MUS*) la nueva ola; **to** ~ **goodbye to sb** decir adiós a uno con la mano; **he** ~**d us over to his table** nos hizo señas (con la mano) para que fuéramos a su mesa.

wave aside, wave away *vt* (*person*): **to** ~ **sb aside** apartar a uno con la mano; (*fig: suggestion, objection*) rechazar; (*doubts*) desechar.

waveband [wāv'band] *n* banda de ondas.

wavelength [wāv'lengkth] *n* longitud *f* de onda.

waver [wā'vûr] *vi* oscilar; (*confidence*) disminuir; (*faith*) flaquear.

wavy [wā'vē] *a* ondulado.

wax [waks] *n* cera ♦ *vt* encerar ♦ *vi* (*moon*) crecer.

waxen [wak'sən] *a* (*fig: pale*) blanco como la cera.

wax paper *n* papel *m* apergaminado.

waxworks [waks'wûrks] *npl* museo *sg* de cera.

way [wā] *n* camino; (*distance*) trayecto, recorrido; (*direction*) dirección *f*, sentido; (*manner*) modo, manera; (*habit*) costumbre *f*; **which** ~? — **this** ~ ¿por dónde? *or* ¿en qué dirección? — por aquí; **on the** ~ (*en route*) en (el) camino; (*expected*) en camino; **to be on one's** ~ estar en camino; **you pass it on your** ~ **home** está en el camino a tu casa; **to be in the** ~ bloquear el camino; (*fig*) estorbar; **to keep out of sb's** ~ esquivar a uno; **to make** ~ (**for sb/sth**) dejar paso (a uno/algo); (*fig*) abrir camino (a uno/algo); **to go out of one's** ~ **to do sth** desvivirse por hacer algo; **to lose one's** ~ perderse, extraviarse; **to be the wrong** ~ **around** estar del *or* al revés; **in a** ~ en cierto modo *or* sentido; **by the** ~ a propósito; **by** ~ **of** (*via*) pasando por; (*as a sort of*) como, a modo de; ~ **in** entrada; ~ **out** salida; **the** ~ **back** el camino de vuelta; **the village is rather out of the** ~ el pueblo está un poco apartado *or* retirado; **it's a long** ~ **away** está muy lejos; **to get one's own** ~ salirse con la suya; "**give** ~" (*Brit AUT*) "ceda el paso"; **no** ~! (*col*) ¡ni pensarlo!; **put it the right** ~ **up** ponlo boca arriba; **he's in a bad** ~ está grave; **to be under** ~ (*work, project*) estar en marcha.

waybill [wā'bil] *n* (*COMM*) hoja de ruta, carta de porte.

waylay [wālā'] *vt* (*irg: like* **lay**) atacar.

wayside [wā'sīd] *n* borde *m* del camino; **to fall by the** ~ (*fig*) fracasar.

way station *n* (*US RAIL*) apeadero; (*fig*) paso intermedio.

wayward [wā'wûrd] *a* díscolo, caprichoso.

WC *n abbr* (*Brit: = water closet*) wáter *m*.

WCC *n abbr* = *World Council of Churches*.

we [wē] *pl pron* nosotros/as; ~ **understand** (nosotros) entendemos; **here** ~ **are** aquí estamos.

weak [wēk] *a* débil, flojo; (*tea, coffee*) flojo, aguado; **to grow** ~(**er**) debilitarse.

weaken [wē'kən] *vi* debilitarse; (*give way*) ceder ♦ *vt* debilitar.

weak-kneed [wēk'nēd] *a* (*fig*) sin voluntad *or* carácter.

weakling [wēk'ling] *n* debilucho/a.

weakly [wēk'lē] *a* enfermizo, débil ♦ *ad* débilmente.

weakness [wēk'nis] *n* debilidad *f*; (*fault*) punto débil.

wealth [welth] *n* (*money, resources*) riqueza; (*of details*) abundancia.

wealth tax *n* impuesto sobre el patrimonio.

wealthy [wel'thē] *a* rico.

wean [wēn] *vt* destetar.

weapon [wep'ən] *n* arma.

wear [wār] *n* (*use*) uso; (*deterioration through use*) desgaste *m*; (*clothing*): **sports/baby**~ ropa de deportes/de niños ♦ *vb* (*pt* **wore**, *pp* **worn**) [wôr, wôrn]) *vt* (*clothes, beard*) llevar; (*shoes*) calzar; (*look, smile*) tener; (*damage: through use*) gastar, usar ♦ *vi* (*last*) durar; (*rub through etc*) desgastarse; **evening** ~ (*man's*) traje *m* de etiqueta; (*woman's*) traje *m* de noche; **to** ~ **a hole in sth** hacer un agujero en algo.

wear away *vt* gastar ♦ *vi* desgastarse.

wear down *vt* gastar; (*strength*) agotar.

wear off *vi* (*pain, excitement etc*) pasar, desaparecer.

wear out *vt* desgastar; (*person, strength*) agotar.

wearable [wār'əbəl] *a* que se puede llevar.

wear and tear *n* desgaste *m*.

wearer [wār'ûr] *n*: **the** ~ **of this jacket** el/la que lleva puesta esta chaqueta.

wearily [wē'rilē] *ad* con cansancio.

weariness [wē'rēnis] *n* cansancio; abatimiento.

wearisome [wē'rēsəm] *a* (*tiring*) cansado, pesado; (*boring*) aburrido.

weary [wēr'ē] *a* (*tired*) cansado; (*dispirited*) abatido ♦ *vt* cansar ♦ *vi*: **to** ~ **of** cansarse de, aburrirse de.

weasel [wē'zəl] *n* (*ZOOL*) comadreja.

weather [weth'ûr] *n* tiempo ♦ *vt* (*storm, crisis*) hacer frente a; **under the** ~ (*fig: ill*) mal, indispuesto; **what's the** ~ **like?** ¿qué tiempo hace?

weather-beaten [weth'ûrbētən] *a* curtido.

weathercock [weth'ûrkák] *n* veleta.

weather forecast *n* boletín *m* meteorológico.

weatherman [weth'ûrman] *n* hombre *m* del tiempo.

weatherproof [weth'ûrproof] *a* (*garment*) impermeable.

weather report n parte m meteorológico.
weather strip(ping) [weth'ûr strip('ing)] n burlete m.
weather vane n = **weathercock**.
weave, pt **wove**, pp **woven** [wēv, wōv, wō'vən] vt (cloth) tejer; (fig) entretejer ♦ vi (fig: pt, pp ~d: move in and out) zigzaguear.
weaver [wē'vûr] n tejedor(a) m/f.
weaving [wē'ving] n tejeduría.
web [web] n (of spider) telaraña; (on foot) membrana; (network) red f.
webbed [webd] a (foot) palmeado.
webbing [web'ing] n (on chair) cinchas fpl.
wed [wed] vt (pt, pp **wedded**) casar ♦ n: **the newly-~s** los recién casados.
Wed. abbr (= Wednesday) miérc.
we'd [wēd] = **we had; we would**.
wedded [wed'id] pt, pp of **wed**.
wedding [wed'ing] n boda, casamiento.
wedding anniversary a aniversario de boda; **silver/golden** ~ bodas fpl de plata/de oro.
wedding day n día m de la boda.
wedding dress n traje m de novia.
wedding present n regalo de boda.
wedding ring n alianza.
wedge [wej] n (of wood etc) cuña; (of cake) trozo ♦ vt acuñar; (push) apretar.
wedge-heeled [wej'hēld] a con suela de cuña.
wedlock [wed'lák] n matrimonio.
Wednesday [wenz'dā] n miércoles m inv.
wee [wē] a (Scottish) pequeñito.
weed [wēd] n mala hierba, maleza ♦ vt escardar, desherbar.
weedkiller [wēd'kilûr] n herbicida m.
weedy [wē'dē] a (person) debilucho.
week [wēk] n semana; **a ~ from today** de hoy en ocho días; **Tuesday ~, a ~ from Tuesday** de martes en una semana; **once/twice a ~** una vez/dos veces a la semana; **this ~** esta semana; **in 2 ~s' time** dentro de 2 semanas; **every other ~** cada 2 semanas.
weekday [wēk'dā] n día m laborable; **on ~s** entre semana, en días laborables.
weekend [wēk'end] n fin m de semana.
weekend case n neceser m.
weekly [wēk'lē] ad semanalmente, cada semana ♦ a semanal ♦ n semanario; **~ newspaper** semanario.
weep, pt, pp **wept** [wēp, wept] vi, vt llorar; (MED: wound etc) supurar.
weeping willow [wē'ping wil'ō] n sauce m llorón.
weft [weft] n (TEXTILES) trama.
weigh [wā] vt, vi pesar; **to ~ anchor** levar anclas; **to ~ the pros and cons** pesar el pro y el contra.
weigh down vt sobrecargar; (fig: with worry) agobiar.
weigh out vt (goods) pesar.

weighing machine [wā'ing məshēn'] n báscula, peso.
weight [wāt] n peso; (on scale) pesa; **to lose/put on** ~ adelgazar/engordar; **~s and measures** pesas y medidas.
weightlessness [wāt'lisnis] n ingravidez f.
weight lifter [wāt'liftûr] n levantador(a) m/f de pesas.
weight limit n límite m de peso.
weighty [wā'tē] a pesado.
weir [wēr] n presa.
weird [wērd] a raro, extraño.
welcome [wel'kəm] a bienvenido ♦ n bienvenida ♦ vt dar la bienvenida a; (be glad of) alegrarse de; **to make sb** ~ recibir or acoger bien a uno; **thank you — you're** ~ gracias — de nada; **you're** ~ **to try** puede intentar cuando quiera; **we** ~ **this step** celebramos esta medida.
weld [weld] n soldadura ♦ vt soldar.
welding [weld'ing] n soldadura.
welfare [wel'fär] n bienestar m; (social aid) asistencia social; **to look after sb's** ~ cuidar del bienestar de uno; **to be on** ~ estar parado.
welfare state n estado benefactor.
welfare work n asistencia social.
well [wel] n fuente f, pozo ♦ ad bien ♦ a: **to be** ~ estar bien (de salud) ♦ excl ¡vaya!, ¡bueno!; **as** ~ (in addition) además, también; **as** ~ **as** además de; **you might as** ~ **tell me** más vale decírmelo; **it would be as** ~ **to ask** más valdría preguntar; ~ **done!** ¡bien hecho!; **get** ~ **soon!** ¡que te mejores pronto!; **to do** ~ (business) ir bien; (in exam) salir bien; **to be doing** ~ ir bien; **to think** ~ **of sb** pensar bien de uno; **I don't feel** ~ no me encuentro or siento bien; ~, **as I was saying** ... bueno, como decía ... .
well up vi brotar.
we'll [wēl] = **we will, we shall**.
well-behaved [welbihāvd'] a modoso.
well-being [wel'bē'ing] n bienestar m.
well-bred [wel'bred'] a bien educado.
well-built [wel'bilt'] a (person) fornido.
well-chosen [wel'chō'zən] a (remarks, words) acertado.
well-deserved [wel'dizûrvd'] a merecido.
well-developed [wel'divel'əpt] a (arm, muscle etc) bien desarrollado; (sense) agudo, fino.
well-disposed [wel'dispōzd'] a: ~ **to(wards)** bien dispuesto a.
well-dressed [wel'drest'] a bien vestido.
well-earned [wel'ûrnd'] a (rest) merecido.
well-groomed [wel'grōōmd'] a de apariencia cuidada.
well-heeled [wel'hēld'] a (col: wealthy) rico.
well-informed [wel'infôrmd'] a (having knowledge of sth) enterado, al corriente.
Wellington [wel'ingtən] n Wellington m.

wellingtons [wel'ingtənz] *npl* (*also:* **Wellington boots**) botas *fpl* de goma.
well-kept [wel'kept'] *a* (*secret*) bien guardado; (*hair, hands, house, grounds*) bien cuidado.
well-known [wel'nōn'] *a* (*person*) conocido.
well-mannered [wel'man'ûrd] *a* educado.
well-meaning [wel'mē'ning] *a* bienintencionado.
well-nigh [wel'nī'] *ad:* ~ **impossible** casi imposible.
well-off [wel'ôf'] *a* acomodado.
well-read [wel'red'] *a* culto.
well-spoken [wel'spō'kən] *a* bienhablado.
well-stocked [wel'stákt'] *a* (*shop, larder*) bien surtido.
well-timed [wel'tīmd'] *a* oportuno.
well-to-do [wel'tədōō'] *a* acomodado.
well-wisher [wel'wishûr] *n* admirador(a) *m/f.*
Welsh [welsh] *a* galés/esa ♦ *n* (*LING*) galés *m*; **the** ~ *npl* los galeses.
Welshman [wel'shmən] *n* galés *m.*
Welsh rarebit [welsh rär'bit] *n* pan *m* con queso tostado.
Welshwoman [welsh'wōōmən] *n* galesa.
welter [wel'tûr] *n* mescolanza, revoltijo.
went [went] *pt of* **go.**
wept [wept] *pt, pp of* **weep.**
were [wûr] *pt of* **be.**
we're [wēr] = **we are.**
weren't [wûr'ənt] = **were not.**
werewolf, *pl* **-wolves** [wär'wōōlf, -wōōlvz] *n* hombre *m* lobo.
west [west] *n* oeste *m* ♦ *a* occidental, del oeste ♦ *ad* al *or* hacia el oeste; **the W**~ el Oeste, el Occidente.
westbound [west'bound] *a* (*traffic, lane*) con rumbo al oeste.
westerly [wes'tûrlē] *a* (*wind*) del oeste.
western [wes'tûrn] *a* occidental ♦ *n* (*CINEMA*) película del oeste.
westernized [wes'tûrnīzd] *a* occidentalizado.
West German *a* de Alemania Occidental ♦ *n* alemán/ana *m/f* (de Alemania Occidental.
West Germany *n* Alemania Occidental.
West Indian *a, n* antillano/a *m/f.*
West Indies [west in'dēz] *npl:* **the** ~ las Antillas, las Islas Occidentales.
westward(s) [west'wûrd(z)] *ad* hacia el oeste.
wet [wet] *a* (*damp*) húmedo; (*soaking* ~) mojado; (*rainy*) lluvioso ♦ *vt:* **to** ~ **one's pants** *or* **o.s.** mojarse; **to get** ~ mojarse; **"~ paint"** 'recién pintado'.
wet blanket *n:* **to be a** ~ (*fig*) ser un/una aguafiestas.
wetness [wet'nis] *n* humedad *f.*
wet rot *n* putrefacción *f* húmeda.
wet suit *n* traje *m* de buzo.
we've [wēv] = **we have.**
whack [wak] *vt* dar un buen golpe a.

whale [wāl] *n* (*ZOOL*) ballena.
whaler [wā'lûr] *n* (*ship*) ballenero.
wharf, *pl* **wharves** [wôrf, wôrvz] *n* muelle *m.*
what [wut] *excl* ¡qué!, ¡cómo! ♦ *a* que ♦ *pron* (*interrogative*) qué, cómo; (*relative, indirect: object*) lo que; (: *subject*) el/la que; **for** ~ **reason?** ¿por qué (razón)?; ~ **are you doing?** ¿qué haces?; ~**'s happening?** ¿qué pasa?; **I don't know** ~ **to do** no sé qué hacer; **I saw** ~ **you did** he visto lo que hiciste; ~ **a mess!** ¡qué lío!; ~ **is it called?** ¿cómo se llama?; ~ **is his address?** ¿cuáles son sus señas?; ~ **will it cost?** ¿cuánto costará?; ~ **about me?** ¿y yo?; ~ **I want is a cup of tea** lo que quiero es una taza de té.
whatever [wutev'ûr] *a:* ~ **book you choose** cualquier libro que elijas ♦ *pron:* **do** ~ **is necessary** haga lo que sea necesario; **no reason** ~ ninguna razón sea la que sea; **nothing** ~ nada en absoluto; ~ **it costs** cueste lo que cueste.
wheat [wēt] *n* trigo.
wheat germ *n* germen *m* de trigo.
wheatmeal [wēt'mēl] *n* (*Brit*) harina integral.
wheedle [wēd'əl] *vt:* **to** ~ **sb into doing sth** engatusar a uno para que haga algo *or* para hacer algo; **to** ~ **sth out of sb** sonsacar algo a uno.
wheel [wēl] *n* rueda; (*AUT: also:* **steering** ~) volante *m*; (*NAUT*) timón *m* ♦ *vt* (*baby carriage etc*) empujar ♦ *vi* (*also:* ~ **around**) dar la vuelta, girar; **four-**~ **drive** tracción *f* en las cuatro ruedas; **front-/rear-**~ **drive** tracción *f* delantera/trasera.
wheelbarrow [wēl'barō] *n* carretilla.
wheelbase [wēl'bās] *n* batalla.
wheelchair [wēl'chär] *n* silla de ruedas.
wheel clamp *n* (*Brit AUT*) cepo.
wheeler-dealer [wē'lûrdē'lûr] *n* negociante *m/f* muy astuto/a.
wheeling [wē'ling] *n:* ~ **and dealing** (*col*) intrigas *fpl.*
wheeze [wēz] *vi* resollar.
when [wen] *ad* cuándo ♦ *conj* cuando; (*whereas*) mientras; **on the day** ~ **I met him** el día que le conocí; **that's** ~ **the train arrives** eso es cuando llega el tren.
whenever [wenev'ûr] *conj* cuando; (*every time*) cada vez que; **I go** ~ **I can** voy siempre *or* todas las veces que puedo.
where [wär] *ad* dónde ♦ *conj* donde; **this is** ~ aquí es donde; ~ **possible** donde sea posible; ~ **are you from?** ¿de dónde es usted?
whereabouts [wär'əbouts] *ad* dónde ♦ *n:* **nobody knows his** ~ nadie conoce su paradero.
whereas [wäraz'] *conj* visto que, mientras.
whereby [wärbī'] *ad* mediante el/la cual *etc.*

whereupon [wärəpân'] *conj* con lo cual, después de lo cual.

wherever [wärev'ûr] *ad* dondequiera que; (*interrogative*) dónde; **sit ~ you like** siéntese donde quiera.

wherewithal [wär'withôl] *n* recursos *mpl*; **the ~ (to do sth)** los medios (para hacer algo).

whet [wet] *vt* estimular.

whether [weth'ûr] *conj* si; **I don't know ~ to accept or not** no sé si aceptar o no; **~ you go or not** vayas o no vayas.

whey [wā] *n* suero.

which [wich] *a* (*interrogative*) qué, cuál; **~ one of you?** ¿cuál de vosotros?; **~ picture do you want?** ¿qué cuadro quieres? ♦ *pron* (*interrogative*) ¿cuál?; (*relative: subject*) que, lo que; (: *object*) el que *etc*, el cual *etc*, lo cual; **after ~** después de lo cual; **~ do you want?** ¿cuál quieres?; **I don't mind ~** no me importa cuál; **the apple ~ is on the table** la manzana que está sobre la mesa; **the chair on ~ you are sitting** la silla sobre la que estás sentado; **he said he knew, ~ is true** el dijo que sabía, lo cual es cierto; **by ~ time** a esas alturas, para entonces; **in ~ case** en cuyo caso.

whichever [wichev'ûr] *a*: **take ~ book you prefer** coja el libro que prefiera; **~ book you take** cualquier libro que coja.

whiff [wif] *n* bocanada; **to catch a ~ of sth** oler algo.

while [wīl] *n* rato, momento ♦ *conj* durante; (*whereas*) mientras; (*although*) aunque ♦ *vt*: **to ~ away the time** pasar el rato; **for a ~** durante algún tiempo; **in a ~** dentro de poco; **all the ~** todo el tiempo; **we'll make it worth your ~** te lo compensaremos generosamente.

whilst [wīlst] *conj* = **while**.

whim [wim] *n* capricho.

whimper [wim'pûr] *n* (*weeping*) lloriqueo; (*moan*) quejido ♦ *vi* lloriquear; quejarse.

whimsical [wim'zikəl] *a* (*person*) caprichoso.

whine [wīn] *n* (*of pain*) gemido; (*of engine*) zumbido ♦ *vi* gemir; zumbar.

whip [wip] *n* látigo; (*POL: person*) *encargado/a de la disciplina partidaria en el parlamento* ♦ *vt* azotar; (*snatch*) arrebatar; (*US CULIN*) batir.

whip up *vt* (*cream etc*) batir (rápidamente); (*col: meal*) preparar rápidamente; (: *stir up: support, feeling*) avivar.

whiplash [wip'lash] *n* (*MED: also*: **~ injury**) latigazo.

whipped cream [wipt krēm] *n* nata *or* crema montada.

whipping boy [wip'ing boi] *n* (*fig*) cabeza de turco.

whip-round [wip'round] *n* (*Brit*) colecta.

whirl [wûrl] *n* remolino ♦ *vt* hacer girar, dar vueltas a ♦ *vi* (*dancers*) girar, dar vueltas; (*leaves, dust, water etc*) arremolinarse.

whirlpool [wûrl'pōōl] *n* remolino.

whirlwind [wûrl'wind] *n* torbellino.

whirr [wär] *vi* zumbar.

whisk [wisk] *n* (*CULIN*) batidor *m* ♦ *vt* (*CULIN*) batir; **to ~ sb away** *or* **off** llevar volando a uno.

whiskers [wis'kûrz] *npl* (*of animal*) bigotes *mpl*; (*of man*) pelo de la barba.

whiskey (*US, Ireland*), **whisky** (*Brit*) [wis'kē] *n* whisky *m*.

whisper [wis'pûr] *n* cuchicheo; (*rumor*) rumor *m*; (*fig*) susurro, murmullo ♦ *vi* cuchichear, hablar bajo; (*fig*) susurrar ♦ *vt* decir en voz muy baja; **to ~ sth to sb** decirle algo al oído a uno.

whispering [wis'pûring] *n* cuchicheo.

whist [wist] *n* (*Brit*) whist *m*.

whistle [wis'əl] *n* (*sound*) silbido; (*object*) silbato ♦ *vi* silbar; **to ~ a tune** silbar una melodía.

whistle-stop [wis'əlstâp] *a*: **~ tour** (*US POL*) gira electoral rápida; (*fig*) recorrido rápido.

Whit [wit] *n* (*Brit*) Pentecostés *m*.

white [wīt] *a* blanco; (*pale*) pálido ♦ *n* blanco; (*of egg*) clara; **to turn** *or* **go ~** (*person*) palidecer, ponerse blanco; (*hair*) encanecer; **the ~s** (*washing*) la ropa blanca; **tennis ~s** ropa *f* de tenis.

whitebait [wīt'bāt] *n* morralla.

white coffee *n* (*Brit*) café *m* con leche.

white-collar worker [wīt'kâl'ûr wûr'kûr] *n* oficinista *m/f*.

white elephant *n* (*fig*) maula.

white goods *npl* (*appliances*) electrodomésticos *mpl* de línea blanca; (*linen etc*) lencería, ropa blanca.

white-hot [wīt'hât'] *a* (*metal*) calentado al (rojo) blanco.

white lie *n* mentirilla.

whiteness [wīt'nis] *n* blancura.

white noise *n* sonido blanco.

whiteout [wīt'out] *n* resplandor *m* sin sombras; (*fig*) masa confusa.

white paper *n* (*POL*) libro rojo.

whitewash [wīt'wâsh] *n* (*paint*) jalbegue *m*, cal *f* ♦ *vt* (*also fig*) encubrir.

whiting [wī'ting] *n* (*pl inv*) (*fish*) pescadilla.

Whit Monday *n* (*Brit*) lunes *m* de Pentecostés.

Whitsun [wit'sən] *n* (*Brit*) Pentecostés *m*.

whittle [wit'əl] *vt*: **to ~ away**, **~ down** ir reduciendo.

whizz [wiz] *vi*: **to ~ past** *or* **by** pasar a toda velocidad.

whizz kid *n* (*col*) prodigio/a.

WHO *n abbr* (= *World Health Organization*) OMS *f*.

who [hōō] *pron* (*relative*) que, el que *etc*, quien; (*interrogative*) quién; (*pl*) quiénes.

whodun(n)it [hōōdun'it] *n* (*col*) novela policíaca.

whoever [hōōev'ûr] *pron*: ~ **finds it** cualquiera *or* quienquiera que lo encuentre; **ask ~ you like** pregunta a quién quieras; ~ **he marries** no importa con quién se case.

whole [hōl] *a* (*complete*) todo, entero; (*not broken*) intacto ♦ *n* (*total*) total *m*; (*sum*) conjunto; ~ **villages were destroyed** pueblos enteros fueron destruidos; **the ~ of the town** toda la ciudad, la ciudad entera; **on the ~, as a ~** en general.

wholefood [hōl'fōōd] *n* alimentos *mpl* integrales.

wholehearted [hōl'hâr'tid] *a* (*support, approval*) total; (*sympathy*) todo.

wholeheartedly [hōl'hâr'tidlē] *ad* con entusiasmo.

wholemeal [hōl'mēl] *a* (*Brit*) = **wholewheat.**

whole milk *n* (*US*) leche *f* cremosa.

whole note *n* (*US MUS*) semibreve *f*.

wholesale [hōl'sāl] *n* venta al por mayor ♦ *a* al por mayor; (*destruction*) sistemático.

wholesaler [hōl'sālûr] *n* mayorista *m/f*.

wholesome [hōl'səm] *a* sano.

wholewheat [hōl'wēt] *a* (*flour, bread*) integral.

wholly [hō'lē] *ad* totalmente, enteramente.

whom [hōōm] *pron* que, a quien; (*interrogative*) ¿a quién?; **those to ~ I spoke** aquéllos a *or* con los que hablé.

whooping cough [wōō'ping kôf] *n* tos *f* ferina.

whoosh [wōōsh] *n*: **it came out with a ~** (*sauce etc*) salió todo de repente; (*air*) salió con mucho ruido.

whopper [wâp'ûr] *n* (*col: lie*) embuste *m*; (: *large thing*): **a ~** uno/a enorme.

whopping [wâp'ing] *a* (*col*) enorme.

whore [hôr] *n* (*col: pej*) puta.

whose [hōōz] *a*: ~ **book is this?** ¿de quién es este libro?; **the man ~ son you rescued** el hombre cuyo hijo salvaste; **the girl ~ sister you were speaking to** la chica con cuya hermana estabas hablando ♦ *pron*: ~ **is this?** ¿de quién es esto?; **I know ~ it is** yo sé de quien es.

why [wī] *ad* por qué; (*interrogative*) por qué, para qué ♦ *excl* ¡toma!, ¡cómo!; **tell me ~** dime por qué, dime la razón; ~ **is he late?** ¿por qué lleva retraso?

whyever [wī'evúr] *ad* (*Brit*) por qué.

WI *n abbr* (*GEO*) = **West Indies;** (*US MAIL*) = **Wisconsin.**

wick [wik] *n* mecha.

wicked [wik'id] *a* malvado, cruel.

wickedness [wik'idnis] *n* maldad *f*, crueldad *f*.

wicker [wik'ûr] *n* (*also*: ~**work**) artículos *mpl* de mimbre.

wicket [wik'it] *n* (*CRICKET*) palos *mpl*.

wide [wīd] *a* ancho; (*area, knowledge*)

vasto, grande; (*choice*) grande ♦ *ad*: **to open ~** abrir de par en par; **to shoot ~** errar el tiro; **it is 3 meters ~** tiene 3 metros de ancho.

wide-angle lens [wīd'ang'gəl lenz] *n* objetivo gran angular.

wide-awake [wīd'əwāk'] *a* bien despierto.

wide-eyed [wīd'īd] *a* con los ojos muy abiertos; (*fig*) ingenuo.

widely [wīd'lē] *ad* (*differing*) muy; **it is ~ believed that ...** hay una convicción general de que ...; **to be ~ read** (*author*) ser muy leído; (*reader*) haber leído mucho.

widen [wī'dən] *vt* ensanchar.

wideness [wīd'nis] *n* anchura; amplitud *f*.

wide open *a* abierto de par en par.

wide-ranging [wīd'rān'jing] *a* (*survey, report*) de gran alcance; (*interests*) muy diversos.

widespread [wīdspred'] *a* (*belief etc*) extendido, general.

widow [wid'ō] *n* viuda.

widowed [wid'ōd] *a* viudo.

widower [wid'ōûr] *n* viudo.

width [width] *n* anchura; (*of cloth*) ancho; **it's 7 meters in ~** tiene 7 metros de ancho.

widthwise [width'wīz] *ad* a lo ancho.

wield [wēld] *vt* (*sword*) manejar; (*power*) ejercer.

wife, *pl* **wives** [wīf, wīvz] *n* mujer *f*, esposa.

wig [wig] *n* peluca.

wiggle [wig'əl] *vt* menear ♦ *vi* menearse.

wiggly [wig'lē] *a* (*line*) ondulado.

wigwam [wig'wâm] *n* tipí *m*, tienda india.

wild [wīld] *a* (*animal*) salvaje; (*plant*) silvestre; (*rough*) furioso, violento; (*idea*) descabellado; (*col: angry*) furioso ♦ *n*: **the ~** la naturaleza; ~**s** *npl* regiones *fpl* salvajes, tierras *fpl* vírgenes; **to be ~ about** (*enthusiastic*) estar *or* andar (*LAm*) loco por; **in its ~ state** en su estado natural.

wild card *n* (*COMPUT*) comodín *m*.

wildcat [wīld'kat] *n* gato montés.

wildcat strike *n* huelga espontánea *or* salvaje.

wilderness [wil'dûrnis] *n* desierto.

wildfire [wīld'fiûr] *n*: **to spread like ~** correr como la pólvora (en reguero).

wild-goose chase [wīld'gōōs' chās] *n* (*fig*) búsqueda inútil.

wildlife [wīld'lif] *n* fauna.

wildly [wīld'lē] *ad* (*roughly*) violentamente; (*foolishly*) locamente; (*rashly*) descabelladamente.

wiles [wīlz] *npl* artimañas *fpl*, ardides *mpl*.

wilful [wil'fəl] *a* (*Brit*) = **willful.**

will [wil] *auxiliary vb*: **he ~ come** vendrá; **you won't lose it, ~ you?** no lo vayas a perder *or* no lo perderás ¿verdad?; (*in conjectures*): **that ~ be the postman** debe ser el cartero; ~ **you sit down** (*politely*) ¿quiere (usted) sentarse?; (*angrily*) ¡siéntate!; **the car won't start** el coche no arranca ♦ *vt* (*pt, pp* **willed**): **to ~ sb to do sth** desear que uno haga algo; **he ~ed himself to go on** con gran fuerza de voluntad, continuó ♦ *n* voluntad *f*; (*testament*) testamento; **against sb's ~** contra la voluntad de uno; **to do sth of one's own free ~** hacer algo por voluntad propia.

willful [wil'fəl] *a* (*action*) deliberado; (*obstinate*) testarudo.

willing [wil'ing] *a* (*with goodwill*) de buena voluntad; complaciente; **he's ~ to do it** está dispuesto a hacerlo; **to show ~** mostrarse dispuesto.

willingly [wil'inglē] *ad* con mucho gusto.

willingness [wil'ingnis] *n* buena voluntad.

will-o'-the-wisp [wil'ōthəwisp'] *n* fuego fatuo; (*fig*) quimera.

willow [wil'ō] *n* sauce *m*.

willpower [wil'pouûr] *n* fuerza de voluntad.

willy-nilly [wil'ēnil'ē] *ad* quiérase o no.

wilt [wilt] *vi* marchitarse.

Wilts [wilts] *abbr* (*Brit*) = *Wiltshire*.

wily [wī'lē] *a* astuto.

wimp [wimp] *n* (*col*) endeble *m/f*, enclenque *m/f*.

win [win] *n* (*in sports etc*) victoria, triunfo ♦ *vb* (*pt, pp* **won** [wun]) *vt* ganar; (*obtain: contract etc*) conseguir, lograr ♦ *vi* ganar, tener éxito.

win over, (*Brit*) **win round** *vt* convencer a.

wince [wins] *vi* encogerse.

winch [winch] *n* torno.

Winchester disk [win'chestûr disk] ® *n* (*COMPUT*) disco Winchester ®.

wind *n* [wind] viento; (*MED*) gases *mpl*; (*breath*) aliento ♦ *vb* [wind] (*pt, pp* **wound** [wound]) *vt* enrollar; (*wrap*) envolver; (*clock, toy*) dar cuerda a; [wind] (*take breath away from*) dejar sin aliento a ♦ *vi* (*road, river*) serpentear; **into** *or* **against the ~** contra el viento; **to get ~ of sth** enterarse de algo; **to break ~** ventosear.

wind down *vt* (*car window*) bajar; (*fig: production, business*) disminuir, bajar.

wind up *vt* (*clock*) dar cuerda a; (*debate*) concluir, terminar.

windbreak [wind'brāk] *n* barrera contra el viento.

windbreaker [wind'brākûr] *n* (*US*) cazadora.

wind erosion *n* erosión *f* del viento.

windfall [wind'fôl] *n* golpe *m* de suerte.

winding [wīn'ding] *a* (*road*) tortuoso.

wind instrument [wind in'strəmənt] *n* (*MUS*) instrumento de viento.

windmill [wind'mil] *n* molino de viento.

window [win'dō] *n* ventana; (*in bank, car, train*) ventanilla; (*in shop etc*) escaparate *m*, vitrina (*LAm*), vidriera (*LAm*); (*COMPUT*) ventanilla.

window box *n* jardinera (de ventana).

window cleaner *n* (*person*) limpiacristales *m inv*.

window dressing *n* decoración *f* de escaparates.

window envelope *n* sobre *m* de ventanilla.

window frame *n* marco de ventana.

window ledge *n* alféizar *m*, repisa (*LAm*).

window pane *n* cristal *m*.

window-shopping [win'dōsháping] *n*: **to go ~** ir a ver *or* mirar escaparates.

windowsill [win'dōsil] *n* alféizar *m*, repisa (*LAm*).

windpipe [wind'pīp] *n* tráquea.

windscreen [wind'skrēn] *etc* (*Brit*) = **windshield** *etc*.

windshield [wind'shēld] *n* parabrisas *m inv*.

windshield washer *n* lavaparabrisas *m inv*.

windshield wiper *n* limpiaparabrisas *m inv*.

windswept [wind'swept] *a* azotado por el viento.

wind tunnel *n* túnel *m* aerodinámico.

windy [win'dē] *a* de mucho viento; **it's ~** hace viento.

wine [wīn] *n* vino ♦ *vt*: **to ~ and dine sb** agasajar *or* festejar a uno.

wine cellar *n* bodega.

wineglass [wīn'glas] *n* copa (para vino).

wine-growing [wīn'grōing] *a* viticultor(a).

wine list *n* lista de vinos.

wine merchant *n* vinatero.

wine tasting *n* degustación *f* de vinos.

wine waiter *n* escanciador *m*.

wing [wing] *n* ala; (*US SPORT*) extremo; (*Brit AUT*) aleta; **~s** *npl* (*THEATER*) bastidores *mpl*.

winger [wing'ûr] *n* (*Brit SPORT*) extremo.

wing mirror *n* (espejo) retrovisor *m*.

wing nut *n* tuerca (de) mariposa.

wingspan [wing'span], **wingspread** [wing'spred] *n* envergadura.

wink [wingk] *n* guiño, pestañeo ♦ *vi* guiñar, pestañear; (*light etc*) parpadear.

winkle [win'kəl] *n* bígaro, bigarro.

winner [win'ûr] *n* ganador(a) *m/f*.

winning [win'ing] *a* (*team*) ganador(a); (*goal*) decisivo; (*charming*) encantador(a).

winning post *n* meta.

winnings [win'ingz] *npl* ganancias *fpl*.

winsome [win'səm] *a* atractivo.

winter [win'tûr] *n* invierno ♦ *vi* invernar.

winter sports *npl* deportes *mpl* de invierno.

wintry [win'trē] *a* invernal.

wipe [wīp] *n*: **to give sth a ~** pasar un trapo sobre algo ♦ *vt* limpiar; **to ~ one's nose** limpiarse la nariz.

wipe off *vt* limpiar con un trapo.

wipe out *vt* (*debt*) liquidar; (*memory*) borrar; (*destroy*) destruir.

wipe up *vt* limpiar.

wire [wī'ûr] *n* alambre *m*; (*ELEC*) cable *m* (eléctrico); (*TEL*) telegrama *m* ♦ *vt* (*house*) poner la instalación eléctrica en; (*also*: ~ **up**) conectar.

wire cutters *npl* cortaalambres *msg inv*.

wire mesh, wire netting *n* tela metálica.

wiretapping [wī'ûrtaping] *n* intervención *f* telefónica.

wiring [wiûr'ing] *n* instalación *f* eléctrica.

wiry [wiûr'ē] *a* enjuto y fuerte.

Wis., Wisc. *abbr* (*US*) = *Wisconsin*.

wisdom [wiz'dəm] *n* sabiduría, saber *m*; (*good sense*) cordura.

wisdom tooth *n* muela del juicio.

wise [wīz] *a* sabio; (*sensible*) juicioso; **I'm none the ~r** sigo sin entender.

  wise up *vi* (*col*): **to ~ up (to sth)** enterarse (de algo).

wisecrack [wīz'krak] *n* broma.

wish [wish] *n* (*desire*) deseo ♦ *vt* desear; (*want*) querer; **best ~es** (*on birthday etc*) felicidades *fpl*; **with best ~es** (*in letter*) saludos *mpl*, recuerdos *mpl*; **to ~ sb goodbye** despedirse de uno; **he ~ed me well** me deseó mucha suerte; **to ~ sth on sb** imponer algo a uno; **to ~ to do/sb to do sth** querer hacer/que uno haga algo; **to ~ for** desear.

wishful [wish'fəl] *n*: **it's ~ thinking** eso sería soñar.

wishy-washy [wish'ēwâshē] *a* (*col: color*) desvaído; (: *ideas, thinking*) insípido.

wisp [wisp] *n* mechón *m*; (*of smoke*) voluta.

wistful [wist'fəl] *a* pensativo; (*nostalgic*) nostálgico.

wit [wit] *n* (*wittiness*) ingenio, gracia; (*intelligence: also*: ~**s**) inteligencia; (*person*) chistoso/a; **to have** *or* **keep one's ~s about one** no perder la cabeza.

witch [wich] *n* bruja.

witchcraft [wich'kraft] *n* brujería.

witch doctor *n* hechicero.

witch-hunt [wich'hunt] *n* (*POL*) caza de brujas.

with [with, with] *prep* con; (*manner, means, cause*): **she's come down ~ the flu** está con gripe; **red ~ anger** rojo de cólera; **to shake ~ fear** temblar de miedo; **to stay ~ friends** estar en casa de amigos; **the man ~ the grey hat** el hombre del sombrero gris; **I am ~ you** (*I understand*) te entiendo.

withdraw [withdrô'] *vb* (*irg: like* **draw**) *vt* retirar, sacar ♦ *vi* retirarse; (*go back on promise*) retractarse; **to ~ money (from the bank)** retirar fondos (del banco); **to ~ into o.s.** ensimismarse.

withdrawal [withdrô'əl] *n* retirada.

withdrawal symptoms *npl* síndrome *m* de abstinencia.

withdrawn [withdrôn'] *a* (*person*) reservado, introvertido, apartado (*LAm*) ♦ *pp of*

withdraw.

wither [with'ûr] *vi* marchitarse.

withered [with'ûrd] *a* marchito, seco.

withhold [withhōld'] *vt* (*irg: like* **hold**) (*money*) retener; (*decision*) aplazar; (*permission*) negar; (*information*) ocultar.

within [within'] *prep* dentro de ♦ *ad* dentro; **~ reach** al alcance de la mano; **~ sight of** a la vista de; **~ the week** antes de acabar la semana; **to be ~ the law** estar dentro de la ley; **~ an hour from now** dentro de una hora.

without [without'] *prep* sin; **to go** *or* **do ~ sth** prescindir de algo; **~ anybody knowing** sin saberlo nadie.

withstand [withstand'] *vt* (*irg: like* **stand**) resistir a.

witness [wit'nis] *n* (*person*) testigo *m/f*; (*evidence*) testimonio ♦ *vt* (*event*) presenciar; (*document*) atestiguar la veracidad de; **~ for the prosecution/defense** testigo de cargo/descargo; **to ~ to (having seen) sth** dar testimonio de (haber visto) algo.

witness stand, (*Brit*) **witness box** *n* tribuna de los testigos.

witticism [wit'əsizəm] *n* dicho ingenioso.

wittily [wit'əlē] *ad* ingeniosamente.

witty [wit'ē] *a* ingenioso.

wives [wīvz] *npl of* **wife**.

wizard [wiz'ûrd] *n* hechicero.

wizened [wiz'ənd] *a* arrugado, marchito.

wk *abbr* = **week**.

Wm. *abbr* = *William*.

WO *n abbr* = **warrant officer**.

wobble [wâb'əl] *vi* tambalearse; (*chair*) ser poco firme.

wobbly [wâb'lē] *a* (*hand, voice*) tembloroso; (*table, chair*) tambaleante, cojo.

woe [wō] *n* desgracia.

woke [wōk] *pt of* **wake**.

woken [wō'kən] *pp of* **wake**.

wolf, *pl* **wolves** [wòòlf, wòòlvz] *n* lobo.

woman, *pl* **women** [wòòm'ən, wim'ən] *n* mujer *f*; **young ~** (mujer *f*) joven *f*; **women's page** (*PRESS*) sección *f* de la mujer.

woman doctor *n* doctora.

woman friend *n* amiga.

womanize [wòòm'ənīz] *vi* ser un mujeriego.

womanly [wòòm'ənlē] *a* femenino.

womb [wòòm] *n* (*ANAT*) matriz *f*, útero.

women [wim'ən] *npl of* **woman**.

Women's (Liberation) Movement *n* (*also*: **women's lib**) Movimiento de Liberación de la Mujer.

won [wun] *pt, pp of* **win**.

wonder [wun'dûr] *n* maravilla, prodigio; (*feeling*) asombro ♦ *vi*: **to ~ whether** preguntarse si; **to ~ at** asombrarse de; **to ~ about** pensar sobre *or* en; **it's no ~ that** no es de extrañarse que.

wonderful [wun'dûrfəl] *a* maravilloso.

wonderfully [wun'dûrfəlē] *ad* maravillosamente, estupendamente.

wonky [wǎng'kē] *a* (*Brit col*: *unsteady*) poco seguro, cojo; (: *broken down*) estropeado.

won't [wōnt] = **will not.**

woo [wōo] *vt* (*woman*) cortejar.

wood [wōod] *n* (*timber*) madera; (*forest*) bosque *m* ♦ *cpd* de madera.

wood alcohol *n* (*US*) alcohol *m* desnaturalizado.

wood carving *n* tallado en madera.

wooded [wōod'id] *a* arbolado.

wooden [wōod'ən] *a* de madera; (*fig*) inexpresivo.

woodland [wōod'land] *n* bosque *m*.

woodpecker [wōod'pekûr] *n* pájaro carpintero.

wood pigeon *n* paloma torcaz.

woodwind [wōod'wind] *n* (*MUS*) instrumentos *mpl* de viento de madera.

woodwork [wōod'wûrk] *n* carpintería.

woodworm [wōod'wûrm] *n* carcoma.

woof [wōof] *n* (*of dog*) ladrido ♦ *vi* ladrar; ~, ~! ¡guau, guau!

wool [wōol] *n* lana; **knitting ~** lana (de hacer punto); **to pull the ~ over sb's eyes** (*fig*) dar a uno gato por liebre.

woolen, (*Brit*) **woollen** [wōol'ən] *a* de lana ♦ *n*: ~**s** géneros *mpl* de lana.

wooly, (*Brit*) **woolly** [wōol'ē] *a* lanudo, de lana; (*fig*: *ideas*) confuso.

word [wûrd] *n* palabra; (*news*) noticia; (*promise*) palabra (de honor) ♦ *vt* redactar; ~ **for** ~ palabra por palabra; **what's the ~ for "pen" in Spanish?** ¿cómo se dice "pen" en español?; **to put sth into ~s** expresar algo en palabras; **to have a ~ with sb** hablar (dos palabras) con uno; **in other ~s** en otras palabras; **to break/keep one's ~** faltar a la palabra/ cumplir la promesa; **to leave ~ (with/for sb) that ...** dejar recado (con/para uno) de que ...; **to have ~s with sb** (*quarrel with*) discutir *or* reñir con uno.

wording [wûr'ding] *n* redacción *f*.

word-perfect [wûrd'pûrfikt] *a* (*speech etc*) sin falta de expresión.

word processing *n* procesamiento de textos.

word processor *n* procesador *m* de textos.

wordwrap [wûrd'rap] *n* (*COMPUT*) salto de línea automático.

wordy [wûr'dē] *a* verboso, prolijo.

wore [wôr] *pt of* **wear.**

work [wûrk] *n* trabajo; (*job*) empleo, trabajo; (*ART, LIT*) obra ♦ *vi* trabajar; (*mechanism*) funcionar, marchar; (*medicine*) ser eficaz, surtir efecto ♦ *vt* (*shape*) trabajar; (*stone etc*) tallar; (*mine etc*) explotar; (*machine*) manejar, hacer funcionar; (*cause*) producir ♦ *cpd* (*day, week*) labora

ble; (*tools, clothes*) de trabajo; **to go to ~** ir a trabajar *or* al trabajo; **to be at ~ (on sth)** estar trabajando (sobre algo); **to set to ~, start ~** ponerse a trabajar; **to be out of ~** estar parado, no tener trabajo; **his life's ~** el trabajo de su vida; **to ~ hard** trabajar mucho *or* duro; **to ~ to rule** (*Brit INDUSTRY*) estar en huelga de brazos caídos; **to ~ loose** (*part*) desprenderse; (*knot*) aflojarse; *see also* **works.**

work off *vt*: **to ~ off one's feelings** desahogarse.

work on *vt fus* trabajar en, dedicarse a; (*principle*) basarse en; **he's ~ing on the car** está reparando el coche.

work out *vi* (*plans etc*) salir bien, funcionar; (*SPORT*) hacer ejercicios ♦ *vt* (*problem*) resolver; (*plan*) elaborar; **it ~s out to $100** suma 100 dólares.

work up *vt*: **he ~ed his way up in the company** ascendió en la compañía mediante sus propios esfuerzos.

workable [wûr'kəbəl] *a* (*solution*) práctico, factible.

workaholic [wûrkəhâl'ik] *n* curroadicto/a.

workbench [wûrk'bench] *n* banco *or* mesa de trabajo.

workbook [wûrk'bōok] *n* cuaderno.

work council *n* comité *m* de empresa.

worked up [wûrkt up] *a*: **to get ~** excitarse.

worker [wûr'kûr] *n* trabajador(a) *m/f*, obrero/a; **office ~** oficinista *m/f*.

work force *n* mano *f* de obra.

work-in [wûrk'in] *n* (*Brit*) ocupación *f* (de la empresa) sin interrupción del trabajo.

working [wûr'king] *a* (*Brit*: *day, week*) laborable; (: *tools, conditions, clothes*) de trabajo; (*wife*) que trabaja; (*partner*) activo.

working capital *n* (*COMM*) capital *m* circulante.

working class *n* clase *f* obrera ♦ *a*: **working-class** obrero.

working knowledge *n* conocimientos *mpl* básicos.

working man *n* obrero.

working model *n* modelo operacional.

working order *n*: **in ~** en funcionamiento.

working week *n* (*Brit*) semana laboral.

work-in-progress [wûrkinprâg'res] *n* (*COMM*) trabajo en proceso.

workload [wûrk'lōd] *n* carga de trabajo.

workman [wûrk'mən] *n* obrero.

workmanship [wûrk'mənship] *n* (*art*) hechura, arte *m*; (*skill*) habilidad *f*, trabajo.

workmate [wûrk'māt] *n* compañero/a de trabajo.

workout [wûrk'out] *n* (*SPORT*) sesión *f* de ejercicios.

work party *n* comisión *f* de investigación, grupo de trabajo.

work permit *n* permiso de trabajo.

works [wûrks] *nsg* (*Brit*: *factory*) fábrica ♦ *npl* (*of clock*, *machine*) mecanismo; **road** ~ obras *fpl*.

worksheet [wûrk'shēt] *n* (*COMPUT*) hoja de trabajo.

workshop [wûrk'shâp] *n* taller *m*.

work station *n* puesto *or* estación *f* de trabajo.

work study *n* (*US SCOL*) práctica estudiantil.

work-to-rule [wûrk'tərōōl'] *n* (*Brit*) huelga de brazos caídos.

work week *n* (*US*) semana laboral.

world [wûrld] *n* mundo ♦ *cpd* (*champion*) del mundo; (*power*, *war*) mundial; **all over the** ~ por todo el mundo, en el mundo entero; **the business** ~ el mundo de los negocios; **what in the** ~ **is he doing?** ¿qué diablos está haciendo?; **to think the** ~ **of sb** (*fig*) tener un concepto muy alto de uno; **to do sb a** ~ **of good** sentar muy bien a uno; **W~ War One/Two** la primera/segunda Guerra Mundial.

World Cup *n* (*SOCCER*) Copa Mundial.

world-famous [wûrldfā'məs] *a* de fama mundial, mundialmente famoso.

worldly [wûrld'lē] *a* mundano.

worldwide [wûrld'wīd] *a* mundial, universal.

worm [wûrm] *n* gusano; (*earth*~) lombriz *f*.

worn [wôrn] *pp of* **wear** ♦ *a* usado.

worn-out [wôrn'out'] *a* (*object*) gastado; (*person*) rendido, agotado.

worried [wûr'ēd] *a* preocupado; **to be** ~ **about sth** estar preocupado por algo.

worrisome [wûr'ēsəm] *a* preocupante, inquietante.

worry [wûr'ē] *n* preocupación *f* ♦ *vt* preocupar, inquietar ♦ *vi* preocuparse; **to** ~ **about** *or* **over sth/sb** preocuparse por algo/uno.

worrying [wûr'ēing] *a* inquietante.

worse [wûrs] *a*, *ad* peor ♦ *n* el peor, lo peor; **a change for the** ~ un empeoramiento; **so much the** ~ **for you** tanto peor para ti; **he is none the** ~ **for it** se ha quedado tan fresco *or* tan tranquilo; **to get** ~, **to grow** ~ empeorar.

worsen [wûr'sən] *vt*, *vi* empeorar.

worse off *a* (*fig*): **you'll be** ~ **this way** de esta forma estarás peor que nunca; **he is now** ~ **than before** ha quedado aun peor que antes.

worship [wûr'ship] *n* (*organized* ~) culto; (*act*) adoración *f* ♦ *vt* adorar; **Your W~** (*Brit*: *to mayor*) señor alcalde; (: *to judge*) señor juez.

worshiper, (*Brit*) **worshipper** [wûr'shipûr] *n* devoto/a.

worst [wûrst] *a* (el/la) peor ♦ *ad* peor ♦ *n* lo peor; **at** ~ en el peor de los casos; **to come off** ~ llevar la peor parte; **if** ~ **comes to** ~, (*Brit*) **if the** ~ **comes to the** ~ en último caso.

worsted [wōōs'tid] *n*: (**wool**) ~ estambre *m*.

worth [wûrth] *n* valor *m* ♦ *a*: **to be** ~ valer; **how much is it** ~? ¿cuánto vale?; **it's** ~ **it** vale *or* merece la pena; **to be** ~ **one's while (to do)** merecer la pena (hacer); **it's not** ~ **the trouble** no vale *or* merece la pena.

worthless [wûrth'lis] *a* sin valor; (*useless*) inútil.

worthwhile [wûrth'wīl'] *a* (*activity*) que merece la pena; (*cause*) loable.

worthy [wûr'thē] *a* (*person*) respetable; (*motive*) honesto; ~ **of** digno de.

would [wōōd] *auxiliary vb*: **she** ~ **come** (ella) vendría; (*emphatic*): **you WOULD say that,** ~**n't you!** tú sí dirías eso, ¿qué no?; (*insistence*): **she** ~**n't behave** no hubo forma de que se portara bien; **he** ~ **have come** él hubiera venido; ~ **you like a cookie?** ¿quieres una galleta?; ~ **you close the door please?** ¿quiere hacer el favor de cerrar la puerta?; **he** ~ **go on Mondays** solía ir los lunes.

would-be [wōōd'bē'] *a* (*pej*) presunto.

wouldn't [wōōd'ənt] = **would not**.

wound *vb* [wound] *pt*, *pp of* **wind** ♦ *n*, *vt* [wōōnd] *n* herida ♦ *vt* herir.

wove [wōv] *pt of* **weave**.

woven [wō'vən] *pp of* **weave**.

WP *n abbr* = **word processing**; **word processor**.

WPC *n abbr* (*Brit*) = **woman police constable**.

wpm *abbr* (= *words per minute*) p.p.m.

wrangle [rang'gəl] *n* riña ♦ *vi* reñir.

wrap [rap] *n* (*stole*) chal *m* ♦ *vt* (*also*: ~ **up**) envolver; **under** ~**s** (*fig*: *plan*, *scheme*) escondido, (*LAm*) tapado.

wrapper [rap'ûr] *n* (*on chocolate etc*) envoltura.

wrapping paper [rap'ing pā'pûr] *n* papel *m* de envolver.

wrath [rath] *n* cólera.

wreak [rēk] *vt* (*destruction*) causar; **to** ~ **havoc (on)** hacer *or* causar estragos (en); **to** ~ **vengeance (on)** vengarse (en).

wreath, ~**s** [rēth, rēthz] *n* (*funeral* ~) corona; (*of flowers*) guirnalda.

wreck [rek] *n* (*ship*: *destruction*) naufragio; (: *remains*) restos *mpl* del barco; (*pej*: *person*) ruina ♦ *vt* destruir, hundir; (*fig*) arruinar.

wreckage [rek'ij] *n* (*remains*) restos *mpl*; (*of building*) escombros *mpl*.

wrecker [rek'ûr] *n* (*US*) camión-grúa *m*.

wren [ren] *n* (*ZOOL*) reyezuelo.

wrench [rench] *n* (*TECH*) llave *f* inglesa; (*tug*) tirón *m* ♦ *vt* arrancar; **to** ~ **sth from sb** arrebatar algo violentamente a uno.

wrest [rest] *vt*: **to** ~ **sth from sb** arrebatar *or* arrancar algo a uno.

wrestle [res'əl] *vi*: **to ~ (with sb)** luchar (con *or* contra uno).

wrestler [res'lûr] *n* luchador(a) *m/f* (de lucha libre).

wrestling [res'ling] *n* lucha libre.

wrestling match *n* partido de lucha libre.

wretch [rech] *n* desgraciado/a, miserable *m/f*; **little ~!** (*often humorous*) ¡pillo!; ¡pícaro!

wretched [rech'id] *a* miserable.

wriggle [rig'əl] *vi* serpentear.

wring *pt*, *pp* **wrung** [ring, rung] *vt* torcer, retorcer; (*wet clothes*) escurrir; (*fig*): **to ~ sth out of sb** sacar algo por la fuerza a uno.

wringer [ring'ûr] *n* escurridor *m*.

wringing [ring'ing] *a* (*also*: **~ wet**) empapado.

wrinkle [ring'kəl] *n* arruga ♦ *vt* arrugar ♦ *vi* arrugarse.

wrinkled [ring'kəld], **wrinkly** [ring'klē] *a* (*fabric, paper, etc*) arrugado.

wrist [rist] *n* muñeca.

wristwatch [rist'wâch] *n* reloj *m* de pulsera.

writ [rit] *n* mandato judicial; **to serve a ~ on sb** notificar un mandato judicial a uno.

write, *pt* **wrote**, *pp* **written** [rīt, rōt, rit'ən] *vt*, *vi* escribir; **to ~ sb a letter** escribir una carta a uno.

write away *vi*: **to ~ away for** (*information, goods*) pedir por escrito *or* carta.

write down *vt* escribir; (*note*) apuntar.

write off *vt* (*debt*) borrar (como incobrable); (*fig*) desechar por inútil; (*smash up*: *car*) destrozar.

write out *vt* escribir.

write up *vt* redactar.

write-off [rīt'ôf] *n* pérdida total; **the car is a ~** (*Brit*) el coche es pura chatarra.

write-protect [rīt'prətekt'] *vt* (*COMPUT*) proteger contra escritura.

writer [rī'tûr] *n* escritor(a) *m/f*.

write-up [rīt'up] *n* (*review*) crítica, reseña.

writhe [rīth] *vi* retorcerse.

writing [rī'ting] *n* escritura; (*hand~*) letra; (*of author*) obras; **in ~** por escrito; **to put sth in ~** poner algo por escrito; **in my own ~** escrito por mí; *see also* **writings**.

writing case *n* (*Brit*) estuche *m* de papel de escribir.

writing desk *n* escritorio.

writing paper *n* papel *m* de escribir.

writings [rī'tingz] *npl* obras *fpl*.

written [rit'ən] *pp of* **write**.

wrong [rông] *a* (*wicked*) malo; (*unfair*) injusto; (*incorrect*) equivocado, incorrecto; (*not suitable*) inoportuno, inconveniente ♦ *ad* mal; equivocadamente ♦ *n* mal *m*; (*injustice*) injusticia ♦ *vt* ser injusto con; (*hurt*) agraviar; **to be ~** (*answer*) estar equivocado; (*in doing, saying*) equivocarse; **it's ~ to steal, stealing is ~** es malo ro-

bar; **you are ~ to do it** estás equivocado en hacerlo, cometes un error al hacerlo; **you are ~ about that, you've got it ~** en eso estás equivocado; **to be in the ~** no tener razón, tener la culpa; **what's ~?** ¿qué pasa?; **what's ~ with the car?** ¿qué le pasa al coche?; **there's nothing ~** no pasa nada; **you have the ~ number** (*TEL*) se ha equivocado (usted) de número; **to go ~** (*person*) equivocarse; (*plan*) salir mal; (*machine*) estropearse.

wrongful [rông'fəl] *a* injusto; **~ dismissal** (*INDUSTRY*) despido improcedente *or* injustificado.

wrongly [rông'lē] *ad* (*answer, do, count*) incorrectamente; (*treat*) injustamente.

wrote [rōt] *pt of* **write**.

wrought [rôt] *a*: **~ iron** hierro forjado.

wrung [rung] *pt*, *pp of* **wring**.

wry [rī] *a* irónico.

wt. *abbr* = **weight**.

WV *abbr* (*US MAIL*) = West Virginia.

W. Va. *abbr* (*US*) = West Virginia.

WY *abbr* (*US MAIL*) = Wyoming.

Wyo. *abbr* (*US*) = Wyoming.

WYSIWYG [wiz'ēwig] *abbr* (*COMPUT*: = *what you see is what you get*) tipo de presentación en un procesador de textos.

X

X, x [eks] *n* (*letter*) X, x *f*: **X for Xmas** X de Xiquena; **if you earn X dollars a year** si ganas X dólares al año.

Xerox [zē'râks] ® *n* (*also*: **~ machine**) fotocopiadora; (*photocopy*) fotocopia ♦ *vt* fotocopiar.

XL *abbr* (= *extra large*) E.

Xmas [eks'mis] *n abbr* = **Christmas**.

X-rated [eks'rātid] *a* (*US*: *movie*) no apto para menores de 18 años.

X-ray [eks'rā] *n* radiografía; **~s** *npl* rayos *mpl* X ♦ *vt* radiografiar a.

xylophone [zī'ləfōn] *n* xilófono.

Y

Y, y [wī] *n* (*letter*) Y, y *f*; **Y for Yoke** Y de Yegua.

yacht [yât] *n* yate *m*.

yachting [yât'ing] *n* (*sport*) balandrismo.

yachtsman [yâts'mən] *n* balandrista *m*.

yachtswoman [yâts'wōōmən] balandrista.

yam [yam] *n* ñame *m*; (*sweet potato*) bata-ta, (*LAm*) camote *m*.

Yank [yangk], **Yankee** [yang'kē] *n* (*pej*) yanqui *m/f*.

yank [yangk] *vt* tirar de, (*LAm*) jalar de ♦ *n* tirón *m*.

yap [yap] *vi* (*dog*) aullar.

yard [yârd] *n* patio; (*US: garden*) jardín *m*; (*measure*) yarda; **lumber** ~ depósito.

yardstick [yârd'stik] *n* (*fig*) criterio, norma.

yarn [yârn] *n* hilo; (*tale*) cuento (chino), historia.

yawn [yôn] *n* bostezo ♦ *vi* bostezar.

yawning [yôn'ing] *a* (*gap*) muy abierto.

yd. *abbr* (= *yard*) yda.

yeah [ye] *ad* (*col*) sí.

year [yēr] *n* año; (*Brit SCOL, UNIV*) curso, clase *f*; **this** ~ este año; ~ **in,** ~ **out** año tras año; **a** *or* **per** ~ al año; **to be 8** ~**s old** tener 8 años; **she's three** ~**s old** tiene tres años; **an eight-**~**-old child** un niño de ocho años (de edad).

yearbook [yēr'bōōk] *n* anuario.

yearling [yēr'ling] *n* (*racehorse*) potro de un año.

yearly [yēr'lē] *a* anual ♦ *ad* anualmente, cada año; **twice** ~ dos veces al año.

yearn [yûrn] *vi*: **to** ~ **for sth** añorar algo, suspirar por algo.

yearning [yûr'ning] *n* ansia, añoranza.

yeast [yēst] *n* levadura.

yell [yel] *n* grito, alarido ♦ *vi* gritar.

yellow [yel'ō] *a, n* amarillo; **at a** ~ **light** (*US AUT*) en el amarillo.

yellow fever *n* fiebre *f* amarilla.

yellowish [yel'ōish] *a* amarillento.

Yellow Sea *n*: **the** ~ el Mar Amarillo.

yelp [yelp] *n* aullido ♦ *vi* aullar.

Yemen [yem'ən] *n* el Yemen.

Yemeni [yem'ənē] *a, n* yemenita *m/f*.

yen [yen] *n* (*currency*) yen *m*.

yeoman [yō'mən] *n*: **Y**~ **of the Guard** ala-bardero de la Casa Real.

yes [yes] *ad, n* sí *m*; **to say/answer** ~ decir/contestar que sí; **to say** ~ **(to)** decir que sí (a), conformarse (con).

yes man *n* pelotillero.

yesterday [yes'tûrdā] *ad, n* ayer *m*; ~ **morning/evening** ayer por la mañana/tarde; **all day** ~ todo el día de ayer; **the day before** ~ antes de ayer, anteayer.

yet [yet] *ad* todavía ♦ *conj* sin embargo, a pesar de todo; ~ **again** de nuevo; **it is not finished** ~ todavía no está acabado; **the best** ~ el/la mejor hasta ahora; **as** ~ hasta ahora, todavía.

yew [yōō] *n* tejo.

YHA *n abbr* (*Brit*: = *Youth Hostel Associa-tion*) ≈ Red *f* Española de Albergues Juve-niles.

Yiddish [yid'ish] *n* yiddish *m*.

yield [yēld] *n* producción *f*; (*AGR*) cosecha; (*COMM*) rendimiento ♦ *vt* producir, dar; (*profit*) rendir ♦ *vi* rendirse, ceder; (*US AUT*) ceder el paso; **a** ~ **of 5%** un rédito del 5 por ciento.

YMCA *n abbr* (= *Young Men's Christian Association*) Asociación *f* de Jóvenes Cris-tianos.

yodel [yōd'əl] *vi* cantar a la tirolesa.

yoga [yō'gə] *n* yoga *m*.

yog(h)ourt, yog(h)urt [yō'gûrt] *n* yogur *m*.

yoke [yōk] *n* (*of oxen*) yunta; (*on shoulders*) balancín *m*; (*fig*) yugo ♦ *vt* (*also:* ~ **to-gether:** *oxen*) uncir, acoplar.

yolk [yōk] *n* yema (de huevo).

yonder [yân'dûr] *ad* allá (a lo lejos).

Yorks *abbr* (*Brit*) = *Yorkshire*.

you [yōō] *pron* tú; (*pl*) vosotros; (*polite form*) usted; (: *pl*) ustedes; (*complement*) te; (: *pl*) os; (*after prep*) tí; (: *pl*) voso-tros; (: *formal*) le/la; (: *pl*) les; (*after prep*) usted; (: *pl*) ustedes; (*one*): ~ **never know** nunca se sabe; (*impersonal*) uno; **fresh air does** ~ **good** el aire fresco te hace bien; ~ **can't do that** eso no se hace; **I'll see** ~ **tomorrow** hasta mañana; **if I was** *or* **were** ~ yo que tú, yo en tu lugar.

you'd [yōōd] = **you had; you would.**

you'll [yōōl] = **you will, you shall.**

young [yung] *a* joven ♦ *npl* (*of animal*) cría; (*people*): **the** ~ los jóvenes, la ju-ventud; **a** ~ **man/lady** un(a) joven; **my** ~**er brother** mi hermano menor; **the** ~**er generation** la nueva generación.

youngster [yung'stûr] *n* joven *m/f*.

your [yōōr] *a* tu; (*pl*) vuestro; (*formal*) su; ~ **house** tu *etc* casa; *see also* **my.**

you're [yōōr] = **you are.**

yours [yōōrz] *pron* tuyo; (: *pl*) vuestro; (*formal*) suyo; **a friend of** ~ un amigo tuyo *etc*; *see also* **faithfully, mine, sincerely, truly.**

yourself [yōōrself'] *pron* (*reflexive*) tú mismo; (*complement*) te; (*after prep*) tí (mismo); (*formal*) usted mismo; (: *com-plement*) se; (: *after prep*) sí (mismo); **you** ~ **told me** me lo dijiste tú mismo; (**all**) **by** ~ sin ayuda de nadie, solo; *see also* **oneself.**

yourselves [yōōrselvz'] *pl pron* vosotros mismos; (*after prep*) vosotros (mismos); (*formal*) ustedes (mismos); (: *comple-ment*) se; (: *after prep*) sí mismos.

youth [yōōth] *n* juventud *f*; (*young man*) (*pl* ~**s** [yōōthz]) joven *m*; **in my** ~ en mi ju-ventud.

youth club *n* club *m* juvenil.

youthful [yōōth'fəl] *a* juvenil.

youthfulness [yōōth'fəlnis] *n* juventud *f*.

youth hostel *n* albergue *m* de juventud.

youth movement *n* movimiento juvenil.

you've [yōōv] = **you have.**
yowl [youl] *n* (*of animal, person*) aullido ♦ *vi* aullar.
yr. *abbr* (= *year*) a.
YT *abbr* (*Canada*) = *Yukon Territory.*
YTS *n abbr* (*Brit*: = *Youth Training Scheme*) plan de inserción profesional juvenil.
yuck [yuk] *excl* (*col*) ¡puaj!
Yugoslav [yōō'gōslåv] *a*, *n* yugoslavo/a *m/f.*
Yugoslavia [yōō'gōslå'vēə] *n* Yugoslavia.
Yugoslavian [yōō'gōslå'vēən] *a* yugoslavo/a.
yuppie [yup'ē] (*col*) *a*, *n* yuppie *m/f.*
YWCA *n abbr* (= *Young Women's Christian Association*) Asociación *f* de Jóvenes Cristianas.

Z

Z, z [zē] *n* (*letter*) Z, z *f*; **Z for Zebra** Z de Zaragoza.
Zaire [zåēr'] *n* Zaire *m.*
Zambia [zam'bēə] *n* Zambia.
Zambian [zam'bēən] *a*, *n* zambiano/a *m/f.*
zany [zā'nē] *a* estrafalario.
zap [zap] *vt* (*COMPUT*) borrar.
zeal [zēl] *n* celo, entusiasmo.
zealot [zel'ət] *n* fanático/a.
zealous [zel'əs] *a* celoso, entusiasta.
zebra [zēb'rə] *n* cebra.
zebra crossing *n* (*Brit*) paso de peatones.

zenith [zē'nith] *n* (*ASTRO*) cénit *m*; (*fig*) apogeo.
zero [zē'rō] *n* cero; **5 degrees below** ~ 5 grados bajo cero.
zero hour *n* hora cero.
zero-rated [zē'rōrā'tid] *a* (*Brit*) de tasa cero.
zest [zest] *n* ánimo, vivacidad *f*; ~ **for living** brío.
zigzag [zig'zag] *n* zigzag *m* ♦ *vi* zigzaguear.
Zimbabwe [zimbâ'bwā] *n* Zimbabwe *m.*
Zimbabwean [zimbâ'bwāən] *a*, *n* zimbabuo/a *m/f.*
zinc [zingk] *n* cinc *m*, zinc *m.*
Zionism [zī'ənizəm] *n* sionismo.
Zionist [zī'ənist] *a*, *n* sionista *m/f.*
zip [zip] *n* (*also*: ~**per**) cremallera, cierre *m* (*LAm*); (*energy*) energía, vigor *m* ♦ *vt* (*also*: ~ **up**) cerrar la cremallera de ♦ *vi*: **to** ~ **along to the shops** ir de compras volando.
zip code *n* (*US*) código postal.
zither [zith'ûr] *n* cítara.
zodiac [zō'dēak] *n* zodíaco.
zombie [zâm'bē] *n* (*fig*): **like a** ~ como un autómata.
zone [zōn] *n* zona.
zoo [zōō] *n* (jardín *m*) zoológico.
zoological [zōəlâj'ikəl] *a* zoológico.
zoologist [zōâl'əjist] *n* zoólogo/a.
zoology [zōâl'əjē] *n* zoología.
zoom [zōōm] *vi*: **to** ~ **past** pasar zumbando; **to** ~ **in** (**on sth/sb**) (*PHOT, CINEMA*) enfocar (algo/a uno) con el zoom.
zoom lens *n* zoom *m.*
zucchini [zōōkē'nē] *n*(*pl*) (*US*) calabacín(ines) *m*(*pl*).
Zulu [zōō'lōō] *a*, *n* zulú *m/f.*